Great Brit
&
Ireland

the
MICHELIN
guide
2014

HOTELS & RESTAURANTS

Contents

A Culinary History

Britain hasn't always been known for its vibrant culinary scene – indeed, the food of the 'masses' started out dull and dreary, with meals driven by need rather than desire. So how did we get to where we are today? Well, it took quite a few centuries…

There's no place like Rome

The Romans kick-started things with their prolific road building, opening up the country and allowing goods to be transported more easily, country-wide. The Vikings brought with them new smoking and drying techniques for preserving fish, and the Saxons, who were excellent farmers, cultivated a wide variety of herbs – used not only for flavouring but to bulk-out stews. They also made butter, cheese and mead (a drink made from fermented honey); with the lack of sugar to sweeten things, honey was very important, and bees were kept in every village. The Normans introduced saffron, nutmeg, pepper, ginger and sugar – ingredients used in the likes of plum pudding, hot cross buns and Christmas cake. They also encouraged the drinking

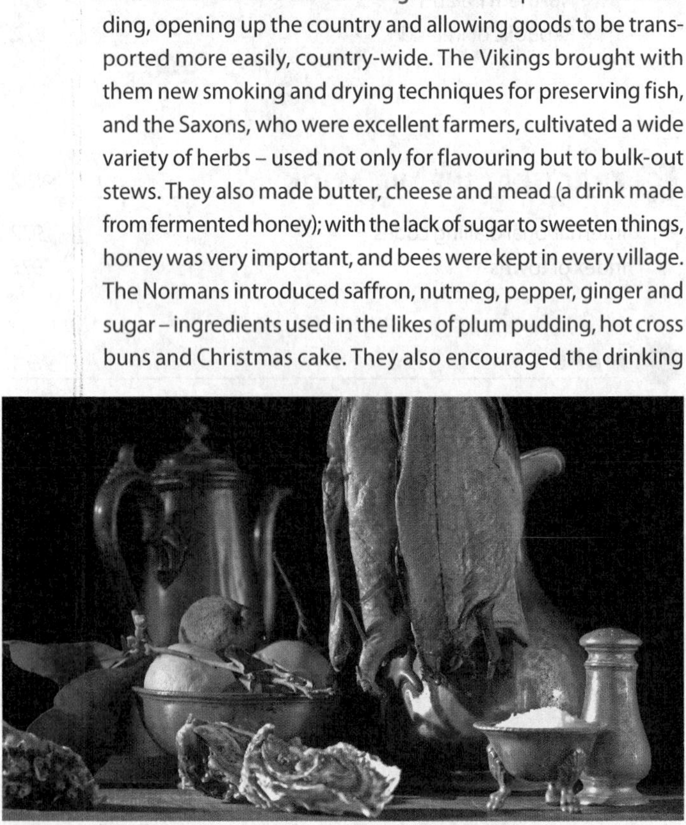

Ian O'Leary/Mode Images/Age Fotostock

of wine. Meat was a luxury reserved for those with money, so the poor were left with bread, cheese and eggs as their staple diet.

Emilio Ereza/easyFotostock/Age Fotostock

The Middle Ages saw the wealthy eating beef, mutton, pork and venison, along with a great variety of birds, including blackbirds, greenfinches, herons and swans; and when the church decreed that meat couldn't be eaten on certain days, they turned to fish. Breakfast was eaten in private; lunch and dinner, in the great hall; and on special occasions they held huge feasts and banquets with lavish spectacles, musicians and entertainment. The poor, meanwhile, were stuck with their simple, monotonous fare: for lunch, cheese and coarse, dark bread made from barley or rye; and in the evening, pottage, a type of stew made by boiling grain, vegetables and, on occasion, some rabbit – if they could catch one.

Sugar and spice...

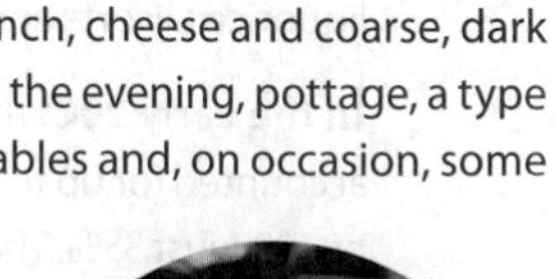

Joanna Wnuk/Zoonar GmbH RM/Age Fotostock

Things really began to take off in Tudor times, with spices being brought back from the Far East, and sugar from the Caribbean. Potatoes and turkeys were introduced from north America; the latter were bred almost exclusively in Norfolk, then driven to London in flocks of 500 or more and fattened up for several days before being sold. The poor baked bread, salted meat, preserved vegetables, made pickles and conserves, and even brewed their own beer. As the water was so dirty, the children drank milk, the adults drank ale, cider or perry, and the rich drank wine.

Little changed until the rise of the British Empire, when new drinks such as tea, coffee and chocolate appeared, and coffee houses started to spring up – places where professionals could meet to read the newspaper and 'talk shop'. More herbs and spices were brought back, this time from India, and exotic fruits such as bananas and pineapples came onto the scene. Despite improvements in farming, the poor continued to eat bread, butter, cheese, potatoes and bacon; butcher's meat remained a luxury.

Import-ant times

Advancements continued to pick up pace in Victorian times. The advent of the railways and steamships made it possible to import cheap grain from North America, and refrigeration units allowed meat to be brought in from Argentina and Australia. The first fish and chip shops opened in the 1860s and the first convenience food in tins and jars went on sale. The price of sugar also began to drop and sweets such as peanut brittle, liquorice allsorts and chocolate bars came into being.

In the early 20C, the cost of food fell dramatically: in 1914 it accounted for up to 60% of a working class family's income and by 1937, just 35%. Then, as things were beginning to look up, the war intervened and staple food items such as meat, sugar, butter, eggs and tea were rationed until long after the war had ended.

The late 20C saw a surge in technological and scientific advancements, and the creation of affordable fridges, freezers and microwave ovens meant that food could be stored for longer and cooked more easily. In an increasingly time-pressured world, convenience and time-saving became key, increasing the popularity of the 'ready meal' and takeaway outlets.

Pierre Lapin/Cephas/Photononstop

As immigration increased, so too did the number of restaurants serving cuisine from different nations. What started as a handful of Indian and Chinese restaurants, has now moved on in the 21C to cover everything from Thai to Turkish, Jamaican to Japanese.

Not only has the range of dining establishments increased but, with the opening up of European borders and the ease of travel and transport, many supermarkets have also started to stock a range of foreign products, from pierogi to paneer.

Food Collection/hemis.fr

The British Aisles

Supermarkets may now offer an endless choice of products but at the same time, an increased interest in health and wellbeing has sparked a trend for using seasonal ingredients from small, local producers – with a focus on reducing food miles. With increasing concerns about the origins of produce and the methods used in mass-production, many people are now turning back to the traditional 'farmers' market' or opting for 'organic' alternatives, where the consumer can trace the product back to its source or be assured of a natural, ethical or sustainable production method.

This can be seen in a true British institution – the pub. Take the traditional Sunday roast, one of the country's favourite meals; some chewy meat and microwaved veg won't cut it anymore – consumers now want to see top quality seasonal ingredients on their plate, sourced from the nearby farmer or the local allotment, and freshly prepared in the kitchen. And chefs are rising to the challenge: exploring new ways of using British ingredients, and reviving and reinventing traditional regional recipes.

In the past Britain may have lagged behind its European neighbours, due, in part, to its having a largely industrial economy. But what is in no doubt today, is that it's certainly making up for lost time. It may not have such a clear culinary identity as say, France or Italy, but it now offers greater choice and diversity by providing chefs with the freedom and confidence to take inspiration from wherever they wish and bring together flavours from across the globe.

The MICHELIN guide's commitments

Experienced in quality

Whether they are in Japan, the USA, China or Europe, our inspectors apply the same criteria to judge the quality of each and every hotel and restaurant that they visit. The Michelin guide commands a worldwide reputation thanks to the commitments we make to our readers – and we reiterate these below:

The MICHELIN guide's commitments:

→ **Anonymous inspections:** our inspectors make regular and anonymous visits to hotels and restaurants to gauge the quality of products and services offered to an ordinary customer. They settle their own bill and may then introduce themselves and ask for more information about the establishment. Our readers' comments are also a valuable source of information, which we can then follow up with another visit of our own.

→ **Independence:** To remain totally objective for our readers, the selection is made with complete independence. Entry into the guide is free. All decisions are discussed with the Editor and our highest awards are considered at a European level.

→ **Selection and choice:** The guide offers a selection of the best hotels and restaurants in every category of comfort and price. This is only possible because all the inspectors rigorously apply the same methods.

→ **Annual updates:** All the practical information, the classifications and awards are revised and updated every single year to give the most reliable information possible.

→ **Consistency:** The criteria for the classifications are the same in every country covered by the MICHELIN guide.

The sole intention of Michelin is to make your travels safe and enjoyable.

Dear Reader,

Dear Reader,

Having kept up-to-date with the latest developments in the hotel and restaurant scene, we are pleased to present this new, improved and updated edition of the Michelin Guide.

Since the very beginning, our ambition has remained the same each year: to accompany you on all of your journeys and to help you choose the best establishments in which to stay and to eat, across all categories of comfort and price; whether that's a friendly guesthouse or luxury hotel, a lively gastropub or fine dining restaurant.

To this end, the Michelin Guide is a tried-and-tested travel planner, its primary objective being to provide first-hand experience for you, our readers. All of the establishments selected have been rigorously tested by our team of professional inspectors, who are constantly seeking out new places and continually assessing those already listed.

Every year the guide recognises the best places to eat, by awarding them one ✿, two ✿✿ or three ✿✿✿ stars. These lie at the heart of the selection and highlight the establishments producing the best quality cuisine – in all styles – taking into account the quality of ingredients, creativity, mastery of techniques and flavours, value for money and consistency.

Other symbols to look out for are the Bib Gourmand ☺ and the Bib Hotel, which point out establishments that represent particularly good value; here you'll be guaranteed excellence but at moderate prices.

We are committed to remaining at the forefront of the culinary world and to meeting the demands of our readers. As such, we are very interested to hear your opinions on the establishments listed in our guide. Please don't hesitate to contact us, as your contributions are invaluable in directing our work and improving the quality of our information.

We continually strive to help you on your journeys.

Thank you for your loyalty and happy travelling with the 2014 edition of the Michelin Guide.

Consult the MICHELIN guide at:
www.ViaMichelin.com

and write to us at:
themichelinguide-gbirl@uk.michelin.com

How to use this guide

TOURIST INFORMATION

Distances from the main towns, tourist offices, local tourist attractions, means of transport, golf courses and leisure activities...

HOTELS

From 🏨🏨🏨🏨🏨 to 🏨, 🏠: categories of comfort.
In red 🏨🏨🏨🏨🏨 ... 🏨, 🏠: the most pleasant.

RESTAURANTS AND PUBS

From XXXXX to X, 🍺: categories of comfort.
In red XXXXX ... X, 🍺: the most pleasant.

STARS

✿✿✿ Worth a special journey.
✿✿ Worth a detour.
✿ A very good restaurant.

GOOD FOOD & ACCOMMODATION AT MODERATE PRICES

Bib Gourmand.
Bib Hotel.

NEW IN THE GUIDE

New establishment in the guide.

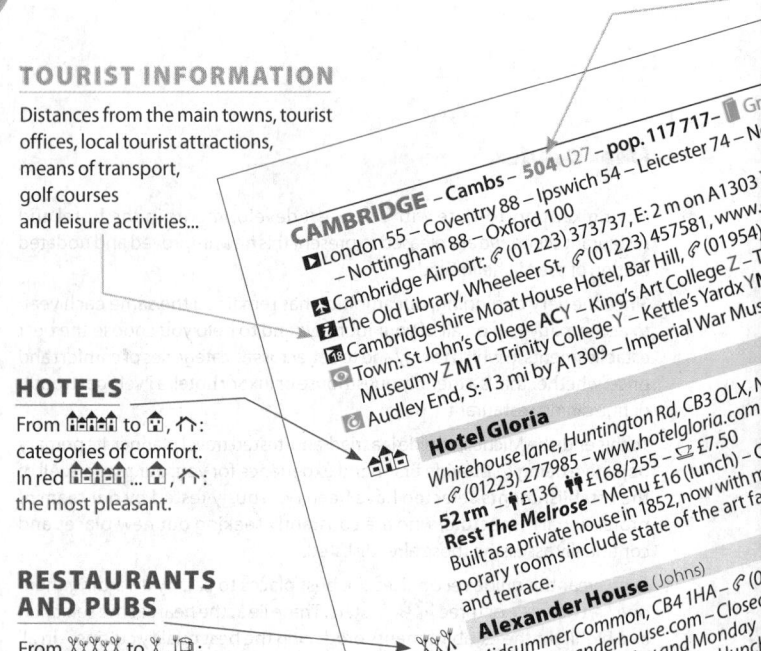

CAMBRIDGE – Cambs – 504 U27 – pop. 117 717 –
London 55 – Coventry 88 – Ipswich 54 – Leicester 74 –
– Nottingham 88 – Oxford 100
Cambridge Airport: ℰ (01223) 373737, E: 2 m on A1303
The Old Library, Wheeler St, ℰ (01223) 457581, www.
Cambridgeshire Moat House Hotel, Bar Hill, ℰ (01954)
Town: St John's College ACY – King's Art College Z –
Museumy Z M1 – Trinity College Y – Kettle's Yardx Y
Audley End, S: 13 mi by A1309 – Imperial War Mus
Hotel Gloria
Whitehouse lane, Huntington Rd, CB3 OLX,
– ℰ (01223) 277985 – www.hotelgloria.com
52 rm – £136 £168/255 – £7.50
Rest The Melrose – Menu £16 (lunch) –
Built as a private house in 1852, now with
porary rooms include state of the art
and terrace.
Alexander House (Johns)
Midsummer Common, CB4 1HA – ℰ
– www.alexanderhouse.com – Closed
1 week spring, Sunday and Monday
Rest – Menu (dinner only and lunch
A river Cam idyll. Chic conservatory
with blissful views over the river.
→ Salad of smoked eel, pig's tro
and pistachios and asparagus.
bois and mint.
ENGLAND
The Roasted Pepper
35 Chesterton Rd, CB4 3AX –
– Closed Christmas-New Yea
Rest – (booking essential)
Personally run Victorian tow
dishes with mild Asian influ
at Histon North: 3 m on B104 –
Blue House with
44 High St, CB3 7HV –
– Closed 2 weeks Christ
22 rm – £38 £60
Red-brick 18C listed fa
overlooks meadow.
preserves. Immacula
CANTERBURY – Kent
London 59 –
Felix Hall
Conifer Drive,
– ℰ (0870) 400

12A2
ridge.gov.uk
Queen's College ACZ
, Duxford, S: 9 mi on M11
Zd
west: 1,5 m by A1307
£25.20/35.50
n and stylish public areas. The contem-
es. Sleek restaurant overlooks garden
Ya
369 245
eeks Christmas, 2 weeks August,
ay-Saturday) £30/50
g room with smart first floor bar and terrace
nd apple purée. Braised turbot with peanuts
lloni of apricot, Strawberry sorbet, fraises des
Yc
23) 351872 – www.roastedpepper.co.uk
Sunday
only) Menu £25
se with smartly clad tables. Classic French and Italian
s, served at reasonable prices.
ambridge
23) 262164 – www.bluehousefarm.com
New Year
ouse on a working farm... with beautiful blue windows; house
garden room for breakfast, including home-made bread and
ooms.
9D2
Great Britain
04 R29 – pop. 47 123 (inc. Frimley)
nton 76 – Dover 15 – Maidstone 28 – Margate 17
2BG, East: 0,75 m off Portsmouth Rd (A325)
– www.felixhall.com
£210 – £6.50
oking essential) (dinner only) £19/28
A carved wooden staircase leads to the bedrooms; some are
others are bright and modern. 19C restau-
Yc

OTHER MICHELIN PUBLICATIONS

References for the Michelin map and Green Guide which cover the area.

LOCATING THE TOWN

Locate the town on the regional map at the end of the guide (map number and coordinates).

QUIET HOTELS

Quiet hotel.

Very quiet hotel.

LOCATING THE ESTABLISHMENT

Located on the town plan (coordinates and letters giving the location).

DESCRIPTION OF THE ESTABLISHMENT

Atmosphere, style, character and specialities.

PRICES

FACILITIES AND SERVICES

Classification & awards

CATEGORIES OF COMFORT

The Michelin guide selection lists the best hotels and restaurants in each category of comfort and price. The establishments we choose are classified according to their levels of comfort and, within each category, are listed in order of preference.

- Luxury in the traditional style
- Top class comfort
- Very comfortable
- Comfortable
- Quite comfortable
- Pubs serving good food
- Other recommended accommodation (Guesthouses, farmhouses and private homes)
- without rest. — This hotel has no restaurant
- with rm — This restaurant also offers accommodation

THE AWARDS

To help you make the best choice, some exceptional establishments have been given an award in this year's Guide. They are marked , , For those awarded a Bib Hotel, the mention "**rm**" appears in blue in the description of the establishment.

THE BEST CUISINE

Michelin stars are awarded to establishments serving cuisine, of whatever style, which is of the highest quality. The cuisine is judged on the quality of ingredients, the skill in their preparation, the combination of flavours, the levels of creativity, the value for money and the consistency of culinary standards.

For every restaurant awarded a star we include 3 specialities that are typical of their cooking style. These specific dishes may not always be available.

Exceptional cuisine, worth a special journey
One always eats extremely well here, sometimes superbly.

Excellent cooking, worth a detour

Very good cooking in its category

GOOD FOOD AND ACCOMMODATION AT MODERATE PRICES

Bib Gourmand
Establishment offering good quality cuisine for under £28 or under €40 in the Republic of Ireland (price of a 3 course meal not including drinks).

Bib Hotel
Establishment offering good levels of comfort and service, with most rooms priced at under £90 or under €115 in the Republic of Ireland (price of a room for 2 people, including breakfast).

PLEASANT HOTELS AND RESTAURANTS

Symbols shown in red indicate particularly pleasant or restful establishments: the character of the building, its décor, the setting, the welcome and services offered may all contribute to this special appeal.

⌂, 🏠 to 🏠🏠🏠🏠🏠	**Pleasant hotels & guesthouses**
🍺, ✗ to ✗✗✗✗✗	**Pleasant restaurants & pubs**

Ⓝ **New establishment in the guide**

OTHER SPECIAL FEATURES

As well as the categories and awards given to the establishment, Michelin inspectors also make special note of other criteria which can be important when choosing an establishment.

LOCATION

If you are looking for a particularly restful establishment, or one with a special view, look out for the following symbols:

- **Quiet hotel**
- **Very quiet hotel**
- **Interesting view**
- **Exceptional view**

WINE LIST

If you are looking for an establishment with an excellent wine list, look out for the following symbol:

Particularly interesting wine list
This symbol might cover the list presented by a sommelier in a luxury restaurant or that of a simple pub or restaurant where the owner has a passion for wine. The two lists will offer something exceptional but very different, so beware of comparing them by each other's standards.

OTHER SPECIAL FEATURES

- **Notable cocktail list**
- **Vegetarian menu**
- **Restaurants offering theatre menus**
- **Open for breakfast**
- **Small plates**

SMOKING

In Great Britain and the Republic of Ireland the law prohibits smoking in all pubs, restaurants and hotel public areas.

Facilities & services

30 rm	Number of rooms
	Lift (elevator)
	Air conditioning (in all or part of the establishment)
	Fast Internet access in bedrooms
	Wi-fi Internet access in bedrooms
	Establishment at least partly accessible to those of restricted mobility
	Special facilities for children
	Meals served in garden or on terrace
Spa	An extensive facility for relaxation and well-being
	Sauna – Exercise room
	Swimming pool: outdoor or indoor
	Garden – Park
18	Tennis court – Golf course and number of holes
	Fishing available to hotel guests. A charge may be made
	Equipped conference room
	Private dining rooms
	Hotel garage (additional charge in most cases)
P	Car park for customers only
	No dogs allowed (in all or part of the establishment)
	Credit cards not accepted
	Nearest Underground station (in London)

Prices

Prices quoted in this guide were supplied in summer 2013 and apply to low and high seasons. They are subject to alteration if goods and service costs are revised. By supplying the information, hotels and restaurants have undertaken to maintain these rates for our readers. In some towns, when commercial, cultural or sporting events are taking place, the hotel rates are likely to be considerably higher. Prices are given in £ sterling, except for the Republic of Ireland where euros are quoted.
All accommodation prices include both service and V.A.T. All restaurant prices include V.A.T. Service is also included when an **s** appears after the prices.
Where no **s** is shown, prices may be subject to the addition of a variable service charge which is usually between 10 % - 15 %.
(V.A.T. does not apply in the Channel Islands).
Out of season, certain establishments offer special rates. Ask when booking.

RESERVATION AND DEPOSITS

Some hotels will require a deposit which confirms the commitment of both the customer and the hotelier. Ask the hotelier to provide you with all the terms and conditions applicable to your reservation in their written confirmation.

ROOMS

rm 🚹 50/90	Lowest price 50 and highest price 90 for a comfortable single room
rm 🚹🚹 70/120	Lowest price 70 and highest price 120 for a double or twin room for 2 people
rm ☕ 55/85	Full cooked breakfast (whether taken or not) is included in the price of the room
☕ 6	Price of breakfast

SHORT BREAKS

Many hotels offer a special rate for a stay of two or more nights which comprises dinner, room and breakfast usually for a minimum of two people. Please enquire with the hotel for rates.

RESTAURANT

Fixed price: lowest price £13, highest price £28, usually for a 2 or 3 course meal. The lowest priced set menu is often only available at lunchtimes.
A la carte meals: the prices represent the range of charges from a simple to an elaborate 3 course meal.

s	Service included
🎭	Restaurants offering lower priced pre and/or post theatre menus

🏠: Dinner in this category of establishment is sometimes communal and meals are not always available every evening. It will generally be a limited menu, served at a set time, to residents only. Lunch is rarely offered. Many will not be licensed to sell alcohol.

Information on localities

GENERAL INFORMATION

✉ **York**	Postal address
501 M27, ⑩	Michelin map and co-ordinates or fold
Great Britain	See the Michelin Green Guide Great Britain
pop. 1057	Population Source : ONS / Office for National Statistics (www.statistics.gov.uk) [census 2011+census 2001 = estim 2008] and CSO/Central Statistics Office (www.cso.ie) [census 2011]
BX **a**	Letters giving the location of a place on a town plan
18	Golf course and number of holes (handicap sometimes required, telephone reservation strongly advised)
✻ ⋞	Panoramic view, viewpoint
✈	Airport
⛴	Shipping line (passengers & cars)
⛴	Passenger transport only
i	Tourist Information Centre

STANDARD TIME

In winter, standard time throughout the British Isles is Greenwich Mean Time (GMT). In summer, British clocks are advanced by one hour to give British Summer Time (BST). The actual dates are announced annually but always occur over weekends in March and October.

TOURIST INFORMATION

STAR-RATING

★★★	Highly recommended
★★	Recommended
★	Interesting
AC	Admission charge

LOCATION

◉	Sights in town
⊙	On the outskirts
N, S, E, W	The sight lies North, South, East or West of the town
A 22	Take road A 22, indicated by the same symbol on the Guide map
2 mi.	Distance in miles (In the Republic of Ireland, kilometres are quoted).

Plan key

- Hotels
- Restaurants

SIGHTS

Place of interest
Interesting place of worship Catholic-Protestant

ROADS

M 1 Motorway
Numbered junctions: complete, limited
Dual carriageway with motorway characteristics
Main traffic artery
A 2 Primary route (GB) and National route (IRL)
One-way street – Unsuitable for traffic or street subject to restrictions
Pedestrian street – Tramway
Piccadilly P Shopping street – Car park – Park and Ride
Gateway – Street passing under arch – Tunnel
15'5 Low headroom (16'6" max.) on major through routes
Station and railway
Funicular – Cable-car
B Lever bridge – Car ferry

VARIOUS SIGNS

Tourist Information Centre
Church/Place of worship - Mosque – Synagogue
Communications tower or mast – Ruins
Garden, park, wood – Cemetery
Stadium - Racecourse - Golf course
Golf course (with restrictions for visitors) – Skating rink
Outdoor or indoor swimming pool
View – Panorama
Monument – Fountain – Hospital – Covered market
Pleasure boat harbour – Lighthouse
Airport – Underground station – Coach station
Ferry services: passengers and cars
Main post office
Public buildings located by letter:
C H J County Council Offices – Town Hall – Law Courts
M T U Museum – Theatre – University, College
POL. Police (in large towns police headquarters)

LONDON

BRENT WEMBLEY Borough – Area
Borough boundary
Congestion Zone – Charge applies Monday-Friday 07.00-18.00
Nearest Underground station to the hotel or restaurant

Awards 2014

Starred establishments 2014

The colour corresponds to the establishment
with the most stars in this location.

London	This location has at least one 3 star restaurant	✻✻✻
Dublin	This location has at least one 2 star restaurant	✻✻
Edinburgh	This location has at least one 1 star restaurant	✻

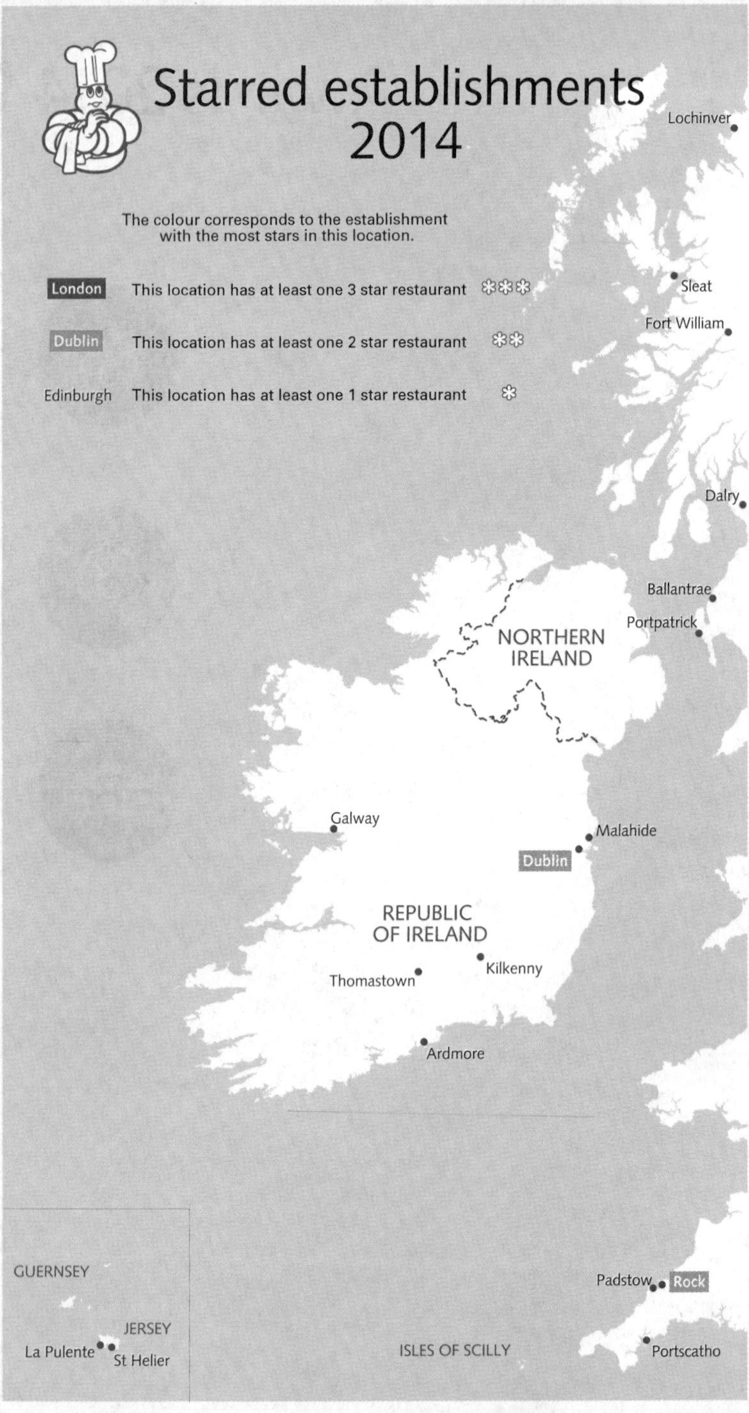

SHETLAND ISLANDS
ORKNEY ISLANDS
Nairn
SCOTLAND
Auchterarder
Peat Inn
Elie
Balloch
Edinburgh
Leith
Summerhouse
Ambleside
Windermere
Ramsgill-in-Nidderdale
Oldstead
Cartmel
Ilkley
South Dalton
Langho
ENGLAND
Birkenhead
Sheffield
Chester
Baslow
Llandrillo
Nottingham
Morston
Hunstanton
Montgomery
Hambleton
Birmingham
Ludlow
Titley
Winchcombe
WALES
Eldersfield
Upper Slaughter
Cambridge
Cheltenham
Woburn
Llanddewi Skirrid
Murcott
Great Milton
Castle Combe
Malmesbury
Marlow
Sprigg's Alley
London
Bristol
Little Bedwyn
Chew Magna
Colerne
Shinfield
Seasalter
Bath
Ripley
East Chisenbury
Bray
Biddenden
Bagshot
Knowstone
Winchester
Cranbrook
Petersfield
Bodiam
Chagford
Dorchester
Emsworth
Royal Tunbridge Wells
Beaulieu
Horsham
Torquay
Cuckfield

Starred establishments

✿✿✿ 2014

→ England

Bray	Fat Duck	
Bray	Waterside Inn	
London / City of Westminster	Alain Ducasse at The Dorchester	
London / Kensington and Chelsea	Gordon Ramsay	

✿✿ 2014

→ England

Bagshot	Michael Wignall at The Latymer	
Cambridge	Midsummer House	
Chagford	Gidleigh Park	
Cheltenham	Le Champignon Sauvage	
Grange-over-Sands / Cartmel	L'Enclume	
London / City of Westminster	Dinner by Heston Blumenthal	**N**
London / City of Westminster	Le Gavroche	
London / City of Westminster	Greenhouse	**N**
London / City of Westminster	Hibiscus	
London / City of Westminster	Hélène Darroze at The Connaught	
London / City of Westminster	Marcus Wareing at The Berkeley	
London / City of Westminster	Sketch (The Lecture Room and Library)	
London / City of Westminster	Square	
London / Kensington and Chelsea	Ledbury	
Malmesbury	The Dining Room	
Marlow	Hand and Flowers	
Nottingham	Restaurant Sat Bains	
Oxford / Great Milton	Le Manoir aux Quat' Saisons	
Rock	Restaurant Nathan Outlaw	

→ Scotland

Auchterarder	Andrew Fairlie at Gleneagles

→ Republic of Ireland

Dublin	Patrick Guilbaud

→ **N** *Newly awarded distinction*

✿ 2014

→ England

Ambleside	The Samling	**N**
Baslow	Fischer's at Baslow Hall	
Bath	Bath Priory	
Bath / Colerne	The Park	
Beaulieu	The Terrace	
Beverley / South Dalton	Pipe and Glass Inn	
Biddenden	West House	
Birkenhead	Fraiche	
Birmingham	Turners	
Birmingham	adam's	**N**
Birmingham	Purnell's	
Birmingham	Simpsons	
Blackburn / Langho	Northcote	
Blakeney / Morston	Morston Hall	
Bodiam	Curlew	
Bourton-on-the-Water / Upper Slaughter	Lords of the Manor	
Bray	Hinds Head	
Bray	Royal Oak	
Bristol	Casamia	
Bristol	wilks	**N**
Cambridge	Alimentum	
Castle Combe	Bybrook	
Chester	Simon Radley at Chester Grosvenor	
Chew Magna	Pony and Trap	
Chinnor / Sprigg's Alley	Sir Charles Napier	
Cranbrook	Apicius	
Cuckfield	Ockenden Manor	
Darlington / Summerhouse	Raby Hunt	
Dorchester	Sienna	
East Chisenbury	Red Lion Freehouse	
Eldersfield	Butchers Arms	
Emsworth	36 on the Quay	
Horsham	The Pass	
Horsham	Restaurant Tristan	
Hunstanton	The Neptune	
Ilkley	Box Tree	
Jersey / La Pulente	Ocean	
Jersey / St Helier	Bohemia	
Jersey / St Helier	Ormer by Shaun Rankin	**N**
Jersey / St Helier	Tassili	
Knowstone	Masons Arms	
London / Bromley	Chapter One	
London / Camden	Dabbous	
London / Camden	Hakkasan Hanway Place	
London / Camden	Pied à Terre	
London / City of London	Club Gascon	
London / City of Westminster	Alyn Williams at The Westbury	
London / City of Westminster	Amaya	
London / City of Westminster	Ametsa with Arzak Instruction	**N**
London / City of Westminster	Apsleys	
London / City of Westminster	Arbutus	

London / City of Westminster	L'Atelier de Joël Robuchon	
London / City of Westminster	L'Autre Pied	
London / City of Westminster	Benares	
London / City of Westminster	Bo London	**N**
London / City of Westminster	Brasserie Chavot	**N**
London / City of Westminster	Galvin at Windows	
London / City of Westminster	Hakkasan Mayfair	
London / City of Westminster	Kai	
London / City of Westminster	Lima	**N**
London / City of Westminster	Locanda Locatelli	
London / City of Westminster	Maze	
London / City of Westminster	Murano	
London / City of Westminster	Nobu	
London / City of Westminster	Nobu Berkeley St	
London / City of Westminster	One Leicester Street	
London / City of Westminster	Pollen Street Social	
London / City of Westminster	Pétrus	
London / City of Westminster	Quilon	
London / City of Westminster	Seven Park Place	
London / City of Westminster	Social Eating House	**N**
London / City of Westminster	Tamarind	
London / City of Westminster	Texture	
London / City of Westminster	Trishna	
London / City of Westminster	Umu	
London / City of Westminster	Wild Honey	
London / City of Westminster	Yauatcha	
London / Hackney (Borough of)	HKK	**N**
London / Hammersmith and Fulham	River Café	
London / Hammersmith and Fulham	Harwood Arms	
London / Hounslow	Hedone	
London / Hounslow	La Trompette	
London / Islington (Borough of)	Angler	**N**
London / Islington (Borough of)	St John	
London / Kensington and Chelsea	Kitchen W8	
London / Kensington and Chelsea	Launceston Place	
London / Kensington and Chelsea	Medlar	
London / Kensington and Chelsea	Outlaw's at The Capital	**N**
London / Kensington and Chelsea	Rasoi	
London / Kensington and Chelsea	Tom Aikens	
London / Richmond-upon-Thames	The Glasshouse	
London / Southwark (Borough of)	Story	**N**
London / Tower Hamlets	Galvin La Chapelle	
London / Tower Hamlets	Viajante	
London / Wandsworth (Borough of)	Chez Bruce	
Ludlow	Mr Underhill's at Dinham Weir	
Marlborough / Little Bedwyn	Harrow at Little Bedwyn	
Marlow	Danesfield House	
Murcott	Nut Tree	
Oakham / Hambleton	Hambleton Hall	
Oldstead	Black Swan	
Padstow	Paul Ainsworth at No.6	
Pateley Bridge / Ramsgill-in-Nidderdale	Yorke Arms	
Petersfield	JSW	
Portscatho	Driftwood	
Reading / Shinfield	L'Ortolan	
Ripley (Surrey)	Drake's	

Royal Tunbridge Wells	Thackeray's
Sheffield	Old Vicarage
Titley	Stagg Inn
Torquay	Room in the Elephant
Whitstable / Seasalter	The Sportsman
Winchcombe	5 North St
Winchester	Black Rat
Windermere	Holbeck Ghyll
Woburn	Paris House

➜ Scotland

Ballantrae	Glenapp Castle
Balloch	Martin Wishart at Loch Lomond
Dalry	Braidwoods
Edinburgh	Castle Terrace
Edinburgh	Number One
Edinburgh	21212
Edinburgh / Leith	Kitchin
Edinburgh / Leith	Martin Wishart
Elie	Sangster's
Fort William	Inverlochy Castle
Lochinver	Albannach
Nairn	Boath House
Peat Inn	The Peat Inn
Portpatrick	Knockinaam Lodge
Skye (Isle of) / Sleat	Kinloch Lodge

➜ Wales

Abergavenny / Llanddewi Skirrid	Walnut Tree
Llandrillo	Tyddyn Llan
Montgomery	The Checkers

➜ Republic of Ireland

Ardmore	House	
Dublin	Chapter One	
Dublin	L'Ecrivain	
Dublin	Thornton's	
Galway	Aniar	
Kilkenny	Campagne	**N**
Malahide	bon appétit	
Thomastown	Lady Helen	**N**

Bib Gourmand 2014

• Places with at least one Bib Gourmand establishment.

SHETLAND ISLANDS
ORKNEY ISLANDS
SCOTLAND
Glasgow
Edinburgh
Peebles
Newcastle-upon-Tyne
North Shields
Durham
Hurworth-on-Tees
Masham
Thornton
Drighlington
Ramsbottom
Ripponden
Bury
ENGLAND
Chester
Nottingham
Stathern
Gedney Dyke
Thorpe Market
Ingham
Kibworth Beauchamp
Wymondham
WALES
Stamford
Bruntingthorpe
Keyston
Stanton
East Haddon
Bury St. Edmunds
Belbroughton
Woolhope
Bourton on the Hill
Aldeburgh
Brecon
Tewkesbury
Cheltenham
Hitchin
Upper South Wraxall
Wootton
Kelvedon
Tetbury
Britwell Salome
Long Ashton
Oxford
Stonor
Hunsdon
London
Wrington
Bristol
Bishopstone
Cookham
Oare
Ramsgate
Wells
Longparish
Preston
West Pennard
Longstock
Candover
Bruton
West Hoathly
Romsey
Donhead-St-Andrew
Droxford
Hove
Rockbeare
Christchurch
Chichester
Brighton
Hastings and St Leonards

Bib Gourmand

Good food at moderate prices

➜ England

Aldeburgh	Lighthouse	
Belbroughton	The Queens	**N**
Bishopstone	Royal Oak	
Blackpool / Thornton	Twelve	
Brighton	Chilli Pickle	
Brighton / Hove	Ginger Pig	
Bristol	Flinty Red	
Bristol / Long Ashton	Bird in Hand	**N**
Britwell Salome	Red Lion	**N**
Bruntingthorpe	The Joiners	
Bruton	At The Chapel	
Bury	Waggon	
Bury St Edmunds	Pea Porridge	
Cheltenham	The Tavern	**N**
Chester	Joseph Benjamin	
Chichester	Amelie and Friends	**N**
Christchurch	Kings Arms	**N**
Cookham	White Oak	
Darlington / Hurworth-on-Tees	Bay Horse	
Donhead St Andrew	The Forester	
Drighlington	Prashad	**N**
Droxford	Bakers Arms	
Durham	Bistro 21	
East Haddon	Red Lion	
Exeter / Rockbeare	Jack in the Green Inn	
Faversham / Oare	Three Mariners	
Gedney Dyke	Chequers	
Hastings and St. Leonards	St Clements	
Henley-on-Thames / Stonor	Quince Tree	
Hitchin	hermitage rd	
Hunsdon	Fox and Hounds	**N**
Ingham	Ingham Swan	
Jersey / Beaumont	Mark Jordan at the Beach	
Kelvedon	George and Dragon	
Keyston	Pheasant	
Kibworth Beauchamp	Lighthouse	**N**
London / Brent	Sushi-Say	
London / Camden	Barrica	
London / Camden	Bradley's	
London / Camden	Gail's Kitchen	**N**
London / Camden	Great Queen Street	
London / Camden	Honey and Co	**N**
London / Camden	Made in Camden	
London / Camden	Market	
London / Camden	Salt Yard	
London / City of Westminster	A. Wong	**N**
London / City of Westminster	Barrafina	
London / City of Westminster	Bocca di Lupo	
London / City of Westminster	Brasserie Zédel	
London / City of Westminster	Copita	
London / City of Westminster	Green Man and French Horn	**N**
London / City of Westminster	Hereford Road	
London / City of Westminster	Kateh	
London / City of Westminster	Koya	
London / City of Westminster	Opera Tavern	
London / City of Westminster	Picture	**N**
London / City of Westminster	Polpo Covent Garden	
London / City of Westminster	Polpo Soho	
London / City of Westminster	Terroirs	
London / Hackney (Borough of)	Empress	
London / Hackney (Borough of)	Princess of Shoreditch	
London / Hammersmith and Fulham	Azou	

➜ **N** *Newly awarded distinction*

London / Islington (Borough of)	Comptoir Gascon
London / Islington (Borough of)	Drapers Arms
London / Islington (Borough of)	500
London / Islington (Borough of)	Medcalf
London / Islington (Borough of)	Morito
London / Islington (Borough of)	Polpo Smithfield **N**
London / Islington (Borough of)	Trullo
London / Kings Cross St Pancras	Grain Store **N**
London / Lambeth	Bistro Union
London / Lambeth	Canton Arms
London / Merton	Fox and Grapes
London / Redbridge	Provender
London / Richmond-upon-Thames	Mango and Silk
London / Richmond-upon-Thames	Simply Thai
London / Southwark (Borough of)	Anchor and Hope
London / Southwark (Borough of)	Del Mercato **N**
London / Southwark (Borough of)	Elliot's
London / Southwark (Borough of)	José
London / Southwark (Borough of)	Zucca
London / Tower Hamlets	Brawn
London / Tower Hamlets	Cafe Spice Namaste
London / Tower Hamlets	Corner Room
London / Tower Hamlets	Galvin Café a Vin
London / Tower Hamlets	St John Bread and Wine
London / Wandsworth (Borough of)	Soif
Longparish	Plough Inn
Longstock	Peat Spade Inn
Marazion / Perranuthnoe	Victoria Inn
Masham	Vennell's
Moreton-in-Marsh / Bourton on the Hill	Horse and Groom
Newcastle upon Tyne	Broad Chare
Newlyn	Tolcarne Inn **N**
North Shields	David Kennedy's River Cafe
Nottingham	Ibérico World Tapas
Oxford	Magdalen Arms
Oxford	Rickety Press **N**
Padstow	Rick Stein's Café
Porthleven	Kota
Preston Candover	Purefoy Arms
Ramsbottom	Hearth of the Ram **N**
Ramsgate	Age and Sons
Ripponden	El Gato Negro **N**
Romsey	Three Tuns
St Ives	Black Rock
Stamford	Jim's Yard
Stanton	Leaping Hare
Stathern	Red Lion Inn
Tetbury	Gumstool Inn
Tewkesbury	Owens
Thorpe Market	Gunton Arms
Upper South Wraxall	Longs Arms **N**
Wells	Old Spot
West Hoathly	Cat Inn
West Pennard	Apple Tree Inn
Woolhope	Butchers Arms
Wootton	Killingworth Castle **N**
Wrington	The Ethicurean
Wymondham	Berkeley Arms

→ Scotland

Benderloch	Hawthorn
Edinburgh	Dogs
Edinburgh	Galvin Brasserie De Luxe **N**
Glasgow	Stravaigin
Kintyre (Peninsula) / Kilberry	Kilberry Inn
Peebles	Osso
Peebles	Restaurant at Kailzie Gardens

→ Wales

Brecon	Felin Fach Griffin

→ Northern Ireland

Ballyclare	Oregano
Belfast	Coppi **N**
Belfast	Home **N**
Holywood	Fontana

→ Republic of Ireland

Carrickmacross	Courthouse
Clonakilty	Deasy's
Clonegall	Sha-Roe Bistro
Dingle	Chart House
Dublin	Pichet
Dublin	Pig's Ear
Dublin / Clontarf	Downstairs
Duncannon	Aldridge Lodge
Kinsale	Fishy Fishy Cafe
Lisdoonvarna	Wild Honey Inn
Malahide	Brasserie at bon appétit **N**

Bib Hotel

Good accommodation at moderate prices

➜ England

Bodmin	Bokiddick Farm
Boston Spa	Four Gables
Bourton-on-the-Water	Coombe House
Bungay / Earsham	Earsham Park Farm
Christchurch	Druid House
Deddington	Old Post House
Devizes	Blounts Court Farm
Doddington	Old Vicarage
Earl Stonham	Bays Farm
Harrogate / Kettlesing	Knabbs Ash
Hartland	Golden Park
Huccombe	Huccombe House
Kirkwhelpington	Shieldhall
Leyburn	Clyde House
Morpeth / Longhorsley	Thistleyhaugh Farm
North Bovey	Gate House
Ouston	Low Urpeth Farm **N**
Penrith	Brooklands
Ripon	Sharow Cross House
Ross-on-Wye / Kerne Bridge	Lumleys
St Keverne	Old Temperance House
Salisbury / Little Langford	Little Langford Farmhouse
Scarborough	Alexander
Sheringham	Ashbourne House
Southend-on-Sea	Beaches **N**
Stow-on-the-Wold	Number Nine
Warwick	Charter House
Wells / Easton (Somerset)	Beaconsfield Farm

➜ Scotland

Anstruther	Spindrift
Auchencairn	Balcary Mews
Ballater	Moorside House
Blairgowrie	Gilmore House
Carnoustie	Old Manor
Dunkeld	Letter Farm
Dyke	Old Kirk
Jedburgh	Willow Court
Kingussie	Hermitage
Montrose	36 The Mall
Mull (Isle of) / Tobermory	Brockville
Peebles	Rowanbrae
Perth	Taythorpe
Pitlochry	Dunmurray Lodge
Skye (Isle of) / Broadford	Tigh an Dochais
Strathpeffer	Craigvar
Thornhill	Gillbank House
Wick	Clachan

➜ Wales

Betws Garmon	Betws Inn
Builth Wells	Rhedyn **N**
Dolgellau	Tyddyn Mawr
Llandudno	Abbey Lodge
Llandudno	Lympley Lodge
Llanwrda	Tŷ Llwyd Hir **N**
Ruthin	Firgrove
Whitton	Pilleth Oaks

➜ Northern Ireland

Bangor	Cairn Bay Lodge
Crumlin	Caldhame Lodge

➜ **N** *Newly awarded distinction*

➜ Republic of Ireland

Ballyvaughan	Drumcreehy House
Bansha	Rathellen House
Carrigans	Mount Royd **N**
Castlegregory	Shores Country House
Donegal	Ardeevin
Dundalk	Rosemount
Kilkenny	Rosquil House **N**
Kinsale / Barrells Cross	Rivermount House
Oughterard	Railway Lodge
Oughterard	Waterfall Lodge
Skull/Schull	Corthna Lodge
Toormore	Fortview House
Tramore	Glenorney

Particularly pleasant hotels & guesthouses

England

London / City of Westminster Berkeley
London / City of Westminster Claridge's
London / City of Westminster Connaught
London / City of Westminster Corinthia
London / City of Westminster Dorchester
London / City of Westminster Four Seasons
London / City of Westminster Mandarin Oriental Hyde Park
London / City of Westminster Ritz
London / City of Westminster Savoy
New Milton Chewton Glen
Oxford / Great Milton Le Manoir aux Quat'Saisons
Taplow Cliveden

England

Ascot Coworth Park
Aylesbury Hartwell House
Bath / Colerne Lucknam Park
Bourton-on-the-Water / Lower Slaughter Lower Slaughter Manor
Chagford Gidleigh Park
Cheltenham Ellenborough Park
Jersey / St Saviour (Jersey) Longueville Manor
London / City of Westminster Bulgari
London / City of Westminster 45 Park Lane
London / City of Westminster Goring
London / City of Westminster Lanesborough
London / City of Westminster One Aldwych
London / City of Westminster Soho
Lyndhurst Lime Wood
Malmesbury Whatley Manor
Newbury Vineyard
North Bovey Bovey Castle
Ston Easton Ston Easton Park

Scotland

Ballantrae Glenapp Castle
Eriska (Isle of) Isle of Eriska
Fort William Inverlochy Castle

Republic of Ireland

Ballyfin Ballyfin
Dublin Merrion
Kenmare Park

England

Amberley Amberley Castle
Bath Bath Priory
Beaulieu Montagu Arms
Bolton Abbey Devonshire Arms Country House
Bourton-on-the-Water / Upper Slaughter Lords of the Manor
Broadway Buckland Manor
Chaddesley Corbett Brockencote Hall
Dedham Maison Talbooth
East Grinstead Gravetye Manor
Egham Great Fosters
Evershot Summer Lodge
Frome Babington House
Gillingham Stock Hill Country House

Guernsey / St Peter Port Old Government House H. and Spa
Jersey / La Pulente Atlantic
London / Camden Covent Garden
London / City of Westminster Charlotte Street
London / City of Westminster Dukes
London / City of Westminster Halkin
London / City of Westminster Stafford
London / Islington (Borough of) South Place
London / Kensington and Chelsea Blakes
London / Kensington and Chelsea The Capital
London / Kensington and Chelsea The Milestone
London / Kensington and Chelsea The Pelham
Newcastle upon Tyne Jesmond Dene House
Oakham / Hambleton Hambleton Hall
Reading Forbury
Royal Leamington Spa Mallory Court
Tetbury Calcot Manor
Ullswater / Pooley Bridge Sharrow Bay Country House
Winchester / Sparsholt Lainston House
Windermere / Bowness-on-Windermere Gilpin H. and Lake House
Yarm Judges Country House
York Middlethorpe Hall

→ Scotland

Blairgowrie Kinloch House
Edinburgh Prestonfield
Gullane Greywalls
Torridon Torridon

→ Wales

Llandudno Bodysgallen Hall
Llangammarch Wells Lake Country House and Spa

→ Republic of Ireland

Ardmore Cliff House
Ballyvaughan Gregans Castle
Dublin / Ballsbridge Dylan
Gorey (Wexford) Marlfield House

→ England

Ambleside The Samling
Bath Queensberry
Bigbury-on-Sea Burgh Island
Bildeston Bildeston Crown
Blakeney / Morston Morston Hall
Brampton Farlam Hall
Brockenhurst The Pig
Cirencester / Barnsley Barnsley House
Helmsley / Harome Pheasant
Lewdown Lewtrenchard Manor
London / Kensington and Chelsea Egerton House
London / Kensington and Chelsea Knightsbridge
London / Kensington and Chelsea The Levin
London / Kensington and Chelsea Number Sixteen
North Walsham Beechwood
Orford Crown and Castle
Portscatho Driftwood
Rowsley Peacock
Rushlake Green Stone House
St Mawes Hotel Tresanton
Salcombe South Sands
Scilly (Isles of) Hell Bay
Southampton / Netley Marsh Hotel TerraVina
Stratford-upon-Avon Arden
Tavistock / Milton Abbot Hotel Endsleigh
Wareham Priory
Windermere Holbeck Ghyll

→ Scotland

Abriachan Loch Ness Lodge
Achiltibuie Summer Isles
Arran (Isle of) Kilmichael Country House
Lochearnhead / Balquhidder Monachyle Mhor
Nairn Boath House
Port Appin Airds
Portpatrick Knockinaam Lodge
Skye (Isle of) / Sleat Kinloch Lodge

→ Wales

Llandudno Osborne House
Machynlleth Ynyshir Hall
Narberth Grove

→ Republic of Ireland

Ballingarry Mustard Seed at Echo Lodge
Kinsale Perryville House

England

Bourton-on-the-Water	Dial House
Bristol	Number 38 Clifton
Chillington	whitehouse
Dartmouth / Kingswear	Nonsuch House
Durham	Gadds Town House
Fivehead	Langford Fivehead
Fowey	Old Quay House
Helmsley / Harome	Cross House Lodge
Jersey / St Helier	Eulah Country House
Keswick / Portinscale	Swinside Lodge
Lynton	Hewitt's - Villa Spaldi
Lynton / Martinhoe	Old Rectory
Pershore / Eckington (Worcs)	Eckington Manor
Porlock	Oaks
Salisbury / Teffont Evias	Howard's House
Southampton	Pig-in the Wall

Scotland

Kelso / Ednam	Edenwater House
Kirkbean	Cavens
Mull (Isle of) / Tiroran	Tiroran House
Pitlochry / Killiecrankie	Killiecrankie House
Tain / Cadboll	Glenmorangie House
Walkerburn	Windlestraw Lodge

Wales

Betws-y-Coed	Tan-y-Foel Country House
Dolgellau	Ffynnon

Republic of Ireland

Bagenalstown	Kilgraney Country House
Castlelyons	Ballyvolane House
Dingle	Emlagh Country House
Lahinch	Moy House

England

Arnside	Number 43
Ash	Great Weddington
Austwick	Austwick Hall
Benenden	Ramsden Farm
Blackpool	Number One St Lukes
Bridport / Burton Bradstock	Norburton Hall
Broad Oak	Fairacres
Broadway	East House
Chipping Campden / Broad Campden	Malt House
Clun	Birches Mill
Cranbrook	Cloth Hall Oast
Dartmouth / Strete	Strete Barton House
Doddington	Old Vicarage
East Hoathly	Old Whyly
Eastbourne	Manse
Hawkshead / Far Sawrey	West Vale
Henley-on-Thames	Falaise House
Ivychurch	Olde Moat House
Lavenham	Lavenham Priory
Lizard	Landewednack House
Lurgashall	Barn
Marazion / Perranuthnoe	Ednovean Farm
Marazion / St Hilary	Ennys
Moreton-in-Marsh	Old School
North Bovey	Gate House
North Lopham	Church Farm House
Padstow	Treann
Padstow	Treverbyn House
Padstow	Woodlands Country House
Pershore	Barn
Pickering	17 Burgate
Pickering / Levisham	Moorlands Country House
Ripon	Sharow Cross House
St Austell	Anchorage House
St Mellion	Pentillie Castle
Stow-on-the-Wold / Lower Swell	Rectory Farmhouse
Tavistock / Chillaton	Tor Cottage
Thursford Green	Holly Lodge
Warkworth	Roxbro House
Wells	Stoberry House
Wold Newton	Wold Cottage

Scotland

Ayr	No.26 The Crescent
Ballantrae	Cosses Country House
Barcaldine	Ardtorna
Connel	Ards House
Drumbeg	Blar na Leisg at Drumbeg House

Edinburgh One Royal Circus
Fort William Grange
Fortrose Water's Edge
Glasgow 15 Glasgow
Grantown-on-Spey Dulaig
Harris (Isle of) / Borve Pairc an t-Srath
Islay (Isle of) / Ballygrant Kilmeny
Kilchrenan Roineabhal
Lewis (Isle of) / Back Broad Bay House
Linlithgow Arden House
Lochinver Ruddyglow Park Country House
Mainland (Orkney Islands) / Harray Holland House
Skirling Skirling House
Skye (Isle of) / Bernisdale Spoons
Strathpeffer Craigvar
Tain / Nigg Wemyss House

➜ Wales

Aberaeron 3 Pen Cei
Anglesey (Isle of) / Beaumaris Cleifiog
Anglesey (Isle of) / Menai Bridge Neuadd Lwyd
Betws-y-Coed / Penmachno Penmachno Hall
Dolfor Old Vicarage
Glynarthen Penbontbren
Pwllheli / Boduan Old Rectory
St Clears Coedllys Country House

➜ Northern Ireland

Ballintoy Whitepark House

➜ Republic of Ireland

Castlegregory Shores Country House
Cong Ballywarren House
Fethard Mobarnane House
Kenmare Sallyport House
Ramelton Moorfield Lodge
Toormore Fortview House

Particularly pleasant restaurants & pubs

➜ England

London / City of Westminster — Alain Ducasse at The Dorchester
London / City of Westminster — Ritz Restaurant

➜ England

Bath / Colerne — The Park
Bourton-on-the-Water / Lower Slaughter — Sixteen58
Bray — Waterside Inn
Chagford — Gidleigh Park
London / City of Westminster — Hélène Darroze at The Connaught
London / City of Westminster — Marcus Wareing at The Berkeley
London / City of Westminster — Sketch (The Lecture Room and Library)
Oxford / Great Milton — Le Manoir aux Quat' Saisons

➜ Scotland

Fort William — Inverlochy Castle

➜ Republic of Ireland

Dublin — Patrick Guilbaud

➜ England

Baslow — Fischer's at Baslow Hall
Birmingham — Simpsons
Blackburn / Langho — Northcote
Bourton-on-the-Water / Upper Slaughter — Lords of the Manor
Cambridge — Midsummer House
Dedham — Le Talbooth
Emsworth — 36 on the Quay
Faversham — Read's
Ilkley — Box Tree
Jersey / La Pulente — Ocean
Jersey / St Saviour (Jersey) — Longueville Manor

Lavenham	Great House
London / City of Westminster	Cut
London / City of Westminster	Delaunay
London / City of Westminster	Dining Room
London / City of Westminster	Greenhouse
London / City of Westminster	Pétrus
London / City of Westminster	Quo Vadis
London / City of Westminster	The Wolseley
London / Hackney (Borough of)	Boundary
London / Hounslow	La Trompette
London / Kensington and Chelsea	Bibendum
London / Tower Hamlets	Galvin La Chapelle
New Milton	Vetiver
Oakham / Hambleton	Hambleton Hall
Padstow	Seafood
Pateley Bridge / Ramsgill-in-Nidderdale	Yorke Arms
Reading / Shinfield	L'Ortolan
Reading / Sonning	French Horn
Skipton / Hetton	Angel Inn and Barn Lodgings
Ston Easton	Sorrel
Welwyn Garden City	Auberge du Lac
Winchester / Sparsholt	Avenue
Windermere / Bowness-on-Windermere	Gilpin H. and Lake House
Winteringham	Winteringham Fields
Woburn	Paris House

➔ Scotland

Ballantrae	Glenapp Castle
Edinburgh	21212
Nairn	Boath House
Peat Inn	The Peat Inn

➔ Wales

Llandrillo	Tyddyn Llan
Llandudno	Dining Room
Llanrhidian	Fairyhill

➔ Republic of Ireland

Dublin	Chapter One
Kenmare	Park

✕✕

➔ England

Alkham	Marquis
Ambleside	The Samling
Arlingham	Old Passage Inn
Ashwater	Blagdon Manor
Bath / Colerne	Brasserie
Blakeney / Morston	Morston Hall
Brockenhurst	The Pig
Bury St Edmunds	Maison Bleue
Cheltenham	Daffodil
Cirencester / Barnsley	The Potager

Folkestone	Rocksalt
Grantham / Great Gonerby	Harry's Place
Grantham / Hough-on-the-Hill	Brownlow Arms
Helmsley / Harome	Pheasant
Kibworth Beauchamp	Lighthouse
Kirkby Lonsdale	Hipping Hall
London / City of Westminster	Angelus
London / City of Westminster	Bar Boulud
London / City of Westminster	Brasserie Chavot
London / City of Westminster	Le Café Anglais
London / City of Westminster	Clos Maggiore
London / City of Westminster	Dinner by Heston Blumenthal
London / City of Westminster	Hawksmoor (Mayfair)
London / City of Westminster	J. Sheekey
London / City of Westminster	Momo
London / City of Westminster	Rules
London / City of Westminster	Wild Honey
London / Hackney (Borough of)	HKK
London / Hammersmith and Fulham	River Café
London / Islington (Borough of)	Angler
London / Kensington and Chelsea	Outlaw's at The Capital
London / Kings Cross St Pancras	Gilbert Scott
Ludlow	Mr Underhill's at Dinham Weir
Lyndhurst	Hartnett Holder and Co
Newquay / Watergate Bay	Fifteen Cornwall
Rowsley	Peacock
St Mawes	Restaurant Tresanton
Salcombe	Beachside
Sark	La Sablonnerie
Southampton / Netley Marsh	Restaurant TerraVina
Tavistock / Milton Abbot	Restaurant Endsleigh
Windermere	Holbeck Ghyll
Yeovil / Barwick	Little Barwick House

➜ Scotland

Gullane	Chez Roux
Lochinver	Albannach
Portpatrick	Knockinaam Lodge
Skye (Isle of) / Dunvegan	Three Chimneys and The House Over-By

➜ Wales

Machynlleth	Ynyshir Hall
Pwllheli	Plas Bodegroes

➜ Northern Ireland

Lisnaskea	Watermill

➜ Republic of Ireland

Aran Islands / Inishmaan	Inis Meáin Restaurant and Suites
Ballyvaughan	Gregans Castle
Clogheen	Old Convent
Dunkineely	Castle Murray House
Durrus	Blairscove House

England

Ashburton	Agaric
Blakeney	Wiveton Farm Café
Bournemouth	West Beach
Bray / Bray Marina	Riverside Brasserie
Bruton	At The Chapel
Falmouth / Maenporth	Cove
Jersey / St Brelades Bay	Oyster Box
London / City of Westminster	Bentley's (Oyster Bar)
London / City of Westminster	Bocca di Lupo
London / City of Westminster	Le Boudin Blanc
London / City of Westminster	Dehesa
London / City of Westminster	J. Sheekey Oyster Bar
London / Islington (Borough of)	Comptoir Gascon
London / Islington (Borough of)	Quality Chop House
London / Richmond-upon-Thames	Petersham Nurseries Café
London / Southwark (Borough of)	Oxo Tower Brasserie
London / Southwark (Borough of)	Zucca
Padstow	Paul Ainsworth at No.6
Padstow	St Petroc's
Plymouth	River Cottage Canteen and Deli
St Ives	Porthminster Beach Café
Shaldon	ODE
Stanton	Leaping Hare
Stowmarket	Buxhall Coach House
Stow-on-the-Wold / Daylesford	Café at Daylesford Organic

Scotland

Edinburgh	Timberyard
Kingairloch	Boathouse
Perth / Stanley	Apron Stage
Thurso / Scrabster	Captain's Galley

Wales

Abergavenny / Llanddewi Skirrid	Walnut Tree

Republic of Ireland

Barna	O'Grady's on the Pier
Clonegall	Sha-Roe Bistro
Dingle	Chart House
Dublin	Locks Brasserie
Kinsale	Fishy Fishy Cafe

England

Alton / Lower Froyle	The Anchor Inn
Ambleside	Drunken Duck Inn
Barnard Castle / Romaldkirk	Rose and Crown
Bath / Combe Hay	Wheatsheaf

Baughurst	Wellington Arms
Beverley / South Dalton	Pipe and Glass Inn
Bolnhurst	Plough at Bolnhurst
Bray	Hinds Head
Burford / Swinbrook	Swan Inn
Cambridge / Little Wilbraham	Hole in the Wall
Cirencester / Barnsley	Village Pub
Cirencester / Sapperton	The Bell
Clipsham	Olive Branch and Beech House
Clitheroe / Wiswell	Freemasons
East Garston	Queen's Arms
Helmsley / Harome	Star Inn
Kendal / Crosthwaite	Punch Bowl Inn
Keyston	Pheasant
Kirkby Lonsdale / Lupton	Plough
Knowstone	Masons Arms
London / Southwark (Borough of)	Garrison
Longstock	Peat Spade Inn
Lydford	Dartmoor Inn
Marlow	Hand and Flowers
Midhurst / Henley	Duke of Cumberland Arms
Northaw	Sun at Northaw
Northleach	Wheatsheaf Inn
Old Warden	Hare and Hounds
Oldstead	Black Swan
Oxford / Fyfield (Oxford)	White Hart
Skipton / Hetton	Angel Inn
Southrop	Swan
Stalisfield Green	Plough
Stockbridge	Greyhound on the Test
Stoke-by-Nayland	Crown
Stow-on-the-Wold / Nether Westcote	Feathered Nest
Sutton-on-the-Forest	Rose and Crown
Thorpe Market	Gunton Arms
Tisbury	Beckford Arms
Woodbridge / Bromeswell	British Larder
Wymondham	Berkeley Arms

→ Wales

Aberaeron	Harbourmaster
Brecon	Felin Fach Griffin
Skenfrith	Bell at Skenfrith

→ Republic of Ireland

Kinsale	Toddies at The Bulman

The Michelin Adventure

It all started with rubber balls! This was the product made by a small company based in Clermont-Ferrand that André and Edouard Michelin inherited, back in 1880. The brothers quickly saw the potential for a new means of transport and their first success was the invention of detachable pneumatic tyres for bicycles. However, the automobile was to provide the greatest scope for their creative talents.

Throughout the 20th century, Michelin never ceased developing and creating ever more reliable and high-performance tyres, not only for vehicles ranging from trucks to F1 but also for underground transit systems and aeroplanes.

From early on, Michelin provided its customers with tools and services to facilitate mobility and make travelling a more pleasurable and more frequent experience. As early as 1900, the Michelin Guide supplied motorists with a host of useful information related to vehicle maintenance, accommodation and restaurants, and was to become a benchmark for good food. At the same time, the Travel Information Bureau offered travellers personalised tips and itineraries.

The publication of the first collection of roadmaps, in 1910, was an instant hit! In 1926, the first regional guide to France was published, devoted to the principal sites of Brittany, and before long each region of France had its own Green Guide. The collection was later extended to more far-flung destinations, including New York in 1968 and Taiwan in 2011.

In the 21st century, with the growth of digital technology, the challenge for Michelin maps and guides is to continue to develop alongside the company's tyre activities. Now, as before, Michelin is committed to improving the mobility of travellers.

MICHELIN TODAY

WORLD NUMBER ONE TYRE MANUFACTURER

- 69 production sites in 18 countries
- 115,000 employees from all cultures and on every continent
- 6,000 people employed in research and development

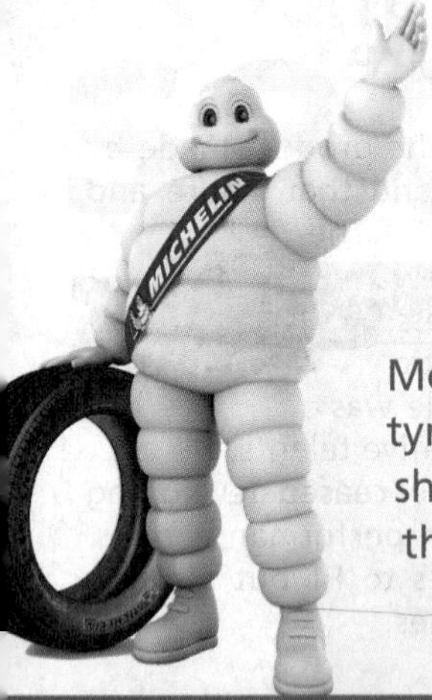

Moving for a world

Moving forward means developing tyres with better road grip and shorter braking distances, whatever the state of the road.

CORRECT TYRE PRESSURE

RIGHT PRESSURE

- Safety
- Longevity
- Optimum fuel consumption

-0,5 bar

- Durability reduced by 20% (- 8,000 km)

-1 bar

- Risk of blowouts
- Increased fuel consumption
- Longer braking distances on wet surfaces

forward together
where mobility is safer

It also involves helping motorists take care of their safety and their tyres. To do so, Michelin organises "Fill Up With Air" campaigns all over the world to remind us that correct tyre pressure is vital.

WEAR

DETECTING TYRE WEAR

MICHELIN tyres are equipped with tread wear indicators, which are small blocks of rubber molded into the base of the main grooves at a height of 1.6 mm. When tread depth is the same level as indicators, the tyres are worn and need replacing.

Tyres are the only point of contact between vehicle and the road, a worn tyre can be dangerous on wet surfaces.

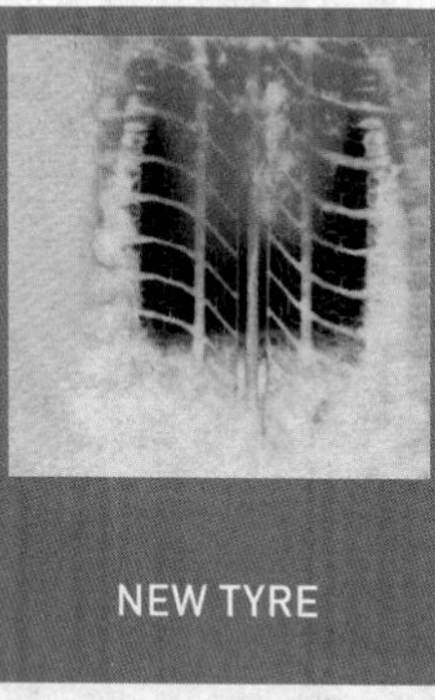

NEW TYRE

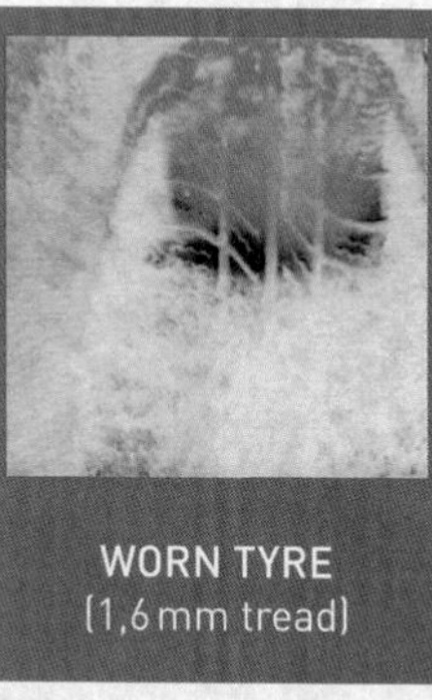

WORN TYRE
(1,6 mm tread)

The photo shows the actual contact zone on wet surfaces.

Moving forward means sustainable mobility

INNOVATION AND THE ENVIRONMENT

By 2050, Michelin aims to cut the quantity of raw materials used in its tyre manufacturing process by half and to have developed renewable energy in its facilities. The design of MICHELIN tyres has already saved billions of litres of fuel and, by extension, billions of tonnes of CO2.

Similarly, Michelin prints its maps and guides on paper produced from sustainably managed forests and is diversifying its publishing media by offering digital solutions to make travelling easier, more fuel efficient and more enjoyable!

The group's whole-hearted commitment to eco-design on a daily basis is demonstrated by ISO 14001 certification.

Like you, Michelin is committed to preserving our planet.

Chat with Bibendum

Go to www.michelin.com/corporate/EN/home
Find out more about Michelin's
history and the latest news.

QUIZ

Michelin develops tyres for all types of vehicles. See if you can match the right tyre with the right vehicle…

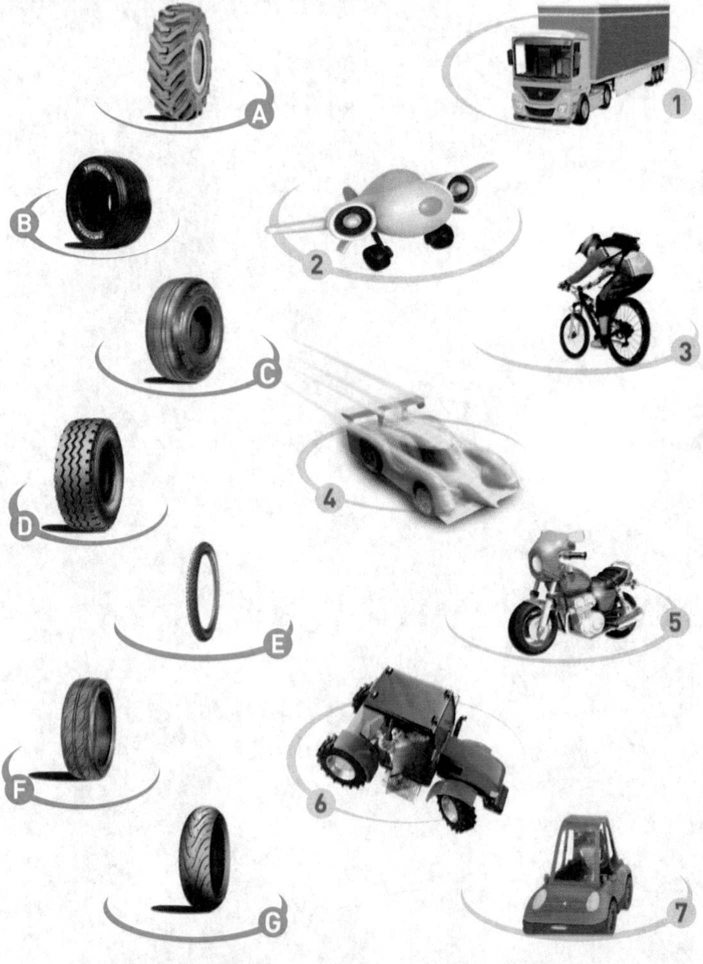

Solution : A-6 / B-4 / C-2 / D-1 / E-3 / F-7 / G-5

Towns

from A to Z

Great Britain

PS
Minster Deli
Oxfam
BRADLEYS
Family Jewellers
NOA
NOA

England

Channel Islands • Isle of Man

ABBERLEY – Worcestershire – **503** M27 – **pop. 654** – ✉ **Worcester** **18** B2

🚇 London 137 mi – Birmingham 27 mi – Worcester 13 mi

Elms ♨ ≼ 🚗 🐾 🔥 📺 ◉ ⑩ 🎧 ⚿ ✕ ☗ rm, ♠ ⚒ 🛜 🅿

Stockton Rd, West : 2 mi on A 443 ✉ *WR6 6AT* – 𝒞 *(01299) 896 666*
– www.theelmshotel.co.uk
23 rm ☑ – 🛏£ 102/204 🛏🛏£ 120/240
Rest *Brookes* – Menu £ 21/39
Rest *Garden Café* – Carte £ 25/42

Impressive Queen Anne house with spacious guest areas where modern colours and fabrics blend with traditional furnishings. Bedrooms are split between the house and the old stables; most boast pleasant country views. Classic dishes in Brookes. All-day menu in the more informal Garden Café, which is child-friendly and set within the pleasant spa.

ABBOTSBURY – Dorset – **503** M32 – **pop. 422** **3** B3

🚇 London 146 mi – Bournemouth 44 mi – Exeter 50 mi – Weymouth 10 mi

◉ Town★★ - Chesil Beach★★ - Swannery★ **AC** – Sub-Tropical Gardens★ **AC**

◉ St Catherine's Chapel★, 0.5 mi uphill (30 mn rtn on foot). Maiden Castle★★ (≼★) NE : 7.5 m

Abbey House without rest ♨ ≼ 🚗 ⚒ 🛜 🅿

Church St ✉ *DT3 4JJ* – 𝒞 *(01305) 871 330* – *www.theabbeyhouse.co.uk*
5 rm ☑ – 🛏£ 75 🛏🛏£ 75/110

Characterful guesthouse-cum-tea-shop in a stunning location beside the ruins of a 15C abbey. Well-kept, classical bedrooms; one has a half-tester and one runs almost the length of the building. Unique Benedictine watermill in the gardens.

ABBOTS RIPTON – Cambridgeshire – **504** T26/27 – see Huntingdon

ABINGDON – Oxfordshire – **503** Q28 – **pop. 36 010** ▯ Great Britain **10** B2

🚇 London 64 mi – Oxford 6 mi – Reading 25 mi

⛴ from Abingdon Bridge to Oxford (Salter Bros. Ltd) 2 daily (summer only)

🛈 Abbey Close, 𝒞 (01235) 52 27 11, www.abingdon.gov.uk

 Drayton Park, Drayton, Steventon Rd, 𝒞 (01235) 55 06 07

◉ Town★ – County Hall★

at Marcham West : 3 mi on A 415

Rafters without rest ⚒ 🛜 🅿

Abingdon Rd, on A 415 ✉ *OX13 6NU* – 𝒞 *(01865) 391 298*
– www.bnb-rafters.co.uk
4 rm ☑ – 🛏£ 55/89 🛏🛏£ 99/130

An unassuming exterior conceals a stylish, modern hotel. Smart bedrooms have a Scandic feel and excellent facilities; one even has a water bed! The friendly owner serves homemade bread and tasty local bacon and sausages for breakfast.

ABINGER COMMON – Surrey – **504** S30 **7** D2

🚇 London 32 mi – Croydon 26 mi – Barnet 62 mi – Ealing 44 mi

🍺 **Abinger Hatch** 🚗 🔥 🅿

Abinger Ln ✉ *RH5 6HZ* – 𝒞 *(01306) 730 737* – *www.theabingerhatch.com*
Rest – Carte £ 18/24

Set in prime walking country, this attractive 18C inn has been lovingly restored and now oozes country gentility. The bar is the best spot to enjoy the flavoursome country cooking, and the outside kitchen is a hit in the warmer months.

ALDEBURGH – Suffolk – **504** Y27 – **pop. 2 654** **15** D3

🚇 London 97 mi – Ipswich 24 mi – Norwich 41 mi

🛈 152 High St, 𝒞 (01728) 45 36 37, www.aldeburgh-uk.com

 Thorpeness Hotel and Golf Course, Thorpeness, 𝒞 (01728) 45 21 76

Wentworth

Wentworth Rd ✉ IP15 5BD – ☎ (01728) 452 312
– www.wentworth-aldeburgh.com
35 rm (dinner included) – £ 79/123 £ 127/280
Rest – Menu £ 13 (weekdays)/25
Carefully furnished, traditional seaside hotel; coast view bedrooms are equipped with binoculars and all have a copy of 'Orlando the Marmalade Cat'; a story set in the area. Formal dining room offers mix of brasserie and classic dishes.

Brudenell

The Parade ✉ IP15 5BU – ☎ (01728) 452 071 – www.brudenellhotel.co.uk
44 rm – £ 100/120 £ 130/335 **Rest** – Carte £ 22/46
Contemporary hotel situated right on the beach, with a relaxed ambience and superb sea views. Bedrooms feature modern bathrooms and up-to-date facilities. Informal, split-level bar/restaurant offers an accessible menu of modern classics to suit every taste.

Lighthouse

77 High St ✉ IP15 5AU – ☎ (01728) 453 377 – www.lighthouserestaurant.co.uk
– Closed lunch 1 January and lunch 26 December
Rest – *(booking essential)* Menu £ 10 – Carte £ 20/35
Popular split-level eatery with bright yellow décor, amiable service and a laid-back feel. Menus change constantly, featuring fish from the boats 200m away and local, seasonal meats and vegetables. Flavoursome, rustic dishes come in generous portions and display subtle Mediterranean influences.

ENGLAND

Aldeburgh Market Cafe

170-172 High St ✉ IP15 5EY – ☎ (01728) 452 520
– www.thealdeburghmarket.co.uk – Closed 25 December
Rest – Carte £ 16/33
Set in a shop brimming with fresh local vegetables and a beautiful array of fresh seafood; the best tables are in the bay window, with views across the street. Well-priced, flavoursome cooking; relaxed, friendly service.

ALDERLEY EDGE – Cheshire East – 502 N24 – pop. 5 280 20 B3

London 187 mi – Chester 34 mi – Manchester 14 mi – Stoke-on-Trent 25 mi
Wilmslow, Mobberley, Great Warford, ☎ (01565) 87 21 48

Alderley Edge

Macclesfield Rd ✉ SK9 7BJ – ☎ (01625) 583 033 – www.alderleyedgehotel.com
50 rm – £ 100/140 £ 135/155 – 1 suite
Rest ***The Brasserie*** **Rest** ***Alderley*** – see restaurant listing
Well-run, early Victorian country house in an affluent village. Smart landscaped gardens; compact, fairly formal interior with modern, leather-furnished guest areas and stylish bedrooms. Good service from dedicated staff.

Alderley – Alderley Edge Hotel

Macclesfield Rd ✉ SK9 7BJ – ☎ (01625) 583 033 – www.alderleyedgehotel.com
– Closed Sunday dinner to non residents
Rest – Menu £ 26/30 – Carte £ 46/48
Smart, formal conservatory restaurant with a long-standing reputation. Modern British dishes display some interesting combinations. Good value lunch and daily evening menus. Excellent wine list with some fine vintage burgundies and clarets.

The Brasserie – Alderley Edge Hotel

Macclesfield Rd ✉ SK9 7BJ – ☎ (01625) 583 033 – www.alderleyedgehotel.com
– Closed Sunday
Rest – Carte £ 23/34
Informal, French-style brasserie with mirrored walls and leather banquettes, on the ground floor of a well-run, busy hotel. Retro British dishes like prawn and crayfish cocktail, scampi in a basket and jam roly poly are given a modern twist.

Wizard Inn
Macclesfield Rd, Southeast : 1.25 mi on B 5087 ✉ SK10 4UB – ✆ (01625) 584 000 – www.ainscoughs.co.uk – Closed 25 December
Rest – Menu £ 10 (weekday dinner) – Carte £ 21/38
Characterful, dog-friendly, 200 year old pub with flag floors, beams and open fires; set next to the Alderley Edge escarpment. The wide-ranging menu offers traditional pub favourites, retro British classics and fish and meat platters.

ALDFIELD – North Yorkshire – 502 P21 – see Ripon

ALFRISTON – East Sussex – 504 U31 – pop. 1 721 – ✉ Polegate 8 A3

London 66 mi – Eastbourne 9 mi – Lewes 10 mi – Newhaven 8 mi

Wingrove House with rm
High St ✉ BN26 5TD – ✆ (01323) 870 276 – www.wingrovehousealfriston.com – Closed 25 December
5 rm – †£ 95/110 ††£ 95/175
Rest – *(dinner only and lunch Saturday and Sunday)* Carte £ 19/34
Imposing colonial-style house; personally run, with relaxed, informal feel. Spacious, contemporary brasserie, wood-floored lounge and pleasant terrace. Modern menu of brasserie dishes served by a bright team. Understated, stylish bedrooms; some with balconies.

George Inn with rm
High St ✉ BN26 5SY – ✆ (01323) 870 319 – www.thegeorge-alfriston.com – Closed 25-26 December
6 rm – †£ 60/80 ††£ 100/140 **Rest** – Carte £ 22/34
Characterful 14C stone and timber pub in a delightful village on the Southdown Way. The traditional blackboard menu changes every 3 months – if you're after a snack, try one of the rustic sharing boards. Comfortable bedrooms have period charm; Bob Hall boasts 13C wattle and daub murals.

ENGLAND

ALKHAM – Kent – 504 X30 – pop. 607 9 D2

London 72 mi – Birmingham 198 mi – Liverpool 291 mi – Leeds 264 mi

Alkham Court without rest
Meggett Ln, Southwest : 1 mi by Alkham Valley Rd ✉ CT15 7DG – ✆ (01303) 892 056 – www.alkhamcourt.co.uk
4 rm – †£ 100/130 ††£ 130/160
Set on a hill and surrounded by mature grounds, a delightful guesthouse with a hot tub, a sauna and a livery yard for 20 horses. Good-sized, homely, well-equipped bedrooms and stylish bathrooms. Large conservatory offers lovely views.

Marquis with rm
Alkham Valley Rd ✉ CT15 7DF – ✆ (01304) 873 410 – www.themarquisatalkham.co.uk – Closed Monday lunch
10 rm – †£ 64/199 ††£ 89/249
Rest – Menu £ 13 (weekday lunch)/55 – Carte £ 24/60
Fashionable former pub with smart bar, stylish dining room and relaxed atmosphere. Accomplished cooking features classical combinations with original touches; portions are generous and presentation is modern. 'Foraging' and 'tasting' menus available. Chic, sexy bedrooms boast luxurious bathrooms.

ALNWICK – Northumberland – 501 O17 – pop. 7 767 Great Britain 24 B2

London 320 mi – Edinburgh 86 mi – Newcastle upon Tyne 34 mi
2 The Shambles, ✆ (01665) 510 665, www.visitalnwick.org.uk
Swansfield Park, ✆ (01665) 60 26 32
Town ★ - Castle★★ **AC**
Dunstanburgh Castle★ **AC**, NE : 8 mi by B 1340 and Dunstan rd (last 2.5 mi on foot)

Greycroft without rest
Croft Pl, via Prudhoe St ✉ NE66 1XU – ✆ (01665) 602 127 – www.greycroft.co.uk – Closed Christmas
6 rm – £ 63/68 £ 95/130
Late 19C house by Alnwick Castle and Gardens. Individually decorated bedrooms have good facilities and homely touches; bright conservatory breakfast room overlooks the walled garden. The welcoming owners will recommend local sights.

Aln House without rest
South Rd, Southeast : 0.75 mi by B 6346 on Newcastle rd ✉ NE66 2NZ – ✆ (01665) 602 265 – www.alnhouse.co.uk – Closed 24-26 December
6 rm – £ 65/80 £ 90/100
Bay windowed, semi-detached Edwardian house with mature front and rear gardens; run by friendly, welcoming owners. Homely lounge and neatly laid breakfast room. Well-kept, individually decorated bedrooms have feature walls and bright décor.

at North Charlton North : 6.75 mi by A 1 – ✉ Alnwick

North Charlton Farm without rest
✉ NE67 5HP – ✆ (01665) 579 443 – www.northcharltonfarm.co.uk – Closed Christmas
3 rm – £ 45 £ 80
Attractive house on working farm with agricultural museum. Offers traditional accommodation. Each bedroom is individually decorated and has countryside views.

at Chathill North : 8.75 mi by A 1 off B 6347

Doxford Hall H. and Spa
rm,
✉ NE67 5DN – ✆ (01665) 589 700 – www.doxfordhall.com
30 rm – £ 93/153 £ 125/245 – 1 suite
Rest ***George Runciman*** – Menu £ 25/30
Extended Georgian house with immaculately kept, formal gardens; a popular venue for weddings. Numerous comfy lounges and a smart spa. Bedrooms mix modern facilities and antique furniture; those in the original house are spacious and contemporary. Traditional menus in the formal, wood-panelled dining room.

ENGLAND

ALSTONEFIELD – Staffordshire – 504 O24 – pop. 274 19 C1

London 157 mi – Birmingham 66 mi – Liverpool 77 mi – Leeds 88 mi

George
✉ DE6 2FX – ✆ (01335) 310 205 – www.thegeorgeatalstonefield.com – Closed 25 December
Rest – Carte £ 23/45
Simply furnished, family-run pub with roaring fire and relaxed, cosy atmosphere. Daily changing menus offer well-priced, down-to-earth dishes; good 'on toast' section at lunch.

ALTON – Hampshire – 504 R30 – pop. 16 051 6 B2

London 53 mi – Reading 24 mi – Southampton 29 mi – Winchester 18 mi
7 Cross and Pillory Lane, ✆ (01420) 8 84 48, www.visit-hampshire.co.uk
Old Odiham Rd, ✆ (01420) 8 20 42

at Lower Froyle Northeast : 4.5 mi by A 31

The Anchor Inn with rm
✉ GU34 4NA – ✆ (01420) 23 261 – www.anchorinnatlowerfroyle.co.uk – Closed 25 December
5 rm – £ 120/160 £ 120/160 **Rest** – Carte £ 24/44
Part-whitewashed, part-tile hung 14C building in pretty countryside, boasting low beams, open fires and bric-a-brac aplenty. Good-sized menus offer classic pub dishes with a refined edge; cooking is hearty and flavoursome. Bedrooms are fittingly characterful.

ALTRINCHAM – Greater Manchester – 502 N23 – pop. 40 695 — 20 B3

London 191 mi – Chester 30 mi – Liverpool 30 mi – Manchester 8 mi

20 Stamford New Rd, (0161) 912 59 31, www.altrincham.org.uk

Altrincham Municipal, Timperley, Stockport Rd, (0161) 928 07 61

Dunham Forest, Oldfield Lane, (0161) 928 26 05

Ringway, Hale Barns, Hale Mount, (0161) 980 26 30

Victoria

29 Stamford St ✉ WA14 1EX – (0161) 613 18 55 – www.thevictoria-altrincham.co.uk – Closed 1 January, 26 December and Sunday dinner

Rest – *(bookings advisable at dinner)* Menu £ 14 (weekday dinner)/20 – Carte £ 26/35

Traditional looking pub in a quiet part of town, with flowers on the windowsills, a few pavement tables and an appealing, single-roomed interior with a wooden bar at its centre. Menu offers light bites and classics with a modern twist.

at Little Bollington Southwest : 3.25 mi on A 56 – ✉ Altrincham

Ash Farm without rest

Park Ln ✉ WA14 4TJ – (0161) 929 92 90 – www.ashfarm.co.uk – Closed 8-28 January

5 rm – †£ 49/67 ††£ 79/94

Red-brick, 18C former farmhouse with pine-furnished breakfast room and comfy lounge with wood-burning stove. Some bedrooms are furnished in a traditional country house style; others are more modern. Large garden. Friendly owners.

ENGLAND

ALVESTON – Warwickshire – 504 O/P27 – see Stratford-upon-Avon

AMBERLEY – West Sussex – 504 S31 – pop. 525 – ✉ Arundel — 7 C2

Great Britain

London 56 mi – Brighton 24 mi – Portsmouth 31 mi

Bignor Roman Villa (mosaics★) **AC**, NW : 3.5 mi by B 2139 via Bury

Amberley Castle

Southwest : 0.5 mi on B 2139 ✉ BN18 9LT – (01798) 831 992 – www.amberleycastle.co.uk

19 rm – †£ 315/680 ††£ 315/680 – 6 suites

Rest *Queen's Room* – see restaurant listing

Stunning 12C castle displaying original stonework, battlements and evidence of a moat. Charming grounds with lovely gardens, lakes and a croquet lawn, matched inside by a characterful array of rooms. Sumptuous bedrooms boast spa baths and a palpable sense of history. Ongoing refurbishments in 2014.

Queen's Room – Amberley Castle Hotel

Southwest : 0.5 mi on B 2139 ✉ BN18 9LT – (01798) 831 992 – www.amberleycastle.co.uk

Rest – *(booking essential)* Menu £ 25/65

Elegant dining room with a barrel-vaulted ceiling, lancet windows and an open fire, set within a stunning 12C castle. Ambitious modern menu; dishes are complex and arrive artfully presented.

AMBLESIDE – Cumbria – 502 L20 – pop. 3 064 Great Britain — 21 A2

London 276 mi – Birmingham 162 mi – Liverpool 93 mi – Leeds 121 mi

Market Cross, (015394) 3 25 82, www.thehubofambleside.co.uk

Central Buildings

Lake Windermere★★ – Dove Cottage, Grasmere★ **AC** AY **A** – Brockhole National Park Centre★ **AC**, SE : 3 mi by A 591 AZ. Wrynose Pass★★, W : 7.5 mi by A 593 AY – Hard Knott Pass★★, W : 10 mi by A 593 AY

AMBLESIDE

Borrans Rd . . . . BY 2
Cheapside . . . . AZ 4
Church St . . . . AZ 6
Compston St . . . . AZ 8
Kelsick Rd . . . . AZ 12
King St . . . . AZ 13
Lake Rd . . . . AZ
Market Pl. . . . . AZ 14
North Rd . . . . AZ 17
Old Lake Rd . . . . AZ 20
St Mary's Lane . . . . AZ 22
Smithy Brow . . . . AZ 23

GRASMERE

Broadgate . . . . BZ 3
Easedale Rd . . . . BZ 10
Swan Lane . . . . AY 24

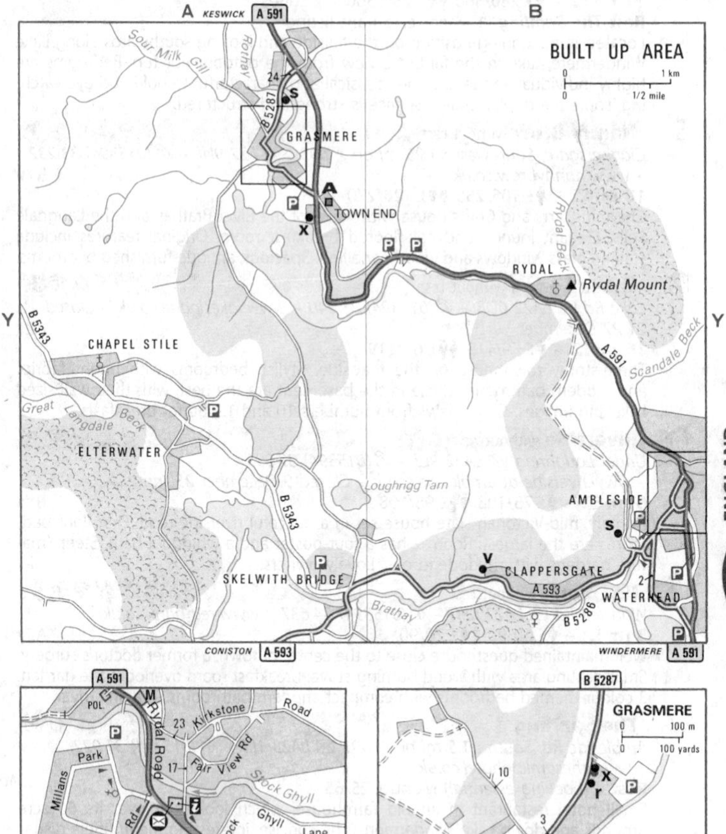

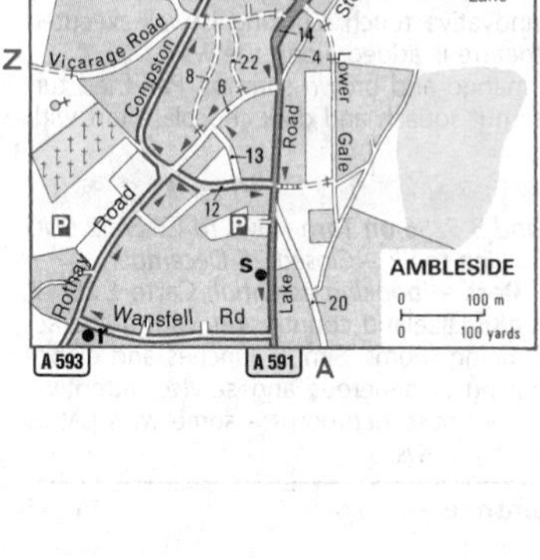

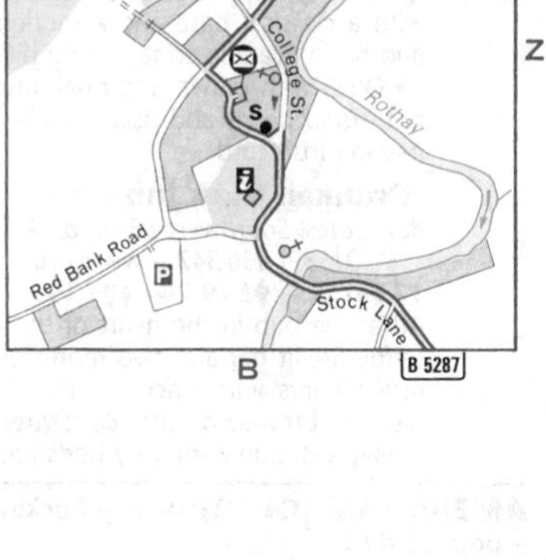

The Samling
Ambleside Rd, South : 1.5 mi on A 591 ✉ LA23 1LR – ✆ (015394) 31 922 – www.thesamlinghotel.co.uk
11 rm – £ 280/560 £ 280/560 – 2 suites
Rest *The Samling* ✿ – see restaurant listing
Located in a stunning position on the fellside and looking southwards along Lake Windermere; take in the fantastic view from the outdoor hot tub. Bedrooms are highly individual and range from classical and characterful to bold and eye-catching; some are duplex suites. Service is strong and structured.

Nanny Brow without rest
Clappersgate, Southwest : 1.25 mi on A 593 ✉ LA22 9NF – ✆ (015394) 33 232 – www.nannybrow.co.uk BY**v**
10 rm – £ 105/255 £ 120/270
Charming Arts and Crafts house with views of the River Brathay and the Langdale Fells. Elegant lounge and oak-floored breakfast room. Original features include stained glass windows and wood panelling. Spacious, antique-furnished bedrooms.

Lakes Lodge without rest
Lake Rd ✉ LA22 0DB – ✆ (015394) 33 240 – www.lakeslodge.co.uk – Closed 21-27 December AZ**s**
16 rm – £ 59/119 £ 69/119
Three-storey townhouse on the roadside. Stylish bedrooms with bright fabrics and modern bathrooms; those in the basement are the best, with their wall-sized Lakeland images. Great views from numbers 10 and 12. Buffet breakfasts.

Riverside without rest
Under Loughrigg ✉ LA22 9LJ – ✆ (015394) 32 395 – www.riverside-at-ambleside.co.uk – Closed 9 December-25 January
6 rm – £ 75/108 £ 98/108 BY**s**
Homely, mid-Victorian slate house set in a peaceful riverside road. First floor bedrooms are the largest; Room 2 has a four-poster and a whirlpool bath. Steep, mature gardens with rhododendrons. Lovely owners.

ENGLAND

Red Bank without rest
Wansfell Rd ✉ LA22 0EG – ✆ (015394) 34 637 – www.red-bank.co.uk
3 rm – £ 60/90 £ 70/90 AZ**r**
Well-maintained guesthouse close to the centre of town; a former doctor's surgery. Small seating area with wood burning stove; breakfast room overlooks the garden. 3 colour-themed bedrooms with compact, modern bathrooms. Tea on arrival.

XX ✿ **The Samling**
Ambleside Rd, South : 1.5 mi on A 591 ✉ LA23 1LR – ✆ (015394) 31 922 – www.thesamlinghotel.co.uk
Rest – *(booking essential)* Menu £ 25/65
Small hotel restaurant in an old farmhouse, which looks out over its 66 acre grounds and down Lake Windermere. The concise, interesting menu offers dishes with a classical base and a modern, innovative touch. Cooking is well-executed and has a Scandic edge; a little bit of theatre is added along the way.
→ Quail with prawn and quail ravioli, mango and brown shrimps. Pan-fried turbot, squid pearls and Asian broth. Butternut squash and dark chocolate tart with passion fruit curd.

Drunken Duck Inn with rm
Barngates, Southwest : 3 mi by A 593 and B 5286 on Tarn Hows rd ✉ LA22 0NG – ✆ (01539) 436 347 – www.drunkenduckinn.co.uk – Closed 25 December
17 rm – £ 79/244 £ 105/325 **Rest** – *(booking essential)* Carte £ 25/47
Attractive pub in the heart of the beautiful Lakeland countryside, with a characterful, fire-lit bar and two more formal dining rooms. Simple lunches and elaborate dinners with prices to match; cooking is generous and service, attentive. Ales are brewed on-site. Boutique, country house bedrooms – some with patios – have extremely squashy beds and country views.

AMERSHAM (Old Town) – Buckinghamshire – 504 S29 – pop. 21 470 — 11 D2
London 34 mi – Birmingham 109 mi – Liverpool 203 mi – Leeds 189 mi
Little Chalfont, Lodge Lane, ✆ (01494) 76 48 77

XX **Artichoke**

9 Market Sq ✉ HP7 0DF – ✆ (01494) 726 611 – www.artichokerestaurant.co.uk – Closed 2 weeks late August, 1 week spring, 1 week Christmas, Sunday and Monday

Rest – *(booking essential at dinner)* Menu £ 22 (weekday lunch)/45 – Carte lunch £ 37/45

16C red-brick house in a picturesque town, with an artichoke etched on its window. A narrow beamed room with cream-painted walls and polished tables leads through to a more modern extension. Ambitious modern dishes arrive nicely presented.

X **Gilbey's**

1 Market Sq ✉ HP7 0DF – ✆ (01494) 727 242 – www.gilbeygroup.com – Closed 24-30 December

Rest – *(booking essential)* Menu £ 20 (weekdays)/28 – Carte £ 31/44

Part of a 17C school, a busy neighbourhood restaurant that's becoming a local institution. It's rooted in tradition, from the furnishings to the food; homemade jams feature at afternoon tea. Three rustic rooms and a delightful terrace.

AMPLEFORTH – North Yorkshire – 502 Q21 – see Helmsley

ANSTEY – Hertfordshire – 504 Q25 — 12 B2

London 38 mi – Croydon 71 mi – Barnet 35 mi – Ealing 47 mi

Anstey Grove Barn without rest

East : 0.5 mi on Meesden rd ✉ SG9 0BJ – ✆ (01763) 848 828 – www.ansteygrovebarn.co.uk

6 rm – †£ 65/100 ††£ 80/100

Converted barn at the centre of what was a working pig farm; fronted by a pleasant rose and herb garden. Large, open-plan lounge and communal breakfast area. Light, airy bedrooms with wood floors; one has a four-poster and a roll-top bath.

APPLEBY-IN-WESTMORLAND – Cumbria – 502 M20 – pop. 2 862 — 21 B2

London 285 mi – Carlisle 33 mi – Kendal 24 mi – Middlesbrough 58 mi

Boroughgate, ✆ (017683) 5 11 77, www.visitcumbria.com

Appleby, Brackenber Moor, ✆ (017683) 5 14 32

Appleby Manor Country House

Roman Rd, East : 1 mi by B 6542 and Station Rd ✉ CA16 6JB – ✆ (017683) 51 571 – www.applebymanor.co.uk – Closed Christmas

31 rm – †£ 75/105 ††£ 150/240 **Rest** – Carte £ 29/40 **s**

Family-run, Victorian gentleman's residence with mature gardens and more recent extensions. Spacious, traditionally styled guest areas; small leisure suite. Bedrooms in the original house are the most characterful. Two-roomed, formal restaurant offers classical menus.

Tufton Arms

Market Sq ✉ CA16 6XA – ✆ (017683) 51 593 – www.tuftonarmshotel.co.uk – Closed 24-27 December

22 rm – †£ 83/123 ††£ 140/210 **Rest** – Carte £ 19/37

16C former coaching inn, in an old market town; popular with fishing and shooting parties. Guest areas include two traditional lounges and a bar. Chic bedrooms are a complete contrast with their bold fabrics and wallpapers. Classical, cane-furnished restaurant offers an easy-going menu.

APPLEDORE – Devon – 503 H30 – pop. 2 187 — 2 C1

London 228 mi – Barnstaple 12 mi – Exeter 46 mi – Plymouth 61 mi

Town★

West Farm without rest

Irsha St, West : 0.25 mi ✉ EX39 1RY – ✆ (01237) 425 269 – www.appledore-devon.co.uk – Closed Christmas-New Year

3 rm – †£ 57/67 ††£ 100

Whitewashed house with mature rear gardens, hidden away among the tiny cottages in this characterful coastal village. Comfortable, traditional sitting room, delightful, antique-furnished dining room and homely bedrooms.

ENGLAND

APPLETREEWICK – North Yorkshire – 502 O21 — 22 B2

London 238 mi – Birmingham 148 mi – Liverpool 87 mi – Leeds 29 mi

Knowles Lodge without rest
South : 1 mi on Bolton Abbey rd ✉ BD23 6DQ – ✆ (01756) 720 228 – www.knowleslodge.com
4 rm – †£ 60 ††£ 100
Unusual, timber-clad, Canadian ranch house, surrounded by 16 acres of meadows and woodland. Simple, well-kept bedrooms with floral fabrics; the top one has super Wharfe Valley views. Comfy lounge and airy, communal breakfast room.

ARKHOLME – Lancashire – 502 M21 — 20 A1

London 254 mi – Birmingham 140 mi – Liverpool 71 mi – Leeds 99 mi

Redwell Inn
Southwest : 3 mi on B 6254 ✉ LA6 1BQ – ✆ (015242) 21 240 – www.redwellinn.net – Closed 25 December, January and Monday-Wednesday
Rest – *(booking advisable)* Carte £ 19/41
Attractive 16C stone inn with a rustic bar and more formal dining room. The son cooks while his parents look after the front of house. Menus offer something for everyone, from a homemade Scotch egg with HP sauce to a classic fish pie.

ARLINGHAM – Gloucestershire – 503 M28 – pop. 377 – ✉ Gloucester — 4 C1

London 120 mi – Birmingham 69 mi – Bristol 34 mi – Gloucester 16 mi

ENGLAND

Old Passage Inn with rm
Passage Rd, West : 0.75 mi ✉ GL2 7JR – ✆ (01452) 740 547 – www.theoldpassage.com – Closed 25-26 December, Sunday dinner and Monday and dinner Tuesday-Wednesday January-February
3 rm – †£ 60/130 ††£ 80/130
Rest – Menu £ 15 (weekday lunch) – Carte £ 35/73
Sweet, green painted former inn by the River Severn – its terrace is a great place to watch the famous Severn Bore. Bright yellow décor, red tiled floors and eye-catching local art for sale. Good-sized seafood menus offer simply prepared dishes of top notch produce. Well-equipped, modern bedrooms boast pleasant views.

ARMSCOTE – Warwickshire – 504 P27 — 19 C3

London 98 mi – Birmingham 45 mi – Liverpool 139 mi – Leeds 145 mi

Willow Corner without rest
✉ CV37 8DE – ✆ (01608) 682 391 – www.willowcorner.co.uk – Restricted opening in winter, minimum 2 night stay weekends in summer
3 rm – †£ 55/70 ††£ 70/85
Creamwashed thatched cottage in a small village, with low-beamed, homely guest areas. Original features include leaded windows, an inglenook fireplace and a stable door. Cottage-style bedrooms boast good facilities and thoughtful touches.

ARNSIDE – Cumbria – 502 L21 – pop. 2 301 — 21 A3

London 257 mi – Liverpool 74 mi – Manchester 69 mi – Bradford 97 mi

Number 43
43 The Promenade ✉ LA5 0AA – ✆ (01524) 762 761 – www.no43.org.uk
6 rm – †£ 120 ††£ 120/180 **Rest** – Menu £ 20
Stylishly converted Victorian townhouse boasting superb estuary and fell views. Contemporary bedrooms have smart bathrooms, quality furnishings, good facilities and come with plenty of extras. Comfortable, open-plan lounge and dining room, where light meat and cheese sharing platters are offered in the evening. Have breakfast on the glass-enclosed terrace.

ARUNDEL – West Sussex – 504 S31 – pop. 3 297 Great Britain — 7 C2

London 58 mi – Brighton 21 mi – Southampton 41 mi – Worthing 9 mi
61 High St, ✆ (01903) 88 22 68, www.arundel.org.uk
Castle★★ AC

XX **Town House** with rm
65 High St ✉ BN18 9AJ – ✆ (01903) 883 847 – www.thetownhouse.co.uk
– Closed 2 weeks Easter, 2 weeks October, 25-26 December, 1 January, Sunday and Monday
4 rm – †£ 75/95 ††£ 95/130 **Rest** – Menu £ 18/30
Early 17C house displaying original sugar glass windows and an impressively ornate Renaissance ceiling with gilded walnut panelling, taken from a Medici palace in Florence. Smartly laid, intimate dining room. Confidently executed, tried-and-tested dishes with a classical base. Quirky, well-equipped bedrooms.

at Burpham **Northeast : 3 mi by A 27 – ✉ Arundel**

Burpham Country House
The Street ✉ BN18 9RJ – ✆ (01903) 882 160 – www.burphamcountryhouse.com
– Closed January and 25-26 December
9 rm – †£ 80/140 ††£ 80/145
Rest – *(closed Sunday-Monday and lunch Tuesday and Saturday)* Carte £ 23/34
Remotely set former hunting lodge, built in 1720; very personally run and with a relaxing atmosphere. Individually styled bedrooms; 6 and 7 are the most comfortable. Pretty dining room and conservatory offer a regularly changing menu of classical dishes. Comprehensive breakfasts.

George & Dragon Inn
Main St ✉ BN18 9RR – ✆ (01903) 883 131 – www.gdinn.co.uk
Rest – Menu £ 13/16 – Carte £ 24/34
Standing close to the green in a peaceful hamlet, this good old English pub has been trading since 1736. The menu features British classics supplemented by pub favourites and daily specials. Sit in the traditional dining room or rustic bar.

ENGLAND

ASCOT – **Windsor and Maidenhead** – **504** R29 – **pop. 15 761** **11** D3
London 37 mi – Birmingham 119 mi – Liverpool 213 mi – Leeds 214 mi
Mill Ride, Ascot, ✆ (01344) 88 67 77

Coworth Park
London Rd, East : 2.75 mi on A 329 ✉ SL5 7SE – ✆ (01344) 876 600
– www.coworthpark.com
70 rm – †£ 215/500 ††£ 215/500 – 21 suites
Rest *Coworth Park* Rest *Barn* – see restaurant listing
17C property set in 246 acres, with its own championship polo pitches. Stylish, comfortable guest areas. Beautiful bedrooms feature bespoke furniture, marble bathrooms and excellent facilities; those in main house are the largest. Superb spa built into the hillside, with a living roof of herbs and flowers.

XXXX **Coworth Park** – Coworth Park Hotel
London Rd, East : 2.75 mi on A 329 ✉ SL5 7SE – ✆ (01344) 876 600
– www.coworthpark.com – Closed Sunday dinner and Monday
Rest – Menu £ 30 (weekday lunch)/40 – Carte approx. £ 75
A bright, elegant restaurant in a beautiful 17C mansion house, with stylish tableware, an eye-catching centrepiece and a lovely terrace offering views over the manicured gardens. Modern, well-presented cooking; professional service.

XX **Ascot Oriental**
East : 2.25 mi on A 329 ✉ SL5 0PU – ✆ (01344) 621 877
– www.ascotoriental.com – Closed 25-26 December
Rest – Menu £ 28/33 – Carte £ 32/47
Professionally run restaurant with calming décor. Extensive menu combines old customer favourites with newer, more original dishes; excellent Cantonese choices. Clean, flavoursome cooking.

XX **Barn** – Coworth Park Hotel
London Rd, East : 2.75 mi on A 329 ✉ SL5 7SE – ✆ (01344) 876 600
– www.coworthpark.com
Rest – Menu £ 25 (weekday lunch)/35 – Carte £ 33/52
A buzzy, informal alternative to this 17C mansion's fine dining restaurant. The rustic room's floor-to-ceiling windows let in plenty of light and offer views over the fields. The menu offers old favourites like steak and fish and chips.

Ascot Grill

6 Hermitage Par, High St ✉ SL5 7HE – ✆ (01344) 622 285 – www.ascotgrill.co.uk – Closed 25-26 December, 1 January and Sunday
Rest – Menu £ 13 (weekday lunch)/32 – Carte £ 20/51
Neighbourhood restaurant with a slick, minimalistic interior featuring leather, silk and velvet; floor-to-ceiling windows open onto a pleasant pavement terrace. Wide-ranging modern grill menu offers steak and seafood. Good value lunches.

ASENBY – North Yorkshire – see Thirsk

ASH – Kent – **504** X30 **9** D2

London 75 mi – Birmingham 199 mi – Liverpool 292 mi – Leeds 265 mi

Great Weddington

Northeast : 0.5 mi by A 257 on Weddington rd ✉ CT3 2AR – ✆ (01304) 813 407 – www.greatweddington.co.uk – Closed Christmas-New Year
4 rm – †£ 75/125 ††£ 90/130 **Rest** – Menu £ 30
A delightful Regency house set in 4½ acres; personally run by charming owners. Spacious, tastefully furnished sitting room featuring antiques, fresh flowers and family photos. Individually decorated bedrooms have a country house style; a family suite is available. Breakfast and evening meals served at a communal antique dining table.

ASHBOURNE – Derbyshire – **502** O24 – **pop. 5 020** Great Britain **16** A2

London 141 mi – Birmingham 45 mi – Manchester 46 mi – Sheffield 52 mi
13 Market Pl, ✆ (01335) 34 36 66, www.visitpeakdistrict.com
Dovedale★★ (Ilam Rock★) NW : 6 mi by A 515

Callow Hall

Mapleton Rd, West : 0.75 mi by Union St (off Market Pl) ✉ DE6 2AA – ✆ (01335) 300 900 – www.callowhall.co.uk
16 rm – †£ 100/180 ††£ 100/180 – 1 suite **Rest** – Carte £ 30/48
Victorian country house in 30 acres of gardens, fields and woodland. Individually styled bedrooms boast original features, spacious bathrooms, and traditional fabrics and furnishings. Daily changing menus feature local produce and classically based dishes, with a few modern touches.

dining room

33 St Johns St ✉ DE6 1GP – ✆ (01335) 300 666 – www.thediningroomashbourne.co.uk – Closed 2 weeks Christmas-New Year, 1 week February-March, 1 week September and Sunday-Wednesday
Rest – *(dinner only) (booking essential)* Menu £ 40/48
Modern, stylish décor blends agreeably with period features, including a cast iron range and a 17C salt safe. Local, seasonal ingredients inform the intricate, modern dishes on the 5 and 8 course tasting menus. Dinner is served at 7pm.

at Shirley Southeast : 5 mi by A 515 and off A 52

Saracen's Head Ⓝ

Church Ln ✉ DE6 3AS – ✆ (01335) 360 330 – www.saracens-head-shirley.co.uk
Rest – Carte £ 20/40
Cosy pub opposite a striking church, in a remote, picturesque village. The bright bar leads to a beamed dining room and an open-fired room hung with local art. A large, oft-changing blackboard menu lists old favourites; portions are large.

ASHBURTON – Devon – **503** I32 – **pop. 3 309** **2** C2

London 192 mi – Birmingham 187 mi – Liverpool 269 mi – Leeds 299 mi
Dartmoor National Park★★

✗ **Agaric** with rm

30 North St ⊠ *TQ13 7QD* – ℰ *(01364) 654 478* – *www.agaricrestaurant.co.uk* – *Closed first 2 weeks August, 2 weeks Christmas, Sunday-Tuesday and Saturday lunch*

4 rm ⊡ – ♦£ 58/70 ♦♦£ 120/140

Rest – *(booking essential)* Menu £ 15 (weekday lunch) – Carte £ 27/42

Rustic neighbourhood restaurant with a small bar, exposed stone walls, a wood-burning stove and shelves and dressers filled with homemade preserves, chutneys and sauces. Good-sized, classically based menus feature Cornish fish and local beef. For the simple bedrooms, check in at the adjoining cookery shop.

ASHFORD – Kent – 504 W30 – pop. 58 936 **9** C2

▶ London 56 mi – Canterbury 14 mi – Dover 24 mi – Hastings 30 mi

Access Channel Tunnel : Eurostar information and reservations ℰ (08705) 186186

🛈 18 The Churchyard, ℰ (01233) 62 91 65, www.visitheartofkent.com

🏠🏠 **Eastwell Manor** ♨ ≼ 🚗 🕭 ⅄ 📺 ● 🐾 14 ✕ 🖾 📶 🏊 🎿 📶 ㉑ 🅿

Eastwell Park, Boughton Lees, North : 3 mi by A 28 on A 251 ⊠ *TN25 4HR* – ℰ *(01233) 213 000* – *www.eastwellmanor.co.uk*

42 rm ⊡ – ♦£ 150 ♦♦£ 180 – 22 suites – ♦♦£ 445

Rest *Manor* – Menu £ 16/32 – Carte £ 37/61

Rest *Pavilion* – ℰ (01233) 213 100 *(closed Sunday dinner)* Carte £ 16/29

Impressive manor house with Tudor origins, surrounded by beautifully manicured gardens and extensive parkland. Rebuilt in 1926 following a fire but some superb plaster ceilings and stone fireplaces remain. Characterful guest areas and luxurious bedrooms. Sizeable spa and golf course. Choice of wood-panelled restaurant complete with pianist or more casual brasserie and terrace.

ASHFORD-IN-THE-WATER – Derbyshire – 502 O24 – ⊠ Bakewell **16** A1

▶ London 164 mi – Birmingham 87 mi – Liverpool 68 mi – Leeds 72 mi

🏠 **Riverside House** 🚗 ✕ rm, 📶 🅿

Fennel St ⊠ *DE45 1QF* – ℰ *(01629) 814 275* – *www.riversidehousehotel.co.uk*

14 rm ⊡ – ♦£ 120/155 ♦♦£ 145/195

Rest *Riverside Room* – Menu £ 12 (weekday lunch)/45

Charming former hunting lodge with gardens running down to the river. Comfortable, individually styled bedrooms named after flowers and birds: Kingfisher is a four-poster, 4 have terraces with doors to the garden and all come with fruit, chocolates, nuts and sherry. Classical dining.

↑ **River Cottage** without rest 🚗 ✕ 📶 🅿 ⇄

Buxton Rd ⊠ *DE45 1QP* – ℰ *(01629) 813 327* – *www.rivercottageashford.co.uk* – *Closed December and January*

4 rm ⊡ – ♦£ 85/100 ♦♦£ 100/125

Traditional stone cottage by the River Wye, with delightful gardens and terrace. Bedrooms blend modern furnishings and antiques; mattresses are handmade. Locally sourced breakfast ingredients and homemade preserves.

ASHPRINGTON – Devon – 503 J32 – **see Totnes**

ASHWATER – Devon – 503 H31 **2** C2

▶ London 217 mi – Plymouth 36 mi – Torbay 62 mi – Exeter 42 mi

✗✗ **Blagdon Manor** with rm ♨ ≼ 🚗 🕭 🕭 📶 🅿

Northwest : 2 mi by Holsworthy rd on Blagdon rd ⊠ *EX21 5DF* – ℰ *(01409) 211 224* – *www.blagdon.com* – *Closed January, Monday, Tuesday and lunch Wednesday*

6 rm ⊡ – ♦£ 90/110 ♦♦£ 145/250

Rest – *(booking essential)* Menu £ 28 (weekday dinner)/40

Former farmhouse with delightful gardens; set in a peaceful rural location and proudly run by husband and wife team. Comfortable restaurant with lovely countryside views and a large flagged terrace for summer dining. Unfussy, seasonal cooking; dishes are classically based, with a modern touch. Immaculately kept, well-equipped bedrooms, with stylish, modern bathrooms.

ENGLAND

ASKRIGG – North Yorkshire – 502 N21 – pop. 1 002 – ✉ Leyburn 22 A1

London 251 mi – Kendal 32 mi – Leeds 70 mi – Newcastle upon Tyne 70 mi

Yorebridge House

Bainbridge, West : 1 mi ✉ DL8 3EE – ✆ (01969) 652 060 – www.yorebridgehouse.com

13 rm – †£ 175/225 ††£ 200/285

Rest – *(closed lunch in winter) (booking essential)* Menu £ 38 (dinner) – Carte £ 25/50

Charmingly restored former school in a lovely setting. Stylish, modern interior with a snug, open-fired bar and sitting room offering country views. Bedrooms feature designer fabrics; those in the annexe have riverside patios and hot tubs. The brasserie offers Yorkshire meats and game in British-based dishes.

ASTON CANTLOW – Warwickshire – 503 O27 – pop. 1 843 19 C3

Great Britain

London 104 mi – Birmingham 30 mi – Leicester 46 mi – Coventry 22 mi

Mary Arden's House★ AC, SE : 2 mi by Wilmcote Lane and Aston Cantlow Rd

King's Head

21 Bearley Rd ✉ B95 6HY – ✆ (01789) 488 242 – www.thekh.co.uk

Rest – Carte £ 20/36

Characterful black and white timbered inn, covered in ivy and set in a picturesque village. Rustic, open-fired bar and country chic restaurant. Menu of pub favourites and British classics with some modern twists; local game is a feature.

ASTON TIRROLD – Oxfordshire 10 B3

London 58 mi – Reading 16 mi – Streatley 4 mi

Sweet Olive at The Chequers Inn

Baker St ✉ OX11 9DD – ✆ (01235) 851 272 – www.sweet-olive.com – Closed 2 weeks February, 3 weeks July, Sunday dinner and Wednesday

Rest – *(booking essential)* Carte £ 28/44

A charming red-brick Victorian pub at the heart of the village; cosy, welcoming and popular with the locals. Gallic owners offer a French-influenced menu of tasty, seasonal dishes and an interesting selection of fine wines.

ATCHAM – Shropshire – 503 L25 – see Shrewsbury

ATTLEBOROUGH – Norfolk – 504 X26 – pop. 6 530 15 C2

London 101 mi – Norwich 19 mi – Ipswich 42 mi – Peterborough 87 mi

Mulberry Tree with rm

Station Rd ✉ NR17 2AS – ✆ (01953) 452 124 – www.the-mulberry-tree.co.uk – Closed 26 December, 1 January and Sunday

7 rm – †£ 79 ††£ 106 **Rest** – Carte £ 25/37

Contemporary bar-cum-restaurant in an imposing brick-built property, with a pleasant terrace and even a bowling green. The bar menu is popular at lunchtime, while the modern à la carte offers attractively presented, globally influenced dishes. Bedrooms are stylish and very comfortable.

AUSTWICK – North Yorkshire – 502 M21 – pop. 467 22 A2

– ✉ Lancaster (lancs.)

London 259 mi – Kendal 28 mi – Lancaster 20 mi – Leeds 46 mi

Traddock

✉ LA2 8BY – ✆ (015242) 51 224 – www.thetraddock.co.uk

12 rm – †£ 85/95 ††£ 95/190 **Rest** – *(booking essential)* Carte £ 26/40

Georgian country house with Victorian additions – once a private residence – named after a horse trading paddock. Traditional interior with bright, airy lounges. Bedrooms boast feature beds, rural views and roll-top baths. Formal dining room serves modern versions of old classics, showcasing local produce.

⌂ **Austwick Hall** without rest 🚗 🕭 🛇 🛜 **P**
✉ *LA2 8BS* – ☏ *(015242) 51 794* – *www.austwickhall.co.uk*
4 rm ⌂ – ♦£ 140/170 ♦♦£ 155/185
Characterful house in a delightful village on the edge of the dales, surrounded by tiered gardens and woodland. Spacious, antique-furnished bedrooms; the Blue Room has a roll-top bath which offers views down the garden. Nothing is too much trouble for the friendly owners. Tea is served on arrival.

⌂ **Wood View** without rest 🚗 📞 **P**
The Green ✉ *LA2 8BB* – ☏ *(015242) 51 190* – *www.woodviewbandb.com*
– *Restricted opening in winter*
5 rm ⌂ – ♦£ 48/65 ♦♦£ 72/80
17C stone cottage in a pleasant village green location. Open-fired lounge and cosy breakfast room with low-beamed ceilings and exposed rafters. Simple, well-kept bedrooms have a mix of furnishings. There's even a bike store for cyclists.

AXBRIDGE – Somerset – **503** L30 – **pop. 2 025** **3** B2
▶ London 142 mi – Bristol 17 mi – Taunton 27 mi – Weston-Super-Mare 11 mi

✗ **Oak House** with rm 🛜
The Square ✉ *BS26 2AP* – ☏ *(01934) 732 444* – *www.theoakhousesomerset.com*
– *Closed 2-4 January, Sunday, Monday and lunch Tuesday-Wednesday*
9 rm – ♦£ 50/110 ♦♦£ 50/110, ⌂ £ 8 **Rest** – Carte £ 28/40
Oak-beamed 17C house overlooking the square, with a relaxed, rustic feel. One menu displays classic dishes with subtle modern touches; the other offers more originality. Cooking is well-judged with good ingredients, clear flavours and some flair. Enthusiastic young team. Comfortable, good value bedrooms.

AXMINSTER – Devon – **503** L31 – **pop. 4 952** **2** D2
▶ London 156 mi – Exeter 27 mi – Lyme Regis 5 mi – Taunton 22 mi
◙ Lyme Regis★ - The Cobb★, SE : 5.5 mi by A 35 and A 3070

✗ **River Cottage Canteen**
Trinity Sq ✉ *EX13 5AN* – ☏ *(01297) 631 715* – *www.rivercottage.net/axminster*
– *Closed 25-26 December and dinner Sunday and Monday*
Rest – Carte £ 20/31
Busy restaurant, deli and coffee shop owned by Hugh Fearnley-Whittingstall. Simple, industrial-style room with mismatched furniture. Blackboards change twice-daily, offering gutsy, flavoursome country cooking and showcasing local produce.

AYLESBURY – Buckinghamshire – **504** R28 – **pop. 69 021** **11** C2
▌ Great Britain
▶ London 46 mi – Birmingham 72 mi – Northampton 37 mi – Oxford 22 mi
🛈 Kings Head Passage off Market Square, ☏ (01296) 33 05 59,
www.visitbuckinghamshire.org
🔟 Weston Turville, New Rd, ☏ (01296) 42 40 84
🔟 Aylesbury Golf Centre, Bierton, Hulcott Lane, ☏ (01296) 39 36 44
◙ Waddesdon Manor★★, NW : 5.5 mi by A 41 – Chiltern Hills★

 Hartwell House 🛇 ⪡ 🚗 🕭 ⌇ 🖵 ⊚ 🕸 ⅃⅋ ✗ 🍴 🛇 🛜 ♨ **P**
Oxford Rd, Southwest : 2 mi on A 418 ✉ *HP17 8NR* – ☏ *(01296) 747 444*
– *www.hartwell-house.com*
46 rm ⌂ – ♦£ 175 ♦♦£ 290 – 10 suites
Rest *Soane* – *(closed lunch 31 December)* Menu £ 25 (weekdays)
– Carte £ 43/60 **s**
Erstwhile residency of Louis XVIII, exiled King of France; now owned by the National Trust. Impressive palatial house in 90 acres of parkland, boasting luxurious lounges, ornate furnishings, an intimate spa and magnificent, antique-filled bedrooms. Afternoon tea is a speciality. Formal restaurant offers good value lunches and traditional country house cooking.

ENGLAND

AYLESFORD – Kent – 504 V30 8 B1

London 37 mi – Maidstone 3 mi – Rochester 8 mi

Hengist

7-9 High St ✉ ME20 7AX – ✆ (01622) 719 273 – www.hengistrestaurant.co.uk – Closed Monday

Rest – *(dinner only and lunch Friday-Sunday)* Menu £ 23 – Carte £ 34/43

Converted 16C townhouse named after one of two Viking brothers who landed in Aylesford in the 5C. Smart ground floor dining room with etched glass, gilded walls and pretty wallpaper. Ambitious, modern cooking; pleasant service.

AYLSHAM – Norfolk – 504 X25 – pop. 5 504 15 D1

London 128 mi – Norwich 13 mi – Ipswich 57 mi – Stevenage 105 mi

Old Pump House without rest

2 Holman Rd ✉ NR11 6BY – ✆ (01263) 733 789 – www.theoldpumphouse.com – Closed Christmas

5 rm – £ 80/98 £ 98/120

Tastefully furnished Georgian house, named after the old village water pump which stands in the square outside. Bedrooms boast fine reproduction oak furniture; one has a four-poster. The owners have a passion for antiques and art.

AYNHO – Northamptonshire – 504 Q28 – pop. 632 16 B3

London 73 mi – Birmingham 66 mi – Leicester 62 mi – Coventry 48 mi

Cartwright

rest,

1-5 Croughton Rd ✉ OX17 3BE – ✆ (01869) 811 885 – www.oxfordshire-hotels.co.uk

21 rm – £ 70/135 £ 75/175

Rest – Menu £ 12 (weekday lunch)/21 – Carte £ 28/36

Cotswold stone former coaching inn dating back to the 16C. Spacious modern bedrooms are split between the main house and courtyard; the former are more characterful, with some timbered ceilings and original fireplaces. Brasserie restaurant serves a traditional menu; the grills and cheeseboard are popular.

AYOT GREEN – Hertfordshire – see Welwyn

AYSGARTH – North Yorkshire – 502 O21 22 A1

London 249 mi – Ripon 28 mi – York 56 mi

George and Dragon Inn with rm

✉ DL8 3AD – ✆ (01969) 663 358 – www.georgeanddragonaysgarth.co.uk – Closed 3 weeks January

7 rm – £ 40/60 £ 90/120 **Rest** – Menu £ 14 (lunch) – Carte £ 20/33

Laid-back coaching inn set in the National Park, close to the breathtaking River Ure waterfalls. Unfussy pub classics include plenty of local meats, game and proper old-fashioned puddings. Comfy, individually styled bedrooms; some with whirlpool baths.

BABBACOMBE – Torbay – 503 J32 – see Torquay

BAGSHOT – Surrey – 504 R29 – pop. 5 247 7 C1

London 37 mi – Reading 17 mi – Southampton 49 mi

Windlesham, Grove End, ✆ (01276) 45 22 20

Pennyhill Park

London Rd, Southwest : 1 mi on A 30 ✉ GU19 5EU – ✆ (01276) 486 156 – www.exclusivehotels.co.uk

112 rm – £ 210/365 £ 375/415, £ 21 – 11 suites

Rest *Michael Wignall at The Latymer* ✿✿ **Rest *Brasserie*** – see restaurant listing

Impressive 19C manor house set in 123 acres. Classical guest areas display modern touches; spacious bedrooms boast period furnishings and great views. Have afternoon tea in the comfy lounge before heading for one of the best spas in Europe.

ENGLAND

Michael Wignall at The Latymer – Pennyhill Park Hotel

London Rd, Southwest : 1 mi on A30 ✉ *GU19 5EU*
– ✆ (01276) 486 156 – www.exclusivehotels.co.uk – Closed 1-16 January, Sunday, Monday, lunch Tuesday and Saturday
Rest – *(booking essential)* Menu £ 32/78
Elegant hotel dining room with oak-clad walls, a glass-enclosed chef's table and top quality place settings. Cooking is confident, precise and uses only the best ingredients. Flavours are clearly defined yet exhibit a delicate edge; innovative, modern combinations marry seamlessly. Efficient service.
→ John Dory, textures of cauliflower. Spring lamb with globe artichoke, girolles and goat's curd. Raspberry financier with nitrogen chocolate, raspberry crémeux and jelly.

Brasserie – Pennyhill Park Hotel

London Rd, Southwest : 1 mi on A 30 ✉ *GU19 5EU – ✆ (01276) 471 774 – www.exclusivehotels.co.uk – Closed Saturday lunch*
Rest – *(buffet lunch)* Menu £ 30 – Carte £ 35/57
Spacious hotel dining room set in an impressive 19C manor house that lies within 123 acres of grounds. Stylish, modern décor with doors opening out onto the garden. Appealing brasserie menu.

BALLASALLA – 502 F21 – pop. 2 304 – see Man (Isle of) – ✉

BAMBURGH – Northumberland – 501 O17 – pop. 582 Great Britain — 24 B1

London 337 mi – Edinburgh 77 mi – Newcastle upon Tyne 51 mi
Castle★ **AC**

Lord Crewe Arms

rest,

Front St ✉ *NE69 7BL – ✆ (01668) 214 243 – www.lordcrewe.co.uk – Closed 6 January-7 February*
17 rm – †£ 70/145 ††£ 90/145
Rest *Wynding Inn* – Carte £ 19/43
Smart 17C former coaching inn, privately owned and superbly set in the shadow of a famous Norman castle. Comfy, cosy bedrooms have a modern feel, yet are in keeping with the age of the building. Characterful stone-walled bar and New England style restaurant serve brasserie dishes. Efficient service.

at Waren Mill West : 2.75 mi on B 1342 – ✉ Belford

Waren House

✉ *NE70 7EE – ✆ (01668) 214 581 – www.warenhousehotel.co.uk*
15 rm – †£ 90/150 ††£ 180/280 – 3 suites
Rest – *(dinner only)* Menu £ 39
Personally run, antique-furnished country house set in beautiful, tranquil gardens. Bedrooms – some named after the owners' family members – mix classic and modern styles: some have four-posters and coastal views. Formal dining room boasts an ornate ceiling; traditional menus showcase local ingredients.

BAMPTON – Devon – 503 J31 – pop. 1 617 — 2 D1

London 189 mi – Exeter 18 mi – Minehead 21 mi – Taunton 15 mi

Bark House

Oakfordbridge, West : 3 mi by B 3227 on A 396 ✉ *EX16 9HZ – ✆ (01398) 351 236 – www.thebarkhouse.co.uk – Closed 1 week January and 1 week November*
5 rm – †£ 45/50 ††£ 80/98
Rest – *(closed Monday) (dinner only and Sunday lunch) (booking essential)* Menu £ 30
Simple, homely hotel with a welcoming feel; once used as a wood store for the local tannery. Traditional, cottagey bedrooms: one leads to a small garden, while another has a balcony. Honest home cooking, coupled with bargains from the owner's wine business.

ENGLAND

Swan with rm
Station Rd ✉ EX16 9NG – ✆ (01398) 332 248 – www.theswan.co – Closed 25-26 December and Monday
3 rm – †£ 60 ††£ 80/85 **Rest** – Carte £ 19/33
Laid-back, modernised, open-plan pub whose history can be traced back to 1450, when it provided accommodation for craftsmen working on the local church. Unfussy pub dishes arrive neatly presented on wooden boards and showcase local produce. Smart, modern bedrooms are found on the 2nd floor.

BANBURY – **Oxfordshire** – **503** P27 – **pop. 43 867** Great Britain **10** B1

London 76 mi – Birmingham 40 mi – Coventry 25 mi – Oxford 23 mi
Spiceball Park Rd, ✆ (01295) 25 98 55, www.visitnorthoxfordshire.com
Cherwell Edge, Chacombe, ✆ (01295) 71 15 91
Upton House★ **AC**, NW : 7 mi by A 422

at Sibford Gower **West : 8 mi by B 4035 – ✉ Banbury**

Wykham Arms
Temple Mill Rd ✉ OX15 5RX – ✆ (01295) 788 808 – www.wykhamarms.co.uk – Closed Monday except bank holidays
Rest – Carte £ 23/32
Thatched stone pub set down country lanes in a small village. Featuring local produce, menus range from bar snacks and lights bites to the full 3 courses. Good range of wines by the glass.

ENGLAND

BARNARD CASTLE – **Durham** – **502** O20 – **pop. 6 714** Great Britain **24** A3

London 258 mi – Carlisle 63 mi – Leeds 68 mi – Middlesbrough 31 mi
Flatts Rd, ✆ (01833) 69 09 09, www.teesdalediscovery.com
Harmire Rd, ✆ (01833) 63 83 55
Bowes Museum★ **AC**
Raby Castle★ **AC**, NE : 6.5 mi by A 688

Homelands
85 Galgate ✉ DL12 8ES – ✆ (01833) 638 757 – www.homelandsguesthouse.co.uk
5 rm – †£ 45/50 ††£ 75/80 **Rest** – Menu £ 10
Victorian terraced house just a short drive from Raby Castle. Pastel-coloured lounge filled with books and photos. Compact, individually furnished bedrooms; the largest and most peaceful is at the end of the long mature garden. Simple, home-cooked dinners of local produce, by arrangement.

at Greta Bridge **Southeast : 4.5 mi off A 66 – ✉ Barnard Castle**

Morritt
✉ DL12 9SE – ✆ (01833) 627 232 – www.themorritt.co.uk
27 rm – †£ 85/120 ††£ 95/130 – 1 suite
Rest *Gilroy's* – see restaurant listing
Rest *Bistro/Bar* – Carte £ 17/24
Attractive 19C inn on the site of an old Roman fort. The characterful interior cleverly blends the old and the new, with lovely parquet floors, antiques and feature bedsteads offset by contemporary décor. Superb spa with a car garage theme. All-day snacks in the bar-bistro; modern menu in the restaurant.

XX **Gilroy's** – Morritt Hotel
✉ DL12 9SE – ✆ (01833) 627 232 – www.themorritt.co.uk
Rest – Menu £ 39
Smart hotel dining room with a lovely parquet floor, wood-panelling and bold splashes of colour here and there. Dishes are modern, attractively presented and employ some complex techniques. Start with a drink by the fire in the cosy lounge.

at Hutton Magna Southeast : 7.25 mi by A 66

Oak Tree Inn
DL11 7HH – (01833) 627 371 – www.theoaktreehutton.co.uk – Closed 24-27 and 31 December, 1 January and Monday
Rest – *(dinner only) (booking essential)* Carte £ 32/40
Small but charming whitewashed pub with six tables flanked by green settles and a bench table for drinkers. It's run by a husband and wife team; he cooks, while she serves. Cooking is hearty and flavoursome with a rustic British style.

at Romaldkirk Northwest : 6 mi by A 67 on B 6277 – Barnard Castle

Rose and Crown with rm
DL12 9EB – (01833) 650 213 – www.rose-and-crown.co.uk – Closed 23-27 December
14 rm – £ 95/125 £ 150/175
Rest – Carte £ 18/29 **s**
Rest *Rose and Crown* – *(dinner only and Sunday lunch)* Menu £ 38 **s** – Carte £ 22/41
Quintessential 18C English inn with atmospheric bar and horse brasses; set by a Saxon church and surrounded by three village greens. Both bar and rear brasserie serve classical fare; more formal restaurant offers seasonally changing four course dinner menu. Bedrooms boast designer décor, flat screen TVs and Bose radios.

BARNSLEY – Gloucestershire – 503 O28 – see Cirencester

BARRASFORD – Northumberland 24 A2

London 309 mi – Newcastle upon Tyne 29 mi – Sunderland 42 mi – Middlesbrough 66 mi

Barrasford Arms with rm
NE48 4AA – (01434) 681 237 – www.barrasfordarms.co.uk – Closed 25-26 December, Sunday dinner, Monday lunch and bank holidays
7 rm – £ 67 £ 87 **Rest** – Menu £ 12 (weekday lunch) – Carte £ 21/31
Personally run, 19C stone inn, close to Kielder Water and Hadrian's Wall. It has a traditional, homely atmosphere, with cosy fires and regular competitions for the locals. Pub classics are served at lunch; followed by more refined dishes at dinner. Bedrooms are modern, comfortable and sensibly priced.

BARTON-ON-SEA – Hampshire – 503 P31 6 A3

London 108 mi – Bournemouth 11 mi – Southampton 24 mi – Winchester 35 mi

Pebble Beach with rm
Marine Dr BH25 7DZ – (01425) 627 777 – www.pebblebeach-uk.com
4 rm – £ 56/70 £ 72/100 **Rest** – Carte £ 27/56
Large, split-level restaurant with an open-plan kitchen, a fish tank and a metal-furnished terrace boasting impressive Solent and Isle of Wight views. Extensive, seasonally changing menus are centred around local seafood. Good-sized bedrooms have a homely feel.

BARWICK – Somerset – 503 M31 – see Yeovil

BASHALL EAVES – Lancashire – 502 M23 – see Clitheroe

BASLOW – Derbyshire – 502 P24 – pop. 1 184 – Bakewell 16 A1

Great Britain

London 158 mi – Birmingham 70 mi – Manchester 35 mi – Sheffield 14 mi

Chatsworth★★★ (Park and Garden★★★) **AC**

Cavendish
Church Ln, on A 619 DE45 1SP – (01246) 582 311 – www.cavendish-hotel.net
23 rm – £ 133/177 £ 169/219, £ 19 – 1 suite
Rest *The Gallery* – see restaurant listing **Rest *Garden Room*** – Carte £ 23/38
Elegant hotel on the Chatsworth Estate, boasting lovely parkland views. Bedrooms have a cosy, country house feel and a contemporary edge; some of the furniture and paintings are from Chatsworth House. Garden Room offers all-day dining and afternoon teas; formal restaurant serves traditionally based menus.

ENGLAND

XXX **Fischer's at Baslow Hall** with rm

Calver Rd, on A 623 ✉ DE45 1RR – ✆ (01246) 583 259 – www.fischers-baslowhall.co.uk – Closed 25-26 and 31 December

10 rm – †£ 105/145 ††£ 155/225 – 1 suite

Rest – *(closed Sunday dinner to non-residents and Monday lunch) (booking essential)* Menu £ 26 (weekday lunch)/72

Fine Edwardian manor house with a country house feel, impressive formal grounds and a walled vegetable garden. The two dining rooms with their ornate ceilings and quality furnishings offer an array of interesting, modern, flavoursome dishes, prepared using skilful, labour intensive techniques. Service is professional. Charming bedrooms; the garden rooms are largest.

→ Tempura of Cornish crab, salmon and langoustine with lightly curried cauliflower purée. Best end of Cumbrian hogget, wild garlic emulsion. Chocolate 'Tree Trunk' with hazelnut granita.

XXX **The Gallery** – Cavendish Hotel

Church Ln, on A 619 ✉ DE45 1SP – ✆ (01246) 582 311 – www.cavendish-hotel.net

Rest – Menu £ 35/50

Contemporary restaurant in an elegant hotel, with views out across the Chatsworth Estate parkland. Dishes have a traditional base but presentation and techniques are more modern. Service is detailed yet personable.

X **Rowley's**

Church St ✉ DE45 1RY – ✆ (01246) 583 880 – www.rowleysrestaurant.co.uk – Closed Sunday dinner and Monday except bank holidays

Rest – *(booking advisable)* Menu £ 20 (lunch and early dinner) – Carte £ 23/51

Stone-built former blacksmith's forge and pub; now a contemporary bar-restaurant set over two floors. Brisk trade at the ground floor bar; more intimate dining upstairs. Classic dishes with modern touches; slick, efficient service.

BASSENTHWAITE – Cumbria – 501 K19 – pop. 433 — 21 A2

London 300 mi – Carlisle 24 mi – Keswick 7 mi

Pheasant — rest,

Southwest : 3.25 mi by B 5291 on Wythop Mill Rd ✉ CA13 9YE – ✆ (017687) 76 234 – www.the-pheasant.co.uk – Closed 24-25 December

15 rm – †£ 90/110 ††£ 140/210

Rest *Bistro* – Carte £ 25/43

Rest *The Fell* – *(dinner only and Sunday lunch)* Menu £ 35 – Carte £ 33/49

Characterful 16C coaching inn with comfy lounges and welcoming open fires. Bedrooms are spacious and retain a classic look appropriate to the building's age; some have lovely country outlooks. Have drinks amongst polished brass in the bar then make for the informal oak-furnished bistro for pub favourites, or for the formal restaurant for modern, daily changing dishes.

Overwater Hall

Northeast : 2.5 mi by A 591, Uldale rd on Overwater rd ✉ CA7 1HH – ✆ (017687) 76 566 – www.overwaterhall.co.uk – Closed 2-16 January

11 rm – †£ 50/160 ††£ 110/185

Rest – *(closed Monday lunch) (light lunch/dinner)* Menu £ 45

Castellated Georgian manor house built in 1811, set in 18 acres of mature gardens. Three good-sized lounges, one with a bar. Large, boldly patterned bedrooms come with rich fabrics, homemade fruit liqueurs and spacious, good quality bathrooms. Formal dining room offers a traditional country house menu.

BATCOMBE – Somerset – 503 M30 – pop. 391 – ✉ Shepton Mallet — 4 C2

London 130 mi – Bournemouth 50 mi – Bristol 24 mi – Salisbury 40 mi

Three Horseshoes Inn with rm

✉ BA4 6HE – ✆ (01749) 850 359 – www.thethreehorseshoesinn.com – Closed 25 December

3 rm – †£ 60/75 ††£ 70/85 **Rest** – Carte £ 18/34

Enthusiastically run former blacksmith's workshop, hidden in a small hamlet off the beaten track, with a characterful beamed interior and a large inglenook fireplace. Menus cover all bases from pork pies and pub classics to more sophisticated dishes. Excellent cheeses. Comfortable, simply furnished bedrooms.

BATH

See city maps on following pages **4** C2

© Ingolf Pompe/Hemis.fr

Bath and North East Somerset – pop. 77 846 – **503** M29 – **504** M29 – Great Britain

London 119 mi – Bristol 13 mi – Southampton 63 mi – Taunton 49 mi

Tourist Information

Abbey Chambers, Abbey Church Yard, ✆(0906) 711 20 00, www.visitbath.co.uk

Golf Courses

Tracy Park, Wick, Bath Rd, ✆(0117) 9 37 18 00

Lansdown, ✆(01225) 42 21 38

Entry Hill, ✆(01225) 83 42 48

SIGHTS

In the town : City★★★ • Royal Crescent★★★ AV • The Circus★★★ AV • Museum of Costume★★★ **AC** AV**M7** • Roman Baths★★ **AC** BX**D** • Holburne Museum★★ **AC** Y**M5** • Pump Room★ BX**B** • Assembly Rooms★ AV • Bath Abbey★ BX • Pulteney Bridge★ BV • Lansdown Crescent★★ Y • Camden Crescent★ Y

On the outskirts : American Museum at Claverton★★ **AC** E : 3 mi by A 36 Y

In the surrounding area : Corsham Court★★ AC, NE : 8.5 mi by A 4 • Dyrham Park★ **AC**, N : 6.5 mi by A 4 and A 46

Royal Crescent

16 Royal Cres ✉ BA1 2LS – ✆ (01225) 823 333 – www.royalcrescent.co.uk
45 rm – ♦£ 199/345 ♦♦£ 440/760 – 12 suites AV**a**
Rest *Dower House* – see restaurant listing
At the centre of the famous sweeping terrace – a masterpiece of Georgian architecture. Open-fired, tiled hall and beautifully proportioned drawing room filled with antiques. Elegant Regency bedrooms; main house rooms are the most luxurious.

Bath Spa

rm,

Sydney Rd ✉ BA2 6JF – ✆ (0844) 879 91 06 – www.macdonaldhotels.co.uk/bathspa
129 rm – ♦£ 135/165 ♦♦£ 195/695, £ 15 – 11 suites Y**z**
Rest *Vellore* – *(dinner only)* Menu £ 45
Rest *Alfresco* – *(lunch only and dinner Friday-Saturday)* Carte approx. £ 25
Charming Georgian mansion set in landscaped gardens, with characterful period lounges and an excellent spa. Spacious bedrooms; the Imperial Suites come with 24-hour butler service. Formal Vellore features impressive Corinthian columns. Alfresco offers an appealing classic grill menu, with lamb chops and steaks a specialty.

ENGLAND

Bath Priory – Bath Priory Hotel
Weston Rd ✉ BA1 2XT – ✆ (01225) 331 922 – www.thebathpriory.co.uk
33 rm – †£ 195/420 ††£ 215/460 – 6 suites Y**c**
Rest *Bath Priory* ✿ – see restaurant listing
Charming Georgian house in a smart residential area near Royal Victoria Park. Comfy, country house interior with elegant, antique-filled lounges, a library and drawing room. Luxurious bedrooms have superb bathrooms and blend the traditional with the modern. A chic spa and excellent service complete the picture.

Homewood Park
Abbey Ln, Hinton Charterhouse, Southeast : 6.5 mi on A 36 ✉ BA2 7TB – ✆ (01225) 723 731 – www.homewoodpark.co.uk
21 rm – †£ 100/275 ††£ 120/310 – 2 suites **Rest** – Carte £ 29/44
18C country house with mature gardens and a fashionable interior. Charming guest areas – many boasting open fires – and contemporary bedrooms with bold colour schemes. Superb spa and treatment facilities. Classical dining split between 3 rooms; modern dishes are stylishly presented.

Queensberry
Russel St ✉ BA1 2QF – ✆ (01225) 447 928 – www.thequeensberry.co.uk
29 rm – †£ 130/190 ††£ 130/255, £ 17 AV**x**
Rest *Olive Tree* – see restaurant listing
A series of Georgian townhouses in one of the oldest parts of the city, run by a friendly, well-versed team. Guest areas include a charming wood-panelled lounge and a chic bar with an extensive array of unusual spirits. Funky, individually designed bedrooms have smart designer touches and a host of extras.

ENGLAND

Francis Ⓝ
rm,
Queen Sq ✉ BA1 2HH – ✆ (01225) 424 105 – www.francishotel.com
98 rm – †£ 149/239 ††£ 169/259 AV**c**
Rest *Brasserie Blanc* – ✆ (01225) 303 860 – Menu £ 16/19 – Carte £ 19/43
Seven Grade I listed townhouses built between 1728 and 1736 by John Wood the Elder, overlooking the picturesque Queen Square. Contemporary interior with boldly coloured furnishings and a funky boutique style. Buzzy, brightly furnished restaurant; the lengthy menu offers satisfying French brasserie classics.

Dukes without rest
Great Pulteney St ✉ BA2 4DN – ✆ (01225) 787 960 – www.dukesbath.co.uk
17 rm – †£ 80/120 ††£ 80/200 – 4 suites BV**n**
Two Grade I listed Palladian-style townhouses built in 1789; now an informal, boutique guesthouse. Bedrooms are named after famous Dukes – some have four-posters. If you've skipped dinner, they offer a late night cheeseboard and port.

Dorian House without rest
1 Upper Oldfield Pk ✉ BA2 3JX – ✆ (01225) 426 336 – www.dorianhouse.co.uk – Closed 24-25 December Z**u**
13 rm – †£ 65/165 ††£ 99/165
Charming 19C townhouse featuring original stained glass and musical memorabilia. Individually decorated bedrooms offer a high level of comfort; 2 have four-posters. Delightful conservatory breakfast room overlooks the garden.

Paradise House without rest
86-88 Holloway ✉ BA2 4PX – ✆ (01225) 317 723 – www.paradise-house.co.uk – Closed 24-25 December AX**s**
11 rm – †£ 69/170 ††£ 69/210
Elegant yet homely 18C house with a beautiful walled garden, set on Beechen Cliff and boasting views over the city. Charming interior with a classical lounge and bedrooms ranging from traditional four-posters to more modern styles.

Apsley House without rest
141 Newbridge Hill ✉ BA1 3PT – ✆ (01225) 336 966 – www.apsley-house.co.uk – Closed 24-25 December Y**x**
12 rm – †£ 65/130 ††£ 75/190
Substantial 18C house built for the Duke of Wellington and still retaining many grand features. High-ceilinged guest areas have large fireplaces and chandeliers. Luxuriously appointed bedrooms display a subtle contemporary style.

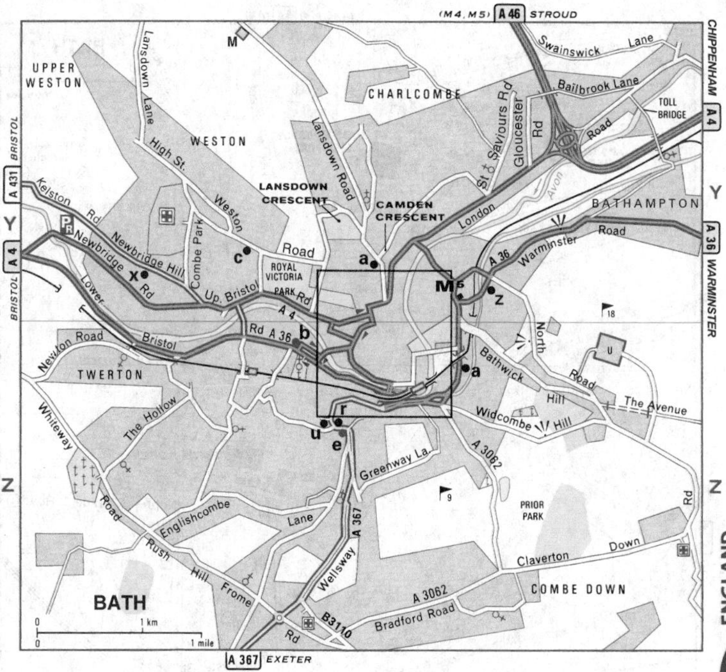

🏠 **Villa Magdala** without rest

Henrietta Rd ✉ *BA2 6LX – ☎ (01225) 466 329 – www.villamagdala.co.uk – Closed 1 week Christmas* BV**r**

20 rm ☕ – 🚹£ 80/150 🚹🚹£ 100/180

Victorian house named after Napier's 1868 victory, in an attractive residential area, overlooking a park. Smart, modern interior with two impressive staircases. Stylish, airy bedrooms have shuttered windows and feature wallpapers.

🏠 **One Three Nine** without rest

139 Wells Rd ✉ *BA2 3AL – ☎ (01225) 314 769 – www.139bath.co.uk – Closed 24-25 December* Z**r**

10 rm ☕ – 🚹£ 59/110 🚹🚹£ 69/170

Detached Victorian house within walking distance of the city centre. A contemporary black and white sitting room and chic breakfast room set the tone. Bedrooms are equally stylish; some have four-poster beds or spa baths.

🏠 **Brindleys** without rest

14 Pulteney Gdns ✉ *BA2 4HG – ☎ (01225) 310 444 – www.brindleysbath.co.uk – Closed 24-26 December* Z**a**

6 rm ☕ – 🚹£ 90/165 🚹🚹£ 110/185

Victorian house tucked away in a residential street and concealing a surprisingly chic interior. Cosy lounge and neatly laid breakfast room. Tastefully decorated bedrooms in colour themes ranging from lavender to monochrome.

🏠 **Hill House** (N) without rest

25 Belvedere ✉ *BA1 5ED – ☎ (01225) 920 520 – www.hillhousebath.co.uk*

6 rm ☕ – 🚹£ 80/120 🚹🚹£ 110/140 Y**a**

A former hotel, pub and wine merchant's, this Georgian townhouse retains much of its original character, but with all the comfort expected by the modern traveller. Good-sized, contemporary bedrooms; those at the rear have city views.

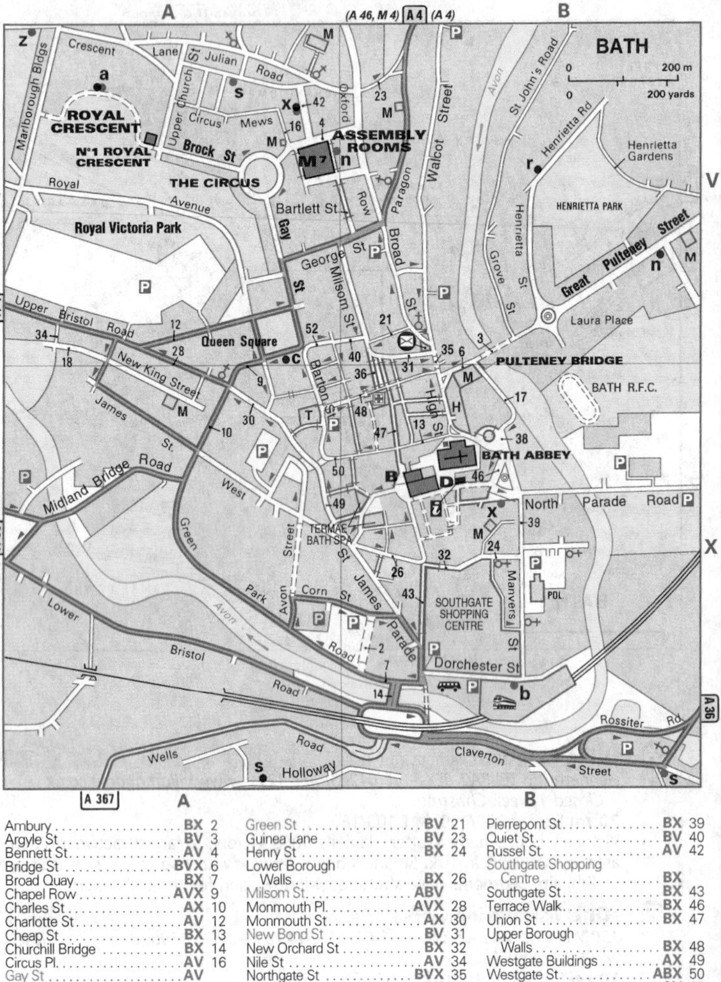

Ambury	BX	2
Argyle St	BV	3
Bennett St	AV	4
Bridge St	BVX	6
Broad Quay	BX	7
Chapel Row	AVX	9
Charles St	AX	10
Charlotte St	AV	12
Cheap St	BX	13
Churchill Bridge	BX	14
Circus Pl.	AV	16
Gay St	AV	
Grand Parade	BX	17
Great Stanhope St	AV	18
Green St	BV	21
Guinea Lane	BV	23
Henry St	BX	24
Lower Borough Walls	BX	26
Milsom St	ABV	
Monmouth Pl.	AVX	28
Monmouth St	AX	30
New Bond St	BV	31
New Orchard St	BX	32
Nile St	AV	34
Northgate St	BVX	35
Old Bond St	BX	36
Orange Grove	BX	38
Pierrepont St	BX	39
Quiet St	BV	40
Russel St	AV	42
Southgate Shopping Centre	BX	
Southgate St	BX	43
Terrace Walk	BX	46
Union St	BX	47
Upper Borough Walls	BX	48
Westgate Buildings	AX	49
Westgate St	ABX	50
Wood St	AV	52
York St	BX	53

XXX **Bath Priory** – Bath Priory Hotel

Weston Rd ✉ *BA1 2XT – ✆ (01225) 331 922*
– www.thebathpriory.co.uk Yc

Rest – Menu £ 25/75

Elegant hotel restaurant made up of several areas: an airy dining room overlooking the gardens; the classical 'Browns' room; and a contemporary orangery and terrace. Cooking is refined and accomplished, delivering robust flavours in interesting, classically based dishes. A superb wine list accompanies.

→ Pan-fried pheasant egg, pork belly and morels. Sea bass with a parsnip and ginger purée and vanilla jus roti. Lemon verbena panna cotta with poached blackcurrant.

XXX **Dower House** - Royal Crescent Hotel
16 Royal Cres ✉ BA1 2LS – ☎ (01225) 823 333 – www.royalcrescent.co.uk
Rest – Menu £ 28 (weekday lunch)/63 AV**a**
Elegant hotel dining room with crisply laid tables, set across the garden in a separate building. Accomplished modern cooking displays a good level of creativity; flavours are well-judged and defined. Service is polite and professional.

XX **Allium Brasserie** Ⓝ
Abbey Hotel, 1 North Par ✉ BA1 1LF – ☎ (01225) 461 603 – www.abbeyhotelbath.co.uk BX**x**
Rest – *(booking advisable)* Menu £ 23 (lunch and early dinner) – Carte £ 32/45
In a grand Georgian terrace is this distinctly modern hotel restaurant, with high ceilings, purple and white décor and vivid contemporary art. Keenly priced, all-day menu. Confident, modern brasserie cooking is skilful and highly original, with influences ranging from Britain to Asia and the Mediterranean.

XX **Olive Tree** – Queensberry Hotel
Russel St ✉ BA1 2QF – ☎ (01225) 447 928 – www.olivetreebath.co.uk
Rest – *(dinner only and lunch Friday-Sunday)* Menu £ 33 (weekdays) – Carte £ 35/52 AV**x**
Stylish, well-run restaurant in the basement of a boutique hotel, with a small bar and three dining rooms - all on different levels. The contemporary décor and artwork are matched by highly ambitious, original cooking in a modern vein.

XX **Menu Gordon Jones**
2 Wellsway ✉ BA2 3AQ – ☎ (01225) 480 871 – www.menugordonjones.co.uk – Closed Sunday and Monday Z**e**
Rest – *(booking essential) (set menu only)* Menu £ 35/55
Tiny restaurant comprising just 8 tables and an open-kitchen. Daily 6 course 'surprise' menu is guided by the latest ingredients available; the chef cooks alone. Dishes are well-balanced, with interesting texture and flavour combinations.

ENGLAND

XX **Mint Room**
Lower Bristol Rd ✉ BA2 3EB – ☎ (01225) 446 656 – www.themintroom.co.uk
Rest – Menu £ 26 – Carte £ 17/26 Z**b**
Smart, spacious restaurant with a distinctly modern, glitzy style. The experienced chef offers an impressive collection of appealing, well-presented dishes which display original and contemporary twists. Service is knowledgeable.

X **Graze** Ⓝ
Unit 5, 9 Brunel Sq ✉ BA1 1SX – ☎ (01225) 429 392 – www.bathales.com
Rest – Menu £ 13 (weekday lunch) – Carte £ 19/43 BX**b**
Buzzy, modern, industrial-style restaurant next to Bath Spa Station, in the Vaults development; its terrace is a must for railway enthusiasts. The grill menu features steak cooked in the Josper oven. Superb ales from their own brewery.

X **Casanis**
4 Saville Row ✉ BA1 2QP – ☎ (01225) 780 055 – www.casanis.co.uk – Closed 25-26 December, 2 weeks January, 1 week July-August, Sunday and Monday
Rest – *(booking essential)* Menu £ 16/18 – Carte £ 26/43 A/BV**n**
Sweet Gallic bistro tucked away in the shadow of the Assembly Rooms; run by a French chef and his charming wife. Small, cosy interior and lovely rear courtyard. Authentic, tasty cooking with a focus on classics from the south west.

Marlborough Tavern
35 Marlborough Buildings ✉ BA1 2LY – ☎ (01225) 423 731 – www.marlborough-tavern.com – Closed 25 December AV**z**
Rest – Menu £ 15 (lunch) – Carte £ 22/44
18C pub on the edge of Victoria Park, close to the Royal Crescent. Chic, fashionable interior with boldly patterned wallpapers and contemporary art. Carefully sourced ingredients feature in pub classics and interesting specials.

Chequers
50 Rivers St ✉ BA1 2QA – ☎ (01225) 360 017 – www.thechequersbath.com
Rest – Menu £ 12 (weekday lunch) – Carte £ 23/42 AV**s**
Set in a smart residential street amid elegant Georgian terraces, with a brightly painted, simply furnished bar. Cooking is sophisticated and presentation, elaborate; lunch is good value and desserts offer something a little different.

White Hart
Widcombe Hill ✉ BA2 6AA – ☎ (01225) 338 053 – www.whitehartbath.co.uk – Closed 25-26 December, Sunday dinner and bank holidays BXs
Rest – *(booking essential at dinner)* Menu £ 13 (weekday lunch) – Carte £ 24/34
Appealing pub on south east edge of the city centre, with a local following and a neighbourhood feel. Generous portions of hearty cooking; smaller tapas plates also popular.

at Box **Northeast : 4.75 mi on A 4 - Y - ✉ Bath**

The Northey with rm
Bath Rd ✉ SN13 8AE – ☎ (01225) 742 333 – www.ohhcompany.co.uk – Closed 25-26 December
5 rm – †£ 89/160 ††£ 99/160 **Rest** – Carte £ 23/49
Traditional-looking, family-run coaching inn with an open-plan interior, a large dining room and a vast bar. Appealing monthly menus feature unfussy, seasonal British cooking. Fish dishes – particularly the mussels – are a strength. Smart, contemporary bedrooms with bathrooms to match.

at Colerne **Northeast : 6.5 mi by A 4 - Y - Batheaston rd and Bannerdown Rd – ✉ Chippenham**

Lucknam Park
North : 0.5 mi on Marshfield rd ✉ SN14 8AZ – ☎ (01225) 742 777 – www.lucknampark.co.uk
37 rm – †£ 345/1170 ††£ 345/1170, £ 25 – 5 suites
Rest ***The Park*** ✿ **Rest** ***Brasserie*** – see restaurant listing
Grand Palladian mansion with a mile-long tree-lined drive, rich, elegant décor, luxurious furnishings and sumptuous fabrics. Extremely comfortable, classically furnished bedrooms. Top class facilities include an impressive modern spa and well-being centre, a renowned equestrian centre and a cookery school.

ENGLAND

The Park – Lucknam Park Hotel
✿
North : 0.5 mi on Marshfield rd ✉ SN14 8AZ – ☎ (01225) 742 777 – www.lucknampark.co.uk – Closed Sunday dinner and Monday
Rest – *(dinner only and Sunday lunch) (booking essential)* Menu £ 70 (weekdays)/90
An aperitif in the elegant library of this impressive mansion is a fine prelude to a formal dinner in the opulent dining room. Service is professional and the kitchen, knowledgeable. Classical menus display modern European influences, with dishes expertly crafted from top quality produce; some from the estate.
→ Poached Scottish lobster, potato mousse, Oscietra caviar and gribiche dressing. Fillet of turbot, buttered iceberg and Cornish crab with hand-rolled macaroni. Glazed passion fruit cream, lemongrass, lime leaf and mango.

Brasserie – Lucknam Park Hotel
North : 0.5 mi on Marshfield rd ✉ SN14 8AZ – ☎ (01225) 742 777 – www.lucknampark.co.uk – Closed 25-26 December and 1 January
Rest – Menu £ 21 (weekday lunch) – Carte £ 25/48
Stylish brasserie in a beautiful courtyard setting in Lucknam Park's state-of-the-art spa, with a spacious bar-lounge and an airy, open-plan dining room with full-length windows. Precise, modern cooking in well-judged combinations; many healthy options are available. Barbecues on the charming terrace in summer.

at Monkton Combe **Southeast : 4.5 mi by A 36 - Y – ✉ Bath**

Wheelwrights Arms with rm
Church Ln ✉ BA2 7HB – ☎ (01225) 722 287 – www.wheelwrightsarms.co.uk
7 rm – †£ 75/85 ††£ 95/150
Rest – Menu £ 12 (weekday lunch) – Carte £ 22/33 **s**
Two charming 18C buildings in a sleepy little village, displaying exposed stone walls, parquet floors and open fires. Wide-ranging, classical menus; specials consist mainly of fish dishes. Set in the old carpenter's workshop, individually designed bedrooms are modern with rustic overtones.

at Combe Hay Southwest : 5 mi by A 367 – ✉ Bath

Wheatsheaf with rm

✉ BA2 7EG – ✆ (01225) 833 504 – www.wheatsheafcombehay.com – Closed 1 week January, 24-25 December, Sunday dinner and Monday except bank holidays

4 rm – †£ 120/150 ††£ 120/150

Rest – Menu £ 15 (weekday lunch) – Carte £ 21/40

A modern take on the classical country pub; remotely set in a pretty village, with chic styling, open fires, comfy sofas and a relaxed atmosphere. Contemporary presentation of flavourful, seasonal dishes. Spacious, modern bedrooms.

BATTLE – East Sussex – **504** V31 – **pop. 5 190** Great Britain **8** B3

London 55 mi – Brighton 34 mi – Folkestone 43 mi – Maidstone 30 mi

Battle and Bexhill TIC, Battle Abbey, High St, ✆ (01424) 77 37 21, www.battle-sussex.co.uk

Town★ – Abbey and Site of the Battle of Hastings★ **AC**

Nobles

17 High St ✉ TN33 OAE – ✆ (01424) 774 422 – www.noblesrestaurant.co.uk – Closed Sunday dinner and Monday

Rest – Menu £ 20 – Carte £ 24/34

A sweet, traditional, personally run restaurant in the heart of the historical high street. Regularly changing menus offer unfussy, classical dishes of local, seasonal produce, with the occasional twist.

BAUGHURST – Hampshire **6** B1

London 61 mi – Camberley 28 mi – Farnborough 27 mi

Wellington Arms with rm

Baughurst Rd, Southwest : 0.5 mi ✉ RG26 5LP – ✆ (0118) 982 01 10 – www.thewellingtonarms.com – Closed Sunday dinner

3 rm – †£ 130/200 ††£ 130/200

Rest – *(booking essential)* Menu £ 16 (weekday lunch) – Carte £ 21/39

Smart, cream pub boasting its own sheep, pigs, chickens, bees, herb beds and vegetable gardens. Produce is strictly local and home-grown/reared/made. Blackboard menus feature 6 dishes per course, which are replaced as produce runs out; cooking is generous and satisfying. Smart, rustic bedrooms come with sheepskin rugs and large, comfortable beds.

BEACONSFIELD – Buckinghamshire – **504** S29 – **pop. 12 292** **11** D3

London 26 mi – Aylesbury 19 mi – Oxford 32 mi – Croydon 37 mi

Beaconsfield Seer Green, ✆ (01494) 67 65 45

Crazy Bear

75 Wycombe End ✉ HP9 1LX – ✆ (01494) 673 086 – www.crazybeargroup.co.uk – Closed 10 May

19 rm – †£ 190/370 ††£ 190/370, £ 12

Rest *Thai* – see restaurant listing

Rest *English* – 73 Wycombe End *(booking advisable)* Menu £ 19 (lunch) – Carte £ 29/71

Discreet, unique hotel with sumptuous, over-the-top styling and idiosyncratic furnishings. 10 moody, masculine bedrooms blend original features with rich fabrics; 7 slightly less flamboyant bedrooms are located over the road. The lavishly styled English restaurant offers extensive menus and uses produce from their farm shop. Sexy Thai serves Asian cuisine.

Thai – Crazy Bear Hotel

73 Wycombe End ✉ HP9 1LX – ✆ (01494) 673 086 – www.crazybeargroup.co.uk – Closed Monday

Rest – *(dinner only) (booking essential)* Menu £ 30/50 – Carte £ 29/71

Part of the Crazy Bear but in a separate building: it's extravagant, sexy and atmospheric, with chandeliers, flock wallpaper, snakeskin handrails and studded leather chairs. Thai dishes dominate, but influences are drawn from all over Asia.

ENGLAND

at Seer Green **Northeast : 2.5 mi by A 355 – ✉ Buckinghamshire**

Jolly Cricketers

24 Chalfont Rd ✉ HP9 2YG – ✆ (01494) 676 308 – www.thejollycricketers.co.uk
Rest – *(Closed Sunday dinner) (booking advisable)* Carte £ 25/43
Charming Victorian pub filled with a host of cricketing memorabilia; even the menu is divided into 'Openers, Main Play and Lower Order'. Warming open fire and friendly staff. Appealing cooking pleasingly balances a selection of classics with more modern choices.

at Wooburn Common **Southwest : 3.5 mi by A 40 – ✉ Beaconsfield**

Chequers Inn

Kiln Ln, Southwest : 1 mi on Bourne End rd ✉ HP10 0JQ – ✆ (01628) 529 575 – www.chequers-inn.com
17 rm – †£ 85/110 ††£ 90/128
Rest – *(closed dinner 25 December and 1 January)* Menu £ 14 (weekday lunch)/29 – Carte £ 28/43
Attractive 17C former inn, which has been family-owned and run since 1975. Good-sized bedrooms have flowery feature walls and old pine furnishings collected from antique shops. Enjoy drinks in the spacious, leather-furnished lounge, snacks in the cosy beamed bar or more ambitious dishes in the restaurant.

BEAMHURST – Staffordshire – see Uttoxeter

BEAMINSTER – Dorset – 503 L31 – pop. 2 791 3 B3

London 154 mi – Exeter 45 mi – Taunton 30 mi – Weymouth 29 mi
Chedington Court, South Perrott, ✆ (01935) 89 14 13

BridgeHouse

3 Prout Bridge ✉ DT8 3AY – ✆ (01308) 862 200 – www.bridge-house.co.uk
13 rm – †£ 95/190 ††£ 125/220
Rest ***Beaminster Brasserie*** – Carte £ 32/42
Hugely characterful 13C former priest's house, with newer extensions. Traditionally furnished, flag-floored lounges boast inglenook fireplaces. Mix of classical and modern bedrooms. Linen-laid restaurant with conservatory and terrace offers brasserie-style menu.

BEARSTED – Kent – 504 V30 – see Maidstone

BEAULIEU – Hampshire – 503 P31 – pop. 726 – ✉ Brockenhurst 6 B2

Great Britain

London 102 mi – Bournemouth 24 mi – Southampton 13 mi – Winchester 23 mi
Town★★ - National Motor Museum★★ **AC**
Buckler's Hard★ (Maritime Museum★ **AC**) SE : 2 m

Montagu Arms

Palace Ln ✉ SO42 7ZL – ✆ (01590) 612 324 – www.montaguarmshotel.co.uk
18 rm – †£ 164/239 ††£ 228/378 – 4 suites
Rest ***The Terrace*** ✿ **Rest** ***Monty's Inn*** – see restaurant listing
Well-run 18C inn which boasts a characterful parquet-floored reception and wood-panelled lounge. Lovely rear gardens are overlooked by a wicker-furnished conservatory and paved terrace. Traditional country house style bedrooms successfully marry antique furniture with modern facilities. Good level of service.

The Terrace – Montagu Arms Hotel

✿
Palace Ln ✉ SO42 7ZL – ✆ (01590) 612 324 – www.montaguarmshotel.co.uk – Closed Tuesday lunch and Monday
Rest – Menu £ 23 (weekday lunch)/70
Traditional dining room of a country house hotel, with a wood-panelled lounge, good-sized, linen-laid tables and polite, efficient service. Precisely prepared, top quality produce is used in refined, classically based dishes with modern touches. Sit on the terrace for a lovely garden outlook.
→ Spiced scallops, cauliflower purée and coriander and cumin velouté. Lamb with confit belly, crispy sweetbread and goat's curd. Salted caramel fondant, crème fraîche and 'Cider Lolly' sorbet.

Monty's Inn - Montagu Arms Hotel

Palace Ln ✉ SO42 7ZL – ✆ (01590) 612 324 – www.montaguarmshotel.co.uk

Rest – Carte £ 23/38

Set within a large red-brick inn in a pleasant town; an informal hotel restaurant serving home-cooked classics. Meats are free range and from nearby farms; eggs are from their own chickens.

BEAUMONT – Saint Peter – 503 P33 – see Channel Islands (Jersey)

BEELEY – Derbyshire – pop. 165 16 B1

London 160 mi – Derby 26 mi – Matlock 5 mi

Devonshire Arms with rm

Devonshire Sq ✉ DE4 2NR – ✆ (01629) 733 259 – www.devonshirebeeley.co.uk

14 rm – †£ 109/209 ††£ 129/239 **Rest** – Carte £ 27/39

Stone inn with a rustic bar and modern extension – close to Chatsworth House and also owned by the Estate. Classical main menu and daily changing game dishes cooked to order or hot off the rotisserie. Tasty afternoon teas. Cosy bedrooms in the main inn; larger, brighter rooms next door.

BELBROUGHTON – Worcestershire – 504 N26 19 C2

London 122 mi – Sheffield 108 mi – Kingston upon Hull 156 mi – Derby 64 mi

The Queens N

Queens Hill ✉ DY9 0DU – ✆ (01562) 730 276
– www.thequeensbelbroughton.co.uk – Closed 25 December

Rest – *(closed Sunday dinner) (bookings advisable at dinner)* Menu £ 18 – Carte £ 23/36

This 16C pub might have been refurbished but its traditional look and feel remains – a conscious effort by the owners to respect the locals' preferences. Refined, attractive dishes range from hearty pub favourites to flavoursome classics.

BELCHFORD – Lincolnshire – 502 T24 – ✉ Horncastle 17 C1

London 169 mi – Horncastle 5 mi – Lincoln 28 mi

Blue Bell Inn

1 Main Rd ✉ LN9 6LQ – ✆ (01507) 533 602 – www.bluebellbelchford.co.uk
– Closed 6-21 January

Rest – Carte £ 15/32

Welcoming pub in a tiny village in the Lincolnshire Wolds. Traditional bar with a copper-topped counter and sofas leads to a bright red dining room. Menus cover all bases, offering honest, home-cooked dishes which are big on flavour.

BELFORD – Northumberland – 501 O17 – pop. 1 177 24 A1

London 335 mi – Edinburgh 71 mi – Newcastle upon Tyne 49 mi

Belford, South Rd, ✆ (01668) 21 33 23

Market Cross

1 Church St ✉ NE70 7LS – ✆ (01668) 213 013 – www.marketcrossbelford.co.uk
– Closed 24-27 December

4 rm – †£ 60/100 ††£ 70/110 **Rest** – Menu £ 19

200 year old stone townhouse close to the medieval cross in the market square; run by friendly, welcoming owners. Bright modern bedrooms come in neutral hues and feature Nespresso machines and complimentary sherry and Lindisfarne Mead. Local produce features at breakfast; dinner is by arrangement.

ENGLAND

BELPER – Derbyshire – 502 P24 – pop. 21 938 — 16 B2

London 141 mi – Birmingham 59 mi – Leicester 40 mi – Manchester 55 mi

at Shottle Northwest : 4 mi by A 517 – ✉ Belper

Dannah Farm Country House without rest
Bowmans Lane, North : 0.25 mi by Alport rd ✉ DE56 2DR – ✆ (01773) 550 273 – www.dannah.co.uk – Closed 24-26 December
8 rm – †£ 85/105 ††£ 165/295
Family-run, 18C stone farmhouse in 154 acres on the Chatsworth Estate; its outbuildings converted into spacious suites and bedrooms. Many have spa baths and the Granary/Studio Suites also have hot tubs and terraces.

BENENDEN – Kent – 504 V30 — 8 B2

London 55 mi – Croydon 49 mi – Barnet 81 mi – Ealing 85 mi

Ramsden Farm without rest
Dingleden Ln, Southeast : 1 mi by B 2086 ✉ TN17 4JT – ✆ (01580) 240 203 – www.ramsdenfarmcottage.co.uk
3 rm – †£ 75/110 ††£ 85/110
Attractive clapperboard house with modern styling, a refreshingly relaxed air and fine countryside views. Spacious, up-to-date bedrooms; luxurious, modern bathrooms with underfloor heating.

BEPTON – West Sussex – see Midhurst

BERKHAMSTED – Hertfordshire – 504 S28 – pop. 18 800 — 12 A2

Great Britain

London 34 mi – Aylesbury 14 mi – St Albans 11 mi

Whipsnade Wild Animal Park★ AC, N : 9.5 mi on A 4251, B 4506 and B 4540

The Gatsby
97 High St ✉ HP4 2DG – ✆ (01442) 870 403 – www.thegatsby.net – Closed 25-26 December
Rest – Menu £ 15 (lunch) – Carte £ 32/47
Charming cinema built in 1938 and sympathetically converted to incorporate a trendy art deco bar and glamorous restaurant. Dine among elegant columns and ornate plasterwork. Menus offer detailed, classically based dishes with modern twists.

BERWICK – East Sussex — 8 A3

London 65 mi – Leeds 271 mi – Sheffield 241 mi – Manchester 280 mi

Restaurant at the English Wine Centre with rm
Alfriston Rd ✉ BN26 5QS – ✆ (01323) 870 164 – www.englishwine.co.uk – Closed last 2 weeks February, Christmas-New Year and Monday
5 rm – †£ 75/120 ††£ 135/175
Rest – *(lunch only and dinner Friday-Saturday) (booking essential)* Carte £ 23/29
A delightful collection of 16 and 17C barns; one houses a shop selling over 140 English wines and this pretty, intimate restaurant where sweet-natured staff serve tasty, traditional English dishes. Spacious, comfortable, modern bedrooms are situated in another barn, with views of the South Downs.

BEVERLEY – East Riding of Yorkshire – 502 S22 – pop. 29 110 – ✉ Kingston-Upon-Hull — 23 D2

Great Britain

London 188 mi – Kingston-upon-Hull 8 mi – Leeds 52 mi – York 29 mi

34 Butcher Row, ✆ (01482) 86 74 30, www.yorkshire.com

The Westwood, ✆ (01482) 86 87 57

Town★ - Minster★★ – St Mary's Church★

XX **Whites** with rm
12a North Bar Without ✉ HU17 7AB – ✆ (01482) 866 121 – www.whitesrestaurant.co.uk – Closed 1 week Christmas, 1 week August, Sunday and Monday
4 rm – 🚹£ 75/125 🚹🚹£ 100/125
Rest – *(dinner only and Saturday lunch) (booking advisable)* Menu £ 23 (weekdays) – Carte approx. £ 36
Small restaurant by the old city walls, its plain décor contrasting nicely with black wood tables and eye-catching glass art. Good value weekday set menu uses lesser-known cuts; à la carte offers more ambitious, complex dishes. Smart, modern bedrooms, some with bespoke furniture; rooftop terrace breakfast.

at Tickton **Northeast : 3.5 mi by A 1035 – ✉ Kingston-Upon-Hull**

Tickton Grange
on A 1035 ✉ HU17 9SH – ✆ (01964) 543 666 – www.beverleyticktongrange.co.uk
21 rm – 🚹£ 85/115 🚹🚹£ 120/175
Rest *Champagne* – see restaurant listing
Warm, welcoming, family-run hotel in a Georgian house – a popular wedding venue. Spacious main sitting room with a grand piano looks out over immaculately kept gardens. Homely bedrooms; those in the converted cottage are more contemporary.

XX **Champagne** – Tickton Grange Hotel
on A 1035 ✉ HU17 9SH – ✆ (01964) 543 666 – www.beverleyticktongrange.co.uk
Rest – Menu £ 27/60 – Carte £ 35/51
Formal hotel restaurant with elegant furnishings. Accomplished, original dishes are presented in a modern style; flavours are distinct and combinations, well-judged. Dishes are more technical than their concise descriptions imply.

at South Dalton **Northwest : 5 mi by A 164 and B 1248 – ✉ Beverley**

Pipe and Glass Inn (James Mackenzie) with rm
West End ✉ HU17 7PN – ✆ (01430) 810 246 – www.pipeandglass.co.uk – Closed 2 weeks January, Sunday dinner and Monday except bank holidays
2 rm – 🚹£ 160 🚹🚹£ 160 **Rest** – Carte £ 21/51
Warm, bustling and inviting pub; very personally run by its experienced owners. Dishes are generously proportioned, carefully executed and flavourful, with judicious use of local, seasonal and traceable produce. Luxurious designer bedrooms boast the latest mod cons and have their own patios overlooking the estate woodland; breakfast is served in your room.
➜ Tartare of sea trout, crowdie and pickled samphire. Rump of lamb with crispy mutton belly and spring vegetable 'hotchpotch'. Raspberry and pistachio Bakewell tart with raspberry ripple ice cream.

BEYTON – **Suffolk** – **504** W27 – **see Bury St Edmunds**

BIBURY – **Gloucestershire** – **503** O28 – **pop. 570** – **✉ Cirencester** **4** D1
Great Britain
London 86 mi – Gloucester 26 mi – Oxford 30 mi
Village★

Swan
✉ GL7 5NW – ✆ (01285) 740 695 – www.cotswold-inns-hotels.co.uk/swan
22 rm – 🚹£ 150/210 🚹🚹£ 170/210 – 4 suites
Rest *Swan Brasserie* – see restaurant listing
Set in a delightful village; an ivy-clad former coaching inn with a trout stream running through its private garden. Cosy lounges and a clubby bar. Bedrooms mix cottagey character and contemporary touches – the best are in the annexes.

ENGLAND

⛪ **Cotteswold House** without rest 🚗 ℅ 🛜 **P**
Arlington, on B 4425 ⊠ GL7 5ND – ℰ (01285) 740 609
– www.cotteswoldhouse.net
3 rm ⌂ – †£ 50/60 ††£ 70/80
Set in a pleasant garden outside the picturesque village. Homely, spotless and
modestly priced bedrooms, comprehensively remodelled behind a Victorian façade. Friendly, welcoming owner.

✗✗ **Swan Brasserie** – Swan Hotel 🚗 🛖 **P**
⊠ GL7 5NW – ℰ (01285) 740 695 – www.cotswold-inns-hotels.co.uk/swan
Rest – Menu £ 15 (weekday lunch) – Carte £ 23/30
Relaxed, modern brasserie within a 17C coaching. It has an unusual floor and log
wall, and opens out onto a lovely flag-stoned courtyard complete with a water
fountain. The menu offers a mix of light bites and brasserie-style dishes.

BIDDENDEN – Kent – **504** V30 – **pop. 2 205** ▌ Great Britain **9** C2
🚇 London 52 mi – Ashford 13 mi – Maidstone 16 mi
🌀 Bodiam Castle★★, S : 10 mi by A 262, A 229 and B 2244 – Sissinghurst Garden★,
W : 3 mi by A 262 – Battle Abbey★, S : 20 mi by A 262, A 229, A 21 and A 2100

⛪ **Barclay Farmhouse** without rest 🚗 ℅ 🛜 **P**
Woolpack Corner, South : 0.5 mi by A 262 on Benenden rd ⊠ TN27 8BQ
– ℰ (01580) 292 626 – www.barclayfarmhouse.co.uk
3 rm ⌂ – †£ 65/70 ††£ 85/90
Farmhouse and barn conversion in an acre of neat gardens complete with a duck
pond. Comfortable bedrooms have French oak flooring and furniture; extra
touches include chocolates on your pillow and fresh milk.

✗ **West House** (Graham Garrett) **P**
⚘ 28 High St ⊠ TN27 8AH – ℰ (01580) 291 341
*– www.thewesthouserestaurant.co.uk – Closed Christmas-New Year, 2
weeks summer, Saturday lunch, Sunday dinner and Monday*
Rest – Menu £ 25 (weekday lunch)/50
Characterful beamed restaurant with contemporary oil paintings and a wood-
burning stove – one of a row of old weavers' cottages in a picturesque village.
Original, modern dishes display global influences and the occasional playful
touch; and top quality ingredients allow the natural flavours to shine through.
→ Duck liver parfait, duck confit and cured foie gras. Duck breast with mushroom tortellini, beetroot and Lapsang duck tea. Milk mousse, honey ice cream
and caramelised chocolate.

🍺 **The Three Chimneys** 🚗 🛖 **P**
Hareplain Rd, West : 1.5 mi by A 262 ⊠ TN27 8LW – ℰ (01580) 291 472
– www.thethreechimneys.co.uk – Closed 25 and dinner 31 December
Rest – (booking essential) Carte £ 24/37
Delightful pub with a charming terrace and garden, dating back to 1420 and
boasting a roaring fire, dimly lit low-beamed rooms and an old world feel. Dishes
are mainly British based; there are some tempting local wines, ciders and ales too.

BIGBURY – Devon – **503** I33 **2** C3
🚇 London 195 mi – Exeter 41 mi – Plymouth 22 mi
🌀 Kingsbridge★, E : 13 mi by B 3392 and A 379

✗ **Oyster Shack** 🛜 **P**
Milburn Orchard Farm, Stakes Hill, East : 1 mi by Easton rd on Tidal rd
*⊠ TQ7 4BE – ℰ (01548) 810 876 – www.oystershack.co.uk – Closed 2 January-1
February*
Rest – (booking essential) Menu £ 12 (weekdays) – Carte approx. £ 37
Former oyster farm with a small oyster bar and lounge, and a large terrace. The
brightly decorated room is hung with fishing nets and centred around a large
fish tank. Cooking is fresh and unfussy, focusing on shellfish and the daily catch.

BIGBURY-ON-SEA – Devon – 503 I33 – pop. 600 – ✉ Kingsbridge 2 C3

London 196 mi – Exeter 42 mi – Plymouth 23 mi

Burgh Island

South : 0.5 mi by hotel transport ✉ *TQ7 4BG – ✆ (01548) 810 514 – www.burghisland.com*

25 rm (dinner included) – £ 310 £ 430/640 – 10 suites

Rest – *(dinner only and Sunday lunch) (bookings essential for non-residents)* Menu £ 48/60

Grade II listed house set on its own island and accessed using the hotel's tractor at high tide. Classical art deco styling throughout, from the bar, lounge and snooker room to the individually designed bedrooms; some rooms have small balconies and most have excellent bay views. Modern daily menus served in the ballroom; Weds and Sat are 1930s themed – dress in black tie.

Henley

Folly Hill ✉ *TQ7 4AR – ✆ (01548) 810 240 – www.thehenleyhotel.co.uk – March-October*

5 rm – £ 85 £ 120/145 **Rest** – *(dinner only) (residents only)* Menu £ 36

Charming hotel affording superb views over Burgh Island and towards Bolt Tail. Homely lounge and wicker-furnished conservatory. Comfortable bedrooms cross New England and English Country styles; Room 6 boasts the best views. Concise, unfussy menus feature locally sourced ingredients.

BILDESTON – Suffolk – 504 W27 15 C3

London 85 mi – Bury St Edmunds 18 mi – Ipswich 15 mi

Bildeston Crown

104 High St ✉ *IP7 7EB – ✆ (01449) 740 510 – www.thebildestoncrown.com*

13 rm – £ 70/120 £ 100/195

Rest – Menu £ 21 (weekday lunch)/45 – Carte £ 33/50

Rest *Ingrams* – *(booking essential)* Menu £ 45/70

Hugely characterful 15C former wool merchants with a lovely rear courtyard. Stylish, modern interior with warm colours and open fires. Bedrooms vary from florally feminine to bright and bold; all are luxurious with designer furniture and chic bathrooms. Sumptuous, formal Ingrams serves creative modern dishes; the charming beamed dining room offers a more classical menu.

BIRKENHEAD – Merseyside – 502 K23 – pop. 83 729 20 A3

London 208 mi – Liverpool 3 mi – Manchester 37 mi – Stoke-on-Trent 52 mi

Access Mersey Tunnels (toll)

to Liverpool and Wallasey (Mersey Ferries) frequent services daily

18 Arrowe Park, Woodchurch, ✆ (0151) 677 15 27

18 Prenton, Golf Links Rd, ✆ (0151) 609 34 26

Fraiche (Marc Wilkinson)

11 Rose Mount, Oxton, Southwest : 2.25 mi by A 552 and B 5151 ✉ *CH43 5SG – ✆ (0151) 652 29 14 – www.restaurantfraiche.com – Closed 25 December, 1-7 July, Monday and Tuesday*

Rest – *(dinner only and lunch Friday-Saturday) (booking essential)* Menu £ 35 (lunch)/65

Stylish, sophisticated restaurant – seating just 10-12 diners – with striking glass friezes and intimate mood lighting. The passionate chef cooks alone and offers a modern six course menu which uses ingredients from around the globe. Dishes feature some unusual combinations and are impressively presented.

→ Feta panna cotta, wild garlic textures and white truffle. Pigeon with cocoa crisp, onion varieties and spinach. White chocolate mousse, passion fruit cream, coffee meringue and lemon balm.

ENGLAND

BIRMINGHAM

See city maps on following pages **19** C2

© Jane Sweeney/Age fotostock

ENGLAND

West Midlands – pop. 935 270 – 503 O26 – **504** O26 – Great Britain

London 122 mi – Bristol 91 mi – Liverpool 103 mi – Manchester 86 mi

Tourist Information

150 New St, ✆(0121) 202 50 00, www.visitbirmingham.com

Airport

Birmingham International Airport : ✆ (0844) 576 6000, E : 6 ½ m. by A 45 DU

Golf Courses

Edgbaston, Church Rd, ✆(0121) 454 17 36

Hilltop, Handsworth, Park Lane, ✆(0121) 554 44 63

Hatchford Brook, Sheldon, Coventry Rd, ✆(0121) 743 98 21

SIGHTS

In the town : City★ • Museum and Art Gallery★★ LY**M2** • Library of Birmingham, Centenary Square KZ • Barber Institute of Fine Arts★★ EX**U**

On the outskirts : Aston Hall★★ FVM

In the surrounding area : Black Country Museum★, Dudley, NW : 10 mi by A 456 and A 4123 AU • Bournville★, SW : 4 mi on A 38 and A 441

INDEX OF STREET NAMES IN BIRMINGHAM

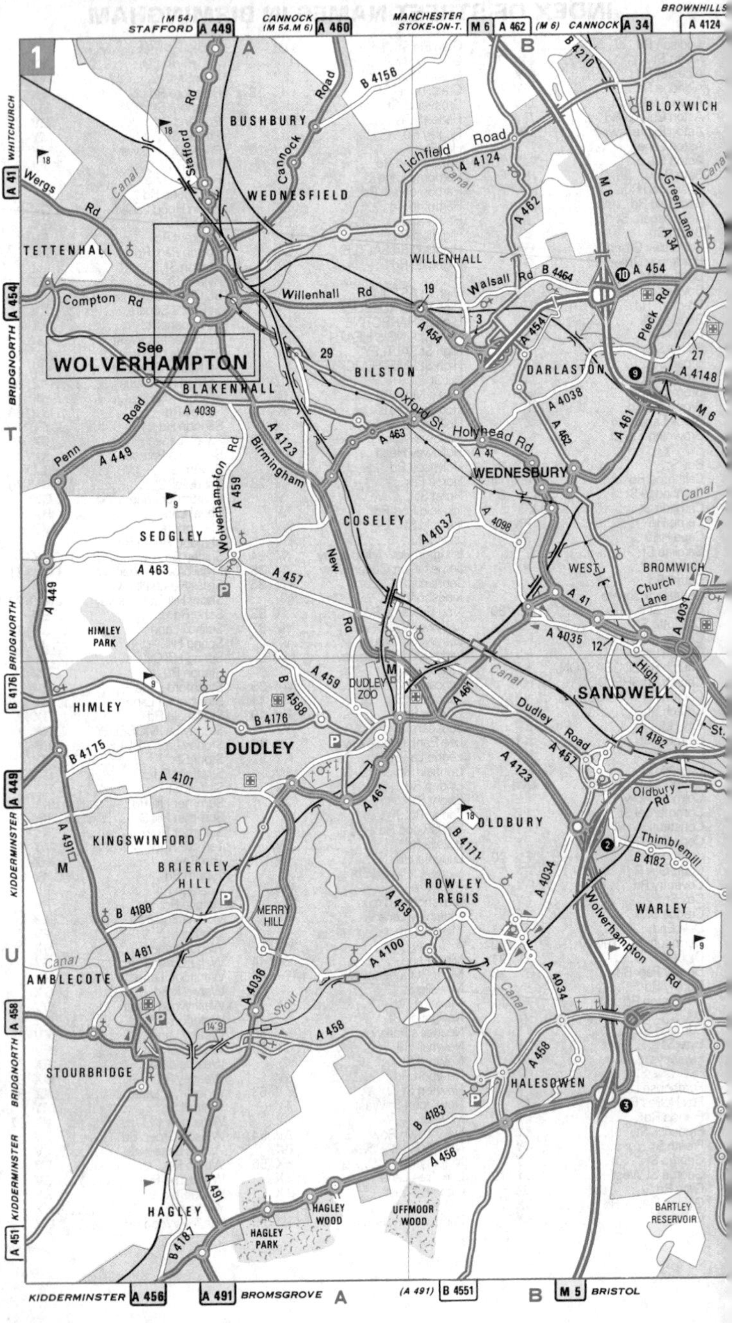
1
(M 54) STAFFORD A 449
CANNOCK (M 54.M 6) A 460
MANCHESTER STOKE-ON-T. M 6 A 462
(M 6) CANNOCK A 34
BROWNHILLS A 4124
A
B
WHITCHURCH A 41
BRIDGNORTH A 454
BRIDGNORTH B 4176
KIDDERMINSTER A 449
BRIDGNORTH A 458
KIDDERMINSTER A 451
T
U
KIDDERMINSTER A 456
A 491 BROMSGROVE
(A 491) B 4551
M 5 BRISTOL
BUSHBURY
WEDNESFIELD
BLOXWICH
TETTENHALL
WILLENHALL
See WOLVERHAMPTON
BLAKENHALL
BILSTON
DARLASTON
WEDNESBURY
SEDGLEY
COSELEY
WEST BROMWICH
HIMLEY PARK
HIMLEY
DUDLEY
DUDLEY ZOO
SANDWELL
KINGSWINFORD
BRIERLEY HILL
MERRY HILL
OLDBURY
ROWLEY REGIS
WARLEY
AMBLECOTE
STOURBRIDGE
HALESOWEN
HAGLEY
HAGLEY WOOD
HAGLEY PARK
UFFMOOR WOOD
BARTLEY RESERVOIR
Wergs Rd
Compton Rd
Stafford Rd
Cannock Road
Lichfield Road
Willenhall Rd
Walsall Rd
Penn Road
Oxford St.
Holyhead Rd
Wolverhampton Rd
Birmingham New Rd
Green Lane
Pleck Rd
Church Lane
High St.
Dudley Road
Oldbury Rd
Thimblemill
Wolverhampton Rd
Canal
Stout
B 4210
B 4156
A 4124
A 462
A 454
B 4464
A 4148
M 6
A 34
A 4039
A 4123
A 459
A 463
A 457
A 4037
A 4098
A 4038
A 461
A 41
A 4035
A 4031
A 4182
B 4588
B 4176
B 4175
A 4101
A 491
B 4171
A 4034
B 4182
B 4180
A 4100
A 4036
A 458
B 4183
A 456
B 4187
18
9
19
3
29
27
12
14'9

BIRMINGHAM AND WOLVERHAMPTON

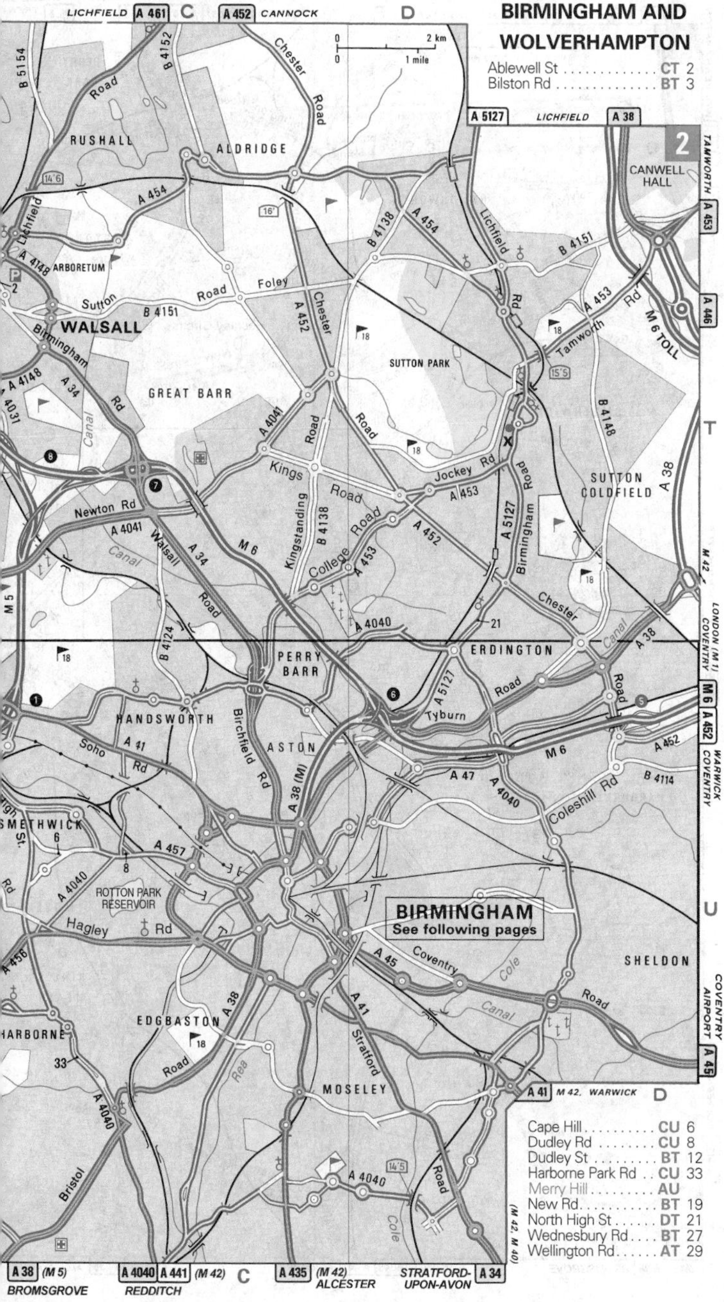

ENGLAND

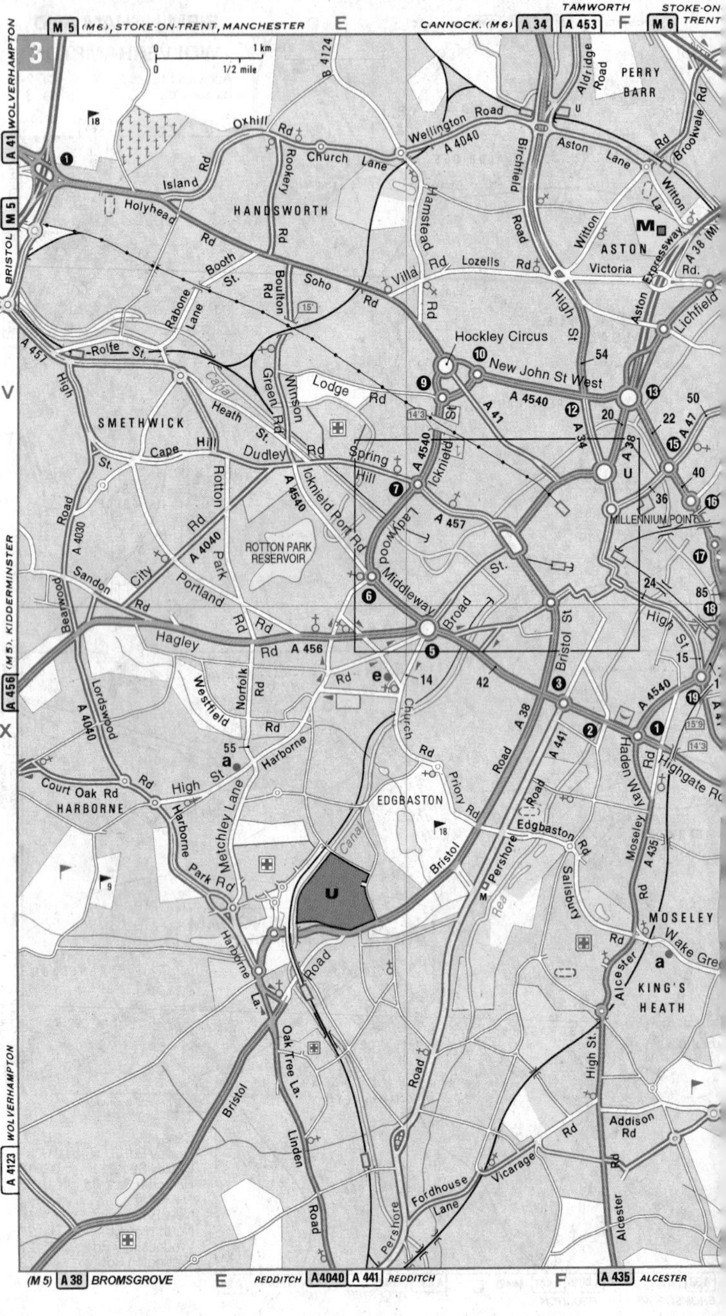

3
M 5 (M6), STOKE-ON-TRENT, MANCHESTER
E
CANNOCK. (M6) A 34
TAMWORTH A 453
F
STOKE-ON-TRENT M 6
0 1 km
0 1/2 mile
A 41 WOLVERHAMPTON
M 5 BRISTOL
V
A 456 (M5). KIDDERMINSTER
X
A 4123 WOLVERHAMPTON
(M 5) A 38 BROMSGROVE
REDDITCH A4040 A 441 REDDITCH
A 435 ALCESTER
PERRY BARR
HANDSWORTH
ASTON
SMETHWICK
ROTTON PARK RESERVOIR
MILLENNIUM POINT
EDGBASTON
HARBORNE
MOSELEY
KING'S HEATH
Hockley Circus
Oxhill Rd
Church Lane
Wellington Road
A 4040
Aldridge Road
Aston Lane
Brookvale Rd
Witton La.
Witton Rd
Aston Expressway
A 38 (M)
Victoria Rd.
Lichfield
Birchfield Road
Hamstead Rd
Lozells Rd
Villa Rd
High St
Island Rd
Holyhead Rd
Rookery Rd
Booth St.
Soho Rd
Boulton Rd
Rabone Lane
Rolfe St.
Canal
A 457
High St
Heath St.
Green Rd
Winson
Lodge Rd
New John St West
A 4540
A 41
A 34
A 38
A 47
Cape Hill
Dudley Rd
Spring Hill
Icknield St
Ladywood
Middleway
Icknield Port Rd
Rotton Rd
Road
A 4030
Sandon Rd
City Rd
Park Rd
Portland Rd
Bearwood Rd
Hagley Rd
A 456
Broad St.
Bristol St
Westfield Rd
Norfolk Rd
Lordswood Rd
A 4040
Harborne
Church Rd
Court Oak Rd
High St
Metchley Lane
Harborne Park Rd
Harborne La.
Priory Rd
Edgbaston Rd
Pershore Road
Bristol Road
A 441
Haden Way
Highgate Rd
Moseley Rd
A 435
Salisbury
Rea
Wake Green
Alcester Rd
Oak Tree La.
Linden Road
Bristol
Road
High St.
Addison Rd
Vicarage Rd
Fordhouse Lane
Pershore
Alcester
U
M
e
a
55
14
42
54
20
22
50
40
36
24
85
15

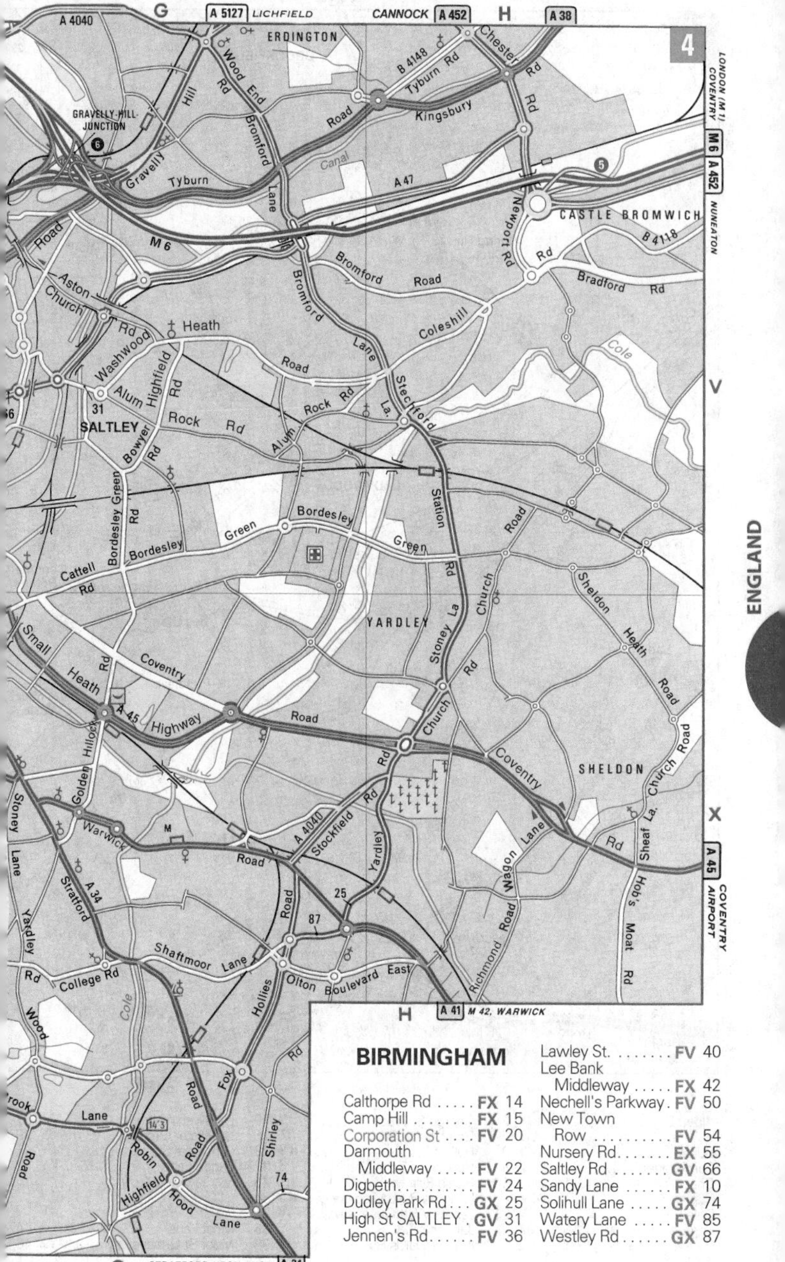

G
A 5127 LICHFIELD
CANNOCK A 452
H
A 38
4
LONDON (M 1) COVENTRY
M 6
A 452
NUNEATON
A 4040
ERDINGTON
GRAVELLY HILL JUNCTION
6
5
Wood End Rd
Hill
Bromford Lane
B 4148
Tyburn Rd
Chester Rd
Road
Kingsbury
Gravelly
Tyburn
Canal
A 47
Newport Rd
CASTLE BROMWICH
B 4118
Road
M 6
Bromford Road
Rd
Bradford Rd
Aston Church Rd
Heath
Coleshill
Washwood
Highfield Rd
Road
Cole
V
Alum Rock Rd
31
SALTLEY
Bowyer Rd
Alum Rock Rd
Stechford La.
Station Rd
Road
Bordesley Green Rd
Bordesley Green
Green
Cattell Rd
Bordesley
Church Rd
Sheldon Heath Road
YARDLEY
Stoney La
Small Heath Rd
Coventry
A 45 Highway
Road
Road
Church Rd
Coventry
SHELDON
Church Road
Golden Hillock
Rd
X
Stoney Lane
Warwick Road
M
A 4040
Stockfield Rd
Yardley
Wagon Lane
Rd
Sheaf La.
A 45
COVENTRY AIRPORT
Stratford A 34
25
87
Hob's Moat Rd
Yardley Rd
Shaftmoor Lane
Road
Richmond Road
College Rd
Olton Boulevard East
Cole
Wood
Hollies
H
A 41 M 42, WARWICK
Fox
Road
Rd
Lane
Road
Shirley
Robin Hood Lane
Highfield
74
G
STRATFORD-UPON-AVON A 34
ENGLAND

BIRMINGHAM

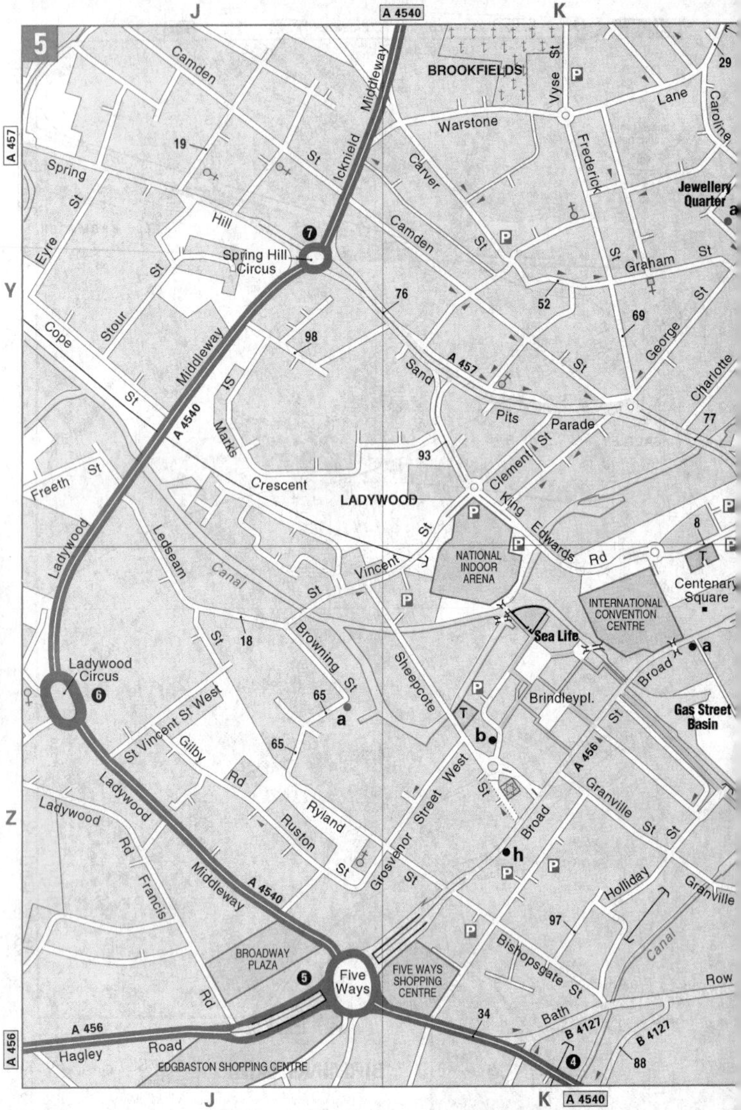
5
J
K
A 4540
A 457
A 456
Y
Z
BROOKFIELDS
Camden
Middleway
Icknield
Vyse
St
Lane
Caroline
29
Warstone
Carver
Frederick
Jewellery
Quarter
Spring
Hill
19
Eyre
Spring Hill
Circus
Stour
Cope
Graham
George
Charlotte
76
52
69
98
Sand
Pits
Parade
77
Marks
Crescent
93
Clement
LADYWOOD
King
Edwards
Rd
8
Freeth
Ledsseam
Canal
Vincent
NATIONAL
INDOOR
ARENA
Centenary
Square
INTERNATIONAL
CONVENTION
CENTRE
Sea Life
Broad
Gas Street
Basin
Browning
Sheepcote
18
Brindleypl.
Ladywood
Circus
65
St Vincent St West
Gilby
Rd
Ryland
Ruston
Grosvenor
Street West
A 4540
Granville
Francis
Holliday
97
Bishopsgate St
BROADWAY
PLAZA
Five
Ways
FIVE WAYS
SHOPPING
CENTRE
Row
Bath
34
B 4127
88
Hagley
Road
EDGBASTON SHOPPING CENTRE

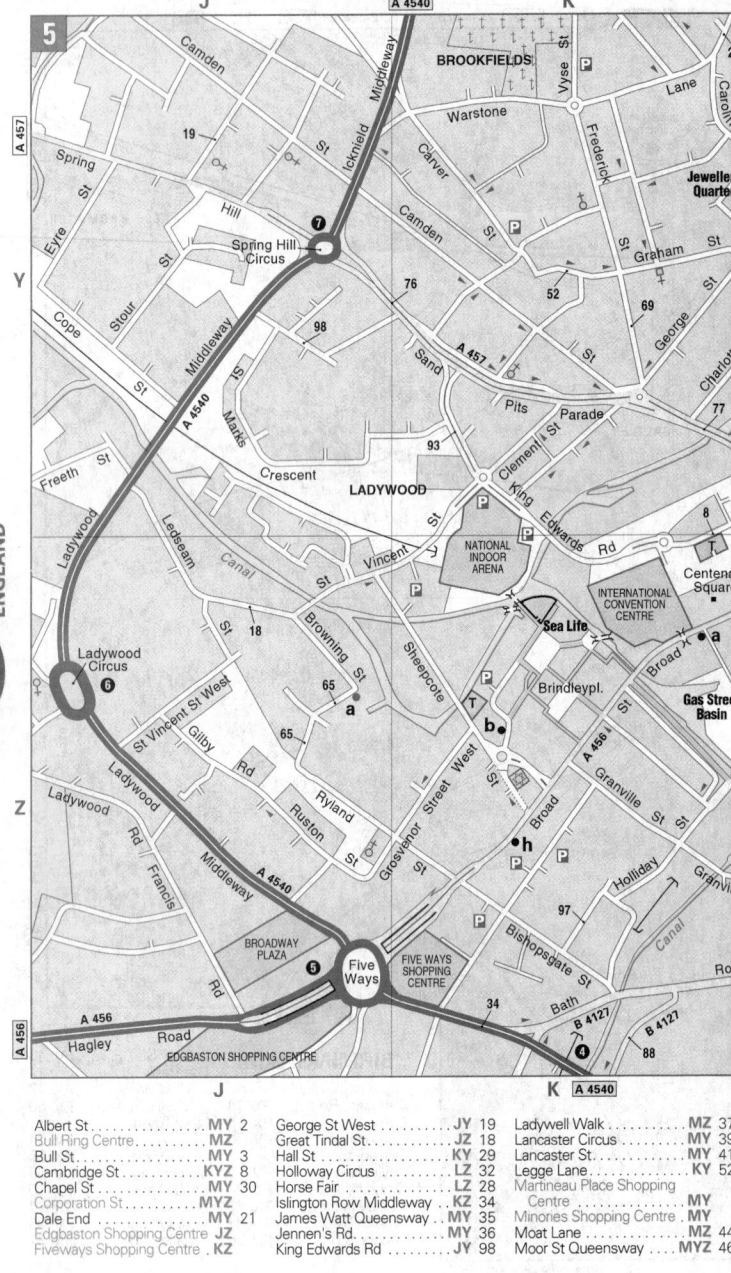

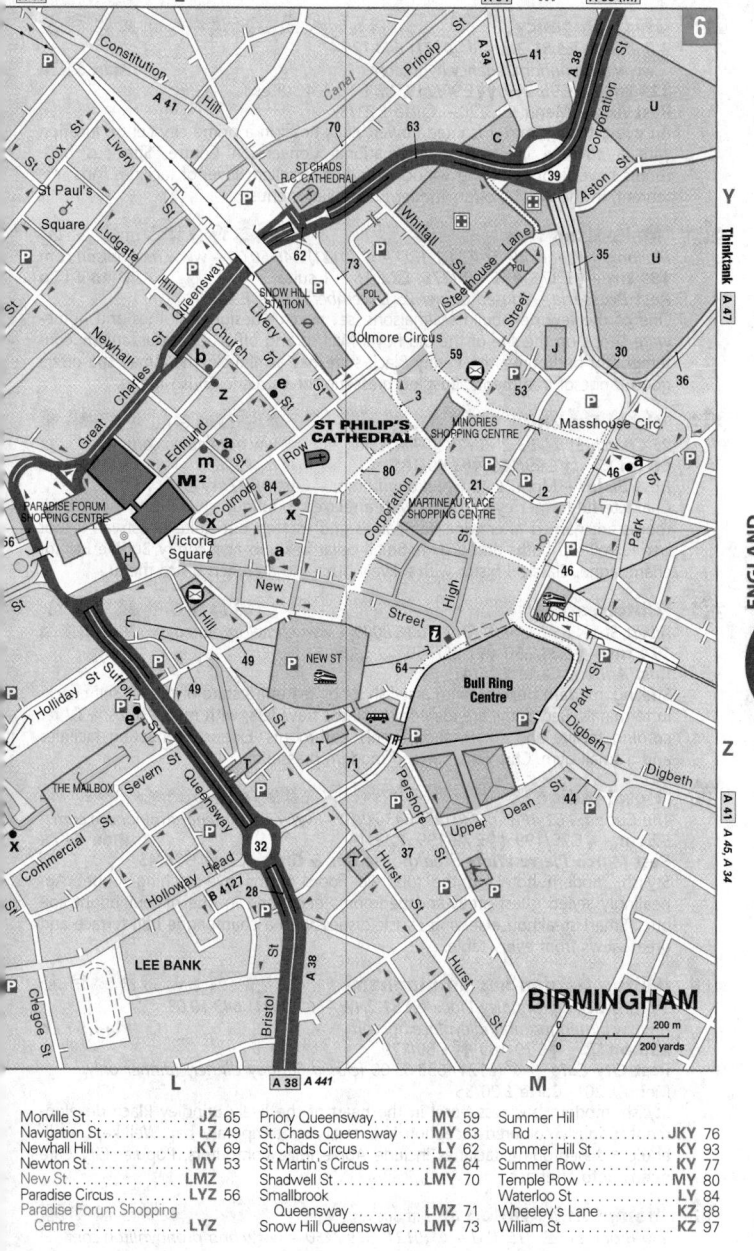

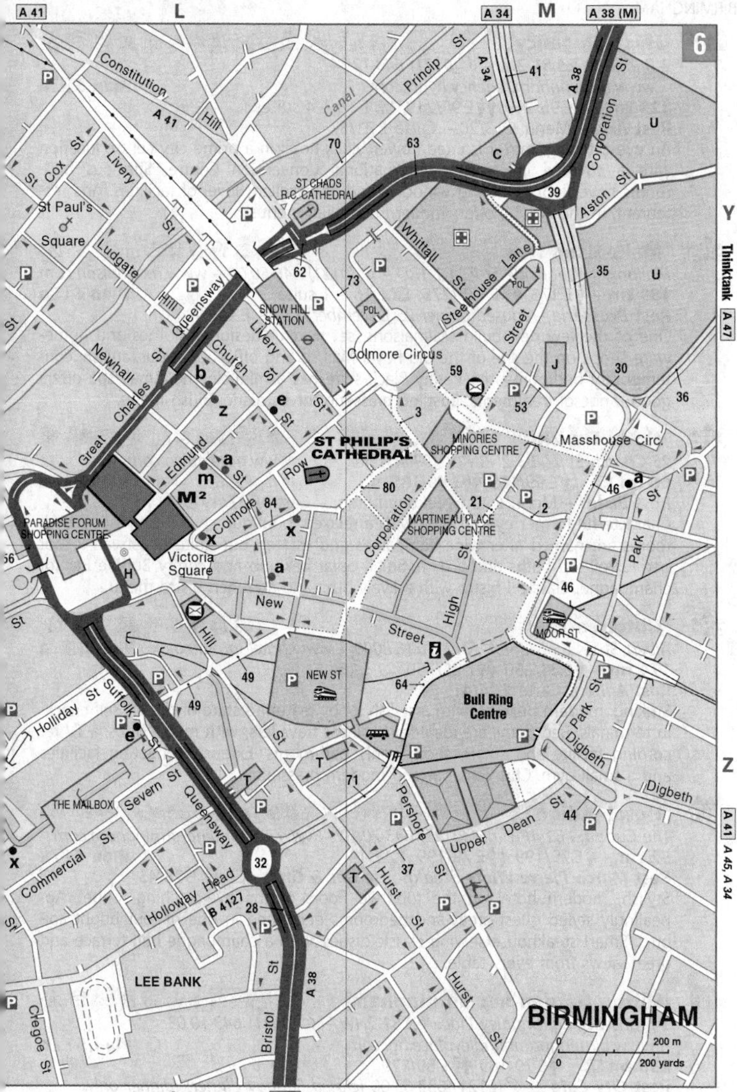

A 41
L
A 34
M
A 38 (M)
6
Constitution Hill
A 41
Canal
Princip St
A 34
41
A 38
Corporation St
U
C
70
63
39
Aston St
Y
Thinktank
A 47
Cox St
Livery St
St Paul's Square
ST CHADS R.C. CATHEDRAL
Ludgate Hill
Whittall St
Steelhouse Lane
62
73
35
U
SNOW HILL STATION
POL
Queensway
Newhall St
Church St
Colmore Circus
Street
J
30
36
59
53
Great Charles St
Edmund St
ST PHILIP'S CATHEDRAL
MINORIES SHOPPING CENTRE
Masshouse Circ.
Row
80
46
Park St
PARADISE FORUM SHOPPING CENTRE
M²
Colmore
84
Corporation St
21
2
MARTINEAU PLACE SHOPPING CENTRE
Victoria Square
High St
46
ENGLAND
New Street
MOOR ST
Hill St
49
NEW ST
64
Bull Ring Centre
Holliday St
Suffolk St
49
Park St
Digbeth
Z
THE MAILBOX
Severn St
Queensway
71
Pershore St
Digbeth
Upper Dean St
44
A 41
A 45, A 34
Commercial St
32
37
Hurst St
Holloway Head
B 4127
28
LEE BANK
Bristol St
A 38
Hurst St
Cregoe St
BIRMINGHAM
200 m
200 yards
L
A 38
A 441
M

Hyatt Regency

2 Bridge St ✉ B1 2JZ – ✆ (0121) 643 12 34 – www.birmingham.regency.hyatt.com **Plan 5** KZ**a**

325 rm – †£ 95/219 ††£ 95/219, ☕ £ 18 – 4 suites

Rest *Aria* – Menu £ 13/20 – Carte £ 21/57

An eye-catching, mirror-fronted, tower block hotel in a prime city centre location with a covered link to the International Convention Centre. Spacious bedrooms have floor to ceiling windows and an excellent level of facilities. Aria restaurant, in the atrium, offers modern European menus.

Malmaison

Mailbox, 1 Wharfside St ✉ B1 1RD – ✆ (0121) 246 50 00 – www.malmaison.com

189 rm – †£ 175 ††£ 175/275, ☕ £ 16 – 1 suite **Plan 6** LZ**e**

Rest *Brasserie* – *(closed dinner 25 December)* Carte £ 24/67

One of the few new-build Malmaisons, set next to designer clothes and homeware shops on the site of the old Royal Mail sorting office. Spacious, stylish, contemporary bedrooms; the Penny Black suite has a mini-cinema. Small spa offers good range of treatments. Bustling brasserie serves rustic British menu.

Hotel Du Vin

25 Church St ✉ B3 2NR – ✆ (08447) 364 250 – www.hotelduvin.com

66 rm ☕ – †£ 99/165 ††£ 99/185 **Plan 6** LY**e**

Rest *Bistro* – Menu £ 20 (weekday lunch) – Carte £ 27/49

Characterful former eye hospital with a relaxed, boutique style. Richly hued bedrooms are named after wine companies and estates; one suite boasts an 8 foot bed, 2 roll-top baths and a gym. Small cellar bar/pub and comfy Bubble Bar for champagne. Classical bistro with a lively buzz and a French bistro menu.

ENGLAND

Hotel La Tour

Albert St ✉ B5 5JE – ✆ (0121) 718 8000 – www.hotel-latour.co.uk **Plan 6** MY**a**

174 rm – †£ 85/250 ††£ 85/250, ☕ £ 16

Rest *Aalto* – Carte £ 24/41

Striking, modern building with a stylish lobby featuring state-of-the-art self check-in terminals. Bedrooms are ideal for business travellers, with media hubs, a TV recording facility and smart, shower-only bathrooms. Extensive meeting facilities and a small gym. Chic café, bar and modern brasserie.

Hotel Indigo

The Cube ✉ B1 1PR – ✆ (0121) 643 20 10 – www.hotelindigobirmingham.com

52 rm – †£ 79/199 ††£ 79/199, ☕ £ 14 **Plan 6** LZ**x**

Rest *Marco Pierre White Steakhouse Bar & Grill* – Carte £ 28/45

Stylish, modern hotel on the top two floors of the eye-catching 'Cube'. Appealingly styled guest areas and bedrooms decorated in one of four bright colours. Smart steakhouse serving classic dishes, with a champagne bar, terrace and great views from every table.

Hilton Garden Inn Birmingham

1 Brunswick Sq, Brindley Place ✉ B1 2HW – ✆ (0121) 643 10 03 – www.birminghambrindleyplace.hgi.com **Plan 5** KZ**b**

238 rm ☕ – †£ 79/169 ††£ 89/179

Rest *City Café* – ✆ (0121) 633 63 00 *(closed Sunday dinner) (dinner only)* Menu £ 20 – Carte £ 20/35

Stylish, modern business hotel in the heart of the lively Brindley Place development. Brightly coloured reception and small, contemporary bar. Well-kept, well-equipped bedrooms; facilities include Apple iMac computers. Popular City Café opens onto a terrace.

Hampton by Hilton (N) without rest

200 Broad St ✉ B15 1SU – ✆ (0121) 329 7450 – www.hamptonbyhilton.com

285 rm ☕ – †£ 49/129 ††£ 49/129 **Plan 5** KZ**h**

The top 17 floors of a modern 20 storey block, close to Brindley Place in the heart of the city. Bedrooms are geared towards business travellers, with good work desks, free wi-fi, comfortable beds and smart, part-marbled bathrooms.

XXX **Simpsons** (Andreas Antona) with rm — AC rest, P
✿
20 Highfield Rd, Edgbaston ✉ B15 3DU – ☎ (0121) 454 34 34 – www.simpsonsrestaurant.co.uk – Closed 25-26 December and bank holidays
4 rm ☕ – †£ 160/225 ††£ 160/225 **Plan 3** EX**e**
Rest – *(closed Sunday dinner)* Menu £ 40 (lunch)/90 – Carte £ 50/59
Smart Georgian mansion with stylish lounges, pleasant garden terrace and summer house. Tables are well-spaced; service is formal and efficient. Classical menu displays Mediterranean influences, contemporary twists and excellent produce. Spacious bedrooms boast French country styling.
➜ Crispy duck egg with smoked salmon and potato foam. Rump of lamb, burnt leek, anchovy and shallot purée. Valrhona chocolate tart with popcorn ice-cream.

XXX **Purnell's** (Glynn Purnell) — AC
✿
55 Cornwall St ✉ B3 2DH – ☎ (0121) 212 97 99 – www.purnellsrestaurant.com – Closed 4-20 August, 1 week Easter, 1 week Christmas, Saturday lunch, Sunday and Monday **Plan 6** LY**b**
Rest – Menu £ 30 (weekday lunch)/80
A well-regarded restaurant with a passionate owner and a keen local following; you are encouraged to relax and enjoy your time here. Start with a drink in the large bar, then move to the sleek dining room. Cooking is modern and refined; the degustation menu is worth a try. Service is smooth and friendly.
➜ Carpaccio of beef with red wine octopus and sweet and sour onions. Slow-cooked lamb, basil emulsion and scorched cucumber. 'Mint Choccy Chip'.

XXX **Opus** — AC
54 Cornwall St ✉ B3 2DE – ☎ (0121) 200 2323 – www.opusrestaurant.co.uk – Closed 24 December-6 January, 19 August-1 September, Saturday lunch, Sunday and bank holidays **Plan 6** LY**z**
Rest – Menu £ 16 (weekdays) – Carte £ 15/38
Very large and popular restaurant with floor to ceiling windows; enjoy an aperitif in the cocktail bar before dining in the stylish main room or at the chef's table in the kitchen. Daily changing menu of modern brasserie dishes.

XXX **Asha's** — AC
12-22 Newhall St ✉ B3 3LX – ☎ (0121) 200 27 67 – www.ashasuk.co.uk – Closed Sunday lunch **Plan 6** LY**m**
Rest – Menu £ 29/55 – Carte £ 19/54
A stylish, passionately run Indian restaurant with exotic décor; owned by renowned artiste/gourmet Asha Bhosle. Extensive menus cover most parts of the Subcontinent, with everything cooked to order. Watch the tandoor chef while you wait.

XX **adam's** N (Adam Stokes) — AC
✿
21a Bennetts Hill ✉ B2 5QP – ☎ (0121) 643 3745 – www.adamsrestaurant.co.uk – Closed 3 weeks Christmas-New Year, 2 weeks July-August, Sunday and Monday
Rest – *(booking advisable)* Menu £ 25/45 **Plan 6** LZ**a**
Smart restaurant with a huge feature photo of a Victorian columned hallway. At lunch there's a two-choice set menu; in the evening they offer a 5 and 9 course tasting selection with wine pairings. Cooking is intricate, original and attractively presented, and relies on top quality seasonal ingredients.
➜ Brown shrimp, leeks and red mustard. Lamb with purple sprouting broccoli and Gentleman's Relish. Milk chocolate, espelette pepper and coffee.

XX **Turners** (Richard Turner) — AC
✿
69 High St, Harborne ✉ B17 9NS – ☎ (0121) 426 44 40 – www.turnersofharborne.com – Closed Sunday, Monday and lunch Tuesday-Thursday **Plan 3** EX**a**
Rest – *(booking essential)* Menu £ 35 (weekdays)/60
Busy neighbourhood restaurant in a suburban parade, smartly decorated with etched mirrors and velvet chairs; there are just 8 neatly set tables. Visually impressive, confidently crafted, flavoursome dishes use top quality seasonal ingredients. Cooking is classically based but has a modern touch.
➜ Duck liver with sweet and sour pineapple, coconut and pain d'épice. New season lamb with caramelised sweetbreads and goat's cheese tortellini. Crème brûlée with strawberry, honeycomb, basil and white balsamic.

ENGLAND

Loves
The Glasshouse, Browning St ✉ B16 8FL – ☎ (0121) 454 51 51 – www.loves-restaurant.co.uk – Closed 2 weeks August, 1 week January, 1 week Easter and Sunday-Tuesday **Plan 5** JZ**a**
Rest – *(dinner only and lunch Friday-Saturday)* Menu £ 30 (weekdays)/68
Spacious restaurant on the ground floor of an apartment block beside the canal basin, run by very welcoming owners. The husband creates original, modern dishes, while his clued-up wife makes recommendations from the interesting wine list.

Carters of Moseley
2c St Mary's Row, Wake Green Rd ✉ B13 9EZ – ☎ (0121) 449 8885 – www.cartersofmoseley.co.uk – Closed 12-27 August, 1-10 January, Monday and Tuesday **Plan 3** FX**a**
Rest – *(booking advisable)* Menu £ 18/30 – Carte £ 29/45 **s**
Stylish neighbourhood restaurant with dark banquette seating, black ash tables and a large wine wall. Modern European cooking features tried-and-tested combinations given a personal twist. Afternoon tea – on Saturdays – is done very well.

Purnell's Bistro
Ground Floor, Newater House, 11 Newhall St ✉ B3 3NY – ☎ (0121) 200 1588 – www.purnellsbistro-gingers.com – Closed 25-30 December and Sunday dinner
Rest – Menu £ 20 – Carte £ 26/35 **Plan 6** LY**a**
Glynn Purnell's newest venture is just around the corner from his eponymous restaurant. This simply styled, low-ceilinged restaurant has a lively front bar and offers clever, modern cooking with original combinations. Friendly service.

Saffron
126 Colmore Row ✉ B3 3AP – ☎ (0121) 212 05 99 – www.saffronbirmingham.co.uk – Closed Saturday lunch and Sunday
Rest – Menu £ 10 (weekday lunch)/27 – Carte £ 18/35 **Plan 6** LY**x**
Smart, modern Indian restaurant in the city centre; ask for a table on the raised area overlooking the street. Refined, flavoursome, authentic Indian food: try the more unusual dishes, like the duck or venison.

Lasan
3-4 Dakota Buildings, James St, St Pauls Sq ✉ B3 1SD – ☎ (0121) 212 36 64 – www.lasan.co.uk – Closed 25 December **Plan 5** KY**a**
Rest – Carte £ 26/46
Smart, professionally run restaurant on the ground floor of a converted warehouse in the Jewellery Quarter. Authentic Indian cooking has a refined edge; try the unusual beef dishes. Efficient, friendly service.

Fumo N
1 Waterloo St ✉ B2 5PG – ☎ (0121) 643 8979 – www.sancarlofumo.co.uk
Rest – *(bookings not accepted)* Carte £ 18/35 **Plan 6** LY**x**
In a smart area beside Louis Vuitton; an elegant Italian restaurant with a 1930s edge and a lovely bar. Tables are closely set and waiters bustle around delivering good value 'cicchetti' – tasty Venetian small plates designed for sharing.

BISHOP'S STORTFORD – Hertfordshire – 504 U28 – pop. 35 325 12 B2

Great Britain

London 34 mi – Cambridge 27 mi – Chelmsford 19 mi – Colchester 33 mi
Stansted Airport : ☎ (0844) 3351803, NE : 3.5 m
2 Market Square, ☎ (01279) 65 58 31, www.bishopsstortford.org
Audley End★★ **AC**, N : 11 mi by B 1383

Lemon Tree
14-16 Water Ln ✉ CM23 2LB – ☎ (01279) 757 788 – www.lemontree.co.uk – Closed 25-27 December, 1 January, 5-11 August and bank holidays
Rest – Menu £ 10 (weekday lunch)/24 – Carte £ 22/52
Friendly little restaurant in a 200 year old house, hidden in the town centre. Characterful interior with a comfy bar-lounge and several beamed dining areas. Seasonal menus of unfussy, classical dishes; good value lunch selection.

ENGLAND

BISHOPSTONE – Swindon – 503 P29 4 D2

London 77 mi – Birmingham 88 mi – Leeds 196 mi – Sheffield 166 mi

Royal Oak

Cues Ln ✉ SN6 8PP – ✆ (01793) 790 481 – www.royaloakbishopstone.co.uk

Rest – Carte £ 23/40

Relaxing country pub with open fires and rustic décor. They assert that 'great food starts off with good farming', and the menu changes according to what's fresh, local and seasonal. Produce comes from the owner's organic farm or is imported from the Abruzzo region of Italy, where the chef has a house.

BLACKAWTON – Devon – 503 I32 – see Dartmouth

BLACKBURN – Blackburn with Darwen – 502 M22 – pop. 105 085 20 B2

London 228 mi – Leeds 47 mi – Liverpool 39 mi – Manchester 24 mi

50-54 Church St, ✆ (01254) 68 80 40, www.visitblackburn.co.uk

Pleasington, ✆ (01254) 20 21 77

Wilpshire, 72 Whalley Rd, ✆ (01254) 24 82 60

Great Harwood, Harwood Bar, Whalley Rd, ✆ (01254) 88 43 91

Clog & Billycock

Billinge End Rd, Pleasington, West : 2 mi by A 677 ✉ BB2 6QB – ✆ (01254) 201 163 – www.theclogandbillycock.com – Closed 25 December

Rest – Carte £ 19/33

Spacious, modern, open-plan pub. Extensive menus offer plenty of choice and display a strong Lancastrian slant; cooking is rustic and generous. Most produce is sourced from within 20 miles.

at Langho North : 4.5 mi on A 666 – ✉ Whalley

Northcote (Nigel Haworth) with rm

Northcote Rd, North : 0.5 mi on A 59 at junction with A 666 ✉ BB6 8BE – ✆ (01254) 240 555 – www.northcote.com

14 rm – †£ 220/245 ††£ 225/280

Rest – Menu £ 28 (weekday lunch)/85 – Carte £ 50/61

Contemporary restaurant with garden views, in a red-brick Victorian house. Refined cooking features classic combinations, showing depth of flavour and a lightness of touch. Traceability and food miles are all-important, with seasonal regional ingredients and local suppliers the stars of the show. Spacious, stylish bedrooms offer good facilities and extra touches.

→ Venison with sheep's milk curd, wild garlic and pickled mushrooms. Crispy coated hake, smoked tartare and marrow bone. Liquid chocolate, carrot and rhubarb with salted walnuts.

at Mellor Northwest : 3.25 mi by A 677 – ✉ Blackburn

Stanley House

Southwest : 0.75 mi by A 677 and Further Lane ✉ BB2 7NP – ✆ (01254) 769 200 – www.stanleyhouse.co.uk

30 rm – †£ 132/222 ††£ 154/252

Rest *Grill on the Hill* – *(closed Monday) (dinner only and Sunday lunch)* Carte £ 27/52

Rest *Mr Fred's* – Carte £ 19/35

Attractive 17C manor house with superb country views and a smart spa boasting four types of sauna. Stylish, individually designed bedrooms: those in the main house feature original beams and mullioned windows; those in the annexe are more contemporary. Stylish Grill on the Hill offers modern favourites and great views towards the coast; simpler fare in Mr Fred's.

Millstone

Church Ln ✉ BB2 7JR – ✆ (01254) 813 333 – www.millstonehotel.co.uk

22 rm – †£ 75/105 ††£ 105/135 – 1 suite **Rest** – Carte £ 21/40

Characterful sandstone inn set in a charming Ribble Valley village. Bedrooms offer modern comforts and a cottagey feel, while the dining room blends contemporary styling with traditional features. Classic dishes change with the seasons; steak is a perennial favourite. Cheery service.

BLACKPOOL – Blackpool – 502 K22 – pop. 142 283 Great Britain 20 A2

London 246 mi – Leeds 88 mi – Liverpool 56 mi – Manchester 51 mi
Blackpool Airport : ✆ (0844) 4827171, S : 3 mi by A 584
1 Clifton St, ✆ (01253) 47 82 22, www.visitblackpool.com
Blackpool Park, North Park Drive, ✆ (01253) 39 79 16
Poulton-le-Fylde, Breck Rd, Myrtle Farm, ✆ (01253) 89 24 44
Tower★ **AC** AY **A**

Plan page 100

Number One South Beach

4 Harrowside West ✉ FY4 1NW – ✆ (01253) 343 900 – www.numberonehotels.com BZ**v**
13 rm – †£ 81/150 ††£ 125/150 – 1 suite
Rest – *(dinner only and Sunday lunch)* Carte £ 23/32
Modernised hotel close to the promenade: run with a passion and featuring bold, bright colour schemes. Striking, contemporary bedrooms – two with four-posters – and superb bathrooms boasting whirlpool baths and TVs. Interesting menus are largely made up of free range, organic and fair trade produce.

Redstone without rest

9 Alexandra Rd ✉ FY1 6BU – ✆ (01253) 283 387 – www.theredstoneblackpool.co.uk – Closed 17-28 December BZ**a**
8 rm – †£ 80/110 ††£ 90/120
A very stylish, intimate hotel close to the famous Pleasure Beach. Small lounge and bijou basement bar. Smartly furnished bedrooms with good mod cons. Breakfast on soufflé omelette or Manx kippers next to a baby grand piano.

Number One St Lukes without rest

1 St Lukes Rd ✉ FY4 2EL – ✆ (01253) 343 901 – www.numberoneblackpool.com AZ**a**
3 rm – †£ 70/100 ††£ 100/140
Boutique guesthouse close to the promenade and Pleasure Beach; run by a very charming owner. Bedrooms are named after the town's piers: 'North' has an African feel and 'Central', a white four-poster and more feminine touch. They also have an outdoor hot tub and mini pitch and putt green.

Langtrys N without rest

36 King Edward Ave ✉ FY2 9TA – ✆ (01253) 352 031 – www.langtrysblackpool.co.uk Y**x**
6 rm – †£ 75/90 ††£ 100/130
Smart guesthouse in a peaceful residential area. Bedrooms have warm fabrics, modern facilities and extras such as robes, clothes brushes and small items travellers often forget. Bathrooms feature underfloor heating and one even has a TV!

at Thornton Northeast : 5.5 mi by A 584 - BY - on B 5412 – ✉ Blackpool

Twelve

Marsh Mill, Fleetwood Rd North, North : 0.5 mi on A 585 ✉ FY5 4JZ – ✆ (01253) 821 212 – www.twelve-restaurant.co.uk – Closed first 2 weeks January and Monday
Rest – *(dinner only and Sunday lunch)* Menu £ 20 (weekdays)/28 – Carte £ 31/49
Spacious restaurant where brick walls, exposed pipework and grey beams contribute to a slightly industrial feel. Passionately run by dynamic owner and friendly team. Good value menus offer interesting, well-executed modern dishes with the odd innovative touch.

Don't confuse the classification ✗ with the stars ✿!
The number of ✗ denotes levels of comfort and service,
while stars are awarded for the best cooking across all categories.

ENGLAND

BLAKENEY - Norfolk - 504 X25 - pop. 1 628 - ✉ Holt 15 C1

London 127 mi – King's Lynn 37 mi – Norwich 28 mi

Blakeney

The Quay ✉ NR25 7NE – ✆ (01263) 740 797 – www.blakeneyhotel.co.uk
64 rm – 🚹£ 99/203 🚹🚹£ 194/290
Rest – *(closed to non-residents 24-28, 31 December and 1 January)* Menu £ 29 (dinner) – Carte £ 20/46
Traditional, privately owned hotel in a great quayside location, affording views over the estuary and salt marshes. Various comfy lounges and a bar with subtle modern touches. Individually designed bedrooms, some with balconies or sea views. Formal dining room offers a good outlook and a wide-ranging menu.

Blakeney House without rest

High St ✉ NR25 7NX – ✆ (01263) 740 561 – www.blakeneyhouse.com – Closed Christmas
8 rm – 🚹£ 55/95 🚹🚹£ 70/150
Substantial Victorian house tucked away in a tranquil spot on the High Street. Spacious, individually decorated, up-to-date bedrooms. Pleasant breakfast room with garden views.

Wiveton Farm Café

West : 0.5 mi on A149 ✉ NR25 7TE – ✆ (01263) 740 515 – www.wivetonhall.co.uk – Easter-October
Rest – *(lunch only and dinner Thursday-Saturday)* Carte £ 19/27
An extension of a farm shop, set down a dusty track and run by a smiley young team. Light breakfasts and tasty, salad-based lunches; weekends see more substantial breakfasts and 'Norfolk' tapas in the evenings. Unfussy preparation of local and farm produce. Glorious farm and coastal views from the terrace.

Moorings

High St ✉ NR25 7NA – ✆ (01263) 740 054 – www.blakeney-moorings.co.uk – Closed 3 weeks January, Tuesday-Thursday November-March, Sunday except bank holidays and Monday dinner
Rest – *(light lunch) (booking essential)* Carte £ 26/37
Bright, relaxed village bistro just a stone's throw from the quay and run by an experienced couple. Light lunches and more substantial dinners featuring unfussy, seasonal dishes in classic combinations; tasty, homemade, old school puddings.

White Horse with rm

4 High St ✉ NR25 7AL – ✆ (01263) 740 574 – www.blakeneywhitehorse.co.uk – Closed 25 December
9 rm – 🚹£ 80/135 🚹🚹£ 110/170 **Rest** – *(booking advisable)* Carte £ 24/35
Attractive brick and flint former coaching inn set by the harbour. The menu champions all things seasonal, local and British, so expect lobsters, crabs, Brancaster oysters and meat from Norfolk estates. Simply furnished, pretty bedrooms come in various shapes and sizes; one has a great view of the marshes.

at Cley next the Sea East : 1.5 mi on A 149 – ✉ Holt

Cley Windmill

The Quay ✉ NR25 7RP – ✆ (01263) 740 209 – www.cleywindmill.co.uk
9 rm – 🚹£ 99/199 🚹🚹£ 99/199
Rest – *(dinner only) (booking essential)* Menu £ 29
Restored 18C redbrick windmill in salt marshes with a viewing gallery: a bird-watcher's paradise. Neatly kept rooms, full of character, in the mill, stable and boatshed. Flagstoned dining room; communal table.

at Wiveton South : 1 mi by A149 on Wiveton Rd

Wiveton Bell with rm

Blakeney Rd ✉ NR25 7TL – ✆ (01263) 740 101 – www.wivetonbell.com
4 rm – 🚹£ 80/120 🚹🚹£ 80/140 **Rest** – *(booking essential)* Carte £ 24/35
Modernised pub featuring beams, stripped floors and wood-burning stoves; with picnic tables out the front and a beautifully landscaped rear terrace. Seasonal menu offers pub classics, carefully crafted from quality local ingredients. Stylish, cosy bedrooms offer smart bathrooms and continental breakfasts.

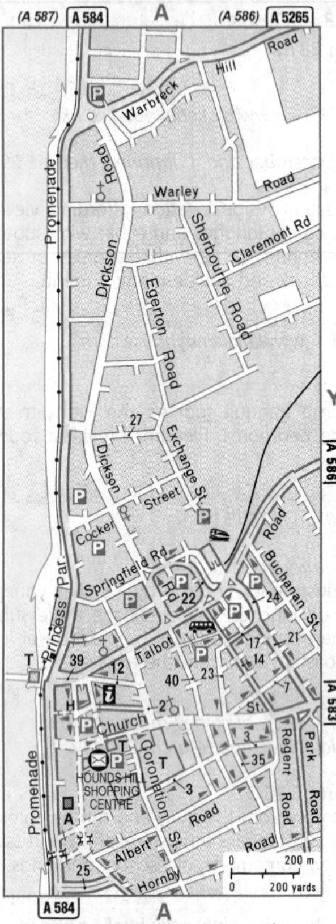

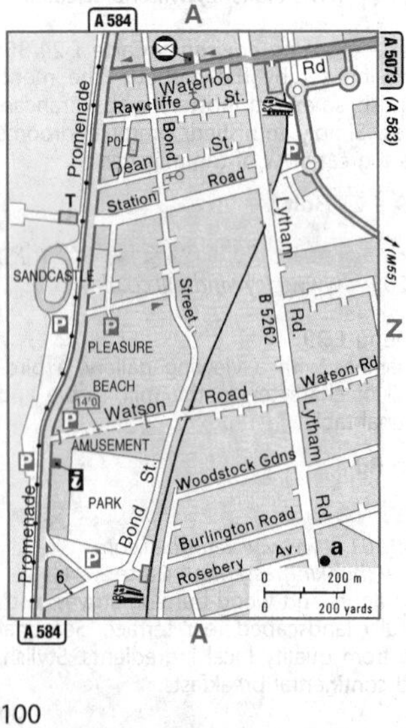

BLACKPOOL

Abingdon St.	AY	2
Adelaide St	AY	3
Ansdell Rd	BZ	4
Blackpool Old Rd	BY	5
Burlington Rd West	AZ	6
Caunce St	AY	7
Central Drive	BZ	8
Cherry Tree Rd	BZ	9
Church St.	AY	
Clifton St	AY	12
Condor Grove	BZ	13
Cookson St	AY	14
Deansgate	AY	15
Garstang Rd West	BY	16
George St	AY	17
Grange Rd	BY	19
Grasmere Rd	BZ	20
Grosvenor St	AY	21
High St	AY	22
Hornby Rd	BY	
Hounds Hill Centre	AY	
King St	AY	23
Lark Hill St	AY	24
New Bonny St	AY	25
North Park Drive	BY	26
Pleasant St	AY	27
Plymouth Rd	BY	28
Poulton Rd	BY	29
Queen's Promenade	BY	
Reads Ave	BZ	32
Rigby Rd	BZ	33
Seaside Way	BZ	34
South King St	AY	35
South Park Drive	BZ	36
Talbot Square	AY	39
Topping St	AY	40
Westcliffe Drive	BY	41

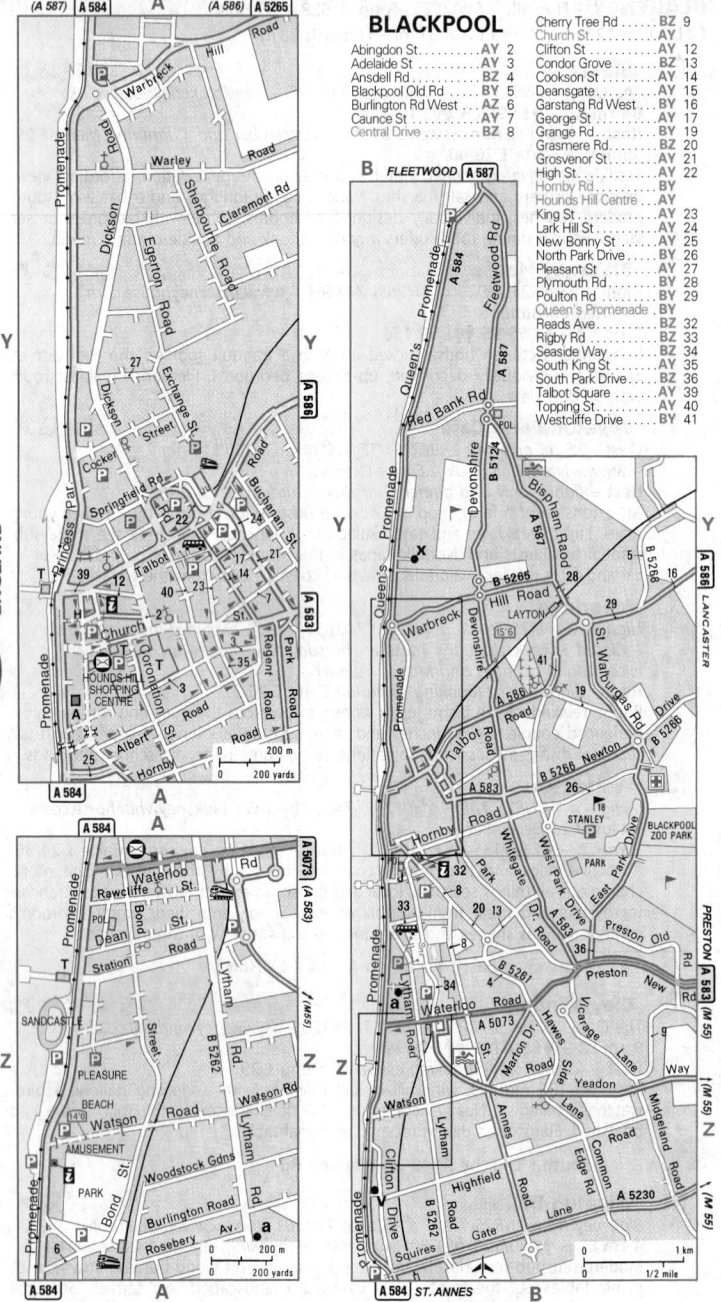

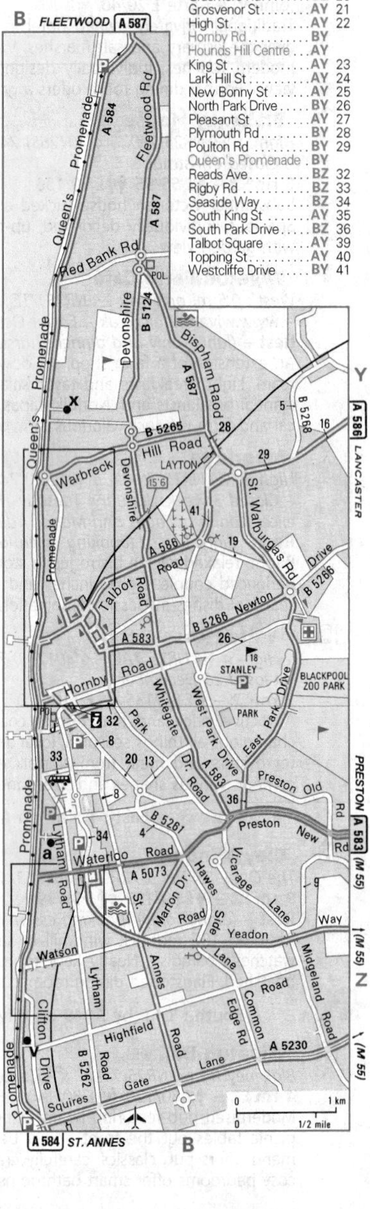

ENGLAND

at Morston West : 1.5 mi on A 149 – ✉ Holt

Morston Hall

The Street ✉ NR25 7AA – ✆ (01263) 741 041 – www.morstonhall.com – Closed 1-25 January and 24-26 December

13 rm – †£ 130/150 ††£ 210/230

Rest *Morston Hall* ✿ – see restaurant listing

Attractive, personally owned country house with manicured gardens, set in a small coastal hamlet. Comfy guest areas display antiques and paintings. Bedrooms are split between the main house and an annexe – the latter are larger, more luxurious and display subtle contemporary touches. Keen, friendly service.

Morston Hall (Galton Blackiston) – Morston Hall Hotel

The Street ✉ NR25 7AA – ✆ (01263) 741 041 – www.morstonhall.com – Closed 1-25 January and 24-26 December

Rest – *(dinner only and Sunday lunch) (booking essential) (set menu only)*
Menu £ 65

Set in an attractive country house surrounded by manicured gardens; choose between a traditionally furnished room or beautiful conservatory. Formal 4 course daily menu (served at 8pm) offers well-balanced, seasonal dishes. Cooking is classically based, sophisticated and exhibits a delicate, modern touch.

→ White turnip with buttermilk, apples and chives. Lightly smoked loin of lamb with wood-fired swede, pearl barley and sage oil. Lemongrass panna cotta, pineapple sorbet, ginger syrup and pistachio snow.

BLANDFORD FORUM – Dorset – 503 N31 – pop. 9 854 — 4 C3

London 124 mi – Bournemouth 17 mi – Dorchester 17 mi – Salisbury 24 mi

1 Greyhound Yard, ✆ (01258) 45 47 70, www.visit-dorset.org.uk

Ashley Wood, Wimbourne Rd, ✆ (01258) 45 22 53

Town★

Kingston Lacy★★ **AC**, SE : 5.5 mi by B 3082 – Royal Signals Museum★, NE : 2 mi by B 3082. Milton Abbas★, SW : 8 mi by A 354 – Sturminster Newton★, NW : 8 mi by A 357

Portman Lodge without rest

Whitecliff Mill St ✉ DT11 7BP – ✆ (01258) 453 727 – www.portmanlodge.co.uk – Closed January

5 rm – †£ 65 ††£ 80/85

Red-brick guesthouse with colourful hanging baskets, comfortable bedrooms and smart bathrooms; it retains some original Victorian features but has been given a fresh, bright feel. Plenty of books and board games to borrow.

at Farnham Northeast : 7.5 mi by A 354 – ✉ Blandford Forum

Farnham Farm House without rest

North : 1 mi by Shaftesbury rd ✉ DT11 8DG – ✆ (01725) 516 254 – www.farnhamfarmhouse.co.uk – Closed 25-26 December

3 rm – †£ 70/80 ††£ 80/90

Cosy, welcoming farmhouse on a working farm; enjoy tea and cake on arrival. Homely, immaculately kept bedrooms with country views. On-site swimming pool and therapy centre. Breakfast on eggs from the hens you see roaming.

at Tarrant Launceston Southeast : 6.5 mi by A 354

Launceston Farm without rest

✉ DT11 8BY – ✆ (01258) 830 528 – www.launcestonfarm.co.uk

6 rm – †£ 65/115 ††£ 90/115

Charming guesthouse on a working farm; the friendly owner's childhood home. Comfy, stylish bedrooms are reached via a wrought iron spiral staircase, and feature period furniture, modern bathrooms and homely extras.

BLEDINGTON – Gloucestershire – 503 P28 – see Stow-on-the-Wold

BLOCKLEY – Gloucestershire – 503 O27 – pop. 1 668 — 4 D1
– ✉ Moreton-In-Marsh

London 91 mi – Birmingham 39 mi – Oxford 34 mi

Lower Brook House

Lower St ✉ GL56 9DS – ✆ (01386) 700 286 – www.lowerbrookhouse.com – Closed January and 16-27 December
6 rm ☕ – 🚹£ 80/190 🚹🚹£ 80/190
Rest – *(closed Sunday) (dinner only)* Carte £ 15/26
Personally run, adjoining 17C Cotswold stone cottages with large inglenooks, exposed beams and flagged floors. Hugely characterful and stylish from every aspect. Individually appointed bedrooms take on a more contemporary style. Imaginative evening menus of local Cotswold produce.

BODIAM – East Sussex – 504 V30 Great Britain — 8 B2

London 58 mi – Cranbrook 7 mi – Hastings 13 mi

Castle★★

Battle Abbey★, S : 10 mi by B 2244, B 2089, A 21 and minor rd – Rye★★, SW : 13 mi by A 268

Curlew

Junction Rd, Northwest : 1.5 mi at junction with B 2244 ✉ TN32 5UY – ✆ (01580) 861 394 – www.thecurlewrestaurant.co.uk – Closed 1-7 January and Monday
Rest – Menu £ 20 (weekday lunch) – Carte £ 34/44
Smart, contemporary restaurant behind a white clapperboard pub façade, with funky cow print wallpaper and a clubby feel. Menus offer precise, modern, well-considered combinations of first class ingredients. The wine lists promotes organic and biodynamic wines. Service is smooth and professional.
➔ Wood pigeon carpaccio, truffle custard and salt-baked artichoke. Fillet and crispy belly of pork with onion purée and wild garlic gnocchi. Blackberry macaroon, lemon curd ice cream and poached blackberries.

ENGLAND

BODMIN – Cornwall – 503 F32 – pop. 12 778 — 1 B2

London 270 mi – Newquay 18 mi – Plymouth 32 mi – Truro 23 mi

Mount Folly, ✆ (01208) 7 66 16, www.bodminlive.com

St Petroc Church★

Bodmin Moor★★ - Lanhydrock★★, S : 3 mi by B 3269 - Blisland★ (Church★), N : 5.5 mi by A 30 and minor roads – Pencarrow★, NW : 4 mi by A 389 and minor roads – Cardinham (Church★), NE : 4 mi by A 30 and minor rd – St Mabyn (Church★), N : 5.5 mi by A 389, B 3266 and minor rd. St Tudy★, N : 7 mi by A 389, B 3266 and minor rd

Trehellas House

Washaway, Northwest : 3 mi on A 389 ✉ PL30 3AD – ✆ (01208) 72 700 – www.trehellashouse.co.uk
12 rm ☕ – 🚹£ 50/75 🚹🚹£ 65/130
Rest – *(dinner only and Sunday lunch)* Carte £ 25/42 **s**
Former posting inn, built by the Lordship of Pencarrow Manor to house officers from the local garrison. Cosy bedrooms with smart wood furnishings and understated décor. Popular restaurant offers extensive menu of local produce with venison a speciality. Good value 'steak and dessert' menu.

Bokiddick Farm without rest

Lanivet, South : 5 mi by A 30 following signs for Lanhydrock and Bokiddick ✉ PL30 5HP – ✆ (01208) 831 481 – www.bokiddickfarm.co.uk – Closed Christmas
5 rm ☕ – 🚹£ 50/55 🚹🚹£ 75/84
Traditional farmhouse on a working dairy farm, where you are guaranteed a very warm welcome. Homely, spotlessly kept bedrooms with fridges – 3 in the main house; 2 larger rooms in the old barn. Hearty breakfasts taken overlooking the garden. Cream tea on arrival.

BOLLINGTON – Cheshire East – 502 N24 – pop. 6 880 – ✉ Cheshire 20 B3

London 178 mi – Birmingham 69 mi – Leeds 58 mi – Manchester 22 mi

XX **Oliver at Bollington Green**

22 High St ✉ SK10 5PH – ☎ (01625) 575 058
– www.oliveratbollingtongreen.com – Closed Sunday dinner and Monday
Rest – *(light lunch) (bookings advisable at dinner)* Menu £ 19 – Carte £ 25/38
Bright neighbourhood restaurant opposite a tiny village green, run by an enthusiastic young couple. Light lunches and an interesting evening à la carte of refined, flavoursome dishes. The breads, ice-creams and chocolates are all homemade.

BOLNHURST – Bedford 12 A1

London 64 mi – Bedford 8 mi – St Neots 7 mi

Plough at Bolnhurst

Kimbolton Rd, South : 0.5 mi on B 660 ✉ MK44 2EX – ☎ (01234) 376 274
– www.bolnhurst.com – Closed 2 weeks January, Sunday dinner and Monday
Rest – Menu £ 16 (weekday lunch)/25 – Carte £ 29/49
Charming whitewashed pub with a rustic bar, a modern restaurant, a lovely garden and a bustling atmosphere. Menus change with the seasons but always feature 28-day aged Aberdeenshire steaks, dishes containing Mediterranean ingredients like Sicilian black olives, and a great selection of wines and cheeses.

BOLTON ABBEY – North Yorkshire – 502 O22 – pop. 117 22 B2

– ✉ Skipton Great Britain

London 216 mi – Harrogate 18 mi – Leeds 23 mi – Skipton 6 mi

Bolton Priory★ AC

Devonshire Arms Country House

✉ BD23 6AJ – ☎ (01756) 710 441
– www.thedevonshirearms.co.uk
40 rm – †£ 110/435 ††£ 160/485 – 2 suites
Rest *Burlington* Rest *Brasserie* – see restaurant listing
Period coaching inn on the Duke and Duchess of Devonshire's 30,000 acre estate, in the Yorkshire Dales. Comfy lounges display part of the owners' vast art collection and dogs are welcome inside. Bedrooms in the wing are bright, modern and compact; those in the main house are more traditional. Popular spa.

XXX **Burlington** – Devonshire Arms Country House Hotel

✉ BD23 6AJ – ☎ (01756) 710 441 – www.burlingtonrestaurant.co.uk – Closed Monday
Rest – *(dinner only and Sunday lunch) (booking essential)* Menu £ 65/75
Elegant, antique-filled hotel dining room hung with impressive oil paintings; sit in the conservatory to overlook the Italian garden. Wide choice of menus includes a vegetarian, pescatarian and tasting selection; dishes are modern, creative and attractively presented. Extensive wine list of mature vintages.

XX **Brasserie** – Devonshire Arms Country House Hotel

✉ BD23 6AJ – ☎ (01756) 710 710 – www.devonshirebrasserie.co.uk
Rest – Carte £ 18/39
Bright, modern hotel brasserie opposite the kitchen garden. Sit on stripy banquettes in the appealing bar or on red velour chairs in the dining room. Extensive à la carte offers satisfying brasserie classics. Attractive wine cellar.

BOLTON-BY-BOWLAND – Lancashire – 502 M/N22 Great Britain 20 B2

London 246 mi – Blackburn 17 mi – Skipton 15 mi

Skipton - Castle★, E : 12 mi by A 59 – Bolton Priory★, E : 17 mi by A 59

Middle Flass Lodge

Settle Rd, North : 2.5 mi by Clitheroe rd on Settle rd ✉ BB7 4NY – ☎ (01200) 447 259 – www.middleflasslodge.co.uk
7 rm – †£ 50/55 ††£ 70/76 **Rest** – Menu £ 25
Friendly, welcoming owners in a delightfully located barn conversion. Plenty of beams add to rustic effect. Pleasantly decorated, comfy rooms with countryside outlook. Blackboard's eclectic menu boasts local, seasonal backbone.

BONCHURCH – Isle of Wight – 504 P32 – see Wight (Isle of)

ENGLAND

BORDON – Hampshire – 504 R30

London 54 mi – Croydon 57 mi – Barnet 67 mi – Ealing 49 mi

Groomes

Frith End, North : 2.75 mi by A 325 on Frith End Sand Pit rd ✉ GU35 0QR – ✆ (01420) 489 858 – www.groomes.co.uk

7 rm – †£ 90/130 ††£ 120/150

Rest – *(dinner only) (residents only, set menu only)* Menu £ 20

Former farmhouse set in 185 acres, with lawned gardens and wood-furnished terrace. Good-sized bedrooms boast modern facilities; some have free-standing roll-top baths. Two tables of eight for communal dining; set menus of home-cooked dishes make use of local produce.

BOREHAM – Essex – 504 V27 – see Chelmsford

BOROUGHBRIDGE – North Yorkshire – 502 P21 – pop. 3 311 — 22 B2

London 215 mi – Leeds 19 mi – Middlesbrough 36 mi – York 16 mi

2 Fishergate, ✆ (01423) 32 33 73, www.boroughbridge.org.uk

thediningroom

20 St James's Sq ✉ YO51 9AR – ✆ (01423) 326 426 – www.thediningroomonline.co.uk – Closed 26 December, 1 January, Sunday dinner, Monday and lunch Tuesday

Rest – *(light lunch Wednesday-Saturday) (booking essential)* Carte £ 30/41

Characterful, bow-fronted cottage with a courtyard terrace. Modern lounge-bar and intimate beamed restaurant. Set price menu offers hearty, boldly flavoured, Mediterranean-influenced dishes.

ENGLAND

at Roecliffe West : 1 mi

Crown Inn with rm

✉ YO51 9LY – ✆ (01423) 322 300 – www.crowninnroecliffe.com

4 rm – †£ 80/90 ††£ 90/120

Rest – Menu £ 17 (weekday lunch)/18 – Carte £ 26/41

Smart 14C inn with stylish country interior, set by a delightful village green. Good-sized menus offer a nice balance of meat and fish, and a dedicated 'meat free' selection. Well-chosen wine list. Smart bedrooms with antique-style furnishings and feature beds.

BOSCASTLE – Cornwall – 503 F31 — 1 B2

London 260 mi – Bude 14 mi – Exeter 59 mi – Plymouth 43 mi

Village★

Poundstock Church★ – Tintagel Old Post Office★

Boscastle House without rest

Tintagel Rd, South : 0.75 mi on B 3263 ✉ PL35 0AS – ✆ (01840) 250 654 – www.boscastlehouse.com – Closed 2 weeks Christmas

6 rm – †£ 55/90 ††£ 75/120

Modern styling in a detached Victorian house with a calm, relaxing air. Bedrooms are light and spacious, with roll-top baths and walk-in showers. Hearty breakfasts with home-baked muffins and banana bread. Tea and cake on arrival.

Old Rectory without rest

St Juliot, Northeast : 2.5 mi by B 3263 ✉ PL35 0BT – ✆ (01840) 250 225 – www.stjuliot.com

4 rm – †£ 45/92 ††£ 65/102

Lovely house with Victorian walled garden. Characterful bedrooms: one with a wood-burning stove; another, a super king sized bed and whirlpool bath. Breakfasts include bacon and sausages from the owner's pigs. Thomas Hardy once stayed here.

BOSHAM – West Sussex – 504 R31 – see Chichester

BOSTON SPA - West Yorkshire - 502 P22 - pop. 5 952 22 B2

London 127 mi – Harrogate 12 mi – Leeds 12 mi – York 16 mi

Four Gables without rest

Oaks Ln, West : 0.25 mi by A 659 ✉ LS23 6DS – ☎ (01937) 845 592 – www.fourgables.co.uk – Closed Christmas-New Year

4 rm – †£ 50/60 ††£ 63/88

Grade II listed Arts and Crafts house hidden down a private road, yet only a short walk from town. Beautifully manicured garden and croquet lawn. Ornate plaster ceiling in lounge; quarry-floored breakfast room with homemade breads, jams and eggs from their own hens. Pretty, cosy bedrooms have good comforts.

BOUGHTON MONCHELSEA - Kent - pop. 2 863 8 B2

London 40 mi – Croydon 42 mi – Barnet 56 mi – Ealing 53 mi

Mulberry Tree

Hermitage Lane, South : 1.5 mi by Park Lane and East Hall Hill ✉ ME17 4DA – ☎ (01622) 749 082 – www.themulberrytreekent.co.uk – Closed first 2 weeks January, Sunday dinner and Monday

Rest – Menu £ 15 (weekdays) – Carte £ 29/38

Stylish restaurant with a smart bar, large terrace and screened kitchen footage. Modern British menus provide a good choice of confidently prepared, imaginatively presented, accomplished dishes, crafted from well-sourced ingredients.

BOURN - Cambridgeshire - 504 T27 - pop. 1 764 14 A3

London 58 mi – Croydon 87 mi – Barnet 44 mi – Ealing 57 mi

Willow Tree

29 High St ✉ CB23 2SQ – ☎ (01954) 719 775 – www.thewillowtreebourn.com

Rest – Carte £ 13/46

Quirky pub with a life-sized cow model outside and gilt mirrors, chandeliers and Louis XV style furniture inside. Menus range from old pub classics to much more ambitious modern dishes; afternoon tea and a 'Deckchair' menu served May-Sept.

BOURNEMOUTH - Bournemouth - 503 O31 - pop. 157 861 4 D3

London 114 mi – Bristol 76 mi – Southampton 34 mi

Bournemouth (Hurn) Airport : ☎ (01202) 364000, N : 5 mi by Hurn - DV

Westover Rd, ☎ (0845) 0 51 17 00, www.bournemouth.co.uk

Queens Park, Queens Park West Drive, ☎ (01202) 30 26 11

Meyrick Park, Central Drive, ☎ (01202) 78 60 00

Compton Acres★★ (English Garden ≤★★★) **AC** AX – Russell-Cotes Art Gallery and Museum★★ **AC** DZ **M1** - Shelley Rooms **AC** EX **M2**

Poole★, W : 4 mi by A 338 – Brownsea Island★ (Baden-Powell Stone ≤★★) **AC**, by boat from Sandbanks BX or Poole Quay – Christchurch★ (Priory Church★) E : 4.5 mi on A 35. Corfe Castle★, SW : 18 mi by A 35 and A 351 – Lulworth Cove★ (Blue Pool★) W : 8 mi of Corfe Castle by B 3070 – Swanage★, E : 5 mi from Corfe Castle by A 351

Plans on following pages

Bournemouth Highcliff Marriott

St Michael's Rd, West Cliff ✉ BH2 5DU – ☎ (01202) 557 702 – www.bournemouthhighcliffmarriott.co.uk rm, CZz

160 rm – †£ 150/275 ††£ 150/360, £ 15

Rest *Highcliff Grill* – ☎ (01202) 200 800 *(dinner only and Sunday lunch)*
Menu £ 34 – Carte £ 28/50 **s**

Set on the clifftop, this grand old seaside hotel has a funicular linking it directly to the beach. Smart guest areas and airy modern bedrooms; some with lovely sea views. Leisure club boasts a tennis court and indoor and outdoor pools. Stylish grill restaurant offers a modern steak and seafood based menu.

ENGLAND

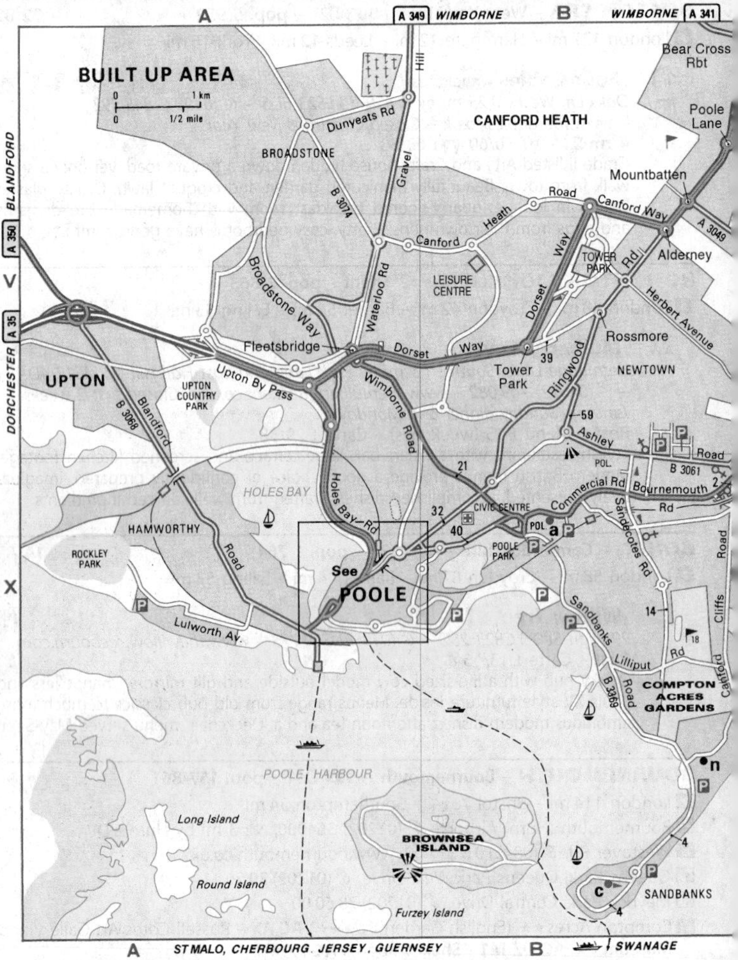

ENGLAND

BOURNEMOUTH AND POOLE

Archway Rd . . . . **BX** 2
Banks Rd . . . . **BX** 4
Boscombe Overcliff Rd . . . . **EX** 6
Boscombe Spa Rd . . . . **DX** 7
Branksome Wood Rd . . . . . **CY** 9
Chessel Ave . . . . **EX** 10
Clarendon Rd . . . . **CX** 12
Commercial Rd . . . . **CY** 13
Compton Ave . . . . **BX** 14
Cranleigh Rd . . . . **EV** 16
Durley Rd . . . . **CZ** 17
Ensbury Park Rd . . . . **CV** 19
Exeter Rd . . . . **CDZ** 20
Fernside Rd . . . . **ABX** 21
Fir Vale Rd . . . . **DY** 23
Gervis Pl . . . . **DY** 24
Gloucester Rd . . . . **EV** 26
Hampshire Centre . . . . **DV**
Hinton Rd . . . . **DZ** 27
Lansdowne Rd . . . . **DY** 30
Lansdowne (The) . . . . **DY** 28
Leven Ave . . . . **CX** 31
Longfleet Rd . . . . **BX** 32
Madeira Rd . . . . **DY** 34
Manor Rd . . . . **EY** 35
Meyrick Rd . . . . **EYZ** 36
Old Christchurch Rd . . . . **DY**
Old Wareham Rd . . . . **BV** 39
Parkstone Rd . . . . **BX** 40
Pinecliff Rd . . . . **CX** 42
Post Office Rd . . . . **CY** 43
Priory Rd . . . . **CZ** 45
Queen's Rd . . . . **CX** 46
Richmond Hill . . . . **CY** 47
Richmond Park Rd . . . . **DV** 48
Russell Cotes Rd . . . . **DZ** 49
St Michael's Rd . . . . **CZ** 51
St Paul's Rd . . . . **EY** 52
St Peter's Rd . . . . **DY** 53
St Stephen's Rd . . . . **CY** 55
St Swithuns Rd South . . . . . **EY** 56
Seabourne Rd . . . . **EV** 57
Seamoor Rd . . . . **CX** 58
Sea View Rd . . . . **BV** 59
Southbourne Grove . . . . **EX** 61
Southbourne Overcliff Drive . . . . **EX** 62
Sovereign Shopping Centre . **EX**
Square (The) . . . . **CY** 63
Suffolk Rd . . . . **CY** 64
Surrey Rd . . . . **CX** 66
Triangle (The) . . . . **CY** 67
Upper Hinton Rd . . . . **DZ** 68
Wessex Way . . . . **CX** 70
Western Rd . . . . **CX** 73
Westover Rd . . . . **DZ** 75
West Cliff Promenade . . . . . **CZ** 71

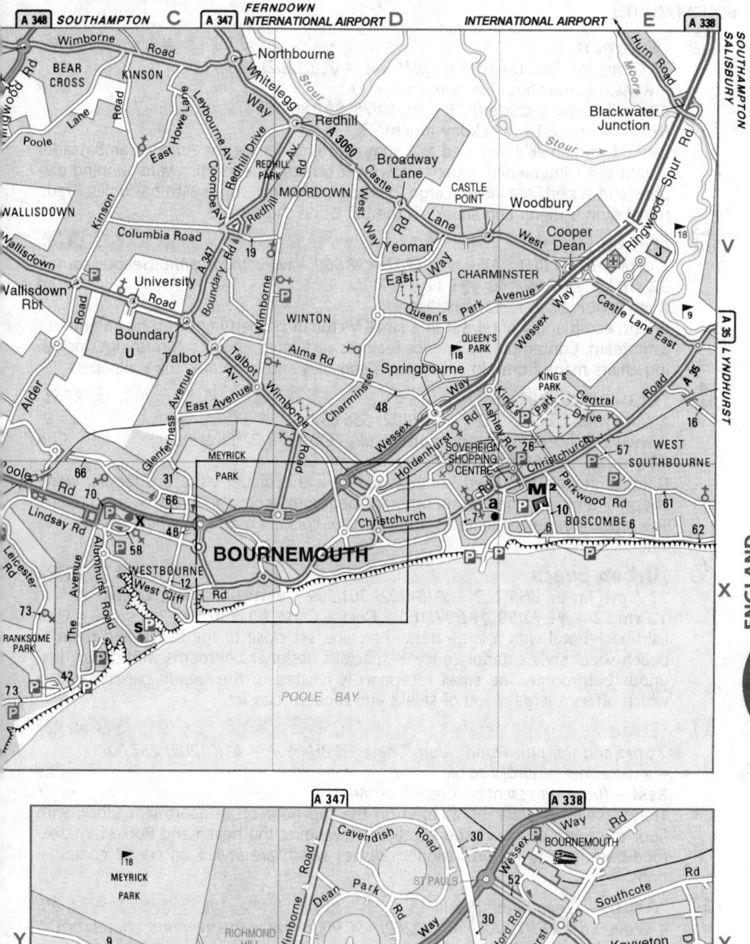
A 348 SOUTHAMPTON
C
A 347 FERNDOWN INTERNATIONAL AIRPORT
D
INTERNATIONAL AIRPORT
E
A 338
SOUTHAMPTON SALISBURY
Wimborne
Road
Northbourne
BEAR CROSS
KINSON
Whitelegg
Way
Stour
Hurn Road
Moors
Blackwater Junction
Redhill
A 3060
Poole
Lane
Road
Leybourne Lane
East Howe Lane
Leybourne Av.
Coombe Av.
Redhill Drive
REDHILL PARK
Av.
Rd
Castle
Broadway Lane
Stour
Spur Rd
Ringwood
WALLISDOWN
Kinson
MOORDOWN
West Way
CASTLE POINT
Woodbury
Columbia Road
Redhill
Boundary Rd
A 347
19
Rd
Lane
West
Cooper Dean
18
V
Wallisdown
Yeoman
East Way
CHARMINSTER
Ringwood
J
Wallisdown Rbt
University
Road
Wimborne
Queen's Park Avenue
Wessex Way
Castle Lane East
9
Road
Boundary
U
WINTON
QUEEN'S PARK
18
A 35
LYNDHURST
Talbot
Talbot Av.
Alma Rd
Springbourne
KING'S PARK
Alder
Glenferness Avenue
East Avenue
Wimborne
Charminster
48
Way
Central Drive
Road
A 35
Wessex
Ashley Rd
King's Park
Holdenhurst Rd
16
Road
WEST SOUTHBOURNE
MEYRICK PARK
26
Christchurch
57
Poole
66
31
SOVEREIGN SHOPPING CENTRE
Rd
70
66
Christchurch
M²
Parkwood Rd
61
Lindsay Rd
X
46
a
7
10
BOSCOMBE
6
6
62
Leicester Rd
58
Alumhurst Road
BOURNEMOUTH
The Avenue
WESTBOURNE
West Cliff
12
Rd
X
73
S
RANKSOME PARK
42
73
POOLE BAY

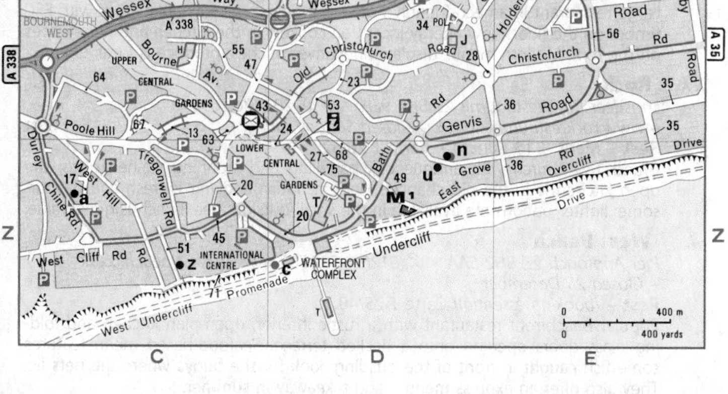
A 347
A 338
Cavendish
Road
30
Wessex Way Rd
BOURNEMOUTH
18
MEYRICK PARK
Wimborne Road
Dean Park Rd
ST PAULS
52
Rd
Southcote
30
Oxford Rd
Holdenhurst
Y
RICHMOND HILL
9
Way
Wessex
Way
Knyveton Road
Derby Rd
Y
Wessex
BOURNEMOUTH WEST
A 338
34
POL
J
56
A 35
Bourne
55
Christchurch
Road
28
Christchurch
Road
A 338
UPPER
47
Av.
64
CENTRAL
Old
23
35
GARDENS
43
53
Rd
36
Road
Poole Hill
67
13
63
Gervis
35
LOWER
n
Drive
Tregonwell Rd
CENTRAL
27
68
Bath
36
Rd Overcliff
Durley
17
West Hill
a
GARDENS
20
75
T
49
u
Grove
East
Chine Rd.
M¹
Drive
Z
20
45
Z
51
INTERNATIONAL CENTRE
Undercliff
West
Cliff
Rd
Rd
z
c
WATERFRONT COMPLEX
71
Promenade
West Undercliff
T
0 400 m
0 400 yards
C
D
E

ENGLAND

Miramar
19 Grove Rd, East Overcliff ✉ BH1 3AL – ✆ (01202) 556 581
– www.miramar-bournemouth.com DZ**u**
43 rm (dinner included) – £ 40/75 £ 80/150
Rest – Menu £ 19 (weekday lunch)/43
Late Edwardian villa intended as a summer residence for the Austrian ambassador – until WW1 intervened. Close to town yet boasting peaceful, award winning gardens and superb sea views. Large, classical bedrooms; some with balconies. Traditional dinner menu and snacks in the bar or on the terrace.

Green House
4 Grove Rd ✉ BH1 3AX – ✆ (01202) 498 900 – www.thegreenhousehotel.com
32 rm – £ 99/140 £ 129/179 DZ**n**
Rest *Arbor* – see restaurant listing
Bright, eco-friendly hotel, set in a small Victorian property and run by an enthusiastic team. Contemporary interior features reclaimed and eco-furnishings, including chairs made from old video game consoles and vegetable ink wallpapers.

Chocolate without rest
5 Durley Rd ✉ BH2 5JQ – ✆ (01202) 556 857
– www.thechocolateboutiquehotel.co.uk – Closed 2-27 December CZ**a**
13 rm – £ 65 £ 90/175
Unique, chocolate-themed hotel owned by a chocolatier who runs regular workshops. Fittingly named, contemporary bedrooms come in browns and creams. The small lounge-bar features an automatic cocktail machine, which even serves 'choctails'.

ENGLAND

Urban Beach
23 Argyll Rd ✉ BH5 1EB – ✆ (01202) 301 509 – www.urbanbeach.co.uk
12 rm – £ 72/99 £ 97/180 **Rest** – Carte £ 17/36 DX**a**
Laid-back hotel with a large decked terrace, set close to the beach and town. A beach shack style exterior conceals spacious designer bedrooms with stylish, luxurious bathrooms. The small reception is located in the trendy bar-cum-bistro, which offers a large menu of steaks and modern classics.

Edge
2 Studland Rd, (4th Floor), Alum Chine ✉ BH4 8JA – ✆ (01202) 757 007
– www.edgerestaurant.co.uk CX**s**
Rest – *(booking essential)* Carte £ 30/44
Trendy, stylish restaurant situated on the top floor of an apartment block, with floor to ceiling windows and excellent views over the beach and Poole bay. Seafood-based menu features modern dishes which are styled on classic combinations.

Arbor – Green House Hotel
4 Grove Rd ✉ BH1 3AX – ✆ (01202) 498 900 – www.thegreenhousehotel.com
Rest – Carte £ 21/33 DZ**n**
Large restaurant in an eco-friendly hotel; it upholds a 'sustainable' ethos with FSC timber on the floors, low energy induction cookers in the kitchen and honey bees on the roof. Modern menus display innovative touches; produce is local.

Rock N
Lansdeer Rd, Westbourne ✉ BH4 9EH – ✆ (01202) 765 696
– www.rockrestaurants.co.uk – Closed Sunday dinner DX**x**
Rest – Menu £ 15 (lunch) – Carte £ 26/52
Grand 18C church with antique oak panelling and stunning stained glass; the open kitchen is in the old chancel. Modern British cooking is fresh and flavoursome; lighter options are available in the small outside area. Lunch is good value.

West Beach
Pier Approach ✉ BH2 5AA – ✆ (01202) 587 785 – www.west-beach.co.uk
– Closed 25 December DZ**c**
Rest – *(booking essential)* Carte £ 25/40
Popular beachfront restaurant with a rustic interior, open-plan kitchen and folding glass doors opening onto a decked terrace. Seafood-based menu features some fish caught in front of the building; look for the buoys where the nets lie. They also offer an express menu – and takeaway in summer.

BOURTON-ON-THE-HILL - Gloucestershire - see Moreton-in-Marsh

BOURTON-ON-THE-WATER - Gloucestershire - 503 O28 4 D1

- pop. 3 093 Great Britain

London 91 mi – Birmingham 47 mi – Gloucester 24 mi – Oxford 36 mi

Town★

Northleach (Church of SS. Peter and Paul★, Wool Merchants' Brasses★), SW : 5 mi by A 429

Dial House without rest

The Chestnuts, High St ✉ *GL54 2AN* – ✆ *(01451) 822 244*
– www.dialhousehotel.com – Closed January
14 rm – †£ 110/140 ††£ 129/169

The oldest house in this charming Cotswold village, with lovely lawned gardens and a tranquil feel. Contemporary guest areas include a comfy lounge and bar. Bedrooms are in the original house, the extensions and a converted cottage; those in the main house have the most character and the best views.

Coombe House without rest

Rissington Rd ✉ *GL54 2DT* – ✆ *(01451) 821 966 – www.coombehouse.net*
– Restricted opening in winter
5 rm – †£ 60/70 ††£ 75/90

Spacious 1920s detached house, not far from the delightful village centre. Traditional lounge and first floor terrace; breakfast room boasts full-length leaded windows overlooking the pleasant garden. Simple but immaculately kept bedrooms offer good comforts.

ENGLAND

at Lower Slaughter Northwest : 1.75 mi by A 429 – ✉ Cheltenham

Lower Slaughter Manor

✉ *GL54 2HP* – ✆ *(01451) 820 456* – *www.lowerslaughter.co.uk*
19 rm – †£ 330/875 ††£ 350/895
Rest *Sixteen58* – see restaurant listing

A beautiful, listed, part-17C manor house in warm Cotswold stone, with delightful grounds. Two charming, antique-furnished drawing rooms with period oil paintings and open fires. Smart, elegant bedrooms are split between the house and the stable block; each one is unique, with its own style and stature.

Slaughters Country Inn

✉ *GL54 2HS* – ✆ *(01451) 822 143* – *www.theslaughtersinn.co.uk*
26 rm – †£ 80/155 ††£ 95/265 – 4 suites
Rest *Bar* – see restaurant listing
Rest – *(dinner only)* Carte £ 22/43

Originally a crammer school for Eton College, this stone-built manor house is a good choice for families – and they welcome dogs too! It's relaxed and understated, with minimalist, modern styling and the cosy bedrooms have feature walls and up-to-date facilities. The restaurant serves classic British dishes.

Sixteen58 Ⓝ – Lower Slaughter Manor

✉ *GL54 2HP* – ✆ *(01451) 820 456* – *www.lowerslaughter.co.uk*
Rest – Menu £ 25 (weekday lunch)/65

Elegant dining room in a fine manor house hotel with sumptuous sitting rooms and delightful grounds. Impressive chandeliers, antique furnishings and immaculately laid tables with beautiful floral displays. Menus offer classic French dishes and the skilful cooking uses modern techniques. Professional service.

Bar Ⓝ – Slaughters Country Inn

✉ *GL54 2HS* – ✆ *(01451) 822 143* – *www.theslaughtersinn.co.uk*
Rest – Carte £ 21/43

A trio of characterful rooms with wonky low ceilings and stone floors; in a hotel in a charming Cotswold village. Appealing menu of hearty, wholesome dishes and puddings that stray from the norm. Have afternoon tea on the beautiful terrace.

at Upper Slaughter **Northwest : 2.5 mi by A 429 – ✉ Bourton-On-The-Water**

Lords of the Manor

✉ *GL54 2JD – ✆ (01451) 820 243 – www.lordsofthemanor.com*
24 rm – †£ 179/445 ††£ 199/495 – 2 suites
Rest ***Lords of the Manor*** ✿ – see restaurant listing
Charming 17C former rectory in a pretty Cotswold village, with beautiful gardens, superb views and a real sense of tranquility. Two luxurious sitting rooms and a bar with a 'nature' colour theme. Bedrooms have a fittingly country house style and subtle contemporary touches. Staff are diligent and affable.

Lords of the Manor – Lords of the Manor Hotel

✉ *GL54 2JD – ✆ (01451) 820 243 – www.lordsofthemanor.com*
Rest – *(dinner only and Sunday lunch) (booking essential)* Menu £ 65/92
Plush, formal dining room in a beautiful country house in a tranquil Cotswold village; enjoy an aperitif in the luxurious sitting rooms. Accomplished, understated dishes use well-judged, classical combinations and are executed using modern techniques. Service is professional and very personable.
→ Foie gras and duck confit set in Monbazillac jelly. Canon of lamb with smoked potato mousseline. Prune and armagnac soufflé with Earl Grey tea mousse.

BOVEY TRACEY – Devon – 503 I32 – pop. 4 514 – ✉ Newton Abbot — 2 C2

London 214 mi – Exeter 14 mi – Plymouth 32 mi
Stover, Bovey Rd, Newton Abbot, ✆ (01626) 35 24 60
St Peter, St Paul and St Thomas of Canterbury Church★
Dartmoor National Park★★

Brookfield House without rest

Challabrook Ln, Southwest : 0.75 mi by Brimley rd ✉ TQ13 9DF – ✆ (01626) 836 181 – www.brookfield-house.com – March-November
3 rm – †£ 53/57 ††£ 76/84
Early Edwardian house on a private road in a peaceful part of town. Set behind electric gates, in two acres of attractive gardens, it has a simple, classically styled interior and large, immaculately appointed bedrooms; popular 'Iris' catches the sun all day.

BOWLAND BRIDGE – Cumbria – ✉ Cumbria — 21 A2_3

London 269 mi – Liverpool 86 mi – Preston 48 mi – Blackpool 60 mi

Hare and Hounds with rm

✉ *LA11 6NN – ✆ (015395) 68 333 – www.hareandhoundsbowlandbridge.co.uk – Closed 25 December*
3 rm – †£ 75/165 ††£ 100/165 **Rest** – Carte £ 20/29
Charming, 17C Lakeland pub in a delightful village. Large front terrace leads through into a rustic, open-fired inner hung with old village photos and hop bines. Menus offer typical, hearty favourites and most produce is locally sourced. Bedrooms are well-equipped and elegant; some boast roll-top baths.

BOWNESS-ON-WINDERMERE – Cumbria – 502 L20 – see Windermere

BOX – Wiltshire – 503 N29 – see Bath

BRABOURNE – Kent – pop. 1 442 — 9 C2

London 61 mi – Bromley 53 mi – Lewisham 56 mi – Stratford 61 mi

Five Bells Inn Ⓝ with rm

✉ *TN25 5LP – ✆ (01303) 813 334 – www.fivebellsinnbrabourne.com*
4 rm – †£ 90/140 ††£ 100/140 **Rest** – Carte £ 23/39
Characterful 16C building: a glorious candlelit hotchpotch of exposed beams, hop bines, open fires, butcher's block tables and an appealing deli. The gutsy menu ranges from eggs Benedict to wood-fired pizzas and fish from the local boats. Service is chatty and welcoming, and the bedrooms, delightfully busy.

BRADFORD-ON-AVON - Wiltshire - 503 N29 - pop. 9 072 4 C2

London 118 mi - Bristol 24 mi - Salisbury 35 mi - Swindon 33 mi

50 St Margarets St, ☎(01225) 86 57 97, www.bradfordonavon.co.uk

Town★★ - Saxon Church of St Lawrence★★ - Tithe Barn★ - Bridge★

Great Chalfield Manor★ (All Saints★) **AC**, NE : 3 mi by B 3109 – Westwood Manor★ **AC**, S : 1.5 mi by B 3109 – Top Rank Tory (←★). Bath★★★, NW : 7.5 mi by A 363 and A 4 – Corsham Court★★ **AC**, NE : 6.5 mi by B 3109 and A 4

Woolley Grange

Woolley Green, Northeast : 0.75 mi by B 3107 on Woolley St ✉ BA15 1TX – ☎(01225) 864 705 – www.woolleygrangehotel.co.uk

25 rm – †£ 119/161 ††£ 140/190 – 6 suites

Rest – Menu £ 39 (dinner) – Carte £ 27/39

Fine Jacobean manor house that's geared towards families, with a crèche, a kids club, a games room and outdoor activities. For adults, there's a chic spa and some lovely country views. Smart bedrooms come in many styles. Accomplished, classical cooking is served in the restaurant and more relaxed orangery.

Bradford Old Windmill

4 Masons Ln, on A 363 ✉ BA15 1QN – ☎(01225) 866 842 – www.bradfordoldwindmill.co.uk – closed November-March

3 rm – †£ 79/105 ††£ 89/115 **Rest** – Menu £ 25 **s**

Converted windmill built in 1807 – surprisingly hidden from the main road – with a unique circular lounge and dining room. Bedrooms are cosy and characterful with whirlpool baths; one has a round bed and another, a queen-sized water bed. Vegetarian country-style dishes use produce from the owners' allotment.

Three Gables

St Margaret's St ✉ BA15 1DA – ☎(01225) 781 666 – www.thethreegables.com – Closed 1-14 January, Sunday and Monday

Rest – Menu £ 18 (lunch) – Carte £ 30/50

Personally and passionately run restaurant in a 350 year old house, with a lovely terrace and charming exposed stone and wattle and daub walls. Skilful, accomplished cooking; interesting, original dishes are based on classical combinations.

at Winsley West : 2 mi by A 363 off B 3108

Stillmeadow without rest

18 Bradford Rd ✉ BA15 2HW – ☎(01225) 722 119 – www.stillmeadow.co.uk – Closed 23 December-2 January

4 rm – †£ 75/100 ††£ 90/100

The name sums it up well, as it has a charming wildflower garden and is located on the edge of a small hamlet. Tasteful furnishings provide a good degree of luxury and comfort. Bedrooms are colour-themed and have thoughtful touches.

BRADWELL - Derbyshire - 504 O24 - pop. 1 728 16 A1

London 170 mi - Birmingham 99 mi - Liverpool 66 mi - Leeds 48 mi

Samuel Fox Country Inn with rm

Stretfield Rd ✉ S33 9JT – ☎(01433) 621 562 – www.samuelfox.co.uk – Closed 3-17 January

4 rm – †£ 85/95 ††£ 120/130

Rest – Menu £ 20 (early dinner) – Carte £ 22/34

Attractive, light-stone building with a dramatic, hilly backdrop: named after an inventor of the steel-ribbed umbrella. Sit in the cosy bar or pleasant restaurant. Dishes hint at the chef's time spent in Andalucia; on Fridays, try the popular 'secret supper' small plates. Bedrooms are homely and well-kept.

BRAITHWAITE - Cumbria - 502 K20 - see Keswick

ENGLAND

BRAMPFORD SPEKE – Devon – see Exeter

London 184 mi – Cardiff 110 mi – Plymouth 50 mi – Torbay 29 mi

BRAMPTON – Cumbria – 501 L19 – pop. 3 965 Great Britain 21 B1

London 317 mi – Carlisle 9 mi – Newcastle upon Tyne 49 mi

Market Pl, (016977) 34 33, www.visitcumbria.com

Talkin Tarn, (016977) 22 55

Hadrian's Wall★★, NW : by A 6077

Farlam Hall

Southeast : 2.75 mi on A 689 ✉ CA8 2NG – (016977) 46 234 – www.farlamhall.co.uk – Closed 5-23 January and 25-30 December

12 rm (dinner included) – †£ 115/145 ††£ 210/270

Rest – *(dinner only) (booking essential)* Menu £ 45

Well-run, family-owned Victorian country house, whose origins can be traced back to the 1600s. Bedrooms are furnished with antiques but also boast flat screen TVs and Bose radios. The sumptuous formal dining room has romantic lake views, a traditional daily menu and attentive service. Enjoy afternoon tea in the comfy lounges overlooking the ornamental gardens.

Good food at moderate prices? Look for the Bib Gourmand ☺.

BRANCASTER STAITHE – Norfolk 15 C1

London 131 mi – King's Lynn 25 mi – Boston 57 mi – East Dereham 27 mi

White Horse with rm

✉ PE31 8BY – (01485) 210 262 – www.whitehorsebrancaster.co.uk

15 rm – †£ 60/80 ††£ 130/170 **Rest** – *(booking essential)* Carte £ 24/33

The rear views over the marshes and Scolt Head Island really make this pub. Choose from old favourites, tapas-style dishes and a few more ambitious offerings on the bar menu; or seasonally changing dishes supplemented by daily specials on the à la carte. Smart, New England style bedrooms – some with terraces.

Jolly Sailors

✉ PE31 8BJ – (01485) 210 314 – www.jollysailorsbrancaster.co.uk

Rest – Carte £ 19/25 **s**

'Eat, Drink and Be Jolly' is their motto and it's easy to do all three at this cosy, unaffected pub with its yesteryear charm. Straightforward, traditional cooking. Kids will love the play area, the ice cream hut and their own special menu.

BRAUGHING – Hertfordshire 12 B2

London 33 mi – Leeds 171 mi – Sheffield 153 mi – Manchester 200 mi

Golden Fleece

20 Green End ✉ SG11 2PG – (01920) 823 555 – www.goldenfleecebraughing.co.uk – Closed 25-26 December and Sunday dinner

Rest – Carte £ 21/33

Proudly run, part-16C pub with a spacious garden, a pretty terrace overlooking the village and striking period features including a vast inglenook fireplace. Tasty, comforting, country-style dishes; gluten and dairy free options.

BRAY – Windsor and Maidenhead – 504 R29 – pop. 8 121 – ✉ Maidenhead 11 C3

London 30 mi – Croydon 37 mi – Barnet 43 mi – Ealing 25 mi

see Maidenhead Plan

XXXX **Waterside Inn** (Alain Roux) with rm

✿✿✿ *Ferry Rd ✉ SL6 2AT – ☎ (01628) 620 691 – www.waterside-inn.co.uk – Closed 26 December-23 January* Xs

11 rm – †£ 220/500 ††£ 220/500 – 2 suites

Rest – *(closed Monday and Tuesday) (booking essential)* Menu £ 60 (weekday lunch)/153 – Carte £ 127/170

An illustrious restaurant in a glorious spot on the bank of the Thames, with an elegant dining room and a delightful terrace ideal for aperitifs. Carefully considered French menus reflect the seasons and dishes range from time-honoured classics to those with a more modern style. Service is charming and expertly structured; bedrooms are chic and luxurious.

→ Tronçonnettes de homard poêlées minute au Porto blanc. Filets de lapereau grillés, sauce à l'armagnac et aux marrons glacés. Péché gourmand selon "Alain".

XXX **Fat Duck**

✿✿✿ *High St ✉ SL6 2AQ – ☎ (01628) 580 333 – www.thefatduck.co.uk – Closed 2 weeks Christmas-New Year, Sunday and Monday* Xe

Rest – *(booking essential) (set menu only)* Menu £ 195

Stylish restaurant in an old, low-beamed pub, owned by Heston Blumenthal. The 14 course menu lists intriguingly named creations such as the 'Sound of the Sea' or the 'BFG', which are presented in theatrical ways and stimulate the senses. Highly original dishes contain excellent contrasts of texture and taste.

→ Mad Hatter's Tea Party. Lamb with cucumber, green pepper and caviar oil. Botrytis cinerea.

XX **Caldesi in Campagna**

Old Mill Ln ✉ SL6 2BG – ☎ (01628) 788 500 – www.caldesi.com – Closed Sunday dinner and Monday Xx

Rest – Menu £ 15 (weekday lunch)/24 – Carte £ 28/53

Welcoming former pub with smart interior, conservatory and decked garden with wood fired oven. Flavoursome Italian cooking displays Ligurian, Tuscan and Sicilian influences.

Hinds Head

✿ *High St ✉ SL6 2AB – ☎ (01628) 626 151 – www.hindsheadbray.com – Closed 25-26 December and Sunday dinner* Xe

Rest – *(booking essential)* Menu £ 22 (weekday lunch) – Carte £ 32/52

Listed 15C pub at the heart of a pretty village; its dark wood panelling and log fires giving it a characterful, almost medieval feel. Prime seasonal produce is used to create rich, satisfying dishes that are down-to-earth, fiercely British, carefully presented and big on flavour. Informed, engaging service.

→ Hash of snails. Veal chop with cabbage, onion and Reform sauce. Caramelised butter loaf with apple and Pomona.

Royal Oak

✿ *Paley Street, Southwest : 3.5 mi by A 308 and A 330 on B 3024 ✉ SL6 3JN – ☎ (01628) 620 541 – www.theroyaloakpaleystreet.com – Closed Sunday dinner*

Rest – Menu £ 25 (weekday lunch) – Carte £ 35/63

A warm and welcoming beamed dining pub, with a smart extension and an elegantly manicured herb garden. The appealing menu champions seasonal British produce. Cooking is skilled, confident and sensibly avoids over-elaboration; fish and game are handled deftly. Formal service provides a sense of occasion.

→ Lasagne of wild rabbit with wood blewits. Peppered haunch of roe deer with creamed spinach and sauce poivrade. Chocolate fondant with toffee sauce and coffee ice cream.

Crown

High St ✉ SL6 2AH – ☎ (01628) 621 936 – www.thecrownatbray.com

Rest – Carte £ 23/38 Xa

Charmingly restored 16C building, formerly 2 cottages and a bike shop. Dark oak columns and low beams in the bar; lighter cottage style dining room. Cooking is robust, flavoursome and British.

ENGLAND

at Bray Marina Southeast : 2 mi by B 3208, A 308 - X - on Monkey Island Lane – ✉ Bray-On-Thames

Riverside Brasserie

(follow road through the marina) ✉ *SL6 2EB – ✆ (01628) 780 553 – www.riversidebrasserie.co.uk – Closed Wednesday-Thursday October-March, Sunday dinner, Monday and Tuesday*

Rest – *(booking essential)* Carte £ 31/44

Well-run restaurant superbly located in a former boathouse on the banks of the Thames. Grab a seat on the attractive terrace, where heaters help extend the summer season. Skilled cooking of modern European classics, with perennial favourites such as crispy pork salad or rib-eye steak. Charming service.

BRAYE – **503** Q33 – see Channel Islands (Alderney)

BRAY MARINA – Buckinghamshire – see Bray

BREARTON – North Yorkshire – pop. 141 — 22 B2

London 216 mi – Leeds 23 mi – Sheffield 67 mi – Manchester 77 mi

Malt Shovel

Main St ✉ *HG3 3BX – ✆ (01423) 862 929 – www.themaltshovelbrearton.co.uk – Closed 25 December, 1 January and Sunday dinner*

Rest – Menu £ 14 (lunch and early dinner) – Carte £ 26/43

Quirky, shabby-chic pub run by the Bleikers, who also own the famous smokehouse. Classical dishes with continental flavours; lots of smoked seasonal produce. Tapas-style small plates at lunch.

BREEDON ON THE HILL – Leicestershire – pop. 958 — 16 B2

– ✉ Castle Donington

London 121 mi – Birmingham 35 mi – Sheffield 57 mi – Manchester 95 mi

Three Horseshoes Inn

44-46 Main St ✉ *DE73 8AN – ✆ (01332) 695 129 – www.thehorseshoes.com – Closed 25-26 December, 1 January and Sunday dinner*

Rest – Carte £ 20/40

Large, highly characterful, whitewashed pub with a pleasant terrace and numerous interlinking rooms featuring cosy fires and intimate corners. Blackboard menus display robust, classical dishes of flavoursome, seasonal produce.

BRENTWOOD – Essex – 504 V29 – pop. 47 593 — 13 C2

London 22 mi – Chelmsford 11 mi – Southend-on-Sea 21 mi

44 High St, ✆ (01277) 20 03 00, www.visitessex.com

Bentley G. & C.C., Ongar Rd, ✆ (01277) 37 31 79

Warley Park, Little Warley, Magpie Lane, ✆ (01277) 22 48 91

Marygreen Manor

London Rd, Southwest : 1.25 mi on A 1023 ✉ *CM14 4NR – ✆ (01277) 225 252 – www.marygreenmanor.co.uk*

44 rm – †£ 75/160 ††£ 75/160, ☕ £ 15

Rest *Tudors* – Menu £ 18 (weekdays) – Carte £ 39/56

Tudor house with 15C origins; once owned by a servant of Catherine of Aragon. Charming open-fired rooms, ornate plaster ceilings and carved wood panelling. Bedrooms split between the house and courtyard; the former, more characterful. Formal restaurant offers elaborate, classically based dishes.

BRIDGNORTH – Shropshire – 502 M26 – pop. 11 891 ▌Great Britain — 18 B2

London 146 mi – Birmingham 26 mi – Shrewsbury 20 mi – Worcester 29 mi

Listley St, ✆ (01746) 76 32 57, www.visitbridgnorth.co.uk

Stanley Lane, ✆ (01746) 76 33 15

Ironbridge Gorge Museum★★ **AC** (The Iron Bridge★★ - Coalport China Museum★★ - Blists Hill Open Air Museum★★ - Museum of the Gorge and Visitor Centre★) NW : 8 mi by B 4373

Casa Ruiz

45 High St. ✉ WV16 4DX – ☎ (01746) 218 084 – www.casaruiz.co.uk
Rest – Menu £ 19/25 – Carte £ 10/28
Follow a steep, narrow staircase up to this small Spanish restaurant, where the atmosphere is unpretentious and the service, friendly. Well-priced, authentic tapas dishes; choose 3 or 4 per person. Iberico hams are a speciality.

at Worfield Northeast : 4 mi by A 454 – ✉ Bridgnorth

Old Vicarage

✉ WV15 5JZ – ☎ (01746) 716 497 – www.oldvicarageworfield.com
14 rm – †£ 65/110 ††£ 85/130
Rest *Orangery* – *(booking essential)* Menu £ 20 – Carte £ 22/39
Red-brick Edwardian former vicarage in a quiet village. Country house styling in the lounge, bar and bedrooms – the latter exhibiting a slightly more contemporary style; some rooms are in the old coach house. The smart restaurant has a tiled floor, glass roof and pleasant garden views.

BRIDPORT – Dorset – 503 L31 – pop. 12 977 3 B3

London 150 mi – Exeter 38 mi – Taunton 33 mi – Weymouth 19 mi
47 South St, ☎ (01308) 42 49 01, www.visit-dorset.org.uk
Bridport and West Dorset, West Bay, East Cliff, ☎ (01308) 42 25 97
Mapperton Gardens★, N : 4 mi by A 3066 and minor rd. Lyme Regis★ - The Cobb★, W : 11 mi by A 35 and A 3052

Roundham House without rest

Roundham Gdns, West Bay Rd, South : 1 mi by B 3157 ✉ DT6 4BD – ☎ (01308) 422 753 – www.roundhamhouse.co.uk – May-November
8 rm – †£ 50/58 ††£ 90/125
Sizeable Edwardian house displaying rich colours and period furnishings. Comfy lounge; modern bedrooms with bold feature walls and good comforts. Elevated position offers pleasant country views.

Bull

34 East St ✉ DT6 3LF – ☎ (01308) 422 878 – www.thebullhotel.co.uk
19 rm – †£ 75/115 ††£ 85/200 **Rest** – Carte £ 25/42
Stylishly refurbished, 16C coaching inn with a grand Victorian ballroom and a well-equipped games room. Chic bedrooms – upstairs and in a mews – are decorated with local auction house finds and artefacts from Parisian flea markets. Appealing classics in the bar; pizzas, pies and ciders in the former stables.

Riverside

West Bay, South : 1.75 mi by B 3157 ✉ DT6 4EZ – ☎ (01308) 422 011 – www.thefishrestaurant-westbay.co.uk – Closed 1 December-13 February, Sunday dinner and Monday except bank holidays
Rest – *(booking essential)* Menu £ 27 (lunch) – Carte £ 24/57
Long-standing seafood restaurant with harbour views; accessed via a bridge. Good value daily menu offers extremely fresh, straightforward dishes crafted from local produce. Plenty of choice.

at Burton Bradstock Southeast : 2 mi by B 3157

Norburton Hall without rest

Shipton Ln, North : 0.25 mi on Shipton Gorge rd ✉ DT6 4NQ – ☎ (01308) 897 007 – www.norburtonhall.com
3 rm – †£ 90/150 ††£ 125/250
Originally a 17C farmhouse; extended and turned into an Arts and Crafts gem in 1902. Woodwork, ornate carvings and period furniture abound. Comfortable bedrooms offer good quality bedding and modern bathrooms. 6 acres of mature grounds, with barbecue available. Charming owners.

BRIGGSWATH – North Yorkshire – 502 S20 – see Whitby

ENGLAND

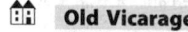

BRIGHTON AND HOVE – Brighton and Hove – 504 T31 – pop. 125 167 Great Britain 8 A3

London 53 mi – Portsmouth 48 mi – Southampton 61 mi

Shoreham Airport : ☎ (01273) 467373, W : 8 mi by A 27 AV

Royal Pavilion Shops, ☎ (01273) 29 25 95, www.visitbrighton.com

The Dyke, Devil's Dyke Rd, Devil's Dyke, ☎ (01273) 85 72 96

Hollingbury Park, Ditchling Rd, ☎ (01273) 55 20 10

Waterhall, Waterhall Rd, ☎ (01273) 50 86 58

Town★★ - Royal Pavilion★★★ **AC** CZ – Seafront★★ – The Lanes★ BCZ – St Bartholomew's★ **AC** CX **B**

Devil's Dyke (<★) NW : 5 mi by Dyke Rd (B 2121) BY

Plans on following pages

Hotel du Vin

2-6 Ship St ✉ BN1 1AD – ☎ (01273) 718 588 – www.hotelduvin.com

49 rm – †£ 115/200 ††£ 150/400, ☕ £ 17 CZ**a**

Rest *Bistro* – *(booking essential)* Carte £ 23/51

Set on the promenade and made up of various different buildings; the oldest being a 17C former arts club. Cavernous, gothic-style bar-lounge and mezzanine lounge with terrace. Comfy, contemporary bedrooms; some in their next door pub. Relaxed brasserie with a hidden courtyard serves French bistro classics.

Drakes

43-44 Marine Par ✉ BN2 1PE – ☎ (01273) 696 934 – www.drakesofbrighton.com

20 rm – †£ 115/145 ††£ 135/295, ☕ £ 13 CZ**u**

Rest *Drakes* – see restaurant listing

Pair of 18C townhouses on the promenade, with stylish interiors and a cocktail bar. Chic, well-equipped bedrooms boast bamboo flooring, wooden feature walls and wet rooms, along with sea or city views. 2 night stay (min.) at weekends.

Myhotel Brighton without rest

17 Jubilee St ✉ BN1 1GE – ☎ (01273) 900 300 – www.myhotels.com

80 rm – †£ 75 ††£ 75/200, ☕ £ 10 CY**z**

Contemporary glass cube set in the heart of town. Wacky, designer interior with a relaxed vibe, a funky bar and a modern coffee shop-cum-breakfast room. Quirky, minimalist bedrooms have the latest technological extras.

Kemp Townhouse without rest

21 Atlingworth St ✉ BN2 1PL – ☎ (01273) 681 400
– www.kemptownhousebrighton.com – Closed 25-26 December CZ**n**

9 rm ☕ – †£ 75/95 ††£ 125/215

Stylish, 19C townhouse with a tastefully decorated breakfast room. Bedrooms have a modern, uncluttered, 'New England' style and compact wet rooms; those facing the front are larger and more comfortable - two are four-posters.

The Twenty One without rest

21 Charlotte St ✉ BN2 1AG – ☎ (01273) 686 450 – www.thetwentyone.co.uk

7 rm ☕ – †£ 60/70 ††£ 95/155 CV**u**

A smart and well-run Regency townhouse in the heart of the city. Compact, modern, immaculately kept bedrooms with bathrobes and a tea tray bursting with goodies. Fresh coffee on arrival. Great choice at breakfast.

Paskins without rest

18-19 Charlotte St ✉ BN2 1AG – ☎ (01273) 601 203 – www.paskins.co.uk

19 rm ☕ – †£ 50/70 ††£ 65/145 CV**u**

Quirky, personally run guesthouse with art deco breakfast room. Small, modern bedrooms are simply furnished and well-kept. Showers only – to save water – and eco-toiletries. Organic breakfast features homemade sausages.

brightonwave without rest

10 Madeira Pl ✉ BN2 1TN – ☎ (01273) 676 794 – www.brightonwave.com
– Closed 23-27 December CZ**s**

8 rm ☕ – †£ 65/70 ††£ 95/120

Personally run Victorian townhouse featuring ever-changing artwork. Contemporary bedrooms: the front facing and garden rooms are the largest and most comfortable. One modern four-poster.

ENGLAND

BRIGHTON AND HOVE

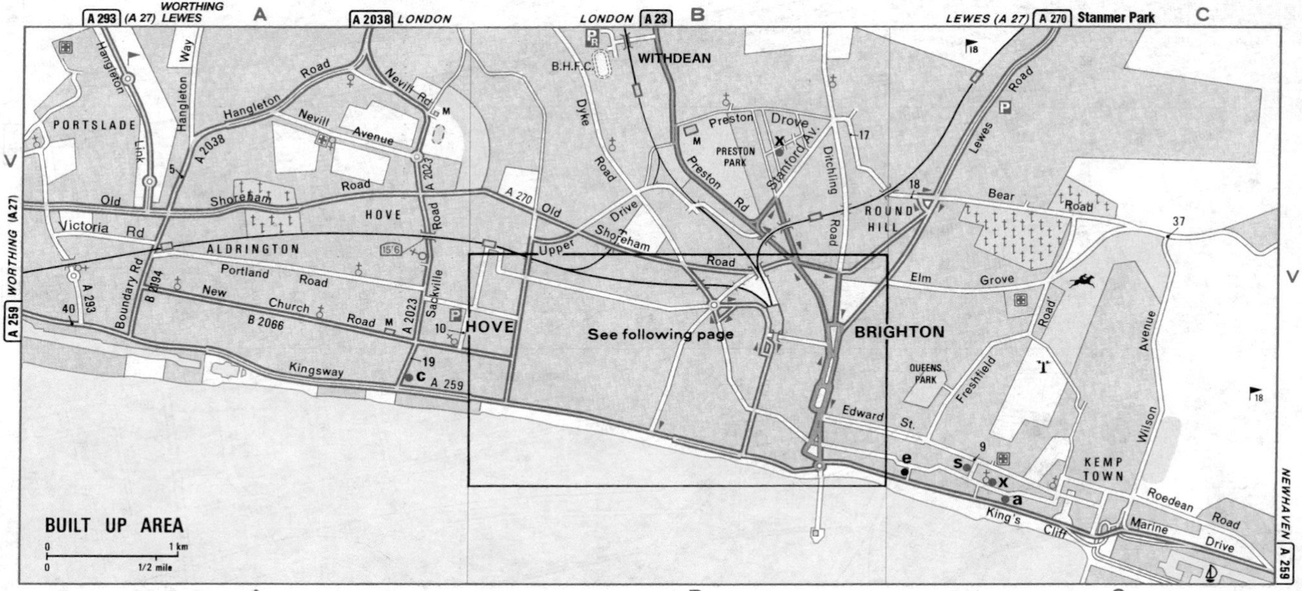

ENGLAND

BRIGHTON
HOVE
ROYAL PAVILION
THE LANES
CHURCHILL SQ. SHOPPING CENTRE
THE BRIGHTON CENTRE
ST. ANN'S WELL GARDENS
CENTRE
A 2073
A 270
A 23
A 259
B 2185
B 2066
(A 27)
B 2120
B 2119
B 2121
B 2122
A 2010
King's Road
Kingsway
Madeira Drive
Marine Parade
Grand Parade
Old Shoreham Road
Dyke Road
Viaduct Road
London Rd
Ditchling
Southover St.
Albion Hill
Sussex St.
Carlton Hill
John St.
Edward St.
James's St.
Trafalgar Street
North Road
Church St.
North St.
Queen's Road
West St.
Buckingham Road
Buckingham Pl.
New England Street
New England Rd
Clifton Hill
Vernon Ter.
Upper North St.
Western Road
Montpelier Road
Preston St.
Davigdor Road
Lansdowne Road
Holland Road
Palmeira Avenue
Selborne Rd
First Avenue
Wilbury Road
Second Av.
Grand Avenue
The Drive
Cromwell Road
Eaton Road
Tisbury Road
Norton Rd
Third Av.
Fourth Av.
Church Road
300 m
300 yards

XX **Drakes** – Drakes Hotel

43-44 Marine Par ✉ BN2 1PE – ☎ (01273) 696 934
– www.therestaurantatdrakes.co.uk CZ**u**
Rest – *(booking advisable)* Menu £ 15/30
Set in the basement of an 18C townhouse hotel. Two small, intimate dining rooms with a soft, moody atmosphere and elegantly laid tables. Menus feature luxury ingredients and have a classical bent. Formal feel, even at lunch.

XX **Gingerman**

21a Norfolk Sq ✉ BN1 2PD – ☎ (01273) 326 688
– www.gingermanrestaurants.com – Closed 2 weeks winter, 25 December and Monday BZ**i**
Rest – *(booking essential)* Menu £ 18 (weekday lunch)/35
Tucked away off the promenade; French and Mediterranean flavours to the fore in a confident, affordable, modern repertoire: genuine neighbourhood feel.

XX **Coal Shed**

8 Boyces St ✉ BN1 1AN – ☎ (01273) 322 998 – www.coalshed-restaurant.co.uk
– Closed 25-26 December BZ**x**
Rest – Carte £ 22/43
A stylish, modern steakhouse hidden away in the Brighton Lanes. Cooking centres around the Josper charcoal oven; they specialise in 35-day aged organic steaks but there's also a wide selection of fish and other tasty dishes.

XX **24 St Georges**

24 St George's Rd ✉ BN2 1ED – ☎ (01273) 626 060 – www.24stgeorges.co.uk
– Closed 25-26 December, 1-2 January, Sunday and Monday CV**x**
Rest – *(dinner only and lunch Saturday and Sunday) (booking advisable)*
Menu £ 16 (weekdays)/32 – Carte £ 25/38
Neighbourhood brasserie on the edge of Kemp Town; its three adjoining rooms have a stylish, contemporary feel. Seasonal menu of technically skilled, classical dishes. Staff are welcoming and knowledgeable.

ENGLAND

X **Chilli Pickle**

17 Jubilee St ✉ BN1 1GE – ☎ (01273) 900 383 – www.thechillipickle.com
– Closed 25-26 December CY**z**
Rest – Menu £ 24 – Carte £ 18/33
Simple, relaxed restaurant with passionate chef, buzzy vibe and friendly, welcoming service. Oft-changing menu of tasty, thoughtfully prepared, authentic Indian dishes, with delicate spicing and good quality ingredients. Great selection of beers and teas; superb ice creams and sorbets.

X **Terre à Terre**

71 East St ✉ BN1 1HQ – ☎ (01273) 729 051 – www.terreaterre.co.uk – Closed 25-26 December and Monday in winter CZ**e**
Rest – *(booking essential)* Menu £ 25/35 – Carte £ 26/33
Relaxed, friendly restaurant decorated in warm burgundy colours. Appealing menu of generous, tasty, original vegetarian dishes which include items from Japan, China and South America. Mini épicerie sells wine, pasta and chutney.

X **Sam's of Brighton**

1 Paston Pl ✉ BN2 1HA – ☎ (01273) 676 222 – www.samsofbrighton.co.uk
– Closed 25 December, Sunday dinner and Monday CV**a**
Rest – Menu £ 15 (lunch and early dinner) – Carte £ 24/36
Simple neighbourhood eatery boasting three enormous candelabras. Simple menu of classical, seasonal dishes. Early brunch on offer at the weekend and a concise à la carte at noon.

X **Blenio Bistro**

87-93 Dyke Rd ✉ BN1 3JE – ☎ (01273) 220 220 – www.bleniobistro.com
– Closed 2 weeks late June-early July, Monday and Tuesday BX**c**
Rest – *(dinner only and lunch Friday-Sunday)* Carte £ 23/38
Friendly, passionately run neighbourhood bistro. Simply furnished, with exposed brick, food-related art and pleasant terrace. Regularly changing menu ranges from snacks to the full 3 courses; locally sourced ingredients to the fore.

Ginger Dog

12 College Pl ✉ BN2 1HN – ✆ (01273) 620 990
– www.gingermanrestaurants.com – Closed 25 December CV**s**

Rest – Menu £ 13 (lunch) – Carte £ 24/35

Charming Victorian pub with a shabby-chic, canine-theme, a welcoming atmosphere and a relaxed feel. Fresh produce is to the fore; dishes are mostly British-based but with the odd nod to Italy. A ginger 'dog' biscuit is served with coffee.

Preston Park Tavern

88 Havelock Rd ✉ BN1 6GF – ✆ (01273) 542 271
– www.prestonparktavern.co.uk – Closed 25 December and 1 January

Rest – Menu £ 13 (weekday lunch) – Carte £ 22/31 BV**x**

Majestic Victorian coaching inn, lovingly restored by a charming couple. Shabby-chic interior with boldly decorated walls. Menus focus on local, sustainable produce and dishes are confidently cooked, well-balanced and bursting with flavour.

at Hove

Graze

42 Western Rd ✉ BN3 1JD – ✆ (01273) 823 707 – www.graze-restaurant.co.uk
– Closed 1-4 January AY**z**

Rest – Menu £ 18/34

Lively neighbourhood eatery with quirky, informal feel and a great private dining room in the basement. Cooking is elaborate and adventurous: good value mid-week menu; 7 course tasting menu – must be ordered in advance at lunch.

ENGLAND

Ginger Pig

3 Hove St ✉ BN3 2TR – ✆ (01273) 736 123 – www.gingermanrestaurants.com
– Closed 25 December AV**c**

Rest – Menu £ 13 (weekday lunch) – Carte £ 23/35

Smart building by the seafront – formerly a hotel – boasting a mortar ship relief and a beautifully restored revolving door. Menus offer precise, flavoursome British dishes and vegetarians are well-catered for. Great value set menus at both lunch and dinner. Service copes well under pressure.

BRISTOL

See city maps on following pages **4** C2

© Bernd Tschakert/imagebroker/Age fotostock

City of Bristol – pop. 371 042 – **503** M29 – **504** M29 – Great Britain

London 121 mi – Birmingham 91 mi

Tourist Information

Harbourside, ✆(0333) 321 01 01, www.visitbristol.co.uk

Airport

Bristol Airport : ✆ (0871) 334 4444, SW : 7 m. by A 38 AX

Bridge

Severn Bridge (toll)

Golf Courses

Short Lodge GC, Carsons Rd, ✆(0117) 956 55 01

Clifton Beggar, Clifton, Bush Lane, Failand, ✆(01275) 39 34 74

SIGHTS

In the town

City★★ • St Mary Redcliffe★★ DZ • At-Bristol★★ CZ • Brandon Hill★★ AX • Georgian House★★ AX**K** • Bristol Museum★★ CZ**M3** • Brunel's ss Great Britain and Maritime Heritage Centre★ **AC** AX**S2** • The Old City★ CYZ : Theatre Royal★★ CZ**T** • Merchant Seamen's Almshouses★ CZ**Q** • St Stephen's Church★ CY**S1** • St John the Baptist★ CY • College Green★ CYZ• City Museum and Art Gallery★ AX**M1**

On the outskirts

Clifton★★ AX •Clifton Suspension Bridge★★ (toll) • RC Cathedral of St Peter and St Paul★★ **F1** • Bristol Zoological Gardens★★ **AC**

In the surrounding area

Bath★★★, SE : 13 mi by A 4 BX

ENGLAND

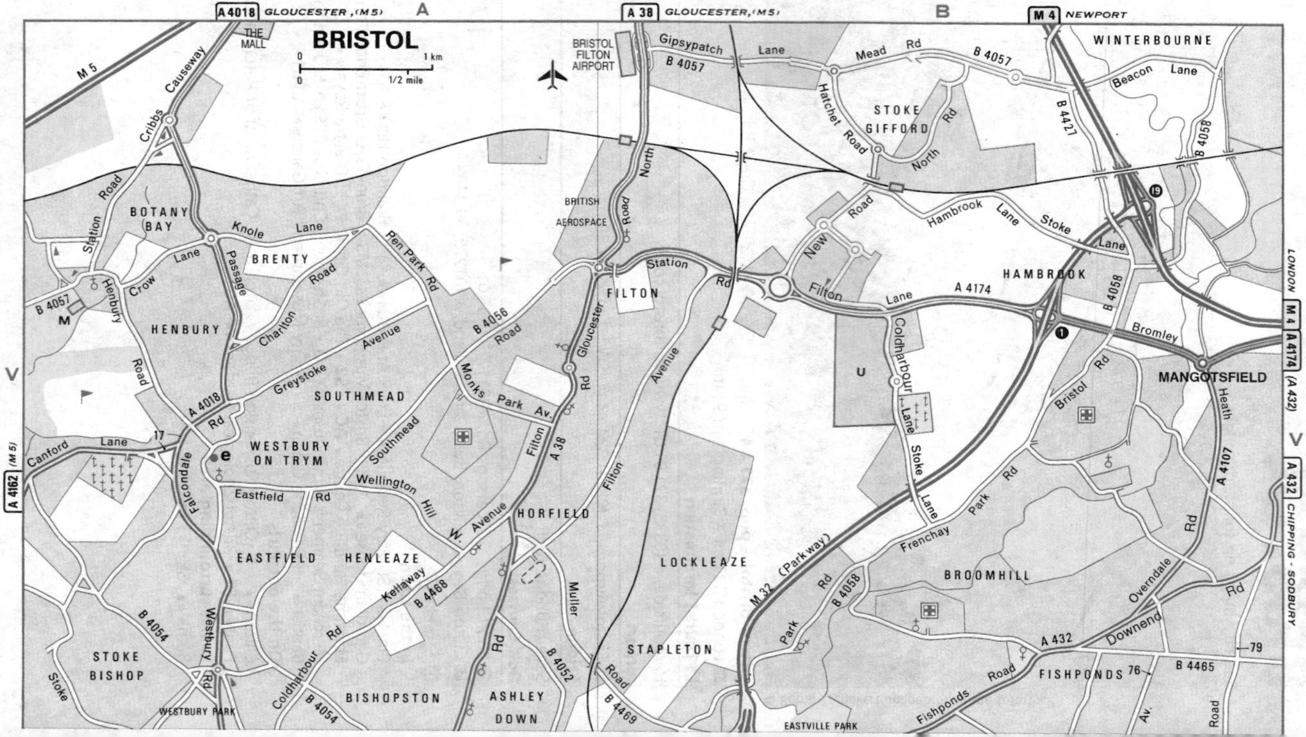
BRISTOL
0 1 km
0 1/2 mile
A 4018 GLOUCESTER, (M5)
A 38 GLOUCESTER, (M5)
M 4 NEWPORT
LONDON M 4 A 4174 (A 432)
A 432 CHIPPING - SODBURY
A 4162 (M 5)
A
B
V
THE MALL
BRISTOL FILTON AIRPORT
BRITISH AEROSPACE
M 5
Cribbs Causeway
Station Road
BOTANY BAY
Knole Lane
Passage
BRENTY
Crow Lane
Henbury
B 4057
HENBURY
Road
Charlton Road
Pen Park Rd
Greystoke Avenue
SOUTHMEAD
A 4018 Rd
WESTBURY ON TRYM
Canford Lane
Falcondale
Eastfield Rd
EASTFIELD
HENLEAZE
Wellington Hill
W. Avenue
Southmead
Monks Park Av.
B 4056 Road
Gloucester Rd
Filton A 38
HORFIELD
Kellaway B 4468
Coldharbour Rd
B 4054
STOKE BISHOP
Stoke
WESTBURY PARK
Westbury Rd
BISHOPSTON
ASHLEY DOWN
Rd
Muller
B 4052
Road B 4469
STAPLETON
LOCKLEAZE
Filton Avenue
Station Rd
FILTON
North Road
Gipsypatch Lane
B 4057
Mead Rd
Hatchet Road
STOKE GIFFORD
North Rd
WINTERBOURNE
Beacon Lane
B 4427
B 4058
New Road
Hambrook Lane
Stoke Lane
HAMBROOK
Filton Lane
A 4174
Coldharbour Lane
Stoke Lane
U
Bromley
MANGOTSFIELD
Heath
A 4107
Bristol Rd
Frenchay Park Rd
M 32 (Parkway)
Park Rd
B 4058
BROOMHILL
Overndale Rd
Downend
A 432
FISHPONDS
Fishponds Road
Av.
Road
B 4465
EASTVILLE PARK
76
79
17
19
1
e
M

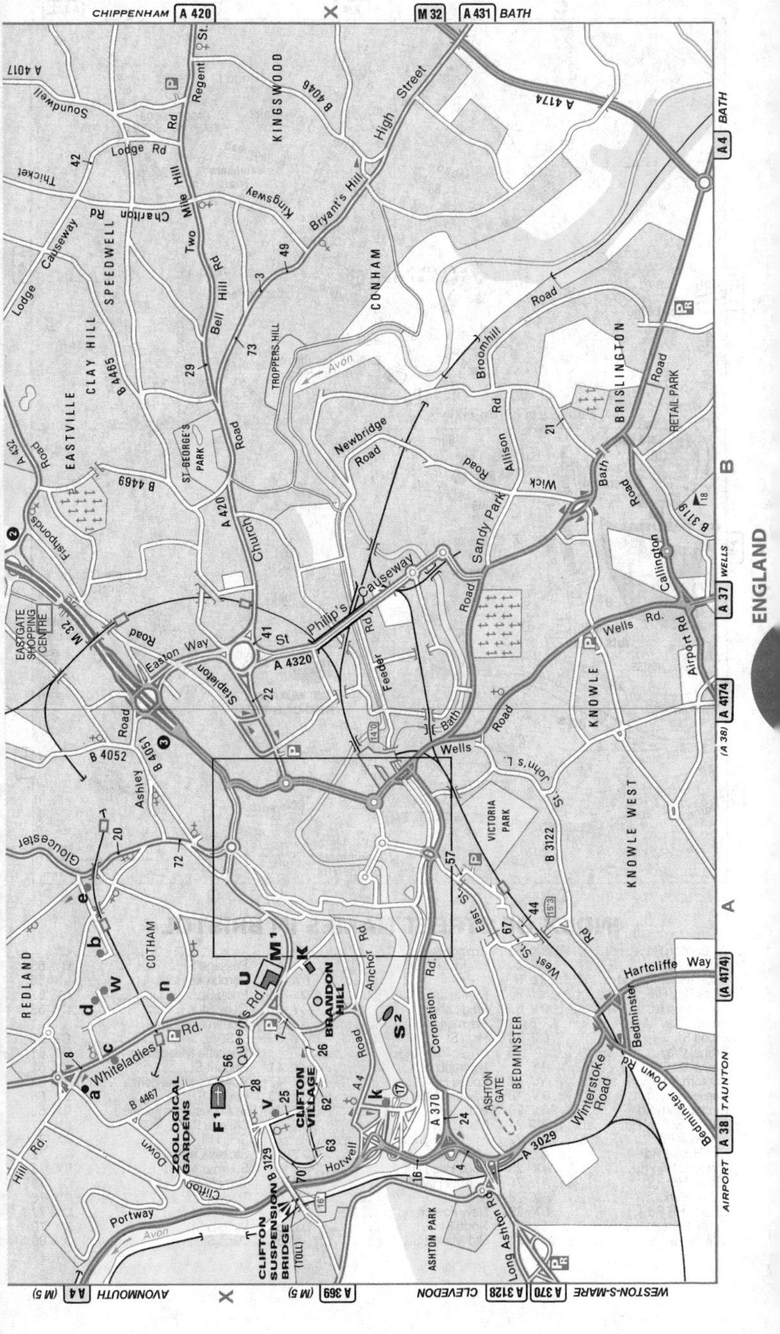
CHIPPENHAM A 420
M 32
A 431 BATH
A 4 BATH
A 37 WELLS
A 4174
(A 38)
(A 4174)
AIRPORT A 38 TAUNTON
WESTON-S-MARE A 370
A 3128 CLEVEDON
A 369 (M 5)
AVONMOUTH A 4 (M 5)
KINGSWOOD
SPEEDWELL
CLAY HILL
EASTVILLE
CONHAM
TROPPERS HILL
ST GEORGE'S PARK
EASTGATE SHOPPING CENTRE
BRISLINGTON
RETAIL PARK
KNOWLE
KNOWLE WEST
VICTORIA PARK
BEDMINSTER
ASHTON GATE
ASHTON PARK
REDLAND
COTHAM
BRANDON HILL
CLIFTON VILLAGE
ZOOLOGICAL GARDENS
CLIFTON SUSPENSION BRIDGE
(TOLL)
Two Mile Hill
Bell Hill Rd
Church Road
Bryant's Hill
High Street
Kingsway
Charlton Rd
Lodge Rd
Soundwell
Regent St.
Lodge Causeway
Fishponds Road
Easton Way
Stapleton Road
St Philip's Causeway
Feeder Rd
Newbridge Road
Broomhill Road
Allison Rd
Wick Road
Sandy Park Road
Bath Road
Wells Road
Wells Rd.
Callington Road
Airport Rd
Hartcliffe Way
Bedminster Down Rd
Winterstoke Road
Coronation Rd.
Anchor Rd
Hotwell Road
Queen's Rd.
Whiteladies Rd.
Gloucester Road
Ashley Road
Clifton Down
Portway
Hill Rd.
Long Ashton Rd
West St.
East St.
John's L.
Avon
ENGLAND
A B

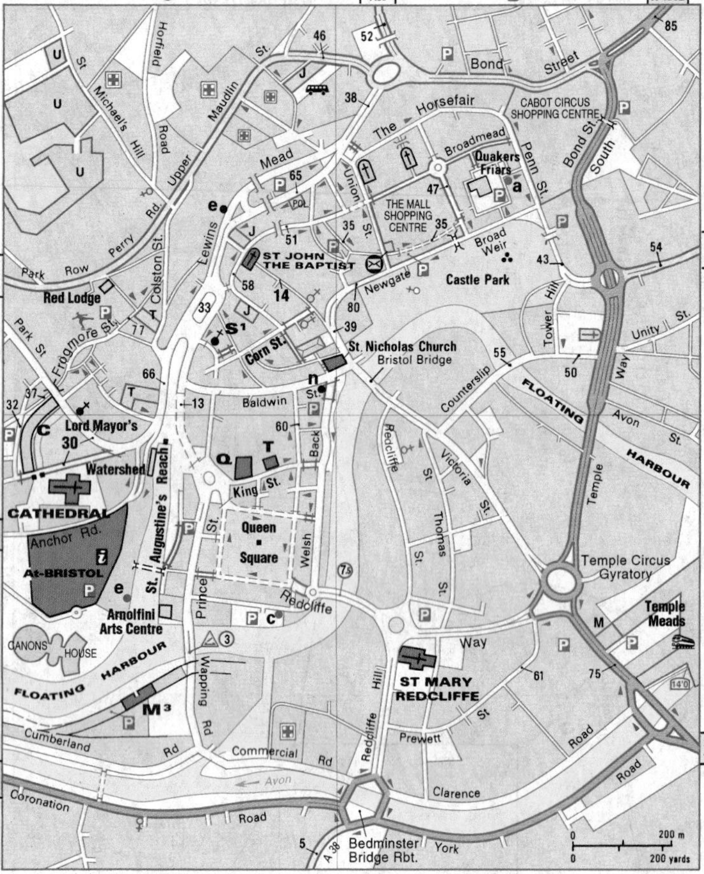

INDEX OF STREET NAMES IN BRISTOL

Hotel du Vin

The Sugar House ✉ *BS1 2NU – ✆ (0844) 736 42 52 – www.hotelduvin.com*
40 rm – †£ 119/325 ††£ 129/345, ☕ £ 15 CY**e**
Rest ***Bistro*** – *(booking essential)* Carte £ 25/71
Characterful 18C former sugar refinery with classical Hotel du Vin styling and a wine-theme running throughout. Dark-hued bedrooms and duplex suites boast Egyptian cotton linen – one room has twin roll-top baths. Cosy lounge-bar; French brasserie with a pleasant courtyard terrace for bistro classics.

Mercure Bristol Brigstow

5-7 Welsh Back ✉ *BS1 4SP – ✆ (0117) 929 10 30 – www.mercure.com*
115 rm – †£ 60/165 ††£ 68/195, ☕ £ 17 – 1 suite CY**n**
Rest ***Ellipse*** – Menu £ 18 **s** – Carte £ 21/41 **s**
Modern city centre hotel overlooking the River Avon. Stylishly furnished, curvaceous bedrooms have bold colour schemes and luxurious bathrooms, with a TV above the bath. Some have balconies; others, coffee machines and river views. Smart, contemporary Ellipse serves a menu of European classics.

Number 38 Clifton without rest

38 Upper Belgrave Rd ✉ *BS8 2XN – ✆ (01179) 466 905*
– www.number38clifton.com AX**a**
9 rm ☕ – †£ 110/195 ††£ 125/210
Built in 1820, this substantial townhouse overlooks both the city and the Clifton Downs. Boutique bedrooms have coloured wood-panelled walls, Roberts radios and smart bathrooms with underfloor heating; the most luxurious are the loft suites, complete with copper baths. The rear terrace makes a great suntrap.

Second Floor at Harvey Nichols

27 Philadelphia St, Quakers Friars, Cabot Circus ✉ *BS1 3BZ – ✆ (0117) 916 8898*
– www.harveynichols.com – Closed 25 December, 1 January, Easter Sunday, Sunday and Monday dinner DY**a**
Rest – Menu £ 20 – Carte £ 30/41
A spacious and elegant light-filled restaurant with stylish gold décor. Good value lunch menu and concise à la carte offering original, modern dishes. Chic lounge bar for cocktails and light bites. Attentive service.

Casamia (Jonray and Peter Sanchez-Iglesias)

38 High St, Westbury-on-Trym, Northwest : 4 mi by A 4018 ✉ *BS9 3DZ*
– ✆ (0117) 959 28 84 – www.casamiarestaurant.co.uk – Closed Sunday and Monday AV**e**
Rest – *(booking essential) (set menu only)* Menu £ 38 (weekday lunch)/88
This minimalistic restaurant with its understated feel puts the emphasis where it belongs: on the food. Like the details in the décor, the set menus – 5 or 7 courses at lunch and 13 courses at dinner – change with the seasons, and the ambitious, skilful and highly innovative cooking uses modern techniques.
→ Spelt with parsley. Lamb, allium stew and mint sauce. Rhubarb fool.

Bordeaux Quay

V Shed, Canons Way ✉ *BS1 5UH – ✆ (0117) 943 12 00*
– www.bordeaux-quay.co.uk – Closed 25-26 December CZ**e**
Rest – Menu £ 19/30 – Carte £ 19/36
A huge harbourside emporium which is 100% organic. The ground floor houses a deli, a bakery, a cookery school, a relaxed bar and a brasserie. The linen-laid restaurant above offers more adventurous Mediterranean-influenced cuisine.

Rockfish Grill

128 Whiteladies Rd ✉ *BS8 2RS – ✆ (0117) 973 73 84 – www.rockfishgrill.co.uk*
– Closed first week January, 25-29 December, Sunday and Monday
Rest – Menu £ 13 (lunch) – Carte £ 24/47 AX**c**
Well-run and busy, with polite, friendly service. Daily changing menus focus on fresh, simply prepared fish and seafood, cooked in the charcoal Josper oven. Owners' fishmongers is adjacent.

ENGLAND

wilks (James Wilkins)
1 Chandos Rd ✉ BS6 6PG – ✆ (0117) 973 79 99 – www.wilksrestaurant.co.uk – Closed 2 weeks January, 2 weeks August, Sunday and Monday AX**d**
Rest – *(booking essential)* Menu £ 19 (lunch and early dinner) – Carte £ 24/38
Appealing neighbourhood restaurant with a relaxed atmosphere and a simple, understated style. Menus are modern and highly original; and dishes are well-balanced and refreshingly lacking in over-adornment, displaying a lightness of touch and a real understanding of flavours. The set menu offers good value.
→ Pan-seared scallops with apple, ginger and celery. Venison haunch, Savoy cabbage, chestnuts and quince. Cocoa meringue, coffee ice cream, almond and vanilla.

Flinty Red
34 Cotham Hill ✉ BS6 6LA – ✆ (0117) 923 87 55 – www.flintyred.co.uk – Closed 1-7 January, 25-28 December, Monday lunch and Sunday AX**n**
Rest – *(booking essential)* Menu £ 10 (lunch) – Carte £ 20/31
Combined effort of two couples; one pair are independent wine merchants, the other, chefs. Simple, rustic interior and friendly, knowledgeable team. Concise daily menu of Mediterranean small plates. Unfussy cooking relies on quality local produce and features some lesser-known cuts. Tempting wine list.

Riverstation
The Grove, Harbourside ✉ BS1 4RB – ✆ (0117) 914 44 34 – www.riverstation.co.uk – Closed 24-26 December CZ**c**
Rest – Menu £ 16 (lunch) – Carte £ 27/38
Great riverside location: watch canal boats pass by from the terrace. Bar offers all day dining with breakfast, brunch and meze plates. Upstairs restaurant offers more substantial modern European fare.

Moreish
6 Chandos Rd ✉ BS6 6PE – ✆ (0117) 970 60 78 – www.moreishrestaurant.co.uk – Closed 25 December AX**w**
Rest – Menu £ 15/21
Unassuming restaurant in a parade of shops; its name is a play on the chef's surname. The great value daily menu offers well-prepared, rustic dishes, from breakfast right through to dinner. Have drinks in the bar or on the small terrace.

Pump House
Merchants Rd ✉ BS8 4PZ – ✆ (0117) 927 2229 – www.the-pumphouse.com – Closed 25 December, Sunday dinner and Monday AX**k**
Rest – Carte £ 27/38
Victorian former pumping station for the adjacent docks; watch the boats go by from the terrace. Cavernous, slightly industrial interior with various levels. Sandwiches and pub classics sit alongside more elaborate dishes on the menu.

Albion Public House and Dining Rooms
Boyces Ave, Clifton Village ✉ BS8 4AA – ✆ (0117) 973 35 22 – www.thealbionclifton.co.uk – Closed 25-26 December AX**v**
Rest – *(booking essential)* Carte £ 20/31
Trendy, Grade II listed pub tucked away down a cobbled street. Fun, friendly and informal, with modern styling and a canopy-covered terrace out front. Unfussy, highly seasonal menu changes twice a day; everything is homemade.

Kensington Arms
35-37 Stanley Rd ✉ BS6 6NP – ✆ (0117) 944 64 44 – www.thekensingtonarms.co.uk – Closed 25-26 December and Sunday dinner AX**b**
Rest – Menu £ 15 (lunch) – Carte £ 22/43
Charming, Victorian-style neighbourhood pub, with a traditional bar and an impressive, high-ceilinged dining room. Daily menus have a strong British and seasonal base; in winter you'll find hearty, nourishing dishes and proper puddings.

ENGLAND

at Long Ashton **Southwest : 2.5 mi by A 370 off B 3128**

Bird in Hand
17 Weston Rd ✉ BS41 9LA – ✆ (01275) 395 222 – www.bird-in-hand.co.uk – Closed 25 December
Rest – *(booking essential at dinner)* Carte £ 20/30
Tiny country pub with eclectic décor, including an antelope's head and a wall covered in pages from Mrs Beeton's Book of Household Management. Concise menu of pub classics at lunch; more interesting dinner menu of tasty, carefully cooked dishes which let local and foraged ingredients speak for themselves.

BRITWELL SALOME – Oxfordshire – pop. 187 11 C2

London 75 mi – Oxford 21 mi – Reading 19 mi

Red Lion N
✉ OX49 5LG – ✆ (01491) 613 140 – www.theredlionbritwellsalome.co.uk – Closed Sunday dinner, Monday and lunch Tuesday
Rest – *(booking essential)* Carte £ 21/38
A 'proper' pub next to the village cricket pitch, run by experienced owners. Well-executed dishes provide plenty of interest, from the tasty nibbles to the pie of the day. There's always plenty of pork, as whole beasts are delivered from the farm next door; the homemade black pudding scotch egg is a must-try.

BROAD CAMPDEN – Gloucestershire – see Chipping Campden

BROAD OAK – East Sussex – 504 V31 8 B3

London 62 mi – Hastings 8 mi – Rye 7 mi

Fairacres without rest
Udimore Rd, on B 2089 ✉ TN31 6DG – ✆ (01424) 883 236 – www.fairacresrye.co.uk – Closed Christmas-New Year
3 rm – †£ 70/100 ††£ 80/150
Charming, listed, 17C cottage in picture-postcard pink, with delightful gardens and a cosy, beamed lounge with an open fire. Gloriously cluttered bedrooms display family knick-knacks and offer many thoughtful extras. Big breakfasts, with homemade bread, and local bacon and sausages.

BROADCLYST – Devon – 503 J31 – see Exeter

BROADSTAIRS – Kent – 504 Y29 – pop. 22 712 9 D1

London 77 mi – Canterbury 18 mi – Ramsgate 2 mi

Belvidere Place without rest
Belvedere Rd ✉ CT10 1PF – ✆ (01843) 579 850 – www.belvidereplace.co.uk
5 rm – †£ 120 ††£ 140/170
Centrally located Georgian house with charming owner, green credentials and eclectic, individual style. Bohemian, shabby-chic lounge boasts a retro football table. Spacious bedrooms mix modern facilities with older antique furnishings.

Burrow House without rest
Granville Rd ✉ CT10 1QD – ✆ (01843) 601 817 – www.burrowhouse.com
4 rm – †£ 95/125 ††£ 95/165
Tastefully restored and subtly modernised Victorian house, close to the seafront. Bedrooms blend contemporary décor and fine antique furniture. They host gourmet weekends by arrangement. Substantial breakfasts.

Albariño
29 Albion St ✉ CT10 1LXG – ✆ (01843) 600 991 – www.albarinorestaurant.co.uk – Closed 23-26 December, 1 January and Sunday
Rest – Menu £ 10 (lunch) – Carte £ 17/23
Run by a husband and wife team and named after her favourite wine. Freshly prepared, full-flavoured tapas dishes; 3 per person will suffice – let the chef choose. Counter seating for 7. Good views of the Channel.

ENGLAND

▶ London 93 mi – Birmingham 36 mi – Cheltenham 15 mi – Oxford 38 mi

🔢 1 Cotswold Court, ✆ (01386) 85 29 37, www.broadway-cotswolds.co.uk

◉ Town ★

🄶 Country Park (Broadway Tower ✳ ★★★), SE : 2 mi by A 44 – Snowshill
Manor★ (Terrace Garden★) **AC**, S : 2.5 m

ENGLAND

Buckland Manor ⅁ ≤ ☕ ꝏ ✗ ⅍ 🛜 **P**
✉ WR12 7LY – ✆ (01386) 852 626 – www.bucklandmanor.com
14 rm ☲ – ♦£ 185/575 ♦♦£ 195/585
Rest – (booking essential) Menu £ 26/29 – Carte £ 41/57 ⅜
Attractive sandstone house with lovely gardens, set behind automatic gates in a
peaceful village. Elegant, stylish interior, with traditionally furnished lounges
boasting big open fires, and comfortable, country house style bedrooms which
blend antique furniture with good mod cons. Formal restaurant with garden
views offers classic cooking.

Lygon Arms ⅁ ☒ ⊕ ℘ ⅍ ✗ ⅌ rm, 🛜 ⅏ **P**
High St ✉ WR12 7DU – ✆ (01386) 852 255 – www.pumahotels.co.uk
78 rm – ♦£ 120/260 ♦♦£ 120/260, ☲ £ 20 – 6 suites
Rest *Luke's* – (closed Monday-Tuesday) Carte £ 24/37
Rest *Great Hall* – (dinner only and Sunday lunch) Menu £ 41
One of the most famous old coaching inns in the country, retaining period features such as wood panelling and inglenook fireplaces, and offering assorted
comfy corners. Bedrooms vary in size and shape; those in the newer wing have
a more contemporary style. Accessible menu in Luke's. 17C minstrels' gallery and
modern European menu in the more formal Great Hall.

Broadway ⅁ ⅌ ⅌ rest, 🛜 **P**
The Green ✉ WR12 7AA – ✆ (01386) 852 401
– www.cotswold-inns-hotels.co.uk/broadway
21 rm ☲ – ♦£ 120/160 ♦♦£ 180/200
Rest *Tattersalls Brasserie* – Carte £ 26/41
16C inn on the village green – once an abbots' retreat – with warmly decorated,
individually styled bedrooms. Relax in the timbered bar with its minstrels' gallery
or have afternoon tea by the inglenook fireplace in the sitting room. The light,
airy, atrium brasserie offers an extensive seasonal menu.

East House without rest ⅁ ⅁ ⅍ 🛜 **P**
162 High St ✉ WR12 7AJ – ✆ (01386) 853 789
– www.vacationcotswolds.co.uk
4 rm ☲ – ♦£ 165/195 ♦♦£ 165/195
Beautifully furnished, 18C former farmhouse in lovely mature gardens, with wood-
burning stoves and a welcoming feel. Sumptuous beamed bedrooms mix antique
furniture with modern technology; superb bathrooms have underfloor heating.
The Jacobean Suite is the biggest room, with a four-poster and garden views.

Windrush House without rest ⅁ ⅍ 🛜 **P**
Station Rd ✉ WR12 7DE – ✆ (01386) 853 577 – www.windrushhouse.com
5 rm ☲ – ♦£ 65/85 ♦♦£ 80/100
Fresh, modern guesthouse with a landscaped garden, set on the main road into a
picturesque village. Welcoming owners. Comfortable, open-plan lounge and individually decorated bedrooms with bold feature walls; some have wrought iron
beds.

Olive Branch without rest 🛜 **P**
78 High St ✉ WR12 7AJ – ✆ (01386) 853 440
– www.theolivebranch-broadway.com
8 rm ☲ – ♦£ 62/68 ♦♦£ 88/98
Welcoming guesthouse run by an experienced husband and wife team. Pleasantly
cluttered bedrooms with thoughtful extras; one has a small veranda. Rustic, characterful dining room with homemade cakes, breads and muesli at breakfast.

✗✗ Russell's with rm ⌂ 🄰 🛜 🖥 🅿

20 High St ⊠ WR12 7DT – ℰ (01386) 853 555 – www.russellsofbroadway.co.uk
– Closed Sunday dinner except before bank holiday and bank holiday Mondays
7 rm ⌸ – **†**£ 85/145 **††**£ 110/300 **Rest** – Menu £ 18 – Carte £ 27/53
Attractive Cotswold stone house in the centre of the village, with a smart, modern, brasserie-style interior and both a front and rear terrace. Seasonal menus of modern dishes, with a well-priced set menu. Casual service. Stylish, modern bedrooms boast good facilities.

BROCKENHURST – Hampshire – 503 P31 – pop. 2 865 ▌ Great Britain 6 A2

▶ London 99 mi – Bournemouth 17 mi – Southampton 14 mi – Winchester 27 mi
🖫 Brockenhurst Manor, Sway Rd, ℰ (01590) 62 33 32
ⓖ New Forest★★ (Rhinefield Ornamental Drive★★, Bolderwood Ornamental
Drive★★)

🏨 Rhinefield House ⤳ 🖨 🄺 ⌂ ⌶ 🛖 🕍 ✗ & 🄰 rm, 🛥 🕻 🕋 🅿

Rhinefield Rd, Northwest : 3 mi ⊠ SO42 7QB – ℰ (01590) 622 922
– www.handpickedhotels.co.uk
50 rm ⌸ – **†**£ 99/190 **††**£ 129/290 – 1 suite
Rest Armada – ℰ (0845) 072 7516 *(dinner only and Sunday lunch)* Menu £ 36
(dinner) – Carte £ 40/56
Rest Grill – ℰ (0845) 072 7516 – Carte £ 27/53
Impressive country house complete with an ornamental pond, parterres and a yew maze, set in 40 acres of tranquil forest parkland. Period features include ornate wooden carvings. Bedrooms boast the latest mod cons; those in the original house are smaller but more characterful. Modern fine dining in traditional Armada or classical grill menu in relaxed conservatory.

ENGLAND

🏨 The Pig ⤳ 🖨 🄺 ✗ 🛜 🅿

Beaulieu Rd, East : 1 mi on B 3055 ⊠ SO42 7QL – ℰ (01590) 622 354
– www.thepighotel.com
26 rm – **†**£ 135/225 **††**£ 135/225, ⌸ £ 15
Rest The Pig – see restaurant listing
Smartly refurbished hotel that follows a philosophy of removing barriers and bringing nature indoors. Divided between the main house and stable block, characterful bedrooms boast distressed wood floors, chunky furnishings and large, squashy beds. The lounges and dining room have a shabby-chic style.

🏨 New Park Manor ⤳ ≪ 🖨 🄺 ⌶ 🖾 🌑 🛖 🛜 🕋 🅿

Lyndhurst Rd, North : 1.5 mi on A 337 ⊠ SO42 7QH – ℰ (01590) 623 467
– www.newparkmanorhotel.co.uk
21 rm ⌸ – **†**£ 115/195 **††**£ 135/315 – 1 suite
Rest The Stag – Menu £ 25/44
Extended, elegantly proportioned former hunting lodge built by Charles II on his return from France. Classic bedrooms in the main house; those in the Forest Wing are more contemporary. Candlelit fine dining.

🏠 Cloud ⌂ ✗ 🛜 🕋 🅿

Meerut Rd ⊠ SO42 7TD – ℰ (01590) 622 165 – www.cloudhotel.co.uk
– Closed 27 December-13 January
18 rm ⌸ – **†**£ 83/90 **††**£ 124/180
Rest Encore – Menu £ 16/30
Well-kept hotel made up of four cottages, set on the edge of a pretty New Forest town; photos attest to the owner's past as a tiller girl. Neat, tidy bedrooms. Busy, linen-laid restaurant with conservatory extension and theatrical theme; traditional menus.

🏠 Cottage Lodge without rest 🖨 & 🛜 🅿

Sway Rd ⊠ SO42 7SH – ℰ (01590) 622 296 – www.cottagelodge.co.uk – Closed
Christmas
15 rm ⌸ – **†**£ 50/110 **††**£ 60/159
Cosy, low-ceilinged former forester's cottage dating back to 1650, in a charming village where New Forest ponies wander freely. Smart, modern bedrooms; some with balconies. Tea and cake are served in the snug beamed bar.

Thatched Cottage
16 Brookley Rd ✉ SO42 7RR – ☎ (01590) 623 090 – www.thatchedcottage.co.uk
6 rm – †£ 50/120 ††£ 70/150
Rest – *(dinner only) (booking essential)* Carte £ 19/35
Characterful thatched cottage built in 1627, edged by a modern decked terrace complete with a pizza oven. Named after teas, bedrooms feature traditional furnishings and thoughtful extras; some have fireplaces or four-posters. The restaurant is crammed with knick-knacks; afternoon tea is popular.

Daisybank Cottage without rest
Sway Rd, South : 0.5 mi on B 3055 ✉ SO42 7SG – ☎ (01590) 622 086 – www.bedandbreakfast-newforest.co.uk
5 rm – †£ 90/115 ††£ 100/135
Cream Arts and Crafts house built in 1902. Stylish, modern bedrooms have smart bathrooms and seating areas; one opens onto an internal courtyard, another, onto a terrace. Aga-cooked breakfasts come in English, Irish and American versions.

The Pig – The Pig Hotel
Beaulieu Rd, East : 1 mi on B 3055 ✉ SO42 7QL – ☎ (01590) 622 354 – www.thepighotel.com
Rest – Carte £ 23/47
Large, Victorian, lean-to conservatory with plants dotted about, an eclectic collection of old tables and chairs, and a bustling atmosphere. The forager and kitchen gardener supply what's best and 90% of ingredients come from within 25 miles. Cooking is unfussy, wholesome and British-based.

BROCKTON – Shropshire 18 B2

London 150 mi – Birmingham 48 mi – Leeds 130 mi – Sheffield 114 mi

Feathers at Brockton
✉ TF13 6JR – ☎ (01746) 785 202 – www.feathersatbrockton.co.uk – Closed 26 December, 1 January, Monday and lunch Tuesday
Rest – Menu £ 13 (lunch and early dinner) – Carte £ 21/33
Rustic 16C pub set in prime walking country, with a snug, characterful inner and relaxing atmosphere. Traditional dishes display some Mediterranean influences and are made using locally sourced produce. The gift shop sells home accessories.

BROMESWELL – Suffolk – see Woodbridge

BROMFIELD – Shropshire – 503 L26 – see Ludlow

BROUGHTON – North Yorkshire 22 A2

London 228 mi – Sheffield 71 mi – Kingston upon Hull 94 mi – Derby 106 mi

Bull
✉ BD23 3AE – ☎ (01756) 792 065 – www.thebullatbroughton.com – Closed 25 December and Monday
Rest – Carte £ 20/32
Part of Ribble Valley Inns, a burgeoning pub company which proudly promotes local and very British ingredients and dishes. This solid, sizeable pub boasts log fires, beams and stone floors.

BROUGHTON GIFFORD – Wiltshire 4 C2

London 109 mi – Bristol 31 mi – Cardiff 64 mi – Southampton 81 mi

The Fox
The Street ✉ SN12 8PN – ☎ (01225) 782 949 – www.thefox-broughtongifford.co.uk – Closed 26 -27 December, 1-2 January and Sunday dinner
Rest – Menu £ 16 (lunch) – Carte £ 25/44
Raising the profile of this pub, both locally and farther afield, has been a labour of love for its young owner. Cooking is simple, unfussy and fresh, using what's in the garden: salad leaves, fruits, chickens and pigs.

BRUNDALL - Norfolk - 504 Y26 - pop. 5 832 15 D2

London 118 mi - Great Yarmouth 15 mi - Norwich 8 mi

Lavender House

39 The Street ✉ *NR13 5AA* – ✆ *(01603) 712 215* – *www.thelavenderhouse.co.uk*
– Closed 26 December-9 January, Sunday dinner and Monday-Wednesday
Rest – *(dinner only and Sunday lunch) (booking advisable)* Menu £ 28/60
Characterful thatched cottage with low beamed ceilings and inglenook fireplaces. Cooking has a rustic, north Italian style – good quality ingredients feature in gutsy dishes and flavours are clearly defined. They also run cookery courses.

BRUNTINGTHORPE - Leicestershire Great Britain 16 B3

London 96 mi - Leicester 10 mi - Market Harborough 15 mi

Leicester - Museum and Art Gallery★, Guildhall★ and St Mary de Castro Church★, N : 11 mi by minor rd and A 5199

The Joiners

Church Walk ✉ *LE17 5QH* – ✆ *(0116) 247 82 58* – *www.thejoinersarms.co.uk*
– Closed Sunday dinner and Monday
Rest – *(booking essential)* Menu £ 15 (lunch) – Carte £ 24/34
Neat and tidy whitewashed pub with a characterful low-beamed interior; run by an enthusiastic husband and wife team. Good value menus offer a mix of refined pub classics and brasserie-style dishes, cooked and presented in a straightforward manner. There's also a wide selection of wines by the glass.

BRUSHFORD - Somerset - 503 J30 - see Dulverton

BRUTON - Somerset - 503 M30 - pop. 2 982 4 C2

London 118 mi - Bristol 27 mi - Bournemouth 44 mi - Salisbury 35 mi

Stourhead★★★ **AC**, W : 8 mi by B 3081

At The Chapel with rm

High St ✉ *BA10 0AE* – ✆ *(01749) 814 070* – *www.atthechapel.co.uk*
8 rm – †£ 100/150 ††£ 100/250 **Rest** – *(booking advisable)* Carte £ 20/40
Stylish, informal restaurant in a former 18C chapel, with a bakery to one side and a wine shop to the other. Well-priced, daily menus offer rustic, Mediterranean-influenced dishes; specialities include wood-fired breads, pizzas and cakes. Luxurious bedrooms have king-sized beds, 46" TVs and Egyptian cotton. Chic club lounge and cocktail bar opens at weekends.

BRYHER - 503 A/B34 - see Scilly (Isles of)

BUCKDEN - Cambridgeshire - 504 T27 - pop. 2 385 - ✉ Huntingdon 14 A2

London 65 mi - Bedford 15 mi - Cambridge 20 mi - Northampton 31 mi

George

High St ✉ *PE19 5XA* – ✆ *(01480) 812 300* – *www.thegeorgebuckden.com*
12 rm – †£ 95/150 ††£ 110/150
Rest *Brasserie* – see restaurant listing
Delightfully restored, part black and white, part red-brick coaching inn. Original flag floors mix with modern furnishings, giving a stylish, understated feel. Tasteful, individually decorated bedrooms are named after famous Georges.

Brasserie - George Hotel

High St ✉ *PE19 5XA* – ✆ *(01480) 812 300* – *www.thegeorgebuckden.com*
Rest – Menu £ 16/22 – Carte £ 25/44
Appealing, well-run brasserie in a stylish hotel, featuring a parquet floor, a glass skylight and a pleasant summer terrace. Monthly menus display a wide range of influences, from classic British dishes to those with a more global edge.

ENGLAND

BUCKHORN WESTON - Dorset 4 C3

London 117 mi – Poole 36 mi – Bath 33 mi – Weymouth 37 mi

Stapleton Arms with rm

Church Hill ✉ SP8 5HS – ✆ (01963) 370 396 – www.thestapletonarms.com – Closed 25 and 26 December

4 rm – †£ 72/96 ††£ 90/120 **Rest** – Carte £ 24/34

A welcoming, well-run pub with a homely, shabby-chic style. Menus showcase pub classics, with the occasional international influence, and snacks like a Scotch egg or pork pie can be wrapped up and taken home. Spacious bedrooms boast Egyptian cotton, smart bathrooms and a mix of modern and antique furnishings.

BUCKINGHAM - Buckinghamshire - 503 Q27 - pop. 12 512 11 C1

Great Britain

London 64 mi – Birmingham 61 mi – Northampton 20 mi – Oxford 25 mi

Silverstone, Stowe, Silverstone Rd, ✆ (01280) 85 00 05

Tingewick Rd, ✆ (01280) 81 55 66

Stowe Gardens★★, NW : 3 mi by minor rd. Claydon House★ **AC**, S : 8 mi by A 413

Villiers

rm, rest,

3 Castle St ✉ MK18 1BS – ✆ (01280) 822 444 – www.oxfordshire-hotels.co.uk

49 rm – †£ 85/140 ††£ 110/190 – 4 suites

Rest *Villiers* – *(closed dinner 25 December)* Menu £ 17 – Carte £ 24/43

Proudly run hotel on a central street in a quaint market town. Bright, modern meetings rooms and a cosy lounge; the bar has a charming open fire. Bedrooms vary in style: all have modern facilities; some have original beams and some are duplex suites. The restaurant serves a mix of classical and modern dishes.

BUCKLAND MARSH - Oxfordshire - pop. 2 243 10 A2

London 76 mi – Faringdon 4 mi – Oxford 15 mi

Trout at Tadpole Bridge with rm

✉ SN7 8RF – ✆ (01367) 870 382 – www.troutinn.co.uk – Closed 25-26 December

6 rm – †£ 85/100 ††£ 130/160 **Rest** – Carte £ 22/40

Smart pub with attractive garden leading down to the Thames. Concise menu consists of classic Gallic dishes with contemporary touches; seafood and game often feature as specials. Comfy bedrooms exceed expectations. Private moorings available.

BUDE - Cornwall - 503 G31 - pop. 3 681 1 B2

London 252 mi – Exeter 51 mi – Plymouth 50 mi – Truro 53 mi

The Crescent, ✆ (01288) 35 42 40, www.visitbude.info

Burn View, ✆ (01288) 35 20 06

The Breakwater★★ – Compass Point (≤★)

Poughill★ (church★★), N : 2.5 mi - E : Tamar River★★ – Kilkhampton (Church★), NE : 5.5 mi by A 39 – Stratton (Church★), E : 1.5 mi – Launcells (Church★), E : 3 mi by A 3072 – Marhamchurch (St Morwenne's Church★), SE : 2.5 mi by A 39 – Poundstock★ (≤★★, church★, guildhouse★), S : 4.5 mi by A 39. Morwenstow (cliffs★★, church★), N : 8.5 mi by A 39 and minor roads - Jacobstow (Church★), S : 7 mi by A 39

Falcon

rest,

Breakwater Rd ✉ EX23 8SD – ✆ (01288) 352 005 – www.falconhotel.com – Closed 25 December

30 rm – †£ 63/83 ††£ 125/165 – 1 suite

Rest – *(bar lunch Monday-Saturday)* Carte £ 21/31 **s**

An imposing whitewashed hotel overlooking the Bude Canal; purportedly the oldest coaching house in North Cornwall, and where Tennyson broke his leg falling over the garden wall. Classically styled bedrooms with contemporary touches. The traditional restaurant and spacious bar are smartly dressed in red velour.

beach at bude without rest
Summerleaze Cres. ✉ EX23 8HL – ✆ (01288) 389 800
– www.thebeachatbude.co.uk – Closed 22 December-5 January
17 rm ☕ – 🚹£ 105/155 🚹🚹£ 125/175
Relaxed, spacious 'New England' style hotel with views over the Atlantic Ocean. Contemporary bedrooms have limed oak furnishings and all the latest mod cons. 'Deluxe' boast roll-top baths and a terrace or balcony; 'Premier' have sea views.

BUDLEIGH SALTERTON – **Devon** – **503** K32 – **pop. 4 801** **2** D2
London 182 mi – Exeter 16 mi – Plymouth 55 mi
Fore St, ✆ (01395) 44 52 75, www.visitbudleigh.com
East Devon, Links Rd, Budleigh Salterton, ✆ (01395) 44 33 70
East Budleigh (Church★), N : 2.5 mi by A 376 – Bicton★ (Gardens★) **AC**, N : 3 mi by A 376

Heath Close
3 Lansdowne Rd, West : 1 mi by A 3178 ✉ EX9 6AH – ✆ (01395) 444 337
– www.heathclose.com
5 rm ☕ – 🚹£ 85 🚹🚹£ 105 **Rest** – Carte £ 19/26
Smart detached house with a lovely rear patio and garden. Stylish, modern interior with an open-plan lounge and dining room. Good-sized bedrooms display personal touches; marble bathrooms have underfloor heating. Welcoming owners offer tea and cake on arrival. Traditional, home-cooked dinners Fri and Sat.

Long Range without rest
5 Vales Rd, by Raleigh Rd ✉ EX9 6HS – ✆ (01395) 443 321
– www.thelongrangehotel.co.uk – Restricted opening in winter
9 rm ☕ – 🚹£ 58/80 🚹🚹£ 96/125
Spotlessly kept guesthouse with a large garden, set on a quiet street. Choice of two lounges; one in a conservatory and complete with a small bar. Unfussy, brightly coloured bedrooms have good facilities; those to the rear can see the sea.

BUNBURY – **502** M24 – **pop. 1 308** – ✉ **Tarporley** **20** A3
London 183 mi – Birmingham 68 mi – Liverpool 39 mi – Sheffield 87 mi

Yew Tree Inn
Long Ln, Spurstow ✉ CW6 9RD – ✆ (01829) 260 274 – www.theyewtreebunbury.com
Rest – Carte £ 20/33
Handsome, part red brick, part black and white timbered pub with a central bar and several smaller, rustic rooms. Extensive menus offer local and homemade produce. Regular themed events; try guest ales accompanied by British tapas on a Friday.

BUNGAY – **Suffolk** – **504** Y26 – **pop. 4 895** Great Britain **15** D2
London 108 mi – Beccles 6 mi – Ipswich 38 mi
Norwich★★ - Cathedral★★, Castle Museum★, Market Place★, NW : 15 mi by B 1332 and A 146

Castle Inn with rm
35 Earsham St ✉ NR35 1AF – ✆ (01986) 892 283 – www.thecastleinn.net
– Closed 25 December and Monday in winter
4 rm ☕ – 🚹£ 65/75 🚹🚹£ 85/95 **Rest** – Menu £ 16 (lunch) – Carte £ 19/34
Sky-blue pub with open-plan dining area and intimate rear bar. Fresh, simple and seasonal country based cooking; the Innkeeper's platter of local produce is a perennial favourite. Tasty homemade cakes and cookies on display. Homely, comfortable bedrooms.

at Earsham **Southwest : 3 mi by A 144 and A 143** – ✉ **Bungay**

Earsham Park Farm without rest
Old Railway Rd, on A 143 ✉ NR35 2AQ – ✆ (01986) 892 180
– www.earsham-parkfarm.co.uk
4 rm ☕ – 🚹£ 52/65 🚹🚹£ 82/104
Appealing red-brick farmhouse on a working farm. Country-style interior displays sculptures and stencilling by the charming owner. Individually furnished bedrooms boast attractive furnishings. Extensive breakfasts include their own homemade bacon, sausages, preserves and muesli.

ENGLAND

BURCOMBE – Wiltshire – see Salisbury

BURFORD – Oxfordshire – 503 P28 – pop. 1 171 — 10 A2

London 76 mi – Birmingham 55 mi – Gloucester 32 mi – Oxford 20 mi
Sheep St, ✆(01993) 82 35 58, www.burfordcotswolds.co.uk
Burford Golf Club, ✆(01993) 82 25 83

Bay Tree

Sheep St ✉ OX18 4LW – ✆(01993) 822 791
– www.cotswold-inns-hotels.co.uk/baytree
21 rm – †£ 160/170 ††£ 180/190 – 3 suites **Rest** – Menu £ 17/33
Characterful, 16C, wisteria-clad house with low beamed ceilings and antique furnishings. Delightful bedrooms split between main house and adjacent cottage. Charming bar and lounges with vast stone fireplaces and a snack menu. Restaurant offers simple, modern dishes overlooking the beautiful landscaped garden.

Burford House

99 High St ✉ OX18 4QA – ✆(01993) 823 151 – www.burfordhouse.co.uk
– Closed 6-13 January
8 rm – †£ 160/180 ††£ 180/220
Rest *Centre Stage* – *(closed dinner Sunday-Tuesday) (light lunch/dinner)*
Menu £ 35
The welcome is warm at this delightful 17C house, where comfortable bedrooms – including three four-posters – mix traditional styling with contemporary touches. A pair of cosy sitting rooms lead to the restaurant, which is decorated with framed posters from famous musicals and serves simple, modern dishes.

XX Bull (N) with rm

105 High St ✉ OX18 4RG – ✆(01993) 823 226 – www.bullatburford.co.uk
13 rm – †£ 60/80 ††£ 75/170 **Rest** – Menu £ 22 (lunch) – Carte £ 26/41
Sympathetically refurbished, 15C former inn on the high street; run with a hefty dose of Gallic charm. Characterful, open-fired reception and rustic, exposed stone walls. Tasty French cooking errs towards the classics, so expect terrines, smoked meats, and game in season. Cosy, characterful bedrooms.

Lamb Inn with rm

Sheep St ✉ OX18 4LR – ✆(01993) 823 155
– www.cotswold-inns-hotels.co.uk/lamb
17 rm – †£ 150/170 ††£ 160/310 **Rest** – Menu £ 25/39
Delightful collection of 15C weavers' cottages with a gloriously cosy feel. The elegant, candlelit dining room offers a tasting menu and an à la carte of classic dishes; a simpler menu is served in the bar and sitting rooms. Chatty service. Charming, individually furnished bedrooms; Rosie has a private garden.

Highway Inn with rm

117 High St ✉ OX18 4RG – ✆(01993) 823 661 – www.thehighwayinn.co.uk
– Closed first 2 weeks January and 25-26 December
9 rm – †£ 85/110 ††£ 89/150 **Rest** – Carte £ 19/39
Characterful, personally run beamed inn dating from 1480. Simple, honest cooking of pub classics, with an emphasis on local produce; tasty nursery puddings. Classic, cosy bedrooms.

at Swinbrook East : 2.75 mi by A 40 – ✉ Burford

Swan Inn with rm

✉ OX18 4DY – ✆(01993) 823 339 – www.theswanswinbrook.co.uk
6 rm – †£ 65/80 ††£ 100/180 **Rest** – Carte £ 25/43
Wisteria-clad, honey-coloured pub on the riverbank boasting a lovely garden filled with fruit trees. Charming interior displays an open oak frame and exposed stone walls hung with old photos. Daily menu features the latest local produce and a modern take on older recipes. Well-appointed bedrooms have a luxurious feel.

BURLTON – Shropshire – ✉ Shrewsbury **18** B1

London 235 mi – Shrewsbury 10 mi – Wrexham 20 mi

Burlton Inn with rm

✉ SY4 5TB – ☎ (01939) 270 284 – www.burltoninn.com – Closed 25-26 December

6 rm – †£ 68/95 ††£ 68/95 **Rest** – Carte £ 18/41

Characterful, 18C whitewashed inn with a pleasant terrace, a colourful flower display and a pretty fountain. Keenly priced menus feature unfussy, classical cooking, with lighter snacks at lunch and more adventurous dishes in the evening. Neat, wood-furnished bedrooms; one has a four-poster bed.

BURNHAM MARKET – Norfolk – **504** W25 – **pop. 898** Great Britain **15** C1

London 128 mi – Cambridge 71 mi – Norwich 36 mi

Lambourne, Dropmore Rd, ☎ (01628) 66 67 55

Holkham Hall★★ **AC**, E : 3 mi by B 1155

Hoste

rest,

The Green ✉ PE31 8HD – ☎ (01328) 738 777 – www.hostearms.co.uk

45 rm – †£ 110/250 ††£ 130/270 – 1 suite

Rest – *(booking advisable)* Carte £ 22/42

Personally and passionately run extended 17C inn, set at the heart of a picturesque village. Smart beauty and wellness spa. Stylish, luxurious bedrooms are split between the main inn and Vine House, just across the green. Extensive restaurant comprises an appealing bar, five dining rooms and a courtyard garden; wide-ranging menu.

Railway Inn without rest

Creake Rd ✉ PE31 8HD – ☎ (01328) 738 777 – www.hostearms.co.uk

8 rm – †£ 65/130 ††£ 65/130

Stylish old station house, complete with a disused platform and a beautifully restored carriage – now a lovely bedroom. Modern lounge; meals are served at the Hoste Arms. Bedrooms have bold feature walls, retro fittings and good facilities.

BURNSALL – North Yorkshire – **502** O21 – **pop. 108** – ✉ Skipton **22** A2

London 223 mi – Bradford 26 mi – Leeds 29 mi

Devonshire Fell

✉ BD23 6BT – ☎ (01756) 729 000 – www.devonshirefell.co.uk

12 rm – †£ 94/184 ††£ 129/219 **Rest** – Carte £ 22/42

Stone-built hotel – once a 19C gentleman's club for mill owners – set in a lovely hillside location and decorated with bold colours and striking, contemporary artwork. Spacious, modern bedrooms have dale views. Modern British menu served in the formal conservatory and funky, open-plan bar and bistro.

Red Lion with rm

✉ BD23 6BU – ☎ (01756) 720 204 – www.redlion.co.uk

25 rm – †£ 60/80 ††£ 83/158 **Rest** – Carte £ 20/37

Appealing stone inn on the riverbank with cosy bar, laid-back lounge and formally dressed dining room. Extensive menus offer local meat/fish/game, pub favourites and daily specials. Classic bedrooms have modern overtones; the annexe rooms are more contemporary.

BURPHAM – West Sussex – **504** S30 – see Arundel

BURRINGTON – Devon – **503** I31 – **pop. 533** **2** C1

London 260 mi – Barnstaple 14 mi – Exeter 28 mi – Taunton 50 mi

Northcote Manor

rm,

Northwest : 2 mi on A 377 ✉ EX37 9LZ – ☎ (01769) 560 501 – www.northcotemanor.co.uk

23 rm – †£ 120/180 ††£ 170/280 – 7 suites

Rest – *(booking essential)* Menu £ 23

Creeper-clad hall in the Torr Valley, dating from 1716. Fine fabrics and antiques in elegant, individually styled rooms; attention to well-judged detail lends air of idyllic calm. Country house restaurant features eye-catching murals.

BURTON BRADSTOCK – Dorset – **503** L31 – see Bridport

ENGLAND

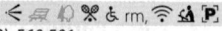

BURY - Greater Manchester - 502 N23 - pop. 60 718 20 B2

London 211 mi - Leeds 45 mi - Liverpool 35 mi - Manchester 9 mi
Market St, (0161) 253 51 11, www.visitbury.com
Greenmount, (01204) 88 37 12

Waggon

131 Bury and Rochdale Old Rd, Birtle, East : 2 mi on B 6222 BL9 6UE – (01706) 622 955 – www.thewaggonatbirtle.co.uk – Closed 2 weeks summer, first week January, Monday and Tuesday
Rest – *(dinner only and lunch Thursday, Friday and Sunday)* Menu £ 16 (lunch and early dinner) – Carte £ 22/40
Unassuming former pub on a busy main road; what matters here is the food, which is both well-cooked and well-priced. Classically based dishes change with the seasons; there's fresh fish daily, an excellent value market menu and popular themed gourmet nights. Young, chatty staff.

BURY ST EDMUNDS - Suffolk - 504 W27 - pop. 36 218 15 C2

Great Britain
London 79 mi - Cambridge 27 mi - Ipswich 26 mi - Norwich 41 mi
6 Angel Hill A, (01284) 76 46 67, www.visit-burystedmunds.co.uk
The Suffolk Golf and Spa Hotel, Fornham St Genevieve, (01284) 70 67 77
Town★ - Abbey and Cathedral★
Ickworth House★ **AC**, SW : 3 mi by A 143

ENGLAND

Angel

3 Angel Hill IP33 1LT – (01284) 714 000 – www.theangel.co.uk
79 rm – £ 90/180 £ 105/195 – 1 suite
Rest ***Eaterie*** – see restaurant listing
Behind the ivy-clad Georgian façade is a stylish, surprisingly contemporary hotel. Comfy lounge with open fire and leather sofas. Individually designed bedrooms; some offer classic four-poster luxury; others, funky wallpaper and iPod docks.

Ounce House without rest

Northgate St IP33 1HP – (01284) 761 779 – www.ouncehouse.co.uk
5 rm – £ 90/95 £ 130/140
Characterful, well-run hotel: two late 19C, red-brick houses knocked into one. Spacious, antique-furnished bedrooms; Barclay, overlooking the walled garden, is the best and those at the back are the quietest. Communal breakfasts.

Maison Bleue

30-31 Churchgate St IP33 1RG – (01284) 760 623 – www.maisonbleue.co.uk – Closed 3 weeks January, 2 weeks summer, Sunday and Monday
Rest – Menu £ 19/33 – Carte £ 33/52
Passionately run neighbourhood restaurant in a converted 17C house, with a smart blue canopy, a semi-open kitchen and sharp, modern décor featuring wood panelling and impressive fish sculptures. Menus focus on seafood; cooking is contemporary in style but with classic influences and Gallic and Asian touches.

Eaterie - Angel Hotel

3 Angel Hill IP33 1LT – (01284) 714 000 – www.theangel.co.uk
Rest – Menu £ 16 (lunch) – Carte dinner £ 24/43
Light and airy two-roomed bistro in attractive 15C coaching inn, where Dickens once stayed. Impressive modern chandelier; owner's collection of contemporary art. Tasty, modern European brasserie-style dishes use much local produce.

Pea Porridge

28-29 Cannon St IP33 1JR – (01284) 700 200 – www.peaporridge.co.uk – Closed 2 weeks summer, last week December, first week January, Sunday-Monday and lunch Tuesday
Rest – *(booking advisable)* Menu £ 17 (weekdays) – Carte £ 24/34
Charming restaurant in cosy 19C brick cottage – a former bakery – well run by husband and wife team. Tasty, seasonal, country-style cooking with a strong Mediterranean bias. Great value lunch menus. Biodynamic and organic old world wines. Efficient service.

at Ixworth Northeast : 7 mi by A 143 – ✉ Bury St Edmunds

XX **Theobalds**
68 High St ✉ IP31 2HJ – ☎ (01359) 231 707 – www.theobaldsrestaurant.co.uk – Closed 1 week early summer, Monday and dinner Sunday
Rest – *(dinner only and lunch Friday and Sunday)* Menu £ 22/30 – Carte £ 31/40
Part-16C cottage with a cosy, fire-lit lounge and a beamed dining room; run by a husband and wife team. Seasonal menus offer heart-warming, well-presented, traditional dishes with a roast for Sunday lunch. Professional service.

at Whepstead South : 4.5 mi by A 143 on B 1066

White Horse
Rede Rd ✉ IP29 4SS – ☎ (01284) 735 760 – www.whitehorsewhepstead.co.uk – Closed 1 week January, 25-26 December and Sunday dinner
Rest – Carte £ 22/30
Cheerfully run 17C village pub; choose between a characterful beamed room and the brighter Gallery with local artists' work. The kitchen's strength lies in the more conventional dishes.

at Horringer Southwest : 3 mi on A 143 – ✉ Bury St Edmunds

Ickworth
✉ IP29 5QE – ☎ (01284) 735 350 – www.ickworthhotel.co.uk
27 rm – †£ 141/220 ††£ 165/325 – 12 suites
Rest *Frederick's* – *(dinner only)* Menu £ 34 **s**
Rest *Conservatory* – Carte £ 18/41
Grand 200 year old mansion set in 1,800 acres: former home to the 7th Marquess of Bristol and now owned by the National Trust. The family-orientated hotel occupies the east wing and features huge, art-filled lounges, antique-furnished bedrooms and luxurious suites. Formal dining in Frederick's. Relaxed meals and high teas in the impressive former orangery.

BURYTHORPE – North Yorkshire – see Malton

BUSHEY – Hertfordshire – **504** S29 – **pop. 17 001** **12** A2

London 18 mi – Luton 21 mi – Watford 3 mi
18 Bushey Hall, Bushey Hall Drive, ☎ (01923) 22 22 53
9 Bushey G. & C.C., High St, ☎ (020) 8950 22 83

Plan : see Greater London (North-West) 1

XX **Alpine**
135 High Rd ✉ WD23 1JA – ☎ (020) 8950 2024 – www.thealpinerestaurant.co.uk – Closed 26-27 December, dinner 25 December and Monday BT**c**
Rest – Menu £ 16/24 – Carte £ 27/38
Long-standing family restaurant with low lighting, bold wallpaper and contemporary fabrics. Honest Italian menu displays influences from Sicily and Emilia-Romagna, ranging from family classics to more modern interpretations; homemade pasta.

BUTTERMERE – Cumbria – **502** K20 – **pop. 139** – ✉ Cockermouth **21** A2

London 306 mi – Carlisle 35 mi – Kendal 43 mi

Wood House
Northwest : 0.5 mi on B 5289 ✉ CA13 9XA – ☎ (017687) 70 208 – www.wdhse.co.uk – March-October
3 rm – †£ 60/70 ††£ 90/110 **Rest** – Menu £ 29 **s**
Charming part-16C house with Victorian additions and lovely gardens, in a wonderfully serene lakeside setting. Welcoming owners, stunning views and no TVs to disturb the peace! Classical lounge and cosy dining room with communal antique table, silver cutlery and cut crystal glassware.

ENGLAND

BUXTON – Derbyshire – 502 O24 – pop. 20 836 16 A1

London 172 mi – Derby 38 mi – Manchester 25 mi – Stoke-on-Trent 24 mi

Pavillion Gardens, St. John's Rd, (01298) 2 51 06, www.visitpeakdistrict.co.uk

The Crescent

Buxton and High Peak, Townend, (01298) 2 62 63

Buxton's Victorian without rest

3A Broad Walk SK17 6JE – (01298) 78 759 – www.buxtonvictorian.co.uk – Closed Christmas-New Year

4 rm – £ 50/60 £ 86/104

Charming townhouse built in 1860 by the Duke of Devonshire, overlooking the boating lake and bandstand in the Pavilion Gardens. Cosy lounge and breakfast room with a large dragon mural. Traditional bedrooms – one has a four-poster.

CALLINGTON – Cornwall – 503 H32 – pop. 4 048 2 C2

London 237 mi – Exeter 53 mi – Plymouth 15 mi – Truro 46 mi

Cadson Manor without rest

Southwest : 2.75 mi by A 390 PL17 7HW – (01579) 383 969 – www.cadsonmanor.co.uk – Closed Christmas

3 rm – £ 65 £ 96

Welcoming guesthouse on a 600 year old working farm, with views over an iron age settlement. Cosy, individually furnished bedrooms feature antiques, fresh flowers and a decanter of sherry. Rayburn-cooked breakfasts include weekly specials.

Langmans

3 Church St PL17 7RE – (01579) 384 933 – www.langmansrestaurant.co.uk – Closed Sunday-Wednesday

Rest – *(dinner only) (booking essential) (set menu only)* Menu £ 40

Quaint, double-fronted shop conversion run by husband and wife team. Pre-dinner drinks in lounge followed by 6 course tasting menu in formal rear dining room. Refined cooking with a good selection of Cornish cheeses.

CALLOW HILL – Worcestershire 19 C3

London 120 mi – Birmingham 26 mi – Coventry 35 mi – Wolverhampton 27 mi

Royal Forester with rm

DY14 9XW – (01299) 266 286 – www.royalforesterinn.co.uk

7 rm – £ 65/75 £ 79/99 **Rest** – Carte £ 22/40

Dating from 1411, with a rustic dining room, a relaxed atmosphere and a bright, contemporary bar with a grand piano. Regularly changing menu of simple, flavourful cooking. Fresh, modern, food-themed bedrooms; Aubergine, Pear and Cherry are the largest.

CALNE – Wiltshire – 503 O29 – pop. 13 789 4 C2

London 91 mi – Bristol 33 mi – Southampton 63 mi – Swindon 17 mi

Bowood House★ AC, (Library ★) SW : 2 mi by A 4 – Avebury★★ (The Stones★, Church★) E : 6 mi by A 4

Bowood

Derry Hill, West : 3 mi by A 4 on Derry Hill rd SN11 9PQ – (01249) 822 228 – www.bowood-hotel.co.uk

43 rm – £ 170/205 £ 185/220

Rest *Shelburne* – *(dinner only and Sunday lunch)* Carte £ 27/50

Rest *Clubhouse Brasserie* – Carte £ 21/38

Smart, professionally run, purpose-built hotel in grounds of Lord and Lady Lansdowne's Estate. Contemporary country house styling. Spacious bedrooms; some with balconies. Modern British cooking in formal Shelburne, with attractive terrace. Brasserie menu in golf clubhouse.

ENGLAND

at Compton Bassett Northeast : 4.5 mi by A 4

White Horse Inn with rm
SN11 8RG – (01249) 813 118 – www.whitehorse-comptonbassett.co.uk
– Closed 2-9 January, Sunday dinner and Monday
8 rm – £ 65/85 £ 85/105 **Rest** – Carte £ 21/39
Truly welcoming 18C pub. The cosy bar has a wood burning stove and jolly atmosphere and there's also a more formal dining room. All-encompassing menus offer everything from a croque monsieur to loin of venison from their own farm. Simple, well-priced bedrooms are set across the large garden.

CAMBER – East Sussex – **504** W31 – see Rye

CAMBRIDGE – Cambridgeshire – **504** U27 – **pop. 116 403** **14** B3
Great Britain
London 55 mi – Coventry 88 mi – Ipswich 54 mi – Kingston-upon-Hull 137 mi
Cambridge City Airport : (01223) 373765, E : 2 mi on A 1303 X
Paes Hill, (0871) 2 26 80 06, www.visitcambridge.org
Cambridge Menzies Hotel, Bar Hill, (01954) 78 00 98
Town★★★ – St John's College★★★ **AC** Y – King's College★★ (King's College Chapel★★★) Z The Backs★★ YZ – Fitzwilliam Museum★★ Z **M1** – Trinity College★★ Y – Clare College★ Z **B** – Kettle's Yard★ Y **M2** – Queen's College★ **AC** Z
Audley End★★, S : 13 mi on Trumpington Rd, A 1309, A 1301 and B 1383 – Imperial War Museum★, Duxford, S : 9 mi on M 11

Plan on next page

Hotel du Vin
15-19 Trumpington St CB2 1QA – (01223) 227 330 – www.hotelduvin.com
41 rm – £ 145/230 £ 295/430 Z**e**
Rest *Bistro* – Carte £ 25/43
Stylish hotel set over a row of 16C and 17C ex-university owned buildings. Original quarry tiled floors and wood-panelled walls feature, along with plenty of passages, nooks and crannies. Chic, modern bedrooms – one even has its own cinema. Clubby bar and an appealing brasserie with a Gallic-led menu.

Hotel Felix
Whitehouse Ln, Huntingdon Rd, Northwest : 1.5 mi by A 1307 CB3 0LX
– (01223) 277 977 – www.hotelfelix.co.uk
52 rm – £ 165/210 £ 200/320
Rest *Graffiti* – see restaurant listing
Set in 3 acres of gardens, a substantial Victorian mansion that was once a private house. Stylish, contemporary lounge and bar hung with modern art. Large, comfortable, boutique bedrooms with good mod cons; only four are in the main house.

Varsity H. & Spa
Thompson's Ln CB5 8AQ – (01223) 306 030 – www.thevarsityhotel.co.uk
48 rm – £ 165/325 £ 165/580 – 2 suites Y**x**
Rest *River Bar Steakhouse & Grill* – *(dinner only and Saturday-Sunday lunch)*
Carte £ 27/46 **s**
Boutique hotel on banks of the River Cam. Smart spa, stylish roof terrace and tranquil lounge with complimentary drinks. Bedrooms have designer bathrooms; some boast coffee machines, fresh orchids and balconies. Informal restaurant set over two floors with a view of the Cam and a menu of steak and fish.

Midsummer House (Daniel Clifford)
Midsummer Common CB4 1HA – (01223) 369 299 – www.midsummerhouse.co.uk
– Closed 2 weeks December, Tuesday lunch, Sunday and Monday Y**a**
Rest – Menu £ 40 (lunch)/95
In an idyllic location on Midsummer Common; the first floor bar overlooks the River Cam. Set 3, 4 or 5 course lunches and 6 or 10 course dinners: visually impressive, carefully crafted dishes use a range of modern techniques, and flavours are clear and pronounced. Service is formal and attentive.
→ Seared scallop, celeriac and truffle purée. Braised turbot with peanuts and hazelnuts. Pistachio soufflé and chocolate sorbet.

ENGLAND

CAMBRIDGE

Bridge St	Y	2
Coldham's Lane	X	5
Corn Exchange St	Z	6
Downing St	Z	7
Free School Lane	Z	12
Grafton Centre	Y	
Hobson St	Y	14
King's Parade	Z	15
Lion Yard Centre	Z	
Madingley Rd	X	16
Magdalene St	Y	17
Market Hill	YZ	18
Market St	Y	19
Milton Rd	Y	20
Newmarket Rd	Y	21
Northampton St	Y	22
Parker St	Z	23
Peas Hill	Z	25
Pembroke St	Z	26
Petty Cury	Z	27
Rose Crescent	Y	28
St Andrew's St	Z	30
St John's St	Y	31
Short St	Y	32
Sidney St	Y	34
Trinity St	Y	36
Trumpington Rd	Z	37
Wheeler St	Z	39

COLLEGES

Christ's	Y	A
Churchill	X	B
Clare	Z	B
Clare Hall	X	N
Corpus Christi	Z	G [1]
Darwin	Z	D
Downing	Z	E [1]
Emmanuel	Z	F
Fitzwilliam	X	G
Gonville and Caius	Y	G [2]
Hugues Hall	Z	K
Jesus	Y	K
King's	Z	
Lucy Cavendish	Y	O [1]
Magdalene	Y	N
Newnham	X	E [2]
New Hall	X	D
Pembroke	Z	N
Peterhouse	Z	O [2]
Queen's	Z	
Robinson	X	K
St Catharine's	Z	R
St Edmund's House	Y	U
St John's	Y	
Selwyn	X	F
Sidney Sussex	Y	P
Trinity	Y	
Trinity Hall	Y	V
Wolfson	X	U

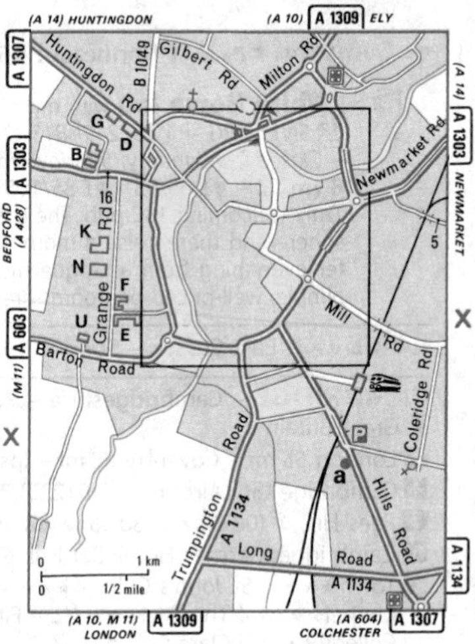

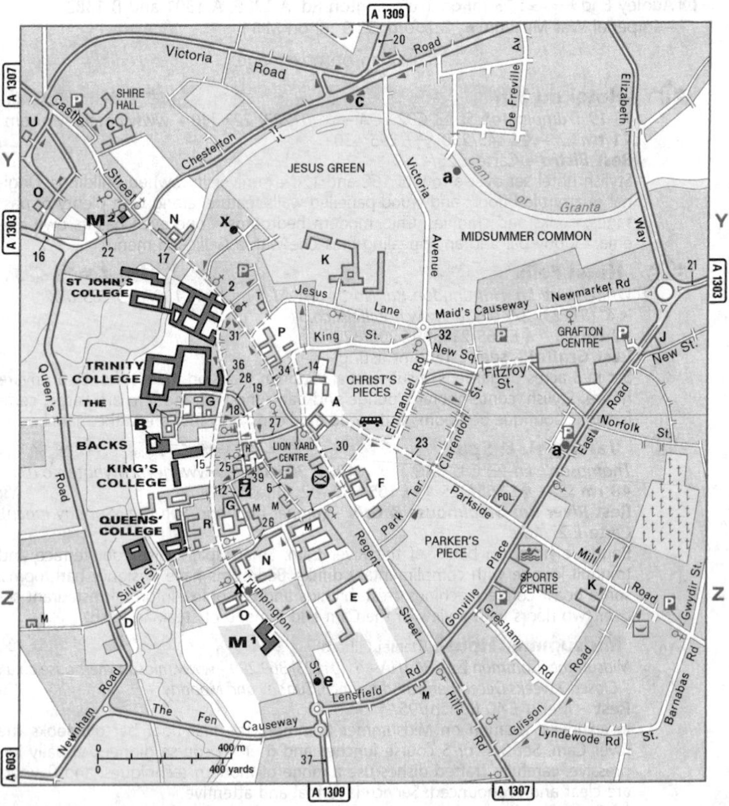

XXX **Alimentum** (Mark Poynton)
152-154 Hills Rd ✉ CB2 8PB – ✆ (01223) 413 000 – www.restaurantalimentum.co.uk – Closed 23-30 December, Sunday May-October and bank holidays Xa
Rest – Menu £ 25 (lunch and early dinner)/85
Sleek, stylish restaurant with a spacious cocktail bar and a striking red and black dining room with bold feature walls. Top quality ingredients are showcased in skilfully crafted dishes. Cooking is classically based, with clearly defined flavours and innovative modern touches. Good value early evening menu.
→ Ballotine of quail, broccoli, peanut and lime. Roast halibut, pumpkin seeds, squash and trompette mushrooms. Apricot and almond Battenberg with apricot sorbet.

XX **Restaurant 22**
22 Chesterton Rd ✉ CB4 3AX – ✆ (01223) 351 880 – www.restaurant22.co.uk – Closed 24 December-2 January, Sunday and Monday Yc
Rest – *(dinner only) (booking essential)* Menu £ 34
Converted Victorian townhouse with a formal dining room; its ten tables set with flowers and candles. Monthly changing, four course set menu of classically based, flavourful cooking. Cheese and fish courses cost extra.

XX **Graffiti** – Hotel Felix
Whitehouse Ln, Huntingdon Rd, Northwest : 1.5 mi by A 1307 ✉ CB3 0LX – ✆ (01223) 277 977 – www.hotelfelix.co.uk
Rest – Menu £ 19 (weekday lunch) – Carte £ 22/34
Dark wood furnished restaurant hung with contemporary art. Cosy fire for colder months and south facing terrace the perfect spot in summer. Interesting modern menu with Mediterranean twists.

ENGLAND

X **Cotto**
183 East Rd ✉ CB1 1BG – ✆ (01223) 302 010 – www.cottocambridge.co.uk – Closed August, 23 December-10 January, Sunday-Tuesday Za
Rest – *(dinner only) (booking essential)* Menu £ 50 **s**
Personally run, first floor restaurant with illuminated canvasses lining the walls. Weekly changing, fixed price menu; classic cooking showcases excellent ingredients. The chef-owner is a chocolatier by trade so the chocolates are a must!

X **Fitzbillies** N
51-52 Trumpington St ✉ CB2 1RG – ✆ (01223) 352 500 – www.fitzbillies.com – Closed dinner Sunday-Wednesday Zx
Rest – Carte £ 24/31
1922 cake shop famed for its Chelsea buns; saved from closure and transformed into a stylish, modern eatery which retains its dark wood, art deco façade. Concise weekly menu offers simple, flavourful dishes. Excellent baked goods.

at Histon North : 3 mi on B 1049 - X – ✉ Cambridge

XX **Phoenix**
20 The Green ✉ CB4 9JA – ✆ (01223) 233 766 – Closed 25-26 December
Rest – Menu £ 20/28 – Carte £ 20/79
Smart Chinese restaurant within an old red-brick pub and overlooking the duck pond on the village green. The vast menu offers Cantonese, Malaysian and Thai dishes, along with plenty of Peking and Sichuan specialities. Friendly service.

at Horningsea Northeast : 4 mi by A 1303 - X - and B 1047 on Horningsea rd – ✉ Cambridge

Crown and Punchbowl with rm
High St ✉ CB25 9JG – ✆ (01223) 860 643 – www.thecrownandpunchbowl.com – Closed 26 December-1 January, dinner Sunday and bank holiday Monday
5 rm – †£ 75/80 ††£ 90/100 **Rest** – Carte £ 25/42
Homely dining pub with beams, open fires and chunky wood tables. Choose from the seasonal à la carte, daily specials or popular 'sausage board'. Cooking is sophisticated and ranges from a traditional blade of beef to more modern fish terrine. Relax on the terrace then head for one of the simple bedrooms.

at Little Wilbraham East : 7.25 mi by A 1303 - X – ✉ Cambridge

Hole in the Wall
2 High St ✉ CB21 5JY – ✆ (01223) 812 282 – www.holeinthewallcambridge.com – Closed 2 weeks January, 1 week September-October, Sunday dinner and Monday
Rest – *(booking advisable)* Menu £ 14 (lunch) – Carte £ 23/33
Charming 16C pub with a cosy, fire-lit, beamed bar. The regularly changing, seasonal menu offers European flavours presented in a modern fashion; dishes are prepared with zeal by the young chefs, one of whom was a past MasterChef finalist. Excellent value lunch menu. Heart-warming, classical desserts.

at Madingley West : 4.5 mi by A 1303 - X – ✉ Cambridge

Three Horseshoes
High St ✉ CB23 8AB – ✆ (01954) 210 221 – www.threehorseshoesmadingley.com
Rest – *(booking advisable)* Carte £ 20/46
Appealing thatched pub with a lively bar and more formal conservatory restaurant. Choose from the interesting bar menu or daily à la carte, which feature attractive modern dishes such as truffled mac and cheese or smoked eel with green tea.

CAMPSEA ASH – Suffolk 15 D3
London 101 mi – Norwich 46 mi – Southend-on-Sea 76 mi – Ipswich 16 mi

Old Rectory
Station Rd ✉ IP13 0PU – ✆ (01728) 746 524 – www.theoldrectorysuffolk.com – Closed 25 December-2 January
7 rm – †£ 75/95 ††£ 95/150
Rest – *(dinner only Monday, Wenesday and Friday) (set menu only)* Menu £ 28
Former Georgian rectory with attractive gardens and stylish, contemporary bedrooms – each with its own theme. The drawing room features old Asian furnishings. Eat in the striking grey dining room in winter or in the conservatory in summer. Dinners are set and are served on Mondays, Wednesdays and Fridays.

CANTERBURY – Kent – 504 X30 – pop. 41 257 Great Britain 9 D2
London 59 mi – Brighton 76 mi – Dover 15 mi – Maidstone 28 mi
Buttermarket, ✆ (01227) 37 81 00, www.canterbury.co.uk
City★★★ - Cathedral★★★ Y - St Augustine's Abbey★★ **AC** YZ **K** – King's School★ Y – Mercery Lane★ Y **12** - Christ Church Gate★ Y **D** – Museum of Canterbury★ **AC** Y **M1** – St Martin's Church★ Y **N** – West Gate Towers★ **AC** Y **R**

Abode Canterbury
30-33 High St ✉ CT1 2RX – ✆ (01227) 766 266 – www.michaelcaines.com
72 rm – †£ 105/500 ††£ 105/500, £ 10 – 1 suite Y**a**
Rest *Michael Caines* – see restaurant listing
Centrally located former coaching inn; heavily beamed, yet with a stylish, boutique feel. Comfy champagne bar and atmospheric first floor lounge. Contemporary bedrooms come in 4 categories: 'Enviable' and 'Fabulous' are the most luxurious.

Magnolia House without rest
36 St Dunstan's Terr. ✉ CT2 8AX – ✆ (01227) 765 121 – www.magnoliahousecanterbury.co.uk – Closed 23-30 December Y**s**
6 rm – †£ 50/55 ††£ 95/125
Small, creamwashed Georgian house in a residential area close to town. The breakfast room overlooks a walled garden and the lounge is filled with local info. Neat, compact bedrooms have flat screen TVs, CD players and fridges.

Michael Caines – Abode Canterbury Hotel
High St ✉ CT1 2RX – ✆ (01227) 826 684 – www.michaelcaines.com – Closed Sunday dinner Y**a**
Rest – Menu £ 15 (lunch) – Carte £ 36/54
Spacious, modern restaurant divided in two by a smart, glass-walled wine cellar. Accomplished, contemporary cooking is stylishly presented, with classic combinations of ingredients interpreted in a modern fashion. Private chef's table.

ENGLAND

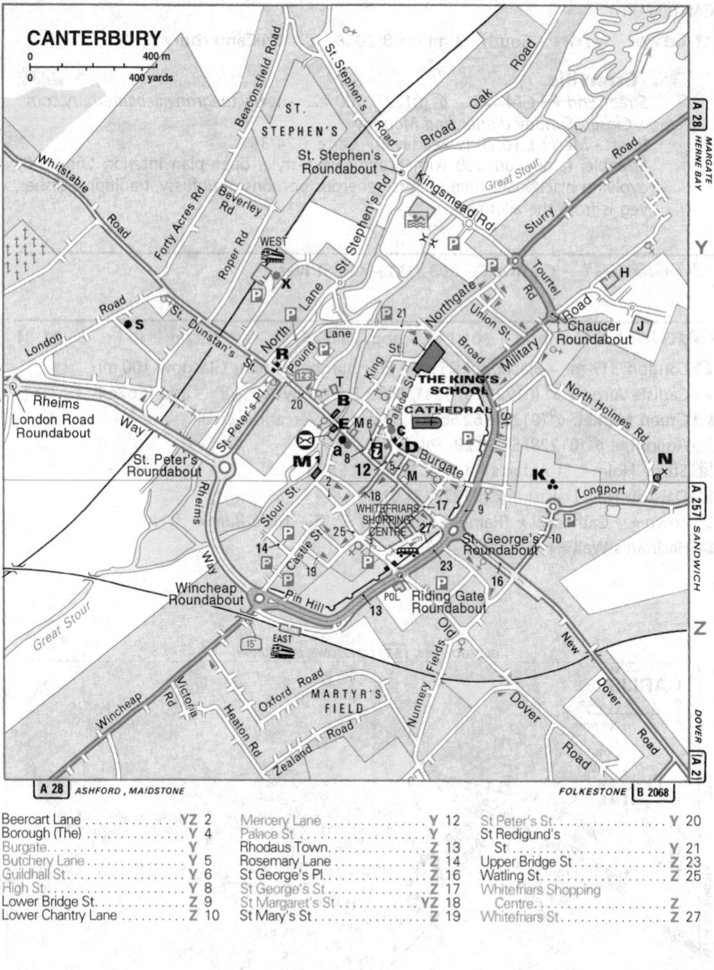

- Beercart Lane YZ 2
- Borough (The) Y 4
- Burgate Y
- Butchery Lane Y 5
- Guildhall St Y 6
- High St Y 8
- Lower Bridge St. Z 9
- Lower Chantry Lane Z 10
- Mercery Lane Y 12
- Palace St Y
- Rhodaus Town Z 13
- Rosemary Lane Z 14
- St George's Pl. Z 16
- St George's St Z 17
- St Margaret's St YZ 18
- St Mary's St Z 19
- St Peter's St Y 20
- St Redigund's St Y 21
- Upper Bridge St. Z 23
- Watling St. Z 25
- Whitefriars Shopping Centre Z
- Whitefriars St Z 27

XX Deesons (N)

25-27 Sun St ✉ CT1 2HX – ✆ (01227) 767 854 – www.deesonsrestaurant.co.uk – Closed 25-26 December Y**c**

Rest – Menu £ 15 (lunch) – Carte £ 28/40

Charming building close to the cathedral. Two period rooms with traditional wood furnishings and funky wallpaper. Traditional, hearty British menu; many ingredients such as the pork, salad, fruit and veg come from the owner's smallholding.

X Goods Shed

Station Rd West, St Dunstans ✉ CT2 8AN – ✆ (01227) 459 153 – www.thegoodsshed.net – Closed 25 December, 1 January, Sunday dinner and Monday Y**x**

Rest – Carte £ 22/43

Daily farmers' market and food hall in an early Victorian locomotive shed, selling an excellent variety of organic, free range and homemade produce. Hearty, rustic, daily changing dishes are served at scrubbed wooden tables.

ENGLAND

at Lower Hardres South : 3 mi on B 2068 - Z – ✉ Canterbury

Granville

Street End ✉ CT4 7AL – ✆ (01227) 700 402 – www.thegranvillecanterbury.com – Closed Sunday dinner and Monday

Rest – Menu £ 16/20 (weekdays) – Carte £ 24/35

Sizeable, family-run pub with Scandinavian-style, open-plan interior. Constantly evolving blackboard menu offers generous portions of unfussy, traditional dishes; veg is from the allotment.

CARBIS BAY – Cornwall – **503** D33 – see St Ives

CARLISLE – Cumbria – 501 L19 – pop. 71 773 ▌Great Britain — 21 B1

London 317 mi – Blackpool 95 mi – Edinburgh 101 mi – Glasgow 100 mi

Carlisle Airport ✆ (01228) 573641, NW : 5.5 mi by A 7 - BY - and B 6264

Green Market, ✆ (01228) 62 56 00, www.discovercarlisle.co.uk

Aglionby, ✆ (01228) 51 30 29

Stony Holme, St Aidan's Rd, ✆ (01228) 62 55 11

Dalston Hall, Dalston, ✆ (01228) 71 01 65

Town★ - Cathedral★ (Painted Ceiling★) AY **E** – Tithe Barn★ BY **A**

Hadrian's Wall★★, N : by A 7 AY

ENGLAND

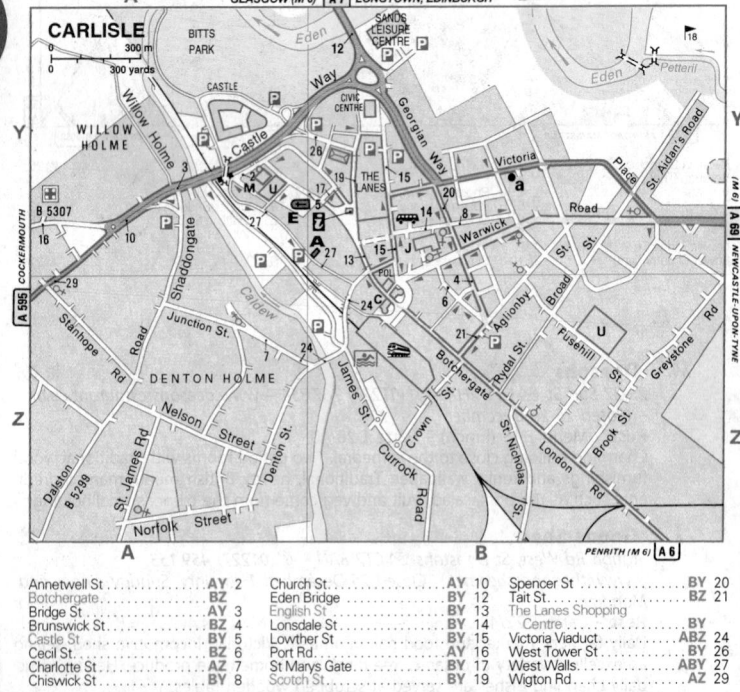

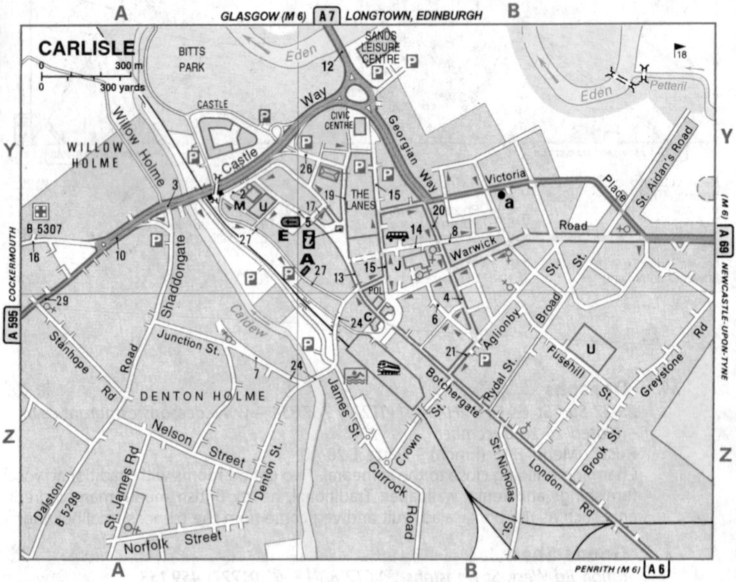

Number Thirty One without rest

31 Howard Pl ✉ CA1 1HR – ✆ (01228) 597 080 – www.number31.co.uk

4 rm – †£ 65 ††£ 85 BY**a**

Terraced Victorian townhouse with bay windows, a sumptuous lounge filled with memorabilia and a plant-strewn terrace. Smart period style throughout. Warm, welcoming bedrooms are comfortably and individually furnished; 'Ruby' is the best.

at Warwick-on-Eden East : 4.5 mi by A 69 - BY

Warwick Hall

Northeast : 0.25 mi on A 69 ✉ CA4 8PG – ✆ (01228) 561 546 – www.warwickhall.org

9 rm – †£ 98 ††£ 126/180 **Rest** – Menu £ 30

Impressive sandstone house in a commanding 270 acre riverside setting. Extremely spacious interior with a charming lobby, sweeping stone staircase and elegant drawing room. Sizeable, period-furnished bedrooms; suites have fires, kitchens and iPod docks. Communal dining from a traditional menu.

CARLYON BAY – Cornwall – 503 F33 – see St Austell

CARTHORPE – North Yorkshire 22 B1

London 228 mi – Leeds 49 mi – Middlesbrough 40 mi – York 34 mi

Fox and Hounds

✉ DL8 2LG – ✆ (01845) 567 433 – www.foxandhoundscarthorpe.co.uk – Closed first 2 weeks January, 25 December, and Monday

Rest – Menu £ 15 (weekdays) – Carte £ 21/42

Traditional country pub with an open-fired bar and a dining room filled with equine, farming and blacksmith paraphernalia. Good-sized menu offers unfussy, home-cooked dishes. Local, organic and homemade products are also for sale.

CARTMEL – Cumbria – 502 L21 – see Grange-over-Sands

CASTLE CARY – Somerset – 503 M30 – pop. 3 056 4 C2

London 127 mi – Bristol 28 mi – Wells 13 mi

at Lovington West : 4 mi by B 3152 and A 371 on B 3153 – ✉ Castle Cary

Pilgrims with rm

✉ BA7 7PT – ✆ (01963) 240 597 – www.thepilgrimsatlovington.co.uk – Closed first 2 weeks October, Sunday dinner, Monday and lunch Tuesday

5 rm – †£ 60/120 ††£ 60/120 **Rest** – Menu £ 22 – Carte £ 31/43

Cosy, hugely characterful restaurant with low-beamed ceilings, flagged floors and a roaring fire; run by a passionate husband and wife team. Well-prepared, classical dishes are made with quality local produce. Comfortable, contemporary bedrooms, luxurious bathrooms and substantial breakfasts.

CASTLE COMBE – Wiltshire – 503 N29 – pop. 347 – ✉ Chippenham 4 C2

London 110 mi – Bristol 23 mi – Chippenham 6 mi

Village★★

Manor House H. and Golf Club

✉ SN14 7HR – ✆ (01249) 782 206 – www.manorhouse.co.uk

41 rm – †£ 205/675 ††£ 205/675 – 7 suites

Rest *Bybrook* ❀ – see restaurant listing

Fine period manor house in 365 acres of formal gardens and parkland. The interior exudes immense charm and style, with characterful oak panelling and a host of open-fired lounges. Uniquely styled, luxurious bedrooms are split between the main house and mews cottages. Book ahead for one of the event days.

Castle Inn

✉ SN14 7HN – ✆ (01249) 783 030 – www.castle-inn.info – Closed 25 December

11 rm – †£ 70/165 ††£ 125/199

Rest – *(bar lunch)* Menu £ 27/33 – Carte £ 21/43

Delightful 12C former inn in a charming village, with two small, cosy lounges and a pubby dining room – where rustic features blend with contemporary touches. Menus range from old favourites to more sophisticated dishes. Bedrooms mix old beams with modern furnishings; some have four-posters.

XXX **Bybrook** – Manor House Hotel and Golf Club
✉ *SN14 7HR* – *℘ (01249) 782 206* – *www.manorhouse.co.uk*
Rest – *(closed Monday lunch)* Menu £ 30 (weekday lunch)/74
Spacious dining room within a charming 14C manor house, in 365 acres of formal gardens and parkland. Large, well-spaced tables are immaculately laid. Menus offer refined, carefully prepared dishes with a classical base and modern overtones, which use local and kitchen garden produce. Smooth service.
➜ Mackerel with celeriac remoulade, pink grapefruit and smoked eel beignet. Pork belly, cheek and fillet with apple purée and shallot mashed potatoes. Crème fraîche parfait, rhubarb granola and pistachios.

CASTLE DONINGTON – Leicestershire – 502 P25 – pop. 5 977 – ✉ Derby 16 B2

London 121 mi – Leeds 82 mi – Sheffield 52 mi – Manchester 96 mi
Nottingham East Midlands Airport : ℘ (0871) 919 9000, S : by B 6540 and A 453

Radisson Blu East Midlands Airport
Herald Way, Pegasus Business Pk, Southeast : 4 mi by A 453
✉ *DE74 2TZ* – *℘ (01509) 670 575* – *www.radissonblu.com*
218 rm – †£ 79/189 ††£ 79/189, £ 18 – 1 suite
Rest *Runway Brasserie* – *(bar lunch)* Carte £ 24/50
An ultra-modern airport hotel with admirable green credentials and a well-equipped gym. Good-sized bedrooms have feature walls, modern facilities and good soundproofing; some boast runway views. A European menu is served in light, airy restaurant; watch the planes taking off and landing while you dine.

CATEL/CASTEL – 503 P33 – see Channel Islands (Guernsey)

CAUNTON – Nottinghamshire – 502 R24 – see Newark-on-Trent

CERNE ABBAS – Dorset – 503 M31 4 C3

London 132 mi – Bristol - 60 mi – Cardiff 115 mi – Southampton 58 mi

New Inn with rm
14 Long St ✉ *DT2 7JF* – *℘ (01300) 341 274* – *www.thenewinncerneabbas.co.uk*
12 rm – †£ 75/145 ††£ 95/160 **Rest** – Carte £ 22/44
Sizeable 16C flint-faced pub set in picture postcard village, with exposed beams, a landscaped courtyard and a vast orchard garden. Freshly prepared, ably cooked dishes make good use of locally sourced produce. Bedrooms are stylish: some are in the main pub and others are in the converted stable block.

CHADDESLEY CORBETT – Worcestershire – 503 N26 18 B2

London 123 mi – Birmingham 26 mi – Leicester 62 mi – Coventry 35 mi

Brockencote Hall
on A 448 ✉ *DY10 4PY* – *℘ (01562) 777 876* – *www.brockencotehall.com*
21 rm – †£ 105/250 ††£ 135/325
Rest *Brockencote Hall* – see restaurant listing
Professionally run, 19C mansion with the feel of a French château; its long driveway leads past a lake and grazing cattle. Inside it's stylish and modern, with a contemporary country house style and bold colour schemes. Bedrooms are spacious and well-equipped and some have pleasant park views.

XXX **Brockencote Hall** – Brockencote Hall Hotel
on A 448 ✉ *DY10 4PY* – *℘ (01562) 777 876* – *www.brockencotehall.com*
Rest – Menu £ 23/43 **s**
Elegant restaurant in an impressive 19C mansion. Start with a drink in the smart conservatory bar, then in summer, head for the terrace. Contemporary purple armchairs are set at smartly laid tables and all overlook the gardens. Concise, daily changing set menus of modern dishes. Polite, formal service.

ENGLAND

CHADWICK END - West Midlands - 503 O26 19 C2

London 106 mi - Birmingham 13 mi - Leicester 40 mi - Stratford-upon-Avon 16 mi

Orange Tree

Warwick Rd, on A 4141 ✉ *B93 0BN* - ✆ *(01564) 785 364*
- www.lovelypubs.co.uk - Closed 25 December and Sunday dinner
Rest - *(booking advisable)* Carte £ 21/37
Impressively smart and well-run pub with 'ski chalet meets New England' styling. Plenty of choice on the menu, with sharing plates, globally influenced dishes and some adventurous combinations. Relaxed, friendly service.

CHAGFORD - Devon - 503 I31 - pop. 1 417 2 C2

London 218 mi - Exeter 17 mi - Plymouth 27 mi
Dartmoor National Park★★

Gidleigh Park

Northwest : 2 mi by Gidleigh Rd ✉ *TQ13 8HH* - ✆ *(01647) 432 367*
- www.gidleigh.com - Closed 5 to 17 January
23 rm - †£ 320/1170 ††£ 345/1195 - 1 suite
Rest *Gidleigh Park* ✿✿ - see restaurant listing
Impressive black & white timbered Arts and Crafts house with lovely mature gardens and Teign Valley views. Luxurious lounges and drawing rooms have a classical country house feel but a contemporary edge. Wonderfully comfortable bedrooms echo this and come in an appealing mix of styles. Superb service.

Gidleigh Park (Michael Caines) - Gidleigh Park Hotel

✿✿

Northwest : 2 mi by Gidleigh Rd ✉ *TQ13 8HH* - ✆ *(01647) 432 367*
- www.gidleigh.com - Closed 5 to 17 January
Rest - *(booking essential)* Menu £ 38/135
Formal, three-roomed restaurant in a beautifully restored Edwardian house in 100 acres of parkland. Classical French menus showcase top quality local produce and vegetables from the kitchen garden in skilfully prepared combinations; the tasting menu features Michael Caines' signature dishes. Superb wine list.
→ Warm salad of native lobster, cardamom, lime and mango vinaigrette. Lamb with boulangère potato and confit shoulder, fennel purée and a tapenade jus. Strawberry mousse, jelly and sorbet with sweet black olive and basil.

22 Mill Street with rm

22 Mill St ✉ *TQ13 8AW* - ✆ *(01647) 432 244 - www.22millst.com*
3 rm - †£ 60/80 ††£ 80/120 **Rest** - *(booking essential)* Menu £ 19
Smart, well-run restaurant in an attractive village in the heart of Dartmoor National Park. A small lounge leads through to the main room with its polished wood tables and leather chairs. Concise menus offer interesting modern dishes. Rustic bedrooms display contemporary touches.

at Sandypark Northeast : 2.25 mi on A 382 - ✉ Chagford

Mill End

on A 382 ✉ *TQ13 8JN* - ✆ *(01647) 432 282 - www.millendhotel.com - Closed 4-17 January*
15 rm - †£ 75/175 ††£ 80/210 - 1 suite
Rest - Menu £ 15 (lunch) - Carte £ 22/37
Whitewashed former mill off a quiet country road: once home to Frank Whittle, inventor of the jet engine. Comfy, cosy lounges with beams and open fires. Contemporary bedrooms have bold feature walls and colourful throws. Bright dining room offers classical dishes prepared using local produce.

Parford Well without rest

on Drewsteignton rd ✉ *TQ13 8JW* - ✆ *(01647) 433 353 - www.parfordwell.co.uk*
3 rm - †£ 55/100 ††£ 85/110
Well-kept guesthouse with superb mature gardens. Homely lounge with a woodburning stove, books and games. Two small breakfast rooms; one communal and one with a table for two. Individually decorated bedrooms offer pleasant country views.

at Easton Northeast : 1.5 mi on A 382 – ✉ Chagford

Easton Court without rest
Easton Cross ✉ TQ13 8JL – ☎ (01647) 433 469 – www.easton.co.uk
5 rm ☕ – 🚹£ 50/60 🚹🚹£ 70/85
Collection of old farm buildings, set back from the road. Homely lounge and breakfast room with a high beamed ceiling. Neat, individually styled bedrooms. The sun rises over the hills in the summer, so breakfast in the garden is a must.

CHANNEL ISLANDS – 503 L/M33

ALDERNEY – Alderney – 503 M33 – pop. 2 400

BRAYE – Alderney 5 B1

Braye Beach
✉ GY9 3XT – ☎ (01481) 824 300 – www.brayebeach.com
27 rm ☕ – 🚹£ 90/180 🚹🚹£ 100/220
Rest – Menu £ 25 (dinner) – Carte £ 25/56 **s**
Stylish hotel on Braye beach, just a stone's throw from the harbour. The vaulted basement houses two lounges and a 19-seater cinema; above is a modern bar with a delightful terrace. Bedrooms are beech-furnished, and some have balconies and bay views. The formal restaurant showcases local island seafood.

GUERNSEY – Guernsey – 503 L32 – pop. 58 867 5 A2

✈ Guernsey Airport ☎ (01481) 237766, Aurigny Air ☎ (01481) 822 886

⛴ from St Peter Port to France (St Malo) and Jersey (St Helier) (Condor Ferries Ltd) 2 weekly – from St Peter Port to France (Dielette) (Manche Iles Express) (summer only) (60 mn) – from St Peter Port to Herm (Herm Seaway) (25 mn) – from St Peter Port to Sark (Isle of Sark Shipping Co. Ltd) (45 mn) – from St Peter Port to Jersey (St Helier) (HD Ferries) (1hr) – from St Peter Port to Jersey (St Helier) (Condor Ferries Ltd) daily

⛴ from St Peter Port to France (St Malo) and Jersey (St Helier) (Condor Ferries Ltd) – from St Peter Port to Jersey (St Helier) and Weymouth (Condor Ferries Ltd)

ℹ North Esplanade, ☎ (01481) 72 35 52, www.visitguernsey.com

👁 Island★ - Pezeries Point★★ – Icart Point★★ – Côbo Bay★★ - St Martin's Point★★ – St Apolline's Chapel★ – Vale Castle★ – Fort Doyle★ - La Gran'mere du Chimquiere★ – Rocquaine Bay★ – Jerbourg Point★

CATEL/CASTEL – Guernsey 5 A2

Cobo Bay rest,
Cobo Coast Rd ✉ GY5 7HB – ☎ (01481) 257 102 – www.cobobayhotel.com – Closed January-February
34 rm ☕ – 🚹£ 49/99 🚹🚹£ 79/199 **Rest** – Carte £ 21/39
Modern hotel set on the peaceful side of the island and well run by the 3rd generation of the family. Bright, stylish bedrooms come with fresh fruit, irons, safes and bathrobes - some have large balconies overlooking the sandy bay. Smart dining room; sit on the spacious terrace for lovely sunset views.

FERMAIN BAY – Guernsey 5 A2

Fermain Valley rest,
Fermain Ln ✉ GY1 1ZZ – ☎ (01481) 235 666 – www.fermainvalley.com
43 rm ☕ – 🚹£ 85/210 🚹🚹£ 100/225
Rest *Valley* – see restaurant listing
Rest *Rock Garden* – *(dinner only) (booking essential)* Carte £ 30/37
Stylish, comfortable hotel with beautiful gardens, hidden in a picturesque valley and affording pleasant bay views through the trees. Well-equipped bedrooms are widely dispersed; the 'Gold' rooms have balconies. Colonial-style bar. Tapas, platters and sushi in Rock Garden; Mediterranean dishes in Valley.

XX **Valley** – Fermain Valley Hotel
Fermain Ln ✉ GY1 1ZZ – ✆ (01481) 235 666 – www.fermainvalley.com
Rest – Menu £ 19/25 **s** – Carte £ 26/35 **s**
Informal hotel restaurant with a beautiful multi-level terrace and lovely sea views; a great spot for breakfast or afternoon tea. Menus are classically based, with a fresh Mediterranean style and a modern edge; local seafood is a feature.

ST MARTIN – **Guernsey** – **pop. 6 267** **5** A2
St Peter Port 2 mi

Bella Luce
La Fosse ✉ GY4 6EB – ✆ (01481) 238 764 – www.bellalucehotel.com – Closed 2-16 January
23 rm – †£ 99/152 ††£ 99/220
Rest *Bella Luce* – Menu £ 21/23 – Carte £ 20/55
Originally a Norman manor house; now a hotel with a cosy beamed bar, a cellar-like lounge and a stylish, intimate interior featuring voluptuous velvets. Opulent bedrooms have modern bathrooms and the pleasant gardens come with a pool. The restaurant offers an eclectic array of modern dishes.

La Barbarie
Saints Bay ✉ GY4 6ES – ✆ (01481) 235 217 – www.labarbariehotel.com – March-October
31 rm – †£ 63/93 ††£ 80/151 – 1 suite
Rest – Menu £ 12 (weekday lunch)/25 – Carte £ 24/37
Attractive, stone-built former priory with an outdoor swimming pool and a cosy, cottagey style. Bedrooms are a mix of classical and modern styles; pay the extra for a spacious, newer room. Characterful bar and lounge with oak beams and an open fire. Traditional dining room features plenty of seafood dishes.

XX **Auberge**
Jerbourg Rd ✉ GY4 6BH – ✆ (01481) 238 485 – www.theauberge.gg – Closed 24 December-1 February and Sunday dinner
Rest – *(booking essential)* Menu £ 23 (weekdays) – Carte £ 26/38
Long-standing restaurant in a great location. Simple interior with a bar and well-spaced tables; concertina doors open onto a lovely terrace, which offers views across to the other islands. Classical menu features plenty of island seafood.

ST PETER PORT – **Guernsey** **5** A2
18 Rohais, St Pierre Park, ✆ (01481) 72 70 39
Town★★ - St Peter's Church★ Z – Hauteville House★ **AC** Z – Castle Cornet★ (≤★) **AC** Z
Saumarez Park★ (Guernsey Folk Museum★), W : 2 mi by road to Catel Z – Little Chapel★, SW : 2.25 mi by Mount Durand road Z

Plan on next page

Old Government House H. & Spa rm,
St Ann's Pl ✉ GY1 2NU – ✆ (01481) 724 921 – www.theoghhotel.com Y**a**
62 rm – †£ 173/245 ††£ 173/500 – 1 suite
Rest *The Curry Room at The Governors* – Menu £ 30
Rest *Brasserie* – ✆ (01481) 738 604 – Menu £ 20 (lunch) – Carte £ 32/49
Fine, classically furnished 18C building, with many of its original features restored, including a glorious ballroom. Individually styled bedrooms have padded walls, modern bathrooms and a personal touch. Relax in the well-equipped spa or outdoor pool. Authentic Indian cooking in The Curry Room. The smart yet informal brasserie has a delightful outside terrace.

Duke of Richmond rm,
Cambridge Pk. ✉ GY1 1UY – ✆ (01481) 726 221 – www.dukeofrichmond.com
75 rm – †£ 145/195 ††£ 145/350 – 1 suite Y**s**
Rest *Leopard* – Menu £ 16/20 **s** – Carte £ 26/45 **s**
Contemporary hotel with a bright, modern reception area and a stylish lounge ideal for afternoon tea. Smart, modern bedrooms; some with balconies. Relax in the secluded pool or on the patio overlooking the 19C Candie Gardens. A chic bar with leopard print furnishings leads to the restaurant and terrace.

ENGLAND

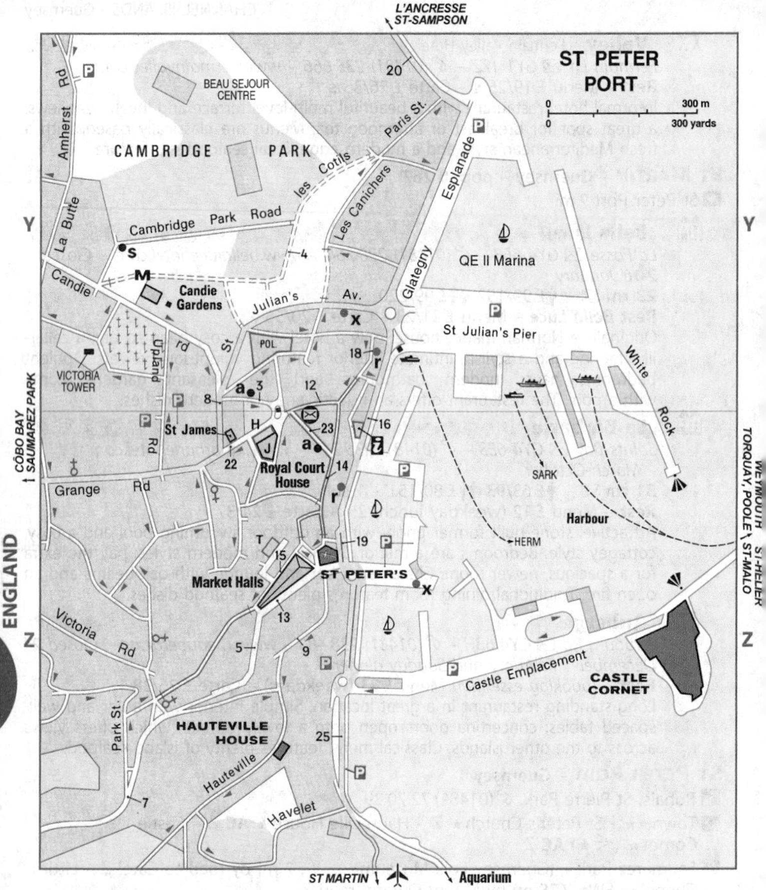

Ann's Place Y 3	Forest Lane Y 12	Quay (The) Z 19
Beauregard Lane Y 4	Fountain Street Z 13	St-George's Esplanade Y 20
Bordage Z 5	High Street Z 14	St-James Street Z 22
Charroterie Z 7	Market Street Z 15	Smith Street Z 23
College Street YZ 8	North Esplanade YZ 16	South Esplanade Z 25
Cornet Street Z 9	Pollet Y 18	

Duke of Normandie

Lefebvre St ✉ GY1 2JP – ✆ (01481) 721 431 – www.dukeofnormandie.com

37 rm ☕ – †£ 49/65 ††£ 100/150 Z**a**

Rest – *(dinner only)* Menu £ 17

Superbly located in the centre of town, with a small private car park and access to a nearby leisure club. Modern, designer bedrooms display bright colours and have a comfy, cosy feel; some are set in the courtyard. The large bar is decorated with maritime memorabilia; the brasserie offers an accessible menu.

Nautique

Quay Steps ✉ GY1 2LE – ✆ (01481) 721 714 – www.lenautiquerestaurant.co.uk – Closed Saturday lunch and Sunday Z**r**

Rest – Menu £ 19 (lunch) – Carte £ 30/52

Quayside former warehouse with a pleasant marina view and a characterful, nautically themed interior; ask for a window seat. Large menu of generously sized, classic dishes, with fish a feature.

Pier 17

Albert Pier ✉ GY1 1AD – ✆ (01481) 720 823 – www.pier17restaurant.com – Closed 25-26 December and Sunday Zx

Rest – Carte £ 24/36

Set at the end of a substantial stone pier in the centre of Guernsey harbour. The conservatory extension affords superb water views and the two terraces catch the last of the sun's rays. Tasty, traditionally based, seasonal dishes.

Red

61 Le Poulet ✉ GY1 1WL – ✆ (01481) 700 299 – www.red.gg – Closed 25 December, lunch Saturday and Sunday Yr

Rest – *(booking essential)* Menu £ 16 (lunch) – Carte £ 21/41

Harbourfront restaurant run by an experienced owner, with a large bar and formal cocktail lounge. Its name refers to red meat – with the large menu focusing on top quality Scottish chargrilled steaks – and red wines, which are a feature.

Swan Inn

St Julian's Ave ✉ GY1 1WA – ✆ (01481) 728 969 – Closed 25 December, Sunday in winter and bank holiday Mondays Yx

Rest – Carte £ 20/22

Smart Victorian pub with a bottle-green façade, a traditional bar complete with a coal fire and a formal first floor dining room. The same menu is served throughout, offering plenty of choice, with hearty main courses and nursery puddings.

ST SAVIOUR – Guernsey
5 A2

St Peter Port 4 mi

Farmhouse

Route des Bas Courtils ✉ GY7 9YF – ✆ (01481) 264 181 – www.thefarmhouse.gg

14 rm – †£ 125/295 ††£ 125/295 **Rest** – Menu £ 16 – Carte £ 26/52

Former farm restyled in a boutique vein. Stylish, sumptuous bedrooms come with hi-tech amenities and the bathrooms have heated floors. The pleasant garden features a pool, a terrace and a kitchen garden. Contemporary cooking has an international edge and uses the island's finest produce in eclectic ways.

KINGS MILLS – Guernsey
5 A2

Fleur du Jardin with rm

Grand Moulins ✉ GY5 7JT – ✆ (01481) 257 996 – www.fleurdujardin.com – Closed dinner 25 December and 1 January

11 rm – †£ 65/135 ††£ 92/185 – 1 suite **Rest** – Carte £ 20/33

Attractive inn with stylish terrace, lovely landscaped gardens and several charming, adjoining rustic rooms. Menu ranges from homemade burgers to sea bass and tasty island seafood specials. Stylish New England themed bedrooms; there's even a heated outdoor pool.

HERM – Herm – 503 M33
5 A2

to Guernsey (St Peter Port) (Herm Seaway) (20 mn)

Le Grand Monceau★

White House

✉ GY1 3HR – ✆ (01481) 750 075 – www.herm.com – April- September

40 rm (dinner included) – †£ 98/170 ††£ 190/300

Rest *Conservatory* – *(booking essential)* Menu £ 17/28 – Carte £ 43/48

Rest *Ship Inn* – *(booking advisable)* Carte £ 19/35

The only hotel on this tranquil, car-free island. Comfy, airy bedrooms are split between the house and various annexes; there are no clocks, TVs or radios. The open-fired lounge offers bay and island views; vast tropical gardens come with tennis courts and a pool. Traditional dining room offers plenty of seafood; popular pub-cum-brasserie serves more modern dishes.

ENGLAND

JERSEY – **C.I.** – **503** L33 – **pop. 85 150** 5 B2

🔼 States of Jersey Airport : 𝒞 (01534) 446 000

🚢 from St Helier to France (St Malo) (Condor Ferries Ltd) (summer only) – from St Helier to France (St Malo) (Condor Ferries Ltd) 3 weekly - from Gorey to France (Carteret) (Manche Iles Express) (summer only) (60mn) – from St Helier to Guernsey (St Peter Port) (Condor Ferries Ltd) (50 mn) – from St Helier to Guernsey (St Peter Port) (Condor Ferries Ltd) daily

🚢 from St Helier to France (St Malo) and Guernsey (St Peter Port) (Condor Ferries Ltd) – from St Helier to Sark (Condor Ferries Ltd) (50 mn) – from St Helier to Guernsey (St Peter Port) and Weymouth (Condor Ferries Ltd)

🗺 St Helier, 𝒞 (01534) 44 88 77, www.jersey.com

🔷 Island★★ - Jersey Zoo★★ **AC** – Jersey Museum★ - Eric Young Orchid Foundation★ – St Catherine's Bay★ (\leqslant★★) – Grosnez Point★ - Devil's Hole★ – St Matthews Church, Millbrook (glasswork★) – La Hougue Bie★ (Neolithic tomb★ **AC**) - Waterworks Valley - Hamptonne Country Life Museum★ – St Catherine's Bay★ (\leqslant★★) – Noirmont Point★

BEAUMONT – **Saint Peter** 5 B2

✗✗ **Mark Jordan at the Beach** \leqslant 🏠 **P**

😊 *La Plage, La Route de la Haule* ✉ *JE3 7YD* – 𝒞 *(01534) 780 180*
– www.markjordanatthebeach.com – Closed 1-21January
Rest – Menu £ 25/28 – Carte £ 26/57
Modern brasserie with a small lounge and bar; a paved terrace with bay views; and a dining room with heavy wood tables, modern seashore paintings and animal ornaments. Menus showcase island produce and fish from local waters. Cooking is refined but hearty, mixing tasty brasserie and restaurant style dishes.

GOREY – **Saint Martin** 5 B2

▶ St Helier 4 mi

🔷 Mont Orgueil Castle★ (\leqslant★★) **AC** – Jersey Pottery★

🏠 **Moorings** \leqslant 🏠 **AC** rest, 📶

Gorey Pier ✉ *JE3 6EW* – 𝒞 *(01534) 853 633* – *www.themooringshotel.com*
15 rm ⬜ – ✝£ 72/150 ✝✝£ 144/185
Rest *Walker's* – see restaurant listing
Rest *Walker's Bistro* – Carte £ 20/26
Keenly run hotel below the ramparts of Mont Orgueil castle, overlooking the harbour. Leather-furnished first floor lounge. Modern bedrooms in cream, brown and purple colour schemes; some have small balconies. Formal restaurant; casual bistro and terrace for comfort dishes and seafood specials.

✗✗ **Walker's** – Moorings Hotel **AC**

Gorey Pier ✉ *JE3 6EW* – 𝒞 *(01534) 853 633* – *www.themooringshotel.com*
Rest – Menu £ 15/23 – Carte £ 33/58
Formal hotel restaurant with a modern lounge, harbour views and local artwork on display. Good value menus offer well-prepared, unashamedly traditional dishes in tried-and-tested combinations and feature the odd personal twist.

✗✗ **Sumas** \leqslant 🏠 **AC**

Gorey Hill ✉ *JE3 6ET* – 𝒞 *(01534) 853 291* – *www.sumasrestaurant.com*
– Closed 23 December-20 January and Sunday dinner
Rest – *(booking essential)* Menu £ 18 (weekdays)/23 – Carte £ 26/48
Well-known restaurant in a yellow-washed house, with a small heated terrace affording lovely views over the harbour. Modern European dishes feature island produce. The monthly changing lunch and midweek dinner menus represent good value.

✗ **Crab Shack Gorey** \leqslant 🏠

La Route de la Cote ✉ *JE3 6DR* – 𝒞 *(01534) 850 830*
– www.jerseycrabshack.com – Closed 25-26 December and 1 January
Rest – *(booking advisable)* Carte £ 20/35
Laid-back, friendly restaurant with a decked terrace and superb views over the harbour. The pared-down, rustic interior is decorated with nautical memorabilia. Unfussy menus have a Mediterranean edge and focus on locally caught seafood.

ENGLAND

Bass and Lobster

Gorey Coast Rd ✉ JE3 6EU – ✆ (01534) 859 590 – www.bassandlobster.com – Closed Monday lunch and Sunday in summer and Monday dinner in winter

Rest – Menu £ 13/21 – Carte £ 27/40

Bright, modern 'foodhouse' close to the beach. Seasonal island produce; fresh, tasty seafood and shellfish dominate the menu. Fantastic oysters; good value lunches. Smooth, effective service.

GREEN ISLAND – Saint Clement 5 B2

Green Island

St Clement ✉ JE2 6LS – ✆ (01534) 857 787 – www.greenisland.je – Closed 23 December-3 January, Sunday dinner and Monday

Rest – *(booking essential)* Menu £ 17/22 – Carte £ 30/46

Friendly, personally run restaurant with a terrace and beachside kiosk; the southernmost restaurant in the British Isles. Mediterranean-influenced dishes and seafood specials showcase island produce. Flavours are bold and perfectly judged.

GROUVILLE – Grouville 5 B2

St Helier 3 mi

Café Poste

La Rue de la ville es Renauds ✉ JE3 9FY – ✆ (01534) 859 696 – www.cafeposte.co.uk – Closed 11-27 November, Monday and Tuesday

Rest – Menu £ 16/19 – Carte £ 30/42

Popular all-day restaurant – formerly a post office – with a vast array of curios, a wood burning stove and a French country kitchen feel. The eclectic Mediterranean menu is supplemented by daily specials and a good value set selection.

LA HAULE – Saint Peter 5 B2

La Haule Manor without rest

St Aubin's Bay ✉ JE3 8BS – ✆ (01534) 741 426 – www.lahaulemanor.com – Closed December-February

16 rm – †£ 75/130 ††£ 106/180

Attractive Georgian house overlooking the fort and bay, with a lovely terrace, a good-sized pool and neat lawned gardens. Stylish guest areas and spacious bedrooms mix modern and antique furnishings; those in the wing are the largest.

LA PULENTE – Saint Brelade 5 B2

St Helier 7 mi

18 Les Mielles G. & C.C., St Ouens Bay, ✆ (01534) 48 27 87

Atlantic

Le Mont de la Pulente, on B 35 ✉ JE3 8HE – ✆ (01534) 744 101 – www.theatlantichotel.com – Closed 3-31 January

50 rm – †£ 100/200 ††£ 150/300 – 1 suite

Rest *Ocean* ✿ – see restaurant listing

Stylish hotel with well-manicured grounds, set in a superb location overlooking St Ouen's Bay. Public areas are understated, with tiled floors, exposed brick, water features and a relaxed, intimate feel. Bedrooms are cool and fresh: some feature a patio; others, a balcony. Attentive, personable staff.

Ocean – Atlantic Hotel

✿

Le Mont de la Pulente, on B 35 ✉ JE3 8HE – ✆ (01534) 744 101 – www.theatlantichotel.com/dining – Closed 3-31 January

Rest – *(booking essential)* Menu £ 25/80

Elegant, well-run dining room with a fresh, understated feel, set in a stunning position overlooking St Ouen's Bay. Delicious, well-crafted dishes make use of fine ingredients from the island and display a real understanding of flavour. Smooth, professional service and a relaxed, friendly atmosphere.

→ Langoustine tails with oyster mayonnaise and Ebène caviar. Pot-roast squab pigeon, crispy leg, pear and blue cheese risotto and raisin purée. Pistachio and olive oil cake, sour cherries and crème fraîche sorbet.

ENGLAND

ROZEL BAY – Saint Martin 5 B2

St Helier 6 mi

Chateau La Chaire

Rozel Valley ✉ *JE3 6AJ – ✆ (01534) 863 354 – www.chateau-la-chaire.co.uk*

14 rm – †£ 95/180 ††£ 105/325 – 2 suites

Rest – Menu £ 18/22 – Carte £ 33/40

Attractive 19C house surrounded by peaceful gardens and mature woodland. Traditionally styled guest areas and more modern, well-equipped bedrooms: 2nd floor rooms are cosy; 1st floor rooms are larger and some have balconies. Formal restaurant with a conservatory and terrace offers classics with a twist.

ST AUBIN – Saint Brelade 5 B2

St Helier 4 mi

Somerville

rest,

Mont du Boulevard, South : 0.75 mi via harbour ✉ *JE3 8AD – ✆ (01534) 741 226 – www.dolanhotels.com*

59 rm – †£ 76/180 ††£ 95/245

Rest *Tides* – Menu £ 22/32 – Carte £ 31/44

Imposing 19C, yellow-washed hotel affording excellent views over the village and bay. Smart, modern guest areas and a well-kept garden with a pleasant poolside terrace. Bright bedrooms vary in shape and size; go for one with a view. Large restaurant offers classical menus and a great outlook.

Panorama without rest

La Rue du Crocquet ✉ *JE3 8BZ – ✆ (01534) 742 429 – www.panoramajersey.com – 20 April- mid October*

14 rm – †£ 52/130 ††£ 104/170

Immaculate hotel with Georgian origins, colourful gardens and stunning views over the fort and bay. Traditional throughout, from the guest areas to the bedrooms. Afternoon tea in the conservatory on arrival; 1,400 teapots are on display.

ST BRELADE'S BAY – Saint Brelade 5 B2

St Helier 6 mi

Fishermen's Chapel (frescoes★)

L'Horizon

rm, rest,

✉ *JE3 8EF – ✆ (01534) 743 101 – www.handpickedhotels.co.uk/lhorizon*

105 rm – †£ 105/155 ††£ 165/215 – 6 suites

Rest *Grill Room* – *(bar lunch Monday-Saturday)* Menu £ 34/48

Long-standing hotel located right on the beachfront and boasting stunning views over the bay. Luxurious interior with extensive guest areas and subtle modern styling. Choose a deluxe bedroom, as they come with balconies and sea views. Stylish, formal restaurant; modern British menus focus on local seafood.

St Brelade's Bay

La Route de la Baie ✉ *JE3 8EF – ✆ (01534) 746 141 – www.stbreladesbayhotel.com*

74 rm – †£ 93/145 ††£ 140/290 – 5 suites

Rest *Bay* – Menu £ 17/34 – Carte £ 28/42

Smart seafront hotel with charming tropical gardens and panoramic views across the bay. A modernised lounge and contemporary bedrooms fit well alongside original parquet floors and ornate plaster ceilings. Excellent health club. Formal restaurant offers impressive sea views and a classical menu.

Oyster Box

La Route de la Baie ✉ *JE3 8EF – ✆ (01534) 850 888 – www.oysterbox.co.uk – Closed 25-26 December, 1 January, dinner Sunday-Monday October-April and Monday lunch*

Rest – *(booking essential)* Carte £ 22/48

Glass-fronted eatery with pleasant heated terrace, set on the promenade and affording superb views over St Brelade's Bay. Stylish, airy interior hung with sail cloths and fishermen's floats. Laid-back, friendly service. Accessible seasonal menu features plenty of fish and shellfish; oysters are a speciality.

✗ Crab Shack St Brelade's Bay ≤ 🍽 AK

La Route de la Baie ⊠ JE3 8EF – ℰ (01534) 850 855 – www.jerseycrabshack.com
– Closed 25-26 December, 1 January and Monday dinner except bank holidays
Rest *– (booking advisable)* Carte £ 20/35
A scaled down version of next door Oyster Box, superbly sited on the beachfront; sit in a cosy booth or on a bench outside. Accessible modern dishes of prime island produce, with seafood a speciality. Relaxed, family-friendly atmosphere.

ST HELIER – Saint Helier 5 B2

🔳 Jersey Museum★ **AC** Z - Elizabeth Castle (≤★) **AC** Z - Fort Regent (≤★ **AC**) Z
🔳 St Peter's Valley - German Underground Hospital★ **AC**, NW : 4 mi by A 1, A 11 St Peter's Valley rd and C 112

Plan on next page

🏨 Grand Jersey ≤ 🔲 ⊛ 🏖 ⅙ 🛗 & rm, AK 🌑 🤍 🔊

The Esplanade ⊠ JE2 3QA – ℰ (01534) 722 301 – www.grandjersey.com
117 rm ☲ – ♦£ 79/125 ♦♦£ 99/240 – 6 suites **Yu**
Rest *Tassili* ❀ – see restaurant listing
Rest *Victoria's* – *(dinner only)* Menu £ 25 – Carte £ 20/40
Welcoming hotel with a large terrace, overlooking St Aubin's Bay. Stylish, modern interior with a chic champagne bar, well-equipped spa and corporate cinema. Contemporary bedrooms come in bold colours; some have balconies and sea views. Fine dining in sophisticated Tassili; brasserie menu in Victoria's.

🏨 Club Hotel & Spa 🔲 ⊛ 🏖 🛗 AK 🌑 🤍 🔊 P

Green St ⊠ JE2 4UH – ℰ (01534) 876 500 – www.theclubjersey.com – *Closed 24-30 December* **Ze**
46 rm ☲ – ♦£ 99/215 ♦♦£ 99/215 – 4 suites
Rest *Bohemia* ❀ – see restaurant listing
Modern hotel with stylish guest areas, an honesty bar and split-level café-cum-breakfast-room. Contemporary bedrooms have floor to ceiling windows and good facilities. Smart spa and a small outdoor pool with a wicker-furnished terrace.

🏨 Royal Yacht 🍽 🔲 ⊛ 🏖 ⅙ 🛗 & rm, AK 🌑 🤍 🔊

Weighbridge ⊠ JE2 3NF – ℰ (01534) 720 511 – www.theroyalyacht.com
111 rm ☲ – ♦£ 145 ♦♦£ 145/280 – 2 suites **Zb**
Rest *Sirocco* – *(dinner only and Sunday lunch)* Menu £ 28 – Carte £ 31/48
Rest *Grill* – *(closed 25 December)* Carte £ 18/30
The unusual combination of an old whitewashed building and a vast, modern extension. Spacious interior boasts a large bar, good conference facilities and a superb spa. Bedrooms are contemporary; the best have balconies and harbour views. Formal, first floor restaurant and terrace with a Mediterranean menu and lovely vistas. Steaks a speciality in the cosy, beamed grill.

🏠 Eulah Country House without rest ≤ 🚗 ⅃ 🏖 🤍 🔊 P

Mont Cochon, Northwest : 2 mi by A 1 on B 27 ⊠ JE2 3JA – ℰ (01534) 626 626
– www.eulah.co.uk – April-September
10 rm ☲ – ♦£ 105/185 ♦♦£ 150/230
Part-Edwardian house with sympathetic extensions, set in lovely mature gardens and overlooking the bay. Small pool and sun terrace. Comfy, classical lounge-cum-breakfast-room filled with antiques and ornaments. Spacious, luxurious bedrooms come with feature beds, modern facilities and superb bay views.

✗✗✗ Bohemia – Club Hotel & Spa & AK 🍽 🔲 ⅏ P

❀ *Green St* ⊠ JE2 4UH – ℰ (01534) 880 588 – www.bohemiajersey.com – *Closed 24-30 December* **Ze**
Rest *– (booking advisable)* Menu £ 25/59
Marble-fronted hotel restaurant with a chic bar and a stylish, candlelit dining room. The emphasis is on tasting menus, with pescatarian and vegetarian options available. Cooking is modern, vibrant and has a lightness of touch; original texture and flavour combinations feature. Charming, attentive service.
➔ Tuna and scallop sashimi salad. Ox cheek and cod. Treacle tart.

ENGLAND

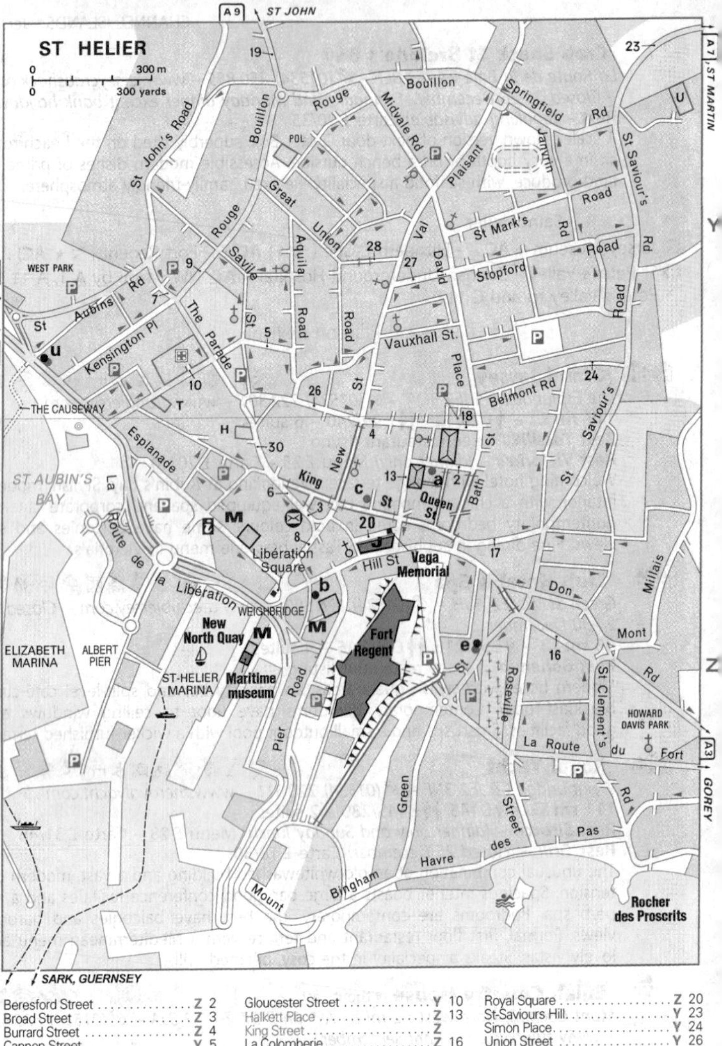

XXX **Tassili** – Grand Jersey Hotel A/C

The Esplanade ✉ JE4 8WD – ✆ (01534) 722 301 – www.grandjersey.com
– Closed 25 December, 1 January, Sunday and Monday Yu

Rest – *(dinner only and lunch Friday-Saturday) (booking essential)* Menu £ 25/67

Small hotel restaurant with an intimate atmosphere, vibrant artwork and a TV showing footage from the kitchen hotplate. Accomplished, innovative modern cooking uses local island produce in precisely executed, interesting and visually impressive combinations. Service is proud and knowledgeable.

➜ Lobster Caesar salad, avocado and shellfish jelly. Olive oil poached cod with chicken hash and 'leek and potato'. Pear pressing with calvados mousse, toffee ice-cream and crumble.

XX **Ormer by Shaun Rankin** N

7-11 Don St ✉ JE2 4TQ – ✆ (01534) 725 100 – www.ormerjersey.com – Closed 2 weeks Christmas-New Year and Sunday **Zo**
Rest – *(booking advisable)* Menu £ 24/30 – Carte £ 42/54
Named after a rare shellfish found in local waters and resembling a French bistro, with distressed blue woodwork, shuttered windows and a pavement terrace. The elegant interior is intimate yet buzzy. Cooking is unfussy, refined and assured, and uses only the very best seasonal island produce.
➜ Lobster ravioli with scallops, ginger, crab and tomato bisque. Lamb shoulder, goat's cheese and honeycomb. Rhubarb soufflé with mascarpone ice cream.

X **Banjo** N with rm

8 Beresford St ✉ JE2 4WN – ✆ (01534) 850 890 – www.banjojersey.com – Closed 25 December **Za**
4 rm – †£ 125/195 ††£ 125/195
Rest – Menu £ 22/25 (lunch) – Carte £ 25/53
Substantial former gentlemen's club with an ornate façade; the banjo belonging to the owners' great grandfather is displayed in a glass-fronted wine cellar. The appealing, wide-ranging menu features everything from brasserie classics to sushi. Stylish bedrooms have Nespresso machines and Bose sound systems.

ST SAVIOUR – Saint Saviour 5 B2

St Helier 1 mi

Longueville Manor

Longueville Rd, on A 3 ✉ JE2 7WF – ✆ (01534) 725 501 – www.longuevillemanor.com – Closed 2-17 January
28 rm – †£ 135/335 ††£ 175/570 – 2 suites
Rest *Longueville Manor* – see restaurant listing
Iconic 13C manor house, which is very personally and professionally run. Comfortable, country house guest areas have a modern edge. Bedrooms come in either classic or contemporary styles and all are well-equipped. Relax in the lovely pool, on the charming terrace or in the 6 acres of delightful gardens.

XXX **Longueville Manor** N – Longueville Manor Hotel

Longueville Rd, on A 3 ✉ JE2 7WF – ✆ (01534) 725 501 – www.longuevillemanor.com – Closed 2-17 January
Rest – *(booking advisable)* Menu £ 23/58 **s** – Carte £ 50/72
Set within a charming manor house; dine in the characterful 15C oak-panelled room, the brighter Garden Room or on the terrace. Daily menus champion island produce; seafood is a feature and many of the ingredients are foraged for or come from the impressive kitchen garden. Classical dishes have a modern edge.

SARK – Sark – 503 L33 5 A2

to Guernsey (St Peter Port) (Isle of Sark Shipping Co. Ltd) (summer only) (45 mn)
to Jersey (St Helier) (Condor Ferries Ltd) (50 mn)
Sark Tourism Visitor Centre, ✆ (01481) 83 23 45, www.sark.info
Island★★ - La Coupáe★★★ – Port du Moulin★★ - Creux Harbour★ – La Seigneurie★ **AC** – Pilcher Monument★ – Hog's Back★

Stocks

✉ GY10 1SD – ✆ (01481) 832 001 – www.stockshotel.com – Closed January-February
23 rm – †£ 210/310 ††£ 225/325 – 5 suites
Rest – Menu £ 15/35 **s** – Carte £ 37/59 **s**
Rest *Stocks Bistro* – Menu £ 25 – Carte £ 28/39
Set facing a wooded valley; a very personally run former farmhouse that's undergone a smart transformation. Immaculately kept, well-equipped, classical bedrooms. Small gym, arty island shop and fantastic wine cellar. Formal gardens have a split-level pool and jacuzzi. Eat in the panelled dining room, in the bistro or on the terrace; local island produce features.

ENGLAND

Aval du Creux

Harbour Hill ✉ *GY10 1SB – ✆ (01481) 832 832 – www.avalducreux.com – Closed 6 October-December*
26 rm ☕ – 🚹£ 99/129 🚹🚹£ 158/270
Rest *Aval du Creux* – see restaurant listing
Pretty hotel close to the harbour, with lovely gardens, a split-level swimming pool and a large terrace. Immaculately kept guest areas. Cosy, very comfortable bedrooms with bespoke furnishings, the latest mod cons and good extras.

Moinerie

✉ *GY10 1SF – ✆ (01481) 832 832 – www.lamoineriehotel.com*
14 rm ☕ – 🚹£ 85/115 🚹🚹£ 158/340
Rest *Moinerie* – ✆ (01481) 832 989 – Menu £ 35
Lovely hotel with a fantastic cobbled drive (the stones were brought in from France), and a cosy bar located in the former dower house. Elegant bedrooms feature fine soft furnishings; most are set around a courtyard and some are split-level. Eat in the large, baronial-style restaurant or delightful garden.

Petit Champ

✉ *GY10 1SF – ✆ (01481) 832 832 – www.hotelpetitchamp.com*
10 rm ☕ – 🚹£ 75/105 🚹🚹£ 145/226 **Rest** – *(dinner only)* Menu £ 35
Small, very remotely set hotel, with commanding views over the sea to the neighbouring islands. Homely interior with a snug lounge and comfy, cosy bedrooms. A truly peaceful place with no TVs or radios; relax in the large gardens or outdoor pool. The simple dining room offers a classically based menu.

ENGLAND

La Sablonnerie with rm

Little Sark ✉ *GY9 OSD – ✆ (01481) 832 061 – www.lasablonnerie.com – mid April-mid October*
22 rm ☕ – 🚹£ 50/98 🚹🚹£ 100/195 – 2 suites
Rest – *(booking essential)* Menu £ 29 – Carte £ 25/47
Charming, whitewashed 16C former farmhouse with beautiful gardens. Cosy, beamed interior with a comfortable lounge for aperitifs. Regularly changing, five course menu offers a classic style of cooking using produce from their own farm. Prompt service. Neat, tidy bedrooms; Room 14, in the former stables, is the best.

Aval du Creux – Aval du Creux Hotel

Harbour Hill ✉ *GY10 1SB – ✆ (01481) 832 936 – www.avalducreux.com – Closed 6 October-December*
Rest – Menu £ 35
Smart hotel restaurant with a large bar, a formal dining room and a delightful terrace that catches the sun all day. Light, fresh, seasonal cooking showcases island produce in unfussy, classical dishes; try the delicious lobsters.

CHANNEL TUNNEL – Kent – 504 X30 – see Folkestone

CHAPEL ROW – West Berkshire 10 B3

London 53 mi – Sheffield 172 mi – Kingston upon Hull 205 mi – Peterborough 119 mi

Bladebone Inn

✉ *RG7 6PD – ✆ (01189) 712 326 – www.thebladeboneinn.com*
Rest – Menu £ 15 (weekday lunch) – Carte £ 25/38
Named after the bone of a mammoth found on the riverbank. Snug, homely interior with open fires. Appealing menu ranges from 'posh' fish finger sandwiches to rabbit with white and black pudding; they grow over 50 herbs in the rough garden.

CHAPEL-EN-LE-FRITH – Derbyshire – 504 O24 – pop. 6 581 16 A1

London 175 mi – Sheffield 27 mi – Manchester 21 mi – Stoke-on-Trent 34 mi

High Croft without rest

Manchester Rd, West : 0.75 mi on B 5470 ✉ *SK23 9UH – ✆ (01298) 814 843 – www.highcroft-guesthouse.co.uk*
4 rm ☕ – 🚹£ 65/75 🚹🚹£ 80/105
Immaculately kept Edwardian house with countryside views; Arts and Crafts features include wood panelling and stained glass windows. Comfortable lounge, elegant breakfast room and period-furnished bedrooms; the Atholl suite is the best.

CHARLTON – West Sussex – 504 R31 7 C2

London 72 mi – Birmingham 165 mi – Leeds 258 mi – Sheffield 228 mi

Fox Goes Free with rm

✉ PO18 0HU – ✆ (01243) 811 461 – www.thefoxgoesfree.com

5 rm – †£ 65/175 ††£ 90/175

Rest – *(closed dinner 26 December)* Carte £ 26/32

Charming 17C flint pub with a superb garden and terrace and lovely outlook. Original features include exposed stone walls, low beamed ceilings and brick floors. Dishes range from simple pub classics to more substantial local offerings, some are to share. Clean, unfussy bedrooms; some with low beamed ceilings.

CHARMOUTH – Dorset – 503 L31 – pop. 1 497 – ✉ Bridport 3 B3

London 157 mi – Dorchester 22 mi – Exeter 31 mi – Taunton 27 mi

White House

2 Hillside, The Street ✉ DT6 6PJ – ✆ (01297) 560 411 – www.whitehousehotel.com – Restricted opening in winter

4 rm – †£ 100/150 ††£ 150/170 **Rest** – *(dinner only)* Carte £ 26/43

Charming Regency house; personally run by a friendly couple. Spacious, comfy bedrooms retain some period features – one has a cast iron bed – and all have modern bathrooms, fresh flowers, iPod docks and seasonal fruit. The wood-furnished dining room offers concise modern menus of local produce.

Abbots House without rest

The Street ✉ DT6 6QF – ✆ (01297) 560 339 – www.abbotshouse.co.uk – Closed last 2 weeks December and January

3 rm – †£ 110/130 ††£ 120/140

Dating back to 1480 – originally an annexe of Forde Abbey. Cosy beamed, panelled lounge; conservatory breakfast room overlooks well-tended gardens and a working model railway. Spacious, stylish bedrooms offer homemade treats and a memento.

CHATHILL – Northumberland – see Alnwick

CHATTON – Northumberland – 502 O17 – pop. 438 24 A1

London 336 mi – Sunderland 63 mi – Newcastle upon Tyne 52 mi – South Shields 57 mi

Chatton Park House without rest

East : 1 mi on B 6348 ✉ NE66 5RA – ✆ (01688) 215 507 – www.chattonpark.com – Closed 23 December-1 February

8 rm – †£ 100/140 ††£ 110/190

Fine 1750s house set in 6 acres of formal gardens and mature grounds. Smart parquet-floored hallway and huge, open-fired sitting room. Spacious bedrooms blend modern décor with original features. Excellent breakfasts use local produce.

CHELMSFORD – Essex – 504 V28 – pop. 99 962 13 C2

London 33 mi – Cambridge 46 mi – Ipswich 40 mi – Southend-on-Sea 19 mi

Unit 3, Dukes Walk, Duke St, ✆ (01245) 28 34 00, www.chelmsford.gov.uk

at Boreham Northeast : 3.5 mi on B 1137 (Springfield Rd)

Lion Inn

rm,

Main Rd ✉ CM3 3JA – ✆ (01245) 394 900 – www.lioninnhotel.co.uk – Closed 26 and 31 December

15 rm – †£ 105/160 ††£ 105/160

Rest – *(bookings not accepted)* Carte £ 19/32

Keenly run, extended former pub with eco-friendly credentials and a French feel. Soundproofed bedrooms blend contemporary fabrics with reproduction furniture. Large open-plan lounge/brasserie with buzzy atmosphere; short menu of appealing, pub-style dishes.

ENGLAND

CHELTENHAM – Gloucestershire – 503 N28 – pop. 106 246 Great Britain 4 C1

London 99 mi – Birmingham 48 mi – Bristol 40 mi – Gloucester 9 mi
77 Promenade, (01242) 52 28 78, www.visitcheltenham.com
Cleeve Hill, (01242) 67 20 25
Cotswold Hills, Ullenwood, (01242) 51 52 64
Town★
Sudeley Castle★ (Paintings★) **AC**, NE : 7 mi by B 4632 A

Ellenborough Park

Southam, Northeast : 2.75 mi on B 4632 ✉ GL52 3NH – (01242) 545 454 – www.ellenboroughpark.com AX**a**
60 rm – †£ 230/875 ††£ 230/875
Rest *Beaufort* Rest *Tudor Club Brasserie* – see restaurant listing
Part-16C, part-timbered manor house, with stone conversions, an understated Indian-themed spa and large grounds stretching down to the racecourse. Beautifully furnished guest areas have an elegant, classical style. Nina Campbell designed bedrooms boast superb bathrooms, the latest mod cons and plenty of extras. Excellent levels of service from a smartly attired team.

Hotel du Vin

Parabola Rd ✉ GL50 3AQ – (01242) 588 450 – www.hotelduvin.com
51 rm – †£ 115/185 ††£ 155/595 – 2 suites BY**c**
Rest *Bistro* – Carte £ 27/78
Attractive Regency house in an affluent residential area next to the Ladies College. Shabby-chic styling with leather-furnished bar and comfy lounge. Individually designed, well-equipped, wine-themed bedrooms; some with baths in the room. French bistro features an eye-catching wine glass chandelier.

Montpellier Chapter

Bayshill Rd ✉ GL50 3AS – (01242) 527 788 – www.themontpellierchapterhotel.com BX**r**
61 rm – †£ 110/300 ††£ 110/400, £ 10
Rest – *(bookings advisable at dinner)* Menu £ 15 (lunch) – Carte £ 21/41
Extended Regency townhouse with retro lounges and large conservatory. Light wood furnished bedrooms come with Nespresso machines, complimentary mini bars and in-room info on an iPod touch. Dine on British dishes at marble-topped tables or on one of two terraces.

Beaumont House without rest

56 Shurdington Rd ✉ GL53 0JE – (01242) 223 311 – www.bhhotel.co.uk AX**u**
16 rm – †£ 69/190 ††£ 89/264
Keenly run Victorian house with comfy drawing room and bar; breakfast room overlooks lawned garden. Refurbished bedrooms are stylish and contemporary with excellent bathrooms.

Lypiatt House without rest

Lypiatt Rd ✉ GL50 2QW – (01242) 224 994 – www.staylypiatt.co.uk
10 rm – †£ 70/95 ††£ 90/130 BZ**c**
A privately owned, serene Victorian house with friendly service. Bedrooms on the top floor with dormer roof tend to be smaller than those on the other floors. Soft, pale colours.

Butlers without rest

Western Rd ✉ GL50 3RN – (01242) 570 771 – www.butlers-hotel.co.uk – Closed Christmas BY**v**
9 rm – †£ 60/85 ††£ 85/110
Personally managed hotel where bedrooms constitute a peaceful haven with stylish drapes and canopies. Rooms named after famous butlers; some overlook wooded garden to rear.

Hanover House without rest

65 St George's Rd ✉ GL50 3DU – (01242) 541 297 – www.hanoverhouse.org – Closed Christmas-New Year and Easter BY**u**
3 rm – †£ 70/80 ††£ 100/110
Early Victorian townhouse, perfectly located for seeing the city. Comfortable family lounge filled with books and portraits; spacious, tastefully furnished bedrooms. Organic breakfasts.

CHELTENHAM

Street	Grid	No.
Berkeley St	CYZ	4
Clarence St	CY	6
Crescent Terrace	BY	7
Deep St	AX	9
Dunalley St	CY	10
Henrietta St	CY	13
High St	BCY	
High St PRESTBURY	AX	14
Keynsham Rd	CZ	15
Knapp Rd	BY	16
Montpellier Ave	BZ	17
Montpellier Walk	BZ	18
North St	CY	20
Norwood Rd	BZ	21
Oriel Rd	CZ	22
Pittville St	CY	26
Portland St	CY	27
Promenade (The)	BZCY	28
Regent Arcade Shopping Centre	CY	
Regent St	CY	29
Rodney Rd	CY	30
Royal Well Rd	BCY	32
St James St	CY	33
St Johns Ave	CY	34
St Margaret's Rd	CY	35
Sandford Mill Rd	CZ	36
Sandford Terrace	CZ	37
Winchcombe St	CY	38

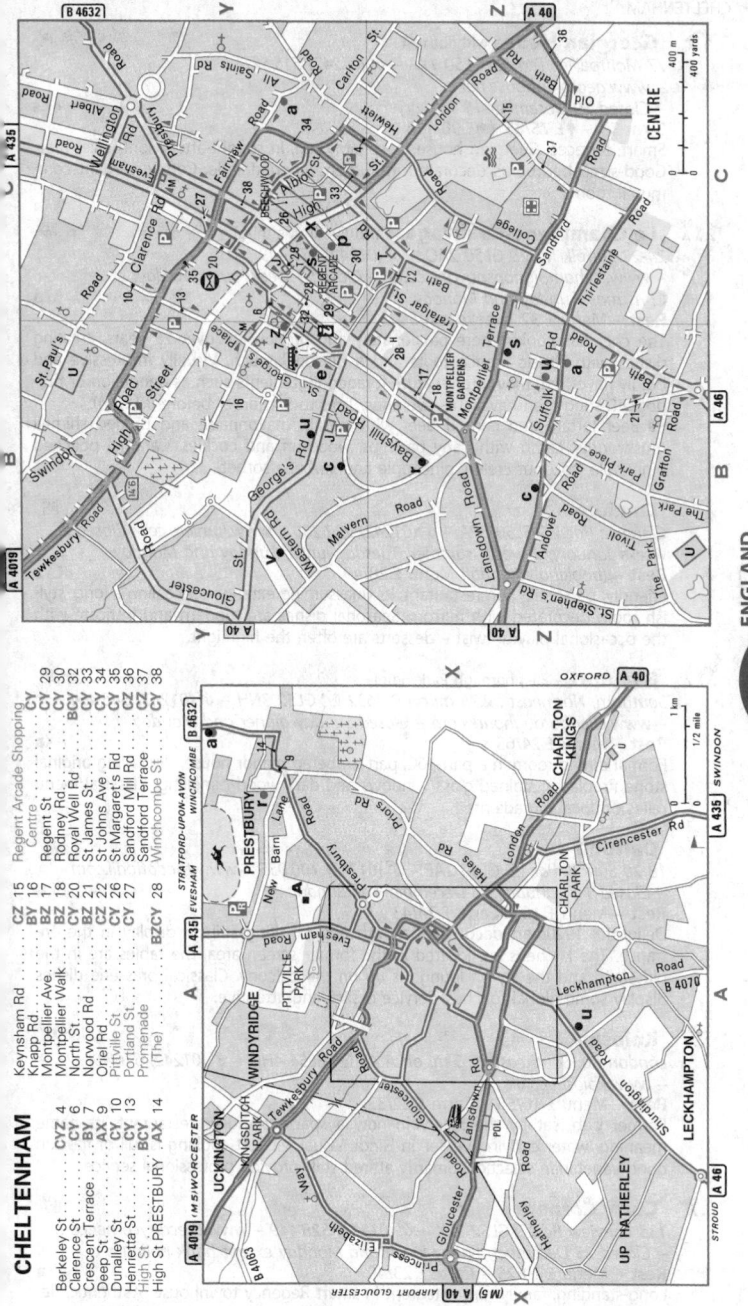

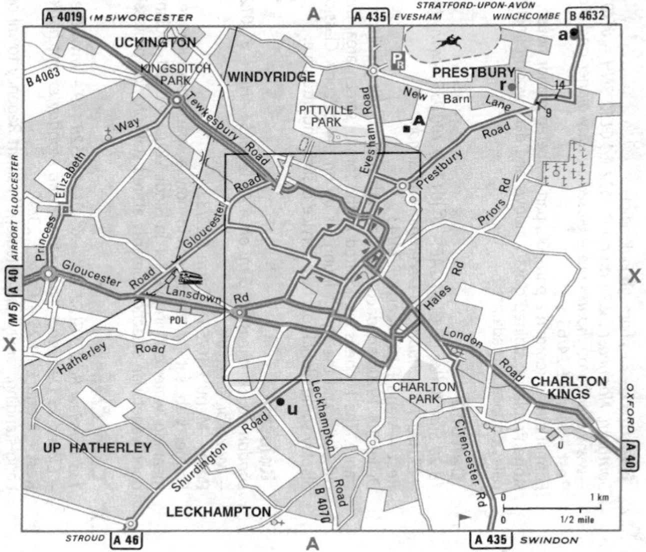

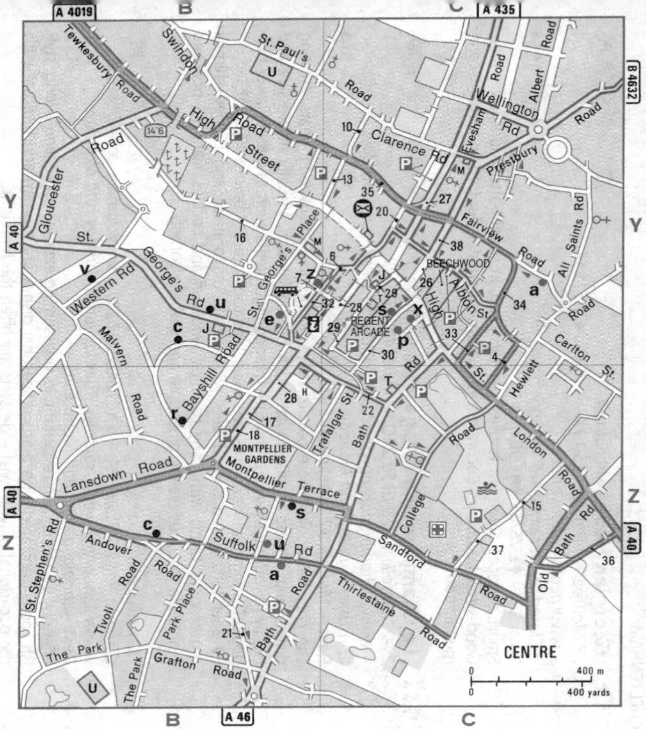

Georgian House without rest

77 Montpellier Terr ✉ GL50 1XA – ✆ (01242) 515 577 – www.georgianhouse.net – Closed 19 December-15 January BZ**s**

3 rm – ♦£ 75/85 ♦♦£ 90/115

Smart, terraced Georgian house, hospitably run, in sought-after Montpellier area. Good-sized bedrooms decorated in authentic period style. Comfy, elegant communal rooms.

Le Champignon Sauvage (David Everitt-Matthias)

24-28 Suffolk Rd ✉ GL50 2AQ – ✆ (01242) 573 449 – www.lechampignonsauvage.co.uk – Closed 3 weeks June, 10 days Christmas, Sunday and Monday BZ**a**

Rest – Menu £ 32 (weekdays)/59

The chef has cooked here passionately and proudly for over 25 years, creating dishes with classic French roots and a personal touch. Visually impressive and boldly flavoured, they often feature foraged ingredients such as dandelion or burdock. Tasting menu available evenings, Tues to Sat (order before 8.15pm).

→ Beef tartare and corned beef with wasabi mayonnaise and pickled shimeji mushrooms. Lamb with baby parsnips, woodruff and cockles. Caramel poached pineapple, coconut cream, pineapple and verbena sorbet.

Lumière

Clarence Par ✉ GL50 3PA – ✆ (01242) 222 200 – www.lumiere.cc – Closed 2 weeks January, 2 weeks summer, Tuesday lunch, Sunday and Monday

Rest – *(booking essential)* Menu £ 28/49 BCY**z**

Friendly, personally run restaurant; its unassuming exterior concealing a long, stylish room decorated with mirrors. Seasonal dishes are modern and intricate with the occasional playful twist – desserts are often the highlight.

Beaufort – Ellenborough Park Hotel

Southam, Northeast : 2.75 mi on B 4632 ✉ GL52 3NH – ✆ (01242) 545 454 – www.ellenboroughpark.com – Closed Sunday dinner and Monday

Rest – Menu £ 24/65 **s** AX**a**

Formal dining room in a part-16C, part-timbered manor house, displaying original stone fireplaces, stained glass windows and dark wood panelling. Classical menu relies on local ingredients.

Daffodil

18-20 Suffolk Par ✉ GL50 2AE – ✆ (01242) 700 055 – www.thedaffodil.com – Closed 1-7 January, 26 December and Sunday BZ**u**

Rest – Menu £ 16 – Carte £ 24/43

Delightful 1920s art deco cinema, with original tiling still on display in the entrance. The kitchens are located in the former screen area, the tables are in the old stalls, and the stylish lounge is up on the balcony. Classical brasserie dishes display some global touches. Service is slick and attentive.

Koloshi (N)

London Rd, Southeast : 2.5 mi on A 40 ✉ GL54 4HG – ✆ (01242) 516 400 – www.koloshi.co.uk

Rest – Menu £ 10/55 – Carte £ 22/33

Former pub, set by the reservoir; now a spacious Indian restaurant, its name meaning 'water carrying vessel' in Hindi. Visual, vibrant cooking is full of flavour; good vegetarian selection. Smartly attired staff provide professional service.

Curry Corner

133 Fairview Rd ✉ GL52 2EX – ✆ (01242) 528 449 – www.thecurrycorner.com – Closed 25 December, Friday lunch and Monday except bank holidays

Rest – Menu £ 10/25 – Carte £ 23/40 CY**a**

Long-standing, family run restaurant in smart Regency townhouse. Authentic, flavoursome dishes from across India, Persia and Bangladesh. Imported spices are ground and roasted every morning.

ENGLAND

Tudor Club Brasserie - Ellenborough Park Hotel

Southam, Northeast : 2.75 mi on B 4632 ✉ GL52 3NH – ✆ (01242) 545 454 – www.ellenboroughpark.com AX**a**

Rest – Carte £ 25/41 **s**

Informal brasserie with low timbered ceiling and wood-clad walls, set within a part-16C, part-timbered manor house. Décor incorporates a sports and 'Cresta Run' theme. Classic brasserie dishes.

Purslane

16 Rodney Rd ✉ GL50 1JJ – ✆ (01242) 321 639 – www.purslane-restaurant.co.uk – Closed 19 January-3 February, 3-18 August, Sunday and Monday

Rest – Menu £ 30 CY**p**

A simple neighbourhood restaurant with a minimalistic feel. Fresh fish and seafood from Scotland and Cornwall are combined with good quality, locally sourced ingredients to produce interesting, modern dishes. Relaxed, efficient service.

Bistrot Coco

30 Cambray Pl ✉ GL50 1JP – ✆ (01242) 534 000 – www.bistrotcoco.co.uk

Rest – Menu £ 15 – Carte £ 21/36 CY**x**

Lovingly refurbished, rustic bistro hidden in the cellars of a terraced Regency house. French oak counter and handmade Parisian-scene ceiling paper in the bar. Cosy, flag-floored dining rooms lead to a heated terrace. Classic bistro menu.

The Tavern

5 Royal Well Pl ✉ GL50 3DN – ✆ (01242) 221 212 – www.thetaverncheltenham.com – Closed 25-27 December BY**e**

Rest – Menu £ 10 (weekday lunch) – Carte £ 13/40

Rustic, all-day eatery with a strong American theme, split over two floors and featuring large tables and bench seating suited to sharing. Stools set around the open kitchen make up the chef's table. Accessible menu offers the likes of sliders, chilli cheese dogs and steaks to share. Chatty service.

Svea

24 Rodney Rd ✉ GL50 1JJ – ✆ (01242) 238 134 – www.sveacafe.co.uk – Closed Sunday, Monday and lunch Tuesday-Wednesday CY**s**

Rest – Carte £ 23/31

A homely city centre café during the day, serving homemade cakes and light snacks; by night, it becomes a restaurant, offering fresh, authentic, classic Swedish dishes. Smorgasbord on the first Saturday of every month.

Royal Oak

The Burgage, Prestbury ✉ GL52 3DL – ✆ (01242) 522 344 – www.royal-oak-prestbury.co.uk – Closed 25-26 December AX**r**

Rest – Carte £ 23/30

This was once owned by batting legend Tom Graveney, hence the 'Pavilion' function room. Lunch offers tasty, satisfying dishes like kedgeree, while dinner steps things up a level. Sit in the cosy bar, dark wood dining room or heated garden.

at Cleeve Hill Northeast : 4 mi on B 4632 - AX – ✉ Cheltenham

Malvern View without rest

✉ GL52 3PR – ✆ (01242) 672 017 – www.malvernview.com – Closed 22-29 December

7 rm – †£ 60/90 ††£ 85/150

Friendly, sandstone house with lovely views across the Malvern countryside towards Cleeve Hill. Boutique-style bedrooms have bold feature walls and modern facilities; smart bathrooms come with rain showers and Egyptian cotton towels.

Cleeve Hill without rest

✉ GL52 3PR – ✆ (01242) 672 052 – www.cleevehill-hotel.co.uk

10 rm – †£ 53/69 ††£ 80/98

Edwardian house in elevated spot; most bedrooms have views across Cleeve Common and the Malvern Hills. Breakfast room is in the conservatory; admire the landscape over coffee.

ENGLAND

at Shurdington Southwest : 3.75 mi on A 46 - AX - ✉ Cheltenham

Greenway

✉ GL51 4UG – ☎ (01242) 862 352 – www.thegreenwayhotelandspa.com
22 rm – †£ 149/209 ††£ 189/329 – 3 suites
Rest *Orchard Brasserie* – Carte £ 19/36
Rest *Garden* – Menu £ 26/50
Ivy-clad, Cotswold stone manor house dating from the 16C, set in 8 acres of peaceful grounds and offering pleasant hill views. Country house interior with comfy drawing rooms and well-equipped, traditional bedrooms. Lovely spa. Oak-panelled restaurant offers classic dishes with modern overtones and overlooks the lily pond; modern Orchard serves a brasserie menu.

at Piff's Elm Northwest : 4 mi on A 4019 - AX

Gloucester Old Spot

Tewkesbury Rd ✉ *GL51 9SY – ☎ (01242) 680 321 – www.thegloucesteroldspot.co.uk*
Rest – Menu £ 13 (lunch) – Carte £ 24/33
Cosy, relaxing inn with a snug, stone-floored bar, a baronial dining room and open fires aplenty. Menus offer tasty, seasonal dishes, with rare breed pork a speciality. Nursery puddings. Cheery, welcoming staff.

CHELWOOD GATE – East Sussex – 504 U31 — 8 A2

London 37 mi – Birmingham 163 mi – Leeds 246 mi – Sheffield 216 mi

ENGLAND

Red Lion

Lewes Rd, on A 275 ✉ *RH17 7DE – ☎ (01825) 791 609*
– www.thecrown-horstedkeynes.co.uk – Closed Sunday dinner and Monday except bank holidays
Rest – Carte £ 23/34
Set on the edge of Ashdown Forest; locals congregate by the fire in the bar but the best place to dine is in the conservatory, overlooking the terrace and garden. The menu concentrates on pub classics, with plenty of game in season.

CHESTER – Cheshire West and Chester – 502 L24 – pop. 80 635 — 20 A3

Great Britain

London 207 mi – Birkenhead 7 mi – Birmingham 91 mi – Liverpool 21 mi
Vicars Lane, ☎ (01244) 40 21 11, www.visitchester.com
Upton-by-Chester, Upton Lane, ☎ (01244) 38 11 83
Curzon Park, ☎ (01244) 67 77 60
City★★ - The Rows★★ B – Cathedral★ B – City Walls★ B
Chester Zoo★ AC, N : 3 mi by A 5116

Plans on following pages

Chester Grosvenor

Eastgate ✉ *CH1 1LT – ☎ (01244) 324 024 – www.chestergrosvenor.com*
– Closed 25-26 December **Ba**
74 rm – †£ 165/276 ††£ 175/276, £ 18 – 6 suites
Rest *Simon Radley at Chester Grosvenor* ✿ **Rest *La Brasserie*** – see restaurant listing
19C hotel with a grand, black and white timbered façade, a stunning Rococo chocolate shop and a buzzy lounge serving all-day snacks. Stylish bedrooms blend traditional furnishings and modern fabrics; luxurious, marble-floored bathrooms.

DoubleTree by Hilton Chester

Warrington Rd, Northeast : 2 mi on A 56 ✉ *CH2 3PD*
– ☎ (01244) 408 800 – www.doubletree-hilton.co.uk/chester **As**
140 rm – †£ 99/203 ††£ 112/216
Rest – Menu £ 20 **s** – Carte £ 23/32 **s**
Rest *Marco Pierre White Steakhouse Bar & Grill* – ☎ (01244) 408 830 – Carte £ 30/46
Smart, stylish hotel offering sleek, spacious bedrooms with super king-sized beds, bright white décor and modern facilities. State-of-the-art conference facilities and superb spa with a well-equipped leisure club. Contemporary steakhouse in the 18C manor house; informal brasserie overlooks the courtyard.

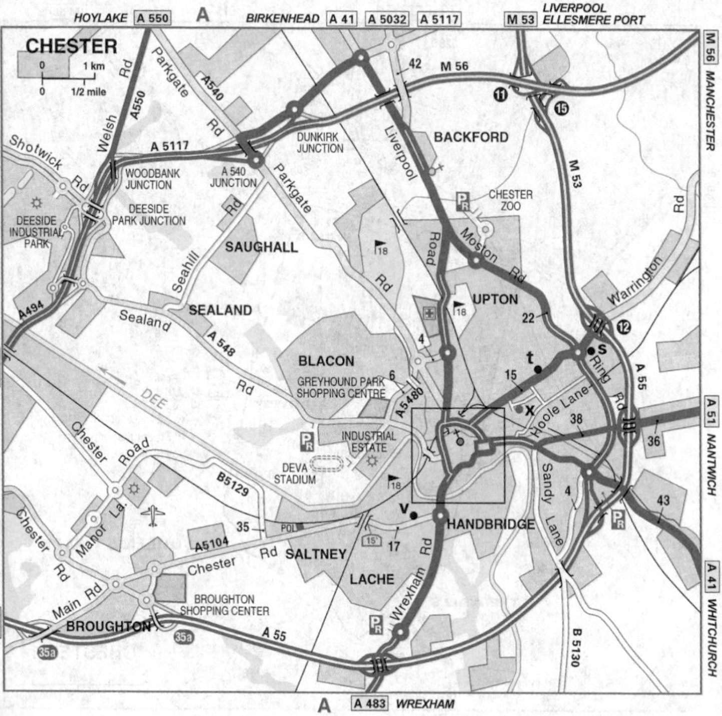

Caldy Valley Rd . . . . A 4
Countess Way . . . . A 5
Deva Link. . . . . A 6
Greyhound Park Shopping Centre . . . . A
Hoole Rd . . . . A 15
Hough Green. . . . . A 17
Long Lane . . . . A 22
Saltney Ferry Rd. A 35
Tarvin Rd . . . . A 36
Vicar's Cross Rd. . . . . A 38
Whitby Lane . . . . A 42
Whitchurch Rd . . . . A 43

ENGLAND

Abode Chester

Grosvenor Rd ✉ CH1 2DJ – ✆ (01244) 347 000 – www.abodehotels.co.uk/chester

84 rm – †£ 79/165 ††£ 79/165, ☕ £ 12 **Bz**

Rest *Michael Caines* – see restaurant listing

Rest *MC Café Bar & Grill* – *(dinner only and lunch Saturday and Sunday)* Carte £ 19/35

Imposing modern hotel opposite the castle and racecourse, just a short walk from the city. Four categories of bedroom: Enviable and Fabulous are the best; ask for a room with a racecourse view. Ground floor café, bar and grill offers a modern brasserie menu.

Green Bough

60 Hoole Rd, on A 56 ✉ CH2 3NL – ✆ (01244) 326 241 – www.greenbough.co.uk – Closed 1 January, 25, 26 and 31 December **At**

15 rm ☕ – †£ 105/125 ††£ 175/215 – 3 suites

Rest *Olive Tree* – *(dinner only)* Menu £ 30/45

Red-brick Victorian house on the edge of the city. Comfy, homely lounge with over 50 whiskies behind the bar. Bedroom styles vary greatly, from traditional country house to bold and contemporary; all have good facilities. Stylish restaurant with a Mediterranean menu; start with canapés in the rooftop garden.

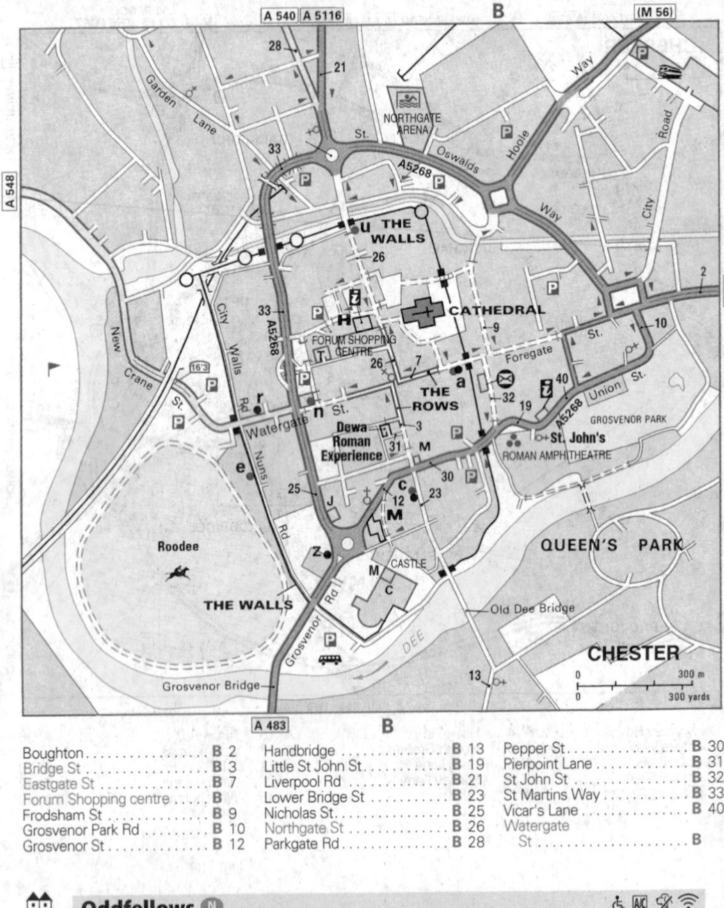

Boughton . . . . B 2
Bridge St . . . . B 3
Eastgate St . . . . B 7
Forum Shopping centre . . . . . B
Frodsham St . . . . B 9
Grosvenor Park Rd . . . . B 10
Grosvenor St . . . . B 12
Handbridge . . . . B 13
Little St John St . . . . B 19
Liverpool Rd . . . . B 21
Lower Bridge St . . . . B 23
Nicholas St . . . . B 25
Northgate St . . . . B 26
Parkgate Rd . . . . B 28
Pepper St . . . . B 30
Pierpoint Lane . . . . B 31
St John St . . . . B 32
St Martins Way . . . . B 33
Vicar's Lane . . . . B 40
Watergate St . . . . B

Oddfellows (N)

20 Lower Bridge St ✉ CH1 1RS – ✆ (01244) 895 700 – www.oddfellowschester.com – Closed 25 December **Bc**

18 rm ☕ – 🛉£ 95/354 🛉🛉£ 115/354

Rest *The Garden by Simon Radley* – see restaurant listing

Originally an Oddfellows Hall built in 1676 to help the poor, but its name also suits its unique, quirky styling. Well-equipped, contemporary bedrooms include some duplex suites: one room has a circular bed; another, a double roll-top bath.

Dragonfly without rest

94 Watergate St ✉ CH1 2LF – ✆ (01244) 346 740 – www.hoteldragonfly.com **Br**

7 rm – 🛉£ 95/375 🛉🛉£ 95/375, ☕ £ 10

Stylish boutique townhouse, where Georgian cornicing and flag and parquet floors blend with contemporary artwork and chic black breakfast tables. Spacious, modern bedrooms boast iPod docks and huge showers.

Mitchell's of Chester without rest

28 Hough Grn, Southwest : 1 mi by A 483 on A 5104 ✉ CH4 8JQ – ✆ (01244) 679 004 – www.mitchellsofchester.com – Closed 23 December-2 January **Av**

3 rm ☕ – 🛉£ 40/55 🛉🛉£ 72/98

Proudly run Victorian house with homely bedrooms, thoughtful extras and smart, compact shower rooms; those on the first floor are the best. Classical lounge complete with a parrot. Spacious breakfast room; try the homemade preserves.

XXXX **Simon Radley at Chester Grosvenor** – Chester Grosvenor Hotel
Eastgate ✉ *CH1 1LT* – *☎ (01244) 324 024*
– *www.chestergrosvenor.com* – *Closed Sunday (except at bank holidays when closed Tuesday) and Monday* Ba
Rest – *(dinner only)* Menu £ 55/90
Elegant restaurant with a fresh, classic feel, a stylish cocktail lounge and an impressive wine cellar. Confident cooking shows respect for ingredients, bringing together clean, clear flavours in sophisticated dishes that display interesting, innovative touches. Formal and detailed service.
→ King scallop with brawn fritter, black ham, toffee apple and quince. Cep dusted beef fillet, Burgundian cheeks, marrow and parsley. Sticky rice with coconut, poached lychee, iced guava and passion fruit.

XX **Michael Caines** – Abode Chester Hotel
Grosvenor Rd ✉ *CH1 2DJ* – *☎ (01244) 405 820* – *www.michaelcaines.com*
– *Closed Sunday* Bz
Rest – Menu £ 15 (lunch) – Carte £ 32/49
Fashionable spot for city dining, located on the fifth floor of a hotel. Menus combine a French base with a modern edge; try the tasting menu to fully appreciate the flavourful, artistic cooking.

XX **Upstairs at the Grill**
70 Watergate St ✉ *CH1 2LA* – *☎ (01244) 344 883* – *www.upstairsatthegrill.co.uk*
– *Closed 1 January* Bn
Rest – *(dinner only and lunch Friday-Sunday)* Carte £ 22/46
Smart restaurant offering prime quality steaks – including rib-eye, sirloin, chateaubriand and rare breeds. Start in the mean, moody cocktail bar, where the cuts are presented and explained, then eat downstairs among the cow paraphernalia.

XX **La Brasserie** – Chester Grosvenor Hotel
Eastgate ✉ *CH1 1LT* – *☎ (01244) 324 024* – *www.chestergrosvenor.com*
– *Closed 25-26 December* Ba
Rest – Menu £ 20 (weekdays) – Carte £ 31/48
Parisian brasserie with a large, hand-painted glass skylight, mirrors, brass rails and colourful light fittings; sit on a leather banquette or in a booth. Refined British, French and Mediterranean dishes are cooked on the Josper grill.

XX **The Garden by Simon Radley** N – Oddfellows Hotel
20 Lower Bridge St ✉ *CH1 1RS* – *☎ (01244) 895 700*
– *www.oddfellowschester.com* – *Closed 25 December* Bc
Rest – Menu £ 15/20 **s** – Carte £ 23/42 **s**
Set in an impressive Georgian hotel; have a drink in the quirky bar then head to the garden-themed restaurant with its bird motifs, flower displays, butterfly-filled glass boxes and large terrace. Unfussy, Mediterranean-influenced menus.

X **Joseph Benjamin**
134-140 Northgate St ✉ *CH1 2HT* – *☎ (01244) 344 295*
– *www.josephbenjamin.co.uk* – *Closed Monday* Bu
Rest – *(lunch only and dinner Thursday -Saturday) (booking essential)* Carte £ 21/32
Personally and passionately run bistro, named after the owners themselves. The simple, light décor mirrors the style of the cooking. The monthly changing menu offers well-judged, satisfying dishes and tasty homemade pastries.

X **Sticky Walnut**
11 Charles St ✉ *CH2 3AZ* – *☎ (01244) 400 400* – *www.stickywalnut.com*
– *Closed 25-26 December, 1-5 January and Sunday dinner* Ax
Rest – *(booking essential at dinner)* Carte £ 24/36
Run by a confident young team, a quirky, slightly bohemian restaurant in a residential parade of shops. Concise menus feature quality ingredients in a mix of British, French and Italian dishes; the breads and pastas are all homemade.

CHESTERFIELD – Derbyshire – 502 P24 – pop. 70 260 Great Britain 16 B1

London 149 mi – Birmingham 72 mi – Liverpool 77 mi – Manchester 44 mi
Grassmoor, North Wingfield Rd, ☎ (01246) 85 60 44
Bolsover Castle★ **AC**, E : 5 mi by A 632

ENGLAND

Casa Ⓝ

Lockoford Ln ✉ S41 7JB – ✆ (01246) 245 999 – www.casahotels.com
100 rm – †£ 90/110 ††£ 99/125
Rest *Cocina* – see restaurant listing
Modern hotel set over 4 floors, with a spacious, open-plan reception, 11 state-of-the-art meeting rooms and a contemporary bar. Sizeable bedrooms are furnished in autumnal colours and have king-sized beds, fridges, irons and useful extras.

Non Solo Vino

417 Chatsworth Rd, Brampton ✉ S40 3AD – ✆ (01246) 276 760 – www.nonsolovino.co.uk – Closed 25 December, 1 January, Sunday dinner and Monday
Rest – Menu £ 17/22 – Carte £ 27/39
It began as a shop specialising in Italian wines and is now also a bright, contemporary restaurant. Adventurous, modern cooking features Italian classics with a twist; the tasting menu can be coupled with a wine tasting menu.

Cocina Ⓝ – Casa Hotel

Lockoford Ln ✉ S41 7JB – ✆ (01246) 245 999 – www.casahotels.com
Rest – *(bar lunch/dinner)* Menu £ 20 – Carte £ 20/36
Stylish hotel restaurant with a well-stocked cocktail bar. Mediterranean menus have a strong Spanish influence; try the tapas or mature steaks from the Josper oven. The beef is organic rare breed and come from the owners' 350 acre farm.

CHEW MAGNA – Bath and North East Somerset – 503 M29 – pop. 1 187 — 4 C2

▶ London 128 mi – Bristol 9 mi – Cardiff 52 mi – Bournemouth 89 mi

Pony & Trap (Josh Eggleton)

Knowle Hill, Newtown, South : 1.25 mi on Bishop Stuttard rd ✉ BS40 8TQ – ✆ (01275) 332 627 – www.theponyandtrap.co.uk – Closed Monday except December and bank holidays and Sunday dinner
Rest – *(booking essential)* Carte £ 23/39
Cosy whitewashed pub in a tiny hamlet; its oversized dining room windows offering lovely country views. Twice-daily menu of extremely fresh, seasonal produce, including locally sourced, hung and smoked meats and fish. Classical cooking with clean, clear flavours.
→ Beetroot salad with ewe's curd, apple and hazelnut. Beef fillet with swede purée, ox tongue, pickled turnips and sweetbreads. Fennel crème brûlée, orange sorbet and chocolate pot with fennel popcorn.

CHICHESTER – West Sussex – 504 R31 – pop. 27 477 Great Britain — 7 C2

▶ London 69 mi – Brighton 31 mi – Portsmouth 18 mi – Southampton 30 mi
29a South St, ✆ (01243) 77 58 88, www.visitchichester.org
Goodwood, Kennel Hill, ✆ (01243) 75 51 33
Chichester Golf Centre, Hunston Village, ✆ (01243) 53 38 33
City★★ – Cathedral★★ BZ **A** – St Mary's Hospital★ BY **D** – Pallant House★ **AC** BZ **M**
Fishbourne Roman Palace★★ (mosaics★) **AC** AZ **R**. Weald and Downland Open Air Museum★★ **AC**, N : 6 mi by A 286 AY

Goodwood

rm, rm,

Northeast : 4 mi by A 285 ✉ PO18 0QB – ✆ (01243) 775 537 – www.goodwood.com
91 rm – †£ 140/335 ††£ 140/335 – 4 suites
Rest *Richmond Arms* – *(dinner only and Sunday lunch)* Carte £ 30/52
Rest *Goodwood Bar & Grill* – Carte £ 26/43
Refurbished hotel on the Goodwood Estate, with luxurious, English-style bedrooms in subtle, contemporary colour schemes; modern furniture and motor racing photos abound. Well-equipped spa. Smart Richmond Arms serves seasonal menu, with many ingredients from the estate. Informal Bar & Grill overlooks the golf course and offers modern classics.

CHICHESTER

Street	Grid	No.
Birdham Rd	AZ	2
Bognor Rd	AZ	3
Chapel St	BY	6
Chartres (Av. de)	BZ	7
Chichester Arundel Rd	AY	8
East Pallant	BZ	9
East St	BZ	
Florence Rd	AZ	10
Hornet (The)	BZ	12
Kingsham Rd	BZ	13
Lavant Rd	AY	14
Little London	BY	15
Market Rd	BZ	16
Northgate	BY	17
North Pallant	BZ	19
North St	BYZ	
Oaklands Way	BY	18
St Jame's	AZ	21
St John's St	BZ	23
St Martin's Square	BY	24
St Pancras	BY	25
St Paul's Rd	BY	27
Sherborne Rd	AZ	28
Southgate	BZ	29
South Pallant	BZ	31
South St	BZ	
Spitalfield Lane	BY	32
Stockbridge Rd	AZ	33
Tower St	BY	35
Via Ravenna	AZ	37
Westhampnett Rd	AYZ	38
West Pallant	BZ	39

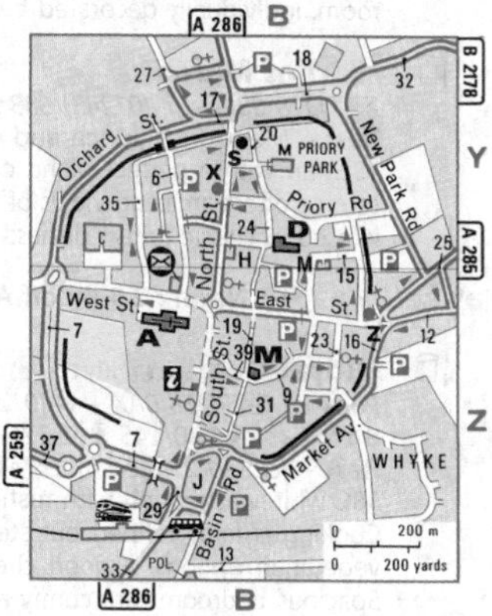

ENGLAND

Ship

57 North St ✉ PO19 1NH – ✆ (01243) 778 000 – www.theshiphotel.net

37 rm – †£ 90/110 ††£ 120/295 BYs

Rest – Menu £ 15/18 – Carte £ 19/36

Grade II listed former home to one of Nelson's men. Some impressive Georgian features remain, including a cantilevered wrought iron staircase. Stylish, up-to-date bedrooms and a spacious, contemporary bar. Airy brasserie offers modern European menu, with meat and game from the nearby estate.

Brasserie Blanc

Richmond House, The Square ✉ PO19 7SJ – ✆ (01243) 534 200 – www.brasserieblanc.com – Closed 25 December BZz

Rest – Menu £ 14/17 – Carte £ 20/41

Classically styled brasserie with lovely terrace, tucked away in a modern cobbled square. Impressive open kitchen and display of artisan provisions for sale. Tasty, rustic French cooking.

Comme ça

67 Broyle Rd ✉ PO19 6BD – ✆ (01243) 788 724 – www.commeca.co.uk – Closed first 2 weeks January, Sunday dinner and Monday AYc

Rest – Menu £ 22/35

A long-standing restaurant in a 17C house, which used to be a prison, but now, with its blue shutters, resembles a French auberge. Traditionally furnished dining room and conservatory. Classic French cooking.

Amelie and Friends

31 North St ✉ PO19 1LY – ✆ (01243) 771 444 – www.amelieandfriends.com – Closed Sunday dinner and Monday-Wednesday dinner January-April

Rest – Menu £ 11/18 – Carte £ 17/33 BYx

Named after the chef's daughter, this simple, modern café is situated in a grand Georgian building, and a counter of freshly baked cakes and meringues entices you in. The stark white, minimalist dining room leads to a heated terrace. Light, unfussy cooking relies on seasonal ingredients. Weekend breakfasts.

at Mid Lavant North : 2 mi on A286

Rooks Hill without rest

Lavant Rd ✉ PO18 0BQ – ✆ (01243) 528 400 – www.rookshill.co.uk
3 rm – †£ 85/125 ††£ 105/175
Grade II listed house with a pleasant view across to the Goodwood estate. Relax on the charming courtyard terrace or next to the wood burner in the cosy sitting room. Individually decorated bedrooms have contemporary touches.

Earl of March

✉ PO18 0BQ – ✆ (01243) 533 993 – www.theearlofmarch.com
Rest – Menu £ 19 (lunch and early dinner) **s** – Carte £ 24/38 **s**
18C inn with a perfect blend of country character and contemporary styling; its terrace offers amazing views of the South Downs. Good quality, seasonal produce is used in classic British dishes.

at East Lavant North : 2.5 mi off A 286 - AY – ✉ Chichester

Royal Oak Inn with rm

Pook Ln ✉ PO18 0AX – ✆ (01243) 527 434 – www.royaloakeastlavant.co.uk
8 rm – †£ 90/145 ††£ 125/340
Rest – *(closed 25 December)* Menu £ 17 (lunch) – Carte £ 27/44
18C whitewashed inn with rustic, laid-back feel; arrive early for a spot by the fire. Cooking is fairly refined but steaks play an important role. There are interesting vegetarian options, a good cheese selection and plenty of wines by the glass. Spacious bedrooms are comfy and well-equipped; breakfast is a treat.

ENGLAND

at Tangmere East : 2 mi by A 27 - AY – ✉ Chichester

Cassons

Arundel Rd, Northwest : 0.25 mi off A 27 (westbound) ✉ PO18 0DU – ✆ (01243) 773 294 – www.cassonsrestaurant.co.uk – Closed 26 December-2 January, lunch Tuesday, Sunday dinner and Monday
Rest – Menu £ 20/28 – Carte £ 31/53
Rustic restaurant with linen-laid tables and exposed brick walls. Set price menus offer generous, hearty dishes with bold flavours. Cooking is classically based but employs modern techniques.

at Bosham West : 4 mi by A 259 - AZ – ✉ Chichester

Millstream

Bosham Ln ✉ PO18 8HL – ✆ (01243) 573 234 – www.millstreamhotel.com
35 rm – †£ 99/109 ††£ 159/179 – 3 suites
Rest – Menu £ 26/34
Rest *Marwick's* – ✆ (01243) 578 599 *(booking advisable)* Menu £ 15/17 – Carte £ 20/38
Genuine, old-fashioned hospitality and classic comforts mean that most guests are on return visits to this pretty hotel, with its well-tended garden and fast-flowing stream. Cosy bar, comfy sitting room and traditionally furnished, immaculately kept bedrooms. Classic menu with modern touches in the light, airy restaurant. Brasserie dishes in contemporary Marwick's.

at Funtington Northwest : 4.75 mi by B 2178 - AY - on B 2146 – ✉ Chichester

Hallidays

Watery Ln ✉ PO18 9LF – ✆ (01243) 575 331 – www.hallidays.info.co.uk – Closed 2 weeks August, 1 week March, 1 week Christmas-New Year, Saturday lunch, Sunday dinner, Monday and Tuesday
Rest – Menu £ 16/29 – Carte lunch £ 30/41
Charming thatched cottage with a low-beamed ceiling and a homely feel. The experienced chef knows about sourcing good, local ingredients and his menu changes weekly. Skilful, classical cooking.

at West Ashling Northwest : 4.5 mi by B 2178 and B 2146

Richmond Arms with rm
Mill Rd ✉ PO18 8EA – ✆ (01243) 572 046 – www.therichmondarms.co.uk – Closed Easter, last week July, last week October, 24 December-11 January, Sunday dinner, Monday and Tuesday
2 rm – †£ 95/110 ††£ 110/125 **Rest** – Carte £ 25/39
Appealing, laid-back country pub opposite a duck pond in a lovely little village. The menu offers a broad mix, from freshly sliced hams and local steaks to game from the family estate in Anglesey; many dishes are cooked on the rotisserie or Japanese robata grill. Two luxurious bedrooms are found above.

CHIDDINGFOLD – Surrey – 504 S30 – pop. 2 128 7 C2

London 47 mi – Guildford 10 mi – Haslemere 5 mi

Swan Inn with rm
Petworth Rd ✉ GU8 4TY – ✆ (01428) 684 688 – www.theswaninnchiddingfold.com
10 rm – †£ 100/180 ††£ 100/180 **Rest** – Carte £ 22/39
Elegant tile-hung pub with 200 year old history and up-to-date interior. Local Surrey set pop in for crab cakes or the 'terrine of the day' at lunch; à la carte changes daily, depending on the latest local produce available. Bedrooms are cool and contemporary.

CHIEVELEY – West Berkshire – 503 Q29 10 B3

London 60 mi – Newbury 5 mi – Swindon 25 mi

Crab at Chieveley with rm
Wantage Rd, West : 2.5mi by School Rd on B 4494 ✉ RG20 8UE – ✆ (01635) 247 550 – www.crabatchieveley.com
14 rm – †£ 85/195 ††£ 85/215 **Rest** – Menu £ 20 (lunch) – Carte £ 28/58
Thatched former inn, a characterful venue, located on a country road lined with wheat fields. Atmospheric restaurant is filled with seafaring memorabilia and offers a seafood-orientated menu. Highly original bedrooms are themed around famous hotels.

ENGLAND

CHILLATON – Devon – 503 H32 – see Tavistock

CHILLINGTON – Devon – 503 I33 2 C3

London 217 mi – Plymouth 26 mi – Torbay 20 mi – Torquay 22 mi

whitehouse
✉ TQ7 2JX – ✆ (01548) 580 505 – www.whitehousedevon.com
6 rm – †£ 170/240 ††£ 190/260
Rest – *(dinner only) (booking advisable)* Carte £ 25/41
Attractive, personally run Georgian house with two spacious lounges. Stylish bedrooms feature bold décor and a mix of modern and retro furnishings; all feature heavy handmade beds and smart bathrooms. The dining room has a large terrace overlooking the lovely lawned gardens and offers a concise modern menu.

CHINNOR – Oxfordshire – 504 R28 – pop. 5 407 Great Britain 11 C2

London 45 mi – Oxford 19 mi – Birmingham 88 mi – Barnet 41 mi
Ridgeway Path★★

at Sprigg's Alley Southeast : 2.5 mi by Bledlow Ridge rd – ✉ Chinnor

Sir Charles Napier
Sprigs Holly ✉ OX39 4BX – ✆ (01494) 483 011 – www.sircharlesnapier.co.uk – Closed 24-26 December, Sunday dinner and Monday except bank holidays
Rest – *(booking advisable)* Menu £ 18 (weekdays) – Carte £ 38/56
Attractive flint pub in a small hillside hamlet, with a hint of eccentricity in its decoration. Pleasant terrace and delightful gardens for summer; log fires and candlelight in winter. Polished and boldly flavoured French based dishes are prepared with obvious skill. Gem of a wine list.
→ Seared foie gras, endive marmalade and black muscat. Yuzu glazed duck, fondant potato, orange and heritage carrots. Chocolate and peanut terrine with salted caramel and mandarin ice cream.

CHIPPING CAMPDEN – Gloucestershire – 503 O27 – pop. 1 943 4 D1

Great Britain

London 93 mi – Cheltenham 21 mi – Oxford 37 mi – Stratford-upon-Avon 12 mi

Old Police Station, (01386) 84 12 06, www.chippingcampdenonline.org

Town★

Hidcote Manor Garden★★ **AC**, NE : 2.5 m

Cotswold House H. and Spa

rest,

The Square ✉ *GL55 6AN* – *(01386) 840 330* – *www.cotswoldhouse.com*

25 rm – £ 120/380 £ 140/400 – 3 suites

Rest *Cotswold Grill* – see restaurant listing

Rest *Dining Room* – *(dinner only) (booking essential)* Menu £ 35

Stylish Regency townhouse with lovely gardens and a fine spiral staircase winding upwards towards luxurious, modern bedrooms. Bright, boldly decorated lounges. Formal dining room with veneer panelling and contemporary artwork offers intricate, modern cooking.

Kings

The Square ✉ *GL55 6AW* – *(01386) 840 256* – *www.kingscampden.co.uk*

18 rm – £ 110/130 £ 130/170

Rest *Kings* – see restaurant listing

Beautiful Cotswold stone townhouse with stylish, boutique interior. Bedrooms in the main house mix antiques with modern facilities and some boast sleigh beds; rooms in the cottage at the end of the garden are more contemporary.

ENGLAND

Seymour House without rest

High St ✉ *GL55 6AG* – *(01386) 840 064* – *www.seymourhousebandb.co.uk* – *Closed Christmas-New Year*

4 rm – £ 80 £ 110/130

Welcoming Cotswold stone house with early 18C origins. Spacious hall, homely lounge and good-sized bedrooms with modern facilities – 3 are in the eaves. Lovely garden and breakfast terrace.

Staddlestones without rest

7 Aston Rd, North : 0.5 mi by B 4081 on B 4035 ✉ *GL55 6HR* – *(01386) 849 288* – *www.staddle-stones.com*

3 rm – £ 75 £ 75/105

Attractive sandstone war veteran's cottage. Individually decorated bedrooms with high level of facilities; large annexed suite boasts comfy lounge and country views. Afternoon tea on arrival.

Kings – Kings Hotel

The Square ✉ *GL55 6AW* – *(01386) 840 256* – *www.kingscampden.co.uk*

Rest – Menu £ 30 – Carte £ 21/29

Appealing restaurant in a stylish boutique townhouse. Rustic interior boasts exposed stone walls, wooden beams and a large inglenook fireplace. Modern British menus use top quality ingredients and dishes are refined and flavoursome.

Cotswold Grill – Cotswold House Hotel and Spa

The Square ✉ *GL55 6AN* – *(01386) 840 330* – *www.cotswoldhouse.com*

Rest – Carte £ 23/40

A relaxed, informal restaurant set in a Regency townhouse hotel. Open all day, it serves breakfast and afternoon tea as well as an appealing, bistro-style menu of modern dishes including steaks, burgers and charcuterie.

Eight Bells Inn with rm

Church St ✉ *GL55 6JG* – *(01386) 840 371* – *www.eightbellsinn.co.uk* – *Closed 25 December*

7 rm – £ 60/85 £ 85/125 **Rest** – Carte £ 25/37

14C pub close to the historic high street in an old wool merchant's town. Cooking is traditionally British – pies are the real thing, puddings are comforting and specials are just that, so arrive early. Bedrooms combine plenty of character with good mod cons.

at Mickleton North : 3.25 mi by B 4035 and B 4081 on B 4632 – ✉ Chipping Campden

Three Ways House

✉ *GL55 6SB – ✆ (01386) 438 429 – www.threewayshousehotel.com*
48 rm – †£ 88/125 ††£ 145/240 **Rest** – Menu £ 15/37
Built in 1870 and renowned as the home of the Pudding Club. Two types of bedroom, split between the original house and modern block; all are very comfy and contemporary – opt for one of the pudding-themed rooms. Informal bar-cum-brasserie boasts antique tiled floor. Formal arcaded dining room offers weekly menu.

at Ebrington East : 2 mi by B 4035

Ebrington Arms with rm

✉ *GL55 6NH – ✆ (01386) 593 223 – www.theebringtonarms.co.uk*
5 rm – †£ 120/140 ††£ 130/150 **Rest** – Carte £ 21/33
Proper village local with beamed, flag-floored bar at its hub, set in charming chocolate box village. Robust, traditional dishes use local ingredients and up-to-date techniques. Bedrooms have country views; Room 3, with four-poster bed and luxury bathroom, is best.

at Paxford Southeast : 3 mi by B 4035 – ✉ Chipping Campden

Churchill Arms with rm

✉ *GL55 6XH – ✆ (01386) 594 000 – www.thechurchillarms.com – Closed 25 December*
4 rm – †£ 60/90 ††£ 80/100 **Rest** – Carte £ 23/36
Traditional stone inn, in a lovely Cotswold village, with a homely, rustic interior, old beams and a large inglenook fireplace. Cooking displays a real mix of influences, from pub classics to more restaurant-style dishes. Cosy bedrooms have good outlooks but silence doesn't reign until closing time.

at Broad Campden South : 1.25 mi by B 4081 – ✉ Chipping Campden

Malt House without rest

✉ *GL55 6UU – ✆ (01386) 840 295 – www.malt-house.co.uk – Closed Christmas-New Year*
7 rm – †£ 85/95 ††£ 120/160
For a rare experience of the countryside idyll, this 16C malting house is a must. Cut flowers from the gardens on view in bedrooms decked out in fabrics to delight the eye.

at Weston-sub-Edge Northwest : 3 mi by B 4081, B 4035 on B 4632

Seagrave Arms with rm

Friday St ✉ *GL55 6QH – ✆ (01386) 840 192 – www.seagravearms.co.uk – Closed first week January, Sunday dinner November-March and Monday*
8 rm – †£ 95/115 ††£ 95/125 **Rest** – Carte £ 25/37
Part Georgian coach house that's been attractively refurbished. Compact but cosy, with open-fired bar, wood-furnished dining rooms and polite, formal service. Concise menu of ambitious, complex, restaurant-style dishes. Stylish, modern bedroom are well-equipped.

CHIPPING NORTON – Oxfordshire – 503 P28 – pop. 5 688 10 A1

London 77 mi – Oxford 22 mi – Stow-on-the-Wold 9 mi

Wild Thyme

10 New St ✉ *OX7 5LJ – ✆ (01608) 645 060 – www.wildthymerestaurant.co.uk – Closed first week January, 1 week spring, Sunday and lunch Monday*
Rest – *(booking advisable)* Menu £ 25 (lunch) – Carte £ 27/47
Friendly restaurant off the high street, with a tiny courtyard garden. Rustic tables; No. 10, in the window, is the best. Wholesome regional British cooking with Mediterranean influences. Local, artisan suppliers; tasty homemade breads.

ENGLAND

CHIPPING ONGAR – Essex – 504 U28 – pop. 5 923 12 B2

London 28 mi – Birmingham 132 mi – Leeds 189 mi – Sheffield 163 mi

XX Smith's

Fyfield Rd ✉ CM5 0AL – ✆ (01277) 365 578 – www.smithsrestaurants.com – Closed 25-26 December and Monday lunch

Rest – *(booking essential)* Menu £ 20/30 – Carte £ 29/52

Long-standing, locally acclaimed seafood restaurant with a buzzy atmosphere. The à la carte and extensive daily set menu offer dishes ranging from Cornish squid to Scottish smoked salmon. Lobster, cooked several ways, is a speciality.

CHIPSTEAD – Kent 8 B1

London 27 mi – Leeds 221 mi – Sheffield 203 mi – Manchester 246 mi

George & Dragon

39 High St ✉ TN13 2RW – ✆ (01732) 779 019 – www.georgeanddragonchipstead.com

Rest – Carte £ 19/34

Superbly set, 400 year old inn with a beamed bar and a wonky-floored upstairs dining room. Delightful garden with terrace and children's play area. The menu is a roll call of seasonal English classics; herbs and salad are home-grown.

CHOBHAM – Surrey – 504 S29 – pop. 2 773 7 C1

London 32 mi – Birmingham 127 mi – Bristol 98 mi – Croydon 31 mi

XXX Stovell's N

125 Windsor Rd, North : 0.75 mi on B 383 ✉ GU24 8QS – ✆ (01276) 858 000 – www.stovells.com – Closed first 2 weeks January, last week August, 26-27 December, Saturday lunch, Sunday dinner and Monday

Rest – *(booking essential)* Menu £ 20/38

Well-run restaurant, which started life as a Tudor farmhouse. Old beams and contemporary furnishings sit side by side. Appealing modern European dishes; the wood-fired grill is a feature, with meats cooked over apple wood and vine cuttings.

CHOLMONDELEY – Cheshire East 20 A3

London 178 mi – Birmingham 65 mi – Leeds 86 mi – Sheffield 90 mi

Cholmondeley Arms with rm

Wrenbury Rd ✉ SY14 8HN – ✆ (01829) 720 300 – www.cholmondeleyarms.co.uk

6 rm – †£ 75 ††£ 90 **Rest** – Carte £ 21/35

The eponymous estate's old schoolhouse, with high, vaulted ceilings, large windows and roaring fires. Modern pub favourites might include calves liver or homemade lamb faggots. Gin lovers will be in clover with more than 140 from which to choose. The 6 comfy bedrooms are in the Old Headmaster's House.

CHORLEY – Lancashire – 502 M23 – pop. 33 424 20 A2

London 222 mi – Blackpool 30 mi – Liverpool 33 mi – Manchester 26 mi

18 Duxbury Park, Duxbury Hall Rd, ✆ (01257) 26 53 80

18 Shaw Hill Hotel G. & C.C., Whittle-le-Woods, Preston Rd, ✆ (01257) 26 92 21

XX Red Cat

Blackburn Rd, Whittle-Le-Woods, Northeast : 2.5 mi on A 674 ✉ PR6 8LL – ✆ (01257) 263 966 – www.theredcat.co.uk – Closed Sunday dinner, Monday and Tuesday

Rest – Menu £ 23 (lunch) – Carte £ 30/47

Restored pub with a series of cosy, rustic rooms displaying old beams, exposed stone and uneven floors. Menus showcase a wealth of local produce and range from a simple two course lunch to a more ambitious, interesting tasting selection.

CHORLTON-CUM-HARDY – Greater Manchester – 502 N23 – see Manchester

ENGLAND

CHRISTCHURCH – Dorset – 503 O31 – pop. 40 208 4 D3

London 111 mi – Bournemouth 6 mi – Salisbury 26 mi – Southampton 24 mi
49 High St, ☎ (01202) 47 17 80, www.visitchristchurch.info
Highcliffe Castle, Highcliffe-on-Sea, 107 Lymington Rd, ☎ (01425) 27 29 53
Riverside Ave, ☎ (01202) 43 64 36
Town★ - Priory★
Hengistbury Head★ (≤★★) SW : 4.5 mi by A 35 and B 3059

Christchurch Harbour

95 Mudeford, East : 2 mi ✉ BH23 3NT – ☎ (01202) 483 434 – www.christchurch-harbour-hotel.co.uk
64 rm – †£ 130/165 ††£ 145/180
Rest *Jetty* – see restaurant listing
Rest – Menu £ 16/24 – Carte £ 21/32
Busy hotel in a great spot, with a pleasant drinks terrace and chic spa. Contemporary styling and plush bedrooms; choose between 'Inland' or 'Harbour'; the latter boasting either a balcony or terrace. Harbour restaurant offers classical dishes with a modern edge; Jetty affords superb views.

Captain's Club

Wick Ferry, Wick Ln ✉ BH23 1HU – ☎ (01202) 475 111 – www.captainsclubhotel.com
17 rm – †£ 179 ††£ 249 – 12 suites
Rest *Tides* – see restaurant listing
Striking modern building with art deco and nautical influences, stylish spa, and floor-to-ceiling windows throughout. Sleek, contemporary bedrooms – some are three-roomed suites. Lovely riverbank location; they have their own boat for hire.

Kings Arms

18 Castle St ✉ BH23 1DT – ☎ (01202) 588 933 – www.thekings-christchurch.co.uk
20 rm (dinner included) – †£ 115/210 ††£ 115/210
Rest *Kings Arms* – see restaurant listing
Lovingly restored Georgian coaching inn, set in the heart of the town and overlooking the castle ruins and the bowling green. The interior is surprisingly contemporary, with a chic, characterful style and well-appointed, boutique bedrooms.

Druid House without rest

26 Sopers Ln ✉ BH23 1JE – ☎ (01202) 485 615 – www.druid-house.co.uk
9 rm – †£ 50/80 ††£ 80/125
Hidden behind an unassuming exterior, a bright, well-kept house that's passionately run and great value for money. Bedrooms are bright and modern; some of those in the newer wing open out onto a small terrace. Excellent breakfasts include a buffet and hot specials such as muffins with poached eggs and bacon.

Tides – Captain's Club Hotel

Wick Ferry, Wick Ln ✉ BH23 1HU – ☎ (01202) 475 111 – www.captainsclubhotel.com
Rest – Menu £ 20/28 – Carte £ 20/40
A laid-back lounge and bar lead to this contemporary hotel restaurant. Head past the wine cave and water feature wall for great river views or sit on the popular terrace. Wide-ranging menus offer classic dishes with a modern edge.

Splinters

12 Church St ✉ BH23 1BW – ☎ (01202) 483 454 – www.splinters.uk.com – Closed 1-10 January, Sunday and Monday
Rest – Menu £ 17/39 – Carte £ 22/32
Traditional, family-run restaurant, so named because of the splinters the owner got when building the booths! Cosy, characterful rooms range from nautical to Parisian bistro in style. Classical cooking, with rich, tasty sauces a feature.

Jetty – Christchurch Harbour Hotel

95 Mudeford, East : 2 mi ✉ BH23 3NT – ☎ (01202) 400 950 – www.thejetty.co.uk
Rest – Menu £ 22/29 – Carte £ 28/49
Contemporary, eco-friendly, hotel restaurant with a dark wood interior and floor-to-ceiling windows offering fantastic sea views. Appealing menus reflect what's available locally, with fish from nearby waters and game from the forest.

✗ **Kings Arms** Ⓝ – Kings Arms Hotel ᴬᶜ
18 Castle St ⊠ BH23 1DT – ℰ (01202) 588 933
– www.thekings-christchurch.co.uk
Rest – Menu £ 15 (lunch and early dinner) – Carte £ 20/30
Smart, spacious hotel brasserie offering gutsy, no frills cooking which is packed with flavour. The Josper grill plays a big role, as does the good value £ 15 weekly changing menu which is made up of produce sourced from within 15 miles. Friday is 'Fizz 'n' Chips' night and they also offer afternoon tea.

CHURCHILL – Oxfordshire – **503** P28 – **pop. 502** – ⊠ **Chipping Norton** **10** A1
▶ London 79 mi – Birmingham 46 mi – Cheltenham 29 mi – Oxford 23 mi

🍴 **Chequers** Ⓝ 🐕 ✦ ♿ 🅿
Church Rd ⊠ OX7 6NJ – ℰ (01608) 659 393 – www.thechequerschurchill.com
– Closed 25 December and dinner 26 December and 1 January
Rest – Carte £ 16/33
Welcoming sandstone pub in the heart of the village; it's a vital part of the community and the owners have got the formula just right. The bar is stocked with local ales; gutsy, traditional dishes include steaks cooked on the Josper grill.

CHURCH ENSTONE – Oxfordshire – ⊠ **Chipping Norton** **10** B1
▶ London 72 mi – Banbury 13 mi – Oxford 38 mi

🍴 **Crown Inn** 🐕 🅿
Mill Ln ⊠ OX7 4NN – ℰ (01608) 677 262 – www.crowninnenstone.co.uk – Closed
25-26 December, 1 January and Sunday dinner
Rest – Menu £ 16 (lunch) – Carte £ 19/32
17C inn set among pretty stone houses in a picturesque village. Meat, fruit and veg come from local farms and seafood is a speciality. Lunch offers pub favourites; tasty puddings are homemade.

CHURCH STRETTON – Shropshire – **502** L26 – **pop. 3 841** **18** B2
▓ Great Britain
▶ London 166 mi – Birmingham 46 mi – Hereford 39 mi – Shrewsbury 14 mi
🔟 Trevor Hill, ℰ (01694) 72 22 81
◱ Wenlock Edge★, E : by B 4371

✗✗ **Studio** 🌣 🐕
59 High St ⊠ SY6 6BY – ℰ (01694) 722 672 – www.thestudiorestaurant.net
– Closed 3 weeks January, 1 week spring, 1 week autumn, Christmas-New Year
and Sunday-Tuesday
Rest – *(dinner only)* Menu £ 30
Cosy, intimate former art studio with a pleasant terrace. Small bar leads to a homely brown and cream dining room hung with bold artwork. Concise, classical menu of carefully prepared, tasty homemade dishes. Friendly owners.

CIRENCESTER – Gloucestershire – **503** O28 – **pop. 15 861** **4** D1
▓ Great Britain
▶ London 97 mi – Bristol 37 mi – Gloucester 19 mi – Oxford 37 mi
🅳 Corinium Museum Park Street, ℰ (01285) 65 41 80, www.cirencester.gov.uk
🔟 Bagendon, Cheltenham Rd, ℰ (01285) 65 24 65
◲ Town★ – Church of St John the Baptist★ – Corinium Museum★ (Mosaic pavements★) **AC**
◱ Fairford : Church of St Mary★ (stained glass windows★★) E : 7 mi by A 417

🏨 **Fleece at Cirencester** Ⓝ 📶
Market Pl ⊠ GL7 2NZ – ℰ (01285) 658 507 – www.thefleececirencester.co.uk
27 rm ⌂ – ♗£ 80/160 ♗♗£ 85/170
Rest *Fleece at Cirencester* – Carte £ 19/41
Charming, centrally located coaching inn with an open-plan coffee shop and a cosy sitting room with an open fire. Spacious, individually furnished, well-kept bedrooms; Rooms 1 and 4 are the best. Simple bistro dining room serves accessible menu, with choices including deli boards and steaks.

ENGLAND

No 12 without rest
12 Park St ✉ GL7 2BW – ☎ (01285) 640 232 – www.no12cirencester.co.uk
4 rm – †£ 80 ††£ 110/130
16C property with Georgian façade, in the centre of a historic Roman town. Delightful rear walled garden. Excellent organic breakfasts. Stylish rooms charmingly blend old and new.

Old Brewhouse without rest
7 London Rd ✉ GL7 2PU – ☎ (01285) 656 099 – www.theoldbrewhouse.com
10 rm – †£ 65/78 ††£ 78/90
17C former brewhouse in busy central spot, with characterful cluttered interior. Cottage-style bedrooms – most with wrought iron beds – or more modern rooms in the extension, set around a small courtyard. Two stone-faced breakfast rooms.

Made by Bob
Unit 6, The Corn Hall, 26 Market Pl ✉ GL7 2NY – ☎ (01285) 641 818 – www.foodmadebybob.com – Closed 25-26 December, 1 January and Sunday
Rest – *(lunch only and dinner Thursday-Friday)* Carte £ 22/34
Large deli crammed with produce and an informal eatery boasting an open kitchen. Everything is homemade or locally sourced, from tasty breakfasts and light lunches to more structured dinners.

Jesse's Bistro
14 Blackjack St ✉ GL7 2AA – ☎ (01285) 641 497 – www.jessesbistro.co.uk – Closed Monday dinner and Sunday
Rest – Carte £ 24/49
Rustic bistro where guests can interact with the team in the open-plan kitchen. Well-crafted, generously proportioned dishes feature fish from Cornwall and meats from their adjoining butcher's shop – many are cooked in the wood-fired oven.

at Barnsley Northeast : 4 mi by A 429 on B 4425 – ✉ Cirencester

Barnsley House
✉ GL7 5EE – ☎ (01285) 740 000 – www.barnsleyhouse.com
18 rm – †£ 262/642 ††£ 280/660 – 7 suites
Rest *The Potager* – see restaurant listing
17C Cotswold manor house with a wonderfully relaxed vibe, set in the midst of beautiful gardens styled by Rosemary Verey. A very stylish interior blends original features with modern touches, from the open-fired lounges to the chic bedrooms; there's also a spa and even a cinema in the grounds.

The Potager – Barnsley House Hotel
✉ GL7 5EE – ☎ (01285) 740 000 – www.barnsleyhouse.com
Rest – Menu £ 21 (lunch) – Carte £ 29/47
Elegant hotel restaurant with a pleasant garden outlook and a laid-back feel. Influencing more than just the name, the kitchen gardens inform what's on the menus each day. Unfussy cooking has Mediterranean overtones; don't miss the freshly baked breads with herb-infused oils and salsa verde.

Village Pub with rm
✉ GL7 5EF – ☎ (01285) 740 421 – www.thevillagepub.co.uk
6 rm – †£ 130/160 ††£ 130/160 **Rest** – Carte £ 24/36
Stylish pub with open fires and cosy feel. Appealing, daily changing menu of modern British dishes, with irresistible nibbles, locally sourced meats, charcuterie from Highgrove and comforting desserts. Individually decorated bedrooms; No. Six has a four-poster.

at Sapperton West : 5 mi by A 419 – ✉ Cirencester

The Bell
✉ GL7 6LE – ☎ (01285) 760 298 – www.bellsapperton.co.uk – Closed 25 December and Sunday dinner January-mid February
Rest – Carte £ 18/40
Set in a pretty village; a charming pub with exposed stone walls, wooden beams, neatly-lawned gardens and paved terraces. The wide-ranging menu offers comforting British classics, seafood specials and the odd international touch. Dishes are rustic yet refined and rely on regional produce.

ENGLAND

CLANFIELD – Oxfordshire – 503 P28 – pop. 1 709 10 A2

London 75 mi – Oxford 24 mi – Ealing 68 mi – Coventry 56 mi

Cotswold Plough

Bourton Rd, on A 4095 ✉ OX18 2RB – ✆ (01367) 810 222 – www.cotswoldploughhotel.com – Closed 24-27 December
11 rm – ♦£ 89/109 ♦♦£ 115/140
Rest *Cotswold Plough* – see restaurant listing
16C wool merchant's house in the heart of a pretty village. Traditional, antique-furnished lounge and a characterful bar with two open fires and 52 types of gin. Spacious bedrooms display modern touches; 3 are four-posters.

Cotswold Plough – Cotswold Plough Hotel

Bourton Rd, on A 4095 ✉ OX18 2RB – ✆ (01367) 810 222 – www.cotswoldploughhotel.com – Closed 24-27 December
Rest – Menu £ 12 (weekday lunch) – Carte £ 22/37
Three-roomed restaurant in a 16C stone-built hotel, with beamed ceilings, polished wood tables and a comfortingly traditional feel. Classically based menus feature steak and game in season. Service is relaxed and informal.

CLAVERING – Essex – 504 U28 – pop. 1 663 – ✉ Saffron Walden 12 B2

London 44 mi – Cambridge 25 mi – Colchester 44 mi – Luton 29 mi

Cricketers with rm

✉ CB11 4QT – ✆ (01799) 550 442 – www.thecricketers.co.uk – Closed 25-26 December
20 rm – ♦£ 68/75 ♦♦£ 70/135 **Rest** – *(booking essential)* Carte £ 20/37
Opposite the cricket pitch in a sleepy village; open fires, exposed beams and polished brass abound. Mainly Italian menu with global influences; tasty homemade pasta, wood-fired specialities and bread baked daily. Fruit, veg and herbs come from the owners' son, Jamie Oliver's, organic garden. Cosy bedrooms.

CLEARWELL – Gloucestershire 4 C1

London 138 mi – Birmingham 85 mi – Bristol 31 mi – Cardiff 46 mi

Tudor Farmhouse

High St ✉ GL16 8JS – ✆ (01594) 833 046 – www.tudorfarmhousehotel.co.uk
23 rm – ♦£ 85/200 ♦♦£ 95/210 **Rest** – Carte £ 22/42
Converted farm buildings in the heart of the Forest of Dean. Character bedrooms in original farmhouse feature beams, uneven floors and antique furniture. More modern bedrooms in two outbuildings. Restaurant offers classic, French-influenced dishes with a twist.

CLEEVE HILL – Gloucestershire – 503 N28 – see Cheltenham

CLENT – Worcestershire – 504 N26 Great Britain 19 C2

London 127 mi – Birmingham 12 mi – Hagley 2 mi

Black Country Museum★, N : 7 mi by A 491 and A 4036 – Birmingham★ - Museum and Art Gallery★★, Aston Hall★★, NE : 10 mi by A 491 and A 456

Bell & Cross

Holy Cross, West : 0.5 mi off A 491 (northbound carriageway) (Bromsgrove rd) ✉ DY9 9QL – ✆ (01562) 730 319 – www.bellandcrossclent.co.uk – Closed 25 December and dinner 26 December and 1 January
Rest – Menu £ 14 (weekdays) – Carte £ 21/34
Charming pub set down a maze of narrow lanes, with colourful window boxes and country views. Lunch offers light bites and pub classics, with more substantial dishes appearing on the à la carte. Influences range from Asia to the Med.

CLEY-NEXT-THE-SEA – Norfolk – 504 X25 – see Blakeney

CLIFTON – Cumbria – 502 L20 – see Penrith

CLIPSHAM – Rutland 17 C2

London 101 mi – Leicester 35 mi – Coventry 72 mi – Nottingham 38 mi

Olive Branch & Beech House with rm

Main St ✉ LE15 7SH – ✆ (01780) 410 355 – www.theolivebranchpub.com

6 rm – †£ 98/113 ††£ 135/195

Rest – *(booking essential)* Menu £ 20/25 – Carte £ 25/42

Stone pub with delightful gardens and real rustic charm. Daily changing menu of classic dishes, with plenty of pasta and game; the provenance of ingredients is listed on the menu. Barn used for regular cookery exhibitions. Stylish bedrooms in the adjacent house include a host of extras.

CLITHEROE – Lancashire – 502 M22 – pop. 14 697 20 B2

London 64 mi – Blackpool 35 mi – Manchester 31 mi

Church Walk, ✆ (01200) 42 55 66, www.visitlancashire.com

18 Whalley Rd, ✆ (01200) 42 26 18

at Wiswell South : 3.75 mi by A 671

Freemasons

8 Vicarage Fold ✉ BB7 9DF – ✆ (01254) 822 218 – www.freemasonsatwiswell.com – Closed 2-14 January and Monday except bank holidays

Rest – Menu £ 20 (lunch and early dinner) – Carte £ 29/55

A delightful pub, hidden away on a narrow lane, with flag floors, low beams and open fires downstairs, and elegant, antique-furnished, country house style dining rooms upstairs. The interesting menu features modern versions of traditional pub dishes and cooking is refined and skilful. Charming service.

at Bashall Eaves Northwest : 3 mi by B6243

Red Pump Inn with rm

Clitheroe Rd ✉ BB7 3DA – ✆ (01254) 826 227 – www.theredpumpinn.co.uk – Closed 1 week January, Monday except bank holidays and Tuesday in winter

3 rm – †£ 65/115 ††£ 75/115

Rest – Menu £ 15 (weekdays) – Carte £ 20/35

One of the oldest pubs in the Ribble Valley, with traditional restaurant, rustic bar and charming fire-lit snug. Local produce features on seasonal menus, with game a speciality. Spacious bedrooms boast good facilities and views of Pendle Hill or Longridge Fell.

ENGLAND

CLOVELLY – Devon – 503 G31 – pop. 439 – ✉ Bideford 1 B1

London 241 mi – Barnstaple 18 mi – Exeter 52 mi – Penzance 92 mi

Village★★

SW : Tamar River★★. Hartland : Hartland Church★ - Hartland Quay★ (viewpoint★★) - Hartland Point ≤★★★, W : 6.5 mi by B 3237 and B 3248 – Morwenstow (Church★, cliffs★★), SW : 11.5 mi by A 39

Red Lion

The Quay ✉ EX39 5TF – ✆ (01237) 431 237 – www.clovelly.co.uk

17 rm (dinner included) – †£ 82/120 ††£ 128/220

Rest – *(dinner only)* Menu £ 30

Traditional inn set in a wonderful location under the cliffs, right on the harbour-front. Good-sized, comfortable bedrooms all have sea views; the newest and largest rooms are in the converted sail loft. Classic dishes and a superb vista in the dining room; lighter snacks in the bar.

CLUN – Shropshire – 503 K26 18 A2

London 173 mi – Church Stretton 16 mi – Ludlow 16 mi

Birches Mill without rest

Northwest : 3 mi by A 488, Bicton rd, Mainstone rd and Burlow rd ✉ SY7 8NL – ✆ (01588) 640 409 – www.birchesmill.co.uk – March-October

3 rm – †£ 74/85 ††£ 84/95

High quality comforts in remote former corn mill: interior has characterful 17C/18C structures. Flagged lounge with lovely inglenook. Simple but tastefully decorated rooms.

COBHAM – Surrey – 504 S30 – pop. 1 586 — 7 D1

London 21 mi – Croydon 19 mi – Barnet 46 mi – Ealing 18 mi

at Stoke D'Abernon Southeast : 1.5 mi on A 245 – ✉ Cobham

Old Plough

2 Station Rd ✉ KT11 3BN – ✆ (01932) 862 244 – www.oldploughcobham.co.uk

Rest – Carte £ 22/34

The fourth venture for this small pub group has a smart yet satisfyingly pubby feel. Sit in a comfy chair in the open-fired bar or at a chunky wood table in the restaurant, and choose from sharing plates or more sophisticated dishes.

COCKERMOUTH – Cumbria – 501 J20 – pop. 7 446 — 21 A2

London 306 mi – Carlisle 25 mi – Keswick 13 mi

Market St, ✆ (01900) 82 26 34, www.cockermouth.org.uk

Embleton, ✆ (017687) 7 62 23

at Lorton Southeast : 4.25 mi by B 5292 – ✉ Cockermouth

Winder Hall Country House

on B 5289 ✉ CA13 9UP – ✆ (01900) 85 107 – www.winderhall.co.uk – Closed January

7 rm – †£ 79/119 ††£ 89/129 **Rest** – *(booking essential)* Carte £ 22/36

Part-Jacobean manor house dating back to 1663, with leaded mullion windows, a relaxed, easy-going feel, and a comfy, characterful lounge and bar. Bedrooms range from olde worlde to more contemporary. The hot tub boasts fell views. Home-cooked meals in the pleasant oak-panelled dining room.

New House Farm

South : 1.25 mi on B 5289 ✉ CA13 9UU – ✆ (0784) 115 98 18 – www.newhouse-farm.com

5 rm – †£ 60/90 ††£ 110/180 **Rest** – Menu £ 32

Part-17C former farmhouse complete with several beamed, open-fired lounges, a hot tub boasting fell views and a tea room in the old cow byres. Richly furnished bedrooms have king or super king sized beds and some feature double jacuzzis; the annexe rooms are the best. Meals are cooked on the Aga.

Old Vicarage

Church Ln, North : 0.5 mi by B 5289 on Lorton Church rd ✉ CA13 9UN – ✆ (01900) 85 656 – www.oldvicarage.co.uk – restricted opening in winter

8 rm – †£ 85/100 ††£ 100/140 **Rest** – Menu £ 30

Charming slate house with lovely gardens and a welcoming owner. Comfy lounge and traditional dining room with fell views and home-cooked dinners. Immaculately kept, sympathetically styled bedrooms; one with a roll-top bath, another with a four-poster – the Coach House rooms have exposed slate walls.

COCKLEFORD – Gloucestershire – ✉ Cheltenham — 4 C1

London 95 mi – Bristol 48 mi – Cheltenham 7 mi

The Green Dragon Inn with rm

✉ GL53 9NW – ✆ (01242) 870 271 – www.green-dragon-inn.co.uk – Closed dinner 25-26 December and 1 January

9 rm – †£ 70/105 ††£ 95/175 **Rest** – *(booking essential)* Carte £ 24/36

Characterful stone pub with huge open fires and carved mice hidden in the woodwork – the hallmark of carpenter Robert 'Mouseman' Thompson. Hearty lunches, unusual starters and generous, meaty mains. Simple, modern bedrooms; one boasts a super king sized bed.

COGGESHALL – Essex – 504 W28 – pop. 3 919 – ✉ Colchester — 13 C2

London 49 mi – Braintree 6 mi – Chelmsford 16 mi – Colchester 9 mi

Baumanns Brasserie

4-6 Stoneham St ✉ CO6 1TT – ✆ (01376) 561 453 – www.baumannsbrasserie.co.uk – Closed first 2 weeks January, Monday and Tuesday

Rest – Menu £ 12/25 – Carte £ 29/47

Characterful 16C building in the market square; its walls packed with pictures and prints. Passionate chef uses quality local produce to create neatly presented, seasonal dishes with modern touches. Friendly service.

at Pattiswick **Northwest : 3 mi by A 120 (Braintree Rd) – ✉ Coggeshall**

Compasses at Pattiswick

Compasses Rd ✉ CM77 8BG – ☎ (01376) 561 322 – www.thegreatpubcompany.co.uk
Rest – Carte £ 19/33
Remote pub with far-reaching views; make the most of these with a seat in the garden. Smart, spacious interior with open fires, chatty staff and a warm, relaxing feel. Wide-ranging menu of traditional English dishes and nursery puddings.

COLERNE – Wiltshire – 503 M29 – see Bath (Bath & North East Somerset)

COLN ST ALDWYNS – Gloucestershire – 503 O28 – pop. 260 – ✉ Cirencester 4 D1

London 101 mi – Bristol 53 mi – Gloucester 20 mi – Oxford 28 mi

New Inn at Coln

✉ GL7 5AN – ☎ (01285) 750 651 – www.new-inn.co.uk
14 rm – †£ 75/150 ††£ 75/190
Rest – *(booking essential)* Menu £ 13/35 – Carte £ 26/45
Charming 16C foliage-clad coaching inn, in a delightful little village. Characterful guest areas and bold modern bedrooms – some with exposed beams, stone walls or brass beds; those in the extension are quieter, with country views. Extensive list of bar meals or more formal menu in contemporary restaurant.

COLSTON BASSETT – Nottinghamshire – 502 R25 – pop. 239 – ✉ Nottingham 16 B2

London 129 mi – Leicester 23 mi – Lincoln 40 mi – Nottingham 15 mi

The Martins Arms

School Ln ✉ NG12 3FD – ☎ (01949) 81 361 – www.themartinsarms.co.uk – Closed dinner 25 December and 1 January
Rest – Carte £ 27/47
Creeper-clad pub in a charming village, with a cosy, fire-lit bar and period furnished dining rooms. The menu has a meaty, masculine base, with a mix of classical and more modern dishes, and plenty of local game in season.

COLTISHALL – Norfolk – 504 Y25 – pop. 2 161 – ✉ Norwich 15 D1

Great Britain

London 125 mi – Norwich 8 mi – Ipswich 54 mi – Lowestoft 31 mi
Norfolk Broads★

Norfolk Mead

Church Loke ✉ NR12 7DN – ☎ (01603) 737 531 – www.norfolkmead.co.uk
12 rm – †£ 115/140 ††£ 125/150
Rest – *(dinner only and Sunday lunch)* Menu £ 30
Former Georgian merchant's house in 8 acres of grounds, complete with an otter lake and a walled garden. Bedrooms are modern and individually styled: one has a jacuzzi; another, a balcony and a roll-top bath. The restaurant has a classical menu and offers views over the meadow to the river.

COLTON – North Yorkshire – see Tadcaster

COLWALL – 501 M27 – see Great Malvern

COLYFORD – Devon – 503 K31 – ✉ Colyton Great Britain 2 D2

London 168 mi – Exeter 21 mi – Taunton 30 mi – Torquay 46 mi
Colyton★ (Church★), N : 1 mi on B 3161 – Axmouth (≤★), S : 1 mi by A 3052 and B 3172

Swallows Eaves

Swan Hill Rd ✉ EX24 6QJ – ☎ (01297) 553 184 – www.swallowseaves.co.uk
7 rm – †£ 75/85 ††£ 95/135
Rest *Reeds* – *(closed Sunday and Monday)* Carte £ 25/33
Smart creamwashed house clad with wisteria, located in the heart of a pretty village close to the marshes. Bright bedrooms come with books, wi-fi and views over the gardens or the Axe Valley. Relax in the lounge or on the terrace. Menus showcase locally sourced produce and display some innovative touches.

ENGLAND

COMBE HAY – Bath and North East Somerset – see Bath

COMPTON BASSETT – Wiltshire – 503 O29 – see Calne

CONGLETON – Cheshire East – 502 N24 – pop. 25 400 Great Britain 20 B3

London 183 mi – Liverpool 50 mi – Manchester 25 mi – Sheffield 46 mi

High St, (01260) 27 10 95, www.cheshirepeakdistrict.com

Biddulph Rd, (01260) 27 35 40

Little Moreton Hall★★ **AC**, SW : 3 mi by A 34

Pecks

Newcastle Rd, Moreton, South : 2.75 mi on A 34 ✉ CW12 4SB – (01260) 275 161 – www.pecksrest.co.uk – Closed 25-30 December, Sunday dinner and Monday

Rest – Menu £ 20/48 – Carte lunch £ 26/53

Airy, modish restaurant with unique style. À la carte lunch; monthly changing 5/7 course set dinner at 8pm sharp. Traditional homemade dishes use good produce and arrive in generous portions.

CONSTABLE BURTON – North Yorkshire – 502 O21 – see Leyburn

CONSTANTINE BAY – Cornwall – 503 E32 – see Padstow

COOKHAM – Windsor and Maidenhead – 504 R29 – pop. 5 304 11 C3

– ✉ **Maidenhead** Great Britain

London 32 mi – High Wycombe 7 mi – Oxford 31 mi – Reading 16 mi

to Marlow, Maidenhead and Windsor (Salter Bros. Ltd) (summer only)

Stanley Spencer Gallery★ **AC**

White Oak

Pound Ln ✉ SL6 9QE – (01628) 523 043 – www.thewhiteoak.co.uk – Closed dinner Sunday and bank holidays

Rest – Menu £ 12/35 – Carte £ 23/54

Contemporary pub close to the common, with a formal dining room and a delightful rear terrace. Appealing, seasonal menus offer largely English dishes, with a few European influences alongside, and cooking is carefully executed and full of flavour. Excellent value daily 'Menu Auberge' and cheery service.

COOKHAM DEAN – Windsor and Maidenhead Great Britain 11 C3

London 32 mi – High Wycombe 7 mi – Oxford 31 mi – Reading 16 mi

Windsor Castle★★★, Eton★★ and Windsor★, S : 5 mi by B 4447, A 4 (westbound) and A 308

Sanctum on the Green

rest,

The Old Cricket Common ✉ SL6 9NZ – (01628) 482 638 – www.sanctumonthegreen.com

9 rm – †£ 99/245 ††£ 99/245

Rest *Luke's Dining Room* – Carte £ 30/36

Hidden away on the side of the green, a part-timbered property with large decked terraces, lovely gardens and a heated outdoor pool. Contemporary furnishings contrast with old beams. Stylish, boutique bedrooms come in bold colours. Two lounges and an open-plan bar and dining area; tasty, classical cooking.

CORBRIDGE – Northumberland – 501 N19 – pop. 2 800 Great Britain 24 A2

London 300 mi – Hexham 3 mi – Newcastle upon Tyne 18 mi

Hill St, (01434) 63 28 15, www.thisiscorbridge.co.uk

Hadrian's Wall★★, N : 3 mi by A 68 – Corstopitum★ **AC**, NW : 0.5 m

Duke of Wellington with rm

rest,

Newton, East : 3 mi by A 6530 ✉ NE43 7UL – (01661) 844 446 – www.thedukeofwellingtoninn.co.uk

7 rm – †£ 80/95 ††£ 95/110

Rest – Menu £ 14 (weekdays) – Carte £ 23/35 **s**

A single track leads to this remote inn which, dating from the early 1600s, is reported to be the county's oldest licensed premises. Rescued by a local, it's now a smart, modern pub offering good food – try the local lamb or roe deer. Stylish, luxurious bedrooms come with characterful exposed beams.

ENGLAND

at Great Whittington North : 5.5 mi by A 68 off B 6318 – ✉ Corbridge

Queens Head Inn

✉ NE19 2HP – ☎ (01434) 672 267 – www.thequeensheadinngw.co.uk – Closed Sunday dinner and Monday
Rest – Carte £ 16/30
Smart dining pub dating from 1615, with a cosy bar and a boldly decorated dining room. Cooking is traditional but has a refined edge and dishes are attractively presented. Lamb is from the next door farm and fish, from nearby North Shields.

CORBY – Northamptonshire – 504 R26 – pop. 49 222 Great Britain 17 C3

London 100 mi – Leicester 26 mi – Northampton 22 mi – Peterborough 24 mi
Priors Hall, Weldon, Stamford Rd, ☎ (01536) 26 07 56
Boughton House★★ AC, S : 5.5 mi by A 6116 and A 43

Hampton by Hilton without rest

Rockingham Leisure Park, Princewood Rd, Northwest : 2.5 mi by Rockingham Rd off A 6116 ✉ NN17 4AP – ☎ (01536) 211 001 – www.hamptonbyhilton.co.uk/corby
88 rm – †£ 49/99 ††£ 59/109
Smart hotel on a business park close to Rockingham Motor Speedway. Modern bedrooms have big comfy beds and are ideal for business travellers; contemporary bathrooms have large walk-in showers. There's a bar and snack shop but no restaurant.

CORFE CASTLE – Dorset – 503 N32 – pop. 1 335 – ✉ Wareham 4 C3

London 129 mi – Bournemouth 18 mi – Weymouth 23 mi
Castle★ (≤★★) AC

Mortons House

45 East St ✉ BH20 5EE – ☎ (01929) 480 988 – www.mortonshouse.co.uk
23 rm – †£ 85/100 ††£ 160 – 2 suites **Rest** – Carte £ 28/44
Elizabethan manor house built in the shape of an "E" to honour the Queen; set next to a castle ruins, with a steam railway running past the garden. Well-kept, classical bedrooms: one with a Victorian bath; four in an annexe, with hi-tech facilities. Lunch in the bar or lounges; dinner in the formal restaurant.

CORNHILL-ON-TWEED – Northumberland – 501 N17 – pop. 317 24 A1

Scotland
London 345 mi – Edinburgh 49 mi – Newcastle upon Tyne 59 mi
Ladykirk (Kirk o'Steil★), NE : 6 mi by A 698 and B 6470

Tillmouth Park

Northeast : 2.5 mi on A 698 ✉ TD12 4UU – ☎ (01890) 882 255 – www.tillmouthpark.co.uk – Closed 2 January-4 April
14 rm – †£ 79/215 ††£ 165/235
Rest *Library* – *(dinner only and Sunday lunch)* Carte £ 24/34
Late Victorian country house in 15 acres; set in prime shooting and fishing country. Welcoming interior with characterful stained glass, grand staircases and traditional guest areas with lovely views. Spacious bedrooms; some four-posters. Wood-panelled restaurant for à la carte dinners and a set Sunday lunch.

Coach House

Crookham, East : 4 mi on A 697 ✉ TD12 4TD – ☎ (01890) 820 293 – www.coachhousecrookham.com – March-November
10 rm – †£ 50/90 ††£ 90/120
Rest – *(dinner only) (bookings essential for non-residents)* Menu £ 24
Keenly run hotel close to the Flodden battleground, consisting of a 1680s dower house and a collection of old farm buildings set around a courtyard. The stable block houses a lounge with an honesty bar and the largest, most modern bedrooms. The cosy breakfast-cum-dining room is in the original house.

CORSE LAWN – Worcestershire – see Tewkesbury (Glos.)

ENGLAND

CORSHAM – Wiltshire – 504 N29 – pop. 11 318 4 C2

London 103 mi – Bristol 31 mi – Cardiff 64 mi – Plymouth 151 mi

Methuen Arms with rm

2 High St ✉ SN13 0HB – ✆ (01249) 717 060 – www.themethuenarms.com

21 rm – †£ 80/115 ††£ 90/180 **Rest** – Menu £ 16/25 – Carte £ 25/48

17C coaching inn set in an attractive little town and named after the family who own Corsham Court. Eat in the 'Little Room' by the bar, the open-fired 'Nott Room' or the characterful restaurant. Good ingredients feature in tasty dishes – dinner steps things up a gear. Comfy, boutique-style bedrooms.

CORTON DENHAM – Somerset – 504 M31 – pop. 210 – ✉ Sherborne 4 C3

London 123 mi – Bristol 36 mi – Cardiff 110 mi – Southampton 84 mi

Queens Arms with rm

✉ DT9 4LR – ✆ (01963) 220 317 – www.thequeensarms.com

8 rm – †£ 80/120 ††£ 100/120 **Rest** – *(booking advisable)* Carte £ 27/35

Relaxed, bohemian pub with open fires and a hotchpotch of tables that include a glass-topped cartwheel. One menu offers pub favourites; the other displays a more interesting array of dishes. Appealing selection of ciders, beers and whiskies. Bedrooms are modern, with good facilities – some have slipper baths.

COTEBROOK – Cheshire West and Chester – see Tarporley

COVERACK – Cornwall – 503 E33 1 A3

London 300 mi – Penzance 25 mi – Truro 27 mi

ENGLAND

Bay

rm,

North Corner ✉ TR12 6TF – ✆ (01326) 280 464 – www.thebayhotel.co.uk – Closed 1-22 December and 3 January-mid March

13 rm (dinner included) – †£ 75/140 ††£ 106/250

Rest – *(dinner only) (bookings essential for non-residents)* Menu £ 29/35

Imposing, family-run country house located in a pretty fishing village and boasting views over the bay. Homely lounge and bar. Spotless, modern bedrooms with a slight New England edge. Dining room and conservatory offer a classical daily menu and local seafood specials.

COWLEY – Gloucestershire – 504 N28 4 C1

London 105 mi – Swindon 28 mi – Gloucester 14 mi – Cheltenham 6 mi

Cowley Manor

✉ GL53 9NL – ✆ (01242) 870 900 – www.cowleymanor.com

22 rm – †£ 185/295 ††£ 205/395 – 8 suites **Rest** – Carte £ 31/45

Impressive Regency manor house in 55 acres, with beautiful formal gardens and a superb spa. Spacious, relaxing guest areas with retro décor, bright colours and unusual fixtures. Appealing, individually styled bedrooms; some with lake views. Traditional menus in the wood-panelled dining room.

COWSHILL – Durham – 502 N19 24 A3

London 295 mi – Newcastle upon Tyne 42 mi – Stanhope 10 mi – Wolsingham 16 mi

Low Cornriggs Farm

Weardale, Northwest : 0.75 mi on A 689 ✉ DL13 1AQ – ✆ (01388) 537 600 – www.cornriggsfarm.co.uk – Closed 20 December-5 January

3 rm – †£ 45 ††£ 68 **Rest** – Menu £ 23 **s**

Extended stone farmhouse dating back 300 years and offering lovely views over Weardale. Cosy flag-floored lounge with an open fire. Dine in the conservatory in summer or the beamed dining room in winter; steak pie is a speciality. Pine-furnished bedrooms have up-to-date facilities and neat, compact bathrooms.

CRADLEY – Herefordshire – see Great Malvern

CRANBROOK – Kent – 504 V30 – pop. 4 225 Great Britain 8 B2

London 53 mi – Hastings 19 mi – Maidstone 15 mi

Stone St, ✆ (01580) 71 25 38, www.cranbrook.org

Sissinghurst Castle★ **AC**, NE : 2.5 mi by A 229 and A 262

Cloth Hall Oast without rest
Coursehorn Ln, East : 1 mi by Tenterden rd ✉ TN17 3NR – ✆ (01580) 712 220 – www.clothhalloast.co.uk – Closed Christmas
3 rm – †£ 65/75 ††£ 90/125
Superbly restored oast house that was rebuilt in 2001. Antiques, family photos and fine artwork fill the drawing room. Bedrooms are well-equipped but retain some original character; one boasts a splendid four-poster bed. Communal breakfasts at an antique table set below restored rafters in the main hall.

Apicius (Tim Johnson)
23 Stone St ✉ TN17 3HE – ✆ (01580) 714 666 – www.restaurant-apicius.co.uk – Closed 2 weeks June-July, 2 weeks Christmas-New Year, Saturday lunch, Sunday dinner, Monday and Tuesday
Rest – Menu £ 27/40
Intimate, personally and passionately run restaurant in a pretty market town; its rustic walls filled with framed menus from the great and the good of the restaurant world. Skilfully prepared dishes use the best local ingredients in classic, tried-and-tested flavour combinations.
→ Crab boudin blanc, tortellini and remoulade. Scallop and bacon brochette with linguini and soya dressing. Medjool date sponge, apricot salad and honey ice cream.

at Sissinghurst Northeast : 1.75 mi by B 2189 on A 262 – ✉ Cranbrook

Rankins
The Street, on A 262 ✉ TN17 2JH – ✆ (01580) 713 964 – www.rankinsrestaurant.com – Closed Monday, Tuesday and bank holidays
Rest – *(dinner only and Sunday lunch) (booking essential)* Menu £ 30
Well-run village restaurant, immaculately kept by knowledgeable, personable owners. Concise set menus display hearty, traditional dishes with the odd Mediterranean touch. Desserts a speciality.

ENGLAND

CRANLEIGH – Surrey – pop. 9 046 7 C2

London 40 mi – Birmingham 150 mi – Leeds 233 mi – Sheffield 203 mi

Richard Onslow with rm
113-117 High St ✉ GU6 8AU – ✆ (01483) 274 922 – www.therichardonslow.co.uk – Closed 25 December
10 rm – †£ 65/85 ††£ 65/85 **Rest** – Menu £ 15 (lunch) – Carte £ 17/39
Friendly, relaxed pub on the high street; its large, airy dining room a contrast to the cosy locals bar with its beams and inglenook fireplace. An accessible menu offers everything from sandwiches and deli boards to roast of the day; dishes are carefully prepared and very tasty. Comfortable, stylish bedrooms.

CRAYKE – North Yorkshire – see Easingwold

CRICKLADE – Wiltshire – 503 029 4 D1

London 89 mi – Birmingham 86 mi – Bristol 54 mi – Cardiff 87 mi

Red Lion with rm
74 High St ✉ SN6 6DD – ✆ (01793) 750 776 – www.theredlioncricklade.co.uk
5 rm – †£ 80 ††£ 80 **Rest** – Carte £ 19/37
Traditional 17C pub, just off the Thames path, offering 10 real ales and 64 speciality beers in the low-beamed bar and beer pairings for every dish in the airy, stone-walled dining room. Classical cooking uses extremely local produce. Comfortable, modern bedrooms are located in the old stables.

CROCKERTON – Wiltshire – see Warminster

CROFT-ON-TEES – North Yorkshire – 502 P20 – see Darlington

CROOKHAM VILLAGE – Hampshire – 504 R30 7 C1

London 43 mi – Sheffield 191 mi – Kingston upon Hull 219 mi – Peterborough 115 mi

Exchequer

Crondall Rd ✉ GU51 5SU – ☎ (01252) 615 336 – www.exchequercrookham.co.uk – Closed 25 December

Rest – Carte £ 22/34

Slick, modern pub with an inviting drinkers' area and a smart conservatory-style room. The menu offers mainly gutsy British staples but there's also a nod to the East; the blackboard best displays the kitchen's abilities. Service is keen.

CROPSTON – Leicestershire – 502 Q25 — 16 B2

London 106 mi – Birmingham 49 mi – Sheffield 67 mi – Leicester 6 mi

Horseshoe Cottage Farm

Roecliffe Rd, Hallgates, Northwest : 1 mi on Woodhouse Eaves rd ✉ LE7 7HQ – ☎ (0116) 235 00 38 – www.horseshoecottagefarm.com

3 rm – †£ 65/70 ††£ 100 **Rest** – Menu £ 20

Well-run, extended farmhouse and outbuildings, beside Bradgate Country Park. Traditional bedrooms with beams, exposed stonework and coordinating fabrics. Small breakfast room and a larger high-ceilinged drawing room, with a solid oak table where communal dinners are served; local and garden produce features.

CROSTHWAITE – Cumbria – 502 L21 – see Kendal

CRUDWELL – Wiltshire – 503 N29 – see Malmesbury

CUCKFIELD – West Sussex – 504 T30 – pop. 3 266 — 7 D2

London 37 mi – Croydon 27 mi – Barnet 51 mi – Ealing 48 mi

Ockenden Manor

Ockenden Ln ✉ RH17 5LD – ☎ (01444) 416 111 – www.ockenden-manor.co.uk

28 rm – †£ 113/205 ††£ 190/395 – 3 suites

Rest *Ockenden Manor* ✿ – see restaurant listing

Part-Elizabethan manor house in 9 acres of parkland with pleasant South Downs views. Elegant drawing room with a grand fireplace; cosy baronial panelled bar. Choice of antique-furnished bedrooms or more stylish rooms above the stunning spa.

Ockenden Manor – Ockenden Manor Hotel

Ockenden Ln ✉ RH17 5LD – ☎ (01444) 416 111 – www.ockenden-manor.co.uk

Rest – *(booking essential)* Menu £ 18 (weekday lunch)/75

Contemporary orangery dining room opening onto the gardens of this part-Elizabethan manor house and affording pleasant views over the parkland and South Downs hills. Passionate chef creates appealing, original menus offering refined, seasonal cooking with well-balanced flavours and good attention to detail.

→ Wood pigeon breast and bon bon with beetroot and hazelnuts. Fillet, cheek and belly of pork with cauliflower, capers and carrots. Oat crème brûlée, orange salad and whisky ice cream.

Cuckoo

1 Broad St ✉ RH17 5LJ – ☎ (01444) 414 184 – www.cuckoorestaurant.co.uk – Closed 1 week January, Sunday dinner and Monday

Rest – Menu £ 15 (lunch) – Carte £ 24/31

Pretty 17C cottage, personally run by an experienced owner; muted, modern décor is enlivened by contemporary artwork. European-influenced dishes have modern touches; save room for the chocolate cheesecake with pineapple and chilli.

CUDDINGTON – Buckinghamshire – 503 M24 Great Britain — 11 C2

London 48 mi – Aylesbury 6 mi – Oxford 17 mi

Waddesdon Manor★★ AC, NE : 6 mi via Cuddington Hill, Cannon's Hill, Waddesdon Hill and A 41

Crown

Aylesbury Rd ✉ HP18 0BB – ☎ (01844) 292 222 – www.thecrowncuddington.co.uk – Closed Sunday dinner

Rest – Carte £ 20/35

Attractive thatched pub in a charming village, with traditional styling and a friendly, welcoming atmosphere. Seasonal menus display hearty comfort food in winter and lighter dishes in summer; the smoked haddock with Welsh rarebit is a hit.

ENGLAND

CURY - Cornwall - 503 E33 - see Helston

CUTNALL GREEN - Worcestershire - 503 N27 - see Droitwich Spa

DARGATE - Kent - see Faversham

DARLEY ABBEY - Derby - 502 P25 - see Derby

DARLINGTON - Darlington - 502 P20 - pop. 86 082 22 B1

London 251 mi - Leeds 61 mi - Middlesbrough 14 mi - Newcastle upon Tyne 35 mi

Teesside Airport : (08712) 242426, E : 6 mi by A 67

Horsemarket, (01325) 38 86 66, www.visitdarlington.com

Blackwell Grange, Briar Close, (01325) 46 44 58

Stressholme, Snipe Lane, (01325) 46 10 02

at Croft-on-Tees South : 4.25 mi on A 167 - ✉ Darlington

Clow Beck House rm,

Monk End Farm, West : 0.75 mi by A 167 off Barton rd ✉ DL2 2SW - (01325) 721 075 - www.clowbeckhouse.co.uk - Closed 24 December-3 January

13 rm - £ 85 £ 135

Rest - *(dinner only) (residents only)* Carte £ 26/41 **s**

Collection of converted farm buildings not far from the River Tees. Welcoming owners and a homely interior. Immaculately kept, tastefully furnished bedrooms come with iPod docks, bathrobes and chocolates; the larger ones have dressing rooms. Home-cooked dinners, with a puzzle supplied while you wait.

at Hurworth-on-Tees South : 5.5 mi by A 167

Rockliffe Hall

✉ DL2 2DU - (01325) 729 999 - www.rockliffehall.com

61 rm - £ 265/295 £ 210/440

Rest *The Orangery* - Menu £ 25/65 **s** - Carte £ 37/95

Rest *Brasserie* - Carte £ 29/49 **s**

Rest *Clubhouse Grill* - Menu £ 22 **s** - Carte £ 26/46 **s**

Impressive red-brick property in 376 acres of grounds, boasting a championship golf course and state-of-the-art leisure facilities. Grand guest areas and characterful bedrooms in the original Victorian house; modern bedrooms in the extensions. Ambitious restaurant menu; light, modern dishes in the airy brasserie; everything from sandwiches to Sunday lunch in the grill.

Bay Horse

45 The Green ✉ DL2 2AA - (01325) 720 663 - www.thebayhorsehurworth.com - Closed 25-26 December and Sunday dinner

Rest - Menu £ 17 (lunch)/25 (weekday dinner) - Carte £ 27/36

Smart village pub with pleasant terrace and gardens. Wide-ranging menu offers largely hearty classics; presentation ranges from simple and rustic to more modern and intricate.

at Summerhouse Northwest : 6.5 mi by A 68 on B 6279

Raby Hunt (James Close) with rm

✉ DL2 3UD - (01325) 374 237 - www.rabyhuntrestaurant.co.uk - Closed 1 week spring, 1 week autumn, 25-26 December, 1 January and Sunday to Tuesday

2 rm - £ 90/135 £ 125/135

Rest - *(booking essential at dinner)* Menu £ 27/75 - Carte dinner £ 40/59

Ivy-clad former inn in a rural hamlet; now a simply but stylishly decorated, family-run restaurant with a small, modern bar and an elegant, wood-floored dining room. The passionate, self-taught chef uses first class ingredients to create a weekly changing menu of unfussy modern dishes, with bold flavours and a confident touch. Comfortable, contemporary bedrooms.

→ Razor clam with peas, morels, almond and brown shrimps. Raby Estate deer with venison ragu, salt-baked beetroot and celeriac. Chocolate bar with popcorn ice cream.

at Headlam Northwest : 8 mi by A 67 – ✉ Gainford

Headlam Hall rm, P
✉ DL2 3HA – ✆ (01325) 730 238 – www.headlamhall.co.uk – Closed 24-27 December
39 rm – †£ 100/110 ††£ 125/135 – 4 suites
Rest – Menu £ 18/23 – Carte £ 24/44
Family owned and run manor house with delightful walled gardens in a secluded countryside setting. Spacious antique-furnished sitting rooms. Well-equipped, traditionally styled bedrooms in the original house; others are more contemporary. Up-to-date leisure facilities. Bright restaurant offers classic dishes.

DARTFORD – Kent – 504 U29 – pop. 56 818 8 B1

London 20 mi – Hastings 51 mi – Maidstone 22 mi
Access Dartford Tunnel and Bridge (toll)

at Wilmington Southwest : 1.5 mi A 225 on B 258 – ✉ Dartford

Rowhill Grange rm, AC rest, P
Southwest : 2 mi on Hextable rd (B 258) ✉ *DA2 7QH – ✆ (01322) 615 136 – www.rowhillgrange.com*
38 rm – †£ 99/190 ††£ 109/290 – 1 suite
Rest *RG'S Grill* – Menu £ 40 (lunch) – Carte dinner £ 31/51
Extended, early 19C thatched house in pretty 15 acre gardens, with smart, modern bedrooms named after flowers or castles. Fantastic spa with 9 treatment rooms, large gym and superb swimming pool; separate infinity pool with waterfall. RG's Grill serves fresh seasonal dishes – try the mixed grill.

DARTMOUTH – Devon – 503 J32 – pop. 6 008 2 C3

London 236 mi – Exeter 36 mi – Plymouth 35 mi
Mayor's Ave, ✆ (01803) 83 42 24, www.discoverdartmouth.com
Town★★ (≤★) - Old Town - Butterwalk★ - Dartmouth Castle (≤★★★) **AC**
Start Point (≤★), S : 13 mi (including 1 mi on foot)

Dart Marina rm, AC rest, P
Sandquay Rd ✉ *TQ6 9PH – ✆ (01803) 832 580 – www.dartmarina.com*
51 rm – †£ 95/155 ††£ 140/200
Rest *River* – *(dinner only and Sunday lunch)* Menu £ 30/38
Relaxed, modern hotel with a small spa and leisure centre; converted from an old boat works and chandlery. Smart, contemporary bedrooms have lovely outlooks over either the river or the marina; many also boast balconies. Stylish, formal restaurant offers up-to-date versions of British classics.

Royal Castle P
11 The Quay ✉ *TQ6 9PS – ✆ (01803) 833 033 – www.royalcastle.co.uk*
25 rm – †£ 100/120 ††£ 149/230 **Rest** – Carte £ 22/37
Iconic 15C coaching inn consisting of two separate buildings joined by a smart glass atrium. Boldly coloured bedrooms offer good comforts – some have jacuzzi baths. Choice of two bars: one for drinkers and one serving all-day dishes. The restaurant offers modern takes on old classics and has great views.

XX **Seahorse** AC
5 South Embankment ✉ *TQ6 9BH – ✆ (01803) 835 147 – www.seahorserestaurant.co.uk – Closed Monday, Sunday dinner and Tuesday lunch*
Rest – *(booking essential)* Menu £ 20 (lunch and early dinner) – Carte £ 29/65
Smart restaurant in a lovely spot on the embankment; sit outside looking over the estuary or inside, beside the glass-walled kitchen. Seafood orientated menus have a Mediterranean bias; whole fish cooked on the Josper grill are a hit.

XX **Annabelles Kitchen**
24 South Embankment ✉ *TQ6 9BB – ✆ (01803) 833 540 – www.annabelleskitchen.co.uk – Closed late January-early February, Sunday, Monday and lunch Tuesday*
Rest – *(dinner only and lunch April-September) (booking essential)* Menu £ 20 (lunch) – Carte £ 28/41
Occupying a prime estuary facing spot is this smart, modern eatery, run by a husband and wife team. Their philosophy is based around sourcing local and seasonal ingredients and keeping the dishes simple.

ENGLAND

Rockfish

8 South Embankment ✉ TQ6 9BH – ☎ (01803) 832 800 – www.rockfishdevon.co.uk – Closed dinner Sunday-Wednesday in winter
Rest – *(bookings not accepted)* Carte £ 20/33
Buzzy 'beach shack' style eatery run by a chatty team. Good old comfort dishes arrive in paper-lined baskets and rely on sustainable produce. Closely set tables have paper cloths proclaiming 'fish so fresh tomorrow's are still in the sea'.

at Kingswear East : via lower ferry – ✉ Dartmouth

Nonsuch House

Church Hill, from lower ferry take first right onto Church Hill before Steam Packet Inn ✉ TQ6 0BX – ☎ (01803) 752 829 – www.nonsuch-house.co.uk
4 rm – †£ 90/135 ††£ 115/180
Rest – *(closed Tuesday, Wednesday and Saturday) (dinner only) (residents only)* Menu £ 38 **s**
Charming Edwardian house run by friendly hands-on owners; boasting lovely views over the castle, town and sea. The bright Mediterranean-style décor blends nicely with original features. Bedrooms are spacious and well-appointed and one has a small balcony. Tea and homemade cake on arrival; local, seasonal cooking and excellent views in the conservatory dining room.

at Strete Southwest : 4.5 mi on A 379 – ✉ Dartmouth

Strete Barton House without rest

Totnes Rd ✉ TQ6 0RU – ☎ (01803) 770 364 – www.stretebarton.co.uk – Closed 2 weeks January
6 rm – †£ 105/160 ††£ 105/160
Attractive, part-16C manor house in a quiet village, with partial views over the rooftops to the sea. Contemporary interior with a personal style; bedrooms have bold feature walls and modern facilities. Homemade cake is served on arrival.

Laughing Monk Ⓝ

Totnes Rd ✉ TQ6 0RN – ☎ (01803) 770 639 – www.thelaughingmonkdevon.co.uk – Closed December and January
Rest – *(dinner only)* Menu £ 24 – Carte £ 24/40
Built in 1839 as the village schoolhouse; the original wooden floor and a huge stone fireplace remain. Tasty, traditional dishes feature meats from nearby farms and seafood from local waters; cooking is unfussy and uses classical pairings.

at Blackawton West : 5.5 mi by A 3122

Normandy Arms Ⓝ with rm

Chapel St ✉ TQ9 7BN – ☎ (01803) 712 884 – www.normandyarms.co.uk – Closed January, Sunday dinner and Monday
3 rm – †£ 85/95 ††£ 85/95
Rest – Menu £ 18 (weekday dinner) – Carte £ 24/37
Pretty little pub with a cosy bar area and a dining room decorated with colourful artwork. Cooking keeps things simple, relying on careful preparation of good quality ingredients to keep flavours clear. Smart, unfussy bedrooms are named after cities in Normandy; the pub's name refers to the Normandy landings.

DATCHWORTH – Hertfordshire – 504 T28 — 12 B2

London 31 mi – Luton 15 mi – Stevenage 6 mi

Coltsfoot Country Retreat

rm,

South 0.75 mi by Bramfield Rd, turning at 'The Horns' ✉ SG3 6SB – ☎ (01438) 212 800 – www.coltsfoot.com
15 rm – †£ 118 ††£ 145/165
Rest – *(closed Sunday) (dinner only) (booking essential)* Carte £ 24/37
A former farmhouse dating back to the 16C; now a contemporary hotel and a popular wedding venue. Spacious bedrooms, some with terraces; Room 15 was where the prize bull was once kept. The bar and restaurant are in a converted barn and offer pleasant country views; menus are classical, with a modern twist.

ENGLAND

Tilbury

Watton Rd ✉ SG3 6TB – ✆ (01438) 815 550 – www.thetilbury.co.uk – Closed Sunday dinner

Rest – Menu £ 14 (lunch) – Carte £ 18/42

Characterful dining pub with a heated terrace; set in a pretty little village and a hit with the locals. Dishes range from good old pub classics to adventurous stuffed lobster; seafood is a speciality and cheese is available by the slice.

DAVENTRY – Northamptonshire – 504 Q27 – pop. 21 731 16 B3

London 79 mi – Coventry 23 mi – Leicester 31 mi – Northampton 13 mi

Norton Rd, ✆ (01327) 70 28 29

Hellidon Lakes H. & C.C., Hellidon, ✆ (01327) 26 25 50

Staverton Park, Staverton, ✆ (01327) 30 20 00

Fawsley Hall

Fawsley, South : 6.5 mi by A 45 off A 361 ✉ NN11 3BA – ✆ (01327) 892 000 – www.fawsleyhall.com

56 rm – †£ 185/190 ††£ 225/245 – 2 suites

Rest *Bess's Brasserie* – see restaurant listing

Rest *Equilibrium* – *(closed Christmas-New Year and Sunday-Wednesday) (dinner only) (booking essential)* Menu £ 59

Set in 2,000 peaceful acres, a luxurious Tudor manor house boasting Georgian and Victorian wings. Cavernous grand hall and exclusive leisure club and spa. Well-appointed bedrooms vary from wing to wing: the most characterful are in the main house. Intimate Equilibrium serves innovative modern dishes; informal Bess's offers brasserie classics.

ENGLAND

Bess's Brasserie – Fawsley Hall Hotel

Fawsley, South : 6.5 mi by A 45 off A 361 ✉ NN11 3BA – ✆ (01327) 892 000 – www.fawsleyhall.com

Rest – Carte £ 22/40

Situated in the heart of an impressive manor house, a smart yet informal dining room boasting an impressive stone fireplace and a courtyard terrace. The wide-ranging menu offers refined brasserie classics with modern twists. Friendly team.

at Staverton Southwest : 2.75 mi by A 45 off A 425 – ✉ Daventry

Colledges House

Oakham Ln, off Glebe Ln ✉ NN11 6JQ – ✆ (01327) 702 737 – www.colledgeshouse.co.uk

4 rm – †£ 68/70 ††£ 95/99 **Rest** – Menu £ 35

17C thatched cottage and barn conversion, run by a friendly, enthusiastic owner. The cosy lounge is filled with antiques and curios; the conservatory is a pleasant spot in summer. Traditional bedrooms have floral fabrics and good extras. Cordon bleu style dinners are taken communally at a solid oak table.

DAYLESFORD – Gloucestershire – 503 O28 – see Stow-on-the-Wold

---

DEAL – Kent – 504 Y30 – pop. 29 248 9 D2

London 78 mi – Canterbury 19 mi – Dover 8 mi – Margate 16 mi

129 High St, ✆ (01304) 36 95 76, www.deal.gov.uk

Walmer & Kingsdown, Kingsdown, The Leas, ✆ (01304) 37 32 56

Dunkerley's

19 Beach St ✉ CT14 7AH – ✆ (01304) 375 016 – www.dunkerleys.co.uk

16 rm – †£ 65/110 ††£ 80/150

Rest *Dunkerley's* – see restaurant listing

Well-located just off the main street, opposite the beach and pier. Simply furnished modern bedrooms with contemporary fabrics and throws: some have feature wallpaper or spa baths. Large bar offers a snack menu.

Number One without rest
1 Ranelagh Rd ✉ CT14 7BG – ✆ (01304) 364 459 – www.numberonebandb.co.uk
4 rm – †£ 65/90 ††£ 85/100
Former boarding house by the promenade, refurbished in a contemporary style. Bedrooms boast bold feature wallpaper, luxury bathrooms and fine bed linen. Delightful breakfast room has ornate light fittings and vast pieces of modern art.

Dunkerley's – Dunkerley's Hotel
19 Beach St ✉ CT14 7AH – ✆ (01304) 375 016 – www.dunkerleys.co.uk
– Closed Monday lunch
Rest – Menu £ 12/29
Traditional hotel restaurant with original stained glass windows and views over the Channel. Cooking is classical and hearty, with plenty of seafood on offer; specials usually come from the day boats. Good range of wines.

at Worth Northwest : 5 mi by A 258

Solley Farm House without rest
The Street ✉ CT14 0DG – ✆ (01304) 613 701 – www.solleyfarmhouse.co.uk
3 rm – †£ 90/95 ††£ 120/140
Attractive 300 year old house overlooking the duck pond; run by a charming, chatty owner. In the beamed lounge, a vast inglenook fireplace takes centre stage; the colour-themed bedrooms come with great extras. Have breakfast on the terrace.

DEDDINGTON – Oxfordshire – 503 Q28 – pop. 1 595 — 10 B1

London 72 mi – Birmingham 46 mi – Coventry 33 mi – Oxford 18 mi

Old Post House without rest
New St, on A 4260 ✉ OX15 0SP – ✆ (01869) 338 978 – www.oldposthouse.co.uk
3 rm – †£ 65 ††£ 90
Charming 17C sandstone house with mullioned windows, a beautiful walled garden and an outdoor pool (for use by prior arrangement). Comfortable open-fired lounge and spacious, classically styled bedrooms. Tea and cake on arrival. Tasty Aga-cooked breakfasts, with homemade preserves for your toast.

DEDHAM – Essex – 504 W28 – pop. 1 847 – ✉ Colchester — 13 D2

Great Britain

London 63 mi – Chelmsford 30 mi – Colchester 8 mi – Ipswich 12 mi
Stour Valley★ – Flatford Mill★, E : 6 mi by B 1029, A 12 and B 1070

Maison Talbooth
Stratford Rd, West : 0.5 mi ✉ C07 6HN – ✆ (01206) 322 367
– www.milsomhotels.com
12 rm – †£ 170/220 ††£ 210/420
Rest *Le Talbooth* – see restaurant listing
Charming, part-Georgian house in rolling countryside, with a modern, country house feel and views over the river valley. Individually decorated bedrooms boast quality furnishings and come in a mix of classical and contemporary styles. Seek out the tennis court and lovely, year-round heated swimming pool.

Milsoms
rest,
Stratford Rd, West : 0.75 mi ✉ CO7 6HW – ✆ (01206) 322 795
– www.milsomhotels.com
15 rm – †£ 120/170 ††£ 120/170 **Rest** – Carte £ 20/44
A late 19C country house with modern additions, overlooking Dedham Vale; its interior is stylish and contemporary, with comfortable and well-equipped 'New England' style bedrooms. All-day dining from an appealing menu in the airy bar restaurant with its huge terrace.

ENGLAND

XXX **Le Talbooth** – Maison Talbooth Hotel

Gun Hill, West : 0.75 mi ✉ CO7 6HP – ✆ (01206) 323 150 – www.milsomhotels.com – Closed Sunday dinner October-May

Rest – Menu £ 31 (weekday lunch) – Carte £ 38/58

Delightful hotel restaurant with numerous private rooms and a lovely terrace, in an attractive riverside setting. To celebrate its 60th birthday, it was cleverly and subtly updated, with a zinc bar and stunning Italian chandeliers. Menus are light and modern, and are accompanied by a well-chosen wine list.

Sun Inn with rm

High St ✉ CO7 6DF – ✆ (01206) 323 351 – www.thesuninndedham.com – Closed 25-26 December

7 rm – £ 85/125 £ 105/150

Rest – Menu £ 16 (weekdays) – Carte £ 21/35

Brightly painted 15C pub in the heart of a picturesque village. Relaxed dining room and beautiful wooden bar stocked with real ales and homemade sausage rolls. Hearty, rustic Italian dishes – many available in two sizes – and a large selection of tasty antipasti. Snug bedrooms; two have a Scandic feel.

DENHAM – Buckinghamshire – 504 S29 – pop. 2 269 Great Britain 11 D3

London 20 mi – Buckingham 42 mi – Oxford 41 mi – Croydon 26 mi

Windsor Castle★★★, Eton★★ and Windsor★, S : 10 mi by A 412

Swan Inn

Village Rd ✉ UB9 5BH – ✆ (01895) 832 085 – www.swaninndenham.co.uk – Closed 25-26 December

Rest – *(booking essential)* Carte £ 20/37

Located in a picture postcard village; a wisteria-clad, red-brick Georgian pub with a pleasant terrace and mature gardens. Menus change with the seasons and offer plenty of interest – the side dishes are appealing and pudding is a must.

ENGLAND

DERBY – Derby – 502 P25 – pop. 253 472 Great Britain 16 B2

London 132 mi – Birmingham 40 mi – Coventry 49 mi – Leicester 29 mi

Nottingham East Midlands Airport, Castle Donington : ✆ (0871) 919 9000, SE : 12 mi by A 6 X

Market Pl, ✆ (01332) 25 58 02, www.visitderby.co.uk

Sinfin, Wilmore Rd, ✆ (01332) 76 63 23

Mickleover, Uttoxeter Rd, ✆ (01332) 51 60 11

Allestree Park, Allestree, Allestree Hall, ✆ (01332) 55 06 16

City★ – Museum and Art Gallery★ (Collection of Derby Porcelain★) YZ **M1** – Royal Crown Derby Museum★ **AC** Z **M2**

Kedleston Hall★★ **AC**, NW : 4.5 mi by Kedleston Rd X

Cathedral Quarter rm,

16 St. Marys Gate ✉ DE1 3JR – ✆ (01332) 546 080 – www.cathedralquarterhotel.com Y**x**

38 rm – £ 55/75 £ 65/140

Rest *Opulence* – *(closed Sunday dinner and Monday) (dinner only and Sunday lunch)* Menu £ 20 – Carte £ 22/40

Boutique-style hotel retaining original features like mosaic floors and marble pillars. Bedrooms vary in size but all are furnished in a contemporary style with pastel shades. First floor Opulence has wood panelling and an 8-seater chef's table. Ambitious modern dishes.

at Darley Abbey North : 2.5 mi off A 6 - X - ✉ Derby

XX **Darleys**

✉ DE22 1DZ – ✆ (01332) 364 987 – www.darleys.com – Closed 25 December-15 January, Sunday dinner and bank holidays

Rest – *(booking advisable)* Menu £ 21 (lunch) – Carte £ 35/41

Popular weir-side restaurant, located in the former canteen of a 19C silk mill. Attractive drinks terrace, modern bar-lounge and traditional dining room. Great value lunches and more ambitious modern European dishes in the evening.

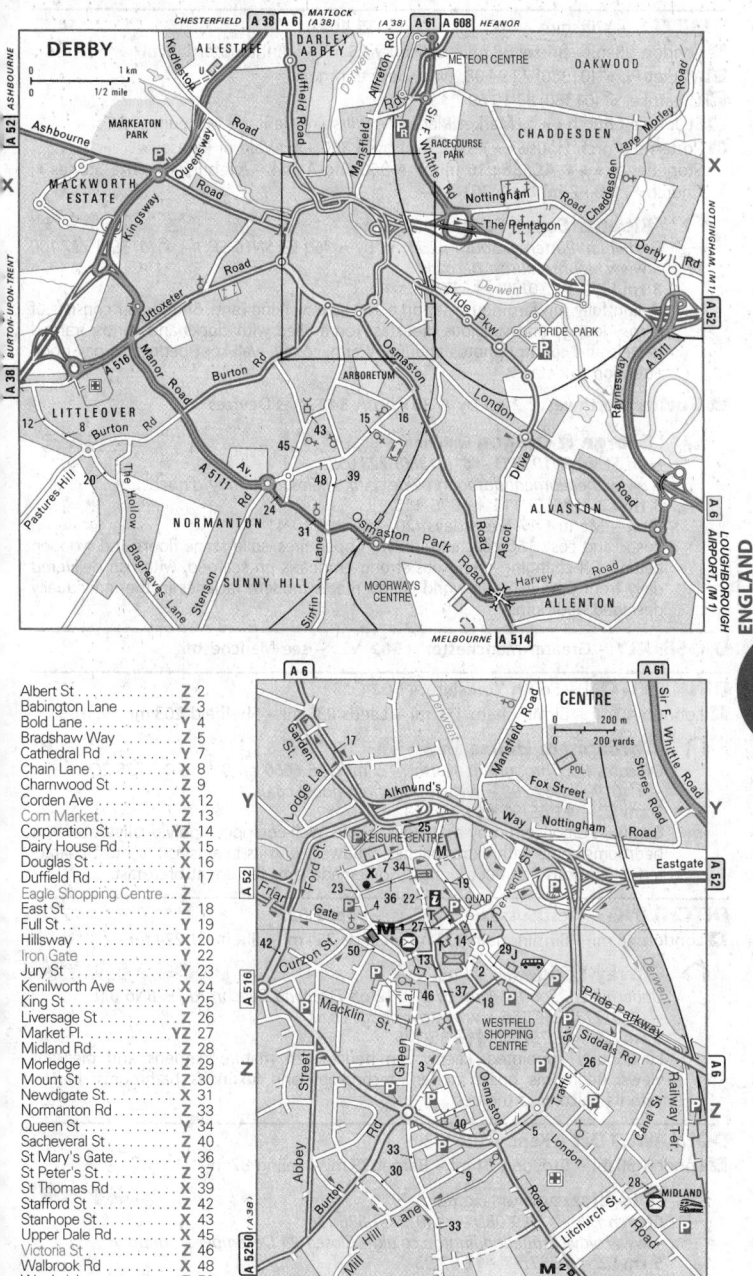

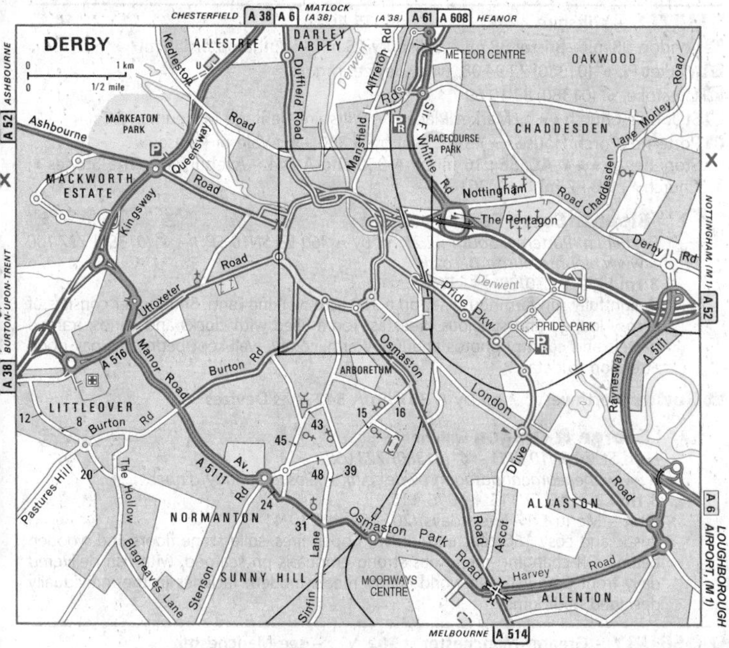

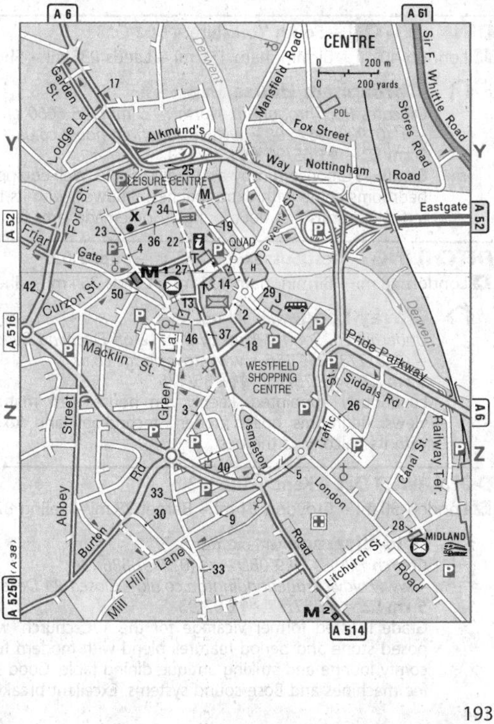

Albert St . . . . Z 2
Babington Lane . . . . Z 3
Bold Lane . . . . Y 4
Bradshaw Way . . . . Z 5
Cathedral Rd . . . . Y 7
Chain Lane . . . . X 8
Charnwood St . . . . Z 9
Corden Ave . . . . X 12
Corn Market . . . . Z 13
Corporation St . . . . YZ 14
Dairy House Rd . . . . X 15
Douglas St . . . . X 16
Duffield Rd . . . . Y 17
Eagle Shopping Centre . . . Z
East St . . . . Z 18
Full St . . . . Y 19
Hillsway . . . . X 20
Iron Gate . . . . Y 22
Jury St . . . . Y 23
Kenilworth Ave . . . . X 24
King St . . . . Y 25
Liversage St . . . . Z 26
Market Pl. . . . . YZ 27
Midland Rd . . . . Z 28
Morledge . . . . Z 29
Mount St . . . . Z 30
Newdigate St . . . . X 31
Normanton Rd . . . . Z 33
Queen St . . . . Y 34
Sacheveral St . . . . Z 40
St Mary's Gate . . . . Y 36
St Peter's St . . . . Z 37
St Thomas Rd . . . . X 39
Stafford St . . . . Z 42
Stanhope St . . . . X 43
Upper Dale Rd . . . . X 45
Victoria St . . . . Z 46
Walbrook Rd . . . . X 48
Wardwick . . . . Z 50

ENGLAND

DEVIZES – Wiltshire – 503 O29 – pop. 15 466 4 C2

London 98 mi – Bristol 38 mi – Salisbury 25 mi – Southampton 50 mi

Market Pl, (01380) 72 94 08, www.devizes.org.uk

Erlestoke, (01380) 83 10 69

St John's Church★★ – Market Place★ – Wiltshire Heritage Museum★ **AC**

Potterne (Porch House★★) S : 2.5 mi by A 360 – E : Vale of Pewsey★. Stonehenge★★★ **AC**, SE : 16 mi by A 360 and A 344 – Avebury★★ (The Stones★, Church★) NE : 7 mi by A 361

Blounts Court Farm without rest

Coxhill Ln, Potterne, South : 2.25 mi by A 360 ✉ SN10 5PH – (01380) 727 180 – www.blountscourtfarm.co.uk

3 rm – £ 50/88 £ 76/88

Delightfully run farmhouse set on a 150 acre working farm. Snug inner consists of a cosy lounge and spacious breakfast room filled with clocks and curios; framed pastels and country photos abound. Warm, comfy, well-kept bedrooms pay good attention to detail.

at Rowde Northwest : 2 mi by A 361 on A 342 – ✉ Devizes

George & Dragon with rm

High St ✉ SN10 2PN – (01380) 723 053 – www.thegeorgeanddragonrowde.co.uk – Closed Sunday dinner

3 rm – £ 75/115 £ 75/115

Rest – Menu £ 17 (weekdays)/20 – Carte £ 19/41

Rustic and cosy 16C coaching inn with open fires, solid stone floors and wooden beams. Oft-changing menu has strong emphasis on seafood, with fish delivered daily from Cornwall. Old-world charm meets modern facilities in the individually designed bedrooms.

DIDSBURY – Greater Manchester – 502 N23 – see Manchester

DINNINGTON – South Yorkshire – 502 Q23 22 B3

London 40 mi – Birmingham 150 mi – Leeds 233 mi – Sheffield 203 mi

Throapham House without rest

Oldcotes Rd, Throapham, North : 1.5 mi by B 6060 on B 6463 ✉ S25 2QS – (01909) 562 208 – www.throapham-house.co.uk

3 rm – £ 65/90 £ 75/100

Comfy 19C house run by a friendly couple. Well-equipped, individually decorated bedrooms come with extra touches; Bradwell, with its beams, is the most characterful. Spacious first floor lounge. Homemade jams feature at breakfast.

DITCHLING – West Sussex – 504 T31 – pop. 2 027 7 D2

London 48 mi – Birmingham 171 mi – Leeds 254 mi – Sheffield 224 mi

Tovey Lodge without rest

Underhill Ln, South : 1 mi by B 2112 off Ditchling Beacon rd ✉ BN6 8XE – (01273) 256 156 – www.toveylodge.co.uk

5 rm – £ 75/155 £ 85/175

Luxuriously appointed, keenly run house with mature gardens and pleasant views. Bedrooms boast modern technology and luxurious bathrooms; Maple, with its balcony, is the best.

DODDINGTON – Kent – 504 W30 9 C2

London 50 mi – Croydon 51 mi – Barnet 73 mi – Ealing 87 mi

Old Vicarage without rest

Church Hill ✉ ME9 0BD – (01795) 886 136 – www.oldvicaragedoddington.co.uk – Closed 24 December-2 January

5 rm – £ 57/72 £ 82/93

Grade II listed former vicarage for the 12C church, where wooden beams, exposed stone and period features blend with modern furnishings. Impressive hall, comfy lounge and striking antique dining table. Good-sized bedrooms boast coffee machines and Bose sound systems. Excellent breakfasts.

DOGMERSFIELD - Hampshire 7 C1

London 44 mi – Farnham 6 mi – Fleet 2 mi

Four Seasons

Dogmersfield Park, Chalky Ln ✉ RG27 8TD – ☎ (01252) 853 000 – www.fourseasons.com/hampshire

111 rm – †£ 260/285 ††£ 260/285, ☕ £ 20 – 22 suites

Rest *Seasons* – *(closed Sunday dinner and Monday) (dinner only and Sunday lunch)* Menu £ 55 – Carte £ 39/62

Attractive, part-Georgian house with pleasant gardens. Luxurious, well-equipped bedrooms; choose one with a view over the extensive parkland. Superb spa in the converted coach house. Contemporary restaurant offers classic dishes presented in a modern style; try the 'Taste of Hampshire' tasting menu.

DONCASTER - South Yorkshire - 502 Q23 - pop. 67 977 23 C3

London 173 mi – Kingston-upon-Hull 46 mi – Leeds 30 mi – Nottingham 46 mi

Robin Hood Airport : ☎ (0871) 220 2210, SE : 7m off A638

38-40 High St, ☎ (01302) 73 43 09, www.visitdoncaster.com

Doncaster Town Moor, Belle Vue, Bawtry Rd, ☎ (01302) 53 31 67

Wheatley, Amthorpe Rd, ☎ (01302) 83 16 55

Owston Park, Owston, Owston Lane, Carcroft, ☎ (01302) 33 08 21

Mount Pleasant

rm, rest,

Great North Rd, Southeast : 6 mi on A 638 ✉ DN11 0HW – ☎ (01302) 868 696 – www.mountpleasant.co.uk – Closed 24-25 December

56 rm ☕ – †£ 79/149 ††£ 99/399 – 2 suites

Rest *Garden* – Menu £ 33 (dinner) – Carte £ 23/45

Well-run hotel with luxurious, individually styled bedrooms – many with feature beds, jacuzzi baths and even saunas; try a room with a glass or five-poster bed. Good range of beauty treatments in the spa. Characterful bar and a formal restaurant with an impressive wall tapestry; extensive, classical menu.

ENGLAND

DONHEAD-ST-ANDREW - Wiltshire - 503 N30 4 C3

London 115 mi – Bournemouth 34 mi – Poole 32 mi – Bath 37 mi

The Forester

Lower St ✉ SP7 9EE – ☎ (01747) 828 038 – www.theforesterdonheadstandrew.co.uk – Closed Sunday dinner

Rest – Menu £ 17 (weekdays) – Carte £ 23/36

Gloriously rustic, 13C thatched pub, hidden down narrow lanes in a delightful village. Exposed stone walls and vast open fires feature throughout. Seasonal menus showcase well-prepared, flavoursome dishes with a classical country base and a refined edge; they also offer a daily seafood selection.

DORCHESTER - Dorset - 503 M31 - pop. 18 248 4 C3

London 135 mi – Bournemouth 27 mi – Exeter 53 mi – Southampton 53 mi

11 Antelope Walk, ☎ (01305) 26 79 92, www.visit-dorset.com

Came Down, ☎ (01305) 81 34 94

Town★ - Dorset County Museum★ **AC**

Maiden Castle★★ (≤★) SW : 2.5 mi – Puddletown Church★, NE : 5.5 mi by A 35. Moreton Church★★, E : 7.5 mi – Bere Regis★ (St John the Baptist Church★ - Roof★★) NE : 11 mi by A 35 – Athelhampton House★ **AC**, NE : 6.5 mi by A 35 - Cerne Abbas★, N : 7 mi by A 352 – Milton Abbas★, NE : 12 mi on A 354 and by-road

Little Court without rest

5 Westleaze, Charminster, North : 1 mi by A 37, turning right at Loders garage ✉ DT2 9PZ – ☎ (01305) 261 576 – www.littlecourt.net

8 rm ☕ – †£ 79/119 ††£ 89/129

Lutyens style house boasting Edwardian wood and brickwork, leaded windows and mature gardens with a pool and tennis court. Bedrooms display original features and modern furnishings; one has a four-poster bed.

Westwood House without rest

29 High St West ✉ DT1 1UP – ✆ (01305) 268 018 – www.westwoodhouse.co.uk – Closed 31 December-5 January

6 rm – †£ 60/75 ††£ 80/95

Georgian townhouse built in 1815 by Lord Illchester. Its sunny drawing room opens onto the conservatory, where a hearty breakfast is served. Bedrooms have bold colours and king-sized beds; family suite on the top floor.

Sienna (Russell Brown)

36 High West St ✉ DT1 1UP – ✆ (01305) 250 022 – www.siennarestaurant.co.uk – Closed 2 weeks spring, 2 weeks autumn, Tuesday lunch, Sunday and Monday

Rest – *(booking essential)* Menu £ 27/65

Unassuming, intimate high street restaurant with just five tables. The 6 course tasting menu features accomplished, carefully crafted dishes. Excellent quality local produce is showcased in superbly flavoured, tried-and-tested combinations. Service is at once professional and friendly.

→ Rump of rose veal, white bean casserole and pickled carrot. Fillet of brill with squid, chorizo, chickpeas and saffron. Rhubarb frangipane tart with orange custard and rhubarb sorbet.

Yalbury Cottage with rm

Lower Bockhampton, East : 3.75 mi by A 35 ✉ DT2 8PZ – ✆ (01305) 262 382 – www.yalburycottage.com – Closed Christmas-15 January

8 rm – †£ 70/85 ††£ 95/120

Rest – *(bar lunch Monday-Saturday)* Menu £ 36

Proudly run restaurant in an old thatched cottage, with a snug beamed lounge and dining room. English tapas at lunch, with locally cured meats, cheese and bread baked in plant pots; gutsy, masculine dishes at dinner, with produce sourced from within 9 miles. Spacious, modern bedrooms are in a newer wing.

ENGLAND

at Winterbourne Steepleton West : 4.75 mi by B 3150 and A 35 on B 3159 – ✉ Dorchester

Old Rectory without rest

✉ DT2 9LG – ✆ (01305) 889 468 – www.theoldrectorybandb.co.uk – Closed 1 week Christmas

4 rm – †£ 60 ††£ 70/100

Attractive house in pretty village; cross the brook and enter mature gardens. Comfy lounge and conservatory breakfast room. Immaculate bedrooms with homely, modern décor and smart bathrooms.

DORKING – Surrey – 504 T30 – pop. 16 071 — 7 D2

London 26 mi – Brighton 39 mi – Guildford 12 mi – Worthing 33 mi

Betchworth Park, Reigate Rd, ✆ (01306) 88 20 52

Two to Four

2-4 West St ✉ RH4 1BL – ✆ (01306) 889 923 – www.2to4.co.uk – Closed 24 December-early January, 1 week spring, 1 week summer, Sunday in summer and Monday

Rest – Menu £ 16 (weekday lunch)/26 – Carte £ 24/46

This 17C, Grade II listed property sports contemporary décor, although beams bear witness to its history and help give it a pleasant rustic feel. Friendly and informal; cosy in the evening. Menu is British at its core but with influences from all over; dishes are unfussy and well-presented.

DORNEY – Buckinghamshire — 11 D3

London 27 mi – Birmingham 111 mi – Bristol 97 mi – Croydon 35 mi

Palmer Arms (N)

Village Rd ✉ SL4 6QW – ✆ (01628) 666 612 – www.thepalmerarms.com

Rest – *(booking advisable)* Carte £ 20/36

Run by a keen young couple and a charismatic chef; it's the food, not the furnishings, that matters here. Menus display a well-balanced mix of pub favourites and more adventurous dishes. The private dining room offers far-reaching views.

DORRIDGE – West Midlands – 503 O26 – ✉ Birmingham 19 C2

London 109 mi – Birmingham 11 mi – Warwick 11 mi

Forest with rm

25 Station Approach ✉ B93 8JA – ✆ (01564) 772 120 – www.forest-hotel.com – Closed 25 December and Sunday dinner

12 rm – †£ 70/99 ††£ 100/130 **Rest** – Menu £ 16 – Carte £ 23/34

Neighbourhood restaurant opposite the railway station with a surprisingly stylish and contemporary interior; choose the bar lounge for simple classics, or head to the dining room for ambitious, modern dishes. Cooking is accomplished and well-judged. Comfortable, contemporary bedrooms.

DOUGLAS – Douglas – 502 G21 – see Man (Isle of)

DOVER – Kent – 504 Y30 – pop. 35 557 Great Britain 9 D2

London 76 mi – Bexley 63 mi – Southend-on-Sea 88 mi – Eastbourne 68 mi

to France (Calais) (P & O Stena Line) frequent services daily (1 h 15 mn) – to France (Calais) (SeaFrance S.A.) frequent services daily (1 h 30 mn) – to France (Boulogne) (SpeedFerries) 3-5 daily (50 mn)

Biggin, ✆ (01304) 20 51 08, www.whitecliffscountry.org.uk

Castle★★ **AC** Y

White Cliffs, Langdon Cliffs, NE : 1 mi on A 2 Z and A 258

Plan on next page

at St Margaret's at Cliffe Northeast : 4 mi by A 258 - Z – ✉ Dover

Wallett's Court Country House

West Cliffe, Northwest : 0.75 mi on Dover rd ✉ CT15 6EW – ✆ (01304) 852 424 – www.wallettscourthotelspa.com

17 rm – †£ 79/170 ††£ 99/230

Rest – *(dinner only and Sunday lunch)* Menu £ 35/40

Heavily beamed, family run, 17C country house with a characterful lounge and comfy bar. Four-poster bedrooms in the main house; rustic rooms in the annexes – the most luxurious are above the pleasant spa. Atmospheric restaurant with smartly laid tables offers ambitious, original, modern menu.

ENGLAND

DOWNTON – Hampshire – 503 P31 – see Lymington

DREWSTEIGNTON – Devon – 503 I31 – pop. 668 2 C2

London 190 mi – Plymouth 56 mi – Torbay 35 mi – Exeter 15 mi

Old Inn with rm

✉ EX6 6QR – ✆ (01647) 281 276 – www.old-inn.co.uk – Closed Sunday-Tuesday

3 rm – †£ 70 ††£ 90

Rest – *(dinner only and lunch Friday-Saturday) (booking essential)* Menu £ 43

Olive green former pub in the centre of a lovely Devonshire village, with two small, cosy dining rooms and a parquet-floored lounge with modern art for sale on the walls and a wood-burning stove in the large inglenook fireplace. The concise menu offers hearty, classical dishes. Bedrooms are simply furnished.

DRIGHLINGTON – West Yorkshire – 502 P22 22 B2

London 196 mi – Leeds 7 mi – Sheffield 41 mi – Manchester 35 mi

Prashad N

137 Whitehall Rd ✉ BD11 1AT – ✆ (0113) 285 20 37 – www.prashad.co.uk – Closed 25 December and 1 January

Rest – *(dinner only and lunch Friday-Sunday)* Carte £ 17/28

Stylish former pub with a vibrant pink and blue colour scheme and wood panels from India fronting the bar; head upstairs to admire the huge picture of a Mumbai street scene. Authentic vegetarian dishes range from enticing street food to original creations with countrywide influences; be sure to try the dosas.

DROITWICH SPA – Worcestershire – 503 N27 – pop. 22 585 19 C3

London 129 mi – Birmingham 20 mi – Bristol 66 mi – Worcester 6 mi

Victoria Sq, ✆ (01905) 77 43 12, www.cotswolds.info

Droitwich G. & C.C., Ford Lane, ✆ (01905) 77 43 44

DOVER

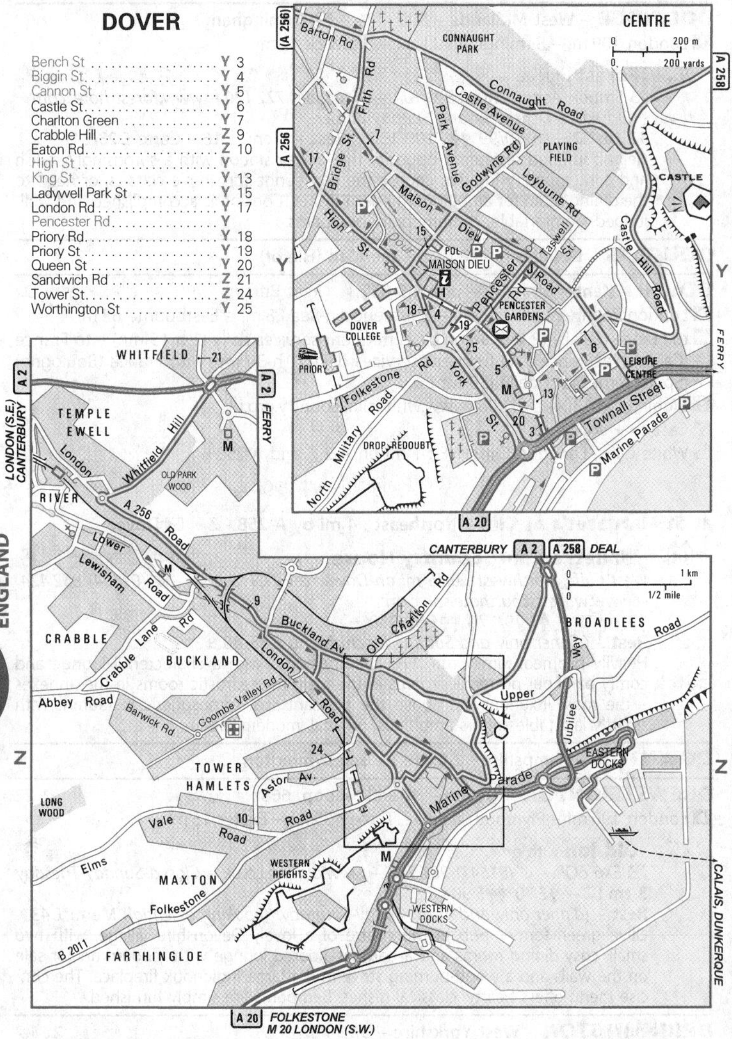

at Cutnall Green North : 3 mi on A 442 – ✉ Droitwich Spa

Chequers

Kidderminster Rd ✉ WR9 0PJ – ✆ (01299) 851 292 – www.chequerscutnallgreen.co.uk – Closed 25 December, dinner 26 December and 1 January

Rest – Menu £ 14 (weekdays) – Carte £ 20/34

Cosy roadside pub, run by the former England football team chef and his wife. Large, Asian-influenced menus offer light bites and pub classics, with more adventurous fish and offal-based specials chalked on the board daily.

at Hadley Heath **Southwest : 4 mi by Ombersley Way, A 4133 and Ladywood rd – ✉ Droitwich Spa**

Old Farmhouse without rest
✉ WR9 0AR – ✆ (01905) 620 837 – www.theoldfarmhouse.uk.com – Closed 23 December-3 January
4 rm – †£ 45/50 ††£ 75/80
Red-brick former farmhouse in a peaceful village, with traditional country house styling. Bedrooms boast good facilities; those in the main house have a cosy, cluttered feel. Communal breakfasts overlooking the lovely garden.

DROXFORD – Hampshire – 504 Q31 — 6 B2

London 79 mi – Southampton 21 mi – Portsmouth 16 mi – Basingstoke 37 mi

Bakers Arms
High St ✉ SO32 3PA – ✆ (01489) 877 533 – www.thebakersarmsdroxford.com
Rest – Menu £ 13 (weekdays) – Carte £ 24/32
Proudly run, traditional village pub with an open-plan bar, leather sofas and a roaring log fire; it also features decorative beer adverts, Victorian photographs and stag heads. Unfussy, filling dishes rely on local produce, with veg grown by the owners and bread baked in-house. Friendly service. Local ales.

DRY DODDINGTON – Lincolnshire – see Grantham

DULVERTON – Somerset – 503 J30 – pop. 1 870 — 3 A2

London 198 mi – Barnstaple 27 mi – Exeter 26 mi – Minehead 18 mi
Village★
Exmoor National Park★★ - Tarr Steps★★, NW : 6 mi by B 3223

Woods
4 Banks Sq ✉ TA22 9BU – ✆ (01398) 324 007 – www.woodsdulverton.co.uk – Closed dinner 26 December and 1 January
Rest – Carte £ 22/34
Former bakery, with a cosy, hugely characterful interior. Tasty, carefully prepared dishes offer more than just the usual pub fare. Provenance is taken seriously, with quality local ingredients including meat from the owner's farm.

at Brushford **South : 1.75 mi on B 3222 – ✉ Dulverton**

Three Acres Country House without rest
✉ TA22 9AR – ✆ (01398) 323 730 – www.threeacresexmoor.co.uk
6 rm – †£ 60/75 ††£ 90/120
Remotely set guesthouse boasting nearly 3 acres of mature gardens/parkland. Comfy lounge, small bar, pine-furnished breakfast room and pleasant terrace. Large, cosy bedrooms with country views.

DUNSTER – Somerset – 503 J30 – pop. 848 — 3 A2

London 185 mi – Minehead 3 mi – Taunton 23 mi
Town★★ - Castle★★ **AC** (upper rooms ≤★) - Water Mill★ **AC** - St George's Church★ - Dovecote★

Exmoor House without rest
12 West St ✉ TA24 6SN – ✆ (01643) 821 268 – www.exmoorhousedunster.co.uk – Closed 3 January-14 February
6 rm – †£ 55/60 ††£ 75/87
Terraced Georgian house on the main street of a historic town; run by warm, welcoming owners. Comfy, chintzy lounge and spacious pine-furnished breakfast room. Cosy, well-kept bedrooms.

ENGLAND

London 267 mi – Leeds 77 mi – Middlesbrough 23 mi – Newcastle upon Tyne 20 mi

Mount Oswald, South Rd, (0191) 386 75 27

City★★★ - Cathedral★★★ (Nave★★★, Chapel of the Nine Altars★★★, Sanctuary Knocker★) B – Oriental Museum★★ **AC** (at Durham University by A 167) B – City and Riverside (Prebends' Bridge ≤★★★ A , Framwellgate Bridge ≤★★ B) – Monastic Buildings (Cathedral Treasury★, Central Tower ≤★) B – Castle★ (Norman chapel★) **AC** B

Hartlepool Historic Quay★, SE : 14 mi by A 181, A 19 and A 179

Gadds Town House

34 Old Elvet DH1 3HN – (0191) 384 10 37 – www.gaddstownhouse.com

11 rm – £ 99/250 £ 99/250 B**x**

Rest *Gadd's Town House* – see restaurant listing

Attractive Georgian townhouse with lavishly decorated rooms: the lounge has purple velvet furnishings and there's a mahogany bar. Sumptuous bedrooms vary from floor to floor but all have good extras and bathrooms with underfloor heating; some have baths in the room; those in the garden annexe have hot tubs.

Farnley Tower

The Avenue DH1 4DX – (0191) 375 00 11 – www.farnley-tower.co.uk – Closed 25 December and 1 January A**c**

13 rm – £ 55/65 £ 69/95

Rest *Gourmet Spot* – (0191) 384 66 55 *(closed 2 January-10 January, Sunday and Monday) (dinner only)* Menu £ 25 (weekdays)/40

Spacious Victorian house hidden away in a quiet residential area overlooking the city; it's privately owned and has a relaxed air about it. Bedrooms vary in shape and size – those offering rooftop views are in demand. Monochrome Gourmet Spot offers ambitious dishes in some unusual combinations.

Cathedral View Town House without rest

212 Lower Gilesgate DH1 1QN – (0191) 386 95 66 – www.cathedralview.com – Closed 20 December-6 January B**n**

5 rm – £ 70/150 £ 85/150

Cosy Georgian townhouse with a terraced garden. The breakfast room offers excellent cathedral views and an extensive menu with daily specials. Smart, modern bedrooms have bold feature walls, coordinating fabrics and good facilities.

Castle View without rest

4 Crossgate DH1 4PS – (0191) 386 88 52 – www.castle-view.co.uk – Closed 15 December-8 January A**e**

5 rm – £ 70/80 £ 100/125

Attractive Georgian townhouse beside a Norman castle on a steep cobbled hill; reputedly a former vicarage. Large bedrooms have modern monochrome colour schemes, good facilities and smart bathrooms. Have breakfast on the terrace in summer.

Bistro 21

Aykley Heads House, Aykley Heads, Northwest : 1.5 mi by A 691 and B 6532 DH1 5TS – (0191) 384 43 54 – www.bistrotwentyone.co.uk – Closed Sunday and bank holidays

Rest – *(booking essential)* Menu £ 19/28

Brightly painted restaurant with an internal courtyard and a herb garden. Formerly a manor house outbuilding, the rustic main room has high windows and French farmhouse styling; the bar is in a smaller vaulted room. Cooking is satisfying and filling, and centres around good old British classics.

Finbarr's

Waddington St, Flass Vale DH1 4BG – (0191) 370 9999 – www.finbarrsrestaurant.co.uk A**x**

Rest – *(booking advisable)* Menu £ 16 (lunch) – Carte £ 24/49

Hidden away in a hotel just outside the city, a spacious restaurant with monochrome photos and well-spaced, smartly laid tables. Modern menus display international influences; the set menu provides good value. Smooth, professional service.

ENGLAND

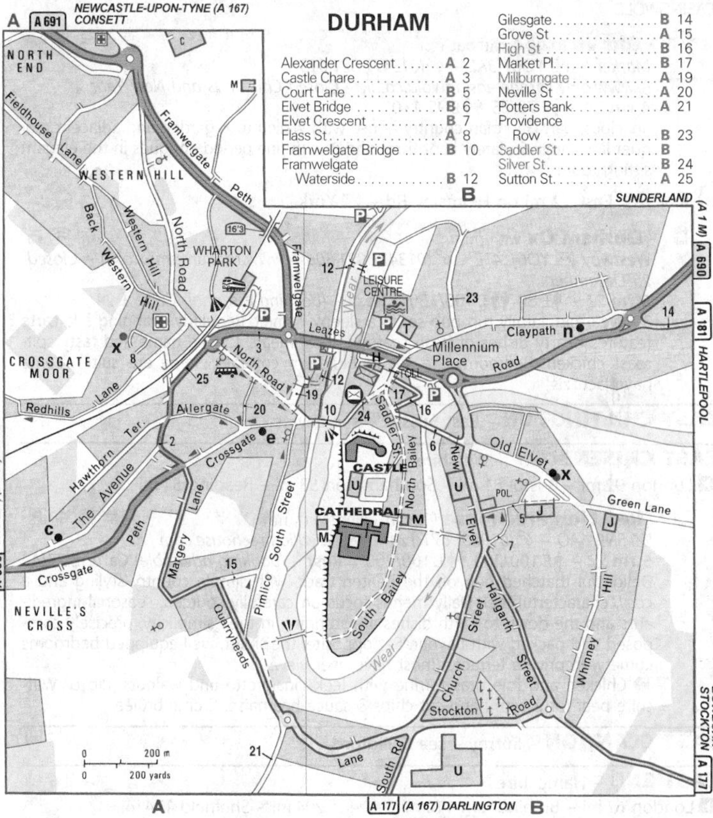

XX **Gadd's Town House** (N) – Gadds Townhouse

34 Old Elvet ✉ DH1 3HN – ✆ (0191) 384 10 37 – www.gaddstownhouse.com

Rest – Carte £ 20/62 Bx

Intimate hotel restaurant with a religious ceiling mural, a leopard print carpet and large purple chairs with gold tassels. Extensive menus are based around classic British dishes; steaks are a speciality and include chateaubriand for two.

EARL STONHAM – Suffolk – 504 X27 15 C3

London 91 mi – Ipswich 12 mi – Colchester 33 mi – Clacton-on-Sea 38 mi

Bays Farm without rest

Forward Grn, Northwest : 1 mi by A1120 on Broad Green rd ✉ IP14 5HU – ✆ (01449) 711 286 – www.baysfarmsuffolk.co.uk

3 rm – †£ 65/80 ††£ 75/90

17C farmhouse with kitchen garden, set in 4 attractive acres. Characterful interior with comfy lounge and beamed dining room. Individually styled bedrooms; annexed 'Hayloft' is the most luxurious. Communal breakfasts of local produce and homemade bread and jam.

EARSHAM – Norfolk – 504 Y26 – see Bungay

EASINGWOLD – North Yorkshire – 502 Q21 – pop. 3 975 – ✉ York 23 C2

London 217 mi – Leeds 38 mi – Middlesbrough 37 mi – York 14 mi

Chapel Lane, ✆ (01347) 82 15 30, www.visit-easingwold.com

Stillington Rd, ✆ (01347) 82 24 74

Old Vicarage without rest
Market Pl ✉ YO61 3AL – ✆ (01347) 821 015
– www.oldvicarage-easingwold.co.uk – Closed Christmas and New Year
4 rm – £ 70/85 £ 95/110
Spacious, part Georgian country house with walled rose garden and adjacent croquet lawn. Immaculately kept throughout with fine period antiques in the elegant sitting room.

at Crayke East : 2 mi on Helmsley Rd – ✉ York

Durham Ox with rm
Westway ✉ YO61 4TE – ✆ (01347) 821 506 – www.thedurhamox.com – Closed 25 December
5 rm – £ 80 £ 100/150 **Rest** – *(booking essential)* Carte £ 24/38
300 year old, family run pub set in a sleepy hamlet. Regularly changing à la carte features hearty dishes of fresh seafood, local meats, Crayke game and tasty spit-roast chicken. Bedrooms are set in old farm cottages; some are suites, some have jacuzzis.

EAST CHILTINGTON – East Sussex – see Lewes

EAST CHISENBURY – Wiltshire 4 D2

London 92 mi – Bristol 51 mi – Southampton 53 mi – Reading 51 mi

Red Lion Freehouse (Guy Manning) with rm
✉ SN9 6AQ – ✆ (01980) 671 124 – www.redlionfreehouse.com
5 rm – £ 100/200 £ 100/200 **Rest** – *(booking advisable)* Carte £ 27/42
Delightful thatched pub off the beaten track, with simple country styling and a cosy, characterful feel. Daily menus focus on carefully sourced, seasonal ingredients and the down-to-earth dishes are stunning in their simplicity, precisely composed and packed with flavour. Set opposite, the smart, well-equipped bedrooms come with private terraces; most have river views.
→ Chicken and foie gras terrine with leek vinaigrette and walnuts. Rib of Wiltshire beef for 2 with hand-cut chips & sauce béarnaise. Crème brûlée.

ENGLAND

EAST CLANDON – Surrey – see Guildford

EAST END – Hampshire 6 B1

London 67 mi – Birmingham 110 mi – Leeds 204 mi – Sheffield 174 mi

East End Arms with rm
Lymington Rd ✉ SO41 5SY – ✆ (01590) 626 223 – www.eastendarms.co.uk
5 rm – £ 71 £ 99/120
Rest – *(closed dinner Sunday and Monday)* Carte £ 18/39
Traditional country pub owned by John Illsley of Dire Straits. Shabby locals bar and classical pine-furnished dining room; great display of music-based photos. Concise menus of satisfying British dishes. Modern, cottage-style bedrooms provide a smart contrast.

EAST GARSTON – West Berkshire 10 B3

London 69 mi – Bristol 58 mi – Hillingdon 56 mi – Ealing 63 mi

Queen's Arms with rm
Newbury St ✉ RG17 7ET – ✆ (01488) 648 757 – www.queensarmshotel.co.uk – Closed 25 December
8 rm – £ 80/120 £ 80/120 **Rest** – Carte £ 24/36
A proudly British inn nestled in the heart of racehorse country, with framed prints, a rustic bar and meaty, satisfying dishes – which range from warming braises to tasty local game. Country pursuits can be arranged and you might even spot a famous trainer or breeder in the bar. Modern bedrooms are kitted out by leading clothing and countrywear companies.

EAST GRINSTEAD – West Sussex – 504 T30 – pop. 26 222 7 D2

London 48 mi – Brighton 30 mi – Eastbourne 32 mi – Lewes 21 mi
18 Copthorne, Borers Arm Rd, ✆ (01342) 71 25 08

Gravetye Manor

Vowels Ln, Southwest : 4.5 mi by B 2110 taking second turn left towards West Hoathly ✉ RH19 4LJ – ✆ (01342) 810 567 – www.gravetyemanor.co.uk
17 rm – †£ 160/200 ††£ 240/430 – 1 suite
Rest – *(booking essential)* Menu £ 30/40 – Carte £ 58/69
A quintessential English country house set in a forest and surrounded by 35 glorious acres of gardens. Ornate Elizabethan ceilings and fireplaces dominate beautifully furnished lounges, perfect for afternoon tea. Luxurious bedrooms boast antique wood furniture. Delightful, wood-panelled dining room; accomplished cooking of classic dishes with subtle modern overtones.

EAST HADDON – Northamptonshire 16 B3

London 76 mi – Birmingham 47 mi – Leicester 32 mi – Coventry 34 mi

Red Lion with rm

rest,

Main St ✉ NN6 8BU – ✆ (01604) 770 223 – www.redlioneasthaddon.co.uk – Closed Sunday dinner
7 rm – †£ 80/95 ††£ 95/110 **Rest** – Carte £ 21/29
Thatched honey-stone inn at the heart of an attractive village, boasting pretty gardens and a pleasing mix of exposed wood, brick and slate. Drinkers are welcome but it's the food that's the focus here: menus offer upgraded pub classics like mutton cottage pie, and they run a cookery school in the adjacent barn. Service is enthusiastic and bedrooms, warm and welcoming.

EAST HENDRED – Oxfordshire – 503 P29 – see Wantage

EAST HOATHLY – East Sussex – 504 U31 – pop. 1 206 8 B3

London 60 mi – Brighton 16 mi – Eastbourne 13 mi – Hastings 25 mi

Old Whyly

✉ BN8 6EL – ✆ (01825) 840 216 – www.oldwhyly.co.uk
3 rm – †£ 80/95 ††£ 95/140 **Rest** – Menu £ 33
Charming red-brick house built in 1760, set in beautiful grounds and very personally run by its delightful owner. Guest areas mix the classic and the contemporary. Bedrooms are individually designed around a theme: choose from Tulip, French or Chinese. Stylish, minimalist dining room with homemade yoghurts and jams at breakfast and daily changing 3 course dinners.

EAST KENNETT – Wiltshire – see Marlborough

EAST LAVANT – West Sussex – see Chichester

EAST WITTERING – West Sussex – 504 R31 – pop. 5 127 7 C3

London 86 mi – Birmingham 178 mi – Leeds 272 mi – Sheffield 242 mi

Samphire

57 Shore Rd ✉ PO20 8DY – ✆ (01243) 672 754 – www.samphireeastwittering.co.uk – Closed January and Sunday
Rest – Menu £ 16 (lunch) – Carte £ 21/36
Modest, keenly run restaurant set 100 metres from the sea and featuring reclaimed wooden furniture. Fresh, locally caught seafood and fish – with a wide range of meat dishes too. Straightforward, tasty, good value cooking.

EAST WITTON – North Yorkshire – 502 O21 – ✉ Leyburn 22 B1

London 238 mi – Leeds 45 mi – Middlesbrough 30 mi – York 39 mi

Blue Lion with rm

✉ DL8 4SN – ✆ (01969) 624 273 – www.thebluelion.co.uk
15 rm – †£ 69/145 ††£ 94/145
Rest – *(booking essential)* Menu £ 16/29 – Carte £ 25/48 **s**
Charming, characterful countryside pub. Daily-changing menu features a tasty mix of classic and modern dishes, all with seasonality and traceability at their core. Bedrooms – in the pub and outbuildings – are warm and cosy.

EASTBOURNE – East Sussex – 504 U31 – pop. 106 562 Great Britain 8 B3

London 68 mi – Brighton 25 mi – Dover 61 mi – Maidstone 49 mi
Cornfield Rd, (01323) 41 54 50, www.visiteastbourne.com
Royal Eastbourne, Paradise Drive, (01323) 74 40 45
Eastbourne Downs, East Dean Rd, (01323) 72 08 27
Eastbourne Golfing Park, Lottbridge Drove, (01323) 52 04 00
Seafront★
Beachy Head★★★, SW : 3 mi by B 2103 Z

Grand

King Edward's Par. ✉ *BN21 4EQ – (01323) 412 345 – www.grandeastbourne.com*
152 rm – †£ 135/200 ††£ 165/230 – 10 suites **Zx**
Rest *Mirabelle* – see restaurant listing
Rest *Garden Restaurant* – Menu £ 23/39 – Carte £ 37/64
Built in 1871 and offering all that its name promises. Retains many original features, including ornate plasterwork, column-lined corridors and a Great Hall. Classical bedrooms; pay extra for a sea view. Delightful gardens and a superb outdoor pool. Lavish lounges, a smart cocktail bar and formal restaurants.

Waterside without rest

11-12 Royal Par ✉ *BN22 7AR – (01323) 646 566*
– www.watersidehoteleastbourne.co.uk **Za**
19 rm – †£ 45/90 ††£ 95/195
Stylish, modern hotel, located on the seafront, with views of the beach and pier. Compact, well-maintained, individually designed bedrooms. Cosy leather sofas and funky wallpaper in the bar.

Manse without rest

7 Dittons Rd ✉ *BN21 1DWH – (01323) 737 851 – www.themansebb.com*
– Closed Christmas-New Year **Zs**
3 rm – †£ 60/65 ††£ 90/100
Lovingly restored Arts and Crafts house – originally a Presbyterian Manse – with many original features including oak panelling, fine fireplaces and beautiful stained glass windows. Good-sized, antique-furnished bedrooms with fresh flowers and thoughtful extras. Delightful owners and great breakfasts.

Brayscroft

13 South Cliff Ave ✉ *BN20 7AH – (01323) 647 005*
– www.brayscrofthotel.co.uk **Zn**
6 rm – †£ 36/42 ††£ 72/84 **Rest** – Menu £ 15
Spacious Edwardian house located close to the seafront, gardens and pier. Traditional lounge and dining room display antiques and Italian artwork. Comfortable, classically styled bedrooms. Evening meals by daily arrangement; tailored to each guest, they feature fresh, local, free range ingredients.

Southcroft

15 South Cliff Ave ✉ *BN20 7AH – (01323) 729 071 – www.southcrofthotel.com*
5 rm – †£ 36/50 ††£ 72/80 **Rest** – Menu £ 14 **Zn**
One of the most important, yet often neglected, elements of a hotel stay is a warm welcome – a fact obviously appreciated by the charming owners of this homely guesthouse. Bedrooms are cosy and well-kept; cooking is hearty and traditional.

Mirabelle – Grand Hotel

King Edward's Par. ✉ *BN21 4EQ – (01323) 412 345*
– www.grandeastbourne.com **Zx**
Rest – *(booking essential)* Menu £ 25/42
Plush fabrics and linen-laid tables with monogrammed silverware; formal dress code and professional team. Seasonal classics or 6 course tasting menu at dinner. Rich, well-executed cooking.

Grand Bocca Ⓝ

12 Grand Hotel Buildings, Compton St ✉ *BN21 4EJ – (01323) 731 662*
– www.grandbocca.com – Closed 25-26 December, Sunday dinner and Monday
Rest – *(booking essential)* Carte £ 17/48 **Zb**
Small but lively eatery with a rustic interior and picnic benches on a pavement terrace. It's all about sharing, with a wide range of picoteo and tapas dishes. Cooking is fresh and flavoursome; the local seafood specials are a highlight.

ENGLAND

EASTBOURNE

Arndale Centre V
Ashford Rd . . . . V 2
Bedfordwell Rd . . . . V 3
Church St . . . . Z 4
Cornfield Rd . . . . V 5
Devonshire Pl. . . . . X 6
Gildredge Rd . . . . V 7
Grove Rd V
Hailsham Rd . . . . Y 8
High St . . . . Z 9
Lewes Rd . . . . Y 13
Lismore Rd . . . . V 14
North St . . . . V 15
Polegate By-Pass . . . . Y 18
St Anthony's Ave. . . . . Y 21
Seaside Rd V
South St V
Station Rd . . . . Y 24
Susan's Rd . . . . V 25
Terminus Rd V
The Goffs . . . . Z 26
Trinity Trees . . . . V 27
Upperton Rd . . . . V, Z 28

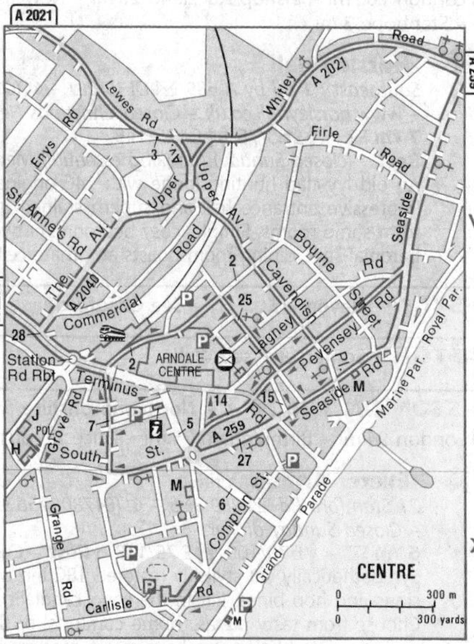

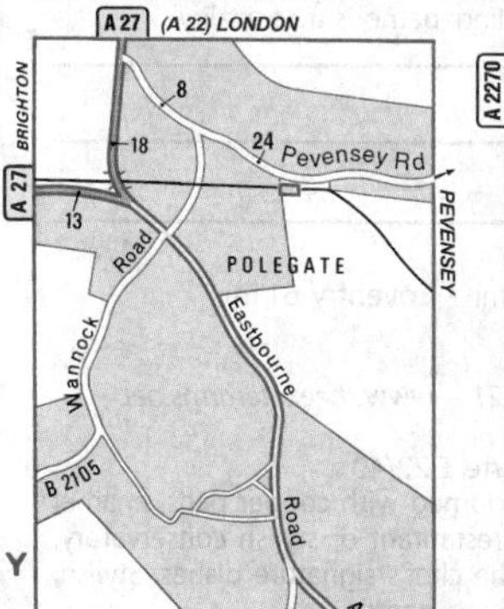
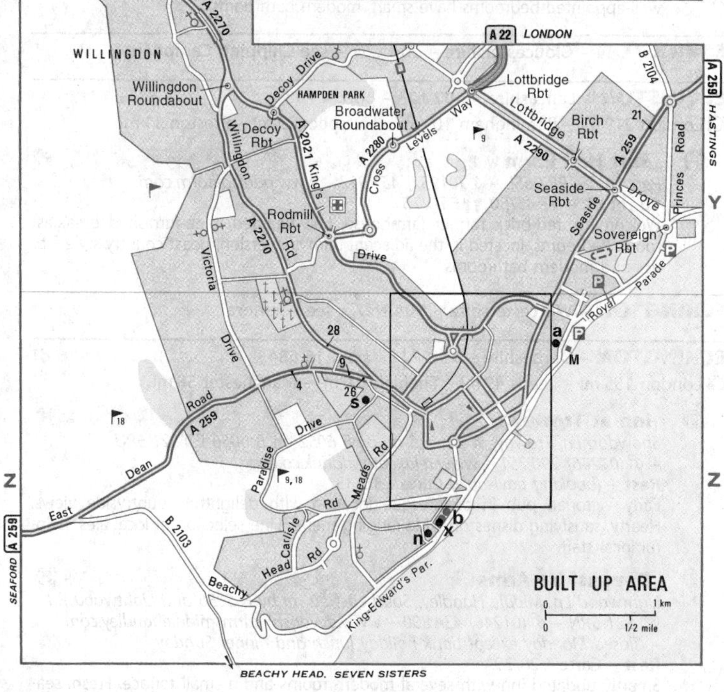

ENGLAND

EASTGATE – Durham – 502 N19 24 A3

London 288 mi – Bishop Auckland 20 mi – Newcastle upon Tyne 35 mi – Stanhope 3 mi

Horsley Hall

Southeast : 1 mi by A 689 ✉ DL13 2LJ – ☎ (01388) 517 239 – www.horsleyhall.co.uk – Closed Christmas-New Year

7 rm – †£ 65/75 ††£ 125/145

Rest – *(closed Sunday) (booking essential)* Menu £ 20/32

An old ivy-clad hunting lodge with 14C origins, built for the Bishop of Durham. Impressive entrance hall and superb stained glass windows; lovely valley views from some rooms. Simple, cosy bedrooms – two with Edwardian bathrooms. The baronial-style dining room boasts an ornate ceiling; game is a speciality.

EASTON – Devon – 503 I31 – see Chagford

EASTON – Somerset – see Wells

EASTON ON THE HILL – Northamptonshire 17 C2

London 94 mi – Birmingham 75 mi – Leicester 30 mi – Coventry 61 mi

Exeter Arms with rm

21 Stamford Rd ✉ PE9 3NS – ☎ (01780) 756 321 – www.theexeterarms.net – Closed Sunday dinner

6 rm – †£ 70/100 ††£ 75/110 **Rest** – Carte £ 22/40

Sympathetically yet stylishly restored 18C inn adorned with copper pans, enamel signs and hop bines. Eat in the snug candlelit restaurant or stylish conservatory. Choose from tasty pizzas, 'home comforts' or the chef's signature dishes. Stylish, well-appointed bedrooms have smart, modern bathrooms.

EBRINGTON – Gloucestershire – 504 O27 – see Chipping Campden

ECCLESTON – Lancashire – 502 L23 – pop. 4 708 20 A2

London 219 mi – Birmingham 103 mi – Liverpool 29 mi – Preston 11 mi

Parr Hall Farm without rest

Parr Ln. ✉ PR7 5SL – ☎ (01257) 451 917 – www.parrhallfarm.com

10 rm – †£ 45/50 ††£ 70/75

Welcoming, red-brick former farmhouse. Low-beamed, pine-furnished breakfast room. Bedrooms, located in the adjacent barn conversion, boast country style fabrics and modern bathrooms.

ECKINGTON – Worcestershire – 504 N27 – see Pershore

ECKINGTON – Derbyshire – 502 P24 – pop. 16 684 16 B1

London 155 mi – Leeds 49 mi – Sheffield 10 mi – Manchester 58 mi

Inn at Troway

Snowdon Ln, Troway, West : 3.5 mi by B 6052 on B 6056 ✉ S21 5RU – ☎ (01246) 290 751 – www.relaxeatanddrink.co.uk

Rest – *(booking advisable)* Carte £ 18/33

Early Victorian pub in picturesque location with delightful countryside views. Hearty, satisfying dishes on wide-ranging menu. Fine selection of local ales; helpful local staff.

Devonshire Arms (N)

Lightwood Ln, Middle Handley, Southeast : 2 mi by B 5056 and Lightwood Rd ✉ S21 5RN – ☎ (01246) 434 800 – www.devonshirearmsmiddlehandley.com – Closed Monday except bank holiday lunch and dinner Sunday

Rest – Carte £ 20/39

Smartly updated inn with several modern rooms and a small terrace. Fresh, seasonal ingredients are at the core of the hearty menu. They like to keep things local, with eggs coming from down the road and meat from the butcher's opposite.

EDINGTON – Wiltshire – 503 N30 — 4 C2

London 105 mi – Bristol 43 mi – Cardiff 76 mi – Southampton 64 mi

Three Daggers with rm

47 Westbury Rd ✉ BA13 4PG – ✆ (01380) 830 940 – www.threedaggers.co.uk

3 rm – †£ 80 ††£ 90/150 **Rest** – Menu £ 12 (lunch) – Carte £ 21/38

Attractive pub with original wood beams and flagstones, and a large conservatory overlooking the garden. The accessible menu features a homemade soup, a pie 'of the day', and the Huntsman's and Fisherman's sharing platters are extremely popular. Charming bedrooms feature bespoke oak furnishings.

EGHAM – Surrey – 504 S29 – pop. 27 666 — 7 C1

London 22 mi – Croydon 24 mi – Barnet 35 mi – Ealing 17 mi

Great Fosters

Stroude Rd, South : 1.25 mi by B 388 ✉ TW20 9UR – ✆ (01784) 433 822 – www.greatfosters.co.uk

46 rm – †£ 195/450 ††£ 195/450, £ 20 – 3 suites

Rest *Tudor Room* – see restaurant listing

Rest *Estate Grill* – Menu £ 27/40 – Carte £ 32/61

Striking Elizabethan manor built as a hunting lodge for Henry VIII, boasting 50 acres of gardens and a beautiful parterre. The charming interior displays characterful original detailing. Bedrooms come with feature beds and a flamboyant touch; those in the annexes are more modern. The Estate Grill specialises in steaks from the Josper grill; fine dining in the Tudor Room.

Tudor Room (N) – Great Fosters Hotel

Stroude Rd, South : 1.25 mi by B 388 ✉ TW20 9UR – ✆ (01784) 433 822 – www.greatfosters.co.uk – Closed 2 weeks January, 2 weeks August, Sunday and Monday

Rest – *(booking advisable)* Menu £ 30/62

Intimate hotel restaurant with mullioned windows and burgundy décor; a large tapestry and a gilt mirror hang on its walls. Cooking is assured, modern and creative. Influences come from across Europe, with the odd Asian touch featuring too.

EGTON – North Yorkshire – 502 S20 — 23 C1

London 250 mi – Birmingham 180 mi – Leeds 72 mi – Sheffield 107 mi

Wheatsheaf Inn

✉ YO21 1TZ – ✆ (01947) 895 271 – www.wheatsheafegton.com – Closed 25 December and Monday

Rest – *(light lunch)* Carte £ 20/26

Family-run, late 19C inn on the edge of the picturesque North Yorkshire Moors. Menu offers a real taste of Yorkshire with fresh, hearty dishes like lamb's kidneys, local steak, Whitby scampi and game from within 2 miles.

Is breakfast included? If it is, the cup symbol appears after the number of rooms.

ELDERSFIELD – Worcestershire — 18 B3

London 124 mi – Birmingham 63 mi – Liverpool 145 mi – Bristol 52 mi

Butchers Arms (James Winter)

Lime Street, Southeast : 1 mi ✉ GL19 4NX – ✆ (01452) 840 381 – www.thebutchersarms.net – Closed 2 weeks early January, 2 weeks late August, Sunday dinner, Monday, lunch Tuesday to Thursday and bank holidays

Rest – *(booking essential)* Carte £ 37/47

Pleasant red-brick pub with a traditional feel, run by a husband and wife team, where everyone comes for the great atmosphere and the terrific food. Everything from bread to ice cream is homemade; the cooking is clever and dishes full of flavour. But hurry, only 25 diners can be accommodated.

→ Middle White pig's cheek with egg yolk ravioli and black pudding. Roast turbot on the bone with saffron risotto. Pink praline and pistachio macaroons with pistachio ice cream.

ELLAND – West Yorkshire – **502** O22 – **pop. 14 554** – ✉ **Halifax** 22 B3

London 204 mi – Bradford 12 mi – Burnley 29 mi – Leeds 17 mi

Hullen Edge, Hammerstones Leach Lane, ✆ (01422) 37 25 05

La Cachette

31 Huddersfield Rd ✉ HX5 9AW – ✆ (01422) 378 833 – www.lacachette-elland.com – Closed 2 weeks August, 27 December-9 January, Sunday and bank holidays

Rest – Menu £ 14/23 – Carte £ 20/47

Long-standing, well-run bistro. Spacious bar and dining rooms display Gallic décor and memorabilia. Extensive choice from daily or weekly menus and specials. Classical, seasonal cooking displays international influences.

ELLEL – Lancashire 20 A1

London 519 mi – Leeds 391 mi – Sheffield 533 mi – Manchester 427 mi

Bay Horse Inn

Bay Horse Ln, Bay Horse, South 1.5 mi by A 6 on Quernmore rd ✉ LA2 0HR – ✆ (01524) 791 204 – www.bayhorseinn.com – Closed Sunday dinner in winter and Monday except bank holiday lunch

Rest – Menu £ 18 (lunch) **s** – Carte £ 20/39 **s**

Cosy, homely pub in a pleasant rural location, with characterful interior and attractive terrace. Seasonal, locally sourced produce is crafted into classic, tried-and-tested dishes. Lancashire cheese board a speciality.

ENGLAND

ELMTON – Derbyshire 16 B1

London 155 mi – Birmingham 78 mi – Leeds 51 mi – Sheffield 21 mi

Elm Tree

✉ S80 4LS – ✆ (01909) 721 261 – www.elmtreeelmton.co.uk – Closed Tuesday

Rest – Menu £ 11 (weekday lunch) – Carte £ 18/38

18C stone pub with a brightly lit bar, characterful beamed rooms, a wood-burning stove and a large garden. The good value menu offers pub classics presented in a modern manner, with all ingredients sourced from within 10 miles.

ELTISLEY – Cambridgeshire – **507** T27 14 A3

London 62 mi – Croydon 73 mi – Barnet 49 mi – Ealing 61 mi

Eltisley

2 The Green ✉ PE19 6TG – ✆ (01480) 880 308 – www.theeltisley.co.uk – Closed Monday in winter and Sunday dinner

Rest – Carte £ 22/40

Chic and stylish gastropub beside a village green. Simple, unfussy cooking relies on quality, local produce to speak for itself; everything from starters to desserts is homemade.

ELTON – Cambridgeshire – **504** S26 14 A2

London 84 mi – Peterborough 11 mi – Bedford 40 mi – Kettering 24 mi

Crown Inn with rm

8 Duck St ✉ PE8 6RQ – ✆ (01832) 280 232 – www.thecrowninn.org

8 rm – †£ 65/75 ††£ 95/120, ☕ £ 8 **Rest** – Menu £ 21/30 – Carte £ 25/38

17C honey-stone pub in a delightful country parish, with a thatched roof, a cosy inglenook fireplace in the bar and a laid-back feel. Extensive menus offer homely British dishes which arrive in generous portions. Bedrooms are smart and individually styled – some have feature beds or roll-top baths.

ELY – Cambridgeshire – **504** U26 – **pop. 13 954** Great Britain 14 B2

London 74 mi – Cambridge 16 mi – Norwich 60 mi

29 St Mary's St, ✆ (01353) 66 20 62, www.visitely.org.uk

107 Cambridge Rd, ✆ (01353) 66 27 51

Cathedral★★ **AC**

Wicken Fen★, SE : 9 mi by A 10 and A 1123

Poets House Ⓝ

St Mary's St ✉ CB7 4EY – ✆ (01353) 887 777 – www.poetshouse.com

21 rm – ♦£ 129/209 ♦♦£ 149/269

Rest ***Dining Room*** – Menu £ 23 – Carte £ 29/46

A series of 19C townhouses opposite the cathedral. The modern bar has views over the pretty walled garden; the dining room blends original features with contemporary décor and serves attractive modern dishes. Spacious, boutique bedrooms come with beautiful bathrooms and extras such as local vodka and gin.

Boathouse

5-5a Annesdale ✉ CB7 4BN – ✆ (01353) 664 388 – www.theboathouseely.co.uk

Rest – Carte £ 18/35

Modern restaurant in a wonderful spot on the banks of the Ouse; nab a table on the terrace if you can. Monthly changing menus offer a wide selection of dishes; their trademark is a fresh fish board with different sides and sauces.

at Little Thetford South : 2.75 mi by A 10 – ✉ Ely

Springfields without rest

Ely Rd, North : 0.5 mi on A 10 ✉ CB6 3HJ – ✆ (01353) 663 637 – www.smoothhound.co.uk/hotels/springfields – Closed Christmas-New Year

3 rm – ♦£ 60 ♦♦£ 75/85

Delightfully run, curio-filled bungalow in pleasant gardens. Immaculately kept bedrooms have different coloured Toile de Joie wallpapers and plenty of extra touches. Enjoy breakfast among the Cranberry Glass collection or in the courtyard.

at Sutton Gault West : 8 mi by A 142 off B 1381 – ✉ Ely

Anchor Inn with rm

✉ CB6 2BD – ✆ (01353) 778 537 – www.anchor-inn-restaurant.co.uk

4 rm – ♦£ 60/90 ♦♦£ 80/155

Rest – Menu £ 14 (weekday lunch)/18 – Carte £ 23/40

Riverside pub dating back to 1650 and the creation of the Hundred Foot Wash. Tempting menu complemented by daily fish specials. For a pleasant river outlook head for the wood-panelled rooms to the front of the bar. Neat, pine-furnished bedrooms include two suites; one with river views.

ENGLAND

EMSWORTH – Hampshire – 504 R31 – pop. 18 310 6 B2

London 75 mi – Brighton 37 mi – Portsmouth 10 mi – Southampton 22 mi

36 on the Quay (Ramon Farthing) with rm

47 South St, The Quay ✉ PO10 7EG – ✆ (01243) 375 592 – www.36onthequay.co.uk – Closed first 2 weeks January, 1 week May, 1 week October and 24-26 December

6 rm – ♦£ 75/90 ♦♦£ 100/120

Rest – *(closed Sunday and Monday) (booking essential)* Menu £ 24/70

Long-standing quayside restaurant run by an experienced chef-owner, with an elegant bar-lounge and an intimate linen-laid restaurant in neutral hues. Concise à la carte of well-executed, classical dishes in flavoursome, tried-and-tested combinations. Friendly, efficient service. Stylish bedrooms offer good comforts; be ready to order your breakfast at check-in.

→ Duck egg, Serrano ham and braised lentils with truffle dressing. Veal roasted in hay, wild nettles, mousseline potato and caramelised onion sauce. Peanut parfait with butterscotch doughnuts and a coffee foam.

Fat Olives

30 South St ✉ PO10 7EH – ✆ (01243) 377 914 – www.fatolives.co.uk – Closed 2 weeks late June, 1 week Christmas, 1 week spring, Sunday and Monday

Rest – *(booking essential)* Menu £ 20 (lunch) – Carte £ 29/41

Sweet terraced restaurant run by a charming couple, in a characterful coastal town. Smart, slightly rustic room with locally crafted tables and upholstered chairs. Classic British dishes with a modern edge rely on small local suppliers.

EPSOM – Surrey – 504 T30 – pop. 64 493 — 7 D1

London 14 mi – Croydon 9 mi – Barnet 29 mi – Ealing 18 mi

Longdown Lane South, Epsom Downs, (01372) 72 16 66

Horton Park G & C.C., Hook Rd, (020) 8393 84 00

Chalk Lane

Chalk Ln, Southwest : 0.5 mi by A 24 and Woodcote Rd ✉ KT18 7BB – (01372) 721 179 – www.chalklanehotel.com

21 rm – £ 85/105 £ 105/150

Rest – *(dinner only and Sunday lunch)* Carte £ 31/50

Personally run hotel in a residential area; comfortable and welcoming, with a charming, traditionally furnished interior to match its Victorian heritage. Individually styled bedrooms – one with a four-poster. More modern dining room serves a menu inspired by classic French cooking.

Le Raj

211 Fir Tree Rd, Epsom Downs, Southeast : 2 mi by B 289 and B 284 on B 291 ✉ KT17 3LB – (01737) 371 371 – www.lerajrestaurant.co.uk

Rest – Carte £ 21/33

A local institution with a larger-than-life owner, a comfortable bar-lounge and a smart, wood-panelled restaurant. Waiters in bow ties and white gloves serve carefully prepared, well-presented, authentic Bangladeshi cooking.

ERMINGTON – Devon – 503 I32 — 2 C2

London 216 mi – Plymouth 11 mi – Salcombe 15 mi

Plantation House with rm

Totnes Rd, Southwest : 0.5 mi on A 3121 ✉ PL21 9NS – (01548) 831 100 – www.plantationhousehotel.co.uk

8 rm – £ 70/95 £ 125/195

Rest – *(dinner only) (bookings essential for non-residents)* Menu £ 36/43 **s**

Georgian former rectory in a pleasant country spot, with a small drinks terrace, an open-fired lounge and two dining rooms: one formal, with black furnishings; one more relaxed, with polished wood tables. Interesting modern menus feature local produce. Stylish bedrooms come with fresh milk and homemade cake.

ESHOTT – see Morpeth

ETTINGTON – Warwickshire – 504 P27 – pop. 953 — 19 C3

London 95 mi – Birmingham 41 mi – Leicester 48 mi – Coventry 23 mi

Chequers Inn

91 Banbury Rd ✉ CV37 7SR – (01789) 740 387 – www.the-chequers-ettington.co.uk – Closed Sunday dinner and Monday

Rest – Carte £ 22/33

Chandeliers, brushed velvet furniture and Regency chairs set at chequered tables mean this is not your typical pub. Menus display a broad international style; dishes range from British classics to Mediterranean and Asian-inspired dishes.

EVERSHOT – Dorset – 503 M31 – pop. 225 – ✉ Dorchester — 4 C3

London 149 mi – Bournemouth 39 mi – Dorchester 12 mi – Salisbury 53 mi

Summer Lodge

rm,

9 Fore St ✉ DT2 0JR – (01935) 482 000 – www.summerlodgehotel.com

24 rm – £ 235/350 £ 235/650 – 4 suites

Rest – *(booking essential)* Menu £ 27/40 – Carte £ 54/60

Attractive former dower house in mature gardens. Country house style guest areas display heavy fabrics and antiques. Individually designed bedrooms boast quality furnishings and marble bathrooms. Exclusive glass-built wellness centre. Formal dining room and conservatory offer classical cuisine. Smart, effective service.

Acorn Inn

28 Fore St ✉ DT2 0JW – (01935) 83 228 – www.acorn-inn.co.uk

10 rm – £ 79/150 £ 99/200 **Rest** – Carte £ 19/38

Historic inn mentioned in 'Tess of the d'Urbervilles'. Individually styled bedrooms boast fabric-covered walls, good facilities and modern bathrooms. Guest areas include a characterful residents' lounge, a locals bar with skittle alley and a classical restaurant.

Wooden Cabbage

East Chelborough, West : 3.25 mi by Beaminter rd and Chelborough rd on East Chelborough rd ✉ DT2 0QA – ✆ (01935) 83 362 – www.woodencabbage.co.uk – Restricted opening in winter

3 rm – †£ 75/90 ††£ 100/120 **Rest** – Menu £ 35

Attractive former gamekeeper's cottage. Spacious guest areas include a cosy dining room used in winter and an airy conservatory used in summer. Pretty bedrooms boast good facilities and lovely countryside views. Meals (by arrangement) feature home-grown produce.

EVESHAM – Worcestershire – 503 O27 – pop. 22 179 19 C3

London 99 mi – Birmingham 30 mi – Cheltenham 16 mi – Coventry 32 mi

The Wood Norton N

rest,

Northwest : 2.5 mi by B 4624 on A 44 ✉ WR11 4YB – ✆ (01386) 765 611 – www.thewoodnorton.com

52 rm – †£ 85/125 ††£ 85/185 – 3 suites

Rest – *(bar lunch Monday-Saturday)* Menu £ 35

Characterful country house in the shadow of the Malvern Hills; once a French duke's hunting lodge and then a BBC training centre. Beautiful wood panelling and parquet floors. Bedrooms in the main house have the best views; those in the mews are more modern. The intimate restaurant overlooks the parterre.

EXETER – Devon – 503 J31 – pop. 109 548 2 D2

London 201 mi – Bournemouth 83 mi – Bristol 83 mi – Plymouth 46 mi

Exeter Airport : ✆ (01392) 367433, E : 5 mi by A 30 V

Princesshay, ✆ (01392) 66 57 00, www.discoverexeter.ne

Downes Crediton, Hookway, ✆ (01363) 77 30 25

City★★ - Cathedral★★ Z – Royal Albert Memorial Museum★ Y

Killerton★★ **AC**, NE : 7 mi by B 3181 V – Ottery St Mary★ (St Mary's★) E : 12 mi by B 3183 - Y - A 30 and B 3174 – Crediton (Holy Cross Church★), NW : 9 mi by A 377

Plans pages 212, 213

Abode Exeter

Cathedral Yard ✉ EX1 1HD – ✆ (01392) 319 955 – www.abodehotels.co.uk

52 rm – †£ 79/145 ††£ 79/145, £ 12 – 1 suite Y**z**

Rest *Michael Caines* – see restaurant listing

Attractive Georgian property in the shadow of the cathedral. Stylish interior with a formal reception, a chic champagne bar and small, well-equipped gym. Smart, boldly coloured bedrooms; some with baths beside the beds or cathedral views. Laid-back all-day café and deli or formal restaurant.

Magdalen Chapter

Magdalen St ✉ EX2 4HY – ✆ (01392) 281 000 – www.themagdalenchapter.com

59 rm – †£ 98/140 ††£ 120/250 Z**a**

Rest *Magdalen Chapter* – see restaurant listing

Converted Victorian eye hospital; now a stylish, modern hotel with a garden and a small spa tucked away to the rear. Chic, understated bedrooms come with mood lighting, espresso machines and iPads loaded with the hotel's information.

Southernhay House

rm,

36 Southernhay East ✉ EX1 1NX – ✆ (01392) 435 324 – www.southernhayhouse.com Z**x**

10 rm – †£ 150/240 ††£ 150/240

Rest – *(closed Sunday dinner) (bookings essential for non-residents)* Menu £ 15 (lunch) – Carte £ 27/50

Attractive Georgian townhouse with original lighting roses and ornate coving. Smart, compact guest areas include a stylish lounge and a bar with bright blue furniture. Warmly decorated bedrooms have sumptuous beds, luxurious fabrics and chic bathrooms. Small dining room offers British-based menus.

ENGLAND

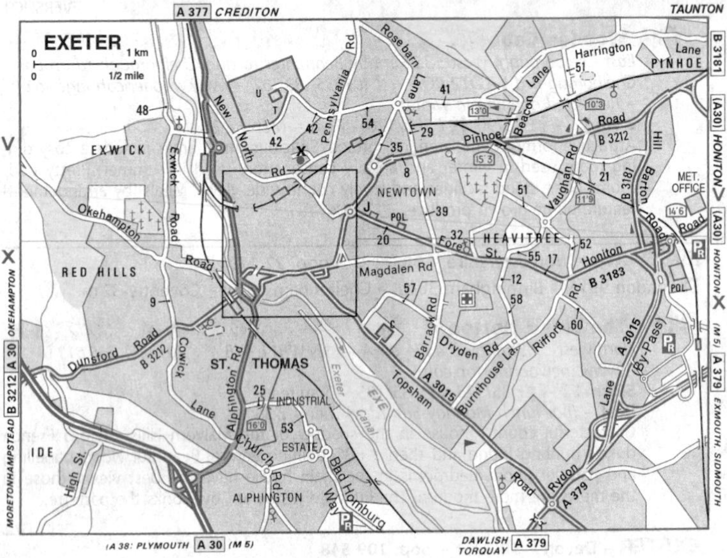

Blackboy Rd	V 8	North St HEAVITREE	X 32	Sweetbriar Lane	VX 52
Buddle Lane	X 9	Old Tiverton Rd	V 35	Trusham Rd	X 53
Butts Rd	X 12	Polsloe Rd	V 39	Union Rd	V 54
East Wonford Hill	X 17	Prince Charles Rd	V 41	Whipton Lane	X 55
Heavitree Rd	VX 20	Prince of Wales Rd	V 42	Wonford Rd	X 57
Hill Lane	V 21	St Andrew's Rd	V 48	Wonford St	X 58
Marsh Barton Rd	X 25	Summer Lane	V 51	Woodwater Lane	X 60
Mount Pleasant Rd	V 29				

XX **Michael Caines** – Abode Exeter Hotel [A/C]
Cathedral Yard ✉ EX1 1HD – ☎ (01392) 223 638 – www.michaelcaines.com – Closed Sunday Y**z**
Rest – Carte £ 36/50
Smart, contemporary restaurant in a famous old hotel; sit by the window for cathedral views. Modern British menus offer flavoursome dishes with lots of ingredients on the plate; lunch represents the best value. Formal service.

XX **Magdalen Chapter** (N) – Magdalen Chapter Hotel
Magdalen St ✉ EX2 4HY – ☎ (01392) 281 000 – www.themagdalenchapter.com
Rest – Menu £ 20/32 – Carte £ 21/43 Z**a**
An impressive steel and glass extension to a 19C hotel, with a curved wood roof, overlooking a delightful terrace. The large menu of brasserie classics mixes British, French, Spanish and Italian influences. Produce is carefully sourced.

Rusty Bike
67 Howell Rd ✉ EX4 4LZ – ☎ (01392) 214 440 – www.rustybike-exeter.co.uk – Closed lunch Monday-Wednesday V**x**
Rest – Carte £ 22/37
Rustic, city centre pub with an eclectic mix of art and a vintage table football game. Hearty, satisfying dishes use West Country produce. They breed their own pigs and all parts of the animal are used; pork dishes are particularly popular.

at Brampford Speke North : 5 mi by A 377

Lazy Toad Inn with rm [P]
✉ EX5 5DP – ☎ (01392) 841 591 – www.thelazytoadinn.co.uk – Closed 3 weeks January, Sunday dinner, Monday and bank holidays
3 rm – †£ 58/78 ††£ 80/100 **Rest** – Carte £ 23/36
Sweet little pub with a cobbled courtyard, which uses vegetables from its own polytunnel and lambs raised on its smallholding. Nibble on homemade pork scratchings while choosing a dish from the interesting Asian-inspired menu. Individually styled bedrooms have king-sized beds and iPod docks.

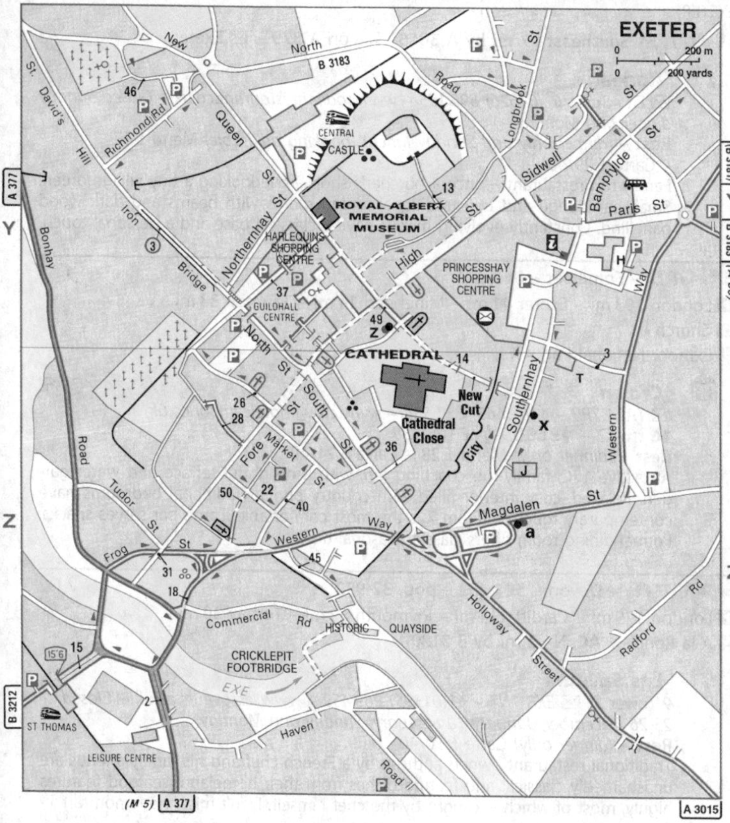

at Broadclyst Northeast : 4.5 mi by B 3212 on B 3181

The HH

✉ *EX5 3ET – ☎ (01392) 461 472 – www.the-hh.co.uk – Closed Christmas-New Year, Sunday and Monday*

Rest – Menu £ 15 (weekday lunch)/30 – Carte £ 32/46

Pleasant little restaurant which resembles a cottage. The interior blends the rustic and the contemporary, with its wooden beams, inglenook fireplace and modern décor. Interesting modern dishes are well presented and flavours are clear.

at Rockbeare East : 7.5 mi by A 3183, A 30 and Clyst Honiton rd - V – ✉ Exeter

Jack in the Green

London Rd ✉ EX5 2EE – ☎ (01404) 822 240 – www.jackinthegreen.uk.com – Closed 25 December-3 January

Rest – Menu £ 25 – Carte £ 18/35

Unassuming whitewashed pub with a warm, welcoming interior. Cooking is taken seriously and they are keen to support local producers. A vast array of menus feature both pub and restaurant style dishes, and you can mix and match between them; the 6 highlighted dishes make up the 'Totally Devon' set menu.

at Kenton Southeast : 7 mi by A 3015 - X - on A 379 – ✉ Exeter

XX **Rodean**

✉ *EX6 8LS – ✆ (01626) 890 195 – www.rodeanrestaurant.co.uk – Closed Sunday dinner and Monday*

Rest – *(dinner only and Sunday lunch) (booking advisable)* Menu £ 17 – Carte £ 29/40

Family-run restaurant – once a butcher's shop – overlooking a tiny village green. Small bar-lounge and two traditional dining rooms with beams and dark wood panelling. Constantly evolving menus have a classical base and a personal touch.

EXFORD – Somerset – 503 J30

3 A2

London 193 mi – Exeter 41 mi – Minehead 14 mi – Taunton 33 mi

Church★

Exmoor National Park★★

Crown

✉ *TA24 7PP – ✆ (01643) 831 554 – www.crownhotelexmoor.co.uk*

16 rm – †£ 60/79 ††£ 105/159

Rest – *(dinner only)* Menu £ 28 – Carte £ 21/40

Attractive 17C, family-run coaching inn, with a delightful terrace and water garden. Relaxed, cosy interior filled with country prints. Traditional bedrooms have contemporary touches; Room 7 is the most comfortable. Large bar serves snacks. Formal dining room offers classic, seasonal dishes.

EXMOUTH – Devon – 503 J32 – pop. 32 972

2 D2

London 175 mi – Cardiff 114 mi – Plymouth 52 mi – Torbay 30 mi

A la Ronde★ **AC**, N : 2 mi by B 3180

X **Les Saveurs** N

9 Tower St ✉ EX8 1NT – ✆ (01395) 269 459 – www.lessaveurs.co.uk – Closed 25-26 December, January-10 February, Sunday and Monday

Rest – *(dinner only)* Carte £ 30/40

Traditional restaurant owned and run by a French chef and his family. Menus are unashamedly classical and feature dishes from their homeland; seafood features highly, most of which is caught by the chef himself. Don't miss the lemon tart.

EXTON – Devon – 503 J30

2 D2

London 176 mi – Exmouth 4 mi – Topsham 3 mi

Puffing Billy

Station Rd ✉ EX3 0PR – ✆ (01392) 877 888 – www.thepuffingbilly.co.uk

Rest – Menu £ 16 (weekdays) – Carte £ 20/37

Bright, modern, open-plan country dining pub with high vaulted ceilings, a semi-circular bar and a friendly, welcoming atmosphere. The eclectic menu offers tasty, globally influenced dishes and local specialities.

FALMOUTH – Cornwall – 503 E33 – pop. 21 635

1 A3

London 308 mi – Penzance 26 mi – Plymouth 65 mi – Truro 11 mi

Prince of Wales Pier, ✆ (01326) 31 23 00, www.discoverfalmouth.co.uk

18 Swanpool Rd, ✆ (01326) 31 12 62

9 Budock Vean Hotel, Mawnan Smith, ✆ (01326) 25 21 02

Town★ – Pendennis Castle★ (≤★★) **AC** B

Glendurgan Garden★★ **AC** - Trebah Garden★, SW : 4.5 mi by Swanpool Rd A – Mawnan Parish Church★ (≤★★) S : 4 mi by Swanpool Rd A – Cruise along Helford River★. Trelissick★★ (≤★★) NW : 13 mi by A 39 and B 3289 A – Carn Brea (≤★★) NW : 10 mi by A 393 A – Gweek (Setting★, Seal Sanctuary★) SW : 8 mi by A 39 and Treverva rd – Wendron (Poldark Mine★) **AC**, SW : 12.5 mi by A 39 - A - and A 394

FALMOUTH

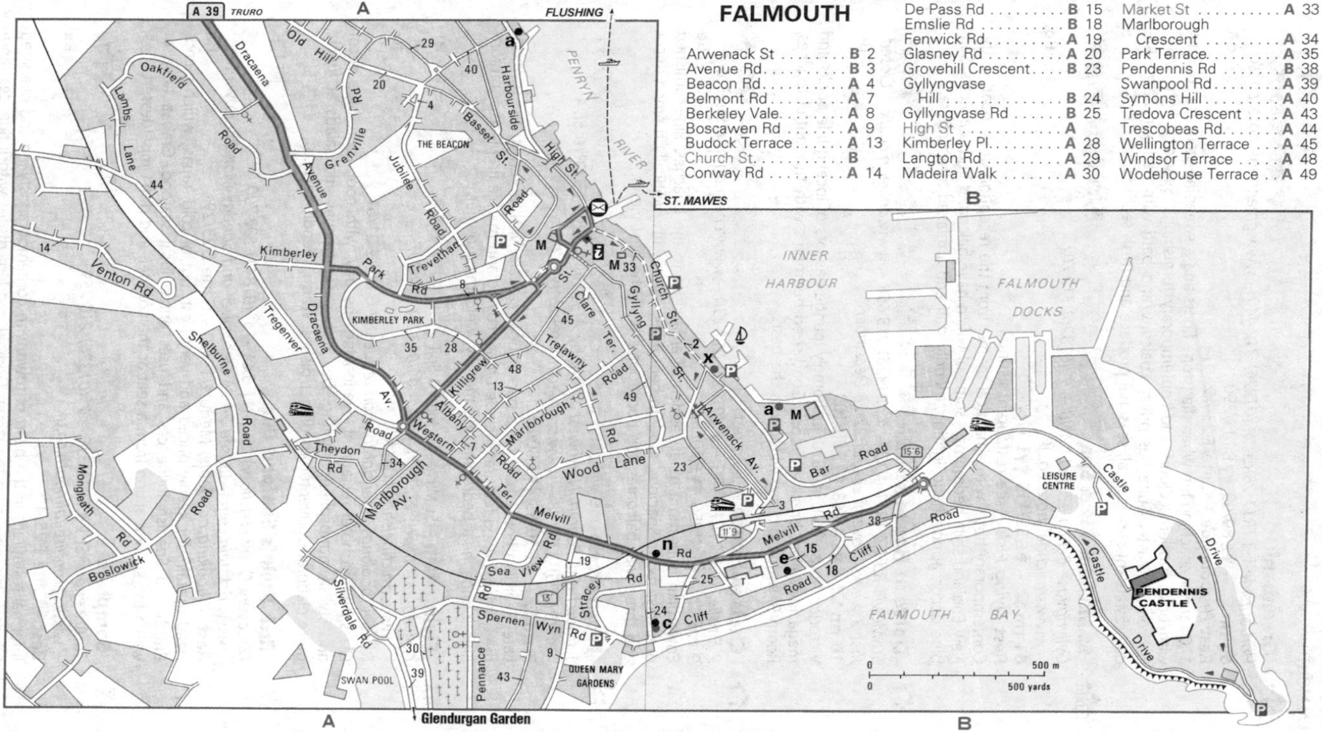

A 39 TRURO
FLUSHING
ST. MAWES
PENRYN RIVER
INNER HARBOUR
FALMOUTH DOCKS
FALMOUTH BAY
THE BEACON
KIMBERLEY PARK
LEISURE CENTRE
PENDENNIS CASTLE
QUEEN MARY GARDENS
SWAN POOL
Glendurgan Garden
Old Hill
Oakfield
Lambs Lane
Dracaena Avenue
Grenville Rd
Basset St.
Harbourside
High St.
Jubilee Road
Trevethan Rd
Kimberley Park Rd
Venton Rd
Tregenver
Shelburne Road
Dracaena Av.
Killigrew St.
Clare Ter.
Trelawny Road
Marlborough Rd
Albany Road
Western Ter.
Wood Lane
Gyllyng St.
Church St.
Arwenack Av.
Bar Road
Castle Drive
Melvill Rd
Cliff Road
Sea View Rd
Stracey Rd
Spernen Wyn Rd
Pennance
Silverdale Rd
Theydon Rd
Marlborough Av.
Mongleath Rd
Boslowick
0 500 m
0 500 yards
A
B

Greenbank

Harbourside ✉ *TR11 2SR – ☎ (01326) 312 440 – www.greenbank-hotel.co.uk* Aa
60 rm – †£ 89/99 ††£ 145/290
Rest *Harbourside* – Carte £ 23/45
17C former coaching inn where flagstone floors and a sweeping staircase contrast with bold, modern colours and contemporary furnishings. Spacious, light wood bedrooms. Master Suite has private balcony and bath with harbour views. All-day restaurant serves local, seasonal produce and fresh seafood.

St Michael's H & Spa

Gyllyngvase Beach ✉ *TR11 4NB – ☎ (01326) 312 707 – www.stmichaelshotel.co.uk* Bc
61 rm – †£ 59/115 ††£ 116/230
Rest *Flying Fish* – see restaurant listing
Contemporary hotel with a nautical theme, from the reception desk 'boat' to the New England style bedrooms – some of which have balconies and sea views. Sea-blue décor, atmospheric lighting, friendly staff and a relaxed atmosphere.

Dolvean House without rest

50 Melvill Rd ✉ *TR11 4DQ – ☎ (01326) 313 658 – www.dolvean.co.uk – Closed first 2 weeks November and 22-28 December* Bn
10 rm – †£ 41/68 ††£ 80/100
Victorian house built in 1870; its homely lounge has lots of local guide books and magazines. Neat breakfast room. Good-sized bedrooms with thoughtful touches; Room 9, with a big bay window, is the best.

Chelsea House without rest

2 Emslie Rd ✉ *TR11 4BG – ☎ (01326) 212 230 – www.chelseahousehotel.com* Be
9 rm – †£ 45/50 ††£ 70/110
Edwardian house in a quiet residential area close to the beaches. Pine-furnished breakfast room. Spacious, modern bedrooms, some with nautically themed décor and three with balconies; top floor rooms have the best views.

Prospect House without rest

1 Church Rd, Penryn, Northwest : 2 mi by A 39 on B 3292 ✉ *TR10 8DA – ☎ (01326) 373 198 – www.prospecthouse-penryn.co.uk*
3 rm – †£ 50/55 ††£ 80/85
Late Georgian house built for a packet boat captain, with a Penryn tea tower in the garden; period features include ornate coving and marble fireplaces. Comfortable lounge, neat bedrooms and friendly, welcoming owner.

Flying Fish – St Michael's Hotel & Spa

Gyllyngvase Beach ✉ *TR11 4NB – ☎ (01326) 312 707 – www.stmichaelshotel.co.uk* Bc
Rest – *(bookings essential for non-residents)* Carte £ 21/61
Glass-fronted hotel restaurant overlooking the bay, with cool, azure-blue décor and stylish, atmospheric lighting. Deli dishes, sandwiches and salads at lunch; more elaborate, adventurous dinner dishes. Warm, friendly service.

Rick Stein's Seafood Bar

Discovery Quay (1st floor) ✉ *TR11 3XA – ☎ (01841) 532 700 – www.rickstein.com – Closed 24-26 December and Sunday-Monday in winter*
Rest – *(booking advisable)* Menu £ 13/20 – Carte £ 23/29 Ba
Head upstairs for keenly priced and very fresh hot or cold 'tapas', which blends British and Spanish influences and uses prime local seafood. Grab a table or watch the kitchen action from a seat at the counter, and don't miss dessert.

Samphire

36 Arwenack St ✉ *TR11 3JF – ☎ (01326) 210 759 – www.samphire-falmouth.co.uk* Bx
Rest – Carte £ 25/41
Informal restaurant in the heart of town with contemporary styling and oversized windows opening onto the street. Original, modern dishes with influences ranging from the Med to Asia. Fresh, local seafood and tasty Sunday roasts.

ENGLAND

at Maenporth Beach South : 3.75 mi by Pennance Rd

Cove

Maenporth Beach ✉ TR11 5HN – ✆ (01326) 251 136 – www.thecovemaenporth.co.uk – Closed 25 December

Rest – Carte £ 23/39

Bright, stylish restaurant in a smart glass-fronted building overlooking the beach, the cove and St Anthony's Head. The modern dining room is decorated in purple and there's a lovely split-level terrace with a retractable roof. Menus are contemporary, with a strong seafood base and some Asian influences.

FARNBOROUGH – Hampshire – **504** R30 – **pop. 57 147** **7** C1

London 41 mi – Reading 17 mi – Southampton 44 mi – Winchester 33 mi

Southwood, Ively Rd, ✆ (01252) 54 87 00

Aviator

Farnborough Rd, Southwest : 1 mi on A 325 ✉ GU14 6EL – ✆ (01252) 555 890 – www.aviatorbytag.com

169 rm – †£ 165/245 ††£ 165/245

Rest *Brasserie* – ✆ (01252) 555 895 – Menu £ 21 (lunch) **s** – Carte £ 27/59 **s**

Eye-catching, modern hotel overlooking Farnborough Airport and boasting an unusual circular atrium, a smart first-floor lounge-bar and a small deli. Sleek, good-sized bedrooms feature light wood, modern facilities and fully tiled bathrooms.

FARNHAM – Dorset – **503** N31 – see Blandford Forum

FARNINGHAM – Kent – **504** U29 **8** B1

London 22 mi – Dartford 7 mi – Maidstone 20 mi

Beesfield Farm without rest

Beesfield Ln, off A 225 ✉ DA4 0LA – ✆ (01322) 863 900 – www.beesfieldfarm.co.uk – Closed 25 December

4 rm – †£ 65/70 ††£ 80/85

Charming house set in 400 acres and packed with photographs and curios. Luxurious, antique-furnished sitting room with an open fire and chandelier; individually styled, quirky, beamed bedrooms. Communal breakfasts feature local honey.

FAR SAWREY – Cumbria – **502** L20 – see Hawkshead

FAVERSHAM – Kent – **504** W30 – **pop. 18 222** **9** C1

London 52 mi – Dover 26 mi – Maidstone 21 mi – Margate 25 mi

13 Preston St, ✆ (01795) 53 45 42, www.faversham.org

Read's with rm

Macknade Manor, Canterbury Rd, East : 1 mi on A 2 ✉ ME13 8XE – ✆ (01795) 535 344 – www.reads.com – Closed 2 weeks early September, 1 week early January, 25-26 December, Sunday and Monday

6 rm – †£ 125/185 ††£ 165/195 **Rest** – Menu £ 25/60

Elegant Georgian house in landscaped grounds, with antique furniture, traditional country house styling and some lovely oil paintings. Classically based dishes make use of seasonal produce from the walled kitchen garden; professional service. Comfortable bedrooms are full of period charm and thoughtful extras give a sense of luxury.

at Dargate East : 6 mi by A 2 off A 299 – ✉ Kent

Dove Inn

Plum Pudding Ln ✉ ME13 9HB – ✆ (01227) 751 360 – www.doveatdargate.co.uk – Closed first week January, 1 week February, Monday except bank holidays, Sunday dinner and Tuesday lunch

Rest – *(booking advisable)* Carte £ 24/37

Attractive Victorian pub with well-tended gardens and cosy rooms. Weekday menus offer enticing nibbles, pub classics and specials. Concise Friday and Saturday menus are much more ambitious.

ENGLAND

at Oare Northwest : 2.5 mi by A2 off B2045 – ✉ Kent

Three Mariners

2 Church Rd ✉ ME13 0QA – ✆ (01795) 533 633 – www.thethreemarinersoare.co.uk – Closed dinner 24-25 December

Rest – Menu £ 12/17 – Carte £ 22/33

Welcoming 500 year old pub set by a small marina in a sleepy hamlet and boasting pleasant views across the marshes to the estuary. Constantly evolving menus offer an appealing mix of carefully prepared, flavoursome dishes; the 'Walkers' and 'Business' set lunches represent excellent value.

FELIXKIRK – North Yorkshire – 502 Q21 – see Thirsk

FERMAIN BAY – 503 L33 – see Channel Islands (Guernsey)

FERRENSBY – North Yorkshire – see Knaresborough

FILKINS – Oxfordshire 10 A2

London 78 mi – Birmingham 72 mi – Manchester 152 mi – Bristol 59 mi

Five Alls (N) with rm

✉ GL7 3JQ – ✆ (01367) 860 875 – www.thefiveallsfilkins.co.uk – Closed 25 December and Sunday dinner

4 rm – †£ 90/110 ††£ 110/160

Rest – Menu £ 20 – Carte £ 26/43

Like its curious logo, this pub has it all: an open-fired bar where they serve snacks and takeaway burgers; a locals bar stocked with fine ales; three antique-furnished dining rooms; and a terrace and a garden with an Aunt Sally area. The menu is satisfyingly traditional and bedrooms are modern and cosy.

FIVEHEAD – Somerset – 503 L30/31 3 B3

London 140 mi – Bristol 63 mi – Cardiff 84 mi – Bournemouth 77 mi

Langford Fivehead

Lower Swell, East : 0.5 mi by Westport rd on Swell rd ✉ TA3 6PH – ✆ (01460) 281 159 – www.langfordfivehead.co.uk – Closed 3-31 January

6 rm – †£ 110/300 ††£ 245/350

Rest – *(closed Sunday-Monday) (dinner only) (bookings essential for non-residents)* Menu £ 36

Beautiful 1453 country house on the Somerset Levels, surrounded by landscaped gardens and very personally run. Tastefully furnished sitting rooms have a classic English style. Luxurious bedrooms are furnished with antiques; one has a particularly impressive ceiling. Dine in a beamed, open-fired room from a concise menu; classic dishes have a subtle modern edge.

FLAUNDEN – Hertfordshire – pop. 5 468 12 A2

London 35 mi – Reading 43 mi – Luton 23 mi – Milton Keynes 42 mi

Bricklayers Arms

Hogpits Bottom ✉ HP3 0PH – ✆ (01442) 833 322 – www.bricklayersarms.com – Closed 25 December

Rest – Menu £ 15 (weekdays) – Carte £ 22/44

Smart pub tucked away in a small hamlet. There are no snacks, just traditional, hearty, French-inspired dishes and old-school puddings. The wine list is a labour of love, featuring boutique Australian wines.

FLETCHING – East Sussex – 504 U30/3 – pop. 1 722 8 A2

London 45 mi – Brighton 20 mi – Eastbourne 24 mi – Maidstone 20 mi

Griffin Inn with rm

✉ TN22 3SS – ✆ (01825) 722 890 – www.thegriffininn.co.uk – Closed 25 December

13 rm – †£ 70/80 ††£ 85/145 **Rest** – Menu £ 25 – Carte £ 25/43

Hugely characterful coaching inn, under the same ownership for over 30 years. There's a sizeable garden and a terrace with a wood-burning oven for summer BBQs. Menus feature British and Italian classics and some Spanish influences. Individually decorated bedrooms are accessed via narrow, sloping corridors.

ENGLAND

FOLKESTONE – Kent – **504** X30 – **pop. 45 273** Great Britain **9** D2

London 76 mi – Brighton 76 mi – Dover 8 mi – Maidstone 33 mi

Access Channel Tunnel : Eurotunnel information and reservations ✆ (08705) 353535

Bouverie Place Shopping Centre, ✆ (01303) 25 85 94, www.discoverfolkestone.co.uk

The Leas★ (≤★) Z

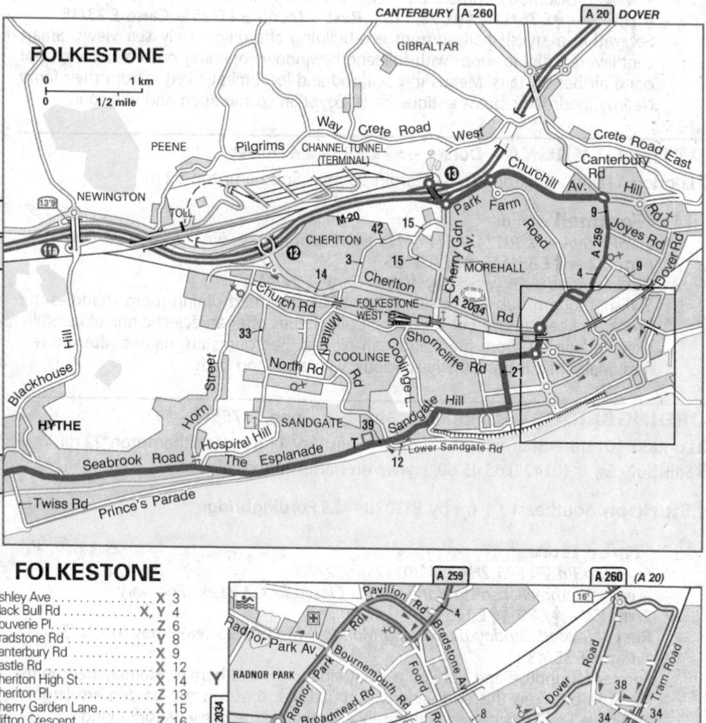

FOLKESTONE

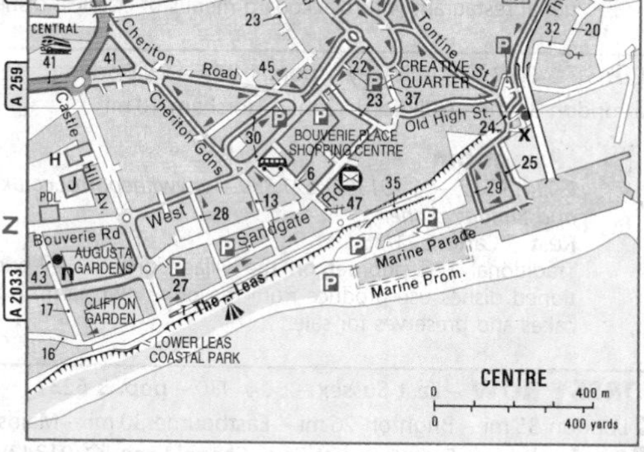

Relish without rest
4 Augusta Gdns ✉ CT20 2RR – ✆ (01303) 850 952 – www.hotelrelish.co.uk – Closed 21 December-2 January Zn
10 rm – ♦£ 88/100 ♦♦£ 98/110
A fine Regency house with a stylish, spacious interior. Contemporary bedrooms are colour-led in name and style, and the breakfast room has a terrace overlooking the gardens. Handy self-service 'coffee and cake' area under the stairs.

Rocksalt with rm — rest,
4-5 Fish Market ✉ CT19 6AA – ✆ (01303) 212 070 – www.rocksaltfolkestone.co.uk – Closed Sunday dinner Zx
4 rm – ♦£ 75/115 ♦♦£ 75/115 **Rest** – Menu £ 17/25 – Carte £ 23/48
Set within a stylish harbourfront eco-building affording lovely sea views. Smart cantilevered dining room with full-length windows opening onto a terrace; semi open air bar upstairs. Menus mix seafood and local meats; veg is from their farm. Nearby, bedrooms boast antique beds, Egyptian cotton linen and wet rooms.

FONTMELL MAGNA – Dorset – 503 N31 – ✉ Dorset 4 C3

London 115 mi – Bristol 60 mi – Cardiff 93 mi – Southampton 52 mi

Fontmell with rm
✉ SP7 0PA – ✆ (01747) 811 441 – www.thefontmell.com – Closed 26 December
6 rm – ♦£ 85/145 ♦♦£ 95/155
Rest – Menu £ 16 (weekdays)/19 – Carte £ 22/41
Stylish, modern pub with a simple front bar; the smart dining room straddles the brook, so keep an eye out for otters. Daily menus offer an eclectic mix of carefully executed dishes, from Mediterranean to Thai. Bedrooms are named after butterflies; Mallyshag is particularly spacious, with a roll-top bath.

ENGLAND

FORDINGBRIDGE – Hampshire – 503 O31 – pop. 5 755 6 A2

London 101 mi – Bournemouth 17 mi – Salisbury 11 mi – Southampton 22 mi
Salisbury St, ✆ (01425) 65 45 60, www.visit-hampshire.co.uk

at Stuckton Southeast : 1 mi by B 3078 – ✉ Fordingbridge

Three Lions
Stuckton Rd ✉ SP6 2HF – ✆ (01425) 652 489 – www.thethreelionsrestaurant.co.uk – Closed last 2 weeks February
7 rm – ♦£ 79 ♦♦£ 125
Rest – *(closed Sunday dinner and Monday)* Menu £ 23 (weekday lunch)/30 – Carte £ 35/48
Former farmhouse and pub, on a quiet lane in a small hamlet. Homely bedrooms are split between this and various outbuildings; those in the garden are largest and have French windows and outdoor seating. Large conservatory lounge. Traditional restaurant with blackboard menus of classical dishes.

FOREST GREEN – Surrey – pop. 1 843 – ✉ Dorking 7 D2

London 34 mi – Guildford 13 mi – Horsham 10 mi

Parrot Inn
✉ RH5 5RZ – ✆ (01306) 621 339 – www.theparrot.co.uk – Closed 25 December and Sunday dinner
Rest – Carte £ 21/35
Traditional 17C pub set on the village green. Well-priced, generously proportioned dishes use produce from the pub's own farm. Homemade bread, cheese, cakes and preserves for sale.

FOREST ROW – East Sussex – 504 U30 – pop. 3 623 8 A2

London 35 mi – Brighton 26 mi – Eastbourne 30 mi – Maidstone 32 mi
Royal Ashdown Forest, Forest Row, Chapel Lane, ✆ (01342) 82 20 18

Ashdown Park

Colemans Hatch Rd, Wych Cross, South : 3.25 mi by A 22 ✉ RH18 5JR – ☎ (01342) 824 988 – www.ashdownpark.com

99 rm – †£ 135/230 ††£ 135/230 – 3 suites

Rest *Anderida* – Menu £ 26/40 – Carte £ 37/54

Impressive Victorian building in extensive parkland. Luxurious country house interior boasts grand staircases, impressive halls and open-fired lounges. Huge bedrooms display antique furniture and feature beds. Formal restaurant offers classical cooking and good estate views.

FOTHERINGHAY Northants – 504 S26 – see Oundle

FOWEY – Cornwall – 503 G32 – pop. 2 064 1 B2

London 277 mi – Newquay 24 mi – Plymouth 34 mi – Truro 22 mi

5 South St, ☎ (01726) 83 36 16, www.fowey.co.uk

Town★★

Gribbin Head (≤★★) 6 mi rtn on foot – Bodinnick (≤★★) - Lanteglos Church★, E : 5 mi by ferry – Polruan (≤★★) SE : 6 mi by ferry – Polkerris★, W : 2 mi by A 3082

Fowey Hall

Hanson Drive, West : 0.5 mi off A 3082 ✉ PL23 1ET – ☎ (01726) 833 866 – www.foweyhallhotel.co.uk

36 rm – †£ 128/213 ††£ 150/300 – 11 suites

Rest – Menu £ 39 (dinner) – Carte £ 29/43 **s**

Striking 19C manor house with ornate, period-furnished lounge and a mix of traditional and modern bedrooms. Families are well-catered for and an informal feel pervades. Oak-panelled restaurant for adults; conservatory for those with children. Set menu has modern touches; less formal à la carte.

Old Quay House

28 Fore St ✉ PL23 1AQ – ☎ (01726) 833 302 – www.theoldquayhouse.com – Closed 18 November-23 December

11 rm – †£ 100/325 ††£ 130/325

Rest *Q* – see restaurant listing

19C former seamen's mission in a pretty harbour village; now a characterful boutique hotel with a friendly, laid-back feel. Bedrooms are individually decorated and have a contemporary, understated style; most have balconies and water views. Be sure to spend some time on the lovely terrace beside the river.

XX **Q** – Old Quay House Hotel

28 Fore St ✉ PL23 1AQ – ☎ (01726) 833 302 – www.theoldquayhouse.com – Closed 18 November-23 December and lunch October-April

Rest – Menu £ 16/38

Light, bright hotel restaurant with wood framed mirrors, wicker furnishings and a glorious terrace with harbour views. Light lunches and more sophisticated dinners of modern, flavoursome dishes; fish is from Looe and shellfish, from Fowey.

X **Bistro**

24 Fore St. ✉ PL23 1AQ – ☎ (01726) 832 322 – www.thebistrofowey.co.uk – Closed 2 weeks January and 2 weeks November

Rest – Menu £ 13 (weekdays)/16 – Carte £ 27/38

Former deli; now a relaxed, cosy, all-day eatery with an upstairs restaurant open in the evening. Modern European dishes range from sandwiches and pasta to bouillabaisse and beef Bourguignon. Good value 'Plat du Jour' menu.

at Golant North : 3 mi by B 3269 – ✉ Fowey

Cormorant

✉ PL23 1LL – ☎ (01726) 833 426 – www.cormoranthotel.co.uk

14 rm – †£ 80/200 ††£ 80/250

Rest – *(bookings essential for non-residents)* Carte £ 28/43

Well-run hotel in a superb waterside position. At only one room deep, all of its bedrooms overlook the estuary; the superior rooms boast balconies. Appealing seasonal menus feature local meats and seafood dishes. Light lunches offered in the formal restaurant or on the terrace.

ENGLAND

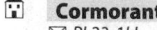

FOXHAM – Wiltshire 4 C2

London 94 mi – Bristol 28 mi – Cardiff 61 mi – Southampton 81 mi

Foxham Inn with rm

rest,

SN15 4NQ – (01249) 740 665 – *www.thefoxhaminn.co.uk* – *Closed 2 weeks early January and Monday*

2 rm – £ 65 £ 80 **Rest** – *(booking advisable)* Carte £ 24/28

Family-run pub in a sleepy Wiltshire village. A semi-covered terrace overlooks the fields and inside there's a cosy bar and a light, airy restaurant in a conservatory extension. Dishes are uniformly priced, and everything from the condiments to the ice creams is homemade. Bedrooms are warm and homely.

FREATHY – Cornwall – see Millbrook

FRESHWATER – Isle of Wight – 504 P31 – see Wight (Isle of)

FRESSINGFIELD – Suffolk – 504 X26 15 D2

London 104 mi – Ipswich 34 mi – Lowestoft 27 mi

Fox & Goose Inn

Church Rd IP21 5PB – (01379) 586 247 – *www.foxandgoose.net* – *Closed 2 weeks early January, 25-30 December and Monday*

Rest – *(booking advisable)* Menu £ 20/45 – Carte approx. £ 34

Attractive 16C pub with wooden beams, open fireplaces and a pleasant terrace overlooking the duck pond. Local cask ales, classic pub dishes and restaurant-style specials in the bar; more original, modern dishes in the upstairs restaurant.

FRILSHAM – West Berkshire – see Yattendon

FRISTON – Suffolk – see Aldeburgh

FRITHSDEN – Hertfordshire – see Hemel Hempstead

FROGGATT – Derbyshire – 502 P24 16 A1

London 167 mi – Bakewell 6 mi – Sheffield 11 mi

Chequers Inn with rm

Hope Valley, on A 625 S32 3ZJ – (01433) 630 231 – *www.chequers-froggatt.com* – *Closed 25 December*

6 rm – £ 85/115 £ 85/115 **Rest** – Carte approx. £ 29

Traditional 16C inn built right into the stone boulders of Froggat Edge and boasting a direct path up to the peak. Cooking is unfussy, tasty and largely classical, with more imaginative specials on the blackboard. Simple, comfortable bedrooms; Number One, to the rear, is the quietest.

FROME – Somerset – 503 M/N30 – pop. 24 171 4 C2

London 118 mi – Bristol 24 mi – Southampton 52 mi – Swindon 44 mi

Babington House

Babington, Northwest : 6.5 mi by A 362 on Vobster rd BA11 3RW – (01373) 812 266 – *www.babingtonhouse.co.uk*

32 rm – £ 360 £ 390/720, £ 16 – 11 suites

Rest *Orangery* – Carte £ 24/37

Behind this country house's classic Georgian façade is a cool, fashionable hotel with bold, stylish colour schemes and a laid-back, bohemian feel. Beautiful spa, with superb fitness area and pool; luxurious lounges and modern, understated, individually designed bedrooms. Newly built but classic-looking Orangery offers an accessible menu of Italian-influenced dishes.

ENGLAND

FULBECK – Lincolnshire 17 C2

London 123 mi – Birmingham 83 mi – Leeds 80 mi – Sheffield 54 mi

Hare & Hounds with rm

The Green ✉ NG32 3JJ – ✆ (01400) 273 322 – www.hareandhoundsfulbeck.com – Closed 25 December and Sunday dinner

8 rm – †£ 55 ††£ 75 **Rest** – Carte £ 22/34

Whitewashed pub with shabby-chic styling, in a charming location next to the church. Concise menus focus on simple pub classics, done well. Friendly, cheerful service; popular jazz evenings. Smart bedrooms with bold wallpaper and bright fabrics are located in the old stable annexe.

FULLER STREET – Essex – 504 V28 – pop. 50 13 C2

London 52 mi – Birmingham 141 mi – Leicester 112 mi – Coventry 123 mi

Square & Compasses

✉ CM3 2BB – ✆ (01245) 361 477 – www.thesquareandcompasses.co.uk – Closed Sunday dinner

Rest – *(booking essential)* Carte £ 20/32

Charming little pub with low beams, wood burning stoves and character aplenty. Unfussy menus of freshly made pub classics and unashamedly traditional puddings; daily blackboards offer locally shot game and fish caught nearby. Friendly team.

FULMER – Buckinghamshire – 504 – pop. 501 11 D3

London 21 mi – Croydon 49 mi – Barnet 30 mi – Ealing 13 mi

Black Horse

Windmill Rd ✉ SL3 6HD – ✆ (01753) 663 183 – www.theblackhorsefulmer.co.uk

Rest – Menu £ 13 (lunch) – Carte £ 21/36

Whitewashed village pub with thick walls, cosy alcoves, a wood-burning stove and a gem of a garden for sunny days. Stylish, formal dining area with delightful portraits; dishes include sharing boards, small plates and grills.

FUNTINGTON – West Sussex – 504 R31 – see Chichester

FYFIELD – Essex 12 B2

London 33 mi – Birmingham 134 mi – Croydon 44 mi – Leicester 111 mi

Queens Head N

Queen St ✉ CM5 0RY – ✆ (01277) 899 231 – www.thequeensheadfyfield.co.uk – Closed 1-7 January, Sunday dinner and Monday

Rest – Menu £ 19 (lunch) – Carte £ 25/39

Characterful village pub with a pretty rear garden leading down to the river. The inviting interior features original 16C beams and fireplaces. Menus change every 2 months and offer a good choice of tasty, restaurant-style dishes.

FYFIELD – Oxfordshire – see Oxford

GATESHEAD – Tyne and Wear – 501 P19 – pop. 78 403 Great Britain 24 B2

London 282 mi – Durham 16 mi – Middlesbrough 38 mi – Newcastle upon Tyne 1 mi

Access Tyne Tunnel (toll)

Prince Consort Rd, ✆ (0191) 433 84 20, www.newcastlegateshead.com

Ravensworth, Wrekenton, Angel View, Long Bank, ✆ (0191) 487 60 14

Heworth, Gingling Gate, ✆ (0191) 469 98 32

Beamish : North of England Open Air Museum★★ **AC**, SW : 6 mi by A 692 and A 6076 BX

Plan : see Newcastle upon Tyne

ENGLAND

at Low Fell South : 2 mi on A 167 - BX – ⊠ Gateshead

Eslington Villa
🍴 🛦 rest, 💥 🛜 🏄 **P.**

8 Station Rd, West : 0.75 mi by Belle Vue Bank, turning left at T junction, right at roundabout then taking first turn right ⊠ NE9 6DR – ℰ (0191) 487 60 17
– www.eslingtonvilla.co.uk – *Closed 25-26 December and 1 January*
18 rm ☑ – ♦£ 60/80 ♦♦£ 85/100 **Rest** – Menu £ 17 (weekday lunch)/26
Comprising two red-brick Victorian houses in the city suburbs. It's well-run by its hand-on owners and has a relaxed atmosphere and a surprisingly large rear garden. Individually styled bedrooms have a contemporary edge. Dine from a traditional menu with modern twists in the dining room or conservatory.

GEDNEY DYKE – Lincolnshire – 504 U25 – ⊠
17 D2

▶ London 112 mi – Birmingham 112 mi – Sheffield 91 mi – Cambridge 32 mi

✗✗ Chequers
🍴 **P.**

Main St ⊠ PE12 0AJ – ℰ (01406) 366 700 – www.the-chequers.co.uk – *Closed Sunday dinner, Monday and Tuesday*
Rest – Menu £ 16 (lunch) – Carte dinner £ 25/31
Formerly a pub, now a stylish, modern restaurant and bar with a smart conservatory extension. The experienced chef creates generously proportioned dishes using the wealth of produce on the doorstep. Lunchtime sees pub-style dishes, while the dinner menu offers greater choice – and at a good price.

GEORGE GREEN – Buckinghamshire
11 D3

▶ London 56 mi – Croydon 49 mi – Barnet 78 mi – Ealing 60 mi

Pinewood
🍴 🍴 🛗 🛦 rm, 🎞 💥 🛜 🏄 **P.**

Wexham Park Ln, Uxbridge Rd, on A 412 ⊠ SL3 6AP – ℰ (01753) 896 400
– www.pinewoodhotel.co.uk – *Closed 24-28 December*
49 rm ☑ – ♦£ 79/139 ♦♦£ 89/159
Rest *Eden* – Carte £ 19/36 **s**
Modern, purpose-built hotel in 4 acres; named after the nearby film studios and within easy reach of the M4, M25 and M40. Good-sized, well-equipped bedrooms are split between the house and an adjacent annexe. The simply decorated dining room serves a wide-ranging menu; go for a pizza from the wood-fired oven.

GERRARDS CROSS – Buckinghamshire – 504 S29 – pop. 19 523
11 D3

▶ London 22 mi – Birmingham 106 mi – Bristol 112 mi – Cardiff 145 mi

🍺 Three Oaks
🍴 🍴 **P.**

Austenwood Ln, Northwest : 0.75 mi by A 413 on Gold Hill rd ⊠ SL9 8NL
– ℰ (01753) 899 016 – www.thethreeoaksgx.co.uk
Rest – Menu £ 12/35 – Carte £ 22/49
Revamped pub with reconditioned furniture to add a lived-in look. Two dining rooms; choose the brighter one overlooking the terrace and garden. Bright young service and satisfying cooking that sticks to the tried-and-tested.

GESTINGTHORPE – Essex – 504 V27
13 C2

▶ London 65 mi – Birmingham 133 mi – Liverpool 226 mi – Leeds 184 mi

🍺 Pheasant 🆕 with rm
🍴 🛦 rm, 🛜 **P.**

South : 0.75 mi by Church St on Halstead rd ⊠ CO9 3AU – ℰ (01787) 465 010
– www.thepheasant.net – *Closed first 2 weeks January*
5 rm ☑ – ♦£ 80/105 ♦♦£ 90/165 **Rest** – Menu £ 15 (lunch) – Carte £ 22/36
A true country inn centring around sustainability, where they grow vegetables and keep chickens and bees. Simple cooking offers traditional, heartwarming dishes and the inviting, low-beamed bar and takeaway fish & chips keep the locals happy. Modern bedrooms feature good quality bedding and country views.

GILLINGHAM – Dorset – 503 N30 – pop. 8 630
4 C3

▶ London 116 mi – Bournemouth 34 mi – Bristol 46 mi – Southampton 52 mi
◎ Stourhead ★★★ **AC**, N : 9 mi by B 3092, B 3095 and B 3092

Stock Hill Country House
Stock Hill, West : 1.5 mi on B 3081 ✉ SP8 5NR – ✆ (01747) 823 626 – www.stockhillhouse.co.uk
8 rm (dinner included) – †£ 100/150 ††£ 195/245
Rest – *(booking essential)* Menu £ 23/40
Well-run, Georgian country house with later extensions, set in attractive mature grounds. Classical lounges boast heavy fabrics and antiques. Bedrooms, in the main house and stables, display a mix of cottagey and contemporary country house styles; all have good facilities. The formal, two-roomed restaurant has its own kitchen garden.

GISBURN – Lancashire – 502 N22 — 20 B2
London 242 mi – Bradford 28 mi – Skipton 12 mi

Park House (N) without rest
13 Church View ✉ BB7 4HG – ✆ (01200) 445 269 – www.parkhousegisburn.co.uk – Closed December and January
6 rm – †£ 55/80 ††£ 70/95
Imposing Victorian house with a classical open-fired drawing room and a small library leading to a hidden stepped garden. Bedrooms mix antique and more modern furnishings. Good breakfast selection; tea and homemade cake served on arrival.

La Locanda (N)
Main St ✉ BB7 4HH – ✆ (01200) 445 303 – www.lalocanda.co.uk – Closed 25 December-1 January, Tuesday lunch and Monday lunch except bank holidays
Rest – Menu £ 10/15 – Carte £ 18/38
Charming low-beamed, flag-floored cottage run by a keen couple. Comfy lounge serving Italian drinks, with the dining room above. Extensive menu of hearty homemade dishes; try the tasty pastas. Good quality local and imported produce.

ENGLAND

GITTISHAM – Devon – 503 K31 – see Honiton

GLINTON – 504 T26 – see Peterborough

GODALMING – Surrey – 504 S30 – pop. 21 514 — 7 C2
London 39 mi – Guildford 5 mi – Southampton 48 mi
18 West Surrey, Enton Green, ✆ (01483) 42 12 75
9 Shillinglee Park, Chiddingfold, ✆ (01428) 65 32 37

La Luna
10-14 Wharf St ✉ GU7 1NN – ✆ (01483) 414 155 – www.lalunarestaurant.co.uk – Closed Sunday and Monday
Rest – Menu £ 17 (lunch) – Carte £ 23/37
Contemporary Italian restaurant whose passionate owner looks after his guests with great enthusiasm. Classic Italian dishes use excellent ingredients. Particularly good selection of authentic antipasti and pasta.

at Lower Eashing West : 1.75 mi by A 3100

Stag on the River with rm
Lower Eashing Rd ✉ GU7 2QG – ✆ (01483) 421 568 – www.stagontherivereashing.co.uk
7 rm – †£ 65/110 ††£ 65/110 **Rest** – Carte £ 25/33
Pretty 16C former mill; sit on the terrace overlooking the old millstream or beside the fire in the appealing beamed and quarry-tiled interior. Choose from sandwiches, pub classics and more interesting dishes such as haddock and bacon rarebit fishcakes. Attractively appointed, modern bedrooms.

GODSHILL – Isle of Wight – 504 Q32 – see Wight (Isle of)

GOLANT Cornwall – 503 G32 – see Fowey

GOLDSBOROUGH – North Yorkshire – see Whitby

GOREY – 503 P33 – see Channel Islands (Jersey)

GORRAN HAVEN – Cornwall – 503 F33 — 1 B3

London 260 mi – Plymouth 53 mi – Torbay 80 mi – Torquay 83 mi

Llawnroc

Chute Ln ✉ *PL26 6NU* – ✆ *(01726) 843 461* – *www.thellawnrochotel.co.uk*
– Closed 25-26 December and restricted opening in winter
18 rm – †£ 92/160 ††£ 115/310
Rest ***Gwineas*** – Carte £ 22/41
Unpretentious boutique hotel that's popular with families – enjoy tea on the terrific terrace. Boldly coloured, well-equipped bedrooms feature plenty of contemporary design touches; bathrooms have drench showers and Voya seaweed toiletries. Unfussy bistro dishes are served in the minimalistic restaurant.

GOUDHURST – Kent – 504 V30 – pop. 2 498 — 8 B2

London 47 mi – Leeds 242 mi – Sheffield 224 mi – Manchester 267 mi

Goudhurst Inn

Cranbrook Rd ✉ *TN17 1DX* – ✆ *(01580) 212 605* – *www.thegoudhurstinn.com*
– Closed Sunday dinner
Rest – Carte £ 21/37
Village pub given a top-to-toe refurbishment; rustic bar, small snug and lovely rear terrace. Seasonal menus offer classic English dishes like steak and kidney pud or sausage and mash, alongside charcuterie boards and old school puddings.

GRANGE-OVER-SANDS – Cumbria – 502 L21 – pop. 4 835 — 21 A3

Great Britain
London 268 mi – Kendal 13 mi – Lancaster 24 mi
Main St, ✆ (015395) 3 40 26, www.grange-over-sands.com
Meathop Rd, ✆ (015395) 3 31 80
Cartmel Priory★, NW : 3 mi

Netherwood

Lindale Rd ✉ *LA11 6ET* – ✆ *(015395) 32 552* – *www.netherwood-hotel.co.uk*
34 rm – †£ 90/110 ††£ 160/190 **Rest** – Menu £ 19/34
Impressive castellated Victorian mansion on the hillside, affording lovely bay views. Traditional guest areas display wood panelling and original features. Simple, well-maintained bedrooms; more contemporary rooms in annexe. Formal dining comes with great outlook.

Clare House

Park Rd ✉ *LA11 7HQ* – ✆ *(015395) 33 026* – *www.clarehousehotel.co.uk*
– Closed 16 December-30 March
18 rm (dinner included) – †£ 96 ††£ 192
Rest – *(booking essential) (bar lunch Monday-Saturday)* Menu £ 36
Family-run Victorian house set in lovely gardens, overlooking Morecambe Bay. Two classical sitting rooms. Stylish, boldly coloured bedrooms in main house; smaller, simpler rooms with balconies in wing. Smart, modern dining room offers traditional daily menus.

at Cartmel Northwest : 3 mi – ✉ Grange-Over-Sands

L'Enclume (Simon Rogan) with rm

Cavendish St ✉ *LA11 6PZ* – ✆ *(015395) 36 362* – *www.lenclume.co.uk*
17 rm – †£ 69 ††£ 159/199
Rest – *(closed lunch Monday-Tuesday) (booking essential)* Menu £ 35/95
Friendly, stone-built former smithy in an attractive village. Inventive, modern cooking uses top quality produce to create dishes with a pleasing lightness and a superb balance of flavours. Home-grown and foraged ingredients feature highly. Comfy, traditional bedrooms are spread about the village; breakfast is taken at Rogan and Company.
→ Cod 'yolk' with sage cream, pea shoots, salt and vinegar. Venison with charcoal oil, mustard and fennel. Sea buckthorn, sweet cheese and malt.

ENGLAND

Rogan and Company
The Square ✉ LA11 6QD – ✆ (015395) 35 917 – www.roganandcompany.co.uk – Closed Sunday
Rest – Menu £ 30/39
Converted cottage by a lovely stream; the informal cousin to L'Enclume. Characterful beamed interior with leather sofas and an open fire. Relaxed, friendly service. Seasonal menus rely on locally sourced produce.

Pig & Whistle (N)
✉ LA11 6PL – ✆ (01539) 536 482 – www.pigandwhistlecartmel.co.uk – Closed Monday and Tuesday
Rest – Carte £ 24/33
Comfy, cosy local in a delightful village. It looks rather like a row of terraced cottages and with three tiny rooms, has an intimate feel. Reasonably priced, traditional pub menus: cooking is honest and careful with bold, defined flavours.

GRANTHAM – Lincolnshire – 502 S25 – pop. 34 592 Great Britain 17 C2
London 113 mi – Leicester 31 mi – Lincoln 29 mi – Nottingham 24 mi
St Peter's Hill, ✆ (01476) 40 61 66, www.granthamuk.com
Belton Park, Londonthorpe Rd, Belton Lane, ✆ (01476) 56 73 99
De Vere Belton Woods H., ✆ (01476) 59 32 00
St Wulfram's Church★
Belton House★ **AC**, N : 2.5 mi by A 607. Belvoir Castle★★ **AC**, W : 6 mi by A 607

at Hough-on-the-Hill North : 6.75 mi by A 607 – ✉ Grantham

Brownlow Arms with rm
rest,
High Rd ✉ NG32 2AZ – ✆ (01400) 250 234 – www.thebrownlowarms.com
6 rm – †£ 65/75 ††£ 98
Rest – *(closed Sunday dinner and Monday) (dinner only and Sunday lunch)* Menu £ 17 (weekdays) – Carte £ 26/44
Characterful former shooting lodge for the nearby Belton Estate, with wood-panelled walls and large open fireplaces. Lengthy menu and specials list offer classically based dishes with modern presentation. Lovely terrace and friendly service. Delightful bedrooms are furnished with contemporary fabrics and period pieces.

at Dry Doddington Northwest : 11 mi by B 1174 and A 1

Wheatsheaf Inn
Main St ✉ NG23 5HU – ✆ (01400) 281 458 – www.wheatsheaf-pub.co.uk – Closed Monday except bank holidays
Rest – Carte £ 19/37
Smartly kept pub overlooking a pretty green, with cosy bar, laid-back restaurant and small courtyard. Simple, unfussy light bites lunch menu; more ambitious à la carte with evening specials.

at Great Gonerby Northwest : 2 mi on B 1174 – ✉ Grantham

Harry's Place
17 High St ✉ NG31 8JS – ✆ (01476) 561 780 – Closed 25 December-1 January, 1 week August, Sunday, Monday and bank holidays
Rest – *(booking essential)* Carte £ 55/67
Long-standing, intimate restaurant in a former farmhouse: it consists of just 3 tables and is personally run by a dedicated and delightful husband and wife team. Warm, welcoming feel, with fresh flowers, candles and antiques. Classically based menus offer 2 choices per course. Good cheese selection.

GRASMERE – Cumbria – 502 K20 – ✉ Ambleside Great Britain 21 A2
London 282 mi – Carlisle 43 mi – Kendal 18 mi
Dove Cottage★ **AC** AY **A**
Lake Windermere★★, SE : by A 591 AZ

Plan : see Ambleside

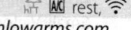

Rothay Garden
Broadgate ✉ *LA22 9RJ – ☎ (015394) 35 334 – www.rothaygarden.com*
30 rm – †£ 107/122 ††£ 155/265 **Rest** – Menu £ 22/40 **s** AY**s**
Slate-built Lakeland house with modern extensions, including a copper-roofed conservatory restaurant and a spa. Stylish, contemporary bedrooms; many with king-sized beds and some with balconies or patios – the Loft Suites are the best. Light, airy restaurant offers lovely outlook and classically based menu.

Daffodil N
Keswick Rd, on A 591 ✉ *LA22 9PR – ☎ (015394) 63 550 – www.daffodilhotel.co.uk*
78 rm – †£ 120/210 ††£ 130/220 **Rest** – Carte £ 23/45 AY**x**
Smart corporate hotel with lake and mountain views, set opposite the Wordsworth Museum. The small spa specialises in Rasul mud treatments. Bedrooms have multi-media panels, Molton Brown toiletries and king, super king or emperor sized beds. Light lunches, followed by hearty, traditional dishes in the evening.

Moss Grove Organic without rest
✉ *LA22 9SW – ☎ (015394) 35 251 – www.mossgrove.com – Closed 24-25 December* BZ**s**
11 rm – †£ 99/154 ††£ 114/169
Large house with a stylish, modern interior, which features some reclaimed furnishings. Funky bedrooms boast king or super-king sized beds, Bose sound systems and whirlpool baths. Organic breakfasts include tasty vegetarian options.

Grasmere
Broadgate ✉ *LA22 9TA – ☎ (015394) 35 277 – www.grasmerehotel.co.uk – Restricted opening in winter* BZ**r**
11 rm – †£ 60/65 ††£ 114/138
Rest – *(dinner only) (booking essential)* Menu £ 30 **s**
Small Victorian house close to the village centre, with the River Rothay running through the garden. Traditional décor in spacious lounge and bar; similarly styled bedrooms are named after writers – some have antique beds. Classically furnished dining room overlooks the garden.

Oak Bank
Broadgate ✉ *LA22 9TA – ☎ (015394) 35 217 – www.lakedistricthotel.co.uk – Closed 2-16 January, 3-14 August and 21-26 December* BZ**x**
14 rm – †£ 44/113 ††£ 87/158
Rest *Oak Bank* – see restaurant listing
Victorian house with pretty rear garden, set on the edge of a famous village. Relax beside a converted range in the sitting room or open-fire in the lounge-bar. Modern bedrooms boast comfortable beds, bold fabrics and bright colours.

XX **Oak Bank** – Oak Bank Hotel
Broadgate ✉ *LA22 9TA – ☎ (015394) 35 217 – www.lakedistricthotel.co.uk – Closed 2-16 January, 3-14 August and 21-26 December* BZ**x**
Rest – *(dinner only) (booking essential)* Menu £ 34
Split-roomed hotel restaurant in a Victorian house, with pleasant conservatory extension overlooking the garden. Concise daily menu features interesting modern dishes crafted from local, seasonal produce. Puddings are classically based.

GRASSINGTON – North Yorkshire – 502 O21 – pop. 1 102 – ✉ Skipton 22 A2

London 240 mi – Bradford 30 mi – Burnley 28 mi – Leeds 37 mi
National Park Centre, Colvend, Hebden Rd, ☎ (01756) 75 16 90, www.grassington.uk.com

Ashfield House
Summers Fold, off Main St ✉ *BD23 5AE – ☎ (01756) 752 584 – www.ashfieldhouse.co.uk – Closed 2 weeks spring and 23-26 December*
8 rm – †£ 72/250 ††£ 100/250
Rest – *(closed Wednesday and Sunday except bank holidays) (dinner only) (booking essential)* Menu £ 36
Bright, cheery hotel with a larger-than-life owner. Formerly three miner's cottages, its beams and mullioned windows blend well with Mediterranean colours in the bedrooms; the cottage to the rear boasts a spiral staircase and terrace. Modern menus feature local produce – vegetarian dishes are a speciality.

ENGLAND

Grassington Lodge without rest
8 Wood Ln ✉ BD23 5LU – ✆ (01756) 752 518 – www.grassingtonlodge.co.uk
12 rm – †£ 60/95 ††£ 70/95
Stone-built house not far from the main square, with a sleek breakfast room and two lounges – one offering complimentary sherry, the other with a large DVD collection and a laptop. Unfussy modern bedrooms; those in the eaves are best.

Grassington House with rm
5 The Square ✉ BD23 5AQ – ✆ (01756) 752 406 – www.grassingtonhousehotel.co.uk – Closed 25 December
9 rm – †£ 95 ††£ 110/130
Rest – Menu £ 17 (lunch and early dinner) – Carte £ 24/40
Georgian house with a large bar-lounge, two dining rooms and delightful service. Classical menus display Mediterranean touches and include their home-bred pork. Smart, modern bedrooms; No.6 has a roll-tap bath in the room. Home-cured bacon or sausages are offered at breakfast and they host regular wine dinners.

GRAVESEND – Kent – 504 V29 – pop. 53 045 8 B1

London 25 mi – Dover 54 mi – Maidstone 16 mi – Margate 53 mi

Barbutis
Old Town Hall, High St ✉ DA11 0AZ – ✆ (01474) 550 030 – www.barbutis.co.uk – Closed Monday and Tuesday
Rest – *(booking advisable)* Carte £ 24/37
'Bearded One' in Italian (and the owner's wife's maiden name), Barbutis is set in an impressive 18C former police station and the old town hall. Piano bar and 4 private dining rooms in what were the cells. Tasty, classic British cooking.

GREAT DUNMOW – Essex – 504 V28 – pop. 5 943 13 C2

London 42 mi – Cambridge 27 mi – Chelmsford 13 mi – Colchester 24 mi

Square 1
15 High St. ✉ CM6 1AB – ✆ (01371) 859 922 – www.square1restaurant.co.uk – Closed 25-26 December and Sunday dinner
Rest – Menu £ 15 (lunch) – Carte £ 22/37
Pretty little whitewashed building; once a 14C monastic reading room. Much original character remains in the form of exposed beams and low ceilings; which contrast with vibrant modern art. Unfussy monthly menu has Mediterranean leanings.

at Great Easton North : 2.75 mi by B 184

Green Man
Mile End Grn, Northeast : 1 mi by B 184 on Mile End Green rd ✉ CM6 2DN – ✆ (01371) 852 285 – www.greenman-lindsell.com – Closed Sunday dinner
Rest – Carte £ 22/45
Modern, family-run restaurant in a former pub, with a rustic bar and a delightful terrace. The smart, beamed restaurant has a formal air. Simple, classical dishes rely on quality produce; portions are large and seafood features highly.

GREAT EASTON – Essex – 504 U28 – see Great Dunmow

GREAT GONERBY – Lincolnshire – 502 S25 – see Grantham

GREAT MALVERN – Worcestershire – 503 N27 – pop. 35 588 18 B3

London 127 mi – Birmingham 34 mi – Cardiff 66 mi – Gloucester 24 mi
21 Church St, ✆ (01684) 89 22 89, www.great-malvern.co.uk

Plan on next page

Cotford
51 Graham Rd ✉ WR14 2HU – ✆ (01684) 572 427 – www.cotfordhotel.co.uk
15 rm – †£ 68/85 ††£ 120/135 Bs
Rest *L'Amuse Bouche* – *(dinner only and Sunday lunch)* Carte £ 26/37
Refurbished, Victorian, gothic stone building in landscaped gardens; built in 1851 for the Bishop of Worcester. Modern but homely guest areas; cosy bedrooms. Contemporary dining room with garden views and a seasonal menu of local, organic produce.

ENGLAND

GREAT MALVERN

Albert Rd South	B	3
Blackmore Park Rd	A	5
Church St.	B	
Clerkenwell Crescent	B	6
Cockshot Rd	B	8
Court Rd	B	12
Croft Bank	A	13
Happy Valley off St Ann's Rd	B	15
Imperial Rd	B	16
Jubilee Drive	A	17
Lygon Bank	B	18
Madresfield Rd	B	20
Moorlands Rd	B	22
North Malvern Rd	B	23
Orchard Rd	B	24
Richmond Rd	B	25
Townsend Way	A	26
Upper Welland Rd	A	27
Walwyn Rd	A	29
Wells Rd	A, B	30
Zetland Rd	B	31

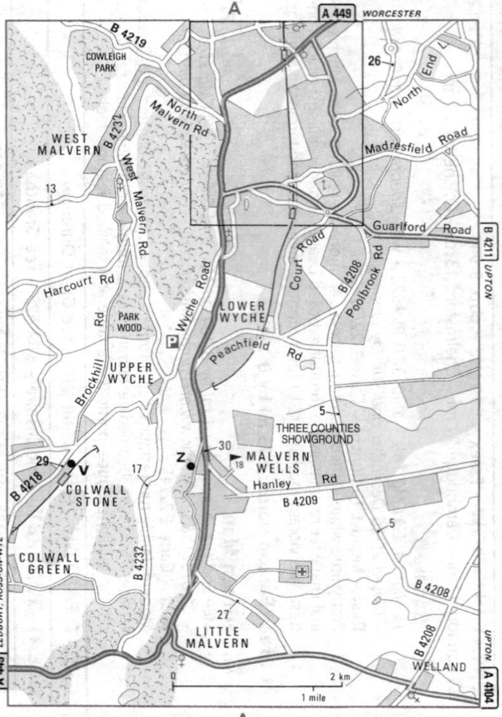

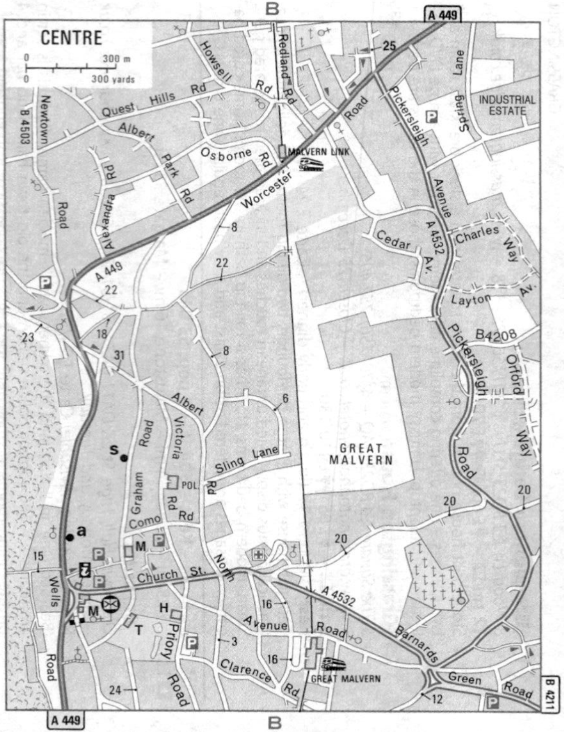

⌂ **Bredon House** without rest ≼ 🚗 📶 **P** ⇄
34 Worcester Rd ✉ WR14 4AA – 𝒞 (01684) 566 990 – www.bredonhouse.co.uk
10 rm ☑ – †£ 55/75 ††£ 85/100 **B**a
Roadside Regency house with spectacular views; on a clear day, you can see
35 miles to Broadway. Simply decorated, with homely touches; rear bedrooms enjoy the vista. Friendly owners provide excellent breakfasts.

at Malvern Wells South : 2 mi on A 449 – ✉ Malvern

🏨 **Cottage in the Wood** ⌘ ≼ 🚗 🏡 &. rm, 🅺 📶 **P**
Holywell Rd ✉ WR14 4LG – 𝒞 (01684) 588 860 – www.cottageinthewood.co.uk
30 rm ☑ – †£ 79/121 ††£ 99/198 **A**z
Rest *Outlook* – Carte £ 21/47 **s**𝄢
Three detached properties with woodland behind, superbly set and boasting
amazing views down the valley. Smart, good-sized bedrooms boast modern soft
furnishings; most rooms have views. Comfortable bar-lounge and a bright restaurant with full-length windows, extensive modern menus and over 700 wines.

at Colwall Southwest : 3 mi on B 4218 – ✉ Great Malvern

🏨 **Colwall Park** 🚗 🅺 rm, ⌘ 📶 ⚗ **P**
Walwyn Rd ✉ WR13 6QG – 𝒞 (01684) 540 000 – www.colwall.co.uk
23 rm ☑ – †£ 79/130 ††£ 100/190 – 1 suite **A**v
Rest *Seasons* – (booking essential) Menu £ 17 (lunch) – Carte £ 21/36
Passionately run, part red-brick, part black and white timbered house with lovely
gardens, nestled in the Malvern Hills. Pleasant lounges. Comfy bedrooms range
from traditional to more contemporary styles. Brasserie menu available in bar or
linen-laid restaurant.

at Cradley West : 4 mi by B 4219 and A 4103

⌂ **Old Rectory** Ⓝ ⌘ 🚗 📶 **P**
✉ WR13 5LQ – 𝒞 (01886) 880 109 – www.oldrectorycradley.com
3 rm ☑ – †£ 100 ††£ 140 **Rest** – Menu £ 38
Welcoming Georgian house in mature gardens; built in 1790 and set right next to
the church. The place is packed with curios and antiques; many of the pictures
were painted by the owner herself. Food plays a big role – jams are homemade,
bacon is home-cured, meats are local and vegetables are from the garden.

GREAT MILTON – Oxfordshire – **503** Q28 – see Oxford

GREAT MISSENDEN – Buckinghamshire – **504** R28 – **pop. 7 980** **11** C2
▶ London 34 mi – Aylesbury 10 mi – Maidenhead 19 mi – Oxford 35 mi

🍴🍴 **La Petite Auberge**
107 High St ✉ HP16 0BB – 𝒞 (01494) 865 370 – www.lapetiteauberge.co.uk
– Closed 2 weeks Christmas, 2 weeks Easter and Sunday except Mothering Sunday
Rest – (dinner only) Carte £ 31/40
Unashamedly traditional in style, this personally run neighbourhood restaurant of-
fers carefully prepared, classic French dishes in an intimate, candlelit atmosphere.
Service is unhurried but efficient.

🍴 **Nags Head** with rm 🚗 📶 **P**
London Rd, Southeast : 1 mi by A 413. ✉ HP16 0DG – 𝒞 (01494) 862 200
– www.nagsheadbucks.com
5 rm ☑ – †£ 75/95 ††£ 75/115
Rest – Menu £ 15 (weekdays) – Carte £ 26/47
Traditional 15C inn whose features include original oak beams and thick brick
walls. Gallic charm mixes with British classics on interesting menus. Cheerful service. Stylish, modern bedrooms; Number One is best. Tasty breakfasts.

ENGLAND

GREAT TOTHAM – Essex – 504 W28 – pop. 720 13 C2

London 59 mi – Croydon 64 mi – Barnet 58 mi – Ealing 70 mi

The Bull with rm

2 Maldon Rd ✉ CM9 8NH – ☎ (01621) 893 385 – www.thebullatgreattotham.co.uk

4 rm – †£ 75 ††£ 85 **Rest** – Menu £ 16 (weekday lunch) – Carte £ 23/39

Dating from the 1500s, this attractively refurbished and modernised roadside pub comes with a lovely terrace and garden. Seasonal dishes look to Europe for their inspiration but there are also some great British classics and a good value lunch menu. Individually decorated bedrooms are located in a cottage.

GREAT WOLFORD – Warwickshire – 503 P27 19 C3

London 84 mi – Birmingham 37 mi – Cheltenham 26 mi

Fox & Hounds Inn with rm

✉ CV36 5NQ – ☎ (01608) 674 220 – www.thefoxandhoundsinn.com – Closed first two weeks January, Sunday dinner and Monday

3 rm – †£ 60 ††£ 80 **Rest** – Carte £ 24/38

A traditional, family-run, cosy country inn, with flagged floors, a large inglenook fireplace and hops hanging from low beamed ceilings. Local, seasonal produce features in rustic pub favourites and some more modern dishes on the daily blackboard menu. Simple, pine-furnished bedrooms offer country views.

GREAT YARMOUTH – Norfolk – 504 Z26 – pop. 58 032 15 D2

Great Britain

London 126 mi – Cambridge 81 mi – Ipswich 53 mi – Norwich 20 mi

25 Marine Parade, ☎ (01493) 84 63 45, www.great-yarmouth.co.uk

Gorleston, Warren Rd, ☎ (01493) 66 19 11

Beach House, Caister-on-Sea, Great Yarmouth & Caister, ☎ (01493) 72 86 99

Norfolk Broads★

Andover House with rm

28-30 Camperdown ✉ NR30 3JB – ☎ (01493) 843 490 – www.andoverhouse.co.uk – Closed 23-30 December and Sunday dinner

20 rm – †£ 77/107 ††£ 77/107 – 4 suites

Rest – *(dinner only residents only Sunday)* Carte £ 29/42 **s**

Modernised, listed Victorian property with a crisp, chic style and friendly, well-drilled service. Constantly evolving à la carte of modern, well-presented and accomplished dishes, with the occasional Asian touch. Simple, modern bedrooms; some with four-posters, some with large bay windows.

GREAT YELDHAM – Essex – 504 V27 – pop. 1 601 13 C2

London 64 mi – Birmingham 129 mi – Leeds 180 mi – Sheffield 154 mi

White Hart with rm

Poole St ✉ CO9 4HJ – ☎ (01787) 237 250 – www.whitehartyeldham.co.uk – Closed dinner 25-26 December and lunch Monday-Tuesday

11 rm – †£ 55/80 ††£ 75/180 **Rest** – *(booking advisable)* Carte £ 30/49

Charming 16C inn with a characterful interior. The large, open-fired bar with its wonky floors and exposed beams serves unfussy favourites, while the elegant restaurant offers a refined, modern menu of skilfully prepared dishes which are full of flavour. Keenly priced bedrooms are cosy and well-maintained.

GREAT WHITTINGTON – Northumberland – 501 O18 – see Corbridge

GREEN ISLAND – 503 P33 – see Channel Islands (Jersey)

GREETHAM – Rutland 17 C2

London 101 mi – Birmingham 86 mi – Liverpool 164 mi – Leeds 98 mi

Wheatsheaf Inn

1 Stretton Rd ✉ LE15 7NP – ☎ (01572) 812 325 – www.wheatsheaf-greetham.co.uk – Closed first 2 weeks January, Monday except bank holidays and Sunday dinner

Rest – Carte £ 20/33

The aroma of fresh bread is the first thing you notice at this simple, family-friendly country pub. Robust modern cooking comes with hints of the Med; cheaper cuts keep prices sensible and desserts are a must. It's run by a charming couple.

GRETA BRIDGE – Durham – 502 O20 – see Barnard Castle

GRETTON – Gloucestershire – see Winchcombe

GRIMSTON – Norfolk – 504 V25 – see King's Lynn

GRINDLETON – Lancashire – 502 M22 – pop. 1 446 20 B2

London 238 mi – Birmingham 125 mi – Leeds 44 mi – Sheffield 85 mi

Duke of York Inn

Brow Top ✉ BB7 4QR – ✆ (01200) 441 266 – www.dukeofyorkgrindleton.com – Closed 25 December, Monday except bank holidays and Tuesday following bank holidays

Rest – Menu £ 16 (weekdays) – Carte £ 23/40

Ivy-clad pub in the heart of the Trough of Bowland, with views to Pendle Hill. Rustic bar and light, contemporary dining room. Excellent choice on seasonal menu, with plenty of regional dishes. Good value set menu.

GRINSHILL – Shropshire – 503 L25 – see Shrewsbury

GROUVILLE – 503 M33 – pop. 4 658 – see Channel Islands (Jersey)

GUILDFORD – Surrey – 504 S30 – pop. 68 230 Great Britain 7 C1

London 33 mi – Brighton 43 mi – Reading 27 mi – Southampton 49 mi

155 High Street, ✆ (01483) 44 43 33, www.visitguildford.com

Clandon Park★★, E : 3 mi by A 246 Z – Hatchlands Park★, E : 6 mi by A 246 Z. Painshill★★, Cobham, NE : 10 m – Polesden Lacey★, E : 13 mi by A 246 Z and minor rd

Plan on next page

Radisson Blu Edwardian Guildford

3 Alexandra Terr, High St ✉ GU1 3DA – ✆ (01483) 792 300 – www.radissonblu-edwardian.com/guildford Yx

183 rm – †£ 99/295 ††£ 99/295, £ 18 – 2 suites

Rest *Scoff & Banter* – ✆ (01483) 792 305 – Menu £ 25 – Carte £ 18/32

Newly built hotel in the heart of the town; notable for its modern design and subtle theatrical theme. Well-soundproofed, contemporary bedrooms offer high levels of comfort and the latest technology. Curvaceous bar, theatre montages, and a menu of British classics with a modern edge in Scoff & Banter.

CAU

274 High St ✉ GU1 3JL – ✆ (01483) 459 777 – www.caurestaurants.com – Closed 25-26 December and 1 January Ys

Rest – *(bookings advisable at dinner)* Carte £ 19/33

The name stands for Carne Argentina Unica and beef reigns supreme; go for a steak, as it's what they do best. Staff are attentive, the atmosphere's lively, prices are reasonable and the surroundings, trendy and bright.

at East Clandon Northeast : 4.75 mi by A 25 off A 246

Queen's Head

The Street ✉ GU4 7RY – ✆ (01483) 222 332 – www.queensheadeastclandon.co.uk

Rest – Carte £ 22/34

Charming 17C pub with a large garden where village celebrations are held. Four rooms feature open fires and bovine-themed pictures. Simple menu offers something for everyone, from sharing boards or ham hock to steak and ale pie or a roast.

at West Clandon Northeast : 4.75 mi by A 25 and A 246 on A 247

Onslow Arms

The Street ✉ GU4 7TE – ✆ (01483) 222 447 – www.onslowarmsclandon.co.uk – Closed 26 December

Rest – Carte £ 18/42

Smartly refurbished pub, with old beams, copper artefacts and open fires giving a clue as to its true age. The same menu is served throughout, offering sharing platters, light bites and more sophisticated dishes in the evening.

GUILDFORD

Bedford Rd . . . . Y 2
Bridge St . . . . Y 3
Castle St. . . . . Y 5
Chertsey St . . . . Y 6
Commercial Rd . . . . Y 8
Eastgate Gardens . . . . Y 9
Friary Bridge. . . . . Y 12
Friary Centre . . . . Y
High St. . . . . Y
Ladymead . . . . Z 13
Leapale Lane . . . . Y 15
Leapale Rd. . . . . Y 16
Leas Rd . . . . Y 17
Market St. . . . . Y 18
Mary Rd . . . . Y 19
Middle Rd. . . . . Z 20
Millbrook . . . . Y 21
New Inn Lane . . . . Z 22
North St . . . . Y
One Tree Hill Rd. . . . . Z 24
Onslow St . . . . Y 25
Park St . . . . Y 27
Quarry St . . . . Y 28
Stoughton Rd. . . . . Z 30
Trood's Lane. . . . . Z 31
Tunsgate . . . . Y 33
Tunsgate Shopping Centre . . . . Y
Warwick's Bench . . . . Y 34
Woodbridge Rd . . . . Z 37

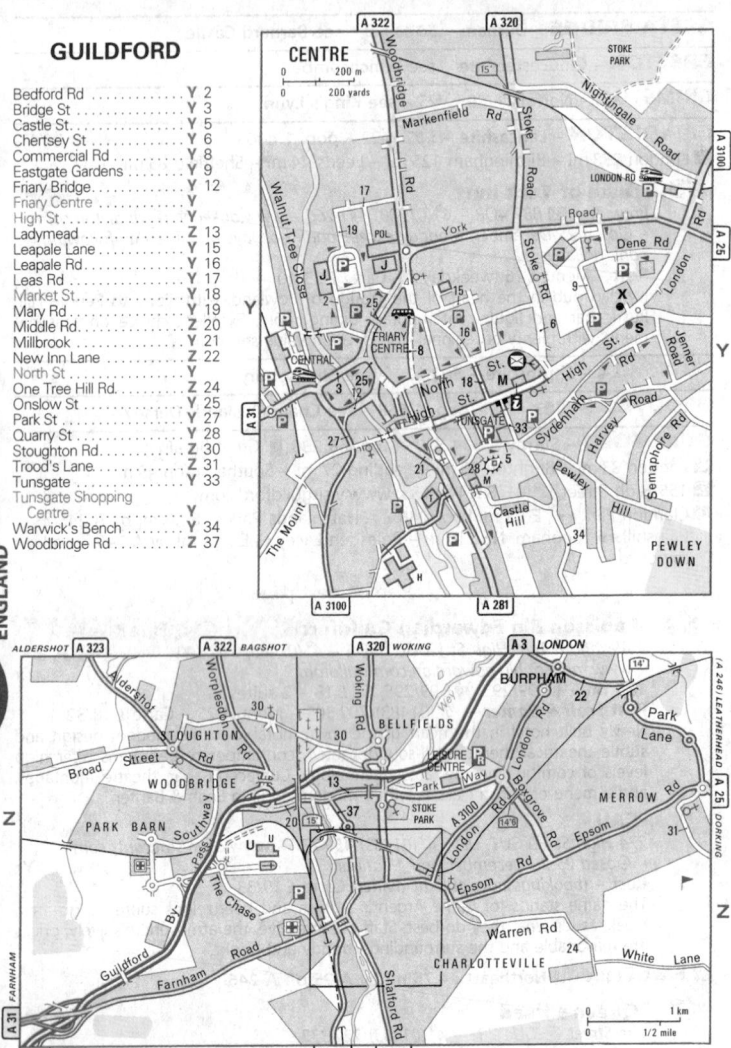

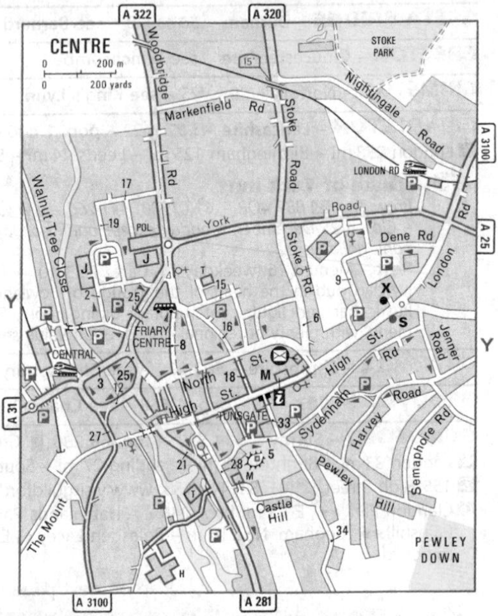

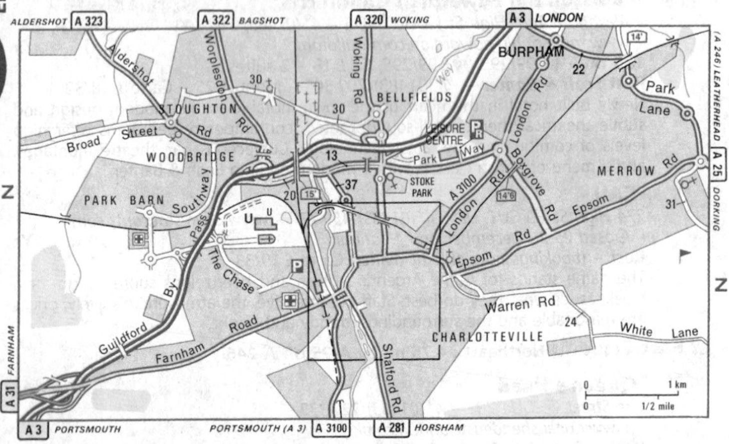

at Shere East : 6.75 mi by A 246 off A 25 - Z – ✉ Guildford

XX **Kinghams**

Gomshall Ln ✉ GU5 9HE – ✆ (01483) 202 168 – www.kinghams-restaurant.co.uk – Closed 25 December-5 January, Sunday dinner and Monday

Rest – Menu £ 17 (weekdays) – Carte £ 29/40

Attractive, creeper-clad, 17C cottage with a cosy, characterful beamed interior and a pleasant terrace. Cooking has a classical foundation, with fish specials and game in season. Be sure to try the 'Medley of Apple'.

GULVAL – Cornwall – **503** D33 – see Penzance

GULWORTHY – Devon – 503 H32 – see Tavistock

HADLEIGH – Suffolk – 504 W27 – pop. 7 124 15 C3

London 72 mi – Cambridge 49 mi – Colchester 17 mi – Ipswich 10 mi

29 High St, (01473) 82 37 78, www.suffolktouristguide.com

Edge Hall without rest

2 High St. ✉ IP7 5AP – (01473) 822 458 – www.edgehall.co.uk – Closed 23-29 December

6 rm – †£ 50/60 ††£ 85/125

Dating back to 1453, with a red-brick Georgian façade and a Queen Anne rear. Elegant, comfortable drawing room. Breakfast room with a bay window overlooking the garden. Spacious, antique-furnished bedrooms; one with a four-poster.

HADLEY HEATH – Worcestershire – see Droitwich Spa

HALFORD – Warwickshire – 503 P27 – pop. 301 19 C3

London 94 mi – Oxford 43 mi – Stratford-upon-Avon 8 mi

Old Manor House without rest

Queens St ✉ CV36 5BT – (01789) 740 264 – www.oldmanor-halford.co.uk – Closed Christmas-New Year

3 rm – †£ 65/80 ††£ 100/110

Characterful part-timbered house in a pleasant spot next to the River Stour. Well-appointed drawing room with garden views and an antique-furnished breakfast room with a large inglenook. Appealing period style bedrooms have rich fabrics.

HALFWAY BRIDGE – West Sussex – 504 R31 – see Petworth

HALIFAX – West Yorkshire – 502 O22 – pop. 83 570 22 B2

London 205 mi – Bradford 8 mi – Burnley 21 mi – Leeds 15 mi

Piece Hall BX, (01422) 36 87 25, www.visitcalderdale.com

18 Halifax Bradley Hall, Holywell Green, (01422) 37 41 08

18 Halifax West End, Highroad Well, Paddock Lane, (01422) 34 18 78

9 Ryburn, Sowerby Bridge, Norland, (01422) 83 13 55

Holdsworth House

rm,

Holdsworth Rd, North : 3 mi by A 629 and Shay Ln ✉ HX2 9TG – (01422) 240 024 – www.holdsworthhouse.co.uk

39 rm – †£ 175 ††£ 210/250 – 4 suites **Rest** – Carte £ 21/51

Attractive 17C property with beautiful gardens – including a parterre – within its old stone walls. Characterful interior displays original wood panelling and mullioned windows. Bedrooms are comfortable and contemporary. Three-roomed restaurant offers brasserie classics and some more refined, local dishes.

XX Design House

Dean Clough (Gate 5) ✉ HX3 5AX – (01422) 383 242 – www.designhouserestaurant.co.uk – Closed 26 December-8 January, Saturday lunch, Sunday and bank holidays

Rest – Menu £ 20 (weekday lunch) – Carte £ 21/42 **s**

Long-standing restaurant in a converted mill complex. Striking modern interior with white tables and bright artwork; smart team offer a warm welcome. Good value menus of tasty classics and some more ambitious modern dishes.

Shibden Mill Inn with rm

Shibden Mill Fold ✉ HX3 7UL – (01422) 365 840 – www.shibdenmillinn.com – Closed dinner 25-26 December and 1 January

11 rm – †£ 90/154 ††£ 111/182

Rest – Menu £ 15 (lunch and early dinner) **s** – Carte £ 22/42 **s**

A former corn mill set in a tranquil, deep-sided valley, with beamed ceilings, welcoming fires and lots of cosy corners. Menus offer plenty of choice, with pub favourites alongside more ambitious dishes. Well-drilled staff. Comfy, individually furnished bedrooms; choose Room 14 if it's luxury you're after.

HALSETOWN – Cornwall – 503 D33 – see St Ives

HALTWHISTLE – Northumberland – 501 M19 – pop. 3 811 — 24 A2

Great Britain

London 335 mi – Carlisle 22 mi – Newcastle upon Tyne 37 mi

Station Rd, (01434) 32 20 02, www.visitnorthumberland.com

Wallend Farm, Greenhead, (01697) 74 73 67

Hadrian's Wall★★, N : 4.5 mi by A 6079 – Housesteads★★ **AC**, NE : 6 mi by B 6318 – Roman Army Museum★ **AC**, NW : 5 mi by A 69 and B 6318 – Vindolanda (Museum★) **AC**, NE : 5 mi by A 69 – Steel Rig (★) NE : 5.5 mi by B 6318

Centre of Britain

Main St NE49 0BH – (01434) 322 422 – www.centre-of-britain.org.uk

12 rm – £ 59/75 £ 70/110 **Rest** – *(dinner only)* Menu £ 20

Yellow-painted former coaching inn in the town centre, with a pele tower dating from the 16C. Simple, well-kept bedrooms; those in the main house are larger and more characterful, while the cosy duplex chalet rooms are ideal for walkers, cyclists and guests with dogs. Traditional menus.

Ashcroft without rest

Lantys Lonnen NE49 0DA – (01434) 320 213 – www.ashcroftguesthouse.co.uk – Closed 25 December

9 rm – £ 65/90 £ 75/104

Imposing Victorian house, formerly a vicarage, with beautifully kept gardens. Family run and attractively furnished throughout creating a welcoming atmosphere. Large bedrooms.

HAMBLE-LE-RICE – Hampshire – 503 Q31 – pop. 3 853 — 6 B2

London 87 mi – Birmingham 149 mi – Leeds 243 mi – Sheffield 213 mi

Bugle

High St SO31 4HA – (023) 8045 3000 – www.buglehamble.co.uk

Rest – *(booking essential)* Carte £ 20/36 **s**

Attractive pub down a cobbled street, its terrace overlooking the marina. Bar menu offers sandwiches, small plates and pub classics. More ambitious à la carte available in the dining room.

HAMBLETON – Rutland – see Oakham

HAMPTON IN ARDEN – West Midlands – 504 O26 – pop. 1 655 — 19 C2

London 113 mi – Birmingham 15 mi – Leicester 39 mi – Coventry 11 mi

Hampton Manor

Shadowbrook Ln B92 0EN – (01675) 446 080 – www.hamptonmanor.eu

16 rm – £ 150 £ 150, £ 15 – 1 suite

Rest ***Peel's*** – see restaurant listing

Early Victorian manor house set in 45 acres; built for the son of Sir Robert Peel. Contemporary décor blends with characterful original plasterwork and wood panelling in the guest areas. Spacious, modern bedrooms boast excellent bathrooms.

Peel's – Hampton Manor Hotel

Shadowbrook Ln B92 0EN – (01675) 446 080 – www.hamptonmanor.eu – Closed Sunday dinner and Monday

Rest – Menu £ 18/42

Contemporary dining room situated in a former stable courtyard of Hampton Manor; with a slate floor, a glass roof and floor to ceiling windows. Modern menus feature some original, ambitious combinations. Service is formal and attentive.

HAMPTON POYLE – Oxfordshire – pop. 106 — 10 B2

London 68 mi – Birmingham 72 mi – Barnet 71 mi – Ealing 57 mi

Bell at Hampton Poyle with rm

rest,

11 Oxford Rd OX5 2QD – (01865) 376 242 – www.thebellathamptonpoyle.co.uk

9 rm – £ 95/125 £ 120/145 **Rest** – Carte £ 22/45

Almost Mediterranean in its style, with a very visual kitchen that includes a wood burning oven. Menu offers everything from meze and charcuterie boards to pub staples and seafood. They have the biggest gin selection in the world! Bright, fresh bedrooms are located above the bar and in a cottage.

HAROME – North Yorkshire – see Helmsley

HARROGATE – North Yorkshire – **502** P22 – **pop. 66 178** **22** B2

Great Britain

London 211 mi – Bradford 18 mi – Leeds 15 mi – Newcastle upon Tyne 76 mi

Crescent Rd, ✆ (01423) 53 73 00, www.harrogate.gov.uk

Forest Lane Head, ✆ (01423) 86 31 58

Pannal, Follifoot Rd, ✆ (01423) 87 26 28

Oakdale, ✆ (01423) 56 71 62

Town★

Fountains Abbey★★★ **AC** :- Studley Royal **AC** (≤★ from Anne Boleyn's Seat) - Fountains Hall (Fa 0.5ade★), N : 13 mi by A 61 and B 6265 AY – Harewood House★★ (The Gallery★) **AC**, S : 7.5 mi by A 61 BZ

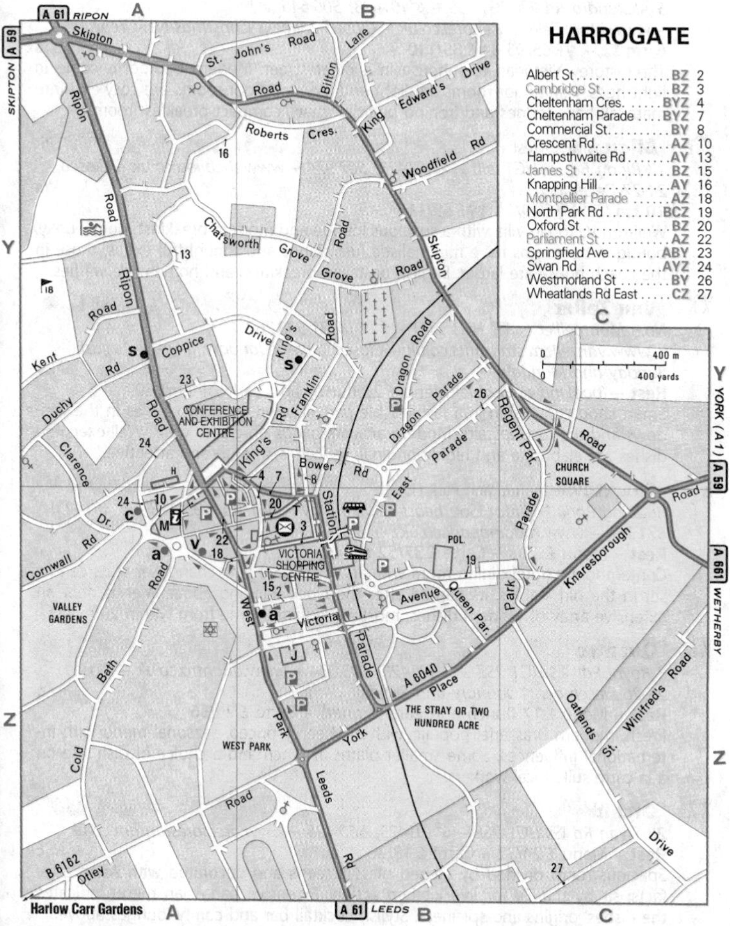

Rudding Park

Rudding Park, Follifoot, Southeast : 3.75 mi by A 661 ✉ HG3 1JH – ✆ (01423) 871 350 – www.ruddingpark.com
90 rm – ♦£ 123/160 ♦♦£ 144/190 – 7 suites
Rest *Clocktower* – see restaurant listing
Extended, Grade I listed Georgian manor house and Victorian church, in 250 acres of mature grounds, with a small spa and cinema. Modern lounges, bars and lovely terraces. The most luxurious bedrooms boast media hubs and touch lighting.

Hotel du Vin

Prospect Pl ✉ HG1 1LB – ✆ (01423) 856 800 – www.hotelduvin.com
48 rm – ♦£ 95/165 ♦♦£ 95/165, £ 16 BZ**a**
Rest *Bistro* – *(closed dinner 25 December)* Carte £ 25/48
Smart, modern hotel in a terrace of Georgian houses overlooking the green. Boutique-style interior with wine-themed décor. Contemporary bedrooms; two in the attic boast huge bathrooms with 'his and hers' roll-top baths. Small basement spa. Stylish bistro with an open courtyard and Gallic brasserie menu.

Brookfield House without rest

5 Alexandra Rd ✉ HG1 5JS – ✆ (01423) 506 646 – www.brookfieldhousehotel.co.uk – Closed 2 weeks Christmas-New Year
6 rm – ♦£ 65/95 ♦♦£ 85/110 BY**s**
Three-storey Victorian townhouse in a quiet street. Modern bedrooms come in light hues – first floor rooms are light and airy, top floor rooms are cosy and intimate; all have fridges and ironing boards. Smart, compact breakfast room.

ENGLAND

Bijou without rest

17 Ripon Rd ✉ HG1 2JL – ✆ (01423) 567 974 – www.thebijou.co.uk – Closed 24-27 December AY**s**
10 rm – ♦£ 49/74 ♦♦£ 59/114
Well-run Victorian villa with a spacious lounge and modern breakfast room. Funky, boutique bedrooms have minimalistic furnishings and thoughtful extras; those in the coach house are larger. English or Italian breakfasts and homemade waffles.

Van Zeller

No.8 Montpellier St ✉ HG1 2TQ – ✆ (01423) 508 762 – www.vanzellerrestaurants.co.uk – Closed 1 week January, 1 week August, Sunday and Monday AZ**v**
Rest – *(booking advisable)* Menu £ 25 (lunch and early dinner)/50
Smart shop conversion in a fashionable part of town, with two tables in the windows and the rest upstairs. Modern artwork hangs on cream walls. Well-executed dishes are elaborate and highly original; service is smooth and attentive.

Clocktower – Rudding Park Hotel

Rudding Park, Follifoot, Southeast : 3.75 mi by A 661 ✉ HG3 1JH – ✆ (01423) 871 350 – www.ruddingpark.co.uk
Rest – Menu £ 37 **s** – Carte £ 37/52 **s**
Contemporary hotel dining room with an impressive pink chandelier at its centre; set in the old stables, its named after the clock hanging above. Menus offer an extensive array of modern dishes; most ingredients come from within 20 miles.

Quantro

3 Royal Par ✉ HG1 2SZ – ✆ (01423) 503 034 – www.quantro.co.uk – Closed 25-26 December, 1 January and Sunday AZ**a**
Rest – Menu £ 17 (lunch and early dinner) – Carte £ 26/36
Fresh, modern brasserie; popular with all. Keenly priced, seasonal menu with international influences. Some smaller plates at lunch and a choice of dish size on à la carte suits local workers.

Orchid

28 Swan Rd ✉ HG1 2SE – ✆ (01423) 560 425 – www.orchidrestaurant.co.uk
Rest – Menu £ 24/32 – Carte £ 18/36 AZ**c**
Spacious room divided by etched glass screens and decorated with Asian artefacts; sit by the TV for live kitchen action. Extensive pan-Asian menu indicates the dishes' origins and spiciness. Stylish cocktail bar and comfy lounges above.

at Kettlesing West : 6.5 mi by A 59 - AY - ✉ Harrogate

Knabbs Ash without rest
Skipton Rd, on A 59 ✉ HG3 2LT – ☎ (01423) 771 040 – www.knabbsash.co.uk
3 rm ☕ – †£ 55/60 ††£ 80/85
Welcoming, stone-built farmhouse set on a smallholding overlooking Nidderdale. Comfy, cosy lounge and pine-furnished breakfast room. Light, airy bedrooms have plain walls, modern fabrics and a complimentary decanter of Madeira. Spacious gardens and grounds.

Cold Cotes without rest
Cold Cotes Rd, Felliscliffe, West : 1 mi by A 59 ✉ HG3 2LW – ☎ (01423) 770 937 – www.coldcotes.com
6 rm ☕ – †£ 50/75 ††£ 50/99
Remotely set former farmhouse in colourful, well-tended gardens; the owners love gardening and run a small plant nursery. Smart bedrooms provide good comforts: those in the house are small suites; Room 6, in the old barn, is the best.

HARTINGTON – Derbyshire – **502** O24 – **pop. 1 604** – ✉ **Buxton** **16** A1
London 168 mi – Derby 36 mi – Manchester 40 mi – Sheffield 34 mi

Biggin Hall
Biggin, Southeast : 2 mi by B 5054 ✉ SK17 0DH – ☎ (01298) 84 451 – www.bigginhall.co.uk
21 rm ☕ – †£ 80/140 ††£ 90/150
Rest – *(booking essential)* Menu £ 13/23 – Carte £ 19/32
Characterful house with traditional, rustic appeal. Many guests follow the Tissington and High Peak Trails: bike storage and picnics are offered. Classical, low-beamed bedrooms in main house; brighter rooms in the barns. Pleasant garden views from dining room. Homely cooking.

HARTLAND – Devon – **503** G31 **1** B1
London 221 mi – Bude 15 mi – Clovelly 4 mi

Golden Park without rest
Southwest : 5 mi by B 3248, A 39, Elmscott rd on Golden Park rd ✉ EX39 6EP – ☎ (01237) 441 254 – www.goldenpark.co.uk – Closed Christmas-New Year and restricted opening in winter
3 rm ☕ – †£ 40/80 ††£ 75/95
Large farmhouse on working arable farm, with lovely mature gardens. Charming owner provides a warm welcome; relax by the open fire in the comfortable lounge. Traditionally furnished bedrooms offer good mod cons; the four-poster is the best. Large communal table for hearty breakfasts.

HARTLEBURY – Worcestershire – **504** N26 – **pop. 2 253** **18** B2
London 135 mi – Birmingham 33 mi – Cardiff 93 mi – Leicester 72 mi

White Hart
✉ DY11 7TD – ☎ (01299) 250 286 – www.thewhitehartinhartlebury.co.uk
Rest – *(closed Monday)* Menu £ 15 (lunch) – Carte £ 21/34
Proudly run pub that's a proper village local. Carefully prepared, classically based dishes rely on quality produce; go for one of the specials from the board. They hold regular curry and pizza nights, as well as an annual beer festival.

HARTLEY WINTNEY – Hampshire **7** C1
London 43 mi – Croydon 46 mi – Barnet 56 mi – Ealing 38 mi

Cricketers Ⓝ
The Green ✉ RG27 8QB – ☎ (01252) 842 166 – www.thecricketers-hartleywintney.co.uk – Closed dinner 25 December
Rest – Carte £ 22/35
Attractive red-brick pub with a pillared entrance, creeping ivy and bright hanging baskets. The daily menu focuses on local ingredients and pub classics, and the tables in front overlook reputedly the oldest cricket pitch in the world.

ENGLAND

HARWICH – Essex – 504 X28 – pop. 20 130 13 D2

London 78 mi – Chelmsford 41 mi – Colchester 20 mi – Ipswich 23 mi

to Denmark (Esbjerg) (DFDS Seaways A/S) 3-4 weekly (20 h) – to The Netherlands (Hook of Holland) (Stena Line) 2 daily (3 h 30 mn)

Parkeston, ✆(01255) 50 61 39, www.touruk.co.uk

Parkeston, Station Rd, ✆(01255) 50 36 16

Pier at Harwich

The Quay ✉ CO12 3HH – ✆ (01255) 241 212 – www.milsomhotels.com

14 rm – †£ 115/135 ††£ 115/195

Rest *Harbourside* – see restaurant listing

Rest *Ha'Penny Pier* – Carte £ 22/35

Victorian hotel in a pleasant quayside spot – built to accommodate rail travellers waiting to board their cruise liners and an ideal place to stay if you're catching the ferry. Stylish, 'New England' style bedrooms; some boast port views. Smart seafood restaurant or casual all-day dining overlooking the pier.

Harbourside – Pier at Harwich Hotel

The Quay ✉ CO12 3HH – ✆ (01255) 241 212 – www.milsomhotels.com

Rest – Menu £ 26 (weekday lunch) – Carte £ 32/61 **s**

Comfortable hotel dining room boasting crisp linen-laid tables and attractive port and North Sea views. Seafood-orientated menu offers everything from the traditional to the more contemporary.

HASTINGS and ST LEONARDS – East Sussex – 504 V31 – pop. 85 828 8 B3

London 65 mi – Brighton 37 mi – Folkestone 37 mi – Maidstone 34 mi

Town Hall, Queen's Sq, Priory Meadow, ✆(0845) 2 74 10 01, www.hastingschoice.co.uk

Beauport Park Golf Course, St Leonards-on-Sea, Battle Rd, ✆(01424) 85 42 45

Zanzibar

9 Eversfield Pl ✉ TN37 6BY – ✆ (01424) 460 109 – www.zanzibarhotel.co.uk AZ**c**

8 rm – †£ 99/145 ††£ 109/235

Rest *Pier Nine* – Menu £ 15 (weekday lunch) – Carte £ 28/42

Stylish boutique hotel in a Victorian townhouse, with large lounge and communal breakfast room. Named and themed after places the owner has visited, bedrooms are furnished to a high standard, with intimate lighting and good mod cons. Delightful garden and terrace. Modern, seasonal cooking with a French base.

Hastings House without rest

9 Warrior Sq. ✉ TN37 6BA – ✆ (01424) 422 709 – www.hastingshouse.co.uk AZ**u**

8 rm – †£ 80/110 ††£ 80/145

Stylish, modern and very comfortable guesthouse just off the promenade; personally run by hospitable owners. Rooms 3, 5 and 7 are the best choice for their size and sea views.

Black Rock House (N) without rest

10 Stanley Rd ✉ TN34 1UE – ✆ (01424) 438 448 – www.hastingsaccommodation.com BZ**a**

5 rm – †£ 90/95 ††£ 130/135

Smart Victorian villa hidden away in the backstreets. Spacious rooms feature stripped wooden floors and stylish, modern furnishings. Individually designed bedrooms are cool and contemporary. Breakfasts showcase locally sourced produce.

Webbe's Rock-a-Nore

1 Rock-a-Nore ✉ TN34 3DW – ✆ (01424) 721 650 – www.webbesrestaurants.co.uk – Closed 24-26 December BY**x**

Rest – Carte £ 21/38

Bright, modern seafood restaurant with an open kitchen, a marble-topped horseshoe bar, and a large terrace overlooking the Stade and its fishing huts. Straightforward cooking offers small plates and classics, dictated by the daily catch.

HASTINGS ST. LEONARDS

Albert Rd	BZ	3
Bourne (The)	BY	4
Cambridge Gardens	BZ	5
Castle Hill Rd	BZ	8
Castle St	BZ	7
Cornwallis Gardens	BZ	9
Cornwallis Terrace	BZ	10
Denmark Pl.	BZ	13
Dorset Pl.	BZ	15
Gensing Rd	AZ	16
George St	BY	18
Grosvenor Crescent	AY	19
Harold Pl.	BZ	20
Havelock Rd	BZ	21
King's Rd	AZ	22
London Rd	AZ	
Marine Court	AZ	23
Middle St	BZ	24
Norman Rd	AZ	
Priory Meadow Shopping Centre	BZ	
Queen's Rd	BZ	
Robertson St	BZ	27
Rock-a-Nore Rd	BY	30
St Helen's Park Rd	BY	31
Sedlescombe Rd South	AY	32
Silchester Rd	AZ	33
Warrior Square	AZ	34
Wellington Pl.	BZ	35
Wellington Square	BZ	36
White Rock Road	BZ	38

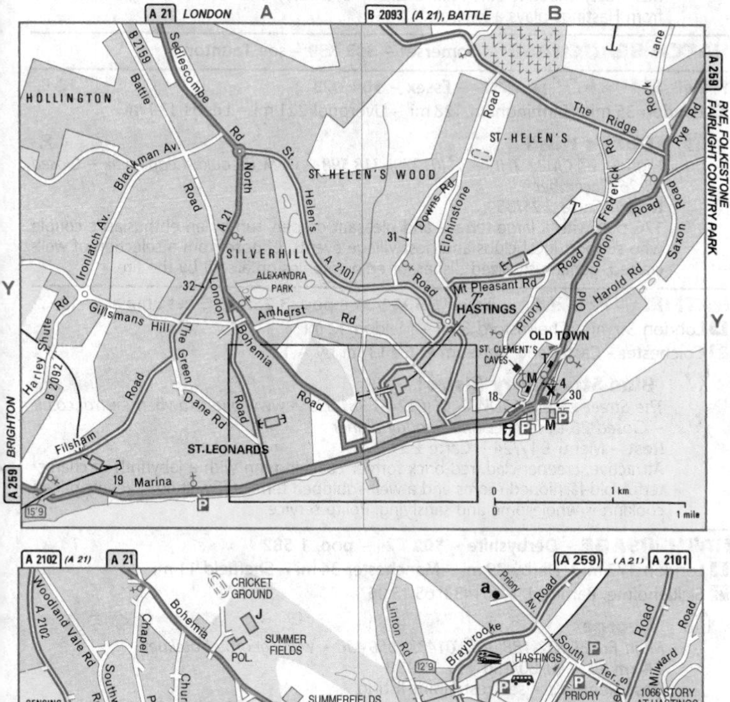

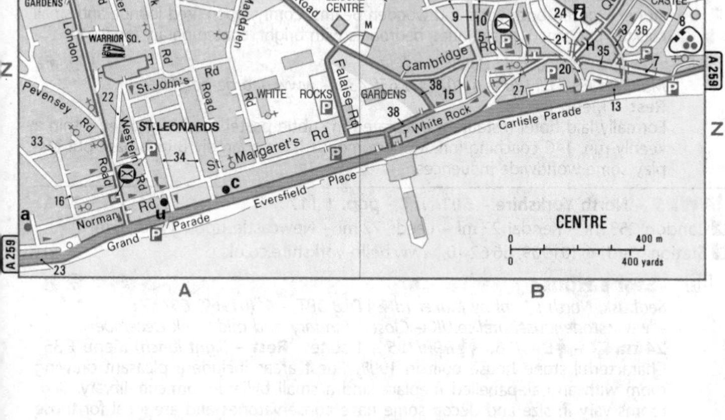

St Clements

3 Mercatoria, St Leonards on Sea ✉ TN38 0EB – ✆ (01424) 200 355 – www.stclementsrestaurant.co.uk – Closed 25-26 December, 1 January, Easter Monday, Sunday dinner and Monday AZ**a**

Rest – Menu £ 19/28 – Carte £ 25/36

Pleasant neighbourhood restaurant with striking local artwork hung on plain walls. Comprehensive à la carte and concise, good value lunch and midweek menus. Tasty modern European cooking is unfussy with a rustic edge. Fresh fish from Hastings plays a key role.

HATCH BEAUCHAMP – Somerset – 503 K30 – see Taunton

HATFIELD BROAD OAK – Essex – 504 U28 12 B2

London 35 mi – Birmingham 128 mi – Liverpool 221 mi – Leeds 179 mi

Duke's Head

High St ✉ CM22 7HH – ✆ (01279) 718 598 – www.thedukeshead.co.uk – Closed 25-26 December

Rest – Carte £ 21/35

17C pub with a large terrace and pleasant garden, run by an enthusiastic couple who support local clubs and host village events. Choose from a selection of well-crafted, generously sized dishes, or enjoy nibbles on a sofa by the fire.

HATFIELD PEVEREL – Essex – 504 V28 – pop. 3 258 Great Britain 13 C2

London 39 mi – Chelmsford 8 mi – Maldon 12 mi

Colchester - Castle and Museum★, E : 13 mi by A 12

Blue Strawberry Bistrot

The Street ✉ CM3 2DW – ✆ (01245) 381 333 – www.bluestrawberrybistrot.co.uk – Closed 26 December and Sunday dinner

Rest – Menu £ 17/24 – Carte £ 21/37

Attractive, creeper-clad, red-brick former coaching inn with a labyrinth of characterful, old-fashioned rooms and a well-equipped terrace. Traditional, keenly priced cooking is wholesome and satisfying. Polite service.

HATHERSAGE – Derbyshire – 502 P24 – pop. 1 582 16 A1

London 177 mi – Derby 39 mi – Manchester 34 mi – Sheffield 11 mi

Sickleholme, Bamford, ✆ (01433) 65 13 06

George

Main Rd ✉ S32 1BB – ✆ (01433) 650 436 – www.george-hotel.net

24 rm – †£ 80/150 ††£ 95/198

Rest *George's* – see restaurant listing

Keenly run 14C coaching inn where modern furnishings blend nicely with traditional stone, exposed brick walls and wooden beams. Comfy, open-fired lounge and small cocktail bar. Smart, pastel-hued bedrooms with bright, contemporary fabrics.

George's – George Hotel

Main Rd ✉ S32 1BB – ✆ (01433) 650 436 – www.george-hotel.net

Rest – Menu £ 20/37

Formally laid hotel restaurant decorated in subtle pastel shades and set within a keenly run, 14C coaching inn. Modern menus have a largely British base but display some worldwide influences.

HAWES – North Yorkshire – 502 N21 – pop. 1 117 22 A1

London 253 mi – Kendal 27 mi – Leeds 72 mi – Newcastle upon Tyne 76 mi

Station Yard, ✆ (01969) 66 62 10, www.hello-yorkshire.co.uk

Stone House

Sedbusk, North : 1 mi by Muker rd ✉ DL8 3PT – ✆ (01969) 667 571 – www.stonehousehotel.co.UK – Closed January and mid-week December

24 rm – †£ 45/160 ††£ 90/185 – 1 suite **Rest** – *(light lunch)* Menu £ 35

Characterful stone house built in 1908. Guest areas include a pleasant drawing room with an oak-panelled fireplace and a small billiard-room-cum-library. Bedrooms vary in size and décor; some have conservatories and are ideal for those with dogs. The traditional beamed dining room offers a classical menu.

ENGLAND

HAWKSHEAD – Cumbria – 502 L20 – pop. 570 – ✉ Ambleside 21 A2

Great Britain

London 283 mi – Carlisle 52 mi – Kendal 19 mi

Main Street, ✆ (015394) 3 69 46, www.hawksheadtouristinfo.org.uk

Village★

Lake Windermere★★ – Coniston Water★ (Brantwood★, on east side), SW : by B 5285

at Far Sawrey Southeast : 2.5 mi on B 5285 – ✉ Ambleside

West Vale without rest

✉ LA22 0LQ – ✆ (015394) 42 817 – www.westvalecountryhouse.co.uk – Closed 25-26 December and restricted opening 3 January-4 February

7 rm – £ 85/105 £ 110/180

Welcoming slate house boasting lovely countryside views; run by keen owners. Two comfy lounges and a smart country house style room for hearty breakfasts. Good-sized bedrooms with warm, comfy, boutique style; 7 and 8, on the top floor, are the best. Tea and cake on arrival, and plenty of extra touches.

HAWNBY – North Yorkshire – 502 Q21 – ✉ Helmsley 23 C1

London 245 mi – Middlesbrough 27 mi – Newcastle upon Tyne 69 mi – York 30 mi

Inn at Hawnby

✉ YO62 5QS – ✆ (01439) 798 202 – www.innathawnby.co.uk – Closed 25 December

9 rm – £ 70/80 £ 90/99 **Rest** – Carte £ 23/37

Homely inn set in a very rural spot in prime walking and shooting country. Classically styled bedrooms are split between the house and barn, and boast good linens and home comforts. Simplicity is key. Pub-style dishes at lunch; more substantial, classical dinners.

at Laskill Northeast : 2.25 mi by Osmotherley rd – ✉ Hawnby

Laskill Country House

Easterside ✉ YO62 5NB – ✆ (01439) 798 265 – www.laskillcountryhouse.co.uk – Closed 24-25 December

3 rm – £ 45 £ 90/120 **Rest** – Menu £ 25

Delightful manor-style house in popular shooting/walking area. Comfy lounge; small function suite. Good-sized bedrooms with countryside views. Communal dining; wholesome home-cooked meals, with meat from the family's farms.

HAWORTH – West Yorkshire – 502 O22 – pop. 6 078 – ✉ Keighley 22 A2

Great Britain

London 213 mi – Burnley 22 mi – Leeds 22 mi – Manchester 34 mi

2-4 West Lane, ✆ (01535) 64 23 29, www.haworth-village.org.uk

Bront Parsonage Museum**AC**

Ashmount Country House

Mytholmes Ln ✉ BD22 8EZ – ✆ (01535) 645 726 – www.ashmounthaworth.co.uk

12 rm – £ 65/125 £ 95/245

Rest – *(dinner only) (bookings essential for non-residents)* Carte £ 23/39

Substantial Victorian house built by the Brontë sisters' physician. Luxurious bedrooms have state-of-the-art bathrooms – some with hot tubs. Original features include impressive stained glass paintings and an intricate plaster ceiling in the dining room; menus mix classics with more modern dishes.

Old Registry

2-6 Main St ✉ BD22 8DA – ✆ (01535) 646 503 – www.theoldregistryhaworth.co.uk – Closed 24-26 December

9 rm – £ 75/120 £ 75/120 **Rest** – Carte £ 22/26

Stone-built former registrar's office at the bottom of the village's cobbled main street. Individually decorated bedrooms feature rich fabrics and antiques; some have four-posters. Eat at simple wooden tables surrounded by Brontë memorabilia; local ingredients feature in traditionally based dishes.

HAYDON BRIDGE – Northumberland – 501 N19 – see Hexham

ENGLAND

HAYLING ISLAND – Hampshire – 504 R31 – pop. 14 842 6 B3

London 77 mi – Brighton 45 mi – Southampton 28 mi

Seven Seafront, www.hayling.co.uk

Links Lane, (023) 9246 44 46

Cockle Warren Cottage without rest

36 Seafront PO11 9HL – (023) 9246 4961 – www.cocklewarren.co.uk

6 rm – £ 65/80 £ 79/90

Set just across the road from the beach, with a fish pond and fountain in the courtyard, Isle of Wight views and a very helpful owner. Comfy bedrooms; the 'Stable' rooms welcome dogs. Conservatory breakfast room overlooks the pool.

HAYWARDS HEATH – West Sussex – 504 T31 – pop. 29 110 Great Britain 7 D2

London 39 mi – Croydon 30 mi – Barnet 53 mi – Ealing 50 mi

Lindfield, East Mascalls Lane, (01444) 48 44 67

Sheffield Park Garden★, E : 5 mi on A 272 and A 275

Jeremy's at Borde Hill

Borde Hill Gdns, North : 1.75 mi by B 2028 and Balcombe Rd on Borde Hill Ln. RH16 1XP – (01444) 441 102 – www.jeremysrestaurant.com – Closed 2-11 January, Monday except lunch on bank holidays and Sunday dinner

Rest – Menu £ 19 (weekdays) – Carte £ 34/41

Converted stable block with exposed rafters, contemporary sculptures, vivid artwork and delightful views towards the Victorian walled garden. Interesting, modern European dishes and a good value 'menu of the day'. Regular gourmet nights.

HEADLAM – Durham – 502 O20 – see Darlington

HEATHROW AIRPORT – Greater London – 504 S29 – see London

HEDDON ON THE WALL – Northumberland 24 A2

London 288 mi – Blaydon 7 mi – Newcastle upon Tyne 8 mi

Close House

Southwest : 2.25 mi by B 6528 NE15 0HT – (01661) 852 255 – www.closehouse.co.uk

35 rm – £ 150/250 £ 150/250 **Rest *Argent D'Or*** – Menu £ 30/45

Stunning Georgian mansion in 300 acres of mature grounds that stretch to the river. Original features blend with modern décor; front bedrooms have views, those to rear are more contemporary. Stylish restaurant offers interesting modern cooking and intimate air.

HEDLEY ON THE HILL – Northumberland 24 A2

London 293 mi – Newcastle upon Tyne 16 mi – Sunderland 26 mi – South Shields 26 mi

Feathers Inn

NE43 7SW – (01661) 843 607 – www.thefeathers.net – Closed first 2 weeks January

Rest – *(closed Monday except bank holidays and Sunday dinner)* Carte £ 20/29

Traditional stone inn set on a steep hill in the heart of a rural village. Daily changing menu of hearty British classics, cooked using carefully sourced, regional produce, with meat and game to the fore. Relaxed, friendly atmosphere.

HELMSLEY – North Yorkshire – 502 Q21 – pop. 1 559 Great Britain 23 C1

London 239 mi – Leeds 51 mi – Middlesbrough 28 mi – York 24 mi

Castlegate, (01439) 77 01 73, www.yorkshire.com

Ampleforth College, Castle Drive, Gilling East, (01439) 78 82 12

Rievaulx Abbey★★ **AC**, NW : 2.5 mi by B 1257

Black Swan

Market Pl YO62 5BJ – (01439) 770 466 – www.blackswan-helmsley.co.uk

46 rm – £ 132/204 £ 144/216 – 1 suite

Rest *Black Swan* – see restaurant listing

One of the country's best known coaching inns, dating back to the 16C and overlooking the historic marketplace. Charming interior with beams, modern lounge-bar and all-day tea shop. Most characterful bedrooms in original building.

Feversham Arms

1-8 High St ✉ YO62 5AG – ✆ (01439) 770 766 – www.fevershamarmshotel.com
33 rm – †£ 110/240 ††£ 180/200 – 22 suites
Rest *Feversham Arms* – see restaurant listing
19C former coaching inn with a lovely stone façade. Relax on the terrace beside the outdoor pool; the spa is superb and boasts a salt vapour room and an ice cave. Be sure to book one of the stylish newer bedrooms; many have stoves or fires.

No.54 without rest

54 Bondgate ✉ YO62 5EZ – ✆ (01439) 771 533 – www.no54.co.uk – Closed Christmas-New Year
3 rm – †£ 70/85 ††£ 100/130
Charming Victorian stone cottage located just off the main square. Simply decorated, cosy bedrooms are well-equipped and set around a rear courtyard. Friendly owner offers communal breakfasts of fresh, local produce.

Carlton Lodge without rest

Bondgate ✉ YO62 5EY – ✆ (01439) 770 557 – www.carlton-lodge.com – Closed January
8 rm – †£ 45/65 ††£ 85/95
Late 19C detached house set just out of town, with a colourful, well-tended garden. Roomy guest areas and homely, immaculately kept bedrooms. The charming owner will provide any local information you should need.

Feversham Arms – Feversham Arms Hotel

1-8 High St ✉ YO62 5AG – ✆ (01439) 770 766 – www.fevershamarmshotel.com
Rest – *(bar lunch Monday-Saturday)* Carte £ 45/60
Modern hotel restaurant with a pleasingly laid-back style. Dishes feature the latest local produce and cooking is refined and accurate; the cheese trolley is a feature. In summer, have lunch in the garden or on the poolside terrace.

Black Swan – Black Swan Hotel

Market Pl ✉ YO62 5BJ – ✆ (01439) 770 466 – www.blackswan-helmsley.co.uk
Rest – *(dinner only and Sunday lunch)* Menu £ 27/36
'Fine dining' restaurant with a subtle, modern style, set within a historic 16C coaching inn. Concise menus are supplemented by daily specials and consist of classically based dishes with some modern twists.

at Nawton East : 3.25 mi on A 170 – ✉ York

Plumpton Court without rest

High St ✉ YO62 7TT – ✆ (01439) 771 223 – www.plumptoncourt.com – Restricted opening January-February
6 rm – †£ 65 ††£ 74/78
17C stone-built house with a small open-fired bar and a homely lounge. Comfy, cosy, simply furnished bedrooms with modern bathrooms. The cottage-style breakfast room offers local bacon and sausages. Relax in the secluded garden.

at Harome Southeast : 2.75 mi by A 170 – ✉ York

Pheasant

Mill St ✉ YO62 5JG – ✆ (01439) 771 241 – www.thepheasanthotel.com
15 rm – †£ 78/150 ††£ 155/265
Rest *Pheasant* – see restaurant listing
An attractive hotel in a picturesque hamlet, with a delightful duck pond and a mill stream close by. Beautiful, very comfortable lounges and spacious, well-furnished bedrooms; Rudland – running the width of the building and with views of the pond – is one of the best. Pleasant service. Excellent breakfasts.

Cross House Lodge

✉ YO62 5JE – ✆ (01439) 770 397 – www.thestaratharome.co.uk
8 rm – †£ 160/270 ††£ 160/270
Rest *Star Inn* – see restaurant listing
Sympathetically converted farm buildings with ultra-stylish, super-smart, individually decorated bedrooms; one boasts a snooker table; another, a bed suspended on ropes. Excellent breakfasts in the dramatic Wheelhouse. Open-plan, split-level lounge and a shop selling tea, cakes and the like.

ENGLAND

XX **Pheasant** - Pheasant Hotel
Mill St ✉ YO62 5JG – ☎ (01439) 771 241 – www.thepheasanthotel.com
Rest – Menu £ 29/36 – Carte £ 37/49
Elegant hotel dining room with both classical and contemporary touches – along with a less formal conservatory and a lovely terrace overlooking the village duck pond. Appealing menus of seasonal dishes with a classical base and a modern touch. Skilful, knowledgeable cooking; smooth, assured service.

Star Inn
High St ✉ YO62 5JE – ☎ (01439) 770 397 – www.thestaratharome.co.uk – Closed Monday lunch except bank holidays
Rest – *(booking essential)* Menu £ 25 (weekdays) – Carte £ 30/56
Thatched 14C pub with a delightful terrace, set in a pretty village; sit in the low-ceilinged bar, the rustic middle room or the brighter, brasserie-like restaurant. Comprehensive, seasonal menu offers classic, generously proportioned dishes; the kitchen garden provides some of the produce.

at Ampleforth Southwest : 4.5 mi . by A 170 off B 1257 – ✉ Helmsley

Shallowdale House
West : 0.5 mi ✉ YO62 4DY – ☎ (01439) 788 325 – www.shallowdalehouse.co.uk – Closed Christmas-New Year
3 rm – †£ 90/105 ††£ 110/135 **Rest** – Menu £ 40
A remotely set, personally run house with a well-tended garden and stunning views of the Howardian Hills. Charming, antique-furnished interior, with an open-fired sitting room and good-sized bedrooms decorated in bright, Mediterranean tones. Four course set menu of home-cooked fare.

ENGLAND

HELPERBY - North Yorkshire – 502 Q21 — 22 B2

London 220 mi – Leeds 36 mi – Sheffield 70 mi – Manchester 81 mi

Oak Tree Inn with rm
Raskelf Rd ✉ YO61 2PH – ☎ (01423) 789 189 – www.theoaktreehelperby.com
6 rm – †£ 80/100 ††£ 120/150 **Rest** – Carte £ 20/33
A pub of two halves, with a large bar, tap room, two snugs and a smarter dining room. Menus offer hearty, generous dishes using ingredients from small local suppliers. Everything is homemade and combinations are familiar and comforting. Smart, modern bedrooms come with 'Yorkie' bars and jacuzzi baths.

HELSTON - Cornwall – 503 E33 – pop. 10 578 — 1 A3

London 280 mi – Birmingham 275 mi – Croydon 288 mi – Barnet 293 mi
The Flora Day Furry Dance★★
Lizard Peninsula★ - Gunwalloe Fishing Cove★, S : 4 mi by A 3083 and minor rd - Culdrose (Flambards Village Theme Park★), SE : 1 mi - Wendron (Poldark Mine★), NE : 2.5 mi by B 3297 – Gweek (Seal Sanctuary★), E : 4 mi by A 394 and minor rd

at Trelowarren Southeast : 4 mi by A 394 and A 3083 on B 3293 – ✉ Helston

X **New Yard**
Trelowarren Estate ✉ TR12 6AF – ☎ (01326) 221 595 – www.trelowarren.com – Closed October-May, Sunday dinner, Monday and Tuesday
Rest – *(bookings advisable at dinner)* Carte £ 24/38
Converted 17C stable building adjoining a craft gallery. Spacious, rustic room with timbered walls and doors opening onto the terrace. Seasonal menu uses quality Cornish produce; breads and ice creams are homemade. Friendly service.

at Cury South : 5 mi by A394 off A3083

Colvennor Farmhouse without rest
✉ TR12 7BJ – ☎ (01326) 241 208 – www.colvennorfarmhouse.com
3 rm – †£ 50/55 ††£ 70/75
Part-17C farmhouse in a peaceful location, boasting a lovely mature garden and paddock to the rear. Homely lounge features a wood burning stove. Simple, wood-furnished bedrooms are of a reasonable size. Linen-laid breakfast room.

HEMEL HEMPSTEAD – Hertfordshire – 504 S28 – pop. 83 118 12 A2

Great Britain

London 30 mi – Aylesbury 16 mi – Luton 10 mi – Northampton 46 mi

Little Hay Golf Complex, Bovingdon, Box Lane, ✆ (01442) 83 37 98

Boxmoor, 18 Box Lane, ✆ (01442) 24 24 34

Whipsnade Wild Animal Park★

at Frithsden **Northwest : 4.5 mi by A 4146 – ✉ Hemel Hempstead**

Alford Arms

✉ HP1 3DD – ✆ (01442) 864 480 – www.alfordarmsfrithsden.co.uk – Closed 25-26 December

Rest – Carte £ 21/37

Attractive Victorian pub beside the village green. The traditional British menu follows the seasons closely, with salads and fish featuring in the summer and game and comfort dishes in the winter; have a look at the tempting specials board.

HEMINGFORD GREY – Cambridgeshire – 504 T27 – see Huntingdon

HENFIELD – West Sussex – 504 T31 – pop. 4 527 7 D2

London 47 mi – Brighton 10 mi – Worthing 11 mi

Ginger Fox

Muddleswood Rd, Albourne, Southwest : 3 mi on A 281 ✉ BN6 9EA – ✆ (01273) 857 888 – www.gingermanrestaurants.com – Closed 25 December

Rest – Carte £ 25/35

Spot the fox running across the thatched roof and you know you're in the right place. Monthly changing menu offers good value, flavourful dishes, with a popular vegetarian tasting plate. Desserts are a highlight, so save space.

HENLADE – Somerset – see Taunton

HENLEY – West Sussex – see Midhurst

HENLEY-IN-ARDEN – Warwickshire – 503 O27 – pop. 2 797 19 C3

London 104 mi – Birmingham 15 mi – Stratford-upon-Avon 8 mi – Warwick 8 mi

Crabmill

Preston Bagot, East : 1 mi on A 4189 ✉ B95 5EE – ✆ (01926) 843 342 – www.thecrabmill.co.uk – Closed Sunday dinner

Rest – *(booking essential)* Menu £ 14 (weekdays) – Carte £ 21/37

Characterful timbered pub with a lawned garden, a peaceful terrace and various beamed snugs and lounges. The good-sized menu offers modern Mediterranean-influenced dishes; start with a tasty sharing plate before an interesting main course.

Bluebell

93 High St ✉ B95 5AT – ✆ (01564) 793 049 – www.bluebellhenley.co.uk

Rest – Menu £ 15/23 – Carte £ 26/34

Part-timbered pub on the high street, displaying an unusual mix of rustic character and formal elegance. The experienced chef uses the best local ingredients in honest, seasonal dishes and there's a wide range of wines, beers and cocktails.

HENLEY-ON-THAMES – Oxfordshire – 504 R29 – pop. 10 513 11 C3

London 40 mi – Oxford 23 mi – Croydon 44 mi – Barnet 46 mi

to Reading (Salter Bros. Ltd) (summer only) daily (2 h 15 mn) – to Marlow (Salter Bros. Ltd) (summer only) daily (2 h 15 mn)

Market Place, ✆ (01491) 57 80 34, www.henley-on-thames.org

Huntercombe, Nuffield, ✆ (01491) 64 12 07

Hotel du Vin

rm, rm,

New St. ✉ RG9 2BP – ✆ (01491) 848 400 – www.hotelduvin.com

43 rm – †£ 130/300 ††£ 130/300, ☕ £ 17 – 2 suites

Rest *Bistro* – Carte £ 26/49

Characterful 1857 building that was formerly the Brakspear Brewery. Stylish bedrooms include airy doubles and duplex suites: one features two roll-top tubs and a great view of the church; others boast heated balconies and outdoor baths. Brasserie classics and a choice of over 700 wines in the bistro.

ENGLAND

Falaise House without rest

37 Market Pl ✉ RG9 2AA – ☎ (01491) 573 388 – www.falaisehouse.com – Closed Christmas

6 rm – †£ 85/105 ††£ 95/115

18C merchant's house, well-located at the top of the marketplace and run by friendly, welcoming owners. Tastefully decorated bedrooms are named after local villages and come in neutral hues. Tasty breakfasts; hot dishes are cooked to order.

Luscombes at The Golden Ball

Lower Assendon, Northwest : 0.75 mi by A 4130 on B 480 ✉ RG9 6AH – ☎ (01491) 574 157 – www.luscombes.co.uk

Rest – Menu £ 15 (weekdays) – Carte £ 29/44

Pretty former pub – now a cosy, comfortable restaurant that's popular with the locals. Appealing menu of tasty, well-executed, modern classics; homemade preserves and afternoon tea are a feature. Friendly, attentive service.

Three Tuns

5 Market Pl ✉ RG9 2AA – ☎ (01491) 410 138 – www.threetunshenley.co.uk – Closed 25 December, Monday except bank holidays and Sunday dinner

Rest – Menu £ 10/17 – Carte £ 24/40

Pretty, red-brick, town centre pub with a lively, open-fired front bar and a formal dining room for a more intimate meal. Seasonal, traditional dishes are well-presented, satisfying and full of flavour. Homemade bread. Friendly service.

at Stonor North : 4 mi by A 4130 on B 480

Quince Tree Café

✉ RG9 6HE – ☎ (01491) 639 039 – www.thequincetree.com

Rest – *(lunch only) (bookings not accepted)* Menu £ 14 (weekdays) – Carte £ 18/33

Charming café with a green oak timber frame and floor to ceiling windows overlooking the herb garden and terrace. Pass through the deli to the modern dining room or up to the mezzanine. Open for breakfast and light, Mediterranean lunches.

Quince Tree

✉ RG9 6HE – ☎ (01491) 639 039 – www.thequincetree.com – Closed 25 December, 1 January and Sunday dinner

Rest – *(booking advisable)* Menu £ 14 (weekday lunch) – Carte £ 24/35

19C brick inn in a delightful setting in a fold of the Chiltern Hills, with smart gardens, a sunny terrace and country-chic décor. Sit in the main room or formal restaurant; the small area opposite the bar is for drinkers. Appealing dishes range from pub classics with a twist to more original, modern dishes.

at Shiplake South : 2 mi on A 4155

Plowden Arms N

Reading Rd ✉ RG9 4BX – ☎ (01189) 402 794 – www.plowdenarmsshiplake.co.uk

Rest – Carte £ 18/37

An appealing pub with a delightful garden; inside, open fires, twinkling tea lights and hop bines set the scene. The large blackboard offers tasty snacks and the interesting main menu features a number of Eliza Acton inspired dishes.

at Shiplake Row South : 3.5mi. by A 4155 by Peppard rd and Binfield Heath rd

Orwells

Shiplake Row ✉ RG9 4DP – ☎ (01189) 403 673 – www.orwellsatshiplake.co.uk – Closed first 2 weeks January, first 2 weeks September, 1 week April, Sunday dinner and Monday except bank holidays

Rest – Menu £ 10 (weekday lunch) – Carte £ 26/48

Dating from the 18C and named after George Orwell, who spent his childhood in the area. It might look like a rural inn but inside it has contemporary décor and a formal feel. Menus mix pub classics with ambitious restaurant-style dishes.

HEREFORD – Herefordshire – **503** L27 – **pop. 54 747** Great Britain **18** B3

London 133 mi – Birmingham 51 mi – Cardiff 56 mi

1 King St, ✆ (01432) 26 84 30, www.visitherefordshire.co.uk

Belmont Lodge, Belmont, Ruckhall Lane, ✆ (01432) 35 26 66

Hereford Municipal, Holmer Rd, ✆ (01432) 34 43 76

Burghill Valley, Burghill, Tillington Rd, ✆ (01432) 76 04 56

City★ - Cathedral★★ (Mappa Mundi★) A **A** – Old House★ A **B**

Kilpeck (Church of SS. Mary and David★★) SW : 8 mi by A 465 B

Castle House

rm,

Castle St ✉ *HR1 2NW – ✆ (01432) 356 321 – www.castlehse.co.uk* A**e**

24 rm – **†**£ 130 **††**£ 150/230 **Rest** – Carte £ 22/39

Smart Georgian house near the cathedral. Bedrooms in the main house come in various sizes and are warmly furnished, with modern facilities. Those in red brick 'Number 25' are more contemporary. The formal restaurant overlooks the garden and the River Wye and serves classic dishes cooked in a modern style.

Brandon Lodge without rest

Ross Rd, South : 1.75 mi on A 49 ✉ *HR2 8BH – ✆ (01432) 355 621 – www.brandonlodge.co.uk*

10 rm – **†**£ 50/65 **††**£ 65/75

Well-run, good value hotel with a welcoming owner. Bedrooms in the main house and in the garden wing; the latter are more spacious, but all have good facilities. Neatly linen-laid breakfast room; comfy bar and lounge.

Somerville House without rest

12 Bodenham Rd ✉ *HR1 2TS – ✆ (01432) 273 991 – www.somervillehouse.net*

12 rm – **†**£ 60/87 **††**£ 77/112 B**x**

Victorian villa with enclosed garden; home-grown apples, plums and pears are used to make breakfast preserves. Spacious first floor rooms; those in the roof are smaller; good facilities include mini-bar. Cathedral and hill views from rear.

ENGLAND

HEREFORD

Aubrey St . . . . . A 3
Berrington St . . . . . A 5
Blueschool St . . . . . A 6
Broad St . . . . . A 7
Church St . . . . . A 12
Commercial Rd . . . . . A 14
Commercial St . . . . . A 13
Eign St . . . . . B 16
Greyfriars Bridge . . . . . A 17

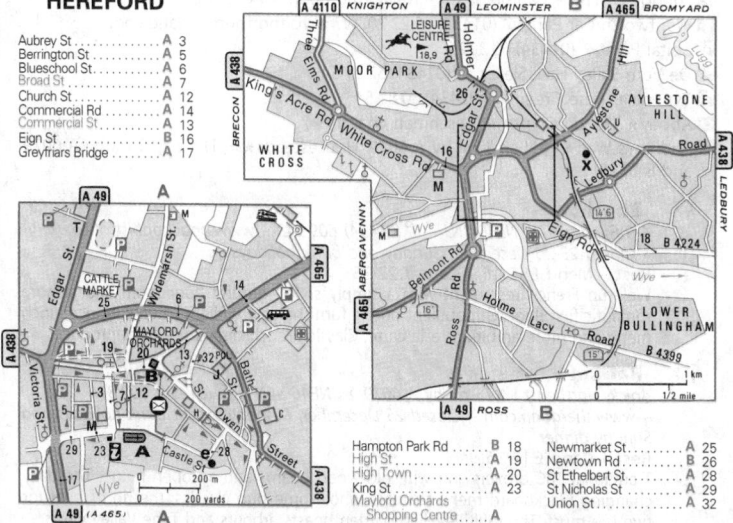

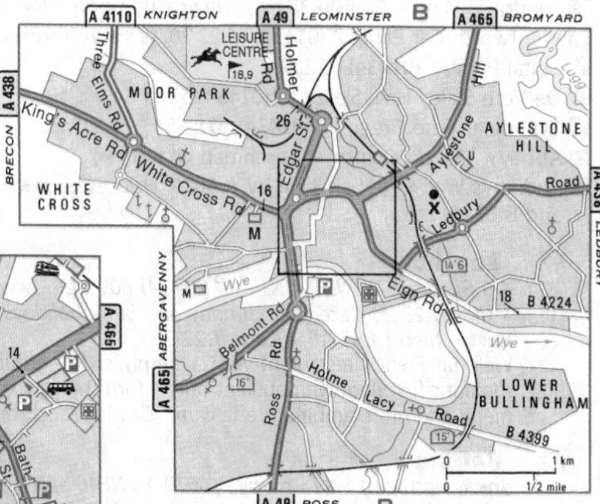

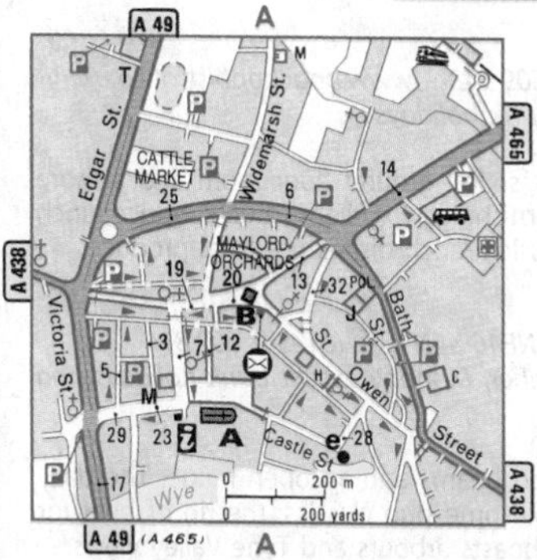

Hampton Park Rd . . . . . B 18
High St . . . . . A 19
High Town . . . . . A 20
King St . . . . . A 23
Maylord Orchards Shopping Centre . . . . . A
Newmarket St . . . . . A 25
Newtown Rd . . . . . B 26
St Ethelbert St . . . . . A 28
St Nicholas St . . . . . A 29
Union St . . . . . A 32

HERNE BAY – Kent – **504** X29 – **pop. 34 747** **9** D1

▶ London 65 mi – Croydon 68 mi – Bromley 59 mi – Enfield 80 mi

X **Le Petit Poisson**

Pier Approach, Central Par. ✉ *CT6 5JN* – ✆ *(01227) 361 199*
*– www.lepetitpoisson.co.uk – Closed Sunday dinner and Monday except bank
holidays when closed Tuesday*
Rest – Carte £ 19/33

Sweet whitewashed building with small terrace, overlooking the pier. Split-level
interior boasts flag floors, exposed brick and eye-catching mosaic art. Concise,
constantly evolving blackboard menus consist of tasty, unfussy seafood dishes.

HERSTMONCEUX – East Sussex – **504** U31 – **pop. 3 898** **8** B3

▶ London 63 mi – Eastbourne 12 mi – Hastings 14 mi – Lewes 16 mi

XXX **Sundial**

Gardner St ✉ *BN27 4LA* – ✆ *(01323) 832 217 – www.sundialrestaurant.co.uk*
– Closed Sunday dinner and Monday
Rest – Menu £ 26 – Carte £ 42/50

A characterful, converted 16C cottage, retaining leaded windows and a beamed
ceiling, with a rustic bar and a formal dining room. Seasonal menus offer rich,
classical French dishes using luxurious ingredients.

at Wartling Southeast : 3.75 mi by A 271 on Wartling rd – ✉ Herstmonceux

⌂ **Wartling Place**

✉ *BN27 1RY* – ✆ *(01323) 832 590 – www.wartlingplace.co.uk*
4 rm ☑ – †£ 85/100 ††£ 125/165 **Rest** – Menu £ 35

Charming, part-Georgian house set in three acres of mature grounds. Homely,
open-fired sitting room and spacious bedrooms – two with four-posters; touches
like DAB radios and iPod docks are a contrast to the antique furniture. Delightful
owner. Communal dining with traditional cooking.

HETTON – North Yorkshire – **502** N21 – **see Skipton**

HEXHAM – Northumberland – **501** N19 – **pop. 10 682** ▌ Great Britain **24** A2

▶ London 304 mi – Carlisle 37 mi – Newcastle upon Tyne 21 mi

🛈 Wentworth Car Park, ✆ (01434) 65 22 20, www.visitnorthumberland.com

🏌 Spital Park, ✆ (01434) 60 30 72

🏌 De Vere Slaley Hall, Slaley, ✆ (01434) 67 31 54

🏌 Tynedale, Tyne Green, ✆ (01434) 60 81 54

◎ Abbey★ (Saxon Crypt★★, Leschman chantry★)

◎ Hadrian's Wall★★, N : 4.5 mi by A 6079. Housesteads★★, NW : 12.5 mi by A 6079
and B 6318

XX **Bouchon**

4-6 Gilesgate ✉ *NE46 3NJ* – ✆ *(01434) 609 943 – www.bouchonbistrot.co.uk*
– Closed 23-26 December, Sunday and bank holidays
Rest – Menu £ 13/16 – Carte £ 22/35

Well-run French restaurant with a simply styled ground floor room and a more
romantic first floor with opulent purple furnishings. Excellent value set price lunch
menu and more ambitious à la carte. Classic French dishes use local produce.

🍴 **Rat Inn**

Anick, Northeast : 1.75 mi by A 6079 ✉ *NE46 4LN* – ✆ *(01434) 602 814*
*– www.theratinn.com – Closed 25 December, Monday except bank holidays and
Sunday dinner*
Rest – Carte £ 19/36

Traditional 18C drovers' inn with old wood beams and an open range. The daily
changing blackboard menu features wholesome pub classics; the rib of beef for
two is a must. The multi-levelled garden boasts arbours and Tyne Valley views.

ENGLAND

at Slaley Southeast : 5.5 mi by B 6306 – ✉ Hexham

Slaley Hall

Southeast : 2.25 mi ✉ NE47 0BX – ✆ (01434) 673 350 – www.devere.co.uk
140 rm – ♀£ 79/179 ♀♀£ 99/219 – 2 suites
Rest *Duke's Grill* – *(closed Sunday-Monday and midweek in winter) (dinner only)* Carte £ 31/60
Rest *Hadrian's Brasserie* – *(dinner only)* Menu £ 27
Rest *Claret Jug* – *(closed November-February)* Carte £ 24/40
Extended Edwardian manor house set in 1,000 acres and boasting two championship golf courses, a spa and extensive leisure facilities. Spacious, stylish guest areas. Largely classical bedrooms, with 'Double Deluxe' being more contemporary. Classical dishes served in formal, cosy Duke's; Brasserie menu in Hadrian's; British favourites offered in clubby Claret Jug.

at Haydon Bridge West : 7.5 mi on A 69 – ✉ Hexham

Langley Castle

Langley-on-Tyne, South : 2 mi by Alston rd on A 686 ✉ NE47 5LU – ✆ (01434) 688 888 – www.langleycastle.com
27 rm – ♀£ 120/210 ♀♀£ 155/279
Rest *Josephine's* – Menu £ 23/43
Rest *Pavillion* – Carte £ 31/48
Impressive 14C castle in 12 acres; its charming guest areas feature stone walls, tapestries and heraldic shields. Superb hidden chapel. Characterful, comfy bedrooms have excellent bathrooms and some have four-posters or window seats; the Castle View rooms are more uniform in style. Classic dining in Josephine's. Grills to the fore in the modern glass extension, Pavillion.

ENGLAND

HEYTESBURY – Wiltshire – **503** N30 – see Warminster

HIGHCLERE – Hampshire – **503** P29 – pop. 2 409 – ✉ Newbury **6** B1

London 69 mi – Newbury 5 mi – Reading 25 mi

Yew Tree with rm

Hollington Cross, Andover Rd, South : 1 mi on A 343 ✉ RG20 9SE – ✆ (01635) 253 360 – www.theyewtree.net
8 rm – ♀£ 95/120 ♀♀£ 95/120 **Rest** – Carte £ 18/48
Attractive 17C whitewashed inn, with a pretty terrace, a welcoming open-fired bar and three low-beamed dining rooms. Classically based dishes come in a choice of sizes and are given modern twists; the vegetarian dishes provide interest. Cosy bedrooms come with good mod cons and smart wet rooms.

HIGHCLIFFE – Dorset – **503** O31 **4** D3

London 112 mi – Bournemouth 10 mi – Salisbury 21 mi – Southampton 26 mi

Lord Bute

179-185 Lymington Rd ✉ BH23 4JS – ✆ (01425) 278 884 – www.lordbute.co.uk
13 rm – ♀£ 110/235 ♀♀£ 110/235 – 2 suites
Rest – *(closed Sunday dinner and Monday)* Menu £ 16/24 – Carte £ 30/46
Some of the bedrooms in this elegant hotel stand where the original 18C entrance lodges to Highcliffe Castle – home to Lord Bute – were once located. Rooms are well-appointed and decorated in a contemporary style. Smart restaurant and courtyard offer classical menus and host jazz and cabaret evenings.

HIGH CROSBY – Cumbria – see Carlisle

HIGHER BURWARDSLEY – Cheshire West and Chester – see Tattenhall

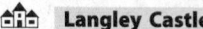

HINDRINGHAM – Norfolk 15 C1

London 118 mi – Fakenham 8 mi – Holt 8 mi

Field House without rest

Moorgate Rd ✉ NR21 0PT – ☎ (01328) 878 726 – www.fieldhousehindringham.co.uk – Closed 20 December-1 February

3 rm – †£ 70/75 ††£ 90/110

Traditional flint house with well-kept gardens and a summer house, in a peaceful hamlet. Comfy lounge opens into a conservatory where extensive, organic breakfasts are served. Tidy, individually styled bedrooms have up-to-date bathrooms.

HINTLESHAM – Suffolk – 504 X27 – see Ipswich

HINTON ST GEORGE – Somerset 3 B3

London 138 mi – Taunton 21 mi – Weymouth 41 mi – Yeovil 13 mi

Lord Poulett Arms with rm

High St ✉ TA17 8SE – ☎ (01460) 73 149 – www.lordpoulettarms.com – Closed 25-26 December and 1 January

4 rm – †£ 60/65 ††£ 85/95 **Rest** – Carte £ 21/38

A wide range of menus mean there's something for everyone at this 17C inn, set on the high street of a picturesque village and featuring a stone-floored, candlelit dining room. The charmingly rustic garden comes with a hammock for a post-prandial snooze; stylish bedrooms boast roll-top or slipper baths.

HISTON – Cambridgeshire – 504 U27 – see Cambridge

ENGLAND

HITCHIN – Hertfordshire – 504 T28 – pop. 33 352 12 A2

London 40 mi – Bedford 14 mi – Cambridge 26 mi – Luton 9 mi

hermitage rd

20-21 Hermitage Rd ✉ SG5 1BT – ☎ (01462) 433 603 – www.hermitagerd.co.uk – Closed 25-26 December

Rest – *(booking essential)* Carte £ 21/33

Pass through the large cocktail bar to the vast, open-plan brasserie with its exposed brick walls, low-level booths and vibrant, buzzy atmosphere. An all-encompassing menu offers something for everyone; start with mussels or oysters – from their own beds – then move onto a grill or meat dish.

Radcliffe Arms

31 Walsworth Rd ✉ SG4 9ST – ☎ (01462) 456 111 – www.radcliffearms.com

Rest – Menu £ 12 (weekday lunch) – Carte £ 23/36

True neighbourhood pub with central bar, gravity fed ales and a good spirit and wine selection. Tasty cooking focuses on well-presented, restaurant-style dishes. Breakfast is served from 8am.

HOCKLEY HEATH – West Midlands – 503 O26 – pop. 1 525 – ✉ Solihull 19 C2

London 117 mi – Birmingham 11 mi – Coventry 17 mi

Nuthurst Grange Country House

Nuthurst Grange Ln, South : 0.75 mi by A 3400 ✉ B94 5NL – ☎ (01564) 783 972 – www.nuthurst-grange.co.uk

19 rm – †£ 100/143 ††£ 128/225

Rest *Kingswood* – see restaurant listing

Attractive, part-Edwardian former farmhouse, next to the M40. Comfortable lounges and spacious, individually furnished, country house style bedrooms; some with four-posters. Lovely mature grounds with a walled herb garden.

Kingswood – Nuthurst Grange Country House Hotel

Nuthurst Grange Ln, South : 0.75 mi by A 3400 ✉ B94 5NL – ☎ (01564) 783 972 – www.nuthurst-grange.co.uk

Rest – Menu £ 20/38

Traditional hotel dining room with a formal ambience and country house styling; the brighter Orangery area is the best place to sit. Seasonal, classically based menus display innovative modern touches, with influences from throughout Europe.

HOLCOMBE – Somerset – 503 M30 — 4 C2

London 119 mi – Birmingham 106 mi – Leeds 228 mi – Sheffield 198 mi

Holcombe Inn with rm

Stratton Rd, West : 0.25 mi on Stratton-on-the-Fosse rd ✉ BA3 5EB – ✆ (01761) 232 478 – www.holcombeinn.co.uk

7 rm – £ 65/100 £ 90/110 **Rest** – Carte £ 19/32

Charming 17C inn set in the heart of the Somerset countryside, with a lovely south-facing garden and a peaceful air. Menus offer quite a range of dishes, from good old pub classics to more sophisticated offerings. Bedrooms are luxuriously appointed; some boast views over Downside Abbey.

HOLFORD – Somerset – 503 K30 – pop. 307 – ✉ Bridgwater Great Britain — 3 B2

London 171 mi – Bristol 48 mi – Minehead 15 mi – Taunton 22 mi

Stogursey Priory Church★★, W : 4.5 mi

Combe House

Southwest : 0.75 mi by Youth Hostel rd ✉ TA5 1RZ – ✆ (01278) 741 382 – www.combehouse.co.uk

18 rm – £ 79/99 £ 89/159 **Rest** – Carte £ 20/35

Smart country house with a lovely garden, in a secluded wooded valley. Stylish, modern interior boasts a pleasant spa. Bright, airy bedrooms feature contemporary fabrics and white furniture, which give them a slightly Scandinavian feel. Split-level restaurant offers classical cooking.

HOLKHAM – Norfolk – 504 W25 — 15 C1

London 124 mi – King's Lynn 32 mi – Norwich 39 mi

Victoria

rm,

Park Rd ✉ NR23 1RG – ✆ (01328) 711 008 – www.holkham.co.uk

10 rm – £ 100/160 £ 120/250 **Rest** – Carte £ 19/44

Located close to the beach, at the gates of Holkham Hall, an extended flint inn with large lawned gardens and pleasant country views. A relaxed, modern style pervades and bedrooms have a stylish, homely feel. Dine on traditional British dishes while overlooking the marshes of the adjacent nature reserve.

HOLMFIRTH – West Yorkshire – 502 O23 – pop. 21 979 — 22 B3

London 187 mi – Leeds 35 mi – Sheffield 32 mi – Manchester 25 mi

Sunnybank

78 Upperthong Ln, Northwest : 0.5 mi by A 6024 ✉ HD9 3BQ – ✆ (01484) 684 065 – www.sunnybankguesthouse.co.uk

3 rm – £ 50/100 £ 60/110 **Rest** – Menu £ 20/25

Attractive Victorian house with lovely gardens, hidden away up a narrow road. Mix of period and modern furnishings, with a smart art deco piano in the lounge and original stained glass on the landing. Cosy bedrooms have a personal touch. Elegant, oak-panelled dining room offers local produce and valley views.

HOLT – Norfolk – 504 X25 – pop. 3 550 — 15 C1

London 124 mi – King's Lynn 34 mi – Norwich 22 mi

Byfords

Shirehall Plain ✉ NR25 6BG – ✆ (01263) 711 400 – www.byfords.org.uk

16 rm – £ 110/125 £ 145/200 **Rest** – Carte £ 22/34

Grade II listed, 15C flint house. Stunning bedrooms come with feature beds, underfloor heating and plenty of extras. Numerous characterful rooms incorporate a deli, a café and a restaurant. Light meals are served during the day and more substantial dishes in the evening; it's a real hit with the locals.

HOLTON – Somerset – 503 M30 – pop. 225 4 C3

London 117 mi – Bristol 35 mi – Cardiff 111 mi – Southampton 76 mi

Old Inn

BA9 8AR – (01963) 32 002 – www.theoldinnholton.co.uk – Closed Sunday dinner

Rest – Carte £ 20/36

The owner of nearby Clinger Farm always fancied being a chef but instead bought this 400 year old pub, added a large restaurant and now delights in seeing the kitchen make good use of his produce; the Josper grill is the star of the show.

HOLYPORT – Windsor and Maidenhead 11 C3

London 30 mi – Birmingham 107 mi – Bristol 93 mi – Croydon 37 mi

Belgian Arms

Holyport St SL6 2JR – (01628) 634 468 – www.thebelgianarms.com – Closed Sunday dinner

Rest – Carte £ 19/35

Pretty, wisteria-clad inn tucked away by a pond, just off the village green. Beamed ceilings and sloping floors feature. Gutsy pub dishes include tempting bar snacks and heartwarming desserts. It's a real locals' local, with lots of events.

The sun's out? Enjoy eating outside on the terrace:

ENGLAND

HONITON – Devon – 503 K31 – pop. 11 213 2 D2

London 186 mi – Exeter 17 mi – Southampton 93 mi – Taunton 18 mi

Lace Walk Car Park, (01404) 4 37 16, www.honiton.com

All Hallows Museum★ **AC**

Ottery St Mary★ (St Mary's★) SW : 5 mi by A 30 and B 3177. Faraway Countryside Park (≤★) **AC**, SE : 6.5 mi by A 375 and B 3174

Holt

178 High St EX14 1LA – (01404) 47 707 – www.theholt-honiton.com – Closed 25-26 December, 1 January, Sunday and Monday

Rest – Carte £ 21/32

Rustic family-run pub providing a 'distinctive and sustainable taste of Devon'. Regularly changing menu of regional and homemade produce; local ales from the family brewery.

Railway with rm

Queen St EX14 1HE – (01404) 47 976 – www.therailwayhoniton.co.uk – Closed 25-26 December, Sunday and Monday

3 rm – †£ 70/80 ††£ 80/90 **Rest** – Carte £ 21/32

Smart, modern pub with a horseshoe bar, an open kitchen and a decked terrace. Authentic, affordable Mediterranean cooking features homemade pastas, brick-fired pizzas and well-cooked steaks. An eclectic wine list and an olive oil top-up service add to the fun, and comfortable bedrooms complete the picture.

at Gittisham Southwest : 3 mi by A 30 – Honiton

Combe House

EX14 3AD – (01404) 540 400 – www.combehousedevon.com – Closed 2 weeks January

16 rm – †£ 190/430 ††£ 215/450 – 3 suites

Rest – *(bookings essential for non-residents)* Menu £ 29/52

Hugely impressive, listed Elizabethan mansion, set down a long drive and boasting wonderful country views. Characterful guest areas display original features and period furnishings. Imposing Great Hall; classical, country house bedrooms. Three dining rooms; menus feature produce from the superb gardens.

HOOK – Hampshire – 504 R30 – pop. 6 471 – ✉ Basingstoke 6 B1

London 47 mi – Oxford 39 mi – Reading 13 mi – Southampton 31 mi

Tylney Hall

Rotherwick, Northwest : 2.5 mi by A 30 and Newnham rd on Ridge Ln
✉ RG27 9AZ – ✆ (01256) 764 881 – www.tylneyhall.co.uk
112 rm – †£ 220/500 ††£ 250/530 – 9 suites
Rest *Oak Room* – Menu £ 25/40 – Carte approx. £ 50
Impressively restored, 19C mansion house in delightful gardens designed by Jekyll. Country house bedrooms boast good facilities; some have private conservatories. Well-appointed spa in former coach house. Classic dishes in formal restaurant with oak panelling, feature fireplaces and ornate plasterwork.

Old House at Home

Newnham Grn ✉ RG27 9AH – ✆ (01256) 762 222
– www.oldhousenewham.co.uk – Closed Sunday dinner
Rest – *(booking advisable)* Carte £ 27/34
Mid-19C former post office tucked away in the corner of a lovely green. The main room is split in two with open fires on both sides; the original bar is cosier. Menus provide plenty of choice from British classics to Asian-inspired dishes.

Hogget

London Rd, (at the junction of A 30 and A 287) ✉ RG27 9JJ – ✆ (01256) 763 009
– www.thehogget.co.uk – Closed 25-26 December
Rest – Carte £ 18/33
Located at the junction of the A30 and A287. Wholesome, honest, flavourful cooking shows a real respect for the locally sourced ingredients, with sensibly priced dishes like pie and mash or slow-cooked lamb shank.

ENGLAND

HOPE – Derbyshire – 502 O23 – ✉ Sheffield 16 A1

London 180 mi – Derby 50 mi – Manchester 31 mi – Sheffield 15 mi

Losehill House

Lose Hill Ln, Edale Rd, North : 1 mi by Edale Rd ✉ S33 6AF – ✆ (01433) 621 219
– www.losehillhouse.co.uk
23 rm – †£ 140/190 ††£ 170/260 **Rest** – Menu £ 20/38
Comfortable, well-kept hotel with a bright, airy, modern feel. Open-plan lounge and bar. Small pool, sauna and outdoor hot tub. Bedrooms all have a view. Formally laid restaurant with superb views up to Win Hill; modern-style dishes, with British cheeses a speciality.

Underleigh House without rest

Losehill Ln, Hope Valley, North : 1 mi by Edale Rd ✉ S33 6AF – ✆ (01433) 621 372 – www.underleighhouse.co.uk – Closed Christmas-New Year and January
5 rm – †£ 70/90 ††£ 90/110
Former Derbyshire longhouse and shippon with far-reaching views; the gregarious owner offers a friendly welcome. Traditional bedrooms, some opening onto the garden. Communal breakfasts include homemade preserves, bread and muesli.

HOPTON HEATH – Shropshire 18 A2

London 162 mi – Birmingham 66 mi – Leeds 152 mi – Sheffield 131 mi

Hopton House without rest

on Clun rd ✉ SY7 0QD – ✆ (01547) 530 885 – www.shropshirebreakfast.co.uk
3 rm – †£ 80/90 ††£ 110/120
Unassuming house backed by a wild flower meadow and the Shropshire Hills. Spacious, stylish bedrooms boast quality beds, sofas and double-ended baths; one has a balcony, one a terrace, and all come with a freshly baked cake.

HORLEY – Surrey – 504 T30 – pop. 22 582 | 7 D2

London 27 mi – Brighton 26 mi – Royal Tunbridge Wells 22 mi

Langshott Manor

Langshott, North : 0.5 mi by A 23 turning right at Chequers H. onto Ladbroke Rd
RH6 9LN – (01293) 786 680 – *www.alexanderhotels.com*
22 rm – £ 99/199 £ 109/209, £ 17 – 1 suite
Rest *Mulberry* – see restaurant listing
Characterful 16C manor house set amidst roses, vines and ponds. Traditional exterior contrasts with contemporary furnishings. Many bedrooms feature fireplaces or four-posters and one has a patio terrace. Smart marble and granite bathrooms.

Mulberry – Langshott Manor Hotel

Langshott, North : 0.5 mi by A 23 turning right at Chequers H. onto Ladbroke Rd
RH6 9LN – (01293) 786 680 – *www.langshottmanor.com*
Rest – Menu £ 15/45 – Carte £ 32/53
Smart hotel dining room set within a charming manor house, which part-dates back to 1540. Good choice of modern, well-presented dishes from the set menu, à la carte or evening tasting menu.

HORNCASTLE – Lincolnshire – 502 T24 – pop. 6 090 | 17 C1

London 143 mi – Lincoln 22 mi – Nottingham 62 mi
Wharf Rd, (01507) 60 11 11, www.horncastleuk.com

Magpies with rm

rest,

71-75 East St LN9 6AA – (01507) 527 004 – www.magpiesrestaurant.co.uk – Closed 26-30 December, first two weeks January, Saturday lunch, Monday and Tuesday
3 rm – £ 70/80 £ 110/130 **Rest** – Menu £ 20/45
Once three 18C cottages, now a cosy, family-run restaurant hosting regular gourmet and wine dinners. Hearty, classically based dishes are attractively presented; tasty homemade canapés and breads; elaborate desserts. Modern bedrooms have floral feature walls and a free-standing bath or double sinks.

HORNDON ON THE HILL – Thurrock – 504 V29 – pop. 1 612 | 13 C3

London 25 mi – Chelmsford 22 mi – Maidstone 34 mi – Southend-on-Sea 16 mi

Bell Inn with rm

High Rd SS17 8LD – (01375) 642 463 – www.bell-inn.co.uk – Closed 25-26 December and bank holidays
27 rm – £ 50/120 £ 50/120 **Rest** – Carte £ 19/40
15C coaching inn, run by the same family for 70 years. Cooking is a step above your usual pub fare, displaying classically based dishes with some modern touches. Pub bedrooms are styled after Victorian mistresses; those in Hill House display thoughtful extras.

HORNING – Norfolk – 504 Y25 | 15 D1

London 121 mi – Great Yarmouth 16 mi – Norwich 11 mi

Bure River Cottage

27 Lower St NR12 8AA – (01692) 631 421 – www.burerivercottagerestaurant.co.uk – Closed 25 December-13 February, Sunday and Monday
Rest – *(dinner only) (booking advisable)* Carte £ 21/50
Friendly restaurant tucked away in a lovely riverside village that's famed for its boating. Informal, L-shaped room with modern tables and chairs. Blackboard menu features fresh, carefully cooked fish and shellfish; much from Lowestoft.

HORNINGSEA – Cambridgeshire – see Cambridge

HORNINGSHAM – Wiltshire – 504 N30 – see Warminster

ENGLAND

HORN'S CROSS – Devon – 503 H31 – ✉ Bideford ▮ Great Britain 2 C1

London 222 mi – Barnstaple 15 mi – Exeter 46 mi

Clovelly★★, W : 6.5 mi on A 39 and B 3237 – Bideford : Bridge★★ - Burton Art Gallery★ **AC** - Lundy Island★★ (by ferry), NE : 7 mi on a 39 and B 3235 – Hartland : Hartland Church★ - Hartland Quay★ (※★★) - Hartland Point ≤★★★, W : 9 mi on A 39 and B 3248 – Great Torrington (Dartington Crystal★ **AC**), SE : 15 mi on A 39 and A 386 – Rosemoor★, SE : 16 mi on A 39, A 386 and B 3220

Roundhouse without rest

West : 1 mi on A 39 ✉ EX39 5DN – ✆ (01237) 451 687 – www.the-round-house.co.uk

3 rm – †£ 50 ††£ 65

Spacious, welcoming guesthouse on the site of a 13C corn mill, with donkeys in the paddock, neat gardens and comfortable, homely guest areas. Immaculately kept bedrooms: ask for the round room (the largest) on the first floor.

HORRINGER – Suffolk – 504 W27 – see Bury St Edmunds

HORSHAM – West Sussex – 504 T30 – pop. 47 804 7 D2

London 39 mi – Brighton 23 mi – Guildford 20 mi – Lewes 25 mi

9 Causeway, ✆ (01403) 21 16 61, www.horsham.gov.uk

Mannings Heath, Fullers, Hammerpond Rd, Mannings Heath, ✆ (01403) 21 02 28

South Lodge

Brighton Rd, Lower Beeding, Southeast : 5 mi on A 281 ✉ RH13 6PS – ✆ (01403) 891 711 – www.exclusivehotels.co.uk

85 rm – †£ 165/330 ††£ 165/330 – 4 suites

Rest *The Pass* ✿ – see restaurant listing

Rest *Camellia* – Menu £ 24/38 – Carte £ 41/57

Victorian mansion set in 93 acres, with intricate carved fireplaces and ornate ceilings. Traditionally styled bedrooms in the main house; those in the modern wing are larger and more luxurious. Classic dishes in Camellia, with its bold wallpaper, gargoyles and wood panelling; unique kitchen dining in The Pass.

The Pass – South Lodge Hotel

✿

Brighton Rd, Lower Beeding, Southeast : 5 mi on A 281 ✉ RH13 6PS – ✆ (01403) 891 711 – www.southlodgehotels.co.uk – Closed first 2 weeks January, Monday and Tuesday

Rest – *(number of covers limited, pre-book)* Menu £ 25/90

A unique experience and ideal for those for whom a chef's table is not enough: sit on luxurious high chairs or banquettes in the hotel's main kitchen and watch all the action. Expect beautifully presented, modern, intricate and balanced dishes, with well-thought-out combinations. Formal service.

→ Crab lasagne with lemon oil, shellfish bisque and tarragon. Lamb belly, rhubarb, grelot onion and morels. Chocolate mousse with cardamom, blood orange and salted caramel.

Restaurant Tristan (Tristan Mason)

✿

Stans Way, East St ✉ RH12 1HU – ✆ (01403) 255 688 – www.restauranttristan.co.uk – Closed 2 weeks late July-early August, 25-26 December, first week January, Sunday and Monday

Rest – Menu £ 24/60

16C property with ground floor coffee shop and heavily beamed upstairs restaurant. Well-presented, classic dishes delivered with a modern touch; ingredients are excellent and flavours, distinct and well-matched. Service is enthusiastic and friendly and the atmosphere, refreshingly relaxed.

→ Scallops, chicken wings with cauliflower caramel, turnip and vanilla. Squab pigeon, beetroot, rhubarb and burnt red onion. Banana tarte Tatin, lemon sauce, caramelised walnut and parsley ice cream.

ENGLAND

at Rowhook **Northwest : 4 mi by A 264 and A 281 off A 29 – ✉ Horsham**

Chequers Inn

✉ RH12 3PY – ✆ (01403) 790 480 – www.thechequersrowhook.com – Closed 25 December and Sunday dinner
Rest – Carte £ 26/40
Part-15C inn with a charming open-fired, stone-floored bar and unusual dining room extension. Chef-owner grows, forages for or shoots the majority of his produce. Classical menus.

HOUGH-ON-THE-HILL – Lincolnshire – see Grantham

HOVE – Brighton and Hove – 504 T31 – see Brighton and Hove

HOVERINGHAM – Nottinghamshire – pop. 308 16 B2

London 135 mi – Birmingham 77 mi – Leeds 74 mi – Sheffield 57 mi

Reindeer Inn

Main St ✉ NG14 7JR – ✆ (01159) 663 629 – www.thereindeerinn.com – Closed Tuesday lunch, Sunday dinner and Monday
Rest – *(booking essential at lunch)* Menu £ 11/23 – Carte £ 24/38
Characterful country inn set next to a cricket pitch, with beams, open fire and a cosy, relaxed atmosphere. Popular with locals. Well-priced menus offer mainly classical dishes.

ENGLAND

HOVINGHAM – North Yorkshire – 502 R21 – ✉ York 23 C2

London 235 mi – Leeds 47 mi – Middlesbrough 36 mi – York 25 mi

Worsley Arms

High St ✉ YO62 4LA – ✆ (01653) 628 234 – www.worsleyarms.co.uk
20 rm – †£ 85/95 ††£ 85/130
Rest – *(dinner only and Sunday lunch)* Carte £ 26/33
Characterful inn with a large walled garden; dating back to 1841 and located in a delightful estate village. Rustic interior with cosy lounges and an open-fired bar. Homely bedrooms are split between the main building and a row of cottages on the green. Formal dining room offers a classical menu.

HUCCOMBE – Devon 2 C3

London 217 mi – Bristol 121 mi – Cardiff 152 mi – Plymouth 30 mi

Huccombe House without rest

✉ TQ7 2EP – ✆ (01548) 580 669 – www.southdevonandb.co.uk
3 rm – †£ 70 ††£ 90
Converted Victorian school – the owner herself once went to school here! Pleasant lounge with high beamed ceilings and huge windows affording countryside views. Large bedrooms with sleigh beds made up with Egyptian cotton linen. Aga-cooked breakfasts at the communal table or on the patio.

HUDDERSFIELD – West Yorkshire – 502 O23 – pop. 146 234 22 B3

London 191 mi – Bradford 11 mi – Leeds 15 mi – Manchester 25 mi
Princes Alexandra Walk, ✆ (01484) 22 32 00, www.huddersfieldonline.org.uk
27 Bradley Park, Bradley Rd, ✆ (01484) 22 37 72
18 Woodsome Hall, Fenay Bridge, ✆ (01484) 60 29 71
18 Outlane, Slack Lane, Off New Hey Rd, ✆ (01422) 37 47 62
18 Meltham, Thick Hollins Hall, ✆ (01484) 85 02 27
18 Fixby Hall, Lightridge Rd, ✆ (01484) 42 62 03
18 Crosland Heath, Felks Stile Rd, ✆ (01484) 65 32 16

Eric's

73-75 Lidgets St, Lindley, Northwest : 3.25 mi by A 629 and Birchencliffe Hill Rd. ✉ *HD3 3JP – ✆ (01484) 646 416 – www.ericsrestaurant.co.uk – Closed Sunday dinner and Monday*

Rest – *(bookings advisable at dinner)* Menu £ 15/22 – Carte £ 28/48

Contemporary neighbourhood restaurant offering seasonal menus of appealing modern dishes packed with bold, distinct flavours. Great value lunch and early evening menu. On selected Saturdays they host brunch or afternoon tea events.

HULLBRIDGE – Essex – pop. 6 050 13 C2_3

London 40 mi – Croydon 46 mi – Barnet 50 mi – Ealing 63 mi

Anchor

Ferry Rd ✉ *SS5 6ND – ✆ (01702) 230 777 – www.theanchorhullbridge.co.uk – Closed 25 December*

Rest – Carte £ 24/37

Modern, informal, open-plan restaurant with a pleasant terrace, a sleek bar and lots of windows to take in the river views. Wide-ranging, seasonal British menu; more adventurous specials at dinner.

HUMSHAUGH – Northumberland – 502 N18 24 A2

London 290 mi – Birmingham 220 mi – Glasgow 132 mi

Carraw without rest

Carraw Farm, Military Rd, West : 5 mi on B 6318 ✉ *NE46 4DB – ✆ (01434) 689 857 – www.carraw.co.uk*

4 rm – †£ 60/65 ††£ 80/98

Converted farmhouse and barn on the foundations of Hadrian's Wall. Two bedrooms with exposed stone walls and beams, and two larger, more modern rooms. Bright, pine-furnished breakfast room, lounge with local info and pleasant country views.

HUNNINGHAM – Warwickshire – pop. 190 19 D3

London 94 mi – Birmingham 36 mi – Liverpool 129 mi – Leeds 125 mi

Red Lion

Main St ✉ *CV33 9DY – ✆ (01926) 632 715 – www.redlionhunningham.co.uk*

Rest – Carte £ 19/32

Charming, part-17C timbered inn set by the River Lemm, displaying over 300 framed American comics and a ceiling-mounted air pipe for delivering orders. The daily menu offers well-crafted, unfussy pub fare, with the occasional modern touch.

HUNSDON – Hertfordshire 12 B2

London 26 mi – Bishop's Stortford 8 mi – Harlow 7 mi

Fox and Hounds

2 High St ✉ *SG12 8NH – ✆ (01279) 843 999 – www.foxandhounds-hunsdon.co.uk – Closed 26 December, Sunday dinner and Monday*

Rest – Menu £ 14 (weekdays) – Carte £ 23/36

Sizeable pub with a rustic interior, a large garden and a terrace. Concise menus offer tasty, unfussy dishes that display a clear understanding of flavours. Pastas are homemade, they smoke their own fish, and desserts are not to be missed.

HUNSTANTON – Norfolk – 502 V25 – pop. 4 505 14 B1

London 120 mi – Cambridge 60 mi – Norwich 45 mi

The Green, ✆ (01485) 53 26 10, www.hunstanton-info.com

Golf Course Rd, ✆ (01485) 53 28 11

The Neptune (Kevin Mangeolles) with rm
85 Old Hunstanton Rd, Old Hunstanton, Northeast : 1.5 mi on A 149
✉ PE36 6HZ – ☎ (01485) 532 122 – www.theneptune.co.uk – Closed 3 weeks January, 2 weeks November, 26 December and Monday
6 rm – †£ 80/130 ††£ 140/150
Rest – *(dinner only and Sunday lunch)* Carte £ 48/58
Very personally run, attractive, red-brick former pub. New England style interior with a rattan-furnished bar and large nautical photographs in the dining room. The constantly evolving menu relies on the latest local produce to arrive at the door. Presentation is modern; service is relaxed and efficient. Comfy bedrooms have Nespresso machines and thoughtful extras.
→ Lobster salad with star anise mousse, pea purée and lobster croquettes. Duck breast with almond praline, butternut squash and red cabbage. Dark chocolate sphere, Horlicks ice cream and hazelnut meringue.

at Thornham Northeast : 4.5 mi on A 149

Orange Tree with rm
High St ✉ PE36 6LY – ☎ (01485) 512 213 – www.theorangetreethornham.co.uk
6 rm – †£ 65/99 ††£ 89/110 **Rest** – Carte £ 25/42 **s**
You're guaranteed a warm welcome at this 17C inn; even your dog will be offered a snack in the laid-back bar. An array of menus offer everything from pub classics to globally-influenced restaurant dishes, via some vegetarian choices and daily specials. Contemporary restaurant and compact, modern bedrooms.

ENGLAND

HUNTINGDON – Cambridgeshire – 504 T26 – pop. 20 600 14 A2

London 69 mi – Bedford 21 mi – Cambridge 16 mi
St. Mary's St, ☎ (01480) 38 85 88, www.visithuntingdonshire.org
Hemingford Abbots, Cambridge Rd, New Farm Lodge, ☎ (01480) 49 50 00

Old Bridge
1 High St ✉ PE29 3TQ – ☎ (01480) 424 300 – www.huntsbridge.com
24 rm – †£ 99/130 ††£ 160/230
Rest *Terrace* – see restaurant listing
Attractive 18C former bank next to the River Ouse; its bright, contemporary décor cleverly blended with the property's original features. Cosy, oak-panelled bar; individually styled, up-to-date bedrooms; and a superbly stocked wine shop.

Terrace – Old Bridge Hotel
1 High St ✉ PE29 3TQ – ☎ (01480) 424 300 – www.huntsbridge.com
Rest – Menu £ 15 (weekday lunch) – Carte £ 29/49 **s**
Light-filled conservatory restaurant with a pleasant terrace, serving an all-encompassing, daily changing menu of brasserie classics. The excellent wine list offers depth, variety and quality, with a fantastic selection by the glass.

at Abbots Ripton North : 6.5 mi by B1514 and A141 on B1090

Abbot's Elm (N) with rm
Moat Ln. ✉ PE28 2PA – ☎ (01487) 773 773 – www.theabbotselm.co.uk
3 rm – †£ 55/85 ††£ 70/85 **Rest** – Menu £ 14/24 – Carte £ 19/42
A modern reconstruction of an attractive 17C pub. The bar offers light bites, hot plates and a 'menu du jour'; later in the week there's also a tasting menu and an à la carte of appealing, hearty dishes served in the formal dining room. Cosy bedrooms come with free wi-fi and fluffy bathrobes.

at Hemingford Grey Southeast : 5 mi by A 1198 off A 14 – ✉ Huntingdon

The Cock
47 High St ✉ PE28 9BJ – ☎ (01480) 463 609 – www.cambscuisine.com
Rest – *(booking essential)* Menu £ 17 (weekday lunch) – Carte £ 22/35
Homely 17C country pub with a spacious dining room, run by an experienced team. Tried-and-tested pub cooking offers good value lunches, an extensive list of daily fish specials and a 'mix and match' homemade sausage and mash board.

HUNWORTH - Norfolk 15 C1

London 129 mi - Norwich 25 mi - East Dereham 17 mi - Taverham 19 mi

Hunny Bell

The Green ✉ NR24 2AA - ✆ (01263) 712 300 - www.thehoneybell.co.uk

Rest - Menu £ 19 - Carte £ 19/35

Sympathetically renovated, 18C whitewashed pub with a smart country interior; set on the village green. Appealing menu of pub classics crafted from local, seasonal produce; even the bar snacks are homemade. Pleasant garden.

HURLEY - Windsor and Maidenhead - pop. 1 712 11 C3

London 35 mi - Maidenhead 5 mi - Reading 18 mi

Olde Bell Inn

High St ✉ SL6 5LX - ✆ (01628) 825 881 - www.theoldebell.co.uk

48 rm - †£ 95/450 ††£ 95/450 - 1 suite

Rest *Olde Bell Inn* - see restaurant listing

Part-12C timbered inn close to the Thames. Charming rear gardens with outside bar, rotisserie and BBQ. Characterful bedrooms in contemporary, minimalist style; all have rocking chairs, sheepskin rugs and good extras. Lovely open-fired bar.

Olde Bell Inn - Olde Bell Inn Hotel

High St ✉ SL6 5LX - ✆ (01628) 825 881 - www.theoldebell.co.uk

Rest - Menu £ 13/30 - Carte £ 25/41

Heavily timbered dining room within a part-12C inn, boasting chunky tables, wood-panelling, tiled floors and a pleasant summer terrace. Interesting seasonal menus have a rustic base; much of the produce comes from the kitchen garden.

Black Boys Inn with rm

Henley Rd, Southwest : 1.5 mi on A 4130 ✉ SL6 5NQ - ✆ (01628) 824 212 - www.blackboysinn.co.uk - Closed Sunday dinner

7 rm - †£ 65/88 ††£ 88/120 **Rest** - Menu £ 13/28 - Carte £ 29/43

Rustic restaurant in a 16C former pub, with exposed beams and a wood burning stove. The experienced owners are avid Francophiles and the concise, traditional French menu reflects this. Polite service. Clean, unfussy bedrooms with thoughtful extras such as books.

HURSTBOURNE TARRANT - Hampshire - 503 P30 - pop. 700 - ✉ Andover 6 B1

London 77 mi - Bristol 77 mi - Oxford 38 mi - Southampton 33 mi

Esseborne Manor

Northeast : 1.5 mi on A 343 ✉ SP11 0ER - ✆ (01264) 736 444 - www.esseborne-manor.co.uk

18 rm - †£ 89/130 ††£ 125/250

Rest *Courtyard* - Menu £ 15/30 **s** - Carte £ 23/34 **s**

Victorian country house set in attractive grounds. Smart, fairly classically decorated bedrooms are split between the house and two cottages; some have whirlpool baths, two have four-posters and one leads out into the herb garden. The restaurant offers modern classics and hosts regular events.

HURSTPIERPOINT - 504 T31 - pop. 6 264 7 D2

London 45 mi - Croydon 35 mi - Barnet 87 mi - Ealing 69 mi

Fig Tree

120 High St ✉ BN6 9PX - ✆ (01273) 832 183 - www.figtreerestaurant.co.uk - Closed 2 weeks January, Tuesday lunch, Sunday dinner and Monday

Rest - Menu £ 19/23 - Carte £ 24/41

Attractive Victorian house in a pretty high street, personally run by a young couple: she looks after diners while he cooks. Carefully priced menus showcase local, seasonal ingredients. Loyal local following.

HURWORTH-ON-TEES - Darlington - 502 P20 - see Darlington

ENGLAND

HUTTON-LE-HOLE – North Yorkshire – **502** R21 – **pop. 162** 23 C1

▶ London 244 mi – Scarborough 27 mi – York 33 mi

⌂ **Burnley House** without rest 🚄 📶 **P**
✉ YO62 6UA – ℰ (01751) 417 548 – www.burnleyhouse.co.uk
8 rm ⌷ – †£ 43/48 ††£ 86/96
A cosy, welcoming guesthouse at the entrance to this picture postcard village on the edge of the moors. Small sitting room with a stone floor, coir carpet and wood-burning stove. Snug, bright bedrooms and a pretty garden.

HUTTON MAGNA – Durham – see Barnard Castle

ICKLESHAM – East Sussex – **504** V/W31 9 C3

▶ London 66 mi – Brighton 42 mi – Hastings 7 mi

⌂ **Manor Farm Oast** without rest 🐾 🚄 ⚵ 📶 **P**
Windmill Ln, South : 0.5 mi ✉ TN36 4WL – ℰ (01424) 813 787
– www.manorfarmoast.co.uk – Closed January and New Year
3 rm ⌷ – †£ 95/105 ††£ 105
Restored, extended oast house built in 1860 and surrounded by orchards and farmland. Original features remain both inside and out. The welcoming beamed lounge has an open fire; homely bedrooms feature large beds – one is completely round.

IDEN GREEN – Kent – **504** V30 8 B2

▶ London 55 mi – Croydon 49 mi – Barnet 81 mi – Ealing 85 mi

⌂ **Waters End Farm** without rest 🐾 🚄 ⚵ 📶 **P**
Standen St, Southeast : 1.25 mi ✉ TN17 4LA – ℰ (01580) 850 731
– www.watersendfarm.co.uk – Closed October-March
5 rm ⌷ – †£ 110/135 ††£ 110/135
Characterful part-timbered, part-brick house, set in 43 peaceful acres. Bedrooms – in converted barns – boast heavy wood furniture and modern facilities. Huge mural of the house in the breakfast room; eat outside on the terrace in summer.

ILFRACOMBE – Devon – **503** H30 – **pop. 10 466** 📗 Great Britain 2 C1

▶ London 218 mi – Barnstaple 13 mi – Exeter 53 mi

◉ Mortehoe★★ : St Mary's Church - Morte Point★, SW : 5.5 mi on B 3343 – Lundy Island★★ (by ferry). Braunton : St Brannock's Church★, Braunton Burrows★, S : 8 mi on A 361 – Barnstaple★ : Bridge★, S : 12 mi on A 3123, B 3230, A 39, A 361 and B 3233

⌂ **Hamptons** without rest ⚵ 📶 **P**
Excelsior Villas, Torrs Pk. ✉ EX34 8AZ – ℰ (01271) 864 246
– www.thehamptonshotel.com
6 rm ⌷ – †£ 75/140 ††£ 75/140
Imposing Victorian villa with individual, bohemian style. Open-plan lounge and breakfast room with honesty bar and DVDs. Well-equipped, individually styled bedrooms are designed by the friendly owner; those to the front boast rooftop views.

⌂ **Westwood** without rest ≤ ⚵ 📶 **P**
Torrs Pk ✉ EX34 8AZ – ℰ (01271) 867 443 – www.west-wood.co.uk
5 rm ⌷ – †£ 75/85 ††£ 85/125
Perched on the hillside overlooking the rooftops, this appealingly styled Victorian house offers warm décor and an eclectic mix of modern and retro furniture. Spacious bedrooms boast bold feature wallpaper; those to the front are the best.

✗✗ **Quay** ≤ 𝔸𝕂
11 The Quay ✉ EX34 9EQ – ℰ (01271) 868 090 – www.11thequay.co.uk – Closed 6-20 January
Rest – Carte £ 20/43
Wander down to the harbourside and this smart red building stands out; inside, it's the artwork of owner Damien Hirst which catches the eye. Well-priced, appealing menu of simple, flavoursome dishes, with local produce to the fore.

La Gendarmerie

63 Fore St ✉ EX34 9ED – ✆ (01271) 865 984 – www.lagendarmerie.co.uk – Closed November, Tuesday-Wednesday October-March and Monday
Rest – *(dinner only) (booking advisable)* Menu £ 29
Once a police station, now a simple little restaurant with exposed stone walls and an intimate feel; personally run by a husband and wife team. Concise, daily changing menu showcases market produce in precise, skilfully executed combinations.

ILKLEY – West Yorkshire – 502 O22 – pop. 13 472 22 B2

London 210 mi – Bradford 13 mi – Harrogate 17 mi – Leeds 16 mi
Station Rd, ✆ (01943) 60 23 19, www.visitbradford.com
Myddleton, ✆ (01943) 60 72 77

Box Tree (Simon Gueller)

37 Church St, on A 65 ✉ LS29 9DR – ✆ (01943) 608 484 – www.theboxtree.co.uk – Closed 1-6 January, 26-30 December, Sunday dinner and Monday
Rest – *(dinner only and lunch Friday-Sunday)* Menu £ 28/70
An iconic restaurant set in two charming sandstone cottages, with a plush, antique-furnished lounge and two luxurious dining rooms; it celebrated 50 years in 2012. Cooking is refined and skilful, with a classical French base, and dishes are light and delicate. Only the best ingredients are used.
→ Glazed veal sweetbreads, morels and truffle jus. Squab pigeon, puy lentils, Alsace bacon and roast shallots. Cherry soufflé with toasted almond ice cream.

ILMINGTON – Warwickshire – 504 O27 Great Britain 19 C3

London 91 mi – Birmingham 31 mi – Oxford 34 mi – Stratford-upon-Avon 9 mi
Hidcote Manor Garden★★, SW : 2 mi by minor rd – Chipping Campden★★, SW : 4 mi by minor rd

Folly Farm Cottage without rest

Back St ✉ CV36 4LJ – ✆ (01608) 682 425 – www.follyfarm.co.uk
3 rm – †£ 55/65 ††£ 64/88
Characterful barn conversion with lovely gardens. The cosy breakfast room has floral fabrics and a cottagey feel; try the 'Folly Challenge'! Traditional beamed bedrooms – one has a four-poster and all have homemade cake. Welcoming owners.

Howard Arms with rm

Lower Green ✉ CV36 4LT – ✆ (01608) 682 226 – www.howardarms.com
8 rm – †£ 85/145 ††£ 95/145 **Rest** – Carte £ 21/47
Delightful 17C Cotswold stone inn on a peaceful village green. Sit in the beamed bar with its inglenook fireplace, in the raised-level dining room or on the lovely terrace. Dishes are hearty and mainly British-based. Bedrooms are warm and cosy: some have antiques; those in the extension are more contemporary.

INGHAM – Norfolk – 504 W27 – pop. 376 15 D1

London 139 mi – Norwich 25 mi – Ipswich 65 mi – Lowestoft 30 mi

Ingham Swan

Sea Palling Rd ✉ NR12 9AB – ✆ (01692) 581 099 – www.theinghamswan.co.uk – Closed 25-26 December, Sunday dinner and Monday in winter
Rest – *(booking essential at dinner)* Menu £ 14 (weekday lunch)/28 **s** – Carte £ 26/47 **s**
Cosy, attractive, thatched 14C pub in the shadow of an 11C church, with an equally characterful beamed interior. Dishes can be quite complex, using plenty of ingredients, albeit in classic combinations.

ENGLAND

INGLETON – North Yorkshire – 502 M21 – pop. 1 641 22 A2

London 266 mi – Kendal 21 mi – Lancaster 18 mi – Leeds 53 mi

Riverside Lodge

24 Main St ✉ LA6 3HJ – ✆ (015242) 41 359 – www.riversideingleton.co.uk – Closed 24-25 December

8 rm – †£ 44/48 ††£ 58/66 **Rest** – Menu £ 17 **s**

19C doctor's house with a homely interior and a snooker table and sauna hidden in the basement. Spacious, pine-furnished bedrooms have modern bathrooms. The conservatory dining room offers views over the dales and the river. Breakfast features homemade preserves and muesli, along with a fish special.

IPSWICH – Suffolk – 504 X27 – pop. 147 226 Great Britain 15 C3

London 77 mi – Redbridge 64 mi – Romford 59 mi – Norwich 45 mi

St Stephens Lane, ✆ (01473) 25 80 70, www.allaboutipswich.com

St Stephens Church

Rushmere, Rushmere Heath, ✆ (01473) 72 56 48

Purdis Heath, Bucklesham Rd, ✆ (01473) 72 89 41

Fynn Valley, Witnesham, ✆ (01473) 78 52 67

Sutton Hoo★, NE : 12 mi by A 12 Y and B 1083 from Woodbridge

Salthouse Harbour

1 Neptune Quay ✉ IP4 1AX – ✆ (01473) 226 789 – www.salthouseharbour.co.uk X**a**

70 rm – †£ 120/180 ††£ 135/195

Rest ***Eaterie*** – see restaurant listing

Stylish converted salt warehouse with good marina views; its trendy lobby-lounge boasting floor to ceiling windows. Modern boutique bedrooms have well-appointed bathrooms; some feature chaise longues, copper slipper baths or balconies.

Kesgrave Hall

Hall Rd, East : 4.75 mi by A 1214 on Bealings rd ✉ IP5 2PU – ✆ (01473) 333 471 – www.kesgravehall.com

22 rm – †£ 125/300 ††£ 125/300 – 1 suite

Rest – *(bookings not accepted)* Carte £ 21/38

White Georgian house built in 1812, with large lawned gardens, an impressive terrace and a 38 acre wood. Stylish lounges have a relaxed, urban-chic feel. Large, luxurious bedrooms boast quality furnishings, modern facilities and stylish bathrooms. Busy, brasserie-style dining room offers European menu.

Trongs (N)

23 St Nicholas St ✉ IP1 1TW – ✆ (01473) 256 833 – Closed 3 weeks August and Sunday X**s**

Rest – Carte £ 21/46

Brightly painted restaurant filled with flowers and candles. The owners are from Hanoi: the parents and one son cook – his brother runs front of house. The extensive menu specialises in vibrant dishes from northern China; try the spring rolls.

Eaterie – Salthouse Harbour Hotel

1 Neptune Quay ✉ IP4 1AX – ✆ (01473) 226 789 – www.salthouseharbour.co.uk X**a**

Rest – Menu £ 18 (weekday lunch) – Carte £ 25/46

Modern brasserie in a converted warehouse hotel; zinc-topped bar, gold pillars, modern art and padded leather booths. Tasty brasserie dishes with Mediterranean influences. Dine on the terrace overlooking the marina.

at Hintlesham West : 5 mi by A 1214 on A 1071 - Y – ✉ Ipswich

Hintlesham Hall

✉ IP8 3NS – ✆ (01473) 652 334 – www.hintleshamhall.com

33 rm – †£ 169/209 ††£ 169/209 – 3 suites

Rest – Menu £ 18 (lunch)/33 **s** – Carte £ 45/62

Impressive Georgian manor house with 16C roots; original features such as ornate plasterwork and gold leaf inlaid cornicing remain. Grand bedrooms in main house; cosy courtyard rooms – some with terraces. Dining in the impressive Salon and wood-panelled Parlour; fresh herbs come from the garden.

IPSWICH

Street	Square	No.
Argyle St	X	2
Back Hamlet	Z	3
Birkfield Drive	Z	5
Bond St	X	6
Bridgwater Rd	Z	7
Buttermarket Centre	X	9
Carr St	X	10
Chevallier St	Y	13
College St	X	15
Corn Hill	X	16
Dogs Head St	X	18
Ellenbrook Rd	Z	19
Falcon St	X	21
Fore Hamlet	Z	22
Franciscan Way	X	24
Friars St	X	25
Grey Friars Rd	X	26
Grove Lane	YZ	28
Handford Rd	X, Y	30
Lloyds Ave	X	31
Lower Orwell St	X	32
Northgate St	X	33
Orwell Pl	X	34
Quadling St	X	35
Queen St	X	37
St Helen's St	X, Y	39
St Margarets St	X	40
St Nicholas St	X	41
St Peter's St	X	42
Salthouse St	X	43
Silent St	X	46
Tavern St	X	
Tower Ramparts Centre	X	47
Upper Orwell St	X	49
Waterworks St	X	51
Westgate St	X	52
Wolsey St	X	53
Yarmouth Rd	Y	54

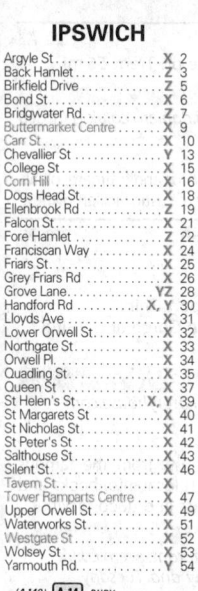

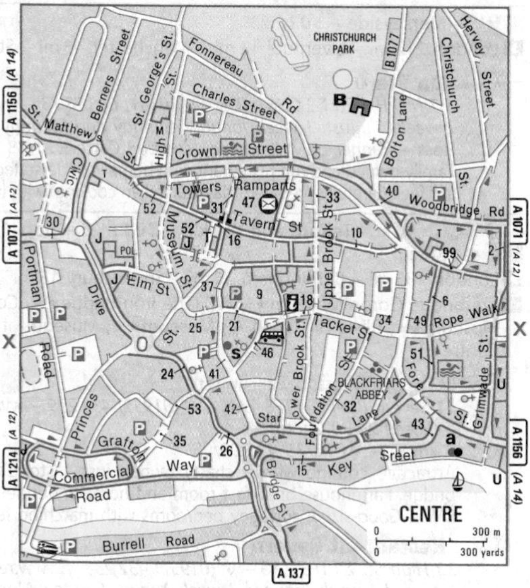

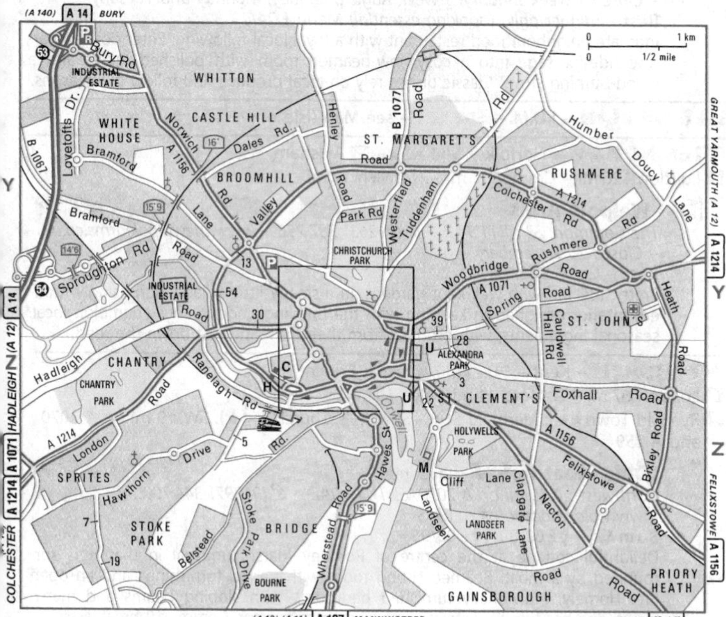

IRBY – Merseyside – 502 K23 — 20 A3

London 212 mi – Liverpool 12 mi – Manchester 46 mi – Stoke-on-Trent 56 mi

XX **Da Piero**

5-7 Mill Hill Rd ✉ CH61 4UB – ✆ (0151) 648 73 73 – www.dapiero.co.uk – Closed 2 weeks August, 1 week January, Sunday and Monday

Rest – *(dinner only) (booking essential)* Carte £ 21/43

Family-owned and run restaurant with homely, understated décor and intimate, pleasant feel. Carefully prepared, classical Italian cooking, with lots of rustic Sicilian dishes.

IRONBRIDGE – Telford and Wrekin – 503 M26 – pop. 1 560 — 18 B2

Great Britain

London 135 mi – Birmingham 36 mi – Shrewsbury 18 mi

Ironbridge Gorge Museum★★ **AC** (The Iron Bridge★★, Coalport China Museum★★, Blists Hill Open Air Museum★★, Museum of the Gorge and Visitor Centre★)

Library House without rest

11 Severn Bank ✉ TF8 7AN – ✆ (01952) 432 299 – www.libraryhouse.com – Closed 24-30 December

4 rm – †£ 70/75 ††£ 90/95

Attractive cottage with a chatty owner, just a stone's throw from the famous bridge. Farmhouse breakfast room and homely lounge with local info, books and DVDs. Good-sized, cottagey bedrooms with matching fabrics and good facilities.

XX **Restaurant Severn**

33 High St. ✉ TF8 7AG – ✆ (01952) 432 233 – www.restaurantsevern.co.uk – Closed 1 week January, 1 week August, Sunday, Monday and Tuesday

Rest – *(dinner only) (booking essential)* Menu £ 24/29

Intimate neighbourhood restaurant with a loyal local following. Enter down a narrow side passage into a cosy, low-beamed room with polished tables and a wood-burning stove. Classic dishes rely on local produce and follow the seasons.

ISLE OF MAN – I.O.M. – 502 G21 – see Man (Isle of)

ITTERINGHAM – Norfolk – 504 X25 – ✉ Aylsham — 15 C1

London 126 mi – Cromer 11 mi – Norwich 17 mi

Walpole Arms

The Common ✉ NR11 7AR – ✆ (01263) 587 258 – www.thewalpolearms.co.uk – Closed 25 December

Rest – Carte £ 18/38

Pretty 18C inn with well-kept gardens, in a sleepy little village. Surprisingly modern interior designed in keeping with the building's age. Menus champion local, seasonal ingredients, with produce from their farm and just down the road.

IVYCHURCH – Kent – 504 W30 Great Britain — 9 C2

London 67 mi – Ashford 11 mi – Rye 10 mi

Rye Old Town★★ : Mermaid St★ - St Mary's Church (≤★), SW : 9 mi on A 2070 and A 259

Olde Moat House without rest

Northwest : 0.75 mi on B 2070 ✉ TN29 0AZ – ✆ (01797) 344 700 – www.oldemoathouse.co.uk

3 rm – †£ 60/80 ††£ 80/95

Delightful cottage at the centre of Romney Marsh; unusual in that it is surrounded by a moat. Beamed sitting room with period furnishings and an open fire. Homely, individually furnished bedrooms with sloping beams and marsh views; one has a four-poster and another, a half-tester. Communal breakfasts.

IXWORTH – Suffolk – 504 W27 – see Bury St Edmunds

KEGWORTH – Leicestershire – 502 Q25 – pop. 3 338 Great Britain — 16 B2

London 123 mi – Leicester 18 mi – Loughborough 6 mi – Nottingham 13 mi

Calke Abbey★, SW : 7 mi by A 6 (northbound) and A 453 (southbound) – Derby★ - Museum and Art Gallery★, Royal Crown Derby Museum★, NW : 9 mi by A 50 – Nottingham Castle Museum★, N : 11 mi by A 453 and A 52

🏠 **Kegworth House** without rest 🖨 ⚓ 🛜 **P**
42 High St ⊠ DE74 2DA – 𝒞 (01509) 672 575 – www.kegworthhouse.co.uk
– Closed Christmas and New Year
11 rm ☑ – †£ 86/150 ††£ 105/206
Charming, family-run, Georgian townhouse with many original features and a pleasant walled garden. Individually furnished bedrooms; Room 11, with its exposed beams and four-poster, is one of the best. Extensive buffet breakfasts.

KELSALE – Suffolk – 504 Y27 – pop. 1 309 – ⊠ Saxmundham 15 D3
▶ London 103 mi – Cambridge 68 mi – Ipswich 23 mi – Norwich 37 mi

⌂ **Mile Hill Barn** without rest 🖨 ⚓ **P** ⇤
Main Rd, North Green, North : 1.5 mi by A 12 on North Green rd. ⊠ IP17 2RJ
– 𝒞 (01728) 668 519 – www.mile-hill-barn.co.uk
3 rm ☑ – †£ 55/85 ††£ 75/100
Traditional 15C Suffolk barn in landscaped gardens. Tea on arrival in impressive raftered lounge. Bedrooms boast feature beds and well-appointed bathrooms. Cosy breakfast room; Aga-cooked breakfasts.

KELVEDON – Essex – 504 W28 – pop. 4 593 13 C2
▶ London 56 mi – Leicester 118 mi – Wandsworth 56 mi – Bromley 55 mi

XX **George & Dragon** 🍴 **P**
🏷️ *Coggleshall Rd, Northwest : 2 mi on B 1024 ⊠ CO5 9PL – 𝒞 (01376) 561 797*
– www.georgeanddragonkelvedon.co.uk – Closed 25 December-2 January,
Sunday and Monday
Rest – Carte £ 23/34
Clean, bright and welcoming former pub with a sleek, contemporary style, encompassing topiary planters, marble tiled floors, antique mirrors, and art deco pictures and statuettes. Simple, well-priced menu with locally caught fish specials. Pretty terrace. Hands-on owners.

KENDAL – Cumbria – 502 L21 – pop. 28 030 ▮ Great Britain 21 B2
▶ London 270 mi – Bradford 64 mi – Burnley 63 mi – Carlisle 49 mi
🏢 25 Stramongate, 𝒞 (01539) 73 58 91, www.madeincumbria.co.uk
🛈 Town Hall
🏟 The Heights, 𝒞 (01539) 72 34 99
🟢 Levens Hall and Garden★ **AC**, S : 4.5 mi by A 591, A 590 and A 6. Lake Windermere★★, NW : 8 mi by A 5284 and A 591

⌂ **Beech House** without rest 🖨 ⚓ 🛜 **P**
40 Greenside, by All Hallows Ln ⊠ LA9 4LD – 𝒞 (01539) 720 385
– www.beechhouse-kendal.co.uk – Closed 1 week Christmas
5 rm ☑ – †£ 60/75 ††£ 80/100
Pretty, three-storey Georgian house set just out of town. Modern, open-plan lounge with comfy sofas and communal breakfast tables. Bright, airy, pine-furnished bedrooms with up-to-date bathrooms. Welcoming owners.

X **Newmoon**
129 Highgate ⊠ LA9 4EN – 𝒞 (01539) 729 254 – www.newmoonrestaurant.co.uk
– Closed 1-7 January, 25-26 December, Sunday and Monday
Rest – (booking advisable) Menu £ 10/13 – Carte £ 22/31
Smart, high street restaurant with ground floor bar, intimate, beamed dining room and a loyal local following. The owner's Turkish heritage is reflected in the menu, which has a strong Mediterranean base; dishes are fresh and colourful.

at Crosthwaite West : 5.25 mi by All Hallows Ln – ⊠ Kendal

🏠 **Punch Bowl Inn** with rm ⇐ 🍴 🛜 **P**
⊠ LA8 8HR – 𝒞 (01539) 568 237 – www.the-punchbowl.co.uk
9 rm ☑ – †£ 85/125 ††£ 105/305 **Rest** – Carte £ 22/40
Charming 17C inn set in the picturesque Lyth Valley, boasting antiques, cosy fires and exposed wood beams; dine either in the rustic bar or the more formal restaurant. Cooking has a classical base but displays some modern touches, and dishes display a degree of complexity that you wouldn't usually find in a pub. Luxury bedrooms boast quality linens and roll-top baths.

ENGLAND

KENILWORTH – Warwickshire – 503 P26 – pop. 22 218 Great Britain **19** C2

London 102 mi – Birmingham 19 mi – Coventry 5 mi – Leicester 32 mi

11 Smalley Pl, (01926) 74 89 00, www.kenilworthweb.co.uk

Castle★ **AC**

Victoria Lodge without rest

180 Warwick Rd CV8 1HU – (01926) 512 020 – www.victorialodgekenilworth.co.uk – Closed 2 weeks Christmas-New Year

10 rm – £ 52/68 £ 75/85

Keenly and proudly run red-brick house with a linen-laid breakfast room and a comfy lounge complete with a piano. Clean, well-maintained bedrooms; some with balconies or patios. Fresh milk and mineral water are in a fridge on the landing.

Beef

11 Warwick Rd CV8 1HD – (01926) 863 311 – www.beef-restaurant.co.uk – Closed last two weeks August, 1 January, 25-26 December and 31 December

Rest – Menu £ 10 (weekday lunch)/21 – Carte £ 26/52

Rustic restaurant boasting exposed brickwork, slate floors and quirky cowhide banquettes. Menus offer robust, hearty dishes; mainly Scottish steaks cooked on the charcoal grill and cuts of beef from American, Argentinean or Wagyu cattle.

KENTON – Devon – 503 J31 – see Exeter

KERNE BRIDGE – Herefordshire – 503 M28 – see Ross-on-Wye

KESSINGLAND – Suffolk – pop. 4 211 **15** D2

London 126 mi – Norwich 28 mi – Ipswich 40 mi – Colchester 66 mi

Old Rectory

157 Church Rd NR33 7SQ – (01502) 742 188 – www.bandblowestoft.co.uk – Closed 19 December-2 January

3 rm – £ 57/64 £ 84/98 **Rest** – Menu £ 25 **s**

1834 rectory retaining original character, a short walk from the beach. Individually furnished bedrooms boast antique furniture and feature beds. Beautiful gardens. Choice of dishes offered at dinner; locally sourced produce includes their own vegetables and eggs.

KESWICK – Cumbria – 502 K20 – pop. 4 984 Great Britain **21** A2

London 294 mi – Carlisle 31 mi – Kendal 30 mi

Market Sq., (017687) 7 26 45, www.keswick.org

Threlkeld Hall, (017687) 7 93 24

Derwentwater★ X – Thirlmere (Castlerigg Stone Circle★), E : 1.5 mi X **A**

Lairbeck

Vicarage Hill CA12 5QB – (017687) 73 373 – www.lairbeckhotel-keswick.co.uk – Closed Christmas-New Year X**a**

14 rm – £ 55/64 £ 110/128

Rest – *(dinner only) (booking essential)* Menu £ 25 **s**

Attractive Victorian house in the suburbs, its mature garden boasting a huge Sequoia Redwood. Original barley-twist staircase, galleried landing and comfy bar-lounge. Bedrooms come in a mix of styles; some, such as Room 4, have lovely views. Daily menu in the traditional dining room.

Howe Keld without rest

5-7 The Heads CA12 5ES – (017687) 72 417 – www.howekeld.co.uk

14 rm – £ 50/95 £ 90/130 Z**s**

A comfortable, well-run guest house with boutique styling and strong eco-credentials. Contemporary bedrooms feature reclaimed wood furnishings. Good breakfasts with homemade granola, Cumbrian air-dried meats and home-baked bread.

Morrel's

34 Lake Rd CA12 5DQ – (017687) 72 666 – www.morrels.co.uk – Closed 24-27 December and Monday Z**x**

Rest – *(dinner only)* Menu £ 20 – Carte £ 21/30

Popular local eatery with scrubbed wood flooring, etched glass dividers and a buzzy atmosphere. Seasonally changing dishes have subtle Mediterranean influences; some come in two sizes. Good value menus.

ENGLAND

KESWICK

Bank St . . . . Z 2
Borrowdale Rd . . . . . Z 3
Brackenrigg Drive . . Z 5
Brundholme Rd . . . . X 6
Chestnut Hill . . . . . . X 8
Church St . . . . Z 10
Crosthwaite Rd . . . . . X 12
Derwent St. . . . . Z 13
High Hill . . . . Z 14
Main St . . . . Z
Manor Brow. . . . . . . X 17
Market Square . . . . . Z 18
Museum Square . . . Z 19
Otley Rd . . . . Z 20
Park Horse Yard . . . . Z 21
Police Station Court . Z 22
Ratcliffe Pl. . . . . Z 23
St Herbert St . . . . . . Z 24
Standish St . . . . Z 25
Station St . . . . Z 26
The Crescent . . . . . . Z 27
The Hawthorns . . . . Y 29
The Headlands . . . . . Z 31
Tithebarn St . . . . Z 32

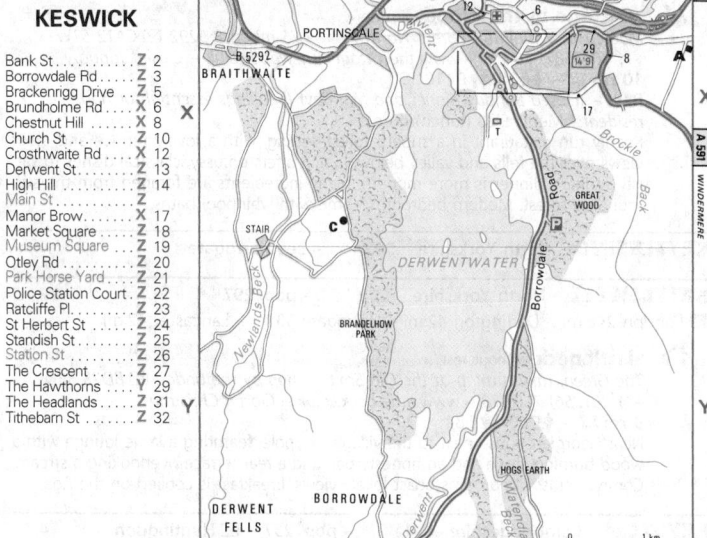

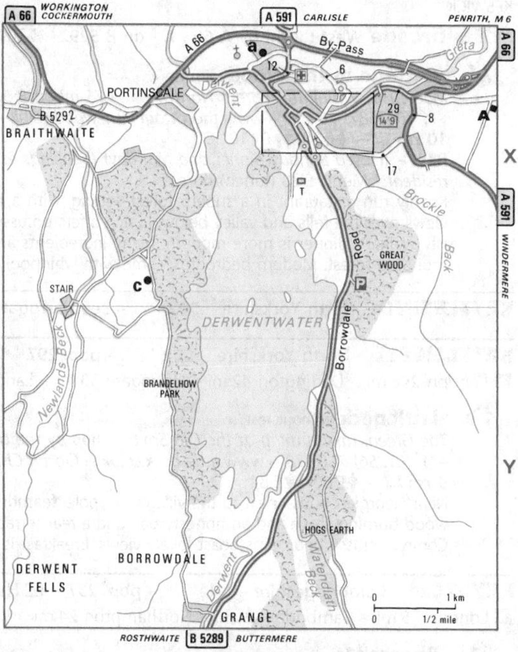

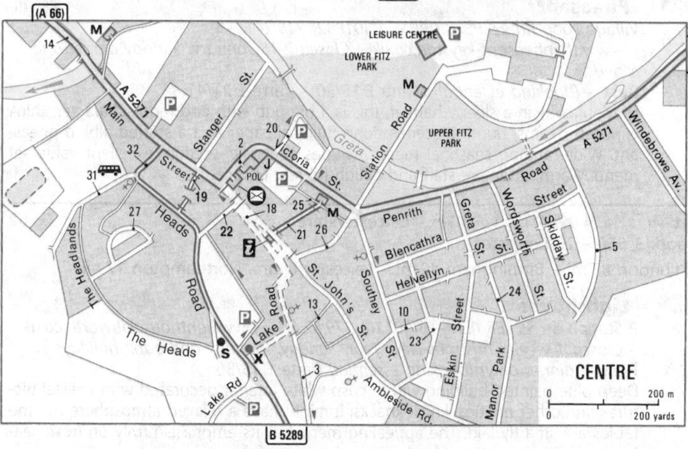

at Portinscale West : 1.5 mi by A 66 – ✉ Keswick

Swinside Lodge

Newlands, South : 1.5 mi on Grange Rd ✉ CA12 5UE – ✆ (017687) 72 948 – www.swinsidelodge-hotel.co.uk – Restricted opening January and December

7 rm (dinner included) – £ 91/123 £ 122/234 Xc

Rest – *(dinner only) (bookings essential for non-residents)* Menu £ 38 **s**

Whitewashed Georgian house in a countryside location, boasting lovely views over the fells. Local info in reception. Two small, traditional country house lounges filled with books and antiques, including an old jukebox. Comfortable bedrooms with homemade biscuits. Formal dining room offers set 4 course menu of classical dishes and a house party atmosphere.

at Braithwaite West : 2 mi by A 66 - X - on B 5292 – ✉ Keswick

XX **Cottage in the Wood** with rm
Magic Hill, Whinlatter Forest, Northwest : 1.75 mi on B 5292 ✉ CA12 5TW – ☎ (017687) 78 409 – www.thecottageinthewood.co.uk – Closed January
10 rm – †£ 88 ††£ 110/190
Rest – *(closed Sunday dinner and Monday) (bookings essential for non-residents)* Menu £ 20 (lunch)/60 **s**
Keenly run restaurant in a superb forest setting, with a lovely terrace and great views over the fells and valley below. Lunch offers unfussy, classical dishes to satisfy walkers; dinner is more modern. Many ingredients are foraged from the surrounding forest. Modern bedrooms; some with whirlpool baths.

KETTLESING – North Yorkshire – **502** P21 – see Harrogate

KETTLEWELL – North Yorkshire – **502** N21 – pop. 297 **22** A2
London 246 mi – Darlington 42 mi – Harrogate 30 mi – Lancaster 42 mi

Littlebeck without rest
The Green, take turning at the Old Smithy shop by the bridge ✉ BD23 5RD – ☎ (01756) 760 378 – www.little-beck.co.uk – Closed Christmas
3 rm – †£ 60 ††£ 84
Neat Georgian house next to the village maypole, featuring a large lounge with a wood burning stove and an honesty bar, and a rear terrace overlooking a stream. Comfy, unfussy bedrooms boast lovely views. Breakfast is cooked on the Aga.

ENGLAND

KEYSTON – Cambridgeshire – **504** S26 – pop. 257 – ✉ Huntingdon **14** A2
London 75 mi – Cambridge 29 mi – Northampton 24 mi

Pheasant
Village Loop Rd ✉ PE28 0RE – ☎ (01832) 710 241 – www.thepheasant-keyston.co.uk – Closed 2-15 January, Sunday dinner and Monday
Rest – *(booking essential)* Menu £ 15/30 – Carte £ 21/41
Hidden away in a sleepy hamlet, this is a big pub with enormous character; think exposed beams, hunting scenes, John Bull wallpaper and a stuffed albino pheasant. Wide-ranging seasonal menu includes a 'classic' section; excellent value set menu. Warm, attentive staff and delightful rear terrace.

KIBWORTH BEAUCHAMP – Leicestershire – **504** Q/R26 **16** B2
– pop. 3 550 – ✉ Leicester
London 85 mi – Birmingham 49 mi – Leicester 6 mi – Northampton 17 mi

XX **Lighthouse**
9 Station St ✉ LE8 0LN – ☎ (0116) 279 62 60 – www.lighthousekibworth.co.uk – Closed 1 week Christmas-New Year, Sunday, Monday and bank holidays
Rest – *(dinner only) (booking essential)* Carte £ 15/36
Deep blue painted building with a crisp white interior decorated with coastal pictures and other nautical knick-knacks; it might have a relaxed atmosphere but the tables are smartly laid. The appealing menu has its emphasis firmly on fresh seafood, offering everything from fish and chips to lobster.

KIBWORTH HARCOURT – Leicestershire – **504** R26 **16** B2
London 101 mi – Leicester 9 mi – Coventry 36 mi – Nottingham 41 mi

X **Boboli**
88 Main St ✉ LE8 0NQ – ☎ (0116) 279 33 03 – www.bobolirestaurant.co.uk – Closed 25-26 December and 1 January
Rest – Menu £ 19 (lunch) – Carte £ 16/44
Buzzy, laid-back restaurant with a sunny terrace; formerly a pub, it has a central bar and dining on three levels. Extensive selection of seasonally inspired dishes; flavours are bold and portions, large. Satisfyingly affordable wines.

KINGHAM – Oxfordshire – 503 P28 – pop. 1 434 10 A1

London 81 mi – Gloucester 32 mi – Oxford 25 mi – Cardiff 91 mi

Mill House

OX7 6UH – (01608) 658 188 – www.millhousehotel.co.uk
21 rm – £ 107/152 £ 120/165 **Rest** – Menu £ 15/33
Privately run house in 10 acres of lawned gardens with a brook flowing through the grounds. Spacious lounge with comfortable armchairs and books. Comfortable, traditionally styled bedrooms. Modern décor suffuses restaurant.

Moat End without rest

The Moat, by West St OX7 6XZ – (01608) 658 090 – www.moatend.co.uk – Closed Christmas and New Year
3 rm – £ 60/70 £ 68/80
Stone-built barn conversion with ponies, hens and countryside views. Cosy sitting room with impressive wood-burning stove. Simple, neatly kept bedrooms. Communal breakfasts include fresh eggs, and bacon and sausages from a local butcher.

Kingham Plough with rm

rest,

The Green OX7 6YD – (01608) 658 327 – www.thekinghamplough.co.uk – Closed 25 December
7 rm – £ 80/110 £ 95/145 **Rest** – Carte £ 28/47
Rustic, laid-back pub and restaurant located on the green in an unspoilt Cotswold village; run by a friendly team and experienced chef-owner. Menus mix modern, gutsy pub dishes with a few more ambitious offerings, and evolve as new ingredients arrive. Comfy bedrooms await: 2 and 4, in the main building, are best.

KING'S LYNN – Norfolk – 502 V25 – pop. 43 547 Great Britain 14 B1

London 103 mi – Cambridge 45 mi – Leicester 75 mi – Norwich 44 mi
Purfleet Quay, (01553) 76 30 44, www.kingslynnonline.com
Eagles, Tilney All Saints, School Rd, (01553) 82 71 47
Houghton Hall★★ **AC**, NE : 14.5 mi by A 148 – Four Fenland Churches★ (Terrington St Clement, Walpole St Peter, West Walton, Walsoken) SW : by A 47

Bankhouse

King's Staithe Sq PE30 1RD – (01553) 660 492 – www.thebankhouse.co.uk
11 rm – £ 80/110 £ 100/140 **Rest** – Carte £ 19/33
Grade II listed Georgian townhouse by the River Ouse: where Barclays Bank was founded. Comfortable bedrooms in various shapes and sizes: all have good facilities and excellent bathrooms; some have a pleasant outlook. Stylish, contemporary bar and brasserie with terrace; modern European menu.

Market Bistro

11 Saturday Market Pl. PE30 5DQ – (01553) 771 483 – www.marketbistro.co.uk – Closed 25-26 December, 1-12 January, Sunday and Monday
Rest – Carte £ 17/33
Set in the historic part of town; original beams and a fireplace remain, but this relaxed, informal bistro is more modern than its 17C exterior suggests. Fresh, unfussy cooking is passionately local and seasonal. Service is friendly.

at Grimston East : 6.25 mi by A 148 – King's Lynn

Congham Hall

Lynn Rd. PE32 1AH – (01485) 600 250 – www.conghamhallhotel.co.uk
26 rm – £ 95/265 £ 125/265 – 1 suite
Rest – Menu £ 18 (weekday lunch) – Carte £ 22/43
Part-Georgian country house in 30 acres of peaceful grounds. Guest areas include a snug bar and a spacious drawing room with a subtle modern style. Opt for one of the lovely Garden Rooms which are close to the smart spa and overlook the formal flower or herb gardens. The restaurant serves modern classics.

KINGS MILLS – see Channel Islands (Guernsey)

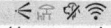

KINGSBRIDGE – Devon – 503 I33 – pop. 5 521 2 C3

London 236 mi – Exeter 36 mi – Plymouth 24 mi – Torquay 21 mi

Thurlestone, ✆ (01548) 56 04 05

Town★ – Boat Trip to Salcombe★★ AC

Prawle Point (≤★★★) SE : 10 mi around coast by A 379

Buckland-Tout-Saints

Goveton, Northeast : 3 mi by A 381 ✉ TQ7 2DS – ✆ (01548) 853 055 – www.tout-saints.co.uk – Closed 17 January-12 February

16 rm – †£ 125/175 ††£ 125/195 – 2 suites

Rest – Menu £ 22/39 – Carte dinner £ 28/45

Appealing Queen Anne mansion set in large, peaceful grounds. Traditional, antique-furnished interior with wood-panelling in many rooms. Bedrooms vary in shape and size; some have a classic country house feel and others are more contemporary. Choice of two dining rooms offering accomplished dishes.

KINGSKERSWELL – Devon – 503 J32 – pop. 4 624 – ✉ Torquay 2 C2

London 199 mi – Exeter 18 mi – Torquay 4 mi

Bickley Mill Inn with rm

Stoneycombe, West : 2 mi by Stoneycombe rd ✉ TQ12 5LN – ✆ (01803) 873 201 – www.bickleymill.co.uk

12 rm – †£ 65/85 ††£ 75/100 **Rest** – Carte £ 20/30

Converted former flour mill with a huge decked terrace, gardens built into the rocky banks and a rustic yet modern feel. Menus are keenly priced and, for the most part, take on a simple, traditional style. Individually designed bedrooms are bold and stylish; Riviera is one of the best.

KINGSTON BAGPUIZE – Oxfordshire – 503 P28 – see Oxford

KINGSWEAR – Devon – 503 J32 – see Dartmouth

KIRKBY FLEETHAM – North Yorkshire – 502 P20 – pop. 556 22 B1

London 234 mi – Liverpool 124 mi – Leeds 53 mi – Sheffield 84 mi

Black Horse Inn with rm

Lumley Ln ✉ DL7 0SH – ✆ (01609) 749 010 – www.blackhorsekirkbyfleetham.com

7 rm – †£ 60/80 ††£ 60/100

Rest – *(closed Sunday dinner) (booking advisable)* Carte £ 21/32

Subtly modernised 18C pub with original beams, a smart new flagged floor, a candlelit bar and a rear dining room. Menus range from tasty sharing boards to flavoursome British classics that are a step above your usual pub fare. Stylish bedrooms come with good comforts and designer bathrooms.

KIRKBY LONSDALE – Cumbria – 502 M21 – pop. 2 076 21 B3

London 259 mi – Carlisle 62 mi – Kendal 13 mi – Lancaster 17 mi

Scaleber Lane, Barbon, ✆ (015242) 7 63 66

Casterton, Sedbergh Rd, ✆ (015242) 7 15 92

Royal (N)

Main St ✉ LA6 2AE – ✆ (01524) 271 966 – www.royalhotelkirkbylonsdale.co.uk

14 rm – †£ 63/135 ††£ 85/180 **Rest** – Carte £ 23/39

Well-run Georgian hotel overlooking a characterful town square. The décor is a mix of modern and shabby-chic, and the owner has a keen eye for detail. Bedrooms are spacious; some have free-standing baths in the room. Snug, open-fired lounge and an all-day brasserie serving classics and wood-fired pizzas.

Plato's (N)

2 Mill Brow ✉ LA6 2AT – ✆ (01524) 274 180 – www.platoskirkbylonsdale.co.uk

8 rm – †£ 65/90 ††£ 80/140 **Rest** – Carte £ 20/34

Georgian-style townhouse once home to Plato Harrison wine merchants. Tastefully decorated bedrooms blend modern furnishings with period charm and come with thoughtful extras. The all-day coffee shop cum café offers an extensive range of modern, international dishes ranging from tapas to tasting boards.

Hipping Hall with rm
Cowan Bridge, Southeast : 2.5 mi on A 65 ✉ LA6 2JJ – ✆ (01524) 271 187 – www.hippinghall.com – Closed 7-10 January
9 rm – †£ 90/172 ††£ 119/229
Rest – *(dinner only and lunch Saturday-Sunday)* Menu £ 55/65
Charming part-15/16C house – a former blacksmith's – named after the stepping (or 'hipping') stones over the beck, which runs past the old washhouse. Smart, airy restaurant with superb beamed ceiling and minstrel's gallery. Well-executed dishes use quality ingredients; the tasting menu is the highlight. Sleek white bedrooms feature deep pile carpets and modern bathrooms.

Sun Inn with rm
6 Market St ✉ LA6 2AU – ✆ (015242) 71 965 – www.sun-inn.info – Closed Monday lunch
11 rm – †£ 76/141 ††£ 99/168
Rest – Menu £ 27 (dinner) – Carte approx. £ 29
17C inn with characterful beamed bar and more formal, smartly furnished restaurant, which comes into its own in the evening. Pub classics and tapas-style small plates at lunch; dinner is a more serious affair. Well-lit, modern bedrooms boast quality linen and thoughtful extras; delicious breakfasts.

at Lupton Northwest : 4.75 mi on A 65 – 502 L21

Plough with rm
Cow Brow ✉ LA6 1PJ – ✆ (015395) 67 700 – www.theploughatlupton.co.uk
5 rm – †£ 95/195 ††£ 115/195 **Rest** – Carte £ 19/33
Homely pub with antique tables, comfy sofas and a cheery, knowledgeable team, set on the main road running from the Lake District to North Yorkshire. Choose from a list of classics or a selection of mix and match small plates, as well as an enticing array of side dishes. Smart, individually styled bedrooms with roll-top baths complete the picture.

ENGLAND

KIRKBY STEPHEN – Cumbria – 502 M20 – pop. 1 832 — 21 B2

London 296 mi – Carlisle 46 mi – Darlington 37 mi – Kendal 28 mi

Augill Castle
Northeast : 4.25 mi by A 685 ✉ CA17 4DE – ✆ (01768) 341 937 – www.stayinacastle.com
14 rm – †£ 100/200 ††£ 160/240
Rest – *(dinner only) (booking essential) (residents only)* Menu £ 30
A carefully restored Victorian folly with antique-furnished bedrooms. Langdale has a four-poster and a roll-top bath; Stable House is ideal for families. Spacious dining room with communal table and ornate plaster ceiling. Set menu of traditional, home-cooked dishes with a modern edge.

KIRKBY THORE – Cumbria – 502 M20 — 21 B2

London 275 mi – Preston 68 mi – Sunderland 68 mi – Newcastle upon Tyne 68 mi

Bridge N
on A66 ✉ CA10 1UZ – ✆ (01768) 362 766 – www.thebridgebistro.co.uk – Closed dinner Sunday-Thursday
Rest – Carte £ 15/31
Remodelled village pub with a large, bright extension and a bistro feel. They open all day and for dinner on Fri and Sat. Cooking has a likeable simplicity, with the odd Asian touch, and there's a tempting display of cakes on the counter.

KIRKBYMOORSIDE – North Yorkshire – 502 R21 – pop. 2 595 — 23 C1

London 244 mi – Leeds 61 mi – Scarborough 26 mi – York 33 mi
Manor Vale, ✆ (01751) 43 15 25

Brickfields Farm without rest
Kirby Mills, East : 0.75 mi . by A 170 on Kirby Mills Industrial Estate rd
✉ YO62 6NS – ☎ (01751) 433 074 – www.brickfieldsfarm.co.uk
7 rm – †£ 60 ††£ 100/130
Red-brick former farmhouse set in 14 acres. Modern bedrooms have lovely bathrooms with walk-in showers: one room is in the main house; the remainder, in the courtyard. Spacious conservatory breakfast room – enjoy local bacon and sausages.

Cornmill without rest
Kirby Mills, East : 0.5 mi by A 170 ✉ YO62 6NP – ☎ (01751) 432 000 – www.kirbymills.co.uk
5 rm – †£ 55/75 ††£ 75/110
Charming 18C cornmill with pleasant courtyard. Spacious, rustic bedrooms set in the old farmhouse and stables. Characterful dining room with mill race running beneath a glass panel.

KIRKWHELPINGTON – Northumberland – 501 N/O18 – pop. 353 — 24 A2

– ✉ Morpeth Great Britain
London 305 mi – Carlisle 46 mi – Newcastle upon Tyne 20 mi
Wallington House★ AC, E : 3.5 mi by A 696 and B 6342

Shieldhall
Wallington, Southeast : 2.5 mi by A 696 on B 6342 ✉ NE61 4AQ – ☎ (01830) 540 387 – www.shieldhallguesthouse.co.uk – Closed Christmas-New Year
4 rm – †£ 60/80 ††£ 80/96 **Rest** – Menu £ 28
Early 17C farmhouse and outbuildings, where Capability Brown's uncle once lived. Mix of rustic and country house guest areas; library-lounge has garden views. Individually styled bedrooms, with furniture handmade by the owner. Beamed, flag-floored dining room for classical British dishes and Aga-cooked breakfasts.

ENGLAND

KIRTLINGTON – Oxfordshire – 503 Q28 — 10 B2

London 70 mi – Bicester 11 mi – Oxford 16 mi

Dashwood rm,
South Green, Heyford Rd ✉ OX5 3HJ – ☎ (01869) 352 707 – www.thedashwood.co.uk – Closed 24 December-6 January
12 rm – †£ 90/130 ††£ 115/160
Rest – *(closed Sunday and Monday lunch)* Carte £ 19/43
Grade II listed former pub and barn, built in classic Cotswold stone; popular with visitors to Bicester Village. Clean, fresh, uncluttered bedrooms are decorated in a contemporary style; Room 1 is the best, with air con and a spacious bathroom. Modern European menu served in informal, ground floor restaurant.

KNARESBOROUGH – North Yorkshire – 502 P21 – pop. 13 380 — 22 B2

London 217 mi – Bradford 21 mi – Harrogate 3 mi – Leeds 18 mi
Market Pl, ☎ (01423) 86 68 86, www.knaresborough.co.uk
Boroughbridge Rd, ☎ (01423) 86 26 90

Newton House without rest
5-7 York Pl ✉ HG5 0AD – ☎ (01423) 863 539 – www.newtonhouseyorkshire.com
12 rm – †£ 55 ††£ 95/115
Listed Georgian townhouse with a spacious lounge and honesty bar. Individually styled bedrooms come with books, sweets and minibars; some are in the old stables. Breakfast includes stewed garden fruit, homemade granola and rare breed bacon.

Gallon House
47 Kirkgate ✉ HG5 8BZ – ☎ (01423) 862 102 – www.gallon-house.co.uk – Closed 24 December-3 January
3 rm – †£ 75/85 ††£ 110/130 **Rest** – Menu £ 36
A charming, elegant property close to the railway station, with impressive views of the Nidd Gorge from its terrace. Compact, well-kept bedrooms. Seasonal menus offer tasty, straightforward cooking, with a good wine list to match.

at Ferrensby Northeast : 3 mi on A 6055

XX **General Tarleton Inn** with rm
Boroughbridge Rd ✉ HG5 0PZ – ✆ (01423) 340 284 – www.generaltarleton.co.uk
13 rm – †£ 75/95 ††£ 129/150 **Rest** – Menu £ 15 – Carte £ 25/41
18C coaching inn with a stylish cocktail bar, a smart restaurant, a wicker-furnished conservatory and a large rear terrace. The menu offers a good range of hearty, classical dishes with a seasonal Yorkshire base. Modern bedrooms feature solid oak furnishings and come with home-baked biscuits.

KNOWSTONE – Devon – ✉ South Molton **2** C1

London 183 mi – Bristol 78 mi – Cardiff 109 mi – Plymouth 78 mi

Masons Arms (Mark Dodson)
✉ EX36 4RY – ✆ (01398) 341 231 – www.masonsarmsdevon.co.uk – Closed first week January, 1 week mid February, 1 week August-September, Sunday dinner and Monday
Rest – *(booking essential)* Menu £ 25 (lunch) – Carte £ 35/47
Pretty 13C thatched inn set in Exmoor's foothills, with a cosy bar and bright dining room featuring a celestial ceiling mural. Experienced owners offer sophisticated cooking of French and British classics using first class local produce. Pronounced, assured flavours. Friendly service.
→ Smoked scallops with wasabi, noodles and vermouth sauce. Red mullet and brill with potato crust, salmon mousse sausage and lemongrass cream. Trio of raspberry desserts.

KNUTSFORD – Cheshire East – 502 M24 – pop. 12 656 **20** B3

London 187 mi – Chester 25 mi – Liverpool 33 mi – Manchester 18 mi
Toft Rd, ✆ (01565) 63 26 11, www.virtual-knutsford.co.uk

XX **Belle Epoque Brasserie** with rm
60 King St ✉ WA16 6DT – ✆ (01565) 633 060 – www.thebelleepoque.com – Closed Sunday dinner
7 rm – †£ 95 ††£ 115
Rest – Menu £ 15 (lunch and early dinner)/30 – Carte £ 24/46
Long-standing restaurant with striking exterior features and an impressive art nouveau interior; look out for the lovely mosaic floor. Relaxed brasserie-style dining, featuring British classics, grills and a few more modern dishes. Bedrooms are stylish and contemporary.

at Mobberley Northeast : 2.5 mi by A 537 on B 5085 – ✉ Knutsford

Hinton without rest
Town Ln, on B 5085 ✉ WA16 7HH – ✆ (01565) 873 484 – www.thehinton.co.uk
6 rm – †£ 48/53 ††£ 68/72
Welcoming cream-washed guesthouse on main road through the village, with a homely, comfortable lounge and bright, well-kept bedrooms offering good facilities. Linen-clad breakfast room; or eat in the conservatory, overlooking the garden.

at Lower Peover Southwest : 3.25 mi by A 50 on B 5081

Bells of Peover
The Cobbles ✉ WA16 9PZ – ✆ (01565) 722 269 – www.thebellsofpeover.com – Closed Monday except bank holidays
Rest – Menu £ 17 (lunch) – Carte £ 23/39
16C coaching inn down a narrow cobbled lane – whose regulars once included Generals Eisenhower and Patton. Cosy, open-fired bar and three tastefully decorated, contemporary dining rooms. The refined, balanced cooking is keenly priced.

at Lach Dennis Southwest : 7 mi by A 50 and B 5081 on B 5082 – ✉ Knutsford

Duke of Portland
Penny's Ln ✉ CW9 8SY – ✆ (01606) 46 264 – www.dukeofportland.com
Rest – Carte £ 19/38
Village inn on the main road; the most popular place to dine is the smart, contemporary room featuring a stag's head. Lengthy menu offers simply prepared dishes of carefully sourced, local produce. Good value set price Sunday lunch.

ENGLAND

KYNASTON – Herefordshire – see Ledbury

LACH DENNIS – Cheshire West and Chester – see Knutsford

LACOCK – Wiltshire – 503 N29 – pop. 1 068 – ✉ Chippenham 4 C2

London 109 mi – Bath 16 mi – Bristol 30 mi – Chippenham 3 mi

Village★★ - Lacock Abbey★ **AC** – High St★, St Cyriac★, Fox Talbot Museum of Photography★ **AC**

At The Sign of the Angel

6 Church St ✉ SN15 2LB – ✆ (01249) 730 230 – www.lacock.co.uk – Closed 24-28 December

6 rm – †£ 85 ††£ 129/159

Rest – Menu £ 15 (weekday lunch)/18 – Carte £ 22/36

Delightful 15C inn with beamed ceilings, wattle and daub walls and open fires, located in charming National Trust village. Traditional, antique-furnished bedrooms are quirky and characterful; Room 5 is particularly pleasant and light. Classic country cooking uses home-grown produce.

LA HAULE – 503 L33 – see Channel Islands (Jersey)

LALEHAM – Surrey 7 C1

London 20 mi – Bristol 110 mi – Cardiff 143 mi – Southampton 63 mi

Three Horseshoes

25 Shepperton Rd ✉ TW18 1SE – ✆ (01784) 455 014 – www.3horseshoeslaleham.co.uk – Closed 26 December

Rest – Menu £ 17/31 – Carte £ 22/33

A pub with 17C origins but 21C sensibilities; take a seat in one of several smart rooms or in the pretty walled garden. The menu's got something for everyone from sandwiches and salads to meaty main courses, pub classics and sharing plates.

LAMESLEY – Tyne and Wear 24 B2

London 273 mi – Sheffield 130 mi – Nottingham 153 mi – York 85 mi

Stables Lodge without rest

South Farm ✉ NE11 0ET – ✆ (0191) 492 17 56 – www.thestableslodge.co.uk

4 rm – †£ 75 ††£ 81/138

Converted stone barn and outbuildings with a comfy, characterful style. Rustic, open-plan guest areas with heavy wood furniture and warm fabrics and colours. Bedrooms are spacious and cosy with modern facilities; one has its own hot tub.

LANCASTER – Lancashire – 502 L21 – pop. 45 952 Great Britain 20 A1

London 252 mi – Blackpool 26 mi – Bradford 62 mi – Burnley 44 mi

Meeting House Lane, ✆ (01524) 58 23 94, www.visitlancashire.com

18 Ashton Hall, Ashton-with-Stodday, ✆ (01524) 75 20 90

9 Lansil, Caton Rd, ✆ (01524) 3 92 69

Castle★ **AC**

Ashton

Wyresdale Rd, Southeast : 1.25 mi by A 6 on Clitheroe rd ✉ LA1 3JJ – ✆ (01524) 68 460 – www.theashtonlancaster.com

5 rm – †£ 95/115 ††£ 115/175 **Rest** – Menu £ 25 **s**

Georgian house in lawned gardens; personally run by friendly owner. Good-sized bedrooms are decorated in bold colours and feature a blend of modern and antique furniture. Small, informal dining room; home-cooked comfort food makes good use of local produce.

LANGAR – Nottinghamshire – 502 R25 16 B2

London 132 mi – Boston 45 mi – Leicester 25 mi – Lincoln 37 mi

Langar Hall

NG13 9HG – (01949) 860 559 – www.langarhall.co.uk
12 rm – £ 89/140 £ 109/199 – 1 suite
Rest – Menu £ 20 – Carte £ 26/51
Georgian Manor set in 23 acres of pastoral land; its antique-furnished bedrooms named after those who've featured in the house's history. Dine by candlelight in the elegant, pillared dining room; cooking is classically based, with fruit and vegetables from the kitchen garden and local game in season.

LANGHO – Lancashire – 502 M22 – see Blackburn

LANGTHWAITE – North Yorkshire – 502 O20 – see Reeth

LA PULENTE – 503 P33 – see Channel Islands (Jersey)

LAPWORTH – Warwickshire – pop. 2 100 19 C2

London 108 mi – Birmingham 23 mi – Leicester 47 mi – Coventry 19 mi

Boot Inn

Old Warwick Rd B94 6JU – (01564) 782 464 – www.bootinnlapworth.co.uk
Rest – *(booking essential)* Menu £ 17 (weekdays) – Carte £ 21/34
Large, buzzy red-brick pub close to the M40, boasting a large terrace, a traditional quarry-floored bar and a modern first floor restaurant. Dishes vary from sandwiches, a picnic board and sharing plates to more sophisticated specials.

LASKILL – North Yorkshire – 502 Q21 – see Hawnby

LASTINGHAM – North Yorkshire – 502 R21 – pop. 87 – York 23 C1

London 244 mi – Scarborough 26 mi – York 32 mi

Lastingham Grange

YO62 6TH – (01751) 417 345 – www.lastinghamgrange.com – closed November-March
11 rm – £ 95/135 £ 150/199
Rest – Menu £ 40 (dinner) – Carte £ 21/36
Delightfully located, family-run, 17C former farmhouse set in 14 acres on the edge of the moors. Pleasantly old-fashioned décor, with plenty of antiques and curios. Well-maintained bedrooms and lovely gardens. Traditional dining room offers a four course set menu of classic dishes.

LAVENHAM – Suffolk – 504 W27 – pop. 1 231 – Sudbury 15 C3

Great Britain

London 66 mi – Cambridge 39 mi – Colchester 22 mi – Ipswich 19 mi
Lady St, (01787) 24 82 07, www.discoverlavenham.co.uk
Town★★ – Church of St Peter and St Paul★

Swan

rest,

High St CO10 9QA – (01787) 247 477 – www.theswanatlavenham.co.uk
45 rm – £ 155 £ 195/350 – 1 suite
Rest *Brasserie* – see restaurant listing
Rest *Gallery* – Menu £ 22 (lunch) **s** – Carte approx. £ 36 **s**
Characterful, 15C former coaching inn with delightful, timbered lounges and a superbly atmospheric bar. Beamed, individually decorated bedrooms boast a subtle contemporary style. The Gallery, with its timbered roof and minstrels' gallery, offers a modern British menu and live piano at weekends.

Lavenham Priory without rest

Water St CO10 9RW – (01787) 247 404 – www.lavenhampriory.co.uk – *Closed Christmas-New Year*
6 rm – £ 87/97 £ 120/183
Part-13C, Grade I listed priory in a historic town, with gorgeous garden and mini parterre. Characterful interior features a vast inglenook fireplace, Elizabethan murals and a Jacobean staircase. Cosy lounge and atmospheric dining room. Heavily beamed bedrooms with feature beds and roll-top or slipper baths.

XXX **Great House** with rm

Market Pl ✉ CO10 9QZ – ✆ (01787) 247 431 – www.greathouse.co.uk – Closed 3 weeks January, 2 weeks summer, Sunday dinner, Monday and lunch Tuesday
3 rm – †£ 95/195 ††£ 135/195, ☕ £ 12 – 2 suites
Rest – Menu £ 19/34 – Carte £ 40/48
Passionately run restaurant on the main square of an attractive town; its impressive Georgian façade concealing a timbered house with 14C origins. Choose between two dining rooms and a smart enclosed terrace. Concise menus offer ambitious dishes with worldwide influences and a French heart. Stylish, contemporary décor blends well with old beams in the bedrooms.

XX **Brasserie** – Swan Hotel

High St ✉ CO10 9QA – ✆ (01787) 247 477 – www.theswanatlavenham.co.uk
Rest – Carte £ 29/43
Well-run hotel restaurant blending smart, modern furnishings with traditional elements of the 15C inn in which it resides. In winter, sit by the fire; in summer, on the terrace overlooking the gardens. Keenly priced classic bistro dishes.

LAWHITTON – Cornwall 2 C2

London 221 mi – Bristol 136 mi – Cardiff 156 mi – Plymouth 26 mi

Primrose Cottage without rest

Southeast : 1.25 mi on B 3362 ✉ PL15 9PE – ✆ (01566) 773 645 – www.primrosecottagesuites.co.uk – Closed Christmas
3 rm ☕ – †£ 70/90 ††£ 90/130
Part-18C house with a friendly owner and lovely gardens leading down to the river. Good-sized bedrooms boast their own entrances, separate sitting rooms and afford great country views. Complimentary wine and homemade cakes; light suppers available in your room.

LEDBURY – Herefordshire – 503 M27 – pop. 8 491 18 B3

London 119 mi – Hereford 14 mi – Newport 46 mi – Worcester 16 mi

Feathers

High St ✉ HR8 1DS – ✆ (01531) 635 266 – www.feathers-ledbury.co.uk
22 rm ☕ – †£ 100/135 ††£ 150/255 – 3 suites
Rest *Quills* – *(dinner only Friday-Saturday and lunch Sunday)* Carte £ 30/43
Rest *Fuggles* – Menu £ 25 (weekday dinner) – Carte £ 30/41
Modernised 16C black and white timbered coaching inn – a clever blend of old and new. Comfortable bedrooms; Lanark House suites are more contemporary in style. Linen-clad Quills boasts chandeliers; Fuggles is more informal. Modern, seasonally changing menus.

at Trumpet Northwest : 3.25 mi on A 438 – ✉ Ledbury

Verzon House

Hereford Rd ✉ HR8 2PZ – ✆ (01531) 670 381 – www.verzonhouse.com – Closed 2-20 January
8 rm ☕ – †£ 110/130 ††£ 150/205 **Rest** – *(bar lunch)* Carte £ 25/43
Pleasantly restored Georgian manor house with a stylish beamed lounge and bar. Smart, modern bedrooms are named after cider apples; most have countryside views and some have a bath in the room. Contemporary restaurant with a countryside outlook and delightful terrace serves classic, hearty British dishes.

ENGLAND

LEEDS

See city maps on following pages **22** B2

West Yorkshire – **pop. 440 055** – **502** P22 – Great Britain

London 204 mi – Liverpool 75 mi – Manchester 43 mi – Newcastle upon Tyne 95 mi

Tourist Information

City Station, ✆(0113) 242 52 42, www.visitleeds.co.uk

Airport

Leeds-Bradford Airport : ✆ (0113) 250 9696, NW : 8 m. by A 65 and A 658 BT

Golf Courses

36 Temple Newsam, Halton, Temple Newsam Rd, ✆(0113) 264 56 24

18 Gotts Park, Armley, Armley Ridge Rd, ✆(0113) 234 20 19

18 Middleton Park, Middleton, Ring Rd, Beeston Park, ✆(0113) 270 04 49

PRACTICAL INFORMATION

SIGHTS

In the town : City★ • Royal Armouries Museum★★★ GZ • City Art Gallery★ **AC** GY**M**

On the outskirts : Kirkstall Abbey★ **AC**, NW : 3 mi by A 65 GY • Temple Newsam★ **AC**, E : 5 mi by A 64 and A 63 CU**D**

In the surrounding area : Harewood House★★ **AC**, N : 8 mi by A 61 CT • Nostell Priory★, SE : 18 mi by A 61 and A 638 • Yorkshire Sculpture Park★, S : 20 mi by M 1 to junction 38 and 1 mi north off A 637 • Brodsworth Hall★, SE : 25 mi by M 1 to junction 40, A 638 and minor rd (right) in Upton

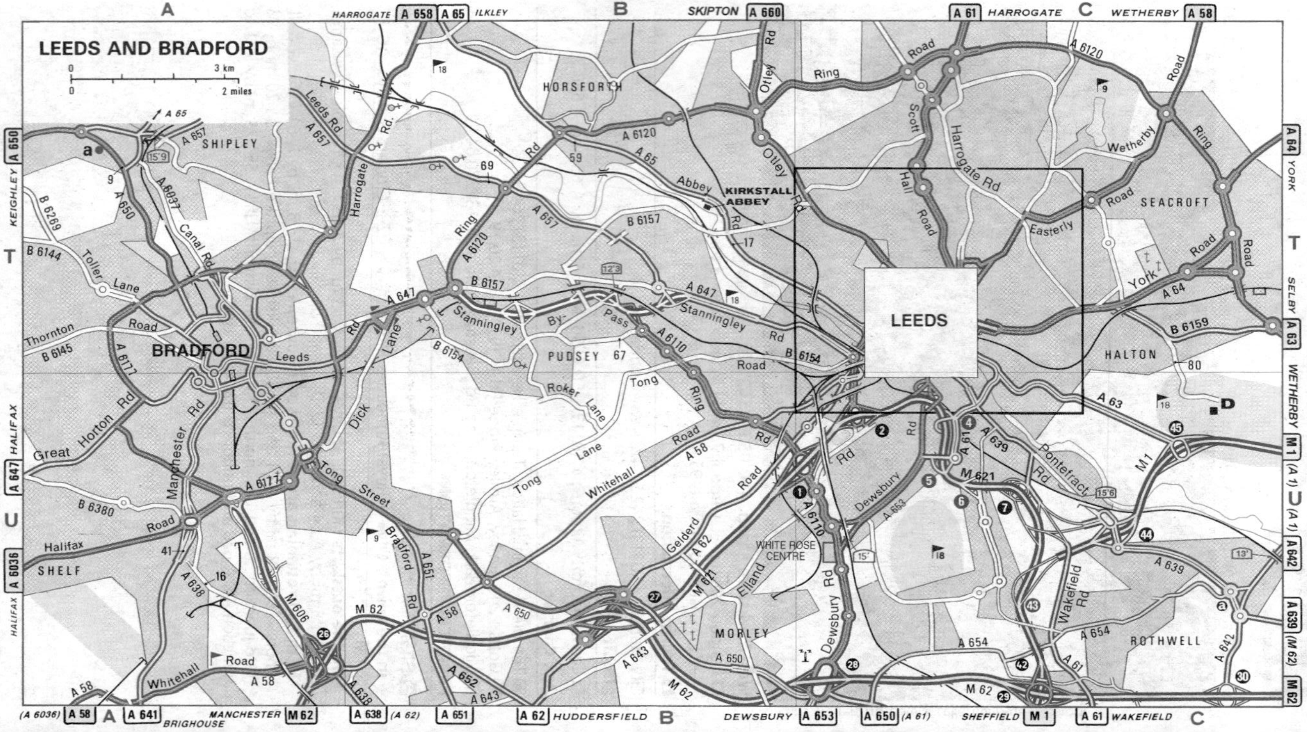
LEEDS AND BRADFORD
0 3 km
0 2 miles
A
B
C
T
U
HARROGATE A 658
A 65 ILKLEY
SKIPTON A 660
A 61 HARROGATE
WETHERBY A 58
A 64 YORK
SELBY A 63
WETHERBY M 1 (A 1)
(A 1) A 642
A 639 (M 62)
M 62
KEIGHLEY A 650
HALIFAX A 647
A 6036 HALIFAX
(A 6036) A 58
A 641 BRIGHOUSE
MANCHESTER M 62
A 638 (A 62)
A 651
A 62 HUDDERSFIELD
DEWSBURY A 653
A 650 (A 61)
SHEFFIELD M 1
A 61 WAKEFIELD
LEEDS
BRADFORD
SHIPLEY
HORSFORTH
KIRKSTALL ABBEY
SEACROFT
HALTON
PUDSEY
MORLEY
ROTHWELL
SHELF
WHITE ROSE CENTRE
Ring Road
Otley Rd
Scott Hall Road
Harrogate Rd
Wetherby Road
Easterly Road
York Road
Abbey Rd
Stanningley Rd
Stanningley By-Pass
Tong Road
Tong Lane
Roker Lane
Whitehall Road
Dewsbury Rd
Pontefract Rd
Wakefield Rd
Elland Road
Gelderd Road
Tong Street
Bradford Rd
Dick Lane
Leeds Rd
Leeds
Canal Rd
Toller Lane
Thornton Road
Great Horton Rd
Manchester Rd
Halifax Road
Harrogate Rd.
Whitehall Road
M 1
M 62
M 621
M 606
A 6120
A 65
A 657
A 647
A 6110
A 6037
A 650
A 6177
A 58
A 61
A 639
A 653
A 654
A 643
A 652
A 651
A 638
A 642
A 64
A 63
A 62
B 6157
B 6154
B 6159
B 6269
B 6144
B 6145
B 6380
a
D

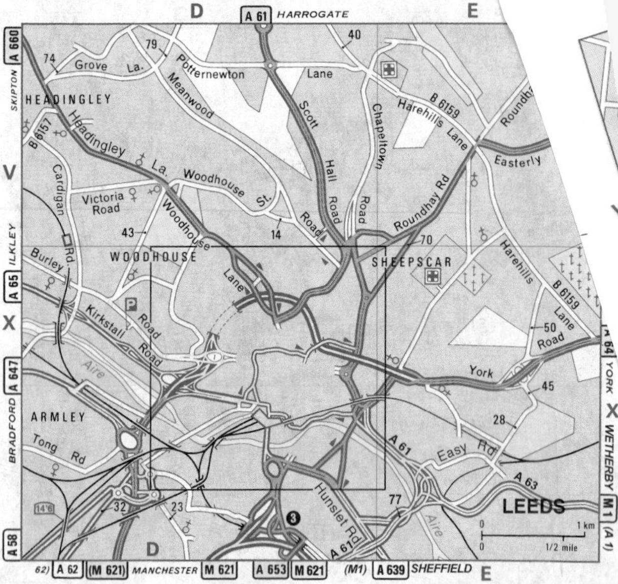

ENGLAND

Malmaison

1 Swinegate ✉ *LS1 4AG – ✆ (0113) 398 10 00 – www.malmaison.com*
100 rm – †£ 139/159 ††£ 139/159, ☕ £ 15 – 1 suite GZ**n**
Rest – Menu £ 16/20 – Carte £ 19/39
Chic, boutique hotel in the former offices of the city's tram and bus department; hence the name of the stylish suite, 'Depot'. Generously sized bedrooms have warm colour schemes and good comforts. Smart, intimate guest areas include a relaxing bar and a modern take on a brasserie.

Doubletree by Hilton

2 Wharf Approach, Granary Wharf ✉ *LS1 4BR – ✆ (0113) 241 10 00 – www.doubletree.com* FZ**c**
333 rm – †£ 69/169 ††£ 69/169, ☕ £ 17 – 6 suites
Rest *City Café* – Carte £ 21/41
Modern business hotel overlooking the canal basin, with photos of the city's industrial landmarks hung on white walls. Well-equipped bedrooms boast iMac TVs and panoramic city views. Relax on the quayside terrace or in the 13th floor sky lounge. The chic restaurant serves modern cuisine.

Quebecs without rest

9 Quebec St ✉ *LS1 2HA – ✆ (0113) 244 89 89 – www.quebecshotel.co.uk – Closed 23-27 December* FZ**a**
43 rm – †£ 70/110 ††£ 80/145, ☕ £ 15 – 2 suites
Interesting 19C building; formerly a Liberal Club. Original features include wood-panelling, an oak staircase and stained glass windows depicting Yorkshire cities. Bedrooms blend the classic with the contemporary and offer good comforts.

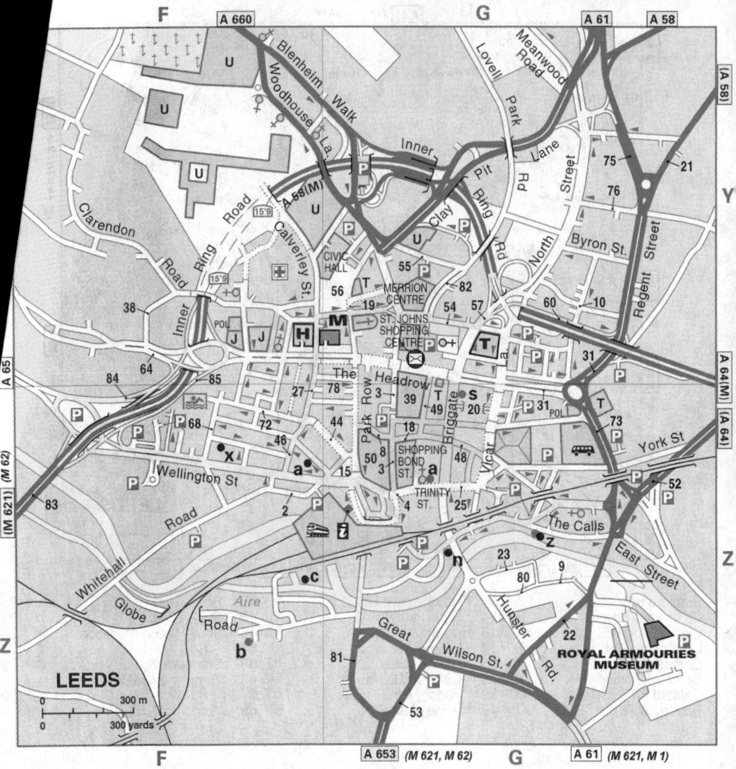

Street	Grid	No.
Aire St.	FZ	2
Albion St	GZ	3
Boar Lane	GZ	4
Bond St	GZ	8
Bowman Lane	GZ	9
Bridge St	GY	10
Briggate	GZ	
City Square	GZ	15
Commercial St	GZ	18
Cookridge St	GY	19
County Arcade	GZ	20
Cross Stamford St	GY	21
Crown Point Rd	GZ	22
Dock St	GZ	23
Duncan St	GZ	25
Eastgate	GZ	31
East Parade	FGZ	27
Hanover Way	FY	38
Headrow Centre	GZ	39
Headrow (The)	GY	
Infirmary St	GZ	44
King St	FZ	46
Kirkgate	GZ	48
Lands Lane	GZ	49
Leeds Shopping Plaza	GZ	50
Marsh Lane	GZ	52
Meadow Lane	GZ	53
Merrion Centre	GY	
Merrion St	GY	54
Merrion Way	GY	55
Millennium Square	GY	56
New Briggate	GY	57
New York Rd	GY	60
Park Lane	FY	64
Queen St	FZ	68
St John's Centre	GY	
St Paul's St	FZ	72
St Peter's St	GZ	73
Sheepscar St South	GY	75
Skinner Lane	GY	76
South Parade	FGZ	78
Trinity St Shopping Centre	GZ	
Victoria Rd	GZ	81
Wade Lane	GY	82
Waterloo St	GZ	80
Wellington Rd	FZ	83
Westgate	FZ	85
West St	FZ	84

New Ellington

23-25a York Pl ✉ *LS1 2EY* – ✆ *(0113) 204 21 50*
– *www.thenewellington.com*
– *Closed 23-27 December* FZ**x**

34 rm – £ 99/150 £ 109/160 – 1 suite
Rest – *(closed Sunday and bank holidays) (dinner only)* Carte £ 27/49

Named after composer and bandleader Duke Ellington, and featuring themed prints and framed sheet music. Classical bedrooms are well-equipped, with fridges, Nespresso machines and numerous audio-visual connections; iPods and games consoles can be borrowed. Basement restaurant offers original modern menus.

42 The Calls

42 The Calls ✉ LS2 7EW – ✆ (0113) 244 00 99 – www.42thecalls.co.uk – Closed 3 days Christmas GZ**z**

38 rm – †£ 75/150 ††£ 85/180, ☕ £ 15 – 3 suites

Rest ***Brasserie Forty 4*** – see restaurant listing

Converted 18C grain mill on the banks of the River Aire. Many of the well-equipped bedrooms display original beams, steel girders or industrial machinery; choose one with a river view. Comprehensive, award-winning breakfasts.

Crafthouse Ⓝ

Trinity Leeds (5th Floor), 70 Boar Ln ✉ LS1 6HW – ✆ (0113) 897 0444 – www.crafthouse-restaurant.co.uk – Closed 25 December GZ**a**

Rest – Menu £ 23 (early dinner) – Carte £ 24/58

Located in the Trinity shopping centre, with a wraparound terrace and rooftop views. It has a dark, moody, masculine feel; the open-plan kitchen and counter take centre stage. Menus offer European classics and meats from the Josper grill.

Fourth Floor at Harvey Nichols

✉ LS1 6AZ – ✆ (0113) 204 80 00 – www.harveynichols.com – Closed 25 December, 1 January, Easter Sunday and dinner Sunday and Monday

Rest – *(booking essential at lunch)* Menu £ 20 – Carte £ 26/65 GZ**s**

Bright, stylish dining room with rooftop views, metal fretwork screens and a Scandic feel; located on the top floor of a chic store. Watch the chefs prepare tasty, modern, globally influenced dishes. Pleasant service is from a smart team.

Angelica Ⓝ

Trinity Leeds (6th Floor), 70 Boar Ln ✉ LS1 6HW – ✆ (0113) 897 0099 – www.angelica-restaurant.co.uk – Closed 25 December GZ**a**

Rest – Carte £ 18/34

Set above its sister 'Crafthouse' and also boasting a terrace and skyline views. A large bar dominates the room and cocktails are a speciality. Cooking is simple, modern and global – sharing plates and seafood from the Raw Bar feature.

Brasserie Forty 4 – 42 The Calls Hotel

44 The Calls ✉ LS2 7EW – ✆ (0113) 234 32 32 – www.brasserie44.com – Closed Sunday and bank holidays GZ**z**

Rest – Menu £ 24 – Carte £ 23/35

Contemporary hotel brasserie and bright, stylish bar in an 18C former warehouse. Tables are spread amongst steel girders; choose one by the window for a river view. Straightforward, up-to-date cooking displays global influences.

Foundry

1 Saw Mill Yard, The Round Foundry ✉ LS11 5WH – ✆ (0113) 245 03 90 – www.thefoundrywinebar.co.uk – Closed first week January, last week August, 25-26 December, Saturday lunch, Sunday and Monday FZ**b**

Rest – Menu £ 13/25 – Carte £ 20/41

Simply styled bistro-cum-wine bar on the site of the legendary steel foundry, with a vaulted ceiling, ornate bar and laid-back feel. Wine box ends and 'squashed' bottles feature. Classic dishes include plenty of specials.

Cross Keys

107 Water Ln, The Round Foundry ✉ LS11 5WD – ✆ (0113) 243 37 11 – www.the-crosskeys.com – Closed 25-26 December and 1 January

Rest – *(booking essential)* Carte £ 22/32 FZ**b**

Traditional brick-built pub: a watering hole for foundry workers in the 19C. Cosy and welcoming with beams, flagged floors and wood-burning stoves. It gets busy, so book ahead. Hearty, straightforward, British cooking; popular Sunday lunch.

LEGBOURNE – Lincolnshire 17 D1

London 151 mi – Kingston upon Hull 48 mi – Nottingham 68 mi – Peterborough 66 mi

XX **Michael Bullamore at The Queens Head** (N)

Station Rd ✉ LN11 8LL – ☎ (01507) 604 803 – www.queensheadlegbourne.co.uk – Closed 2 weeks Christmas-New Year, Monday and Tuesday

Rest – *(booking essential)* Menu £ 30 – Carte £ 20/45

Intimate former pub in a rural setting. Vivid modern wallpaper and bright prints stand out against a lovely original tiled floor. The locally taught chef creates fresh, appealing British dishes and grows herbs and salad in the garden.

LEICESTER – Leicester – 502 Q26 – pop. 300 210 Great Britain 16 B2

London 107 mi – Birmingham 43 mi – Coventry 24 mi – Nottingham 26 mi

East Midlands Airport, Castle Donington : ☎ (0871) 9199000 NW : 22 mi by A 50 - AX - and M 1

51 Gallowtree Gate, ☎ (0844) 888 51 81, www.visitleicester.info

Leicestershire, Evington Lane, ☎ (0116) 273 88 25

Western Park, Scudamore Rd, ☎ (0116) 287 52 11

Humberstone Heights, Gipsy Lane, ☎ (0116) 299 55 70

Guildhall★ BY **B** – Museum and Art Gallery★ CY **M3** – St Mary de Castro Church★ BY **D**

National Space Centre★ N : 2 mi by A 6 - AX - turning east into Corporation Rd and right into Exploration Drive

Plans pages 285, 286

Leicester Marriott

Smith Way, Grove Park, Enderby, Southwest : 4 mi by A 5460 off A 563 at junction 21 of M1 ✉ LE19 1SW – ☎ (0116) 282 01 00 – www.leicestermarriott.co.uk AY**z**

227 rm – †£ 129/149 ††£ 149/159, ☕ £ 16 – 1 suite

Rest *Miix* – *(dinner only and Sunday lunch)* Carte £ 24/36

Purpose-built hotel on a suburban business park. Stylish open-plan guest areas include an atrium lounge and informal café. Uniform bedrooms boast a good level of facilities. Smart executive lounge and excellent leisure club. East meets West in the restaurant; choose from the buffet or an eclectic à la carte.

Belmont

De Montfort St ✉ LE1 7GR – ☎ (0116) 254 47 73 – www.belmonthotel.co.uk – Closed 24-25 December and 1 January CY**c**

75 rm ☕ – †£ 69/99 ††£ 79/119 – 1 suite

Rest *Windows on New Walk* – *(closed Saturday lunch and Sunday dinner)* Menu £ 18 (lunch) – Carte £ 25/39

Friendly, family-run hotel in a city suburb, made up of a collection of houses – each with its own classical style. Spacious guest areas and a contemporary bar. Bedrooms vary in shape and size but all are modern and offer good facilities. Formal restaurant serves classical dishes with a Mediterranean edge.

Hotel Maiyango

13-21 St Nicholas Pl ✉ LE1 4LD – ☎ (0116) 251 88 98 – www.maiyango.com – Closed 25-26 December BY**a**

14 rm ☕ – †£ 90/170 ††£ 90/170 – 1 suite

Rest *Maiyango* – see restaurant listing

Privately owned city centre hotel in a 150 year old shoe factory. Stylish interior with a trendy bar opening onto a terrace overlooking the rooftops. Spacious, individually designed bedrooms boast bespoke wood furniture and a colonial feel.

XX **Chutney Ivy**

41 Halford St ✉ LE1 1TR – ☎ (0116) 251 1889 – www.chutneyivy.com – Closed 25-26 December,1 January, Saturday lunch and Sunday CY**x**

Rest – Menu £ 9 (weekday lunch)/25 – Carte £ 15/33

Keenly run former warehouse with a smart industrial feel; its floor-to-ceiling windows open onto the pavement . Menus mix modern and classic dishes, with influences coming from Hyderabad, Goa and Bengal. Watch the chefs in the open kitchen.

ENGLAND

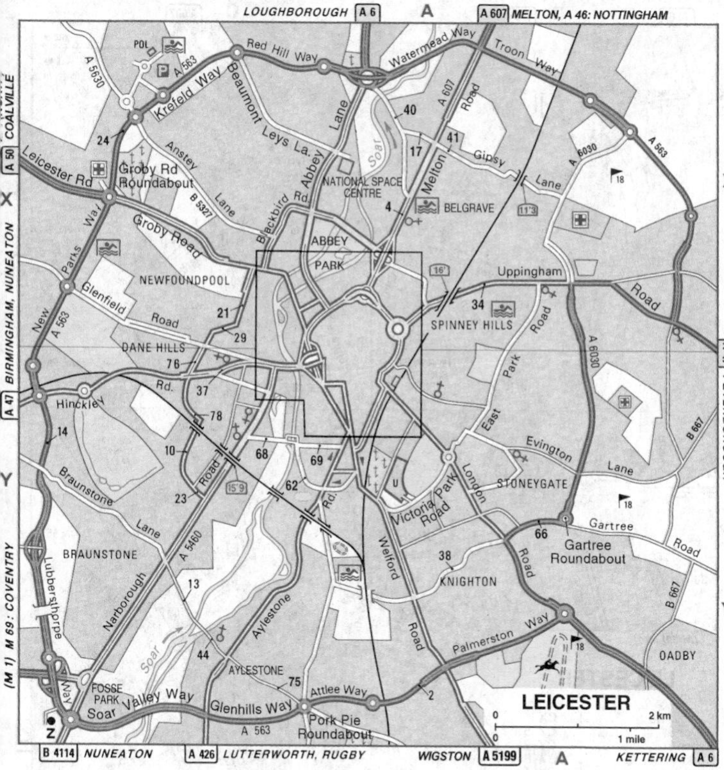

Asquith Way	AY 2	Glenfrith Way	AX 24	Raw Dykes Rd	AY 62
Belgrave Rd	AX 4	Henley Rd	AX 29	Stoughton Rd	AY 66
Braunstone Ave	AY 10	Humberstone Rd	AX 34	Upperton Rd	AY 68
Braunstone Lane East	AY 13	King Richards Rd	AY 37	Walnut St	AY 69
Braunstone Way	AY 14	Knighton Rd	AY 38	Wigston Lane	AY 75
Checketts Rd	AX 17	Loughborough Rd	AX 40	Woodville Rd	AY 76
Fosse Rd North	AX 21	Marfitt St	AX 41	Wyngate Drive	AY 78
Fullhurst Ave	AY 23	Middleton St	AY 44		

XX **Maiyango** – Hotel Maiyango

13-21 St Nicholas Pl ✉ LE1 4LD
– ✆ (0116) 251 88 98 – www.maiyango.com
– Closed 25-26 December and lunch Sunday-Tuesday BY**a**

Rest – Menu £ 20/30

Glass-fronted restaurant in a stylish hotel. Round dark wood booths and silk drapes create an Oriental feel and there's a relaxed, funky vibe. Refined cooking uses local farm and allotment produce, and is Mediterranean and Asian-led.

X **Boot Room**

27-29 Millstone Ln ✉ LE1 5JN – ✆ (0116) 262 25 55
– www.thebootroomeaterie.co.uk
– Closed 2 weeks January, 2 weeks summer, Sunday and Monday BY**x**

Rest – Menu £ 13 (lunch and early dinner)/16
– Carte £ 25/40

Set in an interesting, brick-built former shoe factory; the original cast iron girders and pillars still remain. Simple styling, friendly service and a warm, laid-back feel. Unfussy British cooking with some European and Asian influences.

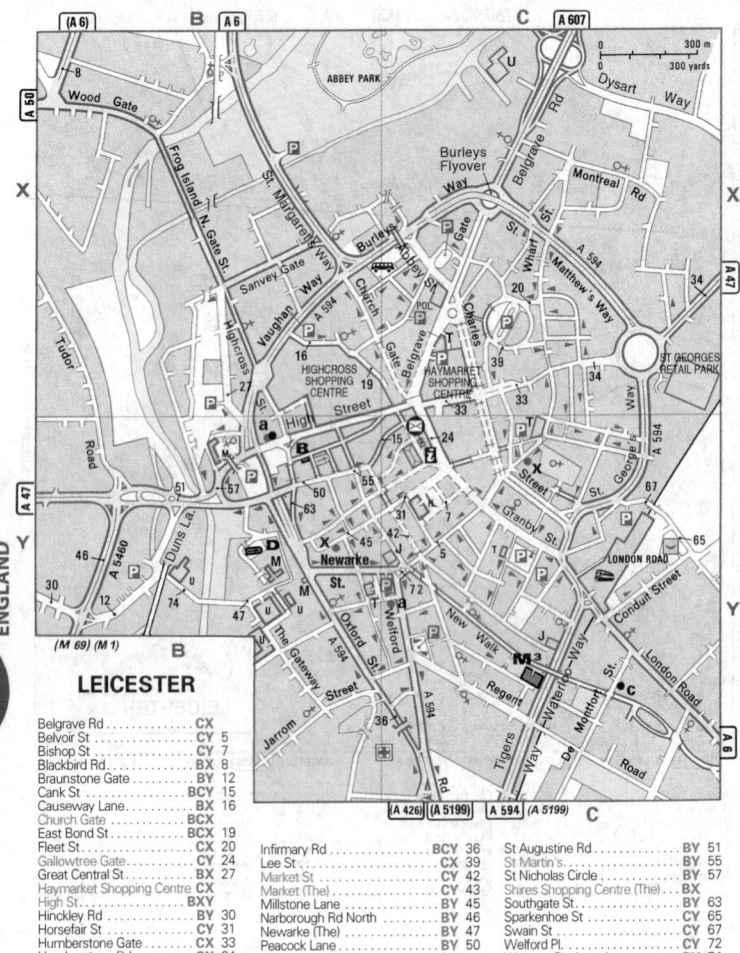

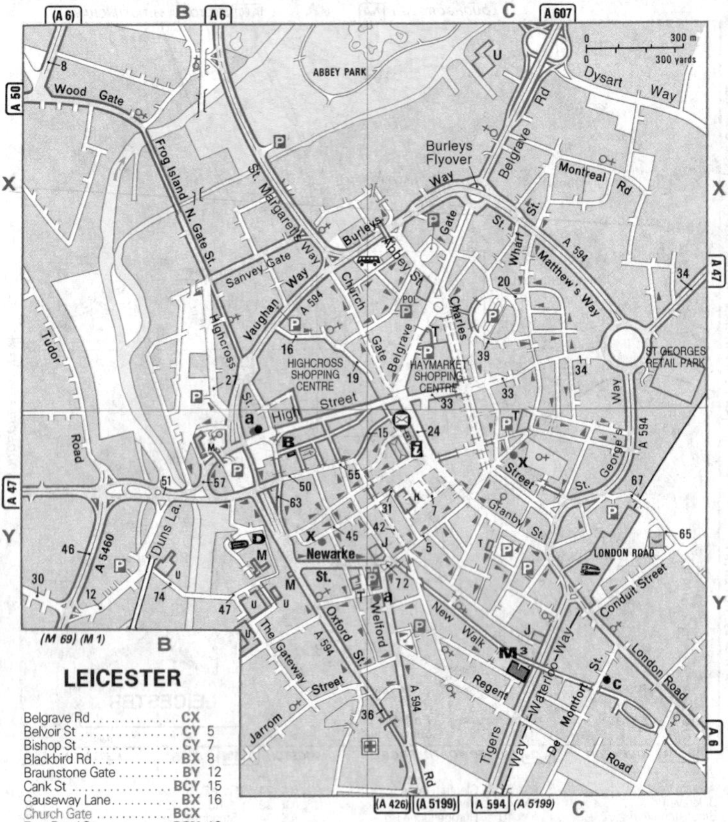

LEICESTER

Shivalli

21 Welford Rd ✉ LE2 7AD – ✆ (0116) 255 01 37 – www.shivallirestaurant.com – Closed 25 December CY**a**

Rest – Carte £ 11/18

Simple, part-panelled restaurant with Indian artefacts on the walls. Appealing South Indian, vegetarian menu with most dishes also suitable for vegans. Tasty, authentic cooking with honest flavours. Good value thalis and buffet lunches.

LEIGH-ON-SEA – Southend-on-Sea – 504 W29 13 C3

London 37 mi – Brighton 85 mi – Dover 86 mi – Ipswich 57 mi

Sandbank

1470 London Rd ✉ SS9 2UR – ✆ (01702) 719 000 – www.sandbankrestaurant.co.uk – Closed Sunday dinner and Monday

Rest – Menu £ 20 (weekdays) – Carte £ 30/39

Former bank in a parade of shops; now a spacious restaurant with a high ceiling, a classic black and white theme and a tropical fish tank in a dramatic feature wall. Wide-ranging menu of well-presented dishes with clear flavours.

LEINTWARDINE – Herefordshire – **503** L26 – ⊠ **Craven Arms** 18 A2

▶ London 156 mi – Birmingham 55 mi – Hereford 24 mi – Worcester 40 mi

XX **Lion** with rm ⛟ 🏠 📶 **P**
⊠ SY7 0JZ – 𝒞 (01547) 540 203 – www.thelionleintwardine.co.uk – Closed 25 December

8 rm ☐ – †£ 75/80 ††£ 100/120 **Rest** – Menu £ 25 – Carte £ 22/35
On the riverside by an attractive medieval bridge and owned by a local mineral water producer. Casual, country style interior with a bar, choice of dining areas, terrace and garden. Classic, satisfying dishes use local produce. Smart, modern bedrooms with good facilities; some have river views.

LEVISHAM – North Yorkshire – **502** R21 – see Pickering

LEWDOWN – Devon – **503** H32 2 C2

▶ London 238 mi – Exeter 37 mi – Plymouth 29 mi

◙ Lydford★★, E : 4 m. Launceston★ - Castle★ (≤★) St Mary Magdalene★, W : 8 mi by A 30 and A 388

🏠 **Lewtrenchard Manor** ⛟ ⛟ 🐾 ⚒ 📶 **P**
South : 0.75 mi by Lewtrenchard rd ⊠ EX20 4PN – 𝒞 (01566) 783 222
– www.lewtrenchard.co.uk

15 rm ☐ – †£ 120/190 ††£ 155/235 – 1 suite
Rest Lewtrenchard Manor – see restaurant listing
Hugely impressive, Grade II listed Jacobean manor house in mature grounds. The characterful, antique-furnished interior features huge fireplaces, ornate oak panelling and intricately designed ceilings. Bedrooms are spacious and well-equipped; those in the coach house are the most contemporary.

XX **Lewtrenchard Manor** – Lewtrenchard Manor Hotel ⛟ 🐾 ⇔ **P**
South : 0.75 mi by Lewtrenchard rd ⊠ EX20 4PN – 𝒞 (01566) 783 222
– www.lewtrenchard.co.uk

Rest – (booking essential) Menu £ 20 (lunch and early dinner)/50
Intimate wood-panelled dining room in a Jacobean manor house. The ambitious, original modern cooking is a surprising contrast to the setting. For a more unique experience book 'Purple Carrot' (the kitchen table) and watch the chefs at work.

LEWES – East Sussex – **504** U31 – **pop. 15 988** ▮ Great Britain 8 A3

▶ London 53 mi – Brighton 8 mi – Hastings 29 mi – Maidstone 43 mi

🅓 187 High St, 𝒞 (01273) 48 34 48, www.enjoysussex.info

🅂 Chapel Hill, 𝒞 (01273) 47 32 45

◙ Town★ (High St★, Keere St★) – Castle (≤★) **AC**

◙ Sheffield Park Garden★ **AC**, N : 9.5 mi by A 275

🏠 **Shelleys** ⛟ 🏠 📶 ⚒ **P**
High St ⊠ BN7 1XS – 𝒞 (01273) 472 361 – www.the-shelleys.co.uk
19 rm ☐ – †£ 110/190 ††£ 130/250 – 1 suite **Rest** – Menu £ 25
Formerly an inn, and before that, a private house dating back to 1577 – owned by the great poet's family. Spacious, classically styled bedrooms include a fourposter and a suite with garden views. The elegant dining room, with its chandeliers and grand proportions, overlooks the lawns.

X **Real Eating Company** 🏠 **AC**
18 Cliffe High St ⊠ BN7 2AJ – 𝒞 (01273) 402 650 – www.real-eating.co.uk
– Closed 25 December and Sunday dinner

Rest – Carte £ 19/33
Light lunches in buzzy atmosphere; more intimate dinners. Fresh, seasonal, local produce cooked in an unfussy style to create honest, tasty dishes, including plenty of British favourites. Fine selection of cakes served during the day.

ENGLAND

at East Chiltington Northwest : 5.5 mi by A 275 and B 2116 off Novington Lane – ✉ Lewes

Jolly Sportsman
Chapel Ln ✉ BN7 3BA – ✆ (01273) 890 400 – www.thejollysportsman.com – Closed 25 December
Rest – *(booking essential)* Menu £ 15/20 – Carte £ 24/39
Grey clapperboard pub that's popular with the locals. Choose from interesting bar bites, good value set menus, a rustic European-based à la carte and blackboard specials; many of the herbs and fruits are from their own polytunnel.

LEYBURN – North Yorkshire – **502** O21 – **pop. 1 844** — **22** B1

London 251 mi – Darlington 25 mi – Kendal 43 mi – Leeds 53 mi

Railway St, ✆ (01748) 82 87 47, www.hello-yorkshire.co.uk

Clyde House without rest
5 Railway St ✉ DL8 5AY – ✆ (01969) 623 941 – www.clydehouse.com – Closed 8-21 January
5 rm – £ 50/60 £ 80/95
18C former coaching inn on the main market square, run by an experienced owner and immaculately kept throughout. Small, cosy sitting room and cottagey breakfast room. Smart, comfortable bedrooms with good quality soft furnishings, hair dryers and bathrobes. Extensive buffet and 'full Yorkshire' breakfasts.

Sandpiper Inn with rm
Market Pl ✉ DL8 5AT – ✆ (01969) 622 206 – www.sandpiperinn.co.uk – Closed Monday
2 rm – £ 75/80 £ 85/90 **Rest** – Carte £ 26/41 **s**
Charming 16C inn just off the square in busy market town. Frequently changing blackboard menus feature fine local produce; simpler dishes and sandwiches at lunchtime. Pleasant bedrooms have a homely feel.

at Constable Burton East : 3.5 mi on A 684 – ✉ Leyburn

Wyvill Arms with rm
✉ DL8 5LH – ✆ (01677) 450 581 – www.thewyvillarms.co.uk – Closed Monday except bank holidays
4 rm – £ 65/85 £ 95/125 **Rest** – Carte £ 21/37 **s**
Intimate, ivy-clad stone pub with pleasant gardens, formerly an 18C farmhouse. Menus offer plenty of choice and feature local, traceable produce in carefully prepared, classical dishes; the tasty mature steaks are a popular choice. Simple, well-kept bedrooms.

LICHFIELD – Staffordshire – **502** O25 – **pop. 28 435** Great Britain — **19** C2

London 128 mi – Birmingham 16 mi – Derby 23 mi

Castle Dyke, ✆ (01543) 41 21 12, www.visitlichfield.co.uk

Lichfield Golf and Country Club, Elmhurst, ✆ (01543) 41 73 33

City★ - Cathedral★★ **AC**

Netherstowe House
Netherstowe Ln, Northeast : 1.75 mi following signs for A 51 and A 38, off Eastern Ave ✉ WS13 6AY – ✆ (01543) 254 270 – www.netherstowehouse.com
15 rm – £ 95/195 £ 95/195 – 8 suites
Rest – Menu £ 20 (weekdays)/35
Rest *Steakhouse Brasserie* – Carte £ 27/40
Extensively restored 19C country house; professionally run by a family team. Period lounges and elegant, luxurious bedrooms come with antique furnishings and original fireplaces; modern apartments with kitchenettes are located in the grounds. The elegant, formal restaurant offers ambitious modern cooking; the atmospheric cellar brasserie specialises in local steaks.

ENGLAND

St Johns House without rest

28 St John St ✉ WS13 6PB – ☎ (01543) 252 080 – www.stjohnshouse.co.uk
9 rm – †£ 70/115 ††£ 115
Impressive Regency townhouse fronted by large columns. Beautiful tiled hallway and a drawing room with ornate cornicing and chandeliers; breakfast is in the old billiard room. Individually styled bedrooms have a modern, understated feel.

Wine House

27 Bird St ✉ WS13 6PW – ☎ (01543) 419 999 – www.thewinehouselichfield.co.uk
Rest – Carte £ 26/51
Smart red-brick restaurant with a loyal local following. There's an open-fired bar at one end and a dining room at the other; it takes its name from the impressive glass wine cellar. Classically based menus have the occasional modern twist.

Chandlers

Corn Exchange, Conduit St ✉ WS13 6JU – ☎ (01543) 416 688 – www.chandlersrestaurant.co.uk – Closed 26 December, 1-4 January and bank holiday Mondays
Rest – Menu £ 15/19 (weekdays) – Carte £ 18/45
Hexagonal building in heart of the city, with spacious, wood-floored restaurant and mezzanine floor for more intimate dining. Menus offer a mix of classic and Mediterranean dishes.

at Wall South : 2.75 mi by A 5127

The Trooper

Watling St ✉ WS14 0AN – ☎ (01543) 480 413 – www.thetrooperwall.co.uk
Rest – Carte £ 25/50
Open fires welcome you into the lounge, where you'll find locals sitting around a central bar; to the rear, an extension leads out onto a huge terrace and garden. Tasty, restaurant-style dishes, supplemented by pub classics at lunch.

LIFTON – Devon – 503 H32 – pop. 964 2 C2

London 238 mi – Bude 24 mi – Exeter 37 mi – Launceston 4 mi
Launceston★ - Castle★ (<★) St Mary Magdalene★, W : 4.5 mi by A 30 and A 388

Arundell Arms

Fore St ✉ PL16 0AA – ☎ (01566) 784 666 – www.arundellarms.com
25 rm – †£ 75/90 ††£ 150/180 **Rest** – Menu £ 23/48 – Carte £ 20/28
Roadside former coaching inn with access to 20 miles of the Tamar River for fishing. Comfortable, characterful bedrooms. Smart bar and restaurant; the latter with views over the garden and terrace. Light lunches available in bar. Classic menus in restaurant.

LINCOLN – Lincolnshire – 502 S24 – pop. 87 065 Great Britain 17 C1

London 140 mi – Bradford 81 mi – Cambridge 94 mi – Kingston-upon-Hull 44 mi
Humberside Airport : ☎ (01652) 688456, N : 32 mi by A 15 - Y - M 180 and A 18
Britain & London Visitor Centre 9 Castle Hill, ☎ (01522) 54 54 58, www.lincolntourism.co.uk
Carholme, Carholme Rd, ☎ (01522) 52 37 25
City★★ - Cathedral and Precincts★★★ **AC** Y – High Bridge★★ Z **9** – Usher Gallery★ **AC** YZ **M1** – Jew's House★ Y – Castle★ **AC** Y
Doddington Hall★ **AC**, W : 6 mi by B 1003 - Z - and B 1190. Gainsborough Old Hall★ **AC**, NW : 19 mi by A 57 - Z - and A 156

Plan on next page

ENGLAND

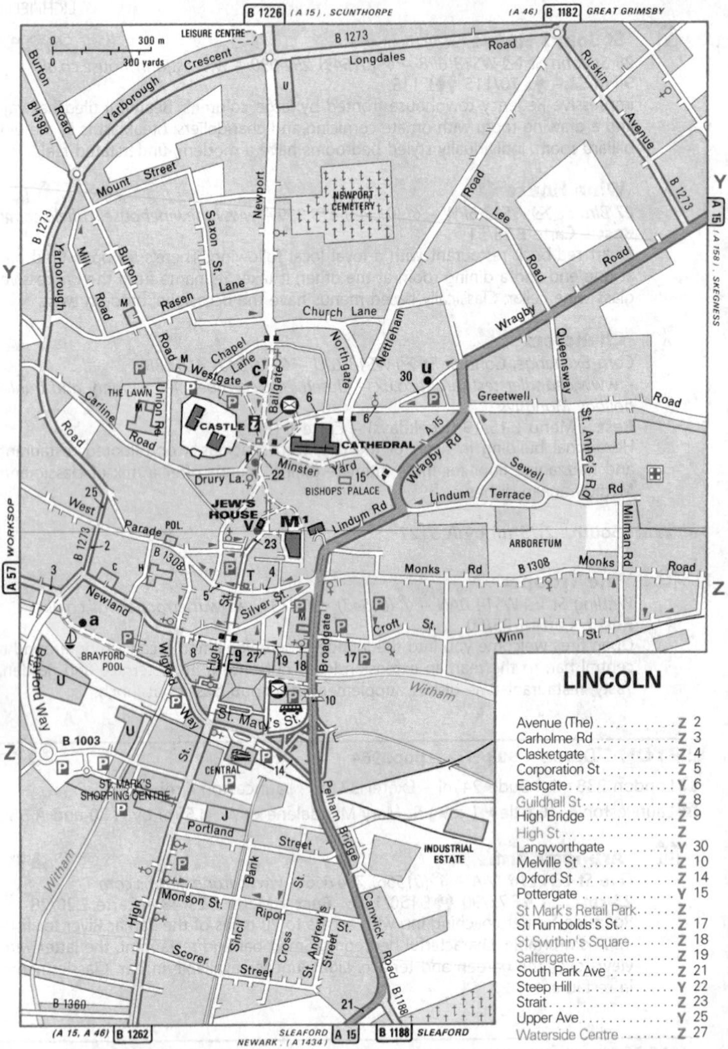

LINCOLN

Doubletree by Hilton Lincoln

Brayford Wharf North ✉ LN1 1YW – ✆ (01522) 565 180 – www.doubletree.com/lincoln **Za**

115 rm – †£ 85/220 ††£ 85/220, ☕ £ 16 – 8 suites

Rest *Electric* – ✆ (01522) 565 182 *(booking advisable)* Menu £ 13 (weekday lunch)/25 – Carte £ 28/50

Modern corporate hotel on the site of the old City of Lincoln Electrical works. Minimalistic bedrooms have sleek, contemporary lines; suites overlook the marina. State-of-the-art conference rooms. Smart brasserie with floor-to-ceiling windows; the modern menu has British influences.

Bail House without rest

34 Bailgate ✉ LN1 3AP – ✆ (01522) 541 000 – www.bailhouse.co.uk

10 rm – †£ 69/99 ††£ 79/109, ☕ £ 10 Yc

Keenly run, part-14C baronial hall with a red-brick Georgian façade and Victorian additions to the rear. Many rooms still have their original wooden beams; one bedroom has an exposed Roman wall and another, a charming brass bedstead. Breakfast is served in the tea rooms next door.

St Clements Lodge without rest

21 Langworthgate ✉ LN2 4AD – ✆ (01522) 521 532 – www.stclementslodge.co.uk

3 rm ☕ – †£ 55 ††£ 70/75 Yu

Cosy, Edwardian-style house close to the cathedral and castle (where you can view the Magna Carta). Cheerful owners offer good old-fashioned hospitality. Spacious, well-equipped bedrooms have pine furnishings and a homely feel.

XX **Jews House**

15 The Strait ✉ LN2 1JD – ✆ (01522) 524 851 – www.jewshouserestaurant.co.uk – Closed 2 weeks January, 2 weeks July, 1 week October, Sunday and Monday

Rest – Carte £ 28/39 Yv

Characterful stone house dating from 1150; reputedly Europe's oldest surviving dwelling. Bold, ambitious dishes display an eclectic mix of influences. Choose from a set menu or tapas at lunch and an à la carte at dinner. Charming service.

Wig & Mitre A/C

30-32 Steep Hill ✉ LN2 1LU – ✆ (01522) 535 190 – www.wigandmitre.com

Rest – Menu £ 14/20 – Carte £ 20/34 Yr

Well-established pub with a cosy bar, period dining rooms and an airy beamed restaurant. Menus offer classical dishes with the odd Mediterranean or Asian influence, alongside daily specials, hearty breakfasts and over 20 wines by the glass.

LISKEARD – Cornwall – 503 G32 – pop. 8 478 1 B2

London 261 mi – Exeter 59 mi – Plymouth 19 mi – Truro 37 mi

Church★

Lanhydrock★★, W : 11.5 mi by A 38 and A 390 – NW : Bodmin Moor★★ - St Endellion Church★★ - Altarnun Church★ - St Breward Church★ - Blisland★ (church★) - Camelford★ – Cardinham Church★ - Michaelstow Church★ - St Kew★ (church★) - St Mabyn Church★ – St Neot★ (Parish Church★★) - St Sidwell's, Laneast★ - St Teath Church★ - St Tudy★ – Launceston★ - Castle★ (<★) St Mary Magdalene★, NE : 19 mi by A 390 and A 388

Pencubitt Country House without rest

Station Rd, South : 0.5 mi by B 3254 on Lamellion rd ✉ PL14 4EB – ✆ (01579) 342 694 – www.pencubitt.com – 6 March-16 November

8 rm ☕ – †£ 60/70 ††£ 85/120

Sympathetically restored Victorian property with delightful views; personally run by charming owners. Comfy bedrooms – Room 3 boasts a balcony and Room 9 features a part-vaulted ceiling and a roll-top bath. The lounge opens onto a veranda.

LISS – Hampshire – 504 R30 – pop. 6 441 7 C2

London 53 mi – Bristol 104 mi – Cardiff 137 mi – Plymouth 184 mi

XX **Madhuban Tandoori** A/C

94 Station Rd ✉ GU33 7AQ – ✆ (01730) 893 363 – www.madhubanrestaurant.co.uk – Closed 25-26 December

Rest – Carte £ 14/25

Smartly furnished restaurant owned by three enthusiastic brothers. The focus is on fresh north Indian dishes; most of which can be prepared to the desired heat (the menu provides a useful glossary of terms). They also sell their sauces.

LITTLE BEDWYN – Wiltshire – 503 P29 – see Marlborough

LITTLE BOLLINGTON – Cheshire East – see Altrincham

LITTLE COXWELL – Oxfordshire 10 A2

London 79 mi – Sheffield 158 mi – Derby 120 mi – York 202 mi

Eagle Tavern with rm

SN7 7LW – (01367) 241 879 – www.eagletavern.co.uk – Closed Sunday dinner and Monday

6 rm – £ 60/80 £ 70/90 **Rest** – Menu £ 22 (dinner) – Carte £ 19/28

Welcoming pub built in 1901 for the farmers of this sleepy hamlet; although it might look slightly different now, a convivial atmosphere still reigns. The self-taught chef cooks the kind of food he himself likes to eat and dishes range from the simple to the complex. Bedrooms are cosy and worth the money.

LITTLE ECCLESTON – Lancashire 20 A2

London 238 mi – Liverpool - 55 mi – Leeds 83 mi – Manchester 51 mi

Cartford Inn with rm

rm,

Cartford Ln PR3 0YP – (01995) 670 166 – www.thecartfordinn.co.uk – Closed 25 December and Monday lunch except bank holidays

14 rm – £ 70/100 £ 100/130 **Rest** – Carte £ 19/39

Tiny 17C coaching inn next to the Pilling Marshes, with a series of cosy little rooms; one overlooking the river. Cooking is in the tried-and-tested vein, offering proper pub classics, with signature dishes under the heading of 'Cartford Favourites'. Choose between quirky or French farmhouse style bedrooms.

ENGLAND

LITTLE LANGFORD – Wiltshire – see Salisbury

LITTLE MARLOW – Buckinghamshire – see Marlow

LITTLE PETHERICK – Cornwall – 503 F32 – see Padstow

LITTLE THETFORD – Cambridgeshire – see Ely

LITTLE WILBRAHAM – Cambridgeshire – see Cambridge

LITTLEHAMPTON – West Sussex – 504 S31 – pop. 55 716 7 C3

London 64 mi – Brighton 18 mi – Portsmouth 31 mi

63-65 Surrey St, (01903) 72 18 66, www.littlehampton.org.uk

Bailiffscourt H. & Spa

Climping St, Climping, West : 2.75 mi by A 259 BN17 5RW – (01903) 723 511 – www.hshotels.co.uk

39 rm (dinner included) – £ 165/480 £ 220/680 **Rest** – Menu £ 19/50

Charming, reconstructed medieval manor in immaculately kept gardens. Bedrooms are split between the main house and the outbuildings; the newer rooms are in the grounds and are more suited to families. Beautiful spa facility. Classic country house cooking served in the formal dining room.

Amberley Court without rest

Crookthorn Ln, Climping, West : 1.75 mi by B 2187 off A 259 BN17 5SN – (01903) 725 131 – Closed mid-December to mid-January

3 rm – £ 55 £ 79/89

Sweet little thatched guesthouse with exposed beams and a homely feel, run by a very welcoming owner. Small breakfast room and open-fired seating area. One of the simple, immaculately kept bedrooms is situated in the grounds.

LIVERPOOL

See city maps on following pages **20** A3

© Yadid Levy/Age fotostock

Merseyside – pop. 449 063 – **502** L23 – **503** L23 – Great Britain

London 219 mi – Birmingham 103 mi – Leeds 75 mi – Manchester 35 mi

Airport

Liverpool John Lennon Airport: ✆ (0871) 521 8484, SE: 6 m. by A 561 BX

Ferries and Shipping Lines

to Birkenhead and Wallasey (Mersey Ferries) frequent services daily.

to Isle of Man (Douglas) (Isle of Man Steam Packet Co. Ltd) 2 daily (2h 30 mn) - to Dublin (P & O Irish Sea) 1-2 daily (8h).

Tunnel

Mersey Tunnels (toll) AX

Golf Courses

Allerton Municipal, Allerton Rd, ✆(0151) 428 10 46

Liverpool Municipal, Kirby, Ingoe Lane, ✆(0151) 546 54 35

Tourist Information

Anchor Courtyard, Albert Dock, ✉ L3 4BS, ✆(0151) 233 20 08, www.visitliverpool.com

SIGHTS

In the town : City★ • The Walker★★ DY**M3** • Liverpool Cathedral★★ EZ • Metropolitan Cathedral of Christ the King★★EY • Albert Dock★CZ

In the surrounding area : Speke Hall★ AC, SE : 8 mi by A 561 BX

ENGLAND

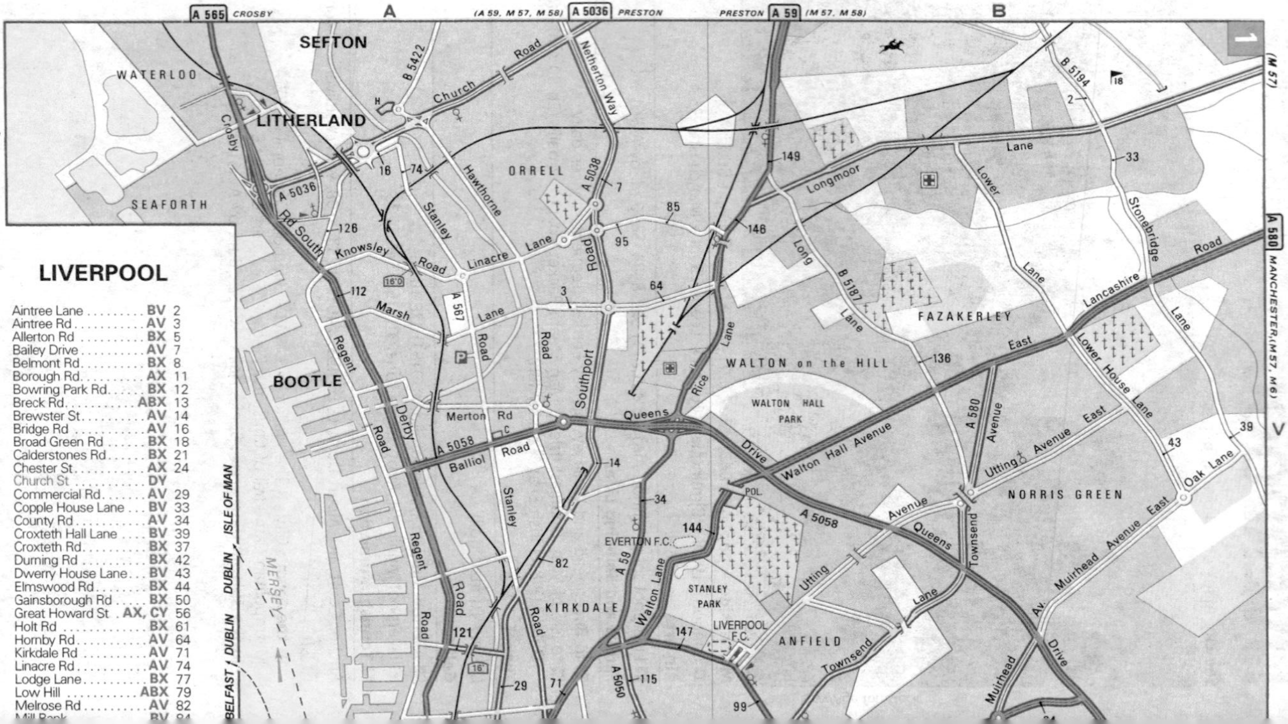

A 565 CROSBY
A
(A 59, M 57, M 58) A 5036 PRESTON
PRESTON A 59 (M 57, M 58)
B
1
(M 57)
A 580 MANCHESTER,(M 57, M 6)
SEFTON
WATERLOO
LITHERLAND
SEAFORTH
ORRELL
BOOTLE
FAZAKERLEY
WALTON on the HILL
WALTON HALL PARK
NORRIS GREEN
KIRKDALE
STANLEY PARK
EVERTON F.C.
LIVERPOOL F.C.
ANFIELD
MERSEY
ISLE OF MAN
DUBLIN
BELFAST
Netherton Way
Church Road
B 5422
Crosby
A 5036
Rd South
Knowsley Road
Stanley
Hawthorne
Linacre Lane
Marsh Lane
A 567
Regent Road
Derby Road
Merton Rd
A 5038
Southport Road
Queens Drive
A 5058
Balliol Road
Stanley Road
A 59
Walton Lane
Rice Lane
Long Lane
B 5187
Longmoor Lane
Lower Lane
Stonebridge Lane
B 5194
Lancashire Road
East Lancashire Road
Lower House Lane
Walton Hall Avenue
A 580
Utting Avenue
Utting Avenue East
Townsend Avenue
Townsend Lane
Queens Drive
Muirhead Avenue
Muirhead Avenue East
Oak Lane
A 5050
POL.

LIVERPOOL

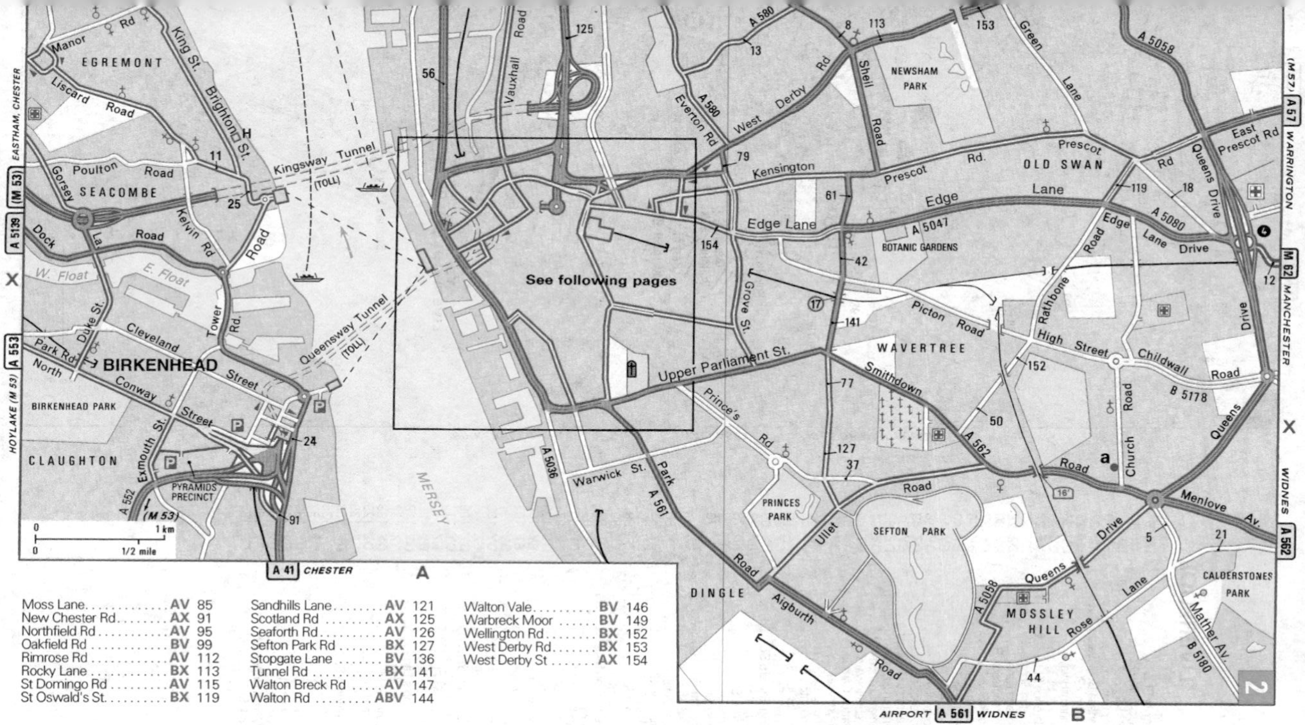

Moss Lane	AV	85	Sandhills Lane	AV	121	Walton Vale	BV	146
New Chester Rd	AX	91	Scotland Rd	AX	125	Warbreck Moor	BV	149
Northfield Rd	AV	95	Seaforth Rd	AV	126	Wellington Rd	BX	152
Oakfield Rd	BV	99	Sefton Park Rd	BX	127	West Derby Rd	BX	153
Rimrose Rd	AV	112	Stopgate Lane	BV	136	West Derby St	AX	154
Rocky Lane	BX	113	Tunnel Rd	BX	141			
St Domingo Rd	AV	115	Walton Breck Rd	AV	147			
St Oswald's St	BX	119	Walton Rd	ABV	144			

LIVERPOOL

Argyle St . . . . DZ 6
Blackburne Pl. . . . . EZ 10
Bold St. . . . . DZ
Brunswick Rd . . . . EY 19
Canada Boulevard . . . . CYZ 22
Canning Pl. . . . . CZ 23
Churchill Way . . . . DY 26
Church St . . . . DY
Clarence St. . . . . EYZ 27
Clayton Square Shopping Centre DY
College Lane. . . . . DZ 28
Commutation Row . . . . DY 30
Cook St . . . . CY 32
Crosshall St. . . . . DY 36
Daulby St. EY 40
Erskine St . . . . EY 45
Fontenoy St . . . . DY 48
Forrest St . . . . DZ 49
George's Dock Lane . . . . CY 51
Grafton St . . . . DZ 53
Great Charlotte St . . . . DY 54
Great Howard St . . . . CY 56
Hatton Garden . . . . DY 57
Haymarket . . . . DY 58
Hood St. . . . . DY 62
Houghton St. . . . . DY 65
Huskisson St. . . . . EZ 66
James St. CY 68
King Edward St. . . . . CY 69
Knight St . . . . EZ 72
Leece St . . . . EZ 73
Lime St . . . . DY
Liver St . . . . CZ 76
London Rd . . . . DEY
Lord St . . . . CDY
Mansfield St. . . . . DEY 80
Mathew St. . . . . CDY 81
Moss St . . . . EY 86
Mount St . . . . EZ 88
Myrtle St . . . . EZ 89
Newington St . . . . DZ 92
New Quay. CY 93
North John St . . . . CY 96
Norton St. EY 97
Parker St . . . . DY 103
Prescot St . . . . EY 105
Prince's Rd . . . . EZ 107
Queen Square . . . . DY
Ranelagh St . . . . DY 108
Renshaw St . . . . DEZ
Richmond St. . . . . DY 109
Roe St . . . . DY 114
St James Pl. . . . . EZ 117
St John's Centre. . . . . DY
St John's Lane . . . . DY 118
School Lane . . . . DYZ 122
Scotland Pl. . . . . DY 123
Sefton St. DZ 129
Seymour St. . . . . EY 130
Skelhorne St. . . . . DY 133
Stanley St. . . . . CDY 135
Suffolk St. . . . . DZ 137
Tarleton St. . . . . DY 139
Victoria St . . . . DY 143
Water St . . . . CY 150
William Brown St. . . . . DY 156
York St. . . . . DZ 157

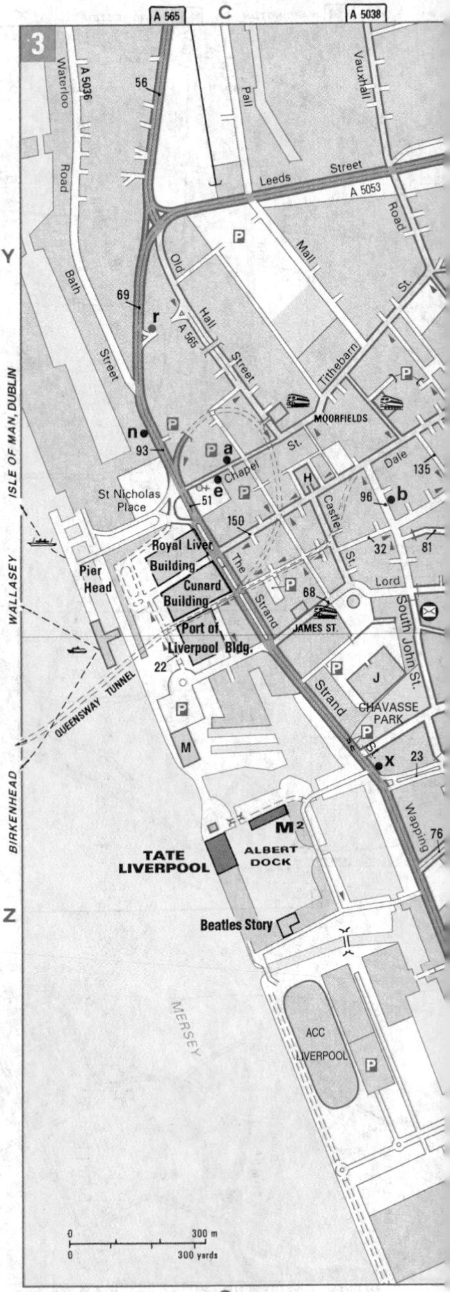

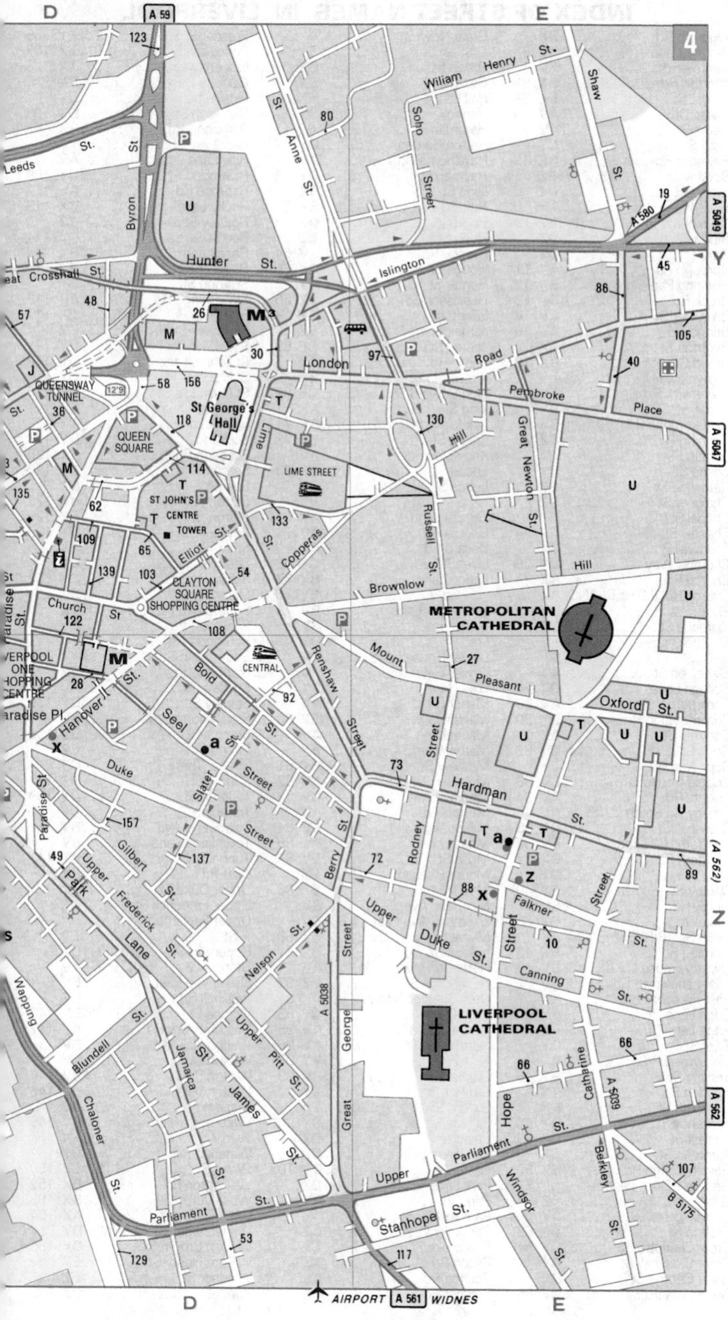
D
A 59
E
4
123
Leeds
St.
St
Byron
U
Hunter
St.
Crosshall
St.
48
57
26
M³
M
J
QUEENSWAY TUNNEL
58
156
30
St George's Hall
36
QUEEN SQUARE
118
114
T
ST JOHN'S CENTRE
TOWER
135
62
109
65
Elliot
St.
54
139
103
CLAYTON SQUARE SHOPPING CENTRE
Church
St
122
108
LIVERPOOL ONE SHOPPING CENTRE
28
Hanover
St.
Paradise Pl.
Paradise St
X
Duke
Bold
Seel
Slater
St.
a
Street
CENTRAL
92
157
Gilbert
St.
137
49
Upper
Frederick
Park
Lane
Wapping
Blundell
St.
Chaloner
Jamaica
St.
James
St.
Nelson
Upper
Pitt
St.
Parliament
129
53
Anne
St.
80
Islington
London
97
Road
Lime
LIME STREET
133
Copperas
Russell
St.
130
Hill
Brownlow
Renshaw
Street
Berry
St.
Mount
27
Pleasant
U
Street
73
Hardman
Rodney
Street
72
88
X
Upper
Duke
St.
Falkner
10
St.
Street
Canning
St.
T
a
Z
A 5038
George
Great
LIVERPOOL CATHEDRAL
66
Hope
Catharine
A 5039
Parliament
St.
Upper
Stanhope
St.
Windsor
St.
117
Berkley
St.
107
B 5175
Soho
Street
William
Henry
St.
Shaw
St.
19
A 580
A 5049
45
Y
86
105
40
Pembroke
Place
Great
Newton
St.
A 5047
Hill
METROPOLITAN CATHEDRAL
Oxford
St.
St.
89
(A 562)
N
A 562
AIRPORT
A 561
WIDNES

ENGLAND

INDEX OF STREET NAMES IN LIVERPOOL

ENGLAND

Hilton
3 Thomas Steers Way ✉ L1 8LW – ✆ (0151) 708 42 00
– www.hilton.co.uk/liverpool **Plan 3** CZ**x**
215 rm – †£ 69/295 ††£ 89/325, ☕ £ 15 – 11 suites
Rest *Exchange* – Menu £ 15/35 – Carte £ 22/48
Spacious, light-filled hotel in a waterfront location, with the latest in modern styling and facilities. Floor to ceiling windows in the bedrooms. Trendy cocktail bar, good conference facilities and a well-equipped gym. Accessible menu of international dishes in Exchange.

Malmaison
rm,
7 William Jessop Way, Princes Dock ✉ L3 1QZ – ✆ (0151) 229 50 00
– www.malmaison.com **Plan 3** CY**n**
130 rm ☕ – †£ 89/225 ††£ 99/250 – 2 suites
Rest *Brasserie* – *(closed Saturday lunch)* Menu £ 16 (dinner) – Carte £ 24/55
Contemporary hotel with a striking stone and black glass façade, overlooking the marina. Chic bedrooms are decorated in sensuous purple or orange tones and boast sunken baths; two are football-themed suites. Sexy, sophisticated bar and an industrial-style brasserie with pop art and a stylish chef's table.

Hope Street
40 Hope St ✉ L1 9DA – ✆ (0151) 709 30 00 – www.hopestreethotel.co.uk
89 rm – †£ 76/680 ††£ 76/680, ☕ £ 17 **Plan 4** EZ**a**
Rest *London Carriage Works* – see restaurant listing
Minimalist, boutique hotel in two interlinking buildings: bedrooms in the former carriage works have a slightly rustic edge, while those in the old police station are more modern. The top floor suites offer stunning city skyline views.

Hard Days Night
rm,
Central Buildings, North John St ✉ L2 6RR – ✆ (0151) 236 19 64
– www.harddaysnighthotel.com – Closed 23-26 December **Plan 3** CY**b**
108 rm – †£ 90/275 ††£ 100/285, ☕ £ 16 – 2 suites
Rest *Blakes* – Menu £ 14 (lunch and early dinner) **s** – Carte dinner £ 28/53 **s**
Unique Beatles themed hotel – their story recounted in artwork from doorstep to rooftop – with contemporary bedrooms featuring original works, and suites styled around Lennon and McCartney. Blakes, named after the designer of the Sgt. Pepper album cover, features a modern brasserie menu.

Hotel Indigo
rm, rm,
10 Chapel St ✉ L3 9AG – ✆ (0151) 559 0111 – www.hotelindigoliverpool.com
151 rm – †£ 60/169 ††£ 60/169, ☕ £ 14 **Plan 3** CY**a**
Rest *Marco Pierre White Steakhouse Bar & Grill* – ✆ (0151) 559 0555 *(closed Saturday lunch)* Menu £ 13/20 – Carte £ 26/47
Smart, modern hotel on the site of a former cotton trading hall and seaman's mission; characterised by its use of vibrant colours. Compact bedrooms have powerful walk-in showers. Staff are smart and cheery. All-day snacks in Cotton Lounge; classic dishes in brightly decorated restaurant.

Hampton by Hilton without rest
Kings Dock Mill, 7 Hurst St ✉ L1 8DA – ✆ (0151) 702 6200
– www.hamptoninn3.hilton.com **Plan 4** DZ**s**
151 rm ☕ – †£ 55/179 ††£ 55/179
Smart, well-priced hotel, a 10min walk from the city centre, offering good modern comforts. It's worth paying a little extra for the 6th floor rooms, which have great views across the river. Buffet breakfasts. Hands-on staff.

base2stay without rest
29 Seel St ✉ L1 4AU – ✆ (0151) 705 2626 – www.base2stay.com **Plan 4** DZ**a**
106 rm – †£ 49/159 ††£ 59/169, ☕ £ 6
Something a little different, this converted 19C mill has rooms ranging from small singles to spacious duplex suites; one with a decked courtyard. All have modern bathrooms and a kitchenette. Pre-order breakfast to be delivered to your room.

ENGLAND

Racquet Club
rest,

Hargreaves Buildings, 5 Chapel St ✉ L3 9AG – ✆ (0151) 236 66 76 – www.racquetclub.org – Closed first week January, 25 December and bank holidays **Plan 3** CY**e**

8 rm – †£ 60/100 ††£ 60/100, ☕ £ 12

Rest ***Ziba*** – *(closed Saturday lunch and Sunday)* Carte £ 22/36 **s**

Ornate Victorian building, formerly a Shipping Agency office and then a gentleman's club, boasting a grand façade and a bohemian style. Bedrooms differ greatly in both layout and décor but most feature antique furniture and eclectic art. Airy restaurant; wide-ranging menu of British dishes.

Panoramic 34

West Tower (34th floor), Brook St ✉ L3 9PJ – ✆ (0151) 236 55 34 – www.panoramic34.com – Closed 25-26 December, 1 January and Monday

Rest – Menu £ 25 (lunch) – Carte £ 30/43 **Plan 3** CY**r**

On the 34th floor of city's highest building, a stylish glass skyscraper with 360° views. Clothed tables, formal service and intimate dinners. Creative, ambitious cooking; excellent value lunch menu.

London Carriage Works – Hope Street Hotel

40 Hope St ✉ L1 9DA – ✆ (0151) 705 22 22 – www.thelondoncarriageworks.co.uk **Plan 4** EZ**a**

Rest – Menu £ 15 (lunch and early dinner) – Carte £ 26/57

Start with a drink in the hotel's lounge-bar, then head to the spacious modern restaurant divided by large shards of glass. The set menu represents the best value, while the à la carte steps things up a gear; both rely on local produce.

60 Hope Street

60 Hope St ✉ L1 9BZ – ✆ (0151) 707 60 60 – www.60hopestreet.com – Closed 26 December, 1 January, Saturday lunch and Sunday dinner **Plan 4** EZ**x**

Rest – Menu £ 25 – Carte £ 29/54

Attractive Grade II listed Georgian house concealing a well-established modern brasserie with bold feature walls and an informal basement wine bar. Interesting regional dishes provide good value.

Spire

1 Church Rd ✉ L15 9EA – ✆ (0151) 734 50 40 – www.spirerestaurant.co.uk – Closed 1-7 January and lunch Saturday-Monday **Plan 2** BX**a**

Rest – Menu £ 15 (weekday lunch) – Carte £ 26/41

Simple neighbourhood restaurant set in the Penny Lane area of the city. Good value, understated menus offer regional and modern European dishes. Flavoursome cooking and friendly service.

Hanover Street Social

Casartelli Building, 16-20 Hanover St ✉ L1 4AA – ✆ (0151) 709 87 84 – www.hanoverstreetsocial.co.uk – Closed 25 December **Plan 4** DZ**x**

Rest – Menu £ 13 (lunch) – Carte £ 20/31

Lively restaurant near the old docks, with a smart, rustic interior featuring a metal-topped cocktail bar and exposed bricks and air ducts. All-day menus offer something for everyone, from small plates and grills to charcuterie and oysters.

Host

31 Hope St ✉ L1 9HX – ✆ (0151) 708 58 31 – www.ho-st.co.uk – Closed 25-26 December **Plan 4** EZ**z**

Rest – Carte £ 20/28

Lively place with a trendy bar and an informal dining area of refectory-style tables. Wide range of Asian-inspired dishes, including Chinese, Japanese, Thai and Vietnamese. Good desserts.

LIZARD – Cornwall – 503 E34
1 A3

London 326 mi – Penzance 24 mi – Truro 29 mi

Lizard Peninsula★ - Mullion Cove★★ (Church★) - Kynance Cove★★ - Cadgwith★ - Coverack★ – Cury★ (Church★) - Gunwalloe Fishing Cove★ - St Keverne (Church★) - Landewednack★ (Church★) – Mawgan-in-Meneage (Church★) - Ruan Minor (Church★) - St Anthony-in-Meneage★

Landewednack House

Church Cove, East : 1 mi by A 3083 ✉ *TR12 7PQ* – *(01326) 290 877*
– *www.landewednackhouse.com*
5 rm – £ 110/190 £ 110/190 **Rest** – Menu £ 38 **s**
Charming, part-17C rectory overlooking Church Cove. Elegant, antique-furnished drawing room. Bedrooms are a mix of shapes and styles but all have a floral theme, a decanter of sherry and sweets. Lovely open-fired dining room with a communal table and cut crystal glassware; menus are discussed with residents. Tea and cake served on arrival.

LOCKERLEY – 503 P30 – pop. 827

6 A2

London 82 mi – Bristol 66 mi – Cardiff 108 mi – Plymouth 146 mi

Kings Arms

Romsey Rd ✉ *SO51 OJF* – *(01794) 340 332* – *www.kingsarmslockerley.co.uk*
Rest – Carte £ 19/32
Cosy, friendly, simply styled pub; its garden has funky wooden pods with heating, lighting and iPod docks. Food-wise they keep things simple and dishes are tasty, hearty and cooked with care; plenty of game in winter.

ENGLAND

LONDON

See city maps on following pages **12** B3

© SIME/Dutton Colin/Simeone/Photononstop

– Great Britain

Tourist Information

Black Rd, ✆(020) 8846 90 00, www.visitlondon.com

Airports

- **Heathrow** ✆ 0844 335 1801 **12** AX Terminal: Bus and Coach services run regularly, each day from Victoria. By Rail: Heathrow Express and Connect from Paddington Underground, daily every 15 minutes.
- **Gatwick** ✆ 0844 335 1802 **13**: by A23 EZ and M23 - Terminal: Coach services from Victoria Coach Station run regularly each day. By Rail: Gatwick Express from Victoria Underground, daily every 15 minutes. Southern Trains every 15 minutes from Victoria, London Bridge and Clapham Junction
- **London City Airport** ✆ (020) 7646 0088 **11** HV
- **Stansted**, at Bishop's Stortford ✆ 0844 335 1803, NE: 34m **11** by M11 JT and A12O.

British Airways, Ticket sales and reservations, Paddington Station London, W2, ✆08700 8509 8500 **36** BX

Medical Emergencies

To contact a doctor for first aid, emergency medical advice and chemists night service: ✆ 07000 372255.

Accident & Emergency: dial 999 for Ambulance, Police or Fire Services.

Shopping

Most stores are found in Oxford Street (Selfridges, M & S), Regent Street (Hamleys, Libertys) and Knightsbridge (Harrods, Harvey Nichols). Open usually Monday to Saturday 9 am to 6 pm. Some open later (8 pm) once a week; Knightsbridge Wednesday, Oxford Street and Regent Street Thursday. Other areas worth visiting include Jermyn Street and Savile Row (mens outfitters), Bond Street (jewellers and haute couture).

Theatres

The "West End" has many major theatre performances and can generally be found around Shaftesbury Avenue. A half-price ticket booth is located in Leicester Square and is open Monday to Saturday 1 pm to 6.30 pm, Sunday and matinée days 12 noon to 6.30 pm. Restrictions apply.

Tipping

When a service charge is included in a bill it is not necessary to tip extra. If service is not included a discretionary 10% is normal.

LONDON

Travel

As driving in London is difficult, it is advisable to take the Underground, a bus or taxi. Taxis can be hailed when the amber light is illuminated.

Congestion Charging

The congestion charge is £ 10 per day on all vehicles (except motor cycles and exempt vehicles) entering the central zone between 7.00 am and 6.00 pm - Monday to Friday except on Bank Holidays.

Payment can be made in advance, on the day, by post, on the Internet, by telephone (0845 900 1234) or at retail outlets.

A charge of up to £ 100 will be made for non-payment.

Further information is available on the Transport for London website - www.tfl.gov.uk

Localities outside the Greater London limits are listed alphabetically throughout the guide.

☉ SIGHTS

Historical Buildings and Monuments

Palace of Westminster★★★39ALX • Tower of London★★★ • London Eye★★★❄ 32 AMV •Banqueting House★★ 31ALV • Buckingham Palace★★ 38AIX • Kensington Palace★★ 27ABV • Lincoln's Inn★★ 32AMT • Lloyds Building★★ 34ARU • Royal Hospital Chelsea★★ 37AGZ • St James's Palace★★ 30AJV • Somerset House★★ 32AMU • South Bank Arts Centre★★ 32AMV • Spencer House★★ 30AIV • The Temple★★ 32ANU • Tower Bridge★★ 34ASV • Albert Memorial★• Gray's Inn★ 32AMV • Guildhall★ 33AQT • Shakespeare's Globe★ 33APV• London Bridge★ 34ARV • Mansion House★ 33AQV • The Monument★❄ 34ARU • Old Admiralty★ 31AKV • Royal Albert Hall★ 36ADX • Royal Exchange★ 34ARU • Royal Opera House★ 31ALU • Theatre Royal★ 31AKV

Churches in the City

St Paul's Cathedral★★★≼ 33APU •St Bartholomew the Great★★ 33APT • Temple Church★★ 32ANU • All Hallows-by-the-Tower★ 34ARU • St Giles Cripplegate★ 33AQT • St Helen Bishopgate★ 34ART

Other Churches

Westminster Abbey★★★ 39ALX • Southwark Cathedral★★ 33AQV • Queens Chapel★ 39AJV • St James's★ 30AJV • St Margaret's★ 39ALX • St Martin-in-the-Fields★ 31ALV

Parks

Regent's Park★★★ 11QZC • Hyde Park★ 29AFV • Kensington Gardens★★ 28 ACV • St James's Park★★31AKV

Streets and Squares

The City★★★ 33AQT •Burlington Arcade★ 30 AIV • Covent Garden★★ 31ALU • The Mall★★ 31AKV • Piccadilly★ 30AIV - Trafalgar Square★★ 31AKV • Whitehall★★ 31 ALV• Bond Street★ 30 AIU• Jermyn Street★ 30AJV • Leicester Square★ 31AKU • Piccadilly Circus★ 31AJU • Shepherd Market★ 30AHV • Victoria Embankment Gardens★ 31ALV

Museums

British Museum★★★ 31AKL • Imperial War Museum★★★ 40ANY • National Gallery★★★ 31AKV • Science Museum★★★ 36ADX • Tate Britain★★★ 39ALY • Victoria and Albert Museum★★★ 36ADY • Wallace Collection★★★ 29AGT • Somerset House★★ 32AMU • Museum of London★★ 33APT • National Portrait Gallery★★ 31AKU • Natural History Museum★★ 36ADY • Sir John Soane's Museum★★ 32AMT • Tate Modern★★≼ 33APV• Madame Tussaud's Waxworks★ 17QZD

Outer London

Brentford 5BX Syon Park★★

Chiswick 6CV Chiswick Mall★★• Chiswick House★ **D** • Hogarth's House★ **E**

Greenwich 7 and 8 GHV Cutty Sark★★ GV**F** •National Maritime Museum★★ GV**M²** • Royal Naval College★★ GV**G** • The Park and Old Royal Observatory★ HV**K**

Hampstead Kenwood House★★ 2 EU**P** •Fenton House★★ 11PZA

Kew 6 CX Royal Botanic Gardens★★★

Kingston upon Thames 5BY Hampton Court Palace★★★

Hendon★ 2 Royal Air Force Museum★★ CT**M³**

Hounslow 5BV Osterley Park★★

Richmond 5 and 6 CX Richmond Park★★❄CX •Ham House★★ BX**V**

Twickenham 5BX Marble Hill House★ **Z** • Strawberry Hill★ **A**

The maps in this section of the Guide are based upon the Ordnance Survey of Great Britain with the permission of the Controller of Her Majesty's Stationery Office. © Crown Copyright 100000247

Alphabetical index of hotels

LONDON

10 Alphabetical index of restaurants

LONDON

LONDON

LONDON

LONDON

Starred Restaurants

Bib Gourmand

Good food at moderate prices

Particularly pleasant hotels

Particularly pleasant restaurants

Restaurants by cuisine type

Greek

Indian

Israeli

Italian

Peruvian

Spanish

Thai

Turkish

Vietnamese

Fish and seafood

Innovative

Meats and grills

LONDON

Other world kitchens

Outside dining

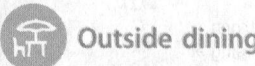

Restaurants open late

Time of last orders in brackets

Amaya (23.30)	XXX ✿	442
Automat (23.45)	X	454
Bentley's (Oyster Bar) (23.30)	X	453
Boisdale of Belgravia (23.30)	XX	480
Boqueria (23.30)	X	423
Brasserie Max (23.30)	XX	383
Brasserie Zédel (00.00)	XX ☺	467
Capote y Toros (23.15)	X	421
Le Caprice (00.00)	XX	463
Cecconi's (23.15)	XXX	449
Ceviche (23.30)	X	471
Chicken Shop (00.00)	X	386
China Tang (23.45)	XXXX	447
Chutney Mary (23.30)	XXX	410
Colbert (23.30)	XX	412
Daphne's (23.30)	XX	411
Dean Street Townhouse Restaurant (23.45)	XX	467
Duck and Waffle (00.00)	XX	391
Eleven Park Walk (23.45)	XXX	410
Floridita (23.30)	XX	467
Hakkasan Hanway Place (00.00)	XX ✿	383
Hakkasan Mayfair (23.30)	XX ✿	451
Haozhan (02.00)	XX	468
Imperial China (23.30)	XXX	466
The Ivy (00.00)	XXX	473
J. Sheekey (00.00)	XX	474
J. Sheekey Oyster Bar (00.00)	X	475
Malabar (23.30)	XX	417
Master and Servant (23.30)	X	395
Momo (23.30)	XX	450
Mr Chow (23.30)	XX	444
Nobu (02.15)	XX ✿	452
Nobu Berkeley St (00.00)	XX ✿	451
Paramount (23.15)	X	384
Plum + Spilt Milk (23.30)	XX	422
Plum Valley (23.15)	XX	467
Poissonnerie (23.30)	XX	411
Refuel (00.00)	XX	468
Roka (23.15)	XX	383
Roka Canary Wharf (23.15)	XX	435
Spuntino (01.00)	X	470
Tendido Cero (23.15)	X	421
Ten Room (00.00)	XX	465
The Wolseley (00.00)	XXX	463
Yauatcha (23.30)	XX ✿	466

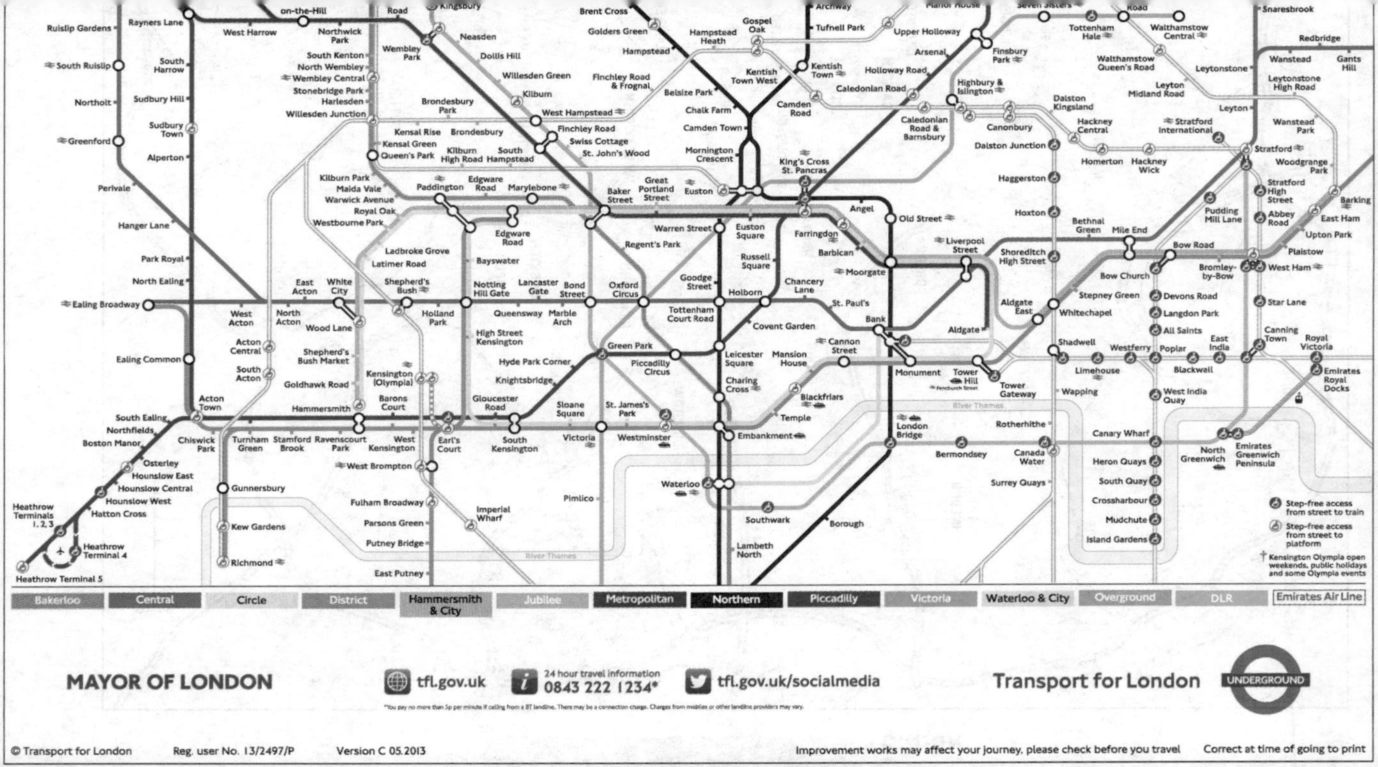

Ruislip Gardens
Rayners Lane
on-the-Hill
West Harrow
Northwick Park
Road
Kingsbury
Brent Cross
Golders Green
Gospel Oak
Hampstead Heath
Hampstead
Archway
Tufnell Park
Kentish Town
Manor House
Upper Holloway
Arsenal
Holloway Road
Caledonian Road
Seven Sisters
Tottenham Hale
Walthamstow Central
Walthamstow Queen's Road
Snaresbrook
Redbridge
Wanstead
Gants Hill
Leytonstone
Leytonstone High Road
Leyton Midland Road
Leyton
Wanstead Park
South Ruislip
South Harrow
Northolt
Sudbury Hill
Sudbury Town
Greenford
Alperton
Perivale
Hanger Lane
Park Royal
North Ealing
Ealing Broadway
Ealing Common
Acton Town
South Ealing
Northfields
Boston Manor
Osterley
Hounslow East
Hounslow Central
Hounslow West
Hatton Cross
Heathrow Terminals 1, 2, 3
Heathrow Terminal 4
Heathrow Terminal 5
Wembley Park
Neasden
Dollis Hill
South Kenton
North Wembley
Wembley Central
Stonebridge Park
Harlesden
Willesden Junction
Willesden Green
Kilburn
Brondesbury Park
Brondesbury
Kensal Rise
Kensal Green
Queen's Park
Kilburn High Road
South Hampstead
West Hampstead
Finchley Road & Frognal
Finchley Road
Swiss Cottage
St. John's Wood
Belsize Park
Chalk Farm
Camden Town
Kentish Town West
Camden Road
Mornington Crescent
Kilburn Park
Maida Vale
Warwick Avenue
Royal Oak
Westbourne Park
Paddington
Edgware Road
Marylebone
Baker Street
Great Portland Street
Euston
King's Cross St. Pancras
Caledonian Road & Barnsbury
Highbury & Islington
Finsbury Park
Canonbury
Dalston Kingsland
Dalston Junction
Hackney Central
Homerton
Hackney Wick
Stratford International
Stratford
Woodgrange Park
Haggerston
Hoxton
Angel
Old Street
Ladbroke Grove
Latimer Road
Bayswater
Warren Street
Euston Square
Regent's Park
Russell Square
Farringdon
Barbican
Moorgate
Liverpool Street
Shoreditch High Street
Bethnal Green
Mile End
Pudding Mill Lane
Stratford High Street
Abbey Road
Barking
East Ham
Upton Park
Plaistow
Bow Road
Bow Church
Bromley-by-Bow
West Ham
East Acton
White City
Shepherd's Bush
Notting Hill Gate
Lancaster Gate
Bond Street
Oxford Circus
Goodge Street
Holborn
Chancery Lane
St. Paul's
Stepney Green
Devons Road
Aldgate East
Whitechapel
Langdon Park
Star Lane
West Acton
North Acton
Wood Lane
Holland Park
Queensway
Marble Arch
Tottenham Court Road
Covent Garden
Bank
Aldgate
All Saints
Canning Town
Royal Victoria
Acton Central
South Acton
Shepherd's Bush Market
Goldhawk Road
Kensington (Olympia)
High Street Kensington
Hyde Park Corner
Knightsbridge
Green Park
Piccadilly Circus
Leicester Square
Charing Cross
Mansion House
Cannon Street
Monument
Tower Hill
Fenchurch Street
Tower Gateway
Shadwell
Limehouse
Westferry
Poplar
Blackwall
East India
Emirates Royal Docks
Wapping
West India Quay
Hammersmith
Barons Court
Gloucester Road
Sloane Square
St. James's Park
Blackfriars
Temple
River Thames
Chiswick Park
Turnham Green
Stamford Brook
Ravenscourt Park
West Kensington
Earl's Court
South Kensington
Victoria
Westminster
Embankment
London Bridge
Bermondsey
Rotherhithe
Canada Water
Canary Wharf
North Greenwich
Emirates Greenwich Peninsula
West Brompton
Gunnersbury
Heron Quays
South Quay
Surrey Quays
Waterloo
Fulham Broadway
Pimlico
Crossharbour
Mudchute
Island Gardens
Imperial Wharf
Parsons Green
Kew Gardens
Southwark
Borough
Putney Bridge
Lambeth North
Richmond
East Putney
Step-free access from street to train
Step-free access from street to platform
† Kensington Olympia open weekends, public holidays and some Olympia events
Bakerloo
Central
Circle
District
Hammersmith & City
Jubilee
Metropolitan
Northern
Piccadilly
Victoria
Waterloo & City
Overground
DLR
Emirates Air Line
MAYOR OF LONDON
tfl.gov.uk
24 hour travel information
0843 222 1234*
tfl.gov.uk/socialmedia
Transport for London
UNDERGROUND
*You pay no more than 5p per minute if calling from a BT landline. There may be a connection charge. Charges from mobiles or other landline providers may vary.
© Transport for London
Reg. user No. 13/2497/P
Version C 05.2013
Improvement works may affect your journey, please check before you travel
Correct at time of going to print

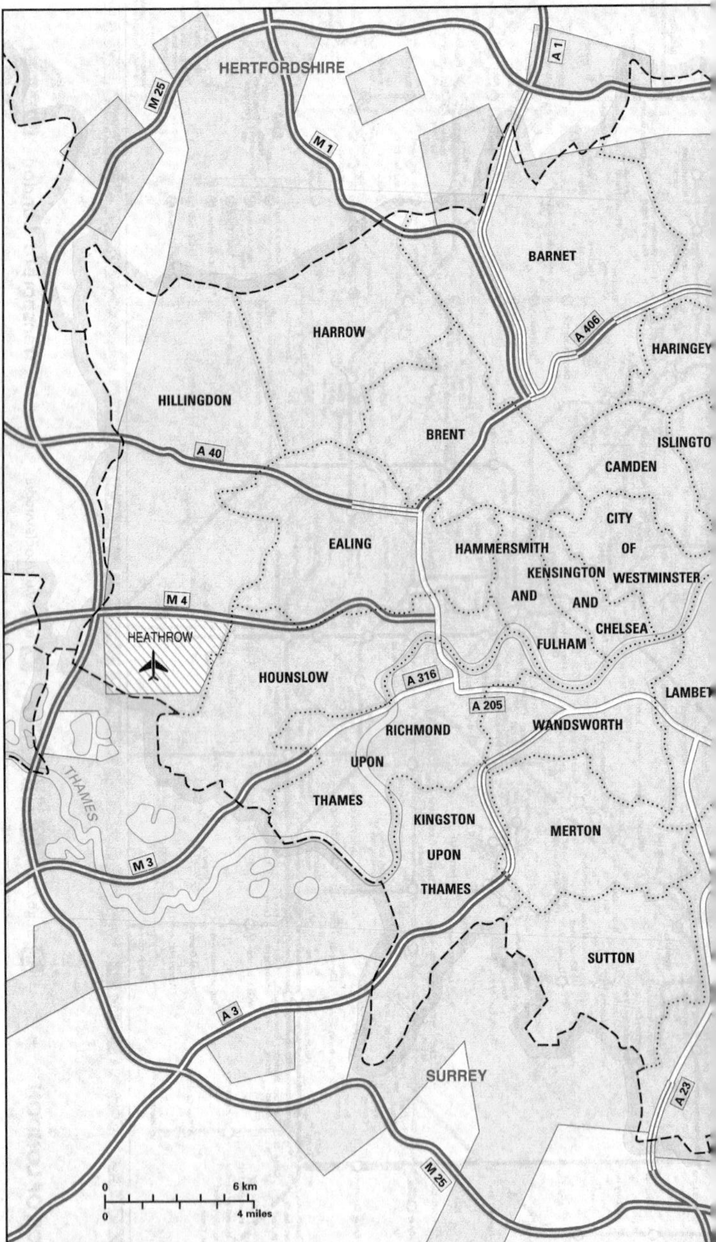
HERTFORDSHIRE
M 25
M 1
A 1
BARNET
HARROW
A 406
HARINGEY
HILLINGDON
BRENT
ISLINGTO
A 40
CAMDEN
CITY
OF
WESTMINSTER
EALING
HAMMERSMITH
AND
FULHAM
KENSINGTON
AND
CHELSEA
M 4
HEATHROW
HOUNSLOW
A 316
A 205
LAMBET
RICHMOND
UPON
THAMES
WANDSWORTH
THAMES
KINGSTON
UPON
THAMES
MERTON
M 3
SUTTON
A 3
SURREY
A 23
M 25
0
6 km
0
4 miles

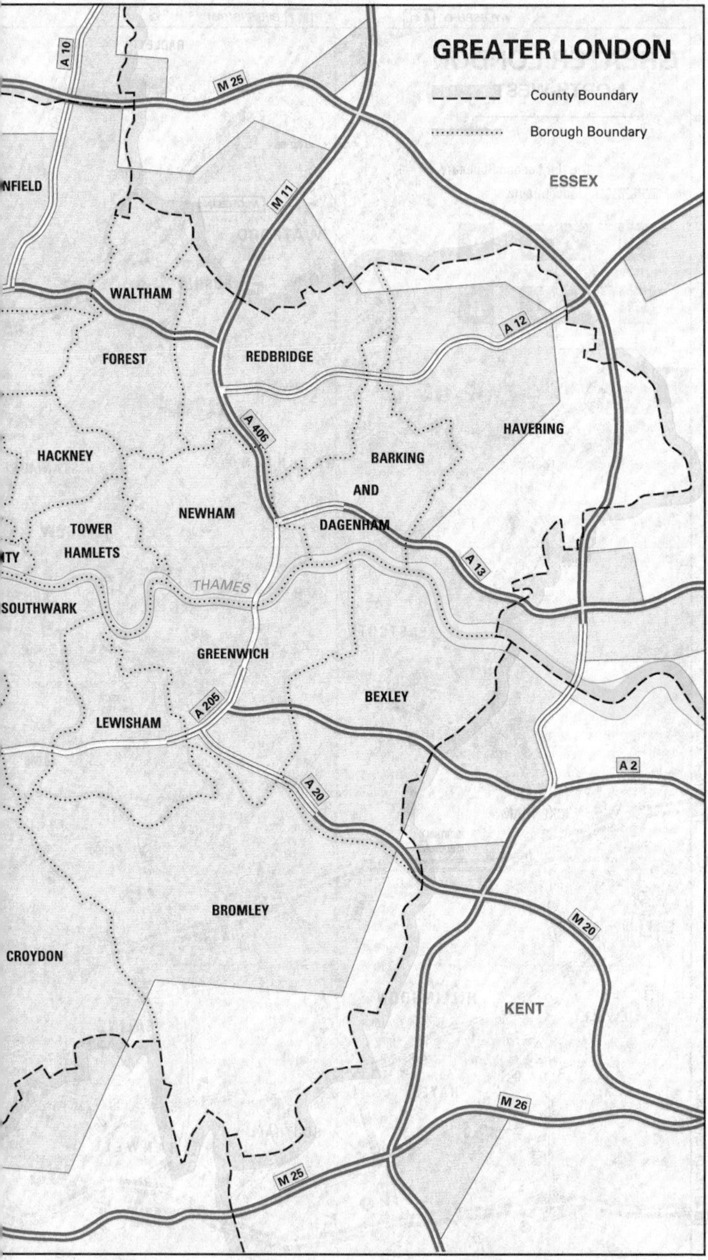
GREATER LONDON
County Boundary
Borough Boundary
ESSEX
NFIELD
WALTHAM
FOREST
REDBRIDGE
HAVERING
HACKNEY
BARKING
AND
DAGENHAM
NEWHAM
TOWER
HAMLETS
TY
THAMES
SOUTHWARK
GREENWICH
BEXLEY
LEWISHAM
BROMLEY
CROYDON
KENT
A 10
M 25
M 11
A 12
A 406
A 13
A 205
A 2
A 20
M 20
M 26
M 25

LONDON

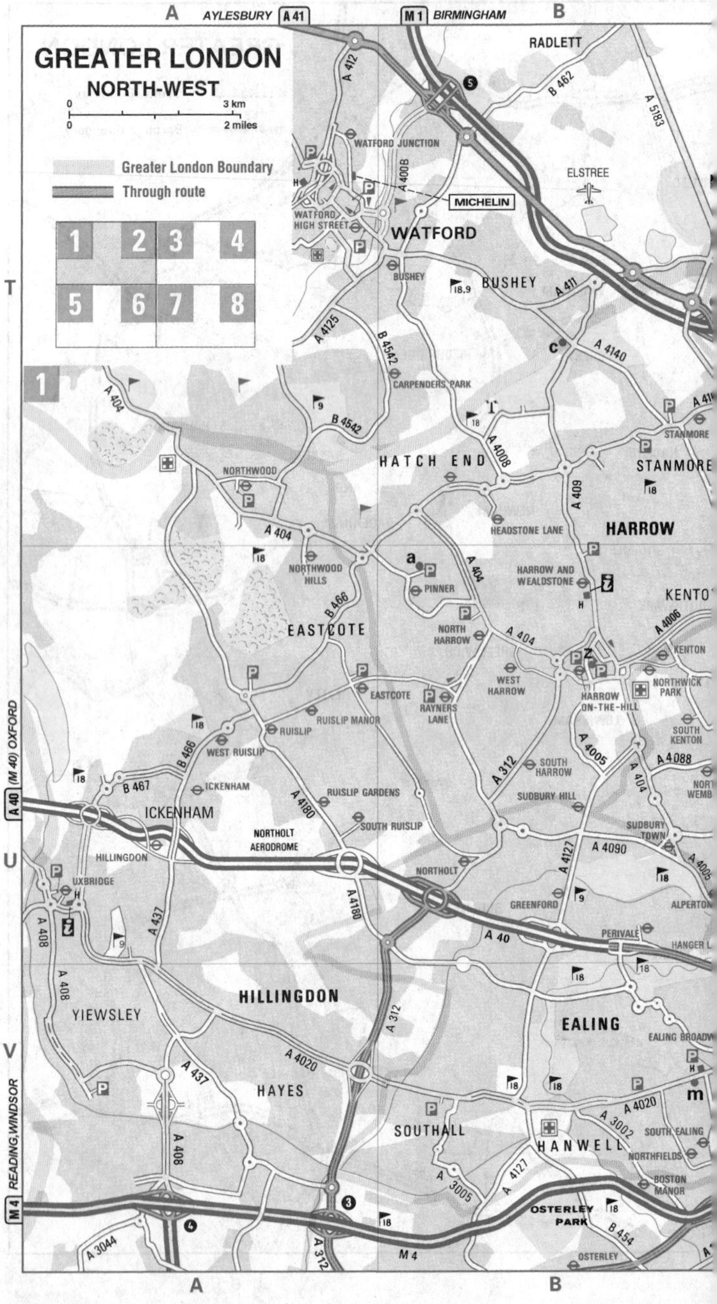
GREATER LONDON
NORTH-WEST
0 3 km
0 2 miles
Greater London Boundary
Through route
1 2 3 4
5 6 7 8
A AYLESBURY A 41
M 1 BIRMINGHAM B
T
U
V
A 40 (M 40) OXFORD
M 4 READING, WINDSOR
RADLETT
ELSTREE
MICHELIN
WATFORD JUNCTION
WATFORD HIGH STREET
WATFORD
BUSHEY
HATCH END
CARPENDERS PARK
STANMORE
HARROW
NORTHWOOD
NORTHWOOD HILLS
PINNER
HEADSTONE LANE
HARROW AND WEALDSTONE
KENTON
EASTCOTE
NORTH HARROW
WEST HARROW
HARROW ON-THE-HILL
NORTHWICK PARK
RAYNERS LANE
RUISLIP MANOR
RUISLIP
WEST RUISLIP
SOUTH KENTON
SOUTH HARROW
ICKENHAM
RUISLIP GARDENS
SUDBURY HILL
SUDBURY TOWN
SOUTH RUISLIP
NORTHOLT AERODROME
NORTHOLT
HILLINGDON
UXBRIDGE
GREENFORD
ALPERTON
PERIVALE
HANGER L
YIEWSLEY
EALING
EALING BROADW
HAYES
SOUTHALL
HANWELL
SOUTH EALING
NORTHFIELDS
BOSTON MANOR
OSTERLEY PARK
OSTERLEY
A 412
A 400B
B 462
A 5183
A 411
A 4125
B 4542
A 4140
A 404
A 4008
A 409
B 466
A 4006
A 312
A 4005
A 4088
B 467
A 4180
A 4127
A 4090
A 437
A 408
A 40
A 4020
A 3002
A 3005
B 454
A 3044
M 4
A B

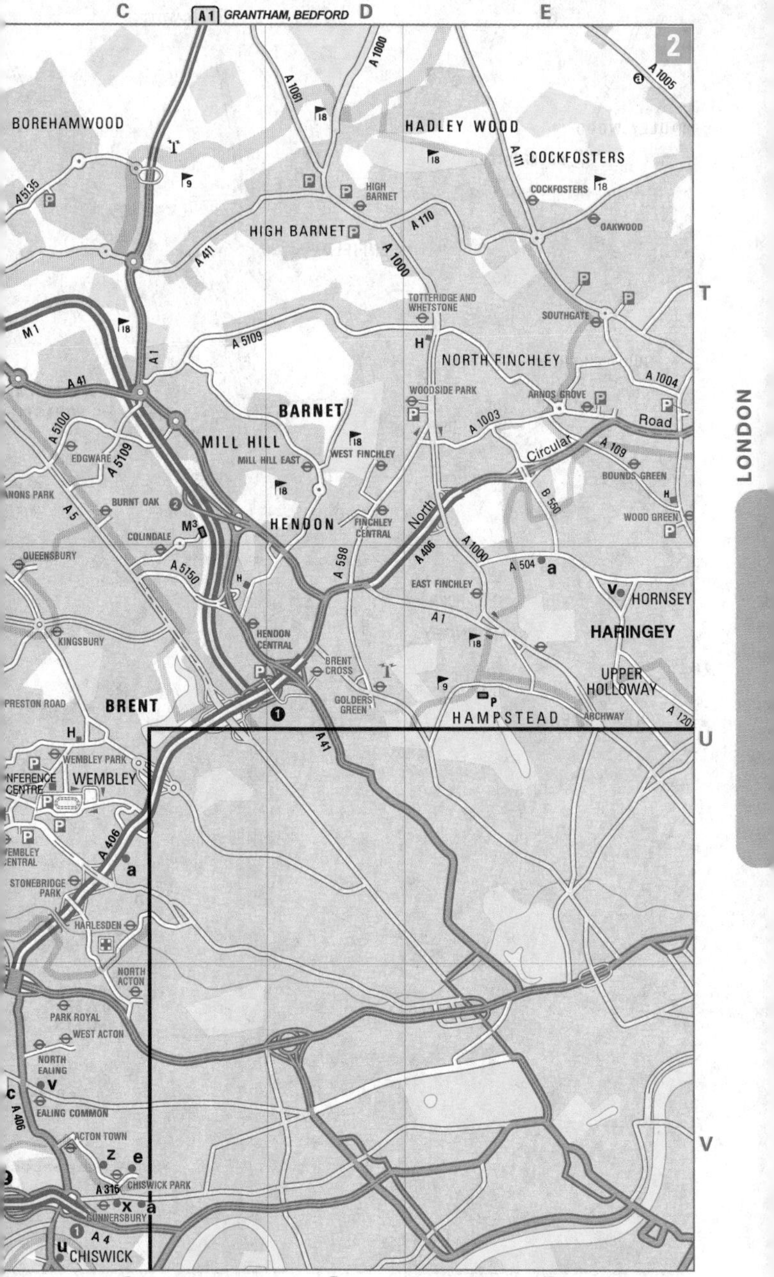

C
A1 GRANTHAM, BEDFORD
D
E
2
A 1005
A 1000
A 1081
BOREHAMWOOD
HADLEY WOOD
A 111
COCKFOSTERS
A5135
HIGH BARNET
COCKFOSTERS
HIGH BARNET
A 110
OAKWOOD
A 411
A 1000
TOTTERIDGE AND WHETSTONE
SOUTHGATE
T
M1
A 5109
A1
NORTH FINCHLEY
A 41
WOODSIDE PARK
ARNOS GROVE
A 1004
A 5100
BARNET
A 1003
Road
MILL HILL
Circular
A 109
EDGWARE
A 5109
MILL HILL EAST
WEST FINCHLEY
BOUNDS GREEN
B 550
ANONS PARK
A 5
BURNT OAK
North
WOOD GREEN
COLINDALE
HENDON
FINCHLEY CENTRAL
QUEENSBURY
A 5150
A 598
A 406
A 1000
A 504
EAST FINCHLEY
HORNSEY
A1
HARINGEY
KINGSBURY
HENDON CENTRAL
BRENT CROSS
UPPER HOLLOWAY
PRESTON ROAD
BRENT
GOLDERS GREEN
HAMPSTEAD
ARCHWAY
A 1201
U
A 41
WEMBLEY PARK
NFERENCE CENTRE
WEMBLEY
EMBLEY CENTRAL
A 406
STONEBRIDGE PARK
HARLESDEN
NORTH ACTON
PARK ROYAL
WEST ACTON
NORTH EALING
A 406
EALING COMMON
ACTON TOWN
V
A 315
CHISWICK PARK
GUNNERSBURY
A 4
CHISWICK
C
D
E
LONDON

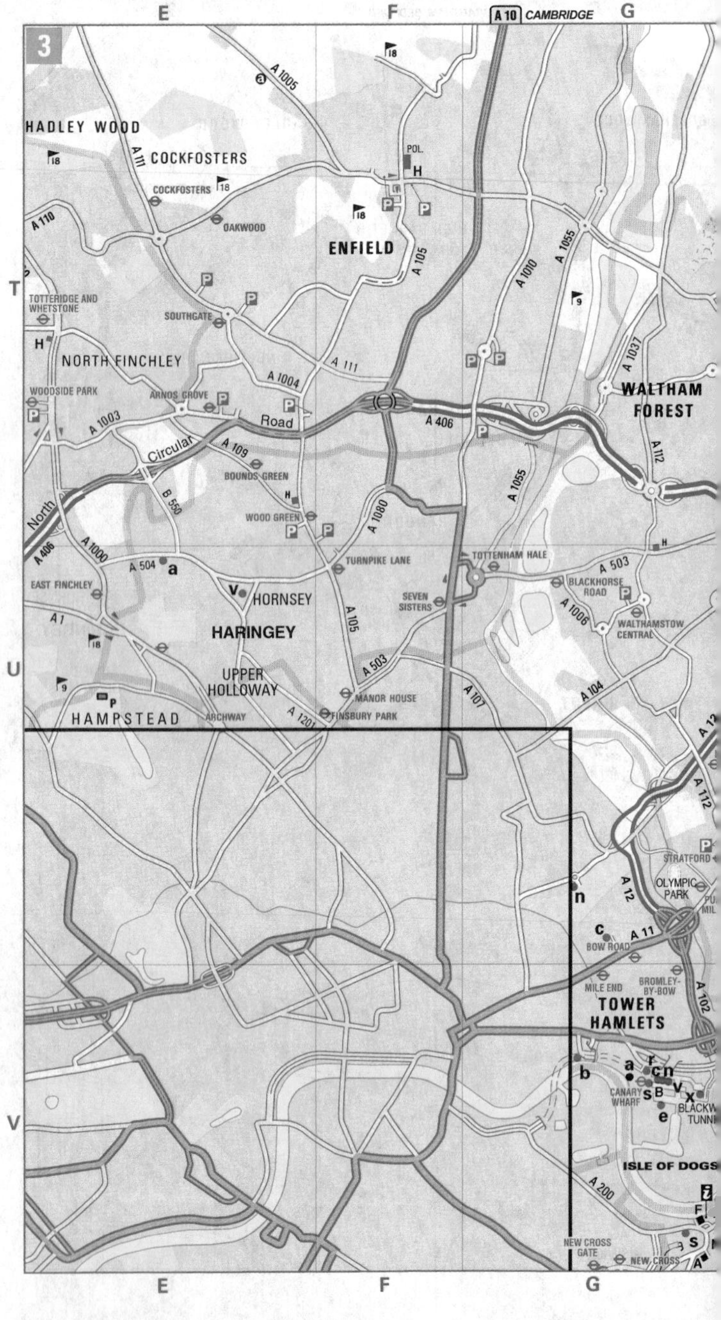

E
F
G
A 10 CAMBRIDGE
3
HADLEY WOOD
COCKFOSTERS
A 111
A 1005
POL.
H
ENFIELD
A 105
A 110
OAKWOOD
A 1010
A 1055
T
TOTTERIDGE AND WHETSTONE
SOUTHGATE
NORTH FINCHLEY
A 111
A 1004
A 1037
WALTHAM FOREST
WOODSIDE PARK
ARNOS GROVE
A 1003
Road
A 406
Circular
A 109
A 112
BOUNDS GREEN
North
B 550
A 1055
WOOD GREEN
A 1080
A 406
A 1000
A 504
a
TURNPIKE LANE
TOTTENHAM HALE
A 503
EAST FINCHLEY
v
HORNSEY
SEVEN SISTERS
BLACKHORSE ROAD
A 1006
A 1
HARINGEY
A 105
WALTHAMSTOW CENTRAL
U
UPPER HOLLOWAY
A 503
A 107
A 104
HAMPSTEAD
ARCHWAY
A 1201
MANOR HOUSE
FINSBURY PARK
A 112
STRATFORD
OLYMPIC PARK
A 12
n
c
BOW ROAD
A 11
MILE END
BROMLEY-BY-BOW
A 102
TOWER HAMLETS
a
b
r
c
n
CANARY WHARF
s
B
v
x
e
BLACKW
TUNN
V
ISLE OF DOGS
A 200
F
NEW CROSS GATE
NEW CROSS
s
A

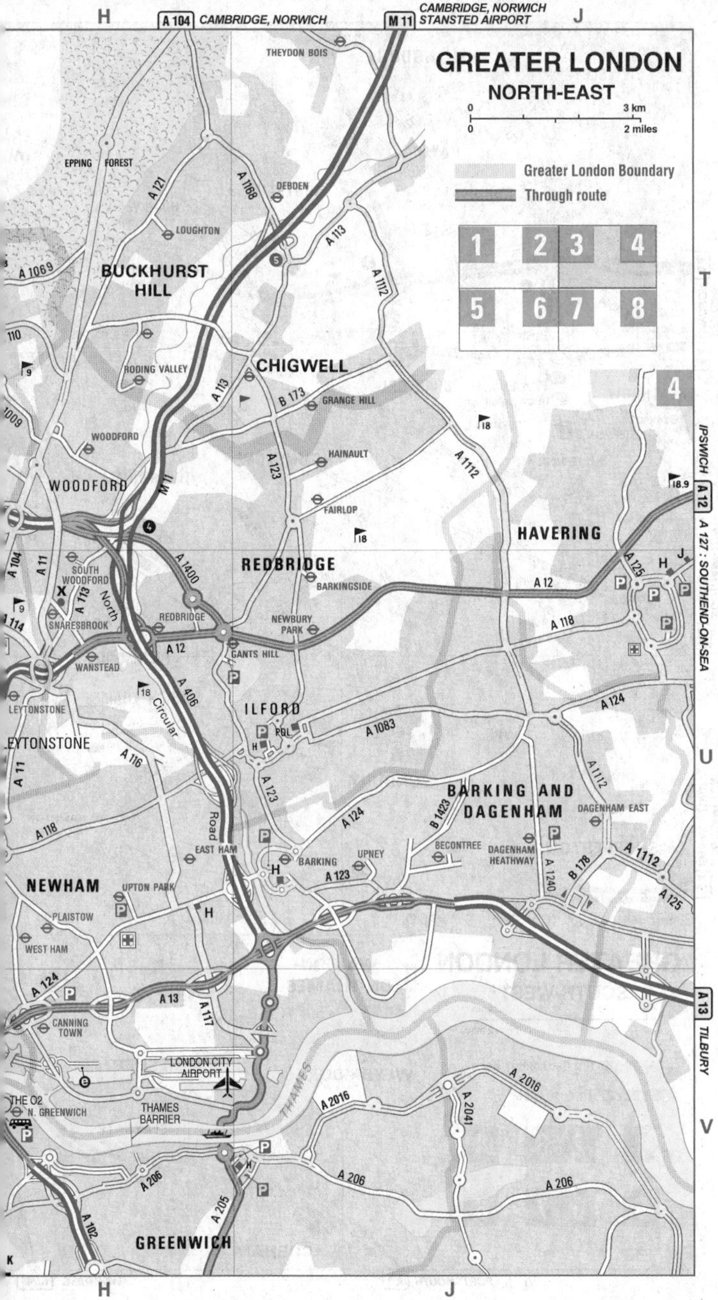
GREATER LONDON
NORTH-EAST
Greater London Boundary
Through route
A 104 CAMBRIDGE, NORWICH
M 11 CAMBRIDGE, NORWICH STANSTED AIRPORT
THEYDON BOIS
EPPING FOREST
DEBDEN
LOUGHTON
BUCKHURST HILL
CHIGWELL
RODING VALLEY
GRANGE HILL
WOODFORD
HAINAULT
FAIRLOP
REDBRIDGE
BARKINGSIDE
SOUTH WOODFORD
SNARESBROOK
NEWBURY PARK
GANTS HILL
WANSTEAD
LEYTONSTONE
ILFORD
HAVERING
BARKING AND DAGENHAM
DAGENHAM EAST
BECONTREE
DAGENHAM HEATHWAY
UPNEY
BARKING
EAST HAM
UPTON PARK
NEWHAM
PLAISTOW
WEST HAM
CANNING TOWN
LONDON CITY AIRPORT
THE O2 N. GREENWICH
THAMES BARRIER
THAMES
GREENWICH
North Circular Road
IPSWICH
A 127 : SOUTHEND-ON-SEA
A 13 TILBURY
LONDON

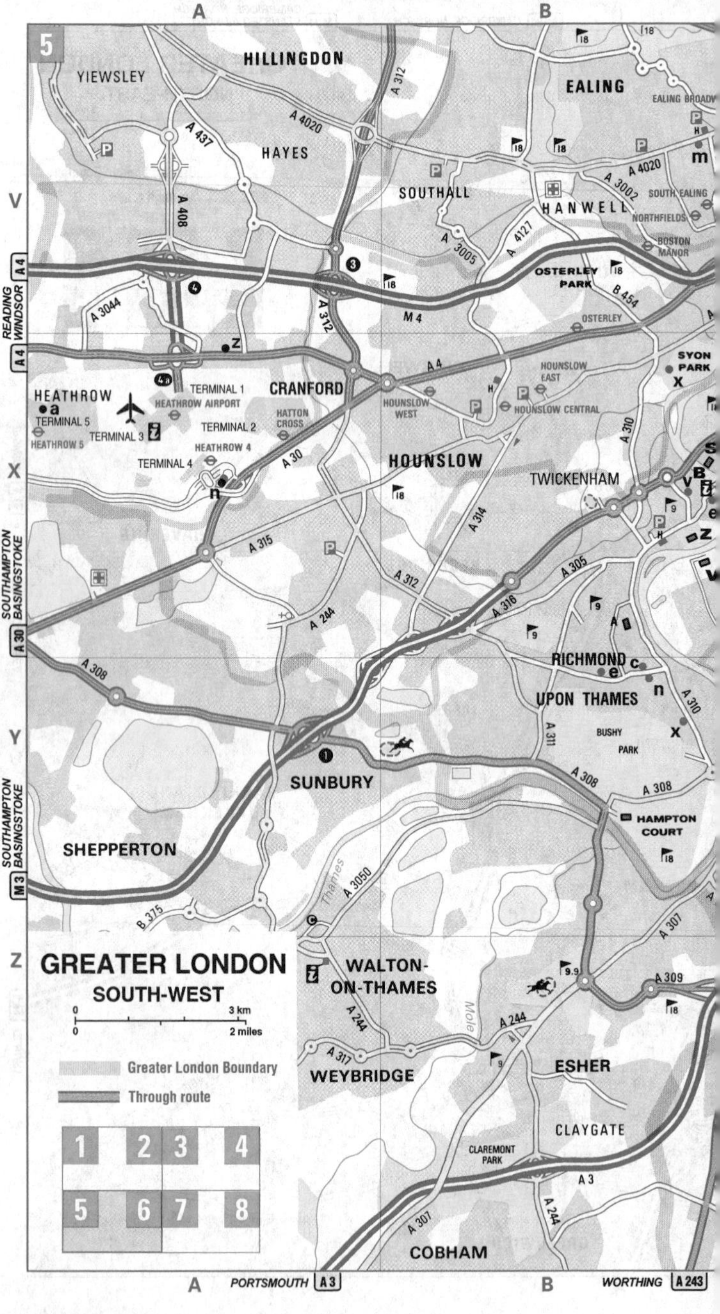
5
HILLINGDON
YIEWSLEY
HAYES
EALING
EALING BROADWAY
SOUTHALL
HANWELL
SOUTH EALING
NORTHFIELDS
BOSTON MANOR
OSTERLEY PARK
OSTERLEY
SYON PARK
HOUNSLOW EAST
HOUNSLOW WEST
HOUNSLOW CENTRAL
HOUNSLOW
CRANFORD
HEATHROW
HEATHROW AIRPORT
TERMINAL 1
TERMINAL 2
TERMINAL 3
TERMINAL 4
TERMINAL 5
HEATHROW 4
HEATHROW 5
HATTON CROSS
TWICKENHAM
RICHMOND UPON THAMES
BUSHY PARK
HAMPTON COURT
SUNBURY
SHEPPERTON
WALTON-ON-THAMES
WEYBRIDGE
ESHER
CLAYGATE
CLAREMONT PARK
COBHAM
Thames
Mole
M 4
A 4
A 30
A 308
A 312
A 4020
A 437
A 408
A 3044
A 315
A 244
A 314
A 316
A 305
A 310
A 311
A 3002
A 3005
A 4127
B 454
A 3050
B 375
A 317
A 307
A 309
A 3
READING WINDSOR
SOUTHAMPTON BASINGSTOKE
M 3
PORTSMOUTH
WORTHING
A 243
A
B
V
X
Y
Z
GREATER LONDON
SOUTH-WEST
0 3 km
0 2 miles
Greater London Boundary
Through route
1 2 3 4
5 6 7 8

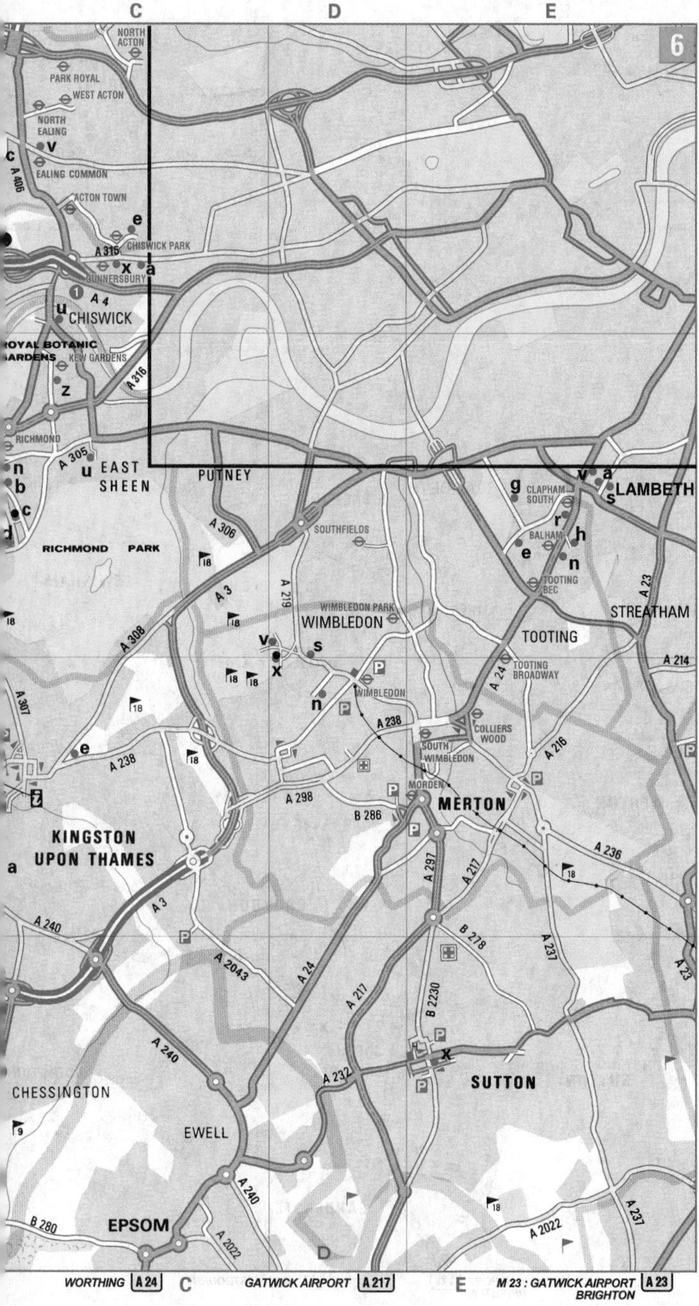
C
D
E
6
V
X
Y
Z
LONDON
NORTH ACTON
PARK ROYAL
WEST ACTON
NORTH EALING
EALING COMMON
ACTON TOWN
CHISWICK PARK
GUNNERSBURY
CHISWICK
ROYAL BOTANIC GARDENS
KEW GARDENS
RICHMOND
EAST SHEEN
PUTNEY
RICHMOND PARK
SOUTHFIELDS
CLAPHAM SOUTH
LAMBETH
BALHAM
TOOTING BEC
STREATHAM
WIMBLEDON PARK
WIMBLEDON
TOOTING
TOOTING BROADWAY
COLLIERS WOOD
SOUTH WIMBLEDON
MORDEN
MERTON
KINGSTON UPON THAMES
SUTTON
CHESSINGTON
EWELL
EPSOM
A 406
A 315
A 4
A 316
A 305
A 306
A 3
A 219
A 308
A 307
A 238
A 298
B 286
A 24
A 214
A 216
A 236
A 297
A 217
A 240
B 278
A 237
A 23
A 2043
B 2230
A 232
B 280
A 2022
WORTHING A 24
GATWICK AIRPORT A 217
M 23 : GATWICK AIRPORT BRIGHTON A 23

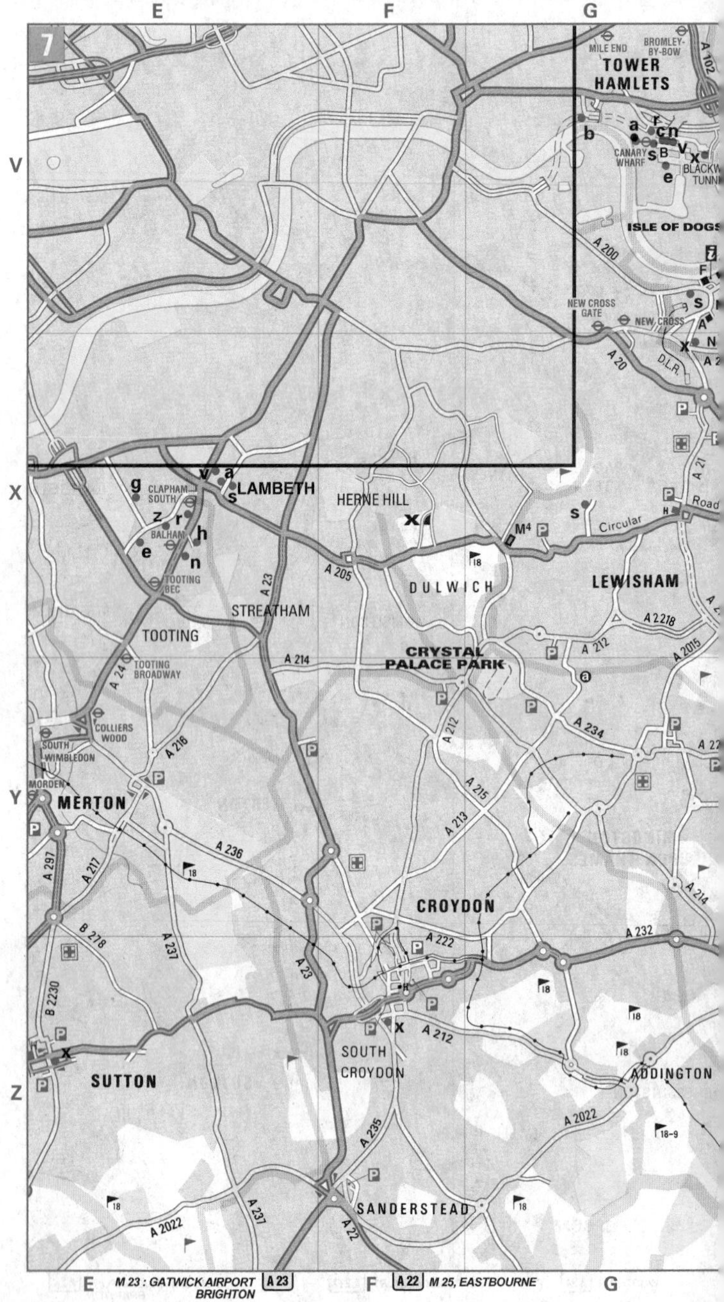
7
E
F
G
V
X
Y
Z
MILE END
BROMLEY-BY-BOW
TOWER HAMLETS
A 102
CANARY WHARF
BLACKW TUNN
ISLE OF DOGS
A 200
NEW CROSS GATE
NEW CROSS
D.L.R.
A 20
CLAPHAM SOUTH
BALHAM
LAMBETH
HERNE HILL
TOOTING BEC
A 205
DULWICH
LEWISHAM
Circular
Road
A 21
A 23
STREATHAM
TOOTING
A 2218
A 212
A 2015
CRYSTAL PALACE PARK
A 214
A 24
TOOTING BROADWAY
COLLIERS WOOD
SOUTH WIMBLEDON
A 216
A 234
MORDEN
MERTON
A 215
A 213
A 236
A 297
A 217
CROYDON
A 214
A 232
B 278
A 237
A 222
B 2230
A 23
A 212
SOUTH CROYDON
ADDINGTON
SUTTON
A 2022
A 235
SANDERSTEAD
A 2022
A 237
A 22
M 23 : GATWICK AIRPORT BRIGHTON
A 23
A 22
M 25, EASTBOURNE

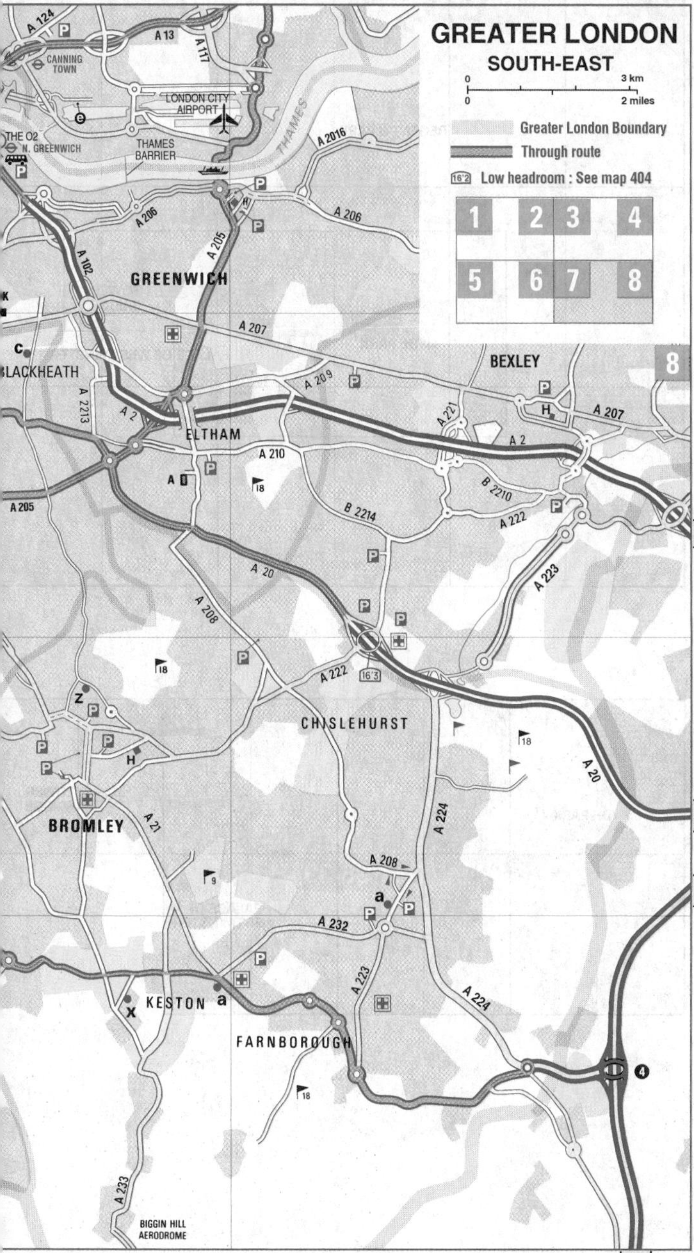
GREATER LONDON
SOUTH-EAST
0 3 km
0 2 miles
Greater London Boundary
Through route
16'2 Low headroom : See map 404
1 2 3 4
5 6 7 8
H
J
V
X
Y
Z
CANNING TOWN
LONDON CITY AIRPORT
THE O2
N. GREENWICH
THAMES BARRIER
THAMES
GREENWICH
BLACKHEATH
ELTHAM
BEXLEY
CHISLEHURST
BROMLEY
KESTON
FARNBOROUGH
BIGGIN HILL AERODROME
A 124
A 13
A 117
A 2016
A 206
A 205
A 102
A 207
A 209
A 2213
A 2
A 221
A 210
B 2210
B 2214
A 222
A 223
A 20
A 208
A 21
A 224
A 232
A 233
16'3
A 2 DOVER
FOLKESTONE A 20
M 25
A 21 : HASTINGS M 25
LONDON

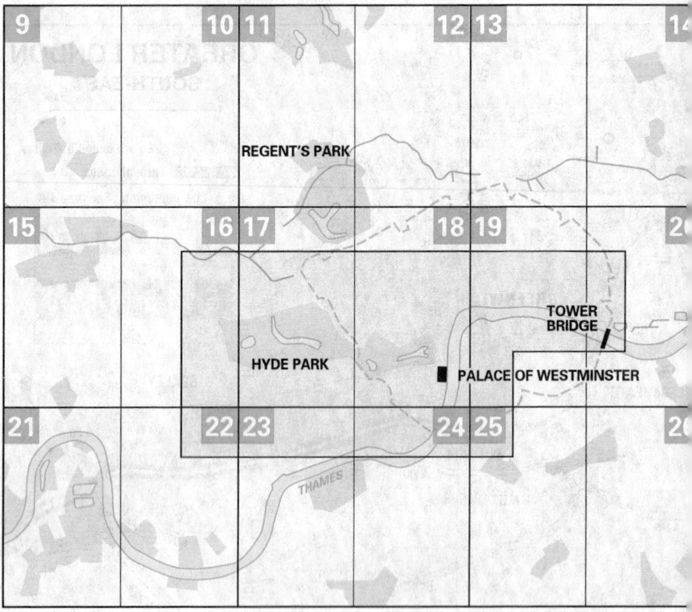
9
10
11
12
13
REGENT'S PARK
15
16
17
18
19
TOWER BRIDGE
HYDE PARK
PALACE OF WESTMINSTER
21
22
23
24
25
THAMES

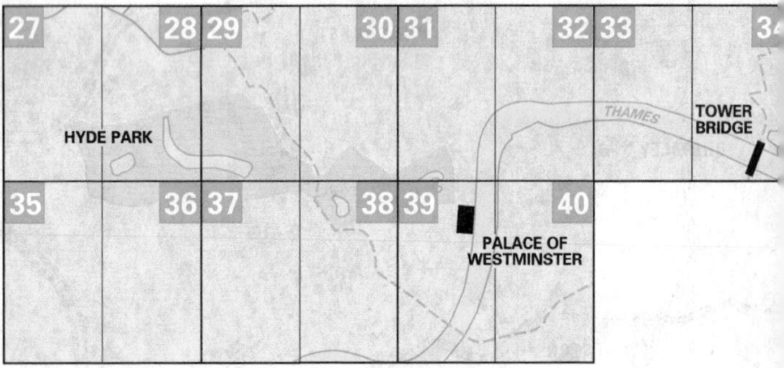
27
28
29
30
31
32
33
HYDE PARK
THAMES
TOWER BRIDGE
35
36
37
38
39
40
PALACE OF WESTMINSTER

INDEX OF STREET NAMES IN LONDON CENTRE

LONDON

ford Gardens 16 MZD
yal Crescent 16 MZE 371
Ann's Rd 16 MZE
Mark's Rd 16 MZD
irland Rd 16 NZD
nclair Rd 16 MZE
xth Ave 16 MZC
therland Ave 16 NZD
alterton Rd 16 NZD 347
arwick Ave 16 OZD
est Cross Route 16 MZE

PLAN 17

sop Pl. 17 QZD 4
omfield Rd 17 OZD
oadley St 17 PZD
fton Gardens 17 PZD
ampton St 17 PZD
ll Rd 17 PZC
sson Grove 17 PZD
aida Ave 17 PZD
orth Carriage Drive 17 PZE
rk Rd 17 QZD
ssmore Rd 17 QZD
John's Wood Rd 17 PZD
arrington Crescent 17 OZD 348

PLAN 18

rnard St 18 SZD 25
ester Rd 18 RZC
ston Rd 18 RZD
zroy Square 18 RZD
eat Ormond St 18 SZD
uilford St 18 SZD
erbrand St 18 SZD 218
unter St 18 SZD 233
dd St 18 SZC
rk Crescent 18 RZD 28
obert St 18 RZC
ssell Square 18 SZD
dmouth St 18 SZD 385
vistock Pl. 18 SZD
vistock Square 18 SZD 409
pper Woburn Pl. 18 SZD 432
oburn Pl. 18 SZD

PLAN 19

ath St 19 VZC
eech St 19 VZD
orough Rd 19 UZE
owling Green Lane 19 UZD 43
unhill Row 19 VZD
althorpe St 19 TZD 65
entral St 19 VZC
hiswell St 19 VZD
ty Rd 19 VZC
erkenwell Rd 19 UZD 474
orporation Row 19 UZD 110
ufferin St 19 VZD 141
ephant and Castle
Shopping Centre 19 UZF
lmouth Rd 19 VZE
nn St 19 VZD 166
oswell Rd 19 UZC
eat Dover St 19 VZE
arper Rd 19 VZE
ng's Cross Rd 19 TZC
ver St 19 VZC
oyd Baker St 19 UZC 265
ng Lane
SOUTHWARK 19 VZE
errick Square 19 VZE
oreland St 19 VZC 293
yddelton St 19 UZC 296
ewington
Causeway 19 VZE 307
ew Kent Rd 19 VZF

Old St 19 VZD
Paul St 19 VZD
Percival St 19 UZD
Pilgrimage St. 19 VZE 349
Rosebery Ave 19 UZD
St John St 19 UZC
Suffolk St. 19 VZE
Tabard St 19 VZE 408
Trinity Church Square 19 VZE
Trinity St. 19 VZE
Whitecross St 19 VZD
Worship St 19 VZD

PLAN 20

Abbey St 20 XZE
Appold St 20 XZD 5
Back Church Rd 20 XZD
Bermondsey St. 20 XZE
Bethnal Green Rd 20 XZD
Bigland St 20 YZD
Brady St. 20 YZD
Brick Lane 20 XZD
Brunel Rd 20 YZE
Cable St. 20 YZD
Cambridge Heath Rd 20 YZD
Cannon Street Rd 20 YZD
Cavell St 20 YZD
Cephas St 20 YZD
Cheshire St 20 XZD
Christian St 20 YZD
Clements Rd 20 YZE
Club Row 20 XZD
Commercial Rd 20 YZD
Curtain Rd 20 XZD 126
Dock St 20 XZD
Drummond Rd 20 YZE
Fielgate St 20 XZD
Globe Rd 20 YZC
Grange Rd 20 XZE
Great Eastern St 20 XZD 192
Highway (The) 20 YZE
Jamaica Rd 20 XZE
Jublilee St 20 YZD
Lower Rd 20 YZE
Luke St 20 XZD
Mile End Rd 20 YZD
New Rd 20 YZD
Old Montague St 20 XZD
Pages Walk 20 XZF
Redman's Rd 20 YZD
Roman Rd 20 YZC
Rovel Rd 20 XZE 75
Salter Rd 20 YZE
Sclater St 20 XZD 470
Shoreditch High St 20 XZD 384
Sidney St 20 YZD
Spa Rd 20 XZE
Stepney Way 20 YZD
Surrey Quay's Rd 20 YZE 377
Tarling St 20 YZD
Thomas Moore St 20 XZE 365
Turin St 20 XZC
Vallance Rd 20 YZD
Vaughan Way 20 XZE
Wapping High St 20 YZE
Wapping Lane 20 YZE
Wapping Wall 20 YZE
Whitechapel Rd 20 XZD

PLAN 21

Banin St. 21 LZF
Barnes High St 21 KZH 404
Bath Rd 21 KZF
Brook Green 21 LZF
Burlington Lane 21 KZG
Castelnau 21 LZG
Chancellor's Rd. 21 LZG 21
Chiswick High Rd 21 KZG
Chiswick Lane 21 KZG
Chiswick Mall 21 KZG
Church Rd RICHMOND
UPON THAMES 21 KZH
Dailing Rd 21 LZF 13
Devonshire Rd 21 KZG
Dorchester Grove 21 KZG 402
Dover House Rd 21 LZH
Erpingham Rd 21 LZH
Ferry Rd. 21 KZG
Glenthorne Rd 21 LZF
Great West Rd 21 KZG
Gwendolen Ave 21 LZH
Hammersmith
Bridge 21 LZG
Hammersmith Bridge
Rd 21 LZG 431
Hertford Ave 21 KZH
Hotham Rd 21 LZH
Howards Lane 21 LZH
King St
HAMMERSMITH 21 KZG
Lonsdale Rd 21 KZG
Lower Richmond Rd 21 LZH
Mill Hill Rd 21 KZH
Prebend Gardens 21 KZF
Priory Lane 21 KZH
Queen's Ride Lower 21 LZH
Rainville Rd 21 LZG
Rannoch Rd 21 LZG
Rocks Lane 21 LZH
Roehampton Lane 21 KZH
Station Rd 21 KZH
Stevenage Rd 21 LZG
Suffolk Rd 21 KZG
Talgarth Rd 21 LZG
Terrace (The) 21 KZH
Turnham Green
Terrace 21 KZG 389
Upper Richmond Rd 21 LZH
Upper Richmond Rd
West 21 KZH
Verdun Rd 21 KZG
Vine Rd 21 KZH
White Hart Lane 21 KZH

PLAN 22

Armoury Way 22 NZH 7
Bagley's Lane 22 OZH
Baron's Court Rd 22 MZG
Bishops Rd 22 NZG
Bishop's Park Rd. 22 MZH
Broomhouse Lane 22 NZH
Carnwath Rd 22 NZH
Charlwood Rd 22 MZH
Clancarty Rd 22 NZH
Crabtree Lane 22 MZG 164
Dawes Rd 22 MZG
Disraeli Rd 22 MZH
Edith Rd. 22 MZG
Estcourt Rd 22 MZG 203
Fairfield St 22 OZH 165
Fawe Park Rd 22 MZH
Filmer Rd. 22 MZG
Finlay St. 22 MZH
Fulham High St 22 MZH 172
Fulham Palace Rd 22 MZG
Gliddon Rd 22 MZG 182
Greyhound Rd 22 MZG
Gunterstone Rd 22 MZG
Halford Rd 22 NZG
Hammersmith Rd 22 MZG
Harwood Rd 22 NZG
Hugon Rd 22 NZH
Hurlingham Rd 22 NZH
Munster Rd 22 MZG
Musard Rd 22 MZG
New King's Rd 22 NZH
Oakhill Rd 22 NZH

PLAN 27

PLAN 28

PLAN 29

PLAN 30

Street	Plan	Grid	No.
Great Portland St	30	AIT	
Great Titchfield St	30	AIT	
Grosvenor Square	30	AHU	
Grosvenor St	30	AHU	
Half Moon St	30	AHV	81
Hamilton Pl.	30	AHV	205
Hanover Square	30	AIU	
Hanover St	30	AIU	
Harley St WESTMINSTER	30	AHT	
Hay's Mews	30	AHV	
Henrietta Pl.	30	AHT	
Hertford St	30	AHV	
Hill St	30	AHV	
Holles St	30	AIT	
Howland St	30	AIT	232
James St	30	AHT	
Kingly St	30	AIU	
King St ST. JAMES'S	30	AIV	
Langham St	30	AIT	
Little Portland St	30	AIT	228
Maddox St	30	AIU	
Margaret St	30	AIT	
Market Pl.	30	AIT	286
Marshall St	30	AIU	
Marylebone High St	30	AHT	
Marylebone Lane	30	AHT	287
Mortimer St	30	AIT	
Mount Row	30	AHU	
New Bond St	30	AHU	
New Cavendish St	30	AHT	
Old Bond St	30	AIV	
Old Burlington St	30	AIU	322
Old Park Lane	30	AHV	
Oxford Circus	30	AIT	
Piccadilly	30	AHV	
Piccadilly Arcade	30	AIV	
Poland St	30	AIT	
Portland Pl.	30	AIT	
Princes St	30	AQU	
Queen Anne St.	30	AHT	
Queen's Walk	30	AIV	
Regent St	30	AIT	
Sackville St	30	AIU	
St George St	30	AIU	
St James's Pl.	30	AIV	116
St James's St	30	AIV	
Savile Row	30	AIU	
Shepherd Market	30	AHV	
Shepherd St	30	AHV	153
South Audley St	30	AHU	
South Molton St	30	AHU	
South St	30	AHV	
Stratton St	30	AIV	168
Thayer St	30	AHT	413
Tilney St	30	AHV	421
Vere St	30	AHU	
Vigo St	30	AIU	
Waverton St	30	AHV	178
Weighouse St.	30	AHU	184
Welbeck St	30	AHT	
Wells St	30	AIT	
Weymouth St	30	AHT	
Wimpole St	30	AHT	

PLAN 31

Street	Plan	Grid	No.
Adam St	31	ALU	
Bateman St	31	AKU	18
Bayley St	31	AKT	260
Bedfordbury	31	ALU	243
Bedford Square	31	AKT	
Bedford St	31	ALU	
Berner's St	31	AJT	
Berwick St	31	AJT	26
Bloomsbury Square	31	ALT	
Bloomsbury St	31	AKT	
Bloomsbury Way	31	ALT	9
Boswell St	31	ALT	
Bow St	31	ALU	
Brewer St	31	AJU	
Broadwick St	31	AJU	
Bury Pl.	31	ALT	
Cambridge Circus	31	AKU	
Carlton Gardens	31	AJV	74
Carlton House Terrace	31	AKV	
Carting Lane	31	ALU	245
Chandos Pl.	31	ALU	
Charing Cross	31	ALV	
Charing Cross Rd	31	AKT	
Charles II St	31	AKV	
Charlotte St	31	AJT	
Cherries St	31	AKT	256
Cockspur St	31	AKV	39
Coventry St	31	AKU	
Cranbourn St	31	AKU	115
Craven St	31	ALV	
Dean St	31	AJT	
Denman St	31	AJU	133
Denmark St	31	AKT	134
Drury Lane	31	ALT	
Duke of York St	31	AJV	143
Duncannon St	31	ALV	147
D'Arblay St	31	AJU	
Earlham St	31	AKU	
Endell St	31	ALT	
Exeter St	31	ALU	
Floral St	31	ALU	
Frith St	31	AKU	
Garrick St	31	ALU	
Gerrard St	31	AKU	174
Glasshouse St SOHO	31	AJU	179
Golden Jubilee Bridge	31	ALV	
Golden Square	31	AJU	
Goodge St	31	AJT	
Gower St	31	AKT	
Great Queen St	31	ALT	
Great Russell St	31	AKT	
Great Windmill St	31	AJU	261
Greek St	31	AKU	
Hanway St	31	AKT	210
Haymarket	31	AKU	
Henrietta St	31	ALU	217
Horse Guards Ave	31	ALV	
Horse Guards Rd	31	AKV	
James St SOHO	31	AJU	
Jermyn St	31	AJV	
John Adam St	31	ALV	238
Kingsway	31	ALT	
King St STRAND	31	ALU	
Leicester Square	31	AKU	
Lexington St	31	AJU	
Lisle St	31	AKU	
Long Acre	31	ALU	
Macklin St	31	ALT	
Maiden Lane	31	ALU	83
Mall (The)	31	AKV	
Monmouth St	31	ALU	88
Museum St	31	ALT	
Neal St	31	ALU	
Newman St	31	AJT	
Newton St	31	ALT	
New Oxford St	31	AKT	
New Row	31	ALU	
Noel St	31	AJU	
Northumberland Ave	31	ALV	
Old Compton St	31	AKU	
Old Gloucester St	31	ALT	
Orange St	31	AKV	
Pall Mall	31	AJV	
Panton St	31	AKU	
Parker St	31	ALT	
Percy St	31	AJT	
Piccadilly Circus	31	AJU	
Richmond Terrace	31	ALV	234
Romilly St	31	AKU	368
Royal Opera Arcade	31	AKV	
Rupert St	31	AKU	
Russell St	31	ALU	
St Giles Circus	31	AKT	
St Giles High St	31	AKT	
St James's Square	31	AJV	
St Martins Lane	31	ALU	
Savoy Pl.	31	ALU	
Shaftesbury Ave	31	AKU	
Shelton St	31	ALU	
Shorts Gardens	31	ALU	
Soho Square	31	AKT	
Southampton Row	31	ALT	4
Southampton St	31	ALU	3
Store St	31	AKT	
Strand	31	ALV	
Tavistock St	31	ALU	
Tottenham Court Rd.	31	AJT	
Trafalgar Square	31	AKV	
Upper St Martin's Lane	31	ALU	4
Villiers St	31	ALV	
Wardour St	31	AJU	
Warwick St	31	AJU	4
Waterloo Pl.	31	AKV	
Wellington St	31	ALU	1
Whitcomb St	31	AKU	1
Whitehall	31	ALV	
Whitehall Court	31	ALV	4
Whitehall Pl.	31	ALV	
Wild St	31	ALU	
William IV St	31	ALV	4

PLAN 32

Street	Plan	Grid	No.
Aldwych	32	AMU	
Arundel St	32	AMU	
Bedford Row	32	AMT	
Belvedere Rd	32	AMV	
Bouverie St	32	ANU	
Bream's Buildings	32	ANT	4
Carey St	32	AMU	
Chancery Lane	32	AMT	
Charterhouse St	32	ANT	
Cornwall Rd	32	ANV	
Cut (The)	32	ANV	
Essex St	32	AMU	
Farringdon Rd	32	ANT	
Fetter Lane	32	ANT	
Fleet St	32	ANU	
Furnival St	32	ANT	2
Gray's Inn Rd	32	ANT	
Greville St	32	ANT	
Halton Garden	32	ANT	
Hatfields	32	ANV	
High Holborn	32	AMT	
Holborn	32	ANT	
Holborn Viaduct	32	ANT	
John Carpenter St	32	ANU	1
Kemble St	32	AMU	
Lancaster Pl.	32	AMU	
Leather Lane	32	ANT	
Lincoln's Inn Fields	32	AMT	
New Fetter Lane	32	ANT	
New Square	32	AMT	
New St Square	32	ANT	28
Portugal St	32	AMU	
Procter St	32	AMT	2
Red Lion Square	32	AMT	
Red Lion St	32	AMT	
Roupel St	32	ANV	
St Andrews St	32	ANT	3
St Bride St	32	ANT	3
Sardinia St	32	AMT	3
Savoy St	32	AMU	2
Serle St	32	AMT	
Shoe Lane	32	ANT	
Stamford St	32	ANV	
Surrey St	32	AMU	1
Temple Ave	32	ANU	
Temple Pl.	32	AMU	

LONDON

LONDON

Gloucester Rd...... 36 ACX
Grenville Pl......... 36 ACY
Harcourt Terrace..... 36 ACZ 477
Harrington Gardens . 36 ACY
Harrington Rd .... 36 ADY
Hollywood Rd .... 36 ACZ
Hyde Park Gate ...... 36 ACX
Kensington Gore...... 36 ACX
King's Rd........... 36 ADZ
Launceston Pl. ...... 36 ACX 259
Little Boltons (The).. 36 ACZ
Manresa Rd .... 36 ADZ
Neville Terrace ...... 36 ADZ 300
Old Church St .... 36 ADZ
Onslow Gardens ... 36 ADZ
Onslow Square...... 36 ADY
Palace Gate......... 36 ACX
Park Walk .... 36 ACZ
Pelham St .... 36 ADY
Prince Consort Rd .. 36 ADX
Prince's Gardens.... 36 ADX 356
Queensberry Pl. ..... 36 ADY 360
Queen's Gate .... 36 ACX
Queen's Gate
  Gardens.......... 36 ACY 198
Queen's Gate Pl..... 36 ACY 363
Queen's Gate
  Terrace.......... 36 ACX
Redcliffe Rd .... 36 ACZ
Roland Gardens ..... 36 ACZ
South Parade .... 36 ADZ
Stanhope Gardens ... 36 ACY
Sumner Pl. .... 36 ADY
Sydney Pl............ 36 ADY 405
Thurloe Pl. .... 36 ADY
Thurloe Square ...... 36 ADY
Tregunter Rd......... 36 ACZ
Vale (The)........... 36 ADZ
Victoria Grove .... 36 ACX
Victoria Rd
  KENSINGTON..... 36 ACX
Wetherby Gardens... 36 ACY

PLAN 37

Basil St .... 37 AFX
Beauchamp Pl. ...... 37 AFX
Belgrave Square .... 37 AGX
Bourne St .... 37 AGY
Bray Pl. .... 37 AFY 45
Britten St........... 37 AEZ
Brompton Rd .... 37 AFX
Cadogan Gardens... 37 AGY 23
Cadogan Gate....... 37 AGY 220
Cadogan Pl.......... 37 AGY
Cadogan Square..... 37 AGY
Cadogan St.......... 37 AFY
Carriage Rd (The) ... 37 AFX
Chelsea Bridge Rd .. 37 AGZ
Chelsea
  Embankment ..... 37 AGZ
Chelsea Manor St... 37 AFZ
Cheltenham Terrace. 37 AGZ
Chesham Pl.......... 37 AGX
Chesham St .... 37 AGY
Chester Row........ 37 AGY
Cheval Pl. .... 37 AFX
Christchurch St..... 37 AFZ
Draycott Ave........ 37 AFY
Draycott Pl.......... 37 AFY
Eaton Pl............ 37 AGY
Egerton Gardens ... 37 AFY 160
Egerton Gardens
  Mews........... 37 AFY 162
Egerton Terrace .... 37 AFY 161
Elystan Pl. .... 37 AFZ
Elystan St .... 37 AEY
Ennismore Gardens . 37 AEX
Flood St............ 37 AFZ
Franklin's Row ..... 37 AGZ

Glebe Pl. .... 37 AEZ
Grosvenor Crescent . 37 AGX
Hans Crescent ..... 37 AFX
Hans Pl. .... 37 AFX
Hans Rd .... 37 AFX
Harriet St........... 37 AGX 214
Hasker St .... 37 AFY
Holbein Mews ..... 37 AGZ 223
Holbein Pl.......... 37 AGY
Ixworth Pl........... 37 AEY
Jubilee Pl. .... 37 AFZ
Knightsbridge ...... 37 AFX
Lennox Gardens.... 37 AFY
Lennox Gardens
  Mews .... 37 AFY 263
Lower Sloane St.... 37 AGY
Lowndes Square ... 37 AGX
Lowndes St .... 37 AGX
Lyall St............ 37 AGY
Markham St .... 37 AFZ
Milner St .... 37 AFY
Montpelier Square .. 37 AFX
Montpelier St ...... 37 AFX
Moore St........... 37 AFY
Mossop St .... 37 AFY
Oakley St.......... 37 AEZ
Ormonde Gate ..... 37 AGZ 329
Pimlico Rd......... 37 AGZ
Pont St .... 37 AFY
Radnor Walk ...... 37 AFZ
Rawlings St........ 37 AFY
Redesdale St ...... 37 AFZ 367
Royal Hospital Rd... 37 AFZ
Rutland Gate....... 37 AEX
St Leonard's Terrace. 37 AGZ
Shawfield St .... 37 AFZ
Sloane Ave .... 37 AFY
Sloane Square...... 37 AGY
Sloane St.......... 37 AGX
Smith St .... 37 AFZ
South Terrace ...... 37 AEY
Sydney St .... 37 AEZ
Symons St .... 37 AGY 407
Tedworth Square ... 37 AFZ
Tite St .... 37 AFZ
Trevor Pl. .... 37 AFX
Trevor Square ..... 37 AFX
Walton St .... 37 AFY
West Halkin St ..... 37 AGX
Whiteheads .... 37 AFY
William St .... 37 AGX 468
Wilton Pl........... 37 AGX

PLAN 38

Alderney St .... 38 AIY
Belgrave Pl.......... 38 AHX
Belgrave Rd .... 38 AIY
Birdcage Walk...... 38 AIX
Bressenden Pl. ..... 38 AIX
Buckingham Gate... 38 AIX
Buckingham Palace
  Rd .... 38 AHY
Carlisle Pl. .... 38 AIY
Castle Lane......... 38 AIX
Chapel St
  BELGRAVIA ..... 38 AHX
Charlwood St ...... 38 AIZ
Chelsea Bridge ..... 38 AHZ
Chester Square...... 38 AHY
Chester St.......... 38 AHX
Churchill Gardens Rd 38 AIZ
Clarendon St........ 38 AIZ
Constitution Hill .... 38 AHX
Cumberland St ..... 38 AIZ
Denbigh St .... 38 AIZ
Duke
  of Wellington Pl... 38 AHX 142
Eaton Square ...... 38 AHY
Ebury Bridge....... 38 AHZ

Ebury Bridge Rd .... 38 AHZ
Ebury St............ 38 AHY
Eccleston Bridge ... 38 AHY 1
Eccleston Square.... 38 AIY
Eccleston St .... 38 AHY
Elizabeth St .... 38 AHY
Francis St .... 38 AIY
Gillingham St....... 38 AIY
Gloucester St ...... 38 AIZ
Grosvenor Gardens . 38 AHX
Grosvenor Pl. ...... 38 AHX
Grosvenor Rd ...... 38 AHZ
Guildhouse St ...... 38 AIY 2
Halkin St .... 38 AHX
Hobart Pl. .... 38 AHX
Hudson's Pl. .... 38 AIY
Hugh St .... 38 AIY
Lower Belgrave St .. 38 AHY
Lower Grosvenor Pl. 38 AIX 2
Lupus St .... 38 AIZ
Palace St.......... 38 AIX
St George's Drive... 38 AIY
South Eaton Pl...... 38 AHY
Sutherland St ...... 38 AHZ
Terminus Pl. .... 38 AIY 4
Upper Belgrave St .. 38 AHX
Vauxhall Bridge Rd .. 38 AIY
Victoria St .... 38 AIX
Warwick Square .... 38 AIY
Warwick Way ...... 38 AHZ
Wilton Rd .... 38 AIY
Wilton St .... 38 AHX

PLAN 39

Abingdon St .... 39 AKY
Albert Embankment. 39 ALY
Artillery Row ...... 39 AJX 8
Atterbury St........ 39 ALZ
Aylesford St .... 39 AKZ
Bessborough
  Gardens......... 39 AKZ
Bessborough St .... 39 AKZ 3
Bridge St .... 39 ALX
Broad Sanctuary .... 39 ALX 5
Caxton St .... 39 AJX
Chichester St ...... 39 AJZ
Claverton St .... 39 AJZ
Dolphin Square..... 39 AJZ
Douglas St......... 39 AKY
Erasmus St .... 39 AKY
Glasshouse St
  LAMBETH....... 39 ALZ 1
Great College St .... 39 ALX
Great George St .... 39 AKX 1
Great Peter St....... 39 AKY
Great Smith St ..... 39 AKX
Greencoat Pl. ...... 39 AJY
Greycoat Pl......... 39 AJY 2
Greycoat St......... 39 AJY
Horseferry Rd ...... 39 AKY
Howick Pl.......... 39 AJY
John Islip St .... 39 AKZ
King Charles St ..... 39 AKX
Lambeth Bridge .... 39 ALY
Marsham St .... 39 AKY
Millbank........... 39 ALZ
Monck St.......... 39 AKY
Montpelier Walk.... 37 AFX
Moreton St .... 39 AJZ
Nine Elms Lane .... 39 AKZ
Old Pye St......... 39 AKX
Page St .... 39 AKY
Palmer St .... 39 AJX
Parlament Square... 39 ALX
Parliament St ...... 39 ALX
Parry St .... 39 ALZ 3
Petty France .... 39 AJX
Ponsonby Pl........ 39 AKZ
Rampayne St ...... 39 AKZ

Regency St . . . . 39 **AKY**
Rochester Row. . . . . 39 **AJY**
St Anne's St . . . . 39 **AKX**
St George's Square . 39 **AJZ**
South Lambeth Rd . . 39 **ALZ** 154
Storeys Gate . . . . 39 **AKX**
Tachbrook St. . . . . . . 39 **AJY**
Thirleby Rd . . . . 39 **AJY** 416
Thorney St. . . . . 39 **ALY**
Tinworth St . . . . 39 **ALZ** 129
Tothill St. . . . . 39 **AKX**
Tufton St . . . . 39 **AKX**
Vauxhall Bridge . . . . . 39 **ALZ**
Vincent Square . . . . . 39 **AJY**
Vincent St . . . . 39 **AKY**
Westminster Bridge . 39 **ALX**

PLAN 40

Baylis Rd . . . . 40 **ANX**
Black Prince Rd. . . . . 40 **AMY**
Braganza St. . . . . 40 **AOZ**
Brook Drive . . . . 40 **ANY**
Chester Way . . . . 40 **ANY**
Clayton St . . . . 40 **ANZ**
Cleaver St . . . . 40 **ANZ**
Cooks St . . . . 40 **AOZ**
Courtenay St . . . . 40 **AMZ**
Dante Rd . . . . 40 **AOY**
De Laune St . . . . 40 **ANZ**
Durham St. . . . . 40 **AMZ** 150
Fitzalan St . . . . 40 **AMY**
Garden Row . . . . 40 **AOX** 173
Harleyford Rd . . . . . . 40 **AMZ**
Hayles St . . . . 40 **AOY**
Hercules Rd . . . . 40 **AMX**
Johnathan St. . . . . . . 40 **AMZ**
Juxon St . . . . 40 **AMY**
Kennington Lane . . . 40 **AMZ**
Kennington Oval . . . . 40 **AMZ**
Kennington Rd . . . . . 40 **ANX**
Kennington Park Rd 40 **ANZ**
Lambeth High St . . . 40 **AMY**
Lambeth Palace Rd . 40 **AMX**
Lambeth Rd . . . . 40 **AMY**
Lambeth Walk . . . . . . 40 **AMY**
London Rd . . . . 40 **AOX**
Lower Marsh . . . . 40 **AMX**
Newburn St . . . . 40 **AMZ**
Pearman St . . . . 40 **ANX**
Ravensdon St . . . . . . 40 **ANZ** 219
Renfrew Rd . . . . 40 **ANY**
St George's Rd . . . . . 40 **ANX**
Sancroft St . . . . 40 **AMZ**
Stannary St . . . . 40 **ANZ**
Tyers St . . . . 40 **AMZ**
Vauxhall St. . . . . 40 **AMZ**
Vauxhall Walk . . . . . . 40 **AMZ**
Walcot Square . . . . . 40 **ANY**
Walnut Tree Walk. . . 40 **AMY**
Webber St. . . . . 40 **ANX**
Westminster Bridge Rd . . . . 40 **AMX**
West Square . . . . 40 **AOY**
Wincoot St . . . . 40 **ANY**
York Rd . . . . 40 **AMX**

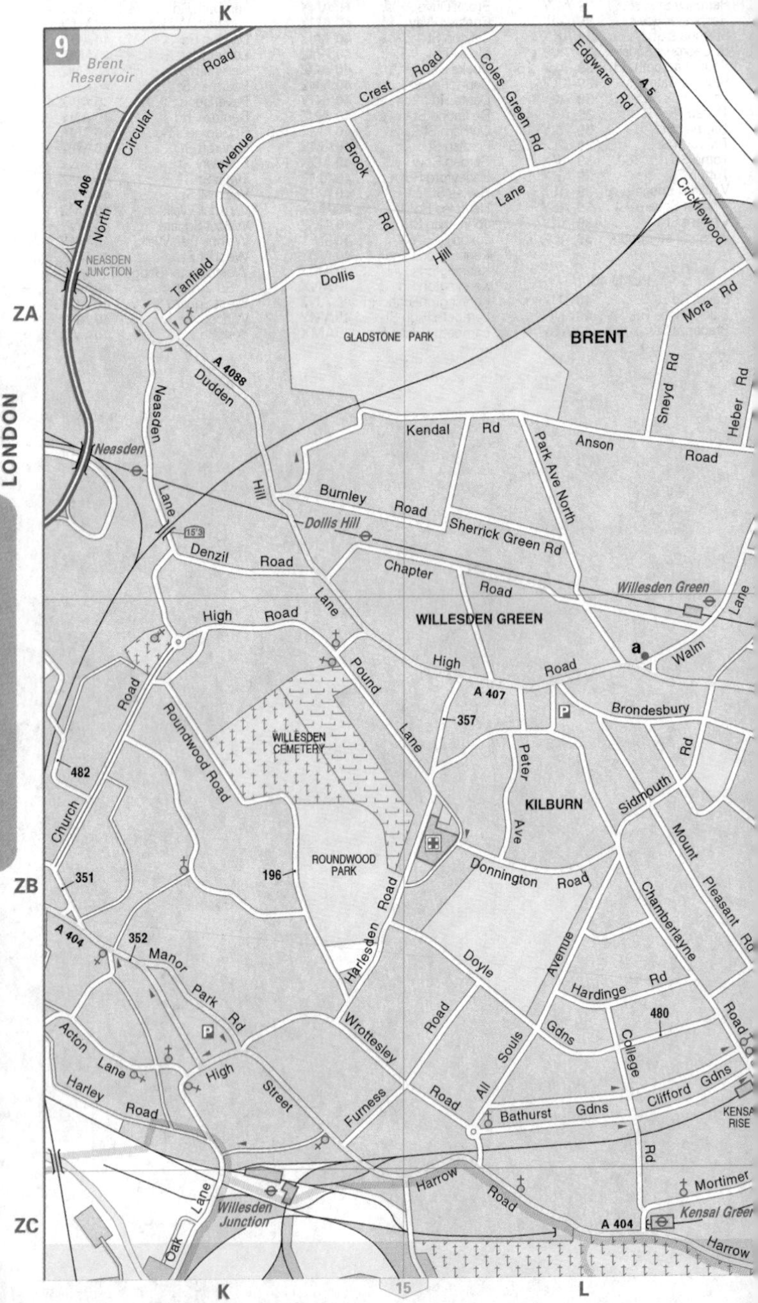
K
L
9
Brent Reservoir
Road
Circular
North
A 406
NEASDEN JUNCTION
Avenue
Tanfield
Crest Road
Brook Rd
Coles Green Rd
Edgware Rd
A 5
Lane
Hill
Dollis
Cricklewood
Mora Rd
ZA
GLADSTONE PARK
BRENT
Sneyd Rd
Heber Rd
A 4088
Dudden
Neasden
Neasden
Lane
Kendal Rd
Park Ave North
Anson Road
LONDON
Hill
Burnley Road
Sherrick Green Rd
Dollis Hill
Denzil Road
Chapter Road
Willesden Green
Lane
WILLESDEN GREEN
High Road
Lane
Walm
a
High Road
A 407
Pound Lane
Road
Roundwood Road
WILLESDEN CEMETERY
357
Brondesbury Rd
Peter Ave
KILBURN
Sidmouth
482
Church
Mount Pleasant Rd
ROUNDWOOD PARK
196
Donnington Road
ZB
351
Road
Chamberlayne
A 404
352
Manor Park Rd
Harlesden
Doyle
Avenue
Hardinge Rd
480
Road
Acton Lane
High Street
Wrottesley Road
Road
Gdns
College
Harley Road
Furness
All Souls
Clifford Gdns
Bathurst Gdns
KENSAL RISE
Rd
Lane
Harrow Road
Mortimer
Willesden Junction
ZC
Oak
A 404
Kensal Green
Harrow
K
15
L

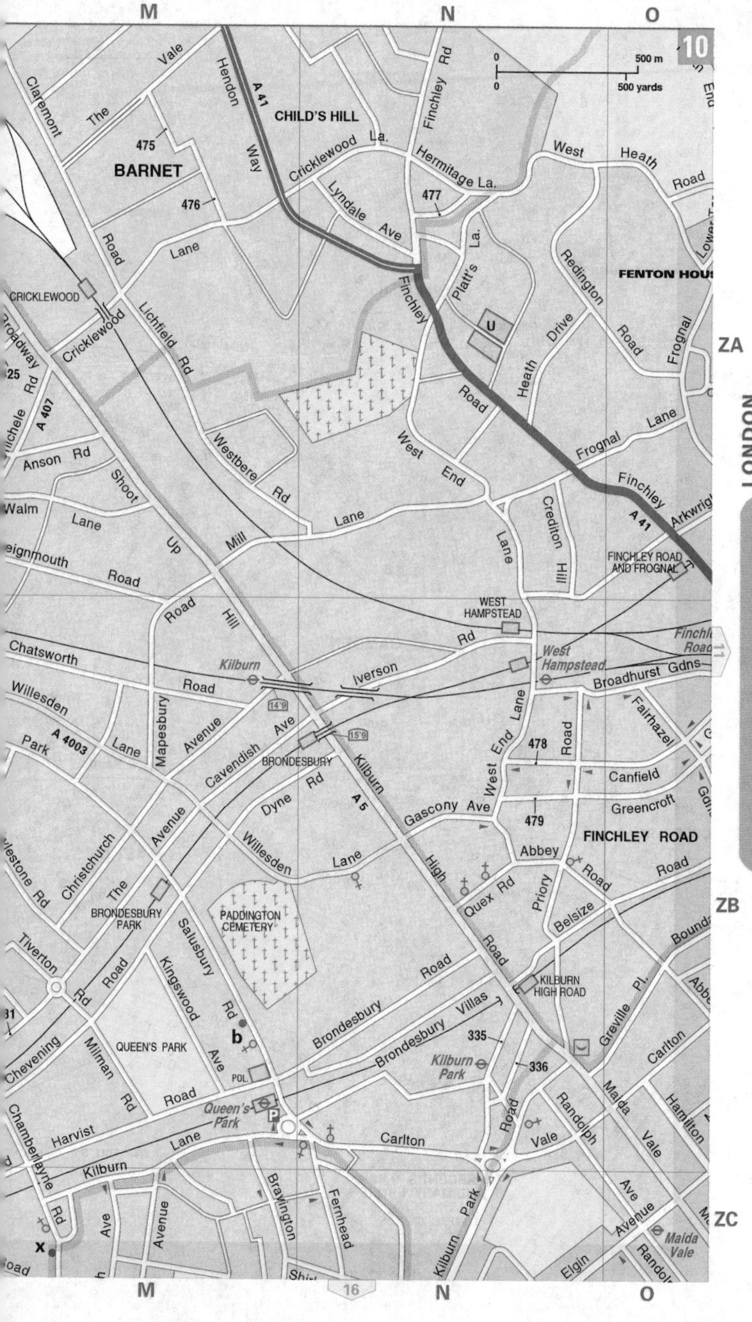
M
N
O
10
0
500 m
500 yards
ZA
ZB
ZC
LONDON
BARNET
CHILD'S HILL
FENTON HOUSE
FINCHLEY ROAD
QUEEN'S PARK
CRICKLEWOOD
WEST HAMPSTEAD
West Hampstead
Kilburn
FINCHLEY ROAD AND FROGNAL
BRONDESBURY
BRONDESBURY PARK
KILBURN HIGH ROAD
Kilburn Park
Queen's Park
Maida Vale
PADDINGTON CEMETERY
POL.
A 41
A 407
A 4003
A 5
475
476
477
478
479
335
336
11
16
b
x
Claremont
The Vale
Hendon Way
Cricklewood La.
Hermitage La.
Lyndale Ave
Finchley Rd
West Heath Road
Platt's La.
Redington Road
Heath Drive
Frognal
Frognal Lane
Finchley Road
Arkwright
Cricklewood Road
Lane
Cricklewood Broadway
Lichfield Rd
Westbere Rd
West End Lane
Anson Rd
Shoot Up Hill
Walm Lane
Mill Lane
Teignmouth Road
Crediton Hill
Chatsworth Road
Iverson Rd
Broadhurst Gdns
Fairhazel
Willesden Lane
Mapesbury
Avenue
Cavendish Ave
Park
Dyne Rd
Kilburn High Road
Canfield
Greencroft
Gascony Ave
Abbey Road
Priory
Quex Rd
Belsize Road
Christchurch Avenue
The
Salusbury Rd
Kingswood Ave
Tiverton Rd
Brondesbury Road
Brondesbury Villas
Greville Pl.
Boundary
Carlton
Hamilton
Milman Rd
Chevening
Chamberlayne Rd
Harvist Road
Kilburn Lane
Carlton Vale
Randolph
Randolph Ave
Maida Vale
Kilburn Park Road
Bravington
Fernhead
Elgin Avenue
Ave
Avenue
Shirland

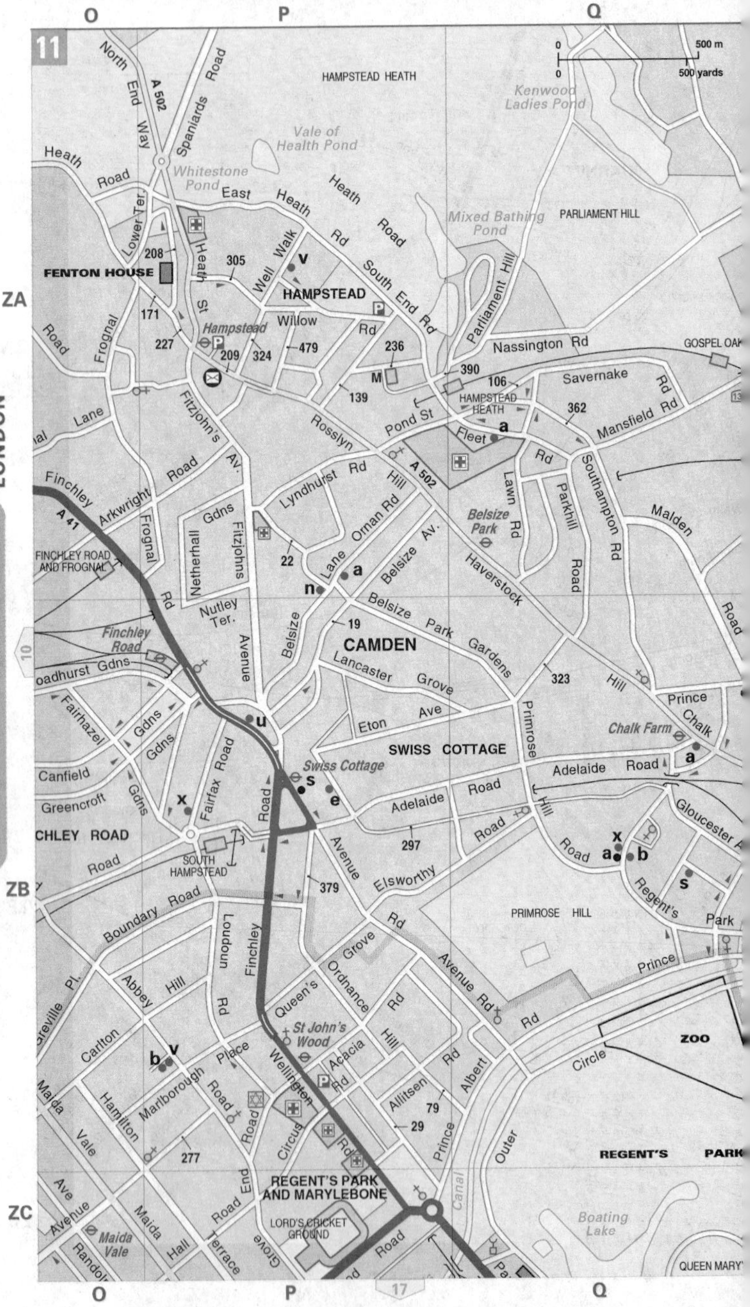
O
P
Q
11
0
500 m
0
500 yards
HAMPSTEAD HEATH
Kenwood Ladies Pond
Vale of Health Pond
Whitestone Pond
Mixed Bathing Pond
PARLIAMENT HILL
North End Way
A 502
Spaniards Road
Heath Road
East Heath Rd
Heath Road
Lower Ter.
Heath St
Well Walk
South End Rd
Parliament Hill
FENTON HOUSE
208
305
171
227
HAMPSTEAD
Willow Rd
Hampstead
209
324
479
236
390
106
Nassington Rd
GOSPEL OAK
Savernake Rd
Mansfield Rd
362
HAMPSTEAD HEATH
Pond St
Fleet Rd
Frognal
Lane
Fitzjohn's Av.
Rosslyn Hill
139
A 502
Lawn Rd
Parkhill Road
Southampton Rd
Malden Road
Finchley Road
A 41
Arkwright Road
Frognal
Netherhall Gdns
Fitzjohns Avenue
Lyndhurst Rd
Oman Rd
Belsize Av.
Belsize Park
Haverstock Hill
FINCHLEY ROAD AND FROGNAL
22
Lane
Nutley Ter.
Belsize Lane
Belsize Park Gardens
19
CAMDEN
Finchley Road
Broadhurst Gdns
Lancaster Grove
323
Prince
Chalk
Chalk Farm
Fairhazel Gdns
Eton Ave
Primrose Hill Rd
SWISS COTTAGE
Fairfax Road
Swiss Cottage
Canfield Gdns
Adelaide Road
Adelaide Road
Greencroft Gdns
Road
Gloucester Av.
FINCHLEY ROAD
SOUTH HAMPSTEAD
297
Road
Road
Regent's Park Road
Avenue
Elsworthy Rd
379
ZA
ZB
ZC
Boundary Road
Loudoun Rd
Finchley
PRIMROSE HILL
Abbey Hill
Grove
Ordnance Hill
Queen's
Avenue Rd
Prince
Greville Pl.
Carlton
St John's Wood
Acacia Rd
Rd
ZOO
Circle
Maida Vale
Hamilton
Marlborough Place
Road
Wellington Road
Allitsen Rd
Albert Rd
79
29
Circus Rd
Prince
Outer
REGENT'S PARK
277
REGENT'S PARK AND MARYLEBONE
Canal
Ave
Avenue
Maida Vale
Maida
Hall
Road End
Terrace
Grove
LORD'S CRICKET GROUND
Road
Boating Lake
QUEEN MARY'S
Randolph
10
17

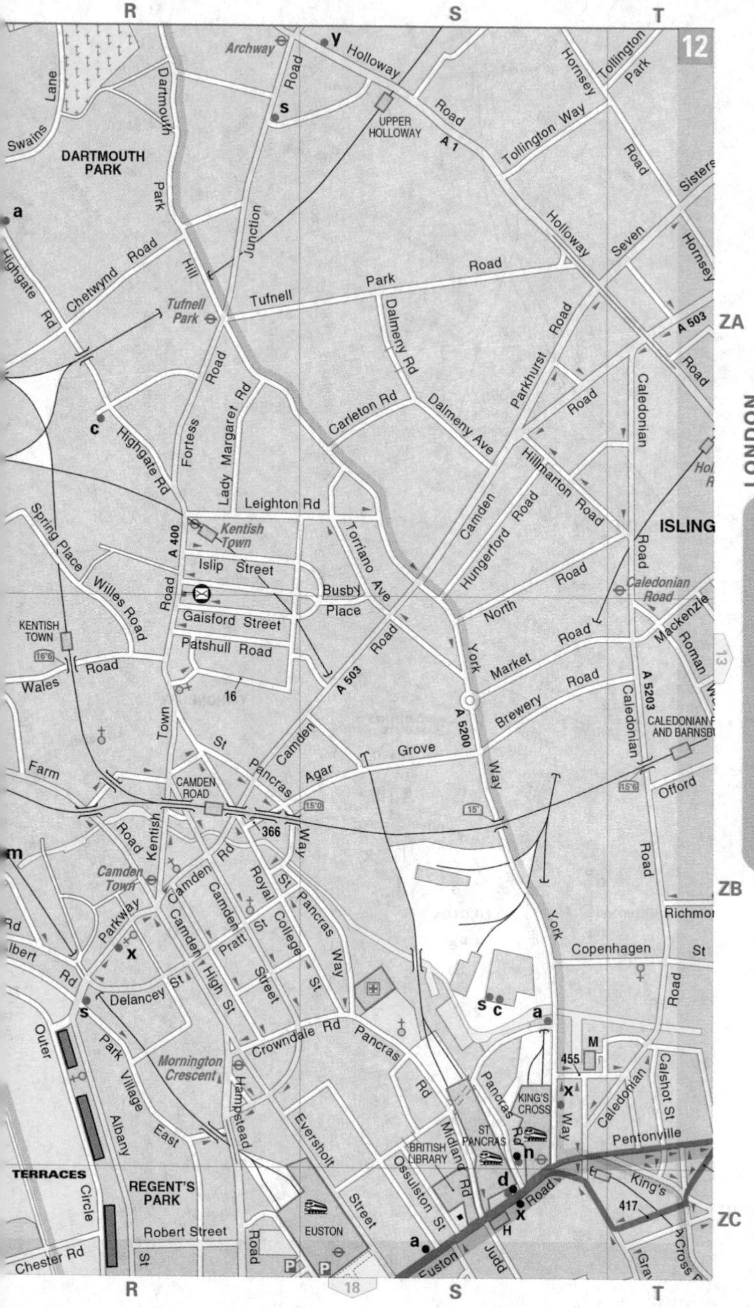
R
S
T
12
Archway
Holloway
Road
UPPER HOLLOWAY
A 1
Hornsey
Tollington
Park
Tollington Way
Sisters
Swains
Lane
DARTMOUTH PARK
Dartmouth
Park
Hill
Junction
Seven
Hornsey
Chetwynd
Highgate
Rd
Tufnell
Tufnell Park
Dalmeny Rd
Parkhurst
A 503
ZA
Caledonian
LONDON
Carleton Rd
Dalmeny Ave
Fortess
Lady Margaret Rd
Highgate Rd
Leighton Rd
Kentish Town
Camden
Hillmarton
Hungerford
ISLING
Spring Place
A 400
Islip Street
Torriano Ave
Caledonian Road
Willes Road
Busby Place
North
Mackenzie
KENTISH TOWN
Gaisford Street
Patshull Road
York
Market
Roman
16'6
Wales
16
A 5200
Brewery
A 5203
CALEDONIAN AND BARNSB
Town
St
Pancras
Camden
Agar
Grove
Farm
CAMDEN ROAD
15'0
15'
15'6
Offord
366
Way
m
ZB
Camden Town
Royal
College
Richmon
Copenhagen
Parkway
Pratt
High St
Delancey St
Street
Crowndale Rd
Outer
Park Village East
Mornington Crescent
Hampstead
Eversholt
Midland Rd
455
M
KING'S CROSS
Calshot St
Pentonville
ST PANCRAS
BRITISH LIBRARY
Ossulston St
Albany
TERRACES
Circle
REGENT'S PARK
Robert Street
Chester Rd
EUSTON
Euston
Judd
King's
417
Cross
Gray
ZC
H
18

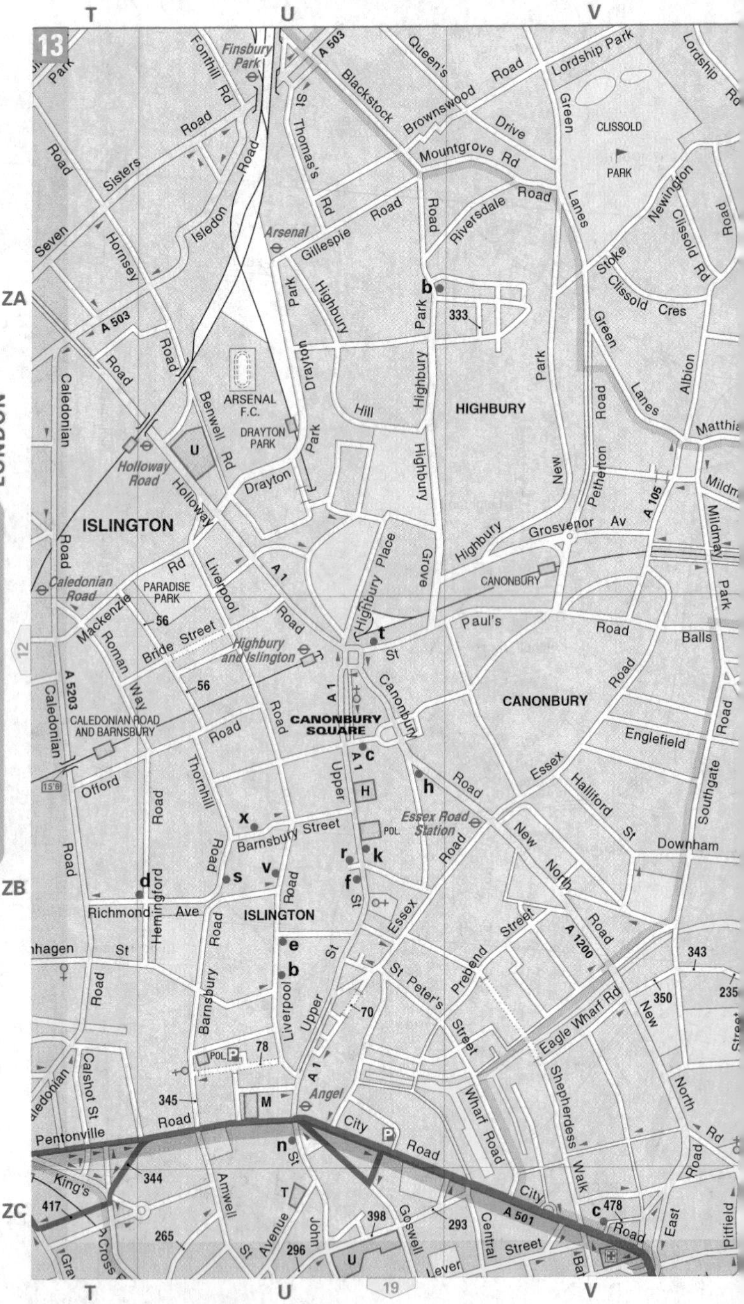

T
U
V
13
Finsbury Park
A 503
Queen's
Lordship Park
Lordship Rd
Fonthill Rd
Park
Blackstock
Brownswood
Road
Drive
St Thomas's
Road
Sisters
Seven
Mountgrove Rd
Green Lanes
CLISSOLD PARK
Rd
Road
Riversdale
Road
Newington
Clissold Rd
Road
Arsenal
Gillespie
Isledon
Hornsey
Stoke
Clissold Cres
ZA
A 503
Highbury Park
333
b
Road
Road
Drayton Park
ARSENAL F.C.
DRAYTON PARK
Benwell Rd
Hill
Highbury
HIGHBURY
New Park Road
Green Lanes
Albion
Matthias
Caledonian Road
Holloway Road
Holloway
U
Drayton
Petherton
A 105
Mildmay
ISLINGTON
Grosvenor Av
Highbury
Caledonian Road
Rd
Liverpool
A 1
Highbury Place
Grove
CANONBURY
Mildmay Park
PARADISE PARK
Mackenzie
56
Road
Highbury
t
Paul's
Road
Balls
Bride Street
Highbury and Islington
St
12
Roman Way
56
Canonbury
CANONBURY
Road
A 5203
Caledonian
CALEDONIAN ROAD AND BARNSBURY
Road
Road
A 1
CANONBURY SQUARE
Englefield
Road
c
A 1
Offord
15'6
Thornhill
Upper
H
h
Road
Essex
Halliford
Southgate
Road
x
Barnsbury Street
Essex Road Station
POL.
New
St
Downham
Road
Road
r
k
Road
North
ZB
d
s
v
f
Road
Hemingford
Richmond Ave
ISLINGTON
St
Essex
Street
A 1200
Road
Road
hagen St
e
St
Prebend
343
b
Road
Barnsbury
Liverpool
Upper
St Peter's
350
235
70
New
Eagle Wharf Rd
Street
Calshot St
POL.
P
78
Street
Shepherdess
Caledonian
345
A 1
Angel
M
Wharf Road
North
Pentonville
Road
City
P
Road
Rd
n
St
Walk
King's
344
T
Road
Amwell
City
ZC
417
Avenue
398
Goswell
293
Central
A 501
c
478
Road
Pitfield
Cross
265
St
John
296
U
Lever
Street
East
Ba
19
T
U
V

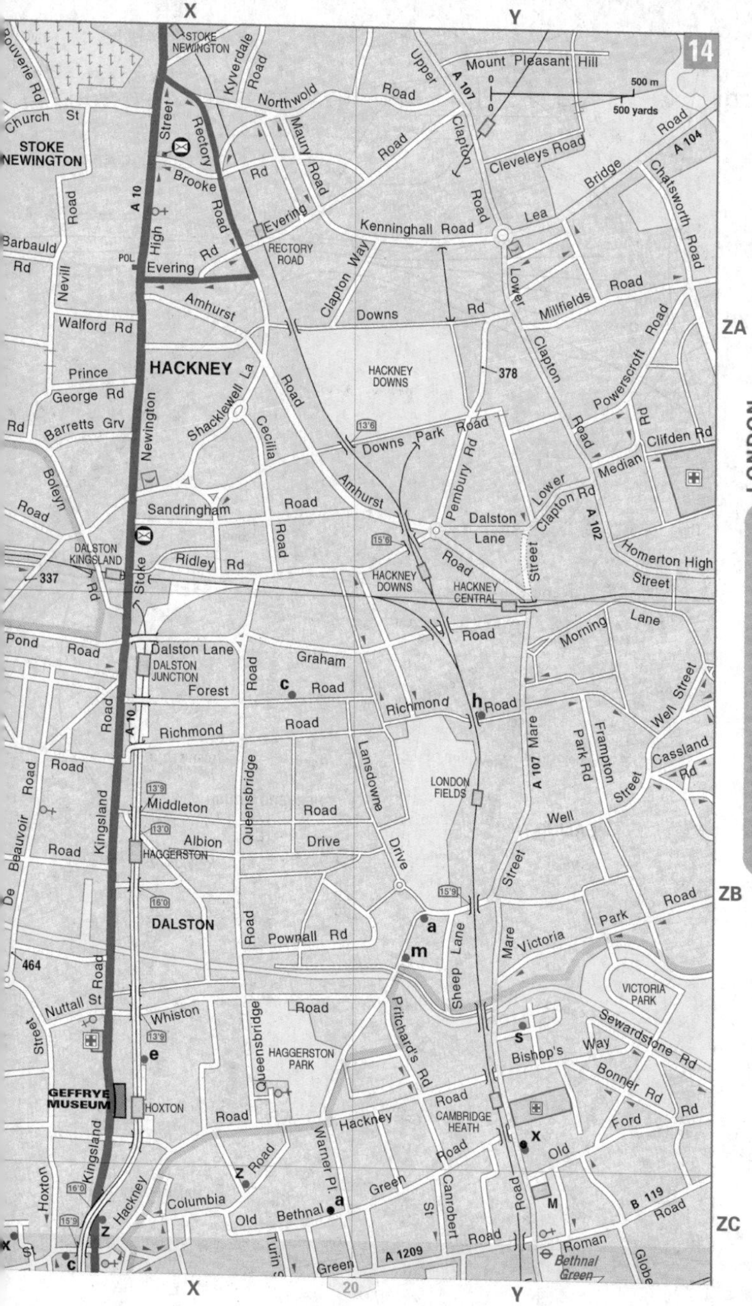
X
Y
14
STOKE NEWINGTON
Kyverdale Road
Northwold Road
Upper Road
Mount Pleasant Hill
A 107
500 m
500 yards
Church St
STOKE NEWINGTON
Rectory Road
Maury Road
Road
Clapton Road
Cleveleys Road
Bridge Road
A 104
Chatsworth Road
Brooke Rd
A 10
High Street
Evering Rd
Kenninghall Road
Lea Bridge
Barbauld Rd
Nevill Road
POL
Evering Rd
RECTORY ROAD
Clapton Way
Lower Clapton
Millfields Road
Amhurst Road
Walford Rd
Downs Rd
ZA
Powerscroft Road
Prince George Rd
HACKNEY
Shacklewell La
HACKNEY DOWNS
378
Barretts Grv
Rd
Newington
Cecilia Road
Downs Park Road
Pembury Rd
Rd
Clifden Rd
Median
Boleyn Road
Amhurst Road
Lower Clapton Rd
A 102
Sandringham Road
Dalston Lane
Road
DALSTON KINGSLAND
Ridley Rd
Homerton High Street
337
Stoke
HACKNEY DOWNS
HACKNEY CENTRAL
Street
Morning Lane
Pond Road
Dalston Lane
Graham Road
DALSTON JUNCTION
Forest Road
c
Well Street
Richmond Road
h
A 10
Richmond Road
A 107 Mare
Park Rd
Frampton
Cassland Rd
Road
Lansdowne Drive
LONDON FIELDS
Middleton Road
Well Street
De Beauvoir Road
Kingsland
Albion Drive
Queensbridge
HAGGERSTON
DALSTON
Pownall Rd
a
m
Sheep Lane
Mare Street
Victoria Park Road
ZB
464
Nuttall St
Whiston Road
Pritchard's Rd
VICTORIA PARK
Sewardstone Rd
s
Bishop's Way
Bonner Rd
e
HAGGERSTON PARK
Queensbridge
GEFFRYE MUSEUM
HOXTON
Road
Hackney Road
CAMBRIDGE HEATH
Ford Rd
x
Old Road
Z Road
Warner Pl.
Green
Canrobert St
Hoxton St
Kingsland
Hackney Road
Columbia
a
Old Bethnal Green
M
B 119 Road
ZC
Turin St
A 1209
Road
Roman Road
Bethnal Green
Globe
20
LONDON

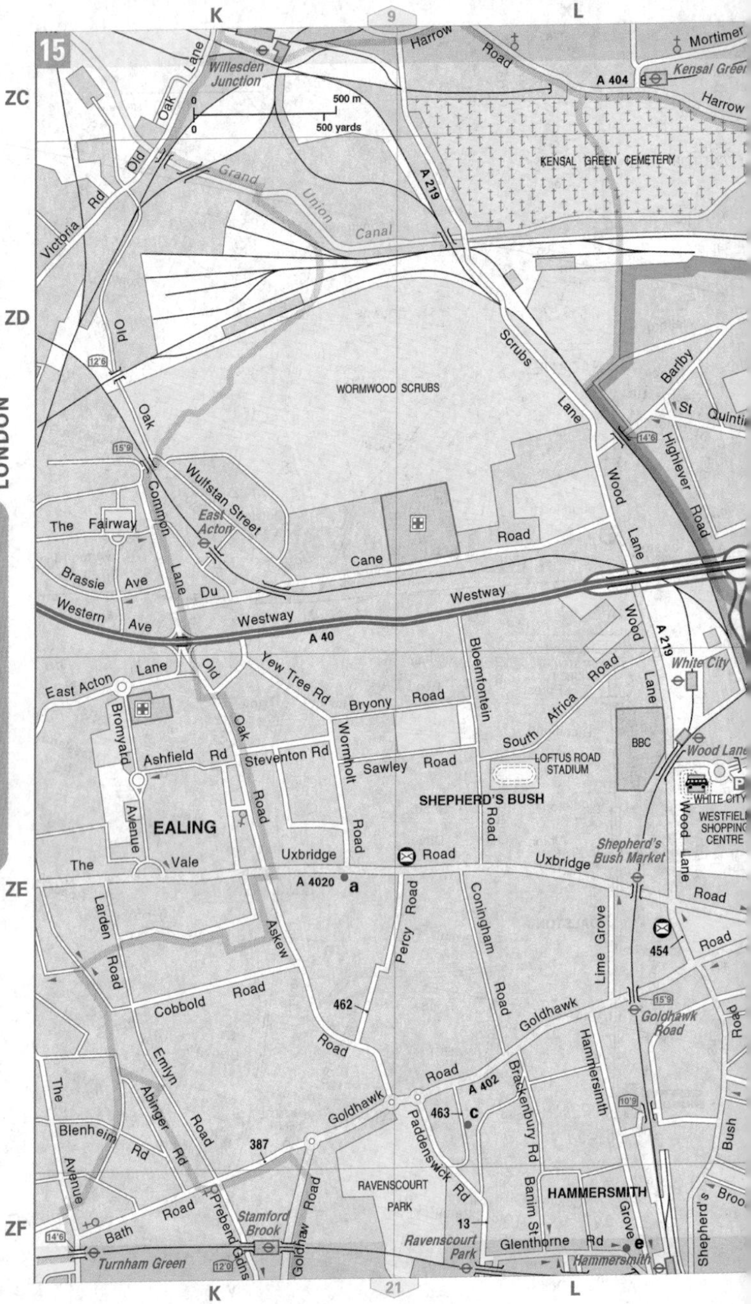

15
K
L
9
21
ZC
ZD
ZE
ZF
0
500 m
0
500 yards
Willesden Junction
Harrow Road
Mortimer
Kensal Green
A 404
Harrow
KENSAL GREEN CEMETERY
Old Oak Lane
Grand Union Canal
A 219
Victoria Rd
Old
12'6
Oak
Scrubs Lane
WORMWOOD SCRUBS
Barlby
St Quintin
14'6
Highlever Road
15'9
Wood Lane
Common Lane
Wulfstan Street
East Acton
The Fairway
Road
Cane
Brassie Ave
Du
Westway
Western Ave
Westway
A 40
A 219
Old
Yew Tree Rd
Bloemfontein
Road
White City
East Acton Lane
Bryony Road
South Africa
Lane
BBC
Bromyard
Ashfield Rd
Oak
Steventon Rd
Wormholt
Sawley Road
LOFTUS ROAD STADIUM
Wood Lane
WHITE CITY
WESTFIELD SHOPPING CENTRE
Avenue
EALING
Road
SHEPHERD'S BUSH
Road
Road
The Vale
Uxbridge
Road
Uxbridge
Shepherd's Bush Market
Wood Lane
A 4020
a
Road
Larden Road
Askew
Percy Road
Coningham Road
Lime Grove
454
Road
Cobbold Road
462
Road
Goldhawk
15'9
Goldhawk Road
Road
Emlyn
Road
A 402
Brackenbury Rd
Hammersmith
The
Abinger
Road
10'9
Goldhawk
463
c
Paddenswick Rd
Bush
Blenheim
Rd
Rd
387
Avenue
Prebend Gdns
Goldhawk Road
RAVENSCOURT PARK
Banim St
HAMMERSMITH
Grove
Shepherd's
Bath Road
Stamford Brook
13
Ravenscourt Park
Glenthorne Rd
e
14'6
Turnham Green
12'0
Hammersmith
K
L

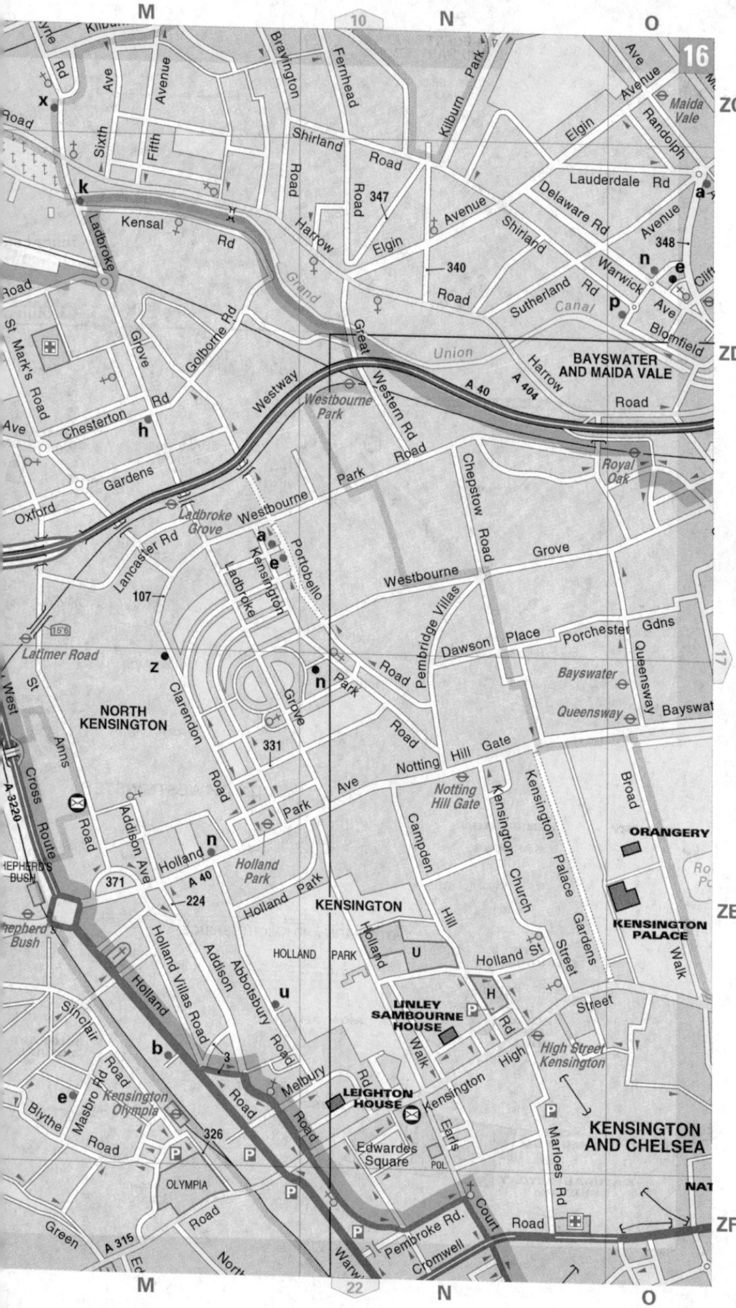
M
N
O
10
16
17
22
ZC
ZD
ZE
ZF
Kensal Rd
Ladbroke Grove
Sixth Ave
Fifth Avenue
Bravington Road
Fernhead Road
Kilburn Park
Shirland Road
Elgin Avenue
Harrow Road
Grand Union Canal
Maida Vale
Randolph Avenue
Lauderdale Rd
Delaware Rd
Warwick Ave
Sutherland Ave
Blomfield Rd
BAYSWATER AND MAIDA VALE
Golborne Rd
Great Western Rd
Westway
A 40
A 404
Westbourne Park
Westbourne Park Road
Royal Oak
Chesterton Rd
Oxford Gardens
St Mark's Road
Ladbroke Grove
Lancaster Rd
Kensington Park Rd
Portobello Road
Chepstow Road
Westbourne Grove
Pembridge Villas
Dawson Place
Porchester Gdns
Queensway
Bayswater
Latimer Road
NORTH KENSINGTON
Clarendon Road
St Anns Road
West Cross Route
A 3220
Notting Hill Gate
Holland Park Ave
Campden Hill
Kensington Church Street
Kensington Palace Gardens
Broad Walk
ORANGERY
KENSINGTON PALACE
Addison Ave
Holland Park
Shepherd's Bush
KENSINGTON
HOLLAND PARK
Holland Villas Road
Addison Road
Abbotsbury Road
Holland Road
Holland Walk
Holland St
LINLEY SAMBOURNE HOUSE
Kensington High Street
High Street Kensington
Melbury Rd
LEIGHTON HOUSE
Edwardes Square
Earls Court Road
Marloes Rd
KENSINGTON AND CHELSEA
Sinclair Road
Masbro Rd
Blythe Road
Kensington Olympia
OLYMPIA
Pembroke Rd.
Cromwell Road
Warwick Road
A 315
North End Road
Green
POL
371
224
107
331
326
340
347
348

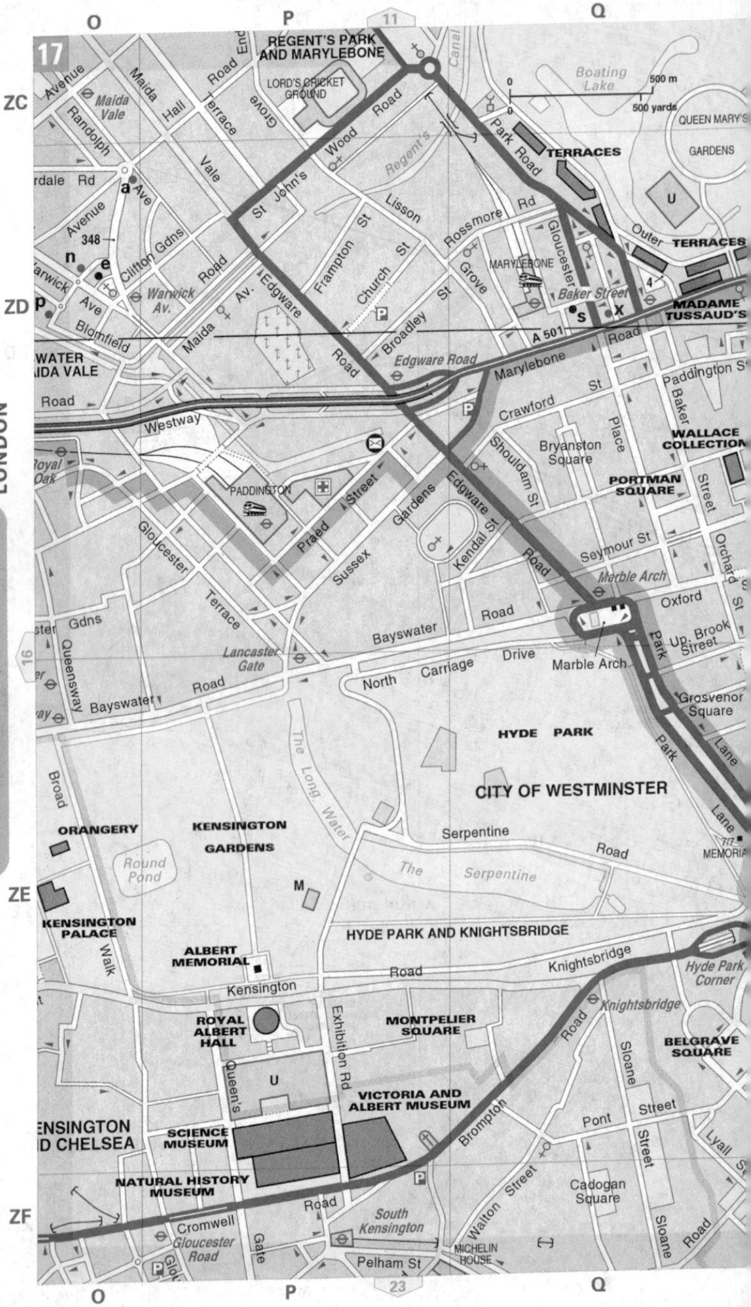
O
P
Q
11
17
ZC
ZD
ZE
ZF
16
23
REGENT'S PARK AND MARYLEBONE
LORD'S CRICKET GROUND
Boating Lake
0
500 m
500 yards
QUEEN MARY'S GARDENS
TERRACES
Outer
TERRACES
U
Park Road
Canal
Regent's
Maida Vale
Randolph
Maida
Hall
Road
Terrace
Grove
Road
Wood
St John's
Vale
Lisson
Rossmore
Rd
Gloucester
Grove
MARYLEBONE
Baker Street
4
MADAME TUSSAUD'S
S
X
rdale Rd
a
Ave
Avenue
348
n
e
Clifton Gdns
Road
Warwick Av.
arwick
Ave
p
Blomfield
Maida
Av.
Edgware
Frampton
St
Church
St
St
Broadley
Road
A 501
Road
WATER
AIDA VALE
Edgware Road
Marylebone
Road
Westway
St
Crawford
Paddington St
Baker
Place
Bryanston Square
WALLACE COLLECTION
Shouldam St
Royal Oak
PADDINGTON
Street
Praed
Gardens
Edgware
PORTMAN SQUARE
Street
Gloucester
Sussex
Kendal St
Road
Seymour St
Orchard St
Marble Arch
Terrace
Road
Oxford
Up. Brook Street
Park
Gdns
ster
Queensway
Bayswater
Lancaster Gate
Drive
Carriage
North
Marble Arch
Road
Bayswater
Grosvenor Square
HYDE PARK
Park
Lane
The Long Water
CITY OF WESTMINSTER
Broad
ORANGERY
KENSINGTON GARDENS
Serpentine
Road
Lane
7/7 MEMORIAL
Round Pond
The Serpentine
M
KENSINGTON PALACE
HYDE PARK AND KNIGHTSBRIDGE
Walk
ALBERT MEMORIAL
Road
Knightsbridge
Hyde Park Corner
Kensington
Knightsbridge
ROYAL ALBERT HALL
MONTPELIER SQUARE
Road
Exhibition Rd
BELGRAVE SQUARE
Queen's
U
Sloane
VICTORIA AND ALBERT MUSEUM
Street
ENSINGTON
D CHELSEA
SCIENCE MUSEUM
Pont
Street
Brompton
Lyall St
Street
NATURAL HISTORY MUSEUM
Walton
Street
Cadogan Square
Road
South Kensington
Cromwell
Gloucester Road
Gate
Sloane
Road
MICHELIN HOUSE
Pelham St

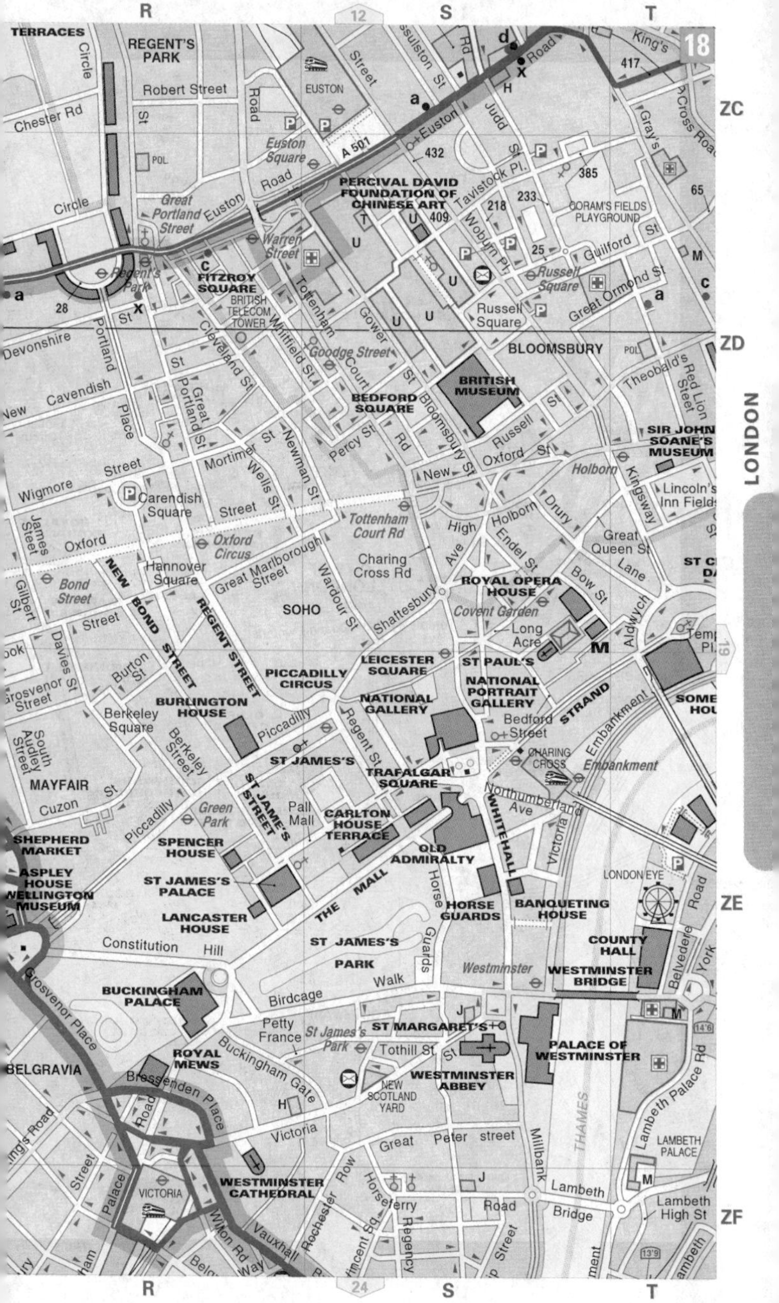

R
S
T
12
18
LONDON
ZC
ZD
ZE
ZF
24
19
TERRACES
REGENT'S PARK
Robert Street
Chester Rd
Circle
Great Portland Street
Euston Road
Euston Square
EUSTON
A 501
Warren Street
Regent's Park
FITZROY SQUARE
BRITISH TELECOM TOWER
PERCIVAL DAVID FOUNDATION OF CHINESE ART
Tavistock Pl.
Judd St
Gray's Inn Road
King's Cross Road
CORAM'S FIELDS PLAYGROUND
Guilford St
Russell Square
Great Ormond St
Woburn Pl.
Devonshire St
Portland Place
New Cavendish St
Great Portland St
Cleveland St
Whitfield St.
Tottenham Court Rd
Goodge Street
Gower St
BLOOMSBURY
BRITISH MUSEUM
Theobald's Rd
Red Lion Street
SIR JOHN SOANE'S MUSEUM
BEDFORD SQUARE
Bloomsbury St
Percy St
Mortimer St
Wells St
Newman St
Wigmore Street
Cavendish Square
James Street
Oxford Street
Oxford Circus
Tottenham Court Rd
Charing Cross Rd
New Oxford St
Holborn
Kingsway
Lincoln's Inn Fields
High Holborn
Drury Lane
Great Queen St
Endell St
Hannover Square
Great Marlborough Street
Wardour St
SOHO
Shaftesbury Ave
ROYAL OPERA HOUSE
Bow St
Aldwych
Covent Garden
Long Acre
Bond Street
NEW BOND STREET
REGENT STREET
Gilbert St
Davies St
Grosvenor Street
Burton St
BURLINGTON HOUSE
PICCADILLY CIRCUS
LEICESTER SQUARE
ST PAUL'S
NATIONAL PORTRAIT GALLERY
NATIONAL GALLERY
STRAND
Embankment
Temple Pl.
Berkeley Square
Berkeley Street
South Audley Street
Piccadilly
Regent St
Bedford Street
CHARING CROSS
ST JAMES'S
TRAFALGAR SQUARE
MAYFAIR
Curzon St
ST JAMES'S STREET
Green Park
Pall Mall
CARLTON HOUSE TERRACE
Northumberland Ave
WHITEHALL
Victoria Embankment
SHEPHERD MARKET
SPENCER HOUSE
OLD ADMIRALTY
APSLEY HOUSE WELLINGTON MUSEUM
ST JAMES'S PALACE
THE MALL
Horse Guards Rd
HORSE GUARDS
BANQUETING HOUSE
LONDON EYE
LANCASTER HOUSE
Constitution Hill
ST JAMES'S PARK
COUNTY HALL
Westminster
WESTMINSTER BRIDGE
Belvedere Road
York Road
BUCKINGHAM PALACE
Birdcage Walk
Grosvenor Place
Petty France
St James's Park
ST MARGARET'S
Tothill St
PALACE OF WESTMINSTER
Lambeth Palace Rd
BELGRAVIA
ROYAL MEWS
Buckingham Gate
NEW SCOTLAND YARD
WESTMINSTER ABBEY
Bressenden Place
THAMES
Victoria Street
Great Peter Street
Millbank
LAMBETH PALACE
WESTMINSTER CATHEDRAL
Rochester Row
Horseferry Road
Lambeth Bridge
Lambeth High St
VICTORIA
Palace Street
Wilton Rd
Vauxhall Bridge Road
Regency St
Vincent Sq.

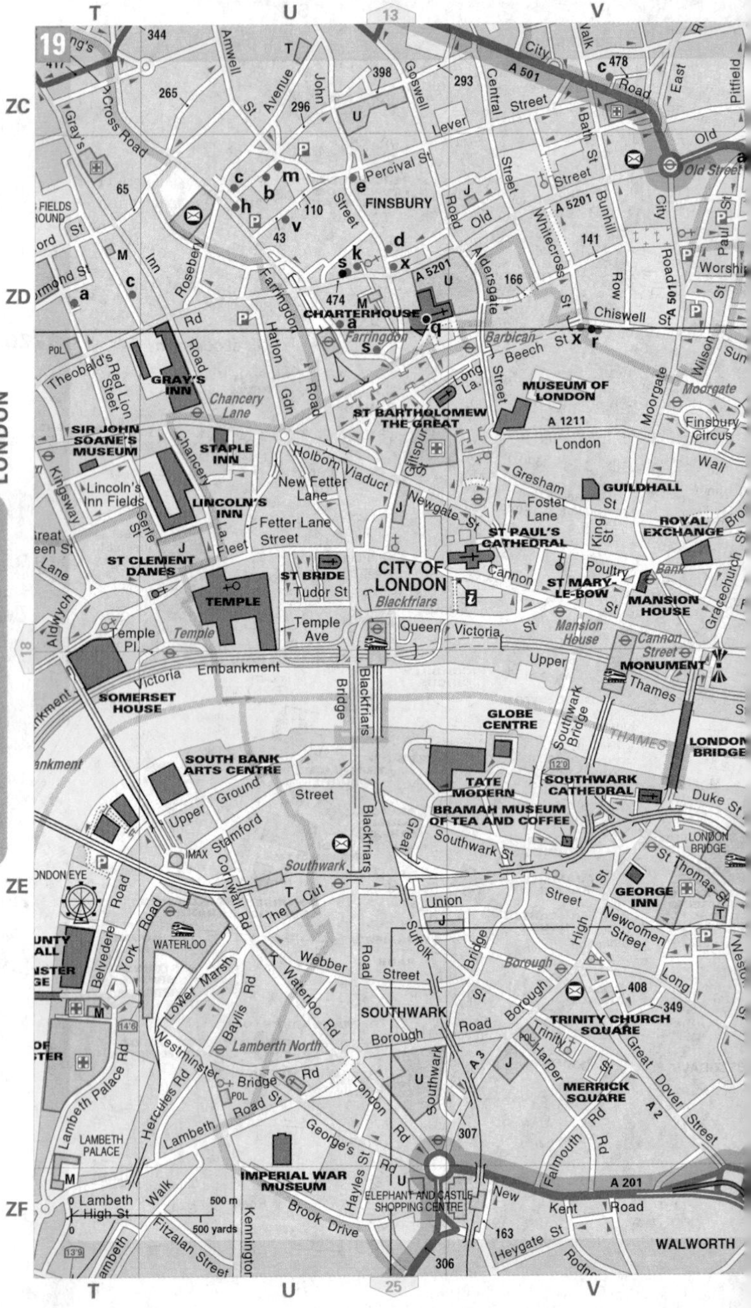
19
T
U
V
ZC
ZD
ZE
ZF
13
18
25
FINSBURY
CHARTERHOUSE
GRAY'S INN
Chancery Lane
ST BARTHOLOMEW THE GREAT
MUSEUM OF LONDON
SIR JOHN SOANE'S MUSEUM
STAPLE INN
LINCOLN'S INN
GUILDHALL
ROYAL EXCHANGE
ST PAUL'S CATHEDRAL
ST CLEMENT DANES
ST BRIDE
CITY OF LONDON
Blackfriars
ST MARY-LE-BOW
MANSION HOUSE
Mansion House
TEMPLE
Temple
Cannon Street
MONUMENT
SOMERSET HOUSE
GLOBE CENTRE
LONDON BRIDGE
THAMES
SOUTH BANK ARTS CENTRE
TATE MODERN
SOUTHWARK CATHEDRAL
BRAMAH MUSEUM OF TEA AND COFFEE
LONDON EYE
IMAX
Southwark
GEORGE INN
WATERLOO
SOUTHWARK
Borough
TRINITY CHURCH SQUARE
Lambeth North
MERRICK SQUARE
LAMBETH PALACE
IMPERIAL WAR MUSEUM
ELEPHANT AND CASTLE SHOPPING CENTRE
WALWORTH
Farringdon
Barbican
Moorgate
Finsbury Circus
Old Street
A 501
A 5201
A 1211
A 3
A 2
A 201
City Road
Goswell Road
Central Street
Aldersgate Street
Whitecross St
Bunhill Row
Chiswell St
Beech St
London Wall
Gresham St
Foster Lane
King St
Poultry
Gracechurch St
Cannon St
Queen Victoria St
Upper Thames St
Victoria Embankment
Holborn Viaduct
Newgate St
New Fetter Lane
Fetter Lane
Fleet Street
Tudor St
Temple Ave
Temple Pl.
Aldwych
Kingsway
Lincoln's Inn Fields
Serle St
Chancery La.
Theobald's Rd
Red Lion Street
Gray's Inn Road
Rosebery Avenue
Farringdon Road
Hatton Gdn
St John Street
Amwell St
Percival St
Lever St
Old Street
Bath St
Pitfield St
East Road
Paul St
Wilson St
Worship St
Blackfriars Bridge
Blackfriars Road
Southwark Bridge
Southwark St
Upper Ground
Stamford St
Cornwall Rd
The Cut
Union Street
Great Suffolk Street
Webber Street
Waterloo Rd
Baylis Rd
Lower Marsh
York Road
Belvedere Road
Westminster Bridge Rd
Lambeth Palace Rd
Hercules Rd
Lambeth Walk
Lambeth Road
London Rd
St George's Rd
Borough High Street
Borough Road
Newcomen Street
Long La.
Great Dover Street
Harper Rd
Trinity St
Falmouth Rd
New Kent Road
Heygate St
Brook Drive
Hayles St
Kennington
Fitzalan Street
Lambeth High St
Duke St
St Thomas St
Southwark Bridge Rd
500 m
500 yards
0

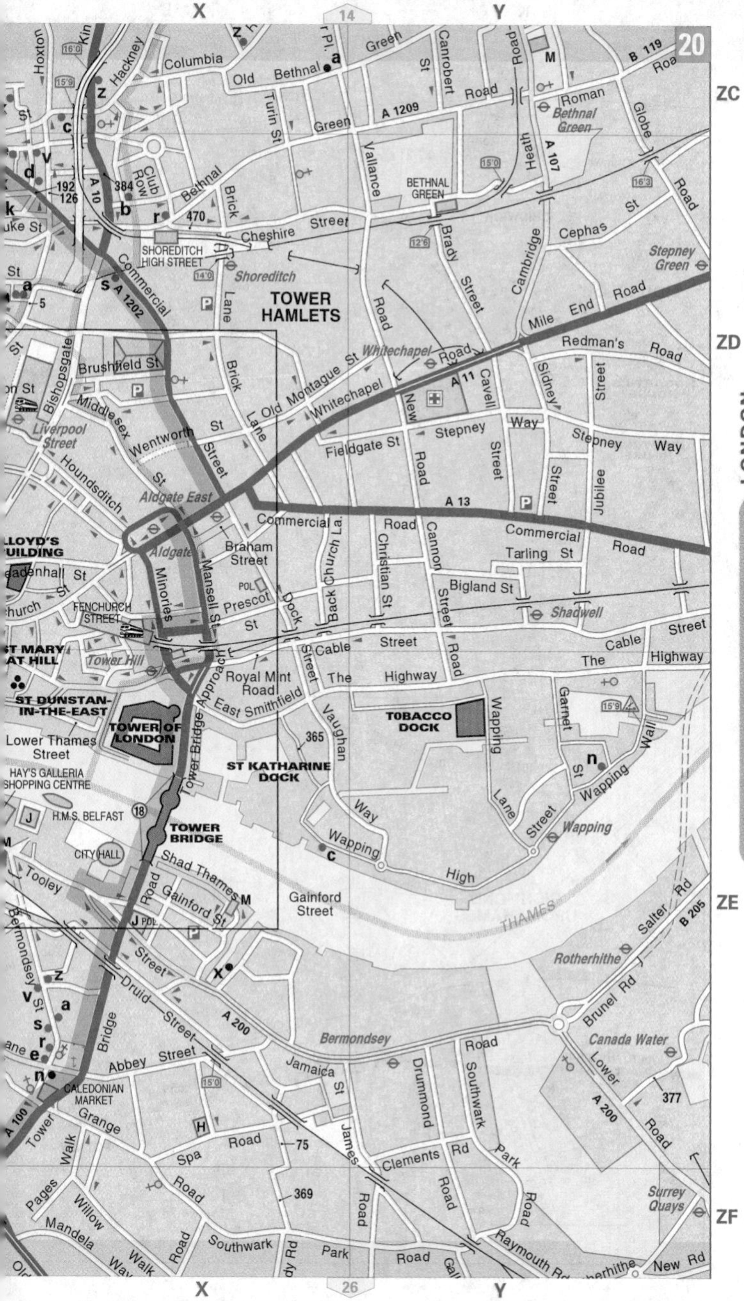
X
Y
14
20
ZC
ZD
ZE
ZF
26
Hoxton
Kingsland
Hackney
Columbia
Old Bethnal Green Road
Turin St
Green
A 1209
Canrobert St
Road
Heath
Roman Road
Bethnal Green
Globe Road
B 119
A 10
A 107
Club Row
Bethnal
Brick Lane
Vallance Road
BETHNAL GREEN
Cheshire Street
Brady Street
Cambridge
Cephas St
Shoreditch
SHOREDITCH HIGH STREET
Commercial
A 1202
TOWER HAMLETS
Stepney Green
Mile End Road
Whitechapel
Redman's Road
Sidney
Cavell Street
A 11
Brushfield St
Bishopsgate
Liverpool Street
Middlesex
Wentworth St
Old Montague St
Stepney Way
Fieldgate St
New Road
Houndsditch
Aldgate East
A 13
Jubilee
Commercial Road
Tarling St
Braham Street
Aldgate
LLOYD'S BUILDING
Leadenhall St
Fenchurch St
FENCHURCH STREET
Minories
Mansell St
Prescot St
Dock
Back Church La.
Christian St
Cannon Street Road
Bigland St
Shadwell
Cable Street
The Highway
ST MARY AT HILL
Tower Hill
Royal Mint Road
East Smithfield
Tower Bridge Approach
ST DUNSTAN-IN-THE-EAST
TOWER OF LONDON
TOBACCO DOCK
Wapping Lane
Garnet St
Wapping Wall
Lower Thames Street
HAY'S GALLERIA SHOPPING CENTRE
ST KATHARINE DOCK
Vaughan Way
365
H.M.S. BELFAST
TOWER BRIDGE
CITY HALL
Wapping High Street
Wapping
Tooley
Shad Thames
Gainford St
Gainford Street
THAMES
Salter Rd
B 205
Rotherhithe
Bermondsey St
Druid Street
A 200
Brunel Rd
Bridge
Bermondsey
Canada Water
Abbey Street
Jamaica St
Drummond Road
Southwark Park Road
Lower Road
377
CALEDONIAN MARKET
Grange
A 100
Tower Bridge Road
Spa Road
75
James
Clements Rd
Surrey Quays
369
Pages Walk
Willow Walk
Mandela Way
Southwark Park Road
Raymouth Rd
Rotherhithe New Rd

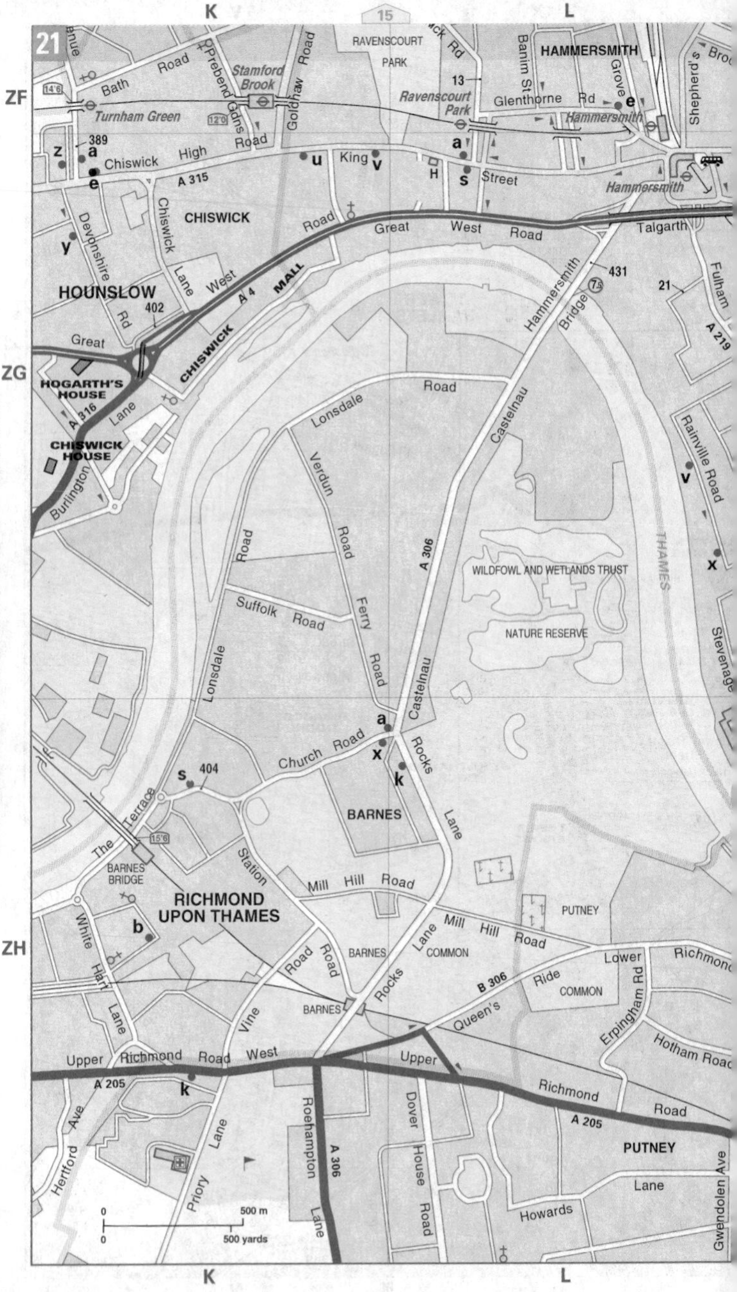
21
15
K
L
ZF
ZG
ZH
HAMMERSMITH
RAVENSCOURT PARK
Ravenscourt Park
Stamford Brook
Turnham Green
Hammersmith
CHISWICK
HOUNSLOW
HOGARTH'S HOUSE
CHISWICK HOUSE
BARNES
BARNES BRIDGE
RICHMOND UPON THAMES
PUTNEY
BARNES COMMON
PUTNEY COMMON
WILDFOWL AND WETLANDS TRUST
NATURE RESERVE
THAMES
Bath Road
Chiswick High Road
King Street
Great West Road
Talgarth
Prebend Gdns
Goldhawk Road
Glenthorne Rd
Banim St
Grove
Shepherd's
Devonshire Rd
Chiswick Lane
West
A 4
MALL
CHISWICK
Great
Lane
A 316
Burlington
Hammersmith Bridge
Fulham
A 219
A 315
Lonsdale Road
Verdun Road
Ferry Road
Suffolk Road
Castelnau
A 306
Rainville Road
Stevenage
Church Road
Rocks Lane
The Terrace
Station Road
Mill Hill Road
Mill Hill Road
White Hart Lane
Vine Road
Queen's Ride
B 306
Lower Richmond
Erpingham Rd
Hotham Road
Upper Richmond Road West
A 205
Upper Richmond Road
A 205
Hertford Ave
Priory Lane
Roehampton Lane
A 306
Dover House Road
Howards Lane
Gwendolen Ave
BARNES
402
389
404
13
431
21
14'6
12'0
15'6
7.5
0
500 m
0
500 yards
a
z
e
u
v
a
s
H
e
y
v
x
a
x
k
s
b
k

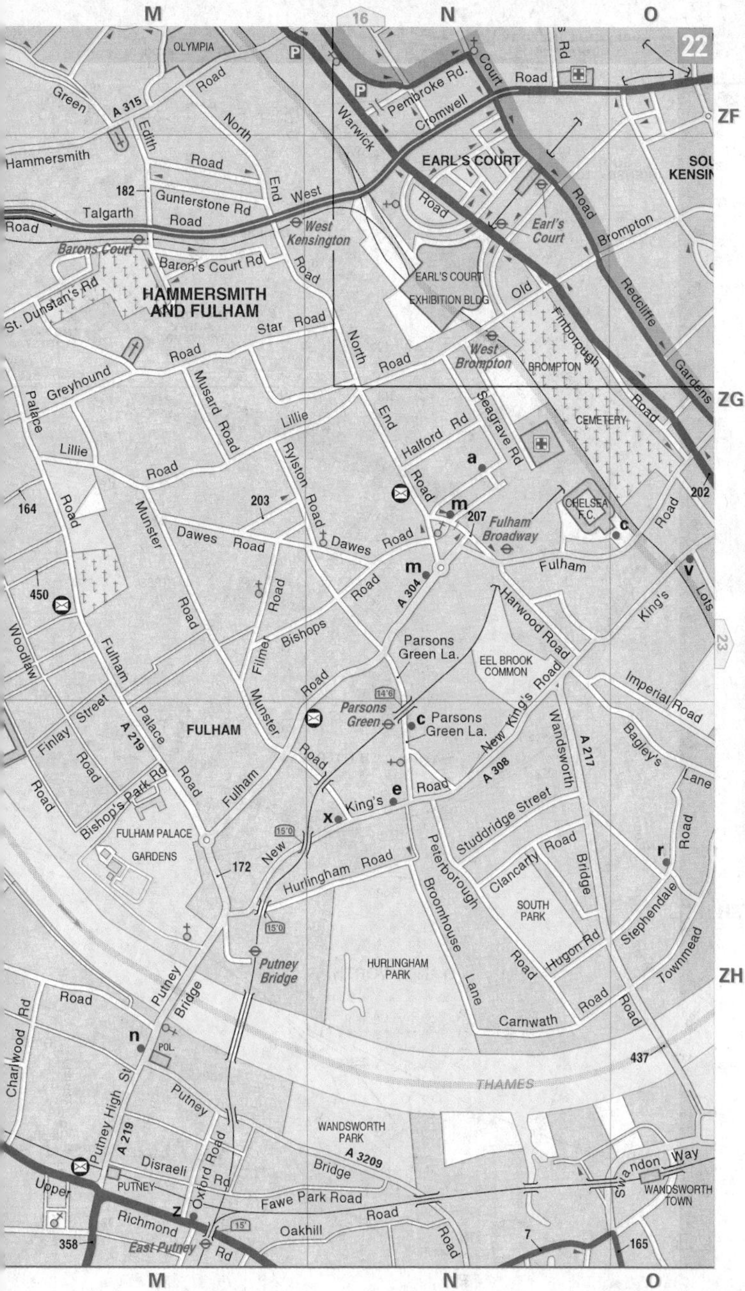
M
N
O
16
22
ZF
ZG
ZH
23
LONDON
OLYMPIA
HAMMERSMITH AND FULHAM
EARL'S COURT
SOUTH KENSINGTON
Earl's Court
West Kensington
Barons Court
West Brompton
Fulham Broadway
Parsons Green
Putney Bridge
East Putney
EARL'S COURT EXHIBITION BLDG
BROMPTON CEMETERY
CHELSEA F.C.
EEL BROOK COMMON
FULHAM
FULHAM PALACE GARDENS
HURLINGHAM PARK
SOUTH PARK
THAMES
WANDSWORTH PARK
WANDSWORTH TOWN
PUTNEY
POL.
A 315
A 304
A 219
A 308
A 217
A 3209
Hammersmith Road
Talgarth Road
Gunterstone Rd
Edith Road
North End Road
West Cromwell Road
Pembroke Rd.
Warwick Road
Earl's Court Road
Old Brompton Road
Brompton Road
Redcliffe Gardens
Finborough Road
Baron's Court Rd
St. Dunstan's Rd
Star Road
Greyhound Road
Musard Road
Lillie Road
Palace Road
Seagrave Rd
Halford Rd
Rylston Road
Dawes Road
Munster Road
Fulham Road
Filmer Road
Bishops Road
Parsons Green La.
Harwood Road
King's Road
Lots Road
Imperial Road
Bagley's Lane
New King's Road
Wandsworth Bridge Road
Woodlaw Road
Fulham Palace Road
Finlay Street
Bishop's Park Rd
Studdridge Street
Clancarty Road
Peterborough Road
Broomhouse Lane
Hurlingham Road
Stephendale Road
Townmead Road
Hugon Rd
Carnwath Road
Putney Bridge
Charlwood Rd
Putney High St
Putney Bridge Road
Disraeli Rd
Oxford Road
Upper Richmond Rd
Fawe Park Road
Oakhill Road
Swandon Way
182
203
164
450
207
202
172
437
358
7
165
14'6
15'0
15'
a
m
c
v
e
x
r
n
z

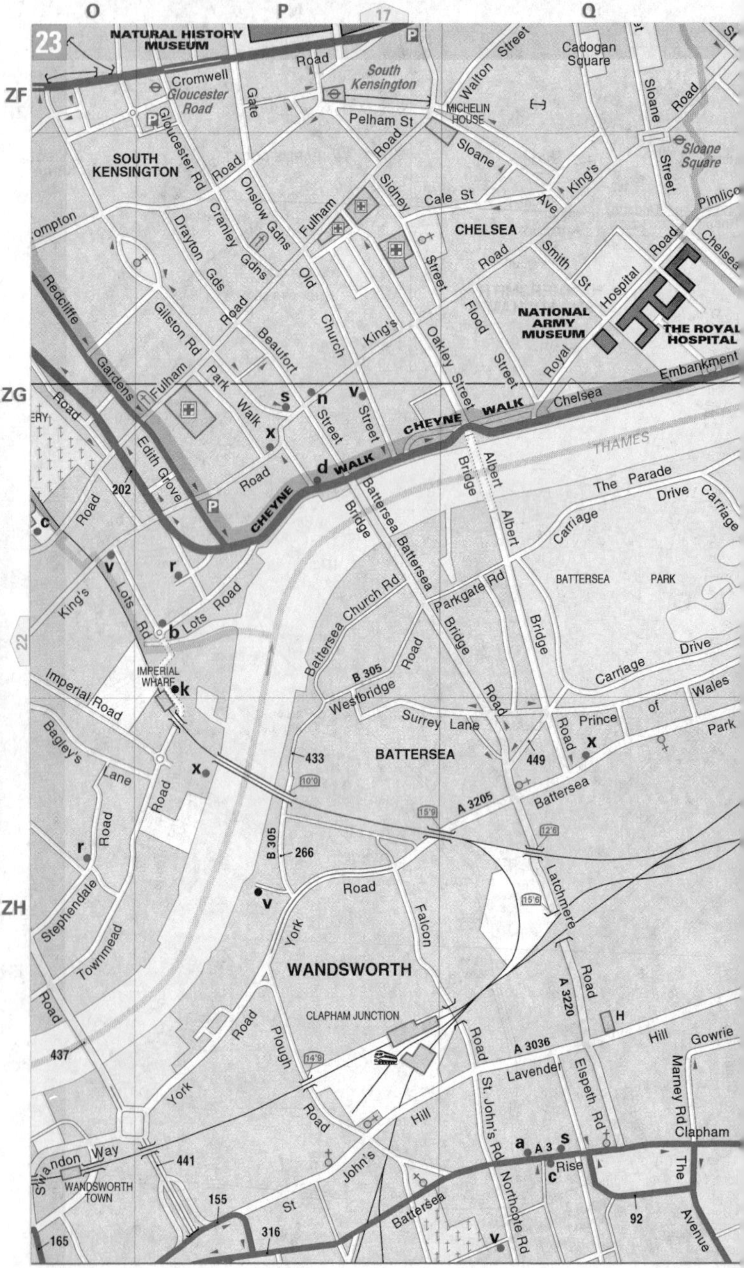
O
P
Q
17
23
NATURAL HISTORY MUSEUM
Cromwell
Gloucester Road
South Kensington
Road
Gate
Walton Street
Cadogan Square
Sloane
Road
MICHELIN HOUSE
Pelham St
Sloane
Sloane Square
SOUTH KENSINGTON
Gloucester Rd
Road
Onslow Gdns
Fulham
Road
Sidney
Cale St
King's
Ave
Street
Pimlico
Brompton
Drayton Gds
Cranley Gdns
CHELSEA
Chelsea
Smith St
Road
Hospital
Redcliffe
Gilston Rd
Road
Old Church
Street
Flood
Beaufort
King's
Oakley
NATIONAL ARMY MUSEUM
THE ROYAL HOSPITAL
Gardens
Fulham
Park Walk
Street
Street
Royal
Embankment
ZF
ZG
ZH
Road
Street
Street
CHEYNE WALK
Chelsea
Edith Grove
THAMES
Bridge
Albert
Road
CHEYNE WALK
The Parade
Drive
Carriage
202
Road
Battersea
Albert
Carriage
Bridge
Battersea
BATTERSEA PARK
Lots Rd
Lots Road
King's
Battersea Church Rd
Parkgate Rd
Bridge
Bridge
22
IMPERIAL WHARF
Imperial Road
B 305
Road
Carriage
Drive
Westbridge
Road
Wales
of
Prince
Surrey Lane
Road
Park
Bagley's Lane
433
BATTERSEA
449
Road
A 3205
Battersea
Road
B 305
266
Latchmere
Stephendale
Townmead
Road
York
Falcon
WANDSWORTH
Road
A 3220
Road
CLAPHAM JUNCTION
H
437
Road
Plough
Road
A 3036
Hill
Gowrie
Lavender
Elspeth Rd
Marney Rd
York
Road
St. John's Rd
Hill
Clapham
Swandon Way
441
John's
A 3
Rise
The
WANDSWORTH TOWN
Northcote Rd
155
St
Battersea
92
Avenue
165
316

R
S
T
18
24
ZF
ZG
ZH
25
WESTMINSTER CATHEDRAL
VICTORIA
Palace
Wilton Rd
Vauxhall Bridge Road
Rochester Row
Horseferry Road
Vincent Sq.
Regency St
Lambeth Bridge
Lambeth High St
Black Prince
TATE BRITAIN
Islip Street
John Islip
Millbank
Albert Embankment
Belgrave
Way
Tachbrook St.
Pimlico
Ebury
Buckingham
Rd
St
Warwick
George's
Dr.
Ebury Bridge Rd
Sutherland Street
Street
Lupus Street
Claverton St.
St George's Square
Vauxhall Bridge
Vauxhall
Vauxhall Walk
Tyers St
Kennington
Harleyford Rd
Lupus
Grosvenor Road
Chelsea Bridge
Bridge Rd
290
Lane
Nine Elms
Fentiman Road
Dorset Rd
North
Queenstown Road
Drive East
361
South
BATTERSEA PARK
Drive
QUEENSTOWN ROAD
NEW COVENT GARDEN MARKET
Wandsworth Road
SOUTH LAMBETH
Lambeth
South Lambeth
420
a
Landsdowne
Way
Stockwell
Clapham
Binfield Rd
Stockwell
Lane
Larkhall
Jeffrey's Road
Lingham St
Stockwell
Sidney Road
A 3036
Union
Road
WANDSWORTH ROAD
Silverthorne Road
Road
Wandsworth
North Street
B 224
Queenstown
Grove
Rectory
Clapham Manor St
CLAPHAM HIGH ST.
A 3
Landor Road
436
Clapham North
Clapham High St
B 221
Bedford Road
CLAPHAM
Cedars Road
426
428
Clapham Common
Triangle Pl.
Common North Side
Long Road
Clapham Park Rd
x
Acre b Lane
Acre Lane
Crescent Lane
Park Hill
King's Ave
Clapham Common South Side
A 24
CLAPHAM COMMON
Brixton
0
500 m
500 yards
R
S
T

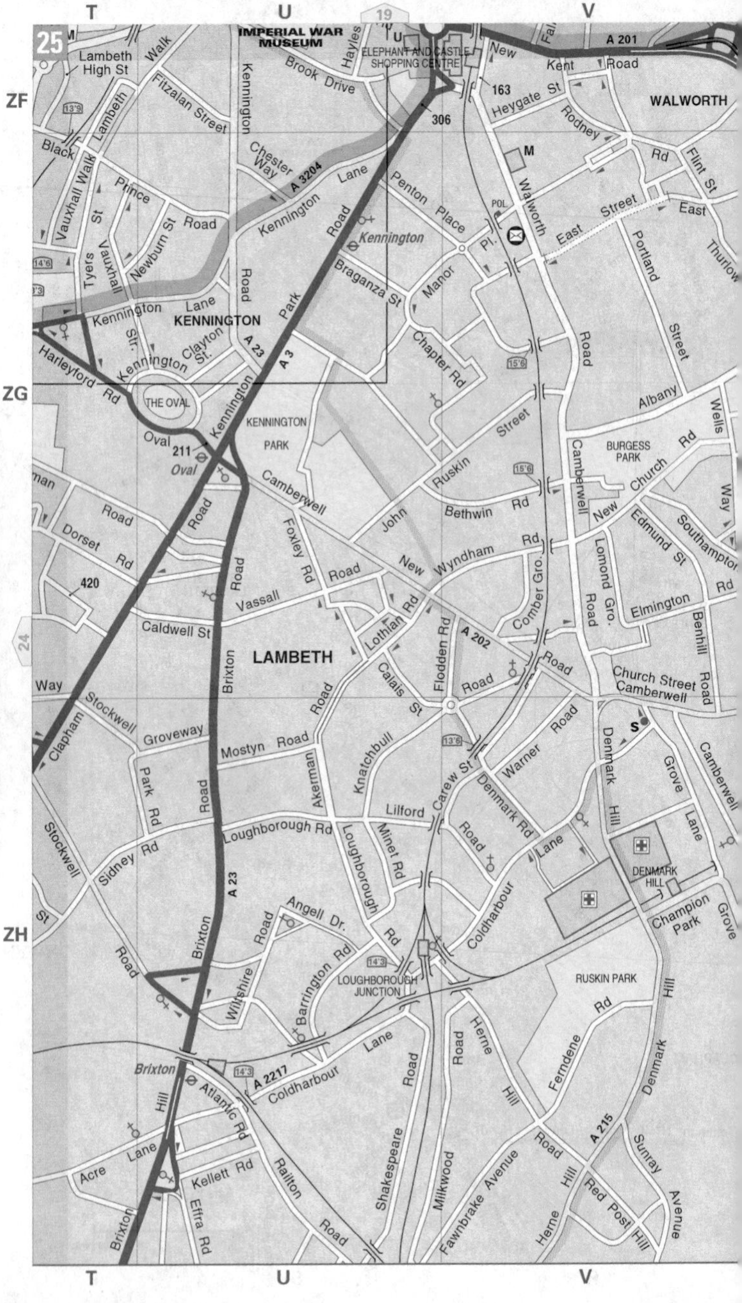
T
U
19
V
25
ZF
ZG
24
ZH
IMPERIAL WAR MUSEUM
ELEPHANT AND CASTLE SHOPPING CENTRE
WALWORTH
KENNINGTON
THE OVAL
KENNINGTON PARK
BURGESS PARK
LAMBETH
DENMARK HILL
RUSKIN PARK
LOUGHBOROUGH JUNCTION
Kennington
Oval
Brixton
A 201
A 3204
A 23
A 3
A 202
A 2217
A 215
163
306
211
420
POL.
M
S
Lambeth High St
Lambeth Walk
Fitzalan Street
Kennington Road
Brook Drive
Hayles
New Kent Road
Heygate St
Rodney Rd
Flint St
East Street
Thurlow
Black
Vauxhall Walk
Prince Road
Newburn St
Tyers St
Vauxhall St
Chester Way
Kennington Lane
Penton Place
Walworth Road
Pl.
Manor Pl.
Braganza St
Portland Street
Kennington Park Road
Chapter Rd
Clayton St.
Kennington Oval
Harleyford Rd
Albany Road
Wells Way
Camberwell Road
Ruskin Street
Bethwin Rd
John Ruskin Street
New Church Rd
Edmund St
Southampton Way
Camberwell New Road
Dorset Rd
Foxley Rd
New Wyndham Rd
Lomond Gro.
Comber Gro.
Elmington Rd
Benhill Road
Vassall Road
Caldwell St
Brixton Road
Lothian Rd
Flodden Rd
Church Street Camberwell
Way
Stockwell
Clapham Road
Groveway
Calais St
Mostyn Road
Akerman Road
Knatchbull Road
Warner Road
Denmark Hill
Grove Lane
Camberwell Grove
Park Rd
Carew St
Lilford Road
Loughborough Rd
Minet Rd
Denmark Rd
Coldharbour Lane
Sidney Rd
Stockwell Road
St
Angell Dr.
Wiltshire Road
Barrington Rd
Loughborough Rd
Champion Park
Grove
Ferndene Rd
Herne Hill
Hill
Atlantic Rd
Coldharbour Lane
Shakespeare Road
Milkwood Road
Sunray Avenue
Red Post Hill
Acre Lane
Kellett Rd
Effra Rd
Railton Road
Fawnbrake Avenue
Brixton Hill
13'9
14'6
15'6
13'6
14'3
13'3

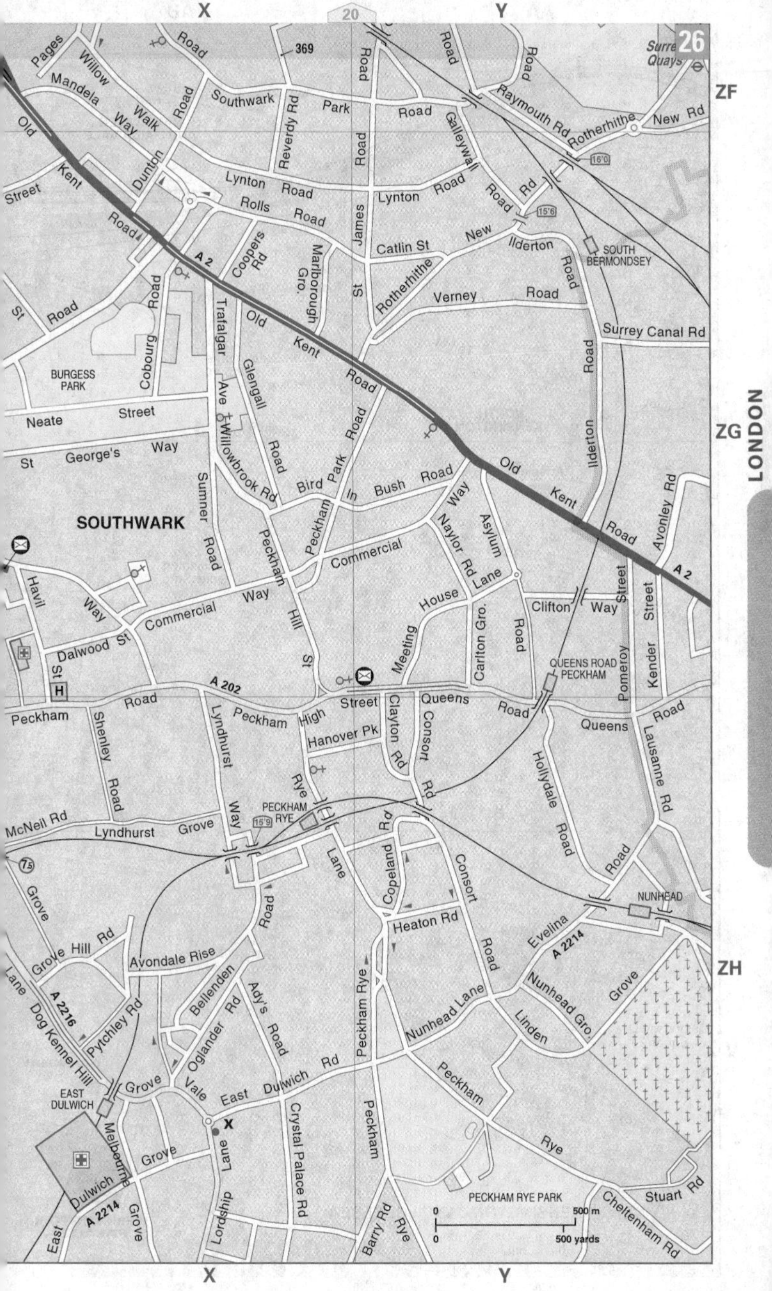
X
20
Y
26
Surrey Quays
ZF
ZG
ZH
LONDON
Pages
Willow
Walk
Road
369
Road
Road
Road
Road
Mandela Way
Southwark Park Road
Reverdy Rd
Galleyway
Raymouth Rd
Rotherhithe New Rd
16'0
Old Kent Road
Street
Dunton Road
Lynton Road
Lynton Road
Rolls Road
Rd
15'6
Ilderton Road
SOUTH BERMONDSEY
A 2
Coopers Rd
Marlborough Gro.
James St
Catlin St
New Rotherhithe
Verney Road
Surrey Canal Rd
St
Road
Cobourg Road
Trafalgar Ave
Old Kent Road
Glengall Road
BURGESS PARK
Neate Street
St George's Way
Willowbrook Rd
Bird In Bush Road
Peckham Park Road
Ilderton Road
Old Kent Road
Avonley Rd
A 2
SOUTHWARK
Sumner Road
Peckham Hill St
Commercial Way
Naylor Rd
Asylum Lane
Way
Havil St
Way
Commercial Way
Meeting House Lane
Clifton Way
Carlton Gro.
Road
Street
Street
Dalwood St
QUEENS ROAD PECKHAM
Pomeroy
Kender
A 202
Peckham Road
Peckham High Street
Queens Road
Queens Road
Shenley Road
Lyndhurst Way
Hanover Pk
Clayton Rd
Consort Rd
Hollydale Road
Lausanne Rd
Rye Lane
PECKHAM RYE
15'9
McNeil Rd
Lyndhurst Grove
Copeland Rd
Consort Road
Road
75
Grove Hill Rd
Road
Heaton Rd
NUNHEAD
Evelina Road
A 2214
Avondale Rise
Lane
Dog Kennel Hill
A 2216
Pytchley Rd
Bellenden Rd
Ady's Road
Peckham Rye
Nunhead Lane
Nunhead Gro
Grove
Linden
Oglander Rd
Grove Vale
East Dulwich Rd
Peckham Rye
EAST DULWICH
Melbourne Grove
X
Lordship Lane
Crystal Palace Rd
Peckham
Dulwich
A 2214
East
Grove
Barry Rd
Rye
PECKHAM RYE PARK
0
500 m
0
500 yards
Stuart Rd
Cheltenham Rd
X
Y

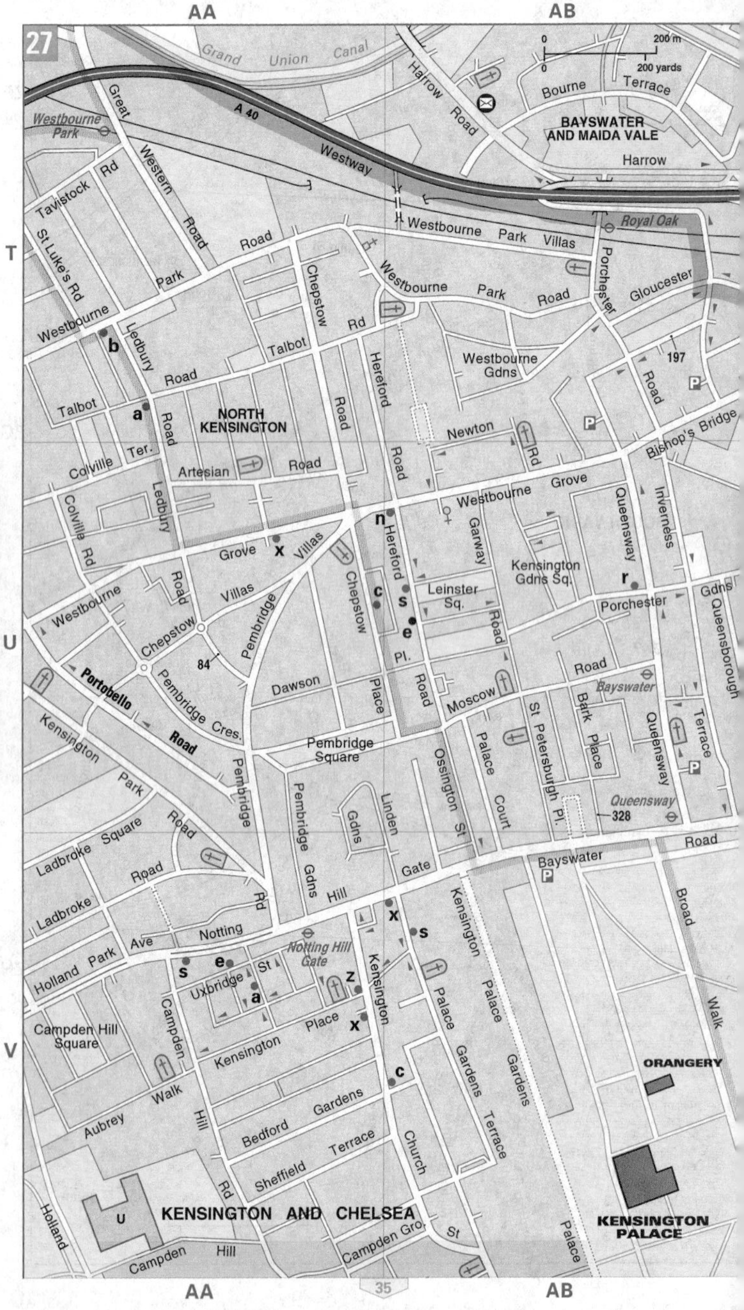
AA
AB
27
Grand Union Canal
0
200 m
200 yards
A 40
Westway
Harrow Road
Bourne Terrace
BAYSWATER AND MAIDA VALE
Harrow
Westbourne Park
Royal Oak
Great Western Road
Tavistock Rd
St Luke's Rd
Westbourne Park Road
Westbourne Park Villas
Westbourne Park Road
Porchester
Gloucester
Chepstow Rd
Talbot Road
Ledbury Road
Westbourne Gdns
197
Talbot
Hereford Road
NORTH KENSINGTON
Newton Rd
Bishop's Bridge
Colville Ter.
Artesian Road
Westbourne Grove
Queensway
Inverness
Colville Rd
Ledbury
Grove Villas
Garway Road
Kensington Gdns Sq.
Leinster Sq.
Porchester Gdns
Queensborough Terrace
Westbourne Villas
Chepstow Villas
Pembridge
Chepstow Pl.
Road
84
Dawson Place
Moscow Road
Bayswater
Bark Place
Portobello Road
Pembridge Cres.
Kensington Park Road
Pembridge Square
Ossington St
Palace Court
St Petersburgh Pl.
Queensway
Pembridge Rd
Pembridge Gdns
Linden Gdns
Queensway
328
Ladbroke Square
Ladbroke Road
Notting Hill Gate
Bayswater Road
Broad Walk
Kensington Palace Gardens
Holland Park Ave
Notting Hill Gate
Uxbridge St
Kensington Church
Kensington Place
Palace Gardens Terrace
Campden Hill Square
Campden Hill Rd
Aubrey Walk
Bedford Gardens
Sheffield Terrace
Church
ORANGERY
Holland
KENSINGTON AND CHELSEA
Campden Gro.
St
Palace
KENSINGTON PALACE
Campden Hill
35
LONDON
T
U
V

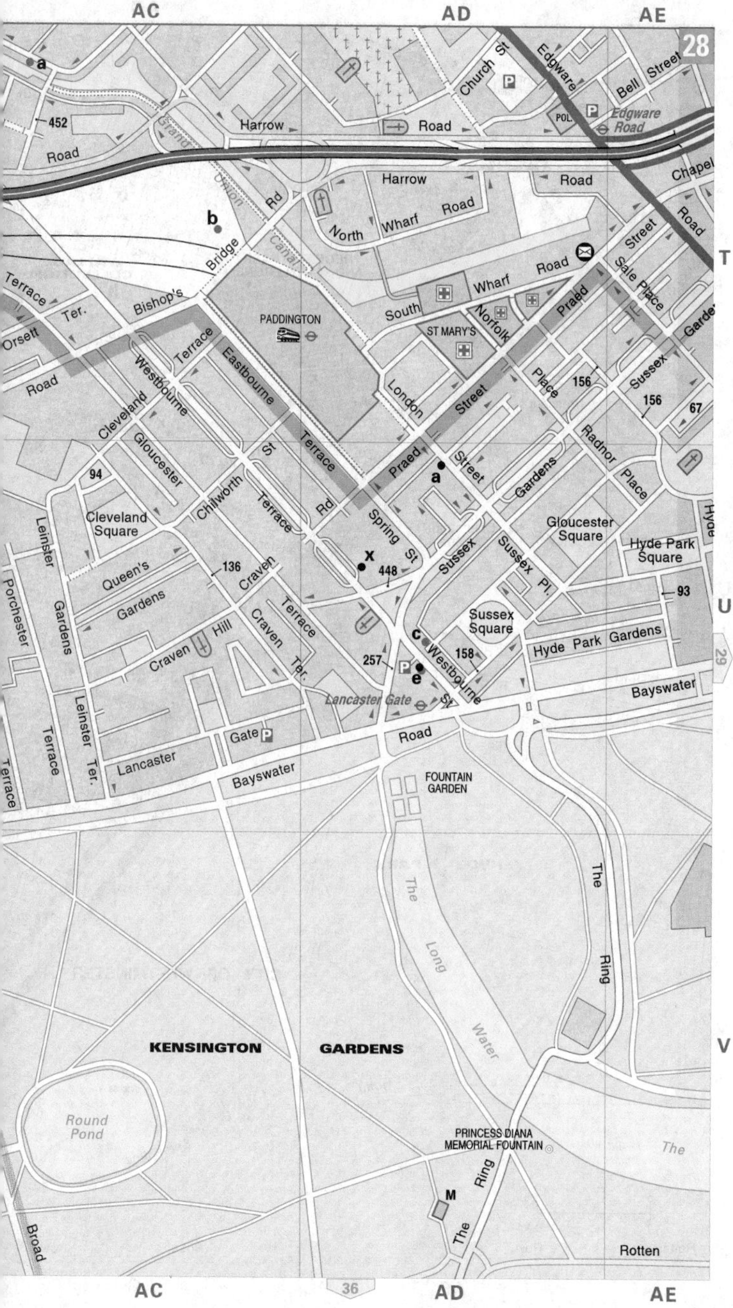

AC
AD
AE
28
T
U
V
29
36
a
452
Road
Harrow
Road
Church St
Edgware
Bell
Street
POL.
Edgware Road
Grand Union Canal
Harrow
Road
Chapel
North
Wharf
Road
Rd
b
Bridge
Bishop's
Terrace
Ter.
Orsett
Road
South
Wharf
Road
Street
Sale Place
Road
PADDINGTON
ST MARY'S
Norfolk
Praed
Garden
Sussex
Westbourne
Terrace
Eastbourne
London
Street
Place
156
156
67
Cleveland
Gloucester
Terrace
Praed
a
Street
Radnor
Place
94
Chilworth
St
Gardens
Cleveland Square
Rd
Terrace
Spring
St
Gloucester Square
Hyde Park Square
Hyde
Leinster
Queen's
136
Craven
x
448
Sussex
Sussex
Pl.
93
Porchester
Gardens
Gardens
Terrace
Craven
Hill
Craven
Terrace
Sussex Square
c
158
Hyde Park Gardens
Craven
Ter.
257
e
Westbourne
St
Lancaster Gate
Bayswater
Leinster
Ter.
Gate
Road
Terrace
Terrace
Lancaster
Bayswater
FOUNTAIN GARDEN
The
Long
Water
The
Ring
KENSINGTON
GARDENS
Round Pond
PRINCESS DIANA MEMORIAL FOUNTAIN
The
Ring
The
M
Broad
Rotten
AC
AD
AE

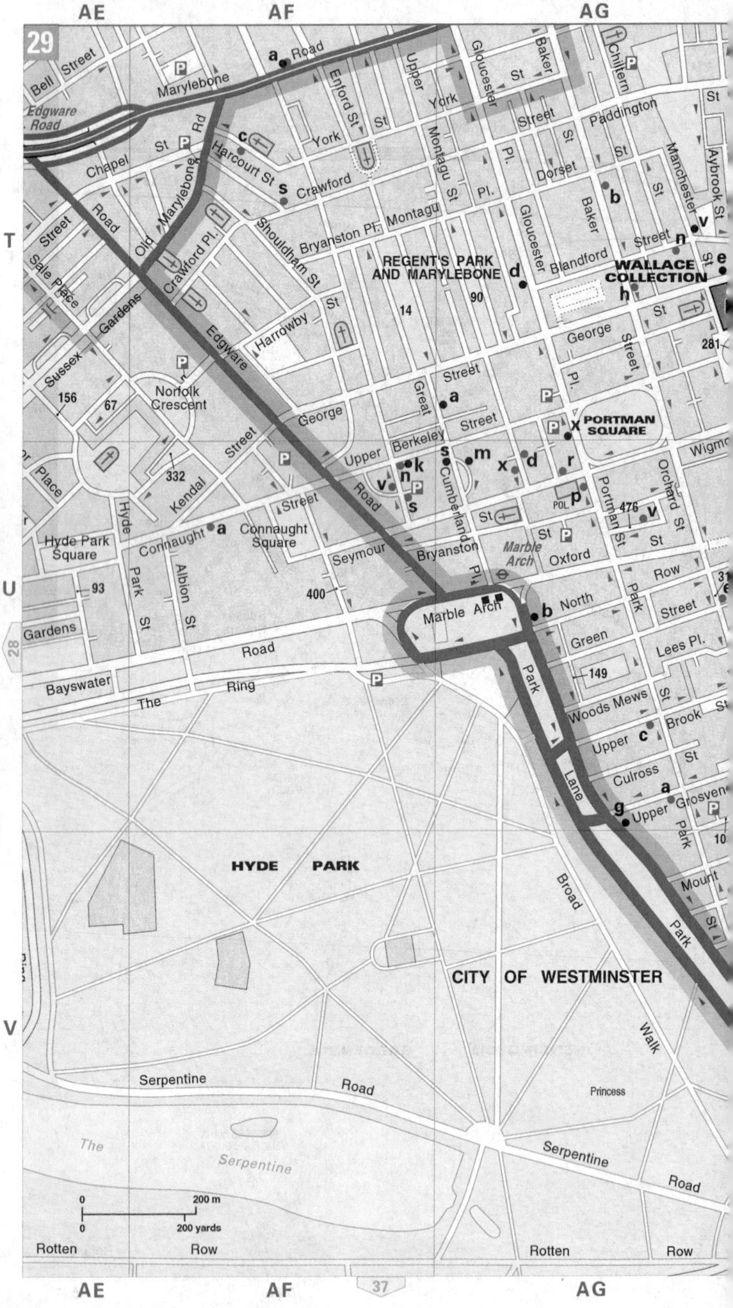
AE
AF
AG
29
T
U
V
28
37
Bell Street
Marylebone Road
Edgware Road
Chapel St
Old Marylebone Rd
Harcourt St
Crawford St
Enford St
York St
Upper Montagu St
Upper York St
Gloucester Pl.
Baker St
Chiltern St
Paddington St
Manchester St
Aybrook St
Dorset St
Montagu Pl.
Gloucester Pl.
Baker St
Blandford Street
Bryanston Pl.
Montagu
Shouldham St
Crawford Pl.
Street
Sale Place
Sussex Gardens
Harrowby St
REGENT'S PARK AND MARYLEBONE
14
90
WALLACE COLLECTION
George St
George Street
Edgware Road
Norfolk Crescent
156
67
332
Great Cumberland Pl.
Upper Berkeley Street
PORTMAN SQUARE
Wigmore
Orchard St
Portman St
476
Kendal Street
Hyde Park Square
Connaught Square
Connaught St
Seymour St
Bryanston St
Marble Arch
Oxford St
Hyde Park St
Albion St
93
400
Gardens
Bayswater Road
The Ring
Marble Arch
North Row
Park Street
Green St
Lees Pl.
149
Woods Mews
Upper Brook St
Culross St
Upper Grosvenor St
Park Lane
Park St
Mount St
Park Lane
HYDE PARK
Broad Walk
CITY OF WESTMINSTER
Serpentine Road
Princess
Serpentine Road
The Serpentine
0 200 m
0 200 yards
Rotten Row
Rotten Row

AH
AI
AJ
30
BRITISH TELECOM TOWER
232
Marylebone High St
Wimpole St
Harley Street
Weymouth St
New Cavendish Street
Portland Place
Great Portland St
Great Cavendish St
Cleveland St
Charlotte St
Goodge St
Foley St
Great Titchfield Street
Langham St
Wells St
Newman St
Berner's St
Welbeck St
Queen Anne Street
Mortimer St
Regent St
Cavendish Sq.
Wigmore St
Henrietta Pl.
Margaret St
Eastcastle Street
Oxford Circus
Oxford St
Holles St
James St
Duke St
Vere St
Argyll St
Poland St
Noel St
D'Arblay St
Wardour St
NEW BOND ST
Princes St
Hannover Sq.
Great Marlborough St
Marshall St
Carnaby St
Kingly St
Broadwick St
Lexington St
Bond St
South Molton St
Binney St
Gilbert St
Davies St
Brook St
Hanover St
Maddox St
George St
Brook's Mews
MAYFAIR
Grosvenor Square
Grosvenor Street
Conduit St
Savile Row
Beak St
Golden Sq.
Brewer St
Bruton Street
Cork St
Vigo St
Adam's Row
Mount Row
Mount Street
South Audley St
Berkeley Square
Dover St
BURLINGTON HOUSE
BURLINGTON ARCADE
OLD BOND ST
Sackville St
Farm St
Hay's Mews
Charles Street
Hill St
Curzon St
Bolton Street
Berkeley St
Albemarle Street
PICCADILLY
PICCADILLY ARCADE
JERMYN ST
ST JAMES'S SQUARE
Duke St
Bury St
King St
Pall Mall
ST JAMES'S ST
Green Park
SHEPHERD MARKET
Queen's Walk
SPENCER HOUSE
GREEN PARK
QUEEN'S CHAPEL
ST JAMES'S PALACE
LANCASTER HOUSE
Hertford St
Brick St
Old Park La.
Park Lane
APSLEY HOUSE WELLINGTON MUSEUM
7/7 MEMORIAL
T
U
V
31
38

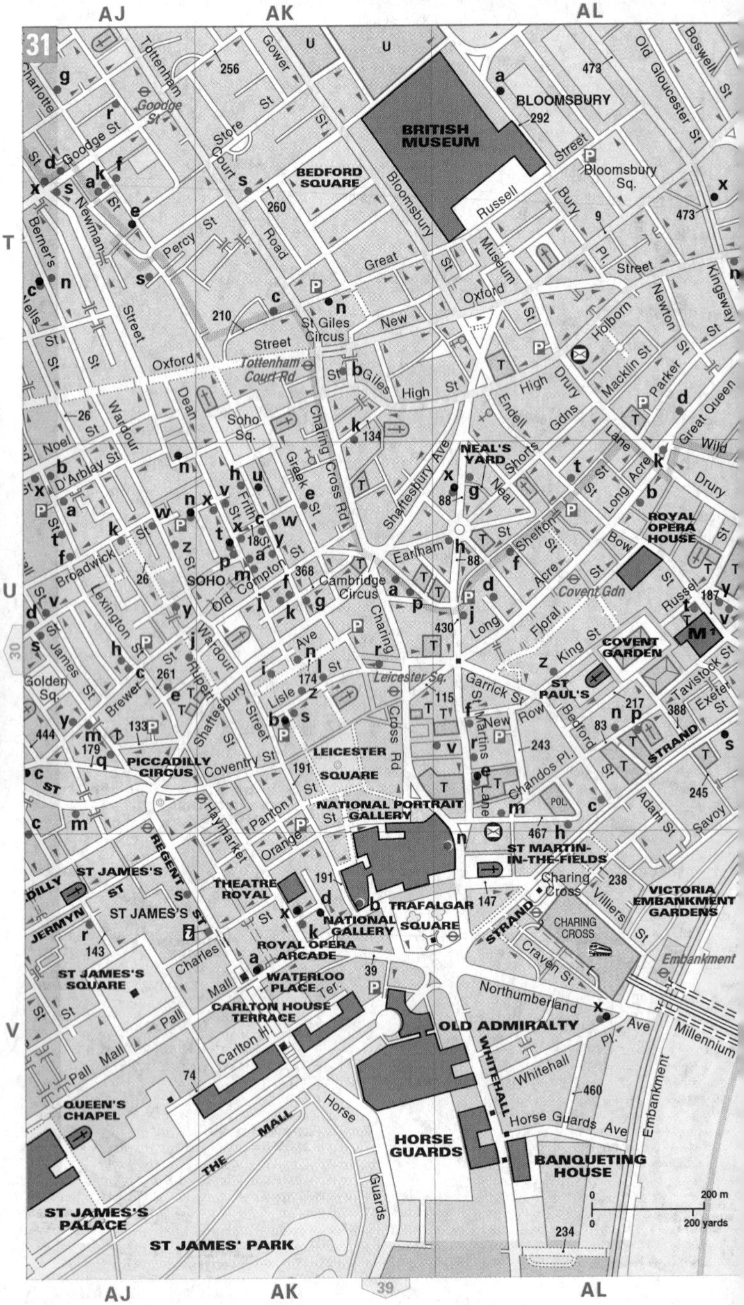
AJ
AK
AL
31
T
U
V
BRITISH MUSEUM
BLOOMSBURY
BEDFORD SQUARE
Bloomsbury Sq.
Goodge St
Tottenham Court Rd
St Giles Circus
SOHO
Soho Sq.
Cambridge Circus
NEAL'S YARD
ROYAL OPERA HOUSE
Covent Gdn
COVENT GARDEN
ST PAUL'S
STRAND
Leicester Sq.
LEICESTER SQUARE
PICCADILLY CIRCUS
NATIONAL PORTRAIT GALLERY
ST MARTIN-IN-THE-FIELDS
Charing Cross
CHARING CROSS
Embankment
VICTORIA EMBANKMENT GARDENS
THEATRE ROYAL
NATIONAL GALLERY
TRAFALGAR SQUARE
ROYAL OPERA ARCADE
WATERLOO PLACE
CARLTON HOUSE TERRACE
OLD ADMIRALTY
WHITEHALL
HORSE GUARDS
BANQUETING HOUSE
ST JAMES'S
ST JAMES'S SQUARE
JERMYN ST
REGENT ST
QUEEN'S CHAPEL
ST JAMES'S PALACE
ST JAMES' PARK
THE MALL
Oxford Street
New Oxford St
Great Russell Street
Charing Cross Rd
Shaftesbury Ave
Haymarket
Pall Mall
Northumberland Ave
Horse Guards Ave
Kingsway
Drury Lane
Long Acre
Floral St
King St
Garrick St
Bedford St
Southampton St
Savoy
Villiers St
Craven St
Coventry St
Old Compton St
Wardour St
Dean St
Frith St
Greek St
Broadwick St
Berwick St
Lexington St
Golden Sq.
Brewer St
Rupert St
Lisle St
Orange St
Charles II St
Carlton H. Ter.
Whitehall Pl.
Embankment
Millennium
Horse Guards
0 200 m
0 200 yards
30
39

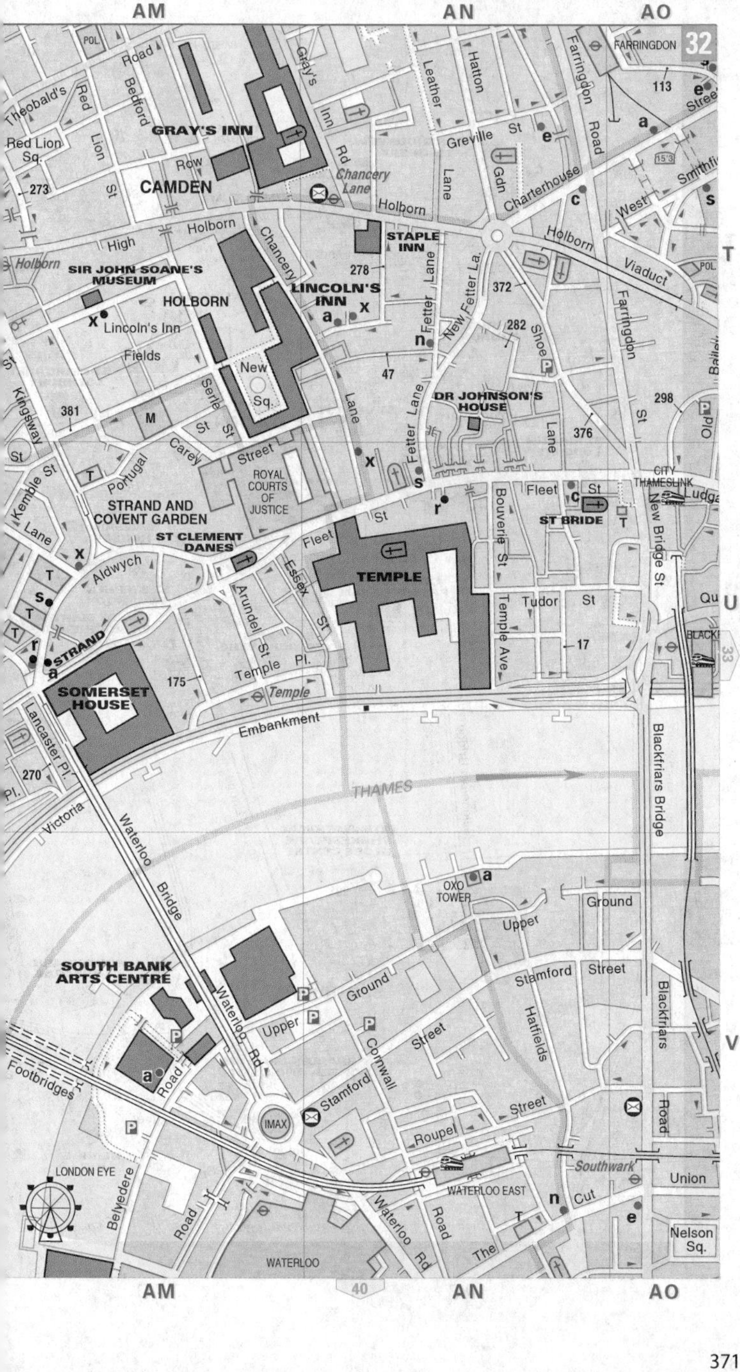
AM
AN
AO
32
FARRINGDON
GRAY'S INN
CAMDEN
Theobald's Rd
Red Lion Sq.
Red Lion St
Bedford Row
Gray's Inn Rd
Chancery Lane
Leather Lane
Hatton Gdn
Greville St
Farringdon Road
Charterhouse St
Holborn
High Holborn
Holborn Viaduct
West Smithfield
STAPLE INN
SIR JOHN SOANE'S MUSEUM
HOLBORN
LINCOLN'S INN
Lincoln's Inn Fields
New Sq.
Fetter Lane
New Fetter La.
Shoe Lane
Farringdon St
DR JOHNSON'S HOUSE
Kingsway
Serle St
Carey Street
Portugal St
ROYAL COURTS OF JUSTICE
Kemble St
STRAND AND COVENT GARDEN
ST CLEMENT DANES
Fleet St
ST BRIDE
CITY THAMESLINK
Ludgate
New Bridge St
Bouverie St
Aldwych
Essex St
Arundel St
TEMPLE
Tudor St
Temple Ave
STRAND
Temple Pl.
Temple
SOMERSET HOUSE
Lancaster Pl.
Embankment
Victoria
BLACKFRIARS
33
THAMES
Blackfriars Bridge
Waterloo Bridge
OXO TOWER
Upper Ground
Stamford Street
SOUTH BANK ARTS CENTRE
Hatfields
Waterloo Rd
Cornwall Road
Blackfriars Road
Footbridges
IMAX
Roupell Street
Southwark
WATERLOO EAST
The Cut
Union
Nelson Sq.
LONDON EYE
Belvedere Road
WATERLOO
40
113
273
278
372
282
47
381
298
376
175
17
270

AO AP AQ

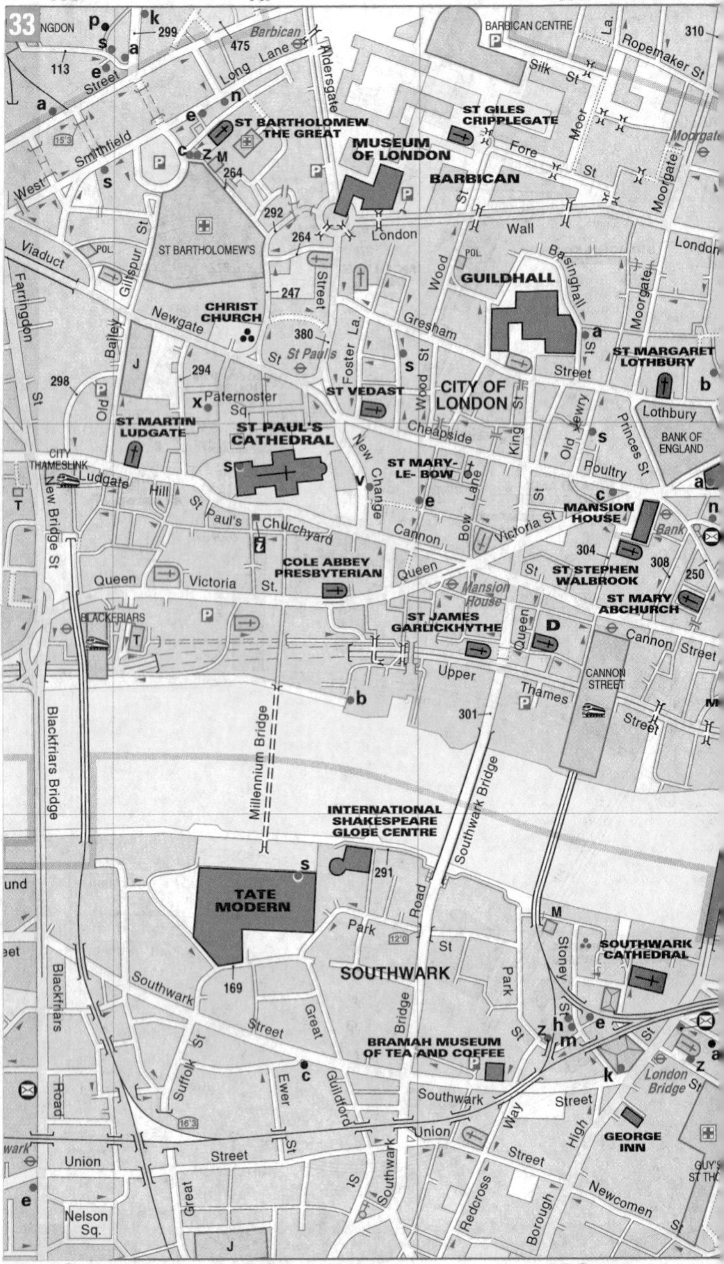

T U V

AO AP AQ

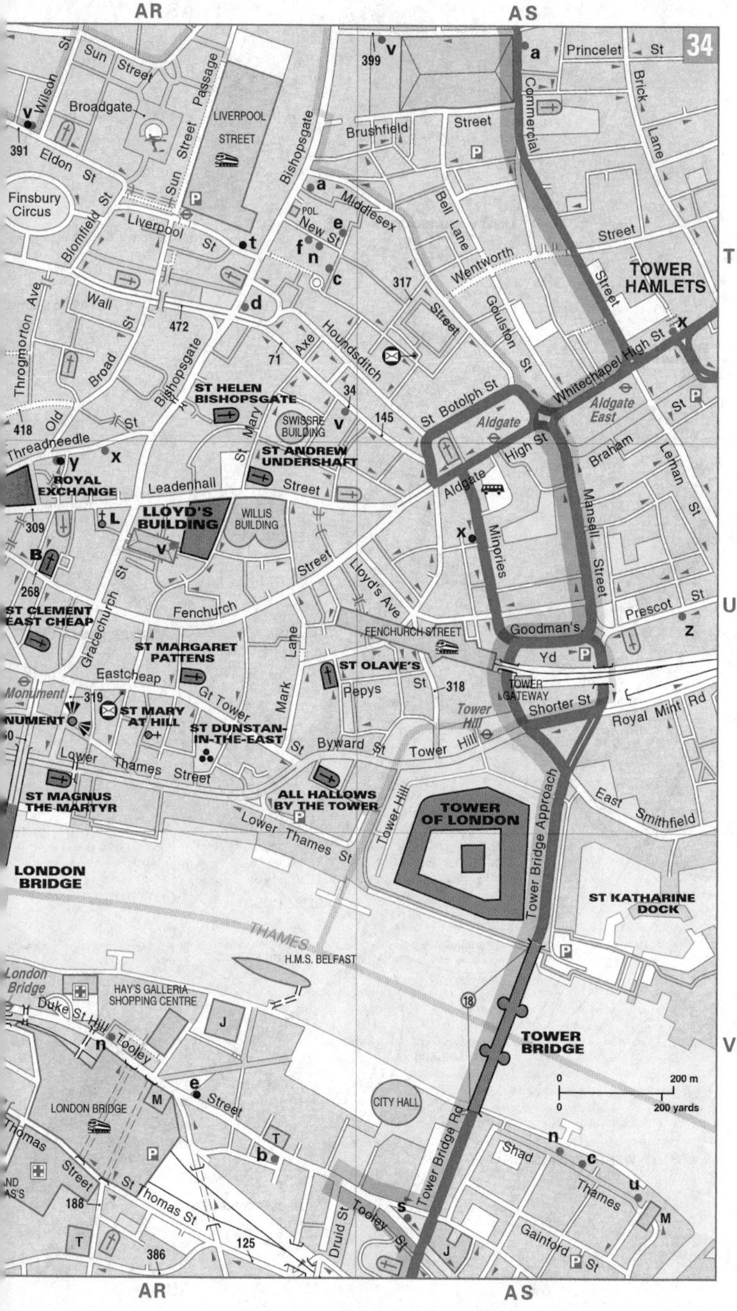
AR
AS
34
Sun Street
Broadgate
Wilson St
Sun Street Passage
LIVERPOOL STREET
391
Eldon St
Finsbury Circus
Blomfield St
Liverpool St
Bishopsgate
Brushfield Street
Princelet St
Commercial Street
Brick Lane
399
Middlesex Street
New St
POL
Bell Lane
Wentworth Street
TOWER HAMLETS
Throgmorton Ave
Wall
Broad St
472
Old Broad St
71
Axe
Houndsditch
317
Goulston St
Whitechapel High St
St Botolph St
Aldgate
Aldgate East
High St
Braham St
Leman St
418
Threadneedle St
ST HELEN BISHOPSGATE
SWISSRE BUILDING
St Mary Axe
145
34
ST ANDREW UNDERSHAFT
ROYAL EXCHANGE
Leadenhall Street
LLOYD'S BUILDING
WILLIS BUILDING
309
Minories
Mansell Street
268
Gracechurch St
Fenchurch Street
Lloyd's Ave
Prescot St
ST CLEMENT EAST CHEAP
ST MARGARET PATTENS
Mark Lane
FENCHURCH STREET
Goodman's Yd
Eastcheap
ST OLAVE'S
Pepys St
318
TOWER GATEWAY
Shorter St
Royal Mint Rd
Monument
319
MONUMENT
ST MARY AT HILL
Gt Tower St
ST DUNSTAN-IN-THE-EAST
Tower Hill
Byward St
Lower Thames Street
ST MAGNUS THE MARTYR
ALL HALLOWS BY THE TOWER
TOWER OF LONDON
Tower Bridge Approach
East Smithfield
Lower Thames St
LONDON BRIDGE
ST KATHARINE DOCK
THAMES
H.M.S. BELFAST
London Bridge
HAY'S GALLERIA SHOPPING CENTRE
Duke St Hill
Tooley Street
18
TOWER BRIDGE
0
200 m
200 yards
CITY HALL
LONDON BRIDGE
Thomas Street
St Thomas St
Tower Bridge Rd
Shad Thames
188
125
386
Druid St
Tooley St
Gainford St
T
U
V

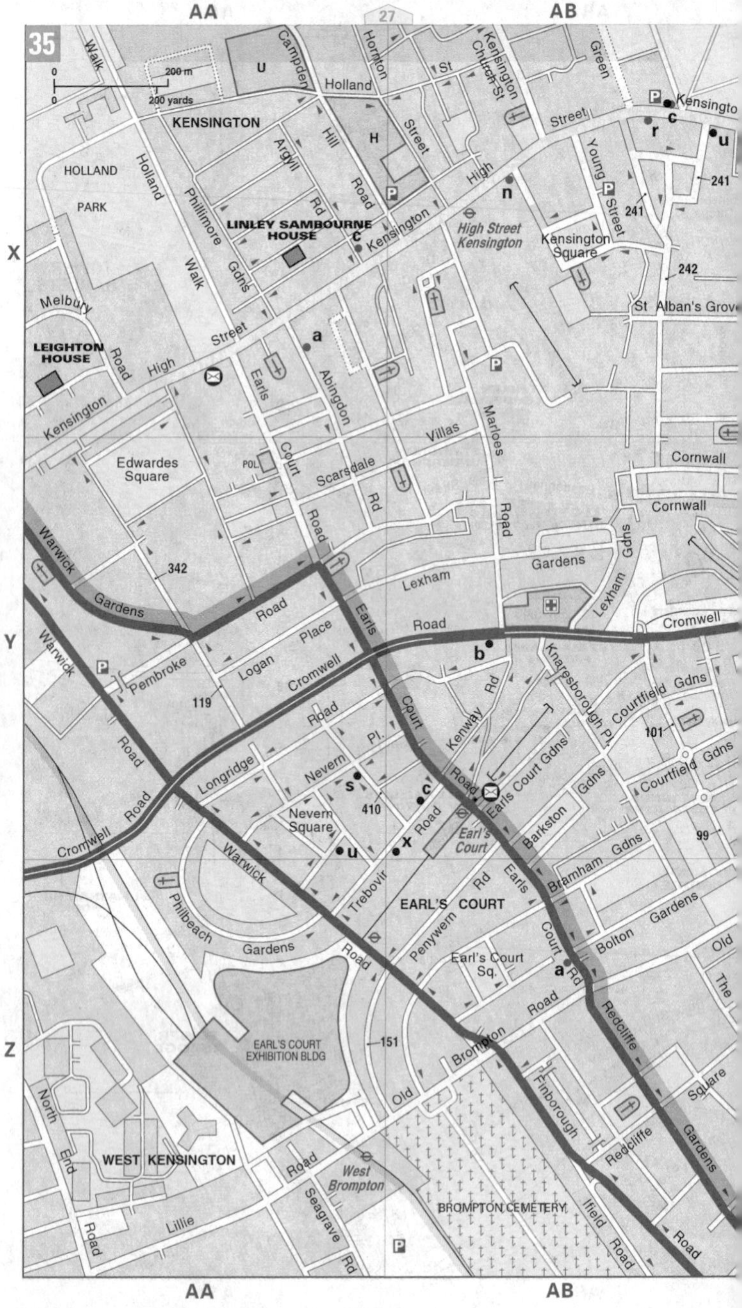
35
27
AA
AB
X
Y
Z
0
200 m
200 yards
KENSINGTON
HOLLAND
PARK
LINLEY SAMBOURNE HOUSE
LEIGHTON HOUSE
High Street Kensington
Kensington Square
Edwardes Square
Nevern Square
EARL'S COURT
Earl's Court
Earl's Court Sq.
EARL'S COURT EXHIBITION BLDG
WEST KENSINGTON
West Brompton
BROMPTON CEMETERY
Campden Hill Road
Holland Street
Hornton Street
Kensington Church St
Kensington High Street
Green
Young Street
Argyll Rd
Phillimore Gdns
Phillimore Walk
Holland Walk
Melbury Road
Earls Court Road
Abingdon Rd
Scarsdale Villas
Marloes Road
St Alban's Grove
Cornwall Gdns
Lexham Gardens
Lexham Gdns
Cromwell Road
Warwick Gardens
Warwick Road
Pembroke Road
Logan Place
Longridge Road
Nevern Pl.
Kenway Rd
Knaresborough Pl.
Courtfield Gdns
Earls Court Gdns
Barkston Gdns
Bramham Gdns
Trebovir Road
Penywern Rd
Philbeach Gardens
Bolton Gardens
Old Brompton Road
Redcliffe Gardens
Redcliffe Square
Finborough Road
Ifield Road
North End Road
Lillie Road
Seagrave Rd
The
Old
POL.
241
242
342
119
410
101
99
151

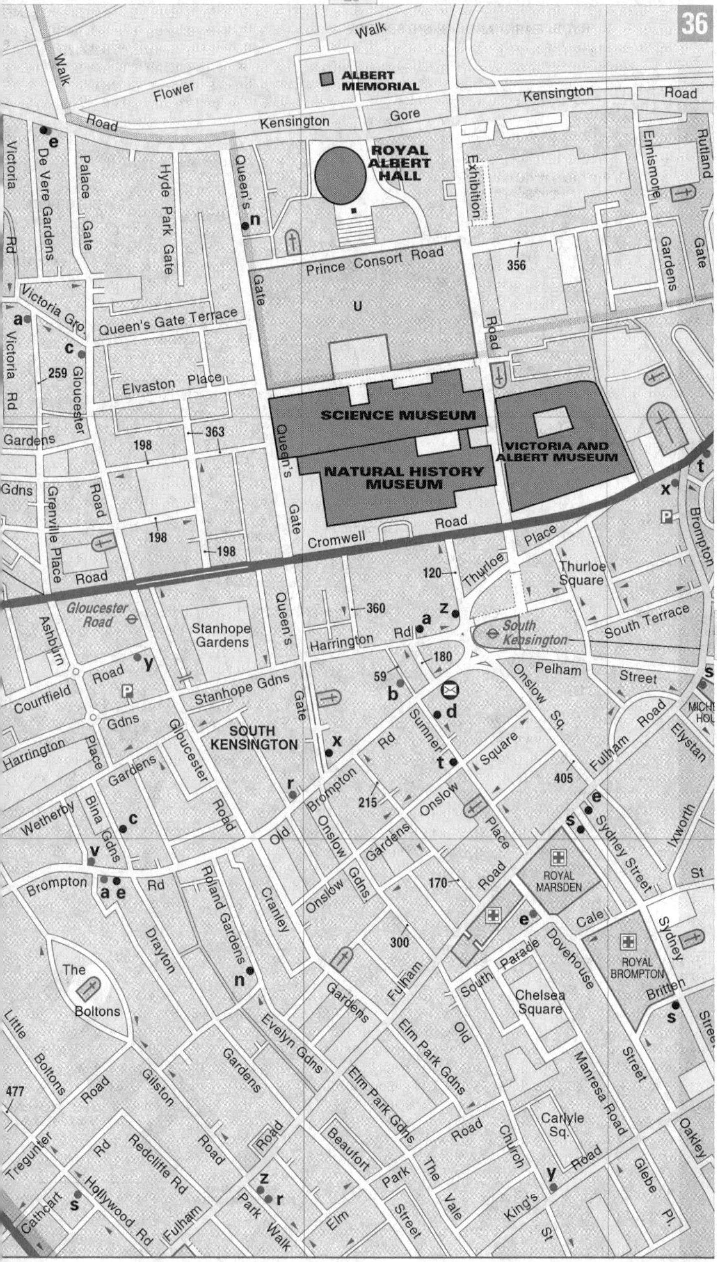
36
28
Walk
ALBERT MEMORIAL
Flower
Kensington Gore
Kensington Road
Road
ROYAL ALBERT HALL
Exhibition Road
Queen's Gate
Prince Consort Road
356
U
Queen's Gate Terrace
Elvaston Place
363
198
SCIENCE MUSEUM
NATURAL HISTORY MUSEUM
VICTORIA AND ALBERT MUSEUM
Cromwell Road
Thurloe Place
Thurloe Square
120
360
Harrington Rd
South Kensington
South Terrace
180
59
Pelham Street
Onslow Sq.
Sumner Place
Onslow Square
Fulham Road
405
Sydney Street
ROYAL MARSDEN
ROYAL BROMPTON
Britten St
Ixworth Pl.
Cale St
Dovehouse St
South Parade
Chelsea Square
Manresa Road
Carlyle Sq.
Oakley St
Glebe Pl.
King's Rd
Old Church Street
The Vale
Elm Park Road
Elm Park Gdns
Elm Park Gardens
Beaufort Street
Park Walk
Evelyn Gdns
Cranley Gardens
Onslow Gdns
Onslow Gardens
Old Brompton Road
215
170
300
Roland Gardens
Drayton Gardens
Gilston Road
The Boltons
Little Boltons
Tregunter Rd
Redcliffe Rd
Hollywood Rd
Cathcart Rd
477
Brompton Rd
Bina Gdns
Wetherby Gardens
Harrington Gardens
Courtfield Road
Gloucester Road
Ashburn Place
Gloucester Road
Stanhope Gardens
Stanhope Gdns
SOUTH KENSINGTON
Grenville Place
Victoria Road
Victoria Gro
De Vere Gardens
Palace Gate
Hyde Park Gate
Gloucester Road
259
Ennismore Gardens
Rutland Gate
Brompton Road
Elystan
MICHE HOU
LONDON
X
Y
Z
37

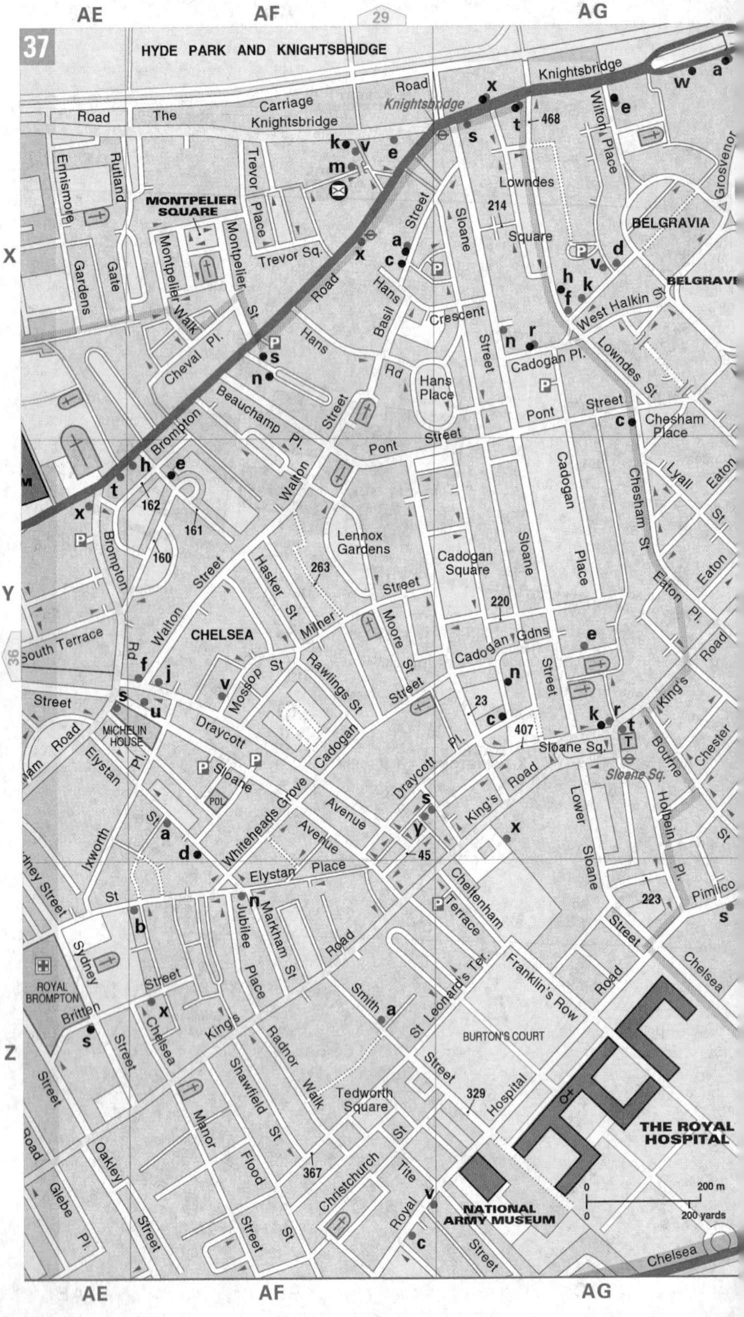

37
HYDE PARK AND KNIGHTSBRIDGE
AE
AF
AG
29
36
X
Y
Z
LONDON
MONTPELIER SQUARE
BELGRAVIA
CHELSEA
MICHELIN HOUSE
ROYAL BROMPTON
BURTON'S COURT
THE ROYAL HOSPITAL
NATIONAL ARMY MUSEUM
Knightsbridge
Sloane Sq.
Lennox Gardens
Cadogan Square
Hans Place
Tedworth Square
0
200 m
200 yards

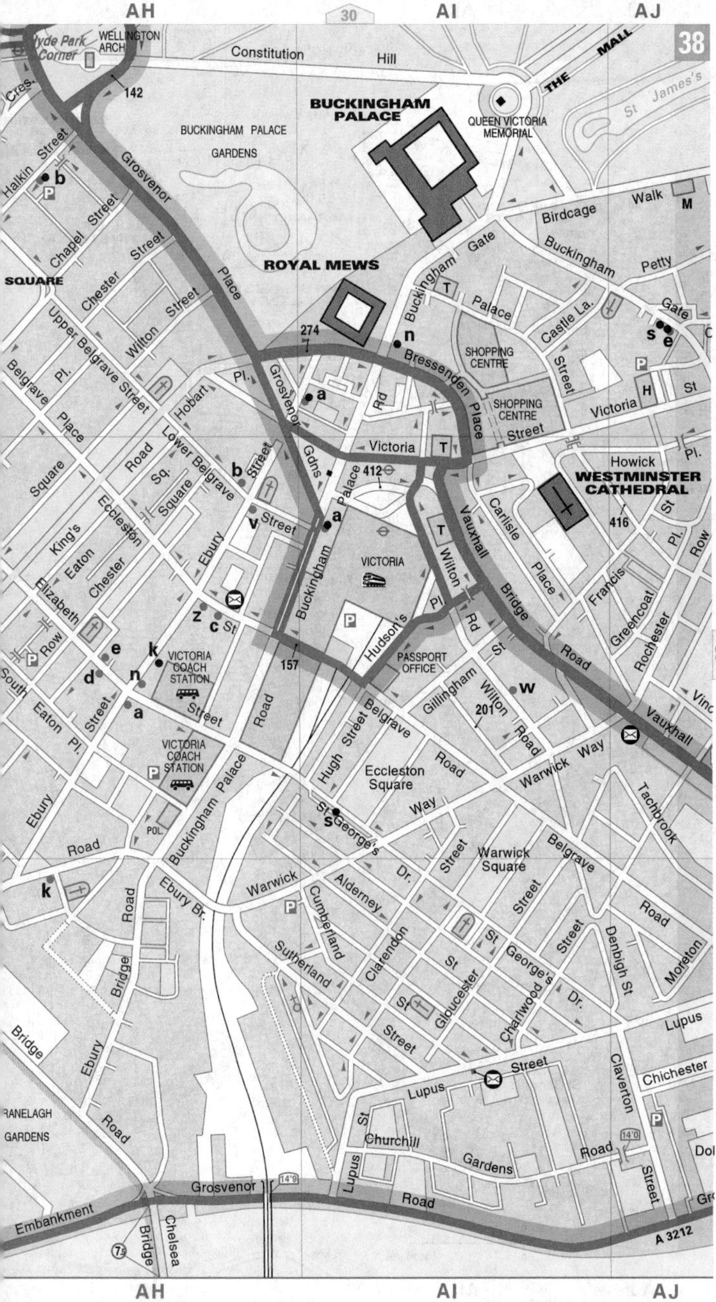

AH
30
AI
AJ
38
Hyde Park Corner
WELLINGTON ARCH
Constitution Hill
THE MALL
142
BUCKINGHAM PALACE
BUCKINGHAM PALACE GARDENS
QUEEN VICTORIA MEMORIAL
St James's
Birdcage Walk
M
Halkin Street
Chapel Street
Grosvenor Place
SQUARE
Chester Street
Wilton Street
Upper Belgrave Street
ROYAL MEWS
Buckingham Gate
Buckingham Palace
Petty
Gate
Castle La.
X
274
n
SHOPPING CENTRE
s
e
Belgrave Place
Pl.
Hobart Pl.
Grosvenor Gdns
a
Bressenden Place
Rd
Street
Victoria Street
H
St
SHOPPING CENTRE
T
Victoria
Howick Pl.
WESTMINSTER CATHEDRAL
Square
Road
Sq.
Lower Belgrave Street
b
Palace
412
Carlisle Place
416
King's
Eccleston
Chester Square
Eaton
Ebury
v
Street
VICTORIA
Vauxhall Bridge Road
Wilton Rd
Francis
Row
Elizabeth
Eaton
Chester
z
c
St
Buckingham
Pl.
Greencoat
Rochester
Y
39
e
k
VICTORIA COACH STATION
Hudson's
Rd
PASSPORT OFFICE
St
P
Row
d
n
157
South Eaton Pl.
Street
a
Street
Road
Gillingham
Belgrave
Wilton Road
201
w
Vincent
Vauxhall
VICTORIA COACH STATION
Buckingham Palace Road
Hugh Street
Belgrave Road
Eccleston Square
Warwick Way
Ebury
POL
St George's Dr.
s
Way
Tachbrook
Road
Warwick
Street
Warwick Square
Belgrave Road
k
Ebury Br.
Alderney
Road
Cumberland
Street
St George's Dr.
Street
Denbigh St
Moreton
Bridge
Sutherland
Clarendon
St
Gloucester
Charlwood
St
Street
Lupus
Bridge
Ebury
Z
Lupus Street
Chichester
Claverton
RANELAGH GARDENS
Road
St
Lupus
Churchill Gardens
Road
14'0
Dol
Street
Lupus St
Grosvenor
14'9
Road
Gr
Embankment
Bridge
Chelsea
A 3212
AH
AI
AJ

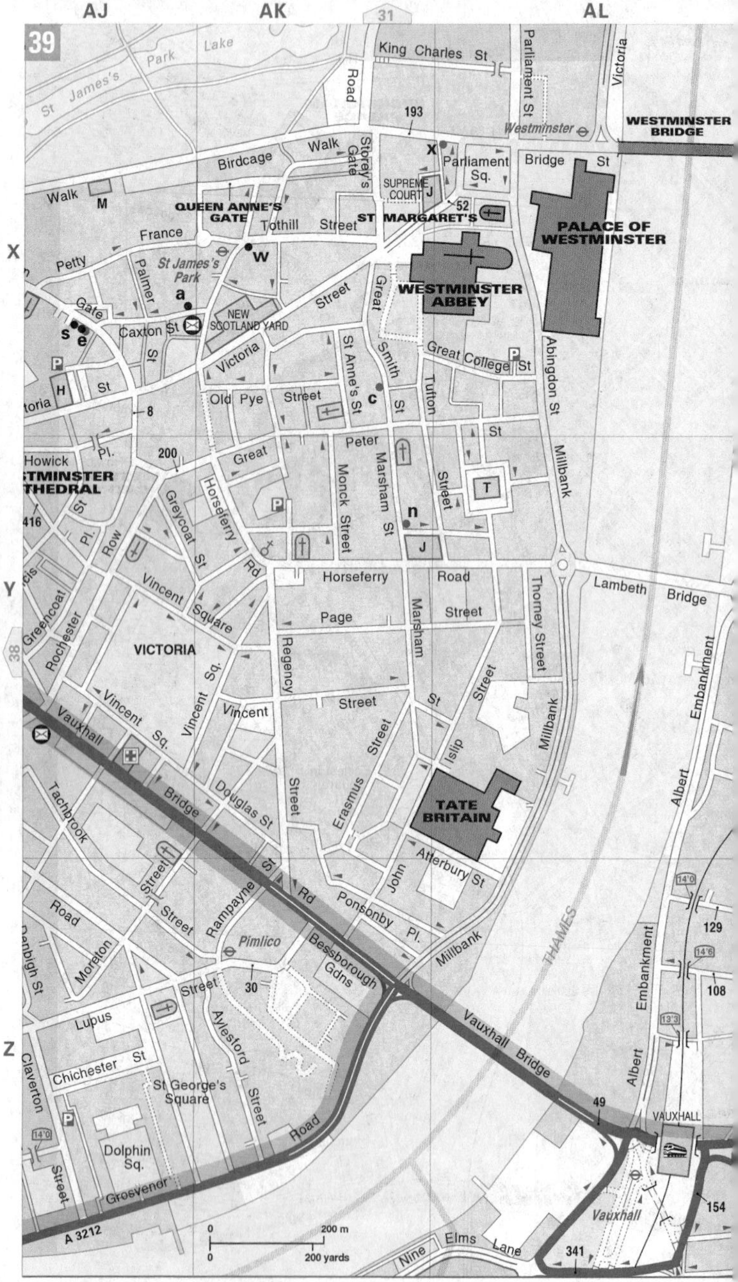
AJ
AK
31
AL
39
Lake
St James's Park
King Charles St
Road
Parliament St
Victoria
193
Westminster
WESTMINSTER BRIDGE
Birdcage Walk
Storey's Gate
X
Parliament Sq.
Bridge St
Walk
M
SUPREME COURT
J
52
QUEEN ANNE'S GATE
Tothill Street
ST MARGARET'S
PALACE OF WESTMINSTER
France
X
Petty
W
St James's Park
Palmer
Great
WESTMINSTER ABBEY
a
Gate
Street
NEW SCOTLAND YARD
Caxton St
s
e
Victoria
Smith
Great College St
St
P
H
St
St Anne's St
Abingdon St
LONDON
toria
Old Pye Street
c
Tufton
8
St
St
Peter
Howick
Pl.
200
Great
Marsham
STMINSTER THEDRAL
Greycoat
Horseferry
Monck Street
Street
T
Millbank
St
P
n
416
Pl.
Row
St
St
Rd
J
Y
Horseferry Road
Lambeth Bridge
Vincent
Square
Page
Street
Greencoat
Rochester
Marsham
Thorney Street
38
VICTORIA
Sq.
Regency
Street
Embankment
Vincent
Street
St
Vincent Sq.
Vincent
Vincent
Street
Islip
Millbank
Vauxhall
Bridge
Douglas St
Street
Erasmus
TATE BRITAIN
Albert
Tachbrook
Street
Atterbury St
John
St
Rd
Ponsonby Pl.
Street
Rampayne
14'0
Road
129
Denbigh St
Moreton
Pimlico
Bessborough Gdns
Millbank
THAMES
14'6
Embankment
30
Street
108
Lupus
Vauxhall Bridge
13'3
Z
St
Chichester
St George's Square
Albert
Claverton
Aylesford
Street
49
VAUXHALL
P
Road
14'0
Dolphin Sq.
Street
Grosvenor
154
Vauxhall
A 3212
0
200 m
0
200 yards
Elms
Lane
Nine
341
AJ
AK
AL

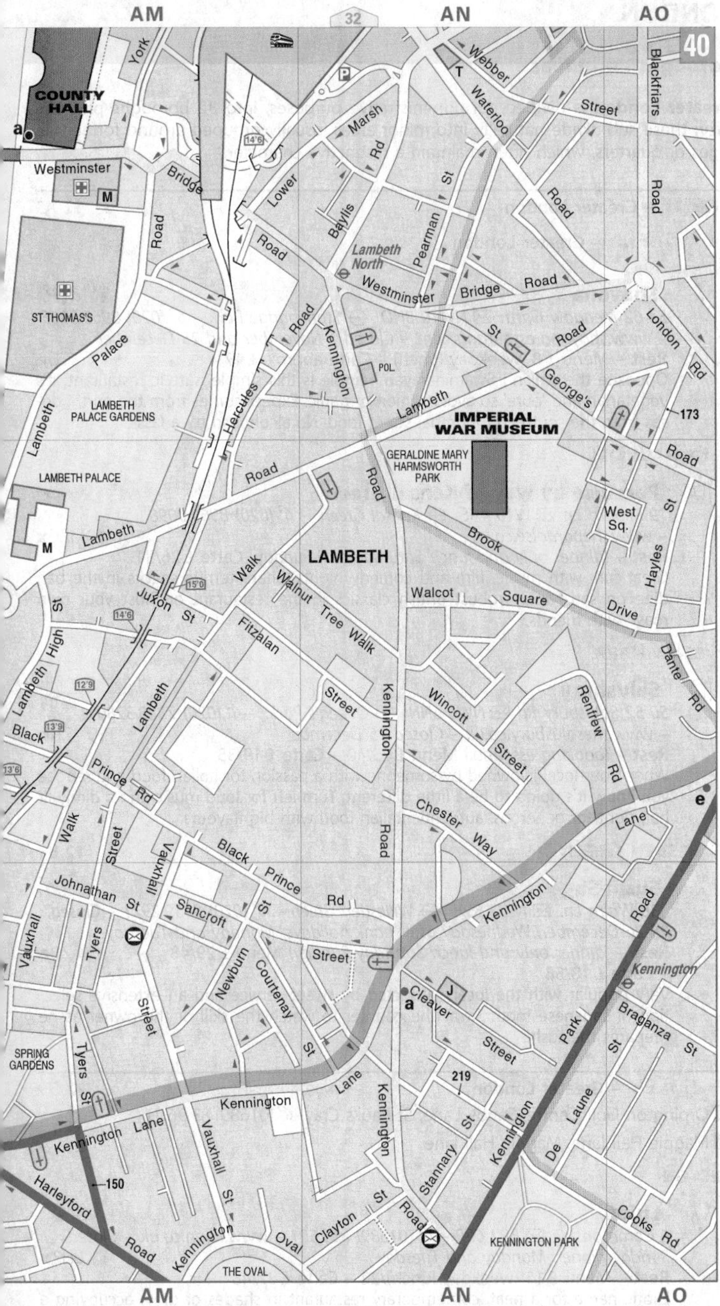
AM
AN
AO
32
40
COUNTY HALL
York
Westminster
M
Bridge
Road
ST THOMAS'S
Palace
LAMBETH PALACE GARDENS
Lambeth
LAMBETH PALACE
Hercules
Lower
Marsh
Baylis
Rd
Lambeth North
Pearman
St
Webber
Waterloo
Road
Street
Blackfriars
Road
X
Westminster
Bridge
Road
London
Rd
Kennington
POL.
St
George's
Road
173
IMPERIAL WAR MUSEUM
GERALDINE MARY HARMSWORTH PARK
Brook
West Sq.
Hayles
St
Lambeth
Road
Lambeth
LAMBETH
Walk
Walnut Tree Walk
Walcot
Square
Drive
Dante
Rd
Y
Juxon
St
Fitzalan
Street
Kennington
Road
Wincott
Street
Renfrew
Rd
Lambeth High St
Black
Prince
Rd
Chester
Way
Lane
e
Lambeth
Walk
Street
Vauxhall
Black
Prince
Rd
Johnathan St
Sancroft
St
Kennington
Road
Vauxhall
Tyers
Newburn
Courtenay
Street
Kennington
a
Cleaver
Street
J
Braganza
St
Z
Park
SPRING GARDENS
Tyers
St
Street
St
Lane
219
Kennington
Kennington
Lane
Vauxhall
St
Kennington
St
Kennington
Stannary
De Laune
Harleyford
150
Road
Kennington
Oval
Clayton
St
Road
KENNINGTON PARK
Cooks
Rd
THE OVAL
AM
AN
AO

LONDON

Boroughs and areas

Greater London is divided, for administrative purposes, into 32 boroughs plus **the City:** these sub-divide naturally into minor areas, usually grouped around former villages or quarters, which often maintain a distinctive character.

BRENT – Greater London 12 A3

CHURCH END – Greater London

X **Shayona** A/C P

54-62 Meadow Garth ✉ NW10 8HD ⊖ Stonebridge Park – ✆ (020) 8965 3365 – www.shayonarestaurants.com – Closed 1 November and 25 December

Rest – Menu £ 8 (weekday lunch) – Carte approx. £ 17 **2**CU**a**

Opposite the striking Swaminarayan Temple is this simple, sattvic restaurant: it's vegetarian and 'pure' so avoids onion or garlic. Expect curries from the north, dosas from the south and Mumbai street food. No alcohol so try a lassi.

LONDON

KENSAL GREEN

Paradise by way of Kensal Green A/C

19 Kilburn Ln ✉ W10 4AE ⊖ Kensal Green. – ✆ (020) 8969 0098 – www.theparadise.co.uk **10**MZC**x**

Rest – *(dinner only and lunch Saturday and Sunday)* Carte £ 26/31

Great fun, with music, film and comedy nights. Share terrific snacks in the bar; dine on satisfyingly robust British classics in the restaurant or 'host your own roast' with friends.

QUEEN'S PARK

Salusbury A/C

50-52 Salusbury Rd ✉ NW6 6NN ⊖ Queen's Park. – ✆ (020) 7328 3286 – www.thesalusbury.co.uk – Closed 25 December **10**MZB**b**

Rest – *(booking essential)* Menu £ 25/40 – Carte £ 19/35

When your local is owned by someone with a passion for Italian food and reggae you know it's going to be a little different. Turn left for loud music and a dimly lit bar; right for generous, authentic Italian food with big flavours.

WILLESDEN GREEN 12 B3

X **Sushi-Say**

33B Walm Ln. ✉ NW2 5SH ⊖ Willesden Green – ✆ (020) 8459 2971 – Closed, 25-26 December, Wednesday after bank holidays, Monday and Tuesday

Rest – *(dinner only and lunch Saturday-Sunday)* Menu £ 29/48 – Carte £ 18/58 **9**LZB**a**

Very popular with the locals, attracted by sweet service and an extensive selection of Japanese food. Sit at the counter to watch the skill of the owner as he prepares the sushi.

BROMLEY – Greater London 12 B3

27 Orpington Golf Centre, Sandy Lane, St Paul's Cray, ✆ (01689) 83 96 77

9 Magpie Hall lane, Magpie Hall lane

KESTON

XX **Lujon** A/C

6 Commonside ✉ BR2 6BP – ✆ (01689) 855 501 – www.lujon.co.uk – Closed Sunday dinner, Monday and Tuesday **8**HZ**x**

Rest – Menu £ 15 (weekday lunch)/22 – Carte £ 27/48

Exotic name for a neat, contemporary restaurant in shades of grey, occupying a pleasant spot overlooking the Common. The European cooking is modern but the combinations of ingredients are reassuringly familiar.

Farnborough

XXX **Chapter One**

Farnborough Common, Locksbottom ✉ BR6 8NF – ✆ (01689) 854 848 – www.chaptersrestaurants.com – Closed 2-4 January **8HZa**

Rest – Menu £ 20/38 – Carte £ 38/53

Long-standing restaurant with many regulars, its stylish bar leading into an elegant, modern dining room. Wide-ranging menus offer keenly priced, carefully prepared modern European dishes; cooking is light and delicate, mixing classic and modern flavours. Assured service.

➜ Smoked haddock kedgeree, curry mayonnaise. Suckling pig with roast artichokes, potato purée and black truffle butter. Custard tart with rhubarb and nutmeg ice cream.

Orpington

XX **Xian**

324 High St. ✉ BR6 0NG – ✆ (01689) 871 881 – Closed 2 weeks April, 25-26 December, Sunday lunch and Monday **8JYa**

Rest – Menu £ 10 (lunch) – Carte £ 15/22

Stylish, modern dining room with banquette seating, bamboo matting on the walls and six super lithographs of the famous Terracotta Warriors of Xian. Appealing menu offers flavoursome, authentic Chinese dishes, with something for everyone.

Sundridge Park

XX **Cinnamon Culture**

46 Plaistow Ln ✉ BR1 3PA – ✆ (020) 8289 0322 – www.cinnamonculture.com – Closed 26 December **8HYz**

Rest – Menu £ 15 (weekdays) – Carte £ 23/36

Former Victorian pub transmogrified into a smart Indian restaurant where the cooking is undertaken with care. A plethora of menus include Tasting and Vegetarian options, as well as a monthly menu focusing on one region.

CAMDEN – Greater London **12 B3**

Belsize Park

XX **XO**

29 Belsize Ln. ✉ NW3 5AS ⊖ Belsize Park – ✆ (020) 7433 0888 – www.rickerrestaurants.com/xo – Closed 25-26 December, 1 January and bank holidays **11PZAa**

Rest – Menu £ 18 (lunch) – Carte £ 20/39

Busy bar behind which is a slick and stylish dining room. Vibrant atmosphere; popular with all the good-looking locals. Japanese, Korean, Thai and Chinese cooking; dishes are best shared.

X **Retsina**

48-50 Belsize Ln ✉ NW3 5AR ⊖ Belsize Park – ✆ (020) 7431 5855 – www.retsina-london.com – Closed 25-26 December, 1 January, Monday lunch and bank holidays **11PZAn**

Rest – Menu £ 19 (lunch) – Carte £ 21/45

Family-run restaurant whose unapologetically traditional menu offers all the Greek classics but the grill and souvla are the stars of the show. Service and atmosphere are both relaxed and friendly.

X **Tandis**

73 Haverstock Hill ✉ NW3 4SL ⊖ Chalk Farm – ✆ (020) 7586 8079 – www.tandisrestaurant.com – Closed 25 December **11QZBx**

Rest – Carte £ 17/24

Enticing Iranian food comes in the form of invigorating 'koresht' stews and succulent 'kababs', along with specialities such as 'sabzi polo' and 'kashke bademjaan'. Contemporary décor.

Covent Garden
10 Monmouth St. ✉ *WC2H 9HB* ⊖ *Covent Garden* – ✆ *(020) 7806 1000*
– www.firmdalehotels.com **31**ALU**x**
58 rm – †£ 315 ††£ 315, ☕ £ 18 – 1 suite
Rest *Brasserie Max* – see restaurant listing
Popular with those of a theatrical bent. Boldly designed, stylish bedrooms, with technology discreetly concealed. Boasts a very comfortable first floor oak-panelled drawing room with its own honesty bar.

Montague on the Gardens
15 Montague St. ✉ *WC1B 5BJ* ⊖ *Holborn* – ✆ *(020) 7637 1001*
– www.montaguehotel.com **31**ALT**a**
112 rm – †£ 186/330 ††£ 204/348, ☕ £ 20 – 12 suites
Rest *Blue Door Bistro* – Menu £ 20/25 – Carte £ 25/58
A traditional but elegant British feel to this period townhouse; its clubby bar and conservatory overlook a secluded, private garden. Individually decorated bedrooms. Bistro divided between two small, pretty rooms.

LONDON

Radisson Blu Edwardian Mercer Street
20 Mercer St ✉ *WC2H 9HD* ⊖ *Covent Garden* – ✆ *(020) 7836 4300*
– www.radissonblu-edwardian.com **31**ALU**d**
137 rm – †£ 234 ††£ 234/318, ☕ £ 23
Rest *The Dial* – Carte £ 18/29
Radisson Edwardian spent considerable funds transforming their former Mountbatten hotel. The bedrooms come with a contemporary look and relaxed restaurant blends in nicely with the theatreland neighbourhood.

Bloomsbury
16-22 Gt Russell St ✉ *WC1B 3LR* ⊖ *Tottenham Court Road*
– ✆ *(020) 7347 1000*
– www.doylecollection.com/bloomsbury **31**AKT**n**
153 rm – †£ 162/426 ††£ 186/450, ☕ £ 20
Rest *Landseer* – Menu £ 21 (early dinner) – Carte £ 30/56
Neo-Georgian building by Edward Lutyens, built for the YWCA in 1929. Now boasts a smart, comfortable interior, from the lobby to the contemporary bedrooms. Restaurant with largely British menu and clubby bar.

DoubleTree by Hilton London - West End
92 Southampton Row ✉ *WC1B 4BH* ⊖ *Russell Square*
– ✆ *(020) 7242 2828 – www.doubletree3hilton.com* **31**ALT**x**
207 rm – †£ 170/230 ††£ 188/248, ☕ £ 19 – 8 suites
Rest – Menu £ 15/24 – Carte £ 28/36
Now a corporate-minded hotel with a contemporary feel – the stained glass windows and original staircase are the only clues to the early 1900s origins of the building. Basement restaurant with a wide ranging menu including grills; or order snacks in the brighter bar just off the foyer.

Pied à Terre
34 Charlotte St ✉ *W1T 2NH* ⊖ *Goodge Street* – ✆ *(020) 7636 1178*
– www.pied-a-terre.co.uk
– Closed last week December-5 January, Saturday lunch, Sunday and bank holidays **31**AJT**f**
Rest – *(booking essential)* Menu £ 38/75
David Moore's Pied à Terre celebrated its 21st birthday in 2012 and remains in rude health. Head Chef Marcus Eaves' cooking is bold and imaginative and the wine list offers over 700 bins, with considerable depth across all major regions. Each year a different artist is commissioned to decorate the room.
→ Marinated scallops with avocado cream. Roast breast and crispy leg of quail, Wye Valley asparagus and foie gras. Hazelnut praline mousse with rum and raisin ice cream.

Hakkasan Hanway Place

8 Hanway Pl. ✉ W1T 1HD ⊖ Tottenham Court Road – ✆ (020) 7927 7000 – www.hakkasan.com – Closed 24-25 December **31**AKT**c**

Rest – Menu £ 29/118 – Carte £ 33/82

Cool and seductive subterranean restaurant, with an air of exclusivity. Innovation and originality have been added to the Cantonese base to create dishes with zip and depth. Lunchtime dim sum is a highlight.

→ Crispy duck salad with pomelo, pine nut and shallot. Stir-fry black pepper rib eye beef with merlot. Hazelnut Jivara bomb with dark chocolate sauce.

Kitchen Table at Bubbledogs

70 Charlotte St ✉ W1T 4QG ⊖ Goodge Street – ✆ (020) 7637 7770 – www.kitchentablelondon.co.uk – Closed 1-14 January, 18-25 April, 19 August-2 September, 23-30 December, Sunday and Monday **30**AJT**g**

Rest – *(dinner only) (booking essential) (set menu only)* Menu £ 78

Unless you've come for a hot dog, skip past the queue and head downstairs. Here you sit at a horseshoe-shaped counter and watch as the chef-owner and his young team cook and introduce around 12 meticulously prepared courses.

Mon Plaisir

19-21 Monmouth St. ✉ WC2H 9DD ⊖ Covent Garden – ✆ (020) 7836 7243 – www.monplaisir.co.uk – Closed Christmas-New Year, Sunday and bank holidays **31**ALU**g**

Rest – Menu £ 15/25 – Carte £ 30/47

This proud French institution opened in the 1940s. Enjoy satisfyingly authentic classics in any of the four contrasting rooms, full of Gallic charm; apparently the bar was salvaged from a Lyonnais brothel.

Roka

37 Charlotte St ✉ W1T 1RR ⊖ Goodge Street – ✆ (020) 7580 6464 – www.rokarestaurant.com – Closed 25 December **31**AJT**k**

Rest – Carte £ 18/89

Bright, atmospheric interior of teak and oak; bustling and trendy feel. Contemporary touches added to Japanese dishes; try specialities from the on-view Robata grill. Capable and chatty service.

Fino

33 Charlotte St, (entrance on Rathbone St.) ✉ W1T 1RR ⊖ Goodge Street – ✆ (020) 7813 8010 – www.finorestaurant.com – Closed Saturday lunch, Sunday and bank holidays **31**AJT**a**

Rest – Menu £ 18 (weekday lunch)/45 – Carte £ 18/31

Seafood is handled especially well in this lively, quite smart and smoothly run basement tapas restaurant. Sensibly divided menu, with dishes designed for sharing. Youthful, helpful service.

Brasserie Max – Covent Garden Hotel

10 Monmouth St. ✉ WC2H 9HB ⊖ Covent Garden – ✆ (020) 7806 1007 – www.firmdalehotels.com **31**ALU**x**

Rest – *(booking essential)* Menu £ 24 – Carte £ 33/69

It's not just shoppers and theatregoers who appreciate this stylish brasserie. Its international menu, grilled specialities, Sunday brunches and afternoon teas have widespread appeal.

Dabbous (Ollie Dabbous)

39 Whitfield St ✉ W1T 2SF ⊖ Goodge Street – ✆ (020) 7323 1544 – www.dabbous.co.uk – Closed 21 December-14 January, 18-22 April, three weeks August, Sunday and Monday **31**AJT**r**

Rest – *(booking essential)* Menu £ 28/59 – Carte £ 22/38

One of the hottest tickets in town – the kitchen adopts the 'less is more' approach; the food comes with elegantly restrained finesse and a bewitching purity. Most have the 7-course menu with its stimulating and sublime combinations of ingredients. The ersatz industrial room has a simple elegance.

→ Avocado, pistachio and lemon balm in a chilled osmanthus infusion. Grilled mackerel, iodized sour cream, samphire and lovage. Fresh milk curds, birch sap, winter fruit and vegetables.

Paramount

Centre Point (32nd floor) 101-103 New Oxford St. ✉ WC1A 1DD ⊖ Tottenham Court Road – ✆ (020) 7420 2900 – www.paramount.uk.net – Closed 25 December

Rest – Menu £ 29 (lunch) – Carte £ 32/54 **31**AKT**b**

Worth the palaver of getting into this Grade II listed building: the views are terrific, especially from the Viewing Gallery bar on the 33rd floor. Modern European cooking. The highest venue in London for afternoon tea.

Kopapa

32-34 Monmouth St ✉ WC2H 9HA ⊖ Covent Garden – ✆ (020) 7240 6076 – www.kopapa.co.uk – Closed 25 December **31**ALU**h**

Rest – *(booking advisable)* Menu £ 18/39 – Carte £ 27/59

Kopapa, a Maori word for a gathering, is Peter Gordon's just-drop-in-anytime place. It's busy but fun, with breakfast morphing into all-day dining. Go for the 'fusion'-inspired dishes - they'll give your taste buds the best workout.

Giaconda Dining Rooms

9 Denmark St. ✉ WC2H 8LS ⊖ Tottenham Court Road – ✆ (020) 7240 3334 – www.giacondadining.com – Closed 2 weeks August, Saturday lunch and Sunday

Rest – Menu £ 19 – Carte £ 18/31 **31**AKT**k**

Now doubled in size but still offering the same value for money. Affable Aussie owner-chef's philosophy is seasonal ingredients prepared with little fuss and lots of flavour. Steak tartare and duck confit remain favourites and how many chefs have the courage to put 'today's staff meal' on their menu?

Gail's Kitchen Ⓝ

11-13 Bayley St ✉ WC1B 3HD ⊖ Goodge Street – ✆ (020) 7323 9694 – www.gailskitchen.co.uk – Closed 25 December **31**AKT**s**

Rest – Carte £ 17/27

From the bakery people comes this engagingly run eatery that occupies a rather small space within the Myhotel. The enticing Mediterranean dishes are prepared with care and designed for sharing; the snacks are great too.

Salt Yard

54 Goodge St. ✉ W1T 4NA ⊖ Goodge Street – ✆ (020) 7637 0657 – www.saltyard.co.uk – Closed 10 days Christmas, Sunday and bank holidays

Rest – Carte £ 14/24 **31**AJT**d**

Ground floor bar and buzzy basement restaurant specialising in good value plates of tasty Italian and Spanish dishes, ideal for sharing; charcuterie a speciality. Super wine list.

Honey & Co Ⓝ

25a Warren St ✉ W1T 5LZ ⊖ Warren Street – ✆ (020) 7388 6175 – www.honeyandco.co.uk – Closed first week January, last week August, Christmas, Monday dinner, Sunday and bank holidays **18**RZD**c**

Rest – *(booking essential)* Menu £ 27 (dinner) – Carte £ 20/29

The husband and wife team at this sweet little café were both Ottolenghi head chefs so expect cooking full of freshness and colour. Influences stretch beyond Israel to the wider Middle East. Open from 8am; packed at night.

Barrica

62 Goodge St ✉ W1T 4NE ⊖ Goodge Street – ✆ (020) 7436 9448 – www.barrica.co.uk – Closed 25-26 December, 1 January, Sunday and bank holidays

Rest – *(booking essential)* Carte £ 12/26 **31**AJT**x**

All the staff at this lively little tapas bar are Spanish, so perhaps it's national pride that makes them run it with a passion lacking in many of their competitors. When it comes to the food authenticity is high on the agenda.

Cigala

54 Lamb's Conduit St. ✉ WC1N 3LW ⊖ Russell Square – ✆ (020) 7405 1717 – www.cigala.co.uk – Closed Christmas **19**TZD**a**

Rest – *(booking essential)* Menu £ 18 (lunch) – Carte £ 24/36

Relaxed surroundings and an accessible menu allow this Spanish restaurant to appeal to a wide audience. Try the grilled black pudding, hams from the open kitchen counter and homemade chorizo, or share a paella.

LONDON

Tsunami

93 Charlotte St. ✉ W1T 4PY ⊖ Goodge Street – ✆ (020) 7637 0050 – www.tsunamirestaurant.co.uk – Closed Saturday lunch and Sunday

Rest – Menu £ 37 – Carte £ 20/48 **s** **30**AITa

Sister to the original in Clapham. Sweet, pretty place, with lacquered walls, floral motif and moody lighting. Contemporary Japanese cuisine is carefully prepared and sensibly priced.

Lady Ottoline

11a Northington St ✉ WC1N 2JF ⊖ Chancery Lane. – ✆ (020) 7831 0008 – www.theladyottoline.com – Closed 24 December-2 January and bank holidays

Rest – Carte £ 22/38 **19**TZDc

Sister to Princess of Shoreditch, this large red-bricked Victorian pub is largely unchanged from when it was called The Kings Arms. Enjoy the same gutsy cooking in the busy bar or the Queen Anne style upstairs dining room.

Camden Town

Market

43 Parkway ✉ NW1 7PN ⊖ Camden Town – ✆ (020) 7267 9700 – www.marketrestaurant.co.uk – Closed 25 December-3 January , Sunday dinner and bank holidays **12**RZBx

Rest – *(booking essential)* Menu £ 10/18 – Carte £ 25/35

Market fresh produce used to create satisfying and refreshingly matter of fact British dishes, at excellent prices that entice plenty of passers-by. Appealing décor of exposed brick walls, old school chairs and zinc-topped tables.

Made in Camden

Roundhouse, Chalk Farm Rd ✉ NW1 8EH ⊖ Chalk Farm – ✆ (020) 7424 8495 – www.madeincamden.com – Closed 25 December, 1-2 January, Sunday dinner and Monday **11**QZBa

Rest – Menu £ 12 (weekday lunch) – Carte £ 23/32

Attached to the Roundhouse is this large bar and dining room where the posters instil curiosity or nostalgia, depending on your age. What sets it apart is the food: small plates in vibrant, unusual and exciting combinations.

York & Albany with rm

127-129 Parkway ✉ NW1 7PS ⊖ Camden Town. – ✆ (020) 7388 3344 – www.gordonramsay.com/yorkandalbany **12**RZBs

10 rm – 🛉£ 205 🛉🛉£ 235/387

Rest – *(booking essential)* Menu £ 22 (weekday lunch) – Carte £ 28/50

The same menu is now served throughout this handsome 1820s John Nash coaching inn; part of Gordon Ramsay's empire. There's everything on offer, from wood-fired pizzas to lamb shoulder or lemon sole. The ground floor has the buzz; the bedrooms have character.

Dartmouth Park

Bull & Last

168 Highgate Rd ✉ NW5 1QS ⊖ Tufnell Park. – ✆ (020) 7267 3641 – www.thebullandlast.co.uk – Closed 24-25 December **12**RZAa

Rest – *(booking essential)* Carte £ 22/44

A busy Victorian pub with plenty of charm and character; the upstairs is a little quieter. Cooking is muscular, satisfying and reflects the time of year; charcuterie is a speciality.

Euston

Pullman London St Pancras

100-110 Euston Rd ✉ NW1 2AJ ⊖ Euston – ✆ (020) 7666 9000 – www.pullmanhotels.com **18**SZCa

312 rm – 🛉£ 395 🛉🛉£ 405, ☕ £ 20 – 2 suites

Rest *Golden Arrow* – *(bar lunch Saturday, Sunday and bank holidays)* Menu £ 30 – Carte £ 18/64

Designed primarily for the business traveller, Pullman is a stylish and modern brand from the Accor group. The open- plan reception and chic lounge lead into a relaxed eatery offering the brasserie classics. State-of-the-art conference facilities include a theatre. Ideally located for Eurostar.

HAMPSTEAD

Wells
30 Well Walk ✉ NW3 1BX ⊖ Hampstead. – ✆ (020) 7794 3785 – www.thewellshampstead.co.uk **11**PZA**v**

Rest – Carte £ 22/40

Part country pub, part city sophisticate; busy ground floor, with more sedate upstairs restaurant. Cooking is hearty in flavour and sophisticated in look, with a pleasing British edge.

HATTON GARDEN

XX Bleeding Heart
Bleeding Heart Yard, off Greville St. ✉ EC1N 8SJ ⊖ Farringdon – ✆ (020) 7242 2056 – www.bleedingheart.co.uk – Closed 24 December-1 January, Saturday, Sunday and bank holidays **32**ANT**e**

Rest – *(booking essential)* Menu £ 25/45 **s** – Carte £ 28/52 **s**

Dickensian yard plays host to this atmospheric, candlelit restaurant; popular with those from The City. Classic French cuisine is the draw, with service that's formal but has personality. Wines from owners' New Zealand estate.

LONDON

HOLBORN

XX Moti Mahal
45 Great Queen St. ✉ WC2B 5AA ⊖ Holborn – ✆ (020) 7240 9329 – www.motimahal-uk.com – Closed 25 December, Saturday lunch, Sunday and bank holidays **31**ALU**k**

Rest – Menu £ 15/25 – Carte £ 25/47

The menu follows the path of the 16C Grand Trunk Road, stretching from Bengal through northern India to the mountains of the northwest frontier. The tandoor features heavily but there's also plenty of unfamiliar dishes to try.

XX Asadal
227 High Holborn ✉ WC1V 7DA ⊖ Holborn – ✆ (020) 7430 9006 – www.asadal.co.uk – Closed 25-26 December, 1 January and Sunday lunch

Rest – Carte £ 20/30 **31**ALT**n**

Sharing is the key in this busy basement, where you'll be oblivious to its unprepossessing location. Hotpots, dumplings and barbeques are the highlights from the easy-to-follow Korean menu. Staff cope well with the evening rush.

X Great Queen Street
32 Great Queen St ✉ WC2B 5AA ⊖ Holborn – ✆ (020) 7242 0622 – Closed Christmas-New Year, Sunday dinner and bank holidays **31**ALT**d**

Rest – *(booking essential)* Carte £ 20/33

The menu is a model of British understatement and is dictated by the seasons; the cooking, confident and satisfying with laudable prices and generous portions. Lively atmosphere and enthusiastic service.

KENTISH TOWN

X Chicken Shop Ⓝ
79 Highgate Rd ✉ NW5 1TL ⊖ Kentish Town – ✆ (020) 3310 2020 – www.chickenshop.com – Closed Sunday dinner **12**RZA**c**

Rest – *(dinner only and lunch Saturday-Sunday) (bookings not accepted)* Carte £ 16/21

Simply great chicken – marinated, steamed and finished over wood and charcoal – with a choice of sides and three desserts. It all happens in a noisy, mildly chaotic basement but it's great fun and good value. Be ready to queue.

PRIMROSE HILL

XX Odette's
130 Regent's Park Rd. ✉ NW1 8XL ⊖ Chalk Farm – ✆ (020) 7586 8569 – www.odettesprimrosehill.com – Closed 25-27 December and 1 January

Rest – Menu £ 15/20 – Carte £ 28/37 **11**QZB**b**

A local institution that has recently lightened up. Warm and inviting interior, with chatty but organised service. Robust and quite elaborate cooking, with chef-owner passionate about his Welsh roots.

Michael Nadra Primrose Hill
42 Gloucester Ave ✉ NW1 8JD ⊖ Camden Town – ☎ (020) 7722 2800 – www.restaurant-michaelnadra.co.uk/primrose – Closed 24-28 December and 1 January **12**RZB**m**

Rest – Menu £ 15 – Carte £ 32/47

Michael Nadra went north for his second branch and took over this unusual, modern building. The menu resembles his Chiswick operation, which means flavours from the Med but also the odd Asian note. The bar offers over 20 martinis.

L'Absinthe
40 Chalcot Rd ✉ NW1 8LS ⊖ Chalk Farm – ☎ (020) 7483 4848 – www.labsinthe.co.uk – Closed August and Christmas **11**QZB**s**

Rest – Menu £ 9/20 – Carte £ 20/37

Lively and enthusiastically run French bistro, with tightly packed tables, spread over two floors. All the favourites, from Lyonnais salad to duck confit. Commendably priced French wine list.

Swiss Cottage

Bradley's
25 Winchester Rd. ✉ NW3 3NR ⊖ Swiss Cottage – ☎ (020) 7722 3457 – www.bradleysnw3.co.uk – Closed Sunday dinner **11**PZB**e**

Rest – Menu £ 18/26 – Carte £ 32/40

A stalwart of the local dining scene and ideal for visitors to the nearby Hampstead Theatre. The thoughtfully compiled and competitively priced set menus of mostly classical cooking draw in plenty of regulars.

Singapore Garden
83 Fairfax Rd. ✉ NW6 4DY ⊖ Swiss Cottage – ☎ (020) 7328 5314 – www.singaporegarden.co.uk – Closed 24-28 December **11**PZB**x**

Rest – Menu £ 30 (dinner) – Carte £ 21/52

A smart, bright and comfortable room, with endearingly enthusiastic service. Your best bet is to pick vibrant and zesty dishes from the list of Singaporean and Malaysian specialities.

Eriki
4-6 Northways Par, Finchley Rd ✉ NW3 5EN ⊖ Swiss Cottage – ☎ (020) 7722 0606 – www.eriki.co.uk **11**PZB**u**

Rest – Menu £ 8 (lunch)/30 – Carte approx. £ 25

The menu offers an invigorating gastronomic tour of all parts of India; vegetarians will be in clover. Vividly coloured, comfortable room with fine tapestries; well-meaning service and lots of regulars.

CITY OF LONDON – Greater London **12** B3

Andaz Liverpool Street
40 Liverpool St. ✉ EC2M 7QN ⊖ Liverpool Street – ☎ (020) 7961 1234 – www.andaz.com **34**ART**t**

267 rm – †£ 126/402 ††£ 162/438, ☕ £ 24 – 3 suites

Rest ***1901*** – see restaurant listing

Rest ***Miyako*** – ☎ (020) 7618 7100 *(closed Christmas, Saturday lunch, Sunday and bank holidays) (booking essential)* Carte £ 16/42

Rest ***Eastway Brasserie*** – ☎ (020) 7618 7400 – Menu £ 17 – Carte £ 21/30

A contemporary and stylish interior hides behind the classic Victorian façade. Bright and spacious bedrooms boast state-of-the-art facilities. Various dining options include a brasserie specialising in grilled meats, a compact Japanese restaurant and a traditional pub.

Threadneedles
5 Threadneedle St. ✉ EC2R 8AY ⊖ Bank – ☎ (020) 7657 8080 – www.hotelthreadneedles.co.uk **34**ARU**y**

74 rm – †£ 355/450 ††£ 355/750, ☕ £ 23

Rest ***Bonds*** – see restaurant listing

A converted bank, dating from 1856, with a stunning stained-glass cupola in the lounge. Bedrooms are very stylish and individual, featuring Egyptian cotton sheets and thoughtful extras.

LONDON

Apex Temple Court

1-2 Serjeant's Inn, Fleet St ✉ *EC4Y 1LL* ⊖ *Blackfriars* – ✆ *(020) 3004 4141*
– www.apexhotels.co.uk **32**ANU**r**
184 rm – †£ 159/360 ††£ 159/360, ☕ £ 20
Rest *Chambers* – Menu £ 17/20 – Carte £ 22/46
Smart, corporate hotel fashioned out of former law firm offices and tucked away in a courtyard. Chambers is a well-kept brasserie with a Mediterranean menu. Four grades of bedroom, but all are bright, light and a good size.

Montcalm London City at The Brewery

52 Chiswell St ✉ *EC1Y 4SD* ⊖ *Barbican* – ✆ *(020) 7614 0100*
– www.themontcalmlondoncity.co.uk **19**VZD**r**
235 rm – †£ 156/240 ††£ 168/360, ☕ £ 22 – 11 suites
Rest *Chiswell Street Dining Rooms* – see restaurant listing
The majority of the contemporary rooms are in the original part of the Whitbread Brewery, built in 1714; ask for a quieter one overlooking the courtyard, or one of the 25 found in one of 4 restored Georgian townhouses across the road.

Hotel Indigo London - Tower Hill

142 Minories ✉ *EC3N 1LS* ⊖ *Aldgate* – ✆ *(020) 7265 1014*
– www.hotelindigo.com/lontowerhill **34**ASU**x**
46 rm – †£ 155/395 ††£ 155/395, ☕ £ 9
Rest – Carte £ 21/35
Quieter than its city location would suggest, this business hotel comes with funky modern bedrooms equipped with iPod docks and coffee machines. Tower Bridge and Tower Hill suites have skyline views. Popular menu in Square Mile brasserie.

Bonds – Threadneedles Hotel

5 Threadneedle St. ✉ *EC2R 8AY* ⊖ *Bank* – ✆ *(020) 7657 8088*
– www.bonds-restaurant.com
– Closed Saturday, Sunday and bank holidays **34**ARU**y**
Rest – Menu £ 24/28 – Carte £ 28/44
With its classical proportions, panelling and Corinthian columns, this Victorian banking hall provides a striking backdrop. Cooking has a classical backbone and a fondness for British produce; sauces are gutsy and flavours assured.

Lutyens

85 Fleet St. ✉ *EC4Y 1AE* ⊖ *Blackfriars* – ✆ *(020) 7583 8385*
– www.lutyens-restaurant.com – Closed 1 week Christmas-New Year, Saturday, Sunday and bank holidays **32**ANU**c**
Rest – Menu £ 22 – Carte £ 28/61
The unmistakable hand of Sir Terence Conran: timeless and understated good looks mixed with functionality and an appealing Anglo-French menu with plenty of classics such as fruits de mer and game in season.

Sauterelle

The Royal Exchange ✉ *EC3V 3LR* ⊖ *Bank* – ✆ *(020) 7618 2483*
– www.royalexchange-grandcafe.co.uk/ – Closed Saturday, Sunday and bank holidays, **33**AQU**a**
Rest – Menu £ 20/45 – Carte £ 34/55
Impressive location on the mezzanine floor of The Royal Exchange; ask for a table looking down over the Grand Café. A largely French-inspired contemporary menu makes good use of luxury ingredients.

1901 – Andaz Liverpool Street Hotel

Liverpool St. ✉ *EC2M 7QN* ⊖ *Liverpool Street* – ✆ *(020) 7618 7000*
– www.andaz.com – Closed Christmas, Saturday lunch, Sunday and bank holidays **34**ART**t**
Rest – Menu £ 30 – Carte £ 36/53
The crisp white decoration and judicious lighting highlight the immense Doric columns, the cornicing and the beautiful cupola above. The menu champions British produce and the cooking is modern and quite ambitious in its reach.

LONDON

XX **Club Gascon** (Pascal Aussignac)
57 West Smithfield ✉ EC1A 9DS ⊖ Barbican – ✆ (020) 7600 6144 – www.clubgascon.com – Closed Christmas-New Year, Saturday lunch, Sunday and bank holidays **33**APT**z**
Rest – *(booking essential)* Menu £ 25/90 – Carte £ 35/48
The gastronomy of Gascony and France's southwest are the starting points but the assured and intensely flavoured cooking also pushes at the boundaries. Marble and huge floral displays create suitably atmospheric surroundings.
➜ Royale of marrow bone, Aquitaine caviar and geraniums. Crackled capon wings, scallop ballotine and lovage. Black olive and chocolate millionaire, lemon gel and thyme ice cream.

XX **Bread Street Kitchen**
10 Bread St ✉ EC4M 9AJ ⊖ St Paul's – ✆ (020) 3030 4050 – www.breadstreetkitchen.com – Closed 25 December **33**AQU**e**
Rest – *(booking advisable)* Carte £ 28/72
Gordon Ramsay's take on NY loft-style dining comes with a large bar, thumping music, an open kitchen and enough zinc ducting to kit out a small industrial estate. For the food, think modern bistro dishes with an element of refinement.

XX **New St Grill** N
16A New St ✉ EC2M 4TR ⊖ Liverpool Street – ✆ (020) 3503 0785 – www.newstreetgrill.com – Closed 23 December-7 January except dinner 31 December, Saturday lunch and Sunday dinner **34**ART**n**
Rest – Carte £ 28/66
D&D converted an 18C warehouse to satisfy our increasing appetite for red meat. They use Black Angus beef; grass-fed British and aged for 28 days, or corn-fed American, aged for 40 days. Start with a drink in the Old Bengal Bar.

XX **1701** N
Bevis Marks Synagogue, Bevis Marks ✉ EC3A 5DQ ⊖ Aldgate – ✆ (020) 7621 1701 – www.restaurant1701.co.uk – Closed Christmas, New Year, Saturday, Sunday and Jewish bank holidays **34**ART**v**
Rest – *(booking advisable)* Menu £ 32 (lunch) – Carte £ 35/51
1701 is the year that Bevis Marks Synagogue was built and the name of this modern, well run kosher restaurant that adjoins it. The talented kitchen has a deft touch and has cleverly brought the classic dishes up to date.

XX **Sushisamba** N
Heron Tower (38th and 39th Floor), 110 Bishopsgate ✉ EC2N 4AY ⊖ Liverpool Street – ✆ (020) 3640 7330 – www.sushisamba.com **34**ART**d**
Rest – *(booking essential)* Carte £ 28/79
Stunning views, a great destination bar and a menu that blends Japanese, Peruvian and Brazilian influences – it may not come cheap but this US import is all about giving its young, fashionable fan base a fun night out.

XX **The Chancery**
9 Cursitor St ✉ EC4A 1LL ⊖ Chancery Lane – ✆ (020) 7831 4000 – www.thechancery.co.uk – Closed 23-30 December, 1 January, Saturday lunch, Sunday and bank holidays **32**ANT**a**
Rest – Menu £ 35/49
An elegant restaurant that's so close to the law courts you'll assume your fellow diners are barristers, jurors, or the recently acquitted. The menu is appealing concise; dishes come with a classical backbone and bold flavours.

XX **Mint Leaf Lounge**
12 Angel Ct, Lothbury ✉ EC2R 7HB ⊖ Bank – ✆ (020) 7600 0992 – www.mintleaflounge.com – Closed 25-26 December, 1 January, Saturday, Sunday and bank holidays **33**AQT**b**
Rest – Menu £ 14 – Carte £ 28/46
Sister branch to the original in St James's. Slick and stylish, with busy bar. Well-paced service of carefully prepared contemporary Indian food, with many of the influences from the south.

LONDON

XX **Vanilla Black**

17-18 Tooks Ct. ✉ EC4A 1LB ⊖ Chancery Lane – ✆ (020) 7242 2622 – www.vanillablack.co.uk – Closed 2 weeks Christmas and bank holidays

Rest – Menu £ 24/38 **32**ANT**x**

Proving that vegetarian food can be flavoursome, creative and satisfying, with a menu that is varied, imaginative and, at times, ambitious. This is a well-run, friendly restaurant with understated décor, run by a husband and wife.

XX **Cinnamon Kitchen**

9 Devonshire Sq ✉ EC2M 4YL ⊖ Liverpool Street – ✆ (020) 7626 5000 – www.cinnamonclub.com – Closed Saturday lunch, Sunday and bank holidays **34**ART**e**

Rest – Menu £ 19/60 – Carte £ 24/63

Sister to The Cinnamon Club. Contemporary Indian cooking, with punchy flavours and arresting presentation. Sprightly service in large, modern surroundings. Watch the action from the Tandoor Bar.

XX **Kenza**

10 Devonshire Sq. ✉ EC2M 4YP ⊖ Liverpool Street – ✆ (020) 7929 5533 – www.kenza-restaurant.com – Closed Saturday lunch, Sunday and bank holidays

Rest – Menu £ 33/50 – Carte £ 29/43 **34**ART**c**

Exotic basement restaurant, with lamps, carvings, pumping music and nightly belly dancing. Lebanese and Moroccan cooking are the menu influences and the food is authentic and accurate.

XX **Cigalon**

115 Chancery Ln ✉ WC2A 1PP ⊖ Chancery Lane – ✆ (020) 7242 8373 – www.cigalon.co.uk – Closed Christmas and New Year, Saturday, Sunday and bank holidays **32**ANU**x**

Rest – Menu £ 13/25 – Carte £ 23/41

Pays homage to the food and wine of Provence, in an appropriately bright space that was a once an auction house. All the classics are here, from bouillabaisse to pieds et paquets. Busy bar in the cellar.

XX **The Mercer**

34 Threadneedle St ✉ EC2R 8AY ⊖ Bank – ✆ (020) 7628 0001 – www.themercer.co.uk – Closed 25-26 December, Saturday, Sunday and bank holidays

Rest – Carte £ 27/60 **34**ARU**x**

Converted bank, with airy feel thanks to high ceilings and large windows. Brasserie-style menu with appealing mix of classics and comfort food. Huge choice of wines available by glass or carafe.

XX **Boisdale of Bishopsgate**

Swedeland Crt, 202 Bishopsgate ✉ EC2M 4NR ⊖ Liverpool Street – ✆ (020) 7283 1763 – www.boisdale.co.uk – Closed Saturday, Sunday and bank holidays **34**ART**a**

Rest – Menu £ 20 – Carte £ 28/61

It's champagne and oysters on the ground floor and Scottish hospitality in the characterful vaulted cellar below. Enjoy smoked salmon, roast haggis and 28-day dry aged cuts of beef, along with live jazz most nights.

XX **The White Swan**

1st Floor, 108 Fetter Ln ✉ EC4A 1ES ⊖ Chancery Lane – ✆ (020) 7242 9696 – www.thewhiteswanlondon.com – Closed 25-26 December, Saturday, Sunday and bank holidays **32**ANT**n**

Rest – Menu £ 27/31 – Carte £ 26/42

The classically educated kitchen uses British ingredients but also flavours from the Med. To reach this clubby, part-panelled first floor room – a haven of serenity – one must fight through the hordes of drinkers on the ground floor.

XX **Manicomio**

6 Gutter Ln ✉ EC2V 8AS ⊖ St Paul's – ✆ (020) 7726 5010 – www.manicomio.co.uk – Closed 1 week Christmas, Saturday, Sunday and bank holidays **33**APT**s**

Rest – Carte £ 27/49

Second branch to follow the first in Chelsea. Regional Italian fare, with top-notch ingredients. Bright and fresh first floor restaurant, with deli-café on the ground floor and bar on top floor.

LONDON

XX **Luc's Brasserie**
17-22 Leadenhall Mkt ✉ EC3V 1LR ⊖ Bank – ✆ (020) 7621 0666 – www.lucsbrasserie.com – Closed Christmas, New Year, Saturday, Sunday and bank holidays **34ARUv**
Rest – *(lunch only and dinner Tuesday-Thursday) (booking essential at lunch)* Menu £ 20 – Carte £ 24/45
Looks down on the Victorian splendour of Leadenhall Market. First appeared in 1890 but re-invigorated this century. The menu is a paean to all things French and every classic dish is there.

XX **Barbecoa**
20 New Change Passage ✉ EC4M 9AG ⊖ St Paul's – ✆ (020) 3005 8555 – www.barbecoa.com – Closed 24-26 December and 1 January **33APUv**
Rest – *(booking essential)* Carte £ 30/55
Set up by Jamie Oliver, to show us what barbecuing is all about. The prime meats, butchered in-house, are just great; go for the pulled pork shoulder with cornbread on the side. By dessert you may be willing to share!

XX **High Timber**
8 High Timber St. ✉ EC4V 3PA ⊖ Mansion House – ✆ (020) 7248 1777 – www.hightimber.com – Closed 23-30 December, 1 January, Saturday dinner, Sunday and bank holidays **33APUb**
Rest – Menu £ 17 (lunch) – Carte £ 26/53
Rustic look to the room, despite being in a modern block, offering river views. Great wine cellar, with large choice from South Africa, the owners' homeland. Cumbrian steaks the speciality.

XX **Goodman City**
11 Old Jewry ✉ EC2R 8DU ⊖ Bank – ✆ (020) 7600 8220 – www.goodmanrestaurants.com – Closed Saturday, Sunday and bank holidays
Rest – Menu £ 22 (lunch) – Carte £ 30/61 **33AQUs**
Steaks, cut to order, are the stars of the show at this sister to the Mayfair original. Choose corn-fed, wet-matured USDA beef or Scottish and Irish grass-fed; plenty of side dishes available too.

XX **Morgan M**
50 Long Ln ✉ EC1A 9EJ ⊖ Barbican – ✆ (020) 7609 3560 – www.morganm.com – Closed 22-30 December, Saturday lunch and Sunday
Rest – Menu £ 22/52 – Carte £ 39/55 **33APTe**
Morgan Meunier, a proud Frenchman from the Champagne region, moved here in 2011 from his long-standing Islington locale. His bold cooking and formal restaurant keep things in a classical vein; popular vegetarian menu.

XX **Chiswell Street Dining Rooms** – Montcalm London City at The Brewery Hotel
56 Chiswell St ✉ EC1Y 4SA ⊖ Barbican – ✆ (020) 7614 0177 – www.chiswellstreetdining.com **19VZDr**
Rest – Menu £ 25 (weekdays) – Carte £ 27/47
The Martin brothers used their Botanist restaurant as the model for this corner of the old Whitbread Brewery. The cocktail bar comes alive at night. Makes good use of British produce, especially fish from nearby Billingsgate.

XX **Duck & Waffle** Ⓝ
Heron Tower (40th floor), 110 Bishopsgate ✉ EC2N 4AY ⊖ Liverpool Street – ✆ (020) 3640 7310 – www.duckandwaffle.com **34ARTd**
Rest – *(booking essential)* Menu £ 65 – Carte £ 28/60
The UK's highest restaurant, on the 40th floor of Heron Tower, is a cheaper and less excitable alternative to Sushisamba one floor down. The menu is varied and offal is done well – try the crispy pig's ears. It's open 24 hours a day.

X **Hispania** Ⓝ
72-74 Lombard St ✉ EC3V 9AY ⊖ Bank – ✆ (020) 7621 0338 – www.hispanialondon.com – Closed Saturday, Sunday and bank holidays
Rest – Carte £ 23/34 **33AQUn**
9,000 square foot of former banking hall given over to the celebration of Spanish gastronomy. The ground floor specialises in authentic, flavoursome tapas; the upstairs à la carte restaurant was due to open as we went to print.

X **Bird of Smithfield** N

26 Smithfield St ✉ EC1A 9LB ⊖ Farringdon – ✆ (020) 7559 5100 – www.birdofsmithfield.com – Closed Christmas, New Year, Sunday dinner and bank holidays **33**AOT**s**

Rest – *(booking essential)* Menu £ 24 (lunch) – Carte £ 22/51

Feels like a private members' club but without the smugness. Five floors of fun include a cocktail bar, lounge, rooftop terrace and small, friendly restaurant. The appealing British menu makes good use of the country's larder.

X **Hawksmoor**

10-12 Basinghall St ✉ EC2V 5BQ ⊖ Bank – ✆ (020) 7397 8120 – www.thehawksmoor.com – Closed 20 December-4 January, Saturday, Sunday and bank holidays

Rest – *(booking essential)* Menu £ 26 (dinner) – Carte £ 39/62 **33**AQT**a**

Fast and furious, busy and boisterous, this handsome room is the backdrop for another testosterone filled celebration of the serious business of beef eating. Nicely aged and rested Longhorn steaks take centre-stage.

X **Fish Market** N

16b New St ✉ EC2M 4TR ⊖ Liverpool Street – ✆ (020) 3503 0790 – www.fishmarket-restaurant.co.uk – Closed 20 December-6 January, Saturday lunch, Sunday and bank holidays

Rest – *(booking advisable)* Menu £ 17 – Carte £ 23/58 **34**ART**f**

How to get to the seaside from Liverpool Street? Simply step into this bright fish restaurant, in an old warehouse of the East India Company, and you'll almost hear the seagulls. The menu is lengthy and the cooking style classic.

X **Chabrot** N

62-63 Long Ln ✉ EC1A 9EJ ⊖ Barbican – ✆ (020) 7796 4550 – www.chabrot.com – Closed Christmas, Saturday lunch and Sunday **33**APT**n**

Rest – Menu £ 20 – Carte £ 24/51

Relive that romantic weekend in Paris here at this reassuringly familiar Gallic bistrot and sister to the original branch in Knightsbridge. Classics like tête de veau, confit de canard and boudin noir are here in all their glory.

X **Cellar Gascon**

59 West Smithfield ✉ EC1A 9DS ⊖ Barbican – ✆ (020) 7600 7561 – www.cellargascon.com – Closed Christmas-New Year, Saturday, Sunday and bank holidays **33**APT**c**

Rest – *(booking essential at lunch)* Menu £ 11 (lunch) – Carte approx. £ 19

It's not unlike a smart tapas bar except it's French and the monthly changing menu has plenty of treats: pâtés, rillettes, hams, cheeses and even some salads for the virtuous; but the Toulouse sausages and the Gascony pie stand out.

X **Vivat Bacchus**

47 Farringdon St ✉ EC4A 4LL ⊖ Farringdon – ✆ (020) 7353 2648 – www.vivatbacchus.co.uk – Closed Christmas and New Year, Saturday, Sunday and bank holidays **32**ANT**c**

Rest – Carte £ 20/44

Wine is the star at this bustling City spot: from 4 cellars come 500 labels and 15,000 bottles. The menu complements the wine: steaks, charcuterie, sharing platters and South African specialities feature along with great cheese.

X **Paternoster Chop House**

Warwick Ct., Paternoster Sq. ✉ EC4M 7DX ⊖ St Paul's – ✆ (020) 7029 9400 – www.paternosterchophouse.co.uk – Closed Christmas, Sunday dinner, Saturday and bank holidays **33**APT**x**

Rest – Menu £ 24 – Carte £ 29/49

Appropriately British menu in a restaurant lying in the shadow of St Paul's Cathedral. Large, open room with full-length windows; busy bar attached. Kitchen uses thoughtfully sourced produce.

28°-50° Fetter Lane

140 Fetter Ln ✉ EC4A 1BT ⊖ Temple – ☎ (020) 7242 8877 – www.2850.co.uk – Closed Saturday, Sunday and bank holidays **32**ANU**s**

Rest – Menu £ 16 (lunch) – Carte £ 22/32

From the owners of Texture comes this cellar wine bar and informal restaurant. The terrific wine list is thoughtfully compiled and the grills, cheeses, charcuterie and European dishes are designed to allow the wines to shine.

Restaurant at St Paul's Cathedral

St Paul's Churchyard ✉ EC4M 8AD ⊖ St Paul's – ☎ (020) 7248 2469 – www.restaurantatstpauls.co.uk – Closed Good Friday and 26 December

Rest – *(lunch only) (booking advisable)* Menu £ 15/26 **33**APU**s**

Tucked away in a corner of the crypt of Sir Christopher Wren's 17C masterpiece, offering respite to tired tourists and weary worshippers. The monthly menu is reassuringly concise, seasonal and a celebration of all things British.

Jugged Hare

42 Chiswell St ✉ EC1Y 4SA ⊖ Barbican. – ☎ (020) 7614 0134 – www.thejuggedhare.com **19**VZD**x**

Rest – *(booking advisable)* Menu £ 27/48 – Carte £ 26/61

Vegetarians may feel ill at ease – and not just because of the taxidermy. The atmospheric dining room, with its open kitchen down one side, specialises in stout British dishes, with meats from the rotisserie a highlight.

CROYDON – Greater London **12** B3

South Croydon

Albert's Table

49b South End ✉ CR0 1BF – ☎ (020) 8680 2010 – www.albertstable.co.uk – Closed Sunday dinner and Monday **7**FZ**x**

Rest – Menu £ 22/45

The owner-chef has a notable pedigree and his surprisingly spacious restaurant, named after his grandfather, deserves success. Service is earnest and the accomplished, modern European cooking defined by its well-judged flavours.

EALING – Greater London **12** A3

West Middlesex, Southall, Greenford Rd, ☎ (020) 8574 34 50

Horsenden Hill, Woodland Rise

Acton Green

Le Vacherin

76-77 South Par ✉ W4 5LF ⊖ Chiswick Park – ☎ (020) 8742 2121 – www.levacherin.com – Closed Monday lunch **6**CV**e**

Rest – Menu £ 23 (weekday lunch)/28 – Carte £ 30/50

Authentic feel to this comfortable brasserie, with its brown leather banquette seating, mirrors and belle époque prints. French classics from snails to duck confit; beef is a speciality.

Duke of Sussex

75 South Par ✉ W4 5LF ⊖ Chiswick Park. – ☎ (020) 8742 8801 – www.realpubs.co.uk **6**CV**e**

Rest – Carte £ 18/33

Bustling Victorian pub, whose striking dining room was once a variety theatre complete with proscenium arch. Stick to the Spanish dishes; stews and cured meats are the specialities. BYO on Mondays.

Ealing

Charlotte's Place

16 St Matthew's Rd ✉ W5 3JT ⊖ Ealing Common – ☎ (020) 8567 7541 – www.charlottes.co.uk – Closed 26 December and 1 January **2**CV**c**

Rest – Menu £ 20/30

Warmly run neighbourhood restaurant opposite the Common; divided between bright ground floor room and cosier downstairs. Menu is an appealing mix of British and Mediterranean influences.

Kiraku

8 Station Par, Uxbridge Rd. ✉ W5 3LD ⊖ Ealing Common – ☎ (020) 8992 2848 – www.kiraku.co.uk – Closed Christmas-New Year, 10 days August, Monday and Tuesday following bank holidays **2CVv**

Rest – Carte £ 15/39

The name of this cute little Japanese restaurant means 'relax and enjoy'; easy with such charming service. Extensive menu includes zensai, skewers, noodles, rice dishes and assorted sushi.

Atari-ya

1 Station Par, Uxbridge Rd ✉ W5 3LD ⊖ Ealing Common – ☎ (020) 8202 2789 – www.atariya.co.uk – Closed bank holiday Mondays **2CVv**

Rest – Carte £ 12/26

Atari-ya are importers and suppliers of fish and assorted Japanese ingredients and so are well-placed to run a few accessibly-priced sushi bars around the capital. Go for nigiri to fully appreciate the texture and flavour of the fish.

Kerbisher & Malt Ⓝ

53 New Broadway ✉ W5 5AH ⊖ Ealing Broadway – ☎ (020) 8840 4418 – www.kerbisher.co.uk **5BVm**

Rest – Carte £ 11/21

The fish and chip shop reinvented...fresh, sustainably sourced fish is cooked to order in rapeseed oil; chips are made from British spuds and fried separately; and packaging is biodegradable. There's another branch in Hammersmith.

The Grove Ⓝ

The Green ✉ W5 5QX ⊖ Ealing Broadway. – ☎ (020) 8567 2439 – www.thegrovew5.co.uk **5BVg**

Rest – Menu £ 23/33

A beast of a pub with an enormous front terrace; inside, it's half bar, half restaurant. The menus change monthly – lunch is standard issue, but at dinner the skilful kitchen uses British ingredients in dishes with a French edge.

GREENWICH – Greater London 12 B3

Inside

19 Greenwich South St ✉ SE10 8NW ⊖ Greenwich (DLR) – ☎ (020) 8265 5060 – www.insiderestaurant.co.uk – Closed 24-28 December, Sunday dinner and Monday **7GXx**

Rest – Menu £ 18/25 – Carte £ 26/37

Inside is tidy, comfortable and uncluttered, although it does take a few diners to generate an atmosphere. On offer is a well-priced set menu, with quite elaborate, largely European cooking.

Rivington Grill

178 Greenwich High Rd ✉ SE10 8NN ⊖ Greenwich (DLR) – ☎ (020) 8293 9270 – www.rivingtongreenwich.co.uk – Closed 25-26 December and lunch Monday-Wednesday **7GVs**

Rest – Menu £ 15 (weekday lunch) – Carte £ 21/44

Spread over two floors and part of the Picturehouse complex. The extensive menu doubles as a placemat and is comfortingly familiar: there are pies, chops, plenty of things 'on toast' and assorted meats cooked on the grill.

HACKNEY – Greater London 12 B3

HACKNEY

Lardo Ⓝ

197-205 Richmond Rd ✉ E8 3NJ – ☎ (020) 8985 2683 – www.lardo.co.uk

Rest – Carte £ 16/60 **14YZBh**

Housed in the striking 1930s Arthaus building, this delightful Italian eatery may boast the ubiquitous faux industrial look but there's nothing bogus about the cooking – the small plates really hit the spot. Try the succulent home-cured meats and the terrific pizzas from the shiny wood-fired oven.

LONDON

X **Market Cafe** Ⓝ

2 Broadway Mkt ✉ E8 4QG ⊖ Bethnal Green – ✆ (020) 7249 9070 – www.market-cafe.co.uk – Closed 25-26 December and 1 January

Rest – Carte £ 22/30 **14**YZB**m**

This former pub by the canal appeals to local hipsters with its retro looks, youthful service team and Italian-influenced menu. Cooking is fresh and generous and uses some produce from the local market; homemade pasta a feature.

Cat & Mutton

76 Broadway Mkt ✉ E8 4QJ ⊖ Bethnal Green. – ✆ (020) 7254 5599 – www.catandmutton.co.uk – Closed 25-26 December **14**YZB**a**

Rest – Carte £ 20/32

The pub's lived-in look, music and relaxed vibe attract a young, local crowd. Satisfying pub food, from a weekly changing menu, delivers on flavour. Regular quiz nights and art classes.

Prince Arthur

95 Forest Rd ✉ E8 3BH ⊖ Bethnal Green. – ✆ (020) 7249 9996 – www.theprincearthurlondonfields.com – Closed 25 December **14**XZB**c**

Rest – *(dinner only and lunch Saturday-Sunday)* Carte £ 25/39

An intimate local pub for local people, with plenty of character. Unpretentious and heart-warming menu, with classics like a pint of prawns and cottage pie; filling puddings.

Empress

130 Lauriston Rd., Victoria Park ✉ E9 7LH ⊖ Mile End. – ✆ (020) 8533 5123 – www.empresse9.co.uk – Closed 25 December and Monday lunch except bank holidays **3**GU**n**

Rest – Menu £ 10 (weekdays) – Carte £ 23/28

Sourdough is from the local baker; the butcher and fishmonger are within walking distance. Dishes like pearl barley and feta risotto demonstrate the kitchen's confidence and ability; prices are good and Sunday lunch a languid affair.

HOXTON

The Hoxton

81 Great Eastern St. ✉ EC2A 3HU ⊖ Old Street – ✆ (020) 7550 1000 – www.hoxtonhotels.com **20**XZD**x**

208 rm – †£ 59/359 ††£ 59/359

Rest ***Hoxton Grill*** – ✆ (020) 7739 9111 – Carte £ 17/44

Industrial-styled urban lodge with a rakish, relaxed air – a hotel run for the convenience of its guests rather than the management. Bedrooms are compact but come with some nice touches. Youthful clientele and even younger staff. Open-plan restaurant with American menu and great cocktails.

X **Fifteen London**

15 Westland Pl ✉ N1 7LP ⊖ Old Street – ✆ (020) 3375 1515 – www.fifteen.net – Closed 25 December **13**VZC**c**

Rest – *(booking essential)* Menu £ 24 (lunch) – Carte £ 30/46

Trainees at Jamie Oliver's charitable restaurant learn about cooking seasonal British food – dishes that have personality and are all about flavour. The same menu is served in the ground floor restaurant and the livelier cellar.

X **Master & Servant** Ⓝ

8-9 Hoxton Sq ✉ N1 6NU ⊖ Old Street – ✆ (020) 7729 4626 – www.masterandservant.co.uk – Closed 25-27 December and Sunday dinner

Rest – Carte £ 22/34 **20**XZC**x**

A fun, lively bistro which is part NYC (ersatz-industrial looks and great cocktails) and part London (it's named after a Depeche Mode song and the underlying culinary inspiration comes from the owner's alma mater, St John).

X **Beagle** Ⓝ

397-400 Geffrye St ✉ E2 8HZ ⊖ Hoxton. – ✆ (020) 7613 2967 – www.beaglelondon.co.uk – Closed lunch Monday-Tuesday **14**XZB**e**

Rest – *(booking essential)* Carte £ 23/35

Occupying three vast converted railway arches: one houses the bar; one the dining room; and the third is the kitchen. The British menu, with touches of Italian, changes twice a day and its contents are determined by the seasons.

SHOREDITCH

XXX **Boundary** with rm

2-4 Boundary St ✉ E2 7DD ⊖ Old Street – ✆ (020) 7729 1051 – www.theboundary.co.uk **20**XZD**b**

17 rm – †£ 170/510 ††£ 170/510, ☕£ 11

Rest – Menu £ 20 (lunch and early dinner) – Carte £ 33/65

Sir Terence Conran has taken a warehouse and created a 'caff' with a bakery and shop, a rooftop terrace and a stylish, good-looking French restaurant serving plenty of cross-Channel classics. Comfy and individual bedrooms.

XXX **L' Anima**

1 Snowden St. ✉ EC2A 2DQ ⊖ Liverpool Street – ✆ (020) 7422 7000 – www.lanima.co.uk – Closed 25 December, Saturday lunch, Sunday and bank holidays **20**XZD**a**

Rest – *(booking essential)* Menu £ 23 (weekday lunch)/35 – Carte £ 35/75

Very handsome room, with limestone and leather creating a sophisticated, glamorous environment. Appealing menu is a mix of Italian classics and less familiar dishes, with the emphasis firmly on flavour. Service is smooth and personable.

XX **HKK** (N)

Broadgate West, 88 Worship St ✉ EC2A 2BE ⊖ Liverpool Street – ✆ (020) 3535 1888 – www.hkklondon.com – Closed 24 December-6 January, Saturday lunch and Sunday **20**XZD**h**

Rest – Menu £ 42/95 – Carte lunch £ 32/62

From the Hakkasan group comes this most sophisticated of Cantonese restaurants. The room is elegant and graceful; the service smooth and assured. Expect the classic flavour combinations but delivered in a modern, refined way.

→ Cherry wood roasted Peking duck. Gai lan, shimeji mushroom and lily bulb in XO sauce. Pineapple fritter, salted lime jelly and vanilla ice cream.

XX **Eyre Brothers**

70 Leonard St ✉ EC2A 4QX ⊖ Old Street – ✆ (020) 7613 5346 – www.eyrebrothers.co.uk – Closed 24 December-4 January, Saturday lunch, Sunday and bank holidays **20**XZD**k**

Rest – Menu £ 18 (lunch) – Carte £ 23/47

Sleek, confidently run and celebrating all things Iberian by drawing on the brothers' memories of their childhood in Mozambique. Delicious hams; terrific meats cooked over lumpwood charcoal. If a larger group, pre-order paella or suckling pig.

X **Rivington Grill**

28-30 Rivington St ✉ EC2A 3DZ ⊖ Old Street – ✆ (020) 7729 7053 – www.rivingtonshoreditch.co.uk – Closed 25-26 December **20**XZD**e**

Rest – Carte £ 22/54

Very appealing 'back to basics' British menu, with plenty of comforting classics including a section 'on toast'. This converted warehouse is popular with the local community of artists.

X **Clove Club** (N)

380 Old St ✉ EC1V 9LT ⊖ Old Street – ✆ (020) 7729 6496 – www.thecloveclub.com – Closed 2 weeks Christmas-New Year, August bank holiday, Monday lunch and Sunday **20**XZC**c**

Rest – *(bookings advisable at dinner)* Menu £ 47 – Carte £ 19/41

Three friends who made their names in 'pop-ups' opened at the rescued Shoreditch Town Hall. So sparse it's bang on trend. Choice in the bar; tasting menu only in the restaurant – of ambitious, original food with some Nordic notes.

X **Tramshed**

32 Rivington St ✉ EC2A 3LX ⊖ Old Street – ✆ (020) 7749 0478 – www.chickenandsteak.co.uk – Closed 24-26 December **20**XZD**v**

Rest – Carte £ 20/44

A striking 1905 Grade II warehouse – with a Damien Hirst tank – is the setting for this stunning brasserie from Mark Hix. Simply choose chicken or beef: a whole Woolley Park Farm free-range chicken or marbled sirloin steak by the 250g.

LONDON

✗ **Beard to Tail** ⓝ &. 🅰🅲 🗄

77 Curtain Rd ⊠ EC2A 3BS ⊖ Old Street – 𝒞 (020) 7729 2966
– www.beardtotail.co.uk – Closed 25-26 December, Easter Sunday and bank holiday
Mondays **20**XZD**d**
Rest – Carte £ 23/37

Meat and whiskey – if you like one or the other, or ideally both, then you'll like this fun, loud place. Housed in a big old industrial warehouse, it specialises in using all parts of the beast; don't miss the BBQ bourbon ribs.

✗ **Viet Grill** ⓝ 🅰🅲 🍷 🗄

58 Kingsland Rd ⊠ E2 8DP ⊖ Old Street – 𝒞 (020) 7739 6686
– www.vietnamesekitchen.co.uk **20**XZC**z**
Rest – Menu £ 10/24 – Carte £ 16/34

Owned by the team behind Cây Tre which means that service is charming and helpful and the Vietnamese food is fresh and authentic. Larger parties should consider ordering one of their 'feast' menus, which require 48 hours' notice.

🍽 **Princess of Shoreditch** 😗
⊛

76-78 Paul St ⊠ EC2A 4NE ⊖ Old Street. – 𝒞 (020) 7729 9270
– www.theprincessofshoreditch.com – Closed 24-27 December **19**VZD**a**
Rest – (booking essential) Carte £ 23/30🕸

There has been a pub on this corner site since 1742 but it is doubtful many of the previous incarnations were as busy or as pleasant as the Princess is today. The best dishes are those with a rustic edge, such as goose rillettes or chicken pie.

<div style="text-align:right;">LONDON</div>

HAMMERSMITH and FULHAM – Greater London **12** B3
FULHAM

✗✗ **Mao Tai** 🅰🅲 🍷 ⊖

58 New Kings Rd, Parsons Grn ⊠ SW6 4LS ⊖ Parsons Green – 𝒞 (020)
7731 2520 – www.maotai.co.uk – Closed 25-26 December **22**NZH**e**
Rest – (dinner only) Carte £ 24/63

Influences from across China inform the modern menu of this stylish, long-standing Chinese restaurant. Divided into two rooms; the front section with the cocktail bar is the more animated.

✗✗ **Blue Elephant** 😗 🅰🅲

The Boulevard, Imperial Wharf ⊠ SW6 2UB – 𝒞 (020) 7751 3111
– www.blueelephant.com – Closed 25-26 December and 1 January,
Rest – (booking advisable) Menu £ 18/55 – Carte £ 27/54 **23**PZH**x**

Relocated from Fulham Road to these swankier and appropriately exotic premises, spread over two floors and with two great riverside terraces. The menu traverses Thailand; curries are a strength.

✗ **Tendido Cuatro** 🅰🅲 🗄

108-110 New Kings Rd ⊠ SW6 4LY ⊖ Parsons Green – 𝒞 (020) 7371 5147
– www.cambiodetercio.co.uk – Closed 2 weeks Christmas and lunch Sunday-Monday
Rest – Carte £ 24/50 **22**NZH**x**

Along with tapas, the speciality is paella. Designed for a hungry two, they vary from seafood to quail and chorizo; cuttlefish ink to vegetarian. Vivid colours used with abandon deck out the busy room.

✗ **Manuka Kitchen** ⓝ 🅰🅲 🗄

510 Fulham Rd ⊠ SW6 5NJ ⊖ Fulham Broadway – 𝒞 (020) 7736 7588
– www.manukakitchen.co.uk – Closed 16-30 August, 25-26 December,
Sunday dinner and Monday **22**NZG**m**
Rest – Carte £ 20/28

The two young owners run their simple little restaurant with great enthusiasm and their prices are keen. Like the magical Manuka honey, the chef is from New Zealand; his menu is varied and his food is wholesome and full of flavour.

✗ **Claude's Kitchen** ⓝ 🍷

51 Parsons Green Ln ⊠ SW6 4JA ⊖ Parsons Green. – 𝒞 (020) 7371 8517
– www.amusebouchelondon.com – Closed Sunday dinner and Monday **22**NZH**c**
Rest – (dinner only and lunch Saturday-Sunday) (booking essential) Carte £ 23/32

Two operations in one converted pub: 'Amuse Bouche' is a well-priced champagne bar; upstairs is an intimate dining room with a weekly changing menu. The cooking is colourful and fresh, with the odd challenging flavour combination.

Harwood Arms

Walham Grove ✉ SW6 1QP ⊖ Fulham Broadway. – ☎ (020) 7386 1847 – www.harwoodarms.com – Closed 24-27 December, 1 January and Monday lunch

Rest – *(booking essential)* Menu £ 20 (weekday lunch) – Carte £ 35/43 **22NZGa**

Its reputation may have spread like wildfire but this remains a proper, down-to-earth pub that just happens to serve really good food. The cooking is very seasonal, proudly British, full of flavour and doesn't seem out of place in this environment. Service is suitably relaxed and friendly.

➜ Crisp pheasant eggs with wild garlic, parsley and ham hock. Roast Berkshire wood pigeon with Yorkshire rhubarb, beetroot and chicory. Bramley apple and cinnamon ice cream with salted caramel.

Malt House with rm

rest,

17 Vanston Pl ✉ SW6 1AY ⊖ Fulham Broadway – ☎ (020) 7084 6888 – www.malthousefulham.co.uk – Closed 25 December **22NZGm**

6 rm – †£ 125/140 ††£ 125/140

Rest – Menu £ 20 (weekday lunch) – Carte £ 26/54

Following the success of the Fox and Grapes in Wimbledon, Claude Bosi (of Hibiscus restaurant) and his brother Cedric spruced up this solidly built 18th century inn, which comes with 6 elegant bedrooms. A very skilled kitchen produces refined dishes that are more typical of a restaurant.

LONDON

Sands End

135-137 Stephendale Rd ✉ SW6 2PR ⊖ Fulham Broadway. – ☎ (020) 7731 7823 – www.thesandsend.co.uk – Closed 25 December **22OZHr**

Rest – *(booking advisable)* Menu £ 14 (weekday lunch) – Carte £ 24/40

Cosy, warm and welcoming little corner pub, offering appealing bar snacks and a thoughtfully put-together menu with a British bias. Game is handled deftly and ingredients are well-sourced.

Hammersmith

River Café (Ruth Rogers)

Thames Wharf, Rainville Rd ✉ W6 9HA ⊖ Barons Court – ☎ (020) 7386 4200 – www.rivercafe.co.uk – Closed 24 December-1 January, Sunday dinner and bank holidays **21LZGv**

Rest – *(booking essential)* Carte £ 51/75

It's all about the natural Italian flavours of the superlative ingredients. The on-view kitchen with its wood-fired oven dominates the stylish riverside room; the contagiously effervescent atmosphere is helped along by very charming service.

➜ Wood roasted langoustines, chilli and oregano. Roast turbot tranche with an anchovy and rosemary sauce and broad beans. Panna cotta with champagne rhubarb.

Potli

319-321 King St ✉ W6 9NH ⊖ Ravenscourt Park – ☎ (020) 8741 4328 – www.potli.co.uk **21KZFv**

Rest – Menu £ 12/30 – Carte £ 18/25

Named after a sort of spiced bouquet garni – apt, since spicing plays a big part at this smart, warmly run Indian restaurant. Food markets across India provide the ideas, with smaller dishes like 'Chicken 65' inspired by street food.

Indian Zing

236 King St. ✉ W6 0RF ⊖ Ravenscourt Park – ☎ (020) 8748 5959 – www.indianzing.co.uk **21LZGa**

Rest – Menu £ 12/15 – Carte £ 20/36

The enthusiastic chef-owner offers well-judged, flavoursome and quite refined Indian cooking from across all parts of the country. Colourful surroundings; keen, if slightly disorganised, service.

Azou

375 King St. ✉ W6 9NJ ⊖ Stamford Brook – ☎ (020) 8563 7266 – www.azou.co.uk – Closed 1 January, 25 December **21KZGu**

Rest – *(dinner only) (booking essential)* Carte £ 20/38

Silks, lanterns and rugs add to the atmosphere of this personally run, North African restaurant. Most come for the excellent tajines, with triple steamed couscous. Much is designed for sharing.

Anglesea Arms

35 Wingate Rd ✉ W6 0UR ⊖ Ravenscourt Park. – ✆ (020) 8749 1291 – www.anglesea-arms.com – Closed 25-26 December **15**LZE**c**

Rest – *(bookings not accepted)* Carte £ 24/40

The daily menu is governed by what its suppliers bring but constants are pig's head terrine, prawns, tarts and seasonal salad. Fish and game are good and try the 'Orb of Joy'. The pub has a cluttered, lived-in look and gets packed.

Hampshire Hog

227 King St ✉ W6 9JT ⊖ Ravenscourt Park. – ✆ (020) 8748 3391 – www.thehampshirehog.com – Closed 24-25 December and Sunday dinner

Rest – Menu £ 15/18 – Carte £ 23/42 **21**LZG**s**

For years the owners ran The Engineer in Primrose Hill. 'The Hog' is a sizeable pub with a great terrace and garden. It offers everything from breakfast, bar snacks and cocktails to an appealing seasonal menu in a roomy dining room.

Havelock Tavern

57 Masbro Rd, Brook Grn ✉ W14 0LS ⊖ Kensington Olympia. – ✆ (020) 7603 5374 – www.havelocktavern.com – Closed 25-26 December **16**MZE**e**

Rest – *(bookings not accepted)* Carte £ 19/29 **s**

Warm, friendly and atmospheric pub with easy-going service and pleasantly mixed clientele. Blackboard menu offers robust, satisfying pub food. Arrive early if you don't want to wait for a table.

LONDON

Crabtree

4 Rainville Rd ✉ W6 9HA ⊖ Barons Court. – ✆ (020) 7385 3929 – www.thecrabtreeW6.co.uk **21**LZG**x**

Rest – Carte £ 24/35

With a beer garden seating over 80 and a separate dining room terrace, this Victorian pub makes great use of its riverside location. Parfaits and terrines are highlights but Veggies are also considered. Service is unhurried.

Dartmouth Castle

26 Glenthorne Rd ✉ W6 0LS ⊖ Hammersmith. – ✆ (020) 8748 3614 – www.thedartmouthcastle.co.uk – Closed 23 December-2 January and Saturday lunch

Rest – Carte £ 20/33 **21**LZF**e**

The Mediterranean exerts quite an influence on the large menu at this popular, welcoming and traditional pub. Spread over two levels but the ground floor is the more atmospheric.

Shepherd's Bush

Princess Victoria

217 Uxbridge Rd ✉ W12 9DH ⊖ Shepherd's Bush. – ✆ (020) 8749 5886 – www.princessvictoria.co.uk – Closed 24-28 December **15**KZE**a**

Rest – Carte £ 23/36

Magnificent Victorian gin palace, with original plasterwork. The kitchen knows its butchery; pork board, homemade sausages and terrines all feature. Excellent wine list, with over 350 bottles.

HARINGEY – Greater London **12** B3

Crouch End

Bistro Aix

54 Topsfield Par, Tottenham Ln ✉ N8 8PT – ✆ (020) 8340 6346 – www.bistroaix.co.uk – Closed 1 January **3**EU**v**

Rest – Menu £ 12/15 – Carte £ 24/45

Dressers, cabinets and contemporary artwork lend an authentic Gallic edge to this bustling bistro, a favourite with many of the locals. Traditionally prepared French classics are the highlights of an extensive menu.

FORTIS GREEN

Clissold Arms
105 Fortis Green ✉ N2 9HR ⊖ East Finchley. – ✆ (020) 8444 4224 – www.clissoldarms.co.uk **3EUa**
Rest – Menu £ 21 (weekdays)/30 – Carte £ 20/45
Reputedly the venue for The Kinks' first gig. Now modernised throughout, with a large rear terrace. Interesting menus, with terrines, whole sea bass and 28-day aged steaks the specialities.

HARROW – Greater London **12 A3**

HARROW ON THE HILL

Incanto
41 High St. ✉ HA1 3HT ⊖ Harrow on the Hill – ✆ (020) 8426 6767 – www.incanto.co.uk – Closed 24-26 December, 1 January, Easter Sunday, Monday and dinner Sunday **1BUz**
Rest – Menu £ 18 (weekday lunch)/24 – Carte £ 27/38
Within Grade II former post office; split-level restaurant to rear of well stocked deli. Well-paced service; Italian bias to the modern cooking from an ambitious kitchen. Notable wine list is predominantly Italian.

PINNER

Friends
11 High St ✉ HA5 5PJ ⊖ Pinner – ✆ (020) 8866 0286 – www.friendsrestaurant.co.uk – Closed 25-26 December, Sunday dinner, Monday and bank holidays **1BUa**
Rest – Menu £ 25/34 – Carte £ 33/42
This characterful, low-beamed restaurant has been proudly and personally run for over 20 years – and has a history stretching back over 500 more. Cooking is classical and carefully done, and the service is well-paced and friendly.

HEATHROW AIRPORT – Greater London **12 A3**

18 Haste Hill, Northwood, The Drive, ✆ (01923) 82 52 24

Sofitel
Terminal 5, Heathrow Airport ✉ TW6 2GD ⊖ Heathrow Terminal 5 – ✆ (020) 8757 7777 – www.sofitel.com **5AXa**
605 rm – †£ 150/270 ††£ 150/270, ☕ £ 20 – 27 suites
Rest *La Belle Époque* – *(closed Saturday lunch and Sunday)* Menu £ 25/45 – Carte £ 39/53
Rest *Vivre* – *(dinner only)* Menu £ 29 – Carte £ 27/51
Smart and well-run contemporary hotel, designed around a series of atriums, with direct access to T5. Crisply decorated, comfortable bedrooms with luxurious bathrooms. Choice of restaurant: international or classic French cuisine.

Hilton London Heathrow Airport Terminal 5
Poyle Rd, Colnbrook, West : 2.5 mi by A 3113 rm,
✉ SL3 OFF – ✆ (01753) 686 860 – www.hilton.com/heathrowterminal5
350 rm – †£ 119/339 ††£ 119/339, ☕ £ 21 – 3 suites
Rest *Mr Todiwala's Kitchen* – see restaurant listing
Rest *Gallery* – Menu £ 29 – Carte £ 30/56
A feeling of light and space pervades this modern, corporate hotel. Soundproofed rooms are fitted to a good standard; the spa offers wide-ranging treatments. Open-plan Gallery for British comfort food.

Hilton London Heathrow Airport
rm,
Terminal 4 ✉ TW6 3AF ⊖ Heathrow Terminal 4 – ✆ (020) 8759 7755 – www.hilton.com/heathrow **5AXn**
398 rm ☕ – †£ 145/323 ††£ 155/333 – 5 suites
Rest *Zen Oriental* – see restaurant listing
Rest *Aromi* – *(closed lunch Saturday, Sunday and bank holidays)* Carte £ 23/51
Group hotel with a striking modern exterior and linked to Terminal 4 by a covered walkway. Good-sized bedrooms, with contemporary styled suites. Casual dining in Aromi which occupies part of the vast atrium.

London Heathrow Marriott
Bath Rd, Hayes ✉ UB3 5AN ⊖ Heathrow Terminal 1,2,3 – ✆ (020) 8990 1100 – www.londonheathrowmarriott.co.uk 5AX **z**

393 rm – †£ 125/219 ††£ 125/219, ☕ £ 18 – 2 suites

Rest *Tuscany* – *(closed Christmas-New Year, Easter and Sunday) (dinner only)* Carte £ 33/57

Rest *Allie's American Grille* – Carte £ 28/58

Built at the end of 20C, this modern, comfortable hotel is centred around a large atrium, with comprehensive business facilities: there is an exclusive Executive floor. Italian cuisine in bright and convivial Tuscany. Grill favourites in Allie's.

Mr Todiwala's Kitchen – Hilton London Heathrow Airport Terminal 5 Hotel
Poyle Rd, Colnbrook, West : 2.5 mi by A 3113 ✉ SL3 OFF – ✆ (01753) 766 482 – www.hilton.com/heathrowterminal5 – Closed Christmas and Sunday

Rest – *(dinner only)* Menu £ 35 – Carte £ 30/49

Secreted within the Hilton is Cyrus Todiwala's appealingly stylish, fresh-looking restaurant. The choice ranges from street food to tandoor dishes, Goan classics to Parsee specialities; order the 'Kitchen menu' for the full experience.

Zen Oriental – Hilton London Heathrow Airport Hotel
Terminal 4 ✉ TW6 3AF ⊖ Heathrow Terminal 4 – ✆ (020) 8759 7755 – www.hilton.com/heathrow – Closed 25-26 December 5AX **n**

Rest – *(booking essential at dinner)* Menu £ 34/47 – Carte £ 23/51

With its capable service and appealing menu of authentically executed classics, Zen Oriental has long been a favourite at the Hilton. Popular for business lunches; busy at dinner with hotel guests.

HOUNSLOW – Greater London 12 A3

High St, ✆ (0845) 456 29 29, www.hounslow.inuklocal.co.uk

Wyke Green, Isleworth, Syon Lane, ✆ (020) 8560 87 77

Airlinks, Southall Lane, ✆ (020) 8561 14 18

Hounslow Heath, Staines Rd, ✆ (020) 8570 52 71

BRENTFORD

Hilton London Syon Park
Park Rd ✉ TW7 6AZ – ✆ (020) 7870 7777 – www.londonsyonpark.com 5BX **x**

137 rm – †£ 239/329 ††£ 239/329, ☕ £ 21 – 1 suite

Rest *Capability* – *(bar lunch)* Carte £ 25/42

A large, impressively decorated, purpose-built hotel in the grounds of Syon House – the London residence of the Duke of Northumberland. Most of the smart, stylish rooms have a terrace or balcony; ask for one overlooking the walled garden. British produce features in the restaurant.

CHISWICK

High Road House
162 Chiswick High Rd ✉ W4 1PR ⊖ Turnham Green – ✆ (020) 8742 1717 – www.highroadhouse.co.uk 21KZG **e**

14 rm – †£ 116/215 ††£ 116/215, ☕ £ 22

Rest *High Road Brasserie* – see restaurant listing

Cool, sleek hotel and club, the latter a slick place to lounge around or play games. Light, bright bedrooms with crisp linen. A carefully appointed, fairly-priced destination.

La Trompette
5-7 Devonshire Rd ✉ W4 2EU ⊖ Turnham Green – ✆ (020) 8747 1836 – www.latrompette.co.uk – Closed 24-26 December 21KZG **y**

Rest – *(booking essential)* Menu £ 28 (lunch and early dinner)/45

Chez Bruce's sister is a delightful neighbourhood restaurant that's now a little roomier. The service is charming and the food terrific. Dishes at lunch are quite simple but great value; the cooking at dinner is a tad more elaborate.

→ Lasagne of braised rabbit and ceps with broad beans and lemon thyme. Skate wing with cauliflower, smoked anchovy and shrimp beurre noisette. Hot chocolate fondant with vanilla ice cream, banana and popcorn.

XX **Hedone** (Mikael Jonsson)
301-303 Chiswick High Rd ✉ W4 4HH ⊖ Chiswick Park – ✆ (020) 8747 0377 – www.hedonerestaurant.com – Closed 2 weeks August, Christmas-New Year, Sunday and Monday **6**CV**x**
Rest – *(dinner only and lunch Thursday-Saturday)* Menu £ 35/55
The Swedish chef-owner's unfussy food relies on the superb quality of the ingredients; he cooks them sympathetically, allowing their natural flavours to shine through. His passion is palpable – as is the enthusiasm of his service team.
➜ Slow-cooked duck's egg, morels, green peas and bell pepper. Roasted squab and beetroot five ways. Apple millefeuille with caramel ice cream.

XX **Michael Nadra**
6-8 Elliott Rd. ✉ W4 1PE ⊖ Turnham Green – ✆ (020) 8742 0766 – www.restaurant-michaelnadra.co.uk – Closed 24-26 December, 1 January and Sunday dinner **21**KZG**z**
Rest – Menu £ 20/49
Enough regulars now appreciate the chef-owner's well-judged cooking for him to finally put his own name above the door of this intimate, friendly restaurant. Balanced and sensibly priced menu.

XX **Charlotte's Bistro**
6 Turnham Green Terr ✉ W4 1QP ⊖ Turnham Green – ✆ (020) 8742 3590 – www.charlottes.co.uk **21**KZG**a**
Rest – *(booking advisable)* Menu £ 16/24
A pleasant, unpretentious bistro; run by a friendly team, with a well-priced menu of flavoursome, well prepared dishes of largely European provenance. Little sister to Charlotte's Place in Ealing.

X **Sam's Brasserie**
11 Barley Mow Passage ✉ W4 4PH ⊖ Turnham Green – ✆ (020) 8987 0555 – www.samsbrasserie.co.uk – Closed 24-26 December **2**CV**a**
Rest – Menu £ 17 (weekdays) – Carte £ 20/38
A former Sanderson wallpaper mill, now a bustling, fun brasserie with Sir Peter Blake artwork adding to the hip feel. Appealing, modern menu; satisfying dishes deliver on flavour. Look out for regular Soul and Jazz evenings.

X **High Road Brasserie** – High Road House Hotel
162 Chiswick High Rd. ✉ W4 1PR ⊖ Turnham Green – ✆ (020) 8742 7474 – www.highroadhouse.co.uk **21**KZG**e**
Rest – *(booking essential)* Carte £ 20/36
Authentic brasserie, with mirrors, panelling and art deco lighting. Despite the high volume of customers, the classic dishes are prepared with care and staff cope well with being busy.

ISLINGTON – Greater London **12** B3

ARCHWAY

X **500**
782 Holloway Rd ✉ N19 3JH ⊖ Archway – ✆ (020) 7272 3406 – www.500restaurant.co.uk – Closed 2 weeks summer and 2 weeks Christmas-New Year **12**SZA**y**
Rest – *(dinner only and lunch Friday-Sunday) (booking essential)* Carte £ 24/32
Small, fun and well-priced Italian that's always busy. Good pastas and bread; the veal chop and rabbit are specialities. The passion of the ebullient owner and keen chef are evident.

St John's Tavern
91 Junction Rd ✉ N19 5QU ⊖ Archway. – ✆ (020) 7272 1587 – www.stjohnstavern.com – Closed 25-26 December and 1 January
Rest – *(dinner only and lunch Friday-Sunday) (booking advisable)* **12**RZA**s**
Carte £ 21/34
Having undergone an English Heritage restoration, the pub is a beacon of hope on stubbornly unchanging Junction Road. Great bar snacks but head to the large, theatre-like dining room for robust English food with nods to the Med.

LONDON

Barnsbury

Roots at N1

115 Hemingford Rd ✉ N1 1BZ ⊖ Caledonian Road – ☎ (020) 7697 4488 – www.rootsatn1.com – Closed 25-26 December, 1 January and Monday

Rest – *(dinner only and Sunday lunch) (booking essential)* **13**UZB**d**

Carte £ 22/34

Opening their own place was the dream of these three friends from India. Their warm, friendly restaurant is known for its refreshingly short menu; tandoori lamb chops and Rogan Josh are the highlights.

Canonbury

Trullo

300-302 St Paul's Rd ✉ N1 2LH ⊖ Highbury & Islington – ☎ (020) 7226 2733 – www.trullorestaurant.com – Closed Christmas-New Year and Sunday dinner

Rest – *(booking essential)* Carte £ 26/34 **13**UZB**t**

Great value Italian food that delivers on flavour ensures that this friendly and relaxed restaurant is always full of contented diners. Terrific antipasti and the charcoal grill dishes are favourites.

Canonbury Kitchen

19 Canonbury Ln ✉ N1 2AS ⊖ Highbury & Islington – ☎ (020) 7226 97 91 – www.canonburykitchen.com – Closed Sunday dinner **13**UZB**c**

Rest – *(dinner only and lunch Saturday-Sunday)* Menu £ 12 – Carte £ 24/35

A bright, local Italian with seating for just 40; exposed brick walls and painted floorboards add to the fresh feel. The kitchen keeps things simple and the menu pricing is prudent.

House

63-69 Canonbury Rd ✉ N1 2DG ⊖ Highbury & Islington. – ☎ (020) 7704 7410 – www.thehouse.islington.com – Closed Monday except bank holidays

Rest – Menu £ 30 (weekdays)/38 – Carte £ 23/35 **13**UZB**h**

Must have one of the smartest terraces of any pub in London. An intimate, laid back feel adds to the appeal. The kitchen handles pub classics and more contemporary dishes equally well. Popular weekend breakfasts and brunches.

Clerkenwell

Malmaison

18-21 Charterhouse Sq ✉ EC1M 6AH ⊖ Barbican – ☎ (020) 7012 3700 – www.malmaison.com **19**UZD**q**

97 rm – †£ 168/359 ††£ 168/359, ☕ £ 19

Rest *Brasserie* – *(closed Saturday lunch)* Carte £ 23/42

Striking early 20C red-brick building overlooking pleasant square. Stylish, comfy public areas. Bedrooms in vivid, bold colours, with plenty of extra touches. Modern brasserie with international menu; grilled meats a highlight.

The Rookery without rest

12 Peters Ln, Cowcross St ✉ EC1M 6DS ⊖ Barbican – ☎ (020) 7336 0931 – www.rookeryhotel.com – Closed 24-26 December **33**AOT**p**

33 rm – †£ 245/285 ††£ 245/285, ☕ £ 12

A row of charmingly restored 18C houses. Wood panelling, stone-flagged flooring, open fires and antique furniture. Highly individual bedrooms, with Victorian bathrooms.

Redhook

89 Turnmill St ✉ EC1M 5QU ⊖ Farringdon – ☎ (020) 7065 6800 – www.redhooklondon.com – Closed 25 December, Sunday, lunch Saturday and Monday bank holidays **19**UZD**a**

Rest – *(bookings advisable at dinner)* Carte £ 19/59

Brooklyn comes to Clerkenwell in the shape of this American-style restaurant specialising in seafood and steaks. Bare brick walls, booths and a faux industrial aesthetic add to the New York feel.

Comptoir Gascon

61-63 Charterhouse St. ✉ EC1M 6HJ ⊖ Farringdon – ☎ (020) 7608 0851 – www.comptoirgascon.com – Closed Christmas-New Year, Sunday, Monday and bank holidays **33**AOT**a**

Rest – *(booking essential)* Menu £ 15 (weekday lunch) – Carte £ 16/30

Buzzy restaurant; sister to Club Gascon. Rustic and satisfying specialities from the SW of France include wine, cheese, bread and especially duck. Further produce on display to take home.

Polpo Smithfield

3 Cowcross St ✉ EC1M 6DR ⊖ Farringdon. – ☎ (020) 7250 0034 – www.polpo.co.uk – Closed Christmas, New Year and Sunday dinner

Rest – Carte £ 14/29 **33**AOT**s**

For his third Venetian-style bacaro, Russell Norman converted an old meat market storage facility; it has an elegantly battered feel. Head first for the Negroni bar downstairs; then over-order tasty, uncomplicated and very satisfying dishes to share. Bookings only taken up to 5.30pm.

St John

26 St John St ✉ EC1M 4AY ⊖ Farringdon – ☎ (020) 7251 0848 – www.stjohnrestaurant.com – Closed Christmas-New Year, Saturday lunch, Sunday dinner and bank holidays, **33**APT**k**

Rest – *(booking essential)* Carte £ 25/57

A glorious celebration of British fare and a champion of 'nose to tail eating'. Utilitarian surroundings and a refreshing lack of ceremony ensure the food is the focus; it's appealingly simple, full of flavour and very satisfying.

➜ Roast bone marrow and parsley salad. Roast grouse, bread sauce and watercress. Eccles cake with Lancashire cheese.

Hix Oyster and Chop House

36-37 Greenhill Rents ✉ EC1M 6BN ⊖ Farringdon – ☎ (020) 7017 1930 – www.hixoysterandchophouse.co.uk – Closed 25-29 December, bank holidays, Saturday lunch and Sunday dinner **33**AOT**e**

Rest – Menu £ 18 (lunch and early dinner) – Carte £ 27/59

Appropriately utilitarian surroundings put the focus on seasonal and often underused British ingredients. Cooking is satisfying and unfussy, with plenty of oysters and aged beef served on the bone.

Vinoteca

7 St John St. ✉ EC1M 4AA ⊖ Farringdon – ☎ (020) 7253 8786 – www.vinoteca.co.uk – Closed 25-26 December, 1 January, bank holidays and Sunday **33**APT**a**

Rest – Carte £ 23/34

This cosy and enthusiastically run 'bar and wine shop' is always busy and full of life. The thrilling wine list is constantly evolving and the classic European dishes, cured meats and cheeses are ideal accompaniments.

FINSBURY

South Place

3 South Pl ✉ EC2M 2AF ⊖ Moorgate – ☎ (020) 3503 0000 – www.southplacehotel.com **34**ART**v**

80 rm – †£ 170/380 ††£ 210/420, ☕ £ 20 – 1 suite

Rest *Angler* – see restaurant listing

Rest *3 South Place* – ☎ (020) 3215 1270 – Menu £ 20 – Carte £ 25/54

Restaurant group D&D's first venture into the hotel business is a stylish affair; unsurprising as its interior was designed by Conran & Partners. Bedrooms are a treat for those with an eye for aesthetics and no detail has been forgotten. The ground floor hosts 3 South Place, a bustling bar and grill.

Zetter

St John's Sq., 86-88 Clerkenwell Rd. ✉ EC1M 5RJ ⊖ Farringdon – ☎ (020) 7324 4444 – www.thezetter.com **19**UZD**s**

72 rm – †£ 162/234 ††£ 162/450, ☕ £ 10

Rest *Bistrot Bruno Loubet* – see restaurant listing

A trendy and discreet converted 19C warehouse with well-equipped bedrooms that come with pleasant touches, such as Penguin paperbacks. The more idiosyncratic Zetter Townhouse across the square is used as an overflow.

Angler – South Place Hotel

3 South Pl EC2M 2AF Moorgate – (020) 3215 1260 – www.anglerrestaurant.com – Closed Saturday lunch and Sunday

Rest – *(booking advisable)* Menu £ 25 – Carte £ 33/61 **34**ARTv

The rooftop restaurant of D&D's South Place hotel is a bright, light and very comfortable space; its adjoining bar and terrace the perfect spot for a pre-prandial cocktail. The menu champions the best of British seafood and the freshness of the ingredients really shines through.

→ Langoustine minestrone with dressed crab on toast. Turbot with red wine braised squid, fennel purée and sea purslane. Hazelnut cake, salted caramel, lime and vanilla sorbet.

Quality Chop House

92-94 Farringdon Rd EC1R 3EA Farringdon – (020) 7278 1452 – www.thequalitychophouse.com – Closed Sunday and bank holidays

Rest – *(booking advisable)* Menu £ 35 – Carte £ 21/32 **19**UZD**h**

Back in the hands of owners who respect its history, this 'progressive working class caterer' is once again championing gusty British grub. It also has a terrific, concise wine list with plenty of gems. The Grade II listed room, with its trademark booths, has been an eating house since 1869.

LONDON

Moro

34-36 Exmouth Mkt EC1R 4QE Farringdon – (020) 7833 8336 – www.moro.co.uk – Closed 23 December-3 January, bank holidays and Sunday dinner

Rest – *(booking essential)* Carte £ 30/39 **19**UZD**m**

A feature of Exmouth Market for over 15 years and still one of its busiest restaurants. Daily changing menu is an appealing and eclectic mix of Mediterranean, Moroccan and Spanish. Friendly T-shirted staff and a fun atmosphere.

Medcalf

40 Exmouth Mkt. EC1R 4QE Farringdon – (020) 7833 3533 – www.medcalfbar.co.uk – Closed 31 December-3 January, Sunday dinner and bank holidays **19**UZD**m**

Rest – *(booking essential)* Menu £ 17 (dinner) – Carte £ 24/30

When Albert Medcalf opened his butcher's in 1912 he probably never thought that a century later it would be home to a busy, hip restaurant. Good use is made of the same sort of quality British produce for which Albert was renowned.

Cicada

132-134 St John St EC1V 4JT Farringdon – (020) 7608 1550 – www.rickerrestaurants.com – Closed 25 December and 1 January

Rest – Carte £ 19/45 **19**UZD**d**

Set in a culinary hotbed, this buzzy restaurant and vibrant bar is spacious, lively and popular for its south east Asian dishes. You can even just pop in for one course and a beer.

The Modern Pantry

47-48 St John's Sq. EC1V 4JJ Farringdon – (020) 7553 9210 – www.themodernpantry.co.uk – Closed 25 August and 25-26 December

Rest – *(booking advisable)* Menu £ 22 (weekday lunch)/27 – Carte £ 25/39 **19**UZD**k**

Fusion cooking that uses complementary flavours to create vibrant, zesty dishes. The simple, crisp ground floor of this Georgian building has the buzz; upstairs is more intimate. Clued-up service.

Bistrot Bruno Loubet – Zetter Hotel

St John's Sq., 86-88 Clerkenwell Rd. EC1M 5RJ Farringdon – (020) 7324 4444 – www.bistrotbrunoloubet.com – Closed 24-26 December to non-residents **19**UZD**s**

Rest – *(booking advisable)* Carte £ 29/36

The trendy Zetter hotel and Bruno Loubet's flavoursome French cooking are a good fit. The classic bistro dishes come with added sophistication; the bright room has plenty of buzz and the service is informed and unhurried.

Morito

32 Exmouth Mkt ✉ EC1R 4QE ⊖ Farringdon – ✆ (020) 7278 7007 – www.morito.co.uk – Closed 24 December-3 January and bank holidays

Rest – *(bookings not accepted)* Carte £ 12/19 **19**UZD**b**

From the owners of next door Moro comes this authentic and appealingly down to earth little tapas bar. Seven or eight dishes between two should suffice but over-ordering is easy and won't break the bank.

Caravan

11-13 Exmouth Market ✉ EC1R 4QD ⊖ Farringdon – ✆ (020) 7833 8115 – www.caravanonexmouth.co.uk – Closed Christmas-New Year and Sunday dinner

Rest – *(booking advisable)* Carte £ 22/33 **19**UZD**c**

A discernible Antipodean vibe pervades this casual eatery, from the laid-back charm of the service to the kitchen's confident combining of unusual flavours. Cooking is influenced by owner's travels – hence the name.

Clerkenwell Kitchen

27-31 Clerkenwell Cl ✉ EC1R 0AT ⊖ Farringdon – ✆ (020) 7101 9959 – www.theclerkenwellkitchen.co.uk – Closed Christmas-New Year, Saturday, Sunday and bank holidays **19**UZD**v**

Rest – *(lunch only) (booking advisable)* Carte £ 17/25

The owner of this simple, friendly, tucked away eatery worked with Hugh Fearnley-Whittingstall and is committed to sustainability. Daily changing, well-sourced produce; fresh, flavoursome cooking.

Naamyaa Café (N)

407 St John St ✉ EC1V 4AB ⊖ Angel – ✆ (020) 3122 0988 – www.naamyaa.com – Closed 25 December **13**UZB**n**

Rest – *(bookings not accepted)* Carte £ 18/28

From restaurateur supreme Alan Yau comes his version of the all-day Thai café. Its sleek look and good value menu of street snacks, nicely balanced curries, soups and zesty salads mean there'll be a queue outside. Try Krating Daeng, as drunk by tuk tuk drivers. There are more branches to come.

Peasant

240 St John St ✉ EC1V 4PH ⊖ Farringdon. – ✆ (020) 7336 7726 – www.thepeasant.co.uk – Closed 25 December-1 January and bank holidays except Good Friday **19**UZD**e**

Rest – *(booking essential)* Menu £ 24 – Carte £ 22/28

This handsome Victorian pub was at the vanguard of the gastropub movement. Share a cheeseboard or meze in the bar or book in the upstairs restaurant for more sophisticated yet equally gutsy cooking.

Well

180 St John St ✉ EC1V 4JY ⊖ Farringdon. – ✆ (020) 7251 9363 – www.downthewell.com – Closed 25-26 December **19**UZD**x**

Rest – Carte £ 23/37

This well-supported local pub from the Martin Brothers comes with the sort of food that is reassuringly familiar yet done well, and service that instils confidence. Eat on the ground floor, rather than in the less welcoming basement.

Highbury

Au Lac

82 Highbury Park ✉ N5 2XE ⊖ Arsenal – ✆ (020) 7704 9187 – www.aulac.co.uk – Closed 24-26 December, 1-2 January and 1 week early August **13**UZA**b**

Rest – *(dinner only and lunch Thursday-Friday)* Carte £ 11/25

Sweet, longstanding Vietnamese restaurant run by two brothers. New dishes are regularly added to the already lengthy but authentic and keenly priced menu, whose dishes exhibit plenty of fresh and lively flavours.

Islington

XX Almeida
30 Almeida St. ✉ N1 1AD ⊖ Angel – ☎ (020) 7354 4777 – www.almeida-restaurant.com – Closed 25 December, 1 January, Sunday dinner and Monday lunch **13**UZB**r**

Rest – Menu £ 17 (weekdays)/34 – Carte £ 33/42

Crisply decorated restaurant dating from 1891. Classically inspired menus with plenty of choice; good value lunch. Interesting French regional wines. Overwhelmingly busy pre/post theatre.

X Ottolenghi
287 Upper St. ✉ N1 2TZ ⊖ Highbury & Islington – ☎ (020) 7288 1454 – www.ottolenghi.co.uk – Closed 25-26 December, dinner Sunday and bank holidays **13**UZB**k**

Rest – *(booking essential)* Carte approx. £ 26

You've bought the book; now see how the dish is meant to taste at Yotam Ottolenghi's deli/restaurant. The freshness is palpable, with flavours from the Med, North Africa and Middle East. You'll never think of salad in the same way.

X Yipin China
70-72 Liverpool Rd ✉ N1 0QD ⊖ Angel – ☎ (020) 7354 3388 – www.yipinchina.co.uk – Closed 25 December **13**UZB**b**

Rest – Carte £ 19/42

Don't be put off by the flashing fairy lights or the pink and cream colour scheme. It's well worth coming here for the spicy, chilli-based dishes from Hunan province that use techniques like smoking and curing.

Drapers Arms
44 Barnsbury St ✉ N1 1ER ⊖ Highbury & Islington. – ☎ (020) 7619 0348 – www.thedrapersarms.com **13**UZB**x**

Rest – *(bookings advisable at dinner)* Carte £ 22/34

Anyone unfamiliar with Britain's bounteous larder should get along to this down-to-earth Georgian pub to enjoy ingredients like lamb's tongues, smoked eel, blade steak and rabbit in dishes that are satisfying, gutsy and affordable.

Albion
10 Thornhill Rd ✉ N1 1HW ⊖ Highbury & Islington. – ☎ (020) 7607 7450 – www.the-albion.co.uk – Closed 1 January **13**UZB**s**

Rest – Carte £ 22/38

A perfectly named Georgian jewel and it's not just its wisteria-covered façade or the warm interior that bring a patriotic tear to the eye. The food has a distinctive British feel – grills and rare breeds take centre stage.

Pig and Butcher (N)
80 Liverpool Rd ✉ N1 0QD ⊖ Angel. – ☎ (020) 7226 8304 – www.thepigandbutcher.co.uk – Closed 25-27 December and Monday-Wednesday lunch **13**UZB**e**

Rest – *(booking advisable)* Carte £ 25/42

Dating from the mid-19C, when cattle drovers taking livestock to Smithfield Market would stop for a swift one, and now fully restored. There's a strong British element to the daily menu; meat is butchered and smoked in-house.

John Salt (N)
131 Upper St. ✉ N1 1QP ⊖ Angel. – ☎ (020) 7704 8955 – www.john-salt.com – Closed 25-26 December and Monday lunch **13**UZB**f**

Rest – *(booking essential)* Carte £ 20/29

It's loud, slightly chaotic, ersatz industrial and all about barbecue – it's so 'on trend' it'll make anyone over 30 feel ancient. There's plenty of originality and influences stretch beyond the US to include Malaysia and Korea.

Barnsbury
209-211 Liverpool Rd ✉ N1 1LX ⊖ Highbury & Islington. – ☎ (020) 7607 5519 – www.thebarnsbury.co.uk – Closed lunch Monday-Wednesday **13**UZB**v**

Rest – Carte £ 13/22

The emphasis here may be on the bar – beer drinking is given due deference and a blackboard lists the guest beers – but that doesn't stop this reliable local turning out gutsy and satisfying food for its many regulars.

LONDON

CHELSEA

Jumeirah Carlton Tower

Cadogan Pl ✉ SW1X 9PY ⊖ Knightsbridge – ✆ (020) 7235 1234 – www.jumeirahcarltontower.com 37AGXr

186 rm – 🛉£ 336/822 🛉🛉£ 336/822, ☕ £ 39 – 30 suites

Rest *Rib Room* – see restaurant listing

Imposing international hotel overlooking a leafy square and just yards from all the swanky boutiques. Well-equipped rooftop health club has great views. Generously proportioned bedrooms boast every conceivable facility.

Wyndham Grand

Chelsea Harbour ✉ SW10 0XG – ✆ (020) 7823 3000 – www.wyndhamgrandlondon.co.uk 23PZGk

158 rm – 🛉£ 228/480 🛉🛉£ 228/480, ☕ £ 24

Rest *Chelsea Riverside Brasserie* – Carte £ 34/62

Modern hotel within an exclusive marina and retail development. Many of the spacious and well-appointed rooms have balconies and views across the Thames. Bright restaurant with wide-ranging menu overlooks the harbour.

Park Tower Knightsbridge

101 Knightsbridge ✉ SW1X 7RN ⊖ Knightsbridge – ✆ (020) 7235 8050 – www.theparktowerknightsbridge.com 37AGXt

258 rm – 🛉£ 289/909 🛉🛉£ 289/909, ☕ £ 27 – 22 suites

Rest *One-O-One* – see restaurant listing

Built in the 1970s in a unique cylindrical shape. The well-equipped bedrooms are all identical in size. Top floor executive rooms come with commanding views of Hyde Park and the city.

The Capital

22-24 Basil St. ✉ SW3 1AT ⊖ Knightsbridge – ✆ (020) 7589 5171 – www.capitalhotel.co.uk 37AFXa

49 rm – 🛉£ 240/350 🛉🛉£ 290/500, ☕ £ 20 – 1 suite

Rest *Outlaw's at The Capital* ✿ – see restaurant listing

This fine, thoroughly British hotel has been under the same private ownership for over 40 years. Known for its discreet atmosphere, conscientious and attentive service and immaculately kept bedrooms courtesy of different designers.

Draycott

26 Cadogan Gdns ✉ SW3 2RP ⊖ Sloane Square – ✆ (020) 7730 6466 – www.draycotthotel.com 37AGYc

35 rm – 🛉£ 174/198 🛉🛉£ 270/354, ☕ £ 22

Rest – *(room service only)*

Charming 19C house with elegant sitting room overlooking tranquil garden for afternoon tea. Bedrooms are individually decorated in a country house style and are named after writers or actors.

Knightsbridge

10 Beaufort Gdns ✉ SW3 1PT ⊖ Knightsbridge – ✆ (020) 7584 6300 – www.knightsbridgehotel.com 37AFXs

44 rm – 🛉£ 235 🛉🛉£ 290/475, ☕ £ 19

Rest – *(room service only)*

Charming and attractively furnished townhouse in a Victorian terrace, with a very stylish, discreet feel. Every bedroom is immaculately appointed and has an individuality of its own; fine detailing throughout.

Egerton House

17-19 Egerton Terr ✉ SW3 2BX ⊖ South Kensington – ✆ (020) 7589 2412 – www.egertonhousehotel.com 37AFYe

28 rm – 🛉£ 276/516 🛉🛉£ 276/516, ☕ £ 29

Rest – *(room service only)* Carte £ 35/55

Compact but comfortable townhouse in a very good location, well-maintained throughout and owned by the Red Carnation group. High levels of personal service make the hotel stand out.

The Levin

28 Basil St. ✉ *SW3 1AS* ⊖ *Knightsbridge – ✆ (020) 7589 6286 – www.thelevinhotel.co.uk* **37**AFX**c**

12 rm – †£ 250/600 ††£ 275/650

Rest *Le Metro* – Carte £ 16/33

A discreet townhouse and sister to The Capital next door. Impressive façade, contemporary interior and comfortable bedrooms in subtle art deco style, with marvellous champagne mini bars. Simple dishes served all day down at Le Metro.

No.11 Cadogan Gardens

11 Cadogan Gdns ✉ *SW3 2RJ* ⊖ *Sloane Square – ✆ (020) 7730 7000 – www.no11cadogangardens.com* **37**AGY**n**

54 rm – †£ 270/499 ††£ 300/529, £ 22 – 5 suites

Rest – *(closed Sunday and Monday)* Menu £ 30

Townhouse hotel fashioned out of four red-brick houses and exuberantly dressed in bold colours and furnishings. Theatrically decorated bedrooms vary in size from cosy to spacious. Basement restaurant with concise, modern menu.

Beaufort

rm,

33 Beaufort Gdns ✉ *SW3 1PP* ⊖ *Knightsbridge – ✆ (020) 7584 5252 – www.thebeaufort.co.uk* **37**AFX**n**

29 rm – †£ 168/240 ††£ 240/336, £ 15 **Rest** – *(room service only)*

A vast collection of English floral watercolours adorn this 19C townhouse, set in a useful location. Modern and co-ordinated rooms. Tariff includes all drinks and afternoon tea.

Sydney House without rest

9-11 Sydney St. ✉ *SW3 6PU* ⊖ *South Kensington – ✆ (020) 7376 7711 – www.sydneyhousechelsea.com – Closed 25-26 December* **36**ADY**s**

21 rm – †£ 150/306 ††£ 150/426, £ 11

Stylish and compact Georgian townhouse made brighter through plenty of mirrors and light wood. Thoughtfully designed bedrooms; Room 43 has its own terrace. Part of the Abode group.

The Sloane Square

rm,

7-12 Sloane Sq. ✉ *SW1W 8EG* ⊖ *Sloane Square – ✆ (020) 7896 9988 – www.sloanesquarehotel.co.uk* **37**AGY**k**

102 rm – †£ 200 ††£ 235, £ 16

Rest *Côte* – Menu £ 14 (lunch and early dinner) – Carte £ 21/32

Well-placed, red-brick hotel boasting bright, contemporary décor. Stylish, co-ordinated bedrooms, with laptops; library of DVDs and games available. Rooms at the back are slightly quieter. The smart brasserie offers Gallic fare and has a lively bar attached.

Gordon Ramsay (Clare Smyth)

68-69 Royal Hospital Rd. ✉ *SW3 4HP* ⊖ *Sloane Square – ✆ (020) 7352 4441 – www.gordonramsay.com – Closed 23-27 December, Saturday and Sunday*

Rest – *(booking essential)* Menu £ 55/95 **37**AFZ**c**

Attention to detail ensures that Gordon Ramsay's flagship restaurant still provides the consummate dining experience. Composed, reassuring and discreet service adds to the calmness of the room; Clare Smyth's cooking is poised, elegant and a little more daring.

→ Coeur de boeuf and tomato tartare with buffalo milk curd and black olives. Isle of Gigha halibut with Atlantic king crab, cauliflower couscous, finger lime and ras el hanout infused broth. Smoked chocolate cigar with blood orange and cardamom ice cream.

Tom Aikens

43 Elystan St. ✉ *SW3 3NT* ⊖ *South Kensington – ✆ (020) 7584 2003 – www.tomaikens.co.uk – Closed Christmas, Saturday lunch, Sunday and bank holidays* **37**AFY**a**

Rest – Menu £ 28/95 – Carte £ 56/73

The look is now much edgier, with oak tables, atmospheric lighting and food-related aphorisms stencilled on the walls. The kitchen follows the culinary zeitgeist by looking to Scandinavia; each striking-looking dish is focused around one main ingredient and presented on a variety of plates and bowls.

→ Homemade ricotta, green olive juice, honey jelly and pine nuts. Braised and roasted piglet belly with aubergine and smoked apple. Candied beetroot, yoghurt parfait, sweetened beets, port syrup.

LONDON

XXX **Bibendum** AC 🍸

Michelin House, 81 Fulham Rd. ✉ SW3 6RD ⊖ South Kensington – ☎ (020) 7581 5817 – www.bibendum.co.uk – Closed dinner 24 December, 25-26 December and 1 January **37**AEY**s**

Rest – Menu £ 27 (weekday lunch)/33 – Carte £ 37/69☆☆

Located on the 1st floor of a London landmark – Michelin's former HQ, dating from 1911. French food comes with a British accent and there's fresh seafood served in the oyster bar below. It's maintained a loyal following for over 20 years.

XXX **Fifth Floor at Harvey Nichols** AC ♲

109-125 Knightsbridge ✉ SW1X 7RJ ⊖ Knightsbridge – ☎ (020) 7235 5250 – www.harveynichols.com – Closed Christmas, Easter and Sunday dinner

Rest – Menu £ 25 – Carte £ 26/42☆☆ **37**AGX**s**

If the revamped food hall hasn't left you sated then try the stylish restaurant on the same floor here at Harvey 'Nics'. It's busy with shoppers at lunch but is more intimate at dinner. The food is light and unfussy.

XXX **Rib Room** – Jumeirah Carlton Tower Hotel ⇔

Cadogan Pl ✉ SW1X 9PY ⊖ Knightsbridge – ☎ (020) 7858 7250 – www.theribroom.co.uk **37**AGX**r**

Rest – Menu £ 29/58 – Carte £ 48/97

Rib of Aberdeen Angus, steaks and other classic British dishes attract a prosperous, international crowd; few of whom appear to have a beef with the prices at this swish veteran.

XXX **Five Fields** 🆕 ⅙ AC ⇔

8-9 Blacklands Terr ✉ SW3 2SP ⊖ Sloane Square – ☎ (020) 7838 1082 – www.fivefieldsrestaurant.com – Closed first 2 weeks January, first 2 weeks August, Sunday and Monday **37**AFY**s**

Rest – (dinner only) Menu £ 45

Expect some rather daring combinations on the plate, along with bold flavours; desserts have a unique identity all of their own. The restaurant may be comparatively small but it comes with a warm, intimate and chic feel.

XXX **Chutney Mary** AC 🏆 🍸 ⇔

535 King's Rd. ✉ SW10 0SZ ⊖ Fulham Broadway – ☎ (020) 7351 3113 – www.realindianfood.com – Closed dinner 25 December **22**OZG**v**

Rest – (dinner only and lunch Saturday-Sunday) Menu £ 21/45 – Carte £ 32/53

Since 1990 it has offered a side order of sophistication along with regional specialities from across India. Wine pairings and cocktails also set it apart. The conservatory is slightly less hectic and away from the larger groups.

XXX **One-O-One** – Park Tower Knightsbridge Hotel AC

101 Knightsbridge ✉ SW1X 7RN ⊖ Knightsbridge – ☎ (020) 7290 7101 – www.oneoonerestaurant.com **37**AGX**t**

Rest – Menu £ 17 (lunch)/59 – Carte £ 49/98

Smart ground floor restaurant; lacking a little in atmosphere but the seafood is good. Much of the produce from Brittany and Norway; don't miss the King crab legs. Small tasting plates also offered.

XXX **Eleven Park Walk** AC ⇔

11 Park Walk ✉ SW10 0AJ ⊖ South Kensington – ☎ (020) 7352 3449 – www.11parkwalk.co.uk – Closed 25 December **36**ACZ**v**

Rest – Carte £ 25/96

What was 'Aubergine' is now a sophisticated Italian; its menu traverses the country but it is the Sardinian specialities that shine. It attracts an equally smart set who appreciate the polished service.

XXX **Baku** AC 🏆 🍽 ⇔

164 Sloane St (1st Floor) ✉ SW1X 9QB ⊖ Knightsbridge – ☎ (020) 7235 5399 – www.bakulondon.com **37**AGX**n**

Rest – Menu £ 18/75 – Carte £ 28/62

Named after the capital city, Baku offers diners the chance to try subtly lightened Azerbaijani cuisine in fairly opulent surroundings. Kebabs, tandir dishes, soups and plenty of sturgeon from the Caspian Sea feature.

XX **Outlaw's at The Capital** N – The Capital Hotel
22-24 Basil St. ✉ SW3 1AT ⊖ Knightsbridge – ✆ (020) 7591 1202 – www.capitalhotel.co.uk – Closed Sunday **37**AFX **a**
Rest – *(booking essential)* Menu £ 25/70 – Carte £ 48/60
Chef Nathan Outlaw brings his award-winning formula up from Cornwall: great seafood where the quality of the fish shines through and the flavours harmonise perfectly. The well-structured wine list features the ever popular Levin Sauvignon Blanc from the owner's own estate in the Loire.
→ Crab meat, celeriac and apple salad. Cod with scampi and rosemary butter and crispy courgettes. Treacle tart, orange syrup and clotted cream.

XX **Rasoi** (Vineet Bhatia)
10 Lincoln St ✉ SW3 2TS ⊖ Sloane Square – ✆ (020) 7225 1881 – www.rasoirestaurant.co.uk – Closed 25-26 December, 1-3 January and Saturday lunch **37**AFY **y**
Rest – Menu £ 22/89
With outposts in Geneva, Mauritius and Dubai, Vineet Bhatia proves that Indian food is as open to innovation and interpretation as any other cuisine. His exotically decorated dining room sits within an archetypical Chelsea townhouse.
→ Scallop and prawn brochette with spring onion risotto. Grilled duck with mushroom khichdi, peppercorn jus and sesame duck confit tikki. Madras coffee cheesecake, amaretto gel, toasted almonds and caramelised banana roll.

XX **Medlar** (Joe Mercer Nairne)
438 King's Rd ✉ SW10 0LJ ⊖ South Kensington – ✆ (020) 7349 1900 – www.medlarrestaurant.co.uk **23**PZG **x**
Rest – Menu £ 26 (weekday lunch)/42
The two young owners, both alumni of Chez Bruce, have created a charming and successful local restaurant. David and his team provide warm, knowledgeable but unobtrusive service; while Joe produces easy-to-eat dishes with a French base and a light touch, where the component flavours marry perfectly.
→ Crab raviolo with samphire, brown shrimps, fondue of leeks and bisque sauce. Under blade fillet with Café de Paris snails, salad, triple-cooked chips and béarnaise. Cannelé with Camp ice cream and molten Congolese chocolate.

XX **Le Colombier**
145 Dovehouse St. ✉ SW3 6LB ⊖ South Kensington – ✆ (020) 7351 1155 – www.le-colombier-restaurant.co.uk **36**ADZ **e**
Rest – Menu £ 20 (lunch) – Carte £ 33/58
Proudly Gallic corner restaurant in an affluent residential area. Attractive enclosed terrace. Bright and cheerful surroundings and service; traditional French cooking.

XX **Racine**
239 Brompton Rd ✉ SW3 2EP ⊖ South Kensington – ✆ (020) 7584 4477 – www.racine-restaurant.com – Closed 25 December **37**AEY **t**
Rest – Menu £ 16 (lunch and early dinner)/20 – Carte £ 30/53
An authentic feel to this French brasserie, with dark leather seats, wood floors and mirrors. The menu provides a roll-call of classic regional specialities, from steak tartare to fruits de mer.

XX **Daphne's**
112 Draycott Ave. ✉ SW3 3AE ⊖ South Kensington – ✆ (020) 7589 4257 – www.daphnes-restaurant.co.uk – Closed 25-26 December **37**AFY **j**
Rest – *(booking essential)* Carte £ 20/55
Established over 40 years ago and a Chelsea institution with a 'celebrity' following. Reliable formula of tried-and-tested Italian classics in a room with a warm, Tuscan feel.

XX **Poissonnerie**
82 Sloane Ave. ✉ SW3 3DZ ⊖ South Kensington – ✆ (020) 7589 2457 – www.poissonnerie-chelsea.co.uk – Closed Easter and 25-26 December
Rest – Menu £ 22 (lunch) – Carte £ 34/48 **37**AFY **u**
A smart, personally run, wood-panelled Chelsea institution since 1946. Its extensive choice of carefully prepared, traditional seafood dishes attracts a smart and loyal following.

XX **Eight over Eight**

392 King's Rd ✉ SW3 5UZ ⊖ South Kensington – ✆ (020) 7349 9934 – www.rickerrestaurants.com – Closed 24-27 December 23PZGs

Rest – Menu £ 14 (weekday lunch)/17 – Carte £ 19/47

Reopened after a fire, with a slightly plusher feel; still as popular as ever with the fashionable crowds. Influences stretch across South East Asia and dishes are designed for sharing.

XX **Bluebird**

350 King's Rd. ✉ SW3 5UU ⊖ South Kensington – ✆ (020) 7559 1000 – www.bluebird-restaurant.co.uk 23PZGn

Rest – Menu £ 20 – Carte £ 22/57

Former industrial space incorporates everything from a wine store to a private members club. Large, buzzy restaurant champions British produce in an appealing menu that has something for everyone.

XX **Le Cercle**

1 Wilbraham Pl. ✉ SW1X 9AE ⊖ Sloane Square – ✆ (020) 7901 9999 – www.lecercle.co.uk – Closed Christmas and New Year, Sunday, Monday and bank holidays 37AGYe

Rest – Menu £ 20/60 – Carte £ 23/33

Deep basement location made into a fashionable spot, with drapes and high ceilings; comes alive more at dinner. Order three or four small plates of the delicate French cooking per person.

XX **Painted Heron**

112 Cheyne Walk ✉ SW10 0DJ ⊖ Gloucester Road – ✆ (020) 7351 5232 – www.thepaintedheron.com – Closed Monday 23PZGd

Rest – Menu £ 20/65 – Carte £ 26/37

Well-supported locally and quite formally run Indian restaurant. Nooks and crannies create an intimate atmosphere. Fish and game dishes are the highlight of the contemporary Indian cooking.

XX **il trillo**

4 Hollywood Rd ✉ SW10 9HY ⊖ Earl's Court – ✆ (020) 3602 1759 – www.iltrillo.net – Closed 2 weeks August and 2 weeks Christmas 36ACZs

Rest – *(dinner only and lunch Saturday-Sunday)* Carte £ 26/49

The Bertuccelli family have been making wine and running a restaurant in the Tuscan Hills for over 30 years. Two of the brothers now run this smart local which showcases the produce and wine from their region. Delightful courtyard.

XX **Colbert** N

50-52 Sloane Sq ✉ SW1W 8AX ⊖ Sloane Square – ✆ (020) 7730 2804 – www.colbertchelsea.com – Closed 25 December and dinner 24 December

Rest – *(booking advisable)* Carte £ 18/56 37AGYt

With its posters, chessboard tiles and red leather seats, Colbert bears more than a passing resemblance to a Parisian pavement café. It's an all-day, every day operation with French classics from croque monsieur to steak Diane.

XX **Manicomio**

85 Duke of York Sq, King's Rd ✉ SW3 4LY ⊖ Sloane Square – ✆ (020) 7730 3366 – www.manicomio.co.uk – Closed 25 December- 1 January

Rest – Menu £ 25 (weekday lunch) – Carte £ 33/45 37AGYx

Modern, busy Italian, popular with shoppers and visitors to the Saatchi Gallery; the simplest dishes are the best ones. The terrific terrace fills quickly. Next door is their café and deli.

XX **Marco**

Stamford Bridge, Fulham Rd. ✉ SW6 1HS ⊖ Fulham Broadway – ✆ (020) 7915 2929 – www.marcorestaurant.org – Closed Christmas, Easter, Sunday and Monday 22OZGc

Rest – *(dinner only) (booking advisable)* Carte £ 32/52

Marco Pierre White's brasserie at Chelsea Football Club offers an appealing range of classics, from British favourites to satisfying French and Italian fare; puddings are a highlight. Comfortable and well-run room.

LONDON

XX **Good Earth** A/C

233 Brompton Rd. ✉ SW3 2EP ⊖ Knightsbridge – ✆ (020) 7584 3658 – www.goodearthgroup.co.uk – Closed 23-31 December 37AFY**h**

Rest – Menu £ 12/39 – Carte £ 27/75

The basement is busier and more popular than the ground floor. Extensive menu makes good use of quality ingredients and offers appealing choice between classic and more unusual dishes.

XX **The Botanist** A/C

7 Sloane Sq ✉ SW1W 8EE ⊖ Sloane Square – ✆ (020) 7730 0077 – www.thebotanistonsloanesquare.com – Closed 25-26 December 37AGY**r**

Rest – Carte £ 29/80

Pass through the busy bar to get to the stylish and comfortable restaurant with its warm and vibrant atmosphere. Appealing and accessible menu delivers unfussy and satisfying dishes.

XX **Joe's** A/C

126 Draycott Ave ✉ SW3 3AH ⊖ South Kensington – ✆ (020) 7225 2217 – www.joseph.co.uk – Closed 25 December and dinner Sunday-Monday

Rest – Menu £ 25/45 – Carte £ 23/43 37AFY**f**

Joe's gives its glamorous customers what they want – Mediterranean influenced favourites and light, healthy dishes. The attractive room is framed by bookcases of wine and magazines, and the good looking staff really do seem to care.

LONDON

X **Foxtrot Oscar** A/C

79 Royal Hospital Rd. ✉ SW3 4HN ⊖ Sloane Square – ✆ (020) 7352 4448 – www.gordonramsay.com/foxtrotoscar – Closed 25 December 37AFZ**v**

Rest – *(booking essential)* Menu £ 25 – Carte £ 27/79

Gordon Ramsay's least known restaurant has a relaxed, local feel, with celebrity photographs adorning its burgundy walls. Bistro cooking, with the Foxtrot Burger a highlight.

X **Henry Root** A/C

9 Park Walk ✉ SW10 0AJ ⊖ South Kensington – ✆ (020) 7352 7040 – www.thehenryroot.com – Closed 25-27 December 36ACZ**z**

Rest – *(booking advisable)* Carte £ 21/32

William Donaldson satirised many of the good and the great of his day through the letters of his alter ego, Henry Root. His name lives on in this cheery local spot, with its appealing menu that includes small plates and charcuterie.

X **Tom's Kitchen**

27 Cale St. ✉ SW3 3QP ⊖ South Kensington – ✆ (020) 7349 0202 – www.tomskitchen.co.uk – Closed 25 December 37AFZ**b**

Rest – Carte £ 27/42

A converted pub, whose white tiles and mirrors help to give it an industrial feel. Appealing and wholesome dishes come in man-sized portions. The eponymous Tom is Tom Aikens.

X **Galvin Demoiselle** A/C

Ground Floor Food Hall, Harrods, 87-135 Brompton Rd ✉ SW1X 7XL ⊖ Knightsbridge – ✆ (020) 7730 1234 – www.galvinrestaurants.com – Closed 25 December and Sunday dinner 37AFX**x**

Rest – *(bookings not accepted)* Menu £ 20 – Carte £ 24/43

The Galvin brothers' café overlooks Harrods food hall. The light, French-accented menu is ideal for the busy shopper. You'll find a different soup each day, salads, charcuterie, cocottes and their popular baked lobster fishcake.

X **Geales** A/C

1 Cale St ✉ SW3 3QT ⊖ South Kensington – ✆ (020) 7965 0555 – www.geales.com – Closed 24-27 and 31 December, 1-2 January and Monday

Rest – Carte £ 23/37 37AFZ**n**

Fish and chips are the main draw at this cosy, warmly run and sweetly decorated spot. Other choices can include fish pie and soft shell crab tempura, along with wholesome, homemade puddings.

Admiral Codrington

17 Mossop St ✉ SW3 2LY ⊖ South Kensington. – ✆ (020) 7581 0005 – www.theadmiralcodrington.com – Closed 24-25 December **37**AFY**v**

Rest – Carte £ 21/66

Busy front bar and a separate, rather smart restaurant with a retractable roof. Head for the more familiar dishes from the monthly-changing menu. Beef is big here and is aged in-house; burgers are very popular. A Chelsea institution.

Chelsea Ram

32 Burnaby St ✉ SW10 0PL ⊖ Fulham Broadway. – ✆ (020) 7351 4008 – www.geronimo-inns.co.uk/thechelsearam – Closed 25 December **23**PZG**r**

Rest – Carte £ 21/35

A proper 'locals' pub; Thursday is steak night and Friday, fish night. Blackboard specials supplement the menu of sturdy pub classics and seasonal dishes. Dining tables wind around the bar, with quieter ones under a glass roof.

Cadogan Arms

298 King's Rd ✉ SW3 5UG ⊖ South Kensington. – ✆ (020) 7352 6500 – www.thecadoganarmschelsea.com – Closed 25-26 December **36**ADZ**y**

Rest – *(bookings advisable at dinner)* Carte £ 20/40

A Victorian corner pub, owned by the Martin brothers, and just as welcoming to drinkers as to diners. The best dishes are the filling, blokey and meaty ones. Original tiling and panelling add to the warmth; pool tables upstairs.

Builders Arms

13 Britten St ✉ SW3 3TY ⊖ South Kensington. – ✆ (020) 7349 9040 – www.geronimo-inns.co.uk **37**AFZ**x**

Rest – *(bookings not accepted)* Carte £ 20/40

Smart looking and busy pub for the Chelsea set; drinkers are welcomed as much as diners. Cooking reveals the effort put into sourcing decent ingredients; rib of beef for two is a favourite. Thoughtfully compiled wine list.

Pig's Ear

35 Old Church St ✉ SW3 5BS ⊖ South Kensington. – ✆ (020) 7352 2908 – www.thepigsear.info **23**PZG**v**

Rest – Carte £ 21/50

Honest pub, with rough-and-ready ground floor bar for lunch; more intimate, wood-panelled upstairs dining room for dinner. Robust, confident and satisfying cooking with a classical bent.

Phoenix

23 Smith St ✉ SW3 4EE ⊖ Sloane Square. – ✆ (020) 7730 9182 – www.geronimo-inns.co.uk/thepheonix – Closed 25 December **37**AFZ**a**

Rest – Carte £ 21/38

Friendly, conscientiously run Chelsea local, where satisfying and carefully prepared pub classics are served in the roomy, civilised bar or in the warm, comfortable dining room at the back.

Lots Road Pub & Dining Room

114 Lots Rd ✉ SW10 0RJ ⊖ Fulham Broadway. – ✆ (020) 7352 6645 – www.lotsroadpub.com **23**PZG**b**

Rest – Carte £ 20/33

It may be a little worn around the edges but when a kitchen occupies half the bar you know they take food seriously. The short menu may seem safe but uses good produce cooked with care and respect. Try the daily 'season's eatings'.

Earl's Court

K + K George

1-15 Templeton Pl ✉ SW5 9NB ⊖ Earl's Court – ✆ (020) 7598 8700 – www.kkhotels.com **35**AAY**s**

154 rm – †£ 150/300 ††£ 180/350 **Rest** – Carte £ 21/36 **s**

Five converted 19C houses overlooking large rear garden. Scandinavian-style rooms with low beds, white walls and light wood furniture. Breakfast room has the garden view. Informal dining in the bar.

LONDON

Twenty Nevern Square without rest
20 Nevern Sq. ✉ SW5 9PD ⊖ Earl's Court – ✆ (020) 7565 9555 – www.twentynevernsquare.co.uk **35**AAY**u**
20 rm ☕ – 🚹£ 80/160 🚹🚹£ 100/330
Privately owned townhouse overlooking an attractive Victorian garden square. It's decorated with original pieces of hand-carved Indonesian furniture; breakfast in a bright conservatory. Some bedrooms have their own terrace.

Mayflower without rest
26-28 Trebovir Rd. ✉ SW5 9NJ ⊖ Earl's Court – ✆ (020) 7370 0991 – www.mayflowerhotel.co.uk **35**ABY**x**
48 rm ☕ – 🚹£ 99/199 🚹🚹£ 129/250
Conveniently placed, friendly establishment with a secluded rear breakfast terrace and basement breakfast room. Individually styled bedrooms with Asian influence.

Amsterdam without rest
7-9 Trebovir Rd. ✉ SW5 9LS ⊖ Earl's Court – ✆ (020) 7370 2814 – www.amsterdam-hotel.com **35**ABY**c**
19 rm – 🚹£ 80/135 🚹🚹£ 90/250, ☕ £ 3
Basement breakfast room and a small secluded garden. The brightly decorated bedrooms are light and airy. Some have smart wood floors; some boast their own balcony.

Garnier Ⓝ
314 Earl's Court Rd ✉ SW5 9QB ⊖ Earl's Court – ✆ (020) 7370 4536 – www.garnier-restaurant-london.co.uk **35**ABZ**a**
Rest – Menu £ 19 – Carte £ 27/53
A wall of mirrors, rows of simply dressed tables and imperturbable service lend an authentic feel to this Gallic brasserie. The extensive menu of comforting French classics is such a good read, you'll find it hard to choose.

LONDON

KENSINGTON

Royal Garden
2-24 Kensington High St ✉ W8 4PT ⊖ High Street Kensington – ✆ (020) 7937 8000 – www.royalgardenhotel.co.uk **35**ABX**c**
394 rm – 🚹£ 160/440 🚹🚹£ 210/490, ☕ £ 25 – 17 suites
Rest *Min Jiang* – see restaurant listing
Rest *Park Terrace* – Menu £ 17/37 – Carte approx. £ 37
A tall, modern hotel with many of its rooms enjoying enviable views over the adjacent Kensington Gardens. All the modern amenities and services, with well-drilled staff. Bright, spacious Park Terrace offers British, Asian and modern European cuisine.

The Milestone
1-2 Kensington Ct ✉ W8 5DL ⊖ High Street Kensington – ✆ (020) 7917 1000 – www.milestonehotel.com **35**ABX**u**
56 rm – 🚹£ 342/450 🚹🚹£ 402/630, ☕ £ 25 – 6 suites
Rest *Cheneston's* – *(bookings essential for non-residents)* Menu £ 25/29 – Carte £ 44/79
Elegant and enthusiastically run hotel with decorative Victorian façade and a very British feel. Charming oak-panelled sitting room is popular for afternoon tea; snug bar in former stables. Meticulously decorated bedrooms offer period detail. Ambitious cooking in discreet Cheneston's restaurant.

Baglioni
60 Hyde Park Gate ✉ SW7 5BB ⊖ High Street Kensington – ✆ (020) 7368 5700 – www.baglionihotels.com **36**ACX**e**
52 rm – 🚹£ 334/530 🚹🚹£ 630, ☕ £ 29 – 15 suites
Rest *Brunello* – see restaurant listing
Opposite Kensington Palace and no escaping the fact that this is an Italian owned hotel. The interior is bold and ornate and there's a trendy basement bar. Stylish bedrooms have a masculine feel and boast impressive facilities.

Launceston Place

1a Launceston Pl ✉ W8 5RL ⊖ Gloucester Road – ✆ (020) 7937 6912 – www.launcestonplace-restaurant.co.uk – Closed 23-29 December, Monday lunch and dinner bank holiday Mondays **36**ACX**a**

Rest – *(bookings advisable at dinner)* Menu £ 25 (weekday lunch)/65

Longstanding intimate neighbourhood restaurant; divided into various areas, where everyone has their favourite spot. The style of food is refined without being dainty and, like most of its customers, sophisticated without being showy.

➜ Cold-smoked and grilled mackerel, variations of cucumber and iced horseradish. Pork belly with tomatoes, broad beans and a dried fig reduction. Virunga chocolate mousse with poached pear, salted caramel and praline soil.

Min Jiang – Royal Garden Hotel

(10th Floor), 2-24 Kensington High St ✉ W8 4PT ⊖ High Street Kensington – ✆ (020) 7361 1988 – www.minjiang.co.uk **35**ABX**c**

Rest – Menu £ 50/70 – Carte £ 25/97

The cooking at this stylish 10th floor Chinese restaurant covers all provinces, but Cantonese and Sichuan dominate. Wood-fired Beijing duck is a speciality. The room's good looks compete with the great views of Kensington Gardens.

LONDON

Belvedere

Holland House, off Abbotsbury Rd. ✉ W8 6LU ⊖ Holland Park – ✆ (020) 7602 1238 – www.belvedererestaurant.co.uk – Closed 26 December and Sunday dinner **16**MZE**u**

Rest – Menu £ 17 (weekdays)/28 – Carte £ 32/46

Former 19C orangery in a delightful position in the middle of the park. On two floors with a bar and balcony terrace and decorated with huge vases of flowers. Modern take on classic dishes.

Kitchen W8

11-13 Abingdon Rd ✉ W8 6AH ⊖ High Street Kensington – ✆ (020) 7937 0120 – www.kitchenw8.com – Closed 25-26 December and bank holidays

Rest – Menu £ 25 (lunch and early dinner) – Carte £ 36/52 **35**AAX**a**

Smart, comfortable restaurant which is not as casual as its name implies, but which does have a pleasant, neighbourhood feel. Skilled kitchen produces balanced dishes free of showiness, with the emphasis on flavour.

➜ Smoked eel with grilled mackerel, golden beetroots and sweet mustard. Loin and raviolo of Pata Negra pork with grapefruit and charred lettuce. Hazelnut parfait with salted caramel ice cream, chocolate brioche, praline and lime.

Brunello – Baglioni Hotel

60 Hyde Park Gate ✉ SW7 5BB ⊖ High Street Kensington – ✆ (020) 7368 5900 – www.baglionihotels.com **36**ACX**e**

Rest – Menu £ 23/29 – Carte £ 39/64

Brunello now seems to have sensibly settled on a kitchen that is less about showiness and more about delivering recognisable Italian classics. This works because there's frankly more than enough drama in the exuberant decoration.

Chakra

157-159 Notting Hill Gate ✉ W11 3LF ⊖ Notting Hill Gate – ✆ (020) 7229 2115 – www.chakralondon.com – Closed 25-26 December, 1 January and Easter Monday **27**AAV**s**

Rest – *(booking advisable)* Menu £ 17/20 – Carte £ 20/42

The influences come from the Royal kitchens of the Maharajahs, particularly those from the North Western province of Lucknow. The spicing is more subtle than usual, the aroma fresher and the presentation more striking.

Babylon

The Roof Gardens, 99 Kensington High St, (entrance on Derry St) ✉ W8 5SA ⊖ High Street Kensington – ✆ (020) 7368 3993 – www.roofgardens.virgin.com – Closed 24-30 December, 1-2 January and Sunday dinner **35**ABX**n**

Rest – Menu £ 22 (weekday lunch)/47 – Carte £ 38/75

Found on the 7th floor and affording great views of the city skyline and an amazing 1.5 acres of rooftop garden. Stylish modern décor in keeping with the contemporary, British cooking.

XX **Clarke's** A/C

124 Kensington Church St ✉ W8 4BH ⊖ Notting Hill Gate – ✆ (020) 7221 9225 – www.sallyclarke.com – Closed Christmas-New Year, Sunday dinner and bank holidays 27ABV**c**

Rest – *(booking advisable)* Menu £ 25 (dinner) – Carte £ 35/44

Forever popular restaurant, serving a choice of dishes boasting trademark fresh, seasonal ingredients and Sally Clarke's famed lightness of touch. Has enjoyed a loyal local following for over 25 years.

XX **Yashin** A/C

1A Argyll Rd. ✉ W8 7DB ⊖ High Street Kensington – ✆ (020) 7938 1536 – www.yashinsushi.com – Closed first Monday in month and Christmas

Rest – *(booking essential)* Menu £ 45/50 – Carte £ 25/80 35AAX**c**

Ask for a counter seat to watch the chefs prepare the sushi; choose 8, 11 or 15 pieces, to be served together. The quality of fish is clear; tiny garnishes and the odd bit of searing add originality.

XX **Zaika** A/C

1 Kensington High St. ✉ W8 5NP ⊖ High Street Kensington – ✆ (020) 7795 6533 – www.zaika-restaurant.co.uk – Closed 25-26 December, 1 January and Monday lunch 35ABX**r**

Rest – Menu £ 18 (weekday lunch)/55 – Carte £ 29/69

Indian artefacts and judicious lighting have been used to make this grand, wood-panelled former bank appear less imposing. The Indian food is contemporary and original; presentation is strong and dishes are quite elaborate.

LONDON

XX **Seventeen** A/C ⇔

17 Notting Hill Gate ✉ W11 3JQ ⊖ Notting Hill Gate – ✆ (020) 7985 0006 – www.seventeen-london.com 27ABV**x**

Rest – Menu £ 29 – Carte £ 15/45

Stylishly kitted out, intimate and moodily lit Chinese restaurant on two floors. The kitchen, behind an eye-catching glass wall, specialises in authentic Sichuan and Shanghainese delicacies.

XX **Cibo**

3 Russell Gdns ✉ W14 8EZ ⊖ Kensington Olympia – ✆ (020) 7371 6271 – www.ciborestaurant.net – Closed 1 week Christmas, Easter and bank holidays

Rest – Menu £ 20 (dinner) – Carte £ 25/42 16MZE**b**

Long-standing neighbourhood Italian with local following. More space at the back of the room. Robust, satisfying cooking; the huge grilled shellfish and seafood platter a speciality.

XX **Malabar** A/C

27 Uxbridge St. ✉ W8 7TQ ⊖ Notting Hill Gate – ✆ (020) 7727 8800 – www.malabar-restaurant.co.uk – Closed 1 week Christmas 27AAV**e**

Rest – *(buffet lunch Sunday)* Menu £ 18/25 **s** – Carte £ 14/31 **s**

Opened in 1983 in a residential Notting Hill street, but keeps up its appearance, remaining fresh and good-looking. Balanced menu of carefully prepared and sensibly priced Indian dishes.

X **Kensington Place** A/C ⇔

201-209 Kensington Church St. ✉ W8 7LX ⊖ Notting Hill Gate – ✆ (020) 7727 3184 – www.kensingtonplace-restaurant.co.uk – Closed Sunday dinner, Monday lunch and bank holidays 27AAV**z**

Rest – Menu £ 17 (weekday lunch) – Carte £ 24/40

Opened in 1987 as a big, boisterous, brasserie; these days a little less noisy but it remains well run. Competitively priced set menu offers a wide choice of modern European dishes.

X **The Shed** N

122 Palace Gardens Terr. ✉ W8 4RT ⊖ Notting Hill Gate – ✆ (020) 7229 4024 – www.theshed-restaurant.com – Closed Sunday dinner and Monday

Rest – Menu £ 35 – Carte £ 12/24 27ABV**s**

It's more than just a shed but does have a higgledy-piggledy charm and a healthy dose of the outdoors. One brother cooks, one manages and the third runs the farm which supplies the produce for the earthy, satisfying dishes.

⅋ Mazi ⌂⌐ 🍴

12-14 Hillgate Rd ✉ *W8 7SR* ⊖ *Notting Hill Gate –* ☏ *(020) 7229 3794*
– www.mazi.co.uk
– Closed 24-26 December and 1-2 January **27**AAV**a**
Rest – Menu £ 13/18 – Carte £ 26/46

It's all about sharing at this simple, bright Greek restaurant where traditional recipes are given a modern twist to create vibrant, colourful and fresh tasting
dishes. The garden terrace at the back is a charming spot in summer.

NORTH KENSINGTON

🏠 The Portobello without rest 🖥 ⅋ 📶

22 Stanley Gdns. ✉ *W11 2NG* ⊖ *Notting Hill Gate –* ☏ *(020) 7727 2777*
– www.portobellohotel.co.uk – Closed 24-29 December **16**NZE**n**
21 rm ☐ – ♦£ 174/234 ♦♦£ 234/384

An attractive Victorian townhouse in an elegant terrace. Original and theatrical
décor. Circular beds, half-testers, Victorian baths: no two bedrooms are the same.

⅋⅋⅋ Ledbury (Brett Graham) ⌐ 🆎

❀❀

127 Ledbury Rd. ✉ *W11 2AQ* ⊖ *Notting Hill Gate –* ☏ *(020) 7792 9090*
*– www.theledbury.com – Closed 25-26 December, August bank holiday and
Monday lunch* **27**AAT**a**
Rest – Menu £ 35/105 – Carte approx. £ 59 🍷

Elegant, understated surroundings with professional, well-organised service but it
still has a neighbourhood feel. Highly skilled kitchen with an inherent understanding of flavour; great ingredients, especially game in season.
→ Buffalo milk curd with Saint-Nectaire and truffle toast. Breast and confit leg of
pigeon with red vegetables and leaves. Burnt cream of lemon thyme with
crushed apples.

⅋⅋ Edera 🆎 ⇔

148 Holland Park Ave. ✉ *W11 4UE* ⊖ *Holland Park –* ☏ *(020) 7221 6090*
– www.edera.co.uk **16**MZE**n**
Rest – Carte £ 33/52

Warm and comfortable neighbourhood restaurant with plenty of local regulars
and efficient, well-marshalled service. Robust cooking has a subtle Sardinian accent and comes in generous portions.

⅋⅋ E&O 🆎 ⅋ 🍴 ⇔

14 Blenheim Cres. ✉ *W11 1NN* ⊖ *Ladbroke Grove –* ☏ *(020) 7229 5454*
– www.rickerrestaurants.com – Closed 25 December **16**MZD**a**
Rest – Menu £ 20/59 – Carte £ 22/55

Mean, moody and cool and that's just the customers. Sophisticated, chic and
noisy, thanks to contented groups of diners. Menus scour the Far East, with
dishes designed for sharing.

⅋ Dock Kitchen

Portobello Dock, 342-344 Ladbroke Grove ✉ *W10 5BU* ⊖ *Ladbroke Grove*
– ☏ *(020) 8962 1610 – www.dockkitchen.co.uk – Closed 24 December-5 January
and Sunday dinner* **16**MZD**k**
Rest – Menu £ 25/55 – Carte £ 28/41

What started as a 'pop-up' became a permanent feature in this open-plan former
Victorian goods yard. The chef's peregrinations inform his cooking, which relies
on simple, natural flavours.

⅋ Electric Diner 🆕 🆎 🖥

191 Portobello Rd ✉ *W11 2ED* ⊖ *Ladbroke Grove –* ☏ *(020) 7908 9696*
– www.electricdiner.com **16**MZD**e**
Rest – (bookings not accepted) Carte £ 22/35

Next to the iconic Electric Cinema is this loud, brash and fun all-day operation
with an all-encompassing menu; the flavours are as big as the portions. The long
counter and red leather booths add to the authentic diner feel.

Bumpkin

209 Westbourne Park Rd ✉ W11 1EA ⊖ Westbourne Park – ✆ (020) 7243 9818 – www.bumpkinuk.com – Closed August bank holiday **27**AAT**b**

Rest – Carte £ 23/39

Converted pea-green pub with casual, clubby feel and wholesome philosophy of cooking seasonal, carefully sourced and organic food. The same modern, Mediterranean-influenced menu is served on both floors.

Granger & Co

175 Westbourne Grove ✉ W11 2SB ⊖ Bayswater – ✆ (020) 7229 9111 – www.grangerandco.com – Closed August bank holiday weekend and 25-26 December **27**AAU**x**

Rest – *(bookings not accepted)* Carte £ 20/44

When Bill Granger moved from sunny Sydney to cool Notting Hill he opened a local restaurant too. He's brought with him that delightful 'matey' service that only Aussies do, his breakfast time ricotta hotcakes and a fresh, zesty menu.

Portobello House (N) with rm

225 Ladbroke Grove ✉ W10 6HQ ⊖ Ladbroke Grove. – ✆ (020) 3181 0920 – www.portobellohouse.com **16**MZD**h**

12 rm – †£ 99/180 ††£ 99/250

Rest – Menu £ 15 (weekday lunch) – Carte £ 19/32

Whether it's a smart pub, bistro or hotel – or all three – may be up for discussion but what is indisputable is that this is a great addition to this end of Ladbroke Grove. The menu is a combination of British stoutness and Italian flair. The bedrooms are comfortable and contemporary.

South Kensington

The Pelham

15 Cromwell Pl ✉ SW7 2LA ⊖ South Kensington – ✆ (020) 7589 8288 – www.thepelhamhotel.co.uk **36**ADY**z**

52 rm – †£ 180/335 ††£ 260/480, £ 18 – 1 suite

Rest *Bistro Fifteen* – Menu £ 20 – Carte £ 19/31

Immaculately kept hotel, with willing staff and a discreet atmosphere. Decoratively it's a mix of English country house and city townhouse, with a panelled sitting room and library with honesty bar. Sweet and intimate basement restaurant with European menu.

Blakes

rest,

33 Roland Gdns ✉ SW7 3PF ⊖ Gloucester Road – ✆ (020) 7370 6701 – www.blakeshotels.com **36**ACZ**n**

47 rm – †£ 215/300 ††£ 263/359 – 8 suites

Rest – Menu £ 25 (lunch) – Carte £ 41/84

Behind the Victorian façade is one of London's first 'boutique' hotels. Dramatic, bold and eclectic décor, with oriental influences and antiques from around the world. Ambitious, Asian-influenced cooking in the intimate restaurant.

Kensington

rm,

109-113 Queen's Gate ✉ SW7 5LR ⊖ South Kensington – ✆ (020) 7589 6300 – www.doylecollection.com **36**ADY**x**

149 rm – †£ 210 ††£ 210, £ 20 – 2 suites

Rest *Aubrey* – Menu £ 21 – Carte £ 27/80

Grand façade to this well-placed, corporate hotel fashioned from several townhouses. Appealing superior rooms and studios; quite compact singles. Pleasant drawing room with fireplace; brasserie-style dining and popular afternoon tea.

Number Sixteen

rm,

16 Sumner Pl. ✉ SW7 3EG ⊖ South Kensington – ✆ (020) 7589 5232 – www.numbersixteenhotel.co.uk **36**ADY**d**

41 rm – †£ 180 ††£ 235, £ 19 **Rest** – *(room service only)*

Elegant and delightfully furnished 19C townhouses in smart neighbourhood. Discreet entrance, comfortable sitting room, charming breakfast terrace and pretty little garden at the back. Bedrooms in an English country house style.

LONDON

Ampersand

10 Harrington Rd ✉ *SW7 3ER* ⊖ *South Kensington.* – ✆ *(020) 7589 5895 – www.ampersandhotel.com* **36ADYa**

111 rm – †£ 150/216 ††£ 150/360, ☕ £ 10 – 5 suites

Rest *Apero* – ✆ (020) 7591 4410 – Menu £ 10/26 – Carte £ 18/32

A bright, elegant converted Victorian hotel in London's cultural centre – the nearby museums inspire the bedroom decoration. Rooms aren't the largest but they're smart and well-lit. Basement restaurant has a Mediterranean menu.

The Cranley

10 Bina Gdns ✉ *SW5 0LA* ⊖ *Gloucester Road* – ✆ *(020) 7373 0123 – www.cranleyhotel.com* **36ACYc**

39 rm – †£ 144/234 ††£ 168/258, ☕ £ 10 – 2 suites

Rest – *(room service only)*

Delightful Regency townhouse combines charm and period details with modern comforts and technology. Individually styled bedrooms; some with four-posters. Breakfast served in bedrooms.

The Rockwell

181-183 Cromwell Rd. ✉ *SW5 0SF* ⊖ *Earl's Court* – ✆ *(020) 7244 2000 – www.therockwell.com* **35ABYb**

40 rm ☕ – †£ 110/130 ††£ 140/190 **Rest** – Menu £ 25 – Carte £ 20/42

Two Victorian houses with open, modern lobby and secluded, south-facing garden terrace. Bedrooms come in bold, warm colours; 'Garden Rooms' have their own patios. Small dining room offers easy menu of modern European staples.

The Gore

190 Queen's Gate ✉ *SW7 5EX* ⊖ *Gloucester Road* – ✆ *(020) 7584 6601 – www.gorehotel.com* **36ACXn**

50 rm – †£ 160/250 ††£ 180/280, ☕ £ 15

Rest *Bistro 190* – *(booking essential)* Menu £ 25/27 – Carte £ 26/98

Idiosyncratic, hip Victorian house close to the Royal Albert Hall, whose charming lobby is covered with pictures and prints. Individually styled bedrooms have plenty of character and fun bathrooms. Bright and casual bistro.

Aster House without rest

3 Sumner Pl. ✉ *SW7 3EE* ⊖ *South Kensington* – ✆ *(020) 7581 5888 – www.asterhouse.com* **36ADYt**

13 rm ☕ – †£ 120/180 ††£ 240/360

An end of terrace Victorian house in a charming neighbourhood and great location for visiting museums. Pretty little rear garden; breakfast served in first floor conservatory. Ground floor bedrooms available.

Bombay Brasserie

Courtfield Rd. ✉ *SW7 4QH* ⊖ *Gloucester Road* – ✆ *(020) 7370 4040 – www.bombaybrasserielondon.com – Closed 25 December* **36ACYy**

Rest – *(bookings advisable at dinner)* Menu £ 24 (weekday lunch) – Carte £ 30/42

Plush new look for this well-run, well-known and comfortable Indian restaurant; very smart bar and conservatory with a show kitchen. More creative dishes now sit alongside the more traditional.

Cassis

232-236 Brompton Rd. ✉ *SW3 2BB* ⊖ *South Kensington* – ✆ *(020) 7581 1101 – www.cassisbistro.co.uk – Closed 25 December* **36AEYx**

Rest – Menu £ 18/35 – Carte £ 25/49

The style of cooking at this colourful, contemporary restaurant has moved away from Provençal and is becoming more Italian – the name may well change to reflect this. The wine list is outstanding and the service smooth.

L'Etranger

36 Gloucester Rd. ✉ *SW7 4QT* ⊖ *Gloucester Road* – ✆ *(020) 7584 1118 – www.etranger.co.uk* **36ACXc**

Rest – *(booking essential)* Menu £ 22 (lunch) – Carte £ 37/94

Eclectic menu mixes French dishes with techniques and flavours from Japanese cooking. Impressive wine and sake lists. Moody and atmospheric room; ask for a corner table.

XX **Cambio de Tercio**

163 Old Brompton Rd. ✉ SW5 0LJ ⊖ Gloucester Road – ✆ (020) 7244 8970 – www.cambiodetercio.co.uk – Closed 25 December 36ACZ **a**

Rest – Carte £ 32/40 s

A longstanding, ever-improving Spanish restaurant. Start with small dishes like the excellent El Bulli inspired omelette, then have the popular Pluma Iberica. There are super sherries and a wine list to prove there is life beyond Rioja.

X **Bumpkin**

102 Old Brompton Rd ✉ SW7 3RD ⊖ Gloucester Road – ✆ (020) 7341 0802 – www.bumpkinuk.com 36ACY **r**

Rest – Carte £ 30/37

Sister to the Notting Hill original with the same pub-like informality and friendly service. The kitchen champions British seasonal produce; the simpler dishes are the best ones.

X **Bangkok**

9 Bute St ✉ SW7 3EY ⊖ South Kensington – ✆ (020) 7584 8529 – www.bangkokrestaurant.co.uk – Closed 24 December-2 January and Sunday

Rest – Carte £ 23/33 36ADY **b**

For over 40 years Bangkok has been providing fresh, authentic and traditional Thai food for its many regulars. The surroundings are pleasantly modest, the prices down-to-earth and the atmosphere warm.

X **Tendido Cero**

174 Old Brompton Rd. ✉ SW5 0LJ ⊖ Gloucester Road – ✆ (020) 7370 3685 – www.cambiodetercio.co.uk – Closed last two weeks December 36ACZ **v**

Rest – Menu £ 30 (dinner) – Carte £ 17/28

Highlights at this busy tapas bar include Galician octopus, white bean stew with chorizo and pork cheeks with potato purée. There are also some unusual dishes, like the mini 'hamburger' made with sardines.

X **Capote y Toros**

157 Old Brompton Road ✉ SW5 0LJ ⊖ Gloucester Road – ✆ (020) 7373 0567 – www.cambiodetercio.co.uk – Closed Christmas, Sunday and Monday

Rest – *(dinner only)* Carte £ 14/39 36ACZ **v**

Expect to queue at this compact and vividly coloured spot which celebrates sherry, tapas, ham...and bullfighting. Sherry is the star; those as yet unmoved by this most underappreciated of wines will be dazzled by the variety.

LONDON

KING'S CROSS ST PANCRAS – Greater London

St Pancras Renaissance

rm,

Euston Rd ✉ NW1 2AR ⊖ King's Cross St Pancras – ✆ (020) 7841 3540 – www.stpancrasrenaissance.co.uk 12SZC **d**

235 rm – †£ 275/400 ††£ 275/400, ☕ £ 26 – 10 suites

Rest *Gilbert Scott* – see restaurant listing

Rest *Booking Office* – ✆ (020) 7841 3566 – Carte £ 26/52

This restored Gothic jewel was built in 1873 as the Midland Grand hotel and reopened in 2011 under the Marriott brand. A former taxi rank is now a spacious lobby and all-day dining is in the old booking office. Luxury suites in Chambers wing; Barlow wing bedrooms are a little more functional.

Great Northern H. London N

Pancras Rd ✉ N1C 4TB ⊖ Kings Cross St Pancras – ✆ (020) 3388 0800 – www.gnhlondon.com 12SZB **n**

91 rm – †£ 245/305 ††£ 245/305, ☕ £ 12 – 1 suite

Rest *Plum + Spilt Milk* – see restaurant listing

Built as a railway hotel in 1854; reborn as a stylish townhouse. Connected to King's Cross' Western Concourse and just metres from Eurostar check-in. Bespoke furniture in each of the modern bedrooms, and a pantry on each floor.

Megaro

23-27 Euston Rd, (entrance on Belgrove St) ✉ *NW1 2SD*
⊖ *King's Cross St Pancras* – ✆ *(020) 7843 2222* – *www.hotelmegaro.co.uk*
49 rm – †£ 175/280 ††£ 175/280, ☕ £ 10 **12SZCx**
Rest *Karpo* – ✆ (020) 7843 2221 – Carte £ 21/47
Contemporary hotel fashioned out of a converted bank. The rooms are unfussy and the bathrooms smart. Daily 'absinthe hour' in the basement bar; simple seasonal modern European menu. Pastries for breakfast from their on-site bakery.

Gilbert Scott – St Pancras Renaissance Hotel

Euston Rd ✉ *NW1 2AR* ⊖ *King's Cross St Pancras* – ✆ *(020) 7278 3888*
– *www.thegilbertscott.co.uk* **12SZCd**
Rest – Menu £ 21 (weekdays)/27 – Carte £ 26/58
Run under the aegis of Marcus Wareing and named after the architect of this Gothic masterpiece, the restaurant has the look of a Grand Salon but the buzz of a brasserie. It celebrates the UK's many regional and historic specialities.

Plum + Spilt Milk – Great Northern Hotel London

Pancras Rd ✉ *N1C 4TB* ⊖ *Kings Cross St Pancras* – ✆ *(020) 3388 0818*
– *www.plumandspiltmilk.com* **12SZBn**
Rest – Carte £ 25/40
Bright brasserie in the Grade II listed Great Northern hotel; ideal for those who've just arrived, or are about to leave, by train. Classic British dishes like potted shrimps and 'pie of the day'. Start with a drink in the GNH bar.

Grain Store

Granary Sq, 1-3 Stable St ✉ *N1C 4AB* ⊖ *King's Cross St Pancras*
– ✆ *(020) 7324 4466* – *www.grainstore.com*
– *Closed 24-25 December, 1 January and Sunday dinner* **12SZBs**
Rest – Menu £ 35 (dinner) – Carte £ 24/29
Big, buzzy 'canteen' from Bruno Loubet and the Zetter hotel people. Eclectic, clever dishes – influenced by Bruno's experiences around the world – are packed with interesting flavours and textures; vegetables often take the lead role.

Shrimpy's

The King's Cross Filling Station, Goods Way ✉ *N1C 4UR*
⊖ *King's Cross St. Pancras* – ✆ *(020) 8880 6111* – *www.shrimpys.co.uk*
– *Closed Christmas* **12SZBa**
Rest – *(booking essential)* Menu £ 18 (lunch) – Carte £ 19/35
Proof that London's restaurant scene is fast moving, thrilling, witty and ephemeral. An old petrol station; no signs; great cocktails; touches of irony; art; lots of deep-frying; soft shell crab burgers; Latin flavours.

Caravan

The Granary Building, 1 Granary Sq. ✉ *N1C 4AA* ⊖ *King's Cross St Pancras*
– ✆ *(020) 7101 7661* – *www.caravankingscross.co.uk* – *Closed Christmas-New Year* **12SZBc**
Rest – *(booking essential)* Carte £ 23/31
This second Caravan pitched up near King's Cross in an old granary warehouse. The industrial-chic look is matched by a great atmosphere – crowds flock here for breakfast, brunch, great coffee, pizza and globally influenced dishes.

Fellow

24 York Way ✉ *N1 9AA* ⊖ *King's Cross St Pancras.* – ✆ *(020) 7833 4395*
– *www.thefellow.co.uk* **12SZBx**
Rest – Carte £ 19/34
Busy, atmospheric pub close to the station with a youthful, local clientele. Confident cooking on the ground floor displays a lightness of touch; boisterous upstairs cocktail bar.

Good food at moderate prices? Look for the Bib Gourmand.

KINGSTON UPON THAMES – Greater London 12 A3

Hampton Court Palace, Hampton Wick, ✆ (020) 8977 24 23

Kingston-upon-Thames

XX **Roz ana**

6-8 Kingston Hill ✉ KT2 7NH – ✆ (020) 8546 6388 – www.roz-ana.com – Closed 25-26 December 6CY**e**

Rest – Menu £ 21/33 – Carte £ 15/37

It may have smart surroundings, a cocktail bar and pleasant service but it is the cooking that marks out this Indian restaurant. Expect vibrant and satisfying dishes from across India, from monkfish Ambat to Chennai prawn Biryani.

Surbiton

XX **The French Table**

85 Maple Rd ✉ KT6 4AW – ✆ (020) 8399 2365 – www.thefrenchtable.co.uk – Closed 25-26 December, Sunday and Monday 6CY**a**

Rest – Menu £ 24 (weekday lunch) – Carte £ 34/50

Husband and wife team run this lively local. Expect zesty and satisfying French-Mediterranean cooking; learn how with Saturday morning cookery lessons. They also run the bakery next door.

LAMBETH – Greater London 12 B3

Brixton

XX **Upstairs**

89b Acre Ln. ✉ SW2 5TN ⊖ Clapham North – ✆ (020) 7733 8855 – www.upstairslondon.com – Closed 22 December-7 January, 13-22 April, 17August-2 September, Sunday and Monday 24SZH**b**

Rest – *(dinner only)* Menu £ 29/41

Spread over two floors of a house; ring the doorbell to gain entry. Enthusiastic, unapologetically Gallic service; fortnightly changing set menu with a chef keen to showcase his technical ability with plenty of original touches.

X **Boqueria**

192 Acre Ln. ✉ SW2 5UL ⊖ Clapham North – ✆ (020) 7733 4408 – www.boqueriatapas.com 24SZH**x**

Rest – *(dinner only and lunch Saturday-Sunday)* Carte £ 10/20

Contemporary tapas bar, named after Barcelona's famous food market. Sit at the counter rather than in the unremarkable dining room. Highlights include the assorted cured hams and an excellent Crema Catalana.

Clapham Common

XX **Trinity**

4 The Polygon ✉ SW4 0JG ⊖ Clapham Common – ✆ (020) 7622 1199 – www.trinityrestaurant.co.uk – Closed 22-29 December, Monday lunch and Sunday dinner 24RZH**a**

Rest – Menu £ 27 (weekday lunch) – Carte £ 32/54

Smartly decorated and smoothly run neighbourhood restaurant; ask for a table by the windows in summer. Sophisticated cooking displays some innovative combinations. Good value lunch menu.

X **Bistro Union**

40 Abbeville Rd ✉ SW4 9NG ⊖ Clapham Common – ✆ (020) 7042 6400 – www.bistrounion.co.uk – Closed Sunday dinner 7EX**s**

Rest – *(booking advisable)* Carte £ 20/29

'Comforting' is the word that comes to mind at this affordable, fun and bustling offspring of Trinity restaurant. The food evokes feelings of nostalgia while simultaneously being bang on-trend. Start with some of their great snacks.

X **Tsunami**

Unit 3, 5-7 Voltaire Rd ✉ SW4 6DQ ⊖ Clapham North – ✆ (020) 7978 1610 – www.tsunamirestaurant.co.uk – Closed 24-26 December 24SZH**a**

Rest – *(dinner only and lunch Saturday-Sunday)* Carte £ 16/48

Stylish and lively surroundings in which to enjoy innovative and original, modern Japanese food. The restaurant enjoys a large, local following and there' s a second branch in Charlotte Street.

Abbeville Kitchen

47 Abbeville Rd ✉ SW4 9JX ⊖ Clapham Common – ✆ (020) 8772 1110 – www.abbevillekitchen.co.uk – Closed Monday lunch **7**EX**a**

Rest – *(bookings advisable at dinner)* Carte £ 21/27

The food is gutsy and wholesome, the choice is varied – it's not often one sees empanadas and braised goat on the same menu – and the prices are fair. The owner has a small boulangerie on this road so the bread's good too.

Rookery

69 Clapham Common South Side ✉ SW4 9DA ⊖ Clapham Common – ✆ (020) 8673 9162 – www.therookeryclapham.co.uk – Closed 25-26 December and Monday lunch **7**EX**v**

Rest – Carte £ 20/33

The on-trend Rookery shows that Soho doesn't have a monopoly on ersatz Brooklyn speakeasies. Come for the impressive selection of artisan beers and a short yet appealing menu; the kitchen delivers some punchy flavours.

East Dulwich

Palmerston

91 Lordship Ln ✉ SE22 8EP ⊖ East Dulwich (Rail). – ✆ (020) 8693 1629 – www.thepalmerston.net **26**XZH**x**

Rest – Menu £ 14 (weekday lunch) – Carte £ 27/64

A brightly run Victorian pub that has a comfortable, lived-in feel and lies at the heart of the local community. The cooking has a satisfying, gutsy edge with meat dishes, especially game, being the highlight.

Kennington

Kennington Tandoori

313 Kennington Rd ✉ SE11 4QE ⊖ Kennington – ✆ (020) 7735 9247 – www.kenningtontandoori.com – Closed 25 December **40**ANZ**a**

Rest – *(booking advisable)* Menu £ 25/28 – Carte £ 18/31

Known as KT, the Hoque family's longstanding Indian restaurant was reinvigorated a couple of years ago when their son Kowsar took over. This stylish spot has a familiar menu of classics but what sets it apart is the skilled execution.

Lobster Pot

3 Kennington Ln. ✉ SE11 4RG ⊖ Kennington – ✆ (020) 7582 5556 – www.lobsterpotrestaurant.co.uk – Closed 1 week Christmas-New Year, Sunday and Monday **40**AOY**e**

Rest – Carte £ 39/65

Family-run, with exuberant décor of fish tanks, portholes and even the sound of seagulls. Classic seafood menu with fruits de mer, plenty of oysters and daily specials. Good crêpes too.

Southbank

London Marriott H. County Hall

rm,

Westminster Bridge Rd ✉ SE1 7PB ⊖ Westminster – ✆ (020) 7928 5200 – www.marriott.co.uk **40**AMX**a**

200 rm – †£ 295/900 ††£ 295/900, ☐ £ 22 – 5 suites

Rest *Gillray's* – ✆ (020) 7902 8000 – Menu £ 35 – Carte £ 27/84

Occupying the historic County Hall building. Many of the spacious and comfortable bedrooms enjoy river and Parliament outlooks. Impressive leisure facilities. World famous views too from Gillray's, which specialises in steaks.

Skylon

1 Southbank Centre, Belvedere Rd ✉ SE1 8XX ⊖ Waterloo – ✆ (020) 7654 7800 – www.skylon-restaurant.co.uk – Closed 25 December and Sunday dinner **32**AMV**a**

Rest – Menu £ 25/43

Ask for a window table here at the Royal Festival Hall. Informal grill-style operation on one side, a more formal and expensive restaurant on the other, with a busy cocktail bar in the middle.

STOCKWELL

Canton Arms

177 South Lambeth Rd ✉ SW8 1XP ⊖ Stockwell. – ✆ (020) 7582 8710 – www.cantonarms.com – Closed Christmas-New Year, Monday lunch, Sunday dinner and bank holidays **24**SZG**a**

Rest – *(bookings not accepted)* Carte £ 19/31

An appreciative crowd of all ages come for the earthy, robust and seasonal British dishes which suit the relaxed environment of this pub so well. Staff are attentive and knowledgeable.

LEWISHAM – Greater London 12 B3

BLACKHEATH

Chapters

43-45 Montpelier Vale ✉ SE3 0TJ – ✆ (020) 8333 2666 – www.chaptersrestaurants.com – Closed 2-3 January **8**HX**c**

Rest – Menu £ 15/18 – Carte £ 19/43

A classic, bustling brasserie that keeps the locals happy, by being open all day and offering everything from Mediterranean-influenced main courses to meats cooked over charcoal. There's also a kids' menu and wines by the pichet.

FOREST HILL

Babur

119 Brockley Rise ✉ SE23 1JP – ✆ (020) 8291 2400 – www.babur.info – Closed dinner 25 December-lunch 27 December **7**GX**s**

Rest – Carte £ 24/32

Good looks and innovative cooking make this passionately run and long-established Indian restaurant stand out. Influences from the south and north west feature most and seafood is a highlight - look out for the 'Treasures of the Sea' menu.

MERTON – Greater London 12 B3

WIMBLEDON

Cannizaro House

West Side, Wimbledon Common ✉ SW19 4UE ⊖ Wimbledon – ✆ (020) 8879 1464 – www.cannizarohouse.com **6**DXY**x**

46 rm – †£ 195/500 ††£ 195/500 – 2 suites

Rest *Cannizaro House* – see restaurant listing

Part-Georgian mansion in charming spot overlooking Wimbledon Common. Modern bedrooms; funky suites; 'Sophia Johnson' has lovely balcony overlooking the park. Local artists' work decorates.

Cannizaro House – Cannizaro House Hotel

West Side, Wimbledon Common ✉ SW19 4UE ⊖ Wimbledon – ✆ (020) 8879 1464 – www.cannizarohouse.com **6**DXY**x**

Rest – Menu £ 29 – Carte £ 32/48

Choose the elegant main room or the more intimate Loggia overlooking the Italian sunken garden. A daily set menu offers simple, modern dishes; the à la carte is more elaborate. A slightly corporate feel but staff keep things light.

Lawn Bistro

67 High St. ✉ SW19 5EE ⊖ Wimbledon – ✆ (020) 8947 8278 – www.thelawnbistro.co.uk – Closed 25-26 December, 1 January and Sunday dinner **6**DXY**s**

Rest – Menu £ 15/38

Casual yet nicely manicured, this attractively decorated bistro sits in the heart of the village. The modern European food is clean and well defined; menus are thoughtfully compiled and the kitchen even does its own butchery.

Light House

75-77 Ridgway ✉ SW19 4ST ⊖ Wimbledon – ✆ (020) 8944 6338 – www.lighthousewimbledon.com – Closed 25-26 December, 1 January and Sunday dinner **6**DY**n**

Rest – Menu £ 14/24 – Carte £ 24/42

The robust and flavoursome Italian dishes provide the highlights of the menu. This large, well lit room attracts plenty of locals and the service remains calm and cheery.

Fox and Grapes with rm

9 Camp Rd ✉ SW19 4UN ⊖ Wimbledon. – ✆ (020) 8619 1300 – www.foxandgrapeswimbledon.co.uk – Closed 25 December 6DX**v**

3 rm – †£ 125 ††£ 125 **Rest** – *(booking advisable)* Carte £ 25/36

Owned by Claude Bosi, chef-owner of Hibiscus, and run by Cedric, his brother. They may be French but they know about 'proper' pub food, from Cumberland sausages and prawn cocktail to wild boar scotch egg. Three cosy bedrooms also available.

REDBRIDGE – Greater London 12 B3

WANSTEAD

Provender

17 High St ✉ E11 2AA ⊖ Snaresbrook – ✆ (020) 8530 3050 – www.provenderlondon.co.uk – Closed 26 December and Sunday dinner

Rest – Menu £ 15 (weekdays) – Carte £ 18/39 4HU**x**

A modern, busy and bustling neighbourhood bistro courtesy of experienced restaurateur Max Renzland. The well-priced French cooking is pleasingly rustic and satisfying, with great charcuterie, appealing salads and well-timed grills.

LONDON

RICHMOND-UPON-THAMES – Greater London 12 B3

Whittaker Ave, ✆ (020) 8940 91 25, www.visitrichmond.co.uk

Richmond Park, Roehampton Gate, ✆ (020) 8876 32 05

Sudbrook Park

BARNES

Sonny's Kitchen

94 Church Rd ✉ SW13 0DQ – ✆ (020) 8748 0393 – www.sonnyskitchen.co.uk

Rest – Menu £ 17/25 – Carte £ 26/43 21KZH**x**

Long-established neighbourhood spot which successfully combines its role as deli, café and restaurant. The latter's menus are full of seasonal goodness and the service is warm and attentive.

Indian Zilla

2-3 Rocks Ln. ✉ SW13 0DB – ✆ (020) 8878 3989 – www.indianzilla.co.uk

Rest – *(dinner only and lunch Saturday-Sunday)* Menu £ 15 (lunch) – Carte £ 12/15 21LZH**k**

Bright, and contemporary restaurant with attentive, friendly service. Modern menu includes a few classics; the authentic, fully-flavoured dishes display a lightness of touch.

Riva

169 Church Rd. ✉ SW13 9HR – ✆ (020) 8748 0434 – Closed 3 weeks August, Christmas-New Year, Saturday lunch and bank holidays 21LZH**a**

Rest – Carte £ 28/54

A restaurant built on customer loyalty; the regulars are showered with attention from the eponymous owner. Gutsy, no-nonsense dishes, full of flavour. Interesting all-Italian wine list.

Georgina's

56 Barnes High St ✉ SW13 9LF – ✆ (020) 8166 5559 – www.georginasrestaurants.com – Closed Sunday dinner 21KZH**s**

Rest – Carte £ 17/29

Dubbed 'Superwoman' by the tabloids, Nicola Horlick has turned her hand to the restaurant business by opening this bright eatery, part café, part informal restaurant. The food is easy to eat, with occasional Middle Eastern hints.

Brown Dog

28 Cross St ✉ SW13 0AP – ✆ (020) 8392 2200 – www.thebrowndog.co.uk – Closed 25 December 21KZH**b**

Rest – Carte £ 23/36

Pretty Victorian pub with a genuine neighbourhood feel; snug bar, intimate dining room and a look that combines the traditional with the modern. Concise, balanced menu delivers wholesome, commendably priced dishes.

EAST SHEEN

Mango & Silk

199 Upper Richmond Rd. West ✉ SW14 8 QT – ✆ (020) 8876 6220 – www.mangoandsilk.com – Closed 25-27 December and Sunday dinner

Rest – *(dinner only and buffet lunch Sunday)* Carte £ 16/24 **21KZHk**

Opened by the late Udit Sarkhel, who did so much to change the image of Indian restaurants in the UK. His influence is evident in the subtle spicing and the fresh, healthy taste of the dishes. Try the daily changing seasonal specials.

Victoria with rm

10 West Temple Sheen ✉ SW14 7RT – ✆ (020) 8876 4238 – www.thevictoria.net

7 rm – £ 120/130 £ 130/140 **6CXu**

Rest – Menu £ 13 (weekdays) – Carte £ 23/40

Beautifully restored pub and a genuine local, playing its part in the community. The kitchen takes its sourcing seriously; eat in the bar or more formal conservatory overlooking the terrace. Recently refurbished bedrooms available.

KEW

The Glasshouse

14 Station Par. ✉ TW9 3PZ ⊖ Kew Gardens – ✆ (020) 8940 6777 – www.glasshouserestaurant.co.uk – Closed 24-26 December and 1 January

Rest – Menu £ 28 (weekday lunch)/43 **6CXz**

Bright and relaxed interior, with a palpable sense of neighbourhood. Balanced and seasonally informed dishes are full of flavour, from a varied and appealing menu influenced mostly by Europe. Service is pleasant and unflappable.

→ Mackerel tartare with baby beetroot, crisp quail eggs, crème fraîche and mustard cress. Guinea fowl breast with curry leaf potato gratin, black lentil sauce and coriander. Valrhona chocolate Jaffa tube with chocolate brownie and burnt orange ice cream.

Kew Grill

10b Kew Grn. ✉ TW9 3BH ⊖ Kew Gardens – ✆ (020) 8948 4433 – www.awtrestaurants.com/kewgrill – Closed 25 December-4 January

Rest – *(booking essential)* Menu £ 14 (weekday lunch) – Carte £ 25/70 **6CVu**

Just off Kew Green, this long, narrow restaurant has a Mediterranean style and feel. Grilled specialities employ top-rate ingredients: the beef is hung for 35 days.

RICHMOND

Petersham

rest,

Nightingale Ln ✉ TW10 6UZ ⊖ Richmond – ✆ (020) 8940 7471 – www.petershamhotel.co.uk – Closed 25-26 December **6CXc**

58 rm – £ 125 £ 175 – 1 suite

Rest *Restaurant at The Petersham* – ✆ (020) 8939 1084 – Menu £ 23 (weekdays) – Carte £ 34/61

Extended over the years, a fine example of Victorian Gothic architecture, with Portland stone and self-supporting staircase. The most comfortable bedrooms overlook the Thames. Formal restaurant in which to enjoy a mix of classic and modern cooking; ask for a window table for terrific park and river views.

Bingham

61-63 Petersham Rd. ✉ TW10 6UT ⊖ Richmond – ✆ (020) 8940 0902 – www.thebingham.co.uk **6CXc**

15 rm – £ 175 £ 195, £ 16

Rest *Bingham Restaurant* – see restaurant listing

A pair of conjoined and restored Georgian townhouses; a short walk from Richmond centre. Ask for a room overlooking the river and garden. Contemporary styled bedrooms; some with four-posters.

Bingham Restaurant – Bingham Hotel

61-63 Petersham Rd. ✉ TW1O 6UT ⊖ Richmond – ✆ (020) 8940 0902 – www.thebingham.co.uk – Closed Sunday dinner **6CXc**

Rest – Menu £ 25/65

Charming spot, especially if you've arrived on foot from along the river; dine on the balcony overlooking the garden or in the more traditional dining room. There's a modern style to the cooking and dishes are visually impressive.

XX **Dysart Arms** (N)

135 Petersham Rd ✉ TW10 7AA – ☎ (020) 8940 8005 – www.thedysartarms.co.uk – Closed 25 December and Sunday dinner

Rest – *(booking advisable)* Menu £ 20 (weekdays) – Carte £ 33/48 **6CXd**

A pub built in the 1900s as part of the Arts and Crafts movement but now run as quite a formal restaurant. The kitchen uses top-notch ingredients and adds subtle Asian tones to a classical base. Occasional musical recital suppers.

X **Petersham Nurseries Café**

Church Ln (off Petersham Rd) ✉ TW10 7AG – ☎ (020) 8940 5230 – www.petershamnurseries.com – Closed 25-26 December and Monday

Rest – *(lunch only) (booking advisable)* Carte £ 37/52 **6CXx**

On a summer's day there can be few more delightful spots for lunch, whether that's on the terrace or in the greenhouse. The kitchen uses the freshest seasonal produce in unfussy, flavoursome dishes that have a subtle Italian accent.

X **Matsuba**

10 Red Lion St ✉ TW9 1RW ⊖ Richmond – ☎ (020) 8605 3513 – Closed 25-26 December, 1 January and Sunday **6CXn**

Rest – Carte £ 21/39

Family-run Japanese restaurant with just 11 tables; understated but well-kept appearance. Extensive menu offers wide range of Japanese dishes, along with bulgogi, a Korean barbecue dish.

X **Swagat**

86 Hill Rise ✉ TW10 6UB ⊖ Richmond – ☎ (020) 8940 75 57 – www.swagatindiancuisine.co.uk – Closed 25-26 December, 1 January and Sunday **6CXb**

Rest – *(dinner only) (booking essential)* Menu £ 30/35 – Carte £ 16/29

A very likeable little Indian restaurant, run by two friends who met while training with Oberoi hotels in India. One partner organises the warm service; the other prepares dishes with a pleasing degree of lightness and subtlety.

TEDDINGTON

XX **Rétro Bistrot**

114-116 High St ✉ TW11 8JB – ☎ (020) 8977 22 39 – www.retrobistrot.co.uk – Closed first 2 weeks August, first 10 days January, Sunday dinner and Monday

Rest – Menu £ 15/23 – Carte £ 26/48 **5BYn**

There's substance as well as style to this French bistrot. The classic bourgeois cuisine is prepared with innate skill; service is warm and effusive and the slick decoration conductive to merrymaking.

XX **Al Borgo**

3 Church Rd. ✉ TW11 8PF – ☎ (020) 8943 4456 – www.alborgo.co.uk – Closed Sunday and bank holidays **5BYe**

Rest – Menu £ 17 (weekdays) – Carte £ 25/49

A refreshingly unpretentious and keenly run Italian restaurant that exudes warmth and bonhomie. Homemade focaccia and pasta are the highlights. Look out too for seasonal offerings such as the black truffle menu.

X **Simply Thai**

196 Kingston Rd. ✉ TW11 9JD – ☎ (020) 8943 9747 – www.simplythai-restaurant.co.uk – Closed 25-26 December and Sunday

Rest – *(dinner only)* Menu £ 19/25 – Carte £ 21/29 **5BYx**

Extremely busy local Thai restaurant; the owner does all the cooking and her passion is clear. New creations sit alongside classics on the large menu. Prices are competitive; service can sometimes struggle to keep up.

King's Head

123 High St ✉ TW11 8HG ⊖ Teddington (Rail). – ☎ (020) 3166 2900 – www.whitebrasserie.com – Closed 25 December **5BYc**

Rest – Menu £ 14/17 – Carte £ 18/34

Britain has its pubs and France its brasseries; The King's Head does its bit for the entente cordiale by combining both. Have a drink in the front bar, then enjoy rustic classics in the rear brasserie.

LONDON

Twickenham

XX **A Cena**

418 Richmond Rd. ✉ TW1 2EB ⊖ Richmond – ✆ (020) 8288 0108 – www.acena.co.uk – Closed Sunday dinner, Monday lunch and bank holidays
Rest – Carte £ 26/39 **5BXe**
Rustic and quite intimate feel to this well-run neighbourhood Italian restaurant. Appealing, seasonal menu covers most of Italy and the generously sized dishes are full of flavour.

XX **Brula**

43 Crown Rd., St Margarets ✉ TW1 3EJ – ✆ (020) 8892 0602 – www.brula.co.uk – Closed 26 December, Sunday dinner and Monday **5BXv**
Rest – *(booking essential)* Menu £ 19/28 – Carte £ 28/43
Traditional in look, with its mirrors and chandeliers but friendly service and popular with the locals. They come for the good value, well-crafted cooking, which is largely French but now comes with a few Spanish and Italian influences.

X **Tangawizi**

406 Richmond Rd., Richmond Bridge ✉ TW1 2EB ⊖ Richmond – ✆ (020) 8891 3737 – www.tangawizi.co.uk – Closed 25-26 December and 1 January
Rest – *(dinner only)* Carte £ 15/32 **5BXe**
Name means Ginger in Swahili. Sleek décor in warm purple with subtle Indian touches. Well-priced, nicely balanced, slowly evolving menus take their influence from north India.

SOUTHWARK – Greater London 12 B3

Level 2, Tate Modern, Bankside, ✆ (020) 7401 52 66, www.visitlondon.com

Bermondsey

Hilton London Tower Bridge rm,

5 More London, Tooley St ✉ SE1 2BY ⊖ London Bridge – ✆ (020) 3002 4300 – www.towerbridge.hilton.com **34ARVe**
245 rm – †£ 199/419 ††£ 199/419, ☕ £ 20
Rest ***The Larder*** – Carte £ 28/48
Rest ***Takara*** – *(closed 27 December- 6 January and Monday)* Carte £ 31/55
Usefully located new-style Hilton hotel with boldly decorated open-plan lobby. Contemporary bedrooms boast well-designed features; 4 floors of executive rooms. The Larder has an international menu; Takara is a sushi bar.

Bermondsey Square rm,

Bermondsey Sq, Tower Bridge Rd ✉ SE1 3UN ⊖ London Bridge – ✆ (020) 7378 2450 – www.bermondseysquarehotel.co.uk **20XZEn**
80 rm – †£ 99/239 ††£ 99/420, ☕ £ 9
Rest ***Gregg's Bar & Grill*** – Menu £ 12/20 – Carte £ 19/40
Cleverly designed hotel in a regenerated square, with subtle '60s influences and a relaxed, hip feel. Well-equipped bedrooms, including stylish loft suites. Grilled meats the focus in the open-plan Gregg's Bar & Grill.

London Bridge rm,

8-18 London Bridge St ✉ SE1 9SG ⊖ London Bridge – ✆ (020) 7855 2200 – www.londonbridgehotel.com **33AQVa**
138 rm – †£ 382 ††£ 395, ☕ £ 17 – 3 suites
Rest ***Londinium*** – *(dinner only)* Carte £ 28/43
In one of the oldest parts of London, independently owned with an ornate façade dating from 1915. Modern interior with classically decorated bedrooms and an impressive gym. Londinium for brasserie dining.

XXX **Le Pont de la Tour**

36d Shad Thames, Butlers Wharf ✉ SE1 2YE ⊖ London Bridge – ✆ (020) 7403 8403 – www.lepontdelatour.co.uk – Closed 26 December and 1 January
Rest – Menu £ 25/30 – Carte £ 37/67 **34ASVc**
Providing, since 1991, seasonal French cooking, an urbane atmosphere and a wonderful riverside location, with views of Tower Bridge. Simpler dishes served in the livelier cocktail bar and grill.

LONDON

XX **Story** N (Tom Sellers)
201 Tooley St. ✉ SE1 2UE ⊖ London Bridge – ☎ (020) 7183 2117 – www.restaurantstory.co.uk – Closed 2 weeks Christmas-New Year, Sunday and Monday **34ASVs**
Rest – *(booking essential)* Menu £ 45/65
Amazing what you can create out of an old public toilet on a traffic island. In what looks like a Nordic eco-lodge, Tom Sellers offers 6 or 10 courses of earthy yet delicate, playful yet easy to eat dishes; go for 10, as 6 is too few. With just 13 tables, getting a booking is another story.
→ Burnt onion, apple gin and thyme. Pigeon, summer truffle and pine. Almond and dill.

XX **Magdalen**
152 Tooley St. ✉ SE1 2TU ⊖ London Bridge – ☎ (020) 7403 1342 – www.magdalenrestaurant.co.uk – Closed bank holidays, Sunday and lunch Saturday **34ARVb**
Rest – Menu £ 16 (weekday lunch) – Carte £ 26/43
The clever sourcing and confident British cooking will leave you satisfied. Add genial service, an affordable lunch menu and a food-friendly wine list and you have the favourite restaurant of many.

X **Zucca**
184 Bermondsey St ✉ SE1 3TQ ⊖ Borough – ☎ (020) 7378 6809 – www.zuccalondon.com – Closed 24 December-7 January, Easter, Sunday dinner and Monday **20XZEs**
Rest – *(booking essential at dinner)* Carte £ 22/33
Bright and buzzy modern room, where the informed Italian cooking is driven by the fresh ingredients, the prices are more than generous and the service is sweet and responsive. The appealing antipasti is great for sharing.

X **Blueprint Café**
Design Museum, Shad Thames, Butlers Wharf ✉ SE1 2YD ⊖ London Bridge – ☎ (020) 7378 7031 – www.blueprintcafe.co.uk – Closed 26-27 December, 1-4 January and Sunday dinner **34ASVu**
Rest – Menu £ 15/30 – Carte £ 27/41
Large retractable windows make the most of the river views from this bright restaurant above the Design Museum. The first change of head chef in 16 years was seamless: the cooking remains light, seasonally pertinent and easy to eat.

X **Village East**
171-173 Bermondsey St ✉ SE1 3UW ⊖ London Bridge – ☎ (020) 7357 60 82 – www.villageeast.co.uk – Closed 25-26 December **20XZEa**
Rest – Menu £ 14 (weekday lunch) – Carte £ 24/60
In a glass-fronted block sandwiched by Georgian townhouses, this trendy restaurant has two loud, buzzy bars and dining areas serving ample portions of modern British fare.

X **Cantina Del Ponte**
36c Shad Thames, Butlers Wharf ✉ SE1 2YE ⊖ London Bridge – ☎ (020) 7403 5403 – www.cantina.co.uk – Closed 25-27 December **34ASVc**
Rest – Menu £ 13/35 – Carte £ 28/43
This Italian stalwart offers an appealing mix of classic dishes and reliable favourites from a sensibly priced menu, in pleasant faux-rustic surroundings. Its pleasant terrace takes advantage of its riverside setting.

X **Butlers Wharf Chop House**
36e Shad Thames, Butlers Wharf ✉ SE1 2YE ⊖ London Bridge – ☎ (020) 7403 3403 – www.chophouse-restaurant.co.uk **34ASVn**
Rest – Carte £ 24/51
Grab a table on the terrace in summer and dine in the shadow of Tower Bridge. Rustic feel to the interior; noisy and fun. The menu focuses on traditional English ingredients and dishes; grilled meats a speciality.

LONDON

Vivat Bacchus London Bridge

4 Hays Ln ✉ SE1 2HB ⊖ London Bridge – ✆ (020) 7234 0891 – www.vivatbacchus.co.uk – Closed Christmas and New Year, Saturday lunch, Sunday and bank holidays **34**ARV **n**

Rest – Carte £ 20/44

Wines from the South African owners' homeland feature strongly and are well-suited to the meat dishes – the strength here. Choose one of the sharing boards themed around various countries, like Italian hams or South African BBQ.

Pizarro

171-173 Bermondsey St ✉ SE1 3UW ⊖ Borough – ✆ (020) 7378 9455 – www.josepizarro.com – Closed 24-28 December **20**XZE **r**

Rest – *(bookings not taken at dinner and weekend lunch)* Menu £ 17 (weekday lunch) – Carte £ 22/31

José Pizarro has a refreshingly simple way of naming his establishments: after José, his tapas bar, comes Pizarro, a larger restaurant a few doors down. Go for the small plates, like prawns with piquillo peppers and jamón.

Antico

214 Bermondsey St ✉ SE1 3TQ ⊖ London Bridge – ✆ (020) 7407 4682 – www.antico-london.co.uk – Closed Sunday dinner and Monday **20**XZE **e**

Rest – Menu £ 15 – Carte £ 21/54

Once an antique warehouse – hence the name – Antico is fun, bright and breezy, with honest and straightforward Italian food; the homemade pasta is good. Check out the seasonal ragu, risotto and sorbet on the blackboard.

José

104 Bermondsey St ✉ SE1 3UB ⊖ London Bridge – ✆ (020) 7403 4902 – www.josepizarro.com – Closed Christmas and Sunday dinner **20**XZE **v**

Rest – *(bookings not accepted)* Carte approx. £ 25

Standing up while eating tapas feels so right, especially at this small, fun bar that packs 'em in like boquerones. Five dishes each should suffice; go for the daily fish dishes from the blackboard. There's a great list of sherries too.

Garrison

99-101 Bermondsey St ✉ SE1 3XB ⊖ London Bridge. – ✆ (020) 7089 9355 – www.thegarrison.co.uk – Closed 25-26 December **20**XZE **z**

Rest – *(booking essential at dinner)* Carte £ 23/37

Known for its charming vintage look, booths and sweet-natured service, The Garrison boasts a warm, relaxed vibe. Open from breakfast until dinner, when a Mediterranean-led menu pulls in the crowd.

CAMBERWELL

Crooked Well

16 Grove Ln ✉ SE5 8SY – ✆ (020) 7252 7798 – www.thecrookedwell.com – Closed Monday lunch **25**VZH **s**

Rest – Carte £ 20/34

Warmly run pub that manages to look both new and lived-in at the same time. The kitchen mixes things up by offering sturdy classics like rabbit and bacon pie alongside more playful dishes such as a deconstructed Peach Melba.

SOUTHWARK

Level 2, Tate Modern, Bankside, ✆ (020) 7401 52 66, www.visitlondon.com

citizenM without rest

20 Lavington St ✉ SE1 0NZ ⊖ Southwark – ✆ (020) 3519 1680 – www.citizenm.com **33**APV **c**

192 rm – †£ 99/199 ††£ 99/199, ☕ £ 12

A new type of budget hotel with an eye for the aesthetic. Relaxing, open-plan lobby with sofas, books, tables, desks and a bar for snacks and drinks. Upstairs, the bedrooms may be pod-like but are well-lit and cleverly designed.

LONDON

XXX **Oxo Tower**

Oxo Tower Wharf (8th floor), Barge House St ✉ SE1 9PH ⊖ Southwark – ✆ (020) 7803 3888 – www.harveynichols.com – Closed 25 December, dinner 24 December and lunch 26 December **32ANVa**

Rest – Menu £ 35/50 – Carte £ 44/75

Rest *Oxo Tower Brasserie* – see restaurant listing

Top of a converted iconic factory, providing stunning views of the Thames and beyond. Stylish, minimalist interior with huge windows. Expect quite ambitious, mostly European, cuisine.

XX **Oblix**

Level 32, The Shard, St Thomas St. ✉ SE1 9RY ⊖ London Bridge – ✆ (020) 7268 6700 – www.oblixrestaurant.com **33AQVz**

Rest – Carte £ 34/61

From the Zuma/Roka people comes this New York grill restaurant, where meat and fish from the rotisserie, grill and Josper oven are the stars of the show. Views are far-reaching and there's live music in the adjacent lounge bar.

XX **Roast**

The Floral Hall, Borough Mkt ✉ SE1 1TL ⊖ London Bridge – ✆ (0845) 034 73 00 – www.roast-restaurant.com – Closed 25 December and 1 January

Rest – *(booking essential)* Menu £ 30 (weekdays)/35 – Carte £ 31/57 **33AQVe**

Known for its British food and for promoting UK producers – not surprising considering the restaurant's in the heart of Borough Market. The 'dish of the day' is often a highlight; service is affable and there's live music at night.

XX **Baltic**

74 Blackfriars Rd ✉ SE1 8HA ⊖ Southwark – ✆ (020) 7928 1111 – www.balticrestaurant.co.uk – Closed 24-27 December and 1 January

Rest – *(bookings advisable at dinner)* Menu £ 27/37 – Carte £ 24/36 **33AOVe**

In this converted 18C coach builder's works you'll find a big, bright restaurant specialising in Eastern European food – from Poland, Russia, Bulgaria, even Siberia. Dumplings and meat dishes stand out, as do the great vodkas.

XX **Del Mercato**

Park St ✉ SE1 9AD ⊖ London Bridge – ✆ (020) 7407 3651 – www.delmercato.co.uk **33AQVz**

Rest – Menu £ 20/30 – Carte £ 18/29

Owned by Vinopolis and occupying 3,000 sq ft of space under railway arches. It comprises a bakery, an espresso bar, a trattoria that does a brisk trade in pizzas and homemade pasta, and a stylish upstairs restaurant with a skilful kitchen and a competitive set menu run alongside the à la carte.

X **Oxo Tower Brasserie**

Oxo Tower Wharf (8th floor), Barge House St ✉ SE1 9PH ⊖ Southwark – ✆ (020) 7803 3888 – www.harveynichols.com – Closed 24 December dinner and 25 December **32ANVa**

Rest – Menu £ 25/60 – Carte £ 34/58

Less formal but more fun than the next-door restaurant. Open-plan kitchen produces modern, colourful and easy-to-eat dishes with influences from the Med. Great views too from the bar.

X **Tate Modern (Restaurant)**

Tate Modern (6th floor), Bankside ✉ SE1 9TG ⊖ Southwark – ✆ (020) 7887 8888 – www.tate.org.uk – Closed 24-26 December **33APVs**

Rest – *(lunch only and dinner Friday-Saturday)* Carte £ 26/40

Ask for a front window table facing St Paul's at this big, bright restaurant on Level 6. The menu is seasonal and the influences largely British; the kitchen has a light touch and each dish comes with a suggested wine pairing.

LONDON

X **Elliot's**

12 Stoney St., Borough Market ✉ SE1 9AD ⊖ London Bridge – ✆ (020) 7407 7436 – www.elliotscafe.com – Closed Sunday and bank holidays
Rest – *(booking advisable)* Carte £ 21/54 **33**AQV**h**
Open from breakfast onwards, this busy and unpretentious café sources most of its ingredients from Borough Market, in which it stands. The appealing menu is concise and the cooking is earthy, pleasingly uncomplicated and very satisfying.

X **Tapas Brindisa**

18-20 Southwark St, Borough Market ✉ SE1 1TJ ⊖ London Bridge – ✆ (020) 7357 8880 – www.tapasbrindisa.com **33**AQV**k**
Rest – *(bookings not accepted)* Carte £ 12/31
A blueprint for many of the tapas bars that subsequently sprung up over London. It has an infectious energy and the well-priced, robust dishes include Galician-style hake and black rice with squid; do try the hand-carved Ibérico hams.

X **Wright Brothers**

11 Stoney St., Borough Market ✉ SE1 9AD ⊖ London Bridge – ✆ (020) 7403 9554 – www.thewrightbrothers.co.uk – Closed dinner 24 December-dinner 28 December, 1-2 January, Easter Sunday and bank holiday Mondays
Rest – *(booking advisable)* Carte £ 29/39 **33**AQV**m**
Originally an oyster wholesaler; now offers a wide range of oysters along with porter, as well as fruits de mer, daily specials and assorted pies. It fills quickly and an air of contentment reigns.

Anchor & Hope

36 The Cut ✉ SE1 8LP ⊖ Southwark. – ✆ (020) 7928 9898 – Closed Christmas-New Year, Sunday dinner, Monday lunch and bank holidays
Rest – *(bookings not accepted)* Carte £ 26/37 **32**ANV**n**
As popular as ever thanks to its congenial feel and lived-in looks but mostly because of the appealingly seasonal menu and the gutsy, bold cooking that delivers on flavour. No reservations so be prepared to wait at the bar.

SUTTON – Greater London **12** B3

Sutton

Oak Sports Centre, Carshalton, Woodmansterne Rd, ✆ (020) 8643 83 63

X **Brasserie Vacherin**

12 High St ✉ SM1 1HN – ✆ (020) 8722 0180 – www.brasserievacherin.co.uk – Closed 25 December **7**EZ**x**
Rest – Menu £ 12/16 – Carte £ 23/64
Relaxed, modern French brasserie with tiled walls, art nouveau posters and deep red banquettes. Good value midweek set price menu and à la carte of French classics. Diligent service.

TOWER HAMLETS – Greater London **12** B3

Bethnal Green

Town Hall

Patriot Sq ✉ E2 9NF ⊖ Bethnal Green – ✆ (020) 7871 0460 – www.townhallhotel.com
97 rm – †£ 174/348 ††£ 174/426, ☕ £ 15 – 1 suite **14**YZB**x**
Rest *Viajante* ✿ **Rest *Corner Room*** – see restaurant listing
Edwardian, former council offices converted into a hotel in 2010. Its period character is balanced with modernity, with individually decorated, understated bedrooms and frequently changing art.

XX **Viajante** – Town Hall Hotel

✿ *Patriot Sq., (entrance on Cambridge Heath Rd) ✉ E2 9NF ⊖ Bethnal Green – ✆ (020) 7871 0461 – www.viajante.co.uk – Closed Monday, Tuesday and bank holidays*
Rest – *(dinner only and lunch Friday-Sunday) (booking essential)* **14**YZB**x**
Menu £ 35/95
Highly innovative and original cooking from Nuno Mendes. Choose 6, 9 or 12 delicate courses, influenced by his travels. A converted Victorian town hall is the unlikely setting for this creative style of cooking; ask to sit in the front room if you want to watch the chefs at work.
➜ Scallops, liquorice and parsley. Dehesa lamb with black quinoa. Frozen pear, cider and pecans.

LONDON

Brawn

49 Columbia Rd. ✉ E2 7RG ⊖ Bethnal Green – ✆ (020) 7729 5692 – www.brawn.co – Closed Christmas and New Year, Sunday dinner, Monday lunch and bank holidays **20**XZD**z**

Rest – Carte £ 19/34

Unpretentious and simply kitted out baby sister to Terroirs; the name captures the essence of the cooking perfectly: it is rustic, muscular and makes very good use of pig. Great local atmosphere and polite, helpful service.

Corner Room – Town Hall Hotel

Patriot Sq ✉ E2 9NF ⊖ Bethnal Green – ✆ (020) 7871 0461 – www.cornerroom.co.uk **14**YZB**x**

Rest – *(bookings not accepted at dinner)* Menu £ 19/23 – Carte approx. £ 28

Nuno Mendes' more accessible and relaxed addendum to his Viajante restaurant is open all day; you can wait for a table at the bar downstairs. The cooking is fresh, equally innovative and, because they use lesser cuts, more affordable.

LONDON

Bistrotheque

23-27 Wadeson St ✉ E2 9DR ⊖ Bethnal Green – ✆ (020) 8983 7900 – www.bistrotheque.com – Closed 24 and 26 December **14**YZB**s**

Rest – *(dinner only and brunch Saturday and Sunday) (booking advisable)* Carte £ 23/34

When the exterior is as irredeemably bleak as this, you just know it's going to be painfully cool inside. This bustling space in a converted sweat shop is great fun; its menu is French-bistro in style. Live music at weekend brunch.

Bow

Morgan Arms

43 Morgan St ✉ E3 5AA ⊖ Bow Road. – ✆ (020) 8980 6389 – www.capitalpubcompany.com/The-Morgan-Arms – Closed 25 December

Rest – Carte £ 21/32 **3**GU**c**

Characterful pub with mismatch of furniture and shabby-chic appeal. Constantly evolving menu offers robust cooking which occasionally uses some unfamiliar ingredients; simpler food is served in the lively bar.

Canary Wharf

Four Seasons

Westferry Circus ✉ E14 8RS ⊖ Canary Wharf – ✆ (020) 7510 1999 – www.fourseasons.com/canarywharf **3**GV**a**

127 rm – †£ 220/400 ††£ 220/400, ☕ £ 27 – 14 suites

Rest *Quadrato* – ✆ (020) 7510 1858 – Carte £ 28/55

Professionally run international hotel geared mainly to the local corporate market. The deluxe rooms boast impressive views across the river. Spacious restaurant, with river-facing terrace and menu that covers all parts of Italy.

Dockmaster's House

1 Hertsmere Rd ✉ E14 8JJ ⊖ Canary Wharf – ✆ (020) 7345 0345 – www.dockmastershouse.com – Closed 25 December-1 January, bank holidays, Saturday lunch and Sunday

Rest – *(booking advisable)* Menu £ 20/55 – Carte £ 24/49 **3**GV**r**

A contemporary overhaul of a three storey Georgian house in the shadow of Canary Wharf's skyscrapers has created this slick operation. Elaborate Indian cooking, although sometimes a little pretentious.

Plateau

Canada Place (4th floor), Canada Square ✉ E14 5ER ⊖ Canary Wharf – ✆ (020) 7715 7100 – www.plateaurestaurant.co.uk – Closed 25 December, 1 January and Sunday **3**GV**n**

Rest – Menu £ 22 – Carte £ 28/54

Impressive open-plan space with dramatic glass walls and ceilings and striking 1950s influenced design. Rotisserie meats in the contemporary Bar & Grill; globally-influenced dishes in the more formal restaurant.

XX **Roka Canary Wharf** A/C

4 Park Pavilion (1st Floor) ✉ E14 5FW ⊖ Canary Wharf – ✆ (020) 7636 5228 – www.rokarestaurant.com – Closed 25 December 3GVv

Rest – *(booking essential)* Carte £ 20/89

You'll be hit by a wall of sound at this large and perennially busy operation in the shadow of Canary Wharf Tower. The meats cooked on the robata grill are highlights of the Japanese menu.

XX **Boisdale of Canary Wharf**

Cabot Pl ✉ E14 4QT ⊖ Canary Wharf – ✆ (020) 7715 5818 – www.boisdale.co.uk – Closed bank holidays 7GVs

Rest – *(booking advisable)* Menu £ 20 – Carte £ 32/75

It's the 1st floor for the relaxed, art deco inspired Oyster bar, with its crustacea, burgers and steaks. The grander 2nd floor has a stage for live jazz (a charge is made) and offers plenty of dishes of a Scottish persuasion.

XX **Goodman Canary Wharf** A/C

Discovery Dock East, 3 South Quay ✉ E14 9RU ⊖ South Quay (DLR) – ✆ (020) 7531 0300 – www.goodmanrestaurants.com – Closed 25-26 December, 1 January, Saturday lunch, Sunday and bank holidays 7GVe

Rest – *(booking advisable)* Menu £ 22 (lunch) – Carte £ 26/75

Whether you like corn or grass fed Scottish fillet, rib on the bone or US strip loin, corn or grass fed, the delightful staff will explain the maturation process; you decide on the cut and weight. A lively brasserie with waterfront views.

XX **Iberica Canary Wharf** A/C

Cabot Sq ✉ E14 4QQ ⊖ Canary Wharf – ✆ (020) 7636 8650 – www.ibericalondon.co.uk – Closed 24-25 December, 1 January and dinner on Sunday and bank holidays 7GVc

Rest – Menu £ 10 (weekday lunch) – Carte £ 18/46

Lively, modern Spanish restaurant whose narrow shop front belies its vast interior; choose the bustle of the ground floor or the quieter mezzanine. The tapas is an appealing mix of the traditional and the more contemporary.

Gun

27 Coldharbour ✉ E14 9NS ⊖ Blackwall (DLR). – ✆ (020) 7515 5222 – www.thegundocklands.com – Closed 25-26 December 7GVx

Rest – Carte £ 25/50

Despite its 21C makeover, this 18C pub, with links to Lord Nelson, hasn't forgotten its roots. Smart dining room; menu a mix of classic and modern. Always busy, especially the large decked area.

LIMEHOUSE

Narrow A/C P

44 Narrow St ✉ E14 8DP ⊖ Limehouse (DLR). – ✆ (020) 7592 7950 – www.gordonramsay.com – Closed 25 December 3GVb

Rest – *(booking essential)* Menu £ 22 – Carte £ 26/50

Terrific river views from this Grade II listed former dockmaster's house; part of Gordon Ramsay's group. Sit in the conservatory and order British classics like Scotch egg, cottage pie, and bread and butter pudding.

SPITALFIELDS

XXX **Galvin La Chapelle**

35 Spital Sq ✉ E1 6DY ⊖ Liverpool Street – ✆ (020) 7299 0400 – www.galvinrestaurants.com – Closed dinner 24-26 December and 1 January

Rest – Menu £ 30 (lunch and early dinner) – Carte £ 43/63 34ASTv

The Victorian splendour of St Botolph's Hall, with its vaulted ceiling, arched windows and marble pillars, lends itself perfectly to its role as a glamorous restaurant. The food is bourgeois French with a sophisticated edge and is bound to satisfy.

→ Smoked eel with caramelised pineapple, parsley and horseradish. Tagine of Bresse pigeon, couscous and harissa sauce. Chilled Valrhona chocolate fondant with banana and yoghurt ice cream.

LONDON

✗✗ Les Trois Garcons AC ✿

1 Club Row ⊠ E1 6JX ⊖ Shoreditch – ✆ (020) 7613 1924
– www.lestroisgarcons.com – Closed 23 December-3 January, Sunday dinner and
bank holidays 20XZD**r**
Rest – (dinner only and lunch Thursday-Friday) Menu £ 22 (weekday lunch)
– Carte £ 29/59
Extraordinarily eccentric decoration, with stuffed animals, twinkling beads, velvet
drapes, chandeliers and handbags hanging from the ceiling. By contrast, the
French food is surprisingly traditional.

✗ Hawksmoor AC ⬤

157 Commercial St ⊠ E1 6BJ ⊖ Shoreditch – ✆ (020) 7426 4850
– www.thehawksmoor.com – Closed 24-27 December, 1 January and Sunday
dinner 20XZD**s**
Rest – (booking essential) Menu £ 26 (lunch and early dinner) – Carte £ 39/62
Unremarkable surroundings and ordinary starters and puds but no matter: this is
all about great British beef, hung for 35 days, from Longhorn cattle in the heart of
the Yorkshire Moors.

✗ Galvin Café a Vin ⬤

35 Spital Sq (entrance on Bishops Sq) ⊠ E1 6DY ⊖ Liverpool Street – ✆ (020)
7299 0404 – www.galvinrestaurants.com – Closed dinner 24 December, 25-26
December and 1 January 34AST**v**
Rest – Menu £ 16/19 – Carte £ 23/32
In the same building as La Chapelle is this simpler but equally worthy operation
from the Galvin brothers. The room may not have the grandeur of next door but
what it does offer is classic French bistro food at very appealing prices.

✗ St John Bread and Wine AC 🗱

94-96 Commercial St ⊠ E1 6LZ ⊖ Shoreditch – ✆ (020) 7251 0848
– www.stjohnbreadandwine.com – Closed Christmas and New Year
Rest – Carte £ 23/30 34AST**a**
Part-wine shop/bakery and local restaurant. Highly seasonal and appealing menu
changes twice a day; cooking is British, uncomplicated and very satisfying. Try the
less familiar dishes.

WAPPING

✗✗ Smith's of Wapping AC

22 Wapping High St ⊠ E1W 1NJ ⊖ Wapping – ✆ (020) 7488 3456
– www.smithsrestaurants.com – Closed 25-26 December, 1 January and Sunday
dinner 20XZE**c**
Rest – (booking advisable) Menu £ 20 (weekdays) – Carte £ 29/58
Having provided seafood to the burghers of Essex for over 50 years, the Smiths
opened this large riverside brasserie in 2011. The kitchen keeps it traditional; the
best dishes are old favourites like dressed crab and Dover sole meunière.

✗ Wapping Food ⬤ P

Wapping Wall ⊠ E1W 3SG ⊖ Wapping – ✆ (020) 7680 2080
– www.thewappingproject.com – Closed 23 December-3 January, Sunday dinner
and bank holidays 20YZE**n**
Rest – Carte £ 28/45
This striking Victorian former hydraulic power station houses an atmospheric restaurant and art gallery. Sit among the old turbines and enjoy robust, straightforward dishes based on what's in season.

WHITECHAPEL

✗✗ Cafe Spice Namaste AC

16 Prescot St. ⊠ E1 8AZ ⊖ Tower Hill – ✆ (020) 7488 9242
– www.cafespice.co.uk – Closed Saturday lunch, Sunday and bank holidays
Rest – Menu £ 35 – Carte £ 25/36 34ASU**z**
Fresh, vibrant and fairly priced Indian cuisine from Cyrus Todiwala, served in a
colourfully decorated room that was once a magistrate's court. Engaging service
from an experienced team.

X **Whitechapel Gallery Dining Room**

77-82 Whitechapel High st. ✉ E1 7QX ⊖ Aldgate East – ✆ (020) 7522 7896 – www.whitechapelgallery.org/dining-room – Closed Christmas-New Year, Monday and dinner Sunday and Tuesday **34AST x**

Rest – *(booking advisable)* Menu £ 28 (dinner) – Carte £ 23/34

Founded in 1901 and best known for exhibiting Picasso's 'Guernica', the gallery underwent a major refit in 2009, which resulted in the creation of this sweet restaurant. Bright, European and Med influenced cooking from an accessible menu.

WANDSWORTH – Greater London **12 B3**

BALHAM

X **Lamberts**

2 Station Par ✉ SW12 9AZ ⊖ Balham – ✆ (020) 8675 2233 – www.lambertsrestaurant.com – Closed 24-26 December, 1-2 January, Sunday dinner and Monday **6EX n**

Rest – Menu £ 18/24 – Carte £ 29/38

Locals come for the relaxed surroundings, hospitable service and tasty, seasonal food. Sunday lunch is very popular. The enthusiasm of the eponymous owner has rubbed off on his team.

X **Harrison's**

15-19 Bedford Hill ✉ SW12 9EX ⊖ Balham – ✆ (020) 8675 6900 – www.harrisonsbalham.co.uk – Closed 24-28 December **6EX h**

Rest – Menu £ 14/26 – Carte £ 24/38

Lively, popular sister to Sam's Brasserie in Chiswick. Open all day, with an appealing list of favourites, from fishcakes to 'Harrison's burgers'. Weekend brunches; kids' menu; good value weekday set menus.

Avalon

16 Balham Hill ✉ SW12 9EB ⊖ Clapham South. – ✆ (020) 8675 8613 – www.theavalonlondon.com – Closed 25-26 December **6EX r**

Rest – *(booking advisable)* Menu £ 23 (dinner) – Carte £ 22/34

Large, bustling and atmospheric pub with an appealing summer terrace. Snacks served in the busy, long bar and an appealingly broad menu offered in the tiled and characterful rear dining room.

BATTERSEA

XX **Chada**

208-210 Battersea Park Rd. ✉ SW11 4ND – ✆ (020) 7622 2209 – www.chadathai.com – Closed Sunday and bank holidays **23QZH x**

Rest – *(dinner only)* Carte £ 22/34

Going strong after 20 years; its striking façade stands out in an otherwise unremarkable street. The welcome is warm, the service polite and the Thai food appealing and keenly priced.

X **Soif**

27 Battersea Rise ✉ SW11 1HG – ✆ (020) 7233 1112 – www.soif.co – Closed Christmas and New Year, bank holidays, Sunday dinner and Monday lunch **23QZH c**

Rest – *(booking essential at dinner)* Carte £ 23/37

Great food, an appealingly louche look and a thoughtful wine list – yes, it's another terrific eaterie from the team behind Terroirs and Brawn. The cooking is robust and satisfying; anything 'piggy' is done particularly well.

X **Entrée**

2 Battersea Rise ✉ SW11 1ED – ✆ (020) 7223 5147 – www.entreebattersea.co.uk – Closed 24-28 December **23QZH s**

Rest – *(dinner only and lunch Saturday-Sunday)* Menu £ 19 (lunch) – Carte £ 26/32

They've gone for a casual bistro look which, along with a basement bar and weekend pianist, hits the right note with locals. Sensibly priced menu mixes French classic and modern European dishes.

LONDON

Lola Rojo

78 Northcote Rd ✉ SW11 6QL – ☎ (020) 7350 2262 – www.lolarojo.net – Closed 25-26 December and lunch 1 January **23**QZH**v**

Rest – *(booking essential)* Carte £ 12/26

Few spots on Northcote Road are as fun as this lively, if cramped Spanish eatery. The owner-chef comes from Valencia so paella is a sure thing but other Catalan tapas specialities are also worth seeking out.

Metrogusto

153 Battersea Park Rd. ✉ SW8 4BX – ☎ (020) 7720 0204 – www.metrogusto.co.uk – Closed 4-17 August, 25-26 December, Easter and Sunday dinner **24**RZG**a**

Rest – Menu £ 12 (weekday lunch) – Carte £ 19/31

Ambro Ianeselli, one of London's most affable restaurateurs, has moved from Islington back to his original Battersea base, along with his art collection. The Italian food is simple and as heart-warming as Ambro's never-ending hospitality.

LONDON

Rosita (N)

124 Northcote Rd ✉ SW11 6QU – ☎ (020) 7998 9093 – www.rositasherry.net – Closed 25-26 December and lunch 1 January **6**EX**g**

Rest – *(dinner only and lunch Friday-Sunday)* Menu £ 15 (lunch) – Carte £ 15/26

From the owners of nearby Lola Roja comes this fun sherry and tapas bar. Dishes include flavoursome meats and seafood cooked by Josper grill. There are many sherries by the glass and suggested pairings with certain dishes.

Hana (N)

60 Battersea Rise ✉ SW11 1EG – ☎ (020) 7228 2496 – www.hanakorean.co.uk – Closed 24-25 December **23**QZH**a**

Rest – Carte £ 18/27

A warm, sweet little Korean restaurant. Yang Yeum chicken and Pa Jeon pancake are popular starters; bibimbap rice dishes burst with flavour; seafood cooked on the barbeque is very good; and they do their own version of Bossam.

Battersea Heliport

Hotel Verta London by Rhombus

rm,

Bridges Wharf ✉ SW11 3BE – ☎ (020) 7801 3500 – www.hotelverta.co.uk **23**PZH**v**

68 rm – †£ 180/360 ††£ 180/360 – 2 suites

Rest *Red Pocket* – ☎ (020) 7801 3535 – Menu £ 30 – Carte £ 26/37

Built in 2010, in a unique riverside location with a heliport. Well-equipped bedrooms; those without views are bigger than those with. Impressive spa facilities. Chinese cuisine served in the contemporary Red Pocket restaurant.

Putney

Enoteca Turi

28 Putney High St ✉ SW15 1SQ ⊖ Putney Bridge – ☎ (020) 8785 4449 – www.enotecaturi.com – Closed 25-26 December, 1 January, Sunday and lunch bank holiday Mondays **22**MZH**n**

Rest – Menu £ 18/33 – Carte £ 27/46

A long-standing owner-run Italian restaurant. Earthy cooking focuses on the northerly regions of Italy. Interesting wine list, with plenty by the glass and carafe.

Prince of Wales

138 Upper Richmond Rd ✉ SW15 2SP ⊖ East Putney. – ☎ (020) 8788 1552 – www.princeofwalesputney.co.uk – Closed 23 December-1 January and Monday lunch except bank holidays **22**MZH**z**

Rest – Carte £ 24/42

Idiosyncratic decoration and good food make this substantial Victorian pub stand out. Daily changing menu reads well and includes British specialities like Cornish sardines as well as Spanish delicacies; simpler menu in the bar.

WANDSWORTH

Chez Bruce (Bruce Poole)

2 Bellevue Rd ✉ SW17 7EG ⊖ Tooting Bec – ✆ (020) 8672 0114
– *www.chezbruce.co.uk* – *Closed 24-26 December and 1 January* **6EXe**
Rest – *(booking essential)* Menu £ 28/45
Flavoursome, uncomplicated French cooking with hints of the Mediterranean prepared with innate skill; well-organised, personable service and an easy-going atmosphere - some of the reasons why Chez Bruce remains a favourite of so many.
➜ Foie gras and chicken liver parfait with toasted brioche, smoked duck, walnuts and pear. Roast cod with olive oil mash, provençale tomato and gremolata. Hot chocolate and almond pudding with praline parfait.

WESTMINSTER (City of) – Greater London 12 B3

BAYSWATER AND MAIDA VALE

Lancaster London

Lancaster Terr ✉ *W2 2TY* ⊖ *Lancaster Gate* – ✆ *(020) 7262 6737*
– *www.lancasterlondon.com* **28ADUe**
416 rm – †£ 130/385 ††£ 166/421, ☕ £ 16 – 22 suites
Rest *Nipa* – see restaurant listing
Rest *Island* – ✆ (020) 7551 6070 – Menu £ 13 (lunch and early dinner)
– Carte £ 19/34
The former Royal Lancaster is an imposing 1960s hotel overlooking Hyde Park. Known for its extensive conference suites. Bedrooms are bright and well-equipped. Island has an accessible, Med-influenced menu, with steaks a highlight.

Hotel Indigo London - Paddington

16 London St ✉ *W2 1HL* ⊖ *Paddington* – ✆ *(020) 7706 4444*
– *www.hotelindigo.com* **28ADUa**
64 rm – †£ 192 ††£ 216/360, ☕ £ 15
Rest *London Street Brasserie* – Carte £ 19/27
You'll find a smart, modern, corporate townhouse behind the imposing period façade. Bright bedrooms come with a feature wall depicting scenes of the local area. All-day menu of steaks, pasta and brasserie classics.

Colonnade without rest

2 Warrington Cres ✉ *W9 1ER* ⊖ *Warwick Avenue* – ✆ *(020) 7286 1052*
– *www.colonnadehotel.co.uk* **17OZDe**
43 rm – †£ 200/480 ††£ 250/600, ☕ £ 15.50
Former hospital in quiet yet easily accessible location. Bedrooms range in size according to grade; all are comfortable and classically furnished with good amenities. Lower floor bar.

Royal Park without rest

3 Westbourne Terr ✉ *W2 3UL* ⊖ *Lancaster Gate* – ✆ *(020) 7479 6600*
– *www.theroyalpark.com* **28ADUx**
48 rm – †£ 227 ††£ 227, ☕ £ 14 – 3 suites
Three attractive 19C townhouses set back from the road, in a pleasant location near Hyde Park. Quiet lounges with period furnishings. Breakfast served in the well-appointed bedrooms.

New Linden without rest

59 Leinster Sq. ✉ *W2 4PS* ⊖ *Bayswater* – ✆ *(020) 7221 4321*
– *www.newlinden.com* **27ABUe**
50 rm ☕ – †£ 65/95 ††£ 79/189
Smart four-storey white stucco façade. Basement breakfast room opens onto summer courtyard. Bedrooms are its strength: flat screen TVs and wooden floors; two split-level family rooms.

Le Café Anglais

8 Porchester Gdns ✉ *W2 4BD* ⊖ *Bayswater* – ✆ *(020) 7221 1415*
– *www.lecafeanglais.co.uk* – *Closed 25-26 December and 1 January*
Rest – Menu £ 20/35 – Carte £ 19/53 **27ABUr**
Big, bustling and contemporary brasserie with art deco styling, within Whiteley's shopping centre. Large, appealing selection of classic brasserie food; the rotisserie is the centrepiece. More casual oyster bar by entrance.

XX **Angelus**

4 Bathurst St ✉ W2 2SD ⊖ Lancaster Gate – ✆ (020) 7402 0083 – www.angelusrestaurant.co.uk – Closed 24 December-2 January 28ADU**c**

Rest – Menu £ 20 (lunch) – Carte £ 40/57

Hospitable owner has created an attractive French brasserie within a 19C former pub, with a warm and inclusive feel. Satisfying and honest French cooking uses seasonal British ingredients.

XX **Nipa** – Lancaster London Hotel

Lancaster Terr ✉ W2 2TY ⊖ Lancaster Gate – ✆ (020) 7551 6039 – www.niparestaurant.co.uk – Closed Christmas-New Year and lunch Saturday-Monday 28ADU**e**

Rest – Menu £ 10/38 – Carte £ 27/45

On the 1st floor and overlooking Hyde Park. Authentic and ornately decorated restaurant offers subtly spiced Thai cuisine. Keen to please staff in traditional silk costumes.

XX **Pearl Liang**

8 Sheldon Sq, Paddington Central ✉ W2 6EZ ⊖ Paddington – ✆ (020) 7289 7000 – www.pearlliang.co.uk – Closed 24 and 25 December 28ACT**b**

Rest – Menu £ 11/25 – Carte £ 13/65

Spacious, business-orientated Chinese restaurant within a corporate development. Extensive choice from a variety of set menus; try the more unusual dishes like jellyfish or pig's trotter.

XX **Colchis**

39 Chepstow Pl ✉ W2 4TS ⊖ Bayswater – ✆ (020) 7221 7620 – www.colchisrestaurant.co.uk – Closed Christmas-New Year 27AAU**c**

Rest – *(dinner only and lunch Saturday-Sunday)* Carte £ 24/45

Hearty Georgian cooking, with its Med and Middle Eastern influences, is celebrated at this former pub. Start with khachapuri (leavened bread with cheese) or lobio mchadit (red kidney bean stew) and then share shashlyk (kebabs).

X **Hereford Road**

3 Hereford Rd ✉ W2 4AB ⊖ Bayswater – ✆ (020) 7727 1144 – www.herefordroad.org – Closed 24 December-3 January and 27-29 August

Rest – *(booking essential)* Menu £ 10 (weekday lunch)/16 – Carte £ 20/30 27ABU**s**

Converted butcher's shop specialising in tasty British dishes without frills, using first-rate, seasonal ingredients; offal a highlight. Booths for six people are the prized seats. Friendly and relaxed feel.

X **Assaggi**

39 Chepstow Pl, (1st Floor) ✉ W2 4TS ⊖ Bayswater – ✆ (020) 7792 5501 – Closed 2 weeks Christmas, Sunday and bank holidays 27AAU**c**

Rest – *(booking essential)* Carte £ 39/56

The pared-down simplicity to this room works well; regulars are given fulsome welcomes and the atmosphere is great. Cooking puts the focus on the quality of the ingredients and the wine list is exclusively Italian.

X **Casa Malevo**

23 Connaught St ✉ W2 2AY ⊖ Marble Arch – ✆ (020) 7402 1988 – www.casamalevo.com – Closed 22-28 December 29AFU**a**

Rest – Carte £ 22/42

Carnivores will be in clover at this friendly Argentinian restaurant, with its bare brick walls and intimate lighting. Most come for the grilled Argentine beef, accompanied by a bottle of Malbec.

X **El Pirata De Tapas**

115 Westbourne Grove ✉ W2 4UP ⊖ Bayswater – ✆ (020) 7727 5000 – www.elpiratadetapas.co.uk – Closed 26-27 August, 24-26 December and 1 January 27ABU**n**

Rest – Menu £ 9/25 – Carte £ 19/38

Contemporary yet warm Spanish restaurant with a genuine neighbourhood feel. Authentic flavours from a well-priced and appealing selection of tapas, ideal for sharing with friends.

Kateh

5 Warwick Pl ✉ W9 2PX ⊖ Warwick Avenue – ☎ (020) 7289 3393
– www.kateh.net **28ACTa**

Rest – *(dinner only and lunch Friday-Sunday) (booking essential)*
Carte £ 19/35

Booking is imperative if you want to join the locals who have already discovered what a little jewel they have in the form of this buzzy, busy Persian restaurant. Authentic stews, expert chargrilling and lovely pastries and teas.

Prince Alfred & Formosa Dining Room

5A Formosa St ✉ W9 1EE ⊖ Warwick Avenue. – ☎ (020) 7286 3287
– www.theprincealfred.com **17OZDn**

Rest – Menu £ 12 (weekdays) – Carte £ 24/36

The Prince Alfred is a striking Victorian pub; sadly, the eating is done in the Formosa Dining Room extension but at least it's a lively room. Cooking has a rustic edge; steaks, pork belly and sticky toffee pudding are perennials.

Waterway

54 Formosa St ✉ W9 2JU ⊖ Warwick Avenue. – ☎ (020) 7266 3557
– www.thewaterway.co.uk **17OZDp**

Rest – Carte £ 23/39

Terrific decked terrace by the canal its most appealing feature. Contemporary interior with busy cocktail bar; menu in separate dining room mixes the classics with more ambitious dishes.

LONDON

BELGRAVIA

Berkeley

Wilton Pl ✉ SW1X 7RL ⊖ Knightsbridge – ☎ (020) 7235 6000
– www.the-berkeley.co.uk **37AGXe**

184 rm – †£ 310/660 ††£ 378/900, ☕ £ 32 – 26 suites
Rest *Marcus Wareing at The Berkeley* ✿✿
Rest *Koffmann's* – see restaurant listing

Discreet and very comfortable hotel with impressive rooftop pool and opulently decorated, immaculately kept bedrooms. Relax in the gilded, panelled Caramel Room or have a drink in the ice cool Blue Bar. Choice of two restaurants.

Lanesborough

Hyde Park Corner ✉ SW1X 7TA ⊖ Hyde Park Corner – ☎ (020) 7259 5599
– www.lanesborough.com **37AGXa**

83 rm – †£ 495/570 ††£ 665/775, ☕ £ 35 – 10 suites
Rest *Apsleys* ✿ – see restaurant listing

Converted in the 1990s from 18C St George's Hospital. Regency-era inspired decoration; lavishly appointed bedrooms come with impressive technological extras and full butler service is offered. Delightfully clubby library bar.

Halkin

5 Halkin St ✉ SW1X 7DJ ⊖ Hyde Park Corner – ☎ (020) 7333 1000
– www.comohotels.com/thehalkin **38AHXb**

41 rm – †£ 324/564 ††£ 504/804, ☕ £ 28 – 6 suites
Rest *Ametsa with Arzak Instruction* ✿ – see restaurant listing

Opened in 1991 as London's first boutique hotel and still looking sharp today. Thoughtfully conceived bedrooms with silk walls and marbled bathrooms; everything at the touch of a button. Abundant Armani-clad staff. Small, discreet bar.

The Wellesley Ⓝ

11 Knightsbridge ✉ SW1X 7LY ⊖ Hyde Park Corner – ☎ (020) 7235 3535
– www.thewellesley.co.uk **37AGXw**

36 rm – †£ 420/2500 ††£ 800/2500, ☕ £ 25 – 15 suites
Rest – Carte £ 50/70

Stylish, elegant townhouse inspired by the jazz age, on the site of the famous Pizza on the Park. Impressive cigar lounge and bar with a super selection of whiskies and cognacs. Smart bedrooms have full butler service; those facing Hyde Park the most prized. Modern Italian food in the discreet restaurant.

Belgraves
20 Chesham Pl ✉ SW1X 8HQ ⊖ Knightsbridge – ✆ (020) 7858 0100 – www.thompsonhotels.com **37AGXc**
85 rm – †£ 359/599 ††£ 359/683, ☕ £ 20 **Rest** – Carte £ 23/60
US group Thompson's first UK venture opened in 2012; an elegant, stylish boutique-style hotel with a hint of bohemia and in a great location. Uncluttered, decent sized bedrooms with oak flooring and lovely marble bathrooms.

Jumeirah Lowndes
21 Lowndes St ✉ SW1X 9ES ⊖ Knightsbridge – ✆ (020) 7823 1234 – www.jumeirah.com **37AGXh**
87 rm – †£ 216/702 ††£ 216/702, ☕ £ 30 – 6 suites
Rest *Lowndes Bar & Kitchen* – Menu £ 15/20 – Carte £ 28/47
Compact yet friendly modern corporate hotel within this exclusive residential area. Good levels of personal service offered. Close to the famous shops of Knightsbridge. Informal restaurant with appealing courtyard terrace.

Marcus Wareing at The Berkeley – Berkeley Hotel
Wilton Pl ✉ SW1X 7RL ⊖ Knightsbridge – ✆ (020) 7235 1200 – www.marcus-wareing.com – Closed 1 January and Sunday **37AGXe**
Rest – Menu £ 30 (weekday lunch)/115
The room is elegant, sophisticated and very comfortable indeed; the Chef's Table is one of the best in town. Marcus Wareing's cooking is now lighter and more modern yet remains underpinned by sound techniques; his dishes display great care and attention, as does the impressive wine list.
→ Mackerel, scallop, pine nut and yuzu. Suckling lamb with beans, oregano and Flower Marie. Horlicks, honey, whisky.

Apsleys – Lanesborough Hotel
Hyde Park Corner ✉ SW1X 7TA ⊖ Hyde Park Corner – ✆ (020) 7333 7254 – www.apsleysrestaurant.com **37AGXa**
Rest – Menu £ 25 (lunch) – Carte £ 60/113
Under the guidance of celebrated chef Heinz Beck from Rome's La Pergola. Exquisite and precise Italian cooking, in a grand, eye-catching but far from intimidating room, designed by Adam Tihany. The serving team are polished and the atmosphere reassuringly upbeat.
→ Fish crudo. Carbonara fagottelli. Chocolate soufflé with vanilla and raspberry.

Pétrus
1 Kinnerton St ✉ SW1X 8EA ⊖ Knightsbridge – ✆ (020) 7592 1609 – www.gordonramsay.com/petrus – Closed Christmas and Sunday **37AGXv**
Rest – Menu £ 35/75
Elegant Gordon Ramsay restaurant, opened in 2010, in stylish tones of silver, oyster and – as a nod to the name – claret. Experienced team bring personality to the service. Elaborate French-based cooking uses top quality ingredients.
→ Scallops with cauliflower, anchovy and caper. Fillet of beef, roast onion braised shin, bone marrow and barolo jus. Chocolate sphere with milk ice cream and honeycomb.

Ametsa with Arzak Instruction N – Halkin Hotel
5 Halkin St ✉ SW1X 7DJ ⊖ Hyde Park Corner – ✆ (020) 7333 1234 – www.comohotels.com/thehalkin – Closed lunch Sunday and Monday
Rest – Menu £ 52/105 – Carte £ 53/69 **38AHXb**
The father and daughter team from the celebrated Arzak restaurant in San Sebastián bring the Basque country to Belgravia. Traditional Basque flavours are presented in a modern way, with much originality and a little playfulness.
→ King prawns with sweetcorn. Lamb with macchiato. 'Moon Rocks'.

Amaya
Halkin Arcade, 19 Motcomb St ✉ SW1X 8JT ⊖ Knightsbridge – ✆ (020) 7823 1166 – www.realindianfood.com – Closed dinner 25 December
Rest – Menu £ 21/80 – Carte £ 37/59 **37AGXk**
Order a selection of small dishes from the tawa griddle, tandoor or sigri grill and finish with a curry or biryani. Dishes like lamb chops are aromatic and satisfying and the cooking is skilled and consistent. This busy Indian restaurant is bright, colourful and lively; ask for a table by the open kitchen.
→ Rock oysters with coconut and ginger moilee sauce. Slow-roasted leg of baby lamb, cumin and garam masala. Blood orange brûlée.

LONDON

Koffmann's - Berkeley Hotel
Wilton Pl ✉ SW1X 7RL ⊖ Knightsbridge – ✆ (020) 7235 1010 – www.the-berkeley.co.uk **37**AGX**e**

Rest – Menu £ 22/28 – Carte £ 39/84

Pierre Koffmann, one of London's most fêted chefs, was enticed out of retirement to open this comfortable, well run and spacious restaurant. Expect classic signature dishes and plenty of gutsy flavours true to his Gascon roots.

Zafferano
15 Lowndes St ✉ SW1X 9EY ⊖ Knightsbridge – ✆ (020) 7235 5800 – www.zafferanorestaurant.co.uk **37**AGX**f**

Rest – *(booking essential)* Carte £ 33/60

Be sure to sit in the more atmospheric main room of this longstanding Italian restaurant. The menu sticks to the tried-and-tested and the cooking is reassuringly familiar to its well-dressed local clientele.

Pantechnicon
10 Motcomb St ✉ SW1X 8LA ⊖ Knightsbridge. – ✆ (020) 7730 6074 – www.thepantechnicon.com – Closed 25 December **37**AGX**d**

Rest – *(booking advisable)* Carte £ 27/63

Urbane, enthusiastically run pub with a busy ground floor and altogether more formal upstairs dining room. Traditional dishes are given a modern twist; oysters and Scottish steaks are perennials.

Hyde Park and Knightsbridge

Mandarin Oriental Hyde Park
66 Knightsbridge ✉ SW1X 7LA ⊖ Knightsbridge – ✆ (020) 7235 2000 – www.mandarinoriental.com/london **37**AGX**x**

194 rm – †£ 354/882 ††£ 354/882, ☕ £ 32 – 25 suites

Rest *Dinner by Heston Blumenthal* ✿✿ **Rest *Bar Boulud*** – see restaurant listing

Built in 1889, this classic international hotel, with its striking façade, remains one of London's grandest. The luxurious bedrooms have a charming English country feel; many enjoy views of Hyde Park. Impressive service levels.

Bulgari
171 Knightsbridge ✉ SW7 1DW ⊖ Knightsbridge – ✆ (020) 7151 1010 – www.bulgarihotels.com/london **37**AFX**k**

85 rm – †£ 528/828 ††£ 588/948, ☕ £ 32 – 7 suites

Rest *Il Ristorante* – Menu £ 30 (lunch) – Carte £ 44/76

Impeccably tailored hotel, opened in 2012, makes stunning use of materials like silver, mahogany, silk and marble. Luxurious bedrooms with sensual curves, sumptuous bathrooms and a great spa – and there is substance behind the style. Down a sweeping staircase to the sleek Italian restaurant.

Dinner by Heston Blumenthal - Mandarin Oriental Hyde Park Hotel
✿✿

66 Knightsbridge ✉ SW1X 7LA ⊖ Knightsbridge – ✆ (020) 7201 3833 – www.dinnerbyheston.com – Closed 2 days Christmas **37**AGX**x**

Rest – Menu £ 36 (weekday lunch) – Carte £ 50/67

Don't come expecting 'molecular gastronomy' – this is all about respect for, and a wonderful renewal of, British food, with just a little playfulness thrown in. Each one of the meticulously crafted and deceptively simple looking dishes comes with a date relating to its historical provenance.

➜ Octopus, smoked sea broth, pickled dulse and lovage. Short rib, smoked anchovy and onion, ox tongue and red wine. Brown bread ice cream, salted butter caramel, pear and malted yeast syrup.

Bar Boulud - Mandarin Oriental Hyde Park Hotel
66 Knightsbridge ✉ SW1X 7LA ⊖ Knightsbridge – ✆ (020) 7201 3899 – www.barboulud.com **37**AGX**x**

Rest – Menu £ 23 – Carte £ 22/55

Daniel Boulud's London outpost is fashionable, fun and frantic. His hometown is Lyon but he built his considerable reputation in New York, so charcuterie, sausages and burgers are the highlights.

XX **Zuma**

5 Raphael St ✉ SW7 1DL ⊖ Knightsbridge – ✆ (020) 7584 1010 – www.zumarestaurant.com – Closed 25 December **37**AFX**m**

Rest – Carte £ 20/96

Now a global brand but this was the original. The glamorous clientele come for the striking surroundings, bustling atmosphere and easy-to-share food. Head for the more modern dishes and those cooked on the robata grill.

XX **Mr Chow**

151 Knightsbridge ✉ SW1X 7PA ⊖ Knightsbridge – ✆ (020) 7589 7347 – www.mrchow.com – Closed 1 January, 24-26 December, Easter Monday dinner and Monday lunch **37**AFX**e**

Rest – Menu £ 26/50 – Carte £ 39/63

Long-standing Chinese restaurant, opened in 1968. Smart clientele, stylish and comfortable surroundings and prompt service from Italian waiters. Carefully prepared and satisfying food.

X **Chabrot**

9 Knightsbridge Grn ✉ SW1X 7QL ⊖ Knightsbridge – ✆ (020) 7225 2238 – www.chabrot.co.uk – Closed 25 December and 1 January **37**AFX**v**

Rest – Carte £ 28/50

In 2011 Thierry Laborde, formerly of Le Gavroche, got together with three friends to open this fervently French and atmospheric bistro. The kitchen looks to France's SW and Basque country for most of its influences.

Mayfair

Dorchester

Park Ln. ✉ W1K 1QA ⊖ Hyde Park Corner – ✆ (020) 7629 8888 – www.thedorchester.com **30**AHV**a**

250 rm – †£ 510/894 ††£ 510/894, ☕ £ 26 – 50 suites

Rest *Alain Ducasse at The Dorchester* ✿✿✿ **Rest *China Tang* Rest *The Grill*** – see restaurant listing

Luxury hotel on a grand scale offering every possible facility. Striking marbled and pillared promenade provides one of the best backdrops to afternoon tea. Impressive spa and bedrooms quintessentially English in style. Exemplary levels of service.

Claridge's

Brook St ✉ W1K 4HR ⊖ Bond Street – ✆ (020) 7629 8860 – www.claridges.co.uk **30**AHU**c**

203 rm – †£ 480/780 ††£ 540/900, ☕ £ 32 – 67 suites

Rest – *(booking essential)* Menu £ 35/41 – Carte £ 49/88

Rightly celebrated for its art deco detailing and one of London's finest hotels. Exceptionally well-appointed and sumptuous bedrooms, all with butler service. Magnificent Foyer for afternoon tea. Gordon Ramsay's restaurant has closed and, as we go to print, its replacement has yet to be revealed.

Connaught

Carlos Pl. ✉ W1K 2AL ⊖ Bond Street – ✆ (020) 7499 7070 – www.the-connaught.co.uk **30**AHU**e**

121 rm – †£ 300/840 ††£ 360/840, ☕ £ 30 – 26 suites

Rest *Hélène Darroze at The Connaught* ✿✿ – see restaurant listing

Rest *Espelette* – ✆ (020) 3147 7100 – Carte £ 38/66

One of London's most famous hotels; restored and renovated but still retaining an elegant British feel. All the luxurious bedrooms come with large marble bathrooms and butler service. There's a choice of two stylish bars and Espelette is an all-day venue for classic French and British dishes.

Four Seasons

Hamilton Pl, Park Ln ✉ W1J 7DR ⊖ Hyde Park Corner – ✆ (020) 7499 0888 – www.fourseasons.com/london/ **30**AHV**v**

193 rm – †£ 800/980 ††£ 800/980, ☕ £ 32 – 33 suites

Rest *Amaranto* – see restaurant listing

Reopened in 2011 after a huge refurbishment project and has raised the bar for luxury hotels. Striking lobby sets the scene; sumptuous bedrooms have a rich, contemporary look and boast every conceivable comfort. Great views from the stunning roof-top spa.

InterContinental
1 Hamilton Pl, Park Ln ✉ W1J 7QY ⊖ Hyde Park Corner – ✆ (020) 7409 3131 – www.london.intercontinental.com **30**AHV**k**
447 rm – †£ 275/790 ††£ 275/790, ☕ £ 28 – 48 suites
Rest *Theo Randall* – see restaurant listing
Rest *Cookbook Café* – Menu £ 18 – Carte £ 35/53
International hotel whose position facing the park is an impressive feature. Everything leads off from the large, open-plan lobby. English-style bedrooms with hi-tech equipment; luxurious suites. Casual, family-friendly Cookbook Café.

London Hilton
22 Park Ln. ✉ W1K 1BE ⊖ Hyde Park Corner – ✆ (020) 7493 8000 – www.hilton.co.uk/londonparklane **30**AHV**e**
453 rm – †£ 219/599 ††£ 219/599, ☕ £ 20 – 56 suites
Rest *Galvin at Windows* ✿ – see restaurant listing
Rest *Podium* – ✆ (020) 7208 4022 – Menu £ 19 – Carte £ 31/63
Rest *Trader Vic's* – ✆ (020) 7208 4113 *(dinner only)* Carte £ 33/62
The bedrooms at this 28 storey hotel, which celebrated 50 years in 2013, now come with a sharper and more contemporary edge. For Polynesian food and a Mai Tai, head to the iconic brand that is Trader's Vic's; for casual, all-day dining, try Podium. Extensive banqueting and conference facilities.

LONDON

Grosvenor House
Park Ln ✉ W1K 7TN ⊖ Marble Arch – ✆ (020) 7499 6363 – www.londongrosvenorhouse.co.uk **29**AGU**g**
494 rm – †£ 249/457 ††£ 249/457, ☕ £ 30 – 52 suites
Rest *JW Steakhouse* – ✆ (020) 7399 8460 – Menu £ 49 – Carte £ 28/72
A large, landmark property occupying a commanding position by Hyde Park. Uniform, comfortable but well proportioned bedrooms in classic Marriott styling. Busy banqueting department boasts the largest ballroom in Europe. JW Steakhouse is the place for beer, bourbon and beef.

45 Park Lane
45 Park Ln ✉ W1K 1PN ⊖ Hyde Park Corner – ✆ (020) 7493 4545 – www.45parklane.com **30**AHV**r**
36 rm – †£ 395/695 ††£ 495/945, ☕ £ 30 – 10 suites
Rest *Cut* – see restaurant listing
It was the original site of the Playboy Club and has been a car showroom but now 45 Park Lane has been reborn as The Dorchester's sister hotel. The bedrooms, all with views over Hyde Park, are wonderfully sensual and the marble bathrooms are beautiful.

Westbury
Bond St ✉ W1S 2YF ⊖ Bond Street – ✆ (020) 7629 7755 – www.westburymayfair.com **30**AIU**z**
246 rm – †£ 270/499 ††£ 270/499, ☕ £ 26 – 13 suites
Rest *Alyn Williams at The Westbury* ✿ – see restaurant listing
Rest *Tsukiji* – ✆ (020) 8382 5066 *(booking advisable)* Menu £ 23 (lunch) – Carte £ 25/38
Now as stylish as when it opened in the 1950s. Smart, comfortable bedrooms with terrific art deco inspired suites. Elegant, iconic Polo bar and bright, fresh sushi bar. All the designer brands outside the front door.

Brown's
Albemarle St ✉ W1S 4BP ⊖ Green Park – ✆ (020) 7493 6020 – www.roccofortehotels.com **30**AIV**d**
117 rm – †£ 426/1116 ††£ 426/1116, ☕ £ 25 – 12 suites
Rest *Hix Mayfair* – see restaurant listing
Opened in 1837 by James Brown, Lord Byron's butler. This urbane and very British hotel with an illustrious past offers a swish bar with Terence Donovan prints, bedrooms in neutral hues and a classic English sitting room for afternoon tea.

London Marriott H. Grosvenor Square
84-86 Duke St ✉ W1K 6JP ⊖ Bond Street – ✆ (020) 7493 1232 – www.marriottgrosvenorsquare.com **30**AHU**s**
237 rm – †£ 239/599 ††£ 239/599, ☐ £ 18 – 11 suites
Rest *Maze Grill* – see restaurant listing
A well-appointed international hotel that benefits from an excellent location in the heart of Mayfair. Bedrooms are specifically equipped for business travellers. Ask for a Balcony room: they have access to a private roof garden.

London Marriott H. Park Lane
140 Park Ln ✉ W1K 7AA ⊖ Marble Arch – ✆ (020) 7493 7000 – www.londonmarriottparklane.co.uk **29**AGU**b**
157 rm – †£ 289/409 ††£ 329/509, ☐ £ 23 – 9 suites **Rest** – Carte £ 28/59
International hotel located close to Hyde Park and the shops of Oxford Street. One of only two hotels on Park Lane with a pool. Smart, generously sized bedrooms are well-equipped; the attractive restaurant overlooks Marble Arch.

Metropolitan
Old Park Ln ✉ W1K 1LB ⊖ Hyde Park Corner – ✆ (020) 7447 1000 – www.metropolitan.como.bz **30**AHV**c**
147 rm – †£ 409 ††£ 439, ☐ £ 22 – 3 suites
Rest *Nobu* ✿ – see restaurant listing
Minimalist interior and a voguish reputation have made this hotel and its Met Bar the favoured choice of pop stars and celebrities. Sleek design and fashionably attired staff set it apart.

Athenaeum
116 Piccadilly ✉ W1J 7BJ – ✆ (020) 7499 3464 – www.athenaeumhotel.com
164 rm – †£ 239/714 ††£ 239/714, ☐ £ 28 – 28 suites **30**AHV**g**
Rest – Menu £ 19/30 – Carte £ 34/63
Refurbished 1920s building opposite the park; its stylish bedrooms come in cool pastel shades and have floor to ceiling windows. Bright restaurant and a bar offering over 270 different whiskies. The hotel also organises events for kids.

Chesterfield
35 Charles St ✉ W1J 5EB ⊖ Green Park – ✆ (020) 7491 2622 – www.chesterfieldmayfair.com **30**AHV**f**
107 rm – †£ 192/360 ††£ 216/504, ☐ £ 23 – 4 suites
Rest *Butlers* – Menu £ 22/26 – Carte £ 37/66
An assuredly English feel to this Georgian house. Discreet lobby leads to a clubby bar and wood panelled library. Individually decorated bedrooms, with some antique pieces. Intimate and pretty restaurant.

Alain Ducasse at The Dorchester – Dorchester Hotel
✿✿✿
Park Ln ✉ W1K 1QA ⊖ Hyde Park Corner – ✆ (020) 7629 8866 – www.alainducasse-dorchester.com – Closed 3 weeks August, first week January, 18-21 April, 26-30 December, Saturday lunch, Sunday and Monday
Rest – Menu £ 60/85 **30**AHV**a**
Luxury and extravagance are the hallmarks of Alain Ducasse's London outpost. The dining room is elegant without being staid; food is modern and refined yet satisfying and balanced. Service is formal, thoughtful and well-organised.
➜ Sauté of lobster, truffled chicken quenelles and pasta. Fillet of beef Rossini with Périgueux sauce. 'Baba like in Monte-Carlo'.

Sketch (The Lecture Room & Library)
✿✿
9 Conduit St (1st floor) ✉ W1S 2XG ⊖ Oxford Circus – ✆ (020) 7659 4500 – www.sketch.uk.com – Closed last 2 weeks August, Saturday lunch, Sunday and Monday **30**AIU**h**
Rest – *(booking essential)* Menu £ 35/95 – Carte £ 88/126
Pierre Gagnaire's London operation is within a striking 18C townhouse which is full of colour, energy and vitality. The sophisticated French cooking is ambitious and elaborate in conception and execution; dishes arrive artfully presented.
➜ 'Perfume of the Earth'. Challans duck. Pierre Gagnaire's 'Grand Dessert'.

XXXX ✿✿ **Hélène Darroze at The Connaught** - Connaught Hotel
Carlos Pl. ✉ W1K 2AL ⊖ Bond Street - ✆ (020) 3147 7200 - www.the-connaught.co.uk - Closed 2 weeks August, 2 weeks January, Sunday and Monday **30**AHU **e**
Rest - *(booking essential)* Menu £ 35/85
Landes and the SW of France inform Hélène Darroze's exquisite cooking, although international influences also play a part. Service is courteous and the dining room is elegant and comfortable, with original mahogany wood panelling.
➜ Duck foie gras with Yorkshire rhubarb chutney and lemon verbena jelly. XXL scallop with tandoori spices, confit carrot and citrus mousseline. Manjari chocolate, ganache and galangal crème brûlée.

XXXX ✿✿ **Le Gavroche** (Michel Roux Jnr)
43 Upper Brook St ✉ W1K 7QR ⊖ Marble Arch - ✆ (020) 7408 0881 - www.le-gavroche.co.uk - Closed Christmas, January, Saturday lunch, Sunday and bank holidays **29**AGU **c**
Rest - *(booking essential)* Menu £ 54/115 - Carte £ 61/156
Classical, rich and indulgent French cuisine is the draw at Michel Roux's renowned London institution. The large, smart basement room has a clubby, masculine feel; service is formal and structured but also has charm.
➜ Mousseline de homard au champagne et caviar. Râble de lapin et galette au parmesan. Palet au chocolat amer et praline croustillant.

LONDON

XXXX ✿✿ **Square** (Philip Howard)
6-10 Bruton St. ✉ W1J 6PU ⊖ Green Park - ✆ (020) 7495 7100 - www.squarerestaurant.com - Closed 24-26 December and Sunday lunch
Rest - Menu £ 35/80 **30**AIU **v**
Confident and accomplished kitchen which understands the importance of sound techniques, prime ingredients and clarity of flavour. The room is comfortable and the buoyant atmosphere prevents things becoming too formal. Good cheeseboard and wine list, which is rooted in the Old World.
➜ Lasagne of crab with a cappuccino of shellfish and champagne foam. Roast leg of lamb with a Jerusalem artichoke gratin. Banana soufflé with milk and granola ice cream.

XXXX ✿ **Alyn Williams at The Westbury** - Westbury Hotel
Bond St ✉ W1S 2YF ⊖ Bond Street - ✆ (020) 7183 6426 - www.alynwilliams.co.uk - Closed Saturday lunch and Sunday **30**AIU **z**
Rest - Menu £ 25/60
Confident, cheery service ensures the atmosphere never strays into terminal seriousness; rosewood panelling and a striking wine display add warmth. The cooking is creative and even playful but however elaborately constructed the dish, the combinations of flavours and textures always work.
➜ Foie gras semifreddo with liquorice and salted hazelnut caramel. Sea bass, grilled lobster, lemon gnocchi and beach vegetables. Banana baba, rum cream and caramelised banana ice cream.

XXXX **China Tang** - Dorchester Hotel
Park Ln ✉ W1K 1QA ⊖ Hyde Park Corner - ✆ (020) 7629 9988 - www.chinatanglondon.co.uk - Closed 25 December **30**AHV **a**
Rest - Menu £ 23 (lunch) - Carte £ 28/79
Sir David Tang's atmospheric, art deco-inspired Chinese restaurant, downstairs at The Dorchester, is always abuzz with activity. Be sure to see the terrific bar, before sharing the traditional Cantonese specialities.

XXX ✿✿ **Greenhouse**
27a Hay's Mews ✉ W1J 5NY ⊖ Hyde Park Corner - ✆ (020) 7499 3331 - www.greenhouserestaurant.co.uk - Closed Saturday lunch, Sunday and bank holidays **30**AHV **m**
Rest - Menu £ 29/110 - Carte £ 80/100
Chef Arnaud Bignon's cooking is confident, balanced and innovative and uses the best from Europe's larder; his dishes exude an exhilarating freshness. The breadth and depth of the wine list is astounding. This is a discreet, sleek and contemporary restaurant with well-judged service.
➜ Cornish crab with mint jelly, cauliflower, apple and curry. Milk-fed veal with Swiss chard, sage and galangal. Orange, saffron, date and filo pastry.

XXX **Cut** – 45 Park Lane Hotel
45 Park Ln ✉ W1K 1PN ⊖ Hyde Park Corner – ✆ (020) 7493 4545 – www.45parklane.com **30**AHV**r**
Rest – *(booking essential)* Menu £ 35 (weekday lunch) – Carte £ 43/124
The first European venture from Wolfgang Puck, the US-based Austrian celebrity chef, is this very slick, stylish and sexy room where glamorous people come to eat meat. The not-inexpensive steaks are cooked over hardwood and charcoal and finished off in a broiler.

XXX **Hibiscus** (Claude Bosi)
✿✿ *29 Maddox St ✉ W1S 2PA ⊖ Oxford Circus – ✆ (020) 7629 2999 – www.hibiscusrestaurant.co.uk – Closed 21 December-7 January, Monday except October-December, Sunday and bank holidays* **30**AIU**s**
Rest – Menu £ 35/88
To best experience Clause Bosi's creative and original cooking, choose 3, 6 or 9 courses and create your own menu from the best of that day's ingredients – or simply let the kitchen decide for you. A new look makes the dining room feel brighter and bigger and has also lightened the atmosphere.
➜ Scallops with an apple and hazelnut crust, pork pie sauce. Sea bream stuffed with morel mushrooms and kaffir lime, morel and coffee fricassee. Hibiscus tarte au chocolate, Indonesian basil ice cream.

XXX **Murano** (Angela Hartnett)
✿ *20 Queen St ✉ W1J 5PP ⊖ Green Park – ✆ (020) 7495 1127 – www.angela-hartnett.com – Closed Christmas and Sunday* **30**AHV**b**
Rest – Menu £ 25/85
Angela Hartnett's Italian influenced cooking exhibits an appealing lightness of touch, with assured combinations of flavours, borne out of confidence in the ingredients. This is a stylish and elegant room with an appealingly fresh feel.
➜ Pumpkin tortelli, sage butter and crushed amaretti. Monkfish with broccoli purée and chicken jus. Rice pudding soufflé with rum and raisin ice cream.

XXX **Galvin at Windows** – London Hilton Hotel
✿ *22 Park Ln (28th floor) ✉ W1K 1BE ⊖ Hyde Park Corner – ✆ (020) 7208 4021 – www.galvinatwindows.com – Closed Saturday lunch and Sunday dinner*
Rest – Menu £ 29/68 **30**AHV**e**
Spectacular views from the 28th floor of the Hilton are not the only draw. The room is contemporary and cleverly laid out; service is attentive and efficient; cooking is confident and detailed and dishes balanced and satisfying.
➜ Scallops with cauliflower and mango chutney. Loin of mutton, onion textures and mini shepherd's pie. Banana soufflé, chocolate and caramelised peanut.

XXX **Benares** (Atul Kochhar)
✿ *12a Berkeley Square House ✉ W1J 6BS ⊖ Green Park – ✆ (020) 7629 8886 – www.benaresrestaurant.com – Closed 24-26 December and 1-2 January*
Rest – Menu £ 35 – Carte £ 45/96 **30**AIU**q**
Modern techniques are used to add contemporary touches to the classical base; the inventive Indian food here continues to evolve. The smart first-floor surroundings match the food in their sophistication. Popular and smart Chef's Table.
➜ Tandoori Ratan. Cod with coconut and curry leaf. Rose and raspberry bhapa doi.

XXX **Tamarind**
✿ *20 Queen St. ✉ W1J 5PR ⊖ Green Park – ✆ (020) 7629 3561 – www.tamarindrestaurant.com – Closed 25-26 December, 1 January and Saturday lunch* **30**AHV**h**
Rest – Menu £ 20/68 – Carte £ 35/60
Makes the best use of its basement location through smoked mirrors, gilded columns and a somewhat exclusive feel. The appealing and enjoyable Indian food is mostly traditionally based; kebabs and curries are the specialities, complemented by carefully judged vegetable dishes.
➜ Scallops with star anise and smoked tomato chutney. Hyderabadi lamb shank with turmeric, yoghurt and browned garlic. Dark chocolate mousse with cinnamon.

LONDON

XXX **Kai**

65 South Audley St ✉ W1K 2QU ⊖ Hyde Park Corner – ✆ (020) 7493 8988 – www.kaimayfair.co.uk – Closed 25-26 December and 1 January **30AHVn**

Rest – *(booking essential)* Menu £ 27 (lunch) – Carte £ 39/90

Carefully prepared Chinese food, from a menu that mixes the classics with more innovative dishes; flavours are authentic and assured. Its smart surroundings are spread over two floors - ask for the ground floor; sweet natured service.

➜ Braised abalone with broccolini. Chilean sea bass with black vinegar syrup. Mango cake, palm sugar ice cream and pandan milkshake.

XXX **Cecconi's**

5a Burlington Gdns ✉ W1S 3EP ⊖ Green Park – ✆ (020) 7434 1500 – www.cecconis.com **30AIUd**

Rest – *(booking essential)* Carte £ 40/49

Branches of this fashionable restaurant are now opening up around the world. Regulars pop in for a bite at the bar; the restaurant prepares the classic dishes with care. Open from breakfast onwards; popular for weekend brunches.

XXX **34**

34 Grosvenor Sq (entrance on South Audley St) ✉ W1K 2HD ⊖ Marble Arch – ✆ (020) 3350 3434 – www.34-restaurant.co.uk/ – Closed 25-26 December

Rest – Carte £ 31/100 **30AHUb**

A wonderful mix of art deco style and Edwardian warmth makes it feel like a glamorous brasserie. Parrilla grill used for beef – a mix of Scottish dry-aged, US prime, organic Argentinian and Australian Wagyu – as well as fish and game.

XXX **The Grill** – Dorchester Hotel

Park Ln. ✉ W1K 1QA ⊖ Hyde Park Corner – ✆ (020) 7629 8888 – www.thedorchester.com **30AHVa**

Rest – Menu £ 27/55 – Carte £ 42/64

A bastion of Britishness, where timeless classics are served alongside more modern creations. The extravagantly kitted out room, bedecked in acres of tartans, is even more memorable.

XXX **Bentley's (Grill)**

11-15 Swallow St. ✉ W1B 4DG ⊖ Piccadilly Circus – ✆ (020) 7734 4756 – www.bentleys.org – Closed 25-26 December and 1 January **30AJUc**

Rest – Menu £ 26 (weekday dinner) – Carte £ 26/63

Entrance into striking bar; panelled staircase to richly decorated restaurant. Carefully sourced seafood or meat dishes enhanced by clean, crisp cooking. Unruffled service.

XXX **Theo Randall** – Intercontinental Hotel

1 Hamilton Pl, Park Ln ✉ W1J 7QY ⊖ Hyde Park Corner – ✆ (020) 7318 8747 – www.theorandall.com – Closed 25-26 December, 1 January, Saturday lunch, Sunday and bank holidays **30AHVk**

Rest – Menu £ 27/33 – Carte £ 45/65

Expect simple, flavoursome and seasonal Italian dishes from the former head chef of the River Café. The pleasingly rustic nature of the food is somewhat at odds with the formal service and the corporate feel of the dining room.

XXX **Scott's**

20 Mount St ✉ W1K 2HE ⊖ Bond Street – ✆ (020) 7495 7309 – www.scotts-restaurant.com – Closed 25-26 December and 1 January

Rest – Carte £ 34/55 **30AHUd**

Stylish yet traditional and one of London's most fashionable addresses, so getting a table can be tricky. Oak panelling is juxtaposed with vibrant artwork from young British artists. Enticing choice of top quality fish and shellfish.

XXX **Corrigan's Mayfair**

28 Upper Grosvenor St. ✉ W1K 7EH ⊖ Marble Arch – ✆ (020) 7499 9943 – www.corrigansmayfair.com – Closed 25-26 December, 1 January and Saturday lunch **29AGUa**

Rest – Menu £ 25 (weekday lunch) – Carte £ 46/83

Richard Corrigan's flagship celebrates British and Irish cooking, with game a speciality. The room is comfortable, clubby and quite glamorous and feels as though it has been around for years.

LONDON

XXX **Sartoria**

20 Savile Row ✉ W1S 3PR ⊖ Green Park – ✆ (020) 7534 7000 – www.sartoria-restaurant.co.uk – Closed 25 December, Saturday lunch, Sunday and bank holidays **30**AIU **b**

Rest – Menu £ 21 – Carte £ 31/55

In the street renowned for English tailoring, a coolly sophisticated and stylish restaurant to suit those looking for classic Italian cooking with some modern touches thrown in. It also comes with confident service.

XXX **Hix Mayfair** – Brown's Hotel

Albemarle St ✉ W1S 4BP ⊖ Green Park – ✆ (020) 7518 4004 – www.roccofortecollection.com **30**AIV **d**

Rest – Menu £ 28/33 – Carte £ 31/63

This wood-panelled dining room is lightened with the work of current British artists. Mark Hix's well-sourced menu of British classics will appeal to the hunter-gatherer in every man.

XXX **Amaranto** – Four Seasons Hotel

Hamilton Pl, Park Ln ✉ W1J 7DR ⊖ Hyde Park Corner – ✆ (020) 7499 0888 – www.fourseasons.com/london/dining **30**AHV **v**

Rest – Menu £ 20/26 – Carte £ 31/70

It's all about flexibility as the Italian influenced menu is served in the stylish bar or comfortable lounge, on the great terrace or in the restaurant decorated in the vivid colours of the amaranth plant.

XX **Wild Honey**

✿ *12 St George St. ✉ W1S 2FB ⊖ Oxford Circus – ✆ (020) 7758 9160 – www.wildhoneyrestaurant.co.uk – Closed 25-26 December and 1 January* **30**AIU **w**

Rest – Menu £ 27/30 (weekdays) – Carte £ 35/51

Skilled kitchen uses seasonal ingredients at their peak to create dishes full of flavour and free from ostentation. Attractive oak-panelled room; personable and unobtrusive service adds to the relaxed feel.

➜ Scottish crab, guacamole and green mango. Roast chicken with new season morels and potato gnocchi. Wild honey ice cream and honeycomb.

XX **Brasserie Chavot** Ⓝ

✿ *41 Conduit St ✉ W1S 2YQ ⊖ Bond Street – ✆ (020) 7183 6425 – www.brasseriechavot.com – Closed 25-26 December* **30**AIU **z**

Rest – Carte £ 30/45

Mosaic flooring, smoked mirrors, red leather seats and sparkling chandeliers add style; a satisfied buzz and great service make it fun. Eric Chavot's ability is obvious in his hearteningly rustic, refreshingly unfussy and hugely enjoyable French classics.

➜ Crab mayonnaise with avocado. Canette à l'orange and caramelised endive. Baba au rhum with crème Chantilly.

XX **Hawksmoor** Ⓝ

5A Air St ✉ W1B 4EA ⊖ Piccadilly Circus – ✆ (020) 7406 3980 – www.thehawksmoor.com/airstreet – Closed 25-26 December **30**AJU **m**

Rest – *(booking advisable)* Menu £ 23/26 – Carte £ 31/54

The best of the Hawksmoors is large, boisterous and has an appealing art deco feel. Expect top quality, 35-day aged Longhorn beef but also great seafood, much of which is charcoal grilled. The delightful staff are well organised.

XX **Momo**

25 Heddon St. ✉ W1B 4BH ⊖ Oxford Circus – ✆ (020) 7434 4040 – www.momoresto.com – Closed 25 December, 1 January and Sunday lunch

Rest – Menu £ 20/52 – Carte £ 31/47 **30**AIU **n**

Lanterns, rugs, trinkets and music contribute to the authentic Moroccan atmosphere; come in a group to better appreciate it. The more traditional dishes are the kitchen's strength.

XX **Pollen Street Social** (Jason Atherton)

8-10 Pollen St ✉ W1S 1NQ ⊖ Oxford Circus – ✆ (020) 7290 7600 – www.pollenstreetsocial.com – Closed 25-26 December, 1-2 January, Sunday and bank holidays **30AIU u**

Rest – *(booking essential)* Menu £ 30 (lunch) – Carte £ 51/64

Jason Atherton's cooking marries innovation and imagination with skilful technique and an innate understanding of good ingredients. Dishes are elaborately constructed but there are never too many flavours. The room is smoothly run but not overly formal. Try their terrific version of a Negroni.

➜ Roasted quail 'brunch' cereals, toast and tea. Salt marsh lamb with Jerusalem artichoke and spiced aubergine. Peanut parfait, cherry yuzu sorbet and nitro peanut.

XX **Hakkasan Mayfair**

17 Bruton St ✉ W1J 6QB ⊖ Green Park – ✆ (020) 7907 1888 – www.hakkasan.com – Closed 25 December **30AIU l**

Rest – *(booking essential)* Carte £ 32/74 **s**

Less a copy, more a sister to the original; a sister who's just as fun but lives in a nicer part of town. This one has a funky, more casual ground floor to go with the downstairs dining room. You can expect the same extensive choice of top quality, modern Cantonese cuisine; dim sum is a highlight.

➜ Crispy duck salad with pomelo, pine nut and shallot. Roasted silver cod with champagne and honey. Hazelnut Jivara bomb with dark chocolate sauce.

LONDON

XX **Bo London** N

4 Mill St ✉ W1S 2AX ⊖ Oxford Circus – ✆ (020) 7493 3886 – www.bolondonrestaurant.com – Closed 24-26 December, Saturday lunch and Sunday **30AIU f**

Rest – Menu £ 27/138

Having made his name in Hong Kong with his 'X-treme Chinese' cuisine, Alvin Leung returned to the city of his birth to open Bo London. His cooking is celebrated for giving traditional Chinese flavours a modern interpretation – here he goes a stage further by taking inspiration from British cuisine.

➜ Sichuan butter poached lobster, roasted corn and peas. Pigeon in an aromatic bouillon, potato and chive jiaozi. 'Beans on toast'- red beans and butter toast ice cream.

XX **Nobu Berkeley St**

15 Berkeley St. ✉ W1J 8DY ⊖ Green Park – ✆ (020) 7290 9222 – www.noburestaurants.com – Closed 25 December, 1 January and lunch Saturday and Sunday **30AIV b**

Rest – *(booking essential)* Menu £ 35/90 – Carte £ 34/73

Offers all the innovative Nobu favourites, along with specialities from the wood oven. Large, lively but smoothly run first floor operation with plenty of glamour; ground floor destination bar. Helpful, well-informed service.

➜ Yellowtail sashimi with jalapeño dressing. Black cod with miso. Chocolate tart with sake kasu ice cream.

XX **Coya** N

118 Piccadilly ✉ W1J 7NW ⊖ Hyde Park Corner – ✆ (020) 7042 7118 – www.coyarestaurant.com – Closed 25 December **30AHV d**

Rest – *(booking advisable)* Menu £ 27 (lunch) – Carte £ 33/53

From the people behind Zuma and Roka comes this lively, loud and enthusiastically run basement restaurant that celebrates all things Peruvian. Try their ceviche and their skewers, as well as their Pisco Sours in the fun bar.

XX **La Petite Maison** N

54 Brooks Mews ✉ W1K 4EG ⊖ Bond Street – ✆ (020) 7495 4774 – www.lpmlondon.co.uk – Closed Christmas-New Year **30AHU m**

Rest – *(booking essential)* Carte £ 31/62 **s**

A little piece of southern France and Ligurian Italy in Mayfair. The slickly run sister to the Nice original has a buzzy, glamorous feel, with prices to match. Just reading the menus of Mediterranean dishes will improve your tan.

XX ✿ **Umu**

14-16 Bruton Pl. ✉ W1J 6LX ⊖ Bond Street – ✆ (020) 7499 8881 – www.umurestaurant.com – Closed Saturday lunch, Sunday and bank holidays

Rest – Menu £ 25/100 – Carte £ 48/122 **30AIUk**

Stylish, discreet interior using natural materials, with central sushi bar. Extensive choice of Japanese dishes; choose one of the seasonal kaiseki menus for the full experience. Over 160 different labels of sake.

➜ Sake-cured Scottish langoustine and tomato jelly. Wood pigeon, enoki sauce and pumpkin purée. Mikan cake with sansho ice cream, Earl Grey tea jam and pomelo.

XX ✿ **Nobu** – Metropolitan Hotel

19 Old Park Ln ✉ W1Y 1LB ⊖ Hyde Park Corner – ✆ (020) 7447 4747 – www.noburestaurants.com **30AHVc**

Rest – *(booking essential)* Menu £ 35 – Carte £ 29/78

Its celebrity clientele ensure this remains one of London's more glamorous spots. Staff are fully conversant in the innovative menu that adds South American influences to Japanese cooking. Has spawned many imitators around the world.

➜ Rock shrimp ceviche. Snow crab with spicy sauce. Chocolate bento box.

XX ✿ **Maze**

10-13 Grosvenor Sq ✉ W1K 6JP ⊖ Bond Street – ✆ (020) 7107 0000 – www.gordonramsay.com/maze **30AHUz**

Rest – Menu £ 25 (lunch) – Carte £ 32/44

Choose a variety of small but expertly formed dishes at this sleek and stylish David Rockwell designed restaurant from the Gordon Ramsay stable. The cooking is contemporary and nicely balanced; four dishes per person should suffice.

➜ Beef fillet tataki, wakame seaweed, pickled onion and ginger. Lobster, tiger prawn and salmon dumpling in a lemongrass broth. Lemon tart with toasted meringue and crème fraîche sorbet.

XX **Maze Grill** – London Marriott Hotel Grosvenor Square

10-13 Grosvenor Sq ✉ W1K 6JP ⊖ Bond Street – ✆ (020) 7495 2211 – www.gordonramsay.com/mazegrill **30AHUs**

Rest – Menu £ 24 (lunch and early dinner) – Carte £ 27/73

An addendum to Maze, with a menu specialising in steaks, from Hereford grass-fed to Wagyu 9th grade; all appealingly served on wooden boards. Individually priced side dishes and sauces can push the bill up.

XX **Goodman**

26 Maddox St ✉ W1S 1QH ⊖ Oxford Circus – ✆ (020) 7499 3776 – www.goodmanrestaurants.com – Closed Sunday and bank holidays

Rest – *(booking essential)* Carte £ 26/73 **30AIUu**

A worthy attempt at recreating a New York steakhouse; all leather and wood and macho swagger. Beef is dry or wet aged in-house and comes with a choice of four sauces; rib-eye the speciality.

XX **Sketch (The Gallery)**

9 Conduit St ✉ W1S 2XG ⊖ Oxford Circus – ✆ (020) 7659 4500 – www.sketch.uk.com – Closed 25-26 December **30AIUh**

Rest – *(dinner only) (booking essential)* Carte £ 37/73

Martin Creed was the artist charged with changing the look of The Gallery and he's made it a vibrant, witty and provocative space. The menus have also been updated and are a mix of original dishes and updated brasserie classics.

XX **Aurelia**

13-14 Cork St ✉ W1S 3NS ⊖ Green Park – ✆ (020) 7409 1370 – www.aurelialondon.co.uk – Closed Sunday dinner **30AIUm**

Rest – Menu £ 25 – Carte £ 27/78

The Roman road that stretched from Rome through southern France and into Spain provides the culinary inspiration. Highlights are meats cooked on the rotisserie. The atmosphere and the aromas are more enticing downstairs.

LONDON

XX **Alloro**

19-20 Dover St ✉ W1S 4LU ⊖ Green Park – ✆ (020) 7495 4768 – www.atozrestaurants.com/alloro – Closed 25 December, Saturday lunch and Sunday

Rest – *(booking essential)* Menu £ 35/45 **30**AIV**r**

Confidently run and smartly dressed Italian with an appealing menu of easy-to-eat dishes; breads and pasta are made in-house. Great atmosphere, especially at busy lunchtimes. Boisterous adjacent baretto.

XX **Hush**

8 Lancashire Ct., Brook St. ✉ W1S 1EY ⊖ Bond Street – ✆ (020) 7659 1500 – www.hush.co.uk – Closed Easter, 25-26 December, 1 January and Sunday

Rest – *(booking essential)* Menu £ 13 (lunch) – Carte £ 23/48 **30**AHU**v**

Appealing and all-purpose European brasserie-style menu served in a busy room with smart destination bar upstairs and plenty of private dining. Tucked away in a charming courtyard, with a pleasant summer terrace.

XX **Mews of Mayfair**

10-11 Lancashire Ct, Brook St, (1st floor) ✉ W1S 1EY ⊖ Bond Street – ✆ (020) 7518 9388 – www.mewsofmayfair.com – Closed 25 December and Sunday dinner

Rest – Carte £ 20/72 **30**AHU**a**

This pretty restaurant, bright in summer and warm in winter, is on the first floor of a mews house, once used as storage rooms for Savile Row. Seasonal menus offer something for everyone.

XX **Sumosan**

26 Albemarle St. ✉ W1S 4HY ⊖ Green Park – ✆ (020) 7495 5999 – www.sumosan.com – Closed lunch Saturday-Sunday and bank holidays

Rest – Menu £ 25 (weekday lunch)/75 – Carte £ 20/101 **30**AIU**e**

Its modern Japanese food and stylish surroundings have been attracting a glamorous crowd for over a decade. The produce is of unimpeachable quality, there's plenty of choice and the kitchen knows how to make a dish look good.

XX **Veeraswamy**

Victory House, 99 Regent St, (entrance on Swallow St.) ✉ W1B 4RS ⊖ Piccadilly Circus – ✆ (020) 7734 1401 – www.realindianfood.com

Rest – Menu £ 18/45 – Carte £ 36/64 **30**AIU**t**

May have opened back in 1926 but this Indian restaurant feels fresh and is awash with vibrant colours and always full of bustle. Skilled kitchen cleverly mixes the traditional with more contemporary creations.

XX **Kiku**

17 Half Moon St. ✉ W1J 7BE ⊖ Green Park – ✆ (020) 7499 4208 – www.kikurestaurant.co.uk – Closed 25-27 December, 1 January, Sunday and lunch on bank holidays **30**AIV**g**

Rest – Menu £ 20/25 – Carte £ 21/84

For over 35 years this earnestly run, authentically styled, family owned restaurant has been providing every style of Japanese cuisine to its homesick Japanese customers, from shabu shabu to sukiyaki, yakitori to teriyaki.

XX **Cafe at Sotheby's**

34-35 New Bond St. ✉ W1A 2AA ⊖ Bond Street – ✆ (020) 7293 5077 – www.sothebys.com/cafe – Closed 3 weeks August, Christmas and New Year, Saturday, Sunday and bank holidays **30**AIU**y**

Rest – *(lunch only) (booking essential)* Carte £ 26/38 **s**

Occupying a cosy space just off the foyer of the famous auction house. The appealing lunch menu changes weekly; the lobster sandwich is a perennial favourite. Service is discreet.

X **Bentley's (Oyster Bar)**

11-15 Swallow St ✉ W1B 4DG ⊖ Piccadilly Circus – ✆ (020) 7734 4756 – www.bentleys.org – Closed 25-26 December and 1 January **30**AJU**c**

Rest – Menu £ 26 (lunch) – Carte £ 26/63

Sit at the counter to watch white-jacketed staff open oysters by the bucket load. Interesting seafood menus feature tasty fish pies; lots of daily specials on blackboard.

LONDON

Le Boudin Blanc

5 Trebeck St ✉ W1J 7LT ⊖ Green Park – ✆ (020) 7499 3292
– www.boudinblanc.co.uk – Closed 24-26 December **30**AHV**q**
Rest – Carte £ 27/56
Appealing, lively French bistro in Shepherd Market, spread over two floors. Satisfying French classics and country cooking is the draw, along with authentic Gallic service. Good value lunch menu.

Little Social

5 Pollen St ✉ W1S 1NE ⊖ Oxford Circus – ✆ (020) 7870 3730
– www.littlesocial.co.uk – Closed Sunday and bank holidays **30**AIU**r**
Rest – *(booking essential)* Menu £ 25 (lunch) – Carte £ 33/41
Jason Atherton's lively French bistro, opposite his Pollen Street Social restaurant, has a clubby feel and an appealing, deliberately worn look. Service is breezy and capable and the food is mostly classic with the odd modern twist.

Great British

14 North Audley St ✉ W1K 6WE ⊖ Marble Arch – ✆ (020) 7741 2233
– www.eatbrit.com – Closed 25 December, 1 January and Sunday dinner
Rest – Menu £ 16 (weekday dinner) – Carte £ 27/40 **29**AGU**e**
As the name suggests, it waves the Union Flag in this most British of London districts. Sausages come with bubble and squeak, fish and chips with curry sauce, and apple crumble with 'proper' custard. They do a great breakfast too.

Automat

33 Dover St. ✉ W1S 4NF ⊖ Green Park – ✆ (020) 7499 3033
– www.automat-london.com – Closed 25 December and 1 January
Rest – Menu £ 33/49 – Carte £ 23/47 **30**AIV**r**
A fun, noisy, New York style brassiere in very British Mayfair. Head straight for what Uncle Sam does best: crab cake, burger, mac 'n' cheese and pecan pie; and ask to sit in the lively room at the back with the open kitchen.

Only Running Footman

5 Charles St ✉ W1J 5DF ⊖ Green Park. – ✆ (020) 7499 2988
– www.therunningfootmanmayfair.com **30**AHV**x**
Rest – Carte £ 24/39
Busy ground floor bar with its appealing menu of pub classics doesn't take bookings. By contrast, upstairs is formal and its menu more European and ambitious but simpler dishes still the best.

Burger & Lobster

29 Clarges St ✉ W1J 7EF ⊖ Green Park. – ✆ (020) 7409 1699
– www.burgerandlobster.com – Closed Christmas and bank holidays
Rest – *(bookings not accepted)* Menu £ 20 **30**AIV**v**
Choose a burger, a lobster or a lobster roll, with chips, salad and sauces, and mousse for dessert – an ingeniously simple idea. The lobsters are Canadian and the burgers 10oz. It's a well organised bunfight in an old pub.

Regent's Park and Marylebone

The Landmark London

222 Marylebone Rd ✉ NW1 6JQ ⊖ Edgware Road – ✆ (020) 7631 8000
– www.landmarklondon.co.uk **29**AFT**a**
291 rm – †£ 276/780 ††£ 276/780, ☕ £ 29 – 9 suites
Rest ***Winter Garden*** – see restaurant listing
Imposing Victorian Gothic building with a vast glass-enclosed atrium, overlooked by many of the modern, well-equipped bedrooms. Choice of relaxed wood panelled cellar bar or more sophisticated Mirror bar.

Langham

1c Portland Pl., Regent St. ✉ W1B 1JA ⊖ Oxford Circus – ✆ (020) 7636 1000
– www.langhamhotels.com **30**AIT**n**
380 rm – †£ 288/852 ††£ 288/852, ☕ £ 30 – 25 suites
Rest ***Roux at The Landau*** – see restaurant listing
Was one of Europe's first purpose-built grand hotels when it opened in 1865. Now back to its best, with its famous Palm Court for afternoon tea, the stylish Artesian bar and bedrooms that are not without personality and elegance.

LONDON

Hyatt Regency London-The Churchill
rm,

30 Portman Sq ✉ *W1H 7BH* ⊖ *Marble Arch* – ✆ *(020) 7486 5800* – *www.london.churchill.hyatt.com* **29**AGT**x**

434 rm – †£ 240/600 ††£ 240/600, ☕ £ 27.50 – 47 suites

Rest *The Montagu* – ✆ (020) 7299 2037 – Menu £ 25 – Carte £ 24/60

Smart well-located property whose best bedrooms overlook the attractive square opposite. Elegant marbled lobby with plenty of staff. Well-appointed and refurbished bedrooms have the international traveller in mind. A British menu and afternoon tea served in The Montagu.

Charlotte Street

15 Charlotte St ✉ *W1T 1RJ* ⊖ *Goodge Street* – ✆ *(020) 7806 2000* – *www.charlottestreethotel.co.uk* **31**AJT**e**

52 rm – †£ 300 ††£ 300, ☕ £ 18 – 4 suites

Rest *Oscar* – ✆ (020) 7907 4005 – Menu £ 23 – Carte £ 31/55

Stylish interior designed with a charming, understated English feel. Impeccably kept and individually decorated bedrooms. Popular in-house screening room. Colourful restaurant whose terrace spills onto Charlotte Street; grilled meats a highlight.

LONDON

Sanderson

50 Berners St ✉ *W1T 3NG* ⊖ *Oxford Circus* – ✆ *(020) 7300 1400* – *www.morganshotelgroup.com* **31**AJT**c**

150 rm – †£ 276/960 ††£ 288/960, ☕ £ 25

Rest *Suka* – see restaurant listing

Designed by Philippe Starck and still attracting a suitably fashionable crowd. Purple Bar dark and moody; Long Bar bright and stylish. Pure white bedrooms with idiosyncratic design touches such as a framed picture...on the ceiling.

Arch
rm,

50 Great Cumberland Pl ✉ *W1H 7FD* ⊖ *Marble Arch* – ✆ *(020) 7724 4700* – *www.thearchlondon.com* **29**AGT**a**

80 rm – †£ 246/360 ††£ 246/360, ☕ £ 22 – 2 suites

Rest *Hunter 486* – ✆ (020) 207 724 0486 – Menu £ 15 (lunch) – Carte £ 22/58

Fashioned out of a row of seven terrace houses and two mews cottages. Plenty of extras and thoughtful touches are found in the comfortable bedrooms. Interesting pieces of art throughout. Casual restaurant doubles as a bar.

Montcalm
rm,

34-40 Great Cumberland Pl. ✉ *W1H 7TW* ⊖ *Marble Arch* – ✆ *(020) 7402 4288* – *www.montcalm.co.uk* **29**AGU**m**

126 rm – †£ 360 ††£ 360/720, ☕ £ 20 – 17 suites

Rest *Grill at the Montcalm* – Menu £ 20 – Carte £ 27/47

Named after an 18C French general, The Montcalm forms part of a crescent of townhouses with a Georgian façade. A top-to-toe refurbishment has created smart and contemporary bedrooms in lively colours. Seasonal British dishes served in Grill at the Montcalm.

Durrants
rest,

26-32 George St ✉ *W1H 5BJ* ⊖ *Bond Street* – ✆ *(020) 7935 8131* – *www.durrantshotel.co.uk* **29**AGT**e**

89 rm – †£ 185 ††£ 240/340, ☕ £ 23 – 3 suites

Rest – *(closed dinner 25 December)* Menu £ 25/35 – Carte £ 32/49

Traditional, privately owned hotel with friendly, long-standing staff. Bedrooms are now brighter in style but still retain a certain English character. Clubby dining room for mix of British classics and lighter, European dishes.

Dorset Square

39-40 Dorset Sq ✉ *NW1 6QN* ⊖ *Marylebone* – ✆ *(020) 7723 7874* – *www.dorsetsquarehotel.co.uk* **17**QZD**s**

38 rm – †£ 195 ††£ 260, ☕ £ 15

Rest *Potting Shed* – Carte £ 23/44

Having reacquired this Regency townhouse, Firmdale refurbished it fully before reopening it in 2012. It has a contemporary yet intimate feel and visiting MCC members will appreciate the cricketing theme, which even extends to the cocktails in their sweet little basement brasserie.

LONDON

Marble Arch by Montcalm without rest

31 Great Cumberland Pl. ✉ W1H 7TA ⊖ Marble Arch – ✆ (020) 7258 0777 – www.themarblearch.co.uk **29AGUs**

42 rm – †£ 173/204 ††£ 204/312, ☕ £ 20

Bedrooms at this 5-storey Georgian townhouse come with the same high standards of stylish, contemporary design as its parent hotel opposite, the Montcalm, but are just a little more compact.

Mandeville

Mandeville Pl ✉ W1U 2BE ⊖ Bond Street – ✆ (020) 7935 5599 – www.mandeville.co.uk **30AHTx**

142 rm – †£ 438 ††£ 462/558, ☕ £ 22.50 – 2 suites

Rest *Reform Social & Grill* – ✆ (020) 7935 5599 – Carte £ 25/41

Usefully located hotel with marbled reception leading into a very colourful and comfortable bar. Stylish rooms have flatscreen TVs and make good use of the space available. Modern British cuisine served in bright restaurant.

No. Ten Manchester Street

10 Manchester St ✉ W1U 4DG ⊖ Baker Street – ✆ (020) 7317 5900 – www.tenmanchesterstreethotel.com **29AGTv**

54 rm – †£ 155/315 ††£ 155/315, ☕ £ 19 – 9 suites

Rest – Menu £ 45 – Carte £ 30/62

Converted Edwardian house in an appealing, central location. Discreet entrance leads into stylish little lounge; semi-enclosed cigar bar also a feature. Neat and well-kept bedrooms.

Sumner without rest

54 Upper Berkeley St ✉ W1H 7QR ⊖ Marble Arch – ✆ (020) 7723 2244 – www.thesumner.com **29AFUk**

19 rm ☕ – †£ 150/270 ††£ 150/270

Two Georgian terrace houses in central location. Comfy, stylish sitting room; basement breakfast room. Largest bedrooms, 101 and 201, benefit from having full-length windows.

Hart House without rest

51 Gloucester Pl ✉ W1U 8JF ⊖ Marble Arch – ✆ (020) 7935 2288 – www.harthouse.co.uk **29AGTd**

15 rm ☕ – †£ 98/145 ††£ 145/195

Within an attractive Georgian terrace and run by the same family for over 35 years. Warm and welcoming service; well-kept, competitively priced bedrooms over three floors.

Locanda Locatelli

XXX ✿

8 Seymour St. ✉ W1H 7JZ ⊖ Marble Arch – ✆ (020) 7935 9088 – www.locandalocatelli.com – Closed 25-26 December and 1 January **29AGUr**

Rest – Carte £ 29/61

Giorgio Locatelli's slick and dapper-looking Italian comes with a celebrity following and a sophisticated atmosphere. Plenty of appealing dishes on the extensive menu, with cooking that is confident, balanced and expertly rendered; pastas and desserts are the stand-out courses.

➜ Scallops, celeriac purée and saffron vinaigrette. Wild sea bass baked in salt and herb crust, escarole, sultanas and pine kernels. Tasting of Amedei chocolate.

Roux at The Landau – Langham Hotel

XXX

1c Portland Pl., Regent St. ✉ W1B 1JA ⊖ Oxford Circus – ✆ (020) 7636 1000 – www.langhamhotels.com – Closed Saturday lunch and Sunday **30AITn**

Rest – Menu £ 35/60 – Carte £ 35/59

Grand, oval-shaped hotel restaurant run under the aegis of the Roux organisation. Classical, French-influenced cooking is the order of the day, but a lighter style of cuisine using the occasional twist is also emerging.

Latium

21 Berners St. ✉ W1T 3LP ⊖ Oxford Circus – ✆ (020) 7323 9123 – www.latiumrestaurant.com – Closed 25-26 December, 1 January, Saturday lunch, Sunday and bank holidays **31**AJT**n**

Rest – Menu £ 17/36

Bright and contemporary surroundings but with warm and welcoming service. Owner-chef from Lazio but dishes come from across Italy, often using British produce. Ravioli is the house speciality.

Orrery

55 Marylebone High St ✉ W1U 5RB ⊖ Regent's Park – ✆ (020) 7616 8000 – www.orrery-restaurant.co.uk **18**RZD**a**

Rest – *(booking essential)* Menu £ 26 (weekday lunch)/60

These are actually converted stables from the 19C but, such is the elegance and style of the building, you'd never know. Featured is elaborate, modern European cooking; dishes are strong on presentation and come with the occasional twist.

Texture (Agnar Sverrisson)

34 Portman St. ✉ W1H 7BY ⊖ Marble Arch – ✆ (020) 7224 0028 – www.texture-restaurant.co.uk – Closed 1-14 August, 1 week Easter, Christmas, New Year, Sunday and Monday **29**AGU**p**

Rest – Menu £ 27/79 – Carte £ 52/77

Technically skilled but light and invigorating cooking from Icelandic chef-owner, who uses ingredients from home. Bright restaurant with high ceiling and popular adjoining champagne bar. Pleasant service from keen staff, ready with a smile.

➜ Norwegian king crab, garlic, ginger and wasabi. Milk-fed veal, artichokes and Tio Pepe sauce. Valrhona white chocolate mousse and ice cream with dill cucumber.

L'Autre Pied

5-7 Blandford St. ✉ W1U 3DB ⊖ Bond Street – ✆ (020) 7486 9696 – www.lautrepied.co.uk – Closed 4 days Christmas, 1 January and Sunday dinner **30**AHT**k**

Rest – Menu £ 26/70 – Carte £ 50/62

Chef Andy McFadden's dishes are elaborate yet easy to eat and provide pleasing contrasts in textures; venison dishes are a particular speciality. This more relaxed sibling to Pied à Terre has a buoyant atmosphere; ask for a table by the window to better enjoy the local 'village' feel.

➜ Scallop ceviche with black quinoa. Roe deer cooked in cocoa and juniper with black pudding, beetroot and watercress. Chocolate pavé, honeycomb, pistachio and tonka bean ice cream.

Galvin Bistrot de Luxe

66 Baker St. ✉ W1U 7DJ ⊖ Baker Street – ✆ (020) 7935 4007 – www.galvinrestaurants.com – Closed dinner 24 December, 25-26 December and 1 January **29**AGT**b**

Rest – Menu £ 20/30 – Carte £ 31/54

Firmly established modern Gallic bistro with ceiling fans, globe lights and wood panelled walls. Satisfying and precisely cooked classic French dishes from the Galvin brothers.

Cotidie

50 Marylebone High St ✉ W1U 5HN ⊖ Baker Street – ✆ (020) 7258 9878 – www.cotidierestaurant.com – Closed Christmas **30**AHT**b**

Rest – Menu £ 27 (lunch) – Carte £ 37/65

'Cotidie' means 'everyday' which refers to the oft-changing menu rather than the style of the Italian food, which is sophisticated and imaginative. The prices and elegant surroundings make this a special occasion restaurant.

Zayna

25 New Quebec St. ✉ W1H 7SF ⊖ Marble Arch – ✆ (020) 7723 2229 – www.zaynarestaurant.co.uk **29**AGU**x**

Rest – Carte £ 20/33

Enthusiastically run, elegant restaurant spread over two floors, with keen owner. Interesting north Indian and Pakistani delicacies; kitchen only uses halal meat and free-range chicken.

XX **Ozer**
5 Langham Pl., Regent St. ✉ W1B 3DG ⊖ Oxford Circus – ☎ (020) 7323 0505 – www.ozer.co.uk **30AITz**
Rest – Menu £ 12/25 – Carte £ 18/44
Come in a group of friends to best appreciate the large bar, the excitable atmosphere and the sharing of healthy food. Go for the authentic specialities such as borek, kofte and the extensive choice of chargrilled meats.

XX **Royal China**
24-26 Baker St ✉ W1U 7AB ⊖ Baker Street – ☎ (020) 7487 4688 – www.royalchinagroup.co.uk **29AGTh**
Rest – Carte £ 22/53
Barbeque meats, assorted soups and stir-fries attract plenty of large groups to this smart and always bustling Cantonese restaurant. Over 40 different types of dim sum served during the day.

XX **Verru**
69 Marylebone Ln ✉ W1U 2PH ⊖ Bond Street – ☎ (020) 7935 0858 – www.verru.co.uk **30AHTa**
Rest – Menu £ 15/18 – Carte £ 33/41
Chef-owner is Estonian so his cooking not only displays a Baltic boldness of flavour but also makes good use of northern European influences. The restaurant is tiny and tucked away but warmly run and smartly dressed.

LONDON

XX **Suka** – Sanderson Hotel
50 Berners St ✉ W1T 3NG ⊖ Oxford Circus – ☎ (020) 7300 5588 – www.morganshotelgroup.com **31AJTc**
Rest – Menu £ 21 – Carte approx. £ 29
Have cocktails in the Sanderson's trendy Long Bar then climb onto one of the high stools here at Suka. Be prepared to share, from a menu that mixes street food with more sophisticated Malaysian offerings.

XX **Archipelago**
53 Cleveland St ✉ W1T 4JJ ⊖ Goodge Street – ☎ (020) 7383 3346 – www.archipelago-restaurant.co.uk – Closed 24-28 December, Saturday lunch, Sunday and bank holidays **30AITe**
Rest – Carte £ 28/37
Eccentrically decorated in the style of an overflowing bazaar. There's an Asian influence to the equally exotic and highly unusual menu which could include crocodile, zebra and wildebeest.

XX **L'Aventure**
3 Blenheim Terr ✉ NW8 0EH ⊖ St John's Wood – ☎ (020) 7624 6232 – www.laventure.co.uk – Closed 2 weeks August, first week January, Saturday lunch, Sunday and bank holidays **11PZBb**
Rest – Menu £ 22/43
Behind the pretty tree-lined entrance you'll find a charming neighbourhood restaurant. Relaxed atmosphere and service by personable owner. Authentic French cuisine.

XX **Winter Garden** – The Landmark London Hotel
222 Marylebone Rd ✉ NW1 6JQ ⊖ Edgware Road – ☎ (020) 7631 8000 – www.landmarklondon.co.uk **29AFTa**
Rest – Menu £ 34 (lunch) – Carte £ 33/57
Dining options north of Marylebone Road can be limited, so the Winter Garden, housed in the vast atrium of the Landmark, is a useful spot for a business lunch. The kitchen has a lightness of touch and the confidence not to overcrowd a plate.

XX **The Providores**
109 Marylebone High St. ✉ W1U 4RX ⊖ Bond Street – ☎ (020) 7935 6175 – www.theprovidores.co.uk – Closed 25-26 December **30AHTy**
Rest – Menu £ 25 (weekday lunch) – Carte £ 35/48
Packed ground floor for tapas; upstairs for innovative fusion cooking, with spices and ingredients from around the world, including Australasia. Starter-sized dishes at dinner allow for greater choice.

XX **Iberica Marylebone** A/C

195 Great Portland St ✉ W1W 5PS ⊖ Great Portland Street – ✆ (020) 7636 8650 – www.ibericalondon.co.uk – Closed 24-26 December, bank holidays and Sunday dinner **18RZDx**

Rest – Menu £ 10 (weekday lunch) – Carte £ 18/46

Some prefer the intimacy of upstairs, others the bustle of the ground floor with its bar and deli. Along with an impressive array of Iberico hams are colourful dishes to share such as glossy black rice with cuttlefish and prawns.

XX **One Blenheim Terrace** A/C

1 Blenheim Terrace ✉ NW8 0EH ⊖ St John's Wood – ✆ (020) 7372 1722 – www.oneblenheimterrace.co.uk – Closed Monday **11PZBv**

Rest – Carte £ 16/51

The young chef owner offers something a little different: some dishes are re-interpretations of '60s and '70s classics, but owe more to modern cooking techniques than nostalgia. The bright room comes with a popular terrace.

XX **Phoenix Palace** A/C

5 Glentworth St. ✉ NW1 5PG ⊖ Baker Street – ✆ (020) 7486 3515 – www.phoenixpalace.co.uk – Closed 25 December **17QZDx**

Rest – *(bookings advisable at dinner)* Menu £ 33 – Carte £ 24/65

The menu may be disconcertingly long at this vast but well-organised Chinese restaurant but the cooking is good, particularly the Cantonese specialities like roast pork belly or fish maw with conpoy and winter melon.

XX **Levant** A/C

Jason Ct., 76 Wigmore St. ✉ W1U 2SJ ⊖ Bond Street – ✆ (020) 7224 1111 – www.levant.co.uk – Closed 25-26 December **30AHTc**

Rest – Menu £ 10/50 – Carte £ 23/71

Come in a group to best enjoy the Lebanese and Middle Eastern specialities; it's worth ordering one of the 'Feast' menus. Belly dancing, a low slung bar, lanterns and joss sticks add to the exotic feel of this basement restaurant.

X **Lima** N A/C

31 Rathbone Pl ✉ W1T 1JH ⊖ Goodge Street – ✆ (020) 3002 2640 – www.limalondon.com – Closed 23 December-3 January and Sunday

Rest – Menu £ 20 (lunch and early dinner) – Carte £ 29/46 **31AJTs**

Lima is one of those restaurants that just makes you feel good about life – and that's even without the Pisco Sours. The Peruvian food at this informal, fun place is the ideal antidote to our recessionary times: it's full of punchy, invigorating flavours and fantastically vivid colours.

➜ Sea bream ceviche, tiger's milk. ají limo pepper and cancha corn. Lamb shoulder 'seco', dried potato and pisco mosto verde. Lucuma fruit ice cream, chocolate powder, annatto and chancaca cream.

X **Trishna** (Karam Sethi) A/C

15-17 Blandford St. ✉ W1U 3DG ⊖ Baker Street – ✆ (020) 7935 5624 – www.trishnalondon.com – Closed 24-28 December and 1-6 January

Rest – Menu £ 20 (lunch)/55 – Carte £ 26/41 **29AGTr**

The coast of southwest India provides many influences at this understated, double-fronted, modern Indian restaurant. The food is balanced, satisfactory and executed with care; be sure to order the wondrously rich Dorset brown crab.

➜ Hariyali bream with green chilli, coriander, tomato and cucumber. Guinea fowl tikka. Cardamom kheer with fig, raisin and pistachio.

X **The Wallace**

Hertford House, Manchester Sq ✉ W1U 3BN ⊖ Bond Street – ✆ (020) 7563 9505 – www.thewallacerestaurant.com – Closed 24-26 December

Rest – *(lunch only and dinner Friday-Saturday)* Menu £ 27 (lunch) – Carte £ 32/43 **29AGTk**

Large glass-roofed courtyard on the ground floor of Hertford House, home to the splendid Wallace Collection. French-influenced menu, with fruits de mer section; terrines are the house speciality.

LONDON

Caffé Caldesi

118 Marylebone Ln. (1st floor) ✉ W1U 2QF ⊖ Bond Street – ✆ (020) 7487 0754 – www.caldesi.com **30**AHT **s**

Rest – Menu £ 15/20 – Carte £ 21/46

Head upstairs at this converted corner pub for generously proportioned, big flavoured classics from across Italy. Stay on the ground floor for a simpler and more accessibly priced menu.

Roti Chai

3 Portman Mews South ✉ W1H 6HS ⊖ Marble Arch – ✆ (020) 7408 0101 – www.rotichai.com – Closed 25 December **29**AGU **v**

Rest – Carte £ 15/31

Representing the new wave of modern, casual Indian restaurants, in appropriately vivid colours. The ground floor is for quick and easy pan-Indian street food; downstairs is swankier and offers a contemporary update of Indian home cooking.

Il Baretto

43 Blandford St. ✉ W1U 7HF ⊖ Baker Street – ✆ (020) 7486 7340 – www.ilbaretto.co.uk – Closed 25-26 December, lunch 31 December and 1 January **29**AGT **n**

Rest – Menu £ 45/75 – Carte £ 25/54

The robata grill is the star of the show at this lively Italian restaurant. The extensive and variably priced menu offers something for everyone, from pizzas to succulent lamb chops. The basement setting adds to the 'local' feel.

28°-50° Marylebone

15-17 Marylebone Ln. ✉ W1U 2NE ⊖ Bond Street – ✆ (020) 7486 7922 – www.2850.co.uk – Closed 25-26 December **30**AHT **c**

Rest – Carte £ 25/36

This second wine bar from the owners of Texture restaurant offers a great choice of wines by the glass and a terrific Collectors' List. Most plump for the grilled meats from the coal burning oven. Service is as bright as the room.

Riding House Café

43-51 Great Titchfield St ✉ W1W 7PQ ⊖ Oxford Circus – ✆ (020) 7927 0840 – www.ridinghousecafe.co.uk – Closed 25-26 December **30**AIT **k**

Rest – Carte £ 22/41

It's less a café, more a large, quirkily designed, all-day New York style brasserie and cocktail bar. The 'small plates' have more zing than the main courses. The 'unbookable' side of the restaurant is the more fun part.

Picture (N)

110 Great Portland St. ✉ W1W 6PQ ⊖ Oxford Circus – ✆ (020) 7637 7892 – www.picturerestaurant.co.uk – Closed 25 December and Sunday **30**AIT **t**

Rest – Carte £ 18/26

An ex Arbutus and Wild Honey triumvirate have created this cool, great-value restaurant. The look may be a little stark but the delightful staff add warmth. The small plates are vibrant and colourful, and the flavours are assured.

Briciole

20 Homer St ✉ W1H 4NA ⊖ Edgware Road – ✆ (020) 7723 0040 – www.briciole.co.uk – Closed 25-26 December **29**AFT **s**

Rest – Carte £ 13/25

Maurizio Morelli opened this fun, all-day Italian as a less expensive and more relaxed alternative to his Latium restaurant. It offers a pleasant local feel and faux-rustic surroundings. Try the homemade sausages and meatballs.

Donostia

10 Seymour Pl ✉ W1H 7ND ⊖ Marble Arch – ✆ (020) 3620 1845 – www.donostia.co.uk – Closed Monday lunch **29**AFU **s**

Rest – Carte £ 14/32

The two young owners were inspired by the food of San Sebastiàn to open this pintxos and tapas bar. Sit at the counter for Basque classics like cod with pil-pil sauce, chorizo from the native pig Kintoa and slow-cooked pig's cheeks.

LONDON

Vinoteca

15 Seymour Pl. ✉ W1H 5BD ⊖ Marble Arch – ✆ (020) 7724 7288 – www.vinoteca.co.uk – Closed 24-26, 31 December, 1 January, bank holiday Mondays and Sunday dinner **29AFUv**

Rest – *(booking advisable)* Carte £ 22/38

Follows the formula of the original: great fun, great wines, gutsy and wholesome food, enthusiastic staff and almost certainly a wait for a table. Influences from sunnier parts of Europe, along with some British dishes.

Zoilo

9 Duke St. ✉ W1U 3EG ⊖ Bond Street – ✆ (020) 7486 9699 – www.zoilo.co.uk

Rest – Carte £ 12/33 **30AHTz**

It's all about sharing so grab a seat at the counter and discover Argentina's regional specialities. Don't miss chewy melted provoleta cheese, beetroot with goat's curd and garrapiñada (a Buenos Aires street snack), and escabeche.

Bonnie Gull

21a Foley St ✉ W1W 6DS ⊖ Goodge Street – ✆ (020) 7436 0921 – www.bonniegull.com **30AITb**

Rest – *(booking essential)* Carte £ 21/39

Sweet Bonnie Gull calls itself a 'seafood shack' – a reference perhaps to its modest beginnings as a pop-up. Start with an order from the raw bar then go for a classic like Cullen Skink, a whole Devon Cock crab or fish and chips.

LONDON

Yalla Yalla

12 Winsley St. ✉ W1W 8HQ ⊖ Oxford Circus – ✆ (020) 7637 4748 – www.yalla-yalla.co.uk – Closed 25-26 December, 1 January and Sunday

Rest – Carte £ 19/29 **30AITv**

Queues form for the Beirut street food which includes zesty mezze and succulent charcoal-grilled lamb dishes. Desserts come from the enticing pastry corner and wines from the Bekaa Valley. Takeaway also available.

Dinings

22 Harcourt St. ✉ W1H 4HH ⊖ Edgware Road – ✆ (020) 7723 0666 – www.dinings.co.uk – Closed Christmas and Sunday **29AFTc**

Rest – *(booking essential)* Carte £ 19/59

It's hard not to be charmed by this sweet little Japanese place, with its ground floor counter and basement tables. Its strengths lie with the more creative, contemporary dishes; sharing is recommended but prices can be steep.

Newman Street Tavern

48 Newman St ✉ W1T 1QQ ⊖ Goodge Street – ✆ (020) 3667 1445 – www.newmanstreettavern.co.uk – Closed bank holidays **30AJTs**

Rest – Carte £ 23/39

The experienced team behind this Edwardian pub have created a warm, welcoming spot. The kitchen celebrates the best of British and the menu is instantly appealing. Eat in the busy bar or in the more sedate first floor dining room.

Grazing Goat with rm

6 New Quebec St ✉ W1H 7RQ ⊖ Marble Arch. – ✆ (020) 7724 7243 – www.thegrazinggoat.co.uk **29AGUd**

8 rm – †£ 195 ††£ 195/225, ☕ £ 7

Rest – *(booking essential at dinner)* Carte £ 28/44

A smart city facsimile of a country pub; it's first-come-first-served in the bar but you can book in the upstairs dining room. Proper pub classics such as pies and Castle of Mey steaks are on offer. Bedrooms with Nordic style bathrooms.

Portman

51 Upper Berkeley St ✉ W1H 7QW ⊖ Marble Arch. – ✆ (020) 7723 8996 – www.theportmanmarylebone.com **29AFUn**

Rest – Menu £ 30/38 – Carte £ 21/35

The condemned on their way to Tyburn Tree gallows would take their last drink here. Now it's an urbane pub with a formal upstairs dining room. The ground floor is more fun for enjoying the down-to-earth menu.

St James's

Ritz

150 Piccadilly ✉ W1J 9BR ⊖ Green Park – ✆ (020) 7493 8181 – www.theritzlondon.com **30AIVc**

133 rm – †£ 315/780 ††£ 360/925, ☕ £ 35 – 45 suites

Rest *Ritz Restaurant* – see restaurant listing

World famous hotel, opened in 1906 as a fine example of Louis XVI architecture and decoration. Elegant Palm Court famed for its afternoon tea. Many of the lavishly appointed and luxurious rooms and suites overlook the park.

Haymarket

1 Suffolk Pl. ✉ SW1Y 4HX ⊖ Piccadilly Circus – ✆ (020) 7470 4000 – www.haymarkethotel.com **31AKVx**

50 rm – †£ 320 ††£ 320, ☕ £ 20 – 3 suites

Rest *Brumus* – see restaurant listing

Smart, spacious hotel in John Nash Regency building, with stylish blend of modern and antique furnishings. Large, comfortable bedrooms in soothing colours. Impressive basement pool often used in photo-shoots.

Sofitel London St James

6 Waterloo Pl. ✉ SW1Y 4AN ⊖ Piccadilly Circus – ✆ (020) 7747 2200 – www.sofitelstjames.com **31AKVa**

183 rm – †£ 288/576 ††£ 288/576, ☕ £ 17 – 8 suites

Rest *Balcon* – see restaurant listing

Great location for this international hotel in a Grade II former bank. The triple-glazed bedrooms are immaculately kept; the spa is one of the best around. The bar is inspired by Coco Chanel; the lounge by an English rose garden.

Dukes

35 St James's Pl. ✉ SW1A 1NY ⊖ Green Park – ✆ (020) 7491 4840 – www.dukeshotel.com **30AIVf**

90 rm – †£ 234/454 ††£ 276/496, ☕ £ 24 – 6 suites

Rest *Thirty Six by Nigel Mendham* – *(closed Sunday dinner and Monday lunch)* Menu £ 32/60 – Carte £ 44/62

The wonderfully located Dukes has been steadily updating its image over the last few years, despite being over a century old. Bedrooms are now fresh and uncluttered and the atmosphere less starchy. The basement restaurant offers a modern menu, with dishes that are original in look and elaborate in construction.

Stafford

16-18 St James's Pl. ✉ SW1A 1NJ ⊖ Green Park – ✆ (020) 7493 0111 – www.kempinski.com/london **30AIVu**

213 rm ☕ – †£ 403/565 ††£ 428/590 – 8 suites

Rest *The Lyttelton* – Carte £ 37/73

Styles itself as a 'country house in the city'; its bedrooms are divided between the main house, converted 18C stables and a more modern mews. Legendary American bar a highlight; traditional British food served in the restaurant.

St James's Hotel and Club

7-8 Park Pl. ✉ SW1A 1LS ⊖ Green Park – ✆ (020) 7316 1600 – www.stjameshotelandclub.com **30AIVk**

55 rm – †£ 260/3000 ††£ 260/3000, ☕ £ 16 – 10 suites

Rest *Seven Park Place* ✿ – see restaurant listing

1890s house in a cul-de-sac, formerly a private club and reopened as a hotel in 2008. Modern, boutique-style interior with over 300 European works of art from the '30s and '40s. Fine finish to the compact but well-equipped bedrooms.

Cavendish

81 Jermyn St ✉ SW1Y 6JF ⊖ Piccadilly Circus – ✆ (020) 7930 2111 – www.thecavendishlondon.com **30AIVp**

228 rm – †£ 179/288 ††£ 179/288, ☕ £ 23 – 2 suites

Rest – *(Closed 24-26 December and lunch Saturday-Sunday)* Menu £ 20 – Carte £ 30/45

There's been a hotel on this site since the 18C; this one was built in the '60s but is smart and contemporary inside. Great location, bistro-style dining with British menu and good views across London from the top 5 floors; a parking space for every room too!

LONDON

XXXXX **Ritz Restaurant** – Ritz Hotel
150 Piccadilly ✉ W1J 9BR ⊖ Green Park – ☎ (020) 7493 8181
– www.theritzlondon.com **30**AIV**c**
Rest – Menu £ 47/55 **s** – Carte £ 66/83 **s**
Grand and lavish restaurant, with Louis XVI decoration, trompe l'oeil and ornate gilding. Delightful terrace over Green Park. Structured, formal service. Classic, traditional dishes are the highlight of the menu. Jacket and tie required.

XXX **Seven Park Place** – St James's Hotel and Club
✿ *7-8 Park Pl ✉ SW1A 1LS ⊖ Green Park – ☎ (020) 7316 1615*
– www.stjameshotelandclub.com – Closed Sunday and Monday **30**AIV**k**
Rest – *(booking essential)* Menu £ 26/72
Small restaurant concealed somewhat within St James's Hotel and divided between two rooms; ask for the gilded back room. The accomplished food has a French base, displays confidence and clarity and uses quality British ingredients.
➜ Seared scallops, braised celeriac purée and smoked bacon. Assiette of lamb. Milk chocolate mousse with gingerbread spices and salted caramel ice cream.

XXX **The Wolseley**
160 Piccadilly ✉ W1J 9EB ⊖ Green Park – ☎ (020) 7499 6996
– www.thewolseley.com – Closed dinner 24 December **30**AIV**q**
Rest – *(booking essential)* Carte £ 24/64
Feels like a grand European coffee house, with pillars and high vaulted ceiling. Appealing menus range from caviar to a hot dog. Open from breakfast and boasts a celebrity following.

XX **Balcon** – Sofitel London St James Hotel
8 Pall Mall. ✉ SW1Y 5NG ⊖ Piccadilly Circus – ☎ (020) 7968 2900
– www.thebalconlondon.com **31**AKV**a**
Rest – Menu £ 15 (weekdays) – Carte £ 26/82
A former banking hall with vast chandeliers and a grand brasserie look. It's open from breakfast onwards and the menu features French classics like snails and cassoulet; try the charcuterie from Wales and France.

XX **Matsuri**
15 Bury St. ✉ SW1Y 6AL ⊖ Green Park – ☎ (020) 7839 1101
– www.matsuri-restaurant.com – Closed 25 December and 1 January
Rest – Menu £ 39/55 – Carte £ 30/126 **30**AIV**w**
Sweet natured service at this longstanding, traditional Japanese stalwart. Teppanyaki is their speciality, with Scottish beef the highlight; sushi counter also available. Good value lunch menus and bento boxes.

XX **Le Caprice**
Arlington House, Arlington St. ✉ SW1A 1RJ ⊖ Green Park – ☎ (020) 7629 2239
– www.le-caprice.co.uk – Closed 25-26 December **30**AIV**h**
Rest – Menu £ 25 (dinner) – Carte £ 27/70
For over 30 years Le Caprice's effortlessly sophisticated atmosphere and surroundings have attracted a confident and urbane clientele. Perennials on their catch-all menu include their famous burger and rich salmon fishcake.

XX **Sake No Hana**
23 St James's St ✉ SW1A 1HA ⊖ Green Park – ☎ (020) 7925 8988
– www.sakenohana.com – Closed 25 December and Sunday **30**AIV**n**
Rest – Menu £ 29/45 – Carte £ 18/91
A modern Japanese restaurant within a Grade II listed '60s edifice – and proof that you can occasionally find good food at the end of an escalator. As with the great cocktails, the menu is best enjoyed when shared with a group.

XX **Franco's**
61 Jermyn St ✉ SW1Y 6LX ⊖ Green Park – ☎ (020) 7499 2211
– www.francoslondon.com – Closed Sunday and bank holidays **30**AIV**i**
Rest – *(booking essential)* Menu £ 18/22 – Carte £ 39/57
Open from breakfast until late, with café at the front leading into smart, clubby restaurant. Menu covers all parts of Italy and includes popular grill section and plenty of classics.

XX Avenue AC ☆ ⊡ ⟷

7-9 St James's St. ✉ *SW1A 1EE* ⊖ *Green Park –* ✆ *(020) 7321 2111*
*– www.avenue-restaurant.co.uk – Closed Saturday lunch, Sunday dinner and
bank Holidays* 30AIV**y**
Rest – Menu £ 20 (weekday lunch)
– Carte dinner £ 26/53

Large canvases have made this large room more colourful and there's greater
warmth from the service too. The menu roams predatorily around the globe and
dishes display a greater degree of depth than one expects.

XX Mint Leaf AC ⊡

Suffolk Pl ✉ *SW1Y 4HX* ⊖ *Piccadilly Circus –* ✆ *(020) 7930 9020*
– www.mintleafrestaurant.com
– Closed 25-26 December and 1 January 31AKV**k**
Rest – Menu £ 14 – Carte £ 28/42

Cavernous and moodily lit basement restaurant incorporating trendy bar with
lounge music and extensive cocktail list. Contemporary Indian cooking with curries the highlight.

XX Al Duca AC ⊡ ⊡

4-5 Duke of York St ✉ *SW1Y 6LA* ⊖ *Piccadilly Circus –* ✆ *(020) 7839 3090*
*– www.alduca-restaurant.co.uk – Closed Easter, 25 December, Sunday and bank
holidays* 31AJV**r**
Rest – Menu £ 17/33

Cooking which focuses on flavour continues to draw in the regulars at this warm
and spirited Italian restaurant. Prices are keen when one considers the central location and service is brisk and confident.

XX Quaglino's AC ⊡ ⟷

16 Bury St ✉ *SW1Y 6AJ* ⊖ *Green Park –* ✆ *(020) 7930 6767*
*– www.quaglinos-restaurant.co.uk – Closed Christmas, Easter Monday and
Sunday* 30AIV**j**
Rest – Menu £ 15/26 – Carte £ 32/75

It may be synonymous with the early '90s but the old girl can still shake it on a
weekend for those wanting a fun night out with a bit of glitz. The kitchen delivers
on brasserie classics like pork belly and duck confit.

XX Brumus – Haymarket Hotel AC ☆ ⊡

1 Suffolk Pl ✉ *SW1Y 4HX* ⊖ *Piccadilly Circus –* ✆ *(020) 7470 4000*
– www.haymarkethotel.com 31AKV**x**
Rest – Menu £ 20 – Carte £ 23/49

Ideally positioned for pre or post theatre dining, when a good value menu is offered. Energetic room, with busy bar attached, and an unthreatening menu of
Mediterranean favourites.

X Portrait ≤ AC

National Portrait Gallery, (3rd floor), St Martin's Pl. ✉ *WC2H 0HE*
⊖ *Charing Cross –* ✆ *(020) 7312 2490 – www.searcys.co.uk – Closed 24-26
December* 31ALV**n**
Rest – *(lunch only and dinner Thursday-Saturday) (booking essential)*
Menu £ 18/35

On the top floor of National Portrait Gallery with rooftop local landmark views: a
charming spot for lunch. Modern British/European dishes; weekend brunch.

X The National Dining Rooms AC

Sainsbury Wing, The National Gallery, Trafalgar Sq ✉ *WC2N 5DN*
⊖ *Charing Cross –* ✆ *(020) 7747 2525 – www.peytonandbyrne.co.uk – Closed
24-26 December* 31AKV**b**
Rest – *(lunch only and Friday dinner)* Menu £ 20 – Carte £ 30/37

Set on the East Wing's first floor, you can tuck into cakes in the bakery or grab
a prime corner table in the restaurant for great views and proudly seasonal British menus.

Shoryu

9 Regent St. ✉ SW1Y 4LR ⊖ Piccadilly Circus – www.shoryuramen.com – Closed Christmas-New Year **31**AJV**s**

Rest – *(bookings not accepted)* Carte £ 11/27

Owned by Japan Centre opposite and specialising in Hakata tonkotsu ramen. The base is a milky broth made from pork bones to which is added hosomen noodles, egg, and assorted toppings. Its restorative powers are worth queuing for.

SOHO

Soho

4 Richmond Mews ✉ W1D 3DH ⊖ Tottenham Court Road – ✆ (020) 7559 3000 – www.sohohotel.com **31**AJU**n**

91 rm – †£ 355 ††£ 355, ☕ £ 20 – 5 suites

Rest *Refuel* – see restaurant listing

Stylish and fashionable hotel that mirrors the vibrancy of the neighbourhood. Boasts two screening rooms, a comfortable drawing room and up-to-the-minute bedrooms; some vivid, others more muted but all with hi-tech extras.

Café Royal

68 Regent St ✉ W1B 4DY ⊖ Piccadilly Circus – ✆ (020) 7406 3333 – www.hotelcaferoyal.com **30**AJU**c**

159 rm – †£ 500/795 ††£ 500/795, ☕ £ 32 – 25 suites

Rest *Ten Room* – Carte £ 28/58

The iconic Café Royal's colourful history goes back to 1865. It's been redeveloped into this luxury hotel, with cool, contemporary bedrooms and stunning bathrooms. The spa is amazing; the rococo Grill Room has been restored to its original splendour and Ten Room serves classic and modern British dishes.

W London

10 Wardour St ✉ W1D 6QF ⊖ Leicester Square – ✆ (0207) 758 10 00 – www.wlondon.co.uk **31**AKU**b**

192 rm – †£ 300 ††£ 384, ☕ £ 27 – 15 suites

Rest *Spice Market* – see restaurant listing

An achingly trendy hotel bang in the heart of Leicester Square. A DJ plays in the lobby lounge at weekends; there's an over-subscribed bar with low slung tables and slick, über cool bedrooms in categories called 'Fantastic or 'Spectacular'. Anyone over 40 will feel slightly bewildered.

Sanctum Soho

20 Warwick St. ✉ W1B 5NF ⊖ Piccadilly Circus – ✆ (020) 7292 6100 – www.sanctumsoho.com **30**AIU**g**

30 rm – †£ 210/240 ††£ 210/240, ☕ £ 15

Rest *No. 20* – *(closed Sunday dinner)* Carte £ 23/46

Plenty of glitz and bling at this funky, self-styled rock 'n' roll hotel, with some innovative touches such as TVs behind mirrors. Rooftop lounge and hot tub. Relaxed and comfortable dining with plenty of classic dishes.

Dean Street Townhouse

69-71 Dean St. ✉ W1D 3SE ⊖ Tottenham Court Road – ✆ (020) 7434 1775 – www.deanstreettownhouse.com **31**AKU**t**

39 rm – †£ 110/440 ††£ 300/440, ☕ £ 13

Rest *Dean Street Townhouse Restaurant* – see restaurant listing

In the heart of Soho where bedrooms range from tiny to bigger; the latter have roll-top baths in the room. All are well designed and come with a good range of extras. Cosy ground floor lounge.

Nadler Soho without rest

10 Carlisle St ✉ W1D 3BR ⊖ Tottenham Court Road – ✆ (020) 3697 3697 – www.thenadler.com

78 rm – †£ 145 ††£ 280/330, ☕ £ 7 – 1 suite

On a quiet lane, but in the heart of Soho, is a townhouse with a concept: no bar nor restaurant, just comfortable, very well-equipped bedrooms, most of which have a small kitchenette. The smart receptionists double as concierge.

LONDON

LONDON

Hazlitt's

6 Frith St ✉ W1D 3JA ⊖ Tottenham Court Road – ✆ (020) 7434 1771 – www.hazlittshotel.com **31**AKU**u**

30 rm – †£ 198/222 ††£ 215/288, ☕ £ 12

Rest – *(room service only)*

Three adjoining early 18C townhouses and former home of the eponymous essayist. Idiosyncratic bedrooms, many with antique furniture and Victorian baths; ask for one of the newer ones.

XXX Quo Vadis

26-29 Dean St ✉ W1D 3LL ⊖ Tottenham Court Road – ✆ (020) 7437 9585 – www.quovadissoho.co.uk – Closed 25-26 December, 1 January and bank holidays **31**AKU**v**

Rest – Menu £ 18/20 – Carte £ 22/41

A stylish, elegant Soho institution dating from the 1920s and now owned by the Hart Brothers. First order some great 'bites' then choose from a menu of satisfying British dishes that includes a daily pie and braised dish along with grilled meats and assorted seafood.

XXX Gauthier - Soho

21 Romilly St ✉ W1D 5AF ⊖ Leicester Square – ✆ (020) 7494 3111 – www.gauthiersoho.co.uk – Closed Monday lunch, Sunday and bank holidays except Good Friday **31**AKU**k**

Rest – Menu £ 18 (lunch) – Carte approx. £ 45

Tucked away from the mischief of Soho is this charming Georgian townhouse, with dining spread over three floors. Alex Gauthier offers assorted menus of his classically based cooking, with vegetarians particularly well looked after.

XXX Aqua Nueva

240 Regent St.(5th floor), (entrance on Argyll St.) ✉ W1B 3BR ⊖ Oxford Circus – ✆ (020) 7478 0540 – www.aqua-london.com **30**AIU**x**

Rest – Menu £ 25 (lunch) – Carte £ 35/59

Large operation on the 5th floor of a former department store. Choose between the elegant main dining room or the more buzzy but equally stylish tapas bar. Spanish food interpreted in a modern style.

XXX Red Fort

77 Dean St. ✉ W1D 3SH ⊖ Tottenham Court Road – ✆ (020) 7437 2525 – www.redfort.co.uk – Closed 25 December, lunch Saturday, Sunday and bank holidays **31**AKU**t**

Rest – *(bookings advisable at dinner)* Menu £ 15/59

A feature in Soho since 1983 but the last makeover gave it a stylish, contemporary look. Balanced Indian cooking uses much UK produce such as Herdwick lamb; look out for more unusual choices like rabbit.

XXX Imperial China

White Bear Yard, 25a Lisle St ✉ WC2H 7BA ⊖ Leicester Square – ✆ (020) 7734 3388 – www.imperialchina-london.com **31**AKU**l**

Rest – *(booking advisable)* Menu £ 20 – Carte £ 17/70

Sharp service and comfortable surroundings are not the only things that set this restaurant apart: the Cantonese cooking exudes freshness and vitality, whether that's the steamed dumplings or the XO minced pork with fine beans.

XX ✿ Yauatcha

15 Broadwick St ✉ W1F 0DL ⊖ Tottenham Court Road – ✆ (020) 7494 8888 – www.yauatcha.com – Closed 24-25 December **31**AJU**k**

Rest – Menu £ 45 – Carte £ 18/49

Refined, delicate and delicious dim sum; ideal for sharing in a group. Stylish surroundings spread over two floors: the lighter, brighter ground floor or the darker, more atmospheric basement. Afternoon teas also a speciality.

➜ Scallop shui mai. Dover sole with shiitake and soya. Jasmine honey with milk chocolate, caramelised honey and almond.

XX **One Leicester Street** with rm
1 Leicester St ✉ WC2H 7BL ⊖ Leicester Square – ✆ (020) 3301 8020 – www.oneleicesterstreet.com **31**AKU**s**
15 rm – †£ 210/340 ††£ 210/340
Rest – *(booking advisable)* Carte £ 20/50
Now shares the same ownership as Town Hall and the look has been softened somewhat from when this was St John. The cooking is still all about seasonality and simplicity, from an appealingly down-to-earth, daily changing menu. Service is bright and cheerful, as indeed are the bedrooms upstairs.
➜ Crab, fennel and sea purslane. Smoked wild sea trout, broad beans and buttermilk. Brown butter and honey tart.

XX **Brasserie Zédel**
20 Sherwood St ✉ W1F 7ED ⊖ Piccadilly Circus – ✆ (020) 7734 4888 – www.brasseriezedel.com – Closed 25 December **31**AJU**q**
Rest – *(booking advisable)* Menu £ 9/20 – Carte £ 14/38
A grand French brasserie, which is all about inclusivity and accessibility, in a bustling subterranean space restored to its original art deco glory. Expect a roll-call of classic French dishes and some very competitive prices.

XX **Bob Bob Ricard**
1 Upper James St ✉ W1F 9DF ⊖ Oxford Circus – ✆ (020) 3145 1000 – www.bobbobricard.com – Closed 25-26 December, 1 January and Sunday
Rest – Carte £ 29/75 **31**AJU**s**
Everyone needs a little glamour now and again and this place provides it. The room may be quite small but it sees itself as a grand salon – ask for a booth. The menu is all-encompassing – oysters and caviar to pies and burgers.

XX **Dean Street Townhouse Restaurant**
69-71 Dean St. ✉ W1D 3SE ⊖ Tottenham Court Road – ✆ (020) 7434 1775 – www.deanstreettownhouse.com **31**AKU**t**
Rest – *(booking essential)* Menu £ 19/28 – Carte £ 26/90
Georgian house now home to a fashionable and very busy bar and restaurant; the Parlour is the less hectic area. Appealingly classic British food includes some retro dishes and satisfying puddings.

XX **Aqua Kyoto**
240 Regent St. (5th floor), (entrance on Argyll St.) ✉ W1F 7EB ⊖ Oxford Circus – ✆ (020) 7478 0540 – www.aqua-london.com **30**AIU**x**
Rest – Menu £ 20 (lunch) – Carte £ 26/88 **s**
The more boisterous of the two large restaurants on the 5th floor of Aqua London, along with a busy bar. Ideally suited to larger groups, as the contemporary Japanese food is designed for sharing.

XX **Floridita**
100 Wardour St ✉ W1F 0TN ⊖ Tottenham Court Road – ✆ (020) 7314 4000 – www.floriditalondon.com – Closed Sunday, Monday and bank holidays
Rest – *(dinner only)* Menu £ 25/38 **31**AJU**z**
Mediterranean tapas on the ground floor; the huge downstairs for live music, dancing and Latin American specialities, from Cuban spice to Argentinean beef. Great cocktails and a party atmosphere.

XX **Vasco and Piero's Pavilion**
15 Poland St ✉ W1F 8QE ⊖ Oxford Circus – ✆ (020) 7437 8774 – www.vascosfood.com – Closed Saturday lunch, Sunday and bank holidays
Rest – *(booking essential at lunch)* Carte £ 25/44 **31**AJU**b**
Celebrated forty years in 2011; its longevity down to its twice-daily changing menu and the simple but effective Umbrian-influenced cooking. The bright room attracts a high proportion of regulars.

XX **Plum Valley**
20 Gerrard St. ✉ W1D 6JQ ⊖ Leicester Square – ✆ (020) 7494 4366 – Closed 23-24 December **31**AKU**i**
Rest – Menu £ 38 – Carte £ 19/37
Its striking black façade make this modern Chinese restaurant easy to spot in Chinatown. Mostly Cantonese cooking, with occasional forays into Vietnam and Thailand; dim sum is the strength.

LONDON

Haozhan

8 Gerrard St ✉ W1D 5PJ ⊖ Leicester Square – ✆ (020) 7434 3838 – www.haozhan.co.uk – Closed 24-25 December **31**AKU**n**

Rest – Menu £ 15/48 – Carte £ 20/78

Interesting fusion-style dishes, with mostly Cantonese but other Asian influences too. Specialities like jasmine ribs or wasabi prawns reveal a freshness that marks this place out from the plethora of Chinatown mediocrity.

Refuel – Soho Hotel

4 Richmond Mews ✉ W1D 3DH ⊖ Tottenham Court Road – ✆ (020) 7559 3007 – www.sohohotel.com **31**AJU**n**

Rest – Menu £ 15 – Carte £ 26/57

At the heart of the cool Soho hotel is their aptly named bar and restaurant. With a menu to suit all moods and wallets, from Dover sole to burgers, and a cocktail list to lift all spirits, it's a fun and bustling spot.

Spice Market – W London Hotel

10 Wardour St ✉ W1D 6QF ⊖ Leicester Square – ✆ (0207) 758 10 00 – www.wlondon.co.uk **31**AKU**b**

Rest – Menu £ 38/48 – Carte £ 20/45

Over two floors and as strikingly decorated and as fun as Jean-Georges Vongerichten's original in Manhattan's Meatpacking district. Influences from across Asia in dishes designed for sharing; curries a highlight.

MASH (N)

77 Brewer St ✉ W1F 9ZN ⊖ Piccadilly Circus – ✆ (020) 7734 2608 – www.mashsteak.dk/restaurants/london – Closed 23-25 December and Sunday lunch **30**AJU**m**

Rest – Menu £ 22/25 – Carte £ 35/71

A team from Copenhagen raised the old Titanic and restored the art deco to create this striking 'Modern American Steak House', offering Danish, Nebraskan and Uruguayan beef. A great bar and slick service add to the grown up feel.

Arbutus

63-64 Frith St. ✉ W1D 3JW ⊖ Tottenham Court Road – ✆ (020) 7734 4545 – www.arbutusrestaurant.co.uk – Closed 25-26 December and 1 January

Rest – *(booking advisable)* Menu £ 18 (weekday lunch) – Carte £ 30/37 **31**AKU**h**

A relaxed setting, enthusiastic service, a terrific wine list that doesn't break the bank, and wonderfully flavoursome cooking – what's not to like? The technically confident kitchen has an innate understanding of the 'less is more' principle along with an inherent understanding of what-goes-with-what.

➜ Squid and mackerel 'burger' with razor clams. Elwy Valley lamb with sweet potato and Madeira braised celery. Egg custard tart with golden sultanas.

Social Eating House (N)

58 Poland St ✉ W1F 7NR ⊖ Oxford Circus – ✆ (020) 7993 3251 – www.socialeatinghouse.com – Closed Christmas, Sunday and bank holidays

Rest – Menu £ 21 (lunch) – Carte £ 29/42 **30**AJU**t**

Jason Atherton creates a bit of Brooklyn in Soho. The bustle and din let you know instantly you're in the right place. The cooking would make Escoffier proud with its 'faites simple' approach; staff are unstuffy and always on the ball.

➜ 'CLT'- crab, lettuce and tomato with roast tomato vinaigrette. Lamb neck fillet, sheep's ricotta potato, garlic and parsley. London honey almond sponge, goat's curd ice cream and orange.

Bocca di Lupo

12 Archer St ✉ WID 7BB ⊖ Piccadilly Circus – ✆ (020) 7734 2223 – www.boccadilupo.com – Closed 24 December-1 January and 25 August

Rest – *(booking essential)* Carte £ 24/35 **31**AJU**e**

Atmosphere, food and service are all best when sitting at the marble counter, watching the chefs at work. Specialities from across Italy come in large or small sizes and are full of flavour and vitality. Try also their Gelato shop opposite.

Dehesa
25 Ganton St ✉ W1F 9BP ⊖ Oxford Circus – ✆ (020) 7494 4170 – www.dehesa.co.uk – Closed 24-25 and 31 December and 1 January
Rest – Carte £ 23/35 **30AIUi**
Repeats the success of its sister restaurant, Salt Yard, by offering tasty, good value Spanish and Italian tapas. Unhurried atmosphere in appealing corner location. Terrific drinks list too.

Barrafina
54 Frith St. ✉ W1D 3SL ⊖ Tottenham Court Road – ✆ (020) 7813 8016 – www.barrafina.co.uk – Closed 25 December and 1 January **31AKUc**
Rest – *(bookings not accepted)* Carte £ 14/33
Centred around a counter with seating for 20; come here if you want authentic Spanish tapas served in a buzzy atmosphere. Seafood is a speciality and the Jabugo ham a must.

Polpo Soho
41 Beak St. ✉ W1F 9SB ⊖ Oxford Circus – ✆ (020) 7734 4479 – www.polpo.co.uk – Closed dinner 24 December, 25-26 and 31 December, 1 January and Sunday dinner **30AJUd**
Rest – *(bookings not taken at dinner)* Carte £ 12/32
A fun and lively Venetian bacaro, with a stripped-down, faux-industrial look. The small plates, from arancini and prosciutto to fritto misto and Cotechino sausage, are so well priced that waiting for a table is worth it.

Copita
27 d'Arblay St ✉ W1F 8EP ⊖ Oxford Circus – ✆ (020) 7287 7797 – www.copita.co.uk – Closed Sunday and bank holidays **30AJUa**
Rest – *(bookings not accepted)* Carte £ 13/20
Perch on one of the high stools or stay standing and get stuck into the daily menu of small, colourful and tasty dishes. Staff add to the atmosphere and everything on the Spanish wine list comes by the glass or copita.

Nopi
21-22 Warwick St. ✉ W1B 5NE ⊖ Piccadilly Circus – ✆ (020) 7494 9584 – www.nopi-restaurant.com – Closed 25-26 December, 1 January and Sunday dinner **30AIUg**
Rest – Carte £ 22/50
The bright, clean look of Yotam Ottolenghi's restaurant matches the fresh, invigorating food. The sharing plates take in the Mediterranean, Middle East and Asia and the veg dishes stand out.

Mele e Pere
46 Brewer St ✉ W1F 9TF ⊖ Piccadilly Circus – ✆ (020) 7096 2096 – www.meleepere.co.uk – Closed 25-26 December, 1 January Easter Sunday and Easter bank holiday Monday **31AJUh**
Rest – Menu £ 18 (dinner) – Carte £ 23/38
Head downstairs – the 'apples and pears'? – to a vaulted, if somewhat hard-edged room with an appealing Vermouth bar. The owner-chef has worked in some decent London kitchens but hails from Verona so expect gutsy Italian dishes.

Wright Brothers Soho
13 Kingly St. ✉ W1B 5PW ⊖ Oxford Circus – ✆ (020) 7434 3611 – www.thewrightbrothers.co.uk – Closed 24-28 December, 1-2 January, Easter Sunday and bank holidays **30AIUz**
Rest – Menu £ 15 – Carte £ 21/55
Bigger than the original in Borough Market, this branch is spread over three levels but the best spot is at the counter on the lower floor. Oysters a speciality but all seafood is handled deftly.

HIX
66-70 Brewer St. ✉ WIF 9UP ⊖ Piccadilly Circus – ✆ (020) 7292 3518 – www.hixsoho.co.uk – Closed 25-26 December **30AJUp**
Rest – Menu £ 18 (lunch) – Carte £ 27/94
The exterior may hint at exclusivity but inside this big restaurant the atmosphere is fun, noisy and sociable. The room comes decorated with the works of eminent British artists. Expect classic British dishes and ingredients.

10 Greek Street

10 Greek St ✉ W1D 4DH ⊖ Tottenham Court Road – ✆ (020) 7734 4677 – www.10greekstreet.com – Closed Christmas, Easter and Sunday **31**AKU **e**

Rest – Carte £ 21/35

With just 28 seats and a dozen at the counter, the challenge is getting a table at this modishly sparse-looking bistro (no bookings taken at dinner). The chef-owner's blackboard menu comes with Anglo, Med and Middle Eastern elements.

Cinnamon Soho

5 Kingly St ✉ W1B 5PF ⊖ Oxford Circus – ✆ (020) 7437 1664 – www.cinnamonsoho.com – Closed bank holidays **30**AIU **a**

Rest – *(bookings not accepted)* Menu £ 18/35 – Carte £ 17/28

This Cinnamon outpost is altogether more fun than its two older siblings. It blends Indian flavours with traditional British dishes, so you can order Rogan Josh shepherd's pie, curried Cullen Skink or Cumbrian lamb biryani.

Tapas Brindisa

46 Broadwick St. ✉ W1F 7AF ⊖ Oxford Circus – ✆ (020) 7534 1690 – www.brindisa.com – Closed dinner 24-27 December **31**AJU **f**

Rest – *(bookings not accepted at dinner)* Menu £ 20 (weekday lunch) – Carte £ 11/29

Sister to the original Tapas Brindisa in Borough Market. Expect the same quality of tapas from these importers of Spanish produce and the same bustling atmosphere. Service is obliging but bookings are not taken.

Burger & Lobster N

36 Dean St ✉ W1D 4PS ⊖ Leicester Square – ✆ (020) 7432 4800 – www.burgerandlobster.com – Closed bank holidays **31**AKU **x**

Rest – Menu £ 20

A sizeable place, yet as busy as the first branch in Mayfair. Choose a lobster roll in a brioche bun, a 1½lb Maine or Canadian lobster, or a 280g burger of Irish or Nebraskan beef. Bookings only taken for parties of 6 or more.

Vinoteca

53-55 Beak St ✉ W1F 9SH ⊖ Oxford Circus – ✆ (020) 3544 7411 – www.vinoteca.co.uk – Closed 24-26 December and 1 January **30**AJU **v**

Rest – *(booking advisable)* Carte £ 18/35

The terrific wine list mixes the classic with the esoteric and emerging markets are also covered. The food isn't forgotten – cured meats and cheeses are a highlight and European dishes like bavette and risotto also hit the spot.

Spuntino

61 Rupert St. ✉ W1D 7PW ⊖ Piccadilly Circus – www.spuntino.co.uk – Closed dinner 24 December, 25-26, 31 December and 1 January **31**AJU **j**

Rest – *(bookings not accepted)* Carte £ 16/23

Influenced by Downtown New York, with its no-booking policy and industrial look. Sit at the counter and order classics like Mac 'n' cheese or mini burgers. The staff, who look like they could also fix your car, really add to the fun.

Bibigo N

58-59 Great Marlborough St ✉ W1F 7JY ⊖ Oxford Circus – ✆ (020) 7042 5225 – www.bibigouk.com **30**AJU **x**

Rest – Menu £ 12 – Carte £ 16/30

The enthusiastically run Bibigo represents Korea's largest food company's first foray into the UK market. Watch the kitchen send out dishes such as kimchi, Bossam (simmered pork belly) and hot stone galbi (chargrilled short ribs).

Imli Street

167-169 Wardour St ✉ W1F 8WR ⊖ Tottenham Court Road – ✆ (020) 7287 4243 – www.imlistreet.com – Closed 25-26 December and 1 January

Rest – *(pre-book at weekends)* Carte approx. £ 16 **31**AJU **w**

Imli has a brighter look these days and comes with a terrific cocktail bar – a great place to wait for a table. The sharing plates are mostly influenced by southern India, although there are also some Indo-Chinese dishes.

LONDON

Ceviche
17 Frith St ✉ W1D 4RG ⊖ Tottenham Court Road – ✆ (020) 7292 2040 – www.cevicheuk.com **31AKUw**
Rest – Carte £ 15/28
Based on a Lima Pisco bar, Ceviche is as loud as it is fun. First try the deliriously addictive drinks based on the Peruvian spirit Pisco, and then share some thinly sliced sea bass or octopus, along with anticuchos skewers.

Cây Tre
42-43 Dean St ✉ W1D 4PZ ⊖ Tottenham Court Road – ✆ (020) 7317 9118 – www.caytresoho.co.uk **31AKUm**
Rest – *(booking advisable)* Menu £ 23/29 – Carte £ 17/28
Bright, sleek and bustling surroundings where Vietnamese standouts include Cha La Lot (spicy ground pork wrapped in betel leaves), slow-cooked Mekong catfish with a well-judged sweet and spicy sauce, and 6 versions of Pho (noodle soup).

Bone Daddies (N)
30-31 Peter St ✉ W1F 0AR ⊖ Piccadilly Circus – ✆ (020) 7287 8581 – www.bonedaddiesramen.com – Closed 25 December **31AJUy**
Rest – *(bookings not accepted)* Carte £ 16/21
Maybe ramen is the new rock 'n' roll. The charismatic Aussie chef-owner feels that combinations are endless when it comes to these comforting bowls. Be ready to queue then share a table. It's a fun place, run by a hospitable bunch.

LONDON

Barshu
28 Frith St. ✉ W1D 5LF ⊖ Leicester Square – ✆ (020) 7287 8822 – www.bar-shu.co.uk – Closed 24-25 December **31AKUg**
Rest – *(booking advisable)* Carte £ 22/49
The fiery and authentic flavours of China's Sichuan Province are the draw here; help is at hand as the menu has pictures. It's decorated with carved wood and lanterns; downstairs is better for groups.

Ba Shan
24 Romilly St. ✉ W1D 5AH ⊖ Leicester Square – ✆ (020) 7287 3266 – Closed 24-25 December **31AKUf**
Rest – *(booking advisable)* Carte £ 15/30
3-4 tables in each of the five rooms. Open all day, serving a mix of 'snack' and 'home-style' dishes, some with Sichuan leanings, others from northern areas and Henan province.

Tonkotsu (N)
63 Dean St ✉ W1D 4QG ⊖ Tottenham Court Road – ✆ (020) 7437 0071 – www.tonkotsu.co.uk **31AKUp**
Rest – *(bookings not accepted)* Carte £ 15/25
Some things are worth queuing for. Good ramen is all about the base stock: 18 hours goes into its preparation here to ensure the bowls of soup and wheat-based noodles reach a depth of flavour that seems to nourish one's very soul.

Ducksoup
41 Dean St ✉ W1D 4PY ⊖ Leicester Square – ✆ (020) 7287 4599 – www.ducksoupsoho.co.uk – Closed bank holidays and Sunday dinner
Rest – Carte £ 22/31 **31AKUa**
It's compact, with bar seating; decoratively it's knowingly underwhelming; and the menu is handwritten each day – yes, every 'on-trend' box is ticked here. Dishes are all about the produce and are confidently unadorned.

Baozi Inn
25-26 Newport Court ✉ WC2H 7JS ⊖ Leicester Square – ✆ (020) 7287 6877 – Closed 24-25 December **31AKUr**
Rest – *(bookings not accepted)* Carte £ 12/14
Baozi, or steamed filled buns, are a good way to start, followed by some fiery Sichuan specialities. Simple, honest and friendly restaurant, just off the main strip of Chinatown.

Beijing Dumpling

23 Lisle St. ✉ WC2H 7BA ⊖ Leicester Square – ✆ (020) 7287 68 88 – Closed 24-25 December **31AKUl**

Rest – Menu £ 16/20 – Carte £ 10/40

This relaxed little place serves freshly prepared dumplings of both Beijing and Shanghai styles. Although the range is not as comprehensive as the name suggests, they do stand out, especially varieties of the famed Siu Lung Bao.

Manchurian Legends

16 Lisle St ✉ WC2H 7BE ⊖ Leicester Square – ✆ (020) 7287 6606 – www.manchurianlegends.com – Closed Christmas **31AKUz**

Rest – Menu £ 14/22 – Carte £ 19/31

Try specialities from a less familiar region of China: Dongbei, the 'north east'. As winters here are long, stews and BBQ are popular, as are pickled ingredients and chilli heat. Further warmth comes from the sweet natured staff.

Koya

49 Frith St ✉ W1D 4SG ⊖ Tottenham Court Road – ✆ (020) 7434 4463 – www.koya.co.uk – Closed Christmas **31AKUy**

Rest – *(bookings not accepted)* Carte £ 13/28

Come for authentic udon noodles, made with wheat kneaded by foot, at this sweetly run, simply adorned place. The dashi base stock is freshly made every day. Be respectful by slurping with abandon.

LONDON

Rosa's

48 Dean St ✉ W1D 5BF ⊖ Leicester Square – ✆ (020) 7494 1638 – www.rosaslondon.com – Closed Easter and Christmas **31AKUj**

Rest – *(booking advisable)* Menu £ 20/30 – Carte £ 21/33

The worn-in, pared down look of this authentic Thai café adds to its intimate feel. Signature dishes include warm minced chicken salad and a sweet pumpkin red curry. Tom Yam soup comes with lovely balance of sweet, sour and spice.

Pitt Cue Co. (N)

1 Newburgh St ✉ W1F 7RB ⊖ Oxford Circus – ✆ (020) 7287 5578 – www.pittcue.co.uk – Closed 25 December, 1 January and Sunday dinner

Rest – *(bookings not accepted)* Carte £ 21/28 **30AJUp**

The owners started out selling their American barbecue from a van before finding this tiny spot. The ribs are smoked in-house for 6 hours before roasting; the pulled pork is excellent. It's messy, filling and fun; be ready to queue.

Strand and Covent Garden

Savoy

Strand ✉ WC2R 0EU ⊖ Charing Cross – ✆ (020) 7836 4343 – www.fairmont.com/savoy **31ALUs**

268 rm – †£ 420 ††£ 420, ☕ £ 30 – 30 suites

Rest *Savoy Grill* – see restaurant listing

Rest *Kaspar's* – Carte £ 31/69

A legendary hotel renewed after a 3 year renovation; its luxurious bedrooms and stunning suites come in Edwardian or art deco styles. Have tea in the Thames Foyer, the hotel's heart, or drinks in the famous American Bar or the moodier Beaufort Bar. Along with the Savoy Grill is Kaspar's, an informal seafood bar and grill which replaced the River restaurant.

One Aldwych

1 Aldwych ✉ WC2B 4RH ⊖ Temple – ✆ (020) 7300 1000 – www.onealdwych.com **32AMUr**

105 rm – †£ 260/435 ††£ 260/435, ☕ £ 26 – 12 suites

Rest *Axis* – see restaurant listing

Rest *Indigo* – ✆ (020) 7300 0400 – Menu £ 20/24 – Carte £ 27/47

Former 19C bank, now a stylish hotel with lots of artwork; the lobby changes its look seasonally and doubles as a bar. Stylish, contemporary bedrooms with the latest mod cons; the deluxe rooms and suites are particularly desirable. Impressive leisure facilities. Light, accessible menu at Indigo.

Waldorf Hilton
Aldwych ✉ WC2B 4DD ⊖ Temple – ✆ (020) 7836 2400 – www.hilton.co.uk/waldorf **32**AMU**s**
298 rm – †£ 199/379 ††£ 199/379, ☕ £ 23 – 11 suites
Rest *Homage* – *(dinner only)* Menu £ 23 – Carte £ 28/66
Impressive curved and columned façade: an Edwardian landmark in a great location. Popular for afternoon tea; relaxed brasserie style dining. On-going refurbishment of bedrooms.

ME London
336-337 Strand ✉ WC2R 1HA ⊖ Temple – ✆ (020) 7395 3400 – www.melondonuk.com **32**AMU**a**
157 rm – †£ 300/600 ††£ 300/600, ☕ £ 25 – 16 suites
Rest *STK* – *(closed 25 December and 1 January)* Menu £ 21/25 – Carte £ 32/92
Rest *Cucina Asellina* – ✆ (020) 7395 3445 – Menu £ 15 (lunch) – Carte £ 25/36
Rest *Radio* – *(closed 25 December and 1 January)* Carte £ 16/28
On the site of the Gaiety theatre and Marconi House, now a striking hotel designed by Fosters + Partners. Eye-catching pyramid shaped reception; bedrooms that are crisply decorated, cleverly lit and very comfortable. Steaks in the glitzy STK; Cucina Asellina offers a contemporary setting for Italian food; Radio has a simple menu and comes with a stunning rooftop bar.

LONDON

St Martins Lane
45 St Martin's Ln ✉ WC2N 3HX ⊖ Charing Cross – ✆ (020) 7300 5500 – www.stmartinslane.com **31**ALU**e**
206 rm – †£ 262/360 ††£ 288/384, ☕ £ 25 – 2 suites
Rest *Asia de Cuba* – see restaurant listing
The unmistakable hand of Philippe Starck is evident at this most contemporary of hotels. Unique and stylish, from the starkly modern lobby to the state-of-the-art bedrooms, which come in a blizzard of white.

Savoy Grill – Savoy Hotel
Strand ✉ WC2R 0EU ⊖ Charing Cross – ✆ (020) 7592 1600 – www.gordonramsay.com/thesavoygrill **31**ALU**s**
Rest – Menu £ 26 (weekday lunch) – Carte £ 33/79
Archives were explored, designers briefed and much money spent, with the result that The Savoy Grill has returned to the traditions that made it famous. As befits the name, it is the charcoal grilling of meats that takes centre stage.

Delaunay
55 Aldwych ✉ WC2B 4BB ⊖ Temple – ✆ (020) 7499 8558 – www.thedelaunay.com – Closed dinner 24 December and 25 December
Rest – *(booking essential)* Carte £ 21/47 **32**AMU**x**
The Delaunay was inspired by the grand cafés of Europe but, despite sharing the same buzz and celebrity clientele as its sibling The Wolseley, is not just a mere replica. The all-day menu is more mittel-European, with great schnitzels and wieners.

The Ivy
1-5 West St ✉ WC2H 9NQ ⊖ Leicester Square – ✆ (020) 7836 4751 – www.the-ivy.co.uk – Closed 25-26 December **31**AKU**p**
Rest – Menu £ 27 – Carte £ 30/68
One of the original celebrity hang-out restaurants; still pulling them in. Appealing menu, from shepherd's pie to fishcakes and nursery puddings. Staff go about their business with alacrity.

Axis – One Aldwych Hotel
1 Aldwych ✉ WC2B 4RH ⊖ Temple – ✆ (020) 7300 0300 – www.onealdwych.com/axis – Closed 16 August-3 September, 20 December-14 January and Saturday lunch **31**AMU**r**
Rest – Menu £ 20/24 – Carte £ 30/49
A spiral marble staircase leading down to this impressively high-ceilinged restaurant adds to the expectation. The menu is a combination of British classics and lighter European choices.

XX **J. Sheekey**

28-34 St Martin's Ct. ✉ WC2 4AL ⊖ Leicester Square – ✆ (020) 7240 2565 – www.j-sheekey.co.uk – Closed 25-26 December **31**ALU**v**

Rest – *(booking essential)* Carte £ 31/69

Festooned with photographs of actors and linked to the theatrical world since opening in 1890. Wood panels and alcove tables add famed intimacy. Accomplished seafood cooking.

XX **Rules**

35 Maiden Ln ✉ WC2E 7LB ⊖ Leicester Square – ✆ (020) 7836 5314 – www.rules.co.uk – Closed 25-26 December **31**ALU**n**

Rest – *(booking essential)* Carte £ 34/60

London's oldest restaurant boasts a fine collection of antique cartoons, drawings and paintings. Tradition continues in the menu, specialising in game from its own estate.

XX **Clos Maggiore**

33 King St ✉ WC2E 8JD ⊖ Leicester Square – ✆ (020) 7379 9696 – www.closmaggiore.com – Closed 24-25 December **31**ALU**z**

Rest – Menu £ 16/49 – Carte £ 32/55

One of London's most romantic restaurants – but be sure to ask for the enchanting conservatory with its retractable roof. The sophisticated French cooking is joined by a wine list of great depth. Good value and very popular pre/post theatre menus.

XX **Les Deux Salons**

40-42 William IV St ✉ WC2N 4DD ⊖ Charing Cross – ✆ (020) 7420 2050 – www.lesdeuxsalons.co.uk – Closed 25-26 December and 1 January

Rest – Menu £ 10/20 – Carte £ 14/46 **31**ALU**m**

Authentic Parisian brasserie complete with smoked mirrors, globe lights and striking mosaic floor. Ground floor is the better salon for atmosphere. Appealing menu mixes French classics, chargrilled meats and the odd British interloper.

XX **Balthazar** (N)

4-6 Russell St. ✉ WC2B 5HZ ⊖ Covent Garden – ✆ (020) 3301 1155 – www.balthazarlondon.com **31**ALU**t**

Rest – *(booking essential)* Carte £ 25/56

Those who know the original Balthazar in Manhattan's SoHo district will find the London version of this classic brasserie uncannily familiar in looks, vibe and food. The Franglais menu keeps it simple and the cocktails are great.

XX ✿ **L'Atelier de Joël Robuchon**

13-15 West St. ✉ WC2H 9NE ⊖ Leicester Square – ✆ (020) 7010 8600 – www.joelrobuchon.co.uk – Closed 25-26 December, 1 January, Sunday and August bank holiday Monday

Rest – Menu £ 28/129 – Carte £ 36/99 **31**AKU**a**

Creative, skilled and occasionally playful cooking; dishes may look delicate but pack a punch. Ground floor Atelier comes with counter seating and chefs on view. More structured La Cuisine upstairs and a cool bar above that.

→ Crab with a citrus dressing and green asparagus. Halibut with rosemary and baby fennel. Manjari chocolate dome, crunchy almonds, cognac ice cream and caramel sauce.

XX **Le Deuxième**

65a Long Acre ✉ WC2E 9JH ⊖ Covent Garden – ✆ (020) 7379 0033 – www.ledeuxieme.com – Closed 24-25 December **31**ALU**b**

Rest – Menu £ 15/28 – Carte £ 28/44

Caters well for theatregoers: opens early, closes late. Buzzy eatery, simply decorated in white with subtle lighting. International menu but emphasis within Europe.

Asia de Cuba - St Martins Lane Hotel

45 St Martin's Ln ✉ WC2N 3HX ⊖ Charing Cross – ✆ (020) 7300 5588 – www.morganshotelgroup.com **31**ALU**e**

Rest – Menu £ 15/23 – Carte £ 35/50

The striking Philippe Starck designed room and the Asian and Cuban inspired cooking appeal to a young, hip crowd. Sharing is the key and that should also include the bill.

J. Sheekey Oyster Bar

33-34 St Martin's Ct. ✉ WC2 4AL ⊖ Leicester Square – ✆ (020) 7240 2565 – www.j-sheekey.co.uk – Closed 25-26 December **31**ALU**v**

Rest – Carte £ 31/65

An addendum to J.Sheekey restaurant. Sit at the bar to watch the chefs prepare the same quality seafood as next door but at slightly lower prices; fish pie and fruits de mer are the popular choices. Open all day.

Hawksmoor

11 Langley St ✉ WC2H 9JG ⊖ Covent Garden – ✆ (020) 7420 9390 – www.thehawksmoor.com – Closed 24-26 and 31 December, 1-2 January and Sunday dinner **31**ALU**f**

Rest – Menu £ 25 (lunch) – Carte £ 39/62

Steaks from Longhorn cattle lovingly reared in North Yorkshire and dry-aged for at least 35 days are the stars of the show. Atmospheric, bustling basement restaurant in former brewery cellars.

Terroirs

5 William IV St ✉ WC2N 4DW ⊖ Charing Cross – ✆ (020) 7036 0660 – www.terroirswinebar.com – Closed 25-26 December, 1 January, Sunday and bank holidays **31**ALU**h**

Rest – Carte £ 24/35

Eat in the ground floor bistro/wine bar or from a slightly different menu two floors below at 'Downstairs at Terroirs'. Flavoursome French cooking, with extra Italian and Spanish influences. Thoughtfully compiled wine list.

Opera Tavern

23 Catherine St. ✉ WC2B 5JS ⊖ Covent Garden – ✆ (020) 7836 3680 – www.operatavern.co.uk – Closed 24-26 and 31 December, 1-2 January and Sunday dinner **31**ALU**y**

Rest – Menu £ 35/45 – Carte approx. £ 26

Shares the same appealing concept of small plates of Spanish and Italian delicacies as its sisters, Salt Yard and Dehesa. All done in a smartly converted old boozer which dates from 1879; ground floor bar and upstairs dining room.

Polpo Covent Garden

6 Maiden Ln. ✉ WC2E 7NA ⊖ Leicester Square – ✆ (020) 7836 8448 – www.polpo.co.uk – Closed 24-26 December **31**ALU**p**

Rest – *(bookings not taken at dinner)* Carte £ 12/32

First Soho, now Covent Garden gets a fun Venetian bacaro. The small plates are surprisingly filling, with delights such as pizzette of white anchovy vying with fennel and almond salad, fritto misto competing with spaghettini and meatballs.

Green Man & French Horn (N)

54 St Martin's Ln ✉ WC2N 4EA Westminster ⊖ Leicester Square – ✆ (020) 7836 2645 – www.greenmanfrenchhorn.co **31**ALU**w**

Rest – Menu £ 10 – Carte £ 21/33

A small old pub so artfully transformed into a bustling French bistro/wine bar, it feels as though it's been here for years. The wine list and menu take their inspiration from the Loire River and Valley; the cooking is comforting and earthy and the wines from small organic and biodynamic growers.

Bedford & Strand

1a Bedford St ✉ WC2E 9HH ⊖ Charing Cross – ✆ (020) 7836 3033 – www.bedford-strand.com – Closed 24 December-2 January, Sunday and bank holidays **31**ALU**c**

Rest – *(booking essential)* Menu £ 18 – Carte £ 20/36

It calls itself a 'wine room and bistro' which neatly sums up both the philosophy and the style of this usefully located basement: interesting wines, reassuringly familiar French and British dishes and relaxed surroundings.

Dishoom

12 Upper St Martin's Ln ✉ WC2H 9FB ⊖ Leicester Square – ✆ (020) 7420 9320 – www.dishoom.com – Closed 24 December dinner, 25-26 December and 1-2 January **31**ALU**j**

Rest – Menu £ 20/35 – Carte £ 10/26

A facsimile of a Bombay café, of the sort opened by Persian immigrants in the early 20C. Try baked roti rolls with chai, vada pav – Bombay's version of the chip butty; a curry or grilled meats. There's another branch in Shoreditch.

Suda

23 Slingsby Pl, St Martin's Courtyard ✉ WC2E 9AB ⊖ Covent Garden – ✆ (020) 7240 8010 – www.suda-thai.com – Closed 25 January **31**ALU**d**

Rest – Carte £ 17/26

This shiny Thai restaurant in a new development may look like a branded chain restaurant but the quality of its food far exceeds one's expectations. Come in a group, sit upstairs, order cocktails and share plenty of dishes.

10 Cases

16 Endell St ✉ WC2H 9BD ⊖ Covent Garden – ✆ (020) 7836 6801 – www.the10cases.co.uk – Closed Easter, Christmas-New Year and bank holidays

Rest – *(booking essential)* Carte £ 25/37 **31**ALU**t**

Cosy and inviting little bistrot offering an unpretentious daily menu of 3 starters, 3 main courses and 3 desserts, along with a very reasonably priced wine list of 10 reds and 10 whites available by the glass, carafe or bottle.

Mishkin's

25 Catherine St ✉ WC2B 5JS ⊖ Covent Garden – ✆ (020) 7240 2078 – www.mishkins.co.uk – Closed 24-26 and 1-2 January **31**ALU**v**

Rest – Carte £ 18/27

The Jewish-American deli, but with cocktails, was the inspiration behind this fun spot from the Polpo people. Lox beigel, chopped liver and salt beef sit alongside nibbles like cod cheek popcorn; the Reuben sandwich hits the spot.

Angel & Crown

58 St Martin's Ln ✉ WC2N 4EA ⊖ Leicester Square. – ✆ (020) 7748 5244 – www.theangelandcrown.com – Closed 25 December **31**ALU**f**

Rest – Carte £ 23/34

Tourist spots and good food are rarely seen together but the gastropub revolution is now creeping into the West End. Enjoy British classics like venison pie or wild boar sausages in the upstairs dining room of this handsome Victorian pub.

VICTORIA

Corinthia

Whitehall Pl. ✉ SW1A 2BD ⊖ Embankment – ✆ (020) 7930 8181 – www.corinthia.com/london **31**ALV**x**

271 rm – †£ 347/1020 ††£ 347/1020, ☕ £ 26 – 23 suites

Rest *Northall* Rest *Massimo* – see restaurant listing

The restored Victorian splendour of this grand, luxurious hotel cannot fail to impress. Tasteful and immaculately finished bedrooms are some of the largest in town; suites come with butlers. The stunning spa is over four floors.

LONDON

Goring

15 Beeston Pl ✉ SW1W 0JW ⊖ Victoria – ✆ (020) 7396 9000 – www.thegoring.com **38**AIX**a**

69 rm – †£ 290/595 ††£ 290/950, ☕ £ 30 – 8 suites

Rest *Dining Room* – see restaurant listing

This very English, very charming and immaculately kept hotel is still owned and run by the Goring family who built it in 1910 – the fourth generation now at the helm. Many of the attractive bedrooms overlook a peaceful garden.

InterContinental London Westminster (N)

22-28 Broadway ✉ SW1H 9JS ⊖ St James's Park – ✆ (020) 3301 8080 – www.intercontinental.com/westminster **39**AKX**w**

256 rm – †£ 249/289 ††£ 249/289, ☕ £ 25 – 45 suites

Rest *Blue Boar Smokehouse* – ✆ (020) 3301 1400 – Carte £ 22/44

Its proximity to the seat of power is a recurring theme at this hotel which opened in 2013. Apart from its façade, little remains of the original 19C building. A cool, crisp reception area sets the tone; bedrooms are stylish and contemporary. The Smokehouse specialises in ribs, pulled pork and steaks.

St James' Court

rm, rm,

45 Buckingham Gate ✉ SW1E 6BS ⊖ St James's Park – ✆ (020) 7834 6655 – www.tajhotels.com/stjamescourt **39**AJX**e**

318 rm – †£ 198/594 ††£ 198/594, ☕ £ 21 – 20 suites

Rest *Quilon* ✿ – see restaurant listing

Rest *Bank* – ✆ (020) 7630 6644 *(closed 25-26 December and 1 January)* Carte £ 27/61

Rest *Bistro 51* – Menu £ 30 – Carte £ 28/44

Built in 1897 as serviced accommodation for visiting aristocrats. Behind the impressive Edwardian façade lies an equally elegant interior. Quietest bedrooms overlook a courtyard. Relaxed, bright Bistro 51 comes with an international menu; Bank offers brasserie classics in a conservatory.

51 Buckingham Gate without rest

51 Buckingham Gate ✉ SW1E 6AF ⊖ St James's Park – ✆ (020) 7769 7766 – www.51-buckinghamgate.com **39**AJX**s**

86 suites – ††£ 300/720, ☕ £ 21

In the courtyard of the Crowne Plaza but offering greater levels of comfort and service. Contemporary in style, suites range from one to nine bedrooms. Butler service available. Restaurants located in adjacent hotel.

Grosvenor

rm,

101 Buckingham Palace Rd ✉ SW1W 0SJ ⊖ Victoria – ✆ (020) 7834 94 94 – www.guoman.com **38**AIY**a**

347 rm ☕ – †£ 160/2500 ††£ 160/2500 – 4 suites

Rest *Grand Imperial* – see restaurant listing

Rest *Brasserie* – ✆ (0871) 376 9038 – Menu £ 16/48 – Carte £ 26/77

Grand old lady returned to her original 1862 splendour after a major refurbishment. Impressive lobby, contemporary bedrooms and a stylish 'Réunion' bar with views across Victoria Station concourse. Classic menu in the brasserie.

St Ermin's

rm,

2 Caxton St. ✉ SW1H 0QW ⊖ St James's Park – ✆ (020) 7222 7888 – www.sterminshotel.co.uk **39**AJX**a**

331 rm – †£ 219/349 ††£ 219/349, ☕ £ 24 – 41 suites

Rest *Caxton Grill* – *(closed lunch Saturday-Sunday)* Carte £ 34/62

Built as an apartment block in 1897 but has spent most of its life as a hotel and is a favoured spot for many a politician. A comprehensive refurbishment restored many of its original features, including the stunning rococo lobby. The restaurant specialises in meat cooked on the Josper grill.

A red **Rest** mention denotes an establishment with an award for culinary excellence, ✿ (star) or ☺ (Bib Gourmand).

LONDON

41 without rest
41 Buckingham Palace Rd. ✉ SW1W 0PS ⊖ Victoria – ✆ (020) 7300 0041 – www.41hotel.com **38**AIX**n**
28 rm – †£ 323/443 ††£ 347/466, ☕ £ 25 – 3 suites
Smart, discreet addendum to The Rubens hotel next door. Attractively decorated and quiet lounge where breakfast is served; comfortable bedrooms boast fireplaces and plenty of extras. Light lunches and dinners for residents only.

The Rubens at The Palace rm,
39 Buckingham Palace Rd ✉ SW1W 0PS ⊖ Victoria – ✆ (020) 7834 6600 – www.rubenshotel.com **38**AIX**n**
161 rm – †£ 179/311 ††£ 191/323, ☕ £ 20 – 1 suite
Rest *Library* – *(dinner only)* Menu £ 33 – Carte £ 30/58
Rest *Old Masters* – *(closed lunch Saturday and Sunday)* Menu £ 25
Rest *bbar* – ✆ (020) 7958 7000 *(closed Sunday and bank holidays)* Menu £ 21 – Carte £ 22/41
Discreet, comfortable hotel in great location for tourists. Constant reinvestment ensures bright and contemporary bedrooms. Old Masters for a buffet-style carvery; 'fine dining' in cosy Library; South African themed bbar.

Eccleston Square rm,
37 Eccleston Sq ✉ SW1V 1PB ⊖ Victoria – ✆ (020) 3489 1001 – www.ecclestonsquarehotel.com **38**AIY**s**
39 rm – †£ 186/252 ††£ 186/252, ☕ £ 12
Rest *Bistrot on the Square* – Menu £ 19 – Carte £ 25/32
Attractive townhouse in a smart square, with a crisp, contemporary interior. Bedrooms are decorated to a high standard and come full of assorted electronic gadgetry. Varied international menu in Bistrot; afternoon tea a feature.

Lord Milner without rest
111 Ebury St ✉ SW1W 9QU ⊖ Victoria – ✆ (020) 7881 9880 – www.lordmilner.com **38**AHY**k**
10 rm – †£ 94/125 ††£ 117/175, ☕ £ 14
A four storey terraced house, with individually decorated bedrooms, three with four-poster beds and all with smart marble bathrooms. Garden Suite is the best room; it has its own patio. Breakfast served in your bedroom.

Dining Room – Goring Hotel
15 Beeston Pl ✉ SW1W 0JW ⊖ Victoria – ✆ (020) 7396 9000 – www.thegoring.com – Closed Saturday lunch **38**AIX**a**
Rest – Menu £ 38/50
Like the hotel in which it is found, The Goring dining room is a paean to Britishness and ideal for those who still like things done 'properly'. The classics are all here, from jugged hare to beef Wellington; served by a smart team in urbane surroundings.

Quilon – Crowne Plaza London - St James Hotel
41 Buckingham Gate ✉ SW1E 6AF ⊖ St James's Park – ✆ (020) 7821 1899 – www.quilon.co.uk – Closed 25 December **39**AJX**e**
Rest – Menu £ 24/58 – Carte £ 30/53
An extensive 2012 makeover left this longstanding restaurant looking slick and contemporary. The elegant surroundings provide the perfect backdrop to chef Sriram Aylur's accomplished and light style of cooking which focuses on India's southwest coast and mixes the modern with the traditional.
→ Fisherman's catch. Braised lamb shank. Spiced chocolate with lentil cappuccino.

Grand Imperial – Grosvenor Hotel
101 Buckingham Palace Rd ✉ SW1W 0SJ ⊖ Victoria – ✆ (020) 7821 8898 – www.grandimperiallondon.com **38**AIY**a**
Rest – Menu £ 16/75 – Carte £ 22/192
Grand it most certainly is, as this elegant restaurant is in the Grosvenor hotel's former ballroom. It specialises in Cantonese cuisine, particularly the version found in Hong Kong; steaming and frying are used to great effect.

XXX Roux at Parliament Square

Royal Institution of Chartered Surveyors, Parliament Sq.
✉ SW1P 3AD ⊖ Westminster – ✆ (020) 7334 3737
– www.rouxatparliamentsquare.co.uk
– Closed 23 December-4 January, Saturday, Sunday and bank holidays
Rest – *(bookings advisable at lunch)* Menu £ 35/65 – Carte £ 42/65 **39**ALX**x**

Light floods through the Georgian windows of this comfortable restaurant within the offices of the Royal Institute of Chartered Surveyors. Carefully crafted, contemporary cuisine, with some interesting flavour combinations.

XXX Northall – Corinthia Hotel

Whitehall Pl. ✉ WC2N 5AE ⊖ Embankment – ✆ (020) 7321 3100
– www.thenorthall.co.uk **31**ALV**x**
Rest – Menu £ 28/30 – Carte £ 29/61

The Corinthia Hotel's British restaurant champions our indigenous produce and its menu is an appealing document. It occupies two rooms: the most appealing is the more modern room which is less formal than the other section.

XXX The Cinnamon Club

30-32 Great Smith St ✉ SW1P 3BU ⊖ St James's Park
– ✆ (020) 7222 2555 – www.cinnamonclub.com
– Closed bank holidays and Sunday **39**AKX**c**
Rest – Menu £ 24/75 – Carte £ 31/60

A plethora of menus is offered at this formally run, busy Indian restaurant housed within the former Westminster Library. Attractively presented, modern food; the tandoori dishes stand out. Buzzy atmosphere; funky basement bar.

XXX Santini

29 Ebury St ✉ SW1W 0NZ ⊖ Victoria – ✆ (020) 7730 4094
– www.santinirestaurant.com – Closed 23-26 December, 1 January and Easter
Rest – Carte £ 30/80 **38**AHY**v**

Santini has looked after its many immaculately coiffured regulars for 30 years. The not inexpensive menu of classic Italian dishes is broadly Venetian in style; the daily specials, pasta dishes and desserts are the standout courses.

XX Tinello

87 Pimlico Rd ✉ SW1W 8PH ⊖ Sloane Square – ✆ (020) 7730 3663
– www.tinello.co.uk – Closed Sunday **37**AGZ**s**
Rest – *(booking essential at dinner)* Carte £ 29/51

Sleekly designed Italian restaurant run by two brothers, both alumni of Locanda Locatelli. Their native Tuscany informs the cooking; the antipasti and 'small eats' sections are very appealing.

XX Osteria Dell' Angolo

47 Marsham St ✉ SW1P 3DR ⊖ St James's Park
– ✆ (020) 3268 1077 – www.osteriadellangolo.co.uk
– Closed Easter, 17-31 August, 23-27 December-1-7 January, Saturday lunch, Sunday and bank holidays **39**AKY**n**
Rest – *(booking essential)* Menu £ 17/28 – Carte £ 30/45

At lunch, this Italian opposite the Home Office is full of bustle and men in suits; at dinner it's a little more relaxed. Staff are personable and the menu is reassuringly familiar; homemade pasta and seafood dishes are good.

XX Il Convivio

143 Ebury St ✉ SW1W 9QN ⊖ Sloane Square
– ✆ (020) 7730 4099 – www.ilconvivio.co.uk
– Closed Christmas-New Year, Easter, bank holidays and Sunday **38**AHY**a**
Rest – Menu £ 18/24 – Carte £ 24/51

Handsome Georgian house, with a retractable roof and Dante's poetry embossed on the walls. All pasta is made on the top floor of the house. Dishes are artfully presented and flavoursome.

XX **Massimo** - Corinthia Hotel

10 Northumberland Ave. ✉ WC2N 5AE ⊖ Embankment – ✆ (020) 7321 3156 – www.corinthia.com/london – Closed Sunday **31**ALV**x**

Rest – Menu £ 28/30 – Carte £ 21/54

Opulent, visually impressive room with an oyster bar on one side. On offer are traditional dishes true to the regions of Italy; fish and seafood dishes stand out. Impressive private dining room comes with its own chef.

XX **Boisdale of Belgravia**

15 Eccleston St ✉ SW1W 9LX ⊖ Victoria – ✆ (020) 7730 6922 – www.boisdale.co.uk – Closed 25 December, Saturday lunch, Sunday and bank holidays **38**AHY**c**

Rest – Menu £ 20 – Carte £ 27/78

A proudly Scottish restaurant with acres of tartan and a charmingly higgledy-piggledy layout. Stand-outs are the smoked salmon and the 28-day aged Aberdeenshire cuts of beef. Live nightly jazz.

XX **The Ebury Restaurant & Wine Bar**

139 Ebury St. ✉ SW1W 9QU ⊖ Victoria – ✆ (020) 7730 5447 – www.eburyrestaurant.co.uk – Closed Christmas-New Year **38**AHY**n**

Rest – Menu £ 19 – Carte £ 28/41

Going strong for over 50 years and as likeable as ever. Some imaginative touches but generally quite classic cooking. Dairy and gluten free menus offered, along with a keenly-priced wine list.

X **A. Wong** (N)

70 Wilton Rd ✉ SW1V 1DE ⊖ Victoria – ✆ (0207) 828 8931 – www.awong.co.uk – Closed 23-27 December, 1-2 January, Sunday and Monday lunch

Rest – *(booking essential)* Menu £ 13/39 – Carte £ 15/24 **38**AIY**w**

Andrew Wong transformed his mother's restaurant into a modern and lively Chinese restaurant. He's taken classics from across China and introduced the odd twist here and there, whilst keeping the original combinations intact.

X **Olivocarne** (N)

61 Elizabeth St ✉ SW1W 9PP ⊖ Sloane Square – ✆ (020) 7730 7997 – www.olivorestaurants.com **38**AHY**d**

Rest – Menu £ 27 (lunch) – Carte £ 28/49

Just when you thought Mauro Sanno had this part of town sown up he opens another restaurant. This one focuses on meat dishes, along with a selection of satisfying Sardinian specialities and is smarter and larger than his others.

X **Olivo**

21 Eccleston St ✉ SW1W 9LX ⊖ Victoria – ✆ (020) 7730 2505 – www.olivorestaurants.com – Closed lunch Saturday-Sunday and bank holidays **38**AHY**z**

Rest – *(booking essential)* Menu £ 24 (lunch) – Carte £ 28/41

Carefully prepared, authentic Sardinian specialities are the highlight at this popular Italian restaurant. Simply decorated in blues and yellows, with an atmosphere of bonhomie.

X **Olivomare**

10 Lower Belgrave St ✉ SW1W 0LJ ⊖ Victoria – ✆ (020) 7730 9022 – www.olivorestaurants.com – Closed bank holidays **38**AHY**b**

Rest – Carte £ 34/48

Expect understated and stylish piscatorial decoration and seafood with a Sardinian base. Fortnightly changing menu, with high quality produce, much of which is available in the deli next door.

LONDON

Thomas Cubitt

44 Elizabeth St ✉ SW1W 9PA ⊖ Sloane Square. – ✆ (020) 7730 6060 – www.thethomascubitt.co.uk **38**AHY**e**

Rest – *(booking essential)* Carte £ 28/40

A pub of two halves: choose the busy ground floor bar with its accessible menu or upstairs for more ambitious, quite elaborate cooking with courteous service and a less frenetic environment.

The Orange with rm

37 Pimlico Rd ✉ SW1W 8NE ⊖ Sloane Square. – ✆ (020) 7881 9844 – www.theorange.co.uk **38**AHZ**k**

4 rm – †£ 195/225 ††£ 195/225, ☕ £ 8

Rest – Carte £ 22/40

The old Orange Brewery is as charming a pub as its stucco-fronted façade suggests. Try the fun bar or book a table in the more sedate upstairs room. The menu has a Mediterranean bias; spelt or wheat based pizzas are a speciality. Bedrooms are stylish and comfortable.

LONDON STANSTED AIRPORT - Essex - 504 U28 — 12 B2
- ✉ Stansted Mountfitchet

London 37 mi - Cambridge 29 mi - Chelmsford 18 mi - Colchester 29 mi

Stansted International Airport : ☎ (0844) 335 1803

Radisson Blu H. London Stansted Airport

Waltham Close, follow signs for short stay parking and car rental returns ✉ *CM24 1PP* - ☎ *(01279) 661 012* - *www.stansted.radissonblu.com*

494 rm - †£ 86/300 ††£ 86/300, ☕ £ 10 - 6 suites

Rest *New York Grill Bar* - *(closed Christmas) (dinner only)* Carte £ 26/63

Rest *Angels' Wine Tower Bar* - Menu £ 24 - Carte £ 19/37

Rest *Fillini* - *(dinner only)* Menu 23 - Carte £ 21/46

Spacious, modern hotel with great facilities and lots of parking, just a stone's throw from the terminal. Smart, well-equipped bedrooms come in 3 colour schemes. The vast atrium is dominated by a 40ft glass wine cellar, where 'Angels' fly up to get your bottle. Choose from snacks in the Tower Bar, Italian fare in Fillini or American steakhouse dishes in the Grill Bar.

LONG ASHTON - North Somerset - 503 M29 - see Bristol

LONG COMPTON - Warwickshire - pop. 705 - ✉ Shipston-On-Stour — 19 C3

London 81 mi - Birmingham 53 mi - Liverpool 147 mi - Bristol 72 mi

Red Lion with rm

Main St ✉ *CV36 5JS* - ☎ *(01608) 684 221* - *www.redlion-longcompton.co.uk*

5 rm ☕ - †£ 60 ††£ 90/140 **Rest** - Carte £ 25/33

18C former coaching inn with flag floors, log fires and a warm, modern feel. Seasonal menu of tasty, home-cooked pub classics, with more adventurous daily specials. Keen service. Good-sized garden and children's play area. Stylish bedrooms have a contemporary, country-chic feel and a good level of facilities.

ENGLAND

LONG CRENDON - Buckinghamshire - 504 Q/R28 - pop. 2 383 — 11 C2
- ✉ Aylesbury

London 50 mi - Aylesbury 11 mi - Oxford 15 mi - Birmingham 82 mi

Angel with rm

47 Bicester Rd ✉ *HP18 9EE* - ☎ *(01844) 208 268* - *www.angelrestaurant.co.uk* - *Closed 24-26 December, 1-2 January and Sunday dinner*

4 rm ☕ - †£ 75 ††£ 110 **Rest** - Menu £ 15/20 - Carte £ 23/50

Sweet former pub with low ceilings and plenty of character. Large, leather-furnished bar and a collection of intimate dining rooms leading to an airy conservatory. Traditional, unfussy, British-based dishes are accompanied by a well-chosen wine list. Bedrooms are cosy and individually decorated.

Mole & Chicken (N) with rm

Easington, North 0.5 mi by Dorton rd ✉ *HP18 8EY* - ☎ *(01844) 208 387* - *www.themoleandchicken.co.uk* - *Closed 25 December*

5 rm ☕ - †£ 85 ††£ 110 **Rest** - Menu £ 15 (weekdays) - Carte £ 26/40

Charming pub built in 1831 as part of a local farm workers' estate, with wonky low ceilings, open fires and a large garden offering commanding country views. The slightly curious menu ranges from classics to dishes influenced by Asia and the Lebanon. Delightful modern bedrooms are in the adjoining house.

LONG MELFORD - Suffolk - 504 W27 - pop. 2 734 Great Britain — 15 C3

London 62 mi - Cambridge 34 mi - Colchester 18 mi - Ipswich 24 mi

Melford Hall★ AC

Black Lion

Church Walk, The Green ✉ *CO10 9DN* - ☎ *(01787) 312 356* - *www.blacklionhotel.net*

10 rm ☕ - †£ 102/136 ††£ 125/175 - 1 suite

Rest *Georgian Room* - see restaurant listing

Rest - Menu £ 16/26 - Carte £ 30/45

Whitewashed Georgian inn with comfortable, classically styled interior. Individually decorated bedrooms named after wines; first floor rooms are more spacious. Wood-panelled Melford bar with deep sofas and open fires; more formal restaurant with terrace. Modern-style classic dishes use the best local produce.

XX **Scutchers** A/C

Westgate St, on A 1092 ✉ CO10 9DP – ✆ (01787) 310 200 – www.scutchers.com – Closed 2 weeks Christmas and Sunday-Thursday

Rest – Carte £ 32/50

Former medieval hall house; now a smart, split-level, personally run restaurant. Traditional dishes use good ingredients and feature tried-and-tested combinations. Well-selected wine list features some top class New and Old World producers.

XX **Georgian Room** – Black Lion Hotel

Church Walk, The Green ✉ CO10 9DN – ✆ (01787) 312 356 – www.blacklionhotel.net

Rest – *(booking advisable)* Menu £ 16/26 – Carte £ 30/45

Intimate, candlelit restaurant in a Georgian inn, with just four tables and a hugely characterful fireplace. Well-executed, modern dishes feature some highly original combinations and local produce is a feature. Service is formal.

LONG SUTTON – Somerset – 503 L30 – ✉ Langport 3 B3

London 131 mi – Bristol 39 mi – Cardiff 83 mi – Bournemouth 64 mi

Devonshire Arms with rm

✉ TA10 9LP – ✆ (01458) 241 271 – www.thedevonshirearms.com – Closed 25-26 December and 1 January

9 rm – †£ 80/135 ††£ 95/135 **Rest** – Carte £ 24/42

Spacious Grade II listed hunting lodge set on village green; contemporary interior, with relaxing, open-plan bar and formal dining room. Locally sourced produce used in seasonal European dishes. Comfortable bedrooms boast excellent quality linen and toiletries.

LONG WHATTON – Leicestershire 16 B2

London 120 mi – Birmingham 43 mi – Liverpool 101 mi – Leeds 84 mi

Royal Oak with rm

The Green ✉ LE12 5BD – ✆ (01509) 843 694 – www.theroyaloaklongwhatton.co.uk

7 rm – †£ 79/95 ††£ 79/95 **Rest** – Menu £ 13 – Carte £ 19/40

Smartly modernised pub in a sleepy village, with a spacious yet cosy bar, an intimate dining room and large grounds. Menus offer plenty of choice, from sharing platters and pub favourites to appealing main courses with a quirky touch. Well-equipped bedrooms are in an adjacent block; one has a whirlpool bath.

LONGHORSLEY – Northumberland – 501 O18 – see Morpeth

LONGPARISH – Hampshire 6 B2

London 67 mi – Bristol 86 mi – Cardiff 119 mi – Plymouth 152 mi

Plough Inn

✉ SP11 6PB – ✆ (01264) 720 358 – www.theploughinn.info – Closed Sunday dinner

Rest – Menu £ 12 (weekdays) – Carte £ 21/37

Red brick and slate pub in a characterful village in the Test Valley, with a smartly laid rustic dining room, a wine cave and a cheese trolley. Appealing menus offer a likeable selection of classics, with a few modern touches; refined, flavourful dishes show respect for their ingredients.

LONGSTOCK – Hampshire – 503 P30 – ✉ Stockbridge 6 B2

London 74 mi – Bristol 77 mi – Cardiff 110 mi – Plymouth 148 mi

Peat Spade Inn with rm

Village St ✉ SO20 6DR – ✆ (01264) 810 612 – www.peatspadeinn.co.uk – Closed 25 December

8 rm – †£ 100/245 ††£ 100/245 **Rest** – *(booking essential)* Carte £ 25/40

Charming 19C inn set in the heart of the Test Valley, with period furnishings, warming fires, welcoming candlelight and a country pursuits theme. Menus offer generous, classically based dishes with bold flavours and a refined style. Stylish bedrooms are split between the inn and annexe; the residents' lounge overlooks the garden and its sunken fire-pit.

ENGLAND

LONGTOWN - Cumbria - 502 L18 21 A1

London 326 mi – Carlisle 9 mi – Newcastle upon Tyne 61 mi

Bessiestown Farm

Catlowdy, Northeast : 8 mi by Netherby St on B 6318 ✉ CA6 5QP – ✆ (01228) 577 219 – www.bessiestown.co.uk – Closed 25 December

5 rm – £ 59 £ 95 **Rest** – Menu £ 20 **s**

Converted farmhouse with spacious, comfortable bedrooms, set on a 150 acre sheep farm close to the English-Scottish border. The light, airy conservatory overlooks a windswept garden. Homemade bread and preserves feature at breakfast. 2 course dinners by arrangement in the bright dining room.

LOOE - Cornwall - 503 G32 - pop. 5 280 1 B2

London 264 mi – Plymouth 23 mi – Truro 39 mi

Fore St, ✆ (01503) 26 20 72, www.visit-southeastcornwall.co.uk

Bin Down, ✆ (01503) 24 02 39

Whitsand Bay Hotel, Torpoint, Portwrinkle, ✆ (01503) 23 02 76

Town★ – Monkey Sanctuary★ **AC**

Barclay House

St Martins Rd, East Looe, East : 0.5 mi by A 387 on B 3253 ✉ PL13 1LP – ✆ (01503) 262 929 – www.barclayhouse.co.uk

12 rm – £ 55/90 £ 80/170 – 1 suite

Rest *Barclay House* – see restaurant listing

Imposing, whitewashed Victorian house in an elevated position; sit on the terrace and take in the view. Guest areas mix the traditional and the modern. Room 7 has an attractive estuary vista and room 9 boasts a balcony and a whirlpool bath.

Beach House without rest

Marine Dr, Hannafore, Southwest : 0.75 mi by Quay Rd ✉ PL13 2DH – ✆ (01503) 262 598 – www.thebeachhouselooe.co.uk – Closed Christmas

5 rm – £ 75/130 £ 90/140

Detached house in a fantastic location, looking out to sea. Personally run, with immaculately kept bedrooms; Fistral, with its balcony and sea views, is the best. In-house beauty therapist; treatments by appointment.

Barclay House – Barclay House Hotel

St Martins Rd, East Looe, East : 0.5 mi by A 387 on B 3253 ✉ PL13 1LP – ✆ (01503) 262 929 – www.barclayhouse.co.uk – Closed Sunday

Rest – *(dinner only)* Menu £ 32/39

Modern restaurant in a hillside hotel; its impressive terrace offering extensive views of the estuary. Seasonal dishes feature seafood from the day boats. Choose from the à la carte or a 6 course tasting menu with matching wine flights.

Trawlers on the Quay

The Quay, East Looe ✉ PL13 1AH – ✆ (01503) 263 593 – www.trawlers-restaurant.co.uk – Closed Monday and Tuesday in winter

Rest – Carte £ 27/42

Bright, contemporary restaurant on the edge of the quay; ask for a window table for great views to West Looe. The menu focuses on seafood and ranges from light lunches up to the full three courses; ambitious, boldly flavoured cooking.

LORTON - Cumbria - 502 K20 - see Cockermouth

LOSTWITHIEL - Cornwall - 503 G32 - pop. 2 602 1 B2

London 244 mi – Bristol 148 mi – Cardiff 179 mi – Plymouth 32 mi

Asquiths

19 North St ✉ PL22 0EF – ✆ (01208) 871 714 – www.asquithsrestaurant.co.uk – Closed first 2 weeks January, Sunday and Monday

Rest – *(dinner only)* Carte £ 23/29

Smartly converted shop with exposed stone walls hung with modern Cornish art, funky lampshades and contemporary styling. Confidently executed dishes feature some original flavour combinations. The atmosphere is relaxed and intimate.

LOUTH - Lincolnshire - **502** T/U23 - **pop. 15 930** **17** D1

London 156 mi - Boston 34 mi - Great Grimsby 17 mi - Lincoln 26 mi

Cannon St., (01507) 60 11 11, www.louthuk.com

Brackenborough
rest,

Cordeaux Corner, Brackenborough, North : 2 mi by A 16 ✉ LN11 0SZ – (01507) 609 169 – www.oakridgehotels.co.uk

24 rm – £ 87/125 £ 102/160 **Rest** – Carte £ 17/31

Contemporary, family-owned hotel with a relaxed feel and a warm, personal style. Spacious, individually designed bedrooms boast the latest mod cons; executive rooms include jacuzzi baths. Sexy cocktail bar. Conservatory lounge-bar and brasserie serve grills and bistro classics with a modern twist.

LOVINGTON - Somerset - **503** M30 - **see Castle Cary**

LOW FELL - Tyne and Wear - **see Gateshead**

LOW ROW - North Yorkshire - **502** N20 - **see Reeth**

LOWER EASHING - Surrey - **see Godalming**

LOWER FROYLE - Hampshire - **see Alton**

LOWER HARDRES - Kent - **504** X30 - **see Canterbury**

LOWER ODDINGTON - Gloucestershire - **see Stow-on-the-Wold**

LOWER PEOVER - Cheshire East - **see Knutsford**

LOWER SLAUGHTER - Gloucestershire - **503** - **see Bourton-on-the-Water**

LOWER SWELL - Gloucestershire - **see Stow-on-the-Wold**

LOWESTOFT - Suffolk - **504** Z26 - **pop. 68 340** Great Britain **15** D2

London 116 mi - Ipswich 43 mi - Norwich 30 mi

Royal Plain, (01502) 53 36 00, www.visit-sunrisecoast.co.uk

Rookery Park, Carlton Colville, (01502) 50 91 90

Norfolk Broads★

Britten House without rest

21 Kirkley Cliff Rd ✉ NR33 0DB – (01502) 573 950 – www.brittenhouse.co.uk

10 rm – £ 50/75 £ 65/95

Fine brick-built Victorian house overlooking the promenade; the birthplace of Benjamin Britten in 1913. Classically furnished bedrooms are named after composers; choose Mozart or Elgar, both of which have sea views.

LUDLOW - Shropshire - **503** L26 - **pop. 9 936** Great Britain **18** B2

London 162 mi - Birmingham 39 mi - Hereford 24 mi - Shrewsbury 29 mi

Castle St, (01584) 87 50 53, www.virtual-shropshire.co.uk

Town★ Z - Castle★ **AC** - Feathers Hotel★ - St Laurence's Parish Church★ (Misericords★) **S**

Stokesay Castle★ **AC**, NW : 6.5 mi by A 49

Plan on next page

Fishmore Hall

Fishmore Rd, North : 1.5 mi by B 4361 and Kidderminster rd on Elm Lodge rd ✉ SY8 3DP – (01584) 875 148 – www.fishmorehall.co.uk

15 rm – £ 75/210 £ 99/250

Rest *Forelles* – see restaurant listing

Whitewashed Georgian mansion in half an acre of mature gardens, just out of town. Original features mix with modern fittings to create a boutique country house feel. Smart bedrooms have bold wallpapers, stylish bathrooms and good views.

ENGLAND

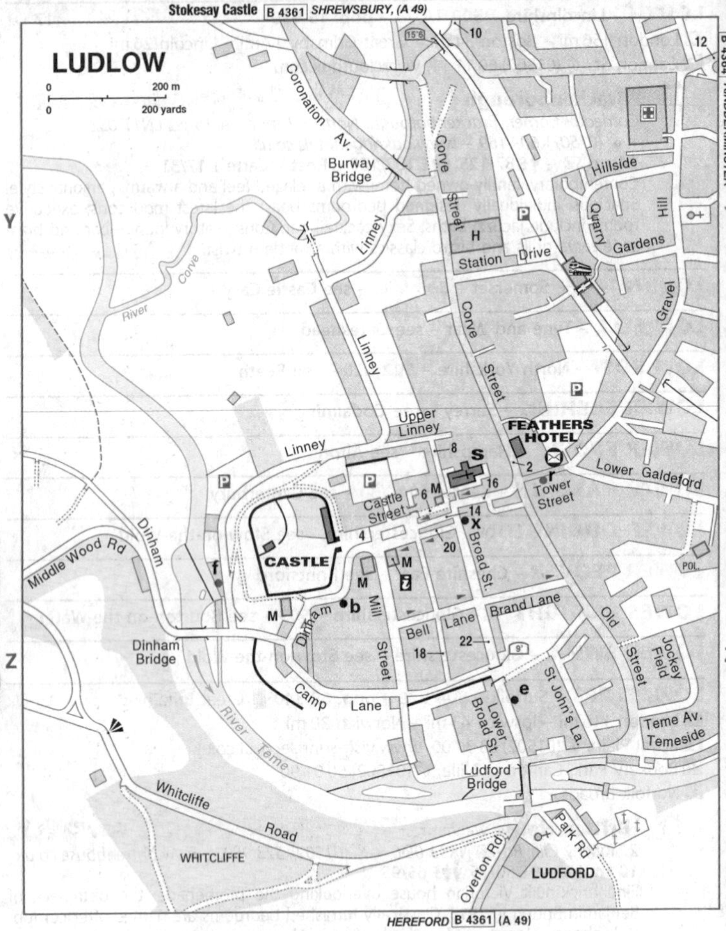

Bull Ring	Z	2	Fishmore Rd	Y	10	Lower Raven Lane	Z	18
Castle Square	Z	4	Henley Rd	Y	12	Market St	Z	20
Church St	Z	6	High St	Z	14	Silk Mill	Z	22
College St	Z	8	King St	Z	16			

Overton Grange

Old Hereford Rd, South : 1.75 mi on B 4361 ✉ *SY8 4AD – ✆ (01584) 873 500 – www.overtongrangehotel.com*

14 rm ☕ – †£ 99/199 ††£ 125/245 **Rest** – *(booking essential)* Menu £ 30/43

Well-maintained Edwardian country house where subtle modern touches sit alongside original features. Well-equipped bedrooms and smart bathrooms. Good-sized pool, sauna and 2 treatment rooms. Dining rooms offer immaculately laid tables and countryside views; cooking has a refined French base.

Symbols shown in red indicate particularly charming establishments.

Dinham Hall

Dinham ✉ SY8 1EJ – ☎ (01584) 876 464 – www.dinhamhall.com Z**b**

13 rm – £ 99/199 £ 129/239

Rest – Menu £ 17 (lunch and early dinner) – Carte £ 27/35

18C former schoolhouse with a pretty walled garden, in a great town centre location. Spacious guest areas filled with antiques and ornaments. Comfy bedrooms boast original features and good mod cons. Formal restaurant offers a concise menu, where classic dishes are given a modern twist.

De Grey's Town House without rest

Broad St ✉ SY8 1NG – ☎ (01584) 872 764 – www.degreys.co.uk – Closed 24-26, 31 December and 1 January Z**x**

9 rm – £ 95/135 £ 110/165

Appealing 1570s building in a central location in this historic market town; check in at the nearby tea room and bakery. Spacious, individually designed bedrooms display original beams, antique furnishings and good modern facilities.

Bromley Court without rest

18-20 Lower Broad St ✉ SY8 1PQ – ☎ (01584) 876 996 – www.ludlowhotels.com

3 rm – £ 85/120 £ 85/120 Z**e**

Three delightful adjoining Tudor cottages, each one comprising of a kitchen, a seating area and a first floor bedroom. Extensive DIY continental breakfasts left in the fridge. Pleasant walled courtyard with wrought iron furnishings.

Forelles – Fishmore Hall Hotel

Fishmore Rd, North : 1.5 mi by B 4361 and Kidderminster rd on Elm Lodge rd ✉ SY8 3DP – ☎ (01584) 875 148 – www.fishmorehall.co.uk

Rest – Menu £ 25/49

Formal hotel restaurant named after the pear tree outside, with lovely garden views from the conservatory. Attractively presented dishes use local produce and modern techniques, and feature good flavour and texture combinations.

Mr Underhill's at Dinham Weir (Chris Bradley) with rm

Dinham ✉ SY8 1EH – ☎ (01584) 874 431 – www.mr-underhills.co.uk – Closed 2 weeks June, 2 weeks October, Christmas and New Year Z**f**

4 rm – £ 195/325 £ 245/375

Rest – *(closed Monday and Tuesday) (dinner only) (booking essential) (set menu only)* Menu £ 68/75

Smart, comfortable restaurant in a stunning location by the weir. Traditionally based menus showcase superlative ingredients in skilfully and accurately prepared dishes, where natural flavours take the lead. Be sure to start your meal with drinks on the pretty terrace. Stylish bedrooms are all 'spa' suites and boast steam showers and garden views.

→ Brill and pickled vegetables with lime and vanilla. Slow-roast duck breast with an orange and green peppercorn jus, walnuts and aubergine. Ludlow blue cheese millefeuille with pear and apple chutney.

French Pantry

15 Tower St. ✉ SY8 1RL – ☎ (01584) 879 133 – www.thefrenchpantry.co.uk – Closed 1-5 January and Sunday Z**r**

Rest – *(booking advisable)* Menu £ 25 (dinner) – Carte lunch £ 23/29

Small épicerie-cum-café-cum-bistro on a paved side street, selling produce and wines imported from the Parisian markets. Authentic French dishes are crafted from local and imported ingredients. Cooking is hearty and full of flavour.

Green Café

Mill on the Green ✉ SY8 1EG – ☎ (01584) 879 872 – www.thegreencafe.co.uk – Closed 23 December-13 February and Monday Z**f**

Rest – *(lunch only)* Carte £ 16/25

Simple little eatery with delightful waterside terrace, set in a charming 14C watermill on the banks of the River Teme. Concise menu of unfussy, daily changing dishes that showcase British ingredients in simple, flavoursome combinations.

at Woofferton South : 4 mi by B 4361 - Z - on A 49 – ✉ Ludlow

Ravenscourt Manor without rest

On A 49 ✉ SY8 4AL – ✆ (01584) 711 905 – www.ravenscourtmanor.com – Closed mid-October-mid-March

3 rm – †£ 55/60 ††£ 75/85

Black and white timbered 16C manor house in 2½ acres of mature gardens. Characterful interior with cosy breakfast room and lounge complete with wood burning stove. Good-sized bedrooms mix antique furnishings and modern facilities.

at Bromfield Northwest : 2.5 mi on A 49 - Y – ✉ Ludlow

Clive with rm

✉ SY8 2JR – ✆ (01584) 856 565 – www.theclive.co.uk – Closed 25-26 December

15 rm – †£ 70/95 ††£ 100/125

Rest – *(booking essential at dinner)* Carte £ 21/37

Large, Georgian former farmhouse. Extensive menu of classically based dishes with local produce to the fore and a mix of British and international influences. Two colourfully decorated dining rooms are hung with contemporary art. Spacious, simply furnished bedrooms are set around a courtyard.

LUND – East Riding of Yorkshire – **502** S22 — **23** C2

London 213 mi – Leeds 61 mi – Sheffield 64 mi – Bradford 67 mi

Wellington Inn

19 The Green ✉ YO25 9TE – ✆ (01377) 217 294 – www.thewellingtoninn.co.uk – Closed 25 December, 1 January and Monday

Rest – Carte £ 27/40

Well-run pub with beamed, open-fired bars and more formal, linen-laid dining rooms. Experienced kitchen uses quality ingredients in dishes that are generous, both in flavour and portion. Efficient service. Good selection of Yorkshire beers.

ENGLAND

LUPTON – Cumbria – **502** L21 – see Kirkby Lonsdale

LURGASHALL – West Sussex – **504** S30 — **7** C2

London 49 mi – Bristol 124 mi – Cardiff 157 mi – Plymouth 197 mi

Barn Ⓝ — rest,

Lower Roundhurst Farm, Jobson's Ln, Northwest : 2.5 mi by Haslemere rd ✉ GU27 3BY – ✆ (01428) 642 535 – www.thebarnatroundhurst.com

6 rm – †£ 109/159 ††£ 120/170 **Rest** – Menu £ 45

Beautifully restored, mid-17C threshing barn, on a 250 acre organic farm in the South Downs. The spacious lounge features fresh flowers, sculptures and modern art. Meals use eggs and meats from the farm, along with other local ingredients. Bedrooms, in the old outbuildings, are stylish and modern, and come with homemade biscuits, iPod docks and luxurious bathrooms.

Noah's Ark Inn

The Green ✉ GU28 9ET – ✆ (01428) 707 346 – www.noahsarkinn.co.uk

Rest – Carte £ 21/35

Quintessentially English pub in a picturesque location right on the village green, overlooking the cricket pitch. Gloriously rustic interior with an inglenook and exposed beams. Wide-ranging menus; tasty, generously proportioned dishes.

LUTON – Luton – **504** S28 – **pop. 185 543** Great Britain — **12** A2

London 35 mi – Cambridge 36 mi – Ipswich 93 mi – Oxford 45 mi

Luton International Airport : ✆ (01582) 405100, E : 1.5 mi X

St George's Sq, ✆ (01582) 40 15 79, www.visitorinformationcentre.luton.towntalk.co.uk

Stockwood Park, London Rd, ✆ (01582) 41 37 04

Whipsnade Wild Animal Park★, West : 8 mi by B 489, signed from M 1 (junction 9) and M 25 (junction 21) X

🏨 Luton Hoo 🦢 ≮ 🚗 🕙 🛆 🖼 ⑳ 🌊 🕰 ℀ 🖥 🛗 ᓕ 🛜 🖼 🅿

The Mansion House, Southeast : 2.5 mi by A 505 on A 1081 ✉ *LU1 3TQ*
– 𝒞 (01582) 734 437 – www.lutonhoo.com
135 rm ☑ – †£ 280/1100 ††£ 280/1100 – 9 suites
Rest Wernher *– (closed Monday and Tuesday)* Menu £ 33/53
Rest Adam's Brasserie *– (closed Sunday dinner)* Carte £ 28/38
Stunning 18C house in over 1,000 acres of gardens; some designed by Capability Brown. The main mansion boasts an impressive hallway, numerous beautifully furnished drawing rooms and classical, luxurious bedrooms. The marble-filled Wernher restaurant offers sophisticated modern cuisine. The old stable block houses the smart spa and the casual, contemporary brasserie.

LYDDINGTON – Rutland – see Uppingham

LYDFORD – Devon – 503 H32 – pop. 1 734 – ✉ Okehampton 2 C2
▶ London 234 mi – Exeter 33 mi – Plymouth 25 mi
◎ Village★★
Ꮆ Dartmoor National Park★★

🍴 Dartmoor Inn with rm 🏠 🛜 🅿

Moorside, East : 1 mi on A 386 ✉ *EX20 4AY – 𝒞 (01822) 820 221*
– www.dartmoorinn.com – Closed Sunday dinner and Monday lunch except bank holidays
3 rm ☑ – †£ 75/85 ††£ 95/115
Rest – Menu £ 18 (weekdays) – Carte £ 22/35
Cosy, rustic pub with friendly staff and a buzzy atmosphere. The numerous rooms have shabby-chic styling: the one with the wood-burning stove is most popular; another houses a boutique selling homewares. Classic dishes are satisfying and full of flavour; see the blackboard for simpler options. Spacious bedrooms are named after the fabrics they feature.

LYME REGIS – Dorset – 503 L31 – pop. 4 406 3 B3
▶ London 160 mi – Dorchester 25 mi – Exeter 31 mi – Taunton 27 mi
🆔 Church St, 𝒞 (01297) 44 21 38, www.lymeregis.org
🔟 Timber Hill, 𝒞 (01297) 44 29 63
◎ Town★ – The Cobb★

🏨 Alexandra ≮ 🚗 🏠 ᓕ 🛜 🅿

Pound St ✉ *DT7 3HZ – 𝒞 (01297) 442 010 – www.hotelalexandra.co.uk – Closed January and Christmas-New Year*
25 rm ☑ – †£ 90 ††£ 177/305 **Rest** – Carte £ 24/38
18C dower house with lovely gardens and superb views over the Cobb and out to sea. Modern lounges and up-to-date bedrooms; No.12 has a large bay window to take in the views. Small terrace and a lookout tower (for hire) in the garden. Modern menus in the formal restaurant; classical dishes in the conservatory.

🏠 1 Lyme Town House without rest 🛜

1 Pound St ✉ *D17 3HZ – 𝒞 (01297) 442 499 – www.1lymetownhouse.co.uk*
– Closed 25-26 December
7 rm ☑ – †£ 90/100 ††£ 100/135
Spacious Georgian townhouse. Contemporary bedrooms boast feature beds: No.7 runs the length of the house and No.5 has rooftop and bay views. All come with dining tables – a hamper of fruits, cereals and pastries is delivered every morning.

℀ Hix Oyster & Fish House ≮ 🏠

Lister Gdns, Cobb Rd ✉ *DT7 3JP – 𝒞 (01297) 446 910*
– www.hixoysterandfishhouse.co.uk – Closed 25-26 December and Monday November-February
Rest *– (booking essential)* Carte £ 23/48
Smart, Scandic-style restaurant with basement chef's table and superb views across Lyme Bay and the Cobb. Seafood menu focuses on fish from the day boats and dishes have a likeable simplicity. Crumpets and tea, am and pm.

ENGLAND

LYMINGTON – Hampshire – 504 P31 – pop. 14 227 — 6 A3

London 103 mi – Bournemouth 18 mi – Southampton 19 mi – Winchester 32 mi
to the Isle of Wight (Yarmouth) (Wightlink Ltd) frequent services daily (30 mn)
New St, (01590) 68 90 00, www.lymington.org

Stanwell House

14-15 High St SO41 9AA – (01590) 677 123 – www.stanwellhouse.com
29 rm – £ 79/99 £ 89/140 – 1 suite
Rest *Seafood at Stanwells* – see restaurant listing
Rest *Bistro* – *(dinner only)* Carte £ 32/44
Neatly painted 18C house in the town centre, run by a friendly owner. Comfy, well-equipped bedrooms: those in the original house are more characterful, those in the extension, more contemporary. Eat in the smart restaurant, wood-furnished bistro with covered courtyard and terrace or trendy wine bar.

Mill at Gordleton

rest,

Silver St, Hordle, Northwest : 3.5 mi by A 337 off Sway Rd SO41 6DJ – (01590) 682 219 – www.themillatgordleton.co.uk – Closed 25 December
9 rm – £ 115/125 £ 150/195 – 1 suite
Rest – Menu £ 19/28 – Carte £ 34/52
Charming, part-17C creeper-clad water mill with delightful terraces and colourful gardens. Comfortable, country house interior shows an eye for detail; bedrooms are extremely cosy. Snacks in the bar, classic dishes with a modern edge in the restaurant and afternoon teas by the river in summer.

Seafood at Stanwells – Stanwell House Hotel

14-15 High St SO41 9AA – (01590) 677 123 – www.stanwellhouse.com
Rest – *(booking essential at dinner)* Carte £ 30/67
Smart, well-run and very popular hotel restaurant serving modern seafood dishes ranging from tapas to platters for two. Unfussy preparation focuses on the main ingredient. At lunch, the menu is offered in the conservatory.

at Downton West : 3 mi on A 337 – Lymington

Olde Barn without rest

Christchurch Rd, East : 0.5 mi on A 337 SO41 0LA – (01590) 644 939 – www.theoldebarn.co.uk
3 rm – £ 50/70 £ 50/75
Converted 17C barn with small, traditional lounge and communal breakfast room. Bedrooms in the barn annexe – a converted dairy – are spotlessly kept, with a homely, cottagey style.

LYMM – Warrington – 502 M23 – pop. 9 554 — 20 B3

London 190 mi – Liverpool 26 mi – Leeds 62 mi – Sheffield 68 mi

Church Green

Higher Ln, on A 56 WA13 0AP – (01925) 752 068 – www.thechurchgreen.co.uk
Rest – *(booking essential)* Carte £ 21/54
Double gable-fronted Victorian pub beside Lymm Dam, with a smart interior, an attractive terrace and a kitchen garden. Appealing menu includes 'pub classics' and 'steak house' sections: choose a cut, then add sauce, garnish and extras.

LYNDHURST – Hampshire – 503 – pop. 2 281 Great Britain — 6 A2

London 95 mi – Bournemouth 20 mi – Southampton 10 mi – Winchester 23 mi
Main Car Park, (023) 8028 22 69, www.thenewforest.co.uk
New Forest Museum and Visitor Centre, (023) 8028 34 44, www.newforestcentre.org.uk
Dibden Golf Centre, Main Rd, (023) 8020 75 08
New Forest, Southampton Rd, (023) 8028 27 52
New Forest★★ (Bolderwood Ornamental Drive★★, Rhinefield Ornamental Drive★★)

ENGLAND

Lime Wood

Beaulieu Rd, Southeast : 1 mi by A 35 on B 3056 ✉ SO43 7FZ – ☎ (023) 8028 7177 – www.limewoodhotel.co.uk

32 rm – †£ 225/375 ††£ 225/375, ☕ £ 19 – 14 suites

Rest *Hartnett Holder & Co* – see restaurant listing

Impressive Georgian mansion with a stunning spa topped by a herb garden roof. Stylish guest lounges have quality fabrics and furnishings; one is set around a courtyard and features a retractable glass roof. Beautifully furnished bedrooms boast luxurious marble-tiled bathrooms, and many have New Forest views.

XX **Hartnett Holder & Co** – Lime Wood Hotel

Beaulieu Rd, Southeast : 1 mi by A 35 on B 3056 ✉ SO43 7FZ – ☎ (023) 8028 7167 – www.limewood.co.uk

Rest – Menu £ 25 (weekday lunch) – Carte £ 28/45

Elegant restaurant in an impressive Georgian mansion, offering views out over the delightful grounds. A central bar divides the room into several different dining areas; sit on the sofas, at the bar counter or in leather tub chairs. The tempting, Italian-based menu features home-smoked charcuterie.

LYNMOUTH – **Devon** – **503** I30 – **see Lynton**

LYNTON – Devon – 503 I30 – pop. 1 870 — 2 C1

London 206 mi – Exeter 59 mi – Taunton 44 mi

Lee Rd, ☎ (01598) 75 22 25, www.lynton-lynmouth-tourism.co.uk

Town★ (<★)

Valley of the Rocks★, W : 1 mi – Watersmeet★, E : 1.5 mi by A 39. Exmoor National Park★★ – Doone Valley★, SE : 7.5 mi by A 39 (access from Oare on foot)

ENGLAND

Hewitt's - Villa Spaldi

North Walk ✉ EX35 6HJ – ☎ (01598) 752 293 – www.hewittshotel.com – Closed October-March

8 rm ☕ – †£ 80/120 ††£ 110/180

Rest – *(dinner only)* Menu £ 29/36 – Carte £ 29/40

Splendid cliffside Arts and Crafts house in mature gardens. Antique-furnished bedrooms with up-to-date facilities, sea views and smart, modern bathrooms. Informal weekday meals in wood-panelled bar; fine dining on Friday and Saturday evenings. High tea, with its homemade scones and excellent tea selection, is a must and the terrace is a delightful spot for breakfast.

St Vincent

Market St, Castle Hill ✉ EX35 6JA – ☎ (01598) 752 720 – www.st-vincent-hotel.co.uk

6 rm ☕ – †£ 40/75 ††£ 60/85 **Rest** – Carte £ 15/19

Whitewashed, Grade II listed Georgian House in the village centre, 200m from the coastal path. Lovely fire-lit lounge with honesty bar and well-kept, uncluttered bedrooms with smart bathrooms. Simple home-cooked meals use local produce where possible. Tea and cakes – outside if sunny.

Castle Hill without rest

Castle Hill ✉ EX35 6JA – ☎ (01598) 752 291 – www.castlehill.biz

7 rm ☕ – †£ 45/75 ††£ 65/95

Stone-built house on the main street of this popular tourist village. Spacious, simply decorated bedrooms; 3 of the 7 have their own sitting area. Lounge with plenty of local info and a large fish tank. Friendly owners.

at Lynmouth East : 1 mi

Shelley's without rest

8 Watersmeet Rd ✉ EX35 6EP – ☎ (01598) 753 219 – www.shelleyshotel.co.uk – Closed November-February

11 rm ☕ – †£ 79/129 ††£ 79/129

A bright, keenly run hotel overlooking the sea; the eponymous poet honeymooned here in 1812. Traditionally styled guest areas include a homely lounge and a formally laid breakfast room with coastal views. Good-sized bedrooms.

Heatherville
Tors Park, by Tors Rd bearing left at the fork ✉ EX35 6NB – ✆ (01598) 752 327 – www.heatherville.co.uk – Closed November-March
6 rm – †£ 90/120 ††£ 95/125 **Rest** – Menu £ 28
Large Victorian house on the side of the valley, with a lovely coastal outlook. Immaculately kept, decently sized bedrooms have warm, traditional décor and fabrics. Comfortable lounge, cosy bar and large, linen-laid dining room where home-cooked meals are served.

at Martinhoe West : 4.25 mi via Coast rd (toll) – ✉ Barnstaple

Old Rectory
✉ EX31 4QT – ✆ (01598) 763 368 – www.oldrectoryhotel.co.uk – Closed November-March
11 rm (dinner included) – †£ 170/215 ††£ 215/260
Rest – *(dinner only residents only)* Menu £ 34
Built in 19C for rector of Martinhoe's 11C church, this quiet country retreat is set in a charming spot, with a well-tended three acre garden and cascading brook. Fresh, bright bedrooms are modern, yet retain period touches: Heddon and Paddock are two of the best. Comfortable dining room; simple home-cooking.

LYTHAM – Lancashire – **502** L22 – **see Lytham St Annes**

LYTHAM ST ANNE'S – Lancashire – **502** L22 – **pop. 41 327** **20** A2

London 237 mi – Blackpool 7 mi – Liverpool 44 mi – Preston 13 mi
St Annes Rd West, ✆ (01253) 72 56 10, www.visitlythamstannes.co.uk
Fairhaven, Ansdell, Oakwood Avenue, ✆ (01253) 73 67 41
St Annes Old Links, Highbury Rd, ✆ (01253) 72 35 97

at Lytham

Rooms without rest
35 Church Rd ✉ FY8 5LL – ✆ (01253) 736 000 – www.theroomslytham.com
5 rm – †£ 100/125 ††£ 125/180
Mid-Victorian terrace on the approach road into this delightful estuary town. Striking, contemporary bedrooms come with good mod cons. Room One (on the top floor) is the largest, with a stone bath as part of the room. Bounteous breakfasts.

at St Anne's

Grand
South Promenade ✉ FY8 1NB – ✆ (01253) 643 424 – www.the-grand.co.uk – Closed 24-26 December
54 rm – †£ 80/180 ††£ 80/180
Rest *Cafe Grand* – see restaurant listing
Keenly run by an experienced local hotelier: the most architecturally pleasing building on the promenade. Contemporary interior with Victorian stained glass windows and grand staircase in situ. Turret rooms have the best views.

Cafe Grand – Grand Hotel
South Promenade ✉ FY8 1NB – ✆ (01253) 643 409 – www.the-grand.co.uk – Closed 24-26 December
Rest – Carte £ 20/43
Contemporary hotel restaurant with a fun, friendly atmosphere and a circular bar counter off to one side. Menus offer an interesting mix of Mediterranean dishes and modern-classics, including tapas and dishes 'a la plancha'.

MADINGLEY – Cambridgeshire – **504** U27 – **see Cambridge**

MAENPORTH – Cornwall – **see Falmouth**

MAIDENCOMBE – Torbay – **503** J32 – **see Torquay**

MAIDENHEAD - Windsor and Maidenhead - 504 R29 - pop. 58 848 11 C3

London 33 mi – Oxford 32 mi – Reading 13 mi
to Marlow, Cookham and Windsor (Salter Bros. Ltd) (summer only) (3 h 45 mn)
St Ives Rd, ✆ (01628) 79 65 02, www.windsor.gov.uk
Bird Hills, Hawthorn Hill, Drift Rd, ✆ (01628) 77 10 30
Shoppenhangers Rd, ✆ (01628) 62 46 93

Plan on next page

Fredrick's

Shoppenhangers Rd ✉ SL6 2PZ – ✆ (01628) 581 000 – www.fredricks-hotel.co.uk – Closed 22-27 December Xc
37 rm – †£ 99/169 ††£ 99/194 – 1 suite
Rest *Fredrick's* – Menu £ 31 – Carte £ 46/58
Red-brick former inn with very stylish, well-equipped spa. Ornate, marble reception with smoked mirrors; wicker-furnished conservatory and comfortable, individually styled bedrooms. Large restaurant boasts chandeliers, full-length windows and elaborate British menus.

Boulters Riverside Brasserie

Boulters Lock Island ✉ SL6 8PE – ✆ (01628) 621 291 – www.boultersrestaurant.co.uk – Closed 26-30 December, Sunday dinner and Monday Vx
Rest – Menu £ 16 (weekdays)/29 – Carte £ 30/37
Stylish modern eatery beside a lock, on a small island in the Thames. Full-length windows open onto the terrace; excellent river views. Hearty yet refined brasserie classics use quality produce.

MAIDEN NEWTON - Dorset - 503 M31 4 C3

London 144 mi – Bristol 93 mi – Cardiff 113 mi – Southampton 66 mi

Le Petit Canard

Dorchester Rd ✉ DT2 0BE – ✆ (01300) 320 536 – www.le-petit-canard.co.uk – Closed 2 weeks January, Sunday dinner and Monday
Rest – *(dinner only and Sunday lunch)* Menu £ 25/33
Double-fronted, beamed former shop with yachting prints, candlelight and a cosy feel. Run by a husband and wife team, it offers a seasonally changing menu of classic dishes; duck and homemade bread feature.

MAIDENSGROVE - Oxfordshire - pop. 1 572 - ✉ Henley-On-Thames 11 C3

London 43 mi – Oxford 23 mi – Reading 15 mi

Five Horseshoes

✉ RG9 6EX – ✆ (01491) 641 282 – www.thefivehorseshoes.co.uk
Rest – Menu £ 12 (weekdays) – Carte £ 22/46
Charming, part-17C inn; a walkers' paradise. The large garden and terrace afford delightful country views and there's a wood-fired oven for bespoke pizzas. Cooking is wholesome, with plenty of meaty dishes and a good value set selection.

MAIDSTONE - Kent - 504 V30 - pop. 89 684 Great Britain 8 B2

London 36 mi – Brighton 64 mi – Cambridge 84 mi – Colchester 72 mi
High St, ✆ (01622) 60 21 69, www.visitmaidstone.com
Tudor Park Hotel, Bearsted, Ashford Rd, ✆ (01622) 73 43 34
Cobtree Manor Park, Boxley, Chatham Rd, ✆ (01622) 75 32 76
Leeds Castle★ **AC**, SE : 4.5 mi by A 20 and B 2163

at Bearsted East : 3 mi by A 249 off A 20 – ✉ Maidstone

Fish On The Green

Church Ln ✉ ME14 4EJ – ✆ (01622) 738 300 – www.fishonthegreen.com – Closed 25 December-26 January, Sunday dinner and Monday
Rest – Menu £ 16 (lunch) – Carte £ 29/45
Tucked away on a corner of the green is this simply decorated restaurant with a pleasant terrace. Professional cooking focuses on fresh, tasty, local fish and seafood. Good value lunch menu; polite, knowledgeable service.

MAIDENHEAD

- Bad Godesberg Way . . . . . Y 2
- Belmont Park Ave . . . . . . V 3
- Blackamoor Lane . . . . . . V 5
- Boyn Hill Ave . . . . Z 6
- Braywick Rd . . . . Z 7
- Bridge St . . . . Y 9
- College Rd . . . . V 13
- Cookham Rd . . . . Y 14
- Crescent (The) . . . . Y 15
- Ferry Rd . . . . X 17
- Frascati Way . . . . YZ 18
- Furze Platt Rd . . . . V 20
- Grenfell Pl. . . . . Z 21
- Gringer Hill . . . . V 22
- Harrow Lane . . . . V 24
- High St . . . . Y
- High St BRAY-ON-THAMES . . . . X 25
- King's Grove . . . . Z 27
- Linden Ave . . . . V 28
- Lower Cookham Rd . . . . . V 29
- Manor Lane . . . . X 31
- Market St . . . . Y 32
- Nicholson's Walk Shopping Centre . . . . . YZ
- Norreys Drive . . . . X 35
- Oldfield Rd . . . . V 36
- Ray Mill Rd West . . . . . . V 39
- Ray St . . . . V 38
- St Ives Rd . . . . Y 41
- St Mark Rd . . . . V 42
- Stafferton Way . . . . Z 43
- Upper Bray Rd . . . . X 45

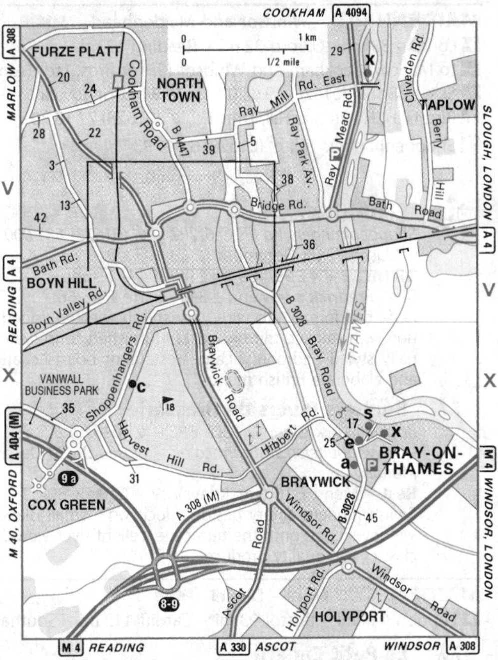

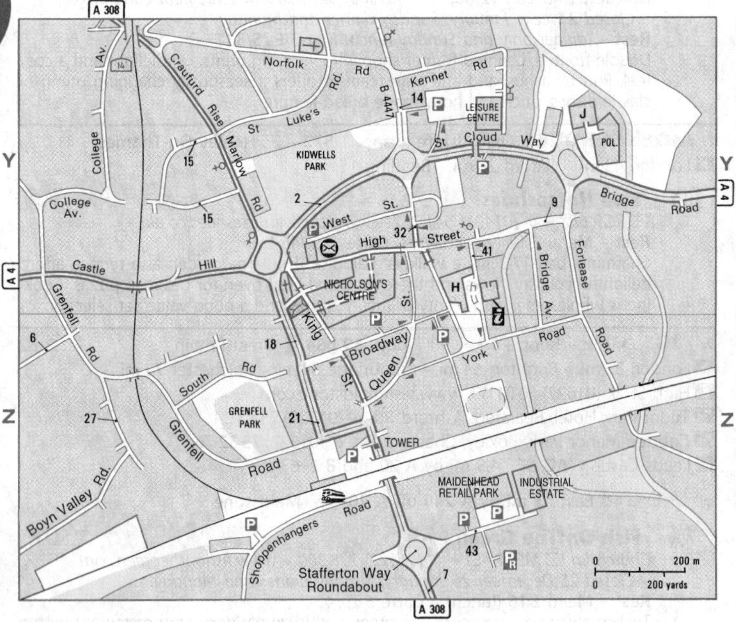

ENGLAND

MALMESBURY – Wiltshire – 503 N29 – pop. 5 094 4 C2

London 108 mi – Bristol 28 mi – Gloucester 24 mi – Swindon 19 mi

Cross Hayes, ✆ (01666) 82 37 48, www.malmesbury.gov.uk

Town★ – Market Cross★★ – Abbey★

Whatley Manor

Easton Grey, West : 2.25 mi on B 4040 ✉ SN16 0RB – ✆ (01666) 822 888 – www.whatleymanor.com

23 rm – †£ 305 ††£ 305/665 – 8 suites

Rest *The Dining Room* ✿✿ **Rest *Le Mazot*** – see restaurant listing

Charming Cotswold stone country house in 12 acres of beautiful formal gardens. Guest areas include a delightful wood-panelled sitting room, a stunning spa, a top class business centre and a private cinema. Luxurious, individually decorated bedrooms have a chic, contemporary feel and sumptuous bathrooms.

Old Bell

Abbey Row ✉ SN16 0BW – ✆ (01666) 822 344 – www.oldbellhotel.com

33 rm – †£ 99/159 ††£ 115/275

Rest *Old Bell* – see restaurant listing

Charming creeper-clad property built in 1220, next to a beautiful abbey. Characterful beamed interior with parquet floors and roaring fires, numerous cosy lounges and a smart bar. Stylish bedrooms in the main house; simpler annexe rooms.

The Dining Room – Whatley Manor Hotel

✿✿

Easton Grey, West : 2.25 mi on B 4040 ✉ SN16 0RB – ✆ (01666) 822 888 – www.whatleymanor.com – Closed Monday and Tuesday

Rest – *(dinner only) (booking essential)* Menu £ 85 **s**

Smart, sophisticated, three-roomed restaurant in an elegant hotel, overlooking the kitchen garden. Original, modern dishes show an excellent appreciation of ingredients and understanding of combinations; cooking is technically skilled and flavours are stunning. Extensive wine list and attentive team.

→ Quail breasts with Morteau sausage, sage and onion purée and deep-fried quails' eggs rolled in chicken crumb. Fillets of turbot with oyster and lime cannelloni, compressed cucumber and champagne caviar sauce. Chicory mousse layered with bitter coffee and mascarpone cream.

Le Mazot – Whatley Manor Hotel

Easton Grey, West : 2.25 mi on B 4040 ✉ SN16 0RB – ✆ (01666) 822 888 – www.whatleymanor.com

Rest – Menu £ 19 (weekday lunch) **s** – Carte £ 28/34 **s**

The less formal dining option at the charming Whatley Manor Hotel. With a comfy laid-back feel, wood panelling and carvings, it brings to mind a traditional Swiss chalet. Dishes are classical, with the occasional Bavarian speciality.

Old Bell – Old Bell Hotel

Abbey Row ✉ SN16 0BW – ✆ (01666) 822 344 – www.oldbellhotel.com

Rest – *(booking essential at dinner)* Menu £ 45 (dinner) – Carte £ 25/39

Elegant dining room in a charming 13C hotel, with mirrors and old portraits hung on aubergine walls and a contemporary lounge-bar. Concise menu of ambitious modern dishes with a classical base; lunch sees reinterpreted brasserie classics.

at Crudwell North : 4 mi on A 429 – ✉ Malmesbury

The Rectory

✉ SN16 9EP – ✆ (01666) 577 194 – www.therectoryhotel.com

12 rm – †£ 95/195 ††£ 105/205 **Rest** – *(dinner only)* Menu £ 27

Classical 18C former rectory with high ceilings, period features and a laid-back feel. Stylish fabrics and contemporary furnishings in the lounge and bar. Bedrooms boast bold feature walls, iPod docks, Roberts radios and some antiques. Oak-panelled dining room offers carefully cooked modern dishes.

Potting Shed Pub

The Street ✉ SN16 9EW – ✆ (01666) 577 833 – www.thepottingshedpub.com

Rest – Carte £ 23/36

Spacious, light-filled pub with contemporary décor, exposed beams and a relaxing feel. Monthly changing menus offer wholesome, satisfying dishes, with vegetables and herbs from their garden.

ENGLAND

MALPAS – Cheshire West and Chester – 502 L24 – pop. 3 684 20 A3

London 177 mi – Birmingham 60 mi – Chester 15 mi – Shrewsbury 26 mi

at Tilston Northwest : 3 mi on Tilston Rd – ✉ Malpas

Tilston Lodge without rest
✉ SY14 7DR – ✆ (01829) 250 223
3 rm – †£ 50/60 ††£ 80/100
Victorian hunting lodge with colourful gardens and welcoming owners. Classical bedrooms feature objets d'art and offer country views; two have four-posters. Spacious lounge and breakfast room. Juices are made from their home-grown apples.

MALTBY – Stockton-on-Tees – 502 Q23 24 B3

London 251 mi – Liverpool 141 mi – Leeds 69 mi – Sheffield 101 mi

Chadwicks Inn
High Ln ✉ TS8 0BG – ✆ (01642) 590 300 – www.chadwicksinnmaltby.co.uk – Closed 26 December, 1 January and Monday
Rest – *(booking advisable)* Menu £ 12/18 – Carte £ 23/43
This pub dates back over 200 years and was a favourite haunt of the Spitfire pilots before their missions. The à la carte features ambitious, intricate dishes, supplemented by a simpler bistro menu. The live acoustic evenings are popular.

MALTON – North Yorkshire – 502 R21 – pop. 5 023 Great Britain 23 C2

London 234 mi – Pickering 9 mi – Scarborough 23 mi

Castle Howard★★, W : 4 mi by minor rd. Rievaulx Abbey★★, NW : 17 mi by B 1257

Talbot
Yorkersgate ✉ YO17 7AJ – ✆ (01653) 639 096 – www.talbotmalton.co.uk
26 rm – †£ 85/245 ††£ 95/345 – 2 suites
Rest *Talbot* – see restaurant listing
Early 18C hunting lodge owned by the Fitzwilliam Estate. Impressive wood staircase and traditional country house guest areas filled with family artefacts and portraits. Individually styled bedrooms; some with 6ft beds and marble bathrooms.

Talbot Ⓝ – Talbot Hotel
Yorkersgate ✉ YO17 7AJ – ✆ (01653) 639 096 – www.talbotmalton.co.uk
Rest – *(bar lunch Monday-Saturday)* Menu £ 25/39 – Carte £ 21/34
Formal, two-roomed hotel restaurant, with a grand, elegant style, chandeliers and fine paintings. Concise menu uses quality local and estate ingredients; classic combinations have a delicate touch and a subtle modern style. Friendly team.

New Malton Ⓝ
2-4 Market Pl ✉ YO17 7LX – ✆ (01653) 693 998 – www.thenewmalton.co.uk – Closed 25-26 December and 1 January
Rest – Carte £ 18/32
18C stone pub with open fires, reclaimed furniture and photos of old town scenes. A good-sized menu offers hearty pub classics with the odd more adventurous dish thrown in; cooking is unfussy and flavoursome with an appealing Northern bias.

at Burythorpe South : 4.25 mi by Pocklington rd

Burythorpe House
✉ YO179LB – ✆ (01653) 658 200 – www.burythorpehouse.co.uk
13 rm – †£ 85/175 ††£ 95/235 **Rest** – *(dinner only)* Menu £ 30
Victorian country house set in 1.5 acres. Lovely large drawing room with open fire and oil paintings. Spacious, uniquely furnished bedrooms come with a host of extras; some are classically styled, others more modern. Traditional cooking served in oak-panelled dining rooms.

MALVERN WELLS – Worcestershire – 503 N27 – see Great Malvern

MAN (Isle of) – I.O.M. – 502 G21 – pop. 80 058 Great Britain 20 B1

from Douglas to Belfast (Isle of Man Steam Packet Co. Ltd) (summer only) (2 h 45 mn) – from Douglas to Republic of Ireland (Dublin) (Isle of Man Steam Packet Co. Ltd) (2 h 45 mn/4 h) – from Douglas to Heysham (Isle of Man Steam Packet Co.) (2 h/3 h 30 mn) – from Douglas to Liverpool (Isle of Man Steam Packet Co. Ltd) (2 h 30 mn/4 h)

Laxey Wheel★★ - Snaefell★ (✵★★★) - Cregneash Folk Museum★

BALLASALLA

Abbey
Rushen Abbey, Mill Road ✉ IM9 3DB – ✆ (01624) 822 393 – www.theabbeyrestraurant.co.im – Closed Monday October-April
Rest – Menu £ 40/60 – Carte £ 19/50
Once a judge's house and a jam factory. Lively, cosy interior has a rug-strewn floor and pre-war furniture; a delightful terrace overlooks the abbey gardens. All-day dishes range from soup to lobster. Breads and desserts are homemade.

DOUGLAS – Douglas – pop. 26 218 20 B1

Ronaldsway Airport : ✆ (01624) 821600, SW : 7 mi
Sea Terminal Buildings, ✆ (01624) 68 67 66, www.iomguide.com
Douglas, Pulrose Park, ✆ (01624) 67 59 52
King Edward Bay, Onchan, Groudle Rd, ✆ (01624) 62 04 30

Sefton
Harris Promenade ✉ IM1 2RW – ✆ (01624) 645 500 – www.seftonhotel.co.im
93 rm – †£ 95/115 ††£ 110/250 – 10 suites
Rest *The Gallery* – *(bar lunch)* Menu £ 20 (weekdays) – Carte £ 28/60
Victorian-fronted promenade hotel, built around unique atrium water garden. Bedrooms may have balconies, look out to sea or have water garden views. Impressive apartment suites. The Gallery, with its boldly coloured Manx art, offers speciality flambé dishes.

Claremont
18-22 Loch Promenade ✉ IM1 2LX – ✆ (01624) 617 068 – www.claremont.im
56 rm – †£ 70/170 ††£ 90/195
Rest *Coast* – Menu £ 13/20 – Carte £ 23/43
Made up of several Victorian seaside hotels. Smart, modern interior: bedrooms have good quality dark wood furnishings, Hungarian duck feather pillows, superb wet rooms, and state-of-the-art TV and audio equipment. Large, brasserie-style restaurant has traditional menus and a cheery team.

Regency
Queens Promenade ✉ IM2 4NN – ✆ (01624) 680 680 – www.regency.im
38 rm – †£ 80/110 ††£ 135/165 – 4 suites
Rest *Stephen Dedman - A Restaurant* – see restaurant listing
Restored Victorian hotel popular with business travellers. Featuring wood panelling and seascape watercolours, guest areas have a classic feel. Bedrooms are more modern and come with mobile phones, PCs and free internet.

Penta without rest
Queens Promenade ✉ IM9 4NE – ✆ (01624) 680 680 – www.regency.im
23 rm – †£ 50/95 ††£ 62/115
Good value hotel with bay views and a complimentary shuttle bus to the financial district. Large, functional bedrooms have computers with free internet. Mediterranean-style breakfast room; access to the bar and restaurant at the Regency.

Inglewood without rest
26 Palace Terr, Queens Promenade ✉ IM2 4NF – ✆ (01624) 674 734 – www.inglewoodhotel-isleofman.com – Closed 1 week November and Christmas-New Year
16 rm – †£ 50/80 ††£ 85/110
Modern hotel at the quieter end of the promenade; the front-facing rooms enjoy views over the bay. Spacious bedrooms have chunky, contemporary furnishings, leather armchairs and modern shower rooms. Well-stocked residents' bar.

XXX **Stephen Dedman - A Restaurant** – Regency Hotel

Queens Promenade ✉ IM2 4NN – ✆ (01624) 680 680 – www.regency.im

Rest – *(dinner only)* Menu £ 28 – Carte £ 36/55

Classical oak-panelled restaurant within the Regency hotel, featuring a collection of original island pictures. Menus are strongly rooted in tradition, with the likes of cheese soufflé, Manx queenies and grilled calves' liver.

XX **JAR**

Admirals House, 11-12 Loch Promenade ✉ IM1 2LX – ✆ (01624) 663 553 – www.jar.co.im – Closed 26-28 December

Rest – Menu £ 18 (weekday lunch)/38 – Carte £ 32/45

Set on the ground floor of a hotel, with a comfy leather-furnished lounge and a pleasant coastal outlook from the front tables. Italian-influenced menus offer clean, unfussy, flavoursome cooking.

XX **Macfarlane's**

24 Duke St ✉ IM1 2AY – ✆ (01624) 624 777 – www.macfarlanes.im – Closed 2 weeks early August, 1 week spring, 1 week Christmas-New Year, Sunday and Monday

Rest – *(dinner only and lunch Thursday-Friday) (booking essential)* Menu £ 15 (weekday lunch)/28 – Carte £ 27/56

Small, simple restaurant in the heart of town, with leather-topped tables and high-sided booths. Unfussy, regularly changing menu relies on fresh local produce, with fish to the fore.

ENGLAND

X **Tanroagan**

9 Ridgeway St ✉ IM1 1EW – ✆ (01624) 612 355 – www.tanroagan.co.uk – Closed 25-26 December and Sunday

Rest – Menu £ 20 (weekday lunch) – Carte £ 31/55

Friendly restaurant off the quayside, with seafaring décor and a cosy feel. Fish from the island's day boats are simply cooked, making the most of their natural flavours. Portions are hearty; bread, desserts and ice creams are homemade.

PORT ERIN – Port Erin – pop. 3 575 20 B1

Rowany Cottier without rest

Spaldrick ✉ IM9 6PE – ✆ (01624) 832 287 – www.rowanycottier.com

5 rm – †£ 50/70 ††£ 80/88

Large, purpose-built house set close to Bradda Glen. Pleasant guest areas have views over Port Erin and the Calf of Man. Bedrooms are simple and well-kept. Locally sourced breakfasts feature homemade bread.

RAMSEY – Ramsey – pop. 7 309 20 B1

River House without rest

North : 0.25 mi by A 9 turning left immediately after bridge ✉ IM8 3DA – ✆ (01624) 816 412 – www.theriverhouse-iom.com

3 rm – †£ 60/80 ††£ 95/115

Attractive Georgian country house in an idyllic riverside setting; its bright, spacious interior filled with antique furnishings and objets d'art. Traditional bedrooms come with floral fabrics, knick-knacks and large baths.

PORT ST MARY – Port Saint Mary – pop. 1 913 20 B1

Aaron House without rest

The Promenade ✉ IM9 5DE – ✆ (01624) 835 702 – www.aaronhouse.co.uk – Closed 20 December, 7 January and Christmas-New Year

6 rm – †£ 49/98 ††£ 70/118

Charming, antique-furnished guesthouse with bay and harbour views and a strong Victorian feel. Comfortable, traditionally styled bedrooms. Afternoon tea served on arrival; interesting choices at breakfast.

MANCHESTER

See city maps on following pages **20** B2

© Peter Erik Forsberg/Age fotostock

ENGLAND

Greater Manchester – **pop. 396 830** – **502** N23 – **503** N23 – **504** N23 – Great Britain

London 202 mi – Birmingham 86 mi – Glasgow 221 mi – Leeds 43 mi

Tourist Information

Manchester Visitor Centre, 45-50 Piccadilly Plaza, Portland St., ✉ M1 4AJ, ✆(0871) 222 82 23, www.visitmanchester.com

Airport

Manchester International Airport : ✆ (08712) 710 711, S : 10 m. by A 5103 - AX - and M 56

Golf Courses

Heaton Park, Prestwich, ✆(0161) 654 98 99

Houldsworth Park, Stockport, Houldsworth St, Reddish, ✆(0161) 442 17 12

SIGHTS

In the town : City★ • Castlefield Urban Heritage Park★ CZ • Town Hall★ CZ • Manchester Art Gallery★ CZ**M2** • Cathedral★ CY • Museum of Science and Industry★ CZ**M** • Imperial War Museum North★, Trafford Park AX**M**

On the outskirts : Whitworth Art Gallery★, S : 1.5 m

In the surrounding area : Quarry Bank Mill★, S : 10 mi off B 5166, exit 5 from M 56

MANCHESTER
LEEDS
M 60
A
A 56
(M 60, M 66) BURY
A 665
BOLTON
A 666
M 60
(M 61)
V
A 6
PRESTON
A 580
LIVERPOOL (M 60, M 62)
(M 60), (M 62)
M 602
A 57
WARRINGTON, (M 62)
X
M 60
LIVERPOOL, (M 61, M62)
A 6144
CHESTER, (M 6)
A 56
M 60
STOCKPORT
A
BIRMINGHAM, AIRPORT, (M 60, M 56, M 6)
0
1 km
0
1 mile
BURY
PRESTWICH
HEATON PARK
HEATON
PARK
PRESTWICH
POL.
Scholes Lane
Sheepfoot Lane
A 6044
BOWKER VALE
Bury Old Road
Hilton Lane
Bury New Road
Middleton Old Road
Leicester Road
97
PENDLEBURY
Agecroft Road
A 6044
Manchester Road
Bolton Road
Station Road
Chorley Road
Partington La.
A 572
A 6
Worsley Road
Manchester Road
Hospital Rd
East Lancashire Road
SALFORD
Great Cheetham Street West
55
A 6010
102
Cromwell Road
A 576
Great Clowes St.
New Road
Claremont Rd
A 6
A 5185
Old Road
Weaste Lane
Langworthy Rd
A 5186
20
Broad St.
Albion Way
A 5063
Eccles
LADYWELL
32
ECCLES
WEST ONE RETAIL PARK
Eccles New
WEASTE
LANGWORTHY Road
M 602
105
15
3
A 6042
Chapel St.
35
POL
A 57
Regent Rd
87
39
48
Centenary Way
ANCHORAGE
HARBOUR CITY
Broadway
TRAFFORD PARK
MEDIA CITY UK
SALFORD QUAYS
LOWRY CENTRE
Trafford Wharf Rd
Trafford Rd
Ordsall Lane
CORNBROOK
EXCHANGE QUAY
POMONA
A 57 (M)
Chorlton Road
A 5103
A 576
Village Way
Wharfside Way
A 5081
A 56
Barton Dock Road
B 5211
Park
Mosley Road
M.U.F.C.
Stretford Road
TRAFFORD BAR
WHITE CITY RETAIL PARK
POL.
A 5067
Talbot Rd.
STRETFORD
OLD TRAFFORD
Seymour Grove
Upper Chorlton Road
81
Moss
Princess
ALEXANDRA PARK
TRAFFORD
Barton Road
15'3
Park Rd
Stretford
Chester Road
FIRSWOOD
Manchester Road
LONGFORD PARK
STRETFORD
Stretford Road
Urmston La.
66
A 5145
CHORLTON-CUM HARDY
A 6010
Road
Edge Lane
Wilbraham Road
High Lane
A 5145
URMSTON
Sandy Lane
Eccles By-Pass
CHESTER RD
ST WERBURGH'S ROAD
Mauldeth Road West
16
9
8
7
Z

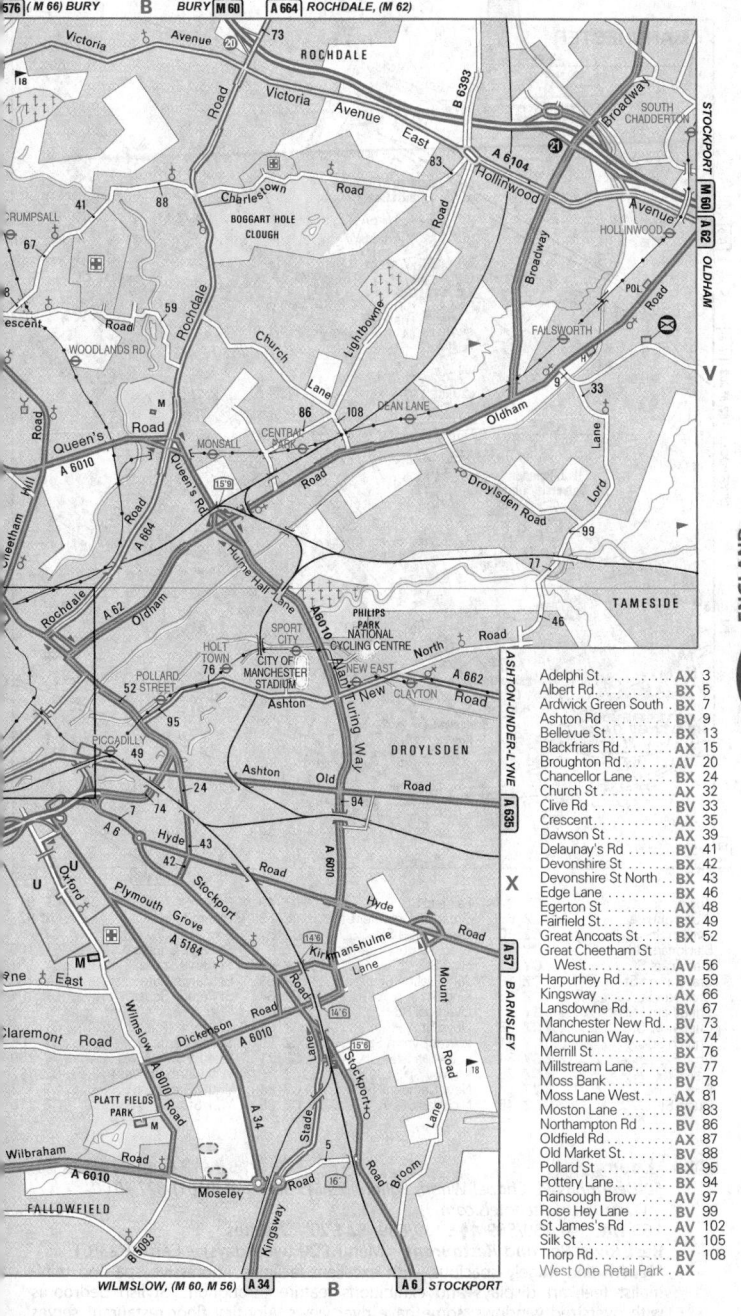

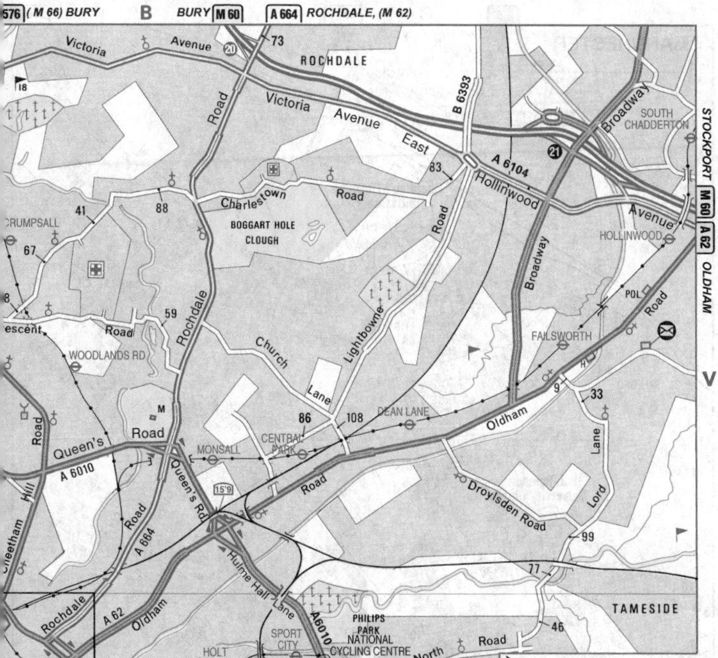

576 (M 66) BURY
B
BURY M 60
A 664 ROCHDALE, (M 62)
Victoria Avenue
ROCHDALE
Victoria Avenue East
B 6393
Broadway
SOUTH CHADDERTON
STOCKPORT M 60
A 62 OLDHAM
A 6104
Hollinwood Avenue
HOLLINWOOD
Charlestown Road
BOGGART HOLE CLOUGH
CRUMPSALL
Rochdale Road
Lightbowne Road
Church Lane
Broadway
FAILSWORTH
POL
WOODLANDS RD
DEAN LANE
Oldham Road
Lane
Lord
Queen's Road
A 6010
MONSALL
CENTRAL PARK
Droylsden Road
Queen's Rd
A 664
Cheetham Hill Road
Hulme Hall Lane
TAMESIDE
V
ENGLAND

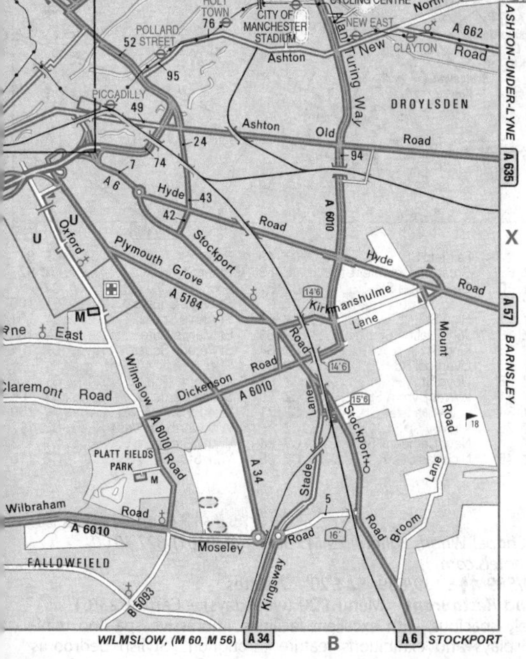

Rochdale
A 62
Oldham
A6010
PHILIPS PARK
NATIONAL CYCLING CENTRE
North Road
SPORT CITY
HOLT TOWN
CITY OF MANCHESTER STADIUM
NEW EAST
A 662
POLLARD STREET
Ashton New Road
CLAYTON
Alan Turing Way
ASHTON-UNDER-LYNE
PICCADILLY
DROYLSDEN
Ashton Old Road
A 635
A 6
Hyde Road
A 6010
X
Oxford
Plymouth Grove
Stockport
A 5184
Kirkmanshulme Lane
A 57
BARNSLEY
Mount Road
Claremont Road
Wilmslow
Dickenson Road
A 6010
Stockport
Lane
PLATT FIELDS PARK
A 6010 Road
A 34
Stade
Lane
Wilbraham Road
A 6010
Moseley Road
Broom
FALLOWFIELD
Kingsway
B 5093
WILMSLOW, (M 60, M 56) A 34
B
A 6 STOCKPORT

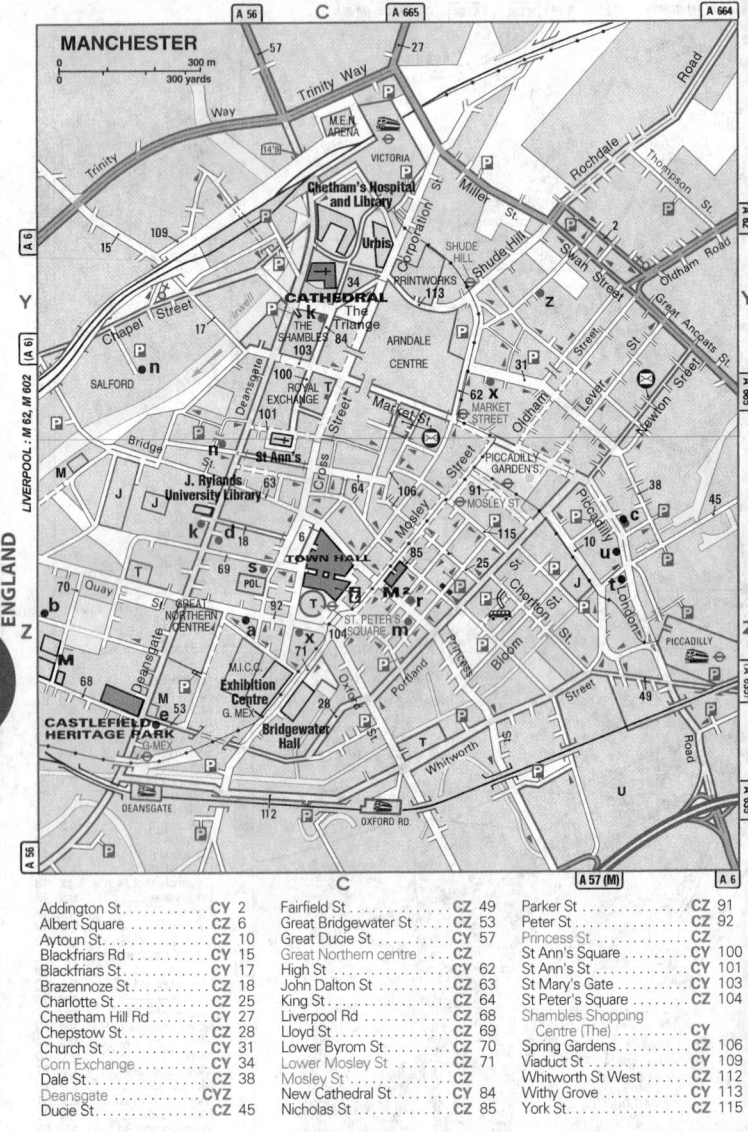

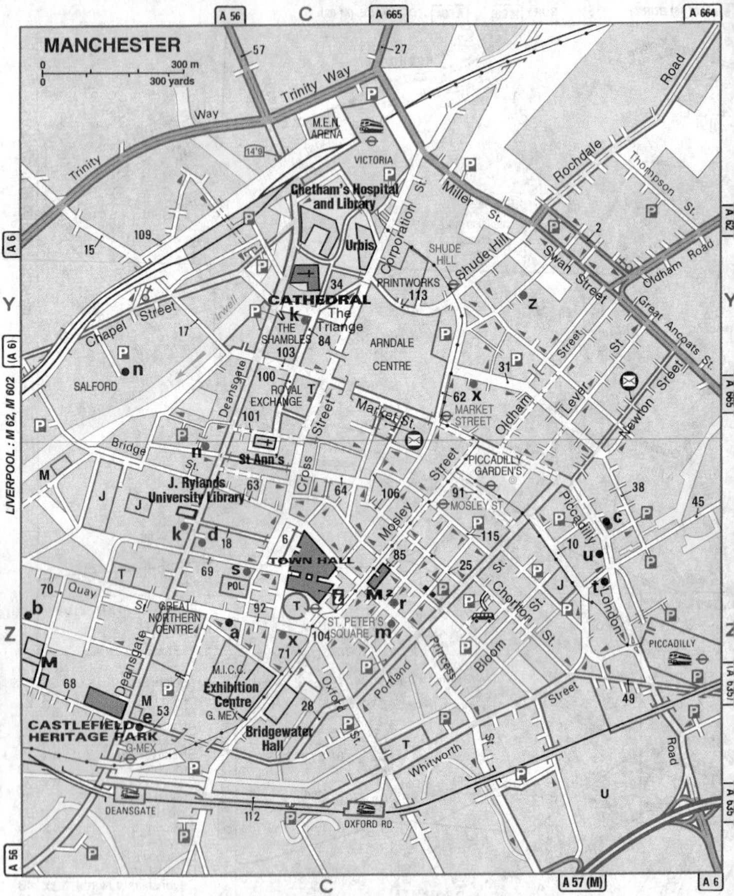

Lowry

rm,

50 Dearmans Pl, Chapel Wharf, Salford ✉ M3 5LH – ✆ (0161) 827 40 00 – www.roccofortehotels.com CY**n**

165 rm – †£ 139/589 ††£ 139/589, ☕ £ 20 – 7 suites

Rest *River Bar and Restaurant* – Menu £ 20 (weekdays) – Carte £ 23/61

Modern and hugely spacious, with excellent facilities, impressive spa and minimalist feel: art displays and exhibitions feature throughout. Stylish bedrooms with oversized windows; some have river views. Airy first floor restaurant serves a wide-ranging menu.

Radisson Edwardian

Free Trade Hall, Peter St ✉ M2 5GP – ☎ (0161) 835 9929 – www.radissonedwardian.com/manchester CZ**a**

263 rm – †£ 89/320 ††£ 99/330, ☕ £ 19 – 4 suites

Rest *Opus One* – Menu £ 25

Rest *Alto* – ☎ (0161) 835 8903 – Menu £ 15 – Carte £ 22/27

14 floor hotel which cleverly incorporates the façade of the former Free Trade Hall. Contemporary bedrooms, some with an outdoor seating area. The Valentino Suite is the best, with superb views. Great basement pool and spa. Opus One offers a seasonally changing, modern menu, and is popular for afternoon tea and cocktails. All-day menu in informal Alto.

Great John Street without rest

Great John St ✉ M3 4FD – ☎ (0161) 831 3211 – www.greatjohnstreet.co.uk

30 rm – †£ 120/178 ††£ 144/420, ☕ £ 17 CZ**b**

Converted schoolhouse; now a stylish, boutique hotel, with a meeting room in the former headmaster's study. All bedrooms are duplex-style suites, with roll-top baths. Outdoor roof terrace. Room service but no restaurant.

Malmaison

Piccadilly ✉ M1 3AQ – ☎ (0161) 278 10 00 – www.malmaison-manchester.com

167 rm – †£ 99/199 ††£ 99/199, ☕ £ 12 – 1 suite CZ**u**

Rest *Smoak Bar & Grill* – ☎ (0161) 278 10 01 – Carte £ 31/67

Old cotton warehouse and dolls hospital joined by a striking granite extension. Stylish bedrooms: some in dark, masculine shades; others in more subtle pastel hues. Uniquely designed suites include Man Utd and Man City themes. Smoak offers a menu inspired by American steakhouses.

ENGLAND

Abode

107 Piccadilly ✉ M1 2DB – ☎ (0161) 247 77 44 – www.abodehotels.co.uk

61 rm – †£ 69/275 ††£ 69/275, ☕ £ 12 CZ**c**

Rest *Michael Caines* – see restaurant listing

Late Victorian cotton merchant's former head office with iron columns and girders still in situ. Relaxed boutique ambience with modern, trendy, open-plan rooms and stylish bathrooms. 5th floor suites; the Johnny Cash is one of the largest.

Doubletree by Hilton Manchester Piccadilly

One Piccadilly Pl, 1 Auburn St ✉ M1 3DG – ☎ (0161) 242 10 00 – www.doubletree.com CZ**t**

285 rm – †£ 79/225 ††£ 79/225, ☕ £ 17 – 1 suite

Rest *City Café* – ☎ (0161) 242 10 20 – Menu £ 25 – Carte £ 33/37

Contemporary glass building with spacious, airy interior and local art on display. Modern bedrooms boast pale hues, iMac computers and excellent entertainment facilities; showers only except top floor suites. Smart, stylish restaurant with appealing, wide-ranging, modern menu.

The French by Simon Rogan Ⓝ

Midland Hotel, Peter St. ✉ M60 2DS – ☎ (0161) 236 333 – www.the-french.co.uk – Closed 10 days August, 1 week Christmas, Sunday, Monday and lunch Tuesday

Rest – *(booking essential)* Menu £ 29/79 CZ**x**

Iconic restaurant with original ornate detailing, crystal chandeliers and an unusual carpet. Creative modern cooking showcases British ingredients, including some from Simon Rogan's own farm. Service is well-paced and knowledgeable.

Wings

1 Lincoln Sq ✉ M2 5LN – ☎ (0161) 834 90 00 – www.wingsrestaurant.co.uk

Rest – *(booking essential at dinner)* Menu £ 31/45 – Carte £ 21/61 CZ**d**

Well-run restaurant off busy square. Narrow room with linen-clad tables, comfy booths, terracotta army replicas and Hong Kong skyline murals. Extensive menu of authentic Cantonese dim sum.

Good food at moderate prices? Look for the Bib Gourmand.

XX **Michael Caines** – Abode Hotel

107 Piccadilly ✉ M1 2DB – ☎ (0161) 200 56 78 – www.michaelcaines.co.uk – Closed Sunday CZ**c**

Rest – Menu £ 15/60 – Carte £ 35/52

Large, lively modern restaurant in a hotel basement, featuring subdued lighting and a sophisticated style. Contemporary British cooking has some Mediterranean influences. The tasting menu comes with matching wine suggestions.

XX **Australasia**

1 The Avenue, Spinningfields ✉ M3 3AP – ☎ (0161) 831 0288 – www.australasia.uk.com – Closed 25-26 December and 1 January

Rest – Carte £ 22/84 CZ**k**

Fun, fashionable basement restaurant on the site of the old Manchester Evening News; come for cocktails, small plates, sushi, designer styling, DJs and a clubby vibe. Vibrant dishes have European/Pacific Rim/Asian influences. Helpful staff.

XX **63 Degrees** (N)

20 Church St ✉ M4 1PN – ☎ (0161) 832 5438 – www.63degrees.co.uk – Closed Sunday and Monday CY**x**

Rest – Menu £ 18 (weekdays)/25 – Carte £ 26/49

Family-run restaurant near Arndale shopping centre. Elegant, contemporary lighting illuminates rustic stencilled walls. The cooking also mixes the classical with the modern, using traditional combinations and the latest techniques.

XX **Second Floor at Harvey Nichols**

21 New Cathedral St ✉ M1 1AD – ☎ (0161) 828 8898 – www.harveynichols.com – Closed 25-28 December, 1 January, Easter Sunday, Sunday and dinner Monday

Rest – Menu £ 25/40 CY**k**

Smart restaurant with stylish, colour-changing lighting and oversized windows offering big wheel and city views. Elaborate modern European menu with interesting twists; good presentation.

XX **Yang Sing**

34 Princess St ✉ M1 4JY – ☎ (0161) 236 22 00 – www.yang-sing.com – Closed 25 December CZ**m**

Rest – Menu £ 15 (weekday lunch)/45 – Carte £ 18/42

Family-run Chinese restaurant spread over 4 floors of an imposing Victorian building, with a '1930s Shanghai' basement room, a classic ground floor and private rooms above. Authentic Cantonese cooking features tasty dim sum at lunch.

XX **San Carlo Cicchetti**

House of Fraser (Ground Floor), Deansgate, (entrance on King St West) ✉ M3 2QG – ☎ (0161) 839 2233 – www.sancarlocicchetti.co.uk – Closed 25 December CZ**n**

Rest – Carte £ 14/29

On the ground floor of House of Fraser department store, with marble counter and striking yellow leather banquettes. Extensive seasonal menu focuses on cicchetti (small plates); choose 5 or 6 per person and share.

X **Second Floor Brasserie at Harvey Nichols**

21 New Cathedral St ✉ M1 1AD – ☎ (0161) 828 88 98 – www.harveynichols.com – Closed 25 December, 1 January, Easter Sunday and dinner Sunday-Monday

Rest – Menu £ 20 (dinner) – Carte £ 19/41 CY**k**

Relaxed, minimalist brasserie and bar, with colour-changing strip lighting and buzzy atmosphere. Extensive menu of modern British dishes, with some lighter meals available. Popular with shoppers.

X **Livebait**

18-22 Lloyd St ✉ M2 5WA – ☎ (0161) 817 4110 – www.livebaitmanchester.com – Closed 25-26 December, 1 January, Sunday and Monday CZ**s**

Rest – Menu £ 14 (lunch and early dinner) – Carte £ 21/36

Set in a grand looking building, with a simply furnished interior and a lively atmosphere. The daily à la carte and good value set menu offer fresh seafood dishes, featuring hand-dived Mull scallops and fish from the Scottish day boats.

ENGLAND

X **Northern Quarter**

108 High St ✉ M4 1HQ – ☎ (0161) 832 71 15 – www.tnq.co.uk – Closed 24-26 December, 1 January and Sunday dinner CY**z**

Rest – *(booking essential at dinner)* Menu £ 14/28 – Carte £ 20/41

Friendly, modern restaurant with floor to ceiling windows. Keenly priced, seasonal menus offer classic dishes presented in a modern style. The three course 'Love Lunch' is very popular – as are the monthly themed evenings.

X **Red N Hot**

56 Faulkner St (1st Floor) ✉ M1 4FH – ☎ (0161) 236 26 50 – www.rednhotgroup.com – Closed 25 December CZ**r**

Rest – Carte £ 15/26

Fiery chilli and pepper infused Sichuan dishes; choose a level of spice – hot, medium or cooler. Signature dish of sliced pork with chilli and pepper. Ducks tongues, stewed frogs legs and pigs intestines are not for the fainthearted.

at Didsbury South : 5.5 mi by A 5103 - AX - on A 5145 – ✉ Manchester

Didsbury House

Didsbury Pk, South : 1.5 mi on A 5145 ✉ M20 5LJ – ☎ (0161) 448 22 00 – www.didsburyhouse.com

27 rm – †£ 90/250 ††£ 90/250, ☕ £ 16 – 2 suites

Rest – *(residents only)* Carte £ 22/34 **s**

Cream-washed Victorian villa – now a boutique townhouse; original features include an impressive stained glass window. Bedrooms are comfortable and stylish with a contemporary edge; some boast roll-top baths. Small basement dining room serves an accessible menu of classic, seasonal dishes.

Eleven Didsbury Park

11 Didsbury Pk, South : 1.5 mi by A 5145 ✉ M20 5LH – ☎ (0161) 448 77 11 – www.elevendidsburypark.com

19 rm – †£ 90/140 ††£ 90/140, ☕ £ 16 – 1 suite

Rest – *(room service only)* Carte £ 22/31 **s**

Comfortable, boutique-style townhouse in pleasant residential setting, with simply furnished breakfast room overlooking delightful garden. Stylish, contemporary bedrooms with warm décor and good facilities; many have tubs in the rooms. Informal all-day menu available as room service only.

X **Jem&I**

1c School Ln ✉ M20 6RD – ☎ (0161) 445 39 96 – www.jemandirestaurant.co.uk

Rest – Menu £ 13/20 – Carte £ 11/32

Simple, unpretentious cream-coloured building tucked away off the high street. Open-plan kitchen; homely, bistro feel. Good value, modern European menus. Polite, friendly service.

at Chorlton-Cum-Hardy Southwest : 4 mi . by A 5103 - AX - on A 6010 – ✉ Manchester

Abbey Lodge without rest

501 Wilbraham Rd ✉ M21 0UJ – ☎ (0161) 862 92 66 – www.abbey-lodge.co.uk

4 rm ☕ – †£ 50/60 ††£ 65/80 AX**z**

Red-brick Edwardian house in the city suburbs; a 'wishing table' provides a splash of colour on the stairwell. Warm, homely bedrooms offer good facilities; Rooms 3 and 4 are the largest. Continental-style buffet in your room.

at Prestwich Northwest : 5 mi on A 56

XX **Aumbry**

2 Church Ln ✉ M25 1AJ – ☎ (0161) 798 58 41 – www.aumbryrestaurant.co.uk – Closed 1 week early January, Sunday and Monday AV**x**

Rest – *(dinner only and lunch Friday-Saturday) (booking essential)* Menu £ 40/55

Intimate neighbourhood restaurant offering a 9 course tasting menu. Well-presented, modern dishes use local, seasonal produce and offer good combinations of flavours. Friendly service.

ENGLAND

MANSFIELD – Nottinghamshire – 502 Q24 – pop. 69 987 16 B1

London 143 mi – Chesterfield 12 mi – Worksop 14 mi

XX **No.4 Wood Street** Ⓝ

4 Wood St ✉ NG18 1QA – ☎ (01623) 424 824 – www.4woodstreet.co.uk – Closed Saturday lunch, Sunday dinner and Monday

Rest – Menu £ 15 (weekday lunch)/35 – Carte £ 21/38

Modern restaurant on the first floor of a converted stone warehouse. Spacious, rustic sitting room and two dining rooms with exposed stone walls and chunky wood furniture. Classical cooking with distinct flavours. Professional service.

MARAZION – Cornwall – 503 D33 – pop. 1 381 – ✉ Penzance 1 A3

London 318 mi – Penzance 3 mi – Truro 26 mi

Praa Sands, Penzance, ☎ (01736) 76 34 45

St Michael's Mount★★ (≤★★) – Ludgvan★ (Church★) N : 2 mi by A 30 – Chysauster Village★, N : 2 mi by A 30 – Gulval★ (Church★) W : 2.5 m – Prussia Cove★, SE : 5.5 mi by A 30 and minor rd

Mount Haven

Turnpike Rd, East : 0.25 mi ✉ TR17 0DQ – ☎ (01736) 710 249 – www.mounthaven.co.uk

18 rm ☕ – †£ 90/200 ††£ 130/230

Rest – *(closed 27-29 December) (bar lunch Monday-Saturday)* Carte £ 26/41

Small hotel overlooking St Michael's Bay, with a spacious bar and a lounge featuring Indian fabrics and artefacts. Contemporary bedrooms come with good modern amenities and most have a balcony and a view. Bright, attractive dining room offers elaborate modern dishes with ambitious flavour combinations.

X **Ben's Cornish Kitchen** Ⓝ

West End ✉ TR17 0EL – ☎ (01736) 719 200 – www.benscornishkitchen.com – Closed 25-26 December, 1 January, Monday lunch and Sunday

Rest – Menu £ 18 (lunch) – Carte dinner £ 25/31

Personally run, rustic little eatery – sit upstairs for views over the rooftops to St Michael's Mount. Unfussy, good value lunches; sophisticated dinners feature some interesting flavour combinations. Each dish has a recommended wine.

at Perranuthnoe Southeast : 1.75 mi by A 394 – ✉ Penzance

Ednovean Farm without rest

✉ TR20 9LZ – ☎ (01736) 711 883 – www.ednoveanfarm.co.uk – Closed Christmas

3 rm ☕ – †£ 90/115 ††£ 90/120

17C granite barn in a tranquil spot overlooking the bay and surrounded by 22 acres of sub-tropical gardens and paddocks. Individually styled bedrooms and locally produced toiletries; the Blue Room has a French bed, a roll-top bath and a terrace. Have a range-cooked breakfast at the oak table or a continental selection in your room. Complimentary sherry in the hall.

Victoria Inn with rm

✉ TR20 9NP – ☎ (01736) 710 309 – www.victoriainn-penzance.co.uk – Closed 25-26 December, 1 January, Monday in winter and Sunday dinner

2 rm ☕ – †£ 50 ††£ 75 **Rest** – Carte £ 22/32

Characterful, pink-washed pub in the heart of the village, with a cosy, homely feel and a suntrap rear terrace. Ever-changing menus showcase local produce, including plenty of seafood from Newlyn; wholesome dishes are neatly presented and vibrantly flavoured with a modern edge. Service is cheery and you'll find modest bedrooms set directly above the pub.

at St Hilary East : 2.5 mi by Turnpike Rd on B 3280 – ✉ Penzance

Ennys without rest

Trewhella Ln ✉ TR20 9BZ – ☎ (01736) 740 262 – www.ennys.co.uk – Closed November-March

5 rm ☕ – †£ 95/145 ††£ 105/165

Delightful 18C granite former tin merchant's house, its lovingly restored interior simply furnished in light colours and displaying Indian artefacts from the charming owner's travels. A grass tennis court and outdoor swimming pool are set in a secluded part of the garden. Complimentary afternoon tea.

MARCHAM - Oxfordshire - 503 P29 - see Abingdon

MARGATE - Kent - 504 Y29 - pop. 58 465 9 D1

London 74 mi – Canterbury 17 mi – Dover 21 mi – Maidstone 43 mi

12-13 The Parade, (0872) 64 61 11, www.visitthanet.co.uk

Reading Rooms without rest

31 Hawley Sq CT9 1PH – (01843) 225 166 – www.thereadingroomsmargate.co.uk

3 rm – £ 99/180 £ 150/180

Passionately run guesthouse with stripped plaster, worn woodwork and unique shabby-chic style. Eclectic bedrooms – one per floor – boast distressed furniture, super comfy beds and huge bathrooms. Extensive breakfasts served in your room.

Ambrette Margate

44 King St CT9 1QE – (01843) 231 504 – www.theambrette.co.uk – Closed 25-26 December and Monday

Rest – Menu £ 15 (lunch) – Carte £ 21/30

Quirky Indian restaurant with modest surroundings. Concise, seasonal menu showcases Kentish produce in an original style; freshly prepared dishes offer well-balanced flavours and subtle spicing.

MARKET DRAYTON - Shropshire - 502 M25 - pop. 10 407 18 B1

London 159 mi – Nantwich 13 mi – Shrewsbury 21 mi

Goldstone Hall

Goldstone, South : 4.5 mi by A 529 TF9 2NA – (01630) 661 202 – www.goldstonehall.com

12 rm – £ 82/100 £ 140/170

Rest – Menu £ 23 (weekdays)/29 **s** – Carte £ 31/66 **s**

Attractive red-brick house with numerous extensions, surrounded by 5 acres of peaceful grounds. Lovely panelled drawing room and characterful beamed seating area with small bar. Classically styled bedrooms have plenty of space and pleasant country views. Modern menus feature kitchen garden produce.

ENGLAND

MARKET RASEN - Lincolnshire - 504 T23 - pop. 3 491 17 C1

London 158 mi – Nottingham 54 mi – Kingston upon Hull 37 mi – Sheffield 53 mi

Advocate Arms with rm

2 Queen St LN8 3EH – (01673) 842 364 – www.advocatearms.couk

10 rm – £ 50/65 £ 80/100, £ 7 **Rest** – Carte £ 21/37

Former hotel close to the market square, with an original revolving door and a smart, modern interior divided by etched glass walls. Lunch sticks to good old pub classics and at dinner, mature local steaks are a speciality; they also serve breakfast and afternoon tea. Bedrooms are spacious and well-equipped.

MARLBOROUGH - Wiltshire - 503 O29 - pop. 7 713 4 D2

London 84 mi – Bristol 47 mi – Southampton 40 mi – Swindon 12 mi

High St, (01225) 774 2 22, www.visitwiltshire.co.uk

The Common, (01672) 51 21 47

Town★

Savernake Forest★★ (Grand Avenue★★★), SE : 2 mi by A 4 – Whitehorse (<★), NW : 5 m – West Kennett Long Barrow★, Silbury Hill★, W : 6 mi by A 4. Ridgeway Path★★ – Avebury★★ (The Stones★, Church★), W : 7 mi by A 4 – Crofton Beam Engines★ **AC**, SE : 9 mi by A 346 – Wilton Windmill★ **AC**, SE : 9 mi by A 346, A 338 and minor rd

Coles

27 Kingsbury Hill SN8 1JA – (01672) 515 004 – www.colesrestaurant.co.uk – Closed 25 December, Sunday and bank holidays except Good Friday

Rest – Menu £ 14/17 – Carte £ 26/33

Cosy, buzzy bistro with a loyal local following. Two rooms feature an eclectic range of memorabilia – including architects' plans and vineyard maps. The menu is equally as diverse, with dishes ranging from fishcakes to monkfish 'ossobuco'.

at Little Bedwyn East : 9.5 mi by A 4 – ✉ Marlborough

XX **Harrow at Little Bedwyn** (Roger Jones)
✉ *SN8 3JP – ☎ (01672) 870 871 – www.theharrowatlittlebedwyn.com – Closed 25 December-4 January and Sunday-Tuesday*
Rest – Menu £ 35/50 – Carte approx. £ 55
Former pub with smartly laid tables and an intimate atmosphere. Flavourful, seasonal cooking is presented in a modern style, whilst still retaining a classical base; produce is top quality and fish plays an important role. The wine list is comprehensive and they also hold regular wine evenings.
➜ Tempura of lobster with spiced sea salt. Fillet of roe deer with duck bon bon and foie gras toffee. Mini dessert platter of lemon.

at West Overton West : 4 mi on A 4

Bell
Bath Rd ✉ SN8 1QD – ☎ (01672) 861 099 – www.thebellwestoverton.co.uk – Closed Monday except bank holidays
Rest – Menu £ 15 (weekdays) – Carte £ 22/42
A simple, friendly pub, rescued from oblivion by a local couple, who hired an experienced pair to run it. The menu mixes pub classics with Mediterranean-influenced dishes; presentation is modern but not at the expense of flavour.

at East Kennett West : 5.25 mi by A4

Old Forge without rest
✉ *SN8 4EY – ☎ (01672) 861 686 – www.theoldforge-avebury.co.uk*
4 rm – †£ 60/75 ††£ 70/85
Converted former smithy with a relaxing, homely feel. Comfortable bedrooms have classic country house style; the family room has pleasant countryside views. Communal breakfast.

ENGLAND

MARLDON – Devon – 503 J32 – pop. 1 798 2 C2

London 193 mi – Plymouth 30 mi – Torbay 3 mi – Exeter 23 mi

Church House Inn
Village Rd ✉ TQ3 1SL – ☎ (01803) 558 279 – www.churchhousemarldon.com – Closed dinner 25-26 December
Rest – Carte £ 22/39
Charming, well-run inn with wooden beams, open fires and original Georgian windows. Extensive choice on blackboard menus, with classically based dishes and some Mediterranean influences. Exotic theme nights and friendly, helpful service.

MARLOW – Buckinghamshire – 504 R29 – pop. 17 522 11 C3

London 35 mi – Aylesbury 22 mi – Oxford 29 mi – Reading 14 mi
to Henley-on-Thames (Salter Bros. Ltd) (summer only) (2 h 15 mn) – to Maidenhead, Cookham and Windsor (Salter Bros. Ltd) (summer only)
31 High St, ☎ (01628) 48 35 97, www.visitbuckinghamshire.org

Danesfield House rest,
Henley Rd, Southwest : 2.5 mi on A 4155 ✉ SL7 2EY – ☎ (01628) 891 010 – www.danesfieldhouse.co.uk
86 rm – †£ 154/224 ††£ 184/305
Rest *Danesfield House* – see restaurant listing
Rest *Orangery* – Menu £ 17 (weekday lunch) – Carte £ 26/44
Stunning house and gardens in Italian Renaissance style, with breathtaking views of the Chilterns and the Thames. Characterful guest areas and a smart spa. Bedrooms at the front are the best; most are traditional and some have four-posters. Charming, informal brasserie offers great views. Intimate restaurant serves intricate, modern fare.

Compleat Angler

Marlow Bridge, Bisham Rd ✉ SL7 1RG – ☎ (0844) 879 91 28 – www.macdonald-hotels.co.uk/compleatangler

64 rm – †£ 125/234 ††£ 135/244 – 3 suites

Rest *Aubergine at the Compleat Angler* – ☎ (01628) 405 405 *(booking essential)* Menu £ 29/50

Rest *Bowaters* – ☎ (01628) 405 406 *(closed Sunday dinner)* Menu £ 25/39

Well-kept hotel in an idyllic spot on the Thames, with views of the weir and the characterful chain bridge. Comfortable, corporate-style bedrooms blend classic furnishings with contemporary fabrics: some have balconies; opt for a Feature Room. Both restaurants afford water views – Aubergine serves ambitious modern European dishes; Bowaters offers British classics.

Danesfield House – Danesfield House Hotel

Henley Rd, Southwest : 2.5 mi on A 4155 ✉ SL7 2EY – ☎ (01628) 891 010 – www.danesfieldhouse.co.uk – Closed 20 August-3 September, 22 December-6 January, Sunday and Monday

Rest – *(dinner only and lunch Thursday-Saturday)* Menu £ 65/82

Elegant, very intimate fine dining restaurant with a huge fireplace, panelled walls, linen-laid tables and a relaxed air. Creative, flavourful, intricate cooking uses modern techniques, making skilful use of excellent quality, seasonal ingredients. Formal service.

→ Sautéed langoustine and mackerel with anchovy and wasabi. Slow-cooked loin of lamb, belly and sweetbreads with charcoaled onion and goat's curd. Iced white chocolate mousse, blackberry purée and dehydrated white chocolate.

Vanilla Pod

31 West St ✉ SL7 2LS – ☎ (01628) 898 101 – www.thevanillapod.co.uk – Closed 24 December-8 January, Sunday, Monday and bank holidays

Rest – *(booking essential)* Menu £ 20/45 **s**

Intimate, well-established restaurant – in T. S. Eliot's former home – with a plush interior and nicely spaced, smartly laid tables. Ambitious cooking has classical French foundations and displays original touches.

Hand and Flowers (Tom Kerridge) with rm

126 West St ✉ SL7 2BP – ☎ (01628) 482 277 – www.thehandandflowers.co.uk – Closed 24-26 December, 1 January and Sunday dinner

4 rm – †£ 140/190 ††£ 140/190

Rest – *(booking essential)* Menu £ 20 (weekday lunch) – Carte £ 42/64

Softly lit pub with low beamed ceilings, flagstone floors and a characterful dining area. The friendly team serve refined, flavoursome dishes created using classical techniques. Ingredients marry perfectly and the simple really is turned into the sublime. Characterful cottage bedrooms are equally meticulous; some have feature baths or outdoor jacuzzis.

→ Smoked haddock omelette with parmesan. Slow-cooked duck breast with Savoy cabbage and duck fat chips. Tonka bean panna cotta with poached rhubarb, ginger wine jelly and rhubarb sorbet.

Royal Oak

Frieth Rd, Bovingdon Green, West : 1.25 mi by A 4155 ✉ SL7 2JF – ☎ (01628) 488 611 – www.royaloakmarlow.co.uk – Closed 25-26 December

Rest – Carte £ 21/38

Part-17C, country-chic pub with a herb garden, a petanque pitch and a pleasant terrace. Set close to the M40 and M4, it's an ideal London getaway. Cooking is British-led; wash down an ox cheek pasty with a pint of local Rebellion ale.

at Little Marlow East : 3 mi on A 4155

Queens Head

Pound Ln ✉ SL7 3SR – ☎ (01628) 482 927 – www.marlowslittlesecret.co.uk – Closed 25-26 December

Rest – Carte £ 26/35

16C pub that's popular with walkers, with keen young partners at its helm and poised, friendly service. The refined à la carte changes regularly and features produce from local farms, forages and shoots; lunch also offers pub classics.

ENGLAND

MARPLE – Greater Manchester – 502 N23 – pop. 23 480 20 B3

London 190 mi – Chesterfield 35 mi – Manchester 11 mi

Springfield without rest

99 Station Rd ✉ SK6 6PA – ✆ (0161) 449 07 21 – www.springfieldhotelmarple.co.uk

8 rm – †£ 60/65 ††£ 65/85

Personally run, part-Victorian house with sympathetic extensions and pleasant rural views. Bright breakfast room; individually styled bedrooms. Useful for visits to the Peak District.

MARSDEN – West Yorkshire – 502 O23 – pop. 3 499 – ✉ Huddersfield 22 A3

London 195 mi – Leeds 22 mi – Manchester 18 mi – Sheffield 30 mi

Olive Branch with rm

✉ HD7 6LU – ✆ (01484) 844 487 – www.olivebranch.uk.com – Closed first 2 weeks January

3 rm – †£ 60/80 ††£ 60/110

Rest – *(dinner only)* Menu £ 20 (weekdays) – Carte £ 23/42

Characterful drovers' inn with stone floors, rustic walls, secluded garden and pleasant views from terrace. Classical, French-influenced menu supplemented by fish specials. Good choice of wines by the glass. Bedrooms are modern, cosy and individually themed.

MARTINHOE – Devon – see Lynton

MARTON – Shropshire Great Britain 18 A2

London 181 mi – Leeds 133 mi – Sheffield 132 mi – Manchester 95 mi

Powis Castle★★★, NW : 7 mi by B 4386 and A 490

Sun Inn

✉ SY21 8JP – ✆ (01938) 561 211 – www.suninn.org.uk – Closed Sunday dinner and lunch Monday-Tuesday

Rest – Carte £ 21/30

Welcoming country pub on the English-Welsh border, with a fire-lit bar and a brightly painted restaurant. The concise menu offers satisfying and comforting home-cooked dishes which include some great fish specials.

MARTON CUM GRAFTON – North Yorkshire 22 B2

London 206 mi – Birmingham 136 mi – Liverpool 103 mi – Leeds 28 mi

Punch Bowl Inn

✉ YO51 9QY – ✆ (01423) 322 519 – www.thepunchbowlmartoncumgrafton.com – Closed 25 December

Rest – Carte £ 21/36

Delightful inn, part-dating from the 14C; arrive early in summer to bag a seat on the terrace. All-encompassing, seasonal menu includes seafood platter and a 'Yorkshire board', with excellent fish and chips and rib-eye steak to die for.

MASHAM – North Yorkshire – 502 P21 – pop. 1 171 – ✉ Ripon 22 B1

London 231 mi – Leeds 38 mi – Middlesbrough 37 mi – York 32 mi

Swinton Park

Swinton, Southwest : 1 mi ✉ HG4 4JH – ✆ (01765) 680 900 – www.swintonpark.com

31 rm – †£ 195/450 ††£ 195/450 – 4 suites

Rest *Samuels* – see restaurant listing

17C castle with Georgian and Victorian additions, set on a 20,000 acre estate. The galleried hall leads to a snooker and a children's play room; antiques and portraits abound. Bedroom styles vary greatly. Try your hand at shooting, fishing, riding, falconry or cooking.

Bank Villa

The Avenue, on A 6108 ✉ HG4 4DB – ✆ (01765) 689 605 – www.bankvilla.com
5 rm – †£ 55/95 ††£ 55/120 **Rest** – Menu £ 20 **s**
Stone-built Georgian villa with a lovely stepped garden; the welcoming owners look after their guests well. Relax in one of two cosy lounges or the conservatory. Comfy bedrooms have modern feature walls; those in the eaves are the most characterful. Unfussy dinners. Homemade yoghurt features at breakfast.

Samuels – Swinton Park Hotel

Swinton, Southwest : 1 mi ✉ HG4 4JH – ✆ (01765) 680 900 – www.swintonpark.com – Closed Monday lunch
Rest – Menu £ 22 (weekday lunch)/60
Beautiful, rococo-style dining room with an ornate gold leaf ceiling and garden views; set within a castle. Well-spaced tables are adorned with lilies. Complex, modern cooking uses produce from the huge kitchen gardens and local suppliers.

Vennell's

7 Silver St ✉ HG4 4DX – ✆ (01765) 689 000 – www.vennellsrestaurant.co.uk – Closed first 2 weeks January, 1 week June, 1 week September, 26-30 December, Sunday dinner and Monday
Rest – *(dinner only and Sunday lunch) (booking essential)* Menu £ 28 **s**
Endearing, personally run restaurant with stylish purple walls and boldly patterned chairs; for a more intimate experience sit downstairs. Seasonal menus offer 4 choices per course. Cooking is well-judged, flavourful and has a modern edge.

MATFEN – Northumberland – 501 O18 – pop. 500 — 24 A2

London 309 mi – Carlisle 42 mi – Newcastle upon Tyne 24 mi

Matfen Hall

✉ NE20 0RH – ✆ (01661) 886 500 – www.matfenhall.com
53 rm – †£ 79/285 ††£ 79/285
Rest *Library* – *(dinner only and Sunday lunch)* Carte £ 32/46
Impressive 19C country mansion: popular as a wedding venue and for its golf course and spa. Spacious, traditional country house style bedrooms have good facilities; some boast four-posters and most offer rural views. Superb Great Hall and pleasant conservatory bar. Formal dining in the original library.

David Kennedy at Vallum N

Military Rd, Southeast : 3 mi by Newcastle rd on B 6318 ✉ NE18 0LL – ✆ (01434) 672 406 – www.vallumfarm.co.uk – Closed 25-26 December, 1-2 January, Sunday dinner and Monday October-March
Rest – Menu £ 13 (lunch and early dinner) – Carte £ 19/34
A converted milking shed with country views, in an artisan producers' collective. Classic British dishes are hearty and flavoursome, with a real emphasis on Northumbrian produce. Good value lunch and early evening menus. Friendly service.

MAWGAN PORTH – Cornwall – 503 E32 – see Newquay

MEDBOURNE – Leicestershire – 504 R26 — 16 B2

London 93 mi – Corby 9 mi – Leicester 16 mi

Homestead House without rest

Ashley Rd ✉ LE16 8DL – ✆ (01858) 565 724 – www.homesteadhouse.co.uk
3 rm – †£ 38 ††£ 60
Well-kept, detached house in an elevated position, with colourful flowerbeds set around an apple tree. Spacious lounge with leather sofas and an open fire. Traditional bedrooms offer good comforts; the two at the front have rural views.

MELLOR – Lancashire – see Blackburn

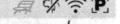

MELLOR - Greater Manchester 20 B3

London 185 mi – Bristol 163 mi – Cardiff 184 mi – Plymouth 277 mi

Oddfellows

Moor End Rd ✉ SK6 5PT – ✆ (0161) 449 7826 – www.oddfellowsmellor.com – Closed Sunday dinner, Monday and Tuesday

Rest – Carte £ 17/33

A complete refurbishment has given Oddies – as it is known locally – a light, uncluttered feel; wood burning stoves add an element of cosiness. The appealing, daily changing menu offers 'British food with a modern twist'.

MELTON MOWBRAY - Leicestershire - 502 R25 - pop. 25 554 16 B2

London 113 mi – Leicester 15 mi – Northampton 45 mi – Nottingham 18 mi

Nottingham Rd, ✆ (01664) 48 09 92, www.goleicestershire.com

Thorpe Arnold, Waltham Rd, ✆ (01664) 56 21 18

Stapleford Park

East : 5 mi by B 676 on Stapleford rd ✉ LE14 2EF – ✆ (01572) 787 000 – www.staplefordpark.com

55 rm – †£ 160/210 ††£ 160/210 – 3 suites

Rest *Grinling Gibbons Dining Room* – *(booking essential)* Carte £ 35/52

Beautiful stately home in 500 acres of landscaped grounds, with grand drawing rooms, a lovely leather-furnished bar, exceedingly comfortable bedrooms and marble bathrooms. The extensive leisure facilities are a replica of those at Buckingham Palace! Ornate rococo dining room; mix of classic and modern dishes.

MERE - Cheshire East - 502 M23 20 B3

London 185 mi – Bristol 152 mi – Cardiff 173 mi – Plymouth 266 mi

Mere

rm,

Chester Rd, on A 556 ✉ WA16 6LJ – ✆ (01565) 830 155 – www.themereresort.co.uk

81 rm – †£ 110/170 ††£ 120/200 – 10 suites

Rest *Browns* – *(dinner only and Sunday lunch)* Menu £ 26/34

Red-brick house set in 150 acres, complete with a lake and a championship golf course. Spacious guest areas include numerous meeting rooms and a smart spa; contemporary bedrooms offer the latest mod cons. Snacks in the spa and golf club; bistro-style menu in the glass-roofed courtyard restaurant.

MEVAGISSEY - Cornwall - 503 F33 - pop. 2 221 1 B3

London 287 mi – Newquay 21 mi – Plymouth 44 mi – Truro 20 mi

Town★★

NW : Lost Gardens of Heligan★

Trevalsa Court

School Hill, East : 0.5 mi ✉ PL26 6TH – ✆ (01726) 842 468 – www.trevalsa-hotel.co.uk – Closed January and December

14 rm – †£ 70/105 ††£ 145/195 **Rest** – *(dinner only)* Menu £ 27/30

Charming Arts and Crafts style house which combines dark wood panelling and stone fireplaces with bright modern art and bold soft furnishings. Well-appointed bedrooms; most with coastal views. Oak-panelled dining room looks onto terrace and garden; concise, set price dinner menu.

MICKLETON - Gloucestershire - 503 O27 - see Chipping Campden

MIDDLETON-IN-TEESDALE - Durham - 502 N20 - pop. 1 143 24 A3

London 260 mi – Carlisle 91 mi – Leeds 124 mi – Middlesbrough 70 mi

10 Market Pl, ✆ (01833) 64 10 01, www.middletonplus.org.uk

Grove Lodge

Hude, Northwest : 0.5 mi on B 6277 ✉ DL12 0QW – ✆ (01833) 640 798 – www.grovelodgeteesdale.co.uk

6 rm – †£ 55 ††£ 82 **Rest** – Menu £ 25

Old Victorian shooting lodge, perched on a hillside overlooking the valley; a place to relax and escape from technology. Traditional lounges furnished with antiques and heavy fabrics. Neat, up-to-date bedrooms; some have private bathrooms. Home-cooked dinners are served in the formally laid dining room.

MIDHURST – West Sussex – 504 R31 – pop. 6 120 7 C2

London 57 mi – Brighton 38 mi – Chichester 12 mi – Southampton 41 mi

North St, ✆ (01730) 81 73 22, www.visitmidhurst.com

Spread Eagle

South St ✉ GU29 9NH – ✆ (01730) 816 911 – www.hshotels.co.uk

39 rm – †£ 85/229 ††£ 85/229 – 2 suites **Rest** – Carte £ 28/44

15C former coaching inn retaining plenty of character in the form of heavy beams, antiques, gleaming brass and inglenook fireplaces. Individually decorated bedrooms; some with four-posters. Well-equipped spa. Formally laid restaurant offers classic dishes presented in a modern style.

The Town House without rest

West St ✉ GU29 9NF – ✆ (01730) 814 931 – www.themidhursttownhouse.com – Closed January-March

4 rm – †£ 65/150 ††£ 85/150

Experience genuine hospitality at this 19C house, set on a side street in the centre of town. Bedrooms are stylish and modern; those at the back are quieter. Communal breakfasts made with good quality local produce.

at Henley North : 4.5 mi by A286

Duke of Cumberland Arms

✉ GU27 3HQ – ✆ (01428) 652 280 – www.dukeofcumberland.com – Closed 25-26 December and dinner Sunday-Monday

Rest – Carte £ 32/48

A hidden gem, with a delightfully low-beamed interior featuring a huge fireplace and flag floors; tiered gardens have babbling brooks, trout ponds and views over the Downs. Appealing, daily changing menu of carefully prepared, seasonal dishes; 2 courses at lunch and 3 at dinner. Charming service.

at Bepton Southwest : 2.5 mi by A 286 on Bepton rd – ✉ Midhurst

Park House

✉ GU29 0JB – ✆ (01730) 819 000 – www.parkhousehotel.com

21 rm – †£ 150/320 ††£ 150/350 – 1 suite

Rest – *(booking essential)* Menu £ 27/38

Comfortable country house with light, modern style and smart spa and leisure facilities. Spacious bedrooms in neutral shades; most have views of well-tended gardens and golf course; some in separate two-storey house. Stylish conservatory restaurant offers modern menus.

at Redford Northwest : 4 mi by A272 then following signs for Redford

Redford Cottage without rest

✉ GU29 0QF – ✆ (01428) 741 242

3 rm – †£ 65/95 ††£ 95

Hospitable owners welcome you to this charming 16C cottage, set in 3 acres of delightful gardens. Cosy beamed lounge with wood burner; traditionally furnished bedrooms. Aga-cooked breakfasts use local ingredients, with many home-made items.

MID LAVANT – West Sussex – 504 R31 – see Chichester

MILFIELD – Northumberland 24 A1

London 336 mi – Glasgow 118 mi – Edinburgh 72 mi – Aberdeen 204 mi

Red Lion Inn with rm

Main Rd ✉ NE71 6JD – ✆ (01668) 216 224 – www.redlionmilfield.co.uk – Closed 1 January, 25 December and dinner 31 December

2 rm – †£ 30 ††£ 60 **Rest** – *(booking advisable)* Carte £ 17/32

Set close to the Scottish border, this former coaching inn really is the heart of the village. It has a traditional look and feel, matched by a classical menu which makes good use of the larders of both Scotland and England – and you definitely won't leave hungry! Bedrooms are fittingly homely.

MILFORD-ON-SEA – Hampshire – 503 P31 – pop. 4 229 6 A3
– ✉ Lymington

London 109 mi – Bournemouth 15 mi – Southampton 24 mi – Winchester 37 mi

ENGLAND

XX **Marine**
Hurst Rd (1st Floor) ✉ SO41 0PY – ✆ (01590) 644 369 – www.themarinerestaurant.co.uk – Closed Monday and Tuesday
Rest – Menu £ 15/35 – Carte £ 24/32
Set above a simple café and below a large roof terrace bar, this contemporary restaurant boasts great views across The Solent to the Isle of Wight. Menus mix traditional and more adventurous, modern dishes; fish is a strength.

X **Verveine** Ⓝ
98 High St ✉ SO41 0QE – ✆ (01590) 642 176 – www.verveine.co.uk – Closed Sunday and Monday
Rest – Menu £ 15 (weekday lunch)/55 – Carte £ 30/53
New England style restaurant fronted by a fishmonger's; sit bedside the open kitchen or in the bright rear dining room. Breads are baked twice-daily, veg is from the raised beds and smoking takes place on-site. The focus is on wonderfully fresh fish and cooking is accurate, original and bursting with flavour.

MILLBROOK – Cornwall – 503 H32 2 C2

London 235 mi – Liskeard 16 mi – Plymouth 23 mi

at Freathy West : 3 mi by B 3247, Whitsand Bay rd on Treninnow Cliff Rd – ✉ Millbrook

X **The View**
East : 1 mi ✉ PL10 1JY – ✆ (01752) 822 345 – www.theview-restaurant.co.uk – Closed February, Monday and Tuesday
Rest – Menu £ 16 (lunch) – Carte £ 30/36
Charming and informal converted café perched on a cliff, with coastal views. Relaxed daytime vibe; more atmospheric in the evening. Assured, confident cooking and friendly service. Plenty of seafood; generous portions. Try the rustic homemade bread.

ENGLAND

MILSTEAD – Kent – pop. 264 9 C1

London 46 mi – Croydon 48 mi – Barnet 68 mi – Ealing 84 mi

Red Lion
Rawling St ✉ ME9 0RT – ✆ (01795) 830 279 – www.theredlionmilstead.co.uk – Closed Sunday and Monday
Rest – *(booking advisable)* Carte £ 17/39
Simple, cosy country pub, personally run by an experienced couple. Ever-changing blackboard menu offers French-influenced country cooking. Dishes are honest, wholesome and richly flavoured.

MILTON – Oxfordshire – 503 P7 – see Banbury

MILTON ABBOT – Devon – 503 H32 – see Tavistock

MILTON KEYNES – Milton Keynes – 504 R27 – pop. 156 148 11 C1

London 56 mi – Bedford 16 mi – Birmingham 72 mi – Northampton 18 mi
The Chapel, The Knoll, Newport Pagnell, ✆ (01908) 614 6 38, www.destinationmiltonkeynes.co.uk
18 Abbey Hill, Two Mile Ash, Monks Way, ✆ (01908) 56 38 45
18 Tattenhoe, Bletchley, Tattenhoe Lane, ✆ (01908) 63 11 13
27 Wavendon Golf Centre, Wavendon, Lower End Rd, ✆ (01908) 28 18 11

Plans on following pages

XX **Brasserie Blanc**
Chelsea House, 301 Avebury Blvd ✉ MK9 2GA – ✆ (01908) 546 590 – www.brasserieblanc.com – Closed 25 December and dinner 26 December and 1 January EZc
Rest – *(booking essential)* Menu £ 14 (weekdays) – Carte £ 20/47
Bustling French brasserie and a small shop, set within a striking modern building and accessed via a revolving 1930s mahogany door. Friendly team and a lively, buzzy atmosphere. Menus focus on tasty, wholesome, classic brasserie dishes.

Jamie's Italian
3-5 Silbury Arcade ✉ MK9 3AG – ☎ (01908) 769 011 – www.jamiesitalian.com – Closed 26-26 December and Easter Sunday EY**a**
Rest – *(booking advisable)* Menu £ 12 (lunch) – Carte £ 15/31
Busy, buzzy restaurant with a laid-back, family-friendly feel. The passionate team serve flavoursome, rustic Italian dishes; all of the pasta is made on-site. For a quieter time, head for the upstairs floor, which opens at the weekend.

MINEHEAD – **Somerset** – **503** J30 – **pop. 11 699** **3** A2

London 187 mi – Bristol 64 mi – Exeter 43 mi – Taunton 25 mi
Warren Rd, ☎ (01643) 70 26 24, www.visitsomerset.co.uk
The Warren, Warren Rd, ☎ (01643) 70 20 57
Town★ - Higher Town (Church Steps★, St Michael's★)
Dunster★★ - Castle★★ **AC** (upper rooms ≤★) Water Mill★ **AC**, St George's Church★, Dovecote★, SE : 2.5 mi by A 39 – Selworthy★ (Church★, ≤★★) W : 4.5 mi by A 39. Exmoor National Park★★ – Cleeve Abbey★★ **AC**, SE : 6.5 mi by A 39

Channel House
Church Path, off Northfield Dr ✉ TA24 5QG – ☎ (01643) 703 229 – www.channelhouse.co.uk – Closed November-February
8 rm – †£ 101 ††£ 162 **Rest** – *(dinner only)* Menu £ 25 **s**
Passionately run, detached Edwardian house in an elevated position, with the sea just visible through its mature gardens. Comfy lounge and a cosy bar. Immaculately kept bedrooms have a modern edge; Rooms 7 and 8 are the most comfortable. Traditional, daily changing dinner menu and comprehensive breakfasts.

Glendower House without rest
30-32 Tregonwell Rd ✉ TA24 5DU – ☎ (01643) 707 144 – www.glendower-house.co.uk – Closed January
11 rm – †£ 38/60 ††£ 60/80
Well-run guesthouse, a few minutes' walk from the seafront. Traditionally furnished lounge. Individually decorated, immaculately kept bedrooms; those upstairs at the front are larger. Good breakfasts, with ingredients from local farms.

MINSTER LOVELL – **Oxfordshire** – **503** P28 **10** A2

London 74 mi – Birmingham 87 mi – Bristol 67 mi – Sheffield 151 mi

Minster Mill without rest
✉ OX29 0RN – ☎ (01993) 774 441 – www.oldswanandminstermill.com
44 rm – †£ 145/355 ††£ 165/395
17C Cotswold stone mill set on the riverbank in a small hamlet. Comfy lounge and minstrels' gallery. Corporate-style bedrooms with contemporary furnishings; the best boast riverside terraces. Meals at sister establishment, the Old Swan.

Old Swan with rm
✉ OX29 0RN – ☎ (01993) 774 441 – www.oldswanandminstermill.com
16 rm – †£ 135/355 ††£ 155/375 **Rest** – *(booking essential)* Carte £ 29/43
Smart inn with parquet floors, roaring open fires and garden games. Large herb plots contribute to unfussy pub classics; tasty daily specials feature fish from the Brixham day boats. Bedrooms boast period furnishings, mod cons and some have feature bathrooms.

MISTLEY – **Essex** – **504** X28 – **pop. 1 684** **13** D2

London 69 mi – Colchester 11 mi – Ipswich 14 mi

Mistley Thorn with rm
High St ✉ CO11 1HE – ☎ (01206) 392 821 – www.mistleythorn.co.uk
8 rm – †£ 85/170 ††£ 120/195 **Rest** – Menu £ 17 – Carte £ 22/40
Simply decorated restaurant in a historic coastal town. The appealing menu offers something for everyone, from local mussels and oysters to steak, arancini or seafood stew; with fish a feature and American and Italian influences evident. Bright, comfortable bedrooms; some with river views.

MITTON – **Lancashire** – **502** M22 – see Whalley

ENGLAND

HORIZONTAL ROADS

Bletcham Way (H10) .... **CX**
Chaffron Way (H7) .... **BX, CV**
Childs Way (H6) .... **BX, CV**
Dansteed Way (H4) .... **ABV**
Groveway (H9) .... **CVX**
Millers Way (H2) .... **AV**
Monks Way (H3) .... **ABV**
Portway (H5) .... **BCV**
Ridgeway (H1) .... **AV**
Standing Way (H8) .... **BX, CV**

MILTON KEYNES

Buckingham Rd .... **BX**
London Rd .... **CUV**
Manor Rd .... **CX**
Marsh End Rd .... **CU**
Newport Rd .... **BV**
Northampton Rd .... **AU**
Stoke Rd .... **CX**
Stratford Rd .... **AV**
Whaddon Way .... **BX**
Wolverton Rd .... **BU**

VERTICAL ROADS

Brickhill St (V10) .... **BU, CX**
Fulmer St (V3) .... **ABX**
Grafton St (V6) .... **BVX**
Great Monks St (V5) .... **AV**
Marlborough St (V8) .... **BV, CX**
Overstreet (V9) .... **BV**
Saxon St (V7) .... **BVX**
Snelshall St (V1) .... **BX**
Tattenhoe St (V2) .... **ABX**
Tongwell St (V11) .... **CVX**
Watling St (V4) .... **AV, BX**

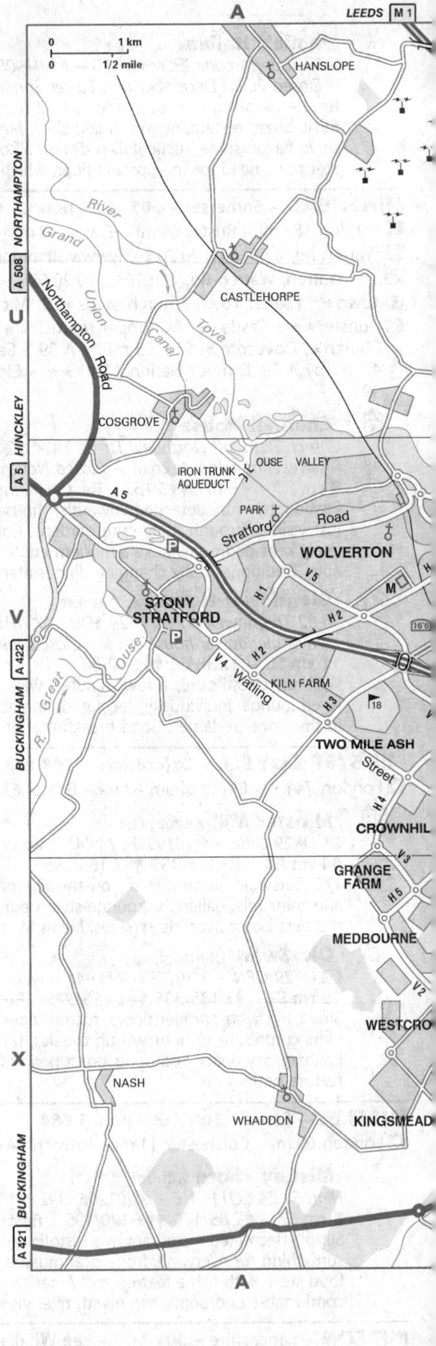

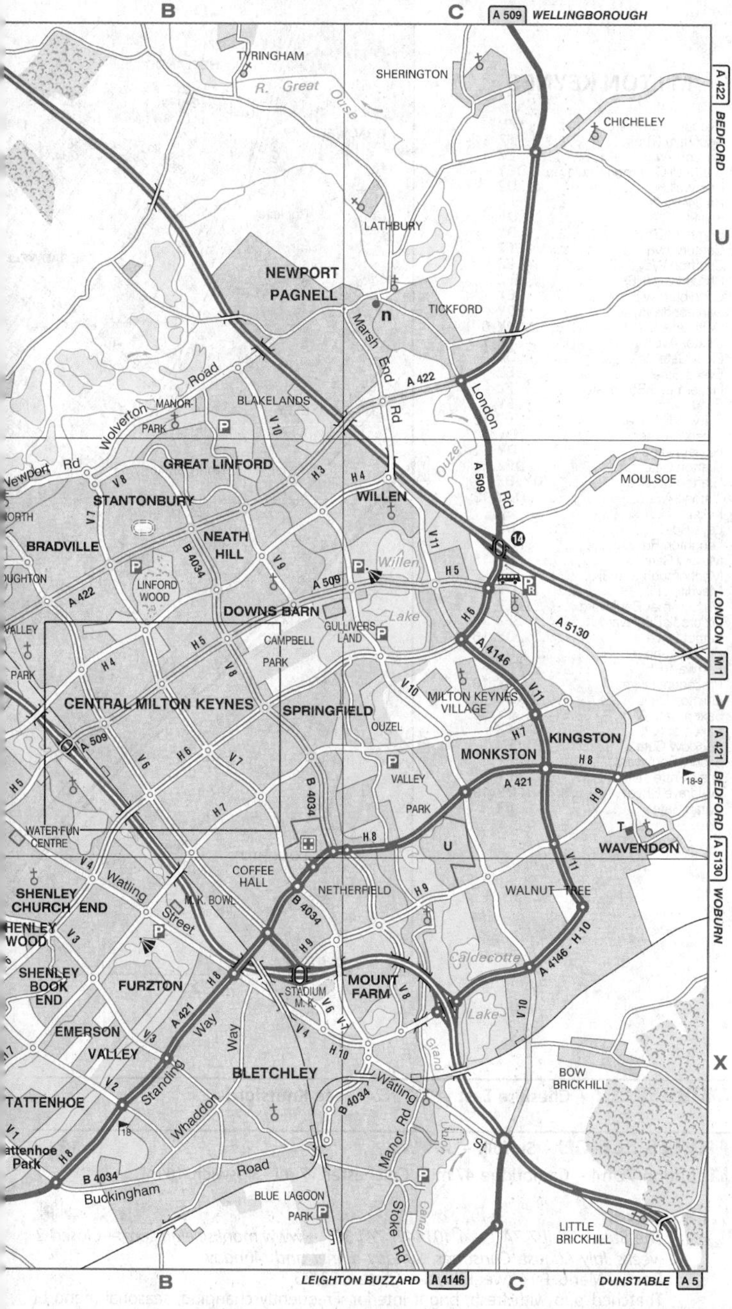

B
C
A 509 WELLINGBOROUGH
TYRINGHAM
R. Great Ouse
SHERINGTON
A 422 BEDFORD
CHICHELEY
LATHBURY
U
NEWPORT PAGNELL
TICKFORD
Marsh End Rd
Wolverton Road
MANOR-PARK
BLAKELANDS
A 422
London Rd
A 509
Ouzel
Newport Rd
GREAT LINFORD
V 10
V 8
H 3
H 4
WILLEN
MOULSOE
STANTONBURY
V 7
NEATH HILL
BRADVILLE
B 4034
V 9
V 11
Willen Lake
H 5
LINFORD WOOD
A 422
A 509
DOWNS BARN
H 6
A 5130
LONDON M 1
GULLIVERS LAND
CAMPBELL PARK
H 5
H 4
V 8
A 4146
V 10
MILTON KEYNES VILLAGE
V 11
CENTRAL MILTON KEYNES
SPRINGFIELD
OUZEL
V
A 509
KINGSTON
MONKSTON
H 7
H 6
V 7
V 6
H 8
A 421 BEDFORD
18-9
H 5
VALLEY PARK
A 421
B 4034
H 9
H 7
WATER-FUN-CENTRE
H 8
U
WAVENDON
A 5130 WOBURN
V 4
COFFEE HALL
NETHERFIELD
H 9
WALNUT TREE
V 11
SHENLEY CHURCH END
Watling Street
M.K. BOWL
B 4034
H 10
A 4146 - H 10
SHENLEY WOOD
V 3
H 9
Caldecotte Lake
SHENLEY BOOK END
FURZTON
H 8
STADIUM M.K.
MOUNT FARM
V 8
V 10
V 6
V 7
A 421
Way
EMERSON VALLEY
V 3
V 4
Way
H 10
Grand
X
BLETCHLEY
Standing
Watling St.
BOW BRICKHILL
V 2
TATTENHOE
B 4034
Manor Rd
V 1
18
Whaddon Road
Tattenhoe Park
H 8
B 4034
Buckingham Road
Union Canal
BLUE LAGOON PARK
Stoke Rd
LITTLE BRICKHILL
B
LEIGHTON BUZZARD A 4146
C
DUNSTABLE A 5

ENGLAND

MILTON KEYNES

Avebury Boulevard	EFY	
Boundary (The)	FZ	3
Boycott Ave	EZ	4
Bradwell Common Boulevard	DEY	
Bradwell Rd	DZ	
Brearley Ave	EFZ	
Brill Pl.	DY	
Burnham Drive	DY	
Century Ave	EFZ	
Chaffron Way (H7)	FZ	
Childs Way (H6)	EFZ	
Conniburrow Boulevard	EY	
Dansteed Way (H4)	DY	
Deltic Ave	DY	6
Dexter Ave	FZ	7
Elder Gate	DZ	9
Evans Gate	EZ	
Fishermead Boulevard	FZ	
Food Centre	FY	
Fulwoods Drive	FZ	10
Gibsons Green	DY	
Glovers Lane	DY	12
Grafton Gate	DEZ	
Grafton St (V6)	DY, EZ	
Ibstone Ave	DEY	13
Kirkstall Pl.	EZ	
Leys Rd	DZ	
Loughton Rd	DY	
Mallow Gate	EY	15
Marlborough St (V8)	FY	
Mayditch Pl.	DY	
Midsummer Boulevard	EFY	
Oldbrook Boulevard	EFZ	
Patriot Drive	DY	16
Pitcher Lane	DZ	
Portway (H5)	EFY	
Precedent Drive	DY	18
Quinton Drive	DY	
Saxon Gate (V7)	EY	
Saxon St (V7)	EY, FZ	
Secklow Gate	FY	
Silbury Boulevard	EFY	
The Centre : MK	EFY	
Walgrave Drive	DY	19
Witan Gate	EZ	

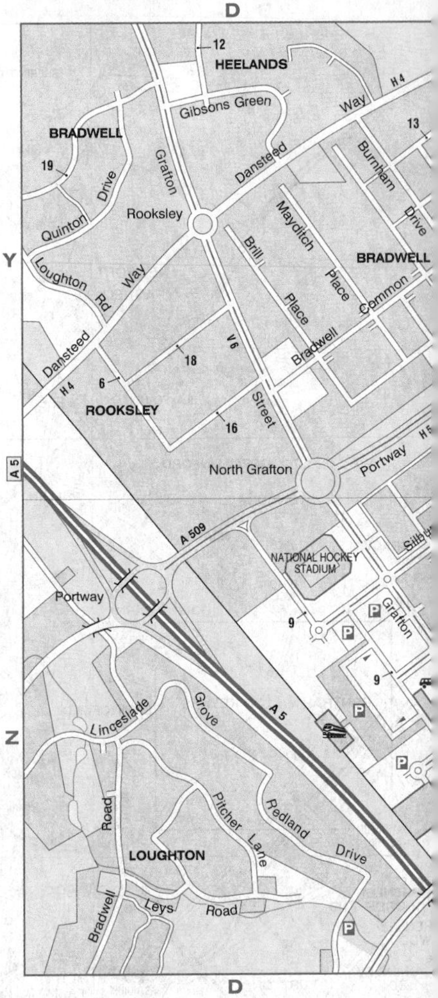

MOBBERLEY – Cheshire East – 502 N24 – see Knutsford

MONKS ELEIGH – Suffolk – 504 W27 15 C3

London 72 mi – Cambridge 47 mi – Colchester 17 mi – Ipswich 16 mi

Swan

The Street ✉ IP7 7AU – ✆ (01449) 741 391 – www.monkseleigh.com – Closed 2 weeks July-August, Christmas, Sunday dinner and Monday

Rest – Menu £ 14 (weekdays) – Carte £ 23/35

Thatched pub with fresh, bright interior. Frequently changing, seasonal menu of generous, flavourful dishes, with the occasional Italian influence; all homemade from local produce.

ENGLAND

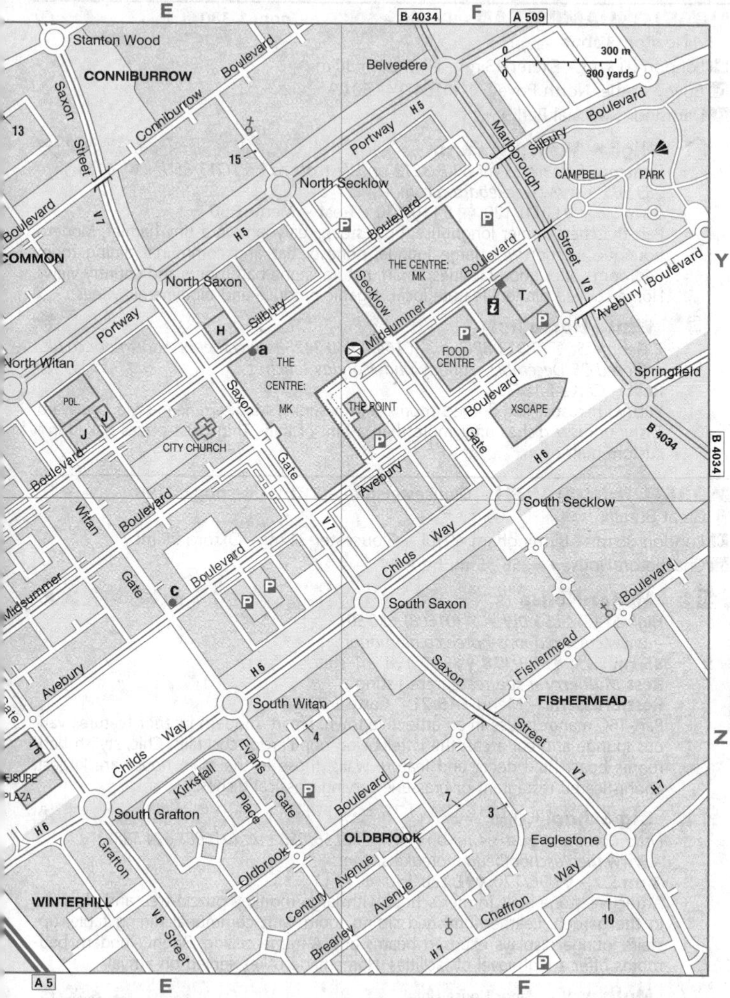

MONKTON COMBE – Bath and North East Somerset – see Bath

MORECAMBE – Lancashire – **502** L21 – **pop. 49 569** **20** A1

London 247 mi – Preston 27 mi – Blackpool 39 mi – Blackburn 34 mi

Midland

Marine Road West ✉ LA4 4BU – ✆ (01524) 424 000 – www.englishlakes.co.uk – Closed Christmas and New Year

44 rm – †£ 77/144 ††£ 94/228 – 2 suites **Rest** – Carte £ 25/42

Iconic 1933 hotel set in a stunning location, with views of Morecambe Bay and the mountains. Art deco styling – original features include a listed staircase. Variously sized, contemporary bedrooms. Modern restaurant offers a superb outlook and plenty of Lancashire produce. Afternoon tea in the conservatory.

MORETONHAMPSTEAD – Devon – 503 I32 – pop. 1 380 2 C2

– ✉ Newton Abbot

London 213 mi – Exeter 13 mi – Plymouth 30 mi

Bovey Castle, North Bovey, ✆ (01647) 44 50 09

Dartmoor National Park★★

Higher Westcott Farm

Westcott, East : 4.25 mi by B 3212 on Westcott rd ✉ TQ13 8SU – ✆ (01647) 253 505 – www.weekebarton.com

5 rm ☕ – †£ 100/120 ††£ 110/130 **Rest** – Menu £ 30

Part-thatched former longhouse, up a steep, leafy lane in a tiny hamlet. Modern, boutique interior with large lounge, honesty bar and communal dining room. Bedrooms offer good facilities, smart, natural stone bathrooms and country views. Home-cooked dinners feature local, organic produce and biodynamic wines.

White Horse Inn

7 George St ✉ TQ13 8PG – ✆ (01647) 440 242 – www.thehorsedartmoor.co.uk – Closed 25 December, Sunday and Monday lunch

Rest – Carte £ 18/38

Pub with rustic, flag-floored rooms and a sunny, Mediterranean-style courtyard. Tasty, unfussy dishes offer more than a hint of Italy. Thin crust pizzas baked in a custom-built oven.

MORETON-IN-MARSH – Gloucestershire – 503 O28 – pop. 3 198 4 D1

Great Britain

London 86 mi – Birmingham 40 mi – Gloucester 31 mi – Oxford 29 mi

Chastleton House★★, SE : 5 mi by A 44

ENGLAND

Manor House

High St ✉ GL56 0LJ – ✆ (01608) 650 501 – www.cotswold-inns-hotels.co.uk/manor

35 rm ☕ – †£ 79/178 ††£ 99/198 – 1 suite

Rest *Mulberry* – see restaurant listing

Rest *Brasserie* – Menu £ 15/21 – Carte £ 22/36

Part-16C manor house in an attractive town. Smart, modern interior features various lounge and bar areas; the latter being popular for cocktails. Chic, stylish bedrooms boast bold décor and feature walls; those in the main house are largest. Sophisticated restaurant or brasserie serving classical dishes.

Old School without rest

Little Compton, East : 4 mi on A 44 ✉ GL56 0SL – ✆ (01608) 674 588 – www.theoldschoolbedandbreakfast.com

4 rm ☕ – †£ 96/120 ††£ 120/150

Attractive stone-built former school with large monkey puzzle tree and chickens in the garden. Leather-furnished sitting room with communal dining table; upstairs lounge displays exposed beams and A-frame ceiling. Bright, modern bedrooms offer a high level of facilities. Homemade cakes served on arrival.

Mulberry – Manor House Hotel

High St ✉ GL56 0LJ – ✆ (01608) 650 501 – www.cotswold-inns-hotels.co.uk/manor

Rest – *(dinner only and Sunday lunch)* Menu £ 39

Formal restaurant with an enclosed walled garden, located in a part-16C manor house. Choose between a modern, adventurous 4 course set menu or a seasonal 8 course tasting menu which features some challenging combinations.

at Bourton-on-the-Hill West : 2 mi on A44 – ✉ Moreton-In-Marsh

Horse & Groom with rm

✉ GL56 9AQ – ✆ (01386) 700 413 – www.horseandgroom.info – Closed 25, 31 December and Sunday dinner

5 rm ☕ – †£ 80 ††£ 120/170 **Rest** – *(booking essential)* Carte £ 22/33

Honey-coloured, Cotswold stone pub in a pretty village high on the hillside, featuring stylish bedrooms and lovely country views. Food is good value, fresh and flavoursome; study the daily blackboard menu then order at the bar. Passionately described beer selection and plenty of wines by the glass.

MORPETH – Northumberland – 501 O18 – pop. 13 555 24 B2

London 301 mi – Edinburgh 93 mi – Newcastle upon Tyne 15 mi

Bridge St, ☎ (01670) 50 07 00, www.visitnorthumberland.com

The Clubhouse, ☎ (01670) 50 49 42

at Eshott North : 8.5 mi by A 1 – ✉ Morpeth

Eshott Hall

✉ NE65 9EN – ☎ (01670) 787 454 – www.eshotthall.co.uk – Closed Christmas-New Year

16 rm – †£ 90/175 ††£ 120/270 **Rest** – Carte £ 39/48

Attractive Georgian manor house in a quiet, rural location – yet only 5min from the A1. Classically stylish guest areas. Smart, modern bedrooms boast warm fabrics, antique furniture and good facilities. Formal dining room offers contemporary menus; local produce includes fruit and veg from the kitchen garden.

at Longhorsley Northwest : 6.5 mi by A 192 on A 697 – ✉ Morpeth

Thistleyhaugh Farm

Northwest : 3.75 mi by A 697 and Todburn rd taking first right turn ✉ NE65 8RG – ☎ (01665) 570 629 – www.thistleyhaugh.co.uk – Closed 25 December-31 January

5 rm – †£ 60/85 ††£ 90 **Rest** – Menu £ 25

Attractive Georgian farmhouse, set off the beaten track on a 750 acre organic farm, with the River Coquet flowing through its grounds. Cosy, open-fired lounge and antique-filled dining room. Spacious, comfortable bedrooms – most have luxurious bathrooms with feature baths. Communal dinners; home-cooking features beef and lamb from the farm. Charming owners.

MORSTON – Norfolk – see Blakeney

MOULSFORD – Oxfordshire – pop. 491 10 B3

London 53 mi – Newbury 16 mi – Reading 13 mi

Beetle & Wedge Boathouse with rm

Ferry Ln ✉ OX10 9JF – ☎ (01491) 651 381 – www.beetleandwedge.co.uk – Closed first week January

3 rm – †£ 75 ††£ 90/100

Rest – *(booking essential)* Menu £ 15 (weekdays) – Carte £ 26/34

Former boathouse named after the beetle (mallet) and wedge (splitter) used in skiff making. It's in a wonderful Thameside location and has a charming terrace and oversized windows ideal for bird watching. Cooking is honest and robust and features dishes from the chargrill. Cosy bedrooms are in an annexe.

MOUSEHOLE – Cornwall – 503 D33 – ✉ Penzance 1 A3

London 321 mi – Penzance 3 mi – Truro 29 mi

Village★

Penwith★★ – Lamorna (The Merry Maidens and The Pipers Standing Stone★) SW : 3 mi by B 3315. Land's End★ (cliff scenery★★★) W : 9 mi by B 3315

Cornish Range with rm

6 Chapel St ✉ TR19 6SB – ☎ (01736) 731 488 – www.cornishrange.co.uk – Closed 2 weeks January-February

3 rm – †£ 65/90 ††£ 80/110

Rest – *(booking essential)* Menu £ 17 (dinner) – Carte £ 21/34

Former pilchard processing cottage hidden away in a backstreet of an old fishing village; bright, modern artwork adorns the walls. Simple brunch and lunch menus, good value early evening selection and a seafood orientated à la carte. Good-sized, comfy bedrooms – one used to be artist Jack Pender's studio.

2 Fore Street

✉ TR19 6PF – ☎ (01736) 731 164 – www.2forestreet.co.uk – Closed January and Monday in winter

Rest – *(booking essential at dinner)* Carte approx. £ 28

Bright, friendly, all-day café and bistro in a pretty harbourside setting; popular with locals and tourists alike. Menus are based on the best of the day's catch and feature simple, unfussy preparations. Brunch is a feature at weekends.

✗ **Old Coastguard** with rm ≤ 🚗 🎤 🔊 & rest, 🔊 **P**
The Parade ✉ TR19 6PR – 𝒞 (01736) 731 222 – www.oldcoastguardhotel.co.uk
– *Closed 25 December and early January*
14 rm ☐ – †£ 83/148 ††£ 110/235
Rest – Menu £ 14 (weekdays) – Carte £ 21/27 **s**
Old coastguard's cottage in a small fishing village, with a laid-back, open-plan interior, a sub-tropical garden and views towards St Clement's Isle. Well-presented
brasserie dishes display a Mediterranean edge; great wine selection. Individually
styled bedrooms – some with balconies, most with sea views.

MULLION – Cornwall – 503 E33 – pop. 1 834 – ✉ Helston 1 A3
🗗 London 287 mi – Birmingham 282 mi – Croydon 295 mi – Barnet 300 mi
🔘 Mullion Cove★★ (Church★) – Lizard Peninsula★
🔘 Kynance Cove★★, S : 5 mi – Cury★ (Church★), N : 2 mi by minor roads. Helston
(The Flora Day Furry Dance★★) (May), N : 7.5 mi by A 3083 – Culdrose (Flambards
Village Theme Park★) **AC**, N : 6 mi by A 3083 – Wendron (Poldark Mine★), N :
9.5 mi by A 3083 and B 3297

🏨 **Polurrian Bay** ≤ 🚗 🕭 🎤 ⅀ 🛋 ✗ & rm, 🚴 🔊 🎏 **P**
✉ TR12 7EN – 𝒞 (01326) 240 421 – www.polurrianhotel.com
41 rm ☐ – †£ 107/226 ††£ 125/265 **Rest** – *(dinner only)* Menu £ 39
Imposing Victorian hotel with 12 acres of grounds, in a commanding clifftop position. Spacious, modern interior is geared towards families, with a crèche, games
room and cinema. Most of the bright bedrooms boast views across Mount's Bay.
Unfussy menus showcase seasonal, local produce.

MURCOTT – Oxfordshire – pop. 1 293 – ✉ Kidlington 10 B2
🗗 London 70 mi – Oxford 14 mi – Witney 20 mi

🍴 **Nut Tree** (Mike North) 🚗 🎤 **P**
✿ *Main St* ✉ OX5 2RE – 𝒞 (01865) 331 253 – www.nuttreeinn.co.uk – *Closed 27
December-2 January, Sunday dinner and Monday (except lunch bank holidays)*
Rest – Menu £ 18 (weekday lunch) – Carte £ 32/51
Traditional thatched pub with a cosy bar and a smart restaurant. The appealing
menus change constantly, relying on the latest seasonal ingredients to arrive at
the door, and produce is organic, free range or wild wherever possible; they
even rear rare breed pigs. Combinations are classical and satisfying.
→ Home-smoked salmon with whipped horseradish cream. Fillet of beef, triple-
cooked chips and tarragon butter. Hot blood orange soufflé.

NAILSWORTH – Gloucestershire – 503 N28 – pop. 5 276 4 C1
🗗 London 110 mi – Bristol 30 mi – Swindon 28 mi

✗✗ **Wild Garlic** with rm 🎤 **AC** rest, 🔊
3 Cossack Sq ✉ GL6 0DB – 𝒞 (01453) 832 615 – www.wild-garlic.co.uk – *Closed
first 2 weeks January, Wednesday lunch, Sunday dinner, Monday and Tuesday*
3 rm ☐ – †£ 75/95 ††£ 95/125 **Rest** – Menu £ 39/49 – Carte £ 28/37
Family-run restaurant in the heart of a market town. Two smart, contemporary,
semi-panelled rooms feature bright food-themed photos and stencilled wallpaper.
Monthly menus reflect the latest local ingredients available; there's also a popular
tasting menu. Stylish, modern bedrooms are well-equipped.

✗ **mark@street**
Market St ✉ GL6 0HL – 𝒞 (01453) 839 251 – www.marketstreetnailsworth.co.uk
– *Closed 2 weeks January, 1 week September, Sunday dinner and Monday*
Rest – *(bookings advisable at dinner)* Menu £ 13 (weekday lunch)/42
– Carte £ 20/35
Small, friendly restaurant on a narrow street. Simple lunch menus are supplemen-
ted by brunch at the weekends. Candlelit dinners offer well-balanced, classical
dishes presented in a modern way; the vegetables are from their allotment.

NANTWICH – Cheshire East – 502 M24 – pop. 13 447 20 A3
🗗 London 176 mi – Chester 20 mi – Liverpool 45 mi – Manchester 40 mi
🛈 Market St, 𝒞 (01270) 61 09 83, www.nantwich.ivisitorguide.com
🔟 Alvaston Hall, Middlewich Rd, 𝒞 (01270) 62 84 73

Rookery Hall

Worleston, North : 2.5 mi by A 51 on B 5074 ✉ CW5 6DQ – ☎ (01270) 610 016 – www.handpicked.co.uk/hotels/rookery-hall
70 rm – †£ 99/136 ††£ 209/236 – 2 suites
Rest – *(dinner only and Sunday lunch) (booking essential)* Menu £ 31 – Carte £ 31/46 **s**
19C property set in pleasant grounds, with considerable extensions. Main building offers characterful, country house bedrooms; more modern rooms are located in the purpose-built rear wing. Smart, impressive spa. Formal, two-roomed, wood-panelled dining room overlooking gardens.

NAWTON – see Helmsley

NETHER BURROW – Lancashire – ✉ Kirkby Lonsdale 20 B1

London 257 mi – Liverpool 73 mi – Leeds 101 mi – Manchester 68 mi

Highwayman

✉ LA6 2RJ – ☎ (01524) 273 338 – www.highwaymaninn.co.uk – Closed Monday and 25 December
Rest – Carte £ 19/32
Sizeable 18C coaching inn with open-fired, stone-floored bar and lovely terrace. A rustic, no-nonsense approach to food makes for well-crafted, flavourful dishes. Produce is local and seasonal, with Lancashire Hot Pot a perennial favourite.

NETHER WESTCOTE – Gloucestershire – see Stow-on-the-Wold

NETLEY MARSH – Hampshire – 503 P31 – see Southampton

NEW MILTON – Hampshire – 503 P31 – pop. 24 324 6 A3

London 106 mi – Bournemouth 12 mi – Southampton 21 mi – Winchester 34 mi
Barton-on-Sea, Milford Rd, ☎ (01425) 61 53 08

Chewton Glen

Christchurch Rd, West : 2 mi by A 337 and Ringwood Rd on Chewton Farm Rd ✉ BH25 6QS – ☎ (01425) 275 341 – www.chewtonglen.com
70 rm – †£ 356/1429 ††£ 377/1450 – 15 suites
Rest *Vetiver* – see restaurant listing
Very professionally run 19C country house, set in 130 acres of New Forest parkland. Impressive spa and a host of outdoor pursuits, including croquet, archery and clay pigeon shooting. Luxurious bedrooms range from classic to contemporary and many have balconies or terraces; opt for a unique Tree House suite.

Vetiver – Chewton Glen Hotel

Christchurch Rd, West : 2 mi by A 337 and Ringwood Rd on Chewton Farm Rd ✉ BH25 6QS – ☎ (01425) 275 341 – www.chewtonglen.com
Rest – Menu £ 25 (weekday lunch) **s** – Carte £ 37/72 **s**
Stylish hotel restaurant comprising 5 impressive rooms, including one with wines displayed in illuminated cases. Modern 7 course tasting menu or accessible à la carte ranging from fish and chips to caviar; weekend specials from the trolley.

NEW ROMNEY – Kent – 504 W31 9 C2

London 71 mi – Brighton 60 mi – Folkestone 17 mi – Maidstone 36 mi

Romney Bay House

Coast Rd, Littlestone, East : 2.25 mi by B 2071 ✉ TN28 8QY – ☎ (01797) 364 747 – www.romneybayhousehotel.co.uk – Closed 1 week Christmas
10 rm – †£ 75/95 ††£ 110/164
Rest – *(closed Sunday, Monday and Thursday) (dinner only) (booking essential) (set menu only)* Menu £ 45
Built by Sir Clough Williams-Ellis in the 1920s, for actress Hedda Hopper, and accessed via a private coast road. Open-fired drawing room with honesty bar; first floor lounge has a telescope and lovely views out to sea. Homely bedrooms. Conservatory dining room offers a daily, seafood-based menu.

ENGLAND

NEWARK-ON-TRENT – Nottinghamshire – 502 R24 – pop. 35 454 17 C1

Great Britain

London 127 mi – Lincoln 16 mi – Nottingham 20 mi – Sheffield 42 mi

Coddington, Newark, (01636) 62 62 82

St Mary Magdalene★

Grange

73 London Rd, South : 0.5 mi on Grantham rd (B 6326) ✉ NG24 1RZ – (01636) 703 399 – www.grangenewark.co.uk – Closed 22 December-6 January

19 rm – ♦£ 75/120 ♦♦£ 85/150

Rest *Cutlers* – *(closed Sunday dinner) (dinner only and Sunday lunch)*
Carte £ 24/34

Personally run hotel with tranquil, award-winning gardens. The main house has mock Tudor gables, a Victorian-style bar and lounge, and a smart restaurant decorated with antique plates and cutlery. Individually styled bedrooms are split between this and a second house, and offer good comforts.

at Norwell North : 7.25 mi by A 1

Willoughby House without rest

Main St ✉ NG23 6JN – (01636) 636 266 – www.willoughbyhousebandb.co.uk

3 rm – ♦£ 60/75 ♦♦£ 85/105

Three-storey, red-brick Georgian farmhouse and converted stables. Chic, stylish interior with a small open-fired lounge and a deep scarlet breakfast room. Bedrooms feature quality furnishings and antiques, along with contemporary art and homemade flapjacks. The owner has an eye for detail.

at Caunton Northwest : 7 mi by A 616 – ✉ Newark-On-Trent

Caunton Beck

Main St ✉ NG23 6AB – (01636) 636 793 – www.wigandmitre.com

Rest – Menu £ 14/17 – Carte £ 21/35

Modern-looking pub with tan coloured bricks, a wrought iron pergola and a large, flower-filled terrace. Menus offer detailed, classically based cooking with Mediterranean influences. They open from 9am Mon-Sat for breakfast.

NEWBIGGIN – Cumbria – 502 L19 – see Penrith

NEWBURY – West Berkshire – 503 Q29 – pop. 32 675 10 B3

London 67 mi – Bristol 66 mi – Oxford 28 mi – Reading 17 mi

Newbury and Crookham, Greenham Common, Bury's Bank Rd, (01635) 4 00 35

Donnington Valley, Donnington, Snelsmore House, Snelsmore Common, (01635) 56 81 40

Plans pages 525, 526

Vineyard

Stockcross, Northwest : 2 mi by A 4 on B 4000 ✉ RG20 8JU – (01635) 528 770 – www.the-vineyard.co.uk AV**b**

49 rm – ♦£ 190/335 ♦♦£ 190/335, £ 21 – 26 suites

Rest *Vineyard* – see restaurant listing

Extended, bay-windowed former hunting lodge with over 1,000 pieces of art and a striking fire and water feature. Some bedrooms have a country house style while others are more contemporary; all boast smart marble bathrooms. The owner also has a vineyard in California, hence the wine-themed 'California Bar'.

Donnington Valley H. & Spa

Old Oxford Rd, Donnington, North : 1.75 mi by A 4 off B 4494 ✉ RG14 3AG – (01635) 551 199 – www.donningtonvalley.co.uk AV**a**

111 rm – ♦£ 114/237 ♦♦£ 129/252

Rest *Winepress* – see restaurant listing

Modern, business-orientated hotel with golf club and 18 hole course. Spacious, stylishly furnished guest areas and wine-themed bar. Smart bedrooms offer a high level of facilities; opt for 'Executive'. Excellent leisure and wellness centre.

ENGLAND

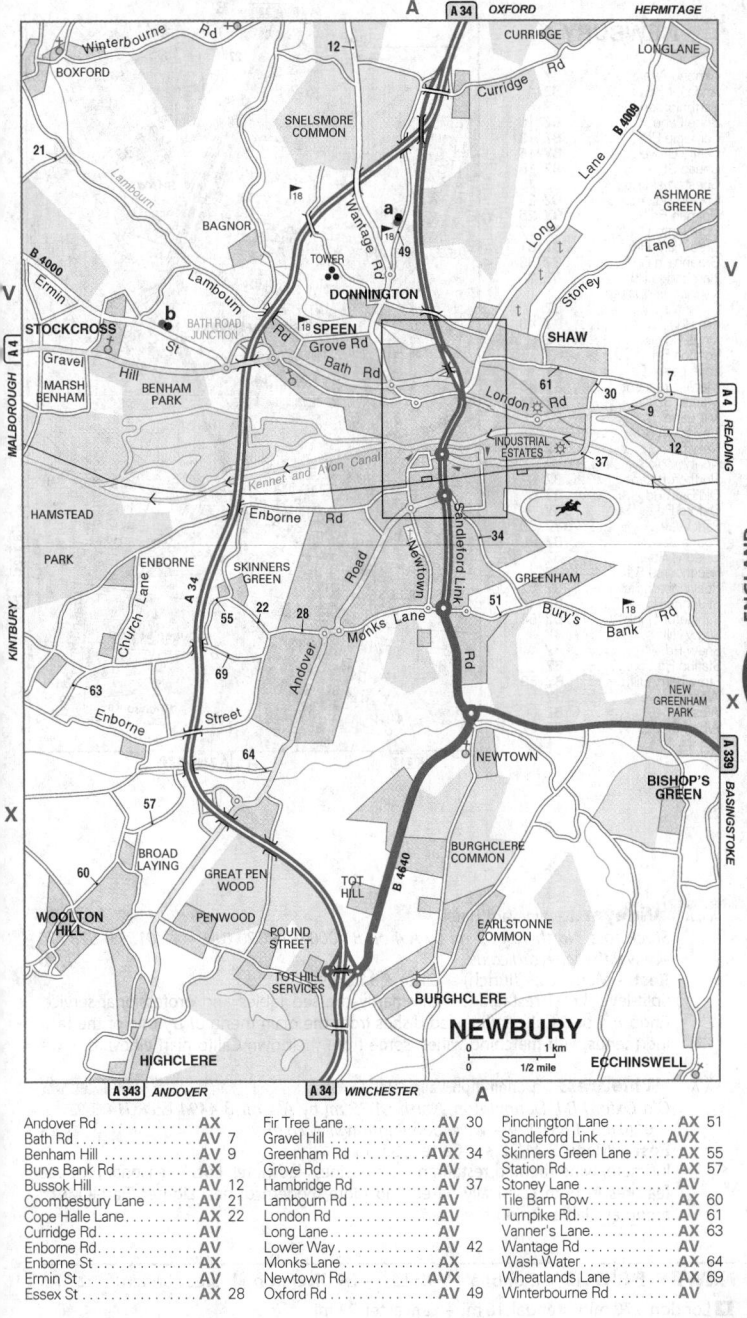

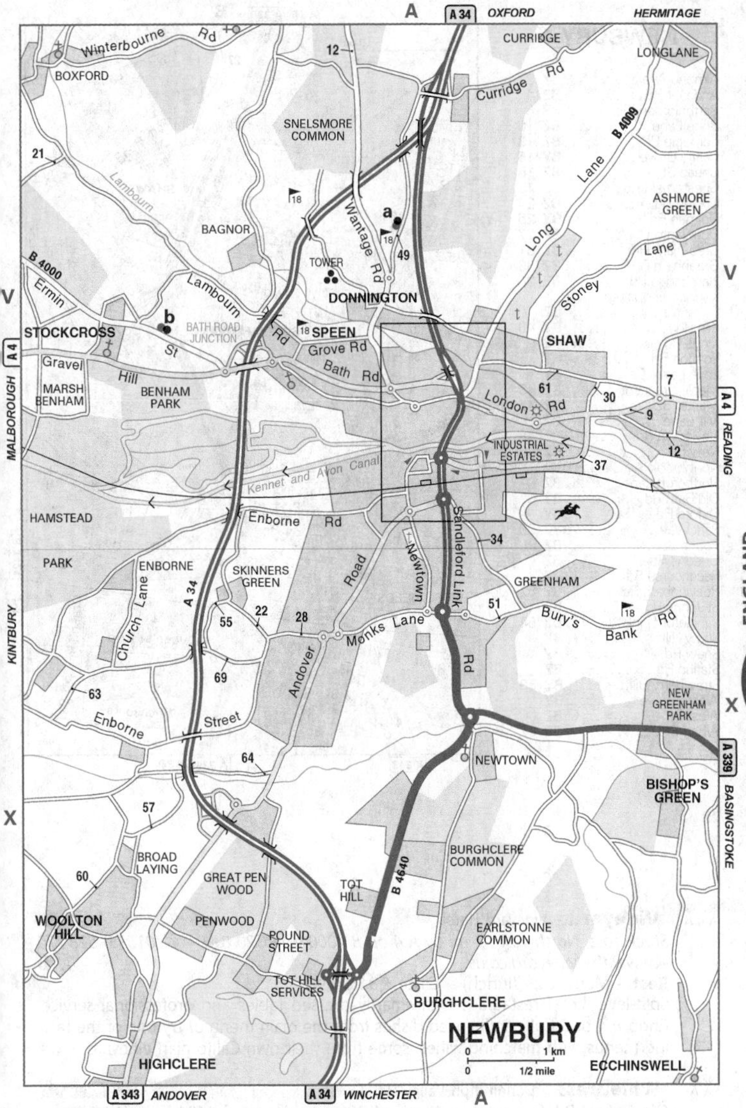

Andover Rd	AX	
Bath Rd	AV	7
Benham Hill	AV	9
Burys Bank Rd	AX	
Bussok Hill	AV	12
Coombesbury Lane	AV	21
Cope Halle Lane	AX	22
Curridge Rd	AV	
Enborne Rd	AV	
Enborne St	AX	
Ermin St	AV	
Essex St	AX	28
Fir Tree Lane	AV	30
Gravel Hill	AV	
Greenham Rd	AVX	34
Grove Rd	AV	
Hambridge Rd	AV	37
Lambourn Rd	AV	
London Rd	AV	
Long Lane	AV	
Lower Way	AV	42
Monks Lane	AX	
Newtown Rd	AVX	
Oxford Rd	AV	49
Pinchington Lane	AX	51
Sandleford Link	AVX	
Skinners Green Lane	AX	55
Station Rd	AX	57
Stoney Lane	AV	
Tile Barn Row	AX	60
Turnpike Rd	AV	61
Vanner's Lane	AX	63
Wantage Rd	AV	
Wash Water	AX	64
Wheatlands Lane	AX	69
Winterbourne Rd	AV	

NEWBURY

Almond Ave . . . . **BY** 3
Andover Rd . . . . **BZ** 4
Bartholomew St . . . . **BZ** 6
Bone Lane . . . . **BZ** 10
Carnegie Rd. . . . . **BZ** 13
Castle Grove . . . . **BY** 15
Cheap St . . . . **BZ** 16
Chesterfield Rd . . . . **BZ** 18
Craven Rd . . . . **BZ** 24
Dolman Rd . . . . **BY** 25
Donnington Link . . . . **BY** 27
Greenham Hill . . . . **BZ** 31
Greenham Rd . . . . **BZ** 33
Hambridge Rd. . . . . **BZ** 36
Kennett Shopping Centre . . . . **BZ**
Kiln Rd . . . . **BY** 40
Kings Rd . . . . **BZ**
London Rd. . . . . **BY**
Love Lane . . . . **BY**
Maple Crescent . . . . **BY** 43
Market St. . . . . **BZ** 45
Mill Lane . . . . **BZ**
Newtown Rd. . . . . **BZ** 48
New Rd . . . . **BZ** 46
Northbrook St . . . . **BYZ**
Northcroft Lane . . . . **BZ**
Old Bath Rd. . . . . **BY**
Oxford Rd . . . . **BY**
Park Way . . . . **BYZ** 50
Pound St . . . . **BZ**
Queens Rd . . . . **BZ**
Racecourse Rd . . . . **BZ**
Rockingham Rd . . . . **BZ** 52
St Johns Rd. . . . . **BZ**
Sandleford Link . . . . **BZ** 54
Shaw Hill . . . . **BY**
Shaw Rd . . . . **BY**
Station Rd . . . . **BZ**
Strawberry Hill . . . . **BY** 58
Western Ave. . . . . **BY**
West St . . . . **BZ** 66
Wharf St . . . . **BZ** 67

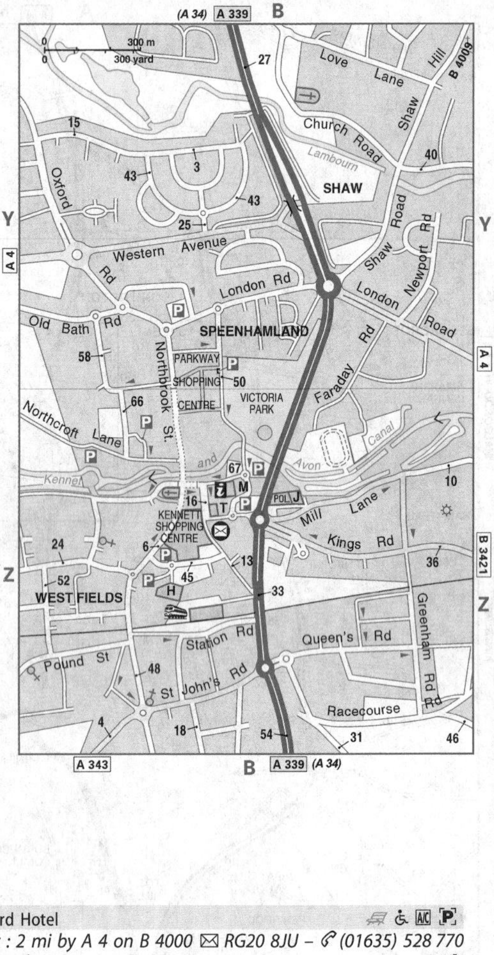

XXX **Vineyard** – Vineyard Hotel

Stockcross, Northwest : 2 mi by A 4 on B 4000 ✉ *RG20 8JU* – ☎ *(01635) 528 770 – www.the-vineyard.co.uk* AV**b**

Rest – Menu £ 29 (lunch) – Carte £ 34/54

Split-level hotel restaurant with smartly dressed tables and professional service. Choose 4 or 5 Gallic-influenced dishes from the main menu or try one of the tasting menus with matching wines; some from their own Californian vineyard.

XX **Winepress** – Donnington Valley Hotel & Spa

Old Oxford Rd, Donnington, North : 1.75 mi by A 4 off B 4494 ✉ *RG14 3AG – ☎ (01635) 551 199 – www.donningtonvalley.co.uk* AV**a**

Rest – Menu £ 24/28 **s** – Carte £ 33/56 **s**

Intimate, wine-themed restaurant in a business-led hotel. Local, seasonal produce features in both classically based and more modern dishes. Lighter 'Bar + Mezz' menu available during the day.

NEWBY BRIDGE – **Cumbria** – **502** L21 – ✉ **Ulverston** Great Britain **21** A3

London 270 mi – Kendal 16 mi – Lancaster 27 mi

Lake Windermere★★

Lakeside

Lakeside, Northeast : 1 mi on Hawkshead rd ✉ *LA12 8AT – ✆ (015395) 30 001 – www.lakesidehotel.co.uk – Closed 3-17 January*
75 rm – £ 125/385 £ 159/395 – 7 suites
Rest *John Ruskin's Brasserie* – see restaurant listing
Rest *Lakeview* – *(dinner only)* Menu £ 42
Superbly situated on the water's edge. Very comfy, traditional guest areas. Smart, modern bedrooms; some with four-posters, feature walls or great views. Contemporary spa, leisure club and good-sized pool. Smart, formal dining room offers traditional menu. Stylish, modern brasserie. Light lunches and afternoon tea in conservatory, with great views over the lake.

Swan

rm, rm,

✉ *LA12 8NB – ✆ (015395) 31 681 – www.swanhotel.com*
51 rm – £ 99/190 £ 99/190
Rest *River Room* – *(dinner only and Sunday lunch)* Carte £ 22/39
Rest *Swan Inn* – Carte £ 21/38
Extended 17C coaching inn overlooking Newby Bridge; set in 10 acres, with gardens and a playground. Chic bedrooms feature bold wallpaper; many overlook the river. Family suites offer dolls houses and PlayStations. River Room's brasserie menu uses quality produce from the Lakes' larder. Swan Inn for pub classics, Cumbrian platters and a wonderful riverside terrace.

Knoll

Lakeside, Northeast : 1.25 mi on Hawkshead rd ✉ *LA12 8AU – ✆ (015395) 31 347 – www.theknoll-lakeside.co.uk – Closed 22-27 and 31 December and 1 January*
10 rm – £ 75/100 £ 95/220
Rest – *(closed Sunday and Monday) (dinner only)* Menu £ 22 **s**
Keenly run, slate-built Edwardian house opposite the lake, with a smart interior that blends classic and modern styles. Comfy, leather-furnished lounge. Good-sized bedrooms with bold décor and modern bathrooms; 'The Retreat' has a private entrance and hot tub. Simple dining room displays heart-themed art.

John Ruskin's Brasserie – Lakeside Hotel

Lakeside, Northeast : 1 mi on Hawkshead rd ✉ *LA12 8AT – ✆ (015395) 30 001 – www.lakesidehotel.co.uk – Closed 3-17 January*
Rest – *(dinner only)* Carte £ 30/44
Stylish brasserie in a superbly situated hotel on the shore of Lake Windermere. Classical brasserie menu. Have a drink in the conservatory or on the terrace to fully appreciate the view.

NEWCASTLE UPON TYNE

See city maps on following pages **24** B2

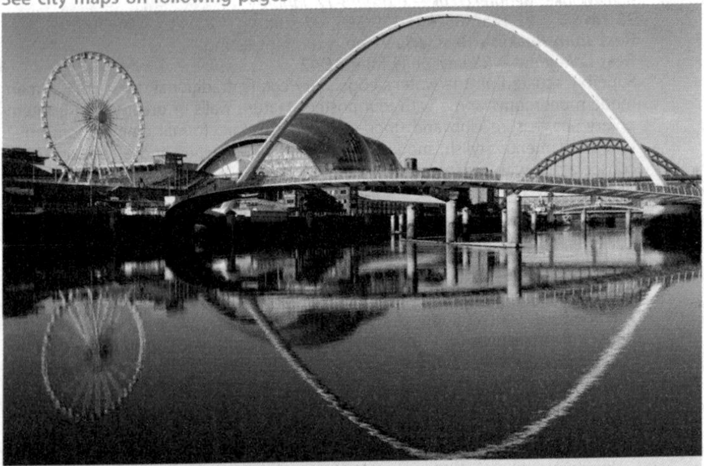

© Eurasia Press/Photononstop

ENGLAND

Tyne and Wear – pop. 163 015 – **501** O19 – **502** O19 – Great Britain

London 276 mi – Edinburgh 105 mi – Leeds 95 mi

Tourist Information

8-9 Central Arcade, ✆(0191) 277 80 00, www.newcastlegateshead.com

Airport

Newcastle Airport : ✆ (0871) 882 1121, NW : 5 m. by A 696 AV

Ferries and Shipping Lines

to Norway (Bergen, Haugesund and Stavanger) (Fjord Line) (approx 26 h) – to The Netherlands (Amsterdam) (DFDS Seaways A/S) daily (15 h)

Tunnel

Tyne Tunnel (toll)

Golf Courses

Broadway East, Gosforth, ✆(0191) 285 05 53

City of Newcatle, Gosforth, Three Mill Bridge, ✆(0191) 285 17 75

SIGHTS

In the town : City★• Quayside★ CZ : Composition★, All Saints Church★ • Castle Keep★ **AC** CZ • Laing Art Gallery and Museum★ **AC** CY**M1** • Great North Museum★ CY**M2** • LIFE Interactive World★ CZ • Gateshead Millennium Bridge★ CZ

On the outskirts : Hadrian's Wall★★, W : by A 69 AV

In the surrounding area : Beamish : North of England Open-Air Museum★★ **AC**, SW : 7 mi by A 692 and A 6076 AX

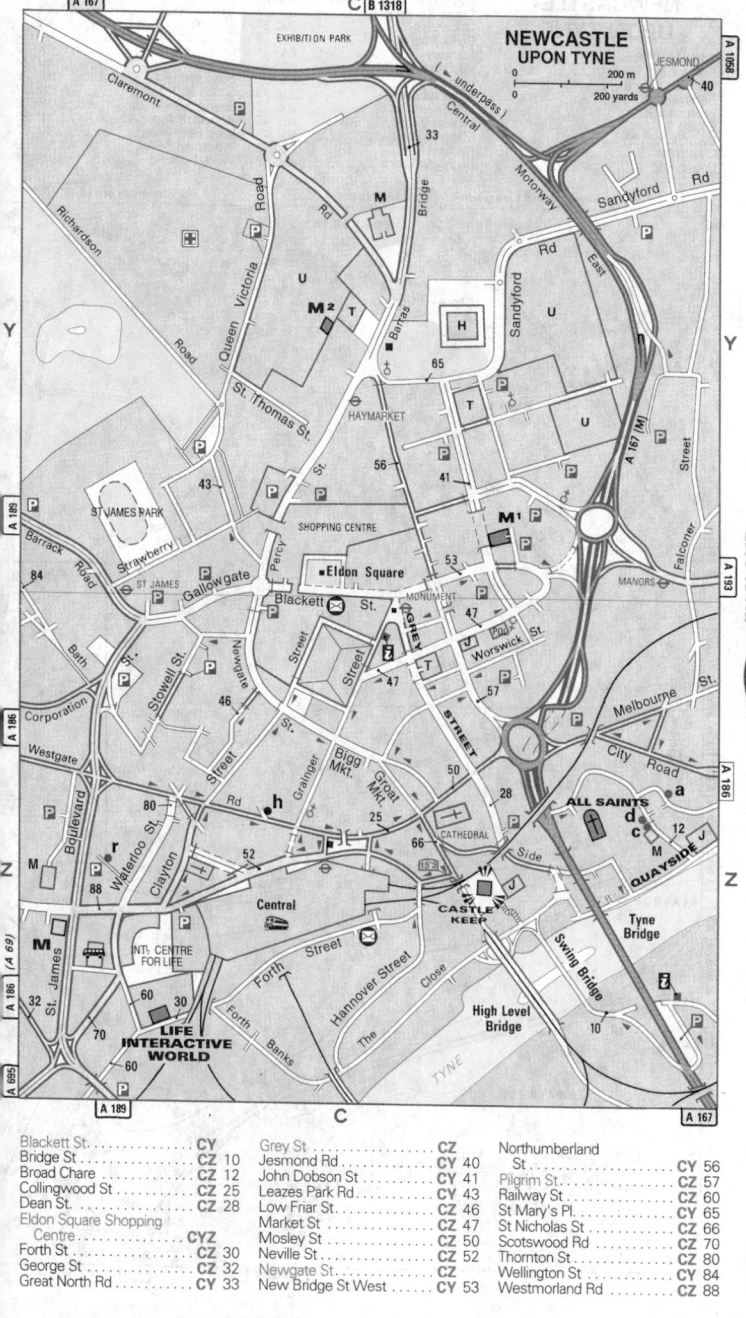

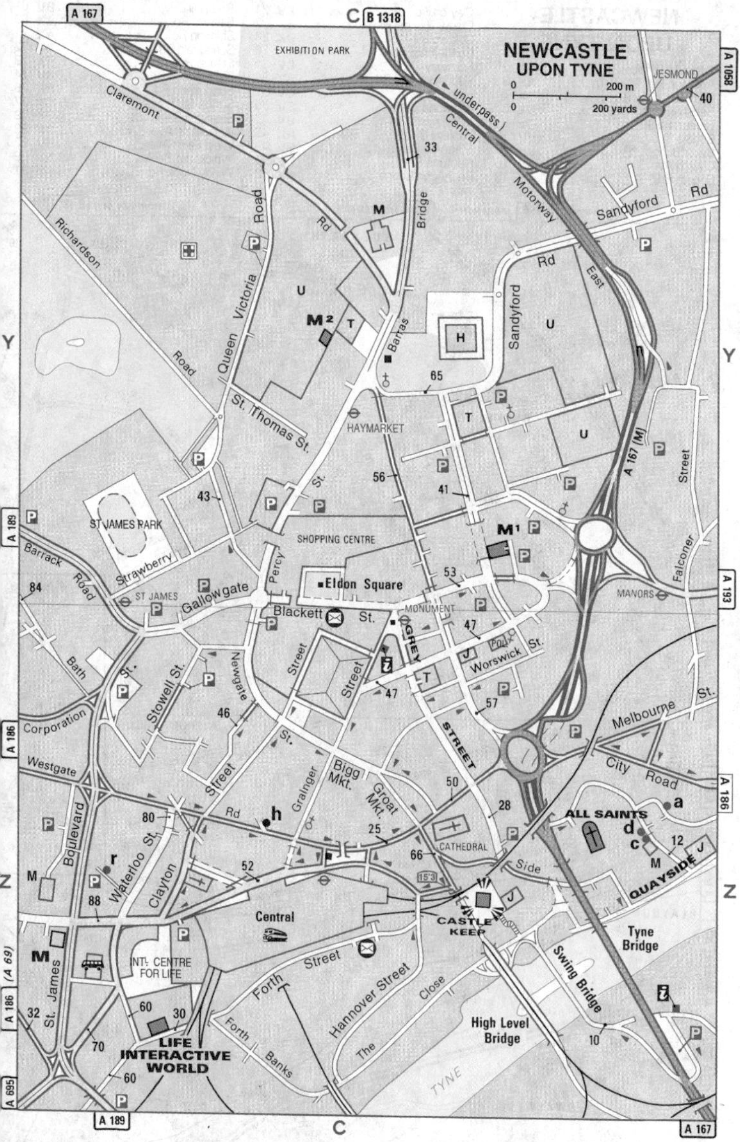

Blackett St. . . . . **CY**
Bridge St . . . . **CZ** 10
Broad Chare . . . . **CZ** 12
Collingwood St . . . . **CZ** 25
Dean St. . . . . **CZ** 28
Eldon Square Shopping
Centre . . . . **CYZ**
Forth St . . . . **CZ** 30
George St . . . . **CZ** 32
Great North Rd . . . . **CY** 33
Grey St . . . . **CZ**
Jesmond Rd . . . . **CY** 40
John Dobson St . . . . **CY** 41
Leazes Park Rd . . . . **CY** 43
Low Friar St. . . . . **CZ** 46
Market St . . . . **CZ** 47
Mosley St . . . . **CZ** 50
Neville St . . . . **CZ** 52
Newgate St. . . . . **CZ**
New Bridge St West . . . . **CY** 53
Northumberland
St . . . . **CY** 56
Pilgrim St. . . . . **CZ** 57
Railway St . . . . **CZ** 60
St Mary's Pl. . . . . **CY** 65
St Nicholas St . . . . **CZ** 66
Scotswood Rd . . . . **CZ** 70
Thornton St. . . . . **CZ** 80
Wellington St . . . . **CY** 84
Westmorland Rd . . . . **CZ** 88

NEWCASTLE-UPON-TYNE

Adelaide Terrace . . . . AX 2
Atkinson Rd . . . . AX 3
Bath St . . . . BX 4
Bensham Rd . . . . AX 6
Benton Bank . . . . BV 8
Buddle St . . . . BV 13
Byker Bridge . . . . BV 15
Church Ave . . . . AV 16
Church Rd . . . . AV 18
Clayton Rd . . . . BV 21
Coldwell Lane . . . . BX 22
Coldwell St . . . . BX 24
Condercum Rd . . . . AX 26
Fossway . . . . BV 31
Haddrick's Mill Rd . . . . BV 36
High St West . . . . BV 37
Jesmond Dene Rd . . . . BV 39
Killingworth Rd . . . . BV 42
Lobley Hill Rd . . . . AX 45
Matthew Bank . . . . BV 49
Neptune Rd . . . . BV 51
Redheugh Bridge . . . . AX 62
Red Hall Drive . . . . BV 61
Saltwell Rd . . . . BX 69
Shipdon Rd . . . . AX 71
Springfield Rd . . . . AV 72
Station Rd . . . . BX 73
Stephenson Rd . . . . BV 74
Sunderland Rd . . . . BX 76
Sutton St . . . . BV 77
Swalwell Bank . . . . ABX 79
Waverdale Ave . . . . BV 83
West Farm Ave . . . . BV 87
Whickham Bank . . . . AX 89
Windy Nook Rd . . . . BX 91

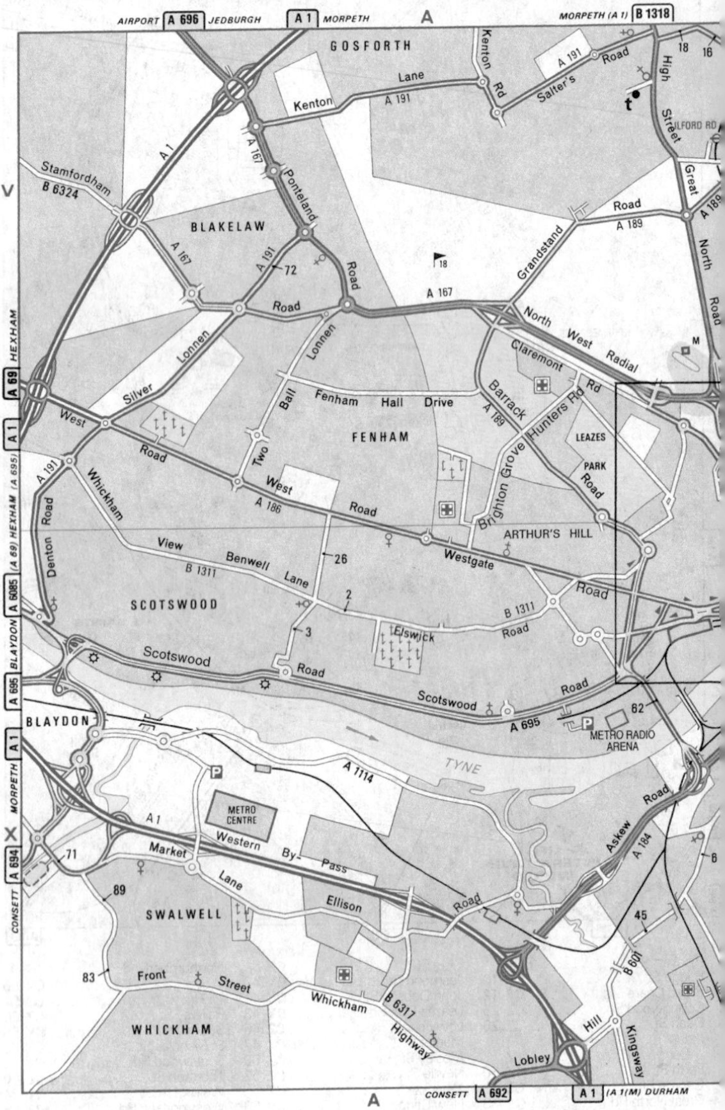

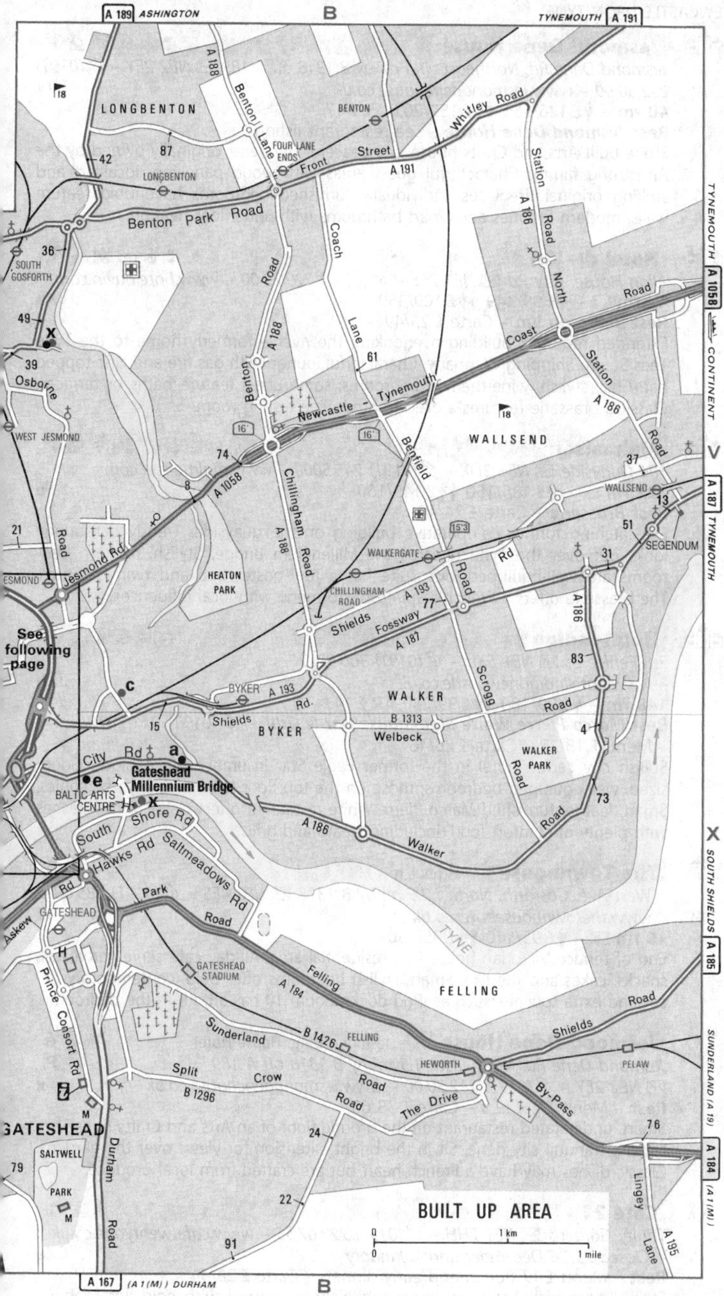
A 189 ASHINGTON
B
TYNEMOUTH A 191
LONGBENTON
A 188
Benton Lane
BENTON
Whitley Road
FOUR LANE ENDS
Front Street
A 191
87
42
LONGBENTON
Benton Park Road
Station Road
North
A 186
Coach Lane
36
SOUTH GOSFORTH
Benton Road
A 188
Coast Road
A 1058
Station Road
A 186
49
X
39
Osborne
WEST JESMOND
61
Newcastle - Tynemouth
Benfield
WALLSEND
74
8
A 1058
Chillingham Road
A 188
37
WALLSEND
13
51
SEGENDUM
21
Road
Jesmond Rd
HEATON PARK
JESMOND
WALKERGATE
Rd
31
CHILLINGHAM ROAD
A 193
77
Road
A 186
Shields
Fossway
A 187
See following page
83
BYKER
A 193
Rd.
WALKER
Scrogg
c
15
Shields
BYKER
B 1313
Welbeck
Road
4
City Rd
a
Gateshead Millennium Bridge
e
BALTIC ARTS CENTRE
X
WALKER PARK
Road
South
Shore Rd
A 186
Walker
Road
73
Hawks Rd
Saltmeadows Rd
Rd
Park Road
GATESHEAD
Askew
TYNE
H
Prince Consort Rd
GATESHEAD STADIUM
A 184
Felling
FELLING
Road
Shields
Sunderland
B 1426
FELLING
HEWORTH
PELAW
Split Crow Road
Road
B 1296
The Drive
By-Pass
GATESHEAD
24
76
SALTWELL PARK
M
79
Durham Road
22
Lingey Lane
A 195
BUILT UP AREA
0 1 km
0 1 mile
91
A 167 (A 1(M)) DURHAM
B
TYNEMOUTH A 1058
CONTINENT
V
A 187 TYNEMOUTH
X
SOUTH SHIELDS A 185
SUNDERLAND (A 19)
A 184 (A 1(M))

ENGLAND

Jesmond Dene House

Jesmond Dene Rd, Northeast : 1.5 mi by B 1318 off A 189 ✉ NE2 2EY – ☎ (0191) 212 30 00 – www.jesmonddenehouse.co.uk BVx

40 rm – †£ 126/151 ††£ 152/202, ☕ £ 17

Rest *Jesmond Dene House* – see restaurant listing

Stone-built Arts and Crafts house in a peaceful city dene; originally owned by the Armstrong family. Characterful guest areas with wood panelling, local art and striking original fireplaces. Individually furnished bedrooms have bold feature walls, modern facilities and smart bathrooms with underfloor heating.

Hotel du Vin

Allan House, City Rd ✉ NE1 2BE – ☎ (0191) 229 22 00 – www.hotelduvin.com BXa

42 rm ☕ – †£ 99/349 ††£ 109/359

Rest *Bistro du Vin* – Carte £ 25/49

Extended red-brick building overlooking the river – formerly home to the Tyne Tees Steam Shipping Company. Characterful lounge with gas fire and zinc-topped bar. Chic, stylish, wine-themed bedrooms; some boast feature baths or terraces. Classical brasserie features a glass-fronted wine tasting room.

Malmaison

104 Quayside ✉ NE1 3DX – ☎ (0191) 245 5000 – www.malmaison.com BXe

122 rm ☕ – †£ 135/150 ††£ 145/160

Rest *Brasserie* – Carte £ 24/44

Eye-catching former co-operative building on the quayside. Trendy bar-lounge looks out over the Tyne towards the Millennium Bridge. Stylish, modern bedrooms are well-equipped; one suite has a four-poster bed and twin bathtubs. The brasserie offers a French-inspired bistro menu with local influences.

ENGLAND

Hotel Indigo (N)

2-8 Fenkle St ✉ NE1 5XU – ☎ (0191) 300 9222 – www.hotelindigonewcastle.co.uk CZh

148 rm – †£ 99/180 ††£ 99/230, ☕ £ 14

Rest *Marco Pierre White Steakhouse Bar & Grill* – ☎ (0191) 211 2870 – Menu £ 18/25 – Carte £ 26/46

Stylish city centre hotel in the former Eagle Star Insurance office block. Good-sized, well-equipped bedrooms; those on the top floor have their own balconies. Smart, leather-furnished Marco Pierre White restaurant offers classic British dishes with plenty of comfort food, including steaks and grills.

The Townhouse (N) without rest

1 West Ave, Gosforth, North : 2.5 mi by B 1318 ✉ NE3 4ES – ☎ (0191) 285 6812 – www.thetownhousehotel.co.uk AVt

10 rm ☕ – †£ 95/110 ††£ 95/150

End of terrace Victorian house in a residential area. All-day café serves breakfast, snacks, cakes and the like. Smart, stylish bedrooms offer bold, contemporary décor and extra touches such as iPod docks; Room 10 has a bath in the bedroom.

Jesmond Dene House (N) – Jesmond Dene House Hotel

Jesmond Dene Rd, Northeast : 1.5 mi by B 1318 off A 189 ✉ NE2 2EY – ☎ (0191) 212 30 00 – www.jesmonddenehouse.co.uk BVx

Rest – Menu £ 26/29 **s** – Carte £ 38/60

Smart, understated restaurant on the ground floor of an Arts and Crafts house hotel in a tranquil city dene. Sit in the bright extension for views over the gardens. Classic dishes may have a French heart but are crafted from local produce.

Café 21

Trinity Gardens ✉ NE1 2HH – ☎ (0191) 222 07 55 – www.cafetwentyone.co.uk – Closed 25-26 December and 1 January CZa

Rest – Menu £ 17 (lunch and early dinner) – Carte £ 28/54

Stylish, open-plan brasserie where subtle greys contrast with bold floral fabrics. Eye-catching zinc-topped bar, smart dining room and efficient service. Appealing British and French classics, with a good value set lunch menu.

David Kennedy's Food Social

The Biscuit Factory, 16 Stoddart St ✉ *NE2 1AN – ✆ (0191) 260 54 11 – www.foodsocial.co.uk – Closed 25-26 December, 1 January and Sunday dinner*

Rest – Menu £ 10 (weekday lunch) – Carte £ 22/38 BV**c**

Set on the ground floor of a contemporary art gallery in the city suburbs; an airy, industrial-style restaurant with exposed brick and pipework, heavy wood furniture and sofas set around a large bar. Hearty cooking has a regional tone.

Caffé Vivo

29 Broad Chare ✉ *NE1 3DQ – ✆ (0191) 232 13 31 – www.caffevivo.co.uk – Closed Sunday, Monday and bank holidays* CZ**d**

Rest – Menu £ 19 – Carte £ 17/38

In a quayside warehouse – with a theatre. Zinc ducting and steel pillars give it an industrial feel, while hams, salamis and oils add a touch of the Mediterranean. Simple, satisfying cooking of classic Italian dishes. Good value lunch menu.

Electric East

Waterloo Square, St James's Boulevard ✉ *NE1 4DN – ✆ (0191) 221 10 00 – www.electric-east.co.uk – Closed 24-26 December, Sunday and Monday*

Rest – *(dinner only and Friday-Saturday lunch)* Menu £ 11 (weekdays) – Carte £ 21/33 CZ**r**

Enter past the tuk tuk into a large bar, then on into a long, narrow room with heavy wood furnishings, lanterns and a simple, rustic, southeast Asian style. Extensive menus mix dishes from Vietnam, China and Japan. Polite, unfussy service.

Broad Chare

25 Broad Chare ✉ *NE1 3DQ – ✆ (0191) 211 2144 – www.thebroadchare.co.uk – Closed 25 December and Sunday dinner* CZ**c**

Rest – *(booking advisable)* Carte £ 17/32

Owned by Terry Laybourne and next to its sister operation, Caffé Vivo. Sit in the snug ground floor bar or upstairs dining room. Choose from a snack menu of 'Geordie Tapas', an appealing 'on toast' selection, hearty daily specials and tasty nursery puddings. Over 40 ales, including some which are custom-made.

ENGLAND

at Newcastle International Airport Northwest : 6.75 mi by A 167 off A 696 - AV – ✉ Newcastle Upon Tyne

Doubletree by Hilton Newcastle International Airport

Woolsington ✉ *NE13 8BZ – ✆ (01661) 824 266 – www.doubletree-newcastle.com*

179 rm – †£ 60/220 ††£ 70/230

Rest *Fratello's* – Carte £ 16/36

A modern, V-shaped building: the closest hotel to the airport. Contemporary bedrooms and compact, well-equipped bathrooms are geared towards the modern business traveller; ask for a room with a runway view. Traditional pub menu in the bar; the restaurant with a terrace serves Mediterranean-influenced dishes.

at Ponteland Northwest : 8.25 mi by A 167 on A 696 - AV – ✉ Newcastle Upon Tyne

Cafe Lowrey

33-35 Broadway, Darras Hall Estate, Southwest : 1.5 mi by B 6323 off Darras Hall Estate rd ✉ *NE20 9PW – ✆ (01661) 820 357 – www.cafelowrey.co.uk – Closed Monday*

Rest – *(dinner only and lunch Friday to Sunday) (booking essential)* Menu £ 19 – Carte £ 26/42

Proudly run bistro in a parade of shops on a residential estate – a real hit with the locals. Simply decorated room with modern artwork and a quarry-tiled floor. Classic menus feature plenty of local produce. Service is polite and friendly.

NEWCASTLE INTERNATIONAL AIRPORT – Tyne and Wear – 502 O18

– see Newcastle Upon Tyne

NEWICK – East Sussex – 504 U31 – pop. 2 129 8 A2

London 57 mi – Brighton 14 mi – Eastbourne 20 mi – Hastings 34 mi

Newick Park

rm,

Southeast : 1.5 mi following signs for Newick Park ✉ BN8 4SB – ✆ (01825) 723 633 – www.newickpark.co.uk

16 rm – †£ 125/245 ††£ 165/285 – 3 suites

Rest – *(booking essential)* Menu £ 18 (weekday lunch)/42

Restored Georgian mansion in 200 acres; its elegant, luxurious feel makes it a popular wedding venue. Welcoming fires and deep sofas in lounges and libraries. Individually decorated bedrooms; some with superb views of the Estate. Formal yet relaxed dining, with ingredients from the walled garden.

NEWLYN – Cornwall – 503 D33 1 A3

London 288 mi – Camborne 16 mi – Saint Austell 44 mi – Falmouth 29 mi

Tolcarne Inn N

Tolcarne Pl ✉ TR18 5PR – ✆ (01736) 363 074 – www.tolcarneinn.co.uk

Rest – Carte £ 20/34

Unassuming 19C pub beside the sea wall. Inside it's narrow and cosy, with old beams, a wood burning stove and a long bar. The experienced chef offers appealing, flavoursome dishes which centre around fresh fish and shellfish that's been landed locally. They host jazz nights every first and third Sunday.

NEWPORT PAGNELL – Milton Keynes – 504 R27 – pop. 14 739 11 C1

London 57 mi – Bedford 13 mi – Luton 21 mi – Northampton 15 mi

Plan : see Milton Keynes

Robinsons

18-20 St John St ✉ MK16 8HJ – ✆ (01908) 611 400 – www.robinsonsrestaurant.co.uk – Closed Sunday dinner and bank holidays

Rest – Menu £ 19 (weekdays)/23 – Carte £ 28/44 CU**n**

Large, striking building with a fire-lit bar-lounge and a split-level dining room. Seasonal menus offer a mix of modern British and Mediterranean dishes; go for the good value set priced menu. The Tuesday steak nights are popular.

NEWQUAY – Cornwall – 503 E32 – pop. 19 562 1 A2

London 291 mi – Exeter 83 mi – Penzance 34 mi – Plymouth 48 mi

Newquay Airport : ✆ (01637) 860600 Y

Marcus Hill, ✆ (01637) 85 40 20, www.visitnewquay.org

Tower Rd, ✆ (01637) 87 20 91

Treloy, ✆ (01637) 87 85 54

Merlin, Mawgan Porth, ✆ (01841) 54 02 22

Penhale Point and Kelsey Head★ (≤★★), SW : by A 3075 Y – Trerice★ **AC**, SE : 3.5 mi by A 392 - Y - and A 3058. St Agnes - St Agnes Beacon★★ (※★★), SW : 12.5 mi by A 3075 - Y - and B 3285

at Watergate Bay Northeast : 3 mi by A 3059 on B 3276 – ✉ Newquay

Watergate Bay N

rm, rest,

On The Beach ✉ TR8 4AA – ✆ (01637) 860 543 – www.watergatebay.co.uk

64 rm – †£ 95/270 ††£ 125/385

Rest *Dining Room* – *(dinner only)* Menu £ 30

Rest *Beach Hut* – Carte £ 20/33

Long-standing beachfront hotel. The fresh, contemporary bedrooms range from standards to family suites; some have freestanding baths with sea views. The beautiful infinity pool and hot tub overlook the beach and there's direct beach access, changing rooms and even a surfboard store. Dine in the bar, in the laid-back, sandy-floored café or in the comfy restaurant.

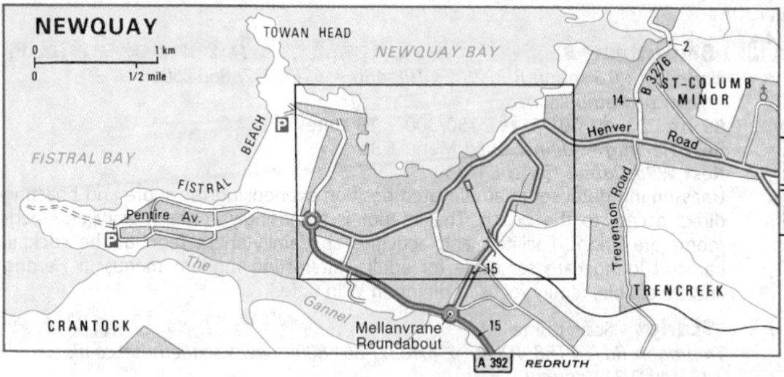

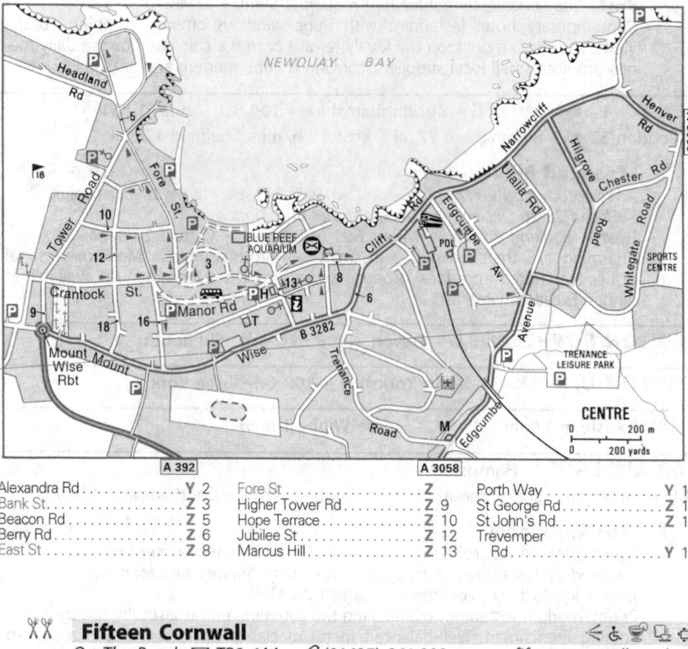

Alexandra Rd . . . . Y 2	Fore St . . . . Z	Porth Way . . . . Y 14
Bank St. . . . . Z 3	Higher Tower Rd . . . . Z 9	St George Rd . . . . Z 16
Beacon Rd . . . . Z 5	Hope Terrace . . . . Z 10	St John's Rd. . . . . Z 18
Berry Rd . . . . Z 6	Jubilee St . . . . Z 12	Trevemper
East St . . . . Z 8	Marcus Hill . . . . Z 13	Rd. Y 15

Fifteen Cornwall

On The Beach ✉ *TR8 4AA – ✆ (01637) 861 000 – www.fifteencornwall.co.uk*
Rest – *(booking essential)* Menu £ 28 (weekday lunch) – Carte £ 18/60
Lively beachfront restaurant with fabulous bay views; a registered charity set up by Jamie Oliver to train local youngsters to be chefs. Unfussy Italian menus feature homemade pasta, steaks from the Josper grill and imported olives and oils – 80% of the produce is from Cornwall. They open for breakfast too.

at Mawgan Porth Northeast : 6 mi by A 3059 on B 3276

Scarlet

Tredragon Rd ✉ *TR8 4DQ – ✆ (01637) 861 800 – www.scarlethotel.co.uk*
– Closed 2-31 January
37 rm – †£ 175/440 ††£ 195/460
Rest ***Scarlet*** – see restaurant listing
Eco-centric, adults only hotel set high on a cliff and boasting stunning coastal views. Modern bar and lounges, and a great spa offering extensive treatments. Bedrooms range from 'Just Right' to 'Indulgent' and have unusual open-plan bathrooms and a cool, Scandic style – every room has a terrace and sea view.

Bedruthan

Northeast : 0.5 mi on B 3276 ✉ *TR8 4BU* – ✆ *(01637) 860 860 – www.bedruthan.com*
89 rm – £ 60/75 £ 150/300 – 10 suites
Rest *Herring* – *(dinner only)* Menu £ 35
Rest *Wild Café* – Carte £ 18/30
Unassuming hotel set in an elevated position overlooking the shore and boasting direct access to the beach. The interior is surprisingly contemporary and bedrooms are bright. Facilities and activities are family-orientated but the cocktail bar and lounge are set aside for adults. Interesting modern menus in Herring and accessible, family focused dining in Wild Café.

Scarlet – Scarlet Hotel

Tredragon Rd ✉ *TR8 4DQ* – ✆ *(01637) 861 800 – www.scarlethotel.co.uk – Closed 2-31 January*
Rest – *(bookings essential for non-residents)* Menu £ 23/43
Contemporary hotel restaurant with huge windows offering stunning coastal views; start with a drink on the lovely terrace or in the chic bar. Concise daily menus promote small local suppliers; cooking is light, modern and seasonal.

NEWTON LONGVILLE – Buckinghamshire – 504 R28 – pop. 1 851 — 11 C1

London 52 mi – Birmingham 77 mi – Bristol 110 mi – Sheffield 126 mi

Crooked Billet

2 Westbrook End ✉ *MK17 0DF* – ✆ *(01908) 373 936 – www.thebillet.co.uk – Closed 25-26 December, Sunday dinner and Monday*
Rest – *(booking advisable)* Menu £ 21 (weekdays) – Carte £ 20/37
Charming 17C thatched pub with smart yet informal interior. Modern, seasonal dishes are crafted from local produce and a 7 course tasting menu is available at dinner. Excellent wine list.

NEWTON POPPLEFORD – Devon – 503 K31 – see Sidmouth

NEWTON-ON-OUSE – North Yorkshire – 502 Q22 – see York

NITON – Isle of Wight – 504 Q32 – see Wight (Isle of)

NOMANSLAND – Hampshire – 503 P31 — 4 D3

London 96 mi – Bournemouth 26 mi – Salisbury 13 mi – Southampton 14 mi

Les Mirabelles

Forest Edge Rd ✉ *SP5 2BN* – ✆ *(01794) 390 205 – www.lesmirabelles.co.uk – Closed 22 December-13 January, 1 week May, Sunday and Monday*
Rest – Menu £ 19 (weekdays) – Carte £ 28/41
Bright, modern restaurant overlooking the common, enthusiastically run by a welcoming Frenchman. Well-balanced menu of classic Gallic dishes and a superb wine list. Friendly atmosphere.

NORTH BOVEY – Devon – 503 I32 – pop. 254 – ✉ Newton Abbot — 2 C2

London 197 mi – Plymouth 41 mi – Torbay 23 mi – Exeter 15 mi
Dartmoor National Park★★

Bovey Castle

Northwest : 2 mi by Postbridge rd, bearing left at fork just out of village ✉ *TQ13 8RE* – ✆ *(01647) 445 000 – www.boveycastle.com*
64 rm – £ 219/239 £ 219/239, £ 15 – 4 suites
Rest *The Edwardian Grill* – Carte £ 34/64
Rest *Castle Bistro* – Carte £ 18/36
Impressive manor house within an extensive country estate, beautifully set in Dartmoor National Park. Relaxed, homely feel and a high degree of comfort throughout. Bedrooms come in pastel hues and with contemporary touches but retain a classic edge. Modern grill-style menu in formal Edwardian Grill or Mediterranean-influenced dishes in Castle Bistro.

ENGLAND

Gate House without rest
just off village green, past "Ring of Bells" public house ✉ *TQ13 8RB – ☎ (01647) 440 479 – www.gatehouseondartmoor.com – Closed 24-26 December*
3 rm – †£ 55 ††£ 84
Charming 15C medieval hall house in the heart of an attractive village, boasting a characterful thatched roof, a large oak door and a lovely country garden with a small pool. Homely lounge, cosy low-beamed breakfast room and simple, spotlessly kept bedrooms, some with moor views. Charming owners.

NORTH CHARLTON – Northumberland – 501 O17 – see Alnwick

NORTH KILWORTH – Leicestershire – 502 Q26 — 16 B3

London 95 mi – Leicester 20 mi – Market Harborough 9 mi

Kilworth House
Lutterworth Rd, West : 0.5 mi on A 4304 ✉ *LE17 6JE – ☎ (01858) 880 058 – www.kilworthhouse.co.uk*
44 rm – †£ 149/215 ††£ 159/240 – 3 suites
Rest *Wordsworth* – *(dinner only and Sunday lunch)* Menu £ 50
Rest *Orangery* – Menu £ 30 – Carte £ 28/40
Impressively restored and extended Victorian mansion in 38 acres of tranquil grounds, which feature a popular open-air theatre. Spacious, classical drawing rooms. Immaculately kept bedrooms with luxurious bathrooms; the largest are in the main house. Traditional menus in the ornate restaurant and light, brasserie-style dishes in the attractive orangery.

NORTH LOPHAM – Norfolk – 504 W26 — 15 C2

London 98 mi – Norwich 34 mi – Ipswich 31 mi – Bury Saint Edmunds 20 mi

Church Farm House
Church Rd ✉ *IP22 2LP – ☎ (01379) 687 270 – www.churchfarmhouse.org – Closed January-February*
3 rm – †£ 50 ††£ 100 **Rest** – Menu £ 30
Characterful thatched farmhouse in the shadow of the village church, with lovely mature gardens and a terrace for summer breakfasts. Comfy conservatory and spacious beamed lounge with antiques and ornaments; traditional bedrooms with complimentary sherry. Home-cooked meals of local produce. Delightful owners.

NORTH MOLTON – Devon – 503 I30 — 2 C1

London 192 mi – Cardiff 118 mi – Plymouth 87 mi – Swansea 153 mi

Heasley House
Heasley Mill, Northwest : 1.25 mi by Heasley Mill rd. ✉ *EX36 3LE – ☎ (01598) 740 213 – www.heasley-house.co.uk – Closed February-mid-March and 24 December-2 January*
7 rm – †£ 110/170 ††£ 150/170
Rest – *(dinner only) (booking essential)* Menu £ 26/32
Former Georgian Dower House in remote Devon village bordering Exmoor National Park. Clean, fresh style with whitewashed walls, rush matting and quirky modern artwork. Tea and cakes on arrival. Simple, wholesome cooking.

NORTH SHIELDS – Tyne and Wear – 502 P18 – pop. 39 042 — 24 B2

London 288 mi – Newcastle upon Tyne 9 mi – Sunderland 14 mi – Middlesbrough 39 mi

Irvins Brasserie
The Richard Irvin Building, Union Quay ✉ *NE30 1HJ – ☎ (0191) 296 32 38 – www.irvinsbrasserie.co.uk – Closed 2 weeks January, Monday and Tuesday*
Rest – Menu £ 12 – Carte £ 19/41
Busy, informal restaurant in an old industrial building on the historic fish quay; brick walls and exposed pipes feature. The experienced chef has worked in a variety of places – menus are appealing and eclectic, with personal twists.

ENGLAND

David Kennedy's River Cafe

51 Bell St, Fish Quay ✉ NE30 1HF – ✆ (0191) 296 61 68 – www.davidkennedysrivercafe.com – Closed 25-26 December, 1-2 January, Monday, Sunday dinner and lunch Tuesday-Wednesday

Rest – *(booking advisable)* Menu £ 10 (lunch and early dinner) – Carte £ 18/28

Laid-back restaurant run by a friendly local team, set above a pub in the North Shields fish quay. The daily changing à la carte offers unfussy, bistro-style dishes of fresh local produce, including fish from the market on the quay. At £ 10 the 3 course set lunch and early dinner menu is a steal.

NORTH WALSHAM – Norfolk – 503 Y25 – pop. 11 845 Great Britain 15 D1

London 133 mi – Norwich 15 mi – Ipswich 61 mi – Lowestoft 34 mi

Blicking Hall★★ **AC**, W : 8.5 mi by B 1145, A 140 and B 1354

Beechwood

20 Cromer Rd ✉ NR28 0HD – ✆ (01692) 403 231 – www.beechwood-hotel.co.uk

17 rm – †£ 88 ††£ 100/160

Rest – *(dinner only and Sunday lunch)* Menu £ 25/39

Attractive, creeper-clad, part-Georgian property, where the keen owners offer a warm welcome. The cosy interior displays original features and a host of memorabilia. Period bedrooms vary in size and comfort – many have feature beds and some have terraces onto the lovely gardens. A '10 Mile Menu' offers local ingredients in modern dishes with influences from the Med.

NORTHALLERTON – North Yorkshire – 502 P20 – pop. 15 517 22 B1

London 238 mi – Leeds 48 mi – Middlesbrough 24 mi – Newcastle upon Tyne 56 mi

Applegarth, ✆ (01609) 77 68 64, www.visit-northallerton.com

at Staddlebridge Northeast : 7.5 mi by A 684 on A 19 at junction with A 172 – ✉ Northallerton

Cleveland Tontine with rm

On southbound carriageway of A 19 ✉ DL6 3JB – ✆ (01609) 882 671 – www.theclevelandtontine.co.uk

7 rm – †£ 90/110 ††£ 110/140

Rest – *(booking essential)* Menu £ 21/25 – Carte £ 23/52

Established basement bistro with a long wooden bar and an airy conservatory. Yorkshire meets France on the classically based menus and steaks remain a favourite. Quirky modern bedrooms boast bold wallpapers and free-standing baths. As we go to print, they are undergoing a refurbishment.

NORTHAW – Hertfordshire – 504 T28 12 B2

London 22 mi – Birmingham 110 mi – Bristol 134 mi – Croydon 57 mi

Sun at Northaw

1 Judges Hill ✉ EN6 4NL – ✆ (01707) 655 507 – www.thesunatnorthaw.co.uk – Closed Sunday dinner and Monday except bank holidays when closed Tuesday

Rest – Menu £ 13 (weekday lunch)/33 – Carte £ 24/42

A restored, whitewashed, part-16C inn which sits by the village green; passionately run and contemporary in style, it's deceptively spacious, with a traditional edge. Hearty, unfussy, flavoursome cooking uses seasonal East of England produce, and beers and ciders are equally local. Friendly service.

NORTHLEACH – Gloucestershire – pop. 1 923 4 D1

London 87 mi – Birmingham 73 mi – Bristol 54 mi – Coventry 47 mi

Wheatsheaf Inn with rm

West End ✉ GL50 3EZ – ✆ (01451) 860 244 – www.cotswoldswheatsheaf.com

14 rm – †£ 130/240 ††£ 130/200

Rest – Menu £ 13 (weekday lunch) – Carte £ 25/84

Smartly refurbished, 17C coaching inn with a pretty tiered terrace and two dining rooms – one either side of the stone-floored, open-fired bar. The same menu is available throughout, offering classical dishes and something to suit every taste. Simple, modern bedrooms have quirky touches and feature interesting French flea market finds; some have baths in the rooms.

NORTON DISNEY - Lincolnshire - 502 R24 17 C1

London 134 mi – Bristol 162 mi – Cardiff 188 mi – Plymouth 276 mi

Brills Farm

Brills Hill, West : 2 mi on Newark Rd ✉ LN6 9JN – ✆ (01636) 892 311 – www.brillsfarm-bedandbreakfast.co.uk – Closed Christmas-New Year

3 rm – †£ 56 ††£ 92 **Rest** – Menu £ 30

Charming Georgian farmhouse in a commanding hilltop position, affording lovely rural views. Antique-furnished drawing room and elegant country bedrooms with period wallpapers and goose down duvets. Tasty, Aga-cooked dinners served at an antique table; bacon comes from their 2,000 acre farm.

NORTON ST PHILIP - Somerset - 503 N30 - pop. 820 - ✉ Bath 4 C2

London 113 mi – Bristol 22 mi – Southampton 55 mi – Swindon 40 mi

The Plaine without rest

✉ BA2 7LT – ✆ (01373) 834 723 – www.theplaine.co.uk

3 rm – †£ 65/95 ††£ 75/125

Charming 17C stone cottages in a delightful village, on the site of the original market place. Snug, beamed interior with an airy breakfast room. Simple bedrooms feature fresh, colour-themed linens. Bubbly owner.

NORWELL - Nottinghamshire - see Newark-on-Trent - ✉

NORWICH - Norfolk - 504 Y26 - pop. 170 285 Great Britain 15 D2

London 109 mi – Kingston-upon-Hull 148 mi – Leicester 117 mi

Norwich Airport : ✆ (0844) 748 0112, N : 3.5 mi by A 140 V

Millennium Plain, ✆ (01603) 21 39 99, ww.visitnorwich.co.uk

The Forum

Royal Norwich, Hellesdon, Drayton High Rd, ✆ (01603) 42 57 12

Marriott Sprowston Manor Hotel, Wroxham Rd, ✆ (0870) 4 00 72 29

Costessy Park, Costessey, ✆ (01603) 74 63 33

Bawburgh, Marlingford Rd, Glen Lodge, ✆ (01603) 74 04 04

City★★ - Cathedral★★ Y – Castle (Museum and Art Gallery★ **AC**) Z – Market Place★ Z

Sainsbury Centre for Visual Arts★ **AC**, W : 3 mi by B 1108 X. Blicking Hall★★ **AC**, N : 11 mi by A 140 - V - and B 1354 – NE : Norfolk Broads★

Plans pages 540, 541

St Giles House

41-45 St Giles St ✉ NR2 1JR – ✆ (01603) 275 180 – www.stgileshousehotel.com

24 rm – †£ 130 ††£ 130 – 3 suites **Rest** – Carte £ 24/40 YZ**a**

Stylish, centrally located hotel with impressive façade, columns and wood panelling. Luxurious 'Deluxe' front suites. Rear bedrooms are quieter and more contemporary. Open-plan lounge/bar/dining room with pleasant terrace serves modern brasserie classics.

38 St Giles without rest

38 St Giles St ✉ NR2 1LL – ✆ (01603) 662 944 – www.38stgiles.co.uk

7 rm – †£ 90/120 ††£ 130/160 Z**x**

City centre Georgian townhouse where boutique styling blends with original features. Elegant, uncluttered bedrooms feature high ceilings and wood panelling, with silk curtains, handmade mattresses and quality linen. Excellent breakfasts.

Catton Old Hall without rest

Lodge Ln, Old Catton, North : 3.5 mi by Catton Grove Rd off St Faiths Rd ✉ NR6 7HG – ✆ (01603) 419 379 – www.catton-hall.co.uk

7 rm – †£ 70/125 ††£ 70/150

Attractive, personally run, 17C merchant's house with a characterful interior. Individually designed bedrooms include 5 feature rooms; Anna Sewell, with exposed rafters and a vast four-poster, is the best.

ENGLAND

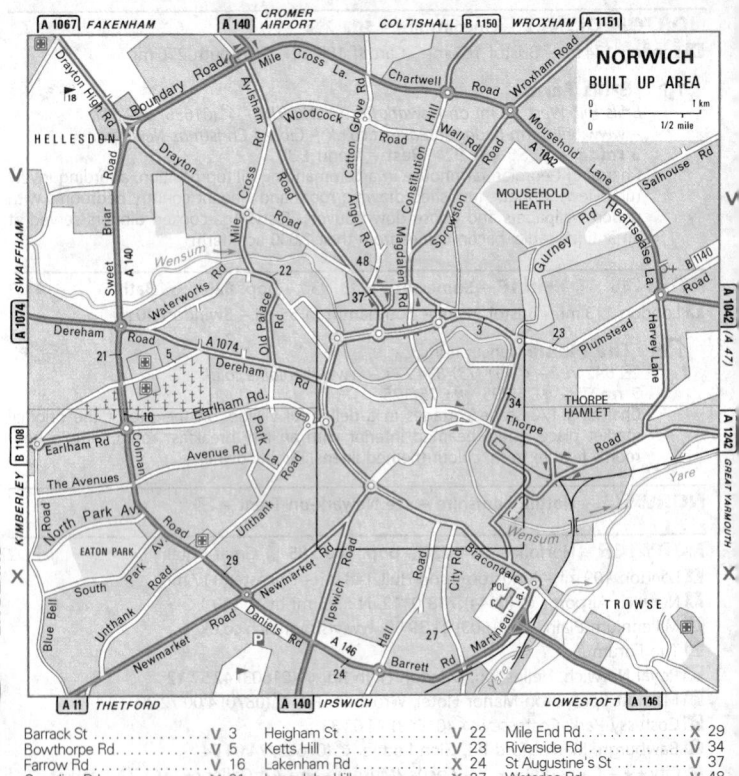

Barrack St	V 3	Heigham St	V 22	Mile End Rd	X 29
Bowthorpe Rd	V 5	Ketts Hill	V 23	Riverside Rd	V 34
Farrow Rd	V 16	Lakenham Rd	X 24	St Augustine's St	V 37
Guardian Rd	V 21	Long John Hill	X 27	Waterloo Rd	V 48

ENGLAND

XX **Roger Hickman's** A/C

79 Upper St Giles St ✉ NR2 1AB – ✆ (01603) 633 522 – www.rogerhickmansrestaurant.com – Closed 1 week August, 1 week Christmas, Sunday and Monday Z**c**

Rest – Menu £ 34/55

Personally run restaurant in a historic part of the city, with soft hues, modern art and romantic corners. Service is attentive yet unobtrusive. Cooking is modern, intricate and displays respect for ingredients' natural flavours.

XX **Bishop's** A/C

8-10 St Andrew's Hill ✉ NR2 1AD – ✆ (01603) 767 321 – www.bishopsrestaurant.co.uk – Closed Sunday and Monday Y**a**

Rest – *(booking essential)* Menu £ 14/32

Intimate restaurant of only eight tables, in a 15C building with a country-chic décor of floral prints, oval mirrors, crystal chandeliers and silk curtains. Simply presented, traditional dishes. Efficient service.

X **Tatlers**

21 Tombland ✉ NR3 1RF – ✆ (01603) 766 670 – www.tatlersrestaurant.co.uk – Closed 25 December and Sunday Y**c**

Rest – Menu £ 20 (weekday lunch) – Carte £ 24/40

Georgian merchant's house close to the cathedral, with high ceilings, bay windows and shabby-chic styling. Satisfying, flavourful bistro classics use the best of local ingredients; service is efficient and polite.

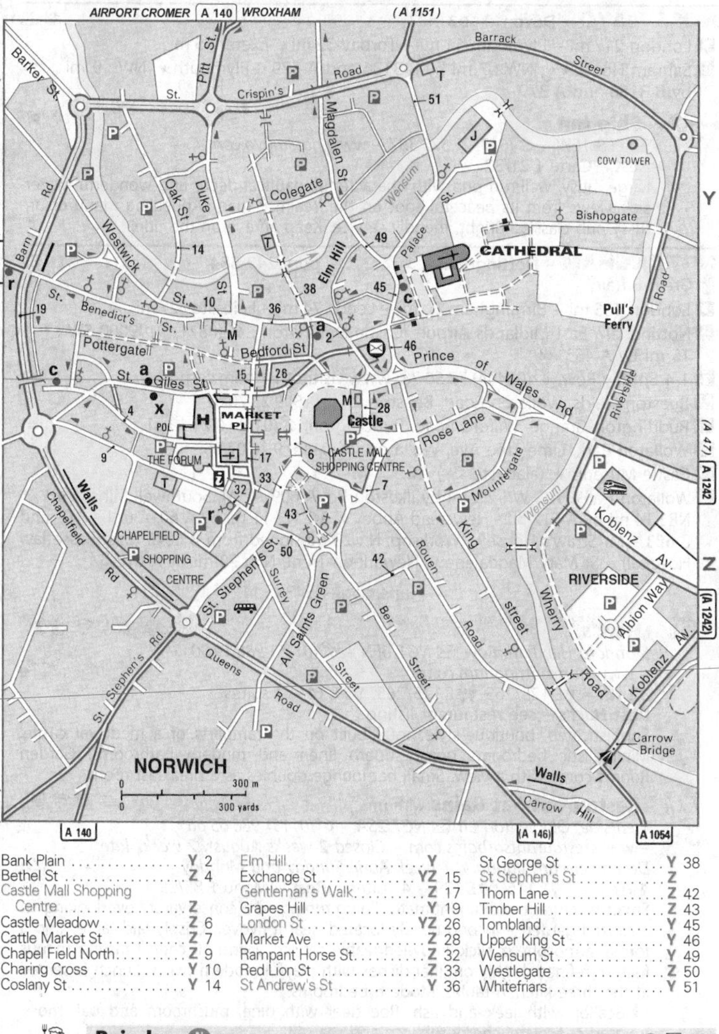

Bank Plain	Y	2	Elm Hill	Y		St George St	Y	38
Bethel St	Z	4	Exchange St	YZ	15	St Stephen's St	Z	
Castle Mall Shopping Centre	Z		Gentleman's Walk	Z	17	Thorn Lane	Z	42
Castle Meadow	Z	6	Grapes Hill	Y	19	Timber Hill	Z	43
Cattle Market St	Z	7	London St	YZ	26	Tombland	Y	45
Chapel Field North	Z	9	Market Ave	Z	28	Upper King St	Y	46
Charing Cross	Y	10	Rampant Horse St	Z	32	Wensum St	Y	49
Coslany St	Y	14	Red Lion St	Z	33	Westlegate	Z	50
			St Andrew's St	Y	36	Whitefriars	Y	51

Reindeer Ⓝ

10 Dereham Rd ✉ NR2 4AY – ✆ (01603) 612 995 – www.thereindeerpub.co.uk – Closed 25-26 December and Monday Y**r**

Rest – Menu £ 23 – Carte £ 20/33

Rustic neighbourhood pub with a keen local following. Plenty of space is kept aside for drinkers, who have 10 real ales to choose from. Straightforward, proudly British cooking employs lesser-used cuts and offers plenty of sharing dishes.

at Stoke Holy Cross South : 5.75 mi by A 140 - X – ✉ Norwich

Wildebeest

82-86 Norwich Rd ✉ NR14 8QJ – ✆ (01508) 492 497 – www.animalinns.co.uk

Rest – *(booking essential)* Menu £ 15 (weekday lunch)/22 – Carte £ 26/46

Unusually decorated pub with African rugs, wooden wild animals and tree trunk tables. An array of menus offer modern British and European flavours. Wednesday steak nights feature cuts from their own herd of cattle. Smart, polite service.

NOSS MAYO – Devon – 503 H33 2 C3

London 217 mi – Plymouth 11 mi – Torbay 32 mi – Exeter 45 mi

Saltram House★★, NW : 7 mi by B 3186 and A 379 – Plymouth★, NW : 9 mi by B 3186 and A 379

Ship Inn

PL8 1EW – (01752) 872 387 – www.nossmayo.com

Rest – Carte £ 21/32

Large, busy, well-run pub with characterful, nautical décor and wonderful waterside views from its peaceful spot on the Yealm Estuary. Appealing menu of unfussy pub classics. Bright, friendly service. Keep an eye on the tide!

NOTTINGHAM – Nottingham – 502 Q25 – pop. 249 584 16 B2

Great Britain

London 135 mi – Birmingham 50 mi – Leeds 74 mi – Leicester 27 mi

Nottingham East Midlands Airport, Castle Donington : (0871) 9199000 SW : 15 mi by A 453 AZ

1-4 Smithy Row, (08444) 77 56 78, www.visitnottingham.com

Beeston Fields, Wollaton Road, Beeston, (0115) 9 25 70 62

Ruddington Grange, Wilford Road, Ruddington, (0115) 9 21 19 51

Wollaton Park, Lime Tree Ave, Wollaton, (0115) 9 70 07 36

Castle Museum★ (alabasters★) **AC**, CZ **M**

Wollaton Hall★ **AC**, W : 2.5 mi by Ilkeston Rd, A 609 AZ **M**. Southwell Minster★★, NE : 14 mi by A 612 BZ - Newstead Abbey★ **AC**, N : 11 mi by A 60, A 611 - AY - and B 683 – Mr Straw's House★, Worksop, N : 20 mi signed from B 6045 (past Bassetlaw Hospital) – St Mary Magdalene★, Newark-on-Trent, NE : 20 mi by A 612 BZ

Plans pages 543, 544

ENGLAND

Hart's

Standard Hill, Park Row NG1 6FN – (0115) 988 19 00 – www.hartsnottingham.co.uk CZ**e**

32 rm – †£ 125/265 ††£ 125/265, £ 14 – 2 suites

Rest *Hart's* – see restaurant listing

Sophisticated, boutique-style hotel built on the ramparts of a medieval castle. Minimalistic bedrooms boast superb linen and modern bathrooms; Garden Rooms come with a view. Small bar-lounge doubles as a breakfast room.

Restaurant Sat Bains with rm

Trentside, Old Lenton Ln NG7 2SA – (0115) 986 65 66 – www.restaurantsatbains.com – Closed 2 weeks August, 2 weeks late December-early January, 1 week April, Sunday and Monday AZ**n**

4 rm – †£ 115 ††£ 129 – 4 suites **Rest** – Menu £ 85/99

Smart restaurant with an intimate dining room and a conservatory overlooking an enclosed garden – incongruously located near a flyover. Crisply laid tables and a formal atmosphere; slick, knowledgeable service. 7 and 10 course tasting menus feature refined, highly original dishes with playful modern twists. Lunch is served at the three kitchen tables. Modern bedrooms.

→ Scallop with leek and ash. Roe deer with pine, mushroom and oak moss. Aerated chocolate, cherry tobacco and sea salt.

Hart's – Hart's Hotel

Standard Ct., Park Row NG1 6GN – (0115) 988 19 00 – www.hartsnottingham.co.uk – Closed 1 January and dinner 25-26 December

Rest – Menu £ 18/24 – Carte £ 25/39 CZ**e**

This light, contemporary restaurant is in the former A&E dept. of the old city hospital – part of the hotel of the same name. Well-priced, flavourful, modern British dishes and professional service. Sit in one of the central booths.

World Service

Newdigate House, Castlegate NG1 6AF – (0115) 847 55 87 – www.worldservicerestaurant.com – Closed 1-7 January and Sunday dinner

Rest – Menu £ 15/25 – Carte £ 27/52 CZ**n**

Double-fronted Georgian property with modern extension and clubby, colonial feel; enter via an Indonesian-inspired courtyard garden. Visually appealing dishes have wide ranging influences, including French, British, Spanish and Asian.

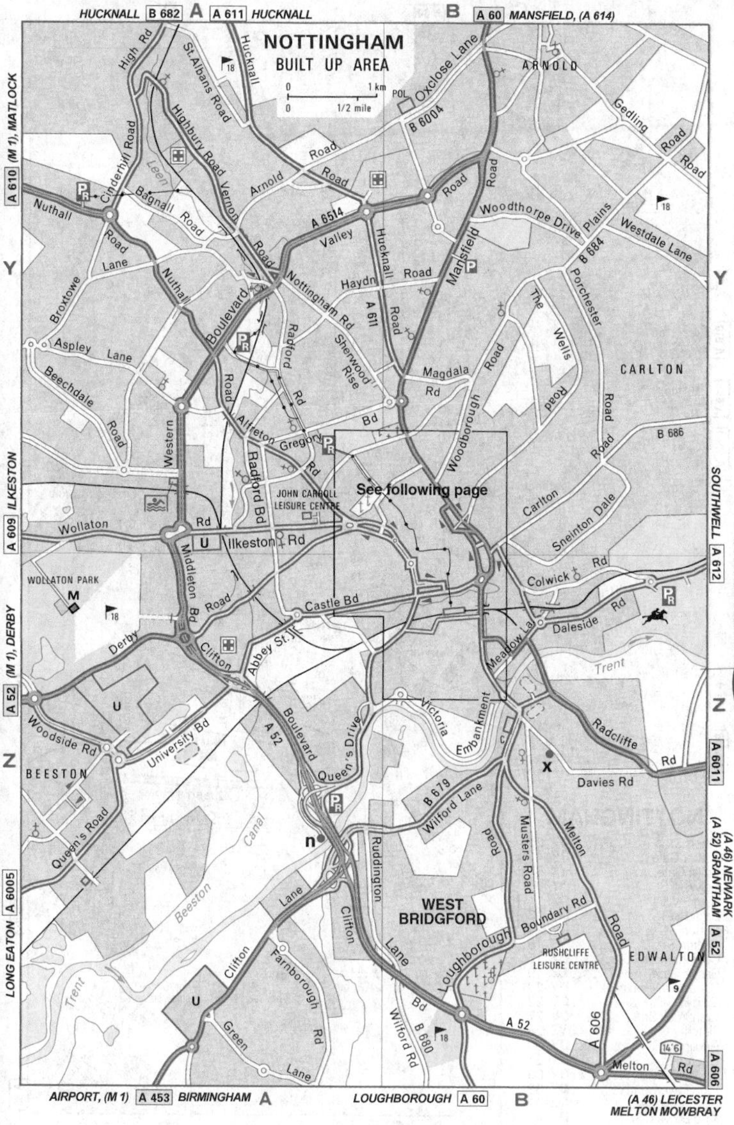

MemSaab

12-14 Maid Marian Way ✉ *NG1 6HS – ☎ (0115) 957 0009*
– www.mem-saab.co.uk – Closed 25 December CY**n**

Rest – *(dinner only)* Carte £ 18/36

Professionally run restaurant dominated by a wooden copy of the Gateway of India. Original, authentic cooking with well-judged spicing and a distinctive North Indian influence. Dishes from the charcoal grill are a highlight.

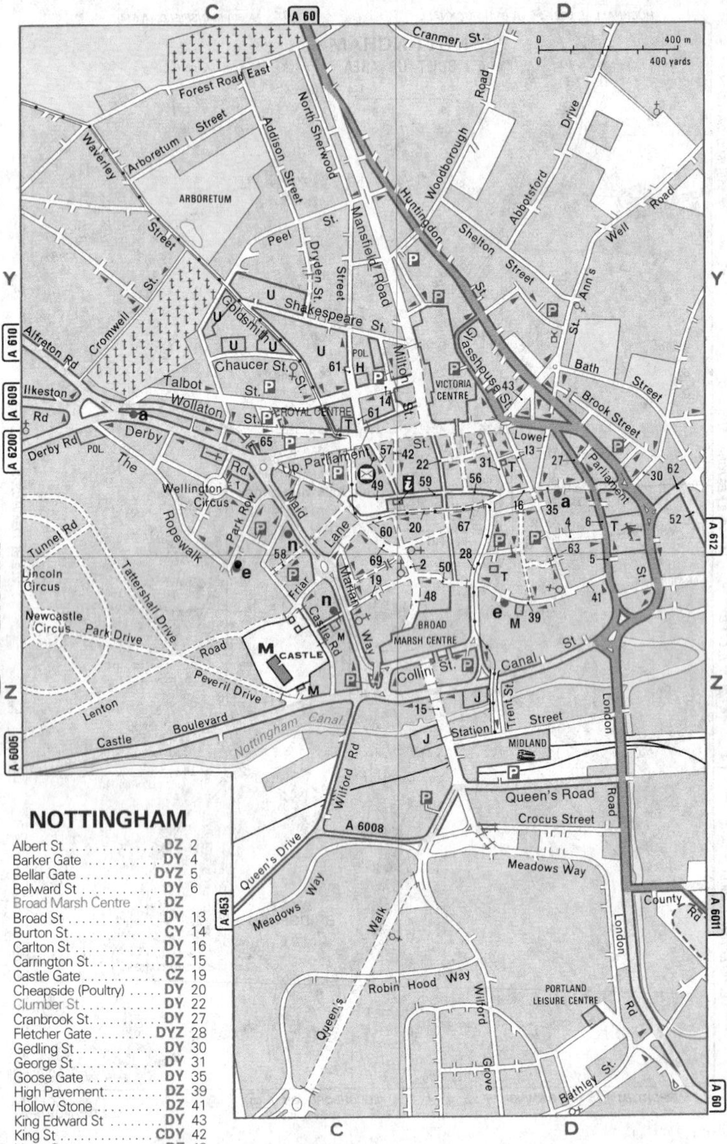

NOTTINGHAM

Albert St	DZ	2
Barker Gate	DY	4
Bellar Gate	DYZ	5
Belward St	DY	6
Broad Marsh Centre	DZ	
Broad St	DY	13
Burton St	CY	14
Carlton St	DY	16
Carrington St	DZ	15
Castle Gate	CZ	19
Cheapside (Poultry)	DY	20
Clumber St	DY	22
Cranbrook St	DY	27
Fletcher Gate	DYZ	28
Gedling St	DY	30
George St	DY	31
Goose Gate	DY	35
High Pavement	DZ	39
Hollow Stone	DZ	41
King Edward St	DY	43
King St	CDY	42
Lister Gate	DZ	48
Long Row	CY	49
Low Pavement	DZ	50
Manvers St	DY	52
Pelham St	DY	56
Queen St	CY	57
St James St	CYZ	58
Smithy Row (Long Row)	DY	59
Southwell Rd	DY	62
South Parade	CY	60
South Sherwood St	CY	61
Stoney St	DYZ	63
Toll House Hill	CY	65
Upper Parliament St	CDY	
Victoria Centre	DY	
Victoria St	DY	67
Wheeler Gate	CYZ	69

Ibérico World Tapas

The Shire Hall, High Pavement ✉ NG1 1HN – ✆ (0115) 941 04 10 – www.ibericotapas.com – Closed Sunday DZe

Rest – *(booking essential at dinner)* Menu £ 12 (weekday lunch) **s** – Carte £ 13/35 **s**

Lively, well-run restaurant hidden away in the basement of the former city jail and law courts, with a vaulted ceiling, colourful Moorish tiles and ornate fretwork. Tapas menu with 'Spanish' and 'World' sections; skilful cooking is full of flavour. Friendly staff offer good recommendations.

Larder on Goosegate (N)

1st Floor, 16-22 Goosegate ✉ NG1 1FE – ✆ (0115) 950 01 11 – www.thelarderongoosegate.co.uk – Closed Sunday, Monday and Tuesday-Wednesday lunch DYa

Rest – Menu £ 14 (weekdays) – Carte £ 23/33

Airy first floor restaurant in a listed Victorian building; sit in the window for a view of the street below. Unfussy dishes are skilfully cooked, good value and very tasty. Delicious steaks. Freshly made cakes.

Lime (N)

4 Upminster Dr, Northwest : 3.5 mi by A 610 and A 6002 ✉ NG16 1PT – ✆ (0115) 975 0005 – www.lime-restaurant.co.uk – Closed 25 December

Rest – *(dinner only)* Carte £ 15/27

Bright, modern Indian restaurant away from the city centre; personally run by the cheery owner. Flavoursome food with distinctive spicing. Non-alcoholic bar, and no corkage fee if you bring your own wine or beer.

at West Bridgford Southeast : 1.75 mi by A 60 - DZ - ✉ Nottingham

escabeche

27 Bridgford Rd ✉ NG2 6AU – ✆ (0115) 981 7010 – www.escabeche.co.uk

Rest – Menu £ 12 (weekdays) **s** – Carte £ 18/27 BZx

Informal, modern, Mediterranean-inspired restaurant with a sunny front terrace. The broad main menu lists vibrant, well-presented tapas dishes, offering a great variety of flavours. Excellent value set menu.

at Plumtree Southeast : 5.75 mi by A 60 - BZ - off A 606 – ✉ Nottingham

Perkins

Old Railway Station, Station Rd ✉ NG12 5NA – ✆ (0115) 937 36 95 – www.perkinsrestaurant.co.uk – Closed Sunday dinner

Rest – *(booking advisable)* Menu £ 14/19 – Carte £ 25/34

Converted Victorian railway station; now a light, modern, airy restaurant; sit in the conservatory overlooking the railway line. Classically based menus include sharing boards and tureens; local produce features.

at Stapleford Southwest : 5.5 mi by A 52 - AZ - ✉ Nottingham

Crème

12 Toton Ln ✉ NG9 7HA – ✆ (0115) 939 74 22 – www.cremerestaurant.co.uk – Closed 25-26 and 31 December, Saturday lunch, Sunday dinner and Monday

Rest – *(booking advisable)* Menu £ 16/20

Well-run neighbourhood restaurant with a spacious, comfortable lounge area and a stylish, modern, formally laid dining room. Seasonally changing, modern British menu; well-presented dishes are served by friendly staff.

at Sherwood Business Park Northwest : 10 mi by A 611 - AY - off A 608 – ✉ Nottingham

Holiday Inn

Lake View Dr ✉ NG15 0DA – ✆ (01623) 727 670 – www.dakotanottingham.co.uk

92 rm – †£ 69/109 ††£ 69/109, ☕ £ 14

Rest *Grill* – Menu £ 10/25 – Carte £ 22/35

Situated close to the M1, in the heart of the business park. Spacious modern bedrooms have bathrooms with walk-in showers (no baths). Executive rooms offer king-sized beds and extras such as bathrobes and chocolates. Spacious restaurant with bar-lounge; international, grill-style menu.

ENGLAND

NUNEATON – Warwickshire – 503 P26 – pop. 70 721 19 D2

London 102 mi – Birmingham 25 mi – Coventry 17 mi

Leathermill Grange without rest

Leathermill Lane, Caldecote, Northwest : 3.5 mi by B 4114 on B 4111
✉ CV10 0RX – ✆ (01827) 714 637 – www.leathermillgrange.co.uk
– Closed 2 weeks Christmas-New Year and 8-14 May
5 rm – †£ 60/70 ††£ 80/90
Red-brick Victorian farmhouse in a peaceful rural spot; the welcoming owners serve homemade cake on arrival. Traditional, pine-furnished bedrooms and a spacious Victoriana-style lounge with rich furnishings. Tasty, Aga-cooked breakfasts.

OAKHAM – Rutland – 502 R25 – pop. 9 620 Great Britain 17 C2

London 103 mi – Leicester 26 mi – Northampton 35 mi – Nottingham 28 mi

Catmose St, ✆ (01572) 75 84 41, www.discover-rutland.co.uk

Oakham Castle★

Rutland Water★, E : by A 606 – Normanton Church★ **AC**, SE : 5 mi by A 603 and minor road East

Barnsdale Lodge

The Avenue, Rutland Water, East : 2.5 mi on A 606 ✉ LE15 8AH
– ✆ (01572) 724 678 – www.barnsdalelodge.co.uk
45 rm – †£ 80/95 ††£ 110/150
Rest – Menu £ 16 (weekday lunch) – Carte £ 23/40
Collection of interconnecting former farm buildings in neat, lawned gardens. Characterful guest areas with York stone flooring in the lounge and bar. Individually designed bedrooms boast good facilities and a country chic style. Classic dishes with Mediterranean influences in the dining room and conservatory.

at Hambleton East : 3 mi by A 606 – ✉ Oakham

Hambleton Hall

✉ LE15 8TH – ✆ (01572) 756 991
– www.hambletonhall.com
17 rm – †£ 195/430 ††£ 260/435 – 1 suite
Rest *Hambleton Hall* ✿ – see restaurant listing
Beautiful Victorian manor house with mature grounds, in a peaceful location overlooking Rutland Water. Classical country house drawing rooms boast heavy drapes, open fires and antiques. Good-sized bedrooms are designed by the owner herself – who is part of the original founding family.

XXX ✿ Hambleton Hall – Hambleton Hall Hotel

✉ LE15 8TH – ✆ (01572) 756 991 – www.hambletonhall.com
Rest – Menu £ 31/72
Formal, traditionally styled dining room in a lovely Victorian manor house, surrounded by mature, peaceful grounds and boasting superb views over Rutland Water. Intricate, highly technical cooking marries together a host of top quality seasonal ingredients in classically based dishes with modern touches.
→ Cornish crab with Granny Smith apple and crab bisque purée. Variations of lamb, mint jelly and a rosemary jus. Lime meringue with chocolate sorbet.

Finch's Arms with rm

Oakham Rd ✉ LE15 8TL – ✆ (01572) 756 575
– www.finchsarms.co.uk
10 rm – †£ 80/100 ††£ 100/130
Rest – Menu £ 16/19 – Carte £ 22/40
Quaint stone inn with a characterful bar, two very stylish dining rooms and a delightful terrace overlooking Rutland Water. Assured, seasonal dishes rely on local produce; desserts are satisfyingly old school and afternoon tea is also an option. Ultra-modern bedrooms complete the picture.

OAKSEY – Wiltshire – 503 N29 — 4 C1

London 98 mi – Cirencester 8 mi – Stroud 20 mi

Wheatsheaf at Oaksey

Wheatsheaf Ln ✉ SN16 9TB – ✆ (01666) 577 348 – www.thewheatsheafatoaksey.co.uk – Closed Sunday dinner and Monday

Rest – Carte £ 19/35

Community pub with a traditional fire-lit bar, a more modern dining room and a cosy snug. Regularly changing menus offer pub classics with a twist, as well as 10 varieties of burger, including one made with Wagyu beef.

OARE – Kent – 504 W30 – see Faversham

OBORNE – Dorset – 503 M31 – see Sherborne

OFFCHURCH – Warwickshire – see Royal Leamington Spa

OLD BASING – Hampshire – 503 Q30 — 6 B1

London 50 mi – Bristol 84 mi – Cardiff 117 mi – Plymouth 169 mi

Crown

The Street ✉ RG24 7BW – ✆ (01256) 321 424 – www.thecrownoldbasing.com – Closed Sunday dinner

Rest – Carte dinner £ 22/33

Popular with locals and with a likeable simplicity to its menus. Choices range from simple snacks to flavoursome, classic dishes like roast chicken. Everything is homemade, from the bread to the fudge that comes with your coffee.

OLD BURGHCLERE – Hampshire – 504 Q29 – ✉ Newbury — 6 B1

London 77 mi – Bristol 76 mi – Newbury 10 mi – Reading 27 mi

Dew Pond

✉ RG20 9LH – ✆ (01635) 278 408 – www.dewpond.co.uk – Closed 2 weeks Christmas-New Year, Sunday and Monday

Rest – *(dinner only)* Menu £ 34

Long-standing, personally run restaurant with attractive country views. Homely lounge; two dining rooms display local art for sale. Classical cooking with French influences. Friendly service.

OLD WARDEN – Central Bedfordshire – 504 S27 – pop. 275 — 12 A1

London 51 mi – Birmingham 89 mi – Bristol 164 mi – Sheffield 134 mi

Hare & Hounds

The Village ✉ SG18 9HQ – ✆ (01767) 627 225 – www.hareandhoundsoldwarden.co.uk – Closed 26 December, 1 January, Sunday dinner and Monday except bank holidays

Rest – Carte £ 24/36

Charming picture postcard pub in an idyllic village, boasting ornate bargeboards and manicured shrubs. Monthly changing à la carte offers hearty, flavoursome dishes; blackboard menu presents choices of a classic pub persuasion. Tasty homemade bread and pasta.

OLDHAM – Greater Manchester – 502 N23 – pop. 103 544 — 20 B2

London 212 mi – Leeds 36 mi – Manchester 7 mi – Sheffield 38 mi

18 Crompton and Royton, Royton, High Barn, ✆ (0161) 624 21 54

18 Werneth, Garden Suburb, Green Lane, ✆ (0161) 624 11 90

18 Lees New Rd, ✆ (0161) 624 49 86

White Hart Inn with rm

51 Stockport Rd, Lydgate ✉ OL4 4JJ – ✆ (01457) 872 566 – www.thewhitehart.co.uk – Closed 26 December

12 rm – †£ 95 ††£ 128

Rest – Menu £ 17 (lunch and early dinner) – Carte £ 26/39

Stone-built inn with exposed beams and open fires, overlooking Saddleworth Moor. Mix of brasserie dishes and pub classics, with a good value lunch and early evening menu; the restaurant à la carte shifts things up a gear. 12 individually styled bedrooms are named after local men of note.

OLDSTEAD – North Yorkshire – 502 Q21 23 C2

London 235 mi – Liverpool 125 mi – Leeds 54 mi – Sheffield 86 mi

Black Swan with rm

YO61 4BL – (01347) 868 387 – www.blackswanoldstead.co.uk – Closed lunch Monday-Wednesday

4 rm – †£ 160/230 ††£ 160/230

Rest – Menu £ 25 (weekdays) – Carte £ 42/54

Owned by a family who've lived and farmed here for generations. Top-rate bar meals in characterful beamed bar; more ambitious dishes in upstairs restaurant. Cooking is modern and highly skilled but satisfyingly unpretentious. Bedrooms boast modern fabrics, antiques, luxurious bathrooms and private patios.

→ Tuna tartare, wasabi, ginger and lime. Lamb 'three ways' with gnocchi and ratatouille. Lemon drizzle cake, strawberry and mascarpone.

OLTON – West Midlands – 502 O26 – see Solihull

OMBERSLEY – Worcestershire – 503 N27 – pop. 2 089 18 B3

London 148 mi – Birmingham 42 mi – Leominster 33 mi

Bishopswood Rd, (01905) 62 07 47

Venture In

Main St WR9 0EW – (01905) 620 552 – Closed 2 weeks February, 2 weeks August, 1 week June, 1 week Christmas, Sunday dinner and Monday

Rest – Menu £ 29/39

Black and white timbered house with 15C origins, exposed beams and a large inglenook fireplace. The concise menu is supplemented by plenty of daily specials; cooking is classically based but has modern overtones and personal twists.

ORFORD – Suffolk – 504 Y27 – pop. 1 153 – Woodbridge 15 D3

London 103 mi – Ipswich 22 mi – Norwich 52 mi

Crown and Castle

IP12 2LJ – (01394) 450 205 – www.crownandcastle.co.uk

21 rm – †£ 120/190 ††£ 135/210 – 1 suite

Rest *Trinity* – see restaurant listing

Refreshingly well-run, mock-Tudor style house with relaxed yet professional service; set next to the 12C castle. Smart guest areas. Modern, individually designed bedrooms with good comforts and stylish bathrooms; some have terraces, others boast distant sea views.

Trinity – Crown and Castle Hotel

IP12 2LJ – (01394) 450 205 – www.crownandcastle.co.uk

Rest – *(closed lunch 31 December) (booking essential at dinner)* Carte £ 28/45

Relaxed dining room with red banquettes, eclectic art and chic, modern bar-lounge. Wide-ranging lunches and more sophisticated dinners. Simple yet precise cooking relies on quality, seasonal ingredients. Friendly, efficient service.

OSMOTHERLEY – North Yorkshire – 502 Q20 – pop. 1 217 – Northallerton 22 B1

London 245 mi – Darlington 25 mi – Leeds 49 mi – Middlesbrough 20 mi

Golden Lion with rm

6 West End DL6 3AA – (01609) 883 526 – www.goldenlionosmotherley.co.uk – Closed 25 December, lunch Monday and Tuesday except bank holidays

5 rm – †£ 65 ††£ 90/100 **Rest** – Carte £ 22/36

18C stone inn set in a historic village in the North York Moors National Park. Low-ceilinged bar with dark wood furnishings. Traditional, satisfying cooking, with filling dishes on the main menu and more ambitious weekly specials. Modern bedrooms have heavy oak furnishings and good facilities.

OTTERBOURNE – Hampshire – 504 P30 6 B2

London 72 mi – Birmingham 134 mi – Bristol 96 mi – Cardiff 129 mi

White Horse

Main Rd ✉ SO21 2EQ – ✆ (01962) 712 830 – www.whitehorseotterbourne.co.uk

Rest – Carte £ 17/43

Smart pub with designer décor, vintage adverts and leather sofas; one side is for drinkers; the other, for diners. Flexible menu with lovely local cheeses, artisan bread, Sunday roasts and afternoon teas. Pleasant terrace; friendly service.

OUNDLE – Northamptonshire – 504 S26 – pop. 5 219 – ✉ Peterborough 17 C3

London 89 mi – Leicester 37 mi – Northampton 30 mi

14 West St, ✆ (01832) 27 43 33, www.northamptonshiretouristguide.com

Benefield Rd, ✆ (01832) 27 32 67

Oundle Mill with rm

Barnwell Rd, South : 1 mi by West St and Mill Rd ✉ PE8 5PB – ✆ (01832) 272 621 – www.oundlemill.co.uk

2 rm – †£ 100/195 ††£ 100/320 **Rest** – Menu £ 13/26 – Carte £ 26/43

17C limestone watermill on the banks of the Nene. Interior fuses original features with strikingly modern new designs, including glass floors looking down to the water. Detailed modern British cooking; locally and ethically sourced produce. Well-appointed bedrooms boast low beams and original mill workings.

at Fotheringhay North : 3.75 mi by A 427 off A 605 – ✉ Peterborough (cambs.)

Castle Farm without rest

✉ PE8 5HZ – ✆ (01832) 226 200 – www.castlefarm-guesthouse.co.uk

5 rm – †£ 45/60 ††£ 85/100

Large 19C, wisteria-clad former farmhouse with lawned gardens leading down to the River Nene. Comfy lounge with deep sofas and a pleasant aspect. Spacious, traditionally styled bedrooms: two are in the wing; the best one is at the front.

Falcon Inn

✉ PE8 5HZ – ✆ (01832) 226 254 – www.thefalcon-inn.co.uk

Rest – Menu £ 14 (weekdays) – Carte £ 26/37

Attractive ivy-clad inn with neat garden and terrace, set in a pretty village. Good-sized menus include unusual combinations and some interesting modern takes on traditional dishes.

ENGLAND

OUSTON – Durham 24 B2

London 197 mi – Cardiff 141 mi – Swansea 177 mi – Gloucester 241 mi

Low Urpeth Farm without rest

North : 1 mi on Kibblesworth rd ✉ DH2 1BD – ✆ (0191) 410 2901 – www.lowurpeth.co.uk

3 rm – †£ 50/62 ††£ 70/87

A stone-built Victorian farmhouse on a working arable farm: a very welcoming place, full of warmth and run with pride. Cakes and biscuits are served on arrival in the traditional, antique-furnished lounge; breakfast features homemade bread and preserves, and the spacious, comfy bedrooms have country views.

OXFORD – Oxfordshire – 503 Q28 – pop. 147 210 Great Britain 10 B2

London 59 mi – Birmingham 63 mi – Brighton 105 mi – Bristol 73 mi

Access Swinford Bridge (toll)

to Abingdon Bridge (Salter Bros. Ltd) (summer only) daily (2 h)

15-16 Broad St, ✆ (01865) 25 22 00, www.visitoxfordandoxfordshire.com

City★★★ - Christ Church★★ (Hall★★ **AC**, Tom Quad★, Tom Tower★, Cathedral★ **AC** - Choir Roof★) BZ – Merton College★★ **AC** BZ - Magdalen College★★ BZ – Ashmolean Museum★★ BY **M1** – Bodleian Library★★ (Ceiling★★, Lierne Vaulting★) **AC** BZ **A1** – St John's College★ BY - The Queen's College★ BZ – Lincoln College★ BZ - Trinity College (Chapel★) BY – New College (Chapel★) **AC**, BZ – Radcliffe Camera★ BZ **P1** – Sheldonian Theatre★ **AC**, BZ **T** – University Museum of National History★ BY **M4** – Pitt Rivers Museum★ BY **M3**

Iffley Church★ AZ **A**. Woodstock : Blenheim Palace★★★ (Park★★★) **AC**, NW : 8 mi by A 4144 and A 34 AY

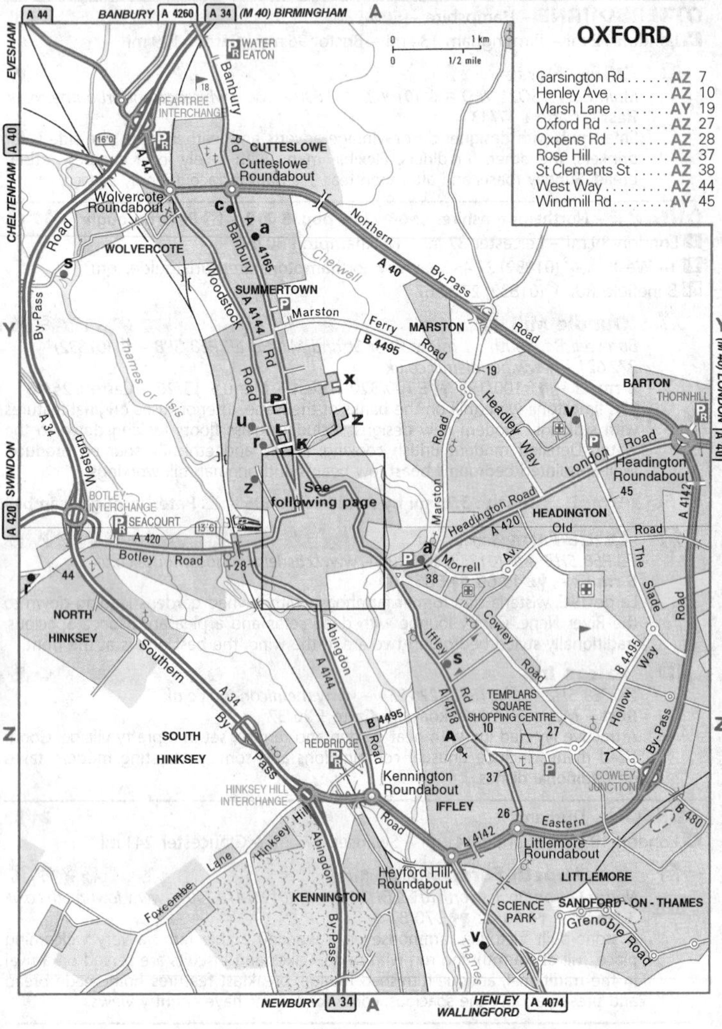

Randolph

Beaumont St. ✉ *OX1 2LN* – ✆ *(0844) 879 91 32*
– *www.macdonaldhotels.co.uk/Randolph*
– *Restricted opening Christmas* BY**n**
151 rm – 🚹£ 159/299 🚹🚹£ 205/309, ☕ £ 15 – 9 suites
Rest ***Randolph*** – see restaurant listing
A grand old lady with her make-up firmly intact, this fine Victorian building offers immense charm and character. Delightful wrought iron stairway; plush period bedrooms. Afternoon tea in the drawing room with its Sir Osbert Lancaster oils.

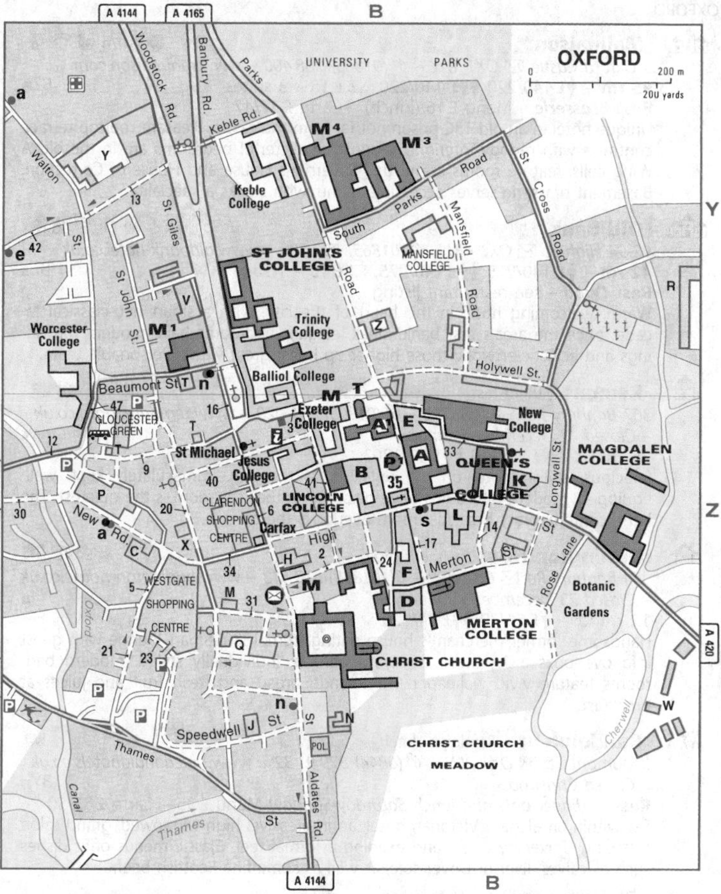

ENGLAND

OXFORD

Blue Boar St . . . . BY 2
Broad St . . . . BZ 3
Castle St . . . . BZ 5
Clarendon Shopping Centre BZ
Cornmarket St. . . . . BZ 6
George St . . . . BZ 9
High St. . . . . BZ
Hythe Bridge St . . . . BZ 12
Little Clarendon St . . . . BY 13
Logic Lane . . . . BZ 14
Magdalen St. . . . . BYZ 16
Magpie Lane . . . . BZ 17
New Inn Hall St. . . . . BZ 20
Norfolk St . . . . BZ 21
Old Greyfriars St . . . . BZ 23
Oriel Square . . . . BZ 24
Park End St . . . . BZ 30
Pembroke St. . . . . BZ 31
Queen St. . . . . BZ 34
Queen's Lane . . . . BZ 33
Radcliffe Square . . . . BZ 35
St Michael St. . . . . BZ 40
Turl St. . . . . BZ 41
Walton Crescent. . . . . BY 42
Westgate Shopping
Centre . . . . BZ
Worcester St. . . . . BZ 47

COLLEGES

All Souls . . . . BZ **A**
Balliol . . . . BY
Brasenose . . . . BZ **B**
Christ Church . . . . BZ
Corpus Christi . . . . BZ **D**
Exeter . . . . BZ
Hertford . . . . BZ **E**
Jesus . . . . BZ
Keble . . . . BY
Lady Margaret Hall . . . . AY **Z**
Linacre . . . . BZ **N**
Lincoln . . . . BZ
Magdalen . . . . BZ
Mansfield . . . . BY
Merton . . . . BZ
New . . . . BZ
Nuffield . . . . BZ **P**
Oriel . . . . BZ **F**
Pembroke . . . . BZ **Q**
Queen's . . . . BZ
St Anne's . . . . AY **K**
St Anthony's . . . . AY **L**
St Catherine's . . . . BY **R**
St Cross . . . . BY **V**
St Edmund
Hall . . . . BZ **K**
St Hilda's . . . . BZ **W**
St Hugh's . . . . AY **P**
St John's . . . . BY
St Peter's . . . . BZ **X**
Sommerville . . . . BY **Y**
Trinity . . . . BY
University . . . . BZ **L**
Wadham . . . . BY **Z**
Wolfson . . . . AY **X**
Worcester . . . . BY

Malmaison
3 Oxford Castle ✉ OX1 1AY – ✆ (01865) 268 400 – www.malmaison.com
95 rm – †£ 140/220 ††£ 140/220, ☕ £ 15 – 3 suites BZ**a**
Rest *Brasserie* – Menu £ 16 (lunch) – Carte £ 27/47
Unique hotel in an old 13C prison not far from the castle. Pleasant rooftop terrace contrasts with moody interior: the most characterful bedrooms are in the old A Wing cells; feature rooms are in the Governor's House and House of Correction. Basement brasserie serves accessible menu, with steaks a speciality.

Old Bank
92-94 High St ✉ OX1 4BJ – ✆ (01865) 799 599 – www.oldbank-hotel.co.uk
42 rm – †£ 140/275 ††£ 140/275, ☕ £ 15 – 1 suite BZ**s**
Rest *Quod* – see restaurant listing
Warm, welcoming hotel in the heart of the city, with a smart neo-classical façade; once the area's first bank. Sleek, elegant bedrooms have modern furnishings and eclectic artwork; those higher up boast great views. Personable team.

Remont without rest
367 Banbury Rd. ✉ OX2 7PL – ✆ (01865) 311 020 – www.remont-oxford.co.uk – Closed 17 December-5 January AY**c**
25 rm ☕ – †£ 75/110 ††£ 89/120
Spacious, stylish hotel on the outskirts of the city. Immaculately kept, well-equipped, modern bedrooms have personality; the rear room is the quietest. The light, contemporary breakfast room overlooks the garden.

Burlington House without rest
374 Banbury Rd ✉ OX2 7PP – ✆ (01865) 513 513 – www.burlington-house.co.uk – Closed 23 December-3 January AY**a**
12 rm ☕ – †£ 66/79 ††£ 84/120
Handsome former merchant's house dating from 1889. Smart lounge with guest info overlooks a Japanese courtyard garden. Individually styled, modern bedrooms feature vivid wallpaper. Homemade bread and fresh fruit and juices at breakfast.

ENGLAND

Randolph Ⓝ – Randolph Hotel
Beaumont St. ✉ OX1 2LN – ✆ (0844) 879 91 32 – www.macdonaldhotels.co.uk – Closed Christmas BY**n**
Rest – *(dinner only and lunch Saturday-Sunday)* Menu £ 35 – Carte £ 35/50
Set within an elegant Victorian hotel; an impressive, high-windowed, grand salon featuring University crests and exuding a formal feel. Classic menus offer dishes such as calves' liver or Dover sole, as well as some fine Scottish beef.

Shanghai 30's
✉ OX1 1RA – ✆ (01865) 242 230 – www.shanghai30s.com BZ**n**
Rest – Menu £ 12/27 – Carte £ 15/34
Delightful, colonial-style restaurant in a characterful 15C building; the rooms are listed and feature wood panelling and ornate plaster ceilings. Menus offer a wide range of authentic Chinese dishes; don't miss the fiery Sichuan section.

Brasserie Blanc
71-72 Walton St. ✉ OX2 6AG – ✆ (01865) 510 999 – www.brasserieblanc.com – Closed 25 December AY**z**
Rest – Menu £ 12 (lunch) – Carte £ 21/41
A bustling brasserie with smartly laid tables; its walls filled with black and white photos of Raymond Blanc and his staff. French country cooking includes all the old favourites. Gluten free menu; children warmly welcomed.

Quod – Old Bank Hotel
92-94 High St ✉ OX1 4BJ – ✆ (01865) 799 599 – www.oldbank-hotel.co.uk BZ**s**
Rest – Menu £ 17 (weekday lunch) – Carte £ 20/41
Lively, Italian-influenced brasserie with a busy, buzzy vibe; set within a city centre hotel and once the banking hall of the area's very first bank. Accessible menu and twice-daily blackboard specials. Lovely decked terrace to the rear.

Branca

111 Walton St. ✉ OX2 6AJ – ✆ (01865) 556 111 – www.branca.co.uk – Closed 25 December BY**a**

Rest – Menu £ 12 (lunch and early dinner) – Carte £ 19/36

Bustling restaurant with a spacious, modern interior and French doors opening onto a courtyard terrace. The menu is a roll call of Italian classics; portions are generous and lunch deals, good value. Friendly young staff; adjoining deli.

Al Shami

25 Walton Cres ✉ OX1 2JG – ✆ (01865) 310 066 – www.al-shami.co.uk

Rest – Menu £ 15/18 – Carte £ 12/21 BY**e**

Smart, established neighbourhood restaurant serving well-priced, tasty Middle Eastern food. Beautiful, ornate ceiling in rear dining room. Lengthy menu offers wide range of authentic Lebanese dishes.

Fishers

36-37 St Clements ✉ OX4 1AB – ✆ (01865) 243 003 – www.fishers-restaurant.com – Closed 25-26 December and 1 January

Rest – Carte £ 20/38 AZ**a**

Long-standing rustic seafood restaurant with a simple, nautical feel. There's something for everyone on the daily changing menu, from traditional fish and chips to roasted sea bass and tomatoes. Classic desserts; friendly service.

Magdalen Arms

243 Iffley Rd ✉ OX4 1SJ – ✆ (01865) 243 159 – Closed 2 weeks August, 24-26 December, 1 January, Monday lunch and bank holidays AZ**s**

Rest – Carte £ 17/32

Buzzy pub that's a hit with the locals, boasting quirky standard lamps, eclectic 1920s posters, board games and a bar billiards table. Tasty, good value dishes change twice daily and are informed by the latest local, seasonal produce to arrive at the door. Try the delicious fresh juices and homemade lemonade.

Rickety Press

67 Cranham St ✉ OX2 6DE – ✆ (01865) 424 581 – www.thericketypress.com – Closed 25-27 December AY**r**

Rest – Carte £ 22/37

Professionally run by three old school friends; a friendly, shabby-chic pub in a residential area, with a cosy bar, a conservatory and a large room filled with wooden pews. Monthly menus use vibrant, seasonal ingredients which provide plenty of flavour, such as Sandy Lane lamb and Cerne Abbas cheddar.

Black Boy

91 Old High St, Headington ✉ OX3 9HT – ✆ (01865) 741 137 – www.theblackboy.uk.com – Closed 26 December and 1 January AY**v**

Rest – Carte £ 22/33

Sizeable pub just off Headington village, serving sensibly priced pub classics with a French edge. Try the homemade breads, mix and match tapas dishes and the popular Sunday roasts. Tuesday is quiz night and Thursday is for jazz-lovers.

at Sandford-on-Thames Southeast : 5 mi by A 4158 – ✉ Oxford

Oxford Thames Four Pillars

rm, rest,

Henley Rd ✉ OX4 4GX – ✆ (01865) 334 444 – www.four-pillars.co.uk/thames AZ**v**

84 rm – †£ 115/220 ††£ 115/220

Rest ***River Room*** – Carte £ 29/39

Extended sandstone cottages and a tithe barn set in 30 acres of peaceful parkland leading to the Thames. The bright College Hall bedrooms are the best; some have garden views and balconies. Great outlook over the river and gardens from the formal restaurant, which serves traditional dishes with a modern edge.

ENGLAND

at Toot Baldon Southeast : 5.5 mi by B 480 - AZ – ✉ Oxford

Mole Inn

✉ *OX44 9NG – ☎ (01865) 340 001 – www.themoleinn.com – Closed 25 December*
Rest – *(booking advisable)* Menu £ 20 – Carte £ 28/34
Popular pub with pleasant terrace and beautiful landscaped gardens. Appealing menu suits all tastes and appetites. Sourcing is taken seriously, so when ingredients are gone, they're gone.

at Great Milton Southeast : 12 mi by A 40 off A 329 - AY – ✉ Oxford

Le Manoir aux Quat' Saisons

Church Rd ✉ OX44 7PD – ☎ (01844) 278 881 – www.manoir.com
32 rm – †£ 545/625 ††£ 545/625 – 17 suites – ††£ 1055/1200
Rest ***Le Manoir aux Quat' Saisons*** ✿✿ – see restaurant listing
Majestic country house offering the ultimate in service levels and guest experience. Extremely comfortable bedrooms – those in the Garden Wing are the most luxurious and have subtle themes. Relax by an open fire in the sumptuous sitting rooms or on the delightful terrace overlooking the pristine gardens.

Le Manoir aux Quat' Saisons (Raymond Blanc)

✿✿

Church Rd ✉ OX44 7PD – ☎ (01844) 278 881 – www.manoir.com
Rest – *(booking essential)* Menu £ 80/155 – Carte £ 112/135
Elegant beamed restaurant with a large conservatory, set in a luxurious hotel. French-inspired cooking uses seasonal garden produce and dishes are prepared with skill, clarity and a lightness of touch. Choose from the monthly à la carte or try the signature dishes on the 9 course menu 'Découverte'.
→ Risotto of spring vegetables, chervil cream. Assiette of piglet with cabbage, onion purée and prune. Exotic fruit raviole, kaffir lime and coconut jus.

ENGLAND

at Kingston Bagpuize Southwest : 7 mi by A 420 AZ – ✉ Oxford

Fallowfields

Faringdon Rd. ✉ OX13 5BH – ☎ (01865) 820 416 – www.fallowfields.com
10 rm – †£ 110/125 ††£ 140/180
Rest ***Fallowfields*** – see restaurant listing
18C manor house in 12 acres of gardens and parkland; they keep an array of animals, from chickens and ducks to suckling pigs and Dexter cows. Spacious bedrooms come in a mix of traditional and more modern styles – all have delightful views.

Fallowfields – Fallowfields Hotel

Faringdon Rd. ✉ OX13 5BH – ☎ (01865) 820 416 – www.fallowfields.com
Rest – *(bookings advisable at dinner)* Menu £ 30/65 – Carte £ 34/60
Light, airy monochrome restaurant in an 18C manor house; overlooking the croquet lawn and paddocks. Elaborate modern cooking showcases produce from the garden and orchard, and meats are from their livestock. Try the 5 course tasting menu.

at Fyfield Southwest : 9.5 mi by A 420 AZ – ✉ Abingdon

White Hart

Main Rd ✉ OX13 5LW – ☎ (01865) 390 585 – www.whitehart-fyfield.com – Closed Monday except bank holidays
Rest – Menu £ 20/30 – Carte £ 27/40
Intriguing 15C former chantry house with a cosy open-fired bar, an impressive flag-floored, vaulted dining room, and a pleasant terrace; along with a minstrels' gallery and a secret tunnel. The diverse range of dishes relies on produce from the vegetable plot; save room for one of the excellent desserts.

OXHILL – Warwickshire – 503 P27 – pop. 303 — 19 C3

London 90 mi – Banbury 11 mi – Birmingham 37 mi

Oxbourne House without rest

✉ *CV35 0RA – ☎ (01295) 688 202 – www.oxbournehouse.com*
3 rm – †£ 60/75 ††£ 80/95
Large brick house in a quiet village, with a lovely mature garden and a tennis court. Elegant, antique-furnished lounge features a wood burning stove. Comfy, immaculately kept bedrooms offer good facilities and extras; one is split-level.

PADSTOW – Cornwall – 503 F32 – pop. 2 449

London 288 mi – Exeter 78 mi – Plymouth 45 mi – Truro 23 mi
North Quay, (01841) 53 34 49, www.padstowlive.com
Trevose, Constantine Bay, (01841) 52 02 08
Town★ - Prideaux Place★
Trevone (Cornwall Coast Path★★) W : 3 mi by B 3276 – Trevose Head★ (★★) W : 6 mi by B 3276. Bedruthan Steps★, SW : 7 mi by B 3276 – Pencarrow★, SE : 11 mi by A 389

Plan on next page

Metropole

Station Rd PL28 8DB – (01841) 532 486 – www.the-metropole.co.uk BYa
58 rm – £ 69/140 £ 69/279
Rest – *(bar lunch Monday-Saturday)* Menu £ 33
Grand 19C hotel perched on a cliff above the old railway station, just a short walk from town. Characterful, well-appointed guest areas. Bedrooms are a mix of traditional and contemporary styles; No.6 boasts great harbour and estuary views. Simply prepared lunches; more elaborate dinners.

Old Custom House Inn

rest,

South Quay PL28 8BL – (01841) 532 359 – www.oldcustomhousepadstow.co.uk BYc
21 rm – £ 100/190 £ 135/220
Rest *Pescadou* – *(booking essential)* Carte £ 27/42 **s**
Well-run, slate hotel; formerly a grain store and exciseman's house. Beauty studio and ice cream parlour. Nautically themed bedrooms feature good mod cons – some have roll-top baths or harbour/estuary views. Traditional bar and open-plan seafood restaurant; watch the chefs at work.

Treverbyn House without rest

Station Rd PL28 8DA – (01841) 532 855 – www.treverbynhouse.com – Closed 25 December-13 February BYe
5 rm – £ 90/125 £ 90/125
Charming Edwardian house built for a wine merchant. Comfortable bedrooms boast polished floors and interesting furniture from local sale rooms. One has a huge roll-top bath and some have harbour views; the Turret Room is best. Breakfast in your bedroom, the dining room or the garden. Delightful owner.

Treann House without rest

24 Dennis Rd PL28 8DE – (01841) 533 855 – www.treannhouse.com – Closed January-March BZn
3 rm – £ 90/120 £ 105/130
Edwardian house set in an elevated position, with first floor views over the Camel Estuary. Chic breakfast room, cool lounge and superb bedrooms which mix antiques with contemporary furnishings to create an understated, elegant style.

Woodlands Country House without rest

Treator, West : 1.25 mi on B 3276 PL28 8RU – (01841) 532 426 – www.woodlands-padstow.co.uk – Closed 20 December-1 February
8 rm – £ 74/94 £ 98/138
Characterful Victorian house with great coastal outlook to rear. Tastefully furnished lounge, breakfast room and honesty bar; pictures, books and objets d'art abound. Comfy, homely bedrooms; Beach is the largest and best. Homemade muesli and hot specials at breakfast.

Althea Library without rest

27 High St, (access via Church St.) PL28 8BB – (01841) 532 717 – www.althealibrary.co.uk – Closed 30 April-1 May and 22-26 December AYg
3 rm – £ 80/98 £ 94/98
Grade II listed former Sunday school and library, just 5min from the harbour. Homely lounge and breakfast room; pine-furnished bedrooms. In summer, the aga-cooked breakfasts are served on the terrace, next to the pond and water feature.

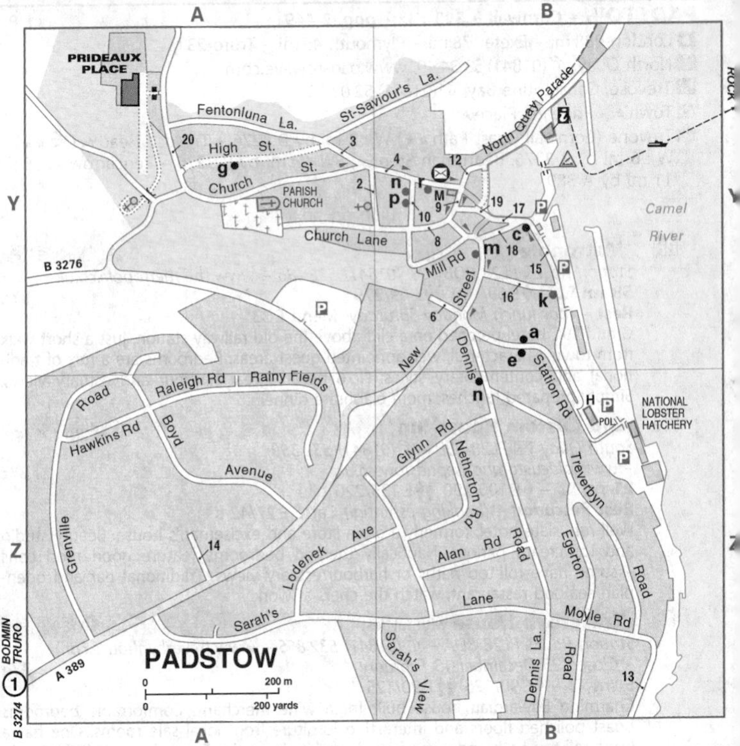

Seafood with rm

AC rest, P

Riverside ✉ PL28 8BY – ✆ (01841) 532 700 – www.rickstein.com
– Closed 24-26 December BY**k**

16 rm – †£ 150/260 ††£ 150/260

Rest – *(booking essential)* Menu £ 39 (lunch) – Carte £ 39/84

Relaxed, stylish seafood restaurant dominated by large stainless steel topped bar. Daily menus of fresh local fish and shellfish. Classic dishes sit alongside those influenced by Rick Stein's travels; perhaps Singapore chilli crab or monkfish vindaloo. New England style bedrooms boast quality furnishings; some have terraces or balconies and estuary views.

Paul Ainsworth at No.6

6 Middle St ✉ PL28 8AP – ✆ (01841) 532 093
– www.number6inpadstow.co.uk
– Closed 6 January-1 February, 24-26 December, Sunday and Monday

Rest – Menu £ 18 (lunch) **s** – Carte £ 46/65 **s** BY**n**

Delightful bright yellow Georgian townhouse with a contemporary interior, set on a harbour backwater. Intimate, candlelit room with contemporary black & white floor tiles. Relaxed air and friendly, enthusiastic service. Modern seasonal cooking displays originality, with refined textures and flavours.

→ Mackerel with celeriac remoulade, Parma ham and cucumber. Saddleback pork, buttered turnips, crackling, scallop and cider apple. Caramelised vanilla loaf with Cornish cream custard and stout.

St Petroc's with rm
4 New St ✉ PL28 8EA – ✆ (01841) 532 700 – www.rickstein.com – Closed 24-26 December BY**m**
10 rm – †£ 150/240 ††£ 150/240
Rest – *(booking essential)* Menu £ 27 – Carte £ 24/47
Attractive house on a steep hill, with an oak-furnished bistro and a front and rear terrace. Menu offers a mix of simply prepared seafood, grills and old-fashioned classics. Smart, well-appointed bedrooms in the house and annexe; small lounge and quiet library.

Rick Stein's Café with rm
10 Middle St ✉ PL28 8AP – ✆ (01841) 532 700 – www.rickstein.com – Closed 24-26 December BY**p**
3 rm – †£ 100/150 ††£ 100/150
Rest – *(booking essential at dinner)* Menu £ 22 – Carte £ 22/30
Deceptively large café hidden behind a tiny shop front on a side street. Concise, seasonally changing menu of tasty, unfussy cooking with influences from Thailand, Morocco and the Med. Homemade bread and great value set menus. Comfy, simply furnished bedrooms; breakfast in café or small courtyard garden.

Margot's
11 Duke St ✉ PL28 8AB – ✆ (01841) 533 441 – Closed January, 24-31 December, Sunday and Monday BY**r**
Rest – *(dinner only and lunch May-September) (booking essential)* Carte £ 26/37
Small yellow and blue bistro with a relaxed atmosphere and a loyal local following. Daily menus feature the latest seasonal produce in classical bistro-style dishes; cooking is rustic and flavoursome. Dinner also offers a tasting menu.

at Little Petherick South : 3 mi on A 389 – ✉ Wadebridge

Molesworth Manor without rest
✉ PL27 7QT – ✆ (01841) 540 292 – www.molesworthmanor.co.uk – Closed November-January
9 rm – †£ 85/125 ††£ 115/125
Part 16C and 17C former rectory set in mature gardens and run by affable owners. Elegant drawing room with honesty bar; spacious bedrooms boast period features, roll top baths and large walk in showers. Homemade preserves at breakfast.

at St Issey South : 3.5 mi on A 389 – ✉ Wadebridge

Higher Trevorrick Country House without rest
Northwest : 0.75 mi by Burgois rd on Sea Mills and Trevorrick rd. ✉ PL27 7QH – ✆ (01841) 540 943 – www.higher-trevorrick.co.uk – Closed early November-February
4 rm – †£ 109/136 ††£ 109/136
Restored property with spectacular first floor views out over the Camel Estuary and towards Rock. Spacious, well-kept bedrooms. Experienced, personable owners offer tea and biscuits on arrival. Breakfast in conservatory. No children policy.

at St Merryn West : 2.5 mi by A 389 on B 3276 – 503 F32 – ✉ Padstow

Cornish Arms
Churchtown ✉ PL28 8ND – ✆ (01841) 532 700 – www.rickstein.com
Rest – *(bookings not accepted)* Carte £ 20/29
Popular with locals – one of them was Rick Stein, who liked it so much, he now leases it! Nicely priced menu of pub classics, with seafood specials, Sunday roasts and nursery puddings. Cosy, beamed bar; light, airy dining room.

at Constantine Bay West : 4 mi by B 3276 – ✉ Padstow

Treglos rm, rest,
✉ PL28 8JH – ✆ (01841) 520 727 – www.tregloshotel.com – Closed December-13 February
42 rm – †£ 74/105 ††£ 148/209 – 4 suites
Rest – *(bar lunch Monday-Saturday)* Menu £ 32
Family-owned, whitewashed property with tiered lawns looking down to the sea. Spacious guest areas include a comfortable lounge and a traditional bar. Classically styled bedrooms with modern touches; many have balconies and a sea view. Dress smartly for dinner in the formal restaurant; traditional menus.

ENGLAND

PAINSWICK – Gloucestershire – 503 N28 – pop. 1 666 Great Britain 4 C1

London 107 mi – Bristol 35 mi – Cheltenham 10 mi – Gloucester 7 mi

Town★

Cotswolds 88

Kemps Ln ✉ GL6 6YB – ✆ (01452) 813 688 – www.cotswolds88hotel.com – Closed 2-16 January

17 rm – †£ 99/395 ††£ 99/395

Rest *Juniper* – see restaurant listing

Stone-built, Regency-style house in a delightful village; the interior couldn't be more of a contrast, with its vivid colour schemes, vibrant furnishings and striking objets d'art. Unique, stylish bedrooms. Attractive gardens and terrace.

Juniper – Cotswolds 88 Hotel

Kemps Ln ✉ GL6 6YB – ✆ (01452) 813 688 – www.cotswolds88hotel.com – Closed 2-16 January

Rest – Menu £ 15 (weekday lunch)/45

Striking restaurant in a fine Regency hotel; its bold décor includes black and white carpets, electric-red wallpaper, faux snakeskin tables and vibrant red leather chairs. Seasonal, modern cooking showcases up-to-date techniques.

PATELEY BRIDGE – North Yorkshire – 502 O21 – pop. 2 504 22 B2

– ✉ Harrogate Great Britain

London 225 mi – Leeds 28 mi – Middlesbrough 46 mi – York 32 mi

18 High St, ✆ (01423) 71 11 47, www.aboutbritain.com

Fountains Abbey★★★ AC - Studley Royal AC (< ★ from Anne Boleyn's Seat) - Fountains Hall (Fa 0.5ade★), NE : 8.5 mi by B 6265

at Ramsgill-in-Nidderdale Northwest : 5 mi by Low Wath Rd – ✉ Harrogate

Yorke Arms (Frances Atkins) with rm

✉ HG3 5RL – ✆ (01423) 755 243 – www.yorke-arms.co.uk

16 rm – †£ 200/250 ††£ 290/430 – 4 suites

Rest – *(closed Sunday dinner to non-residents)* Menu £ 35 (weekday lunch) – Carte £ 47/70

Charming, part-17C former shooting lodge overlooking the village green and run in a friendly, professional manner. Traditional, antique-furnished restaurant with a beamed ceiling and open fires. Measured and accomplished classical cooking demonstrates a good understanding of flavours; presentation is contemporary. Bedrooms have a subtle modern style and good comforts.

→ Red mullet, crevette and clam with black pudding biscuit. Squab with morel, pistachio tapenade, beetroot and lime. Lychee soufflé, jasmine tea sorbet and almond pastry.

PATRICK BROMPTON – North Yorkshire – 502 P21 – ✉ Bedale 22 B1

London 242 mi – Newcastle upon Tyne 58 mi – York 43 mi

Elmfield House without rest

Arrathorne, Northwest : 2.25 mi by A 684 on Richmond rd ✉ DL8 1NE – ✆ (01677) 450 558 – www.elmfieldhouse.co.uk

5 rm – †£ 70/75 ††£ 82/90

Spacious guesthouse set in peaceful farmland, surrounded by livery stables, a fishing lake and a 14 acre forest. Vast conservatory lounge-cum-breakfast-room with simple, cottagey décor. Cosy, well-kept bedrooms are warm and welcoming.

Mill Close Farm without rest

✉ DL8 1JY – ✆ (01677) 450 257 – www.millclose.co.uk – Closed January and December

3 rm – †£ 40/60 ††£ 80/95

Modernised farmhouse with a walled garden and a summerhouse. Bedrooms blend contemporary furnishings with traditional features and have an uncluttered, homely feel; two boast whirlpool baths.

PATTISWICK – Essex – see Coggeshall

PAULERSPURY – Northamptonshire – 503 R27 – see Towcester

PAXFORD – Gloucestershire – 504 O27 – see Chipping Campden

PENN - Buckinghamshire - 504 R/S29 - pop. 3 779 11 D2

London 31 mi - High Wycombe 4 mi - Oxford 36 mi

Old Queens Head

Hammersley Ln ✉ HP10 8EY - ✆ (01494) 813 371
- www.oldqueensheadpenn.co.uk - Closed 25-26 December
Rest - Carte £ 20/36
Lively pub with characterful rustic feel, part-dating back to 1666; head for the old barn. Menus offer generous, hearty dishes and some appealing sides. Homemade puddings are a must.

PENRITH - Cumbria - 501 L19 - pop. 14 471 21 B2

London 290 mi - Carlisle 24 mi - Kendal 31 mi - Lancaster 48 mi
Middlegate, ✆ (01768) 86 74 66, www.penrithtown.co.uk
Salkeld Rd, ✆ (01768) 89 19 19

Brooklands without rest

2 Portland Pl ✉ CA11 7QN - ✆ (01768) 863 395
- www.brooklandsguesthouse.com - Closed Christmas and New Year
6 rm - †£ 40/60 ††£ 78/88
Victorian terraced house located close to the town centre, run by warm, welcoming owners. Traditional, antique-furnished hall and smart breakfast room with marble-topped tables. Homely, pine-furnished bedrooms boast good modern facilities; one has a four-poster.

at Temple Sowerby East : 6.75 mi by A 66 - ✉ Penrith

Temple Sowerby House

✉ CA10 1RZ - ✆ (01768) 361 578 - www.templesowerby.com - Closed Christmas
12 rm - †£ 95/110 ††£ 140/160
Rest - *(dinner only) (booking essential)* Menu £ 34
Attractive, red-brick Georgian mansion with spacious, classically styled guest areas. Traditional country house bedrooms boast antique furnishings and contemporary facilities. Enthusiastic owners. Ambitious, modern menus of local, seasonal produce served overlooking enclosed, lawned gardens.

at Clifton Southeast : 3 mi on A 6

George and Dragon with rm

✉ CA10 2ER - ✆ (01768) 865 381 - www.georgeanddragonclifton.co.uk
- Closed 26 December
12 rm - †£ 79/119 ††£ 95/155
Rest - Carte £ 22/38
Whitewashed coaching inn with a characterful 18C bar and modern, brasserie-style restaurant. Appealing dishes feature vegetables from the garden, game from the moors and organic meats from the Lowther Estate farms. Modern bedrooms showcase furniture and paintings from the family's collection.

at Newbiggin West : 3.5 mi by A 66 - ✉ Penrith

Old School

✉ CA11 0HT - ✆ (01768) 483 709 - www.theold-school.com - Closed 21 December-1 January
3 rm - †£ 40/45 ††£ 85/90
Rest - Menu £ 12
Grey-stone Victorian schoolhouse in a small village. Compact, traditionally styled guest areas. Classical bedrooms are named after the colour of their décor - red, green and blue - the latter is the largest and has the best outlook. Home-cooked meals eaten at a communal oak table.

PENZANCE – Cornwall – **503** D33 – **pop. 20 255** **1** A3

London 319 mi – Exeter 113 mi – Plymouth 77 mi – Taunton 155 mi

Access Access to the Isles of Scilly by helicopter, British International Heliport (01736) 364296, Fax (01736) 363871

to the Isles of Scilly (Hugh Town) (Isles of Scilly Steamship Co. Ltd) (summer only) (approx. 2 h 40 mn)

Welcome to West Cornwall Centre, Station Rd, (01736) 335 5 30, www.westcornwall.org.uk

Town★ - Outlook★★★ – Western Promenade (≤★★★) YZ – National Lighthouse Centre★ **AC** Y – Chapel St★ Y – Maritime Museum★ **AC** Y **M1** – Penlee House Gallery and Museum★, **AC**

St Buryan★★ (church tower★★), SW : 5 mi by A 30 and B 3283 - Penwith★★ – Trengwainton Garden★★, NW : 2 mi – Sancreed - Church★★ (Celtic Crosses★★) - Carn Euny★, W : 3.5 mi by A 30 Z – St Michael's Mount★★ (≤★★), E : 4 mi by B 3311 - Y - and A 30 – Gulval★ (Church★), NE : 1 mi - Ludgvan★ (Church★), NE : 3.5 mi by A 30 - Chysauster Village★, N : 3.5 mi by A 30, B 3311 and minor rd – Newlyn★ - Pilchard Works★, SW : 1.5 mi by B 3315 Z - Lanyon Quoit★, NW : 3.5 mi by St Clare Street – Men-an-Tol★, NW : 5 mi by B 3312 - Madron Church★, NW : 1.5 mi by St Clare Street Y. Morvah (≤★★), NW : 6.5 mi by St Clare Street Y – Zennor (Church★), NW : 6 mi by B 3311 Y – Prussia Cove★, E : 8 mi by B 3311 - Y - and A 394 – Land's End★ (cliff scenery★★★), SW : 10 mi by A 30 Z – Porthcurno★, SW : 8.5 mi by A 30, B 3283 and minor rd

Hotel Penzance

Britons Hill ✉ TR18 3AE – (01736) 363 117 – www.hotelpenzance.com – Closed 2-12 January Y**c**

25 rm – †£ 89/165 ††£ 135/205

Rest ***Bay*** – see restaurant listing

Two adjoining Edwardian merchants' houses in a residential street, overlooking the harbour, the bay and St Michael's Mount. Choice of period lounges. Bedrooms range from classical to modern in their styling; four have Juliet balconies.

Abbey

Abbey St ✉ TR18 4AR – (01736) 366 906 – www.theabbeyonline.co.uk – Closed 20-28 December and 4 January-14 February Y**u**

8 rm – †£ 90/140 ††£ 100/200

Rest ***Slipway*** – see restaurant listing

17C townhouse in powder blue, with tranquil walled gardens and distant harbour views. Relaxed, slightly quirky atmosphere with a shabby-chic charm. Lovely antique-filled sitting room and bright, well-kept bedrooms; No.1 is the best.

Chy-An-Mor without rest

15 Regent Terr ✉ TR18 4DW – (01736) 363 441 – www.chyanmor.co.uk – Closed December-February Y**e**

9 rm – †£ 40/45 ††£ 80/95

Georgian townhouse overlooking the promenade; its name meaning 'House of the Sea'. Bedrooms boast lovely soft furnishings; two have 6ft cast iron beds. Airy breakfast room offers homemade muffins, Scotch pancakes and granola sundaes.

Summer House

Cornwall Terr ✉ TR18 4HL – (01736) 363 744 – www.summerhouse-cornwall.com – Closed 3 October-24 March Z**s**

5 rm – †£ 90/150 ††£ 120/150 **Rest** – Menu £ 30

Bright blue Regency townhouse with a Mediterranean-style terraced garden. Spacious yellow lounge has a light, airy feel. Contemporary bedrooms: many with a nautical theme; one with a small seating area. Pleasant dining room with a trompe l'oeil; light suppers during the week, more formal menu at the weekend.

Bay – Hotel Penzance

Britons Hill ✉ TR18 3AE – (01736) 366 890 – www.thebaypenzance.co.uk – Closed 2-12 January Y**c**

Rest – *(bookings essential for non-residents)* Menu £ 18/34

All-day, brasserie-style hotel restaurant, with a small terrace overlooking the harbour. Wide-ranging menus display the odd Asian and Mediterranean influence; dinner is more adventurous. Local produce includes an all-Cornish cheese board.

ENGLAND

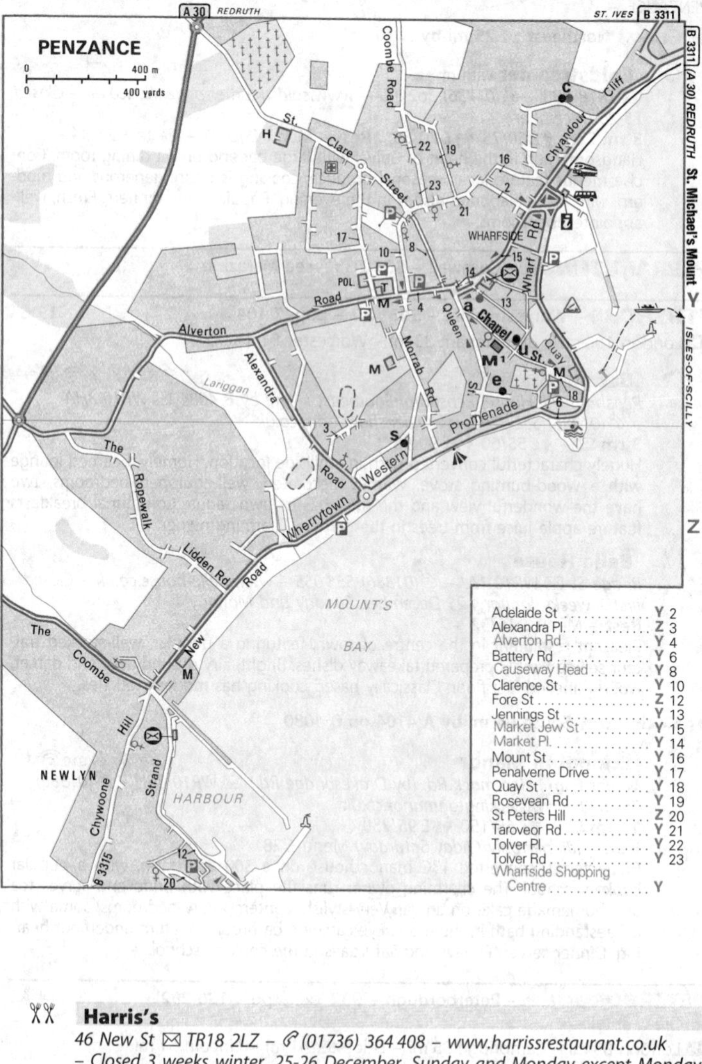

Adelaide St	Y	2
Alexandra Pl.	Z	3
Alverton Rd	Y	4
Battery Rd	Y	6
Causeway Head	Y	8
Clarence St	Y	10
Fore St	Z	12
Jennings St	Y	13
Market Jew St	Y	15
Market Pl.	Y	14
Mount St	Y	16
Penalverne Drive	Y	17
Quay St	Y	18
Rosevean Rd	Y	19
St Peters Hill	Z	20
Taroveor Rd	Y	21
Tolver Pl.	Y	22
Tolver Rd	Y	23
Wharfside Shopping Centre	Y	

ENGLAND

XX **Harris's**

46 New St ✉ TR18 2LZ – ☎ (01736) 364 408 – www.harrissrestaurant.co.uk – Closed 3 weeks winter, 25-26 December, Sunday and Monday except Monday dinner June-September Y**a**

Rest – Carte £ 34/47

Long-standing, split-level restaurant with a spiral staircase and an unusual Welsh black metal plate ceiling; run by a keen husband and wife. Classical cooking uses seasonal Cornish produce; try the steamed lobster when it's in season.

XX **Slipway** – Abbey Hotel

Abbey St ✉ TR18 4AR – ☎ (01736) 333 714 – www.theslipway.co.uk – Closed 20-28 December, 4 January-14 February and lunch Sunday-Monday

Rest – *(booking essential at dinner)* Menu £ 20/30 – Carte £ 19/37 Y**u**

Start with drinks in the rustic bar then head to the stylish restaurant of this town-house hotel. During the day, they serve small plates of world street food; at night, they offer modern British cuisine.

at Gulval Northeast : 1.25 mi by A 30

Coldstreamer with rm

TR18 3BB – (01736) 362 072 – www.coldstreamer-penzance.co.uk – Closed 25-26 December

3 rm – £ 60/75 £ 70/85 **Rest** – Menu £ 15/21 – Carte £ 21/34

Handsome pub in the heart of Gulval with large bar and bright dining room. Concise menus feature local, seasonal produce; cooking is clean, generous and modern, with more elaborate dishes in the evening. Popular wine dinners. Fresh, well-appointed bedrooms.

PERRANUTHNOE – **Cornwall** – **503** D33 – **see Marazion**

PERSHORE – **Worcestershire** – **503** N27 – **pop. 7 104** **19** C3

London 106 mi – Birmingham 33 mi – Worcester 8 mi

Barn without rest

Pensham Hill House, Pensham, Southeast : 1 mi by B 4084 WR10 3HA – (01386) 555 270 – www.pensham-barn.co.uk

3 rm – £ 55/60 £ 90/95

Hugely characterful converted barn in a hillside location. Homely, beamed lounge with a wood-burning stove. Warmly decorated, well-equipped bedrooms; two have the wonderful view and the third has its own sauna. Communal breakfasts feature apple juice from trees in the garden. Charming owner.

Belle House

Bridge St WR10 1AJ – (01386) 555 055 – www.belle-house.co.uk – Closed first 2 weeks January, 25 December, Sunday and Monday

Rest – Menu £ 16/32 **s**

Pleasant restaurant in the centre of town, featuring a popular, well-stocked traiteur selling freshly prepared takeaway dishes. Bright, airy ground floor and darker, wood-panelled first floor. Classically based cooking has modern touches.

at Eckington South : 4 mi by A 4104 on B 4080

Eckington Manor rm,

Manor Farm, Hammock Rd, (by Drakesbridge Rd.) WR10 3BH – (01386) 751 600 – www.eckingtonmanor.co.uk

14 rm – £ 65/150 £ 95/250

Rest – *(dinner only Friday-Saturday)* Menu £ 28

Characterful, converted 13C manor house on a 300 acre farm, with a popular cookery school. The charming owner runs the place with pride and serves tea and homemade cake on arrival. Very stylish, contemporary bedrooms; some with a freestanding bath in the room. Eye-catching bathrooms feature underfloor heating. Dinner served Fridays and Saturdays in the cookery school.

PETERBOROUGH – **Peterborough** – **502** T26 – **pop. 136 292** **14** A2

Great Britain

London 85 mi – Cambridge 35 mi – Leicester 41 mi – Lincoln 51 mi

Bridge St, (01733) 45 23 36, www.visitpeterborough.com

Thorpe Wood, Nene Parkway, (01733) 26 77 01

Peterborough Milton, Milton Ferry, (01733) 38 04 89

Orton Meadows, Ham Lane, (01733) 23 74 78

Cathedral★★ **AC** Y

Clarkes

10 Queen St PE1 1PA – (01733) 892 681 – www.clarkespeterborough.co.uk – Closed first 2 weeks January, lunch 25-26 December, Sunday and Monday

Rest – Menu £ 15 (weekday lunch)/40 Y**x**

Smart restaurant set on a square in the heart of the city. Enjoy a drink in the bar or make for the private courtyard in summer. Cooking is ambitious, modern and seasonal. It's formally run by a husband and wife team.

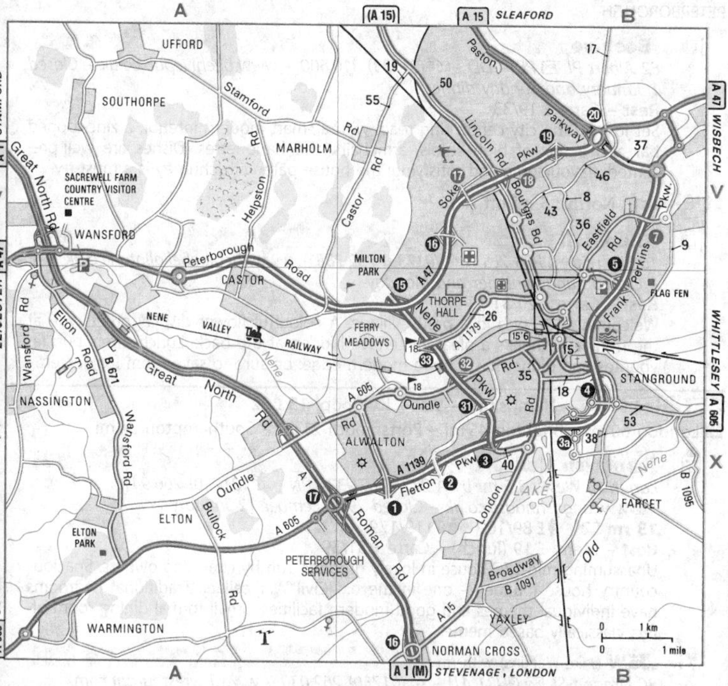

PETERBOROUGH

Bridge St	Z	
Cattle Market Rd	Y	2
Church St	YZ	
City Rd	Y	3
Cowgate	Y	5
Cross St.	Z	6
Dogsthorpe Rd	BV	8
Edgerley Drain Rd	BV	9
Embankment Rd	Z	12
Exchange St	Y	13
Fletton Ave	BX	15
Geneva St	Y	16
Guntons Rd	BV	17
High St	BX	18
Hurn Rd	BV	19
Longthorpe Parkway	BX	26
Long Causeway	Y	25
Market Way	Y	28
Midgate	Y	29
New Rd	BX	35
Park Rd	BV	36
Paston Parkway	BV	37
Peterborough Rd	BX	38
Phorpres Way	BX	40
Queensgate Shopping Centre	Y	
Rivergate	Z	42
Rivergate Shopping Centre	Z	
St Paul's Rd	BV	43
Thorpe Rd	Y	45
Welland Rd	BV	46
Wentworth St	Z	48
Werrington Parkway	BV	50
Wheelyard	Y	52
Whittlesey Rd	BX	53
Woodcroft Rd	BV	55

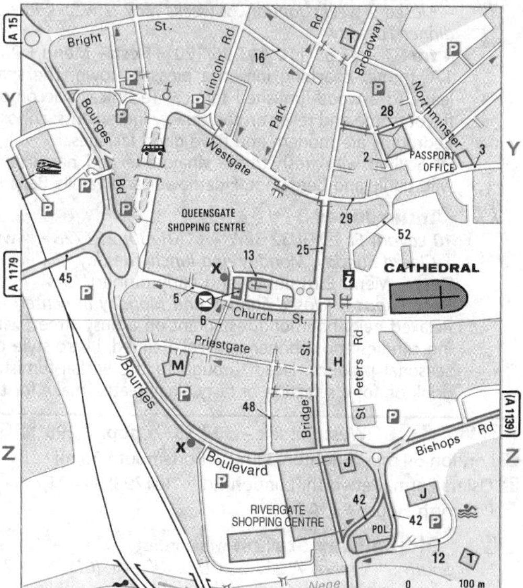

Beehive

62 Albert Pl ✉ PE1 1DD – ✆ (01733) 310 600 – www.beehivepub.co.uk – Closed 1 January and Sunday dinner Zx

Rest – Carte £ 19/33

Set just off the city centre ring road, with a smart modern interior, a zinc-topped bar and a mix of high stools, armchairs and banquettes. Dishes are well-presented, flavoursome and satisfying; the house pâté with chutney is a must-try.

at Glinton North : 5 mi off A 15

Blue Bell N

10 High St ✉ PE6 7LS – ✆ (01733) 252 285 – www.thebluebellglinton.co.uk – Closed Sunday dinner and Monday

Rest – Carte £ 20/31

Welcoming 18C pub in a pretty village. A colourful flower display greets you at the front and there's a pleasant terrace hidden at the back. Lunch offers pub favourites and dinner has a more modern edge; be sure to save room for dessert.

PETERSFIELD – Hampshire – 504 R30 – pop. 13 092 7 C2

London 60 mi – Brighton 45 mi – Portsmouth 21 mi – Southampton 34 mi

Langrish House

Langrish, West : 3.5 mi by A 272 ✉ GU32 1RN – ✆ (01730) 266 941 – www.langrishhouse.co.uk – Closed 29 December-12 January

13 rm – †£ 89/109 ††£ 119/179

Rest – Menu £ 19 (lunch) – Carte £ 31/39

Unassuming mid-17C house in lovely grounds; run by charming owners. Spacious country house lounges – one in the old Civil War cellars. Traditional bedrooms have individual themes and good modern facilities. Small formal dining room offers classically based menus.

JSW (Jake Watkins) with rm

20 Dragon St ✉ GU31 4JJ – ✆ (01730) 262 030 – www.jswrestaurant.com – Closed 2 weeks January, 2 weeks May, 2 weeks July and Sunday dinner-Tuesday

4 rm – †£ 85/110 ††£ 95/120 **Rest** – Menu £ 20 (weekday lunch)/75 **s**

17C former coaching inn, in a pleasant town. The spacious beamed restaurant leads to a wood-furnished terrace. Technically accomplished cooking is refined, flavoursome and relies on top quality ingredients: choose from an array of menus. Bedrooms are modern and have good facilities.

→ Scallop with fresh truffle vinaigrette and nasturtium. Textures of lamb with wild garlic and bergamot. Elderflower and vanilla Bellini.

Annie Jones

10 Lavant St ✉ GU32 3EW – ✆ (01730) 262 728 – www.anniejones.co.uk – Closed Sunday, Monday and lunch Tuesday

Rest – Menu £ 18 (lunch and early dinner)/35 **s**

Rest *Tapas* – *(closed Sunday and Monday in winter)* Carte £ 15/25

Relaxed neighbourhood restaurant on a busy street, with deep red décor, flickering candles and a bohemian feel. Refined, bistro-style cooking uses good quality seasonal produce. Head through to the wicker-furnished terrace and bar for a drink or, for a selection of tasty small plates, make for the tapas bar.

PETWORTH – West Sussex – 504 S31 – pop. 2 298 Great Britain 7 C2

London 54 mi – Brighton 31 mi – Portsmouth 33 mi

Osiers Farm, Petworth, London Rd, ✆ (01798) 34 40 97

Petworth House★★ AC

Old Railway Station without rest

South : 1.5 mi by A 285 ✉ GU28 0JF – ✆ (01798) 342 346 – www.old-station.co.uk – Closed 23-26 December

10 rm – †£ 58/150 ††£ 78/230

The perfect place for train enthusiasts: 8 of the 10 bedrooms are sited in genuine Pullman carriages; wonderfully restored, with impressive marquetry and sited at what was the platform of the station house. Check in at the ticket booth.

ENGLAND

Leconfield
New St ✉ GU28 0AS – ☎ (01798) 345 111 – www.theleconfield.co.uk – Closed Sunday dinner and Monday except bank holidays
Rest – Menu £ 21/29 – Carte £ 31/48
Attractive, red-brick 19C building; inside it resembles a stylish brasserie – tastefully furnished, with a formal restaurant, a timbered first floor dining room and a cobbled courtyard terrace. Concise menu of refined, classic dishes.

Badgers
Coultershaw Bridge, South : 1.5 mi on A 285 ✉ GU28 0JF – ☎ (01798) 342 651 – www.badgerspetworth.co.uk – Closed 25 December
Rest – Carte £ 22/37
Homely pub close to the river, boasting log fires, fresh flowers and candles. Eclectic menus offer robust, flavoursome cooking with international influences. In summer, lobster is a speciality.

at Tillington West : 1 mi on A272

Horse Guards Inn with rm
Upperton Rd ✉ GU28 9AF – ☎ (01798) 342 332 – www.thehorseguardsinn.co.uk – Closed 25 December
3 rm – †£ 85/120 ††£ 85/130 **Rest** – Carte £ 19/38
In an elevated spot in the heart of a quiet village sits this pretty mid-17C inn; which is equally charming on the inside as it is out. Local seafood stands out and some of the vegetables come from their own patch. Young, friendly service. Simple, rustic bedrooms, with a family room in the cottage opposite.

at Halfway Bridge West : 3 mi on A 272 – ✉ Petworth

Halfway Bridge with rm
✉ GU28 9BP – ☎ (01798) 861 281 – www.halfwaybridge.co.uk
7 rm – †£ 80/190 ††£ 120/190 **Rest** – Menu £ 20 – Carte £ 29/50
17C roadside pub with several cosy and wonderfully atmospheric, fire-lit rooms, set on the edge of Cowdray Park. Traditional pub dishes and nursery puddings. Beamed bedrooms are set in converted stables and, like the pub, blend rustic charm with modern fittings and facilities.

PICKERING – North Yorkshire – 502 R21 – pop. 6 616 23 C1

London 237 mi – Middlesbrough 43 mi – Scarborough 19 mi – York 25 mi

White Swan Inn
Market Pl ✉ YO18 7AA – ☎ (01751) 472 288 – www.white-swan.co.uk
21 rm – †£ 105/155 ††£ 139/179 – 2 suites **Rest** – Carte £ 26/44
Well-run former coaching inn, with its bar and lounges decorated in modern hues. Appealing bedrooms boast good mod cons and smart bathrooms; those in the outbuildings have heated stone floors and one even has a bath in the lounge. Brasserie-style restaurant offers classical menus.

17 Burgate without rest
✉ YO18 7AU – ☎ (01751) 473 463 – www.17burgate.co.uk – Closed January and restricted opening in winter
5 rm – †£ 70/120 ††£ 80/120
Restored 17C townhouse with colourful gardens, run by a charming and experienced couple. The lounge boasts an honesty bar and a large inglenook fireplace; the breakfast room has Mackintosh-style chairs. Spacious bedrooms are furnished in a comfy, modern style: two have subtle oriental themes.

Bramwood without rest
19 Hall Garth ✉ YO18 7AW – ☎ (01751) 474 066 – www.bramwoodguesthouse.co.uk – Closed 16 December-1 February
8 rm – †£ 48 ††£ 75/82
Georgian townhouse with pretty gardens, set close to town. Cosy, homely interior with a fire-lit lounge and tea served on arrival. Have breakfast in the large kitchen beside china-filled dressers or in the more formal dining room. Comfy, cottagey bedrooms. The owners go the extra mile to please.

ENGLAND

at Levisham Northeast : 6.5 mi by A 169 – ✉ Pickering

Moorlands Country House
✉ *YO18 7NL – ☎ (01751) 460 229 – www.moorlandslevisham.co.uk – Closed November-April, minimum 2 night stay*
4 rm – ♦£ 90/120 ♦♦£ 140/180 **Rest** – Menu £ 25
19C restored vicarage in the heart of the national park, boasting superb views down the valley. Spacious, well-maintained interior with a classically decorated lounge and flowery wallpapers. Comfortable bedrooms boast rich colour schemes; one has a four-poster bed. Traditional three course dinners. Menu changes daily.

at Sinnington Northwest : 4 mi by A 170 – ✉ York

Fox and Hounds with rm
Main St ✉ YO62 6SQ – ☎ (01751) 431 577 – www.thefoxandhoundsinn.co.uk – Closed 25-27 December
10 rm – ♦£ 59/94 ♦♦£ 70/170 **Rest** – Carte £ 22/43
Pretty 18C inn in a sleepy hamlet, with spacious, homely, individually decorated bedrooms: well-located for visiting the moors. Formal dining room, residents lounge and cosy bar with exposed beams and hanging hop bines. Big portions of proper, hearty, Yorkshire cooking. Service is a strength.

PICKHILL – North Yorkshire – 502 P21 – pop. 412 – ✉ Thirsk 22 B1

London 229 mi – Leeds 41 mi – Middlesbrough 30 mi – York 34 mi

Nags Head Country Inn with rm
✉ *YO7 4JG – ☎ (01845) 567 391 – www.nagsheadpickhill.co.uk – Closed 25 December*
12 rm – ♦£ 50/70 ♦♦£ 60/97 **Rest** – Carte £ 16/32
Quirky pub close to the A1; it has a rustic open-fired bar filled with framed ties and a dining area hung with hunting scenes. Classic dishes are listed on blackboards, alongside local cheeses; game season is the best time to visit, as the owner likes to shoot. Cosy bedrooms are set in the pub and an annexe.

ENGLAND

PIFF'S ELM – Gloucestershire – see Cheltenham

PILLERTON PRIORS – Warwickshire – 503 P27 – pop. 123 – ✉ Stratford-Upon-Avon 19 C3

London 93 mi – Birmingham 43 mi – Liverpool 137 mi – Leeds 141 mi

Fulready Manor without rest
South : 0.75 mi on Halford rd ✉ CV37 7PE – ☎ (01789) 740 152 – www.fulreadymanor.co.uk
3 rm – ♦£ 105/125 ♦♦£ 105/125
Delightful castellated manor house overlooking a lake, in 125 acres of tranquil arable farmland. Spacious, well-appointed lounge with lovely views. Antique-furnished bedrooms – two have four-poster beds and one is located in the tower.

PLUMTREE – Nottinghamshire – see Nottingham

PLYMOUTH – Plymouth – 503 H32 – pop. 255 858 2 C2

London 242 mi – Bristol 124 mi – Southampton 161 mi

Access Tamar Bridge (toll) AY

Plymouth City (Roborough) Airport : ☎ (01752) 204090, N : 3.5 mi by A 386 ABY

to France (Roscoff) (Brittany Ferries) 1-3 daily (6 h) – to Spain (Santander) (Brittany Ferries) 2 weekly (approx 24 h)

3-5 The Barbican, ☎ (01752) 30 63 30, www.visitplymouth.co.uk

Plymouth Mayflower

Staddon Heights, Plymstock, ☎ (01752) 40 24 75

Elfordleigh Hotel G. & C.C., Plympton, Colebrook, ☎ (01752) 34 84 25

Town★ - Smeaton's Tower (<★★) **AC** BZ **T1** – Royal Citadel (ramparts <★★) **AC** BZ – City Museum and Art Gallery★ BZ **M1**

Saltram House★★ **AC**, E : 3.5 mi BY **A** - Tamar River★★ – Anthony House★ **AC**, W : 5 mi by A 374 – Mount Edgcumbe (<★) **AC**, SW : 2 mi by passenger ferry from Stonehouse AZ. NE : Dartmoor National Park★★ – Buckland Abbey★★ **AC**, N : 7.5 mi by A 386 ABY

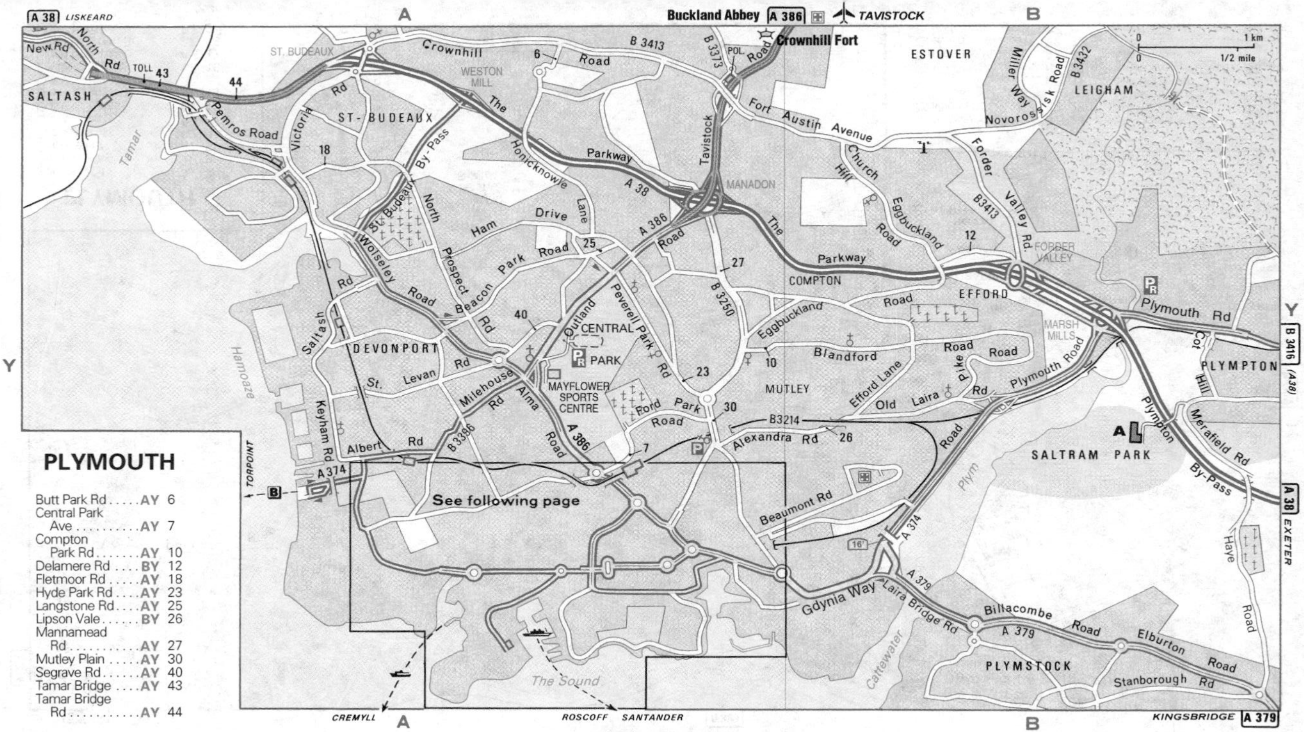
A 38 LISKEARD
A
Buckland Abbey A 386 TAVISTOCK
B
Crownhill Fort
ESTOVER
LEIGHAM
0 1 km
0 1/2 mile
Miller Way
B 3432
Novorossisk Road
New Rd
North Rd
TOLL 43
44
SALTASH
ST. BUDEAUX
Crownhill
6
Road
B 3413
B 3373
POL.
Road
WESTON MILL
St - BUDEAUX
Pemros Road
Victoria Rd
18
Tamar
The Parkway
Honicknowle Lane
Tavistock
MANADON
Fort Austin Avenue
Church Hill
Eggbuckland Road
Forder Valley Rd.
B3413
FORDER VALLEY
St Budeaux By-Pass
North Prospect Rd
Ham Drive
Park Road
25
A 38
A 386
Road
The Parkway
12
27
COMPTON
EFFORD
Wolseley Road
Beacon Park Road
Saltash Rd
DEVONPORT
40
Outland
CENTRAL PARK
Peverell Park Rd
B 3250
Eggbuckland
Road
MARSH MILLS
Plymouth Rd
Y
B 3416 (A38)
Cot Hill
PLYMPTON
Hamoaze
St. Levan Rd
Milehouse Rd
Alma Road
MAYFLOWER SPORTS CENTRE
Ford Park Road
23
30
Blandford
10
MUTLEY
Efford Lane
Old Laira Rd
Pike Road
Plymouth Road
Keyham Rd
Albert Rd
B 3396
A 386
7
Alexandra Rd
B3214
26
Road
SALTRAM PARK
Plympton By-Pass
Merafield Rd
A 374
TORPOINT
B
See following page
Beaumont Rd
Plym
A 374
16'
A 38 EXETER
Haye Road
PLYMOUTH
Gdynia Way
Laira Bridge Rd
A 379
Billacombe Road
A 379
Elburton Road
Stanborough Rd
PLYMSTOCK
Cattewater
The Sound
CREMYLL
ROSCOFF SANTANDER
KINGSBRIDGE A 379

PLYMOUTH

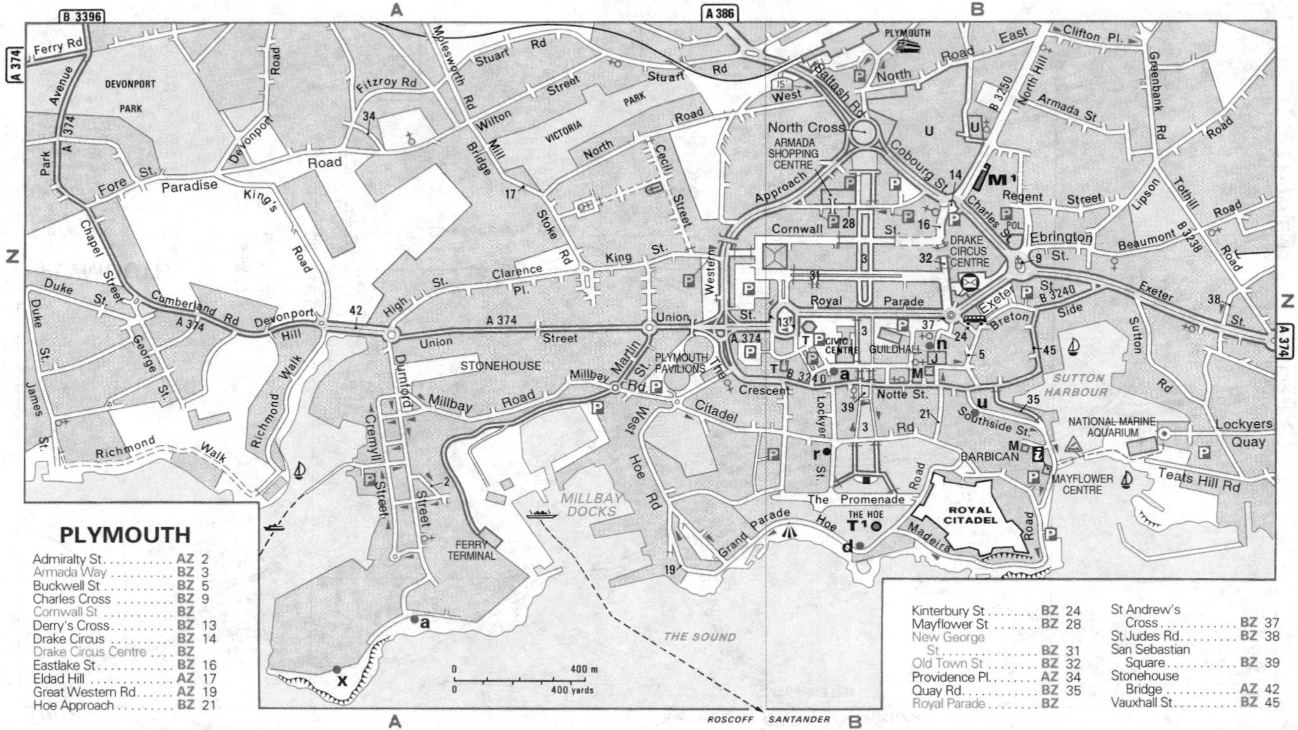

PLYMOUTH

Admiralty St.	AZ	2
Armada Way	BZ	3
Buckwell St.	BZ	5
Charles Cross	BZ	9
Cornwall St	BZ	
Derry's Cross	BZ	13
Drake Circus	BZ	14
Drake Circus Centre	BZ	
Eastlake St.	BZ	16
Eldad Hill	AZ	17
Great Western Rd.	AZ	19
Hoe Approach	BZ	21
Kinterbury St	BZ	24
Mayflower St	BZ	28
New George St.	BZ	31
Old Town St	BZ	32
Providence Pl.	AZ	34
Quay Rd.	BZ	35
Royal Parade	BZ	
St Andrew's Cross	BZ	37
St Judes Rd.	BZ	38
San Sebastian Square	BZ	39
Stonehouse Bridge	AZ	42
Vauxhall St.	BZ	45

Bowling Green without rest
9-10 Osborne Pl, Lockyer St, The Hoe ✉ PL1 2PU – ☎ (01752) 209 090 – www.thebowlingreenplymouth.com BZ**r**
12 rm – ♦£ 50/60 ♦♦£ 75
Georgian terraced house set near the site of the legendary game Drake played while waiting for the Spanish Armada. Comfy lounge-cum-breakfast room and conservatory extension. Simple, high-ceilinged bedrooms; some with views over the Hoe.

Tanners
Prysten House, Finewell St ✉ PL1 2AE – ☎ (01752) 252 001 – www.tannersrestaurant.com – Closed 21 December-12 January, Sunday and Monday BZ**n**
Rest – *(booking essential)* Menu £ 17/20 (weekdays) **s** – Carte £ 34/42 **s**
Hugely characterful building with a modern lounge and decked courtyard; reputedly the oldest house in the city. Stone-faced walls, mullioned windows and an illuminated well feature. Interesting menus have modern touches and personal twists.

Rhodes @ The Dome (N)
Hoe Rd ✉ PL1 2NZ – ☎ (01752) 266 600 – www.rhodesatthedome.co.uk – Closed 25-26 December BZ**d**
Rest – Menu £ 14/17 – Carte £ 19/48
Contemporary restaurant with a stunning panoramic view over Plymouth Sound; start off with a cocktail beneath the vast cupola. The menu offers unfussy, fairly priced brasserie classics; from a burger to a smoked salmon croque monsieur.

Artillery Tower
Firestone Bay ✉ PL1 3QR – ☎ (01752) 257 610 – www.artillerytower.co.uk – Closed Saturday lunch, Sunday and Monday AZ**a**
Rest – *(booking essential at lunch)* Carte £ 25/54
Uniquely set in a 500 year old former defence tower overlooking Plymouth Sound. Circular dining room with exposed stoned walls and traditional furniture and fabrics. Menus offer a concise selection of classically based dishes.

Barbican Kitchen
Black Friars Distillery, 60 Southside St ✉ PL1 2LQ – ☎ (01752) 604 448 – www.barbicankitchen.com – Closed 25-26 December and dinner 31 December BZ**u**
Rest – *(booking advisable)* Menu £ 15 (lunch and early dinner) – Carte £ 18/41 **s**
Informal eatery set in the Plymouth Gin Distillery, comprising two long, narrow rooms with vibrant pink chairs and green banquettes. Brasserie menus offer a good selection of simply cooked dishes, with classic comfort food to the fore.

Chloe's
Gill Akaster House, Princess St ✉ PL1 2EX – ☎ (01752) 201 523 – www.chloesrestaurant.co.uk – Closed 24 December-2 January, Sunday and Monday BZ**a**
Rest – Menu £ 19 (early dinner)/40 – Carte £ 34/46
Friendly neighbourhood restaurant with a small paved terrace, an airy, open-plan interior and a nightly pianist. Cooking is hearty and satisfying, featuring good old French classics; the lunch and early evening menus are good value.

River Cottage Canteen & Deli
No 1 Brew House, Royal William Yard ✉ PL1 3QQ – ☎ (01752) 252 702 – www.rivercottage.net/canteens/plymouth – Closed 25-26 December, Sunday dinner and Monday dinner except in summer AZ**x**
Rest – *(booking essential)* Carte £ 21/34
Large, buzzy restaurant featuring reclaimed wood, exposed stone, a deli and a terrace; set in the old docks and boasting views over the Sound. Appealing menus offer gutsy, satisfying dishes; produce is local, wild, organic and sustainable.

ENGLAND

at Plympton St Maurice East : 6 mi by A 374 on B 3416 - BY - ✉ Plymouth

St Elizabeth's House

Longbrook St ✉ PL7 1NJ – ✆ (01752) 344 840 – www.stelizabeths.co.uk – Closed 24-26 December
14 rm – †£ 89/129 ††£ 99/139 – 1 suite
Rest – Menu £ 12/30 – Carte dinner £ 22/47
Modern, boutique-style hotel – a former convent – with stylish lounge and pewter-topped bar. Good-sized bedrooms offer up-to-date facilities; their stark décor given splashes of colour by eye-catching fabrics. Smart dining room overlooks the garden; classical cooking with a modern twist.

PLYMPTON ST MAURICE Devon – Plymouth – 503 H32 – see Plymouth

---

POLPERRO – Cornwall – 503 G33 – ✉ Looe 1 B2

London 238 mi – Birmingham 223 mi – Bristol 142 mi – Cardiff 173 mi
Village★

Trenderway Farm without rest

Northeast : 2 mi by A 387 ✉ PL13 2LY – ✆ (01503) 272 214 – www.trenderwayfarm.co.uk
7 rm – †£ 95/189 ††£ 95/189
16C farmhouse and outbuildings in 206 acres of working farmland. Well-appointed bedrooms in mix of styles; some with seating areas and kitchenettes. Cream tea on arrival; Aga-cooked breakfasts.

ENGLAND

PONTELAND – Northumberland – 501 O19 – see Newcastle upon Tyne

---

POOLE – Poole – 503 O31 – pop. 144 800 4 C3

London 116 mi – Bournemouth 4 mi – Dorchester 23 mi – Southampton 36 mi
to France (Cherbourg) (Brittany Ferries) 1-2 daily May-October (4 h 15 mn) day (5 h 45 mn) night – to France (St Malo) (Brittany Ferries) daily (8 h) – to France (St Malo) (Condor Ferries Ltd)
Poole Quay, ✆ (01202) 25 32 53, www.pooletourism.com
Parkstone, Links Rd, ✆ (01202) 70 71 38
Bulbury Woods, Lytchett Minster, Bulberry Lane, ✆ (01929) 45 95 74
Town★ (Waterfront **M1** , Scaplen's Court **M2**)
Compton Acres★★, (English Garden ≤★★★) **AC**, SE : 3 mi by B 3369 BX (on Bournemouth town plan) – Brownsea Island★ (Baden-Powell Stone ≤★★) **AC**, by boat from Poole Quay or Sandbanks BX (on Bournemouth town plan)

Plan : see Bournemouth

Hotel du Vin

7-11 Thames St. ✉ BH15 1JN – ✆ (0844) 748 92 65 – www.hotelduvin.com
38 rm – †£ 99/165 ††£ 99/395, £ 13 **a**
Rest *Bistro* – Carte £ 22/40
Strikingly extended Queen Anne property in the heart of the old town. Smart guest areas with eye-catching, wine-themed murals. Stylish, modern bedrooms are named after wine or champagne houses; one boasts an 8ft bed and twin roll-top baths. Local produce features in classical French dishes; 300 bin wine list.

Harbour Heights

Haven Rd, Sandbanks, Southeast : 3 mi by A 35 and B 3369 ✉ BH13 7LW – ✆ (01202) 707 272 – www.harbourheights.com **BXn**
38 rm – †£ 109/189 ††£ 119/199
Rest *Harbar Bistro* – Menu £ 21/30 – Carte £ 28/65
1920s whitewashed hotel, perched on the hillside, overlooking Poole Bay and Brownsea Island; the modern lounge-bar boasts a superb three-tiered terrace which makes the most of the view. Contemporary bedrooms come with good mod cons and smart bathrooms. The open-plan restaurant serves a modern menu.

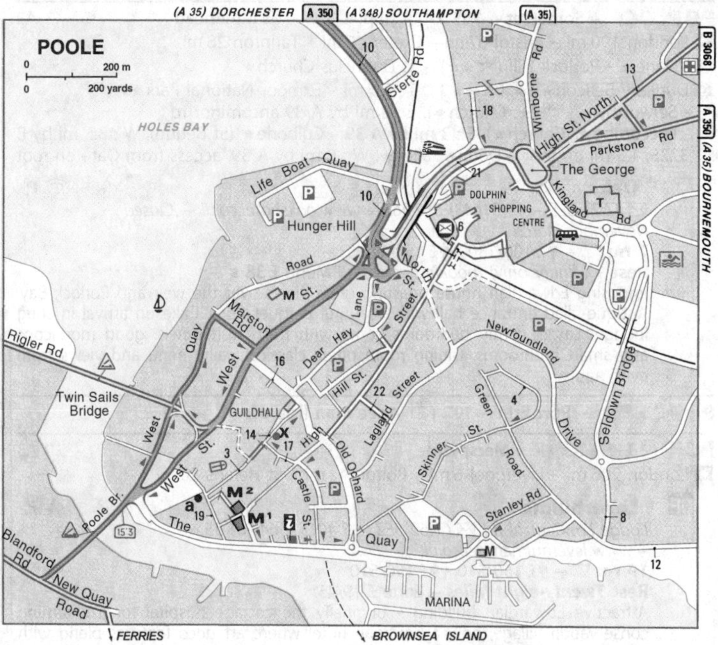

XX **Cafe Shore** Ⓝ

10-14 Banks Rd, Sandbanks, Southeast : 3.5 mi by A 35 and B 3369 ✉ BH13 7QB – ✆ (01202) 707 271 – www.cafeshore.co.uk – Closed 25 December

Rest – Menu £ 15 (weekdays) – Carte £ 25/60 BX**c**

Stylish restaurant on the Sandbanks Peninsula, with a drinks terrace, a trendy lounge-bar and a softly lit dining room offering great views across the harbour. Extensive modern menus lean towards well-executed fresh fish dishes and steaks.

XX **Isabel's**

32 Station Rd, Lower Parkstone ✉ BH14 8UD – ✆ (01202) 747 885 – www.isabelsrestaurant.co.uk – Closed 25-26 December, 1 January, Sunday and Monday BX**a**

Rest – *(dinner only) (booking essential)* Menu £ 24/33 – Carte £ 31/40

Lovingly run restaurant in a former chemist's shop; its old shelving still in situ. Red-hued dining room with booths and banquettes; Mediterranean-style basement room opens onto the garden. Extensive selection of hearty French dishes.

XX **Guildhall Tavern** A/C

15 Market Street ✉ BH15 1NB – ✆ (01202) 671 717 – www.guildhalltavern.co.uk – Closed 1 week January, first two weeks July, 1 week October, Sunday and Monday **x**

Rest – Menu £ 17 (weekday lunch)/25 – Carte £ 28/47

Blue and white French restaurant opposite the Guildhall, in a characterful part of the old town. Bright, cheery interior has a nautical theme; the charming team run monthly gourmet evenings. Tasty, traditional seafood dishes are the draw.

POOLEY BRIDGE – **Cumbria** – **501** L20 – **see Ullswater**

PORLOCK – Somerset – **503** J30 – pop. 1 395 – ⊠ **Minehead** **3** A2

▶ London 190 mi – Bristol 67 mi – Exeter 46 mi – Taunton 28 mi

◉ Village★ - Porlock Hill (← ★★) - St Dubricius Church★

◙ Dunkery Beacon★★★ (← ★★★), S : 5.5 mi – Exmoor National Park★★
- Selworthy★ (← ★★, Church★), E : 2 mi by A 39 and minor rd
- Luccombe★ (Church★), E : 3 mi by A 39 – Culbone★ (St Beuno), W : 3.5 mi by B
3225, 1.5 mi on foot – Doone Valley★, W : 6 mi by A 39, access from Oare on foot

🏠 Oaks ← 🚗 ℀ 🛜 🅿

⊠ TA24 8ES – ℰ (01643) 862 265 – www.oakshotel.co.uk – *Closed November-March*
7 rm ⊵ – ♦£ 100/130 ♦♦£ 150/170
Rest – *(dinner only) (booking essential)* Menu £ 38 **s**
Imposing Edwardian house boasting great views over the weir and Porlock Bay. Antique-filled entrance hall with beautiful parquet floor. Cake on arrival in snug lounge. Large, comfy bedrooms come with fresh fruit bowls, good mod cons and smart bathrooms. Dining room offers classical daily menu and views from every table.

PORT ERIN – Port Erin – **502** F21 – see Man (Isle of)

PORT SUNLIGHT – Merseyside – **502** L23 **20** A3

▶ London 206 mi – Liverpool 6 mi – Bolton 42 mi – St Helens 20 mi

🏨 Leverhulme 🚗 ❤ ℀ 🛜 🏋 🅿

Lodge Ln, Central Rd ⊠ CH62 5EZ – ℰ (0151) 644 66 55
– www.leverhulmehotel.co.uk
19 rm ⊵ – ♦£ 150/510 ♦♦£ 150/510
Rest *Twenty-eight Miles* – Carte £ 19/45
Attractive Edwardian building – originally the cottage hospital for a charming conservation village; now a boutique hotel where art deco features blend with contemporary styling. Well-equipped bedrooms and modern bathrooms. The restaurant serves tapas-style dishes; ingredients are sourced from within 28 miles.

PORT ST MARY – Port Saint Mary – **502** F/G21 – see Man (Isle of)

PORTHLEVEN – Cornwall – pop. 3 190 **1** A3

▶ London 284 mi – Helston 3 mi – Penzance 12 mi

✗✗ Kota with rm 🛜

😊 Harbour Head ⊠ TR13 9JA – ℰ (01326) 562 407 – www.kotarestaurant.co.uk
– *Closed 1 January-10 February, 25-26 December, Sunday and Monday*
2 rm ⊵ – ♦£ 50/70 ♦♦£ 65/90
Rest – *(dinner only)* Menu £ 21 – Carte £ 27/38
Welcoming 18C harbourside granary; its name meaning 'shellfish' in Maori. Cottagey interior with thick stone walls, a tiled floor and a mix of wood furnishings. Menus offer a mix of unfussy and more elaborate dishes, and display subtle Asian influences courtesy of the owner's Chinese and Malaysian background; many of the ingredients are foraged for. Simple bedrooms.

PORTINSCALE – Cumbria – see Keswick

PORTSCATHO – Cornwall – **503** F33 – ⊠ **Truro** **1** B3

▶ London 298 mi – Plymouth 55 mi – Truro 16 mi

◙ St Just-in-Roseland Church★★, W : 4 mi by A 3078 – St Anthony-in-Roseland
(← ★★) S : 3.5 m

🏨 Driftwood 🌊 ← 🚗 ℀ 🛜 🅿

Rosevine, North : 2 mi by A 3078 ⊠ TR2 5EW – ℰ (01872) 580 644
– www.driftwoodhotel.co.uk – *Closed 7 December-6 February*
15 rm ⊵ – ♦£ 145/230 ♦♦£ 190/270
Rest *Driftwood* ❀ – see restaurant listing
Charming clifftop hotel looking out over mature grounds, which stretch down to the shore and a private beach. Stylish, contemporary guest areas are decorated with pieces of driftwood. Smart bedrooms – in the main house and annexed cottages – have a good level of modern facilities; some have decked terraces.

Rosevine

Rosevine, North : 2 mi by A 3078 ✉ TR2 5EW – ✆ (01872) 580 206 – www.rosevine.co.uk – Closed January

15 suites – ††£ 135/385, ☕ £ 10

Rest – *(closed Sunday dinner October-May) (bar lunch) (bookings essential for non-residents)* Menu £ 25/32 – Carte £ 26/46

Dramatically refurbished and extended country house overlooking the sea. Cool, contemporary, neutrally hued inner. Stylish, modern bedrooms boast kitchenettes. Strongly family orientated services; kids have their own lounge. All-day brasserie uses local produce.

Driftwood – Driftwood Hotel

Rosevine, North : 2 mi by A 3078 ✉ TR2 5EW – ✆ (01872) 580 644 – www.driftwoodhotel.co.uk – Closed 7 December-6 February

Rest – *(dinner only) (booking essential)* Menu £ 50/85

Bright, New England style restaurant in an attractive house in a peaceful clifftop setting; it's delightfully run by a friendly, efficient team and boasts superb views out to sea. Unfussy, modern, seasonally pertinent dishes display technical adroitness and feature excellent flavour and texture combinations.

→ Poached ray wing, cucumber nori, white radish and spiced cuttlefish consommé. Hake with lobster tortellini, braised fennel, barbecue mussels and seaweed. Spiced pineapple, toasted coconut meringue, lemongrass and lime sorbet.

PORTSMOUTH and SOUTHSEA – Portsmouth – 503 Q31 — 6 B3

– **pop. 207 461** Great Britain

London 78 mi – Brighton 48 mi – Salisbury 44 mi – Southampton 21 mi

to the Isle of Wight (Ryde) (Wightlink Ltd) frequent services daily (15 mn) – from Southsea to the Isle of Wight (Ryde) (Hovertravel Ltd) frequent services daily (10 mn)

to France (St Malo) (Brittany Ferries) daily (8 h 45 mn) day (10 h 45 mn) night – to France (Caen) (Brittany Ferries) 2-4 daily (6 h) day (6 h 45 mn) night – to France (Cherbourg) (Brittany Ferries) 2 daily (5 h) day, (7 h) night – to France (Le Havre) (LD Lines) daily (5 h 30 mn/7 h 30 mn) – to France (Cherbourg) (Brittany Ferries) 1-2 daily (2 h 45 mn) – to France (Caen) (Brittany Ferries) 2-4 daily (3 h 45 mn) – to Spain (Bilbao) (P & O European Ferries Ltd) 1-2 weekly (35 h) – to Guernsey (St Peter Port) and Jersey (St Helier) (Condor Ferries Ltd) daily except Sunday (10 hrs) – to the Isle of Wight (Fishbourne) (Wightlink Ltd) frequent services daily (35 mn)

Southsea, ✆ (023) 9282 67 22, www.visitportsmouth.co.uk

Southsea, Burrfields Rd, ✆ (023) 9266 86 67

Crookhorn Lane, Waterlooville, Widley, ✆ (023) 9237 22 10

Southwick Park, Southwick, Pinsley Drive, ✆ (023) 9238 01 31

City★ – Naval Portsmouth BY : H.M.S. Victory★★★ **AC**, The Mary Rose★★, National Museum of the Royal Navy★★ **AC** – Old Portsmouth★ BYZ : The Point (≤★★) - St Thomas Cathedral★ – Southsea (Castle★ **AC**) AZ – Royal Marines Museum, Eastney★ **AC**, AZ **M1**

Portchester Castle★ **AC**, NW : 5.5 mi by A 3 and A 27 AY

Plans pages 574, 575

Clarence without rest

Clarence Rd, Southsea ✉ PO5 2LQ – ✆ (023) 9287 6348 – www.theclarencehotel.co.uk – Closed 24 December-10 January AZ**c**

8 rm ☕ – †£ 95/225 ††£ 95/245

Red-brick, bay windowed house a short walk from the sea. Variously sized bedrooms feature contemporary décor, a good level of facilities, superb modern bathrooms and pleasing extra touches.

Retreat without rest

35 Grove Rd South, Southsea ✉ PO5 3QS – ✆ (023) 9235 3701 – www.theretreatguesthouse.co.uk CZ**e**

4 rm ☕ – †£ 85/105 ††£ 85/105

Grade II listed Arts and Crafts house not far from the university; built for the local mayor in 1889. Original terrazzo floors and stained glass windows. Relaxed, spacious inner with stylish, understated décor. One four-poster room.

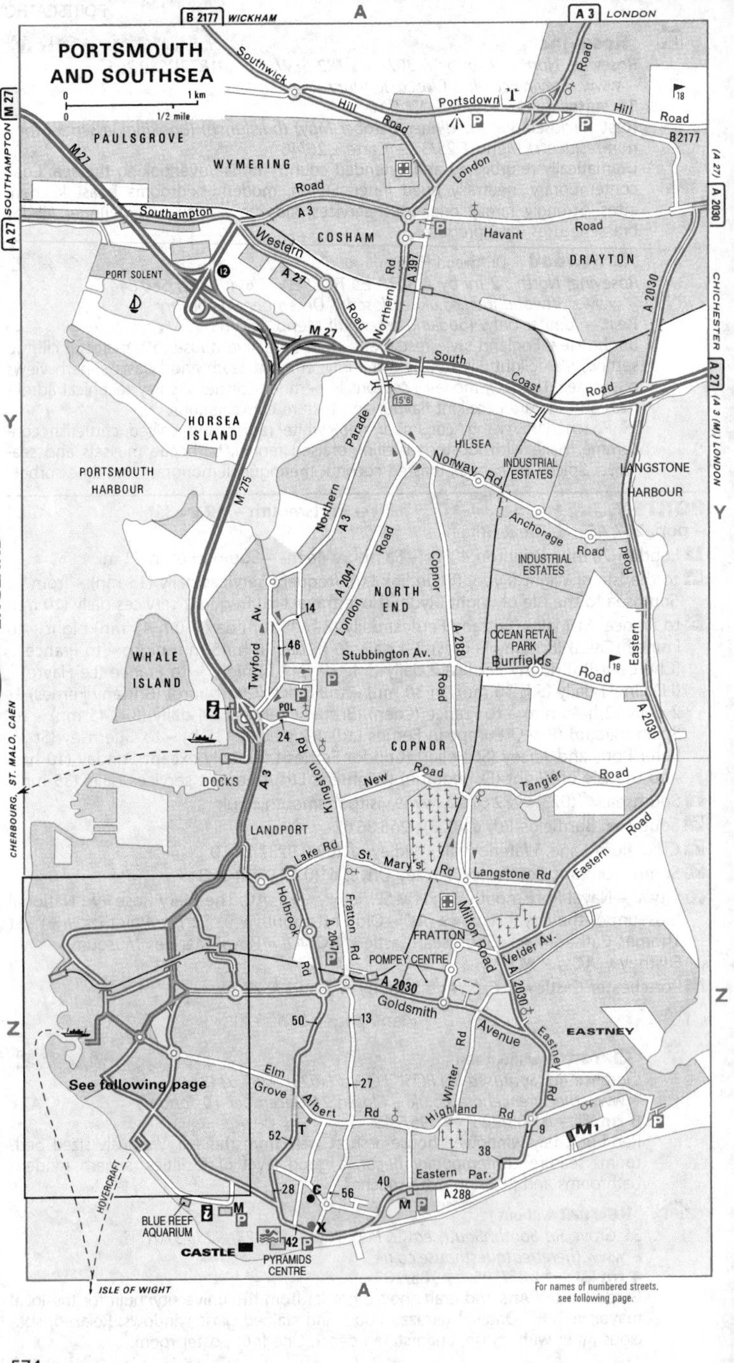
PORTSMOUTH AND SOUTHSEA
0 1 km
0 1/2 mile
B 2177 WICKHAM
A 3 LONDON
A 27 SOUTHAMPTON M 27
(A 27) A 2030 CHICHESTER
A 27 (A 3 (M)) LONDON
PAULSGROVE
WYMERING
COSHAM
DRAYTON
PORT SOLENT
HORSEA ISLAND
PORTSMOUTH HARBOUR
WHALE ISLAND
HILSEA
INDUSTRIAL ESTATES
LANGSTONE HARBOUR
NORTH END
OCEAN RETAIL PARK
COPNOR
DOCKS
LANDPORT
FRATTON
POMPEY CENTRE
EASTNEY
See following page
BLUE REEF AQUARIUM
CASTLE
PYRAMIDS CENTRE
HOVERCRAFT
ISLE OF WIGHT
CHERBOURG, ST. MALO, CAEN
Southwick Hill Road
Portsdown Hill Road
London Road
Southampton Road
Western Road
Havant Road
Northern Rd
A 397
South Coast Road
Northern Parade
Norway Rd.
Anchorage Road
London Road
A 2047
Copnor Road
A 288
Twyford Av.
Stubbington Av.
Burrfields Road
Eastern Road
A 2030
New Road
Tangier Road
Kingston Rd
Lake Rd
St. Mary's Rd
Langstone Rd
Holbrook Rd
Fratton Rd
Milton Road
Velder Av.
Goldsmith Avenue
Eastney Rd
Winter Rd
Elm Grove
Albert Rd
Highland Rd
Eastern Par.
POL
M1
For names of numbered streets, see following page.

ENGLAND

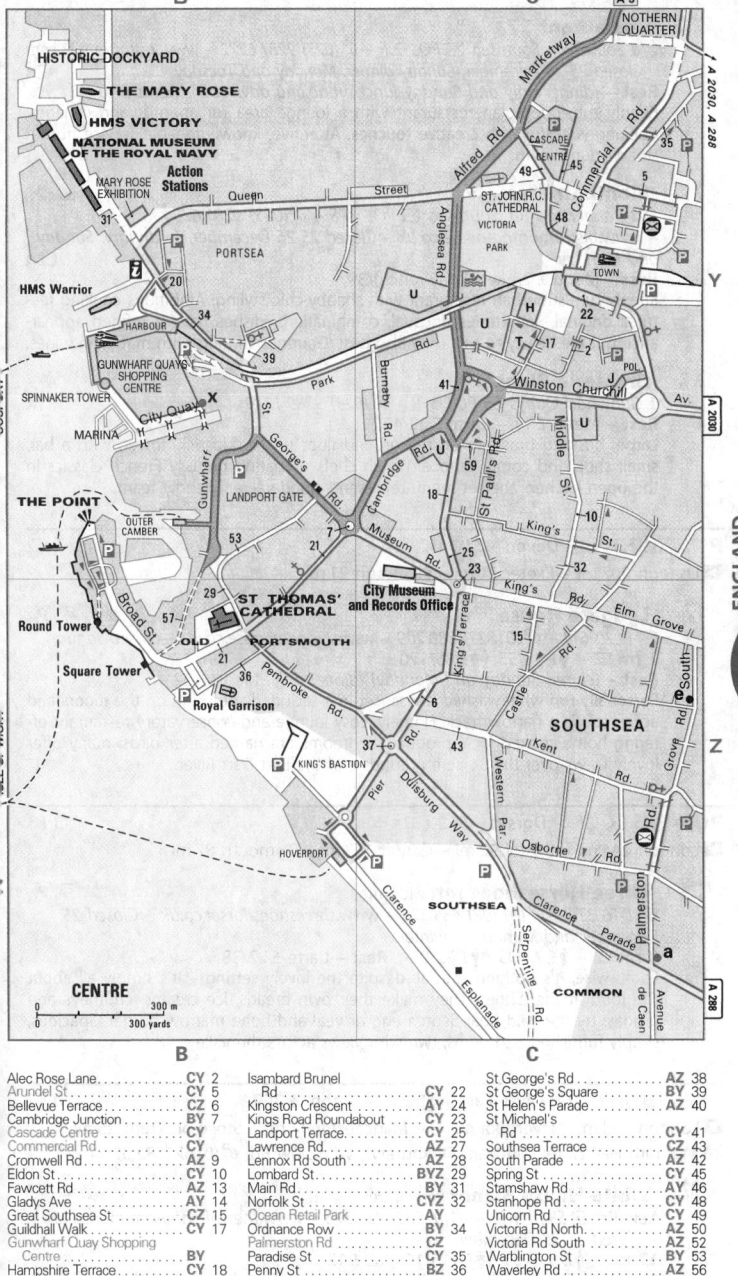

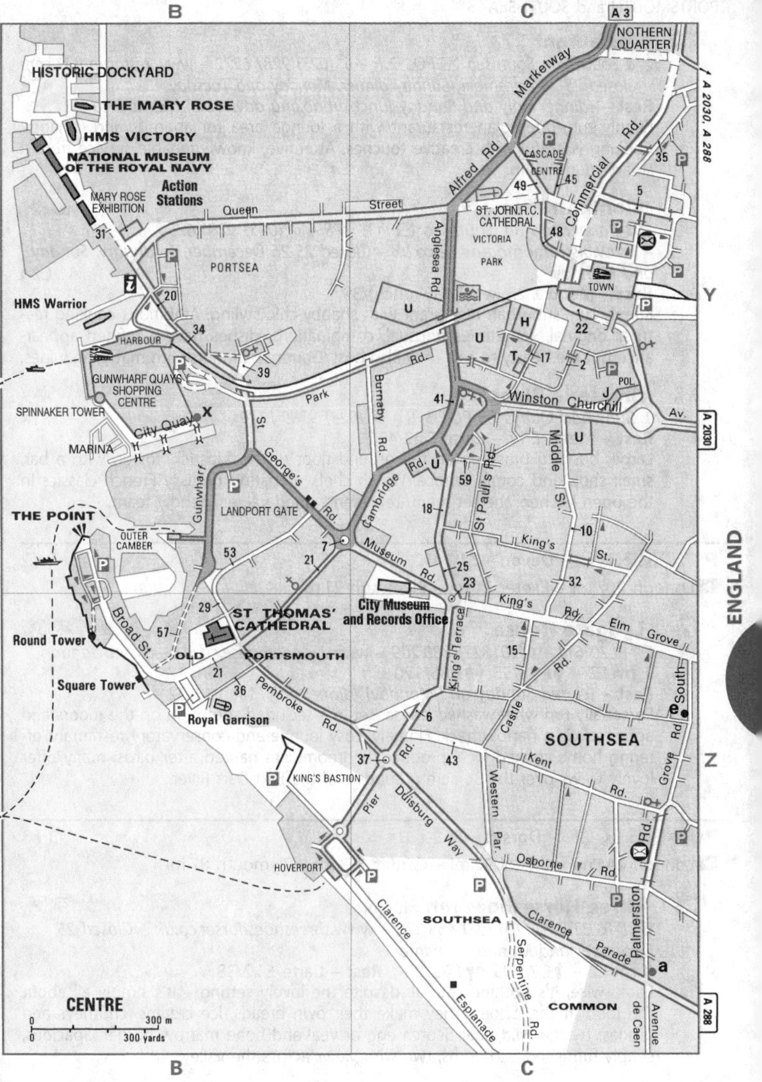

Alec Rose Lane	CY	2
Arundel St	CY	5
Bellevue Terrace	CZ	6
Cambridge Junction	BY	7
Cascade Centre	CY	
Commercial Rd	CY	
Cromwell Rd	AZ	9
Eldon St	CY	10
Fawcett Rd	AZ	13
Gladys Ave	AY	14
Great Southsea St	CZ	15
Guildhall Walk	CY	17
Gunwharf Quay Shopping Centre	BY	
Hampshire Terrace	CY	18
Hard (The)	BY	20
High St	BYZ	21
Isambard Brunel Rd	CY	22
Kingston Crescent	AY	24
Kings Road Roundabout	CY	23
Landport Terrace	CY	25
Lawrence Rd	AZ	27
Lennox Rd South	AZ	28
Lombard St	BYZ	29
Main Rd	BY	31
Norfolk St	CYZ	32
Ocean Retail Park	AY	
Ordnance Row	BY	34
Palmerston Rd	CZ	
Paradise St	CY	35
Penny St	BZ	36
Pier Road Roundabout	CZ	37
Pompey Centre	AZ	
St George's Rd	AZ	38
St George's Square	BY	39
St Helen's Parade	AZ	40
St Michael's Rd	CY	41
Southsea Terrace	CZ	43
South Parade	AZ	42
Spring St	CY	45
Stamshaw Rd	AY	46
Stanhope Rd	CY	48
Unicorn Rd	CY	49
Victoria Rd North	AZ	50
Victoria Rd South	AZ	52
Warblington St	BY	53
Waverley Rd	AZ	56
White Hart Rd	BYZ	57
Wiltshire St	CY	59

XX **Restaurant 27**

27a South Par, Southsea ✉ PO5 2JF – ✆ (023) 9287 6272 – www.restaurant27.com – Closed 25-26 December, Sunday dinner, Monday and Tuesday AZ**x**

Rest – *(dinner only and Sunday lunch) (booking advisable)* Menu £ 40

Keenly run, open-plan restaurant with a lounge area for aperitifs and canapés. Cooking is skilful with creative touches. Attentive, knowledgeable service from a smart young team.

XX **Montparnasse**

103 Palmerston Rd, Southsea ✉ PO5 3PS – ✆ (023) 9281 6754 – www.bistromontparnasse.co.uk – Closed 25-26 December, 1 January, Sunday and Monday CZ**a**

Rest – Menu £ 22 (weekday lunch)/39

Keenly run, suburban restaurant with shabby-chic styling. Ambitious cooking features original, sometimes unusual, combinations; dishes have a refined appearance but are hearty to eat. They also host 'Gourmet' dinners with matching wines.

XX **Brasserie Blanc**

1 Gunwharf Quays ✉ PO1 3FR – ✆ (023) 9289 1320 BY**x**

Rest – Menu £ 17 – Carte £ 22/43

Large, bustling brasserie on the ground floor of the 'Lipstick' tower, with a bar, small shop and comfy terrace. Watch chefs preparing unfussy French classics in the open kitchen: the set menu represents good value. Friendly team.

ENGLAND

POSTBRIDGE – Devon – 503 I32 — 2 C2

London 207 mi – Exeter 21 mi – Plymouth 21 mi

Lydgate House

✉ PL20 6TJ – ✆ (01822) 880 209 – www.lydgatehouse.co.uk – Closed January

7 rm – †£ 43/55 ††£ 85/120

Rest – *(closed Sunday and Monday) (dinner only)* Menu £ 22

Personally run whitewashed house, set in a secluded spot high on the moors and accessed via a narrow track. Homely, cosy lounge and conservatory restaurant offering home-cooked local produce. Bedrooms are named after birds; many offer lovely views over the 36 acre grounds and the East Dart River.

POWERSTOCK – Dorset – 503 L31 — 3 B3

London 144 mi – Bristol 92 mi – Cardiff 113 mi – Plymouth 87 mi

Three Horseshoes Inn with rm

✉ DT6 3TF – ✆ (01308) 485 328 – www.threeshoesdorset.co.uk – Closed 25 December and Monday in winter

3 rm – †£ 75/95 ††£ 75/95 **Rest** – Carte £ 22/38

Looks-wise, it's nothing special, despite the lovely setting – it's simply all about the food at the 'Shoes. They make their own breads, ice creams, chutneys and pickles; try the wild boar Scotch egg or veal and bone marrow burger. Spacious, simply furnished bedrooms; two with views across the valley.

PRESTBURY – Cheshire East – 502 N24 – pop. 3 269 — 20 B3

London 184 mi – Liverpool 43 mi – Manchester 17 mi – Stoke-on-Trent 25 mi

Mottram Hall Hotel, Mottram St Andrews, Wilmslow Rd, ✆ (01625) 82 00 64

White House Manor without rest

New Rd ✉ SK10 4HP – ✆ (01625) 829 376 – www.thewhitehousemanor.co.uk – Closed 25-26 December

12 rm – †£ 85/105 ††£ 115/150, £ 12

Attractive Georgian house with mature lawned garden and sheltered terrace. Nicely furnished lounge boasts an honesty bar. Beautifully appointed bedrooms display quality furnishings; Crystal has a four-poster and a feature bathroom.

PRESTON CANDOVER – Hampshire – 504 Q30 6 B2

London 59 mi – Croydon 67 mi – Barnet 72 mi – Ealing 54 mi

Purefoy Arms

Alresford Rd ✉ RG25 2EJ – ✆ (01256) 389 777 – www.thepurefoyarms.co.uk – Closed 26 December, 1 January, Sunday dinner and Monday

Rest – Menu £ 18 (weekday lunch) – Carte £ 23/33

Dating from the 1860s, this once crumbling pub was thoughtfully restored and is run by a charming, young but experienced couple. There are hints of Spain on the menu, especially in the bar nibbles; prices are very competitive and the focus is on flavour.

PRESTWICH – Greater Manchester – 503 N23 – see Manchester

PULHAM MARKET – Norfolk – 504 X26 – pop. 919 – ✉ Diss 15 C2

London 106 mi – Cambridge 58 mi – Ipswich 29 mi – Norwich 16 mi

Old Bakery without rest

Church Walk ✉ IP21 4SL – ✆ (01379) 676 492 – www.theoldbakery.net – Closed Christmas-New Year

5 rm – ♦£ 60/80 ♦♦£ 80/95

Pretty 16C former bakery just off the village green. Characterful interior features exposed beams and inglenooks: homely lounge and breakfast room; good-sized bedrooms with modern facilities. Don't miss the 'baker's breakfast'.

PURTON – Wiltshire – 503 O29 – pop. 3 328 – ✉ Swindon 4 D2

London 94 mi – Bristol 41 mi – Gloucester 31 mi – Oxford 38 mi

Pear Tree at Purton

Church End, South : 0.5 mi by Church St on Lydiard Millicent rd ✉ SN5 4ED – ✆ (01793) 772 100 – www.peartreepurton.co.uk – Closed 26 December

17 rm – ♦£ 119/149 ♦♦£ 119/149 – 2 suites **Rest** – Menu £ 23/36 **s**

Heavily extended, personally run, 16C vicarage in 7 acres of grounds, which include mature gardens and a vineyard used for making their own wine. Comfortably and traditionally furnished throughout; some bedrooms have balconies or terraces. Conservatory offers a classical menu and garden views.

RADNAGE – Buckinghamshire – see Stokenchurch

RAINHAM – Medway – 504 U29 9 C1

London 14 mi – Basildon 16 mi – Dartford 9 mi

Barn

507 Lower Rainham Rd, North : 1.75 mi by Station Rd ✉ ME8 7TN – ✆ (01634) 361 363 – www.thebarnrestaurant.co.uk – Closed 25-26 December, 1 January, Saturday lunch, Sunday dinner, Monday and bank holidays

Rest – Menu £ 25 (weekday lunch) **s** – Carte £ 35/48 **s**

Black and white timbered, 18C Essex barn, reconstructed on this site. Heavily beamed, rustic dining room and upstairs lounge. Good choice of frequently changing menus. Elaborate seasonal cooking comes in generous portions.

RAMSBOTTOM – Greater Manchester – 502 N23 – pop. 17 352 20 B2

London 223 mi – Blackpool 39 mi – Burnley 12 mi – Leeds 46 mi

ramsons

18 Market Pl ✉ BL0 9HT – ✆ (01706) 825 070 – www.ramsons-restaurant.com – Closed 1 January, 26 December, Sunday dinner, Monday and lunch Tuesday

Rest – *(booking essential)* Menu £ 20 (dinner) – Carte £ 25/45

Intimate, two-roomed restaurant run by passionate owner. Array of menus includes 6 and 10 course tasting options. Clean, refined, Italian-influenced cooking mixes quality local and imported produce.

ENGLAND

Sanmini's
7 Carrbank Lodge, Ramsbottom Ln ✉ BL0 9DJ – ✆ (01706) 821 831 – www.sanminis.com – Closed Monday
Rest – *(dinner only and Sunday lunch) (booking essential)* Menu £ 18 (weekdays)/35 – Carte £ 16/31
Charming little restaurant in Victorian gatehouse. Neatly presented, authentic south Indian dishes with gentle spicing; every one is made from scratch. Family are doctors, so it's healthy too.

Hearth of the Ram N
13 Peel Brow ✉ BL0 0AA – ✆ (01706) 828 681 – www.hearthoftheram.com
Rest – Carte £ 15/35
Rustic former pub with characterful original features, a friendly team and a laid-back feel. The experienced chef offers a good value menu – choose from enticing pies and platters during the day and more sophisticated dishes in the evening. Cooking is classically based but has a light, modern touch.

RAMSBURY – Wiltshire – 503 P29 – pop. 1 540 — 4 D2

London 73 mi – Bristol 53 mi – Cardiff 86 mi – Plymouth 172 mi

Bell with rm
The Square ✉ SN8 2PE – ✆ (01672) 520 230 – www.thebellramsbury.com – Closed 25 December
9 rm – †£ 110/150 ††£ 110/150
Rest – Menu £ 19 (weekday lunch)/25 – Carte £ 25/37
Charming 16C pub with stylish, well-appointed bedrooms. Dine on pub favourites among hop-covered beams in the bar or sit on smart tartan banquettes in the crisply laid dining room and choose from more ambitious, accomplished dishes. 'Café Bella' is a popular spot with the locals.

RAMSEY – Ramsey – 502 G21 – see Man (Isle of)

RAMSGATE – Kent – 504 Y30 – pop. 37 967 — 9 D1

London 77 mi – Southend-on-Sea 89 mi – Ipswich 128 mi

Age & Sons
Charlotte Ct ✉ CT11 8HE – ✆ (01843) 851 515 – www.ageandsons.co.uk – Closed 2-16 January, Sunday dinner and Monday except lunch on bank holidays when closed Tuesday
Rest – Menu £ 13/16 (weekdays) – Carte £ 21/37
Attractive converted wine warehouse in centre of town. Sexy basement bar; rustic ground floor café; more formal 1st floor restaurant and lovely terrace. Interesting modern menu of gutsy, flavourful cooking. Charming service.

RAMSGILL-IN-NIDDERDALE – North Yorkshire – 502 O21 – see Pateley Bridge

RAVENSTONEDALE – Cumbria – 502 M20 – pop. 886 — 21 B2

London 272 mi – Bristol 247 mi – Cardiff 268 mi – Plymouth 361 mi

Black Swan
✉ CA17 4NG – ✆ (01539) 623 204 – www.blackswanhotel.com
15 rm – †£ 55/125 ††£ 75/125 **Rest** – Menu £ 15/17 – Carte £ 20/35
Set in a rural village, a part-Victorian, family-run inn with a huge garden and a babbling beck. Cosy, antique-furnished bedrooms; Room 15 is the best, with its four-poster, wood-burning stove and roll-top bath. Menus feature filling pub classics, supplemented by restaurant-style specials in the evening.

King's Head with rm
✉ CA17 4NH – ✆ (01539) 623 050 – www.kings-head.com – Closed 25 December
6 rm – †£ 65/75 ††£ 80/98 **Rest** – Carte £ 20/33
Whitewashed inn consisting of four 17C cottages; its smart interior featuring polished timbers, a flagged floor and a wood-burning stove. Well-prepared, appealingly presented, tasty dishes; eat in the garden, with a view of the babbling beck. Comfortable, elegant bedrooms.

ENGLAND

READING - Reading - 503 Q29 - pop. 232 662 11 C3

London 43 mi - Brighton 79 mi - Bristol 78 mi - Croydon 47 mi
Access Whitchurch Bridge (toll)
to Henley-on-Thames (Salter Bros. Ltd) (summer only)
Calcot Park, Calcot, Bath Rd, (0118) 942 71 24

Plan on next page

Forbury
rm, rest,
26 The Forbury RG1 3EJ - (0118) 952 77 70 - www.theforburyhotel.co.uk
23 rm - £ 174/234 £ 246/306 Y**c**
Rest *Cerise* - Carte £ 29/46
Former civic hall overlooking Forbury Square Gardens; now a very stylish town house hotel. Eye-catching artwork features in all the stunningly individualistic bedrooms. Stylish basement cocktail bar/restaurant where clean, crisp, modern cooking holds sway.

Malmaison
rm,
Great Western House, 18-20 Station Rd RG1 1JX - (0118) 956 23 00 - www.malmaison.com Y**e**
75 rm - £ 89/250 £ 89/250, £ 16
Rest *Brasserie* - Menu £ 16/20 - Carte £ 26/63
Converted railway hotel with stylish lounges, rich contemporary décor and a funky feel. Named after famous trains, smart bedrooms display bold colours, a high level of facilities and quirky touches; one even has its own train set. Informal brasserie features exposed pipework and a glass-fronted wine cellar.

Holiday Inn
rm,
Wharfedale Rd, Winnersh Triangle, Southeast : 4.5 mi by A 4 and A 3290 off Winnerish rd RG41 5TS - (0118) 944 04 44 - www.meridianleisurehotels.com/reading
174 rm - £ 49/189 £ 49/189
Rest *Caprice* - (0118) 944 42 18 - Menu £ 19/23 - Carte £ 28/42
Modern, purpose-built hotel, conveniently located for the M4. Spacious, open-plan guest areas, smart function facilities and a well-equipped leisure club. Uniform bedrooms come with good facilities and compact, up-to-date bathrooms. Snacks served in the lounge; split-level brasserie offers an extensive menu.

Beech House without rest
60 Bath Rd RG30 2AY - (0118) 959 19 01 - www.beechhousehotel.com
15 rm - £ 75/95 £ 85/105 X**a**
Red-brick Victorian house with slightly Gothic exterior. Neat garden, terrace and summer house. Traditionally furnished throughout, with antiques and period ornaments. Pleasant, well-equipped bedrooms.

Forbury's
1 Forbury Sq RG1 3BB - (0118) 957 40 44 - www.forburys.co.uk - Closed 26-27 December, 1-2 January and Sunday Y**a**
Rest - Menu £ 14/39 - Carte £ 25/51
In a city centre square near the law courts, with a pleasant terrace, a leather-furnished bar-lounge and a smart, spacious dining room decorated with wine paraphernalia. Menus offer French-inspired dishes. Popular monthly wine events.

London Street Brasserie
2-4 London St RG1 4PN - (0118) 950 50 36 - www.londonstbrasserie.co.uk - Closed 25 December Z**c**
Rest - *(booking essential)* Menu £ 16/36 - Carte £ 28/47
Intimate 200 year old building which was once a post office; the two decked terraces and some of the first floor tables overlook the River Kennett. The extensive menu offers something for everyone and dishes are stout and satisfying.

Enjoy good food without spending a fortune! Look out for the Bib Gourmand symbol to find restaurants offering good food at special prices!

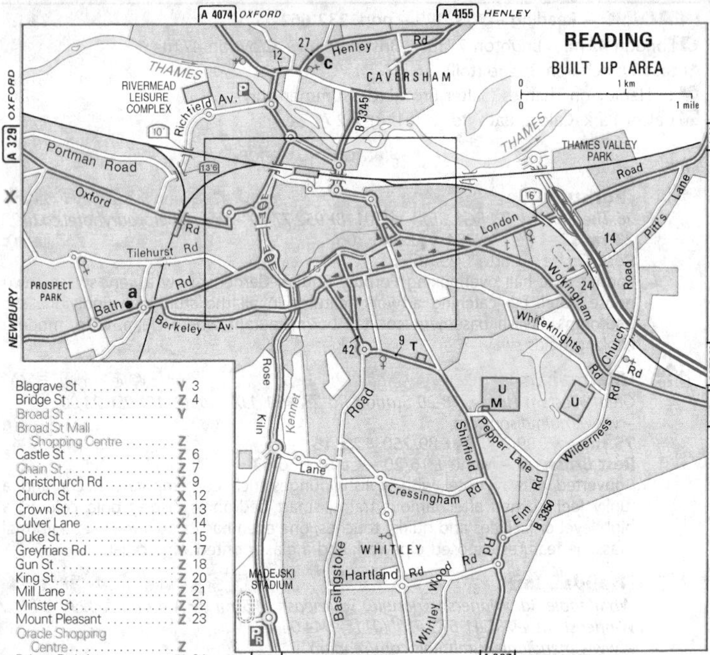

- Blagrave St . . . . Y 3
- Bridge St . . . . Z 4
- Broad St . . . . Y
- Broad St Mall Shopping Centre . . . . Z
- Castle St . . . . Z 6
- Chain St. . . . . Z 7
- Christchurch Rd . . . . X 9
- Church St . . . . X 12
- Crown St. . . . . Z 13
- Culver Lane . . . . X 14
- Duke St . . . . Z 15
- Greyfriars Rd. . . . . Y 17
- Gun St . . . . Z 18
- King St . . . . Z 20
- Mill Lane . . . . Z 21
- Minster St . . . . Z 22
- Mount Pleasant . . . . Z 23
- Oracle Shopping Centre . . . . Z
- Palmer Park Ave. . . . . X 24
- Prospect St. . . . . X 27
- Queen Victoria St. . . . . Y 28
- St Mary's Butts. . . . . Z 29
- Station Hill. . . . . Y 30
- Station Rd . . . . Y 31
- Tilehurst Rd . . . . Z 33
- Tudor Rd . . . . Y 34
- Valpy St . . . . Y 37
- Watlington St. . . . . Z 40
- West St . . . . Y 41
- Whitley St . . . . X 42

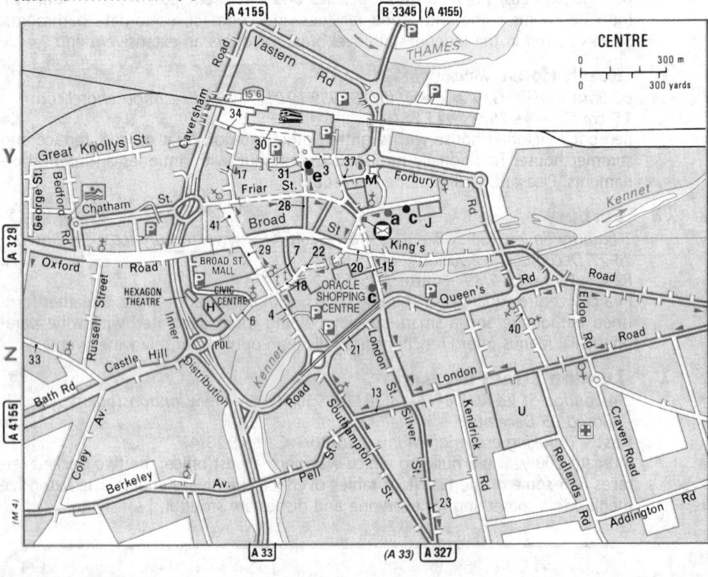

at Sonning-on-Thames Northeast : 4.25 mi by A 4 on B 4446

French Horn with rm

✉ RG4 6TN – ✆ (0118) 969 22 04 – *www.thefrenchhorn.co.uk* – *Closed 1-3 January and dinner 25-26 December*
21 rm – †£ 125/170 ††£ 160/215 – 4 suites
Rest – *(booking essential)* Menu £ 27 (weekdays) – Carte £ 35/70 **s**
Beautifully located on a bank of the Thames fringed with weeping willows; splendid rear terrace. Formal dining room with delightful view of the river and gardens offers classical menu of dishes from yesteryear; a gueridon trolley adds to the theatre. Cosy, traditionally decorated bedrooms; some in an annexe.

at Shinfield South : 4.25 mi on A 327 - X – ✉ Reading

L'Ortolan

Church Ln ✉ *RG2 9BY* – ✆ *(0118) 988 85 00* – *www.lortolan.com* – *Closed 25 December-3 January, Sunday and Monday*
Rest – Menu £ 28/71
Beautiful, red-brick former vicarage with stylish, modern décor, several private dining rooms and a conservatory-lounge overlooking a lovely garden. Cooking is confident and passionate, with well-crafted, classically based dishes showing flair, originality and some playful, artistic touches.
→ Sesame-crusted tuna loin, watermelon and sweet soy. Goosnargh chicken, leg ravioli, asparagus, sherry and crème fraîche. Bay leaf panna cotta, blueberry compote, olive oil and blueberry sorbet.

REDDITCH – Worcestershire – 503 O27 – pop. 74 803 19 C2

London 111 mi – Birmingham 15 mi – Cheltenham 33 mi – Stratford-upon-Avon 15 mi
Alcester St, ✆ (01527) 6 08 06, www.ukinformationcentre.com
Abbey Hotel G. & C.C., Dagnell End Rd, ✆ (01527) 40 66 00
Lower Grinsty, Callow Hill, Green Lane, ✆ (01527) 54 30 79
Pitcheroak, Plymouth Rd, ✆ (01527) 54 10 54

Old Rectory

Ipsley Lane, Ipsley ✉ *B98 0AP* – ✆ *(01527) 523 000* – *www.theoldrectory-hotel.co.uk* – *Closed 25-31 December*
10 rm – †£ 87/156 ††£ 117/175
Rest – *(closed Friday-Sunday) (booking essential)* Menu £ 20/25
Part-Elizabethan, part-Georgian former rectory in well-tended gardens. Spacious guest areas have a country house feel. Comfortable, individually styled bedrooms blend traditional décor with modern facilities. Formal dining in bright conservatory restaurant.

REDFORD – West Sussex – see Midhurst

REETH – North Yorkshire – 502 O20 – pop. 939 – ✉ Richmond 22 B1

London 253 mi – Leeds 53 mi – Middlesbrough 36 mi – Newcastle upon Tyne 61 mi
The Green, ✆ (01748) 88 40 59, www.reeth.org

Burgoyne

On The Green ✉ *DL11 6SN* – ✆ *(01748) 884 292* – *www.theburgoyne.co.uk* – *Closed 24-26 December and Monday-Thursday in January*
9 rm – †£ 113/193 ††£ 130/210 – 1 suite
Rest – *(dinner only) (booking essential)* Menu £ 18/39
Late Georgian hotel with a cosy, comforting feel; set in a lovely spot overlooking the village green and the Yorkshire Dales. The two lounges are filled with antiques and vases of lilies. Bedrooms are individually styled and traditionally appointed. The elegant dining room offers an all-encompassing menu.

ENGLAND

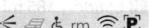

at Low Row West : 4 mi on B 6270

🍴📗 **Punch Bowl Inn** with rm 📶 🛜 **P**
✉ *DL11 6PF* – 𝒞 *(01748) 886 233* – *www.pbinn.co.uk* – *Closed 25 December*
11 rm ☐ – **♦**£ 80/105 **♦♦**£ 95/115 **Rest** – Carte £ 20/34
A traditional 17C stone-built inn with a contrastingly modern, shabby-chic interior. It's a popular stop-off for walkers, who can refuel on classic dishes like lamb
shank or beef and red wine casserole. Supremely comfortable bedrooms are decorated in a fresh, modern style; all have views over Swaledale.

at Langthwaite Northwest : 3.25 mi on Langthwaite rd – ✉ Reeth

🍴📗 **Charles Bathurst Inn** with rm 🦢 ≤ 🛜 🛜 **P**
✉ *DL11 6EN* – 𝒞 *(01748) 884 567* – *www.cbinn.co.uk* – *Closed 25 December*
19 rm ☐ – **♦**£ 81/107 **♦♦**£ 99/125 **Rest** – Carte £ 21/35
Characterful 18C hostelry set in a peaceful hillside village, boasting commanding
rural views. The daily menu, inscribed on a mirror, offers refined yet hearty classical British dishes. Bedrooms are spacious and extremely comfy.

REIGATE – Surrey – **504** T30 – **pop. 47 602** 7 D2
🅓 London 26 mi – Brighton 33 mi – Guildford 20 mi – Maidstone 38 mi

🍴🍴 **Tony Tobin @ The Dining Room** 🆎
59a High St ✉ *RH2 9AE* – 𝒞 *(01737) 226 650* – *www.tonytobinrestaurants.co.uk*
– *Closed 23 December-3 January, Saturday lunch, Sunday dinner and bank
holidays*
Rest – Menu £ 25 (weekdays)/39 – Carte £ 41/49
Chic, contemporary restaurant with a comfortable atmosphere and professional
staff. Cooking demonstrates the chef's classical background whilst also incorporating some international influences. Most plump for the 5 course tasting menu.

🍴 **Barbe** 🆎
71 Bell St ✉ *RH2 7AN* – 𝒞 *(01737) 241 966* – *www.labarbe.co.uk* – *Closed 26-28
December, 1 January, Saturday lunch, Sunday dinner and bank holiday Mondays*
Rest – Menu £ 20/35
Long-standing French bistro with cheery owner and huge local following. Two
main dining areas strewn with Gallic memorabilia. Simply laid, tightly packed tables. Classical, bi-monthly menu.

RETFORD – Nottinghamshire – **502** R24 – **pop. 20 679** 16 B1
🅓 London 148 mi – Lincoln 23 mi – Nottingham 31 mi – Sheffield 27 mi
🅵 40 Grove St, 𝒞 (01777) 86 07 80, www.visitnottingham.com

🏠 **Barns** without rest 🦢 🚗 🛝 🛜 **P**
Morton Farm, Babworth, Southwest : 2.25 mi by A 620 on B 6420 ✉ *DN22 8HA*
– 𝒞 *(01777) 706 336* – *www.thebarns.co.uk* – *Closed Christmas-New Year*
6 rm ☐ – **♦**£ 39/68 **♦♦**£ 64/75
18C barn with a pleasant garden and well-kept, traditionally styled interior. Neat,
oak-beamed breakfast room with old dressers and a fireplace. Tidy, country-style
bedrooms have waxed pine furnishings; one has a four-poster.

RHYDYCROESAU – Shropshire – **503** K25 18 A1
🅓 London 185 mi – Bristol 135 mi – Cardiff 132 mi – Plymouth 249 mi

🏠 **Pen-Y-Dyffryn** 🦢 ≤ 🚗 🛜 **P**
✉ *SY10 7JD* – 𝒞 *(01691) 653 700* – *www.peny.co.uk*
12 rm ☐ – **♦**£ 89/99 **♦♦**£ 120/180
Rest – *(dinner only) (booking essential)* Menu £ 30/37
Early Victorian rectory in a peaceful countryside setting, with a pretty garden and
lovely views. Classical guest areas feature antique furnishings; bedrooms have
good facilities and contemporary fabrics – coach house rooms have their own terrace. Daily menus use local and organic produce.

ENGLAND

RIBCHESTER – Lancashire – 502 M22 – pop. 1 654 — 20 B2

London 229 mi – Blackburn 7 mi – Manchester 41 mi

Angels

Fleet Street Ln, Northwest : 1.5 mi by B 6245 (Longridge Rd) ✉ PR3 3ZA – ✆ (01254) 820 212 – www.angelsribchester.co.uk – Closed Monday and lunch Tuesday, Wednesday and Saturday

Rest – Menu £ 15/45 – Carte £ 33/47

Smartly converted roadside pub with a cocktail bar and comfy lounge seating. Two formally dressed dining rooms, with a grand piano played on Friday evenings. Classic dishes with a modern edge; tasty, well-balanced and good value.

RICHMOND – North Yorkshire – 502 O20 – pop. 8 178 Great Britain — 22 B1

London 243 mi – Leeds 53 mi – Middlesbrough 26 mi – Newcastle upon Tyne 44 mi

Victoria Rd, ✆ (01748) 828 7 42, www.guide2richmond.com

Bend Hagg, ✆ (01748) 82 53 19

Catterick, Leyburn Rd, ✆ (01748) 83 32 68

Town★ - Castle★ **AC** – Georgian Theatre Royal and Museum★

The Bowes Museum★, Barnard Castle, NW : 15 mi by B 6274, A 66 and minor rd (right) – Raby Castle★, NE : 6 mi of Barnard Castle by A 688

Millgate House without rest

3 Millgate ✉ DL10 4JN – ✆ (01748) 823 571 – www.millgatehouse.com

4 rm – †£ 85/110 ††£ 110/145

Georgian guesthouse with a beautiful garden leading down to the river. A wonderful collection of silver, grandfather clocks and antiques fills the house. Comfy bedrooms; the lounge and breakfast room offer commanding river and castle views.

Frenchgate with rm

59-61 Frenchgate ✉ DL10 7AE – ✆ (01748) 822 087 – www.thefrenchgate.co.uk

9 rm – †£ 88/138 ††£ 118/250

Rest – Menu £ 34 (dinner) – Carte lunch £ 19/36

Part-dating from the 17C, with two open-fired lounges filled with vivid art, a simply furnished dining room and a lovely terrace and walled garden. Modern, ambitious dishes. Immaculately kept, well-equipped bedrooms; breakfast features local bacon and sausages, and preserves made from berries picked nearby.

RINGWOOD – Hampshire – 503 O31 – pop. 13 387 — 6 A2

London 102 mi – Bournemouth 11 mi – Salisbury 17 mi – Southampton 20 mi

Moortown Lodge without rest

244 Christchurch Rd, South : 1 mi on B 3347 ✉ BH24 3AS – ✆ (01425) 471 404 – www.moortownlodge.co.uk

7 rm – †£ 76/96 ††£ 76/96

Welcoming Georgian hunting lodge built in 1760, on a busy road at the edge of the forest. The large main room has soft seating and neatly laid breakfast tables. Bedrooms have good comforts; the largest ones come with feature beds.

RIPLEY – North Yorkshire – 502 P21 – pop. 193 – ✉ Harrogate — 22 B2

London 213 mi – Bradford 21 mi – Leeds 18 mi – Newcastle upon Tyne 79 mi

Boar's Head

✉ HG3 3AY – ✆ (01423) 771 888 – www.boarsheadripley.co.uk

25 rm – †£ 85/125 ††£ 100/150

Rest *Brasserie* – Carte £ 21/34

18C creeper-clad coaching inn, set in an estate-owned village and reputedly furnished from the next door castle's attics. Family portraits and knick-knacks fill the lounges. Comfy, individually furnished bedrooms; some in the courtyard or adjacent house. All-encompassing menu served in various rooms.

ENGLAND

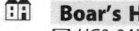

RIPLEY – Surrey – 504 S30 – pop. 2 041 7 C1

London 24 mi – Croydon 22 mi – Barnet 46 mi – Ealing 28 mi

Drake's (Steve Drake)

The Clock House, High St ✉ GU23 6AQ – ✆ (01483) 224 777 – www.drakesrestaurant.co.uk – Closed 2 weeks August, 1 week January, 1 week Christmas, Tuesday lunch, Sunday and Monday

Rest – Menu £ 28/60

Red-brick Georgian building with a large clock to the front and a drinks terrace overlooking a beautiful garden to the rear. The panelled bar leads to an elegant dining room with garden views. Choose either a 'surprise' or set menu; cooking is creative, very visual and pushes the boundaries.

→ Veal tongue with soft poached egg, bone marrow, asparagus and hay. Grey mullet, oyster mayonnaise, shrimp butter, turnip and miso emulsion. Pear in brown butter, goat's milk, crystallised vodka, and hibiscus ice cream.

RIPON – North Yorkshire – 502 P21 – pop. 17 795 Great Britain 22 B2

London 222 mi – Leeds 26 mi – Middlesbrough 35 mi – York 23 mi

Minster Rd, ✆ (01765) 60 46 25, www.visitripon.org

Ripon City, Palace Rd, ✆ (01765) 60 36 40

Town★ - Cathedral★ (Saxon Crypt) **AC**

Fountains Abbey★★★ **AC** :- Studley Royal **AC** (≤★ from Anne Boleyn's Seat) - Fountains Hall (Fa 0.5ade★), SW : 2.5 mi by B 6265 – Newby Hall (Tapestries★) **AC**, SE : 3.5 mi by B 6265

Old Deanery

Minster Rd ✉ HG4 1QS – ✆ (01765) 600 003 – www.theolddeanery.co.uk – Closed 1 January and 25-26 December

11 rm – †£ 90/110 ††£ 105/155

Rest – *(closed Sunday dinner)* Menu £ 18 (weekday lunch)/20 – Carte £ 18/27

Attractive former deanery opposite Ripon Cathedral. Inside, modern furnishings blend with older features – climb the 18C oak staircase to comfy, up-to-date bedrooms; some with beams, Victorian-style baths and cathedral views. Large, simply furnished bar offers a menu of complex dishes.

Sharow Cross House

Dishforth Rd, Sharow, Northeast : 1.75 mi by A 61 on Sharow rd ✉ HG4 5BQ – ✆ (01765) 609 866 – www.sharowcrosshouse.co.uk – Closed 23 December-2 January

3 rm – †£ 65/75 ††£ 80/100 **Rest** – Menu £ 28

Late Victorian villa; originally a country residence for a soap manufacturer. Characterful interior with spacious, light-filled rooms; tea is served in the comfy lounge on arrival. Tastefully furnished bedrooms come with thoughtful extras and the master room offers cathedral views. Choose your dinners in advance from a series of seven set menus.

at Aldfield Southwest : 3.75 mi by B 6265 – ✉ Ripon

Bay Tree Farm without rest

✉ HG4 3BE – ✆ (01765) 620 394 – www.baytreefarm.co.uk

6 rm – †£ 50/65 ††£ 80/90

18C sandstone barn with a farmhouse-style interior, smartly furnished bedrooms and pleasant country views. The open-fired lounge is hung with farm implements and opens onto the garden. The welcoming owner always makes time to stop and chat.

RIPPONDEN – West Yorkshire – 502 O22 – pop. 3 784 22 A3

London 200 mi – Bristol 195 mi – Cardiff 216 mi – Plymouth 309 mi

El Gato Negro

1 Oldham Rd ✉ HX6 4DN – ✆ (01422) 823 070 – www.elgatonegrotapas.co.uk – Closed 7-21 January, one week June-July, first week October, Sunday and Monday

Rest – *(dinner only and Saturday lunch) (booking essential)* Carte approx. £ 24

Laid-back former pub in a small valley town; the eye-catching modern exterior conceals two warm, rustic rooms with stone walls and open fires. Appealing Spanish menus feature refined, carefully prepared, authentic tapas dishes; the chef visits Spain regularly. Knowledgeable staff guide you through the menu.

ROADE – Northamptonshire – 504 R27 – pop. 2 254 — 16 B3

London 66 mi – Coventry 36 mi – Leicester 42 mi – Northampton 5 mi

Roade House with rm

AC rest, P

16 High St ✉ NN7 2NW – ✆ (01604) 863 372 – www.roadehousehotel.co.uk – Closed 26-30 December, Sunday dinner and bank holiday Mondays

10 rm – £ 70/82 £ 82/90 **Rest** – Menu £ 21 (lunch) – Carte £ 28/38

Personally run, former village pub and schoolhouse, with open-fired lounge and simple, linen-laid dining room. Crafted from local produce, set lunch and à la carte dinner menus offer classical cooking with modern touches. Pleasant bedrooms are furnished in pine.

ROCHDALE – Greater Manchester – 502 N23 – pop. 95 796 — 20 B2

London 224 mi – Blackpool 40 mi – Burnley 11 mi – Leeds 45 mi

The Esplanade, ✆ (01706) 92 49 28, www.manchesterscountryside.com

18 Bagslate, Edenfield Rd, ✆ (01706) 64 38 18

18 Marland, Bolton Rd, Springfield Park, ✆ (01706) 64 98 01

27 Castle Hawk, Castleton, Chadwick Lane, ✆ (01706) 64 08 41

Peacock Room at The Crimble

AC P

Crimble Ln, Bamford, West : 2 mi on B 6222 ✉ OL11 4AD – ✆ (01706) 368 591 – www.thedeckersgroup.com – Closed Saturday lunch, Sunday dinner, Monday and Tuesday

Rest – Menu £ 14/20 – Carte £ 26/40

Large, mirror-ceilinged dining room with vast chandeliers, candelabras, crisp linen and an elegant lounge, set in a landmark Victorian house. Constantly evolving menus and modern presentation.

Nutters

AC P

Edenfield Rd, Norden, West : 3.5 mi on A 680 ✉ OL12 7TT – ✆ (01706) 650 167 – www.nuttersrestaurant.com – Closed 30 December, 6-7 January and Monday

Rest – Menu £ 17 (weekday lunch) – Carte £ 26/41

A restaurant of 2 halves: the top part is smart, with a modern, minimalistic feel. The lower part is more traditionally styled. Complex modern British dishes have international influences. Can't decide? Go for the 6 course 'Surprise' menu.

ROCK – Cornwall – 503 F32 – pop. 4 593 – ✉ Wadebridge — 1 B2

London 266 mi – Newquay 24 mi – Tintagel 14 mi – Truro 32 mi

Pencarrow★, SE : 8.5 mi by B 3314 and A 389

St Enodoc

P

✉ PL27 6LA – ✆ (01208) 863 394 – www.enodoc-hotel.co.uk – Closed late December-January

20 rm – £ 144/257 £ 160/285 – 4 suites

Rest *Restaurant Nathan Outlaw* ✿✿

Rest *Seafood & Grill* – see restaurant listing

Beautifully located hotel boasting stunning bay views. Strong New England theme throughout with pastel painted woodwork and stripy sofas. Comfy guest areas and modern, well-appointed bedrooms.

Restaurant Nathan Outlaw – St Enodoc Hotel

✿✿ P

✉ PL27 6LA – ✆ (01208) 863 394 – www.nathan-outlaw.com – Closed 21 December-31 January, Sunday and Monday

Rest – *(dinner only) (booking essential) (set menu only)* Menu £ 99/120

Highlight of St Enodoc Hotel is this stylish, modern restaurant of just nine tables, with understated décor which puts the spotlight on the accomplished cooking. Top quality fresh fish is their focus and dishes are simple yet superbly crafted with delicate, defined flavours. Friendly, professional service.

→ Cured brill, blood orange and tarragon. Lemon sole with crispy oyster and Jerusalem artichoke. Passion fruit and coconut ice cream sandwich.

ENGLAND

XX **Dining Room**
Pavilion Buildings, Rock Rd ✉ *PL27 6JS – ☎ (01208) 862 622 – www.thediningroomrock.co.uk – Closed 2 weeks January-February, 2 weeks November, Monday except bank holidays and Tuesday*
Rest – *(dinner only) (booking essential)* Carte £ 34/46
Immaculately kept restaurant with a small terrace and friendly team. Flavoursome, classically based cooking features local, seasonal produce; everything is homemade, including the butter. Good value set lunches – dinner is more of an event.

X **Seafood & Grill** – St Enodoc Hotel
✉ *PL27 6LA – ☎ (01208) 863 394 – www.nathan-outlaw.com – Closed 21 December-31 January*
Rest – Carte £ 34/65
All day, split-level restaurant and bar overlooking the Camel Estuary and opening out onto a lovely rear terrace. Menus feature light offerings and simply executed steak and seafood dishes; the use of local ingredients is key.

at Trebetherick North : 1 mi by Trewint Lane

St Moritz rm, P
✉ *PL27 6SD – ☎ (01208) 862 242 – www.stmoritzhotel.co.uk*
30 rm – †£ 79/128 ††£ 105/170 – 15 suites
Rest – *(dinner only in winter)* Carte £ 31/46
Rest *Sea Side* – *(lunch only)* Carte £ 24/32
Art deco style hotel with leisure club, indoor and outdoor swimming pools and a 6 room spa. Contemporary bedrooms have a minimalistic style and spacious bathrooms. Suites have an open plan lounge, a kitchen and balconies with estuary views. Modern brasserie serves a simple, flavoursome menu of unfussy dishes. Informal, poolside restaurant, Sea Side.

ENGLAND

ROCKBEARE – **Devon** – **see Exeter**

ROECLIFFE – **North Yorkshire** – **see Boroughbridge**

ROGATE – **West Sussex** – **504** R30 – **pop. 1 785** – ✉ **Petersfield (hants.)** 7 C2
London 63 mi – Brighton 42 mi – Guildford 29 mi – Portsmouth 23 mi

Mizzards Farm without rest P
Southwest : 1 mi by Harting rd ✉ *GU31 5HS – ☎ (01730) 821 656 – Closed Christmas and New Year*
3 rm – †£ 55/65 ††£ 80/92
17C farmhouse with delightful grounds and gardens. The main hall features an impressive wooden staircase which leads to 3 individually furnished bedrooms; two are classic and cosy, the other is rather more grand, with a sumptuous bathroom.

ROMALDKIRK – **Durham** – **502** N20 – **see Barnard Castle**

ROMSEY – **Hampshire** – **503** P31 – **pop. 17 386** Great Britain 6 A2
London 82 mi – Bournemouth 28 mi – Salisbury 16 mi – Southampton 8 mi
13 Church St, ☎ (01794) 51 29 87, www.manchesterscountryside.com
18 Dunwood Manor, Awbridge, Danes Rd, ☎ (01794) 34 05 49
18 Nursling, ☎ (023) 8073 46 37
27 Wellow, East Wellow, Ryedown Lane, ☎ (01794) 32 28 72
Abbey★ (interior★★)
Broadlands★ **AC**, S : 1 m

White Horse
Market Pl ✉ *SO51 8ZJ – ☎ (01794) 512 431 – www.silkshotels.com*
31 rm – †£ 85/95 ††£ 115/135, £ 15
Rest *Silks Brasserie* – Menu £ 17 (weekdays) – Carte £ 24/42
Smartly refurbished coaching inn, one of only 12 in the country to have continuously served as a hotel since the 14C. Guest areas feature beams, exposed brick and inglenook fireplaces. Well-equipped modern bedrooms include two duplex suites. Comfy bar and modern brasserie; extensive menu to suit all tastes.

Ranvilles Farm House without rest
Ower, Southwest : 2 mi on A 3090 (southbound carriageway) ✉ SO51 6AA – ✆ (023) 8081 4481 – www.ranvilles.com – Closed 25 December
5 rm ☕ – †£ 35/45 ††£ 70/80
Attractive, part-16C former farmhouse in mature grounds. Spacious beamed interior has a cottagey, country house feel. Comfortable lounge boasts an antique breakfast table. Good-sized bedrooms have a homely feel.

Three Tuns
58 Middlebridge St ✉ SO51 8HL – ✆ (01794) 512 639 – www.the3tunsromsey.co.uk
Rest – Carte £ 22/33
This delightful pub, dating back to the 1720s, now has the tenants it deserves. It oozes charm, with a beamed bar and panelled dining room offering a 'proper' pub menu of steak and kidney pie, honey-glazed ham and Hampshire rhubarb crumble.

ROSS-ON-WYE – Herefordshire – 503 M28 – pop. 10 085 — 18 B3

Great Britain

London 118 mi – Gloucester 15 mi – Hereford 15 mi – Newport 35 mi
Edde Cross St, ✆ (01989) 56 27 68, www.wyenot.com
Market House★ – Yat Rock (<★)
SW : Wye Valley★ – Goodrich Castle★ **AC**, SW : 3.5 mi by A 40

Wilton Court
Wilton Ln, Wilton, West : 0.75 mi by B 4260 ✉ HR9 6AQ – ✆ (01989) 562 569 – www.wiltoncourthotel.com – Closed 2-15 January
10 rm ☕ – †£ 100/155 ††£ 125/175 **Rest** – Menu £ 17/33 – Carte £ 30/41
Attractive, part-Elizabethan house out of the town centre, on the banks of the River Wye. Traditionally styled, comfortable bedrooms have good facilities; those to the front have a river view. Tasty breakfasts with homemade preserves. Choice of two dining rooms; classic menus utilise local produce.

at Walford South : 3 mi on B 4234

Mill Race
✉ HR9 5QS – ✆ (01989) 562 891 – www.millrace.info
Rest – Carte £ 21/32
Surprisingly modern pub in a small country village. Cooking is simple, letting local ingredients speak for themselves. Regular theme nights, with pizzas cooked twice-weekly on the terrace; food and wine available to take away.

at Kerne Bridge South : 4.25 mi on B 4234 – ✉ Ross-On-Wye

Lumleys without rest
✉ HR9 5QT – ✆ (01600) 890 040 – www.thelumleys.co.uk
3 rm ☕ – †£ 50/65 ††£ 65/75
Double-fronted brick house with colourful gardens; formerly the village pub, now a cosy, characterful guesthouse run with love and care. Cluttered, homely bedrooms, comfy lounge, and drying room for walkers. Well-located for the Wye Valley and Forest of Dean.

ROTHBURY – Northumberland – 501 O18 – pop. 1 963 – ✉ Morpeth — 24 A2

Great Britain

London 311 mi – Edinburgh 84 mi – Newcastle upon Tyne 29 mi
Church St, ✆ (01669) 62 08 87, www.visitnorthumberland.com
Cragside House★ (interior★) **AC**

Farm Cottage without rest
Thropton, West : 2.25 mi on B 6341 ✉ NE65 7NA – ✆ (01669) 620 831 – www.farmcottageguesthouse.co.uk – Closed 1 week Christmas
4 rm ☕ – †£ 60/65 ††£ 70/90
18C stone cottage run by friendly owners – one of them was born here! Cosy, open-fired lounge filled with curios and a small breakfast room overlooking the garden. Traditional, homely bedrooms; the one in the annexe is the most modern.

ENGLAND

Thropton Demesne Farmhouse without rest
Thropton, West : 2.5 mi on B 6341 ✉ NE65 7LT – ✆ (01669) 620 196 – www.throptondemesne.co.uk – Closed January
3 rm – £ 50 £ 75
Extended stone farmhouse with lovely valley views. Comfy lounge and conservatory; bright, well-kept bedrooms with good facilities – one has a private bathroom. Artwork is by the chatty owner. Homemade bread and marmalade at breakfast.

ROWDE – **Wiltshire** – **503** N29 – **see Devizes**

ROWHOOK – **West Sussex** – **see Horsham**

ROWSLEY – **Derbyshire** – **502** P24 – **pop. 451** – ✉ **Matlock** Great Britain **16** A1

London 157 mi – Derby 23 mi – Manchester 40 mi – Nottingham 30 mi
Chatsworth★★★ (Park and Garden★★★) **AC**, N : by B 6012

Peacock
Bakewell Rd ✉ DE4 2EB – ✆ (01629) 733 518 – www.thepeacockatrowsley.com – Closed 24-26 December
15 rm – £ 90/135 £ 160/275
Rest *Peacock* – see restaurant listing
Characterful 17C former Dower House to the Duchess of Rutland, with gardens leading down to the river. Snug, open-fired sitting room and antique-furnished bedrooms with good facilities; one has a four-poster. The charming bar boasts exposed stone walls and old wood-panelling, and serves snacks. Lovely team.

East Lodge
✉ DE4 2EF – ✆ (01629) 734 474 – www.eastlodge.com
12 rm – £ 100/220 £ 100/220
Rest *East Lodge* – see restaurant listing
17C hunting lodge in 10 acres of landscaped gardens, with ponds and a fountain. Elegant, well-appointed guest areas. Smart bedrooms – several with four-posters – have good views and state-of-the-art bathrooms; some with TVs.

Peacock – Peacock Hotel
Bakewell Rd ✉ DE4 2EB – ✆ (01629) 733 518 – www.thepeacockatrowsley.com – Closed 24-26 December and Sunday dinner
Rest – Menu £ 17 (lunch) – Carte dinner £ 47/61
Elegant hotel restaurant which mixes old stone mullioned windows, Mousey Thompson oak furnishings and antique oil paintings with modern lighting and contemporary art. Classical dishes at lunch; more complex, elaborate combinations featuring lots of ingredients in the evening. Attentive, formal service.

East Lodge – East Lodge Hotel
✉ DE4 2EF – ✆ (01629) 734 474 – www.eastlodge.com
Rest – Menu £ 20/40 – Carte £ 25/53
Formal, traditionally furnished dining room in a country house hotel, serving classic dishes with a modern touch. Chef's table for up to 8 diners: 5 or 8 course tasting menus showcase the kitchen's skills.

ROYAL LEAMINGTON SPA – **Warwickshire** – **503** P27 – **pop. 61 595** **19** D3

London 99 mi – Birmingham 23 mi – Coventry 9 mi – Leicester 33 mi
The Parade, ✆ (01926) 74 27 62, www.royal-leamington-spa.co.uk
Leamington and County, Whitnash, Golf Lane, ✆ (01926) 42 59 61

Mallory Court
Harbury Ln, Bishop's Tachbrook, South : 2.25 mi by B 4087 (Tachbrook Rd) ✉ CV33 9QB – ✆ (01926) 330 214 – www.mallory.co.uk
31 rm – £ 125/450 £ 159/525
Rest *Dining Room at Mallory* Rest *Brasserie at Mallory* – see restaurant listing
Charming, part-Edwardian house in Lutyens' style, with lovely gardens to the rear. Classical lounges display fine antiques and quality furnishings; more modern extension houses the function room. Fresh flowers and fruit feature in the smart bedrooms, which are styled in keeping with the building's age.

ENGLAND

ROYAL LEAMINGTON SPA

Adelaide Rd V
Avenue Rd . . . . . V 2
Bath St . . . . . V 3
Beauchamp Ave . . . . . U
Beauchamp Hill . . . . . U 4
Binswood St . . . . . U 6
Brandon Parade . . . . . U 10
Church Hill . . . . . UV 16
Clarendon Ave . . . . . U
Clarendon Pl . . . . . U 18
Dale St . . . . . UV
Hamilton Terrace . . . . . V 21
High St . . . . . V 22
Holly Walk . . . . . U
Kenilworth Rd . . . . . U
Leam Terrace V
Leicester St . . . . . U
Lillington Ave . . . . . U
Lillington Rd . . . . . U
Lower Ave . . . . . V 28
Newbold Terrace . . . . . V 30
Northumberland Rd . . . . . U 33
Old Warwick Rd V
Parade . . . . . UV
Priory Terrace . . . . . V 37
Radford Rd V
Regent Grove . . . . . UV 40
Regent St . . . . . UV
Royal Priors Shopping Centre . . . . . U
Rugby Rd . . . . . U
Russell Terrace V
Spencer St . . . . . V 44
Tachbrook Rd . . . . . V 47
Victoria Terrace . . . . . V 49
Warwick St . . . . . U
Willes Rd . . . . . UV

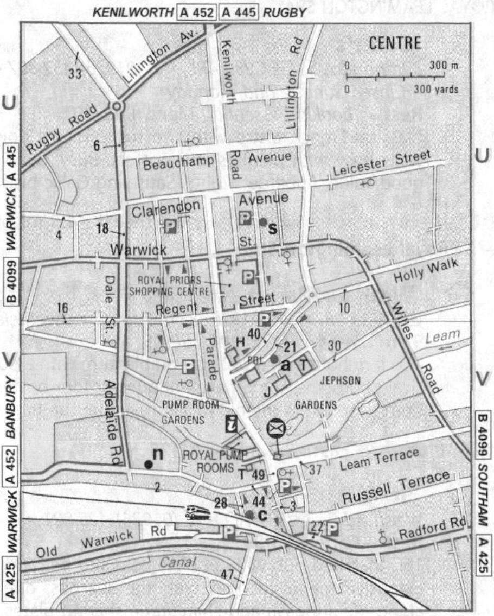

ENGLAND

Adams without rest
22 Avenue Rd ✉ CV31 3PQ – ✆ (01926) 450 742 – www.adams-hotel.co.uk
– Closed 23 December-2 January V**n**
12 rm – †£ 68/83 ††£ 79/99
Attractive detached Regency house with bay windows on either side. Bedrooms are classically styled and come with extra touches; the four at the rear are smaller but quieter. Smart bar-lounge with ornate cornicing. Extensive breakfasts.

XXX **Dining Room at Mallory** – Mallory Court Hotel
Harbury Ln, Bishop's Tachbrook, South : 2.25 mi by B 4087 (Tachbrook Rd)
✉ CV33 9QB – ✆ (01926) 330 214 – www.mallory.co.uk – Closed Saturday lunch
Rest – *(booking essential)* Menu £ 33/85
Elegant, wood-panelled dining room hidden within a charming country house and looking out over delightful gardens. Daily menus feature modern dishes with a classical base. Herbs, vegetables and soft fruits are from the kitchen garden.

XX **Restaurant 23**
34 Hamilton Terr ✉ CV32 4LY – ✆ (01926) 422 422 – www.restaurant23.co.uk
– Closed 25-26 December, 1 January and Sunday dinner V**a**
Rest – *(booking advisable)* Menu £ 21/25 – Carte £ 37/52
Smart restaurant with a chic cocktail bar and a stylish, elegant dining room, which is intimately candlelit at dinner. Modern cooking has classical European tendencies and is attractively presented. Top quality ingredients are the focus.

XX **Emperors**
Bath Pl. ✉ CV31 3BP – ✆ (01926) 313 030 – www.emperorsrestaurant.co.uk
– Closed 25-26 December, 1 January, Sunday and bank holiday Mondays
Rest – *(booking advisable)* Menu £ 18 – Carte £ 16/35 **s** V**c**
Tucked away in a backstreet, this old warehouse is now a smart restaurant with black chairs, red banquettes and emperors' jackets on the walls. The extensive Chinese menu specialises in Peking and Cantonese dishes, especially seafood.

XX **Brasserie at Mallory** – Mallory Court Hotel
Harbury Ln, Bishop's Tachbrook, South : 2.25 mi by B 4087 (Tachbrook Rd)
✉ CV33 9QB – ✆ (01926) 453 939 – www.mallory.co.uk – Closed Sunday dinner
Rest – *(booking essential)* Carte £ 23/35
Smart brasserie in a part-Edwardian country house. The bar has striking black art deco features and the airy, conservatory style dining room looks out over the pretty walled garden. The wide-ranging modern British menu follows the seasons.

Oscar's
39 Chandos St ✉ CV32 4RL – ✆ (01926) 452 807 – www.oscarsfrenchbistro.co.uk – Closed Sunday and Monday Us
Rest – *(booking essential)* Menu £ 12/29
Classical French bistro with two rustic rooms downstairs and a third above; the walls busy with pictures and posters. Busy, buzzy atmosphere, especially on the good value 'Auberge' nights. Satisfying Gallic bistro dishes. Friendly service.

at Weston under Wetherley Northeast : 4.5 mi by A 445 on B 4453 – ✉ Royal Leamington Spa

Wethele Manor without rest
✉ CV33 9BZ – ✆ (01926) 831 772 – www.wethelemanor.com
9 rm – †£ 65/75 ††£ 75/105
16C farmhouse on a 250 acre arable farm with a pond, an orchard and lamas! Classical bedrooms: some have antiques or four-posters; the family rooms are duplex. Comfy lounge in the old milking parlour; the timbered breakfast room has a well.

at Offchurch East : 3.5 mi by A 425

Stag
Welsh Rd ✉ CV33 9AQ – ✆ (01926) 425 801 – www.thestagatoffchurch.com
Rest – Carte £ 23/39
16C thatched pub with a boldly coloured bar and two modern dining rooms. The extensive menu changes with the seasons, offering generous, classical dishes, alongside antipasti and charcuterie sharing plates. Service is efficient.

ENGLAND

ROYAL TUNBRIDGE WELLS – Kent – 504 U30 – pop. 59 083 8 B2
Great Britain
London 36 mi – Brighton 33 mi – Folkestone 46 mi – Hastings 27 mi
The Pantiles, ✆ (01892) 51 56 75, www.visittunbridgewells.com
Langton Rd, ✆ (01892) 52 30 34
The Pantiles★ B 26 – Calverley Park★ B

Hotel du Vin
Crescent Rd ✉ TN1 2LY – ✆ (08447) 489 266 – www.hotelduvin.com
34 rm – †£ 125/450 ††£ 135/460 Bc
Rest *Bistro* – *(booking essential)* Carte £ 26/46
Attractive 18C property in the town centre, boasting southerly views over the park. Wine-themed throughout, with comfy lounge, clubby bar and even its own vineyard. Contemporary bedrooms; some have baths in the room and emperor-sized beds. Popular bistro offers wide-ranging British and international dishes.

Danehurst without rest
41 Lower Green Rd, Rusthall, West : 1.75 mi by A 264 ✉ TN4 8TW – ✆ (01892) 527 739 – www.danehurst.net – Closed 20 December-2 January Ae
4 rm – †£ 79/125 ††£ 90/175
Quiet Victorian house with terrace and koi carp pond, set in residential area. Quality furnishings and good attention to detail in bedrooms. Comfy lounge, library and conservatory breakfast room with homemade bread and jam.

Thackeray's
85 London Rd ✉ TN1 1EA – ✆ (01892) 511 921 – www.thackerays-restaurant.co.uk – Closed Sunday dinner and Monday
Rest – Menu £ 19/29 (weekdays) – Carte £ 43/50 Bn
Grade II listed clapperboard house; once home to the author, Thackeray. Two stylish, contemporary dining rooms and a delightful terrace; original features include lovely oak flooring. Exacting, skilful cooking with clear, well-defined flavours: classical dishes display modern elements.
→ Coq au vin ballotine with Parma ham, crisp wing and creamed porcini mushrooms. Wild duck with pear purée and port braised turnips. Apricot and tonka bean soufflé.

ROYAL TUNBRIDGE WELLS

- Benhall Mill Rd . . . . A 3
- Bishop's Down . . . . A 4
- Calverley Rd . . . . B
- Crescent Rd . . . . B 9
- Fir Tree Rd . . . . A 10
- Grosvenor Rd . . . . B 12
- Hall's Hole Rd . . . . A 13
- High Rocks Lane . . . . A 16
- High St . . . . B 14
- Hungershall Park Rd . . . . . . A 17
- Lansdowne Rd . . . . B 18
- Lower Green Rd . . . . A 20
- Major York's Rd . . . . A 21
- Monson Rd . . . . B 22
- Mount Ephraim . . . . A, B 23
- Mount Ephraim Rd . . . . B 24
- Mount Pleasant Rd . . . . B 25
- Pantiles (The) . . . . B 26
- Prospect Rd . . . . A 27
- Royal Victoria Pl. Shopping Centre . . . . B
- Rusthall Rd . . . . A 28
- St John's Rd . . . . B 29
- Tea Garden Lane . . . . A 30
- Vale Rd . . . . B 33
- Victoria Rd . . . . B 34
- Warwick Park . . . . B 35

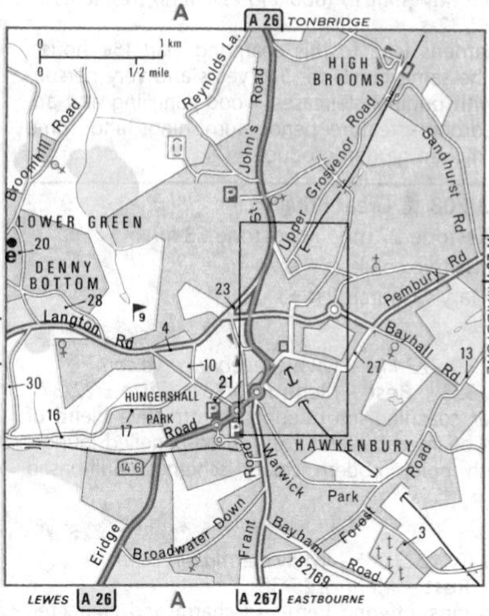

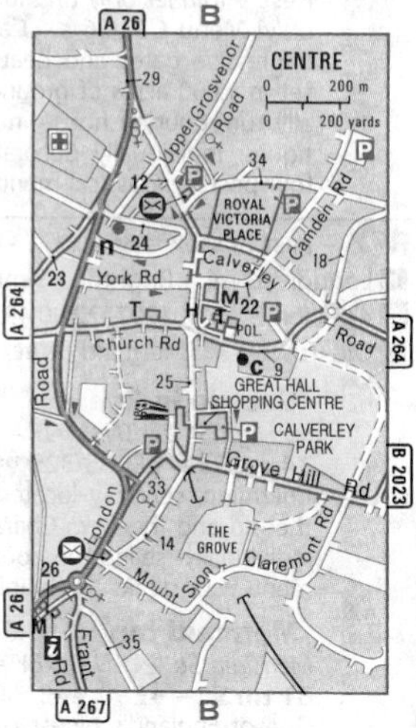

at Speldhurst Northwest : 3.5 mi by A 26 - A

George & Dragon

Speldhurst Hill ✉ *TN3 0NN* – ✆ *(01892) 863 125 – www.speldhurst.com*

Rest – Menu £ 23/29 – Carte £ 22/39

Hugely characterful Wealden Hall house dating back to 1212 and boasting an impressive beamed ceiling and an unusual Queen's post. Generous cooking uses local, organic produce, offering pub classics alongside more elaborate dishes.

ROZEL BAY – Saint Martin – 503 P33 – see Channel Islands (Jersey)

RUNSWICK BAY – North Yorkshire – ✉ Whitby 23 C1

London 285 mi – Middlesbrough 24 mi – Whitby 9 mi

Cliffemount

✉ *TS13 5HU* – ✆ *(01947) 840 103 – www.cliffemounthotel.co.uk*

20 rm ☕ – †£ 75/115 ††£ 115/180

Rest – *(dinner only and light lunch)* Menu £ 25/30 – Carte £ 23/51

Perched on the clifftop, with amazing views down to the bay – watch the sun rise and set from the delightful garden. Simply furnished bedrooms share the view and some have balconies or patios. Snacks served in the bar; classical dishes featuring local meats and seafood in the dining room.

ENGLAND

RUSHLAKE GREEN – East Sussex – 504 U31 – ✉ Heathfield 8 B2

London 54 mi – Brighton 26 mi – Eastbourne 13 mi

Stone House

(Northeast corner of the green) ✉ *TN21 9QJ – (01435) 830 553 – www.stonehousesussex.co.uk – Closed 23 December-2 January and 17 February-16 March*

7 rm – †£ 110/140 ††£ 214/280 – 2 suites

Rest – *(dinner only and lunch mid-May-August) (booking essential) (residents only)* Menu £ 32/36 **s** – Carte £ 22/32 **s**

Impressive gates and beautiful gardens lead to this charming, part-15C house, set in 1,000 acres of grounds; in the same family for 500 years and very personally run. Country house interior with original staircases, wood-panelling and antiques. Individually decorated bedrooms feature period furnishings and some four-posters. Classical menus use kitchen garden produce.

RYE – East Sussex – 504 W31 – pop. 3 708 Great Britain 9 C2

London 61 mi – Brighton 49 mi – Folkestone 27 mi – Maidstone 33 mi

4/5 Lion St, (01797) 22 90 49, www.visitrye.co.uk

Old Town★★ : Mermaid Street★, St Mary's Church (<★)

George in Rye

98 High St. ✉ *TN31 7JT – (01797) 222 114 – www.thegeorgeinrye.com*

34 rm – †£ 135/325 ††£ 135/325 **Rest** – Menu £ 16/33 – Carte £ 22/37

Charming, centrally located former coaching inn offering an attractive blend of the old and the new. Characterful beamed bar and cosy, wood-panelled lounge. Individually styled bedrooms with bold, modern colour schemes. Grill-based menu with steaks the highlight.

Mermaid Inn

Mermaid St. ✉ *TN31 7EY – (01797) 223 065 – www.mermaidinn.com*

31 rm – †£ 90 ††£ 150/220 **Rest** – Menu £ 25/38

One of England's oldest coaching inns, offering immense charm and character, from its heavy beams and tapestries to its priests' holes, false stairways and carved wooden fireplaces. The owner has been looking after guests here for nearly 3 decades. Formal dining features mainly local fish and game.

Jeake's House without rest

Mermaid St. ✉ *TN31 7ET – (01797) 222 828 – www.jeakeshouse.com*

11 rm – †£ 75/79 ††£ 116/140

Three 17C houses joined together over time, set down a cobbled lane. A former wool store and Quaker meeting place, it is set apart by its substantial charm. Characterful breakfast room; beamed, antique-furnished bedrooms.

Oaklands without rest

Udimore Rd, Southwest : 1.25mi on B 2089 ✉ *TN31 6AB – (01797) 229 734 – www.oaklands-rye.co.uk*

3 rm – †£ 80/90 ††£ 95/120

Delightfully set Edwardian house with lovely gardens and town, coast and white cliff views. Guest areas feature souvenirs from the owner's travels – the breakfast table is an Omani front door. Immaculately kept bedrooms; 2 are four-posters.

Willow Tree House without rest

113 Winchelsea Rd., South : 0.5 mi on A 259 ✉ *TN31 7EL – (01797) 227 820 – www.willow-tree-house.com*

6 rm – †£ 80 ††£ 90/130

Restored 300 year old house – a former boathouse and shipyard – on the main road into town. Spacious, tastefully furnished bedrooms, conservatory style breakfast room and cosy sitting room with rustic walls.

Ambrette

24 High St ✉ *TN31 7JF – (01797) 222 043 – www.theambrette.co.uk – Closed Monday*

Rest – Menu £ 15 (lunch) – Carte dinner £ 22/31

Set in a historic building with a fine Georgian façade and an elegant, formal interior: sister to the Margate restaurant of the same name. Skilful, modern, subtly flavoured interpretations of traditional Indian dishes.

ENGLAND

Webbe's at The Fish Café

17 Tower St. ✉ TN31 7AT – ✆ (01797) 222 226 – www.webbesrestaurants.co.uk – Closed 24 December-10 January
Rest – Carte £ 22/40
Relaxed café in former antiques warehouse, with terracotta-coloured brick walls, open-plan kitchen and small counter. Extensive menu of simply prepared seafood from Rye/Hastings day boats.

Tuscan Kitchen

8 Lion St ✉ TN31 7LB – ✆ (01797) 223 269 – www.tuscankitchenrye.co.uk – Closed 13-31 January, first week November, Wednesday and Saturday lunch and Monday- Tuesday except July-September
Rest – *(booking advisable)* Carte £ 21/35
Centrally located, with dark wood tables, studded leather chairs, Italian memorabilia and even a stuffed wild boar. Rustic, classical cooking with everything homemade. The olive oil comes from the family farm in Tuscany.

Ship Inn with rm

The Strand ✉ TN31 7DB – ✆ (01797) 222 233 – www.theshipinnrye.co.uk
10 rm – £ 80/100 £ 90/110 **Rest** – Carte £ 22/34
16C former warehouse with shabby, slightly wacky styling and extremely laid-back feel. Carefully prepared, rustic dishes arrive in generous, flavoursome portions and ingredients are well-sourced. Compact bedrooms boast unusual feature walls and bold styling.

at Camber **Southeast : 4.25 mi by A 259 – ✉ Rye**

Gallivant

New Lydd Rd. ✉ TN31 7RB – ✆ (01797) 225 057 – www.thegallivanthotel.com
20 rm – £ 115/170 £ 115/170
Rest *Beach Bistro* – see restaurant listing
Laid-back hotel opposite Camber Sands, run by a keen, friendly team. Small lounge and terrace with slightly bohemian feel. Bedrooms come in blues and whites, with distressed wood furniture and good modern facilities; four are studio-style.

Beach Bistro – Gallivant Hotel

New Lydd Rd. ✉ TN31 7RB – ✆ (01797) 225 057 – www.thebeachbistro.com
Rest – Carte £ 22/39
Informal hotel restaurant displaying distressed wood furniture and white and blue hues, set opposite Camber Sands. All-day menus have local seafood to the fore. Pleasant covered terrace.

RYHALL – Rutland – 504 S25 — 17 C2

London 94 mi – Sheffield 81 mi – Kingston upon Hull 98 mi – Rotherham 78 mi

Wicked Witch

Bridge St ✉ PE9 4HH – ✆ (01780) 763 649 – www.ryhallwitch.co.uk – Closed Sunday dinner and Monday
Rest – Menu £ 15/23 – Carte £ 27/47
Former pub; now a glitzy, modern restaurant with a relaxed formality. Seasonal menus follow the décor's lead, offering modern dishes with an emphasis on presentation. Combinations are ambitious and original, with wide-ranging influences.

ST ALBANS – Hertfordshire – 504 T28 – pop. 80 068 Great Britain — 12 A2

London 27 mi – Cambridge 41 mi – Luton 10 mi
Market Pl, ✆ (01727) 86 45 11, www.allaboutstalbans.com
18 Batchwood Hall, Batchwood Drive, ✆ (01727) 83 33 49
27 Redbourn, Kinsbourne Green Lane, ✆ (01582) 79 34 93
City★ - Cathedral★ BZ – Verulamium★ (Museum★ **AC** AY)
Hatfield House★★ **AC**, E : 6 mi by A 1057

Plans on following pages

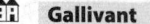

St Michael's Manor

St Michael's Village, Fishpool St ✉ *AL3 4RY* – ✆ *(01727) 864 444* – *www.stmichaelsmanor.com* AY**d**

29 rm – †£ 120/135 ††£ 135/155 – 1 suite

Rest *Lake* – see restaurant listing

Part-16C William and Mary manor house with well-kept gardens and lake views. Characterful guest areas display contemporary touches. Traditionally styled bedrooms are well-appointed; the annexe rooms are more modern – some have terraces.

Lake – St Michael's Manor Hotel

St Michael's Village, Fishpool St ✉ *AL3 4RY* – ✆ *(01727) 864 444* – *www.stmichaelsmanor.com* AY**d**

Rest – Menu £ 17 – Carte £ 36/46

Spacious, airy conservatory in a family owned manor house, which looks out over well-tended gardens and a lake. Daily changing dishes feature contemporary twists; the Lake Menu represents good value. Formal service from a chatty team.

Good food at moderate prices? Look for the Bib Gourmand.

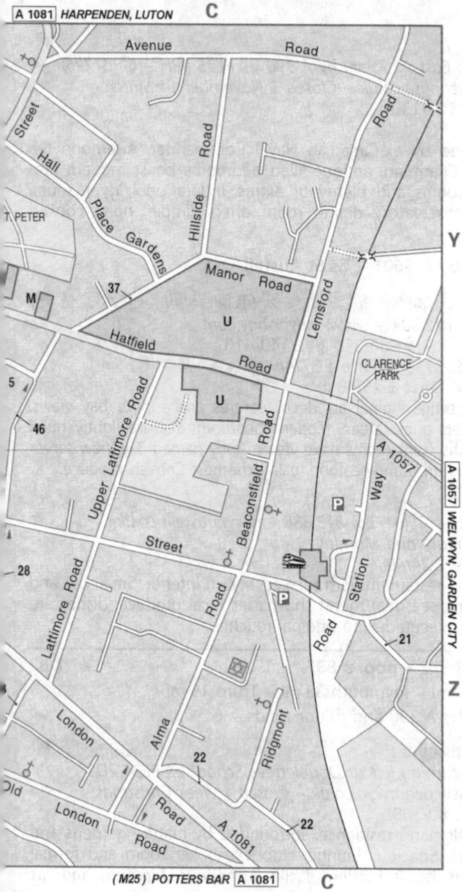

Abbey Mill Lane	AZ	
Albert St	BZ	
Alma Rd	CZ	
Avenue Rd	CY	
Beaconsfield Rd	CYZ	
Belmont Hill	BZ	
Branch Rd	AY	
Bricket Rd	BCYZ	5
Britton Ave	BY	6
Carlisle Ave	BCY	8
Catherine St	BY	
Chequer St	BZ	10
Church Crescent	ABY	11
Cottonmill Lane	BCZ	13
Dalton St	BY	15
Drovers Way	BY	16
Etna Rd	BY	18
Fishpool St	AYZ	
Folly Ave	BY	20
Folly Lane	ABY	
Grange St	BY	
Grimston Rd	CZ	21
Grosvenor Rd	CZ	22
Hall Pl. Gardens	CY	
Hatfield Rd	CY	
High St	BZ	
Hillside Rd	CY	
Holywell Hill	BZ	
Lattimore Rd	CZ	
Lemsford Rd	CY	
London Rd	BCZ	
Lower Dagnall St	BYZ	26
Maltings Shopping Centre	BZ	
Manor Rd	CY	
Market Pl.	BZ	29
Marlborough Rd	CZ	28
Mount Pleasant	AY	
New England St	AY	
Normandy Rd	BY	
Old London Rd	CZ	
Portland St	AY	
Ridgemont Rd	CZ	
Russell Ave	BY	35
St Peter's Rd	CY	37
St Peter's St	BCY	
Sopwell Lane	BZ	
Spencer St	BY	39
Spicer St College	BYZ	40
Station Way	CZ	
Thorpe Rd	BZ	42
Upper Dagnall St	BYZ	44
Upper Lattimore Rd	CYZ	
Upper Marlborough Rd	CYZ	46
Verulam Rd	ABY	
Victoria St	BCZ	
Watson's Walk	CZ	48
Welclose St	AYZ	49
Worley Rd	BY	

ENGLAND

Sukiyaki

✉ AL3 5EG – ✆ (01727) 865 009 – *Closed 2 weeks in summer, 1 week Christmas, Sunday and Monday* BY**e**

Rest – *(dinner only)* Menu £ 22/29 – Carte £ 15/31

A simply decorated restaurant with a pared-down Japanese style and a very amiable owner, who entertains children with her origami. Concise, authentic menu, with set 'sukiyaki', 'tempura' and 'tonkatsu' options – no sushi or noodles here!

ST ANNE'S – Lancashire – 502 K22 – see Lytham St Anne's

ST AUBIN – 503 P33 – see Channel Islands (Jersey)

ST AUSTELL – Cornwall – 503 F32 – pop. 22 658 1 B2

London 281 mi – Newquay 16 mi – Plymouth 38 mi – Truro 14 mi

Carlyon Bay, ✆ (01726) 81 42 50

Holy Trinity Church★

St Austell Bay★★ (Gribbin Head★★) E : by A 390 and A 3082 – Carthew : Wheal Martyn China Clay Heritage Centre★★ **AC**, N : 2 mi by A 391 – Mevagissey★★ - Lost Gardens of Heligan★, S : 5 mi by B 3273 – Charlestown★, SE : 2 mi by A 390 – Eden Project★★, NE : 3 mi by A 390 at St Blazey Gate. Trewithen★★★ **AC**, NE : 7 mi by A 390 – Lanhydrock★★, NE : 11 mi by A 390 and B 3269 – Polkerris★, E : 7 mi by A 390 and A 3082

Anchorage House

Nettles Corner, Boscundle, East : 2.75 mi by A 390 ✉ *PL25 3RH – ✆ (01726) 814 071 – www.anchoragehouse.co.uk – Closed 1 November-14 March*

5 rm – †£ 75/80 ††£ 100/130

Rest – Menu £ 20

Modern guesthouse owned by ex-Canadian Naval Commander. Afternoon tea served in comfy lounge. Charming, antique-filled bedrooms boast modern fabrics, state-of-the-art bathrooms and plenty of extras. Indoor pool, gym, sauna and chill out lounge. Conservatory dining room offers simple, home-cooked dishes. Lovely owners.

at Carlyon Bay East : 2.5 mi by A 3601 – ✉ St Austell

Carlyon Bay

rest,

✉ *PL25 3RD – ✆ (01726) 812 304 – www.carlyonbay.com*

86 rm (dinner included) – †£ 80/310 ††£ 140/410

Rest *Bay View* – Menu £ 22/38 – Carte £ 37/48

Rest *Taste* – *(dinner only)* Carte £ 25/48

Imposing 1920s hotel boasting original art deco features and superb bay views. Large, traditionally furnished guest areas. Modern bedrooms feature lightly hued fabrics: rear rooms are bright; front rooms have views. Aptly named Bay View serves unfussy classics. Taste offers grills and seafood, using the best Cornish produce.

Austell's

10 Beach Rd. ✉ *PL25 3PH – ✆ (01726) 813 888 – www.austells.co.uk – Closed first 2 weeks January and Monday*

Rest – Menu £ 25 – Carte £ 24/40

Keenly run, neighbourhood restaurant with relaxed, stylish interior. Small bar and open-plan kitchen. Modern, seasonal menu showcases local produce; dishes are elaborate and confidently executed, with original touches.

ENGLAND

ST BLAZEY – Cornwall – 503 F32 – pop. 8 837 — 1 B2

London 276 mi – Newquay 21 mi – Plymouth 33 mi – Truro 19 mi

Eden Project★★, NW; 1.5 mi by A 390 and minor roads

Penarwyn House without rest

South : 0.75 mi by A 390 turning left at Doubletrees School ✉ *PL24 2DS – ✆ (01726) 814 224 – www.penarwyn.co.uk – Closed 1 week Christmas*

3 rm – †£ 70/105 ††£ 80/160

Whitewashed former gentleman's residence, surrounded by mature gardens and run by welcoming owners. Spacious lounge, clubby snooker room and formal breakfast room. Bedrooms boast modern facilities, antique furniture and art deco touches.

ST BRELADE'S BAY – 503 P33 – see Channel Islands (Jersey)

ST EWE – Cornwall – 503 F33 — 1 B3

London 258 mi – Bristol 161 mi – Cardiff 192 mi – Plymouth 46 mi

Lower Barn

rm,

Bosue, North : 1.25 mi by Crosswyn rd, St Austell rd and signed off St. Mawes rd ✉ *PL26 6ET – ✆ (01726) 844 881 – www.bosue.co.uk or lower barns.co.uk*

4 rm – †£ 65/75 ††£ 75/130 **Rest** – Menu £ 35

The gregarious owner extends a warm welcome at this stylishly converted 18C granite barn; formerly part of the Heligan Estate, set in 2 acres. Modern, brightly furnished bedrooms have a South American feel and a hot tub on the decking overlooks the garden. Set menu of home-cooked dishes.

ST HELENS – 504 Q31 – see Wight (Isle of)

ST HELIER – 503 P33 – see Channel Islands (Jersey)

ST HILARY – Cornwall – see Marazion

ST ISSEY – Cornwall – 503 F32 – see Padstow

ST IVES - Cornwall - 503 D33 - pop. 9 866 1 A3

London 319 mi – Penzance 10 mi – Truro 25 mi

The Guildhall, Street-an-Pol, ☎ (01736) 79 62 97, www.stivestic.co.uk

Tregenna Castle H., ☎ (01736) 79 52 54

West Cornwall, Lelant, ☎ (01736) 75 34 01

Town★★ - Barbara Hepworth Museum★★ **AC** Y **M1** – Tate St Ives★★ (<★★) - St Nicholas Chapel (<★★) Y – Parish Church★ Y **A**

S : Penwith★★ Y. St Michael's Mount★★ (<★★) S : 10 mi by B 3306 - Y - B 3311, B 3309 and A 30

Plan on next page

Blue Hayes without rest

Trelyon Ave ✉ TR26 2AD – ☎ (01736) 797 129 – www.bluehayes.co.uk – Closed November-February Y**u**

6 rm – †£ 100/110 ††£ 170/240

Built in 1922 for Professor Whitnall, a surgeon friend of Edward III. Comfortable bedrooms: one with French doors onto a roof terrace; another with four-poster and balcony. Single course dinner available. Breakfast on the terrace in summer.

Primrose Valley without rest

Porthminster Beach ✉ TR26 2ED – ☎ (01736) 794 939 – www.primroseonline.co.uk – Closed Christmas and January Y**r**

9 rm – †£ 65/230 ††£ 75/240

Edwardian terraced villa with a trendy bar and an open-plan lounge and breakfast room. Individually furnished bedrooms boast good mod cons; Room 3 has a terrace with views over the beach and the roomy suite features a slipper bath.

No.1 St Ives without rest

1 Fern Glen, (on The Stennack) ✉ TR26 1QP – ☎ (01736) 799 047 – www.no1stives.co.uk Y**x**

4 rm – †£ 70/130 ††£ 85/145

Chic, contemporary guesthouse offering stylish, immaculately kept bedrooms; two with sea views. Cosy minimal sitting room. Open-plan kitchen/breakfast room. Laid-back owners.

11 Sea View Terrace without rest

11 Sea View Terr ✉ TR26 2DH – ☎ (01736) 798 440 – www.11stives.co.uk

3 rm – †£ 75/90 ††£ 100/140 Y**a**

Three-storey Edwardian villa with a small terrace, a cosy bay-windowed lounge and a compact rear breakfast room. Spacious, contemporary bedrooms; one has a south-facing sun-terrace and two have great views over the harbour and bay.

Alba

Old Lifeboat House, The Wharf ✉ TR26 1LF – ☎ (01736) 797 222 – www.thealbarestaurant.com – Closed 25-26 December Y**d**

Rest – *(dinner only)* Menu £ 17/20 – Carte £ 23/43

Former lifeboat station in great location overlooking the harbour; sit upstairs in the window at tables 5, 6 or 7. The same à la carte and set menus are offered at both lunch and dinner. Dishes are European in base, with a modern slant.

Porthminster Beach Café

Porthminster Beach ✉ TR26 2EB – ☎ (01736) 795 352 – www.porthminstercafe.co.uk – Closed January and December 25 Y**p**

Rest – *(booking advisable)* Carte £ 21/40

Charming 1930s beach house in a superb location overlooking Porthminster Sands. Nautical styling with pine furniture, Cornish artwork and a large heated terrace. Seasonal seafood menu of unfussy, vibrantly flavoured dishes. Many herbs grown in the garden opposite. Relaxed, friendly service.

Black Rock

Market Pl ✉ TR26 1RZ – ☎ (01736) 791 911 – www.theblackrockstives.co.uk – Closed November-February, Sunday and restricted opening in winter

Rest – *(dinner only) (booking advisable)* Menu £ 17 – Carte £ 24/32 Y**v**

Formerly the owner's father's hardware shop; now a relaxed, modern bistro featuring a slate floor, a semi-open kitchen and contemporary artwork. The regularly changing menu places its emphasis on fresh, local seafood and cooking is gutsy, rustic and big on flavour. Relaxed, friendly service.

ENGLAND

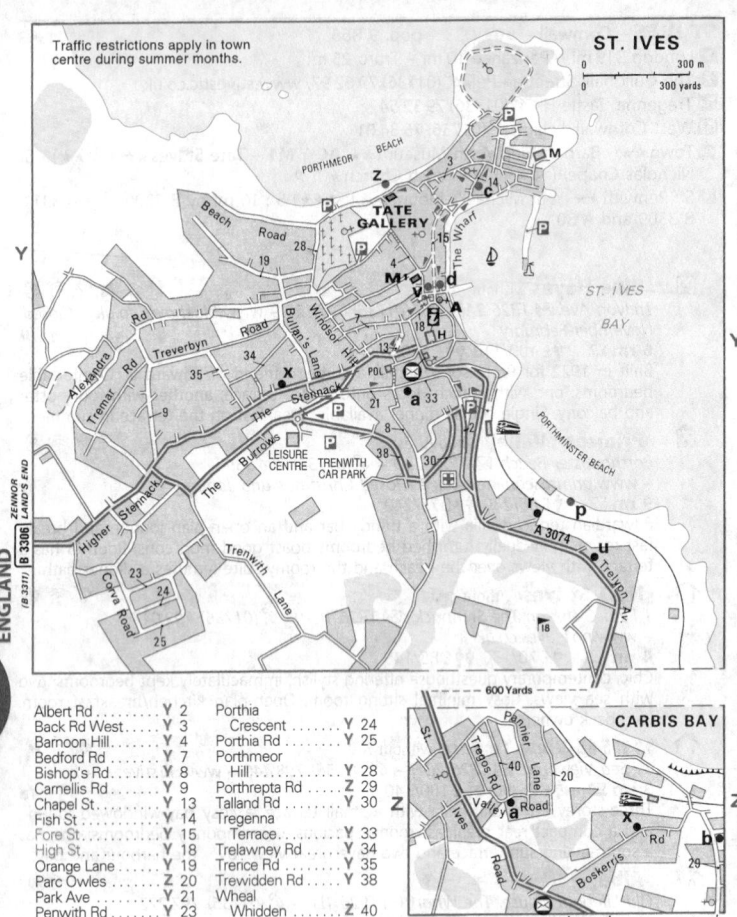

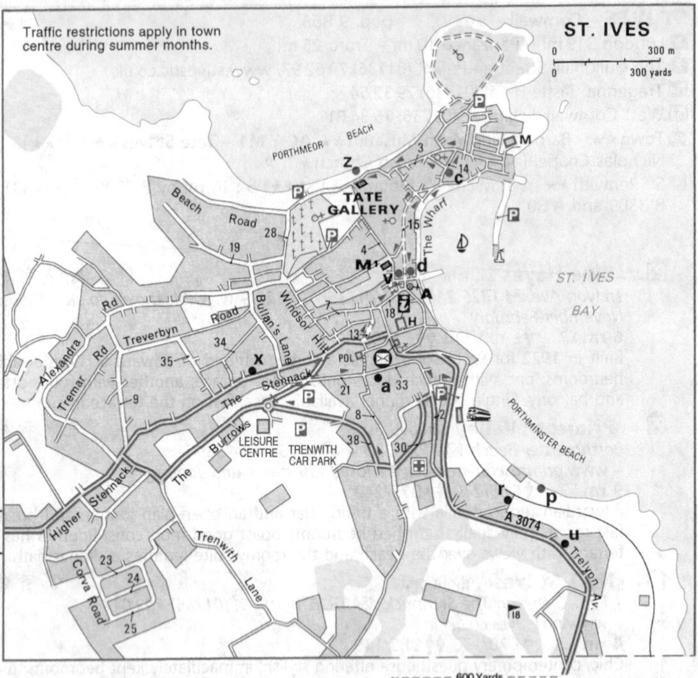

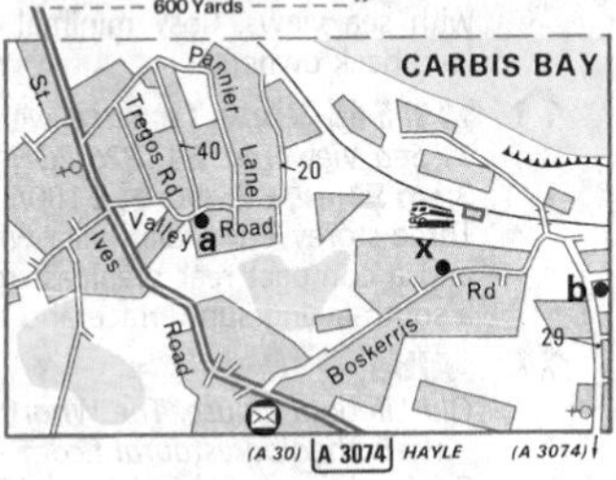

Albert Rd	Y 2	Porthia Crescent	Y 24
Back Rd West	Y 3	Porthia Rd	Y 25
Barnoon Hill	Y 4	Porthmeor Hill	Y 28
Bedford Rd	Y 7	Porthrepta Rd	Z 29
Bishop's Rd	Y 8	Talland Rd	Y 30
Carnellis Rd	Y 9	Tregenna Terrace	Y 33
Chapel St	Y 13	Trelawney Rd	Y 34
Fish St	Y 14	Trerice Rd	Y 35
Fore St	Y 15	Trewidden Rd	Y 38
High St	Y 18	Wheal Whidden	Z 40
Orange Lane	Y 19		
Parc Owles	Z 20		
Park Ave	Y 21		
Penwith Rd	Y 23		

seagrass

Fish St ✉ TR26 1LT – ✆ (01736) 793 763 – www.seagrass-stives.com – Closed dinner 25 December, Sunday and Monday November-April except bank holidays

Rest – *(booking advisable)* Menu £ 17 (dinner) – Carte £ 29/42 Y**c**

Personally run with a reassuring efficiency, this first floor restaurant just off Harbour Beach puts Cornish produce centre stage, with a menu of classic dishes cooked in a modern style. Marble-topped bar; modern décor.

Porthmeor Café Bar

Porthmeor Beach ✉ TR26 1JZ – ✆ (01736) 793 366 – www.porthmeor-beach.co.uk – Closed November-March Y**z**

Rest – *(booking essential)* Carte £ 16/36

Simple little beachfront café; a very popular spot, as all of the tables have a view. Service is friendly and the atmosphere, laid-back. Menus are largely made up of Mediterranean small plates but offer a few more substantial dishes too.

at Carbis Bay South : 1.75 mi on A 3074 – ✉ St Ives

Boskerris
Boskerris Rd ✉ TR26 2NQ – ☎ (01736) 795 295 – www.boskerrishotel.co.uk – Closed mid-November-mid-February
15 rm – ♦£ 94/165 ♦♦£ 125/255 Zx
Rest – *(closed Sunday) (dinner only) (residents only)* Carte £ 25/34
Contemporary hotel with panoramic views of Carbis Bay and the coastline. Contemporary lounge-bar with French styling and doors onto the terrace. Uncluttered bedrooms have a cool, modern style; some have roll-top baths and iPod docks. Enthusiastic young owners. Concise menu of good, honest home-cooking.

Beachcroft Ⓝ without rest
Valley Rd ✉ TR26 2QS – ☎ (01736) 794 442 – www.beachcroftstives.co.uk – Closed November-March except New Year
5 rm – ♦£ 110/150 ♦♦£ 140/180 Za
Set in an elevated position, with stunning views across the bay. Contemporary interior with subtle 1920s touches. Comfy, understated bedrooms have bespoke furnishings and luxurious bathrooms. Have your breakfast on the delightful terrace.

Headland House Ⓝ without rest
Headland Rd ✉ TR26 2NS – ☎ (01736) 796 647 – www.headlandhousehotel.co.uk – Closed November-February
7 rm – ♦£ 85/130 ♦♦£ 89/145 Zb
Substantial house built in 1901, with a decked terrace, an attractive garden and a lovely conservatory breakfast room. Contemporary, New England style décor; cake is served every afternoon in the lounge. The sea is at the end of the road.

at Halsetown Southwest : 1.5 mi on B 3311

Halsetown Inn Ⓝ
✉ TR26 3NA – ☎ (01736) 795 583 – www.hasletowninn.co.uk – Closed Sunday dinner
Rest – Carte £ 21/30
Relaxed, slightly quirky pub, a short drive from St Ives. There are various little areas to sit in, as well as a lovely suntrap of a terrace. Menus are appealing, offering lots of Mediterranean and also some globally influenced dishes.

ST KEVERNE – Cornwall – 503 E33 – pop. 1 843 1 A3

London 302 mi – Penzance 26 mi – Truro 28 mi

Old Temperance House without rest
The Square ✉ TR12 6NA – ☎ (01326) 280 986 – www.oldtemperancehouse.co.uk
4 rm – ♦£ 59 ♦♦£ 85
Pretty pink-washed cottage framed by olive trees. The interior is contemporary and immaculately kept; bright bedrooms display thoughtful touches. Fresh fruit and produce from the local butcher features at breakfast.

Greenhouse
6 High St. ✉ TR12 6NN – ☎ (01326) 280 800 – www.tgor.co.uk – Closed last 2 weeks January
Rest – *(dinner only and occasional Sunday lunch) (booking advisable)*
Carte £ 20/35
Simple eatery in a sleepy little village, where they sell their own bread and meringues. Daily blackboard menus are centred around local, organic and gluten free produce; cooking is unfussy and flavoursome. Seafood is a feature.

ST KEW – Cornwall – see Wadebridge

ST LAWRENCE – 503 P33 – see Channel Islands (Jersey)

ST MARGARET'S AT CLIFFE – Kent – 504 Y30 – see Dover

ST MARTIN – 503 P33 – see Channel Islands (Guernsey)

ST MARTIN'S – 503 B34 – see Scilly (Isles of)

ST MARY'S – 503 B34 – see Scilly (Isles of)

ST MAWES – Cornwall – 503 E33 – ✉ Truro
1 B3

London 299 mi – Plymouth 56 mi – Truro 18 mi

Town★ - Castle★ AC (≤★)

St Just-in-Roseland Church★★, N : 2.5 mi by A 3078

Hotel Tresanton

27 Lower Castle Rd ✉ TR2 5DR – ☎ (01326) 270 055 – www.tresanton.com – Closed 2 weeks January

34 rm – †£ 171/234 ††£ 190/550 – 4 suites

Rest *Restaurant Tresanton* – see restaurant listing

Collection of old fishermen's cottages and a former yacht club. Elegant, nautically themed guest areas include an intimate bar and a movie room. Understated bedrooms, some in cottages, have a high level of facilities and superb sea views. Lovely split-level terrace shares the outlook. Delightful team.

Idle Rocks (N)

Harbourside ✉ TR2 5AN – ☎ (01326) 270 270 – www.idlerocks.com – Closed 9-22 January

20 rm – †£ 140/285 ††£ 150/295

Rest *The Water's Edge* – Carte £ 26/62

Boutique hotel on the waterfront, with fabulous views over the harbour and the estuary. Bedrooms have been thoughtfully designed and feature subtle seaside-themed décor; most share the lovely bay vista. Relax on the south-facing terrace, where you could see the night's seafood being landed by the local boats.

Nearwater without rest

Polvarth Rd., East : 0.5 mi on A 3078 ✉ TR2 5AY – ☎ (01326) 279 278 – www.nearwaterstmawes.co.uk – Closed Christmas

3 rm – †£ 80/95 ††£ 90/110

Modern, purpose-built guesthouse with small lawned garden, set on the main road of a popular coastal town. Open-plan lounge and breakfast room with real fires and subtle nautical theme. Smart, New England style bedrooms offer good mod cons.

Restaurant Tresanton – Hotel Tresanton

27 Lower Castle Rd ✉ TR2 5DR – ☎ (01326) 270 055 – www.tresanton.com – Closed 2 weeks January

Rest – *(booking essential)* Menu £ 22/28 – Carte £ 31/51

Appealing hotel restaurant boasting a large terrace and superb bay views; popular for its Sunday BBQs and live jazz band. Bright interior with nautical theme and attractive mosaic flooring. Daily menus offer unfussy dishes crafted from quality local produce; seafood is a feature. Polite, efficient service.

Watch House (N)

1 The Square ✉ TR2 5DJ – ☎ (01326) 270 038 – www.watchhousestmawes.co.uk – Closed January and Monday-Tuesday except June-September

Rest – Menu £ 22/37

Old Customs and Excise watch house on the quayside, with a nautically styled interior, friendly service and harbour views. Light lunches and substantial dinners; unfussy cooking follows a Mediterranean theme – try the tasty fish specials.

ST MELLION – Cornwall
2 C2

London 225 mi – Bristol 129 mi – Cardiff 160 mi – Plymouth 13 mi

Pentillie Castle

Southeast : 1 mi by A 388 on Cargreen rd ✉ PL12 6QD – ☎ (01579) 350 044 – www.pentillie.co.uk

9 rm – †£ 140/220 ††£ 140/220 **Rest** – Menu £ 28

17C house – later transformed into a castle – set in 2,000 acres overlooking the river. Classical guest areas include a dining room with a crystal chandelier; traditional menus require a minimum of 6 guests. Spacious, elegant bedrooms with antique furnishings, luxurious bathrooms and some great views.

ST MERRYN – Cornwall – 503 F32 – see Padstow

ST OSYTH – Essex – 504 X28 – pop. 4 119
13 D2

London 83 mi – Croydon 88 mi – Barnet 81 mi – Ealing 94 mi

Park Hall without rest

Park Hall, East : 1.5 mi on B 1027 ✉ CO16 8HG – ☎ (01255) 820 922 – www.parkhall.info

3 rm ☕ – 🚹£ 70/110 🚹🚹£ 110/190

14C antique-filled former monastery in 600 acres of arable farmland, with 5 acres of grounds, where peacocks roam free. Traditionally styled rooms come with many thoughtful extras.

ST PETER PORT – 503 P33 – see Channel Islands (Guernsey)

ST SAVIOUR – 503 P33 – see Channel Islands (Jersey)

ST SAVIOUR – 503 P33 – see Channel Islands (Guernsey)

SALCOMBE – Devon – 503 I33 – pop. 1 893
2 C3

London 243 mi – Exeter 43 mi – Plymouth 27 mi – Torquay 28 mi

Market St, ☎ (01548) 84 39 27, www.salcombeinformation.co.uk

Sharpitor (Overbecks Museum and Garden★) (≤★★) **AC**, S : 2 mi by South Sands Z. Prawle Point (≤★★★) E : 16 mi around coast by A 381 - Y - and A 379

South Sands

Bolt Head, Southwest : 1.25 mi ✉ TQ8 8LL – ☎ (01548) 845 900 – www.southsands.com

Zx

27 rm ☕ – 🚹£ 135/315 🚹🚹£ 150/375 – 5 suites

Rest *Beachside* – see restaurant listing

Stylish hotel by the water's edge, with a subtle New England theme running throughout and South Sands views. Small, modern bar and lounges. Smart bedrooms have heavy wood furnishings and good facilities; opt for one with a balcony.

SALCOMBE

Allenhayes Rd	Y 2
Bonaventure Rd	Y 3
Buckley St	Y 4
Camperdown Rd	Y 7
Church St	Y 8
Coronation Rd	Y 9
Devon Rd	Y 13
Fore St	Y
Fortescue Rd	Z 14
Grenville Rd	Y 15
Herbert Rd	Z 18
Knowle Rd	Y 19
Moult Rd	Z 20
Newton Rd	Y 23
Sandhills Rd	Z 24
Shadycombe Rd	Y 25

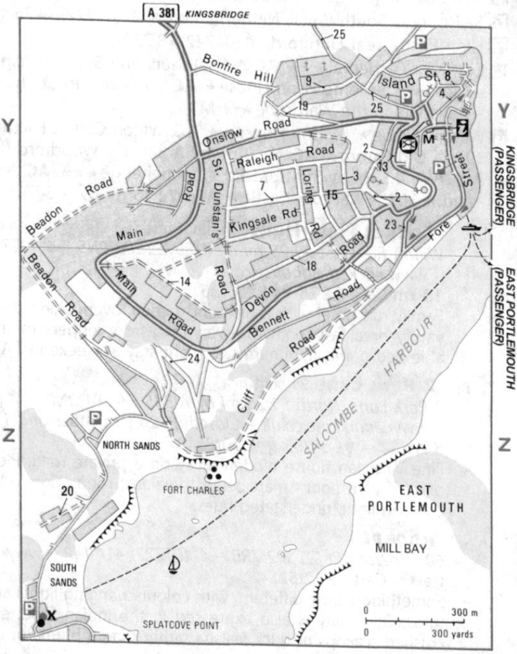

XX **Beachside** – South Sands Hotel
Bolt Head, Southwest : 1.25 mi ✉ TQ8 8LL – ✆ (01548) 859 000 – www.southsands.com
Rest – Carte £ 29/46 **Zx**
Large, airy, hotel restaurant with full-length windows opening onto a delightful decked terrace overlooking the bay. Modern, daily changing menus offer a good mix of unfussy, flavoursome dishes, with plenty of fresh seafood options.

at Soar Mill Cove Southwest : 4.25 mi by A 381 - Y - via Malborough village – ✉ Salcombe

Soar Mill Cove
✉ TQ7 3DS – ✆ (01548) 561 566 – www.soarmillcove.co.uk – Closed January
32 rm – †£ 125/175 ††£ 135/215 **Rest** – Menu £ 15/43 – Carte £ 24/35
Family-run hotel built from local slate and stone; delightfully set above a secluded cove. Relax in the modern lounge or smart bar. Spacious bedrooms come in bright, contemporary styles; half have private patios and sea views. Blue-hued restaurant offers a modern menu and a lovely outlook from every table.

SALE – Greater Manchester – 502 N23 – pop. 55 234 – ✉ Manchester 20 B3

London 212 mi – Liverpool 36 mi – Manchester 6 mi – Sheffield 43 mi
Sale Lodge, Golf Rd, ✆ (0161) 973 16 38

Cornerstones without rest
230 Washway Rd, (on A 56) ✉ M33 4RA – ✆ (0161) 283 69 09 – www.cornerstonesguesthouse.com – Closed Christmas
9 rm – †£ 35/55 ††£ 60/65, £ 7
Substantial red-brick Victorian house with neat garden, in leafy suburban location. Slightly wacky interior with bohemian-style lounge and breakfast room. Bedrooms range from retro to modern.

SALISBURY – Wiltshire – 503 O30 – pop. 42 728 4 D3

London 91 mi – Bournemouth 28 mi – Bristol 53 mi – Southampton 23 mi
Fish Row, ✆ (01722) 33 49 56, www.visitwiltshire.co.uk
Salisbury & South Wilts., Netherhampton, ✆ (01722) 74 26 45
High Post, Great Durnford, ✆ (01722) 78 23 56
City★★ - Cathedral★★★ **AC** Z – Salisbury and South Wiltshire Museum★ **AC** Z **M2** – Close★ Z : Mompesson House★ **AC** Z **A** – Sarum St Thomas Church★ Y **B** – Redcoats in the Wardrobe★ Z **M1**
Wilton Village★ (Wilton House★★ **AC**, Wilton Carpet Factory★ **AC**), W : 3 mi by A 30 Y – Old Sarum★ **AC**, N : 2 mi by A 345 Y – Woodford (Heale House Garden★) **AC**, NW : 4.5 mi by Stratford Rd Y. Stonehenge★★★ **AC**, NW : 10 mi by A 345 - Y - and A 303 – Wardour Castle★ **AC**, W : 15 mi by A 30 Y

Cricket Field House without rest
Wilton Rd, West : 1.25 mi on A 36 ✉ SP2 9NS – ✆ (01722) 322 595 – www.cricketfieldhouse.co.uk
18 rm – †£ 75 ††£ 95/135
Family-run hotel with a pleasant garden, overlooking the cricket ground. Conservatory breakfast room for everything from kippers to smoked salmon. Comfortable bedrooms; minimum two night stay at weekends, April-October.

2 Park Lane without rest
2 Park Lane, North : 1.25 mi by A 345 ✉ SP1 3NP – ✆ (01722) 321 001 – www.2parklane.co.uk – Closed 25-26 December and 1 January
5 rm – †£ 55/65 ††£ 70/85
Fine Victorian house hidden away on a private road. Pleasant entranceway with original tiled floor; smart period breakfast room. Comfortable, modern bedrooms come in light, understated hues.

XX **Anokaa**
60 Fisherton St ✉ SP2 7RB – ✆ (01722) 414 142 – www.anokaa.com
Rest – Carte £ 22/52 **Ye**
Something a little different, with colour-changing lights and interesting water features. Originality is also expressed in the Indian food: expect dishes like spiced crushed scallops or duck jaalsha rather than a bhuna or a balti.

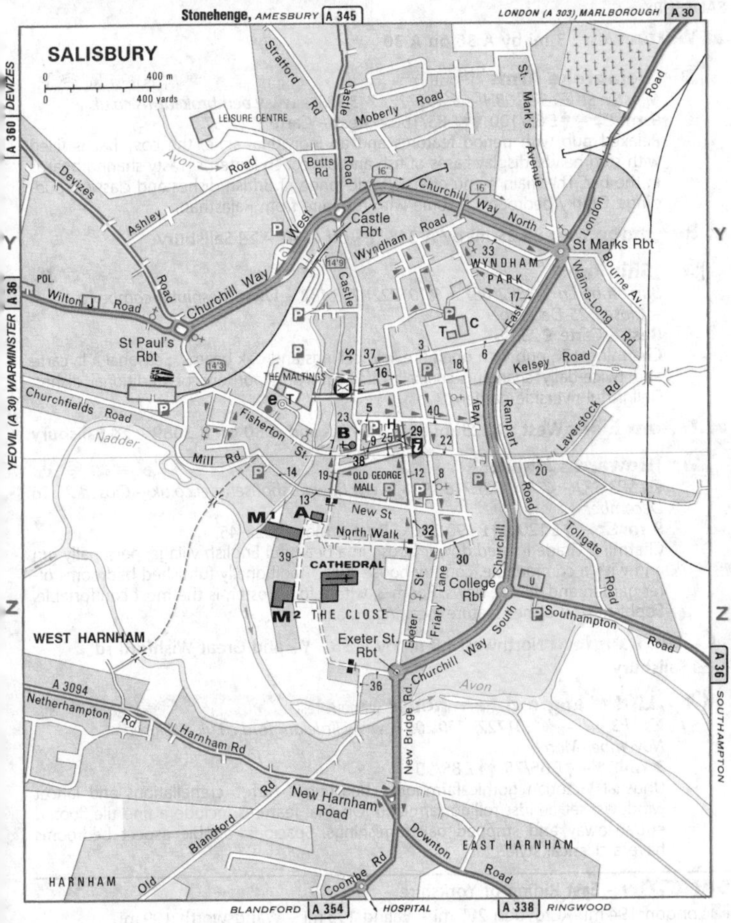

Bedwin St . . . . Y 3
Blue Boar Row . . . . Y 5
Bourne Hill . . . . Y 6
Bridge St . . . . YZ 7
Brown St . . . . Z 8
Butcher Row . . . . Y 9
Catherine St . . . . Z 12
Crane Bridge Rd . . . . Z 14
Crane St . . . . Z 13
Endless St . . . . Y 16
Estcourt Rd . . . . Y 17
Greencroft St . . . . Y 18
High St . . . . Z 19
Maltings Shopping Centre (The) . . . . . Y
Milford Hill . . . . Z 20
Milford St . . . . Y 22
Minster St . . . . Y 23
New Canal . . . . Z 25
Old George Mall Shopping Centre . . . . Z
Queen St . . . . Y 29
St Ann St . . . . Z 30
St John St . . . . Z 32
St Mark's Rd . . . . Y 33
St Nicholas Rd . . . . Z 36
Scots Lane . . . . Y 37
Silver St . . . . YZ 38
West Walk . . . . Z 39
Winchester St . . . . Y 40

at Upper Woodford North : 6.75 mi by A 360 - Y

Bridge Inn

SP4 6NU – (01722) 782 323 – www.thebridgewoodford.co.uk – Closed 25 December and Sunday dinner January-February

Rest – Carte £ 23/38

Light, airy pub on the banks of the River Avon; its garden an alfresco delight. Light bites lunch menu and classic à la carte; fresh, tasty dishes like homemade burger, fishcakes or pork belly are neatly presented on wood or slate.

ENGLAND

at Wilton West : 3 mi by A 36 on A 30

Pembroke Arms Ⓝ with rm

Minster St ✉ *SP2 0BH – ✆ (01722) 743 328 – www.pembrokearms.co.uk*
9 rm ☕ – †£ 65/100 ††£ 85/160 **Rest** – Carte £ 27/37
Relaxed pub with period features and an individual style; the cosy bar is filled with stag heads, display cases of fish and old coach lanterns. Tasty sharing boards in the bar. The main menu offers a wide-range of British dishes and classical puddings. Quirky bedrooms – some with furniture from Rajasthan.

at Burcombe West : 5.25 mi by A 36 - Y - off A 30 – ✉ Salisbury

Ship Inn

Burcombe Ln ✉ *SP2 0EJ – ✆ (01722) 743 182 – www.theshipburcombe.co.uk – Closed 25 December*
Rest – Carte £ 23/38
Charming 17C pub with open fire, low ceilings and oak beams. Seasonal à la carte and twice-daily changing specials offer satisfying portions of traditional dishes. Delightful riverside garden.

at Teffont Evias West : 10.25 mi by A 36 - Y - and A 30 on B 3089 – ✉ Salisbury

Howard's House

✉ *SP3 5RJ – ✆ (01722) 716 392 – www.howardshousehotel.co.uk – Closed 25-26 December*
9 rm ☕ – †£ 120 ††£ 190/210 **Rest** – Menu £ 20/45
Charming Grade II listed dower house in a beautiful English village; personally run and with a comfortable, country house style. Traditionally furnished bedrooms offer garden and village views; Room 3, with a four-poster, is the most comfortable. Sophisticated dishes feature local ingredients.

ENGLAND

at Little Langford Northwest : 8 mi by A 36 - Y - and Great Wishford rd – ✉ Salisbury

Little Langford Farmhouse without rest

✉ *SP3 4NP – ✆ (01722) 790 205 – www.littlelangford.co.uk – Closed November-March*
3 rm ☕ – †£ 65/75 ††£ 85/90
Unusual Victorian gothic farmhouse boasting a turret, crenellations and lancet windows; set amidst rolling farmland. Original features include a fine tile-floored entranceway and stripped oak furnishings. Spacious, double aspect bedrooms have a classical style.

SANCTON – East Riding of Yorkshire – 502 S22 — 23 C2

London 194 mi – Croydon 205 mi – Ealing 193 mi – Wandsworth 199 mi

Star Ⓝ

King St ✉ *YO43 4QP – ✆ (01430) 827 269 – www.thestaratsancton.co.uk – Closed Monday*
Rest – Menu £ 16 (weekday lunch) – Carte £ 21/44
Personally run pub in a small village, with a cosy bar and two smart dining rooms. Choose from hearty pub classics or boldly flavoured dishes which display a little more imagination. The menus proudly list the ingredients' local suppliers.

SANDBACH – Cheshire East – 502 – pop. 17 630 — 20 B3

London 177 mi – Liverpool 44 mi – Manchester 28 mi – Stoke-on-Trent 16 mi
18 Malkins Bank, ✆ (01270) 76 59 31

Old Hall

High St ✉ *CW11 1AL – ✆ (01270) 758 170 – www.oldhall-sandbach.co.uk*
Rest – Carte £ 22/36
Total restoration of this 17C black and white former manor house has created a smart new look, whilst retaining original features like oak panelling and timber beams. The daily menu focuses on keenly priced pub classics.

SANDFORD-ON-THAMES – Oxfordshire – see Oxford

SANDIACRE – Derbyshire 16 B2

London 123 mi – Birmingham 46 mi – Leeds 75 mi – Sheffield 45 mi

La Rock

4 Bridge St ✉ NG10 5QT – ☎ (0115) 939 9833 – www.larockrestaurant.co.uk – Closed 26 December-mid-January, 2 weeks summer, Sunday dinner-Wednesday lunch

Rest – Menu £ 25 (lunch) – Carte £ 25/42

Charming, rustic restaurant with an airy feel; dining is split over two floors – upstairs you'll find exposed brick walls and antler chandeliers. Cooking combines classical flavours with modern techniques; local fruits are well used.

SANDIWAY – Cheshire West and Chester – 502 M24 – pop. 4 299 20 A3 – ✉ Northwich

London 191 mi – Liverpool 34 mi – Manchester 22 mi – Stoke-on-Trent 26 mi

Nunsmere Hall

Tarporley Rd, Southwest : 1.5 mi A 556 on A 49 ✉ CW8 2ES – ☎ (01606) 889 100 – www.nunsmere.co.uk

36 rm – †£ 105/200 ††£ 135/340

Rest *Crystal* – see restaurant listing

Built in 1904 for Sir Aubrey Brocklebank, chairman of Cunard Line shipping. Attractive gardens and lovely terrace; several sumptuous lounges and a maritime-themed bar. Spacious, individually furnished bedrooms, some with modern touches.

Crystal – Nunsmere Hall Hotel

Tarporley Rd, Southwest : 1.5 mi by A 556 on A 49 ✉ CW8 2ES – ☎ (01606) 889 100 – www.nunsmere.co.uk

Rest – *(booking essential)* Menu £ 23/35

Long, narrow hotel dining room with traditional styling and views over the terrace and garden. Simply prepared, classically based dishes have strong, gutsy flavours; be sure to try the homemade bread to start and chocolates to finish.

SANDSEND – North Yorkshire – 502 R/S20 – see Whitby

SANDWICH – Kent – 504 Y30 – pop. 4 398 Great Britain 9 D2

London 72 mi – Canterbury 13 mi – Dover 12 mi

Guildhall, ☎ (01304) 61 35 65, www.discoversandwich.co.uk

Town★

Bell at Sandwich

The Quay ✉ CT13 9EF – ☎ (01304) 613 388 – www.bellhotelsandwich.co.uk

37 rm – †£ 90/95 ††£ 99/110

Rest *Old Dining Room* – see restaurant listing

Substantial Victorian property with a cool modern interior, located next to the River Stour. Clubby, intimate bar; airy conservatory for coffee and light meals. Stylish, modern bedrooms come in cool pastel shades; some overlook the river.

Old Dining Room – Bell at Sandwich Hotel

The Quay ✉ CT13 9EF – ☎ (01304) 626 992 – www.bellhotelsandwich.co.uk

Rest – Carte £ 23/33

Hotel dining room of grand proportions, set within a coolly modernised Victorian property overlooking the River Stour. Classical cooking relies on seasonal ingredients sourced from local suppliers, including lots of seafood and fish.

SANDYPARK – Devon – 503 I31 – see Chagford

SAPPERTON – Gloucestershire – see Cirencester

SAWDON – North Yorkshire – see Scarborough

ENGLAND

SAWLEY – Lancashire – 502 M22 – pop. 237 20 B2

London 242 mi – Blackpool 39 mi – Leeds 44 mi – Liverpool 54 mi

Spread Eagle with rm

BB7 4NH – (01200) 441 202 – www.spreadeaglesawley.co.uk – Closed dinner 25 December and 1 January

7 rm – £ 70/90 £ 85/135 **Rest** – Carte £ 26/30

Stylishly made-over, but still very much at the heart of the community. Gutsy, flavourful cooking, with a menu of pub favourites available in two sizes; plus platters, tapas-style nibbles and daily changing specials. Comfortable bedrooms feature smart, modern bathrooms.

SCARBOROUGH – North Yorkshire – 502 S21 – pop. 38 364 23 D1

Great Britain

London 253 mi – Kingston-upon-Hull 47 mi – Leeds 67 mi – Middlesbrough 52 mi

Brunswick, Westborough- Harbourside, Sandside, (01723) 38 36 36, www.discoveryorkshirecoast.co.uk

Scarborough North Cliff, North Cliff Ave, Burniston Rd, NW : 2 mi. by A 165, (01723) 35 53 97

Scarborough South Cliff, Deepdale Ave, S : 1 mi. by A 165, off Filey Rd, (01723) 37 47 37

Robin Hood's Bay★, N : 16 mi on A 171 and minor rd to the right (signposted) – Whitby Abbey★, N : 21 mi on A 171 – Sledmere House★, S : 21 mi on A 645, B 1249 and B 1253 (right)

ENGLAND

Crown Spa

rm, rest,

8-10 Esplanade YO11 2AG – (01723) 357 400 – www.crownspahotel.com

114 rm – £ 48/250 £ 59/250, £ 15 – 1 suite Zn

Rest *Taste* – (01723) 357 439 – Menu £ 15/24 **s** – Carte £ 23/37 **s**

19C landmark hotel, in a prime position on the headland of a Victorian seaside town. Contemporary guest areas, superb leisure facilities and state-of-the-art meeting rooms. Smart bedrooms feature bespoke furnishings and the latest mod cons. Informal, bistro-style dining is split over four different rooms.

Beiderbecke's

rest,

1-3 The Crescent YO11 2PW – (01723) 365 766 – www.beiderbeckes.com

27 rm – £ 85/120 £ 130/170 – 1 suite Zs

Rest *Marmalade's* – (01723) 350 349 – Carte £ 20/35

Set at the top of the town in a Georgian parade, and named after the famous jazz musician. Large, simply furnished bar and function room. Good-sized bedrooms, some with four-posters; those at the front have garden and sea views. The brasserie offers a large, classical menu which features Yorkshire produce.

Ox Pasture Hall

Lady Edith's Dr, Raincliffe Woods, West : 3.25 mi by A 171 following signs for Raincliffe Woods YO12 5TD – (01723) 365 295 – www.oxpasturehallhotel.com

32 rm – £ 80/129 £ 89/219

Rest *Courtyard* – see restaurant listing

Rest *Bistro* – Menu £ 15 (lunch) **s** – Carte £ 22/30 **s**

Charming, creeper-clad, part-17C farmhouse, in 17 acres of landscaped gardens and grounds. Stylish, contemporary guest areas and well-equipped bedrooms; those in the main house are more characterful, those in the courtyard, smarter. Modern menu in the formal restaurant; hearty, unfussy dishes in the bistro.

Alexander

33 Burniston Rd YO12 6PG – (01723) 363 178 – www.alexanderhotelscarborough.co.uk – Closed October-March Ya

8 rm – £ 47/57 £ 70/87

Rest – *(closed Sunday) (dinner only)* Menu £ 20 **s**

1930s red-brick house at the popular North Beach end of town. Well-kept, classically styled lounge. Contemporary bedrooms with flat-screen TVs, good comforts and a clean, uncluttered style; some boast feature walls. The linen-laid dining room offers a 3 choice set menu and local seafood is a feature. Traditional cocktail bar.

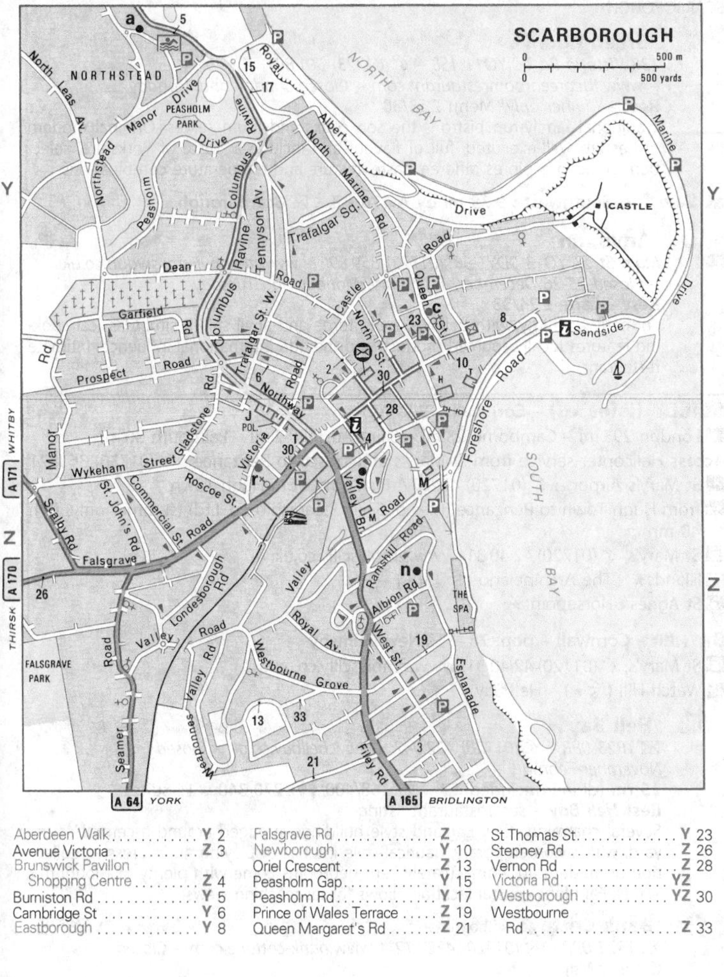

Aberdeen Walk	Y	2	Falsgrave Rd	Z		St Thomas St	Y	23
Avenue Victoria	Z	3	Newborough	Y	10	Stepney Rd	Z	26
Brunswick Pavillon Shopping Centre	Z	4	Oriel Crescent	Z	13	Vernon Rd	Z	28
Burniston Rd	Y	5	Peasholm Gap	Y	15	Victoria Rd	YZ	
Cambridge St	Y	6	Peasholm Rd	Y	17	Westborough	YZ	30
Eastborough	Y	8	Prince of Wales Terrace	Z	19	Westbourne Rd	Z	33
			Queen Margaret's Rd	Z	21			

XXX **Courtyard** – Ox Pasture Hall Hotel

Lady Edith's Dr., Raincliffe Woods, West : 3.25 mi by A 171 following signs for Raincliffe Woods ✉ YO12 5TD – ✆ (01723) 365 295 – www.oxpasturehallhotel.com – Closed Monday and Tuesday

Rest – Menu £ 18 (lunch) – Carte £ 31/42 **s**

Elegant hotel dining room with large, immaculately laid tables, efficient service and pleasant courtyard views. Cooking is careful and precise and dishes are full of flavour. The excellent homemade breads and tasty desserts are a must.

XX **Lanterna**

33 Queen St ✉ YO11 1HQ – ✆ (01723) 363 616 – www.lanterna-ristorante.co.uk – Closed last 2 weeks October, 25-26 December, 1 January and Sunday

Rest – *(dinner only)* Carte £ 30/91 Y**c**

Long-standing, passionately run neighbourhood restaurant with homely décor and a loyal local following. Extensive menu of classic Italian dishes and a sizeable truffle selection – but go for one of the expertly cooked fish specials.

Green Room

138 Victoria Rd ✉ YO11 1SL – ☎ (01723) 501 801 – www.thegreenroomrestaurant.com – Closed Sunday and Monday

Rest – *(dinner only)* Menu £ 13/30 Z**r**

Traditional family-run bistro – the son cooks and mum serves. Original modern dishes are well-executed, full of flavour and include a 'Taste of Yorkshire' selection. Cooking explores different taste, texture and temperature combinations.

at Sawdon Southwest : 9.75 mi by A 170 - Z – ✉ Scarborough

Anvil Inn

Main St ✉ YO13 9DY – ☎ (01723) 859 896 – www.theanvilinnsawdon.co.uk – Closed 25-26 December, 1 January, Monday and Tuesday

Rest – Carte £ 24/38

Formerly a smithy, with bellows, tools, forge and anvil still in situ. Classical cooking features locally sourced produce and the odd international influence. Intimate restaurant.

SCILLY (Isles of) – Cornwall – 503 A/B34 1 A3

London 295 mi – Camborne 23 mi – Saint Austell 52 mi – Falmouth 36 mi

Access Helicopter service from St Mary's and Tresco to Penzance : ☎ (01736) 363871

St Mary's Airport : ☎ (01720) 422677, E : 1.5 mi from Hugh Town

from Hugh Town to Penzance (Isles of Scilly Steamship Co. Ltd) (summer only) (2 h 40 mn)

St Mary's, ☎ (01720) 42 40 31, www.simplyscilly.co.uk

Islands★ - The Archipelago (≤★★★)

St Agnes : Horsepoint★

ENGLAND

BRYHER – Cornwall – pop. 78 – ✉ New Grimsby 1 A3

St Mary's, ☎ (01720) 42 40 31, www.simplyscilly.co.uk

Watch Hill (≤★) – Hell Bay★

Hell Bay

✉ TR23 0PR – ☎ (01720) 422 947 – www.hellbay.co.uk – Closed November-February

25 rm (dinner included) – †£ 168/400 ††£ 270/340 – 14 suites

Rest *Hell Bay* – see restaurant listing

Several charming, New England style buildings arranged around a central courtyard, with a contemporary, nautical-style interior displaying an impressive collection of modern art. Immaculately kept bedrooms come with plenty of thoughtful extras. Fabulous coastal location allows for far-reaching views.

Bank Cottage without rest

✉ TR23 0PR – ☎ (01720) 422 612 – www.bank-cottage.com – Closed October-May

4 rm – †£ 56 ††£ 56

Friendly guesthouse with a well-tended, sub-tropical garden, a koi carp pond and even a rowing boat. Lounge boasts an honesty bar and artefacts from shipwrecks. Bedrooms are simple and compact – one has a roof terrace. Free use of kitchen.

Hell Bay – Hell Bay Hotel

✉ TR23 0PR – ☎ (01720) 422 947 – www.hellbay.co.uk – Closed November-February

Rest – *(booking essential)* Menu £ 39 (dinner) – Carte lunch £ 23/37

Hotel restaurant with a relaxed 'boat house' feel. Light, Mediterranean-influenced lunches in the bar, courtyard or terrace. Dinner steps things up a gear, with unfussy, modern dishes displaying fresh ingredients and clear flavours.

ST MARY'S – Cornwall – pop. 1 607 1 A3

St Mary's, ☎ (01720) 42 40 31, www.simplyscilly.co.uk

Carn Morval, ☎ (01720) 42 26 92

Gig racing★★ - Garrison Walk★ (≤★★) – Peninnis Head★ – Hugh Town - Museum★

Star Castle
The Garrison ✉ TR21 0JA – ✆ (01720) 422 317 – www.star-castle.co.uk – Closed 2 January-10 February
37 rm (dinner included) – †£ 99/159 ††£ 176/388 – 4 suites
Rest *Castle Dining Room* – *(dinner only)* Menu £ 29
Rest *Conservatory* – *(closed November-March) (dinner only)* Menu £ 29
Elizabethan castle in the shape of an 8-pointed star. Well-appointed, classical bedrooms and brighter garden suites – some with harbour or island views. 17C staircase leads from the stone ramparts to the charming Dungeon bar. Fabulous fireplace and kitchen garden produce in the Dining Room. Seafood menus in the Conservatory.

Atlantic
Hugh St, Hugh Town ✉ TR21 0PL – ✆ (01720) 422 417 – www.atlantichotelscilly.co.uk – Closed November-February
25 rm (dinner included) – †£ 75/110 ††£ 180/280
Rest – *(bar lunch)* Menu 20
Former Customs Office in a charming bay setting, affording lovely views across the harbour. Bedrooms – accessed through twisty passages – are well-equipped, and many share the view. Comfortable lounge and small bar. Wicker-furnished restaurant offers an accessible menu.

Evergreen Cottage without rest
Parade, Hugh Town ✉ TR21 0LP – ✆ (01720) 422 711 – www.evergreencottageguesthouse.co.uk – Closed 1 week February and Christmas-New Year
5 rm – †£ 39/50 ††£ 80/82
300 year old captain's cottage in the heart of town, with colourful, welcoming window boxes. The interior is cosy, with a small, low-ceilinged lounge and breakfast room. The oak-furnished bedrooms are compact but spotlessly kept.

ENGLAND

TRESCO – **Cornwall** – **pop. 167** – ✉ **New Grimsby** **1** A3
St Mary's, ✆ (01720) 42 40 31, www.simplyscilly.co.uk
Island★ - Abbey Gardens★★ **AC** (Lighthouse Way ←★★)

Sea Garden Cottages
Old Grimsby ✉ TR24 0QQ – ✆ (01720) 422 849 – www.tresco.co.uk – Restricted opening in winter
9 rm – †£ 135/235 ††£ 135/235
Rest *The Ruin* – ✆ (01720) 424 849 *(booking essential)* Carte £ 23/39
Smart aparthotel divided into New England style 'cottages': each has an open-plan kitchen and lounge and a first floor bedroom; all offer stunning views over St Martin's, Old Grimsby Quay and Blockhouse Point from their terraces and balconies. Relaxed, beachside restaurant serves a Mediterranean menu.

New Inn
New Grimsby ✉ TR24 0QQ – ✆ (01720) 422 849 – www.tresco.co.uk
16 rm – †£ 55/180 ††£ 110/240 **Rest** – *(booking essential)* Carte £ 20/35
Stone-built inn boasting a large terrace, an appealing outdoor pool and pleasant coastal views. Bedrooms are bright, fresh and very comfy. Regular live music events attract guests from near and far. The hugely characterful bar and restaurant offer accessible menus.

SCUNTHORPE – **North Lincolnshire** – **502** S23 – **pop. 72 660** **23** C3
London 167 mi – Leeds 54 mi – Lincoln 30 mi – Sheffield 45 mi
Humberside Airport : ✆ (01652) 688456, E : 15 mi by A 18
18 Ashby Decoy, Burringham Rd, ✆ (01724) 84 29 13
9 Kingsway, ✆ (01724) 84 09 45
18 Grange Park, Messingham, Butterwick Rd, ✆ (01724) 76 29 45

XXX **San Pietro**

11 High St East ✉ DN15 6UH – ✆ (01724) 277 774 – www.sanpietro.uk.com – Closed first week January, 25-26 December, Monday lunch, Sunday dinner and bank holiday Mondays

Rest – Menu £ 18/50 – Carte £ 29/51

Smart restaurant with a chic bar-lounge, housed in a 19C listed windmill. Seasonal menus offer skilfully cooked dishes with Italian and Mediterranean influences; desserts are a highlight. Professional service from a smartly attired team.

SEAHOUSES – Northumberland – 501 P17 Great Britain 24 B1

London 328 mi – Edinburgh 80 mi – Newcastle upon Tyne 46 mi

Seafield Rd, ✆ (01665) 72 08 84, www.seahouses.org

Beadnell Rd, ✆ (01665) 72 07 94

Farne Islands★ (by boat from harbour)

Olde Ship

9 Main St ✉ NE68 7RD – ✆ (01665) 720 200 – www.seahouses.co.uk – Closed December-February

17 rm – †£ 47 ††£ 94/130

Rest – *(bar lunch Monday-Saturday)* Carte £ 19/29 **s**

A long-standing, stone-built, family-run inn in a popular seaside town; full to bursting with nautical memorabilia. This cosy former farmhouse offers comfy, individually designed bedrooms; those in the annexe are bigger, with better views but less character. Formal dining room serves simple, traditional menu.

St Cuthbert's House Ⓝ without rest

192 Main St, Southwest : 0.5 mi by Beadnell rd on North Sunderland rd ✉ NE68 7UB – ✆ (01665) 720 456 – www.stcuthbertshouse.com – Restricted opening in winter

6 rm – †£ 75/90 ††£ 100/120

Former Georgian Presbyterian chapel, with comfortable modern bedrooms, a homely lounge and a wood-furnished breakfast room; large arched windows and many original features remain. The friendly, welcoming owners often host music nights.

SEASALTER – Kent – 504 X29 – see Whitstable

SEAVIEW – Isle of Wight – 503 Q31 – see Wight (Isle of)

SEER GREEN – Buckinghamshire – see Beaconsfield

SETTLE – North Yorkshire – 502 N21 – pop. 3 621 22 A2

London 238 mi – Bradford 34 mi – Kendal 30 mi – Leeds 41 mi

Cheapside, ✆ (01729) 82 51 92, www.settle.org.uk

Giggleswick, ✆ (01729) 82 52 88

X **Brasserie** Ⓝ

The Courtyard, South : 1.5 mi on A 65 ✉ BD24 9JY – ✆ (01729) 892 900 – www.brasserieinthecourtyard.co.uk – Closed 25 December and 1 January

Rest – *(lunch only)* Carte £ 19/28

Characterful barn conversion with a cheese shop, a wine merchant's, a gallery and more; all set around a courtyard. The stylish restaurant offers breakfast, home-made pastries, snacks and afternoon tea. Book ahead for a Sunday joint for 6.

SHAFTESBURY – Dorset – 503 N30 – pop. 6 665 4 C3

London 115 mi – Bournemouth 31 mi – Bristol 47 mi – Dorchester 29 mi

8 Bell St, ✆ (01747) 85 35 14, www.shaftesburydorset.com

Gold Hill★ (<★) – Local History Museum★ **AC**

Wardour Castle★ **AC**, NE : 5 m

ENGLAND

Fleur de Lys

Bleke St ✉ SP7 8AW – ✆ (01747) 853 717 – www.lafleurdelys.co.uk – Closed 2 weeks January

8 rm – †£ 80/105 ††£ 100/160

Rest – *(closed lunch Monday-Tuesday and Sunday dinner)* Menu £ 33

Keenly run, ivy-clad stone house in a lovely market town. Comfortable, well-kept bedrooms are named after grape varieties; each comes with its own laptop. Cosy lounge features a mahogany bar. Dine from traditional menus in the L-shaped restaurant or on the wood-furnished terrace.

Retreat without rest

47 Bell St ✉ SP7 8AE – ✆ (01747) 850 372 – www.the-retreat.co.uk – Closed 28 December-4 February

9 rm – †£ 50/65 ††£ 80/87

Pretty Georgian house on a narrow street in a delightful market town; built for a local doctor on the old site of a school for poor boys. Wood-furnished breakfast room and immaculately kept bedrooms with good facilities. Charming owner.

SHALDON – Devon – 503 J32 – pop. 1 628 2 D2

London 188 mi – Exeter 16 mi – Torquay 7 mi – Paignton 13 mi

ODE

21 Fore St ✉ TQ14 0DE – ✆ (01626) 873 977 – www.odetruefood.co.uk – Closed 2 weeks February, 2 weeks October, 25-26 December, Sunday-Tuesday and bank holidays

Rest – *(dinner only) (booking essential)* Menu £ 35/40

Proudly run neighbourhood restaurant in a glass-fronted Georgian house on a narrow village street. It has a strong sustainable and organic ethos, sourcing recycled glassware, biodynamic wines and produce from small local suppliers and foragers. Simple dishes are precisely prepared and attractively presented.

SHALFLEET – 504 P31 – see Wight (Isle of) – ✉ Isle Of Wight

SHANKLIN – Isle of Wight – 503 Q32 – see Wight (Isle of)

SHEFFIELD – South Yorkshire – 502 P23 – pop. 409 189 22 B3

Great Britain

London 174 mi – Leeds 36 mi – Liverpool 80 mi – Manchester 41 mi

14 Norfolk Row Y, ✆ (0114) 221 19 00, www.spinsheffield.com

Beauchief, Abbey Lane, ✆ (0114) 236 72 74

Concord Park, Shiregreen Lane, ✆ (0114) 257 73 78

Abbeydale, Dore, Twentywell Lane, ✆ (0114) 236 07 63

Cutlers' Hall★ CZ **A** – Cathedral Church of SS. Peter and Paul CZ **B** : Shrewsbury Chapel (Tomb★)

Magna★ **AC**, NE : 3 mi by A 6178 - BY - and Bessemer Way

Plans pages 612, 613

Leopold without rest

2 Leopold St ✉ S1 2GZ – ✆ (0114) 252 40 00 – www.leopoldhotelssheffield.com – Closed 24-30 December CZ**a**

90 rm – †£ 79/149 ††£ 79/249, £ 10 – 14 suites

Evidence of this hotel's past can be seen in the boy's grammar school photos hung throughout and in the Victorian wood-panelling in its meeting rooms. Contemporary bedrooms have fridges and iPod docks; some overlook the rear courtyard.

Westbourne House without rest

25 Westbourne Rd ✉ S10 2QQ – ✆ (0114) 266 01 09 – www.westbournehousehotel.com AZ**c**

8 rm – †£ 55/70 ††£ 75/80

Red-brick Victorian house in a quiet residential suburb, run by welcoming owners. Comfy sitting room with original fireplace and cornicing; breakfast room overlooks mature gardens. Traditionally furnished bedrooms have thoughtful extras.

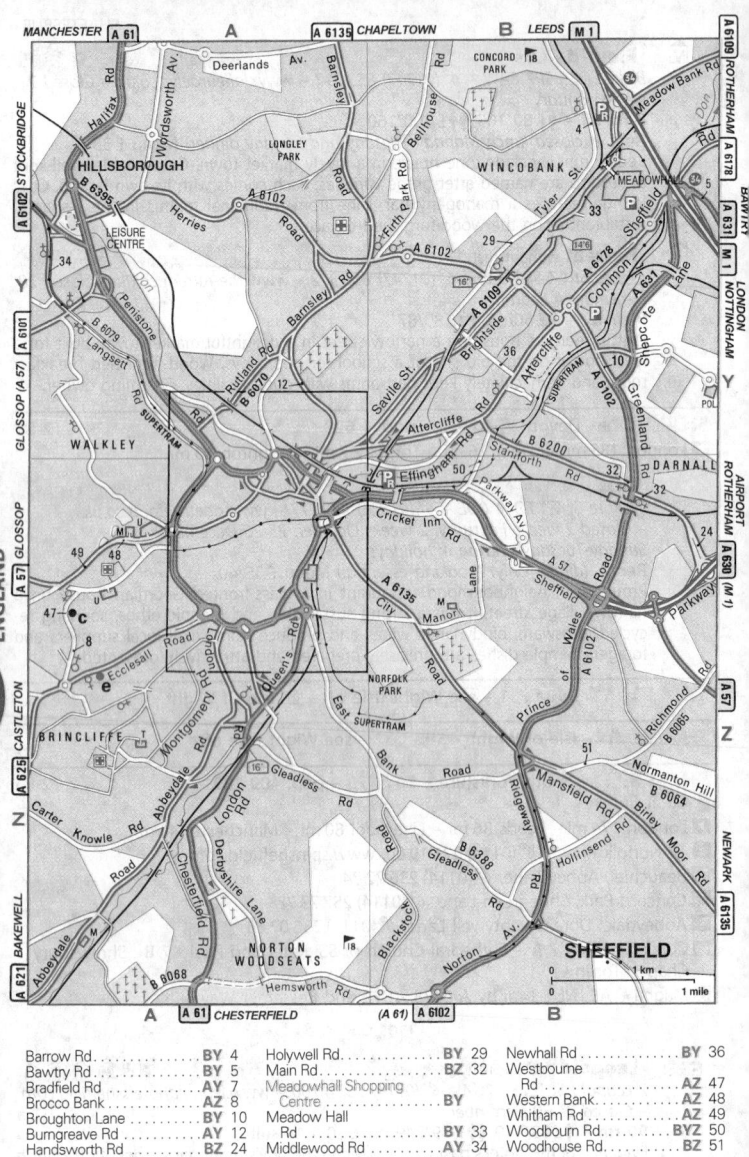

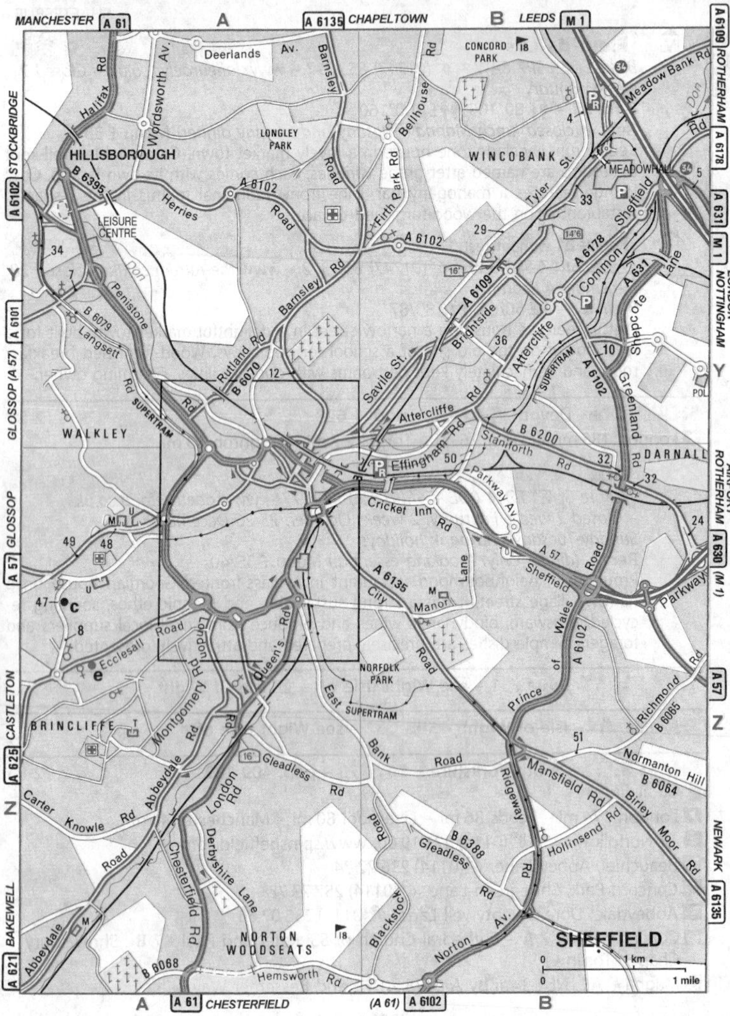

Barrow Rd . . . . BY 4	Holywell Rd. . . . . BY 29	Newhall Rd . . . . BY 36
Bawtry Rd . . . . BY 5	Main Rd. . . . . BZ 32	Westbourne Rd . . . . AZ 47
Bradfield Rd . . . . AY 7	Meadowhall Shopping Centre . . . . BY	Western Bank. . . . . AZ 48
Brocco Bank . . . . AZ 8	Meadow Hall Rd . . . . BY 33	Whitham Rd . . . . AZ 49
Broughton Lane . . . . BY 10	Middlewood Rd . . . . AY 34	Woodbourn Rd. . . . . BYZ 50
Burngreave Rd . . . . AY 12		Woodhouse Rd. . . . . BZ 51
Handsworth Rd . . . . BZ 24		

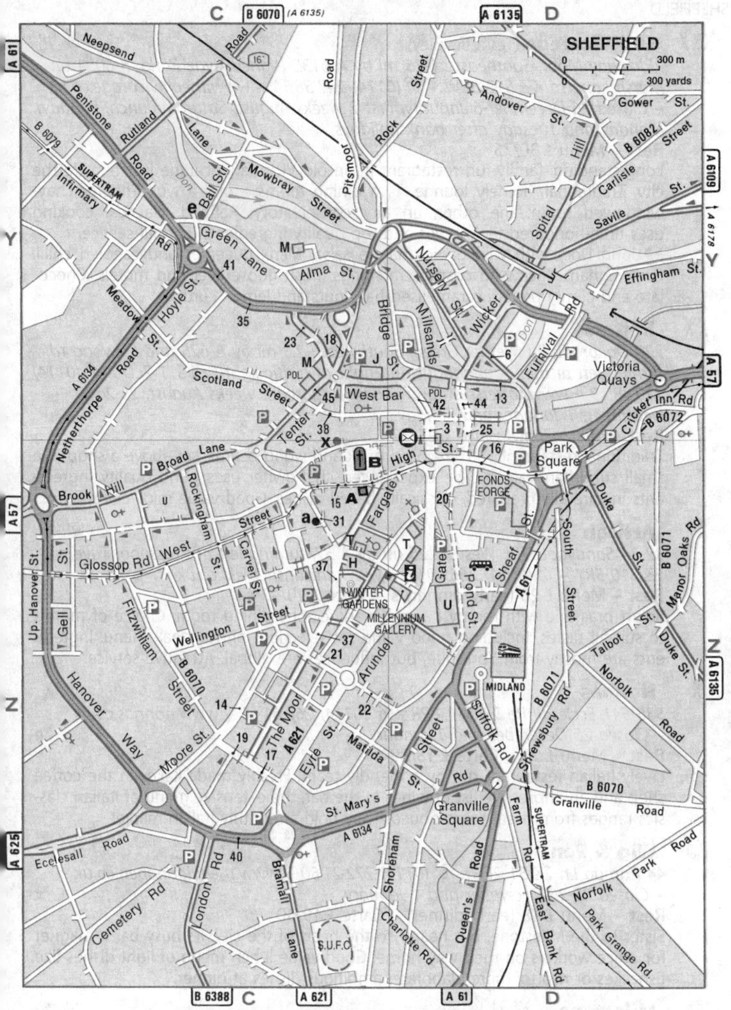

Angel St	DY	3
Blonk St	DY	6
Castle Gate	DY	13
Charter Row	CZ	14
Church St	CZ	15
Commercial St	DZ	16
Corporation St	CY	18
Cumberland St	CZ	17
Fargate	CZ	
Fitzwilliam Gate	CZ	19
Flat St	DZ	20
Furnival Gate	CZ	21
Furnival St	CZ	22
Gibraltar St	CY	23
Haymarket	DY	25
High St	DZ	
Leopold St	CZ	31
Moorfields	CY	35
Pinstone St	CZ	37
Queen St	CY	38
St Mary's Gate	CZ	40
Shalesmoor	CY	41
Snig Hill	DY	42
Waingate	DY	44
West Bar Green	CY	45
West St	CZ	

Old Vicarage (Tessa Bramley)

Ridgeway Moor, Southeast : 6.75 mi by A 6135 (signed Hyde Park), B 6054 on Marsh Lane rd. ✉ S12 3XW – ✆ (0114) 247 58 14 – www.theoldvicarage.co.uk – Closed 26 December-6 January, first 2 weeks August, Saturday lunch, Sunday, Monday and Tuesday after bank holidays

Rest – Menu £ 30/75

Long-standing, family-run restaurant in an old Victorian vicarage just outside the city. Traditional, homely lounge. Two dining rooms – one a wood-floored, bay-windowed room, the other, an airy conservatory. Refined, classical cooking uses time-honoured techniques and top quality ingredients. Formal service.

➜ John Dory with wild garlic, mango salsa, Manx queenies and candied chilli. Gressingham duck with crispy scratchings, fresh goose liver and morels. Chocolate and cumin parfait, caramelised hazelnuts and lemon curd.

Rafters

220 Oakbrook Rd, Nether Green, Southwest : 2.5 mi by A 625 and Fulwood rd, turning left at mini roundabout and right at traffic lights ✉ S11 7ED – ✆ (0114) 230 48 19 – www.raftersrestaurant.co.uk – Closed 2 weeks August, 25-26 December, 1 January and Sunday

Rest – *(dinner only)* Carte £ 25/37

Traditional restaurant with exposed brick and wood beams, set above a shop in a small suburban parade. The experienced chef-owner uses good quality ingredients in carefully prepared, classically based dishes. Good value midweek menu.

Artisan

32-34 Sandygate Rd, West : 2.25 mi by A 57, turning left at Crosspool Tavern ✉ S10 5RY – ✆ (0114) 266 60 96 – www.artisansheffield.co.uk

Rest – Menu £ 20 (early dinner) **s** – Carte £ 20/47 **s**

Smart brasserie with roomy bar and dark, clubby dining room. Choice of menus to suit all tastes, including good value set selections and a steak menu. Ingredients are mostly from Yorkshire, but influences are global. Attentive service.

Nonnas

535-541 Ecclesall Rd ✉ S11 8PR – ✆ (0114) 268 61 66 – www.nonnas.co.uk – Closed 25 December and 1 January AZ**e**

Rest – Menu £ 25 – Carte £ 18/59

Lively Italian restaurant run by a friendly team. Freshly made cakes in the coffee shop and an impressive list of wines in the bar; the extensive menu of Italian classics ranges from pasta to ossobuco. They hold a monthly Italian market.

Wig & Pen

44 Campo Ln ✉ S1 2EG – ✆ (0114) 272 21 50 – www.the-wigandpen.co.uk – Closed 25-26 December and 1 January CY**x**

Rest – Menu £ 18 (early dinner) – Carte £ 19/30

Sister to the Milestone, but nearer to the heart of the city; its busy bar a magnet for office workers on their way home. Good value lunch menu of light dishes like fishcakes or risotto; more elaborate, ambitious dishes at dinner.

Milestone

84 Green Ln ✉ S3 8SE – ✆ (0114) 272 83 27 – www.the-milestone.co.uk – Closed 25-26 December and 1 January CY**e**

Rest – Menu £ 15 (weekday lunch) – Carte £ 23/30

Spacious 18C pub in a recently regenerated area of the city. The hearty gastro menu offers modern dishes with their emphasis firmly on seasonal, organic, locally sourced ingredients; presentation mixes the traditional and the contemporary.

at Totley Southwest : 5.5 mi on A 621 - AZ – ✉ South Yorkshire

Cricket Inn

Penny Ln, (off Hillfoot Rd) ✉ S17 3AZ – ✆ (0114) 236 52 56 – www.cricketinn.co.uk

Rest – Menu £ 15 (weekdays) – Carte £ 17/35

Hidden away next to the cricket pitch, with open fires and rustic wood floors. Wide-ranging, Yorkshire-based menu offers bar snacks through to grills and roasts. Hearty, wholesome cooking.

ENGLAND

SHEFFORD – Central Bedfordshire – 504 S27 – pop. 3 319 12 A1

London 48 mi – Bedford 10 mi – Luton 16 mi – Northampton 37 mi

Black Horse with rm

rest, rest,

Ireland, Northwest : 1.5 mi by Northbridge St and B 658 on Ireland rd ✉ SG17 5QL – ✆ (01462) 811 398 – www.blackhorseireland.com – Closed 25-26 December, 1 January and Sunday dinner

2 rm – †£ 55 ††£ 55 **Rest** – Carte £ 23/34

It may look traditional from the outside, but inside this pub is as stylish and modern as you can get, with marble floors, a granite bar and hi-tech fittings. The eclectic menu offers generous dishes ranging from suet pies to confit of duck or sea bass. Set in the garden, bedrooms are comfy and cosy.

SHELLEY – West Yorkshire – 502 O23 22 B3

London 185 mi – Bristol 197 mi – Cardiff 218 mi – Plymouth 311 mi

Three Acres

rm, rest,

Roydhouse, Northeast : 1.5 mi on Flockton rd ✉ HD8 8LR – ✆ (01484) 602 606 – www.3acres.com – Closed 25-26 December and 1 January

17 rm – †£ 83 ††£ 125/180 **Rest** – *(booking essential)* Carte £ 30/52

Well-established, traditional stone inn perched on top of the moors, with two smart meeting rooms and warmly decorated, modern bedrooms; those in the adjacent cottages are quieter and more contemporary. Busy bar and a maze of charmingly cluttered, low-beamed dining rooms; extensive, classical menu.

SHEPTON MALLET – Somerset – 503 M30 – pop. 8 830 4 C2

London 127 mi – Bristol 20 mi – Southampton 63 mi – Taunton 31 mi

The Mendip, Gurney Slade, ✆ (01749) 84 05 70

Town★ - SS. Peter and Paul's Church★

Downside Abbey★ (Abbey Church★) N : 5.5 mi by A 37 and A 367. Longleat House★★★ **AC**, E : 15 mi by A 361 and B 3092 – Wells★★ - Cathedral★★★, Vicars' Close★, Bishop's Palace★ **AC** (<★★) W : 6 mi by A 371 – Wookey Hole★ (Caves★ **AC**, Papermill★) W : 6.5 mi by B 371 – Glastonbury★★ - Abbey★★ (Abbot's Kitchen★) **AC**, St John the Baptist★★, Somerset Rural Life Museum★ **AC** – Glastonbury Tor★ (<★★★) SW : 9 mi by B 3136 and A 361 - Nunney★, E : 8.5 mi by A 361

Charlton House

rm, rest,

East : 1 mi on A 361 ✉ BA4 4PR – ✆ (01749) 342 008 – www.bannatyne.co.uk

28 rm – †£ 95/400 ††£ 95/400 **Rest** – Menu £ 22/35

Fine 17C house previously owned by Mulberry and now by Duncan Bannatyne: influences from both are evident. Smart boutique styling, with a touch of informality; individually furnished bedrooms feature luxurious bathrooms. Superb spa. Carefully prepared, modern European dishes served in conservatory.

SHERBORNE – Dorset – 503 M31 – pop. 9 939 4 C3

London 128 mi – Bournemouth 39 mi – Dorchester 19 mi – Salisbury 36 mi

Digby Rd, ✆ (01935) 81 53 41, www.sherbornetown.com

Higher Clatcombe, ✆ (01935) 81 22 74

Town★ - Abbey★★ – Castle★ **AC**

Sandford Orcas Manor House★ **AC**, NW : 4 mi by B 3148 – Purse Caundle Manor★ **AC**, NE : 5 mi by A 30. Cadbury Castle (<★★) N : 8 mi by A 30 – Parish Church★, Crewkerne, W : 14 mi on A 30

The Green

3 The Green ✉ DT9 3HY – ✆ (01935) 813 821 – www.greenrestaurant.co.uk – Closed 25-26 December, Sunday and Monday

Rest – Menu £ 22 (weekdays) – Carte £ 28/44

Pretty Grade II listed stone property at the top of the hill, with a traditional bistro style, an inglenook fireplace and ecclesiastical panelling. Concise à la carte and a good value set lunch; classical, confident, satisfying cooking.

at Oborne **Northeast : 2 mi by A 30 – ✉ Sherborne**

Grange

✉ *DT9 4LA – ✆ (01935) 813 463 – www.thegrangeatoborne.co.uk*
18 rm – †£ 99/120 ††£ 118/200 **Rest** – Menu £ 21/35
Family-run, stone-built country house in pretty village; dating back 200 years. Comfy guest areas overlook attractive mature gardens. Spacious bedrooms boast good facilities; some have balconies or patios. Menus showcase the latest local, seasonal ingredients.

SHERE – Surrey – 504 S30 – see Guildford

SHERINGHAM – Norfolk – 504 X25 – pop. 7 143 15 C1

London 136 mi – Cromer 5 mi – Norwich 27 mi

Ashbourne House without rest

1 Nelson Rd ✉ NR26 8BT – ✆ (01263) 821 555
– www.ashbournehousesheringham.co.uk – Closed 21-27 December
3 rm – †£ 50/55 ††£ 70/75
Well-appointed guesthouse in an elevated position; its large, landscaped garden has access to the clifftop. Comfortable bedrooms: two with coastal views. Impressive fireplace in the wood-panelled breakfast room.

SHERWOOD BUSINESS PARK – Nottinghamshire – see Nottingham

SHILTON – Warwickshire – 503 P26 – ✉ Coventry 19 D2

London 97 mi – Bristol 99 mi – Cardiff 131 mi – Plymouth 213 mi

Barnacle Hall without rest

Shilton Ln., West : 1 mi by B 4029 following signs for garden centre ✉ CV7 9LH – ✆ (024) 7661 2629 – www.barnaclehall.co.uk – Closed 24 December-2 January
3 rm – †£ 40/50 ††£ 70/80
Welcoming farmhouse in mature gardens, on a 170 acre arable farm. Traditional, beamed interior with a comfy, fire-lit lounge and 16C origins; spacious bedrooms offer pleasant country views. Hearty, home-cooked, communal breakfasts.

SHINFIELD – Wokingham – 504 R29 – see Reading

SHIPLAKE – Oxfordshire – 504 R29 – see HENLEY-ON-THAMES

SHIPLAKE ROW – Oxfordshire – see Henley-on-Thames

SHIPLEY – West Yorkshire – 502 O22 – pop. 28 162 22 B2

London 216 mi – Bradford 4 mi – Leeds 12 mi

18 Northcliffe, High Bank Lane, ✆ (01274) 58 40 85

18 Bingley, Beckfoot Lane, Cottingley Bridge, ✆ (01274) 56 86 52

plan : see Leeds

Zaara's

34-38 Bradford Rd ✉ BD18 3NT – ✆ (01274) 588 114 – www.zaaras.com
– Closed 25 December and Monday except bank holidays AT**a**
Rest – *(dinner only)* Menu £ 13 (weekdays) – Carte £ 13/21
Modern Indian restaurant with an intimate red colour scheme, wooden feature wall and smart black furnishings. The owner and chefs specialise in dishes from their home region, Punjab; try the dry curries, homemade paneer or karahi dishes.

SHIPSTON-ON-STOUR – Warwickshire – 503 P27 – pop. 4 456 19 C3

London 87 mi – Leeds 146 mi – Sheffield 116 mi – Manchester 139 mi

George

High St ✉ CV36 4AJ – ✆ (01608) 661 453 – www.georgehotelshipston.com
16 rm – †£ 60/85 ††£ 65/90 **Rest** – Menu £ 12/23 – Carte £ 21/35
Red-brick coaching inn at the centre of a busy market town, with a shabby-chic interior, a leather-furnished library and an open-fired bar. Modern, minimalistic bedrooms are named after foods and feature striking food-themed headboards. Seasonal Mediterranean and English based menus in the smart dining room.

SHIRLEY – Derbyshire – **502** O26 – see Ashbourne

SHOTTLE – Derbyshire – see Belper

SHREWSBURY – Shropshire – **502** L25 – pop. 64 684 Great Britain **18** B2

London 164 mi – Birmingham 48 mi – Chester 43 mi – Derby 67 mi

Barker St, ✆ (01743) 28 12 00, www.visitshrewsbury.com

Condover, ✆ (01743) 87 29 77

Meole Brace, ✆ (01743) 36 40 50

Abbey★ **D**

Ironbridge Gorge Museum★★ **AC** (The Iron Bridge★★ - Coalport China Museum★★ - Blists Hill Open Air Museum★★ – Museum of the Gorge and Visitor Centre★) SE : 12 mi by A 5 and B 4380

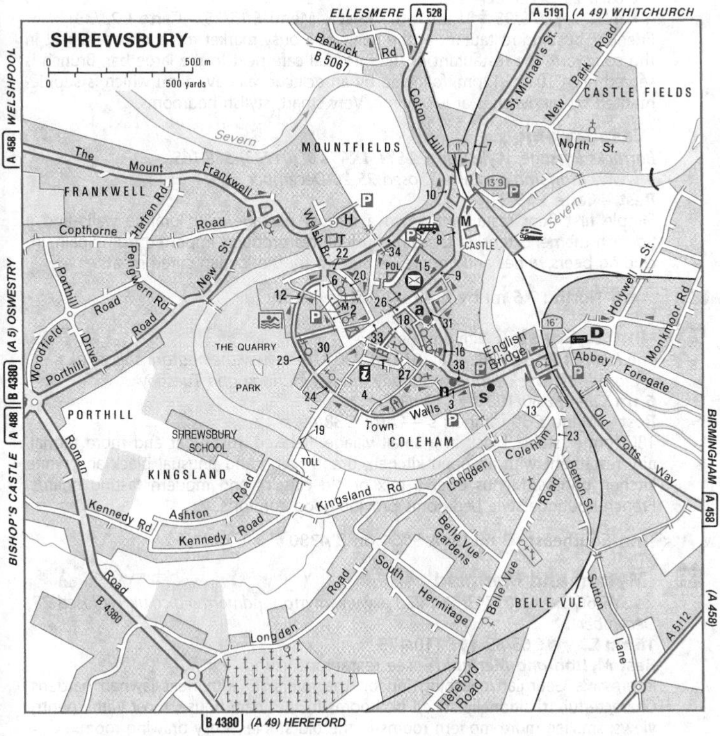

Barker St	2	Coleham Head	13	Pride Hill	26
Beeches Lane	3	Darwin Centre	15	Princess St	27
Belmont	4	Dogpole	16	St Chad's Terrace	29
Bridge St	6	High St	18	St John's Hill	30
Castle Foregate	7	Kingsland Bridge	19	St Mary's St	31
Castle Gates	8	Mardol	20	Shoplatch	33
Castle St	9	Mardol Quay	22	Smithfield Rd	34
Chester St	10	Moreton Crescent	23	Wyle Cop	38
Claremont Bank	12	Murivance	24		

Lion and Pheasant
49-50 Wyle Cop ✉ SY1 1XJ – ✆ (01743) 770 345 – www.lionandpheasant.co.uk – Closed 25 December **s**
23 rm – †£ 79/119 ††£ 99/219 **Rest** – Carte £ 23/44
Collection of adjoining 16C and 18C townhouses, located on a famous medieval street. Modern, minimalist décor throughout: bedrooms, designed by the owner's daughter, vary in shape and size and have a French boutique feel. Bistro-style menu is offered at wooden tables over several dining rooms.

Pinewood House without rest
Shelton Pk, The Mount, Northwest : 1.5 mi on A 458 ✉ SY3 8BL – ✆ (01743) 364 200 – Closed 21-29 December
3 rm – †£ 50 ††£ 64/70
Lovely Edwardian property on the edge of town, converted from three coach houses. Fresh, uncluttered feel throughout, with large, light-filled drawing room and flowers all around. One split-level bedroom with bathroom in the old dovecote. Communal breakfasts.

Mad Jack's with rm
15 St. Mary's St. ✉ SY1 1EQ – ✆ (01743) 358 870 – www.madjacks.uk.com – Closed 25 December **a**
4 rm – †£ 70/95 ††£ 90/150 **Rest** – Menu £ 15/25 – Carte £ 23/38
Friendly, bustling restaurant at the heart of a busy market town; choose a seat in the courtyard, the restaurant or the informal café next to the large bar. Brunch is served from 10am -12pm, followed by an eclectic, all-day menu which is supplemented by sandwiches at lunchtime. Very smart, stylish bedrooms.

Casa Naranjo
Barracks Passage, Wyle Cop ✉ SY1 1XA – ✆ (01743) 588 165 – www.casanaranjo.co.uk – Closed 25-26 December **n**
Rest – Carte £ 19/31
Simple first floor restaurant down a narrow passage, with orange walls and a Spanish theme. Extensive tapas menu features products imported from Spain, including beers, wines and liquors; be sure to try the Iberian cured meats.

ENGLAND

at Grinshill North : 7.5 mi by A 49 – ✉ Shrewsbury

Inn at Grinshill with rm
The High St ✉ SY4 3BL – ✆ (01939) 220 410 – www.theinnatgrinshill.co.uk – Closed first week January, Sunday dinner, Monday and Tuesday
6 rm – †£ 80/100 ††£ 100/140
Rest – Menu £ 30 (dinner) **s** – Carte £ 38/49 **s**
18C former stable block in a small village. Relaxed, rustic bar and more formal, airy restaurant with an open kitchen, grand piano and unusual black and white kitchen photos. Menus offer a mix of old classics and modern tasting boards. French boutique style bedrooms provide good comforts.

at Atcham Southeast : 3 mi by A 5064 on B 4380

Mytton and Mermaid
✉ SY5 6QG – ✆ (01743) 761 220 – www.myttonandmermaid.co.uk – Closed 25 December
16 rm – †£ 65/85 ††£ 110/175
Rest *Mytton and Mermaid* – see restaurant listing
Impressive Georgian coaching inn on the riverside, with neat lawned gardens. Characterful, traditionally styled bedrooms in the main house, most with country views; smaller, more modern rooms in the old stables. Cosy drawing room.

Mytton and Mermaid – Mytton and Mermaid Hotel
✉ SY5 6QG – ✆ (01743) 761 220 – www.myttonandmermaid.co.uk – Closed 25 December
Rest – Carte £ 23/40
Choose between three dining areas: the casual bar, the bustling bistro-style dining room or the pleasant outside terrace. The same extensive menu is served throughout, offering tasty, classically based dishes and daily specials.

SHREWTON – Wiltshire – 503 O30 – pop. 1 648 — 4 D2

London 91 mi – Bristol 53 mi – Southampton 52 mi – Reading 69 mi

Rollestone Manor

Southeast : 0.5 mi on A 360 ✉ SP3 4HF – ✆ (01980) 620 216 – www.rollestonemanor.com – Closed 25-26 December

7 rm – †£ 80/100 ††£ 85/105

Rest – *(dinner only) (bookings essential for non-residents)* Carte £ 18/41

Grade II listed former farmhouse set on main road, just out of the village. Good-sized, antique-furnished bedrooms offer modern facilities. Traditional lounge. Two-roomed restaurant for classic dishes at linen-laid tables.

SHURDINGTON – Gloucestershire – 503 N28 – see Cheltenham

SHUTFORD – Oxfordshire — 10 B1

London 84 mi – Birmingham 51 mi – Sheffield 121 mi – Leicester 58 mi

George & Dragon

Church Lane, ✉ OX15 6PG – ✆ (01295) 780 320 – www.thegeorgeanddragon.com

Rest – Menu £ 15 (weekday dinner) – Carte £ 20/38

Lovely 13C, Grade II listed pub in a pretty village. It's built into a hill, 12 foot beneath St Martin's Church, so when you order at the bar, you're as good as underground! Dishes display a refined simplicity and showcase local produce.

SIBFORD GOWER – Oxfordshire – see Banbury

SIDFORD – Devon – 503 K31 – see Sidmouth

SIDLESHAM – West Sussex – 504 R31 — 7 C3

London 84 mi – Bristol 137 mi – Cardiff 170 mi – Plymouth 187 mi

Landseer House without rest

Cow Ln, South : 1.5 mi by B 2145 and Keynor Lane ✉ PO20 7LN – ✆ (01243) 641 525 – www.landseerhouse.co.uk

6 rm – †£ 85/120 ††£ 85/175

Tastefully furnished guesthouse, with numerous antiques and pleasant views of the surrounding wetlands. Contemporary bedrooms; go for Room 1 – the most luxurious. Those in the garden have their own terraces and kitchens.

Crab & Lobster with rm

Mill Ln ✉ PO20 7NB – ✆ (01243) 641 233 – www.crab-lobster.co.uk

5 rm – †£ 80/185 ††£ 145/250

Rest – *(booking advisable)* Menu £ 20 (weekday lunch) – Carte £ 30/51

Historic inn, in a wonderful setting on a nature reserve, with pretty gardens and a light, relaxed feel. Seasonal menu focuses on seafood. Very comfy bedrooms have a modern, minimalist style; one has its own garden and an open-fired stove.

SIDMOUTH – Devon – 503 K31 – pop. 12 066 — 2 D2

London 176 mi – Exeter 14 mi – Taunton 27 mi – Weymouth 45 mi

Ham Lane, ✆ (01395) 51 64 41, www.visitsidmouth.co.uk

Cotmaton Rd, ✆ (01395) 51 34 51

Bicton★ (Gardens★) **AC**, SW : 5 m

Riviera

The Esplanade ✉ EX10 8AY – ✆ (01395) 515 201 – www.hotelriviera.co.uk – Closed 2 January-12 February

26 rm (dinner included) – †£ 109/199 ††£ 198/378

Rest – Menu £ 30/42 – Carte £ 30/54

Long-standing, family-run hotel with characterful Regency façade. Superbly kept classical guest areas; fresh flowers and friendly staff abound. Smart bedrooms in rich blues and gold, some with a view. Traditional menus have a modern edge. Cream teas a speciality.

at Sidford **North : 2 mi – ✉ Sidmouth**

XX **Salty Monk** with rm
Church St, on A 3052 ✉ EX10 9QP – ✆ (01395) 513 174 – www.saltymonk.co.uk – Closed January, 2 weeks November and lunch Monday-Wednesday
6 rm – £ 85/120 £ 130/180
Rest – *(booking essential)* Menu £ 45 (dinner) – Carte £ 24/43
Smart, proudly run restaurant with a characterful, homely lounge, set in a former 16C salt house. Local produce used in classical cooking with the occasional modern twist. Traditional bedrooms offer antique furniture alongside flat screen TVs. Mini spa facility with garden hot tub.

at Newton Poppleford **Northwest : 4 mi by B 3176 on A 3052 – ✉ Sidmouth**

XX **Moores'**
6 Greenbank, High St ✉ EX10 0EB – ✆ (01395) 568 100 – www.mooresrestaurant.co.uk – Closed first two weeks January, Sunday dinner and Monday
Rest – Menu £ 16/29 **s**
Two 18C cottages set back from the main road, run by a charming husband and wife team. Small, two-roomed restaurant and a conservatory extension. Concise, classical menus rely on local produce; fish and game are specialities.

SINNINGTON – **North Yorkshire** – **502** R21 – **see Pickering**

SISSINGHURST – **Kent** – **504** V30 – **see Cranbrook**

ENGLAND

SITTINGBOURNE – **Kent** – **504** W29 – **pop. 39 974** 9 C1
London 44 mi – Canterbury 18 mi – Maidstone 15 mi – Sheerness 9 mi

Hempstead House
London Rd, Bapchild, East : 2 mi on A 2 ✉ ME9 9PP – ✆ (01795) 428 020 – www.hempsteadhouse.co.uk
34 rm – £ 85/110 £ 110/160
Rest *Lakes* – see restaurant listing
Privately run, red-brick Victorian house with extensions, in pleasant landscaped gardens. Cosy, wood-panelled lounges. Classical bedrooms in main house; more contemporary rooms with the latest mod cons above the truly luxurious spa.

XX **Lakes** – Hempstead House Hotel
London Rd, Bapchild, East : 2 mi on A 2 ✉ ME9 9PP – ✆ (01795) 428 020 – www.hempsteadhouse.co.uk
Rest – *(residents only Sunday dinner)* Menu £ 15/28 – Carte £ 31/39
Set within a red-brick Victorian hotel in pleasant landscaped gardens, a formal conservatory restaurant featuring Georgian columns, crystal chandeliers and linen-laid tables. Classical menus. Homely, open-fired sitting room for drinks.

SKIPTON – **North Yorkshire** – **502** N22 – **pop. 14 313** Great Britain 22 A2
London 217 mi – Kendal 45 mi – Leeds 26 mi – Preston 36 mi
35 Coach St, ✆ (01756) 79 28 09, www.skiptonweb.co.uk
Short Lee Lane, off NW Bypass, ✆ (01756) 79 39 22
Castle★ **AC**

at Hetton **North : 5.75 mi by B 6265 – ✉ Skipton**

XXX **Angel Inn and Barn Lodgings** with rm
✉ BD23 6LT – ✆ (01756) 730 263 – www.angelhetton.co.uk – Closed 4 days January
9 rm – £ 125/150 £ 140/190
Rest *Angel Inn* – see restaurant listing
Rest – *(dinner only and Sunday lunch) (booking essential)* Menu £ 13 – Carte £ 26/43
Formal restaurant comprising two smartly laid dining rooms with an intimate, romantic feel; now something of a local institution and surprisingly busy considering its rural location. Classically based cooking displays a few modern touches. Attentive, professional team. Antique-furnished bedrooms in the 'Barn Lodgings'; more modern rooms in 'Sycamore Bank' cottage.

Angel Inn
✉ BD23 6LT – ✆ (01756) 730 263 – www.angelhetton.co.uk – Closed 4 days January
Rest – *(booking essential)* Carte £ 26/43
18C stone inn, its characterful interior featuring old beams, wood-burning stoves and log fires. Despite its rural location, it's a popular place, and the staff cope well with the numbers. Seasonally changing menus offer hearty dishes of local produce and even some Yorkshire tapas.

SLALEY – **Northumberland** – **see Hexham**

SLAPTON – **Devon** – **503** J33 — 2 C3
London 223 mi – Plymouth 30 mi – Torbay 26 mi – Exeter 50 mi
Dartmouth★★, N : 7 mi by A 379 – Kingsbridge★, W : 7 mi by A 379

Tower Inn with rm
Church Rd ✉ TQ7 2PN – ✆ (01548) 580 216 – www.thetowerinn.com – Closed first 2 weeks January and Sunday dinner in winter
3 rm – †£ 60/65 ††£ 75/90 **Rest** – Carte £ 21/32
Charming pub overlooked by the ruins of a chantry tower (leave your car in the village and walk the narrow lane). Menus differ between services and offer pub food with a twist: maybe fish and chips in vodka batter at lunch or sea bass with crab dumplings in the evening. Simple bedrooms await.

SNAINTON – **North Yorkshire** – **502** S21 — 23 C2
London 241 mi – Pickering 8 mi – Scarborough 10 mi

Coachman Inn with rm
Pickering Rd West, West : 0.5 mi by A 170 on B 1258 ✉ YO13 9PL – ✆ (01723) 859 231 – www.coachmaninn.co.uk – Closed dinner 25 December
6 rm – †£ 80 ††£ 90/110 **Rest** – Carte £ 20/31
Grade II listed coaching inn with a rustic bar and spacious linen-laid restaurant – which is run with some formality. Cooking is classical but presentation is modern and refined. Simpler pub favourites offered at lunch. Bedrooms are smart and spacious.

SNAPE – **Suffolk** – **504** Y27 – **pop. 1 509** — 15 D3
London 113 mi – Ipswich 19 mi – Norwich 50 mi

Crown Inn with rm
Bridge Rd ✉ IP17 1SL – ✆ (01728) 688 324 – www.snape-crown.co.uk
2 rm – †£ 70/90 ††£ **Rest** – Carte £ 19/37
The affable young owners of this characterful 15C former smugglers' inn raise various animals out the back, providing much of the meat for their constantly evolving menus; they also grow many of the fruit and vegetables. Rustic bedrooms have beamed ceilings and sloping floors.

SNETTISHAM – **Norfolk** – **504** V25 – **pop. 2 145** — 14 B1
London 113 mi – King's Lynn 13 mi – Norwich 44 mi

Rose and Crown with rm
Old Church Rd ✉ PE31 7LX – ✆ (01485) 541 382 – www.roseandcrownsnettisham.co.uk
16 rm – †£ 70/90 ††£ 90/110 **Rest** – Carte £ 19/35
14C pub featuring a warren of rooms with uneven floors and low beamed ceilings. Gutsy cooking uses locally sourced produce, with globally influenced dishes alongside trusty pub classics. Impressive children's adventure fort. Modern bedrooms are decorated in sunny colours, and offer a good level of facilities.

SOAR MILL COVE – **Devon** – **503** I33 – **see Salcombe**

SOLIHULL – **West Midlands** – **503** O26 – **pop. 94 753** — 19 C2
London 109 mi – Birmingham 7 mi – Coventry 13 mi – Warwick 13 mi
Homer Rd, ✆ (0121) 704 61 30, www.solihull.gov.uk

ENGLAND

AT OLTON Northwest : 2.5 mi on A 41 – ✉ Solihull

XX **Rajnagar** AC

256 Lyndon Rd., Northeast : 1 mi by Richmond rd. ✉ B92 7QW – ✆ (0121) 742 81 40 – www.rajnagar.com

Rest – *(dinner only)* Menu £ 10 (weekdays) – Carte £ 21/36

Large Indian restaurant with bold, slightly kitsch décor; its name means 'The Place of the Kings'. Extensive menus offer some popular dishes like tikka masala and dopiaza, but try the chef's specials for something a little different.

SOMERTON – Somerset – 503 L30 – pop. 4 133 3 B2

London 138 mi – Bristol 32 mi – Taunton 17 mi

Town★ - Market Place★ (cross★) – St Michael's Church★

Long Sutton★ (Church★★) SW : 2.5 mi by B 3165 – Huish Episcopi (St Mary's Church Tower★★) SW : 4.5 mi by B 3153 – Lytes Cary★, SE : 3.5 mi by B 3151 – Street - The Shoe Museum★, N : 5 mi by B 3151. Muchelney★★ (Parish Church★★) SW : 6.5 mi by B 3153 and A 372 – High Ham (<★★, St Andrew's Church★), NW : 9 mi by B 3153, A 372 and minor rd – Midelney Manor★ **AC**, SW : 9 mi by B 3153 and A 378

Lynch Country House without rest

4 Behind Berry ✉ TA11 7PD – ✆ (01458) 272 316 – www.thelynchcountryhouse.co.uk

9 rm – †£ 65/80 ††£ 80/115

Personally run Regency house with mature grounds that incorporate some unusual plants and a lake frequented by a variety of wildfowl. Traditional country house interior with a conservatory breakfast room and individually decorated bedrooms.

SONNING-ON-THAMES – Wokingham – 504 R29 – see Reading

SOUTH CAVE – East Riding of Yorkshire – 502 S22 – pop. 3 109 23 C2

London 203 mi – Leeds 50 mi – Sheffield 54 mi – Bradford 57 mi

XX **Boars Nest Farmhouse** < P

Rudstone, North : 2 mi by A 1034 on B 1230 ✉ HU15 2AH – ✆ (01482) 445 577 – www.theboarsnesthull.com – Closed 3-15 January, Sunday dinner and Monday

Rest – Menu £ 14/20

Former farmhouse in an elevated position overlooking the Humber Estuary. Inside there's a wacky mix of rustic beams, old fireplaces and contemporary art. The regularly changing menu offers tasty modern classics with the odd humorous touch.

SOUTH DALTON – East Riding of Yorkshire – see Beverley

SOUTH POOL – Devon – ✉ 2 C3

London 218 mi – Plymouth 26 mi – Torbay 25 mi – Exeter 46 mi

Millbrook Inn

✉ TQ7 2RW – ✆ (01548) 531 581 – www.millbrookinnsouthpool.co.uk

Rest – Menu £ 12 (weekday lunch) – Carte £ 24/45

Characterful, passionately run, shabby-chic pub squeezed between the houses on a narrow village street. Choice of cosy, low-beamed interior or two terraces. Cooking is traditional and hearty with Mediterranean influences.

SOUTH RAUCEBY – Lincolnshire – 502 S24/2 – pop. 335 17 C2

London 131 mi – Sheffield 68 mi – Leicester 54 mi – Kingston upon Hull 69 mi

Bustard Inn P

44 Main St ✉ NG34 8QG – ✆ (01529) 488 250 – www.thebustardinn.co.uk – Closed 1 January, Sunday dinner and Monday except bank holidays

Rest – Menu £ 17 (weekday lunch) – Carte £ 22/48

Grade II listed inn set in a peaceful hamlet, with a light and airy flag-floored bar and a spacious, beamed restaurant. Good value lunch menu and a more ambitious à la carte offering modern-style, English dishes.

ENGLAND

SOUTH SHIELDS – Tyne and Wear – 503 P19 – pop. 82 854 — 24 B2

London 278 mi – Bristol 297 mi – Cardiff 318 mi – Plymouth 411 mi

Harbour Lights

101 Lawe Rd ✉ NE33 2AJ – ✆ (0191) 456 0124

Rest – Menu £ 16 (lunch) – Carte £ 20/30

Simply furnished pub perched above the River Tyne, with great views over the Tynemouth Piers to the North Sea. Menus offer pub classics, along with some more adventurous specials at weekends. Fish comes from the North Shields fish quay.

SOUTHAMPTON – Southampton – 503 P31 – pop. 241 261 — 6 B2

Great Britain

London 87 mi – Bristol 79 mi – Plymouth 161 mi

Access Itchen Bridge (toll) AZ

Southampton/Eastleigh Airport : ✆ (0844) 481 7777, N : 4 mi BY

to Hythe (White Horse Ferries Ltd) frequent services daily (12 mn) – to the Isle of Wight (Cowes) (Red Funnel Ferries) frequent services daily (approx. 22 mn)

to the Isle of Wight (East Cowes) (Red Funnel Ferries) frequent services daily (55 mn)

9 Civic Centre Rd, ✆ (023) 8083 33 33, www.visit-southampton.co.uk

Southampton Municipal, Bassett, Golf Course Rd, ✆ (023) 8076 05 46

Stoneham, Bassett, Monks Wood Close, ✆ (023) 8076 92 72

Chilworth, Main Rd, ✆ (023) 8074 05 44

Old Southampton AZ : Bargate★ **B** - Tudor House Museum★ **M1**

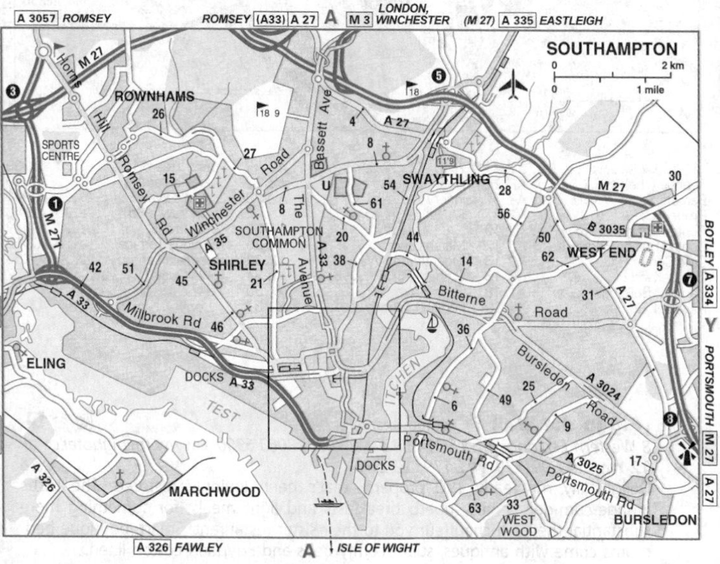

Street		No.
Basset Green Rd	AY	4
Botley Rd	AY	5
Bridge Rd	AY	6
Burgess Rd	AY	8
Butts Rd	AY	9
Cobden Ave	AY	14
Coxford Rd	AY	15
Hamble Lane	AY	17
Highfield Lane	AY	20
Hill Lane	AY	21
Kane's Hill	AY	24
Kathleen Rd	AY	25
Lordswood Rd	AY	27
Lords Hill Way	AY	26
Mansbridge Rd	AY	28
Moorgreen Rd	AY	30
Moor Hill	AY	31
Newtown Rd	AY	33
Peartree Ave	AY	36
Portswood Rd	AY	38
Redbridge Rd	AY	42
St Denys Rd	AY	44
Shirley High Rd	AY	45
Shirley Rd	AY	46
Spring Rd	AY	49
Swaythling Rd	AY	50
Tebourba Way	AY	51
Thomas Lewis Way	AY	54
Townhill Way	AY	56
Welbeck Ave	AY	61
Westend Rd	AY	62
Weston Lane	AY	63

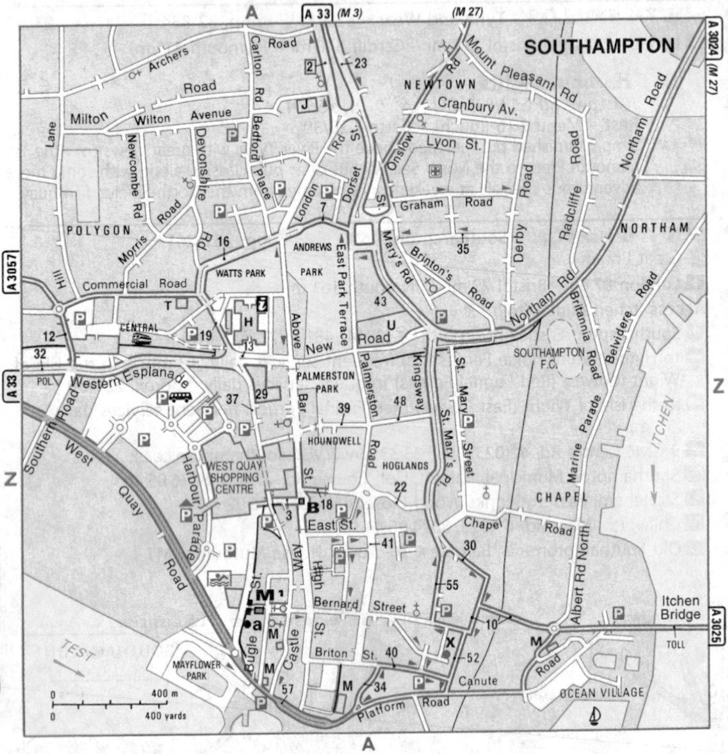

Pig in the Wall Ⓝ without rest

8 Western Esplanade ✉ SO14 2AZ – ✆ (023) 8063 6900 – www.thepighotel.co.uk

12 rm – †£ 99/179 ††£ 179, ☕ £ 10 AZ**a**

Delightfully run, early 19C property that's been lovingly restored. The rustic lounge-cum-deli serves superb breakfasts and light meals; for something more substantial they will chauffeur you to their sister restaurant. Smart, boutique bedrooms come with antiques, super-comfy beds and Egyptian cotton linen.

White Star Tavern, Dining and Rooms with rm

28 Oxford St ✉ SO14 3DJ – ✆ (023) 8082 1990 – www.whitestartavern.co.uk – Closed 25-26 December AZ**x**

14 rm – †£ 75/175 ††£ 75/175, ☕ £ 8 **Rest** – Carte £ 19/40

Eye-catching black pub with vast windows and smart pavement terrace, set in the lively maritime district. Choice of all day tapas-style small plates or modern British à la carte of meaty dishes. Smart, modern bedrooms boast good facilities and extra touches.

at Netley Marsh **West : 6.5 mi by A 33 off A 336**

Hotel TerraVina

174 Woodlands Rd ✉ SO40 7GL – ✆ (023) 8029 3784
– www.hotelterravina.co.uk
11 rm – †£ 150/185 ††£ 165/265
Rest *Restaurant TerraVina* – see restaurant listing
Neat and friendly Victorian red-brick house with wood-clad extensions, in a peaceful New Forest location. Comfy lounge and good-sized bar. Brown and orange hues create a relaxed Mediterranean feel. Bedrooms boast superb bedding, good facilities and thoughtful extras; some have roof terraces.

Restaurant TerraVina – Hotel TerraVina

174 Woodlands Rd ✉ SO40 7GL – ✆ (023) 8029 3784
– www.hotelterravina.co.uk
Rest – Menu £ 21/65 – Carte £ 29/45
Modern hotel restaurant with an open-plan kitchen, a glass-fronted wine cave and a large, covered terrace. Lunch sticks to the classics; dinner introduces some imaginative, modern dishes and a 6 course tasting menu. An ambitious 9 or 12 course tasting menu is available in the 'Dining Room' 3 days a week.

SOUTH CADBURY – Somerset – 503 M30 – see Castle Cary

SOUTHEND-ON-SEA – Southend-on-Sea – 504 W29 – pop. 160 257 13 C3

London 39 mi – Cambridge 69 mi – Croydon 46 mi – Dover 85 mi
Southend-on-Sea Airport : ✆ (01702) 608100, N : 2 m
Western Esplanade, ✆ (01702) 21 51 20, www.visitsouthend.co.uk
18 Belfairs, Leigh-on-Sea, Eastwood Road North, ✆ (01702) 52 53 45
18 Ballards Gore G. & C.C., Gore Rd, Canewdon, ✆ (01702) 25 89 17
27 Garon Park Golf Complex, Garon Park, Eastern Ave, ✆ (01702) 60 17 01

Beaches without rest

192 Eastern Esplanade, Thorpe Bay ✉ SS1 3AA – ✆ (01702) 586 124
– www.beachesguesthouse.co.uk
7 rm – †£ 45/75 ††£ 70/90
Attractive terraced guesthouse on the promenade, boasting fine views over Thorpe Bay and the Thames Estuary. Individually decorated bedrooms are comfortable and well-furnished; those to the front have balconies and afford the best views. Good buffet breakfasts.

Pier View without rest

5 Royal Terr. ✉ SS1 1DY – ✆ (01702) 437 900 – www.pierviewguesthouse.co.uk
8 rm – †£ 55/110 ††£ 80/140
Georgian townhouse in an elevated position overlooking the promenade, estuary and pier. Individually decorated, very comfortable bedrooms; a front sea view room is a must. First floor breakfast room features original cornicing and fireplace.

SOUTHPORT – Merseyside – 502 K23 – pop. 91 404 20 A2

London 221 mi – Liverpool 25 mi – Manchester 38 mi – Preston 19 mi
112 Lord St, ✆ (01704) 53 33 33, www.visitsouthport.com
18 Southport Golf Links, Park Road West, ✆ (01704) 53 52 86

Vincent

98 Lord St. ✉ PR8 1JR – ✆ (01704) 883 800 – www.thevincenthotel.com
63 rm – †£ 93/209 ††£ 103/219 – 4 suites
Rest *V-Café* – see restaurant listing
Striking glass, steel and stone hotel beside the gardens and bandstand. Stylish, boutique interior with chic bar, fitness room and spa. Sleek, modern bedrooms come in dark colours, boasting Nespresso machines and deep Japanese soaking tubs.

V-Café – Vincent Hotel
98 Lord St. ✉ PR8 1JR – ☎ (01704) 883 800 – www.thevincenthotel.com
Rest – Menu £ 15 (weekday dinner) – Carte £ 20/50
Relaxed café in a striking modern hotel, its glass façade overlooking the street. Open all-day and offering everything from sushi at the counter to 3 courses of globally influenced dishes.

Bistrot Vérité
7 Liverpool Rd, Birkdale, South : 1.5 mi by A 565 ✉ PR8 4AR – ☎ (01704) 564 199 – www.bistrotverite.co.uk – Closed 1 week summer, 1 week winter, 25-26 December, 1 January, Sunday and Monday
Rest – *(booking essential)* Carte £ 21/36
Simple neighbourhood bistro with panelled walls and candles; sit on the red banquette which runs down one side. Gutsy, traditional French cooking, with desserts a speciality. Friendly, efficient service.

SOUTHROP – Gloucestershire – 503 O28 — 4 D1

London 87 mi – Birmingham 77 mi – Bristol 60 mi – Sheffield 146 mi

Swan with rm
✉ GL7 3NU – ☎ (01367) 850 205 – www.theswanatsouthrop.co.uk
3 rm – †£ 120 ††£ 160 **Rest** – Menu £ 17 (weekdays) – Carte £ 26/45
Delightful Virginia creeper clad inn set in a quintessential Cotswold village in the Leach Valley. With its characterful low-beamed rooms and charming service, it's popular with locals and visitors alike. Dishes are mainly British-based and feature garden produce; try the delicious homemade bread. Three delightful cottages (2 night stay min.) are just down the road.

ENGLAND

SOUTHWOLD – Suffolk – 504 Z27 – pop. 3 858 — 15 D2

London 108 mi – Great Yarmouth 24 mi – Ipswich 35 mi – Norwich 34 mi
69 High St, ☎ (01502) 72 47 29, www.exploresouthwold.co.uk
The Common, ☎ (01502) 72 32 34

Swan rm, P
Market Pl. ✉ IP18 6EG – ☎ (01502) 722 186 – www.adnams.co.uk
42 rm – †£ 110/125 ††£ 185/205 – 2 suites
Rest – Menu £ 35 (dinner) – Carte lunch £ 22/32
Attractive 17C coaching inn set in the town centre. Subtle modernisations and stylish touches in cosy lounge and bar. Mix of bedrooms: some traditional, some boldly coloured, some charming. Grand dining room with portraits and chandeliers; modern European menu.

Crown with rm P
90 High St ✉ IP18 6DP – ☎ (01502) 722 275 – www.adnams.co.uk
15 rm – †£ 135/150 ††£ 160/255 **Rest** – Carte £ 28/54
17C Georgian-fronted former coaching inn with appealing, relaxed style, buzzing atmosphere and nautically themed locals bar. Modern, seasonal menu served in all areas. Contemporary, individually styled bedrooms; those at the rear are the quietest.

SOWERBY BRIDGE – West Yorkshire – 502 O22 – pop. 9 901 — 22 A2
– ✉ Halifax

London 211 mi – Bradford 10 mi – Burnley 35 mi – Manchester 32 mi

Gimbals N
76 Wharf St ✉ HX6 2AF – ☎ (01422) 839 329 – www.gimbals.co.uk – Closed 25-27 December, 1-2 January, Sunday and Monday
Rest – *(dinner only)* Menu £ 17/20 – Carte £ 22/36
Personally and passionately run restaurant on the high street of a former mill town; look out for the eye-catching illuminated window display. Modern monthly menus have subtle Mediterranean influences and the desserts are a real highlight.

SPARKWELL – Devon 2 C2

London 210 mi – Bristol 114 mi – Cardiff 145 mi – Plymouth 10 mi

Treby Arms

PL7 5DD – (01752) 837 363 – www.thetrebyarms.co.uk – Closed 25-26 December and 1 January

Rest – *(booking essential)* Menu £ 16 (lunch) – Carte £ 27/45

It might be hidden away in a tiny hamlet but it's a very busy place, so you'll need to book. Enticing menus feature tempting bar snacks and carefully prepared modern dishes; the 6 course 'taster' menu best demonstrates the chef's talent.

SPARSHOLT – Hampshire – 503 P30 – see Winchester

SPEEN – Buckinghamshire – 504 R28 – Princes Risborough 11 C2

London 41 mi – Aylesbury 15 mi – Oxford 33 mi – Reading 25 mi

XX Old Plow

Flowers Bottom, West : 0.5 mi by Chapel Hill and Highwood Bottom HP27 0PZ – (01494) 488 300 – www.theoldplow.co.uk – Closed August, 1 week late May, Christmas, Sunday and Monday

Rest – Carte £ 28/46

Characterful roadside inn with low beams and open fires; sit in the dining room or more casual bistro. Cooking is classically based, featuring mature local steaks and seafood arriving daily from Brixham. They celebrated 25 years in 2013.

SPELDHURST – Kent – 504 U30 – see Royal Tunbridge Wells

SPRIGG'S ALLEY – Oxfordshire – see Chinnor

STADDLE BRIDGE – North Yorkshire – see Northallerton

STADHAMPTON – Oxfordshire – 503 Q28 – pop. 718 10 B2

London 53 mi – Aylesbury 18 mi – Oxford 10 mi

Crazy Bear

Bear Ln, off Wallingford rd OX44 7UR – (01865) 890 714 – www.crazybeargroup.co.uk – Closed 29 June

17 rm – †£ 100/410 ††£ 100/410

Rest *Thai* – see restaurant listing

Rest *English* – Menu £ 15 (lunch) – Carte £ 24/46

Wacky converted pub with a red London bus reception, a characterful bar, a smart glasshouse and even a Zen garden. Sumptuous, quirky bedrooms are spread about the place; some have padded walls and infinity baths. The flamboyant English restaurant with mirrored walls serves classic British and French dishes.

XX Thai – Crazy Bear Hotel

Bear Ln, off Wallingford rd OX44 7UR – (01865) 890 714 – www.crazybeargroup.co.uk – Closed 29 June

Rest – *(booking essential)* Menu £ 40/50 – Carte £ 26/45

Cosy, casual hotel restaurant in an intimate basement room, with ornate silk hangings and just 8 polished brass tables. Flavoursome, authentic dishes are skilfully prepared by a Thai chef; the 9, 11 and 13 course set menus are popular.

STAFFORD – Staffordshire – 502 N25 – pop. 63 681 19 C1

London 142 mi – Birmingham 26 mi – Derby 32 mi – Shrewsbury 31 mi

Eastgate St, (0871) 7 16 19 32, www.enjoystaffordshire.com

Stafford Castle, Newport Rd, (01785) 22 38 21

Moat House

rm,

Lower Penkridge Rd, Acton Trussell, South : 3.75 mi by A 449 ST17 0RJ – (01785) 712 217 – www.moathouse.co.uk – Closed 25 December

41 rm – †£ 135 ††£ 155 – 1 suite

Rest *Orangery* – Menu £ 18/30 – Carte £ 34/50

Professionally run, part-timbered, 15C manor house, with lawned gardens, a moat, a pond and a canal. Plenty of lounge space including a rustic, beamed bar. Good-sized bedrooms are traditional in look, with up-to-date facilities. Smart, contemporary Orangery offers modern menus.

Pillar
The Post House, 35 Greengate St, (1st floor) ✉ *ST16 2HZ – ✆ (01785) 231 450 – www.pillarrestaurant.co.uk – Closed Sunday*
Rest – *(dinner only)* Carte £ 20/44
Red-brick former post office with a modern ground floor bistro, an intimate cocktail bar and a trendy club. Smart, formal first floor dining room features eye-catching lampshades and an open kitchen. Classic cooking has a modern touch.

STALISFIELD GREEN
9 C2

London 51 mi – Bristol 169 mi – Cardiff 202 mi – Plymouth 261 mi

Plough
✉ *ME13 0HY – ✆ (01795) 890 256 – www.stalisfieldgreen.com – Closed Monday except bank holidays*
Rest – Menu £ 14 (weekdays) – Carte £ 25/36
Remotely set, 15C pub with thick walls, exposed beams, farming implements and hop bines. Evening candlelight intensifies the pub's rustic charm – as do the friendly staff. Hearty portions of country-style cooking, with local meats a speciality. An impressive range of Kent wine and real ale.

STAMFORD – Lincolnshire – 502 S26 – pop. 22 574 Great Britain
17 C2

London 92 mi – Leicester 31 mi – Lincoln 50 mi – Nottingham 45 mi
27 St Mary's St, ✆ (01780) 75 56 11, www.stamford.co.uk
Town★★ - St Martin's Church★ – Lord Burghley's Hospital★ – Browne's Hospital★ **AC**
Burghley House★★ **AC**, SE : 1.5 mi by B 1443

ENGLAND

George of Stamford
71 St Martins ✉ *PE9 2LB – ✆ (01780) 750 750 – www.georgehotelofstamford.com*
47 rm – £ 95/110 £ 185/245 – 1 suite
Rest *Garden Room* – see restaurant listing
Rest – Menu £ 25 (weekday lunch)/31 – Carte £ 30/54
Historic coaching inn dating back over 900 years and still offering good, old-fashioned hospitality. Plenty of seating options in various bars, lounges, the courtyard and walled garden. Bedrooms have a surprisingly contemporary feel. Formal oak-panelled restaurant requires smart dress; menu has a modern edge.

William Cecil
High St, St Martins ✉ *PE9 2LJ – ✆ (01780) 750 070 – www.thewilliamcecil.co.uk*
27 rm – £ 95/325 £ 110/375 – 1 suite **Rest** – Carte £ 28/54
Extended 17C cream-stone rectory, named after the 1st Baron Burghley, with access through the garden to the estate. Contemporary, shabby-chic, panelled interior. Colonial-style bedrooms feature wood carvings and pastoral scene wallpaper. Restaurant has intimate, Regency-style booths and a classical menu.

Crown
All Saints Pl. ✉ *PE9 2AG – ✆ (01780) 763 136 – www.thecrownhotelstamford.co.uk*
28 rm – £ 70/165 £ 75/165 **Rest** – Carte £ 23/41
Former coaching inn set in historic market town. Main house bedrooms have a funky, boutique style; those in the Town House are larger with a more classical feel. Dine in the modern cocktail bar, in one of the cosy lounges or in the quieter rear dining room.

Jim's Yard
3 Ironmonger St, off Broad St ✉ *PE9 1PL – ✆ (01780) 756 080 – www.jimsyard.biz – Closed last week July, first week August, 25 December-10 January, Sunday and Monday*
Rest – Menu £ 15/20 – Carte £ 21/35
Two 18C houses with a covered courtyard, tucked away in the town centre. Choose between the small ground floor conservatory which opens onto the terrace or the more intimate beamed dining room up in the eaves. Daily menus of appealing classical dishes and great value lunches. Friendly team.

Garden Room – George of Stamford Hotel
71 St Martin's ✉ PE9 2LB – ✆ (01780) 750 750
– www.georgehotelofstamford.com
Rest – *(bookings not accepted)* Carte £ 24/43
Informal, all-day restaurant within a 900 year old coaching inn. Extensive, traditional menu with seafood a highlight – accompanied by a steak counter in winter and a salad bar in summer. The enclosed courtyard is a popular spot.

Bull & Swan with rm
St Martins ✉ PE9 2LJ – ✆ (01780) 766 412 – www.thebullandswan.co.uk
7 rm – †£ 80/375 ††£ 100/425 **Rest** – Carte £ 25/47
Stone-built former hall house converted to an inn during the 1600s and still the only pub south of the river. Characterful beamed bar and smarter dining room. Menu ranges from sharing slates to regional classics and locally sourced steaks. Stylish, individually designed bedrooms boast Egyptian cotton sheets.

STANFORD DINGLEY – West Berkshire 10 B3

London 52 mi – Sheffield 168 mi – Nottingham 130 mi – Bristol 69 mi

Bull Inn (N) with rm
Cock Ln ✉ RG7 6LS – ✆ (01189) 744 582 – www.thebullinnstanforddingley.co.uk
5 rm – †£ 60 ††£ 60, £ 12 **Rest** – Carte £ 22/58
Set in a lovely rural spot, the 15C Bull Inn has it all. It's a real family affair, with dad fixing it up, mum adding arty touches and their daughter running the show. Sit in the rustic bar or dramatically papered dining rooms. The 'beer tapas' is a nice touch and comfy bedrooms complete the picture.

STANSTED MOUNTFITCHET – Essex – 504 U28 – pop. 5 311 12 B2

London 38 mi – Birmingham 125 mi – Croydon 59 mi – Barnet 37 mi

Chimneys without rest
44 Lower St, on B 1351 ✉ CM24 8LR – ✆ (01279) 813 388
– www.chimneysguesthouse.co.uk
4 rm – †£ 58/66 ††£ 82
Charming 17C house with low-beamed ceilings, a cosy lounge and snug breakfast room. Bedrooms have a modern, cottagey style, displaying pine furnishings and homely touches. Tasty breakfast offerings might include Manx kippers or smoked haddock with poached eggs.

STANTON – Suffolk – 504 W27 – pop. 2 073 15 C2

London 88 mi – Cambridge 38 mi – Ipswich 40 mi – King's Lynn 38 mi

Leaping Hare
Wyken Vineyards, South : 1.25 mi by Wyken Rd ✉ IP31 2DW – ✆ (01359) 250 287 – www.wykenvineyards.co.uk – Closed 25 December-5 January
Rest – *(lunch only and dinner Friday-Saturday) (booking essential)*
Menu £ 19/24 – Carte £ 22/40
Beautiful, 17C timber-framed barn with a lovely terrace, at the centre of a 7 acre vineyard. Interesting all-day light bites and accomplished weekly menu. Carefully judged cooking relies on well-sourced, seasonal ingredients; many from their own farm. Farmers' market on Saturdays.

STAPLEFORD – Nottinghamshire – 504 Q25 – see Nottingham

STATHERN – Leicestershire – 502 R25 – ✉ Melton Mowbray 16 B2

London 119 mi – Birmingham 69 mi – Sheffield 62 mi – Leicester 24 mi

Red Lion Inn
2 Red Lion St ✉ LE14 4HS – ✆ (01949) 860 868 – www.theredlioninn.co.uk
– Closed Sunday dinner and Monday
Rest – *(booking essential)* Menu £ 18 (weekdays) – Carte £ 21/39
Large, creamwashed village pub. Good value menus offer straightforward pub classics, alongside well-presented, refined restaurant-style dishes. Produce is sourced from their kitchen garden and local suppliers; the map on the back of the menu emphasis their proximity. Service is friendly and attentive.

ENGLAND

STAVERTON – 503 I32 2 C2

London 220 mi – Exeter 20 mi – Torquay 33 mi

Kingston House

Northwest : 1 mi on Kingston rd ✉ *TQ9 6AR – ℘ (01803) 762 235 – www.kingston-estate.co.uk – Closed Christmas-New Year*

3 rm – †£ 110 ††£ 180/200 **Rest** – Menu £ 25/40

Attractive Georgian house in a peaceful rural spot. Two traditional drawing rooms; original features and antiques abound. Spacious bedrooms feature heavy fabrics, four-posters and views over the parterre garden; some have their original baths. Small, formal dining room serves classical, home-cooked dishes.

STAVERTON – 504 Q27 – see Daventry

STILTON – Cambridgeshire – 504 T26 – pop. 2 500 – ✉ Peterborough 14 A2

London 76 mi – Cambridge 30 mi – Northampton 43 mi – Peterborough 6 mi

Bell Inn

Great North Rd ✉ *PE7 3RA – ℘ (01733) 241 066 – www.thebellstilton.co.uk – Closed 25 December*

22 rm – †£ 80/120 ††£ 108/140

Rest *Galleried Restaurant* – *(closed Sunday dinner and bank holidays except 26 December and 1 January) (dinner only and Sunday lunch)* Menu £ 25/30 – Carte £ 21/37

Historic coaching inn run by a hospitable, hands-on owner. Characterful beamed lounge and comfortable bedrooms with a traditional feel: some have four-posters; the three newest are in the former smithy, overlooking the garden. The first floor restaurant offers a seasonal menu with strong classical base.

Village Bar (at Bell Inn)

Great North Rd ✉ *PE7 3RA – ℘ (01733) 241 066 – www.thebellstilton.co.uk – Closed 25 December*

Rest – Carte £ 21/37 **s**

17C coaching inn where Stilton cheese was born; dine in the characterful bar or more modern bistro. Classically based menus offer plenty of choice and Stilton cheese appears in many of the dishes, from starters through to desserts.

STOCKBRIDGE – Hampshire – 503 P30 – pop. 570 6 B2

London 75 mi – Salisbury 14 mi – Southampton 19 mi – Winchester 9 mi

Greyhound on the Test N with rm

31 High St ✉ *SO20 6EY – ℘ (01264) 810 833 – www.thegreyhoundonthetest.co.uk*

7 rm – †£ 70 ††£ 100/125

Rest – *(booking advisable)* Menu £ 18 (weekday lunch) – Carte £ 23/44

Eye-catching pub with mustard-coloured walls, a red tiled roof and over a mile of River Test fishing rights to the rear. Low beams and wood burning stoves abound, and elegant décor gives it a French bistro feel. Menus offer an appealing range of well-presented, classically based, refined brasserie-style dishes. Homely bedrooms have walk-in showers and quality bedding.

STOCKPORT – Greater Manchester – 502 N23 – pop. 136 082 20 B3

London 201 mi – Liverpool 42 mi – Leeds 50 mi – Sheffield 52 mi

Damson

113 Heaton Moor Rd, Northwest : 2.25 mi by A 6, Heaton Rd, A 5145 and Bank Hall Rd ✉ *SK4 4HY – ℘ (0161) 432 46 66 – www.damsonrestaurant.co.uk – Closed 26 December and 1 January*

Rest – Menu £ 19/46 – Carte £ 22/42

Smart, modern, glass-fronted restaurant on a corner site, with a pavement terrace, damson walls, velvet chairs and rustic tables. Appealing menu of traditional dishes with modern touches. Attentive, formal service.

ENGLAND

STOCKSFIELD – Northumberland – 502 O19 24 A2

London 280 mi – Cardiff 320 mi – Swansea 346 mi – Telford 220 mi

Locksley without rest

45 Meadowfield Rd, Southeast : 2 mi by A 695 and New Ridley Road
NE43 7PY – (01661) 844 778 – www.locksleybedandbreakfast.co.uk
3 rm – £ 35 £ 65/70
Welcoming, immaculately kept house in a peaceful location: a good base for discovering the Tyne Valley. Homely lounge with a piano and a gas-fired stove. Spacious bedrooms have superb bathrooms; family and ground floor rooms are available.

STOKE BY NAYLAND – Suffolk – 504 W28 15 C3

London 70 mi – Bury St Edmunds 24 mi – Cambridge 54 mi – Colchester 11 mi

Crown with rm rm,

CO6 4SE – (01206) 262 001 – www.crowninn.net – Closed 25-26 December
11 rm – £ 95/225 £ 130/225 **Rest** – Carte £ 18/34
Smart, relaxed pub in a great spot overlooking the Box and Stour river valleys. Globally influenced menus feature the latest produce from local farms and estates, with seafood specials sourced from the east coast. Well-priced wine list with over 25 wines by the glass. Spacious, stylish bedrooms with king or super king sized beds; some have French windows and terraces.

STOKE D'ABERNON – Surrey – 504 S30 – see Cobham

STOKE HOLY CROSS – Norfolk – 504 X26 – see Norwich

STOKE POGES – Buckinghamshire – 504 S29 – pop. 4 112 11 D3

London 23 mi – Bristol 99 mi – Croydon 44 mi

Stoke Park, Park Rd, (01753) 71 71 71

Stoke Park

Park Rd, Southwest : 0.75 mi on B 416 SL2 4PG – (01753) 717 171
– www.stokepark.com – Closed 25-26 December
49 rm – £ 285/1500 £ 285/1500, £ 22 – 1 suite
Rest *Humphry's* – see restaurant listing
Grade I listed Palladian property – once home to the Penn family, who created England's first country club. Extensive sporting activities and impressive spa; characterful guest areas. Luxurious 'feature' or chic, contemporary bedrooms.

Stoke Place rm,

Stoke Green, South : 0.5 mi by B 416 SL2 4HT – (01753) 534 790
– www.stokeplace.co.uk – Closed 24 December-8 January
39 rm – £ 95/220 £ 95/220
Rest *Garden Room* – *(closed Sunday lunch)* Menu £ 20/45
17C Queen Anne mansion, set by a large lake and surrounded by 22 acres of delightful gardens and parkland. Quirky guest areas display bold wallpapers and original furnishings. Bedrooms are uniquely styled; those in the garden are simpler.

Humphry's – Stoke Park Hotel

Park Rd SL2 4PG – (01753) 717 171 – www.humphrysrestaurant.co.uk
– Closed 25-26 December
Rest – *(booking essential)* Menu £ 25/58 – Carte lunch £ 40/64
Impressive hotel dining room named after 18C landscape gardener Humphry Repton, who designed the surrounding gardens; the lake and parkland views are superb. Classically based dishes are presented in a modern style. Service is professional.

STOKE ROW – Oxfordshire 11 C3

London 45 mi – Henley-on-Thames 6 mi – Reading 10 mi

Cherry Tree Inn with rm rest,

RG9 5QA – (01491) 680 430 – www.thelittleangel.co.uk
4 rm – £ 60/80 £ 75/110 **Rest** – Carte £ 20/36
Cosy and relaxing 400 year old inn with four intimate dining areas. Classic pub dishes sit alongside more modern creations on the monthly changing à la carte and the seasonal, fish-based blackboard menu. Food is full of flavour and served by attentive staff. Stylish bedrooms are named after fruit trees.

STOKENCHURCH – Buckinghamshire – 504 R29 – pop. 3 949 **11** C2

London 42 mi – High Wycombe 10 mi – Oxford 18 mi

at Radnage Northeast : 1.75 mi by A 40 – ✉ Stokenchurch

Three Horseshoes Inn with rm
Bennett End, North : 1.25 mi by Town End rd. ✉ HP14 4EB – ✆ (01494) 483 273 – www.thethreehorseshoes.net
6 rm – †£ 80/100 ††£ 90/150
Rest – Menu £ 21 (weekdays) – Carte £ 23/39
Attractive pub with lovely terrace, in a fantastic hillside location. Classically prepared dishes display French touches. Lighter offerings at lunch; à la carte or tapas at dinner. Good choice for Sunday lunch. Comfortable yet minimalistic bedrooms have character beds and modern bathrooms; Molières is best.

STOKE-ON-TRENT – Stoke-on-Trent – 502 N24 – pop. 259 252 **19** C1

Great Britain

London 162 – Birmingham 46 – Leicester 59 – Liverpool 58

City Centre, ✆ (01782) 23 60 00, www.visitstoke.co.uk

Greenway Hall, Stockton Brook, ✆ (01782) 50 31 58

Parkhall, Weston Coyney, Hulme Rd, ✆ (01782) 59 95 84

The Potteries Museum and Art Gallery★ Y **M** – Gladstone Pottery Museum★ **AC** V

The Wedgwood Story★ **AC**, S : 7 mi on A 500, A 34 and minor rd V. Little Moreton Hall★★ **AC**, N : 10 mi by A 500 on A 34 U – Biddulph Grange Garden★, N : 7 mi by A 52, A 50 and A 527 U

Plans pages 632, 633

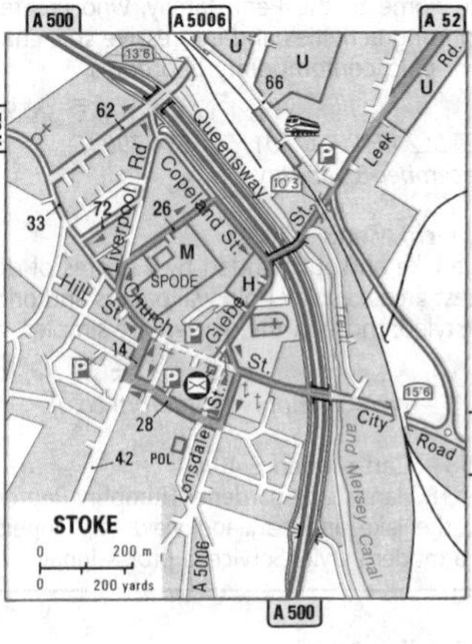

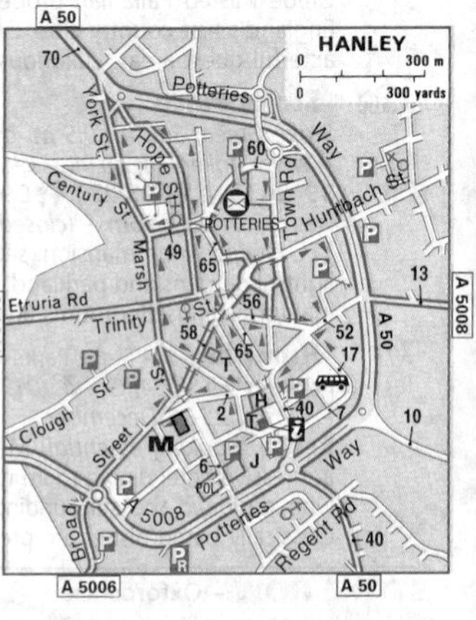

HANLEY

Albion St	Y	2
Bethesda St	Y	6
Birch Terrace	Y	7
Botteslow St	Y	10
Bucknall New Rd	Y	13
Charles St	Y	17
Lichfield St	Y	40
New Hall St	Y	49
Old Hall St	Y	52
Parliament Row	Y	55
Percy St	Y	56
Piccadilly	Y	58
Potteries Shopping Centre	Y	
Quadrant Rd	Y	60
Stafford St	Y	65
Vale Pl.	Y	70

STOKE-ON-TRENT

Campbell Pl.	X	14
Church St	X	
Elenora St	X	26
Fleming Rd	X	28
Hartshill Rd	X	33
London Rd	X	42
Shelton Old Rd	X	62
Station Rd	X	66
Vale St	X	72

STOKE-ON-TRENT NEWCASTLE-UNDER-LYME

Alexandra Rd . . . . U 3
Bedford Rd . . . . U 4
Brownhills Rd . . . . U 12
Church Lane . . . . U 19
Cobridge Rd . . . . U 21
Davenport St. . . . . U 23
Elder Rd . . . . U 24
Etruria Vale Rd . . . . U 27
Grove Rd. . . . . V 30
Hanley Rd . . . . U 31
Heron St . . . . V 34
Higherland. . . . . V 37
High St . . . . U 35
Manor St. . . . . V 44
Mayne St . . . . V 45
Moorland Rd. . . . . U 48
Porthill Rd . . . . U 59
Snow Hill . . . . U 63
Stoke Rd. . . . . U 68
Strand (The). . . . . V 69
Victoria Park Rd . . . . U 75
Victoria Pl. Link . . . . V 76
Watlands View . . . . U 77
Williamson St . . . . U 78
Wolstanton Link Rd. . . . . U 80

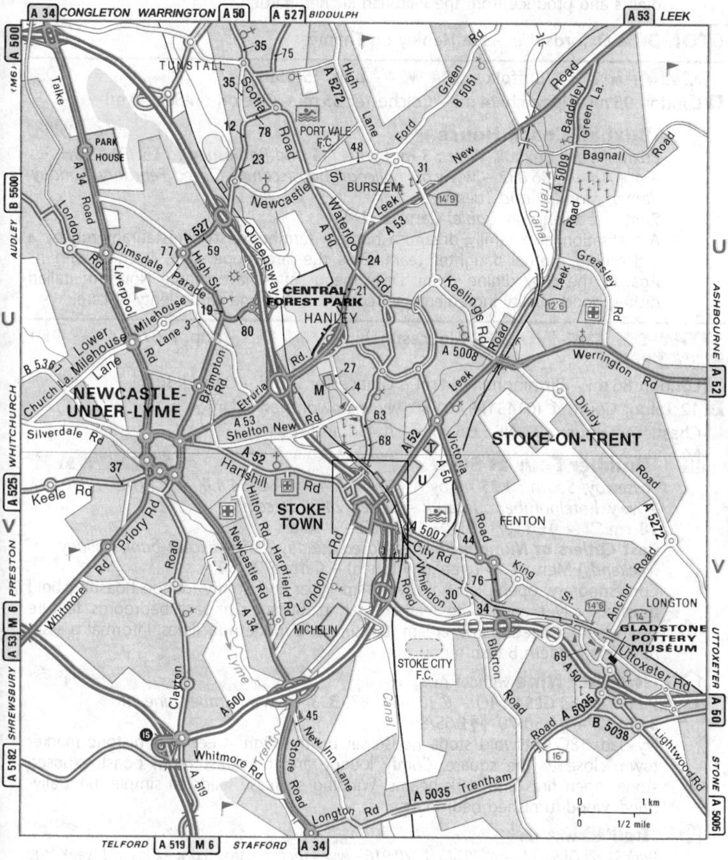

STON EASTON - Somerset - 503 M30 - pop. 579 4 C2

London 131 mi - Bath 12 mi - Bristol 11 mi - Wells 7 mi

Ston Easton Park

BA3 4DF - (01761) 241 631 - www.stoneaston.co.uk
22 rm - †£ 110/185 ††£ 135/345 - 2 suites
Rest ***Sorrel*** - see restaurant listing
Striking aristocratic Palladian mansion, in 36 acres of attractive grounds designed by Humphrey Repton. Fine rooms of epic proportions are filled with antiques, curios and impressive floral arrangements. Stylish, individually designed bedrooms - many with coronet or four-poster beds - one is set in a cottage.

Sorrel – Ston Easton Park Hotel
BA3 4DF – (01761) 241 631 – www.stoneaston.co.uk
Rest – *(bookings essential for non-residents)* Menu £ 23/50
Set in a striking Palladian mansion surrounded by 36 acres of parkland, this elegant, formal restaurant features high ceilings and panelled walls, with crisp white linen on the tables and professional service. Classical menus offer luxurious ingredients and produce from the Victorian kitchen garden.

STONOR – Oxfordshire – see Henley-on-Thames

STOWMARKET – Suffolk – 504 W27 – pop. 15 059 15 C3

London 95 mi – Ipswich 14 mi – Colchester 35 mi – Clacton-on-Sea 40 mi

Buxhall Coach House
Buxhall Vale, Buxhall, West : 3 mi by B 1115 and Rattlesden rd IP14 3DH – (01449) 736 032 – www.buxhallcoachhouse.com – Closed February, Sunday dinner, Monday and Tuesday
Rest – *(booking advisable)* Carte £ 31/45
A realisation of a family dream: a homely, farmhouse-style restaurant run by a welcoming mother-daughter team. Pass the large, open-plan kitchen with its Aga, to the cosy dining room. Daily menus offer flavoursome Northern Italian dishes; good quality ingredients are cooked simply and with plenty of care.

STOW-ON-THE-WOLD – Gloucestershire – 503 O28 – pop. 2 074 4 D1

Great Britain

London 86 mi – Birmingham 44 mi – Gloucester 27 mi – Oxford 30 mi

12 Talbot Court, (01451) 87 01 50, www.stowonthewold.info

Chastleton House★★, NE : 6.5 mi by A 436 and A 44

ENGLAND

Number Four at Stow
Fosseway, South : 1.25 mi by A 429 on A 424 GL54 1JX – (01451) 830 297 – www.hotelnumberfour.co.uk – Closed 24-29 December
18 rm – †£ 110/150 ††£ 125/165 – 4 suites
Rest *Cutlers at Number Four* – *(closed Sunday dinner except bank holiday weekends)* Menu £ 16 (weekday lunch) – Carte £ 28/50
Contemporary, open-plan hotel with small bar and comfy lounge boasting bold brushed velvet and white leather seating. Bright, compact bedrooms feature smart leather headboards, cream furniture and modern facilities. Informal brasserie offers modern British menu.

Number Nine without rest
9 Park St GL54 1AQ – (01451) 870 333 – www.number-nine.info
3 rm – †£ 50/70 ††£ 65/80
Ivy-clad, 18C Cotswold stone house set on the high street of a historic market town, close to the square. Comfy lounge and breakfast room boast exposed stone, open fires and dark beams. Winding staircase leads to simple, neutrally-hued, wood-furnished bedrooms.

Bell with rm
Park St GL54 1AJ – (01451) 870 916 – www.thebellatstow.com – Closed 1 week May
5 rm – †£ 70/120 ††£ 70/120 **Rest** – Carte £ 21/35
Cotswold stone inn with welcoming open fires, at the centre of a delightful market town. Menus offer plenty of choice and portions are hearty; meat comes from the local butcher, the fish board changes daily and puddings are heartwarming. Comfortable bedrooms, some with country views, complete the picture.

at Lower Oddington East : 3 mi by A 436 – Stow-On-The-Wold

Fox Inn with rm
GL56 0UR – (01451) 870 555 – www.foxinn.net
3 rm – †£ 75/100 ††£ 85/110
Rest – *(booking essential)* Menu £ 17 – Carte £ 24/37
Personally run, creeper-clad inn in a peaceful Cotswold village. Its five rooms each have their own character; the stone-walled Old Kitchen is the best. The daily menu keeps things fresh, and mixes British classics and Mediterranean influences. Comfortable bedrooms feature a cuddly toy fox.

at Daylesford East : 3.5 mi by A 436 – ✉ Stow-On-The-Wold

Café at Daylesford Organic

✉ GL56 0YG – ✆ (01608) 731 700 – www.daylesfordorganic.com – Closed 25-26 December and 1 January

Rest – *(lunch only and dinner Friday-Saturday) (booking essential)* Carte £ 18/29

Stylish café attached to the rear of a farm shop, its rustic interior boasting an open charcoal grill and wood-fired oven. Menus showcase an interesting array of home-cooked dishes. Everything is organic, with much of the produce coming from the farm itself.

at Bledington Southeast : 4 mi by A 436 on B 4450 – ✉ Kingham

Kings Head Inn with rm

The Green ✉ OX7 6XQ – ✆ (01608) 658 365 – www.kingsheadinn.net

12 rm – †£ 75/100 ††£ 95/135 **Rest** – Carte £ 22/40

Charming 16C former cider house on a picturesque village green, bisected by a stream filled with bobbing ducks. Traditional weekly menus offer game in season and usually some fish specials. The large bar with its vast inglenook fireplace creates a wonderful atmosphere and the cosy bedrooms – split between the pub and the courtyard – finish it off perfectly.

at Nether Westcote Southeast : 4.75 mi by A 429 and A 424

Feathered Nest with rm

✉ OX7 6SD – ✆ (01993) 833 030 – www.thefeatherednestinn.co.uk – Closed 25 December

4 rm – †£ 105/135 ††£ 150/200

Rest – *(closed Monday except bank holidays) (booking advisable)* Menu £ 20 (weekday lunch) – Carte £ 39/52

This pub offers something for everyone with its laid-back bar, rustic snug, casual conservatory and formal dining room. Sit on quirky horse saddle stools and choose from the bar menu or sample more complex dishes at elegant antique tables; the wine list features over 200 bins. Comfy bedrooms boast antiques, quality linens and roll-top baths. The views are superb.

at Lower Swell West : 1.25 mi on B 4068 – ✉ Stow-On-The-Wold

Rectory Farmhouse without rest

by Rectory Barns Rd ✉ GL54 1LH – ✆ (01451) 832 351 – www.rectoryfarmhouse.yolasite.com – Closed Christmas-New Year

3 rm – †£ 75/85 ††£ 98/105

Charming 17C stone-built farmhouse; to the rear, a terrace overlooks the lovely enclosed garden with its pond and water feature. Relax in the characterful beamed lounge; the cottagey bedrooms have good facilities and extras. Aga-cooked breakfasts are taken in the country kitchen, conservatory or garden.

Good food at moderate prices? Look for the Bib Gourmand ㊕.

STRATFORD-UPON-AVON – Warwickshire – 503 P27 – pop. 23 138 Great Britain 19 C3

London 96 mi – Birmingham 23 mi – Coventry 18 mi – Leicester 44 mi

Bridgefoot, ✆ (01789) 26 42 93, www.discover-stratford.com

Tiddington Rd, ✆ (01789) 20 57 49

Menzies Welcombe Hotel & GC, Warwick Rd, ✆ (01789) 41 38 00

Stratford Oaks, Snitterfield, Bearley Rd, ✆ (01789) 73 19 80

Town★★ - Shakespeare's Birthplace★ **AC**, AB

Mary Arden's House★ **AC**, NW : 4 mi by A 3400 A. Ragley Hall★ **AC**, W : 9 mi by A 422 A

Plan on next page

STRATFORD-UPON-AVON

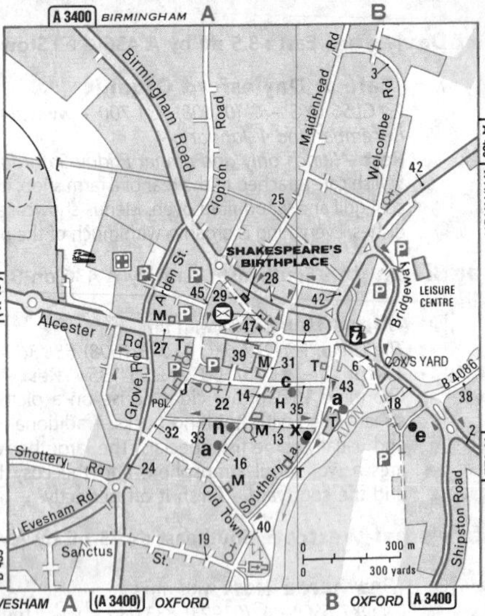

ENGLAND

Welcombe H. Spa and Golf Club

rest,

Warwick Rd, Northeast : 1.5 mi on A 439
✉ *CV37 0NR* – ✆ *(01789) 295 252* – *www.menzieshotels.co.uk*
78 rm ☕ – 🚹£ 113/225 🚹🚹£ 123/235 – 5 suites
Rest *Trevelyan* – *(closed lunch Saturday and bank holidays)* Menu £ 21/35 – Carte £ 35/46

Imposing Jacobean-style house built in 1866, featuring a golf course and a superb spa and leisure club. Well-proportioned, wood panelled guest areas with marble fireplaces. Grand, well-equipped bedrooms; the best are in the main house. The bar and restaurant overlook an impressive parterre and water feature.

Ettington Park

rm,

Alderminster, Southeast : 6.5 mi on A 3400 ✉ *CV37 8BU* – ✆ *(01789) 450 123* – *www.handpickedhotels.co.uk/ettingtonpark*
48 rm ☕ – 🚹£ 113/227 🚹🚹£ 123/337
Rest *Oak Room* – *(bar lunch Monday-Saturday)* Menu £ 40/75 **s** – Carte £ 46/60 **s**

Impressive neo-Gothic mansion surrounded by lovely gardens. Characterful guest areas have vaulted ceilings and ornate rococo plasterwork. 'Feature' bedrooms boast original fireplaces and four-posters; other rooms are more contemporary. The Oak Room – named after its smart panelling – offers a modern menu.

Arden

Waterside ✉ *CV37 6BA* – ✆ *(01789) 298 682* – *www.theardenhotelstratford.com*
45 rm ☕ – 🚹£ 105/275 🚹🚹£ 145/395 B**x**
Rest *Waterside Brasserie* – see restaurant listing

Set in a great location opposite the RSC theatre, with pretty gardens and a split-level terrace overlooking the river. Smart bar-lounge and a second plush lounge for afternoon tea. Twisty corridors lead to stylish modern bedrooms in green, cream and gold colour schemes; one has a roll-top bath in the room.

White Sails without rest

85 Evesham Rd, Southwest : 1 mi on B 439 ✉ *CV37 9BE* – ✆ *(01789) 550 469* – *www.white-sails.co.uk* – *Closed January*
5 rm ☕ – 🚹£ 85/110 🚹🚹£ 85/132

Detached Edwardian house; look out for the 'Sail' signs. Leather-furnished lounge with local info, a Nespresso machine and a decanter of sherry. Smart bedrooms with superb bathrooms and good extras. Comprehensive buffet breakfasts.

Cherry Trees without rest
Swan's Nest Ln ✉ CV37 7LS – ✆ (01789) 292 989
– www.cherrytrees-stratford.co.uk **Be**
3 rm – †£ 85/95 ††£ 110/125
Unassuming guesthouse with a Japanese-style garden, located just over the River Avon. First floor breakfast room, where homemade bread and granola are served. Comfortable bedrooms come with plenty of extras; two have small conservatories.

Waterside Brasserie – Arden Hotel
Waterside ✉ CV37 6BA – ✆ (01789) 298 682 – www.theardenhotelstratford.com
Rest – Menu £ 20 – Carte £ 24/41 **Bx**
Contemporary hotel brasserie with green velvet chairs, deep purple banquettes and Georgian-style doors opening onto a terrace overlooking the river. Quality crockery and crystal glassware. Well-presented British brasserie classics.

Rooftop
Royal Shakespeare Theatre, Waterside ✉ CV37 6BB – ✆ (01789) 403 449
– www.rsc.org.uk/eat – Closed 25 December and Sunday dinner **Ba**
Rest – Menu £ 18 (lunch) – Carte £ 25/35
Modern, open-plan restaurant with a lovely terrace, set on top of the Royal Shakespeare Theatre and boasting views over the canal basin, river and gardens. Interesting modern menu with classic British undertones; attractive presentation.

No 9 Church St.
9 Church St ✉ CV37 6HB – ✆ (01789) 415 522 – www.no9churchst.com – Closed 25 December-3 January, Sunday and bank holidays **Aa**
Rest – Menu £ 13 (lunch and early dinner) – Carte dinner £ 23/43 **s**
Cosy little restaurant within a 400 year old townhouse, a little off the main streets. The experienced chef-owner has returned home to offer honest, flavoursome British cooking with a modern twist. Classical puddings and friendly service.

Church Street Town House with rm
16 Church St ✉ CV37 6HB – ✆ (01789) 262 222
– www.churchstreettownhouse.com **An**
12 rm – †£ 100/170 ††£ 110/180
Rest – Menu £ 12 (weekdays) – Carte £ 25/40
Handsome, part-17C property opposite the school that Shakespeare attended. Bright, bold restaurant with an open kitchen and a zinc-topped bar. Appealing, wide-ranging menu with Mediterranean-influences; good value lunch and pre-theatre choices. Funky bedrooms display rich colours and silver furnishings.

Lambs
12 Sheep St ✉ CV37 6EF – ✆ (01789) 292 554 – www.lambsrestaurant.co.uk
– Closed 25-26 December and lunch Monday-Tuesday **Bc**
Rest – Menu £ 14 – Carte £ 20/42
Attractive 16C house with an interesting history; dine on one of several intimate levels, surrounded by characterful beams and original features. The classic bistro menu lists simply, carefully prepared favourites and daily fish specials.

at Alveston East : 2 mi by B 4086 - B – ✉ Stratford-Upon-Avon

Baraset Barn
1 Pimlico Ln, off B 4086 ✉ CV37 7RJ – ✆ (01789) 295 510
– www.barasetbarn.co.uk – Closed 1 January and Sunday dinner
Rest – Menu £ 14 (weekdays) – Carte £ 25/43
Modernised barn offering something for everyone, with its original features, contemporary furnishings and large terraces. The good-sized menu also caters for one and all, and includes a tasty rotisserie selection and daily fish specials.

STRETE – Devon – see Dartmouth

STRETTON - Staffordshire - 502 P25 19 C1

London 134 mi - Bristol 126 mi - Cardiff 147 mi - Plymouth 240 mi

Dovecliff Hall

Dovecliff Rd ✉ DE13 0DJ - ☎ (01283) 531 818 - www.dovecliffhallhotel.co.uk
15 rm - †£ 60/120 ††£ 60/120 **Rest** - *(closed Sunday dinner)* Carte £ 23/44
Imposing red-brick Georgian manor house in 7 acres of gardens, overlooking the River Dove. Characterful guest areas with antiques and drapes. Bedrooms combine traditional styling with modern facilities and all have pleasant country views. Menu of classics in the orangery restaurant.

STRETTON - Rutland 17 C2

London 100 mi - Bristol 150 mi - Cardiff 177 mi - Plymouth 264 mi

Jackson Stops Inn

Rookery La ✉ LE15 7RA - ☎ (01780) 410 237 - www.thejacksonstops.com - Closed Monday except bank holidays and Sunday dinner
Rest - Menu £ 14 (lunch) - Carte £ 28/41
Lovely stone and thatch pub with several different areas - a small open-fired bar, a cosy barn and a restaurant. Dishes are rooted in tradition but display some interesting touches. Locally reared and smoked meats are a feature.

STUCKTON - Hampshire - see Fordingbridge

STUDLAND - Dorset - 503 O32 - pop. 471 4 C3

London 135 mi - Bournemouth 25 mi - Southampton 53 mi - Weymouth 29 mi

Shell Bay

Ferry Rd, North : 3 mi or via car ferry from Sandbanks ✉ BH19 3BA - ☎ (01929) 450 363 - www.shellbay.net - Closed November-February
Rest - *(booking essential)* Carte £ 22/33
Airy, simply furnished seafood restaurant with a decked terrace; superbly set on the waterfront and boasting views over the harbour to Brownsea Island - all tables have a view. Classical daily menu displays some Mediterranean influences.

SUMMERHOUSE - Darlington - see Darlington

SUNBURY ON THAMES - Surrey - 504 S29 - pop. 27 415 7 C1

London 16 mi - Croydon 38 mi - Barnet 44 mi - Ealing 10 mi

Indian Zest

21 Thames St ✉ TW16 5QF - ☎ (01932) 765 000 - www.indianzest.co.uk - Closed dinner 25 December and lunch 26 December
Rest - Menu £ 11/32 - Carte £ 19/32
Pleasant restaurant with two small terraces, in a building dating back over 450 years. Pretty interior with black and white photos of Colonial India and a fine array of polo mallets. Large, interesting dishes originate from all over India.

SUNNINGDALE - Windsor and Maidenhead - 504 S29 11 D3

London 33 mi - Croydon 39 mi - Barnet 46 mi - Ealing 22 mi

Bluebells

Shrubbs Hill, London Rd, Northeast : 0.75 mi on A 30 ✉ SL5 0LE - ☎ (01344) 622 722 - www.bluebells-restaurant.com - Closed 1-12 January, 25-26 December, Sunday dinner and Monday
Rest - Menu £ 19 (weekdays)/27 - Carte £ 35/55
Smart, well-manicured façade matched by sophisticated interior of deep green. Large rear terrace, deck and garden. Modern British cooking with original starting point.

SUNNISIDE - Tyne and Wear 24 B2

London 283 mi - Newcastle upon Tyne 6 mi - Sunderland 16 mi - Middlesbrough 41 mi

Hedley Hall without rest
Hedley Lane, South : 2 mi by A 6076 ✉ NE16 5EH – ✆ (01207) 231 835 – www.hedleyhall.com – Closed Christmas-New Year
4 rm – †£ 58/70 ††£ 90
Stone-built former farmhouse in a quiet location close to the Beamish Open Air Museum. Formal, linen-laid breakfast room and a comfy lounge with a large conservatory extension. Good-sized bedrooms offer pleasant countryside views.

SUTTON COLDFIELD – West Midlands – 503 O26 – pop. 105 452 — 19 C2

London 124 mi – Birmingham 8 mi – Coventry 29 mi – Nottingham 47 mi
18 Pype Hayes, Walmley, Eachelhurst Rd, ✆ (0121) 351 10 14
18 Boldmere, Monmouth Dr., ✆ (0121) 354 33 79
18 110 Thornhill Rd, ✆ (0121) 580 78 78
36 The Belfry, Wishaw, Lichfield Rd, ✆ (01675) 47 03 01

Plan : see Birmingham

Don Diego
5 Manor Rd ✉ B73 6EJ – ✆ (0121) 355 5354 – www.dondiegobirmingham.co.uk – Closed 25 December and 1 January **Plan 2** DT **x**
Rest – Menu £ 20/25 – Carte £ 10/28
Run by a Spanish husband and wife, with a tiled floor and coral-coloured walls. Large menus offer a good range of authentic tapas dishes; choose 3-4 per person. Carefully imported ingredients include cured meats, wines, beers, and brandies.

SUTTON COURTENAY – Oxfordshire – 504 Q29 – pop. 2 413 — 10 B2

London 72 mi – Bristol 77 mi – Coventry 70 mi

Fish
4 Appleford Rd ✉ OX14 4NQ – ✆ (01235) 848 242 – www.thefishatsuttoncourtenay.co.uk – Closed January, Monday except bank holidays and Sunday dinner
Rest – Menu £ 14 (weekdays) – Carte £ 23/44
Robust, seasonal country cooking: escargots and crème brûlée meet steak and kidney pie and profiteroles on Franco-Anglo menu. Neat garden and bright conservatory. Charming service.

SUTTON GAULT – Cambridgeshire – 504 U26 – see Ely

SUTTON-ON-THE-FOREST – North Yorkshire – 502 P21 – pop. 281 — 23 C2

London 230 mi – Kingston-upon-Hull 50 mi – Leeds 52 mi – Scarborough 40 mi

Rose & Crown
Main St ✉ YO61 1DP – ✆ (01347) 811 333 – www.theroseandcrownyork.co.uk – Closed first 3 weeks January, Sunday dinner and Monday
Rest – *(booking essential)* Menu £ 19 (lunch and early dinner) **s** – Carte £ 25/38 **s**
Welcoming pub in a beautiful village, surrounded by some delightful Georgian country houses. There's a rustic bar and an elegant restaurant which leads through to a conservatory and a superb terrace. Menus offer plenty of choice, from hearty, classically based dishes through to afternoon tea.

SWAFFHAM – Norfolk – 504 W26 – pop. 6 734 Great Britain — 15 C2

London 97 mi – Cambridge 46 mi – King's Lynn 16 mi – Norwich 27 mi
Oxburgh Hall★★ **AC**, SW : 7.5 m

Strattons (N)
4 Ash Cl. ✉ PE37 7NH – ✆ (01760) 723 845 – www.strattonshotel.com – Closed 16-27 December
14 rm – †£ 92/200 ††£ 130/230
Rest *Rustic* – *(booking essential at lunch)* Carte £ 32/43
Laid-back, eco-friendly hotel, in an eye-catching 17C villa with Victorian additions. Quirky, individually styled bedrooms are spread about the place; some are duplex or have terraces or courtyards. The rustic basement restaurant serves modern British dishes; on quieter days, breakfast is taken in their deli.

SWETTENHAM – Cheshire East – pop. 248 20 B3

London 177 mi – Birmingham 63 mi – Liverpool 43 mi – Leeds 79 mi

Swettenham Arms

CW12 2LF – (01477) 571 284 – *www.swettenhamarms.co.uk*

Rest – Carte £ 21/44

Traditional pub with beaten copper bar, open fires, horse brasses and lavender meadow. Seasonal menu provides plenty of choice, ranging from sharing platters and pub classics to carefully prepared, well-presented restaurant-style dishes.

SWINBROOK – Oxfordshire – 503 P28 – see Burford

SYDLING ST NICHOLAS 4 C3

London 142 mi – Bristol 92 mi – Cardiff 113 mi – Southampton 67 mi

Greyhound with rm

26 High St DT2 9DP – (01300) 341 303 – www.dorsetgreyhound.co.uk

6 rm – £ 80/90 ££ 90/100 **Rest** – Carte £ 23/39

Set in a lovely village amongst flint and thatch houses, with a gurgling trout stream behind. Sit in the rustic bar, the conservatory or the linen-laid dining room with its sunken well; and choose from a very modern, seasonal menu. Contemporary bedrooms come with fishing nets, torches and wellies.

TADCASTER – North Yorkshire – 502 Q22 – pop. 6 548 22 B2

London 206 mi – Harrogate 16 mi – Leeds 14 mi – York 11 mi

at Colton Northeast : 3 mi by A 659 off A 64 – Tadcaster

Ye Old Sun Inn with rm

Main St LS24 8EP – (01904) 744 261 – www.yeoldsuninn.co.uk – Closed 26 and 31 December

3 rm – £ 75 ££ 100 **Rest** – Menu £ 20 – Carte £ 20/39

Rustic, family-run pub with warming open fires and a small deli. Owners are great ambassadors of local suppliers and seasonal produce, and give regular cookery demonstrations. Smart bedrooms are located in the house next door.

TANGMERE – West Sussex – 504 R31 – see Chichester

TAPLOW – Buckinghamshire – 504 R29 11 C3

London 33 mi – Maidenhead 2 mi – Oxford 36 mi – Reading 12 mi

Cliveden

North : 2 mi by Berry Hill SL6 0JF – (01628) 668 561 – www.clivedenhouse.co.uk

38 rm – £ 252/1572 ££ 252/1572 – 8 suites

Rest *Terrace Dining Room* – Menu £ 28 (weekdays)/63

Stunning 19C stately home in a superb location, boasting views over the parterre and the National Trust gardens towards the Thames. The opulent interior boasts sumptuous, antique-filled lounges and luxuriously appointed bedrooms; go for one in the main house. Journey in style in one of their vintage launches, then dine from a classical menu in the restaurant.

Taplow House

rm,

Berry Hill SL6 0DA – (01628) 670 056 – www.taplowhouse.com

32 rm – £ 100/205 ££ 105/225

Rest *Berry's* – Carte £ 28/51

Rest *Woofy's* – *(dinner only)* Carte £ 22/31

Georgian house built in 1751 – its expansive gardens boasting Europe's tallest tulip tree, which was reputedly planted by Elizabeth I. Characterful guest areas and well-equipped bedrooms cleverly blend modern and period furnishings. Formal, classical cooking in Berry's; snacks and steaks in Woofy's.

TARPORLEY – Cheshire West and Chester – 502 L/M24 – pop. 2 634 20 A3

London 186 mi – Chester 11 mi – Liverpool 27 mi – Shrewsbury 36 mi

Portal G & C.C., Cobblers Cross Lane, (01829) 73 39 33

Portal Premier, Forest Rd, (01829) 73 38 84

at Cotebrook Northeast : 2.5 mi on A 49 – ✉ Tarporley

Fox and Barrel
Foxbank ✉ CW6 9DZ – ✆ (01829) 760 529 – www.foxandbarrel.co.uk – Closed dinner 25-26 December and 1 January
Rest – Carte £ 16/36
Well-run pub with wood-panelled walls, heaving bookshelves and a smart terrace. The constantly evolving menu offers originality and interest, with sensibly priced dishes arriving neatly presented and generously sized.

TARRANT LAUNCESTON – Dorset – see Blandford Forum

TARR STEPS – Somerset – **503** J30 **3** A2

London 191 mi – Taunton 31 mi – Tiverton 20 mi
Tarr Steps★★ (Clapper Bridge★★)

Tarr Farm Inn with rm
✉ TA22 9PY – ✆ (01643) 851 507 – www.tarrfarm.co.uk – Closed 1-10 February
9 rm – †£ 75/90 ††£ 100/150 **Rest** – Carte £ 20/39
Cosy, beamed pub in an idyllic riverside spot, overlooking a 1000 BC, stone-slab clapper bridge. If it's sunny, head for the garden for afternoon tea; if not, make for the narrow bar or cosy restaurant for everything from potted shrimps and sharing boards to Devon Ruby steak. Comfy, well-equipped bedrooms.

TATTENHALL – Cheshire West and Chester – **502** L24 – **pop. 1 860** **20** A3

London 200 mi – Birmingham 71 mi – Chester 10 mi – Liverpool 29 mi

Higher Huxley Hall without rest
Red Lane , North : 2.25 mi on Huxley rd ✉ CH3 9BZ – ✆ (01829) 781 484 – www.huxleyhall.co.uk – Closed Christmas
4 rm – †£ 70/75 ††£ 88/95
Attractive, part-13C farmhouse boasting an original Elizabethan staircase and field and castle views. Classical, open-fired lounge and linen-laid breakfast room. Homely bedrooms with good facilities.

at Higher Burwardsley Southeast : 1 mi – ✉ Tattenhall

Pheasant Inn with rm
✉ CH3 9PF – ✆ (01829) 770 434 – www.thepheasantinn.co.uk
12 rm – †£ 65/115 ††£ 85/135 **Rest** – Carte £ 19/40
Well-run, modern pub set atop a sandstone escarpment, with views across the Cheshire Plains. The daily menu focuses on simple pub classics, with no-nonsense cooking and clear, gutsy flavours. Spacious, beamed bedrooms in the main building; more modern rooms with views in the barn. Staff are keen to please.

TAUNTON – Somerset – **503** K30 – **pop. 58 241** **3** B3

London 168 mi – Bournemouth 69 mi – Bristol 50 mi – Exeter 37 mi
Paul St, ✆ (01823) 33 63 44, www.visitsomerset.co.uk
Taunton Vale, Creech Heathfield, ✆ (01823) 41 22 20
Vivary, Vivary Park, ✆ (01823) 28 92 74
Taunton and Pickeridge, Corfe, ✆ (01823) 42 15 37
Town★ - St Mary Magdalene★ V – Somerset County Museum★ **AC** V **M** – St James'★ U – Hammett St★ V **25** – The Crescent★ V – Bath Place★ V **3**
Trull (Church★), S : 2.5 mi by A 38 – Hestercombe Gardens★, N : 5 mi by A 3259 BY and minor roads to Cheddon Fitzpaine. Bishops Lydeard★ (Church★), NW : 6 mi – Wellington : Church★, Wellington Monument (<★★), SW : 7.5 mi by A 38 – Combe Florey★, NW : 8 mi – Gaulden Manor★ **AC**, NW : 10 mi by A 358 and B 3227

Plan on next page

ENGLAND

TAUNTON

Bath Pl. . . . . V 3
Billetfield . . . . V 6
Billet St. . . . . V 4
Birch Grove . . . . U 7
Bishop's Hull Rd . . . . AZ 9
Bridge St . . . . U 12
Bridge (The) . . . . U 10
Burton Pl. . . . . V 13
Cann St . . . . V 15
Chritchard Parkway . . . BYZ 45
Cleveland St . . . . U 16
Comeytrowe Lane . . . . . AZ 18
Corporation St . . . . V 19
County Walk Shopping Centre V
Duke St . . . . V 21
East St V
Fore St . . . . V 22
Hamilton Rd . . . . BZ 24
Hammet St . . . . V 25
High St V
Hurdle Way . . . . V 27
Ilminster Rd . . . . BZ 28
Magdalene St . . . . V 30
Middleway . . . . AZ 31
North St . . . . V 33
Obridge Viaduct . . . . BY 34
Old Market Shopping Centre V
Portland St . . . . U 36
Priory Ave . . . . U 37
Shoreditch Rd . . . . BZ 39
Shuttern . . . . V 40
Silver St South . . . . V, Z 42
Upper High St . . . . V 43
Upper Wood St . . . . U 44
Wellington New Rd . . . . . AZ 46
Wilton St . . . . V 48
Winchester St . . . . U 49
Wood St . . . . U 51

ENGLAND

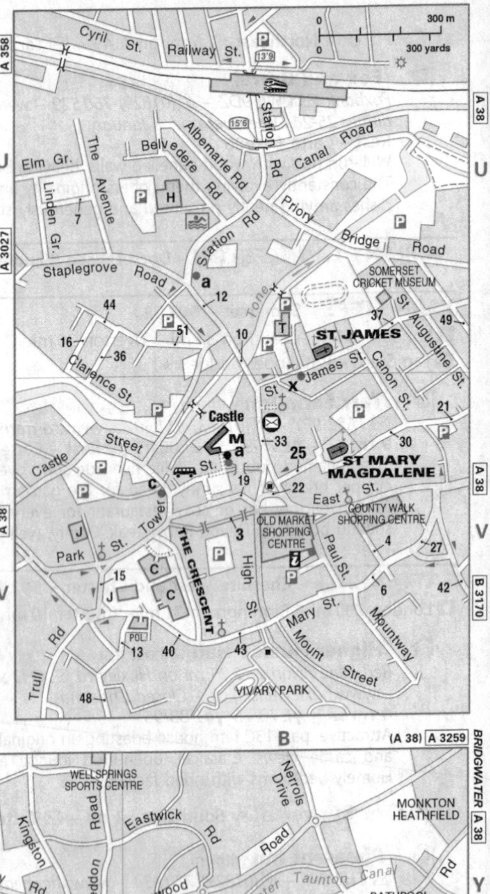

U
V
A
B

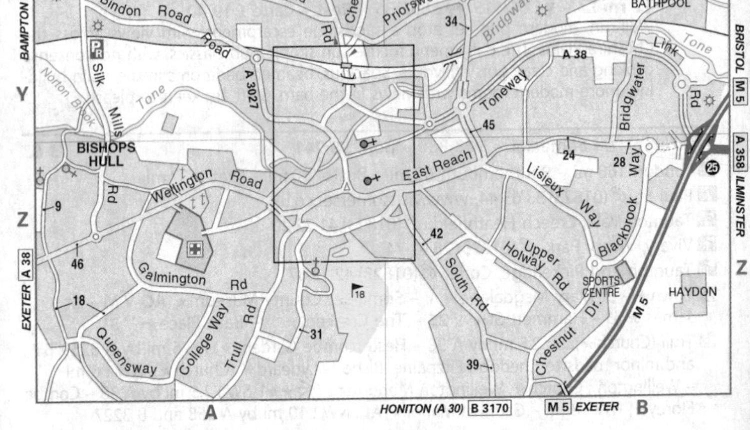

Y
Z
A
B

Castle

Castle Green ✉ *TA1 1NF* – ✆ *(01823) 272 671* – *www.the-castle-hotel.com*
44 rm – †£ 89/99 ††£ 155/200, ☕ £ 13 — V**a**
Rest *Castle Bow Bar & Grill* – see restaurant listing
Rest *Brazz* – ✆ (01823) 252 000 – Carte £ 21/34
Part-12C, wisteria-clad Norman castle with impressive gardens, a keep and two wells. It's been run by the Chapman family for three generations and retains a fittingly traditional style. Well-kept, individually decorated bedrooms. Castle Bow serves modern dishes; relaxed Brazz offers brasserie classics.

Castle Bow Bar & Grill – Castle Hotel

Castle Green ✉ *TA1 1NF* – ✆ *(01823) 328 328* – *www.castlebow.com* – *Closed Sunday dinner, Monday and Tuesday* — V**a**
Rest – *(dinner only and Sunday lunch) (booking advisable)* Menu £ 34
Elegant, art deco style restaurant in the old snooker room of a Norman castle. Regularly changing menus showcase top quality regional produce. Well-balanced dishes are classically based yet refined and feature some playful modern touches.

Mint and Mustard

10 Station Rd ✉ *TA1 1NH* – ✆ *(01823) 330 770* – *www.mintandmustard.com* – *Closed 25-26 December and 1 January* — U**a**
Rest – Menu £ 15/35 – Carte £ 15/32
Smart glass doors lead to a teak-furnished lounge and a contemporary, split-level restaurant in shades of green and mustard. Thalis and curries at lunch; highly original, modern dishes at dinner. The Keralan specialities are a highlight.

Willow Tree

3 Tower Ln ✉ *TA1 4AR* – ✆ *(01823) 352 835* – *www.thewillowtreerestaurant.com* – *Closed January, August, Sunday, Monday and Thursday* — V**c**
Rest – *(dinner only) (booking essential)* Menu £ 28 (weekdays)/33
Converted 17C townhouse with intimate dining rooms, exposed beams and large inglenook. Bi-monthly menu blends a classical base with artful, innovative ideas. Friendly, efficient service.

Augustus

3 The Courtyard, St James St. ✉ *TA1 1JR* – ✆ *(01823) 324 354* – *www.augustustaunton.co.uk* – *Closed 23 December-2 January, Sunday and Monday*
Rest – *(booking essential)* Carte £ 19/36 — V**x**
Simple little bistro set in a small courtyard and run by an experienced chef. Good-sized menu of hearty, unfussy dishes which mix French, British and some Asian influences – supplemented by blackboard specials. Bright and breezy service.

at Henlade East : 3.5 mi on A 358 - BZ – ✉ Taunton

Mount Somerset

Lower Henlade, South : 0.75 mi by Stoke Rd ✉ *TA3 5NB* – ✆ *(01823) 442 500* – *www.mountsomersethotel.co.uk*
19 rm ☕ – †£ 95/155 ††£ 100/270
Rest *Somerset Dining Room* – *(booking advisable)* Menu £ 14 (weekday lunch)/49
Fine Regency country house with formal gardens, set in four acres. Elegant bedrooms, excellent bathrooms and spacious, modern sitting rooms. Capacious dining room with immaculately set tables. Menus offer a mix of traditional and modern dishes.

at Hatch Beauchamp Southeast : 6 mi by A 358 - BZ – ✉ Taunton

Farthings

Village Rd ✉ *TA3 6SG* – ✆ *(01823) 480 664* – *www.farthingshotel.co.uk*
12 rm ☕ – †£ 75/155 ††£ 86/225
Rest – *(bookings essential for non-residents)* Carte £ 31/48 **s**
Extended Georgian house in mature, well-tended gardens, with a small bar and a cosy, country house style lounge; many original features remain. Charming, antique-filled bedrooms – the master rooms are particularly comfortable. Two-roomed restaurant offers constantly evolving, classical menu.

ENGLAND

TAVISTOCK – Devon – 503 H32 – pop. 11 018 2 C2

London 239 mi – Exeter 38 mi – Plymouth 16 mi
Bedford Sq, ✆ (01822) 61 29 38, www.tavistockpeople.co.uk
Down Rd, ✆ (01822) 61 23 44
Hurdwick, Tavistock Hamlets, ✆ (01822) 61 27 46
Morwellham★ **AC**, SW : 4.5 m. E : Dartmoor National Park★★ – Buckland Abbey★★ **AC**, S : 7 mi by A 386 – Lydford★★, N : 8.5 mi by A 386

Browns

80 West St ✉ PL19 8AQ – ✆ (01822) 618 686 – www.brownsdevon.co.uk
20 rm – £ 60/70 £ 80/240
Rest *Brasserie* – see restaurant listing
Smart townhouse hotel in former coaching inn – the oldest licensed premises in town. Bedrooms take on a modern style while still retaining original features; those in the old coach house are best. Polite, efficient service.

Rockmount without rest

Drake Rd ✉ PL19 0AX – ✆ (01822) 611 039 – www.rockmount-tavistock.com
5 rm – £ 55/70 £ 80/110
1920s house with a contrastingly contemporary interior, set beside the Tavistock viaduct and overlooking the town's rooftops. Individually furnished bedrooms are compact but come with plenty of extras. Breakfast is brought to your room.

ENGLAND

Gorton's

19 Plymouth Rd ✉ PL19 8AU – ✆ (01822) 617 581
– www.gortons-tavistock.co.uk – Closed 22-30 December, 1 week January, 1 week April, 1 week June, 1 week October, Sunday, Monday and lunch Tuesday
Rest – *(booking essential)* Menu £ 20 (weekday lunch)/42
Regulars at his previous place of work persuaded experienced restaurateur Peter Gorton to open this eponymous restaurant. An elegant and intimate establishment, it offers tasty classical cooking which uses quality local produce.

Brasserie – Browns Hotel

80 West St ✉ PL19 8AQ – ✆ (01822) 618 686 – www.brownsdevon.co.uk
Rest – *(booking essential)* Menu £ 20/35 – Carte £ 20/45
Set on the ground floor of an old coaching inn; have a drink in the beamed, flag-floored bar with its open fires and comfy leather sofas before heading into the similarly rustic restaurant for tasty, modern brasserie dishes.

Cornish Arms

15 West St ✉ PL19 8AN – ✆ (01822) 612 145
– www.thecornisharmstavistock.co.uk – Closed dinner 24 December
Rest – Carte £ 23/42
A refurbished yet still pleasingly traditional pub, filled with regulars playing darts and watching football. The talented chef offers tasty bar snacks, a mix of classic and modern main dishes, and attractive, sophisticated desserts.

at Gulworthy West : 3 mi on A 390 – ✉ Tavistock

Horn of Plenty with rm

rm, rest,

Gulworthy, Northwest : 1 mi by B 3362 ✉ PL19 8JD – ✆ (01822) 832 528
– www.thehornofplenty.co.uk
10 rm (dinner included) – £ 120/250 £ 165/295 **Rest** – Menu £ 25/50
Attractive, creeper-clad country house in a peaceful location, boasting lovely moor and valley views. The elegant formal dining room offers a good value, seasonal modern menu and an impressive outlook. Service is friendly. Bedrooms are luxurious and well-equipped; some have balconies or terraces.

Good food at moderate prices? Look for the Bib Gourmand.

at Milton Abbot Northwest : 6 mi on B 3362 – ✉ Tavistock

Hotel Endsleigh
Southwest : 1 mi ✉ PL19 0PQ – ✆ (01822) 870 000 – www.hotelendsleigh.com – Closed 2 weeks January
16 rm – †£ 167/257 ††£ 185/360 – 3 suites
Rest *Restaurant Endsleigh* – see restaurant listing
Restored Regency lodge in an idyllic rural setting; spacious guest areas offer wonderful countryside views and have a warm, classical style with a contemporary edge. Comfortable, antique-furnished bedrooms boast an understated elegance; choose one overlooking the magnificent gardens.

Restaurant Endsleigh – Hotel Endsleigh
Southwest : 1 mi ✉ PL19 0PQ – ✆ (01822) 870 000 – www.hotelendsleigh.com – Closed 2 weeks January
Rest – *(bookings essential for non-residents)* Menu £ 28/40
Elegant, wood-panelled restaurant in a peacefully located hotel; ask for a window table for superb countryside views. Classic cooking with a modern edge; dishes are neatly presented and flavoursome, with local produce to the fore. Attentive service, with a pleasant degree of informality.

at Chillaton Northwest : 6.25 mi by Chillaton rd – ✉ Tavistock

Tor Cottage without rest
Southwest : 0.75 mi by Tavistock rd, turning right at bridle path ✉ PL16 0JE – ✆ (01822) 860 248 – www.torcottage.co.uk – Closed mid-December-1 February
5 rm – †£ 98 ††£ 150/155
Remotely set cottage set in 28 hillside acres, with peaceful gardens and lovely outdoor pool. Bedrooms, most in converted outhouses, boast small kitchenettes and wood burning stoves. Breakfast is taken on the terrace or in the conservatory. Charming owner.

ENGLAND

TEFFONT EVIAS – Wiltshire – see Salisbury

TEIGNMOUTH – Devon – 503 J32 – pop. 14 799 — 2 D2

London 216 mi – Exeter 16 mi – Torquay 8 mi
Sea Front, ✆ (01626) 21 56 66, www.visitsouthdevon.co.uk

Thomas Luny House without rest
Teign St, follow signs for the Quays, off the A 381 ✉ TQ14 8EG – ✆ (01626) 772 976 – www.thomas-luny-house.co.uk
4 rm – †£ 60/75 ††£ 80/102
Georgian merchant's house with an attractive walled garden. Classical lounge and antique-filled breakfast room; tea and cake served on arrival. Traditional bedrooms; one with a four-poster. Quality breakfasts and home-grown figs in season.

TEMPLE SOWERBY – Cumbria – 502 M20 – see Penrith

TETBURY – Gloucestershire – 503 N29 – pop. 5 250 Great Britain — 4 C1

London 113 mi – Bristol 27 mi – Gloucester 19 mi – Swindon 24 mi
33 Church St, ✆ (01666) 50 35 52, www.visittetbury.co.uk
Westonbirt, ✆ (01666) 88 02 42
Westonbirt Arboretum★ **AC**, SW : 2.5 mi by A 433

Calcot Manor
Calcot, West : 3.5 mi on A 4135 ✉ GL8 8YJ – ✆ (01666) 890 391 – www.calcotmanor.co.uk
35 rm – †£ 252/277 ††£ 280/385 – 1 suite
Rest *Gumstool Inn* – see restaurant listing
Rest *Conservatory* – *(booking essential)* Carte £ 25/47
Impressive collection of converted farm buildings in a peaceful country setting, comprising ancient barns, old stables and a characterful farmhouse. Comfortable lounges and stylish bedrooms with good mod cons; outbuildings house a crèche, conference rooms and a superb spa complex. Interesting modern dishes in the formal conservatory; popular pub in the grounds.

Gumstool Inn – Calcot Manor Hotel
West : 3.5 mi on A 4135 ✉ GL8 8YJ – ✆ (01666) 890 391 – www.calcotmanor.co.uk
Rest – *(booking essential)* Carte £ 21/30
Set in the grounds of 700 year old Calcot Manor, an attractive outbuilding which cleverly blends an old farmhouse style with a more modern edge. Wide-ranging British menu showcases the latest meats and fish to arrive at the door; a flexible format offers snacks, two sizes of starter and hearty main courses.

Trouble House
Cirencester Rd, Northeast : 2 mi on A 433 ✉ GL8 8SG – ✆ (01666) 502 206 – www.troublehousetetbury.co.uk – Closed 25 December, Sunday dinner and Monday
Rest – Menu £ 12 (weekday lunch) – Carte £ 20/39
Unassuming roadside pub with shabby, homely style, where you'll discover a warm welcome and tasty food. Dishes range from sardines on toast to rib of beef for two. Daily specials usually feature fish.

TEWKESBURY – Gloucestershire – 503 N28 – pop. 9 978 4 C1
Great Britain

London 108 mi – Birmingham 39 mi – Gloucester 11 mi
100 Church St, ✆ (01684) 85 50 40, www.visitcotswoldsandsevernvale.gov.uk
Tewkesbury Park Hotel, Lincoln Green Lane, ✆ (01684) 29 54 05
Town★ – Abbey★★ (Nave★★, vault★)
St Mary's, Deerhurst★, SW : 4 mi by A 38 and B 4213

ENGLAND

Owens
73 Church St ✉ GL20 5RX – ✆ (01684) 292 703 – www.eatatowens.co.uk – Closed Sunday dinner and Monday
Rest – Menu £ 12 (weekday lunch) – Carte £ 19/40
Simple, rustic restaurant with a characterful low-beamed interior, an open fire and just 10 tables; in a charming 15C house set in the shadows of Tewkesbury Abbey. Concise, good value seasonal menu of French and British dishes; clean, unfussy, flavoursome cooking and friendly, efficient service.

at Corse Lawn Southwest : 6 mi by A 38 and A 438 on B 4211 – ✉ Gloucester

Corse Lawn House
✉ GL19 4LZ – ✆ (01452) 780 771 – www.corselawn.com – Closed 24-26 December
18 rm ☕ – 🚹£ 75/95 🚹🚹£ 120/160 – 3 suites
Rest *Corse Lawn House* – see restaurant listing
Rest *Bistro* – Menu £ 20 **s** – Carte £ 26/45 **s**
Elegant Grade II listed Queen Anne house, with a pond in front, just off the village green. Traditionally appointed lounges boast open fires and antiques; spacious bedrooms have a cottagey style. Large pool in glass-enclosed outbuilding. Formal restaurant and characterful bistro-cum-bar with simpler menu.

Corse Lawn House – Corse Lawn House Hotel
✉ GL19 4LZ – ✆ (01452) 780 771 – www.corselawn.com – Closed 24-26 December
Rest – Menu £ 26/34 **s** – Carte £ 28/54 **s**
Formally laid restaurant set within an elegant Grade II listed Queen Anne house, affording pleasant views over the rear gardens. Good-sized menus offer classically based dishes. Helpful team.

THIRSK – North Yorkshire – 502 P21 – pop. 9 099 22 B1

London 227 mi – Leeds 37 mi – Middlesbrough 24 mi – York 24 mi
49 Market Pl, ✆ (01845) 52 27 55, www.visit-thirsk.com
Thirsk & Northallerton, Thornton-Le-Street, ✆ (01845) 52 51 15

at Felixkirk Northeast : 3 mi by A 170

Carpenter's Arms with rm
✉ YO7 2DP – ✆ (01845) 537 369 – www.thecarpentersarmsfelixkirk.com
10 rm – £ 99/120 £ 120/185 **Rest** – Carte £ 21/39
A proper village pub with 18C origins, set in a village mentioned in the Domesday Book. Choose from blackboard specials or a wide-ranging menu of seasonal dishes, and be sure to save room for pudding. Stylishly appointed, well-equipped bedrooms overlook the Vale of Mowbray – as does the lovely terrace.

at Asenby Southwest : 5.25 mi by A 168 – ✉ Thirsk

Crab Manor
Dishforth Rd ✉ YO7 3QL – ✆ (01845) 577 286 – www.crabandlobster.co.uk
17 rm – £ 90 £ 160 – 3 suites
Rest *Crab and Lobster* – see restaurant listing
Well-run, quirky hotel, set in acres of mature grounds. Stylish bedrooms are split between a Georgian manor house and Scandinavian log cabins, and are themed around famous hotels of the world; all have access to private or shared hot tubs.

Crab and Lobster – Crab Manor Hotel
Dishforth Rd ✉ YO7 3QL – ✆ (01845) 577 286 – www.crabandlobster.com
Rest – Menu £ 20 (lunch) – Carte £ 28/46
Charming thatched pub with characterful, quirky interior. Extensive menu features plenty of seafood – from fish soup to whole lobster – as well as traditional British dishes.

THORNBURY – South Gloucestershire – 503 M29 – pop. 11 969 – ✉ Bristol 4 C1

London 128 mi – Bristol 12 mi – Gloucester 23 mi – Swindon 43 mi

Thornbury Castle
Castle St ✉ BS35 1HH – ✆ (01454) 281 182 – www.thornburycastle.co.uk
26 rm – £ 90/120 £ 170/220 – 3 suites
Rest *Tower* – see restaurant listing
Impressive 16C castle with a vineyard, hidden away in a surprisingly tranquil spot in the centre of town. Luxurious library with high ceiling and open fire. Baronial bedrooms, with beams and four-posters.

Tower – Thornbury Castle Hotel
Castle St ✉ BS35 1HH – ✆ (01454) 281 182 – www.thornburycastle.co.uk
Rest – Menu £ 15 (weekday lunch)/50
Sited in a tower within the main 16C part of Thornbury Castle; a small, partly wood-panelled, circular room decorated in deep red, with coats of arms and an impressive fireplace. Elegantly laid tables; elaborate, modern dishes.

THORNHAM – Norfolk – 504 V25 – see Hunstanton

THORNTON – Lancashire – 502 K22 – see Blackpool

THORNTON HOUGH – Merseyside – 502 K24 – ✉ Wirral 20 A3

London 215 mi – Birkenhead 12 mi – Chester 17 mi – Liverpool 12 mi

Thornton Hall N
on B 5136 ✉ CH63 1JF – ✆ (0151) 336 3938 – www.thorntonhallspa.com – Closed 1 January
62 rm – £ 79/159 £ 79/159, £ 14 – 1 suite
Rest *Lawns* – see restaurant listing
Extended manor house on the Wirral Peninsula. Wood panelling and stained glass feature in the main house, along with some luxurious bedrooms – the remainder are more contemporary, with balconies or terraces. Impressively equipped spa.

Mere Brook House without rest
Thornton Common Rd, East : 1.5 mi by B 5136 ✉ CH63 OLU – ✆ (07713) 189 949 – www.merebrookhouse.co.uk – Closed 20 December-2 January
8 rm – £ 80/120 £ 90/130
Restored Victorian house with colourful gardens and beehives which provide their honey. Bedrooms mix modern fabrics with traditional furnishings; stay in the original house or the newer cottage which has its own lounge and pantry kitchen.

ENGLAND

XX **Lawns** N – Thornton Hall Hotel

on B 5136 ✉ CH63 1JF – ✆ (0151) 336 3938 – www.thorntonhallspa.com – Closed 1 January

Rest – Menu £ 17 (weekday lunch) – Carte £ 28/54

Grand hotel restaurant with oak-panelled walls, overlooking the lawns; formerly the house's billiard room. Chandeliers hang from the embossed leather ceiling. Elaborate modern cooking shows respect for local ingredients. Friendly service.

THORPE MARKET – **Norfolk** – **504** X25 – ✉ **North Walsham** 15 D1

London 134 mi – Norwich 20 mi – Ipswich 63 mi – Lowestoft 39 mi

Gunton Arms with rm

Gunton Park, South : 1 mi on A 149 ✉ NR11 8TZ – ✆ (01263) 832 010 – www.theguntonarms.co.uk – Closed 25 December

8 rm – †£ 85/155 ††£ 95/165 **Rest** – *(booking advisable)* Carte £ 18/43

Charming pub overlooking the Gunton Estate deer park. Enjoy a tasty homemade snack over a game of pool or darts in the flag-floored bar, or make for a gnarled wood table by the fireplace in the Elk Room. Dishes are fiercely seasonal; some are cooked over the fire. Elegant bedrooms have a country house feel.

THRIPLOW – **Cambridgeshire** 14 B3

London 54 mi – Croydon 65 mi – Barnet 41 mi – Ealing 54 mi

Green Man N

2 Lower St ✉ SG8 7RJ – ✆ (01763) 208 855 – www.greenmanthriplow.com – Closed Sunday dinner and Monday

Rest – Carte £ 20/34

Laid-back, 19C pub in the heart of a pretty village, with a lovely suntrap garden; it was bought by 153 of the local residents and then put out to tender! Tasty, pub-style dishes display global influences. They brew their own beers too.

ENGLAND

THURLESTONE – **Devon** – **503** I33 2 C3

London 214 mi – Plymouth 21 mi – Torbay 23 mi – Exeter 43 mi

Thurlestone N rm, rest,

✉ TQ7 3NN – ✆ (01548) 560 382 – www.thurlestone.co.uk

65 rm – †£ 95/130 ††£ 190/310 – 6 suites

Rest *Margaret Amelia* – *(dinner only and Sunday lunch)* Menu £ 40 – Carte £ 26/44

Rest *Village Inn* – *(closed 25 December)* Carte £ 20/36

Long-standing, family-friendly hotel with a subtle contemporary style, superb sea views and plenty of activities. Have afternoon tea in the comfy drawing room or relax on the terrace overlooking the manicured grounds. Ask for a room with a view; some even come with children's beds. Refined, traditional dishes in Margaret Amelia and pub fare in the cosy Village Inn.

THURSFORD GREEN – **Norfolk** 15 C1

London 120 mi – Fakenham 7 mi – Norwich 29 mi

Holly Lodge

The Street ✉ NR21 0AS – ✆ (01328) 878 465 – www.hollylodgeguesthouse.co.uk

3 rm – †£ 70/100 ††£ 90/120 **Rest** – Menu £ 20

Remotely set 18C house with delightful gardens and nice pond. Individually themed bedrooms are located in the old stable block and boast exposed beams, feature beds and numerous extra touches. Communal breakfasts, in smart conservatory, use local and homemade produce. Home-cooked dinners from daily changing set menu.

TICEHURST – **East Sussex** – **504** V30 – **pop. 3 118** – ✉ **Wadhurst** 8 B2

London 49 mi – Brighton 44 mi – Folkestone 38 mi – Hastings 15 mi

Dale Hill, ✆ (01580) 20 01 12

Bell with rm
High St ✉ TN5 7AS – ✆ (01580) 200 234 – www.thebellinticehurst.com
7 rm – †£ 110/155 ††£ 110/155
Rest – *(booking advisable)* Menu £ 14 (weekday lunch) – Carte £ 22/39
With top hats as lampshades, tubas in the loos and a private dining room called 'the stable with a table', 'quirky' is this 16C coaching inn's middle name. Seasonal menus offer proper, tasty pub food, and rustic bedrooms – each with their own silver birch tree – share the pub's idiosyncratic charm.

TICKTON – East Riding of Yorkshire – 502 S22 – see Beverley

TILFORD – Surrey 7 C2

London 43 mi – Bristol 101 mi – Cardiff 134 mi – Bournemouth 70 mi

Duke of Cambridge
Tilford Rd ✉ GU10 2DD – ✆ (01252) 792 236
– www.dukeofcambridgetilford.co.uk – Closed 25 December
Rest – Carte £ 24/33
18C pub in the heart of the forest, with a rustic, flag-floored bar, a cosy snug and an appealing heated terrace covered by an impressive oak-beamed roof. Menu offers everything from deli boards and pub classics to more adventurous dishes.

TILLINGTON – West Sussex – 504 S31 – see Petworth

TILSTON – Cheshire West and Chester – 502 L24 – see Malpas

TISBURY – Wiltshire – 503 N30 – pop. 2 056 4 C3

London 103 mi – Bristol 45 mi – Cardiff 87 mi – Torbay 98 mi

Beckford Arms with rm
Fonthill Gifford, Northwest : 2 mi by Greenwich Rd ✉ SP3 6PX – ✆ (01747) 870 385 – www.beckfordarms.com – Closed 25 December
10 rm – †£ 95/175 ††£ 95/175 **Rest** – *(booking essential)* Carte £ 23/32
Charming 18C inn offering something a little different. Beamed dining room, rustic bar and lovely country house sitting room – where films are screened on Sundays. Delightful terrace and garden with hammocks, petanque pitch and dog bath. Tasty, unfussy classics and country-style dishes; try the homemade pork scratchings. Tasteful bedrooms provide thoughtful comforts.

TITCHMARSH – Northamptonshire – 504 S26 17 C3

London 79 mi – Bristol 137 mi – Plymouth 255 mi – Bournemouth 161 mi

Wheatsheaf
1 North St ✉ NN14 3DH – ✆ (01832) 732 203
– www.thewheatsheafattitchmarsh.co.uk – Closed Sunday dinner
Rest – Menu £ 18 (weekday lunch) – Carte £ 17/37
Remotely set, 17C honey-stone inn with a delightful bar, two smart dining rooms and a spacious garden and terrace. Wildlife photography brightens the walls. Proper pub cooking uses quality seasonal ingredients and everything is homemade.

TITCHWELL – Norfolk – 504 V25 – pop. 99 15 C1

London 128 mi – King's Lynn 25 mi – Boston 56 mi – Wisbech 36 mi

Titchwell Manor
✉ PE31 8BB – ✆ (01485) 210 221 – www.titchwellmanor.com
27 rm – †£ 65/150 ††£ 115/250
Rest – Menu £ 45 (dinner) – Carte £ 24/46 **s**
Attractive red-brick former farmhouse. Stylish interior with bare floorboards, leather sofas and seaside photos. Classical bedrooms in the main house; more stylish rooms in the grounds. Informal bar and terrace. Smart conservatory restaurant with a modern 7 course tasting menu.

ENGLAND

TITLEY – Herefordshire – 503 L27 – ✉ Kington 18 A3

London 176 mi – Plymouth 196 mi – Torbay 175 mi – Exeter 159 mi

Stagg Inn (Steve Reynolds) with rm

✉ HR5 3RL – ✆ (01544) 230 221 – www.thestagg.co.uk – Closed 2 weeks January-February, first 2 weeks November, 25-26 December, Sunday dinner and Monday

6 rm – †£ 75/140 ††£ 100/140 **Rest** – *(booking essential)* Carte £ 26/43

Part-medieval, part-Victorian pub with a delightfully cosy interior. Cooking is fittingly straightforward, relying on classically based recipes, careful preparation and top quality produce. Menus are short, simple and to the point, while dishes themselves are truly satisfying. Bedrooms in the pub are snug but can be noisy; opt for one in the former vicarage.

→ Cured salmon with Cornish crab. Slow-cooked belly pork, pig's head, little gem lettuce and noisette potatoes. Rhubarb compote, jelly, custard and soft meringue.

TOLLARD ROYAL – Wiltshire 4 C3

London 118 mi – Bristol 63 mi – Southampton 40 mi – Portsmouth 59 mi

King John Inn with rm

✉ SP5 5PS – ✆ (01725) 516 207 – www.kingjohninn.co.uk – Closed 25 December

8 rm – †£ 110/160 ††£ 120/170 **Rest** – Carte £ 27/34

Creeper-clad Victorian pub in a pretty village, with a smart, spacious, open-plan interior. Daily changing, classically based menus, with game a speciality. Contemporary bedrooms mix modern facilities with antique furniture; some are in the coach house opposite.

ENGLAND

TOOT BALDON – Oxfordshire – see Oxford

TOPSHAM – Devon – 503 J31 – pop. 3 545 – ✉ Exeter 2 D2

London 175 mi – Torbay 26 mi – Exeter 4 mi – Torquay 24 mi

Salutation Inn Ⓝ with rm

68 Fore St ✉ EX3 0HL – ✆ (01392) 873 060 – www.saltationtopsham.co.uk

6 rm – †£ 110/200 ††£ 125/225

Rest – *(light lunch) (booking essential at dinner)* Menu £ 38/92

1720s coaching inn with a surprisingly contemporary interior. The glass-covered courtyard serves breakfast, light lunches and afternoon tea. The stylish dining room offers nicely balanced, weekly 5, 7 and 9 course set menus of well-judged modern cooking. Bedrooms are similarly up-to-date and understated.

La Petite Maison

35 Fore St ✉ EX3 0HR – ✆ (01392) 873 660 – www.lapetitemaison.co.uk – Closed 2 weeks autumn, 1 week April, 26-30 December, Sunday and Monday

Rest – *(booking essential at lunch)* Menu £ 39

Cosy two-roomed restaurant in a charming riverside village, with bright décor and eye-catching Peter Blake art. Seasonally evolving menus features meat from the village butcher's and cheese from the nearby shop. Friendly, welcoming owners.

TORQUAY – Torbay – 503 J32 – pop. 62 968 2 C-D2

London 223 mi – Exeter 23 mi – Plymouth 32 mi

5 Vaughan Parade, ✆ (01803) 21 12 11, www.torquay.com

St Marychurch, Petitor Rd, ✆ (01803) 32 74 71

Torbay★ – Kent's Cavern★ **AC** CX **A**

Paignton Zoo★★ **AC**, SE : 3 mi by A 3022 - Cockington★, W : 1 mi AX

Plans on following pages

Marstan without rest

Meadfoot Sea Rd ✉ TQ1 2LQ – ✆ (01803) 292 837 – www.marstanhotel.co.uk – Closed November-February except 23 December-2 January CX**a**

9 rm – †£ 50/75 ††£ 69/150

Keenly run townhouse in a quiet area of the town, with a pool, hot tub and suntrap terrace. Comfortable, modern bedrooms boast good facilities. Substantial breakfasts include homemade granola and exotic fruit salad.

Somerville without rest

515 Babbacombe Rd. ✉ TQ1 1HJ – ☎ (01803) 294 755
– www.somervillehotel.co.uk CX**u**
9 rm – †£ 60/105 ††£ 70/160
Comfortable hotel, an easy walk down the hill into town. Open-plan lounge and breakfast room filled with ornaments. Modern, slightly kitsch bedrooms with antique French furniture and good mod cons; Room 12 has direct access to the garden.

Kingston House without rest

75 Avenue Rd ✉ TQ2 5LL – ☎ (01803) 212 760
– www.kingstonhousetorquay.co.uk – Closed 20 December-6 January
5 rm – †£ 65/70 ††£ 80/90 BY**n**
Enthusiastically run, Victorian guesthouse. Bedrooms offer good facilities and come with thoughtful touches such as locally made chocolates. Comfy lounge and a breakfast room overlooking the courtyard. Homemade scones served on arrival.

Room in the Elephant (Simon Hulstone)

3-4 Beacon Terr, (1st Floor) ✉ TQ1 2BH – ☎ (01803) 200 044
– www.elephantrestaurant.co.uk – Closed October-Easter, Sunday and Monday
Rest – *(dinner only) (set menu only)* Menu £ 70 CZ**e**
First floor restaurant in an elegant Georgian terrace overlooking Torbay and the marina, with a Colonial-style cocktail bar and a simply decorated dining room. The tasting menu offers appealing, flavoursome, classical combinations with no unnecessary elaboration, and the ingredients are top notch.
→ Crab with chicken skin and pickled cucumber. Modbury venison, haunch bon bon, garlic, capers, celeriac purée and onion ash. Soy and apple tarte Tatin, pomona ice cream.

Orange Tree

14-16 Parkhill Rd ✉ TQ1 2AL – ☎ (01803) 213 936
– www.orangetreerestaurant.co.uk – Closed 2 weeks January, 2 weeks November, 26-27 December, Sunday and Monday CZ**u**
Rest – *(dinner only) (booking essential)* Carte £ 27/43
Modern, split-level restaurant with a homely feel, set down a narrow town centre backstreet. The seasonally evolving menu is made up classically based, French-influenced dishes, which are carefully prepared and rely on fresh, local produce.

Brasserie

3-4 Beacon Terr ✉ TQ1 2BH – ☎ (01803) 200 044
– www.elephantrestaurant.co.uk – Closed 3 weeks January, Sunday and Monday
Rest – Menu £ 17 (weekday lunch) – Carte £ 28/44 CZ**e**
Light, airy brasserie underneath 'Room in the Elephant', displaying an intriguing mix of nautical colours and Indian artefacts. Menus revolve around the seasons; cooking is fresh and simple. Good value wines and an upstairs cocktail bar.

Number 7

7 Beacon Terr. ✉ TQ1 2BH – ☎ (01803) 295 055 – www.no7-fish.com – Closed 2 weeks February, 1 week November, Christmas-New Year, Monday November-May and Sunday October-June CZ**e**
Rest – *(dinner only and lunch Wednesday-Saturday) (booking advisable)* Carte £ 23/41
Personally and passionately run bistro located on the ground floor of a Regency house. The walls are covered with fish-related photos and artefacts, as well as extensive blackboard menus of fresh seafood from the Brixham day boats.

at Maidencombe North : 3.5 mi by A 379 - BX – ✉ Torquay

Orestone Manor

Rockhouse Ln ✉ TQ1 4SX – ☎ (01803) 328 098 – www.orestonemanor.com – Closed 3-30 January
11 rm – †£ 70/120 ††£ 80/200
Rest – Menu £ 19 (weekdays) – Carte £ 21/44
Characterful house set among thick shrubbery and mature trees. Colonial feel throughout with dark wood furniture and Oriental and African artefacts. Individually designed bedrooms: some with feature beds; most have sea or country views. Classical menus – dine in the restaurant, conservatory or on the terrace.

ENGLAND

TORBAY
TORQUAY-PAIGNTON

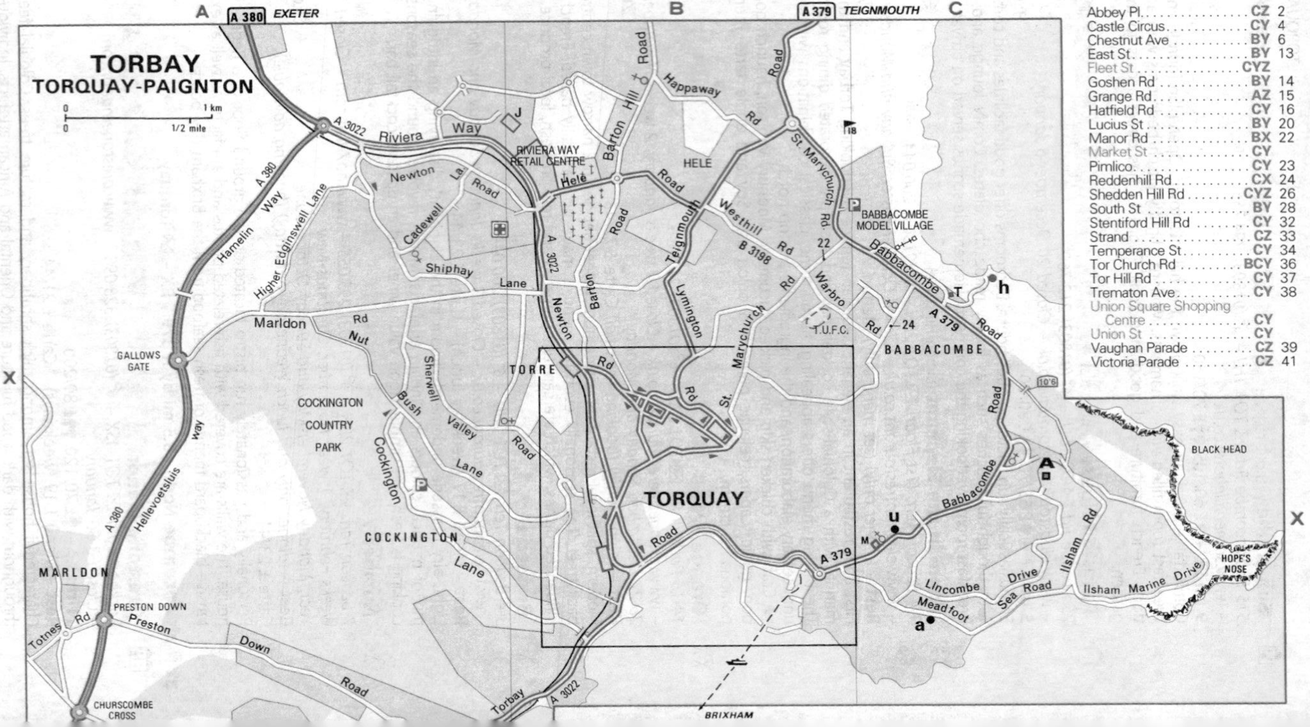

Abbey Pl.	CZ	2
Castle Circus	CY	4
Chestnut Ave	BY	6
East St	BY	13
Fleet St	CYZ	
Goshen Rd	BY	14
Grange Rd	AZ	15
Hatfield Rd	CY	16
Lucius St	BY	20
Manor Rd	BX	22
Market St	CY	
Pimlico	CY	23
Reddenhill Rd	CX	24
Shedden Hill Rd	CYZ	26
South St	BY	28
Stentiford Hill Rd	CY	32
Strand	CZ	33
Temperance St	CY	34
Tor Church Rd	BCY	36
Tor Hill Rd	CY	37
Trematon Ave	CY	38
Union Square Shopping Centre	CY	
Union St	CY	
Vaughan Parade	CZ	39
Victoria Parade	CZ	41

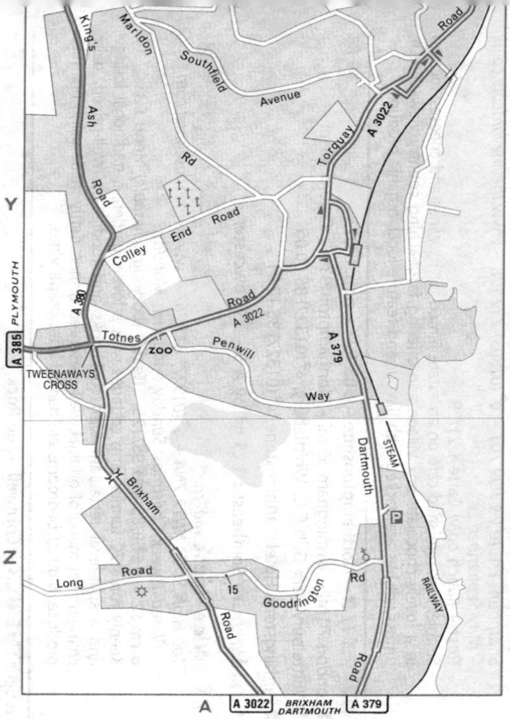
King's Ash Road
Marldon
Southfield Avenue
Rd
Colley End Road
Torquay
A 3022
Road
A 3022
A 380
PLYMOUTH
A 385
Totnes
ZOO
TWEENAWAYS CROSS
Penwill Way
A 379
Dartmouth Road
STEAM RAILWAY
Brixham Road
Long Road
15
Goodrington Rd
Y
Z
A
A 3022
BRIXHAM DARTMOUTH
A 379

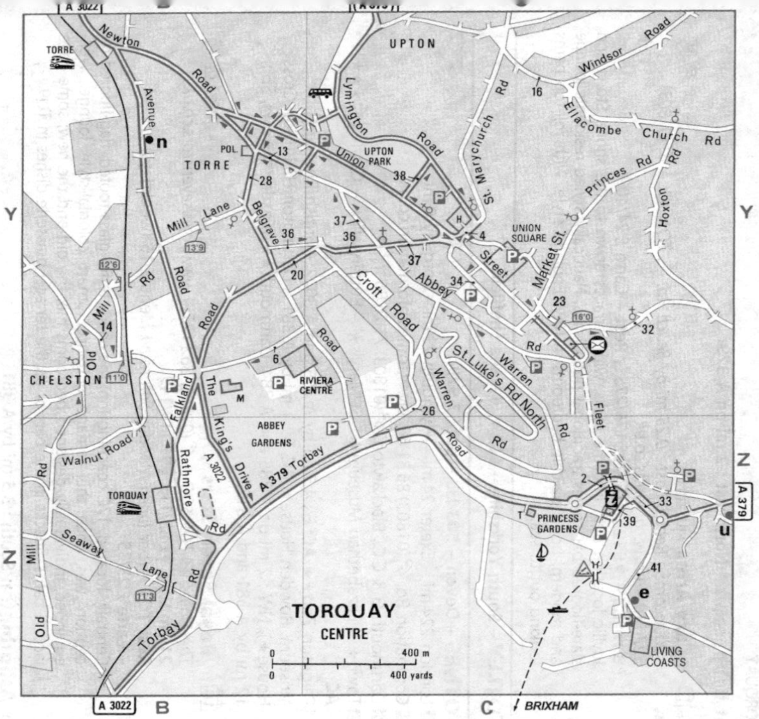
A 3022
TORRE
Newton Road
Avenue
n
UPTON
Lymington Road
Union
UPTON PARK
POL
TORRE
13
28
38
St. Marychurch Rd
16
Windsor Road
Ellacombe Church Rd
Princes Rd
Hoxton Rd
Mill Lane
Belgrave
36
37
4
H
UNION SQUARE
Street
Market St.
Rd
Road
20
Croft Road
Abbey
34
23
Rd
32
Fleet
Mill
14
CHELSTON
Old
6
RIVIERA CENTRE
Falkland
The King's Drive
M
ABBEY GARDENS
Warren Rd
St.Luke's Rd North
Warren
26
Rd
Road
Walnut Road
Rathmore
A 3022
A 379 Torbay
TORQUAY
Rd
Seaway Lane
Rd
Torbay
Mill
Old
2
33
139
PRINCESS GARDENS
T
41
e
u
LIVING COASTS
A 379
TORQUAY
CENTRE
0 400 m
0 400 yards
Y
Z
A 3022
B
C
BRIXHAM

ENGLAND

at Babbacombe Northeast : 2 mi on A 379

Cary Arms with rm
Babbacombe Beach, East : 0.25 mi by Beach Rd. ✉ *TQ1 3LX* – ✆ *(01803) 327 110* – *www.caryarms.co.uk* CX**h**
8 rm – †£ 125/175 ††£ 175/275 **Rest** – Carte £ 24/40
Idyllic location built into the rocks, with terraces down to the shore. Stone and slate-floored bar serves traditional pub dishes. Nautically styled residents lounge and modern, boutique-chic bedrooms in New England style, with roll-top baths looking out to sea.

TOTLEY – South Yorkshire – **502** P24 – see Sheffield

TOTNES – Devon – **503** I32 – pop. 7 929 **2** C2

London 224 mi – Exeter 24 mi – Plymouth 23 mi – Torquay 9 mi
Coronation Rd, ✆ (01803) 86 31 68, www.totnesinformation.co.uk
Dartmouth G & C.C., Blackawton, ✆ (01803) 71 26 86
Town★ – Elizabethan Museum★ - St Mary's★ – Butterwalk★ – Castle (≤★★★) **AC**
Paignton Zoo★★ **AC**, E : 4.5 mi by A 385 and A 3022 – British Photographic Museum, Bowden House★ **AC**, S : 1 mi by A 381 – Dartington Hall (High Cross House★), NW : 2 mi on A 385 and A 384. Dartmouth★★ (Castle ≤★★★), SE : 12 mi by A 381 and A 3122

Royal Seven Stars
The Plains ✉ *TQ9 5DD* – ✆ *(01803) 862 125* – *www.royalsevenstars.co.uk*
21 rm – †£ 85/115 ††£ 119/149
Rest *TQ9* – *(bar lunch Monday-Saturday)* Menu £ 16 (weekdays) – Carte £ 23/35
Centrally located, 17C coaching inn; the characterful glass-roofed, flag-floored reception was once the carriage entrance. Smart colonial-style lounge. Well-equipped, individually designed bedrooms mix the old and the new; some have jacuzzi baths. Snacks in the bars or on the terrace; brasserie dishes in TQ9.

at Ashprington South : 3.5 mi by A 381

Vineyard Café
Sharpham Estate ✉ *TQ9 7UT* – ✆ *(01803) 732 178* – *www.thevineyardcafe.co.uk* – *May-September*
Rest – *(lunch only)* Carte £ 21/29
Simple, teak-furnished café on an estate famed for its wines and cheeses; located in a lovely chocolate box village and offering far-reaching country views. Fresh, unfussy dishes are packed with flavour and feature local, organic produce.

TOWCESTER – Northamptonshire – **503** R27 – pop. 8 073 **16** B3

London 70 mi – Birmingham 50 mi – Northampton 9 mi – Oxford 36 mi
Whittelbury Park G. & C.C., Whittlebury, ✆ (01327) 85 00 00
Farthingstone Hotel, Farthingstone, ✆ (01327) 36 12 91

at Paulerspury Southeast : 3.25 mi by A 5 – ✉ Towcester

Vine House with rm
100 High St ✉ *NN12 7NA* – ✆ *(01327) 811 267* – *www.vinehousehotel.com* – *Closed 1 week Christmas, Sunday and lunch Monday*
6 rm – †£ 69/85 ††£ 95/125 **Rest** – *(booking advisable)* Menu £ 31
Keenly run, 17C former farm cottages with a lovely garden, a traditional lounge and a split-level restaurant with cookbooks and foodie art. Well-priced, daily changing set menu of original, well-presented dishes; deftly made using first-rate produce. Modest bedrooms are named after grape vines.

TREBETHERICK – Cornwall – see Rock

TRELOWARREN – Cornwall – see Helston

TRENT - Dorset - 503 M31 **4** C3

London 128 mi – Southampton 67 mi – Bristol 39 mi – Bournemouth 46 mi

Rose & Crown with rm
rest,

DT9 4SL – (01935) 850 776 – *www.roseandcrowntrent.co.uk*

3 rm – £ 70/85 £ 75/110 **Rest** – Carte £ 20/32

Pretty part-thatched pub dating from the 14C, with an equally charming, rustic interior and a lovely garden. Nothing here is too much trouble for the affable team. The experienced chef offers a plethora of menus; cooking is modern British with a twist. Chic bedrooms have small terraces and country views.

TRESCO – 503 B34 – see Scilly (Isles of)

TRISCOMBE – Somerset – 503 K30 **3** B2

London 163 mi – Bristol 50 mi – Swansea 116 mi – Exeter 42 mi

Blue Ball Inn with rm

TA4 3HE – (01984) 618 242 – *www.blueballinn.info – Closed 25-26 December, dinner 1 January, Monday and Sunday dinner in autumn and winter*

3 rm – £ 55/90 £ 75/110 **Rest** – Carte £ 26/38

Characterful former barn in the Quantock Hills; rustic and cosy with exposed rafters and open fires. Lunchtime sandwiches and pub classics provide fuel for passing walkers; dinner sees well-presented, original, modern dishes. Lovely tiered garden and stylish, comfortable bedrooms in a pretty thatched annexe.

TROUTBECK – Cumbria – 502 L20 – see Windermere

TRUMPET – Herefordshire – see Ledbury

TRURO – Cornwall – 503 E33 – pop. 20 920 **1** B3

London 295 mi – Exeter 87 mi – Penzance 26 mi – Plymouth 52 mi

Municipal Buildings, Boscawen St, (01872) 27 45 55, www.tourism.truro.gov.uk

18 Treliske, (01872) 27 26 40

18 Killiow, Kea, Killiow, (01872) 27 02 46

Royal Cornwall Museum★★ **AC**

Trelissick Garden★★ (<★★) **AC**, S : 4 mi by A 39 – Feock (Church★) S : 5 mi by A 39 and B 3289. Trewithen★★★, NE : 7.5 mi by A 39 and A 390 – Probus★ (tower★ - garden★) NE : 9 mi by A 39 and A 390

Mannings
rm, AC rest,

Lemon St TR1 2QB – (01872) 270 345 – www.manningshotels.co.uk – Closed Christmas

42 rm – £ 65/79 £ 85/99

Rest *Mannings* – (01872) 247 900 *(closed Sunday lunch)* Carte £ 22/43

Imposing hotel located in the city centre, close to the cathedral. Boutique bedrooms are bright, modern and stylish; spacious apartment-style rooms in the neighbouring mews boast over-sized beds and galley kitchens. Chic cocktail bar. Stylish restaurant offers eclectic, all-day menu.

Tabb's

85 Kenwyn St TR1 3BZ – (01872) 262 110 – www.tabbs.co.uk – Closed 1 week January, 1 week October, Saturday lunch, Sunday and Monday

Rest – Menu £ 20 (lunch) – Carte £ 30/38

Series of pleasant slate-floored rooms in a small former pub. Appealing menu of refined dishes, where quality produce shines through. Chef is a passionate chocolatier and duck is a speciality.

Bustophers
AC

62 Lemon St TR1 2PN – (01872) 279 029 – www.bustophersbarbistro.co.uk – Closed 25-26 December and 1 January

Rest – Menu £ 14 (dinner) – Carte £ 20/49

Busy, informal wine bar-bistro just off the town centre, with central bar and open kitchen. Seasonal menus champion Cornish produce and offer a mix of modern and classic dishes, with some Mediterranean touches.

Saffron
5 Quay St ✉ TR1 2HB – ✆ (01872) 263 771 – www.saffronrestauranttruro.co.uk – Closed 25-26 December, Monday dinner January-June, Sunday and bank holidays
Rest – Menu £ 13 (dinner) – Carte £ 22/36
Keenly run restaurant in the heart of town, close to the cathedral. Simply appointed, rustic inner with hearty, flavoursome cooking to match. Extensive menus showcase seasonal Cornish produce.

TUDDENHAM – Suffolk – 504 V27 – pop. 400 — 14 B2
London 76 mi – Birmingham 120 mi – Sheffield 152 mi – Croydon 96 mi

Tuddenham Mill with rm
High St ✉ IP28 6SQ – ✆ (01638) 713 552 – www.tuddenhammill.co.uk
15 rm – †£ 130/180 ††£ 185/395
Rest – Menu £ 25 (lunch) – Carte dinner £ 32/40
Delightful 18C watermill overlooking the old millpond. Stylish bar with mill workings in situ; beamed restaurant with black furnishings above. Cooking uses innovative techniques, displaying quality seasonal produce in unusual combinations. Trendy bedrooms are located in the mill and attractive outbuildings.

TURNERS HILL – West Sussex – 504 T30 – pop. 1 534 — 7 D2
London 33 mi – Brighton 24 mi – Crawley 7 mi

Alexander House
rm, rest,
East St, East : 1 mi on B 2110 ✉ RH10 4QD – ✆ (01342) 714 914 – www.alexanderhouse.co.uk
38 rm – †£ 220 ††£ 255, £ 20 – 5 suites
Rest *AG's* – *(dinner only and Sunday lunch) (booking essential)* Carte £ 51/63
Rest *Reflections Brasserie* – Carte £ 36/53
Stunning 18C country house in extensive grounds; once owned by Percy Shelley's family. Comfy guest areas and a superb spa with 25 treatment rooms and a Grecian basement pool. Spacious, well-equipped bedrooms – some with four-poster beds, claw-foot baths or double showers. Accomplished cooking in formal AG'S; modern brasserie classics in more contemporary Reflections.

ENGLAND

TWO BRIDGES – Devon – 503 I32 – ✉ Yelverton — 2 C2
London 226 mi – Exeter 25 mi – Plymouth 17 mi
Dartmoor National Park★★

Prince Hall
East : 1 mi on B 3357 ✉ PL20 6SA – ✆ (01822) 890 403 – www.princehall.co.uk
8 rm – †£ 75/180 ††£ 95/180
Rest – *(booking essential) (bar lunch Monday-Saturday)* Menu 43 **s**
Remotely set hotel with welcoming interior. Cosy lounges boast real fires and eclectic art. Comfy, homely bedrooms display subtle modern touches and smart bathrooms; some overlook the moor. Small bar. Bright restaurant with wood burning stove and classical menus.

TYNEMOUTH – Tyne and Wear – 501 P18 – pop. 17 056 — 24 B2
London 290 mi – Newcastle upon Tyne 8 mi – Sunderland 7 mi

Grand
14 Grand Par. ✉ NE30 4ER – ✆ (0191) 293 6666 – www.grandhotel-uk.com
45 rm – †£ 75/165 ††£ 85/195
Rest *Victoria* – *(closed Sunday dinner)* Menu £ 13/25
Victorian hotel with superb sea views: once the Duchess of Northumberland's holiday home. Impressive carved staircase and sizeable guest areas boasts ornate coving and pillars. Mix of simply furnished and more comfortable bedrooms; 222 has a four-poster and jacuzzi. Classical dining room with a menu to match.

Martineau without rest
57 Front St ✉ NE30 4BX – ☎ (0191) 257 90 38 – www.martineau-house.co.uk – Closed 24-27 December
4 rm – †£ 75/85 ††£ 95/99
Attractive 18C red-brick house named after Harriet Martineau. Cosy, individually furnished bedrooms come with thoughtful extras; two boast pleasant Tyne views. Superb communal breakfasts with a river and South Shields outlook.

UCKFIELD – East Sussex – 504 U31 – pop. 15 374 — 8 A2

London 45 mi – Brighton 17 mi – Eastbourne 20 mi – Maidstone 34 mi

Horsted Place
Little Horsted, South : 2.5 mi by B 2102 and A 22 on A 26 ✉ TN22 5TS – ☎ (01825) 750 581 – www.horstedplace.co.uk – Closed first week January
20 rm – †£ 105/360 ††£ 105/360 – 5 suites
Rest – *(closed Saturday lunch)* Menu £ 22/38
Impressive country house in Victorian Gothic style, surrounded by parkland. Fully tiled entrance hall leads to impressive main gallery; ornate sitting rooms furnished with fine antiques. Bedrooms are individually styled; the best have dual aspect. Formal 19C dining room offers daily menu of classical dishes.

UFFORD – Suffolk – 504 Y27 — 15 D3

London 91 mi – Bristol 221 mi – Bournemouth 211 mi – Poole 215 mi

Ufford Crown
High St ✉ IP13 6EL – ☎ (01394) 461 030 – www.theuffordcrown.com – Closed Tuesday
Rest – Carte £ 20/34
Welcoming former coaching inn run by an enthusiastic husband and wife team. Dishes change daily and range from a pork belly sandwich to chargrilled duck hearts or rib of Ketley beef for 4. Portions are generous and service is keen.

UFFORD – Peterborough – pop. 163 — 14 A2

London 90 mi – Leicester 38 mi – Coventry 69 mi – Nottingham 50 mi

White Hart with rm
Main St ✉ PE9 3BH – ☎ (01780) 740 250 – www.whitehartufford.co.uk
6 rm – †£ 70/95 ††£ 75/100 **Rest** – Carte £ 23/41
Delightful 17C inn with super sun-trap of a terrace and garden. Eat in the cosy bar, rustic restaurant or lovely conservatory. Menus offer a broad range of dishes, with much of the meat coming from their own farm. Sweet, individually styled bedrooms; one is a four-poster and those outside allow dogs to stay.

ULLSWATER – Cumbria – 502 L20 – pop. 1 199 – ✉ Penrith — 21 B2

London 296 mi – Carlisle 25 mi – Kendal 31 mi – Penrith 6 mi
Beckside Car Park, Glenridding, Penrith, ☎ (017684) 8 24 14, www.ullswater.co.uk

at Pooley Bridge on B 5320 – ✉ Penrith

Sharrow Bay Country House
South : 2 mi on Howtown Rd ✉ CA10 2LZ – ☎ (017684) 86 301 – www.sharrowbay.co.uk
24 rm – †£ 100/200 ††£ 200/400 – 3 suites
Rest *Sharrow Bay Country House* – see restaurant listing
Long-standing, celebrated Victorian villa set in mature gardens and woodland; beautifully located on the shores of Lake Ullswater. Traditional country house style throughout, with very charming drawing rooms and a sense of tranquility. Comfortable bedrooms come with a classic, cottagey feel.

XXX **Sharrow Bay Country House** – Sharrow Bay Country House Hotel
South : 2 mi on Howtown Rd ✉ CA10 2LZ – ☎ (017684) 86 301 – www.sharrowbay.co.uk
Rest – *(booking essential)* Menu £ 28 (weekdays)/75
Two delightful dining rooms set in a beautifully located, traditional country house; 'Lakeside' has superb views out over Lake Ullswater. Service is formal and dishes, as classic as they come; don't miss the sticky toffee pudding.

ENGLAND

at Watermillock on A 592 – ✉ Penrith

Rampsbeck Country House
✉ *CA11 0LP* – ✆ *(017684) 86 442* – *www.rampsbeck.co.uk*
19 rm – †£ 98/177 ††£ 145/300 – 1 suite
Rest ***Rampsbeck Country House*** – see restaurant listing
18C country house in mature grounds, affording lovely views over Ullswater and the fells. Spacious guest areas boast heavy fabrics and antique furniture; contemporary country house bedrooms feature good facilities and marble bathrooms.

Rampsbeck Country House – Rampsbeck Country House Hotel
✉ *CA11 0LP* – ✆ *(017684) 86 442* – *www.rampsbeck.co.uk*
Rest – *(booking essential)* Menu £ 32/60 **s**
Elegant hotel restaurant with good-sized tables and beautiful lake and fell views. The oft-changing set menu offers well-prepared classical dishes presented in a modern manner; take your canapés and coffee in one of the drawing rooms.

UPPER SLAUGHTER – **Gloucestershire** – **503** O28 – **see Bourton-on-the-Water**

UPPER SOUTH WRAXALL – **Wiltshire** **4** C2
London 201 mi – Birmingham 326 mi – Liverpool 419 mi – Leeds 393 mi

Longs Arms N
✉ *BA15 2SB* – ✆ *(01225) 864 450* – *www.thelongsarms.com* – *Closed 2 weeks January-February, Sunday dinner and Monday*
Rest – *(booking essential)* Carte £ 22/35
Handsome, bay-windowed, Bath stone pub opposite a medieval church in a sleepy village. Traditional British dishes are full-flavoured, hearty and satisfying; everything is homemade and they smoke their own meats and fish. Dine in the characterful area in front of the bar. Warm, friendly service.

UPPER WOODFORD – **Wiltshire** – **503** O30 – **see Salisbury**

UPPINGHAM – **Rutland** – **504** R26 – **pop. 3 947** **17** C2
London 101 mi – Leicester 19 mi – Northampton 28 mi – Nottingham 35 mi

Lake Isle with rm
rest,
16 High St East ✉ *LE15 9PZ* – ✆ *(01572) 822 951* – *www.lakeisle.co.uk* – *Closed 26 December-2 January, Sunday dinner and Monday lunch*
12 rm – †£ 60/70 ††£ 80/110 **Rest** – *(light lunch)* Carte £ 26/37
Pleasant town centre property accessed via a narrow passageway, with small, characterful lounge and heavy wood furnishings. Light lunches and much more elaborate dinners with modern influences and the odd Asian touch. Bedrooms boast good facilities and extras: superior are the largest, with whirlpool baths.

at Lyddington South : 2 mi by A 6003 – ✉ Uppingham

Marquess of Exeter with rm
52 Main St ✉ *LE15 9LT* – ✆ *(01572) 822 477* – *www.marquessexeter.co.uk* – *Closed 25 December*
17 rm – †£ 80/100 ††£ 100/125
Rest – Menu £ 14 (lunch) – Carte £ 25/32
Attractive 16C thatched pub with a cosy bar, characterful exposed beams, inglenook fireplaces and a rustic dining room. The daily changing menu offers tasty, classical combinations of local, home-grown and home-reared produce. Comfortable bedrooms are located across the car park.

Old White Hart with rm
51 Main St ✉ *LE15 9LR* – ✆ *(01572) 821 703* – *www.oldwhitehart.co.uk* – *Closed 25 December and Sunday dinner in winter*
10 rm – †£ 65/75 ††£ 90/100 **Rest** – Carte £ 22/37
This pub offers all you'd expect from a traditional 17C coaching inn – and a lot more besides. It's got the chocolate box village setting, the open fires and the seasonal menu of hearty, classic dishes; but also gives you a relaxing ambience, charming service, a 10-piste petanque pitch and stylish bedrooms.

UPTON SCUDAMORE – **Wiltshire** – **503** N30 – **see Warminster**

ENGLAND

UTTOXETER – Staffordshire – 503 O25 – pop. 12 023 19 C1

London 150 mi – Birmingham 41 mi – Stafford 16 mi

at Beamhurst Northwest : 3 mi on A 522 – ✉ Uttoxeter

Gilmore at Strine's Farm

Beamhurst ✉ ST14 5DZ – ✆ (01889) 507 100 – www.restaurantgilmore.com – Closed 1 week Easter, 1 week January, 1 week July-August, 1 week October-November, Monday, Tuesday and dinner Sunday.

Rest – *(dinner only and lunch Thursday, Friday and Sunday) (booking essential)* Menu £ 25/40

Converted farmhouse with three beamed rooms; the one by the kitchen with the quarry tiled flooring is the most popular. Homely décor and personal touches throughout. Traditionally based cooking makes use of local produce.

VENTNOR – Isle of Wight – 503 Q32 – see Wight (Isle of)

VERYAN – Cornwall – 503 F33 – pop. 877 – ✉ Truro 1 B3

London 291 mi – St Austell 13 mi – Truro 13 mi

Village★

Nare rest,

Carne Beach, Southwest : 1.25 mi ✉ TR2 5PF – ✆ (01872) 501 111 – www.narehotel.co.uk

37 rm – †£ 140/268 ††£ 270/768 – 7 suites

Rest *Quarterdeck* – see restaurant listing

Rest *The Dining Room* – *(dinner only and Sunday lunch) (booking essential)* Menu £ 50

Personally run country house hotel boasting a stunning bay outlook. Classical bedrooms: some with patios/balconies; most with a view. Have afternoon tea in the drawing room and canapés in the bar in the evening. Outdoor pool and hot tub. Classical daily menu in The Dining Room or lighter dishes in Quarterdeck.

Quarterdeck – Nare Hotel

Carne Beach, Southwest : 1.25 mi ✉ TR2 5PF – ✆ (01872) 500 000 – www.narehotel.co.uk

Rest – *(bookings essential for non-residents)* Carte £ 31/55

Informal restaurant in a personally run country house, with large black and white prints on the walls and a nautical theme. The menu offers a range of classic dishes, with local seafood a highlight.

VIRGINSTOW – Devon – 503 H31 2 C2

London 227 mi – Bideford 25 mi – Exeter 41 mi – Launceston 11 mi

Percy's

Coombeshead Estate, Southwest : 1.75 mi on Tower Hill rd ✉ EX21 5EA – ✆ (01409) 211 236 – www.percys.co.uk

7 rm – †£ 90/170 ††£ 140/230

Rest – *(dinner only) (booking essential) (set menu only)* Menu £ 40

Stone house in 130 acres of fields and woodland. The owners grow veg, breed racehorses, rear pigs and sheep and sell wool, skins and produce. Spacious, comfy bedrooms in former barn - some have jacuzzi baths. Set menu of traditional dishes in formal dining room; ingredients from the estate.

WADDESDON – Buckinghamshire – 504 R28 – pop. 1 865 11 C2

– ✉ Aylesbury Great Britain

London 51 mi – Aylesbury 5 mi – Northampton 32 mi – Oxford 31 mi

Chiltern Hills★

Waddesdon Manor★★, S : 0.5 mi by A 41 and minor rd – Claydon House★, N : by minor rd

Five Arrows with rm

High St ✉ HP18 0JE – ✆ (01296) 651 727 – www.thefivearrows.co.uk

12 rm – †£ 75/100 ††£ 99/235

Rest – Menu £ 14 (weekday lunch) – Carte £ 24/40

Half-timbered Victorian building on the Rothschild Estate, with Elizabethan chimney stacks, attractive gabling and mullioned windows. Individually styled, antique-furnished bedrooms are split between the main house and courtyard. The traditional restaurant serves classical menus and local game in season.

ENGLAND

WADEBRIDGE – Cornwall – 503 F32 – pop. 6 222 — 1 B2

London 245 mi – Plymouth 41 mi – Torbay 68 mi – Torquay 88 mi

at St Kew Northeast : 4.5 mi by A 39

St Kew Inn
PL30 3HB – (01208) 841 259 – *www.stkewinn.co.uk*
Rest – Carte £ 23/36
Characterful country pub in quintessentially English location. Wide-ranging menu of fresh, tasty dishes and St Austell beer in wooden casks. Attractive garden with picnic tables and heaters.

WALBERSWICK – Suffolk – 504 Y27 – pop. 1 648 — 15 D2

London 115 mi – Norwich 31 mi – Ipswich 31 mi – Lowestoft 16 mi

Anchor with rm
Main St IP18 6UA – (01502) 722 112 – www.anchoratwalberswick.com – Closed 25 December
10 rm – †£ 110/125 ††£ 125/150 **Rest** – Carte £ 26/33
An Arts and Crafts building with a sizeable garden and seaward views. Global flavours alongside British classics on interesting menu; careful cooking uses local, seasonal produce. Excellent beers and wines. Simple chalet bedrooms; impressive breakfasts.

WALFORD – Herefordshire – see Ross-on-Wye

WALL – STS Staffordshire – 504 O26 – see Lichfield

WALTHAM ABBEY – Essex – 504 U28 – pop. 17 675

London 17 mi – Croydon 26 mi – Barnet 13 mi – Ealing 21 mi

XX **Parsons** N
58 Sun St EN9 1EJ – (01992) 700 655 – www.parsonsrestaurant.com – Closed 1-5 January
Rest – Menu £ 17/28 – Carte £ 22/43
Large converted pub with an equally sizeable terrace; owned by an experienced chef and two master butchers. Good value menus of unfussy, well-known dishes. The plain walls are hung with bright pictures and there's good disabled access.

WANTAGE – Oxfordshire – 504 P29 – pop. 9 452 — 10 B3

London 71 mi – Oxford 16 mi – Reading 24 mi – Swindon 21 mi
19 Church St, (01235) 76 01 76, www.wantage.com

at East Hendred West : 4.5 mi by A 417 – Oxfordshire

Eyston Arms
High St OX12 8JY – (01235) 833 320 – www.eystonarms.co.uk – Closed 25 December and Sunday dinner
Rest – Carte £ 27/39
Set in a characterful, largely estate-owned village; a modern dining pub with scrubbed tables, tiled floors and exposed brickwork. Diverse menus offer popular antipasti boards, unfussy main dishes and desserts with a twist. Welcoming team.

WAREHAM – Dorset – 503 N31 – pop. 2 568 — 4 C3

London 123 mi – Bournemouth 13 mi – Weymouth 19 mi
South St, (01929) 55 27 40, www.visit-dorset.com
Town★ – St Martin's★★
Blue Pool★ **AC**, S : 3.5 mi by A 351 – Bovington Tank Museum★ **AC**, Woolbridge Manor★, W : 5 mi by A 352. Moreton Church★★, W : 9.5 mi by A 352 – Corfe Castle★ (≤★★) **AC**, SE : 6 mi by A 351 – Lulworth Cove★, SW : 10 mi by A 352 and B 3070 – Bere Regis★ (St John the Baptist Church★), NW : 6.5 mi by minor rd

Priory
Church Grn ✉ BH20 4ND – ✆ (01929) 551 666 – www.theprioryhotel.co.uk
18 rm – †£ 168/296 ††£ 210/370 – 2 suites
Rest – Menu £ 45 (dinner) – Carte £ 34/52
Charming, privately run part 16C priory, friendly and discreetly cosy. Well-equipped rooms. Manicured four-acre gardens lead down to River Frome: luxury suites in boathouse. Charming restaurant beneath stone vaults of undercroft.

Gold Court House without rest
St John's Hill ✉ BH20 4LZ – ✆ (01929) 553 320 – www.goldcourthouse.co.uk – Closed Christmas
3 rm – †£ 60 ††£ 85
Attractive Georgian house in a small square off the high street; built in 1762, it was once a goldsmith's and set next to the mint. Antique-furnished lounge and traditional bedrooms with private bathrooms. The cellar dates from Saxon times.

WAREN MILL – Northumberland – 501 O17 – see Bamburgh

WARKWORTH – Northumberland – 502 P17

24 B2

London 316 mi – Alnwick 7 mi – Morpeth 24 mi

Roxbro House without rest
5 Castle Terr ✉ NE65 0UP – ✆ (01665) 711 416 – www.roxbrohouse.co.uk – Closed 24-28 December
6 rm – †£ 50/70 ††£ 99/150
Elegant and opulent; suitable adjectives to describe these two houses in the shadow of Warkworth Castle, where individually styled, boutique bedrooms mix modern facilities with antique furniture. Comfy lounges; one with an honesty bar.

WARMINGHAM – Cheshire East

20 B3

London 174 mi – Birmingham 61 mi – Manchester 33 mi – Bristol 143 mi

Bear's Paw with rm
School Ln ✉ CW11 3QN – ✆ (01270) 526 317 – www.thebearspaw.co.uk
17 rm – †£ 95/120 ††£ 105/140 **Rest** – Carte £ 20/38
Handsome 19C inn with a spacious, wood-panelled bar and a huge array of local ales. The menu will please all appetites, with everything from nibbles, salads and deli boards to European dishes, pub favourites and steak you can cook yourself on a hot stone. Stylish, good value bedrooms.

WARMINSTER – Wiltshire – 503 N30 – pop. 17 486

4 C2

London 111 mi – Bristol 29 mi – Exeter 74 mi – Southampton 47 mi
Central Car Park, ✆ (01985) 21 85 48, www.visitwiltshire.co.uk
Longleat House★★★ **AC**, SW : 3 m. Stonehenge★★★ **AC**, E : 18 mi by A 36 and A 303 – Bratton Castle (<★★) NE : 6 mi by A 350 and B 3098

Bishopstrow and Spa
Boreham Rd, Southeast : 1.5 mi on B 3414 ✉ BA12 9HH – ✆ (01985) 212 312 – www.bishopstrow.co.uk
31 rm – †£ 99/220 ††£ 145/220 – 3 suites
Rest ***Mulberry*** – Menu £ 19 (weekday lunch) – Carte £ 28/37
Georgian country house retaining classic styling in its sitting rooms and main hall. In contrast is the stunning glass 'conservatory' which overlooks the terrace and manicured gardens. Stylish, contemporary bedrooms and well-equipped spa. Spacious, elegant restaurant serves classic dishes with a modern edge.

Weymouth Arms Ⓝ with rm
12 Emwell St ✉ BA12 8JA – ✆ (01985) 216 995 – www.weymoutharms.co.uk – Closed Sunday dinner and Monday lunch
6 rm – †£ 65/75 ††£ 75/85, £ 7 **Rest** – Carte £ 21/37
Grade II listed building with plenty of history. It's immensely characterful, with original wood panelling, antiques and lithographs, as well as two fireplaces originally intended for nearby Longleat House. Cooking is fresh and fittingly traditional. Cosy bedrooms have charming original fittings.

ENGLAND

at Upton Scudamore **North : 2.5 mi by A 350 – ✉ Warminster**

Angel Inn with rm
✉ BA12 0AG – ✆ (01985) 213 225 – www.theangelinn.co.uk
10 rm – £ 85 £ 95
Rest – Menu £ 10 (weekday lunch) – Carte £ 24/34
Dependable village local with cottagey dining room and lovely terrace. Menus are fairly formal and classical, offering the likes of home-cured gravadlax, roast duck, venison steak and old-fashioned puddings. Individually themed bedrooms are cosy and well-kept.

at Heytesbury **Southeast : 3.75 mi by B 3414 – ✉ Warminster**

Resting Post without rest
67 High St ✉ BA12 0ED – ✆ (01985) 840 204 – www.therestingpost.co.uk
3 rm – £ 50/60 £ 70/85
This attractive 17C listed cottage is the village's former post office and shop; look out for the mail box on the wall outside. Cosy, neat bedrooms feature up-to-date bathrooms. Traditional English breakfasts.

Angel Inn
High St ✉ BA12 0ED – ✆ (01985) 840 330 – www.theangelheytesbury.co.uk
Rest – Carte £ 19/38
Pretty, family-run, 16C pub with open fires and beams; it boasts a typically English feel, emphasised by the locals and their dogs. Flavoursome dishes come in generous portions and make use of fresh, regional produce.

ENGLAND

at Crockerton **South : 2 mi by A 350**

Bath Arms with rm
Clay St, on Shearwater rd ✉ BA12 8AJ – ✆ (01985) 212 262 – www.batharmscrockerton.co.uk – Closed dinner 25-26 December
2 rm – £ 80/110 £ 80/110 **Rest** – Carte £ 18/29
Down-to-earth pub on the Longleat Estate. Daily changing menu features classic pub dishes, snacks and grills, along with a selection of daily specials; try the legendary 'sticky' beef with braised red cabbage. Two ultra-spacious, contemporary bedrooms, amusingly named 'Left' and 'Right'.

at Horningsham **Southwest : 5 mi by A 362 – ✉ Wiltshire**

Bath Arms with rm
Longleat ✉ BA12 7LY – ✆ (01985) 844 308 – www.batharms.co.uk
16 rm – £ 75/175 £ 95/185 **Rest** – Carte £ 29/37
Charming pub within the Longleat estate, with open fire in bar, grand dining room and delightful terrace. Appealing menus offer something for everyone; produce is locally sourced, much of it from the estate. Quirky, comfortable, individually themed bedrooms.

WARTLING – East Sussex – 504 V31 – see Herstmonceux

WARWICK – Warwickshire – 503 P27 – pop. 23 350 Great Britain 19 C3

London 96 mi – Birmingham 20 mi – Coventry 11 mi – Leicester 34 mi
Jury St, ✆ (01926) 49 22 12, www.visitwarwick.co.uk
Warwick Racecourse, ✆ (01926) 49 43 16
Town★ - Castle★★ **AC** Y – Leycester Hospital★ **AC** Y **B** – Collegiate Church of St Mary★ (Tomb★) Y **A**

Charter House without rest
87 West St ✉ CV34 6AH – ✆ (01926) 496 965 – Closed 1 week Christmas Y**c**
3 rm – £ 65/69 £ 85/95
Hugely characterful timbered house dating from 1480 and used as an officers' billet by Cromwell's troops in 1641; there is a tunnel connecting the house to the castle! The pretty breakfast room has a flag floor and wattle and daub walls. Well-appointed bedrooms feature heavy fabrics and come with good extras.

WARWICK-ROYAL LEAMINGTON SPA

Birmingham Rd . . . . Z 7
Bowling Green St . . . . Y 9
Brook St. Y 12
Butts (The) . . . . Y 13
Castle Hill . . . . Y 15
Church St. . . . . Y 17
High St . . . . Y 23
Jury St . . . . Y
Lakin Rd. . . . . Y 25
Linen St . . . . Y 26
Market Pl. . . . . Y 29
Old Square . . . . Y 35
Old Warwick Rd . . . . Z 36
Radford Rd. . . . . Z 39
Rock (The) . . . . Y 32
St John's Rd . . . . Y 42
St Nicholas Church St . . . . Y 43
Shires Retail Park . . . . Z
Smith St. . . . . Y
Swan St . . . . Y 46
Theatre St . . . . Y 48
West St . . . . Y 50

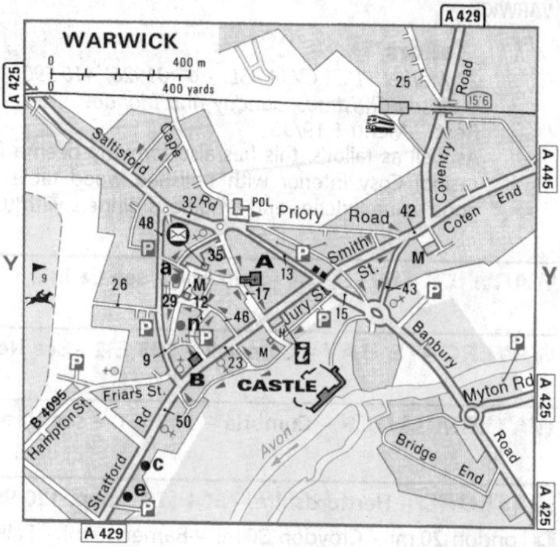

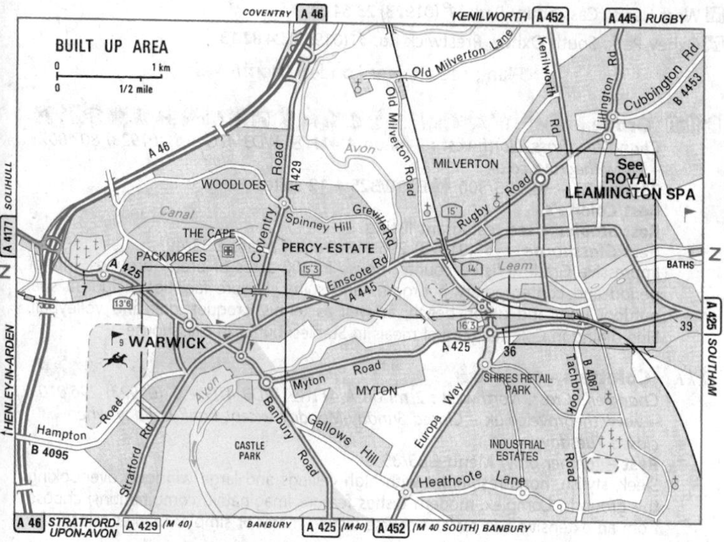

ENGLAND

Park Cottage without rest

113 West St ✉ CV34 6AH – ✆ (01926) 410 319 – www.parkcottagewarwick.co.uk – Closed 23-30 December Y**e**

7 rm – £ 55/70 £ 70/89

15C cross-wing house with wattle and daub walls; set within the grounds of Warwick Castle and originally belonging to the Earl – the 300 year old yew tree was used to make longbows. Cottagey breakfast room and spacious bedrooms with extras.

Saffron Gold

Unit 1, Westgate House, Market St ✉ CV34 4DE – ✆ (01926) 402 061 – www.saffrongoldwarwick.co.uk Y**n**

Rest – *(dinner only)* Carte £ 14/42

Smoothly run by the friendly owner and his attentive team, a modern Indian restaurant with a split-level dining room adorned with contemporary art. Extensive menus offer interesting, authentic cooking, with Goan fish dishes a highlight.

✗ **Tailors** Ⓝ
22 Market Pl ⊠ CV34 4SL – ℰ (01926) 410 590 – www.tailorsrestaurant.co.uk
– Closed Christmas, Sunday and Monday Y**a**
Rest – Menu £ 19/36
As well as tailor's, this has also formerly been a fishmonger's, a butcher's and a casino! Cosy interior with polished wood tables and a brick fireplace. Simple, good value lunches and ambitious dinners with unusual flavour combinations.

WARWICK-ON-EDEN – Cumbria – see Carlisle

WATERGATE BAY – Cornwall – **503** E32 – see Newquay

WATERMILLOCK – Cumbria – **502** L20 – see Ullswater

WATFORD – Hertfordshire – **504** S29 – **pop.** 120 960 **12** A2

▶ London 20 mi – Croydon 30 mi – Barnet 13 mi – Ealing 19 mi

🔟 West Herts., Cassiobury Park, ℰ (01923) 23 64 84

🔟 Oxhey Park, South Oxhey, Prestwick Rd, ℰ (01923) 24 82 13

Plan : see Greater London (North-West) 2

🏨🏨🏨 **Grove** ⟨icons⟩
Chandler's Cross, Northwest : 2 mi on A 411 ⊠ WD3 4TG – ℰ (01923) 807 807
– www.thegrove.co.uk
217 rm ⌑ – ♦£ 285/300 ♦♦£ 310/325 – 12 suites
Rest *Colette's*
Rest *Stables* – see restaurant listing
Rest *Glasshouse* – ℰ (01923) 296 010 *(buffet)* Menu £ 33/49
Impressive Grade II listed country house in 300 acres of pretty grounds. Mix of period and contemporary bedrooms and suites. Leisure facilities include a spa, outdoor pool and urban beach; as well as tennis, croquet, golf and volleyball. Fine dining in Colette's; casual meals in Stables; buffet in Glasshouse.

✗✗✗ **Colette's** – Grove Hotel ⟨icons⟩
Chandler's Cross, Northwest : 2 mi on A 411 ⊠ WD3 4TG – ℰ (01923) 296 010
– www.thegrove.co.uk – Closed Sunday-Monday except bank holiday when closed Tuesday
Rest – *(dinner only)* Menu £ 65/85
Sleek, stylish, hotel restaurant with high ceilings and large windows overlooking the grounds. Complex, modern dishes feature imaginative combinations; choose from an extensive à la carte, 7 course tasting menu or simpler market selection.

✗✗ **Clarendon** ⟨icons⟩
Redhall Ln, Chandlers Cross, West : 5 mi by A 412, Baldwins Lane and Sarratt Rd
⊠ WD3 4LU – ℰ (01923) 270 009 – www.theclarendon.co.uk – Closed 25 December
Rest – Carte £ 21/41 ⟨icon⟩
A former pub deep in country lanes; now a vibrantly decorated, modern restaurant with contemporary art and an open kitchen. Tasty modern British classics and good old-fashioned puddings. Attentive service.

✗✗ **Stables** – Grove Hotel ⟨icons⟩
Chandler's Cross, Northwest : 2 mi on A 411 ⊠ WD3 4TG – ℰ (01923) 296 010
– www.thegrove.co.uk
Rest – Carte £ 27/43
Informal, New England style restaurant in the clubhouse of an impressive Grade II listed country house. It boasts its own sports bar and pleasant views over the course, and offers a grill menu.

ENGLAND

WATLINGTON – Oxfordshire – 504 Q29 – pop. 2 139 11 C2

London 45 mi – Birmingham 89 mi – Bristol 88 mi – Sheffield 153 mi

Fat Fox Inn with rm

13 Shireburn St ✉ OX49 5BU – ✆ (01491) 613 040 – www.thefatfoxinn.co.uk – Closed dinner 25 December and 1 January

9 rm – †£ 79/99 ††£ 89/109 **Rest** – Carte £ 18/26

In the heart of a busy market village; a 19C pub run with honesty and integrity by experienced owners. The menu reflects what they themselves like to eat, covering all bases from potted mackerel to pheasant pie. Fight the cats for a seat by the wood burning range, then settle in to one of the cosy bedrooms.

WATTON – Norfolk – 504 W26 – pop. 7 435 15 C2

London 95 mi – Norwich 22 mi – Swaffham 10 mi

Café at Brovey Lair with rm rest,

Carbrooke Rd., Ovington, Northeast : 1.75 mi by A 1075 ✉ IP25 6SD – ✆ (01953) 882 706 – www.broveylair.com – Closed 25 December and 1 January

3 rm – †£ 135 ††£ 150 **Rest** – *(booking essential 2 days in advance, lunch by arrangement) (set menu only)* Menu £ 53

Keenly run restaurant with integral kitchen. Unique dinner party style dining from single-choice seafood menu, where ambitious dishes display largely Asian and Mediterranean influences. Well-appointed bedrooms sit beside a pool and terrace in lovely gardens.

WEDMORE – Somerset – 503 L30 3 B2

London 155 mi – Bristol 23 mi – Cardiff 67 mi – Plymouth 100 mi

Swan with rm rest,

Cheddar Rd ✉ BS28 4EQ – ✆ (01934) 710 337 – www.theswanwedmore.com – Closed 25 December and Sunday dinner

6 rm – †£ 85/120 ††£ 85/120 **Rest** – *(booking essential)* Carte £ 22/38

Spacious, airy pub with a large wood-furnished bar, a cosy leather seating area and a comfy restaurant. The chef previously worked at River Cottage, so expect good British ingredients that match the seasons appearing in unfussy, flavoursome dishes. Stylish bedrooms complete the picture.

WELLINGHAM – Norfolk – 504 W25 15 C1

London 120 mi – King's Lynn 29 mi – Norwich 28 mi

Manor House Farm without rest

✉ PE32 2TH – ✆ (01328) 838 227 – www.manor-house-farm.co.uk

3 rm – †£ 65/75 ††£ 100/120

Attractive, wisteria-clad farmhouse with large gardens, set by a church in a beautifully peaceful spot. Spacious, airy bedrooms are located in the former stables. Home-grown and home-reared produce is served at breakfast.

WELLS – Somerset – 503 M30 – pop. 11 312 4 C2

London 132 mi – Bristol 20 mi – Southampton 68 mi – Taunton 28 mi

Wells Museum, 8 Cathedral Green, ✆ (01749) 67 17 70, www.wellssomerset.com

18 East Horrington Rd, ✆ (01749) 67 50 05

City★★ – Cathedral★★★ – Bishop's Palace★ (≤★★) **AC** – St Cuthbert★

Glastonbury★★ - Abbey★★ (Abbot's Kitchen★) **AC**, St John the Baptist★★, Somerset Rural Life Museum★ **AC**, Glastonbury Tor★ (≤★★★), SW : 5.5 mi by A 39 – Wookey Hole★ (Caves★ **AC**, Papermill★), NW : 2 m. Cheddar Gorge★★ (Gorge★★, Caves★, Jacob's Ladder ✻★) - St Andrew's Church★, NW : 7 mi by A 371 – Axbridge★★ (King John's Hunting Lodge★, St John the Baptist Church★), NW : 8.5 mi by A 371

Swan rm,

11 Sadler St ✉ BA5 2RX – ✆ (01749) 836 300 – www.swanhotelwells.co.uk

52 rm – †£ 100/122 ††£ 124/157 – 1 suite

Rest *15c A.D.* – Menu £ 12 (weekday lunch) – Carte £ 28/38

15C former coaching inn with a good outlook onto the famous cathedral; its charming interior has subtle, contemporary touches, particularly in the lounge and bar. Comfortable, stylish, well-equipped bedrooms and opulent 'Cathedral Suite'. Formal, wood-panelled restaurant serves classic dishes.

Beryl without rest

East : 1.25 mi by B 3139 off Hawkers Lane ✉ BA5 3JP – ✆ (01749) 678 738 – www.beryl-wells.co.uk – Closed 23-26 December

13 rm ☕ – 🚹£ 75/95 🚹🚹£ 90/150

Fine 19C country house in mature gardens, overlooking the town and run by a charming owner. Delightful, antique-filled drawing room. Individually styled bedrooms: some have four-posters; 'Master and Butterfly' is the best.

Stoberry House Ⓝ without rest

Stoberry Park, Northeast : 0.5 mi by A 39 on College Rd ✉ BA5 3LD – ✆ (01749) 672 906 – www.stoberry-park.co.uk

5 rm ☕ – 🚹£ 75/125 🚹🚹£ 95/145

18C coach house with a delightful walled garden, overlooking Glastonbury Tor. Large lounge with a baby grand piano and antique furniture. Breakfast is an event, with 7 homemade breads, a porridge menu and lots of cooked dishes. Immaculately kept bedrooms come with fresh flowers, chocolates and a pillow menu.

Old Spot

12 Sadler St ✉ BA5 2SE – ✆ (01749) 689 099 – www.theoldspot.co.uk – Closed 1 week Christmas, Monday, Sunday dinner and Tuesday lunch

Rest – Menu £ 19 (weekdays)/23 – Carte £ 24/40

Simple, understated, city centre restaurant with a light, airy feel; its plain walls hung with framed menus and opening out to boast stunning cathedral views at the rear. Well-executed, classical dishes rely on flavoursome English produce. Preparation is kept simple.

at Easton Northwest : 3 mi on A 371 – ✉ Wells

Beaconsfield Farm without rest

✉ BA5 1DU – ✆ (01749) 870 308 – www.beaconsfieldfarm.co.uk – Closed 23 December-2 January

3 rm ☕ – 🚹£ 70/85 🚹🚹£ 70/90

Former farmhouse hidden away in the foothills of the Mendips and run by a personable owner. Snug, homely interior with comfy lounge and pleasant breakfast room overlooking the grounds. Well-kept, cottage-style bedrooms; ask for the four-poster.

WELLS-NEXT-THE-SEA – Norfolk – 504 W25 – pop. 2 451 15 C1

London 122 mi – Cromer 22 mi – Norwich 38 mi

Crown

The Buttlands ✉ NR23 1EX – ✆ (01328) 710 209 – www.flyingkiwiinns.co.uk

12 rm ☕ – 🚹£ 80/155 🚹🚹£ 100/175

Rest *Crown* – Carte £ 23/36

Characterful 16C former coaching inn located in the centre of town, overlooking the green. Individually styled bedrooms blend classical furniture with more modern décor and facilities. Dine from an accessible menu in the charming bar, orangery or dining room.

Machrimore without rest

Burnt St, on A 149 ✉ NR23 1HS – ✆ (01328) 711 653 – www.machrimore.co.uk

4 rm ☕ – 🚹£ 65 🚹🚹£ 84/88

Cross the delightful gardens with their illuminated water features to this collection of converted farm outbuildings. Bedrooms are well-equipped and come with quality furniture and private patios. Photos of old Wells feature throughout.

at Wighton Southeast : 2.5 mi by A 149

Meadowview without rest

53 High St ✉ NR23 1PF – ✆ (01328) 821 527 – www.meadow-view.net

5 rm ☕ – 🚹£ 70/90 🚹🚹£ 90/110

Set in the centre of a peaceful village, this smart, modern guesthouse is the perfect place to unwind, as its neat garden boasts a hot tub and a comfy seating area overlooking a meadow. Breakfast is cooked on the Aga in the country kitchen.

ENGLAND

WELWYN – Hertfordshire – 504 T28 – pop. 10 512 12 B2

London 31 mi – Bedford 31 mi – Cambridge 31 mi

Tewin Bury Farm

Southeast : 3.5 mi by A 1000 on B 1000 ✉ AL6 0JB – ✆ (01438) 717 793 – www.tewinbury.co.uk

29 rm – £ 124 £ 139/159

Rest *Tewin Bury Farm* – see restaurant listing

A collection of converted farm buildings on a 400 acre working farm, next to a nature reserve. Rustic interior with comfy oak-furnished bedrooms in various wings. The function room is in an impressive tithe barn beside the old mill race.

Tewin Bury Farm – Tewin Bury Farm Hotel

Southeast : 3.5 mi by A 1000 on B 1000 ✉ AL6 0JB – ✆ (01438) 717 793 – www.tewinbury.co.uk

Rest – Carte £ 25/38

Rustic hotel restaurant in an old timber chicken shed on a working farm. Modern interior with brick walls, an open kitchen, a smart bar and a large terrace. Well-executed, classical dishes display modern touches.

at Ayot Green Southwest : 2.5 mi by B 197

Waggoners

Brickwall Close ✉ AL6 9AA – ✆ (01707) 324 241 – www.thewaggoners.co.uk

Rest – *(booking advisable)* Menu £ 17/25 – Carte £ 25/39

Charming 17C pub on the edge of the Brocket Hall Estate. Sit in the delightfully simple open-fired bar or very formal dining room. Choose from unfussy bar snacks or a much more ambitious French-based à la carte, with prices to match.

WELWYN GARDEN CITY – Hertfordshire – 504 T28 – pop. 43 512 12 B2

London 25 mi – Croydon 35 mi – Barnet 11 mi – Ealing 24 mi

Panshanger Golf Complex, Old Herns Lane, ✆ (01707) 33 33 12

Auberge du Lac

Brocket Hall, West : 3 mi by A 6129 on B 653 ✉ AL8 7XG – ✆ (01707) 368 888 – www.brocket-hall.co.uk – Closed 27 December-18 January, Sunday and Monday

Rest – Menu £ 40/80 – Carte £ 37/65

You have to be buzzed in at the gates to reach this charming, part-18C former hunting lodge, in a delightful lakeside spot in the grounds of Brocket Hall. Cooking is technically adept, with ambitious flavour combinations. Sit in the interactive 'Cloudy Bay' private room to both see and hear the chefs at work.

WENTBRIDGE – West Yorkshire – 502 Q23 – ✉ Pontefract 22 B3

London 183 mi – Leeds 19 mi – Nottingham 55 mi – Sheffield 28 mi

Wentbridge House

Old Great North Rd. ✉ WF8 3JJ – ✆ (01977) 620 444 – www.wentbridgehouse.co.uk

41 rm – £ 105/190 £ 135/220

Rest *Fleur de Lys* – *(dinner only and Sunday lunch)* Carte £ 34/55

Rest *Wentbridge Brasserie* – Menu £ 16 (weekday lunch) – Carte £ 23/42

Personally run, bay-windowed house, dating back to the 19C and surrounded by 20 acres of immaculate gardens. Bedrooms are a mix of characterful, wood-panelled period styles and spacious modern designs with up-to-date facilities. Classical menu in formal restaurant; smart brasserie serves more modern dishes.

WEST ASHLING – West Sussex – see Chicester

WEST BAGBOROUGH – Somerset – 503 K30 3 B2

London 161 mi – Bristol 57 mi – Cardiff 88 mi – Plymouth 82 mi

Rising Sun Inn with rm

✉ TA4 3EF – ✆ (01823) 432 575 – www.risingsuninn.info – Closed 25 December

2 rm – £ 65 £ 95 **Rest** – Carte £ 20/36

Traditional-looking pub in the Quantock Hills, with several little rooms, a pleasing mix of old tables and chairs, smart slate floors and bright modern art. Menus offer plenty of choice, from typical pub-style light bites to more sophisticated classics. Two contemporary bedrooms offer great views.

WEST BRIDGFORD – Nottinghamshire – 502 Q25 – see Nottingham

WEST CLANDON – Surrey – see Guildford

WEST DIDSBURY – Greater Manchester – see Manchester

WEST END – Surrey – 504 S29 – pop. 4 135 – ✉ Guildford 7 C1

London 37 mi – Bracknell 7 mi – Camberley 5 mi – Guildford 8 mi

The Inn @ West End

42 Guildford Rd, on A 322 ✉ GU24 9PW – ✆ (01276) 858 652 – www.the-inn.co.uk
Rest – Menu £ 14/28 – Carte £ 27/44
A big-hearted pub offering genuine hospitality and a lively atmosphere. Wide-ranging menus offer generously proportioned, seasonal dishes with robust flavours and original touches. The wine shop specialises in European wines.

WEST HATCH – Wiltshire 4 C3

London 104 mi – Birmingham 131 mi – Sheffield 225 mi – Leicester 162 mi

Pythouse Kitchen Garden Shop and Café

✉ SP3 6PA – ✆ (01747) 870 444 – www.pythousekitchengarden.co.uk – Closed 25-26 December. 1 January and Tuesday
Rest – *(lunch only and dinner Thursday-Saturday) (booking advisable)*
Carte £ 19/34
Simple, rustic café in a former potting shed, serving breakfast, coffee, lunch and afternoon tea; order in the well-stocked shop. Tasty, unfussy cooking uses seasonal produce from the charming 18C walled garden. Save room for some cake!

ENGLAND

WEST HOATHLY – West Sussex – pop. 2 121 7 D2

London 36 mi – Bristol 141 mi – Croydon 26 mi – Barnet 78 mi

Cat Inn with rm

Queen's Sq ✉ RH19 4PP – ✆ (01342) 810 369 – www.catinn.co.uk – Closed 25 December and Sunday dinner
4 rm – †£ 90/110 ††£ 110/150 **Rest** – Carte £ 22/39
Popular with the locals and very much a village pub, with beamed ceilings, pewter tankards, open fires and plenty of cosy corners. Carefully executed, good value cooking focuses on tasty pub classics like locally smoked ham, egg and chips or steak, mushroom and ale pie. Service is friendly and efficient – and four tastefully decorated bedrooms complete the picture.

WEST KIRBY – Merseyside – 502 K23 Great Britain 20 A3

London 219 mi – Chester 19 mi – Liverpool 12 mi
Liverpool★ - Cathedrals★★, The Walker★★, Merseyside Maritime Museum★ and Albert Dock★, E : 13.5 mi by A 553

Peel Hey

Frankby Rd, Frankby, East : 2.25 mi by A 540 on B 5139 ✉ CH48 1PP – ✆ (0151) 677 90 77 – www.peelhey.com
10 rm – †£ 65/75 ††£ 85/115, £ 10
Rest – *(closed 25 December and 1 January) (dinner only and Sunday lunch)*
Menu £ 19/24
Personally run, detached 19C house with attractive bedrooms; those to the rear are quieter, with countryside views. Comfortable conservatory and pleasant lawned garden. Simple evening meals and Sunday lunch.

WEST LULWORTH – Dorset – 503 N32 – ✉ Wareham 4 C3

London 129 mi – Bournemouth 21 mi – Dorchester 17 mi – Weymouth 19 mi
Lulworth Cove★

Bishops Ⓝ

Lulworth Cove ✉ BH20 5RQ – ☎ (01929) 400 552 – www.bishopscottage.co.uk
3 rm ☕ – 🚹£ 90/110 🚹🚹£ 150/180 **Rest** – Carte £ 17/26
Attractive cottage part-dating from the 17C, set on the hillside in a pretty village and looking over the Jurassic Coast. Sizeable, very contemporary bedrooms with stylish bathrooms. Rustic bar with a wood-burning stove. Pre-book dinner in the dining room, which doubles as a vegetarian café during the day.

WEST MALLING – Kent – 504 V30 – pop. 2 144 — 8 B1

London 35 mi – Maidstone 7 mi – Royal Tunbridge Wells 14 mi
Addington, Maidstone, ☎ (01732) 84 47 85

Swan

35 Swan St. ✉ ME19 6JU – ☎ (01732) 521 910 – www.loveswan.co.uk – Closed 1-2 January
Rest – *(booking essential)* Menu £ 15 – Carte £ 25/46
Informal 15C former coaching inn where original beams blend with stylish, contemporary furnishings. Nicely appointed bar and comfy lounge are located upstairs. Modern European menus offer flavoursome combinations; side dishes are required.

WEST MEON – Hampshire – 504 Q30 — 6 B2

London 74 mi – Southampton 27 mi – Portsmouth 21 mi – Basingstoke 32 mi

Thomas Lord

High St ✉ GU32 1LN – ☎ (01730) 829 444 – www.thomaslord.co.uk – Closed 25 December
Rest – Carte £ 24/43
Named after the founder of Lord's Cricket Ground; memorabilia abounds among the shabby-chic styling. Locally sourced produce informs oft-changing menu of tasty British dishes.

WEST OVERTON – Wiltshire – 503 O29 – see Marlborough

WEST PENNARD – Somerset – 503 M30 — 4 C2

London 130 mi – Bristol 28 mi – Cardiff 82 mi – Bournemouth 70 mi

Apple Tree Inn

East : 1.5 mi on A 361 ✉ BA6 8ND – ☎ (01749) 890 060 – www.appletreeglastonbury.co.uk – Closed 25 December, 7-14 January and Monday except bank holiday lunch
Rest – Menu £ 12/20 – Carte £ 21/34
Unassuming little pub with beams, flagged floors, a thatched bar and a skittle alley. Blackboards list sandwiches, pub classics and tasty homemade snacks, while the main menu offers braises and confits, plus a few more innovative dishes.

WEST TANFIELD – North Yorkshire – 502 P21 – pop. 551 – ✉ Ripon — 22 B2

London 237 mi – Darlington 29 mi – Leeds 32 mi – Middlesbrough 39 mi

Old Coach House without rest

2 Stable Cottage, North Stainley, Southeast : 1 mi on A 6108 ✉ HG4 3HT – ☎ (01765) 634 900 – www.oldcoachhouse.info
8 rm ☕ – 🚹£ 69/109 🚹🚹£ 79/119
Smart 18C former coach house, nestled between the dales and the moors. Bedrooms – in two main buildings – differ in size, but all have a bright, modern style and are furnished by local craftsmen. The breakfast room overlooks the pleasant courtyard garden and fountain.

ENGLAND

WEST WITTON – North Yorkshire – 502 O21 – ✉ Leyburn 22 B1

London 241 mi – Kendal 39 mi – Leeds 60 mi – Newcastle upon Tyne 65 mi

Wensleydale Heifer

✉ DL8 4LS – ☎ (01969) 622 322 – www.wensleydaleheifer.co.uk

13 rm – †£ 80/180 ††£ 120/220 **Rest** – Menu £ 20 – Carte £ 32/44

Pretty, whitewashed former pub on the main street of the village. Quirky, themed bedrooms boast quality linen and the latest mod cons. Characterful lounge has a roaring fire. Dine in the fish bar or at clothed tables in the beamed restaurant; cooking has a strong seafood base.

WESTONBIRT – Gloucestershire – 503 N29 4 C1

London 104 mi – Bristol 24 mi – Cardiff 57 mi – Plymouth 144 mi

Hare & Hounds

On A 433 ✉ GL8 8QL – ☎ (01666) 881 000 – www.cotswold-inns-hotels.co.uk – Closed 6 January

43 rm – †£ 98/138 ††£ 138/158 – 3 suites

Rest *Beaufort* – *(dinner only and Sunday lunch)* Menu £ 39

Rest *Jack Hare's* – Menu £ 14 – Carte £ 22/36

Smart former farmhouse with lovely gardens, set between Highgrove House and the National Arboretum. Country house style interior with several lounges and a small library. Bedrooms blend modern fabrics with period furniture; half are in the outbuildings. Formal Beaufort serves classically based dishes with a modern edge; Jack Hare's offers a pub-style menu and real ales.

WESTON-SUB-EDGE – Gloucestershire – see Chipping Campden

WESTFIELD – East Sussex – 504 V31 – pop. 1 509 8 B3

London 66 mi – Brighton 38 mi – Folkestone 45 mi – Maidstone 30 mi

Wild Mushroom

Woodgate House, Westfield Ln., Southwest : 0.5 mi on A 28 ✉ TN35 4SB – ☎ (01424) 751 137 – www.webbesrestaurants.co.uk – Closed 1 week October, 1-10 January, 25-26 December, Sunday dinner, Monday and Tuesday

Rest – *(booking essential)* Menu £ 17 (weekdays)/34 – Carte £ 24/41

Rural roadside house with classical dining room and intimate conservatory bar. Good value French/European menus feature well-presented, tried-and-tested combinations. Tasting menu available.

WESTLETON – Suffolk – 504 Y27 – pop. 1 317 – ✉ Saxmundham 15 D2

London 97 mi – Cambridge 72 mi – Ipswich 28 mi – Norwich 31 mi

Westleton Crown with rm

The Street ✉ IP17 3AD – ☎ (01728) 648 777 – www.westletoncrown.co.uk

34 rm – †£ 90/100 ††£ 95/215 **Rest** – Carte £ 24/37

Good-looking, 17C former coaching inn with an appealing terrace and garden, set in a pretty little village. Welcoming beamed bar with open fires – venture further in for the more modern conservatory. The same seasonally pertinent menu is served throughout. Uncluttered bedrooms boast smart bathrooms.

WESTON-SUPER-MARE – North Somerset – 503 K29 – pop. 78 044 3 B2

London 147 mi – Bristol 24 mi – Taunton 32 mi

Beach Lawns, ☎ (01934) 88 88 00, www.visitsomerset.co.uk

Worlebury, Monks Hill, ☎ (01934) 62 57 89

Seafront (≤★★) BZ

Axbridge★★ (King John's Hunting Lodge★, St John the Baptist Church★) SE : 9 mi by A 371 - BY - and A 38 – Cheddar Gorge★★ (Gorge★★, Caves★, Jacob's Ladder ✻★) – Clevedon★ (≤★★, Clevedon Court★), NE : 10 mi by A 370 and M 5 – St Andrew's Church★, SE : 10.5 mi by A 371

ENGLAND

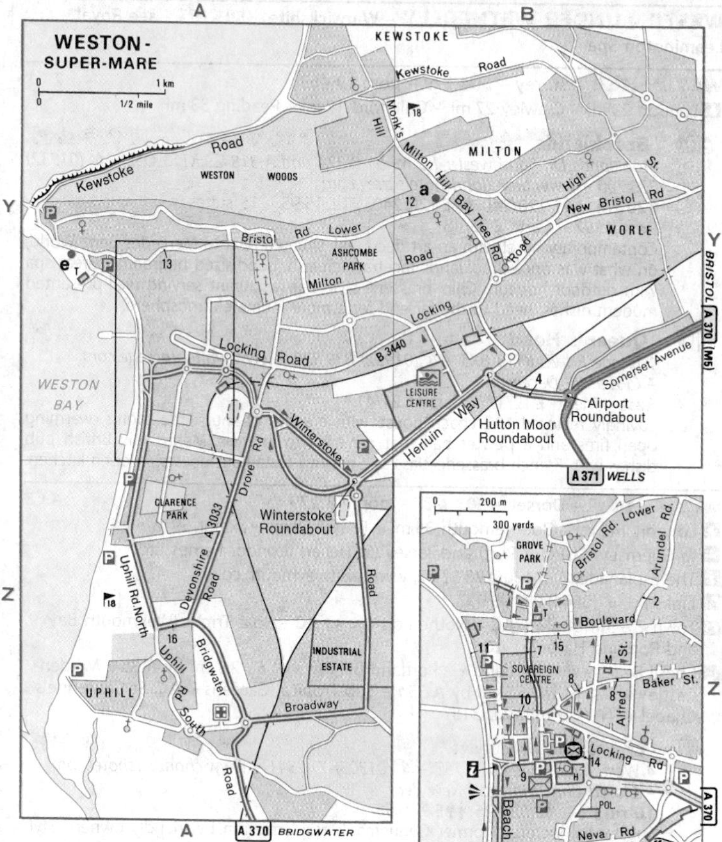

ENGLAND

XX Duets

103 Upper Bristol Rd. ✉ BS22 8ND – ✆ (01934) 413 428 – www.duets.co.uk – Closed 1 week spring, 1 week summer, 1 week winter, Sunday dinner, Monday and Tuesday BY**a**

Rest – Menu £ 22/31

A husband and wife team duet here, with him in the kitchen and her out front; there's also always a duet dish on the menu. It's comfortable and traditionally furnished; ask for the window table. Carefully prepared, classic seasonal dishes.

XX Cove

Birnbeck Rd ✉ BS23 2BX – ✆ (01934) 418 217 – www.the-cove.co.uk – Closed 25 December AY**e**

Rest – Menu £ 15 (weekday lunch) – Carte £ 20/33

Stylish, modern restaurant on the promenade; every table has bay views. Light bites at lunch. More formal dinner menu offers carefully cooked European dishes with modern touches. Open for breakfast every day. Keen, helpful service.

WESTON UNDER WETHERLEY – Warwickshire – 503 P27 – see Royal Leamington Spa

WEYBRIDGE – Surrey – 504 S29 – pop. 19 463 7 C1

London 23 mi – Crawley 27 mi – Guildford 17 mi – Reading 33 mi

Brooklands

rm,

Brooklands Dr, Southwest : 1.5 mi by B 374 and A 318 ✉ *KT13 OSL – ✆ (01932) 335 700 – www.brooklandshotelsurrey.com*

120 rm – †£ 120/240 ††£ 120/240, £ 15.95 – 15 suites

Rest *1907* – Carte £ 23/48

Contemporary hotel with an art deco feel, situated next to Mercedes Benz World, on what was once Brooklands racetrack. Stylish, good-sized bedrooms. Great spa with outdoor hot tub. Chic, brasserie-style bar/restaurant serving well-presented modern dishes; head to the far end for a more intimate atmosphere.

Queen's Head

1 Bridge Rd ✉ *KT13 8XS – ✆ (01932) 839 820 – www.whitebrasserie.com – Closed 25 December*

Rest – Menu £ 12/17 – Carte £ 21/41

Lovingly restored 18C coach house with a series of snug little rooms, warming open fires and a pewter bar, that can't fail to impress. Menus mix British pub dishes with French brasserie classics. Spacious restaurant boasts an open-kitchen.

WEYMOUTH – Dorset – 503 M32 – pop. 48 279 4 C3

London 142 mi – Bournemouth 35 mi – Bristol 68 mi – Exeter 59 mi

to Guernsey (St Peter Port) and Jersey (St Helier) (Condor Ferries Ltd)

The Esplanade, ✆ (01305) 78 57 47, www.visitweymouth.co.uk

Links Rd, ✆ (0844) 980 99 09

Town★ – Timewalk★ **AC** – Nothe Fort (<★) **AC** – Boat Trip★ (Weymouth Bay and Portland Harbour) **AC**

Chesil Beach★★ – Portland★ - Portland Bill (✳★★) S : 2.5 mi by A 354. Maiden Castle★★ (<★) N : 6.5 mi by A 354 – Sub-Tropical Gardens★ **AC**, St Catherine's Chapel★) NW : 9 mi by B 3157

ENGLAND

Chandlers without rest

4 Westerhall Rd ✉ *DT4 7SZ – ✆ (01305) 771 341 – www.chandlershotel.com – Closed Christmas and New Year*

10 rm – †£ 62/125 ††£ 97/155

Substantial Victorian former Gentleman's residence run by friendly owners. Stylish, modern interior with a comfy lounge and airy breakfast room. Bedrooms come with neutral walls and colourful soft furnishings.

Crab House Café

Ferryman's Way, Portland Rd, Wyke Regis ✉ *DT4 9YU – ✆ (01305) 788 867 – www.crabhousecafe.co.uk – Closed 15 December-31 January and Sunday dinner-Tuesday in winter*

Rest – *(booking essential)* Carte £ 21/61

Simple wood building by the sea, with an open-plan kitchen, tables under the eaves and a sunny patio. Unfussy seafood dishes with fish from Looe and oysters from their farm next door; crab is a specialty and comes with an apron and hammer.

WHALLEY – Lancashire – 502 M22 – pop. 3 230 – ✉ Blackburn 20 B2

London 233 mi – Blackpool 32 mi – Burnley 12 mi – Manchester 28 mi

Long Leese Barn, Clerkhill, ✆ (01254) 82 22 36

Food by Breda Murphy

Abbots Ct, 41 Station Rd ✉ *BB7 9RH – ✆ (01254) 823 446 – www.foodbybredamurphy.com – Closed 24 December-7 January, Sunday and Monday*

Rest – *(lunch only)* Carte £ 22/30

Opposite the station, with a smart shop selling gadgets and books and a deli counter for takeaway meals, cakes and coffee. Bright, modern restaurant offers tasty, home-cooked lunches and charming service; open for dinner once a month.

at Mitton Northwest : 2.5 mi on B 6246 – ✉ Whalley

Three Fishes
Mitton Rd ✉ BB7 9PQ – ☏ (01254) 826 888 – www.thethreefishes.com – Closed 25 December
Rest – *(bookings not accepted)* Carte £ 19/33
Spacious, modern country inn offering an extensive, seasonally changing menu which celebrates Lancastrian produce. Family-friendly, with a children's menu and a popular Sunday roast.

WHEPSTEAD – Suffolk – 504 W27 – see Bury St Edmunds

WHIMPLE – Devon – 503 J31 2 D2

London 166 mi – Bristol 81 mi – Cardiff 112 mi – Plymouth 52 mi

Woodhayes Country House without rest
Woodhayes Ln ✉ EX5 2TQ – ☏ (01404) 823 120 – www.woodhayescountryhouse.co.uk
6 rm – †£ 90/160 ††£ 90/160
18C yellow-washed house with mature grounds, in a peaceful village. Small comfy lounge, where tea and cake are served on arrival. Good-sized bedrooms with simple, neutral décor and modern facilities. Order breakfast the night before.

WHITBY – North Yorkshire – 502 S20 – pop. 13 594 Great Britain 23 C1

London 257 mi – Middlesbrough 31 mi – Scarborough 21 mi – York 45 mi
Langborne Rd, ☏ (01723) 38 36 37, www.visitwhitby.com
Low Straggleton, Sandsend Rd, ☏ (01947) 60 06 60
Abbey★

Raithwaite Hall rm, rm,
Sandsend Rd, West : 2 mi on A 197 ✉ YO21 3ST – ☏ (01947) 661 662 – www.raithwaitehall.com
73 rm – †£ 119/399 ††£ 119/399 – 7 suites
Rest ***Brace*** – *(bar lunch Monday-Saturday)* Carte £ 24/52
Modern resort hotel in 80 acres of delightful parkland, complete with a carp lake. Stylish, well-equipped bedrooms; some are duplex suites with wooden floors and ideal for dog owners. Smart spa and meeting rooms. Dine in the large bar or in Brace, which specialises in 45-day matured steaks.

Bagdale Hall
1 Bagdale ✉ YO21 1QL – ☏ (01947) 602 958 – www.bagdale.co.uk
14 rm – †£ 70/220 ††£ 90/220 **Rest** – *(dinner only)* Carte £ 17/38
Charming Tudor manor house built in 1516, featuring carved wood fireplaces, mullioned windows and antique furnishings. Period bedrooms – some with four-posters – and smart bathrooms; more modern rooms in a rear wing. Spacious dining room with 19C Delft tiles from Holland and a traditional menu.

Dillons of Whitby without rest
14 Chubb Hill Rd ✉ Y021 1JU – ☏ (01947) 600 290 – www.dillonsofwhitby.co.uk
5 rm – †£ 70/95 ††£ 75/105
Built in a Victorian style for an old sea captain and set opposite the beautiful Pannett Park. Charming interior with immaculately kept, individually styled bedrooms featuring fine Egyptian cotton. Great choice at breakfast.

Green's
13 Bridge St ✉ YO22 4BG – ☏ (01947) 600 284 – www.greensofwhitby.com – Closed 25-26 December and 1 January
Rest – *(booking essential)* Carte £ 22/40
Established eatery near the quay. Lively bistro atmosphere downstairs and a more formal room above. Menus feature grills and local seafood: blackboards name the skipper and his daily catch; the mussels are particularly good.

ENGLAND

at Sandsend **Northwest : 3 mi on A 174 – ✉ Whitby**

XX **Estbek House** with rm

East Row ✉ YO21 3SU – ✆ (01947) 893 424 – www.estbekhouse.co.uk – Closed January-9 February

5 rm – †£ 80/125 ††£ 125/190 **Rest** – *(dinner only)* Carte £ 34/52

Personally run Regency house close to the beach, with a lovely front terrace and elegant dining room. Basement bar overlooks the kitchens and doubles as a breakfast room. Menus offer unfussy dishes of sustainable wild fish from local waters. Smart bedrooms come with stylish bathrooms.

at Goldsborough **Northwest : 6 mi by A 174**

X **Fox & Hounds**

✉ YO21 3RX – ✆ (01947) 893 372 – www.foxandhoundsgoldsborough.co.uk – Closed Christmas and Sunday-Tuesday

Rest – *(dinner only)* Carte £ 30/44

Former village pub with a homely, cottagey style, set in tiny coastal hamlet. Constantly evolving menu features local produce and unfussy cooking, with an emphasis on fresh fish and seafood.

WHITEHAVEN – Cumbria – **502** J20 – pop. 24 978 — 21 A2

London 332 mi – Carlisle 39 mi – Keswick 28 mi – Penrith 47 mi

XX **Zest**

Low Rd, South : 0.5 mi on B 5345 (St Bees) ✉ CA28 9HS – ✆ (01946) 692 848 – www.zestwhitehaven.com – Closed 25 December, 1 January and Sunday-Tuesday

Rest – *(dinner only)* Carte £ 18/36

Unassuming exterior conceals a stylish, red-hued room with a lively atmosphere, spotted chairs, striped banquettes and booths. Large, modern menu with an Asian edge and blackboard specials. Unfussy, flavoursome cooking.

ENGLAND

WHITEWELL – Lancashire – **502** M22 – pop. 5 617 – ✉ Clitheroe — 20 B2

London 281 mi – Lancaster 31 mi – Leeds 55 mi – Manchester 41 mi

Inn at Whitewell with rm

Forest of Bowland ✉ BB7 3AT – ✆ (01200) 448 222 – www.innatwhitewell.com

23 rm – †£ 88/169 ††£ 210/240 **Rest** – Carte £ 21/41

14C creeper-clad inn, high on the banks of the River Hodder, with panoramic valley views. Atmospheric bar and more formal restaurant. Classic menus of regionally inspired dishes. Spacious bedrooms; some traditional in style, with four-posters and antique baths.

WHITSTABLE – Kent – **504** X29 – pop. 30 195 — 9 C1

London 68 mi – Dover 24 mi – Maidstone 37 mi – Margate 12 mi

7 Oxford St, ✆ (0871) 7 16 24 49, www.canterbury.co.uk

X **JoJo's**

2 Herne Bay Rd ✉ CT5 2LQ – ✆ (01227) 274 591 – www.jojosrestaurant.co.uk – Closed Sunday dinner, Monday, Tuesday and lunch Wednesday

Rest – Carte £ 12/33

Spacious, rustic restaurant with simple wooden tables, a stove heater and an open kitchen with counter seating. Meze-style dishes might include cured meats, koftas or calamari. Terrace, coffee shop and deli.

X **Whitstable Oyster Company**

Royal Native Oyster Stores, Horsebridge ✉ CT5 1BU – ✆ (01227) 276 856 – www.whitstableoystercompany.com – Closed 25-26 December and Monday-Thursday November-January

Rest – *(booking essential)* Carte £ 30/52

Former oyster warehouse right by the sea. Large, rough, wood-furnished interior with great informal atmosphere. Blackboard displays simply prepared seafood dishes. Fresh oysters at the counter; try those from their own beds from Sept-April.

Pearson's Arms

The Horsebridge, Sea Wall ✉ CT5 1BT – ✆ (01227) 773 133 – www.pearsonsarmsbyrichardphillips.co.uk – Closed Monday and dinner Sunday and Tuesday

Rest – Menu £ 11 (weekday lunch) – Carte £ 23/37

Characterful refurbished pub in a great spot, with the Thames Estuary stretched out in front. Busy ground floor bar for nibbles like jellied eels; top floor dining room serves reassuringly familiar dishes, with Kentish produce to the fore.

at Seasalter Southwest : 2 mi by B 2205 – ✉ Whitstable

The Sportsman (Steve Harris)

Faversham Rd, Southwest : 2 mi following coast rd ✉ CT5 4BP – ✆ (01227) 273 370 – www.thesportsmanseasalter.co.uk – Closed 25-26 December, Sunday dinner and Monday

Rest – *(booking advisable)* Carte £ 33/40

An unassuming pub by the sea wall; the décor may be modest but the food is top class. The concise daily menu is informed by the latest produce to arrive at the door. Preparation is precise; flavours, well-judged; and presentation, original. A tasting menu can be requested upon booking. Fish is a strength.

➜ Slip sole grilled in seaweed butter. Roast rump of lamb with mint sauce. Rhubarb sorbet and burnt cream.

WHITTLESFORD – Cambridgeshire – 504 U27 — 14 B3

London 50 mi – Cambridge 11 mi – Peterborough 46 mi

Tickell Arms (N)

1 North Rd ✉ CB2 4NZ – ✆ (01223) 833 025 – www.cambscuisine.com

Rest – Menu £ 14 (weekday lunch) – Carte £ 22/42

17C former pub named after a notorious, self-made squire – whose coat of arms still adorn the walls. Sit in the open-fired bar, rustic dining room or airy conservatory. Seasonal British and European cooking; good value midweek lunches.

WICKHAM – Hampshire – 503 Q31 – pop. 1 915 — 6 B2

London 74 mi – Portsmouth 12 mi – Southampton 11 mi – Winchester 16 mi

Old House

The Square ✉ PO17 5JG – ✆ (01329) 835 870 – www.oldhousehotel.co.uk – Closed 19-20 May

12 rm – †£ 75 ††£ 100/175

Rest – *(closed Sunday dinner)* Menu £ 20 (lunch) – Carte £ 31/46

Lovely, creeper-clad, Queen Anne townhouse built in 1707. Characterful bedrooms; some with original fireplaces, all with modern furnishings. Those in the garden have a slightly Mediterranean feel, boasting tiled floors and large bathrooms. Small restaurant and airy conservatory offer modern takes on classics.

WIGHT (Isle of) – Isle of Wight – 503 P/Q31 – pop. 138 500 — 6 A/B 3

Great Britain

from Ryde to Portsmouth (Hovertravel Ltd) frequent services daily (10 mn) – from Ryde to Portsmouth (Wightlink Ltd) frequent services daily (15 mn) – from East Cowes to Southampton (Red Funnel Ferries) frequent services daily (22 mn)

from East Cowes to Southampton (Red Funnel Ferries) frequent services daily (1 h) – from Yarmouth to Lymington (Wightlink Ltd) frequent services daily (30 mn) – from Fishbourne to Portsmouth (Wightlink Ltd) frequent services daily (35 mn)

Island★★

Osborne House, East Cowes★★ **AC** – Carisbrooke Castle, Newport★★ **AC** (Keep ≤★) – Brading★ (Roman Villa★ **AC**, St Mary's Church★, Nunwell House★ **AC**) – Shorwell : St Peter's Church★ (wall paintings★)

BONCHURCH – Isle of Wight 6 B3

Pond Café

PO38 1RG – (01983) 855 666 – www.thehambrough.com/the-pond-cafe – Closed Tuesday

Rest – *(booking advisable)* Menu £ 20 – Carte £ 26/48

Intimate neighbourhood eatery with an attractive terrace overlooking the duck pond. Bistro-style interior with tablecloths and candles in the evenings. Mediterranean-influenced menus change with the seasons and rely on island produce.

GODSHILL – Isle of Wight 6 B3

Taverners

High St PO38 3HZ – (01983) 840 707 – www.thetavernersgodshill.co.uk – Closed first 3 weeks January

Rest – Carte £ 18/26

Whitewashed pub with cosy bar and two large dining rooms. Cooking is fresh and tasty, mixing traditional pub classics with more ambitious daily specials. Local island produce is a feature.

NITON – Isle of Wight 6 B3

Hermitage

Dolcoppice Ln, St Catherines Down, Whitwell, North : 3 mi by Newport rd PO38 2PD – (01983) 730 010 – www.hermitage-iow.co.uk – Closed 20 December-1 February

10 rm – †£ 70/100 ††£ 90/150 **Rest** – *(dinner only)* Carte £ 18/38

Large 19C country house set in pleasant rural location and surrounded by 12 acres of gardens and woodland. Traditionally styled drawing room and peaceful lounge; individually designed, well-equipped bedrooms. Elegant dining room has a contemporary edge but sticks to the classics when it comes to the food.

ENGLAND

ST HELENS – Isle of Wight 6 B3

Dans Kitchen

Lower Green Rd PO33 1TS – (01983) 872 303 – www.danskitcheniow.co.uk – Closed 3 weeks January, 1 week June, 1 week October, Sunday, Monday and Tuesday lunch

Rest – Carte £ 26/41

Old corner shop in a lovely location overlooking the village green. Simple wood furnishings, scatter cushions and nautical pictures feature. Traditional, hearty dishes showcase island produce; blackboard specials include the daily catch.

SEAVIEW – Isle of Wight – pop. 2 286 6 B3

Priory Bay

Priory Dr, Southeast : 1.5 mi by B 3330 PO34 5BU – (01983) 613 146 – www.priorybay.co.uk

20 rm – †£ 90/225 ††£ 160/300 – 2 suites

Rest *Island Room* – *(closed Sunday-Tuesday) (dinner only)* Menu £ 55

Rest *Priory Oyster* – Menu £ 20 (lunch) – Carte £ 22/41

Peacefully located medieval priory overlooking the sea, with a romantic, shabby-chic interior, spacious guest areas and a relaxed vibe. Bedrooms have good facilities and range in style from classical country house to nautical. The formal 'Island Room' boasts impressive 1810 murals and a modern menu. 'Priory Oyster' specialises in seafood and opens onto a terrace.

Don't expect guesthouses to provide the same level of service as a hotel. They are often characterised by a warm welcome and décor which reflects the owner's personality. Those shown in red are particularly pleasant.

Seaview

High St ✉ PO34 5EX – ✆ (01983) 612 711 – www.seaviewhotel.co.uk – Closed 24-27 December

28 rm – ♦£ 105/125 ♦♦£ 125/150 – 3 suites

Rest *The Restaurant and Sunshine Room* – *(dinner only and lunch during summer) (booking essential)* Menu £ 30 (dinner) – Carte £ 20/35

Long-standing, bay-windowed hotel covered in foliage. Interesting nautical-themed décor with paintings and model ships throughout. Smart, modern bedrooms come in various styles; some are located in annexes. One bright and one more intimate dining room; classical cooking.

SHALFLEET – Isle of Wight

New Inn

Mill Rd ✉ PO30 4NS – ✆ (01983) 531 314 – www.thenew-inn.co.uk

Rest – Carte £ 17/39

Characterful pub on the main Newport to Yarmouth road, with inglenook fireplaces, slate floors and simple, scrubbed wood tables. Proper pub dishes are proudly made with island produce; lots of locally caught fish and seafood.

SHANKLIN – Isle of Wight – pop. 8 055 — 6 B3

Newport 9 mi

67 High St, ✆ (01983) 81 38 13, www.visitshanklin.co.uk

The Fairway, Lake Sandown, ✆ (01983) 40 32 17

Rylstone Manor

Rylstone Gdns ✉ PO37 6RG – ✆ (01983) 862 806 – www.rylstone-manor.co.uk – Closed 28 November-10 February

9 rm – ♦£ 70/120 ♦♦£ 140/160 **Rest** – *(dinner only)* Menu £ 35

Originally a gift from the Queen to one of her physicians: an attractive part-Victorian house close to the historic gardens. Classical interior boasts heavy fabrics and warm, cosy feel. Bedrooms combine antique furniture and modern facilities. Formal dining room.

Foxhills without rest

30 Victoria Ave ✉ PO37 6LS – ✆ (01983) 862 329 – www.foxhillsofshanklin.co.uk

8 rm – ♦£ 55/98 ♦♦£ 98/118

Large, stone-built house in leafy residential avenue. Spacious, Victorian-styled lounge and modern breakfast room; comfy bedrooms in pastel hues. Jacuzzi, spa and beauty treatments available.

VENTNOR – Isle of Wight – pop. 6 257 — 6 B3

Newport 10 mi

Steephill Down Rd, ✆ (01983) 85 33 26

Royal

Belgrave Rd ✉ PO38 1JJ – ✆ (01983) 852 186 – www.royalhoteliow.co.uk – Closed 2 weeks January

53 rm – ♦£ 110/200 ♦♦£ 180/260

Rest – *(closed Sunday lunch July-September) (dinner only and Sunday lunch)* Menu £ 40

Large Victorian building with mature lawned gardens and heated outdoor pool. Modern touches in lounge and bar. Traditionally styled bedrooms with good facilities: premier rooms are larger; some have lovely sea views. Modern menu served in formal dining room.

XX Hambrough with rm

rest,

Hambrough Rd ✉ PO38 1SQ – ✆ (01983) 856 333 – www.thehambrough.com – Closed 3 weeks January, 2 weeks November, Sunday dinner, Monday and Tuesday lunch

7 rm – ♦£ 160/330 ♦♦£ 160/350 **Rest** – *(booking essential)* Menu £ 29/55

Eye-catching clifftop villa with a leather-furnished lounge and two warm, stylish dining rooms boasting excellent sea views. Good quality ingredients feature in refined, modern dishes. Service is polite and knowledgeable. Smart, comfortable bedrooms feature quality linens and espresso machines.

ENGLAND

WOOTTON BRIDGE – Isle of Wight – pop. 3 618 — 6 B3

Lakeside Park
High St. ✉ *PO33 4LJ – ✆ (01983) 882 266 – www.lakesideparkhotel.com*
44 rm – †£ 112/175 ††£ 112/175
Rest *Oyster Room* – *(dinner only Wednesday-Saturday and Sunday lunch) (booking essential)* Carte £ 36/45
Rest *Brasserie* – Menu £ 14 (lunch) – Carte £ 17/37
Unassuming, purpose-built hotel with good leisure facilities, owned by a local builder. Stylish, well-equipped bedrooms; some with terraces. Eat in the smart fine dining restaurant or in the split-level brasserie and bar-lounge, with its large decked terrace and views over the lake.

YARMOUTH – Isle of Wight – pop. 855 — 6 A3

Newport 10 mi

George
Quay St ✉ *PO41 0PE – ✆ (01983) 760 331 – www.thegeorge.co.uk*
19 rm – †£ 99/138 ††£ 190/288 – 1 suite
Rest *Brasserie* – see restaurant listing
Smart 17C townhouse that blends subtle modern touches with characterful period features. Bedrooms have up-to-date facilities: one has a large wet room and opens onto the garden; another boasts a sizeable balcony and excellent Solent views.

Brasserie – George Hotel
Quay St ✉ *PO41 0PE – ✆ (01983) 760 331 – www.thegeorge.co.uk*
Rest – Carte £ 30/41
Contemporary hotel restaurant with pewter bar and small heated terrace. Modern menu offers some interesting combinations, with a tasting option in the evening. Tasty homemade bread and daily fish specials, with local game dishes in season.

ENGLAND

WIGHTON – Norfolk – 504 W25 – see Wells-Next-The-Sea

WILLIAN – Hertfordshire – 504 T28 – pop. 326 — 12 B2

London 38 mi – Croydon 48 mi – Barnet 24 mi – Ealing 37 mi

Fox
✉ *SG6 2AE – ✆ (01462) 480 233 – www.foxatwillian.co.uk*
Rest – Carte £ 20/36
Set right in the heart of the village, a bright, airy pub that's always bustling. Dishes are modern with some Asian influences and there's a good choice of seafood and game in season; if you just can't decide, try 'The Fox Slate' for two.

WILTON – Wiltshire – 504 O30 – see Salisbury

WIMBORNE MINSTER – Dorset – 503 O31 – pop. 14 844 — 4 C3

London 112 mi – Bournemouth 10 mi – Dorchester 23 mi – Salisbury 27 mi
29 High St, ✆ (01202) 88 61 16, www.visit-dorset.org.uk
Town★ - Minster★ - Priest's House Museum★ **AC**
Kingston Lacy★★ **AC**, NW : 3 mi by B 3082

Les Bouviers with rm
Arrowsmith Rd, Canford Magna, Southeast : 2.25 mi by A 349 on A 341 ✉ *BH21 3BD – ✆ (01202) 889 555 – www.lesbouviers.co.uk – Closed Sunday dinner*
6 rm – †£ 88/183 ††£ 94/215 **Rest** – Menu £ 21/46
Formerly a private residence, now a two-roomed restaurant overlooking a terrace and large lawned grounds. Small leather-furnished lounge and a large rear function room. The formal team serve complex dishes from traditionally based menus. Smart, comfortable, slightly kitsch bedrooms.

Tickled Pig Ⓝ
26 West Borough ✉ BH21 1NF – ✆ (01202) 886 778 – www.thetickledpig.co.uk – Closed 25-26 December
Rest – Carte £ 22/35
Charmingly run shop conversion in the heart of a pretty market town. Modern, country style interior with a laid-back feel and a lovely rear terrace. Daily brown paper menus feature home-grown veg and home-reared pork; their mantra is 'taking food back to its roots'. Cooking is vibrant, flavourful and unfussy.

WINCHCOMBE – Gloucestershire – 503 O28 – pop. 3 682 — 4 D1

London 100 mi – Birmingham 43 mi – Gloucester 26 mi – Oxford 43 mi
High St, ✆ (01242) 60 29 25, www.winchcombewelcomeswalkers.com

5 North St (Marcus Ashenford)
5 North St ✉ GL54 5LH – ✆ (01242) 604 566 – www.5northstreetrestaurant.co.uk – Closed 2 weeks January, 1 week August, Monday, Tuesday lunch and Sunday dinner
Rest – Menu £ 41/50
Long-standing neighbourhood restaurant that's very personally run by a husband and wife team. Characterful low-beamed ceilings and burgundy walls create an intimate feel. Menus change with the seasons and feature British ingredients in largely classical combinations. Dishes are precise, well-crafted and full of flavour.
→ Marinated scallops with crab, sweetcorn and iced horseradish. Suckling pig, confit onion potato and cider. Vanilla and mango ripple ice cream with golden raisin purée.

Wesley House with rm
High St ✉ GL54 5LJ – ✆ (01242) 602 366 – www.wesleyhouse.co.uk – Closed 26 December, Sunday dinner and Monday
5 rm – †£ 65/95 ††£ 75/110 **Rest** – Menu £ 15/40 – Carte £ 25/49
Characterful 15C house on the main street. Dine beside the inglenook fireplace in the beamed bar, or in the smart rear dining room with its glass roof. Classical, flavourful cooking and relaxed, cheery service. Cosy bedrooms have a comfortingly traditional feel. Simpler meals are served next door.

Lion Inn Ⓝ with rm
North St ✉ GL54 5PS – ✆ (01242) 603 300 – www.thelioninnwinchcombe.co.uk
6 rm – †£ 110/165 ††£ 140/180
Rest – *(booking advisable)* Menu £ 12 (weekday lunch) – Carte £ 26/39
Located in the heart of this historic town, close to Sudeley Castle; a 15C Cotswold stone inn with chic, country style décor and a pleasant terrace and garden. Menus change daily and are guided by the latest seasonal produce available.

at Gretton Northwest : 2 mi by B 4632 and B 4078

Royal Oak Ⓝ
✉ GL54 5EP – ✆ (01242) 604 999 – www.royaloakgretton.co.uk
Rest – Carte £ 20/32
In summer, head for the large garden, with its chickens, kid's play area, tennis court and passing steam trains; in winter, sit in one of two snug dining rooms or in the conservatory. Local produce features in honest, traditional dishes.

WINCHELSEA – East Sussex – 504 W31 Great Britain — 9 C3

London 64 mi – Brighton 46 mi – Folkestone 30 mi
Town★ – St Thomas Church (effigies★)

Strand House
Tanyard's Ln., East : 0.25 mi on A 259 ✉ TN36 4JT – ✆ (01797) 226 276 – www.thestrandhouse.co.uk
13 rm – †£ 55/125 ††£ 65/195
Rest – *(closed Sunday-Thursday) (dinner only)* Menu £ 35 **s**
Part-timbered, low-beamed house dating from the 14 and 15C; mind your head! Spacious, open-fired sitting room with a slightly medieval feel. Some bedrooms are themed and some have four-posters; 3 more spacious, modern rooms in the garden annexe. Elegant dining room offers simple home cooking.

ENGLAND

WINCHESTER – Hampshire – **503** P30 – **pop. 44 706** Great Britain **6** B2

London 72 mi – Bristol 76 mi – Oxford 52 mi – Southampton 12 mi

High Street, (01962) 84 05 00, www.visitwinchester.co.uk

City★★ - Cathedral★★★ **AC** B – Winchester College★ **AC** B **B** – Castle Great Hall★ B **D** – God Begot House★ B **A**

St Cross Hospital★★ **AC** A

Winchester

rm, rm,

Worthy Ln SO23 7AB – (01962) 709 988 – www.thewinchesterhotel.co.uk

96 rm – †£ 85/165 ††£ 95/175 A**w**

Rest *Hutton's Brasserie* – Menu £ 19/24

Stylishly refurbished business hotel within walking distance of the town centre. Bright, fresh interior with modern bedrooms, a well-equipped gym and small pool. Open-plan foyer leads to the bar and restaurant, the latter serving a mix of grills and international favourites.

Hotel du Vin

rm,

14 Southgate St SO23 9EF – (01962) 841 414 – www.hotelduvin.com

24 rm – †£ 119/190 ††£ 119/190, £ 15 B**c**

Rest *Bistro* – *(booking essential)* Carte £ 25/48

Attractive Georgian house dating from 1715; the first ever Hotel du Vin. Relax in the lounge or champagne bar. Bedrooms – split between the house and garden – are stylish, minimalist and well-equipped; some have baths in the room. Characterful split-level bistro offers unfussy French cooking.

Giffard House without rest

50 Christchurch Rd SO23 9SU – (01962) 852 628 – www.giffardhotel.co.uk – Closed 24 December-2 January B**s**

13 rm – †£ 73/126 ††£ 97/134

Imposing Victorian house in a quiet road. Spacious, classically styled guest areas include a comfy drawing room, modern bar and formal breakfast room. Individually styled bedrooms boast quality furnishings and good facilities.

29 Christchurch Road without rest

29 Christchurch Rd. SO23 9SU – (01962) 868 661 – www.bedbreakfastwinchester.co.uk B**v**

3 rm – †£ 60/75 ††£ 90/100

Modern, Regency style guesthouse in attractive residential area close to town. Comfortable lounge and communal, linen-laid breakfast room. Simple bedrooms with plain walls and floral drapes.

Chesil Rectory

Chesil St. SO23 0HU – (01962) 851 555 – www.chesilrectory.co.uk – Closed 25-26 December and 1 January B**r**

Rest – Menu £ 20 (lunch and early dinner) – Carte £ 26/40

Timbered 15C house on edge of the town centre; its characterful interior taking in beamed ceilings and a large inglenook fireplace. Appealing menu of classically based dishes.

Brasserie Blanc

19-20 Jewry St SO23 8RZ – (01962) 810 870 – www.brasserieblanc.com

Rest – *(booking advisable)* Menu £ 14/17 – Carte £ 21/43 B**x**

Spacious, split-level brasserie in the city centre, with a bustling, informal atmosphere, two small terraces and an open-plan kitchen on the first-floor. Extensive menus feature classical French dishes and local specials.

Black Rat

88 Chesil St. SO23 0HX – (01962) 844 465 – www.theblackrat.co.uk – Closed 2 weeks December-January, 1 week spring and 1 week autumn

Rest – *(dinner only and lunch Saturday-Sunday)* Menu £ 23 (lunch) – Carte £ 36/43 B**a**

This unassuming building conceals a quirky, bohemian-style interior with a small bar, a lounge and a two-roomed restaurant. Refined, classically based cooking displays Mediterranean influences and modern twists. The four wicker-roofed booths on the rear terrace are an unusual feature.

→ Smoked duck breast with goat's cheese mousse, dandelion and candied walnuts. Wood pigeon, pork belly and black pudding, baby leeks and salt-baked kohlrabi. Cherry blossom jelly, kumquats, yoghurt sorbet and shortbread.

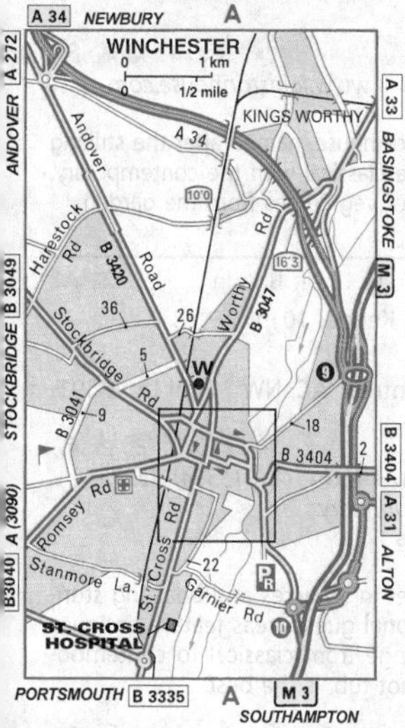

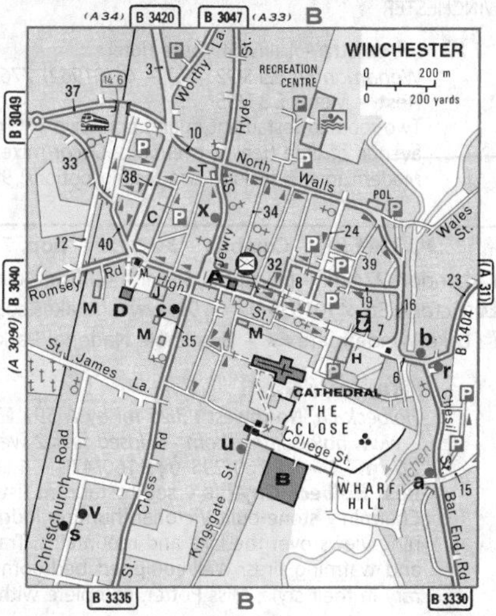

Alresford Rd	A	2	Eastgate St	B	16	St George's St	B	32
Andover Rd	B	3	Easton Lane	A	18	St Paul's Hill	B	33
Bereweeke Rd	A	5	East Hill	B	15	St Peter's St	B	34
Bridge St	B	6	Friarsgate	B	19	Southgate St	B	35
Broadway (The)	B	7	High St	B		Stockbridge Rd	B	37
Brooks Shopping Centre	B	8	Kingsgate Rd	A	22	Stoney Lane	A	36
Chilbolton Ave	A	9	Magdalen Hill	B	23	Sussex St	B	38
City Rd	B	10	Middle Brook St	B	24	Union St	B	39
Clifton Terrace	B	12	Park Rd	A	26	Upper High St	B	40

Wykeham Arms with rm

75 Kingsgate St ✉ *SO23 9PE – ✆ (01962) 853 834 – www.wykehamarmswinchester.co.uk* Bu

14 rm ☕ – 🚹£ 84/99 🚹🚹£ 144/159

Rest – *(booking essential)* Menu £ 18/35 – Carte £ 25/43

Appealingly shabby, 18C red-brick inn tucked away on a cobbled street and packed with memorabilia. Dishes range from simple soups, pies and pastas to more elaborate lobster. Bedrooms have good facilities: those upstairs are characterful; those opposite, quieter.

No.5 Bridge Street with rm

5 Bridge St ✉ *SO23 0HN – ✆ (01962) 863 838 – www.no5bridgestreet.co.uk – Closed 25 December* Bb

6 rm – 🚹£ 90/110 🚹🚹£ 100/125, ☕ £ 11.50 **Rest** – Carte £ 16/41

Roadside pub with a fashionable, modern feel; head to the dining room at the back for table service and a view of the open kitchen. Sections on the Mediterranean-influenced menu include 'small plates' and 'British charcuterie and cheese'. Simply styled, comfortable bedrooms – those at the front hear the traffic.

at Sparsholt Northwest : 3.5 mi by B 3049 - A - ✉ Winchester

Lainston House

Woodman Ln ✉ *SO21 2LT – ✆ (01962) 776 088 – www.lainstonhouse.com*

52 rm – 🚹£ 195/245 🚹🚹£ 195/245, ☕ £ 21 – 3 suites

Rest ***Avenue*** – see restaurant listing

Impressive 17C William and Mary manor house with attractive gardens and a striking avenue of lime trees in the grounds. Guest areas include a clubby, wood-panelled drawing room, a modern country house lounge and a small gym. Spacious bedrooms vary from classical to contemporary; all boast good facilities.

XXX **Avenue** – Lainston House Hotel
Woodman Ln ✉ SO21 2LT – ✆ (01962) 776 088 – www.lainstonhouse.com
Rest – Menu £ 33/55
Two-roomed restaurant in an impressive 17C manor house, named after the striking avenue of lime trees it overlooks. Décor mixes the classical with the contemporary. Modern menus include two tasting options; 90% of veg comes from the garden.

WINDERMERE – Cumbria – 502 L20 – pop. 7 941 Great Britain 21 A2

London 274 mi – Blackpool 55 mi – Carlisle 46 mi – Kendal 10 mi
Victoria St, ✆ (015394) 4 64 99, www.golakes.co.uk
Lake Windermere★★ – Brockhole National Park Centre★ **AC**, NW : 2 mi by A 591

Holbeck Ghyll
Holbeck Ln, Northwest : 3.25 mi by A 591 ✉ LA23 1LU – ✆ (015394) 32375 – www.holbeckghyll.com – Closed first 2 weeks January
26 rm – †£ 160/295 ††£ 160/470 – 4 suites
Rest *Holbeck Ghyll* ❀ – see restaurant listing
Charming, stone-built Victorian hunting lodge, set in 15 acres and boasting stunning views over the lake and mountains. Traditional guest areas feature antiques and warming fires. Well-equipped bedrooms range from classical to contemporary in their style; Miss Potter, complete with a hot tub, is the best.

Miller Howe
rest, rest,
Rayrigg Rd ✉ LA23 1EY – ✆ (015394) 42 536 – www.millerhowe.com – Closed 2 weeks January Y**s**
15 rm (dinner included) – †£ 80/150 ††£ 160/250 – 2 suites
Rest – *(booking essential)* Menu £ 25/45 – Carte £ 36/56
Superbly situated Victorian villa in mature gardens, looking down the lake to the mountains. Arts and Crafts furnishings feature in the guest areas; take in the fabulous view from the conservatory. Comfy, classical bedrooms have a contemporary edge. Traditional menus are served in the split-level dining room.

Windermere Suites without rest
New Rd ✉ LA23 2LA – ✆ (015394) 47 672 – www.windermeresuites.co.uk
8 rm – †£ 150/295 ††£ 180/295 Y**e**
Spacious Edwardian house with a seductive interior. Funky, sexy bedrooms boast bold modern décor, iPod docks and walk-in wardrobes. Huge bathrooms feature TVs and colour-changing lights. Breakfast is served in your room.

Cedar Manor
Ambleside Rd ✉ LA23 1AX – ✆ (015394) 43 192 – www.cedarmanor.co.uk – Closed 3-23 January and 14-26 December Y**m**
10 rm – †£ 100/170 ††£ 120/350 **Rest** – *(dinner only)* Menu £ 40
Victorian house with ecclesiastical influences – built by a former minister, with a cedar tree in the garden. Contemporary country house bedrooms display locally made furniture; some have spa baths or views and the Coach House suite has a private terrace. Appealing menus of local produce.

Jerichos
College Rd ✉ LA23 1BX – ✆ (015394) 42 522 – www.jerichos.co.uk Y**z**
10 rm – †£ 45/55 ††£ 75/125 **Rest** – *(dinner only)* Carte £ 29/52
Traditional Victorian slate house in the town centre, with a contrastingly contemporary interior. The lounge is decorated in silver and the smart modern bedrooms have bold feature walls and good facilities; those on the first floor are larger. Concise, constantly evolving menus feature elaborate dishes.

Howbeck without rest
New Rd ✉ LA23 2LA – ✆ (015394) 44 739 – www.howbeck.co.uk Y**e**
11 rm – †£ 75/175 ††£ 120/225
Smart slate house close to the town centre. Comfy leather-furnished lounge with honesty bar. Stylish, modern bedrooms; some with four-posters or jacuzzi baths. The 'Retreat Suite' with its private entrance, spa bath and patio is best.

ENGLAND

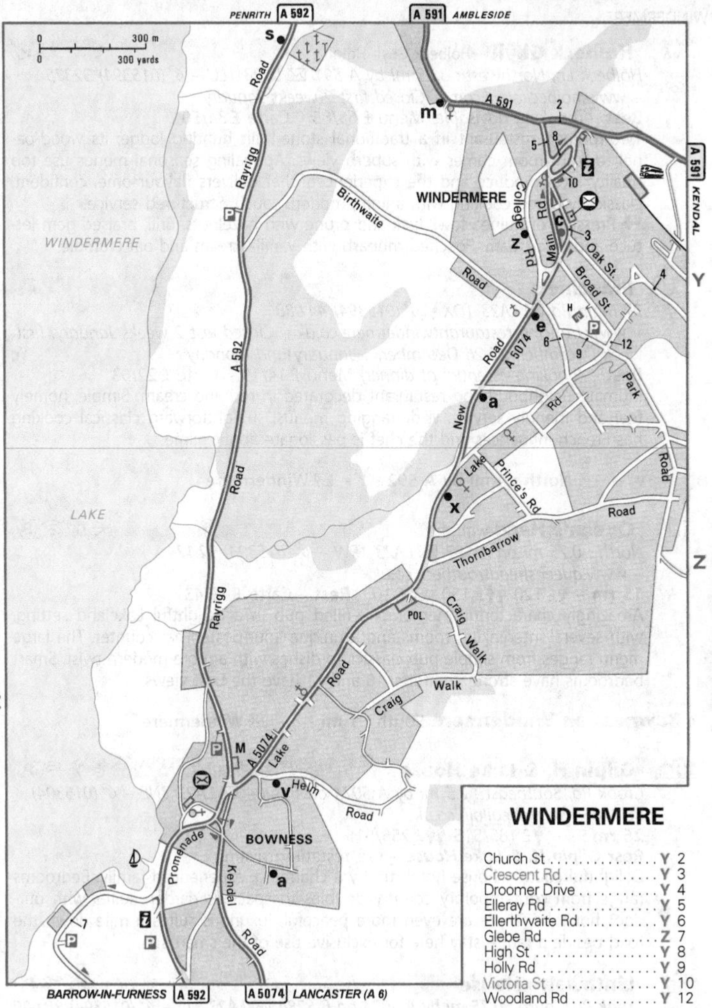

Newstead without rest

New Rd ✉ LA23 2EE – ✆ (015394) 44 485 – www.newstead-guesthouse.co.uk
– Closed 1-28 December Y**a**
9 rm ☕ – 🚹£ 50/80 🚹🚹£ 68/98
Imposing Victorian house with spacious, classical interior; original features include servants' bells, ornate coving and marble fireplaces. Traditional bedrooms have sinks in the rooms; some boast four-posters.

Fir Trees without rest

Lake Rd ✉ LA23 2EQ – ✆ (015394) 42 272 – www.fir-trees.co.uk Z**x**
9 rm ☕ – 🚹£ 55/65 🚹🚹£ 68/96
Reputedly built as a vicarage in 1888, this welcoming guesthouse boasts an original staircase and a lovely tile-floored hallway. The spacious interior includes simple, comfy bedrooms and a wood-furnished breakfast room.

XX ✿ **Holbeck Ghyll** – Holbeck Ghyll Hotel
Holbeck Ln, Northwest : 3.25 mi by A 591 ✉ LA23 1LU – ☎ (015394) 32375 – www.holbeckghyll.com – Closed first 2 weeks January
Rest – *(booking advisable)* Menu £ 65/85 – Carte £ 34/50
Two-roomed restaurant in a traditional stone-built hunting lodge; its wood-panelled front room comes with superb views. Appealing seasonal menus use top quality local produce and the experienced chef delivers flavoursome, confident, classically based cooking with a light, modern touch. Structured service.
➜ Pressing of guinea fowl, leek and prune with hazelnuts. Brill, braised gem lettuce and cider foam. Poached rhubarb with vanilla cream and oat crumble.

X **Francine's**
27 Main Rd ✉ LA23 1DX – ☎ (015394) 44 088 – www.francinesrestaurantwindermere.co.uk – Closed last 2 weeks January, first week December, 25-26 December, 1 January and Monday Y**c**
Rest – *(booking essential at dinner)* Menu £ 14/19 – Carte £ 22/53
Intimate neighbourhood restaurant decorated in red and cream. Simple, homely feel and friendly service. Wide-ranging menus; straightforward classical cooking has French influences and the chef is passionate about game.

at Troutbeck North : 4 mi by A 592 - Y – ✉ Windermere

Queen's Head with rm
North : 0.75 mi on A 592 ✉ LA23 1PW – ☎ (015394) 32 174 – www.queensheadtroutbeck.co.uk
15 rm – 🛉£ 120 🛉🛉£ 150, ☕ £ 10 **Rest** – Carte £ 19/43
Amazingly characterful, memorabilia-filled pub in a delightful Lakeland setting, with several interlinking rooms and a unique 'four-poster' bar counter. The large menu ranges from simple pub classics to dishes with a more modern twist. Smart bedrooms have strong comforts; 10 and 11 have the best views.

ENGLAND

at Bowness-on-Windermere South : 1 mi - Z – ✉ Windermere

Gilpin H. & Lake House
Crook Rd, Southeast : 2.5 mi by A 5074 on B 5284 ✉ LA23 3NE – ☎ (015394) 88 818 – www.thegilpin.co.uk
26 rm ☕ – 🛉£ 185/515 🛉🛉£ 255/515
Rest *Gilpin H. & Lake House* – see restaurant listing
Delightful country house hotel run by a charming, experienced family. Bedrooms range from contemporary country doubles to spacious garden suites with outdoor hot tubs. There are even more peaceful, luxurious suites a mile down the road beside a tarn – stay here for exclusive use of the smart spa.

Linthwaite House
Crook Rd, South : 0.75 mi by A 5074 on B 5284 ✉ LA23 3JA – ☎ (015394) 88 600 – www.linthwaite.com
30 rm ☕ – 🛉£ 90/150 🛉🛉£ 118/550
Rest *Linthwaite House* – see restaurant listing
Set in a peaceful spot overlooking the lake and fells, with stylish lounges and a funky bar with a fish tank in the wall. Smart bedrooms boast mood lighting, modern bathrooms and iPod docks; Room 31 has a telescope and a retractable window.

Lindeth Howe rm,
Lindeth Dr., Longtail Hill, South : 1.25 mi by A 5074 on B 5284 ✉ LA23 3JF – ☎ (015394) 45 759 – www.lindeth-howe.co.uk – Closed 3-12 January
34 rm ☕ – 🛉£ 95 🛉🛉£ 170/360 – 2 suites
Rest *The Dining Room* – Menu £ 18/45 – Carte £ 32/46
Attractive country house once bought by Beatrix Potter for her mother. Homely, clubby bar and lounge; pleasant views from the drawing room. Traditional bedrooms – the top floor boasts the best views, while the suites are more contemporary. Large, classically styled restaurant with menus to match.

Angel Inn rm,
Helm Rd ✉ LA23 3BU – ✆ (015394) 44 080 – www.theangelinnbowness.com
– Closed 24-25 December **Zv**
13 rm – 🚹£ 50/120 🚹🚹£ 70/190 **Rest** – Carte £ 21/41
Cream-washed pub off the main street, boasting contemporary bedrooms with iPod docks and flat screen TVs; the largest in an annexed 18C cottage with lake views. Minimalistic dining room, semi-open-plan bar with a log fire, and a wood-furnished, terraced garden. Classic pub-style dishes and sharing plates.

Dome House without rest
Brantfell Rd ✉ LA23 3AE – ✆ (015394) 45 667
– www.domehouselakedistrict.co.uk **Za**
4 rm – 🚹£ 70/175 🚹🚹£ 120/500
Futuristic-looking house with a domed, grass-covered roof and superb lake views – once featured on 'Grand Designs'. Modern, minimalistic bedrooms with balconies, iPod docks and flat screen TVs. Breakfast hamper delivered to your room.

Fair Rigg without rest
Ferry View, South : 0.5 mi on A 5074 ✉ LA23 3JB
– ✆ (015394) 43 941 – www.fairrigg.co.uk
– Closed January-March
6 rm – 🚹£ 45/64 🚹🚹£ 60/90
Late 19C house run by friendly owners and affording distant lake and hill views. Neat, linen-laid breakfast room; enjoy Cumbrian sausages and bacon. Spacious, immaculately kept bedrooms with quality furniture and up-to-date facilities.

Gilpin H. & Lake House – Gilpin Hotel & Lake House
Crook Rd, Southeast : 2.5 mi by A 5074 on B 5284 ✉ LA23 3NE
– ✆ (015394) 88 818 – www.thegilpin.co.uk
Rest – *(booking essential)* Menu £ 30/58
A series of intimate, individually styled dining rooms in a charming country house hotel; the Garden Room is perhaps the most pleasant. Start with an aperitif in the comfy lounge or the funky bar. Modern, very attractively presented dishes provide a fitting sense of occasion. Service is excellent.

Linthwaite House – Linthwaite House Hotel
Crook Rd, South : 0.75 mi by A 5074 on B 5284 ✉ LA23 3JA – ✆ (015394) 88 600
– www.linthwaite.com
Rest – *(residents only Christmas and New Year)* Menu £ 20/52
Contemporary restaurant in a traditional country house. Sit in the intimate Mirror Room with its romantic booths or in the airy, bay-windowed former billiard room. Daily menus showcase Lakeland produce; cooking is modern and flavoursome.

at Winster South : 4 mi on A 5074 – ✉ Windermere

Brown Horse Inn with rm
on A 5074 ✉ LA23 3NR – ✆ (015394) 43 443 – www.thebrownhorseinn.co.uk
9 rm – 🚹£ 50/90 🚹🚹£ 80/150 **Rest** – Carte £ 19/36
Shabby-chic coaching inn with a lovely split-level terrace. Seasonal menus feature unfussy, generous dishes and more adventurous specials. Much of the produce is from their fields out the back. Bedrooms are a mix of classic and boutique styles; some have terraces.

WINDLESHAM – Surrey – 504 S29 – pop. 4 103 7 C1

London 40 mi – Reading 18 mi – Southampton 53 mi

Brickmakers
Chertsey Rd, East : 1 mi on B 386 ✉ GU20 6HT – ✆ (01276) 472 267
– www.thebrickmakerswindlesham.co.uk
Rest – Menu £ 24 (dinner) – Carte £ 20/31
Beamed ceilings, wooden floors and open fires contribute to this 400 year old pub's charm and rusticity; its garden is the place to be in summer. Sandwiches, light bites and pub classics at lunch; more substantial dishes in the evening.

ENGLAND

WINDSOR – Windsor and Maidenhead – 504 S29 – pop. 32 444 11 D3

Great Britain

London 28 mi – Reading 19 mi – Southampton 59 mi

to Marlow, Maidenhead and Cookham (Salter Bros. Ltd) (summer only)

The Old Booking Hall, Central Station, Thames St, (01753) 74 39 00, www.windsor.gov.uk

Town★ – Castle★★★ : St George's Chapel★★★ **AC** (stalls★★★), State Apartments★★ **AC**, North Terrace (★★) Z – Eton College★★ **AC** (College Chapel★★, Wall paintings★) Z

Windsor Park★ **AC** Y

Macdonald Windsor

rm,

23 High St. SL4 1LH – (01753) 483 100 – www.macdonald-hotels.co.uk/windsor

120 rm – £ 120/225 £ 120/225, £ 15.50 – 2 suites **Zr**

Rest ***Caleys*** – Carte £ 23/46

Opened in 2010 in a former department store. Attractive open-plan guest areas in striking grey, cream and silver; small but state-of-the-art meeting rooms. Contemporary bedrooms with warm hues and high level of facilities. Modern brasserie with menus to match.

Sir Christopher Wren's House

rest,

Thames St SL4 1PX – (01753) 442 400 – www.sarova.com **Ze**

95 rm – £ 90/250 £ 115/270, £ 16 – 1 suite

Rest – Menu £ 32 **s** – Carte £ 25/50 **s**

Characterful house on the riverbank by Windsor Bridge; built by Wren in 1676 as his family home. Traditional guest areas and smart gym. Mix of classical and modern bedrooms: some in annexes; some with balconies and river views. Popular, modern restaurant with lovely Thames outlook.

ENGLAND

Royal Adelaide

46 Kings Rd SL4 2AG – (01753) 863 916 – www.theroyaladelaide.com

42 rm – £ 69/125 £ 75/225 **Rest** – Carte £ 20/43 **Zv**

Three adjoining Georgian houses with light blue painted façade, built for Queen Adelaide. Bedrooms vary in shape and size, and all are decorated in an individual, traditional style. Dining room offers international, brasserie-style menu.

Christopher

rm, rm,

110 High St, Eton SL4 6AN – (01753) 852 359 – www.thechristopher.co.uk

34 rm – £ 100/144 £ 140/200, £ 12 **Rest** – Carte £ 18/33 **Za**

17C former coaching inn close to Eton College and perfect for walking to the castle. Contemporary bedrooms are split between main building and a mews annexe. International menus display North African influences.

65 Degrees at Windsor Grill

65 St Leonards Rd SL4 3BX – (01753) 859 658 – www.awtrestaurants.com – Closed 25 December-5 January, Sunday and bank holidays **Zx**

Rest – *(light Lunch)* Carte £ 25/52

Rustic Victorian property owned by Antony Worrall Thompson. Wide-ranging menu displays classic comfort dishes, including well-flavoured hung beef, and pork and chicken from his own farm.

Greene Oak

Oakley Greene, West : 3 mi by A 308 on B 3024 SL4 5UW – (01753) 864 294 – www.thegreeneoak.co.uk

Rest – *(booking advisable)* Menu £ 15/35 – Carte £ 21/51

It's on a busy junction and is an unusual shade of green but don't let that put you off, as the friendly welcome, pretty terrace and modern interior more than make up for it. Constantly evolving comfort dishes rely on quality produce.

WINFORTON – Herefordshire – 503 L27 18 A3

London 175 mi – Plymouth 188 mi – Torbay 167 mi – Exeter 151 mi

Winforton Court without rest

HR3 6EA – (01544) 328 498 – www.winfortoncourt.co.uk – Closed 23-27 December

3 rm – £ 70/93 £ 88/108

Characterful, part-timbered house with 16C origins: once the court of 'Hanging' Judge Jeffries; now with an art gallery run by the welcoming owner. Bedrooms have a warm, rustic style. Locally pressed fruit juices at breakfast.

WINDSOR

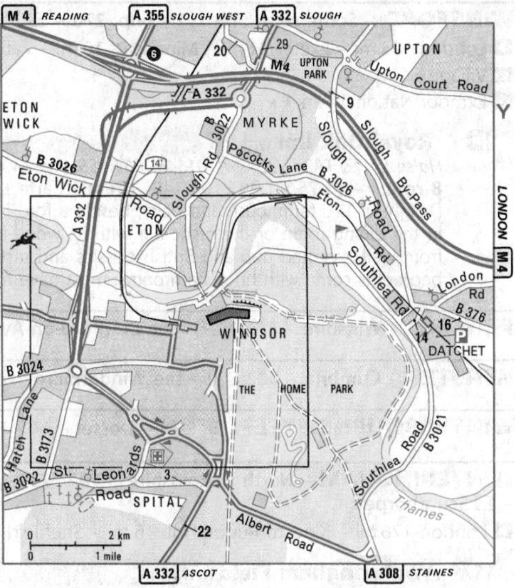

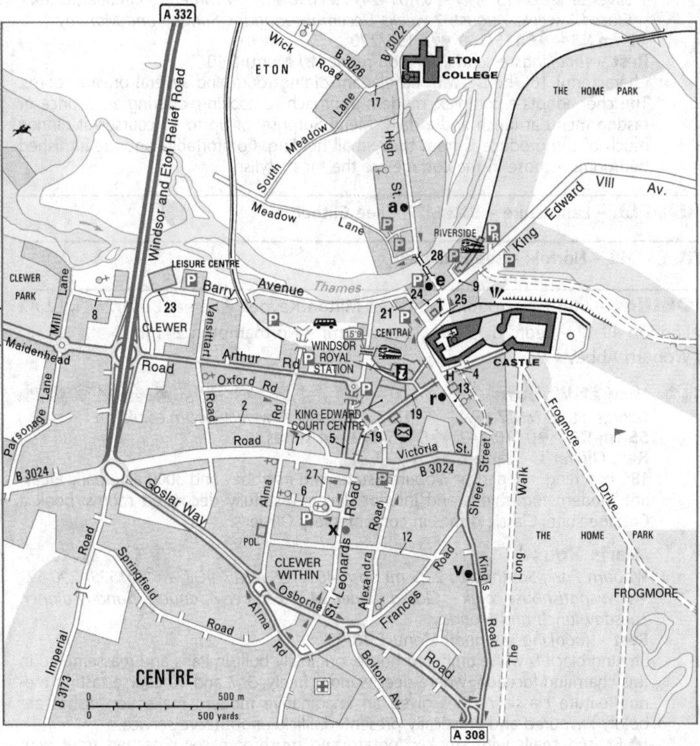

ENGLAND

WINSFORD – Somerset – 503 J30 – pop. 270 – ✉ Minehead 3 A2

London 194 mi – Exeter 31 mi – Minehead 10 mi – Taunton 32 mi

Village★

Exmoor National Park★★

Royal Oak Inn with rm

Halse Ln ✉ TA24 7JE – ☎ (01643) 851 455 – www.royaloakexmoor.co.uk

8 rm – †£ 75/90 ††£ 100/140 **Rest** – Carte £ 22/35

Delightful 12C farmhouse and dairy, beside a ford in a charming little village. Sit in the dining room or the rustic bar with its wood-furnished dining area; choose from well-executed pub and British classics and tasty desserts. Spacious, country bedrooms come with huge bathrooms; most have four-poster beds.

WINSLEY – Wiltshire – 503 N29 – see Bradford-on-Avon

WINSTER – Cumbria – 502 L20 – see Windermere

WINTERBOURNE STEEPLETON – Dorset – 503 M31 – see Dorchester

WINTERINGHAM – North Lincolnshire – 502 S22 – pop. 4 714 – ✉ Scunthorpe 23 C3

London 176 mi – Kingston-upon-Hull 16 mi – Sheffield 67 mi

Winteringham Fields with rm

1 Silver St ✉ DN15 9ND – ☎ (01724) 733 096 – www.winteringhamfields.co.uk – Closed 3 weeks August, 2 weeks December-January, Sunday and Monday

11 rm – †£ 115/160 ††£ 155/220

Rest – *(bookings essential for non-residents)* Menu £ 40/79

Characterful 16C house with an elegant dining room and several private rooms. The chef adopts a complex, modern approach to cooking, offering a set price or tasting menu at lunch and a daily 'Menu Surprise' of up to 10 courses at dinner; much of the produce is from their small holding. Comfortable, antique-furnished bedrooms - those in the cottage are the most stylish.

WISWELL – Lancashire – 502 M22 – see Clitheroe

WIVETON – Norfolk – see Blakeney

WOBURN – 504 S28 – pop. 1 534 – ✉ Milton Keynes Great Britain 12 A2

London 49 mi – Bedford 13 mi – Luton 13 mi – Northampton 24 mi

Woburn Abbey★★

Inn at Woburn

rm, rest,

George St ✉ MK17 9PX – ☎ (01525) 290 441 – www.woburn.co.uk/inn

55 rm – †£ 110/142 ††£ 115/172 – 4 suites

Rest *Olivier's* – Carte £ 26/37

18C coaching inn, part of Woburn Estate with its abbey and 3000 acre park. Pleasant modern furnishings and interior décor. Tastefully decorated rooms: book a Cottage suite. Classic dishes in contemporary Olivier's.

Paris House

Woburn Park, Southeast : 2.25 mi on A 4012 ✉ MK17 9QP – ☎ (01525) 290 692 – www.parishouse.co.uk – Closed dinner 24 December-7 January, Sunday dinner, Tuesday lunch and Monday

Rest – *(booking essential)* Menu £ 36/95

Striking black & white timbered house; originally built in Paris and reassembled in this charming location, where deer wander freely. 5, 7 and 10 course tasting menus feature classic recipes given an imaginative modern makeover; dishes are boldly flavoured and artistically presented. Slick, unobtrusive service.

→ Braised snails with smoked potato and mushroom soil. Poached trout with pea tortellini, compressed cucumber and lobster dashi. Frangelico parfait with goat's milk ice cream.

ENGLAND

Birch

20 Newport Rd, North : 0.5 mi on A 5130 ✉ MK17 9HX – ☏ (01525) 290 295 – www.birchwoburn.com – Closed 25-26 December, 1 January and Sunday dinner
Rest – *(booking essential)* Carte £ 22/38
Long-standing former pub with a traditional façade and more modern interior. With its wood-panelled walls, the glass-roofed restaurant has a New England feel. The large menu offers a range of European dishes, along with grills by the ounce.

WOBURN SANDS – Milton Keynes – 504 S27 – pop. 4 963 — 11 D1

London 53 mi – Leeds 150 mi – Sheffield 120 mi – Manchester 163 mi

Purple Goose

61 High St ✉ MK17 8QY – ☏ (01908) 584 385 – www.thepurplegoose.co.uk – Closed 2 weeks January, Sunday dinner and Monday
Rest – *(dinner only and lunch Thursday-Sunday) (booking advisable)* Menu £ 19 (lunch) – Carte £ 28/50
Simple, family-run restaurant split over two floors, with white walls and purple detailing. Menus mix classical and modern dishes and change every 6 weeks; some unusual flavour combinations feature. Most wines are available by the glass.

Don't confuse the classification X with the stars ✿!
The number of X denotes levels of comfort and service,
while stars are awarded for the best cooking across all categories.

WOKING – Surrey – 504 S30 – pop. 62 796 — 7 C1

London 31 mi – Croydon 25 mi – Barnet 44 mi – Ealing 26 mi

London House

134 High St, Old Woking, Southeast : 2 mi by A 320 on A 247 ✉ GU22 9JN – ☏ (01483) 750 610 – www.londonhouseoldwoking.co.uk – Closed 1-8 January, 4-19 August, Sunday dinner and Monday
Rest – *(dinner only and lunch Thursday-Sunday)* Menu £ 36 (dinner) – Carte lunch £ 26/29
Friendly neighbourhood restaurant in a 17C red-brick former post office; oil lamps create an element of intimacy. The classically trained French chef offers well-presented, satisfying dishes with interesting, modern touches.

Red Lion

High St, Northwest : 1.5 mi by A 324 ✉ GU21 4SS – ☏ (01483) 768 497 – www.redlionhorsell.co.uk – Closed 26 December
Rest – *(booking advisable)* Carte £ 22/34
Sit on a sofa in the open-fired bar or amongst Brooklands racing memorabilia in the rustic beamed dining room; or head out to the terrace and landscaped garden. Dishes range from pub classics to some more unusual combinations.

WOLD NEWTON – East Riding of Yorkshire — 23 D2

London 229 mi – Bridlington 25 mi – Scarborough 13 mi

Wold Cottage

South : 0.5 mi on Thwing rd ✉ YO25 3HL – ☏ (01262) 470 696 – www.woldcottage.com
6 rm ☕ – 🚹£ 70/75 🚹🚹£ 90/120 **Rest** – Menu £ 28
Fine Georgian manor house and an extensive collection of outbuildings, in 300 acres of peaceful farmland. Personal items abound in the homely, tastefully furnished interior. Sizeable bedrooms boast luxurious soft furnishings and antiques; some have four-posters – the courtyard rooms are simpler. Formal communal dining. Hearty British dishes showcase garden produce.

WOLVERCOTE – Oxfordshire – 504 Q28 – see Oxford

WOLVERHAMPTON – Staffordshire – 502 N26 – pop. 251 462 19 C2

London 132 mi – Birmingham 15 mi – Liverpool 89 mi – Shrewsbury 30 mi

18 Queen Sq, ✆ (01902) 31 20 51, www.wolverhampton.co.uk

XX Bilash

No 2 Cheapside ✉ WV1 1TU – ✆ (01902) 427 762 – www.thebilash.co.uk – Closed 25-26 December and Sunday Bc

Rest – Menu £ 11/23 – Carte £ 19/45

Long-standing, personally-run restaurant with several family generations involved. Appealing menu of freshly cooked Indian dishes and tempting specials. Strictly local and homemade produce.

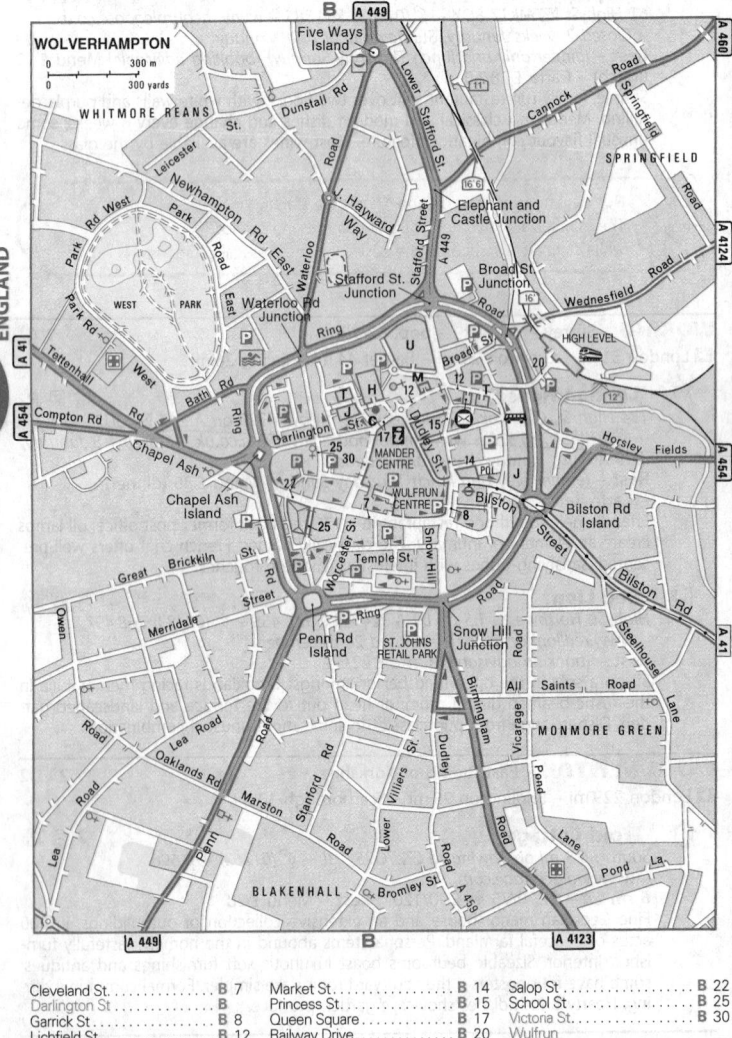

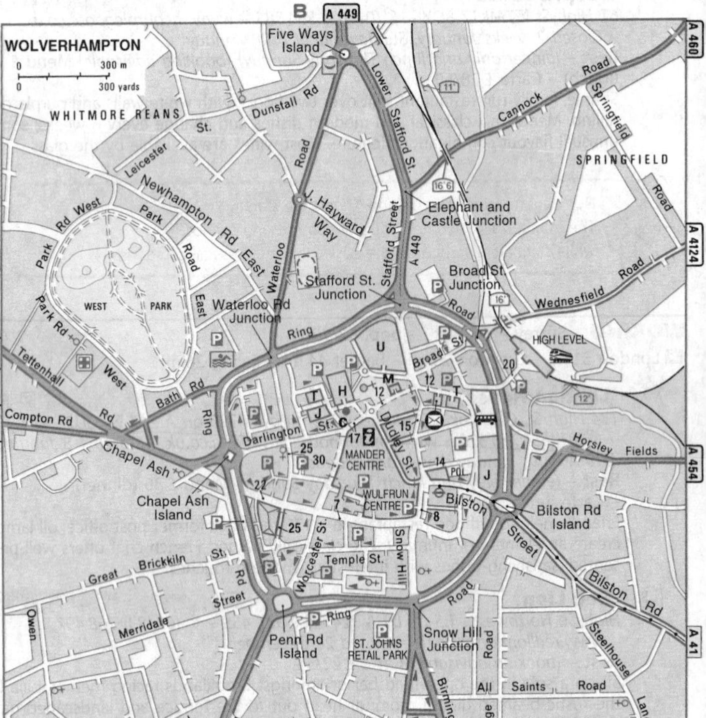

Cleveland St. . . . . B 7
Darlington St . . . . B
Garrick St . . . . B 8
Lichfield St . . . . B 12
Mander Centre . . . . B
Market St . . . . B 14
Princess St. . . . . B 15
Queen Square . . . . B 17
Railway Drive . . . . B 20
St Johns Retail Park . . . . B
Salop St . . . . B 22
School St . . . . B 25
Victoria St. . . . . B 30
Wulfrun Centre . . . . B

WOOBURN COMMON – Buckinghamshire – 504 S29 – see Beaconsfield

WOODBRIDGE – Suffolk – 504 X27 – pop. 10 956 15 D3

London 81 mi – Great Yarmouth 45 mi – Ipswich 8 mi – Norwich 47 mi

Cretingham, Grove Farm, ✆ (01728) 68 52 75

Seckford, Great Bealings, Seckford Hall Rd, ✆ (01394) 38 80 00

Seckford Hall
rm, rest,

Southwest : 1.25 mi by A 12 ✉ IP13 6NU – ✆ (01394) 385 678 – www.seckford.co.uk

32 rm – †£ 78/103 ††£ 124/160, ☕ £ 14 – 7 suites **Rest** – Carte £ 24/40

Reputedly once visited by Elizabeth I, a part Tudor country house set in attractive gardens. Charming traditionally panelled public areas. Comfortable bedrooms. Local lobster proudly served in smart dining room.

Riverside

Quayside ✉ IP12 1BH – ✆ (01394) 382 587 – www.theriverside.co.uk – Closed 25-26 December, 1 January and Sunday dinner

Rest – *(booking advisable)* Carte £ 25/34

A restaurant, cinema and theatre in one, with a set menu whose price includes entrance to a film. Light and airy, with floor to ceiling windows and a marble-topped counter displaying freshly baked bread. Wide range of well-crafted dishes.

Crown with rm

Thoroughfare ✉ IP12 1AD – ✆ (01394) 384 242 – www.thecrownatwoodbridge.co.uk

10 rm ☕ – †£ 90/125 ††£ 120/180 **Rest** – Menu £ 24 – Carte £ 24/40

Modern dining pub in the town centre, with smart granite-floored bar and four different dining areas. Extensive menu makes good use of local produce. Well-presented, rustic cooking and polite, friendly service. Stylish, contemporary bedrooms boast good facilities.

at Bromeswell Northeast : 2.5 mi by B 1438 off A 1152

British Larder

Orford Rd, on A 1152 ✉ IP12 2PU – ✆ (01394) 460 310 – www.britishlardersuffolk.co.uk – Closed Sunday dinner and Monday January-March

Rest – Menu £ 18 (weekday lunch) – Carte £ 24/67

Once down-at-heel, this 17C pub has been modernised in looks and transformed into a beacon for local Suffolk produce, courtesy of its enthusiastic owners who have a passion for all things local. Skilled cooking uses ingredients thoughtfully; wine events and cookery classes are held regularly.

WOODHOUSE EAVES – Leicestershire – 502 Q25 16 B2
– ✉ Loughborough

London 110 mi – Birmingham 43 mi – Liverpool 109 mi – Leeds 91 mi

Woodhouse

43 Maplewell Rd ✉ LE12 8RG – ✆ (01509) 890 318 – www.thewoodhouse.co.uk – Closed Sunday dinner and Monday

Rest – Menu £ 16/38

Unassuming restaurant with a smart bar-lounge and striking artwork hung on pale green walls. Choose from a tasting menu or a good value market menu; classical combinations use modern techniques and are given a personal twist.

WOODSTOCK – Oxfordshire – 503 P28 – pop. 2 389 Great Britain 10 B2

London 65 mi – Gloucester 47 mi – Bristol 78 mi – Barnet 68 mi

Park St, ✆ (01993) 81 32 76, www.woodstock-oxfordshire.co.uk

Blenheim Palace★★★ (Park★★★) AC

Bear

Park St. ✉ OX20 1SZ – ✆ (0844) 879 91 43 – www.macdonaldhotels.co.uk/bear

54 rm ☕ – †£ 114/240 ††£ 129/260 – 8 suites

Rest ***Bear*** – Menu £ 20/35 – Carte £ 33/57

Characterful 13C coaching inn with exposed stone walls, charming oak beams and open fires. Extremely comfy, well-equipped bedrooms are spread about the house and courtyard; pay the extra for an executive. Cosy first floor sitting room and a light, airy restaurant with a large fireplace and food-themed art.

ENGLAND

Feathers
Market St ✉ OX20 1SX – ✆ (01993) 812 291 – www.feathers.co.uk
21 rm – †£ 199/319 ††£ 199/319 – 5 suites
Rest – *(booking essential)* Menu £ 20/55 – Carte £ 36/51
Stylish 17C house boasting individually styled bedrooms with boutique twists: some have feature walls; others, modern art and bold fabrics. Bar-lounge and lovely walled terrace offer a casual menu and a fabulous gin selection. Formal dining room serves classically based dishes with a creative, original edge.

Kings Arms
19 Market St ✉ OX20 1SU – ✆ (01993) 813 636
– www.kingshotelwoodstock.co.uk
15 rm – †£ 80 ††£ 150
Rest *Atrium* – Carte £ 23/37
Keenly run, contemporary hotel in the heart of a busy market town. The immaculately kept interior shows a good eye for detail; the sleek, stylish bedrooms are named after English kings. Have a snack in the cosy open-fired bar or robust, flavoursome British dishes in the black and white tiled dining room.

WOOFFERTON – Shropshire – 503 L26 – see Ludlow

WOOLER – Northumberland – 502 N17 – pop. 1 857 — 24 A1

London 330 mi – Alnwick 17 mi – Berwick-on-Tweed 17 mi

Firwood without rest
Middleton Hall, South : 1.75 mi by Earle rd on Middleton Hall rd ✉ NE71 6RD – ✆ (01668) 283 699 – www.firwoodhouse.co.uk – Closed 1 December-13 February
3 rm – †£ 60 ††£ 90
Bay-windowed former hunting lodge in a peaceful setting with lovely countryside views. Beautiful original tiled hall; warm, comfy lounge. Spacious, simply furnished, period-style bedrooms. Friendly owners are a fount of local knowledge.

ENGLAND

WOOLHOPE – Herefordshire — 18 B3

London 138 mi – Birmingham 70 mi

Butchers Arms
✉ HR1 4RF – ✆ (01432) 860 281 – www.butchersarmswoolhope.co.uk – Closed 1 week January, 25 December, Sunday dinner and Monday except bank holidays
Rest – Carte £ 21/31
Owned by Stephen Bull, this is an attractive, half-timbered 16C inn, with a pretty garden by a babbling brook and a lively bar with low-slung beams and open fires. Daily changing menu of honest, well-priced, regional dishes; with local lamb and cheese the highlights. Try the twice-baked goat's cheese soufflé.

WOOTTON – Oxfordshire — 10 B2

London 61 mi – Birmingham 81 mi – Bristol 68 mi – Croydon 71 mi

Killingworth Castle Ⓝ
Glympton Rd ✉ OX20 1EJ – ✆ (01993) 811 401 – www.thekillingworthcastle.com
Rest – Carte £ 21/33
Rescued from dereliction by experienced owners; a 'proper' village pub with exposed stone walls, open fires and rustic furnishings. Menus are interesting and provide good value – particularly the daily special – and ingredients are seasonal and locally sourced. You will leave feeling suitably fortified.

WOOTTON BRIDGE – 503 P31 – see Wight (Isle of)

WORCESTER – Worcestershire – 503 N27 – pop. 96 959 — 18 B3

Great Britain
London 124 mi – Birmingham 26 mi – Bristol 61 mi – Cardiff 74 mi
High St, ✆ (01905) 72 63 11, www.visitworcestershire.org
Perdiswell Park, Bilford Rd, ✆ (01905) 75 46 68
City★ – Cathedral★★ – Royal Worcester Porcelain Works★ (Museum of Worcester Porcelain★) M
The Elgar Trail★

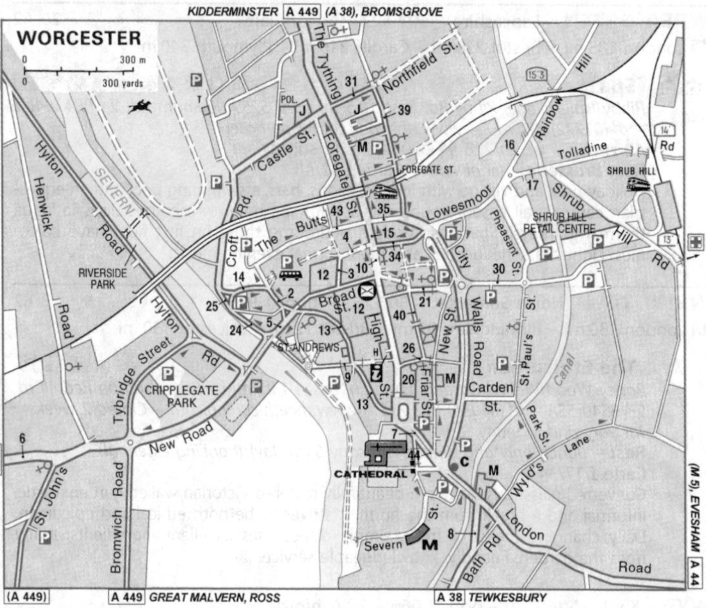

All Saints Rd	2	Deansway	13	Pump St	26
Angel Pl.	3	Dolday	14	St Martin's Gate	30
Angel St	4	Foregate (The)	15	St Mary's St	31
Bridge St.	5	High St		St Nicholas St.	34
Broad St		Lowesmoor Pl.	16	Sansome St	35
Bromyard Rd	6	Lowesmoor Terrace	17	Sansome Walk	39
College St.	7	Lychgate Shopping Centre	20	Shambles (The)	40
Commandery Rd	8	Mealcheapen St	21	Shaw St	43
Copenhagen St	9	North Parade	24	Shrub Hill Retail Centre	
Cross (The)	10	North Quay	25	Sidbury	44
Crown Gate Centre	12				

Bindles

55 Sidbury ✉ WR1 2HU – ✆ (01905) 611 120 – www.bindles.co.uk **c**

Rest – Menu £ 12 (lunch and early dinner) – Carte £ 19/32

Modern, boldly decorated brasserie, set on a busy junction and run by a friendly team. Sit in the small dining area next to the lounge, in the larger upstairs room or on the terrace. Fresh, tasty, classic dishes have a Mediterranean edge.

WORFIELD – Shropshire – see Bridgnorth

WORKSOP – Nottinghamshire – 502 Q24 – pop. 39 072 16 B1

London 160 mi – Sheffield 20 mi – Nottingham 37 mi – Rotherham 17 mi

Browns without rest

Old Orchard Cottage, Holbeck, Southwest : 4.5 mi by A 60 ✉ S80 3NF – ✆ (01909) 720 659 – www.brownsholbeck.co.uk – Closed 24-26 December

3 rm – †£ 59/69 ††£ 81/91

Cross the ford to this keenly run, cosy cottage, which dates back to 1730. Lovely garden with mature fruit trees. Bedrooms are in the old cow shed; all have four-posters and open onto a large decked terrace. Appealing breakfast menu.

WORTH – Kent – 504 Y30 – see Deal

WREA GREEN – Lancashire – **502** L22 – ✉ **Kirkham** **20** A2

▶ London 185 mi – Bristol 226 mi – Cardiff 246 mi – Plymouth 340 mi

🏨 **Spa** ⚲ ⬭ ⬭ ◻ ◉ ⋔ Ⅰ₅ ⅍ ☷ ⅖ rm, ₳ ⅍ ⬙ **P**
Ribby Hall Village, Ribby Rd, East : 0.5 mi on B 5259 (Kirkham Rd) ✉ *PR4 2PR*
– ℰ (01772) 674 477 – www.ribbyhall.co.uk/spa-hotel
42 rm ⌷ – ♦£ 80/228 ♦♦£ 90/440 – 12 suites
Rest *Brasserie* *– (light lunch)* Carte £ 32/48
Holiday park and village with lodges, shops, bars, a swimming pool and an equestrian centre – all based around this superb spa hotel, which specialises in 'aqua
thermal journeys'. Spacious, modern bedrooms; those on first floor have balconies. Light brasserie lunches and more formal evening meals.

WRINGTON – North Somerset – **503** L29 – **pop. 1 995** **3** B2

▶ London 130 mi – Birmingham 99 mi – Bristol 12 mi – Leicester 130 mi

✗ **The Ethicurean** ⬚ ⬚ ₳ ⬙ **P**
🙂 *Barley Wood Walled Garden, Long Ln, East : 1.25 mi by School Rd on Redhill rd*
✉ *BS40 5SA – ℰ (01934) 863 713 – www.theethicurean.com – Closed 2 weeks*
January and Monday
Rest *– (lunch only and dinner Thursday-Saturday) (booking essential)*
Carte £ 17/34
Converted glasshouse within a beautifully restored Victorian walled garden: rustic,
informal and a break from the norm, it strives to be both ethical and epicurean.
Daily changing menu of fresh, simple dishes uses excellent ingredients; many
from the garden. Friendly, knowledgeable service.

WYE – Kent – **504** W30 – **pop. 2 066** – ✉ **Ashford** **9** C2

▶ London 60 mi – Canterbury 10 mi – Dover 28 mi – Hastings 34 mi

✗✗ **Wife of Bath** with rm ⬚ ⬙ **P**
4 Upper Bridge St ✉ *TN25 5AF – ℰ (01233) 812 232 – www.thewifeofbath.com*
– Closed Sunday dinner, Tuesday lunch except December and Monday
5 rm ⌷ – ♦£ 75 ♦♦£ 95/115
Rest *– (booking advisable)* Menu £ 17 (weekdays)/28 – Carte £ 35/49
18C house with an attractive brick façade; its charming interior boasting exposed
beams and an open fire. The eclectic menu offers classic dishes executed in a
modern style. Simple, stylish bedrooms include a four-poster. Those in the annexe
are smaller but more characterful.

WYMESWOLD – Leicestershire – **502** R25 **16** B2

▶ London 120 mi – Birmingham 47 mi – Liverpool 109 mi – Leeds 91 mi

✗ **hammer & pincers** ⓝ ⬚ **P**
5 East Rd ✉ *LE12 6ST – ℰ (01509) 880 735 – www.hammerandpincers.co.uk*
– Closed 25 December, Sunday dinner and Monday
Rest *–* Menu £ 18/35 – Carte dinner £ 25/44
Formerly the village forge – the old water pump can still be seen at the back of
the rustic restaurant. Classically based dishes in original combinations; the 7
course grazing menu is more modern and creative. Smooth, friendly service.

WYMONDHAM – Leicestershire – **504** R25 – **pop. 600** **17** C2

▶ London 107 mi – Birmingham 70 mi – Liverpool 138 mi – Leeds 100 mi

🍴 **Berkeley Arms** ⬚ ⬙ **P**
🙂 *59 Main St* ✉ *LE14 2AG – ℰ (01572) 787 587 – www.theberkeleyarms.co.uk*
– Closed first 2 weeks January, 10 days summer, Sunday dinner and Monday
Rest *–* Menu £ 19 (weekdays)/22 – Carte £ 21/40
Attractive 16C village pub run by an enthusiastic, experienced local couple. Turn
left for the low-beamed bar or right for the slightly more formal dining room.
Gutsy, satisfying dishes rely on local produce. Choose from daily changing bar
snacks or a more adventurous à la carte. Relaxed, personable service.

ENGLAND

WYNYARD – Stockton-on-Tees **24** B3

London 250 mi – Leeds 72 mi – Bradford 74 mi – Sunderland 24 mi

Wynyard Hall (N)

✉ *TS22 5NF* – *☎ (01740) 644 811* – *www.wynyardhall.co.uk*

25 rm – £ 160/240 £ 160/240 – 2 suites

Rest ***Wellington*** – Menu £ 32/55

Impressive Georgian mansion built for the Marquis of Londonderry; its smart spa overlooks a lake. Traditional bedrooms in the main house and more modern lodges spread about the vast grounds. Classical guest areas feature stained glass, open fires and antiques. Formal dining room offers an ambitious menu.

WYTON – Cambridgeshire – see Huntingdon

YARM – Stockton-on-Tees – **502** P20 – **pop. 8 929** **24** B3

London 239 mi – Leeds 61 mi – Bradford 63 mi – Sunderland 34 mi

Judges Country House

Kirklevington Hall, Kirklevington, South : 1.5 mi on A 67 ✉ *TS15 9LW* – *☎ (01642) 789 000* – *www.judgeshotel.co.uk*

21 rm – £ 99/190 £ 130/220

Rest ***Judges Country House*** – see restaurant listing

Victorian former judge's house with wood panelling, antiques and ornaments, set in well-kept gardens. Traditional country house bedrooms offer a high level of facilities, bright modern bathrooms and extra touches such as fresh fruit, flowers and even a goldfish! Welcoming atmosphere; pleasant service.

Judges Country House (N) – Judges Country House

Kirklevington Hall, Kirklevington, South : 1.5 mi on A 67 ✉ *TS15 9LW* – *☎ (01642) 789 000* – *www.judgeshotel.co.uk*

Rest – Menu £ 31/55

Formal, two-roomed restaurant on the ground floor of a traditional country house hotel; the conservatory extension has a lovely outlook over the lawns. Modern, well-prepared dishes are simple and straightforward, yet full of flavour.

Muse (N)

104b High St ✉ *TS15 9AU* – *☎ (01642) 788 558* – *www.museyarm.com* – *Closed 25 December, 1 January and Sunday dinner*

Rest – *(booking advisable)* Menu £ 16 (lunch and early dinner) – Carte £ 21/43

Smart, modern continental café: bright and busy, with a pavement terrace in the summer. Extensive menu offers international brasserie dishes from lunchtime salads to pasta and grills; very good value set price menu of simpler dishes.

YARMOUTH – Isle of Wight – **503** P31 – see Wight (Isle of)

YATTENDON – West Berkshire – **503** Q29 – **pop. 288** – ✉ **Newbury** **10** B3

London 54 mi – Bristol 68 mi – Croydon 61 mi – Barnet 67 mi

Royal Oak with rm

The Square ✉ *RG18 0UF* – *☎ (01635) 201 325* – *www.royaloakyattendon.com*

10 rm – £ 85/130 £ 85/130

Rest – *(booking advisable)* Menu £ 13 (weekday lunch) – Carte £ 24/39

Eye-catching red-brick pub with attractive gardens, in picture postcard village close to the M4; a beamed bar with roaring fire at its hub. Honest British dishes and traditional puddings; Sunday roast of 28-day aged rib of beef. Comfy bedrooms in country house style.

at Frilsham South : 1 mi by Frilsham rd on Bucklebury rd – ✉ **Yattendon**

Pot Kiln

✉ *RG18 0XX* – *☎ (01635) 201 366* – *www.potkiln.org* – *Closed 25 December and Tuesday*

Rest – Menu £ 14 (weekday lunch) – Carte £ 29/37

Pleasant pub in prime game country. Flavoursome British dishes arrive in unashamedly gutsy portions. Chef-owner stalks or gathers much of the produce himself. Fish is from Looe or local rivers.

YEOVIL – Somerset – 503 M31 – pop. 41 871 3 B3

London 130 mi – Bristol 42 mi – Cardiff 86 mi – Southampton 77 mi
Hendford, ✆(01935) 84 59 46, www.yeoviltown.com
Sherborne Rd, ✆(01935) 42 29 65
St John the Baptist★
Monacute House★★ AC, W : 4 mi on A 3088 – Fleet Air Arm Museum, Yeovilton★★ AC, NW : 5 mi by A 37 – Tintinhull House Garden★ AC, NW: 5.5 mi – Ham Hill (≤★★) W : 5.5 mi by A 3088 – Stoke sub Hamdon (parish church★) W : 5.25 mi by A 3088. Muchelney★★ (parish church★★) NW : 14 mi by A 3088, A 303 and B 3165 – Lytes Cary★, N : 7.5 mi by A 37, B 3151 and A 372 – Sandford Orcas Manor House★, NW : 8 mi by A 359 – Cadbury Castle (≤★★) NE : 10.5 mi by A 359 – East Lambrook Manor★ AC, W : 12 mi by A 3088 and A 303

Lanes
West Coker, Southwest : 3 mi on A 30 ✉ BA22 9AJ – ✆(01935) 862 555 – www.laneshotel.net
30 rm – †£ 90 ††£ 130/150 **Rest** – Menu £ 17 (lunch) – Carte £ 17/30
18C former rectory with modern extensions, set in pleasant walled grounds. Airy interior boasts modern meeting rooms, a laid-back lounge and a large bar. Relax in the smart leisure suite or on the croquet lawn. Stylish bedrooms come with up-to-date bathrooms. Modern bistro dishes in the striking dining room.

at Barwick South : 2 mi by A 30 off A 37 – ✉ Yeovil

Little Barwick House with rm — rest, P
✉ BA22 9TD – ✆(01935) 423 902 – www.littlebarwickhouse.co.uk – Closed 3 weeks Christmas-New Year, Sunday, Monday and lunch Tuesday
6 rm – †£ 75 ††£ 210/290 **Rest** – *(booking essential)* Menu £ 29/45
Attractive Georgian dower house on the outskirts of town, run by a hospitable husband and wife team. Relax on deep sofas before heading into the elegant dining room with its huge window and heavy drapes. Cooking is classical, satisfying and full of flavour – a carefully chosen wine list accompanies. Charming, comfortably furnished bedrooms, each with its own character.

YORK – York – 502 Q22 – pop. 198 900 Great Britain 23 C2

London 280 mi – Sunderland 15 mi – Newcastle upon Tyne 8 mi – Middlesbrough 39 mi
Museum St, ✆(01904) 55 00 99, www.visityork.org
Strensall, Lords Moor Lane, ✆(01904) 49 18 40
Heworth, Muncastergate, Muncaster House, ✆(01904) 42 46 18
City★★★ – Minster★★★ (Stained Glass★★★, Chapter House★★, Choir Screen★★) CDY – National Railway Museum★★★ CY – The Walls★★ CDXYZ – Castle Museum★ AC DZ **M2** – Jorvik Viking Centre★ AC DY **M1** – Fairfax House★ AC DY **A** – The Shambles★ DY **54**

Cedar Court Grand H. & Spa — rm, P
Station Rise ✉ YO1 6HT – ✆(01904) 380 038 – www.cedarcourtgrand.co.uk
107 rm – †£ 135/300 ††£ 135/300, £ 15 – 13 suites CY**v**
Rest *Grill Room* – Carte £ 30/52
Early 20C building – the former offices of the North Eastern Railway Co. – where original features blend with contemporary décor. Impressive spa and leisure facilities in cellar. Spacious bedrooms. Modern menu served in Grill Room, with views of the castle walls.

Middlethorpe Hall — rm, P
Bishopthorpe Rd, South : 1.75 mi ✉ YO23 2GB – ✆(01904) 641 241 – www.middlethorpe.com
29 rm – †£ 149/169 ††£ 199/249 – 9 suites
Rest – *(booking essential)* Menu £ 26 (weekday lunch) **s** – Carte £ 41/56 **s**
A fine William and Mary House dating from 1699 and set in 30 acres of mature gardens and parkland next to the Knavesmire Racecourse. Elegant sitting room with French-style furnishings, oil paintings and floral arrangements. Traditional, antique-furnished bedrooms. Classical cooking makes use of luxury ingredients as well as produce grown in the garden.

YORK

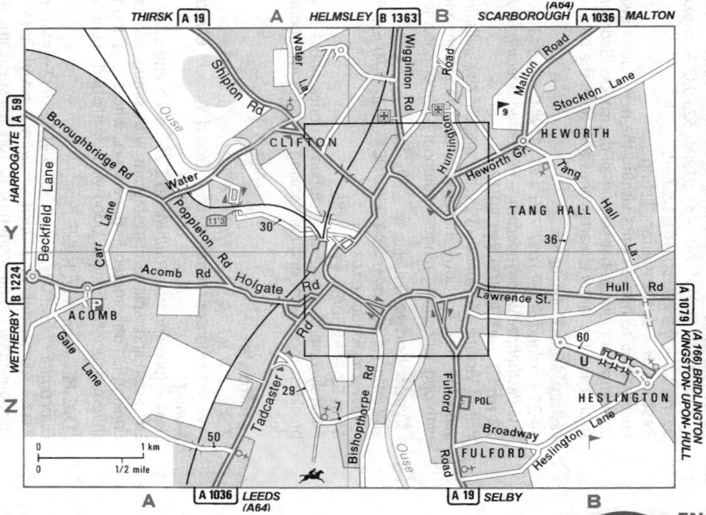

THIRSK A 19
HELMSLEY B 1363
(A64) SCARBOROUGH A 1036
MALTON
HARROGATE A 59
WETHERBY B 1224
A 1036 LEEDS (A64)
A 19 SELBY
A 1079
(A 166) BRIDLINGTON KINGSTON-UPON-HULL
CLIFTON
HEWORTH
TANG HALL
HESLINGTON
FULFORD
ACOMB
Shipton Rd
Wigginton Rd
Huntington Road
Malton Road
Stockton Lane
Boroughbridge Rd
Water La.
Water
Poppleton Rd
Acomb Rd
Holgate Rd
Beckfield Lane
Carr Lane
Gale Lane
Tadcaster Rd
Bishopthorpe Rd
Fulford Road
Broadway
Heslington Lane
Lawrence St.
Hull Rd
Hall La.
Tang
Heworth Gr.
Ouse
POL.
1 km
1/2 mile

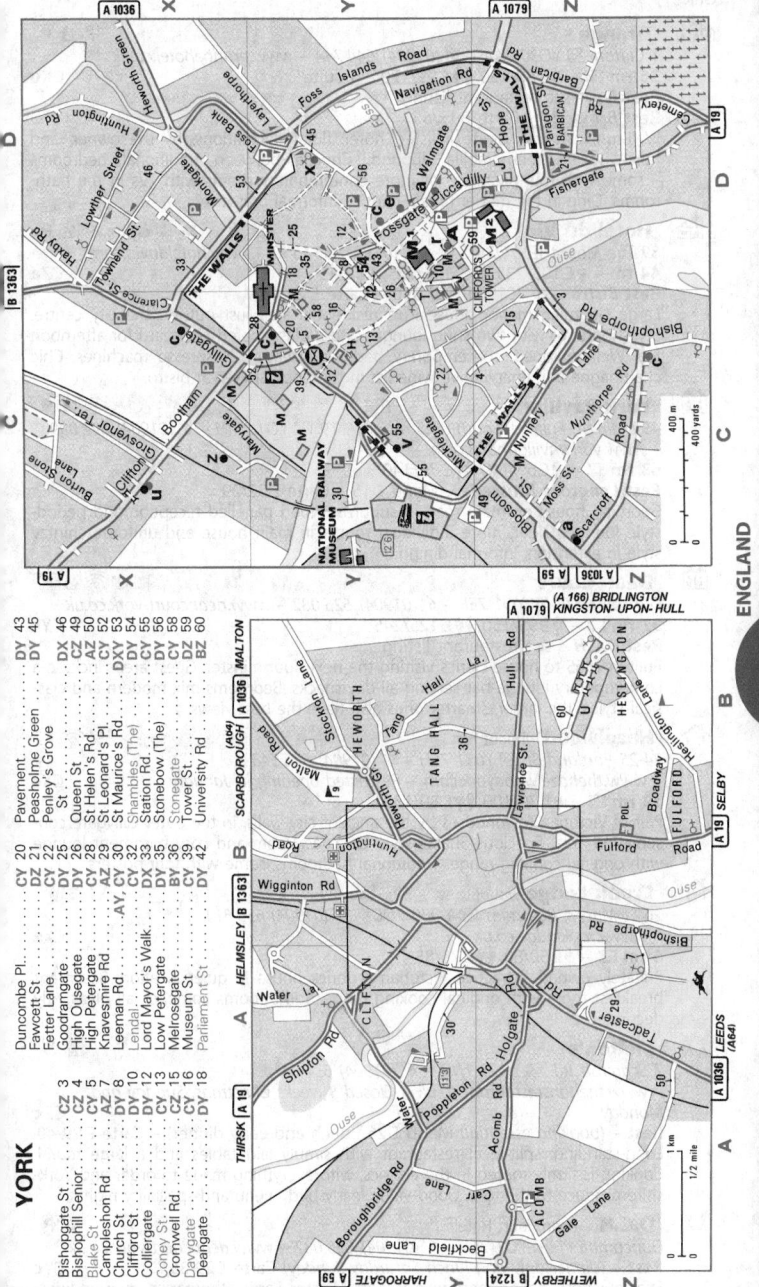

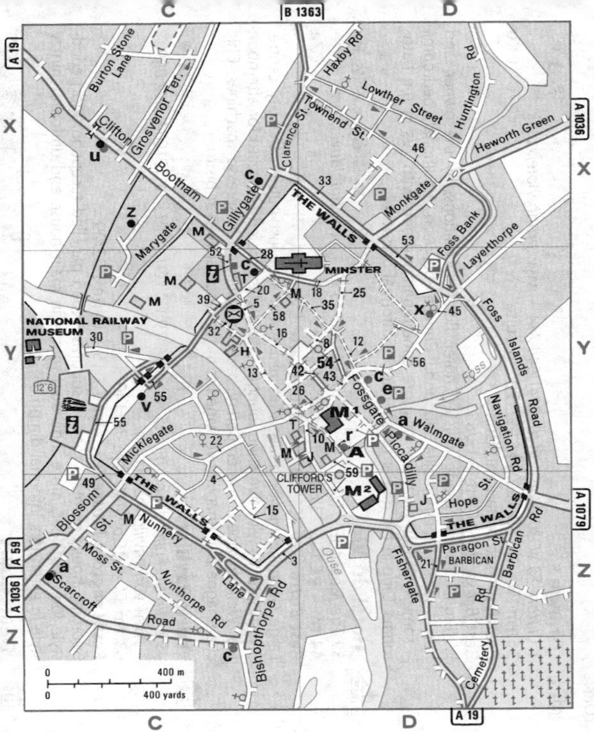

B 1363
A 19
A 1036
A 1079
A 59
NATIONAL RAILWAY MUSEUM
MINSTER
THE WALLS
CLIFFORD'S TOWER
BARBICAN
Clifton
Burton Stone Lane
Grosvenor Ter.
Bootham
Marygate
Gillygate
Clarence St.
Haxby Rd
Lowther Street
Townend St.
Huntington Rd
Heworth Green
Monkgate
Foss Bank
Layerthorpe
Foss Islands Road
Navigation Rd
Foss
Fossgate
Walmgate
Piccadilly
Hope St.
Paragon St.
Barbican Rd
Fishergate
Cemetery Rd
Micklegate
Blossom St.
Nunnery Lane
Moss St.
Scarcroft Road
Nunthorpe Rd
Bishopthorpe Rd
Ouse
400 m
400 yards

Grange
1 Clifton ✉ YO30 6AA – ✆ (01904) 644 744 – www.grangehotel.co.uk
36 rm – †£ 89/150 ††£ 99/170 – 1 suite CX**u**
Rest *Ivy* – see restaurant listing
Rest *Brasserie* – Carte £ 13/55
Well-run, classical, Grade II listed hotel; floral decorations, by the owner, and horse racing memorabilia abound. Choose between traditional bedrooms – some with four-posters – or more contemporary rooms with TVs in the bathrooms. Dine in the modern restaurant or informal brasserie.

Hotel du Vin rm,
89 The Mount ✉ YO24 1AX – ✆ (01904) 557 350 – www.hotelduvin.com
44 rm – †£ 105/225 ††£ 105/225, £ 15 CZ**a**
Rest *Bistro* – ✆ (01904) 567 350 – Carte £ 23/43
Large Georgian manor house in a residential area just outside the city centre. Stylish interior with two snug lounges and a glass-roofed courtyard for afternoon tea. Well-equipped, contemporary bedrooms feature Nespresso machines. Chic champagne bar; imaginative wine list in the popular French bistro.

York Pavilion rm,
45 Main St, Fulford, South : 1.5 mi on A 19 ✉ YO10 4PJ – ✆ (01904) 622 099 – www.yorkpavilionhotel.com
63 rm – †£ 69/140 ††£ 79/140
Rest *Langtons Brasserie* – Menu £ 15 – Carte £ 22/29
Georgian house on main road in suburbs. Wood panelled reception and period-style lounge. Older, more individual rooms in main house and uniform, chintzy style in extension. Informal dining.

Dean Court
Duncombe Pl ✉ YO1 7EF – ✆ (01904) 625 082 – www.deancourt-york.co.uk
37 rm – †£ 95/150 ††£ 125/245 CY**c**
Rest *D.C.H* – see restaurant listing
Built in 1865 to house clerics visiting the next door minster. Guest areas include a contemporary lounge-bar serving all-day snacks. Bedrooms mix modern and classical styles; the larger, smarter ones also have the best views.

Hazelwood without rest
24-25 Portland St ✉ Y031 7EH – ✆ (01904) 626 548 – www.thehazelwoodyork.com – Restricted opening in January CX**c**
12 rm – †£ 70/100 ††£ 80/135
Pair of Victorian townhouses by the ancient city walls, in the outer Gillygate conservation area. Spacious Shaker-style breakfast room and cosy basement lounge with original cooking range. Traditional bedrooms; some with four-posters.

Crook Lodge without rest
26 St Mary's, Bootham ✉ YO30 7DD – ✆ (01904) 655 614 – www.crooklodge.co.uk CX**z**
6 rm – †£ 50/80 ††£ 75/85
Privately owned, attractive Victorian redbrick house in quiet location. Basement breakfast room with original cooking range. Some rooms compact, all pleasantly decorated.

Melton's
7 Scarcroft Rd ✉ YO23 1ND – ✆ (01904) 634 341 – www.meltonsrestaurant.co.uk – Closed 3 weeks Christmas, Sunday and Monday CZ**c**
Rest – *(booking essential)* Menu £ 26 (lunch and early dinner) – Carte £ 29/40
Long-standing, split-level restaurant with simply laid tables and a large mural. Cooking is firmly rooted in the classics, with everything made to order and Yorkshire produce to the fore. Good value 'early bird' menu and speciality nights.

D.C.H – Dean Court Hotel
Duncombe Pl ✉ YO1 7EF – ✆ (01904) 625 082 – www.deancourt-york.co.uk
Rest – *(dinner only and lunch Saturday-Sunday)* Carte £ 29/35 CY**c**
Spacious hotel dining room next to York Minster. Large lithographs, modern lighting and stylish tableware catch the eye. Tasty, modern cooking uses plenty of local produce: the rib of beef for two, carved at the table, is a highlight.

ENGLAND

Ivy – Grange Hotel
1 Clifton ✉ YO30 6AA – ✆ (01904) 644 744 – www.grangehotel.co.uk – Closed Sunday dinner CX**u**
Rest – Carte £ 15/45
Bright, three-roomed restaurant with bold artwork and colourful murals, set in a keenly run hotel. The classically based British menu relies on local produce and offers ambitious dishes with a modern edge; grills are a feature.

Blue Bicycle with rm
34 Fossgate ✉ YO1 9TA – ✆ (01904) 673 990 – www.thebluebicycle.com – Closed 24-26 December, 1-7 January and lunch 27 December DY**e**
6 rm – £ 145/175 £ 145/175
Rest – *(dinner only and lunch Thursday-Sunday and December) (booking essential)* Carte £ 29/45
Split-level restaurant with Mediterranean-style dining room and cosy bar. Menus offer modern classics: some simple, some more elaborate in style. Smart, studio style bedrooms in rear mews, each with a kitchen; create your own breakfast from the ingredients provided.

Le Langhe
Peasholme Grn ✉ YO1 7PW – ✆ (01904) 622 584 – www.lelanghe.co.uk – Closed first 2 weeks January, 25-27 December, 31 March-1 April, Sunday and bank holidays DY**x**
Rest – *(lunch only and dinner Friday-Saturday) (booking advisable)*
Menu £ 23/38 – Carte dinner approx. £ 33
Well-established eatery consisting of an upmarket deli – selling imported Italian produce and a great array of wines – and a small dining room and terrace offering an extensive selection of fresh, unfussy Italian dishes, including homemade pasta and gelato. Formal upstairs dining room open Fri and Sat.

Melton's Too
25 Walmgate ✉ YO1 9TX – ✆ (01904) 629 222 – www.meltonstoo.co.uk – Closed 25-26 December, 1 January and dinner 24 and 31 December
Rest – Menu £ 13 (lunch and early dinner) – Carte £ 19/26 DY**a**
Café-bistro 'descendant' of Melton's restaurant. Located in former saddlers shop with oak beams and exposed brick walls. Good value eclectic dishes, with tapas a speciality.

at Newton-on-Ouse Northwest : 8 mi by A 19 - AY

Dawnay Arms
✉ YO30 2BR – ✆ (01347) 848 345 – www.thedawnayatnewton.co.uk – Closed first week January, Sunday dinner and Monday except bank holidays
Rest – Carte £ 25/43
Handsome whitewashed pub with stone floors, low beams, open fires and country art. Delightful dining room has views over the terrace and garden to the river. Hearty pub classics at lunch; more complex dinners. Local game plays a big part.

ZENNOR – Cornwall – 503 D33 1 A3

London 289 mi – Camborne 17 mi – Saint Austell 45 mi – Falmouth 33 mi

Gurnard's Head with rm
Treen, West : 1.5 mi on B 3306 ✉ TR26 3DE – ✆ (01736) 796 928 – www.gurnardshead.co.uk – Closed 24-25 December and 4 days early January
7 rm – £ 85/130 £ 100/170
Rest – *(booking advisable)* Menu £ 15 (lunch) – Carte £ 25/33
Remotely located, dog-friendly pub, with stone floors, shabby-chic décor, blazing fires and a relaxed, cosy feel. Menus rely on regional and foraged produce, and the wine list offers some interesting choices by the glass. Comfortable beds feature good quality linen and colourful throws.

ENGLAND

Scotland

ABERDEEN Aberdeen City – 501 K12 – pop. 165 968 [illegible]

Edinburgh 126 mi – London 528 mi – Dundee 65 mi – Dunfermline 12 mi

Aberdeen Airport, Dyce : 6 (0844) 481 6666, NW : 7 mi by A 96 X

to Shetland Islands (Lerwick) and to Orkney Islands (Stromness) (P and O Scottish Ferries) [illegible] daily

23 Union St, 6 (01224) [illegible] 28, www.aberdeen-grampian.com

Hazlehead, Hazlehead Park, 6 (01224) 32 18 30

Royal Aberdeen, Bridge of Don, Links Rd, 6 (01224) 702 571

[illegible] Rd, 6 (01224) 87 13 86

[illegible] – Old Aberdeen ★★ X – St Machar's Cathedral ★★ (West Front ★★ [illegible]) – Art Gallery ★★ (Macdonald Collection ★★) [illegible] M – Mercat Cross ★★ Y B – King's College Chapel ★ (Crown Spire ★★, medieval [illegible]) – Provost Skene's House ★ (painted ceilings ★★) [illegible] – Maritime Museum ★ [illegible] – Marischal College ★ Y U

[illegible] Balgownie ★, by Don St X. S : Deeside ★★ – Crathes [illegible] Gardens ★★ [illegible] 16 mi by A 93 X – Dunnottar Castle ★★ [illegible] 18 mi by A 90 – Pitmedden Garden ★★, [illegible] 14 mi by A 90 on B 999 X – Castle Fraser ★ (exterior ★★) AC, W : 16 mi by A 944 X – Fyvie Castle ★ [illegible] on A 947

Marcliffe H. and Spa

North Deeside Rd AB15 9YA – 6 (01224) 861 000 – www.marcliffe.com

41 rm – [illegible] 150/380 [illegible] 160/380 – 2 suites

Rest Conservatory – Carte [illegible]

Professionally run, modern country house in 11 acres of mature woodland. Traditionally styled bedrooms have antique furnishings and extensive facilities. Good selection of malts and afternoon tea in the comfy bar. Conservatory dining room with an open kitchen and a classic menu; steaks are a highlight.

Malmaison

49-53 Queens Rd AB15 4YP – 6 (01224) 327 370 – www.malmaison.com

79 rm – [illegible] – [illegible] 15

Rest Brasserie – Menu £ 18 (lunch) – Carte £ 20/41

In a smart city suburb and built around a period property, now the height of urban chic. Black, slate-floored reception adorned with bagpipes and kilts, stylish bar with a whisky cellar. Funky, modern bedrooms have atmospheric lighting. High-ceilinged brasserie serves modern dishes, with steaks a speciality.

The Marcliffe

[illegible] Langstane Pl [illegible] – 6 (01224) 212 123 – www.thebauhaus.co.uk

39 rm [illegible] 35/115 [illegible] 65/150 – 1 suite

Rest – Menu £ 28 (lunch) – Carte dinner £ 21/28

Modern hotel just off the main street, its dark frontage and minimalist, [illegible] famous school of design. Quality fittings, stylish [illegible] rooms with crisp, clean lines and uncluttered feel – [illegible] restaurant [illegible] modern [illegible]

[illegible]

[illegible] AB15 [illegible] – 6 (01224) 323 505 – [illegible]

[illegible]

[illegible] 105/170 [illegible] – Rest – Carte £ 18/[illegible]

Extended Edwardian style hotel in leafy suburb, a good choice for the business traveller. Warm and friendly, with an up-to-date interior. Bedrooms are well kept and bright; those on the top floor are the largest and some have cityscape views. Comfortable dining room serving tried and tested Scottish classics.

Fusion

10 North Silver St [illegible] AB10 1RL – 6 (01224) 652 959 – www.fusionbarbistro.com

– Closed 1-4 January, Sunday and Monday

Rest – Menu £ 21/28

Modernised granite townhouse featuring a light, airy bar with striking lime green furniture and a more intimate mezzanine restaurant. Grazing and grill served at lunch and in the bar in the evening; concise set price restaurant dinner [illegible]

ABERDEEN – Aberdeen City – 501 N12 – pop. 165 568 Scotland 28 D1

Edinburgh 126 mi – London 528 mi – Dundee 65 mi – Dunfermline 112 mi

Aberdeen Airport, Dyce : ✆ (0844) 481 6666, NW : 7 mi by A 96 X

to Shetland Islands (Lerwick) and via Orkney Islands (Stromness) (P and O Scottish Ferries) 1-2 daily

23 Union St, ✆ (01224) 28 88 28, www.aberdeen-grampian.com

Hazelhead, Hazelhead Park, ✆ (01224) 32 18 30

Royal Aberdeen, Bridge of Don, Links Rd, ✆ (01224) 70 25 71

Balnagask, St Fitticks Rd, ✆ (01224) 87 12 86

City★★ - Old Aberdeen★★ X – St Machar's Cathedral★★ (West Front★★★, Heraldic Ceiling★★★) X **A** – Art Gallery★★ (Macdonald Collection★★) Y **M** – Mercat Cross★★ Y **B** – King's College Chapel★ (Crown Spire★★★, medieval fittings★★★) X **D** – Provost Skene's House★ (painted ceilings★★) Y **E** – Maritime Museum★ Z **M1** – Marischal College★ Y **U**

Brig o' Balgownie★, by Don St X. SW : Deeside★★ - Crathes Castle★★ (Gardens★★★) **AC**, SW : 16 mi by A 93 X – Dunnottar Castle★★ **AC** (site★★★), S : 18 mi by A 90 X – Pitmedden Garden★★, N : 14 mi by A 90 on B 999 X – Castle Fraser★ (exterior★★) **AC**, W : 16 mi by A 944 X - Fyvie Castle★, NW : 26.5 mi on A 947

Marcliffe H. and Spa
rest, AC rest, P

North Deeside Rd ✉ AB15 9YA – ✆ (01224) 861 000 – www.marcliffe.com Xr

41 rm ☕ – 👤£ 150/360 👥£ 160/360 – 2 suites

Rest *Conservatory* – Carte £ 34/85 **s**

Professionally run, modern country house in 11 acres of mature woodland. Traditionally styled bedrooms have antique furnishings and extensive facilities. Good selection of malts and afternoon tea in the comfy bar. Conservatory dining room with an open kitchen and a classic menu; steaks are a highlight.

Malmaison
AC rest, P

49-53 Queens Rd ✉ AB15 4YP – ✆ (01224) 327 370 – www.malmaison.com Xv

79 rm – 👤£ 99/219 👥£ 119/289, ☕ £ 15

Rest *Brasserie* – Menu £ 14 (lunch) – Carte £ 26/41

In a smart city suburb and built around a period property; now the height of urban chic. Black, slate-floored reception adorned with bagpipes and kilts; stylish bar with a whisky cellar. Funky, modern bedrooms have atmospheric lighting. High-ceilinged brasserie serves modern dishes, with steaks a speciality.

bauhaus
AC rest,

52-60 Langstane Pl. ✉ AB11 6EN – ✆ (01224) 212 122 – www.thebauhaus.co.uk Zr

39 rm ☕ – 👤£ 85/115 👥£ 85/150 – 1 suite

Rest – Menu £ 28 (lunch) – Carte dinner £ 22/28

Modern hotel just off the main street, its functional, minimalist style in keeping with the Bauhaus school of design. Trendy lounge; stylish, colour-coded bedrooms with sharp, clean lines and uncluttered feel – Gropius and Kandinsky are the best. First-floor restaurant offers a menu of modern classics.

Atholl
rm, P

54 King's Gate ✉ AB15 4YN – ✆ (01224) 323 505 – www.atholl-aberdeen.co.uk – Closed 1 January Xs

34 rm ☕ – 👤£ 105/140 👥£ 140/155 **Rest** – Carte £ 18/35

Extended baronial-style hotel in a leafy suburb: a good choice for the business traveller. Warm and friendly, with an up-to-date interior. Bedrooms are well-kept and bright; those on the top floor are the largest and some have cityscape views. Comfortable dining room serving tried-and-tested Scottish classics.

XX Fusion
AC

10 North Silver St ✉ AB10 1RL – ✆ (01224) 652 959 – www.fusionbarbistro.com – Closed 1-4 January, Sunday and Monday Zc

Rest – Menu £ 13/28

Modernised granite townhouse featuring a light, airy bar with striking lime green furniture and a more intimate mezzanine restaurant. Grazing and grill served at lunch and in the bar in the evening; concise set price restaurant dinner menu.

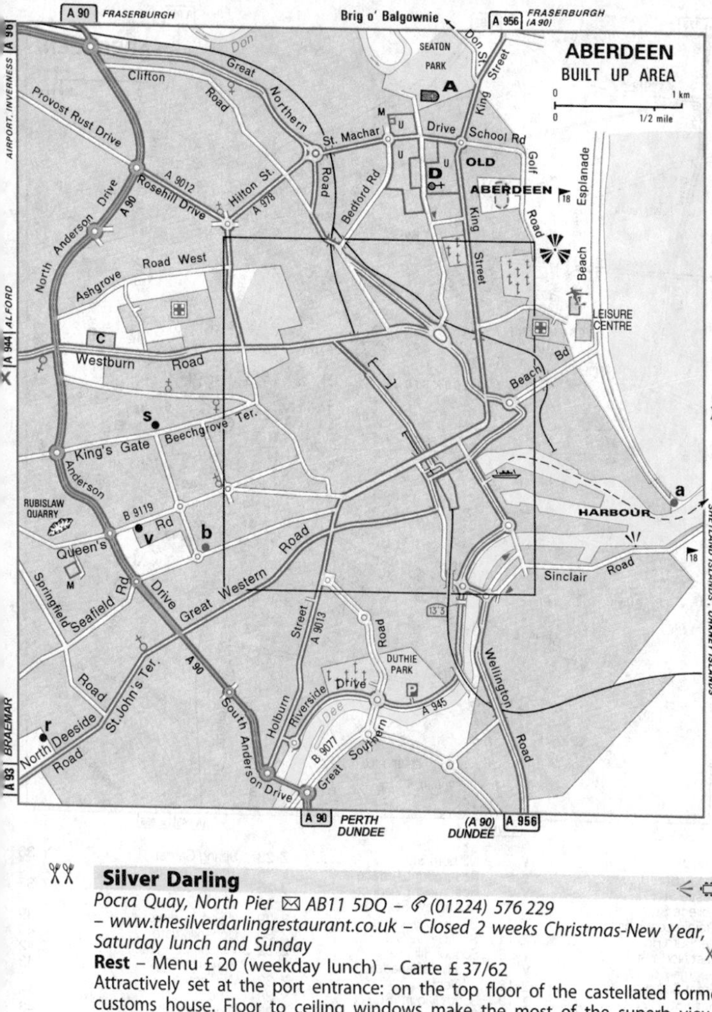

Silver Darling

Pocra Quay, North Pier ✉ *AB11 5DQ* – ✆ *(01224) 576 229*
– *www.thesilverdarlingrestaurant.co.uk* – *Closed 2 weeks Christmas-New Year, Saturday lunch and Sunday* X**a**

Rest – Menu £ 20 (weekday lunch) – Carte £ 37/62

Attractively set at the port entrance: on the top floor of the castellated former customs house. Floor to ceiling windows make the most of the superb views. Neatly presented, classical dishes; excellent quality seafood is a highlight.

Stella

28 Adelphi ✉ *AB11 5BL* – ✆ *(01224) 211 414* – *www.wearebeetroot.co.uk*
– *Closed Sunday* Z**s**

Rest – Menu £ 13/40

Cosy, intimate bistro hidden away down a side street, with simple, bright décor and a neighbourhood feel. Seasonally changing menus focus on quality ingredients; original, modern dishes, with fish a speciality.

Rendezvous at Nargile

106-108 Forest Ave ✉ *AB15 4UP* – ✆ *(01224) 323 700*
– *www.rendezvousatnargile.co.uk* – *Closed 25-26 December and 1-2 January*

Rest – Menu £ 16 (lunch and early dinner) – Carte £ 21/34 X**b**

Bright, refreshing neighbourhood restaurant set opposite the Rendezvous Gallery. All-day menus offer plenty of choice, with cooking influenced by the Mediterranean and in particular, Turkey. Banquet meals are a highlight. Cheerful service.

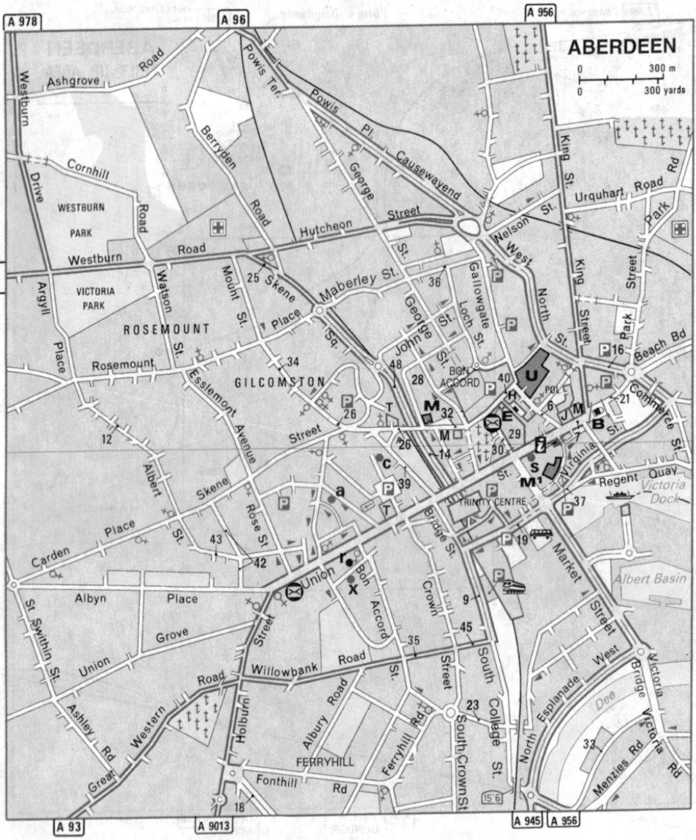

Bon Accord Centre	Y		Millburn St	Z	23	Spring Garden	Y	36
Broad St	Y	6	Rosemount Terrace	Y	25	Trinity Centre	Z	
Castle St	Y	7	Rosemount Viaduct	Y	26	Trinity Quay	Z	37
College St	Z	9	St Andrew St	Y	28	Union St	Z	
Craigie Loanings	Y	12	St Nicholas Centre	Y	29	Union Terrace	Z	39
Denburn Rd	YZ	14	St Nicholas St	YZ	30	Upperkirkgate	Y	40
East North St	Y	16	School Hill	YZ	32	Victoria St	Z	42
George St	Y		South Esplanade West	Z	33	Waverley Pl	Z	43
Great Southern Rd	Z	18	South Mount St	Y	34	Wellington Pl	Z	45
Guild St	Z	19	Springbank Terrace	Z	35	Woolmanhill	Y	48
Justice St	Y	21						

Yatai (N)

53 Langstane Pl ✉ AB11 6EN – ✆ (01224) 592 355 – www.yatai.co.uk – Closed 25-26 December, 1-2 January, Sunday and Monday **Zx**

Rest – *(booking advisable)* Carte £ 15/50

Atmospheric Japanese restaurant in the style of a laid-back izakaya. The ground floor has a wooden counter and a robata grill; upstairs is airy and intimate. Menus offer tasty, authentic dishes – the sushi, sashimi and maki are highlights.

Yorokobi by CJ

51 Huntly St ✉ AB10 1TH – ✆ (01224) 566 002 – www.yorokobibycj.co.uk – Closed 23-31 December, 1-2 January, 22-28 July and Sunday **Za**

Rest – *(booking advisable)* Carte £ 15/45

Popular Japanese restaurant with a name meaning 'joyous bliss'; C is for chef and J is for Jang, who takes on that role. Flavourful, authentic, good value Japanese and Korean dishes; try one of the sizzling platters or a Korean pot dish.

ABERFELDY – Perth and Kinross – 501 I14 – pop. 1 895 28 C2

Edinburgh 76 mi – Glasgow 78 mi – Dundee 57 mi – Paisley 87 mi

at Fortingall West : 8 mi by B 846 on Fortingall rd

Fortingall

PH15 2NQ – (01887) 830 367 – www.fortingall.com
10 rm – £ 100/120 £ 170/220
Rest – *(bar lunch Monday-Saturday)* Menu £ 35
Stylish Arts and Crafts house on a tranquil private estate, boasting lovely country views. Delightful interior with a snug, open-fired bar and two cosy sitting rooms filled with Scottish country knick-knacks. Bedrooms are modern but in keeping with the building's age. Traditional menu in the huge restaurant.

ABRIACHAN – Highland – 501 G11 – pop. 120 30 C2

Edinburgh 567 mi – London 167 mi – Dundee 148 mi – Dunfermline 153 mi

Loch Ness Lodge without rest

Brachla, on A 82 IV3 8LA – (01456) 459 469 – www.loch-ness-lodge.com – Closed December-January
7 rm – £ 95/140 £ 165/330
Personally run, modern country house, set in an elevated spot in 18 acres of immaculately kept grounds, overlooking Loch Ness. A classic-contemporary style features throughout. Spacious bedrooms have a high level of facilities and come with extras such as sherry. Afternoon tea is served on arrival.

ACHILTIBUIE – Highland – 501 D9 30 C1

Edinburgh 243 mi – Inverness 84 mi – Ullapool 25 mi

Summer Isles

IV26 2YG – (01854) 622 282 – www.summerisleshotel.com – Closed November-March
13 rm – £ 115/175 £ 155/310 – 3 suites
Rest *Summer Isles (Bar)* – see restaurant listing
Rest – *(booking essential) (set menu only)* Menu £ 58
Remotely located hotel, with magnificent views over the eponymous islands. Individually styled, comfortable bedrooms are split between main house and various converted outbuildings. Pleasant restaurant, with polished, well-set tables offers a daily set menu of modern dishes, with the emphasis on seafood.

Summer Isles (Bar) – Summer Isles Hotel

IV26 2YG – (01854) 622 282 – www.summerisleshotel.com – Closed November-March
Rest – *(bookings not accepted)* Carte £ 18/45
19C former crofters' bar with two snug rooms, a large garden and a small terrace with glorious views. Concise, daily menus have a strong seafood base. Baguettes, salads and platters are supplemented by blackboard specials in the evening.

ALTNAHARRA – Highland – 501 G9 – Lairg Scotland 30 C1

Edinburgh 223 mi – London 627 mi – Inverness 68 mi

Ben Loyal★★, N : 10 mi by A 836 – Ben Hope★ (★★★) NW : 14 m

Altnaharra

IV27 4UE – (01549) 411 222 – www.altnaharra.com – Closed November-January
14 rm – £ 65 £ 150 **Rest** – *(bar lunch)* Menu £ 32
Extended former drovers' inn dating back to the 1600s, with a cosy, homely interior and good-sized bedrooms with tartan décor. The small locals bar serves simple lunches; while the open-fired restaurant offers a classical menu. The nearby estate offers shooting, fishing and stalking.

ALYTH – Perth and Kinross – 501 J14 – pop. 2 301 28 C2

Edinburgh 63 mi – Aberdeen 69 mi – Dundee 16 mi – Perth 21 mi

Pitcrocknie, (01828) 63 22 68

SCOTLAND

Tigh Na Leigh
22-24 Airlie St ✉ PH11 8AJ – ✆ (01828) 632 372 – www.tighnaleigh.co.uk – Closed 2 December-7 February
5 rm – 🚹£ 52 🚹🚹£ 98/124 **Rest** – *(dinner only) (residents only)* Menu £ 25
Imposing Victorian house run in a professional yet relaxed manner. Surprisingly modern interior with spacious, inviting guest areas. Contemporary bedrooms boast feature beds and great bathrooms; some have spa baths. The superb kitchen garden informs the unfussy modern menu; lovely garden view while dining.

ANNAN – Dumfries and Galloway – pop. 8 389 26 C3

Edinburgh 79 mi – London 321 mi – Glasgow 84 mi – Liverpool 141 mi

Del Amitri
95a High St ✉ DG12 6DJ – ✆ (01461) 201 999 – www.del-amitri.co.uk – Closed 1-14 November, 1-7 January and Monday
Rest – *(dinner only and Sunday lunch)* Carte £ 23/29
Above a fish and chip shop on the main street. Dark walls provide an intimate feel and tables are elegantly laid. Interesting, intricate dishes are skilfully prepared and packed with local produce: the chef has close ties with his suppliers.

ANNBANK – South Ayrshire – 501 G17 – pop. 854 25 B2

Edinburgh 84 mi – Ayr 6 mi – Dumfries 54 mi – Paisley 34 mi

Enterkine House
Southeast : 0.5 mi on B 742 (Coylton rd) ✉ KA6 5AL – ✆ (01292) 520 580 – www.enterkine.com
15 rm – 🚹£ 70/120 🚹🚹£ 80/195 – 1 suite
Rest – *(booking essential)* Menu £ 17/35
Country house surrounded by 350 acres of countryside; originally built for the MacKay family in the 1930s and now a popular wedding venue. Spacious, individually furnished bedrooms; most with estate views. The Bothy is a honeymooners' cottage in the garden. Bright restaurant serves modern dishes.

SCOTLAND

ANSTRUTHER – Fife – 501 L15 – pop. 3 442 Scotland 28 D2

Edinburgh 46 mi – Dundee 23 mi – Dunfermline 34 mi
Harbourhead, ✆ (01333) 31 10 73, www.visitscotland.com
Marsfield Shore Rd, ✆ (01333) 31 09 56
Scottish Fisheries Museum★★ **AC**
The East Neuk★★ – Crail★★ (Old Centre★★, Upper Crail★) NE : 4 mi by A 917. Kellie Castle★ **AC**, NW : 7 mi by B 9171, B 942 and A 917

Spindrift
Pittenweem Rd ✉ KY10 3DT – ✆ (01333) 310 573 – www.thespindrift.co.uk – Closed January and 24-26 December
8 rm – 🚹£ 45/60 🚹🚹£ 66/90 **Rest** – Menu £ 25
Detached Victorian house on the edge of the village, originally owned by a tea clipper captain. Comfy lounge with honesty bar. Cosy, individually furnished bedrooms, some with distant sea views – opt for the top floor Captain's Cabin. Cooking relies on local produce, with seafood from East Neuk to the fore.

APPLECROSS – Highland – 501 C11 29 B2

Edinburgh 233 mi – London 607 mi – Glasgow 210 mi – Liverpool 427 mi

Applecross Walled Garden
North : 0.5 mi ✉ IV54 8ND – ✆ (01520) 744 440 – www.applecrossgarden.co.uk – Closed November-January
Rest – Carte £ 17/31
Set in a former potting shed in a 17C walled garden; where much of the produce is grown. Simple interior with a small counter displaying homemade cakes. Light lunches and daily specials; original, North African influenced dishes at dinner.

Applecross Inn with rm

Shore St ✉ IV54 8LR – ☎ (01520) 744 262 – www.applecross.uk.com – Closed 25 December and 1 January

7 rm ☕ – 🚹£ 75/85 🚹🚹£ 130/140 **Rest** – *(booking essential)* Carte £ 19/42

Unpretentious inn with friendly service and a bustling atmosphere; take the scenic route over the hair-raising, single-track Bealach na Ba, with its stunning views and hairpin bends to reach it. Dine on the freshest of seafood, often caught within sight of the door. Simple bedrooms have marvellous sea views.

ARBROATH – Angus – 501 M14 – pop. 22 785 — 28 D2

Edinburgh 72 mi – Dundee 17 mi – Montrose 12 mi

Old Vicarage without rest

2 Seaton Rd, Northeast : 0.75 mi by A 92 and Hayshead Rd ✉ DD11 5DX – ☎ (01241) 430 475 – www.theoldvicaragebandb.co.uk

3 rm ☕ – 🚹£ 60/70 🚹🚹£ 80/90

Detached 19C house with curios and antiques filling every room – look out for the lovely grandfather clock. Immaculately kept bedrooms have a Victorian feel; some have abbey views. Glorious buffet breakfasts include smokies from the quay.

ARCHIESTOWN – Moray – 501 K11 — 28 C1

Edinburgh 194 mi – Aberdeen 62 mi – Inverness 49 mi

Archiestown

The Square ✉ AB38 7QL – ☎ (01340) 810 218 – www.archiestownhotel.co.uk – Closed 2 January-10 February and 23-29 December

11 rm ☕ – 🚹£ 90 🚹🚹£ 120/200 **Rest** – Menu £ 15/30

Welcoming hotel overlooking the square in a planned Victorian village; ideal for fishermen and visitors to the Whisky Trail. Spacious, comfy sitting rooms with open fires. Classically styled bedrooms; many have country views. Intimate restaurant with feature wall serves traditional menu with Scottish touches.

ARDCHATTAN – Argyll and Bute — 27 B2

Edinburgh 123 mi – London 494 mi – Glasgow 98 mi – Belfast 146 mi

Blarcreen House

East : 1 mi past Ardchattan Priory and gardens on Bonawe rd ✉ PA37 1RG – ☎ (01631) 750 272 – www.blarcreenhouse.com – Closed Christmas and New Year

3 rm ☕ – 🚹£ 70/80 🚹🚹£ 100/110 **Rest** – Menu £ 30

Friendly Victorian former farmhouse set in a tranquil location down a single track and boasting superb views over Loch Etive. Homely lounge and comfy bedrooms: two with four-posters and double-aspects; all with robes, fridges and fresh milk. Lovely dining room offers a daily menu of home-cooked dishes.

ARDHASAIG – Western Isles – 501 Z10 – see Lewis and Harris (Isle of)

ARDUAINE – Argyll and Bute – 501 D15 – ✉ Oban ▮ Scotland — 27 B2

Edinburgh 141 mi – Glasgow 105 mi – Paisley 98 mi – Greenock 105 mi

Loch Awe★★, E : 12 mi by A 816 and B 840

Loch Melfort

✉ PA34 4XG – ☎ (01852) 200 233 – www.lochmelfort.co.uk – Closed 2 weeks January and mid-week November-March

25 rm ☕ – 🚹£ 75/135 🚹🚹£ 90/268

Rest *Asknish Bay* – see restaurant listing

Rest *Chartroom II* – Carte £ 18/65

Large hotel next to the beautiful Arduaine Gardens, affording superb views out over the bay and Sound of Jura. Modern lounges with tartan/nautical themes. Bigger bedrooms in the main house; great outlook from private terraces in the wing. Simple, largely seafood menu in Chartroom II; more formal Asknish Bay.

SCOTLAND

XX **Asknish Bay** - Loch Melfort Hotel
✉ PA34 4XG – ✆ (01852) 200 233 – www.lochmelfort.co.uk – *Closed 2 weeks January and mid-week November-March*
Rest – *(dinner only)* Menu £ 40 – Carte £ 27/50
Formal hotel restaurant in a beautiful setting, with panoramic views of the bay. Menus focus on the freshest seafood available, with Loch Fyne langoustines, Islay scallops and Gigha halibut; carnivores are also well-catered for.

ARRAN (Isle of) – North Ayrshire – 501 E17 – pop. 5 058 ▌ Scotland 25 A2

Edinburgh 83 mi – London 414 mi – Glasgow 37 mi – Liverpool 234 mi
from Brodick to Ardrossan (Caledonian MacBrayne Ltd) 4-6 daily (55 mn) – from Lochranza to Kintyre Peninsula (Claonaig) (Caledonian MacBrayne Ltd) frequent services daily (30 mn)
Island★★ - Brodick Castle★★ **AC**

BRODICK – North Ayrshire – pop. 621 25 A2

Welcome Centre, ✆ (01770) 30 37 76, www.visitscotland.com
Brodick, ✆ (01770) 30 23 49
Machrie Bay, ✆ (01770) 85 02 32

Auchrannie rm,
Northwest : 0.75 mi by Shore Rd. ✉ KA27 8BZ – ✆ (01770) 302 234 – www.auchrannie.co.uk
64 rm – †£ 80/120 ††£ 99/239 – 2 suites
Rest *Eighteen69* – *(closed November-Easter, Sunday and Monday) (dinner only)* Carte £ 25/45
Rest *Brambles* – Carte £ 21/38
Rest *Cruize* – Carte £ 17/30
Mini resort hotel set in 96 acres and offering a good range of family orientated leisure facilities. Built in 1869, the old dower house boasts well-equipped, classical and contemporary bedrooms; family rooms are located in the resort house. Smart conservatory restaurant offers fine dining menu; Brambles serves seafood and grills; all-day Cruize is ideal for families.

Kilmichael Country House
Glen Cloy, West : 1 mi by Shore Rd, taking left turn opposite Golf Club
✉ KA27 8BY – ✆ (01770) 302 219 – www.kilmichael.com – *Closed November-Easter*
8 rm – †£ 78/98 ††£ 130/205
Rest – *(closed Monday and Tuesday) (dinner only) (bookings essential for non-residents) (set menu only)* Menu £ 45
Sympathetically restored 17C house - reputedly the oldest house on the Isle of Arran - delightfully located in a peaceful glen and surrounded by mountains. Comfy, antique-furnished bedrooms; those in the converted stable block offer a little more comfort and privacy. Daily changing four course menu of accomplished cooking served in a classically decorated dining room.

Douglas
✉ KA27 8AW – ✆ (01770) 302 968 – www.thedouglashotel.co.uk
21 rm – †£ 65/105 ††£ 75/220
Rest *Bistro* – *(bar lunch)* Carte £ 22/34
Stylish, modern hotel with attractive pink granite façade, set just past the ferry terminal. Spacious, light-filled bedrooms are decorated in a contemporary style; most have a sea view and room 202 has a large roof terrace. Informal, pubby bar. Smart bistro offers classical French dishes with a modern twist.

LAMLASH – North Ayrshire – pop. 1 010 – ✉ Brodick

Lamlash, ✆ (01770) 60 02 96

Glenisle
Shore Rd. ✉ KA27 8LY – ✆ (01770) 600 559 – www.glenislehotel.com
13 rm – †£ 80/83 ††£ 115/195 **Rest** – Carte £ 14/36
Attractive whitewashed Victorian property, formerly an inn, boasting views over the bay to Holy Island. Open-plan bar-lounge and small snug. Bright, airy bedrooms come in natural hues; one covers the whole top floor and has a roll-top bath. Rustic dining room with terrace offers fresh, simple, homely cooking.

SCOTLAND

LOCHRANZA - North Ayrshire

Apple Lodge

✉ KA27 8HJ – ✆ (01770) 830 229 – www.applelodgearran.co.uk – Closed 15 December-15 January

4 rm – †£ 50 ††£ 78 **Rest** – Menu £ 25

Former manse with attractive gardens, in a quiet hamlet surrounded by mountains. Traditionally decorated, comfortable and personally run, with many regular guests. Bedrooms have pleasant views; Apple Cottage is a self-contained garden suite. 3 course menu of classic, home-cooked dishes served by candlelight.

ASCOG - Argyll and Bute - **501** E16 - see Bute (Isle of)

AUCHENCAIRN - Dumfries and Galloway - **501** I19 **25** B3
- ✉ Castle Douglas

Edinburgh 94 mi - Dumfries 21 mi - Stranraer 60 mi

Balcary Mews without rest

Balcary Bay, Southeast : 2 mi on Balcary rd ✉ DG7 1QZ – ✆ (01556) 640 276 – www.balcarymews.co.uk – Closed mid-December to mid-January

3 rm – †£ 60/80 ††£ 80/90

Former mews for the neighbouring country house, boasting superb views over Balcary Bay and the Solway Firth. Lovely garden with a gate down to the shore. Neat sun lounge and traditional bedrooms; all have views. Homemade bread and jam feature at breakfast.

AUCHTERARDER - Perth and Kinross - **501** I15 - **pop. 3 945** **28** C2
Scotland

Edinburgh 55 mi - London 438 mi - Aberdeen 102 mi - Glasgow 46 mi

18 Ochil Rd, ✆ (01764) 66 28 04

9 Dunning, Rollo Park, ✆ (01764) 68 47 47

Tullibardine Chapel★, NW : 2 m

Gleneagles

Southwest : 2 mi by A 824 on A 823 ✉ PH3 1NF – ✆ (01764) 662 231 – www.gleneagles.com

232 rm – †£ 225/435 ††£ 225/435 – 16 suites

Rest *Andrew Fairlie at Gleneagles* ✿✿ – see restaurant listing

Rest *Strathearn* – ✆ (01764) 694 270 – Menu £ 60

Rest *Deseo* – ✆ (01764) 694 270 *(closed dinner 31 December)* Carte £ 23/82

World-famous resort hotel with renowned championship golf course. Excellent leisure facilities include state-of-the-art spa, popular equestrian centre and gun-dog school. Majestic art deco styling, elegant interior and luxurious bedrooms. Strathearn offers classical menu and superb estate views. All-day Deseo serves Mediterranean-influenced dishes, including tapas.

Cairn (N)

Orchill Rd, West : 0.5 mi by Townhead Rd and Western Rd ✉ PH3 1LX – ✆ (01764) 662 634 – www.cairnlodge.co.uk

14 rm – †£ 99/225 ††£ 99/225

Rest *Grill Room* – see restaurant listing

Glitzy lodge with pleasant gardens and a monochrome theme; the younger sister to Gleneagles. Large bar with tub chairs and an inner hall with a piano. Bedrooms are modern and stylish, with black ash furnishings and Nespresso machines.

Andrew Fairlie at Gleneagles - Gleneagles Hotel

✿✿

Southwest : 2 mi by A 824 on A 823 ✉ PH3 1NF – ✆ (01764) 694 267 – www.andrewfairlie.co.uk – Closed 5-30 January, 24-25 December and Sunday

Rest – *(dinner only)* Menu £ 95/125

Elegant restaurant hung with portraits of its famous chef. The à la carte focuses on refined French classics, with a signature dish of home-smoked lobster. The 8 course dégustation menu showcases dishes 'en miniature' and the Menu du Marché, the latest seasonal produce. Accomplished, carefully balanced cooking is coupled with professional, good-humoured service.

→ Home-smoked lobster, lime and herb butter. Roast loin of roe deer, dauphine potatoes and sauce grand veneur. Pineapple soufflé, coconut milk and rum ice cream.

SCOTLAND

Grill Room – Cairn Hotel

Orchill Rd, West : 0.5 mi by Townhead Rd and Western Rd ✉ PH3 1LX – ✆ (01764) 662 634 – www.cairnlodge.co.uk

Rest – Carte £ 21/64

Chic hotel restaurant with an elegant bar and a large dining room with boldly papered or studded leather walls, twisty chandeliers and sumptuous leather seating. Wide ranging menu of burgers, grills and steaks, alongside a tapas selection.

AVIEMORE – Highland – 501 I12 – pop. 2 397 Scotland 30 D3

Edinburgh 129 mi – Inverness 29 mi – Perth 85 mi

Grampian Rd, ✆ (08452) 25 51 21, www.visitcairngorms.com

Town★

The Cairngorms★★ (≤★★★) - ✳★★★ from Cairn Gorm, SE : 11 mi by B 970 – Landmark Visitor Centre (The Highlander★) **AC**, N : 7 mi by A 9 – Highland Wildlife Park★ **AC**, SW : 7 mi by A 9

Old Minister's Guest House

Rothiemurchus, Southeast : 1 mi on B 970 ✉ PH22 1QH – ✆ (01479) 812 181 – www.theoldministershouse.co.uk

5 rm – †£ 95/115 ††£ 100/140 **Rest** – Menu £ 30

Stone-built former manse dating from 1895, with unusual carved wooden animals and pretty gardens leading down to a river. Smart lounge with deep sofas and an honesty bar; spacious, well-appointed bedrooms. Home-cooked dinners use local ingredients – breakfast includes French toast and eggs Benedict.

SCOTLAND

AYR – South Ayrshire – 501 G17 – pop. 45 840 Scotland 25 A2

Edinburgh 82 mi – London 395 mi – Glasgow 36 mi – Belfast 69 mi

22 Sandgate, ✆ (01292) 29 03 00, www.visitscotland.com

18 Seafield, Doonfoot Rd, Belleisle Park, ✆ (01292) 44 12 58

18 Dalmilling, Westwood Ave, ✆ (01292) 26 38 93

9 Doon Valley, Patna, Hillside, ✆ (01292) 53 16 07

Alloway★ (Burns Cottage and Museum★ **AC**) S : 3 mi by B 7024 BZ. Culzean Castle★ **AC** (setting★★★, Oval Staircase★★) SW : 13 mi by A 719 BZ

Western House

Ayr Racecourse, Craigie Rd ✉ KA8 0HA – ✆ (01292) 294 990 – www.westernhousehotel.co.uk BZ**w**

48 rm – †£ 80/190 ††£ 80/190 – 1 suite

Rest *The Jockey Club* – Carte £ 22/32

Attractive country house designed by Lutyens and set on Ayr racecourse. Tastefully styled bedrooms are named after racecourses; those in the original house are the largest and most luxurious. Wood-panelled lounge/bar. Restaurant offers appealing menu of British classics based around Ayrshire ingredients.

No.26 The Crescent without rest

26 Bellevue Cres ✉ KA7 2DR – ✆ (01292) 287 329 – www.26crescent.co.uk – Closed 22-26 December BZ**c**

5 rm – †£ 45/77 ††£ 77/97

Well-run Victorian terraced house, displaying a pleasing mix of traditional features – such as original fireplaces – and smart, modern décor. Comfortable throughout, with individually furnished bedrooms; the best one has a four-poster. Cosy breakfast room; smoked haddock and poached eggs are a speciality.

Coila without rest

10 Holmston Rd ✉ KA7 3BB – ✆ (01292) 262 642 – www.coila.co.uk AY**u**

4 rm – †£ 35/60 ††£ 55/80

Comfortable, traditionally furnished Victorian house on the edge of town, proudly decorated with the owners' personal ornaments and family photos. Homely sitting room and well-kept bedrooms; those to the rear are quieter.

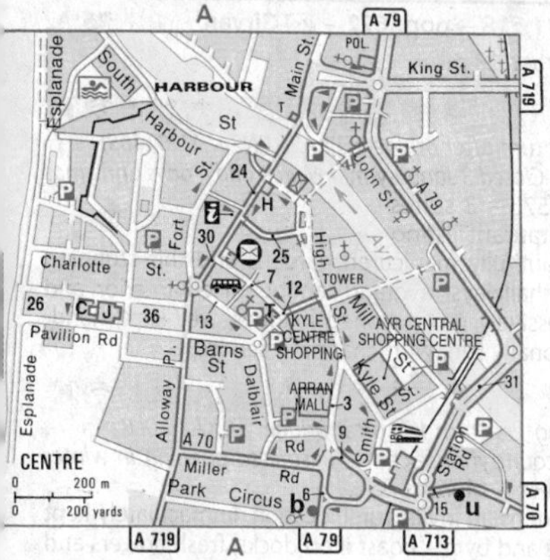

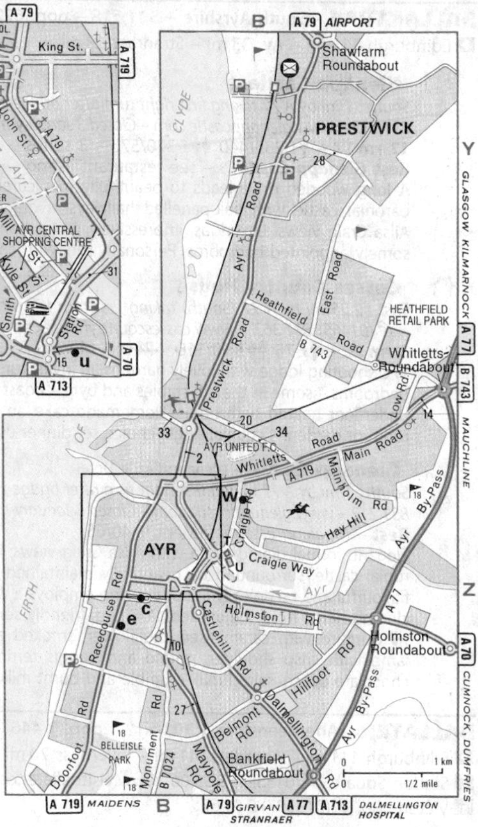

AYR AND PRESTWICK

The Beresford

22 Beresford Terr. ✉ *KA7 2EG – ✆ (01292) 280 820 – www.theberesfordayr.co.uk*

Rest – Menu £ 10 (lunch) – Carte £ 14/31 AY**b**

Start with a cocktail in the downstairs bar, before tucking into the likes of pizza, pasta, seafood or steak, followed by pastries and ice cream sundaes in the spacious, buzzing brasserie. The first floor is an art gallery during the week.

BACK – **Western Isles** – **501** B9 – **see Lewis and Harris (Isle of)**

BALLACHULISH – **Highland** – **501** E13 – **pop. 615** Scotland **30** C3

Edinburgh 117 mi – Inverness 80 mi – Kyle of Lochalsh 90 mi – Oban 38 mi

Loan sern, ✆ (01855) 81 18 66, www.glencoetourism.co.uk

Glen Coe★★, E : 6 mi by A 82

Ardno House without rest

Lettermore, Glencoe, West : 3.5 mi by A 82 on A 828 ✉ *PH49 4JD – ✆ (01855) 811 830 – www.ardnohouse.co.uk – Closed November-February*

4 rm – †£ 40/68 ††£ 70/84

Modern, spotlessly kept guesthouse in an elevated position, with a fine view of Loch Linnhe and the Morven Hills. Spacious, pine-furnished bedrooms named after Scottish clans and tartans. Traditional cooked breakfasts.

BALLANTRAE - South Ayrshire - 501 E18 - pop. 672 - ✉ Girvan 25 A2

Edinburgh 115 mi - Ayr 33 mi - Stranraer 18 mi

Glenapp Castle

South : 1 mi by A 77 taking first right turn after bridge ✉ KA26 0NZ - ✆ (01465) 831 212 - www.glenappcastle.com - Closed 3 January-mid-March and 4 days Christmas

17 rm - £ 235/440 £ 370/575 - 3 suites

Rest *Glenapp Castle* - see restaurant listing

A long wooded drive leads to beautifully manicured gardens and this stunning baronial castle with oak-panelled hallways, a grand, antique-filled interior and Ailsa Craig views. Luxurious, impressively proportioned lounges; well-kept, handsomely appointed bedrooms. Personally run, with charming service.

Cosses Country House

East : 2.25 mi by A 77 (South) taking first turn left after bridge ✉ KA26 0LR - ✆ (01465) 831 363 - www.cossescountryhouse.com - Restricted opening in winter

3 rm - £ 75 £ 90/110 **Rest** - Menu £ 35

17C shooting lodge with lovely gardens, in idyllic rural location. Immaculately kept bedrooms - some in the old stables and byre - boast iPod docks, fresh flowers and underfloor heated bathrooms. Homemade cake on arrival in the kitchen, dining room or garden. 4 course, single-choice set dinner uses local and garden produce.

Glenapp Castle - Glenapp Castle Hotel

South : 1 mi by A 77 taking first right turn after bridge ✉ KA26 0NZ - ✆ (01465) 831 212 - www.glenappcastle.com - Closed 3 January-mid-March and 4 days Christmas

Rest - *(booking essential)* Menu £ 40/65

Elegant, formal dining room with Ailsa Craig views; in a luxuriously furnished baronial castle, surrounded by beautifully maintained gardens. Confident, focused, flavourful and technically adept cooking employs a wealth of local ingredients, including herbs from the garden. Polished, friendly service.

→ Gurnard with caramelised cauliflower, smoked almonds and truffle. Pavé of lamb with crisp shoulder, potato and haggis terrine, and roasting juices. Dark chocolate délice, salted milk crumble and burnt milk ice cream.

SCOTLAND

BALLATER - Aberdeenshire - 501 K12 - pop. 1 446 28 C1

Edinburgh 111 mi - Aberdeen 41 mi - Inverness 70 mi - Perth 67 mi

Station Square, ✆ (013397) 5 53 06, www.visitballater.com

Victoria Rd, ✆ (013397) 5 55 67

Darroch Learg

Braemar Rd ✉ AB35 5UX - ✆ (013397) 55 443 - www.darrochlearg.co.uk - Closed last 3 weeks January and Christmas

12 rm - £ 95/160 £ 140/250

Rest *Conservatory* - see restaurant listing

Victorian country house affording superb views over the Dee Valley and the Grampians. Personally run by the second family generation, it boasts comfy, open-fired, antique-furnished lounges and traditional, individually designed bedrooms.

Auld Kirk without rest

Braemar Rd ✉ AB35 5RQ - ✆ (013397) 55 762 - www.theauldkirk.com - Closed Christmas

7 rm - £ 70 £ 95/105

Striking granite building - a church from 1870-1938; the bar-lounge still has the original stained glass windows. Bright, modern bedrooms with bold furnishings. Comprehensive breakfasts; the 'spirit of ecstasy' sculpture is a talking point!

Moorside House without rest

26 Braemar Rd ✉ AB35 5RL - ✆ (013397) 55 492 - www.moorsidehouse.co.uk - Closed October-Easter

9 rm - £ 40/45 £ 60/65

Traditional 19C former manse with a large garden, simple, homely bedrooms and a comfortable lounge filled with books about the local area. Original Victorian features include ornate cornicing and an attractive pine staircase. Hearty breakfasts feature homemade bread, muffins, muesli and preserves.

XX **Conservatory** – Darroch Learg Hotel
Braemar Rd ✉ AB35 5UX – ✆ (013397) 55 443 – www.darrochlearg.co.uk
– Closed last 3 weeks January and Christmas
Rest – *(dinner only)* Menu £ 45
Conservatory dining room in a Victorian country house, boasting attractive mountain views from the majority of its smartly laid tables. The concise menu showcases quality seasonal ingredients in carefully judged, well-crafted modern dishes.

BALLOCH – West Dunbartonshire – 501 G15 – ✉ Alexandria Scotland 25 B1

Edinburgh 72 mi – Glasgow 20 mi – Stirling 30 mi
Balloch Rd, ✆ (08707) 20 06 07, www.explore-callander.com
N : Loch Lomond★★

Cameron House
Loch Lomond, Northwest : 1.5 mi by A 811 on A 82 rm,
✉ G83 8QZ – ✆ (01389) 755 565 – www.cameronhouse.co.uk
132 rm – †£ 195/685 ††£ 195/685 – 12 suites
Rest *Martin Wishart at Loch Lomond* ✿
Rest *Camerons Grill*
Rest *Boat House* – see restaurant listing
Rest *Claret Jug* – Menu £ 20 (dinner) – Carte £ 16/34
Extensive Victorian house and timeshare lodges, set in 250 acres on the shore of Loch Lomond. Excellent leisure facilities include a health club, spa, golf course and use of a launch and seaplane. Moody, modern bedrooms; traditional suites. British classics in The Claret Jug; named after the Open Golf Trophy.

XXX ✿ **Martin Wishart at Loch Lomond** – Cameron House Hotel
Loch Lomond, Northwest : 1.5 mi by A 811 on A 82
✉ G83 8QZ – ✆ (01389) 722 504 – www.martinwishartlochlomond.co.uk
– Closed 1-14 January, Monday and Tuesday
Rest – *(dinner only and lunch Saturday-Sunday) (booking essential)* Menu £ 29/70
Smart, formal restaurant in a resort hotel on the banks of Loch Lomond, with superb water and mountain views. Seasonal, modern menus showcase Scottish ingredients in well-judged combinations; cooking is accomplished and technically precise. 6 course tasting menu available. Professional, personable service.
→ Razor clams and pork jowl with cauliflower cream and shellfish cappuccino. Saddle of roe deer, king oyster mushrooms and sauce grand veneur. Lemon curd and passion fruit jelly, citrus marshmallow.

XX **Camerons Grill** – Cameron House Hotel
Loch Lomond, Northwest : 1.5 mi by A 811 on A 82 ✉ G83 8QZ – ✆ (01389) 722 582 – www.cameronhouse.co.uk – Closed 26 December
Rest – *(dinner only)* Menu £ 35 – Carte £ 27/67
Contemporary, leather-furnished grill restaurant located within an extensive Victorian house, where 250 acres of grounds lead down to Loch Lomond. They specialise in steaks cooked on the Josper grill.

XX **Boat House** – Cameron House Hotel
Loch Lomond, Northwest : 1.5 mi by A 811 on A 82 ✉ G83 8QZ – ✆ (01389) 722 585 – www.cameronhouse.co.uk
Rest – Carte £ 26/41
Set in the grounds of Cameron House, on the loch shore, this casual restaurant has a true New England feel and looks out towards the jetty. The Mediterranean menu offers unfussy dishes, including fresh Loch Fyne seafood.

BALLYGRANT – Argyll and Bute – 501 B16 – see Islay (Isle of)

BALMACARA – Highland 29 B2

Edinburgh 197 mi – London 573 mi – Glasgow 177 mi – Manchester 388 mi

Balmacara Mains without rest
Glaick, West : 0.75 mi by A 87 ✉ IV40 8DN – ✆ (01599) 566 240 – www.ontheloch.com
8 rm – †£ 60/75 ††£ 105/120
Old farmhouse in a superb lochside location between the castle and Skye Bridge. Modern lounge with a wood-burning stove; split-level breakfast room offers the likes of Skye smoked haddock. Light oak furnished bedrooms and marble bathrooms.

SCOTLAND

BALMEDIE – Aberdeenshire – 501 N12 – pop. 1 653 — 28 D1

Edinburgh 137 mi – Aberdeen 7 mi – Peterhead 24 mi

Cock and Bull with rm

Ellon Rd, Blairton, North : 1 mi on A 90 ✉ AB23 8XY – ✆ (01358) 743 249 – www.thecockandbull.co.uk

8 rm – †£ 85/120 ††£ 95/120 **Rest** – Carte £ 20/41

Quirky pub with a profusion of knick-knacks; dine in the cosy, open-fired lounge, the formal dining room or the airy conservatory. Menus offer a mix of pub classics and well-presented, restaurant style dishes. Some of the contemporary bedrooms are in a nearby annexe; there's a complimentary shuttle service.

BALQUHIDDER – Stirling – 501 G14 – see Lochearnhead

BANCHORY – Aberdeenshire – 501 M12 – pop. 6 034 Scotland — 28 D2

Edinburgh 118 mi – Aberdeen 17 mi – Dundee 55 mi – Inverness 94 mi

Bridge St, ✆ (01330) 82 20 00, www.visitbanchory.com

Kinneskie, Kinneskie Rd, ✆ (01330) 82 23 65

Torphins, Bog Rd, ✆ (013398) 8 21 15

Crathes Castle★★ (Gardens★★★) **AC**, E : 3 mi by A 93 – Cairn o'Mount Road★ (≤★★), S : by B 974. Dunnottar Castle★★ (site★★★) **AC**, SW : 15.5 mi by A 93 and A 957 – Aberdeen★★, NE : 17 mi by A 93

Raemoir House

North : 2.5 mi by A 980 ✉ AB31 4ED – ✆ (01330) 824 884 – www.raemoir.com

20 rm – †£ 120/150 ††£ 180/240

Rest – *(bar lunch Monday-Saturday)* Carte £ 30/48

Impressive Scottish country house in an idyllic rural spot. Original features include an intricately carved counter in the bar and pitch pine panelling in the drawing room. Classical bedrooms have been subtly modernised. Elegant dining room serves daily menu featuring classically based dishes with a modern twist.

Tor-Na-Coille (N)

Inchmarlo Rd, West : 0.5 mi on A 93 ✉ AB31 4AB – ✆ (01330) 822 242 – www.tornacoille.com

25 rm – †£ 70/85 ††£ 95/160 **Rest** – Menu £ 19 (lunch) – Carte £ 30/36

Well-run mansion dating from 1873 and surrounded by mature grounds. The décor blends the modern with the classic and original cornicing, fireplaces and staircases feature. Bedrooms boast stylish wallpapers and bright, bold furnishings. The intimate restaurant showcases Scottish produce in modern dishes.

Cow Shed

Raemoir Rd, North : 1.5 mi on A 980 ✉ AB31 5QB – ✆ (01330) 820 813 – www.cowshedrestaurant.co.uk – Closed 1-7 January and Monday

Rest – *(dinner only and lunch Friday-Sunday) (booking advisable)* Carte £ 28/51

Impressive modern building with a cavernous dining room and countryside views. Simple, good value lunches, followed by more ambitious evening menus, with an abundance of meat and game from the surrounding estates. Cookery classes available.

BARCALDINE – Argyll and Bute – 501 D14 — 27 B2

Edinburgh 124 mi – London 495 mi – Glasgow 98 mi – Leeds 317 mi

Ardtorna without rest

Mill Farm, Southwest : 1.5mi on A 828 ✉ PA37 1SE – ✆ (01631) 720 125 – www.ardtorna.co.uk

4 rm – †£ 100/175 ††£ 125/200

Ultra-modern guesthouse in a stunning spot, with lovely views of the lochs and mountains, and amazing sunsets. Immaculate bedrooms have well-stocked fridges and plenty of space in which to relax; perhaps with a complimentary glass of Baileys or whisky. The charming owners offer archery lessons.

BARRA (Isle of) – Western Isles – 501 X13 – ✉ Castlebay — 29 A3

Edinburgh 126 mi – London 497 mi – Glasgow 101 mi – Liverpool 317 mi

from Castlebay to Oban (Caledonian MacBrayne Ltd) daily (5 h) - from Castlebay to Lochboisdale (Caledonian MacBrayne Ltd) 3 weekly (1 h 40 mn) - from Barra to Eriskay (Caledonian MacBrayne Ltd) 5 daily (40 mn)

CASTLEBAY – Western Isles **29** A3

🏨 **Castlebay** ⇐ 🕭 rm, 🤶 ⑩ 🅿

✉ HS9 5XD – 𝓒 (01871) 810 223 – www.castlebayhotel.com – Closed 21 December-6 January

15 rm ⌂ – †£49/60 ††£79/170 **Rest** – (bar lunch) Carte £19/35

Homely hotel boasting excellent castle and island views – the hub of the island community. Bedrooms mix styles: newer rooms feature subtle tartan fabrics; Mac-Neil has harbour views. Cosy lounge and busy locals bar. Linen-clad dining room serves seafood specials.

🏠 **Grianamul** without rest ⇐ 🚗 🕭 🤶 🅿

✉ HS9 5XD – 𝓒 (01871) 810 416 – www.isleofbarraaccommodation.com – Closed October-March

3 rm ⌂ – †£40 ††£70

Set at the heart of a small hamlet; a homely guesthouse run by caring owners. Bright, clean, spacious bedrooms. Comfortable lounge and sunny breakfast room, where huge breakfasts are served.

NORTH BAY – Western Isles **29** A3

🏠 **Heathbank** ⇐ 🚗 🕭 🤶 🤶 🅿

✉ HS9 5YQ – 𝓒 (01871) 890 266 – www.barrahotel.co.uk – Closed December-February

5 rm ⌂ – †£62 ††£98 **Rest** – (booking essential) (bar lunch) Carte £16/34

Former Presbyterian Church, now a smart, modern hotel that's popular with locals and visitors alike. Fresh, up-to-date bedrooms. Bright, airy bar that forms the hotel's hub and, along with the dining room, serves straightforward, local seafood orientated menus.

BENDERLOCH – Argyll and Bute – **501** E14 – ✉ **Connel** **27** B2

▶ Edinburgh 120 mi – London 491 mi – Glasgow 94 mi – Liverpool 311 mi

🍴 **Hawthorn** ⒶⒸ 🅿

🍴 5 Keil Crofts, Northwest : 0.5 mi by A 828 on Tralee rd ✉ PA37 1QS – 𝓒 (01631) 720 777 – www.thehawthornrestaurant.co.uk – Closed Monday

Rest – (dinner only and lunch Friday-Sunday) Carte £18/41

Keenly run restaurant in a 300 year old croft house, in a glorious rural spot. Exposed stone walls mix with contemporary touches to create a pleasant modern-rustic style. They open for lunch, high tea and dinner, serving carefully prepared, flavoursome dishes.

BERNISDALE – Highland – **501** A/B11 – **see Skye (Isle of)**

BETTYHILL – Highland – **501** H8 **30** C1

▶ Edinburgh 246 mi – London 647 mi – Glasgow 260 mi – Manchester 462 mi

🍴 **Côte du Nord** 🅿 ⇙

The School House, Kirtomy, East : 4 mi by A 836 ✉ KW14 7TB – 𝓒 (01641) 521 773 – www.cotedunord.co.uk – Closed October-March, Sunday-Tuesday and Thursday

Rest – (dinner only) (booking essential) Menu £39

Intimate restaurant of just 3 tables; converted from an old school house by a local doctor cum self-taught chef. Modern, innovative cooking; 12 course 'surprise' menu features local and foraged ingredients, and salt from reduced seawater.

BISHOPTON – Renfrewshire – **501** G16 **25** B1

▶ Edinburgh 59 mi – Dumbarton 9 mi – Glasgow 13 mi

🏨 **Mar Hall** 📶 ⇐ 🚗 ⑩ 🔳 🌐 🛁 ⅃ 🅋 🕭 rm, ⒶⒸ rest, 🤶 🤶 🅫 🅿

Earl of Mar Dr, Northeast : 1 mi on B 815 ✉ PA7 5NW – 𝓒 (0141) 812 99 99 – www.marhall.com

53 rm ⌂ – †£115/225 ††£115/225 – 2 suites

Rest Cristal – (dinner only) Menu £35 – Carte £30/48

Rest Il Posto – (closed Tuesday and Wednesday) Menu £16 – Carte £19/29

Impressive Gothic mansion – a former hospital – on the banks of the Clyde; popular for weddings and with good links to Glasgow city/airport. Well-equipped spa; championship golf course. Spacious, contemporary bedrooms; ask for a 'Deluxe' with a river view. Enjoy afternoon tea in the cavernous Grand Hall. Cristal offers a classic French menu; Italian fare in Il Posto.

BLAIRGOWRIE – Perth and Kinross – 501 J14 – pop. 7 965 Scotland 28 C2

Edinburgh 60 mi – Dundee 19 mi – Perth 16 mi

26 Wellmeadow, (01250) 87 29 60, www.perthshire.co.uk

Scone Palace★★ **AC**, S : 12 mi by A 93

Kinloch House

West : 3 mi on A 923 PH10 6SG – (01250) 884 237 – www.kinlochhouse.com – Closed 12-29 December

15 rm – £ 100/250 £ 210/325 – 1 suite

Rest *Kinloch House* – see restaurant listing

Imposing ivy-clad country house in a tranquil, elevated setting, with beautiful walled gardens to the rear and 25 acres of grounds. Smart oak-panelled hall and a vast array of welcoming guest areas complete with log fires and antiques. Classical bedrooms are well-appointed and immaculately maintained.

Heathpark House without rest

Coupar Angus Rd, Rosemount, Southeast : 0.75 mi on A 923 PH10 6JT – (01250) 870 700 – www.heathparkhouse.com – Closed 24-26 December and 1 January

3 rm – £ 60 £ 80

19C house in 1.75 acres of mature grounds; the owners have spent 10 years renovating it. The two enormous sitting rooms have ornate cornicing; the large, homely bedrooms are accessed via an antique pine staircase. Tasty breakfast specials.

Gilmore House without rest

Perth Rd, Southwest : 0.5 mi on A 93 PH10 6EJ – (01250) 872 791 – www.gilmorehouse.co.uk

3 rm – £ 45/50 £ 70/80

Proudly run, stone-built house with a pretty, flower-filled entrance. Antlers, deer heads and old lithographs fill the walls. The first floor lounge has a good outlook; complimentary sherry and whisky are left out for a traditional nightcap. Immaculately kept modern bedrooms and plentiful breakfasts.

XXX Kinloch House – Kinloch House Hotel

West : 3 mi on A 923 PH10 6SG – (01250) 884 237 – www.kinlochhouse.com – Closed 12-29 December

Rest – Menu £ 26/53

Formal hotel dining room with twinkling chandeliers and smartly dressed tables. Start with drinks in the clubby bar or cosy, open-fired sitting room. The latest local, seasonal produce informs the daily menu – maybe West Coast crab or Perthshire venison. Dishes are well-crafted, traditional and flavoursome.

Dalmore Inn

Perth Rd, Southwest : 1.5 mi on A 93 PH10 6QB – (01250) 871 088 – www.dalmoreinn.com – Closed 25 December and 1-2 January

Rest – Carte £ 20/38

Vivid yellow pub with a surprisingly stylish interior, where brightly coloured walls are juxtaposed with old stonework. Cooking is good value, unfussy and full of flavour, and everything is freshly prepared to order using Scottish produce.

BORVE – Western Isles – 501 Y10 – see Lewis and Harris (Isle of)

BOWMORE – Argyll and Bute – 501 B16 – see Islay (Isle of)

BRAEMAR – Aberdeenshire – 501 J12 – pop. 500 Scotland 28 C2

Edinburgh 85 mi – Aberdeen 58 mi – Dundee 51 mi – Perth 51 mi

Mar Rd AZ, (013397) 4 16 00, www.braemarscotland.co.uk

Cluniebank Rd, (013397) 4 16 18

Lin O'Dee★, W : 5 mi

Callater Lodge without rest

9 Glenshee Rd AB35 5YQ – (013397) 41 275 – www.callaterlodge.co.uk – Closed 1 week Christmas

6 rm – £ 40 £ 80

Victorian granite house on the village outskirts, with a classically furnished interior, tartan carpets and stag's heads. Bright breakfast room and comfy lounge with local info. Fresh, individually styled bedrooms; some with valley views.

BROADFORD - Highland - 501 C12 - see Skye (Isle of)

BRODICK - North Ayrshire - 501 E17 - see Arran (Isle of)

BRORA - Highland - 501 I9 - pop. 1 140 30 D2

Edinburgh 234 mi - Inverness 78 mi - Wick 49 mi

Golf Rd, ✆ (01408) 62 14 17

Royal Marine

Golf Rd ✉ KW9 6QS - ✆ (01408) 621 252 - www.royalmarinebrora.com

21 rm - †£ 97/135 ††£ 140/200

Rest *Lorimer's* - *(bar lunch Monday-Saturday)* Carte £ 27/39

Cream-washed Arts and Crafts house, set next to a top golf course. Leather-furnished lounges and a wood-floored bar. Smart, modern, country house bedrooms with warm fabrics and a good level of facilities. Formal linen-laid restaurant offers traditional Scottish menus.

BUNCHREW - Highland - see Inverness

BURRAY - Orkney Islands - 501 L7 - see Orkney Islands (Mainland)

CADBOLL - Highland - see Tain

CALLANDER - Stirling - 501 H15 - pop. 2 754 Scotland 28 C2

Edinburgh 52 mi - Glasgow 43 mi - Oban 71 mi - Perth 41 mi

Ancaster Sq, ✆ (01877) 33 03 42, www.visitscottishheartlands.com

Rob Roy and Trossachs Visitor Centre

Aveland Rd, ✆ (01877) 33 00 90

Town★

The Trossachs★★★ (Loch Katrine★★) - Hilltop Viewpoint★★★ (✱★★★) W : 10 mi by A 821

Roman Camp

Main St ✉ FK17 8BG - ✆ (01877) 330 003 - www.romancamphotel.co.uk

15 rm - †£ 100/175 ††£ 155/255 - 3 suites

Rest *Roman Camp* - see restaurant listing

Pretty pink house - a former 17C hunting lodge - set by the river among well-tended gardens. Traditional bedrooms with a subtle contemporary edge and smart, marble-tiled bathrooms. Characterful panelled library and chapel. Charming service.

Westerton without rest

Leny Rd ✉ FK17 8AJ - ✆ (01877) 330 147 - www.westertonbnb.co.uk - Closed November-Easter

3 rm - †£ 80/120 ††£ 85/125

Sweet stone house run by delightful owners. Vast sweeping garden with mature trees and colourful azaleas. Open-plan lounge and breakfast room; tasty breakfasts feature fresh, local produce. Spotless bedrooms with DVD players and wi-fi.

Roman Camp - Roman Camp Hotel

Main St ✉ FK17 8BG - ✆ (01877) 330 003 - www.romancamphotel.co.uk

Rest - Menu £ 30/54 - Carte £ 55/77

Enjoy drinks and canapés in the characterful lounge or library of this charming riverside hotel, before dinner in the formal restaurant. Ambitious, modern, well-presented cooking; choose the tasting menu for the best value.

Mhor Fish

75-77 Main St ✉ FK17 8DX - ✆ (01877) 330 213 - www.mhor.net - Closed 10 days November, 25-26 December, 1 January and Monday except bank holidays

Rest - Carte £ 13/25

On one side, a classic take-away chippie; on the other, a funky modern café with a fish counter displaying the day's catch. Tasty chips cooked in beef dripping; pies and bread from their nearby bakery. All-day menu; more ambitious specials.

CARINISH - Western Isles - 501 Y11 - see Uist (Isles of)

CARNOUSTIE – Angus – 501 L14 – pop. 10 561 — 28 D2

Edinburgh 46 mi – London 438 mi – Glasgow 46 mi – Aberdeen 102 mi

21 High St, (01241) 85 96 20, www.angusanddundee.co.uk

Carnoustie Championship Course, Links Par, (01241) 80 22 70

Burnside, Links Par, (01241) 80 22 90

Buddon Links, Links Par, (01241) 80 22 80

Old Manor without rest

Panbride, Northeast : 1.25 mi by A 930 on Panbride Rd DD7 6JP – (01241) 854 804 – www.oldmanorcarnoustie.com – Closed 2 weeks Christmas-New Year

5 rm – £ 60/80 £ 75/80

Sizeable house built in 1765 – formerly a manse – commanding great views over patchwork fields to the sea beyond. Comfortable lounge and a good-sized breakfast room. Spotlessly kept bedrooms come with quality bedding, biscuits and chocolates; 'Balmoral' and 'Dunotter' boast superb outlooks.

CARRADALE – Argyll and Bute – 501 D17 – see Kintyre (Peninsula)

CASTLE DOUGLAS – Dumfries and Galloway – 501 I19 – pop. 3 671 — 25 B3

Scotland

Edinburgh 98 mi – Ayr 49 mi – Dumfries 18 mi – Stranraer 57 mi

Market Hill, (01556) 50 26 11, www.visitscotland.com

Abercromby Rd, (01556) 50 28 01

Threave Garden★★ **AC**, SW : 2.5 mi by A 75 – Threave Castle★ **AC**, W : 1 mi

Douglas House without rest

63 Queen St DG7 1HS – (01556) 503 262 – www.douglas-house.com – Closed Christmas

4 rm – £ 39/55 £ 77/82

Attractive 19C stone-built house, set close to the high street. Open-plan lounge and breakfast room. Comfy, individually decorated bedrooms with contemporary feel. Extensive breakfast menu.

CASTLEBAY – Western Isles – 501 X12/1 – see Barra (Isle of)

CHIRNSIDE – The Scottish Borders – 501 N16 – pop. 1 204 – Duns — 26 D1

Edinburgh 52 mi – Berwick-upon-Tweed 8 mi – Glasgow 95 mi – Newcastle upon Tyne 70 mi

Chirnside Hall

East : 1.75 mi on A 6105 TD11 3LD – (01890) 818 219 – www.chirnsidehallhotel.com – Closed March

10 rm – £ 95/170 £ 170/185

Rest – *(dinner only) (booking essential)* Menu £ 35

Sizeable 1834 country house with lovely revolving door; boasting beautiful views over the Cheviots. Grand lounges with original cornicing and huge fireplaces. Cosy, classical bedrooms, some have four-posters. Local, seasonal dishes in traditional dining room.

COLONSAY (Isle of) – Argyll and Bute – 501 B15 – pop. 106 — 27 A2

Edinburgh 122 mi – London 493 mi – Glasgow 97 mi – Liverpool 313 mi

from Scalasaig to Oban (Caledonian MacBrayne Ltd) 3 weekly (2 h) – from Scalasaig to Kintyre Peninsula (Kennacraig) via Isle of Islay (Port Askaig) (Caledonian MacBrayne Ltd) weekly

Colonsay, (01951) 20 02 90

SCALASAIG – Argyll and Bute – Colonsay — 27 A2

Colonsay

PA61 7YP – (01951) 200 316 – www.colonsayestate.co.uk – Closed November-mid March

9 rm – £ 70 £ 85/145 **Rest** – *(bar lunch)* Carte £ 19/35

Listed building from mid-18C; a thoroughly rural, remote setting. Public areas include excellent photos of local scenes and the only bar on the island. Bright, modern rooms. Welcoming, informal dining room.

SCOTLAND

COMRIE – Perth and Kinross – 501 I14 – pop. 1 926 28 C2

Edinburgh 66 mi – Glasgow 56 mi – Oban 70 mi – Perth 24 mi

Comrie, Laggan Braes, (01764) 67 00 55

Royal

Melville Sq ✉ PH6 2DN – (01764) 679 200 – www.royalhotel.co.uk – Closed 25-26 December

11 rm – †£ 90/110 ††£ 150/190

Rest *Royal* – see restaurant listing

Charming coaching inn dating back to the 18C and set at the heart of a riverside town. Cosy bar and lovely open-fired library with squashy sofas. Well-appointed bedrooms; some with four-posters and antiques. Relaxed, personable service.

Royal – Royal Hotel

Melville Sq ✉ PH6 2DN – (01764) 679 200 – www.royalhotel.co.uk – Closed 25-26 December

Rest – Carte £ 26/41

Intimate dining room and a bright conservatory, set within a stylishly decorated coaching inn. Concise menu of classically based dishes with modern touches. Produce is seasonal and locally sourced; the mussels and steaks are superb.

CONNEL – Argyll and Bute – 501 D14 – ✉ Oban 27 B2

Edinburgh 118 mi – Glasgow 88 mi – Inverness 113 mi – Oban 5 mi

Ards House without rest

on A 85 ✉ PA37 1PT – (01631) 710 255 – www.ardshouse.com – Closed Christmas-New Year

4 rm – †£ 55/65 ††£ 80/100

Attractive house with equally welcoming, hospitable owner. Large, homely lounge packed with books and antiques. Cosy, personally decorated bedrooms show good attention to detail; small bathrooms boast locally made toiletries. Excellent breakfasts with fresh fruit and delicious roasted coffee.

SCOTLAND

CRIEFF – Perth and Kinross – 501 I14 – pop. 6 579 Scotland 28 C2

Edinburgh 60 mi – Glasgow 50 mi – Oban 76 mi – Perth 18 mi

High St, (01764) 65 25 78, www.crieffandstrathearn.co.uk

Perth Rd, (01764) 65 29 09

Muthill, Peat Rd, (01764) 68 15 23

Town★

Drummond Castle Gardens★ **AC**, S : 2 mi by A 822. Scone Palace★★ **AC**, E : 16 mi by A 85 and A 93

Merlindale without rest

Perth Rd, on A 85 ✉ PH7 3EQ – (01764) 655 205 – www.merlindale.co.uk – Closed mid-December-February

3 rm – †£ 60/80 ††£ 85/95

Spacious manor house with a comfy lounge, a well-stocked library and a dark wood furnished room for family-style breakfasts. Immaculate bedrooms have classical furnishings, heavy floral drapes and large bathrooms; some boast roll-top baths.

Yann's at Glenearn House with rm

Perth Rd, on A 85 ✉ PH7 3EQ – (01764) 650 111 – www.yannsatglenearnhouse.com – Closed 1 week October and 25 December

6 rm – †£ 65 ††£ 90 **Rest** – Carte £ 22/38

Busy restaurant in a Victorian house, with a delightful lounge and a large bistro-style dining room hung with French prints. Gallic cooking makes good use of Scottish produce and Savoyard sharing dishes are a speciality. Comfy, cosy bedrooms have good facilities and a relaxed, bohemian style. Pleasant team.

at Muthill South : 3 mi by A 822

X **Barley Bree** with rm

6 Willoughby St ✉ PH5 2AB – ✆ (01764) 681 451 – www.barleybree.com – Closed Christmas-New Year, Monday and Tuesday

6 rm – †£ 70/75 ††£ 110/150 **Rest** – *(booking advisable)* Carte £ 30/42 **s**

Intimate converted coaching inn at the centre of a busy village, with a spacious fire-lit sitting room and a dining room hung with angling memorabilia. Rustic, classical cooking utilises local ingredients and arrives in generous portions. Service is friendly and bedrooms are comfortable and well-thought-out.

CRINAN – Argyll and Bute – 501 D15 – ✉ Lochgilphead ▌Scotland 27 B2

Edinburgh 137 mi – Glasgow 91 mi – Oban 36 mi

Hamlet★

Kilmory Knap (Macmillan's Cross★) SW : 14 m

Crinan

✉ PA31 8SR – ✆ (01546) 830 261 – www.crinanhotel.com – Closed Christmas and January

20 rm – †£ 65/110 ††£ 130/270

Rest *Westward* – see restaurant listing

Rest *Seafood Bar* – Carte £ 20/34

Built in the 19C to accommodate the Laird of Jura's business associates and boasting lovely Sound views. Simply furnished bedrooms – some with balconies and views. Small coffee shop sells homemade cakes; superb 3rd floor bar with terrace. Larger, wood-panelled bar offers an appealing menu of seafood dishes.

XX **Westward** – Crinan Hotel

✉ PA31 8SR – ✆ (01546) 830 261 – www.crinanhotel.com – Closed Christmas and January

Rest – *(dinner only)* Menu £ 45

Set within a welcoming, family-run hotel and boasting lovely views over the loch and Sound of Jura. Concise seafood-based menus rely on local and island produce. Homemade chocolates to finish.

CULLODEN – Highland – 501 H11 – see Inverness

CULNAKNOCK – Highland – 501 B11 – see Skye (Isle of)

CUPAR – Fife – 501 K15 – pop. 8 506 28 C2

Edinburgh 45 mi – Dundee 15 mi – Perth 23 mi

XX **Ostler's Close**

25 Bonnygate ✉ KY15 4BU – ✆ (01334) 655 574 – www.ostlersclose.co.uk – Closed 2 weeks April, 2 weeks October, 25-26 December, 1-2 January, Sunday and Monday

Rest – *(dinner only and Saturday lunch)* Menu £ 29/35

Long-standing, personally run restaurant down a narrow alley just off the main street. Three cosy rooms decorated in warm reds; friendly, chatty service. Concise, traditional menus with beef and seafood to the fore and a Mediterranean edge.

CURRIE – City of Edinburgh – 501 K16 – see Edinburgh

DALKEITH – Midlothian – 501 K16 – pop. 11 566 26 C1

Edinburgh 6 mi – London 374 mi – Glasgow 51 mi – Manchester 208 mi

Sun Inn with rm

Lothian Bridge, Southwest : 2 mi by A 6094 and B 6392 on A 7 ✉ EH22 4TR – ✆ (0131) 663 24 56 – www.thesuninnedinburgh.co.uk – Closed 26 December and 1 January

5 rm – †£ 55/100 ††£ 55/150 **Rest** – Menu £ 15/18 – Carte £ 19/42

17C former blacksmith's with two large, open-fired rooms; their wood and stone-faced walls hung with modern black and white photos. Extensive menus feature good quality local produce; lunch keeps things simple but appealing. Smart bedrooms boast handmade furniture and Egyptian cotton linen.

DALRY – North Ayrshire – 501 F16 25 A1

Edinburgh 70 mi – Ayr 21 mi – Glasgow 25 mi

Lochwood Farm Steading without rest

Southwest : 5 mi by A 737 and Saltcoats rd ✉ KA21 6NG – ✆ (01294) 552 529 – www.lochwoodfarm.co.uk – Closed Christmas and New Year

4 rm – †£ 100/135 ††£ 100/135

Remote farmhouse on a 100 acre working dairy farm, boasting impressive panoramic views. Luxuriously appointed bedrooms are split between an old barn and a rustic wood house – two have private hot tubs. Breakfast is served by candlelight!

Braidwoods (Keith Braidwood)

Drumastle Mill Cottage, Southwest : 1.5 mi by A 737 on Saltcoats rd ✉ KA24 4LN – ✆ (01294) 833 544 – www.braidwoods.co.uk – Closed 25 December-25 January, 2 weeks September, Sunday dinner, Monday, Tuesday lunch and Sunday from May-mid September

Rest – *(booking essential)* Menu £ 23/50

Former crofter's cottage hidden away in the countryside; personally run by experienced owners. Cosy and charming, with just a handful of tables in each of its two rooms. Concise menu of confident, classical cooking uses quality seasonal ingredients; dishes have clear flavours. Great value lunch.

→ Roast quail breast with confit of leg on black pudding with roast beetroot. Pan-fried turbot on crushed peas and warm tartar sauce. Iced heather honey parfait with mango and tayberry coulis and puff candy.

DEERNESS – see Orkney Islands (Mainland)

DINGWALL – Highland – 501 G11 – pop. 5 026 30 C2

Edinburgh 172 mi – Inverness 14 mi – Glasgow 182 mi – Aberdeen 115 mi

Café India Brasserie

Lockhart House, Tulloch St ✉ IV15 9JZ – ✆ (01349) 862 552 – www.cafeindiadingwall.co.uk – Closed 25 December

Rest – Menu £ 13 (weekday lunch) – Carte £ 20/31

Well-run Indian restaurant close to the town centre. Small lounge and several dining areas separated by etched glass screens. Good range of authentic, regional dishes, with tasty Thalis, set menus for 2+ and good value two course lunches.

DINNET – Aberdeenshire – 501 L12 28 D1

Edinburgh 114 mi – London 517 mi – Glasgow 134 mi – Bradford 325 mi

Glendavan House without rest

Northwest : 3 mi by A 97 on B 9119 ✉ AB34 5LU – ✆ (01339) 881 610 – www.glendavanhouse.com

3 rm – †£ 85/95 ††£ 110/150

Set in 9 acres overlooking Loch Davan, this former shooting lodge is somewhere to 'get away from it all'. 2 of the 3 bedrooms are very large suites; all are tastefully furnished with antiques and memorabilia. Delicious communal breakfasts.

DORNOCH – Highland – 501 H10 – pop. 1 206 Scotland 30 D2

Edinburgh 219 mi – Inverness 63 mi – Wick 65 mi

Castle St, ✆ (08452) 25 51 21, www.visitdornoch.com

Royal Dornoch, Golf Rd, ✆ (01862) 81 02 19

Town ★

Highfield House without rest

Evelix Rd ✉ IV25 3HR – ✆ (01862) 810 909 – www.highfieldhouse.co.uk

4 rm – †£ 65 ††£ 85/90

Welcoming guesthouse with immaculately kept gardens and pleasant summer house. Spacious interior boasts conservatory style lounge and smart breakfast room. Comfy bedrooms have good facilities.

DOUNBY – 501 K16 – see Orkney Islands (Mainland)

DRUMBEG – Highland – 501 E9 30 C1

Edinburgh 262 mi – Inverness 105 mi – Ullapool 48 mi

Blar na Leisg at Drumbeg House

Take first right on entering village from Kylesku direction ✉ IV27 4NW – ✆ (01571) 833 325 – www.blarnaleisg.com

5 rm – †£ 72/144 ††£ 144/175 **Rest** – Menu £ 58

Remotely set Edwardian house affording lovely loch views. Large, open-fired sitting room filled with a vast array of books; spacious, luxuriously appointed bedrooms. Impressive modern art collection includes lots of Bauhaus works. Smart, contemporary dining room; Highland beef and game birds a speciality.

DRUMNADROCHIT – Highland – 501 G11 – pop. 813 – ✉ Milton 30 C2

Scotland

Edinburgh 172 mi – Inverness 16 mi – Kyle of Lochalsh 66 mi

Loch Ness★★ – Loch Ness Monster Exhibition★ **AC** – The Great Glen★

Drumbuie Farm without rest

Drumbuie, East : 0.75 mi by A 82 ✉ IV63 6XP – ✆ (01456) 450 634 – www.loch-ness-farm.co.uk – Closed December-January

3 rm – †£ 50 ††£ 68/70

Friendly guesthouse set above Loch Ness, on a 120 acre sheep and cattle farm. Traditional lounge with a stuffed cow head and whisky barrel; breakfast room offers panoramic views. Simple, pine-furnished bedrooms; two boast body jet showers.

SCOTLAND

DUISDALEMORE – Highland – see Skye (Isle of)

DUMFRIES – Dumfries and Galloway – 501 J18 – pop. 30 859 Scotland 26 C3

Edinburgh 80 mi – Ayr 59 mi – Carlisle 34 mi – Glasgow 79 mi

64 Whitesands, ✆ (01387) 25 38 62, www.visitdumfriesandgalloway.co.uk

Dumfries & Galloway, Maxwelltown, 2 Laurieston Ave, ✆ (01387) 25 35 82

Dumfries & County, Edinburgh Rd, Nunfield, ✆ (01387) 25 35 85

Crichton, Bankend Rd, ✆ (01387) 24 78 94

Town★ – Midsteeple★ A **A**

Lincluden College (Tomb★) **AC**, N : 1.5 mi by College St A. Drumlanrig Castle★★ (cabinets★) **AC**, NW : 16.5 mi by A 76 A – Shambellie House Museum of Costume (Costume Collection★) S : 7.25 mi by A 710 A - Sweetheart Abbey★ **AC**, S : 8 mi by A 710 A – Caerlaverock Castle★ (Renaissance fa 0.5ade★★) **AC**, SE : 9 mi by B 725 B – Glenkiln (Sculptures★) W : 9 mi by A 780 - A - and A 75

Hazeldean House without rest

4 Moffat Rd ✉ DG1 1NJ – ✆ (01387) 266 178 – www.hazeldeanhouse.com **Bu**

6 rm – †£ 35/45 ††£ 60/65

Victorian villa built in 1898. Lovely garden; curio-filled lounge and conservatory breakfast room. Victorian-themed bedrooms, 3 with four-posters; basement room has a nautical cabin style.

Hamilton House without rest

12 Moffat Rd ✉ DG1 1NJ – ✆ (01387) 266 606 – www.hamiltonhousedumfries.co.uk – Closed 24 December-3 January **Bc**

7 rm – †£ 40/50 ††£ 60/70

Converted Victorian townhouse next to the bowls club. Large conservatory lounge; neat breakfast tables overlook the tennis courts. Large bedrooms combine the classical and the contemporary.

DUMFRIES

Aldermanhill Rd .... B 2
Bank St .... A 3
Buccleuch St .... A 4
Cardoness St .... B 5
Cassalands .... A 6
Castle Douglas Rd .... A 8
Castle St .... A 7
Catherine St .... B 9
Corberry Ave .... A 10
Cornwall Mount Rd .... B 12
Cuckoo Bridge Retail Park . A
Friars Vennel .... A 13
Galloway St .... A 14
Glebe St .... B 15
Great King St .... A 16
Hermitage Drive .... A 17
High St .... A 18
Loreburn Centre .... A 20
Loreburn St .... A 21
Nith St .... AB 22
Queensberry St .... A 24
Queen St .... B 23
Rae St .... B 26
St Mary's St .... B 27
St Michael St .... B 28
St Michael's Bridge Rd .... A 30
Shakespeare St .... B 31
Union St .... A 32
Whitesands .... A 34

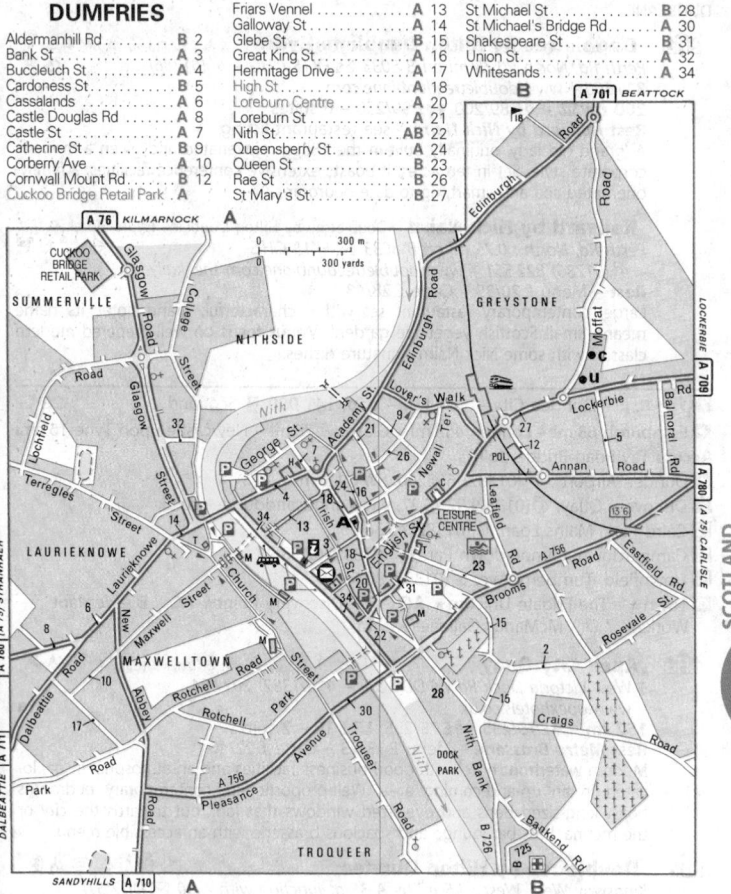

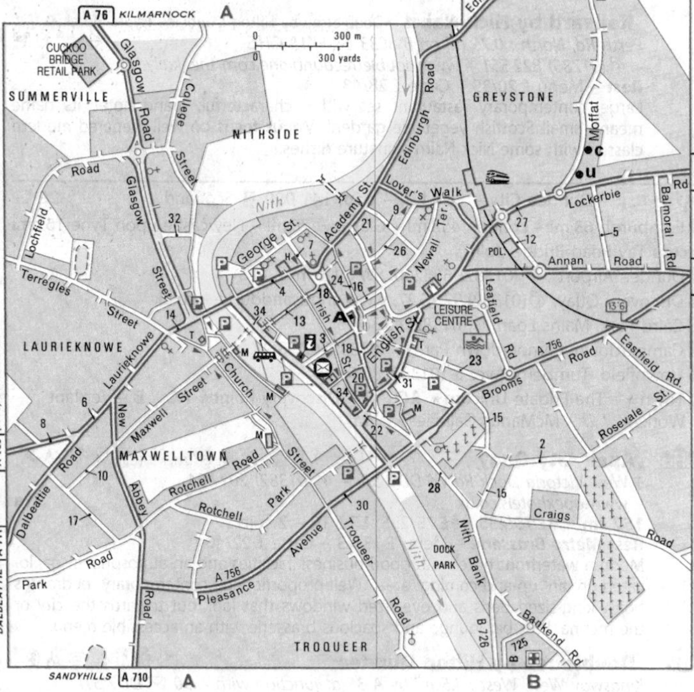

DUNBAR – East Lothian – **501** M15 – **pop. 9 375** **26** D1

▶ Edinburgh 30 mi – London 369 mi – Glasgow 76 mi – Leeds 190 mi

Creel

The Harbour, 25 Lamer St ✉ EH42 1HG
– ✆ (01368) 863 279 – www.creelrestaurant.co.uk
– Closed Sunday dinner-Wednesday lunch

Rest – *(booking essential)* Menu £ 15/27

Unassuming former pub in a working harbour. Wood panelled walls and polished tables are brightened by a welcoming team. Experienced chef uses lesser known cuts from local suppliers and transforms them into good value, full-flavoured dishes.

DUNBLANE – Stirling – **501** I15 – **pop. 7 911** Scotland **28** C2

▶ Edinburgh 42 mi – Glasgow 33 mi – Perth 29 mi

Town★ – Cathedral★★ (west front★★)

Doune★ (castle★ **AC**) W : 4.5 mi by A 820

⌂ Doubletree by Hilton Dunblane Hydro ≤ ⌗ ⌂ 🛁 ⌂ ⌂ ᴦ
Perth Rd, North : 0.75 mi on B 8033 ⊠ FK15 OHG – ℰ (01786) 🏊 **P**
826 600 – www.doubletreedunblane.com
200 rm ⊇ – †£ 89/200 ††£ 99/250 – 6 suites
Rest *Kailyard by Nick Nairn* – see restaurant listing
A 'grand old lady' originally built in the 1800s; rejuvenated and given a modern, corporate style. Set in ten acres, it boasts extensive conference facilities, a family-orientated spa and smart, up-to-date bedrooms.

✗✗ Kailyard by Nick Nairn – Doubletree by Hilton Dunblane Hydro Hotel
Perth Rd, North : 0.75 mi on B 8033 ⊠ FK15 OHG ≤ ⌗ ⌂ **P**
– ℰ (01786) 822 551 – www.doubletreedunblane.com/the_kailyard
Rest – Menu £ 20/35 – Carte £ 28/48
Large, contemporary restaurant set within characterful, grand hotel; its name means 'small Scottish vegetable garden'. Menus focus on well-prepared modern classics with some Nick Nairn signature dishes.

DUNDEE – Dundee City – **501** L14 – pop. **141 090** ▌ Scotland **28** C2
▶ Edinburgh 63 mi – London 458 mi – Glasgow 76 mi – Newcastle upon Tyne 163 mi
Access Tay Road Bridge (toll) Y
✈ Dundee Airport : ℰ (01382) 662200, SW : 1.5 mi Z
ℹ Discovery Quay, ℰ (01382) 52 75 27, www.angusanddundee.co.uk
▣ᴮ Caird Park, Mains Loan, ℰ (01382) 45 36 06
▣ᴮ Camperdown, Camperdown Park, ℰ (01382) 62 33 98
▣ᴮ Downfield, Turnberry Ave, ℰ (01382) 82 55 95
◉ Town★ - The Frigate Unicorn★ **AC** Y **A** – Discovery Point★ **AC** Y **B** – Verdant Works★ Z **D** – McManus Galleries★ Y **M**

⌂ Apex City Quay ≤ 🖥 ⌂ ⌂ 🛁 ⌂ 🐾 rm, 🅺 rest, 🐾 ᴦ 🏊 **P**
1 West Victoria Dock Rd ⊠ DD1 3JP – ℰ (01382) 202 404
– www.apexhotels.co.uk Y**a**
152 rm – †£ 75/235 ††£ 75/235, ⊇ £ 10 – 2 suites
Rest *Metro Brasserie* – Menu £ 13/23 – Carte £ 22/40
Modern waterfront hotel with good business facilities and an atmospheric spa; located in an up-and-coming area. Well-proportioned, contemporary bedrooms boast king-sized beds and oversized windows that look out towards the city or the marina. Vast bar-lounge and spacious brasserie with an accessible menu.

⌂ Doubletree by Hilton Dundee ⌗ 🖥 ⌂ 🛁 ⌂ ᴦ 🏊 **P**
Kingsway West, West : 4.5 mi by A 85 at junction with A 90 ⊠ DD2 5JT
– ℰ (01382) 641 122 – www.dundeedoubletree.co.uk
92 rm – †£ 69/189 ††£ 69/189, ⊇ £ 15
Rest *Maze* – see restaurant listing
Charming granite country house – formerly a private residence – dating from 1870 and surrounded by smart landscaped gardens. Sizeable modern bedrooms with good facilities. Small gym, three conference suites and a 24hr business centre.

✗✗ Playwright 🅺 ⊜
11 Tay Sq, South Tay St. ⊠ DD1 1PB – ℰ (01382) 223 113
– www.theplaywright.co.uk – Closed 25-26 December, 1-3 January and Sunday
Rest – Menu £ 13/20 – Carte £ 39/47 Y**x**
Smart, modern bar and restaurant in an imposing 19C grey-stone building beside the Rep Theatre. Seasonal menus offer modern interpretations of classical dishes and everything from the bread to ice cream is made in-house. Great value lunch.

✗✗ Maze – Doubletree by Hilton Dundee ⌗ **P**
Kingsway West, West : 4.5mi by A 85 at junction with A 90 ⊠ DD2 5JT
– ℰ (01382) 641 122 – www.thelandmarkdundee.co.uk
Rest – Carte £ 24/36
Named after the box hedge maze that it overlooks, an elegant, L-shaped conservatory in a country house hotel; a real hit with the locals. Scottish ingredients are to the fore, with local salmon, cheeses and mature steaks all featuring.

SCOTLAND

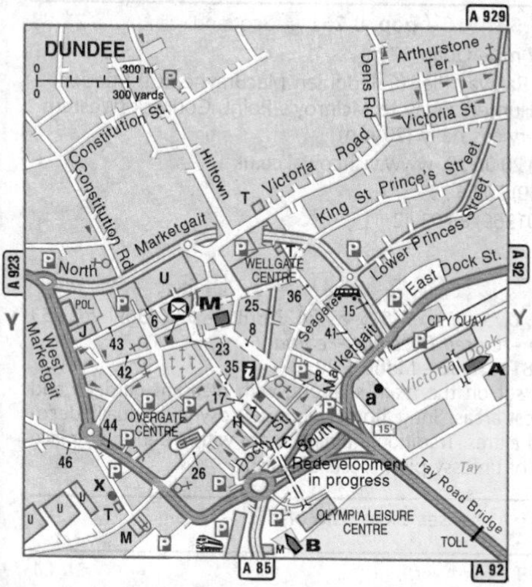

Albert St . . . . Z 2
Bell St . . . . Y 6
City Quay . . . . Y
City Square . . . . Y 7
Commercial St . . . . Y 8
Coupar Angus Rd . . . . Z 9
Douglas Rd . . . . Z 10
Drumgeith Rd . . . . Z 12
Dudhope Terrace . . . . Z 13
East Dock St . . . . Z 14
East Marketgait . . . . Y 15
Greendykes Rd . . . . Z 16
High St . . . . Y 17
Kingsway East Shopping Centre . . . . Z
Kingsway West Shopping Centre . . . . Z
Logie St . . . . Z 18
Mains Rd . . . . Z 21
Meadowside . . . . Y 23
Moncur Crescent . . . . Z 24
Murraygate . . . . Y 25
Nethergate . . . . Y 26
Old Glamis Rd . . . . Z 32
Overgate Centre . . . . Y
Provost Rd . . . . Z 34
Reform St . . . . Y 35
St Andrews St . . . . Y 36
Strathmartine Rd . . . . Z 40
Trades Lane . . . . Y 41
Ward Rd . . . . Y 42
Wellgate Centre . . . . Y
West Bell St . . . . Y 43
West Marketgait . . . . Y 44
West Port . . . . Y 46

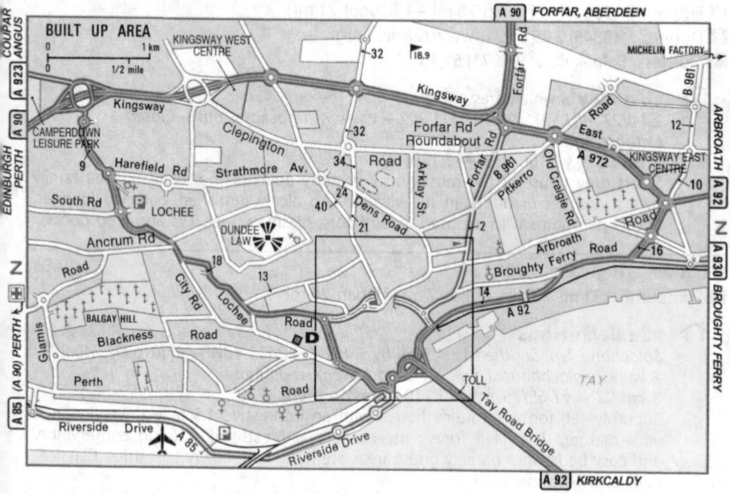

DUNKELD – Perth and Kinross – **501** J14 – **pop. 1 005** Scotland **28** C2

Edinburgh 58 mi – Aberdeen 88 mi – Inverness 98 mi – Perth 14 mi

The Cross, (01350) 72 76 88, www.dunkeldandbirnam.co.uk

Dunkeld & Birnam, Fungarth, (01350) 72 75 24

Village★ - Cathedral Street★

Letter Farm without rest

Loch of the Lowes, Northeast : 3 mi by A 923 on Loch of Lowes rd PH8 0HH – (01350) 724 254 – www.letter-farm.co.uk – Closed November-April

3 rm – £ 45/50 £ 72/90

Traditional farmhouse on a family-run stock farm, nestled between Butterstone Loch and the Loch of Lowes Nature Reserve. Welcoming open-fired lounge and homely communal breakfast room. Comfy, immaculately kept bedrooms come with king-sized beds and nice extras touches; the only TV is in the lounge.

DUNOON – Argyll and Bute – **501** F16 – **pop. 8 251** Scotland **27** B3

Edinburgh 73 mi – Glasgow 27 mi – Oban 77 mi

from Dunoon Pier to Gourock Railway Pier (Caledonian MacBrayne Ltd) frequent services daily (20 mn) – from Hunters Quay to McInroy's Point, Gourock (Western Ferries (Clyde) Ltd) frequent services daily (20 mn)

7 Alexandra Parade, (08707) 20 06 29, www.visitcowal.co.uk

Cowal, Ardenslate Rd, (01369) 70 56 73

Innellan, Knockamillie Rd, (01369) 83 02 42

The Clyde Estuary★

Dhailling Lodge rm,

155 Alexandra Par, North : 0.75 mi on A 815 PA23 8AW – (01369) 701 253 – www.dhaillinglodge.com – Closed December-February

7 rm – £ 40 £ 76/81 **Rest** – Menu £ 20

Proudly run Victorian villa set on the main seafront, with pleasant gardens and nice bay views from its guest areas. Snug, homely lounge; cosy, individually decorated bedrooms with good extras. Traditional dining room with a period fireplace and a classical daily menu of unfussy pies, roasts and fish.

DUNVEGAN – Highland – **501** A11 – **see Skye (Isle of)**

DURNESS – Highland – **501** F8 **30** C1

Edinburgh 266 mi – Thurso 78 mi – Ullapool 71 mi

Durine, (0845) 2 25 51 21, www.durness.org

Durness, Balnakeil, (01971) 51 13 64

Mackay's without rest

IV27 4PN – (01971) 511 202 – www.visitmackays.com – Closed October-April

7 rm – £ 100/135 £ 129/169

Smart grey house at the most north westerly point of the mainland; the family own a number of places in the village. Two nicely furnished, oak-clad lounges. Lovely bedrooms with exposed wood floors, plasma screen TVs and iPod docks.

DUROR – Highland – **501** E14 **29** B3

Edinburgh 131 mi – Ballachulish 7 mi – Oban 26 mi

Bealach House

Salachan Glen, Southeast : 4.5 mi by A 828 PA38 4BW – (01631) 740 298 – www.bealachhouse.co.uk – Closed November-January

3 rm – £ 65/75 £ 90/110 **Rest** – Menu £ 30

Superbly set, former crofter's house with an impressive 1.5 mile driveway lined with mature, deer-filled forest: the scenery is breathtaking. Snug conservatory and cosy bedrooms; homely guest areas are hung with Lowry tapestries. Classical, daily changing menu.

DYKE – Moray – **501** J11

Edinburgh 163 mi – London 564 mi – Aberdeen 81 mi – Glasgow 177 mi

Old Kirk without rest

Northeast : 0.5 mi IV36 2TL – (01309) 641 414 – www.oldkirk.co.uk

3 rm – £ 50/60 £ 76/88

A peacefully set, converted 1856 church, surrounded by grain fields. Airy interior, with a cosy library and a comfortable, open-fired lounge displaying an original stained glass window. Charming, individually decorated bedrooms boast original stonework and arched windows; one has a carved four-poster.

EDDLESTON – The Scottish Borders – **501** K16 – **see Peebles**

EDINBANE – Highland – **501** A11 – **see Skye (Isle of)**

SCOTLAND

EDINBURGH

See city maps on following pages **26** C1

City of Edinburgh – pop. 451 851 – 501 K16 – Scotland

Tourist Information

3 Princes St, ✆(08452) 255 1 21, www.edinburgh.org

Airport

Edinburgh Airport : ✆ (0844) 481 8989, W : 6 m. by A 8 AV

Golf Courses

Braid Hills, Braid Hills Rd, ✆(0131) 447 66 66
Carrick Knowe, Glendevon Park, ✆(0131) 3 37 10 96
Duddingston, Duddingston Road West, ✆(0131) 661 76 88

SIGHTS

In the town : City★★★ • Edinburgh International Festival★★★ (August) • Royal Museum of Scotland★★★ EZ**M2** • National Gallery of Scotland★★ DY**M4** • Royal Botanic Garden★★★ AV • The Castle★★★ **AC** DYZ • Abbey and Palace of Holyroodhouse★★ **AC** BV • New Town★★ CY**14** • The Georgian House★ **AC** CY**D** • Scottish National Portrait Gallery★ EY**M6** • Dundas House★ EY**E**) • Scottish National Gallery of Modern Art★ AV**M1** • Scott Monument★ ≤**AC** EY**F** • Craigmillar Castle★ **AC**, SE : 3 mi by A 7 BX • Dean Gallery★ AV opposite **M1** • Royal Yacht Britannia★ BV

On the outskirts : Edinburgh Zoo★★ **AC** AV • The Royal Observatory ≤★ **AC** BX

In the surrounding area : Rosslyn Chapel★★ **AC** S : 7.5 mi by A 701 - BX - and B 7006 • Forth Bridges★★, NW : 9.5 mi by A 90 AV • Hopetoun House★★ **AC**, NW : 11.5 mi by A 90 - AV - and A 904

SCOTLAND

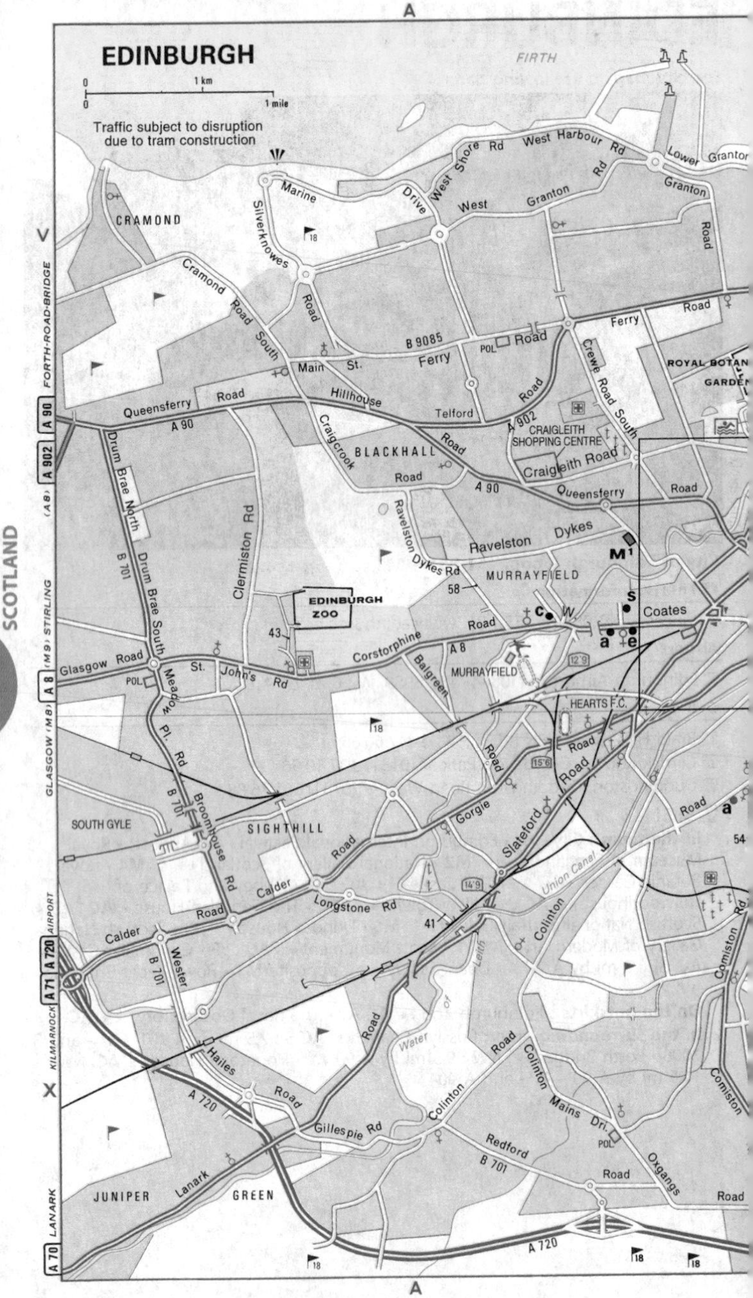
EDINBURGH
0
1 km
1 mile
Traffic subject to disruption due to tram construction
FIRTH
A
V
X
CRAMOND
Marine Drive
Silverknowes Road
West Shore Rd
West Harbour Rd
Lower Granton
West Granton Road
Granton Road
Cramond Road South
Ferry Road
B 9085
POL
Main St.
Hillhouse Road
Crewe Road South
ROYAL BOTAN
GARDEN
Queensferry Road
A 90
Telford Road
A 902
CRAIGLEITH SHOPPING CENTRE
Craigleith Road
Craigcrook Road
BLACKHALL
Queensferry Road
Drum Brae North
Drum Brae South
B 701
Clermiston Rd
Ravelston Dykes Rd
Ravelston Dykes
MURRAYFIELD
EDINBURGH ZOO
58
43
M1
c
W
S
Coates
a
e
Glasgow Road
St. John's Rd
Corstorphine Road
A 8
Balgreen Road
MURRAYFIELD
HEARTS F.C.
Meadow Pl. Rd
Broomhouse Rd
SOUTH GYLE
SIGHTHILL
Gorgie Road
Slateford Road
Union Canal
Calder Road
Longstone Rd
Wester Hailes Road
Colinton Road
Comiston Rd
41
54
Water of Leith
Colinton Mains Dri.
Oxgangs Road
Redford Road
Gillespie Rd
A 720
Lanark Road
JUNIPER GREEN
FORTH-ROAD-BRIDGE
A 90
A 902
(A8) (M9) STIRLING
GLASGOW (M8)
A 8
SCOTLAND
AIRPORT
A 720
A 71
KILMARNOCK
LANARK
A 70

Bruntsfield Pl.	BX	8
Cameron Toll Centre	BX	
Commercial St	BV	15
Constitution St	BV	17
Craigleith Shopping Centre	AV	
Craigmillar Park	BX	20
Duddingston Park	BV	28
Gilmerton Dykes St	BX	34
Great Junction St	BV	36
Howden Hall Rd	BX	40
Inglis Green Rd	AX	41
Kaimes Rd	AV	43
Morningside Rd	AX	54
Murrayfield Rd	AV	58
Newtoft St	BX	60
North Junction St	BV	62
Ocean Terminal Shopping Centre	BV	
Portobello High St	BV	67
Salamander St	BV	76

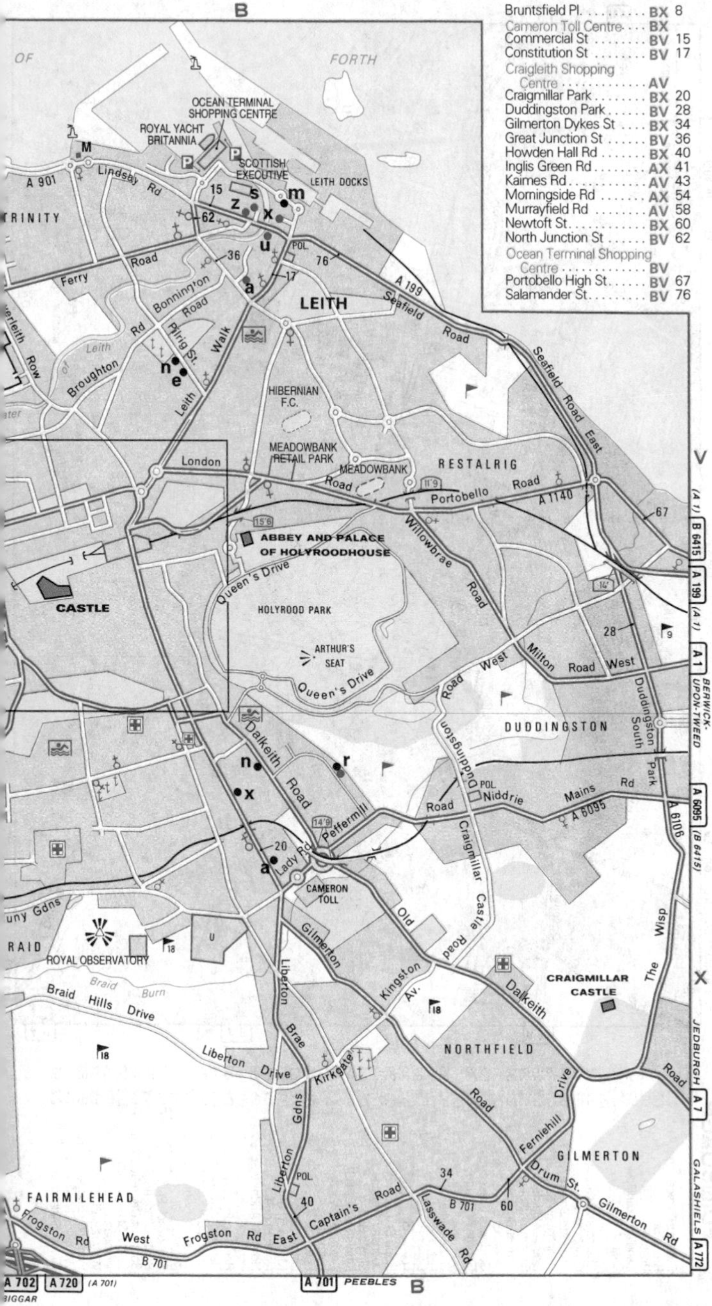

EDINBURGH

Bernard Terrace	EZ	3
Bread St	DZ	6
Bristo Pl.	EZ	7
Candlemaker Row	EZ	9
Castlehill	DZ	10
Castle St	DY	
Chambers St	EZ	12
Chapel St	EZ	13
Charlotte Square	CY	14
Deanhaugh St	CY	23
Douglas Gardens	CY	25
Drummond St	EZ	27
Forrest Rd	EZ	31
Frederick St	DY	
Gardner's Crescent	CZ	32
George IV Bridge	EZ	33
George St	DY	
Grassmarket	DZ	35
Hanover St	DY	
High St	EYZ	37
Home St	DZ	38
Hope St	CY	39
Johnston Terrace	DZ	42
King's Bridge	DZ	44
King's Stables Rd	DZ	45
Lawnmarket	EYZ	46
Leith St	EY	47
Leven St	DZ	48
Lothian St	EZ	51
Mound (The)	DY	55
North Bridge	EY	61
North St Andrew St	EY	66
Princes St	DY	
Raeburn Pl.	CY	69
Randolph Crescent	CY	71
St Andrew Square	EY	73
St James Centre	EY	
St Mary's St	EY	75
Shandwick Pl.	CYZ	77
South Charlotte St	DY	78
South St David St	DEY	79
Spittal St	DZ	83
Victoria St	EZ	84
Waterloo Pl.	EY	87
Waverley Bridge	EY	89
Waverley Market	EY	
West Maitland St	CZ	92

Traffic subject to disruption due to tram construction

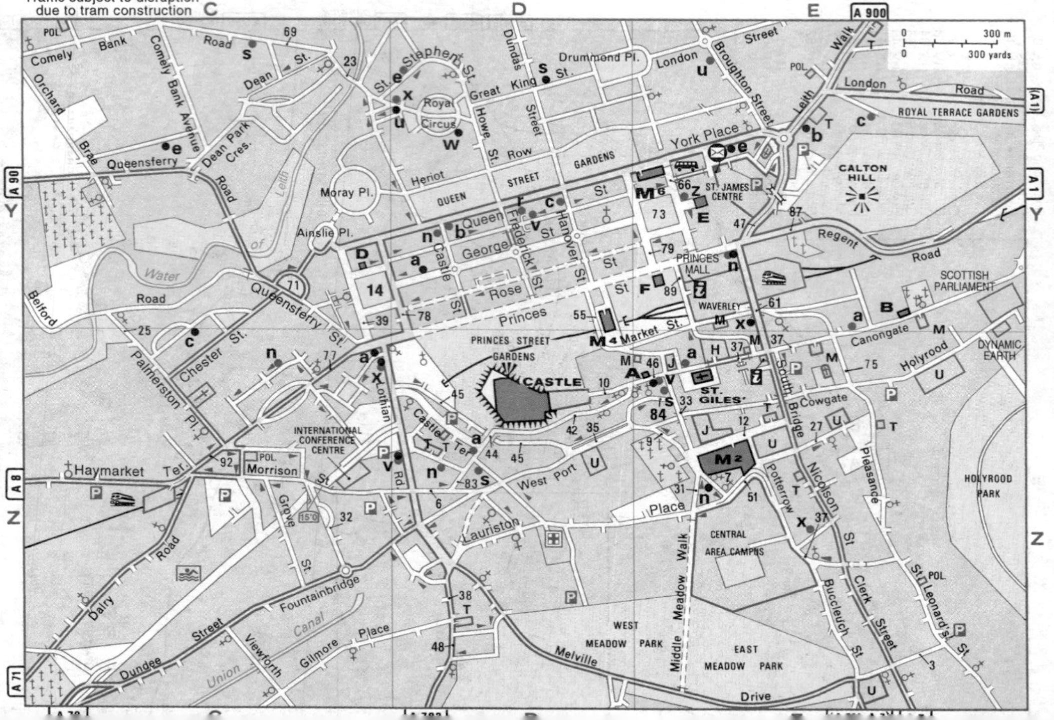

Balmoral

1 Princes St ✉ EH2 2EQ – ✆ (0131) 556 24 14 – www.thebalmoralhotel.com
188 rm – †£ 190/435 ††£ 190/435, ☕ £ 21 – 20 suites EY**n**
Rest *Number One* ✿ – see restaurant listing
Rest *Hadrian's* – ✆ (0131) 557 50 00 – Menu £ 15/24 – Carte £ 24/50
Renowned Edwardian hotel which provides for the modern traveller whilst retaining its old-fashioned charm. Live harp music accompanies the traditional afternoon teas. Bedrooms are classically styled but have a subtle contemporary edge; JK Rowling completed the final Harry Potter book in one of the suites! Luxurious modern dining or brasserie classics in delightful Hadrian's.

Sheraton Grand H. & Spa

1 Festival Sq ✉ EH3 9SR – ✆ (0131) 229 91 31 – www.sheratonedinburgh.co.uk
269 rm – †£ 170/595 ††£ 170/595, ☕ £ 20 – 10 suites CDZ**v**
Rest *One Square* – see restaurant listing
Spacious, modern hotel which has undergone a top-to-toe refurbishment. Sleek, stylish bedrooms boast strong comforts, the latest mod cons and smart bathrooms with mood lighting. An impressive four-storey glass cube houses the stunning spa.

Caledonian Ⓝ

Princes St ✉ EH1 2AB – ✆ (0131) 222 8888 – www.thecaledonianedinburgh.com
241 rm ☕ – †£ 159/399 ††£ 159/399 – 7 suites CZ**x**
Rest *Galvin Brasserie De Luxe* ☺ **Rest *The Pompadour by Galvin*** – see restaurant listing
Smartly refurbished hotel in what was once the Princes Street railway terminus; the stylish cocktail bar is in the arrivals hall. Sumptuous modern bedrooms with excellent facilities; ask for a castle view. The first Guerlain spa in the UK.

Prestonfield

Priestfield Rd ✉ EH16 5UT – ✆ (0131) 225 78 00 – www.prestonfield.com
28 rm ☕ – †£ 295 ††£ 295 – 5 suites BX**r**
Rest *Rhubarb* – see restaurant listing
17C country house in a pleasant rural spot, with an opulent, dimly lit interior displaying warm colours, fine furnishings and old tapestries; one of the most romantic hotels around. Various elegant lounges and a whisky room. Unique, luxurious bedrooms boast a high level of modern facilities. Excellent service.

Howard

34 Great King St ✉ EH3 6QH – ✆ (0131) 557 35 00 – www.thehoward.com
18 rm ☕ – †£ 120/240 ††£ 140/320 – 3 suites DY**s**
Rest *Atholl* – *(booking essential)* Carte £ 30/52
A series of three Georgian townhouses with comfortable period lounges and many characterful original features still in situ. Bedrooms vary in size and have classic furnishings and a contemporary edge; every room is assigned a butler. Formal dining from modern menus in the elegant restaurant.

Hotel Missoni

1 George IV Bridge ✉ EH1 1AD – ✆ (0131) 220 66 66 – www.hotelmissoni.com
136 rm ☕ – †£ 130/450 ††£ 150/450 – 7 suites EZ**v**
Rest *Cucina* – see restaurant listing
Striking, modern hotel; the first from this Milan fashion house, whose trademark stripes feature throughout. Funky bar. Boldly coloured bedrooms with clever design features, complimentary mini bars and smart, black mosaic floored bathrooms.

Scotsman

20 North Bridge ✉ EH3 1TR – ✆ (0131) 556 55 65
– www.thescotsmanhotel.co.uk EY**x**
69 rm ☕ – †£ 130/215 ††£ 160/305 – 2 suites
Rest *North Bridge Brasserie* – ✆ (0131) 622 29 00 – Menu £ 30 (lunch and early dinner) – Carte £ 24/47
Characterful Victorian hotel within the old Scotsman newspaper offices. Lovely period guest areas feature wood panelling and stained glass; traditional bedrooms are accessed via a marble staircase. Good business and leisure facilities. The stylish brasserie boasts a beautiful ceiling and a minstrels' gallery.

Channings

12-16 South Learmonth Gdns ✉ *EH4 1EZ* – ✆ *(0131) 315 2226* – *www.channings.co.uk* CY**e**

41 rm – †£ 85/145 ††£ 120/240 – 3 suites

Rest – *(closed Sunday dinner and Monday) (dinner only and lunch Friday-Sunday)* Menu £ 26

Set over five adjoining Edwardian townhouses; a cosy, tastefully furnished property run by a friendly team. Traditionally styled drawing rooms and bedrooms; the newer ones are themed after Shackleton, who used to live in one of the houses. The formal basement restaurant serves appealing Gallic classics.

Hotel du Vin

11 Bristo Pl ✉ *EH1 1EZ* – ✆ *(0131) 247 49 00* – *www.hotelduvin.com/edinburgh* EZ**n**

47 rm – †£ 109/170 ††£ 119/180

Rest *Bistro* – Carte £ 25/38

Boutique hotel featuring unique modern murals and dark wood, wine-themed bedrooms; located close to the Royal Mile. Guest areas include a whisky snug offering 300 spirits and a mezzanine bar with a wine tasting room and glass-fronted cellars. The classical bistro offers traditional European-based cooking.

Tigerlily

125 George St ✉ *EH2 4JN* – ✆ *(0131) 225 50 05* – *www.tigerlilyedinburgh.co.uk* – *Closed 25 December* DY**a**

33 rm – †£ 135/210 ††£ 135/430

Rest – Menu £ 15 (weekdays) – Carte £ 22/43

Classical Georgian townhouse concealing a funky, boutique interior. Large, individually designed bedrooms are luxurious, boasting seductive lighting, quality furnishings and superb wet rooms. The busy open-plan bar and dining room have similarly stylish modern décor and offer a worldwide menu.

Glasshouse without rest

2 Greenside Pl ✉ *EH1 3AA* – ✆ *(0131) 525 82 00* – *www.theetoncollection.co.uk* – *Closed 24-26 December* EY**b**

65 rm – †£ 115/475 ††£ 115/475, £ 19

A striking combination of a 150 year old church and sleek glass, topped by an impressive two acre roof garden. Stylish bedrooms feature floor to ceiling windows and lots of wood and leather; the suites open onto a sweeping balcony. Instead of a restaurant there's an honesty bar and 3 course room service.

Nira Caledonia

10 Gloucester Pl ✉ *EH3 6EF* – ✆ *(0131) 225 27 20* – *www.niracaledonia.com* DY**u**

28 rm – †£ 126/195 ††£ 159/425

Rest – *(dinner only)* Menu £ 25 – Carte £ 26/42

Two luxurious townhouses with romantic interiors and stunningly restored staircases. Bedrooms boast top class furnishings and are decorated in gold, black and silver colour schemes; some have jacuzzis in the rooms. The sleek, modern dining room – in the main house – offers meats cooked on the Josper grill.

Rutland

1-3 Rutland St ✉ *EH1 2AE* – ✆ *(0131) 229 34 02* – *www.therutlandhotel.com* – *Closed 24-25 December* CZ**a**

13 rm – †£ 140/315 ††£ 140/315, £ 10 – 1 suite

Rest – Menu £ 13 (lunch) – Carte £ 26/52

Boutique hotel occupying a commanding position at the top of Princes Street. Stylish modern bedrooms have bold décor and large slate-floored shower rooms; ask for a castle view. A few doors down is the two-roomed suite. Muffins welcome you on arrival. The contemporary restaurant styles itself on a steakhouse.

Chester Residence without rest

9 Rothesay Pl ✉ *EH3 7SL* – ✆ *(0131) 226 2075* – *www.chester-residence.com* CZ**c**

23 suites – ††£ 135/550, £ 9

Collection of townhouses boasting one and two bedroomed suites complete with fully equipped kitchens. State-of-the-art facilities include video entry and integrated sound systems. They can even arrange for a chef to cook in your room!

SCOTLAND

Hotel Indigo Ⓝ
51-59 York Pl ✉ EH1 3JD – ✆ (0131) 556 5577
– www.hiedinburgh.co.uk EY**e**
60 rm – †£ 99/299 ††£ 99/399
Rest – Menu £ 20 (early dinner) – Carte £ 24/43
Five interconnecting Georgian townhouses; one was previously a famous tea and coffee merchant's. Contemporary décor throughout. Bedrooms have bold feature walls, good amenities and powerful showers – those at the front are larger. Simple bistro serves an accessible all-day menu; afternoon tea is popular.

Dunstane House Ⓝ
4 West Coates, Haymarket ✉ EH12 5JQ – ✆ (0131) 337 61 69
– www.dunstanehotels.co.uk – Closed 23-27 December AV**s**
20 rm – †£ 75/135 ††£ 98/198
Rest *Skerries* – *(dinner only)* Carte £ 20/38
Grand house with well-tended gardens; once a training centre for the Royal Bank of Scotland. Guest areas retain original Victorian features – including elegant woodwork – and the smart, modern bedrooms are warm and calming. Informal whisky bar; the restaurant champions local produce, especially seafood.

Dunstane City without rest
5 Hampton Terr, Haymarket ✉ EH12 5JD – ✆ (0131) 337 61 69
– www.dunstanehotels.co.uk AV**s**
18 rm – †£ 89/169 ††£ 99/249
Traditional Victorian house with contrastingly modern feature wallpapers, black granite tiled floors and large chandeliers. Stylish, wood-furnished bedrooms offer good facilities; some even boast jacuzzis. Extensive buffet breakfasts.

Kingsburgh House without rest
2 Corstorphine Rd ✉ EH12 6HN – ✆ (0131) 313 16 79
– www.thekingsburgh.co.uk AV**c**
6 rm – †£ 89/145 ††£ 99/170
Attractive Victorian villa with keen, hands-on owners. Comfy lounge and formally laid breakfast room with ornate coving. Warm, classically styled bedrooms feature antiques, modern facilities and good extras; some have four-poster beds.

Kildonan Lodge
27 Craigmillar Pk. ✉ EH16 5PE – ✆ (0131) 667 27 93
– www.kildonanlodgehotel.co.uk – Closed 25-26 December BX**a**
12 rm – †£ 79/179 ††£ 89/179
Rest – *(closed Sunday) (dinner only) (booking essential)* Carte £ 20/33
Large detached Victorian house on the main road into the city. Cosy drawing room with an open fire and an honesty bar. Comfy, traditionally furnished bedrooms: some have four-posters or jacuzzis; those in the basement are more contemporary. Appealing, classical dishes feature plenty of Scottish produce.

One Royal Circus without rest
1 Royal Circus ✉ EH3 6TL – ✆ (0131) 625 6669
– www.oneroyalcircus.com DY**w**
5 rm – †£ 129/199 ††£ 138/258
Stunning Georgian house at the end of a crescent; designed by William Playfair in 1823. Spacious interior with a billiard room and two first floor lounges boasting ornate plasterwork, a grand piano and a bar. Stylish, understated bedrooms and marble bathrooms; those on the second floor are the brightest.

94 DR without rest
94 Dalkeith Rd ✉ EH16 5AF – ✆ (0131) 662 92 65 – www.94dr.com
– Closed 4-18 January and 25-26 December BX**n**
6 rm – †£ 90/125 ††£ 100/160
Victorian terraced house on the main road into the city. Brightly tiled hallway leads to a retro lounge with an honesty bar. Lovely breakfast conservatory opens onto a decked terrace. Stylish, well-equipped bedrooms have Scottish touches.

23 Mayfield without rest
23 Mayfield Gdns ✉ EH9 2BX – ✆ (0131) 667 5806 – www.23mayfield.co.uk
8 rm – †£ 65/95 ††£ 80/160 BX**x**
Lovingly restored Victorian house with a very welcoming, helpful owner and an outdoor hot-tub. Spacious lounge has an honesty bar and a collection of old and rare books. Sumptuous bedrooms come with coordinated soft furnishings, some mahogany features and luxurious bathrooms. Extravagant breakfast choices.

Millers64 without rest
64 Pilrig St ✉ EH6 5AS – ✆ (0131) 454 3666 – www.millers64.co.uk – Closed 15-17 November BV**e**
3 rm – †£ 75/85 ††£ 85/150
Modernised Victorian terraced house, in an up and coming part of town. The smart, spacious bedrooms are all suites and boast good quality linens and extras. Communal breakfasts include a hot daily special and homemade pastries.

Kew House without rest
1 Kew Terr, Murrayfield ✉ EH12 5JE – ✆ (0131) 313 07 00 – www.kewhouse.com – Closed January and 25-26 December AV**a**
7 rm – †£ 75/96 ††£ 99/175
Warm, welcoming stone-built house with a neat lounge and a wood-furnished breakfast room; set in a great location for Murrayfield Stadium. Modern, immaculately kept bedrooms come with chocolates, a decanter of sherry and fresh flowers.

SCOTLAND

Ardmor House without rest
74 Pilrig St ✉ EH6 5AS – ✆ (0131) 554 4944 – www.ardmorhouse.com
5 rm – †£ 60/95 ††£ 90/155 BV**n**
Comfortable, laid-back guesthouse on a quiet residential street. Bedrooms range in size and boast bright décor, original plaster ceilings and granite fireplaces. Homemade preserves and cakes at breakfast. The owner has good local knowledge.

Number One – Balmoral Hotel
1 Princes St ✉ EH2 2EQ – ✆ (0131) 557 67 27 – www.restaurantnumberone.com – Closed 25-26 December and 2 weeks mid-January EY**n**
Rest – *(dinner only)* Menu £ 68
A stylish, long-standing restaurant in the basement of a grand Edwardian hotel. Richly upholstered banquettes and red lacquered walls give it a plush, luxurious feel. Cooking is modern, intricate and very visually impressive, and prime Scottish ingredients are key. Service is professional and has personality.
→ Poached scallops, Ibérico ham, pea, yuzu and kombu. Dry-aged beef with dark ale onions and Barwheys cheese. Pineapple and coconut millefeuille, banana and rum sorbet.

21212 (Paul Kitching) with rm
3 Royal Terr ✉ EH7 5AB – ✆ (0131) 523 1030 – www.21212restaurant.co.uk – Closed 10 days January and 10 days summer EY**c**
4 rm – †£ 95/325 ††£ 95/325
Rest – *(closed Sunday and Monday)* Menu £ 20/68 **s**
Stunningly refurbished Georgian townhouse designed by Thomas Playfair. The glass-fronted kitchen is the focal point of the stylish, high-ceilinged dining room. '21212' reflects the number of dishes per course; cooking is skilful, innovative and features some quirky combinations. Plush first floor lounge and luxurious bedrooms; some with views over the Firth of Forth.
→ Smoked chicken with spinach and rosemary cream. Fillet of beef with baked spicy beans, corned beef and basil roots. Strawberry meringue float, mango lassi and rice pudding.

Can't choose between two similar establishments in the same town?
We list them in order of preference,
within each category.

XXX **Castle Terrace** (Dominic Jack)
33-35 Castle Terr ✉ EH1 2EL – ☎ (0131) 229 12 22
– www.castleterracerestaurant.com – Closed Christmas, New Year, Sunday and Monday DZ**a**
Rest – Menu £ 27/75 – Carte £ 48/68
In the shadow of the castle, an understatedly stylish restaurant with a gilded ceiling and an attractive bar-lounge. Refined cooking showcases seasonal local produce in an assured, unfussy manner, following a 'nature to plate' philosophy.
➜ Spelt risotto with crispy ox tongue and finely sliced pork collar. Saddle of roe deer with celery, celeriac, apple and walnuts. Toffee soufflé with a cinnamon crumble and ginger ice cream.

XXX **The Pompadour by Galvin** N – Caledonian Hotel
Princes St ✉ EH1 2AB – ☎ (0131) 222 8975 – www.galvinrestaurants.com
– Closed first two weeks January, 26 December, dinner 25 December, Sunday and Monday CZ**x**
Rest – (dinner only) Menu £ 58
First floor hotel restaurant overlooking the castle, which opened in the 1920s and is modelled on a classic French salon. Gallic dishes showcase Scottish produce, using techniques introduced by Escoffier, executed with a lightness of touch.

XXX **Rhubarb** – Prestonfield Hotel
Priestfield Rd ✉ EH16 5UT – ☎ (0131) 225 13 33 – www.prestonfield.com
Rest – Menu £ 30 – Carte £ 35/68 BX**r**
Sumptuous, richly decorated dining rooms set within a romantic 17C country house; so named as this was the first place in Scotland where rhubarb was grown. Concise menu of modern dishes with some innovative touches. Interesting wine list.

SCOTLAND

XX **The Honours**
58A North Castle St ✉ EH2 3LU – ☎ (0131) 220 2513 – www.thehonours.co.uk
– Closed 2-3 January, Sunday and Monday DY**n**
Rest – Menu £ 19/20 – Carte £ 29/55
Owned by a well-established chef; a bustling brasserie with a smart, stylish interior and a pleasingly informal atmosphere. Menus take their influences from across Europe but have a French leaning and always offer some Scottish dishes.

XX **Mark Greenaway** N
69 North Castle St ✉ EH2 3LJ – ☎ (0131) 226 1155 – www.markgreenaway.com
– Closed 25-26 December, 1 January, Sunday and Monday DY**p**
Rest – (booking advisable) Menu £ 20 (lunch and early dinner) – Carte £ 33/49
Set in an old bank on a corner site in the New Town; they store the wine in the old vault! The cosy dining room has a brasserie look and a formal feel. Menus range from 'set' to 'surprise'; the complex modern dishes have global influences.

XX **Galvin Brasserie De Luxe** N – Caledonian Hotel
Princes St, (entrance on Rutland St) ✉ EH1 2AB – ☎ (0131) 222 8988
– www.galvinrestaurants.com CZ**x**
Rest – Menu £ 19 (lunch and early dinner) – Carte £ 27/37
Accurately described by its name: a simply styled restaurant which looks like a brasserie of old but with the addition of a smart shellfish counter and fairly formal service. Appealing daily menu of French classics and a concise, good value set selection; dishes are refined, flavoursome and well-proportioned.

XX **Ondine**
2 George IV Bridge (first floor) ✉ EH1 1AD – ☎ (0131) 226 18 88
– www.ondinerestaurant.co.uk – Closed 1 week early January and 24-26 December EZ**s**
Rest – Menu £ 18 (lunch and early dinner) – Carte £ 31/79
Smart, lively restaurant dominated by granite-topped bar and crustacean counter. Classic menus showcase prime Scottish seafood. Straightforward, tasty cooking. Well-structured service.

XX **Forth Floor at Harvey Nichols**

30-34 St Andrew Sq ✉ EH2 2AD – ✆ (0131) 524 83 50 – www.harveynichols.com – Closed 25 December, 1 January, Sunday and Monday dinner EY**z**

Rest – Menu £ 30 (lunch and early dinner) – Carte £ 32/44

Buzzy eatery with wonderful Firth of Forth views. Dine on ambitious dishes in the restaurant or old favourites in the all-day bistro. There's also a seafood bar, a tapas bar, a sushi counter and a conveyor belt of champagne and chocolates.

XX **Mulroy** Ⓝ

11A-13A William St ✉ EH3 7NG – ✆ (0131) 225 6061 – www.themulroy.co.uk

Rest – Menu £ 17 (lunch and early dinner)/40 CZ**n**

Located in the basement of a West End optician's and named after a famous Scottish battlefield. Three surprisingly light and airy rooms, tastefully decorated with antiques and watercolours. Dishes are French-based, with some unusual twists.

XX **Cucina** – Hotel Missoni

1 George IV Bridge ✉ EH1 1AD – ✆ (0131) 220 66 66 – www.hotelmissoni.com

Rest – Menu £ 15 (lunch and early dinner) – Carte £ 23/51 EZ**v**

Stylish mezzanine restaurant with a buzzy atmosphere, set among the trademark stripes of this fashion house hotel. Classic Italian dishes served on boldly patterned china; some sharing plates. Large bar offers cocktails and prosecco on tap.

XX **Angels with Bagpipes**

343 High St, Royal Mile ✉ EH1 1PW – ✆ (0131) 220 1111 – www.angelswithbagpipes.co.uk – Closed 24-26 December EZ**a**

Rest – Menu £ 14 (lunch) – Carte £ 25/41

Small, split-level restaurant, just across from St Giles Cathedral on the Royal Mile. Simple interior; some tables overlook a rear courtyard. Seasonal menus change every six weeks, offering a mix of unfussy classics and more modern dishes.

SCOTLAND

XX **One Square** – Sheraton Grand Hotel & Spa

1 Festival Sq ✉ EH3 9SR – ✆ (0131) 221 64 22 – www.onesquareedinburgh.co.uk

Rest – Carte £ 23/53 CDZ**v**

So named because it covers one side of the square, this smart hotel restaurant offers casual all-day dining and views towards Edinburgh Castle. The all-encompassing menu offers dishes ranging from a club sandwich to a grill selection.

X **Timberyard** Ⓝ

10 Lady Lawson St ✉ EH3 9DS – ✆ (0131) 221 1222 – www.timberyard.co – Closed Christmas, 1 week April, 1 week October, Sunday and Monday

Rest – *(booking essential)* Menu £ 18 (lunch and early dinner) DZ**s**
– Carte £ 26/36

Trendy warehouse restaurant; its spacious, rustic interior incorporating wooden floors and wood-burning stoves. Scandic-influenced menu offers 'bites', 'small' and 'large' sizes, with some home-smoked dishes and an emphasis on distinct, punchy flavours. Cocktails are made with vegetable purées and foraged herbs.

X **Cafe Fish**

15 North West Circus Pl ✉ EH3 6SX – ✆ (0131) 225 44 31 – www.cafefish.net – Closed 25 December, Sunday dinner and Monday DY**x**

Rest – Carte £ 23/43

Family-run restaurant in a delightfully converted 1930s bank, with high ceilings, a fine parquet floor, an open kitchen and a pleasant west-facing decked area. Daily changing menu of excellent quality, sustainable Scottish seafood.

X **L'Escargot Bleu**

56 Broughton St ✉ EH1 3SA – ✆ (0131) 557 16 00 – www.lescargotbleu.co.uk – Closed Sunday except July and August EY**u**

Rest – Menu £ 13 (lunch and early dinner) – Carte £ 26/40

Authentic French bistro offering boldly flavoured, regional French favourites; sit in the front room with its large windows and buzzy atmosphere. Dishes may be fiercely French but ingredients champion local produce from artisan producers.

Dogs

110 Hanover St (1st Floor) ✉ EH2 1DR – ✆ (0131) 220 1208 – www.thedogsonline.co.uk – Closed 25 December and 1 January DY**c**

Rest – Carte £ 19/27

Cosy, slightly bohemian-style eatery on the first floor of a classic Georgian mid-terrace, with two high-ceilinged, shabby chic dining rooms and an appealing bar. Robust, good value comfort food is crafted from local, seasonal produce; sharing dishes and Scottish staples such as Arbroath Smokies feature.

Bon Vivant

55 Thistle St ✉ EH2 1DY – ✆ (0131) 225 3275 – www.bonvivantedinburgh.co.uk – Closed 25-26 December and 1 January DY**v**

Rest – Carte £ 18/32

Relaxed eatery in the city backstreets, with a dimly lit interior, tightly packed tables and a cheery, welcoming team. The appealing, twice daily menu has strong Mediterranean influences; start with some of the £ 1 bite-sized nibbles.

Purslane

33a St Stephen St ✉ EH3 5AH – ✆ (0131) 226 3500 – www.purslanerestaurant.co.uk – Closed 25-26 December, 1 January and Monday DY**e**

Rest – *(booking essential)* Menu £ 16/26

Set in the basement of a Georgian house in a residential area; an intimate restaurant of just 9 tightly packed tables, with wallpaper featuring a pine tree motif. The chef prepares modern dishes using well-practiced techniques.

Field (N)

41 West Nicholson St ✉ EH8 9DB – ✆ (0131) 667 7010 – www.fieldrestaurant.co.uk – Closed Sunday and Monday EZ**x**

Rest – Menu £ 15 (lunch and early dinner) – Carte £ 21/27

Small, rustic restaurant run by two young owners; the 8 tables are overlooked by a huge canvas of a prized cow. The appealing menu changes slightly each day, offering unfussy, traditional dishes with the focus firmly on the main ingredient.

Kanpai (N)

8-10 Grindlay St ✉ EH3 9AS – ✆ (0131) 228 1602 – www.kanpaisushi.co.uk – Closed Monday DZ**n**

Rest – Carte £ 15/29

Uncluttered, modern Japanese restaurant with a smart sushi bar and cheerful service. Colourful, elaborate dishes have clean, well-defined flavours; the menu is designed to help novices feel confident and experts feel at home.

Bia Bistrot

19 Colinton Rd ✉ EH10 5DP – ✆ (0131) 452 84 53 – www.biabistrot.co.uk – Closed first week January, 1 week July, Sunday and Monday AX**a**

Rest – Menu £ 11 (lunch and early dinner) – Carte £ 20/33

Good value neighbourhood bistro with a buzzy vibe and a simple modern style; set in a smart residential area. Unfussy, flavoursome dishes range in their influences due to the friendly owners' Irish-Scottish and French-Spanish heritages.

Café St Honoré

34 North West Thistle Street Ln. ✉ EH2 1EA – ✆ (0131) 226 22 11 – www.cafesthonore.com – Closed 24-26 December and 1-2 January

Rest – *(booking essential)* Menu £ 20/25 – Carte £ 29/46 DY**r**

Long-standing French bistro, hidden away down a side street. The interior is cosy, with wooden marquetry, mirrors on the walls and tightly packed tables. Traditional Gallic menus use Scottish produce and they even smoke their own salmon.

Wedgwood

267 Canongate ✉ EH8 8BQ – ✆ (0131) 558 87 37 – www.wedgwoodtherestaurant.co.uk – Closed 25-26 December and 2-24 January EY**a**

Rest – Menu £ 16 (lunch) – Carte £ 30/48

Atmospheric, split-level bistro, hidden away at the bottom of the Royal Mile; it's personally run by a friendly team and a hit with the locals. Well-presented, seasonal dishes feature produce foraged for from the surrounding countryside.

SCOTLAND

The Scran & Scallie N

1 Comely Bank Rd, Stockbridge ✉ EH4 1DT – ✆ (0131) 332 6281 – www.scranandscallie.com – Closed 25-26 December CY**s**

Rest – *(booking advisable)* Carte £ 24/35

A more casual venture from Tom Kitchin and Dominic Jack, with a wood furnished bar and a dining room which blends rustic and contemporary décor. Extensive menus follow a 'Nature to Plate' philosophy and focus on the classical and the local.

at Leith

Malmaison

1 Tower Pl ✉ EH6 7DB – ✆ (0844) 693 0652 – www.malmaison.com

100 rm – †£ 99/325 ††£ 99/325, ☕ £ 12 BV**m**

Rest *Brasserie* – Menu £ 20 (lunch and early dinner) – Carte £ 25/66

Impressive former seamens' mission located on the quayside; the first of the Malmaison hotels. The décor is a mix of bold stripes and contrasting black and white themes. Comfy, well-equipped bedrooms; one with a four-poster and a tartan roll-top bath. Intimate bar and a popular French brasserie and terrace.

Martin Wishart

54 The Shore ✉ EH6 6RA – ✆ (0131) 553 35 57 – www.martin-wishart.co.uk – Closed 31 December-14 January, 25-26 December, Sunday and Monday

Rest – *(booking essential)* Menu £ 29/75 BV**u**

Elegant modern restaurant with immaculately set tables and attentive, professional service. Three 6 course menus - Tasting, Seafood and Vegetarian - and a concise à la carte. Fine ingredients are used in well-judged, flavourful combinations. Dishes display a classical base and elaborate, original touches.

→ Ox tongue tart with Vivaldi potato, comté and truffle sauce. Fillet of red mullet, Finnan haddock potato mousseline and red wine sauce. Valrhona caramelia chocolate cremeux, passion fruit sorbet, caramelized hazelnuts and praline.

Kitchin (Tom Kitchin)

78 Commercial Quay ✉ EH6 6LX – ✆ (0131) 555 17 55 – www.thekitchin.com – Closed Christmas, New Year, Sunday and Monday BV**z**

Rest – *(booking essential)* Menu £ 27/75 – Carte £ 55/99

'From nature to plate' is the motto of this passionate and focused chef, so expect refreshingly honest, seasonal cooking which shows great skill and clarity of flavours. The converted dockside warehouse has been given a plush, sumptuous feel - without over-formality - and service is confident and keen.

→ Razor clams with diced vegetables and chorizo. Braised shin of Orkney beef 'ossobuco' style. Baked cheesecake with poached Yorkshire rhubarb, jelly and rhubarb sorbet.

Plumed Horse

50-54 Henderson St ✉ EH6 6DE – ✆ (0131) 554 55 56 – www.plumedhorse.co.uk – Closed 2 weeks summer, 1 week Easter, Christmas-early January, Sunday and Monday BV**a**

Rest – Menu £ 24/69

Personally run restaurant with ornate ceiling, vivid paintings, an intimate feel and formal service. Well-crafted, classical cooking with strong, bold flavours and good use of Scottish ingredients.

Mithas

7 Dock Pl ✉ EH6 6LU – ✆ (0131) 554 0008 – www.mithas.co.uk – Closed Monday BV**s**

Rest – Menu £ 16/35 – Carte £ 21/50

Smart, three-roomed Indian restaurant with booth seating. The large selection of menus centres on tasty kebabs and vibrant griddled dishes but there are also many vegetarian options; the set menus offer the best value. Attentive team.

Ship on the Shore

24-26 The Shore ✉ EH6 6QN – ✆ (0131) 555 04 09 – www.theshipontheshore.co.uk – Closed 24-26 December BV**x**

Rest – Carte £ 27/41

Smart period building on the quayside, modelled on the Royal Yacht Britannia and filled with nautical memorabilia. The seafood-orientated menu offers fresh, simply prepared, classic dishes and platters; try the smoked salmon at breakfast.

at Currie Southwest : 5 mi on A 70 – ✉ City Of Edinburgh

Violet Bank House without rest

167 Lanark Rd West ✉ EH14 5NZ – ☎ (0131) 451 51 03
– www.violetbankhouse.co.uk
3 rm – †£ 65/85 ††£ 120/140
200 year old cottage in a conservation zone, with attractive gardens running down to the river. Homely, individually decorated bedrooms have a host of thoughtful extras. Impressive breakfasts feature everything from pancakes to kedgeree.

at Kirknewton Southwest : 7 mi by A 71 - AX – ✉ Edinburgh

Dalmahoy H. & Country Club

Northwest : 2 mi on A 71 ✉ EH27 8EB rm, rest,
– ☎ (0131) 333 18 45 – www.marriottdalmahoy.co.uk
215 rm – †£ 69/249 ††£ 79/249, £ 16 – 2 suites
Rest *Pentland* – *(dinner only and Sunday lunch)* Carte £ 30/46
Rest *Zest* – Carte £ 20/39
Extended Georgian mansion boasting two championship golf courses and extensive leisure facilities. Country house style guest areas and well-equipped, bedrooms; the best, in the main house, are a blend of the old and the new. Traditional, formal dining and good views over the 1,000 acre grounds in Pentland; laid-back all-day menus in bright, modern Zest.

at Ingliston West : 7 mi on A 8

Norton House rest,

✉ EH28 8LX – ☎ (0131) 333 12 75 – www.handpicked.co.uk
83 rm – †£ 112/204 ††£ 122/214 – 5 suites
Rest *Ushers* – see restaurant listing
Rest *Brasserie* – Carte £ 25/41
19C country house in mature grounds, close to Edinburgh Airport. Classical bedrooms in the main house and stylish, modern executive rooms in the extension. The impressive oak staircase and country house lounges contrast with a state-of-the-art spa. Dine in the intimate restaurant or relaxed brasserie.

XX **Ushers** N – Norton House Hotel

✉ EH28 8LX – ☎ (0131) 333 12 75 – www.handpicked.co.uk – Closed January-February and Sunday-Tuesday
Rest – *(dinner only) (booking essential)* Carte £ 37/45
Intimate hotel restaurant named after former owners of the house. Elaborate cooking uses top quality seasonal ingredients. Choose from the gourmet menu or concise weekly à la carte. Techniques are modern and combinations, original.

EDNAM – The Scottish Borders – see Kelso

ELGIN – Moray – **501** K11 – **pop. 20 527** Scotland **28** C1

Edinburgh 198 mi – Aberdeen 68 mi – Fraserburgh 61 mi – Inverness 39 mi
Cooper Park, ☎ (01343) 562 6 08, www.visitscotland.com
Moray, Lossiemouth, Stotfield Rd, ☎ (01343) 81 20 18
Hardhillock, Birnie Rd, ☎ (01343) 54 23 38
Hopeman, Moray, ☎ (01343) 83 05 78
Town★ - Cathedral★ (Chapter house★★)**AC**
Glenfiddich Distillery★, SE : 10 mi by A 941

Mansion House

The Haugh, via Haugh Rd ✉ IV30 1AW – ☎ (01343) 548 811
– www.mansionhousehotel.co.uk – Closed 25 December
23 rm – †£ 97/113 ††£ 154/183 **Rest** – Carte £ 19/32
Sizeable Victorian country house in pleasant gardens. Grand inner with beautiful Georgian-style drawing room featuring a grand piano; snooker table in the 'wee bar'. Luxurious bedrooms - some with sleigh beds, four-posters or river views. Classically furnished, formal dining room offers eclectic mix of dishes.

SCOTLAND

Pines without rest
East Rd, East : 0.5 mi on A 96 ✉ IV30 1XG – ✆ (01343) 552 495 – www.thepinesguesthouse.com
6 rm – £ 50/60 £ 60/75
Charming Victorian villa featuring original tiled floors and stained glass windows. Homely lounge and comfortable, traditionally styled bedrooms; Room 4 is the best with its antique four-poster bed. Highland products at breakfast.

ELIE – Fife – 501 L15 – pop. 942 28 D2

Edinburgh 44 mi – Dundee 24 mi – St Andrews 13 mi

Sangster's (Bruce Sangster)
51 High St ✉ KY9 1BZ – ✆ (01333) 331 001 – www.sangsters.co.uk – Closed January-mid February, 1 week November, 25-26 December, Sunday dinner, Monday and Tuesday November-March
Rest – *(dinner only and Sunday lunch) (booking essential)* Menu £ 40
Sweet little restaurant in a sleepy coastal hamlet; run by a husband and wife team. The well-respected, experienced chef uses Fife's natural larder and willingly embraces new ideas. Appealing, flavoursome dishes are carefully executed: the simplest dishes are the best; desserts are more modern.
→ Pig's cheek croquette with Stornoway black pudding. Sea bass on nutty cabbage, crushed Ratte potatoes and a tapenade citrus foam. Salted caramel, peanut and chocolate tart with poached pear, praline and vanilla ice cream.

ERISKA (Isle of) – Argyll and Bute – 501 D14 – ✉ Oban 27 B2

Edinburgh 127 mi – Glasgow 104 mi – Oban 12 mi

Isle of Eriska rm, rest,
Benderloch ✉ PA37 1SD – ✆ (01631) 720 371 – www.eriska-hotel.co.uk – Closed 3-20 January
23 rm – £ 200/350 £ 350/500 – 7 suites
Rest – *(dinner only) (booking essential)* Menu £ 50
19C baronial mansion on private island, boasting fantastic views over Lismore and the mountains. Classically styled, open-fired guest areas display modern touches. Comfy bedrooms feature bright fabrics and hi-tech equipment. Superb spa and leisure facilities. Contemporary dining room offers concise, daily changing menu with a modern edge.

EUROCENTRAL – North Lanarkshire 25 B1

Edinburgh 34 mi – London 397 mi – Glasgow 12 mi – Paisley 20 mi

Dakota rm,
1-3 Parklands Ave ✉ ML1 4WQ – ✆ (01698) 835 440 – www.dakotahotels.co.uk
92 rm – £ 99/129 £ 99/129, £ 13
Rest *Grill* – Carte £ 24/52
Sleek black hotel visible from the M8: perfect for the image-conscious business traveller. Spacious bedrooms offer free wi-fi, king-sized beds and smart, modern shower rooms. Classic dishes served in the open-plan Grill restaurant, which is decorated with huge, blown-up pictures from 'The Eagle' comic.

FAIRLIE – North Ayrshire – 501 F16 – pop. 1 510 25 A1

Edinburgh 79 mi – London 434 mi – Douglas 199 mi – Belfast 78 mi

Catch at Fins
Fencebay Fisheries, Fencefoot Farm, South : 1.5 mi on A 78 ✉ KA29 0EG – ✆ (01475) 568 989 – www.fencebay.co.uk – Closed 25-26 December, 1-2 January, Sunday dinner-Wednesday
Rest – *(booking essential)* Carte £ 18/36
You can eat in the cosy bothy or spacious conservatory at this longstanding, simply furnished restaurant, complete with smokery and farm shop. Menus offer unfussy dishes of fresh fish and shellfish, alongside their own beech-smoked products.

FIONNPHORT – Argyll and Bute – 501 A15 – see Mull (Isle of)

FLODIGARRY – Highland – 501 B11 – see Skye (Isle of)

FOCHABERS - Moray - 501 K11 - pop. 1 499 28 C1

Edinburgh 175 mi - London 580 mi - Aberdeen 56 mi - Inverness 48 mi

Trochelhill Country House without rest

West : 2.75 mi by A 96 off B 9015 ✉ IV32 7LN - ✆ (01343) 821 267 - www.trochelhill.co.uk

3 rm - £ 70 £ 110

Whitewashed Victorian house; well-run by friendly owners who serve tea and cake on arrival. Spacious bedrooms feature modern bathrooms with walk-in showers; 2 have roll-top baths. Breakfast includes haggis, black pudding and homemade bread.

FORT AUGUSTUS - Highland - 501 F12 - pop. 508 30 C3

Edinburgh 158 mi - London 535 mi - Glasgow 138 mi - Manchester 350 mi

The Lovat

✉ PH32 4DU - ✆ (01456) 459 250 - www.thelovat.com

28 rm - £ 60/235 £ 70/275

Rest - *(closed Sunday-Tuesday November-March) (dinner only) (booking advisable)* Menu £ 45

Rest *Brasserie* - Carte £ 23/42

Professionally run, Victorian house with well-tended, lawned gardens and a charming interior featuring old wood panelling and original fireplaces. Elegant drawing room and a comfy lounge complete with a piano. Contemporary bedrooms come with fruit and biscuits. Modern versions of classic dishes in the brasserie; ambitious, intricate set menu in the formal restaurant.

FORT WILLIAM - Highland - 501 E13 - pop. 8 979 Scotland 30 C3

Edinburgh 133 mi - Glasgow 104 mi - Inverness 68 mi - Oban 50 mi

15 High St, ✆ (0845) 2 25 51 21, www.visit-fortwilliam.co.uk

North Rd, ✆ (01397) 70 44 64

Town★

The Road to the Isles★★ (Neptune's Staircase (<★★), Glenfinnan★ <★, Arisaig★, Silver Sands of Morar★, Mallaig★), NW : 46 mi by A 830 - Ardnamurchan Peninsula★★ - Ardnamurchan Point (<★★), NW : 65 mi by A 830, A 861 and B 8007 - SE : Ben Nevis★★ (<★★) - Glen Nevis★

Inverlochy Castle

Torlundy, Northeast : 3 mi on A 82 ✉ PH33 6SN - ✆ (01397) 702 177 - www.inverlochycastlehotel.com

18 rm - £ 280/695 £ 450/695 - 1 suite

Rest *Inverlochy Castle* ✿ - see restaurant listing

Striking castellated house in beautiful grounds, boasting stunning views over the loch to Ben Nevis. Classical country house interior with sumptuous open-fired lounges and a grand hall with an impressive ceiling mural. Elegant bedrooms offer the height of luxury; mod cons include mirrored TVs and laptops.

Distillery Guesthouse without rest

North Rd. ✉ PH33 6LR - ✆ (01397) 700 103 - www.stayinfortwilliam.co.uk - Closed 1 week Christmas

10 rm - £ 55/75 £ 76/89

Smart hotel - formerly 3 distillery workers' cottages - at the foot of Ben Nevis. Comfy lounge with shortbread, whisky and books about the area. Landscaped gardens; terrace boasts lovely views.

Grange without rest

Grange Rd., South : 0.75 mi by A 82 and Ashburn Lane ✉ PH33 6JF - ✆ (01397) 705 516 - www.thegrange-scotland.co.uk - Closed November-mid March

3 rm - £ 120/130 £ 120/130

Delightful Victorian house with attractive garden and immaculate interior, set in a quiet residential area. Beautiful lounge displays fine fabrics; lovely breakfast room boasts Queen Anne style chairs. Bedrooms are extremely well appointed, with smart bathrooms.

Ashburn House without rest

18 Achintore Rd., South : 0.5 mi on A 82 ✉ PH33 6RQ – ☎ (01397) 706 000 – www.highland5star.co.uk

6 rm – †£ 50/55 ††£ 90/120

Attractive Victorian house with comfy lounge and conservatory breakfast room. Bright, modern pine-furnished bedrooms; Room 2 is largest and has the best view. Homemade shortbread on arrival.

The Gantocks without rest

Achintore Rd., South : 1 mi on A 82 ✉ PE33 6RN – ☎ (01397) 702 050 – www.fortwilliam5star.co.uk – Closed December and January

3 rm – †£ 100/110 ††£ 110/130

Whitewashed bungalow with loch views; run by experienced owners. Spacious, modern bedrooms boast king-sized beds, large baths and nice toiletries. Unusual offerings and water views at breakfast.

Inverlochy Castle

Torlundy, Northeast : 3 mi on A 82 ✉ PH33 6SN – ☎ (01397) 702 177 – www.inverlochycastlehotel.com

Rest – *(booking essential)* Menu £ 38/67

Formal restaurant in a striking castle at the foot of Ben Nevis, boasting stunning loch views. Choice of two smart candlelit dining rooms filled with period sideboards and polished silver. Traditional dishes are executed with care and precision, and feature top quality Scottish produce. Lighter menu at lunch.

→ Loch Linnhe langoustines with crispy chicken, tomato and parmesan. Loin and confit shoulder of lamb with tapenade gnocchi and goat's cheese beignets. Hot banana crumble soufflé with malted milk chocolate ice cream.

Lime Tree An Ealdhain with rm

Achintore Rd ✉ PH33 6RQ – ☎ (01397) 701 806 – www.limetreefortwilliam.co.uk – Closed November and 24-26 December

9 rm – †£ 60/120 ††£ 80/120 **Rest** – *(dinner only)* Menu £ 30

Attractive 19C former manse; now an informally run restaurant, art gallery and hotel. The appealingly rustic dining room boasts exposed beams and an open kitchen, and offers fresh modern cooking. Bedrooms are simply furnished and well-priced; ask for one with a view of Loch Linnhe.

Crannog

Town Pier ✉ PH33 6DB – ☎ (01397) 705 589 – www.crannog.net – Closed 25-26 December and 1 January

Rest – *(booking essential)* Menu £ 13 (lunch) – Carte £ 27/39

Popular seafood restaurant with a brightly painted roof; set on the town pier above Loch Linnhe. Simply furnished, boat-like interior; the best tables are in the window. Fresh, local fish and shellfish; good value lunch menu.

FORTINGALL – Perth and Kinross – 501 H14 – see Aberfeldy

FORTROSE – Highland – 501 H11 – pop. 1 174

30 C2

Edinburgh 166 mi – London 571 mi – Inverness 12 mi – Elgin 48 mi

Water's Edge without rest

Canonbury Ter, on A 832 ✉ IV10 8TT – ☎ (01381) 621 202 – www.watersedge.uk.com – Closed mid-October-March

3 rm – †£ 115/125 ††£ 120/150

Personally run guest house with attractive gardens and superb views over the Moray Firth. Immaculately kept guest areas. Three 1st floor rooms have French windows onto terrace.

GALSON – Western Isles – 501 A8 – see Lewis and Harris (Isle of)

GATTONSIDE – The Scottish Borders – see Melrose

GLASGOW

See city maps on following pages 25 B1

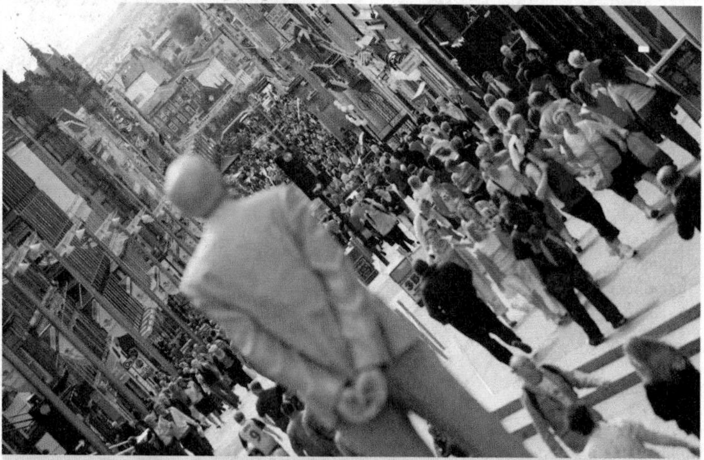

Glasgow City – **pop. 578 776** – **501** H16 – **502** H16 – Scotland

Edinburgh 46 mi – London 399 mi – Belfast 58 mi – Bangor 69 mi

Tourist Information

11 George Sq, (0141) 204 44 00, www.visitscotland.com

Airports

Glasgow Airport : (0844) 481 5555, W : 8 m. by M 8, AV
Access to Oban by helicopter

Golf courses

Littlehill, Auchinairn Rd, (0141) 2 76 07 04
Rouken Glen, Thornlibank, Stewarton Rd, (0141) 638 70 44
Linn Park, Simshill Rd, (0141) 633 03 77

SIGHTS

In the town : City★★★ • Cathedral★★★ ≤ DZ • The Burrell Collection★★★ AXM1 • Hunterian Art Gallery★★ AC CYM4 • Museum of Transport★★ AVM6 • Art Gallery and Museum Kelvingrove★★ CY • Pollok House★ AXD • Tolbooth Steeple★ DZ • Hunterian Museum★CYM5 • City Chambers★ DZC • Glasgow School of Art★ AC CYM3 • Necropolis ≤★ DYZ • Gallery of Modern Art★

On the outskirts : Paisley Museum and Art Gallery★, W : 4 mi by M 8 AV

In the surrounding area : The Trossachs★★★, N : 31 mi by A 879 - BV -, A 81 and A 821 • Loch Lomond★★, NW : 19 mi by A 82 AV

SCOTLAND

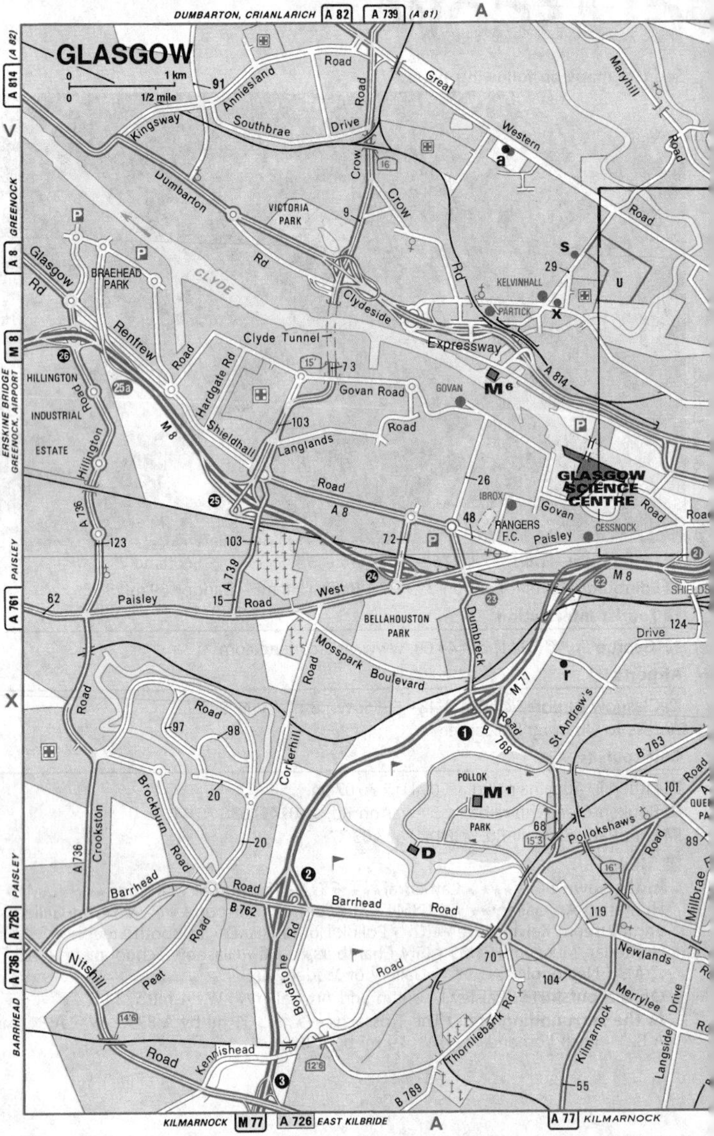
GLASGOW
0 1 km
0 1/2 mile
DUMBARTON, CRIANLARICH
A 82
A 739
(A 81)
A
V
X
(A 82)
A 814
GREENOCK
A 8
M 8
ERSKINE BRIDGE
GREENOCK. AIRPORT
PAISLEY
A 761
PAISLEY
A 726
A 736
BARRHEAD
KILMARNOCK
M 77
A 726
EAST KILBRIDE
A 77
KILMARNOCK
Anniesland
Road
Road
Southbrae
Drive
Kingsway
Great
Western
Road
Maryhill
Road
Crow
Crow
Rd
Dumbarton
Rd
VICTORIA
PARK
Glasgow
Rd
BRAEHEAD
PARK
CLYDE
Clydeside
Expressway
A 814
KELVINHALL
PARTICK
U
Clyde Tunnel
Renfrew
Road
Hardgate Rd
Govan Road
GOVAN
Road
Shieldhall
Langlands
HILLINGTON
INDUSTRIAL
ESTATE
Hillington
Road
A 736
M 8
Road
A 8
IBROX
RANGERS
F.C.
Govan
Paisley
Road
CESSNOCK
GLASGOW
SCIENCE
CENTRE
M 8
SHIELDS
A 739
Paisley
Road
West
Road
BELLAHOUSTON
PARK
Dumbreck
Mossparks
Boulevard
Road
Drive
M 77
St Andrew's
Road
B 768
B 763
Road
POLLOK
PARK
Corkerhill
Road
Road
Brockburn
Road
Crookston
A 736
Barrhead
Road
B 762
Barrhead
Road
Pollokshaws
Road
Millbrae
Nitshill
Peat
Road
Road
Boydstone
Rd
Road
Newlands
Merrylee
Drive
Thornliebank Rd
Kilmarnock
Langside
Drive
Road
Kennishead
B 769
16
15'
15'3
16'
14'6
12'6
91
9
29
73
103
26
48
72
103
123
62
15
124
97
98
20
20
68
101
89
119
70
104
55
a
s
x
r
M6
M1
D
1
2
3
21
22
23
24
25
25a
26

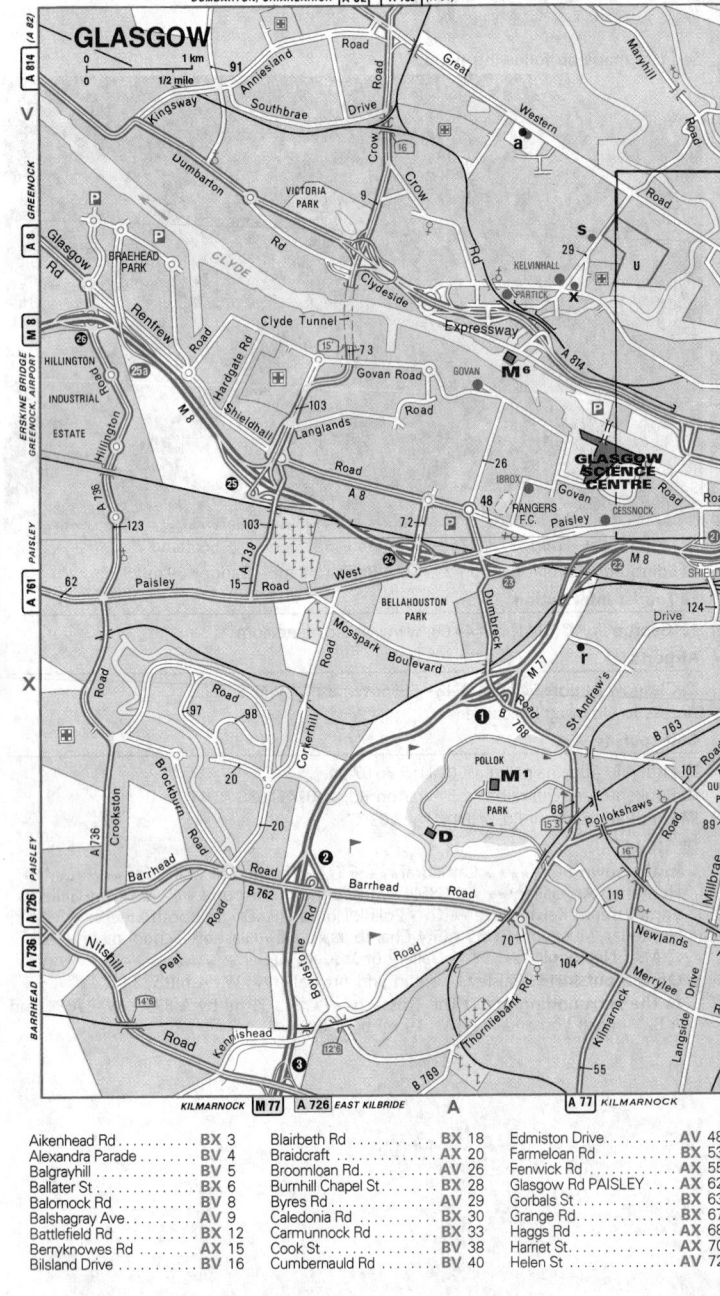

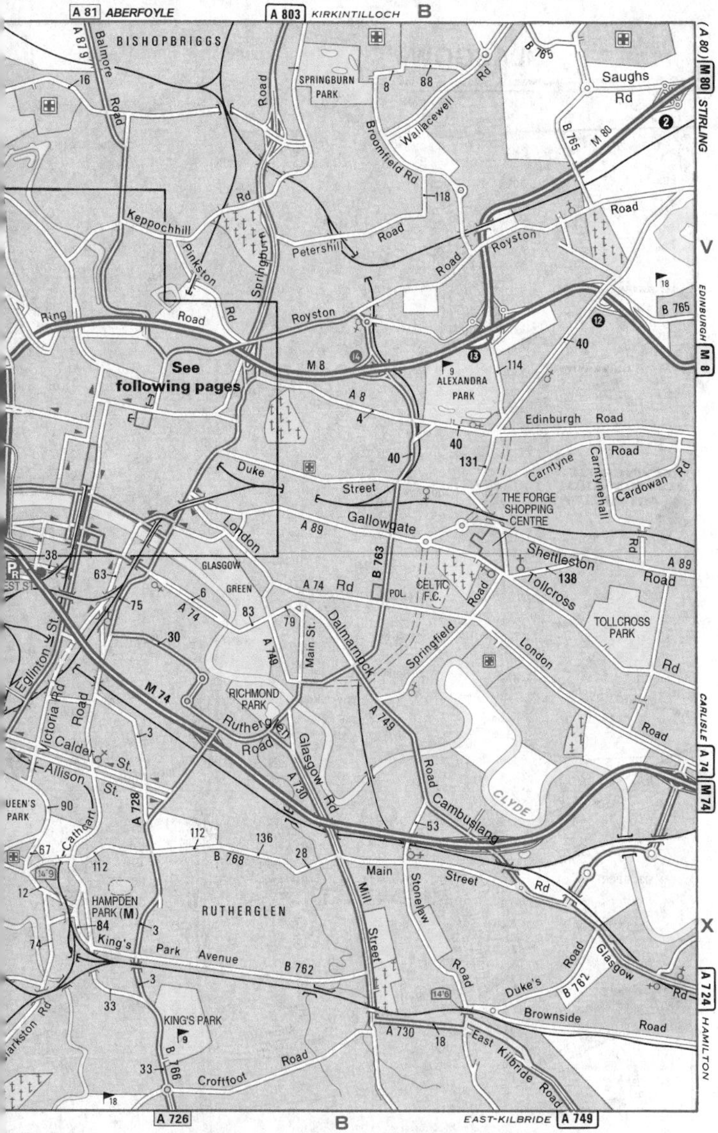
A 81 ABERFOYLE
A 803 KIRKINTILLOCH
B
(A 80) M 80 STIRLING
BISHOPBRIGGS
SPRINGBURN PARK
Saughs Rd
Balmore Road
Wallacewell Rd
Broomfield Rd
Keppochhill Rd
Pinkston Rd
Springburn Road
Petershill Road
Royston Road
Ring Road
See following pages
M 8
ALEXANDRA PARK
Edinburgh Road
V
EDINBURGH M 8
Duke Street
Gallowgate
Carntyne Road
Carntynehall Rd
Cardowan Rd
THE FORGE SHOPPING CENTRE
Shettleston Road
Tollcross Road
TOLLCROSS PARK
CELTIC F.C.
GLASGOW GREEN
A 74 Rd
London Road
Springfield Road
Dalmarnock Road
RICHMOND PARK
Rutherglen Road
Glasgow Rd
Eglinton St.
Victoria Rd
Calder St.
Allison St.
QUEEN'S PARK
Cathcart
M 74
CLYDE
Cambuslang Road
CARLISLE A 74 M 74
Main Street
Mill Street
Stonelaw Road
HAMPDEN PARK (M)
RUTHERGLEN
King's Park Avenue
B 762
B 768
X
Duke's Road
Glasgow Rd
Brownside Road
A 724 HAMILTON
KING'S PARK
Croftfoot Road
East Kilbride Road
A 730
A 726
B
EAST-KILBRIDE A 749
SCOTLAND

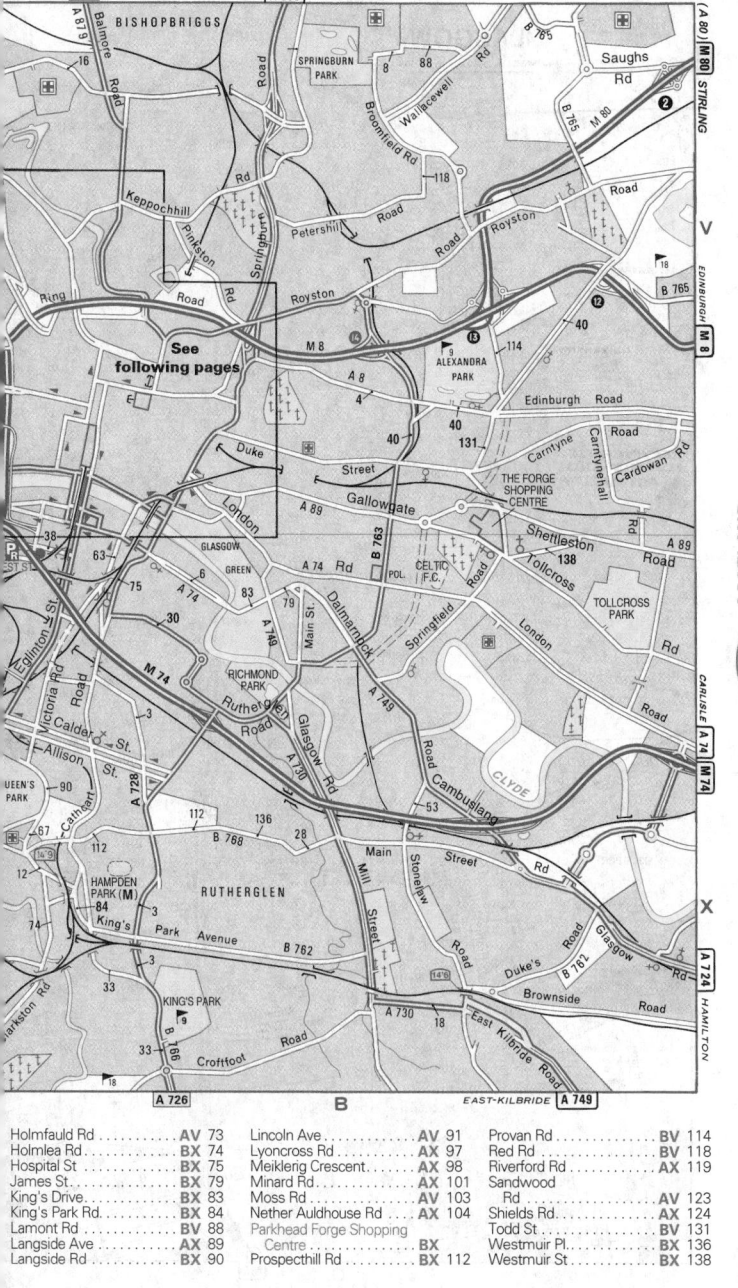

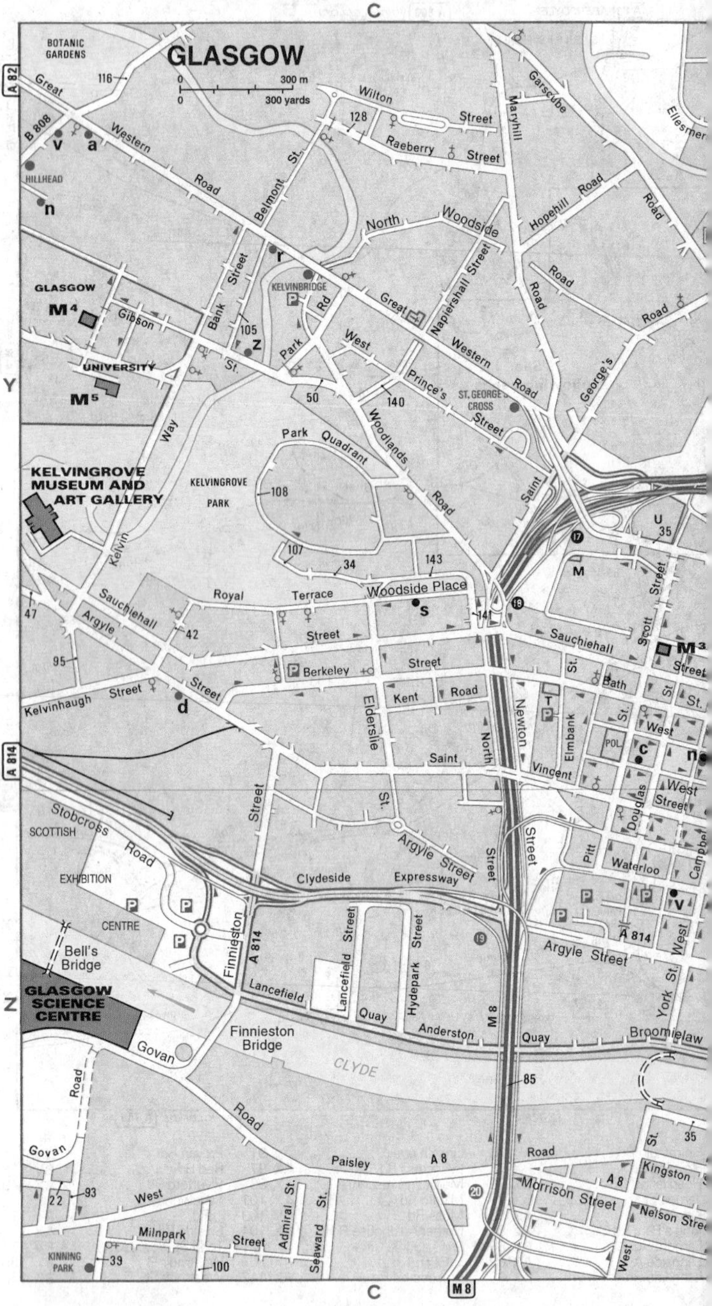

GLASGOW
0 300 m
0 300 yards
C
Y
Z
BOTANIC GARDENS
HILLHEAD
GLASGOW
M4
UNIVERSITY
M5
KELVINGROVE MUSEUM AND ART GALLERY
KELVINGROVE PARK
KELVINBRIDGE
ST. GEORGE'S CROSS
SCOTTISH EXHIBITION CENTRE
Bell's Bridge
GLASGOW SCIENCE CENTRE
Finnieston Bridge
CLYDE
KINNING PARK
A 82
B 808
A 814
A 8
M 8
Great Western Road
Gibson St.
Bank Street
Belmont St.
Wilton Street
Raeberry Street
North Woodside Road
Napiershall Street
Maryhill Road
Garscube Road
Hopehill Road
Ellesmere
George's Road
Park Rd
West Prince's Street
Woodlands Road
Park Quadrant
Kelvin Way
Saint George's Road
Royal Terrace
Woodside Place
Sauchiehall Street
Argyle Street
Berkeley Street
Kent Road
Kelvinhaugh Street
Elderslie St.
Saint Vincent Street
North Street
Newton Street
Elmbank St.
Bath St.
Scott Street
West Regent St.
West Street
Douglas St.
Pitt Street
Waterloo Street
Campbell
Stobcross Road
Finnieston Street
Clydeside Expressway
Lancefield Street
Lancefield Quay
Hydepark Street
Anderston Quay
Broomielaw
York St.
West St.
Govan Road
Paisley Road West
Milnpark Street
Admiral St.
Seaward St.
Kingston St.
Morrison Street
Nelson Street
POL
v a n r z s d c n V U M T P
116 128 105 50 140 108 107 34 143 141 47 42 95 35 85 22 93 39 100
17 18 19 20

SCOTLAND

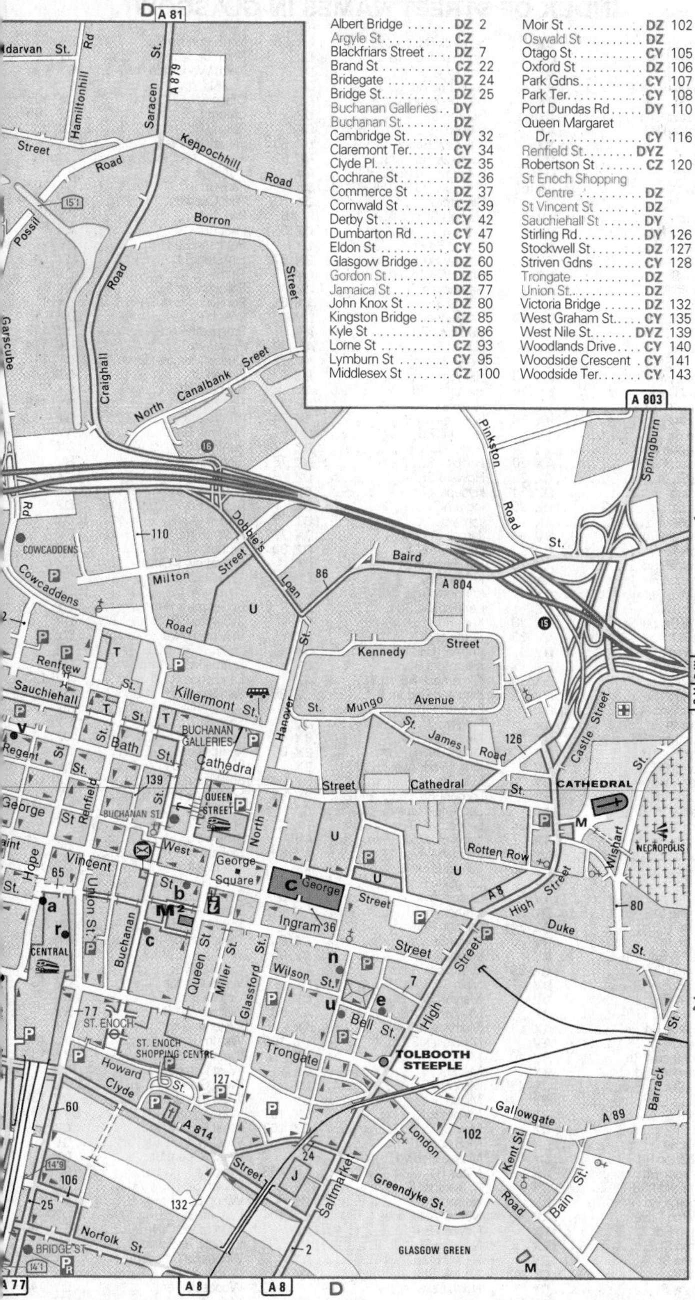

D
A 81
A 879
Saracen St.
Hamiltonhill Rd
Keppochhill Road
Borron Street
Possil Road
Craighall Road
Garscube Rd
North Canalbank Street
Dobbie's Loan
Pinkston Road
Springburn
A 803
Baird St.
A 804
Milton Street
Cowcaddens
COWCADDENS
Kennedy Street
St. Mungo Avenue
St. James Road
Killermont St.
Hanover St.
Renfrew St.
Sauchiehall St.
Bath St.
Regent St.
BUCHANAN GALLERIES
Cathedral Street
CATHEDRAL
Castle Street
NECROPOLIS
Wishart St.
Rotten Row
QUEEN STREET
BUCHANAN ST
George St
Renfield St
West Nile St
North Hanover St
St Vincent St.
George Square
George Street
Ingram St
High Street
Duke St.
Hope St.
Union St.
Buchanan St
Queen St
Miller St.
Glassford St.
Wilson St.
Bell St.
CENTRAL
ST. ENOCH
ST. ENOCH SHOPPING CENTRE
Trongate
TOLBOOTH STEEPLE
Howard St.
Clyde St.
A 814
Gallowgate
A 89
London Road
Kent St.
Bain St.
Barrack St.
Saltmarket
Greendyke St.
Stockwell Street
Norfolk St.
BRIDGE ST
GLASGOW GREEN
A 77
A 8
M 8
Y
Z

INDEX OF STREET NAMES IN GLASGOW

Hotel du Vin at One Devonshire Gardens

1 Devonshire Gdns ✉ G12 0UX – ✆ (0844) 736 42 56 – www.hotelduvin.com
49 rm – †£ 109/379 ††£ 109/379, ☕ £ 18 – 4 suites AV**a**
Rest *Bistro* – see restaurant listing
Collection of adjoining townhouses boasting original 19C stained glass, wood panelling and a labyrinth of corridors. Furnished in dark, opulent shades but with a modern, country house air. Luxurious bedrooms; one with a small gym and sauna.

Blythswood Square

11 Blythswood Sq ✉ G2 4AD – ✆ (0141) 248 88 88 – www.blythswoodsquare.com CY**n**
100 rm ☕ – †£ 120/200 ††£ 160/260 – 7 suites
Rest *Blythswood Square* – see restaurant listing
Stunning property on delightful Georgian square; formerly the Scottish RAC HQ. Modern décor contrasts with original fittings. Dark, moody bedrooms and marble bathrooms; Penthouse Suite displays a bed adapted from a snooker table. Smart spa.

Radisson Blu

rm,

301 Argyle St. ✉ G2 8DL – ✆ (0141) 204 33 33 – www.radissonblu.co.uk/hotel-glasgow DZ**d**
247 rm ☕ – †£ 95/205 ††£ 105/215 – 1 suite
Rest *Collage* – *(closed Sunday lunch)* Menu £ 18 (lunch and early dinner) – Carte £ 27/50
Stylish commercial hotel with an impressive glass atrium. Bedrooms come in three styles - Modern, City, and Gallery - all are spacious and contemporary, with a Scandinavian edge. The restaurant has a central buffet area and an all-encompassing menu; Peter Blake's artwork decorates the walls.

SCOTLAND

Malmaison

rm,

278 West George St ✉ G2 4LL – ✆ (0141) 572 10 00 – www.malmaison.com
72 rm – †£ 80/210 ††£ 80/210, ☕ £ 11 – 8 suites CY**c**
Rest *Brasserie* – Menu £ 18 (lunch and early dinner) – Carte £ 26/46
Impressive-looking, former Episcopal church, with moody, masculine décor. Stylish, boldly coloured bedrooms offer good facilities; some are duplex. Named after Billy Connolly, the Big Yin Suite has a roll-top bath in the room. Characterful, intimate brasserie in the old vaults; French-influenced menus.

Grand Central

rm,

99 Gordon St ✉ G1 3SF – ✆ (0141) 240 37 00 – www.grandcentralhotel.co.uk
186 rm ☕ – †£ 79/269 ††£ 79/269 – 3 suites DZ**a**
Rest *Tempus* – ✆ (0141) 240 37 70 *(dinner only)* Menu £ 18 (weekdays) – Carte £ 19/36
Renowned hotel built into the main station; the first TV signal broadcast from London was to this hotel. Smart bedrooms aimed at corporate market. Original plasterwork in ballroom; marble floors in champagne bar. Contemporary restaurant boasts Murano chandeliers.

Hotel Indigo

rm,

75 Waterloo St ✉ G2 7DA – ✆ (0141) 226 77 00 – www.hotelindigoglasgow.com
94 rm – †£ 95/260 ††£ 95/390, ☕ £ 14 CZ**v**
Rest *Limelight Grill* – Menu £ 18 (lunch and early dinner) – Carte £ 23/45
Stylish, corporate hotel in a grand building dating from 1892,which started life as the city's first power station. Bright colour schemes and photos of city sights in the well-equipped bedrooms; each floor has a different theme. The huge, vibrantly decorated restaurant offers an accessible menu.

Sherbrooke Castle

rest,

11 Sherbrooke Ave, Pollokshields ✉ G41 4PG – ✆ (0141) 427 42 27 – www.sherbrooke.co.uk – Closed 1 January AX**r**
17 rm ☕ – †£ 80/110 ††£ 80/260 – 1 suite
Rest *Morrisons* – Menu £ 18 (lunch and early dinner) – Carte £ 19/46
19C pink granite castle, in an attractive leafy suburb. Original features include an impressive staircase and stained glass windows. Large bedrooms add a touch of the present day and the garden suites provide additional home comforts. The panelled, open-fired dining room offers an all-encompassing menu.

Arthouse without rest
129 Bath St ✉ G2 2SZ – ☎ (0141) 221 67 89 – www.thearthouseglasgow.co.uk – Closed 24-26 December DY**v**
59 rm – †£ 160 ††£ 170/190
Former education authority offices, featuring an original wood-panelled lift in an impressive tiled stairwell. Modern bedrooms in 4 grades – comfortable, desirable, envious and fabulous – with pictures of city landmarks on the headboards.

Grasshoppers Ⓝ without rest
Caledonian Chambers (6th Floor), 87 Union St ✉ G1 3TA – ☎ (0141) 222 2666 – www.grasshoppersglasgow.com DZ**r**
29 rm – †£ 75/105 ††£ 85/125
Unusually located, on the 6th floor of the Victorian railway station building; the lounge overlooks what is the largest glass roof in Europe. Stylish, well-designed bedrooms with bespoke Scandinavian-style furnishings and Scottish art. Smart, compact shower rooms. Three course suppers for residents only.

15 Glasgow without rest
15 Woodside Pl. ✉ G3 7QL – ☎ (0141) 332 12 63 – www.15glasgow.com – Closed 25 December and 3 January CY**s**
5 rm – †£ 99/155 ††£ 99/165
Delightful Victorian townhouse on a quiet square, run by a charming, professional owner. Original features include mosaic floors and ornate cornicing. Extremely spacious, luxurious bedrooms have top quality furnishings and underfloor heating in the bathrooms. Cooked breakfast trays are delivered to your door.

SCOTLAND

Brian Maule at Chardon d'Or
176 West Regent St. ✉ G2 4RL – ☎ (0141) 248 38 01 – www.brianmaule.com – Closed 25 December, 1 January, Sunday and bank holidays CY**b**
Rest – Menu £ 19 (lunch and early dinner) – Carte £ 42/54
Georgian townhouse in the city's heart, with original pillars, ornate carved ceilings and white walls hung with vibrant modern art. Classical cooking with a modern edge; luxurious ingredients and large portions. Friendly, efficient service.

Bistro – Hotel du Vin at One Devonshire Gardens
1 Devonshire Gdns ✉ G12 OUX – ☎ (0844) 736 42 56 – www.hotelduvin.com – Closed Saturday lunch AV**a**
Rest – Menu £ 16 (lunch and early dinner) – Carte £ 35/54
Elegant oak-panelled restaurant in a luxurious hotel. The three rooms are dark, moody and richly appointed, and there's a lovely lounge and whisky snug. Choose from well-prepared classics or more ambitious offerings on the degustation menu.

Rogano
11 Exchange Pl. ✉ G1 3AN – ☎ (0141) 248 4055 – www.roganoglasgow.com – Closed 1 January DZ**c**
Rest – Menu £ 22/45 – Carte £ 33/84
City institution established over 75 years ago. Charming art deco interior with marquetry reputedly from the craftsmen who fitted the Queen Mary. Formal service and a largely seafood-based menu. Keenly priced dishes in the basement café.

Gamba
225a West George St. ✉ G2 2ND – ☎ (0141) 572 08 99 – www.gamba.co.uk – Closed 25 December and first 2 weeks January DZ**x**
Rest – Menu £ 21 (lunch and early dinner) – Carte £ 25/52
Tucked away in a basement but well-known by the locals. Appealing seafood menu of unfussy, classical dishes with the odd Asian influence; lemon sole is a speciality. Cosy bar-lounge and contemporary dining room hung with fish prints.

Cail Bruich
725 Great Western Rd. ✉ G12 8QX – ☎ (0141) 334 62 65 – www.cailbruich.co.uk – Closed 1 week winter, 1 week spring, 26 December, 1 January and Monday
Rest – Menu £ 19 (lunch and early dinner) – Carte £ 28/43 CY**a**
High ceilinged room with large pictures of produce. Run by two brothers; its name means 'to eat well'. Menus range from a good value 'Market' selection to 'Tasting' options. Mix of classic and modern dishes from a young, ambitious team.

XX **Blythswood Square** - Blythswood Square Hotel
11 Blythswood Sq ✉ G2 4AD – ✆ (0141) 248 88 88 – www.blythswoodsquare.com CY**n**
Rest – Menu £ 19 (lunch and early dinner) – Carte £ 26/58
Stylish hotel restaurant in the old ballroom of the former RAC building. Chic in black and white, with a zinc-topped bar and Harris Tweed banquettes. Classic menu with meats from the Josper grill; desserts showcase kitchen's ambitious side.

XX **La Parmigiana**
447 Great Western Rd, Kelvinbridge ✉ G12 8HH – ✆ (0141) 334 06 86 – www.laparmigiana.co.uk – Closed 25-26 December, 1 January and Sunday dinner CY**r**
Rest – *(booking essential)* Menu £ 17 (lunch) – Carte £ 25/47
Unashamedly classic in terms of décor and its dishes, this well-regarded, professionally run Italian restaurant celebrated its 35th birthday in 2013. Red walls, white linen and efficient service. Refined cooking delivers bold flavours.

XX **Ubiquitous Chip**
12 Ashton Ln ✉ G12 8SJ – ✆ (0141) 334 5007 – www.ubiquitouschip.co.uk – Closed 25 December and 1 January CY**n**
Rest – *(bookings advisable at dinner)* Menu £ 20 (lunch and early dinner) – Carte £ 28/66
An iconic establishment on a cobbled street. The restaurant – with its ponds, fountains and greenery – offers modern classics which showcase local ingredients, while the mezzanine-level brasserie serves tasty Scottish favourites.

XX **Two Fat Ladies in the City**
118a Blythswood St ✉ G2 4EG – ✆ (0141) 847 00 88 – www.twofatladiesrestaurant.com CY**e**
Rest – Menu £ 16 (lunch and early dinner) – Carte £ 26/42
Intimate seafood restaurant which resembles an old-fashioned brasserie, with its wooden floor, banquettes and local art. Classic dishes are straightforward in style – but with fish this fresh, it doesn't need to be complicated.

XX **Urban**
23-25 St Vincent Pl. ✉ G1 2DT – ✆ (0141) 248 56 36 – www.urbanbrasserie.co.uk – Closed 25 December and 1 January DZ**b**
Rest – Menu £ 17 (early dinner) – Carte £ 25/51
Imposing 19C building; formerly home to the Bank of England. Sizeable bar and cosy wood-panelled lounge. Grand dining room with booths, vibrant artwork and an impressive illuminated glass and wrought iron ceiling. Classic British dishes.

X **Stravaigin**
28 Gibson St, ✉ G12 8NX – ✆ (0141) 334 26 65 – www.stravaigin.co.uk – Closed 25 December and 1 January CY**z**
Rest – *(booking essential at dinner)* Menu £ 15/30 – Carte £ 18/31
Well-run, long-standing restaurant with a bustling bar, dining set over three levels and a relaxed, shabby-chic style. Interesting menus uphold the motto 'think global, eat local', with dishes ranging from carefully prepared Scottish favourites to tasty Asian-inspired fare. They hold monthly 'thali' nights.

X **Two Fat Ladies West End**
88 Dumbarton Rd ✉ G11 6NX – ✆ (0141) 339 1944 – www.twofatladiesrestaurant.com – Closed 25-26 December and 1-2 January
Rest – Menu £ 15 (lunch and early dinner) – Carte £ 23/36 AV**x**
Quirky neighbourhood restaurant – the first in the Fat Ladies group – with red velour banquettes, bold blue and gold décor, and a semi open plan kitchen in the window. Cooking is simple and to the point, focusing on classical fish dishes.

X **Central Market** N
51 Bell St ✉ G1 1NX – ✆ (0141) 552 09 02 – www.centralmarketglasgow.com
Rest – Carte £ 20/31 DZ**e**
A trendy, informal 'café, restaurant and deli', with a huge plate glass façade, a horseshoe bar counter and an open kitchen. Appealing menu of tasty straightforward dishes, from jugged kippers or oysters to ox cheek stew or whole sea bream.

SCOTLAND

Dhabba
44 Candleriggs ✉ G1 1LE – ✆ (0141) 553 12 49 – www.thedhabba.com – Closed 25 December and 1 January DZ**u**
Rest – Menu £ 10/25 – Carte £ 16/39
Stylish, modern restaurant in the heart of the Merchant City; its walls decorated with huge photos of Indian street scenes. Menus focus on northern India, with interesting breads and lots of tandoor dishes – the speciality is 'dum pukht'.

La Famiglia Ⓝ
111 Cleveden Rd, Northwest : 3.5 mi by Great Western Rd (A 82) ✉ G12 0JU – ✆ (0141) 334 0111 – www.lafamigliarestaurant.co.uk – Closed Monday
Rest – Carte £ 18/35
Pleasant shop conversion in the older part of the city – its walls filled with black and white family photos. Simple, rustic Italian lunches feature the likes of risotto and arancini; dinner is slightly more modern and complex.

Hanoi Bike Shop Ⓝ
8 Ruthven Ln, (off Byres Road) ✉ G12 9BG – ✆ (0141) 334 71 65 – www.thehanoibikeshop.co.uk AV**s**
Rest – Carte £ 16/21
Relaxed Vietnamese café; head to the lighter upstairs room with its fine array of lanterns. Simple menu of classic Vietnamese dishes including street food like rice paper summer rolls. Charming, knowledgeable staff offer recommendations.

SCOTLAND

La Vallée Blanche
360 Byres Rd, (1st floor) ✉ G12 8AW – ✆ (0141) 334 33 33 – www.lavalleeblanche.com – Closed 25-26 December, 1 January and Monday
Rest – Menu £ 13 (lunch and early dinner) – Carte £ 21/41 CY**v**
First floor restaurant with wood-clad walls, stag antler lights and simple wooden tables, giving it the feel of a ski chalet. Menus offer classic French dishes, from pork rillettes to coq au vin. Friendly service.

Dakhin
89 Candleriggs ✉ G1 1NP – ✆ (0141) 553 25 85 – www.dakhin.com – Closed 25 December and 1 January DZ**n**
Rest – Menu £ 10 (lunch) – Carte £ 14/29
It's all about the cooking at this modest, brightly decorated restaurant: authentic, southern Indian dishes might include seafood from Kerala, lamb curry from Tamil Nadu, and their speciality, dosas – available with a variety of fillings.

The Finnieston Ⓝ
1125 Argyle St ✉ G3 8ND – ✆ (0141) 222 28 84 – www.thefinniestonbar.com – Closed 24-26 December CY**d**
Rest – Carte £ 22/55
Small, cosy pub specialising in Scottish seafood and gin cocktails; with an intriguing ceiling, a welcoming fire and lots of booths. Dishes are light, tasty and neatly presented, relying on just a few ingredients so that flavours are clear.

GLENDEVON – Perth and Kinross – 501 I/J15 28 C2

▶ Edinburgh 37 mi – London 434 mi – Glasgow 43 mi – Aberdeen 109 mi

Tormaukin Inn with rm
✉ FK14 7JY – ✆ (01259) 781 252 – www.tormaukinhotel.co.uk – Closed 25 December
11 rm – †£ 60/80 ††£ 60/80 **Rest** – Carte £ 20/39
Characterful inn run by a truly welcoming team. Huge granite fireplace, dark, beamed bar and spacious, classical dining room. Carefully executed dishes are largely traditional, with the odd contemporary offering; tasty homemade bread and ice cream. Tartan-floored bedrooms spread between the inn, a stable block and a chalet.

GLENROTHES – Fife – 501 K15 – pop. 38 679 Scotland 28 C2

Edinburgh 33 mi – Dundee 25 mi – Stirling 36 mi

Glenrothes Golf Club, Golf Course Rd, (01592) 75 45 61

Balbirnie Park, Markinch, (01592) 61 20 95

Auchterderran, Cardenden, Woodend Rd, (01592) 72 15 79

Falkland★ (Palace of Falkland★ AC, Gardens★ AC) N : 5.5 mi by A 92 and A 912

Balbirnie House

rest,

Balbirnie Park, Markinch, Northeast : 1.75 mi by A 911 and A 92 on B 9130
KY7 6NE – (01592) 610 066 – www.balbirnie.co.uk

31 rm – £ 100 £ 175 – 1 suite

Rest *Orangery* – *(closed dinner Monday-Tuesday)* Menu £ 24/35

Rest *Bistro* – Carte £ 19/31

Stunning Palladian mansion with formal gardens and extensive parkland. Large, well-furnished drawing rooms in country house style; period features abound. Luxurious, comfortable bedrooms come in varying sizes. Elegant glass-roofed Orangery serves classics with a twist. Basement Bistro offers French favourites.

GRANDTULLY – Perth and Kinross 28 C2

Edinburgh 70 mi – London 475 mi – Glasgow 84 mi – Dundee 51 mi

Inn on the Tay with rm

PH9 0PL – (01877) 840 760 – www.theinnonthetay.co.uk

6 rm – £ 70 £ 80/110 **Rest** – Carte £ 18/32

Smart, modern inn on the banks of the Tay; have coffee and homemade cake in the snug bar or head to the large dining room for superb views over the water. Choose from pub favourites on the bar menu or more ambitious dishes on the main menu. The owners are cheery and welcoming and the bedrooms, comfy and cosy.

GRANTOWN-ON-SPEY – Highland – 501 J12 – pop. 2 166 30 D2

Edinburgh 143 mi – Inverness 34 mi – Perth 99 mi

54 High St, (01479) 28 22 42, www.visitgrantown.co.uk

Golf Course Rd, (01479) 87 20 79

Abernethy, Nethy Bridge, (01479) 82 13 05

Culdearn House

Woodlands Terr PH26 3JU – (01479) 872 106 – www.culdearn.com

6 rm – £ 69/79 £ 138/158

Rest – *(dinner only) (booking essential)* Menu £ 40

Granite house built in 1860 by Lord Seafield for one of his four daughters; its small garden home to a family of red squirrels. Elegant, open-fired lounge and spacious bedrooms are furnished in period styles. Formal dining room offers a classical daily menu which features quality Scottish ingredients.

Dulaig without rest

Seafield Ave PH26 3JF – (01479) 872 065 – www.thedulaig.com – Closed 20 December-9 January

3 rm – £ 110/120 £ 150/160

Small, detached, personally run guesthouse, built in 1910 and tastefully furnished with original Arts and Crafts pieces. Modern fabrics and an uncluttered feel in the comfortable bedrooms. Tea and homemade cake on arrival. Communal breakfasts include home-baked bread and muffins.

GULLANE – East Lothian – 501 L15 – pop. 2 172 Scotland 26 C1

Edinburgh 20 mi – London 384 mi – Belfast 124 mi – Dundee 81 mi

Dirleton★ (Castle★) NE : 2 mi by A 198

Greywalls

Duncur Rd, Muirfield, Northeast : 0.75 mi by A 198 EH31 2EG – (01620) 842 144 – www.greywalls.co.uk

23 rm – £ 80/105 £ 230/320

Rest *Chez Roux* – see restaurant listing

Long-standing, classic Edwardian country house by Lutyens, in a superb location adjoining the famous Muirfield golf course. Constantly re-inventing itself and providing assured, professional service, it boasts spacious, antique-furnished bedrooms and delightful formal gardens designed by Jekyll.

SCOTLAND

XX **La Potinière**

Main St ✉ EH31 2AA – ✆ (01620) 843 214 – www.lapotiniere.co.uk – Closed January, 25-26 December, Sunday dinner October-May, Monday, Tuesday and bank holidays

Rest – *(booking essential)* Menu £ 20/43

Sweet little restaurant with white walls and striking red curtains. Concise, regularly changing menus of carefully prepared, classical dishes; lunch is good value and their homemade bread is renowned. The two owners share the cooking.

XX **Chez Roux** – Greywalls Hotel

Duncur Rd, Muirfield, Northeast : 0.75 mi by A 198 ✉ EH31 2EG – ✆ (01620) 842 144 – www.greywalls.co.uk

Rest – *(bookings essential for non-residents)* Menu £ 27 (lunch and early dinner) – Carte £ 31/53

Set in a classic country house hotel but with a pleasant, modern feel; enjoy an aperitif in the lounge or in the delightful, Jekyll-designed gardens before dining with a superb view over the Muirfield golf course. Classical French menus have a Roux signature style and feature tried-and-tested classics.

HARRAY – 501 K6 – see Orkney Islands (Mainland)

HARRIS – Highland – 501 Z10 – see Lewis and Harris (Isle of)

INGLISTON – City of Edinburgh – 501 J16 – see Edinburgh

INNERLEITHEN – The Scottish Borders – 501 K17 – pop. 2 586 26 C2

Edinburgh 31 mi – Dumfries 57 mi – Glasgow 60 mi

Caddon View

14 Pirn Rd. ✉ EH44 6HH – ✆ (01896) 830 208 – www.caddonview.co.uk – Closed 25-26 December

8 rm – †£ 50/55 ††£ 80/110

Rest – *(closed Sunday and Monday) (dinner only)* Menu £ 20

Substantial Victorian house run by hospitable couple. Individually decorated bedrooms with modern touches; spacious Yarrow, and Moorfoot with its view, are the best. Bright, airy dining room; regularly changing menu of local produce from the Tweed Valley.

INVERGARRY – Highland – 501 F12 – ✉ Inverness Scotland 30 C3

Edinburgh 159 mi – Fort William 25 mi – Inverness 43 mi – Kyle of Lochalsh 50 mi

The Great Glen★

Glengarry Castle

On A 82 ✉ PH35 4HW – ✆ (01809) 501 254 – www.glengarry.net – Closed 4 November-20 March

26 rm – †£ 72/172 ††£ 106/192 **Rest** – *(dinner only)* Menu £ 33 **s**

Family-run Victorian house, named after the ruined castle in its 60 acre grounds. Two large, open-fired sitting rooms; stuffed wild animals abound. Classical, individually styled bedrooms, some with original art deco baths. Formal dining from 4 course Scottish menu.

Invergarry

On A 87 ✉ PH35 4HJ – ✆ (01809) 501 206 – www.invergarryhotel.co.uk

12 rm – †£ 60/90 ††£ 75/135 **Rest** – Carte £ 25/39

Welcoming hotel in the style of a traditional inn. Smaller, quirky bedrooms in the eaves; first floor superior rooms offer more space and luxury. Comfy lounge featuring shotguns, open fires and tartan carpets. Flavourful cooking focuses on fresh Highland produce.

INVERGORDON - Highland - 501 H10 30 C2

Edinburgh 178 mi - London 582 mi - Inverness 24 mi - Elgin 60 mi

Birch Tree

Delney Riding Centre, Northeast : 3.75 mi on A 9 ✉ IV18 0NP - ✆ (01349) 853 549 - www.the-birch-tree.com - Closed February, Sunday and Monday

Rest - Menu £ 16/25 - Carte £ 24/29

Friendly little restaurant located within a rural riding school. The good value, set price lunch menu is followed by a more ambitious à la carte and a popular 'steak' menu. Cooking is classically based and relies on Scottish ingredients.

INVERKEILOR - Angus - 501 M14 - pop. 902 - ✉ Arbroath 28 D2

Edinburgh 85 mi - Aberdeen 32 mi - Dundee 22 mi

Gordon's with rm

32 Main St ✉ DD11 5RN - ✆ (01241) 830 364 - www.gordonsrestaurant.co.uk - Closed 2 weeks January, lunch Tuesday and Saturday

5 rm - †£ 55/85 ††£ 110/130 **Rest** - *(booking essential)* Menu £ 28/50

Long-standing, passionately run restaurant; the wife oversees the service and the husband and son are in the kitchen. Charming stone walls, open fires and exposed beams. Concise menu of carefully prepared, classic dishes which use local seasonal produce. Well-kept bedrooms - the courtyard suite is the best.

INVERMORISTON - Highland - 501 G12 30 C2

Edinburgh 164 mi - London 541 mi - Belfast 192 mi - Dundee 146 mi

Tigh na Bruach without rest

Southwest : 0.5 mi on A 82 ✉ IV63 7YE - ✆ (01320) 351 349 - www.tighnabruach.com - Restricted opening in winter

3 rm - †£ 75/98 ††£ 100/130

Superbly set on the lochside; its name meaning 'House on the Bank'. Traditional breakfast room. Comfy bedrooms with doors opening onto private terraces, which boast stunning views over neatly tended gardens to Loch Ness and the mountains.

SCOTLAND

INVERNESS - Highland - 501 H11 - pop. 41 237 Scotland 30 C2

Edinburgh 156 mi - Aberdeen 107 mi - Dundee 134 mi

Inverness Airport, Dalcross : ✆ (01667) 464000, NE : 8 mi by A 96 Y

Castle Wynd, ✆ (01463) 23 43 53, www.visithighlands.com

18 Culcabock Rd, ✆ (01463) 23 98 82

18 Torvean, Glenurquhart Rd, ✆ (01463) 22 56 51

Town★ - Museum and Art Gallery★ Y **M**

Loch Ness★★, SW : by A 82 Z - Clava Cairns★, E : 9 mi by Culcabock Rd, B 9006 and B 851 Z - Cawdor Castle★ **AC**, NE : 14 mi by A 96 and B 9090 Y

Plan on next page

Rocpool Reserve

14 Culduthel Rd ✉ IV2 4AG - ✆ (01463) 240 089 - www.rocpool.com

11 rm - †£ 150/395 ††£ 185/395 Z**r**

Rest *Chez Roux* - see restaurant listing

Stylish boutique hotel with a chic lounge and sexy, split-level bar. Minimalist bedrooms come with emperor-sized beds and are graded 'Hip', 'Chic', 'Decadent' and 'Extra Decadent'; some have iPod docks, terraces, hot tubs or saunas.

Glenmoriston Town House

20 Ness Bank ✉ IV2 4SF - ✆ (01463) 223 777 - www.glenmoristontownhouse.com - Closed 8-9 January Z**x**

31 rm - †£ 75/109 ††£ 95/189

Rest *Abstract* - see restaurant listing

Rest *Contrast* - Menu £ 10 (lunch and early dinner) - Carte £ 18/42

Two stylish townhouses next to the river. Bedrooms in the main house are contemporary and minimalistic; those in the annexe have solid wood beds and wicker chairs. Have drinks in the cocktail bar; then choose an Asian or Mediterranean-inspired dish in the brasserie or a modern dish in the formal restaurant.

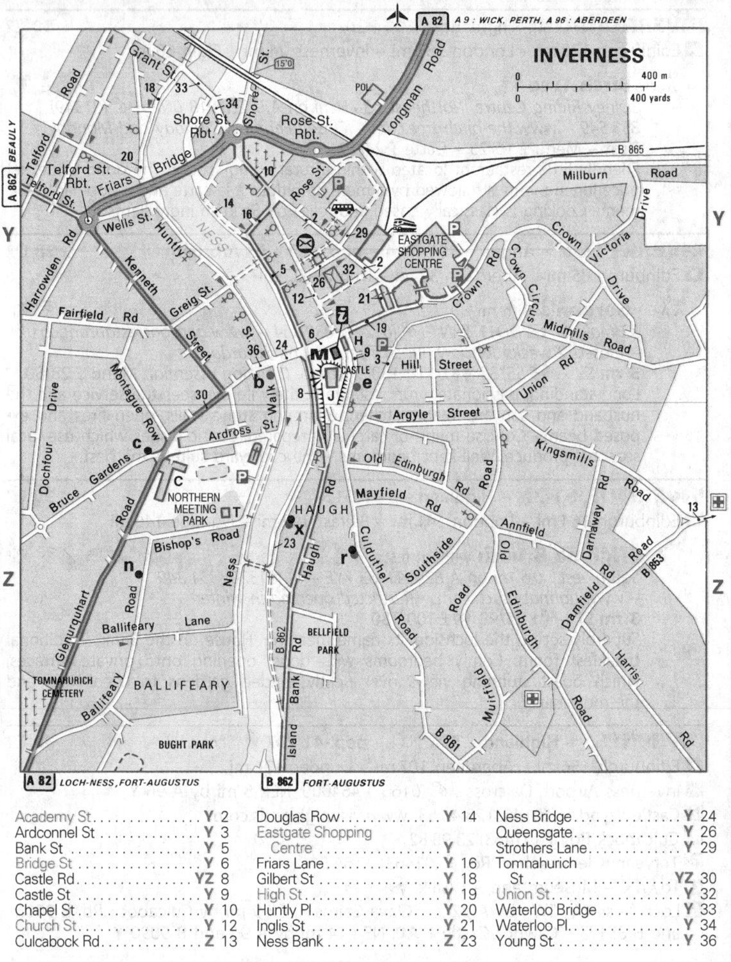

Academy St	Y 2	Douglas Row	Y 14	Ness Bridge	Y 24
Ardconnel St	Y 3	Eastgate Shopping Centre	Y	Queensgate	Y 26
Bank St	Y 5	Friars Lane	Y 16	Strothers Lane	Y 29
Bridge St	Y 6	Gilbert St	Y 18	Tomnahurich St	YZ 30
Castle Rd	YZ 8	High St	Y 19	Union St	Y 32
Castle St	Y 9	Huntly Pl.	Y 20	Waterloo Bridge	Y 33
Chapel St	Y 10	Inglis St	Y 21	Waterloo Pl.	Y 34
Church St	Y 12	Ness Bank	Z 23	Young St	Y 36
Culcabock Rd	Z 13				

Trafford Bank without rest

96 Fairfield Rd, West: 0.75 mi by A 82 and Harrowden Rd ✉ IV3 5LL – ✆ (01463) 241 414 – www.traffordbankguesthouse.co.uk – Closed mid-December-mid-February

5 rm ☕ – †£ 75/110 ††£ 90/128

19C house with a modern, bohemian style. Original features include a tiled entrance and cast iron banister. Bedrooms come with iPod docks, robes and decanters of sherry. Breakfast arrives on local china and includes haggis and tattie scones.

Ballifeary Guest House without rest

10 Ballifeary Rd ✉ IV3 5PJ – ✆ (01463) 235 572 – www.ballifearyguesthouse.co.uk – Closed 24-28 December Z**n**

7 rm ☕ – †£ 40/65 ††£ 70/85

Pleasant house set away from the town centre, with a homely sitting room and comfortable, immaculately kept bedrooms. Smart breakfast room set with crisp linen and polished glassware; local produce includes salmon, kippers and cheeses.

Moyness House without rest
6 Bruce Gdns ✉ IV3 5EN – ☎ (01463) 233 836 – www.moyness.co.uk – Closed 24-26 December **Zc**
6 rm – †£ 60/90 ††£ 69/110
Detached Victorian villa framed by neatly clipped hedges. Period lounge with lots of local info; immaculately kept breakfast room. Variously sized bedrooms come with thoughtful extras, including ear plugs; the first floor rooms are the best.

Abstract – Glenmoriston Town House Hotel
20 Ness Bank ✉ IV2 4SF – ☎ (01463) 223 777 – www.abstractrestaurant.com – Closed Sunday and Monday **Zx**
Rest – *(dinner only)* Menu £ 55 – Carte £ 37/51
Intimate hotel restaurant with abstract ink pictures on dark wood panelled walls and a contemporary, minimalistic style. Original, innovative modern menus feature ambitious flavour combinations. Pianist on Friday and Saturday nights.

Rocpool
1 Ness Walk ✉ IV3 5NE – ☎ (01463) 717 274 – www.rocpoolrestaurant.com – Closed 25-26 December, 1-3 January and Sunday **Yb**
Rest – Menu £ 17 (weekday lunch) – Carte £ 24/44
Well-run restaurant on the banks of the River Ness; close to town and popular with the locals. Modern, modish interior. Wide-ranging menus offer vibrant, colourful dishes that are full of flavour and have a distinct Mediterranean edge.

Chez Roux – Rocpool Reserve Hotel
14 Culduthel Rd ✉ IV2 4AG – ☎ (01463) 240 089 – www.rocpool.com
Rest – Menu £ 25 (lunch and early dinner) – Carte £ 30/45 **Zr**
Smart, modern restaurant consisting of three rooms; their walls hung with photos of the Roux brothers' early days. Well-spaced polished tables and formal, professional service. French-inspired brassiere menu of robust, flavoursome dishes.

Café 1
Castle St ✉ IV2 3EA – ☎ (01463) 226 200 – www.cafe1.net – Closed 25-26 December, 1-2 January and Sunday **Ye**
Rest – Carte £ 21/39
Bustling bistro opposite the castle. Small bar and two dining rooms with walnut veneer topped tables. Good value set lunch; more elaborate à la carte with an Asian and Mediterranean edge. Pork, beef and lamb comes from their own croft.

at Culloden East : 3 mi by A 96 - Y – ✉ Inverness

Culloden House
✉ IV2 7BZ – ☎ (01463) 790 461 – www.cullodenhouse.co.uk – Closed 25-26 December
28 rm – †£ 100/175 ††£ 135/270 – 3 suites
Rest *Adams Dining Room* – Menu £ 20/50 – Carte £ 34/57
Imposing Palladian mansion in 40 acres; requisitioned by Bonnie Prince Charlie as his HQ prior to the famous battle. Grand interior with high ceilings, chandeliers and Adam's plaster reliefs. Well-proportioned bedrooms; many with antiques and views of the grounds. Formal restaurant offers traditional menus.

at Bunchrew West : 3 mi on A 862 - Y – ✉ Inverness

Bunchrew House
✉ IV3 8TA – ☎ (01463) 234 917 – www.bunchrewhousehotel.com
16 rm – †£ 110/230 ††£ 120/240 **Rest** – Menu £ 24/40
Impressive 17C Scottish mansion, in a beautiful spot on the shore of Beauly Firth. Clubby, cosy, open-fired bar and intimate, wood-panelled drawing room. Good-sized, traditionally styled bedrooms; one with a four-poster, another with estuary views. Classical restaurant, with a menu to match and garden views.

ISLAY (Isle of) – Argyll and Bute – 501 B16 27 A3

Edinburgh 164 mi – London 518 mi – Greenock 117 mi – Irvine 132 mi

Port Ellen Airport : ✆ (01496) 302361

from Port Askaig to Isle of Jura (Feolin) (Caledonian MacBrayne Ltd) frequent services daily (approx. 4 mn) – from Port Ellen or Port Askaig to Kintyre Peninsula (Kennacraig) (Caledonian MacBrayne Ltd) 1-2 daily – from Port Askaig to Oban via Isle of Colonsay (Scalasaig) (Caledonian MacBrayne Ltd) weekly – from Port Askaig to Isle of Colonsay (Scalasaig) and Kintyre Peninsula (Kennacraig) (Caledonian MacBrayne Ltd) weekly

The Square, Main St, Bowmore, ✆ (01496) 81 02 54, www.islayinfo.com

Port Ellen, 25 Charlotte St, ✆ (01496) 30 00 94

BALLYGRANT – Argyll and Bute 27 A3

Kilmeny Country House without rest

Southwest : 0.5 mi on A 846 ✉ PA45 7QW – ✆ (01496) 840 668 – www.kilmeny.co.uk – Closed Christmas-New Year

5 rm – †£ 90/120 ††£ 120/155

Delightful house in 350 acres of working farmland. Large lounge with a mock open fire and a fine array of books about Islay. Superb bedrooms have beautiful feature beds, lovely tartans, tweeds and woollens woven on the island, and thoughtful extras. Welcoming owner.

BOWMORE – Argyll and Bute 27 A3

Harbour Inn with rm

The Square ✉ PA43 7JR – ✆ (01496) 810 330 – www.harbour-inn.com

7 rm – †£ 95/125 ††£ 135/165

Rest – Menu £ 38/50 – Carte £ 29/48

Traditional restaurant with pleasant bar and chunky wooden tea tables covered in deep blue cloths. Classical cooking uses fresh local seafood and island meats. Bedrooms are brightly decorated. Two cosy residents' lounges afford fantastic bay and island views.

PORT CHARLOTTE – Argyll and Bute 27 A3

Port Charlotte

Main St ✉ PA48 7TU – ✆ (01496) 850 360 – www.portcharlottehotel.co.uk – Closed 24-26 December

10 rm – †£ 110 ††£ 190 **Rest** – *(bar lunch)* Carte £ 22/40

Waterside hotel packed full of modern art. Large lounge with wood burning stove; cosy bar hung with old island photos. Bedrooms display traditional furniture and modern colour schemes; most have a sea view. Good mix of meat and fish dishes in the restaurant.

PORT ELLEN – Argyll and Bute 27 A3

Glenegedale House without rest

Northwest : 4.75 mi on A 846 ✉ PA42 7AS – ✆ (01496) 300 400 – www.glenegedalehouse.co.uk – Closed Christmas and New Year

6 rm – †£ 90/110 ††£ 130

Well-run hotel opposite the airport. Immaculately kept, individually styled bedrooms feature designer fabrics. Choice of two sitting rooms, both displaying leather sofas, coffee tables and an array of curios.

JEDBURGH – The Scottish Borders – 501 M17 – pop. 4 090 Scotland 26 D2

Edinburgh 48 mi – Carlisle 54 mi – Newcastle upon Tyne 57 mi

Murray's Green, ✆ (01835) 86 31 70, www.visitscotland.com

Jedburgh, Dunion Rd, ✆ (01835) 86 35 87

Town★ - Abbey★★ **AC** – Mary Queen of Scots House Visitor Centre★ **AC** – The Canongate Bridge★

Waterloo Monument (✻★★) N : 4 mi by A 68 and B 6400

Willow Court without rest 🛏 🎛 🤶 **P** ⇄
 The Friars ✉ TD8 6BN – ℰ (01835) 863 702 – www.willowcourtjedburgh.co.uk
3 rm ☐ – †£ 70/75 ††£ 80/86
Contemporary guesthouse looking out over the town's rooftops. Comfortable ground floor bedrooms offer a light, stylish space, with flat screen TVs, iPod docks and DVD players, as well as smart, modern bathrooms. Communal breakfasts, with eggs from their own hens.

KELSO – The Scottish Borders – **501** M17 – **pop. 5 740** 🛢 Scotland **26** D2

▶ Edinburgh 44 mi – Hawick 21 mi – Newcastle upon Tyne 68 mi
🇮 The Square, ℰ (01835) 86 31 70, www.kelso.bordernet.co.uk
🖾 Golf Course Rd, ℰ (01573) 22 30 09
◉ Town★ - The Square★★ – ≼★ from Kelso Bridge
Ⓖ Tweed Valley★★ - Floors Castle★ **AC**, NW : 1.5 mi by A 6089.
Mellerstain★★ (Ceilings★★★, Library★★★) **AC**, NW : 6 mi by A 6089 – Waterloo Monument (≼★★), SW : 7 mi by A 698 and B 6400 – Jedburgh Abbey★★ **AC**, SW : 8.5 mi by A 698 - Dryburgh Abbey★★ **AC** (setting★★★), SW : 10.5 mi by A 6089, B 6397 and B 6404 – Scott's View★★, W : 11 mi by A 6089, B 6397, B 6404 and B 6356 – Smailholm Tower★ (≼★★), NW : 6 mi by A 6089 and B 6397 - Lady Kirk (Kirk o'Steil★), NE : 16 mi by A 698, A 697, A 6112 and B 6437

 Roxburghe 🛏 ≼ 🛏 🕭 🍴 🛢 🖾 🤶 🕿 **P**
Heiton, Southwest : 3.5 mi by A 698 ✉ TD5 8JZ – ℰ (01573) 450 331
– www.roxburghe-hotel.com
22 rm ☐ – †£ 109/195 ††£ 109/195 – 2 suites
Rest – Menu £ 18/38 – Carte £ 36/59 **s**
Characterful Jacobean-style mansion owned by the Duke of Roxburghe, set in extensive parkland and boasting a fly fishing school and golf course. Plush, cosy guest areas display antiques and heirlooms. Feature bedrooms are the most luxurious; courtyard rooms are more modern. Formal fine dining.

 Ednam House ≼ 🛏 🤶 🕿 🖾 **P**
Bridge St ✉ TD5 7HT – ℰ (01573) 224 168 – www.ednamhouse.com – *Closed 24 December-9 January*
32 rm ☐ – †£ 80/115 ††£ 128/180
Rest – Menu £ 25 (dinner) – Carte £ 29/43
Long-standing, fishing-orientated hotel on the banks of the Tweed; in the family since 1928 and now run by the 3rd generation. Grand drawing rooms and classically styled bedrooms boast a timeless elegance. The bar has a mural of the river, while the dining room overlooks it. Much of the produce is homemade.

at Ednam North : 2.25 mi on B 6461 – ✉ **Kelso**

 Edenwater House 🛏 ≼ 🛏 🎛 (☜) **P**
Off Stichill rd ✉ TD5 7QL – ℰ (01573) 224 070 – www.edenwaterhouse.co.uk
– *Closed 1 January-12 March*
5 rm ☐ – †£ 70/80 ††£ 95/115
Rest – *(closed Sunday-Monday) (dinner only)* Menu £ 40
Delightful house run by charming couple, boasting a lovely garden and stream. Antique-filled lounges and comfy, classical bedrooms with tasteful décor and antique furniture. Pleasant dining room overlooks a meadow and offers a traditional, daily changing set menu.

KENMORE – Perth and Kinross – **501** I14 – **pop. 596** 🛢 Scotland **28** C2
▶ Edinburgh 82 mi – London 469 mi – Glasgow 78 mi – Aberdeen 126 mi
🖾 Taymouth Castle, Aberfeldy, ℰ (01887) 83 02 28
🖾 Mains of Taymouth, ℰ (01887) 83 02 26
◉ Village★
Ⓖ Loch Tay★★. Ben Lawers★★, SW : 8 mi by A 827

SCOTLAND

Kenmore
rest,

The Square ✉ PH15 2NU – ✆ (01887) 830 205 – www.kenmorehotel.com
39 rm – †£ 79/129 ††£ 89/139
Rest *Grill Room* – Menu £ 16/25 – Carte £ 21/64
Smart hotel standing on the banks of the Tay; dating from 1572 and reputedly Scotland's oldest inn. The snug 'Poet's Parlour' bar displays Burns' original pencilled verse above its open fire. Bedrooms are cosy and well-kept. The Grill Room offers a large menu of juicy Scottish steaks and grills.

KILBERRY – Argyll and Bute – 501 D16 – see Kintyre (Peninsula)

KILCHRENAN – Argyll and Bute – 501 E14 – ✉ Taynuilt Scotland 27 B2

Edinburgh 117 mi – Glasgow 87 mi – Oban 18 mi
Loch Awe★★, E : 1.25 m

Ardanaiseig

Northeast : 4 mi ✉ PA35 1HE – ✆ (01866) 833 333 – www.ardanaiseig.com
19 rm – †£ 100/185 ††£ 100/185, £ 17 – 1 suite
Rest – *(booking essential)* Menu £ 50
Stunningly located, laid-back country house boasting a vast azalea-filled estate and lovely views down the loch. The large sitting room features impressive columns; bedrooms come in a mix of styles – the Boat Shed is the best. The elegant dining room offers modern dishes and water views.

Roineabhal without rest

✉ PA35 1HD – ✆ (01866) 833 207 – www.roineabhal.com – Closed Christmas-New Year
3 rm – †£ 75 ††£ 100
Rustic stone and log house – built by its charming owners, who provide tea and homemade biscuits on arrival. Relaxing lounge with open fire. Immaculate bedrooms; two up a spiral staircase. Guest bathroom has roll-top bath. Top quality local produce served in homely breakfast room. Riverside garden.

KILLIECRANKIE – Perth and Kinross – 501 I13 – see Pitlochry

KILLIN – Stirling – 501 H14 – pop. 666 Scotland 27 B2

Edinburgh 72 mi – Dundee 65 mi – Oban 54 mi – Perth 43 mi
Falls of Dochart, ✆ (08707) 20 06 27, www.visitscotland.com
Killin, ✆ (01567) 82 03 12
Loch Tay★★, Ben Lawers★★, NE : 8 mi by A 827

Ardeonaig N
rm,

South Loch Tay Side, Northeast : 6.75 mi on South Loch Tay rd ✉ FK21 8SU – ✆ (01567) 820 400 – www.ardeonaighotel.co.uk – Closed first 3 weeks in January
17 rm (dinner included) – †£ 160/320 ††£ 200/360
Rest – *(restricted menu Monday-Tuesday residents only) (bookings essential for non-residents) (set menu only)* Menu £ 29/50
Much extended former inn, stunningly set on the south side of Loch Tay, looking out to Ben Lawers mountain. Choose a bedroom in the main house, in the courtyard, or in one of the garden shielings. Cosy bar; charming library. The dining room has the air of a South African manor house and cooking is modern and seasonal, with a refined edge. Formal, professional service.

KILMARNOCK – East Ayrshire – 501 G17 – pop. 43 588 Scotland 25 B2

Edinburgh 64 mi – Ayr 13 mi – Glasgow 25 mi
Dean Castle (arms and armour★, musical instruments★)

Hogarth's @ The Craigie Inn N

5 Main St, Craigie, Southwest : 6 mi by A 7038 and A 77 off B 730 ✉ KA1 5LY – ✆ (01563) 860 286 – www.craigieinnhogarths.co.uk
Rest – Menu £ 19/24 – Carte £ 23/41
Former pub in a tiny Ayrshire hamlet; its décor a blend of the rustic and the more contemporary. Menus follow suit, with a mix of classics and more modern dishes; portions are large and flavours, pronounced.

KINCLAVEN – Perth and Kinross – 501 J14 – pop. 394 – ✉ Stanley 28 C2

Edinburgh 55 mi – London 456 mi – Belfast 127 mi – Dundee 21 mi

Ballathie House

Stanley ✉ PH1 4QN – ☎ (01250) 883 268 – www.ballathiehousehotel.com

38 rm – †£ 95/135 ††£ 190/270 – 3 suites **Rest** – Menu £ 24/48 **s**

Well-established, mid-19C former shooting lodge, set on a peaceful estate of several hundred acres, on the banks of the River Tay. Comfortable guest areas and individually furnished bedrooms: some with floral themes; some more contemporary. Concise country house menu showcases seasonal, regional produce.

KINGAIRLOCH – Highland – 501 D14 29 B3

Edinburgh 139 mi – London 514 mi – Greenock 113 mi

Boathouse

✉ PH33 7AE – ☎ (01967) 411 232 – www.kingairloch.co.uk – Closed 29 October-28 March and Sunday dinner-Wednesday

Rest – *(booking advisable)* Carte £19/36

Converted Victorian boathouse on the shore of Loch a'Choire in the heart of the 17,000 acre Kingairloch Estate. Appealing dishes use full-flavoured venison from the estate, langoustines from Loch Linnhe, wild salmon from Cuil Bay, and seasonal herbs and vegetables from the kitchen garden.

KINGUSSIE – Highland – 501 H12 – pop. 1 410 Scotland 30 C3

Edinburgh 117 mi – Inverness 41 mi – Perth 73 mi

Gynack Rd, ☎ (01540) 66 16 00

Highland Wildlife Park★ AC, NE : 4 mi by A 9. Aviemore★, NE : 11 mi by A 9 – The Cairngorms★★ (≤★★★) - ✳★★★ from Cairn Gorm, NE : 18 mi by B 970

Hermitage

Spey St ✉ PH21 1HN – ☎ (01540) 662 137 – www.thehermitage-scotland.com – Closed 20 December-4 January

5 rm – †£ 38/60 ††£ 68/90 **Rest** – Menu £ 25 **s**

Traditional Victorian house built from stone and slate; formerly a doctor's surgery. Spacious garden affords great views of the Cairngorm Mountains and Ruthven Barracks. Warm, cosy lounge and comfy bedrooms; one has a super-king-sized bed and wet room. Simple dining room offers daily menu of home-cooked local produce.

Cross at Kingussie with rm

Tweed Mill Brae, Ardbroilach Rd ✉ PH21 1LB – ☎ (01540) 661 166 – www.thecross.co.uk – Closed January and Christmas

8 rm – †£ 50/100 ††£ 90/140 **Rest** – *(booking essential)* Menu £ 18/50 **s**

19C tweed mill in four acres of wooded grounds. Enjoy drinks on the terrace or in the first floor lounge then head to the smart dining room with is low beams, antiques and ornaments. Cooking is modern British/Scottish and is attractively presented. Pleasant, pine-furnished bedrooms have thoughtful extras.

KINTILLO – Perth and Kinross – see Perth

KINTYRE (Peninsula) – Argyll and Bute – 501 D16 Scotland 27 B3

Edinburgh 165 mi – London 515 mi – Dundee 164 mi – Paisley 111 mi

Campbeltown Airport : ☎ (01586) 553797

from Claonaig to Isle of Arran (Lochranza) (Caledonian MacBrayne Ltd) frequent services daily (30 mn) – from Kennacraig to Isle of Islay (Port Ellen or Port Askaig) (Caledonian MacBrayne Ltd) 1-3 daily – from Kennacraig to Oban via Isle of Colonsay (Scalasaig) and Isle of Islay (Port Askaig) 3 weekly

Machrihanish, Campbeltown, ☎ (01586) 81 02 13

Dunaverty, Campbeltown, Southend, ☎ (01586) 83 06 77

Gigha, Isle of Gigha, ☎ (01583) 50 52 42

Carradale★ – Saddell (Collection of grave slabs★)

SCOTLAND

CARRADALE – Argyll and Bute 27 B3

Dunvalanree

Port Righ Bay ✉ PA28 6SE – ✆ (01583) 431 226 – www.dunvalanree.com
5 rm – ♦£ 70 ♦♦£ 115 **Rest** – *(dinner only)* Menu £ 24
1930s Arts and Crafts house with gardens and a terrace overlooking the beach and the Sound. Characterful interior with many original features. Unfussy, individually furnished bedrooms – one in Mackintosh style; some with views. Homely cooking has a traditional, seafood base.

KILBERRY – Argyll and Bute 27 A3

Kilberry Inn with rm

✉ PA29 6YD – ✆ (01880) 770 223 – www.kilberryinn.com – Closed January-mid-March, Christmas and Monday
5 rm – ♦£ 75 ♦♦£ 130 **Rest** – *(booking essential at dinner)* Carte £ 24/37
Remotely set, rustic country inn with wooden beams, stone walls, open fires and mix of bare and linen-laid tables. Classical dishes are crafted from carefully sourced local produce; meat and fish are smoked in-house. Well-stocked bar. Comfy, modern bedrooms are named after nearby islands; one has an outdoor hot tub.

TARBERT – Argyll and Bute 27 B3

Tarbert, Kilberry Rd, ✆ (01880) 82 05 65

Anchor

Harbour St ✉ PA29 6UB – ✆ (01880) 820 577 – www.lochfyne-scotland.co.uk
12 rm – ♦£ 65/95 ♦♦£ 90/120
Rest *Sea Bed* – Carte £ 20/46
Smart, blue, mid-terraced house; once a church and later, a cinema. Modern interior with bright bedrooms, king-sized beds and smart bathrooms; half of the rooms have views over the harbour. Informal, all-day bar-cum-restaurant offers good old favourites and tasty seafood specials.

SCOTLAND

KIRKBEAN – Dumfries and Galloway – 501 J19 Scotland 26 C3

Edinburgh 92 mi – Dumfries 13 mi – Kirkcudbright 29 mi

Sweetheart Abbey★, N : 5 mi by A 710. Threave Garden★★ and Threave Castle★, W : 20 mi by A 710 and A 745

Cavens

✉ DG2 8AA – ✆ (01387) 880 234 – www.cavens.com – Closed January-February
6 rm – ♦£ 80/150 ♦♦£ 120/170
Rest – *(dinner only)* Menu £ 25 – Carte £ 30/41
Attractive 18C country house in 20 acres of mature grounds. Relax in the cosy, book-filled 'Green Room' or elegant drawing room with its grand piano. Luxurious 'Estate' bedrooms boast views over the Solway Firth, while the comfy 'Country' rooms have a simpler style. Linen-clad dining room offers an unfussy, daily menu of local produce; complimentary afternoon tea.

KIRKCUDBRIGHT – Dumfries and Galloway – 501 H19 – pop. 3 190 25 B3

Scotland

Edinburgh 105 mi – London 369 mi – Glasgow 90 mi – Liverpool 185 mi

Harbour Sq, ✆ (01557) 33 04 94, www.kirkcudbright.co.uk

Stirling Crescent, ✆ (01557) 33 03 14

Town★

Dundrennan Abbey★ **AC**, SE : 5 mi by A 711

Selkirk Arms

High St ✉ DG6 4JG – ✆ (01557) 330 402 – www.selkirkarmshotel.co.uk – Closed 26 December and dinner 25 December
16 rm – ♦£ 79/84 ♦♦£ 90/110 – 2 suites
Rest *Artistas* – see restaurant listing
Well-run, 18C former coaching inn, where Robert Burns reputedly wrote the Selkirk Grace. Spacious, comfortable bedrooms; some recently refurbished. Light lunches in the cosy, busy bar, which displays paintings of local scenes.

Gladstone House
48 High St ✉ DG6 4JX – ✆ (01557) 331 734 – www.kirkcudbrightgladstone.com – Closed 2 weeks January-February and Christmas
3 rm – †£ 60 ††£ 75 **Rest** – Menu £ 28
Attractive 18C former merchant's house with friendly owners. Comfy, antique-furnished lounge. Simple, pastel-hued bedrooms with seating areas by the windows and views over the rooftops. 3 course dinner of local produce, tailored around guests' preferences.

Artistas – Selkirk Arms Hotel
High St ✉ DG6 4JG – ✆ (01557) 330 402 – www.selkirkarmshotel.co.uk – Closed 26 December and dinner 25 December
Rest – Menu £ 29 (dinner) – Carte £ 21/35
Formal restaurant in a traditional former coaching inn. Extensive menu offers regional ingredients in classic combinations; Galloway Beef and Kirkcudbright scallops feature. A carved copy of the Selkirk Grace hangs proudly on the wall.

KIRKNEWTON – West Lothian – 501 J16 – see Edinburgh

KIRKWALL – 501 L7 – see Orkney Islands (Mainland)

KYLESKU – Highland – 501 E9 Scotland 30 C1

Edinburgh 256 mi – Inverness 100 mi – Ullapool 34 mi
Loch Assynt★★, S : 6 mi by A 894

Kylesku
✉ IV27 4HW – ✆ (01971) 502 231 – www.kyleskuhotel.co.uk – Closed November-February
8 rm – †£ 65/90 ††£ 95/120
Rest *Kylesku (Bar)* – see restaurant listing
Rest – *(dinner only)* Carte £ 16/43
Delightfully located 17C coaching inn, set beside 2 sea-lochs in a peaceful village. Take in the spectacular panoramic views from the cosy lounge, the restaurant and most of the homely bedrooms. Cooking centres around fresh Highland game and locally landed seafood.

Kylesku (Bar) – Kylesku Hotel
✉ IV27 4HW – ✆ (01971) 502 231 – www.kyleskuhotel.co.uk – Closed November-February
Rest – Carte £ 16/43
Cosy, homely bar with friendly staff, a relaxed atmosphere and breathtaking views of Loch Glendhu and the spectacular surrounding scenery. The menu focuses on fresh seafood, which is landed daily in front of the inn.

LAIRG – Highland – 501 G9 – pop. 857 30 C2

Edinburgh 218 mi – Inverness 61 mi – Wick 72 mi
Sutherland, ✆ (01549) 40 21 60, www.visitscotland.com

Park House
✉ IV27 4AU – ✆ (01549) 402 208 – www.parkhousesporting.com – Closed Christmas-New Year
4 rm – †£ 60/65 ††£ 90/95 **Rest** – Menu £ 25
Victorian sporting lodge offering fishing and field sports, its walls fittingly hung with rods and hunting prints. Cosy, open-fired sitting room and good-sized, homely bedrooms. Dining room offers loch views and a classical menu. Game and seafood feature highly.

LANGASS – Western Isles – see Uist (Isles of)

LEITH – City of Edinburgh – 501 K16 – see Edinburgh

LERWICK – 501 Q3 – see Shetland Islands (Mainland)

SCOTLAND

LEWIS and HARRIS (Isle of) – 501 A9 ▯ Scotland

🚢 from Stornoway to Ullapool (Mainland) (Caledonian MacBrayne Ltd) 2/3 daily (2 h 40 mn) – from Tarbert to Isle of Skye (Uig) (Caledonian MacBrayne Ltd) 1-2 daily (1 h 45 mn) – from Leverburgh to North Uist (Otternish) (Caledonian MacBrayne Ltd) (3-4 daily) (1 h 10 mn)

👁 Callanish Standing Stones★★ – Carloway Broch★ – St Clement's Church, Rodel (tomb★)

LEWIS – Western Isles 29 A1
▶ Edinburgh 210 mi – London 611 mi – Belfast 282 mi – Dundee 192 mi

BACK – Western Isles

⌂ **Broad Bay House** ≼ 🚗 & rm, 🎬 🛜 **P**
Northeast : 1 mi on B 895 ⊠ *HS2 0LQ –* ℰ *(01851) 820 990*
– www.broadbayhouse.co.uk – Restricted opening in winter
4 rm 🖵 – ♦£ 99/139 ♦♦£ 139/179 **Rest** – Menu £ 35
Delightful guesthouse with a decked terrace and a garden leading down to the beach. Luxurious interior features an open-plan, Scandinavian-style lounge and a dining area with panoramic views. Modern, oak-furnished bedrooms come with super king sized beds, sliding doors onto private terraces and great extras. Extensive hot and cold breakfasts and tasty 4 course dinners.

GALSON – Western Isles 29 B1

⌂ **Galson Farm** ⌘ ≼ 🚗 🍴 🛜 **P**
South Galson ⊠ *HS2 0SH –* ℰ *(01851) 850 492 – www.galsonfarm.co.uk*
4 rm 🖵 – ♦£ 50 ♦♦£ 86/100 **Rest** – Menu £ 27
Welcoming guesthouse in a wonderfully remote location, boasting views out across the Atlantic. Traditional, homely guest areas and cosy bedrooms. The owner also operates the village post office from just inside the porch. Freshly prepared, home-cooked meals.

STORNOWAY – Western Isles 29 B1

🛈 26 Cromwell St, ℰ (01851) 70 30 88, www.visitscotland.com
📷 Lady Lever Park, ℰ (01851) 70 22 40

⌂ **Braighe House** without rest ≼ 🚗 🎬 🛜 **P**
20 Braighe Rd, Southeast : 3 mi on A 866 ⊠ *HS2 0BQ –* ℰ *(01851) 705 287*
– www.braighehouse.co.uk – April-September
4 rm 🖵 – ♦£ 70/130 ♦♦£ 90/149
Smart dormer bungalow with a neat garden and a relaxed, modern interior. Immaculately kept bedrooms come with mineral water and chocolates; Deluxe rooms have sleigh beds and sea outlooks. Complimentary port. Diverse, appealing breakfasts.

UIG – Western Isles

✗✗ **Auberge Carnish** with rm ⌘ ≼ & rm, 🛜 **P**
5 Carnish, Southwest : 3.25 mi ⊠ *HS2 9EX –* ℰ *(01851) 672 459*
– www.aubergecarnish.co.uk
4 rm 🖵 – ♦£ 115/125 ♦♦£ 130/145
Rest – *(dinner only) (booking essential)* Menu £ 34
Modern, timber-clad building with decking all around, set in an idyllic position above the sweeping sands of Uig Bay. Lewis produce features in satisfying, classically based dishes with a twist; daily specials are usually seafood-based. Spacious, minimalist bedrooms have stylish bathrooms and stunning views.

HARRIS – Western Isles 29 A1
▶ Edinburgh 261 mi – London 638 mi – Belfast 289 mi – Dundee 242 mi

ARDHASAIG – Western Isles 29 A1

✗✗ **Ardhasaig House** with rm ⌘ ≼ 🛜 **P**
⊠ *HS3 3AJ –* ℰ *(01859) 502 500 – www.ardhasaig.co.uk – Closed November*
6 rm 🖵 – ♦£ 45/60 ♦♦£ 45/80 **Rest** – *(dinner only) (booking essential)* Menu £ 38
Purpose-built house that's been in the family for over 100 years. Modern, airy bar-lounge; flag-floored dining room with antique tables and dramatic bay/mountain views. Set menu offers local meats and seafood. Cosy bedrooms; the one in the stone lodge is the best.

BORVE - Western Isles

Pairc an t-Srath

HS3 3HT – (01859) 550 386 – *www.paircant-srath.co.uk* – *Closed 2 weeks October-November*

4 rm – £ 50/80 £ 100 **Rest** – Menu £ 35

Welcoming guesthouse on a working croft, with views out over the Sound of Taransay. Comfy, open-fired lounge has a chaise longue; the intimate dining room offers delicious home-cooked meals and wonderful vistas. Extremely friendly owners serve tea and homemade cake on arrival. Immaculate bedrooms feature smart oak furniture and brightly coloured Harris Tweed fabrics.

SCALPAY - Western Isles

29 B2

Hirta House without rest

HS4 3XZ – (01859) 540 394 – *www.hirtahouse.co.uk*

3 rm – £ 65/70 £ 65/75

Simple, characterful guesthouse in a small fishing village. Loch and mountain views from the lounge and conservatory. One traditional four-poster bedroom; two more modern rooms - one with a round bed. Nautically themed breakfast room.

SCARISTA - Western Isles

29 A2

Scarista House

HS3 3HX – (01859) 550 238 – *www.scaristahouse.com* – *Closed 21 December-31 January*

6 rm – £ 125/155 £ 210/235

Rest – *(dinner only) (booking essential) (set menu only)* Menu £ 50

19C former manse boasting amazing bay and mountain views. Caring owners; cosy, homely interior with open-fired library and drawing room. Traditional bedrooms, those at the rear are best. Classically inspired menu features garden produce.

TARBERT - Western Isles

29 A2

Ceol na Mara without rest

7 Direcleit, South : 1 mi by A 859 HS3 3DP – (01859) 502 464 – *www.ceolnamara.com*

3 rm – £ 80/100 £ 80/100

Former crofter's cottage - one of only three on the island with three storeys. Spacious, homely interior. Various well-kept lounges and good-sized, comfy bedrooms. Stunning lochside location.

LEWISTON - Highland - 501 G12 Scotland

30 C2

Edinburgh 172 mi – London 553 mi – Belfast 205 mi – Dundee 153 mi

Loch Ness★★ – The Great Glen★

Woodlands without rest

East Lewiston IV63 6UJ – (01456) 450 356 – *www.woodlands-lochness.co.uk* – *Closed November-March*

3 rm – £ 55/65 £ 65/80

Welcoming, purpose-built bungalow with a large decked terrace. Good-sized, pine-furnished bedrooms come with DVD players and comfy chairs. A simple breakfast room overlooks the spacious lawned garden and offers a good range of hot dishes.

Loch Ness Inn with rm

rm,

IV63 6UW – (01456) 450 991 – *www.staylochness.co.uk*

12 rm – £ 65/85 £ 75/112 **Rest** – Carte £ 19/36

Contemporary inn with a small locals bar serving pub classics and a two-roomed restaurant with exposed stone walls, bright timbered beams and a wood burning stove. Hearty, robust, flavoursome dishes champion Scottish produce. Spacious, comfortable, individually styled bedrooms.

SCOTLAND

LINLITHGOW – West Lothian – 501 J16 – pop. 13 048 Scotland — 26 C1

Edinburgh 19 mi – London 421 mi – Glasgow 35 mi – Aberdeen 125 mi

High St, ✆ (01506) 77 53 20, www.visitscotland.com

Braehead, ✆ (01506) 84 25 85

West Lothian, Airngath Hill, ✆ (01506) 82 60 30

Town★★ – Palace★★ **AC** : Courtyard (fountain★★), Great Hall (Hooded Fireplace★★), Gateway★ – Old Town★ – St Michaels★

Cairnpapple Hill★ **AC**, SW : 5 mi by A 706 – House of the Binns (plasterwork ceilings★) **AC**, NE : 4.5 mi by A 803 and A 904. Hopetoun House★★ **AC**, E : 7 mi by A 706 and A 904 – Abercorn Parish Church (Hopetoun Loft★★) NE : 7 mi by A 803 and A 904

Arden House without rest

Belsyde, Southwest : 2.25 mi on A 706 ✉ EH49 6QE – ✆ (01506) 670 172 – www.ardencountryhouse.com – Restricted opening in winter

3 rm – †£ 58/100 ††£ 80/110

Purpose built guesthouse bordering a 105 acre sheep farm. Tea and cake on arrival. Spacious, tastefully styled bedrooms boast modern, slate-floored bathrooms and plenty of extras like fresh flowers and magazines. Tasty, wide-ranging breakfasts are a highlight. Welcoming owner pays great attention to detail.

Champany Inn with rm

Northeast : 2 mi on A 803 at junction with A 904 ✉ EH49 7LU – ✆ (01506) 834 532 – www.champany.com – Closed 25-26 December, 1-2 January, Saturday lunch and Sunday

16 rm – †£ 99/125 ††£ 109/125 **Rest** – Menu £ 26/46 – Carte £ 49/75

Set in a collection of whitewashed cottages; the traditional restaurant was once a flour mill, hence its unusual shape. The focus is on meat and wine – 21-day aged Aberdeen Angus beef is a speciality. There's also a well-stocked wine shop, a second, more laid-back restaurant and tartan-themed bedrooms.

Livingston's

52 High St ✉ EH49 7AE – ✆ (01506) 846 565 – www.livingstons-restaurant.co.uk – Closed 2 weeks January, 1 week June, 1 week October, Sunday and Monday

Rest – Menu £ 21/41

Long-standing, family-run restaurant tucked away off the high street. Conservatory-like dining room with large garden and terrace; friendly, efficient service. Modern cooking with some bold flavours and innovative touches.

LOANS – South Ayrshire – 501 G17 – see Troon

LOCHALINE – Highland – 501 C14 — 29 B3

Edinburgh 162 mi – Craignure 6 mi – Oban 7 mi

Whitehouse

✉ PA80 5XT – ✆ (01967) 421 777 – www.thewhitehouserestaurant.co.uk – Closed November-Easter, Sunday and Monday

Rest – Menu £ 17 (lunch) – Carte £ 26/54

Understated, wood-panelled restaurant in remote headland village. Constantly evolving blackboard menu of local seafood, game and garden produce. Unfussy, flavoursome cooking. Hands-on owners.

LOCHEARNHEAD – Stirling – 501 H14 Scotland — 28 C2

Edinburgh 65 mi – Glasgow 56 mi – Oban 57 mi – Perth 36 mi

at Balquhidder Southwest : 5 mi by A84 – ✉ Stirling

Monachyle Mhor

West : 4 mi ✉ FK19 8PQ – ✆ (01877) 384 622 – www.mhor.net – Closed 5-25 January

14 rm – †£ 186/256 ††£ 195/265

Rest *Monachyle Mhor* – see restaurant listing

Eye-catching, pink former farmhouse, located in a beautiful, very remote valley. Contemporary furnishings blend with original features in the reception, lounge and bar. Smart, modern bedrooms boast slate-tiled bathrooms; those in the main house are smaller but afford great views over the Braes of Balquhidder.

Monachyle Mhor – Monachyle Mhor Hotel
West : 4 mi ✉ FK19 8PQ – ✆ (01877) 384 622 – www.mhor.net – Closed 5-25 January
Rest – *(booking essential)* Menu £ 28/50
Rurally set restaurant in a pink-painted hotel; sit in the snug library or enjoy the valley view from the conservatory. Well-presented dishes champion Scottish produce and are strong on flavour with a modern edge.

LOCHINVER – Highland – 501 E9 – pop. 470 – ✉ Lairg Scotland 30 C1

Edinburgh 251 mi – Inverness 95 mi – Wick 105 mi
Kirk Lane, ✆ (01506) 832 2 22, www.visitscotland.com
Village★
Loch Assynt★★, E : 6 mi by A 837

Inver Lodge
Iolaire Rd ✉ IV27 4LU – ✆ (01571) 844 496 – www.inverlodge.com – Closed November-April
21 rm ☕ – 🛉£ 120/200 🛉🛉£ 220/480
Rest *Chez Roux* – see restaurant listing
Well-run hotel on the hillside, overlooking a quiet fishing village. Spacious open-fired lounge, elegant bar and billiard room. Smart bedrooms with good mod cons and great bay/island views.

Ruddyglow Park Country House without rest
Loch Assynt, Northeast : 6.75 mi on A 837 ✉ IV27 4HB – ✆ (01571) 822 216 – www.ruddyglowpark.com – Closed December-February
3 rm ☕ – 🛉£ 100/150 🛉🛉£ 120/200
Yellow-washed house in a superb location, boasting fantastic loch and mountain views. Spacious guest areas are filled with antiques, paintings and silverware. A high level of facilities and extras feature in the classically styled bedrooms; the room in the modern log cabin offers extra privacy.

Albannach (Colin Craig and Lesley Crosfield) with rm
Baddidarroch, West : 1 mi by Baddidarroch rd ✉ IV27 4LP – ✆ (01571) 844 407 – www.thealbannach.co.uk – Closed Tuesday and Wednesday November to mid-March, except Christmas-New Year and Monday
5 rm (dinner included) ☕ – 🛉£ 180/220 🛉🛉£ 252/375
Rest – *(dinner only) (bookings essential for non-residents) (set menu only)* Menu £ 65
Substantial 19C Scottish house in a remote location, boasting exceptional bay and mountain views from the conservatory, terrace and garden. Traditional 5 course dinners rely on top quality local produce, with seafood from the harbour below and Scottish beef the specialities. Contemporary bedrooms are spread about the building; one boasts a private terrace and a hot tub.
→ Wild turbot mousseline with langoustines. Saddle of roe deer, candied beetroot, potato galette and wild bramble sauce. Caramelised pear tart, pear crisp and pear gelato.

Chez Roux – Inver Lodge Hotel
Iolaire Rd ✉ IV27 4LU – ✆ (01571) 844 496 – www.inverlodge.com – Closed November-April
Rest – *(dinner only)* Menu £ 43
Romantic restaurant hung with photos of the eponymous brothers and boasting well-spaced tables that take in fantastic bay and mountain views. Regularly changing, classical French menus.

LOCHMADDY – Western Isles – 501 Y11 – see Uist (Isles of)

LOCHRANZA – North Ayrshire – 501 E16 – see Arran (Isle of)

LUSS – Argyll and Bute – 501 G15 – pop. 402 Scotland 27 B2

Edinburgh 89 mi – Glasgow 26 mi – Oban 65 mi
Village★
E : Loch Lomond★★

SCOTLAND

Loch Lomond Arms (N)

Main Rd ✉ G83 8NY – ✆ (01436) 860 420 – www.lochlomondarmshotel.com
14 rm – †£ 80/100 ††£ 100/140 **Rest** – Carte £ 20/40
Retaining the warmth and character of an old inn, this hotel offers individual, contemporary bedrooms. Lomond and Colquhoun are the most luxurious: the former has a four-poster bed; the latter, superb views. Wide-ranging menu: dine in the open-fired bar, the relaxed dining room or the more formal library.

MELROSE – **The Scottish Borders** – **501** L17 – **pop. 1 656** Scotland **26** D2

Edinburgh 38 mi – London 347 mi – Glasgow 84 mi – Aberdeen 170 mi
Abbey St, ✆ (01835) 86 31 70, www.visitscotland.com
Melrose, Dingleton, Dingleton Rd, ✆ (01896) 82 28 55
Town★ - Abbey★★ (decorative sculpture★★★) **AC**
Eildon Hills (✳★★★) – Scott's View★★ – Abbotsford★★ **AC**, W : 4.5 mi by A 6091 and B 6360 – Dryburgh Abbey★★ **AC** (setting★★★), SE : 4 mi by A 6091 – Tweed Valley★★. Bowhill★★ **AC**, SW : 11.5 mi by A 6091, A 7 and A 708 – Thirlestane Castle (plasterwork ceilings★★) **AC**, NE : 21 mi by A 6091 and A 68

Burts

Market Sq. ✉ TD6 9PL – ✆ (01896) 822 285 – www.burtshotel.co.uk – Closed 6-12 January and 26 December
20 rm – †£ 70/85 ††£ 133/143 **Rest** – Carte £ 29/43
Characterful coaching inn on the main square; run by the same family for two generations. Appealing bedrooms blend contemporary furnishings with original features. Cosy bar serves old classics; formal dining room offers a mix of modern and traditional dishes.

Townhouse

Market Sq. ✉ TD6 9PQ – ✆ (01896) 822 645 – www.thetownhousemelrose.co.uk – Closed 13-20 January and 26 December
11 rm – †£ 90/145 ††£ 128/145
Rest – Menu £ 19 (dinner) – Carte £ 22/40
Former home of Catherine Spence and contemporary sibling to nearby Burts. Stylish bedrooms are decorated in black and purple and display bold feature walls; some rooms come with a shower only. Trendy all day café-cum-bar or more formal dining room and courtyard offering top Border ingredients.

at Gattonside North : 2 mi by B 6374 on B 6360 – ✉ Melrose

Fauhope House without rest

East : 0.25 mi by B 6360 taking unmarked lane to the right of Monkswood Rd at edge of village ✉ TD6 9LU – ✆ (01896) 823 184 – www.fauhopehouse.com
3 rm – †£ 60/70 ††£ 90/110
Charming 19C house by the Tweed, overlooking Melrose – its delightful gardens stretching for 15 acres. Quirky interior displays an eclectic mix of art and antiques. Bedrooms are all very different; some boast stylish bold colour schemes.

MEMUS – **Angus** **28** D2

Edinburgh 76 mi – London 478 mi – Belfast 159 mi – Dundee 21 mi

Drovers Inn

✉ DD8 3TY – ✆ (01307) 860 322 – www.the-drovers.com – Closed 25-26 December
Rest – Menu £ 10 (weekdays) – Carte £ 23/39
Attractive Highland inn in an extremely remote spot, with a delightful beamed interior and an open-fired bar. The wide-ranging menu is good value for money and showcases local, seasonal produce; game and vegetables come from the estate.

MOFFAT – **Dumfries and Galloway** – **501** J17 – **pop. 2 135** Scotland **26** C2

Edinburgh 61 mi – Carlisle 43 mi – Dumfries 22 mi – Glasgow 60 mi
Churchgate, ✆ (01683) 22 06 20, www.visitmoffat.co.uk
Coatshill, ✆ (01683) 22 00 20
Grey Mare's Tail★★, NE : 9 mi by A 708

Hartfell House

Hartfell Cres. ✉ DG10 9AL – ✆ (01683) 220 153 – www.hartfellhouse.co.uk – Closed 1 week autumn, 1 week January and Christmas

7 rm – †£ 40/45 ††£ 65/75

Rest ***Lime Tree*** – see restaurant listing

Keenly run Victorian house in quiet crescent. Original features include parquet floors and ornate cornicing. Comfy lounge boasts nice southerly aspect. Large, traditionally decorated bedrooms.

Bridge House

Well Rd, East : 0.75 mi by Selkirk rd (A 708) taking left hand turn before bridge ✉ DG10 9JT – ✆ (01683) 220 558 – www.bridgehousemoffat.co.uk – Closed 25 December-February

7 rm – †£ 55 ††£ 70/100 **Rest** – Menu £ 28

Large Victorian house on a quiet residential road, run by experienced owners and affording beautiful valley views. Relax in deep sofas in the comfortable lounge. Bedrooms are individually decorated; those to the front are the biggest. The dining room displays lovely cornicing and offers traditional fare.

Well View

Ballplay Rd, East : 0.75 mi by Selkirk rd (A 708) ✉ DG10 9JU – ✆ (01683) 220 184 – Closed 5-14 May

3 rm – †£ 40/60 ††£ 70/90 **Rest** – Menu £ 35

Substantial 19C house located in a peaceful suburb, boasting spacious, traditionally styled bedrooms and good comforts. Formerly a restaurant, dinner is still a key focus here. The daily changing 4 course set menu is taken at a communal table; wine is included.

Brodies

Altrive Pl ✉ DG10 9EB – ✆ (01683) 222 870 – www.brodiesofmoffat.co.uk – Closed 25-26 December

Rest – Menu £ 11 (early dinner) – Carte £ 20/34

Large, laid-back, modern eatery that caters for all appetites – serving snacks, light lunches, afternoon tea, more substantial dinners and all-day brunch on Sundays. Cooking has a traditional base and features fresh, local ingredients.

Lime Tree – Hartfell House Hotel

Hartfell Cres. ✉ DG10 9AL – ✆ (01683) 220 153 – www.hartfellhouse.co.uk – Closed 1 week October, Christmas, Sunday and Monday

Rest – *(dinner only) (booking essential)* Menu £ 28

Small hotel restaurant with smartly laid tables, open fire and attractive marquetry. Large bay window looks down the valley. Good value weekly menu features tasty, well-presented classics.

MONTROSE – Angus – 501 M13 – pop. 10 845 Scotland 28 D2

Edinburgh 92 mi – Aberdeen 39 mi – Dundee 29 mi

Panmure Place, ✆ (01674) 67 32 32, www.visitmontrose.co.uk

Traill Drive, ✆ (01674) 67 29 32

Edzell Castle★ (The Pleasance★★★) **AC**, NW : 17 mi by A 935 and B 966 – Cairn O'Mount Road★ (≤★★) N : 17 mi by B 966 and B 974 – Brechin (Round Tower★) W : 7 mi by A 935 – Aberlemno (Aberlemno Stones★, Pictish sculptured stones★) W : 13 mi by A 935 and B 9134

36 The Mall without rest

36 The Mall, North : 0.5 mi by A 92 at junction with North Esk Road ✉ DD10 8SS – ✆ (01674) 673 646 – www.36themall.co.uk

3 rm – †£ 55/65 ††£ 65/80

Large, immaculately kept former manse, run by warm, welcoming owners. Homely, characterful interior with tastefully styled, high-ceilinged bedrooms and a lovely conservatory overlooking the lawned garden. Good buffet selection and cooked choices in the communal breakfast room.

MUIR OF ORD – Highland – 501 G11 – pop. 1 812 30 C2

Edinburgh 173 mi – Inverness 10 mi – Wick 121 mi

Great North Rd, ✆ (01463) 87 08 25

Dower House

Highfield, North : 1 mi on A 862 ✉ IV6 7XN – ✆ (01463) 870 090 – www.thedowerhouse.co.uk – Closed November and Christmas-New Year
4 rm – †£ 85/120 ††£ 140/160
Rest – *(dinner only) (residents only)* Menu £ 38
Personally run, part-17C house with charming mature gardens. Characterful guest areas include an antique-furnished dining room and a small, open-fired lounge with fresh flowers and shelves crammed with books. Comfy bedrooms; one with a bay window overlooking the garden. Traditional, daily set menu.

MULL (Isle of) – Argyll and Bute – 501 B/C14 – pop. 2 667 Scotland 27 A2

Edinburgh 141 mi – London 512 mi – Belfast 163 mi – Dundee 136 mi
from Fionnphort to Isle of Iona (Caledonian MacBrayne Ltd) frequent services daily (10 mn) – from Pierowall to Papa Westray (Orkney Ferries Ltd) (summer only) (25 mn)
from Craignure to Oban (Caledonian MacBrayne Ltd) frequent services daily (45 mn) – from Fishnish to Lochaline (Mainland) (Caledonian MacBrayne Ltd) frequent services daily (15 mn) – from Tobermory to Isle of Tiree (Scarinish) via Isle of Coll (Arinagour) (Caledonian MacBrayne Ltd) 3 weekly (2 h 30 mn) – from Tobermory to Kilchoan (Caledonian MacBrayne Ltd) 4 daily (summer only) (35 mn)
Craignure, ✆ (08707) 20 06 10, www.holidaymull.co.uk
Craignure, Scallastle, ✆ (01688) 30 25 17
Island★ - Calgary Bay★★ – Torosay Castle **AC** (Gardens★ ≤★)
Isle of Iona★ (Maclean's Cross★, St Oran's Chapel★, St Martin's High Cross★, Infirmary Museum★ **AC** (Cross of St John★))

FIONNPHORT – Argyll and Bute 27 A2

Ninth Wave

Bruach Mhor, East : 0.75 mi by A 849 ✉ PA66 6BL – ✆ (01681) 700 757 – www.ninthwaverestaurant.co.uk – Closed November-Easter and Monday
Rest – *(dinner only) (booking essential)* Menu £ 42/60
Converted farm building with stylish, modern décor and trinkets from the owner's travels. Daily menu focuses on local seafood and has Asian and global influences. Herbs are foraged for and they catch the crabs and lobsters every morning.

TIRORAN – Argyll and Bute 27 A2

Tiroran House

✉ PA69 6ES – ✆ (01681) 705 232 – www.tiroran.com
10 rm – †£ 110/165 ††£ 175/220 **Rest** – *(light lunch)* Menu £ 36
Stunning 19C whitewashed house with a welcoming owner, set in 17 acres of parkland that run down to the water's edge. Charming, antique-filled interior with two open-fired lounges and immaculate, highly individual bedrooms. The dining room is split into a conservatory and a darker, more clubby area, and offers concise, daily changing menus.

TOBERMORY – Argyll and Bute – pop. 980 27 A2

Erray Rd, ✆ (01688) 30 23 87

Tobermory

53 Main St ✉ PA75 6NT – ✆ (01688) 302 091 – www.thetobermoryhotel.com – Closed 4 November-24 March
16 rm – †£ 49/108 ††£ 98/128
Rest – *(closed Monday) (dinner only)* Menu £ 25
Converted fishermen's cottages right on the quayside, not far from the local distillery. Small lounge and a popular dining room with a seafaring feel. Bedrooms vary in size but most have a pleasant harbour view. Concise menu of seasonal island produce, including homemade burgers and brasserie-style specials.

Sonas House without rest

The Fairways, North : 0.5 mi by Black Brae and Erray Rd following signs for the golf club ✉ PA75 6PS – ✆ (01688) 302 304 – www.sonashouse.co.uk – March-October
3 rm – †£ 70/100 ††£ 90/125
Set in an elevated position above Tobermory, with views over the Sound of Mull. Choose a bedroom in the main house or in the annexe studio; all come with a host of extras and superb views. The lovely swimming pool is open year-round.

Brockville without rest

Raeric Rd, by Back Brae and Erray Rd ✉ *PA75 6RS* – ✆ *(01688) 302 741 – www.brockville-tobermory.co.uk*

3 rm – £ 55/75 £ 75/90

Welcoming guesthouse with a warm, homely feel; run by a friendly owner with plenty of local knowledge. Extremely spacious bedrooms offer good modern facilities and everything you could want. The communal breakfast room boasts pleasant sea views; menus change daily and feature plenty of fresh fruits.

Highland Cottage with rm

Breadalbane St, via B 8073 ✉ *PA75 6PD* – ✆ *(01688) 302 030 – www.highlandcottage.co.uk – Closed 15 October-1 April*

6 rm – £ 95/125 £ 135/165

Rest – *(dinner only) (bookings essential for non-residents)* Menu £ 40

Long-standing, personally run restaurant in an intimate cottage, where family antiques and knick-knacks abound. Classical linen-laid dining room and a homely lounge. Traditional daily menu with a seafood base features plenty of local produce. Bedrooms are snug and individually styled.

MUTHILL – Perth and Kinross – 501 I15 – pop. 675 – see Crieff

---

NAIRN – Highland – 501 I11 – pop. 8 418 Scotland 30 D2

Edinburgh 172 mi – Aberdeen 91 mi – Inverness 16 mi

Seabank Rd, ✆ (01667) 45 32 08

Nairn Dunbar, Lochloy Rd, ✆ (01667) 45 27 41

Forres (Sueno's Stone★★) E : 11 mi by A 96 and B 9011 - Cawdor Castle★ **AC**, S : 5.5 mi by B 9090 – Brodie Castle★ **AC**, E : 6 mi by A 96. Fort George★, W : 8 mi by A 96, B 9092 and B 9006

Golf View rest,

Seabank Rd ✉ *IV12 4HD* – ✆ *(01667) 452 301 – www.crerarhotels.com*

42 rm – £ 90/160 £ 100/180 – 1 suite

Rest *Fairways* – *(dinner only)* Menu £ 33 **Rest *Links Brasserie*** – Carte £ 27/46

Set on the coast, between two golf courses, with pleasant gardens and Moray Firth vistas. Large lounge, clubby bar and smart spa. Spacious bedrooms have Stag-style furnishings; one has a whirlpool bath and views from its four-poster bed. Traditional menus in the part-panelled dining room and airy brasserie.

Boath House

Auldearn, East : 2 mi on A 96 ✉ *IV12 5TE* – ✆ *(01667) 454 896 – www.boath-house.com*

8 rm – £ 190/260 £ 230/335

Rest *Boath House* ✿ – see restaurant listing

Owned by a charming couple, an elegant 1825 neo-classical mansion framed by Corinthian columns. Inside it cleverly blends contemporary furnishings and restored original features; most of the art is for sale. Elegant, intimate bedrooms – one has his and hers roll-top baths and some have views of the lake.

Cawdor House

7 Cawdor St ✉ *IV12 4QD* – ✆ *(01667) 455 855 – www.cawdorhousenairn.co.uk – Closed 21 December-14 January*

7 rm – £ 55/80 £ 76/96

Comfy 19C former manse whose original features blend with contemporary styling. Cosy lounge with a log fire; variously sized bedrooms are clean and uncluttered. The friendly owners are a font of local knowledge. Simple dining room with set menu dinners by arrangement.

Boath House – Boath House Hotel

✿

Auldearn, East : 2 mi on A 96 ✉ *IV12 5TE* – ✆ *(01667) 454 896 – www.boath-house.com*

Rest – *(set menu only at dinner) (booking essential)* Menu £ 30/70 **s**

Elegant oval dining room in an early 19C mansion, with floor to ceiling windows affording lake views. Well-balanced modern menus showcase the chef's skill and understanding; cooking is accomplished, with vivid presentation and interesting flavours. Much of the produce is from their garden, orchard and bees.

➜ Foie gras with apple and meringue. Roe deer, salsify, shallots and pennywort. Rhubarb, pistachio and beetroot.

SCOTLAND

NEW CUMNOCK – East Ayrshire – 501 H17 – pop. 3 165 25 B2

Edinburgh 66 mi – London 378 mi – Glasgow 42 mi – Hamilton 36 mi

Lochside House

rest,

Northwest : 1.5 mi on A 76 ✉ KA18 4PN – ✆ (01290) 333 000 – www.lochside-hotel.com

34 rm – †£ 80/90 ††£ 110/130 – 3 suites

Rest *Afton* – Carte £ 18/34

19C former shooting lodge for the Marquis of Bute, impressively located on the side of a small loch, surrounded by acres of countryside. Stylish, contemporary interior, with an attractive spa, comfortable bedrooms and luxurious suites. The restaurant offers a range of classic dishes and panoramic loch views.

NEWTON STEWART – Dumfries and Galloway – 501 G19 – pop. 3 573 Scotland 25 B3

Edinburgh 131 mi – Dumfries 51 mi – Glasgow 87 mi – Stranraer 24 mi

Dashwood Sq, ✆ (01671) 40 24 31, www.newtonstewart.org

Minnigaff, Kirroughtree Ave, ✆ (01671) 40 21 72

Wigtownshire County, Glenluce, Mains of Park, ✆ (01581) 30 04 20

Galloway Forest Park★, Queen's Way★ (Newton Stewart to New Galloway) N : 19 mi by A 712

Kirroughtree House

Northeast : 1.5 mi by A 75 on A 712 ✉ DG8 6AN – ✆ (01671) 402 141 – www.kirroughtreehouse.co.uk – Closed 2 January-1 February

17 rm – †£ 95/130 ††£ 160/270 – 2 suites

Rest – *(booking essential)* Menu £ 18/35 **s**

Impressive 1719 mansion in landscaped gardens, overlooking the woods and bay. Grand interior with vast open-fired hall and impressive staircase. Traditionally styled bedrooms with plenty of extras. Concise 4 course menu of quality produce in classic combinations.

NIGG – 501 H10 – see Tain

NORTH BAY – Western Isles – see Barra (Isle of)

NORTH BERWICK – East Lothian – 501 L15 – pop. 6 223 Scotland 26 D1

Edinburgh 141 mi – London 512 mi – Belfast 163 mi – Dundee 136 mi

1 Quality St, ✆ (01620) 89 21 97, www.northberwickuk.com

North Berwick, Beach Rd, West Links, ✆ (01620) 89 03 12

Glen, East Links, Tantallon Terrace, ✆ (01620) 89 27 26

North Berwick Law (✻★★★) S : 1 mi - Tantallon Castle★★ (clifftop site★★★) **AC**, E : 3.5 mi by A 198 – Dirleton★ (Castle★ **AC**) SW : 2.5 mi by A 198. Museum of Flight★, S : 6 mi by B 1347 – Preston Mill★, S : 8.5 mi by A 198 and B 1047 – Tyninghame★, S : 7 mi by A 198 – Coastal road from North Berwick to Portseton★, SW : 13 mi by A 198 and B 1348

Glebe House without rest

Law Rd ✉ EH39 4PL – ✆ (01620) 89 2608 – www.glebehouse-nb.co.uk – Closed Christmas and New Year

3 rm – †£ 80/85 ††£ 120

Spacious, welcoming Georgian house with walled gardens and views over the town and sea. Classical, country house drawing room and antique communal breakfast table. Comfortable, well-furnished bedrooms.

Canty Bay House

rm,

Canty Bay, West : 2.5 mi on A 198 ✉ EH39 5PL – ✆ (01620) 248 216 – www.cantybayhouse.co.uk – Closed Christmas-New Year

4 rm – †£ 90/150 ††£ 130/150 **Rest** – Menu £ 35

Small house perched on a clifftop, overlooking Tantallon Castle ruins, Bass Rock and the Firth of Forth. The smart interior has good quality furnishings and a snooker table. Two of the bedrooms open onto a small roof terrace. Communal breakfasts offer a large selection; simple suppers are served on request.

NORTH QUEENSFERRY - Fife - 501 J15 - pop. 1 102 28 C3

Edinburgh 13 mi – London 416 mi – Glasgow 47 mi – Aberdeen 116 mi

Wee Restaurant

17 Main St ✉ KY11 1JT – ✆ (01383) 616 263 – www.theweerestaurant.co.uk – Closed 25-26 December, 1-2 January and Monday

Rest – Menu £ 20/34 **s**

Simple, quarry-floored restaurant in the shadow of the Forth Rail Bridge. Fresh Scottish ingredients are served in neatly presented, classical combinations. Lunch represents the best value.

NORTH UIST - Western Isles - 501 X/Y11 - see Uist (Isles of)

OBAN - Argyll and Bute - 501 D14 - pop. 8 243 Scotland 27 B2

Edinburgh 123 mi – Dundee 116 mi – Glasgow 93 mi – Inverness 118 mi

Access Access to Glasgow by helicopter

to Isle of Mull (Craignure) (Caledonian MacBrayne Ltd) (45 mn) – to Isle of Tiree (Scarinish) via Isle of Mull (Tobermory) and Isle of Coll (Arinagour) (Caledonian MacBrayne Ltd) – to Isle of Islay (Port Askaig) and Kintyre Peninsula (Kennacraig) via Isle of Colonsay (Scalasaig) (Caledonian MacBrayne Ltd) (summer only) – to Isle of Lismore (Achnacroish) (Caledonian MacBrayne Ltd) 2-3 daily (except Sunday) (55 mn) – to Isle of Colonsay (Scalasaig) (Caledonian MacBrayne Ltd) 3 weekly (2 h)

Argyll Sq, ✆ (08707) 20 06 30, www.oban.org.uk

Glencruitten, Glencruitten Rd, ✆ (01631) 56 28 68

Loch Awe★★, SE : 17 mi by A 85 – Bonawe Furnace★, E : 12 mi by A 85 – Cruachan Power Station★ **AC**, E : 16 mi by A 85 – Seal and Marine Centre★ **AC**, N : 14 mi by A 828

Manor House

Gallanach Rd. ✉ PA34 4LS – ✆ (01631) 562 087 – www.manorhouseoban.com – Closed 25-26 December

11 rm – †£ 105/180 ††£ 115/225 **Rest** – *(bar lunch)* Menu £ 39

18C dower house, formerly part of the Argyll Estate. Country house style interior offers traditional comforts; spacious lounge and rustic bar boast delightful bay and harbour views. Individually styled bedrooms. Concise daily menu served in formal dining room.

Glenburnie House without rest

Corran Esplanade ✉ PA34 5AQ – ✆ (01631) 562 089 – www.glenburnie.co.uk – Closed December-February

12 rm – †£ 50/60 ††£ 90/120

Bay-windowed house on main esplanade, affording great bay and island views. Period features include a delightful staircase and etched glass widows; antiques abound. Comfy, good-sized bedrooms.

Coast

✉ PA34 5NT – ✆ (01631) 569 900 – www.coastoban.com – Closed 25-26 December and Sunday lunch

Rest – Menu £ 13 (lunch and early dinner) – Carte £ 24/38

Busy high street restaurant in a former bank with a high ceiling, stripped wooden floor and khaki fabric strips on the walls. Unfussy, modern cooking with good seasoning; local produce is key. 'Light bite' lunches are a steal.

Ee-usk

The North Pier ✉ PA34 5QD – ✆ (01631) 565 666 – www.eeusk.com – Closed 2 weeks January and 25-26 December

Rest – Carte £ 22/56

Long-standing seafood restaurant run by experienced owners, located on the harbourfront and offering great views over the bay from its floor to ceiling windows. Extensive menus focus on simply prepared, fresh local fish and shellfish.

SCOTLAND

ONICH – Highland – 501 E13 – ✉ Fort William **29** B3

Edinburgh 123 mi – Glasgow 93 mi – Inverness 79 mi – Oban 39 mi

Lochleven Seafood Café

Lochleven, Southeast : 6.5 mi by A 82 on B 863 ✉ PH33 6SA – ☎ (01855) 821 048 – www.lochlevenseafoodcafe.co.uk – Restricted opening in winter

Rest – *(bookings advisable at dinner)* Carte £ 22/56 **s**

Stunning lochside location looking toward Glencoe Mountains. Extremely fresh, simply prepared seafood; shellfish platter and razor clams a speciality. Themed evenings in winter.

ORKNEY ISLANDS – 501 K/L7 – pop. 20 238 Scotland

see Kirkwall

from Burwick (South Ronaldsay) to John O'Groats (John O'Groats Ferries) 2-4 daily (40 mn) (summer only)

service between Isle of Hoy (Longhope), Isle of Hoy (Lyness), Isle of Flotta and Houton (Orkney Ferries Ltd) – from Stromness to Scrabster (P & O Scottish Ferries) (1-3 daily) (2 h) – from Stromness to Shetland Islands (Lerwick) and Aberdeen (Northlink Ferries) 1-2 daily – from Kirkwall to Westray, Stronsay via Eday and Sanday (Orkney Ferries Ltd) – from Tingwall to Wyre via Egilsay and Rousay (Orkney Ferries Ltd) – from Kirkwall to Shapinsay (Orkney Ferries Ltd) (25 mn) – from Stromness to Isle of Hoy (Moness) and Graemsay (Orkney Ferries Ltd) – from Kirkwall to North Ronaldsay (Orkney Ferries Ltd) weekly (2 h 40 mn) - from Kirkwall to Invergordon (Orcargo Ltd) daily (8 h 30 mn) – from Houton to Isle of Hoy (Lyness), Flotta and Longhope (Orkney Ferries Ltd), Gill's Bay to St Margaret's Hope (Pentland Ferries) (1hr) 3 times a day.

West Castle St., Kirkwall, ✉ KW15 1GU, ☎ (01856) 87 28 56

Old Man of Hoy★★★ – Islands★★ – Maes Howe★★ **AC** – Skara Brae★★ **AC** – Kirkbuster Museum and Corrigal Farm Museum★ **AC** – Brough of Birsay★ **AC** – Birsay (<★) – Ring of Brodgar★ – Unstan Cairn★

SCOTLAND

MAINLAND – Orkney Islands **31** A3

Edinburgh 277 mi – London 677 mi – Belfast 349 mi – Dundee 258 mi

BURRAY – Orkney Islands **31** A3

Sands

✉ KW17 2SS – ☎ (01856) 731 298 – www.thesandshotel.co.uk – Closed 1-3 January and 25-26 December

8 rm – †£ 60/80 ††£ 80/100 **Rest** – Carte £ 19/30

Converted 19C herring packing store in small hamlet overlooking Scapa Flow. Pleasant bedrooms boast smart bathrooms. Bar with pool table and dartboard offers traditional menu. Dining room serves more refined dishes, featuring island produce and lots of shellfish.

DEERNESS – Orkney Islands

Northfield without rest

West : 2 mi turning left by village shop ✉ KW17 2QL – ☎ (01856) 741 353 – www.orkneybedandbreakfast.com

3 rm – †£ 50/70 ††£ 70

Set down a bumpy lane, right by the water's edge, with views across to some of the smaller islands. Horses, ducks and chickens can be found in the peaceful grounds. Cosy, homely, tastefully furnished bedrooms; one with views from the bed.

DOUNBY – Orkney Islands **31** A3

Ashleigh without rest

Howaback Rd, South : 0.75 mi by A986 ✉ KW17 2JA – ☎ (01856) 771 378 – www.ashleigh-orkney.com – Closed 20 December-10 January

4 rm – †£ 40/45 ††£ 74/80

Purpose-built house in the heart of the island's countryside, boasting loch and mountain views. Large breakfast room and lounge filled with guidebooks. Good-sized bedrooms with modern facilities.

HARRAY – Orkney Islands 31 A3

Merkister

Off A 986 ✉ KW17 2LF – ✆ (01856) 771 366 – www.merkister.com – Closed 23 December-4 January

16 rm ☕ – †£ 65/125 ††£ 100/225 **Rest** – *(bar lunch)* Carte £ 22/42 **s**

Family-run, lochside hotel affording wonderful water and mountain views. Comfortable, well-kept bedrooms; those outside have their own terraces and gardens. Snug, open-fired bar serves snacks. Dining room offers strictly Orkney-based produce and a scenic backdrop.

Holland House without rest

On St Michael's Church rd ✉ KW17 2LQ – ✆ (01856) 771 400 – www.hollandhouseorkney.co.uk – Closed 7 December-12 January and restricted opening in winter

3 rm ☕ – †£ 48/60 ††£ 96

Converted manse run by a welcoming owner, with commanding views throughout. Open-fired lounge – packed with local art and handmade furniture – stone-floored breakfast room and conservatory. Spotless bedrooms with a host of extras and great attention to detail.

KIRKWALL – Orkney Islands Scotland 31 A3

Kirkwall Airport : ✆ (01856) 886210, S : 3.5 mi

West Castle St, ✆ (01856) 87 28 56, www.visitorkney.com

Grainbank, ✆ (01856) 87 24 57

Kirkwall★★ - St Magnus Cathedral★★ – Western Mainland★★, Eastern Mainland (Italian Chapel★) - Earl's Palace★ **AC** – Tankerness House Museum★ **AC** – Orkney Farm and Folk Museum★

Ayre

Ayre Rd. ✉ KW15 1QX – ✆ (01856) 873 001 – www.ayrehotel.co.uk – Closed 25 December and 1 January

51 rm ☕ – †£ 76/95 ††£ 100/130 **Rest** – *(bar lunch)* Carte £ 18/45

Well-run hotel close to the harbour. Formerly 3 Victorian houses, now a traditionally styled hotel with comfortable bedrooms – the newer extension rooms are biggest and best. Spacious bar filled with locals. Dining room offers sizeable menu of Orcadian produce.

Lynnfield

Holm Rd ✉ KW15 1SU – ✆ (01856) 872 505 – www.lynnfieldhotel.com – Closed 1-7 January and 25-26 December

10 rm ☕ – †£ 75/100 ††£ 100/155 – 3 suites

Rest – *(bar lunch)* Carte £ 22/42

Spacious hotel with cosy sitting rooms, Orcadian furniture and a fine range of Scotch whiskies. Supremely comfortable bedrooms; two with four-posters. Formal dining room with large conservatory affording great views of the countryside. Seasonal menus.

Avalon House without rest

Carness Rd, Northeast : 1.5 mi by Shore St. ✉ KW15 1UE – ✆ (01856) 876 665 – www.avalon-house.co.uk – Closed Christmas-New Year

5 rm ☕ – †£ 45/55 ††£ 62/72

Modern, purpose-built guesthouse in a pleasant residential area. Lounge filled with maps and books about the islands. Good-sized bedrooms with simple, homely feel. Nice coastal outlook.

Foveran with rm

St Ola, Southwest : 3 mi on A 964 ✉ KW15 1SF – ✆ (01856) 872 389 – www.foveranhotel.co.uk – Restricted opening October-April

8 rm ☕ – †£ 75/85 ††£ 110/116 **Rest** – *(dinner only)* Carte £ 22/41

Spacious restaurant boasting superb panoramic views over Scapa Flow and the south islands. Traditional menu features local, seasonal produce, including Orcadian lamb/beef and plenty of fresh seafood. Homely, well-kept bedrooms display simple colour schemes.

SCOTLAND

ST MARGARET'S HOPE – Orkney Islands 31 A3

XX **Creel** with rm

Front Rd ✉ *KW17 2SL – ✆ (01856) 831 311 – www.thecreel.co.uk – Closed October-March, Sunday and Monday*

3 rm – †£ 70/75 ††£ 95/110 **Rest** – *(dinner only)* Menu £ 33

Long-standing, family-run restaurant in seafront village. Spacious dining room is hung with local oils and prints. Daily changing menu displays a fresh, traditional seafood base. Comfortable, cosy bedrooms boast modern, co-ordinated furnishings and bay views.

STROMNESS – Orkney Islands ▮ Scotland 31 A3

Town★ - Pier Gallery (collection of abstract art★)

X **Hamnavoe**

35 Graham Pl, off Victoria St ✉ *KW16 3BY – ✆ (01856) 850 606 – Closed Monday and restricted opening in winter*

Rest – *(dinner only) (booking essential)* Carte £ 27/39

Homely restaurant in a sleepy harbourside town; its name meaning 'Safe Haven'. Its plain walls are dotted with local oils and open fires. Unfussy home cooking utilises fresh market produce and dishes are hearty and full of flavour.

ISLE OF WESTRAY – Orkney Islands 31 A2

Edinburgh 289 mi – London 690 mi – Belfast 361 mi – Dundee 270 mi

PIEROWALL – Orkney Islands 31 A2

No 1 Broughton without rest

✉ *KW17 2DA – ✆ (01857) 677 726 – www.no1broughton.co.uk – Closed 24-25 December*

3 rm – †£ 45/60 ††£ 60/70

19C pink-washed house on the waterside, with views over Pierowall Bay and out to Papa Westray. Comfortable lounge and conservatory; simple, homely bedrooms with modern bathrooms. Sauna on request. Dry stone walling courses also available!

PEAT INN – Fife 28 D2

Edinburgh 44 mi – London 447 mi – Belfast 134 mi – Dundee 16 mi

XXX **The Peat Inn** (Geoffrey Smeddle) with rm

✉ *KY15 5LH – ✆ (01334) 840 206 – www.thepeatinn.co.uk – Closed 2 weeks January, Christmas, Sunday and Monday*

8 rm – †£ 125/165 ††£ 185/215

Rest – *(booking essential)* Menu £ 19/65 – Carte £ 30/53

Whitewashed former pub with a log fire in the lounge and a cosy, well-dressed restaurant – ask for a table overlooking the floodlit gardens. Accomplished, classical cooking has subtle modern touches and local ingredients to the fore. Stylish, split-level bedrooms in a separate stone building, with plenty of extras and breakfast served in-room. Charming, professional staff.

→ Oyster panna cotta, Avruga caviar and cauliflower purée. Shoulder and stuffed cutlet of lamb, roast kidney and olive crushed potatoes. Rhubarb, ginger and crowdie cheesecake, poached rhubarb and rhubarb sorbet.

PEEBLES – The Scottish Borders – 501 K17 – pop. 8 065 ▮ Scotland 26 C2

Edinburgh 24 mi – London 382 mi – Glasgow 53 mi – Aberdeen 151 mi

High St, ✆ (01835) 86 31 70, www.peebles.info

Kirkland St, ✆ (01721) 72 01 97

Tweed Valley★★. Traquair House★★ **AC**, SE : 7 mi by B 7062 – Rosslyn Chapel★★ **AC**, N : 16.5 mi by A 703, A 6094, B 7026 and B 7003

Cringletie House

Edinburgh Rd, North : 3 mi on A 703 ✉ EH45 8PL – ☎ (01721) 725 750 – www.cringletie.com – Closed 3-31 January
13 rm – †£ 99/245 ††£ 99/260 – 1 suite
Rest ***Sutherland Room*** – Menu £ 35/55 **s**
A handsome, early Victorian shooting lodge with a baronial feel, set in acres of gardens and parkland. Bedrooms – named after border towns – have views of the gardens. Formal dining under a stunning 1902 ceiling fresco; quality local produce includes herbs and veg from the walled garden.

Rowanbrae without rest

103 Northgate ✉ EH45 8BU – ☎ (01721) 721 630 – www.aboutscotland.co./peebles/rowanbrae – March-November
3 rm – †£ 45 ††£ 65
Cosy Victorian villa close to town, with a pretty terrace and surprisingly spacious interior. Long-standing owners provide a warm welcome and a snug, homely atmosphere reigns. Pleasant, well-kept bedrooms have a modern edge, courtesy of their soft furnishings. Original cornices and pine woodwork feature.

Osso

Innerleithen Rd ✉ EH45 8BA – ☎ (01721) 724 477 – www.ossorestaurant.com – Closed 1 January, 25 December, dinner Tuesday and Wednesday in winter except December and dinner Sunday and Monday,
Rest – Carte £ 20/33
By day, a bustling coffee shop serving a bewildering array of light snacks and daily specials. By night, a more sophisticated restaurant offering a great value, regularly changing menu of tasty, well-presented dishes, with the occasional Asian influence. Friendly, attentive service.

Restaurant at Kailzie Gardens

Kailzie Estate, East : 2 mi on B7062 ✉ EH45 9HT – ☎ (01721) 722 807 – www.kailzie.com – Closed 1-24 January, Monday and Tuesday October-March
Rest – *(lunch only) (booking advisable)* Carte £ 15/32
Rustic eatery in the old stables of a large estate, surrounded by semi-formal gardens, a fishery and an osprey viewing centre. Homemade cakes, pastries and tasty Scandic open sandwiches at lunch. Classical, flavoursome cooking on the weekly main menu, which features local meats and cheeses.

at Eddleston North : 4.5 mi on A 703

Horseshoe Inn with rm

Edinburgh Rd ✉ EH45 8QP – ☎ (01721) 730 225 – www.horseshoeinn.co.uk – Closed 2 weeks January, Monday except bank holidays and Sunday
8 rm – †£ 90/110 ††£ 130/150 **Rest** – Menu £ 22 (lunch) – Carte £ 30/44
Former roadside inn; now a smart, columned restaurant with elegant tableware and formal, white-gloved service. The sophisticated à la carte and tasting menu offer ambitious, well-presented dishes which take their influences from across Europe. Chic, modern bedrooms are located in the annexe.

SCOTLAND

PERTH – **Perth and Kinross** – **501** J14 – **pop. 44 513** Scotland **28** C2

Edinburgh 44 mi – Aberdeen 86 mi – Dundee 22 mi – Dunfermline 29 mi
West Mill St, ☎ (01738) 45 06 00, www.perthshire.co.uk
Craigie Hill, Cherrybank, ☎ (01738) 62 08 29
King James VI, Moncreiffe Island, ☎ (01738) 62 51 70
Murrayshall, New Scone, ☎ (01738) 55 48 04
North Inch, c/o Perth & Kinross Council, 35 Kinncoll St, ☎ (01738) 63 64 81
City★ – Black Watch Regimental Museum★ Y **M1** – Georgian Terraces★ Y – Museum and Art Gallery★ Y **M2**
Scone Palace★★ **AC**, N : 2 mi by A 93 Y – Branklyn Garden★ **AC**, SE : 1 mi by A 85 Z – Kinnoull Hill (←★) SE : 1.25 mi by A 85 Z – Huntingtower Castle★ **AC**, NW : 3 mi by A 85 Y – Elcho Castle★ **AC**, SE : 4 mi by A 912 - Z - and Rhynd rd. Abernethy (11C Round Tower★), SE : 8 mi by A 912 - Z - and A 913

Plan on next page

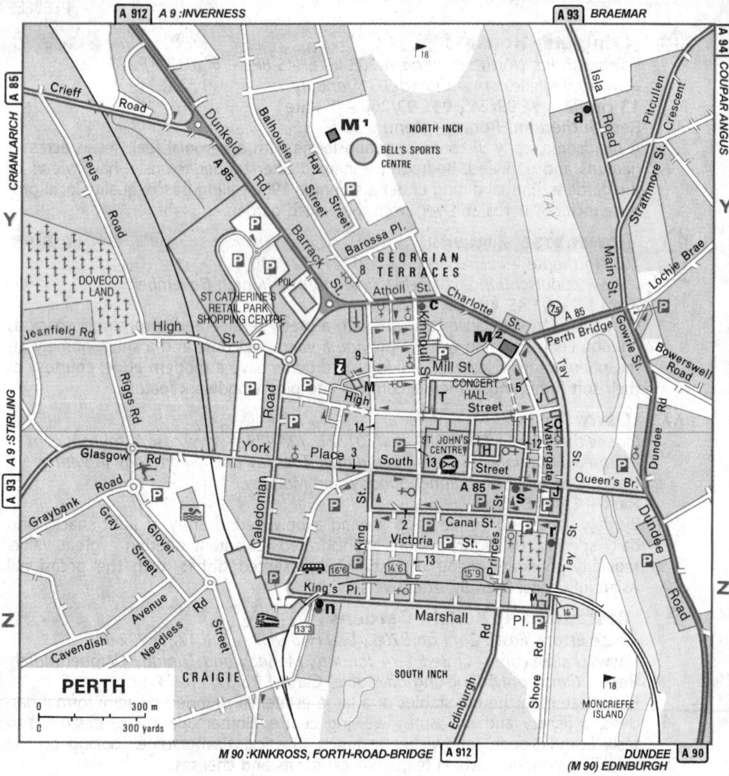

Parklands

2 St Leonard's Bank ✉ PH2 8EB – ✆ (01738) 622 451
– www.theparklandshotel.com – Closed 26 December-6 January Zn
15 rm – †£ 93/149 ††£ 115/199
Rest 63@Parklands – see restaurant listing
Rest *No.1 The Bank* – Carte £ 22/43

Located close to the railway station, a personally run, extended Georgian house with a contemporary interior. Spacious modern bedrooms have good facilities and sizeable bathrooms; those to the front have pleasant views over the park. Modern menu in the intimate 63@Parklands; informal dining in No.1 The Bank.

Taythorpe without rest

Isla Rd, North : 1 mi on A 93 ✉ PH2 7HQ – ✆ (01738) 447 994
– www.taythorpe.co.uk Ya
3 rm – †£ 45/65 ††£ 75

Modern, stone-built house run by a bubbly owner; superbly located close to Scone Palace, the city and the racecourse. Large, cosy sitting room hung with homely pictures and salmon fishing maps; pleasant communal breakfast room where tasty Scottish dishes are served. Appealing, immaculately kept bedrooms.

XX **63 Tay Street**

63 Tay St ✉ PH2 8NN – ✆ (01738) 441 451 – www.63taystreet.co.uk – Closed 1-7 January, 9-15 July, 26-31 December, Sunday, Monday and lunch Tuesday-Wednesday Z**r**

Rest – Menu £ 26/40

Well-established riverside restaurant with bold modern artwork and an attentive team. Good value lunches and a choice of grill or gourmet dinners; the latter where the cooking really comes into its own. The wine list has over 250 bins.

XX **Deans @ Let's Eat**

77-79 Kinnoull St ✉ PH1 5EZ – ✆ (01738) 643 377 – www.letseatperth.co.uk – Closed first 2 weeks January, 1 week October, Sunday and Monday

Rest – Menu £ 21 (early dinner) – Carte £ 21/40 Y**c**

Bottle-green restaurant close to the theatre and the concert hall. Comfortable lounge and a friendly, chatty team. All-encompassing menus, with seasonal deals and special events; passionate, classically based cooking has an ambitious edge.

XX **63@Parklands** – Parklands Hotel

2 St Leonard's Bank ✉ PH2 8EB – ✆ (01738) 622 451 – www.63atparklands.com – Closed 25 December-5 January, Tuesday and Wednesday Z**n**

Rest – *(dinner only)* Menu £ 35

Intimate conservatory restaurant with a relaxed lounge, set within a privately run hotel. The gourmet-style 5 course menu offers one or two choices per course and changes weekly; cooking is modern and features some interesting combinations.

X **Pig Halle** Ⓝ

38 South St ✉ PH2 8PG – ✆ (01738) 248 784 – www.pighalle.co.uk – Closed 1 January and Monday Z**s**

Rest – Carte £ 20/36

Lively bistro; the square, marble-floored room tightly packed with tables and dominated by a mirror stencilled with a Paris Metro map. Menus list all the Gallic favourites. The adjoining deli serves wood-fired pizzas and tasty baguettes.

SCOTLAND

at Stanley North : 7 mi off A9 (Inverness)

X **Apron Stage**

5 King St ✉ PH1 4ND – ✆ (01738) 828 888 – www.apronstagerestaurant.co.uk – Closed 1 week May, 1 week September and Sunday-Wednesday

Rest – *(dinner only)* Carte £ 23/33

Lovely little restaurant in a small village, consisting of a cosy room with formally laid tables and an open-kitchen to the rear. Appealing, weekly menu mixes Scottish, French and Asian influences in generous, flavoursome portions.

at Kintillo Southeast : 4.5 mi off A912

X **Roost**

Forgandenny Rd ✉ PH2 9AZ – ✆ (01738) 812 111 – www.theroostrestaurant.co.uk – Closed 1-16 January, 25-26 December, Monday and dinner Sunday, Tuesday and Wednesday

Rest – Menu £ 18 (lunch) – Carte £ 22/40

Converted hen house in the heart of the village, with a rustic modern interior. Well-crafted, classical dishes display Mediterranean touches and feature local meats and veg from the garden; desserts are a highlight. Run by a friendly team.

PIEROWALL – **501** K6 – **see Orkney Islands (Isle of Westray)**

PITLOCHRY – **Perth and Kinross** – **501** I13 – **pop. 2 906** Scotland **28** C2

▶ Edinburgh 71 mi – Inverness 85 mi – Perth 27 mi

ℹ 22 Atholl Rd, ✆ (01796) 47 22 15, www.pitlochry.org

18 Pitlochry Estate Office, ✆ (01796) 47 27 92

◎ Town★

◎ Blair Castle★★ **AC**, NW : 7 mi by A 9 A – Queen's View★★, W : 7 mi by B 8019 A – Falls of Bruar★, NW : 11 mi by A 9 A

Plan on next page

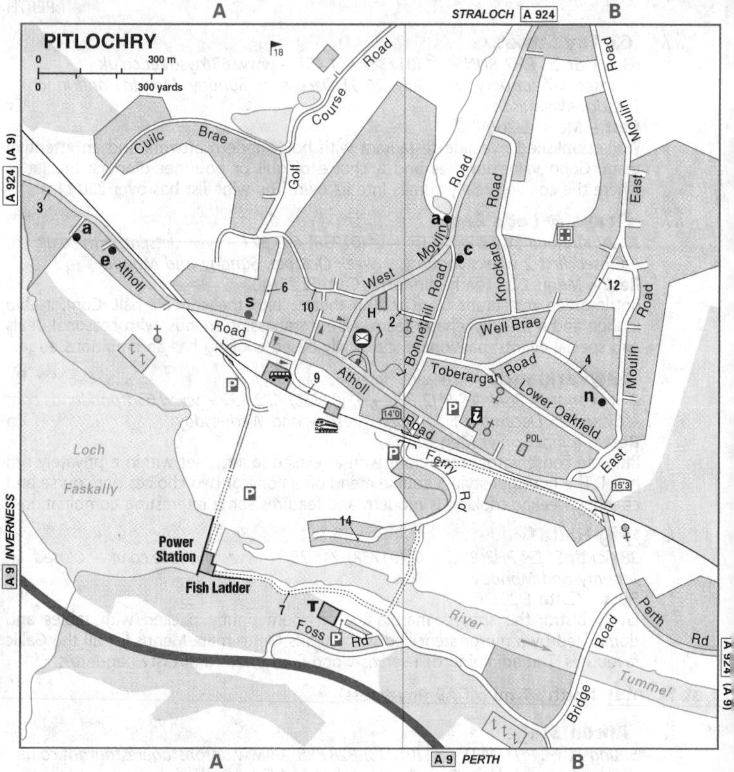

Church Rd	AB 2	Larchwood Rd	A 6	Strathview Terrace	A 10
Clunie Bridge Rd	A 3	Port Na Craig Rd	A 7	Tom Na Moan Rd	B 12
Higher Oakfield	B 4	Station Rd	A 9	Tummel Crescent	A 14

Green Park

Clunie Bridge Rd ✉ PH16 5JY – ✆ (01796) 473 248 – www.thegreenpark.co.uk
– Closed 17-27 December Aa

51 rm ☕ – 🚹£ 71/83 🚹🚹£ 142/166

Rest – *(booking essential at dinner) (bar lunch)* Menu £ 23

Long-standing, family-run hotel on the shore of Loch Faskally; many of its guests return year after year. Well-appointed lounges offer stunning loch and countryside views. Bedrooms vary in style; the largest and most modern are in the newer wing. A traditional dinner is included in the price of the room.

East Haugh House

Southeast : 1.75 mi off A 924 (Perth Rd) ✉ PH16 5TE
– ✆ (01796) 473 121 – www.easthaugh.co.uk
– Closed 1 week Christmas

13 rm ☕ – 🚹£ 79/178 🚹🚹£ 99/248

Rest ***Two Sisters*** – see restaurant listing

17C turreted house in two acres of gardens; originally part of the Atholl Estate. Traditionally appointed bedrooms – named after fishing flies – are split between the house and two lodges. They also own fishing rights to Dalmarnock Beat.

Craigmhor Lodge and Courtyard N without rest

27 West Moulin Rd ✉ PH16 5EF – ☎ (01796) 472 123
– www.craigmhorlodge.co.uk – Closed Christmas **Ba**

12 rm – †£ 55/100 ††£ 79/140

Spacious, cosy house just out of town, with an airy breakfast room where local fruits, bacon and sausages are served. Well-kept modern bedrooms are set in the courtyard – some have balconies. Supper hampers can be delivered to your room.

Craigatin House and Courtyard without rest

165 Atholl Rd ✉ PH16 5QL – ☎ (01796) 472 478 – www.craigatinhouse.co.uk
– Closed Christmas **Ae**

14 rm – †£ 80/107 ††£ 90/117

Built in 1822 as a doctor's house; now a stylish boutique hotel. The stunning open-plan lounge and breakfast room centres around a wood burning stove and overlooks the garden. Contemporary, minimalist bedrooms – some in the old stables.

Beinn Bhracaigh without rest

14 Higher Oakfield ✉ PH16 5HT – ☎ (01796) 470 355
– www.beinnbhracaigh.com – Closed 21-26 December **Bn**

12 rm – †£ 59/119 ††£ 69/129

Spacious stone house built in 1880 and run by passionate owners. Immaculately kept interior with good comforts; most rooms boast lovely views of the Tummel Valley. Breakfast includes French toast and pancakes with maple syrup and bacon.

Dunmurray Lodge without rest

72 Bonnethill Rd ✉ PH16 5ED – ☎ (01796) 473 624 – www.dunmurray.co.uk
– mid March-mid November **Bc**

4 rm – †£ 45/60 ††£ 70/80

Imposing 19C former doctor's surgery, set close to the town and boasting views across to the mountains. Cosy, open-fired lounge and snug, well-equipped bedrooms with co-ordinating décor; the best outlooks are from the front. Bright, breakfast room – choose from a huge array of very locally sourced produce.

Two Sisters – East Haugh House Hotel

Southeast : 1.75 mi off A 924 (Perth Rd) ✉ PH16 5TE – ☎ (01796) 473 121
– www.easthaugh.co.uk – Closed 1 week Christmas and lunch in winter

Rest – Carte £ 22/54

Charming fishermens' bar and a bright, laid-back restaurant, located in a lovely 17C stone house. The seasonal Scottish menu is served in both areas; cooking is clean and exact, with fish and game to the fore and tasty home-baked breads.

Auld Smiddy Inn

154 Atholl Rd ✉ PH16 5AG – ☎ (01796) 472 356 – www.auldsmiddyinn.co.uk
– Closed last week January-first week February and 25-26 December

Rest – Carte £ 18/40 **As**

Old blacksmith's forge with a small, colourful garden and a large terrace and courtyard. It has a likeable simplicity, with polished slate floors and wood burning stoves. Summer menus feature fish and salads; winter menus, hearty classics.

at Killiecrankie Northwest : 4 mi by A 924 - A - and B 8019 on B 8079
– ✉ Pitlochry

Killiecrankie

✉ PH16 5LG – ☎ (01796) 473 220 – www.killiecrankiehotel.co.uk – Closed 3 January-15 March

11 rm – †£ 90/150 ††£ 180/220 **Rest** – *(bar lunch)* Menu £ 42

Whitewashed former vicarage built in 1840 and set in 4.5 acres of mature, rhododendron-filled grounds with a small kitchen garden to the rear. Charming open-fired lounge and a bar with a walnut-topped counter. Well-appointed bedrooms offer everything you might want. Choose from light suppers and more traditional dishes. Excellent levels of service.

PLOCKTON – **Highland** – **501** D11 Scotland **29** B2

Edinburgh 210 mi – Inverness 88 mi

Village★

Wester Ross★★★

SCOTLAND

Plockton Hotel with rm
41 Harbour St ✉ IV52 8TN – ✆ (01599) 544 274 – www.plocktonhotel.co.uk
15 rm – †£ 55 ††£ 130 **Rest** – Carte £ 17/37
A one-time ships' chandlery with a distinctive black-tiled exterior and stunning views over Loch Carron to the mountains beyond. Cooking is honest and hearty with a strong Scottish influence, so expect haggis and whisky or herring in oatmeal – and don't miss the Plockton prawns. Simple, comfortable bedrooms.

POOLEWE – Highland – 501 D10 29 B2

Edinburgh 230 mi – London 635 mi – Inverness 76 mi – Elgin 112 mi

Pool House
✉ IV22 2LD – ✆ (01445) 781 272 – www.pool-house.co.uk
– Mid-March-mid-November
4 rm – †£ 170/230 ††£ 190/295
Rest – *(closed Monday dinner) (dinner only) (residents only, set menu only)* Menu £ 35
Unique, Victorian house by the water's edge; family-run, in a guesthouse rather than a hotel style. Bedrooms are all large suites – each individually themed with incredible attention to detail. Large billiards room, a country house lounge and a bar. The formal restaurant offers a classical, seasonal menu.

PORT APPIN – Argyll and Bute – 501 D14 – ✉ Appin 27 B2

Edinburgh 136 mi – Ballachulish 20 mi – Oban 24 mi

Airds
✉ PA38 4DF – ✆ (01631) 730 236 – www.airds-hotel.com – Closed 1-12 December and Monday-Tuesday November-February
11 rm – †£ 169/326 ††£ 179/394
Rest – *(booking essential)* Menu £ 19/53
Former ferry inn boasting loch/mountain views and a warm, welcoming interior. Two sumptuously furnished, open-fired sitting rooms display antiques. Intimate, floral-themed bedrooms provide good comforts. Excellent views from the well-laid dining room. Classical cooking has a modern edge; 7 course tasting menu available at dinner.

SCOTLAND

PORT CHARLOTTE – Argyll and Bute – 501 A16 – see Islay (Isle of)

PORT ELLEN – Argyll and Bute – 501 B17 – see Islay (Isle of)

PORTMAHOMACK – Highland – 501 I10 30 D2

Edinburgh 194 mi – Dornoch 21 mi – Tain 12 mi

Oystercatcher with rm
Main St ✉ IV20 1YB – ✆ (01862) 871 560 – www.the-oystercatcher.co.uk – Closed November-February, Sunday dinner, Wednesday lunch, Monday and Tuesday
3 rm – †£ 45/78 ††£ 77/108
Rest – *(booking essential)* Menu £ 36 (dinner) **s** – Carte lunch £ 20/42 **s**
Set in a lovely spot in a tiny fishing village, with lobster pots hanging outside. One formal and one rustic room, with walls crammed with memorabilia. Menus offer fresh seafood in some unusual combinations; the boats that land the fish can be seen by the jetty. Modest bedrooms; nearly 20 choices at breakfast.

PORTPATRICK – Dumfries and Galloway – 501 E19 – pop. 585 – ✉ Stranraer 25 A3

Edinburgh 141 mi – Ayr 60 mi – Dumfries 80 mi – Stranraer 9 mi

Golf Course Rd, ✆ (01776) 81 02 73

Knockinaam Lodge
Southeast : 5 mi by A 77 off B 7042 ✉ DG9 9AD – ✆ (01776) 810 471
– www.knockinaamlodge.com
10 rm (dinner included) – †£ 180/355 ††£ 300/460
Rest *Knockinaam Lodge* – see restaurant listing
Charming country house, superbly set in its own private cove, with the sea at the bottom of the garden. Classical guest areas include a wood-panelled bar and open-fired sitting rooms; a relaxed atmosphere pervades. Traditional, antique-furnished bedrooms; 'Churchill' boasts its original 100 year old bath.

Knockinaam Lodge – Knockinaam Lodge Hotel
Southeast : 5 mi by A 77 off B 7042 ✉ *DG9 9AD* – ✆ *(01776) 810 471*
– www.knockinaamlodge.com
Rest – *(booking essential) (set menu only)* Menu £ 30/65
Set in a charming Victorian house in its own private cove, a classically furnished, golden-hued dining room with crisp linen on the tables and lovely sea views. Carefully judged, daily 4 course menus; dishes showcase top quality seasonal ingredients in unfussy, well-balanced, classically based combinations.
➜ Sea bass with pickled fennel and red pepper emulsion. Fillet of Angus beef, baby vegetables, wild garlic and port sauce. Millefeuille of Scottish raspberries.

PORTREE – **Highland** – **501** B11 – **see Skye (Isle of)**

RANNOCH STATION – **Perth and Kinross** – **501** G13 **27** B2
Edinburgh 108 mi – Kinloch Rannoch 17 mi – Pitlochry 36 mi

Moor of Rannoch
✉ *PH17 2QA* – ✆ *(01882) 633 238* – *www.moorofrannoch.co.uk* – *Closed November-mid February*
5 rm – †£ 65/70 ††£ 100/110 **Rest** – *(dinner only)* Menu £ 29
The ultimate in hiking getaways, this 19C hotel is perched high on the moor, in the middle of nowhere. The views are delightful, the whole place has a serene feel and wildlife is in abundance. Bedrooms are cosy and the open-fired guest areas have jigsaws, not TVs. Rustic cooking uses Scottish ingredients.

RATAGAN – **Highland** **29** B2
Edinburgh 186 mi – London 563 mi – Belfast 214 mi – Dundee 168 mi

Grants at Craigellachie
✉ *IV40 8HP* – ✆ *(01599) 511 331* – *www.housebytheloch.co.uk* – *Restricted opening October-Easter*
4 rm – †£ 70/123 ††£ 100/185 **Rest** – Carte £ 26/47
Set in an idyllic spot beside Loch Duich and named after the eponymous local gamekeeper. Compact, pine-furnished bedrooms in the main house; the larger annexe rooms are more comfortable but don't have water views. Small conservatory restaurant with a Mediterranean-influenced menu. Good malt whisky selection.

ST ANDREWS – **Fife** – **501** L14 – **pop. 17 944** Scotland **28** D2
Edinburgh 51 mi – Dundee 14 mi – Stirling 51 mi
70 Market St, ✆ (01334) 47 20 21, www.visitscotland.com
The Duke's, Craigtoun, ✆ (01334) 47 02 14
Old Course, Pilmour House, ✆ (01334) 46 66 66
Fairmont St Andrews, ✆ (01334) 83 70 00
City★★ • Cathedral★ (✻★★) **AC**B • British Golf Museum **AC**AM1 • St Andrews Preservation Trust BM2 • St Andrews Aquarium **AC**AM3 • MUSA University of St Andrews Museum BM4 • West Port★A
Leuchars (parish church★), NW : 6 mi by A 91 and A 919. The East Neuk★★, SE : 9 mi by A 917 and B 9131 B – Crail★★ (Old Centre★★, Upper Crail★) SE : 9 mi by A 917 B – Kellie Castle★ **AC**, S : 9 mi by B 9131 and B 9171 B – Ceres★, SW : 9 mi by B 939 - E : Inland Fife★ A

Plan on next page

Old Course H. Golf Resort & Spa
Old Station Rd ✉ *KY16 9SP* – ✆ *(01334) 474 371*
– www.oldcoursehotel.co.uk A**b**
144 rm – †£ 220/440 ††£ 250/470 – 15 suites
Rest ***Road Hole*** **Rest** ***Sands Grill*** – see restaurant listing
Vast resort hotel on a world-famous championship golf course, overlooking the bay. Spacious guest areas with stylish Scottish theme; superb spa, leisure and meeting facilities. Chic, comfortable bedrooms: some sumptuous, some contemporary.

ST ANDREWS

Abbey St . . . . **B** 2
Abbey Walk . . . . **B** 3
Alexandra Pl. . . . . **A** 5
Alfred Pl. . . . . **A** 6
Bridge St. . . . . **A** 7
Butts Wynd . . . . **B** 9
Castle St . . . . **B** 10
Church St . . . . **AB** 13
Ellice Pl. . . . . **A** 15
Gibson Pl. . . . . **A** 17
Gillespie Terrace . . . . **A** 18
Greenside Pl. . . . . **B** 20
Gregory Lane . . . . **B** 21
Gregory Pl. . . . . **B** 22
Greyfriars Garden . . . . **A** 24
Hepburn Gardens . . . . **A** 25
Link Crescent . . . . **A** 27
Murray Park . . . . **A** 28
Murray Pl. . . . . **A** 29
Pilmour Links . . . . **A** 31
Pilmour Pl. . . . . **A** 32
Playfair Terrace . . . . **A** 34
Queen's Gardens . . . . **A** 35
Queen's Terrace . . . . **B** 36
St Mary's Pl. . . . . **A** 37
Union St . . . . **B** 38

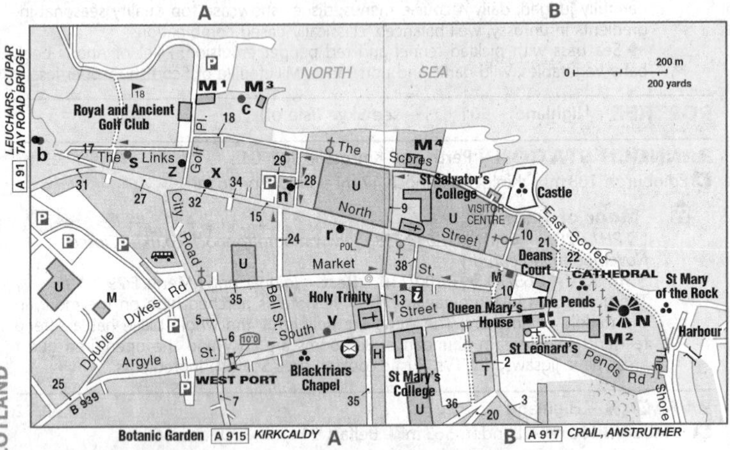

Fairmont St Andrews

Southeast : 3.5 mi on A 917 ✉ *KY16 8PN* – *(01334) 837 000*
– *www.fairmont.com/standrews*
209 rm – £ 159/299 £ 159/299
Rest *Squire* – *(dinner only)* Menu £ 29 – Carte £ 29/39
Rest *Esperante* – *(closed Monday-Tuesday) (dinner only)* Menu £ 65
– Carte £ 34/64
Modern, purpose-built property set in 520 acres. Spacious guest areas display a subtle Scottish theme. Extensive conference and leisure facilities, with two golf courses, a superb spa and a wellness centre. Well-appointed bedrooms feature tartan and driftwood; Deluxe rooms are worth it for the view. Informal Squire in vast atrium. Modern menus in Esperante.

Rufflets Country House

Strathkinness Low Rd, West : 1.5 mi on B 939 ✉ *KY16 9TX* – *(01334) 472 594*
– *www.rufflets.co.uk* – *Closed 4-20 January*
24 rm – £ 125/260 £ 160/300 – 2 suites
Rest *Terrace* – *(bar lunch Monday-Saturday)* Menu £ 40
This modern country house hotel has been owned by the same family for over 60 years. Set in well-tended gardens, it features stylish, contemporary bedrooms. Modern interpretations of classic dishes are served in the restaurant at dinner, with a simpler, more traditional lunch menu offered in the bar and library.

Six Murray Park without rest

6 Murray Pk. ✉ *KY16 9AW* – *(01334) 473 319* – *www.sixmurraypark.co.uk*
9 rm – £ 65/80 £ 85/140 A**n**
Victorian terraced property with smart window boxes. Modern bedrooms boast bold feature walls and good facilities, including flat screen TVs and iPod docks. Hot daily specials are taken in the linen-laid, leather-furnished breakfast room.

Fairways without rest

8a Golf Pl. ✉ *KY16 9JA* – *(01334) 479 513* – *www.fairwaysofstandrews.co.uk*
3 rm – £ 80/100 £ 100/150 A**z**
The closest guesthouse in town to the famous 'Old Course'. Bedrooms are contemporary and offer good modern facilities; the top floor room boasts a balcony which overlooks the 18th hole.

Five Pilmour Place without rest

5 Pilmour Pl. ✉ KY16 9HZ – ✆ (01334) 478 665 – www.5pilmourplace.com – Closed 18 December-6 January Ax

7 rm – †£ 65/125 ††£ 85/160

Terraced Victorian house with neatly lawned rear garden. Flag-floored hall leads to bright lounge and communal breakfast room. Bedrooms range in size and come with boldly coloured feature walls and good facilities; one has a claw-foot bath.

Aslar House without rest

120 North St ✉ KY16 9AF – ✆ (01334) 473 460 – www.aslar.com – Closed December, January and first week July Ar

6 rm – †£ 65/85 ††£ 90/100

Victorian terraced house in the town centre, run by a friendly, enthusiastic couple. Open-plan lounge and breakfast room. Neat, tidy bedrooms offer good modern facilities. Largest rooms are at the top; one has a lounge inside the turret.

Seafood

Bruce Embankment, The Scores ✉ KY16 9AB – ✆ (01334) 479 475 – www.theseafoodrestaurant.com – Closed 25-26 December and 1 January

Rest – *(booking essential)* Menu £ 22/49 Ac

Unusual glass cube overhanging the beach, offering commanding bay views. Immaculate interior with black and white photos and an open kitchen. Dishes are seafood-based; try the daily special of 'fruits de mer' of local fish and shellfish.

Road Hole – Old Course Hotel Golf Resort & Spa

Old Station Rd ✉ KY16 9SP – ✆ (01334) 474 371 – www.oldcoursehotel.co.uk – Closed January, February, Sunday and Monday Ab

Rest – Menu £ 17 (lunch) – Carte £ 24/49

Formally run restaurant within a smart golf resort and spa; dine with a full view of the 18th hole, the clubhouse and the beach. Modern versions of classic dishes use local produce; watch the chefs in the open kitchen while you eat.

Rocca Bar & Grill

Rusacks Hotel, The Links ✉ KY16 9JQ – ✆ (01334) 472 549 – www.roccagrill.com – Closed Sunday November-December As

Rest – *(dinner only) (booking essential)* Carte £ 31/56

Vibrant brasserie run by an experienced owner. Funky bar and vividly decorated dining room with views over the Old Course's 18th hole. Appealing menu of Scottish produce with 'classics', 'pasta' and 'steak' sections; interesting desserts.

Adamson

127 South St ✉ KY16 9UH – ✆ (01334) 479 191 – www.theadamson.com – Closed 25-26 December Av

Rest – Menu £ 27/43 – Carte £ 20/58

Family-run restaurant in a historic former Post Office. Stylish, modern interior with contemporary artwork hung on exposed brick walls. The confident chef prepares tasty local seafood and appealing meat dishes cooked on the Josper grill.

Sands Grill – Old Course Hotel Golf Resort & Spa

Old Station Rd ✉ KY16 9SP – ✆ (01334) 474 371 – www.oldcoursehotel.co.uk

Rest – *(dinner only)* Carte £ 23/51 Ab

Informal grill restaurant located in a stylish golf resort and spa next to St Andrews golf course. Menus comprise mainly of seafood and steak dishes, with all meats cooked in the Josper grill.

ST BOSWELLS – The Scottish Borders – 501 L17 – pop. 1 199 — 26 D2

– ✉ Melrose ▌Scotland

Edinburgh 39 mi – Glasgow 79 mi – Hawick 17 mi – Newcastle upon Tyne 66 mi

St Boswells, ✆ (01835) 82 35 27

Dryburgh Abbey★★ **AC** (setting★★★), NW : 4 mi by B 6404 and B 6356 – Tweed Valley★★. Bowhill★★ **AC**, SW : 11.5 mi by A 699 and A 708

SCOTLAND

Buccleuch Arms
The Green ✉ TD6 0EW – ✆ (01835) 822 243 – www.buccleucharms.com – Closed 24-25 December
19 rm – †£ 73/95 ††£ 79/120 **Rest** – Carte £ 18/35
Long-standing, period coaching inn offering popular golfing, fishing and shooting breaks. Comfy, cosy bedrooms display co-ordinated headboards and soft furnishings. Semi-panelled, fire-lit bar and more formal dining room; choose from an extensive menu of classics, game and daily specials.

Whitehouse rm,
Northeast : 3 mi on B 6404 ✉ TD6 0ED – ✆ (01573) 460 343 – www.whitehousecountryhouse.com
3 rm – †£ 80/85 ††£ 120/130 **Rest** – Menu £ 30
Former dower house built in 1872 by the Duke of Sutherland, with a cosy, country house feel. Traditionally furnished bedrooms boast excellent views across the estate. Many people come for the on-site shooting and fishing; wild salmon and local game – including venison – feature at dinner.

Clint Lodge
North : 2.25 mi by B 6404 on B 6356 ✉ TD6 0DZ – ✆ (01835) 822 027 – www.clintlodge.co.uk
5 rm – †£ 60/90 ††£ 110/120 **Rest** – Menu £ 33
Former shooting lodge with superb river and hill views. Characterful interior boasts antiques and fishing memorabilia. Traditionally decorated bedrooms; luxurious No. 4 and south facing rooms are the best. Daily changing 5 course dinner served at beautiful table.

SCOTLAND

ST FILLANS – Perth and Kinross – 501 H14 — 28 C2
Edinburgh 65 mi – Lochearnhead 8 mi – Perth 29 mi

Achray House
✉ PH6 2NF – ✆ (0560) 368 42 52 – www.achrayhouse.com – Closed December and January
8 rm – †£ 60/134 ††£ 104/184
Rest – *(closed Monday-Tuesday November-March) (dinner only)* Menu £ 34
Superbly located Edwardian villa offering stunning views over Loch Earn. Bright breakfast room and an inviting lounge with open fires and a polished Douglas Fir floor. Modern bedrooms have bespoke pine furnishings and contemporary bathrooms. Simple restaurant offers global dishes crafted from local produce.

ST MARGARET'S HOPE – 501 L7 – see Orkney Islands (Mainland)

ST MONANS – Fife – 501 L15 – pop. 3 965 — 28 D2
Edinburgh 47 mi – Dundee 26 mi – Perth 40 mi – Stirling 56 mi

XX **Craig Millar @ 16 West End**
16 West End ✉ KY10 2BX – ✆ (01333) 730 327 – www.16westend.com – Closed Monday-Tuesday March-September and restricted opening October-March
Rest – *(booking essential)* Menu £ 18/42
Unassuming former pub with attractive interior and charming team. Characterful lounge and smart, linen-laid restaurant with small terrace and great views over the harbour and sea. Experienced chef offers clean, refined, flavoursome dishes.

SANQUHAR – Dumfries and Galloway – 501 I17 – pop. 2 028 — 25 B2
Edinburgh 57 mi – London 362 mi – Dundee 113 mi – Paisley 56 mi

XX **Blackaddie House** with rm
Blackaddie Rd ✉ DG4 6JJ – ✆ (01659) 50 270 – www.blackaddiehotel.co.uk
8 rm – †£ 70/75 ††£ 100/190
Rest – *(booking essential at lunch)* Menu £ 30/52
Former manse with 16C origins, set by the river. Lunch offers good value classics; dinner is more elaborate and features complex, original cooking. Ingredients are luxurious and dishes, well-presented. Bedrooms are named after game birds; ask for Grouse, which has a four-poster bed.

SCALASAIG – Argyll and Bute – 501 B15 – see Colonsay (Isle of)

SCALPAY – **Western Isles** – **501** A10 – **see Lewis and Harris (Isle of)**

SCARISTA – **Western Isles** – **501** Y10 – **see Lewis and Harris (Isle of)**

SCOURIE – **Highland** – **501** E8 – ✉ **Lairg** Scotland **30** C1

Edinburgh 245 mi – London 646 mi – Belfast 317 mi – Dundee 226 mi

Cape Wrath★★★ (≤★★) **AC**, N : 31 mi (including ferry crossing) by A 894 and A 838 – Loch Assynt★★, S : 17 mi by A 894

Eddrachilles

Badcall Bay, South : 2.5 mi on A 894 ✉ IV27 4TH – ✆ (01971) 502 080 – www.eddrachilles.com – Closed October-March

11 rm – £ 77/80 £ 104/110 **Rest** – *(bar lunch)* Menu £ 25

Remotely set, converted 18C manse, with views of the countryside, Badcall Bay and its islands. Snug bar and flag-floored breakfast room; cosy, well-kept bedrooms. Delightful outlook from the conservatory dining room, which offers a daily menu with a strong French slant. Meats are cured on-site.

SCRABSTER – **Highland** – **501** J8 – **see Thurso**

SHETLAND ISLANDS – 501 P/Q3 – pop. 21 800 Scotland

Sumburgh Airport : ✆ (01950) 460905, S : 25 mi of Lerwick by A 970 - Tingwall Airport: 01595) 840246, NW: 6m. of Lerwick by A971

from Foula to Walls (Shetland Islands Council) 1-2 weekly (2 h 30 mn) – from Fair Isle to Sumburgh (Shetland Islands Council) 1-2 weekly (2 h 40 mn)

from Lerwick (Mainland) to Aberdeen and via Orkney Islands (Stromness) (P and O Scottish Ferries) – from Vidlin to Skerries (Shetland Islands Council) booking essential 3-4 weekly (1 h 30 mn) – from Lerwick (Mainland) to Skerries (Shetland Islands Council) 2 weekly (booking essential) (2 h 30 mn) – from Lerwick (Mainland) to Bressay (Shetland Islands Council) frequent services daily (7 mn) – from Laxo (Mainland) to Isle of Whalsay (Symbister) (Shetland Islands Council) frequent services daily (30 mn) – from Toft (Mainland) to Isle of Yell (Ulsta) (Shetland Islands Council) frequent services daily (20 mn) – from Isle of Yell (Gutcher) to Isle of Fetlar (Oddsta) and via Isle of Unst (Belmont) (Shetland Islands Council) – from Fair Isle to Sumburgh (Mainland) (Shetland Islands Council) 3 weekly (2 h 40 mn)

Islands★ - Up Helly Aa (last Tuesday in January) – Mousa Broch★★★ **AC** (Mousa Island) – Jarlshof★★ - Lerwick to Jarlshof★ (≤★) – Shetland Croft House Museum★ **AC**

MAINLAND – **Shetland Islands** **31** B2

Edinburgh 141 mi – London 543 mi – Belfast 224 mi – Dundee 86 mi

LERWICK – **Shetland Islands** – **pop. 6 830** Scotland **31** B2

Lerwick, ✆ (08452) 255 1 21, www.visitscotland.com

Shetland, Gott, Dale, ✆ (01595) 84 03 69

Clickhimin Broch★

Gulber Wick (≤★), S : 2 mi by A 970

Kveldsro House

Greenfield Pl ✉ ZE1 0AQ – ✆ (01595) 692 195 – www.shetlandhotels.com – Closed 25-26 December and 1-2 January

17 rm – £ 110 £ 135

Rest – *(bar lunch Monday-Saturday)* Carte £ 23/38 **s**

Spacious Georgian house hidden in the town centre; its name means 'evening peace'. Cosy sitting room with original ceiling mouldings, comfy bar with views of the islands and traditionally styled bedrooms. Menus offer mainly island produce; portions are hearty.

SCOTLAND

VEENSGARTH – **Shetland Islands** **31** B2

Herrislea House

ZE2 9SB – (01595) 840 208 – www.herrisleahouse.co.uk – Closed 12 December-8 January
9 rm – £ 88/110 £ 130/145
Rest – *(dinner only) (booking essential)* Carte £ 21/38
Large, family-run hotel set just out of town. Unusual African hunting theme with mounted antlers, animal heads and skins on display. Cosy, individually designed bedrooms; some with valley views. Fresh cooking uses local produce and meats from the family crofts.

SHIELDAIG – **Highland** – **501** D11 – **Strathcarron** Scotland **29** B2

Edinburgh 226 mi – London 627 mi – Perth 178 mi – Greenock 209 mi
Wester Ross★★★

Tigh An Eilean

IV54 8XN – (01520) 755 251 – www.tighaneilean.co.uk – Restricted opening in winter
11 rm – £ 75 £ 150
Rest – *(booking essential) (bar lunch)* Menu £ 40 (dinner) – Carte £ 16/33
Rest *Coastal Kitchen* – Carte approx. £ 25
Personally run hotel in a charming lochside setting, with fine views over the Shieldaig Islands. Two small, cottagey lounges and well-kept, compact bedrooms – most with views. Linen-laid restaurant offers traditional, daily changing dishes; informal Coastal Kitchen serves a wide-ranging, all-day menu.

SKIRLING – **The Scottish Borders** – **501** J17 – **Biggar** Scotland **26** C2

Edinburgh 29 mi – Glasgow 45 mi – Peebles 16 mi
Biggar★ - Gladstone Court Museum★, Greenhill Covenanting Museum★, S : 3 mi by A 72 and A 702. New Lanark★★, NW : 16 mi by A 72 and A 73

Skirling House

ML12 6HD – (01899) 860 274 – www.skirlinghouse.com – Closed January, February and 1 week November-December
5 rm – £ 75/95 £ 120/190 **Rest** – Menu £ 30
Delightful Arts and Crafts house set on the green in an attractive hamlet. Charming bedrooms come with good extras. The drawing room boasts a beautiful carved Florentine ceiling and an eclectic range of antiques and memorabilia. The 4 course daily menu is served in the conservatory or cosy dining room; accomplished cooking relies on home-grown produce.

SKYE (Isle of) – **Highland** – **501** B11 – **pop. 9 232** Scotland **29** B2

from Mallaig to Isles of Eigg, Muck, Rhum and Canna (Caledonian MacBrayne Ltd) (summer only) – from Mallaig to Armadale (Caledonian MacBrayne Ltd) (summer only) 1-2 weekly (30 mn)
from Mallaig to Armadale (Caledonian MacBrayne Ltd) 1-5 daily (30 mn) – from Uig to North Uist (Lochmaddy) or Isle of Harris (Tarbert) (Caledonian MacBrayne Ltd) 1-3 daily (1 h 50 mn) – from Sconser to Isle of Raasay (Caledonian MacBrayne Ltd) 9-10 daily (except Sunday) (15 mn)
Island★★ - The Cuillins★★★ – Skye Museum of Island Life★ **AC**
N : Trotternish Peninsula★★ – W : Duirinish Peninsula★ – Portree★

BERNISDALE – **Highland**

Spoons without rest

75 Aird Bernisdale IV51 9NU – (01470) 532 217 – www.thespoonsonskye.com – Closed mid-November-mid-March
3 rm – £ 115/135 £ 140/160
Luxurious, purpose-built guesthouse in unspoilt hamlet, with airy, wood-floored lounge and breakfast room overlooking the loch. Bedrooms are individually decorated in a crisp, modern style and provide every conceivable extra. Superb 3 course breakfasts, with eggs from the charming owners' chickens.

BROADFORD – Highland
29 B2

↑ **Tigh an Dochais**
⟨ ⟷ ⌘ 🛜 P

13 Harrapool, on A 87 ✉ IV49 9AQ – 𝒞 (01471) 820 022
– www.skyebedbreakfast.co.uk – March-October
3 rm ⌂ – †£ 75 ††£ 90 **Rest** – Menu £ 25
Striking house with award-winning architecture, overlooking Broadford Bay and
the Applecross Peninsula. Comfy lounge has well-stocked bookshelves. Modern,
minimalist bedrooms boast superb views and good facilities, including underfloor
heating and plenty of extras. Communal, home-cooked meals by arrangement.

CULNAKNOCK – Highland

✗ **Glenview** with rm
🛜 P

✉ IV51 9JH – 𝒞 (01470) 562 248 – www.glenviewskye.co.uk – Closed January,
December, Sunday and Monday
5 rm ⌂ – †£ 70/75 ††£ 120/125
Rest – (dinner only) (booking essential) Menu £ 35
Simple little restaurant – formerly the village shop – with a cheerful host and an
appealing vintage style. The daily dinner menu offers two choices per course, featuring local produce in unfussy, flavoursome dishes. Bedrooms have retro-style
touches; breakfast is a highlight – try the blueberry pancakes.

DUISDALEMORE – Highland
29 B2

🏠 **Duisdale House**
⟨ ⟷ ⌘ 🌙 ⌘ 🛜 P

Sleat, on A 851. ✉ IV43 8QW – 𝒞 (01471) 833 202 – www.duisdale.com
19 rm ⌂ – †£ 110/150 ††£ 147/320 – 1 suite
Rest – Menu £ 13/45 – Carte £ 20/41
Stylish, up-to-date hotel with lawned gardens, hot tub and coastal views. Comfortable bedrooms boast bold décor, excellent bathrooms and a pleasing blend
of contemporary and antique furniture. Modern cooking makes good use of local
produce. Smart uniformed staff.

SCOTLAND

DUNVEGAN – Highland
29 B2

↑ **Roskhill House** without rest
⟷ ⌘ 🛜 P

Roskhill, Southeast : 2.5 mi by A 863 ✉ IV55 8ZD – 𝒞 (01470) 521 317
– www.roskhillhouse.co.uk – Closed 15 December-2 February
5 rm ⌂ – †£ 59/70 ††£ 74/98
Welcoming 19C croft house with small garden, set in peaceful location close to
the water. Formerly the old post office, the lounge boasts exposed stone, wooden
beams and an open fire. Fresh, bright bedrooms have a contemporary edge and
smart, modern bathrooms.

✗✗ **Three Chimneys & The House Over-By** with rm
⟨ ⟷ & rest, 🛜 P

Colbost, Northwest : 5.25 mi by A 863 on B 884.
✉ IV55 8ZT – 𝒞 (01470) 511 258 – www.threechimneys.co.uk
– Closed December, 1-23 January and Sunday lunch mid September-April
6 rm ⌂ – †£ 195/295 ††£ 195/295
Rest – (dinner only and lunch April-October) (booking essential) Menu £ 37/90
Immaculately kept crofter's cottage in a stunning lochside setting. Three characterful, low-beamed dining rooms display contemporary artwork. Modern Scottish
menus showcase local ingredients and seafood is a highlight. 7 course tasting
menu available at dinner. Split-level bedrooms are spacious and stylishly understated; the residents' lounge has a great outlook.

EDINBANE – Highland
29 B2

🏠 **Greshornish House**
⟨ ⟷ ⌘ 🌙 ✗ 🛜 P

North : 3.75 mi by A 850 in direction of Dunvegan ✉ IV51 9PN – 𝒞 (01470)
582 266 – www.greshornishhouse.com – Restricted opening in winter
6 rm ⌂ – †£ 70/155 ††£ 100/185
Rest – (closed Monday and Tuesday in winter) (light lunch) (booking essential)
Menu £ 38
Early 18C lochside house. Relax in the comfy panelled drawing room or in the old
billiard room with its snooker table, piano, books and games. Country house style
bedrooms – some with four-posters or loch views. Breakfast is in the conservatory; seasonal, island dinners are taken in the candlelit dining room.

FLODIGARRY – Highland 29 B2

Flodigarry Country House

IV51 9HZ – (01470) 552 203 – www.flodigarry.co.uk – Restricted opening in winter
18 rm – £ 80/170 £ 80/170
Rest – *(booking essential) (bar lunch Monday-Saturday)* Menu £ 25 – Carte £ 31/59 **s**
Victorian house and cottage annexe, which was once Flora MacDonald's home. Comfortable, antique-filled interior with excellent island views; the gardens run down to the coast. Cosy, homely bedrooms. Characterful bar and dining room offer a classical menu.

PORTREE – Highland 29 B2

Bayfield Rd, (08452) 25 51 21, www.visitscotland.com

Cuillin Hills

rm,

Northeast : 0.75 mi by A 855 IV51 9QU – (01478) 612 003 – *www.cuillinhills-hotel-skye.co.uk*
26 rm – £ 130/200 £ 200/320
Rest *View* – Carte £ 28/49
Yellow-washed 19C hunting lodge, in 15 acres of gardens and grounds overlooking the bay and hills. Comfortable lounge and stylish open-plan bar. Bedrooms offer good facilities; the best are to the front. Relaxed brasserie or formal dining room offering a good outlook and modern menus.

Bosville

Bosville Terr IV51 9DG – (01478) 612 846 – *www.bosvillehotel.co.uk*
20 rm – £ 56/130 £ 69/350
Rest *Bistro* – Carte £ 17/33
Boldly painted, purpose-built hotel in the town centre. Wood-furnished bar – formerly the village bank – and small, traditionally decorated, first floor lounge. Modern bedrooms with co-ordinated fabrics and good facilities. Accessible menu served in popular bistro.

SCOTLAND

SLEAT – Highland 30 C1

Kinloch Lodge

IV43 8QY – (01471) 833 214 – www.kinloch-lodge.co.uk
19 rm (dinner included) – £ 99/199 £ 159/249 – 7 suites
Rest *Kinloch Lodge* – see restaurant listing
17C hunting lodge in a terrific lochside setting, surrounded by heather-strewn moorland. Traditional country house interior with comfy, antique-filled lounges. Individually styled bedrooms are split between the main house and annexe – they have a similarly classical feel and boast good facilities and extras.

Kinloch Lodge – Kinloch Lodge Hotel

IV43 8QY – (01471) 833 214 – www.kinloch-lodge.co.uk
Rest – *(booking essential)* Menu £ 30/75 **s**
Traditional, country house restaurant in a 17C lochside hunting lodge. Menus showcase local island produce; choose between a tasting selection and a daily changing set menu. Cooking is classically based but displays some clever modern touches. Good service and a well-written wine list complete the picture.
→ Home-cured organic salmon, crispy leeks and beetroot espuma. Sirloin of beef, slow-roast beef cheek and tongue and caramelised onions. Passion fruit parfait with toasted poppy seed caramel, banana and lime ice cream.

STRUAN – Highland 29 B2

Ullinish Country Lodge

West : 1.5 mi by A 863 IV56 8FD – (01470) 572 214 – *www.theisleofskye.co.uk – Closed January, Christmas and New Year*
6 rm – £ 85/110 £ 110/160
Rest *Ullinish Country Lodge* – see restaurant listing
Personally run, 18C former hunting lodge in a windswept location, affording lovely loch and mountain views. Comfortable lounge filled with ornaments and books about the area. Warmly decorated bedrooms boast good facilities and extras.

XX **Ullinish Country Lodge** - Ullinish Country Lodge Hotel
West : 1.5 mi by A 863 ✉ IV56 8FD – ✆ (01470) 572 214 – www.theisleofskye.co.uk – Closed January, Christmas and New Year
Rest – *(dinner only) (booking essential)* Menu £ 48
Formal hotel dining room with traditional tartan fabrics, a masculine style and a house party atmosphere. The daily changing, 2-choice set menu uses quality local ingredients; dishes are modern and inventive, and combinations are ambitious.

TEANGUE – Highland
29 A2

Toravaig House
Knock Bay, on A 851 ✉ IV44 8RE – ✆ (01471) 820 200 – www.skyehotel.co.uk
9 rm – †£ 150/250 ††£ 190/250 **Rest** – *(booking essential)* Menu £ 23/48
Stylish whitewashed house with neat gardens, set on the road to the Mallaig ferry. Cosy, open-fired lounge with baby grand piano and heavy fabrics. Individually designed bedrooms boast quality materials and furnishings. Good service with extras. Two-roomed restaurant offers concise, classical menu of island produce.

WATERNISH – Highland
29 A2

X **Loch Bay Seafood**
1 MacLeod Terr, Stein ✉ IV55 8GA – ✆ (01470) 592 235 – www.lochbay-seafood-restaurant.co.uk – Closed November-Easter, Sunday and Monday
Rest – *(dinner only and lunch Wednesday-Thursday) (booking essential)*
Carte £ 25/35
Whitewashed cottage in a tiny hamlet overlooking the loch. Small room with low-backed chairs and benches. Concise menu of simply prepared seafood and blackboard specials. Friendly service.

Stein Inn with rm
MacLeod Terr, Stein ✉ IV55 8GA – ✆ (01470) 592 362 – www.stein-inn.co.uk – Closed 1 January and 25 December
5 rm – †£ 43/57 ††£ 74/110 **Rest** – Carte £ 16/34
Family-run inn – the oldest on Skye; sit on the grassy terrace or in the cosy bar. Fresh, locally caught seafood dominates the menu; maybe sweet shrimps, rollmop herrings or half a lobster. Simple, comfy bedrooms have superb views to the Outer Hebrides instead of a TV, and the bar offers over 90 whiskies.

SCOTLAND

SLEAT – Highland – see Skye (Isle of)

SORN – East Ayrshire – 501 H17
25 B2

Edinburgh 67 mi – Ayr 15 mi – Glasgow 35 mi

Sorn Inn with rm
35 Main St ✉ KA5 6HU – ✆ (01290) 551 305 – www.sorninn.com – Closed 6-16 January and Monday
4 rm – †£ 40/55 ††£ 55/90 **Rest** – Menu £ 14 (weekdays) – Carte £ 20/28
Very much a family affair at this unassuming inn set in a small village – the father checks you in and the son cooks. Choose either the smart bar or larger dining room. Extensive menu includes a variety of British dishes plus a choice of more elaborate international offerings. Neat, simple bedrooms represent good value.

SPEAN BRIDGE – Highland – 501 F13
30 C3

Edinburgh 143 mi – Fort William 10 mi – Glasgow 94 mi – Inverness 58 mi

The Kingdom of Scotland, by Fort William, Inverness-shirev, ✆ (0845) 2 25 51 21, www.visitscotland.com

Spean Bridge GC, Station Rd, ✆ 077 471 4 70 90

Corriegour Lodge
Loch Lochy, North : 8.75 mi on A 82 ✉ PH34 4EA – ✆ (01397) 712 685 – www.corriegour-lodge-hotel.com – Closed November-22 March
11 rm – †£ 110/130 ††£ 160/190 **Rest** – *(dinner only)* Menu £ 50
19C hunting lodge with pretty gardens, in a great lochside location; the owner's father is the local gamekeeper. Homely, curio-filled sitting room and comfy bedrooms with good quality beds, linens and fabrics. Every dining table has a loch view; the classical 4 course menu features local meats.

Distant Hills without rest
Roy Bridge Rd, East : 0.5 mi on A86 ✉ *PH34 4EU* – *(01397) 712 452*
– *www.distanthillsspeanbridge.co.uk*
7 rm – £ 60/86 £ 76/98
Welcoming guesthouse with friendly owners, who suggest walks and provide packed lunches. French windows in large lounge lead to stream-side seating. Modern bedrooms. Wide-ranging breakfasts.

Corriechoille Lodge rm,
East : 2.75 mi on Corriechoille rd ✉ *PH34 4EY* – *(01397) 712 002*
– *www.corriechoille.com* – *Closed November-March*
4 rm – £ 44/50 £ 68/80 **Rest** – Menu £ 26
Charming, part-18C house in remote location, boasting large gardens and views over the Grey Corries and Aonach Mor. Comfy lounge and spacious, pine-furnished bedrooms; two wooden bothy lodges provide more intimacy. Homely cooking; the fish is smoked on site.

Russell's at Smiddy House with rm
Roybridge Rd ✉ *PH34 4EU* – *(01397) 712 335* – *www.smiddyhouse.com*
– *Closed Monday to non residents*
4 rm – £ 75/95 £ 85/115
Rest – *(restricted opening in winter) (dinner only and Sunday lunch) (booking essential)* Carte £ 30/44
Passionately run restaurant in an appealing Highland village. Snug lounge and two intimate, candlelit dining rooms. Tasty, classic dishes use locally sourced Highland ingredients. Cosy, immaculately kept and well-equipped bedrooms boast comfy beds and fine linens.

SCOTLAND

Old Pines with rm rm,
Northwest : 1.5 mi by A 82 on B 8004 ✉ *PH34 4EG* – *(01397) 712 324*
– *www.oldpines.co.uk* – *Closed November-January*
7 rm – £ 60/80 £ 90/120
Rest – *(bookings essential for non-residents)* Carte £ 25/37
Log cabin style building that blends well with the Highland scenery. Comfy lounge; simple dining room with tables arranged around the windows. Classical menus offer lots of local seafood and beef. Up-to-date, pine-furnished bedrooms feature traditional quilts.

SPITTAL – Highland – 501 J8 — 30 D1

Edinburgh 253 mi – London 654 mi – Belfast 325 mi – Dundee 234 mi

Auld Post Office without rest
on A 9 ✉ *KW1 5XR* – *(01847) 841 391* – *www.auldpostoffice.com*
3 rm – £ 55/60 £ 69/79
Greatly extended former post office, set in a remote spot on a road that cuts across the moors. Homely lounge with a wood-burning stove. Cosy, well-furnished bedrooms open onto a colourful garden and have compact, modern shower rooms.

SPITTAL OF GLENSHEE – Perth and Kinross – 501 J13 — 28 C2

– ✉ **Blairgowrie** Scotland
Edinburgh 79 mi – London 489 mi – Glasgow 98 mi – Livingston 81 mi
Glenshee (✻★★) (chairlift **AC**)

Dalmunzie Castle
✉ *PH10 7QG* – *(01250) 885 224* – *www.dalmunzie.com* – *Closed January and December*
17 rm – £ 105/150 £ 140/240 **Rest** – *(bar lunch)* Menu £ 45
Edwardian hunting lodge on a stunning 6,500 acre estate, encircled by mountains and run by a keen team; the open hall has a large window looking towards the snow-capped peaks. Bedrooms and lounges have a traditional feel. The cosy bar stocks over 100 whiskies and the dining room offers pretty valley views.

STANLEY – Perth and Kinross – 501 J14 – see PERTH

STEVENSTON – North Ayrshire – 501 F17 – pop. 9 129 25 A2

Edinburgh 82 mi – Ayr 19 mi – Glasgow 36 mi

Ardeer Farm Steading without rest

Ardeer Mains Farm, East : 0.75 mi by A 738 and B 752 taking fist left onto Kilwinning rd ✉ KA20 3DD – ✆ (01294) 465 438 – www.ardeersteading.co.uk

6 rm – †£38 ††£50

Converted, family-owned farm buildings on the edge of a 100 acre working farm. Large, leather-furnished lounge and breakfast room boast pleasant country views. Spacious, comfy, up-to-date bedrooms. Complimentary pick-up from the station.

STIRLING – Stirling – 501 I15 – pop. 31 978 Scotland 28 C2

Edinburgh 37 mi – Dunfermline 23 mi – Falkirk 14 mi – Glasgow 28 mi

41 Dumbarton Rd, ✆ (08707) 20 06 20, www.visitstirling.org

Town★★ – Castle★★ **AC** (Site★★★, external elevations★★★, Stirling Heads★★, Argyll and Sutherland Highlanders Regimental Museum★) B – Argyll's Lodging★ (Renaissance decoration★) B **A** – Church of the Holy Rude★ B **B**

Wallace Monument (✻★★) NE : 2.5 mi by A 9 - A - and B 998. Dunblane★ (Cathedral★★, West Front★★), N : 6.5 mi by A 9 A

STIRLING

Barnton St. B 2
Borestone Crescent A 3
Causewayhead Rd A, B 4
Cornton Rd A 7
Corn Exchange Rd B 5
Coxithill Rd A 8
Drummond Pl. B 9
Dumbarton Rd B 10
Goosecroft Rd B 12
King St B 13
Leisure Centre B
Murray Pl. B 15
Newhouse A 16
Park Pl. A 18
Port St. B
Queen St B 20
Randolph Terrace A 22
St John St. B 23
St Mary's Wynd B 24
Seaforth Pl. B 25
Shirra's Brae Rd A 26
Spittal St B 27
Thistle Centre B
Union St B 28
Upper Craigs B 29
Weaver Row A 31

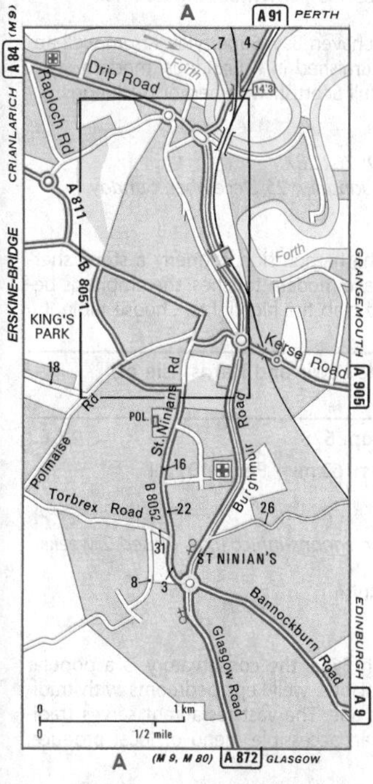

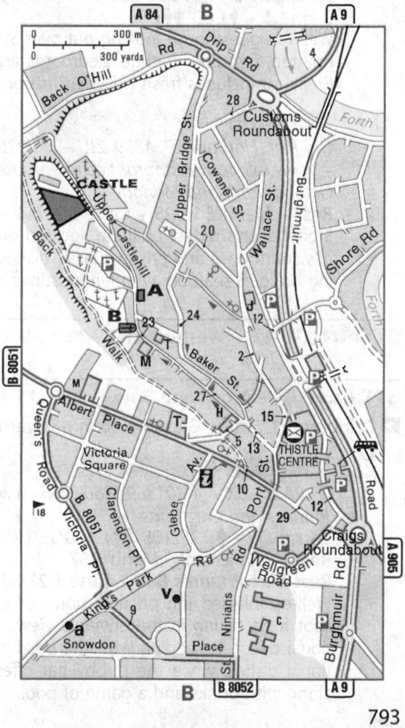

Park Lodge
32 Park Terr ✉ FK8 2JS – ✆ (01786) 474 862 – www.parklodge.net – Closed Christmas and New Year Ba
9 rm – †£ 70/85 ††£ 90/120 **Rest** – *(closed Sunday)* Menu £ 18/28 **s**
Lovely part-Georgian, part-Victorian, creeper-clad house, with mature garden and fruit trees to the rear. Warm, intimate bar and sitting room. Traditional, individually designed bedrooms; the four-poster room is particularly popular. Formal dining room has a beautiful ornate ceiling and traditional menu.

Number 10 without rest
10 Gladstone Pl ✉ FK8 2NN – ✆ (01786) 472 681 – www.cameron-10.co.uk Bv
3 rm – †£ 45/60 ††£ 50/70
Light-stone Victorian townhouse in a quiet street, with an attractive garden and a surprisingly spacious interior. Individually furnished bedrooms have good facilities. Linen-laid breakfast room features ornate coving; choose the porridge.

West Plean House without rest
South : 3.5 mi on A 872 (Denny rd) ✉ FK7 8HA – ✆ (01786) 812 208 – www.westpleanhouse.com – Closed 15 December-15 January
4 rm – †£ 50/55 ††£ 85/90
Attractive house with a long history – its latest extensions added in 1803 – next to a working farm. Beautiful tiled hall, classic country house lounge and communal breakfast room. Warm, traditionally styled bedrooms. Pleasant walled garden.

SCOTLAND

STONEHAVEN – Aberdeenshire – 501 N13 – pop. 11 464 Scotland 28 D2

Edinburgh 111 mi – Glasgow 130 mi – Dundee 50 mi – Aberdeen 15 mi
Dunnottar Castle★★, S : 1.5 mi by A 92

Beachgate House without rest
Beachgate Ln ✉ AB39 2BD – ✆ (01569) 763 155 – www.beachgate.co.uk
5 rm – †£ 80 ††£ 95
Well-run guesthouse looking out over Stonehaven Bay. Super views from well-appointed, first floor lounge. Bedrooms are furnished in a luxurious, modern style. Breakfast includes fresh poached fish or a full Scottish with hen or duck eggs.

Tolbooth
Old Pier, Harbour ✉ AB39 2JU – ✆ (01569) 762 287 – www.tolbooth-restaurant.co.uk – Closed January, 25 December, Sunday October-April and Monday
Rest – Menu £ 16/25 – Carte £ 29/44
Stonehaven's oldest building, located on the harbourside: formerly a store, sheriff's courthouse and prison. Classic dishes have modern touches; the emphasis being on local seafood, with langoustines and crab the highlights. Choose table 3.

STORNOWAY – Western Isles – 501 A9 – see Lewis and Harris (Isle of)

STRACHUR – Argyll and Bute – 501 E15 – pop. 628 27 B2

Edinburgh 112 mi – Glasgow 66 mi – Inverness 162 mi – Perth 101 mi

Creggans Inn
✉ PA27 8BX – ✆ (01369) 860 279 – www.creggans-inn.co.uk – Closed 2 weeks January and Christmas
14 rm – †£ 75/105 ††£ 100/160 – 1 suite
Rest – *(dinner only)* Menu £ 37
Rest *Mac Phunn's Bar* – Carte £ 21/37
Well-established inn on the shores of Loch Fyne; the conservatory is a popular spot for a taking in the enviable view. Spacious, well-kept bedrooms with traditional décor in keeping with the building's age. The vast restaurant serves traditional dishes, while the pubby bar offers an accessible menu of local produce, along with drinks and a game of pool.

Inver Cottage
Strathlaclan, Southwest : 6.5 mi by A 886 on B 8000 ✉ PA27 8BU – ✆ (01369) 860 537 – www.invercottage.com – Closed late December-March, Monday and Tuesday except July-August
Rest – Carte £ 23/41
Lochside former crofter's cottage boasting water and mountain views. Small bar and casual tables for drinks or afternoon tea; simple, airy restaurant. Constantly evolving menu uses only local produce.

STRATHPEFFER – Highland – 501 G11 – pop. 918 — 30 C2

Edinburgh 173 mi – London 573 mi – Belfast 245 mi – Dundee 154 mi
Pump Room Museum, ✆ (01997) 42 14 15, www.visitscotland.com
Strathpeffer Spa, Golf Course Rd, ✆ (01997) 42 12 19

Craigvar without rest
The Square ✉ IV14 9DL – ✆ (01997) 421 622 – www.craigvar.com – Closed 23 December-12 January
3 rm – †£ 55/65 ††£ 86/90
Proudly run by a charming owner, an attractive Georgian house overlooking the main square of a delightful spa village. Traditional guest areas include a comfy lounge and an antique-furnished breakfast room. Spacious bedrooms have a modern edge and plenty of personal touches. Good breakfast selection.

STRATHYRE – Stirling – 501 H15 – ✉ Callander Scotland — 27 B2

Edinburgh 62 mi – Glasgow 53 mi – Perth 42 mi
The Trossachs★★★ (Loch Katrine★★) SW : 14 mi by A 84 and A 821 – Hilltop viewpoint★★★ (✳★★★) SW : 16.5 mi by A 84 and A 821

Creagan House with rm
On A 84 ✉ FK18 8ND – ✆ (01877) 384 638 – www.creaganhouse.co.uk – Closed 15 January-13 March, 6-21 November, Christmas, Wednesday and Thursday
5 rm – †£ 75/95 ††£ 130 **Rest** – *(dinner only)* Menu £ 35
Long-standing, personally run restaurant in a 17C farmhouse. Snug sitting rooms lead to a baronial-style dining room with a vast fireplace and handmade local china. Traditional cooking uses Perthshire's natural larder; the 'Smokie in a Pokie' is a speciality. Watch red squirrels from the comfy, cosy bedrooms.

STROMNESS – 501 K7 – see Orkney Islands (Mainland)

STRONTIAN – Highland – 501 D13 — 29 B3

Edinburgh 139 mi – Fort William 23 mi – Oban 66 mi
Acharacle, ✆ (08452) 25 51 21, www.visitscotland.com

Kilcamb Lodge
✉ PH36 4HY – ✆ (01967) 402 257 – www.kilcamblodge.co.uk – Closed January and restricted opening in winter
10 rm (dinner included) – †£ 120/200 ††£ 220/375
Rest – Menu £ 50 – Carte £ 23/41
Charming lochside hunting lodge, with 19 acres of gardens and woodland running down to a private shore. Traditional interior boasts rich fabrics, log fires and up-to-date bedrooms. Formal restaurant offers a traditional menu; seafood and game feature highly.

STRUAN – Highland – see Skye (Isle of)

SWINTON – The Scottish Borders – 501 N16 – pop. 472 – ✉ Duns — 26 D2

Edinburgh 49 mi – London 351 mi – Newcastle upon Tyne 74 mi – Darlington 110 mi

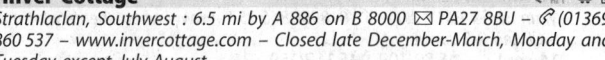

Wheatsheaf with rm
Main St ✉ TD11 3JJ – ✆ (01890) 860 257 – www.wheatsheaf-swinton.co.uk
– Closed 2-3 January
14 rm ☕ – 🚹£ 89/109 🚹🚹£ 119/159
Rest – *(dinner only and lunch Saturday and Sunday) (booking advisable)*
Carte £ 22/43
Substantial stone inn overlooking the village green. The extensive dinner menu offers ambitious dishes; specials feature seafood from Eyemouth, and meat comes from the surrounding border farms and is smoked on-site. Lunch is served only at weekends. Bedrooms are spacious, cosy and well-equipped.

TAIN – Highland – 501 H10 – pop. 4 540 — 30 D2

Edinburgh 191 mi – Inverness 35 mi – Wick 91 mi
Tain, Chapel Rd, ✆ (01862) 89 23 14
Tarbat, Portmahomack, ✆ (01862) 87 12 78

Golf View House without rest
13 Knockbreck Rd ✉ IV19 1BN – ✆ (01862) 892 856
– www.tainbedandbreakfast.co.uk
5 rm ☕ – 🚹£ 45/55 🚹🚹£ 65/80
Well-cared-for Victorian manse close to the golf course, boasting a neat lawned garden and views over the mountains and out to sea. The bright, fresh interior features modern, uncluttered bedrooms and a homely lounge and breakfast room.

at Nigg Southeast : 7 mi by A 9, B 9175 and Pitcalnie Rd.

Wemyss House
Bayfield, South : 1 mi past church ✉ IV19 1QW – ✆ (01862) 851 212
– www.wemysshouse.com
3 rm ☕ – 🚹£ 95/105 🚹🚹£ 95/105 **Rest** – Menu £ 38
Remote, rurally set guesthouse with charming owners, well-maintained gardens and pleasant views. Cosy sitting room with grand piano. Spacious, immaculately kept bedrooms. Freshly prepared dishes use local ingredients. Excellent quality breakfasts.

at Cadboll Southeast : 8.5 mi by A 9 and B 9165 (Portmahomack rd) off Hilton rd – ✉ Tain

Glenmorangie House
Fearn ✉ IV20 1XP – ✆ (01862) 871 671 – www.theglenmorangiehouse.com
– Closed January
12 rm (dinner included) ☕ – 🚹£ 235 🚹🚹£ 370/400
Rest – *(dinner only) (bookings essential for non-residents) (set menu only)*
Menu £ 55
Charming 17C house owned by the famous distillery. Antiques, hand-crafted local furnishings and open peat fires feature; there's even a small whisky tasting room. Luxuriously appointed bedrooms show good attention to detail; those in the courtyard cottages are suites. Communal dining from classical Scottish menu.

TALMINE – Highland – 501 G8 – ✉ Lairg — 30 C1

Edinburgh 245 mi – London 651 mi – Inverness 92 mi – Elgin 128 mi

Cloisters without rest
Church Holme ✉ IV27 4YP – ✆ (01847) 601 286 – www.cloistertal.demon.co.uk
– Closed Christmas-New Year
3 rm ☕ – 🚹£ 38 🚹🚹£ 65
Converted church boasting great views over Tongue Bay and the Rabbit Islands. Homely interior packed with memorabilia. Leather-furnished lounge, snug breakfast area and simple, well-kept bedrooms.

TARBERT – Argyll and Bute – 501 D16 – see Kintyre (Peninsula)

TARBERT – Western Isles – 501 Z10 – see Lewis and Harris (Isle of)

SCOTLAND

TARBET – Argyll and Bute – 501 F15 – ✉ Arrochar 27 B2

Edinburgh 88 mi – Glasgow 42 mi – Inverness 138 mi – Perth 78 mi

Lomond View Country House without rest
On A 82 ✉ G83 7DG – ✆ (01301) 702 477 – www.lomondview.co.uk
3 rm – †£ 60/70 ††£ 80/90
Purpose-built guesthouse which lives up to its name: there are stunning loch views. Spacious sitting room. Light and airy breakfast room. Sizeable, modern bedrooms.

TAYVALLICH – Argyll and Bute – 501 D15 – ✉ Lochgilphead 27 B2

Edinburgh 148 mi – Glasgow 103 mi – Inverness 157 mi

Tayvallich Inn
✉ PA31 8PL – ✆ (01546) 870 282 – www.tayvallichinn.com – Closed Monday November-March
Rest – Carte £ 18/44
Dine in the bar, the more formal dining room or on the decked terrace, with views over the bay. Menu focuses on locally caught fish and shellfish, but also lists classic pub dishes like steak and chips.

TEANGUE – Highland – 501 C12 – see Skye (Isle of)

THORNHILL – Dumfries and Galloway – 501 I18 – pop. 1 633 25 B2

Scotland

Edinburgh 64 mi – Ayr 44 mi – Dumfries 15 mi – Glasgow 63 mi
Drumlanrig Castle★★ (cabinets★) AC, NW : 4 mi by A 76

Gillbank House without rest
8 East Morton St ✉ DG3 5LZ – ✆ (01848) 330 597 – www.gillbank.co.uk
6 rm – †£ 60 ††£ 80
Red-stone house built in 1895; originally the Jenner family holiday home. Lovely stained glass front door, spacious, light-filled interior and airy breakfast room with distant hill views. Large, simply furnished bedrooms: two with feature beds; all with wet rooms.

THURSO – Highland – 501 J8 – pop. 7 196 Scotland 30 D1

Edinburgh 289 mi – Inverness 133 mi – Wick 21 mi
from Scrabster to Stromness (Orkney Islands) (P and O Scottish Ferries) (2 h)
Riverside, ✆ (0845) 2 25 51 21, www.visitscotland.com
Newlands of Geise, ✆ (01847) 89 38 07
Strathy Point★ (<★★★) W : 22 mi by A 836

Forss House
Forss, West : 5.5 mi on A 836 ✉ KW14 7XY – ✆ (01847) 861 201 – www.forsshousehotel.co.uk – Closed 24 December-2 January
14 rm – †£ 97/130 ††£ 130/185 **Rest** – *(dinner only)* Carte £ 25/40 **s**
Traditional Scottish hotel centred around fishing and offering timeshares on the river. Rods and mounted fish sit beside deer heads and open fires. Good-sized bedrooms – annexe rooms are most modern. Elegant dining room serves classic menu; seafood a speciality.

Pennyland House without rest
Northwest : 0.75 mi on A 9 ✉ KW14 7JU – ✆ (01847) 891 194 – www.pennylandhouse.co.uk – Closed Christmas
5 rm – †£ 60 ††£ 70
Old farmhouse built in 1780; where the founder of the Boys' Brigade was born. Simple, stylishly furnished bedrooms with quality oak furnishings, golf course pictures and modern bathrooms. Open-plan lounge-cum-dining room with harbour views.

SCOTLAND

Murray House

1 Campbell St ✉ KW14 7HD – ✆ (01847) 895 759 – www.murrayhousebb.com – Closed Christmas-New Year, minimum 2 night stay

5 rm – £ 30/60 £ 60/70 **Rest** – Menu £ 15

Family-run Victorian house in a great central location. Small lounge and breakfast room. Bright, compact bedrooms with modern shower rooms; two on the second floor are suitable for families. Home-cooked dinners must be pre-ordered; packed breakfasts and lunches available. Minimum two night stay.

at Scrabster **Northwest : 2.25 mi on A 9**

Captain's Galley

The Harbour ✉ KW14 7UJ – ✆ (01847) 894 999 – www.captainsgalley.co.uk – Closed 25-26 December, 1-2 January, Sunday and Monday

Rest – *(dinner only) (booking essential)* Menu £ 49

Rustic seafood restaurant on the pier, with a vaulted stone dining room, a cosy lounge and an old chimney from its former ice house days. Classical daily menu; the owner was once a fisherman, so has excellent local contacts – he keeps some of his produce in creels in the harbour.

TIGHNABRUAICH – Argyll and Bute – 501 E16 **27** B3

Edinburgh 113 mi – Glasgow 63 mi – Oban 66 mi

Royal An Lochan

Shore Rd ✉ PA21 2BE – ✆ (01700) 811 239 – www.theroyalanlochan.co.uk

11 rm – £ 75/125 £ 75/150 **Rest** – Carte £ 25/36 **s**

Spacious 19C hotel located in a peaceful village, overlooking the Kyles of Bute. Comfortable bedrooms; some with excellent outlooks. The characterful bar with its nautical theme serves a snack menu, while the formal conservatory restaurant offers water views and seasonal seafood dishes.

SCOTLAND

TIRORAN – Argyll and Bute – 501 B14 – see Mull (Isle of)

TOBERMORY – Argyll and Bute – 501 B14 – see Mull (Isle of)

TORRIDON – Highland – 501 D11 – ✉ Achnasheen Scotland **29** B2

Edinburgh 234 mi – Inverness 62 mi – Kyle of Lochalsh 44 mi

Wester Ross★★★

Torridon

South : 1.5 mi on A 896 ✉ IV22 2EY – ✆ (01445) 791 242 – www.thetorridon.com – Closed January and Monday-Tuesday November-March

18 rm – £ 230/465 £ 230/465 – 2 suites

Rest – *(bar lunch) (booking essential)* Menu £ 55 **s**

Family-run former hunting lodge built in 1887 by Lord Lovelace; set in 40 acres, with superb loch and mountain views. Delightful interior with wood-panelling, ornate ceilings and a peat fire. Mix of contemporary and a few classic bedrooms – all are spacious, with top quality furnishings and feature baths. Clubby bar and a smart dining room with a modern daily menu.

Torridon Inn with rm rest,

South : 1.5 mi on A 896 ✉ IV22 2EY – ✆ (01445) 791 242 – www.thetorridon.com – Closed mid-December-January and Monday-Thursday November, February and March

12 rm – £ 104 £ 104 **Rest** – Carte £ 19/36 **s**

Tranquil inn geared towards those who enjoy outdoor pursuits. Timbered bar features stags' antlers and an ice axe; restaurant overlooks gardens and loch. Satisfying walkers' favourites mix with more elaborate dishes on the menu. Simply furnished, modern bedrooms; the larger ones are ideal for families.

TROON – South Ayrshire – 501 G17 – pop. 14 766 **25** A2

Edinburgh 77 mi – Ayr 7 mi – Glasgow 31 mi

to Northern Ireland (Larne) (P and O Irish Sea) 2 daily

Troon Municipal, Harling Drive, ✆ (01292) 31 24 64

Lochgreen House

Monktonhill Rd, Southwood, Southeast : 2 mi on B 749 ✉ KA10 7EN – ✆ (01292) 313 343 – www.costley-hotels.co.uk
39 rm – †£ 145/175 ††£ 170/190 – 1 suite
Rest *Tapestry* – see restaurant listing
Coastal Edwardian country house in neat, mature gardens. Sumptuous, classically furnished lounge with an extensive range of malt whiskies. Cosy, traditional bedrooms in main house; those in newer extension are larger and more luxurious.

Tapestry – Lochgreen House Hotel

Monktonhill Rd, Southwood, Southeast : 2 mi on B 749 ✉ KA10 7EN – ✆ (01292) 313 343 – www.costley-hotels.co.uk
Rest – Menu £ 22/40
Cavernous room with rafters, mirrors and chandeliers, in an Edwardian country house hotel. Fixed price or 10 course tasting menus; tasty, original dishes have modern presentation and a strong Scottish base. Formal service.

at Loans East : 2 mi on A 759 – ✉ Troon

Highgrove House

Old Loans Rd, East : 0.25 mi on Dundonald rd ✉ KA10 7HL – ✆ (01292) 312 511 – www.costleyhotels.co.uk
9 rm – †£ 69 ††£ 110 **Rest** – Menu £ 17 (early dinner) – Carte £ 25/41
Hillside property with a stunning panoramic view of the coastline and the Isle of Arran. Comfortable, contemporary bedrooms; Room 1 is the best. Clubby dining room with floor to ceiling windows and a smart, friendly team; sit in one of the plush booths at the top. Classic menus focus on seafood and grills.

TURNBERRY – South Ayrshire – 501 F18 – ✉ Girvan Scotland 25 A2

Edinburgh 97 mi – London 416 mi – Glasgow 51 mi – Carlisle 108 mi
Culzean Castle★ **AC** (setting★★★, Oval Staircase★★) NE : 5 mi by A 719

Turnberry

rest,
On A 719 ✉ KA26 9LT – ✆ (01655) 331 000 – www.luxurycollection.com/turnberry
149 rm – †£ 165/325 ††£ 185/345 – 4 suites
Rest *1906* – see restaurant listing
Rest *James Miller Room* – *(closed Sunday and Monday) (dinner only) (booking essential)* Menu £ 65
Rest *Tappie Toorie* – Carte £ 23/36
Resort-style, Edwardian railway hotel boasting a smart spa and 3 championship golf courses. Spacious interior with a light, contemporary style. Luxurious bedrooms; suites have stunning coast and course views. French classics in 1906; ambitious, modern offerings in intimate James Miller and pub favourites in simpler Tappie Toorie.

1906 – Turnberry Hotel

On A 719 ✉ KA26 9LT – ✆ (01655) 331 000 – www.luxurycollection.com/turnberry
Rest – *(dinner only)* Carte £ 34/84
Named after the year that the Turnberry opened, this smart hotel restaurant boasts lovely views across the sea. Classical French menus feature dishes true to the spirit of Auguste Escoffier.

UDNY GREEN – Aberdeenshire 28 D1

Edinburgh 140 mi – London 543 mi – Belfast 218 mi – Dundee 80 mi

Eat on the Green

✉ AB41 7RS – ✆ (01651) 842 337 – www.eatonthegreen.co.uk – Closed Monday, Tuesday and Saturday lunch
Rest – *(booking essential)* Menu £ 27 (lunch) – Carte £ 34/49
Attractive former inn overlooking the village green, with a cosy lounge and two traditionally furnished dining rooms. Well-presented, classically based dishes change with the seasons. Professional, friendly service.

UIG – Western Isles – 501 Y9 – see Lewis and Harris (Isle of)

UIST (Isles of) – 501 X/Y11 – pop. 3 510

from Lochmaddy to Isle of Skye (Uig) (Caledonian MacBrayne Ltd) 1-3 daily (1 h 50 mn) – from Otternish to Isle of Harris (Leverburgh) (Caledonian MacBrayne Ltd) (1 h 10 mn)

NORTH UIST – Western Isles – 501 X/Y10

CARINISH – Western Isles 29 A2

Temple View

HS6 5EJ – (01876) 580 676 – www.templeviewhotel.co.uk – Closed Christmas

10 rm – £ 65 £ 105 **Rest** – Carte £ 17/31 **s**

Victorian house with an uncluttered interior and a homely style. Small bar, sitting room and sun lounge. Simple, comfortable bedrooms: those to the rear have moor views; those at the front overlook the sea or the 13C ruins of Trinity Temple. Cosy dining room offers popular seafood specials.

LANGASS – Western Isles 29 A2

Langass Lodge rm,

HS6 5HA – (01876) 580 285 – www.langasslodge.co.uk – Closed 1 January, 24-25 and 31 December

11 rm – £ 65/95 £ 95/145 **Rest** – *(bar lunch)* Menu £ 36

Former Victorian shooting lodge nestled in heather-strewn hills and boasting distant loch views. Characterful bedrooms in main house; more modern, spacious rooms with good views in wing. Eat in comfy bar or linen-clad dining room from simple, seafood based menu.

LOCHMADDY – Western Isles 29 A2

Hamersay House rm,

HS6 5AE – (01876) 500 700 – www.hamersay-house.co.uk – Closed 23 December-7 January

11 rm – £ 69/119 £ 80/149

Rest – *(closed Sunday October-March) (dinner only)* Carte £ 17/35

Stylish hotel with sleek, boutique style. Well-equipped gym, sauna and steam room. Chic, modern bedrooms offer good facilities. Forward-thinking owner continually reinvests. Smart bar and dining room; menus display plenty of seafood. Bikes available for hire.

SCOTLAND

ULLAPOOL – Highland – 501 E10 – pop. 1 308 Scotland 30 C2

Edinburgh 215 mi – London 616 mi – Inverness 58 mi – Elgin 94 mi

to Isle of Lewis (Stornoway) (Caledonian MacBrayne Ltd) (2 h 40 mn)

20 Argyle St B, (0845) 2 25 51 21, www.ullapool.com

Town★

Wester Ross★★★ - Loch Broom★★. Falls of Measach★★, S : 11 mi by A 835 and A 832 - Corrieshalloch Gorge★, SE : 10 mi by A 835 – Northwards to Lochinver★★, Morefield (★★ of Ullapool), ★ Loch Broom

Point Cottage without rest

22 West Shore St IV26 2UR – (01854) 613 702 – www.ullapoolbedandbreakfast.co.uk – Closed Christmas-New Year

3 rm – £ 40/65 £ 65/80

18C former fisherman's cottage on the shore of Loch Broom; the Stornoway ferry passes in front. Compact, modern bedrooms with muted tweeds, contemporary art and good views. Small lounge and breakfast room; pre-order from a large selection.

Ardvreck without rest

Morefield Brae, Northwest : 2 mi by A 835 IV26 2TH – (01854) 612 028 – www.ardvreckhouse.com – Closed December-February

10 rm – £ 40/45 £ 78/80

Modern house set away from the town centre, affording amazing views over Loch Broom to the mountains. Simply furnished bedrooms with tartan touches and local watercolours on the walls. The friendly owner is eager to please.

VEENSGARTH – see Shetland Islands (Mainland)

WALKERBURN – The Scottish Borders – pop. 647 26 C2

Edinburgh 30 mi – London 362 mi – Aberdeen 161 mi – Hartlepool 120 mi

Windlestraw Lodge

On A 72 ✉ EH43 6AA – ☎ (01896) 870 636 – www.windlestraw.co.uk – Closed 1 week February, 25 December and 1 January

6 rm – †£ 105 ††£ 160/200 **Rest** – *(dinner only)* Menu £ 45

Attractive Arts and Crafts property built in 1906, boasting original fireplaces, old plaster ceilings and great valley views. Stylish, tastefully modernised bedrooms. Comfy bar, plush lounge and attractive, wood-panelled dining room offering daily changing menu.

WATERNISH – Highland – 501 A11 – see Skye (Isle of)

WESTRAY (Isle of) – 501 K/L6 – see Orkney Islands

WICK – Highland – 501 K8 – pop. 9 713 Scotland 30 D1

Edinburgh 282 mi – Inverness 126 mi

Wick Airport : ☎ (01955) 602215, N : 1 m

Whitechapel Rd, ☎ (0845) 2 25 51 21, www.visitscotland.com

Reiss, ☎ (01955) 60 27 26

Duncansby Head★ (Stacks of Duncansby★★) N : 14 mi by A 9 – Grey Cairns of Camster★ (Long Cairn★★) S : 17 mi by A 9 – The Hill O'Many Stanes★, S : 10 mi by A 9

Clachan without rest

13 Randolph Pl, South Rd, South : 0.75 mi on A 99 ✉ KW1 5NJ – ☎ (01955) 605 384 – www.theclachan.co.uk – Closed 2 weeks Christmas-New Year

3 rm – †£ 60/65 ††£ 76/80

Smart detached house on the edge of town, a short drive from the Queen Mother's former holiday residence, the Castle of Mey. Stylish, well-kept bedrooms blend oak furnishings with tartan fabrics. Black and white photos of the town's herring fishing days decorate the cosy dining room. Extensive breakfasts.

Bord De L'Eau

2 Market St (Riverside) ✉ KW1 4AR – ☎ (01955) 604 400 – Closed 25-26 December, 1-2 January, Sunday lunch and Monday

Rest – Carte £ 24/38

Long-standing riverside bistro with simple dining room and conservatory. Framed Eiffel Tower prints and French posters on the walls. Authentic, classic Gallic dishes; plenty of local seafood.

WORMIT – Fife – 501 L14 28 C2

Edinburgh 53 mi – London 455 mi – Aberdeen 70 mi – Gateshead 162 mi

Scotscraig, Tayport, Golf Rd, ☎ (01382) 55 25 15

View

Naughton Rd ✉ DD6 8NE – ☎ (01382) 542 287 – www.view-restaurant.co.uk – Closed 25-26 December, 1-2 January and Monday

Rest – Menu £ 18 (lunch) – Carte £ 20/35

Unassuming former pub in a small village, boasting superb views over the Tay Bridge to Dundee. Extensive menu and daily specials board offer homemade small plates that can be served in succession or all at once; quality ingredients.

ABERAERON (Aber Aeron) – **Ceredigion** – **503** H27 – **pop. 1 520** **33** B3

London 231 mi – Cardiff 104 mi – Birmingham 138 mi – Liverpool 124 mi

Ty Mawr Mansion Country House

Cilcennin, East : 5 mi by A 482 ✉ SA48 8DB – ✆ (01570) 470 033 – www.tymawrmansion.co.uk – Closed 27 December-20 January

9 rm – †£ 99/140 ††£ 120/280 – 1 suite

Rest – *(closed Sunday dinner) (dinner only)* Menu £ 30

Grade II listed Georgian stone mansion in 12 acres of delightful grounds. Several well-appointed lounges with high ceilings; spacious bedrooms boast marble bathrooms and a good level of facilities. The small basement cinema offers dining packages and the smart restaurant offers bold, widely-influenced dishes.

3 Pen Cei without rest

3 Quay Par ✉ SA46 0BT – ✆ (01545) 571 147 – www.pencei.co.uk – Closed 25-26 December

5 rm – †£ 85/90 ††£ 100/140

Vibrant blue house on the harbourfront; formerly the Packet Steam Company HQ. Stylish modern bedrooms are named after local rivers: those to the front overlook the water; Aeron has a free-standing bath and large walk-in shower. Good choices at breakfast, from fruit salad to smoked salmon and scrambled eggs.

Llys Aeron without rest

Lampeter Rd, on A 482 ✉ SA46 0ED – ✆ (01545) 570 276 – www.llysaeron.co.uk – Closed 25-26 December

3 rm – †£ 50/75 ††£ 80/120

Charmingly run Georgian guesthouse with a conservatory lounge and a breakfast room overlooking the pleasant walled garden. Bedrooms come in neutral colour schemes and have modern bathrooms. For breakfast, choose from extensive Aga-cooked options, as well as local honey and homemade granola and preserves.

Harbourmaster with rm

rest,

Quay Par ✉ SA46 0BA – ✆ (01545) 570 755 – www.harbour-master.com – Closed 25 December

13 rm – †£ 65/240 ††£ 110/250

Rest – Menu £ 30 (dinner) – Carte £ 30/44

Vibrant blue inn with a New England style bar-lounge, a modern dining room and lovely harbour views. Choose between the bar menu or a more substantial evening à la carte and a list of daily specials. Bedrooms, split between the house and a nearby cottage, are comfy and brightly decorated; some boast terraces.

ABERDOVEY (Aberdyfi) – **Gwynedd** – **503** H26 – **pop. 869** **32** B2

London 230 mi – Dolgellau 25 mi – Shrewsbury 66 mi

Snowdonia National Park★★★

Llety Bodfor without rest

Bodfor Terr ✉ LL35 0EA – ✆ (01654) 767 475 – www.lletybodfor.co.uk – Closed 10-31 January

8 rm – †£ 50/70 ††£ 95/150, £ 12

Two 19C seafront houses with a relaxed atmosphere and stylish interior design. Spacious, contemporary bedrooms come with bay views and kitchenettes; guests can also prepare snacks in the pantry. Breakfast is served three doors down.

ABERGAVENNY (Y-Fenni) – **Monmouthshire** – **503** L28 – **pop. 14 055** **33** C4

London 163 mi – Cardiff 31 mi – Gloucester 43 mi – Newport 19 mi

Monmouth Rd, ✆ (01873) 85 32 54, www.abergavenny.org.uk

Monmouthshire, Llanfoist, ✆ (01873) 85 26 06

Town★ - St Mary's Church★ (Monuments★★)

Brecon Beacons National Park★★ – Blaenavon Ironworks★, SW : 5 mi by A 465 and B 4246. Raglan Castle★ **AC**, SE : 9 mi by A 40

WALES

Llansantffraed Court

Llanvihangel Gobion, Southeast : 6.5 mi by A 40 and B 4598 off old Raglan rd
✉ NP7 9BA – ✆ (01873) 840 678 – www.llch.co.uk
21 rm – †£ 100/120 ††£ 135/185
Rest *The Court* – see restaurant listing
Attractive William and Mary style country house with an ornamental lake, in 20 acres of grounds. Traditional guest areas include a two-roomed lounge and a large bar. Dark-hued bedrooms – the corner rooms have both mountain and valley views.

Angel

15 Cross St ✉ NP7 5EN – ✆ (01873) 857 121 – www.angelabergavenny.com – Closed 25 December
36 rm – †£ 111/220 ††£ 111/220 – 2 suites
Rest *Oak Room* – *(closed dinner 24-31 December)* Menu £ 25 (lunch and early dinner) – Carte £ 19/43
Keenly run, family-owned, Georgian coaching inn and outbuildings. Characterful guest areas have a contemporary, shabby-chic feel. Mix of traditional and more contemporary bedrooms. Smart brasserie with oak furniture offers a classical menu with international influences. Afternoon tea in the Wedgewood Room.

The Court – Llansantffraed Court Hotel

Llanvihangel Gobion, Southeast : 6.5 mi by A 40 and B 4598 off old Raglan rd
✉ NP7 9BA – ✆ (01873) 840 678 – www.llch.co.uk
Rest – Menu £ 15/30 – Carte £ 30/47
Contemporary restaurant in a William and Mary style country house, with large photos of local scenes. Dishes have a classical British base but are given a modern twist; fruit, veg and herbs are from the walled garden. Interesting wine list.

WALES

at Llanddewi Skirrid Northeast : 3.25 mi on B 4521 – ✉ Abergavenny

Walnut Tree (Shaun Hill)

✉ NP7 8AW – ✆ (01873) 852 797 – www.thewalnuttreeinn.com – Closed 1 week Christmas, Sunday and Monday
Rest – *(booking essential)* Menu £ 28 (weekday lunch) – Carte £ 32/47
A reinvigorated, long-standing Welsh institution, set in a wooded valley and always bustling with regulars. Start with drinks in the flag-floored lounge-bar. Classic, seasonal dishes are well-priced and refreshingly simple, eschewing adornment and letting the ingredients speak for themselves.
→ Calves' sweetbreads with sauerkraut. Turbot, mussels and clams in spiced broth. Orange and almond cake.

at Cross Ash Northeast : 8.25 mi on B 4521

1861

West : 0.5 mi on B 4521 ✉ NP7 8PB – ✆ (01873) 821 297 – www.18-61.co.uk – Closed first 2 weeks January, Sunday dinner and Monday
Rest – Menu £ 25/35 – Carte £ 34/46
Part-timbered Victorian pub; now a cosy restaurant with a smart lounge, a red brick fireplace and contemporary furnishings. Choose from a set selection, a 7 course tasting menu or the à la carte. Classically based cooking has modern twists.

at Nant-Y-Derry Southeast : 6.5 mi by A 40 off A 4042 – ✉ Abergavenny

Foxhunter

✉ NP7 9DN – ✆ (01873) 881 101 – www.thefoxhunter.com – Closed 25-26 December, 1 January, Sunday dinner and Monday
Rest – Menu £ 28 (lunch) – Carte £ 32/43
Attractive stone-built former station master's house with a small kitchen garden where they grow some of the produce. The characterful dining room features flagged floors and wood burning stoves. Cooking is hearty, unfussy and classical.

ABERGELE – Conwy – 503 J24 – pop. 17 574 32 C1

London 229 mi – Cardiff 182 mi – Liverpool 51 mi – Manchester 75 mi

at Betws-yn-Rhos Southwest : 4.25 mi by A 548 on B 5381

Ffarm Country House
rm,

LL22 8AR – (01492) 680 448 – *www.ffarmcountryhouse.co.uk*

7 rm – £ 79 £ 98/138

Rest – *(dinner only) (booking essential)* Carte £ 18/24

A Gothic-style building which really stands out in this small village. Beautiful tiled hall and grand drawing room. Bedrooms, named after wine regions, have sleek bathrooms and a stylish, modern edge; Cape and Champagne are 2 of the largest.

ABERSOCH – Gwynedd – 502 G25 – pop. 805 – Pwllheli 32 B2

London 265 mi – Caernarfon 28 mi – Shrewsbury 101 mi

Golf Rd, (01758) 71 26 36

Lleyn Peninsula★★ – Plas-yn-Rhiw★ **AC**, W : 6 mi by minor roads. Bardsey Island★, SW : 15 mi by A 499 and B 4413 – Mynydd Mawr★, SW : 17 mi by A 499, B 4413 and minor roads

Venetia with rm

Lon Sarn Bach LL53 7EB – (01758) 713 354 – www.venetiawales.com – Closed 5 January-13 February, 24-26 December, Sunday lunch July-August and Sunday dinner

5 rm – £ 65/133 £ 80/148

Rest – *(dinner only and Sunday lunch)* Carte £ 22/43

Double-fronted house once owned by a sea captain, with a minimalist bar-lounge and a contemporary dining room with lime and aubergine seating. Classic Italian dishes are presented in a distinctly modern style. Friendly, efficient service. Chic, well-equipped bedrooms; one has a Jacuzzi with a waterproof TV.

at Bwlchtocyn South : 2 mi – Pwllheli

Porth Tocyn

LL53 7BU – (01758) 713 303 – www.porthtocynhotel.co.uk – Easter-early November

17 rm – £ 75/90 £ 100/180

Rest – *(buffet lunch Sunday) (bar lunch Monday-Saturday)* Menu £ 44

High on the headland overlooking Cardigan Bay, a traditional hotel that's been in the family for three generations. Relax in the cosy lounges or explore the many leisure and children's facilities. Homely, modernised bedrooms; some with balconies or sea views. Menus offer interesting, soundly executed dishes.

ABERYSTWYTH (Aberestuuth) – Ceredigion – 503 H26 32 B2 – pop. 23 408

London 238 mi – Chester 98 mi – Fishguard 58 mi – Shrewsbury 74 mi

Terrace Rd, (01970) 61 21 25, www.aberystwyth-online.co.uk

Bryn-y-Mor, (01970) 61 51 04

Town★★ - The Seafront★ – National Library of Wales (Permanent Exhibition★)

Vale of Rheidol★★ (Railway★★ **AC**) - St Padarn's Church★, SE : 1 mi by A 44. Devil's Bridge (Pontarfynach)★, E : 12 mi by A 4120 – Strata Florida Abbey★ **AC** (West Door★), SE : 15 mi by B 4340 and minor rd

Nanteos N
rm,

Rhydyfelin, Southeast : 4 mi by A 487 off A 4120 SY23 4LU – (01970) 600 522 – www.nanteos.com

15 rm – £ 125/200 £ 150/300 – 1 suite

Rest *Nightingale* – Menu £ 40 (dinner) – Carte lunch £ 23/34

Impressive Georgian house in a peaceful wooded valley surrounded by mountains. Original flag flooring and ornate coving feature; breakfast is in the characterful old kitchen. Stylish, boldly coloured bedrooms come with antiques, modern facilities and super bathrooms. Classical menus feature Welsh produce.

Gwesty Cymru
19 Marine Terr ✉ SY23 2AZ – ✆ (01970) 612 252 – www.gwestycymru.com – Closed 21-30 December
8 rm – †£ 67/133 ††£ 87/153
Rest – *(closed Tuesday lunch) (booking essential)* Carte £ 22/34
Grade II listed Georgian townhouse on the seafront, with a brightly painted exterior and a terrace overlooking the bay. Thoughtfully designed, modern bedrooms vary in size and décor – all are colour themed, with smart bathrooms. Small, stylish basement bar and dining room; ambitious, adventurous dishes.

ANGLESEY (Isle of) (Sir Ynys Môn) – **Isle of Anglesey** – **503** G/H24 **32** B1
– **pop. 68 900**
London 270 mi – Cardiff 205 mi – Liverpool 92 mi – Birkenhead 86 mi

BEAUMARIS – **Isle of Anglesey** – **503** H24 – ✉ **Isle Of Anglesey** **32** B1
London 253 mi – Birkenhead 74 mi – Holyhead 25 mi
Baron Hill, ✆ (01248) 81 02 31
Town★★ - Castle★ **AC**
Anglesey★★ – Penmon Priory★, NE : 4 mi by B 5109 and minor roads. Plas Newydd★ **AC**, SW : 7 mi by A 545 and A 4080

Ye Olde Bull's Head Inn
Castle St ✉ LL58 8AP – ✆ (01248) 810 329 – www.bullsheadinn.co.uk – Closed 24-25 December
26 rm – †£ 85/90 ††£ 105/175
Rest *Brasserie* Rest *Loft* – see restaurant listing
Characterful 1670s coaching inn with a vast inglenook fireplace in the lounge. Bedrooms in the main house are traditional and named after Dickens' characters; those in the adjacent townhouse are more colourful and contemporary.

Cleifiog without rest
Townsend ✉ LL58 8BH – ✆ (01248) 811 507 – www.cleifiogbandb.co.uk – Closed Christmas-early January
3 rm – †£ 60/80 ††£ 90/110
Delightful seafront guesthouse overlooking the mountains and the Menai Strait; run by a welcoming owner. Watercolours hang on wood-panelled walls in the cosy, antique-furnished lounge. Comfortable bedrooms have fine linens and large bathrooms. Excellent communal breakfasts feature tasty fresh juices.

Churchbank Ⓝ without rest
28 Church St ✉ LL58 8AB – ✆ (01248) 810 353 – www.bedandbreakfastanglesey.com
3 rm – †£ 55/65 ††£ 75/85
Georgian guesthouse with a homely, antique-furnished interior and modern day comforts. Cosy bedrooms look out over the large walled garden and the church opposite; one has a private bathroom. Helpful, amiable owner and hearty breakfasts.

Loft – Ye Olde Bull's Head Inn Hotel
Castle St ✉ LL58 8AP – ✆ (01248) 810 329 – www.bullsheadinn.co.uk – Closed 25-26 December, 1 January, Sunday and Monday
Rest – *(dinner only)* Menu £ 43
Formal restaurant housed under the eaves of an old coaching inn, with a plush, open-fired lounge and an elegant dining room with exposed beams and immaculately laid candlelit tables. Ambitious dishes feature lots of different ingredients.

Cennin
13 Castle St ✉ LL58 8AP – ✆ (01248) 811 230 – www.restaurantcennin.com – Closed 25-26 December, Tuesday dinner in winter, Sunday dinner and Monday
Rest – *(dinner only and Sunday lunch)* Carte £ 32/43
First floor neighbourhood restaurant above a deli and café; its name is Welsh for 'leeks'. The chef is from the island and champions seasonal, local produce; meat comes from the owners farms and includes the signature Welsh Black beef.

Brasserie – Ye Olde Bull's Head Inn Hotel
Castle St ✉ LL58 8AP – ✆ (01248) 810 329 – www.bullsheadinn.co.uk – Closed 25-26 December and dinner 1 January
Rest – *(bookings not accepted)* Carte £ 23/34
Large brasserie in the old stables of a charming 17C coaching inn, overlooking a courtyard. It has a Welsh slate floor, a fireplace built from local stone and a relaxed, modern feel. The international menu features lots of daily specials.

LLANERCHYMEDD – Isle of Anglesey – ✉ Isle Of Anglesey 32 B1

Llwydiarth Fawr without rest
North : 1 mi on B 5111 ✉ LL71 8DF – ✆ (01248) 470 321 – www.llwydiarthfawr.com
4 rm – †£ 45/65 ††£ 85
Lovely Georgian house surrounded by 1,000 acres of farmland. Well-kept interior with an impressive hallway and an open-fired drawing room. Bedrooms are classically furnished, with smart wallpapers and colourful throws adding a modern edge.

LLANGAFFO – Isle of Anglesey – ✉ 32 B1

Outbuildings Ⓝ
Bodowyr Farmhouse, Southeast : 1.5 mi by B 4419 turning left at crossroads and left again by post box. ✉ LL60 6NH – ✆ (01248) 430 132 – www.theoutbuildings.co.uk
5 rm – †£ 75 ††£ 90 **Rest** – Menu £ 30
Tastefully converted former granary, offering fantastic views over Snowdonia. Have afternoon tea in the cosy, open-fired lounge. Stylish, modern bedrooms come with local artwork and smart bathrooms; for a romantic hideaway, choose the Pink Hut. The large dining room offers simple three course dinners.

MENAI BRIDGE – Isle of Anglesey – ✉ Isle Of Anglesey 32 B1

Plas Rhianfa Ⓝ
Glyn Garth, East : 1 mi on A 545 ✉ LL59 5NS – ✆ (01248) 713 656 – www.plasrhianfa.com
16 rm – †£ 130/150 ††£ 130/200 **Rest** – Menu £ 22/36
Built in 1849 and a smaller copy of the Château de Chenonceau. Formal gardens lead down to the Menai Strait and boast fantastic views over Snowdonia. The striking Victorian interior displays original wood panelling, stained glass and turrets, which contrast with bold modern colour schemes. Formal dining.

Neuadd Lwyd
Penmynydd, Northwest : 4.75 mi by B 5420 on Eglwys St Gredifael Church rd ✉ LL61 5BX – ✆ (01248) 715 005 – www.neuaddlwyd.co.uk – Closed 30 November-20 January
4 rm – †£ 130/180 ††£ 150/200 **Rest** – Menu £ 42
Carefully restored former Victorian rectory with an impressive easterly panorama of countryside and mountains; now a stylish and personally run country house. Comfortable, beautifully furnished lounge and luxurious, individually appointed bedrooms. Dinner here is a special event and makes good use of seasonal, local produce. Breakfast is equally as tasty.

Sosban & The Old Butchers Ⓝ
Trinity House, 1A High St ✉ LL59 5EE – ✆ (01248) 208 131 – www.sosbanandtheoldbutchers.com – Closed January-mid February, Christmas-New Year and Sunday-Wednesday
Rest – *(dinner only) (booking essential) (surprise menu only)* Menu £ 39
Brightly painted restaurant with smart awnings; inside, one wall displays the Welsh slate and hand-painted tiles from its days as a butcher's shop. A well-balanced, four course surprise menu offers boldly flavoured, carefully cooked dishes.

Dylan's Ⓝ
St George's Rd ✉ LL59 5DE – ✆ (01248) 716 714 – www.dylansrestaurant.co.uk – Closed 25-26 December
Rest – *(bookings advisable at dinner)* Carte £ 19/39
An old boat yard timber store; now a smart, busy, two-storey eatery by the water's edge, overlooking Bangor. Extensive menus offer everything from homemade cakes and weekend brunch to sourdough pizzas. Find a spot on the terrace if you can.

RHOSCOLYN – **Isle of Anglesey** – ✉ **Isle Of Anglesey**

White Eagle

✉ *LL65 2NJ* – ✆ *(01407) 860 267* – *www.white-eagle.co.uk*
Rest – Carte £ 21/39
Spacious pub with cosy bar, modern dining room, decked terrace and stunning sea views. Monthly menu offers everything from sandwiches and salads to pub classics and more sophisticated fare.

VALLEY – **Isle of Anglesey** – ✉ **Isle Of Anglesey**

Cleifiog Uchaf

off Spencer Rd ✉ *LL65 3AB* – ✆ *(01407) 741 888* – *www.cleifoguchaf.co.uk*
8 rm – †£ 45/72 ††£ 85/125
Rest – *(closed Sunday-Wednesday) (dinner only)* Carte £ 22/40
Smartly restored 16C longhouse, looking towards Holyhead and ideally situated for walking the coastal path. Stylish bedrooms come with character beds and good mod cons; the best are the ground floor suites. The slate-floored, bistro-style dining room offers unfussy, classically based dishes of local produce.

BALA – **Gwynedd** – **503** J25 – **pop. 1 980** – ✉ **Gwynedd** **32** B2

London - 213 mi – Cardiff 160 mi – Liverpool 75 mi – Stoke-on-Trent 84 mi

Abercelyn Country House without rest

Llanycil, Southwest : 1 mi on A 494 ✉ *LL23 7YF* – ✆ *(01678) 521 109*
– *www.abercelyn.co.uk* – *February-October*
3 rm – †£ 53/60 ††£ 70/90
Attractive former rectory with a brook running through the pleasant garden. Period charm blends with modern touches and up-to-date facilities; bedrooms are warmly decorated bedrooms and the lounge is cosy. The owner knows the Fells well.

BEAUMARIS – **504** H24 – **see Anglesey (Isle of)**

BEDDGELERT (Bedkelerd) – **Gwynedd** – **502** H24 – **pop. 535** **32** B1

London 249 mi – Caernarfon 13 mi – Chester 73 mi

Snowdonia National Park★★★ - Aberglaslyn Pass★, S : 1.5 mi on A 498

Sygun Fawr Country House

Northeast : 0.75 mi by A 498 ✉ *LL55 4NE* – ✆ *(01766) 890 258*
– *www.sygunfawr.co.uk* – *Closed 3 January-10 February and 16-27 December*
12 rm – †£ 60 ††£ 82/107
Rest – *(closed Monday and Thursday to non-residents) (dinner only) (booking essential)* Carte £ 20/27
Part-16C stone house, halfway up a mountain and boasting views over the valley. Charming open-fired interior with a snug sitting room and a spacious conservatory. Good-sized bedrooms have a cosy, homely feel. Traditional dining room serves hearty, regional dishes; Mon and Thurs they offer simpler suppers.

BENLLECH – **502** H24 – **see Anglesey (Isle of)**

BETWS GARMON – **Gwynedd** **32** B1

London 249 mi – Cardiff 168 mi – Birmingham 135 mi – Sheffield 154 mi

Betws Inn

Northwest : 1 mi on A 4085 ✉ *LL54 7YY* – ✆ *(01286) 650 324*
– *www.betws-inn.co.uk*
3 rm – †£ 60/80 ††£ 65/85 **Rest** – Menu £ 28 **s**
Rustic former coaching inn surrounded by the towering mountains of Snowdonia. Superb inglenook fireplace on display in the cosy lounge; exposed stone walls and a pine dresser in the breakfast room. Warm, beamed bedrooms boast half-tester or four-poster beds and modern bathrooms – one is on two levels. Home-cooked meals showcase local produce and lamb features highly.

WALES

BETWS-Y-COED - Conwy - 502 I24 - pop. 848 32 B1

London 226 mi - Holyhead 44 mi - Shrewsbury 62 mi

Royal Oak Stables, ✆(01690) 71 04 26, www.betws-y-coed.co.uk

Clubhouse, ✆(01690) 71 05 56

Town★

Snowdonia National Park★★★. Blaenau Ffestiniog★ (Llechwedd Slate Caverns★ **AC**), SW : 10.5 mi by A 470 - The Glyders and Nant Ffrancon (Cwm Idwal★), W : 14 mi by A 5

Tan-y-Foel Country House

East : 2.5 mi by A 5, A 470 and Capel Garmon rd on Llanwrst rd ✉ LL26 ORE - ✆(01690) 710 507 - www.tyfhotel.co.uk - Closed Christmas-New Year, restricted opening January

6 rm - †£ 99/145 ††£ 125/245

Rest - *(closed Sunday and Monday) (dinner only) (booking essential)*
Menu 50

Personally run, part-16C country house in 4 acres of grounds, affording stunning views over the Vale of Conwy and Snowdonia. The snug lounge and breakfast room display traditional features. Modern, individually styled bedrooms have smart bathrooms; the spacious loft room has a vaulted ceiling. Much of the produce used at dinner is grown in the owners' greenhouse.

Pengwern without rest

Allt Dinas, Southeast : 1.5 mi on A 5 ✉ LL24 0HF - ✆(01690) 710 480 - www.snowdoniaaccommodation.co.uk - Closed 19 December-2 January

3 rm - †£ 55/67 ††£ 70/82

Cosy Victorian house with stunning mountain and valley views. Warm, well-proportioned bedrooms are named after famous artists and retain charming original features like the old fireplaces. Comfy lounge. Communal breakfasts.

Bryn Bella without rest

Lôn Muriau, Llanrwst Rd, Northeast : 1 mi by A 5 on A 470 ✉ LL24 0HD - ✆(01690) 710 627 - www.bryn-bella.co.uk

5 rm - †£ 70/80 ††£ 75/85

Comfy, well-kept guesthouse with a pleasant garden, valley views and every conceivable extra in the bedrooms. Keen, friendly owners provide reliable local info. Hearty cooked breakfasts feature fresh, tasty eggs from their rescued hens.

at Penmachno Southwest : 4.75 mi by A 5 on B 4406 - ✉ Betws-Y-Coed

Penmachno Hall

on Ty Mawr rd ✉ LL24 0PU - ✆(01690) 760 410 - www.penmachnohall.co.uk - Closed Christmas-New Year

3 rm - †£ 75/100 ††£ 90/100 **Rest** - Menu £ 18/38

Former rectory built in 1862, set in a pleasant valley location and boasting delightful views. Breakfast-cum-sitting room filled with books; eclectic art collection and lovely mature gardens. Boldly coloured bedrooms, personally decorated by the friendly owners, contain a host of thoughtful extras. Traditional menus, with 2 courses on weekdays and 5 on Saturdays.

BETWS-YN-RHOS - Conwy - 502 J24 - see Abergele

BODUAN - Gwynedd - see Pwllheli

BRECHFA - Carmarthenshire - 503 H28 33 B3

London 216 mi - Cardiff 71 mi - Birmingham 183 mi - Liverpool 164 mi

Ty Mawr Country

✉ SA32 7RA - ✆(01267) 202 332 - www.wales-country-hotel.co.uk

6 rm - †£ 70/75 ††£ 115/130

Rest - *(dinner only) (booking essential)* Menu £ 24

16C stone-built farmhouse, set in the centre of the village next to the river. It's personally run and boasts charm and character aplenty, with exposed bricks, wooden beams, open fires, a comfy lounge and pine-furnished bedrooms. The modern menu has Welsh twists and produce is homemade or from the valley.

BRECON – Powys – **503** J28 – **pop. 7 901** **33** C3

London 171 mi – Cardiff 40 mi – Carmarthen 31 mi – Gloucester 65 mi

Cattle Market Car Park, (01874) 62 24 85, www.breconbeacons.org

Cradoc, Penoyre Park, (01874) 62 36 58

Newton Park, Llanfaes, (01874) 62 20 04

Town★ - Cathedral★ **AC** – Penyclawdd Court★

Brecon Beacons National Park★★. Llanthony Priory★★, S : 8 mi of Hay-on-Wye by B 4423 - Dan-yr-Ogof Showcaves★ **AC**, SW : 20 mi by A 40 and A 4067 – Pen-y-Fan★★, SW : by A 470

Peterstone Court

rest,

Brecon Rd, Llanhamlach, Southeast : 4 mi by B 4601 on A 40 LD3 7YB – (01874) 665 387 – www.peterstone-court.com

12 rm – £ 100/145 £ 100/225 **Rest** – Menu £ 15/23 – Carte £ 26/41

Large Georgian house with a lovely mountain backdrop. Two comfy, characterful lounges. Sizeable, traditional bedrooms in the main house; those in the old stables are duplex-style. Two-roomed restaurant has lovely views and a terrace overlooking the swimming pool; extensive, classical menus of local produce.

Felin Glais

Aberyscir, West : 4 mi by Cradoc rd turning right immediately after bridge LD3 9NP – (01874) 623 107 – www.felinglais.co.uk – Closed 25 December

4 rm – £ 85/95 £ 85/95 **Rest** – Menu £ 40 **s**

17C stone barn and mill, set in a tranquil hamlet and run with pride. Spacious interior has a pleasant 'lived in' feel; cosy, homely bedrooms have toiletries and linen from Harrods. Large beamed lounge; dine here, at the communal table, or in the conservatory in summer. Lengthy menu – order two days ahead.

Felin Fach Griffin with rm

Felin Fach, Northeast : 4.75 mi by B 4602 off A 470 LD3 0UB – (01874) 620 111 – www.felinfachgriffin.co.uk – Closed 24-25 December and early January

7 rm – £ 75/100 £ 115/160 **Rest** – Menu £ 21/28 – Carte £ 26/34

Set in picturesque countryside; a rather unique pub with bright paintwork, colourful art and an extremely laid back atmosphere. Following the motto "simple things, done well", the attractively presented dishes are straightforward, tasty and refined. Pleasant bedrooms come with comfy beds but no TVs.

BRIDGEND (Pen-y-Bont) – **Bridgend** – **503** J29 – **pop. 39 429** **33** B4

London 177 mi – Cardiff 20 mi – Swansea 23 mi

Bridgend Designer Outlet Village, (01656) 65 49 06, www.bridgend.gov.uk

Great House

High St, Laleston, West : 2 mi on A 473 CF32 0HP – (01656) 657 644 – www.great-house-laleston.co.uk

12 rm – £ 85/110 £ 125/150

Rest *Leicester's* – *(closed Sunday dinner and bank holidays)* Menu £ 20 (lunch and early dinner) – Carte £ 22/49

Welcoming 15C, Grade II listed property; the home of the Lordship of Laleston and reputedly a gift from Elizabeth I to the Earl of Leicester. Characterful bar and lounge. Individually styled bedrooms with extras; those in the coach house are most modern. Restaurant offers a seasonal menu of regional produce.

BUILTH WELLS (Llanfair-ym-Muallt) – **Powys** – **503** J27 **33** C3
– **pop. 2 640**

London 191 mi – Cardiff 63 mi – Brecon 20 mi – Swansea 58 mi

Rhedyn

Cilmery, West : 4 mi on A 483 LD2 3LH – (01982) 551 944 – www.rhedynguesthouse.co.uk

3 rm – £ 80 £ 90 **Rest** – Menu £ 28

Former forester's cottage with a small garden and pleasant country views, run by very welcoming owners. Tiny lounge with a bookcase full of local info and DVDs; cosy communal dining room where home-cooked, local market produce is served. Good-sized, modern bedrooms feature heavy wood furnishings, good facilities and quirky touches. Tea and cake are served on arrival.

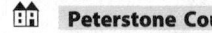

BWLCHTOCYN - Gwynedd - 502 G25 - see Abersoch

CAERNARFON - Gwynedd - 502 H24 - pop. 10 134 32 B1

London 249 mi - Birkenhead 76 mi - Chester 68 mi - Holyhead 30 mi

Castle St., (01286) 67 22 32, www.caernarfononline.co.uk

Aberforeshore, Llanfaglan, (01286) 67 37 83

Town★★ - Castle★★★ **AC**

Snowdonia National Park★★★

Plas Dinas

South : 2.5 mi on A 487 ✉ LL54 7YF – (01286) 830 214 – www.plasdinas.co.uk – Closed Christmas and New Year

9 rm – £ 99/199 £ 99/275

Rest – *(closed Sunday and Monday) (dinner only) (residents only)* Menu £ 30

Former family home of Lord Snowdon, set in large gardens and filled with antiques, historical documents and family portraits. Spacious drawing room with an open fire and a piano. Smart bedrooms boast designer touches and immaculate bathrooms. Concise menu of unfussy, hearty dishes in the simple dining room.

at Seion Northeast : 5.5 mi by A 4086 and B 4366 on Seion rd – ✉ Gwynedd

Ty'n Rhos Country House

Southwest : 0.75 mi ✉ LL55 3AE – (01248) 670 489 – www.tynrhos.co.uk

19 rm – £ 70/80 £ 85/165

Rest – *(dinner only and Sunday lunch)* Menu £ 38

Personally run former farmhouse with a large conservatory and a cosy lounge with an inglenook fireplace. Comfortable, modern bedrooms; some have balconies or terraces and others, their own garden. The formal restaurant offers pleasant views over Anglesey; classically based dishes are presented in modern ways.

at Dolydd South : 3.5 mi by A 487

Y Goeden Eirin

✉ LL54 7EF – (01286) 830 942 – www.ygoedeneirin.co.uk – Closed Christmas-New Year

3 rm – £ 60/75 £ 80/90 **Rest** – Menu £ 28

Cosy stone cottage with interesting furniture, eclectic artwork and a slightly bohemian feel. The bedroom in the main house has views of both the mountains and the sea; bedrooms in the old outbuildings have slate floors, stable doors and small kitchen areas. Tasty home-cooked breakfasts.

at Llanrug East : 3 mi on A 4086 – ✉ Caernarfon

Seiont Manor N

✉ LL55 2AQ – (01286) 673 366 – www.handpickedhotels.co.uk

28 rm – £ 75/185 £ 95/265 **Rest** – Menu £ 25/37

Small manor house in a peaceful location; follow the nature trails or fish on the river in the 150 acre grounds. Spacious, modern country bedrooms – some with Juliet balconies or terraces. Have afternoon tea in one of the lounges, a light meal in the conservatory or modern classics in the formal restaurant.

CARDIFF

See city maps on following pages **33** C4

© Chris Warren/Sime/Photononstop

Cardiff – **pop. 322 192** – **503** K29 – Wales

London 155 mi – Birmingham 110 mi – Bristol 46 mi – Coventry 124 mi

Tourist Information

The Old Library, The Hayes, Working St, ✆(0870) 1 21 12 58, www.visitcardiff.com

Airport

Cardiff (Wales) Airport : ✆ (01446) 711111, SW : 8 m. by A 48 AX

Golf Courses

Dinas Powis, Old Highwalls, ✆(029) 2051 27 27

SIGHTS

In the town : City★★★ • National Museum and Gallery★★★ **AC** BY • Castle★ **AC** BZ • Llandaff Cathedral★ AV**B** • Cardiff Bay★ (Techniquest★ **AC**) AX

On the outskirts : Museum of Welsh Life★★ **AC**, St Fagan's, W : 5 mi by A 4161 AV • Castell Coch★★ **AC**, NW : 5 mi by A 470 AV

In the surrounding area : Caerphilly Castle★★ **AC**, N : 7 mi by A 469 AV • Dyffryn Gardens★ **AC**, W : 8 mi by A 48 AX

St David's H. & Spa

Havannah St, Cardiff Bay ✉ *CF10 5SD* – ✆ *(02920) 454 045* – *www.principal-hayley.com/thestdavids* CU**a**

142 rm – †£ 85/748 ††£ 95/748 – 12 suites

Rest ***Tempus at Tides*** – Carte £ 25/45

Modern, purpose-built hotel on the waterfront, affording lovely 360° views. Good-sized, minimalist bedrooms have a slightly funky feel; all boast balconies and bay outlooks. Smart spa features seawater pools and a dry floatation tank. Stylish restaurant with superb terrace views serves modern British dishes.

Hilton Cardiff

Kingsway ✉ *CF10 3HH* – ✆ *(029) 2064 6300* – *www.hilton.com/cardiff*

197 rm – †£ 119/149 ††£ 129/159 – 4 suites BZ**x**

Rest ***Razzi*** – Menu £ 13 (lunch) – Carte dinner £ 21/52

Imposing former tax office in the city centre, with excellent views of the castle, law courts and city hall. Large atrium; well-equipped function rooms and leisure club. Spacious bedrooms are a touch functional – some have great outlooks. Conservatory-style restaurant offers a Mediterranean-influenced menu.

CARDIFF

Atlas Rd . . . . AX 3
Barry Rd . . . . AX 4
Bridge Rd . . . . AV 5
Cathedral Rd . . . . AVX 7
Clarence Rd . . . . AX 16
Cogan Hill . . . . AX 18
Cowbridge Rd West . . AX 22
James St. . . . . AX 33
Kelston Rd. . . . . AV 35
Llandennis Rd . . . . AV 37
Merthyr Rd . . . . AV 41
Ninian Park Rd . . . . AX 48
Penhill Rd . . . . AV 51
Penline Rd. . . . . AV 52
Pen-y-Land Rd . . . . AV 53
St Fagans Rd . . . . AV 57
Tyn-y-Parc Rd . . . . AV 65
Ty-Wern Rd. . . . . AV 64
Wellington St . . . . AX 66

Park Plaza

Greyfriars Rd ✉ *CF10 3AL – ✆ (029) 20 111 111 – www.parkplazacardiff.com – Closed 25-26 December* BYs

129 rm – †£ 89/210 ††£ 89/280, ☕ £ 13

Rest ***Laguna Kitchen and Bar*** – ✆ (029) 2011 1103 – Menu £ 10/13 – Carte £ 21/38

Formerly municipal offices, now a light, airy hotel with a stylish lounge, extensive conference facilities and a vast leisure centre boasting a smart, stainless steel pool and 8 treatment rooms. Stark, modern bedrooms have laptop safes and slate bathrooms. Informal brasserie serves international dishes.

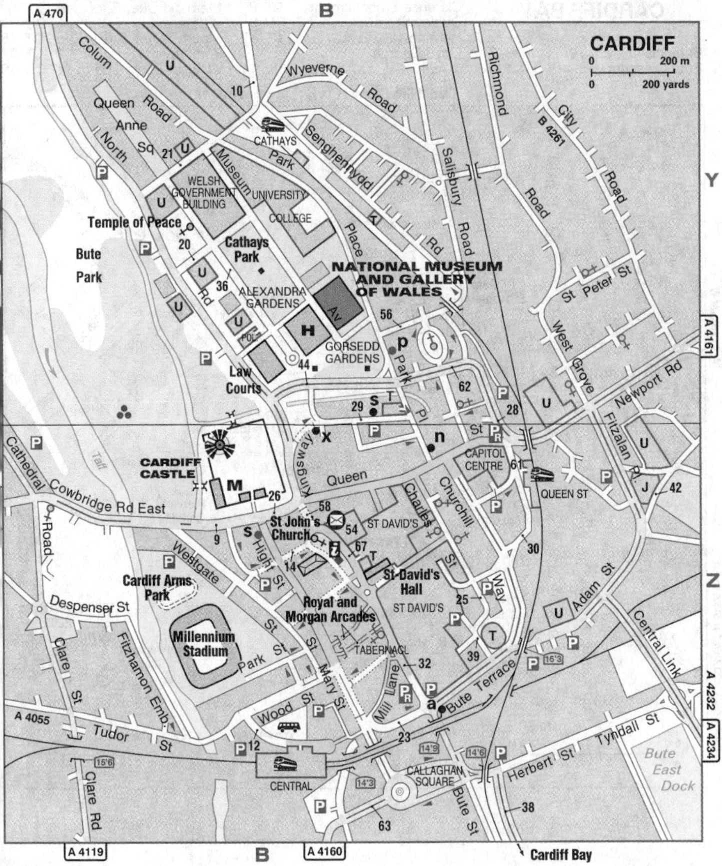

Radisson Blu Cardiff

Meridian Gate, Bute Terr. ✉ *CF10 2FL* – ✆ *(029) 2045 4777* – *www.radissonblu.com/hotel-cardiff* BZ**a**

215 rm – †£ 79/169 ††£ 89/179

Rest *Filini* – *(closed Sunday) (dinner only)* Menu £ 23 – Carte £ 19/46

Large glass building in great central location. Spacious, modern guest areas, excellent meeting facilities and smart bar. Modern, slightly minimalist bedrooms in three styles – Fresh, Fashion and Chic – all boast slate-tiled bathrooms and city views. Simply furnished restaurant offers accessible Italian menu.

WALES

CARDIFF BAY

Britannia Quay . . . . **CU** 2
Bute Crescent . . . . **CT** 4
Clarence Embankment . . . **CT** 8
Dudley St . . . . **CU** 9
Hemingway Rd. . . . . **CT** 12
Lloyd George Ave . . . . **CT** 14
Mermaid Quay Shopping Centre. . . . . **CU**
Mount Stuart Square . . . . **CT** 15
Pomeroy St. . . . . **CT** 17
Windsor Esplanade . . . . . **CU** 19

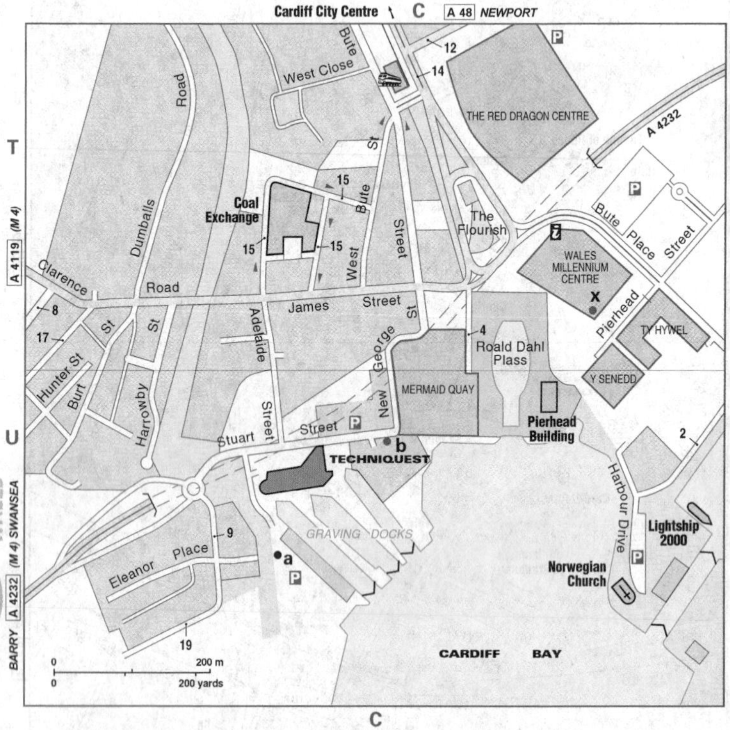

Parc

Park Pl ✉ CF10 3UD – ✆ (0871) 376 9011 – www.thistle.com/theparchotel
140 rm – £ 69/109 £ 69/129 – 1 suite BZ**n**
Rest *Social* – ✆ (029) 2078 5593 – Menu £ 20 – Carte £ 22/31
Centrally located, commercial hotel with striking décor; hidden behind a classic Victorian façade. Marble-tiled lobby and fashionable bar. Stylish, contemporary bedrooms feature bright white décor and offer good facilities; those to the rear are quieter. Accessible menus in smart restaurant.

Lincoln House without rest

118-120 Cathedral Rd ✉ CF11 9LQ – ✆ (029) 2039 5558 – www.lincolnhotel.co.uk AV**e**
24 rm – £ 70/125 £ 90/150
Two lovingly restored Victorian houses on the main road into town: family owned and run, with a classic style and contemporary touches. Bedrooms offer a high level of facilities; some feature four-posters and those to the rear are quieter.

Park House N

20 Park Pl. ✉ CF10 3DQ – ✆ (029) 2022 4343 – www.parkhouseclub.com – Closed 25-26 December, 1 January, Sunday and Monday BY**p**
Rest – Menu £ 21 (lunch) – Carte £ 43/46
Striking building designed by William Burgess in the late 1800s, set overlooking Gorsedd Gardens. The oak-panelled dining room has a formal air. Menus are modern – each dish is matched with a wine from the impressive New World list.

XX **Purple Poppadom** Ⓝ

185a Cowbridge Rd East ✉ CF11 9AJ – ✆ (029) 2022 0026 – www.purplepoppadom.com – Closed 25-26 December and 1 January

Rest – Menu £ 14/40 – Carte £ 18/34 AX**n**

Smart, modern, first floor Indian restaurant with bold purple décor. Classic combinations are cooked in a modern style and given a personal twist; dishes are refined and flavoursome, with seafood being particularly popular.

X **Woods Brasserie**

The Pilotage Building, Stuart St, Cardiff Bay ✉ CF10 5BW – ✆ (029) 2049 2400 – www.knifeandforkfood.co.uk/woods – Closed 25-26 December, bank holidays and Sunday dinner September-April CU**b**

Rest – *(booking essential at dinner)* Menu £ 17 (weekdays)/35 – Carte £ 18/44

An extended, stone-built former river pilots' building featuring a bright, contemporary conservatory dining room and a popular first floor terrace with views over Cardiff Bay. Constantly evolving menus offer unfussy modern brasserie dishes.

X **'Bully's**

5 Romilly Cres. ✉ CF11 9NP – ✆ (029) 2022 1905 – www.bullysrestaurant.co.uk – Closed Sunday dinner, Monday and Tuesday AX**x**

Rest – Menu £ 10 (weekday lunch) – Carte £ 24/44

Welcoming neighbourhood bistro run by a passionate, hands-on owner. Simply furnished interior boasts a fascinating array of memorabilia. Classical cooking displays a strong Gallic edge; carefully prepared dishes feature quality ingredients.

X **Potted Pig** Ⓝ

27 High St ✉ CF10 1PU – ✆ (029) 2022 4817 – www.thepottedpig.com – Closed 23 December-3 January and Monday BZ**s**

Rest – Menu £ 12 (weekday lunch) – Carte £ 20/44

Atmospheric restaurant in a stripped back former bank vault, with brick walls, barrel ceilings and a utilitarian feel. Lesser-known products and cuts of meat used in robust, tasty dishes. Pork is popular and gin cocktails, a speciality.

WALES

X **Mint & Mustard**

134 Whitchurch Rd ✉ CF14 3LZ – ✆ (029) 2062 0333 – www.mintandmustard.com – Closed 25-26 December AV**n**

Rest – *(booking essential at dinner)* Menu £ 38 – Carte £ 16/32

A well-run, welcoming neighbourhood Indian restaurant with a modern, laid-back feel; try to get a table in the front room. The chef's training in Kerala is reflected in the extensive menu of original, authentic dishes with well-balanced spicing.

X **La Cuina** Ⓝ

11 Kings Rd ✉ CF11 9BZ – ✆ (029) 2019 0265 – www.lacuina.co.uk – Closed 25-27 December, Sunday and Monday AX**v**

Rest – Menu £ 28 (dinner) – Carte £ 14/25

A smart, well-stocked ground floor deli sells top quality Spanish produce; the simple, rustic upstairs restaurant serves authentic, flavourful Spanish dishes with strong Catalonian influences. Tapas at lunch and on Tues/Weds evenings.

X **Ffresh**

Wales Millennium Centre, Bute Plas, Cardiff Bay ✉ CF10 5AL – ✆ (029) 2063 6465 – www.ffresh.org.uk – Closed 25 December, Mondays in low season and Sunday dinner CT**x**

Rest – Menu £ 17 (lunch and early dinner) – Carte £ 22/47

Located within the striking, modern 'Wales Millennium Centre', overlooking the piazza and frequented by theatregoers. Large, airy interior with a relaxed atmosphere. Simple, classical cooking is founded on fresh Welsh ingredients.

The Conway

53 Conway Rd ✉ CF11 9NW – ✆ (029) 20 224 373 – www.knifeandforkfood.co.uk/conway AV**a**

Rest – Carte £ 20/30

Pleasant neighbourhood pub offering everything from a pint and a bowl of chips over the rugby to a full 3 course meal with wine. A pleasingly simple approach to food sees foraged and local allotment produce showcased in tasty pub classics.

CARMARTHEN - Carmarthenshire - 503 H28 - pop. 14 648 33 B3

London 219 mi - Fishguard 47 mi - Haverfordwest 32 mi - Swansea 27 mi

113 Lammas St, (01267) 23 15 57, www.visitcarmarthenshire.co.uk

Kidwelly Castle★ - National Botanic Garden★

at Felingwm Uchaf Northeast : 8 mi by A 40 on B 4310 - Carmarthen

Allt y Golau Uchaf without rest

North : 0.5 mi on B 4310 SA32 7BB - (01267) 290 455 - www.alltygolau.com - Closed 20 December-2 January

3 rm - £ 45 £ 70

Converted farmhouse dating from 1812, set up a steep slope on a two acre smallholding. Well-kept, rustic interior; the neat, pine-furnished bedrooms have a homely feel. Extensive breakfasts feature local meats and eggs from their own hens.

at Llanllawddog Northeast : 8 mi by A485

Glangwili Mansion without rest

SA32 7JE - (01267) 253 735 - www.glangwilimansion.co.uk - Closed 24-25 December

4 rm - £ 100/120 £ 115/135

Part-17C mansion rebuilt in a Georgian style, set in a great location on the edge of the forest. The spacious interior features sleek tiled floors, contemporary artwork, an airy lounge and bright, bold bedrooms with modern oak furnishings.

at Nantgaredig East : 5 mi by A 4300 on A 4310 - Carmarthen

WALES

Y Polyn

South : 1 mi on B 4310 SA32 7LH - (01267) 290 000 - www.ypolynrestaurant.co.uk - Closed Sunday dinner and Monday

Rest - *(booking advisable)* Menu £ 40 (dinner) - Carte lunch £ 21/30

Welcoming dining pub in a great rural location by a stream. Hearty, wholesome dishes are classically based with modern touches. À la carte or 'express' lunch and fixed price dinners.

COLWYN BAY (Bae Colwyn) - Conwy - 502 I24 - pop. 30 269 32 B1

London 237 mi - Birkenhead 50 mi - Chester 42 mi - Holyhead 41 mi

Information Point, Cayley Promenade, Rhos-on-Sea, (01492) 54 87 78, www.ukinformationcentre.com/north-wales

18 Abergele, Tan-y-Goppa Rd, (01745) 82 40 34

9 Old Colwyn, Woodland Ave, (01492) 51 55 81

Welsh Mountain Zoo★ **AC** (<★)

Bodnant Garden★★ **AC**, SW : 6 mi by A 55 and A 470

Pen-y-Bryn

Pen-y-Bryn Rd, Upper Colwyn Bay, Southwest : 1 mi by B 5113 LL29 6DD - (01492) 533 360 - www.penybryn-colwynbay.co.uk - Closed dinner 26 December and 1 January

Rest - Carte £ 22/37

Modern, laid-back pub set on a residential street; its unassuming façade concealing impressive bay views. Extensive all-day menu ranges from pub classics to more adventurous fare.

at Rhos-on-Sea Northwest : 1 mi - Colwyn Bay

Plas Rhos House without rest

53 Cayley Promenade LL28 4EP - (01492) 543 698 - www.plasrhos.co.uk - April-October

5 rm - £ 58/75 £ 80/110

Smartly refurbished 19C house with a pleasant terrace, on a small street overlooking the sea. Cosy lounge and bright, cheery breakfast room. Bedrooms have modern bathrooms and thoughtful extras such as chocolates and a decanter of sherry.

CONWY – Conwy – **502** I24 – **pop. 3 847** **32** B1

🚆 London 241 mi – Caernarfon 22 mi – Chester 46 mi – Holyhead 37 mi

🛈 Conwy Castle Visitor Centre, 𝒞 (01492) 59 22 48,
www.touristnetuk.com/wa/northwales

🖸 Penmaenmawr, Conway Old Rd, 𝒞 (01492) 62 33 30

◉ Town★★ - Castle★★ **AC** – Town Walls★★ - Plas Mawr★★

◎ Snowdonia National Park★★★ – Bodnant Garden★★ **AC**, S : 8 mi by A 55 and A
470 – Conwy Crossing (suspension bridge★)

🏨 Castle 📶 🛜 ♨ P

High St ⊠ LL32 8DB – 𝒞 (01492) 582 800 – www.castlewales.co.uk
28 rm 🛏 – ✚£ 70/95 ✚✚£ 120/250 – 1 suite
Rest *Dawson's* – Carte £ 24/40
Friendly, family-run former coaching inn whose distinctive granite and red-brick
façade, added in the late 19C, gives it a Victorian appearance. Bedrooms vary in
style; some have a country house feel, while others are more modern. Wide-ranging menu available in both the restaurant and the cosy bar-lounge.

✗✗ Signatures 🛜 P

*Aberconwy Resort and Spa, Northwest 1.5 mi by A 547 ⊠ LL32 8GA – 𝒞 (01492)
583 513 – www.signaturesrestaurant.co.uk – Closed Monday and Tuesday*
Rest – (dinner only) (booking advisable) Menu £ 22 – Carte £ 33/41
Stylish, contemporary restaurant with elegantly laid tables and a well-versed
team; unusually set in a holiday park close to the sea. Menus showcase classically
based dishes with a modern edge; several are marked out as 'signature' dishes.

🏚 Groes Inn with rm ≤ 🚗 🛜 🛜 ♨ P

South : 3 mi on B 5106 ⊠ LL32 8TN – 𝒞 (01492) 650 545 – www.groesinn.com
14 rm 🛏 – ✚£ 100/200 ✚✚£ 130/230 **Rest** – Carte £ 19/36
Characterful inn, beautifully set overlooking the estuary, in the foothills of Snowdonia. Local Welsh and British dishes arrive in neat, generous portions; more adventurous restaurant menu. Tastefully styled bedrooms boast views; some have
terraces and balconies.

at Rowen South : 3.5 mi by B 5106

🏠 Tir Y Coed 🐾 🚗 P

⊠ LL32 8TP – 𝒞 (01492) 650 219 – www.tirycoed.com
7 rm (dinner included) 🛏 – ✚£ 189/238 ✚✚£ 209/258
Rest – (dinner only) (bookings essential for non-residents) Carte £ 29/39
Late 19C house in a secluded valley at the foothills of Snowdonia. With mature
gardens which are a haven for wildlife, this is an ideal spot for those who have
come away to unwind. Cosy bedrooms feature smart, modern bathrooms. The intimate dining room offers a daily menu of tried-and-tested classics.

CORWEN – Denbighshire – **502** J25 **32** C2

🚆 London 201 mi – Cardiff 148 mi – Liverpool 46 mi – Stoke-on-Trent 65 mi

✗ Bison Grill at Rhug Estate ⓝ 🛜 ♿ 🔲 P

*Rhug Estate Farm Shop, West : 1.5 mi on A 5 ⊠ LL21 0EH – 𝒞 (01490) 411 100
– www.rhug.co.uk – Closed 25 December and 1 January*
Rest – (lunch only) Carte £ 20/40
State-of-the-art farm shop built using local materials and eco-friendly fixtures. The
smart brasserie serves breakfast, snacks and Aberdeen Angus and bison steaks;
you can also purchase organically reared estate meats and Welsh goodies.

COWBRIDGE (Y Bont Faen) – **The Vale of Glamorgan** – **503** J29 **33** B4
– **pop. 3 616**

🚆 London 170 mi – Cardiff 15 mi – Swansea 30 mi

✗✗ Huddarts

*69 High St ⊠ CF71 7AF – 𝒞 (01446) 774 645 – Closed 1 week Christmas-New
Year, 1 week summer, 1 week autumn, Sunday dinner and Monday*
Rest – Menu £ 20 (lunch) – Carte £ 26/34
Honest restaurant in an ancient market town; the husband cooks and the wife
looks after the friendly service. Traditional décor with a stone fireplace and colour-
ful tapestries. Carefully executed, classic dishes with good presentation.

CRICCIETH – Gwynedd – 502 H25 – pop. 1 826 32 B2

London 249 mi – Caernarfon 17 mi – Shrewsbury 85 mi

Ednyfed Hill, ☎ (01766) 52 21 54

Lleyn Peninsula★★ – Ffestiniog Railway★★

Bron Eifion

rest,

West : 1 mi on A 497 ✉ LL52 OSA – ☎ (01766) 522 385 – www.broneifion.co.uk

18 rm – †£ 95/135 ††£ 135/185

Rest *Garden* – Menu £ 20 (weekday lunch) – Carte £ 31/42

Characterful country house built in 1883 for a wealthy slate merchant; the feature staircase is constructed from Oregon pitch pine, which he brought back from the USA. Spacious modern bedrooms; some with carved wooden beds from the Middle East. Lovely garden views and an extensive menu in the restaurant.

CRICKHOWELL (Crucywel) – Powys – 503 K28 – pop. 2 166 33 C4

London 169 mi – Abergavenny 6 mi – Brecon 14 mi – Cardiff 40 mi

Beaufort St, ☎ (01873) 81 19 70, www.crickhowellinfo.org.uk

Brecon Beacons National Park★★. Llanthony Priory★★, NE : 10 mi by minor roads

Gliffaes Country House

West : 3.75 mi by A 40 ✉ NP8 1RH – ☎ (01874) 730 371 – www.gliffaeshotel.com – Closed 2 January-1 February

23 rm – †£ 100 ††£ 112/265 **Rest** – Menu £ 22/42 **s**

Impressive country house built in 1886 in semi-Italianate style, set in 32 acres of delightful grounds that lead down to the river. Spacious, well-appointed lounges and great views from terrace. Smart, individually styled bedrooms; some with balconies. Victorian-style restaurant; menus showcase Welsh produce.

Bear

High St ✉ NP8 1BW – ☎ (01873) 810 408 – www.bearhotel.co.uk

36 rm – †£ 77/129 ††£ 95/167 – 1 suite

Rest *Bear* – see restaurant listing

Well-maintained 15C coaching inn full of nooks and crannies. Comfortable bedrooms, some with jacuzzis; most characterful are in main house and feature beams, four-posters and fireplaces.

Glangrwyney Court without rest

Southeast : 2 mi on A 40 ✉ NP8 1ES – ☎ (01873) 811 288 – www.glancourt.co.uk

8 rm – †£ 75/135 ††£ 90/135

Passionately run country house with Georgian origins, featuring a large lounge and a high-ceilinged breakfast room. Fresh flowers and objets d'art cover every surface. Bedrooms boast rich fabrics, good facilities and country views.

Ty Gwyn without rest

Brecon Rd ✉ NP8 1DG – ☎ (01873) 811 625 – www.tygwyn.com – March-October

3 rm – †£ 40/50 ††£ 68/80

Proudly run whitewashed guesthouse with a stream running through the pretty garden; take it all in from the conservatory breakfast room. Simple, traditionally styled bedrooms. The owners have good local knowledge – one is a certified guide!

Bear

High St ✉ NP8 1BW – ☎ (01873) 810 408 – www.bearhotel.co.uk – Closed 25 December

Rest – *(bookings not accepted)* Carte £ 20/37

Well-maintained 15C coaching inn, adorned with hanging baskets and full of nooks and crannies. Menu offers honest pub classics alongside more elaborate specials. Welcoming staff.

CROSS ASH – Monmouthshire – see Abergavenny

CROSSGATES – Powys – 503 J27 – see Llandrindod Wells

DEGANWY – Conwy – 502 I24 – see Llandudno

DENBIGH – Denbighshire – 502 J24 – pop. 8 272 32 C1

London 215 mi – Cardiff 162 mi – Swansea 151 mi – Telford 70 mi

Castle House without rest

Bull Ln ✉ LL16 3LY – ✆ (01745) 816 860 – www.castlehousebandb.co.uk – Closed Christmas

4 rm – †£ 85 ††£ 140/160

By the ruins of the 16C cathedral, overlooking the Vale of Clwyd; its gardens incorporate the ancient town walls. Spacious bedrooms retain period character and the décor blends the old and new. Afternoon tea by the fire or in the garden.

DINAS CROSS – Pembrokeshire – see Newport (Pembrokeshire)

DOLFOR – Powys – 503 K26 32 C2

London 199 mi – Cardiff 93 mi – Oswestry 34 mi – Ludlow 39 mi

Old Vicarage

North : 1.5 mi by A 483 ✉ SY16 4BN – ✆ (01686) 629 051 – www.theoldvicaragedolfor.co.uk – Closed Christmas-New Year

4 rm – †£ 65/75 ††£ 95/110 **Rest** – Menu £ 25

Extended 19C red-brick house – formerly a vicarage – with large gardens where they grow the produce used in their home-cooked meals. Classical, country house style lounge and dining room. Cosy bedrooms – named after local rivers – mix period furnishings with bright modern colours. Chutney, preserves and soaps are for sale and afternoon tea is served on arrival.

DOLGELLAU – Gwynedd – 502 I25 – pop. 2 407 32 B2

London 221 mi – Birkenhead 72 mi – Chester 64 mi – Shrewsbury 57 mi

Eldon Sq, ✆ (01341) 42 28 88, www.dolgellau-snowdonia.co.uk

Hengwrt Estate, Pencefn Rd, ✆ (01341) 42 26 03

Town★

Snowdonia National Park★★★ - Cadair Idris★★★ - Precipice Walk★, NE : 3 mi on minor roads

Penmaenuchaf Hall

Penmaenpool, West : 1.75 mi on A 493 (Tywyn Rd) ✉ LL40 1YB – ✆ (01341) 422 129 – www.penhall.co.uk – Closed 12-22 December and 4-19 January

14 rm – †£ 118/185 ††£ 174/268 **Rest** – Menu £ 19/43 – Carte £ 35/43

Personally run Victorian house with wood panelling, ornate ceilings and original stained glass windows. Bedrooms cleverly blend the traditional and the modern; some have balconies overlooking the beautiful grounds, mountains and estuary. Friendly staff and a family feel. Formal conservatory dining room.

Ffynnon without rest

Love Ln, (off Cader Rd) ✉ LL40 1RR – ✆ (01341) 421 774 – www.ffynnontownhouse.com

6 rm – †£ 100/215 ††£ 150/215

Spacious Victorian house which once operated as a cottage hospital. Original features and period furnishings abound, offset by stylish modern designs which pay great attention to detail. Keep your wine and snacks in the pantry and dine on homemade crumpets in the morning. They even have an outdoor hot tub.

Y Meirionnydd

Smithfield Sq ✉ LL40 1ES – ✆ (01341) 422 544 – www.themeirionnydd.com

5 rm – †£ 60/75 ††£ 89/135

Rest – *(dinner only) (bookings essential for non-residents)* Menu £ 25

Double-fronted house in the heart of a small town; Gwynedd was known as Meirionnydd up until the 1970s. Simple, modern, homely style with a small bar and a snug basement restaurant. Bedrooms are decorated in subtle hues and have very comfy beds. Hearty breakfasts and traditional dinners with a modern twist.

Tyddyn Mawr without rest
Islawdref, Cader Rd, Southwest : 2.5 mi by Tywyn rd on Cader Idris rd
✉ LL40 1TL – ✆ (01341) 422 331 – www.wales-guesthouse.co.uk – Closed December-January
3 rm – £ 60 £ 80/82
A peaceful haven on a secluded sheep farm; located at the foot of Cader Idris mountain and boasting stunning views. Immaculately kept bedrooms have hand-made Welsh furnishings and plenty of extras; one has a balcony, another, a terrace. Great hospitality. 5 course breakfasts beside the impressive inglenook.

at Llanelltyd Northwest : 2.25 mi by A 470 on A 496

Mawddach
✉ LL40 2TA – ✆ (01341) 424 020 – www.mawddach.com – Closed 2 weeks November, 1 week January, 1 week spring, Sunday dinner, Monday and Tuesday
Rest – Carte £ 25/35
Stylish barn conversion run by two brothers and set on the family farm. The terrace and airy first floor dining room offer superb views over the mountains and estuary. Unfussy cooking uses farm-bred meats and displays Italian influences.

DOLYDD – Gwynedd – see Caernarfon

FELINGWM UCHAF – Carmarthenshire – see Carmarthen

FISHGUARD – Pembrokeshire – 503 F28 – pop. 3 193 — 33 A3

London 265 mi – Cardiff 114 mi – Gloucester 176 mi – Holyhead 169 mi
to Republic of Ireland (Rosslare) (Stena Line) 2-4 daily (1 h 50 mn/3 h 30 mn)
The Square, ✆ (01437) 77 66 36, www.visitpembrokeshire.com
Pembrokeshire Coast National Park★★

Manor Town House without rest
11 Main St ✉ SA65 9HG – ✆ (01348) 873 260 – www.manortownhouse.com – Closed 24-26 December
6 rm – £ 65/85 £ 85/105
Well-run, listed Georgian townhouse, boasting fabulous harbour views. Stylish, elegant lounges and individually designed, antique-furnished bedrooms; some in art deco and some in Victorian styles. Tasty breakfasts; charming owners.

GARTH – Powys – 503 J27 — 33 B3

London 195 mi – Belfast 242 mi – Londonderry 285 mi – Craigavon 231 mi

The Fron N
Southeast : 2 mi on Upper Chapel Rd ✉ LD4 4BL – ✆ (01591) 620 515 – www.thefron.co.uk
3 rm – £ 80 £ 80/110 **Rest** – Menu £ 29
Set in a peaceful hillside location, this stone-built house offers wonderful views over the Elan Valley and the Cambrian Hills; admire the vista from the hot tub. Good-sized bedrooms have heavy wood furniture, warm fabrics and modern bathrooms. Traditional, home-cooked dishes use local and market produce.

GLYNARTHEN – Ceredigion — 33 B3

London 231 mi – Birmingham 152 mi – Bristol 131 mi – Leicester 185 mi

Penbontbren without rest
Glynarthen, North : 1 mi taking first left at cross roads then next left onto unmarked lane ✉ SA44 6PE – ✆ (01239) 810 248 – www.penbontbren.com – Closed Christmas
5 rm – £ 75/95 £ 95/110
Converted farm buildings surrounded by an attractive landscaped garden and 35 acres of rolling countryside. Spacious, stylish bedrooms; each has a sitting room, a mini bar, a coffee machine and a patio. The smart breakfast room features exposed stone, bold wallpaper, Portmeirion china and an extensive menu.

GRESFORD – Wrexham – 502 L24 – see Wrexham

WALES

HARLECH – Gwynedd – 502 H25 – pop. 1 233 32 B2

London 241 mi – Chester 72 mi – Dolgellau 21 mi

High St, (01766) 78 06 58, www.harlech-snowdonia.co.uk

Royal St David's, (01766) 78 02 03

Castle★★ **AC**

Snowdonia National Park★★★

Castle Cottage with rm

Pen Llech, by B 4573 ✉ LL46 2YL – (01766) 780 479
– www.castlecottageharlech.co.uk – Closed 3 weeks November

7 rm – £ 85/125 £ 130/175

Rest – *(dinner only) (booking essential)* Menu £ 40

Sweet little cottage behind Harlech Castle, with a cosy yet surprisingly contemporary interior. Start with canapés and an aperitif in the lounge; the table is yours for the evening. Classical menus feature local produce and modern touches. Spacious bedrooms have smart bathrooms and stunning mountain views.

HAVERFORDWEST (Hwlffordd) – Pembrokeshire – 503 F28 33 A3
– pop. 13 367

London 250 mi – Fishguard 15 mi – Swansea 57 mi

Old Bridge, (01437) 76 31 10, www.visitpembrokeshire.com

Arnolds Down, (01437) 76 35 65

Scolton Museum and Country Park★

Pembrokeshire Coast National Park★★. Skomer Island and Skokholm Island★, SW : 14 mi by B 4327 and minor roads

Lower Haythog Farm without rest

Spittal, Northeast : 5 mi on B 4329 ✉ SA62 5QL – (01437) 731 279
– www.lowerhaythogfarm.co.uk

4 rm – £ 50 £ 75/85

Welcoming guesthouse with mature gardens, part-dating from the 14C and set on a working dairy farm. Cosy bedrooms feature bespoke cherry wood furniture and organic toiletries. Homely lounge and pleasant conservatory. Aga-cooked breakfasts.

Paddock

Northeast : 5 mi on B 4329 ✉ SA62 5QL – (01437) 731 531
– www.thepaddockwales.co.uk

3 rm – £ 60/70 £ 75/90 **Rest** – Menu £ 24

Contemporary guesthouse on a working dairy farm. Comfortable lounge with books, board games and a wood-burning stove. Modern bedrooms feature chunky wood furniture and sleigh beds made up with Egyptian cotton linen. Home-cooked meals rely on local and market produce; the eggs are from their own hens.

HAWARDEN (Penarlâg) – Flintshire – 502 K24 – pop. 1 858 32 C1

London 205 mi – Chester 9 mi – Liverpool 17 mi – Shrewsbury 45 mi

Glynne Arms N

3 Glynne Way ✉ CH3 3NS – (01244) 569 988 – www.theglynnearms.co.uk

Rest – Carte £ 20/40

200 year old coaching inn opposite Hawarden Castle; owned by the descendants of PM William Gladstone. Choose from 'Family Classics', steaks from the estate or more modern dishes with ambitious flavour combinations. Desserts are a highlight.

HOWEY – Powys – see Llandrindod Wells

KNIGHTON (Trefyclawdd) – Powys – 503 K26 – pop. 2 851 33 C3

London 162 mi – Birmingham 59 mi – Hereford 31 mi – Shrewsbury 35 mi

West St, (01547) 52 87 53, www.visitknighton.co.uk

Ffrydd Wood, (01547) 52 86 46

Town★

Offa's Dyke★, NW : 9.5 m

Milebrook House
Ludlow Rd, Milebrook, East : 2 mi on A 4113 ✉ LD7 1LT – ✆ (01547) 528 632 – www.milebrookhouse.co.uk
10 rm – †£ 79/86 ††£ 124/136
Rest – *(closed Sunday dinner and Monday December-February and Monday lunch)* Menu £ 14 (lunch) – Carte £ 30/39
Part-Georgian dower house surrounded by superb formal gardens filled with exotic plants; located in the Teme Valley and once home to explorer Wilfred Thesiger. Well-appointed lounges and spacious, comfortable bedrooms furnished in a country house style. Traditional restaurant showcases kitchen garden produce.

LAMPHEY – **Pembrokeshire** – **503** F28 – **see Pembroke**

LLANARMON DYFFRYN CEIRIOG – **Wrexham** – **502** K25 — **32** C2
– ✉ **Llangollen (denbighshire)**
London 196 mi – Chester 33 mi – Shrewsbury 32 mi

Hand at Llanarmon with rm
✉ LL20 7LD – ✆ (01691) 600 666 – www.thehandhotel.co.uk – Closed 25 December
13 rm – †£ 50/68 ††£ 90/128 **Rest** – Menu £ 19 (lunch) – Carte £ 21/36
Rustic, personally run inn with stone walls, open fires and ancient beams, providing a warm welcome and wholesome meals to travellers through the lush Ceiriog Valley. Generous portions of fresh, flavoursome cooking. Cosy bedrooms offer hill views and modern bathrooms; most have a roll-top bath.

WALES

LLANDDERFEL – **Gwynedd** – **pop. 4 500** — **32** C2
London 210 mi – Cardiff 157 mi – Birmingham 97 mi – Liverpool 72 mi

Palé Hall
Palé Estate ✉ LL23 7PS – ✆ (01678) 530 285 – www.palehall.co.uk
17 rm – †£ 90/155 ††£ 125/210 – 2 suites **Rest** – Menu £ 25/35
Impressive Victorian house with lovely marquetry, fine oil paintings and a Scottish hunting lodge feel. Beautiful wood-panelled hall and traditional lounges; bedrooms boast period fireplaces and antique furniture. Classical menu in the elegant dining room. They even produce their own hydro-electricity here!

LLANDDEWI SKIRRID – **Monmouthshire** – **see Abergavenny**

LLANDEILO – **Carmarthenshire** – **503** I28 – **pop. 1 731** — **33** B3
London 218 mi – Brecon 34 mi – Carmarthen 15 mi – Swansea 25 mi
Town★ - Dinefwr Park★ **AC**
Brecon Beacons National Park★★ – Black Mountain★, SE : by minor roads – Carreg Cennen Castle★ **AC**, SE : 4 mi by A 483 and minor roads

Plough Inn
Rhosmaen, Northeast : 1 mi on A 40 ✉ SA19 6NP – ✆ (01558) 823 431 – www.ploughrhosmaen.com – Closed 26 December
23 rm – †£ 70/80 ††£ 90/120
Rest – Menu £ 28 (lunch and early dinner) – Carte £ 22/39
Powder blue inn with a contemporary interior and pleasant country views. Stylish, wood-furnished bedrooms feature good modern facilities; the best come with balconies and whirlpool baths. Small bar and gym. Various different rooms are used for informal lunches and more substantial dinners.

Fronlas without rest
7 Thomas St. ✉ SA19 6LB – ✆ (01558) 824 733 – www.fronlas.com
4 rm – †£ 55/100 ††£ 65/120
Old Edwardian house furnished in a very contemporary style. Smart bedrooms display funky wallpapers, bold fabrics and stylish bathrooms. They operate an admirable sustainable ethos with solar panels, recycling bins and organic breakfasts.

LLANDENNY – **Monmouthshire** – **503** L28 – **see Usk**

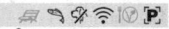

LLANDOVERY – Carmarthenshire – 503 I28 – pop. 2 235 33 B3

London 207 mi – Cardiff 61 mi – Swansea 37 mi – Merthyr Tydfil 34 mi

New White Lion

43 Stone St ✉ SA20 0BZ – ✆ (01550) 720 685 – www.newwhitelion.co.uk – Closed 25-27 December

6 rm – £ 90 ££ 120/145 **Rest** – *(dinner only)* Menu £ 22

Laid-back, Grade II listed former pub, in a small town – now a stylish hotel. Comfortable lounge with an honesty bar. Smart, individually designed bedrooms are named after folklore characters and boast contemporary fabrics and furnishings. Cosy designer restaurant, where menus feature seasonal local produce.

LLANDRILLO – Denbighshire – 502 J25 – pop. 1 048 – ✉ Corwen 32 C2

London 210 mi – Chester 40 mi – Dolgellau 26 mi – Shrewsbury 46 mi

Tyddyn Llan (Bryan Webb) with rm

✉ LL21 0ST – ✆ (01490) 440 264 – www.tyddynllan.co.uk – Closed last 2 weeks January

13 rm – £ 110/140 ££ 140/280

Rest – *(dinner only and lunch Friday-Sunday) (booking essential)* Menu £ 26/55 – Carte £ 41/53

Attractive former shooting lodge in a rural, valley location, surrounded by lovely gardens and run by a committed husband and wife. Spacious country house lounge and two interconnecting dining rooms. Hearty, satisfying cooking is based around the classics, with daily changing menus providing extensive choice. Smart, luxurious bedrooms offer a good level of facilities.

→ Dressed langoustine and crab with a fennel and pea shoot salad. Rack of lamb with an artichoke, pea and broad bean stew. Steamed ginger pudding and custard.

LLANDRINDOD WELLS – Powys – 503 J27 – pop. 5 024 33 C3

London 204 mi – Brecon 29 mi – Carmarthen 60 mi – Shrewsbury 58 mi

Memorial Gardens, ✆ (01597) 82 26 00, www.llandrindod.co.uk

Llandrindod Wells, The Clubhouse, ✆ (01597) 82 38 73

Elan Valley★★ (Dol-y-Mynach and Claerwen Dam and Reservoir★★, Caban Coch Dam and Reservoir★, Garreg-ddu Viaduct★, Pen-y-Garreg Reservoir and Dam★, Craig Goch Dam and Reservoir★), NW : 12 mi by A 4081, A 470 and B 4518

Metropole

rm, rest,

Temple St ✉ LD1 5DY – ✆ (01597) 823 700 – www.metropole.co.uk

112 rm – £ 89/126 ££ 100/150 – 2 suites

Rest – *(dinner only and Sunday lunch)* Carte £ 19/37 **s**

Rest *Spencer's* – Carte £ 19/37 **s**

Large green hotel run for many years by the Baird-Murray family; popular with both leisure and business guests courtesy of its many lounges, conference rooms and leisure facilities. Spacious bedrooms offer good amenities; the tower rooms are popular. Smart brasserie with extensive classical menus; bright fine dining restaurant showcases local produce.

at Crossgates Northeast : 3.5 mi on A 483 – ✉ Llandrindod Wells

Guidfa House without rest

✉ LD1 6RF – ✆ (01597) 851 241 – www.guidfahouse.co.uk

6 rm – £ 70/90 ££ 90/120

Georgian gentleman's residence with a pleasant garden, smart breakfast room and period lounge displaying an original cast iron rose on the ceiling. Bright, airy bedrooms; the best is in the coach house. Friendly owners serve tea on arrival.

at Howey South : 1.5 mi by A 483 – ✉ Llandrindod Wells

Acorn Court without rest

Chapel Rd, Northeast : 0.5 mi ✉ LD1 5PB – ✆ (01597) 823 543 – www.acorncourt.co.uk – Closed 24-27 December

3 rm – £ 40/80 ££ 75/85

Chalet-style house set in 40 acres, with views over rolling countryside towards a river and lake. Welcoming owner and a real family feel. Spacious, well-kept bedrooms come with good extras. Try the Welsh whisky porridge for breakfast.

WALES

LLANDUDNO – Conwy – **502** I24 – **pop. 15 324** **32** B1

London 243 mi – Birkenhead 55 mi – Chester 47 mi – Holyhead 43 mi

Mostyn St, (01492) 57 75 77, www.visitllandudno.org.uk

Rhos-on-Sea, Penrhyn Bay, (01492) 54 96 41

72 Bryniau Rd, West Shore, (01492) 87 53 25

Hospital Rd, (01492) 87 64 50

Town★ - Pier★ B – The Great Orme★ (panorama★★, Tramway★, Ancient Copper Mines★ **AC**) AB

Bodnant Garden★★ **AC**, S : 7 mi by A 470 B

Bodysgallen Hall

rm,

Royal Welsh Way, Southeast : 2 mi on A 470 ✉ LL30 1RS – (01492) 584 466 – www.bodysgallen.com

31 rm – †£ 159/349 ††£ 179/425 – 21 suites

Rest *Dining Room* – see restaurant listing

Rest *1620* – *(closed Sunday)* Menu £ 17 (dinner) – Carte £ 19/30 **s**

Stunning, National Trust owned country house with a 13C tower, 200 acres of delightful gardens and parkland, and a superb outlook to the mountains beyond. Welcoming, open-fired hall and characterful wood-panelled lounge. Antique-furnished bedrooms: some set in cottages and some affording splendid Snowdon views. Simple, traditional dishes served in the 1620 bistro.

Empire

rm,

73 Church Walks ✉ LL30 2HE – (01492) 860 555 – www.empirehotel.co.uk – Closed 20-31 December A**e**

57 rm – †£ 80/130 ††£ 115/140 – 1 suite

Rest *Watkins and Co.* – *(dinner only and Sunday lunch)* Menu £ 23

Family-run hotel – a former Victorian shopping arcade – with a grand columned façade, its interior hung with chandeliers and Russell Flint prints. Well-equipped gym and good-sized pool. Smartly dressed bedrooms with sleek, modern bathrooms; No. 72 is the most spacious. Set price menu in elegant Watkins.

Osborne House

17 North Par ✉ LL30 2LP – (01492) 860 330 – www.osbornehouse.co.uk – Closed 20-30 December A**c**

6 rm – †£ 150/210 ††£ 150/210

Rest *Osborne's Cafe and Grill* – see restaurant listing

Smart townhouse overlooking the bay. All of the bedrooms are large, luxurious suites and have stunning, almost whimsical styles; they boast canopied beds, spacious sitting rooms with Victorian fireplaces and marble bathrooms with double-ended, roll-top baths.

St Tudno

North Par ✉ LL30 2LP – (01492) 874 411 – www.st-tudno.co.uk A**c**

18 rm – †£ 75/85 ††£ 98/310 – 1 suite

Rest *Terrace* – see restaurant listing

Long-standing, personally run seaside hotel, set opposite the old Victorian pier. Classical sitting room and warm bar-lounge afford bay views. Well-kept, warmly furnished bedrooms with mini-bars; some have four-posters and whirlpool baths.

Escape Boutique B&B without rest

48 Church Walks ✉ LL30 2HL – (01492) 877 776 – www.escapebandb.co.uk – Closed 1 week Christmas A**n**

9 rm – †£ 74/125 ††£ 89/140

Attractive Arts and Crafts house with stained glass windows, parquet floors and a chic, modern interior that sets it apart. Stylish lounge and spacious, contemporary bedrooms; those on the top floor have a stunning view of the bay.

Bryn Derwen without rest

34 Abbey Rd ✉ LL30 2EE – (01492) 876 804 – www.bryn-derwen.co.uk – Closed January A**v**

9 rm – †£ 50/56 ††£ 78/100

Well-run, welcoming house built in 1878 for a wealthy family. Original features remain, including an ornate pitch pine staircase. Well-appointed lounge and spacious, individually designed bedrooms. Beauty salon offers a range of treatments.

WALES

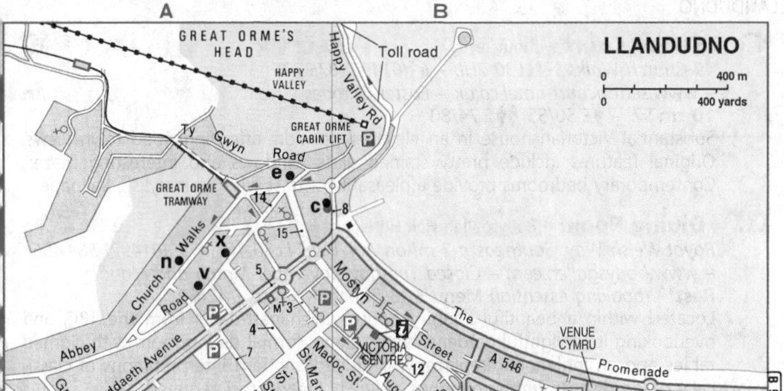

Chapel St . . . . **A** 3
Deganwy Ave . . . . **A** 4
Gloddaeth St. . . . . **A** 5
Maelgwyn Rd . . . . **A** 7
Mostyn Champneys Retail Park . . . . **B**
Mostyn St . . . . **B**
North Parade . . . . **AB** 8
Oxford Rd . . . . **B** 10
Trinity Square. . . . . **B** 12
Tudno St . . . . **A** 14
Tudor Crescent . . . . **B** 13
Upper Mostyn St . . . . **A** 15
Vaughan St . . . . **B** 16
Victoria Centre. . . . . **B**

WALES

Lympley Lodge without rest

Colwyn Rd, East : 2.5 mi on B 5115 ✉ LL30 3AL – ☎ (01492) 549 304 – www.lympleylodge.co.uk – Closed mid-December-mid January

3 rm – 🚹£ 50/55 🚹🚹£ 80/85

Detached Victorian house close to the Little Orme headland; built in 1870 as a summer residence for a local family. Antique-filled lounge with views of the headland and bay. Individually themed bedrooms come with good extras and sea outlooks. Hearty breakfasts of local produce taken at antique tables.

Abbey Lodge without rest

14 Abbey Rd ✉ LL30 2EA – ☎ (01492) 878 042 – www.abbeylodgeuk.com – Closed November-February
A**x**

4 rm – 🚹£ 45 🚹🚹£ 80

Welcoming terraced property – built in the early 1850s as a gentleman's residence and retaining its Victorian style. Individually decorated bedrooms with modern touches; all have baths. Cosy lounge and communal breakfasts from an extensive menu. Pleasant rear garden boasts views up to the Great Orme.

Sefton Court without rest
49 Church Walks ✉ LL30 2HL – ☎ (01492) 875 235
– www.seftoncourt-hotel.co.uk – Easter-October An
10 rm ☕ – 🛉£ 50/55 🛉🛉£ 74/80
Substantial Victorian house in an elevated position, affording good town views. Original features include pretty stained glass windows and interesting friezes. Contemporary bedrooms provide a pleasant contrast with their stylish wallpapers.

Dining Room – Bodysgallen Hall Hotel
Royal Welsh Way, Southeast : 2 mi on A 470 ✉ LL30 1RS – ☎ (01492) 584 466
– www.bodysgallen.com – Closed Tuesday November-March and Monday
Rest – *(booking essential)* Menu £ 25 (lunch) – Carte £ 42/60
Located within a beautiful country house which part-dates from the 13C, and overlooking its delightful gardens, is this grand, formal dining room with clothed tables and an inglenook fireplace. Well-judged, modern interpretations of classically based dishes; simpler offerings at lunch. Smart dress required.

Terrace – St Tudno Hotel
North Par ✉ LL30 2LP – ☎ (01492) 874 411 – www.st-tudno.co.uk Ac
Rest – Menu £ 23 (lunch) – Carte £ 33/43 **s**
Smart, uniquely styled restaurant with murals of Lake Como running the length of the wall and chandeliers adorned with flowers. Set within a personally run seaside hotel and offering a modern, seasonal menu. Professional service.

Osborne's Cafe and Grill – Osborne House Hotel
17 North Par ✉ LL30 2LP – ☎ (01492) 860 330 – www.osbornehouse.co.uk
– Closed 20-30 December Ac
Rest – Menu £ 21 (lunch and early dinner) – Carte £ 21/32
Victorian-style, all-day hotel restaurant with an opulent lounge and an ornate dining room boasting Corinthian columns, gilded mirrors and chandeliers. All-encompassing menu ranges from tasty afternoon tea to flavourful British classics.

WALES

at Deganwy South : 2.75 mi on A 546 - A – ✉ Llandudno

Quay H. & Spa
Deganwy Quay ✉ LL31 9DJ – ☎ (01492) 564 100 – www.quayhotel.co.uk
74 rm ☕ – 🛉£ 85/165 🛉🛉£ 95/185 – 19 suites
Rest ***Grill Room*** – see restaurant listing
Smart hotel by the Conwy Estuary, in a modern marina development. Large guest areas have superb outlooks over the harbour and castle. Extensive meeting facilities; excellent pool and spa. Contemporary bedrooms and penthouses with balconies.

Grill Room – Quay Hotel & Spa
Deganwy Quay ✉ LL31 9DJ – ☎ (01492) 564 100 – www.quayhotel.co.uk
Rest – Menu £ 20/30 – Carte £ 38/77
Smart designer restaurant with a cosy bar, a large glass wine cave and a superb terrace looking over the estuary to Conwy Castle. Extensive menus offer locally sourced meat, seafood and grill dishes; good value set option at lunch.

LLANDWROG – Gwynedd – 503 H24 – see Caernarfon

LLANDYBIE – Carmarthenshire – 503 I28 – pop. 2 635 — 33 B4

London 204 mi – Birmingham 122 mi – Bristol 97 mi – Leicester 192 mi

Valans
Primrose House, 29 High St ✉ SA18 3HX – ☎ (01269) 851 288
– www.valans.co.uk – Closed 24 December-3 January, Sunday and Monday
Rest – *(booking advisable)* Menu £ 12/23 – Carte £ 15/40
Simple little restaurant run by a local and his wife, with a bright red, white and black colour scheme. Fresh, unfussy dishes rely on local produce and offer classical flavour combinations. Good value light lunches; more elaborate dinners.

LLANDYRNOG – Denbighshire – 503 J/K24 — 32 C1

London 211 mi – Cardiff 158 mi – Birmingham 98 mi – Liverpool 34 mi

Pentre Mawr

North : 1.25 mi by B 5429 taking left hand fork after 0.75 mi ✉ LL16 4LA – ☎ (01824) 790 732 – www.pentremawrcountryhouse.co.uk – Closed Christmas, Monday and Tuesday

11 rm – †£ 110/150 ††£ 130/190 **Rest** – Menu £ 35

Unusual guesthouse on a 200 acre estate. Bedrooms in the Georgian house have a classical feel and boast jacuzzi baths – those in the outbuildings are more contemporary; there are also 6 luxurious African lodges with hot tubs. Characterful, antique-filled guest areas and modern conservatory. Classical cooking.

LLANELLI – Carmarthenshire – 503 H28 – pop. 46 357 — 33 B4

London 202 mi – Cardiff 54 mi – Swansea 12 mi

Sosban

The Pump House, North Dock ✉ SA15 2LF – ☎ (01554) 270 020 – www.sosbanrestaurant.com – Closed 25 December and Sunday dinner

Rest – Menu £ 15 – Carte £ 25/40

Built in 1872 to house a pumping engine for the adjacent docks. Impressively restored interior with a relaxed lounge-bar and airy dining room with exposed stone walls. Large à la carte offers tasty, well-prepared dishes; good value lunches.

LLANELLTYD – Gwynedd – 503 I25 – see Dolgellau

LLANERCHYMEDD – 502 G24 – see Anglesey (Isle of)

LLANFAIRFECHAN – Conwy – 502 I24 – pop. 3 653 – ✉ Conwy — 32 B1

London 247 mi – Cardiff 200 mi – Swansea 166 mi – Telford 107 mi

Grove without rest

Ffordd Aber, West : 0.75 m on Bangor rd ✉ LL33 OHR – ☎ (01248) 369 111 – www.thegrovenorthwales.co.uk

3 rm – †£ 50/81 ††£ 60/90

Originally built for an Edwardian cockle merchant, this house has been tastefully modernised, retaining its period features and showcasing the owners' collection of books, antiques and Welsh porcelain. Cosy bedrooms are named after rivers.

LLAN FFESTINIOG – Gwynedd — 32 B2

London 234 mi – Bangor 35 mi – Wrexham 52 mi

Llechwedd Slate Caverns★ **AC** N : 4 mi by A 470

Cae'r Blaidd Country House

North : 0.75 mi by A 470 on Blaenau Rd ✉ LL41 4PH – ☎ (01766) 762 765 – www.caerblaidd.fsnet.co.uk – Closed January

3 rm – †£ 55 ††£ 85 **Rest** – *(dinner only)* Menu £ 20 **s**

Sizeable Victorian house in a remote setting, boasting original features and panoramic mountain views. Spacious guest areas and light, airy bedrooms – two with superb outlooks. The welcoming owners are also mountain guides. Daily changing dishes of local produce are served at a large communal table.

LLANFIHANGEL – Powys – see Llanfyllin

LLANFIHANGEL-Y-CREUDDYN – Ceredigion – 503 I26 — 33 B3

London 235 mi – Cardiff 109 mi – Birmingham 121 mi – Liverpool 123 mi

Y Ffarmers

✉ SY23 4LA – ☎ (01974) 261 275 – www.yffarmers.co.uk – Closed first week January, Monday except bank holidays, and Sunday dinner

Rest – Carte £ 20/32

Life in this remote, picturesque valley revolves around the passionately run village pub. Sit in the locals bar or the homely restaurant which opens onto the garden. Regional and valley produce features in satisfying, original dishes.

LLANFYLLIN – Powys – 502 K25 – pop. 1 267 — 32 C2

London 188 mi – Chester 42 mi – Shrewsbury 24 mi – Welshpool 11 mi

Pistyll Rhaeadr★, NW : 8 mi by A 490, B 4391, B 4580 and minor roads

X **Seeds**
5 Penybryn Cottages, High St ✉ SY22 5AP – ✆ (01691) 648 604 – Closed Wednesday in winter and Sunday-Tuesday
Rest – Menu £ 28 (dinner) – Carte lunch £ 20/30
Converted 16C red-brick cottages in a sleepy village; run with pride by a friendly husband and wife team. Cosy, pine-furnished room with an old range and a country kitchen feel. Unfussy, classical dishes and comforting homemade desserts.

at Llanfihangel Southwest : 5 mi by A 490 and B 4393 on B 4382 – ✉ Llanfyllin

Cyfie Farm
South : 1.5 mi by B 4382 ✉ SY22 5JE – ✆ (01691) 648 451 – www.cyfiefarm.co.uk – Closed November-February
3 rm – †£ 90/110 ††£ 115/140 **Rest** – Menu £ 32
17C longhouse and barn conversions, set in a great spot and boasting far-reaching views across the valley. Mix of bedrooms and self-catering cottages; some with beams and wood-burning stoves. Spacious lounges and communal dining, with porridge cooked overnight on the Aga and cordon bleu dinners.

LLANGAFFO – see Anglesey (Isle of)

LLANGAMMARCH WELLS – Powys – 503 J27 — 33 B3

London 200 mi – Brecon 17 mi – Builth Wells 8 mi – Cardiff 58 mi

Lake Country House and Spa
East : 0.75 mi ✉ LD4 4BS – ✆ (01591) 620 202 – www.lakecountryhouse.co.uk — rm,
31 rm – †£ 75/145 ††£ 125/195 – 8 suites
Rest – *(booking essential)* Menu £ 23/39 – Carte lunch £ 18/29
Extended, part-timbered 19C country house in 50 acres of mature gardens and parkland, with a pond, a lake and a river. Comfortable lounges and well-appointed bedrooms with antiques and extras; some are set in the lodge. The impressive spa overlooks the river. Breakfast is in the orangery; the elegant restaurant is perfect for a classical, candlelit dinner.

LLANGENNITH – Swansea – 503 H29 — 33 B4

London 207 mi – Cardiff 61 mi – Swansea 17 mi – Newport 71 mi

Blas Gŵyr (N)
✉ SA3 1HU – ✆ (01792) 386 472 – www.blasgwyr.co.uk
4 rm – †£ 90/110 ††£ 100/120 **Rest** – Menu £ 25
Converted farm buildings on the Gower Peninsula. Smart, well-equipped bedrooms are set around a courtyard and feature local fabrics and slate bathrooms with underfloor heating. The small stone-walled coffee shop cum dining room serves simple, often Tuscan-based dinners; cockles are popular at breakfast.

LLANGOLLEN – Denbighshire – 502 K25 – pop. 3 093 — 32 C2

London 194 mi – Chester 23 mi – Holyhead 76 mi – Shrewsbury 30 mi
Castle St, ✆ (01978) 86 08 28, www.llangollen.org
18 Vale of Llangollen, Holyhead Rd, ✆ (01978) 86 09 06
Town★ - Railway★ **AC** - Plas Newydd★ **AC**
Pontcysyllte Aqueduct★★, E : 4 mi by A 539 - Castell Dinas Bran★, N : by footpath – Valle Crucis Abbey★ **AC**, N : 2 mi by A 542. Chirk Castle★★ **AC** (wrought iron gates★), SE : 7.5 mi by A 5 – Rug Chapel★ **AC**, W : 11 mi by A 5 and A 494

XX **Manorhaus Llangollen** (N) with rm
10 Hill St ✉ LL20 8EU – ✆ (01978) 860 775 – www.manorhaus.com
6 rm – †£ 83/125 ††£ 115/180 **Rest** – *(dinner only)* Menu £ 26/37
Stylish dining room in a double-fronted Victorian house in the centre of town. Weekly changing dinner menu of carefully cooked, classical dishes with some adventurous flavours; Welsh ingredients include the cheese platter. Funky, modern bar lounge. Smart, contemporary bedrooms and a hot tub with a view.

LLANGRANNOG – Ceredigion – 503 G27 33 B3

London 241 mi – Caerdydd / Cardiff 96 mi – Aberystwyth / Aberyswyth 30 mi – Caerfyrddin / Carmarthen 28 mi

Grange without rest

Pentregat, Southeast : 3 mi by B 4321 on A 487 ✉ SA44 6HW – ✆ (01239) 654 121 – www.grangecountryhouse.co.uk – restricted opening in winter

4 rm – †£ 55/60 ††£ 80/90

Traditional Georgian manor house with a pretty breakfast room and individually decorated bedrooms which feature brass beds and cast iron slipper baths. On arrival, the hospitable owner welcomes you with a pot of tea beside the fire.

LLANGYBI – Monmouthshire – 503 L29 – see Usk

LLANLLAWDDOG – Carmarthenshire – see Carmarthen

LLANRHIDIAN – Swansea – 503 H29 32 B4

London 198 mi – Birmingham 146 mi – Bristol 95 mi – Leicester 190 mi

Fairyhill with rm

Reynoldston, West : 2.5 mi by Llangennith Rd ✉ SA3 1BS – ✆ (01792) 390 139 – www.fairyhill.net – Closed 1-24 January and 25-26 December

8 rm – †£ 160/260 ††£ 180/280 **Rest** – Menu £ 20/45

Attractive Georgian country house with a lake and well-manicured gardens; take it all in from the red and gold dining room or from the terrace. Modern menus rely on seasonal Gower produce. Spacious bedrooms blend the traditional and the contemporary and come with good facilities. Charming guest areas include a cosy bar and contemporary lounge with a piano.

LLANRUG – Gwynedd – 502 H24 – see Caernarfon

LLANSANFFRAID GLAN CONWY – Conwy – 502 I24 – see Conwy

LLANWRDA – Carmarthenshire – 503 I28 33 B3

London 199 mi – Cardiff 65 mi – Swansea 33 mi – Newport 64 mi

Tŷ Llwyd Hir without rest

North : 2 mi by A 482 turning right at caravan park ✉ SA19 8AS – ✆ (01550) 777 362 – www.bandbwestwales.co.uk

3 rm – †£ 65/70 ††£ 80/90

Follow the long track past the old farm buildings to reach this lovely slate guesthouse on the hillside, which overlooks the Black Mountains in the Brecon Beacons National Park. Smart, modern rooms mix the old and the new. The friendly owners keep three donkeys and the brood of hens supply the breakfast eggs.

LLANWRTYD WELLS – Powys – 503 J27 – pop. 649 33 B3

London 214 mi – Brecon 32 mi – Cardiff 68 mi – Carmarthen 39 mi

The Square, ✆ (01591) 61 06 66, www.llanwrtyd.com

Abergwesyn-Tregaron Mountain Road★, NW : 19 mi on minor roads

Lasswade Country House

Station Rd ✉ LD5 4RW – ✆ (01591) 610 515 – www.lasswadehotel.co.uk

7 rm – †£ 55/75 ††£ 70/120 **Rest** – *(dinner only)* Menu £ 35

Very proudly run Edwardian house, set on the edge of the town. Homely, book-filled lounge and conservatory breakfast room. Comfy, uncluttered bedrooms come in light hues and have pleasant country views. Smart dining room with polished wood tables; the traditional menu promotes local, sustainable produce.

Carlton Riverside with rm

Irfon Cres ✉ LD5 4SP – ✆ (01591) 610 248 – www.carltonriverside.com – Closed 23-30 December and Sunday

4 rm – †£ 50 ††£ 65/100 **Rest** – *(dinner only)* Carte £ 23/44

Traditional stone building in the centre of the village, with two comfy lounges and a small bar filled with books and modern art. Well-spaced tables in the dining room, which overlooks the River Irfon. Concise menu utilises local produce; classic dishes have a modern touch. Neat, tidy, well-priced bedrooms.

WALES

LLECHRYD – Pembrokeshire – 503 G27 33 A3

London 238 mi – Cardiff 93 mi – Swansea 53 mi – Newport 102 mi

Hammet House

SA43 2QA – (01239) 682 382 – www.hammethouse.co.uk

14 rm – £ 95/140 £ 130/180 **Rest** – Menu £ 40 – Carte £ 24/49

Attractive Georgian house built for former Sheriff of London Sir Benjamin Hammet. It has contemporary monochrome styling, quirky furnishings and a relaxed, bohemian feel. Bedrooms boast locally handmade beds, good facilities and views over the grounds. The smart restaurant offers appealing modern menus.

LLYSWEN – Powys – 503 K27 – Brecon 33 C3

London 188 mi – Brecon 8 mi – Cardiff 48 mi – Worcester 53 mi

Brecon Beacons National Park★★

Llangoed Hall

Northwest : 1.25 mi on A 470 LD3 0YP – (01874) 754 525 – www.llangoedhall.com

23 rm – £ 150/190 £ 190/500

Rest – *(booking essential)* Menu £ 29/60 **s**

Homely country house by the River Wye, built by Sir Clough Williams-Ellis and restored by the late Sir Bernard and Laura Ashley. Spacious lounges and bedrooms mix period and modern furnishings. The impressive art collection includes pieces by Whistler. Formal country house dining room serves modern dishes.

MACHYNLLETH – Powys – 503 I26 – pop. 2 147 32 B2

London 220 mi – Shrewsbury 56 mi – Welshpool 37 mi

Penrallt St, (01654) 70 24 01, www.ukinformationcentre.com/central-wales

Felingerrig, (01654) 70 20 00

Town★ - Celtica★ **AC**

Snowdonia National Park★★★ - Centre for Alternative Technology★★ **AC**, N : 3 mi by A 487

Ynyshir Hall

Eglwysfach, Southwest : 6 mi on A 487 SY20 8TA – (01654) 781 209 – www.ynyshir-hall.co.uk – closed January

10 rm – £ 150/495 £ 205/600 – 4 suites

Rest *Ynyshir Hall* – see restaurant listing

Smartly refurbished part-Georgian house, set within a 1,000 acre RSPB reserve and run with pride and passion. Comfortable lounges are decorated with the owner's eye-catching artwork. Bedrooms are stylish and contemporary yet retain a fittingly country house feel; two of the suites are situated in the grounds.

Ynyshir Hall – Ynyshir Hall Hotel

Eglwysfach, Southwest: 6 mi on A 487 SY20 8TA – (01654) 781 209 – www.ynyshirhall.co.uk – closed January

Rest – *(booking essential)* Menu £ 25/90

Small restaurant in a smart Georgian house; a popular spot with the locals. Enjoy an aperitif by the fire in one of the lounges before heading to the formal dining room. Traditional combinations of ingredients come with personal modern twists; the soufflés are a hit. Service is professional and friendly.

MENAI BRIDGE – 502 H24 – see Anglesey (Isle of)

MOLD (Yr Wyddgrug) – Flintshire – 502 K24 – pop. 9 568 32 C1

London 211 mi – Chester 12 mi – Liverpool 22 mi – Shrewsbury 45 mi

Earl Rd, (01352) 75 93 31, www.visitmold.com

Old Padeswood, Station Rd, Old Padeswood, (01244) 54 77 01

Padeswood & Buckley, Station Lane, The Caia, (01244) 55 05 37

Caerwys, (01352) 72 12 22

St Mary's Church★

Tower without rest
Nercwys, South : 1 mi by B 5444, Nercwys rd on Treuddyn rd ✉ Cl
– ✆ (01352) 700 220 – www.towerwales.co.uk – Closed 12 Decemb
3 rm – †£ 70/95 ††£ 85/110
Impressive fortified house with pond and extensive grounds, dating from 1465 and in family almost as long. Huge high-ceilinged bedrooms boast character beds, antiques and vast modern showers.

Glasfryn
Raikes Ln, Sychdyn, North : 1 mi by A 5119 on Civic Centre rd (Theatr Clwyd) ✉ CH7 6LR – ✆ (01352) 750 500 – www.glasfryn-mold.co.uk – Closed 25 December
Rest – Carte £ 19/31
Sizeable red-brick pub with Arts and Crafts styling and a terrace with a pleasant town outlook. Menus offer plenty of choice, from pub favourites to culinary classics. Portions are generous, prices are sensible and service is swift.

Tavern
Mold Rd, Alltami, Northeast : 2.5 mi by A 5119 on A 494 ✉ CH7 6LG – ✆ (01244) 550 485 – www.tavernrestaurant.co.uk
Rest – Carte £ 21/31
Modern-looking pub with heavy tables, leather chairs and a formal feel; in contrast, the cooking is hearty and comforting. Daily specials, particularly the market fish, prove popular; the 'Chef's Choice' and tasting menus are more refined.

Don't confuse the classification X with the stars ✿!
The number of X denotes levels of comfort and service,
while stars are awarded for the best cooking across all categories.

MONMOUTH (Trefynwy) – Monmouthshire – 503 L28 – pop. 8 547 — 33 C4

London 135 mi – Abergavenny 19 mi – Cardiff 40 mi
Town★

at Penallt South : 5 mi by B 4293

The Inn at Penallt Ⓝ with rm
✉ NP25 4SE – ✆ (01600) 772 765 – www.theinnatpenallt.co.uk – Closed 1-20 January, Sunday dinner and Monday except bank holidays
4 rm – †£ 45/58 ††£ 75 **Rest** – Menu £ 16 (lunch) – Carte £ 27/38
Proudly and personally run pub. Its neutrally hued rooms are furnished with heavy wood; for the best views, make for the conservatory. Menus offer good-sized dishes with classical roots. Bread is baked daily and the ice creams are homemade. Bedrooms are cosy, neat and tidy with modern facilities.

at Rockfield Northwest : 2.5 mi on B 4233 – ✉ Monmouth

Stonemill
West : 1 mi on B 4233 ✉ NP25 5SW – ✆ (01600) 716 273 – www.thestonemill.co.uk – Closed 2 weeks January, 25-26 December, Sunday dinner and Monday
Rest – Menu £ 16/25 – Carte £ 29/42
Attractive 16C cider mill with exposed timbers and an old millstone at the centre of the characterful, rustic restaurant. Good value set menus are supplemented by a more ambitious evening à la carte. Dishes are hearty and classically based.

MONTGOMERY (Trefaldwyn) – Powys – 503 K26 – pop. 1 059 — 32 C2

London 194 mi – Birmingham 71 mi – Chester 53 mi – Shrewsbury 30 mi
Town★

The Checkers (Stéphane Borie) with rm
Broad St ✉ SY15 6PN – ✆ (01686) 669 822 – www.thecheckersmontgomery.co.uk – Closed 2 weeks January, 1 week autumn, 25-26 December, Sunday, Monday and lunch Tuesday-Wednesday
5 rm – †£ 100/136 ††£ 125/170 **Rest** – Menu £ 65/85 – Carte £ 31/59 **s**
Charming 18C former coaching inn, set in the main square of a hilltop town, with a characterful beamed lounge and a stylish restaurant split over two rooms. Monthly changing menus of classical dishes that are executed with a deft touch; flavours are sharply defined. Elegant, antique-furnished bedrooms.
→ Pithiviers of wild rabbit and foie gras, roasted walnuts and port jus. Ragout of Dover sole with langoustines, broad beans and vermouth. Agen prune and armagnac soufflé with vanilla ice cream.

NANTGAREDIG – Carmarthenshire – 503 H28 – see Carmarthen

NANT-Y-DERRY – Monmouthshire – see Abergavenny

NARBERTH – Pembrokeshire – 503 F28 – pop. 1 869 — 33 A4

London 234 mi – Cardiff 88 mi – Swansea 51 mi – Rhondda 79 mi

Grove
Molleston, South : 2 mi by A 478 on Herons Brook rd ✉ SA67 8BX – ✆ (01834) 860 915 – www.thegrove-narberth.co.uk
20 rm – †£ 150/290 ††£ 150/290 – 6 suites
Rest – Menu £ 22/78 **s** – Carte approx. £ 49
Set in a charming rural location, the Grove comprises a 15C longhouse and an immaculately whitewashed property with Stuart and Victorian additions. Bedrooms blend boldly coloured walls and bright fabrics with more traditional furnishings; the spacious bathrooms boast every modern amenity. Seasonal menus offer creative, contemporary dishes with a classical base.

Canaston Oaks without rest
Canaston Bridge, West : 3 mi by B 4314 and A 40 on A 4075 ✉ SA67 8DE – ✆ (01437) 541 254 – www.canastonoaks.co.uk
7 rm – †£ 85/115 ††£ 98/160
Converted longhouse and outbuildings in 35 acres of gardens and grasslands leading down to the river. Set around a courtyard water feature, the wood-furnished bedrooms boast fridges and DVD players; some have jacuzzis, others, patios.

NEWCASTLE EMLYN – Carmarthenshire – 503 G27 – pop. 1 700 — 33 B3

London 232 mi – Birmingham 156 mi – Bristol 121 mi – Leicester 189 mi

Gwesty'r Emlyn
Bridge St ✉ SA38 9DU – ✆ (01239) 710 317 – www.gwestyremlynhotel.co.uk
28 rm – †£ 80/100 ††£ 115/160 – 1 suite
Rest – Menu £ 10/36 – Carte £ 21/40
300 year old coaching inn set in the centre of town and concealing a surprisingly modern interior. Guest areas include a stylish lounge, a snug bar, a small fitness room and a sauna; bedrooms are contemporary and well-equipped. The smart restaurant offers a classic menu centred around local produce.

NEWPORT – Newport – 503 L29 – pop. 116 143 — 33 C4

London 145 mi – Bristol 31 mi – Cardiff 12 mi – Gloucester 48 mi
John Frost Sq, ✆ (01633) 84 29 62, www.newport.gov.uk
Caerleon, Broadway, ✆ (01633) 42 03 42
Parc, Coedkernew, Church Lane, ✆ (01633) 68 09 33
Museum and Art Gallery★ AX **M** - Transporter Bridge★ **AC** AY - Civic Centre (murals★) AX
Caerleon Roman Fortress★★ **AC** (Fortress Baths★ - Legionary Museum★ - Amphitheatre★), NE : 2.5 mi by B 4596 AX – Tredegar House★★ (Grounds★ - Stables★), SW : 2.5 mi by A 48 AY. Penhow Castle★, E : 8 mi by A 48 AX

Celtic Manor Resort

Coldra Woods, East : 3 mi on A 48 ✉ NP18 1HQ – ✆ (01633) 413 000 – www.celtic-manor.com

409 rm – †£ 119/329 ††£ 142/366 – 19 suites

Rest *Terry M* – see restaurant listing

Rest *Rafters* – ✆ (01633) 410 262 – Menu £ 16 (lunch) – Carte dinner £ 25/63 **s**

Rest *Olive Tree* – ✆ (01633) 410 262 *(dinner only and Sunday lunch)* Menu £ 33 **s**

Rest *Le Patio* – ✆ (01633) 410 262 *(dinner only)* Carte £ 28/52 **s**

Vast resort hotel in 1,400 acres, boasting 3 golf courses, an impressive pool and spa, two floors of function rooms and even a shopping arcade. Mix of classical and modern bedrooms, which range from standard to presidential suites. Modern fine dining in Terry M; grills in Rafters, in the clubhouse; buffet and carvery in Olive Tree; and a French bistro menu in Le Patio.

Terry M – Celtic Manor Resort Hotel

Coldra Woods, East : 3 mi on A 48 ✉ NP18 1HQ – ✆ (01633) 413 000 – www.celtic-manor.com – Closed 6-28 January, Monday and Tuesday

Rest – Menu £ 23/50 **s**

Named after the owner of the huge hotel in which it's set. Comfy lounge for aperitifs and canapés; bright, contemporary dining room with well-spaced tables and cream leather chairs. Menus are modern and ambitious, and service is formal.

NEWPORT (Trefdraeth) – Pembrokeshire – 503 F27 – pop. 1 162 — 33 A3

London 258 mi – Fishguard 7 mi

Long St, ✆ (01239) 82 09 12, www.newport-pembs.co.uk

Newport Links, ✆ (01239) 82 02 44

Pembrokeshire Coast National Park★★

Cnapan

East St, on A 487 ✉ SA42 0SY – ✆ (01239) 820 575 – www.cnapan.co.uk – Closed January-mid-March and 25-26 December

5 rm – †£ 50/60 ††£ 80/90

Rest – *(closed Tuesday) (dinner only) (booking essential)* Menu £ 26

Keenly run, part-Georgian house in a busy coastal village. The traditionally furnished lounge and bar have a homely feel. Well-maintained, compact bedrooms are being updated in a clean, modern style. The candlelit restaurant opens onto a large garden and offers an extensive home-cooked menu.

Llys Meddyg with rm

East St ✉ SA42 0SY – ✆ (01239) 820 008 – www.llysmeddyg.com – Closed first 2 weeks January and Sunday-Monday in winter

8 rm – †£ 85 ††£ 100/180 **Rest** – *(dinner only)* Carte £ 28/40

Centrally located restaurant with a kitchen garden and a slightly bohemian style. Eat in the formal dining room or characterful, laid-back cellar bar; the owner's father's art is displayed throughout. Cooking showcases local produce in ambitious, complex dishes. Contemporary bedrooms have a Scandinavian-style.

at Dinas Cross West : 3.25 mi on A 487

Y Garth Ⓝ without rest

Cae Tabor, via unnamed road opposite bus stop. ✉ SA42 0XR – ✆ (01348) 811 777 – www.bedandbreakfast-pembrokeshire.co.uk – Closed 1 week Christmas

3 rm – †£ 50/105 ††£ 85/105

Welcoming pink-washed guesthouse in a small village. Comfy lounge with a conservatory extension where homemade cakes are served on arrival. Stylish bedrooms have bright, bold décor; Strumble Head has views to the peninsula it's named after.

...TOWN – Powys – **503** K26 – **pop. 10 358** – ✉ **Blaenau Gwent** **32** C2

...London 194 mi – Cardiff 98 mi – Birmingham 81 mi – Wolverhampton 69 mi

Highgate without rest

Bettws Cedewain, Northeast : 2.5 mi by B 4568 off B 4389 ✉ SY16 3LF – ✆ (01686) 623 763 – www.highgatebandb.co.uk – Closed Christmas-New Year

4 rm – ♦£ 45/60 ♦♦£ 80/90

Timbered farmhouse built in 1631, with stables, colourful gardens and superb views across rolling fields. Tastefully furnished, it boasts good-sized bedrooms and a warm, welcoming feel. Homemade breads and preserves feature at breakfast.

OLD RADNOR (Pencraig) – **Powys** – **503** J27 – **pop. 400** **33** C3

London 180 mi – Cardiff 81 mi – Birmingham 86 mi – Liverpool 121 mi

Harp Inn with rm

✉ LD8 2RH – ✆ (01544) 350 655 – www.harpinnradnor.co.uk – Closed Monday except bank holidays and lunch Tuesday-Friday - restricted opening in winter

5 rm – ♦£ 55/60 ♦♦£ 90 **Rest** – Carte £ 20/32

This 15C stone inn welcomes drinkers and diners alike. The charming, flag-floored rooms boast open fires and beams hung with hop bines, and the terrace offers glorious views. 'Seasonality' and 'sustainability' are key, and menus are concise but original. Simple bedrooms come with wonderful views.

PEMBROKE (Penfro) – **Pembrokeshire** – **503** F28 – **pop. 7 214** **33** A4

London 252 mi – Carmarthen 32 mi – Fishguard 26 mi

Access Cleddau Bridge (toll)

to Republic of Ireland (Rosslare) (Irish Ferries) 2 daily (4 h) – to Republic of Ireland (Cork) (Swansea Cork Ferries) daily (8 h 30 mn)

Commons Rd, ✆ (01646) 62 23 88, www.pembrokeshire.gov.uk

Pembroke Dock, Military Rd, ✆ (01646) 62 14 53

Town★★ - Castle★★ **AC**

Pembrokeshire Coast National Park★★ - Carew Castle★ **AC**, NE : 4 mi by A 4075. Bosherston (St Govan's Chapel★), S : 7 mi by B 4319 and minor roads – Stack Rocks★, SW : 9 mi by B 4319 and minor roads

Poyerston Farm without rest

Cosheston, Northeast : 2.75 mi by A 4075 on A 477 ✉ SA72 4SJ – ✆ (01646) 651 347 – www.poyerstonfarm.co.uk – Closed December and January

3 rm – ♦£ 45/55 ♦♦£ 75/85

Victorian farmhouse with well-tended gardens, set on a 220 acre working dairy farm. Intimate breakfast room, airy conservatory and cosy lounge; immaculate bedrooms have light oak furnishings and extras. Warm welcome from experienced owner.

at Lamphey East : 1.75 mi on A 4139 – ✉ Pembroke

Lamphey Court

✉ SA71 5NT – ✆ (01646) 672 273 – www.lampheycourt.co.uk

39 rm – ♦£ 125/135 ♦♦£ 155/165

Rest – Menu £ 25 (dinner) – Carte £ 20/30

Impressive Georgian mansion, fronted by columns and surrounded by mature parkland. Typical country house feel throughout, from the classical lounge to the well-kept bedrooms with mahogany furnishings. Smart modern spa and leisure facilities. Dine in the informal orangery or traditional dining room.

PENARTH – **The Vale of Glamorgan** – **503** K29 – **pop. 23 245** **32** C4

London 152 mi – Birmingham 111 mi – Bristol 47 mi – Leicester 149 mi

Pier 64

Penarth Marina ✉ CF64 1TT – ✆ (029) 2000 0064 – www.pier64.co.uk – Closed Christmas and Sunday dinner

Rest – Menu £ 13 (lunch) – Carte £ 29/40

Modern, wood-clad, all-day restaurant, set on stilts in an enviable harbour location. Light, airy interior with a smart bar and huge windows giving every table a view. Accessible menu features plenty of seafood and 28 day dry-aged steaks.

The Pilot

67 Queens Rd ✉ CF64 1DJ – ✆ (029) 2071 0615 – www.knifeandforkfood.co.uk/pilot
Rest – Carte £ 18/29
A neat dining pub that's part of the local community. Regulars gather in the front room; diners head to the rear. A good-sized blackboard menu mixes hearty, honest pub dishes with more adventurous offerings. Ingredients are laudably local.

PENMACHNO – Conwy – **502** I24 – see Betws-y-Coed

PENNAL – Gwynedd

32 B2

London 222 mi – Birmingham 108 mi – Liverpool 90 mi – Leeds 158 mi

Riverside

✉ SY20 9DW – ✆ (01654) 791 285 – www.riversidehotel-pennal.co.uk
Rest – Menu £ 10 – Carte £ 17/34
Enter under the 'Glan Yr Afron' (Riverside) sign, then make for the 'Cwtch' with its wood-burning stove. Despite its Grade II listing, it has a bright modern feel. Hearty, no-nonsense pub classics are full of flavour and keenly priced.

PORTHCAWL – Bridgend – 503 I29 – pop. 15 640

33 B4

London 183 mi – Cardiff 28 mi – Swansea 18 mi
John St, ✆ (01656) 78 66 39, www.bridgend.gov.uk
Glamorgan Heritage Coast★

Foam Edge without rest

9 West Dr ✉ CF36 3LS – ✆ (01656) 782 866 – www.foam-edge.co.uk – Closed 25 December
3 rm – †£ 45/80 ††£ 75/90
A smart, modern, semi-detached house – a family home – set next to the promenade, with great views over the Bristol Channel. Spacious, stylish bedrooms offer good facilities. Comfortable lounge and communal breakfasts.

WALES

PORTMEIRION – Gwynedd – 502 H25

32 B2

London 245 mi – Caernarfon 23 mi – Colwyn Bay 40 mi – Dolgellau 24 mi
Village★★★ **AC**
Snowdonia National Park★★★ - Lleyn Peninsula★★ – Ffestiniog Railway★★ **AC**

Portmeirion

✉ LL48 6ER – ✆ (01766) 770 000 – www.portmerion-village.com – Closed 2 weeks November
26 rm – †£ 79/269 ††£ 109/289 – 18 suites
Rest – *(booking essential)* Menu £ 24/38 – Carte £ 37/57
A unique, Italianate village built on a private peninsula and boasting wonderful estuary views – the life work of Sir Clough Williams-Ellis. There's an appealing 1930s hotel and snug, well-appointed bedrooms, which are spread about the village. The dining room has an art deco feel and a lovely parquet floor.

Castell Deudraeth

rest,

✉ LL48 6EN – ✆ (01766) 772 400 – www.portmeirion-village.com
11 rm – †£ 109/199 ††£ 139/239 – 3 suites
Rest *Grill* – Carte £ 26/42
Impressive crenellated manor house at the entrance to the Italianate village; its name means 'castle of two beaches'. Huge modern bedrooms have stylish bathrooms and kitchen areas. Have cocktails by the fire then head to the grill for brasserie classics and lovely views of the walled garden and the sea.

PWLLGLOYW – Powys – see Brecon

PWLLHELI – Gwynedd – 502 G25 – pop. 3 861

32 B2

London 261 mi – Aberystwyth 73 mi – Caernarfon 21 mi
Station Sq, ✆ (01758) 61 30 00, www.ukinformationcentre.com/north-wales
Golf Rd, ✆ (01758) 70 16 44
Lleyn Peninsula★★

XX **Plas Bodegroes** with rm
Northwest : 1.75 mi on A 497 ✉ LL53 5TH – ✆ (01758) 612 363 – www.bodegroes.co.uk – Closed December-February
10 rm ☕ – 🚹£ 100/130 🚹🚹£ 120/180
Rest – *(closed Monday except bank holidays) (dinner only and Sunday lunch) (booking essential)* Menu £ 23/45
Set in a charming location, at the end of a winding drive, a delightful Grade II listed Georgian house surrounded by colourful gardens. An eclectic collection of local art decorates the dining room. The friendly, long-standing team serve well-presented modern dishes with clear flavours and the occasional innovative touch. Contemporary bedrooms have a Scandic style.

at Boduan Northwest : 3.75 mi on A 497 – ✉ Pwllheli

Old Rectory without rest
✉ *LL53 6DT – ✆ (01758) 721 519 – www.theoldrectory.net – Closed Christmas*
3 rm ☕ – 🚹£ 80/95 🚹🚹£ 75/105
Lovely part-Georgian family home with well-tended gardens and a paddock. Comfy lounge features a carved wood fireplace; communal breakfasts at a large table include plenty of fresh fruits. Tastefully decorated, homely bedrooms overlook the garden and come with complimentary chocolates and sherry or sloe gin.

RHOSCOLYN – 503 G24 – see Anglesey (Isle of)

RHOS-ON-SEA – Conwy – 502 I24 – see Colwyn Bay

RHYL – Denbighshire – 502 J24 – pop. 24 889 32 C1

London 228 mi – Cardiff 181 mi – Birmingham 114 mi – Wolverhampton 108 mi
Rhuddlan Castle★★, S : 3 mi by A 525 – Bodelwyddan★★, S : 5 mi by A 525 and minor rd – St Asaph Cathedral★, S : 5 mi by A 525. Llandudno★, W : 16 mi by A 548, A 55 and B 5115

XX **Barratt's at Ty'n Rhyl** with rm
167 Vale Rd., South : 0.5 mi on A 525 ✉ LL18 2PH – ✆ (01745) 344 138 – www.barrattsoftynrhyl.co.uk – Closed 28 September-7 October
3 rm ☕ – 🚹£ 75 🚹🚹£ 95
Rest – *(dinner only and Sunday lunch) (booking essential)* Carte approx. £ 40
Rhyl's oldest house boasts comfortable lounges with rich oak panelling. Dine in either the conservatory or original house. Ambitious cooking displays a classic base. Bedrooms are individually designed.

ROCKFIELD – Monmouthshire – 503 L28 – see Monmouth

ROWEN – Conwy – see Conwy

RUTHIN (Rhuthun) – Denbighshire – 502 K24 – pop. 5 218 32 C1

London 210 mi – Birkenhead 31 mi – Chester 23 mi – Liverpool 34 mi
Ruthin-Pwllglas, ✆ (01824) 70 22 96
Llandyrnog (St Dyfnog's Church★), Llanrhaeder-yng-Nghinmeirch (Jesse Window★★), N : 5.5 mi by A 494 and B 5429. Denbigh★, NW : 7 mi on A 525

Firgrove
Llanfwrog, West : 1.25 mi by A 494 on B 5105 ✉ LL15 2LL – ✆ (01824) 702 677 – www.firgrovecountryhouse.co.uk – March-October
3 rm ☕ – 🚹£ 60/85 🚹🚹£ 80/110 **Rest** – Menu £ 35
Attractive stone-built cottage set in stunning gardens. Sit in the snug by the cosy inglenook fireplace in winter or in the delightful, plant-filled glasshouse in summer. Two comfortable four-poster bedrooms and a self-contained cottage offer pleasant valley views. The owners join guests for hearty, home-cooked dinners which showcase locally sourced farm produce.

Eyarth Station without rest

Llanfair Dyffryn Clwyd, South : 1.75 mi by A 525 ✉ LL15 2EE – ✆ (01824) 703 643 – www.eyarthstation.co.uk – Closed January-February

6 rm ☕ – 🚹£ 50 🚹🚹£ 75

Former railway station, with the old platform at heart of the house and the tracks running under the conservatory. Simple pine-furnished bedrooms feature railway memorabilia. Panoramic windows in the lounge offer great rural views.

Manorhaus Ruthin with rm

10 Well St ✉ LL15 1AH – ✆ (01824) 704 830 – www.manorhaus.com

8 rm ☕ – 🚹£ 83/123 🚹🚹£ 115/170

Rest – *(dinner only and lunch Saturday-Sunday by arrangement)* Menu £ 33

Georgian townhouse which retains its period character whilst also boasting a stylish, 'of-the-moment' feel. Formally laid conservatory dining room serves classically based, seasonal dishes, presented in a modern style. Cocktail bar, basement cinema and regularly changing art. Cosy, cleverly designed bedrooms.

On the Hill

1 Upper Clwyd St ✉ LL15 1HY – ✆ (01824) 707 736 – www.onthehillrestaurant.co.uk – Closed 1-7 January, 25-26 December, 1 January, Sunday and Monday

Rest – *(booking essential)* Menu £ 16 (lunch) – Carte £ 22/29

Immensely charming 16C house in a busy market town; a real family-run business. It has characterful sloping floors, exposed beams and a buzzy, bistro atmosphere. The accessible menu offers keenly priced, internationally influenced classics.

ST ASAPH – Denbighshire – 503 J24 – pop. 3 491 — 32 C1

London 223 mi – Cardiff 176 mi – Liverpool 46 mi – Manchester 69 mi

Tan-yr-Onnen without rest

Waen, East : 1.5 mi by A 55 and B 5429 on Trefnant rd ✉ LL17 0DU – ✆ (01745) 583 821 – www.northwalesbreaks.co.uk – Closed 25-26 December

6 rm ☕ – 🚹£ 75/95 🚹🚹£ 95/135

Extended modern building with pleasant gardens; its name means 'house under the tree'. Spacious tastefully furnished bedrooms: the ground floor rooms have French windows and terraces; the first floor rooms come with their own sitting rooms.

ST CLEARS – Carmarthenshire – 503 G28 – pop. 1 587 — 33 B3

London 221 mi – Cardiff 76 mi – Swansea 37 mi – Llanelli 33 mi

Coedllys Country House without rest

Llangynin, Northwest : 3.5 mi by A 40 turning first left after 30 mph sign on entering village. ✉ SA33 4JY – ✆ (01994) 231 455 – www.coedllyscountryhouse.co.uk – Closed 22-28 December

4 rm ☕ – 🚹£ 65/75 🚹🚹£ 90/100

Lovely country house in a peaceful hillside location, complete with a sanctuary where they keep rescued animals – the hens provide the eggs at breakfast. Comfy, traditional guest areas and charming, antique-furnished bedrooms with good mod cons and binoculars for bird watchers. Welsh cakes served on arrival.

ST DAVIDS (Tyddewi) – Pembrokeshire – 503 E28 – pop. 1 959 – ✉ Haverfordwest — 33 A3

London 266 mi – Carmarthen 46 mi – Fishguard 16 mi

Oriel Y Parc, ✆ (01437) 72 03 92, www.stdavids.co.uk

St Davids City, Whitesands Bay, ✆ (01437) 72 17 51

Town★ – Cathedral★★ - Bishop's Palace★ **AC**

Pembrokeshire Coast National Park★★

WALES

Ramsey House

Lower Moor, Southwest : 0.5 mi on Porth Clais rd ✉ SA62 6RP – ✆ (01437) 720 321 – www.ramseyhouse.co.uk – Closed January, December and restricted opening November and February

6 rm – †£ 70/115 ††£ 105/115 **Rest** – Menu £ 40

Unassuming house on the edge of the UK's smallest city. Stylish modern bedrooms have coastal views, bold décor and a boutique style; the smart shower rooms feature aromatherapy toiletries. A comfy lounge leads through to the wood-furnished dining room, where tasty, attractively presented dishes are served.

Cwtch

22 High St ✉ SA62 6SD – ✆ (01437) 720 491 – www.cwtchrestaurant.co.uk – Closed 1 January and 6-31 January, 25- 26 December , Sunday-Tuesday November-March

Rest – *(dinner only) (booking advisable)* Menu £ 15/30

Popular, laid-back restaurant; its name meaning 'hug'. The three rustic dining rooms boast stone walls, crammed bookshelves and log-filled alcoves. Classical British dishes arrive in generous portions and service is polite and friendly.

ST GEORGE (Llan Sain Siôr) – Conwy

32 C1

London 227 mi – Cardiff 180 mi – Dublin 62 mi – Birmingham 113 mi

Kinmel Arms with rm

The Village ✉ LL22 9BP – ✆ (01745) 832 207 – www.thekinmelarms.co.uk – Closed Sunday and Monday

4 rm – †£ 115/175 ††£ 115/175 **Rest** – Carte £ 24/40

Early 17C stone inn, hidden away in a hamlet by the entrance to Kinmel Hall, with a delightful open-fired bar and two spacious dining areas. Lunch offers pub favourites, while dinner is more complex; home-grown herbs and fruit feature. Stylish, contemporary bedrooms boast large kitchenettes for breakfast.

WALES

SAUNDERSFOOT – Pembrokeshire – 503 F28 – pop. 2 946

33 A4

London 241 mi – Cardiff 90 mi – Pembroke 12 mi

St Brides Spa

St Brides Hill ✉ SA69 9NH – ✆ (01834) 812 304 – www.stbridesspahotel.com

46 rm – †£ 125/195 ††£ 150/320 – 6 suites

Rest *Cliff* – see restaurant listing

Nautically styled hotel overlooking the harbour and bay, featuring wood panelling and contemporary Welsh art. The stylish spa boasts an outdoor infinity pool. Well-appointed bedrooms come in cream and blue hues and boast smart bathrooms.

Cliff – St Brides Spa Hotel

St Brides Hill ✉ SA69 9NH – ✆ (01834) 812 304 – www.stbridesspahotel.com

Rest – Carte £ 28/39

Smart yet casual restaurant in a New England style hotel, boasting beautiful decked terraces and stunning views over the bay. Extensive lunch menu; dinner is more refined, offering modern British dishes with local produce to the fore.

SEION – Gwynedd – see Caernarfon

SENNYBRIDGE (Pontsenni) – Powys

33 B3

London 189 mi – Cardiff 43 mi – Birmingham 127 mi – Liverpool 147 mi

Blaencar Farm without rest

South : 1.5 mi by Defynnog Road off A 4067 ✉ LD3 8HA – ✆ (01874) 636 610 – www.blaencar.co.uk – Closed 25 December

3 rm – †£ 45/55 ††£ 70/90

Stone house on a 450 acre working farm; its name meaning 'Mouth of the Brook'. Superb welcome from the friendly, hands-on owner, who is a font of local knowledge. Traditional breakfast room, homely lounge and simple, comfortable bedrooms.

SKENFRITH – Monmouthshire – 503 L28 33 C4

London 135 mi – Hereford 16 mi – Ross-on-Wye 11 mi

Bell at Skenfrith with rm

✉ NP7 8UH – ☎ (01600) 750 235 – www.skenfrith.co.uk – *Closed Tuesday November-Easter*

11 rm – †£ 75/120 ††£ 110/220

Rest – *(booking essential)* Menu £ 18 (weekday lunch)/26 – Carte £ 29/42

Well-run pub in a verdant valley, offering hearty, classical cooking with the occasional ambitious twist and using ingredients from the organic kitchen garden. There's an excellent choice of champagnes and cognacs, and service is warm and unobtrusive. Super-comfy bedrooms have an understated elegance.

SWANSEA – Swansea – 503 I29 – pop. 175 204 33 B4

London 191 mi – Birmingham 136 mi – Bristol 82 mi – Cardiff 40 mi

Plymouth St, ☎ (01792) 46 83 21, www.swansea.info

Morriston, 160 Clasemont Rd, ☎ (01792) 79 65 28

Clyne, Mayals, 120 Owls Lodge Lane, ☎ (01792) 40 19 89

Langland Bay, ☎ (01792) 36 17 21

Town★ - Maritime Quarter★ B – Maritime and Industrial Museum★ B – Glynn Vivian Art Gallery★ B – Guildhall (British Empire Panels★ A **H**)

Gower Peninsula★★ (Rhossili★★), W : by A 4067 A. The Wildfowl and Wetlands Trust★, Llanelli, NW : 6.5 mi by A 483 and A 484 A

Plans pages 841, 842

SWANSEA

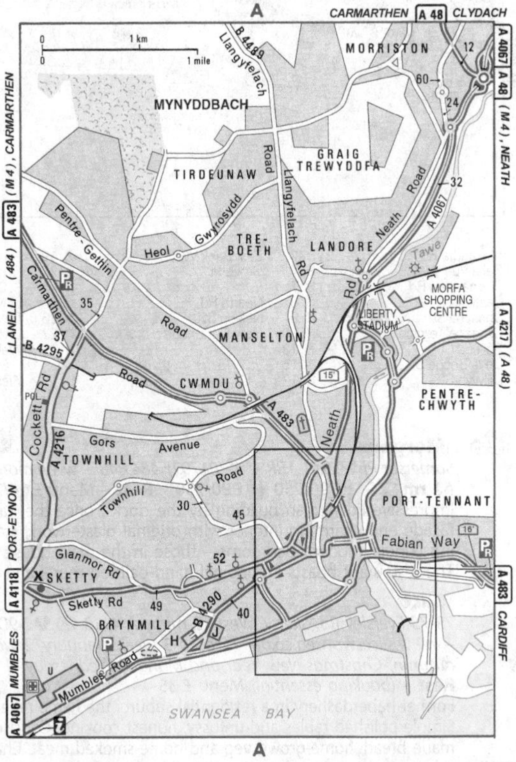

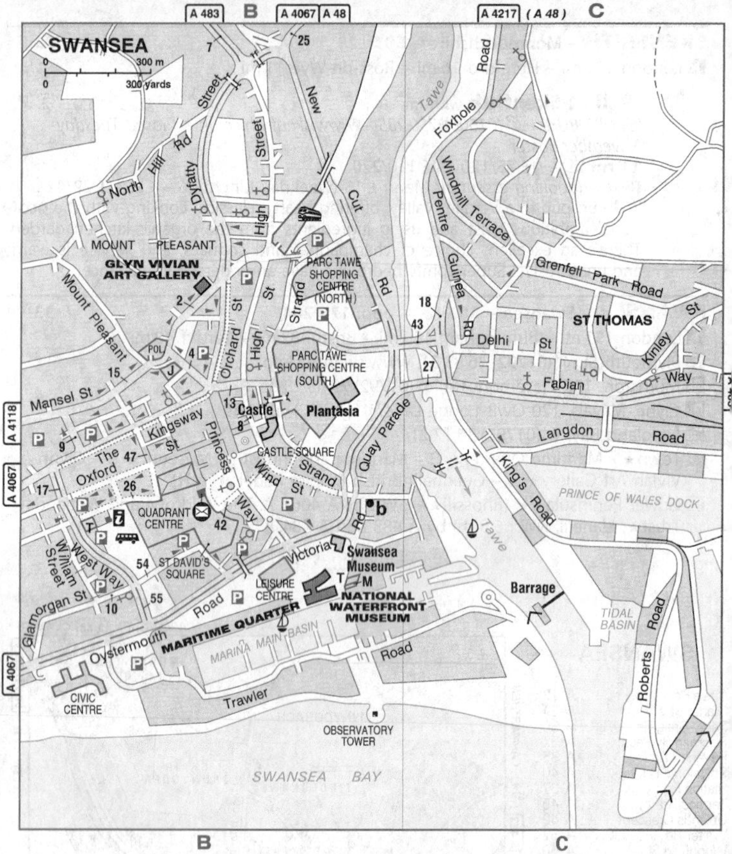

- Alexandra Rd . . . . **B** 2
- Belle Vue Way . . . . **B** 4
- Carmarthen Rd . . . . **B** 7
- Castle St . . . . **B** 8
- Christina St . . . . **B** 9
- Clarence Terrace . . . . **B** 10
- College St . . . . **B** 13
- De la Beche St . . . . **B** 15
- Dillwyn St. . . . . **B** 17
- East Bank Way . . . . **C** 18
- Grove Pl. . . . . **B** 22
- Kingsway (The) . . . . **B**
- Nearth Rd . . . . **B** 25
- Nelson St. . . . . **B** 26
- New Cut Bridge . . . . **C** 27
- Oxford St . . . . **B**
- Parc Tawe Shopping Centre . . . . **B**
- Princess Way. . . . . **B**
- Quadrant Centre . . . . **B**
- St David's Square . . . . **B**
- St Mary's Square. . . . . **B** 42
- Tawe Bridge. . . . . **C** 43
- Union St. . . . . **B** 47
- Wellington St . . . . **B** 54
- West Way . . . . **B** 55

Morgans

Somerset Pl ✉ *SA1 1RR – ✆ (01792) 484 848 – www.morganshotel.co.uk*

42 rm ☕ – 🛉£ 90/250 🛉🛉£ 90/250 **Rest** – Menu £ 14/22 B**b**

Impressive Edwardian building by the docks; once the harbour offices. Beautiful façade and charming interior with original plasterwork, stained glass and a soaring cupola. Modern bedrooms – those in the main house are the most spacious. The restaurant boasts an original hand-painted mural and a modern menu.

Slice

73-75 Eversley Rd, Sketty, West : 2 mi by A 4118 ✉ *SA2 9DE – ✆ (01792) 290 929 – www.sliceswansea.co.uk – Closed 3 weeks January, 2 weeks summer, 2 weeks autumn, Christmas-New Year and Monday-Wednesday* A**x**

Rest – *(booking essential)* Menu £ 35

Former haberdashery in a residential suburb; the name reflecting its tapered shape. Simple polished tables and unfussy, honest cooking. Concise menus feature home-made bread, home-grown veg and home-smoked meat. Chatty, friendly service.

TREDUNNOCK – Newport – **503** L29 – see Usk

TREMEIRCHION – Denbighshire – **502** J24 – ✉ St Asaph **32** C1

London 225 mi – Chester 29 mi – Shrewsbury 59 mi

Bach-Y-Graig without rest

Southwest : 2 mi by B 5429 off Denbigh rd ✉ LL17 0UH – ☎ (01745) 730 627 – www.bachygraig.co.uk

3 rm – †£ 48/50 ††£ 75/84

Welcoming 16C red-brick farmhouse, on a 200 acre working farm. The three decently sized bedrooms boast countryside views; antique furniture sits alongside mod cons like flat-screen TVs. Traditional lounges. Communal breakfasts.

USK – Monmouthshire – **503** L28 – **pop. 2 318** **33** C4

London 144 mi – Bristol 30 mi – Cardiff 26 mi – Gloucester 39 mi

Alice Springs, Usk, Kemeys Commander, ☎ (01873) 88 07 08

Raglan Castle★ **AC**, NE : 7 mi by A 472, A 449 and A 40

Glen-Yr-Afon House rest,

Pontypool Rd ✉ NP15 1SY – ☎ (01291) 672 302 – www.glen-yr-afon.co.uk – Closed 24-26 December

28 rm – †£ 99/123 ††£ 136/159

Rest *Clarkes* – Carte £ 22/38

Olive-green, extended Victorian villa just across the bridge from town. Comfortable, traditionally styled guest areas overlook the well-tended gardens. Mix of country house and more modern bedrooms; one is a four-poster. Wood-panelled, two-roomed restaurant serves traditional dishes made with Welsh produce.

at Llandenny Northeast : 4.25 mi by A 472 off B 4235 – ✉ Usk

Raglan Arms

✉ NP15 1DL – ☎ (01291) 690 800 – www.theraglanarms.co.uk – Closed 25-26 December, Sunday dinner and Monday

Rest – Carte £ 21/34

Cosy, stone-built village pub with fireside sofas, simply laid tables and fresh flowers. Local produce employed in unfussy seasonal dishes, with a good balance of flavours. Lunchtime main courses offer particularly good value.

at Llangybi South : 2.5 mi on Llangybi rd – ✉ Ceredigion

White Hart with rm

✉ NP15 1NP – ☎ (01633) 450 258 – www.thewhitehartvillageinn.com – Closed Monday except bank holidays and Sunday dinner

1 rm – †£ 65/95 ††£ 95/110

Rest – Menu £ 19 (weekday dinner)/45 – Carte £ 25/40

Characterful pub with a priest's hole, 11 fireplaces from the 1600s and an interesting history. Choose from an adventurous à la carte of well-prepared, precisely presented dishes or a slightly simpler set menu; most produce is from within 10 miles. There's only one bedroom – a double with an adjoining single.

at Tredunnock South : 4.75 mi by Llangybi rd – ✉ Newport

Newbridge on Usk with rm rest,

East : 0.5 mi ✉ NP15 1LY – ☎ (01633) 451 000 – www.newbridgeonusk.co.uk

6 rm – †£ 78/192 ††£ 92/212 **Rest** – Menu £ 20 (lunch) – Carte £ 29/41

200 year old inn by a bridge over the River Usk; choose from several dining areas set over two levels or sit on the terrace to have the snack menu. Classic British cooking has a modern twist; sharing plates are popular and include a crumble dessert. The smart, comfortable bedrooms are in a separate block.

VALLEY – **503** G24 – see Anglesey (Isle of)

WHITEBROOK – Monmouthshire – see Monmouth

WHITTON – Powys – **503** J27 – **pop. 300** **33** C3

London 185 mi – Cardiff 84 mi – Birmingham 84 mi – Liverpool 108 mi

Pilleth Oaks without rest

Northwest : 1.25 mi on B 4356 ✉ LD7 1NP – ✆ (01457) 560 272 – www.pillethoaks.co.uk – Closed 26 May- 9 June

3 rm – †£ 45 ††£ 70/80

Double-gabled country house set in 100 acres, overlooking two lakes and the surrounding hills. Traditional, antique-filled interior with an elegant lounge and comfortable bedrooms; one has a balcony and great views. The welcoming owner offers tea on arrival and communal breakfasts at a smart oak table.

WOLF'S CASTLE (Cas-Blaidd) – **Pembrokeshire** – **503** F28 – **pop. 616** **33** A3 – ✉ **Haverfordwest**

London 258 mi – Fishguard 7 mi – Haverfordwest 8 mi

Pembrokeshire Coast National Park★★

Wolfscastle Country H.

✉ SA62 5LZ – ✆ (01437) 741 225 – www.wolfscastle.com – Closed 24-26 December

20 rm – †£ 82/105 ††£ 118/150 **Rest** – Carte £ 22/39

Former manor house that's been greatly expanded over the years; a popular place for weddings and conferences. Bedrooms are modern, well-equipped and have very comfy beds – some are four-posters. Eat in the formal restaurant, the bright and airy brasserie or on the terrace. Friendly, efficient service.

WALES

WREXHAM (Wrecsam) – **Wrexham** – **502** L24 – **pop. 42 576** **32** C1

London 192 mi – Chester 12 mi – Liverpool 35 mi – Shrewsbury 28 mi

Lambpit St, ✆ (01978) 29 20 15, www.wrexham.gov.uk

Chirk, ✆ (01691) 77 44 07

Clays Golf Centre, Bryn Estyn Rd, ✆ (01978) 66 14 06

Moss Valley, Moss Rd, ✆ (01978) 72 05 18

St Giles Church★

Erddig★★ **AC** (Gardens★★), SW : 2 m – Gresford (All Saints Church★), N : 4 mi by A 5152 and B 5445

at Gresford **Northeast : 3 mi by A 483 on B 5445**

Pant-yr-Ochain

Old Wrexham Rd, South : 1 mi ✉ LL12 8TY – ✆ (01978) 853 525 – www.pantyrochain-gresford.co.uk

Rest – Carte £ 20/32

Classic country manor house with mature, manicured gardens leading down to a lake. Daily changing menu offers hearty, wholesome, all-day dishes, ranging from pub classics to more modern fare.

Ireland

Northern Ireland

ANNAHILT = Eanach Eilte – **Lisburn** – **712** N/O4 – **see Hillsborough**

ARMAGH (Ard Mhacha) – **Armagh** – **712** M4 **35** C3

Belfast 39 mi – Dungannon 13 mi – Portadown 11 mi

St Patrick's Cathedral★ (Anglican) - St Patrick's Cathedral★ (Roman Catholic) - The Mall★ : Armagh County Museum★ **AC**, Royal Irish Fusiliers Museum★ **AC**

Navan Fort★ **AC** W : 2 mi by A 28. The Argory★ **AC** N : 10 mi by A 29 and minor road right

Moody Boar

Palace Stables, Palace Demense, South : 0.5 mi off A 3. ✉ BT60 4EL – ℘ (028) 3752 9678 – www.themoodyboar.com – Closed Easter Sunday, 25-26 December

Rest – Menu £ 15 (weekdays) – Carte £ 19/36

Set in the stables of the former Primate of All Ireland's house and run by a young team. Characterful, rustic interior with a vaulted ceiling, a stone floor and booths in the old stalls. Wide choice of classic dishes with personal touches.

Uluru Bistro

16-18 Market St ✉ BT61 7BX – ℘ (028) 3751 8051 – www.ulurubistro.com

Rest – *(booking essential)* Menu £ 17 (weekdays) – Carte £ 22/36

Modern, split-level bistro in the shadow of St Patrick's Cathedral. The Australian chef cooks tasty Mediterranean and Asian dishes, along with a few of his native meats such as crocodile, kangaroo and ostrich; veg is from their poly-tunnel.

BALLINTOY – **Moyle** – **712** M2 **35** C1

Belfast 59 mi – Ballycastle 8 mi – Londonderry 48 mi – Lisburn 67 mi

Whitepark House without rest

150 Whitepark Rd, West : 1.5 mi on A 2 ✉ BT54 6NH – ℘ (028) 2073 1482 – www.whiteparkhouse.com – mid February-October

4 rm – †£ 80 ††£ 120

Charming 18C house near the Giant's Causeway, decorated with lovely wall hangings, framed silks and other artefacts from the personable owner's travels. Large, open-fired lounge where cakes are served on arrival. Bright, antique-furnished bedrooms have four-posters or half testers and smart modern bathrooms.

BALLYCLARE (Bealach Cláir) – **Newtownabbey** – **712** N/O3 **35** D2 – **pop. 8 770**

Belfast 14 mi – Newtownabbey 6 mi – Lisburn 23 mi

Oregano

29 Ballyrobert Rd, South : 3.25 mi by A 57 on B 56 ✉ BT39 9RY – ℘ (028) 9084 0099 – www.oreganorestaurant.co.uk – Closed 11-13 July, 24-27 December, Saturday lunch and Monday

Rest – Menu £ 18 (weekdays)/25 – Carte £ 22/37

Unassuming Victorian house in a countryside setting; the interior is a real contrast with its modern bar and dining room, featuring bold, colourful wallpaper and contemporary art. Local produce is used in unfussy, flavoursome brasserie dishes with some Mediterranean influences. Polite, well-organised service.

BALLYMENA (An Baile Meánach) – **Ballymena** – **712** N3 **35** C2 – **pop. 28 717** Ireland

Belfast 27 mi – Dundalk 78 mi – Larne 21 mi – Londonderry 51 mi

1-29 Bridge St, ℘ (028) 2563 59 00, www.ballymena.gov.uk

128 Raceview Rd, ℘ (028) 2586 12 07

Antrim Glens★★★ - Murlough Bay★★★ (Fair Head ≤★★★), NE : 32 mi by A 26, A 44, A 2 and minor road - Glengariff Forest Park★★ **AC** (Waterfall★★), NW : 13 mi by A 43 – Glengariff★, NE : 18 mi by A 43 - Glendun★, NE : 19 mi by A 43, B 14 and A2 – Antrim (Round Tower★) S : 9.5 mi by A 26

at Galgorm West : 3 mi on A 42

Galgorm Resort and Spa rest,
136 Fenaghy Rd, West : 1.5 mi on Cullybacky rd ✉ BT42 1EA – ✆ (028) 2588 1001 – www.galgorm.com
75 rm – £ 175 £ 175
Rest *River Room* – see restaurant listing
Rest *Gillies* – Carte £ 23/41
Rest *Fratelli* – ✆ (028) 2588 1001 *(closed Monday except in summer) (dinner only and lunch Saturday-Sunday)* Carte £ 17/24
Victorian manor house with newer extensions, set in large grounds. Stylish interior with plenty of lounge space, a huge function capacity and an excellent leisure club with a superb outdoor spa pool. Modern bedrooms boast state-of-the-art facilities; some have balconies. Extensive all-day menus served in characterful Gillies; informal Fratelli offers Italian fare.

River Room – Galgorm Resort and Spa Hotel
136 Fenaghy Rd, West : 1.5 mi on Cullybacky rd ✉ BT42 1EA – ✆ (028) 2588 1001 – www.galgorm.com – Closed Monday and Tuesday
Rest – *(dinner only)* Menu £ 45
Formal, warmly decorated dining room set on the ground floor of a stylishly furnished, whitewashed Victorian manor house, with good views across the River Maine. Refined, classically based cooking and attentive service.

BANGOR (Beannchar) – **North Down** – **712** O/P4 – **pop. 62 840** **35** D2
Ireland

Belfast 15 mi – Newtownards 5 mi
34 Quay St, ✆ (028) 9127 00 69, www.bangor-local.com
North Down Heritage Centre★
Ulster Folk and Transport Museum★★ **AC**, W : 8 mi by A 2. Newtownards : Movilla Priory (Cross Slabs★) S : 4 mi by A 21 - Mount Stewart★★★ **AC**, SE : 90 mi by A 21 and A 20 – Scrabo Tower (★★) S : 6.5 mi by A 21 – Ballycopeland Windmill★, SE : 10 mi by B 21 and A 2, turning right at Millisle – Strangford Lough★ (Castle Espie Centre★ **AC** - Nendrum Monastery★) - Grey Abbey★ **AC**, SE : 20 mi by A 2, A 21 and A 20

Clandeboye Lodge
10 Estate Rd, Clandeboye, Southwest : 3 mi by A 2 and Dundonald rd following signs for Blackwood Golf Centre ✉ BT19 1UR – ✆ (028) 9185 2500 – www.clandeboyelodge.com – Closed 24-26 December
43 rm – £ 70/90 £ 85/150
Rest *Clan Brasserie* – *(dinner only and Sunday lunch)* Menu £ 20 – Carte £ 21/36
Well-run property on the site of a former estate school house. A popular wedding venue, it is surrounded by 4 acres of woodland and well-placed for country and coast. Airy, open-plan guest areas and contemporary bedrooms with a high level of facilities. Accessible menu served in Clan Brasserie.

Salty Dog N
10-12 Seacliff Rd ✉ BT20 5EY – ✆ (028) 9127 0696 – www.saltydogbangor.com
15 rm – £ 60/85 £ 80/110
Rest – *(booking advisable)* Menu £ 15 (lunch)/19 – Carte £ 23/44
Boutique hotel in a pair of bay-windowed, red-brick Victorian townhouses overlooking Bangor Marina and Belfast Lough. Contemporary bedrooms vary greatly in shape and size; go for one of the larger front rooms with a view. Bistro with terrace, serving a mix of classics and more ambitious dishes.

Cairn Bay Lodge without rest
278 Seacliffe Rd, East : 1.25 mi by Quay St ✉ BT20 5HS – ✆ (028) 9146 7636 – www.cairnbaylodge.com
7 rm – £ 50/60 £ 80/90
Large, whitewashed Edwardian house just out of the town centre, overlooking the bay. Comfy guest areas feature unusual objets d'art and ornaments; spacious, individually styled bedrooms boast plenty of extras. Friendly owners leave homemade cake on the landing. Small beauty and therapy facility.

Shelleven House without rest

59-61 Princetown Rd ✉ BT20 3TA – ✆ (028) 9127 1777 – www.shellevenhouse.com – Closed 23-28 December

10 rm ☕ – 🚹£ 40/70 🚹🚹£ 75/90

Double-fronted, three-storey, Victorian end terrace, in smart residential area near the marina. Open-plan lounge and breakfast room; excellent breakfasts. Well-kept bedrooms vary in shape and size; front rooms boast great coastal views.

Boat House

Seacliff Rd ✉ BT20 5HA – ✆ (028) 9146 9253 – www.theboathouseni.co.uk – Closed 1 January, Monday and Tuesday

Rest – Menu £ 20 (lunch)/60 – Carte £ 33/46

This delightful stone-built former lifeboat station houses an intimate dining room with a harbourside terrace. Ambitious, modern menus have the occasional Dutch twist and the experienced owners (brothers) source quality local produce.

Coyle's

44 High St ✉ BT20 5AZ – ✆ (028) 9127 0362 – www.coylesbistro.co.uk – Closed 25 December

Rest – Menu £ 25 (early dinner) – Carte £ 26/32

Friendly, laid-back pub; a great place for a quiet drink or a good meal with family and friends. The modern ground floor bar offers pub classics and some international influences; upstairs, the restaurant menu steps things up a gear.

BELFAST

See city maps on following pages

35 D2

© IIC/Design Pics RM/Age fotostock

Belfast – **pop. 258 659** – **712** O4 – Ireland

Dublin 103 mi – Londonderry 70 mi

Tourist Information

47 Donegal Pl, (028) 9024 66 09, www.gotobelfast.com

Airports

Belfast International Airport, Aldergrove : (028) 9448 4848, W : 15 ½ m. by A 52 AY

George Best Belfast City Airport : (028) 9093 9093

Ferries and Shipping Lines

to Isle of Man (Douglas) (Isle of Man Steam Packet Co. Ltd) (summer only) (2 h 45 mn) – to Stranraer (Stena Line) 4-5 daily (1 h 30 mn/3 h 15 mn), (Seacat Scotland) March-January (90 mn) – to Liverpool (Norfolkline Irish Sea) daily (8 h 30 mn)

Golf Courses

Balmoral, 518 Lisburn Rd, (028) 9038 15 14

Belvoir Park, Newtonbreda, 73 Church Rd, (028) 90 49 16 93

Fortwilliam, Downview Ave, (028) 9037 07 70

SIGHTS

In the town : City★ • Ulster Museum★ AZ**M1** • City Hall★ BY • Donegall Square★ BY**20** • Botanic Gardens★AZ • St Anne's Cathedral★ BX • Crown Liquor Saloon★ BY • Sinclair Seamen's Church★ BX • St Malachy's Church★ BY

In the surrounding area : Carrickfergus Castle★★ **AC** NE : 9.5 mi by A 2

On the outskirts : Belfast Zoological Gardens★★ AC, N : 5 mi by A 6 AY

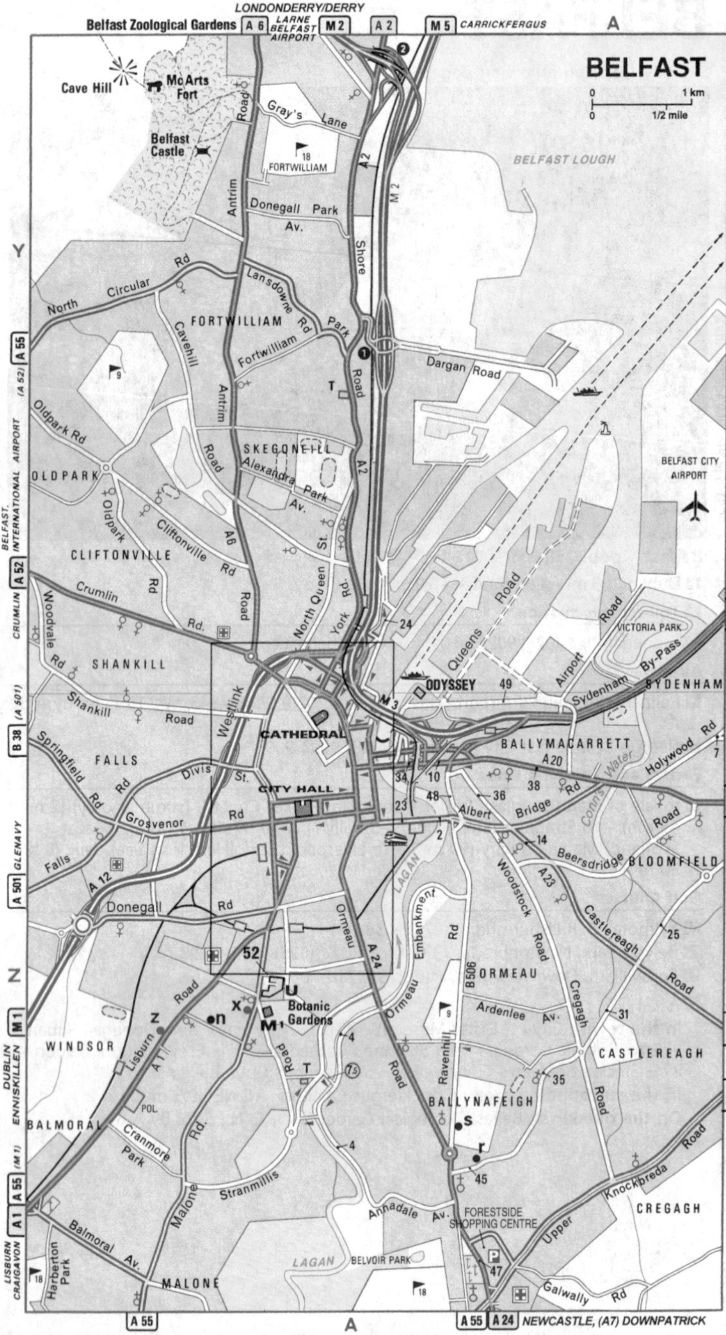

BELFAST
0 1 km
0 1/2 mile
LONDONDERRY/DERRY
Belfast Zoological Gardens
A 6
LARNE
BELFAST
AIRPORT
M 2
A 2
M 5
CARRICKFERGUS
A
Cave Hill
McArts Fort
Belfast Castle
FORTWILLIAM
Gray's Lane
Antrim Road
Donegall Park Av.
Shore Road
BELFAST LOUGH
North Circular Rd
Lansdowne Rd
Park
Fortwilliam
Cavehill
Dargan Road
Oldpark Rd
OLDPARK
SKEGONEILL
Alexandra Park Av.
BELFAST CITY AIRPORT
Cliftonville Rd
CLIFTONVILLE
North Queen St.
York Rd.
Crumlin Rd.
Woodvale Rd
SHANKILL
Queens Road
Airport Road
VICTORIA PARK
Sydenham By-Pass
SYDENHAM
ODYSSEY
Shankill Road
Westlink
CATHEDRAL
BALLYMACARRETT
Holywood Rd
Springfield Rd
FALLS
Divis St.
CITY HALL
Connswater
Grosvenor Rd
Albert Bridge Rd
Beersbridge
BLOOMFIELD
Falls
A 12
Donegall Rd
Woodstock Road
Castlereagh Road
Ormeau Embankment
LAGAN
52
ORMEAU
Botanic Gardens
Lisburn Road
A 24
WINDSOR
Ardenlee Av.
Cregagh Road
CASTLEREAGH
Ormeau Road
Ravenhill Road
BALLYNAFEIGH
POL.
BALMORAL
Cranmore Park
Malone Rd.
Stranmillis Road
Knockbreda Road
Upper
CREGAGH
Annadale Av.
FORESTSIDE SHOPPING CENTRE
Balmoral Av.
Harberton Park
LAGAN
BELVOIR PARK
MALONE
Galwally Rd
A 55
A 55 A 24 NEWCASTLE, (A7) DOWNPATRICK
NORTHERN IRELAND
A 55 (A 52) BELFAST INTERNATIONAL AIRPORT
A 52 CRUMLIN
B 38 (A 501)
A 501 GLENAVY
M 1 DUBLIN ENNISKILLEN
A 55 (M 1)
A 1 LISBURN CRAIGAVON
A 2 BANGOR
A 20 NEWTOWNARDS
A 23 (A 55)
A 55
Y
Z

BELFAST
0 200 m
0 200 yards
A 52
A 6
B
A 2
M 2
X
Y
Z
A 1
A 55
A 24
(A 2, A 20)
A 2
A 20
A 23
Crumlin Rd
Westlink
CLIFTON HOUSE
Frederick St
Great George's St
Donegall
York
Nelson St
Corporation St
SINCLAIR SEAMEN'S CHURCH
M 3
LAGAN
Peters Hill
Carrick Hill
North Street
Millfield
Townsend St
ST ANNE'S CATHEDRAL
Royal Av
Street
CASTLECOURT SHOPPING CENTRE
Divis Street
Castle St
Castle Pl
VICTORIA SQUARE SHOPPING CENTRE
Donegall Pl
WEIR
Belfast Waterfront Hall
POL.
Durham St
College Sq
CITY HALL
Chichester St
Royal Courts of Justice
Victoria
May St
Oxford St
Grosvenor Road
Opera
St George's Market
GREAT VICTORIA
Great Victoria St
Bedford St
CROWN LIQUOR SALOON
ULSTER HALL
Adelaide St
Alfred Street
ST MALACHY'S CHURCH
Cromac Street
Bruce St.
Ormeau Av.
Sandy Row
Dublin Road
Ormeau Road
Pass
Donegall Road
Donegall Pass
CITY HOSPITAL
BOTANIC
Botanic Av.
Lisburn Road
University Road
University Street

INDEX OF STREET NAMES IN BELFAST

Merchant

16 Skipper St ✉ *BT1 2DZ* – ✆ *(028) 9023 4888* – *www.themerchanthotel.com*
62 rm ☕ – 🚹£ 150/250 🚹🚹£ 160/260 – 2 suites BX**x**
Rest *Great Room* – see restaurant listing
Rest *Berts* – *(dinner only and lunch Saturday-Sunday)* Menu £ 20 – Carte £ 23/36
Former Ulster Bank HQ with an impressive Victorian façade. Bedrooms are plush and intimately styled; those in the annexe have an art deco theme. The rooftop gym comes with an outdoor hot tub and a skyline view; afterwards relax in the swish cocktail bar. Fine dining room and classic brasserie with live jazz.

Fitzwilliam

Great Victoria St ✉ *BT2 7BQ* – ✆ *(028) 9044 2080* – *www.fitzwilliamhotelbelfast.com* BY**e**
130 rm ☕ – 🚹£ 190/200 🚹🚹£ 200/210 – 1 suite
Rest *Fitzwilliam* – see restaurant listing
Stylish hotel by the Grand Opera House. Smart modern bedrooms have striking colour schemes, contemporary furnishings and good facilities; the higher up you go, the better the grade. Informal dining in the bar and afternoon tea in the lobby.

Malmaison

rest,

34-38 Victoria St ✉ *BT1 3GH* – ✆ *(0844) 693 06 50* – *www.malmaison.com*
64 rm – 🚹£ 99/180 🚹🚹£ 99/180, ☕ £ 16 – 2 suites BY**v**
Rest *Brasserie* – Menu £ 20 – Carte £ 24/64
Converted Victorian seed warehouse with an ornate exterior. Original features blend with modern furnishings. The dark-hued reception leads to a snug bar; stylish bedrooms offer good facilities – one boasts a 7′ bed and a snooker table. French menus offered in the distressed wood, beach hut style brasserie.

Radisson Blu
3 Cromac Pl, Cromac Wood, Ormeau Rd ✉ BT7 2JB – ☎ (028) 9043 4065 – www.radissonblu.co.uk/hotelbelfast BY**z**
120 rm – †£ 170 ††£ 170 – 1 suite
Rest *Filini* – *(closed Sunday dinner)* Menu £ 14/26 – Carte £ 24/46
Stylish hotel with spacious, open-plan guest areas; on the site of the former city gasworks. Smart, modern bedrooms come in Urban or Nordic styles and offer a high level of facilities, including underfloor heating in the bathrooms. Mediterranean-influenced menus in Filini, with its floor to ceiling windows.

Ten Square
10 Donegall Sq South ✉ BT1 5JD – ☎ (028) 9024 1001 – www.tensquare.co.uk – Closed 25 December BY**x**
22 rm – †£ 65/150 ††£ 65/170
Rest *Grill Room* – Menu £ 23/32 – Carte £ 20/38
Sizeable Victorian property in the town centre, hidden behind the city hall. Stylish, modern bedrooms display bold feature walls and offer a good level of facilities. The vibrant bar has a pavement terrace and entertainment at weekends. The Grill Room offers something for everyone on its extensive menu.

Malone Lodge rest,
60 Eglantine Ave ✉ BT9 6DY – ☎ (028) 9038 8000 – www.malonelodgehotelbelfast.com AZ**n**
53 rm – †£ 75/125 ††£ 90/150 – 2 suites
Rest *Green Door* – Carte £ 16/34
Well-run, privately owned townhouse, in a peaceful Victorian terrace. Smart, spacious bedrooms are spread over various annexes and range from corporate rooms to presidential suites and apartments. State-of-the-art function rooms include a large ballroom. Characterful bar and next door grill restaurant.

Crescent Townhouse
13 Lower Cres ✉ BT7 1NR – ☎ (028) 9032 3349 – www.crescenttownhouse.com – Closed 1 January, 11-12 July and 24-26 December BZ**x**
17 rm – †£ 55/75 ††£ 65/85
Rest *Metro Brasserie* – see restaurant listing
A Regency-style townhouse run by a welcoming team. Snug first floor lounge hung with oils. Smart, spacious bedrooms are split between the old house and extension; all are well-equipped and some boast four-posters and huge bathrooms.

Ravenhill House without rest
690 Ravenhill Rd ✉ BT6 0BZ – ☎ (028) 9020 7444 – www.ravenhillhouse.com – Closed 1-7 January, 7-15 July, 27 August-2 September and 20-31 December
5 rm – †£ 55/60 ††£ 75/85 AZ**s**
Red-brick Victorian house set in the city suburbs. Bright, homely lounge and wood-furnished breakfast room; colourful bedrooms boast good facilities. Organic breakfasts feature homemade muesli and the wheat for the bread is home-milled.

Roseleigh House without rest
19 Rosetta Park, South : 1.5 mi by A 24 (Ormeau Rd) ✉ BT6 0DL – ☎ (028) 9064 4414 – www.roseleighhouse.co.uk – Closed Easter and Christmas AZ**r**
6 rm – †£ 45/50 ††£ 65/80
Victorian bay-windowed house in a residential area by the Belvoir Park golf course; the friendly owner really makes guests feel welcome. Small lounge with lots of local info and a linen-laid breakfast room. Simple, well-kept bedrooms.

XXX **Great Room** – Merchant Hotel
16 Skipper St ✉ BT1 2DZ – ☎ (028) 9023 4888 – www.themerchanthotel.com
Rest – Menu £ 25/28 – Carte dinner £ 35/52 BX**x**
Grand old banking hall – set behind the impressive Victorian façade of the former Ulster Bank HQ – featuring ornate gold coving and plasterwork and original stained glass windows. Classic British dishes come with a Mediterranean edge.

NORTHERN IRELAND

XX **James Street South**

21 James St South ✉ BT2 7GA – ✆ (028) 9043 4310 – www.jamesstreetsouth.co.uk – Closed Easter Monday, 12-17 July, 25-26 December, 1 January and Sunday BY**b**

Rest – Carte £ 26/41

Smart sidestreet restaurant with a Victorian façade, a bright dining room and a semi-open kitchen. Classical cooking relies on quality natural produce, prepared simply so that flavours shine through. Service is efficient and organised.

XX **Shu**

253 Lisburn Rd ✉ BT9 7EN – ✆ (028) 9038 1655 – www.shu-restaurant.com – Closed 1 January, 11-13 July, 24-26 December and Sunday AZ**z**

Rest – Menu £ 14 (lunch)/31 – Carte £ 23/40

A well-established neighbourhood restaurant with a modern look and a lively, vibrant atmosphere. Menus are guided by seasonality and the ambitious, modern British dishes have international influences. Good value set price menu.

XX **Deanes**

36 Howard St ✉ BT1 6PF – ✆ (028) 9033 1134 – www.michaeldeane.co.uk – Closed 25-26 December, 1 January, 12 July, Easter Monday and Sunday

Rest – Menu £ 20 – Carte £ 25/45 BY**n**

Long-standing restaurant consisting of a smart modern brasserie – serving classically based dishes of local produce – and a small seafood bar offering a concise selection of fresh fish and shellfish. Service is polite and organised.

XX **Fitzwilliam** – Fitzwilliam Hotel

Great Victoria St ✉ BT2 7BQ – ✆ (028) 9044 2080 – www.fitzwilliamhotelbelfast.com BY**e**

Rest – *(dinner only) (booking essential)* Menu £ 25/30 – Carte £ 28/42

Bright, three-roomed restaurant on the first floor of a stylish hotel. If you're in a group choose one of the large communal tables; if you're a couple, opt for one of the intimate booths. Concise menus feature modern Irish dishes.

X **Bar + Grill at James Street South**

21 James St South ✉ BT2 7GA – ✆ (028) 9560 0700 – www.belfastbargrill.co.uk – Closed 1 January, 12 July, and 25-26 December BY**b**

Rest – *(booking advisable)* Carte £ 21/40

Vibrant modern bistro with a high ceiling, a marble floor, red brick walls and warehouse-style windows. Classic brasserie menus; the grill dishes are a hit and the succulent steaks are served on boards and come with a choice of sauces.

X **Deanes at Queens**

1 College Gdns ✉ BT9 6BQ – ✆ (028) 9038 2111 – www.michaeldeane.co.uk – Closed 1 January, 31 March-1 April, 12 July, 25-26 December and Sunday dinner AZ**x**

Rest – Menu £ 18/28 – Carte £ 20/34

Bright, bustling brasserie with a nice terrace and a retro style; large pictures of the chef's suppliers hang on the walls. Cooking is simple and focuses on flavours – classic brasserie dishes have modern twists. Polite, structured service.

X **Deanes Deli**

42-44 Bedford St ✉ BT2 7FF – ✆ (028) 9024 8800 – www.michaeldeane.co.uk – Closed Easter, 1 January, 12 July, 25-26 December, and Sunday BY**a**

Rest – Menu £ 16 – Carte £ 21/34

Glass-fronted city centre eatery. One side is a smart restaurant offering an appealing menu of classical dishes with some Asian and Mediterranean influences. The other side acts as a coffee shop by day and a buzzy tapas bar by night.

X **Home** N

22 Wellington Pl ✉ BT1 6GE – ✆ (028) 9023 4946 – www.homepopup.com – Closed Monday dinner BY**r**

Rest – Menu £ 19 (weekday dinner) – Carte £ 20/32

Popular restaurant with a deli and café to the front, and a simple, rustic dining room to the rear. Cooking is straightforward, focusing on tasty, refined versions of dishes that are often prepared at home. Informal, efficient service.

NORTHERN IRELAND

Ginger Bistro

7-8 Hope St ✉ BT2 5EE – ✆ (028) 9024 4421 – www.gingerbistro.com – Closed Christmas, New Year, Easter, 5 days mid-July, lunch Monday, Sunday and bank holidays BYZ**d**

Rest – Carte £ 23/38

Rustic neighbourhood bistro close to the Grand Opera House. The two rooms feature bright modern artwork and bespoke fish-themed paintings. Good-sized menus feature simply cooked Irish ingredients and display some Asian influences.

Coppi Ⓝ

St Annes Sq ✉ BT1 2LD – ✆ (028) 9031 1959 – www.coppi.co.uk – Closed 25 December BX**z**

Rest – Carte £ 15/37

Set on the ground floor of a purpose built property in the Cathedral Quarter. It's big and buzzy, with rustic furnishings and leather booths, and staff are bright and friendly. The menu is Mediterranean with strong Italian influences and the home-made pastas are a must; start with a selection of cicchetti.

Il Pirata Ⓝ

279-281 Upper Newtownards Rd, East : 3 mi on A 2 ✉ BT4 3JF – ✆ (028) 9067 3421

Rest – Menu £ 13 (weekdays)/16 – Carte £ 15/25

Rustic restaurant with scrubbed wooden floors and an open kitchen. Mediterranean-influenced menus offer an extensive range of mainly Italian small plates; 3 or 4 dishes per person (plus dessert) should suffice. Bright, friendly service.

Mourne Seafood Bar

34-36 Bank St ✉ BT1 1HL – ✆ (02890) 248 544 – www.mourneseafood.com – Closed 24-26 December, 1 January, 17 March, Easter Sunday-Monday and dinner Sunday BY**c**

Rest – *(booking essential at dinner)* Carte £ 18/31

Popular, split-level seafood restaurant with a small shop, a large rear bar and a cookery school. Blackboard menus offer a huge array of freshly prepared dishes; go for the specials or the Carlingford oysters accompanied by a pint of stout.

Metro Brasserie – Crescent Townhouse Hotel

13 Lower Cres ✉ BT7 1NR – ✆ (028) 9032 3349 – www.crescenttownhouse.com – Closed 24-26 December, 1 January and 11-12 July BZ**x**

Rest – *(dinner only)* Menu £ 11 – Carte £ 22/32

Smart, modern brasserie in a Regency-style townhouse hotel. Classic brasserie menus; contemporary cooking adds a modern twist. Trendy Metro Bar for light lunches, small plates and sharing platters; live music in the evenings.

Potted Hen Bistro Ⓝ

11 Edward St, St Anne's Sq ✉ BT1 2LR – ✆ (028) 9023 4554 – www.thepottedhen.co.uk BX**v**

Rest – Menu £ 18/25 – Carte £ 21/32

Set in a redeveloped area of the city is this informal, two-floored bistro with exposed pipework, bright modern décor and a lively buzz. Extensive, classically based menus offer appealingly presented, unfussy dishes. Friendly service.

Molly's Yard

1 College Green Mews, Botanic Ave ✉ BT7 1LW – ✆ (028) 9032 2600 – www.mollysyard.co.uk – Closed 11-12 July, 24-26 December, 1 January and Sunday BZ**s**

Rest – *(booking essential)* Menu £ 16 (weekday dinner)/29 – Carte £ 25/35

Split-level bistro in a former coach house and stables, with exposed brickwork and a pleasant courtyard. Simple lunches and more ambitious dinners with classical combinations given a personal twist. Fine selection of ales and stouts.

BRYANSFORD – **Down** – **702** O5 – **see Newcastle**

BUSHMILLS (Muileann na Buaise) – Moyle – 712 M2 – pop. 1 319 35 C1

– ✉ Bushmills ▮ Ireland

▶ Belfast 57 mi – Ballycastle 12 mi – Coleraine 10 mi

Bushfoot, Portballintrae, 50 Bushfoot Rd, ✆ (028) 2073 13 17

Giant's Causeway★★★ (Hamilton's Seat ≤★★) N : 2 mi by A 2 and minor road - Dunluce Castle★★ **AC** W : 3 mi by A 2 – Carrick-a-rede Rope Bridge★★★ **AC**, E : 8 mi by A 2 – Magilligan Strand★★, W : 18 mi by A 2, A 29 and A 2 - Gortmore Viewpoint★★, SW : 23 mi by A 2, A 29, A 23 and minor road from Downhill – Downhill★ (Mussenden Temple★), W : 15 mi by A 2, A 29 and A 2

Bushmills Inn

9 Dunluce Rd ✉ BT57 8QG – ✆ (028) 2073 3000 – www.bushmillsinn.com

41 rm ☕ – †£ 88/158 ††£ 128/398

Rest – *(carvery lunch Sunday)* Carte £ 24/40

Proudly run, part-17C whitewashed inn that successfully blends the old with the new. The conference room features a state-of-the-art cinema. Up-to-date bedrooms are split between the original house and an extension. Have a drink beside the peat fire in the old whiskey bar before dining on classic dishes.

Causeway Lodge Ⓝ without rest

52 Moycraig Rd, Dunseverick, East : 5 mi by A 2 and Drumnagee Rd ✉ BT57 8TB – ✆ (028) 2073 0333 – www.causewaylodge.com

5 rm ☕ – †£ 80/100 ††£ 90/140

Set inland from the Giant's Causeway, in a peaceful location. Guest areas come with polished wood floors, leather furnishings and artwork of local scenes. Spacious, boutique bedrooms have bold feature walls and a high level of facilities.

NORTHERN IRELAND

CASTLEDAWSON – Magherafelt – 712 M3 35 C2

▶ Belfast 34 mi – Antrim 17 mi – Ballymena 23 mi

The Inn Castledawson

47 Main St ✉ BT45 8AA – ✆ (028) 7946 9777 – www.theinncastledawson.com – Closed 4 days Christmas

10 rm ☕ – †£ 70/90 ††£ 90/120

Rest *The Inn Castledawson* – see restaurant listing

Personally run, 200 year old inn with spacious, individually styled, modern bedrooms, which overlook either the courtyard or the River Moyola. Some have super-king or emperor beds; the best is Room 9, with its Juliet balcony.

The Inn Castledawson – The Inn at Castledawson Hotel

47 Main St ✉ BT45 8AA – ✆ (028) 7946 9777 – www.theinncastledawson.com – Closed 4 days Christmas

Rest – Carte £ 21/34

Spacious restaurant with beamed ceilings, linen-laid tables and framed black and white photos, set within a 200 year old inn which has views over the River Moyola. Simple lunches and a more ambitious evening menu of modern British dishes.

COLERAINE (Cúil Raithin) – Coleraine – 712 L2 – pop. 24 089 35 C1

▮ Ireland

▶ Belfast 53 mi – Ballymena 25 mi – Londonderry 31 mi – Omagh 65 mi

Railway Rd, ✆ (028) 7034 47 23, www.causewaycoastandglens.com

Castlerock, 65 Circular Rd, ✆ (028) 7084 83 14

Brown Trout, 209 Agivey Rd, Aghadowey, ✆ (028) 7086 82 09

Giant's Causeway★★★ (Hamilton's Seat ≤★★), NE : 14 mi by A 29 and A2 - Dunluce Castle★★ **AC**, NE : 8 mi by A 29 and A 2 – Carrick-a-rede-Rope Bridge★★★ **AC**, NE : 18 mi by A 29 and A2 – Benvarden★ **AC** E : 5 mi by B 67 – Magilligan Strand★★, NW : 8 mi by A 2 - Gortmore Viewpoint★★, NW : 12 mi by A 2 and minor road from Downhill - Downhill★**AC** (Mussenden Temple★), NE : 7 mi by A 2

Greenhill House without rest
24 Greenhill Rd, Aghadowey, South : 9 mi by A 29 on B 66 ✉ BT51 4EU – ✆ (028) 7086 8241 – www.greenhill-house.co.uk – March-October
4 rm ☕ – †£ 45 ††£ 70
Long-standing guesthouse with mature gardens and a traditional country house style. Spacious open-fired lounge and linen-laid breakfast room; heavy drapes, antiques and ornaments feature. Simple, well-kept bedrooms. Chatty, welcoming owner.

COMBER (An Comar) – Ards – 712 O4 – pop. 8 933 — 35 D2

Belfast 10 mi – Newtownards 5 mi – Lisburn 17 mi

Anna's House without rest
Tullynagee, 35 Lisbarnett Rd., Southeast : 4 mi by A 22 ✉ BT23 6AW – ✆ (028) 9754 1566 – www.annashouse.com – Closed Christmas-New Year
4 rm ☕ – †£ 60/70 ††£ 90/110
An extended farmhouse with welcoming owners, superb views, a cosy, contemporary lounge and good-sized bedrooms featuring modern bathrooms. Snug breakfast room with a wood burning stove: filling organic breakfasts use local produce.

Lisbarnett House Ⓝ
181 Killinchy Rd, Lisbane, Southeast : 3.5 mi on A 22 ✉ BT23 5NE – ✆ (028) 9754 1589 – www.lisbarnetthouse.com
Rest – Menu £ 13 (weekdays)/20 – Carte £ 17/34
Neat, modern-looking building in the centre of a small village, with an adjoining off licence. Cooking is robust and satisfying and their ethos is 'local is best'; try one of the Irish Dexter beef dishes, which range from burgers to steaks.

CRUMLIN (Cromghlinn) – Antrim – 712 N4 – pop. 4 259 — 35 C2

Belfast 14 mi – Ballymena 20 mi

Ballyrobin
144-146 Ballyrobin Rd, North : 7 mi by A 52 and A 26 on A 57 ✉ BT29 4EG – ✆ (028) 9442 2211 – www.ballyrobincountrylodge.com – Closed 25 December
21 rm – †£ 52/101 ††£ 67/101, ☕ £ 9 **Rest** – Carte £ 25/36
Smart, country style lodge – a former farmhouse – just a stone's throw from the airport and offering a week's free parking. Stylish, modern bedrooms. Dine on international dishes in one of the cosy rooms in the original pub building or in the conservatory-style extension.

Caldhame Lodge without rest
102 Moira Rd, Nutts Corner, Southeast : 2 mi on A 26 ✉ BT29 4HG – ✆ (028) 9442 3099 – www.caldhamelodge.co.uk
7 rm ☕ – †£ 45/55 ††£ 65/70
Purpose-built guesthouse near the airport, with a pleasant mix of lawns and paved terracing. Comfy guest areas include a conservatory breakfast room and a lounge filled with family photos. Good-sized, individually decorated bedrooms are immaculately kept and feature warm fabrics and iPod docking stations.

DERRY/LONDONDERRY = Doire – Sligo – 712 K2/3 – see Londonderry

DONAGHADEE (Domhnach Daoi) – Ards – 712 P4 – pop. 6 470 — 35 D2

Ireland

Belfast 18 mi – Ballymena 44 mi

Warren Rd, ✆ (028) 9188 36 24

Ballycopeland Windmill★ **AC** S : 4 mi by A 2 and B 172. Mount Stewart★★★ **AC**, SW : 10 mi by A 2 and minor road SW – Movilla (cross slabs★), Newtownards, SW : 7 mi by B 172

Grace Neill's
33 High St ✉ BT21 0AH – ✆ (02891) 884 595 – www.graceneills.com – Closed 25 December
Rest – Menu £ 9/50 – Carte £ 16/34
Traditional beamed pub – reputedly the oldest in Ireland – dating from 1611 and decorated with antiques and pictures of old Donaghadee. The extensive, classical menu offers hearty, flavoursome cooking. Dishes are rustic yet refined.

Pier 36 with rm — rest,

36 The Parade ✉ BT21 0HE – ✆ (028) 9188 4466 – www.pier36.co.uk – Closed 25 December

6 rm – †£ 50/80 ††£ 70/100

Rest – Menu £ 16 (weekday dinner) – Carte £ 20/47

Spacious family-run pub, set on the quayside, opposite a lighthouse, overlooking the picturesque harbour. Extensive menus feature a mix of classic, modern and international influences, with good weekday deals and plenty of fresh, local seafood. Bright, modern bedrooms; some with great sea and harbour views.

DUNDRUM (Dún Droma) – Down – 712 O5 – pop. 1 065 Ireland 35 D3

Belfast 29 mi – Downpatrick 9 mi – Newcastle 4 mi

Castle★ **AC**

Castlewellan Forest Park★★ **AC**, W : 4 mi by B 180 and A 50 - Tollymore Forest Park★ **AC**, W : 3 mi by B 180 - Drumena Cashel and Souterrain★, W : 4 mi by B 180

Carriage House without rest

71 Main St ✉ BT33 0LU – ✆ (028) 4375 1635 – www.carriagehousedundrum.com

3 rm – †£ 45/50 ††£ 75/80

Sweet, lilac-washed terraced house with colourful window boxes. Homely lounge with books and local info. Simple, antique-furnished bedrooms; some affording pleasant bay views. Breakfast in the conservatory, overlooking the pretty garden.

Buck's Head Inn

77-79 Main St ✉ BT33 0LU – ✆ (028) 4375 1868 – Closed 24- 25 December and Monday from October-March

Rest – Menu £ 20 (weekday dinner)/30 – Carte lunch £ 19/30

Converted village pub. Have drinks in the lounge then head for the front room with its cosy booths and open fire, or the rear room which overlooks the garden. Unfussy, traditional lunches and more ambitious dinners; seafood is a strength.

Mourne Seafood Bar

10 Main St ✉ BT33 0LU – ✆ (028) 4375 1377 – www.mourneseafood.com – Closed dinner 24 December, 25 December and Monday-Wednesday in Winter

Rest – *(booking essential)* Carte £ 19/29

Friendly, rustic restaurant on the main street of a busy coastal town. Simple, wood-furnished dining room with nautically themed artwork. Classic menus centre around seafood, with oysters and mussels from the owners' beds the specialities.

DUNGANNON (Dún Geanainn) – Dungannon – 712 L4 35 C2 – pop. 11 139 Ireland

Belfast 42 mi – Ballymena 37 mi – Dundalk 47 mi – Londonderry 60 mi

The Argory★, S : 5 mi by A 29 and east by minor rd. Ardboe Cross★, NW : 17 mi by A 45, B 161 and B 73 – Springhill★ **AC**, NE : 24 mi by A 29 – Sperrin Mountains★ : Wellbrook Beetling Mill★ **AC**, NW : 22 mi by A 29 and A 505 - Beaghmore Stone Circles★, NW : 24 mi by A 29 and A 505

Grange Lodge

7 Grange Rd, Moy, Southeast : 3.5 mi by A 29 ✉ BT71 7EJ – ✆ (028) 8778 4212 – www.grangelodgecountryhouse.com – Closed 20 December-1 February

5 rm – †£ 65/74 ††£ 82/89 **Rest** – Menu £ 40

Attractive Georgian country house surrounded by mature, well-kept gardens, ideal for afternoon tea. Antique-furnished guest areas display fine sketches and lithographs. Snug, well-appointed bedrooms are immaculately kept and have good extras. The flower-filled dining room serves classically based Irish dishes.

NORTHERN IRELAND

ENNISKILLEN (Inis Ceithleann) - Fermanagh - 712 J4 - pop. 15 855 34 A2

Ireland

Belfast 84 mi - Londonderry 60 mi - Craigavon 62 mi - Portadown 59 mi

Wellington Rd, (028) 6632 31 10, www.enniskillen.com

Castlecoole, (028) 6632 52 50

Castle Coole★★★ **AC**, SE : 1 m - Florence Court★★ **AC**, SW : 8 mi by A 4 and A 32 - Marble Arch Caves and Forest Nature Reserve★ **AC**, SW : 10 mi by A 4 and A 32. NW by A 26 : Lough Erne★★ : Cliffs of Magho Viewpoint★★★ **AC**- Tully Castle★ **AC** - N by A 32, B 72, A 35 and A 47 : Devenish Island★ **AC** - Castle Archdale Forest Park★ **AC** - White Island★ - Janus Figure★

Lough Erne Resort

rest,

Belleek Rd, Northwest : 4 mi by A 4 on A 46 ✉ BT93 7ED - (028) 6632 3230 - www.locherneresort.com

126 rm - £ 90/130 £ 110/200 - 6 suites

Rest *Catalina* - *(dinner only and Sunday lunch)* Menu £ 25/40 - Carte £ 27/38

Rest *Lochside Bar and Grill* - Menu £ 15 (lunch)/35

Vast, luxurious golf and leisure resort on a peninsula between two loughs. Bedrooms have a classical style and are extremely well-appointed; the suites and lodges are dotted about the grounds. Relax in the beautiful Thai spa or the huge pool with its stunning mosaic wall. Ambitious, contemporary dining and lough views in Catalina; steaks and grills in the clubhouse.

Manor House

Killadeas, North : 7.5 mi by A 32 on B 82 ✉ BT94 1NY - (028) 6862 2200 - www.manorhousecountryhotel.com

81 rm - £ 80/110 £ 86/159 - 2 suites

Rest *Belleek* - *(closed Monday- Friday lunch and Sunday dinner in winter)* Menu £ 21/39

Rest *Cellar Door* - Carte £ 20/37

Impressive yellow-washed manor house overlooking Lough Erne and surrounded by mature grounds. Comfy, stylish guest areas mix the traditional and the contemporary. Bedrooms range from characterful in the main house to very smart and modern in the extensions. Formal dining room with ornate plasterwork and classical menus; more casual all-day dining in the old vaults.

Cedars

301 Killadeas Rd., Irvinestown, North : 10 mi by A 32 on B 82 ✉ BT94 1PG - (028) 6862 1493 - www.cedarsguesthouse.com - Closed 1 week Christmas

10 rm - £ 45/75 £ 70/100

Rest *Rectory Bistro* - *(closed Monday-Tuesday) (dinner only and Sunday lunch)* Carte £ 19/29

Spacious converted 19C rectory with pleasant lawned gardens. The two traditional lounges have heavy fabrics and antique furnishings. Bedrooms are simple and wood-furnished; those at the front are larger and have country views. The large, rustic bistro offers extensive menus; sit in the conservatory room.

GALGORM Antrim - Ballymena - 712 N3 - see Ballymena

HILLSBOROUGH (Cromghlinn) - Lisburn - 712 N4 - pop. 3 400 35 C2

Ireland

Belfast 12 mi - London 358 mi - Lisburn 4 mi - Craigavon 21 mi

The Square, (028) 9268 97 17, www.discovernorthernireland.com

Town★ - Fort★

Rowallane Gardens★ **AC**, Saintfield, E : 10 mi by B 178 and B 6. The Argory★, W : 25 mi by A 1 and M 1

Parson's Nose

48 Lisburn St ✉ BT26 6AB - (028) 9268 3009 - www.theparsonsnose.co.uk - Closed 25 December

Rest - *(booking advisable)* Menu £ 18/22 - Carte £ 15/32

Characterful Georgian property built by the first Marquis of Downshire. Rustic, open-fired bar; restaurant above overlooks a lake in the castle grounds. Unashamedly traditional menus and generous portions; the daily fish specials are a hit.

Plough Inn
3 The Square ✉ BT26 6AG – ☎ (028) 9268 2985 – www.theploughhillsbrough.co.uk – Closed 25 December
Rest – Menu £ 10/22 – Carte £ 21/29
Family-run, 18C coaching inn that's three establishments in one: a bar with an adjoining dining room; a café-cum-bistro; and a seafood restaurant. Dishes range from light snacks and pub classics to more modern, international offerings.

at Annahilt **Southeast : 4 mi on B 177 – ✉ Hillsborough**

Fortwilliam without rest
210 Ballynahinch Rd, Northwest : 0.25 mi on B 177 ✉ BT26 6BH – ☎ (028) 9268 2255 – www.fortwilliamcountryhouse.com
3 rm – †£ 50 ††£ 70
Attractive bay-windowed farmhouse with neat gardens, surrounded by 80 acres of land. Homely lounge and a country kitchen with an Aga. Traditional bedrooms have flowery fabrics, antiques and country views; two have private bathrooms.

Pheasant
410 Upper Ballynahinch Rd, North : 1 mi on Lisburn rd ✉ BT26 6NR – ☎ (028) 9263 8056 – www.thepheasantrestaurant.co.uk – Closed 12 July and 25-26 December
Rest – Menu £ 10/24 – Carte £ 20/36
Sizeable creamwashed pub with Gothic styling, Guinness-themed artwork and a typically Irish feel. Internationally influenced menus showcase local, seasonal produce, with seafood a speciality in summer and game featuring highly in winter.

HOLYWOOD (Ard Mhic Nasca) – North Down – 712 O4 — 35 D2

– pop. 12 037 Ireland

Belfast 7 mi – Bangor 6 mi

Holywood, Demesne Rd, Nuns Walk, ☎ (028) 9042 21 38

Cultra : Ulster Folk and Transport Museum★★ **AC**, NE : 1 mi by A 2

Culloden rest,
142 Bangor Rd, East : 1.5 mi on A 2 ✉ BT18 0EX – ☎ (028) 9042 1066 – www.hastingshotels.com
105 rm – †£ 145/180 ††£ 165/240 – 4 suites
Rest *Mitre* – *(dinner only and Sunday lunch)* Menu £ 45 (dinner) – Carte £ 30/48
Rest *Cultra Inn* – ☎ (028) 9042 5840 – Carte £ 19/39
An extended Gothic mansion overlooking Belfast Lough, with well-maintained gardens full of modern sculptures, and a smart spa. Charming, traditional, antique-furnished guest areas have open fires and fine ceiling frescoes. Characterful bedrooms offer good facilities. Classical menus and good views in formal Mitre; Cultra Inn is an informal grill restaurant.

Rayanne House
60 Demesne Rd, by My Lady's Mile Rd ✉ BT18 9EX – ☎ (028) 9042 5859 – www.rayannehouse.com
10 rm – †£ 75/85 ††£ 115/135
Rest – *(closed 23 December-5 January) (dinner only) (residents only)* Menu £ 49 – Carte £ 35/49
Keenly run, part-Victorian house in a residential area. Homely, antique-filled guest areas. Smart, country house bedrooms with a modern edge; those to the front offer the best views. Ambitious, seasonal dishes in formal dining room; try the Titanic tasting menu – a version of the last meal served on the ship.

Beech Hill without rest
23 Ballymoney Rd, Craigantlet, Southeast : 4.5 mi by A 2 on Craigantlet rd ✉ BT23 4TG – ☎ (028) 9042 5892 – www.beech-hill.net
3 rm – †£ 55/60 ††£ 90/100
Antique-furnished guesthouse in a lovely countryside setting; personally run by the friendly owner – a local magistrate. Comfortable lounge and traditional, individually styled bedrooms with fresh flowers. Communal breakfasts.

XX **Fontana**

61A High St ✉ BT18 9AE – ✆ (028) 9080 9908 – Closed 25-26 December, 1-2 January, Saturday lunch, Sunday dinner and Monday

Rest – Menu £ 20 (weekday dinner) – Carte £ 20/36

A favourite with the locals is this smart, modern, first floor restaurant; accessed down a narrow, town centre passageway and decorated with contemporary art. Menus offer British and Mediterranean dishes, with local seafood and steaks a speciality. Good value set menus are available at both lunch and dinner.

KILLINCHY – Ards – 712 O4 — 35 D2

Belfast 16 mi – Newtownards 11 mi – Lisburn 17 mi – Bangor 16 mi

XXX **Balloo House - Restaurant** AC P

1 Comber Rd, (1st floor), West : 0.75 mi on A 22 ✉ BT23 6PA – ✆ (028) 9754 1210 – www.balloohouse.com – Closed 25 December, Sunday and Monday

Rest – *(dinner only) (booking essential)* Menu £ 27 (weekdays)/50 – Carte £ 34/40

Intimate, formally laid, first floor restaurant with high beamed ceilings and exposed stone walls; set in a rural location. Classically based menus see tried-and-tested combinations given a personal touch, with proud use of local produce.

LARNE (Latharna) – Larne – 712 O3 – pop. 18 228 Ireland — 35 D2

Belfast 23 mi – Ballymena 20 mi

to Fleetwood (Stena Line) daily (8 h) – to Cairnryan (P & O Irish Sea) 3-5 daily (1 h/2 h 15 mn)

Narrow Gauge Rd, ✆ (028) 2826 00 88, www.larne.gov.uk

Cairndhu, Ballygally, 192 Coast Rd, ✆ (028) 2858 39 54

SE : Island Magee (Ballylumford Dolmen★), by ferry and 2 mi by B 90 or 18 mi by A 2 and B 90. NW : Antrim Glens★★★ - Murlough Bay★★★ (Fair Head ≤★★★), N : 46 m by A 2 and minor road – Glenariff Forest Park★★ **AC** (Waterfall★★), N : 30 mi by A 2 and A 43 - Glenariff★, N : 25 mi by A 2 - Glendun★, N : 30 mi by A 2 – Carrickfergus (Castle★★ - St Nicholas' Church★), SW : 15 mi by A 2

Manor House without rest P

23 Olderfleet Rd, Harbour Highway ✉ BT40 1AS – ✆ (028) 2827 3305 – www.themanorguesthouse.com – Closed 25-26 December

8 rm – †£ 30/35 ††£ 55/60

Large Victorian house filled with antiques; the owner has been here nearly 50 years. Lounge boasts immense Chinese vase and gilded art; snug dining room has flocked walls. Cosy, immaculate bedrooms reached via original carved staircase.

LIMAVADY (Léim an Mhadaidh) – Limavady – 712 L2 – pop. 12 135 — 34 B1

Ireland

Belfast 62 mi – Ballymena 39 mi – Coleraine 13 mi – Londonderry 17 mi

7 Connell St, ✆ (028) 7776 03 07, www.limavady.gov.uk

Benone Par Three, Benone, 53 Benone Ave, ✆ (028) 7775 05 55

Sperrin Mountains★ : Roe Valley Country Park★ **AC**, S : 2 mi by B 68 - Glenshane Pass★, S : 15 mi by B 68 and A 6

XX **Lime Tree**

60 Catherine St ✉ BT49 9DB – ✆ (028) 7776 4300 – www.limetreerest.com – Closed 1 week July, 25-26 December, Sunday and Monday

Rest – *(dinner only and lunch Thursday-Friday)* Menu £ 19 (early dinner) – Carte £ 18/35

Keenly run neighbourhood restaurant; its traditional exterior concealing a modern room with purple velvet banquettes and colourful artwork. Unfussy, classical cooking features meats and veg from the village; try the homemade wheaten bread.

LISNASKEA – Fermanagh – 712 J5 – pop. 2 739 34 B3

Belfast 82 mi – Dublin 91 mi – Londonderry 67 mi – Omagh 33 mi

XX **Watermill** with rm rest,
Kilmore Quay, Southwest: 3 mi by B 127 ✉ BT92 0DT – ✆ (028) 6772 4369 – Closed January
7 rm – †£ 59/69 ††£ 79/89
Rest – *(closed Monday and Tuesday) (dinner only and lunch Saturday and Sunday) (booking advisable)* Menu £ 20 – Carte £ 22/45
Charming red-brick cottage with a thatched roof, a delightful terrace and superb water gardens flowing down to Lough Erne – where you can hire one of their fishing boats. Characterful, rustic interior with smartly laid tables and a 25,000 litre aquarium; classical Gallic menu. Comfy, airy bedrooms have stone floors and heavy wood furnishings; some look over the water.

LONDONDERRY/DERRY (Doire) – Derry – 712 K2/3 – pop. 90 651 34 B1

Ireland

Belfast 70 mi – Dublin 146 mi

City of Derry Airport : ✆ (028) 7181 0784, E : 6 mi by A 2

44 Foyle St, ✆ (028) 7126 72 84, www.derryvisitor.com

City of Derry, 49 Victoria Rd, ✆ (028) 7134 63 69

Town★ - City Walls and Gates★★ – Guildhall★ **AC** – Long Tower Church★ – St Columb's Cathedral★ **AC** – Tower Museum★ **AC**

Grianan of Aileach★★ (≤★★) (Republic of Ireland) NW : 5 mi by A 2 and N 13. Ulster-American Folk Park★★, S : 33 mi by A 5 - Ulster History Park★ **AC**, S : 32 mi by A 5 and minor road – Sperrin Mountains★ : Glenshane Pass★ (≤★★), SE : 24 mi by A 6 - Sawel Mountain Drive★ (≤★★), S : 22 mi by A 5 and minor roads via Park – Roe Valley Country Park★ **AC**, E : 15 mi by A 2 and B 68 – Beaghmore Stone Circles★, S : 52 mi by A 5, A 505 and minor road

City rest,
Queens Quay ✉ BT48 7AS – ✆ (028) 7136 5800 – www.cityhotelderry.com – Closed 24-26 December
158 rm – †£ 82/152 ††£ 89/159 – 5 suites
Rest *Thompson's* – *(bar lunch Monday-Saturday)* Menu £ 14/21 **s** – Carte £ 24/31 **s**
Large, centrally located hotel overlooking the Peace Bridge on the River Foyle. Well-maintained, modern interior with a comfortable lounge and a well-equipped leisure centre. Smart bedrooms; those on the upper floors have great outlooks. Informal brasserie affords pleasant water views.

Beech Hill Country House
32 Ardmore Rd, Southeast : 3.5 mi by A 6 ✉ BT47 3QP – ✆ (028) 7134 9279 – www.beech-hill.com – Closed 24-25 December
32 rm – †£ 95/235 ††£ 125/235 – 2 suites
Rest *Ardmore* – Menu £ 22 (lunch)/30 **s**
Once a US marine camp, this 18C house is now a welcoming hotel and popular wedding venue. Characterful guest areas feature ornate coving and antiques. Country house bedrooms in the original building; others are more modern and spacious. Dine from traditional menus overlooking the lake and water wheel.

Ramada H. Da Vinci's rest,
15 Culmore Rd, North : 1 mi on A 2 (Foyle Bridge rd) ✉ BT48 8JB – ✆ (028) 7127 9111 – www.davincishotel.com – Closed 25 December
70 rm – †£ 70/100 ††£ 70/120, £ 9
Rest *Grill Room* – *(dinner only and Sunday lunch)* Menu £ 18 – Carte £ 18/32
Set beside a characterful Irish pub – now the trendy hotel bar – at the northern edge of the city. Photos of stars who've stayed here fill one wall. Well-equipped, uniform bedrooms improve with grade. Charming brasserie displays rustic beams and exposed brickwork.

XX **Browns**
1 Bonds Hill,Waterside, East : 1 mi by A 2 ✉ BT47 6DW – ✆ (028) 7134 5180 – www.brownsrestaurant.com – Closed Monday, Saturday lunch and Sunday dinner
Rest – *(booking advisable)* Menu £ 20 (dinner) – Carte £ 28/40
Smart neighbourhood restaurant with a plush lounge and an intimate dining room featuring monochrome photos and some banquette seating. Cooking is modern and technically adept, relying on local produce, home-baking and home-smoking.

MAGHERA (Machaire Rátha) – Magherafelt – 712 L3 – pop. 3 711 35 C2

Belfast 40 mi – Ballymena 19 mi – Coleraine 21 mi – Londonderry 32 mi

Ardtara Country House

8 Gorteade Rd, Upperlands, North : 3.25 mi by A 29 off B 75 ✉ BT46 5SA – ✆ (028) 7964 4490 – www.ardtara.com – Closed 25-26 December

9 rm – †£ 65/75 ††£ 100/130

Rest – *(booking essential at lunch)* Menu £ 32

Small country house in a peaceful setting; its traditional lounges and conservatory extension full of ornaments collected by the owners on their travels. Antique-furnished bedrooms have modern touches; most have lovely garden views. Formal dining room with an interesting hunting mural serves classic menu.

MAGHERAFELT – Magherafelt – pop. 8 881 35 C2

Belfast 76 mi – Dublin 117 mi – Londonderry 5 mi – Craigavon 75 mi

Church Street

23 Church St ✉ BT45 6AP – ✆ (028) 7932 8083 – www.churchstreetrestaurant.co.uk – Closed 7-17 January, 1 week July, Monday and Tuesday

Rest – Menu £ 10/14 – Carte £ 21/27

Located on the main street of a busy country town, a long, narrow restaurant with a mix of bistro, pew and high-backed seating, and a smart private dining room above. Unfussy, classically based dishes rely on good quality local produce.

NEWCASTLE (An Caisleán Nua) – Down – 712 O5 – pop. 7 444 35 D3

Ireland

Belfast 32 mi – Londonderry 101 mi

10-14 Central Promenade, ✆ (028) 4372 22 22, www.newcastle.gov.uk

Castlewellan Forest Park★★ **AC**, NW : 4 mi by A 50 – Tolymore Forest Park★ **AC**, W : 3 mi by B 180 – Dundrum Castle★ **AC**, NE : 4 mi by A 2. Silent Valley Reservoir★ (<★) - Spelga Pass and Dam★ - Kilbroney ForestPark (viewpoint★) – Annalong Marine Park and Cornmill★ **AC**, S : 8 mi by A 2 – Downpatrick : Cathedral★ **AC**, Down Country Museum★ **AC**, NE : 20 mi by A 2 and A 25

Slieve Donard

Downs Rd ✉ BT33 0AH – ✆ (028) 4372 1066 – www.hastingshotels.com

178 rm – †£ 80/170 ††£ 110/220 – 4 suites

Rest *Oak* – Carte £ 31/43

Rest *Percy French* – Carte £ 18/53

Rest *Lighthouse Lounge* – Carte £ 18/31

Grand railway hotel set right beside the beach and boasting its own museum, superb leisure facilities and excellent sea and mountain views. Spacious modern guest areas and stylish bedrooms with good mod cons. Smart spa with a pool overlooking the beach. Classical menu in formal Oak; accessible fare in informal Percy French; casual all-day dining in Lighthouse Lounge.

Burrendale H. & Country Club

rest,

51 Castlewellan Rd, North : 1 mi on A 50 ✉ BT33 0JY – ✆ (028) 4372 2599 – www.burrendale.com

68 rm – †£ 80 ††£ 140 – 1 suite **Rest** – Menu £ 18/30 – Carte £ 16/31 **s**

Privately owned hotel between the Mourne Mountains and the Irish Sea, close to the Royal County Down golf course. Well-equipped modern bedrooms. Good leisure facilities and a vast spa offering a comprehensive range of treatments. Large, open-plan bar and lounge, with informal dining from extensive menus.

Vanilla

67 Main St ✉ BT33 0AE – ✆ (028) 4372 2268 – www.vanillarestaurant.co.uk – Closed 25-27 December and 1 January and Wednesday dinner in winter

Rest – Menu £ 15 (weekdays) – Carte £ 24/39

Contemporary restaurant; its black canopy standing out amongst the town centre shops. The long, narrow room is flanked by brushed velvet banquettes and polished tables. Attractively presented, internationally influenced, modern dishes.

NORTHERN IRELAND

at Bryansford Northwest : 2.75 mi on B 180. – 712 O5

Tollyrose Country House without rest
15 Hilltown Rd, Southwest : 0.5 mi on B 180 ✉ BT33 0PX – ✆ (028) 4372 6077 – www.tollyrose.com
6 rm – ♂£ 45 ♂♂£ 75
Purpose-built guesthouse beside the Tollymore Forest Park, at the foot of the Mourne Mountains. Simple, modern bedrooms come in neutral hues; those on the top floor have the best views. Lots of local info in the lounge. Friendly owners.

NEWTOWNARDS (Baile Nua na hArda) – Ards – 712 O4 – pop. 27 821 35 D2

Belfast 10 mi – Bangor 144 mi – Downpatrick 22 mi

Edenvale House without rest
130 Portaferry Rd, Southeast : 2.75 mi on A 20 ✉ BT22 2AH – ✆ (028) 9181 4881 – www.edenvalehouse.com – Closed Christmas-New Year
3 rm – ♂£ 50 ♂♂£ 100
Attractive Georgian farmhouse with a charming owner and pleasant lough and mountain views. Traditionally decorated, with a comfy drawing room and a wicker-furnished sun room. Spacious, homely bedrooms boast good facilities.

PORTRUSH (Port Rois) – Coleraine – 712 L2 – pop. 6 372 Ireland 35 C1

Belfast 58 mi – Coleraine 4 mi – Londonderry 35 mi

Sandhill Drive, ✆ (028) 7082 33 33, www.portrush.org.uk

Royal Portrush, Dunluce Rd, ✆ (028) 7082 23 11

Giant's Causeway★★★ (Hamilton's Seat ≤★★, E: 9 m by A 2) - Carrick-a-rede Rope Bridge★★★, E: 14 mi by A 2 and B 15 - Dunluce Castle★★ **AC**, E: 3 mi by A 2 – Gortmore Viewpoint★★, E: 14 mi by A 29, A 2 and minor road - Magilligan Strand★★, E: 13 mi by A 29 and A 2 – Downhill★ (Mussenden Temple★), E: 12 mi by A 29 and A 2

Beulah without rest
16 Causeway St ✉ BT56 8AB – ✆ (028) 7082 2413 – www.beulahguesthouse.com – mid Feb-October
9 rm – ♂£ 35/60 ♂♂£ 60/80
Double-fronted terraced house in a seaside town, run by a charming, chatty owner with plenty of local knowledge. Comfy, spotlessly kept bedrooms have compact bathrooms. The house speciality at breakfast is pancakes with maple syrup.

PORTSTEWART (Port Stióbhaird) – Coleraine – 712 L2 35 C1

Belfast 60 mi – Ballymena 32 mi – Coleraine 6 mi

York
2 Station Rd, on A2 ✉ BT55 7DA – ✆ (028) 7083 3594 – www.theyorkportstewart.co.uk – closed 25 December
8 rm – ♂£ 79/115 ♂♂£ 95/145 **Rest** – Carte £ 14/27
Smart hotel overlooking the North Coast. The marble-floored reception with its grand piano leads to a red-hued cocktail bar and a rustic locals bar which hosts live music events. Well-equipped modern bedrooms; those at the front are the largest, with terraces and excellent views. Busy, informal restaurant.

WARRENPOINT (An Pointe) – Newry and Mourne – 712 N5 – pop. 7 000 35 C3

Belfast 44 mi – Newry 7 mi – Lisburn 37 mi

Restaurant 23
Balmoral Hotel (1st floor), 13 Seaview ✉ BT34 3NJ – ✆ (028) 4175 3222 – www.restaurant23.com – Closed 25 December
Rest – Menu £ 15 (weekdays)/28 – Carte £ 27/33
Modern restaurant on the first floor of a seafront hotel, with a trendy bar and lounge, and views over Carlingford Lough. Precise, well-executed cooking has elaborate, sometimes flamboyant presentation. Service is professional.

Republic of Ireland

ABBEYLEIX (Mainistir Laoise) – **Laois** – **712** J9 – **pop. 1 827** **39** C2
Ireland
Dublin 96 km – Kilkenny 35 km – Limerick 108 km
Abbeyleix, Rathmoyle, ☎ (0502) 3 14 50
Emo Court★★ **AC**, N : 17 km by R 425 and R 419 – Rock of Dunamase★, NE : 10 km by R 425 and N 80 – Stradbally Steam Museum★ **AC**, NE : 19 km by R 425 and R 427 – Timahoe Round Tower★, NE : 15 km by R 430 and a minor road

Preston House with rm
Main St – ☎ (057) 873 14 32 – www.prestonhouse.ie – Closed 25-28 December, Sunday dinner and Monday
6 rm – € 75/95 € 95/120 **Rest** – Menu € 25 – Carte € 34/60
18C former school; very personally run by its two experienced owners. Have homemade cake or a light lunch in the cosy tearoom. The relaxed, informal restaurant offers set, à la carte and tasting menus – cooking is modern and features some original combinations. Simple, comfy bedrooms complete the picture.

ACHILL ISLAND (Acaill) – **Mayo** – **712** B5/6 Ireland **36** A2
Dublin 288 km – Castlebar 54 km – Galway 144 km
Achill Sound, ☎ (098) 4 53 84, www.achilltourism.com
Achill Island, Keel, ☎ (098) 4 34 56
Island★

DOOGORT (Dumha Goirt) – **Mayo** – ✉ **Achill Island**

Gray's rest,
– ☎ (098) 43 244 – www.grays-guesthouse.ie – April - September
14 rm – € 35/46 € 70/80 **Rest** – Menu € 26
Two adjoining whitewashed houses; one displaying an old clock face from its former life as a mission. Well-kept, modest bedrooms have small shower rooms and colourful throws and cushions. Striking artwork of local island scenes adorns the dining room walls. Simple dinners often feature the catch of the day.

ADARE (Áth Dara) – **Limerick** – **712** F10 – **pop. 1 106** Ireland **38** B2
Dublin 210 km – Killarney 95 km – Limerick 16 km
Mains St, ☎ (061) 39 62 55, www.ireland-travel-guide.com
Town★ – Adare Friary★ - Adare Parish Church★
Rathkeale (Castle Matrix★ **AC** - Irish Palatine Heritage Centre★) W : 12 km by N 21 – Newcastle West★, W : 26 km by N 21 – Glin Castle★ **AC**, W : 46.5 km by N 21, R 518 and N 69

Adare Manor H. and Golf Resort
– ☎ (061) 605 200 – www.adaremanor.com – Closed 24-26 December
62 rm – € 190/500 € 190/500
Rest *Oakroom* – see restaurant listing
Rest *Carriage House* – Menu € 30 (weekdays) – Carte € 28/48
Part-19C Gothic mansion in 840 acres of riverside parkland: home to the Irish Open. Spacious, elaborately decorated guest areas. The most characterful bedrooms are in the main house and boast fireplaces, wood-panelling and ornate plasterwork. Dine in grand, formal Oakroom or more casual Carriage House.

Dunraven Arms
Main St – ☎ (061) 605 900 – www.dunravenhotel.com
86 rm – € 100 € 145/295
Rest *Maigue* – see restaurant listing
Greatly extended Irish coaching inn dating from 1792, with various small lounges, a busy bar and an annexed conference suite. Good-sized, classical bedrooms – some with four-posters and colourful garden outlooks. Lovely swimming pool.

Oakroom – Adare Manor Hotel and Golf Resort
– ☎ (061) 605 200 – www.adaremanor.com – Closed 24-26 December
Rest – *(dinner only)* Carte € 50/65
Grand hotel dining room with a beautiful drawing room and an intimate conservatory boasting an ornate ceiling and pleasant river views. Elegantly laid tables and formal service. Classically based menus showcase quality Irish ingredients.

XX **Wild Geese**

Rose Cottage – ✆ (061) 396 451 – www.thewild-geese.com – Closed 2 weeks January, 24-26 December , Sunday dinner and Monday
Rest – *(dinner only and Sunday lunch) (booking essential)* Menu € 25/47
Long-standing restaurant located in a delightful terrace of thatched cottages, on the main street of a pretty village. The atmosphere is intimate and cosy, and the service, friendly. Traditional menus make good use of local produce.

XX **Maigue** – Dunraven Arms Hotel

Main St – ✆ (061) 396 633 – www.dunravenhotel.com
Rest – *(bar lunch Monday-Saturday)* Carte € 26/41
Traditional hotel dining room with crystal chandeliers, a formal feel and professional service. Menus focus on Irish produce and are firmly rooted in tradition; a trolley features at every service, offering the likes of prime rib of beef.

ARAN ISLANDS (Oileáin Árann) – Galway – 712 C/D8 – pop. 1 280 38 B1

Ireland

Dublin 260 km – Galway 43 km – Limerick 145 km – Ennis 111 km
Access Access by boat from Galway city or by boat from Kilkieran, Rossaveel or Fisherstreet (Clare) and by aeroplane from Inverin
Inis Mor, ✆ (099) 6 12 63, www.discoverireland.ie/islands
Cill Ronain
Islands★ – Inishmore (Dún Aonghasa★★★)

INISHMORE – Galway

Óstán Árann

Kilronan – ✆ (099) 61 104 – www.aranislandshotel.com – closed November-Mid February
22 rm – † € 59/79 †† € 78/118
Rest – *(bar lunch)* Menu € 11/20 **s** – Carte € 25/36 **s**
Comfortable, family-owned hotel with great view of harbour. Bustling bar with live music most nights in high season. Spacious, up-to-date bedrooms are decorated in bright colours. Traditional dishes served in wood-floored restaurant.

Pier House

Kilronan – ✆ (099) 61 417 – www.pierhousearan.com – closed January and December
12 rm – † € 50/80 †† € 70/100 **Rest** – Carte € 26/39
Brightly painted hotel in great location overlooking Kilronan pier, not far from the ferry point and the village centre; take advantage of the outlook from the comfy lounge. Cosy bedrooms come with good mod cons and some share the view. The intimate restaurant offers a concise, accessible menu.

Ard Einne Guesthouse

Killeany – ✆ (099) 61 126 – www.ardeinne.com – Closed January and December
8 rm – † € 90 †† € 90/120 **Rest** – Menu € 27
Close to the airport, an attractive chalet-style guesthouse set back on a hill and boasting superb views of Killeany Bay; relax in the comfy lounge while taking it all in. Uniformly decorated bedrooms have pine furnishings and afford great outlooks. Homely cooking with a menu featuring lots of island fish.

INISHMAAN – Galway 38 B1

XX **Inis Meáin Restaurant & Suites** with rm

– ✆ (086) 826 60 26 – www.inismeain.com – Closed October-March, 2 night minimum stay
4 rm – † € 237/400 †† € 237/400
Rest – *(closed Sunday-Tuesday) (dinner only) (booking essential)* Carte € 26/57
Set on a beautiful island, this futuristic stone building is inspired by the surrounding landscapes and features limed walls, sage banquettes and panoramic views. Cooking is modern, tasty and satisfyingly straightforward, showcasing island ingredients, including seafood caught in currachs and hand-gathered urchins. Minimalist bedrooms feature natural furnishings.

INISHEER - Galway 38 B1

South Aran House

– ✆ (099) 75 073 – www.southaran.com – restricted opening in winter

4 rm – 🚹 € 48 🚹🚹 € 78 **Rest** – Carte € 30/35

Simple guesthouse on the smallest of the Aran Islands, where traditional living still reigns. With its whitewashed walls and tiled floors, it has a slight Mediterranean feel; bedrooms are homely, with wrought iron beds and modern amenities. Their next door restaurant serves breakfast, snacks and hearty meals.

ARDMORE (Aird Mhór) – Waterford – 712 I12 – pop. 435 39 C3

Dublin 240 km – Waterford 71 km – Cork 60 km – Kilkenny 123 km

Cliff House

Middle Rd – ✆ (024) 87 800 – www.thecliffhousehotel.com – Closed 24-26 December

39 rm – 🚹 € 150/170 🚹🚹 € 180/495 – 3 suites

Rest *House* – see restaurant listing

Rest *Bar* – Menu € 32/40 – Carte € 33/45

Stylish hotel on the cliffside, offering superb bay views. Slate walls, Irish fabrics and bold colours feature throughout; the lower floor houses a lovely spa. Modern bedrooms boast backlit glass artwork and smart bathrooms – all have a view and some have balconies. Extensive menu in the delightful bar and terrace; more accomplished, inventive dishes in the restaurant.

House – Cliff House Hotel

Middle Rd – ✆ (024) 87 800 – www.thecliffhousehotel.com – Closed 24-26 December

Rest – *(closed Tuesday in winter, Sunday except bank holiday weekends and Monday) (dinner only)* Menu € 68/115 – Carte approx. € 68

Smart hotel restaurant, where full length windows provide every table with an impressive coastal view. Local and garden produce features in concise menus; cooking is technically strong and complex. Creative, original dishes combine good flavours and textures; try the luxurious 'specialities' set menu.

→ Ballotine of cured salmon with pickled vegetables and horseradish. Rack of lamb, loin and sweetbreads with goat's cheese, garlic and broad beans. Dark chocolate, coffee, olive oil and sea salt.

ARTHURSTOWN (Colmán) – Wexford – 712 L11 – pop. 135 39 D2

Dublin 166 km – Cork 159 km – Limerick 162 km – Waterford 42 km

Dunbrody Country House

– ✆ (051) 389 600 – www.dunbrodyhouse.com – Closed 21-27 December and Monday-Tuesday except July-August

16 rm – 🚹 € 155/180 🚹🚹 € 205/220 – 6 suites

Rest *Harvest Room* – see restaurant listing

Part-Georgian former hunting lodge; once owned by the Marquis of Donegal and now by celebrity chef, Kevin Dundon, who runs his cookery school here. Comfy lounge-bar with a marble-topped counter. Spacious bedrooms furnished in a period style.

Harvest Room – Dunbrody Country House Hotel

– ✆ (051) 389 600 – www.dunbrodyhouse.com – Closed 21-27 December

Rest – *(dinner only and Sunday lunch) (booking essential)* Menu € 35/80

Light, spacious, classically styled restaurant in keeping with the Georgian country house hotel in which it is sited; bright rugs and vividly coloured seats add a modern touch. Classic dishes feature produce from their own kitchen garden.

ASHFORD (Áth na Fuinseog) – Wicklow – 712 N8 – pop. 1 449 39 D2

Dublin 43 km – Rathdrum 17 km – Wicklow 6 km

Ballyknocken House

Glenealy, South : 4.75 km on L 1096 – ✆ (0404) 44 627 – www.ballyknocken.com – March-November

7 rm – 🚹 € 79/119 🚹🚹 € 99/119 **Rest** – Menu € 45

Part-Victorian house with neat gardens and adjoining cookery school, located next to the family farm. Traditional lounge and good-sized bedrooms with antique furnishings, modern feature walls and bright fabrics; some have claw-foot baths. Traditional dishes of local produce at gingham-clothed tables.

Dublin 120 km – Galway 92 km – Limerick 120 km – Roscommon 32 km
St Peter's Sq, ✆ (090) 647 21 07, www.athlonechamber.ie
Hodson Bay, ✆ (090) 6 49 20 73
Clonmacnois★★★ (Grave Slabs★, Cross of the Scriptures★) S : 21 km by N 6 and N 62 – N : Lough Ree (Ballykeeran Viewpoint★)

Sheraton Athlone
Gleeson St – ✆ (090) 645 1000 – www.sheratonathlone.com – Closed 25 December
167 rm – 🚹 € 99/105 🚹🚹 € 118/210 **Rest** – Menu € 40 – Carte € 26/43
Modern hotel built around a smart shopping centre. The bedroom grade increases with the floor number – all have excellent mod cons and some offer super lough views – the best rooms are in the 11-storey glass tower. Very smart leisure, spa and aquatics area. Eat in the restaurant, laid-back café or chic bar.

Shelmalier House without rest
Retreat Rd., Cartrontroy, East : 2.5 km by Dublin rd (N 6) – ✆ (090) 647 22 45 – www.shelmalierhouse.com – closed December-February
7 rm – 🚹 € 40 🚹🚹 € 70
Well-run guesthouse with neat gardens, homely décor and strong green credentials. Clean, comfortable bedrooms – Room 1 is the best. Extensive breakfasts often include a daily special such as pancakes. Relax in the sauna or hot tub.

Left Bank Bistro
Fry Pl – ✆ (090) 649 44 46 – www.leftbankbistro.com – Closed 1 week Christmas, Sunday and Monday
Rest – Menu € 15 (weekday lunch)/25 – Carte € 28/46
Keenly run bistro with an airy interior, rough floorboards, brick walls and an open-plan kitchen. Extensive menus offer an eclectic mix of dishes, from Irish beef and local fish specials right through to Asian-inspired fare.

Kin Khao
Abbey Ln. – ✆ (090) 649 88 05 – www.kinkhaothai.ie – Closed 24-26 December
Rest – *(dinner only and lunch Wednesday-Friday and Sunday)* Menu € 10 (lunch)/30
Vivid yellow building with red window frames, hidden down a side street near the castle. Small downstairs bar; tapestries in main room. Good choice of authentic Thai dishes and daily specials – try the owner's recommendations.

at Glasson Northeast : 8 km on N 55 – ✉ Athlone

Glasson Golf H. & Country Club
West : 2.75 km – ✆ (090) 648 51 20 – www.glassoncountryhouse.ie – Closed 24-25 December rm,
65 rm – 🚹 € 85/150 🚹🚹 € 100/300
Rest – *(bar lunch)* Menu € 26 (lunch)/55 **s** – Carte € 27/52 **s**
Greatly extended period house with views over the golf course and Lough Ree; the owner was born here and several family generations are now involved. Golfing memorabilia fills the walls. Bedrooms are spacious and modern; some have huge balconies and all have a view. Classical menu served in the dining room.

Wineport Lodge
Southwest : 1.5 km – ✆ (090) 643 90 10 – www.wineport.ie – Closed 24-26 December
30 rm – 🚹 € 99/169 🚹🚹 € 109/290
Rest – *(dinner only and Sunday lunch)* Menu € 35/69 – Carte € 46/56
Superbly set hotel, with the bedroom wing following the line of the lough shore and each luxurious room boasting a waterside terrace or balcony – it's worth paying extra for the Captain's Suite. Two treatment rooms and a rooftop hot tub for relaxation. Extensive menus utilise seasonal produce.

Glasson Stone Lodge without rest
– ✆ (090) 648 50 04 – *www.glassonstonelodge.com* – *May-October*
6 rm – € 50/55 € 75/80
Smart guesthouse with a baronial appearance, built from local Irish limestone. Pine features strongly throughout; bedrooms boast thoughtful extras and locally made furniture. Breakfast includes homemade bread and fruit from the garden.

Fatted Calf
– ✆ (090) 648 52 08 – *www.thefattedcalf.ie* – *Closed Good Friday, 25 December and Monday except bank holidays*
Rest – Menu € 20 (weekdays) – Carte € 28/46
Well-run pub with attractive wood-panelled bar hung with original Guinness and Gilbey's signs and a locals snug complete with pool table. Dishes range from handmade sausages to local rabbit terrine; tasty specials feature in the evening.

AUGHRIM (Eachroim) – Wicklow – 712 N9 – pop. 1 364 — 39 D2

Dublin 74 km – Waterford 124 km – Wexford 96 km
Ballinasloe, ✆ (090) 9 76 39 39, www.wicklowtourism.ie

Brooklodge H & Wells Spa
Macreddin Village, North : 3.25 km – ✆ (0402) 36 444
– *www.brooklodge.com* – *Closed 24-25 December*
86 rm – € 90/150 € 120/195 – 4 suites
Rest ***Strawberry Tree*** **Rest** ***Armento*** – see restaurant listing
Sprawling hotel in 180 peaceful acres in the Wicklow Valley. Flag-floored reception, comfy lounge, informal café and pub. Smart, modern bedrooms with large bathrooms; some in an annexe, along with the conference rooms. State-of-the-art spa.

Strawberry Tree – Brooklodge Hotel
Macreddin Village, North : 3.25 km – ✆ (0402) 36 444 – *www.brooklodge.com*
– *Closed 24-25 December*
Rest – *(dinner only)* Menu € 65/85
Ireland's only certified organic restaurant: formal, with an intimate, atmospheric feel, it is set on a village-style hotel estate. Menus feature wild and organic ingredients sourced from local artisan suppliers.

Armento – Brooklodge Hotel
Macreddin Village, North : 3.25 km – ✆ (0402) 36 444 – *www.brooklodge.com*
– *Closed 24-25 December*
Rest – *(dinner only)* Menu € 30/35
Informal Italian restaurant set in a smart hotel on a secluded 180 acre estate. Southern Italian menus feature artisan produce imported from Armento and pizzas cooked in the wood-fired oven.

BAGENALSTOWN (Muine Bheag) – Carlow – 712 L9 – pop. 2 775 — 39 D2

Dublin 101 km – Carlow 16 km – Kilkenny 21 km – Wexford 59 km

Kilgraney Country House without rest
South : 6.5 km by R 705 (Borris Rd) – ✆ (059) 977 52 83
– *www.kilgraneyhouse.com* – *Closed November-February and Monday-Wednesday*
6 rm – € 110/135 € 150/200
Georgian country house which adopts a truly holistic approach. Period features blend with modern, minimalist furnishings and the mood is calm and peaceful. It boasts a small tea room, a craft gallery and a spa with a relaxation room, along with pleasant herb, vegetable, zodiac and monastic gardens.

BALLINA (Béal an Átha) – Mayo – 712 E5 – pop. 10 490 Ireland — 36 B2

Dublin 241 km – Galway 117 km – Roscommon 103 km – Sligo 59 km
Cathedral Rd AY, ✆ (096) 7 08 48, www.towns.mayo-ireland.ie
Mossgrove, Shanaghy, ✆ (096) 2 10 50
Rosserk Abbey★, N : 6.5 km by R 314. Moyne Abbey★, N : 11.25 km by R 314 - Pontoon Bridge View (≤★), S : 19.25 km by N 26 and R 310 – Downpatrick Head★, N : 32 km by R 314

REPUBLIC OF IRELAND

Mount Falcon

Foxford Rd, South : 6.25 km on N 26 – ☎ (096) 74 472 – www.mountfalcon.com – Closed 24-26 December

32 rm – € 120/160 € 140/200 – 1 suite

Rest *Kitchen* – *(bar lunch Monday-Saturday)* Menu € 28 – Carte € 35/56

Classic country house built in 1872, with golf, cycling, fishing and archery available in its 100 acre grounds. Characterful bedrooms in the main house; spacious, contemporary rooms in the extension. Clubby bar. The restaurant is in the old kitchens and offers updated French classics. Relaxed service.

Ice House

The Quay Village, Northeast : 2.5 km by N 59 – ☎ (096) 23 500 – www.theicehouse.ie – Closed 24-26 December

32 rm – € 95/135 € 99/180

Rest – *(dinner only and Sunday lunch)* Menu € 45 – Carte € 42/63

A former ice vault for local fishermen; now a modern hotel offering great river and woodland views. Feature bedrooms have fireplaces and a traditional feel – the rest are modern and named after ice crystals; the spa suites are the largest. The restaurant opens onto a terrace with two hot tubs. Modern menus.

Crockets on the Quay

The Quay, Northeast : 2.5 km by N 59 – ☎ (096) 75 930 – www.crocketsonthequay.ie – Closed 24-26 December and Good Friday

Rest – *(dinner only and lunch Saturday-Sunday)* Carte € 21/45

Vibrant orange pub with a lively atmosphere. Generously proportioned dishes include tasty Irish steaks. They host regular poker, quiz and traditional Irish music nights and for sports fans, there are plasma screen TVs in the garden.

BALLINASLOE (Béal Átha na Sluaighe) – Galway – 712 H8 – pop. 6 449 Ireland 36 B3

Dublin 146 km – Galway 66 km – Limerick 106 km – Roscommon 58 km

Bridge St, ☎ (0909) 64 26 04, www.ballinasloe.com

Rossgloss, ☎ (0905) 4 21 26

Mountbellew, ☎ (090) 9 67 92 59

Clonfert Cathedral★ (west doorway★★), SW : by R 355 and minor roads. Turoe Stone, Bullaun★, SW : 29 km by R 348 and R 350 – Loughrea (St Brendan's Cathedral★), SW : 29 km by N 6 – Clonmacnoise★★★ (grave slabs★, Cross of the Scriptures★) E : 21 km by R 357 and R 444

Moycarn Lodge and Marina

Shannonbridge Rd, Southeast : 2.5 km by N 6 off R 357 – ☎ (090) 964 50 50 – www.moycarnlodge.ie – Closed 25 December

15 rm – € 49/69 € 69/99 **Rest** – Carte € 17/29

Purpose-built hotel run by friendly owners; its pleasant gardens and terrace overlooking the river, where there's free berthing for guests. Light, airy bedrooms – five open onto a large shared balcony offering pleasant river views. Rustic bar and restaurant serve an accessible menu of traditional dishes.

BALLINGARRY (Baile an Gharraí) – Limerick – 712 F10 – pop. 527 Ireland 38 B2

Dublin 227 km – Killarney 90 km – Limerick 29 km

Kilmallock★ (Kilmallock Abbey★, Collegiate Church★), SE : 24 km by R 518 – Lough Gur Interpretive Centre★ **AC**, NE : 29 km by R 519, minor road to Croom, R 516 and R 512 – Monasteranenagh Abbey★, NE : 24 km by R 519 and minor road to Croom

Mustard Seed at Echo Lodge

– ☎ (069) 68 508 – www.mustardseed.ie – Closed late January-mid February and 24-26 December

16 rm – € 120/165 € 180/320 – 2 suites

Rest – *(dinner only)* Menu € 42 (weekdays)/60

Brightly painted former convent with an exuberant owner, well-kept gardens and an interior filled with antique furnishings, paintings, books, magazines and fresh flowers. The main house bedrooms are furnished in a period style; those in the former school house are brighter and more modern. Dinner is an occasion – boldly flavoured cooking shows respect for the produce.

REPUBLIC OF IRELAND

BALLSBRIDGE = Droichead na Dothra – **Dublin** – **712** N8 – **see Dublin**

BALLYBUNION (Baile an Bhuinneánaigh) – **Kerry** – **712** D10 **38** A2
– **pop. 1 354** Ireland

Dublin 283 km – Limerick 90 km – Tralee 42 km

Ballybunnion, Sandhill Rd, (068) 2 71 46

Rattoo Round Tower★, S : 10 km by R 551. Ardfert★, S : 29 km by R 551, R 556 and minor road W – Banna Strand★, S : 28 km by R 551 – Carrigafoyle Castle★, NE : 21 km by R 551 – Glin Castle★ **AC**, E : 30.5 km by R 551 and N 69

Teach de Broc Country House rest,

Link Rd, South : 2.5 km by Golf Club rd – (068) 27 581
– www.ballybuniongolf.com – closed November-February
14 rm – € 85/100 € 110/145
Rest *Strollers* – *(dinner only and Sunday lunch)* Menu € 25 – Carte € 22/46
Stylish house by the Ballybunion golf course. Spacious, modern interior boasts a nicely furnished bar-lounge with outdoor seating. Bedrooms are extremely comfortable and have smart bathrooms. Elegant dining room with smartly laid tables offers wide-ranging menu.

19th Lodge without rest

South : 2.75 km by Golf Club rd – (068) 27 592
– www.ballybuniongolflodge.com – Closed Christmas and restricted opening in winter
14 rm – € 70/120 € 95/160
Set overlooking the fairways of the famed course and filled with golfing memorabilia. Comfy ground floor lounge; pleasant, classical décor throughout. Executive bedrooms boast both showers and spa baths. Substantial breakfasts.

REPUBLIC OF IRELAND

BALLYCASTLE (Baile an Chaisil) – **Mayo** – **712** D5 – **pop. 215** **36** B2
Ireland

Dublin 267 km – Galway 140 km – Sligo 88 km

Cáide Fields★, **AC**, NE : 8 km by R 314

Stella Maris Country House rm,

Northwest : 3 km by R 314 – (096) 43 322 – www.StellaMarisIreland.com – 25 April-September
12 rm – € 125/177 € 192/240
Rest – *(dinner only) (booking essential)* Carte € 31/52
Former coastguard station and convent; now a homely hotel. Simple bedrooms display period furnishings and religious samplers that were left behind. The conservatory runs the length of the building and looks over the water. Snug, open-fired bar and a cosy dining room offering a daily menu of local ingredients.

BALLYCONNELL (Báal Atha Conaill) – **Cavan** – **712** J5 – **pop. 1 061** **37** C2

Dublin 143 km – Drogheda 122 km – Enniskillen 37 km

Slieve Russell, (049) 952 64 58

Slieve Russell

Southeast : 2.75 km on N 87 – (049) 952 64 44 – www.slieverussell.ie
222 rm – € 92/105 € 125/152 – 2 suites
Rest *Conall Cearnach* – *(July-September) (dinner only and Sunday lunch)*
Menu € 28/38 **s** – Carte € 34/57 **s**
Rest *Setanta* – Menu € 30 (dinner)/37 **s** – Carte € 29/49 **s**
Well-run hotel with immaculate gardens, an impressive mock-Georgian façade and good facilities for families, golfers and businesspeople. Bedrooms overlook the grounds and are large and luxurious, with every mod con. The restaurants are named after Irish folk heroes – Conall Cearnach offers classical dishes and stylish Setanta serves a European menu.

BALLYCOTTON (Baile Choitín) – **Cork** – **712** H12 – **pop. 476** **39** C3
Ireland

Dublin 265 km – Cork 43 km – Waterford 106 km

Cloyne Cathedral★, NW : by R 629

Bayview
– ✆ (021) 464 67 46 – *www.thebayviewhotel.com* – *closed November-March*
35 rm – 🚹 € 80/145 🚹🚹 € 80/145, ☕ €15 – 2 suites
Rest *Capricho* – *(bar lunch Monday-Saturday)* Menu € 28/45 – Carte € 39/51
A series of cottages in an elevated position, with superb views over the bay, the harbour and the island opposite. Two cosy lounges; one on each floor. Spacious bedrooms with floral fabrics and sea views – many have Juliet balconies. Ambitious modern menus; ask for a seat in one of the bay windows.

BALLYFARNAN (Béal Átha Fearnáin) – Roscommon – 712 H5 – pop. 205

37 C2

Dublin 111 km – Roscommon 42 km – Sligo 21 km – Longford 38 km

Kilronan Castle
Southeast : 3.5 km on Keadew rd – ✆ *(071) 961 80 00* – *www.kilronancastle.ie*
84 rm ☕ – 🚹 € 135/155 🚹🚹 € 179/279
Rest *Douglas Hyde* – *(dinner only and Sunday lunch)* Menu € 59 – Carte € 47/68
Impressively restored castle with characterful sitting rooms, a library and a palm court; wood panelling, antiques and oil paintings feature throughout. Smart leisure club and hydrotherapy centre. Opulent red and gold bedrooms offer a high level of comfort. The formal dining room offers a classical menu.

BALLYFIN – Laois – 712 J8

39 C1

Dublin 69 km – Portlaoise 11 km – Cork 114 km – Limerick 67 km

Ballyfin
– ✆ *(057) 875 58 66* – *www.ballyfin.com* – *closed January-February*
15 rm (dinner included) ☕ – 🚹 € 350/600 🚹🚹 € 600/1600 – 2 suites
Rest – *(residents only)*
Immaculate Regency mansion built in 1820 and set in 600 acres. Stunning interior with a drawing room decorated in gold leaf, a library featuring 7,000 old books and elegant, antique-furnished bedrooms boasting marble bathrooms. The 4 course tasting menu is served in the State dining room. Excellent service.

BALLYLICKEY (Béal Átha Leice) – Cork – 712 D12 – ✉ Bantry

38 A3

Ireland

Dublin 347 km – Cork 88 km – Killarney 72 km

Bantry Bay, Donemark, ✆ (027) 5 05 79

Bantry Bay★ - Bantry House★ **AC**, S : 5 km by R 584. Glengarriff★ (Ilnacullin★★, access by boat) NW : 13 km by N 71 - Healy Pass★★ (<★★) W : 37 km by N 71, R 572 and R 574 – Slieve Miskish Mountains (<★★) W : 46.75 km by N 71 and R 572 – Lauragh (Derreen Gardens★ **AC**) NW : 44 km by N 71, R 572 and R 574 – Allihies (copper mines★) W : 66.75 km by N 71, R 572 and R 575 -- Garnish Island (<★) W : 70.75 km by N 71 and R 572

Seaview House
– ✆ *(027) 50 073* – *www.seaviewhousehotel.com* – *mid March-mid November*
25 rm ☕ – 🚹 € 75/95 🚹🚹 € 120/160
Rest – *(dinner only and Sunday lunch)* Menu € 35/45
Well-run Victorian house that upholds tradition in both its décor and its service. Pleasant drawing room, cosy bar and antique-furnished bedrooms; some with sea views. The attractive gardens lead down to the shore of the bay. A classical menu is served at elegant polished tables laid with silver tableware.

Ballylickey House without rest
– ✆ *(027) 50 071* – *www.ballylickeymanorhouse.com* – *May-September*
6 rm ☕ – 🚹 € 90/100 🚹🚹 € 110/180
Pretty country house with an outdoor pool and beautiful gardens reaching down to the sea. Spacious, individually furnished bedrooms are split between the house and garden chalets. The period-style breakfast room displays attractive artwork.

BALLYLIFFIN (Baile Lifín) – Donegal – 712 J2 – pop. 461 37 C1

Dublin 174 km – Lifford 46 km – Letterkenny 39 km

Ballyliffin Lodge

Shore Rd – (074) 937 82 00 – www.ballyliffinlodge.com – Closed 25 December

40 rm – € 80/120 € 110/190 **Rest** – Menu € 18/25 – Carte € 27/40

Remote hotel with well-kept gardens, affording a superb outlook over countryside to the beach. Bedrooms offer good facilities; ask for one facing the front. Relax in the lovely spa and pool, or enjoy afternoon tea with a view in the lounge. Informal, bistro-style dining, with international menus.

BALLYMACARBRY (Baile Mhac Cairbre) – Waterford – 712 I11 39 C2

– pop. 132 – Clonmel Ireland

Dublin 190 km – Cork 79 km – Waterford 63 km

Clonmel★ (St Mary's Church★, County Museum★ AC), N : 16 km by R 671 – Lismore★ (Castle Gardens★ AC, St Carthage's Cathedral★), SW : 26 km by R 671and N 72 – W : Nier Valley Scenic Route★★

Hanora's Cottage

Nire Valley, East : 6.5 km by Nire Drive rd on Nire Valley Lakes rd – (052) 613 61 34 – www.hanorascottage.com – Closed 1 week Christmas

10 rm – € 55/65 € 110/220

Rest – *(closed Sunday and bank holiday Mondays) (dinner only and Sunday lunch) (booking essential)* Menu € 39

Dating back to 1891 and named after the owner's grandmother, to whom it once belonged. Relax on the terrace by the river or explore the nearby Comeragh Mountains. Spacious, brightly painted bedrooms have characterful furnishings and most boast whirlpool baths. The comfy dining room offers a classical menu.

Glasha Farmhouse

Northwest : 4 km by R 671 – (052) 613 61 08 – www.glashafarmhouse.com – Closed December

6 rm – € 60/70 € 100 **Rest** – Menu € 25

Large farmhouse between the Knockmealdown and Comeragh Mountains. Guest areas include a cosy lounge, an airy conservatory and a pleasant patio. Bedrooms are comfortable and immaculately kept; some have jacuzzis. The welcoming owner has good local knowledge. Home-cooked meals, with picnic lunches available.

BALLYMORE EUSTACE (An Baile Mór) – Kildare – 712 J2 39 D1

– pop. 872

Dublin 48 km – Naas 12 km – Drogheda 99 km

Ballymore Inn

– (045) 864 585 – www.ballymoreinn.com

Rest – Menu € 21/34 – Carte € 28/45

Remote village pub with spacious bar and Parisian brasserie style dining area. Generous portions include tasty homemade bread, pizzas, tarts and pastries. Small artisan producers favoured.

BALLYNAHINCH (Baile na hInse) – Galway – 712 C7 – Recess 36 A3

Ireland

Dublin 225 km – Galway 66 km – Westport 79 km

Connemara★★★ – Roundstone★, S : by R 341 – Cashel★, SE : by R 341 and R 340

Ballynahinch Castle

– (095) 31 006 – www.ballynahinch-castle.com – Closed February and Christmas

37 rm – € 160/350 € 170/450 – 3 suites

Rest *Owenmore* – *(dinner only) (booking essential)* Menu € 60 **s** – Carte € 32/75

Part-17C grey-stone castle and extensive grounds, set in an unrivalled riverside location. Log-fired entrance, well-appointed sitting rooms and modern country house style bedrooms with up-to-date facilities. The pub attracts the locals; the restaurant offers classical 4 course dinners and water views.

BALLYVAUGHAN (Baile Uí Bheacháin) – Clare – 712 E8 – pop. 258 38 B1

Ireland

Dublin 240 km – Ennis 55 km – Galway 46 km

The Burren★★ (Scenic Route★★, Aillwee Cave★ AC (Waterfall★★), Corcomroe Abbey★, Poulnabrone Portal Tomb★) – Kilfenora (Crosses★, Burren Centre★ AC), S : 25 km N 67 and R 476. Cliffs of Moher★★★, S : 32 km by N 67 and R 478

Gregans Castle

Southwest : 6 km on N 67 – (065) 707 70 05 – www.gregans.ie – 14 February-22 November

20 rm – € 155/195 € 205/245 – 3 suites

Rest *Gregans Castle* – see restaurant listing

Well-run, part-18C country house with superb views of The Burren and Galway Bay. The open-fired hall leads to a cosy, rustic bar-lounge and an elegant sitting room. Bedrooms are furnished with antiques: two open onto the garden and one is in the old kitchen and features a panelled ceiling and a four-poster.

Drumcreehy House without rest

Northeast : 2 km on N 67 – (065) 707 73 77 – www.drumcreehyhouse.com – Closed 25-26 December and restricted opening in winter

12 rm – € 60 € 100

Brightly painted house overlooking Galway Bay. The interior is warm and welcoming, with rug-covered wood floors, peat fires and an honesty bar. The cosy bedrooms are named after flowers found on the Burren and feature bold colours and German stripped pine furnishings. Excellent continental buffet breakfasts.

Ballyvaughan Lodge without rest

– (065) 707 72 92 – www.ballyvaughanlodge.com – Closed 25-26 December

11 rm – € 45/60 € 75/85

Welcoming guesthouse with a colourful flower display and a decked terrace. The vaulted, light-filled lounge features a locally made flower chandelier; bedrooms boast co-ordinating fabrics. Breakfast uses quality farmers' market produce.

Gregans Castle – Gregans Castle Hotel

Southwest : 6 km on N 67 – (065) 707 70 05 – www.gregans.ie – 14 February-22 November

Rest – *(bar lunch) (booking advisable)* Menu €69 **s**

Have an aperitif in the drawing room of this country house hotel before heading through to the restaurant, where you can look across to Galway Bay. Interesting modern dishes have clean, clear flavours and showcase the latest local produce.

BALTIMORE (Dún na Séad) – Cork – 712 D13 – pop. 347 Ireland 38 A3

Dublin 344 km – Cork 95 km – Killarney 124 km

Sherkin Island★ (by ferry) – Castletownshend★, E : 20 km by R 595 and R 596 – Glandore★, E : 26 km by R 595, N 71 and R 597

Casey's of Baltimore

rest,

East : 0.75 km on R 595 – (028) 20 197 – www.caseysofbaltimore.com – Closed 21-26 December

14 rm – € 90/110 € 100/160 **Rest** – Menu €25 – Carte €27/63 **s**

Extended 19C pub with a terracotta façade, well located near the seashore. Comfy lounge and simple pine-furnished bedrooms with good facilities. You're guaranteed a warm welcome from the family owners. The restaurant and beer garden overlook the bay; classical menus, and traditional music at the weekend.

Slipway without rest

The Cove, Southwest : 0.75 km – (028) 20 134 – www.theslipway.com – May-September

4 rm – € 55/70 € 72/80

Laid-back guesthouse in a lovely spot. The open-fired lounge is hung with tapestries made by the charming owner and the breakfast room leads onto a veranda with stunning views over the bay. Modest, well-kept bedrooms feature fresh flowers.

BANDON (Droichead na Bandan) - Cork - 712 F12 - pop. 1 917 38 B3

Dublin 181 km - Cork 20 km - Carrigaline 28 km - Cobh 33 km

Kilbrogan House without rest

Kilbrogan Hill, North : 1 km on Macroom rd (R 589) – (023) 884 49 35 – www.kilbrogan.com – March-October

4 rm – € 50/55 € 80/90

Georgian townhouse set above the town, boasting a stunning original staircase, fine cornicing and a turn-of-the-century conservatory overlooking pleasant gardens. Simple, antique-furnished bedrooms. Breakfast is cooked on the Aga.

Chapelsteps

St. Patrick's Pl – (023) 885 2581 – www.chapelsteps.ie – Closed 25-26 December, Monday and Tuesday

Rest – Menu € 29 (early dinner) – Carte € 15/45

Vibrant brasserie next to the steps of the church. The smart, boldly papered interior is divided into several different areas and enticing home-baked goods top the counter. Modern bistro cooking, with Black Angus steaks a speciality.

Poacher's Inn

Clonakilty Rd, Southwest : 1.5 km on N 71 – (023) 884 1159 – www.poachersinnbandon.com

Rest – Menu € 24 (weekday dinner)/35 – Carte € 25/44

Cosy neighbourhood pub that's popular with the locals. There's a wood-panelled bar, a cosy snug, and an upstairs restaurant which opens later in the week. Many dishes come in a choice of sizes and West Cork seafood takes centre stage.

BANSHA - South Tipperary - 712 H10 - pop. 349 39 C2

Dublin 121 km - Clonmel 21 km - Cork 59 km - Limerick 31 km

Rathellen House without rest

Southeast : 3.5 km. by N 24 on Coopers Cottage rd – (062) 54 376

6 rm – € 65 € 90/120

Set in a peaceful location, a very comfortable Georgian-style property with a classic country house feel. Variously-sized bedrooms feature antique furnishings and pleasant country or mountain outlooks, and the bathrooms boast heated floors.

BANTRY (Beanntraí) Cork - Cork - 712 D12 38 A3

Dublin 215 km - Cork 53 km - Killarney 49 km - Macroom 34 km

O'Connors

Wolf Tone Sq – (027) 55 664 – www.oconnorsbantry.com – Closed Monday and Tuesday November-April

Rest – *(booking essential)* Menu € 10 (lunch)/25 – Carte € 27/41

Well-run harbourside restaurant, with a compact, bistro-style interior featuring model ships in the windows and modern art on the walls. The menu focuses on local seafood bought directly from the small fishing boats in the harbour.

BARNA (Bearna) - Galway - 712 E8 - pop. 1 878 36 B3

Dublin 227 km - Galway 9 km

Twelve

rest,

Barna Crossroads – (091) 597 000 – www.thetwelvehotel.ie

48 rm – € 90/140 € 100/155 – 10 suites

Rest *Upstairs @ West* – see restaurant listing

Rest *The Pins* – Menu € 25 – Carte € 24/44 **s**

An unassuming exterior hides a keenly run boutique hotel complete with a bakery, a pizza kitchen and a deli. Stylish, modern bedrooms have large gilt mirrors, mood lighting and designer 'seaweed' toiletries; some even boast cocktail bars! Innovative menus in Upstairs @ West; modern European dishes in The Pins.

Upstairs @ West - Twelve Hotel

Barna Crossroads – (091) 597 000 – www.thetwelvehotel.ie – Closed Monday

Rest – *(dinner only)* Menu € 25 (weekdays)/39 **s** – Carte € 29/52 **s**

Stylish first floor restaurant in a smart boutique hotel, with a chic champagne bar, booth seating and an moody, intimate feel. Seasonal menus offer ambitious, innovative dishes, showcasing meats and seafood from the 'West' of Ireland.

O'Grady's on the Pier
– *(091) 592 223 – www.ogradysonthepier.com – Closed 24-26 December*
Rest – *(booking essential)* Carte € 28/51
Smartly painted white and powder blue building on the water's edge, with views across Co. Clare and a charming interior with real fires and fresh flowers. Fish is from Galway or Kinsale; go for the daily catch, which could be classically presented or may have a modern twist. Cheerful, attentive service.

BARRELLS CROSS – **Cork** – **712** G12 – **see Kinsale**

BEAUFORT = Lios an Phúca – **Kerry** – **712** D11 – **see Killarney**

BIRR (Biorra) – **Offaly** – **712** I8 – **pop. 4 428** Ireland — **39** C1
Dublin 140 km – Athlone 45 km – Kilkenny 79 km – Limerick 79 km
Wilmer Rd, (057) 912 09 23, www.heritagetowns.com
18 The Glenns, (057) 9 12 00 82
Town★ – Birr Castle Demesne★★ **AC** (Telescope★★)
Clonfert Cathedral★ (West doorway★★), NW : 24 km by R 439, R 356 and minor roads – Portumna★ (Castle★ **AC**), W : 24 km by R 489 – Roscrea★ (Damer House★ **AC**) S : 19.25 km by N 62 – Slieve Bloom Mountinas★, E : 21 km by R 440

Maltings without rest
Castle St – (057) 912 13 45 – www.themaltingsbirr.com
8 rm – € 40/45 € 70
Characterful stone-built house once used to store malt in the production of Guinness. Set over the river, its breakfast-room-cum-lounge overlooks the castle grounds. Simple, pine furnished bedrooms. Homemade soda bread, scones and jams.

BLACKLION (An Blaic) – **Cavan** – **712** I5 – **pop. 229** — **34** A3
Dublin 194 km – Drogheda 170 km – Enniskillen 19 km
9 Blacklion, Toam, (071) 9 85 30 24

MacNean House with rm — rest,
Main St – (071) 985 30 22 – www.macneanrestaurant.com – Closed January
19 rm – € 50/96 € 67/96
Rest – *(closed Monday-Tuesday and Sunday dinner) (dinner only and Sunday lunch) (booking essential)* Menu € 60/87
Stylish restaurant in a smart townhouse, with a chic lounge and a plush dining room. Choose between a 6 or 9 course set menu – cooking is ambitious and uses complex techniques, and dishes are attractively presented. Charming, knowledgeable service team. Bedrooms are a mix of modern and country styles.

BLARNEY (An Bhlarna) – **Cork** – **712** G12 – **pop. 2 437** – ✉ **Cork** — **38** B3
Ireland
Dublin 268 km – Cork 9 km
Blarney Castle★★ **AC** – Blarney Castle House★ **AC**

Killarney House without rest
Station Rd, Northeast : 1.5 km on Carrignavar rd. – (021) 438 18 41 – www.killarneyhouseblarney.com
6 rm – € 40/45 € 58/65
Well-kept, friendly guesthouse on the edge of town, with immaculate gardens, simple, spacious bedrooms, comfortable lounges and a wood-furnished breakfast room. Extensive breakfast menu includes the full Irish.

at Tower West : 3.25 km on R 617 – ✉ **Cork**

Ashlee Lodge without rest
– *(021) 438 53 46 – www.ashleelodge.com – Closed 20 December-20 January*
10 rm – € 70/140 € 89/160
Smart hotel with a cosy lounge featuring a wood burning stove, board games and an honesty bar. Comfortable bedrooms offer all you could want; some have whirlpool baths. Outdoor hot tub, sauna and in-room treatments. Extensive breakfasts.

BORRIS - Carlow - 712 L10 - pop. 646 39 D2

Dublin 121 km – Carlow 36 km – Waterford 66 km

Step House

– ✆ *(059) 977 32 09 – www.stephousehotel.ie – Closed 9-26 January and 25 December*

20 rm – € 75/85 € 130/190 – 1 suite

Rest *Cellar* – see restaurant listing

Welcoming, family-run, Georgian townhouse in a small heritage village. Spacious, modern bedrooms; most have lovely mountain views and the penthouse boasts a terrace. Comfy bar, named after the year in which the hotel was originally built.

Cellar – Step House Hotel

– ✆ *(059) 977 32 09 – www.stephousehotel.ie – Closed 9-26 January and 25 December*

Rest – *(closed Monday-Tuesday) (bar lunch)* Menu € 28 – Carte € 36/48

Atmospheric hotel restaurant with vaulted ceilings and archways; set in the kitchens of the old McMurrough Kavanagh Estate dower house. Interesting modern menu of local and artisan ingredients.

BOYLE (Mainistir na Búille) - Roscommon - 712 H6 - pop. 1 459 36 B2

Ireland

Dublin 168 km – Roscommon 43 km – Galway 103 km

King House, ✆ (071) 966 21 45, www.visitboyle.net

King House★ **AC**

Boyle Abbey★ **AC**, E : 2 km by N 4 – Lough Key Forest Park★ **AC**, E : 3.25 km by N 4. Arigna Scenic Drive★ (≤★), NE : 20 km by N 4, R 280 and R 207 – Curlew Mountains (≤★), NW : 3.5 km by N 4

Lough Key House Ⓝ

Southeast : 3.75 km by R 294 on N 4 – ✆ (071) 966 21 61 – www.loughkeyhouse.com – Closed 2 January-16 March

5 rm – € 49/59 € 85/98 **Rest** – Menu € 30

Run by a welcoming owner, a stone-built Georgian house with mature grounds, next to Lough Key Forest Park. Homely guest areas with antiques and ornaments; bedrooms in the original house are the best, with antique four-posters and warm fabrics. Formal communal dining room – produce is local or from the garden.

Rosdarrig House without rest

Carrick Rd, East : 1.5 km on R 294 – ✆ (071) 966 20 40 – www.rosdarrig.com – April -October

5 rm – € 35/40 € 65/70

Neat house on the edge of town, close to the abbey, where friendly owners offer genuine Irish hospitality. Two comfy, homely lounges and a linen-laid breakfast room. Pleasant bedrooms with flowery fabrics overlook the garden.

BRIDGE END - Donegal - 712 J2 - pop. 497 37 C1

Dublin 158 km – Lifford 25 km – Belfast 78 km – Londonderry 5 km

Harrys

– ✆ *(074) 936 85 44 – www.harrys.ie – Closed 24-26 December and Good Friday*

Rest – Menu € 22 (dinner) – Carte € 23/39

Long-standing, passionately run restaurant with open-plan interior and modern bistro feel. Menus evolve with the seasons, offering flavoursome, classically prepared dishes. Traceability is key, with much produce from their walled garden.

BUNDORAN (Bun Dobhráin) - Donegal - 712 H4 - pop. 1 781 37 C2

Ireland

Dublin 259 km – Donegal 27 km – Sligo 37 km

Main St, ✆ (071) 9 84 25 39, www.discoverbundoran.com

Creevykeel Court Cairn★, S : 5 km by N 15 – Rossnowlagh Strand★★, N : 8.5 km by N 15 and R 231

Fitzgerald's

– ✆ (071) 984 13 36 – *www.fitzgeraldshotel.com* – *restricted opening in winter*
16 rm – € 55/85 € 90/140
Rest ***Bistro*** – *(closed Monday-Tuesday) (dinner only)* Menu € 25 **s** – Carte € 28/39 **s**
Family-owned hotel in a popular seaside town overlooking Donegal Bay. Characterful guest areas feature tiled floors, stained glass windows and a wood burning stove. Bedrooms are pastel coloured; those facing the sea are the ones to choose. Informal, split-level bistro offers extensive menus of comfort dishes.

BUNRATTY (Bun Raite) – Clare – 712 F9 Ireland 38 B2

Dublin 207 km – Ennis 24 km – Limerick 13 km
Town★★ – Bunratty Castle★★

Bunratty Manor

– ✆ (061) 707 984 – *www.bunrattymanor.ie* – *Closed 23-28 December*
20 rm – € 69/89 € 79/140
Rest – *(dinner only and Sunday lunch)* Menu € 27 – Carte € 31/45
Smart hotel close to a castle and a folk park, in a busy tourist town. Comfy lounge has walls adorned with horse racing memorabilia. Good-sized, brightly decorated bedrooms display colourful fabrics. Traditional bar and restaurant with a courtyard offer a classical set menu and more imaginative à la carte.

CAHERLISTRANE (Cathair Loistreáin) – Galway – 712 E7 36 B3

Dublin 256 km – Ballina 74 km – Galway 42 km

Lisdonagh House

Northwest : 4 km by R 333 off Shrule rd – ✆ (093) 31 163 – *www.lisdonagh.com* – *May-October*
9 rm – € 90/98 € 90/180
Rest – *(dinner only) (residents only, set menu only)* Menu € 25/49
Ivy-clad Georgian house with pleasant lough views. The traditional country house interior boasts eye-catching murals and open-fired lounges. Antique-furnished bedrooms have marble bathrooms; the first floor rooms are larger and brighter. The grand dining room offers 5 course dinners and simpler suppers.

CAHERSIVEEN (Cathair Saidhbhín) – Kerry – 712 B12 – pop. 1 168 38 A2

Ireland
Dublin 355 km – Killarney 64 km
Ring of Kerry★★

QC's with rm

3 Main St – ✆ (066) 947 22 44 – *www.qcbar.com* – *Closed 2 weeks November, Monday-Wednesday in winter*
5 rm – € 65/75 € 79/99
Rest – *(booking advisable)* Menu € 20 (dinner)/45 – Carte € 26/56
Cosy little pub with characterful flagged floors, exposed stone walls and a strong nautical theme. Seafood-orientated menus offer fresh, unfussy classics and some more unusual daily specials; the family also own a local fish wholesalers. Spacious, well-equipped bedrooms are located just around the corner.

O'Neill's (The Point) Seafood Bar

Renard Point, Southwest : 4.5 km by N 70 – ✆ (066) 947 21 65 – *Closed January-February*
Rest – *(bookings not accepted)* Carte € 29/40
In a great location beside Valentia Island ferry terminal, and run by the O'Neill family for over 150 years. Generous portions of locally landed seafood; salmon comes from a nearby smokehouse. No chips, desserts or credit card payments.

CAMPILE (Ceann Poill) – Wexford – 712 L11 – pop. 411 Ireland 39 D2

Dublin 154 km – Waterford 35 km – Wexford 37 km
Dunbrody Abbey★, S : 3.25 km by R 733 – J F Kennedy Arboretum★, N : 3.25 km by R 733. Tintern Abbey★, SE : 12.75 km by R 733 – Duncannon Fort★, S : 12.75 km by R 733

REPUBLIC OF IRELAND

Kilmokea Country Manor rm, rest,
West : 8 km by R 733 and Great Island rd – ✆ (051) 388 109 – www.kilmokea.com – Closed January and December
6 rm – € 75/95 € 85/120
Rest – *(bookings essential for non-residents)* Menu € 50 (dinner) – Carte lunch € 19/31
Georgian rectory set in 20 acres, 7 of which are formal gardens open to the public. Small antique-furnished drawing room with oils and piano. Bedrooms, some in the old coach house, are more contemporary. Conservatory tea rooms and smart restaurant with daily changing classical menu of organic garden produce.

CAPPOQUIN (Ceapach Choinn) – Waterford – 712 I11 – pop. 759 — 39 C2
Ireland

Dublin 219 km – Cork 56 km – Waterford 64 km

Lismore★ (Lismore Castle Gardens★ **AC**, St Carthage's Cathedral★), W : 6.5 km by N 72. The Gap★ (<★) NW : 14.5 km by R 669

Richmond House with rm
Southeast : 0.75 km on N 72 – ✆ (058) 54 278 – www.richmondhouse.net – Closed Christmas-New Year and Monday-Friday January-February
9 rm – € 60/80 € 100/150
Rest – *(dinner only)* Menu € 28 (early dinner)/55
Imposing Georgian house built in 1704 for the Earl of Cork and Burlington, and filled with family curios. Have a drink in the cosy lounge before heading to the cove-ceilinged dining room. Cooking is classically based; be sure to try the delicious local lamb. Cosy bedrooms are decorated in period styles.

at Millstreet East : 11.25 km by N 72 on R 671 – ✉ Cappoquin

Castle Country House without rest
– ✆ (058) 68 049 – www.castlecountryhouse.com – Closed November-March
5 rm – € 50/60 € 80/100
The restored wing of a 16C castle, set on a working dairy and beef farm. The setting is idyllic, with mountain views and a stream running through the colourful gardens. Bedrooms boast period furniture and king or emperor-sized beds.

CARAGH LAKE (Loch Cárthaí) – Kerry – 712 C11 Ireland — 38 A2

Dublin 341 km – Killarney 35 km – Tralee 40 km

Dooks, Glenbeigh, ✆ (066) 9 76 82 05

Lough Caragh★

Iveragh Peninsula★★ (Ring of Kerry★★)

Ard-Na-Sidhe rm,
– ✆ (066) 976 91 05 – www.ardnasidhe.com – Closed November-5 May
18 rm – € 160/270 € 180/290
Rest – *(dinner only) (booking essential)* Carte € 34/67
1913 Arts and Crafts house on the shores of Lough Caragh, surrounded by mountains. A subtle yet stylish modernisation has emphasised many original features, with oak-panelled walls, flag floors and smart, antique-furnished bedrooms. The restaurant offers classical dishes with subtle modern twists.

Carrig Country House
– ✆ (066) 976 91 00 – www.carrighouse.com – Closed November-March
17 rm – € 125/145 € 150/190 – 1 suite
Rest – *(dinner only) (booking essential)* Menu € 45 – Carte € 32/50
Victorian former hunting lodge set down a wooded drive, located on the lough shore and surrounded by mountains. Cosy, country house interior with traditionally furnished guest areas. Individually decorated bedrooms boast antique furnishings. Beautiful views from the dining room; fresh, country house cooking.

CARLINGFORD (Cairlinn) – Louth – 712 N5 – pop. 1 045 Ireland — 37 D2

Dublin 106 km – Dundalk 21 km

Town★

Windy Gap★, NW : 12.75 km by R 173 – Proleek Dolmen★, SW : 14.5 km by R 173

Four Seasons rest,

– ✆ (042) 937 35 30 – *www.4seasonshotelcarlingford.ie – Weekends only in January*
59 rm – € 55/95 € 69/170
Rest – *(bar lunch)* Menu € 25 – Carte € 25/40
Purpose-built hotel on the edge of the village, with a lovely mountain backdrop. Large leisure centre; open-plan bar. Well-equipped bedrooms; 'Executives' are of a good size, with a separate bath and shower. Ask for a room with lough views. Informal bistro overlooks the garden with its wrought iron pergola.

Beaufort House without rest

– ✆ *(042) 937 38 79 – www.beauforthouse.net*
6 rm – € 65/120 € 78/120
Modern house on the shores of the lough. Spacious lounge displays local art and old maritime charts; large, comfortable bedrooms boast water or mountain views. Welcoming owners also run a sailing school.

Carlingford House without rest

– ✆ *(042) 937 31 18 – www.carlingfordhouse.com – Closed 2 January-6 February and Christmas*
5 rm – € 65/100 € 90/120
Early Victorian house close to the old ruined abbey; the owner was born and has always lived here. Smart, understated bedrooms have good mod cons and are immaculately kept. Pleasant breakfast room; tasty locally smoked salmon and bacon.

Bay Tree with rm

Newry St – ✆ (042) 938 3848 – www.belvederehouse.ie – Closed 24-26 December, Monday and Tuesday
7 rm – € 55/65 € 80/90
Rest – *(dinner only and Sunday lunch) (booking essential)* Menu € 21 (weekdays)/24 – Carte € 29/44
Neighbourhood restaurant fronted by bay trees and decorated with wood, branches and hessian. Attractively presented, well-balanced modern dishes feature herbs and salad from the garden and seafood from nearby Carlingford Lough. Service is polite and organised. Simple bedrooms are located upstairs.

REPUBLIC OF IRELAND

CARLOW (Ceatharlach) – Carlow – 712 L9 – pop. 13 698 — 39 D2

Dublin 80 km – Kilkenny 37 km – Wexford 75 km
College St, ✆ (059) 9 13 15 54, www.carlowtourism.com
Carlow, Dublin Rd, Deer Park, ✆ (059) 9 13 16 95

Barrowville Town House without rest

Kilkenny Rd, South : 0.75 km on N 9 – ✆ (059) 914 33 24 – www.barrowville.com – Closed 24-26 December
7 rm – € 40/60 € 70/100
Attractive Georgian house on the main road into town. Comfortable, characterful drawing room with heavy fabrics, period ornaments and a grand piano. Breakfast is in the conservatory, overlooking the pretty garden. Spacious, brightly decorated bedrooms offer a good level of comfort and modern facilities.

CARNAROSS (Carn na Ros) – Meath – 712 L6 – ✉ Kells — 37 D3

Dublin 69 km – Cavan 43 km – Drogheda 48 km

Forge

Pottlereagh, Northwest : 7 km by R 147 and N 3 on L 7112 – ✆ (046) 924 50 03 – www.theforgerestaurant.ie – Closed 1 week February, 1 week August, 24-26 and 31 December, dinner Sunday, Monday and Tuesday
Rest – *(dinner only and Sunday lunch)* Menu € 25/37 – Carte € 33/47
Stone-built former forge in rural Meath; its atmospheric interior features flagged flooring and warm red décor. Two fairly priced menus offer hearty dishes made from local produce, with pork and bacon from the pigs in the garden.

CARNE - Wexford - 712 M11 39 D3

Dublin 169 km - Waterford 82 km - Wexford 21 km

Lobster Pot

Ballyfane - (053) 913 11 10 - www.lobsterpotwexford.ie - Closed 1 January-10 February, 24-26 December, Good Friday and Monday except bank holidays

Rest - Carte € 24/56

Popular pub filled with a characterful array of memorabilia. Large menus feature tasty, home-style cooking. Fresh seafood dishes are a must try, with oysters and lobster cooked to order the specialities. No children after 6pm.

CARRICKMACROSS (Carraig Mhachaire Rois) - Monaghan - 712 L6 - pop. 1 978 Ireland 37 D2

Dublin 92 km - Dundalk 22 km

Nuremore Hotel & CC, (042) 9 66 14 38

Dún a' Rí Forest Park★, SW : 8 km by R 179 - St Mochta's House★, E : 7 km by R 178 and minor road S

Nuremore

South : 2.25 km by R 178 on old N 2 - (042) 966 14 38 - www.nuremore.com

72 rm - € 100/220 € 120/265

Rest *Nuremore* - see restaurant listing

Long-standing Victorian house with extensive gardens and golf course. Classical interior with formal bar and comfy lounge serving three-tiered afternoon tea. Good leisure facilities and smart pool. Peaceful bedrooms; many have rural views.

Nuremore - Nuremore Hotel

South : 2.25 km by R 178 on old N 2 - (042) 966 14 38 - www.nuremore.com

Rest - *(dinner only and lunch Saturday-Sunday)* Carte € 28/46

Traditional split-level dining room within a well-established Victorian hotel. Formally set, linen-laid tables are well-spaced and service is attentive. Menus showcase luxurious seasonal ingredients and dishes are stylishly presented.

Courthouse

1 Monaghan St - (042) 969 28 48 - www.courthouserestaurant.ie - Closed 1 week January, 25-26 December, Good Friday, Monday except bank holidays and Tuesday

Rest - *(pre-book at weekends)* Menu € 20 (weekdays)/25 - Carte € 27/44 **s**

Relaxed, rustic restaurant featuring wooden floors, exposed ceiling rafters and bare brick; ask for table 20, by the window. Great value menus offer carefully prepared, flavourful dishes which are a lesson in self-restraint - their simplicity being a key part of their appeal. Friendly, efficient service.

CARRICK-ON-SHANNON (Cora Droma Rúisc) - Leitrim - 712 H6 - pop. 3 980 Ireland 37 C2

Dublin 156 km - Ballina 80 km - Galway 119 km - Roscommon 42 km

Visitor Information Centre The Marina, (0719) 62 01 70, www.carrickonshannon.ie

Carrick-on-Shannon, Woodbrook, (071) 966 70 15

Town★

Lough Rynn Demesne★

Landmark

rest,

on N 4 - (071) 962 22 22 - www.thelandmarkhotel.com - Closed 24-25 December

60 rm - € 69/115 € 100/170

Rest *Boardwalk Café* - Carte € 21/28

Large, modern hotel next to the Shannon, with a water feature in reception and duck-themed pictures throughout; a popular venue for weddings. Bright, bold bedrooms with good facilities. Stylish cocktail lounge with a stunning contemporary design. Informal dining and pleasant river views in Boardwalk.

Oarsman
Bridge St – ✆ (071) 962 1733 – www.theoarsman.com – Closed 25-26 December, Good Friday, Sunday and Monday
Rest – Menu € 26/40 – Carte € 27/46
Traditional, family-run pub filled with pottery, bygone artefacts and fishing tackle. Cooking is simple and produce, locally sourced. Comfortable restaurant area opens later in the week.

CARRIGALINE (Carraig Uí Leighin) – Cork – 712 G12 – pop. 14 775 38 B3

Dublin 262 km – Cork 14 km
Fernhill, ✆ (021) 437 22 26

Carrigaline Court rest,
Cork Rd – ✆ (021) 485 21 00 – www.carrigcourt.com – Closed 23-26 December
91 rm – € 85/105 € 100/120 – 2 suites
Rest *The Bistro* – *(closed Good Friday) (bar lunch)* Menu € 13/35 – Carte € 22/40 **s**
Purpose-built hotel in the heart of town. Excellent leisure centre boasting a 20m pool and well-equipped events facilities. Luxurious suites and spacious, modern bedrooms with queen-sized beds. Atmospheric bar for snacks and light meals; formal restaurant has eclectic décor and an international menu.

CARRIGANS (An Carraigain) – Donegal – 712 J3 – pop. 336 37 C1

Dublin 225 km – Donegal 66 km – Letterkenny 230 km – Sligo 124 km

Mount Royd without rest
– ✆ (074) 914 01 63 – www.mountroyd.com – Closed 1 week Christmas and restricted opening in winter
4 rm – € 40 € 70
Remotely set, creeper-clad house with well-tended gardens, lovely rear terrace and fountain. Immaculately kept throughout with snug lounge and pleasant breakfast room. Cosy bedrooms; one leading to a terrace. Tasty, locally smoked salmon.

CASHEL (Caiseal) – South Tipperary – 712 I10 – pop. 2 275 Ireland 39 C2

Dublin 162 km – Cork 96 km – Kilkenny 55 km – Limerick 58 km
Heritage Centre, Town Hall, Main St, ✆ (062) 6 25 11, www.cashel.ie
Town★★★ – Rock of Cashel★★★ **AC** – Cormac's Chapel★★ – Round Tower★ – Museum★ – Cashel Palace Gardens★ – GPA Bolton Library★ **AC**
Holy Cross Abbey★★, N : 14.5 km by R 660 – Athassel Priory★, W : 8 km by N 74. Caher (Castle★★, Swiss Cottage★), S : 18 km by N 8 – Glen of Aherlow★, W : 21 km by N 74 and R 664

Cashel Palace
Main St – ✆ (062) 62 707 – www.cashel-palace.ie – Closed 24-27 December
20 rm – € 91/125 € 124/224
Rest – *(bar lunch)* Menu € 25/55 – Carte € 35/48
Queen Anne house, once home to an archbishop, with pleasant gardens and path leading to the famous rock. Pillared entrance hall and high-ceilinged guest areas with ornate plasterwork and open fires. Traditional bedrooms; some in the old coach house. Characterful vaulted bar, buttery and elegant restaurant.

Baileys of Cashel rm,
42 Main St – ✆ (062) 61 937 – www.baileyshotelcashel.com – Closed 23-28 December
20 rm – € 65/80 € 90/120 **Rest** – Carte € 23/43
Extended Georgian townhouse, used as a grain store during the Irish famine. Small lounge with a library and spacious, contemporary bedrooms, furnished to a high standard. Popular cellar bar offers live music and traditional dishes. More contemporary restaurant serves modern European cooking.

Aulber House without rest
Deerpark, Golden Rd, West : 0.75 km on N 74 – ✆ (062) 63 713 – www.aulberhouse.com – March- October
11 rm – € 50/65 € 75/90
Within walking distance of the Rock of Cashel and the 13C Cistercian abbey ruins. Well-kept gardens with a wooden gazebo. Comfy, open-fired lounge. Bespoke mahogany staircase leads to an open-plan landing; many rooms have king-sized beds.

Chez Hans
Rockside, Moor Ln. – ✆ (062) 61 177 – www.chezhans.net – Closed last 2 weeks January, 24-26 December, Sunday and Monday
Rest – *(dinner only) (booking essential)* Menu € 33 – Carte € 41/62
Imposing former Synod Hall built in 1861, with stained glass lancet windows and vast, high-ceilinged inner. Carefully prepared and creatively presented dishes rely on local produce.

Cafe Hans
Rockside, Moore Lane St – ✆ (062) 63 660 – Closed 2 weeks late January, 1 week October, 25 December, Sunday and Monday
Rest – *(lunch only) (bookings not accepted)* Carte € 24/33
Just down the road from The Rock of Cashel, a vibrant, popular eatery set next to big sister 'Chez Hans' and run by the same family. Closely set tables and art-covered walls. Tasty, unfussy dishes crafted from local ingredients. Arrive early as you can't book.

REPUBLIC OF IRELAND

CASHEL (An Caiseal) – Galway – 712 C7 Ireland 36 A3

Dublin 278 km – Galway 66 km
Town★
Connemara★★★

Cashel House rest,
– ✆ (095) 31 001 – www.cashel-house-hotel.com – Closed 1 January-mid February
30 rm – € 70/115 € 180/230
Rest – *(bar lunch Monday-Saturday) (booking essential)* Menu € 32/58
Whitewashed country house built in 1840, surrounded by delightful gardens (gardening courses are available). Plenty of peaceful little seating areas; china and knick-knacks abound. The rear bedrooms are biggest – those higher up have better views. Formal dining room and elegant conservatory. Classical menus.

CASTLEBALDWIN (Béal Átha na gCarraigíní) – Sligo – 712 G5 36 B2

– ✉ Boyle (roscommon) Ireland
Dublin 190 km – Longford 67 km – Sligo 24 km
Carrowkeel Megalithic Cemetery (★★), S : 4.75 km. Arigna Scenic Drive★, N : 3.25 km by N 4 - Lough Key Forest Park★ **AC**, SE : 16 km by N 4 – View of Lough Allen★, N : 14.5 km by N 4 on R 280 – Mountain Drive★, N : 9.5 km on N 4 – Boyle Abbey★ **AC**, SE : 12.75 km by N 4 - King House★, SE : 12.75 km by N 4

Cromleach Lodge
Ballindoon, Southeast : 5.5 km – ✆ (071) 916 51 55 – www.cromleach.com
57 rm – € 70/130 € 80/200
Rest ***Moira's*** – see restaurant listing
Remotely located hotel with superb views over Lough Arrow and the Carrowkeel Cairns. Comfy split-level lounge and bar. Large, luxurious bedrooms in either a modern or classic style; some have balconies or terraces. Stylish, exclusive spa.

Moira's – Cromleach Lodge Hotel
Ballindoon, Southeast : 5.5 km – ✆ (071) 916 51 55 – www.cromleach.com
Rest – *(dinner only and Sunday lunch)* Menu € 39 – Carte € 39/60
Smart, modern hotel restaurant with a glass-fronted kitchen, brushed velvet booths, and lough and country views. Good-sized menus offer classically based dishes with personal twists; local growers and producers are credited on the menu.

CASTLEGREGORY (Caisleán Ghriaire) – Kerry – 712 B11 – pop. 243 38 A2

Dublin 330 km – Dingle 24 km – Killarney 54 km

Shores Country House without rest

Conor Pass Rd, Cappateige, Southwest : 6 km on A 560 – ✆ (066) 713 91 95 – www.shorescountryhouse.com – Closed 2 December-10 January

6 rm – € 45/90 € 70/100

Modern guesthouse, beautifully set in an elevated position between Stradbally Mountain and a spectacular beach. The friendly owner has added a touch of fun to the place. Stylish bedrooms, some with antique beds; all with good attention to detail. Room 3 has a balcony. Plush breakfast room.

CASTLELYONS (Caisleán Ó Liatháin) – Cork – 712 H11 – pop. 292 38 B2

Dublin 219 km – Cork 30 km – Killarney 104 km – Limerick 64 km

Ballyvolane House

rest,

Southeast : 5.5 km by Midleton rd on Britway rd – ✆ (025) 36 349 – www.ballyvolanehouse.ie – Closed 24 December-4 January, restricted opening in winter

6 rm – € 125/135 € 190/230 **Rest** – *(dinner only)* Menu € 38

Stately 18C Italianate mansion surrounded by lovely gardens, lakes and woodland; children can help feed the hens, collect the eggs, pet the donkeys or go on a tractor tour. Comfy guest areas and bedrooms match the period style of the house, and family antiques and memorabilia feature throughout. The walled garden and latest farm produce guide what's on the menu.

CASTLEMARTYR (Baile na Martra) Cork – Cork – 712 H12 39 C3 – pop. 1 277

Dublin 174 km – Cork 20 km – Ballincollig 25 km – Carrigaline 24 km

Castlemartyr

– ✆ (021) 421 90 00 – www.castlemartyrresort.ie

81 rm – € 195 € 205 – 28 suites

Rest ***Bell Tower*** – see restaurant listing

Impressive 17C manor house in 220 acres, complete with lakes, castle ruins, a golf course and a stunning spa. Columned, parquet-floored hall and a superb old ceiling in the bar. Luxurious bedrooms have marble bathrooms and every mod con.

Bell Tower – Castlemartyr Hotel

– ✆ (021) 421 90 00 – www.castlemartyrresort.ie

Rest – *(bookings essential for non-residents) (bar lunch)* Menu € 63 **s**

Formal hotel dining room in a grand 17C manor house. Sit in the Bell Tower for the best views over the 220 acres grounds; the adjoining Garden Room is lighter and airier. Cooking is modern and sophisticated but with a strong classical base.

CASTLEPOLLARD (Baile na gCros) – Westmeath – 712 K6 37 C3 – pop. 1 042

Dublin 63 km – Mullingar 13 km – Tullamore 37 km – Édenderry 36 km

Lough Bishop House

Derrynagarra, Collinstown, South : 6 km by R 394 taking L 5738 opposite church and school after 4 km – ✆ (044) 966 13 13 – www.loughbishophouse.com – Closed Christmas-New Year

3 rm – € 55/70 € 110 **Rest** – Menu € 30

Charming 18C farmhouse on a tranquil, south-facing hillside. The hospitable owners and their dogs greet you, and tea and cake are served on arrival in the cosy lounge. Simple bedrooms have neat shower rooms and no TVs. Communal dining – home-cooked dishes include meats and eggs from their own farm.

CASTLETOWNSHEND (Baile an Chaisleáin) – Cork – 712 E13 38 B3 – pop. 187 Ireland

Dublin 346 km – Cork 95 km – Killarney 116 km

Glandore★, NE : 10 km R 596 – Sherkin Island★ **AC**, W : 15 km by R 596 and R 595 and ferry

Mary Ann's
Main St – ☎ (028) 36 146 – www.westcorkweek.com/maryanns – Closed 9 January-1 February, 24-26 December and Monday-Tuesday October-March
Rest – *(dinner only)* Carte €25/50
Bold red pub set up a steep, narrow street in a sleepy village. Dine in the rustic bar, the linen-laid restaurant or the lovely garden; be sure to visit the art gallery. All-encompassing menus often feature seafood and several Asian dishes.

CAVAN (An Cabhán) – Cavan – 712 J6 – pop. 3 649 ▮ Ireland 37 C2

Dublin 114 km – Drogheda 93 km – Enniskillen 64 km
Central Library, 1st Floor, Farnham St, ☎ (049) 4 33 19 42, www.cavantourism.com
Killykeen Forest Park★, W : 9.5 km by R 198

Radisson Blu Farnham Estate
Farnham Estate, Northwest : 3.75 km on R 198 – ☎ (049) 437 77 00 – www.farnhamestate.com
rest, P
158 rm – 🛉 €99/170 🛉🛉 €109/210 – 4 suites
Rest *Botanica* – *(bar lunch Monday-Saturday)* Menu €40
Set in extensive parkland, boasting every conceivable outdoor activity and an impressive spa. Original Georgian features are combined with contemporary furnishings. Luxury bedrooms offer superb views. Traditional menus feature local, seasonal ingredients.

Cavan Crystal
Dublin Rd, East : 2.5 km on R 212 – ☎ (049) 436 0600 – www.cavancrystalhotel.com – Closed 26-28 December
P
85 rm – 🛉 €75/105 🛉🛉 €160/240
Rest *Opus One* – see restaurant listing
Modern hotel next to – and owned by – the Cavan Crystal factory. Impressive atrium and spacious, stylish lounge-bar. Good meeting and leisure facilities. Up-to-date, red and black bedrooms in uniform designs.

Opus One – Cavan Crystal Hotel
Dublin Rd, East : 2.5 km on R 212 – ☎ (049) 436 0600 – www.cavancrystalhotel.com – Closed 26-28 December
AC P
Rest – *(light lunch)* Carte €29/45
Contemporary first floor restaurant in a smart hotel. Fresh, unfussy dishes at lunch; more ambitious dishes with unusual combinations and textures in the evening. Quality ingredients used in modern techniques.

at Cloverhill North : 12 km by N 3 on N 54 – ✉ Belturbet

Olde Post Inn with rm
rest, AC rest, P
– ☎ (047) 55 555 – www.theoldepostinn.com – Closed 24-27 December and Monday
6 rm – 🛉 €65 🛉🛉 €100/110
Rest – *(dinner only and Sunday lunch)* Menu €33/55
Enjoy a fireside aperitif in the characterful, flag-floored bar or the wood-framed conservatory of this red-brick former post office. The well-established restaurant serves traditional cooking made with Irish produce, wherein classic flavour combinations are given a modern twist. Contemporary bedrooms.

CLAREMORRIS (Clár Chlainne Mhuiris) – Mayo – 712 E/F6 – pop. 3 412 36 B2

Dublin 149 km – Castlebar 18 km – Galway 39 km – Newbridge 41 km

McWilliam Park
rm, AC rest, P
Knock Rd, East : 2 km on N 60 – ☎ (094) 937 80 00 – www.mcwilliampark.ie
103 rm – 🛉 €120/170 🛉🛉 €140/220 – 2 suites
Rest – *(carvery lunch Monday-Saturday)* Menu €20 (lunch) **s** – Carte €27/44 **s**
Popular, purpose-built hotel, named after an 18C landowner and located on the outskirts of town, close to the airport. Spacious, modern bedrooms; pay the extra for a VIP upgrade. Numerous meeting and events rooms. Carvery offered in the bar; wide-ranging menu in the restaurant. Breakfasts are cooked to order.

CLIFDEN (An Clochán) - **Galway** - **712** B7 - **pop. 2 056** Ireland **36** A3

Dublin 291 km - Ballina 124 km - Galway 79 km

Galway Rd, (095) 2 11 63, www.clifden.galway-ireland.ie

Connemara★★★, NE : by N 59 - Sky Road★★ (<★★), NE : by N 59 - Connemara National Park★, NE : 1.5 km by N 59 - Killary Harbour★, NE : 35 km by N 59 - Kylemore Abbey★ **AC**, N : 18 km by N 59

Clifden Station House

rm,

- (095) 21 699 - www.clifdenstationhouse.com - Closed 24-25 December

78 rm - € 75/115 € 130/210 **Rest** - Menu € 30

Purpose-built hotel beside the old Galway-Clifden railway line, in a modern residential and leisure complex, with a residents-only kids club, gym and wellness centre. Spacious, uniform bedrooms have good facilities. Local seafood orientated menus in the restaurant. Classic pub dishes in the Signal Bar.

Ardagh

rest,

Ballyconneely Rd, South : 3 km. on R 341 - (095) 21 384
- www.ardaghhotel.com - Closed November-Easter

19 rm - € 75/105 € 100/150

Rest - *(bar lunch)* Menu € 40/55 - Carte € 37/52

Neat, modern hotel overlooking a small bay. Choice of three lounges. Pleasant bedrooms; many with bold fabrics and colourful headboards designed by the owner - some with sofas and armchairs from which to admire the views. Bright restaurant affords an excellent outlook; seafood is a speciality.

Dolphin Beach Country House

Lower Sky Rd, West : 5.5 km. by Sky Rd - (095) 21 204
- www.dolphinbeachhouse.com - Closed November-March

9 rm - € 55/85 € 100/150

Rest - *(dinner only) (residents only)* Menu € 35 **s**

Terracotta-coloured former farmhouse in a peaceful hillside location. The interior is styled like a Mediterranean villa, with bright décor and red stone tiles. Good-sized bedrooms display artwork by the friendly owner. Traditional home-cooked meals and wonderful bay views from the dining room.

Quay House without rest

Beach Rd - (095) 21 369 - www.thequayhouse.com - Closed November-mid March

14 rm - € 75/95 € 125/150

Creamwashed former harbourmaster's house and monastery, overlooking the bay. Relaxed, bohemian interior with antiques and wild animal memorabilia. Comfortable, spacious bedrooms; those in the wing have kitchenettes. Homemade bread and local cheese feature at breakfast.

Sea Mist House without rest

- (095) 21 441 - www.seamisthouse.com - Closed November-March

4 rm - € 50/75 € 80/110

Centrally located, stone-built house with pleasant gardens, a homely lounge and a bright conservatory breakfast area. Spacious, modern bedrooms boast colourful co-ordinating fabrics and fresh flowers; no TVs. Eclectic Irish art collection.

Buttermilk Lodge without rest

Westport Rd - (095) 21 951 - www.buttermilklodge.com - Closed November-February

11 rm - € 45/65 € 70/100

Immaculate guesthouse filled with bovine memorabilia. Homely, colour co-ordinated bedrooms; games, hot drinks and a real turf fire in the lounge. Friendly owners offer local info, packed lunches and walking tours. Extensive breakfasts.

Tower View without rest

Lower Sky Rd, West : 4 km by Sky Rd - (095) 21 965
- www.towerview.clifden.com - Closed October-April

3 rm - € 40/45 € 70/75

Modern, yellow-painted house overlooking Clifden Bay and the whitewashed tower known locally as the White Lady. Well-priced, cosy bedrooms are spotlessly kept, with plain décor, bright fabrics and fully tiled bathrooms; all have good views.

CLOGHEEN (An Chloichín) – South Tipperary – 712 I11 – pop. 491 39 C2

Dublin 122 km – Tipperary 23 km – Clonmel 21 km – Dungarvan 28 km

XX **Old Convent** with rm

Mount Anglesby, Southeast : 0.5 km on R 668 (Lismore rd) – (052) 746 55 65 – www.theoldconvent.ie – Closed 24 December-31 January and Sunday-Wednesday except bank holidays

7 rm – € 125 € 170

Rest – *(dinner only) (booking essential) (set menu only)* Menu € 65

A substantial former convent on the edge of the village, featuring some delightful stained glass windows – dine in the vast, candlelit former chapel. Set 8 course daily menu with some unusual flavours combinations. Smart. comfortable bedrooms have good quality linens. Help yourself to goodies from the pantry.

CLONAKILTY (Cloich na Coillte) – Cork – 712 F13 – pop. 4 000 38 B3

Ireland

Dublin 310 km – Cork 51 km

25 Ashe St, (023) 8 83 32 26, www.clonakilty.ie

Dunmore, Muckross, (023) 3 46 44

West Cork Regional Museum★ AC

Courtmacsherry★, E : 12 km by R 600 and R 601 – Timoleague Friary★, E : 8 km by R 600. Carbery Coast★ (Drombeg Stone Circle★, Glandore★, Castletownshend★) by N 71 and R 597

Inchydoney Island Lodge and Spa

South : 5.25 km by N 71 following signs for Inchydoney Beach – (023) 883 31 43 – www.inchydoneyisland.com – Closed 24- 25 December rest,

67 rm – € 125/175 € 158/250 – 4 suites

Rest *Gulfstream* – see restaurant listing

Rest *Dunes Bistro* – Carte € 25/49 **s**

Superbly located on a remote headland and boasting stunning views over the beach and out to sea. Contemporary bedrooms come with balconies or terraces and all you could ask for. The smart spa boasts a seawater pool. Dine in the formal restaurant or from an accessible menu in the nautically styled bistro-bar.

XX **Gulfstream** – Inchydoney Island Lodge and Spa Hotel

South : 5.25 km by N 71 following signs for Inchydoney Beach – (023) 883 31 43 – www.inchydoneyisland.com – Closed 24-25 December

Rest – *(dinner only and Sunday lunch)* Menu € 59

Formal, nautically styled restaurant set on the first floor of a vast hotel and offering superb views over the beach and out to sea. Modern menus highlight produce from West Cork and feature plenty of fresh local seafood. Smooth service.

Deasy's

Ring, Southeast : 3 km – (023) 883 57 41 – Closed 24-26 December, Good Friday,Sunday dinner,Monday and Tuesday dinner

Rest – Menu € 32 – Carte € 31/47

An appealing pub in a picturesque hamlet, offering lovely views out across the bay. Its gloriously dated maritime interior is decorated with framed fish prints and boat propellers. Menus are dictated by the seasons and the latest catch from the local boats; try the tasty Thai coconut fish soup.

An Súgán with rm

41 Wolfe Tone St – (023) 883 3719 – www.ansugan.com – Closed 25-26 December and Good Friday

7 rm – € 45/60 € 70/100

Rest – Menu € 30 (dinner)/38 – Carte € 21/52

Charming, personally run, salmon-pink pub with characterful dining rooms. Menus are based around daily arrivals of fresh local fish and seafood; some meat dishes also feature. Bedrooms are in the old harbourmaster's house and boast bold feature walls and flat screen TVs.

CLONEGALL (Cluain na nGall) – **Carlow** – **712** M9 – **pop. 245** **39** D2

Dublin 73 km – Carlow 20 km – Kilkenny 39 km – Wexford 30 km

Sha-Roe Bistro

Main St – (053) 937 56 36 – Closed January, 1 week April, 1 week October, Sunday dinner, Monday and Tuesday

Rest – *(dinner only and Sunday lunch) (booking essential)* Menu € 34 – Carte € 31/42

Rurally located restaurant with a good reputation, set in a pretty little cottage and run by an keen, friendly couple. Rustic lounge and a small dining room with an enormous inglenook and a kitchen table. Flavoursome, classical cooking of local produce; the cheese comes from the weekly farmers' market.

CLONMEL (Cluain Meala) – **South Tipperary** – **712** I10 – **pop. 15 793** **39** C2

Ireland

Dublin 174 km – Cork 95 km – Kilkenny 50 km – Limerick 77 km

Lyreanearla, Mountain Rd, (052) 2 40 50

Town★ - County Museum★, St Mary's Church★

Fethard★, N : 13 km by R 689. Nier Valley Scenic Route★★ - Ahenny High Crosses★, E : 30.5 km by N 24 and R 697 - Ormond Castle★, E : 33.75 km by N 24

Stonehouse

29 Thomas St – (052) 612 88 77 – www.stonehouserestaurant.ie – Closed 25- 26 December, 1 January, Sunday and Monday

Rest – Menu € 29 – Carte € 39/53

Smartly refurbished mill with bright décor and a pianist on Friday and Saturday nights. Cooking is complex, with lots of ingredients on the plate; the simpler dishes are often the best, and the tasting desserts are well worth a try.

CLONTARF = Cluain Tarbh – **Dublin** – **712** N7 – **see Dublin**

CLOVERHILL = Droim Caiside – **Cavan** – **712** J5 – **see Cavan**

COBH (An Cóbh) – **Cork** – **712** H12 – **pop. 6 500** Ireland **38** B3

Dublin 264 km – Cork 24 km – Waterford 104 km

Ballywilliam, (021) 81 23 99

Town★ – St Colman's Cathedral★ – Lusitania Memorial★

Fota Island★ (Fota House★★ **AC**, Fota Wildlife Park★ **AC**), N : 6.5 km by R 624 – Cloyne Cathedral★, SE : 24 km by R 624/5, N 25, R 630 and R 629

Knockeven House

Rushbrooke, West : 2 km by R 624 – (021) 481 17 78 – www.knockevenhouse.com – Closed 24-26 December

4 rm – € 65/75 € 90/100 **Rest** – Menu € 35

Double-fronted Victorian house with high ceilings and lovely cornicing; in the town that was the last port of call for the Titanic. Large period bedrooms come with antiques, feature beds and modern bathrooms. Communal breakfasts and dinners are taken at an antique table and afternoon tea is served from 2-5pm.

CONG (Conga) – **Mayo** – **712** E7 – **pop. 178** Ireland **36** A3

Dublin 257 km – Ballina 79 km – Galway 45 km

Old Courthouse , (094) 9 54 65 42, www.congtourism.com

Town★

Lough Corrib★★. Ross Errilly Abbey★ (Tower ★) – Joyce Country★★ (Lough Nafooey★) W : by R 345

Ashford Castle

– (094) 954 60 03 – www.ashford.ie

83 rm – € 175/415 € 195/435 – 3 suites

Rest ***Cullen's at the Cottage*** – see restaurant listing

Rest ***George V Room*** – *(dinner only)* Menu € 67 – Carte € 54/74

Hugely impressive lochside castle dating from 1228, surrounded by a moat and formal gardens. Handsome, antique-furnished guest areas. Well-appointed bedrooms display warm fabrics; some have four-posters. Activities include archery, falconry and clay pigeon shooting. Elegant George V requires a jacket and tie; casual meals in Cullen's.

Lisloughrey Lodge

The Quay, Southeast : 2.25 km by R 345 off R 346 – (094) 954 54 00 – www.lisloughreylodge.com – Closed January and 24-28 December

50 rm – € 120/190 € 130/200 – 9 suites

Rest *Wilde's* – *(dinner only and Sunday lunch)* Menu € 38/45

Extended Georgian house offering lovely views down to Lough Corrib and once home to the Estate Manager of Ashford Castle. Stylish, modern bedrooms; most overlook a large courtyard and some are duplex. Facilities include a 'Wii' room and an outside sauna and hot tub. Modern menus in the four-roomed restaurant.

Ballywarren House rest,

East : 3.5 km on R 346 – (094) 954 69 89 – www.ballywarrenhouse.com – Closed 1 week spring and 1 week autumn

3 rm – € 98/136 € 124/160 **Rest** – Menu € 45 **s**

Passionately run guesthouse with a lovely oak staircase and a galleried landing. Open-fired guest areas feature chunky pine furnishings, squashy sofas and plenty to read. Bedrooms have luxurious linens and come with complimentary sherry and chocolates. Aga-cooked breakfasts and flavoursome homemade dinners. The charming owners ensure every guest's stay is special.

Michaeleen's Manor without rest

Quay Rd, Southeast : 1.5 km by R 346 – (094) 954 60 89 – www.quietman-cong.com

6 rm – € 45 € 75

'The Quiet Man' was filmed in the village over 60 years ago and this house pays homage – with black and white stills on the walls and rooms named after various characters. Homely lounges and brightly decorated bedrooms. Friendly owners.

Cullen's at the Cottage – Ashford Castle Hotel

– (094) 954 53 32 – www.ashford.ie

Rest – Carte € 27/48

Relaxed, all-day restaurant in an imposing castle. In winter, it operates from the vaulted basement; in summer, from a thatched cottage with lovely views from the outside tables. Modern, bistro-style menu; the sharing boards are popular.

REPUBLIC OF IRELAND

CORK (Corcaigh) – Cork – 712 G12 – pop. 119 230 Ireland **38** B3

Dublin 253 km – Limerick 99 km

Cork Airport : (021) 4313131, S : 6.5 km by L 42 X

to France (Roscoff) (Brittany Ferries) weekly (14 h/16 h) – to Pembroke (Swansea Cork Ferries) 2-6 weekly (8 h 30 mn)

Grand Parade, (021) 4 25 51 00, www.cork-guide.ie

Douglas, (021) 4 89 10 86

Mahon, Blackrock, Cloverhill, (021) 4 29 25 43

Monkstown, Parkgarriffe, (021) 4 84 13 76

City★★ – Shandon Bells★★ Y, St Fin Barre's Cathedral★★ **AC** Z, Cork Public Museum★ X **M** – Grand Parade★ Z , South Mall★ Z , St Patrick Street★ Z , Crawford Art Gallery★ Y – Elizabethan Fort★ Z

Dunkathel House★ **AC**, E : 9.25 km by N 8 and N 25 X. Fota Island★ (Fota House★★ **AC**, Fota Wildlife Park★ **AC**), E : 13 km by N 8 and N 25 X – Cobh★ (St Colman's Cathedral★, Lusitania Memorial★) SE : 24 km by N 8, N 25 and R 624 X

Plans pages 897, 898

Hayfield Manor

Perrott Ave, College Rd – (021) 484 59 00 – www.hayfieldmanor.ie

88 rm – € 159/380 € 169/380 – 4 suites Xz

Rest *Orchids* Rest *Perrotts* – see restaurant listing

Luxurious country house with wood-panelled hall, impressive staircase and antique-furnished drawing rooms; the perfect spot for afternoon tea. Plush bedrooms have plenty of extras, including putting machines. Well-equipped residents spa.

Enjoy good food without spending a fortune! Look out for the Bib Gourmand symbol to find restaurants offering good food at special prices!

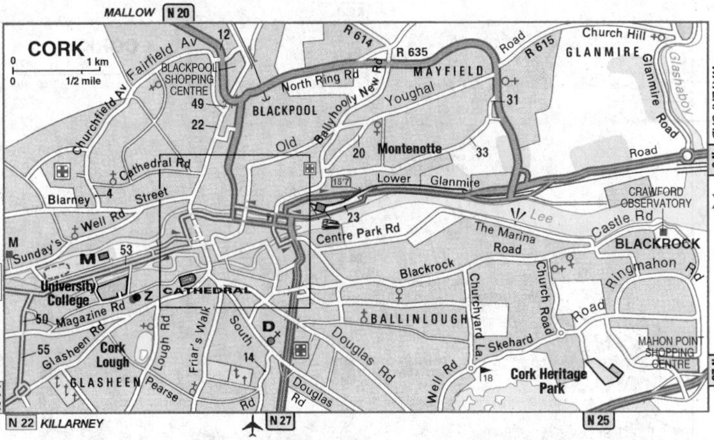

Baker's Rd	X 4	Great William O'Brien St	X 22	Thomas Davis St	X 49
Commons Rd	X 12	Horgan Quay	X 23	Victoria Cross Rd	X 50
Curragh Rd	X 14	Lower Mayfield Rd	X 31	Western Rd	X 53
Gardiner's Hill	X 20	Middle Glanmire Rd	X 33	Wilton Rd	X 55

River Lee

rest,

Western Rd. – (021) 425 27 00 – www.doylecollection.com – Closed 24-25 December
182 rm – € 99/279 € 99/279, €18 Z**a**
Rest *Weir Bistro* – Menu € 35 – Carte € 31/50
Modern, purpose-built hotel, 5min walk from the city centre. Large leisure centre with a gym, a 20m pool, and activity and treatment rooms. One whole floor consists of meeting rooms. Uniform bedrooms offer good facilities. Large bar and terrace, and a modern dining room with an unfussy menu and weir views.

Lancaster Lodge without rest

Lancaster Quay, Western Rd – (021) 425 11 25 – www.lancasterlodge.com – Closed 23-28 December Z**d**
48 rm – € 76/126 € 76/126, €10
Purpose-built hotel next to the River Lee and within easy walking distance of the town centre. Spacious, bright bedrooms with bold fabrics and modern artwork; the executive suites have whirlpool baths. A good choice for the business traveller.

Orchids – Hayfield Manor Hotel

Perrott Ave, College Rd – (021) 484 59 00 – www.hayfieldmanor.ie – Closed Monday-Wednesday and Sunday dinner X**z**
Rest – *(dinner only and Sunday lunch) (booking essential)* Menu € 39 (lunch)/80 – Carte € 39/65
Sophisticated formal dining room in a well-appointed country house. Pillars dominate the room, which is laid with crisp white tablecloths. Menus offer refined dishes with some modern twists.

Les Gourmandises

17 Cook St – (021) 425 19 59 – www.lesgourmandises.ie – Closed Sunday dinner Z**v**
Rest – *(dinner only and Sunday lunch) (booking essential)* Menu € 30/45
Well-run restaurant with a spacious, high-ceilinged dining room that was formerly a Turkish bath. The experienced chef produces accomplished, detailed dishes with a classical French base and original touches.

Perrotts – Hayfield Manor Hotel

Perrott Ave, College Rd – (021) 484 59 00 – www.hayfieldmanor.ie – Closed 25 December X**z**
Rest – Menu € 27/55 – Carte € 28/79
Conservatory restaurant overlooking the gardens of a luxurious country house. Smart but comfortably furnished, with adjoining wood-panelled bar. Menu offers a modern take on brasserie classics.

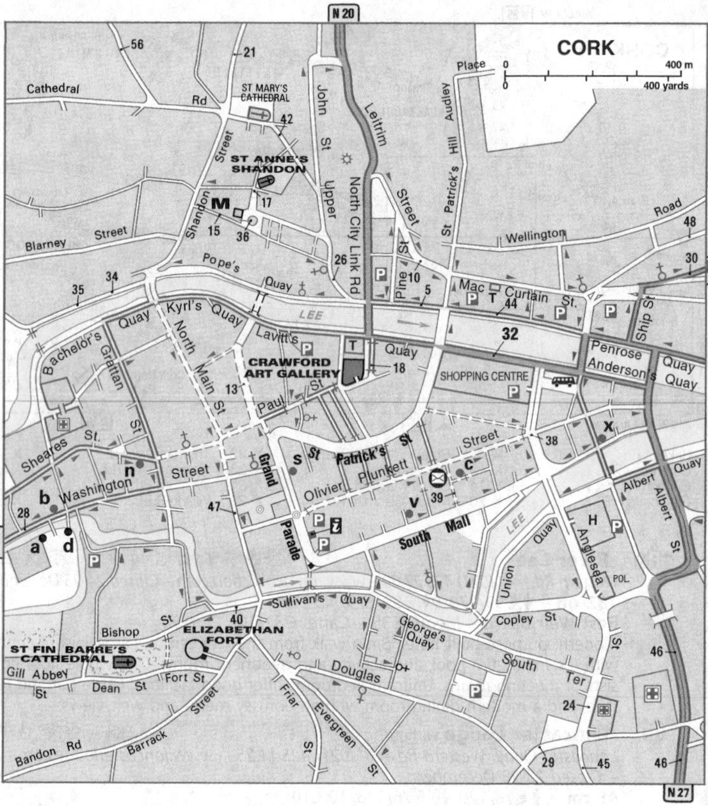

Buttermarket	Y 36	Langford Row	Z 29	Pembroke St	Z 39
Camden Pl.	Y 5	Lower Glanmire Rd	Y 30	Proby's Quay	Z 40
Coburg St	Y 10	Merchant Quay Shopping Centre	Y	Roman St	Y 42
Corn Market St	Y 13	Merchant's Quay	Y 32	St Patrick's Quay	Y 44
Dominic St	Y 15	Newsom's Quay	Y 34	St Patrick's St	Z
Eason Hill	Y 17	North Main Street	YZ	Southern Rd	Z 45
Emmet Pl.	Y 18	North Mall	Y 35	South City Link Rd	Z 46
Gerald Griffin St	Y 21	Olivier Plunkett St	Z	South Main St	Z 47
Infirmary Rd	Z 24	Parnell Pl.	Z 38	Summer Hill	Y 48
John Redmond St	Y 26			Wolfe Tone St	Y 56
Lancaster Quay	Z 28				

XX Oysters (N)

Clarion Hotel, Lapps Quay – ✆ (021) 427 3777 – www.oysters.ie – Closed 2 weeks January, 23-28 December, Sunday, Monday, and bank holidays Z**x**

Rest – Menu €35 – Carte €37/55

Set within the Clarion hotel and, surprisingly, Corks only seafood restaurant! Modern room with a fish tank and central booths. Creative dishes use a classical base and add unusual modern twists. Presentation is bold and service, smooth.

XX Jacques

23 Oliver Plunket St – ✆ (021) 427 73 87 – www.jacquesrestaurant.ie – Closed 25 December-3 January, Sunday, Monday dinner and bank holidays Z**c**

Rest – *(dinner only)* Menu €24 (dinner) – Carte €31/48

Personally run restaurant with a cosy, intimate feel; hidden away in the centre of town. Seasonal, Irish-inspired menu: honest regional cooking uses quality local ingredients and has clear, defined flavours. Friendly, helpful service.

Cafe Paradiso with rm

16 Lancaster Quay, Western Rd – ✆ (021) 427 79 39 – www.cafeparadiso.ie – Closed 25-28 December, Sunday and Monday **Zb**
2 rm – € 100/150 € 100/150
Rest – *(dinner only and lunch Friday-Saturday) (booking essential)*
Menu € 20/40
Stylish little restaurant with a grey and green colour scheme, friendly service and intimate atmosphere. Extensive choice of interesting, original, vegetarian dishes which feature plenty of different flavours and textures. Spacious, modern bedrooms come in bright, bold colours.

Fenn's Quay

5 Sheares St – ✆ (021) 427 95 27 – www.fennsquay.net – Closed 24-27 December, 1 January, Sunday and bank holidays **Zn**
Rest – Menu € 23 (dinner) – Carte € 24/45
Modest little bistro with whitewashed brick walls, closely set tables and a loyal following. Simple, flavoursome cooking offers light lunches and more substantial dishes at dinner; pop in for morning coffee or afternoon tea.

Farmgate Café

English Market (1st floor), Princes St – ✆ (021) 427 81 34 – www.farmgate.ie – Closed 25-27 December, Sunday and bank holidays **Zs**
Rest – *(lunch only)* Carte € 18/32
Popular, long-standing eatery above a bustling 200 year old market; turn right for self-service or left for the bistro. Daily menus use produce from the stalls below and are supplemented by the latest catch. Dishes are hearty and homemade.

at Cork Airport South : 6.5 km by N 27 - X – ✉ Cork

Cork International Airport Hotel

rm,

Gate 2 – ✆ (021) 454 98 00 – www.corkinternationalairporthotel.com – Closed 24-27 December
145 rm – € 79/160 € 79/190, €15 – 4 suites
Rest *Strata* – *(bar lunch Monday-Saturday)* Menu € 25 – Carte € 21/45 **s**
Quirky, modern, design-led hotel, with an aviation theme; a stone's throw from the airport terminal. Very spacious bedrooms offer good facilities for the modern business traveller. Strata contains the fuselage of a plane with authentic airline seating, and offers an appealing, international menu.

CORK AIRPORT = Aerfort Chorcai Cork – Cork – 712 G12 – see Cork

---

CORROFIN (Cora Finne) – Clare – 712 E9 – pop. 689 38 B1

Dublin 228 km – Gort 24 km – Limerick 51 km

Fergus View without rest

Kilnaboy, North : 3.25 km on R 476 – ✆ (066) 837 606 – www.fergusview.com – Closed November-February
6 rm – € 42/45 € 72/76
Charming bay-windowed house – in the family for four generations; the delightful owners offer superb hospitality. Open-fired lounge, cosy breakfast room and country views. Bright, superbly kept bedrooms: smart but tiny bathrooms; no TVs.

CROMANE – Kerry – 712 C11 – pop. 125 38 A2

Dublin 201 km – Tralee 23 km – Cork 73 km – Limerick 78 km

Jacks Coastguard

– ✆ (066) 976 91 02 – www.jackscromane.com – Closed 7 January-9 February, Monday-Wednesday except June-October and Tuesday
Rest – Menu € 28/55 – Carte € 28/62
Remote coastguard station; now a bright, glitzy restaurant offering panoramic bay views. Seafood-orientated menus offer well-presented, classic combinations; concise selection at lunch. Smart bar-lounge features live piano at weekends.

REPUBLIC OF IRELAND

CROOKHAVEN (An Cruachán) – Cork – 712 C13 – pop. 1 669 — 38 A3

Dublin 373 km – Bantry 40 km – Cork 120 km

Galley Cove House without rest

West : 0.75 km on R 591 – (028) 35 137 – www.galleycovehouse.com – Closed November-20 March

4 rm – € 40/50 € 70/90

Detached house just outside the town, affording superb southerly views over the sea towards Fastnet Rock. Conservatory breakfast room and simple, pine-furnished bedrooms with bright colour schemes; all have a sea outlook. Hospitable owners.

CROSSHAVEN – Cork – 712 H12 – pop. 2 093 — 38 B3

Dublin 170 km – Cork 15 km – Limerick 78 km – Galway 140 km

Cronin's

– (021) 483 18 29 – www.croninspub.com – Closed 25 December and Good Friday,

Rest – *(lunch only and dinner Thursday-Saturday)* Carte € 28/40

In the family since 1970, a classic Irish pub now run by the 3rd generation. Interesting artefacts and boxing memorabilia. Unfussy seafood dishes feature local produce. Limited opening in restaurant, which offers more ambitious fare.

CROSSMOLINA (Crois Mhaoilíona) – Mayo – 712 E5 – pop. 930 — 36 B2

Ireland

Dublin 252 km – Ballina 10 km

Errew Abbey★, SE : 9.5 km by R 315. Cáide Fields★ **AC**, N : 24 km by R 315 and R 314 W – Killala★, NE : 16 km by R 315 and minor road – Moyne Abbey★, NE : 18 km by R 115, minor road to Killala, R 314 and minor road – Rosserk Abbey★, NE : 18 km by R 115, minor road to Killala, R 314 and minor road

Enniscoe House

rest,

Castlehill, South : 3.25 km on R 315 – (096) 31 112 – www.enniscoe.com – Closed 7 January-31 March and 1 November-27 December

6 rm – € 130/150 € 220/260

Rest – *(dinner only) (booking essential)* Menu € 40 **s**

Classic Georgian manor, part-dating from 1740 and overlooking Lough Conn; the formal walled garden, heritage museum and tea shop are open to the public. Generously proportioned rooms are filled with antiques and family portraits. Traditional set menu of home-grown ingredients served in the formal dining room.

DINGLE (An Daingean) – Kerry – 712 B11 – pop. 1 965 Ireland — 38 A2

Dublin 347 km – Killarney 82 km – Limerick 153 km

Town★ – St Mary's Church★ – Diseart (stained glass★ **AC**)

Gallarus Oratory★★, NW : 8 km by R 559 – NE : Connor Pass★★ – Kilmalkedar★, NW : 9 km by R 559. Dingle Peninsula★★ – Connor Pass★★, NE : 8 km by minor road – Stradbally Strand★★, NE : 17 km via Connor Pass – Corca Dhuibhne Regional Museum★ **AC**, NW : 13 km by R 559 – Blasket Islands★, W : 21 km by R 559 and ferry from Dunquin

Emlagh Country House without rest

– (066) 915 23 45 – www.emlaghhouse.com – Closed November-16 March

10 rm – € 90/120 € 160/220 — Y**d**

Built to resemble a Georgian country house, with mock period features. Personally run, it has a comfortable, relaxing feel. Large, luxurious bedrooms are colour-themed around local plants and boast antique furnishings and feature beds; choose from a sea view or terrace. Homemade breads and jams at breakfast.

Castlewood House without rest

The Wood – (066) 915 27 88 – www.castlewooddingle.com – Closed 5 January-10 February, and 6-27 December — Y**w**

12 rm – € 65/105 € 90/184

Spacious house overlooking the harbour. Modern bedrooms; all with whirlpool baths – extras include robes, slippers and chocolates. Extensive breakfast buffet and wide range of cooked options; don't miss the bread and butter pudding.

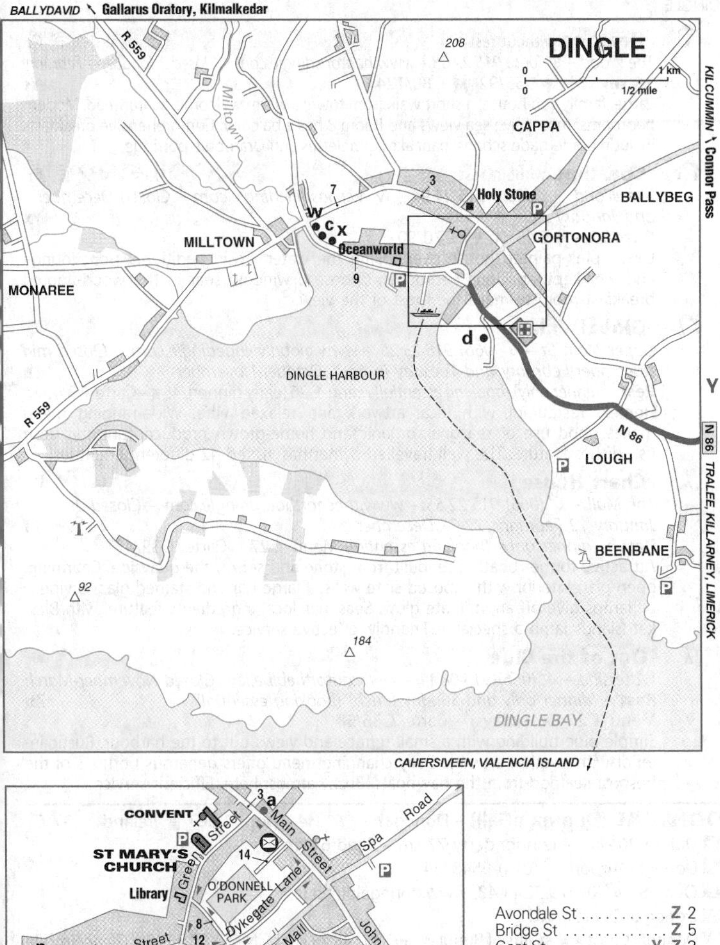

Avondale St	Z 2
Bridge St	Z 5
Goat St	Y, Z 3
Grey's Lane	Z 8
High Road (The)	Y 7
Holy Ground	Z 12
Orchard Lane	Z 14
Tracks (The)	Z 17
Wood (The)	Y 9

Greenmount House without rest

Gortonora – ✆ (066) 915 14 14 – www.greenmounthouse.ie – Closed 15-27 December Zc

15 rm – € 50/120 € 80/150

Well-run hotel in an elevated position above the town, with views of the hills and harbour. Comfy lounges and spacious, modern bedrooms; some have balconies and others, small terraces. Excellent breakfasts with a view.

⌂ **Heatons** without rest
The Wood – ℰ (066) 915 22 88 – www.heatonsdingle.com – Closed 2 January-1 February
16 rm ☑ – **†** € 55/92 **††** € 80/124 Yc
Large, family-run house, a short walk from town; a warm welcome guaranteed. Modern
bedrooms; most have sea views and Room 8 has a balcony. Comprehensive breakfasts
include homemade scones, pancakes, omelettes and Drambuie porridge.

⌂ **Coastline** without rest
*The Wood – ℰ (066) 915 24 94 – www.coastlinedingle.com – Closed December
and January* Yx
8 rm ☑ – **†** € 45/60 **††** € 70/90
Large, pink-painted house overlooking the water. Cosy, traditional front lounge
and well-kept, spacious bedrooms. Choose a window seat in the wood-floored
breakfast room to make the most of the view.

※※ **Global Village**
*Upper Main St – ℰ (066) 915 23 25 – www.globalvillagedingle.com – Closed mid
November-February and Tuesday in April, October-November* Za
Rest – (dinner only) (booking essential) Menu € 26 (early dinner)/45 **s** – Carte € 34/52 **s**
Homely restaurant with local artwork and relaxed vibe. Wide-ranging menu
makes good use of seasonal, organic and home-grown produce; fantastic fresh
fish dishes feature. The well-travelled owner has visited 42 different countries!

※ **Chart House**
*The Mall – ℰ (066) 915 22 55 – www.thecharthousedingle.com – Closed 2
January-12 February, 22-27 December* Zf
Rest – (dinner only) (booking essential) Menu € 27 – Carte € 32/47
Attractive former boathouse, built from stone and set on the quayside. Charming,
open-plan interior with exposed slate walls, a large bar and stained glass dividers;
oil lamps give off an intimate glow. Seasonal, local ingredients feature, with Blas-
ket Islands lamb a speciality. Friendly, effective service.

※ **Out of the Blue**
Waterside – ℰ (066) 915 08 11 – www.outoftheblue.ie – Closed November-March
Rest – (dinner only and Sunday lunch) (booking essential) Zn
Menu € 27 (weekdays) – Carte € 36/53
Simple blue building with a small terrace and views out to the harbour. Rustic in-
terior with nautical artwork. Daily changing menu offers generous portions of the
freshest seafood from the day boats. Buzzy atmosphere. Efficient service.

DONEGAL (Dún na nGall) – **Donegal** – **712** H4 – **pop. 2 607** ▮ Ireland **37** C1
▶ Dublin 264 km – Londonderry 77 km – Sligo 64 km
🛫 Donegal Airport ℰ (074) 9548284
ℹ Quay St, ℰ (074) 9 72 11 48, www.donegaldirect.ie
◎ Donegal Castle★ **AC**
◎ Donegal Coast★★ - Cliffs of Bunglass★★, W : 48.25 km by N 56 and R 263 – Glencolmcille
Folk Village★★ **AC**, W : 53 km by N 56 and R 263 - Rossnowlagh Strand★★, S : 35.5 km by
N 15 and R 231 – Trabane Strand★, W : 58 km by N 56 and R 263

🏨 **Solis Lough Eske Castle**
*Northeast : 6.5 km by N15 – ℰ (074) 972 51 00 – www.solisloughheskecastle.com
– Closed Sunday-Wednesday November-March*
97 rm ☑ – **†** € 195/420 **††** € 195/420 – 1 suite
Rest *Cedars* – see restaurant listing
Beautifully restored 17C castle with extensions, surrounded by 43 sculpture-filled
acres. Fantastic spa; swimming pool overlooks an enclosed garden. Mix of contem-
porary and antique-furnished bedrooms; garden suites are worth the extra cost.

🏨 **Harvey's Point**
*Lough Eske, Northeast : 7.25 km. by Killybegs rd – ℰ (074) 972 22 08
– www.harveyspoint.com – restricted opening in winter*
64 rm ☑ – **†** € 149/209 **††** € 198/240 – 4 suites
Rest *Harvey's Point* – see restaurant listing
Sprawling, family-run hotel in a peaceful loughside setting, with traditional guest
areas and huge, very comfortable bedrooms in a country house style; these offer
a high level of facilities and most have a lovely countryside outlook.

⚭ **Ardeevin** without rest ☒ ≼ 🚗 🛜 🖭 ⊟
Lough Eske, Barnesmore, Northeast : 9 km by N 15 following signs for Lough
Eske Drive – 𝒞 (074) 972 17 90 – www.ardeevin.tripod.com – Closed
November-18 March
6 rm ☑ – ✝ € 50 ✝✝ € 70
Friendly, brightly painted house set in peaceful gardens and boasting beautiful
views over Lough Eske; personally run by the friendly owner. Warm, pleasantly
cluttered guest areas are filled with ornaments and curios. Individually designed
bedrooms display quality furnishings and thoughtful extras.

XXX **Harvey's Point** – Harvey's Point Hotel ≼ 🚗 🕭 🛜 🖭 P
Lough Eske, Northeast : 7.25 km. by Killybegs rd – 𝒞 (074) 972 22 08
– www.harveyspoint.com – Closed Monday-Thursday 4 November-April
Rest – (dinner only) Menu € 50
Formal, traditional restaurant set on the ground floor of a family-owned, country
house hotel; its semi-circular windows affording delightful views of the lough.
Classic dishes make use of local Donegal produce. Attentive service.

XX **Cedars** – Solis Lough Eske Castle Hotel 🚗 🕭 ⅋ 🖭 ✿ P
Northeast : 6.5 km by N15 – 𝒞 (074) 972 51 00 – www.solislougheskecastle.com
– Closed Sunday dinner-Wednesday November-March
Rest – (dinner only and Sunday lunch) Menu € 55
Stylish, modern restaurant in a 17C castle close to the lough, with romantic
booths to the rear and a slate terrace boasting views over the lawns and wood-
land. Small menu with international influences, but Donegal produce to the fore.

DOOGORT = Dumha Goirt – **Mayo** – **712** B5/6 – **see Achill Island**

DOOLIN (Dúlainm) – **Clare** – **712** D8 ▮ Ireland **38** B1

🚇 Dublin 275 km – Galway 69 km – Limerick 80 km

🗺 The Burren★★ (Cliffs of Moher★★★, Scenic Route★★, Aillwee Cave★ **AC**
(Waterfall★★), Poulnabrone Portal Tomb★, Corcomroe Abbey★, Kilfenora
Crosses★, Burren Centre★ **AC**)

XX **Cullinan's** with rm 🚗 🛜 P
– 𝒞 (065) 707 41 83 – www.cullinansdoolin.com – Closed mid December-mid
February, Sunday dinner and Wednesday
10 rm ☑ – ✝ € 40/70 ✝✝ € 60/100
Rest – (closed November-April) (dinner only) (booking essential) Menu € 28
(early dinner) – Carte € 33/46
Run by a keen husband and wife team; an orange building in the middle of the
Burren, with two walls of full length windows making the most of the view. Clas-
sical, comforting cooking uses Irish produce and portions are generous. Comfy,
pine-furnished bedrooms; some overlook the River Aille.

DOONBEG – **Clare** – **712** D9 – **pop. 272** **38** B2

🚇 Dublin 286 km – Inis 45 km – Galway 115 km – Limerick 91 km

🏨 **Lodge at Doonbeg** 🅝 ☒ ≼ 🚗 🕭 🕭 🛜 🖼 🛗 ⅋ 🖭 rm, ⅋ 🛜 P
Northeast : 9 km on N 67 – 𝒞 (065) 905 5600 – www.doonbeggolfclub.com
– Closed 19-26 December
75 suites ☑ – ✝✝ € 225/400
Rest Long Room – Carte € 39/56
Rest Darby's – Carte € 28/52
Smart resort complex owned by the group who built Doonbeg golf course. Stylish, sumptuous bedrooms and suites are spread about the grounds: some are duplex and feature fully fitted kitchens; all have spacious marble bathrooms and are
extremely comfortable. The Long Room offers fine dining with sea views; Darby's
brasserie, in the clubhouse, has a traditional menu.

Morrissey's Ⓝ with rm — rest,
– ✆ (065) 905 5304 – *www.morrisseysdoonbeg.com* – *Closed January, February, 2 weeks November and Monday*
6 rm – € 45/55 € 80/100
Rest – *(dinner only and Sunday lunch)* Carte € 26/36
Smartly refurbished pub in a small coastal village; its terrace overlooking the river and the castle ruins. The menu may be simple but cooking is careful and shows respect for ingredients – locally caught fish and shellfish feature heavily. Bedrooms are modern and they have bikes and even a kayak for hire.

DROGHEDA (Droichead Átha) – Louth – 712 M6 – pop. 30 393 — 37 D3

Ireland

Dublin 46 km – Dundalk 35 km
Mayoralty St, ✆ (041) 9 83 70 70, www.drogheda.ie
Seapoint, Termonfeckin, ✆ (041) 9 82 23 33
Towneley Hall, Tullyallen, ✆ (041) 984 22 29
Town★ – Drogheda Museum★ – St Laurence Gate★
Monasterboice★★, N : 10.5 km by N 1 – Boyne Valley★★, on N 51 – Termonfeckin★, NE : 8 km by R 166. Newgrange★★★, W : 5 km by N 51 on N 2 – Mellifont Old Abbey★ **AC** - Knowth★

The D — rest,
Scotch Hall, Marsh Rd. – ✆ *(041) 987 77 00* – *www.thedhotel.com* – *Closed Christmas*
104 rm – € 69/170 € 79/250, € 13
Rest – Menu € 10 (lunch)/35 – Carte € 20/47
Smart, modern hotel, in an office and shopping complex on the south bank of the river. Spacious, open-plan guest areas are minimalist in style, with colourful furniture. Decently sized, slightly stark bedrooms; those overlooking the river are the most popular. Informal restaurant; characterful Irish pub.

Scholars Townhouse
King St, by West St and Lawrence St turning left at Lawrence's Gate – ✆ *(041) 983 54 10* – *www.scholarshotel.com* – *Closed 25-26 December*
16 rm – € 65/100 € 79/150 **Rest** – Menu € 36 – Carte € 26/71
19C former priest's house: now a well-run, privately owned hotel with smart wood panelling and ornate coving featuring throughout. Appealing bar and cosy lounge; comfortable, well-kept bedrooms. Dine on classically based dishes under an impressive mural of the Battle of Boyne.

Eastern Seaboard Bar & Grill Ⓝ
1 Bryanstown Centre, Dublin Rd, Southeast : 2.5 km. by N 1 taking first right after railway bridge – ✆ *(041) 980 25 70* – *www.easternseaboard.ie* – *Closed Good Friday and 25 December*
Rest – Carte € 17/44
A lively, buzzy bistro; its name a reference to its location within Ireland and also a nod to the East Coast of the USA, which influences its extensive menus. Open-plan, with concrete floors and exposed pipework giving an industrial feel.

The Kitchen Ⓝ
2 South Quay – ✆ *(041) 983 4630* – *www.kitchenrestaurant.ie* – *Closed 1-3 January, 3-16 September, 25-27 December and Monday-Tuesday*
Rest – *(light lunch)* Carte € 23/34
Glass-fronted riverfront eatery. By day, a café serving homemade cakes, pastries, salads and sandwiches; by night, a more interesting, mainly Eastern Mediterranean menu is served, with influences from North Africa and the Middle East.

REPUBLIC OF IRELAND

DUBLIN

See city maps on following pages

39 D1

© IIC/Design Pics RM/Age fotostock

REPUBLIC OF IRELAND

Dublin – **pop. 527 612** – **712** N7 – Ireland

Belfast 166 km – Cork 248 km – Londonderry 235 km

Tourist Information

Suffolk St, ☎(01) 605 77 00, www.visitdublin.com

Airport

Dublin Airport : ☎ (01) 814 1111, N : 9 km by N 1 BS

Ferries

to Holyhead (Irish Ferries) 4 daily (3 h 15 mn) – to Holyhead (Stena Line) 1-2 daily (3 h 45 mn) – to the Isle of Man (Douglas) (Isle of Man Steam Packet Co. Ltd) (2 h 45 mn/4 h 45 mn) – to Liverpool (P & O Irish Sea) (8 h)

Golf Courses

Elm Park, Donnybrook, Nutley House, ☎(01) 269 34 38

Milltown, Lower Churchtown Rd, ☎(01) 497 60 90

Royal Dublin, Dollymount, North Bull Island, ☎(01) 833 63 46

SIGHTS

In the town : City★★★ • Trinity College★★ JY • Old Library★★★ • Christ Church Cathedral★★ HY • St Patrick's Cathedral★★ HZ • National Museum★★ KZ • National Gallery★★ KZ • Newman House★★ JZ • Custom House★★ KX • Kilmainham Gaol Museum★★ AT**M6** • Phoenix Park★★ AS • National Botanic Gardens★★ BS • Tailors' Hall★ HY • City Hall★ HY • Temple Bar★ HJY • Liffey Bridge★ JY • Merrion Square★ KZ • Number Twenty-Nine★ KZ**D** • Grafton Street★ JYZ • Powerscourt Centre★ JY • O'Connell Street★ JX • Hugh Lane Municipal Gallery of Modern Art★ JX**M4** • Bluecoat School★ BS**F** • Guinness Museum★ BT**M7**

On the outskirts : The Ben of Howth ≤★, NE : 9.5 km by R 105 CS

In the surrounding area : Powerscourt★★ **AC**, S : 22.5 km by N 11 and R 117 EV • Russborough House★★★, SW : 35.5 km by N 81 BT

DUBLIN

Adelaïde Rd	BT	3
Alfie Byrne Rd	CS	5
Bath Ave	CT	9
Benburb St	BS	15
Berkeley Rd	BS	16
Botanic Rd	BS	19
Canal Rd	BT	30
Clanbrassil St	BT	40
Conyngham Rd	AS	48
Denmark St	BS	52
Donnybrook Rd	CT	54
Dorset St	BS	55
Drimnagh Rd	AT	57
Eglinton Rd	CT	63
Grand Parade	BT	72
Inchicore Rd	AT	79
Infirmary Rd	AS	81
James St	BT	84
Leeson St Upper	BT	94
Macken St	BST	99
Morehampton Rd	BT	108
Mount St Upper	BT	112
Palmerston Park	BT	123
Phibsborough Rd	BS	132
Rathmines Rd Upper	BT	135
Ringsend Rd	CT	139
St Agnes Rd	AT	141
St Alphonsus Rd	BS	144
St John's Rd West	AS	147
Sandford Rd	BT	151
Shelbourne Rd	CT	157
Shrewsbury Rd	CT	159
South Circular Rd	AS	162
Suir Rd	AT	168
Terenure Rd East	BT	172
Thomas St West	BT	174
Victoria Quay	BS	178
Western Way	BS	184
Wolfe Tone Quay	BS	195

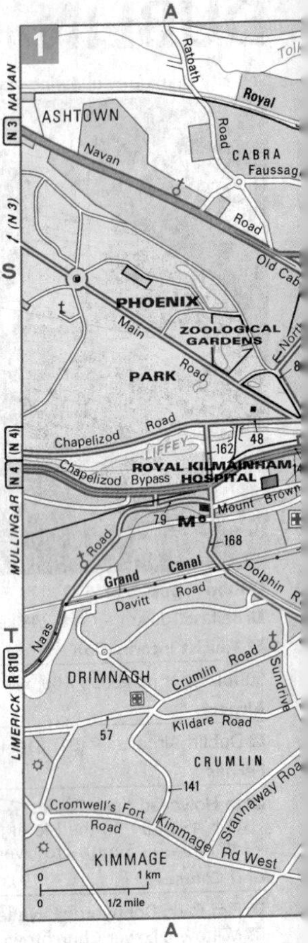

Shelbourne

27 St Stephen's Grn. ✉ D2 – ✆ (01) 663 45 00 – www.theshelbourne.ie **Plan 6** JZ**c**

262 rm – € 198/650 € 198/690 – 12 suites

Rest *Saddle Room* – see restaurant listing

Famed hotel dating from 1824, overlooking an attractive green; this is where the 1922 Irish Constitution was signed. Elegant guest areas and classical architecture; it even has a tiny museum. The bar and lounge are THE places to go for drinks and afternoon tea. Chic spa and characterful, luxurious bedrooms.

Merrion

rm,

Upper Merrion St ✉ D2 – ✆ (01) 603 06 00 – www.merrionhotel.com **Plan 6** KZ**e**

142 rm – € 485 € 505, €29 – 10 suites

Rest *Cellar* – ✆ (01) 603 06 30 – Menu € 23/30 **s** – Carte dinner € 36/71 **s**

Rest *Cellar Bar* – Carte € 30/45 **s**

A classic Georgian façade conceals this luxury hotel; its opulent drawing rooms filled with antique furniture and fine artwork. Enjoy 'art afternoon tea' with a view of the formal parterre garden. Stylish bedrooms have an understated, classic feel and smart marble bathrooms. Compact spa with impressive pool. Accessible menu in the restaurant and barrel-ceilinged bar.

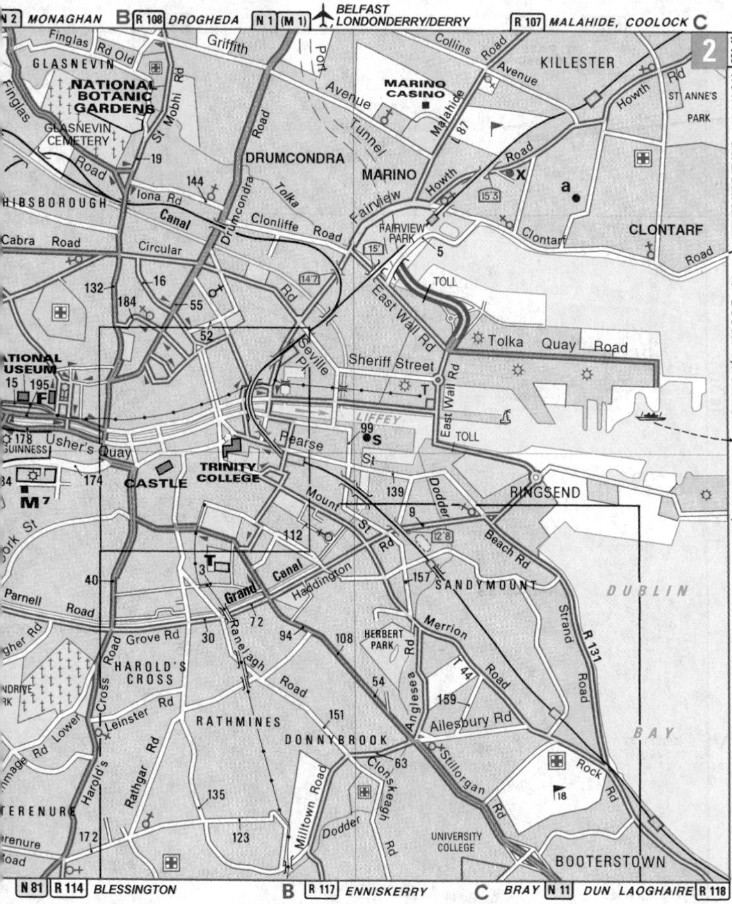

The Westbury

rm,

Grafton St ✉ *D2* – ✆ *(01) 679 1122* – *www.doylecollection.com* **Plan 6** JY**x**

185 rm – € 200/520 € 200/520, € 25 – 20 suites

Rest *Wilde* – *(closed Sunday and Monday) (dinner only)* Menu € 35/41 – Carte € 38/67

Rest *Café Novo* – *(closed 25 December)* Carte € 23/41

Well-run hotel with a stylish bar, a comfy lounge (popular for afternoon tea) and state-of-the-art conference facilities; modern artwork features throughout. Well-equipped, elegant bedrooms come in browns and creams. Excellent service. Formal Wilde offers a modern Irish menu; Café Novo serves old favourites.

Westin

Westmoreland St ✉ *D2* – ✆ *(01) 645 10 00* – *www.thewestindublin.com* **Plan 6** JY**n**

163 rm – € 179/409 € 179/409, € 20 – 13 suites

Rest *Exchange* – *(closed Monday)* Menu € 25 – Carte € 27/48

Rest *Mint* – *(closed Sunday lunch)* Carte € 26/49

Built in 1860 as a bank; now a smart hotel set over 6 period buildings, with comfy lounges, impressive conference rooms and good facilities. Bedroom styles range from classic, with mahogany furniture, to contemporary, with leather furnishings and media hubs. Modern European cooking in semi-formal Exchange. Accessible menu in The Mint, which was once the bank's vaults.

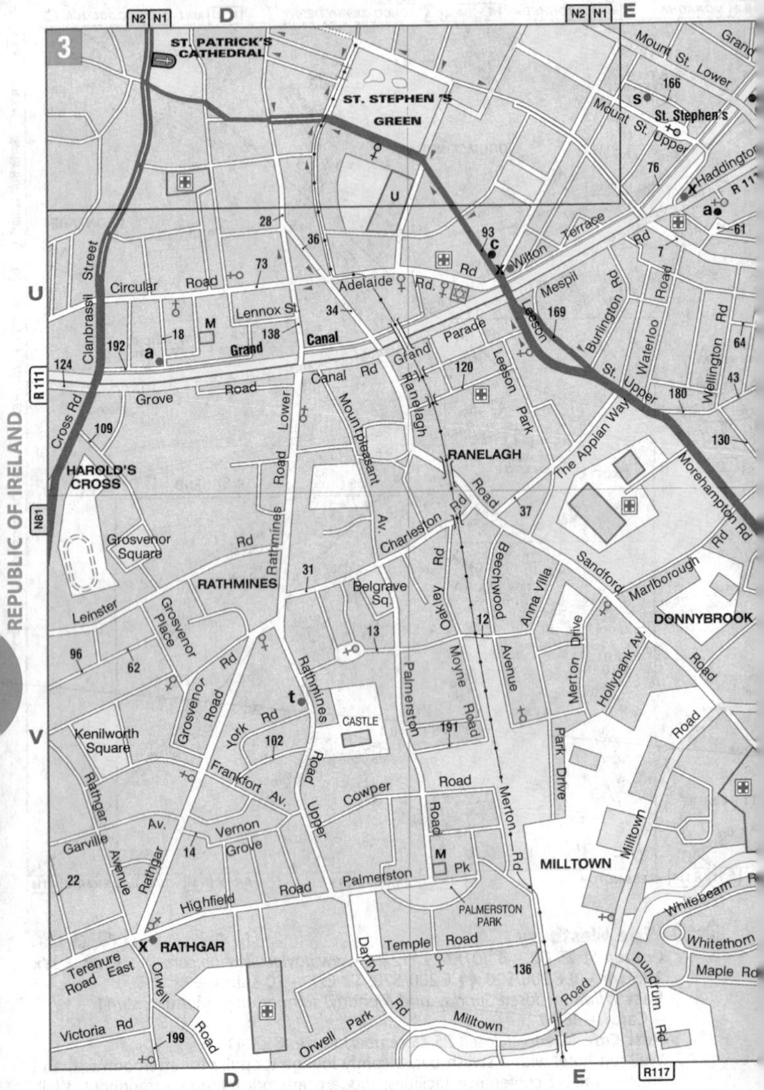
3
N2 N1
D
E
ST. PATRICK'S CATHEDRAL
ST. STEPHEN'S GREEN
Mount St. Lower
Mount St. Upper
Grand
166
S
St. Stephen's
76
Haddington
R 111
a
61
93
c
X
Wilton
Terrace
Rd
7
U
28
36
73
Circular
Road
Adelaide
Rd.
Rd
Mespil
Burlington
Rd
Road
Rd
Clanbrassil
Street
Lennox St
34
169
Leeson
M
18
138
Canal
Grand
192
a
Parade
Waterloo
Wellington
64
124
R111
Grand
Canal
Rd
120
Leeson
Park
St.
Upper
43
180
Cross Rd
Grove
Road
Lower
Mountpleasant
Ranelagh
109
The Appian Way
130
HAROLD'S CROSS
RANELAGH
Road
Rathmines
Road
Av.
Charleston
Rd
37
Morehampton Rd
N81
Grosvenor Square
Rd
Beechwood
Sandford
Rd
RATHMINES
31
Belgrave Sq.
Oakley
Rd
12
Anna Villa
Marlborough
Leinster
Grosvenor Place
13
Avenue
Merton Drive
Hollybank Av.
DONNYBROOK
96
62
Rd
Road
REPUBLIC OF IRELAND
Grosvenor
Road
t
Rathmines
Palmerston
Moyne
Road
Road
York
Rd
CASTLE
191
Park Drive
V
Kenilworth Square
102
Frankfort
Av.
Road
Upper
Cowper
Road
Merton
Rd
Rathgar
Av.
Vernon
Grove
Road
Milltown
Garville
Avenue
Rathgar
14
M
Pk
MILLTOWN
22
Road
Palmerston
Whitebeam
Highfield
PALMERSTON PARK
X
RATHGAR
Temple
Road
Dartry
Whitethorn
Terenure Road East
Orwell
136
Dundrum
Maple Rd
Road
Rd
Victoria Rd
Road
Orwell
Park
Milltown
Rd
199
R117

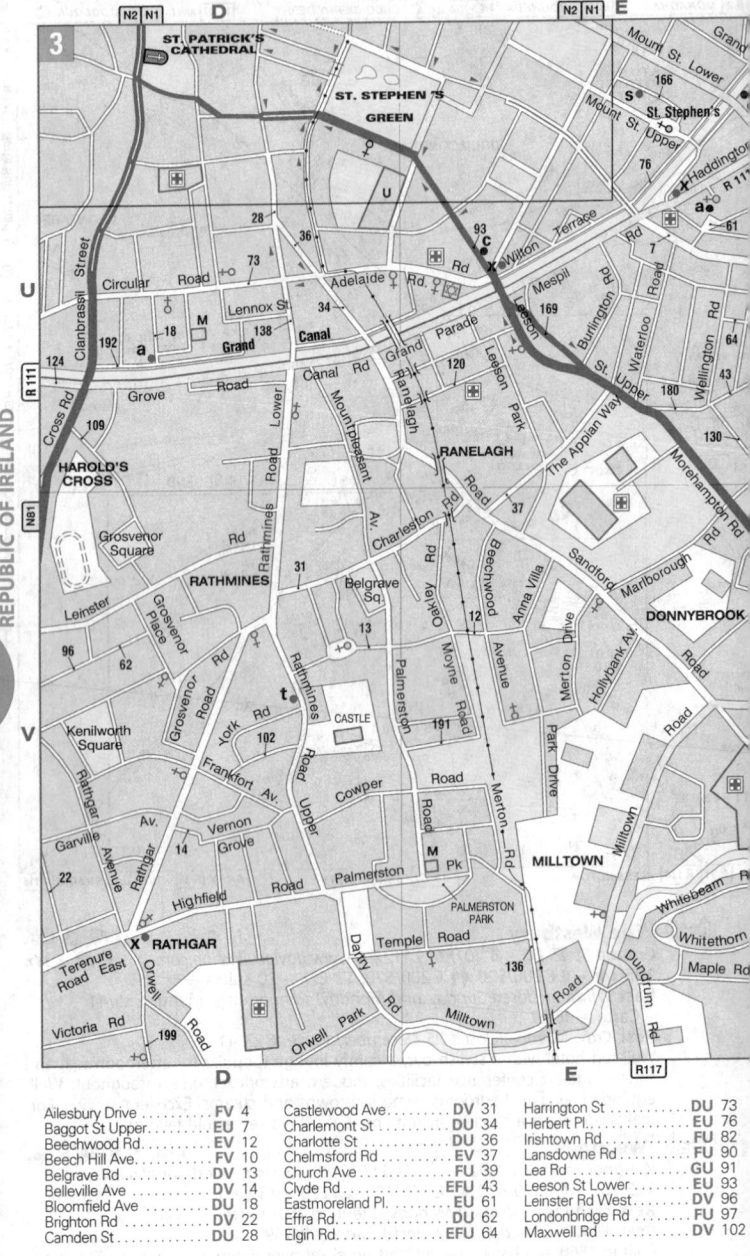

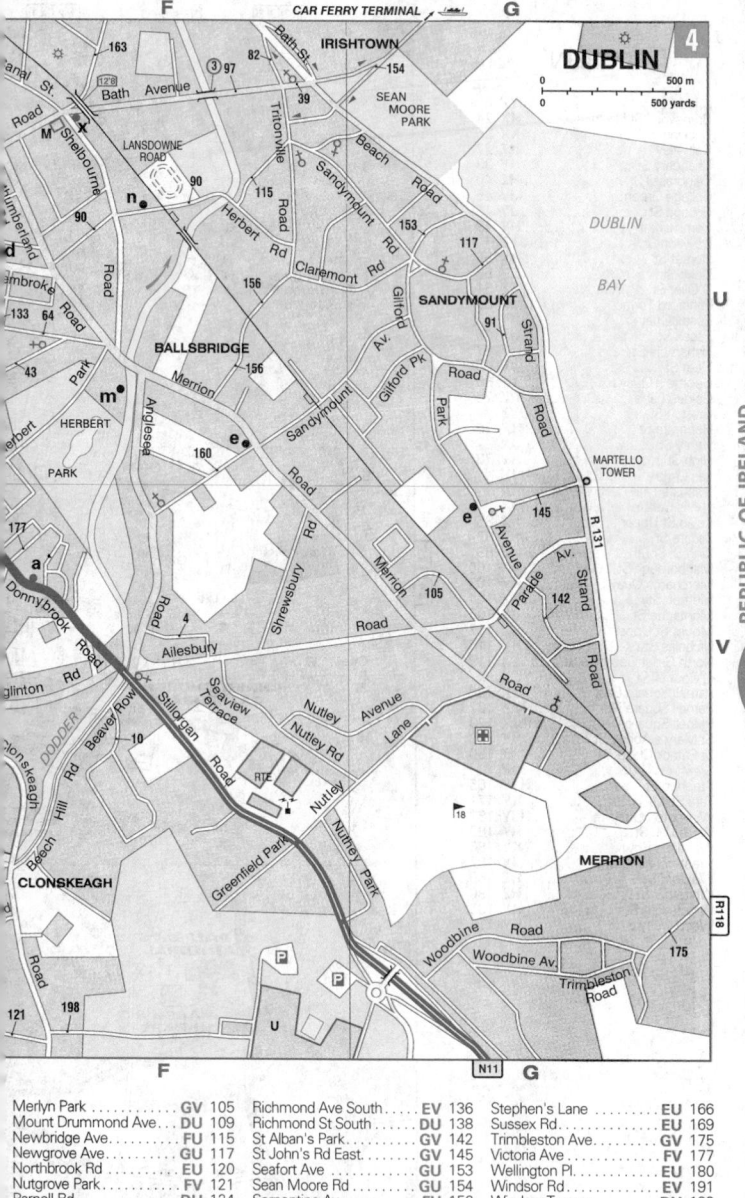

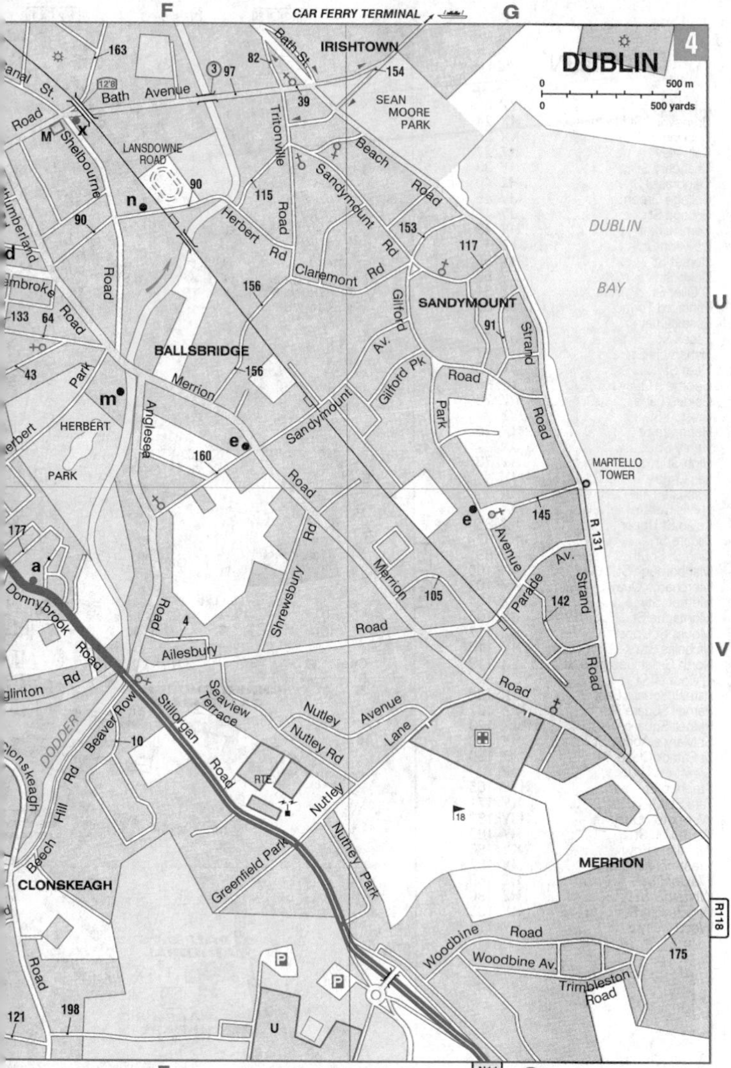

CAR FERRY TERMINAL
DUBLIN
4
0 500 m
0 500 yards
F
G
U
V
IRISHTOWN
SEAN MOORE PARK
DUBLIN BAY
SANDYMOUNT
BALLSBRIDGE
LANSDOWNE ROAD
HERBERT PARK
MARTELLO TOWER
CLONSKEAGH
MERRION
RTE
Bath Avenue
Bath St.
Tritonville Road
Beach Road
Sandymount Rd
Herbert Rd
Claremont Rd
Gilford Av.
Gilford Pk
Shelbourne Road
Merrion Road
Sandymount Road
Anglesea Road
Shrewsbury Rd
Ailesbury Road
Donnybrook Road
Eglinton Rd
Stillorgan Road
Seaview Terrace
Nutley Avenue
Nutley Rd
Nutley Lane
Nutley Park
Greenfield Park
Beaver Row
Clonskeagh Rd
Beech Hill Rd
DODDER
Strand Road
Park Avenue
Parade Av.
R 131
R118
N11
Woodbine Road
Woodbine Av.
Trimbleston Road
REPUBLIC OF IRELAND

DUBLIN

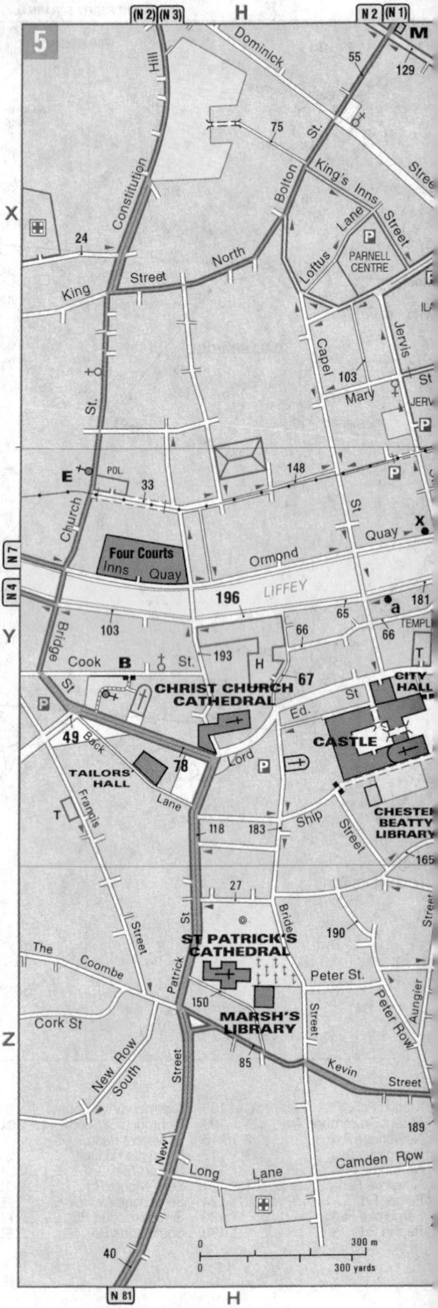

5
H
X
Y
Z
Constitution Hill
Dominick St.
Bolton St.
King's Inns Street
Loftus Lane
PARNELL CENTRE
King Street North
Capel St
Jervis St
Mary St
Church St.
POL.
Four Courts
Inns Quay
Ormond Quay
LIFFEY
Bridge St
Cook St.
CHRIST CHURCH CATHEDRAL
CITY HALL
Ed. St
CASTLE
Lord Ed.
Back Lane
TAILORS' HALL
Francis Street
Ship Street
CHESTER BEATTY LIBRARY
St Patrick St.
Bride St
ST PATRICK'S CATHEDRAL
MARSH'S LIBRARY
Peter St.
Peter Row
Aungier Street
The Coombe
Cork St
New Row South
New Street
Kevin Street
Long Lane
Camden Row
300 m
300 yards

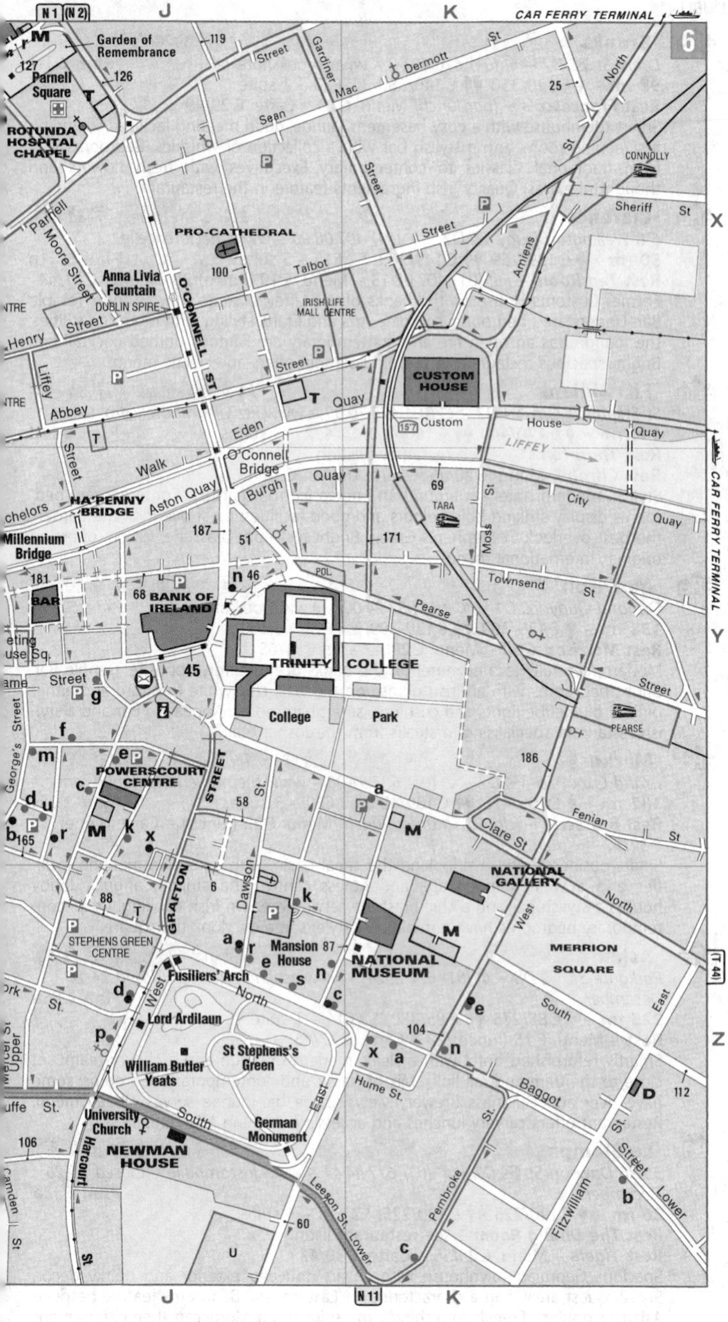

N 1
N 2
J
K
CAR FERRY TERMINAL
6
Garden of Remembrance
Parnell Square
ROTUNDA HOSPITAL CHAPEL
PRO-CATHEDRAL
Anna Livia Fountain
DUBLIN SPIRE
O'CONNELL ST
IRISH LIFE MALL CENTRE
CUSTOM HOUSE
CONNOLLY
Sheriff St
X
Amiens
Talbot
Street
Sean Mac Dermott St
Gardiner Street
North
Parnell
Moore Street
Henry Street
Liffey Street
Abbey Street
Eden Quay
Custom House Quay
LIFFEY
O'Connell Bridge
Burgh Quay
Aston Quay
HA'PENNY BRIDGE
Bachelors Walk
Millennium Bridge
City Quay
TARA
Moss St
Townsend St
Pearse Street
POL
BANK OF IRELAND
TRINITY COLLEGE
College Park
PEARSE
Y
CAR FERRY TERMINAL
Meeting House Sq.
Dame Street
George's Street
POWERSCOURT CENTRE
GRAFTON STREET
Dawson St.
Clare St
Fenian St
NATIONAL GALLERY
Merrion Square North
Merrion Square West
MERRION SQUARE
Merrion Square South
Merrion Square East
STEPHENS GREEN CENTRE
Mansion House
NATIONAL MUSEUM
Fusiliers' Arch
Lord Ardilaun
St Stephens's Green
William Butler Yeats
St Stephen's Green West
St Stephen's Green North
St Stephen's Green East
St Stephen's Green South
Hume St.
Baggot Street Lower
T 44
Z
University Church
NEWMAN HOUSE
German Monument
Harcourt St
Leeson St. Lower
Pembroke St.
Fitzwilliam St.
Upper Mercer St
Cuffe St.
Camden St
York St.
N 11

Brooks

Drury St ✉ *D2 – ✆ (01) 670 40 00 – www.brookshotel.ie* **Plan 6** JY**r**
98 rm – € 120/350 € 140/380, € 20 – 1 suite
Rest *Francesca's* – *(bar lunch)* Menu € 23 – Carte € 29/49
Smart townhouse with a cosy basement lounge, good meeting facilities, including a screening room, and a stylish bar with a collection of whiskies. Bedrooms vary from traditional Classics to contemporary Executives with fresh flowers and thoughtful extras. Quality Irish ingredients feature in the restaurant.

Clarence

rm, rest,

6-8 Wellington Quay ✉ *D2 – ✆ (01) 407 08 00 – www.theclarence.ie*
50 rm – € 139/259 € 149/269, € 15 – 5 suites **Plan 5** HY**a**
Rest *Tea Room* – ✆ (01) 407 08 13 – Menu € 19 (lunch)/28 – Carte € 21/44
Former Customs House on the banks of the Liffey; a stone's throw from Temple Bar. Understated bedrooms combine Arts and Crafts styling with modern facilities; the lounge has an open fire and contemporary art. Famous domed cocktail bar. Bright, spacious restaurant in the old ballroom offers an eclectic menu.

Fitzwilliam

rest,

St Stephen's Grn ✉ *D2 – ✆ (01) 478 70 00 – www.fitzwilliamhotel.com*
140 rm – € 170/440 € 190/460, € 22 – 3 suites **Plan 6** JZ**d**
Rest *Thornton's* ✿ – see restaurant listing
Rest *Citron* – Menu € 20/25 – Carte dinner € 38/48
Stylish, modern hotel set around an impressive roof garden. Contemporary bedrooms display striking bold colours and good facilities: most overlook the garden; the best overlook St Stephen's Green. Bright first floor brasserie, Citron, offers an original, international menu.

Morrison N

Ormond Quay ✉ *D1 – ✆ (01) 887 24 00 – www.morrisonhotel.ie* **Plan 5** HY**x**
138 rm – € 139/399 € 139/399, € 15 – 3 suites
Rest *Morrison Grill* – Menu € 20 – Carte € 31/65
Modern, centrally located hotel on the banks of the Liffey, opposite Temple Bar. Bright bedrooms with an Irish phrase on the wall, chic white furniture and either pink or blue cube lights and cushions; smart bathrooms. Appealing bar and a stylish restaurant specialising in steaks from the Josper grill.

Marker N

rm,

Grand Canal Sq. ✉ *D2 – ✆ (01) 687 51 00 – www.themarkerhoteldublin.com*
187 rm – € 159/425 € 189/455, € 20 – 3 suites **Plan 2** CS**s**
Rest *Brasserie* – *(closed Saturday lunch)* Menu € 22 (lunch) – Carte dinner € 32/52
Smart business hotel overlooking the canal basin, with extensive meeting facilities and a well-equipped spa and fitness centre. The striking angular lobby houses a stylish bar and a chic brasserie serving modern Irish cooking. Crisp, contemporary bedrooms have a minimalist style; some overlook the square.

Ashling

rm, rest,

Parkgate St. ✉ *D8 – ✆ (01) 677 2324 – www.ashlinghotel.ie – Closed 24-26 December* **Plan 2** BS**a**
225 rm – € 85/275 € 85/380, € 14 – 1 suite
Rest – Menu € 15 (lunch)/28 – Carte € 27/46
Smartly refurbished hotel with a sleek, modern frontage and a cheery team; set close to the tram and rail links. Mix of classic and contemporary bedrooms; some have river and Guinness Brewery views. Large bar-lounge serves all-day menu. Restaurant offers carvery lunches and accessible evening à la carte.

La Stampa

35-36 Dawson St ✉ *D2 – ✆ (01) 677 44 44 – www.lastampa.ie – Closed 25-26 December* **Plan 6** JZ**a**
36 rm – € 120/225 € 120/225, € 15 – 1 suite
Rest *The Dining Room* – see restaurant listing
Rest *Tigers* – Menu € 25/55 – Carte € 30/47
Spacious Georgian townhouse with an art nouveau exterior and quirky décor. Stylish guest areas and a characterful Far Eastern spa. Bedrooms feature bespoke Asian or opulent French furnishings; the suite has a Moroccan theme. Basement restaurant offers pan-Asian dishes and turns into a nightclub at weekends.

Number 31 without rest
31 Leeson Cl. ✉ *D2* – ✆ *(01) 676 50 11* – *www.number31.ie* **Plan 3** EU**c**
21 rm ☕ – 🚹 € 110/180 🚹🚹 € 150/220
Unusual and very individual property – once home to architect Sam Stevenson. It's classically styled around the 1960s, with a striking sunken lounge; the most modern bedrooms are found in the Georgian house across the terraced garden.

Kellys without rest
First Floor, 36 South Great George's St ✉ *D2* – ✆ *(01) 648 0010* – *www.kellysdublin.com* **Plan 6** JY**b**
16 rm ☕ – 🚹 € 75 🚹🚹 € 75/260
Shabby-chic hotel set among trendy boutiques and bars, in a bustling area. Stripped paint and white emulsioned walls hung with funky artwork; airy, open-plan lounge and bar; spacious, minimalist bedrooms. Breakfast in the restaurant below.

XXXX ✿✿ **Patrick Guilbaud** (Guillaume Lebrun) A/C
21 Upper Merrion St ✉ *D2* – ✆ *(01) 676 41 92* – *www.restaurantpatrickguilbaud.ie* – *Closed 25-26 December, 18 April, Sunday and Monday* **Plan 6** KZ**e**
Rest – *(booking essential)* Menu € 50 (lunch)/165
Luxurious lounge and stylish restaurant in an elegant Georgian house; the eponymous owner has run it for over 30 years. Accomplished, original cooking has a classical French base elevated by touches of modernity. Dishes are well-crafted and visually stunning with a superb balance of textures and flavours. Professional, knowledgeable service.
→ Lobster ravioli, coconut scented lobster cream, toasted almonds and split curry dressing. Mellow spiced lamb fillet with piquillo pepper and fregola sarda. Assiette of Valrhona chocolate desserts.

XXXX **Shanahan's on the Green** A/C
119 St Stephen's Grn ✉ *D2* – ✆ *(01) 407 09 39* – *www.shanahans.ie* – *Closed 25-27 December, Good Friday and Sunday* **Plan 6** JZ**p**
Rest – *(dinner only and Friday lunch) (booking essential)* Menu € 45 (early dinner) – Carte € 59/82
Georgian townhouse overlooking the green; the basement 'Oval Office' bar features one of JFK's old rocking chairs. Very comfortable, formal dining beneath a fine rococo ceiling. Generous portions; aged Irish Angus beef is a speciality.

XXX ✿ **Thornton's** (Kevin Thornton) – Fitzwilliam Hotel A/C
128 St Stephen's Grn. ✉ *D2* – ✆ *(01) 478 70 08* – *www.thorntonsrestaurant.com* – *Closed 10 days Christmas-New Year, Sunday, Monday and lunch Tuesday-Wednesday* **Plan 6** JZ**d**
Rest – Menu € 45/120
Elegant restaurant overlooking St Stephen's Green, on the first floor of the Fitzwilliam Hotel. Stylish, contemporary décor with eye-catching photographic montages. Concise, monthly changing à la carte menu; technically adept, modern cooking features classic combinations. 5 or 8 course tasting menu.
→ Dublin Bay prawns with truffle sabayon and prawn bisque. Wicklow venison with Sichuan pepper and Valrhona chocolate sauce. Clementine tartlet with lemon verbena sauce and bourbon vanilla ice cream.

XXX ✿ **Chapter One** (Ross Lewis) A/C
The Dublin Writers Museum, 18-19 Parnell Sq ✉ *D1* – ✆ *(01) 873 22 66* – *www.chapteronerestaurant.com* – *Closed 2 weeks August, 2 weeks Christmas, Sunday, Monday and bank holidays* **Plan 6** JX**r**
Rest – *(booking essential)* Menu € 29/65 **s**
Stylish basement restaurant under the Writers Museum, with a modern lounge and two smart dining rooms hung with specially commissioned art. Various set and tasting menus offer flavoursome, classically based dishes prepared using modern techniques; the kitchen table offers its own menu. Pleasant, formal service.
→ Pig's tail stuffed with smoked bacon, langoustines and basil purée. Halibut, salt-baked celeriac and rope mussels in a cider dressing. Rhubarb poached in black pepper with a maple syrup baked custard.

XXX ✿ **L'Ecrivain** (Derry Clarke)
109a Lower Baggot St ✉ D2 – ✆ (01) 661 19 19 – www.lecrivain.com – Closed Sunday and bank holidays **Plan 6** KZ**b**
Rest – *(dinner only and lunch Thursday-Friday) (booking essential)*
Menu €35/65 – Carte €64/80
A well-regarded and busy restaurant which offers a 'fine dining' experience at an affordable price. Piano bar, whiskey-themed private dining room, mezzanine and attractive terrace. Refined cooking uses superb ingredients and has a classic foundation with touches of modernity. Service is formal with personality.
→ Scallops with apple meringue, sea buckthorn and apple. Fillet of beef, braised short ribs, shallot and buttermilk purée. Smoked chocolate ganache with chocolate and currant parfait.

XXX **Forty One**
41 St. Stephen's Grn. ✉ D2 – ✆ (01) 662 00 00 – www.restaurantfortyone.ie – Closed Good Friday, 25-30 December, Sunday and Monday **Plan 6** KZ**x**
Rest – *(booking advisable)* Menu €35/75 – Carte €57/72
Intimate, richly furnished restaurant on the first floor of an attractive, creeper-clad townhouse, in a corner of St Stephen's Green. Accomplished, classical cooking features luxurious Irish ingredients and personal, modern touches.

XXX **Greenhouse**
Dawson St ✉ D2 – ✆ (01) 676 7015 – www.thegreenhouserestaurant.ie – Closed 2 weeks July , 2 weeks Christmas, Sunday and Monday **Plan 6** JZ**r**
Rest – Menu €25 (weekday lunch)/86
Stylish restaurant with bold turquoise chairs and smooth service. Choice of three menus – one a 'Surprise' and two with suggested wine flights. Attractive, flavoursome dishes feature original combinations and many have Scandinavian touches.

XXX **One Pico**
5-6 Molesworth Pl ✉ D2 (eamonnoreillys@gmail.com) – ✆ (01) 676 03 00 – www.onepico.com – Closed bank holidays **Plan 6** JZ**k**
Rest – Menu €25 (lunch)/39 – Carte €46/69
Stylish, modern restaurant tucked away on a back street; a well-regarded place that's a regular haunt for MPs. Muted colour scheme, mirrors and comfy banquettes; Classic French cooking offers plenty of flavour.

XX **Bang**
11 Merrion Row ✉ D2 – ✆ (01) 400 42 29 – www.bangrestaurant.com – Closed Sunday-Tuesday lunch and bank holidays **Plan 6** KZ**a**
Rest – Menu €15 (lunch)/40 – Carte €35/57
Stylish, three floor restaurant with a pale blue colour scheme: the basement is intimate, the ground floor, light, and the top floor, elegant. Good value lunch and early evening menus; more luxurious, modern dishes on the à la carte.

XX **Saddle Room** – Shelbourne Hotel
27 St Stephen's Grn. ✉ D2 – ✆ (01) 663 45 00 – www.theshelbourne.ie
Rest – Menu €22 (weekday lunch)/60 – Carte €34/103 **Plan 6** JZ**c**
Renowned restaurant with a history as long as that of the hotel in which it stands. The warm, inviting room features intimate gold booths and a crustacea counter. The menu offers classic dishes and grills; West Cork beef is a speciality.

XX **Pearl Brasserie**
20 Merrion St Upper ✉ D2 – ✆ (01) 661 35 72 – www.pearl-brasserie.com – Closed 25 December and Sunday **Plan 6** KZ**n**
Rest – Menu €22 (weekdays)/43 – Carte €33/56
Formal basement restaurant with a small bar-lounge and two surprisingly airy dining rooms; sit in a stylish booth in one of the old coal bunkers. Choose from modern menus of elaborate, stylishly presented dishes and a simpler market menu.

XX **Fade St. Social-Restaurant** N
4-6 Fade St ✉ D2 – ✆ (01) 604 00 66 – www.fadestsocial.com – Closed 25-26 December and Good Friday **Plan 6** JY**u**
Rest – Menu €25/50 – Carte €25/55
Have cocktails on the terrace then head for the big, modern brasserie with its raised open kitchen. Dishes use Irish ingredients but have a Mediterranean feel; they specialise in sharing dishes and large cuts of meat such as chateaubriand.

XX **Cliff Townhouse** with rm

22 St Stephen's Grn ✉ D2 – ✆ (01) 638 39 39 – www.theclifftownhouse.com – Closed 25-27 December and 1 January **Plan 6** JZ**s**

9 rm – € 110/200 € 130/220

Rest – *(booking advisable)* Menu € 25 (weekdays)/65 – Carte € 27/73

Impressive Georgian townhouse overlooking the green. Large dining room with blue leather seating and a marble-topped oyster counter. Seafood-orientated menus offer plenty of choice, from fish and chips to seafood platters or market specials. Bedrooms display contemporary colour schemes and good comforts.

XX **Pichet**

14-15 Trinity St ✉ D2 – ✆ (01) 677 10 60 – www.pichetrestaurant.ie – Closed 25-26 December and Sunday except before bank holidays **Plan 6** JY**g**

Rest – *(booking essential)* Menu € 25 (lunch and early dinner) – Carte € 36/54

Popular brasserie with an open-plan kitchen, an enclosed terrace and a buzzy atmosphere; run by a friendly team. Neat, flavoursome, modern European cooking. Wines are available by the glass or in a 500ml 'pichet'. The front café-cum-bar offers light snacks and cocktails, and they open for breakfast too.

XX **Brasserie Le Pont**

25 Fitzwilliam Pl ✉ D2 – ✆ (01) 669 4600 – www.brasserielepont.ie – Closed 26 December- 1 January , Saturday lunch and Monday dinner **Plan 3** EU**x**

Rest – *(bookings advisable at dinner)* Menu € 26 (lunch)/45 – Carte € 28/52

In the basement of a Georgian townhouse; enjoy lunch at the counter or grab one of the booths for more privacy. Gallic cooking has a classical base but is presented in a light, modern manner. Resident jazz band plays Friday and Saturday.

XX **Dax**

23 Pembroke St Upper ✉ D2 – ✆ (01) 676 14 94 – www.dax.ie – Closed Easter, 10 days Christmas, Saturday lunch, Sunday and Monday **Plan 6** KZ**c**

Rest – *(booking essential)* Menu € 24 (weekday lunch)/35 – Carte € 38/59

Simple, rustic restaurant, well-hidden in the old cellar of a Georgian terraced house near Fitzwilliam Square. Classical Gallic-inspired menus include a seven course 'surprise' selection; a few more modern twists are evident at dinner.

XX **Dobbin's**

15 Stephen's Ln , (via Stephen's Pl off Lower Mount St) ✉ D2 – ✆ (01) 661 95 36 – www.dobbins.ie – Closed 24 December-2 January, Saturday lunch, Sunday dinner, Mondays except December and bank holidays **Plan 3** EU**s**

Rest – *(booking essential)* Menu € 25/35 – Carte € 37/54

Hidden away in a back alley. A small bar leads through to a long, narrow room with cosy leather booths, which opens into a spacious conservatory with a terrace. Good value lunch and early evening menus; cooking is in the classical vein.

XX **Peploe's**

16 St Stephen's Grn. ✉ D2 – ✆ (01) 676 31 44 – www.peploes.com – Closed 25-26 December, Good Friday and lunch bank holidays **Plan 6** JZ**e**

Rest – *(booking essential)* Menu € 25 (dinner)/50 – Carte € 34/55

Atmospheric cellar restaurant – formerly a bank vault – named after the artist. Comfy room with a warm, clubby feel and a large mural depicting the owner. The well-drilled team present Mediterranean dishes and an old world wine list.

XX **Town**

21 Kildare St ✉ D2 – ✆ (01) 662 4800 – www.townbarandgrill.com – Closed Good Friday, 25-27 December, Sunday and bank holidays **Plan 6** JZ**n**

Rest – Menu € 22/49 – Carte € 37/55

Located in the old cellars of a famous city wine merchant, with a surprisingly spacious interior hung with modern Irish art. The experienced chef produces understated modern dishes with a classical base and a light, fresh style.

XX **The Dining Room** N – La Stampa Hotel

35-36 Dawson St ✉ D2 – ✆ (01) 677 44 44 – www.lastampa.ie – Closed 25-26 December **Plan 6** JZ**a**

Rest – Menu € 28 (weekdays)/65 – Carte € 35/52

One of the most impressive dining rooms in Dublin. A former ballroom of the La Stampa hotel, it has a high curved ceiling with a glass mosaic at its centre. The smart team deliver ambitious, interesting modern dishes to crisply laid tables.

REPUBLIC OF IRELAND

Locks Brasserie

1 Windsor Terr. ✉ *D8 – ✆ (01) 420 05 55 – www.locksbrasserie.com – Closed 25-28 December and bank holiday Mondays* **Plan 3 DUa**

Rest – *(dinner only and lunch Thursday-Sunday)* Menu € 25/43 – Carte € 37/58

Relaxed, neighbourhood restaurant on a quiet corner site. The pastel-hued room is full of natural light, with comfy banquette seating and a cocktail bar. The appealing menu features modern European dishes in some innovative combinations. Good value seasonal market menu. Professional, engaging service.

Pig's Ear

4 Nassau St ✉ *D2 – ✆ (01) 670 38 65 – www.thepigsear.ie – Closed first week January, Sunday and bank holidays* **Plan 6 KYa**

Rest – *(booking essential)* Menu € 22 (weekday lunch)/45 – Carte € 33/46

Well-established restaurant in a Georgian townhouse, overlooking Trinity College. Floors one and two are bustling dining areas with porcine-themed memorabilia and hearty bistro dishes; floor three is a Scandinavian-style private room with a chef's counter and a more ambitious 12 course tasting menu.

Fade St. Social-Gastro Bar

4-6 Fade St ✉ *D2 – ✆ (01) 6040 066 – www.fadestreetsocial.com* **Plan 6 JYu**

Rest – *(booking essential)* Menu € 25/50 – Carte € 20/54

Buzzy restaurant with an almost frenzied feel. It's all about a diverse range of original, interesting small plates, from a bacon and cabbage burger to a lobster hot dog. Eat at the kitchen counter or on leather cushioned 'saddle' benches.

La Maison

15 Castlemarket ✉ *D2 – ✆ (01) 672 7258 – www.lamaisonrestaurant.ie – Closed 24 December-5 January* **Plan 6 JYc**

Rest – Menu € 22 (lunch and early dinner) – Carte € 28/56

Sweet little French bistro with tables on the pavement and original posters advertising French products. The experienced, Breton-born chef-owner offers carefully prepared, seasonal Gallic classics, brought to the table by a personable team.

Rustic Stone

17 South Great George's St ✉ *D2 – ✆ (01) 707 9596 – www.rusticstone.ie – Closed 25-26 December and 1 January* **Plan 6 JYm**

Rest – Menu € 25 – Carte € 29/54

Split-level restaurant offering something a little different. Good quality ingredients are cooked simply to retain their natural flavours and menus focus on healthy and special dietary options; some meats and fish arrive on a sizzling stone.

Fallon & Byrne

11-17 Exchequer St ✉ *D2 – ✆ (01) 472 10 00 – www.fallonandbyrne.com – Closed Good Friday, 25-26 December* **Plan 6 JYf**

Rest – Menu € 25 (dinner)/40 – Carte € 33/55

A former telephone exchange: now a large, busy, New York style food emporium with a basement wine shop. French-inspired, bistro-style first floor restaurant with banquettes and mirrors; seasonal menu of brasserie classics.

L'Gueuleton

1 Fade St ✉ *D2 – ✆ (01) 675 37 08 – www.lgueuleton.com – Closed 25-27 December, 1 January and Good Friday* **Plan 6 JYd**

Rest – *(bookings not accepted)* Menu € 35 – Carte € 30/51

Rustic restaurant with beamed ceilings, Gallic furnishings, a shabby-chic bistro feel and a large pavement terrace. Flavoursome cooking features good value, French country classics which rely on local, seasonal produce. Service is friendly.

Camden Kitchen

3a Camden Mkt, Grantham St ✉ *D8 – ✆ (01) 476 01 25 – www.camdenkitchen.ie – Closed 24-26 December, Sunday and Monday* **Plan 6 JZx**

Rest – Menu € 19 (lunch)/24 – Carte € 27/46

Simple, modern, neighbourhood bistro set over two floors; watch the owner cooking in the open kitchen. Tasty dishes use good quality Irish ingredients prepared in classic combinations. Relaxed, friendly service from a young team.

Saba

26-28 Clarendon St ✉ D2 – ✆ (01) 679 2000 – www.sabadublin.com – Closed Good Friday and 25-26 December **Plan 6 JYk**

Rest – Menu € 14 (weekday lunch)/35 – Carte € 21/44

Trendy, buzzy Thai restaurant and cocktail bar. Simple, stylish rooms with refectory tables, banquettes and amusing photos. Fresh, visual, authentic cooking from an all-Thai team, with a few Vietnamese dishes and some fusion cooking too.

Port House

64a South William St ✉ D2 – ✆ (01) 677 0298 – www.porthouse.ie – Closed 25-26 December **Plan 6 JYe**

Rest – *(bookings not accepted)* Menu € 10

Characterful Spanish tapas bar serving a vast array of authentic, flavoursome dishes. The rustic candlelit interior features exposed bricks, a semi-vaulted ceiling and tightly packed tables. The tasty meats, cheeses and olives are imported.

at Ballsbridge

Four Seasons

rest,

Simmonscourt Rd. ✉ D4 – ✆ (01) 665 4000 – www.fourseasons.com/dublin

196 rm – † € 185/435 †† € 185/435, ☕ €20 – 40 suites **Plan 4 FUe**

Rest – Carte € 21/66 **s**

Imposing hotel on the edge of the RDS arena. Elegant guest areas, state-of-the-art meeting rooms and impressive ballrooms boast ornate décor, antiques and Irish art. Spacious, classical bedrooms have marble bathrooms and plenty of extras. A wide-ranging menu is served in the lounge and the Reading Room.

Dylan

rm, rest,

Eastmoreland Pl ✉ D4 – ✆ (01) 660 30 00 – www.dylan.ie – Closed 24-26 December **Plan 3 EUa**

44 rm – † € 189/395 †† € 189/395, ☕ €21

Rest – Menu € 24/40 – Carte € 32/56

Victorian nurses home with a sympathetically styled extension, set on a quiet side road; its funky, boutique interior makes vibrant use of colour. Tasteful, individually decorated bedrooms offer a host of extras; those in the original building are more spacious. Warm, stylish restaurant, with a zinc-topped bar and summer terrace, serves modern Irish dishes.

Herbert Park

rest, rest,

✉ D4 – ✆ (01) 667 2200 – www.herbertparkhotel.ie **Plan 4 FUm**

153 rm – † € 99/250 †† € 109/295, ☕ €20 – 2 suites

Rest ***The Pavilion*** – Menu € 29

Striking modern building with a stark white, open plan, marble-floored lobby displaying eye-catching art. Comfortable bedrooms with plenty of natural light; choose an executive room for more luxury. Chic terrace lounge and bar. The Pavilion restaurant serves classic dishes and has park views.

Schoolhouse

2-8 Northumberland Rd ✉ D4 – ✆ (01) 667 5014 – www.schoolhousehotel.com – Closed 24-26 December **Plan 3 EUe**

31 rm ☕ – † € 99/269 †† € 109/279

Rest – Menu € 23 (dinner) – Carte € 18/42

Dating back to 1861 and formerly the St Stephens Parochial School. Spacious, well-kept bedrooms – most in the extension – boast William Morris designed fabrics and locally built Mackintosh-style furniture; some have half-tester beds. Busy bar with vaulted ceiling; formal restaurant serves classic dishes.

Ariel House without rest

50-54 Lansdowne Rd ✉ D4 – ✆ (01) 668 5512 – www.ariel-house.net – Closed 22-28 December **Plan 4 FUn**

37 rm ☕ – † € 69/199 †† € 79/270

Close to the Aviva Stadium and a DART station; a personally run Victorian townhouse with comfy, traditional guest areas and antique furnishings. Warmly decorated bedrooms have modern facilities and smart bathrooms; some feature four-posters.

REPUBLIC OF IRELAND

Aberdeen Lodge without rest

53-55 Park Ave. ✉ *D4 – ☎ (01) 283 8155 – www.halpinsprivatehotels.com*

16 rm ☕ – 🚹 € 90/109 🚹🚹 € 129/169 **Plan 4** GV**e**

Two Edwardian townhouses knocked through into a hotel; in a smart suburban street, minutes' from the sea and a DART Station. Comfy lounge, warm, homely atmosphere and classically furnished, well-equipped bedrooms – some with garden views.

Pembroke Townhouse without rest

88 Pembroke Rd ✉ *D4 – ☎ (01) 66 00 277 – www.pembroketownhouse.ie – Closed 2 weeks Christmas-New Year* **Plan 4** FU**d**

48 rm – 🚹 € 99/299 🚹🚹 € 99/320, ☕ €15

Friendly, traditionally styled hotel set in 3 Georgian houses. Small lounge with honesty bar and pantry. Sunny breakfast room offering homemade bread, cakes and biscuits. Variously sized, neutrally hued bedrooms; go for a duplex room.

Asador Ⓝ

1 Victoria House, Haddington Rd ✉ *D4 – ☎ (01) 254 5353 – www.asador.ie – Closed Monday* **Plan 3** EU**x**

Rest – Carte € 30/52

Themed around the chargrill (or 'asador'); watch the chefs in the open-plan kitchen. Fresh, tasty cooking has South American and Spanish influences. On your own? Try the counter. In a group? Go for one of the curvaceous booths.

Chop House

2 Shelbourne Rd ✉ *D4 – ☎ (01) 660 23 90 – www.thechophouse.ie*

Rest – Carte € 28/48 **Plan 4** FU**x**

Imposing pub close to the stadium, with a small side terrace, a dark bar and a bright, airy conservatory. The relaxed lunchtime menu is followed by more ambitious dishes in the evening, when the kitchen really comes into its own.

REPUBLIC OF IRELAND

at Donnybrook

Mulberry Garden

Mulberry Ln, off Donnybrook Rd ✉ *D4 – ☎ (01) 269 3300 – www.mulberrygarden.ie – Closed Sunday-Wednesday* **Plan 4** FV**a**

Rest – *(dinner only and Sunday lunch in summer) (booking essential)* Menu € 40/60

Delightful restaurant hidden away in the city suburbs; its interesting L-shaped dining room set around a small courtyard terrace. Choice of two dishes per course on the weekly menu; original modern cooking relies on tasty local produce.

at Rathmines

Zen

89 Upper Rathmines Rd ✉ *D6 – ☎ (01) 497 94 28 – www.zenrestaurant.ie – Closed 25-27 December* **Plan 3** DV**t**

Rest – *(dinner only and Friday lunch)* Menu € 15/30 – Carte € 23/31

Long-standing, family-run restaurant, unusually set in an old church hall – at the centre of the plush, elegant interior is a huge sun embellished with gold leaf. Imaginative Chinese cooking centres around Cantonese and spicy Sichuan cuisine.

at Dublin Airport North : 10.5 km by N 1 - BS - and M 1 – ✉ Dublin

Carlton H. Dublin Airport rest,

Old Airport Rd, Cloughran, South : 2 km on R 132 – ☎ (01) 866 7500 – www.carlton.ie/dublinairport – Closed 24-26 December

100 rm – 🚹 € 69/195 🚹🚹 € 79/250, ☕ €14 – 1 suite

Rest *Kittyhawks* – *(carvery lunch)* Menu € 20 (dinner)/59 – Carte € 22/52

Modern, purpose-built, business hotel with a spacious marbled reception and comfy guest areas. Up-to-date bedrooms have good facilities and smart bathrooms. Some rooms overlook the airfield; some have balconies. Informal all-day brasserie offers lunchtime carvery and a wide-ranging evening menu.

🏨 Bewleys
Baskin Ln, East : 4 km on N 32 – ℰ *(01) 871 1000* – www.bewleyshotels.com
469 rm – ♦ €69/169, ♦♦ €69/169, ⌾ €10
Rest *The Brasserie* – *(carvery lunch)* Menu €25 – Carte €29/50
Eight-floor hotel with good conference facilities, plenty of parking and a free courtesy bus to and from the airport. Spacious, up-to-date bedrooms. All-day dining in the comfortable lobby bar and lounge. The Brasserie offers a buffet and carvery lunch, with a wide-ranging evening à la carte.

at Clontarf Northeast : 5.5 km by R 105 – ✉ Dublin

🏰 Clontarf Castle
Castle Ave. ✉ D3 – ℰ *(01) 833 2321* – www.clontarfcastle.ie **Plan 2 CSa**
111 rm ⌾ – ♦ €109/450, ♦♦ €119/450
Rest *Fahrenheit Grill* – *(dinner only)* Menu €25/45 – Carte €29/43
A historic castle, dating back to 1172, with modern extensions; well-located in a quiet residential area close to the city. Contemporary bedrooms are decorated with bold, warm colours. Fahrenheit offers grilled local meats and seafood in a medieval ambience.

✗✗ Downstairs
Hollybrook Park ✉ D3 – ℰ *(01) 833 8883* – www.downstairs.ie – *Closed 25-26 December and Good Friday* **Plan 2 CSx**
Rest – *(dinner only and Sunday lunch)* Menu €23 (lunch)/30 – Carte €32/44
Basement restaurant located beneath a bar, in a lovely neighbourhood close to the sea. It's spacious and contemporary in style, with an attractive tiled bar and a display of wooden wine cases. Menus offer an eclectic mix of dishes and the refined, balanced cooking shows respect for natural flavours.

at Dundrum Southeast : 8 km by N 11 - CT – ✉ Dublin

✗✗ Ananda
Sandyford Rd, Dundrum town centre ✉ D14 – ℰ *(01) 296 00 99*
– www.anandarestaurant.ie – *Closed 25-26 December*
Rest – *(dinner only and lunch Friday-Sunday)* Menu €17 (lunch)/50
– Carte €30/58
Meaning 'bliss' in ancient Sanskrit, and located in a shopping mall, is this stylish restaurant with a smart cocktail bar/lounge and attractive fretwork. Accomplished, original, modern Indian cooking. Attentive, professional service.

✗✗ First Floor at Harvey Nichols
Sandyford Rd, Dundrum Town Centre ✉ D16 – ℰ *(01) 291 0488*
– www.harveynichols.com – *Closed 25 December, dinner Saturday, Sunday and Monday*
Rest – Menu €25 (lunch and early dinner) – Carte €25/45
Striking glass and steel building housing a sexy cocktail bar dressed in red and pink and an airy dining area with blue leather banquettes and a vast feature light. Tasty, modern, brasserie-style cooking and plenty of wines by the glass.

Fancy a last minute break?
Check hotel websites to take advantage of price promotions.

at Sandyford Southeast : 12 km by N 11 and R 112 off R 133 - CT – ✉ Dublin

🏨 Beacon
Beacon Court, Sandyford Business Region ✉ D18 – ℰ *(01) 291 5000*
– www.thebeacon.com – *Closed 24-26 December*
88 rm – ♦ €80/250, ♦♦ €99/250, ⌾ €15 – 1 suite
Rest *My Thai* – Carte €25/38 **s**
Ultra-stylish hotel in a modern glass building; its stunning entrance lobby features mirrored walls and a bed for sitting on. Stark white bedrooms and luxurious, glass-walled bathrooms. Low-key meeting rooms. Modish Crystal bar. Funky, relaxed My Thai serves authentic Asian dishes.

XX **China Sichuan**

The Forum, Ballymoss Rd. ✉ *D18 – ✆ (01) 293 5100 – www.china-sichuan.ie – Closed 25-31 December, Good Friday, lunch Saturday and bank holidays*

Rest – Menu €15 (weekday lunch)/45 – Carte €29/54

Established in 1979 and now run by the third generation of the family. Smart, modern interior matched by creative menus, where Irish produce is used in tasty Chinese dishes: largely Cantonese classics with some Sichuan specialities.

at Foxrock **Southeast : 13 km by N 11 - CT – ✉ Dublin**

XX **Bistro One**

3 Brighton Rd ✉ *D18 – ✆ (01) 289 7711 – www.bistro-one.ie – Closed 25 December-3 January, Sunday and Monday*

Rest – *(booking essential)* Menu €25 (weekdays) – Carte €29/49

Long-standing neighbourhood bistro above a parade of shops; run by a father-daughter team and a real hit with the locals. Good value daily menus – dishes range from traditional Irish to Italian. They produce their own Tuscan olive oil.

at Rathgar **South : 3.75 km by N 81**

X **Bijou**

46 Highfield Rd ✉ *D6 – ✆ (01) 496 1518 – www.bijourathgar.ie – Closed 25-26 December* **Plan 3** DV**x**

Rest – Carte €31/46

Friendly, two-floored restaurant with a heated terrace and a clubby feel; the experienced owners also run the nearby deli. Local ingredients feature in accomplished, full-flavoured, classically based dishes with modern touches.

DUBLIN AIRPORT = Aerfort Bhaile Átha Cliath – Fingal – 712 N7 – see Dublin

DUNBOYNE (Dún Búinne) – Meath – 712 M7 – pop. 6 959 37 D3

Dublin 17 km – Drogheda 45 km – Newbridge 54 km

Dunboyne Castle

– ✆ (01) 801 35 00 – www.dunboynecastlehotel.com

145 rm – †€85/240 ††€105/360 – 4 suites

Rest ***Ivy Brasserie*** – *(dinner only and Sunday lunch)* Menu €20 (dinner)/25 – Carte €30/48

Georgian house with vast, modern extensions and formal gardens, set in 20 acres. Large, relaxing spa has 18 treatment rooms and uses organic Irish seaweed products. Spacious bedrooms boast good mod cons; some have balconies. Informal dining in Ivy Brasserie, which offers classically based Irish dishes.

DUNCANNON (Dún Canann) – Wexford – 712 L11 – pop. 328 39 D2

Ireland

Dublin 167 km – New Ross 26 km – Waterford 48 km

Fort★ **AC**

Dunbrody Abbey★ **AC**, N : 9 km by R 733 – Kilmokea Gardens★ **AC**, N : 11 km by R 733 – Tintern Abbey★ **AC**, E : 8 km by R 737 and R 733. Kennedy Arboretum★ **AC**, N : 21 km by R 733

XX **Aldridge Lodge** with rm

South : 2 km on Hook Head rd – ✆ (051) 389 116 – www.aldridgelodge.com – Closed 3 weeks January and 24-25 December

3 rm – †€45 ††€90

Rest – *(closed Monday and Tuesday) (dinner only and Sunday lunch) (booking essential)* Menu €28/39 **s**

New-build house run by cheery owners. The constantly evolving menu offers tasty homemade bread and veg from the kitchen garden. The focus is good value fish and shellfish – the owner's father is a local fisherman – with some Asian and fusion influences. Simply furnished bedrooms come with hot water bottles and home-baked cookies.

DUNDALK (Dún Dealgan) – Louth – 712 M5/6 – pop. 31 149 37 D2

Ireland

Dublin 82 km – Drogheda 35 km

Killinbeg, Killin Park, (042) 9 33 93 03

Dún a' Rí Forest Park★, W : 34 km by R 178 and R 179 – Proleek Dolmen★, N : 8 km by N 1 R 173

Crowne Plaza

Green Park, South : 2.75 km by R 132 – (042) 939 49 00 – www.cpdundalk.ie – Closed 24-25 December

129 rm – € 84/149 € 84/149 – 1 suite

Rest *Farenheit Grill* – *(closed Sunday-Wednesday) (bar lunch Monday-Saturday)* Menu € 25 **s** – Carte € 22/46 **s**

Modern, 14-storey hotel tower block, close to the business park, with a stylish ground floor bar/lounge and good conference facilities. Uniform bedrooms boast a high level of facilities and countryside views; ask for one higher up. 13th floor restaurant offers a seasonal brasserie menu and a 360° vista.

Rosemount without rest

Dublin Rd, South : 2.5 km on R 132 – (042) 933 58 78 – www.rosemountireland.com – Closed 22-27 December

10 rm – € 45/50 € 70/75

Attractive guesthouse fronted by a delightful flower-filled garden and run by a welcoming couple. Laura Ashley and Brown Thomas fabrics and furnishings feature throughout. Snug, individually styled and spotlessly kept bedrooms. Tea and cake on arrival; freshly cooked breakfasts in the morning.

Left Bank

43-44 Park St – (042) 933 88 51 – www.leftbankdundalk.com – Closed 25-26 December, Monday and Tuesday lunch

Rest – Menu € 14 (dinner)/35 – Carte € 30/44

Well-run bistro in a busy market town. Large bar and raised dining room with tightly packed tables and booth seating; chiller cabinet offers homemade pastries and cakes to take home. All-purpose menus offer carefully prepared, hearty dishes.

at Jenkinstown Northeast : 9 km by N 52 on R 173

Fitzpatricks

Rockmarshall, Southeast : 1 km – (042) 937 61 93 – www.fitzpatricks-restaurant.com – Closed 25 December, Good Friday and Monday November-March except bank holidays

Rest – Menu € 28 (weekdays) – Carte € 26/47

Hugely characterful pub with beautiful flower displays and intriguing memorabilia. Extensive menu of hearty, flavoursome dishes and plenty of classics; local seafood and steaks a speciality.

DUNDRUM = Dún Droma – Dún Laoghaire-Rathdown – 712 N8 – see Dublin

DUNFANAGHY (Dún Fionnachaidh) – Donegal – 712 I2 – pop. 312 37 C1

– Letterkenny Ireland

Dublin 277 km – Donegal 87 km – Londonderry 69 km

Dunfanaghy, Letterkenny, (074) 913 63 35

Horn Head Scenic Route★, N : 4 km. Doe Castle★, SE : 11.25 km by N 56 – The Rosses★, SW : 40.25 km by N 56 and R 259

Mill with rm

rest,

Southwest : 0.75 km on N 56 – (074) 913 69 85 – www.themillrestaurant.com – Mid March-December

6 rm – € 60 € 100/120

Rest – *(closed Monday) (dinner only)* Menu € 40

Converted flax mill on the waterside, with lovely garden edged by reeds and great view of Mount Muckish. Homely inner with conservatory lounge and knick-knacks on display throughout. Antique-furnished dining room has a classical Georgian feel. Traditional menus showcase seasonal ingredients and fish features highly. Cosy, welcoming bedrooms come in individual designs.

DUNGARVAN (Dún Garbhán) – **Waterford** – **712** J11 – **pop. 7 991** 39 C3
Ireland

Dublin 190 km – Cork 71 km – Waterford 48 km

Knocknagrannagh, ✆ (058) 4 16 05

Gold Coast, Ballinacourty, ✆ (058) 4 22 49

East Bank (Augustinian priory, ≤★)

Ringville (≤★), S : 13 km by N 25 and R 674 – Helvick Head★ (≤★), SE : 13 km by N 25 and R 674

XX **Tannery** with rm — AC rest,

10 Quay St, via Parnell St – ✆ (058) 45 420 – www.tannery.ie – Closed 3 weeks January, 25-26 December and Good Friday

14 rm – † € 50/65 †† € 90/110

Rest – *(dinner only and lunch Friday and Sunday)* Menu € 30/65 – Carte € 32/49

Characterful 19C tannery with a high ceiling, rustic girders and modern décor. Menus are concise and offer dishes ranging from the simple to the more imaginative (maybe crab crème brûlée). They also run a renowned cookery school. Stylish bedrooms come in contemporary, New England and French farmhouse styles.

DUNKINEELY (Dún Cionnaola) – **Donegal** – **712** G4 – **pop. 375** 37 C1

Dublin 156 km – Lifford 42 km – Sligo 53 km – Ballybofey 28 km

XX **Castle Murray House** with rm — P

St John's Point, Southwest : 1.5 km by N 56 on St John's Point rd – ✆ (074) 973 70 22 – www.castlemurray.com – Closed January-mid February, 24-26 December, and Monday-Tuesday in winter

10 rm – † € 60/75 †† € 110/140

Rest – *(dinner only and Sunday lunch light lunch in summer)* Menu € 35 (dinner)/60

Established restaurant in a delightful coastal location, offering great castle, sea and sunset views. Start in the snug bar with its seafaring memorabilia then move to the spacious dining room, large conservatory or vast decked terrace. The classical menu features mussels and oysters from the bay. Stylish bedrooms have gilt mirrors, plush fabrics and very comfy beds.

DUN LAOGHAIRE (Dún Laoghaire) – **Dún Laoghaire-Rathdown** – **712** N8 – **pop. 23 857** Ireland 39 D1

Dublin 12 km – Belfast 176 km – Cork 265 km – Lisburn 164 km

to Holyhead (Stena Line) 4-5 daily (1 h 40 mn)

Dun Laoghaire, Eglinton Park, ✆ (01) 280 39 16

≤★★ of Killiney Bay from coast road south of Sorrento Point

XX **Rasam**

18-19 Glasthule Rd, 1st Floor (above Eagle House pub) – ✆ (01) 230 0600 – www.rasam.ie – Closed 25-26 December and Good Friday **e**

Rest – *(dinner only)* Menu € 20 (weekday dinner)/50 – Carte € 30/52

The perfume of rose leaves greets you, as you head up to the plush lounge and contemporary restaurant. Fresh, authentic Indian dishes come in original combinations and are cooked from scratch; they even dry roast and blend their own spices.

X **Cavistons** — AC

58-59 Glasthule Rd – ✆ (01) 280 9245 – www.cavistons.com – Closed Sunday and Monday **a**

Rest – *(lunch only and dinner Friday and Saturday) (booking essential)* Menu € 19 – Carte € 28/47

A landmark in the town: a fresh fish shop, a well-stocked deli and a cosy bistro in one. Simple décor, with ten wooden tables and a mermaid mural. Fresh, carefully cooked fish and seafood. Swift, friendly service.

DUN LAOGHAIRE

REPUBLIC OF IRELAND

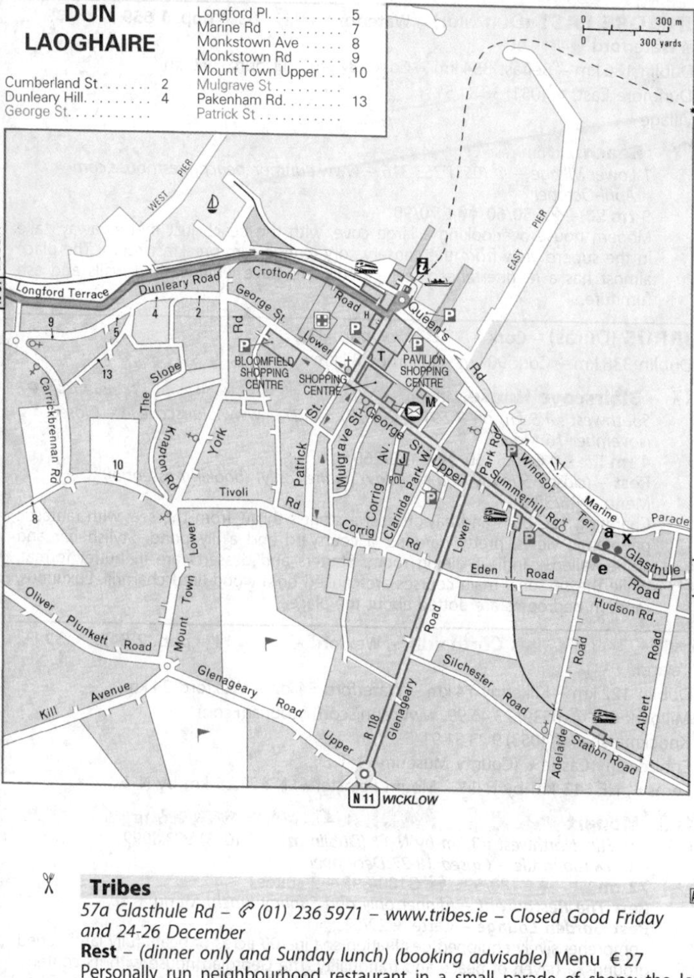

✗ **Tribes** 🄰🄲

57a Glasthule Rd – ℰ (01) 236 5971 – www.tribes.ie – Closed Good Friday and 24-26 December

x

Rest – *(dinner only and Sunday lunch) (booking advisable)* Menu € 27
Personally run neighbourhood restaurant in a small parade of shops; the long narrow room is filled with colourful art and adornments. Good value menus offer plenty of choice and an eclectic range of influences, along with a modern touch.

DUNLAVIN (Dún Luáin) – Wicklow – 712 L8 – pop. 830 39 D2

▶ Dublin 50 km – Kilkenny 71 km – Wexford 98 km

🄸🄸 Rathsallagh, ℰ (045) 40 33 16

🄷🄷 **Rathsallagh House** ⚭ ⪕ 🚗 🜨 ⤳ ✗ 🄵🄰 ⅃ rest. 🛜 🚶 🄿

Southwest : 3.25 km on Grangecon rd – ℰ (045) 403 112 – www.rathsallagh.com – Closed mid week November-March

29 rm ⊻ – 🜨 € 145/200 🜨🜨 € 145/250 – 1 suite

Rest – *(dinner only and Sunday lunch) (bookings essential for non-residents)* Carte € 29/49

Collection of converted 18C stables and farm buildings in a peaceful, rural location. Extensive grounds include a golf course and a working farm to the rear. Characterful, open-fired lounges and cottagey bar; spacious country house bedrooms with good facilities. Large formal restaurant serves classic dishes.

DUNMORE EAST (Dún Mór) – Waterford – **712** L11 – pop. **1 559**　　39 C2
– ✉ Waterford ▯ Ireland

▶ Dublin 186 km – Belfast 354 km – Cork 137 km – Lisburn 342 km

▦ Dunmore East, ✆ (051) 38 31 51

◉ Village★

⌂　**Beach** without rest　　≤ & ⅍ 🛜 **P**
1 Lower Village – ✆ (051) 383 316 – www.dunmorebeachguesthouse.com
– April-October
9 rm ☕ – ♦ € 50/60 ♦♦ € 70/90
Modern house overlooking a large cove, with the beach just metres away; take
in the superb view from the conservatory lounge-cum-breakfast room. The place
almost has a Mediterranean feel – bedrooms have whitewashed walls and ash
furniture.

DURRUS (Dúras) – Cork – **712** D13 – pop. **334**　　38 A3

▶ Dublin 338 km – Cork 90 km – Killarney 85 km

✗✗　**Blairscove House** with rm　　⅍ ≤ 🛋 🛜 **P**
Southwest : 1.5 km on R 591 – ✆ (027) 61 127 – www.blairscove.ie – Closed
November-16 March
4 rm ☕ – ♦ € 105/160 ♦♦ € 150/260
Rest – (closed Sunday and Monday) (dinner only) (booking essential)
Menu € 46/58 **s**
Charming 18C barn and hayloft, just a stone's throw from the sea, with fantastic
panoramic views, pretty gardens, a courtyard and a lily pond. Stylish bar and
stone-walled, candlelit dining room. Starters and desserts are in buffet format,
while the seasonal main courses are cooked on a wood-fired chargrill. Luxurious,
modern bedrooms are dotted about the place.

ENNISCORTHY (Inis Córthaidh) – Wexford – **712** M10 – pop. **2 842**　　39 D2
▯ Ireland

▶ Dublin 122 km – Kilkenny 74 km – Waterford 54 km – Wexford 24 km

🄳 Millpark Rd, ✆ (0539) 23 46 99, www.enniscorthytourism.com

▦ Knockmarshal, ✆ (053) 9 23 31 91

◉ Enniscorthy Castle★ (County Museum★)

◙ Ferns★, NE : 13 km by N 11 – Mount Leinster★, N : 27.25 km by N 11

🏨　**Monart**　　⅍ 🛋 🕭 🍴 🔲 ⊛ 🕭 Ƚ₆ 🛗 & rm, 🅇 rest, ⅍ **P**
The Still, Northwest : 3 km by N 11 (Dublin rd) – ✆ (053) 923 8999
– www.monart.ie – Closed 18-27 December
72 rm ☕ – ♦ € 180/595 ♦♦ € 180/895 – 2 suites
Rest *The Restaurant* – (dinner only and Sunday lunch) Menu € 40
Rest *Garden Lounge* – Carte € 29/51
Comprehensively equipped destination spa in 100 acres of beautifully landscaped
grounds; a haven of peace and tranquillity. The Georgian house with its contemporary glass extension houses spacious, stylish bedrooms with a terrace or balcony. The Restaurant serves light, modern dishes; the minimalistic Garden Lounge
offers global dishes in a more informal environment.

⌂　**Ballinkeele House**　　⅍ ≤ 🛋 🕭 ⅍ 🛜 **P**
Ballymurn, Southeast : 10 km by R 744 and Vinegar Hill rd on Curracloe rd
– ✆ (053) 913 81 05 – www.ballinkeele.ie – Closed November-February
5 rm ☕ – ♦ € 95/105 ♦♦ € 150/170　　**Rest** – Menu € 30 **s**
Impressive Georgian house in 300 acres; family-run with traditional Irish hospitality. Grand, antique-filled sitting rooms. Bedrooms vary from cosy twins to luxurious doubles with four-posters. Four course, communal dinners feature produce
from the garden. Homemade breads and fruit compotes for breakfast.

ENNISKERRY (Áth an Sceire) – Wicklow – **712** N8 – pop. **1 811**　　39 D1
▯ Ireland

▶ Dublin 24 km – Belfast 204 km – Cork 273 km – Lisburn 192 km

▦ Powerscourt, Powerscourt Estate, ✆ (01) 204 60 33

◉ Powerscourt★★ **AC** (Waterfall★★, **AC**)

Ritz Carlton
West : 1.5 km by Powerscourt rd – ✆ (01) 274 88 88 – www.ritzcarlton.com
200 rm – † € 190/290 †† € 220/350, ☕ €29 – 93 suites – †† € 290/500
Rest *Gordon Ramsay at Powerscourt* – see restaurant listing
Rest *Sugar Loaf lounge* – Carte € 30/52
Rest *McGills* – Carte € 32/42
Impressive curved building overlooking Sugar Loaf Mountain. Stylish guest areas, state-of-the-art conference facilities and superb spa. Luxurious bedrooms with marble bathrooms; some have balconies. Activities include archery and falconry. Luxurious lounge-bar with a view offers a concise menu of classic dishes. McGills is a traditional Irish pub with a menu to match.

Ferndale N without rest
– ✆ (01) 286 35 18 – www.ferndalehouse.com – Closed 24-25, 31 December and 1 January
4 rm ☕ – † € 50 †† € 80
Homely guesthouse filled with family artefacts; located in the centre of the village, close to Powerscourt House and Gardens. The simple bedrooms are fairly priced. The splendid 1 acre garden has lots of seating and a large water feature.

Gordon Ramsay at Powerscourt – Ritz Carlton Hotel
West : 1.5 km by Powerscourt rd – ✆ (01) 274 93 77 – www.ritzcarlton.com – Closed Monday
Rest – *(dinner only and lunch Saturday-Sunday)* Menu € 33 – Carte € 49/61
Elegant yet relaxed restaurant set in an impressive estate hotel; it boasts superb mountain views, a kitchen chef's table and a beautiful terrace. Accomplished modern cooking in the Ramsay vein showcases the best of Irish ingredients.

FANORE – Clare – 712 E8 38 B1

Dublin 253 km – Inis 51 km – Galway 65 km – Limerick 92 km

Vasco
West : 1 km on R 477 – ✆ (065) 707 60 20 – www.vasco.ie – Mid March-October
Rest – Carte € 26/35
Remotely set restaurant opposite the seashore, with a minimalist interior and a glass-screened terrace. The keen owners collect the latest produce on their drive in; the daily menu ranges from sandwiches and cake to soup and light dishes.

FENNOR – Waterford – 712 K11 39 C2

Dublin 115 km – Waterford 12 km – Cork 75 km – Limerick 89 km

Copper Hen
Mother McHugh's Pub – ✆ (051) 330 300 – www.thecopperhen.ie – Closed 1 week January, 25-26 December, Monday-Wednesday and Sunday dinner
Rest – *(dinner only and Sunday lunch) (booking advisable)* Menu € 22/25
Simple, likeable little restaurant above a pub, with rustic décor and a brightly coloured fireplace; set on the coast road from Tramore to Dungarven. Keenly priced menus offer hearty, unfussy classics. The owners raise their own pigs.

FETHARD (Fiodh Ard) – South Tipperary – 712 I10 – pop. 1 541 39 C2

Ireland

Dublin 161 km – Cashel 16 km – Clonmel 13 km

Cashel★★★ : Rock of Cashel★★★ **AC** (Cormac's Chapel★★, Round Tower★), Museum★ **AC**, Cashel Palace Gardens★, GPA Bolton Library★ **AC**, NW : 15 km by R 692 – Clonmel★ : County Museum★ **AC**, St Mary's Church★, S : 13 km by R 689

Mobarnane House
North : 8 km. by Cashel rd on Ballinure rd – ✆ (052) 613 19 62 – www.mobarnanehouse.com – March-October
3 rm ☕ – † € 110/130 †† € 160/200 **Rest** – Menu € 55 **s**
Lovingly restored house with a Georgian façade; set in 15 acres of grounds complete with a small lake and walks. Classically styled interior with period furnishings; the best bedrooms also have small sitting rooms. Formal set dinners are served around a large mahogany table in the beautiful dining room.

REPUBLIC OF IRELAND

FOTA ISLAND (Oileán Fhóta) – Cork – 712 H12 38 B3

Dublin 263 km – Cork 17 km – Limerick 118 km – Waterford 110 km

Fota Island

– ✆ *(021) 488 37 00 – www.fotaisland.ie – Closed 25 December*
123 rm – € 138/237 € 153/252 – 8 suites
Rest *Fota* – *(bar lunch)* Carte € 21/54
A resort hotel set within Ireland's only wildlife park. Extensive business and leisure facilities include a golf course and a state-of-the-art spa. Bedrooms are spacious and well-appointed, and most have island views. The stylish restaurant offers modern takes on classical dishes.

FOXROCK = Carraig an tSionnaigh – Dún Laoghaire-Rathdown – 712 N7

– see Dublin

FURBOGH/FURBO (Na Forbacha) – Galway – 712 E8 – pop. 1 236 36 A3

Dublin 219 km – Belfast 333 km – Cork 209 km – Lisburn 321 km

Connemara Coast

– ✆ *(091) 592 108 – www.sinnotthotels.com – Closed 15-27 December*
141 rm – € 100/225 € 280/350 – 3 suites
Rest *The Gallery* – *(bar lunch)* Menu € 39 **s** – Carte € 27/51 **s**
Over the years this has been transformed from a small house into an extensive hotel. Colonial-style lobby; smart bedrooms feature locally made furniture and offer superb views over the bay and The Burren. Dine in the bar or restaurant looking down the gardens to the water's edge; the latter is adults only.

GALWAY (Gaillimh) – Galway – 712 E8 – pop. 75 529 Ireland 36 B3

Dublin 217 km – Limerick 103 km – Sligo 145 km

Carnmore Airport : ✆ (091) 755569, NE : 6.5 km

Discover Ireland Centre, Aras Failte, Forster St, ✆ (091) 53 77 00, www.discoverireland.ie

Galway, Salthill, Blackrock, ✆ (091) 52 20 33

City★★ – St Nicholas' Church★ BY - Roman Catholic Cathedral★ AY – Eyre Square : Bank of Ireland Building (sword and mace★) BY

NW : Lough Corrib★★. W : by boat, Aran Islands (Inishmore - Dun Aenghus★★★) BZ - Thoor Ballylee★, SE : 33.75 km by N 6 and N 18 D – Dunguaire Castle, Kinvarra★ **AC**, S : 25.75 km by N 6, N 18 and N 67 D – Aughnanure Castle★, NW : 25.75 km by N 59 - Oughterard★ (<★★), NW : 29 km by N 59 - Knockmoy Abbey★, NE : 30.5 km by N 17 and N 63 D – Coole Park (Autograph Tree★), SE : 33.75 km by N 6 and N 18 D - St Mary's Cathedral, Tuam★, NE : 33.75 km by N 17 D – Loughrea (St Brendan's Cathedral★), SE : 35.5 km by N 6 D - Turoe Stone★, SE : 35.5 km by N 6 and north by R 350

Plans on following pages

Radisson Blu H. & Spa

Lough Atalia Rd – ✆ *(091) 538 300 – www.radissonhotelgalway.com* **Da**
261 rm – € 115/400 € 135/400 – 2 suites
Rest *Marinas* – Menu € 22/35 – Carte € 27/45
Rest *Raw* – ✆ (091) 538 212 *(dinner only) (booking advisable)* Menu € 35 – Carte approx. € 30
Corporate hotel overlooking a lough, with a striking atrium and vast meeting facilities. Spacious, modern bedrooms; those on the 5th floor have balconies and share a small business lounge. The spa has a thermal suite and a unique salt cave. Marinas offers international dishes, with a 'Food Market Buffet' at lunch; Raw serves sushi and raw meats.

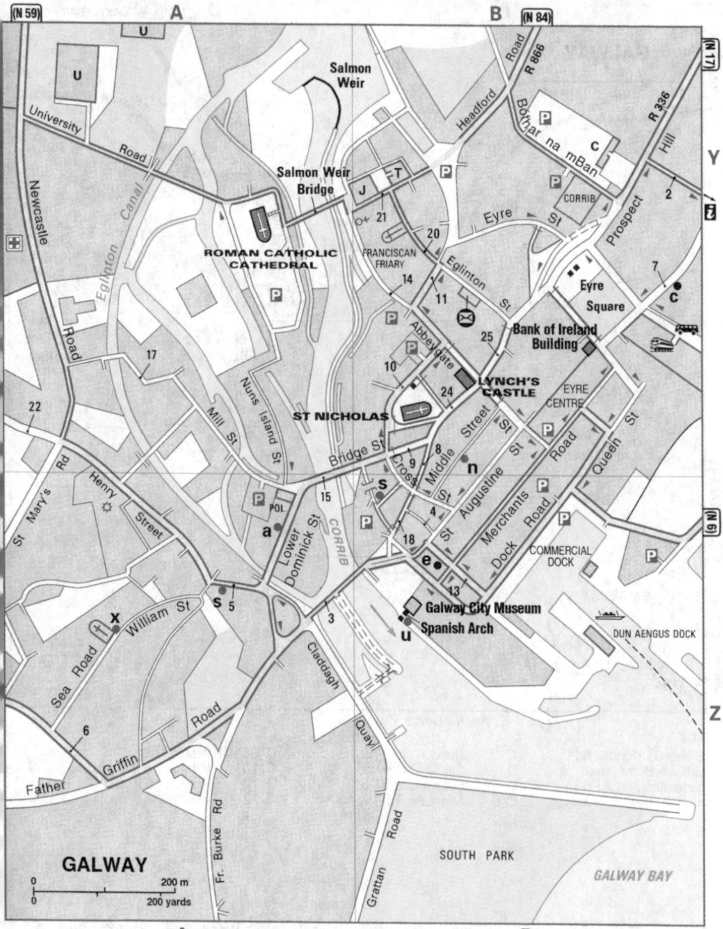

Bothar Ui Eithir	BY	2	Main Guard St	BY	9	Quay St	BZ	18
Claddagh Bridge	AZ	3	Market St	BY	10	St Francis St	BY	20
Corrib Shopping Centre	BY		Mary St	BY	11	St Vincent's Ave	BY	21
Courthouse St	BZ	4	Newton Smith	BY	14	Shantalla Rd	AY	22
Father Griffin Ave	AZ	6	New Dock St	BZ	13	Shop St	BY	24
Forster St	BY	7	O'Brien Bridge	AY	15	Upper Dominick St	AZ	5
High St	BY	8	Presentation St	AY	17	William St	BY	25

G

Wellpark, Dublin Rd – ✆ *(091) 865 200* – *www.theghotel.ie* – *Closed 23-26 December*

Dg

101 rm – † € 135/500 †† € 150/520 – 2 suites

Rest *Gigi's* – *(dinner only and Sunday lunch)* Menu € 25 (lunch) – Carte € 32/54

Boutique hotel featuring boldly coloured walls hung with flamboyant mirrors designed by Irish milliner Philip Treacy. Bright, spacious bedrooms have a more calming feel. The spa has a thermal suite and a relaxation room overlooking a walled bamboo garden. The colourful restaurant served modern Irish dishes.

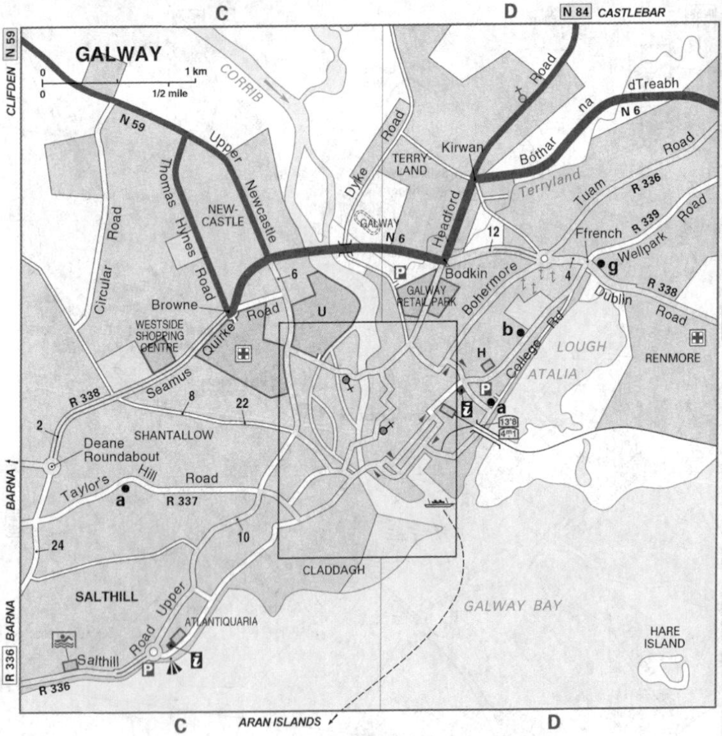

Bishop O'Donnell Rd .... C 2
Galway Retail Park .... D
Moneenageisha Rd .... D 4
Newcastle Rd Lower .... C 6
Rahoon Rd................ C 8
Salthill Rd Lower........... C 10
Sean Mulvoy Rd .... D 12
Shantalla Rd............... C 22
Threadneedle Rd........................ C 24
Westside Shopping Centre C

Clayton

Ballybrit, East : 4 km on N 6 – ✆ (091) 721 900 – www.clayton.ie – Closed 20-27 December

195 rm – € 89/149 € 99/279

Rest – *(dinner only)* Menu € 35 – Carte € 35/60

Stylish hotel on the edge of the city, close to the famous racecourse. Modern guest areas and smart white bedrooms with sleek dark furnishings; go for a spacious 4th floor executive with a country or city view. The bar doubles as a lunchtime carvery and the restaurant offers a simple, traditional menu.

Ardilaun

Taylor's Hill – ✆ (091) 521 433 – www.theardilaunhotel.ie – Closed 23-26 December

C**a**

125 rm – € 74/150 € 99/290 – 4 suites

Rest *Camilaun* – *(dinner only and Sunday lunch)* Menu € 40

Rest *Blazer's Bar and Bistro* – Menu € 28 – Carte € 18/36

Enlarged Georgian house with extensive leisure facilities, surrounded by 5 acres of colourful gardens. It's been family owned and run since 1962 and has a homely, traditional style. Bedrooms are spacious; ask for a newer room. Smart bar and restaurant with a sheltered terrace and classic seafood-based menus.

Park House

Forster St, Eyre Sq – ☎ (091) 564 924 – www.parkhousehotel.ie – Closed 24-26 December BY**c**

84 rm – † € 69/349 †† € 99/349

Rest – Menu € 33 (weekday dinner)/42 – Carte € 30/56

Popular grey-stone hotel in city centre. Marble reception and comfy seating areas. Boss Doyle's Bar is busy and spacious. Dark wood bedrooms with rich, soft fabrics. Strong international flavours define restaurant menus.

House

Lower Merchants Rd – ☎ (091) 538 900 – www.thehousehotel.ie – Closed 24 and 25 December BZ**e**

40 rm – † € 89/189 †† € 99/229 – 1 suite

Rest – *(bar lunch Monday-Saturday)* Menu € 25 (early dinner) – Carte € 22/39

Unassuming hotel with a surprisingly luxurious interior. Smart bedrooms are decorated with eye-catching Italian fabrics and feature quality linens. Service is professional yet friendly. Spacious guest areas include a laid-back lounge, and a bar and dining room serving modern day classics, coffee and cocktails.

Ardawn House without rest

College Rd. – ☎ (091) 568 833 – www.ardawnhouse.com – Closed 15-27 December D**b**

8 rm – † € 45/95 †† € 75/140

Located next to the stadium and the greyhound track, with the city just a stroll away. Good-sized bedrooms are clean and fresh, with modern fabrics. A small lounge leads to a breakfast room laid with silver-plated cutlery. Friendly owners.

Seafood Bar @Kirwan's

Kirwan's Ln – ☎ (091) 568 266 – www.kirwanslane.com – Closed 25-28 December, Sunday dinner in winter and Sunday lunch BZ**s**

Rest – Carte € 30/52

Well-regarded, long-standing restaurant with a large terrace, in an old medieval lane. Lively brasserie atmosphere, with dining on two levels. Modern menus have a classical base; most dishes consist of tasty seafood – go for the specials.

Vina Mara

19 Middle St – ☎ (091) 561 610 – www.vinamara.com – Closed 25-27 December

Rest – Menu € 18 (lunch)/24 – Carte € 27/42 BY**n**

Bistro-style restaurant in the heart of the city, with a rich Mediterranean colour scheme. Modern Irish cooking has a fresh style, clearly defined flavours and relies on quality local ingredients; vegetarians are also well-catered for.

Aniar

53 Lower Dominick St – ☎ (091) 535 947 – www.aniarrestaurant.ie – Closed 25-26 December, Sunday and Monday AZ**a**

Rest – *(dinner only) (booking essential)* Menu € 60 – Carte € 51/58

Intimate restaurant with a cool, Scandic feel and a knowledgeable serving team. Large blackboards list the produce of the month; dishes are stylish, modern and interesting, featuring contrasting textures and plenty of foraged ingredients.

→ Brown crab, hazelnut and tarragon. Pork neck, beetroot, chicory and pear. Selection of Irish cheese, chutney and rye crisp.

Oscar's Seafood Bistro Ⓝ

Dominick St – ☎ (091) 582 180 – www.oscarsbistro.ie – Closed Sunday except bank holidays AZ**s**

Rest – *(dinner only)* Menu € 15 (weekday dinner) – Carte € 24/45

Very welcoming bistro in a bohemian part of the city. The intimate interior is striking red with fabrics on the ceiling and richly upholstered banquettes. Choose something from the daily blackboard menu, which lists the catch of the day.

Kai

22 Sea Rd – ☎ (091) 526 003 – www.kaicaferestaurant.com – Closed Sunday- Monday in winter and bank holidays AZ**x**

Rest – Carte € 33/45

Lovely, laid-back restaurant with a gloriously cluttered interior and old scrubbed floorboards on the walls. Morning cakes morph into fresh, simple lunches, then afternoon tea and tasty dinners. Produce is organic, free range and traceable.

Ard Bia at Nimmos

Spanish Arch – ✆ (091) 561 114 – www.ardbia.com – Closed 25-26 December
Rest – *(light lunch) (booking essential at dinner)* Carte € 31/48 BZ**u**
Buzzy, bohemian restaurant where tables occupy every nook and cranny. They sell homemade cakes, bread and artisan products. Menus blend Irish, Mediterranean and Middle Eastern influences; the provenance of the ingredients takes precedence.

GARRYKENNEDY – North Tipperary – 712 G9 39 C2

Dublin 176 km – Killaloe 14 km – Youghal 2 km

Larkins

– ✆ (067) 23 232 – www.larkins.ie – Closed 25 December, Good Friday and Monday-Tuesday November-April
Rest – Menu € 18/30 – Carte € 23/39
Thatched, whitewashed pub in a charming loughside location. Traditional interior plays host to folk music sessions and Irish dancers. Simple, unfussy bar menu; more ambitious à la carte.

GARRYVOE (Garraí Uí Bhuaigh) – Cork – 712 H12 – pop. 560 39 C3

– ✉ Castlemartyr
Dublin 259 km – Cork 37 km – Waterford 100 km

Garryvoe

– ✆ (021) 464 67 18 – www.garryvoehotel.com – Closed 25 December
82 rm – † € 80/145 †† € 80/145, ☕ €15 – 1 suite
Rest *Samphire* – *(dinner only and Sunday lunch)* Carte € 38/50
Rest *Lighthouse Bistro* – Carte € 29/46
Modernised hotel with a well-equipped fitness centre, overlooking Ballycotton Bay. The contemporary interior features plenty of natural wood and slate. Bedrooms are spacious and comfortable; most boast balconies and sea views. Formal Samphire offers a modern menu of Irish produce. The relaxed Lighthouse Bistro serves simple pub classics.

GLASLOUGH (Glasloch) – Monaghan – 712 L5 – ✉ Monaghan 37 D2

Dublin 133 km – Monaghan 11 km – Belfast 91 km – Lisburn 79 km

Castle Leslie without rest

Castle Leslie Estate – ✆ (047) 88 100 – www.castleleslie.com – Closed 24-27 December
20 rm ☕ – † € 140/280 †† € 170/310
Impressive castle set in 1,000 acres of parkland: home to the 4th generation of the Leslie family. Ornate, comfortable, antique-furnished guest areas and traditional, country house style bedrooms. Dine in Snaffles restaurant in The Lodge.

Lodge at Castle Leslie Estate

– ✆ (047) 88 100 – www.castleleslie.com
29 rm ☕ – † € 100/170 †† € 130/200 – 1 suite
Rest *Snaffles* – *(dinner only)* Menu € 65
Extended former hunting lodge to the main castle; set within 1,000 acres, in mature grounds and gardens. Estate horses for hire in the excellent equestrian centre. Stylish bedrooms; some with balconies. Charming, rustic bar and a mezzanine restaurant offering an extensive menu of modern Mediterranean dishes.

GLASSON – Westmeath – 702 I7 – see Athlone

GOLEEN (An Góilín) – Cork – 712 C13 38 A3

Dublin 230 km – Cork 74 km – Killarney 67 km

Heron's Cove

The Harbour – ✆ (028) 35 225 – www.heronscove.com – Closed Christmas
5 rm ☕ – † € 60/90 †† € 70/100 **Rest** – Menu € 28 – Carte € 32/49
Long-standing guesthouse hidden away in a pretty location, with views over a tiny harbour. Bedrooms are tidy and pleasantly furnished: all overlook the waterfront and most have a balcony – if you're lucky you might see herons at the water's edge. The busy restaurant offers seasonal menus of local produce.

REPUBLIC OF IRELAND

GOREY (Guaire) – Wexford – 712 N9 – pop. 3 463 Ireland 39 D2

Dublin 93 km – Waterford 88 km – Wexford 61 km

Main St, ℰ (055) 942 12 48, www.discoverireland.ie

Courtown, Kiltennel, ℰ (055) 2 51 66

Ferns★, SW : 17.75 km by N 11

Marlfield House

Courtown Rd, Southeast : 1.5 km on R 742 – ℰ (053) 942 11 24 – www.marlfieldhouse.com – Closed 3 January-February

19 rm – † € 90/115 †† € 210/670

Rest – *(closed Monday-Tuesday in November-December) (dinner only and Sunday lunch)* Menu € 35 (weekday dinner)/64

Attractive Regency house surrounded by large informal gardens and woodland. Various stylish, classical lounges and drawing rooms with warm décor, heavy fabrics and antiques. Well-appointed bedrooms in period styles, with a good level of facilities and pleasant views over the grounds. Smart dining room and orangery offer refined, traditional dishes with a modern touch.

GRAIGUENAMANAGH (Gráig na Manach) – Kilkenny – 712 L10 – pop. 1 543 Ireland 39 D2

Dublin 125 km – Kilkenny 34 km – Waterford 42 km – Wexford 26 km

Duiske Abbey★★ **AC**

Jerpoint Abbey★★ **AC**, W : 15 km by R 703 and N 9 – Inistioge★, SW : 8 km by minor road – Kilfane Glen and Waterfall★ **AC**, SW : 17 km by R 703 and N 9

Waterside with rm

The Quay – ℰ (059) 972 42 46 – www.watersideguesthouse.com – Closed November-February

10 rm – † € 49/59 †† € 70/90

Rest – *(closed Monday-Thursday) (dinner only and Sunday lunch)* Menu € 27 (dinner) – Carte € 25/35

1871 stone-built corn store at the foot of Brandon Hill and the Blackstairs Mountains, overlooking the River Barrow. Bright, modern bar and restaurant. Concise à la carte offers modern Irish-influenced dishes with Mediterranean touches. Simply furnished bedrooms have exposed beams and pleasant river views.

GREYSTONES (Na Clocha Liatha) – Wicklow – 712 N8 – pop. 10 173 Ireland 39 D1

Dublin 32 km – Wicklow 22 km – Rathmines 31 km – Dundalk 128 km

Greystones, ℰ (01) 287 41 36

Killruddery House and Gardens★ **AC**, N : 5 km by R 761 – Powerscourt★★ (Waterfall★★) **AC**, NW : 10 km by R 761, minor road, M 11 and minor road via Enniskerry. Wicklow Mountains★★

Chakra by Jaipur

Meridian Point Centre (1st floor), Church Rd – ℰ (01) 201 72 22 – www.jaipur.ie – Closed 25 December

Rest – *(dinner only and Sunday lunch)* Menu € 16/30 – Carte € 34/51

Smart, spacious Indian restaurant with warm exotic hues and carved wooden statues, unusually set in a suburban shopping centre. Three themed set menus and an à la carte: accomplished, modern dishes feature original spicing and flavours.

A Caviston N

1 Westview, Church Rd – ℰ (01) 287 7637 – www.acaviston.ie – Closed Christmas-New Year and bank holidays

Rest – *(lunch only and Friday dinner) (booking essential)* Menu € 20/30 – Carte € 29/56

Through a superbly filled deli and past a comprehensive fish counter is this modestly furnished, family-run café and restaurant decorated with local art. Tasty fresh fish and shellfish are simply prepared in classical ways.

GWEEDORE (Gaoth Dobhair) – **Donegal** – **712** H2 — **37** C1

Dublin 278 km – Donegal 72 km – Letterkenny 43 km – Sligo 135 km

Gweedore Court

on N 56 – (074) 953 29 00 – www.gweedorecourthotel.ie – Closed January and 21-27 December

60 rm – € 69/89 € 99/130

Rest – *(bar lunch Monday-Saturday)* Menu € 30

Privately owned, whitewashed hotel in a rural location, with spacious, comfortable lounges and a well-equipped leisure club. Bedrooms to the front have views over the River Clady to the forests and mountains; feature rooms boast four-posters. Traditional dining room with a menu to match.

HORSE AND JOCKEY (An Marcach) – **North Tipperary** – **712** I10 — **39** C2

Dublin 146 km – Cashel 14 km – Thurles 9 km

Horse and Jockey

– (0504) 44 192 – www.horseandjockeyhotel.com – Closed 24-26 December

69 rm – € 75/95 € 99/119 – 1 suite

Rest ***Silks*** – Menu € 25/40 – Carte € 27/44 **s**

Extended former pub in an area surrounded by racehorse trainers' stables and racecourses. Spacious, modern bedrooms and a superb spa; stylish, state-of-the-art lecture theatre and meeting rooms. The delightful coffee shop sells homemade cakes. The characterful bar and restaurant serve unfussy Irish dishes.

HOWTH (Binn Éadair) – **Fingal** – **712** N7 – **pop. 8 186** – **Dublin** — **39** D1

Ireland

Dublin 22 km – Swords 17 km – Belfast 172 km – Cork 276 km

Deer Park Hotel, Howth Castle, (01) 832 60 39

The Cliffs★ (★)

Aqua

1 West Pier – (01) 832 0690 – www.aqua.ie – Closed Good Friday, 25-26 December, and Monday-Tuesday in winter

Rest – Menu € 20 (weekday lunch)/75 – Carte € 38/53

Smart restaurant at the end of Howth's busy West Pier, with superb views across the Sound to Lambay Island. It has a cosy, open-fired bar-lounge with exposed brickwork, and a seafood-based menu which keeps things pleasingly traditional.

King Sitric with rm

rest,

East Pier – (01) 832 5235 – www.kingsitric.ie – Closed 25-26 December

8 rm – € 110/145 € 150/205

Rest – *(closed dinner Sunday, Tuesday and bank holidays) (dinner only and Sunday lunch)* Menu € 28/37 – Carte € 30/90

A long-standing establishment in a former harbourmaster's house, overlooking the water. Dine in the laid-back ground floor café or in the formal first floor restaurant. Seafood is the order of the day, with lobster a speciality. Bedrooms are named after lighthouses; those on the first floor have better views.

INISHMAAN = Inis Meáin – **Galway** – **712** D8 – **see Aran Islands**

INISHMORE = Árainn – **Galway** – **712** C/D8 – **see Aran Islands**

INISTIOGE (Inis Tíog) – **Kilkenny** – **712** K10 – **pop. 260** — **39** C2

Dublin 82 km – Kilkenny 16 km – Waterford 19 km – Wexford 33 km

Inn @ Ballilogue Clochán without rest

Ballilogue, The Rower, Southeast : 12 km by R 700 on Ballilogue rd – (051) 423 857 – www.ballilogueclochan.com – Closed Christmas-New Year

6 rm – € 115/130 € 130/190

An unconventional, passionately run guesthouse created by an Irish designer from a collection of old farm buildings. Variously sized bedrooms have a distinctly modern and minimalistic style – which contrasts with the rustic exteriors.

JENKINSTOWN = Baile Sheinicín – **Louth** – **see Dundalk**

KANTURK (Ceann Toirc) – **Cork** – **712** F11 – **pop. 2 263** Ireland **38** B2

Dublin 259 km – Cork 53 km – Killarney 50 km – Limerick 71 km

Fairy Hill, ☎ (029) 5 05 34

Town★ - Castle★

Glenlohane

Southeast : 4 km. by R 576 and R 580 on L1043 – ☎ (029) 50 014 – www.glenlohane.com

3 rm – € 85 € 170 **Rest** – Menu € 50

Grand Georgian country house set in 230 acres – which has been in the family for over 250 years. Traditional interior hung with portraits and paintings. Colour-themed bedrooms; 'Blue' has an antique four-poster and bathtub. Cosy library and drawing room. Open-fired dining room for home-cooked dinners.

KEEL = An Caol – **Mayo** – **712** B5/6 – **see Achill Island**

KENMARE (Neidín) – **Kerry** – **712** D12 – **pop. 2 175** Ireland **38** A3

Dublin 338 km – Cork 93 km – Killarney 32 km

Heritage Centre, ☎ (064) 664 12 33, www.kenmare.com

Kenmare, ☎ (064) 4 12 91

Town★

Ring of Kerry★★ - Healy Pass★★ (≤★★), SW : 30.5 km by R 571 and R 574 AY – Mountain Road to Glengarriff (≤★★) S : by N 71 AY - Slieve Miskish Mountains (≤★★), SW : 48.25 km by R 571 AY – Gougane Barra Forest Park★★, SE : 16 km AY - Lauragh (Derreen Gardens★ **AC**), SW : 23.5 km by R 571 AY – Allihies (Copper Mines★), SW : 57 km by R 571 and R 575 AY – Garnish Island (≤★), SW : 68.5 km by R 571, R 575 and R 572 AY

KENMARE

Back Lane . . . . . BY 2
Cromwell's Bridge . . . . . AY
Davitt's Place. . . . . AY
Downing's Row . . . . . BY 5
East Park St. . . . . AY 7
Finnihy Bridge . . . . . AY
Henry St . . . . . AY
Henry's Lane . . . . . ABY 8
Killarney Rd . . . . . AY
Main St. . . . . . BY
Market St . . . . . AY
New St . . . . . AY
Old Bridge St. . . . . AY 12
Railway Rd . . . . . BY
Rock St . . . . . BY 14
Shelborne St. . . . . BY
The Square . . . . . AY

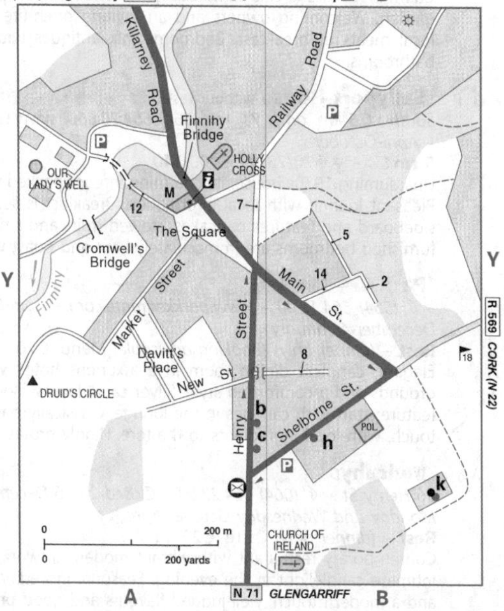

Park

– ✆ (064) 664 12 00 – www.parkkenmare.com – April-October and 25 December-4 January BYk

46 rm – € 220/275 € 290/550

Rest *Park* – see restaurant listing

Grand country house dating from 1897, offering superb views over the bay and the hills. Elegant interior with open fires, a cosy cocktail lounge and a charming drawing room filled with portraits and antiques. Tastefully furnished bedrooms have smart marble bathrooms. The stylish spa adds a modern touch.

Sheen Falls Lodge

Southeast : 2 km. by N 71 – ✆ (064) 664 16 00 – www.sheenfallslodge.ie – Closed January

66 rm – € 90/250 € 140/300 – 9 suites

Rest *La Cascade* – *(closed 28 June) (dinner only)* Menu € 53/95 – Carte € 65/95

Luxurious hotel in an idyllic spot, where the waterfalls drop away into the bay. Welcoming, wood-fired lobby, book-filled library and a lovely indoor pool; the well-appointed bedrooms overlook the falls. Light lunches in the cocktail bar and a classical menu with a modern touch in the formal restaurant.

Brook Lane rm, rest,

North : 1.5 km. by N 71 on N 70 – ✆ (064) 664 20 77 – www.brooklanehotel.com

21 rm – € 75/140 € 100/210

Rest *Casey's* – Menu € 25/45 – Carte € 22/47

Stylish, personally run hotel close to the town centre. Contemporary bedrooms offer a good level of comfort and range from 'Standard' to 'Luxury', the latter boasting impressive fabric headboards and designer touches. Informal bar and restaurant offer classic Irish and seafood dishes; regular live music.

Shelburne Lodge without rest

East : 0.75 km. on R 569 (Cork Rd) – ✆ (064) 664 10 13 – www.shelburnelodge.com – April-October

8 rm – € 70/95 € 110/150

Charming, wisteria-clad farmhouse with sweeping lawns, box hedges and a herb garden. Welcoming owners and an inviting open-fire. Home-baked breads and local meats at breakfast. Bedrooms mix antiques with modern colours; simple bathrooms.

Sallyport House without rest

South : 0.5 km. on N 71 – ✆ (064) 664 20 66 – www.sallyporthouse.com – April-October

5 rm – € 70/75 € 100/140

Unassuming 1930s house; its charming interior packed with antiques and Irish art. Pleasant lounge with local information. Breakfast is served from the characterful sideboard and features pancakes, stewed fruits and smoked salmon. Traditionally furnished bedrooms are immaculately kept and boast water views.

Park – Park Hotel

– ✆ (064) 664 12 00 – www.parkkenmare.com – April-October and 25 December-4 January BYk

Rest – *(dinner only) (booking advisable)* Menu € 70

Elegant, candlelit dining room in a luxurious hotel, with good views over the grounds and a comforting style. Silver candelabras, cloches and gueridon trolleys feature; start with canapés in the lounge. Classically based dishes have a modern touch, with local ingredients to the fore. Highly professional team.

Mulcahys

36 Henry St – ✆ (064) 664 23 83 – Closed 24-26 December, Tuesday, and Monday and Wednesday October-April AYc

Rest – *(dinner only)* Carte € 29/46

Contemporary restaurant with vibrant modern artwork, exposed stone walls and intimate candlelight in the evening. Seasonal ingredients are prepared with care and a modern touch; well-judged flavours and good presentation.

REPUBLIC OF IRELAND

Lime Tree

Shelbourne St. – ✆ (064) 664 12 25 – www.limetreerestaurant.com – Easter-October and weekends in winter BY**h**

Rest – *(dinner only)* Menu € 35/40 – Carte € 34/51

19C property that's taken on many guises over the years. The characterful, rustic interior features exposed stone walls, an open fire and even its own art gallery. Unfussy dishes feature quality local ingredients in generous portions.

Boathouse Bistro

Dromquinna, West : 4.75 km by N 71 on N 70 – ✆ (064) 664 2889 – www.dromquinnamanor.com – Closed January, 2 weeks December and Monday-Wednesday in winter

Rest – *(booking advisable)* Carte € 29/44

Converted boathouse in the grounds of Dromquinna Manor; set on the waterside and overlooking the peninsula and the mountains. It has a nautical, New England style and a laid-back vibe. Menus are simple, appealing and focus on seafood.

Packie's

Henry St – ✆ (064) 664 15 08 – Closed mid-January-mid-February, Monday in winter and Sunday AY**b**

Rest – *(dinner only) (booking essential)* Carte € 25/53

Popular little restaurant in the town centre, with two rustic, bistro-style rooms, exposed stone walls, tiled floors and an interesting collection of modern Irish art. Cooking is honest, fresh and seasonal; the seafood specials are a hit.

REPUBLIC OF IRELAND

KILBRITTAIN (Cill Briotáin) – Cork – 712 F12 – pop. 196 38 B3

Dublin 289 km – Cork 38 km – Killarney 96 km

Glen Country House without rest

Southwest : 6.5 km. by R 600 – ✆ (023) 884 98 62 – www.glencountryhouse.com – May-mid October

5 rm – € 60/75 € 120/130

Victorian house set in 300 acres; the same family have farmed the land for over 350 years and are now in their 10th generation! Comfy open-fired lounge and breakfast room with antique furniture; smart bedrooms have distant sea views.

KILCOLGAN (Cill Cholgáin) – Galway – 712 F8 – ✉ Oranmore 36 B3

Dublin 208 km – Belfast 322 km – Cork 179 km – Lisburn 310 km

Moran's Oyster Cottage

The Weir, Northwest : 2 km. by N 18 – ✆ (091) 796 113 – www.moransoystercottage.com – Closed Good Friday and 24-26 December

Rest – Carte € 27/48

Attractive whitewashed pub with golden thatch, hidden away in a tiny hamlet – a very popular place in summer. Largely cold seafood dishes, with oysters a speciality and tasty homemade bread.

KILCULLEN – Kildare – 712 L8 – pop. 3 473 39 D1

Dublin 48 km – Naas 12 km – Rathmines 50 km – Navan 88 km

Fallon's

Main St – ✆ (045) 481 260 – www.fallonb.ie

Rest – Menu € 28 (dinner) – Carte € 21/40

A 'proper' bar with a long wooden counter and a flagged floor; albeit one with a boutique colour scheme! The experienced chef offers a wide range of dishes, from pie of the day to grilled salmon, followed by tasty homemade puddings.

Dublin 114 km – Cork 138 km – Killarney 185 km – Limerick 111 km
Shee Alms House, (056) 7 75 15 00, www.kilkennytourism.ie
Glendine, (056) 776 54 00
Callan, Geraldine, (056) 772 51 36
Castlecomer, Drumgoole, (056) 444 11 39
Town★★ – St Canice's Cathedral★★ – Kilkenny Castle and Park★★ **AC** – Black Abbey★ – Rothe House★
Jerpoint Abbey★★ **AC**, S : 19.25 km by R 700 and N 9 – Kilfane Glen and Waterfall★ **AC**, S : 21 km by R 700 and N 9 – Kells Priory★, S : 12.5 km by R 697 – Dunmore Cave★ **AC**, N: 11.25 km by N 77 and N 78

Kilkenny rm, rest,
College Rd, Southwest : 1.25 km at junction with N 76 – (056) 776 20 00 – www.hotelkilkenny.ie
138 rm – € 75/130 € 100/190
Rest *Taste* – *(dinner only and Sunday lunch)* Menu € 25/30 **s**
Unassuming modern property just outside the city centre, with contrastingly stylish, contemporary interior. Well-equipped leisure centre and smart function rooms. Funky colour schemes feature throughout. Bright bedrooms have a slightly kitsch style. Mediterranean-influenced menus in pink-hued restaurant.

Pembroke N
Patrick St – (056) 778 35 00 – www.pembrokekilkenny.com – Closed 24-25 December
74 rm – € 70/169 € 79/219
Rest *Stathams* – *(bar lunch Monday-Saturday)* Menu € 10/25 – Carte € 22/39
A usefully located business hotel with a stylish, contemporary look. Spacious, comfortable bedrooms; those at the back are a little quieter and offer views of the castle. Well-equipped business centre. Light lunches in the bar; traditional dinners in the modern restaurant with its appealing courtyard terrace.

Butler House without rest
15-16 Patrick St. – (056) 776 57 07 – www.butler.ie – Closed 23-29 December
14 rm – € 60/180 € 89/195
Beautifully restored Georgian house with some fine original features, a delightful formal garden and views of Kilkenny castle. Large, comfortable, up-to-date bedrooms. Breakfast is served in the adjacent Design Museum.

Rosquil House without rest
Castlecomer Rd, Northwest : 1 km – (056) 772 14 19 – www.rosquilhouse.com
7 rm – € 40/60 € 70/90
Purpose-built guesthouse on the main road out of the city. Comfy, leather-furnished lounge filled with books and local information; linen-laid breakfast room to the rear. Simply furnished bedrooms. Welcoming owners.

Ristorante Rinuccini
1 The Parade – (056) 776 15 75 – www.rinuccini.com – Closed 26-27 December
Rest – Menu € 23 (dinner) – Carte € 30/51
Set in the basement of a townhouse and named after the 17C papal nuncio, this family-owned restaurant is well-known locally. Classic Italian cuisine with home-made ravioli a speciality. Some tables have views through to the wine cellar.

Zuni with rm
26 Patrick St – (056) 772 39 99 – www.zuni.ie – Closed 25-26 December
13 rm – € 60/90 € 75/130 **Rest** – Carte € 30/43
Small wood-furnished café-bar opening out into a chic, light, modern restaurant with mirrored walls, leather panels and a heated terrace. Eclectic modern menus of Irish produce; desserts are a high point. Comfortable black and white bedrooms continue the smart, contemporary theme.

XX **Campagne** (Garrett Byrne)

5 The Arches, Gashouse Ln. – ✆ (056) 777 28 58 – www.campagne.ie – Closed 2 weeks January, Sunday dinner and Monday
Rest – *(dinner only and lunch Friday-Sunday) (booking advisable)*
Menu € 24/47 **s** – Carte € 36/49 **s**
Stylish, relaxed restaurant with vibrant, contemporary art and smart booths, hidden close to the railway arches, away from the city centre. Modern cooking has a classic base, and familiar combinations are delivered with an assured touch. Popular early bird menu. Well-run, with friendly, efficient service.
→ Ham hock terrine with piccalilli, baby gem and walnut toast. John Dory, creamed broad beans and bacon, tomato confit. Chocolate tart with berries and vanilla ice cream.

X **Foodworks** (N)

7 Parliament St – ✆ (056) 777 76 96 – www.foodworks.ie
Rest – Menu € 17 (lunch) – Carte € 22/38
A former bank in the town centre: a high-ceilinged, airy space with a bright, fresh look which matches the style of the cooking. Unfussy dishes use quality local produce, including pork and vegetables from the experienced chef-owner's farm.

KILLALOE (Cill Dalua) – Clare – 712 G9 – pop. 1 292 Ireland 38 B2

Dublin 175 km – Ennis 51 km – Limerick 21 km – Tullamore 93 km
Town★ – St Flannan's Cathedral★
Graves of the Leinstermen (<★), N : 7.25 km by R 494 – Castleconnell★, S : 16 km by R 494 and R 466 – Clare Glens★, S : 24 km by R 494, R 504 and R 503. Nenagh (Castle★), NE : 19.25 km by R 496 and N 7 – Holy Island★ **AC**, N : 25.75 km by R 463 and boat from Tuamgraney

XX **Cherry Tree**

Lakeside, Ballina, follow signs for Lakeside Hotel – ✆ (061) 375 688 – www.cherrytreerestaurant.ie – Closed first week January, Good Friday, 25-26 December, Sunday dinner and Monday
Rest – Menu € 26/35 – Carte € 30/45
Modern restaurant with interesting local art hung on brightly coloured walls, and views across Lough Derg. Choose from an array of classical menus; dishes are well-balanced, seasonal and nicely presented. Service is cheery and welcoming.

KILLARNEY (Cill Airne) – Kerry – 712 D11 – pop. 12 740 Ireland 38 A2

Dublin 304 km – Cork 87 km – Limerick 111 km – Waterford 180 km
Kerry (Farranfore) Airport : ✆ (066) 976 4644, N : 15.25 km by N 22
Beech Rd, ✆ (064) 663 16 33, www.killarney.ie
Mahoney's Point, ✆ (064) 3 10 34
Town★★ – St Mary's Cathedral★ CX
Killarney National Park★★★ (Muckross Friary★, Muckross House and Farms★) AZ - Gap of Dunloe★★, SW : 9.5 km by R 562 AZ – Ross Castle★ **AC**, S : 1.5 km by N 71 and minor rd – Torc Waterfall★, S : 8 km by N 71 BZ. Ring of Kerry★★ – Ladies View★★, SW : 19.25 km by N 71 BZ – Moll's Gap★, SW : 25 km by N 71 BZ

Plans on following pages

Europe

Fossa, West : 4.75 km. by Port Rd on N 72 – ✆ (064) 667 13 00 – www.theeurope.com – Closed 16 December-8 February
187 rm – † € 200/270 †† € 220/290 – 6 suites
Rest *Panorama* Rest *Brasserie* – see restaurant listing
Vast hotel in a superb lakeside location, boasting views over Lough Leane and Macgillycuddy's Reeks. Opulent guest areas, impressive events facilities and a sublime three-level spa. Bedrooms are lavishly appointed; some overlook the lake.

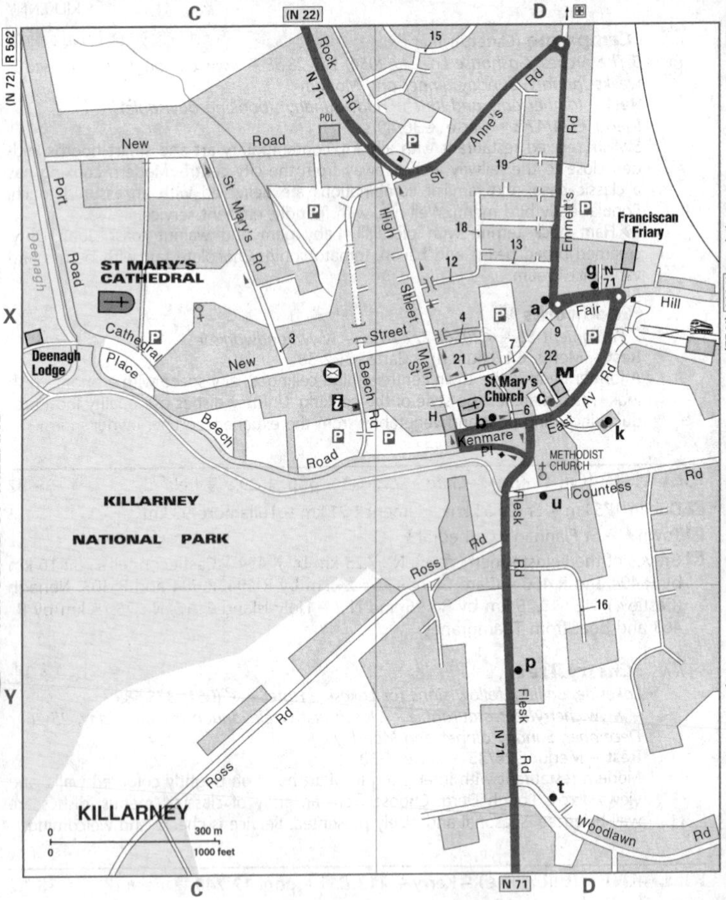

Killarney Park

– ☎ (064) 663 55 55 – www.killarneyparkhotel.ie – *Closed 23-27 December*

68 rm – † € 250/350 †† € 250/350 – 3 suites DX**k**

Rest *Park* – see restaurant listing

Large, luxurious hotel run by a well-versed team. Plush library and lavish drawing room; lunches in the clubby, wood-panelled bar. Bedrooms range in style, mixing modern furnishings with original features. Smart spa and leisure facilities.

Aghadoe Heights H. and Spa

Northwest : 4.5 km. by N 22 off L 2109 – ☎ (064) 663 17 66

– www.aghadoeheights.com – weekends only November-April

74 rm – † € 160/180 †† € 250/300 – 2 suites

Rest *Lake Room* – see restaurant listing

Striking, glass-fronted hotel looking out over lakes, mountains and countryside. Modern interior with an impressive spa and a stylish cocktail bar complete with an evening pianist. Bedrooms are spacious; many have balconies or terraces.

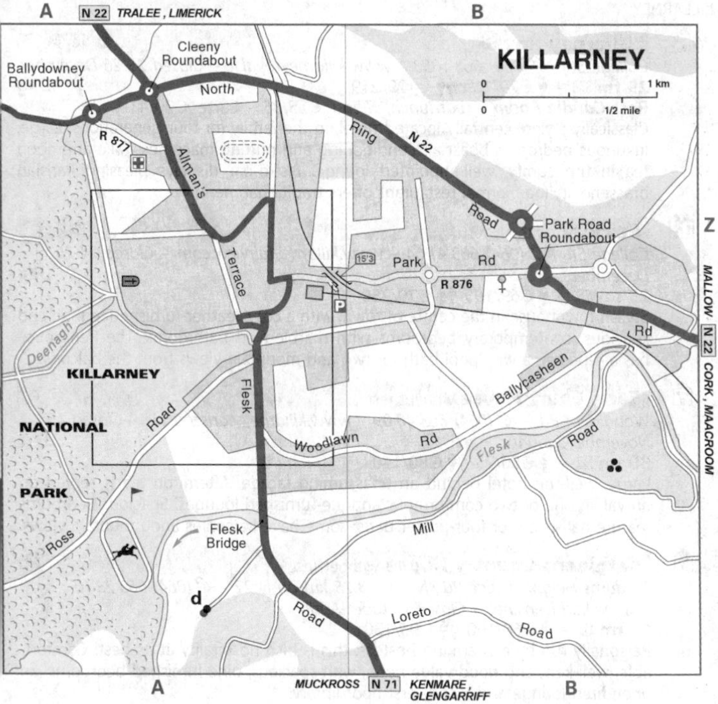

Ross

– ✆ (064) 663 18 55 – *www.theross.ie* – *weekends only November-March*

29 rm – † € 90/130 †† € 110/220 DX**b**

Rest *Cellar One* – Menu € 22/29 – Carte € 26/45

Striking, modern hotel in the centre of town, overlooking the famous 'Killarney Horse and Carriage Tours' HQ. Contemporary bar-lounge with multi-level design. Stylish, boldly coloured bedrooms are comfy and well-equipped. Vibrant basement restaurant features curved timbers, intimate lighting and global menu.

Cahernane House

Muckross Rd – ✆ *(064) 663 18 95* – *www.cahernane.com* – *Closed December-February* AZ**d**

38 rm – † € 95/145 †† € 150/190 – 1 suite

Rest *Herbert Room* – see restaurant listing

Fine Victorian house built in 1877, set in a peaceful location and affording westerly mountain views. Characterful open-fired library and drawing room with stags' heads, portraits and antiques. Bedrooms range from classical to contemporary.

Randles Court

rest,

Muckross Rd – ✆ *(064) 663 53 33* – *www.randlescourt.com* – *Closed 2 January-10 February* DY**p**

75 rm – † € 50/100 †† € 70/300

Rest *Checkers* – *(dinner only and lunch Saturday-Sunday)* Menu € 35 – Carte € 28/46

Family-run hotel in a gabled Edwardian mansion; built as a rectory in 1906. Delightful, antique-furnished lounge with deep sofas and a coal fire. Comfy bedrooms with good facilities; those in newer wing are more modern. Characterful, checker-floored restaurant; traditional menu of local produce.

Killarney Royal

College St – ☎ (064) 663 1853 – www.killarneyroyal.ie – Closed 25-26 December
29 rm – € 79/169 € 129/219 DX**g**
Rest ***Candle Room*** – *(bar lunch)* Menu € 25/35 – Carte € 20/41
Classically styled, centrally located hotel; in the family for four generations. Large, luxurious bedrooms boast air conditioning and putting machines. Take afternoon tea in the comfy, well-appointed lounge. Bistro-bar displays pleasing Parisian brasserie styling. Formal restaurant offers traditional menu.

Fairview without rest

College St. – ☎ (064) 663 41 64 – www.killarneyfairview.com – Closed 24-25 December DX**a**
29 rm – € 69/195 € 79/250
Stylish townhouse in the centre of town, with a cosy, leather-furnished lounge and spacious, contemporary bedrooms with marble-tiled bathrooms. The Penthouse has a 4-poster, a whirlpool bath for two and mountain views from the balcony.

Earls Court House without rest

Woodlawn Rd. – ☎ (064) 663 40 09 – www.killarney-earlscourt.ie – Closed 15 November-January DY**t**
30 rm – € 50/75 € 80/140
Large, well-run hotel behind an unassuming façade. Afternoon tea is served on arrival, in one of two comfortable, antique-furnished lounges. Spacious bedrooms feature half-tester or four-poster beds; some have balconies and mountain views.

REPUBLIC OF IRELAND

Kathleens Country House without rest

Madams Height, Tralee Rd., North : 3.75 km on N 22 – ☎ (064) 663 28 10 – www.kathleens.net – Closed October-April
17 rm – € 60/100 € 95/130
Personally run by a charming hostess: this is Irish hospitality at its best! Comfortable, well-kept and good value hotel, with spacious, pine-furnished bedrooms, an open-fired lounge and a cosy first floor library.

Killarney Lodge without rest

Countess Rd. – ☎ (064) 663 64 99 – www.killarneylodge.net – 11 March-September DX**u**
16 rm – € 60/100 € 90/130
Well-located on the edge of the town centre. Spacious, immaculately kept, well-furnished bedrooms; No. 12 boasts lovely mountain views. Bright and airy breakfast room where homemade bread and scones feature. Afternoon tea on arrival.

Panorama – Europe Hotel

Fossa, West : 4.75 km. by Port Rd on N 72 – ☎ (064) 667 13 00 – www.theeurope.com – Closed 16 December-8 February
Rest – *(closed Sunday dinner)* Carte € 33/61
Large, formal restaurant with a contemporary style, set in a luxurious hotel. Panoramic windows afford superb views across the lough towards the mountains. Creative modern menus follow the seasons and use the very best of Irish produce.

Park – Killarney Park Hotel

– ☎ (064) 663 55 55 – www.killarneyparkhotel.ie – Closed 23-27 December
Rest – *(dinner only)* Menu € 55 – Carte € 35/55 DX**k**
Elegant restaurant boasting chandeliers, ornate cornicing and smartly laid tables, set in an impressive hotel. Classic menus with some modern combinations; Irish meats are a feature and the tasting menu a highlight. Nightly pianist in summer.

Lake Room – Aghadoe Heights Hotel and Spa

Northwest : 4.5 km. by N 22 off L 2109 – ☎ (064) 663 17 66 – www.aghadoeheights.com – weekends only November-April
Rest – *(dinner only) (bar lunch)* Menu € 50 – Carte € 35/66
Smart restaurant in a contemporary hotel; its two different levels making the most of the panoramic water and mountain view. Classical dishes showcase local produce and are executed with a modern touch; there's the odd French influence too.

XX **Brasserie** - Europe Hotel

Fossa, West : 4.75 km. by Port Rd on N 72 – ✆ (064) 667 13 00 – www.theeurope.com – Closed 16 December-8 February

Rest – Carte €33/61 **s**

Set in a sumptuous lakeside hotel; a modern take on a classical brasserie, with lough and mountain views – head for the terrace in warmer weather. The accessible all-day menu ranges from soup and salads to steaks cooked on the open grill.

XX **Herbert Room** – Cahernane House Hotel

Muckross Rd – ✆ (064) 663 18 95 – www.cahernane.com – Closed December-February AZ**d**

Rest – *(closed Sunday-Monday except in summer) (dinner only) (booking advisable)* Carte €40/56

Set in a fine Victorian house; start with a drink in the atmospheric cellar bar then head for the traditional, two-roomed restaurant with its large fireplace and mountain views. Well-judged, classically based dishes display modern touches.

XX **Cucina Italiana**

17 St Anthonys Pl – ✆ (064) 662 65 75 – Closed 10 January- 28 February and Tuesday in winter DX**c**

Rest – *(dinner only) (booking advisable)* Carte €39/61

Charming, split-level restaurant tucked away in a side street, with frosted glass screens and a spiral staircase. Refined, tasty Italian dishes use top quality produce and are presented in an unfussy, modern style. Smooth, friendly service.

at Beaufort West : 9.75 km by N 72 off Glencar rd – ✉ Killarney

The Dunloe

Southeast : 2.5 km on Dunloe Golf Course rd – ✆ (064) 664 41 11 – www.thedunloe.com – Closed 13 October-17 April

102 rm ☕ – 🚹 €160/210 🚹🚹 €180/230 – 2 suites

Rest *Oak* – *(dinner only)* Carte €28/57 **s**

Rest *Garden Café* – Carte €28/56

Creeper-clad hotel in 65 acres, with a continental feel and superb views of the Gap of Dunloe and Macgillycuddy's Reeks. Several spacious lounges and bars. Classical bedrooms, most with balconies and views; the suites have steam rooms. Good-sized pool and stables. Formal dining room and all-day brasserie.

KILLORGLIN (Cill Orglan) – Kerry – 712 C11 – pop. 1 627 Ireland — 38 A2

Dublin 333 km – Killarney 19 km – Tralee 26 km

Killorglin, Stealroe, ✆ (669) 761 979

Lough Caragh★, SW : 9 km by N 70 and minor road S. Ring of Kerry★★

X **Giovannelli**

Lower Bridge St – ✆ (087) 123 13 53

Rest – *(dinner only)* Carte €24/48

Unassuming restaurant hidden in the town centre, with a traditional osteria-style interior. Concise, daily changing blackboard menu offers a mix of Italian and Irish dishes; the pastas are homemade and the herbs come from the owners garden.

X **Sol y Sombra** Ⓝ

Old Church of Ireland, Lower Bridge St – ✆ (066) 976 23 47 – www.solysombra.ie – Closed 7 January-7 February and Tuesday dinner in winter

Rest – *(closed Sunday-Monday)* Menu €16 – Carte €26/37

Spanish restaurant in an imposing 19C former church, with a cavernous interior, stained glass windows and church pews. Fresh, vibrant cooking: go for the raciones, designed for sharing – 3 per person will suffice. Live music is a feature.

KILMALLOCK (Cill Mocheallóg) – Limerick – 712 G10 – pop. 1 635 — 38 B2

Ireland

Dublin 212 km – Limerick 34 km – Tipperary 32 km

Abbey★ - Collegiate Church★

Lough Gur Interpretive Centre★ **AC**, N : 16 km by R 512 and minor road – Monasteranenagh Abbey★, N : 24 km by R 512 to Holycross and minor road W

Flemingstown House
Southeast : 4 km on R 512 – ✆ (063) 98 093 – www.flemingstown.com – closed November-January
5 rm ☕ – 🚹 € 50/55 🚹🚹 € 90/100 **Rest** – Menu € 35
Proudly run, creeper-clad house at the centre of a 200 acre working farm. The cosy, homely interior is filled with family knick-knacks and the scent of peat wafts from the open fires. Attractive, antique-furnished bedrooms have country views. Satisfying home-cooked dishes are served in the comfy dining room.

KINLOUGH (Cionn Locha) – Leitrim – 712 H4 – pop. 1 018 — 37 C2

Dublin 220 km – Ballyshannon 11 km – Sligo 34 km

Courthouse with rm
– ✆ (071) 984 23 91 – www.thecourthouserest.com – *Closed Monday-Wednesday in winter and Tuesday*
4 rm ☕ – 🚹 € 35/45 🚹🚹 € 70
Rest – *(dinner only and Sunday lunch) (booking essential)* Menu € 25/30 – Carte € 24/46
Boldly painted former courthouse with a pretty stained glass entrance. The Sardinian owner-chef creates extensive, seasonal menus of honest, authentic Italian dishes; some produce is imported and local seafood features. The atmosphere is informal and the service, friendly. Bedrooms are neat and good value.

KINSALE (Cionne tSáile) – Cork – 712 G12 – pop. 2 198 Ireland — 38 B3

Dublin 276 km – Belfast 444 km – Cork 25 km – Lisburn 432 km
Pier Rd, ✆ (021) 4 77 22 34, www.kinsale.ie
Town★★ – St Multose Church★ Y – Kinsale Regional Museum★ **AC** Y **M1**
Kinsale Harbour★ (<★ from St Catherine's Anglican Church, Charles Fort★). Carbery Coast★, W : 61 km by R 600

Perryville House without rest
Long Quay – ✆ (021) 477 27 31 – www.perryvillehouse.com – Closed November-15 April Y**f**
22 rm ☕ – 🚹 € 150/250 🚹🚹 € 160/300
Luxuriously appointed house in the heart of town, overlooking the harbour and named after the family that built it in 1820. Two antique-furnished drawing rooms, a smart boutique and a tea shop. Tastefully styled bedrooms; 'Luxury' boast feature beds, chic bathrooms and harbour views. Comprehensive breakfasts.

Blue Haven — rest, AC rest
3-4 Pearse St – ✆ (021) 477 22 09 – www.bluehavenkinsale.com – Closed 25 December Y**c**
17 rm ☕ – 🚹 € 55/110 🚹🚹 € 70/150
Rest *Fish Market* – Menu € 25 (lunch)/38 – Carte € 25/45
Rest *Bistro* – Menu € 22/38 – Carte € 25/44
Small but well-established hotel right in the heart of town; its cosy, vibrant interior featuring interesting artwork. Chic, clubby lounge. Comfortable bedrooms are named after vineyards and have a subtle contemporary edge. The all-day bistro resembles the hull of an upturned boat and the restaurant specialises in seafood from local waters.

Old Bank Town House without rest
10-11 Pearse St. – ✆ (021) 477 40 75 – www.oldbankhousekinsale.com – Closed 23-26 December Y**d**
17 rm ☕ – 🚹 € 59/95 🚹🚹 € 70/170
Substantial Georgian house in the heart of town. A food store and café, where breakfast is served, occupy the ground floor; above them is a cosy, classically furnished lounge. Bedrooms are traditional – No.17 has great harbour views.

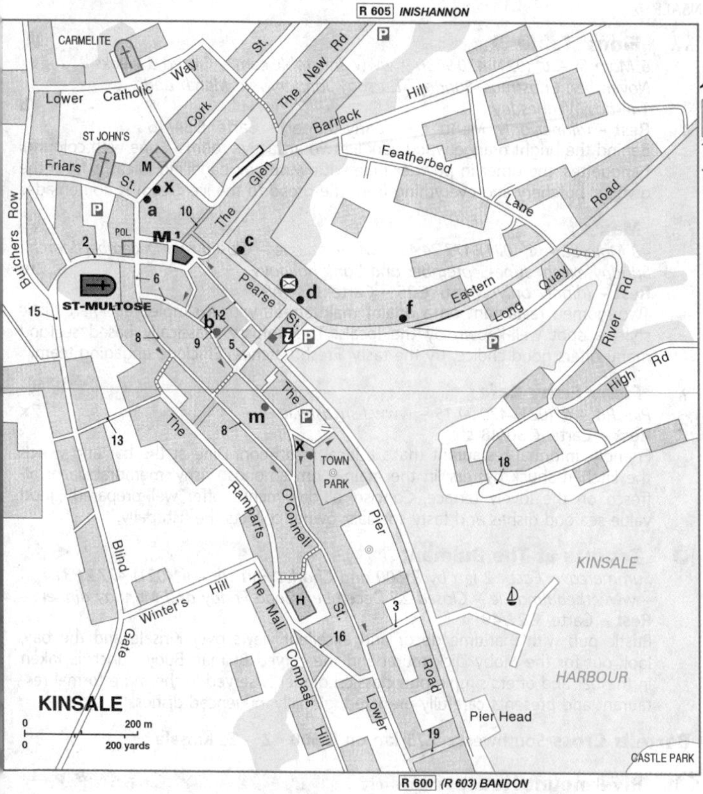

Church St. . . . . **Y** 2
Denis Quay . . . . **Z** 3
Emmet St . . . . **Y** 5
Guardwell . . . . **Y** 6
Higher O'Connel St . . . . **YZ** 8
Main St . . . . **Y** 9
Market Pl. . . . . **Y** 10
Market Quay . . . . **Y** 12
Ramparts Lane . . . . **Z** 13
Rose Abbey . . . . **Y** 15
St John's Hill . . . . **Z** 16
Seilly Walk . . . . **Z** 18
World's End . . . . **Z** 19

Old Presbytery without rest
43 Cork St. – ✆ (021) 477 20 27 – www.oldpres.com – Closed mid-November- mid-March Y**a**
9 rm ☕ – 🚹 € 60/100 🚹🚹 € 90/180
18C building once housing priests from the nearby church; a few ecclesiastical pieces remain. Cosy lounge with a piano and gramophone; the breakfast room boasts some unusual chairs. Bedrooms feature brass or cast iron beds and Irish pine.

Desmond House without rest
42 Cork St. – ✆ (021) 477 35 35 – www.desmondhousekinsale.com – April-October Y**x**
4 rm ☕ – 🚹 € 70/140 🚹🚹 € 100/140
Built by a Spanish merchant in 1780 and once belonging to the church – it still displays a tiny altar on the landing. Homemade bread and scones feature in the attractive, parquet-floored breakfast room. Comfortable bedrooms boast jacuzzis.

XX **Finns' Table** (N)

6 Main St – ℰ (021) 470 9636 – www.finnstable.com – Closed 3 weeks November, Christmas, Sunday-Thursday January-mid March and Tuesday-Wednesday **Yb**

Rest – *(dinner only)* Menu € 33 (early dinner) – Carte € 34/46

Behind the bright orange woodwork lie two attractive rooms – one with colourful banquettes, the other in powder blue with wine box panelling. Meat is from the owners' butchery and everything from the bread to the ice cream is homemade.

XX **Max's**

48 Main St. – ℰ (021) 477 24 43 – www.maxs.ie – Closed mid-December-March, Sunday except June-September and bank holidays **Zm**

Rest – *(dinner only)* Menu € 25 – Carte € 34/49

Two-roomed restaurant on a quaint main street, with a simple yet smart rustic style; a spot well-known by the locals! The unfussy, classically based seafood menu offers good choice, try the tasty 'Fresh Catches'. Efficient, engaging team.

X **Fishy Fishy Cafe**

Pier Rd – ℰ (021) 470 04 15 – www.fishyfishy.ie **Zx**

Rest – Carte € 30/48 **s**

Friendly, informal restaurant that's a local institution. Dine at the bar and watch the kitchen shuck oysters; in the main room amongst 'fishy' memorabilia or al-fresco on the lovely terrace. Concise, all-day menus offer well-prepared, good value seafood dishes and tasty specials; owner collects the fish daily.

Toddies at The Bulman

Summercove, East : 2 km by R 600 and Charles Fort rd. – ℰ (021) 477 21 31 – www.thebulman.ie – Closed 25 December, Good Friday and Monday dinner

Rest – Carte € 27/49

Rustic pub with maritime décor and excellent views over Kinsale and the bay; look out for the Moby Dick mural and the carved Bulman Buoy. Lunch is taken in the bar and offers simple pub classics; dinner is served in the more formal restaurant and presents carefully prepared, globally influenced dishes.

at Barrells Cross Southwest : 5.75 km on R 600 - Z – ✉ Kinsale

Rivermount House without rest

North : 0.75 km on L 7302 – ℰ (021) 477 80 33 – www.rivermount.com – Closed 10 November- 13 March

6 rm – † € 55/85 †† € 85/100

Spacious, purpose-built dormer bungalow overlooking the countryside and the river, yet not far from town. It has a distinctive modern style throughout, with attractive embossed wallpapers and quality furnishings. Bold, well-appointed bedrooms display high attention to detail and have immaculate bathrooms.

KNOCK (An Cnoc) – Mayo – 712 F6 – pop. 811 Ireland — 36 B2

Dublin 212 – Galway 74 – Westport 51

Ireland West Airport, Knock : ℰ (094) 9368100, NE : 14.5 km by N 17

Town Centre, ℰ (094) 9 38 81 93, www.discoverireland.ie

Basilica of our Lady, Queen of Ireland★

Museum of Country Life★★ **AC**, NW : 26 km by R 323, R 321 and N 5

Hotels see : ***Cong*** *SW : 58 km by N 17, R 331 R 334 and R 345*

LAHINCH (An Leacht) – Clare – 712 D9 – pop. 642 Ireland — 38 B1

Dublin 260 km – Galway 79 km – Limerick 66 km

Lahinch, ℰ (065) 7 08 10 03

Spanish Point, Miltown Malbay, ℰ (065) 7 08 42 19

Cliffs of Moher★★★ – Kilfenora (Burren Centre★ **AC**, High Crosses★), NE : 11 km by N 85 and R 481

REPUBLIC OF IRELAND

Vaughan Lodge

Ennistymon Rd – ✆ (065) 708 11 11 – www.vaughanlodge.ie – Closed November-March
22 rm – € 100/155 € 130/210
Rest – *(closed Sunday and Monday) (dinner only)* Menu € 45 – Carte € 37/76
Stylish roadside hotel with a bright, modern interior, a leather-furnished lounge and a great selection of malts behind the bar. The smart, spacious bedrooms come in eye-catching colour schemes and offer good facilities. There are many golf courses nearby. The dining room serves a menu of modern classics.

Moy House

Southwest : 3 km on N 67 (Milltown Malbay rd) – ✆ (065) 708 28 00 – www.moyhouse.com – Closed November-April
9 rm – € 145/175 € 160/360
Rest – *(dinner only) (set menu only)* Menu € 55
18C Italianate clifftop villa, overlooking the bay and run by a friendly, attentive team. Homely guest areas include a small library and an open-fired drawing room with an honesty bar; antiques, oil paintings and heavy fabrics feature throughout. Individually designed, classical bedrooms boast good extras and most have views. Formal dining is from a 5 course set menu.

LEENANE (An Líonán) – Galway – 712 C7 – ✉ Clifden Ireland 36 A3

Dublin 278 km – Ballina 90 km – Galway 66 km
Killary Harbour★
Joyce Country★★ – Lough Nafooey★, SE : 10.5 km by R 336 – Aasleagh Falls★, NE : 4 km. Connemara★★★ – Lough Corrib★★, SE : 16 km by R 336 and R 345 – Doo Lough Pass★, NW : 14.5 km by N 59 and R 335

Delphi Lodge

Northwest : 13.25 km by N 59 on Louisburgh rd – ✆ (095) 42 222 – www.delphilodge.ie
12 rm – € 140/195 € 230/350
Rest – *(dinner only) (set menu only)* Menu € 55
A former shooting lodge of the Marquis of Sligo, in a lovely loughside spot on a 1,000 acre estate. Bright, simple bedrooms with smart bathrooms. 'Special Experience' days, free bike hire and a large walkers' drying room. Communal dining from a set menu; guests are encouraged to mingle in the drawing room.

LEIGHLINBRIDGE (Leithghlinn an Droichid) – Carlow – 712 L9 – pop. 828 39 D2

Dublin 63 km – Carlow 8 km – Kilkenny 16 km – Athy 22 km

Lord Bagenal

Main St – ✆ (059) 977 40 00 – www.lordbagenal.com – Closed 25-26 December
39 rm – € 65/85 € 90/150
Rest – *(carving lunch)* Menu € 25/35 – Carte € 27/43
Striking hotel on the banks of the River Barrow. It was originally just a tiny coaching inn – be sure to head to the characterful original bar for a comforting, classical dish and a pint of Guinness in front of the peat fire. Vast modern extensions house the rest of the guest areas and the modern bedrooms.

LETTERFRACK (Leitir Fraic) – Galway – 712 C7 Ireland 36 A3

Dublin 304 km – Ballina 111 km – Galway 91 km
Connemara★★★ - Sky Road★★ (≤★★) – Connemara National Park★ – Kylemore Abbey★, E : 4.75 km by N 59

Rosleague Manor

West : 2.5 km. on N 59 – ✆ (095) 41 101 – www.rosleague.com – Closed mid-November-mid-March
20 rm – € 85/125 € 130/250 **Rest** – *(dinner only)* Menu € 32/46
Creeper-clad country house in mature grounds, boasting excellent bay and mountain views. Large, classically styled bedrooms. Cosy, antique-filled drawing rooms with open fires; wicker-furnished conservatory for afternoon tea and evening drinks. The formal dining room overlooks the gardens.

REPUBLIC OF IRELAND

LETTERKENNY (Leitir Ceanainn) – **Donegal** – **712** I3 – **pop. 15 387** Ireland **37** C1

Dublin 241 km – Londonderry 34 km – Sligo 116 km

Neil T Blaney Rd, ☎ (074) 9 12 11 60, www.letterkennyguide.com

Dunfanaghy, ☎ (074) 913 63 35

Glenveagh National Park★★ (Gardens★★), NW : 19.25 km by R 250, R 251 and R 254 – Grianan of Aileach★★ (≤★★) NE : 28 km by N 13 – Church Hill (Glebe House and Gallery★ **AC**) NW : 16 km by R 250

Radisson Blu rest,

Paddy Harte Rd – ☎ (074) 919 44 44 – www.radissonblu.ie/hotel-letterkenny

114 rm – € 84/120 € 99/219

Rest *Brasserie Tribeca* – *(dinner only)* Menu € 28 **s** – Carte € 26/45 **s**

Purpose-built hotel set on a shopping and retail park close to the city centre; its reception displays photos of the stars who have stayed here. Uniform bedrooms with modern bathrooms. Good leisure club. Spacious bar serves light meals and snacks; popular, brasserie-style dining room offers dishes to match.

LIMERICK (Luimneach) – **Limerick** – **712** G9 – **pop. 57 106** Ireland **38** B2

Dublin 195 km – Cork 99 km – Galway 102 km – Waterford 127 km

Shannon Airport : ☎ (061) 712000, W : 25.75 km by N 18 Z

Arthur's Quay, ☎ (061) 3 17 52 2Y, www.limericktourist.com

City★★ - St Mary's Cathedral★ Y – Hunt Museum★★ **AC** Y - Georgian House★ **AC** Z – King John's Castle★ **AC** Y - Limerick Museum★ Z **M2** – John Square★ Z **20** – St John's Cathedral★ Z

Bunratty Castle★★ **AC**, W : 12 km by N 18 – Cratloe Wood (≤★) NW : 8 km by N 18 Z. Castleconnell★, E : 11.25 km by N 7 - Lough Gur Interpretive Centre★ **AC**, S : 17.75 km by R 512 and R 514 Z – Clare Glens★, E : 21 km by N 7 and R 503 Y – Monasteranenagh Abbey★, S : 21 km by N 20 Z

Savoy rm,

Henry St – ☎ (061) 448 700 – www.savoylimerick.com Z**e**

94 rm – € 99/255 € 99/255, € 18

Rest *Market Square Brasserie* – *(closed Sunday and Monday) (dinner only) (booking essential)* Menu € 25 (lunch)/39 – Carte € 33/58

Corporate hotel named after the theatre that previously stood on the site. Spacious guest areas and bar; good-sized, uniform bedrooms with smart, modern bathrooms. The hands-on owner and his charming team provide good old-fashioned hospitality. The modern, open-plan dining room offers something for everyone.

Limerick Strand

Ennis Rd – ☎ (061) 421 800 – www.limerickstrandhotel.ie Y**z**

184 rm – € 99/299 € 99/299

Rest *River* – see restaurant listing

Commercial hotel with extensive, state-of-the-art function and leisure facilities. Modern bedrooms are uniformly styled and come with good amenities; go for an executive, which has a balcony. The terraced bar overlooks the River Shannon.

Absolute H. & Spa rm,

Sir Harry's Mall – ☎ (061) 463 600 – www.absolutehotel.com Y**a**

99 rm – € 65/150 € 65/150

Rest *ABG* – Carte € 20/36

Set on the edge of the city and designed in the style of an old mill to reflect the area's industrial heritage. Inside it's contrastingly stylish, with well-thought-out bedrooms, modern meeting rooms and a pleasant spa and leisure centre. The restaurant serves a traditional menu and overlooks the river.

Radisson Blu H. & Spa rest,

Ennis Rd, Northwest : 6.5 km by N 18 – ☎ (061) 456 200 – www.radissonblu.ie/hotel-limerick

153 rm – € 79/149 € 89/159 – 2 suites

Rest *Porters* – *(buffet lunch)* Menu € 12/28 – Carte € 26/40

Modern, well-run hotel by the city bypass – which makes a good base for those wanting to stay outside the city or close to Shannon Airport. Spacious, uniform bedrooms. Excellent spa with 10 treatment rooms and a relaxation suite. The restaurant serves buffet lunches and traditional dinners.

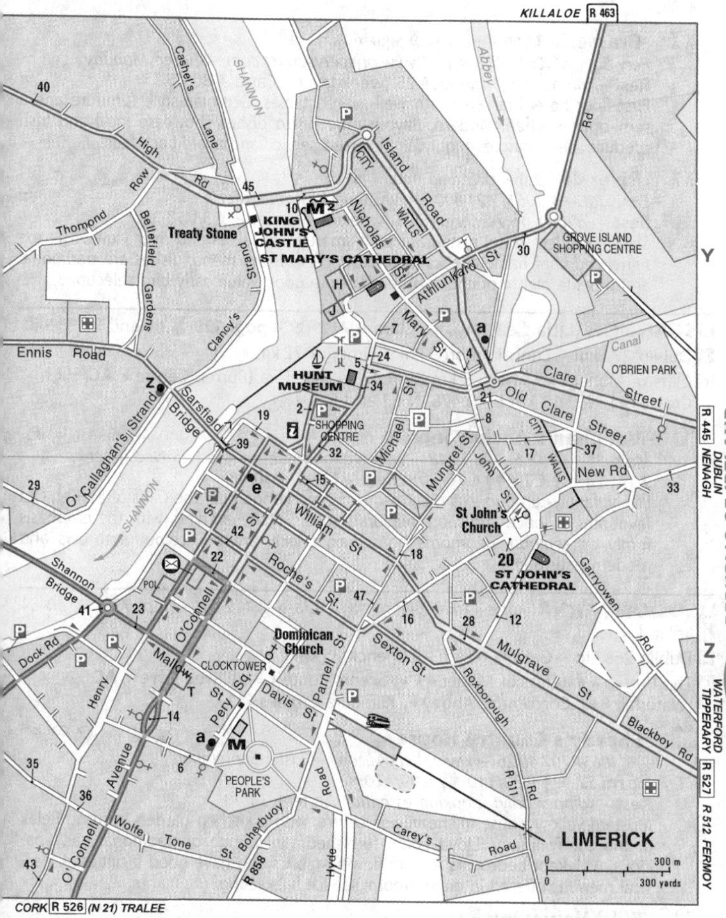

Arthur Quay . . . . Y 2
Arthur Quay Shopping Centre . . . . Y
Baal's Bridge . . . . Y 4
Bank Pl. . . . . Y 5
Barrington St . . . . Z 6
Bridge St . . . . Y 7
Broad St. . . . . Y 8
Castle St . . . . Y 10
Cathedral Pl. . . . . Z 12
Charlotte's Quay . . . . Y 13
Cruises St. . . . . Z 15
Gerald Griffen St . . . . Z 16
Grattan St. . . . . Y 17
Grove Island Shopping Centre . . . . Y
High St . . . . Z 18
Honan's Quay . . . . Y 19
John Square . . . . Z 20
Lock Quay . . . . Y 21
Lower Cecil St . . . . Z 22
Lower Mallow St. . . . . Z 23
Mathew Bridge . . . . Y 24
Newtown Mahon . . . . Z 28
North Circular Rd . . . . Z 29
O'Connell St . . . . Z
O'Dwyer Bridge . . . . Y 30
Patrick St . . . . YZ 32
Penniwell Rd . . . . Z 33
Roches St . . . . Z
Rutland St . . . . Y 34
St Alphonsus St . . . . Z 35
St Gerard St . . . . Z 36
St Lelia St . . . . YZ 37
Sarfield St . . . . Y 39
Sexton St North . . . . Y 40
Shannonside Roundabout . . . . Z 41
Shannon St . . . . Z 42
South Circular Rd . . . . Z 43
The Crescent . . . . Z 14
Thomond Bridge . . . . Y 45
Wickham St . . . . Z 47
William St . . . . Z

No 1 Pery Square

Pery Sq – ✆ *(061) 402 402* – *www.oneperysquare.com* – *Closed 25-26 December*
20 rm ☕ – 🚹 € 135/165 🚹🚹 € 135/195 – 1 suite **Za**
Rest *Brasserie One* – see restaurant listing
Charming Georgian house with well-proportioned rooms and a beautiful spa. Elegant bedrooms display antique furnishings and have a luxurious feel. The open-plan lounge features a coffee shop, and there's a wine shop in the cellar.

XX **Brasserie One** – No 1 Pery Square Hotel
Pery Sq – ✆ (061) 402 402 – www.oneperysquare.com – Closed Monday
Rest – *(dinner only)* Menu € 25 (weekdays) – Carte € 30/45 Z**a**
First floor hotel brasserie with well-spaced tables, Georgian-style furniture and a semi-open kitchen. Modern, flavoursome bistro dishes showcase local and Irish produce; beef features highly. Well-versed service and a laid-back feel.

XX **River** (N) – Limerick Strand Hotel
Ennis Rd – ✆ (061) 421 800 – www.limerickstrandhotel.ie Y**z**
Rest – *(dinner only)* Menu € 23 (weekdays) – Carte € 33/58
Stylish, modern hotel restaurant with smartly laid tables and river views. The experienced chef name-checks local producers on the menu; dishes are traditional and provide plenty of choice. There's also a good value early bird selection.

LISCANNOR (Lios Ceannúir) – Clare – 712 D9 – pop. 129 Ireland 38 B1

Dublin 272 km – Ennistimmon 9 km – Limerick 72 km

Cliffs of Moher★★★, NW : 8 km by R 478 – Kilfenora (Burren Centre★ **AC**, High Crosses★), NE : 18 km by R 478, N 67 and R 481

Vaughan's Anchor Inn with rm rest, **P**
Main St – ✆ (065) 708 15 48 – www.vaughans.ie – Closed 25 December
7 rm – € 70 € 70/80 **Rest** – Carte € 30/48
Lively, family-run pub in a picturesque fishing village near the Cliffs of Moher. Old favourites at lunch and more elaborate meals in the evening, with the emphasis firmly on seafood. Bedrooms boast bright local artwork, colourful throws and modern bathrooms.

LISDOONVARNA (Lios Dúin Bhearna) – Clare – 712 E8 – pop. 739 38 B1

Ireland

Dublin 268 km – Galway 63 km – Limerick 75 km

The Burren★★ (Cliffs of Moher★★★, Scenic Route★★, Aillwee Cave★ **AC** (Waterfall★★), Corcomroe Abbey★, Kilfenora Crosses★)

Sheedy's Country House rm, **P**
– ✆ (065) 707 40 26 – www.sheedys.com – Easter-September
11 rm – € 80/110 € 99/170
Rest – *(dinner only) (booking essential)* Carte € 33/48
Mustard-yellow house in the village centre, with a kitchen garden in front. Relax in the comfy library, Lloyd Loom furnished sun lounge or traditional bar. Spacious, well-kept bedrooms feature flowery fabrics and have good facilities. A classical menu is offered in dining room; service is exacting.

Wild Honey Inn with rm
South : 0.5 km on Ennistimon rd – ✆ (065) 707 43 00 – www.wildhoneyinn.com – Closed first week January-12 February, 24-26 December, and restricted opening November-December and February-April
14 rm – € 50/55 € 80/100
Rest – *(closed lunch Monday and Tuesday) (bookings not accepted)*
Carte € 29/45
Three-storey building at the end of a short terrace, located close to the limestone landscape of The Burren and the Cliffs of Moher. Menus stick with the classics and champion local produce, particularly seafood. Flavours are bold and presentation is modern. Bedrooms are simply furnished; two open onto the walled courtyard. Have breakfast overlooking the garden.

LISTOWEL (Lios Tuathail) – Kerry – 712 D10 – pop. 4 205 Ireland 38 B2

Dublin 270 km – Killarney 54 km – Limerick 75 km – Tralee 27 km

St John's Church, ✆ (068) 2 25 90, www.listowel.ie

Ardfert★ **AC**, SW : 32 km by N 69 and minor roads via Abbeydorney – Banna Strand★, SW : 35 km by N 69 and minor roads via Abbeydorney – Carrigafoyle Castle★, N : 17 km by R 552 and minor road – Glin Castle★ **AC**, N : 24 km by N 69 – Rattoo Round Tower★, W : 19 km by R 553, R 554 and R 551

REPUBLIC OF IRELAND

✗ **Allo's Bistro** with rm 📶
41-43 Church St – 𝒞 (068) 22 880 – www.allosbarbistro-townhouse.com
– Closed Sunday and Monday except bank holidays
3 rm 🛏 – ♦ € 50/70 ♦♦ € 50/70 **Rest** – *(booking essential)* Carte € 24/47
Former pub dating back to 1873; now a simple, well-run and characterful restaurant. Series of homely rooms and friendly, efficient service. Wide-ranging menus rely on regional produce, with theme nights on Thursdays and an adventurous gourmet menu at weekends. Individual, antique-furnished bedrooms.

LONGFORD (An Longfort) – **Longford** – 712 I6 – **pop. 8 002** 37 C3
◘ Dublin 124 km – Drogheda 120 km – Galway 112 km – Limerick 175 km
🔼 Market Square, 𝒞 (043) 4 25 77, www.longfordtourism.ie

🏠 **Viewmount House** 🌿 🚗 ë 📶 🅿
Dublin Rd, Southeast : 1.5 km by R 393 – 𝒞 (043) 334 19 19
– www.viewmounthouse.com
12 rm 🛏 – ♦ € 55/65 ♦♦ € 110/130
Rest *VM* – see restaurant listing
Georgian house in 4 acres of mature grounds, with a charming period style. Original features include an ornate vaulted ceiling in the breakfast room. Bedrooms are traditionally styled and furnished with antiques; opt for a duplex room.

✗✗✗ **VM** 🅝 – Viewmount House Hotel 🚗 ë 🅿
Dublin Rd, Southeast : 1.5 km by R 393 – 𝒞 (043) 334 19 19
– www.viewmounthouse.com
Rest – *(closed Good Friday, 25-26 December, Sunday dinner, Monday and Tuesday)* *(dinner only and Sunday lunch)* Menu € 28/53
Formal hotel restaurant in the old stables of a Georgian house, overlooking a Japanese garden. Classical lounge and a smart, rustic dining room with stone-faced walls. Interesting, original modern menus; orchard and garden produce features.

MALAHIDE (Mullach Íde) – **Fingal** – 712 N7 – **pop. 15 846** ▮ Ireland 39 D1
◘ Dublin 19 km – Cork 274 km – Galway 224 km – Waterford 185 km
🔼 Beechwood, The Grange, 𝒞 (01) 846 16 11
◉ Castle ★★
🔵 Newbridge House ★ **AC**, N : 8 km by R 106, M1 and minor road

✗✗✗ **bon appétit** (Oliver Dunne) 🄰🄲
🍀 *9 St James Terr – 𝒞 (01) 845 0314 – www.bonappetit.ie – Closed first 2 weeks January, first 2 weeks August, Wednesday lunch and Sunday-Tuesday*
Rest – *(booking essential)* Menu € 30/80
Set in a delightful Georgian terrace; ring the bell for entry. Have an aperitif in the subtly lit bar then head for the elegant first floor dining room with its ornate cornicing, crisp linen and detailed service. The concise menu offers well-judged, expertly executed classical dishes with distinct flavours.
➜ Guinea fowl and black pudding boudin, hen's egg and bacon. Best end and pressed shoulder of lamb with asparagus and Jerusalem artichoke. Coffee panna cotta with a Baileys and white chocolate mousse.

✗✗ **Brasserie at bon appétit** 🄰🄲 ▦
😊 *9 St James Terr – 𝒞 (01) 845 0314 – www.bonappetit.ie – Closed 25-26 December*
Rest – *(dinner only and Sunday lunch)* *(booking essential)* Menu € 20/30 – Carte € 29/49
Buzzy basement brasserie below the more formal 'bon appétit'. Appealing, classical cooking with a French accent; dishes are prepared with care and precision and are very satisfying. Pleasant, efficient service and good value 'meal deals'. Selection of small plates in the trendy, dimly lit bar.

✗✗ **Jaipur** 🄰🄲
5 St James Terr – 𝒞 (01) 845 5455 – www.jaipur.ie – Closed 25 December
Rest – *(dinner only)* Menu € 21 – Carte € 33/46
Basement restaurant in terraced Georgian parade. Tasty, contemporary Indian cooking with Tandoori Jhinga (large prawns marinated in Indian spices) a speciality. Friendly, efficient service.

MALLOW (Mala) – **Cork** – **712** F11 – **pop. 8 578** Ireland **38** B2

Dublin 240 km – Cork 34 km – Killarney 64 km – Limerick 66 km

Ballyellis, (022) 2 11 45

Town★ – St James' Church★

Annes Grove Gardens★, E : 17.75 km by N 72 and minor rd – Buttevant Friary★, N : 11.25 km by N 20 – Doneraile Wildlife Park★ **AC**, NE : 9.5 km by N 20 and R 581 – Kanturk★ (Castle★), W : 16 km by N 72 and R 576

Longueville House

West : 5.5 km by N 72 – (022) 47 156 – www.longuevillehouse.ie – Closed 24-27 December, Monday-Tuesday and restricted opening in winter

20 rm – € 119/179 € 169/199

Rest *Presidents* – *(dinner only and Sunday lunch) (booking essential)*

Menu € 38/70

Part-Georgian manor house built in William and Mary style, with pleasant views over Dromineen Castle. Lovely stone-tiled hall, superb flying staircase and stunning drawing room. Well-appointed bedrooms boast antique furniture. Grand restaurant; traditional menus use produce from the kitchen garden and estate.

MIDLETON (Mainistir na Corann) – **Cork** – **712** H12 – **pop. 3 733** **39** C3

Dublin 259 km – Cork 19 km – Waterford 98 km

Jameson Heritage Centre, (021) 4 61 37 02, www.midletononline.com

East Cork, Gortacrue, (021) 4 63 16 87

Cloyne Cathedral★ **AC**, S : 8 km by R 630 and R 629

Farmgate Restaurant & Country Store

Coolbawn – (021) 463 27 71 – www.farmgate.ie – Closed 24 December-3 January, Sunday and Monday

Rest – *(bookings advisable at dinner)* Menu € 45 (dinner) – Carte € 30/52

Friendly food store with a bakery, a rustic two-roomed restaurant and a courtyard terrace. Light lunches offer soups, sandwiches and tarts; dinner features regional fish and meats – the chargrilled steaks are popular. Cakes served all day.

MILLSTREET = Sráid an Mhuilinn – **Waterford** – **712** I11 – **see Cappoquin**

MOHILL (Maothail) – **Leitrim** – **712** I6 – **pop. 928** **37** C2

Dublin 98 km – Carrick-on-Shannon 11 km – Cavan 41 km – Castlerea 44 km

Lough Rynn Castle

rm, AC

Southeast : 4 km by R 201 off Drumlish rd – (071) 963 27 00 – www.loughrynn.ie

43 rm – € 89/165 € 109/195

Rest *Sandstone* – *(dinner only and Sunday lunch)* Menu € 26/52 – Carte € 40/98

18C country house with superb gardens and peaceful grounds; popular for weddings. Numerous lounges and a baronial hall with original parquet flooring and an impressive fireplace. Large, well-appointed bedrooms – those in the main house are the most characterful. Formal dining room; ambitious French cuisine.

Lough Rynn Country House without rest

Southeast : 3.5 km. by R 201 off Drumlish rd – (071) 963 2121 – www.loughrynnbandb.ie

5 rm – € 45 € 90

Stone house on a country road, boasting lovely views over Lough Rynn; three of the homely bedrooms share the view and one has a small balcony. Comfy lounge and cottagey breakfast room. Guest are welcomed with home-baked scones or muffins.

MULLINGAR (An Muileann gCearr) – **Westmeath** – **712** J/K7 **37** C3 – **pop. 9 414** Ireland

Dublin 79 km – Cork 242 km – Galway 146 km – Waterford 177 km

Market Sq., (0449) 34 86 50, www.midirelandtourism.ie

Belvedere House and Gardens★ **AC**, S : 5.5 km by N 52. Fore Abbey★, NE : 27.25 km by R 394 – Multyfarnhan Franciscan Friary★, N : 12.75 km by N 4 – Tullynally★ **AC**, N : 21 km by N 4 and R 394

Mullingar Park
Dublin Rd, East : 2.5 km on Dublin Rd (N 4) – ☎ (044) 933 7500 – www.mullingarparkhotel.com – Closed 25-26 December
94 rm – † €80/105 †† €120/220 – 1 suite
Rest – Menu €30 (dinner) **s** – Carte €32/42 **s**
Large, contemporary hotel close to a business park and the main road to Dublin – a popular conference venue. Well-equipped, modern bedrooms in a uniform style. Comprehensive leisure facilities. Horseshoe bar-lounge and spacious formal dining room offering classical Irish cooking.

Marlinstown Court without rest
Dublin Rd, East : 2.5 km on Dublin Rd (N 4) – ☎ (044) 934 00 53 – www.marlinstowncourt.com – Closed 23-27 December
5 rm – † €40/45 †† €70/75
Clean, tidy guesthouse close to the N4; a very homely, personal option for staying away. The light, airy lounge opens into a pleasant pine-furnished breakfast room overlooking the garden. Bedrooms are simply and brightly decorated.

MULRANNY (An Mhala Raithní) – Mayo – 712 C6 — 36 A2

Dublin 270 km – Castlebar 35 km – Westport 29 km

Mulranny Park
on N 59 – ☎ (098) 36 000 – www.mulrannyparkhotel.ie – Closed 7-21 January and 25-26 December
61 rm – † €75/110 †† €110/190 – 20 suites
Rest *Nephin* – *(dinner only and Sunday lunch)* Menu €40 (dinner) **s** – Carte €27/65 **s**
1897 railway hotel with stunning views of Clew Bay and Achill Island, and its own causeway to the beach. Modern, slightly minimalist bedrooms; the two-bedroomed suites are ideal for families. Impressive leisure and conference facilities. All-day snacks in the bar; modern menu in the restaurant. Charming team.

MURRISK – Mayo – 712 D6 — 36 A2

Dublin 260 km – Castlebar 25 km – Galway 95 km

Tavern Ⓝ
– ☎ (098) 64 060 – www.tavernmurrisk.com – Closed Good Friday and 25 December
Rest – Carte €22/42
Vibrant pink pub with designer colours, leather banquettes and quirky basket lampshades. Wide-ranging dishes display a touch of refinement; the meats and seafood are local and the daily cheesecake is a must. Staff are smart and attentive.

NAAS (An Nás) – Kildare – 712 L/M8 – pop. 20 044 Ireland — 39 D1

Dublin 30 km – Kilkenny 83 km – Tullamore 85 km
Kerdiffstown, Naas, ☎ (045) 87 46 44
Russborough★★★ **AC**, S : 16 km by R 410 and minor road – Castletown House★★ **AC**, NE : 24 km by R 407 and R 403

Killashee House H. & Villa Spa
Kilcullen Rd, South : 3 km on R 448 – ☎ (045) 879 277 – www.killasheehouse.com – Closed 25-26 December
141 rm – † €100/270 †† €130/300 – 12 suites
Rest *Turners* – *(dinner only Friday-Saturday)* Menu €45
Rest *Jack's* – Menu €10 (weekday lunch)/30 – Carte €22/45
Impressive part-1860s hunting lodge, surrounded by vast grounds and boasting spacious, traditionally styled guest areas, good event facilities and a superb leisure club and spa. Country house style bedrooms – those in the main building are the most characterful. Turners offers elegant fine dining overlooking the garden. Family-friendly brasserie menu in informal Jack's.

Vie de Châteaux

The Harbour – ✆ (045) 888 478 – www.viedechateaux.ie – Closed 24 December-5 January, lunch Saturday, Monday-Tuesday and bank holidays
Rest – *(booking essential)* Menu € 19 (lunch)/29 – Carte € 28/50
Stylish, popular restaurant with a terrace, an open-plan kitchen and a brasserie feel; a stone's throw from the canal. Concise, keenly priced menu moves with the seasons; mainly French dishes but with some Mediterranean influences.

at Two Mile House Southwest : 6.5 km by R 448

Brown Bear

– ✆ (045) 883 561 – www.thebrownbear.ie – Closed Monday, Tuesday and 24-27 December
Rest – *(dinner only and lunch Saturday-Sunday)* Menu € 20/27 – Carte € 29/45
Smart restaurant in a small village, boasting a pubby locals bar and leather-furnished dining room with a subtle brasserie feel. Decide between two menus: a two-choice set selection or a complex, ambitious à la carte with a Gallic twist.

NAVAN (An Uaimh) – Meath – 712 L7 – pop. 24 851 Ireland 37 D3

Dublin 48 km – Drogheda 26 km – Dundalk 51 km
Moor Park, Mooretown, ✆ (046) 2 76 61
Royal Tara, Bellinter, ✆ (046) 902 52 44
Brú na Bóinne : Newgrange★★★ **AC**, Knowth★, E : 16 km by minor road to Donore – Bective Abbey★, S : 6.5 km by R 161 – Tara★ **AC**, S : 8 km by N 3. Kells★ (Round Tower and High Crosses★★, St Columba's House★), NW : by N 3 – Trim★ (castle★★), SW : 12.75 km by R 161

Ma Dwyers without rest

Dublin Rd, South : 1.25 km on R 147 – ✆ (046) 907 79 92 – www.madwyers.com – Closed 24-27 December
26 rm – † € 40 †† € 65
Surprisingly spacious detached house on the main road into town. Simple, brightly painted interior with a comfy lounge and large breakfast room. Good value bedrooms in an up-to-date, uniform style; bathrooms are shower only.

NEW QUAY (Bealaclugga) – Clare Ireland

Dublin 240 km – Ennis 55 km – Galway 46 km
Aillwee Cave★ **AC**, S : 10 km by N 67 and R 480 – Corcomroe Abbey★, S : 4.75 km by N 67 – Dunguaire Castle★ **AC**, NE : 15 km by N 67

Mount Vernon

Flaggy Shore, North : 0.75 km on coast rd – ✆ (065) 707 8126 – www.mountvernon.ie – Closed November-March
5 rm – † € 120/145 †† € 190/230 **Rest** – Menu € 50
Charming whitewashed house with a pretty walled garden, set close to the beach and affording lovely views. Antiques and eclectic curios fill the guest areas; spacious bedrooms have their own personalities – two open onto a terrace. Simply cooked dinners rely on fresh, local produce. Warm, welcoming owners.

Linnane's Lobster Bar N

New Quay Pier – ✆ (065) 707 8120 – www.linnanesbar.com – Closed Good Friday, Christmas Day and Monday-Thursday October-Easter
Rest – Carte € 21/38
Simple but likeable place, with peat fires and full-length windows which open onto a terrace. They specialise in fresh, tasty fish and shellfish; watch the local boats unload their catch – some of which is brought straight to the kitchen.

NEWMARKET-ON-FERGUS (Cora Chaitlín) – Clare – 712 F7 – pop. 1 542 Ireland 38 B2

Dublin 219 km – Ennis 13 km – Limerick 24 km
Dromoland Castle, ✆ (061) 36 84 44
Bunratty Castle★★ **AC**, S : 10 km by N 18 – Craggaunowen Centre★ **AC**, NE : 15 km by minor road towards Moymore – Knappogue Castle★ **AC**, NE : 12 km N 18 and minor roads via Quin – Quin Friary★ **AC**, N : 10 km by N 18 and minor road to Quin

Dromoland Castle
Northwest : 2.5 km on R 458 – (061) 368 144 – www.dromoland.ie
99 rm – € 240/464 € 240/464, €29 – 5 suites
Rest *Earl of Thomond* – *(dinner only)* Menu € 70 – Carte € 58/71
Rest *Fig Tree* – Carte € 27/50
Impressive 16C castle in 450 acres, with a championship golf course and equestrian and falconry centres. Various richly appointed, antique-filled, country house lounges. Smart 'feature' bedrooms cleverly blend the old and new; the courtyard rooms are more traditional. Modern classics under crystal chandeliers in the formal restaurant; more casual dining in Fig Tree.

NEWPORT (Baile Uí Fhiacháin) – Mayo – 712 D6 – pop. 590 36 A2

Ireland

Dublin 264 km – Ballina 59 km – Galway 96 km

Westport, (098) 2 57 11, www.mayo-ireland.ie

Burrishoole Abbey★, NW : 3.25 km by N 59 – Furnace Lough★, NW : 4.75 km by N 59. Achill Island★, W : 35 km by N 59 and R 319

Newport House
– (098) 41 222 – www.newporthouse.ie – Closed November-18 March
14 rm – € 120/165 € 190/280 **Rest** – *(dinner only)* Menu € 65
Delightful creeper-clad mansion with lovely gardens and river views; they also own Lough Beltra, nearby. Large drawing room with family portraits; traditional, antique-filled bedrooms. The grand staircase is topped by a domed cupola. Dinner is a highlight, with salmon a speciality and a notable wine list.

OUGHTERARD (Uachtar Ard) – Galway – 712 E7 – pop. 1 305 36 A3

Ireland

Dublin 232 km – Cork 223 km – Galway 25 km – Waterford 253 km

Main Street, (091) 55 28 08, www.oughterardtourism.com

Gortreevagh, (091) 55 21 31

Town★

Lough Corrib★★ (Shore road - NW - ★★) – Aughnanure Castle★ **AC**, SE : 3.25 km by N 59

Currarevagh House
Northwest : 6.5 km on Glann rd – (091) 552 312 – www.currarevagh.com – Closed November-March
12 rm – € 80/95 € 140/170
Rest – *(dinner only) (set menu only)* Menu € 48
Classically furnished Victorian manor house, in 180 acres bordering Lough Corrib. Run by the same family for over 100 years; it has a very 'lived-in' feel and offers a real 'county house' experience. Have afternoon tea by the fire or take a picnic out on the boat. Set dinners of unfussy, flavoursome dishes.

Ross Lake House
Rosscahill, Southeast : 7.25 km by N 59 – (091) 550 109 – www.rosslakehotel.com – Closed November-15 March
13 rm – € 97/105 € 134/170 – 2 suites
Rest – *(dinner only)* Menu € 43
Personally run Georgian country house with attractive gardens, set in a wooded estate. Traditionally styled bedrooms; Strefens suite and Killaguile are the best. Begin the evening in the cocktail bar before dining by candlelight at smartly set, cloth-clad tables.

Railway Lodge without rest
West : 0.75 km by Costello rd taking first right onto unmarked road – (091) 552 945 – www.railwaylodge.net
4 rm – € 50/60 € 90/110
Stylish house in a remote farm setting, with views across the countryside and a beautifully kept, elegantly furnished interior. Bedrooms come with stripped pine furnishings and have a keen eye for detail. The charming owner offers good local recommendations. Homemade bread and scones; tea served on arrival.

REPUBLIC OF IRELAND

Waterfall Lodge without rest
West : 0.75 km on N 59 – (091) 552 168 – www.waterfalllodge.net
6 rm – € 50 € 80
Heavily restored Victorian house run by an infectiously enthusiastic owner. A fishing river runs through the garden – look out for jumping salmon! Sympathetically styled bedrooms with rug-covered floors and modern bathrooms; some have four-posters. Pancakes, French toast and smoked salmon at breakfast.

PORTMAGEE (An Caladh) – Kerry – 712 A12 – pop. 375 Ireland 38 A2

Dublin 365 km – Killarney 72 km – Tralee 82 km
Ring of Kerry★★

Moorings rest,
– (066) 947 71 08 – www.moorings.ie – Closed 24-25 December
16 rm – € 60/100 € 90/140
Rest – *(closed Monday except bank holidays) (bar lunch)* Carte € 32/48
Cosy, personally run hotel overlooking the harbour and bridge, and made up a series of little cottages. First floor lounge offers great views, as do some of the pleasant bedrooms; 4 and 6 boast jacuzzis. Characterful bar with music nights. Nautically themed restaurant with seafood straight from local boats.

PORTLAOISE (Port Laoise) – Laois – 712 K8 – pop. 14 613 39 C2

Dublin 88 km – Carlow 40 km – Waterford 101 km

Ivyleigh House without rest
Bank Pl, Church St – (057) 862 20 81 – www.ivyleigh.com – Closed 25 December
6 rm – € 50/75 € 80/160
Traditional listed Georgian property in the city centre, run by a welcoming owner. Comfy lounge and communal dining area, with antiques and ornaments displayed throughout. Good-sized bedrooms are decorated in a period style. Homemade breads, preserves, muesli and a Cashel blue cheesecake special at breakfast.

PORTMARNOCK (Port Mearnóg) – Fingal – 712 N7 – pop. 8 979 39 D1

Ireland

Dublin 16 km – Belfast 165 km – Cork 271 km – Galway 221 km
Malahide Castle★★ **AC**, N : 4 km by R 124 – Ben of Howth★, S : 8 km by R 124 – Newbridge House★ **AC**, N : 16 km by R 124, M 1 and minor road east

Portmarnock H. and Golf Links rest,
Strand Rd – (01) 846 0611 – www.portmarnock.com – Closed 24-27 December
138 rm – € 79/139 € 89/159, €17 – 3 suites
Rest *Osborne Brasserie* – Menu € 25 (dinner) – Carte € 19/33 **s**
Much-extended 19C house, previously owned by the Jameson family of whiskey fame, and set on its own championship golf course. Well-maintained, classically styled bedrooms; those in the newer wing are larger and more contemporary – ask for a sea view. Traditional menus served in the smart brasserie.

RAMELTON (Ráth Mealtain) /Rathmelton – Donegal – 712 J2 – pop. 1 212 Ireland 37 C1

Dublin 248 km – Donegal 59 km – Londonerry 43 km – Sligo 122 km
Town★

Moorfield Lodge N without rest
Aughnagaddy Glebe, Moorfield, South : 3.25 km on R 245 – (074) 915 2655 – www.moorfieldlodge.com – Closed December-January
3 rm – € 100/110 € 110/150
Striking, modern house run by a welcoming owner. Bright, stylish bedrooms with underfloor heating, floor to ceiling windows and Egyptian cotton sheets. Room 1 has its own terrace, a double Jacuzzi bath and a TV built into the bathroom tiles. Communal breakfasts are served around an antique table.

Ardeen without rest
bear left at the fork in the village centre and left at T junction – ✆ (074) 915 12 43 – www.ardeenhouse.com – Closed October-Easter
5 rm – € 45 € 90
A Victorian house on the edge of the village, with peaceful gardens and a river nearby. Welcoming owner and homely, personally styled interior. Open-fired lounge with local info; communal breakfasts. Simple, well-kept bedrooms without TVs.

RATHGAR – **Dublin** – **712** N8 – **see Dublin**

RATHMINES = **Ráth Maonais** – **Dublin** – **712** N8 – **see Dublin**

RATHMULLAN (**Ráth Maoláin**) – **Donegal** – **712** J2 – **pop. 518** **37** C1
– ✉ **Letterkenny** Ireland
Dublin 265 km – Londonderry 58 km – Sligo 140 km
Otway, Saltpans, ✆ (074) 915 16 65
Knockalla Viewpoint★, N : 12.75 km by R 247 – Rathmelton★, SW : 11.25 km by R 247

Rathmullan House rm,
North : 0.5 mi on R 247 – ✆ (074) 915 81 88 – www.rathmullanhouse.com – Closed 6 January-10 February, restricted opening in winter
34 rm – € 70/170 € 140/250
Rest ***Weeping Elm*** – *(bar lunch)* Menu € 45/55
Family-run, part-19C house set by Lough Swilly. Country house style bedrooms in the original house; those in the extension are more modern and come with balconies or private terraces. The formal dining room has views over the grounds; traditional menus feature produce from the kitchen garden.

RATHNEW = **Ráth Naoi** – **Wicklow** – **712** N8 – **see Wicklow**

RIVERSTOWN (**Baile idir Dhá Abhainn**) – **Sligo** – **712** G5 – **pop. 374** **36** B2
Dublin 189 km – Cork 309 km – Lisburn 193 km – Craigavon 170 km

Coopershill
– ✆ (071) 916 51 08 – www.coopershill.com – Closed November-March
8 rm – € 134/157 € 198/244
Rest – *(dinner only) (booking essential)* Menu € 49
Magnificent Georgian house run by the 7th generation of the same family; set on a working farm within a 500 acre estate. Spacious guest areas showcase original furnishings – now antiques – and family portraits adorn the walls. Warm, country house style bedrooms. Formal dining amongst polished silverware.

ROSCOMMON (**Ros Comáin**) – **Roscommon** – **712** H7 – **pop. 5 693** **36** B3
Ireland
Dublin 151 km – Galway 92 km – Limerick 151 km
Harrison Hall, ✆ (090) 6 62 63 42, www.visitroscommon.com
Moate Park, ✆ (09066) 2 63 82
Castle★
Castlestrange Stone★, SW : 11.25 km by N 63 and R 362 – Strokestown★ (Famine Museum★ **AC**, Strokestown Park House★ **AC**), N : 19.25 km by N 61 and R 368 – Castlerea : Clonalis House★ **AC**, NW : 30.5 km by N 60

Abbey
on N 63 (Galway rd) – ✆ (090) 662 62 40 – www.abbeyhotel.ie – Closed 24-26 December
50 rm – € 75/150 € 100/190 **Rest** – Menu € 30/50 – Carte € 26/40
Part-18C, family-run manor house with a castellated façade; overlooking the ruins of the 13C abbey. The most characterful bedrooms are in the original house; some boast feature beds and roll-top baths. Good function and leisure facilities. Dine from the carvery in the large bar, or in the formal restaurant.

ROSSLARE (Ros Láir) – Wexford – 712 M11 – pop. 1 547 Ireland 39 D2

Dublin 167 km – Waterford 80 km – Wexford 19 km

Kilrane, (053) 3 32 32, www.rosslare.ebookireland.com

Rosslare Strand, (053) 913 22 03

Irish Agricultural Museum, Johnstowon Castle★★ **AC**, NW : 12 km by R 740, N 25 and minor road. Kilmore Quay★, SW : 24 km by R 736 and R 739 – Saltee Islands★, SW : 24 km by R 736, R 739 and ferry

Kelly's Resort

rest,

– (053) 913 21 14 – www.kellys.ie – Closed December-16 February

118 rm – € 77/105 € 154/209

Rest *La Marine* – see restaurant listing

Rest *Beaches* – Menu € 24/44

It started life in 1895 as a beachfront 'refreshment house'; now it's a sprawling leisure-orientated hotel run by the 4th generation of the Kelly family. Various lounges, large bar and sizeable spa. Well-appointed bedrooms; the newer rooms being the largest. Formal Beaches offers an exceptional wine list.

La Marine – Kelly's Resort Hotel

– (053) 913 21 14 – www.kellys.ie – Closed December-16 February

Rest – Menu € 20/27 – Carte € 26/39

Bistro-style restaurant located within a large beachfront hotel, boasting an open-kitchen and glass-fronted wine cellar. A large zinc-topped bar from France takes centre stage, while the menu offers a selection of tasty brasserie classics.

ROSSLARE HARBOUR (Calafort Ros Láir) – Wexford – 712 N11 – pop. 1 123 39 D2

Dublin 169 km – Waterford 82 km – Wexford 21 km

to France (Cherbourg and Roscoff) (Irish Ferries) (17 h/15 h) – to Fishguard (Stena Line) 1-4 daily (1 h 40 mn/3 h 30 mn) – to Pembroke (Irish Ferries) 2 daily (3 h 45 mn)

Kilrane, (053) 3 32 32, www.rosslareharbour.ie

Archways N

Rosslare Rd, Tagoat , West : 6.25 Km on N 25 – (053) 915 81 11 – www.thearchways.ie – Closed 1-3 January

6 rm – € 49/60 € 70/90 **Rest** – Menu € 15/30

Spanish villa style bungalow, conveniently located for Rosslare harbour. Contemporary bedrooms feature coffee machines and smart bathrooms, with colour schemes themed around a single piece of art from a local artist. Daily changing set three course dinners use the best of seasonal, local produce.

ROUNDSTONE (Cloch na Rón) – Galway – 712 C7 – pop. 245 36 A3

Ireland

Dublin 293 km – Galway 76 km – Ennis 144 km

Town★

Connemara★★★: Sky Road, Clifden★★, W : 24 km by R 341 and minor road – Cashel★, E : 15 km by R 341 – Connemara National Park★ **AC**, N : 40 km by R 341 and N 59 – Kylemore Abbey★ **AC**, N : 44 km by R 341 and N 59

O'Dowds

– (095) 35 809 – www.odowdsseafoodbar.com – Closed 25 December

Rest – *(booking advisable)* Menu € 20 – Carte € 17/48

Busy pub in pretty harbourside town; popular with tourists and locals alike. Owned by the O'Dowd family for over 100 years, it specialises in fresh, simply cooked fish and shellfish. Sit in the cosy, fire-lit bar or wood-panelled restaurant.

ROUNDWOOD - **Wicklow** - **712** N9 - **pop. 833** 39 D2

Dublin 25 km - Wicklow 12 km - Belfast 137 km - Limerick 144 km

Byrne & Woods

Main St - (01) 281 70 78 - www.byrneandwoods.com - Closed 25-26 December

Rest - Carte € 24/42

Arguably the second highest pub in Ireland, set up in the Wicklow Mountains. 'Byrne' is a cosy bar with a wood-burning stove; dimly lit 'Woods' has leather and dark wood furnishings and a clubby feel. Cooking is fresh and straightforward.

SANDYFORD = Áth an Ghainimh - **Dún Laoghaire-Rathdown** - **712** N8 - see **Dublin**

SHANAGARRY (An Seangharraí) - **Cork** - **712** H12 - **pop. 414** 39 C3

- ✉ **Midleton** Ireland

Dublin 262 km - Cork 40 km - Waterford 103 km

Cloyne Cathedral★, NW : 6.5 km by R 629

Ballymaloe House

Northwest : 2.5 km on R 629 - (021) 465 25 31 - www.ballymaloe.ie - Closed 2 weeks January and 24-26 December

29 rm - € 115/135 € 180/260

Rest - *(booking essential)* Menu € 36/70

With its pre-18C origins, this is the very essence of a country manor house. Family-run for 3 generations, it boasts numerous traditionally styled guest areas, comfortable, classical bedrooms and a famed cookery school. The 5 course daily menu offers local, seasonal produce.

SKULL (An Scoil) - **Cork** - **712** D13 Ireland 38 A3

Dublin 363 km - Cork 104 km - Killarney 103 km

Coosheen, Schull, Coosheen, (077) 2 81 82

Town★

Mount Gabriel (<★), N : 3 km by minor road. Sherkin Island★ (by ferry)

Corthna Lodge without rest

West : 1 km by R 592 off L 4406 (Coast Rd) - (028) 28 517 - www.corthna-lodge.net - Closed 16 September-14 April

6 rm - € 60/75 € 75/95

Modern house with large gardens, a sauna hut, a hot tub and a Japanese bridge, set in a remote location out of town. Immaculately kept bedrooms are spacious and cosy, with a homely style. The minimalist breakfast room features a great coffee machine. There's also a dining hut in the garden beside the BBQ.

SLANE - **Meath** - **712** M6 - **pop. 1 349** 37 B3

Dublin 34 km - Navan 8 km - City Centre 35 km - Craigavon 69 km

Tankardstown

Northwest : 6 km by N 51 off R 163 - (041) 982 46 21 - www.tankardstown.ie - Closed 25-26 December

12 rm - € 100/200 € 200/350 - 6 suites

Rest ***Brabazon*** - see restaurant listing

Fine Georgian manor house on a mature country estate; extensively restored to a luxurious level. Large, antique-furnished bedrooms in the main house - some with silk-lined walls. The smart, modern courtyard rooms have kitchens.

Conyngham Arms

- (041) 988 4444 - www.conynghamarms.ie - Closed 25 December

15 rm - € 70/80 € 110/130 **Rest** - Carte € 19/26

17C coaching inn close to a castle, in a small but busy town - set on the main street but with a hidden rear garden. Appealing, informal, French boutique styling. Bedrooms have good facilities; some boast sleigh beds or four-posters. Dine in the bar or restaurant, on produce sourced from within 25 miles.

Brabazon – Tankardstown Hotel
Northwest : 6 km by N 51 off R 163 – (041) 982 46 21 – www.tankardstown.ie – Closed 25-26 December
Rest – *(closed Monday-Tuesday) (dinner only and Sunday lunch)* Menu € 35 (dinner) – Carte € 26/39
Relaxed, rustic restaurant set in former piggery of the manor house, with modern interior, painted wooden tables and pleasant terrace overlooking the landscaped courtyard. Contemporary cooking makes use of good quality ingredients.

SLIGO (Sligeach) – Sligo – 712 G5 – pop. 17 568 Ireland 36 B2

Dublin 214 km – Belfast 203 km – Dundalk 170 km – Londonderry 138 km
Sligo Airport, Strandhill : (071) 9168280
Temple St, (071) 9 16 12 01, www.sligotourism.ie
Rosses Point, (071) 917 71 34
Town★★ – Abbey★ **AC** – Model Arts and the Niland Gallery★ **AC**
SE : Lough Gill★★ – Carrowmore Megalithic Cemetery★ **AC**, SW : 4.75 km – Knocknarea★ (< ★★) SW : 9.5 km by R 292. Drumcliff★, N : by N 15 - Parke's Castle★ **AC**, E : 14.5 km by R 286 – Glencar Waterfall★, NE : 14.5 km by N 16 – Creevykeel Court Cairn★, N : 25.75 km by N 15

Tree Tops without rest
Cleveragh Rd, South : 1.25 km by Dublin rd – (071) 916 23 01 – www.sligobandb.com – Closed 20 December-7 January
4 rm – € 40/45 € 70/76
Unassuming whitewashed house in a residential area, with immaculately kept bedrooms, a cosy lounge and a smart breakfast room overlooking the garden. The owners are chatty and welcoming, and they have an interesting Irish art collection.

Montmartre
Market Yard – (071) 916 99 01 – www.montmartrerestaurant.ie – Closed 5-30 January, Sunday and Monday
Rest – *(dinner only)* Menu € 24 (early dinner)/37 – Carte € 25/45
Smart, modern restaurant in the shadow of the cathedral, with a tiled exterior and wooden blinds. The French chefs prepare classic Gallic menus which follow the seasons. The all-French wine list features interesting, lesser-known wines.

Hargadons
4/5 O'Connell St – (071) 915 3709 – www.hargadons.com
Rest – *(closed Sunday) (bookings not accepted)* Carte € 17/27
Hugely characterful pub with sloping floors, narrow passageways, dimly lit ante-rooms and a lovely "Ladies' Room" complete with its own serving hatch. Cooking is warming and satisfying, offering the likes of Irish stew or bacon and cabbage.

at Strandhill West : 4 mi on R 292 – ✉

Strandhill Lodge & Suites without rest
Top Hill – (071) 912 21 22 – www.strandhilllodgeandsuites.ie
18 rm – € 59/119 € 69/149
Modern guesthouse with a comfy lounge and a small breakfast room. Standard bedrooms look inland; go for one with a patio or a balcony overlooking the rooftops to the Atlantic. The suites have small kitchens and are ideal for longer stays.

SPANISH POINT (Rinn na Spáinneach) – Clare – 712 D9 38 B2
– ✉ Milltown Malbay

Dublin 275 km – Galway 104 km – Limerick 83 km

Red Cliff Lodge with rm
– (065) 708 57 56 – www.redclifflodge.ie – Closed November-Easter
6 rm – € 90/115 € 120/190 **Rest** – Menu € 26 – Carte € 31/46
Thatched cottage in a superb spot on the headland; later extensions have created a U-shaped arrangement around a courtyard. Bright, eye-catching décor and elegantly set tables. Light lunches; modern classics with a touch of flair at dinner.

STEPASIDE – Dún Laoghaire-Rathdown 39 D1

Dublin 10 km – Dún Laoghaire 7 km – Belfast 121 km – Cork 164 km

Box Tree

Enniskerry Rd ✉ *D18 – (01) 205 20 25 – www.theboxtree.ie – Closed Good Friday and 25-26 December*

Rest – Menu € 24/25 – Carte € 38/51

Modern eatery beneath a small, new-build apartment block. The attractive restaurant serves good value menus of unfussy, classical dishes. On the other side of the bar is the Wild Boar, which serves slightly lighter offerings.

STRAFFAN (Teach Srafáin) – Kildare – 712 M8 – pop. 635 Ireland 39 D1

Dublin 29 km – Belfast 192 km – Cork 238 km – Lisburn 180 km

Naas, Kerdiffstown, (045) 87 46 44

Castletown House, Celbridge★ **AC**, NW : 7 km by R 406 and R 403

K Club

– (01) 601 72 00 – www.kclub.ie – Closed 2 weeks January

69 rm – € 255/455 € 355/555, € 29 – 9 suites

Rest *River Room* – *(dinner only and Sunday lunch)* Menu € 63

Rest *Legends* – Menu € 49 – Carte € 40/63

Rest *Kwam Suk* – Carte € 38/41

A golf resort with two championship courses, an extensive spa and beautiful formal gardens stretching down to the Liffey. The fine 19C house has elegant, antique-filled guestrooms and luxurious, traditional bedrooms. Grand, formal River Room offers refined, classic dishes. Smart Legends has a brasserie menu. Kwam Suk serves mainly Thai and Malaysian dishes.

Barberstown Castle

North : 0.75 km – (01) 628 81 57 – www.barberstowncastle.ie – Closed January and 24-26 December

57 rm – € 150/200 € 160/200

Rest *Barton Rooms* – *(closed Sunday-Thursday) (dinner only) (bookings essential for non-residents) (residents only)* Menu € 49

Rest *Tea Rooms* – Carte € 24/43

Set within 20 acres of grounds; a 13C castle with whitewashed Georgian and Victorian extensions – a popular venue for weddings. Large, luxurious country house bedrooms feature good facilities; many have four-poster beds and garden outlooks. Dine on traditional dishes in the informal, conservatory style bistro or from French menus in the Georgian house and stone keep.

STRANDHILL – Sligo – see Sligo

TERMONBARRY – Roscommon – 712 I6 – pop. 366 Ireland 37 C3

Dublin 130 km – Galway 137 km – Roscommon 35 km – Sligo 100 km

Strokestown★ (Famine Museum★ **AC**, Strokestown Park House★ **AC**), NW : by N 5

Keenan's

– (043) 332 60 52 – www.keenans.ie – Closed 25-26 December

12 rm – € 70/85 € 99/130

Rest – *(closed Sunday dinner)* Menu € 25/35 – Carte € 22/45

Modern extension to a characterful village pub; run by the 5th generation of the same family. Cosy residents lounge and breakfast room. Stylish black and white bedrooms with compact bathrooms; some have balconies overlooking the Shannon. Large restaurant offers classic menus; the bar serves pub favourites.

THOMASTOWN (Baile Mhic Andáin) – South Tipperary – 712 K10 – pop. 1 837 – ✉ Kilkenny Ireland 39 C2

Dublin 124 km – Kilkenny 17 km – Waterford 48 km – Wexford 61 km

Jerpoint Abbey★★, SW : 3 km by N9 – Graiguenamanagh★ (Duiske Abbey★★ **AC**), E : 16 km by R 703 – Inistioge★, SE : 8 km by R 700 – Kilfane Glen and Waterfall★ **AC**, SE : 5 km by N 9

Mount Juliet
Southwest : 5.5 km by N 9 on R 4286 – ✆ (056) 777 3000 – www.mountjuliet.ie
58 rm – 🛉 € 99/389 🛉🛉 € 260/389 – 13 suites
Rest *Lady Helen* ✿ – see restaurant listing
Rest *Kendals Brasserie* – *(closed Monday and Wednesday) (bar lunch)*
Carte € 29/57
Georgian gem situated in 1,500 acres, with a Jack Nicklaus designed golf course, a spa, an equestrian centre and even a stud farm. Bedrooms range from traditional in the main house to two-roomed garden lodges and smaller but equally comfy rooms in the former hunting stables. Grand restaurant; simple French dishes in the brasserie and light lunches in the clubhouse bar.

Abbey House without rest
Jerpoint Abbey, Southwest : 2 km on N 9 – ✆ (056) 772 41 66 – www.abbeyhousejerpoint.com – Closed 20-30 December
6 rm – 🛉 € 50/70 🛉🛉 € 80/100
Attractive whitewashed Victorian house with a neat, lawned garden and a friendly, hospitable owner; set opposite the ruins of Jerpoint Abbey. Traditionally styled lounge with plenty of local info. Simple bedrooms with antique furniture.

Lady Helen – Mount Juliet Hotel
Southwest : 5.5 km by N 9 on R 4286 – ✆ (056) 777 3000 – www.mountjuliet.ie – Closed Sunday and Tuesday
Rest – *(dinner only) (booking essential)* Menu € 55/75
Classical hotel restaurant consisting of two grand rooms with beautiful stucco-work, overlooking the River Nore. Accomplished cooking uses ingredients from the estate, the county and the nearest coast. Original, modern dishes are well-prepared, attractively presented and feature some stimulating combinations.
→ Scallops with cauliflower, sea lettuce and chicken consommé. Squab with almond milk, date purée and roasting juices. Coconut parfait, caramelised pineapple and muscovado sugar sponge.

TOORMORE (An Tuar Mór) – Cork – 712 D13 – pop. 207 – ✉ Goleen 38 A3

Dublin 355 km – Cork 109 km – Killarney 104 km

Fortview House without rest
Gurtyowen, Northeast : 2.5 km on R 591 (Durrus rd) – ✆ (028) 35 324 – www.fortviewhousegoleen.com – Closed October-April
3 rm – 🛉 € 50 🛉🛉 € 100
Well-kept guesthouse on a 120 acre dairy farm, run by a very bubbly owner. It has a rustic, country feel courtesy of its stone walls, timbered ceilings, coir carpets and aged pine furniture. Breakfast is an event, with home-baked scones and bread, eggs from their hens and other local products all featuring.

TOWER – Cork – 712 G12 – see Blarney

TRALEE (Trá Lí) – Kerry – 712 C11 – pop. 20 814 Ireland 38 A2

Dublin 297 km – Killarney 32 km – Limerick 103 km
Denny St, ✆ (066) 7 12 12 88, www.tralee.ie
Kerry - The Kingdom★ AC
Blennerville Windmill★ AC, SW : 3.25 km by N 86 – Ardfert★, NW : 8 km by R 551. Banna Strand★, NW : 12.75 km by R 551 - Crag Cave★ AC, W : 21 km by N 21 – Rattoo Round Tower★, N : 19.25 km by R 556

Grand
rest,
Denny St – ✆ (066) 712 14 99 – www.grandhoteltralee.com – Closed 25 December
43 rm – 🛉 € 55/85 🛉🛉 € 70/170
Rest – Menu € 25 (dinner) – Carte € 22/43
Opened in 1928 and located right in the heart of this bustling town. Small first floor lounge and comfy, contemporary bedrooms; those to the rear are quietest. Traditional bar, once the post office, is a popular spot, offering hearty all-day dishes. Global menu and Irish specialities in classical dining room.

Brook Manor Lodge without rest
Fenit Rd, Spa, Northwest : 3.5 km by R 551 on R 558 – (066) 712 04 06 – www.brookmanorlodge.com – Closed November-mid-March
8 rm – € 55/85 € 85/110
Spacious detached house with views to the Slieve Mish Mountains; good for those who like golf, hiking or fishing. Traditionally styled lounge and airy conservatory breakfast room. Immaculately kept bedrooms; those at the back have the view.

TRAMORE (Trá Mhór) – Waterford – 712 K11 – pop. 9 722 Ireland 39 C2

Dublin 177 km – Belfast 345 km – Cork 123 km – Lisburn 333 km
Dunmore East★, E : 18 km by R 675, R 685 and R 684

Glenorney without rest
Newtown, Southwest : 1.5 km by R 675 – (051) 381 056 – www.glenorney.com – Closed December-February
6 rm – € 50/80 € 80/90
Smart yellow house with pretty gardens, set on the hillside, overlooking the bay. A homely lounge leads through to a dark wood furnished breakfast room where you can have pancakes, French toast and homemade preserves. Bedrooms are simply furnished, and the book-filled sun lounge is a pleasant place to relax.

TRIM (Baile Átha Troim) – Meath – 712 L7 – pop. 1 441 Ireland 37 D3

Dublin 43 km – Drogheda 42 km – Tullamore 69 km
Castle St, (046) 9 43 72 27, www.meathtourism.ie
County Meath, Newtownmoynagh, (046) 943 14 63
Trim Castle★★ – Town★
Bective Abbey★, NE : 6.5 km by R 161

Trim Castle
rest,
Castle St – (046) 948 30 00 – www.trimcastlehotel.com – Closed 25 December
68 rm – € 65/165 € 65/200
Rest – *(closed Sunday-Thursday) (dinner only)* Menu € 25
Modern family hotel opposite the castle, complete with a café, a homeware shop and a delightful roof garden with a great outlook. Good-sized bedrooms in contemporary hues – the front rooms share the view. Informal dining in the bar; traditional European dishes in the stylish first floor dining room.

Highfield House without rest
Maudlins Rd. – (046) 943 63 86 – www.highfieldguesthouse.com – Closed 21 December-2 February
10 rm – € 55/58 € 80/85
Substantial 18C stone house close to the river and the oldest Norman castle in Ireland. Well-appointed lounge and breakfast room, boldly coloured bedrooms and a delightful terraced courtyard. Comprehensive breakfasts; scones on arrival.

TWO MILE HOUSE – see Naas

VIRGINIA – Cavan – 712 K6 – pop. 2 282 37 C3

Dublin 89 km – Monaghan 76 km – Belfast 153 km – Craigavon 99 km

St Kyrans N
Dublin Rd, South : 2.25 km. on N 3 – (049) 854 70 87 – www.stkyrans.com – Closed 6-30 January and 24-27 December
8 rm – € 55/70 € 80/100
Rest – *(closed Monday-Wednesday lunch)* Menu € 28 (weekday dinner) – Carte € 29/49
Rurally set, off the main road, this hotel may be plain on the outside but it's a different story on the inside. There's a stylish lounge, modernised bedrooms – five with lough views – and a smart, linen-laid restaurant overlooking Lough Ramor. The menu offers classic dishes with an Irish heart.

REPUBLIC OF IRELAND

WATERFORD (Port Láirge) – **Waterford** – **712** K11 – **pop. 46 732** **39** C2

Ireland

Dublin 154 km – Cork 117 km – Limerick 124 km

Waterford Airport, Killowen : (051) 846600

The Granary, The Quay, Cork Rd, (051) 87 58 23, www.waterfordtourism.com

Newrath, (051) 87 67 48

Town★ - City Walls★ - Waterford Treasures★ **AC** Y

Waterford Crystal★, SW : 2.5 km by N 25 Y. Duncannon★, E : 19.25 km by R 683, ferry from Passage East and R 374 (south) Z – Dunmore East★, SE : 19.25 km by R 684 Z – Tintern Abbey★, E : 21 km by R 683, ferry from Passage East, R 733 and R 734 (south) Z

Waterford Castle H. and Golf Resort

The Island, Ballinakill, East : 4 km by R 683, Ballinakill Rd and private ferry – (051) 878 203 – www.waterfordcastle.com – Closed 24-26 December and restricted opening in January

19 rm – € 89/149 € 198/278 – 5 suites

Rest ***Munster Dining Room*** – see restaurant listing

Attractive part-15C castle and lodges, set on a charming 320 acre private island in the river. The carved stone and wood-panelled hall displays antiques and old tapestries. Elegant, classical bedrooms boast characterful period bathrooms.

Athenaeum House

Christendom, Ferrybank, Northeast : 1.5 km by R 771 – (051) 833 999 – www.athenaeumhousehotel.com – Closed 25-28 December and January

28 rm – € 66/150 € 80/180 – 3 suites Z**n**

Rest ***Zaks*** – see restaurant listing

Bright yellow, part-Georgian house, hidden on the quieter side of the River Suir and well-run by a family team. Simple, open-fired lounge and smart, modern bedrooms. Relax on the long terrace or admire the river views from the gardens.

Fitzwilton

Bridge St – (051) 846 900 – www.fitzwiltonhotel.ie – Closed 23-28 December

89 rm – € 55/119 € 58/265, €10 Y**b**

Rest ***Chez K's*** – Menu € 19/22 – Carte € 27/45

Close to the Guinness brewery and the main bridge, with a modern glass façade and a chic bar. Bedrooms are spacious, good value and come with everything you might need, including an iron and ironing board; those at the back are the quietest. The restaurant offers international dishes made from Irish produce.

Foxmount Country House without rest

Passage East Rd, Southeast : 7.25 km by R 683, off Cheekpoint rd – (051) 874 308 – www.foxmountcountryhouse.com – Closed mid October-mid March

4 rm – € 55 € 110

Striking Georgian mansion in a delightful 150 acre farm setting; it's immaculately kept, with classical styling and charming hosts. Bedrooms are named after flowers: Honeysuckle and Bluebell are two of the best. Good communal breakfasts.

Munster Dining Room – Waterford Castle Hotel and Golf Resort

The Island, Ballinakill, East : 4 km by R 683, Ballinakill Rd and private ferry – (051) 878 203 – www.waterfordcastle.com – Closed 24-26 December and restricted opening in January

Rest – *(bar lunch Monday-Saturday)* Menu € 40 (weekdays) – Carte lunch € 49/65

Beautiful oak wood panelled hotel dining room, featuring an ornate ceiling and a delightful hand-carved fireplace. Classically based menus feature bold flavours and name-check local producers. Formal service and live piano accompaniment.

La Palma on The Mall Ⓝ

20 The Mall – (051) 879 823 – www.lapalma.ie – Closed 25-26 December, 1 January, 16 March, 18 April and Sunday Z**a**

Rest – *(dinner only) (booking essential)* Menu € 30 (weekdays) – Carte € 28/55

Established restaurant by the Waterford Crystal factory, that has many repeat customers. Cosy lounge, boldly papered dining rooms and a funky bar. Classic Italian cooking with delicious antipasti, superb ravioli and tasty homemade gelato.

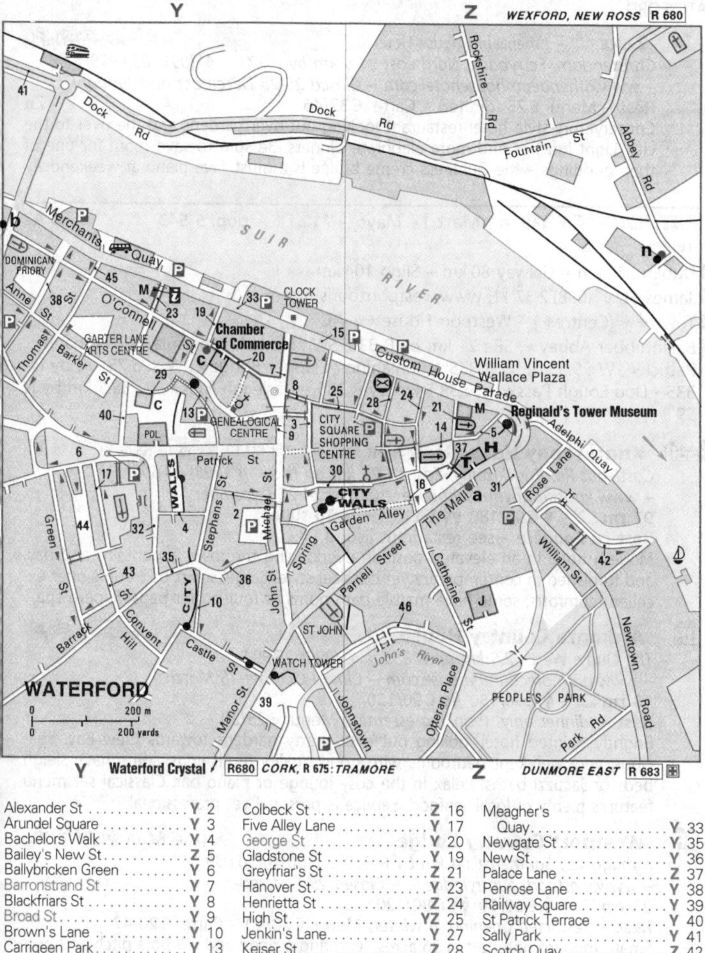

Street	Grid	No.
Alexander St	Y	2
Arundel Square	Y	3
Bachelors Walk	Y	4
Bailey's New St	Z	5
Ballybricken Green	Y	6
Barronstrand St	Y	7
Blackfriars St	Y	8
Broad St	Y	9
Brown's Lane	Y	10
Carrigeen Park	Y	13
Cathedral Square	Z	14
City Square Shopping Centre	YZ	
Coal Quay	Y	15
Colbeck St	Z	16
Five Alley Lane	Y	17
George St	Y	20
Gladstone St	Y	19
Greyfriar's St	Z	21
Hanover St	Y	23
Henrietta St	Z	24
High St	YZ	25
Jenkin's Lane	Y	27
Keiser St	Z	28
King's Terrace	Y	29
Lady Lane	YZ	30
Lombard St	Z	31
Mayors Walk	Y	32
Meagher's Quay	Y	33
Newgate St	Y	35
New St	Y	36
Palace Lane	Z	37
Penrose Lane	Y	38
Railway Square	Y	39
St Patrick Terrace	Y	40
Sally Park	Y	41
Scotch Quay	Z	42
Shortcourse	Y	43
Trinity Square	Y	44
Vulcan St	Y	45
Water Side	Z	46

XX **La Bohème**

2 George's St – ✆ (051) 875 645
– www.labohemerestaurant.ie
– Closed 25-27 December, Sunday, Monday and bank holidays Y**c**
Rest – *(dinner only) (booking essential)* Menu €24 (early dinner)/35 – Carte €36/56

Characterful, candlelit restaurant in the vaulted cellars of a fine Georgian house; start with an aperitif in the stone-floored bar. The French chefs offer a bewildering array of classic Gallic dishes, which include daily market specials.

X **Zaks** (N) – Athenaeum House Hotel

Christendom, Ferrybank, Northeast : 1.5 km by R 771 – ☎ (051) 833 999 – www.athenaeumhousehotel.com – Closed 25-28 December and January

Rest – Menu € 25 (dinner) – Carte € 32/46 Zn

Conservatory-style hotel restaurant looking out over gardens and the river to the city. Light lunches and more elaborate dinners. Be sure to save room for one of their puddings – the Guinness crème brûlée is a must. Live piano at weekends.

WESTPORT (Cathair na Mart) – Mayo – 712 D6 – pop. 5 543 36 A2

Ireland

Dublin 262 km – Galway 80 km – Sligo 104 km

James St, ☎ (098) 2 57 11, www.westporttourism.com

Town★★ (Centre★) – Westport House★★ AC

Ballintubber Abbey★, SE : 21 km by R 330. SW : Murrisk Peninsula★★ – Croagh Patrick★, W : 9.5 km by R 335 – Bunlahinch Clapper Bridge★, W : 25.75 km by R 335 - Doo Lough Pass★, W : 38.5 km by R 335 – Aasleagh Falls★, S : 35.5 km by N 59

REPUBLIC OF IRELAND

Knockranny House H. & Spa

Castlebar Rd, Knockranny, East : 1.25 km on N 5 – ☎ (098) 28 600 – www.knockrannyhousehotel.ie – Closed 24-27 December

97 rm – € 90/180 € 110/190 – 10 suites

Rest *La Fougère* – see restaurant listing

Modern hotel in an elevated position overlooking the town, mountains and bay, and furnished in contemporary yet classical style. Large, smart bedrooms offer excellent comforts; some have marble bathrooms or four-poster beds. Superb spa.

Ardmore Country House

The Quay, West : 2.5 km on R 335 – ☎ (098) 25 994 – www.ardmorecountryhouse.com – Closed October-15 March

13 rm – € 90/150 € 90/150

Rest – *(dinner only) (booking essential)* Menu € 25/30

Brightly painted hotel looking out over pretty gardens towards Clew Bay. Spacious, very well-kept bedrooms with good quality furnishings; some have sleigh beds or Jacuzzi baths. Relax in the cosy lounge or piano bar. Classical set menu features plenty of local seafood. Service is personal yet professional.

Westport Country Lodge

Aghagower, Southeast : 4 km by R 330 – ☎ (098) 56 030 – www.westportcountrylodge.ie – Closed 25 December

21 rm – € 59/99 € 80/120

Rest – *(restricted opening in winter)* Menu € 20/40 – Carte € 20/47

Smart, modern hotel set in 36 acres, featuring a pond and a 9 hole pitch and putt course. Rooms have big beds and good mod cons; many also have views out across the countryside towards Croagh Patrick. Contemporary bar and dining room; all-day dining includes brunch and afternoon tea.

Augusta Lodge without rest

Golf Links Rd, North : 0.75 km by N 59 – ☎ (098) 28 900 – www.augustalodge.ie – closed 23-27 December

9 rm – € 45/65 € 60/95

Family run guesthouse with a small pitch and putt course on the front lawn and golfing memorabilia covering every surface inside. Simple, brightly coloured bedrooms have a homely feel. The welcoming owner has good local knowledge.

XXX **La Fougère** – Knockranny House Hotel & Spa

Castlebar Rd, Knockranny, East : 1.25 km on N 5 – ☎ (098) 28 600 – www.knockrannyhousehotel.ie – Closed 24-27 December

Rest – *(dinner only) (booking advisable)* Menu € 54/72 – Carte € 55/63

Spacious hotel restaurant with a large bar, several different seating areas and huge windows offering views to Croagh Patrick Mountain. The three menus feature fresh, local produce, including langoustines from the bay below. Formal service.

An Port Mór

Brewery Pl, Bridge St – ☎ (098) 26 730 – www.anportmor.com – Closed 24-26 December, Monday except July-August and bank holidays
Rest – *(dinner only)* Menu € 22/29 – Carte € 26/46
Tucked away down a small alleyway and named after the chef's home village. Compact interior with shabby-chic, Mediterranean-style décor. Classically based menu showcases local produce in elaborate dishes; seafood specials on the blackboard.

Sheebeen

Rosbeg, West : 3 km on R 335 – ☎ (098) 26 528 – www.croninssheebeen.com – Closed Good Friday, 25 December and lunch weekdays November-mid March
Rest – Carte € 23/40
Pretty thatched pub with lovely bay and Croagh Patrick views. Hearty, unfussy dishes feature mussels, oysters and lobsters from the bay, and lamb and beef from the fields nearby. Sit outside, in the rustic bar or in first floor dining room.

WEXFORD (Loch Garman) – Wexford – 712 M10 – pop. 19 913 39 D2

Ireland

Dublin 141 km – Kilkenny 79 km – Waterford 61 km

Crescent Quay, ☎ (053) 2 31 11, www.wexfordweb.com

Mulgannon, ☎ (053) 4 22 38

Town★ - Main Street★ YZ - Franciscan Friary★ Z – St Iberius' Church★ Y **D** - Twin Churches★ Z

Irish Agricultural Museum, Johnstown Castle★★ **AC**, SW : 7.25 km X – Irish National Heritage Park, Ferrycarrig★ **AC**, NW : 4 km by N 11 V – Curracloe★, NE : 8 km by R 741 and R 743 V. Kilmore Quay★, SW : 24 km by N 25 and R 739 (Saltee Islands★ - access by boat) X – Enniscorthy Castle★ (County Museum★ **AC**) N : 24 km by N 11 V

Plans on following pages

Whites

rm,

Abbey St – ☎ (053) 912 23 11 – www.whitesofwexford.ie – Closed 24-27 December Y**a**
157 rm – † € 75/125 †† € 79/189 – 5 suites
Rest *Terrace* – *(bar lunch)* Menu € 20 – Carte € 19/32 **s**
Striking angular hotel built around a paved central courtyard; its spacious lobby decorated with local art. Tranquillity spa, coffee shop and library bar. Modern, minimalistic bedrooms; executives are larger with water views. Internationally influenced menu of traditional dishes in the contemporary restaurant.

Ferrycarrig

rm, rest,

Ferrycarrig, Northwest : 4.25 km on N 11 – ☎ (053) 912 09 99 – www.ferrycarrighotel.ie V**a**
102 rm – † € 60/100 †† € 90/300 – 4 suites
Rest *Reeds* – Menu € 25 (dinner)/30 – Carte € 27/41
Sitting pretty on the banks of the Slaney estuary and popular with families is this purpose built hotel with a busy leisure centre. The comfortable bedrooms have superb views and superior rooms have balconies. Waterside bar serves an all-day menu. Spacious Reeds offers traditional fare; ask for a window seat.

Rathaspeck Manor without rest

Rathaspeck, Southwest : 6.5 km by R 730 off Murntown rd – ☎ (053) 914 16 72 – www.rathaspeckmanor.ie – Closed November-December X**k**
4 rm – † € 100/160 †† € 100/160
Georgian house with its own 18 hole golf course. Comfortable first floor drawing room. Large, luxurious, individually furnished bedrooms with impressive bathrooms featuring underfloor heating; Father Albert's Room is the most comfortable.

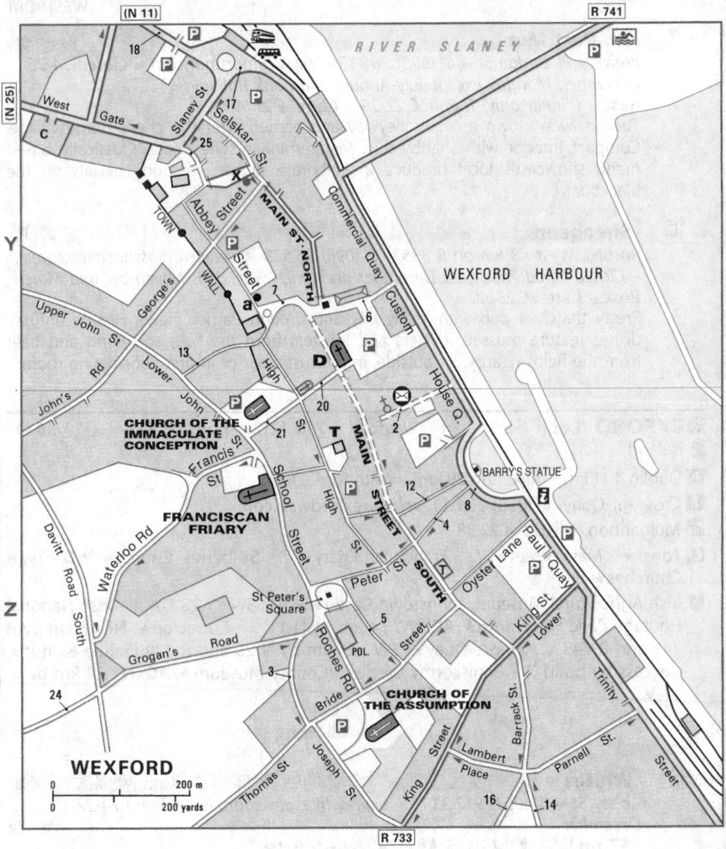

Anne St. . . . Z 2	Henrietta St . . . Z 12	Redmond Rd . . . Y 18
Carrigeen St . . . Z 3	John's Gate St. . . . Y 13	Rowe St Lower. . . . YZ 20
Cinema Lane . . . Z 4	Kevin Barry St . . . Z 14	Rowe St Upper . . . Z 21
Clifford St . . . Z 5	Main St North . . . Y	Selskar St. . . . Y
Common Quay St. . . . Y 6	Main St South. . . . Z	Summerhill Rd. . . . Z 24
Cornmarket . . . Y 7	Michael St . . . Z 16	Temperance Row . . . Y 25
Crescent Quay. . . . Z 8	Redmond Pl. . . . Y 17	

Killiane Castle without rest

Drinagh, South : 5.5 km by R 730 off N 25 – (053) 915 88 85 – www.killianecastle.com – Closed mid-November-mid-March

8 rm – € 60/75 € 100/125

A 17C house and 12C castle on a family-owned dairy farm. Individually decorated, antique-furnished bedrooms look out over the surrounding farmland. Breakfast includes pork from their own pigs, home-laid eggs and homemade bread and yoghurt.

McMenamin's Townhouse without rest

6 Glena Terr – (053) 914 64 42 – www.wexford-bedandbreakfast.com – Closed 10-31 December X**n**

4 rm – € 50 € 90

Homely Victorian townhouse retaining many original features. Friendly, hands-on owners. Comfortable bedrooms; some with half-testers or four-posters. Legendary breakfasts include homemade breads, preserves, omelettes and drop scones.

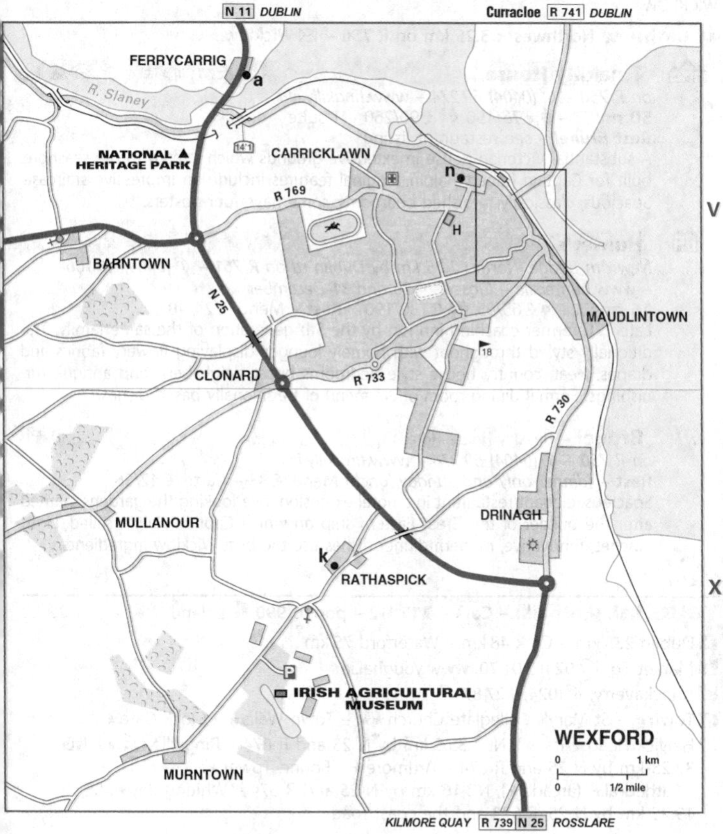

X **Greenacres Bistro**

Selskar – ✆ (053) 91 22 975 – www.greenacres.ie – Closed 25-26 December and Good Friday Y**x**

Rest – *(light lunch)* Menu € 21 (dinner) – Carte € 33/63

Light, airy bistro with a deli and patisserie selling cheese, charcuterie, pastries and breads. Salads and platters at lunch; flavoursome modern dishes at dinner. Well-priced French wines fill the shelves: choose from over 1,300!

WICKLOW (Cill Mhantáin) – **Wicklow** – **712** N9 – **pop. 6 761** **39** D2

Ireland

Dublin 53 km – Waterford 135 km – Wexford 108 km

Fitzwilliam Sq, ✆ (0404) 6 91 17, www.visitwicklow.ie

Mount Usher Gardens, Ashford★ **AC**, NW : 6.5 km by R 750 and N 11 – Devil's Glen★, NW : 12.75 km by R 750 and N 11. Glendalough★★★ (Lower Lake★★★, Upper Lake★★, Cathedral★★, Round Tower★★, St Kevin's Church★★, St Saviour's Priory★) – W : 22.5 km by R 750, N 11, R 763, R 755 and R 756 – Wicklow Mountains★★ (Wicklow Gap★★, Sally Gap★★, Avondale★, Meeting of the Waters★, Glenmacnass Waterfall★, Glenmalur★, – Loughs Tay and Dan★)

at Rathnew Northwest : 3.25 km on R 750 – ✉ Wicklow

Tinakilly House
on R 750 – ✆ (0404) 69 274 – www.tinakilly.ie
50 rm – € 75/150 € 90/260 – 1 suite
Rest *Brunel* – see restaurant listing
A substantial Victorian house in extensive grounds which stretch to the seashore: built for Captain Robert Halpin. Original features include an impressive staircase. Spacious, classically furnished bedrooms; some have four-posters.

Hunter's
Newrath Bridge, North : 1.25 km by Dublin rd on R 761 – ✆ (0404) 40 106 – www.hunters.ie – Closed 24-26 and 31 December
16 rm – € 65/95 € 130/190 **Rest** – Menu € 24/48
Late 17C former coaching inn run by the 5th generation of the same family. Traditionally styled throughout with homely lounges displaying flowery fabrics and drapes. Neat, country house style bedrooms boast sleigh beds and antique furnishings. Formal dining room offers menu of traditionally based dishes.

Brunel – Tinakilly House Hotel
on R 750 – ✆ (0404) 69 274 – www.tinakilly.ie
Rest – *(dinner only and Sunday lunch)* Menu € 33 – Carte € 42/56
Spacious, elegant restaurant in a hotel extension, overlooking the gardens: named after the builder of the Great Eastern ship on which Captain Halpin sailed. Light lunches; innovative, modern dinner dishes use the best Wicklow ingredients.

YOUGHAL (Eochaill) – Cork – 712 I12 – pop. 6 990 Ireland 39 C3

Dublin 235 km – Cork 48 km – Waterford 75 km

Market Sq, ✆ (024) 2 01 70, www.youghal.ie

Knockaverry, ✆ (024) 9 27 87

Town★ – St Mary's Collegiate Church★★ – Town Walls★ - Clock Gate★

Helvick Head★ (★), NE : 35.5 km by N 25 and R 674 – Ringville (★), NE : 32.25 km by N 25 and R 674 – Ardmore★ - Round Tower★ - Cathedral★ (arcade★), N : 16 km by N 25 and R 674 – Whiting Bay★, SE : 19.25 km by N 25, R 673 and the coast road

Aherne's with rm
163 North Main St – ✆ (024) 92 424 – www.ahernes.com – Closed 23-27 December
12 rm – € 80/120 € 120/180
Rest – *(bar lunch)* Menu € 10 (lunch)/29 – Carte € 34/59
Traditional seafood restaurant dating from 1910, passionately run by the third family generation. Lunch in one of the bars; dinner in the restaurant. Fish and shellfish are from the local boats – hot buttered lobster is a speciality. Antique-furnished bedrooms, some with balconies; comfy, open-fired lounge.

The MICHELIN Guide

A collection to savour!

Belgique • België & Luxembourg
Deutschland
España & Portugal
France
Great Britain & Ireland
Italia
Nederland • Netherlands
Suisse • Schweiz • Svizzera
Main Cities of Europe

Also:

Chicago
Hokkaido
Hong Kong • Macau
Kyoto • Osaka • Kobe • Nara
Tokyo • Yokohama • Shonan
London
New York City
Paris
San Francisco

International Dialling Codes

Note: When making an international call, do not dial the first (0) of the city code (except for calls to Italy).

from \ to	A	B	CH	CZ	D	DK	E	FIN	F	GB	GR
A Austria		0032	0041	00420	0049	0045	0034	00358	0033	0044	0030
B Belgium	0043		0041	00420	0049	0045	0034	00358	0033	0044	0030
CH Switzerland	0043	0032		00420	0049	0045	0034	00358	0033	0044	0030
CZ Czech Republic	0043	0032	0041		0049	0045	0034	00358	0033	0044	0030
D Germany	0043	0032	0041	00420		0045	0034	00358	0033	0044	0030
DK Denmark	0043	0032	0041	00420	0049		0034	00358	0033	0044	0030
E Spain	0043	0032	0041	00420	0049	0045		00358	0033	0044	0030
FIN Finland	0043	0032	0041	00420	0049	0045	0034		0033	0044	0030
F France	0043	0032	0041	00420	0049	0045	0034	00358		0044	0030
GB United Kingdom	0043	0032	0041	00420	0049	0045	0034	00358	0033		0030
GR Greece	0043	0032	0041	00420	0049	0045	0034	00358	0033	0044	
H Hungary	0043	0032	0041	00420	0049	0045	0034	00358	0033	0044	0030
I Italy	0043	0032	0041	00420	0049	0045	0034	00358	0033	0044	0030
IRL Ireland	0043	0032	0041	00420	0049	0045	0034	00358	0033	0044	0030
J Japan	00143	00132	00141	001420	00149	00145	00134	001358	00133	00144	00130
L Luxembourg	0043	0032	0041	00420	0049	0045	0034	00358	0033	0044	0030
N Norway	0043	0032	0041	00420	0049	0045	0034	00358	0033	0044	0030
NL Netherlands	0043	0032	0041	00420	0049	0045	0034	00358	0033	0044	0030
PL Poland	0043	0032	0041	00420	0049	0045	0034	00358	0033	0044	0030
P Portugal	0043	0032	0041	00420	0049	0045	0034	00358	0033	0044	0030
RUS Russia	81043	81032	81041	810420	81049	81045	81034	810358	81033	81044	81030
S Sweden	0043	0032	0041	00420	0049	0045	0034	00358	0033	0044	0030
USA	01143	01132	01141	001420	01149	01145	01134	01358	01133	01144	01130

H	I	IRL	J	L	N	NL	PL	P	RUS	S	USA	
0036	0039	00353	0081	00352	0047	0031	0048	00351	007	0046	001	**A Austria**
0036	0039	00353	0081	00352	0047	0031	0048	00351	007	0046	001	**B Belgium**
0036	0039	00353	0081	00352	0047	0031	0048	00351	007	0046	001	**CH Switzerland**
0036	0039	00353	0081	00352	0047	0031	0048	00351	007	0046	001	**CZ Czech Republic**
0036	0039	00353	0081	00352	0047	0031	0048	00351	007	0046	001	**D Germany**
0036	0039	00353	0081	00352	0047	0031	0048	00351	007	0046	001	**DK Denmark**
0036	0039	00353	0081	00352	0047	0031	0048	00351	007	0046	001	**E Spain**
0036	0039	00353	0081	00352	0047	0031	0048	00351	007	0046	001	**FIN Finland**
0036	0039	00353	0081	00352	0047	0031	0048	00351	007	0046	001	**F France**
0036	0039	00353	0081	00352	0047	0031	0048	00351	007	0046	001	**GB United Kingdom**
0036	0039	00353	0081	00352	0047	0031	0048	00351	007	0046	001	**GR Greece**
	0039	00353	0081	00352	0047	0031	0048	00351	007	0046	001	**H Hungary**
0036		00353	0081	00352	0047	0031	0048	00351	007	0046	001	**I Italy**
0036	0039		0081	00352	0047	0031	0048	00351	007	0046	001	**IRL Ireland**
00136	00139	001353		001352	00147	00131	00148	001351	007	001146	0011	**J Japan**
0036	0039	00353	0081		0047	0031	0048	00351	007	0046	001	**L Luxembourg**
0036	0039	00353	0081	00352		0031	0048	00351	007	0046	001	**N Norway**
0036	0039	00353	0081	00352	0047		0048	00351	007	0046	001	**NL Netherlands**
0036	0039	00353	0081	00352	0047	0031		00351	007	0046	001	**PL Poland**
0036	0039	00353	0081	00352	0047	0031	048		007	0046	001	**P Portugal**
81036	81039	810353	81081	810352	81047	81031	81048	810351		81046	8101	**RUS Russia**
0036	0039	00353	0081	00352	0047	0031	0048	00351	007		001	**S Sweden**
01136	01139	011353	01181	011352	01147	01131	01148	011351	0117	011146		**USA**

Index of towns

O. Forir/MICHELIN

D

H

O

P

Q

R

T — Page

Y

Z

Maps

Regional maps of listed towns

Map Key

Places with at least one

- ● hotel or restaurant
- ✿ starred establishment
- « Bib Gourmand » restaurant
- « Bib Hotel »
- particularly pleasant restaurant
- particularly pleasant pub
- particularly pleasant hotel
- particularly pleasant guesthouse
- particularly quiet hotel

Distances in miles

(except for the Republic of Ireland: km). The distance is given from each town to other nearby towns and to the capital of each region as grouped in the guide. To avoid excessive repetition some distances have only been quoted once – you may therefore have to look under both town headings.
The distances quoted are not necessarily the shortest but have been based on the roads which afford the best driving conditions and are therefore the most practical.

	Belfast	Cork	Dublin	Dundalk	Galway	Killarney	Limerick	Londonderry	Omagh	Sligo	Tullamore
Cork	263										
Dublin	104	158									
Dundalk	52	210	52								
Galway	201	124	130	148							
Killarney	293	55	189	242	131						
Limerick	226	62	121	174	64	69					
Londonderry	72	298	147	99	172	292	226				
Omagh	69	264	112	64	157	252	186	35			
Sligo	125	202	130	120	88	208	142	85	68		
Tullamore	134	127	63	81	78	138	72	161	128	96	
Waterford	207	76	102	156	142	121	79	243	209	186	87

130 Miles

Dublin - Sligo

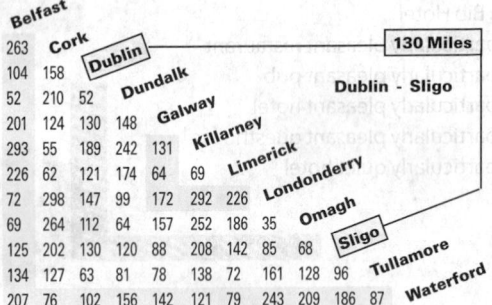

Distances between major towns/cities

Edinburgh - Southampton

425 Miles

	Aberdeen	Ayr	Birmingham	Blackpool	Brighton	Bristol	Cambridge	Cardiff	Carlisle	Coventry	Dover	Dumfries	Dundee	Edinburgh	Glasgow	Inverness	Ipswich	Kingston-upon-Hull	Leeds	Leicester	Liverpool	London	Manchester	Middlesbrough	Newcastle	Norwich	Nottingham	Oban	Oxford	Plymouth	Portsmouth	Sheffield	Southampton	Stoke-on-Trent	Swansea
Ayr	182
Birmingham	424	287
Blackpool	329	192	127
Brighton	596	459	178	299
Bristol	505	368	88	208	158
Cambridge	488	350	100	221	119	168
Cardiff	526	389	108	229	191	45	204
Carlisle	230	93	194	100	366	276	257	295
Coventry	441	303	22	143	158	94	81	120	212
Dover	604	467	202	323	105	196	120	227	376	180
Dumfries	210	59	228	134	400	310	291	329	34	245	409
Dundee	66	111	348	253	520	430	412	449	154	365	530	135
Edinburgh	127	83	292	198	466	374	351	393	98	310	469	79	56
Glasgow	146	37	291	197	463	373	354	392	97	309	472	78	76	47
Inverness	106	207	449	354	620	531	512	550	255	466	629	235	139	158	171
Ipswich	539	401	151	272	127	208	55	240	310	133	128	343	464	404	406	564
Kingston-upon-Hull	376	262	138	139	258	227	142	246	171	124	259	203	305	245	266	424	195
Leeds	355	217	121	85	259	210	150	229	126	120	268	159	280	220	222	380	203	63
Leicester	443	306	44	146	165	118	70	149	215	25	185	248	367	307	310	469	123	100	99
Liverpool	353	216	98	56	270	180	191	172	125	115	294	157	276	221	220	378	244	127	73	118
London	538	400	119	240	53	119	61	151	309	98	77	342	458	398	405	563	78	189	196	104	213
Manchester	348	211	87	51	259	169	162	188	120	104	283	152	272	216	215	373	215	96	43	107	35	200
Middlesbrough	289	186	175	132	314	264	199	283	95	174	317	127	218	158	190	320	252	91	66	150	142	246	112
Newcastle	235	149	207	141	346	296	231	315	60	206	349	91	163	121	154	266	284	127	99	182	174	278	144	39
Norwich	512	375	160	241	169	230	63	265	284	141	170	316	437	377	379	537	46	155	174	119	227	116	187	224	257
Nottingham	413	276	54	124	193	144	88	163	185	53	206	217	338	278	280	438	141	84	73	28	111	131	82	125	158	123
Oban	182	130	385	290	556	467	447	486	191	402	565	171	118	123	98	110	500	360	315	398	314	498	312	284	248	473	377
Oxford	498	360	79	201	108	74	90	106	269	60	144	302	421	366	365	523	140	175	169	77	173	58	161	225	257	151	102	459
Plymouth	619	482	202	322	215	121	266	151	391	208	287	424	543	488	486	645	306	341	322	232	294	217	283	378	410	328	255	581	194
Portsmouth	579	442	161	282	50	123	133	154	351	141	140	384	503	448	446	605	161	257	251	159	255	75	243	306	339	195	183	541	84	172
Sheffield	390	253	91	103	229	180	124	199	162	90	242	195	315	255	257	415	177	66	41	70	90	167	50	102	135	150	44	351	143	293	224
Southampton	563	425	144	265	63	78	130	137	334	124	151	367	486	425	429	588	171	240	235	142	237	81	226	289	322	192	167	524	67	153	20	205
Stoke-on-Trent	382	245	45	85	217	127	139	146	154	62	241	186	305	250	249	407	191	128	92	62	57	158	45	161	193	199	54	343	119	240	200	81	183
Swansea	524	387	143	227	227	80	239	42	296	156	263	328	448	392	391	549	277	283	234	186	172	187	196	320	352	300	197	485	142	187	190	236	173	183
Wick	206	307	549	454	720	631	612	650	355	566	729	335	239	258	271	104	665	524	479	562	478	662	476	421	366	637	541	213	622	744	704	516	686	507	649

For distances refer to the colour key in the table

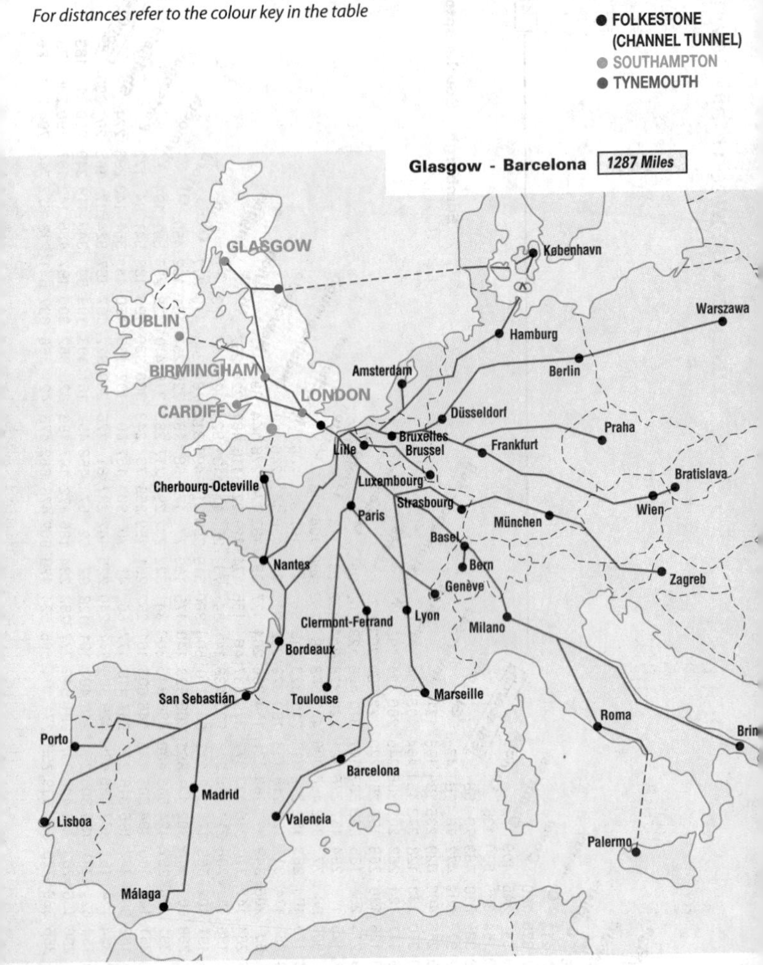

Birmingham	Cardiff	Dublin	Glasgow	London	
226	449	381	481	297	**Amsterdam**
1016	1042	1172	1287	891	**Barcelona**
624	650	779	894	498	**Basel**
773	798	928	1043	647	**Berlin**
684	710	839	954	558	**Bern**
543	530	504	1001	605	**Bordeaux**
1059	1085	1215	1330	934	**Bratislava**
1449	1475	1649	1764	1326	**Brindisi**
318	344	474	589	193	**Bruxelles-Brussel**
161	119	316	447	76	**Cherbourg**
637	662	792	907	511	**Clermont-Ferrand**
442	468	598	713	317	**Düsseldorf**
566	592	721	836	440	**Frankfurt am Main**
663	688	818	933	537	**Genève**
665	691	821	936	540	**Hamburg**
855	881	1010	1125	729	**København**
264	290	420	535	139	**Lille**
1266	1253	478	1725	1329	**Lisboa**
452	477	607	722	326	**Luxembourg**

Birmingham	Cardiff	Dublin	Glasgow	London	
667	693	823	938	542	**Lyon**
971	958	927	1429	1033	**Madrid**
1305	1292	1261	1763	1367	**Málaga**
861	887	1017	1132	736	**Marseille**
833	859	1014	1104	707	**Milano**
790	816	946	1061	665	**München**
364	322	296	650	279	**Nantes**
1359	1385	1514	1629	1189	**Palermo**
369	395	525	640	244	**Paris**
1164	1151	285	1622	1226	**Porto**
879	904	1034	1149	753	**Praha**
1234	1259	1389	1504	1066	**Roma**
691	678	651	1149	753	**San Sebastián**
580	606	736	851	455	**Strasbourg**
795	820	950	1065	669	**Toulouse**
1028	1015	989	1499	1103	**Valencia**
1107	1133	1263	1378	982	**Warszawa**
1006	1032	1162	1277	881	**Wien**
1119	1145	1274	1389	993	**Zagreb**

Great Britain & Ireland in 39 maps

36 37
REPUBLIC OF IRELAND
IRISH SEA
20
CHESHIRE, LANCASHIRE, ISLE OF MAN
22 23
YORKSHIRE
Blackpool
Bradford
Leeds
Kingston upon Hull
Dublin
Manchester
Liverpool
Birkenhead
Sheffield
16 17
DERBYSHIRE, LEICESTERSHIRE, NORTHAMPTONSHIRE, RUTLAND, LINCOLNSHIRE, NOTTINGHAMSHIRE
Stoke-on-Trent
38 39
REPUBLIC OF IRELAND
32 33
WALES
Nottingham
Wolverhampton
Leicester
Norwich
18 19
HEREFORDSHIRE, WORCESTERSHIRE, SHROPSHIRE, STAFFORDSHIRE, WARWICKSHIRE
Birmingham
Coventry
14 15
NORFOLK, SUFFOLK, CAMBRIDGESHIRE
Cork
Northampton
Ipswich
10 11
OXFORDSHIRE, BUCKINGHAMSHIRE
BEDFORDSHIRE, HERTFORDSHIRE, ESSEX
CELTIC SEA
Cardiff
Bristol
Reading
12 13
LONDON
Southend-on-Sea
SOMERSET, DORSET, GLOUCESTERSHIRE, WILTSHIRE
Southampton
CORNWALL, DEVON, ISLES OF SCILLY
3 4
8 9
5
Alderney
1 2
Guernsey
Bournemouth
Portsmouth
Brighton
EAST SUSSEX, KENT
HAMPSHIRE, ISLE OF WIGHT, SURREY, WEST SUSSEX
Plymouth
FRANCE
6 7
ENGLISH CHANNEL
LA MANCHE
Jersey
Isles of Scilly
CHANNEL ISLANDS

1 Cornwall, Devon, Isles of Scilly

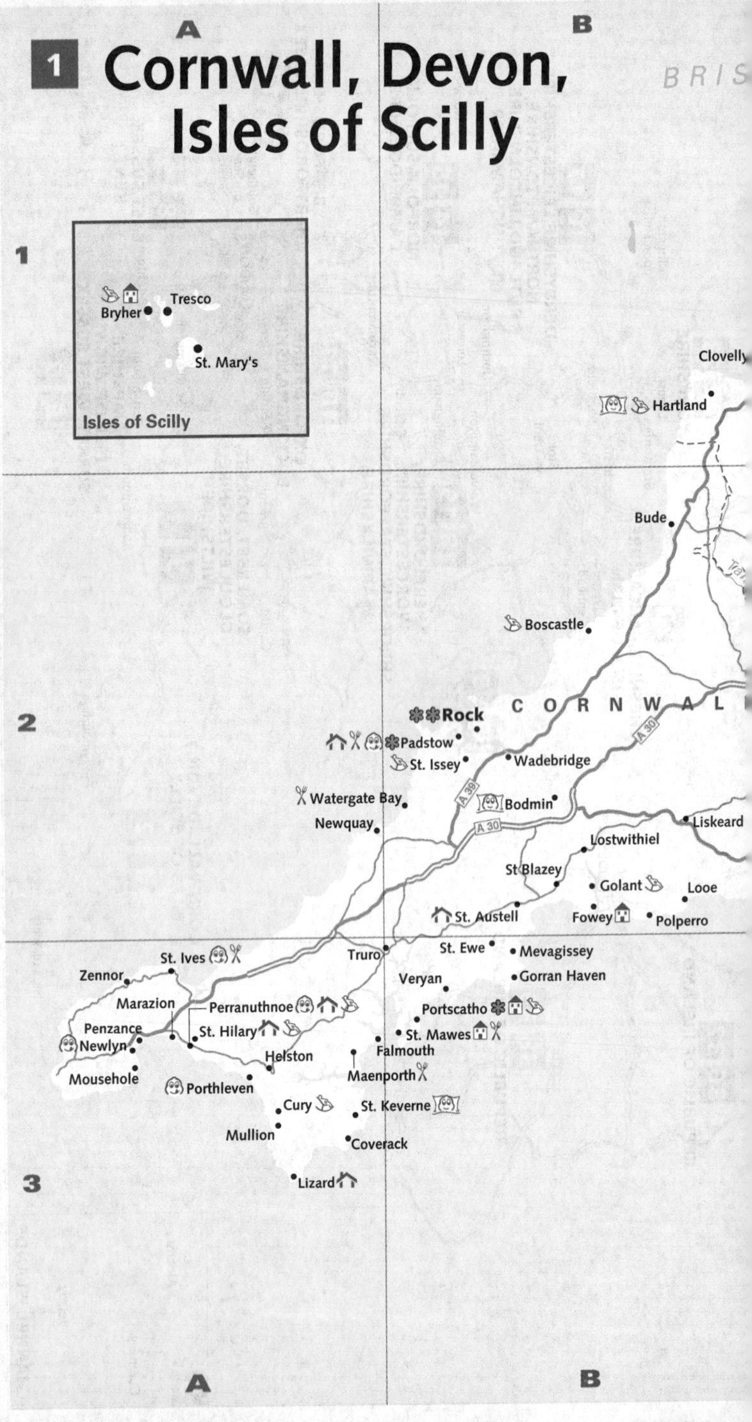
A
B
BRIS
1
2
3
Isles of Scilly
Tresco
Bryher
St. Mary's
Clovelly
Hartland
Bude
Boscastle
CORNWAL
Rock
Padstow
St. Issey
Wadebridge
A 30
A 39
Watergate Bay
Bodmin
Newquay
Liskeard
Lostwithiel
St Blazey
Golant
Looe
St. Austell
Fowey
Polperro
St. Ives
Truro
St. Ewe
Mevagissey
Zennor
Veryan
Gorran Haven
Marazion
Perranuthnoe
Portscatho
Penzance
St. Hilary
St. Mawes
Newlyn
Falmouth
Helston
Mousehole
Maenporth
Porthleven
Cury
St. Keverne
Mullion
Coverack
Lizard
A
B

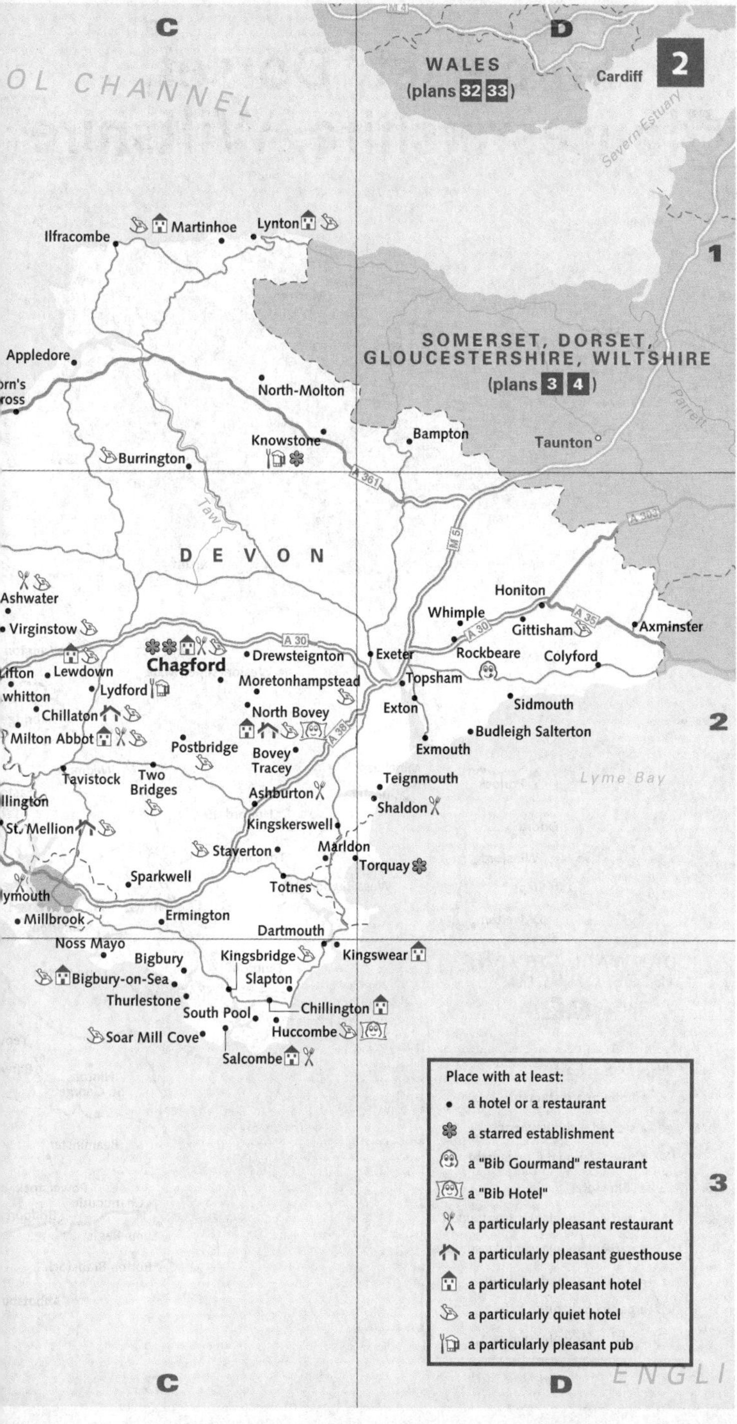

C
D
2
WALES
(plans 32 33)
Cardiff
Severn Estuary
OL CHANNEL
1
Martinhoe
Lynton
Ilfracombe
SOMERSET, DORSET, GLOUCESTERSHIRE, WILTSHIRE
(plans 3 4)
Appledore
North-Molton
Parrett
Knowstone
Bampton
Taunton
Burrington
A 361
Taw
A 303
M 5
DEVON
Ashwater
Honiton
Whimple
A 35
Virginstow
Gittisham
Axminster
A 30
A 30
Chagford
Drewsteignton
Exeter
Rockbeare
Colyford
Lewdown
Moretonhampstead
Topsham
Lydford
Sidmouth
Chillaton
North Bovey
Exton
2
Milton Abbot
Budleigh Salterton
Postbridge
A 38
Bovey Tracey
Exmouth
Tavistock
Two Bridges
Teignmouth
Lyme Bay
Ashburton
Shaldon
St. Mellion
Kingskerswell
Staverton
Marldon
Torquay
Sparkwell
Totnes
Millbrook
Ermington
Dartmouth
Noss Mayo
Kingswear
Bigbury
Kingsbridge
Bigbury-on-Sea
Slapton
Thurlestone
Chillington
South Pool
Soar Mill Cove
Huccombe
Salcombe
Place with at least:
a hotel or a restaurant
a starred establishment
a "Bib Gourmand" restaurant
a "Bib Hotel"
a particularly pleasant restaurant
a particularly pleasant guesthouse
a particularly pleasant hotel
a particularly quiet hotel
a particularly pleasant pub
3
ENGLI
C
D

3 Somerset, Dorset, Gloucestershire, Wiltshire

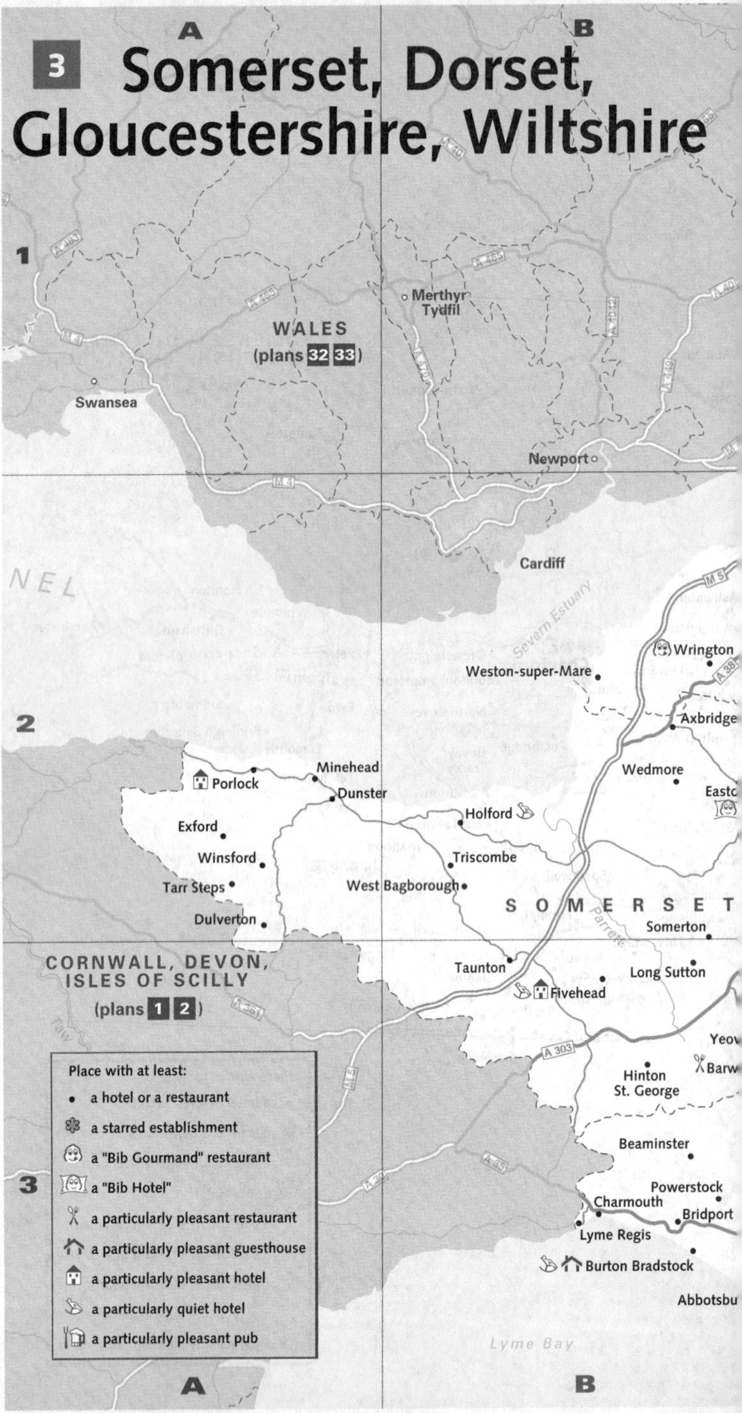

4
C
D
1
2
3
HEREFORDSHIRE, WORCESTERSHIRE, SHROPSHIRE, STAFFORDSHIRE, WARWICKSHIRE
(plans 18 19)
GLOUCESTERSHIRE
OXFORDSHIRE, BUCKINGHAMSHIRE
(plans 10 11)
WILTSHIRE
HAMPSHIRE, ISLE OF WIGHT, SURREY, WEST SUSSEX
(plans 6 7)
DORSET
Chipping Campden
Broad Campden
Blockley
Tewkesbury
Bourton on the Hill
Moreton-in-Marsh
Winchcombe
Stow-on-the-Wold
Loxer Swell
Daylesford
Cheltenham
Upper Slaughter
Lower Slaughter
Nether Westcote
Bourton-on-the-Water
Cowley
Cockleford
Arlingham
Northleach
Clearwell
Painswick
Barnsley
Bibury
Sapperton
Coln St. Aldwyns
Southrop
Nailsworth
Cirencester
Thames
R. Wye
Tetbury
Thornbury
Westonbirt
Oaksey
Cricklade
Malmesbury
Purton
Bishopstone
Bristol
Foxham
Castle Combe
Long Ashton
Colerne
Ramsbury
Chew Magna
Bath
Corsham
Calne
Marlborough
Box
Lacock
Upper South Wraxall
Monkton Combe
Broughton Gifford
Little Bedwyn
Newbury
Combe Hay
Bradford-on-Avon
Avon
Devizes
Ston Easton
Norton St. Philip
East Chisenbury
Edington
Holcombe
Wells
Shepton Mallet
Frome
Warminster
West Pennard
Shrewton
Batcombe
Bruton
Little Langford
Castle Cary
Teffont Evias
Gillingham
Tisbury
Salisbury
Holton
West Hatch
Corton Denham
Buckhorn Weston
Shaftesbury
Donhead-St-Andrew
Trent
Sherborne
Fontmell Magna
Tollard Royal
Nomansland
Farnham
Evershot
Blandford Forum
Southampton
Sydling St. Nicholas
Cerne Abbas
Wimborne Minster
Maiden Newton
Bournemouth
Dorchester
Poole
Highcliffe
Wareham
Christchurch
West Lulworth
Studland
Isle of Wight
Corfe Castle
Weymouth
A 40
M 5
A 417
A 48
M 50
M 4
A 36
A 303
A 34
A 31
A 35
M 27

Channel Islands 5

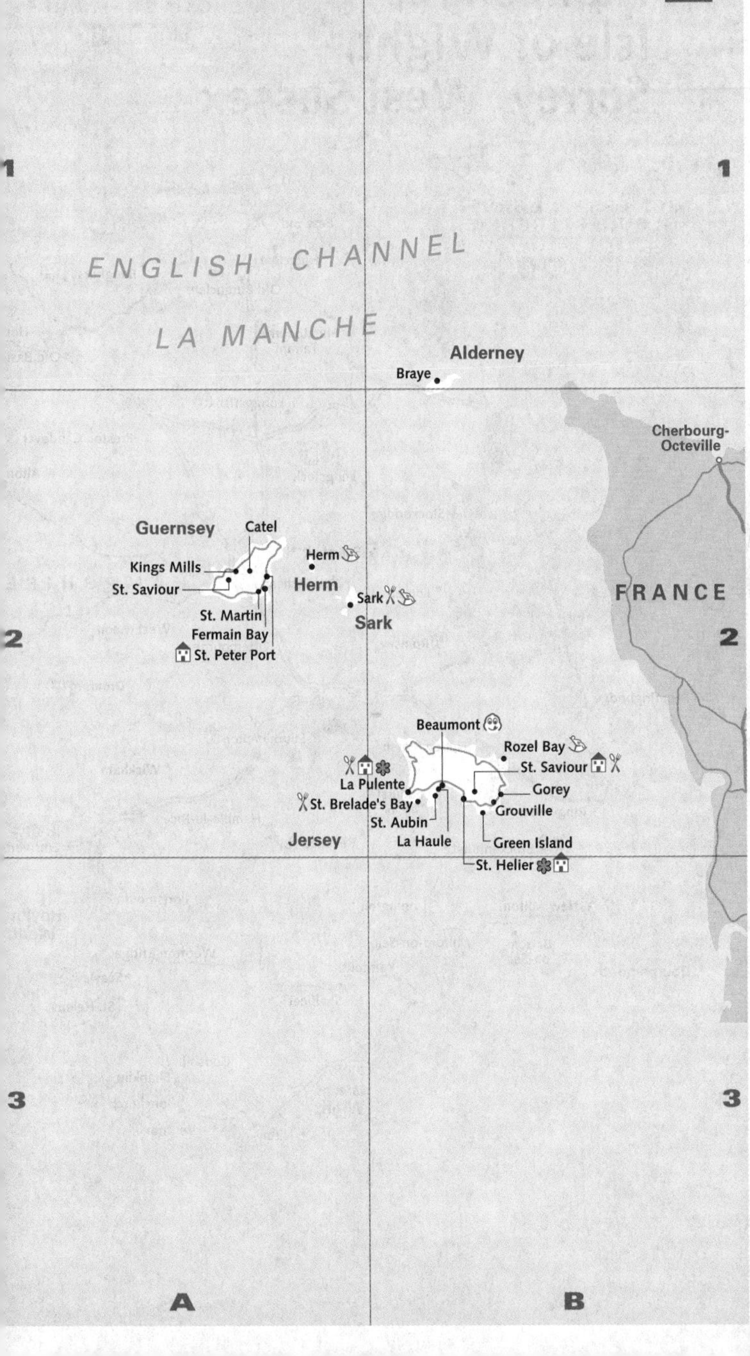

6 Hampshire, Isle of Wight, Surrey, West Sussex

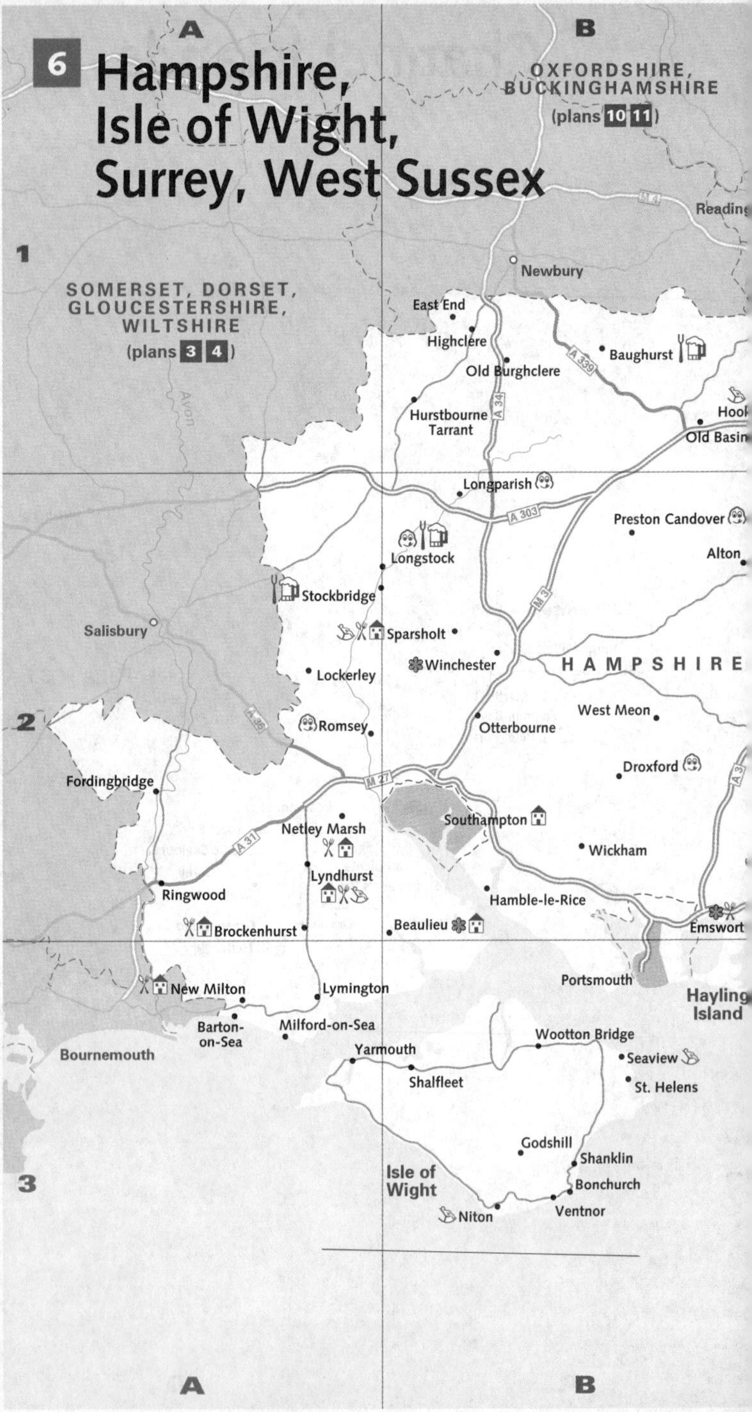

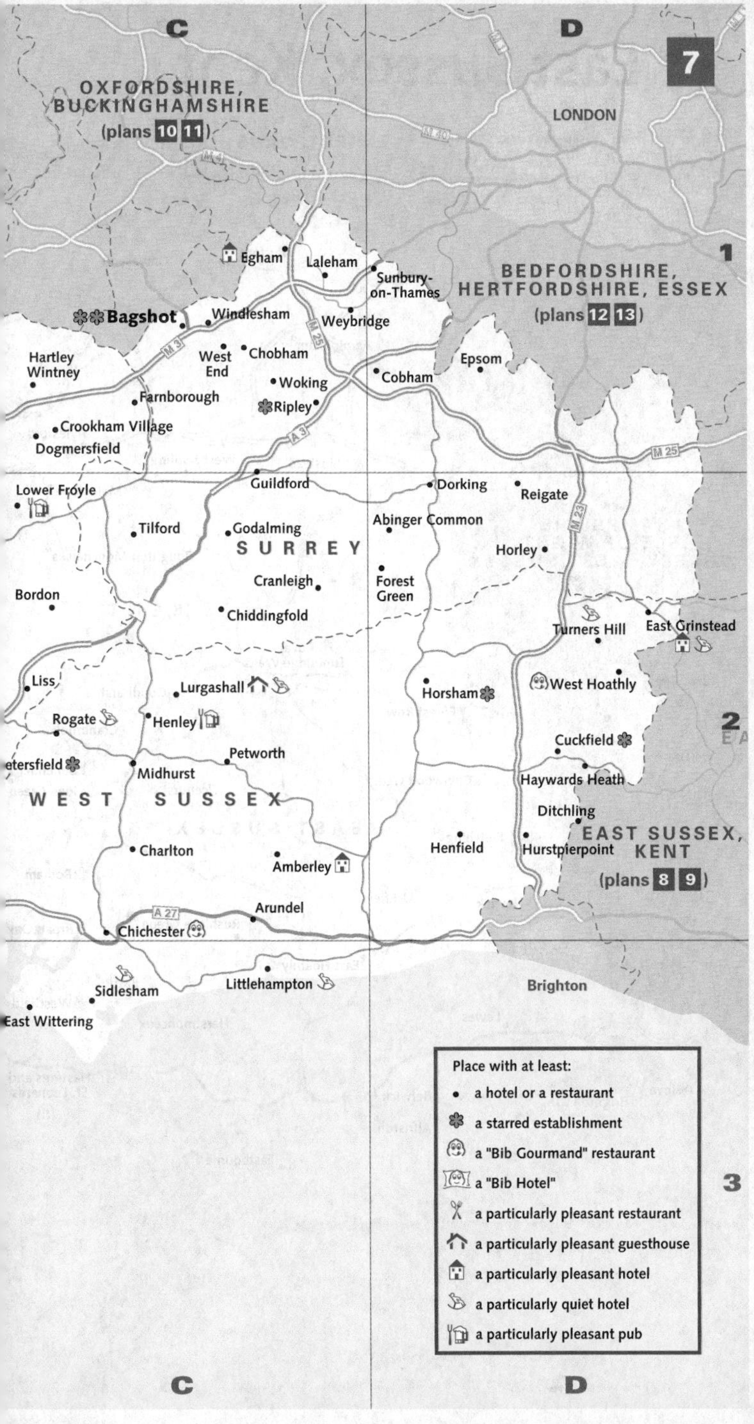
C
D
7
OXFORDSHIRE, BUCKINGHAMSHIRE
(plans 10 11)
LONDON
M 40
M 4
M 3
M 25
A 3
M 23
A 27
BEDFORDSHIRE, HERTFORDSHIRE, ESSEX
(plans 12 13)
1
Egham
Laleham
Sunbury-on-Thames
Bagshot
Windlesham
Weybridge
Hartley Wintney
West End
Chobham
Epsom
Woking
Cobham
Farnborough
Ripley
Crookham Village
Dogmersfield
Guildford
Dorking
Reigate
Lower Froyle
Abinger Common
Tilford
Godalming
SURREY
Horley
Cranleigh
Forest Green
Bordon
Chiddingfold
Turners Hill
East Grinstead
Liss
Lurgashall
Horsham
West Hoathly
Rogate
Henley
2
Cuckfield
Petersfield
Petworth
Midhurst
Haywards Heath
WEST SUSSEX
Ditchling
EAST SUSSEX, KENT
Charlton
Henfield
Hurstpierpoint
Amberley
(plans 8 9)
Arundel
Chichester
Littlehampton
Brighton
Sidlesham
East Wittering
Place with at least:
a hotel or a restaurant
a starred establishment
a "Bib Gourmand" restaurant
a "Bib Hotel"
a particularly pleasant restaurant
a particularly pleasant guesthouse
a particularly pleasant hotel
a particularly quiet hotel
a particularly pleasant pub
3
C
D

8 East Sussex, Kent

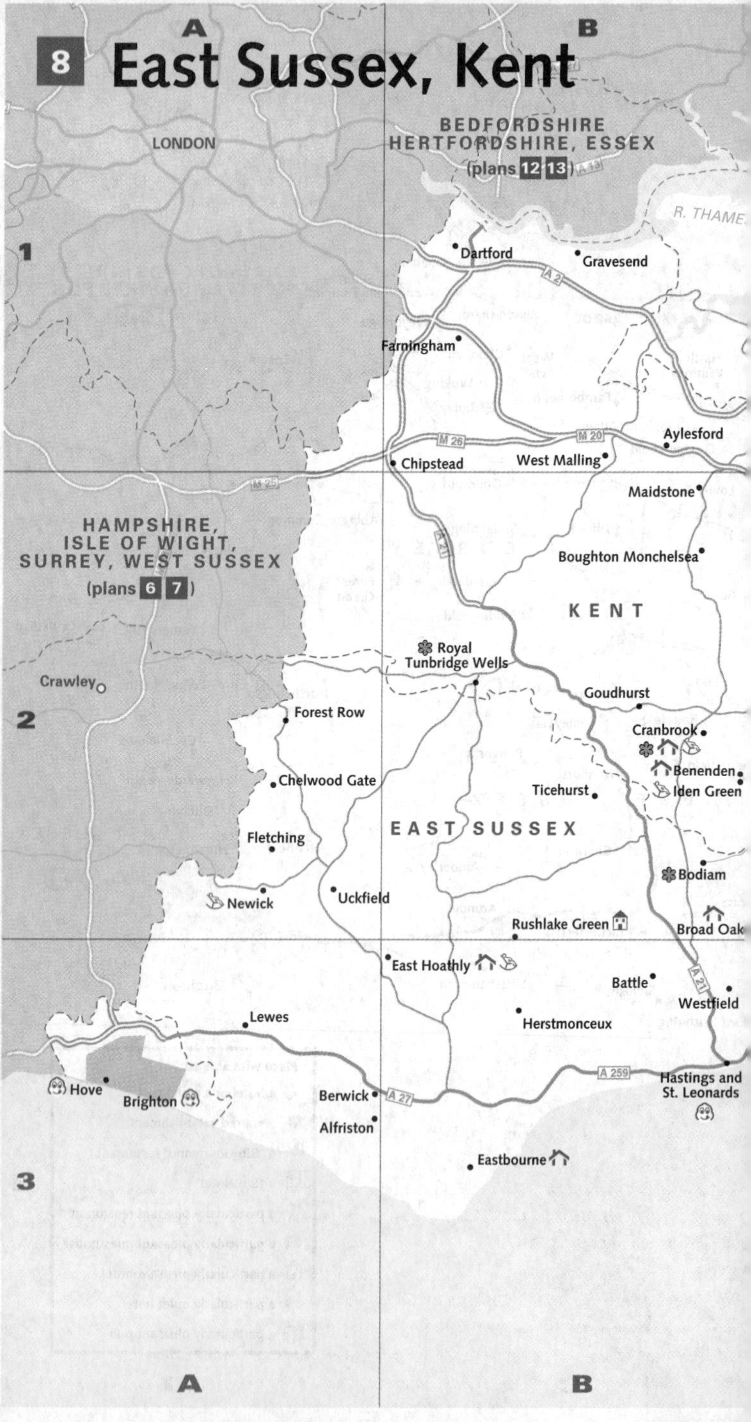

C
D
9
BEDFORDSHIRE
HERTFORDSHIRE, ESSEX
(plans 12 13)
Southend-on-Sea
1
Herne Bay
Margate
Whitstable
A 299
Broadstairs
Rainham
Seasalter
Sittingbourne
Oare
Ramsgate
Faversham
Milstead
M 2
Doddington
Canterbury
Ash
Sandwich
Stalisfield Green
KENT
A 2
A 256
Deal
Wye
Ashford
Brabourne
Alkham
Biddenden
M 20
Dover
2
Folkestone
A 259
Ivychurch
New Romney
Rye
Winchelsea
Icklesham
Place with at least:
a hotel or a restaurant
a starred establishment
a "Bib Gourmand" restaurant
a "Bib Hotel"
a particularly pleasant restaurant
a particularly pleasant guesthouse
a particularly pleasant hotel
a particularly quiet hotel
a particularly pleasant pub
3
DOVER
C
D

10 Oxfordshire, Buckinghamshire

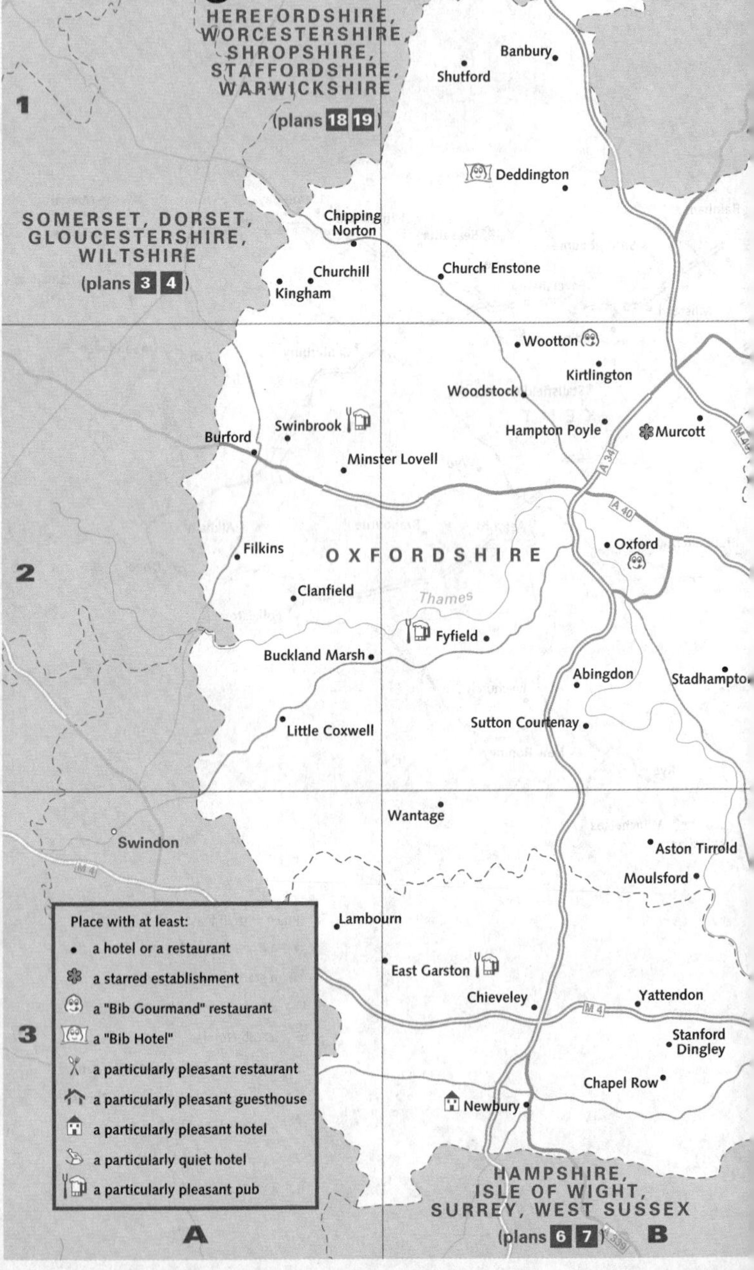

11
C
D
DERBYSHIRE, LEICESTERSHIRE, NORTHAMPTONSHIRE, UTLAND, LINCOLNSHIRE, NOTTINGHAMSHIRE
(plans 16 17)
A 428
Newport Pagnell
Milton Keynes
M 1
BEDFORDSHIRE HERTFORDSHIRE, ESSEX
(plans 12 13)
1
Woburn Sands
Buckingham
Gt. Ouse
Newton Longville
A 6
A 5
BUCKINGHAMSHIRE
Luton
Waddesdon
Aylesbury
Cuddington
Long Crendon
BEDFORDSHIRE HERTFORDSHIRE, ESSEX
(plans 12 13)
2
A 41
Great Milton
Chinnor
Speen
Great Missenden
Sprigg's Alley
Amersham
Watlington
Stokenchurch
Watford
Britwell Salome
Penn
Stonor
Maidensgrove
Beaconsfield
Gerrards Cross
Marlow
Denham
Stoke Row
Cookham
Cookham Dean
Stoke Poges
Fulmer
Henley-on-Thames
Hurley
Taplow
Maidenhead
M 40
George Green
BRAY
M 4
Dorney
Holyport
Bray Marina
Sonning
Windsor
3
Reading
Ascot
Shinfield
Sunningdale
HAMPSHIRE, ISLE OF WIGHT, SURREY, WEST SUSSEX
(plans 6 7)
M 3
C
D

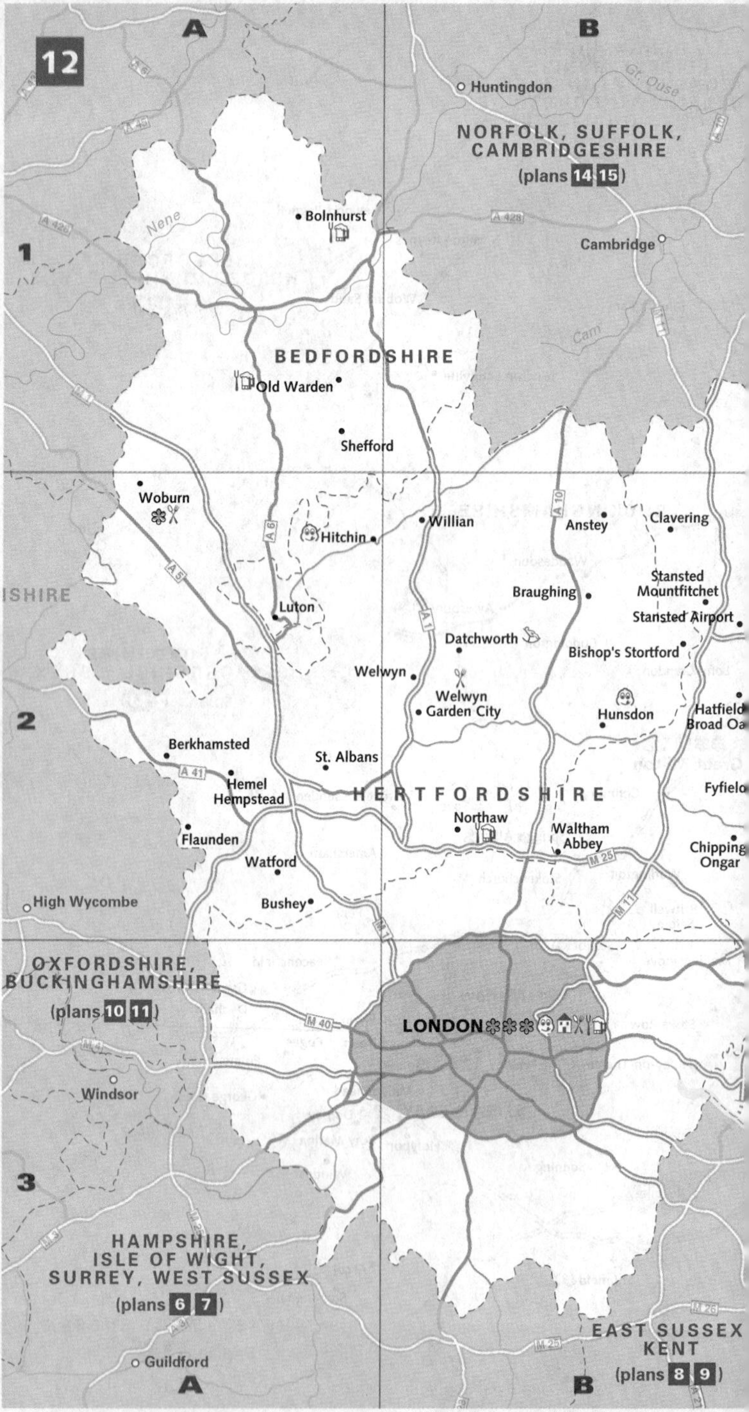
12
A
B
Huntingdon
Gr. Ouse
NORFOLK, SUFFOLK,
CAMBRIDGESHIRE
(plans 14 15)
A 6
A 45
A 428
A 10
Nene
Bolnhurst
Cambridge
1
Cam
BEDFORDSHIRE
Old Warden
Shefford
M 1
Woburn
Willian
Anstey
Clavering
A 10
A 6
Hitchin
A 5
Stansted
Mountfitchet
ISHIRE
Braughing
Luton
A 1
Stansted Airport
Datchworth
Bishop's Stortford
Welwyn
Welwyn
Garden City
Hunsdon
2
Hatfield
Broad Oa
Berkhamsted
St. Albans
A 41
Hemel
Hempstead
HERTFORDSHIRE
Fyfield
Northaw
Flaunden
Waltham
Abbey
Chipping
Ongar
Watford
M 25
High Wycombe
Bushey
M 11
M 1
OXFORDSHIRE,
BUCKINGHAMSHIRE
(plans 10 11)
M 40
LONDON
M 4
Windsor
3
M 25
M 3
HAMPSHIRE,
ISLE OF WIGHT,
SURREY, WEST SUSSEX
(plans 6 7)
M 26
A 3
M 25
EAST SUSSEX
KENT
Guildford
(plans 8 9)
A
B

Bedfordshire, Hertfordshire, Essex

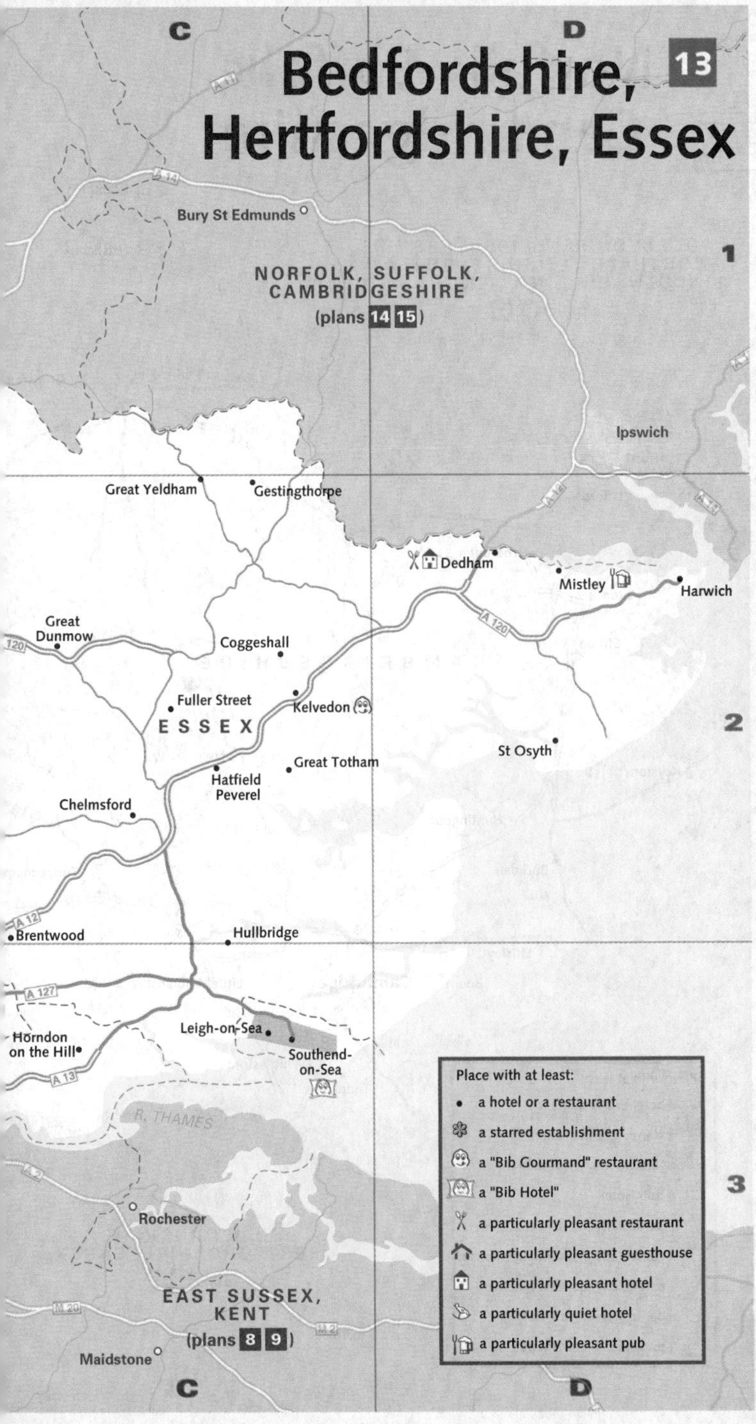

14 Norfolk, Suffolk, Cambridgeshire

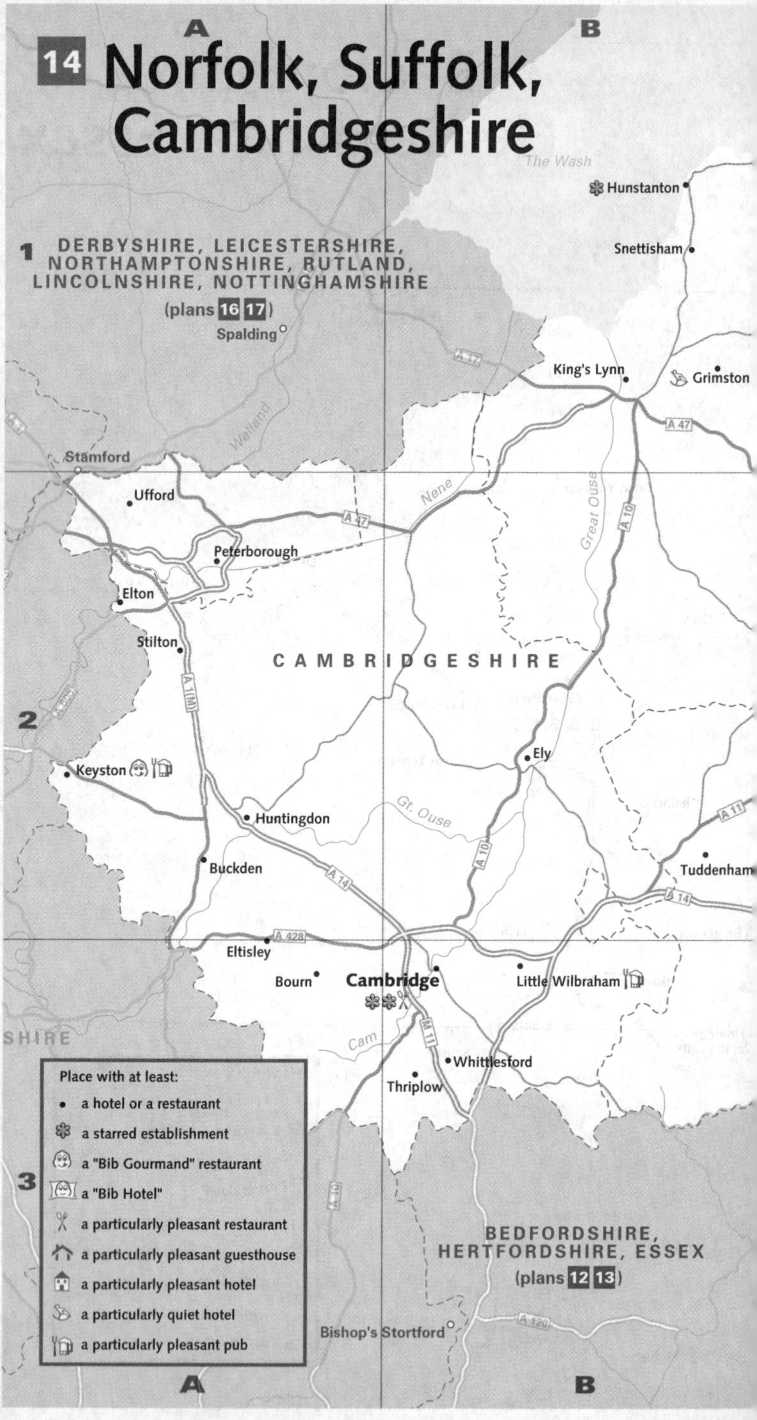

C
D
15
ancaster Staithe
Holkham
Wells-next-the-Sea
Blakeney
Sheringham
chwell
Burnham Market
Morston
Holt
Hindringham
Hunworth
Thursford Green
Thorpe Market
Itteringham
Aylsham
North Walsham
Ingham
Wellingham
NORFOLK
Coltishall
Horning
1
Swaffham
Norwich
A 47
Bure
Brundall
Great Yarmouth
Yare
Watton
A 11
A 12
Attleborough
Earsham
Lowestoft
Bungay
2
Pulham Market
North Lopham
Kessingland
Waveney
Fressingfield
Stanton
Southwold
Walberswick
Bury St Edmunds
Westleton
Kelsale
Earl Stonham
Stowmarket
SUFFOLK
Snape
Aldeburgh
A 12
Campsea Ash
Lavenham
Ufford
Bromeswell
Bildeston
Orford
Monks Eleigh
Woodbridge
Long Melford
Ipswich
Hadleigh
3
Stoke-by-Nayland
A 12
A 14
Harwich
A 120
Colchester
C
D

16
A
B
Manchester
Barnsley
Doncaster
YORKSHIRE
(plans 22 23)
Rotherham
Sheffield
Derwent
CHESHIRE,
LANCASHIRE,
ISLE OF MAN
(plan 20)
1
Hope
Hathersage
Bradwell
Chapel-en-le-Frith
Buxton
Froggatt Edge
Baslow
Eckington
Worksop
Retford
Elmton
Chesterfield
Ashford-in-the-Water
Beeley
Rowsley
DERBYSHIRE
Hartington
Mansfield
NOTTINGHAMSHIRE
Stoke-on-Trent
Ashbourne
Belper
Hoveringham
R. Trent
Nottingham
Sandiacre
Derby
Langa
Colston Bassett
Stathern
HEREFORDSHIRE,
WORCESTERSHIRE,
SHROPSHIRE,
STAFFORDSHIRE,
WARWICKSHIRE
(plans 18 19)
2
Castle Donington
Kegworth
Breedon on the Hill
Long Whatton
Wymeswold
Melton Mowbray
Woodhouse Eaves
LEICESTERSHIRE
Cropston
Leicester
Wolverhampton
Kibworth Harcourt
Kibworth Beauchamp
Medbourne
Birmingham
Bruntingthorpe
North Kilworth
Coventry
NORTHAMPTONSHIRE
East Haddon
Daventry
Northampton
3
Roade
Towcester
Aynho
Gt. Ouse
CESTERSHIRE
A 628
A 616
M 1
A 57
A 1
A 6
A 61
A 614
M 1
A 52
A 50
A 606
A 46
A 6
A 47
A 6
A 14
A 45
A 5
A 43
Place with at least:
a hotel or a restaurant
a starred establishment
a "Bib Gourmand" restaurant
a "Bib Hotel"
a particularly pleasant restaurant
a particularly pleasant guesthouse
a particularly pleasant hotel
a particularly quiet hotel
a particularly pleasant pub

Derbyshire, Leicestershire, Northamptonshire, Rutland, Lincolnshire, Nottinghamshire

18 Herefordshire, Worcestershire, Shropshire, Staffordshire, Warwickshire

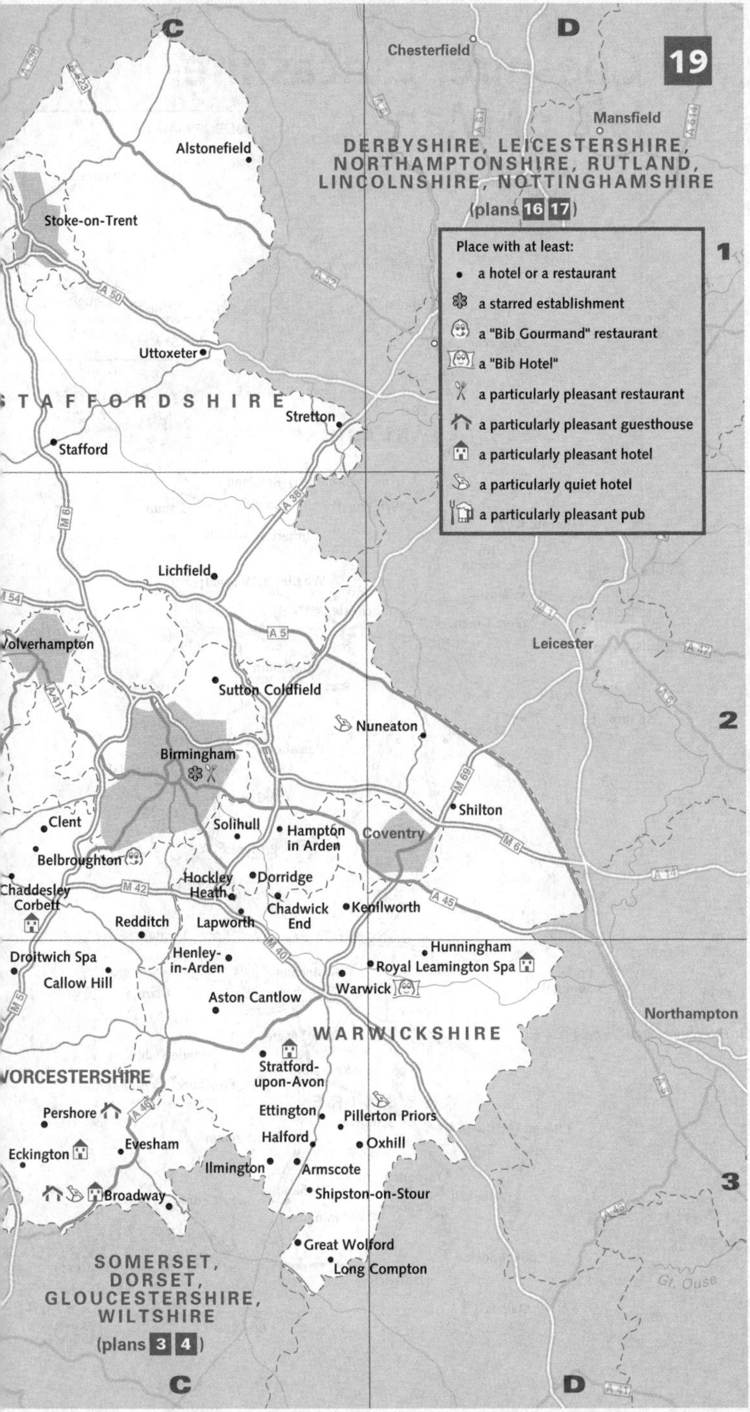
19
C
D
Chesterfield
Mansfield
DERBYSHIRE, LEICESTERSHIRE,
NORTHAMPTONSHIRE, RUTLAND,
LINCOLNSHIRE, NOTTINGHAMSHIRE
(plans 16 17)
Place with at least:
a hotel or a restaurant
a starred establishment
a "Bib Gourmand" restaurant
a "Bib Hotel"
a particularly pleasant restaurant
a particularly pleasant guesthouse
a particularly pleasant hotel
a particularly quiet hotel
a particularly pleasant pub
1
2
3
Alstonefield
Stoke-on-Trent
A 50
A 52
A 523
Uttoxeter
STAFFORDSHIRE
Stretton
Stafford
M 6
A 38
Lichfield
A 5
Wolverhampton
Leicester
A 47
A 41
Sutton Coldfield
Nuneaton
Birmingham
M 69
Shilton
Clent
Solihull
Hampton in Arden
Coventry
M 6
Belbroughton
Chaddesley Corbett
Hockley Heath
Dorridge
M 42
A 14
Chadwick End
Kenilworth
A 45
Redditch
Lapworth
M 40
Hunningham
Droitwich Spa
Henley-in-Arden
Royal Leamington Spa
Callow Hill
Warwick
Aston Cantlow
M 5
Northampton
WARWICKSHIRE
Stratford-upon-Avon
WORCESTERSHIRE
Pershore
A 46
Ettington
Pillerton Priors
Halford
Oxhill
Eckington
Evesham
Ilmington
Armscote
Broadway
Shipston-on-Stour
A 43
Great Wolford
Long Compton
Gt. Ouse
SOMERSET,
DORSET,
GLOUCESTERSHIRE,
WILTSHIRE
(plans 3 4)
A 41

20 Cheshire, Lancashire, Isle of Man

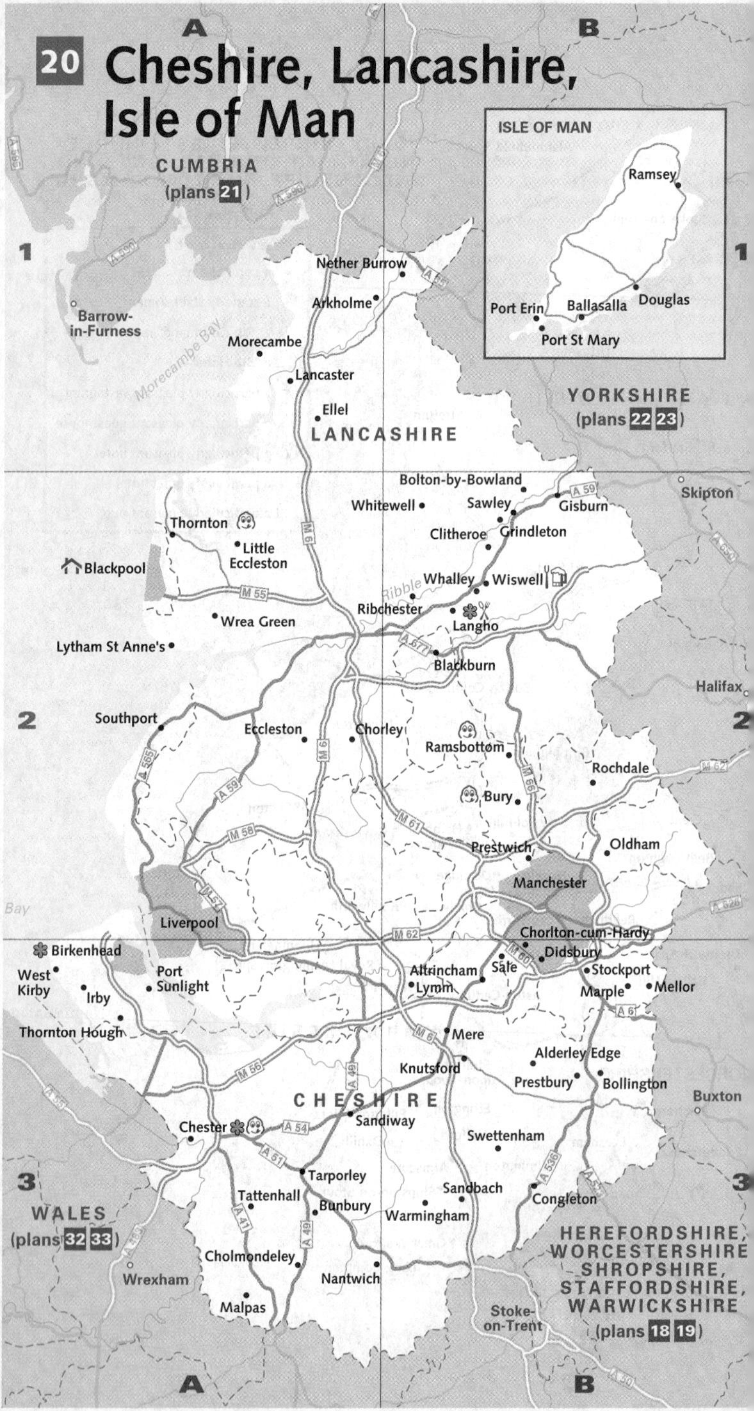

Cumbria 21

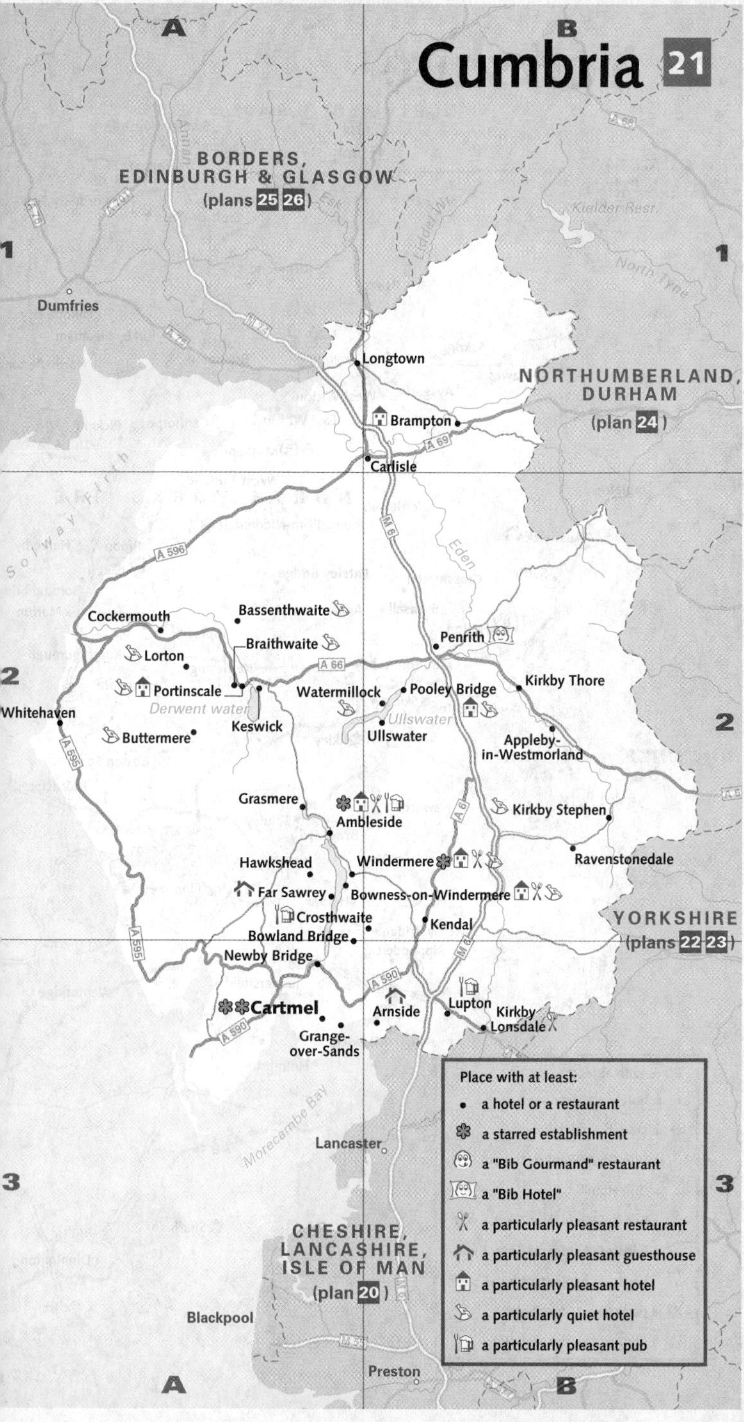
A
B
BORDERS,
EDINBURGH & GLASGOW
(plans 25 26)
NORTHUMBERLAND,
DURHAM
(plan 24)
YORKSHIRE
(plans 22-23)
CHESHIRE,
LANCASHIRE,
ISLE OF MAN
(plan 20)
1
2
3
Dumfries
Kielder Resr.
North Tyne
Longtown
Brampton
Carlisle
A 69
A 596
Solway Firth
Eden
M 6
Cockermouth
Bassenthwaite
Braithwaite
Lorton
Portinscale
Derwent water
Keswick
Whitehaven
Buttermere
A 66
Penrith
Watermillock
Pooley Bridge
Ullswater
Kirkby Thore
Appleby-
in-Westmorland
A 595
Grasmere
Ambleside
A 6
Kirkby Stephen
Ravenstonedale
Hawkshead
Windermere
Far Sawrey
Bowness-on-Windermere
Crosthwaite
Kendal
Bowland Bridge
Newby Bridge
A 590
Cartmel
Arnside
Lupton
Kirkby
Lonsdale
Grange-
over-Sands
Morecambe Bay
Lancaster
Blackpool
Preston
M 55
Place with at least:
a hotel or a restaurant
a starred establishment
a "Bib Gourmand" restaurant
a "Bib Hotel"
a particularly pleasant restaurant
a particularly pleasant guesthouse
a particularly pleasant hotel
a particularly quiet hotel
a particularly pleasant pub

22 Yorkshire

C
D
23
1
2
3
Middlesbrough
Runswick Bay
Whitby
Egton
Hawnby
Hutton-
le-Hole
Lastingham
Levisham
Kirkbymoorside
Scarborough
Helmsley
Harome
Pickering
Oldstead
Snainton
Hovingham
A 64
Wold Newton
Easingwold
Malton
Sutton-
on-the-Forest
A 19
York
EAST RIDING
OF
YORKSHIRE
Lund
A 1079
South Dalton
Derwent
Sancton
Beverley
South
Cave
Kingston
upon Hull
A 164
M 62
R. Ouse
River Humber
Winteringham
A 15
NORTH
LINCOLNSHIRE
Scunthorpe
NORTH EAST
LINCOLNSHIRE
Doncaster
M 18
M 180
R. Trent
A 1
DERBYSHIRE, LEICESTERSHIRE,
NORTHAMPTONSHIRE, RUTLAND,
LINCOLNSHIRE, NOTTINGHAMSHIRE
(plans 16 17)
Louth
C
D

Northumberland, Durham 24

25 Borders, Edinburgh & Glasgow

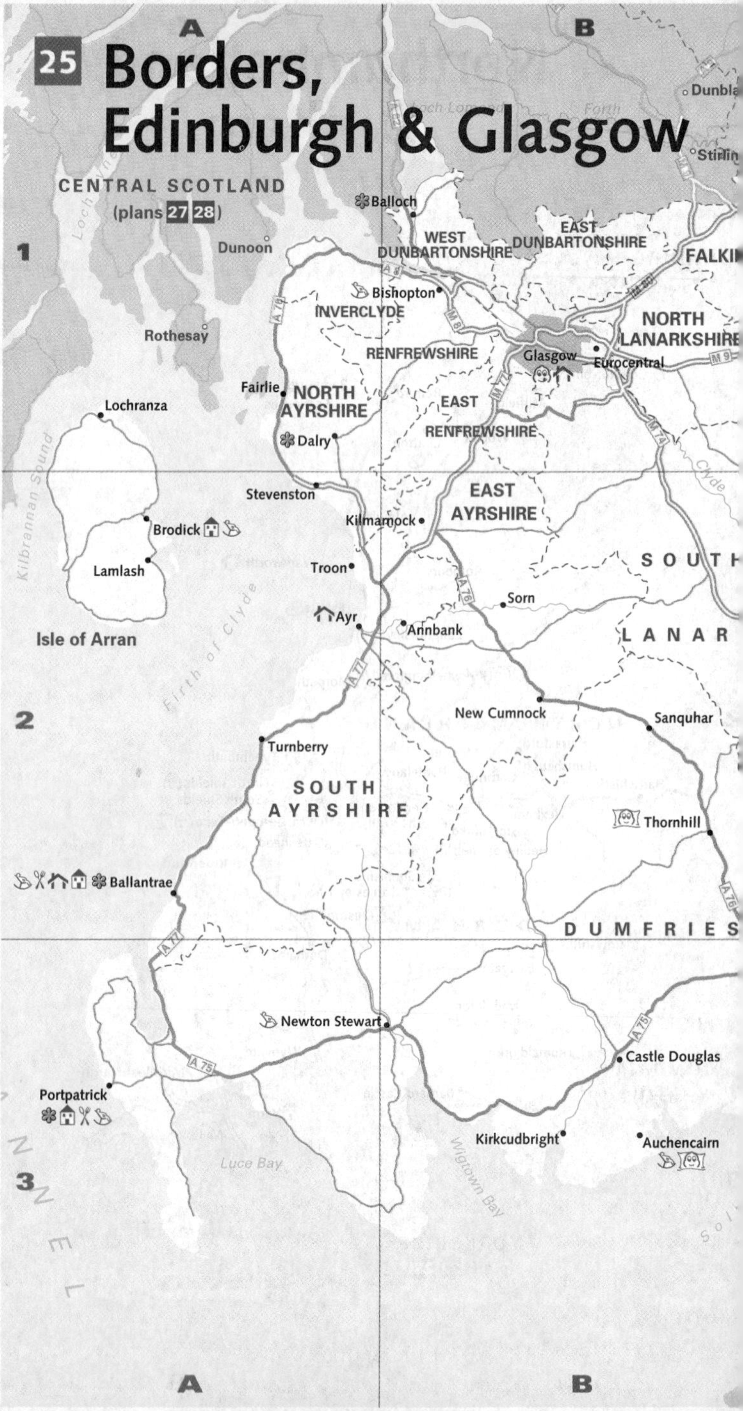

C
St. Andrews
D
CENTRAL SCOTLAND (plans 27 28)
Kirkcaldy
Firth of Forth
Dunfermline
North Berwick
Gullane
1
Dunbar
Linlithgow
Leith
Ingliston
Edinburgh
Kirknewton
Currie
Dalkeith
EAST LOTHIAN
WEST LOTHIAN
MIDLOTHIAN
Chirnside
SCOTTISH
BORDERS
Swinton
R. Tweed
Peebles
Skirling
Walkerburn
Innerleithen
Tweed
Melrose
Ednam
Kelso
St. Boswells
Wooler
Teviot
Jedburgh
2
Moffat
NORTHUMBERLAND, DURHAM
(plan 24)
Annan
Esk
Kielder Resr.
Liddel Wr.
North Tyne
AND GALLOWAY
umfries
Annan
irkbean
Carlisle
Eden
CUMBRIA
(plan 21)
3
Penrith
Keswick
Derwent water
Ullswater
C
D
Place with at least:
a hotel or a restaurant
a starred establishment
a "Bib Gourmand" restaurant
a "Bib Hotel"
a particularly pleasant restaurant
a particularly pleasant guesthouse
a particularly pleasant hotel
a particularly quiet hotel
a particularly pleasant pub

27 Central Scotland

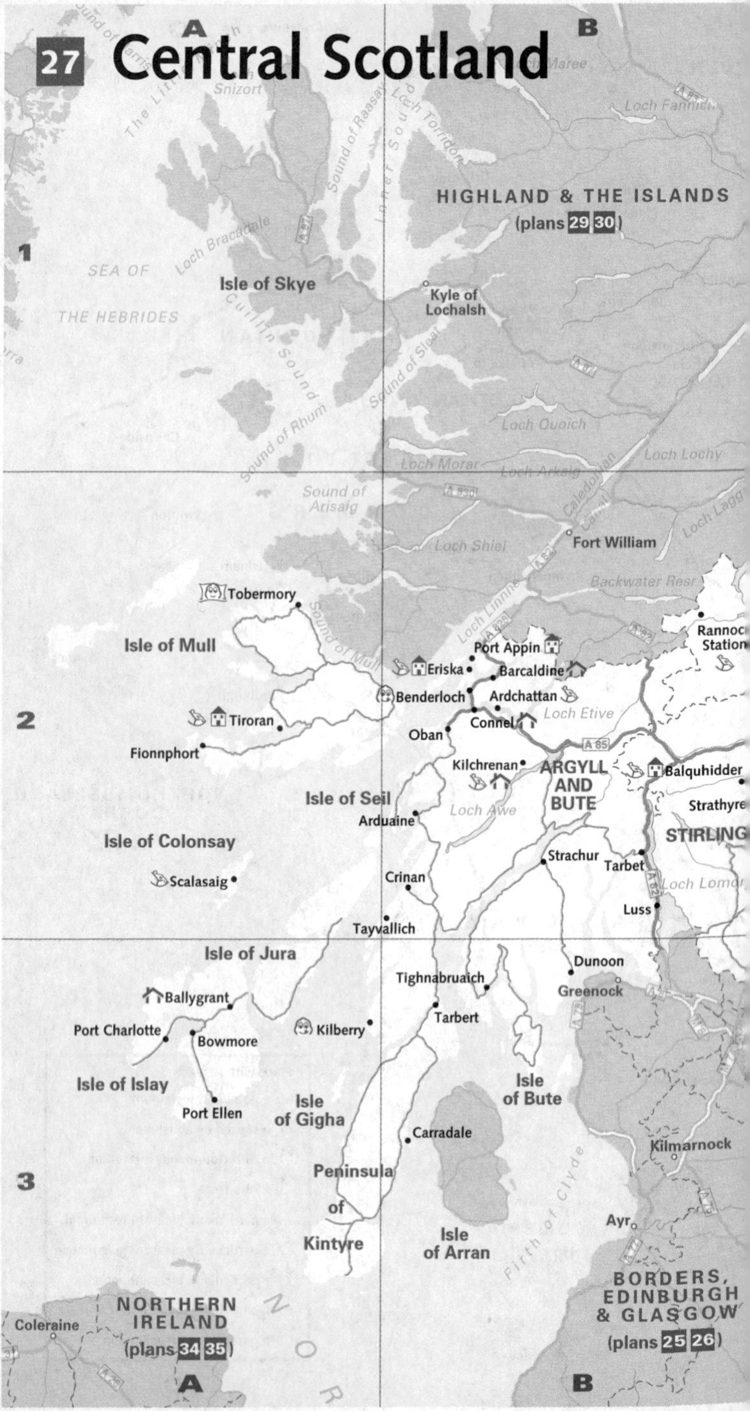

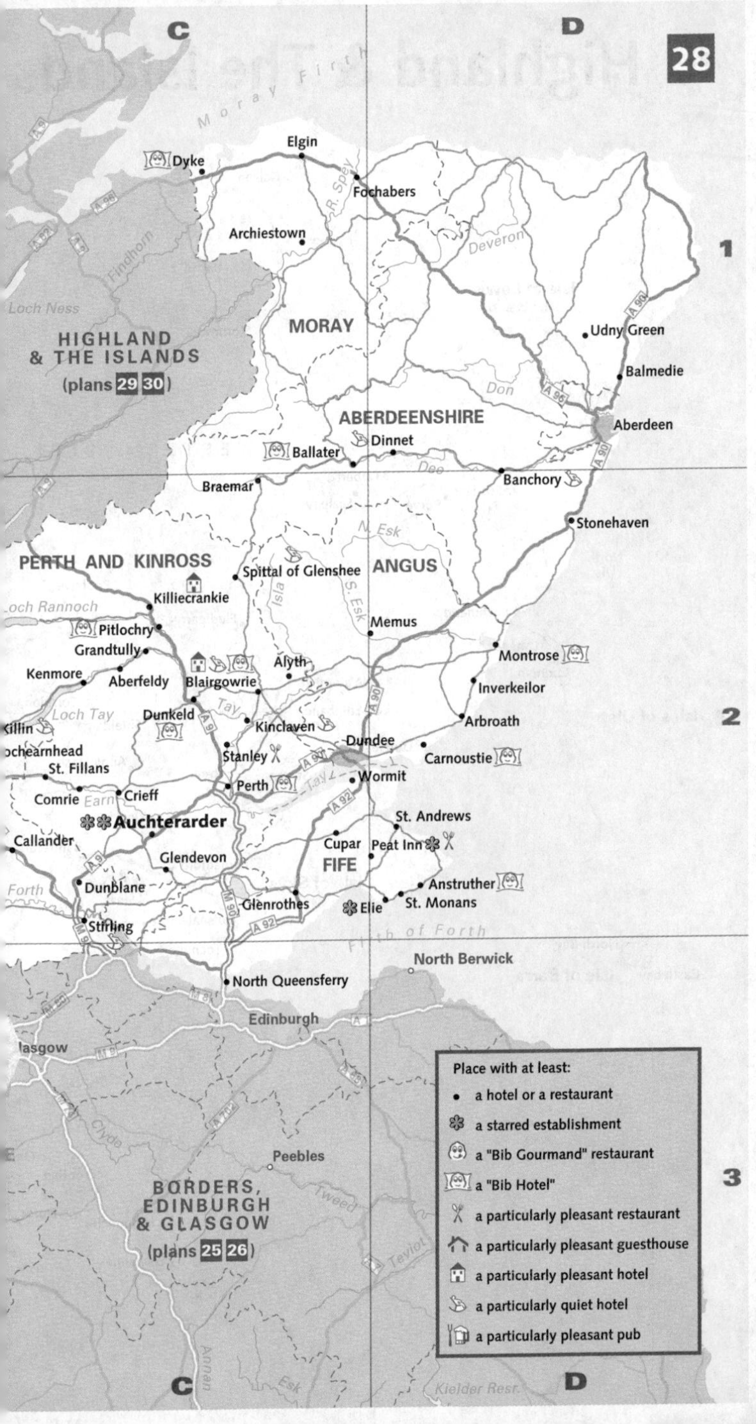
C
D
Moray Firth
1
2
3
Elgin
Dyke
Fochabers
R. Spey
Archiestown
Findhorn
Deveron
Loch Ness
HIGHLAND
& THE ISLANDS
(plans 29 30)
MORAY
Udny Green
Balmedie
Don
ABERDEENSHIRE
Aberdeen
Dinnet
Ballater
Dee
Braemar
Banchory
Stonehaven
N. Esk
PERTH AND KINROSS
Spittal of Glenshee
ANGUS
Isla
S. Esk
Killiecrankie
Loch Rannoch
Memus
Pitlochry
Grandtully
Montrose
Alyth
Kenmore
Aberfeldy
Blairgowrie
Inverkeilor
Tay
Loch Tay
Dunkeld
Kinclaven
Arbroath
Killin
Lochearnhead
Stanley
Dundee
Carnoustie
St. Fillans
Wormit
Perth
Comrie
Earn
Crieff
Auchterarder
St. Andrews
Callander
Cupar
Peat Inn
Glendevon
FIFE
Forth
Dunblane
Anstruther
Glenrothes
Elie
St. Monans
Stirling
Firth of Forth
North Berwick
North Queensferry
Edinburgh
Glasgow
Clyde
Peebles
Tweed
BORDERS,
EDINBURGH
& GLASGOW
(plans 25 26)
Teviot
Annan
Esk
Kielder Resr.
A 9
A 96
A 82
A 90
A 92
M 90
M 9
M 8
A 702
Place with at least:
a hotel or a restaurant
a starred establishment
a "Bib Gourmand" restaurant
a "Bib Hotel"
a particularly pleasant restaurant
a particularly pleasant guesthouse
a particularly pleasant hotel
a particularly quiet hotel
a particularly pleasant pub

29 Highland & The Islands

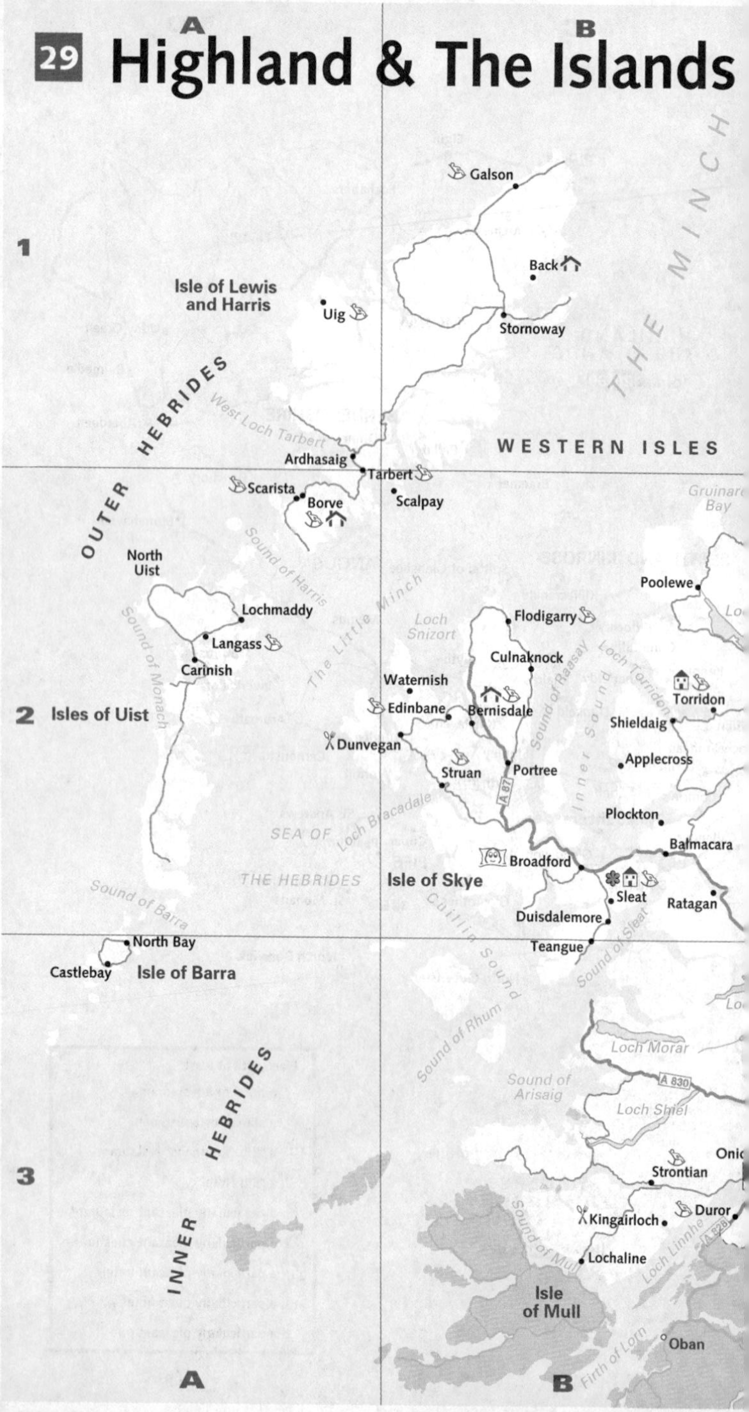

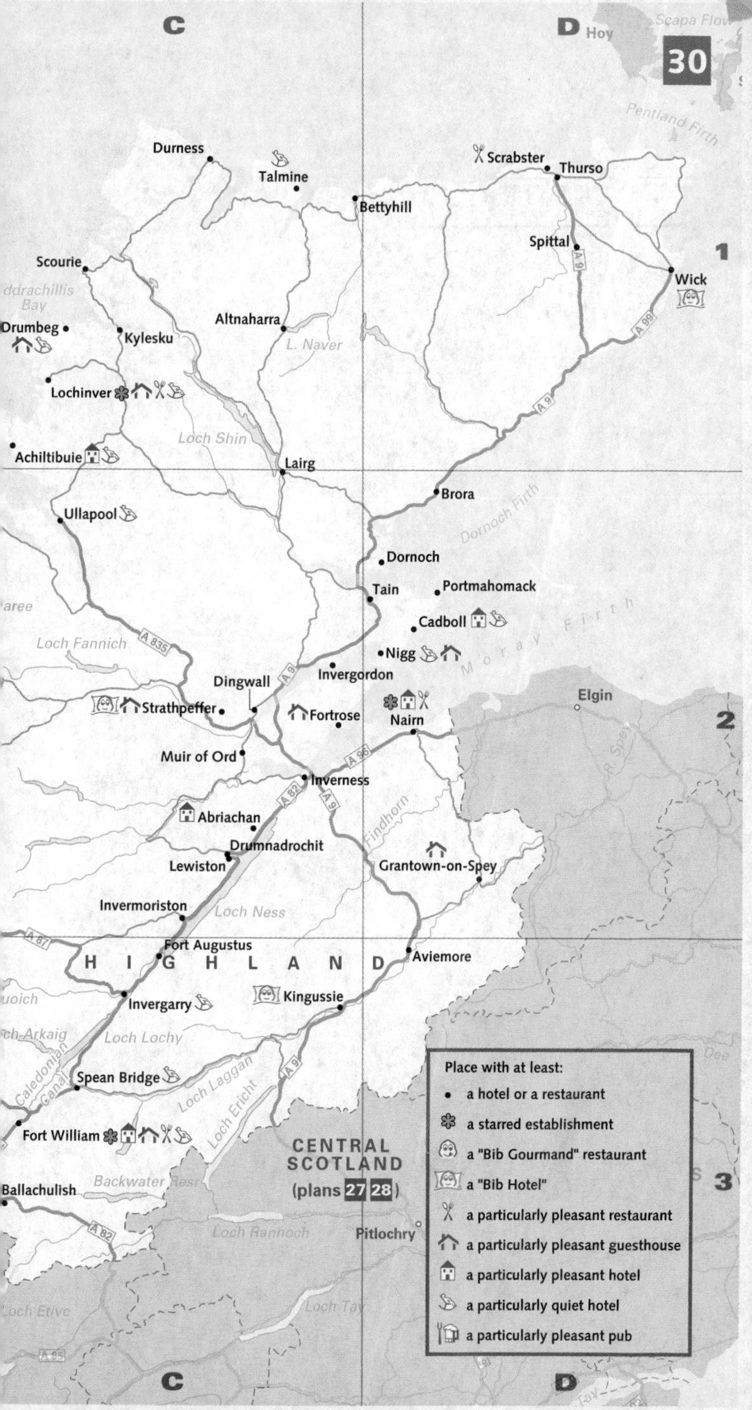
C
D
Hoy
Scapa Flow
Pentland Firth
Durness
Talmine
Scrabster
Thurso
Bettyhill
Spittal
1
Wick
Scourie
ddrachillis Bay
Drumbeg
Kylesku
Altnaharra
L. Naver
Lochinver
Loch Shin
Achiltibuie
Lairg
A 9
A 99
Brora
Dornoch Firth
Ullapool
Dornoch
Tain
Portmahomack
aree
Cadboll
Loch Fannich
A 835
Nigg
Moray Firth
Invergordon
Dingwall
Strathpeffer
Fortrose
Nairn
Elgin
2
R. Spey
Muir of Ord
A 96
Inverness
A 82
Abriachan
Findhorn
Drumnadrochit
Lewiston
Grantown-on-Spey
Invermoriston
Loch Ness
A 87
Fort Augustus
HIGHLAND
Aviemore
uoich
Invergarry
Kingussie
ch Arkaig
Loch Lochy
Caledonian Canal
Spean Bridge
Loch Laggan
Loch Ericht
Fort William
CENTRAL SCOTLAND
(plans 27 28)
Backwater Resr
Ballachulish
Loch Rannoch
Pitlochry
Loch Etive
Loch Tay
A 85
Dee
3
Tay
Place with at least:
a hotel or a restaurant
a starred establishment
a "Bib Gourmand" restaurant
a "Bib Hotel"
a particularly pleasant restaurant
a particularly pleasant guesthouse
a particularly pleasant hotel
a particularly quiet hotel
a particularly pleasant pub

Shetland & Orkney

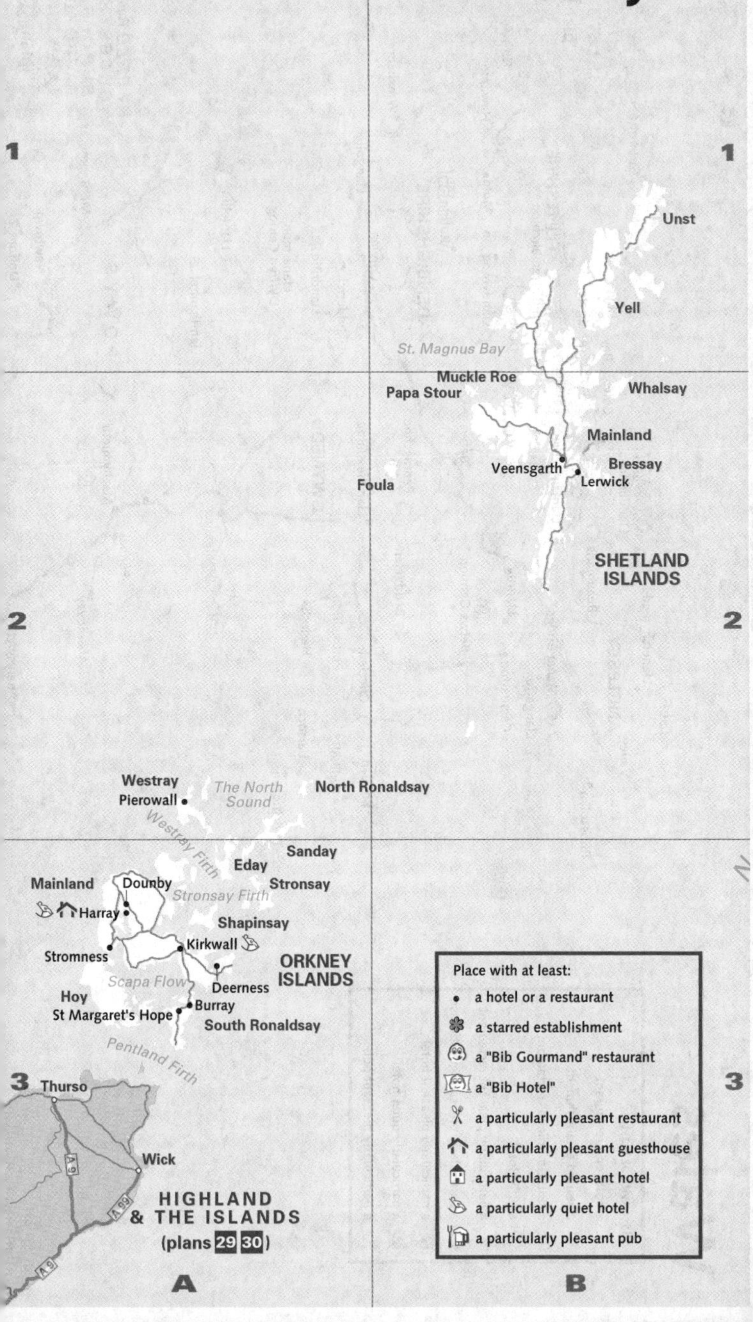

Wales

Place with at least:

- • a hotel or a restaurant
- a starred establishment
- a "Bib Gourmand" restaurant
- a "Bib Hotel"
- a particularly pleasant restaurant
- a particularly pleasant guesthouse
- a particularly pleasant hotel
- a particularly quiet hotel
- a particularly pleasant pub

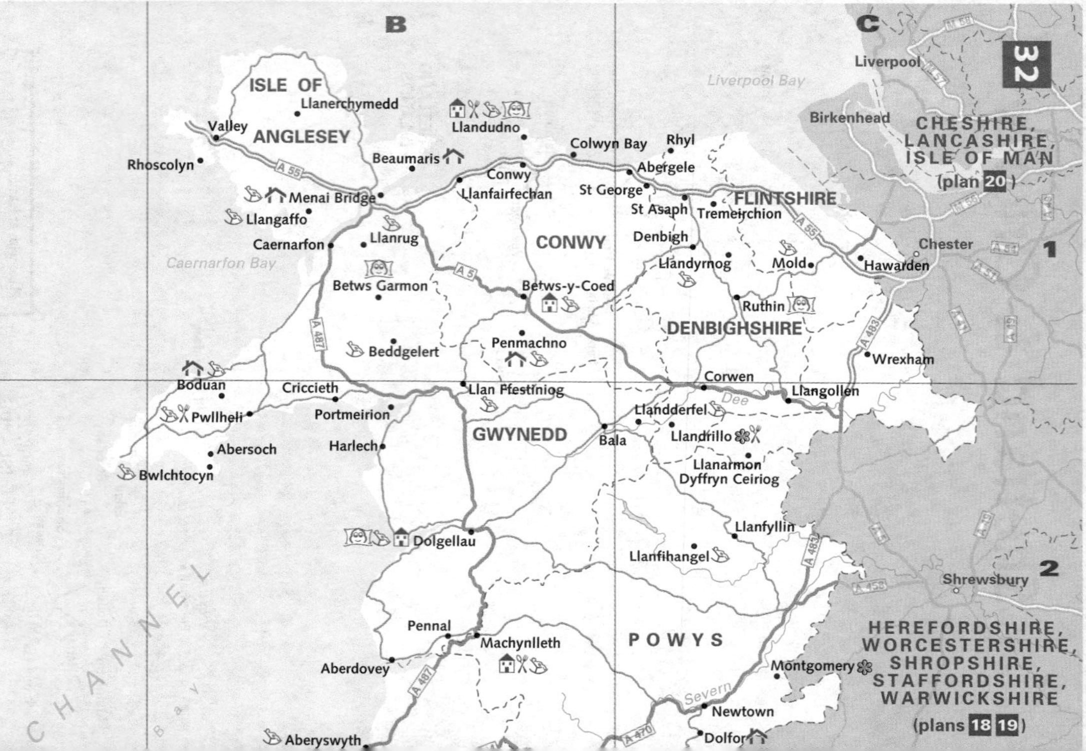

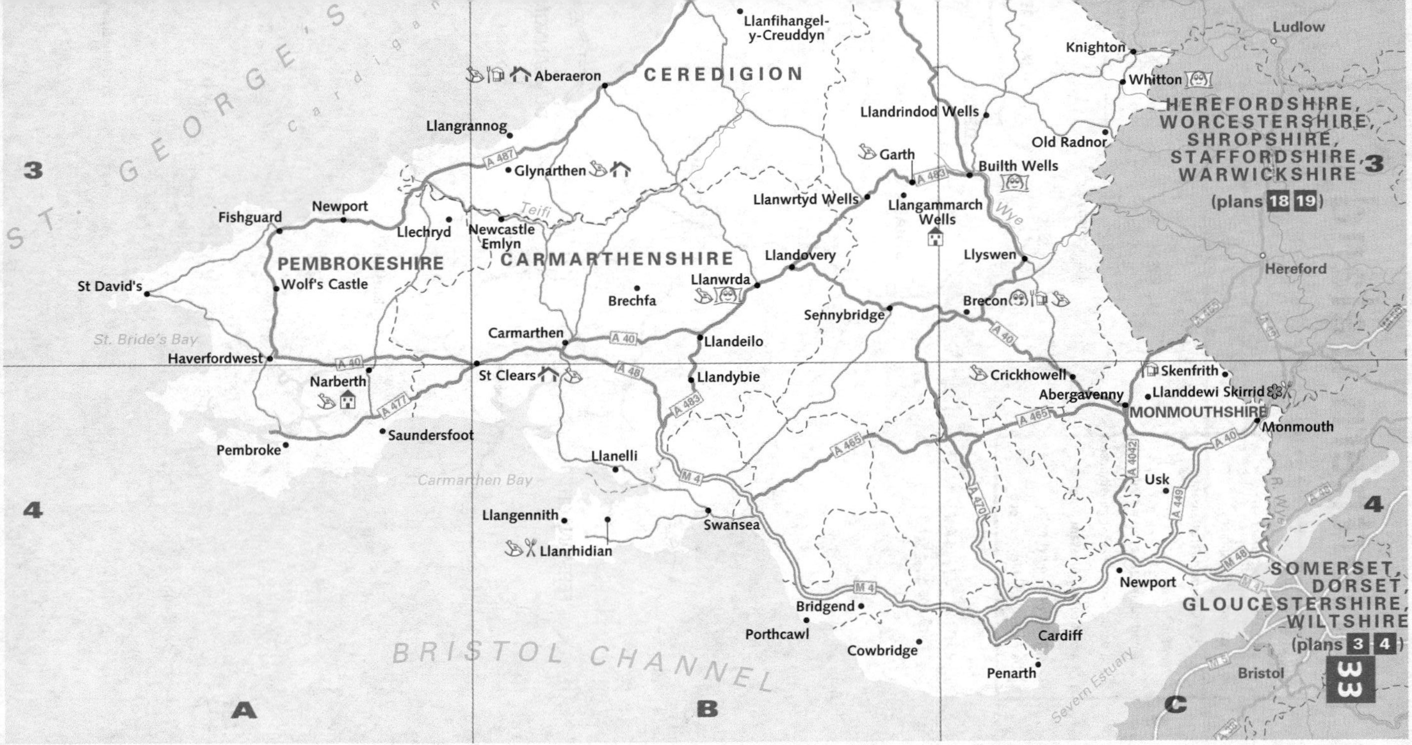
ST GEORGE'S
Cardigan
Llanfihangel-y-Creuddyn
Aberaeron
CEREDIGION
Knighton
Ludlow
Whitton
HEREFORDSHIRE, WORCESTERSHIRE, SHROPSHIRE, STAFFORDSHIRE, WARWICKSHIRE
(plans 18 19)
Llandrindod Wells
Llangrannog
Old Radnor
Garth
Builth Wells
Glynarthen
A 487
A 483
Llanwrtyd Wells
Llangammarch Wells
Newport
Fishguard
Llechryd
Newcastle Emlyn
Teifi
Wye
PEMBROKESHIRE
CARMARTHENSHIRE
Llandovery
Llyswen
Hereford
St David's
Wolf's Castle
Llanwrda
Brechfa
Sennybridge
Brecon
St. Bride's Bay
Carmarthen
A 40
Llandeilo
Haverfordwest
Narberth
St Clears
A 48
Llandybie
Crickhowell
Skenfrith
Abergavenny
Llanddewi Skirrid
MONMOUTHSHIRE
Monmouth
A 477
A 483
A 465
Saunderfoot
Pembroke
Llanelli
Carmarthen Bay
M 4
A 470
A 4042
Usk
A 449
R. Wye
Llangennith
Swansea
Llanrhidian
Newport
M 48
SOMERSET, DORSET, GLOUCESTERSHIRE, WILTSHIRE
(plans 3 4)
Bridgend
Porthcawl
Cowbridge
Cardiff
Penarth
BRISTOL CHANNEL
Severn Estuary
Bristol
A
B
C
3
4

34 Northern Ireland

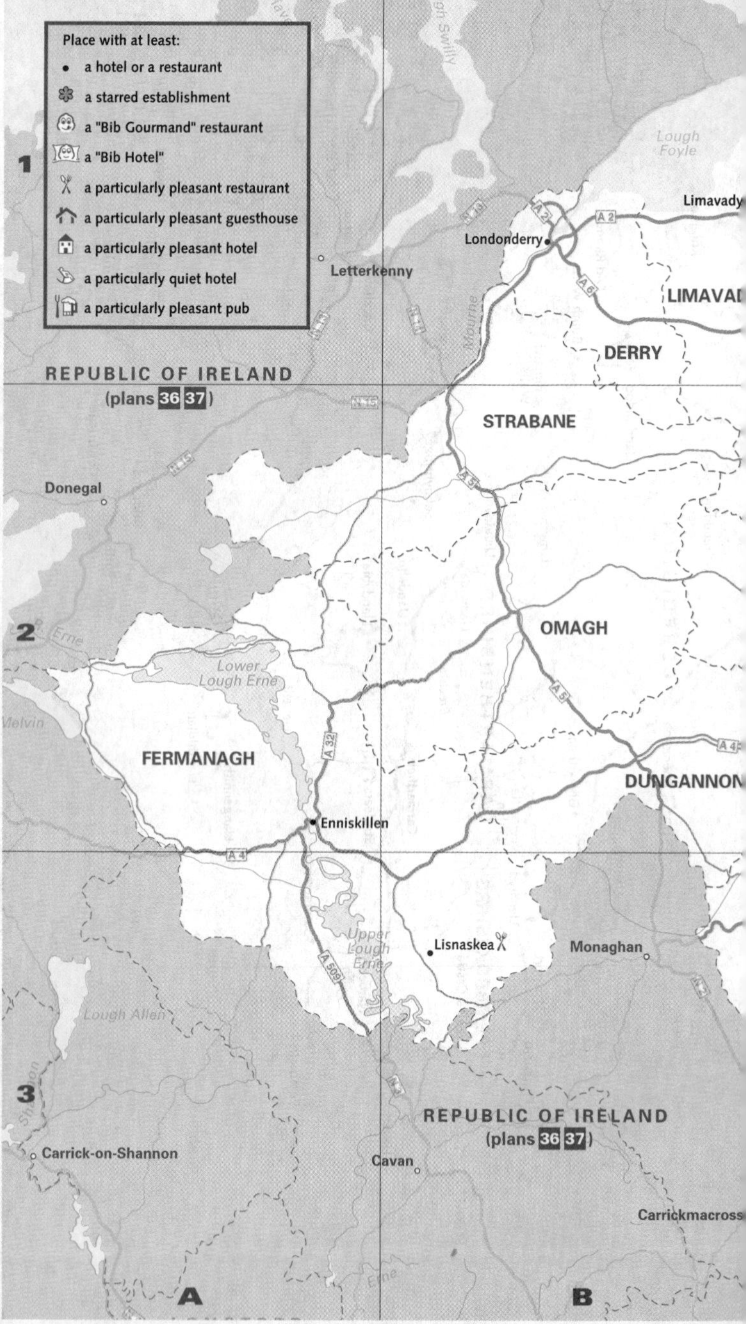

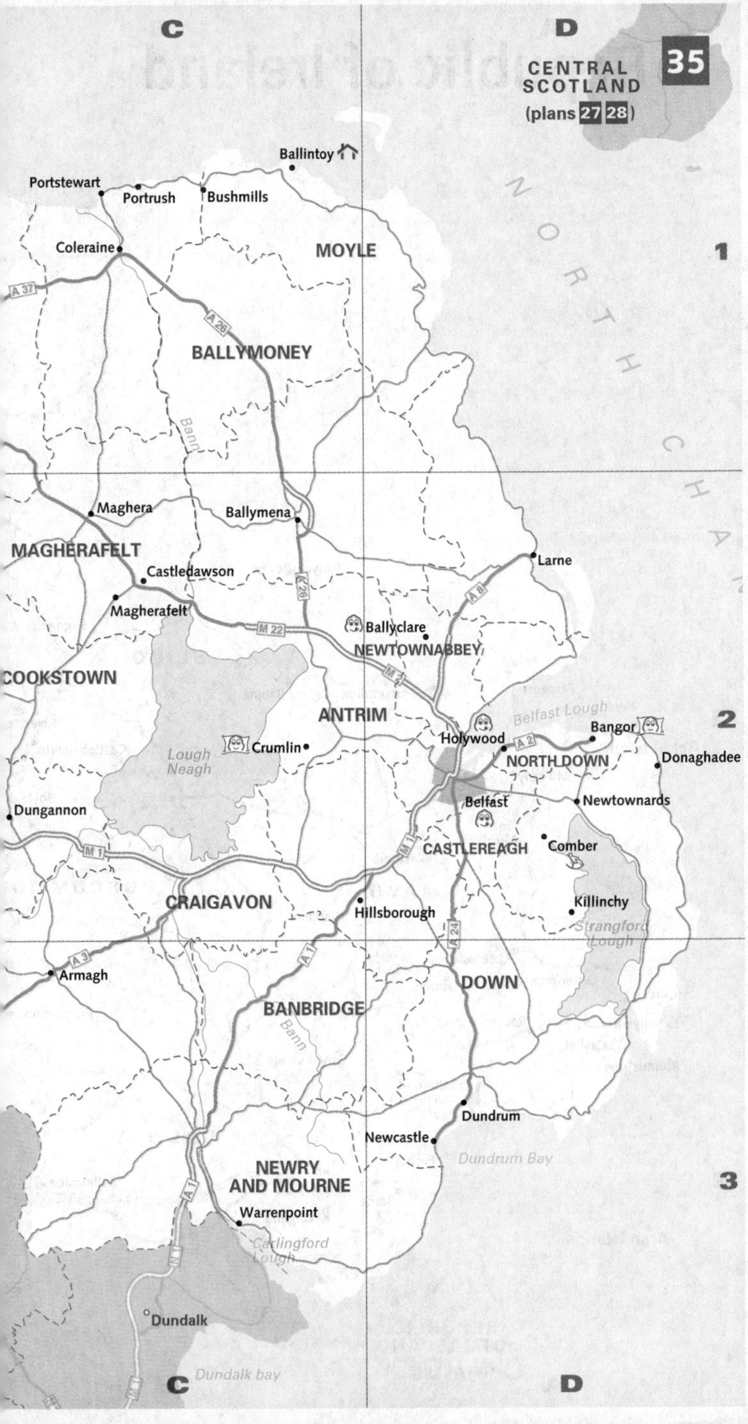
C
D
35
CENTRAL SCOTLAND
(plans 27 28)
NORTH CHANNEL
Ballintoy
Portstewart
Portrush
Bushmills
Coleraine
MOYLE
A 37
A 26
BALLYMONEY
Bann
Maghera
Ballymena
MAGHERAFELT
Larne
Castledawson
A 26
A 8
Magherafelt
M 22
Ballyclare
NEWTOWNABBEY
COOKSTOWN
M 2
ANTRIM
Belfast Lough
Bangor
Holywood
Crumlin
Lough Neagh
A 2
Donaghadee
NORTH DOWN
Belfast
Newtownards
Dungannon
M 1
M 1
CASTLEREAGH
Comber
CRAIGAVON
Hillsborough
Killinchy
Strangford Lough
A 24
A 3
A 1
Armagh
DOWN
BANBRIDGE
Bann
Dundrum
Newcastle
Dundrum Bay
NEWRY AND MOURNE
A 1
Warrenpoint
Carlingford Lough
Dundalk
Dundalk bay
1
2
3

36 Republic of Ireland

38 Republic of Ireland

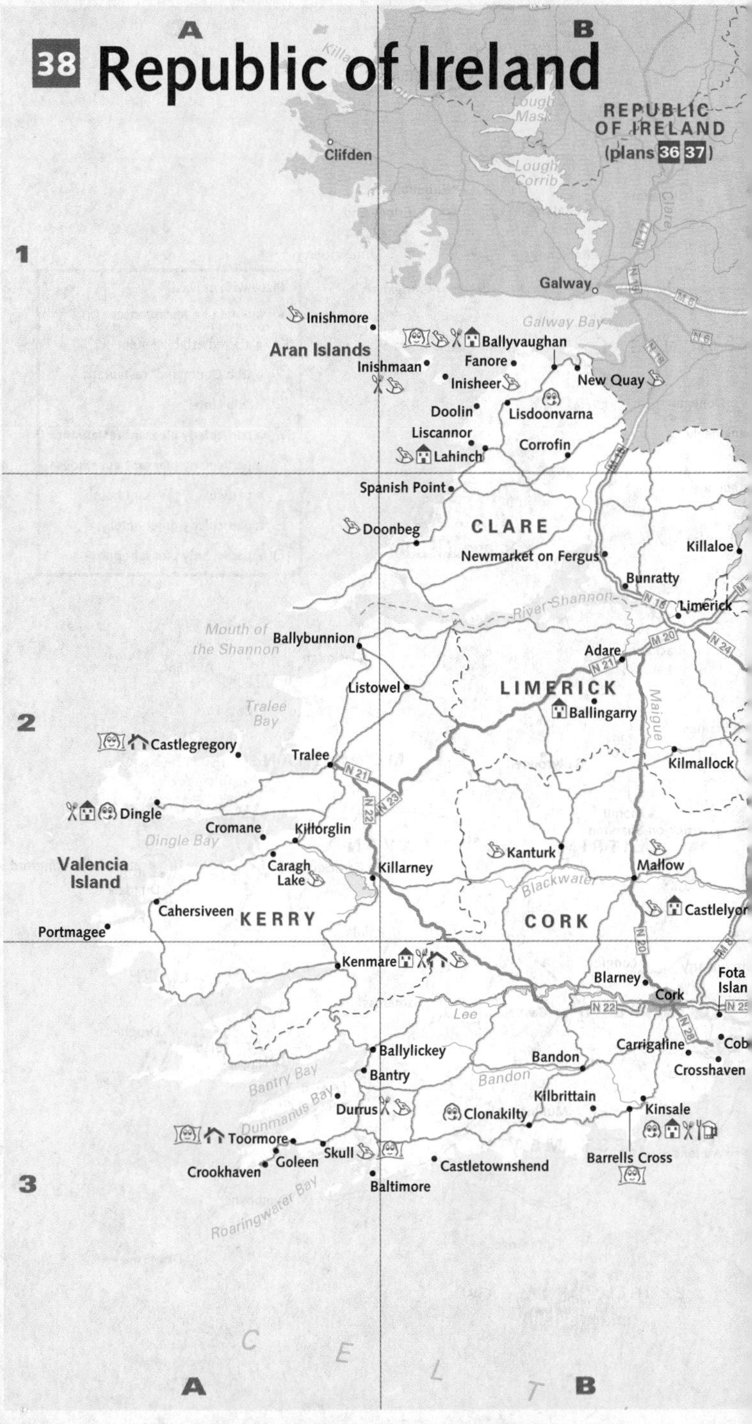
A
B
REPUBLIC OF IRELAND (plans 36 37)
Lough Mask
Lough Corrib
Clifden
Clare
1
Galway
Galway Bay
Inishmore
Aran Islands
Ballyvaughan
Fanore
Inishmaan
Inisheer
New Quay
Doolin
Lisdoonvarna
Liscannor
Corrofin
Lahinch
Spanish Point
Doonbeg
CLARE
Killaloe
Newmarket on Fergus
Bunratty
River Shannon
Limerick
Mouth of the Shannon
Ballybunnion
Adare
Listowel
LIMERICK
Ballingarry
Tralee Bay
Maigue
2
Castlegregory
Tralee
Kilmallock
Dingle
Cromane
Killorglin
Dingle Bay
Kanturk
Valencia Island
Caragh Lake
Killarney
Mallow
Blackwater
Cahersiveen
KERRY
CORK
Castlelyons
Portmagee
Kenmare
Blarney
Fota Island
Cork
Lee
Ballylickey
Carrigaline
Cobh
Bandon
Crosshaven
Bantry
Bantry Bay
Bandon
Dunmanus Bay
Kilbrittain
Durrus
Clonakilty
Kinsale
Toormore
Skull
Goleen
Crookhaven
Castletownshend
Barrells Cross
3
Baltimore
Roaringwater Bay
C E L T
A
B

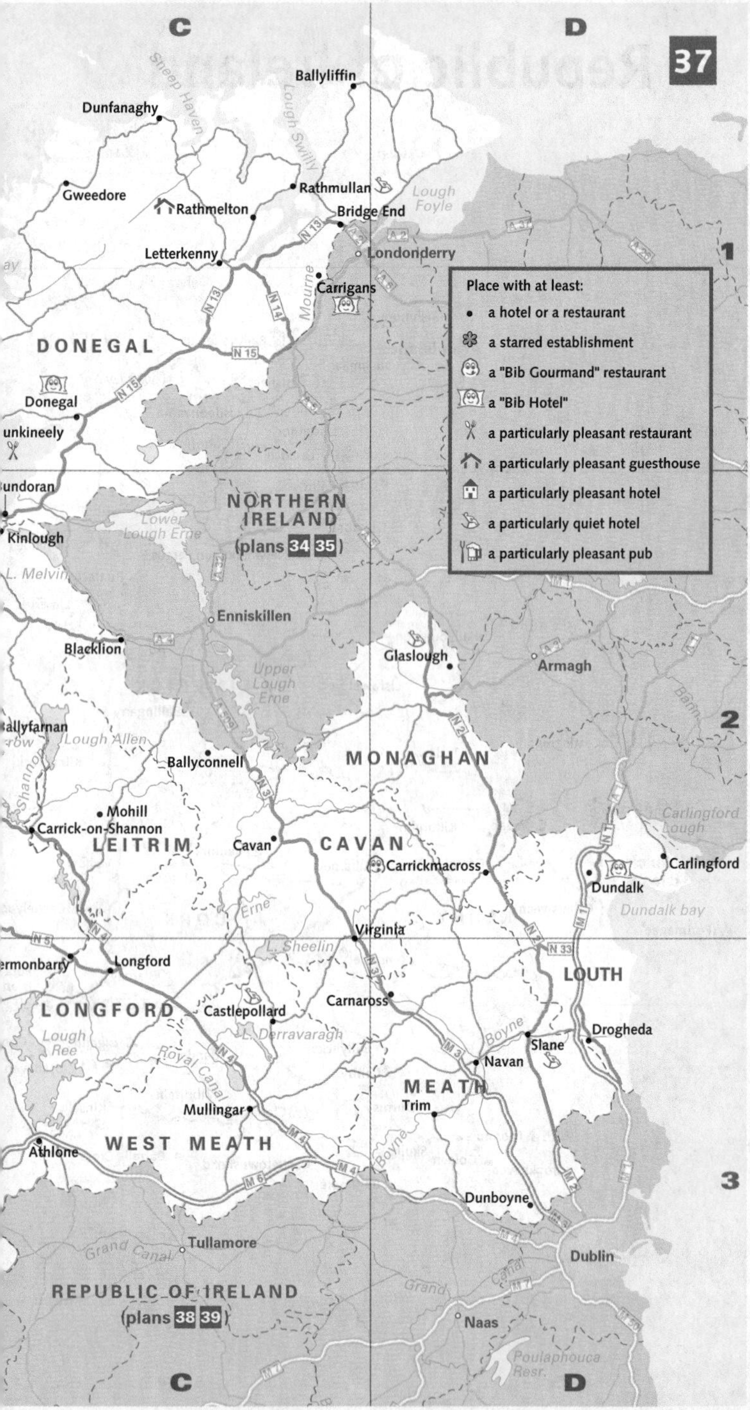
C
D
1
2
3
Place with at least:
a hotel or a restaurant
a starred establishment
a "Bib Gourmand" restaurant
a "Bib Hotel"
a particularly pleasant restaurant
a particularly pleasant guesthouse
a particularly pleasant hotel
a particularly quiet hotel
a particularly pleasant pub
Ballyliffin
Dunfanaghy
Sheep Haven
Lough Swilly
Gweedore
Rathmullan
Lough Foyle
Rathmelton
Bridge End
Letterkenny
Londonderry
Carrigans
Mourne
DONEGAL
Donegal
Dundoran
Kinlough
NORTHERN IRELAND
(plans 34 35)
Lower Lough Erne
Enniskillen
Blacklion
Upper Lough Erne
Glaslough
Armagh
Bann
Lough Allen
Shannon
Ballyconnell
MONAGHAN
Mohill
Carrick-on-Shannon
LEITRIM
Cavan
CAVAN
Carrickmacross
Carlingford Lough
Carlingford
Dundalk
Dundalk bay
Erne
Virginia
L. Sheelin
Longford
LONGFORD
Castlepollard
Carnaross
LOUTH
Lough Ree
L. Derravaragh
Royal Canal
Boyne
Slane
Drogheda
Navan
MEATH
Trim
Mullingar
Athlone
WEST MEATH
Dunboyne
Tullamore
Grand Canal
Dublin
REPUBLIC OF IRELAND
(plans 38 39)
Naas
Poulaphouca Resr.
N 13
N 14
N 15
N 5
N 4
N 3
N 2
N 33
N 1
M 1
M 2
M 3
M 4
M 6
M 7
A 2
A 5
A 4
A 32
A 509